ISBN 978-0-259-48876-7
PIBN 10819467

THE

HOLY BIBLE,

CONTAINING THE

OLD AND NEW TESTAMENTS.

THE TEXT

CAREFULLY PRINTED FROM THE MOST CORRECT COPIES OF THE PRESENT

AUTHORIZED TRANSLATION,

INCLUDING THE

MARGINAL READINGS AND PARALLEL TEXTS:

WITH

A COMMENTARY AND CRITICAL NOTES;

DESIGNED AS A HELP TO A BETTER UNDERSTANDING OF THE SACRED WRITINGS:

BY ADAM CLARKE, LL.D., F.S.A., &c.

A NEW EDITION, WITH THE AUTHOR'S FINAL CORRECTIONS.

FOR WHATSOEVER THINGS WERE WRITTEN AFORETIME WERE WRITTEN FOR OUR LEARNING; THAT WE, THROUGH PATIENCE AND COMFORT OF THE SCRIPTURES, MIGHT HAVE HOPE.—Rom. xv. 4.

THE OLD TESTAMENT.

VOLUME I.—GENESIS TO DEUTERONOMY.

New-York:
PUBLISHED BY G. LANE & C. B. TIPPETT,
FOR THE METHODIST EPISCOPAL CHURCH: 200 MULBERRY-STREET.
JAMES COLLORD, PRINTER.
1846.

GENERAL PREFACE.

THE different nations of the earth, which have received the Old and New Testaments as a Divine revelation, have not only had them carefully translated into their respective languages, but have also agreed in the propriety and necessity of illustrating them by *comments*. At first, the insertion of a *word* or *sentence* in the margin, explaining some particular word in the text, appears to have constituted the whole of the comment. Afterwards, these were mingled with the text, but with such marks as served to distinguish them from the words they were intended to illustrate; sometimes the comment was *interlined* with the text, and at other times it occupied a space at the bottom of the page.

Ancient comments written in all these various ways I have often seen; and a Bible now lies before me, written, probably, before the time of *Wiclif*, where the glosses are all *incorporated* with the text, and only distinguished from it by a *line* underneath; the line evidently added by a later hand. As a matter of curiosity I shall introduce a few specimens.

And seide, Wath, or wele, I am chaufid. I sawe the fiir. Isa. xliv. 16.

He eete haye as an oxe, and with dewe of heben his body was informid or defoulid, till his heris wexiden into licnesse of eglis, and his naylis as naylis or clees of briddis. Dan. iv. 33.

He that is best in hem is as a palyure, that is a scharp busche, or a thistel or firse. Micah vii. 4.

He schal baptise or christend you, with the hooly goost and fiir, whos whynwinge clothe or fan in his hond. Matt. iii. 11, 12.

Who ever schal leebe his wiif, gebe he to her a lybel, that is, a lytil book of forsakinge. Matt. v. 31.

Blynde men seen, crokid men wandren, mesels ben maad clene, deef men heeren, deed men rysen agein, pore men ben taken to prechynge of the gospel, or been maad kepers of the gospel. Matt. xi. 5.

I schal bolke out, or telle out thingis hid fro making of the world. Matt. xiii. 35.

Zee serpentis fruytis of burrowyngis of eddris that sleen her modris, how schuln zee flee fro the dome of helle. Matt. xxiii. 33.

Heroude tetraarcha, that is, prince of the fourth parte. Luke iii. 1.

Habynge your conbersacioun or liif good amonge hethen men. 1 Pet. ii. 12.

Zee schuln rescebe the unwelewable crown of glorie, or that schal neber faade. 1 Pet. v. 4.

Anoynt thin eegen with coluryo, that is, medicinal for eegen maad of diverse erbis, that thou see. Rev. iii. 18.

Comments written in this way have given birth to multitudes of the *various readings* afforded by ancient manuscripts; for the notes of distinction being omitted or neglected, the *gloss* was often considered as an integral part of the text, and entered accordingly by succeeding copyists.

This is particularly remarkable in the *Vulgate*, which abounds with explanatory words and phrases, similar to those in the preceding quotations. In the *Septuagint* also, traces of this custom are easily discernible, and to this circumstance many of its *various readings* may be attributed.

In proportion to the distance of time from the period in which the sacred oracles were delivered, the necessity of comments became more apparent; for the political state of the people to whom the Scriptures were originally given, as well as that of the surrounding nations, being in the lapse of time essentially changed, hence was found the necessity of *historical* and *chronological notes*, to illustrate the facts related in the sacred books.

Did the nature of this preface permit, it might be useful to enter into a detailed history of commentators and their works, and show by what gradations they proceeded from simple *verbal* glosses to those colossal accumulations in which *the words of God* lie buried in the *sayings of men*. But this at present is impracticable; a short sketch must therefore suffice.

Perhaps the most ancient comments containing merely verbal glosses were the *Chaldee Paraphrases*, or *Targums*, particularly those of ONKELOS on the *Law*, and JONATHAN on the *Prophets;* the former written a short time before the Christian era, the latter about fifty years after the incarnation. These comments are rather *glosses* on *words*, than an *exposition* of *things;* and the former is little more than a *verbal* translation of the Hebrew text into pure *Chaldee*.

The TARGUM YERUSHLEMEY is written in the manner of the two former, and contains a paraphrase, in very corrupt Chaldee, on select parts of the five books of Moses.

The *Targum* ascribed to JONATHAN *ben* UZZIEL embraces the whole of the Pentateuch, but is disgraced with the most ridiculous and incredible fables.

Among the *Jews*, several eminent commentators appeared at different times, besides the *Targumists* already mentioned, who endeavoured to illustrate different parts of the Law and the Prophets.—PHILO JUDÆUS may be reckoned among these; his works contain several curious treatises in explication of different parts of the Hebrew Scriptures. He flourished about A. D. 40.

JOSEPHUS may be fairly ranked among commentators; the first twelve books of his Jewish Antiquities are a regular paraphrase and comment on the political and ecclesiastical history of the Jews as given in the Bible, from the foundation of the world to the time of the *Asmoneans* or *Maccabees*. He flourished about A. D. 80.

It is well known that the MISHNAH, or oral law of the Jews, is a pretended comment on the five books of Moses. This was compiled from innumerable traditions by *Rabbi Judah Hakkadosh*, probably about the year of our Lord 150.

The TALMUDS, both of *Jerusalem* and *Babylon*, are a comment on the *Mishnah*. The former was compiled about A. D. 300, the latter about 200 years after.

Chaldee Targums, or Paraphrases, have been written on all the books of the Old Testament; some parts of the book of *Ezra*, and the book of *Daniel*, excepted; which, being originally written in *Chaldee*, did not require for the purpose of being read during the captivity any farther explanation. When the London Polyglot was put to press no Targum was found on the two books of Chronicles; but after that work was printed, a Targum on these two books was discovered in the university of Cambridge, and printed at Amsterdam, with a Latin translation, 4to, 1715, by Mr. *D. Wilkins*. It is attributed to *Rabbi Joseph the Blind*, who flourished about A. D. 400.

The MASORETS were the most extensive Jewish commentators which that nation could ever boast. The system of *punctuation*, probably invented by them, is a *continual gloss* on the Law and Prophets; their *vowel points*, and prosaic and metrical *accents*, &c., give every word to which they are affixed a peculiar kind of meaning, which in their *simple* state multitudes of them can by no means bear. The vowel points alone add *whole conjugations* to the language. This system is one of the most artificial, particular, and extensive comments ever written on the word of God; for there is not one *word* in the Bible that is not the subject of a particular gloss through its influence. This school is supposed to have commenced about 450 years before our Lord, and to have extended down to A. D. 1030. Some think it did not commence before the *fifth* century.

Rabbi SAADIAS GAON, about A. D. 930, wrote a commentary upon Daniel, and some other parts of Scripture; and translated in a literal and very faithful manner the whole of the Old Testament into the Arabic language. The *Pentateuch* of this translation has been printed by Erpenius, *Lugd. Bat.* 1622, 4to. A MS. copy of *Saadias's* translation of the Pentateuch, probably as old as the author, is now in my own library.

Rabbi SOLOMON JARCHI or *Isaaki*, who flourished in A. D. 1140, wrote a commentary on the whole Bible, so completely obscure in many places, as to require a very large comment to make it intelligible.

In 1160 ABEN EZRA, a justly celebrated Spanish rabbin, flourished; his commentaries on the Bible are deservedly esteemed both by Jews and Gentiles.

Rabbi MOSES *ben* MAIMON, commonly called *Maimonides*, also ranks high among the Jewish commentators; his work entitled *Moreh Nebochim*, or *Teacher of the Perplexed*, is a very excellent illustration of some of the most difficult words and things in the sacred writings. He flourished about A. D. 1160.

Rabbi DAVID KIMCHI, a Spanish Jew, wrote a very useful comment on most books of the Old Testament: his comment on the Prophet *Isaiah* is peculiarly excellent. He flourished about A. D. 1220.

Rabbi Jacob BAAL HATTURIM flourished A. D. 1300, and wrote short notes or observations on the Pentateuch, principally cabalistical.

Rabbi Levi ben GERSHOM, a Spanish Jew and physician, died A. D. 1370. He was a very voluminous author, and wrote some esteemed comments on different parts of Scripture, especially the *five books* of *Moses*.

Rabbi ISAAC ABARBANEL or ABRAVANEL, a Portuguese Jew, who was born A. D. 1437, and died A. D. 1508, also wrote extensive commentaries on the Scriptures, which are highly esteemed by the Jews.

RABBINOO ISAIAH wrote select notes or observations on the books of Samuel.

Rabbi Moses Mendelssohn, a German Jew, born at Dissau, in 1729, was one of the most learned Jews that has flourished since the days of the prophets; a man to whose vast mental powers was added a very amiable disposition, and truly philanthropic heart. He wrote Nesibut Hashshalom, i. e., the Path of Peace; the five books of Moses, with a commentary, and German translation; Ritual laws of the Jews; the Psalms of David in verse; also, on the being of a God; the Immortality of the Soul, and several philosophical works. He died at Berlin in 1786. See a well-written life of this great man by M. *Samuels:* 8vo. Lond. 1825.

GENERAL PREFACE.

For farther information on the subject of Jewish and rabbinical writers, I must refer my readers to the **Bibliotheca Magna Rabbinica** of *Bartolocci*, begun in 1675, and finished in 1693, four vols. folio. In this work the reader will find an ample and satisfactory account of all Jewish writers and their works from the giving of the law, A. M. 2513, B. C. 1491, continued down to A. D. 1681. This work is digested in *alphabetical* order, and contains an account of upwards of 1,300 Jewish authors and their works, with a confutation of their principal objections and blasphemies against the Christian religion; together with frequent demonstrations that Jesus Christ is the promised Messiah, drawn, not only from the sacred writings, but from those also of the earlier and most respectable rabbins themselves: each of the volumes is enriched with a great variety of dissertations on many important subjects in Biblical literature. This work, left unfinished by its author, was completed by *Imbonati*, his disciple, who added a fifth volume, entitled *Bibliotheca Latino-Hebraica*, containing an ample alphabetical account of all the Latin authors who have written either against the Jews or on Jewish affairs. Romæ, 1694. These two works are very useful, and the authors may be deservedly ranked among *Biblical critics* and *commentators*. Bartolocci was born at Naples in 1613, and died at Rome, where he was Hebrew professor, in 1687.

Most of the Jewish comments being written in the corrupt Chaldee dialect, and in general printed in the *rabbinical character*, which few, even among scholars, care to read, hence they are comparatively but little known. It must be however allowed that they are of great service in illustrating the *rites* and *ceremonies* of the Mosaic law; and of great use to the Christians in their controversies with the Jews.

As some of my readers may wish to know where the chief of these comments may be most easily found, it will give them pleasure to be informed that the *Targums* or Chaldee paraphrases of **Onkelos** and **Jonathan**; the *Targum* **Yerushlemey**; the **Masorah**; the comments of **Radak**, i. e. *Rabbi David Kimchi;* **Rashi**, i. e. *Rabbi Solomon Jarchi;* **Ralbag**, i. e. *Rabbi Levi ben Gershom;* **Rambam**, i. e. *Rabbi Moses ben Maimon, or Maimonides;* **Rashag**, i. e. *Rabbi Saadias Gaon;* **Aben Ezra**, with the scanty observations of *Rabbi Jacob* **Baal Hatturim**, on the five books of Moses; and those of *Rabbi* **Isaiah** on the two books of Samuel, are all printed in the second edition of Bomberg's Great Bible: Venice, 1547, &c., 2 vols. folio; the most useful, the most correct, and the most valuable Hebrew Bible ever published. It may be just necessary to say, that *Radak, Rashi, Ralbag*, &c., are technical names given to these rabbins from the *initials* of their proper names, with some interposed vowels, as RaDaK, stands for Rabbi David Kimchi; RaShI, for Rabbi Solomon Jarchi; RaLBaG, for Rabbi Levi Ben Gershom; and so of the rest. The *Targums* of *Onkelos* and *Jonathan* are printed also in the three first volumes of the *London Polyglot*, with a generally correct literal Latin version. The *Targum* ascribed to *Jonathan ben Uzziel*, and the *Targum Yerushlemey* on the Pentateuch, are printed with a literal Latin version, in the *fourth* volume of the above work. The *Mishnah* has been printed in a most elegant manner by *Surenhusius:* Amsterdam, 1698, 6 vols. folio, with a Latin translation, and an abundance of notes.

Christian commentators, both ancient and modern, are vastly more numerous, more excellent, and better known, than those among the Jews. On this latter account I may be well excused for passing by many which have all their respective excellences, and mentioning only a few out of the vast multitude, which are either more eminent, more easy of access, or better known to myself.

These comments may be divided into *four* distinct classes: 1. Those of the *Primitive Fathers* and *Doctors* of the *Church;* 2. Those written by *Roman Catholics;* 3. Those written by *Protestants*, and, 4. *Compilations* from both, and *collections* of *Biblical critics*.

Class I.—Primitive Fathers and Doctors.

Tatian, who flourished about A. D. 150, wrote a *Harmony* of the four Gospels, perhaps the first thing of the kind ever composed: the genuine work is probably lost, as that extant under his name is justly suspected by the learned.

In this class **Origen** occupies a distinguished place: he was born A. D. 185, and wrote much on the Scriptures: his principal works are unfortunately lost: many of his Homilies still remain, but they are so replete with metaphorical and fanciful interpretations of the sacred text, that there is much reason to believe they have been corrupted since his time. Specimens of his mode of interpreting the Scriptures may be seen in the ensuing comment. See on Exod. ii.

Hyppolitus wrote many things on the Scriptures, most of which are lost: he flourished about A. D. 230.

Chrysostom is well known and justly celebrated for his learning, skill, and eloquence, in his Homilies on the sacred writings, particularly the *Psalms*. He flourished A. D. 344.

Jerome is also well known: he is author of what is called the *Vulgate*, a Latin version from the Hebrew and Greek of the whole Old and New Testaments, as also of a very valuable comment on all the Bible. He flourished A. D. 360.

Ephraim Syrus, who might be rather said to have *mourned* than to have *flourished* about A. D. 360, has written some very valuable expositions of particular parts of Scripture. They may be found in his works, Syr. and Gr., published by Asseman, Romæ, 1737, &c., 6 vols. folio.

To AUGUSTINE, a laborious and voluminous writer, we are indebted for much valuable information on the sacred writings. His expositions of Scripture, however, have been the subjects of many acrimonious controversies in the Christian Church. He has written upon a number of abstruse and difficult points, and in several cases not in a very lucid manner; and hence it is not to be wondered at if many of his commentators have mistaken his meaning. Some strange things drawn from his writings, and several things in his creed, may be attributed to the tincture his mind received from his *Manichean* sentiments; for it is well known that he had embraced, previously to his conversion to Christianity, the doctrine of the *two principles*, one *wholly evil*, and the other *wholly good;* to whose energy and operation all the *good* and *evil* in the world were attributed. These two opposite and conflicting beings he seems, in some cases, unwarily to unite in one God; and hence he and many of his followers appear to have made the ever-blessed God, the fountain of all justice and holiness, the author, not only of all the good that is in the world, (for in this there can be but one opinion,) but of all the *evil* likewise; having reduced it to a necessity of existence by a predetermining, unchangeable, and eternal decree, by which all the actions of angels and men are appointed and irrevocably established. St. Augustine died A. D. 430.

GREGORY the *Great*, who flourished about A. D. 600, has written commentaries which are greatly esteemed, especially among the Catholics.

THEOPHYLACT has written a valuable comment on the Gospels, Acts, and St. Paul's Epistles. He flourished A. D. 700.

VENERABLE BEDE flourished A. A. 780, and wrote comments (or rather collected those of others) on the principal books of the Old and New Testaments, which are still extant.

RABANUS MAURUS, who flourished A. D. 800, was one of the most voluminous commentators since the days of Origen. Besides his numerous comments published in his works, there is a glossary of his on the whole Bible in MS., in the imperial library at Vienna.

WALAFRIDUS STRABUS composed a work on the Old and New Testaments, entitled *Biblia Sacra cum Glossa Ordinaria*, which is properly a *Catena* or collection of all comments of the Greek and Latin Fathers prior to his time. Strabus constantly endeavours to show the literal, historical, and moral sense of the inspired writers. The best edition of this valuable work was printed at Antwerp in 1684, 6 vols. folio. The author died in his forty-third year, A. D. 846.

It would be very easy to augment this list of Fathers and Doctors by the addition of many respectable names, but my limits prevent me from entering into any detail. A few scanty additional notices of authors and their works must suffice.

SALONIUS, bishop of Vienna, who flourished in 440, wrote a very curious piece, entitled a Mystical Explanation of the *Proverbs of Solomon*, in a dialogue between himself and his brother Veranius: the latter asks questions on every important subject contained in the book, and the former answers and professes to solve all difficulties. He wrote also an Exposition of *Ecclesiastes*.

PHILO, bishop of the Carpathians, wrote on *Solomon's Song*.

JUSTUS, bishop of Orgelitanum, or *Urgel*, wrote a mystical explanation of the same book. He died A. D. 540.

And to APONIUS, a writer of the *seventh* century, a pretty extensive and mystical exposition of this book is attributed. It is a continued allegory of *the marriage between Christ and his Church.*

To *Aponius* and the preceding writers most modern expositors of Solomon's Song stand considerably indebted, for those who have never seen these ancient authors have generally borrowed from others who have closely copied their mode of interpretation.

Among the opuscula of THEOPHILUS, bishop of Antioch, is found an allegorical exposition of the *four Gospels*. Theophilus flourished about the middle of the *second* century.

VICTOR, presbyter of Antioch, wrote a very extensive comment on St. *Mark's* Gospel, in which many very judicious observations may be found.

THEODULUS, a presbyter of Cœlesyria, about A. D. 450 wrote a comment on the *Epistle to the Romans*.

REMIGIUS, bishop of Auxerre, who flourished about the end of the ninth century, wrote a comment on the *twelve Minor Prophets*.

SEDULIUS HYBERNICUS wrote a Collectanea on all the *Epistles of St. Paul*, in which there are many useful things. When he flourished is uncertain.

PRIMASIUS, bishop of Utica, in Africa, and disciple of St. Augustine, wrote also a comment on all *St. Paul's Epistles*, and one on the book of *Revelation*. He flourished A. D. 550.

And to ANDREAS, archbishop of Cæsarea, in Cappadocia, we are indebted for a very extensive comment on the *Apocalypse*, which is highly extolled by Catholic writers, and which contains a sufficient quantum of mystical interpretations.

All these writers, with others of minor note, may be found in the *Bibliotheca Veterum Patrum*, &c., by *De la* BIGNE, folio, par. 1624, vol. i. Any person who is fond of ecclesiastical antiquity will find himself gratified even by a superficial reading of the preceding authors; for they not only give their own sentiments on the subjects they handle, but also those of accredited writers who have flourished long before their times.

Class II.—Catholic Commentators.

Among the *Catholic* writers many valuable commentators are to be found; the chief of whom are the following:—*Hugo de Sancto* Clara, or *Hugh de St.* Cler, flourished in 1200. He was a Dominican monk and cardinal, and wrote a commentary on the whole Bible, and composed a *Concordance*, probably the first regular work of the kind, in which he is said to have employed not less than 500 of his brethren to write for him.

Nicholaus de Lyra or *Lyranus*, Anglice, Nicholas *Harper*, wrote short comments on the whole Bible, which are allowed to be very judicious, and in which he reprehends many reigning abuses. It is supposed that from these Martin Luther borrowed much of that light which brought about the Reformation. Hence it has been said,

Si Lyra non lyrasset,
Lutherus non saltasset.

"If Lyra had not *harped* on profanation,
Luther had never *planned* the reformation."

Lyra flourished in 1300, and was the first of the Christian commentators, since St. Jerome, who brought rabbinical learning to illustrate the sacred writings. His postils may be found in the *Glossa Ordinaria* of *Walafrid Strabus*, already mentioned.

John Menochius, who flourished in the sixteenth century, has published short notes on all the Scriptures; they are generally esteemed very judicious and satisfactory.

Isidore Clarius, bishop of Fuligni in Umbria, in 1550, wrote some learned notes on the Old and New Testaments: he is celebrated for an eloquent speech delivered before the council of Trent in favour of the *Vulgate*. His learned defence of it contributed no doubt to the canonization of that Version.

John Maldonat wrote notes on particular parts of the Old and New Testaments, at present little read.

Cornelius *a* Lapide is one of the most laborious and voluminous commentators since the invention of printing. Though he has written nothing either on the *Psalms* or *Job*, yet his comment forms no less than 16 vols. folio; it was printed at Venice, 1710. He was a very learned man, but cites as *authentic* several *spurious* writings. He died in 1637.

In 1693–4, Father Quesnel, Priest of the Oratory, published in French, at Brussels, *Moral Reflections on the New Testament*, in 8 vols. 12mo. The author was a man of deep piety; and were it not for the rigid Jansenian predestinarianism which it contains, it would, as a *spiritual comment*, be invaluable. The work was translated into English by the Rev. Richard Russel, and published in 4 vols. 8vo., London, 1719, &c. In this work the reader must not expect any elucidation of the difficulties, or indeed of the text, of the New Testament; the design of Father Quesnel is to draw spiritual uses from his text, and apply them to moral purposes. His reflections contain many strong reprehensions of reigning abuses in the Church, and especially among the clergy. It was against this book that Pope Clement XI. issued his famous constitution *Unigenitus*, in which he condemned *one hundred and one* propositions taken out of the Moral Reflections, as dangerous and damnable heresies. In my notes on the New Testament I have borrowed several excellent reflections from Father *Quesnel's* work. The author died at Amsterdam, December 2, 1719, aged 86 years.

Dom Augustin Calmet, a Benedictine, published what he terms *Commentaire Litteral*, on the whole of the Old and New Testaments. It was first printed at Paris, in 26 vols. 4to., 1707-1717; and afterwards in 9 vols. folio, Paris, Emery, Saugrain, and Martin, 1719-1726. It contains the Latin text of the *Vulgate* and a French translation, in collateral columns, with the notes at the bottom of each page. It has a vast apparatus of prefaces and dissertations, in which immense learning, good sense, sound judgment, and deep piety, are invariably displayed. Though the Vulgate is his text, yet he notices all its variations from the *Hebrew* and *Greek* originals, and generally builds his criticisms on *these*. He quotes all the *ancient* commentators, and most of the modern, whether Catholic or Protestant, and gives them due credit and praise. His illustrations of many difficult texts, referring to idolatrous customs, rites, ceremonies, &c., from the Greek and Roman classics, are abundant, appropriate, and successful. His *tables, maps, plans,* &c., are very judiciously constructed, and consequently very useful. This is without exception the best comment ever published on the sacred writings, either by Catholics or Protestants, and has left little to be desired for the completion of such a work. It is true its scarcity, voluminousness, high price, and the language in which it is written, must prevent its ever coming into common use in our country; but it will ever form one of the most valuable parts of the private library of every Biblical student and divine. From this judicious and pious commentator I have often borrowed; and his contributions form some of the best parts of my work. It is to be lamented that he trusted so much to his *printers*, in consequence of which his work abounds with typographical *errors*, and especially in his learned quotations. In almost every case I have been obliged to refer to the originals themselves. When once written he never revised his sheets, but

put them at once into the hands of his printer. This was a source of many mistakes; but for the following I cannot account. In his notes on Numb. xii. 2, he adds the following clause: *Dominus iratus est,* Le Seigneur se suit en colere, on which he makes the following strange observation: Cela n'est dans l'Hebreu, ni dans les Septante, ni dans le Chaldeen. On which Houbigant remarks: *Potuit addere nec in Samaritano codice, nec in ejus interprete, nec in ipso Vulgato, nec in utroque Arabe. Ut difficile sit divinare unde hæc verba Aug. Calmet deprompserit: nec miror talia multa excidisse in scriptore qui chartas suas, prima manu scriptas, non prius retractabat, quam eas jam misisset ad typographos.* The fact is, the words are not in the *Bible* nor in any of its versions.

In 1753, *Father* HOUBIGANT, a Priest of the Oratory, published a *Hebrew Bible,* in 4 vols. folio, with a Latin Version, and several critical notes at the end of each chapter. He was a consummate Hebraician and accurate critic; even his conjectural emendations of the text cast much light on many obscure passages, and not a few of them have been confirmed by the MS. collections of *Kennicott* and *De Rossi.* The work is as invaluable in its *matter* as it is high in *price* and difficult to be obtained. To this edition the following notes are often under considerable obligation.

CLASS III.—PROTESTANT COMMENTATORS.

Sebastian MUNSTER, first a Cordelier, but afterwards a Protestant, published a Hebrew Bible, with a Latin translation, and short critical notes at the end of each chapter. His Bible has been long neglected, but his notes have been often republished in large collections. He died in 1552.

The Bible in Latin, printed at *Zurich,* in 1543, and often afterwards in folio, has a vast many scholia or marginal notes, which have been much esteemed (as also the Latin version) by many divines and critics. The compilers of the notes were *Leo de Juda, Theodore Bibliander, Peter Cholin, Ralph Guatier,* and *Conrad Pelicanus.*

TREMELLIUS, a converted Jew, with *Junius* or *du Jon,* published a very literal Latin version of the Hebrew Bible with short critical notes, folio, 1575. It has often been reprinted, and was formerly in high esteem. *Father Simon* accuses him unjustly of putting in *pronouns* where none exist in the Hebrew: had he examined more carefully he would have found that *Tremellius* translates the *emphatic article* by the *pronoun* in Latin, and it is well known that it has this power in the Hebrew language. *Father Simon's* censure is therefore not well founded.

John PISCATOR published a laborious and learned comment on the Old and New Testaments, in 24 vols. 8vo., Herborn, 1601–1616. Not highly esteemed.

John DRUSIUS was an able commentator; he penetrated the literal sense of Scripture, and in his Animadversions, Hebrew Questions, Explanations of Proverbs, Observations on the Rites and Customs of the Jews, he has cast much light on many parts of the sacred writings. He died at Francker, in 1616, in the 66th year of his age.

Hugo GROTIUS, or *Hugh le Groot,* has written notes on the whole of the Old and New Testaments. His learning was very extensive, his erudition profound, and his moderation on subjects of controversy highly praiseworthy. No man possessed a more extensive and accurate knowledge of the Greek and Latin writers, and no man has more successfully applied them to the illustration of the sacred writings. To give the literal and genuine sense of the sacred writings is always the laudable study of this great man; and he has not only illustrated them amply, but he has defended them strenuously, especially in his treatise *On the Truth of the Christian Religion,* a truly classical performance that has never been answered, and never can be refuted. He has also written a piece, which has been highly esteemed by many, *On the Satisfaction of Christ.* He died in 1645, aged 62 years.

LOUIS DE DIEU wrote animadversions on the Old and New Testaments, in which are many valuable things. He was a profound scholar in Greek, Hebrew, Chaldee, Persian, and Syriac, as his works sufficiently testify. He died at Leyden, in 1642.

Desiderius ERASMUS is well known, not only as an able *editor* of the Greek Testament, but also as an excellent commentator upon it. The *first edition* of this *sacred* BOOK was published by him in Greek and Latin, folio, 1516; for though the Complutensian edition was printed in 1514, it was not published till 1522. For many years the notes of Erasmus served for the foundation of all the comments that were written on the New Testament, and his Latin version itself was deemed an excellent comment on the text, because of its faithfulness and simplicity. Erasmus was one of the most correct Latin scholars since the Augustan age. He died in 1536. I need not state that in some cases he appeared so indecisive in his religious creed, that he has been both claimed and disavowed by Protestants and Catholics.

JOHN CALVIN wrote a commentary on all the Prophets and the Evangelists, which has been in high esteem among Protestants, and is allowed to be a very learned and judicious work. The decided and active part which he took in the Reformation is well known. To the doctrine of human merit, indulgences, &c., he, with *Luther,* opposed the doctrine of justification by grace

through faith, for which they were strenuous and successful advocates. The peculiar doctrines which go under the name of Mr. *Calvin*, from the manner in which they have been defended by some and opposed by others, have been the cause of much dissension among Protestants, of which the enemies of true religion have often availed themselves. Mr. Calvin is allowed by good judges to have written with great purity both in Latin and French. He died in 1564.

Mr. DAVID MARTIN, of Utrecht, not only translated the whole of the Old and New Testaments into French, but also wrote short notes on both, which contain much good sense, learning, and piety. Amsterdam, 1707, 2 vols. folio.

Dr. *Henry* HAMMOND is celebrated over Europe as a very learned and judicious divine. He wrote an extensive comment on the *Psalms*, first published in 1659, and on the whole of the *New Testament*, in 1653. In this latter work he imagines he sees the *Gnostics* every where pointed at, and he uses them as a universal *menstruum* to dissolve all the difficulties in the text. He was a man of great learning and critical sagacity, and as a divine ranks high in the Church of England. He died in 1660.

Theodore BEZA not only published the Greek Testament, but wrote many excellent notes on it. The best edition of this work is that printed at Cambridge, folio, 1642.

Dr. *Edward* WELLS published a very useful Testament in Greek and English, in several parcels, with notes, from 1709 to 1719, in which, 1. The Greek text is amended according to the best and most ancient readings. 2. The common English translation rendered more agreeable to the original. 3. A paraphrase, explaining the difficult expressions, design of the sacred writers, &c. 4. Short Annotations. This is a judicious, useful work.

Of merely critical comments on the Greek Testament, the most valuable is that of *J. James* WETSTEIN, 2 vols. folio, Amsterdam, 1751–2. Almost every peculiar form of speech in the sacred text he has illustrated by quotations from the Jewish, Greek, and Roman writers. But the indistinctness of his quotations causes much confusion in his notes.

Mr. HARDY published a Greek Testament with a great variety of useful notes, chiefly extracted from Poole's Synopsis. The work is in 2 vols. 8vo., London, 1768, and is a very useful companion to every Biblical student. It has gone through two editions, the first of which is the best; but it must be acknowledged that the Greek text in both is inexcusably incorrect. The Rev. Mr. Valpy has given a new edition of this work, with additional scholia, and a correct Greek text.

Mr. HENRY AINSWORTH, one of that class of the ancient *Puritans* called *Brownists*, made a new translation of the *Pentateuch*, *Psalms*, and *Canticles*, which he illustrated with notes, folio, 1639. He was an excellent Hebrew scholar, and made a very judicious use of his rabbinical learning in his comment, especially on the five books of Moses. To his notes on the Pentateuch I am often under obligation.

The notes of the *Assembly of Divines*, in 2 vols. folio, 1654, have been long in considerable estimation. They contain many valuable elucidations of the sacred text.

Mr. *J. Caryl's* exposition of the book of Job, in two immense vols. folio, 1676, another by *Albert Schultens*, and a third by *Chapelowe*, on the same book, contain a vast deal of important matter, delivered in general by the two latter in the dullest and most uninteresting form.

Mr. MATTHEW POOLE, a non-conformist divine, has published a commentary on the Scriptures, in 2 vols. folio. The notes, which are mingled with the text, are short, but abound with good sense and sound judgment. He died in Holland, in 1679.

Dr. JOHN LIGHTFOOT was a profound scholar, a sound divine, and a pious man. He brought all his immense learning to bear on the sacred volumes, and diffused light wherever he went. His historical, chronological, and topographical remarks on the Old Testament, and his *Talmudical Exercitations* on the New, are invaluable. His works were published in *two* large vols. folio, 1684. He died in 1675. A new edition of these invaluable works, with many *additions* and *corrections*, has been published by the Rev. *J. R. Pitman*, A. M., in 13 vols. 8vo., London, 1825.

On the plan of Dr. Lightfoot's HORÆ HEBRAICÆ, or *Talmudical Exercitations*, a work was undertaken by *Christian Schoettgenius* with the title *Horæ Hebraicæ et Talmudicæ in universum Novum Testamentum, quibus Horæ Jo. Lightfooti in Libris historicis supplentur, Epistolæ et Apocalypsis eodem modo illustrantur, &c.* Dresdæ, 1733, 2 vols. 4to. This is a learned and useful work, and *supplies* and *completes* the work of Dr. Lightfoot. The Horæ Hebraicæ of *Lightfoot* extend no farther than the first Epistle to the Corinthians; the work of *Schoettgen* passes over the same ground as a *Supplement*, without touching the things already produced in the English work; and then *continues* the work on the same plan to the end of the New Testament. It is both *scarce* and *dear*.

Mr. RICHARD BAXTER published the New Testament with notes, 8vo., 1695. The notes are interspersed with the text, and are very short, but they contain much sound sense and piety. A good edition of this work was published in the same form by Mr. R. Edwards, London, 1810.

Dr. SIMON PATRICK, bishop of Ely, began a comment on the Old Testament, which was

finished by Dr. *Lowth;* to which the New Testament, by Dr. *Whitby*, is generally added to complete the work. Dr. Whitby's work was first published in 1703, and often since, with many emendations. This is a valuable collection, and is comprised in six vols. folio. *Patrick* and *Lowth* are always judicious and solid, and *Whitby* is learned, argumentative, and thoroughly *orthodox.*

The best comment on the New Testament, taken in all points of view, is certainly that of *Whitby*. He is said to have embraced Socinianism previously to his death, which took place in 1726.

Mr. ANTHONY PURVER, one of the people called Quakers, translated the whole Bible into English, illustrated with critical notes, which was published at the expense of Dr. J. Fothergill, in 1764, two vols. folio. This work has never been highly valued; and is much less literal and simple than the habits of the man, and those of the religious community to which he belonged, might authorize one to expect.

The Rev. WILLIAM BURKITT, rector of Dedham, in Essex, has written a very useful commentary on the New Testament, which has often been republished. It is both pious and practical, but not distinguished either by depth of learning or judgment. The pious author died in 1703.

The Rev. MATTHEW HENRY, a very eminent dissenting minister, is author of a very extensive commentary on the Old and New Testaments, five vols. folio, and one of the most popular works of the kind ever published. It is always orthodox, generally judicious, and truly pious and practical, and has contributed much to diffuse the knowledge of the Scriptures among the common people, for whose sakes it was chiefly written. A new edition of this work, by the Rev. *J. Hughes*, of Battersea, and the Rev. *G. Burder*, of London, corrected from innumerable errors which have been accumulating with every edition, has been lately published.

As I apply the term *orthodox* to persons who differ considerably in their religious creed on certain points, I judge it necessary once for all to explain my meaning. He who holds the doctrine of the fall of man, and through it the universal corruption of human nature; the Godhead of our blessed Redeemer; the atonement made by his obedience unto death; justification through faith alone in his blood; the inspiration of the Holy Spirit, regenerating and renewing the heart, is generally reputed *orthodox*, whether in other parts of his creed he be Arminian or Calvinist. WHITBY and HENRY held and defended all these doctrines in their respective comments, therefore I scruple not to say that both were *orthodox*. With their opinions in any of their other works I have no concern.

Dr. JOHN GILL, an eminent divine of the Baptist persuasion, is author of a very diffuse com mentary on the Old and New Testaments, in nine vols. folio. He was a very learned and good man, but has often lost sight of his better judgment in spiritualizing his text.

Dr. PHILIP DODDRIDGE's Family Expositor, 4to., 1745, often republished, is (with the exception of his *paraphrase*) a very judicious work. It has been long highly esteemed, and is worthy of all the credit it has among religious people.

Paraphrases, which mix up men's words with those of God, his Christ, his Holy Spirit, and his apostles, are in my opinion dangerous works. Through such, many of the common people are led into a *loose* method of quoting the sacred text. I consider the practice, except in very select cases, as highly unbecoming. The republic of letters would suffer no loss if every work of this kind on the Holy Scriptures were abolished. Dr. Whitby, by the insertion of mere *words* in brackets and in another character, has done all that should be done, and vastly outdone the work of Dr. Doddridge.

To Dr. Z. PEARCE, bishop of Rochester, we are indebted for an invaluable commentary and notes on the Four Gospels, the Acts, and the First Epistle to the Corinthians, two vols. 4to., 1777 The deep learning and judgment displayed in these notes are really beyond all praise.

Dr. CAMPBELL's work on the Evangelists is well known, and universally prized. So is also Dr. MACKNIGHT's translation of the Epistles, with notes. Both these works, especially the former, abound in sound judgment, deep erudition, and a strong vein of correct critical acumen.

Mr. LOCKE and Dr. BENSON are well known in the republic of letters; their respective works on different parts of the New Testament abound with judgment and learning.

The Rev. J. WESLEY published a selection of notes on the Old and New Testaments, in four vols. 4to., Bristol, 1765. The notes on the Old Testament are allowed, on all hands, to be meagre and unsatisfactory; this is owing to a circumstance with which few are acquainted. Mr. Pine, the printer, having set up and printed off several sheets in a type much larger than was intended, it was found impossible to get the work within the prescribed limits of *four volumes*, without retrenching the notes, or cancelling what was already printed. The former measure was unfortunately adopted, and the work fell far short of the expectation of the public. This account I had from the excellent author himself. The notes on the New Testament, which have gone through several editions, are of a widely different description; though short, they are always judicious, accurate, spiritual, terse, and impressive; and possess

the happy and rare property of leading the reader immediately to God and his own heart. A new edition of this work, with considerable additions, has been lately published by the Rev. *Joseph Benson*, from whose learning, piety, and theological knowledge, much has been reasonably expected. The work has been very useful, and has been widely dispersed.

The late unfortunate Dr. WILLIAM DODD published a commentary on the Old and New Testaments, in three vols. folio, London, 1770. Much of it is taken from the comment of *Father Calmet*, already described; but he has enriched his work by many valuable notes which he extracted from the inedited papers of Lord Clarendon, Dr. Waterland, and Mr. Locke. He has also borrowed many important notes from Father Houbigant. This work, as giving in general the true sense of the Scriptures, is by far the best comment that has yet appeared in the *English* language. The late lamented Dr. Gosset, of famous bibliographical memory, told me that he "had furnished Dr. Dodd with the MS. collections of Dr. Waterland and others; that Dr. Dodd was employed by the London booksellers to edit this work; and it was by far the best of these works which might be said to be *published by the yard*."

A work, entitled *An Illustration of the Sacred Writings*, was published by Mr. *Goadby*, at Sherbourne: it contains many judicious notes, has gone through several editions, and, while it *seems* to be orthodox, is written entirely on the *Arian* hypothesis.

The Rev. THOMAS COKE, LL.D. has lately published a commentary on the Old and New Testaments, in six vols. 4to. This is, in the main, a reprint of the work of Dr. Dodd, with several retrenchments, and some additional reflections. Though the major part of the *notes*, and even the *dissertations* of Dr. Dodd are here republished; yet all the marginal readings and parallel texts are entirely omitted. The absence of these would be inexcusable in any Bible beyond the size of a *duodecimo*. Of their importance see pp. 19 and 20 of this preface. Dr. Coke's edition is in general well printed, has some good maps, and has had a very extensive sale. The original work of Dodd was both scarce and dear, and therefore a new edition became necessary; and had the whole of the original work, with the marginal readings, parallel texts, &c., been preserved, Dr. Coke's publication would have been much more useful. Dr. Coke should have acknowledged whence he collected his materials, but on this point he is totally silent.

The Rev. T. SCOTT, rector of Aston Sandford, has published a commentary on the Old and New Testaments, in five vols. 4to. The author's aim seems to be, *to speak plain truth to plain men;* and for this purpose he has interspersed a multitude of practical observations all through the text, which cannot fail, from the spirit of sound piety which they breathe, of being very useful.

The late Dr. *Priestley* compiled a body of notes on the Old and New Testaments, in 3 vols. 8vo., published at Northumberland in America, 1804. Though the doctor keeps his own creed (Unitarianism) continually in view, especially when considering those texts which other religious people adduce in favour of theirs, yet his work contains many valuable notes and observations, especially on the philosophy, natural history, geography, and chronology of the Scriptures; and to these subjects few men in Europe were better qualified to do justice.

A new translation of Job, and one of the books of Canticles, has been published by Dr. *Mason Good*, both replete with learned notes of no ordinary merit.

In closing this part of the list, it would be unpardonable to omit a class of eminently learned men, who, by their labours on select parts of the Scriptures, have rendered the highest services both to religion and literature.

Samuel Bochart, pastor of the Protestant Church at Caen in Normandy, wrote a very learned and accurate work on the geography of the sacred writings, entitled *Phaleg* and *Canaan*, and another on the Natural History of the Bible, entitled *Hierozoicon*, by both of which, as well as by several valuable dissertations in his works, much light is thrown on many obscure places in the sacred writings. The best collection of his works is supposed to be that by Leusden and *Villemandy*, three vols. folio. L. Bat. 1712.

Dr. *I. James Scheuchzer*, professor of medicine and the mathematics in the university of Zurich, is author of a very elaborate work on the Natural History of the Bible, entitled *Physica Sacra*, which has been printed in *Latin*, *German*, and *French*, and forms a regular comment on all the books of the Bible where any subject of natural history occurs.

The very learned author has availed himself of all the researches of his predecessors on the same subject, and has illustrated his work with 750 engravings of the different subjects in the animal, vegetable, and mineral kingdoms, to which there is any reference in the Scriptures. The German edition was published in 1731, in 15 vols. folio, the Latin edition in 1731, and the French in 1732, 8 vols. folio, often bound in 4. The work is as rare as it is useful and elegant.

The late Rev. Mr. *Thomas Harmer* published a very useful work, entitled "Observations on various Passages of Scripture," in which he has cast much light on many difficult texts that relate to the customs and manners, religious and civil, of the Asiatic nations, by quotations from the works of ancient and modern travellers into different parts of the East, who have described

those customs, &c., as still subsisting. The best edition of this work was published in four vols. 8vo., 1808, with many additions and corrections by the author of the present commentary.

Campegius Vitringa wrote a learned and most excellent comment on the book of the Prophet Isaiah, in 2 vols. folio; the best edition of which was printed in 1724. He died in 1722.

Dr. R. Lowth, bishop of London, is the author of an excellent work, entitled, Isaiah: *A New Translation, with a preliminary Dissertation, and Notes critical, philological, and explanatory*. 4to., Lond. 1779, first edition. The preliminary dissertation contains a fund of rare and judicious criticism. The translation, formed by the assistance of the ancient versions collated with the best MSS. of the Hebrew text, is clear, simple, and yet dignified. The concluding notes, which show a profound knowledge of Hebrew criticism, are always judicious, and generally useful.

The late Archbishop of Armagh, Dr. Newcome, has published a translation of the minor prophets, with learned notes: it is a good work, but creeps slowly after its great predecessor. He has also published a translation of the New Testament, with notes, not much esteemed.

On the same plan the Rev. Dr. Blayney translated and published the Prophet Jeremiah, with notes, 1784.

John Albert Bengel is author of an edition of the New Testament, with *various readings*, and such a judicious division of it into paragraphs as has never been equalled, and perhaps never can be excelled. He wrote a very learned comment on the *Apocalypse*, and short notes on the New Testament, which he entitled *Gnomon Novi Testamenti, in quo ex nativa verborum vi, simplicitas profunditas, concinnitas, salubritas sensuum Cœlestium indicatur.* In him were united two rare qualifications—the deepest piety and the most extensive learning.

A commentary on the same plan, and with precisely the *same title*, was published by *Phil. David Burkius*, on the twelve minor prophets, 4to., Heilbronnæ, 1753, which was followed by his *Gnomon Psalmorum*, 2 vols. 4to., Stutgardiæ, 1760. These are in many respects valuable works, written in a pure strain of piety, but rather too much in a technical form. They are seldom to be met with in this country, and are generally high priced.

The late pious bishop of Norwich, *Dr. Horne*, published the book of Psalms with notes, which breathe a spirit of the purest and most exalted piety.

Herman Venema is known only to me by a comment on Malachi, some dissertations on sacred subjects, an ecclesiastical history, correct editions of some of Vitringa's Theological Tracts, and a most excellent and extensive *Commentary on the Psalms*, in 6 vols. 4to., printed Leovardiæ, 1762-7. Through its great scarcity the work is little known in Great Britain. What was said by David of Goliah's sword has been said of Venema's commentary on the Book of Psalms, "There is none like it."

Ern. Frid. Car. Rosenmülleri, Ling. Arab. in Acad. Lips. Professoris, &c., Scholia *in* Vetus *Testamentum*. Edit. secunda emendatior, Lips. 1795-1812, 11 vols. 8vo. Scholia in *Novum* Testamentum. Edit. quinta auctior et emendatior, 1801-1808, 5 vols. 8vo., Nuremberg. This is a very learned and useful work, but rather too diffuse for Scholia. In the Scholia on the Old Testament Rosenmüller has not meddled with the historical books.

Class IV.—Compilations and Collections.

On the fourth Class, containing compilations and *critical collections*, a few words must suffice. Among the compilations may be ranked what are termed *Catenæ* of the Greek and Latin Fathers; these consist of a connected series of different writers on the same text. The work of *Galafridus*, or *Walafridus Strabus*, already described, is of this kind; it contains a Catena or connected series of the expositions of all the Fathers and Doctors prior to his time. A very valuable *Catena* on the Octateuch, containing the comments of about fifty Greek Fathers, has been published at Leipsig, 1792, in 2 vols. folio; it is all in Greek, and therefore of no use to common readers. The work of *Venerable Bede*, already noticed, is professedly of the same kind.

Father *De la Haye*, in what was called the *Biblia Magna*, 1643, 5 vols. folio, and afterwards *Biblia Maxima*, 1660, 19 vols. folio, besides a vast number of critical Dissertations, Prefaces, &c., inserted the whole notes of *Nicholas de Lyra*, *Menochius*, *Gagneus*, *Estius*, and the Jesuit *Tirin*.

Several *minor* compilations of this nature have been made by needy writers, who, wishing to get a little money, have without scruple or ceremony borrowed from those whose reputation was well established with the public; and by taking a little from one, and a little from another, pretended to give the *marrow* of all. These pretensions have been rarely justified: it often requires the genius of a voluminous original writer to make a faithful abridgment of his work; but in most of *these* compilations the love of money is much more evident than the capacity to do justice to the original author, or the ability to instruct and profit mankind. To what a vast number of these minor compilations has the excellent work of Mr. Matthew Henry given

birth! every one of which, while professing to lop off his *redundancies*, and supply his *deficiencies*, falls, by a semi-diameter of the immense orb of literature and religion, short of the eminence of the author himself.

The most important *collection* of Biblical critics ever made was that formed under the direction of *Bishop Pearson*, *John Pearson*, *Anthony Scattergood*, and *Francis Gouldman*, printed by *Cornelius Bee*, London, 1660, in 9 vols. folio, under the title of Critici Sacri, intended as a companion for the Polyglot Bible, published by Bishop Walton, in 1657. This great work was republished at Amsterdam, with additions, in 12 vols. folio, in 1698. Two volumes called *Thesaurus Dissertationum Elegantiorum, &c.*, were printed as a supplement to this work, at Amsterdam, in 1701-2. Of this supplement it may be said, it is of less consequence and utility than is generally supposed, as the substance of several treatises in it is to be found in the preceding volumes. The work contains a vast variety of valuable materials for critics, chronologists, &c.

The principal critics on the Old Testament, contained in the foreign edition of this great collection, which is by far the most complete, are the following: Sebastian Munster, Paul Fagius, Francis Vatablus, Claudius Badwellus, Sebastian Castalio, Isidore Clarius, Lucas Brugensis, Andrew Masius, John Drusius, Sextinus Amama, Simeon de Muis, Philip Codurcus, Rodolph Baynus, Francis Forrerius, Edward Lively, David Hœschelius, Hugo Grotius, Christopher Cartwright, Cornelius a Lapide, and John Pricæus.

Besides the above, who are regular commentators on the Old Testament, there are various important *Dissertations* and *Tracts*, on the principal subjects in the law and prophets, by the following critics: Joseph Scaliger, Lewis Capellus, Martin Helvicus, Alberic Gentilis, Moses bar Cepha, Christopher Helvicus, John Buteo, Matthew Hostus, Francis Moncæius, Peter Pithœus, George Rittershusius, Michael Rothardus, Leo Allatius, Gaspar Varrerius, William Schickardus, Augustin Justinianus, Bened. Arias Montanus, Bon. Corn. Bertramus, Peter Cunæus, Caspar Waser, and Edward Brerewood.

On the New Testament the following commentators are included: Sebastian Munster, Laurentius Valla, *James Revius*, *Desiderius Erasmus*, Francis Vatablus, Sebastian Castalio, Isidore Clarius, Andrew Masius, *Nicolas Zegerus*, Lucas Brugensis, *Henry Stephens*, John Drusius, Joseph Scaliger, *Isaac Casaubon*, *John Camero*, *James Capellus*, Lewis Capellus, *Otho Gualtperius*, *Abraham Schultetus*, Hugo Grotius, and John Pricæus.

Dissertations on the most important subjects in the New Testament inserted here were written by Lewis Capellus, *Nicolas Faber*, William Klebitius, *Marquard Freherus*, *Archbishop Usher*, Matthew Hostus, *I. A. Van-der-Linden*, *Claudius Salmasius* under the feigned name of *Johannes Simplicius*, *James Gothofridus*, Philip Codurcus, Abraham Schultetus, *William Ader*, John Drusius, *Jac. Lopez Stunica*, Desider. Erasmus, *Angelus Caninius*, Peter Pithœus, *Nicephorus*, patriarch of Constantinople, *Adriani* Isagoge cum notis Dav. Hœschelii, B. C. Bertram, *Anton. Nebrissensis*, *Nicholas Fuller*, *Samuel Petit*, *John Gregory*, Christ. Cartwright, *John Cloppenburg*, and *Pet. Dan. Huet*. Those marked in *italics* are not included in the critics on the Old Testament. The *Thesaurus Dissertationum Exegeticarum*, published as a supplement to this work by *Theod. Hasæus* and *Conrad Ikenius*, in 2 vols. folio, contains upwards of *one hundred and fifty* additional writers. Such a constellation of learned men can scarcely be equalled in any age or country.

Mr. *Matthew Poole*, whose *English* comment has been already noticed, conceiving that the Critici Sacri might be made more useful by being methodized, with immense labour formed the work well known among divines by the title of *Synopsis Criticorum*, a general view of the critics, viz., those in the nine volumes of the *Critici Sacri* mentioned above. The printing of this work began in 1669, and was finished in 1674, 5 vols. folio. Here the critics no longer occupy *distinct* places as they do in the *Critici Sacri*, but are all consolidated, one general comment being made out of the whole, the names of the writers being referred to by their initials in the margin. To the critics above named Mr. Poole has added several others of equal note, and he refers also to the most important *versions*, both ancient and modern. The learned author spent ten years in compiling this work. In point of size, the work of Mr. Poole has many advantages over the Critici Sacri; but no man who is acquainted with both works will ever prefer the synopsis to the original.

Perhaps no city in the world can boast of having produced, in so short a period, so many important works on the sacred writings as the city of London; works which, for difficulty, utility, critical and typographical correctness, and expense, have never been excelled. These are, 1. The *Polyglot*, 6 vols. folio; begun in 1653, and finished in 1657. 2. The *Critici Sacri*, in 9 vols. folio, 1660. 3. *Castell's Heptaglot* Lexicon, compiled for the Polyglot Bible, 2 vols. folio, 1669. 4. The *Synopsis Criticorum*, 5 vols. folio; begun in 1669, and finished in 1674. These works, printed in *Hebrew*, *Chaldee*, *Samaritan*, *Syriac*, *Arabic*, *Æthiopic*, *Persian*, *Greek*, and *Latin*, forming 22 vast vols. folio, were begun and finished in this city by the *industry* and at the *expense* of a few English divines and noblemen, in the comparatively short compass of

about twenty years! To complete its eminence in *Biblical literature*, and to place itself at the head of all the cities in the universe, *London* has only to add a *new* and *improved* edition of its own POLYGLOT, with the additional *versions* which have come to light since the publication of the original work.

To the above list might be added those who have illustrated the sacred writings by passages drawn from Josephus and the Greek and Roman classics, among which the following are worthy of particular regard: *Jo. Tobiæ* KREBSII Observationes in Nov. Testam. *è Flav.* JOSEPHO, 8vo., Lips. 1754. *Geo. Dav.* KYPKE Observationes in Novi Fœderis Libros, ex *auctoribus*, potissimum *Græcis*, &c., 2 vols. 8vo., Vratislaviæ, 1755. *Georgii* RAPHELII Annotationes in *Sacram Scripturam, &c.*, Lugd. 1747, 2 vols. 8vo. *Krebs* throws much light on different facts and forms of speech in the New Testament by his quotations from Josephus. *Kypke* does the same by an appeal to the Greek writers in general. And *Raphelius* gives historical elucidations of the Old, and philological observations on the New Testament, drawn particularly from *Xenophon, Polybius, Arrian*, and *Herodotus*.

To these might be added several excellent names who have rendered considerable services to sacred literature and criticism by their learned labours: Sir *Norton Knatchbull's* Observations, *Hallett's* Critical Notes, *Bowyer's* Conjectures, *Leigh's* Annotations, &c., &c.; to whom may be added those who have illustrated innumerable passages, obscure and difficult, in lexicons and dictionaries for the Hebrew Bible and Greek Testament: *Buxtorf, Cocceius, Mintert, Pasor, Schoettgenius, Stockius, Krebs, Calmet, Leusden, Robinson, Michaelis*, Edward *Leigh, Schulz*, Dr. *Taylor, Schleusner*, and *Parkhurst*, a particular account of whom would far exceed the limits of this preface; but *Schleusner*, as a lexicographer for the New Testament, is far beyond my praise.

I have already apprized the reader that I did not design to give a *history of commentators*, but only a *short sketch;* this I have done, and am fully aware that different readers will form different opinions of its execution; some will think that writers of comparatively little eminence are inserted, while several of acknowledged worth are omitted. This may be very true; but the judicious reader will recollect that it is a sketch and not a complete history that is here presented to his view, and that the *important* and *non-important* are terms which different persons will apply in opposite senses, as they may be prejudiced in favour of different writers. I have given my opinion, as every honest man should, with perfect deference to the judgment of others, and shall be offended with no man for differing from me in any of the opinions I have expressed on any of the preceding authors or their works. I could easily swell this list with many *foreign* critics, but as far as I know them I do not in general like them; besides, they are not within the reach of common readers, though many of them stand, no doubt, deservedly high in the judgment of learned men.

Having said thus much on *commentaries* in general, it may be necessary to give some account of that now offered to the public, the grounds on which it has been undertaken, and the manner in which it has been compiled.

At an early age I took for my motto Prov. xviii. 1: *Through desire a man, having separated himself, seeketh and intermeddleth with all wisdom.* Being convinced that the Bible was the source whence all the principles of *true wisdom*, wherever found in the world, had been derived, my *desire* to comprehend adequately its great design, and to penetrate the meaning of all its parts, led me to *separate myself* from every pursuit that did not lead, at least indirectly, to the accomplishment of this end; and while *seeking and intermeddling with* different branches of human knowledge, as my limited means would permit, I put each study under contribution to the object of my pursuit, endeavouring to make every thing subservient to the information of my own mind, that, as far as Divine Providence might think proper to employ me, I might be the better qualified to instruct others. At first I read and studied, scarcely committing any thing to paper, having my own edification alone in view, as I could not then hope that any thing I wrote could be of sufficient importance to engage the attention or promote the welfare of the public. But as I proceeded I thought it best to note down the result of my studies, especially as far as they related to the *Septuagint*, which about the year 1785 I began to read regularly, in order to acquaint myself more fully with the phraseology of the New Testament, as I found that this truly venerable version was that to which the evangelists and apostles appear to have had constant recourse, and from which in general they make their quotations. The study of this version served more to illuminate and expand my mind than all the theological works I had ever consulted. I had proceeded but a short way in it before I was convinced that the prejudices against it were utterly unfounded, and that it was of incalculable advantage toward a proper understanding of the literal sense of Scripture, and am astonished that the study of it should be so generally neglected. About nine years after this, my health having been greatly impaired by the severity of my labours, and fearing that I should soon be obliged to relinquish my public employment, I formed the purpose of writing short notes on the New Testament, collating the common printed text with all the versions and collections from MSS. to which I could have

access. Scarcely had I projected this work when I was convinced that another was *previously* necessary, viz., a careful perusal of the *original text*. I began this work, and soon found that it was perfectly possible to *read* and not understand. Under this conviction I sat down determining to *translate* the whole before I attempted any comment, that I might have the sacred text the more deeply impressed on my memory.

I accordingly began my translation, collating the *original text* with all the *ancient* and with several of the *modern versions*, carefully weighing the value of the most important *various readings* found in those versions, as well as those which I was able to collect from the most authentic copies of the Greek text. A worse state of health ensuing, I was obliged to remit almost all application to study, and the work was thrown aside for nearly two years. Having returned to it when a state of comparative convalescence took place, I found I had not gone through the whole of my *preliminary* work. The New Testament I plainly saw was a *comment* on the Old; and to understand *such* a comment, I knew it was absolutely necessary to be well acquainted with the original *text*. I then formed the plan of reading consecutively a portion of the Hebrew Bible daily. Accordingly I began to read the Old Testament, noting down on the different books, chapters, and verses, such things as appeared to me of most importance, intending the work as an *outline* for one on a more extensive scale, should it please God to spare my life and give me health and leisure to complete it. In this preliminary work I spent a little more than *one year* and *two months*, in which time I translated every sentence, Hebrew and Chaldee, in the Old Testament. In such a work it would be absurd to pretend that I had not met with many difficulties. I was attempting to illustrate the most ancient and most learned book in the universe, replete with allusions to arts that are lost, to nations that are extinct, to customs that are no longer observed, and abounding in modes of speech and turns of phraseology which can only be traced out through the medium of the cognate Asiatic languages. On these accounts I was often much perplexed, but I could not proceed till I had done the utmost in my power to make every thing plain. The frequent occurrence of such difficulties led me closely to examine and compare all the original texts, versions, and translations, as they stand in the London Polyglot, with some others not inserted in that work; and from these, especially the Samaritan, Chaldee Targums, Septuagint, and Vulgate, I derived the most assistance, though all the rest contributed their quota in cases of difficulty.

Almost as soon as this work was finished I began my comment on the four gospels, and notwithstanding the preparations already made, and my indefatigable application early and late to the work, I did not reach the end of the fourth Evangelist till eighteen months after its commencement. Previously to this I had purposed to commit what I had already done to the press; but when I had all my arrangements made, a specimen actually set up and printed, and advertisements circulated, a sudden rise in the price of paper, which I fondly hoped would not be of long continuance, prevented my proceeding. When this hope vanished, another work on the Scriptures by a friend was extensively announced. As I could not bear the thought of even the most distant appearance of opposition to any man, I gave place, being determined not to attempt to divide the attention of the public mind, nor hinder the general spread of a work which for aught I knew might supersede the necessity of mine. That work has been for some time completed, and the numerous subscribers supplied with their copies. My plan however is untouched; and still finding from the call of many judicious friends, and especially of my brethren in the ministry, who have long been acquainted with my undertaking and its progress, that the religious public would gladly receive a work on the plan which I had previously announced, I have, after much hesitation, made up my mind; and, in the name of God, with a simple desire to add my mite to the treasury, having recommenced the revisal and improvement of my papers, I now present them to the public. I am glad that Divine Providence has so ordered it that the publication has been hitherto delayed, as the years which have elapsed since my first intention of printing have afforded me a more ample opportunity to reconsider and correct what I had before done, and to make many improvements.

Should I be questioned as to my specific object in bringing this work before the religious world at a time when works of a similar nature abound, I would simply answer, I wish to do a little good also, and contribute *my* quota to enable men the better to understand the records of their salvation. That I am in hostility to no work of this kind, the preceding pages will prove; and I have deferred my own as long as in prudence I can. My tide is turned; life is fast ebbing out; and what I do in this way I must do *now*, or relinquish the design for ever. This I would most gladly do, but I have been too long and too deeply pledged to the public to permit me to indulge my own feelings in this respect. Others are doing much to elucidate the Scriptures; I wish them all God's speed. I also will show my opinion of these Divine records, and do a little in the same way. I wish to assist my fellow labourers in the vineyard to lead men to HIM who is the fountain of all excellence, goodness, truth, and happiness; to magnify his law and make it honourable; to show the wonderful provision made in his GOSPEL for the recovery and salvation of a sinful world; to prove that GOD's great design is to make his creatures happy; and that

such a salvation as it becomes God to give, and such as man needs to receive, is *within the grasp of every human soul.*

He who carefully and conscientiously receives the truths of Divine revelation, not merely as a *creed*, but in reference to his *practice*, cannot fail of being an ornament to civil and religious society. It is my endeavour therefore to set these truths fairly and fully before the eyes of those who may be inclined to consult my work. I do not say that the principles contained in *my creed*, and which I certainly have not studied to conceal, are *all* essentially necessary to every man's salvation; and I should be sorry to unchristianize any person who may think he has Scriptural evidence for a faith in several respects different from mine. I am sure that all sincere Christians are agreed on what are called the essential truths of Divine revelation; and I feel no reluctance to acknowledge that men eminent for wisdom, learning, piety, and usefulness, have differed among themselves and from me in many points which I deem of great importance. While God bears with and does us good, we may readily bear with each other. The hostility of others I pass by. The angry and malevolent are their own tormentors. I remember the old adage: "Let *envy* alone, and it will punish itself."

Of the COPY of the sacred text used for this work it may be necessary to say a few words. It is stated in the title that the text "is taken from the most correct copies of the present authorized version." As several use this term who do not know its meaning, for their sakes I shall explain it. A resolution was formed, in consequence of a request made by Dr. Reynolds, head of the *nonconformist* party, to King James I., in the *conference* held at *Hampton Court*, 1603, that a new translation, or rather a revision of what was called the *Bishops' Bible*, printed in 1568, should be made. *Fifty-four* translators, divided into *six* classes, were appointed for the accomplishment of this important work. *Seven* of these appear to have died before the work commenced, as only *forty-seven* are found in Fuller's list. The *names* of the *persons*, the *places* where employed, and the proportion of *work* allotted to each class, and the *rules* laid down by King James for their direction, I give chiefly from Mr. Fuller's Church History, Book x., p. 44, &c.

Before I insert this account, it may be necessary to state Dr. Reynolds's request in the Hampton Court conference, and King James's answer.

Dr. *Reynolds*. "May your Majesty be pleased that the Bible be new translated, such as are extant not answering the original?" [*Here he gave a few examples.*]

Bishop of *London*. "If every man's humour might be followed, there would be no end of translating."

The *King*. "I profess I could never yet see a Bible well translated in English; but I think that of all, that of *Geneva* is the worst. I wish some special pains were taken for a uniform translation, which should be done by the best learned in both universities, then reviewed by the bishops, presented to the *privy council*, lastly ratified by royal authority, to be read in the whole Church, and no other."

The bishop of London in this, as in every other case, opposed Dr. Reynolds, till he saw that the project pleased the king, and that he appeared determined to have it executed. In consequence of this resolution, the following learned and judicious men were chosen for the execution of the work.

WESTMINSTER.—10.

THE PENTATEUCH: THE STORY FROM JOSHUA TO THE FIRST BOOK OF THE CHRONICLES EXCLUSIVELY.

Dr. ANDREWS, Fellow and Master of Pembroke Hall in Cambridge; then Dean of Westminster, afterwards Bishop of Winchester.
Dr. OVERALL, Fellow of Trinity Coll., Master of Kath. Hall, in Cambridge; then Dean of St. Paul's, afterwards Bishop of Norwich.
Dr. SARAVIA.
Dr. CLARKE, Fellow of Christ Coll. in Cambridge, Preacher in Canterbury.
Dr. LAIFIELD, Fellow of Trin. in Cambridge, Parson of St. Clement Danes. Being skilled in architecture, his judgment was much relied on for the fabric of the Tabernacle and Temple.
Dr. LEIGH, Archdeacon of Middlesex, Parson of All-hallows, Barking.
Master BURGLEY.
Mr. KING.
Mr. THOMPSON.
Mr. BEDWELL, of Cambridge, and (I think) of St. John's, Vicar of Tottenham, near London.

CAMBRIDGE.—8.

FROM THE FIRST OF THE CHRONICLES, WITH THE REST OF THE STORY, AND THE HAGIOGRAPHA, VIZ., JOB, PSALMS, PROVERBS, CANTICLES, ECCLESIASTES.

Master EDWARD LIVELY.
Mr. RICHARDSON, Fellow of Emman., afterwards D. D., Master, first of Peter-house, then of Trin. College.
Mr. CHADERTON, afterwards D. D., Fellow first of Christ Coll., then Master of Emmanuel.
Mr. DILLINGHAM, Fellow of Christ Coll., beneficed at ——— in Bedfordshire, where he died a single and a wealthy man.
Mr. ANDREWS, afterwards D. D., brother to the Bishop of Winchester, and Master of Jesus Coll.
Mr. HARRISON, the Rev. Vice-master of Trinity Coll.
Mr. SPALDING, Fellow of St. John's in Cambridge, and Hebrew Professor therein.
Mr. BING, Fellow of Peter-house, in Cambridge, and Hebrew Professor therein.

OXFORD.—7.

THE FOUR GREATER PROPHETS, WITH THE LAMENTATIONS, AND THE TWELVE LESSER PROPHETS.

Dr. HARDING, President of Magdalen Coll.
Dr. REYNOLDS, President of Corpus Christi Coll.
Dr. HOLLAND, Rector of Exeter Coll. and King's Professor.
Dr. KILBY, Rector of Lincoln Coll. and Regius Professor.
Master SMITH, afterwards D. D., and Bishop of Gloucester. He made the learned and religious Preface to the Translation.
Mr. BRETT, of a worshipful family, beneficed at Quainton, in Buckinghamshire.
Mr. FAIRCLOWE.

CAMBRIDGE.—7.

THE PRAYER OF MANASSEH, AND THE REST OF THE APOCRYPHA.

Dr. DUPORT, Prebend of Ely, and Master of Jesus Coll.
Dr. BRAINTHWAIT, first Fellow of Emmanuel, then Master of Gonvil and Caius Coll.
Dr. RADCLYFFE, one of the Senior Fellows of Trin. Coll.
Master WARD, Emman., afterwards D. D., Master of Sidney Coll. and Margaret Professor
Mr. DOWNS, Fellow of St. John's Coll. and Greek Professor.
Mr. BOYCE, Fellow of St. John's Coll., Prebend of Ely, Parson of Boxworth in Cambridgeshire.
Mr. WARD, Regal, afterwards D. D., Prebend of Chichester, Rector of Bishop-Waltham, in Hampshire.

OXFORD.—8.

THE FOUR GOSPELS, ACTS OF THE APOSTLES, APOCALYPSE.

Dr. RAVIS, Dean of Christ Church, afterwards Bishop of London.
Dr. ABBOTT, Master of University Coll., afterwards Archbishop of Canterbury.
Dr. EEDES.
Mr. THOMSON.
Mr. SAVILL.
Dr. PERYN.
Dr. RAVENS.
Mr. HARMER.

WESTMINSTER.—7.

THE EPISTLES OF ST. PAUL, AND THE CANONICAL EPISTLES.

Dr. BARLOWE, of Trinity Hall, in Cambridge, Dean of Chester, afterwards Bishop of Lincoln.
Dr. HUTCHENSON.
Dr. SPENCER.
Mr. FENTON.
Mr. RABBET.
Mr. SANDERSON.
Mr. DAKINS.

"Now, for the better ordering of their proceedings, his Majesty recommended the following rules, by them to be most carefully observed.

1. The ordinary Bible read in the Church, commonly called the *Bishops' Bible*, to be followed, and as little altered as the original will permit.
2. The names of the prophets, and the holy writers, with their other names in the text, to be retained, as near as may be, according as they are vulgarly used.
3. The old ecclesiastical words to be kept, viz., the word *Church* not to be translated *Congregation, &c.*
4. When any word hath divers significations, that to be kept which hath been most commonly used by the most eminent fathers, being agreeable to the propriety of the place, and the analogy of faith.
5. The division of the chapters to be altered either not at all, or as little as may be, if necessity so require.
6. No marginal notes at all to be affixed, but only for the explanation of the Hebrew or Greek words, which cannot, without some circumlocution, so briefly and fitly be expressed in the text.
7. Such quotations of places to be marginally set down, as shall serve for the fit reference of one scripture to another.
8. Every particular man of each company to take the same chapter, or chapters; and having translated or amended them severally by himself, where he thinks good, all to meet together, confer what they have done, and agree for their part what shall stand.
9. As any one company hath despatched any one book in this manner, they shall send it to the rest, to be considered of seriously and judiciously; for his Majesty is very careful in this point.
10. If any company, upon the review of the book so sent, shall doubt or differ upon any places, to send them word thereof, note the places, and therewithal send their reasons; to which, if they consent not, the difference to be compounded at the general meeting, which is to be of the chief persons of each company, at the end of the work.
11. When any place of special obscurity is doubted of, letters to be directed by authority, to send to any learned in the land, for his judgment in such a place.
12. Letters to be sent from every bishop to the rest of his clergy, admonishing them of this translation in hand; and to move and charge as many as, being skilful in the tongues, have taken pains in that kind, to send his particular observations to the company, either at *Westminster, Cambridge*, or *Oxford.*
13. The directors in each company to be the Deans of *Westminster* and *Chester* for that place; and the King's Professors in Hebrew and Greek in each university.
14. These translations to be used, when they agree better with the text than the Bishops' Bible, viz., { TINDAL'S, MATTHEWS', COVERDALE'S, WHITCHURCH, GENEVA.

"Besides the said directions before-mentioned, three or four of the most ancient and grave divines in either of the universities, not employed in translating, to be assigned by the vice-chancellor, upon conference with the rest of the heads, to be overseers of the translations, as well Hebrew as Greek, for the better observation of the *fourth* rule above specified.

"And now after long expectation and great desire," says Mr. Fuller, "came forth the new translation of the Bible (most beautifully printed) by a *select* and *competent* number of *divines* appointed for that purpose; not being too many, lest one should trouble another; and yet many, lest many things might haply escape them. Who neither coveting praise for expedition, nor fearing reproach for slackness, (seeing in a business of moment none deserve blame for convenient slowness,) had expended almost *three years* in the work, not only examining the *channels* by the *fountain, translations* with the *original*, which was absolutely necessary, but also comparing *channels* with *channels*, which was abundantly useful in the Spanish, Italian, French, and Dutch (German) languages. These, with *Jacob, rolled away the stone from the mouth of the well of life;* so that now, even *Rachel's* weak women may freely *come* both to *drink* themselves *and water the flocks of* their *families* at the same.

"Leave we then those worthy men now all gathered to their fathers and gone to God, however they were requited on earth, well rewarded in heaven for their worthy work. Of whom, as also of that gracious KING that employed them, we may say, *Wheresoever the Bible shall be preached or read in the whole world, there shall also this that they have done be told in memorial of them.*" Ibid. p. 57, &c.

The character of James I. as a *scholar* has been greatly underrated. In the Hampton Court conference he certainly showed a clear and ready comprehension of every subject brought before

him, together with extensive reading and a remarkably sound judgment. For the *best translation* into any language we are indebted under God to King James, who was called a *hypocrite* by those who had no *religion*, and a *pedant* by persons who had not half his *learning*. Both piety and justice require that, while we are thankful to God for the gift of his word, we should revere the memory of the man who was the instrument of conveying the water of life through a channel by which its purity has been so wonderfully preserved. As to politics, he was, like the rest of the Stuart family, a tyrant.

Those who have compared most of the European translations with the original, have not scrupled to say that the *English translation of the Bible, made under the direction of King James I., is the most accurate and faithful of the whole.* Nor is this its only praise; the translators have seized the very *spirit* and *soul* of the original, and expressed this almost everywhere with pathos and energy. Besides, our translators have not only made a *standard translation*, but they have made their translation the *standard of our language;* the English tongue in their day was not equal to such a work, "but God enabled them to stand as upon Mount *Sinai*," to use the expression of a learned friend, "and *crane up* their country's language to the dignity of the originals, so that after the lapse of 200 years the English Bible is, with very few exceptions, the standard of the purity and excellence of the English tongue. The *original* from which it was taken is, alone, superior to the Bible translated by the authority of King James."* This is an opinion in which my heart, my judgment, and my conscience, coincide.†

* These are the words of the late Miss Freeman Shepherd, a very learned and extraordinary woman, and a rigid papist.

† It is not unknown that, at the Hampton Court conference, several alterations were proposed by Dr. Reynolds and his associates to be made in the *Liturgy* then in common use, as well as in the *Bible*. These however were in general objected to by the king, and only a few changes made, which shall be mentioned below. While on this part of the subject it may not be unacceptable to the reader to hear how the present *Liturgy* was compiled, and who the persons were to whom this work was assigned; a work almost universally esteemed by the devout and pious of every denomination, and the greatest effort of the *Reformation*, next to the translation of the Scriptures into the English language. The word LITURGY is derived, according to some, from λιτη, *prayer*, and εργον, *work*, and signifies literally the *work* or *labour of prayer* or *supplication;* and he who *labours* not in his prayers prays not at all: or more properly λειτουργια, from λειτος, *public* or *common*, and εργον, *work*, denoting the *common* or *public work of prayer, thanksgiving, &c.*, in which it is the duty of every person to engage; and from λιτανευω, to *supplicate*, comes λιται, *prayers*, and hence Λιτανεια, LITANY, *supplication*, a *collection of prayers* in the Liturgy or public service of the Church. Previously to the reign of Henry VIII. the Liturgy was all said or sung in *Latin*, but the *Creed*, the *Lord's Prayer*, and the *Ten Commandments*, in 1536 were translated into *English*, for the use of the common people, by the king's command. In 1545 the *Liturgy* was also *permitted* in *English*, as Fuller expresses it, "and this was the farthest *pace* the Reformation *stept* in the reign of Henry VIII."

In the first year of Edward VI., 1547, it was recommended to certain grave and learned bishops, and others then assembled, by order of the king, at Windsor Castle, to draw up a *communion service*, and to revise and reform all other offices in the Divine service; this service was accordingly printed and published, and strongly recommended by special letters from *Seymour*, Lord Protector, and the other lords of the council. The persons who compiled this work were the following:—

1. THOMAS CRANMER, Archbishop of *Canterbury*.
2. *George Day*, Bishop of *Chichester*.
3. *Thomas Goodrick*, Bishop of *Ely*.
4. *John Skip*, Bishop of *Hereford*.
5. *Henry Holbeach*, Bishop of *Lincoln*.
6. NICHOLAS RIDLEY, Bishop of *Rochester*.
7. *Thomas Thirlby*, Bishop of *Westminster*.
8. Doctor *May*, Dean of *St. Paul's*.
9. *John Taylor*, then Dean, afterwards Bishop, of *Lincoln*.
10. Doctor *Haines*, Dean of *Exeter*.
11. Doctor *Robinson*, afterwards Dean of *Durham*.
12. Doctor *John Redman*, Master of *Trinity* College, *Cambridge*.
13. Doctor *Richard Cox*, then Almoner to the King, and afterwards Bishop of *Ely*.

It is worthy of remark that as the *first translators* of the Scriptures into the *English language* were several of them persecuted *unto death* by the papists, so some of the *chief* of those who translated the *Book of Common Prayer*, (Archbishop *Cranmer* and Bishop *Ridley*) were burnt alive by the same cruel faction.

This was what Mr. Fuller calls the *first edition of the Common Prayer*, published in 1548. Some objections having been made to this work by Mr. John Calvin abroad, and some learned men at home, particularly in reference to the *Commemoration of the Dead*, the use of *Chrism*, and *Extreme Unction*, it was ordered by a statute in parliament (5 and 6 of Edward VI.) *that it should be faithfully and godly perused, explained, and made fully perfect.* The chief alterations made in consequence of this order were these: the *General Confession* and *Absolution* were added, and the *Communion Service* was made to begin with the *Ten Commandments*, the use of *oil* in *Confirmation* and *Extreme Unction* was left out, also *Prayers for the Dead*, and *certain expressions* that had a tendency to countenance the doctrine of *transubstantiation*.

The same persons to whom the compiling of the Communion Service was intrusted were employed in this revision, which was completed and published in 1553. On the accession of Queen Mary this Liturgy was abolished, and the Prayer Book, as it stood in the last year of Henry VIII., commanded to be used in its place. In the first year of the reign of Queen Elizabeth, 1559, the former Liturgy was restored, but it was subjected to a farther revision, by which some few passages were altered, and the petition in the Litany for being delivered from the tyranny and all the detestable enormities of the bishop of Rome left out, in order that conscientious Catholics might not be prevented from joining in the common service. This being done, it was presented to parliament, and by them received and established; and the Act for Uniformity, which is usually printed with the Liturgy, published by the queen's authority, and sent throughout the nation. The persons employed in this revision were the following:—

1. Master *Whitehead*, once Chaplain to Queen *Anna Bullein*.
2. *Matthew Parker*, afterwards Archbishop of *Canterbury*.
3. *Edmund Grindall*, afterwards Bishop of *London*.
4. *Richard Cox*, afterwards Bishop of *Ely*.
5. *James Pilkington*, afterwards Bishop of *Durham*.
6. Doctor *May*, Dean of *St. Paul's* and Master of *Trinity* College, *Cambridge*.
7. Sir *Thomas Smith*, Principal Secretary of State.

This Bible was begun in 1607, but was not completed and published till 1611; and there are copies of it which in their titlepages have the dates 1612 and 1613. This translation was corrected, and many parallel texts added, by Dr. Scattergood, in 1683; by Dr. Lloyd, bishop of London, in 1701; and afterwards by Dr. Paris, at Cambridge; but the most complete revision was made by Dr. *Blayney* in the year 1769, under the direction of the vice-chancellor and delegates of the University of Oxford, in which, 1. The *punctuation* was thoroughly revised; 2. The *words* printed in *italics* examined and corrected by the Hebrew and Greek originals; 3. The *proper names*, to the etymology of which *allusions* are made in the text, translated, and entered in the margin; 4. The *heads* and *running titles* corrected; 5. Some material errors in the *chronology* rectified; and 6. The *marginal references* re-examined, corrected, and their number greatly increased. Copies of this revision are those which are termed above *the most correct copies of the present authorized version;* and it is this revision *re-collated, re-examined,* and *corrected* from typographical inaccuracies in a great variety of places, that has been followed for the *text* prefixed to these *notes*. But, besides these corrections, I have found it necessary to re-examine all the *italics;* by those I mean the words interspersed through the text, avowedly not in the original, but thought necessary by our translators to complete the sense, and accommodate the idioms of the Hebrew and Greek to that of the English language. See the sixth rule, p. 16. In these I found gross corruptions, particularly where they have been changed for Roman characters, whereby words have been attributed to God which he never spoke.

The *Punctuation*, which is a matter of no small importance to a proper understanding of the sacred text, I have examined with the greatest care to me possible: by the insertion of commas where there were none before; putting semicolons for commas, the better to distinguish the members of the sentences; changing colons for semicolons, and vice versa; and full points for colons, I have been in many instances enabled the better to preserve and distinguish the sense, and carry on a narration to its close, without interrupting the reader's attention by the intervention of improper stops.

The *References* I have in many places considerably augmented, though I have taken care to reprint all that Dr. Blayney has inserted in his edition, of which I scruple not to say, that as far as they go, they are the best collection ever edited, and I hope their worth will suffer nothing by the additions I have made.

After long and diligently weighing the different systems of *Chronology*, and hesitating which to adopt, I ultimately fixed on the system commonly received; as it appeared to me on the whole, though encumbered with many difficulties, to be the least objectionable. In fixing the dates of particular transactions I have found much difficulty; that this was never done in any edition of the Bible hitherto offered to the public, with any tolerable correctness, every person acquainted with the subject must acknowledge. I have endeavoured carefully to fix the date of each transaction *where* it occurs, and where it could be ascertained, showing throughout the whole of the Old Testament the year of the world, and the year before Christ, in which it happened. From the beginning of Joshua I have introduced the years before the *building of Rome*

Of these Drs. *Cox* and *May* were employed on the first edition of this work, as appears by the preceding list.

In the first year of King James, 1604, another revision took place, and a few alterations were made, which consisted principally in the *addition* of some *prayers* and *thanksgivings*, some *alteration* in the *Rubrics* relative to the *Absolution*, to the *Confirmation*, and to the office of *Private Baptism*, with the *addition* of that *part* of the *Catechism* which contains the *Doctrine of the Sacraments*. The other additions were, *A Thanksgiving for divers Benefits, A Thanksgiving for Fair Weather, A Thanksgiving for Plenty, A Thanksgiving for Peace and Victory*, and *A Thanksgiving for Deliverance from the Plague*. See the Instrument in *Rymer*, vol. xvi. p. 565, &c. When the work was thus completed, a royal proclamation was issued, bearing date March 1, 1604, in which the king gave an account of the Hampton Court conference, the alterations that had been made by himself and his clergy in the Book of Common Prayer, commanding it, and none other, to be used throughout the kingdom. See the Instrument, *Rymer*, vol. xvi., p. 575.

In this state the Book of Common Prayer continued till the reign of Charles II., who, the 25th of October, 1660, "granted his commission, under the great seal of England, to several bishops and divines to review the Book of Common Prayer, and to prepare such alterations and *additions* as they thought fit to offer." In the following year the king assembled the convocations of both the provinces of *Canterbury* and *York*, and "authorized the presidents of those convocations, and other the bishops and clergy of the same, to review the said Book of Common Prayer," &c., requiring them, "after mature consideration, to make such alterations and *additions* as to them should seem meet and convenient." This was accordingly done, several prayers and some whole services added, and the whole published, with the *Act of Uniformity*, in the 14th of Charles II., 1661; since which time it has undergone no farther revision. These several *additions* have made the public service too long, and this is the principal cause why this part of Divine worship is not better attended. This excellent service is now burdensome through its extreme length; and the clergy shorten their sermons, making them superficial, to prevent too much weariness in their congregations. After being an hour and a half at *prayers*, they dismiss their audience with fifteen or twenty minutes' *preaching;* thus the people are not sufficiently instructed. This is a short history of a work which all who are acquainted with it deem superior to every thing of the kind produced either by ancient or modern times.

It would be disingenuous not to acknowledge that the chief of those prayers were in use in the Roman Catholic Church from which the Church of England is reformed; and it would betray a want of acquaintance with ecclesiastical antiquity to suppose that those prayers and services originated in that Church, as several of them were in use from the first ages of Christianity, and many of the best of them before the name of *pope* or *popery* was known in the earth.

till the seven hundred and fifty-third year before Christ, when the foundation of that city was laid, and also introduced the *Olympiads* from the time of their commencement, as both these eras are of the utmost use to all who read the sacred writings, connected with the histories of the times and nations to which they frequently refer. And who that reads his Bible will not be glad to find at what time of the sacred history those great events fell out, of which he has been accustomed to read in the Greek and Roman historians? This is a gratification which the present work will afford from a simple inspection of the margin, at least as far as those facts and dates have been ascertained by the best chronologists.

In the *Pentateuch* I have not introduced either the years of Rome or the Olympiads, because the transactions related in the Mosaic writings are in general too remote from these eras to be at all affected by them; and I judged it early enough to commence with them at the time when Israel was governed by the *Judges*. But as the exodus from Egypt forms a very remarkable era in the Jewish history, and is frequently referred to in the historical books, I have entered this also, beginning at the 12th of Exodus, A. M. 2513, and have carried it down to the building of Solomon's temple. This, I conceive, will be of considerable use to the reader.

As to *Marginal Readings*, I could with very little trouble have added many hundreds, if not thousands; but as I made it a point of conscience strictly to adhere to the *present authorized version* in the *text*, I felt obliged by the same principle scrupulously to follow the *Marginal Readings*, without adding or omitting *any*. Had I inserted *some of my own*, as some others have done, then my text would be no longer *the text of the authorized version*, but an *altered* translation; for the Marginal Readings constitute an integral part, properly speaking, of the authorized version; and to add any thing would be to *alter* this version, and to omit any thing would be to render it *imperfect*. When Dr. Blayney revised the present version in 1769, and proposed the insertion of the translations of some proper names, to the etymology of which reference is made in the text, so scrupulous was he of making any change in this respect that he submitted all his proposed alterations to a select Committee of the University of Oxford, the Vice-chancellor, and the Principal of Hertford College, and Mr. Professor *Wheeler;* nor was even the slightest change made but by their authority. All this part, as well as the entire text, I must, therefore, to be consistent with my proposals, leave conscientiously as I found them, typographical errors and false italics excepted. Whatever *emendations* I have proposed, either from myself or others, I have included among the *Notes*.

That the *Marginal Readings*, in our authorized translation, are essential to the integrity of the version itself, I scruple not to assert; and they are of so much importance as to be in several instances preferable to the *Textual Readings* themselves. Our conscientious translators, not being able in several cases to determine which of two meanings borne by a word, or which of two words found in different copies, should be admitted into the text, adopted the measure of receiving *both*, placing one in the *margin* and the other in the *text*, thus leaving the reader at liberty to adopt either, both of which in their apprehension stood nearly on the same authority. On this very account the marginal readings are essential to our version, and I have found, on collating many of them with the originals, that those in the *margin* are to be preferred to those in the *text* in the proportion of at least *eight* to *ten*.

To the *Geography* of the sacred writings I have also paid the utmost attention in my power. I wished in every case to be able to ascertain the ancient and modern names of places, their situation, distances, &c., &c.; but in several instances I have not been able to satisfy myself. I have given those opinions which appeared to me to be best founded, taking frequently the liberty to express my own doubts or dissatisfaction. I must therefore bespeak the reader's indulgence, not only in reference to the work in general, but in respect to several points both in the Scripture *geography* and *chronology* in particular, which may appear to him not satisfactorily ascertained; and have only to say that I have spared no pains to make every thing as correct and accurate as possible, and hope I may, without vanity, apply to myself on these subjects, with a slight change of expression, what was said by a great man of a great work: "For negligence or deficience, I have perhaps not need of more apology than the nature of the work will furnish; I have left that inaccurate which *can* never be made exact, and that imperfect which *can* never be completed."—JOHNSON. For particulars under these heads I must refer to Dr. *Hales*' elaborate and useful work, entitled, *A new Analysis of Chronology*, 2 vols. 4to., 1809–10.

The *Summaries* to each chapter are entirely written for the purpose, and formed from a careful examination of the chapter, verse by verse, so as to make them a faithful Table of Contents, constantly referring to the verses themselves. By this means all the subjects of each chapter may be immediately seen, so as in many cases to preclude the necessity of consulting a Concordance.

In the *Heads* or head lines to each page I have endeavoured to introduce as far as the room would admit, the chief subject of the columns underneath, so as immediately to catch the eye of the reader.

Quotations from the original texts I have made as sparingly as possible; those which are intro-

duced I have endeavoured to make plain by a literal translation, and by putting them in European characters. The reader will observe that though the *Hebrew* is here produced *without the points*, yet the reading given in European characters is *according to the points*, with very few exceptions. I have chosen this *middle way* to please, as far as possible, the opposers and friends of the *Masoretic* system.

The *controversies* among religious people I have scarcely ever mentioned, having very seldom referred to the creed of any sect or party of Christians; nor have I produced any opinion merely to confute or establish it. I simply propose *what I believe to be the meaning of a passage*, and maintain *what I believe to be the truth*, but scarcely ever in a *controversial* way. I think it quite possible to give my own views of the doctrines of the Bible, without introducing a single sentence at which any Christian might reasonably take offence; and I hope that no provocation which I may receive shall induce me to depart from this line of conduct.

It may be expected by some that I should enter at large into the proofs of the *authenticity of Divine Revelation*. This has been done amply by others; and their works have been published in every form, and, with a very laudable zeal, spread widely through the public; on this account I think it unnecessary to enter professedly into the subject, any farther than I have done in the "Introduction to the four Gospels and Acts of the Apostles," to which I must beg to refer the reader. The different portions of the sacred writings against which the shafts of infidelity have been levelled, I have carefully considered, and I hope sufficiently defended, in the places where they respectively occur.

For a considerable time I hesitated whether I should attach to each chapter what are commonly called *reflections*, as these do not properly belong to the province of the *commentator*. It is the business of the *preacher*, who has the literal and obvious sense before him, to make reflections on select passages, providential occurrences, and particular histories; and to apply the doctrines contained in them to the hearts and practices of his hearers. The chief business of the commentator is critically to examine his text, to give the true meaning of every passage in reference to the context, to explain words that are difficult or of dubious import, illustrate local and provincial customs, manners, idioms, laws, &c., and from the whole to collect the great design of the inspired writer.

Many are of opinion that it is an easy thing to write *reflections on the Scriptures*; my opinion is the reverse; *common-place* observations, which may arise on the surface of the latter, may be easily made by any person possessing a little common sense and a measure of piety; but reflections, such as *become the oracles of God*, are properly *inductive reasonings* on the *facts* stated or the *doctrines* delivered, and require, not only a clear head and a sound heart, but such a compass and habit of philosophic thought, such a power to discern the end from the beginning, the *cause* from its *effect*, (and where several causes are at work to ascertain their *respective* results, so that every effect may be attributed to its true cause,) as falls to the lot of but few men. Through the flimsy, futile, and false dealing of the immense herd of spiritualizers, metaphor-men, and allegorists, pure religion has been often disgraced. Let a man put his reason in ward, turn conscience out of its province, and throw the reins on the neck of his fancy, and he may write—reflections without end. The former description of reflections I rarely attempt for want of adequate powers; the latter, my reason and conscience prohibit; let this be my excuse with the intelligent and pious reader. I have, however, in this way, done what I could. I have generally, at the close of each chapter, summed up in a few particulars the *facts* or *doctrines* contained in it; and have endeavoured to point out to the reader the spiritual and practical use he should make of them. To these *inferences*, *improvements*, or whatever else they may be called, I have given no specific name; and of them can only say, that he who reads them, though he may be sometimes disappointed, will not always lose his labour. At the same time I beg leave to inform him that I have not deferred spiritual uses of important texts to the end of the chapter; where they should be noticed in the occurring verse I have rarely passed them by.

Before I conclude, it may be necessary to give some account of the *original* VERSIONS of the sacred writings, which have been often consulted, and to which occasional references are made in the ensuing work. These are the *Samaritan*, *Chaldaic*, *Æthiopic*, *Septuagint*, with those of *Aquila*, *Symmachus*, and *Theodotion*; the *Syriac*, *Vulgate*, *Arabic*, *Coptic*, *Persian*, and *Anglo-Saxon*.

The SAMARITAN *text* must not be reckoned among the *versions*. It is precisely the same with the Hebrew, only fuller; having preserved many letters, words, and even whole sentences, sometimes several verses, which are not extant in any Hebrew copy with which we are acquainted. In all other respects it is the same as the Hebrew, only written in what is called the Samaritan character, which was probably the ancient Hebrew, as that now called the Hebrew character was probably borrowed from the Chaldeans.

1. The SAMARITAN *version* differs widely from the *Samaritan text*; the latter is pure Hebrew, the former is a literal version of the Hebreo-Samaritan text, into the Chaldaico-Samaritan dialect. *When* this was done it is impossible to say, but it is allowed to be very ancient, consider-

ably prior to the Christian era. The language of this version is composed of pure Hebrew, Syro-Chaldaic, and Cuthite terms. It is almost needless to observe that the Samaritan text and Samaritan version extend no farther than the five books of Moses; as the Samaritans received no other parts of the sacred writings.

2. The CHALDAIC version or TARGUMS have already been described among the commentators. Under this head are included the Targum of *Onkelos* upon the whole *law;* the *Jerusalem* Targum on select parts of the five books of Moses; the Targum of *Jonathan ben Uzziel* also upon the Pentateuch; the Targum of Jonathan upon the prophets; and the Targum of Rabbi *Joseph* on the books of Chronicles; but of all these the Targums of *Onkelos* on the *law*, and *Jonathan* on the *prophets*, are the most ancient, the most literal, and the most valuable. See page 1 and 2 of this preface.

3. The SEPTUAGINT translation of all the versions of the sacred writings has ever been deemed of the greatest importance by *competent* judges. I do not, however, design to enter into the controversy concerning this venerable version; the history of it by Aristæus I consider in the main to be a mere fable, worthy to be classed with the tale of *Bel and the Dragon*, and the stupid story of *Tobit and his Dog*. Nor do I believe, with many of the fathers, that "*seventy* or *seventy-two* elders, six out of each of the twelve tribes, were employed in the work; that each of these translated the whole of the sacred books from Hebrew into Greek while confined in separate cells in the island of Pharos;" or that they were so particularly inspired by God that every species of error was prevented, and that the seventy-two copies, when compared together, were found to be precisely the *same*, verbatim et literatim. My own opinion, on the controversial part of the subject, may be given in a few words: I believe that the five books of Moses, the most correct and accurate part of the whole work, were translated from the Hebrew into Greek in the time of *Ptolemy Philadelphus*, king of Egypt, about 285 years before the Christian era; that this was done, not by *seventy-two*, but probably by *five* learned and judicious men, and that when completed it was examined, approved, and allowed as a faithful version, by the *seventy* or *seventy-two* elders who constituted the *Alexandrian Sanhedrim;* and that the other books of the Old Testament were done at different times by different hands, as the necessity of the case demanded, or the providence of GOD appointed. It is pretty certain, from the quotations of the *evangelists*, the *apostles*, and the *primitive fathers*, that a *complete version* into Greek of the whole Old Testament, probably called by the name of the *Septuagint*, was made and in use before the Christian era; but it is likely that some of the books of that ancient version are now lost, and that some others, which now go under the name of the Septuagint, were the production of times posterior to the incarnation.

4. The Greek versions of *Aquila, Symmachus*, and *Theodotion*, are frequently referred to. Aquila was first a *heathen*, then a *Christian*, and lastly a *Jew*. He made a translation of the Old Testament into Greek so very literal, that St. Jerome said it was a good *dictionary* to give the genuine meaning of the Hebrew words. He finished and published this work in the twelfth year of the reign of the Emperor Adrian, A. D. 128.

5. *Theodotion* was a Christian of the *Ebionite* sect, and is reported to have begun his translation of the Hebrew Scriptures into Greek merely to serve his own party; but from what remains of his version it appears to have been very literal, at least as far as the idioms of the two languages would bear. His translation was made about the year of our Lord 180. All this work is lost, except his version of the book of the Prophet *Daniel*, and some *fragments*.

6. *Symmachus* was originally a *Samaritan*, but became a convert to Christianity as professed by the *Ebionites*. In forming his translation he appears to have aimed at giving the *sense* rather than a *literal version* of the sacred text. His work was probably completed about A. D. 200.

These three versions were published by Origen in his famous work entitled, *Hexapla*, of which they formed the *third, fourth*, and *sixth* columns. All the remaining fragments have been carefully collected by Father Montfaucon, and published in a work entitled, *Hexapla Origenis quæ supersunt, &c.* Paris, 1713. 2 vols. folio. Republished by *C. F. Bahrdt*, Leips. 1769, 2 vols. 8vo.

7. The *Æthiopic* version comprehends only the New Testament, the Psalms, some of the minor Prophets, and a few fragments of other books. It was probably made in the *fourth* century.

8. The *Coptic* version includes only the five books of Moses, and the New Testament. It is supposed to have been made in the *fifth* century.

9. The *Syriac* version is very valuable and of great authority. It was probably made as early as the *second* century; and some think that a Syriac version of the Old Testament was in existence long before the Christian era.

10. A Latin version, known by the name of the ITALA, *Italic* or *Antehieronymian*, is well known among learned men; it exists in the Latin part of the *Codex Bezæ* at Cambridge, and in several other MSS. The text of the four gospels in this version, taken from four MSS. more than a thousand years old, was published by *Blanchini*, at Rome 1749, 4 vols. folio, and a larger

collection by *Sabathier*, Rheims, 1743, 3 vols. folio. This ancient version is allowed to be of great use in Biblical criticism.

11. The *Vulgate*, or Latin version, was formed by *Saint Jerome*, at the command of Pope Damasus, A. D. 384. Previously to this there were a great number of Latin versions made by different hands, some of which Jerome complains of as being extremely corrupt and self-contradictory. These versions, at present, go under the general name of the old *Itala* or *Antehieronymian*, already noticed. Jerome appears to have formed his text in general out of these, collating the whole with the Hebrew and Greek, from which he professes to have translated several books entire. The New Testament he is supposed to have taken wholly from the original Greek; yet there are sufficient evidences that he often regulated even this text by the ancient Latin versions.

12. The *Anglo-Saxon* version of the *four Gospels* is supposed to have been taken from the ancient *Itala* some time in the eighth century; and that of the Pentateuch, Joshua, Judges, and Job, from the *Vulgate*, by a monk called Ælfric, in the ninth century. The former was printed at *Dort*, in conjunction with the *Gothic* version, by *F. Junius*, 1665, 4to.; the latter, by *Edward Thwaites*, *Oxford*, 1698, 8vo.; but in this version many verses, and even whole chapters, are left out; and the Book of Job is only a sort of abstract, consisting of about five pages.

13. The *Arabic* is not a very ancient version, but is of great use in ascertaining the signification of several Hebrew words and forms of speech.

14. The *Persian* includes only the five Books of Moses and the four Gospels. The former was made from the Hebrew text by a Jew named *Yacoub Toosee;* the latter, by a Christian of the Catholic persuasion, *Simon Ibn Yusuf Ibn Ibraheem al Tubreezee*, about the year of our Lord 1341.

These are the principal versions which are deemed of authority in settling controversies relative to the text of the original. There are some others, but of less importance; such as the Slavonic, Gothic, Sahidic, and Armenian; for detailed accounts of which, as also of the preceding, as far as the New Testament is concerned, I beg leave to refer the reader to *Michaelis's Lectures*, in the translation, with the notes of the Rev. Dr. *Herbert Marsh*, and to the General Preface to the Gospels and Acts; and for farther information concerning *Jewish* and *Christian* commentators, he is requested to consult *Bartoloccius's Bibliotheca Rabbinica*, and the *Bibliotheca Theologica* of Father *Calmet*.

In the preceding list of commentators I find I have omitted to insert in its proper place a work with which I have been long acquainted, and which for its piety and erudition I have invariably admired, viz.: "*A plaine discovery of the whole Revelation of Saint John; set downe in two Treatises:* The one searching and proving *the true interpretation thereof:* The other applying the same paraphrastically and historically to the text. Set foorth by John Napeir L. of *Marchestoun, younger.* Whereunto are annexed certaine Oracles of Sibylla, agreeing with the Revelation and other places of Scripture. Edinburgh, printed by Robert Waldegrave, printer to the King's Majestie, 1593. Cum privilegio Regali, 8vo.

When the reader learns that the author of this little work was the famous Baron of Marchestoun, the inventor of the logarithms, a discovery which has been of incalculable use in the sciences of astronomy, practical geometry, and navigation, he will be prepared to receive with respect what so great a genius has written upon a book that, above all others in the sacred code, seems to require the head and hand of the soundest divine and mathematician. The work is dedicated "to the right excellent, high and mighty Prince James VI., King of Scottes," afterwards James I., King of England; and in the Epistle Dedicatorie, the author strongly urges him to complete the reformation begun in his own empire, that he might be a ready instrument in the hand of God in executing judgment on the papal throne, which he then supposed to be near the time of its final overthrow. The first treatise is laid down in *thirty-six* propositions relating to the seals, trumpets, vials, and thunders.

In the *third*, *fifth*, and *sixth* propositions, he endeavours to prove that each trumpet or vial contains 245 years; that the *first* began A. D. 71. The *second* A. D. 316. The *third* A. D. 561. The *fourth* A. D. 806. The *fifth* A. D. 1051. The *sixth* A. D. 1296. The *seventh* A. D. 1541. See Propos. vi. And in Propos. x. he shows that, as the last trumpet or vial began in 1541, consequently, as it contains 245 years, it should extend to A. D. 1786. "Not that I mean," says the noble writer, "that that age or yet the world shall continew so long, because it is said, that for the elect's sake the time shall be shortened; but I mean that if the world were to indure, that seventh age should continew untill the yeare of Christ, 1786." Taking up this subject again, in Propos. xiv., he endeavours to prove, by a great variety of calculations formed on the 1335 days mentioned by Daniel, chap. xii. 11, and the period of the three thundering angels, Rev. viii. and ix., that by the former it appears the day of judgment will take place in A. D. 1700, and by the latter, in 1688, whence it may be confidently expected that this awful day shall take place between these two periods!

We, who have lived to A. D. 1830, see the fallacy of these predictive calculations; and with

such an example before us of the miscarriage of the first mathematician in Europe, in his endeavours to solve the prophetical periods marked in this most obscure book, we should proceed in such researches with humility and caution, nor presume to ascertain the times and the seasons which the Father has reserved in his own power. I may venture to affirm, so very plausible were the reasonings and calculations of Lord Napeir, that there was scarcely a Protestant in Europe, who read his work, that was not of the same opinion. And how deplorably has the event falsified the predictions of this *eminent* and *pious* man! And yet, unawed by his miscarriage, *calculators* and *ready-reckoners*, in every succeeding age, on less specious pretences, with minor qualifications, and a less vigorous opinion, have endeavoured to soar where Napeir sunk! Their labours, however well intended, only serve to increase the records of the weakness and folly of mankind. *Secret* things belong to God; those that are *revealed*, to us and to our children. Writers who have endeavoured to illustrate different prophecies in the Apocalypse by *past* events, and those that are *now* occurring, are not included in this censure. Some respectable names in the present day have rendered considerable service to the cause of Divine revelation, by the careful and pious attention they have paid to this part of the subject; but when persons attempt to speak of what is yet to come, they begin to *prophesy* and are soon lost.

ADAM CLARKE.

P. S. On Gen. ii. 4, I have hinted that our Saxon ancestors have translated the *Dominus* of the Vulgate by Hlaford, Loverd, or Lord. This is not to be understood of the fragments of the translations of the Old and New Testament which have reached our times, for in them *Dominus* when connected with *Deus* is often *omitted*, and the word God substituted for both; at other times they use the Dano-Saxon Drihten, both for יהוה *Jehovah*, and אדני *Adonai;* and in the New Testament, Drihten is generally used for Κυριος, *Lord*, at other times, Hlaford. It seems to have been applied as a title of respect to men: see Matt. xii. 8; xiii. 27; xvii. 25, 26, 27, 31, 32, 34; xxi. 30. Afterwards it was applied to the Supreme Being also; and the title *Lord* continues to be given to both indifferently to the present day, and sometimes both indifferently even in the same discourse. Thus in the Saxon homily in Dom. 1., Quadr. Bedæ Hist. Eccles., lib. iv., c. 9: Man sceal hine gebiddan to his Drihtne ⁊ him anum ƿeorðian: He ana is soð Hlaford and soð God. "Man shall pray to his Lord (Drihtne) and him alone serve: He only is true Lord (Hlaford) and true God." Hlaford belongs more especially to the Anglo-Saxon Drihtne, to the Dano-Saxon. In Danish Drotten is generally used for Lord.

PREFACE TO THE BOOK

OF

GENESIS.

EVERY believer in Divine revelation finds himself amply justified in taking for granted that the Pentateuch is the work of Moses. For more than 3000 years this has been the invariable opinion of those who were best qualified to form a correct judgment on this subject. The Jewish Church, from its most remote antiquity, has ascribed the work to no other hand; and the Christian Church, from its foundation, has attributed it to the Jewish lawgiver alone. The most respectable heathens have concurred in this testimony, and Jesus Christ and his apostles have completed the evidence, and have put the question beyond the possibility of being doubted by those who profess to believe the Divine authenticity of the New Testament. As to those who, in opposition to all these proofs, obstinately persist in their unbelief, they are worthy of little regard, as argument is lost on their unprincipled prejudices, and demonstration on their minds, because ever wilfully closed against the light. When they have *proved* that Moses is *not* the author of this work, the advocates of Divine revelation will reconsider the grounds of their faith.

That there are a few things in the Pentateuch which *seem* to have been added by a later hand there can be little doubt; among these some have reckoned, perhaps without reason, the following passage, Gen. xii. 6: "And the Canaanite was then in the land;" but see the note on this place. Num. xxi. 14, "In the book of the wars of the Lord," was probably a marginal note, which in process of time got into the text; see the note on this passage also. To these may be added the *five first verses* of Deuteronomy, chap. i; the *twelfth* of chap. ii; and the *eight* concluding verses of the last chapter, in which we have an account of the death of Moses. These last words could not have been added by Moses himself, but are very probably the work of Ezra, by whom, according to uninterrupted tradition among the Jews, the various books which constitute the canon of the Old Testament were collected and arranged, and such expository notes added as were essential to connect the different parts; but as *he* acted under Divine inspiration, the additions may be considered of equal authority with the text. A few other places might be added, but they are of little importance and are mentioned in the notes.

The book of GENESIS, Γενεσις, has its name from the title it bears in the *Septuagint*, Βιβλος Γενεσεως, (chap. ii. ver. 4,) which signifies *the book of the Generation*; but it is called in Hebrew בראשית *Bereshith*, "*In the beginning*," from its initial word. It is the most ancient history in the world; and, from the great variety of its singular details and most interesting accounts, is as far superior in its value and importance to all others, as it is in its antiquity. This book contains an account of the creation of the world, and its first inhabitants; the original innocence and fall of man; the rise of religion; the invention of arts; the general corruption and degeneracy of mankind; the universal deluge; the repeopling and

division of the earth; the origin of nations and kingdoms; and a particular history of the *patriarchs* from *Adam* down to the death of *Joseph;* including a space, at the lowest computation, of 2369 years.

It may be asked how a detail so circumstantial and minute could have been preserved when there was no *writing* of any kind, and when the earth, whose history is here given, had already existed more than 2000 years. To this inquiry a very satisfactory answer may be given. There are only *three* ways in which these important records could have been preserved and brought down to the time of Moses: viz., *writing*, *tradition*, and *Divine revelation.* In the antediluvian world, when the life of man was so protracted, there was comparatively little need for *writing* of any kind, and perhaps no alphabetical writing then existed. *Tradition* answered every purpose to which writing in any kind of characters could be subservient; and the necessity of erecting *monuments* to perpetuate public events could scarcely have suggested itself, as during those times there could be little danger apprehended of any important fact becoming obsolete, as its history had to pass through very few hands, and all these *friends* and *relatives* in the most proper sense of the terms; for they lived in an insulated state under a patriarchal government.

Thus it was easy for Moses to be satisfied of the truth of all he relates in the book of *Genesis*, as the accounts came to him through the medium of very few persons. From *Adam* to *Noah* there was but *one man* necessary to the correct transmission of the history of this period of 1656 years. Now this history was, without doubt, perfectly known to Methuselah, who lived to see them both. In like manner *Shem* connected *Noah* and *Abraham*, having lived to converse with both; as *Isaac* did with *Abraham* and *Joseph*, from whom these things might be easily conveyed to *Moses* by *Amram*, who was contemporary with *Joseph*. See the *plate*, chap. xi. Supposing, then, all the curious facts recorded in the book of *Genesis* had no other authority than the *tradition* already referred to, they would stand upon a foundation of credibility *superior* to any that the most reputable of the ancient Greek and Latin historians can boast. Yet to preclude all possibility of mistake, the unerring Spirit of God directed Moses in the selection of his *facts* and the ascertaining of his *dates*. Indeed, the narrative is so simple, so much like truth, so consistent everywhere with itself, so correct in its dates, so impartial in its biography, so accurate in its philosophical details, so pure in its morality, and so benevolent in its design, as amply to demonstrate that it never could have had an *earthly* origin. In this case, also, Moses constructed every thing according to the pattern which God showed him in the mount.

THE FIRST BOOK OF MOSES,

CALLED

GENESIS.

Year before the common era of Christ, 4004.—Julian Period, 710.—Cycle of the Sun, 10.—Dominical Letter, B.—Cycle of the Moon, 7.—Indiction, 5.—Creation from Tisri or September, 1

CHAPTER I.

First day's work—*Creation of the heavens and the earth*, 1, 2. *Of the light and its separation from the darkness*, 3–5. Second day's work—*The creation of the firmament, and the separation of the waters above the firmament from those below it*, 6–8. Third day's work—*The waters are separated from the earth and formed into seas, &c.*, 9, 10. *The earth rendered fruitful, and clothed with trees, herbs, grass, &c.*, 11–13. Fourth day's work—*Creation of the celestial luminaries intended for the measurement of time, the distinction of periods, seasons, &c.*, 14; *and to illuminate the earth*, 15. *Distinct account of the formation of the sun, moon, and stars*, 16–19. Fifth day's work—*The creation of fish, fowls, and reptiles in general*, 20. *Of great aquatic animals*, 21. *They are blessed so as to make them very prolific*, 22, 23. Sixth day's work—*Wild and tame cattle created, and all kinds of animals which derive their nourishment from the earth*, 24, 25. *The creation of man in the image and likeness of God, with the dominion given him over the earth and all inferior animals*, 26. *Man or Adam, a general name for human beings, including both male and female*, 27. *Their peculiar blessing*, 28. *Vegetables appointed as the food of man and all other animals*, 29, 30. *The judgment which God passed on his works at the conclusion of his creative acts*, 31.

A. M. 1.
B. C. 4004.

IN the [a] beginning [b] God created
the heaven and the earth.
2 [c] And the earth was without form and
void; and darkness *was* upon the
face of the deep. [d] And the Spirit
of God moved upon the face of the waters

[a] Prov. viii. 22, 23, 24; Mark xiii. 19; John i. 1, 2; Heb. i. 10.—[b] 1 Chron. xvi. 26; Neh. ix. 6; Psa. viii. 3; xxxiii. 6; xxxix. 11, 12; cxvi. 5; cii. 25; civ. 24; cxv. 15; cxxi. 2; cxxiv. 8; cxxxiv. 3; cxxxvi. 5; cxlvi. 6; Prov. iii. 19; viii. 26, 27, &c.; Eccles. xii. 1; Isa. xxxvii. 16; xlii. 5; xliv. 24; li. 16; lxv. 17; Jer. x. 12; xxxii. 17; li. 15; Zech. xii. 1; Acts iv. 24; xiv. 15; xvii. 24; Rom. i. 20; Eph. iii. 9; Col. i. 16, 17; Heb. i. 2; xi. 3; 2 Pet. iii. 5; Rev. i. 8; iii. 14; iv. 11; x. 6; xiv. 7; xxi. 6; xxii. 13.—[c] Isa. xlv. 18; Jer. iv. 23.—[d] Psa. civ. 30; Isa. xl. 13, 14.

NOTES ON CHAP. I.

Verse 1. בראשית ברא אלהים את השמים ואת הארץ *Bereshith bara Elohim eth hashshamayim veeth haarets; GOD in the beginning created the heavens and the earth.*

Many attempts have been made to define the term GOD: as to the word itself, it is pure Anglo-Saxon, and among our ancestors signified, not only the Divine Being, now commonly designated by the word, but also *good*; as in their apprehensions it appeared that *God* and *good* were correlative terms; and when they thought or spoke of him, they were doubtless led from the word itself to consider him as THE GOOD BEING, a fountain of infinite benevolence and beneficence towards his creatures.

A general definition of this great First Cause, as far as human words dare attempt one, may be thus given: The eternal, independent, and self-existent Being: the Being whose purposes and actions spring from himself, without foreign motive or influence: he who is absolute in dominion; the most pure, the most simple, and most spiritual of all essences; infinitely benevolent, beneficent, true, and holy: the cause of all being, the upholder of all things; infinitely happy, because infinitely perfect; and eternally self-sufficient, needing nothing that he has made: illimitable in his immensity, inconceivable in his mode of existence, and indescribable in his essence; known fully only to himself, because an infinite mind can be fully apprehended only by itself. In a word, a Being who, from his infinite wisdom, cannot err or be deceived; and who, from his infinite goodness, can do nothing but what is eternally just, right, and kind. Reader, such is the God of the Bible; but how widely different from the God of most human creeds and apprehensions!

The original word אלהים *Elohim*, God, is certainly the plural form of אל *El*, or אלה *Eloah*, and has long

A. M. 1.
B. C. 4004.

3 [e] And God said, [f] Let there be
light: and there was light.
4 And God saw the light that *it was* good:
and God [g] divided [h] the light
from the darkness.
5 And God called the light [i] Day, and the

[e] Psa. xxxiii. 6, 9; cxlviii. 5.——[f] Job xxxvi. 30; xxxviii. 19; Psa. xcvii. 11; civ. 2; cxviii. 27; Isa. xlv. 7; lx. 19; John i. 5, 9; iii. 19; 2 Cor. iv. 6; Eph. v. 8; 1 Tim. vi. 16; 1 John i. 5; ii. 8.——[g] 2 Cor. vi. 14.——[h] Heb. *between the light and between the darkness.*——[i] Chap. viii. 22; Psa. xix. 2; lxxiv. 16; civ. 20; Jer. xxxiii. 20; 1 Cor. iii. 13; Eph. v. 13; 1 Thess. v. 5.

been supposed, by the most eminently learned and pious men, to imply a *plurality* of Persons in the Divine nature. As this plurality appears in so many parts of the sacred writings to be confined to *three* Persons, hence the doctrine of the TRINITY, which has formed a part of the creed of all those who have been deemed sound in the faith, from the earliest ages of Christianity. Nor are the *Christians* singular in receiving this doctrine, and in deriving it from the first words of Divine revelation. An eminent Jewish rabbin, Simeon ben Joachi, in his comment on the sixth section of Leviticus, has these remarkable words: "Come and see the mystery of the word Elohim; there are *three degrees*, and each degree by itself *alone*, and yet notwithstanding they are all *one*, and *joined together* in *one*, and are not divided from each other." See *Ainsworth*. He must be strangely prejudiced indeed who cannot see that the doctrine of a Trinity, and of a Trinity in unity, is expressed in the above words. The verb ברא *bara*, he created, being joined in the singular number with this plural noun, has been considered as pointing out, and not obscurely, the *unity* of the Divine Persons in this work of creation. In the ever-blessed Trinity, from the infinite and indivisible unity of the persons, there can be but one will, one purpose, and one infinite and uncontrollable energy.

"Let those who have any doubt whether אלהים *Elohim*, when meaning the true God, Jehovah, be *plural* or not, consult the following passages, where they will find it joined with adjectives, verbs, and pronouns *plural*.

"Gen. i. 26; iii. 22; xi. 7; xx. 13; xxxi. 7, 53; xxxv. 7.

"Deut. iv. 7; v. 23; Josh. xxiv. 19; 1 Sam. iv. 8; 2 Sam. vii. 23; Psa. lviii. 12; Isa. vi. 8; Jer. x. 10; xxiii. 36.

"See also Prov. ix. 10; xxx. 3; Psa. cxlix. 2; Eccl. v. 7; xii. 1; Job v. 1; Isa. vi. 3; liv. 5; lxii. 5; Hos. xi. 12, or xii. 1; Mal. i. 6; Dan. v. 18, 20; vii. 18, 22."—PARKHURST.

As the word *Elohim* is the term by which the Divine Being is most generally expressed in the Old Testament, it may be necessary to consider it here more at large. It is a maxim that admits of no controversy, that every noun in the Hebrew language is derived from a *verb*, which is usually termed the *radix* or root, from which, not only the noun, but all the different flections of the verb, spring. This radix is the third person singular of the preterite or past tense. The *ideal* meaning of this root expresses some essential property of the thing which it designates, or of which it is an appellative. The root in *Hebrew*, and in its sister language, the Arabic, generally consists of *three* letters, and every word must be traced to its root in order to ascertain its genuine meaning, for there alone is this meaning to be found. In Hebrew and Arabic this is essentially necessary, and no man can safely criticise on any word in either of these languages who does not carefully attend to this point.

I mention the *Arabic* with the *Hebrew* for two reasons. 1. Because the two languages evidently spring from the same source, and have very nearly the same mode of construction. 2. Because the deficient roots in the Hebrew Bible are to be sought for in the Arabic language. The reason of this must be obvious, when it is considered that the whole of the Hebrew language is lost except what is in the Bible, and even a part of this book is written in Chaldee. Now, as the *English* Bible does not contain the whole of the *English language*, so the Hebrew Bible does not contain the whole of the Hebrew. If a man meet with an English word which he cannot find in an ample concordance or dictionary to the Bible, he must of course seek for that word in a general English dictionary. In like manner, if a particular form of a Hebrew word occur that cannot be traced to a root in the Hebrew Bible, because the word does not occur in the third person singular of the past tense in the Bible, it is expedient, it is perfectly lawful, and often indispensably necessary, to seek the deficient root in the Arabic. For as the Arabic is still a living language, and perhaps the most copious in the universe, it may well be expected to furnish those terms which are deficient in the Hebrew Bible. And the reasonableness of this is founded on another maxim, viz., that either the Arabic was derived from the Hebrew, or the Hebrew from the Arabic. I shall not enter into this controversy; there are great names on both sides, and the decision of the question in either way will have the same effect on my argument. For if the *Arabic* were derived from the Hebrew, it must have been when the Hebrew was a *living* and *complete* language, because such is the Arabic now; and therefore all its essential roots we may reasonably expect to find there: but if, as Sir William Jones supposed, the *Hebrew* were derived from the Arabic, the same expectation is justified, the deficient roots in Hebrew may be sought for in the *mother* tongue. If, for example, we meet with a term in our ancient English language the meaning of which we find difficult to ascertain, common sense teaches us that we should seek for it in the *Anglo-Saxon*, from which our language springs; and, if necessary, go up to the *Teutonic*, from which the Anglo-Saxon was derived. No person disputes the legitimacy of this measure, and we find it in constant practice. I make these observations at the very threshold of my work, because the necessity of acting on this principle (seeking deficient Hebrew roots in the Arabic) may often occur, and I wish to speak *once for all* on the subject.

The first sentence in the Scripture shows the propriety of having recourse to this principle. We have

A. M. 1.
B. C. 4004.

darkness he called Night. [k] And the evening and the morning were the first day.

[k] Heb. *and the evening was and the morning was.*

6 And God said, [l] Let there be a [m] firmament in the midst of the waters, and let it divide the waters from the waters.

A. M. 1.
B. C. 4004.

[l] Job xxvi. 7; xxxvii. 18; Psa. xix. 1; civ. 2; cxxxvi. 6; cl. 1; Jer. x. 12; li. 15.——[m] Heb. *expansion.*

seen that the word אלהים *Elohim* is plural; we have traced our term *God* to its source, and have seen its signification; and also a general definition of the *thing* or *being* included under this term, has been tremblingly attempted. We should now trace the *original* to its *root*, but this root does not appear in the Hebrew Bible. Were the Hebrew a *complete* language, a pious reason might be given for this omission, viz., "As God is without beginning and without cause, as his being is infinite and *underived*, the Hebrew language consults strict propriety in giving no *root* whence his name can be *deduced*." Mr. Parkhurst, to whose pious and learned labours in Hebrew literature most Biblical students are indebted, thinks he has found the root in אלה *alah, he swore, bound himself by oath;* and hence he calls the ever-blessed Trinity אלהים *Elohim*, as *being bound by a conditional oath to redeem man, &c., &c.* Most pious minds will revolt from such a definition, and will be glad with me to find both the *noun* and the *root* preserved in Arabic. Allah الله is the common name for God in the Arabic tongue, and often the emphatic اللهم is used. Now both these words are derived from the root *alaha*, he *worshipped, adored, was struck with astonishment, fear,* or *terror;* and hence, *he adored with sacred horror* and *veneration*, cum sacro horrore ac veneratione coluit, adoravit.—Wilmet. Hence *ilahon*, fear, veneration, and also *the object of religious fear*, the *Deity*, the supreme God, the *tremendous Being*. This is not a new idea; God was considered in the same light among the ancient Hebrews; and hence Jacob swears by the *fear* of his father Isaac, Gen. xxxi. 53. To complete the definition, Golius renders *alaha, juvit, liberavit,* et *tutatus fuit*, "he succoured, liberated, kept in safety, or defended." Thus from the *ideal* meaning of this most expressive root, we acquire the most correct notion of the Divine nature; for we learn that God is the *sole object of adoration;* that the perfections of his nature are such as must *astonish* all those who piously contemplate them, and fill with *horror* all who would dare to give his glory to *another*, or break his commandments; that consequently he should be *worshipped* with *reverence* and *religious fear;* and that every sincere worshipper may expect from him *help* in all his weaknesses, trials, difficulties, temptations, &c.; *freedom* from the power, guilt, nature, and consequences of sin; and to be *supported, defended*, and saved to the uttermost, and to the end.

Here then is one proof, among multitudes which shall be adduced in the course of this work, of the importance, utility, and necessity of tracing up these sacred words to their *sources;* and a proof also, that subjects which are supposed to be out of the reach of the common people may, with a little difficulty, be brought on a level with the most ordinary capacity.

In the beginning] Before the creative acts mentioned in this chapter all was ETERNITY. *Time* signifies *duration* measured by the revolutions of the heavenly bodies: but prior to the creation of these bodies there could be no measurement of duration, and consequently no *time;* therefore *in the beginning* must necessarily mean the commencement of time which followed, or rather was produced by, God's creative acts, as an effect follows or is produced by a cause.

Created] Caused existence where previously to this moment there was no being. The rabbins, who are legitimate judges in a case of verbal criticism on their own language, are unanimous in asserting that the word ברא *bara* expresses the commencement of the existence of a thing, or egression from nonentity to entity. It does not in its *primary* meaning denote the *preserving* or *new forming* things that had previously existed, as some imagine, but *creation* in the proper sense of the term, though it has some other acceptations in other places. The supposition that God formed all things out of a pre-existing, eternal nature, is certainly absurd, for if there had been an eternal nature besides an eternal God, there must have been two self-existing, independent, and eternal beings, which is a most palpable contradiction.

את השמים *eth hashshamayim.* The word את *eth*, which is generally considered as a *particle*, simply denoting that the word following is in the accusative or oblique case, is often understood by the rabbins in a much more extensive sense. "The particle את," says Aben Ezra, "signifies the *substance* of the thing." The like definition is given by Kimchi in his *Book of Roots*. "This particle," says Mr. Ainsworth, "having the *first* and *last* letters of the Hebrew alphabet in it, is supposed to comprise the *sum* and *substance* of *all things*." "The particle את *eth* (says Buxtorf, Talmudic Lexicon, sub voce) with the cabalists is often mystically put for the *beginning* and the *end*, as Α alpha and Ω omega are in the Apocalypse." On this ground these words should be translated, "God in the beginning created the *substance* of the heavens and the *substance* of the earth," i. e. the *prima materia*, or first elements, out of which the heavens and the earth were successively formed. The Syriac translator understood the word in this sense, and to express this meaning has used the word ܝܬ *yoth*, which has this signification, and is very properly translated in Walton's Polyglot, esse, *cœli* et esse *terræ*, "the *being* or *substance* of the heaven, and the *being* or *substance* of the earth." St. Ephraim Syrus, in his comment on this place, uses the same Syriac word, and appears to understand it precisely in the same way. Though the Hebrew words are certainly no more than the notation of a *case* in most places, yet understood here in the sense above, they argue a wonderful philosophic accuracy in the statement of Moses, which brings before us, not a *finished* heaven and earth, as every other trans-

a

A. M. 1.
B. C. 4004.

7 And God made the firmament, [n] and divided the waters which *were* under the firmament from the waters which *were* [o] above the firmament: and it was so.

A. M. 1.
B. C. 4004.

[n] Prov. viii. 28.

[o] Psa. cxlviii. 4.

lation appears to do, though afterwards the process of their formation is given in detail, but merely the *materials* out of which God built the whole system in the six following days.

The heaven and the earth.] As the word שמים *shamayim* is plural, we may rest assured that it means more than the *atmosphere*, to express which some have endeavoured to restrict its meaning. Nor does it appear that the atmosphere is particularly intended here, as this is spoken of, ver. 6, under the term *firmament.* The word *heavens* must therefore comprehend the whole *solar system*, as it is very likely the whole of this was created in these six days; for unless the earth had been the *centre* of a system, the reverse of which is sufficiently demonstrated, it would be unphilosophic to suppose it was created independently of the other parts of the system, as on this supposition we must have recourse to the almighty power of God to suspend the influence of the earth's gravitating power till the fourth day, when the sun was placed in the centre, round which the earth began then to revolve. But as the design of the inspired penman was to relate what especially belonged to our world and its inhabitants, therefore he passes by the rest of the planetary system, leaving it simply included in the plural word *heavens.* In the word *earth* every thing relative to the terraqueaerial globe is included, that is, all that belongs to the solid and fluid parts of our world with its surrounding atmosphere. As therefore I suppose the whole solar system was created at this time, I think it perfectly in place to give here a general view of all the planets, with every thing curious and important hitherto known relative to their revolutions and principal affections.

A GENERAL VIEW OF THE WHOLE SOLAR SYSTEM.

TABLE I.—THE REVOLUTIONS, DISTANCES, &c., &c., OF ALL THE PRIMARY PLANETS

Names.	Periodical Revolution.					Siderial Revolution.					Mean distance from the Sun in English miles.	Least distance from the Earth in English miles.	Greatest distance from the Earth in English miles.	Diameter in English miles.
	Yrs.	d.	h.	m.	s.	Yrs.	d.	h.	m.	s.				
Sun											. . .	93,908,984	97,118,538	886,473
Mercury	0	87	23	14	33	0	87	23	15	40	36,973,282	58,540,512	132,487,077	3,191
Venus	0	224	16	41	27	0	224	16	49	11	69,088,240	26,425,554	164,602,034	7,630
Earth	1	0	5	48	48	1	0	6	9	12	95,513,794	. . .	. . .	7,954
Moon	0	27	7	43	5	0	27	7	43	12	95,513,794	222,920	254,084	2,172
Mars	1	321	22	18	27	1	321	23	30	36	145,533,667	50,019,873	241,047,462	4,135
Jupiter	11	315	14	39	2	11	317	14	27	11	496,765,289	401,251,495	592,279,083	86,396
Saturn	29	161	19	16	15	29	174	1	51	11	911,141,442	815,627,647	1,006,655,236	79,405
Sat. Ring	29	161	19	16	15	29	174	1	51	11	911,141,442	815,525,205	1,006,757,678	185,280
Herschel	83	52	4	0	0	83	150	18	0	0	1,822,575,228	1,727,061,434	1,918,089,022	34,457

Names.	Proportionate bulk, the Earth being 1.	Time of rotation upon their axis.	Inclination of the axis to the equator.	Attractive power or density, the Earth being 1.	Hourly motion in their orbit, in English miles.
Sun	1,384,462	25d. 14h. 8m. 0s.	. . .	351,886	. . . .
Mercury	$\frac{1}{15}$th	unknown	unknown	$\frac{4}{23}$ths	111,256
Venus	$\frac{8}{9}$ths	0 23 21 0	uncertain	$\frac{95}{100}$ths	81,398
Earth	1	0 23 56 4	23° 28′ 0″	1	75,222
Moon	$\frac{1}{49}$th	27 7 43 5	1 43 0	$1\frac{15}{500}$ths	2,335
Mars	$\frac{1}{7}$th	1 0 39 22	28 42 0	$\frac{1}{5}$th	56,212
Jupiter	1281 greater	0 9 55 33	3 22 0	$330\frac{3}{5}$	30,358
Saturn	995 greater	0 10 16 1	30 0 0	$103\frac{7}{10}$	22,351
Sat. Ring	. . .	0 10 32 15	30 0 0	. . . . :	22,351
Herschel	$80\frac{1}{2}$ greater	unknown	unknown	$17\frac{3}{4}$	15,846

The following Celestial Bodies, commonly called Planets, revolving between Jupiter and Mars, have been recently discovered: all that is known of their Magnitude, Surface, Diameter, and Distance, I here subjoin.

Names.	Mean distance from the Sun.	Least distance from Earth.	Greatest dist. from Earth.	Diameter.	Proportional bulk.	Proportional surface.
Ceres	250,000,000	155,000,000	345,000,000	160	$\frac{1}{125000}$th	$\frac{1}{360}$th
Pallas	270,000,000	175,000,000	365,000,000	110	$\frac{1}{380000}$th	$\frac{1}{3300}$th
Juno	285,000,000	190,000,000	385,000,000	119	$\frac{1}{375000}$th	$\frac{1}{4500}$th
Vesta	unknown	unknown	unknown	unknown	unknown	unknown

TABLE II.—SATELLITES OF JUPITER.

Satellite	Periodic Revolution.	Synodic Revolution.	Distance from Jupiter in semi-diameters of Jupiter.	Dist. from Jupiter in parts of the ecliptic, at Jupiter's mean dist. from Earth.	Diameter, the Earth being 1.	Magnitude, the Earth being 1.	Distance from Jupiter in English miles.
	d. h. m. s.	d. h. m. s.		′ ″			
I.	1 18 27 $33\frac{476}{1000}$	1 18 28 $35\frac{9479}{10000}$	$5\frac{67}{100}$	1 51	$1\frac{2}{35}$	$1\frac{13}{30}$	245,000
II.	3 13 13 $41\frac{929}{1000}$	3 13 17 $53\frac{7489}{10000}$	9	2 57	$0\frac{32}{27}$	$0\frac{6}{10}$	389,000
III.	7 3 42 $32\frac{879}{1000}$	7 3 59 $35\frac{8675}{10000}$	$14\frac{19}{50}$	4 42	$1\frac{1}{49}$	$1\frac{3}{25}$	621,000
IV.	16 16 32 $8\frac{491}{1000}$	16 18 51 $7\frac{917}{10000}$	$25\frac{3}{10}$	8 16	$0\frac{77}{100}$	$0\frac{33}{50}$	1,093,000

Satellite	Greatest semi-duration of eclipse.	Greatest semi-diameter of Jupiter's shadow that the satellite passes through.	Least distance from the Earth in English miles.	Mean distance from the Earth in English miles.	Greatest distance from the Earth in English miles.
	h. m. s.	° ′ ″			
I.	1 7 55	9 35 37	401,006,562	496,765,289	592,524,016
II.	1 25 40	6 1 33	400,862,713	496,765,289	592,667,865
III.	1 47 0	3 43 58	400,630,308	496,765,289	592,900,270
IV.	2 23 0	2 8 2	400,158,586	496,765,289	593,371,992

TABLE III.—SATELLITES OF SATURN.

Satellite	Periodic Revolution.	Synodic Revolution.	Dist. from Sat. in semi-diameters of Saturn.	Dist. from Saturn in semi-diameters of the ring of Saturn.	Distance from Saturn in parts of the ecliptic at Saturn's mean distance from the Earth.	Distance from Saturn in English miles.	Nearest approach to the Earth in English miles.
	d. h. m. s.	d. h. m. s.			′ ″		
VII.	0 22 37 23	0 22 37 30	$3\frac{1}{25}$	$1\frac{3}{10}$	0 $28\frac{1}{2}$	112,000	815,515,647
VI.	1 8 53 9	1 8 53 24	$3\frac{476}{500}$	$1\frac{69}{100}$	0 37	140,000	815,487,647
I.	1 21 18 $26\frac{111}{500}$	1 21 18 $54\frac{389}{500}$	$4\frac{893}{1000}$	$2\frac{97}{1000}$	0 $43\frac{1}{2}$	172,000	815,455,647
II.	2 17 44 $51\frac{177}{1000}$	2 17 45 $51\frac{13}{1000}$	$6\frac{134}{500}$	$2\frac{343}{500}$	0 56	217,000	815,410,647
III.	4 12 25 $11\frac{1}{10}$	4 12 27 $55\frac{239}{1000}$	$8\frac{377}{500}$	$3\frac{94}{125}$	1 18	315,000	815,312,647
IV.	15 22 41 $13\frac{52}{1000}$	15 23 15 $20\frac{175}{1000}$	$20\frac{295}{1000}$	$8\frac{339}{500}$	3 0	709,000	814,918,647
V.	79 7 53 $42\frac{339}{500}$	79 22 3 $12\frac{883}{1000}$	$59\frac{77}{500}$	$25\frac{174}{500}$	8 $42\frac{1}{2}$	2,126,000	813,501,647

TABLE IV.—SATELLITES OF HERSCHEL, OR THE GEORGIUM SIDUS.

Satellite.	Periodic Revolution.	Synodic Revolution.	Dist. from Herschel in semi-diameters of Herschel.	Dist. from Herschel in parts of the ecliptic, at the mean dist. of Herschel from Earth.	Distance from Herschel in English miles.	Least distance from Earth in English miles.	Greatest distance from Earth in English miles.
	d. h. m. s.	d. h. m. s.		′ ″			
I.	5 21 23 22	5 21 25 0	$13\frac{1443}{10000}$	0 $25\frac{1}{2}$	226,450	1,726,834,984	1,918,315,472
II.	8 16 57 43	8 17 1 19	$17\frac{103}{10000}$	0 33	293,053	1,726,768,381	1,918,382,075
III.	10 22 58 20	10 23 4 0	$19\frac{8969}{10000}$	0 $38\frac{3}{5}$	342,784	1,726,718,650	1,918,431,806
IV.	13 10 56 29	13 11 5 1	$22\frac{7835}{10000}$	0 $42\frac{1}{5}$	392,514	1,726,668,920	1,918,481,536
V.	38 0 39 4	38 1 49 0	$45\frac{507}{1000}$	1 $28\frac{2}{5}$	785,028	1,726,276,406	1,918,874,050
VI.	107 7 35 10	107 16 40 0	$91\frac{134}{1000}$	2 $56\frac{4}{5}$	1,570,057	1,725,491,377	1,919,659,079

OBSERVATIONS ON THE PRECEDING TABLES.

In Table I. the quantity of the periodic and sidereal revolutions of the planets is expressed in common years, each containing 365 days; as, e. g., the tropical revolution of Jupiter is, by the table, 11 years, 315 days, 14 hours, 39 minutes, 2 seconds; *i. e.*, the exact number of days is equal to 11 years multiplied by 365, and the extra 315 days added to the product, which make in all 4330 days. The *sidereal* and *periodic* times are also set down to the nearest second of time, from numbers used in the construction of the tables in the third edition of M. de la Lande's Astronomy. The columns containing the *mean distance* of the planets from the sun in English miles, and their *greatest* and *least distance* from the earth, are such as result from the best observations of the two last transits of Venus, which gave the solar parallax to be equal to 8 three-fifth seconds of a degree; and consequently the earth's diameter, as seen from the sun, must be the double of 8 three-fifth seconds, or 17 one-fifth seconds. From this last quantity, compared with the apparent diame-

A. M. 1. B. C. 4004.

8 And God called the firmament
Heaven. And the evening and
the morning were the second day.
9 And God said, [p] Let the waters under the
heaven be gathered together unto
one place, and let the dry *land*
appear: and it was so.
10 And God called the [q] dry *land* Earth;

[p] Job xxvi. 10; xxxviii. 8; Psalm xxiv. 2; xxxiii. 7; xcv. 5; civ. 9; cxxxvi. 5, 6; Proverbs viii. 29; Ecclesiastes i. 7; Jonah i. 9; 2 Peter iii. 5.——[q] 2 Peter iii. 5.

ters of the planets, as seen at a distance equal to that of the earth at her main distance from the sun, the *diameters of the planets in English miles*, as contained in the seventh column, have been carefully computed. In the column entitled "*Proportion of bulk*, the earth being 1," the whole numbers express the number of times the other planet contains more cubic miles, &c., than the earth; and if the number of cubic miles in the earth be given, the number of cubic miles in any planet may be readily found by multiplying the cubic miles contained in the earth by the number in the column, and the product will be the quantity required.

This is a small but accurate sketch of the vast solar system; to describe it fully, even in all its *known* revolutions and connections, in all its astonishing energy and influence, in its wonderful plan, structure, operations, and results, would require more volumes than can be devoted to the commentary itself.

As so little can be said here on a subject so vast, it may appear to some improper to introduce it at all; but to any observation of this kind I must be permitted to reply, that I should deem it unpardonable not to give a general view of the solar system in the very place where its creation is first introduced. If these works be stupendous and magnificent, what must He be who formed, guides, and supports them all by the *word* of his power! Reader, stand in awe of this God, and sin not. Make him thy friend through the Son of his love; and, when these heavens and this earth are no more, thy soul shall exist in consummate and unutterable felicity.

See the remarks on the *sun, moon,* and *stars,* after verse 16.

Verse 2. *The earth was without form and void*] The original term תהו *tohu* and בהו *bohu,* which we translate *without form and void,* are of uncertain etymology; but in this place, and wherever else they are used, they convey the idea of *confusion* and *disorder.* From these terms it is probable that the ancient Syrians and Egyptians borrowed their gods, *Theuth* and *Bau,* and the Greeks their *Chaos.* God seems at first to have created the elementary principles of all things; and this formed the grand mass of matter, which in this state must be without *arrangement,* or any distinction of parts: a vast collection of indescribably confused materials, of nameless entities strangely mixed; and wonderfully well expressed by an ancient heathen poet:—

Ante mare et terras, et, quod tegit omnia, cœlum,
Unus erat toto naturæ vultus in orbe,
Quem dixere Chaos; rudis indigestaque moles,
Nec quicquam nisi pondus iners; congestaque eodem
Non bene junctarum discordia semina rerum. Ovid.

Before the seas and this terrestrial ball,
And heaven's high canopy that covers all,
One was the face of nature, if a face;
Rather, a rude and indigested mass;
A lifeless lump, unfashion'd and unframed,
Of jarring seeds, and justly Chaos named.
Dryden.

The most ancient of the Greeks have spoken nearly in the same way of this crude, indigested state of the primitive chaotic mass.

When this congeries of elementary principles was brought together, God was pleased to spend six days in assimilating, assorting, and arranging the materials, out of which he built up, not only the earth, but the whole of the solar system.

The Spirit of God] This has been variously and strangely understood. Some think a *violent wind* is meant, because רוח *ruach* often signifies *wind,* as well as *spirit,* as *πνευμα* does in Greek; and the term *God* is connected with it merely, as they think, to express the *superlative* degree. Others understand by it an *elementary fire.* Others, the *sun,* penetrating and drying up the earth with his rays. Others, the *angels,* who were supposed to have been employed as *agents* in creation. Others, a certain *occult* principle, termed the *anima mundi* or *soul of the world.* Others, a *magnetic attraction,* by which all things were caused to gravitate to a common centre. But it is sufficiently evident from the use of the word in other places, that the Holy Spirit of God is intended; which our blessed Lord represents under the notion of *wind,* John iii. 8; and which, as a *mighty rushing wind* on the day of pentecost, filled the house where the disciples were sitting, Acts ii. 2, which was immediately followed by their speaking with other tongues, because they were filled with the *Holy Ghost,* ver. 4. These scriptures sufficiently ascertain the sense in which the word is used by Moses.

Moved] מרחפת *merachepheth,* was *brooding* over; for the word expresses that tremulous motion made by the hen while either *hatching* her eggs or *fostering* her young. It here probably signifies the communicating a *vital* or *prolific* principle to the waters. As the idea of *incubation,* or hatching an egg, is implied in the original word, hence probably the notion, which prevailed among the ancients, that the world was generated from an *egg.*

Verse 3. *And God said, Let there be light*] יהי אור ויהי אור YEHI OR, *vaihi or.* Nothing can be conceived more dignified than this form of expression. It argues at once uncontrollable authority, and omnific power; and in human language it is scarcely possible to conceive that God can speak more like himself. This passage, in the Greek translation of the Septuagint, fell in the way of Dionysius Longinus, one of the

A. M. 1.
B. C. 4004.

and the gathering together of the
waters called he Seas: and God
saw that *it was* good.

11 And God said, Let the earth
[r] bring forth [s] grass, the herb yielding seed, *and* the fruit-tree yielding [t] fruit

A. M. 1.
B. C. 4004.

[r] Heb. vi. 7.

[s] Heb. *tender grass.*——[t] Luke vi. 44.

most judicious Greek critics that ever lived, and who is highly celebrated over the civilized world for a treatise he wrote, entitled Περι 'Υψους, Concerning the SUBLIME, both in prose and poetry; of this passage, though a heathen, he speaks in the following terms:— *Ταυτῃ και ὁ των Ιουδαιων θεσμοθετης (ουχ ὁ τυχων ανηρ,) επειδη την του θειου δυναμιν κατα την αξιαν εχωρησε, κᾀξεφηνεν· ευθυς εν τῃ εισβολῃ γραψας των νομων,* ΕΙΠΕΝ 'Ο ΘΕΟΣ, *φησι, τι;* ΓΕΝΕΣΘΩ ΦΩΣ· *και εγενετο.* ΓΕΝΕΣΘΩ ΓΗ· *και εγενετο.* "So likewise the Jewish lawgiver (who was no ordinary man) having conceived a just idea of the Divine power, he expressed it in a dignified manner; for at the beginning of his laws he thus speaks: GOD SAID—*What?* LET THERE BE LIGHT! *and there was light.* LET THERE BE EARTH! *and there was earth.*"—Longinus, sect. ix. edit. *Pearce.*

Many have asked, "How could light be produced on the *first day*, and the *sun*, the fountain of it, not created till the *fourth* day?" With the various and often unphilosophical answers which have been given to this question I will not meddle, but shall observe that the original word אור signifies not only *light* but *fire*, see Isa. xxxi. 9; Ezek. v. 2. It is used for the SUN, Job xxxi. 26. And for the *electric fluid* or LIGHTNING, Job xxxvii. 3. And it is worthy of remark that it is used in Isa. xliv. 16, for the *heat*, derived from אש *esh*, the *fire*. *He burneth part thereof in the fire* (כמו אש *bemo esh*:) *yea, he warmeth himself, and saith, Aha! I have seen the fire,* ראיתי אור *raithi ur*, which a modern philosopher who understood the language would not scruple to translate, I have received caloric, or an additional portion of the matter of *heat*. I therefore conclude, that as God has diffused the matter of *caloric* or *latent heat* through every part of nature, without which there could be neither vegetation nor animal life, that it is *caloric* or *latent heat* which is principally intended by the original word.

That there is *latent light*, which is probably the same with *latent heat*, may be easily demonstrated: take two pieces of smooth rock crystal, agate, cornelian or flint, and rub them together briskly in the dark, and the latent light or matter of caloric will be immediately produced and become visible. The light or caloric *thus* disengaged does not operate in the same powerful manner as the heat or *fire* which is produced by striking with flint and steel, or that produced by *electric* friction. The existence of this *caloric*—latent or *primitive light*, may be ascertained in various other bodies; it can be produced by the flint and steel, by rubbing two hard sticks together, by hammering cold iron, which in a short time becomes red hot, and by the strong and sudden compression of atmospheric air in a tube. Friction in general produces both *fire* and *light*. God therefore created this universal agent on the first day, because without it no operation of nature could be carried on or perfected.

Light is one of the most astonishing productions of the creative skill and power of God. It is the grand medium by which all his other works are discovered, examined, and understood, so far as they can be known. Its immense diffusion and extreme velocity are alone sufficient to demonstrate the being and wisdom of God. Light has been proved by many experiments to travel at the astonishing rate of 194,188 miles in *one second* of time! and comes from the sun to the earth in *eight minutes* $11\frac{43}{50}$ *seconds*, a distance of 95,513,794 English miles.

Verse 4. *God divided the light from the darkness.*] This does not imply that *light* and *darkness* are two distinct substances, seeing *darkness* is only the *privation* of light; but the words simply refer us by anticipation to the rotation of the earth round its own axis once in *twenty-three hours, fifty-six minutes, and four seconds*, which is the cause of the distinction between day and night, by bringing the different parts of the surface of the earth successively into and from under the solar rays; and it was probably at this moment that God gave this rotation to the earth, to produce this merciful provision of day and night. For the *manner* in which light is supposed to be produced, see ver. 16, under the word *sun*.

Verse 6. *And God said, Let there be a firmament*] Our translators, by following the *firmamentum* of the Vulgate, which is a translation of the στερεωμα of the Septuagint, have deprived this passage of all sense and meaning. The Hebrew word רקיע *rakia*, from רקע *raka*, *to spread out as the curtains of a tent or pavilion*, simply signifies an *expanse* or *space*, and consequently that circumambient space or expansion separating the clouds, which are in the higher regions of it, from the seas, &c., which are below it. This we call the *atmosphere, the orb of atoms* or inconceivably small particles; but the word appears to have been used by Moses in a more extensive sense, and to include the whole of the planetary vortex, or the space which is occupied by the whole *solar system*.

Verse 10. *And God called the dry* land *Earth; and the gathering together of the waters called he Seas*] These two constitute what is called the *terraqueous globe*, in which the earth and the water exist in a most judicious proportion to each other. Dr. Long took the papers which cover the surface of a seventeen inch terrestrial globe, and having carefully separated the land from the sea, he weighed the two collections of papers accurately, and found that the sea papers weighed three hundred and forty-nine grains, and the land papers only one hundred and twenty-four; by which experiment it appears that nearly *three-fourths* of the surface of our globe, from the arctic to the antarctic polar circles, are covered with water. The doctor did not weigh the parts within the polar circles, because

A. M. 1.
B. C. 4004.

after his kind, whose seed *is* in
itself, upon the earth: and it
was so.
12 And the earth brought forth grass, *and*
herb yielding seed after his kind,
[u] and the tree yielding fruit, whose
seed *was* in itself, after his kind: and God
saw that *it was* good.

A. M. 1.
B. C. 4004.

[u] Luke, chap. vi. 44.

there is no certain measurement of the proportion of land and water which they contain. This proportion of *three-fourths* water may be considered as too great, if not useless; but Mr. Ray, by most accurate experiments made on evaporation, has proved that it requires so much aqueous *surface* to yield a sufficiency of vapours for the purpose of cooling the atmosphere, and watering the earth. See Ray's *Physico-theological Discourses*.

An eminent chemist and philosopher, Dr. *Priestley*, has very properly observed that it seems plain that Moses considered the whole terraqueous globe as being created in a *fluid* state, the earthy and other particles of matter being mingled with the water. The present form of the earth demonstrates the truth of the Mosaic account; for it is well known that if a soft or elastic globular body be rapidly whirled round on its axis, the parts at the poles will be flattened, and the parts on the equator, midway between the north and south poles, will be raised up. This is precisely the shape of our earth; it has the figure of an *oblate spheroid*, a figure pretty much resembling the shape of an *orange*. It has been demonstrated by admeasurement that the earth is flatted at the poles and raised at the equator. This was first conjectured by Sir Isaac Newton, and afterwards confirmed by M. Cassini and others, who measured several degrees of latitude at the equator and near the north pole, and found that the difference perfectly justified Sir Isaac Newton's conjecture, and consequently confirmed the Mosaic account. The result of the experiments instituted to determine this point, proved that the diameter of the earth at the equator is greater by more than *twenty-three* and *a half* miles than it is at the poles, allowing the *polar* diameter to be $\frac{1}{334}$th part shorter than the *equatorial*, according to the recent admeasurements of several degrees of latitude made by Messrs. Mechain and Delambre.—*L' Histoire des Mathem.* par M. de la Lande, tom. iv., part v., liv. 6.

And God saw that it was *good.*] This is the judgment which God pronounced on his own works. They were *beautiful* and *perfect* in their kind, for such is the import of the word טוב *tob.* They were in weight and measure perfect and entire, lacking nothing. But the reader will think it strange that this approbation should be expressed *once* on the *first*, *fourth*, *fifth*, and *sixth* days; *twice* on the *third*, and not at all on the *second!* I suppose that the words, *And God saw that it was good*, have been either lost from the conclusion of the eighth verse, or that the clause in the tenth verse originally belonged to the eighth. It appears, from the Septuagint translation, that the words in question existed originally at the close of the eighth verse, in the copies which they used; for in that version we still find, *Και ειδεν ὁ Θεος ὁτι καλον· And God saw that it was good.* This reading, however, is not acknowledged by any of Kennicott's or De Rossi's MSS., nor by any of the other versions. If the account of the second day stood originally as it does now, no satisfactory reason can be given for the omission of this expression of the Divine approbation of the work wrought by his wisdom and power on that day.

Verse 11. *Let the earth bring forth grass—herb—fruit-tree, &c.*] In these general expressions all kinds of vegetable productions are included. *Fruit-tree* is not to be understood here in the restricted sense in which the term is used among us; it signifies all trees, not only those which bear fruit, which may be applied to the use of men and cattle, but also those which had the power of propagating themselves by seeds, &c. Now as God delights to manifest himself in the *little* as well as in the *great*, he has shown his consummate wisdom in every part of the *vegetable* creation. Who can account for, or comprehend, the structure of a single tree or plant? The roots, the stem, the woody fibres, the bark, the rind, the air-vessels, the sap-vessels, the leaves, the flowers, and the fruits, are so many mysteries. All the skill, wisdom, and power of men and angels could not produce a single grain of *wheat!* A serious and reflecting mind can see the grandeur of God, not only in the immense *cedars* on Lebanon, but also in the endlessly varied *forests* that appear through the microscope in the mould of cheese, stale paste, &c., &c.

Verse 12. *Whose seed was in itself*] Which has the power of multiplying itself by seeds, slips, roots, &c., *ad infinitum;* which contains in itself all the rudiments of the future plant through its endless generations. This doctrine has been abundantly confirmed by the most accurate observations of the best modern philosophers. The astonishing power with which God has endued the vegetable creation to multiply its different species, may be instanced in the seed of the *elm*. This tree produces *one thousand five hundred* and *eighty-four millions* of seeds; and *each of these seeds* has the power of producing the *same number*. How astonishing is this produce! At first *one* seed is deposited in the earth; from this one a tree springs, which in the course of its vegetative life produces *one thousand five hundred* and *eighty-four millions of seeds*. This is the *first* generation. The *second* generation will amount to *two trillions, five hundred* and *nine thousand* and *fifty-six billions*. The *third* generation will amount to *three thousand nine hundred* and *seventy-four quadrillions, three hundred* and *forty-four thousand seven hundred* and *four trillions!* And the *fourth* generation from these would amount to *six sextillions, two hundred* and *ninety-five thousand three hundred* and *sixty-two quintillions, eleven thousand one hundred* and *thirty-six quadrillions!* Sums too immense for the human mind to conceive; and, when we allow the most confined space in which a tree can grow, it

A. M. 1. B. C. 4004.

13 And the evening and the morning were the third day.

14 And God said, Let there be [v]lights in the firmament of the heaven, to divide [w]the day from the night; and let them be for signs, and [x]for seasons, and for days, and years.

15 And let them be for lights in the firmament of the heaven, to give light upon the earth: and it was so.

16 And God [y]made two great lights; the greater light [z]to rule the day, and [a]the lesser light to rule the night: *he made* [b]the stars also.

[v]Deut. iv. 19; Psa. lxxiv. 16; cxxxvi. 7.——[w]Heb. *between the day and between the night.*——[x]Psa. lxxiv. 17; civ. 19.

[y]Psa. cxxxvi. 7, 8, 9; cxlviii. 3, 5.——[z]Heb. *for the rule of the day.*——[a]Psa. viii. 3.——[b]Job xxxviii. 7.

appears that the seeds of the *third* generation from one elm would be many *myriads* of times more than sufficient to stock the whole superfices of all the planets in the solar system! But plants multiply themselves by *slips* as well as by *seeds.* Sir Kenelm Digby saw in 1660 a plant of barley, in the possession of the fathers of the Christian doctrine at Paris, which contained 249 stalks springing from one root or grain, and in which he counted upwards of 18,000 grains. See my experiments on *Tilling* in the Methodist Magazine.

Verse 14. *And God said, Let there be lights, &c.*] One principal office of these was to divide between day and night. When night is considered a state of comparative *darkness,* how can lights divide or distinguish it? The answer is easy: The sun is the monarch of the day, which is the state of light; the moon, of the night, the state of darkness. The rays of the sun, falling on the atmosphere, are refracted and diffused over the whole of that hemisphere of the earth immediately under his orb; while those rays of that vast luminary which, because of the earth's smallness in comparison of the sun, are diffused on all sides beyond the earth, falling on the opaque disc of the moon, are reflected back upon what may be called the lower hemisphere, or that part of the earth which is opposite to the part which is illuminated by the sun: and as the earth completes a revolution on its own axis in about twenty-four hours, consequently each hemisphere has alternate day and night. But as the solar light reflected from the face of the moon is computed to be 50,000 times less in intensity and effect than the light of the sun as it comes directly from himself to our earth, (for light *decreases* in its intensity as the distance it travels from the sun *increases,*) therefore a sufficient distinction is made between day and night, or light and darkness, notwithstanding each is ruled and determined by one of these *two great lights;* the moon ruling the night, i. e., reflecting from her own surface back on the earth the rays of light which she receives from the sun. Thus both hemispheres are to a certain degree illuminated: the one, on which the sun shines, completely so; this is *day:* the other, on which the sun's light is reflected by the moon, partially; this is *night.* It is true that both the planets and fixed stars afford a considerable portion of light during the night, yet they cannot be said to *rule* or to predominate by their light, because their rays are quite lost in the superior splendour of the moon's light.

And let them be for signs] לאתת *leothoth.* Let them ever be considered as continual tokens of God's tender care for man, and as standing proofs of his continual *miraculous* interference; for so the word אות *oth* is often used. And is it not the almighty energy of God that upholds them in being? The sun and moon also serve as *signs* of the different changes which take place in the atmosphere, and which are so essential for all purposes of agriculture, commerce, &c.

For seasons] מועדים *moadim;* For the determination of the times on which the *sacred festivals* should be held. In this sense the word frequently occurs; and it was right that at the very opening of his revelation God should inform man that there were certain festivals which should be annually celebrated to his glory. Some think we should understand the original word as signifying *months,* for which purpose we know the moon essentially serves through all the revolutions of time.

For days] Both the hours of the day and night, as well as the different lengths of the days and nights, are distinguished by the longer and shorter spaces of time the sun is above or below the horizon.

And years.] That is, those grand divisions of time by which all *succession* in the vast lapse of duration is distinguished. This refers principally to a complete revolution of the earth round the sun, which is accomplished in 365 days, 5 hours, 48 minutes, and 48 seconds; for though the revolution is that of the earth, yet it cannot be determined but by the heavenly bodies.

Verse 16. *And God made two great lights*] Moses speaks of the sun and moon here, not according to their *bulk* or *solid contents,* but according to the *proportion of light* they shed on the earth. The expression has been cavilled at by some who are as devoid of mental capacity as of candour. "The moon," say they, "is not a *great* body; on the contrary, it is the very smallest in our system." Well, and has Moses said the contrary? He has said it is a *great* LIGHT; had he said otherwise he had not spoken the truth. It is, in reference to the earth, next to the sun himself, the *greatest light* in the solar system; and so true is it that the moon is a *great light,* that it affords more light to the earth than all the planets in the solar system, and all the innumerable stars in the vault of heaven, put together. It is worthy of remark that on the *fourth* day of the creation the sun was formed, and then "first tried his beams athwart the gloom profound;" and that at the conclusion of the *fourth millenary* from the creation, according to the Hebrew, the Sun of righteousness shone upon the world, as deeply sunk in that mental darkness produced by sin as the ancient world was, while teeming darkness held the dominion, till the sun was created as the dispenser of light. What would the natural world be without the

A. M. 1.
B. C. 4004.

17 And God set them in the
firmament of the heaven, to give
light upon the earth,
18 And to [c] rule over the day, and over the
night; and to divide the light from the
darkness: and God saw that *it was*
good.
19 And the evening and the morning were
the fourth day.
20 And God said, Let the waters bring

A. M. 1.
B. C. 4004.

[c] Jeremiah, chap. xxxi. 35.

sun? A howling waste, in which neither animal nor vegetable life could possibly be sustained. And what would the moral world be without Jesus Christ, and the light of his word and Spirit? Just what those parts of it now are where his light has not yet shone: "dark places of the earth, filled with the habitations of cruelty," where error prevails without end, and superstition, engendering false hopes and false fears, degrades and debases the mind of man.

Many have supposed that the *days* of the creation answer to so many thousands of years; and that as God created all in *six* days, and rested the *seventh*, so the world shall last *six thousand* years, and the *seventh* shall be the eternal rest that remains for the people of God. To this conclusion they have been led by these words of the apostle, 2 Pet. iii. 8: *One day is with the Lord as a thousand years; and a thousand years as one day.* Secret things belong to God; those that are revealed to us and our children.

He made *the stars also.*] Or rather, *He made the lesser light, with the stars, to rule the night.* See Claudian *de Raptu* PROSER.. lib. ii., v. 44.

Hic Hyperionis solem de semine nasci
Fecerat, et pariter lunam, sed dispare forma,
Auroræ noctisque duces.

From famed Hyperion did he cause to rise
The sun, and placed the moon amid the skies,
With splendour robed, but far unequal light,
The radiant leaders of the day and night.

OF THE SUN.

On the nature of the sun there have been various conjectures. It was long thought that he was a vast *globe of fire* 1,384,462 times larger than the earth, and that he was continually emitting from his body innumerable millions of *fiery* particles, which, being extremely divided, answered for the purpose of *light* and *heat* without occasioning any *ignition* or *burning*, except when collected in the focus of a convex lens or burning glass. Against this opinion, however, many serious and weighty objections have been made; and it has been so pressed with difficulties that philosophers have been obliged to look for a theory less repugnant to nature and probability. Dr. Herschel's discoveries by means of his immensely magnifying telescopes, have, by the general consent of philosophers, added a *new habitable world* to our system, which is the SUN. Without stopping to enter into *detail*, which would be improper here, it is sufficient to say that these discoveries tend to prove that what we call the *sun* is only the *atmosphere* of that luminary; "that this atmosphere consists of various *elastic fluids* that are more or less lucid and transparent; that as the clouds belonging to our earth are probably decompositions of some of the elastic fluids belonging to the atmosphere itself, so we may suppose that in the vast atmosphere of the sun, similar decompositions may take place, but with this difference, that the decompositions of the elastic fluids of the sun are of a *phosphoric* nature, and are attended by lucid appearances, by giving out light." The body of the sun he considers as hidden generally from us by means of this luminous atmosphere, but what are called the *maculæ* or *spots* on the sun are real *openings* in this atmosphere, through which the *opaque body* of the sun becomes visible; that this atmosphere itself is not *fiery* nor *hot*, but is the instrument which God designed to act on the caloric or latent heat; and that heat is only produced by the solar light acting upon and combining with the caloric or matter of fire contained in the air, and other substances which are heated by it. This ingenious theory is supported by many plausible reasons and illustrations, which may be seen in the paper he read before the Royal Society. On this subject see the note on ver. 3.

OF THE MOON.

There is scarcely any doubt now remaining in the philosophical world that the moon is a *habitable globe*. The most accurate observations that have been made with the most powerful telescopes have confirmed the opinion. The *moon* seems, in almost every respect, to be a body similar to our earth; to have its surface diversified by hill and dale, mountains and valleys, rivers, lakes, and seas. And there is the fullest evidence that our earth serves as a moon to the moon herself, differing only in this, that as the earth's surface is *thirteen times* larger than the moon's, so the moon receives from the earth a light *thirteen times* greater in splendour than that which she imparts to us; and by a very correct analogy we are led to infer that all the *planets* and their *satellites*, or attendant moons, are *inhabited*, for matter seems only to exist for the sake of intelligent beings.

OF THE STARS.

The STARS in general are considered to be *suns*, similar to that in our system, each having an appropriate number of *planets* moving round it; and, as these stars are innumerable, consequently there are innumerable worlds, all dependent on the power, protection, and providence of God. Where the stars are in great abundance, Dr. Herschel supposes they form *primaries* and *secondaries*, i. e., suns revolving about *suns*, as planets revolve about the sun in our system. He considers that this must be the case in what is called the *milky way*, the stars being there in prodigious quantity. Of this he gives the following proof:

A. M. I. B. C. 4004. forth abundantly the [d] moving creature that hath [e] life, and [f] fowl *that*
may fly above the earth in the [g] open firmament of heaven.
21 And [h] God created great whales,
and every living creature that moveth,
which the waters brought forth abundantly,
after their kind, and every winged fowl
after his kind: and God saw that *it was*
good.
22 And God blessed them, saying, A. M. I. B. C. 4004.
[i] Be frutiful, and multiply, and fill
the waters in the seas; and let fowl multiply in
the earth.
23 And the evening and the morning were
the fifth day.
24 And God said, Let the earth bring forth
the living creature after his kind, cattle, and
creeping thing, and beast of the earth after
his kind: and it was so.

[d] Or, *creeping.*——[e] Heb. *soul.*——[f] Heb. *let fowl fly.*——[g] Heb. *face of the firmament of heaven.*

[h] Chapter vi. 20; vii. 14; viii. 19; Psalm civ. 26.——[i] Chapter viii. 17.

On August 22, 1792, he found that in forty-one minutes of time not less than 258,000 stars had passed through the field of view in his telescope. What must God be, who has made, governs, and supports so many worlds! For the *magnitudes, distances, revolutions, &c.*, of the *sun, moon, planets*, and their *satellites*, see the preceding TABLES.

Verse 20. *Let the waters bring forth abundantly*] There is a meaning in these words which is seldom noticed. Innumerable millions of animalcula are found in water. Eminent naturalists have discovered not less than 30,000 in a single drop! How inconceivably small must each be, and yet each a perfect animal, furnished with the whole apparatus of bones, muscles, nerves, heart, arteries, veins, lungs, viscera in general, animal spirits, &c., &c. What a proof is this of the manifold wisdom of God! But the *fecundity* of fishes is another point intended in the text; no creatures are so prolific as these. A TENCH lay 1,000 eggs, a CARP 20,000, and Leuwenhoek counted in a middling sized COD 9,384,000! Thus, according to the purpose of God, the *waters bring forth abundantly.* And what a merciful provision is this for the necessities of man! Many hundreds of thousands of the earth's inhabitants live for a great part of the year on *fish* only. Fish afford, not only a wholesome, but a very nutritive diet; they are liable to few diseases, and generally come in vast quantities to our shores when in their greatest perfection. In this also we may see that the kind *providence* of God goes hand in hand with his creating energy. While he manifests his wisdom and his power, he is making a permanent provision for the sustenance of man through all his generations.

Verse 21. *And God created great whales*] התנינם הגדלים *hattanninim haggedolim.* Though this is generally understood by the different versions as signifying *whales*, yet the original must be understood rather as a *general* than a *particular* term, comprising all the great aquatic animals, such as the various species of whales, the porpoise, the dolphin, the monoceros or narwal, and the shark. God delights to show himself in *little* as well as in *great* things: hence he forms animals so minute that 30,000 can be contained in one drop of water; and others so *great* that they seem to require almost a whole *sea* to float in.

Verse 22. *Let fowl multiply in the earth.*] It is truly astonishing with what care, wisdom, and minute skill God has formed the different genera and species of birds, whether intended to live chiefly on land or in water. The structure of a single *feather* affords a world of wonders; and as God made the fowls *that they might fly in the firmament of heaven*, ver. 20, so he has adapted the *form* of their bodies, and the structure and disposition of their plumage, for that very purpose. The head and neck in flying are drawn principally within the breastbone, so that the whole under part exhibits the appearance of a ship's hull. The wings are made use of as sails, or rather oars, and the tail as a helm or rudder. By means of these the creature is not only able to preserve the centre of gravity, but also to go with vast speed through the air, either straight forward, circularly, or in any kind of angle, upwards or downwards. In these also God has shown his skill and his power in the *great* and in the *little*—in the vast *ostrich* and *cassowary*, and in the beautiful *humming-bird*, which in plumage excels the splendour of the peacock, and in size is almost on a level with the *bee*.

Verse 24. *Let the earth bring forth the living creature, &c.*] נפש חיה *nephesh chaiyah;* a general term to express all creatures endued with animal life, in any of its infinitely varied gradations, from the half-reasoning *elephant* down to the stupid *potto*, or lower still, to the *polype*, which seems equally to share the vegetable and animal life. The word חיתו *chaitho*, in the latter part of the verse, seems to signify all *wild* animals, as lions, tigers, &c., and especially such as are *carnivorous*, or live on *flesh*, in contradistinction from *domestic* animals, such as are *graminivorous*, or live on grass and other vegetables, and are capable of being tamed, and applied to domestic purposes. See on ver. 29. These latter are probably meant by בהמה *behemah* in the text, which we translate *cattle*, such as *horses, kine, sheep, dogs, &c.* *Creeping thing*, רמש *remes*, all the different genera of *serpents, worms*, and such animals as have no feet. In *beasts* also God has shown his wondrous skill and power; in the vast *elephant*, or still more colossal *mammoth* or *mastodon*, the whole race of which appears to be extinct, a few skeletons only remaining. This animal, an astonishing effect of God's power, he seems to have produced merely to show what he could do, and after suffering a few of them to propagate, he extinguished the race by a merciful providence, that they might not destroy both man and beast. The mammoth appears to have been a *carnivorous* animal, as the structure of the

A. M. 1.
B. C. 4004.

25 And God made the beast of the earth after his kind, and cattle
after their kind, and every thing that creepeth
upon the earth after his kind: and God saw
that *it was* good.
26 And God said, [k] Let us make man in our
image, after our likeness: and [l] let them have
dominion over the fish of the sea,
and over the fowl of the air, and over
the cattle, and over all the earth, and over every
creeping thing that creepeth upon the earth.
27 So God created man in his *own* image,
[m] in the image of God created he him; [n] male
and female created he them.

[k] Chap. v. 1; ix. 6; Psa. c. 3; Eccles. vii. 29; Acts xvii. 26, 28, 29; 1 Cor. xi. 7; Eph. iv. 24; Col. iii. 10; James iii. 9. — [l] Chap. ix. 2; Psa. viii. 6. — [m] 1 Cor. xi. 7. — [n] Chap. v. 2; Mal. ii. 15; Matt. xix. 4; Mark x. 6.

teeth proves, and of an immense size; from a considerable part of a skeleton which I have seen, it is computed that the animal to which it belonged must have been nearly *twenty-five* feet high, and *sixty* in length! The bones of one toe are entire; the toe upwards of three feet in length. But this skeleton might have belonged to the *megalonyx*, a kind of *sloth*, or *bradypus*, hitherto unknown. Few elephants have ever been found to exceed eleven feet in height. How wondrous are the works of God! But his skill and power are not less seen in the beautiful *chevrotin*, or *tragulus*, a creature of the antelope kind, the smallest of all *bifid* or cloven-footed animals, whose delicate limbs are scarcely so large as an ordinary goose quill; and also in the *shrew mouse*, perhaps the smallest of the many-toed quadrupeds. In the *reptile* kind we see also the same skill and power, not only in the immense snake called *boa constrictor*, the mortal foe and conqueror of the royal tiger, but also in the *cobra de manille*, a venomous serpent, only a little larger than a common sewing needle.

Verse 25. *And God made the beast of the earth after his kind, &c.*] Every thing both in the animal and vegetable world was made *so* according to its kind, both in *genus* and *species*, as to produce *its own kind* through endless generations. Thus the several races of animals and plants have been kept distinct from the foundation of the world to the present day. This is a proof that all future generations of plants and animals have been seminally included in those which God formed in the beginning.

Verse 26. *And God said, Let us make man*] It is evident that God intends to impress the mind of man with a sense of something extraordinary in the formation of his body and soul, when he introduces the account of his creation thus; Let US make man. The word אדם *Adam*, which we translate *man*, is intended to designate the *species* of animal, as חיתו *chaitho*, marks the *wild beasts* that live in general a solitary life; בהמה *behemah*, *domestic* or gregarious animals; and רמש *remes*, all kinds of *reptiles*, from the largest snake to the microscopic eel. Though the same kind of organization may be found in man as appears in the lower animals, yet there is a variety and complication in the parts, a delicacy of structure, a nice arrangement, a judicious adaptation of the different members to their great offices and functions, a dignity of mien, and a perfection of the whole, which are sought for in vain in all other creatures. See chap. iii. 22.

In our image, after our likeness] What is said above refers only to the *body* of man, what is here said refers to his *soul*. This was made in the *image* and *likeness* of God. Now, as the Divine Being is infinite, he is neither limited by parts, nor definable by passions; therefore he can have no *corporeal image* after which he made the body of man. The image and likeness must necessarily be intellectual; his mind, his soul, must have been formed after the nature and perfections of his God. The human mind is still endowed with most extraordinary capacities; it was more so when issuing out of the hands of its Creator. God was now producing a spirit, and a spirit, too, formed after the perfections of his own nature. God is the fountain whence this spirit issued, hence the stream must resemble the spring which produced it. God is holy, just, wise, good, and perfect; so must the soul be that sprang from him: there could be in it nothing impure, unjust, ignorant, evil, low, base, mean, or vile. It was created after the image of God; and that image, St. Paul tells us, consisted in *righteousness*, *true holiness*, and *knowledge*, Eph. iv. 24; Col. iii. 10. Hence man was *wise* in his *mind*, *holy* in his *heart*, and *righteous* in his *actions*. Were even the word of God silent on this subject, we could not infer less from the lights held out to us by reason and common sense. The text tells us he was the work of ELOHIM, the Divine Plurality, marked here more distinctly by the plural pronouns US and OUR; and to show that he was the masterpiece of God's creation, all the persons in the Godhead are represented as united in counsel and effort to produce this astonishing creature.

Gregory Nyssen has very properly observed that the superiority of man to all other parts of creation is seen in this, that all other creatures are represented as the effect of God's *word*, but man is represented as the *work* of God, according to plan and consideration: *Let* US *make* MAN *in our* IMAGE, *after our* LIKENESS. See his Works, vol. i., p. 52, c. 3.

And let them have dominion] Hence we see that the *dominion* was not the *image*. God created man capable of governing the world, and when fitted for the office, he fixed him in it. We see God's tender care and parental solicitude for the comfort and well-being of this masterpiece of his workmanship, in creating the world previously to the creation of man. He prepared every thing for his subsistence, convenience, and pleasure, before he brought him into being; so that, comparing little with great things, the house was built, furnished, and amply stored, by the time the destined tenant was ready to occupy it.

It has been supposed by some that God speaks here to the angels, when he says, Let *us* make man; but to make this a likely interpretation these persons must

A. M. 1.
B. C. 4004.

28 And God blessed them, and
God said unto them, [o] Be fruitful,
and multiply, and replenish the earth, and
subdue it; and have dominion over the fish
of the sea, and over the fowl of the air, and
over every living thing that [p] moveth upon the
earth.
29 And God said, Behold, I have given
you every herb [q] bearing seed, which *is* upon
the face of all the earth, and every tree, in the
which *is* the fruit of a tree yielding
seed; [r] to you it shall be for meat.
30 And to [s] every beast of the earth, and to
every [t] fowl of the air, and to every thing that
creepeth upon the earth, wherein *there is* [u] life,
I have given every green herb for meat: and
it was so.
31 And [v] God saw every thing that he had
made, and, behold, *it was* very good. And the
evening and the morning were the sixth day.

A. M. 1.
B. C. 4004.

---

[o] Chap. ix. 1, 7; Lev. xxvi. 9; Psa. cxxvii. 3; cxxviii. 3, 4.—[p] Heb. *creepeth.*—[q] Heb. *seeding seed.*—[r] Chap. ix. 3; Job xxxvi. 31; Psa. civ. 14, 15; cxxxvi. 25; cxlvi. 7; Acts xiv. 17.—[s] Psa. cxlv. 15, 16; cxlvii. 9.—[t] Job xxxviii. 41.—[u] Heb. *a living soul.*—[v] Psa. civ. 24; Lam. iii. 38; 1 Tim. iv. 4.

---

prove, 1. That angels were then created. 2. That angels could assist in a work of creation. 3. That angels were themselves made in the image and likeness of God. If they were not, it could not be said, *in* OUR *image*, and it does not appear from any part in the sacred writings that any creature but *man* was made in the image of God. See the note on Psalm viii. 5.

Verse 28. *And God blessed them*] Marked them as being under his especial protection, and gave them power to propagate and multiply their own kind on the earth. A large volume would be insufficient to contain what we *know* of the excellence and perfection of man, even in his present degraded fallen state. Both his body and soul are adapted with astonishing wisdom to their *residence* and *occupations;* and also the *place* of their residence, as well as the surrounding objects, in their diversity, colour, and mutual relations, to the mind and body of this lord of the creation. The contrivance, arrangement, action, and re-action of the different parts of the body, show the admirable skill of the wondrous Creator; while the various powers and faculties of the mind, acting on and by the different organs of this body, proclaim the *soul's* Divine origin, and demonstrate that he who was made in the image and likeness of God, was a transcript of his own excellency, destined to know, love, and dwell with his Maker throughout eternity.

Verse 29. *I have given you every herb—for meat.*] It seems from this, says an eminent philosopher, that man was originally intended to live upon *vegetables* only; and as no change was made in the structure of men's bodies after the flood, it is not probable that any change was made in the articles of their food. It may also be inferred from this passage that no animal whatever was originally designed to prey on others; for nothing is here said to be given to any beast of the earth besides *green herbs.*—Dr. Priestley. Before sin entered into the world, there could be, at least, no *violent deaths,* if any death at all. But by the particular structure of the teeth of animals God prepared them for that kind of aliment which they were to subsist on after the FALL.

Verse 31. *And, behold,* it was *very good.*] טוב מאד *tob meod, Superlatively,* or *only good;* as good as they could be. The plan wise, the work well executed, the different parts properly arranged, their nature, limits, mode of existence, manner of propagation, habits, mode of sustenance, &c., &c., properly and permanently established and secured; for every thing was formed to the utmost perfection of its nature, so that nothing could be added or diminished without encumbering the operations of matter and spirit on the one hand, or rendering them inefficient to the end proposed on the other; and God has so done all these marvellous works as to be glorified *in* all, *by* all, and *through* all.

And the evening and the morning were the sixth day.] The word ערב *ereb,* which we translate *evening,* comes from the root ערב *arab,* to *mingle;* and properly signifies that state in which neither *absolute darkness* nor *full light* prevails. It has nearly the same grammatical signification with our *twilight,* the time that elapses from the setting of the sun till he is eighteen degrees below the horizon, and the last eighteen degrees before he arises. Thus we have the morning and evening twilight, or *mixture* of light and darkness, in which neither prevails, because, while the sun is within eighteen degrees of the horizon, either after his setting or before his rising, the atmosphere has power to refract the rays of light, and send them back on the earth. The Hebrews extended the meaning of this term to the whole duration of night, because it was ever a *mingled* state, the moon, the planets, or the stars, tempering the darkness with some rays of light. From the *ereb* of Moses came the Ερεβος, *Erebus,* of Hesiod, Aristophanes, and other heathens, which they *deified* and made, with *Nox* or night, the parent of all things.

The morning—בקר *boker;* From בקר *bakar,* he *looked out;* a beautiful figure which represents the morning as *looking out* at the east, and illuminating the whole of the upper hemisphere.

The evening and the morning were the sixth day.—It is somewhat remarkable that through the whole of this chapter, whenever the division of days is made, the evening always precedes the morning. The reason of this may perhaps be, that darkness was pre-existent to light, (verse 2, *And darkness was upon the face of the deep,*) and therefore time is reckoned from the first act of God towards the creation of the world, which took place before light was called forth into existence. It is very likely, for this same reason, that the Jews began their day at six o'clock in the evening in imitation of Moses's division of time in this chapter. *Cæsa-*

in his Commentaries makes mention of the same peculiarity existing among the Gauls: *Galli se omnes ab Dite patre prognatos prædicant: idque ab Druidibus proditum dicunt: ob eam causam spatia omnis temporis, non numero dierum, sed noctium, finiunt; et dies natales, et mensium et annorum initia sic observant, ut noctem dies subsequatur;* De Bell. Gall. lib. vi. Tacitus likewise records the same of the Germans: *Nec dierum numerum, ut nos, sed noctium computant: sic constituant, sic condicunt, nox ducere diem videtur;* De Mor. Germ. sec. ii. And there are to this day some remains of the same custom in England, as for instance in the word *se'nnight* and *fortnight.* See also Æschyl. Agamem. ver. 273, 287.

Thus ends a chapter containing the most extensive, most profound, and most sublime truths that can possibly come within the reach of the human intellect. How unspeakably are we indebted to God for giving us a revelation of his WILL and of his WORKS! Is it possible to know the mind of God but from himself? It is impossible. Can those things and services which are worthy of and pleasing to an infinitely pure, perfect, and holy Spirit, be ever found out by *reasoning* and *conjecture?* Never! for the Spirit of God alone can know the mind of God; and by this Spirit he has revealed himself to man; and in this revelation has taught him, not only to know the glories and perfections of the Creator, but also his own origin, duty, and interest. Thus far it was essentially necessary that God should reveal his WILL; but if he had not given a revelation of his WORKS, the origin, constitution, and nature of the universe could never have been adequately known. *The world by wisdom knew not God;* this is demonstrated by the writings of the most learned and intelligent heathens. They had no just, no rational notion of the origin and design of the universe. Moses alone, of all ancient writers, gives a consistent and rational account of the creation; an account which has been confirmed by the investigation of the most accurate philosophers. But *where* did he learn this? "In Egypt." That is impossible; for the Egyptians themselves were destitute of this knowledge. The remains we have of their old historians, all posterior to the time of Moses, are egregious for their contradictions and absurdity; and the most learned of the Greeks who borrowed from them have not been able to make out, from their conjoint stock, any consistent and credible account. Moses has revealed the mystery that lay hid from all preceding ages, because he was taught it *by the inspiration of the Almighty.*

READER, thou hast now before thee the most ancient and most authentic history in the world; a history that contains the first written discovery that God has made of himself to mankind; a discovery of his own *being,* in his *wisdom, power,* and *goodness,* in which *thou* and the whole human race are so intimately concerned. How much thou art indebted to him for this discovery he alone can teach thee, and cause thy heart to feel its obligations to his wisdom and mercy. *Read* so as to understand, for these things were written for thy learning; therefore *mark* what thou readest, and *inwardly digest*—deeply and seriously meditate on, what thou hast marked, and *pray* to the Father of lights that he may open thy understanding, that thou mayest know these holy Scriptures, which are able to make thee wise unto salvation.

God made thee and the universe, and governs all things according to the counsel of his will; that will is infinite goodness, that counsel is unerring wisdom. While under the direction of this counsel, thou canst not err; while under the influence of this will, thou canst not be wretched. Give thyself up to his teaching, and submit to his authority; and, after guiding thee *here* by his counsel, he will at last bring thee to his glory. Every object that meets thy eye should teach thee reverence, submission, and gratitude. The earth and its productions were made for *thee;* and the providence of thy heavenly Father, infinitely diversified in its operations, watches over and provides for thee. Behold the firmament of his power, the sun, moon, planets, and stars, which he has formed, not for himself, for he needs none of these things, but for his intelligent offspring. What endless gratification has he designed thee in placing within thy reach these astonishing effects of his wisdom and power, and in rendering thee capable of searching out their wonderful relations and connections, and of knowing himself, the source of all perfection, by having made thee in his own image, and in his own likeness! It is true thou *art* fallen; but he has found out a ransom. God so loved thee in conjunction with the world that he gave his only-begotten Son, that whosoever believeth on him should not perish, but have everlasting life. Believe on HIM; through him *alone* cometh salvation; and the fair and holy image of God in which thou wast created shall be again restored; he will build thee up as at the first, restore thy judges and counsellors as at the beginning, and in thy second creation, as in thy first, will pronounce thee to be *very good,* and thou shalt show forth the virtues of him by whom thou art created anew in Christ Jesus. Amen.

CHAPTER II.

The seventh day is consecrated for a Sabbath, and the reasons assigned, 1–3. *A recapitulation of the six days' work of creation,* 4–7. *The garden of Eden planted,* 8. *Its trees,* 9. *Its rivers, and the countries watered by them,* 10–14. *Adam placed in the garden, and the command given not to eat of the tree of knowledge on pain of death,* 15–17. *God purposes to form a companion for the man,* 18. *The different animals brought to Adam that he might assign them their names,* 19, 20. *The creation of the woman,* 21, 22. *The institution of marriage,* 23, 24. *The purity and innocence of our first parents,* 25.

A. M. 1.
B. C. 4004.

THUS the heavens and the earth
were finished, and [a] all the
host of them.
2 [b] And on the seventh day God ended his work
which he had made; and he rested on the seventh day from all his work which he had made.
3 And God [c] blessed the seventh day, and
sanctified it; because that in it he
had rested from all his work which
God [d] created and made.
4 [e] These *are* the generations of the hea
vens and of the earth when they were created,
in the day that the Lord God made the earth
and the heavens,

A. M. 1.
B. C. 4004.

[a] Psa. xxxiii. 6.——[b] Exod. xx. 11; xxxi. 17; Deut. v. 14; Heb. iv. 4.——[c] Neh. ix. 14; Isa. lviii. 13.——[d] Heb. *created to make*.——[e] Chap. i. 1; Psa. xc. 1, 2.

NOTES ON CHAP. II.

Verse 1. *And all the host of them.*] The word *host* signifies literally an *army*, composed of a number of companies of soldiers under their respective leaders; and seems here elegantly applied to the various celestial bodies in our system, placed by the Divine wisdom under the influence of the *sun*. From the original word צבא *tsaba*, a host, some suppose the *Sabeans* had their name, because of their paying Divine honours to the heavenly bodies. From the Septuagint version of this place, πας ὁ κοσμος αυτων, *all their ornaments*, we learn the true meaning of the word κοσμος, commonly translated *world*, which signifies a *decorated* or *adorned* whole or system. And this refers to the beautiful order, harmony, and regularity which subsist among the various parts of creation. This translation must impress the reader with a very favourable opinion of these ancient Greek translators; had they not examined the works of God with a philosophic eye, they never could have given this turn to the original.

Verse 2. *On the* SEVENTH *day God ended, &c.*] It is the general voice of Scripture that God finished the whole of the creation in SIX days, and rested the *seventh!* giving us an example that we might labour *six* days, and rest the seventh from all manual exercises. It is worthy of notice that the Septuagint, the Syriac, and the Samaritan, read the *sixth* day instead of the *seventh;* and this should be considered the genuine reading, which appears from these versions to have been originally that of the Hebrew text. How the word *sixth* became changed into *seventh* may be easily conceived from this circumstance. It is very likely that in ancient times all the numerals were signified by *letters*, and not by words at full length. This is the case in the most ancient Greek and Latin MSS., and in almost all the rabbinical writings. When these numeral letters became changed for words at full length, two letters nearly similar might be mistaken for each other; ו *vau* stands for *six*, ז *zain* for *seven;* how easy to mistake these letters for each other when writing the words at full length, and so give birth to the reading in question.

Verse 3. *And God blessed the seventh day*] The original word ברך *barach*, which is generally rendered *to bless*, has a very extensive meaning. It is frequently used in Scripture in the sense of *speaking good of* or *to* a person; and hence literally and properly rendered by the Septuagint ευλογησεν, from ευ, *good* or *well*, and λεγω, *I speak*. So God has spoken *well* of the Sabbath, and *good to them* who conscientiously observe it. *Blessing* is applied both to God and man: when God is said to bless, we generally understand by the expression that he *communicates* some good; but when man is said *to bless God*, we surely cannot imagine that he *bestows* any gifts or confers any benefit on his Maker. When God is said to *bless*, either in the Old or New Testament, it signifies his *speaking good* TO *man;* and this comprises the whole of his exceeding great and precious *promises*. And when man is said to *bless God*, it ever implies that he *speaks good* OF *him*, for the giving and fulfilment of his promises. This observation will be of general use in considering the various places where the word occurs in the sacred writings. Reader, God blesses thee when by his promises he *speaks good* TO *thee;* and thou dost bless him when, from a consciousness of his kindness to thy body and soul, thou art thankful to him, and *speakest good* OF his name.

Because that in it he had rested] שבת *shabath, he rested;* hence *Sabbath*, the name of the seventh day, signifying *a day of rest*—rest to the body from labour and toil, and rest to the soul from all worldly care and anxieties. He who labours with his *mind* by worldly schemes and plans on the Sabbath day is as culpable as he who labours with his *hands* in his accustomed calling. It is by the authority of God that the Sabbath is set apart for rest and religious purposes, as the six days of the week are appointed for labour. How wise is this provision! It is essentially necessary, not only to the body of man, but to all the animals employed in his service: take this away and the labour is too great, both man and beast would fail under it. Without this consecrated day religion itself would fail, and the human mind, becoming sensualized, would soon forget its origin and end. Even as a *political* regulation, it is one of the wisest and most beneficent in its effects of any ever instituted. Those who habitually disregard its moral obligation are, to a man, not only good for nothing, but are wretched in themselves, a curse to society, and often end their lives miserably. See the notes on Exod. xx. 8; xxiii. 12; xxiv. 16; and xxxi. 13; to which the reader is particularly desired to refer.

As God formed both the mind and body of man on principles of *activity*, so he assigned him proper employment; and it is his decree that the *mind* shall improve by exercise, and the *body* find increase of vigour and health in honest *labour*. He who idles away his time in the *six* days is equally culpable in the sight of God as he who works on the *seventh*. The idle person is ordinarily clothed with rags, and the Sabbath-breakers frequently come to an ignominious death. Reader, beware.

Verse 4. *In the day that the Lord God made, &c.*] The word יהוה *Yehovah* is for the first time mentioned

A. M. 1.
B. C. 4004.

5 And every [f] plant of the field
before it was in the earth, and
every herb of the field before it grew: for the
Lord God had not [g] caused it to rain upon the
earth, and *there was* not a man [h] to till the
ground.
6 But [i] there went up a mist from the earth,
and watered the whole face of the
ground.
7 And the Lord God formed man [k] *of* the
[l] dust of the ground, and [m] breathed into his
[n] nostrils the breath of life; and [o] man became
a living soul.
8 And the Lord God planted [p] a garden

A. M. 1.
B. C. 4004.

[f] Chap. i. 12; Psa. civ. 14.——[g] Job xxxviii. 26, 27, 28.
[h] Chap. iii. 23.——[i] Or, *a mist which went up from*, &c.——[k] Heb.
dust of the ground.——[l] Chap. iii. 19, 23; Psa. ciii. 14; Eccles.
xii. 7; Isa. lxiv. 8; 1 Cor. xv. 47.——[m] Job xxxiii. 4; Acts xvii.
25.——[n] Chap. vii. 22; Isa. ii. 22.——[o] 1 Cor. xv. 45.——[p] Chap.
xiii. 10; Isa. li. 3; Ezek. xxviii. 13; Joel ii. 3.

here. What it signifies see on Exod. xxxiv. 5, 6. Wherever this word occurs in the sacred writings we translate it Lord, which word is, through respect and reverence, always printed in capitals. Though our English term *Lord* does not give the particular meaning of the original word, yet it conveys a strong and noble sense. *Lord* is a contraction of the Anglo-Saxon hlaford, *Hlaford*, afterwards written Loverd, *Loverd*, and lastly *Lord*, from hlaf, bread; hence our word *loaf*, and ford, *ford*, to supply, to give out. The word, therefore, implies the *giver of bread*, i. e., he who deals out all the necessaries of life. Our ancient English noblemen were accustomed to keep a continual open house, where all their vassals, and all strangers, had full liberty to enter and eat as much as they would; and hence those noblemen had the honourable name of *lords*, i. e., *the dispensers of bread*. There are about *three* of the ancient nobility who still keep up this honourable custom, from which the very name of their nobility is derived. We have already seen, chap. i. 1, with what judgment our Saxon ancestors expressed *Deus*, the Supreme Being, by the term *God;* and we see the same judgment consulted by their use of the term *Lord* to express the word *Dominus*, by which terms the Vulgate version, which they used, expresses *Elohim* and *Jehovah*, which we translate Lord God. God is the *good Being*, and Lord is *the dispenser of bread*, the giver of every good and perfect gift, who liberally *affords* the bread that perisheth to every man, and has amply provided the bread that endures unto eternal life for every human soul. With what propriety then does this word apply to the Lord Jesus, who is emphatically called *the bread of life; the bread of God which cometh down from heaven, and which is given for the life of the world!* John vi. 33, 48, 51. What a pity that this most impressive and instructive meaning of a word in such general use were not more extensively known, and more particularly regarded! See the postscript to the *general preface*. I know that Mr. H. *Tooke* has endeavoured to render this derivation contemptible; but this has little weight with me. I have traced it through the most accredited writers in *Saxony* and on *Saxon* affairs, and I am satisfied that *this* and *this only*, is its proper etymology and derivation.

Verse 5. *Every plant of the field before it was in the earth*] It appears that God created every thing, not only perfect as it respects its nature, but also in a state of *maturity*, so that every vegetable production appeared at once in full growth; and this was necessary that man, when he came into being, might find every thing ready for his use.

Verse 6. *There went up a mist*] This passage appears to have greatly embarrassed many commentators. The plain meaning seems to be this, that the aqueous vapours, ascending from the earth, and becoming condensed in the colder regions of the atmosphere, fell back upon the earth in the form of *dews*, and by this means an equal portion of moisture was distributed to the roots of plants, &c. As Moses had said, ver 5, that *the Lord had not caused it to rain upon the earth*, he probably designed to teach us, in verse 6, *how* rain is produced, viz., by the condensation of the aqueous vapours, which are generally through the heat of the sun and other causes raised to a considerable height in the atmosphere, where, meeting with cold air, the watery particles which were before so small and light that they could float in the air, becoming *condensed*, i. e., many drops being driven into one, become too heavy to be any longer suspended, and then, through their own gravity, fall down in the form which we term *rain*.

Verse 7. *God formed man of the dust*] In the most distinct manner God shows us that man is a *compound* being, having a body and soul distinctly, and separately created; the body out of the dust of the earth, the soul immediately breathed from God himself. Does not this strongly mark that the soul and body are not the *same thing?* The body derives its origin from the *earth*, or as עפר *aphar* implies, the *dust;* hence because it is earthly it is decomposable and perishable. Of the soul it is said, *God breathed into his nostrils the breath of life;* נשמת חיים *nishmath chaiyim*, the breath of lives, i. e., animal and intellectual. While this breath of God expanded the lungs and set them in play, his inspiration gave both spirit and understanding.

Verse 8. *A garden eastward in Eden*] Though the word עדן *Eden* signifies *pleasure* or *delight*, it is certainly the name of a place. See chap. iv. 16; 2 Kings xix. 12; Isa. xxxvii. 12; Ezek. xxvii. 23; Amos i. 5. And such places probably received their name from their *fertility, pleasant situation, &c.* In this light the Septuagint have viewed it, as they render the passage thus: Εφυτευσεν ὁ Θεος παραδεισον εν Εδεν, *God planted a paradise in Eden.* Hence the word paradise has been introduced into the New Testament, and is generally used to signify a place of exquisite pleasure and delight. From this the ancient heathens borrowed their ideas of the *gardens of the Hesperides*, where the trees bore golden fruit; the gardens of *Adonis*, a word which is evidently derived from the Hebrew עדן *Eden;* and hence the origin of *sacred gardens*

a

A. M. 1. B. C. 4004. [q] eastward in [r] Eden; and there
[s] he put the man whom he had
formed.
9 And out of the ground made the LORD
God to grow [t] every tree that is pleasant to
the sight, and good for food; [u] the tree of life
also in the midst of the garden, A. M. 1. B. C. 4004.
[v] and the tree of knowledge of good
and evil.
10 And a river went out of Eden to water
the garden; and from thence it was parted,
and became into four heads.

[q] Chap. iii. 24.—[r] Chap. iv. 16; 2 Kings xix. 12; Ezek. xxvii. 23.—[s] Ver. 15.—[t] Ezek. xxxi. 8.
[u] Chap. iii. 22; Prov. iii. 18; xi. 30; Rev. ii. 7; xxii. 2, 14.—[v] Ver. 17.

or enclosures dedicated to purposes of devotion, some comparatively innocent, others impure. The word *paradise* is not *Greek;* in *Arabic* and *Persian* it signifies a garden, a vineyard, and also the place of the blessed. The Mohammedans say that God created the جنت الفردوس *Jennet al Ferdoos,* the garden of paradise, from light, and the prophets and wise men ascend thither. Wilmet places it after the root فرد *farada,* to *separate,* especially a person or place, for the purposes of devotion, but supposes it to be originally a Persian word, *vox originis Persicæ quam in sua lingua conservarunt* Armeni. As it is a word of doubtful origin, its etymology is uncertain.

Verse 9. *Every tree that is pleasant to the sight, &c.*] If we take up these expressions literally, they may bear the following interpretation: the tree pleasant to the sight may mean every beautiful tree or plant which for *shape, colour,* or *fragrance,* delights the senses, such as flowering shrubs, &c.

And good for food] All fruit-bearing trees, whether of the pulpy fruits, as apples, &c., or of the kernel or nut kind, such as dates, and nuts of different sorts, together with all *esculent vegetables.*

The tree of life] חיים *chaiyim;* of *lives,* or life-giving tree, every *medicinal* tree, herb, and plant, whose healing virtues are of great consequence to man in his present state, when through sin diseases of various kinds have seized on the human frame, and have commenced that process of dissolution which is to reduce the body to its primitive *dust.* Yet by the use of these *trees of life*—those different vegetable medicines, the health of the body may be preserved for a time, and death kept at a distance. Though the exposition given here may be a general meaning for these general terms, yet it is likely that *this tree of life* which was placed *in the midst of the garden* was intended as an emblem of that life which man should ever live, provided he continued in obedience to his Maker. And probably the use of this tree was intended as the *means* of preserving the body of man in a state of continual vital energy, and an antidote against death. This seems strongly indicated from chap. iii. 22.

And the tree of knowledge of good and evil.] Considering this also in a merely literal point of view, it may mean any tree or plant which possessed the property of increasing the knowledge of what was in nature, as the esculent vegetables had of increasing bodily vigour; and that there are some aliments which from their physical influence have a tendency to strengthen the understanding and invigorate the rational faculty more than others, has been supposed by the wisest and best of men; yet here much more seems intended, but *what* is very difficult to be ascertained. Some very eminent men have contended that the passage should be understood *allegorically!* and that the tree of the knowledge of good and evil means simply that *prudence,* which is a mixture of knowledge, care, caution, and judgment, which was prescribed to regulate the whole of man's conduct. And it is certain that to *know good and evil,* in different parts of Scripture, means such knowledge and discretion as leads a man to understand what is *fit* and *unfit,* what is not proper to be done and what *should* be performed. But how could the acquisition of such a faculty be a sin? Or can we suppose that such a faculty could be wanting when man was in a state of perfection? To this it may be answered: The prohibition was intended to *exercise* this faculty in man that it should constantly teach him this moral lesson, that there were some things fit and others unfit to be done, and that in reference to this point the tree itself should be both a constant teacher and monitor. The eating of its fruit would not have increased this moral faculty, but the prohibition was intended to exercise the faculty he already possessed. There is certainly nothing unreasonable in this explanation, and viewed in this light the passage loses much of its obscurity. Vitringa, in his dissertation *De arbore prudentiæ in Paradiso, ejusque mysterio,* strongly contends for this interpretation. See more on chap. iii. 6.

Verse 10. *A river went out of Eden, &c.*] It would astonish an ordinary reader, who should be obliged to consult different commentators and critics on the *situation of the terrestrial Paradise,* to see the vast variety of opinions by which they are divided. Some place it in the third heaven, others in the fourth; some within the orbit of the moon, others in the moon itself; some in the middle regions of the air, or beyond the earth's attraction; some on the earth, others under the earth, and others within the earth; some have fixed it at the north pole, others at the south; some in Tartary, some in China; some on the borders of the Ganges, some in the island of Ceylon; some in Armenia, others in Africa, under the equator; some in Mesopotamia, others in Syria, Persia, Arabia, Babylon, Assyria, and in Palestine; some have condescended to place it in *Europe,* and others have contended it either exists not, or is invisible, or is merely of a spiritual nature, and that the whole account is to be spiritually understood! That there was such a *place* once there is no reason to doubt; the description given by Moses is too *particular* and *circumstantial* to be capable of being understood in any *spiritual* or *allegorical* way. As well might we contend that the *persons* of Adam and Eve were *allegorical,* as that the *place* of their residence was such.

A. M. 1. B. C. 4004.

11 The name of the first *is* Pison: that *is* it which compasseth [w] the whole land of Havilah, where *there is* gold;

12 And the gold of that land *is* good; [x] there *is* bdellium and the onyx stone.

13 And the name of the second river *is* Gihon: the same *is* it that compasseth the whole land of [y] Ethiopia.

14 And the name of the third river *is* [z] Hiddekel: that *is* it which goeth [a] toward the east of Assyria. And the fourth river *is* [b] Euphrates.

15 And the LORD God took [c] the man, and [d] put him into the garden of Eden to dress it, and to keep it.

16 And the LORD God commanded the man, saying, Of every tree of the garden [e] thou mayest freely eat;

17 [f] But of the tree of the knowledge of good and evil, [g] thou shalt not eat of it: for in the day that thou eatest thereof [h] thou shalt surely [i] die.

18 And the LORD God said, *It is* not good that the man should be alone; [k] I will make him a help [l] meet for him.

[w] Chap. xxv. 18; 1 Sam. xv. 17.——[x] Num. xi. 7; Exod. xvi. 31.——[y] Heb. *Cush*.——[z] Dan. x. 4.——[a] Or, *eastward to Assyria*; chap. x. 22.——[b] Deut. i. 7; xi. 24; Rev. ix. 14.——[c] Or, *Adam*.——[d] Ver. 8.——[e] Heb. *eating thou shalt eat*.——[f] Ver. 9.

[g] Chap. iii. 1, 3, 11, 17.——[h] Chap. iii. 3, 19; Rom. vi. 23; 1 Cor. xv. 56; James i. 15; 1 John v. 16.——[i] Heb. *dying thou shalt die*.——[k] Ch. iii. 12; 1 Cor. xi. 9; 1 Tim. ii. 13.——[l] Heb. *as before him*.

The most probable account of its situation is that given by Hadrian Reland. He supposes it to have been in Armenia, near the sources of the great rivers *Euphrates*, *Tigris*, *Phasis*, and *Araxes*. He thinks *Pison* was the *Phasis*, a river of Colchis, emptying itself into the Euxine Sea, where there is a city called *Chabala*, the pronunciation of which is nearly the same with that of Havilah, or חוילה *Chavilah*, according to the Hebrew, the *vau* ו being changed in Greek to *beta* *β*. This country was famous for *gold*, whence the fable of the *Golden Fleece*, attempted to be carried away from that country by the heroes of Greece. The *Gihon* he thinks to be the *Araxes*, which runs into the Caspian Sea, both the words having the same signification, viz., a *rapid motion*. The land of Cush, washed by the river, he supposes to be the country of the *Cussæi* of the ancients. The *Hiddekel* all agree to be the *Tigris*, and the other river *Phrat*, or פרת *Perath*, to be the *Euphrates*. All these rivers rise in the same tract of mountainous country, though they do not arise from one head.

Verse 12. *There is bdellium* (בדלח *bedolach*) and *the onyx stone*, אבן השהם *eben hashshoham.*] Bochart thinks that the bedolach or bdellium means the *pearl-oyster*; and *shoham* is generally understood to mean the *onyx*, or species of *agate*, a precious stone which has its name from ονυξ, a *man's nail*, to the colour of which it nearly approaches. It is impossible to say what is the precise meaning of the original words; and at this distance of time and place it is of little consequence.

Verse 15. *Put him into the garden—to dress it, and to keep it.*] Horticulture, or gardening, is the first kind of employment on record, and that in which man was engaged while in a state of perfection and innocence. Though the garden may be supposed to produce all things *spontaneously*, as the whole vegetable surface of the earth certainly did at the creation, yet dressing and tilling were afterwards necessary to maintain the different kinds of plants and vegetables in their perfection, and to repress luxuriance. Even in a state of innocence we cannot conceive it possible that man could have been happy if *inactive*. God gave him work to do, and his employment contributed to his happiness; for the structure of his body, as well as of his mind, plainly proves that he was never intended for a merely contemplative life.

Verse 17. *Of the tree of the knowledge—thou shalt not eat*] This is the *first positive precept* God gave to man; and it was given as a test of obedience, and a proof of his being in a *dependent*, *probationary* state. It was necessary that, while constituted lord of this lower world, he should know that he was only God's *vicegerent*, and must be accountable to him for the use of his mental and corporeal powers, and for the use he made of the different creatures put under his care. The man from whose mind the strong impression of this dependence and responsibility is erased, necessarily loses sight of his origin and end, and is capable of any species of wickedness. As God is sovereign, he has a right to give to his creatures what commands he thinks proper. An intelligent creature, without a *law* to regulate his conduct, is an absurdity; this would destroy at once the idea of his dependency and accountableness. Man must ever feel God as his sovereign, and act under his authority, which he cannot do unless he have a *rule* of conduct. This rule God gives; and it is no matter of what kind it is, as long as obedience to it is not beyond the powers of the creature who is to obey. God says: There is a certain fruit-bearing tree; thou shalt not eat of *its* fruit; but of all the other fruits, and they are all that are necessary, for thee, thou mayest freely, liberally eat. Had he not an absolute right to say so? And was not man bound to obey?

Thou shalt surely die.] מות תמות *moth tamuth*; Literally, *a death thou shalt die*; or, *dying thou shalt die*. Thou shalt not only die spiritually, by losing the life of God, but from that moment thou shalt become mortal, and shalt continue in a *dying state* till thou *die*. This we find literally accomplished; every moment of man's life may be considered as an act of *dying*, till soul and body are separated. Other meanings have been given of this passage, but they are in general either fanciful or incorrect.

Verse 18. It is *not good that the man should be*

A. M. 1.
B. C. 4004.

19 [m] And out of the ground the LORD God formed every beast of the field and every fowl of the air; and [n] brought *them* unto [o] Adam to see what he would call them: and whatsoever Adam called every living creature, that *was* the name thereof.

20 And Adam [p] gave names to all cattle, and to the fowl of the air, and to every beast of the field; but for Adam there was not found a help meet for him.

21 ¶ And the LORD God caused a [q] deep sleep to fall upon Adam, and he slept: and he took one of his ribs, and closed up the flesh instead thereof:

22 And the rib, which the LORD God had taken from man, [r] made he a woman, and [s] brought her unto the man.

23 And Adam said, This *is* now [t] bone of my bones, and flesh of my flesh: she shall be called [u] Woman, because she was [v] taken out of [w] Man.

[m] Chap. i. 20, 24.——[n] Psa. viii. 6; see chap. vi. 20.——[o] Or, *the man.*——[p] Heb. *called.*——[q] Chap. xv. 12; 1 Sam. xxvi. 12. [r] Heb. *builded.*

[s] Prov. xviii. 22; Heb. xiii. 4.——[t] Chap. xxix. 14; Judg. ix 2; 2 Sam. v. 1; xix. 13; Eph. v. 30.——[u] Heb. *Isha.*——[v] 1 Cor xi. 8.——[w] Heb. *Ish.*

alone] לבדו *lebaddo;* only himself. *I will make him a help meet for him;* עזר כנגדו *ezer kenegdo,* a help, a counterpart of himself, one formed from him, and a perfect resemblance of his person. If the word be rendered scrupulously literally, it signifies one *like,* or *as himself,* standing *opposite to* or *before him.* And this implies that the woman was to be a perfect resemblance of the man, possessing neither inferiority nor superiority, but being in all things *like* and *equal* to himself. As man was made a social creature, it was not proper that he should be alone; for to be alone, i. e. without a matrimonial companion, *was not good.* Hence we find that *celibacy* in general is a thing that *is not good,* whether it be on the side of the man or of the woman. Men may, in opposition to the declaration of God, call this a state of excellence and a state of perfection; but let them remember that the word of God says the *reverse.*

Verse 19. *Out of the ground, &c.*] Concerning the formation of the different kinds of animals, see the preceding chapter.

Verse 20. *And Adam gave names to all cattle*] Two things God appears to have had in view by causing man to name all the cattle, &c. 1. To show him with what comprehensive powers of mind his Maker had endued him; and 2. To show him that no creature yet formed could make him a suitable companion. And that this twofold purpose was answered we shall shortly see; for,

1. *Adam gave names;* but how? From an intimate knowledge of the nature and properties of each creature. Here we see the perfection of his knowledge; for it is well known that the names affixed to the different animals in Scripture always express some prominent feature and essential characteristic of the creatures to which they are applied. Had he not possessed an intuitive knowledge of the grand and distinguishing properties of those animals, he never could have given them such names. This one circumstance is a strong proof of the original perfection and excellence of man, while in a state of innocence; nor need we wonder at the account. Adam was the work of an infinitely wise and perfect Being, and the *effect* must resemble the *cause* that produced it.

2. Adam was convinced that none of these creatures could be a suitable companion for *him,* and that therefore he must continue in the state that *was not good,* or be a farther debtor to the bounty of his Maker; for among all the animals which he had named *there was not found a help meet for him.* Hence we read,

Verse 21. *The Lord God caused a deep sleep to fall upon Adam, &c.*] This was neither *swoon* nor *ecstasy,* but what our translation very properly terms *a deep sleep.*

And he took one of his ribs] It is immaterial whether we render צלע *tsela* a rib, or a part of his *side,* for it may mean *either:* some part of man was to be used on the occasion, whether *bone* or *flesh* it matters not; though it is likely, from verse 23, that a part of *both* was taken; for Adam, knowing how the woman was formed, said, This is *flesh* of my *flesh,* and *bone* of my *bone.* God could have formed the woman out of the dust of the earth, as he had formed the man; but had he done so, she must have appeared in his eyes as a distinct being, to whom he had no natural relation. But as God formed her out of *a part of the man himself,* he saw she was of the same nature, the same identical flesh and blood, and of the same constitution in all respects, and consequently having equal powers, faculties, and rights. This at once ensured his affection, and excited his esteem.

Verse 23. *Adam said, This* is *now bone of my bones, &c.*] There is a very delicate and expressive meaning in the original which does not appear in our version. When the different *genera* of creatures were brought to Adam, that he might assign them their proper names, it is probable that they passed in pairs before him, and as they passed received their names. To this circumstance the words in this place seem to refer. Instead of *this now is* זאת הפעם *zoth happaam,* we should render more literally *this turn,* this creature, which now passes or appears before me, is flesh of my flesh, &c. The creatures that had *passed* already before him were not suitable to him, and therefore it was said, *For Adam there was not a help meet found,* ver. 20; but when the woman came, formed out of himself, he felt all that attraction which consanguinity could produce, and at the same time saw that she was in her person and in her mind every way suitable to be his companion. See *Parkhurst,* sub voce.

She shall be called Woman] A literal version of

A. M. 1. B. C. 4004.

24 [x] Therefore shall a man leave his father and his mother, and shall cleave unto his wife; and they shall be one flesh.

25 [y] And they were both naked, the man and his wife, and were not [z] ashamed.

A. M. 1. B. C. 4004.

[x] Chap. xxxi. 15; Psa. lxv. 10; Matt. xix. 5; Mark x. 7; 1 Cor. vi. 16; Eph. v. 31.

[y] Chapter iii. 7, 10, 11.——[z] Exodus xxxii. 25; Isaiah xlvii. 3.

the Hebrew would appear strange, and yet a literal version is the only proper one. איש *ish* signifies *man*, and the word used to express what we term *woman* is the same with a feminine termination, אשה *ishshah*, and literally means *she-man*. Most of the ancient versions have felt the force of the term, and have endeavoured to express it as literally as possible. The intelligent reader will not regret to see some of them here. The *Vulgate* Latin renders the Hebrew *virago*, which is a feminine form of *vir*, a man. Symmachus uses ανδρις, *andris*, a female form of ανηρ, *aner*, a man. Our own term is equally proper when understood. *Woman* has been defined by many as compounded of *wo* and *man*, as if called *man's wo* because she tempted him to eat the forbidden fruit; but this is *no* meaning of the original word, nor could it be intended, as the transgression was not then committed. The truth is, our term is a proper and literal translation of the original, and we may thank the discernment of our Anglo-Saxon ancestors for giving it. ƿombman, of which *woman* is a contraction, means the *man with the womb*. A very appropriate version of the Hebrew אשה *ishshah*, rendered by terms which signify *she-man*, in the versions already specified. Hence we see the propriety of Adam's observation: *This* creature *is flesh of my flesh, and bone of my bones; therefore shall she be called* WOMBMAN, or female man, *because she was taken out of man*. See *Verstegan*. Others derive it from ƿifman or ƿifman, man's wife or *she-man*. Either may be proper, the first seems the most likely.

Verse 24. *Therefore shall a man leave his father and his mother*] There shall be, by the order of God, a more intimate connection formed between the man and woman, than can subsist even between parents and children.

And they shall be one flesh.] These words may be understood in a twofold sense. 1. *These two shall be one flesh*, shall be considered as *one body*, having no separate or independent rights, privileges, cares, concerns, &c., each being equally interested in all things that concern the marriage state. 2. These two shall be *for the production* of one flesh; from their union a posterity shall spring, as exactly resembling themselves as they do each other. Our Lord quotes these words, Matt. xix. 5, with some variation from this text: *They* TWAIN *shall be one flesh*. So in Mark x. 8. St. Paul quotes in the same way, 1 Cor. vi. 16, and in Eph. v. 31. The Vulgate Latin, the Septuagint, the Syriac, the Arabic, and the Samaritan, all read the word TWO. That this is the genuine reading I have no doubt. The word שניהם *sheneyhem, they two* or *both of them*, was, I suppose, omitted at first from the Hebrew text, by mistake, because it occurs *three* words after in the following verse, or more probably it originally occurred in the 24th verse, and not in the 25th; and a copyist having found that he had written it twice, in correcting his copy, struck out the word in the 24th verse instead of the 25th. But of what consequence is it? In the controversy concerning polygamy, it has been made of very great consequence. *Without* the word, some have contended a man may have *as many wives as he chooses*, as the terms are indefinite, THEY *shall be, &c.*, but *with* the word, marriage is restricted. A man can have in legal wedlock but ONE *wife* at the same time.

We have here the first institution of marriage, and we see in it several particulars worthy of our most serious regard. 1. God pronounces the state of celibacy to be a *bad state*, or, if the reader please, *not a good one;* and the Lord God said, *It is not good for man to be alone.* This is GOD's judgment. Councils, and fathers, and doctors, and synods, have given a different judgment; but on such a subject they are worthy of no attention. The word of God abideth for ever. 2. God made the woman *for* the man, and thus he has shown us that every son of Adam should be united to a daughter of Eve to the end of the world. See on 1 Cor. vii. 3. God made the woman *out* of the man, to intimate that the closest union, and the most affectionate attachment, should subsist in the matrimonial connection, so that the man should ever consider and treat the woman as a *part of himself:* and as no one ever hated his own flesh, but nourishes and supports it, so should a man deal with his wife; and on the other hand the woman should consider that the man was not made *for her*, but that she was made *for the man*, and derived, under God, her being from him; therefore the wife should see that she reverence her husband, Eph. v. 33. The 23d and 24th verses contain the *very words* of the marriage ceremony: *This is flesh of my flesh, and bone of my bone, therefore shall a man leave his father and his mother, and shall cleave unto his wife, and they two shall be one flesh.* How happy must such a state be where God's institution is properly regarded, where the parties are married, as the apostle expresses it, *in the Lord;* where each, by acts of the tenderest kindness, lives only to prevent the wishes and contribute in every possible way to the comfort and happiness of the other! Marriage might still be what it *was* in its original institution, pure and suitable; and in its first exercise, affectionate and happy: but how few such marriages are there to be found! *Passion*, turbulent and irregular, not *religion; custom*, founded by these irregularities, not *reason; worldly prospects*, originating and ending in selfishness and earthly affections, not in *spiritual ends*, are the grand producing causes of the great majority of matrimonial alliances. How then can such turbid and bitter *fountains* send forth pure and sweet waters? See the ancient allegory of *Cupid* and *Psyche*, by which marriage is so happily illustrated, explained in the notes on Matt. xix. 4–6.

Verse 25. *They were both naked, &c.*] The weather

a

was perfectly temperate, and therefore they had no need of clothing, the circumambient air being of the same temperature with their bodies. And as sin had not yet entered into the world, and no part of the human body had been put to any improper use, therefore there was no *shame*, for shame can only arise from a consciousness of sinful or irregular conduct.

Even in a state of *innocence*, when all was perfection and excellence, when God was clearly discovered in all his works, every *place* being his *temple*, every *moment* a *time of worship*, and every *object* an *incitement* to religious reverence and adoration—even *then*, God chose to consecrate a *seventh part* of time to his more especial worship, and to hallow it unto his own service by a perpetual decree. Who then shall dare to reverse this order of God? Had the religious observance of the Sabbath been never proclaimed till the proclamation of the law on Mount Sinai, then it might have been conjectured that this, like several other ordinances, was a shadow which must pass away with that dispensation; neither extending to future ages, nor binding on any other people. But this was not so. God gave the Sabbath, *his first ordinance*, to man, (see the *first precept*, ver. 17,) while all the nations of the world were seminally included in him, and while he stood the father and representative of the whole human race; therefore the Sabbath is not for one nation, for one time, or for one place. It is the fair type of heaven's eternal day—of the state of endless blessedness and glory, where human souls, having fully regained the Divine image, and become united to the *Centre* and Source of all perfection and excellence, shall *rest* in God, unutterably happy through the immeasurable progress of duration! Of this consummation every returning Sabbath should at once be a type, a remembrancer, and a foretaste, to every pious mind; and these it must be to all who are taught of God.

Of this rest, *the garden of Eden*, that paradise of God formed for man, appears also to have been a type and pledge; and the institution of marriage, the cause, bond, and cement of the social state, was probably designed to prefigure that harmony, order, and blessedness which must reign in the kingdom of God, of which the condition of our first parents in the garden of paradise is justly supposed to have been an expressive emblem. What a pity that this heavenly institution should have ever been perverted! that, instead of becoming a sovereign help to all, it is now, through its prostitution to animal and secular purposes, become the destroyer of millions! Reader, every connection thou formest in life will have a strong and sovereign influence on thy future destiny. Beware! an unholy cause, which from its peculiar nature must be ceaselessly active in every muscle, nerve, and passion, cannot fail to produce incessant effects of sin, misery, death, and perdition. Remember that thy earthly connections, no matter of what kind, are not formed merely for *time*, whatsoever thou mayest intend, but also for *eternity*. With what caution therefore shouldst thou take every step in the path of life! On this ground, the observations made in the preceding notes are seriously recommended to thy consideration.

CHAPTER III.

Satan, by means of a creature here called the serpent, *deceives Eve*, 1–5. *Both she and Adam transgress the Divine command, and fall into sin and misery*, 6, 7. *They are summoned before God, and judged*, 8–13. *The creature called the serpent is degraded and punished*, 14. *The promise of redemption by the incarnation of Christ*, 15. *Eve sentenced*, 16. *Adam sentenced*, 17. *The ground cursed, and death threatened*, 18, 19. *Why the woman was called Eve*, 20. *Adam and Eve clothed with skins*, 21. *The wretched state of our first parents after their fall, and their expulsion from the garden of Paradise*, 22–24

A. M. 1. B. C. 4004.

NOW [a] the serpent was [b] more subtle than any beast of the field which the Lord God had made. And he said unto the woman, [c] Yea,

[a] Rev. xii. 9; xx. 2.—[b] Matt. x. 16; 2 Cor. xi. 3. — [c] Heb. *Yea, because*, &c.

NOTES ON CHAP. III.

Verse 1. *Now the serpent was more subtle*] We have here one of the most difficult as well as the most important narratives in the whole book of God. The last chapter ended with a short but striking account of the perfection and felicity of the first human beings, and this opens with an account of their transgression, degradation, and ruin. That man is in a *fallen* state, the history of the world, with that of the life and miseries of every human being, establishes beyond successful contradiction. But *how*, and by what *agency*, was this brought about? Here is a great mystery; and I may appeal to all persons who have read the various comments that have been written on the Mosaic account, whether they have ever yet been satisfied on this part of the subject, though convinced of the fact itself. *Who* was the *serpent*? of what *kind*? In what *way* did he seduce the first happy pair? These are questions which *remain yet to be answered*. The whole account is either a *simple narrative* of *facts*, or it is an *allegory*. If it be a historical relation, its literal meaning should be sought out; if it be an *allegory*, no attempt should be made to explain it, as it would require a direct revelation to ascertain the sense in which it should be understood, for fanciful illustrations are endless. Believing it to be a *simple relation* of *facts* capable of a satisfactory explanation, I shall take it up on this ground; and, by a careful examination of the original text, endeavour to fix the meaning, and show the propriety and con-

A. M. 1.
B. C. 4004.

hath God said, Ye shall not eat of
every tree of the garden?
2 And the woman said unto the serpent,
We may eat of the fruit of the
trees of the garden:
3 [d] But of the fruit of the tree which *is* in

[d] Genesis, chap. ii. 17.

sistency of the Mosaic account of the fall of man. The chief difficulty in the account is found in the question, Who was the *agent* employed in the seduction of our first parents?

The word in the text which we, following the Septuagint, translate *serpent*, is נחש *nachash*; and, according to *Buxtorf* and others, has *three* meanings in Scripture. 1. It signifies to *view* or *observe attentively*, to *divine* or *use enchantments*, because in them the augurs *viewed attentively* the *flight* of *birds*, the *entrails* of *beasts*, the *course* of the *clouds*, &c.; and under this head it signifies to *acquire knowledge by experience*. 2. It signifies *brass*, *brazen*, and is translated in our Bible, not only *brass*, but *chains*, *fetters*, *fetters of brass*, and in several places *steel*; see 2 Sam. xxii. 35; Job xx. 24; Psa. xviii. 34; and in one place, at least, *filthiness* or *fornication*, Ezek. xvi. 36. 3. It signifies a *serpent*, but of what kind is not determined. In Job xxvi. 13, it seems to mean the *whale* or *hippopotamus*: *By his spirit he hath garnished the heavens, his hand hath formed the crooked serpent*, נחש ברח *nachash bariach*: as ברח *barach* signifies to *pass on* or *pass through*, and בריח *beriach* is used for a *bar* of a gate or door *that passed through rings*, &c., the idea of *straightness* rather than *crookedness* should be attached to it here; and it is likely that the *hippopotamus* or *sea-horse* is intended by it.

In Eccles. x. 11, the creature called *nachash*, of whatever sort, is compared to the *babbler*: *Surely the serpent* (נחש *nachash*) *will bite without enchantment; and a babbler is no better.*

In Isa. xxvii. 1, the *crocodile* or *alligator* seems particularly meant by the original: *In that day the Lord—shall punish leviathan the piercing serpent*, &c. And in Isa. lxv. 25, the same creature is meant as in Gen. iii. 1, for in the words, *And dust shall be the serpent's meat*, there is an evident allusion to the text of Moses. In Amos ix. 3, the *crocodile* is evidently intended: *Though they be hid in the bottom of the sea, thence will I command the serpent*, (הנחש *hannachash*,) *and he shall bite them.* No person can suppose that any of the *snake* or *serpent* kind can be intended here; and we see from the various acceptations of the word, and the different senses which it bears in various places in the sacred writings, that it appears to be a sort of *general term* confined to no one sense. Hence it will be necessary to examine the root accurately, to see if its ideal meaning will enable us to ascertain the animal intended in the text. We have already seen that נחש *nachash* signifies to *view attentively*, to *acquire knowledge* or *experience by attentive observation*; so נחשתי *nichashti*, Gen. xxx. 27: *I have learned by experience*; and this seems to be its most general meaning in the Bible. The original word is by the Septuagint translated οφις, a *serpent*, not because this was its *fixed* determinate meaning in the sacred writings, but because it was the best that occurred to the translators: and they do not seem to have given themselves much trouble to understand the meaning of the original, for they have rendered the word as variously as our translators have done, or rather our translators have followed *them*, as they give nearly the same significations found in the Septuagint: hence we find that οφις is as frequently used by them as *serpent*, its supposed literal meaning, is used in our version. And the New Testament writers, who seldom quote the Old Testament *but from the Septuagint translation*, and often do not *change* even a word in their quotations, copy this version in the use of this word. From the Septuagint therefore we can expect no light, nor indeed from any other of the ancient versions, which are all *subsequent* to the Septuagint, and some of them actually made from it. In all this uncertainty it is natural for a serious inquirer after truth to look *everywhere* for information. And in such an inquiry the Arabic may be expected to afford some help, from its great similarity to the Hebrew. A root in this language, very nearly similar to that in the text, seems to cast considerable light on the subject. خنس *chanas* or *khanasa* signifies *he departed*, *drew off*, *lay hid*, *seduced*, *slunk away*; from this root come اخنس *akhnas*, خنسا *khanasa*, and خنوس *khanoos*, which all signify an *ape*, or *satyrus*, or any creature of the *simia* or ape genus. It is very remarkable also that from the same root comes خناس *khanas*, the DEVIL, which appellative he bears from that meaning of خنس *khanasa*, he *drew off*, *seduced*, *&c.*, because he *draws* men *off* from righteousness, *seduces* them from their obedience to God, &c., &c. See *Golius*, sub voce. Is it not strange that the *devil* and the *ape* should have the same name, derived from the same root, and that root so very similar to the word in the text? But let us return and consider what is said of the creature in question. *Now the nachash was more subtle*, ערום *arum*, more wise, cunning, or prudent, *than any beast of the field which the Lord God had made.* In this account we find, 1. That whatever this *nachash* was, he stood at the *head* of all inferior animals for wisdom and understanding. 2. That he *walked erect*, for this is necessarily implied in his punishment—*on thy belly* (i. e., on all fours) *shalt thou go.* 3. That he was *endued with the gift of speech*, for a conversation is here related between him and the woman. 4. That he was also endued with the *gift of reason*, for we find him reasoning and disputing with Eve. 5. That these things were *common to this creature*, the woman no doubt having often seen him walk erect, talk, and reason, and therefore she testifies *no kind of surprise* when he accosts her in the language related in the text; and indeed from the manner in which this is introduced it appears to be only a *part* of a conversation that had passed between them on the occasion: *Yea, hath God said, &c.*

Had this creature never been known to speak before

A. M. 1.
B. C. 4004.

the midst of the garden, God hath said, Ye shall not eat of it, neither shall ye touch it, lest ye die.

4 [a] And the serpent said unto the woman, Ye shall not surely die:

[a] Ver. 13; 2 Cor. xi. 3; 1 Tim. ii. 14.

his addressing the woman at this time and on this subject, it could not have failed to excite her *surprise*, and to have filled her with *caution*, though from the purity and innocence of her nature she might have been incapable of being affected with *fear*. Now I apprehend that none of these things can be spoken of a *serpent* of any species. 1. None of them ever *did* or ever *can* walk erect. The tales we have had of two-footed and four-footed serpents are justly exploded by every judicious naturalist, and are utterly unworthy of credit. The very name *serpent* comes from *serpo*, to creep, and therefore to such it could be neither *curse* nor *punishment* to go on their bellies, i. e., *to creep on*, as they had done from their creation, and must do while their race endures. 2. They have no *organs* for *speech*, or any kind of articulate sound; they can only *hiss*. It is true that an *ass* by miraculous influence may speak; but it is not to be supposed that there was any miraculous interference here. God did not qualify this creature with speech for the occasion, and it is not intimated that there was any *other agent* that did it; on the contrary, the text intimates that *speech* and *reason* were natural to the *nachash:* and is it not in reference to this the inspired penman says, *The nachash was more subtle* or *intelligent than all the beasts of the field that the Lord God had made?* Nor can I find that the *serpentine genus* are remarkable for *intelligence*. It is true the *wisdom of the serpent* has passed into a proverb, but I cannot see on what it is founded, except in reference to the passage in question, where the *nachash*, which we translate *serpent*, following the Septuagint, shows so much intelligence and cunning: and it is very probable that our Lord alludes to this very place when he exhorts his disciples to be *wise*—prudent or intelligent, *as serpents*, φρονιμοι ὡς οἱ οφεις· and it is worthy of remark that he uses the same term employed by the Septuagint in the text in question: Οφις ην φρονιμωτατος, *the serpent was more prudent or intelligent* than all the beasts, &c. All these things considered, we are obliged to seek for some other word to designate the *nachash* in the text, than the word *serpent*, which on every view of the subject appears to me inefficient and inapplicable. We have seen above that *khanas*, *akhnas*, and *khanoos*, signify a creature of the *ape* or *satyrus* kind. We have seen that the meaning of the root is, he *lay hid, seduced, slunk away, &c.;* and that *khanas* means the *devil*, as the inspirer of evil, and seducer from God and truth. See *Golius* and *Wilmet.* It therefore appears to me that a creature of the *ape* or *ouran outang* kind is here intended; and that Satan made use of this creature as the *most proper* instrument for the accomplishment of his murderous purposes against the life and soul of man. Under this creature he *lay hid*, and by this creature he *seduced* our first parents, and *drew off* or *slunk away* from every eye but the eye of God. Such a creature answers to every part of the description in the text: it is evident from the structure of its limbs and their muscles that it might have been originally designed to walk *erect*, and that nothing less than a sovereign controlling power could induce them to put down *hands* in every respect formed like those of man, and walk like those creatures whose claw-armed paws prove them to have been designed to walk on all fours. Dr. *Tyson* has observed, in his anatomy of an *ouran outang*, that the seminal vessels passed between the two coats of the peritoneum to the scrotum, as in man; hence he argues that this creature was designed to walk erect, as it is otherwise in all quadrupeds. Philos. Trans., vol. xxi., p. 340 The subtlety, cunning, endlessly varied pranks and tricks of these creatures, show them, *even now*, to be more subtle and more *intelligent* than any other creature, man alone excepted. Being *obliged* now to walk on all fours, and gather their food from the ground, they are literally obliged to *eat the dust;* and though exceedingly cunning, and careful in a variety of instances to separate that part which is wholesome and proper for food from that which is not so, in the article of *cleanliness* they are lost to all sense of propriety; and though they have every means in their power of cleansing the aliments they gather off the ground, and from among the dust, yet they never in their savage state make use of any, except a slight rub against their side, or with one of their hands, more to see what the article is than to cleanse it. Add to this, their utter aversion to *walk upright;* it requires the utmost discipline to bring them to it, and scarcely any thing irritates them more than to be obliged to do it. Long observation on some of these animals enables me to state these facts.

Should any person who may read this note object against my conclusions, because apparently derived from an Arabic word which is not exactly similar to the Hebrew, though to those who understand both languages the similarity will be striking; yet, as I do not insist on the *identity* of the terms, though important consequences have been derived from less likely etymologies, he is welcome to throw the whole of this out of the account. He may then take up the Hebrew root only, which signifies to *gaze, to view attentively, pry into, inquire narrowly, &c.*, and consider the passage that appears to compare the *nachash* to the *babbler*, Eccles. x. 11, and he will soon find, if he have any acquaintance with creatures of this genus, that for *earnest, attentive watching, looking, &c.*, and for *chattering* or *babbling*, they have no fellows in the animal world. Indeed, the ability and propensity to chatter is all they have left, according to the above hypothesis, of their original gift of speech, of which I suppose them to have been deprived at the fall as a part of their punishment.

I have spent the longer time on this subject, 1. Because it is exceedingly obscure; 2. Because no interpretation hitherto given of it has afforded me the smallest satisfaction; 3. Because I think the above mode of accounting for every part of the whole trans

A. M. 1. B. C. 4004.

5 For God doth know that in the
day ye eat thereof, then [f] your
eyes shall be opened; and ye shall be as
gods, knowing good and evil.

6 And when the woman saw that
the tree *was* good for food, and that
it *was* [g] pleasant to the eyes, and a tree to be
desired to make *one* wise, she took of the

A. M. 1. B. C. 4004.

[f] Ver. 7; Acts xxvi. 18.

[g] Heb. *a desire.*

action is consistent and satisfactory, and in my opinion removes many embarrassments, and solves the chief difficulties. I think it can be no solid objection to the above mode of solution that Satan, in different parts of the New Testament, is called the *serpent*, the *serpent that deceived Eve by his subtlety*, the *old serpent*, *&c.*, for we have already seen that the New Testament writers have borrowed the word from the *Septuagint*, and the Septuagint themselves use it in a *vast variety* and *latitude of meaning;* and surely the *ouran outang* is as likely to be the animal in question as נחש *nachash* and οφις *ophis* are likely to mean at once a *snake*, a *crocodile*, a *hippopotamus*, *fornication*, a *chain*, a *pair of fetters*, a *piece of brass*, a *piece of steel*, and a *conjurer;* for we have seen above that all these are acceptations of the original word. Besides, the New Testament writers seem to lose sight of the animal or instrument used on the occasion, and speak only of Satan himself as the cause of the transgression, and the instrument of all evil. If, however, any person should choose to differ from the opinion stated above, he is at perfect liberty so to do; I make it no article of faith, nor of Christian communion; I crave the same liberty to judge for myself that I give to others, to which every man has an indisputable right; and I hope no man will call me a heretic for departing in this respect from the common opinion, which appears to me to be so embarrassed as to be altogether unintelligible. See farther on ver. 7–14, &c.

Yea, hath God said] This seems to be the continuation of a discourse of which the preceding part is not given, and a proof that the creature in question was endued with the gift of reason and speech, for no surprise is testified on the part of Eve.

Verse 3. *Neither shall ye touch it*] Did not the woman *add* this to what God had before spoken? Some of the Jewish writers, who are only serious on comparative trifles, state that as soon as the woman had asserted this, the serpent pushed her against the tree and said, "See, thou hast *touched* it, and art still alive; thou mayest therefore safely *eat* of the fruit, for surely thou shalt not die."

Verse 4. *Ye shall not surely die*] Here the *father of lies* at once appears; and appears too in flatly contradicting the assertion of God. The tempter, through the *nachash*, insinuates the impossibility of her dying, as if he had said, God has created thee immortal, thy death therefore is impossible; and God knows this, for as thou livest by the *tree of life*, so shalt thou get increase of wisdom by the *tree of knowledge*.

Verse 5. *Your eyes shall be opened*] Your understanding shall be greatly enlightened and improved; *and ye shall be as gods*, כאלהים *kelohim*, like God, so he word should be translated; for what idea could our first parents have of *gods* before idolatry could have had any being, because sin had not yet entered into the world? The Syriac has the word in the *singular* number, and is the only one of all the versions which has hit on the true meaning. As the original word is the same which is used to point out the Supreme Being, chap. i. 1, so it has here the same signification; and the object of the tempter appears to have been this: to persuade our first parents that they should, by eating of this fruit, become wise and powerful as God, (for *knowledge is power*,) and be able to exist for ever, independently of him.

Verse 6. *The tree* was *good for food*] 1. The fruit appeared to be wholesome and nutritive. *And that it* was *pleasant to the eyes*. 2. The beauty of the fruit tended to whet and increase appetite. *And a tree to be desired to make* one *wise*, which was, 3. An additional motive to please the palate. From these three sources all natural and moral evil sprang: they are exactly what the apostle calls the *desire of the flesh;* the tree was good for food: *the desire of the eye;* it was pleasant to the sight: and *the pride of life;* it was a tree to be desired to make one wise. God had undoubtedly created our first parents not only very wise and intelligent, but also with a great capacity and suitable propensity to increase in knowledge. Those who think that Adam was created so perfect as to preclude the possibility of his increase in knowledge, have taken a very false view of the subject. We shall certainly be convinced that our first parents were in a state of sufficient perfection when we consider, 1. That they were endued with a vast capacity to obtain knowledge. 2. That all the means of information were within their reach. 3. That there was no hinderance to the most direct conception of occurring truth. 4. That all the objects of knowledge, whether natural or moral, were ever at hand. 5. That they had the strongest propensity to know; and, 6. The greatest pleasure in knowing. To have God and nature continually open to the view of the soul; and to have a soul capable of viewing both, and fathoming endlessly their unbounded glories and excellences, without hinderance or difficulty; what a state of perfection! what a consummation of bliss! This was undoubtedly the state and condition of our first parents; even the present ruins of the state are incontestable evidences of its primitive excellence. We see at once how transgression came; it was natural for them to desire to be increasingly wise. God had implanted this desire in their minds; but he showed them that this desire should be gratified in a *certain way;* that *prudence* and *judgment* should always regulate it; that they should carefully examine what God had opened to their view; and should not pry into what he chose to conceal. He alone who knows all things knows *how much* knowledge the soul needs to its perfection and increasing happiness, in *what* subjects this may be legitimately sought, and *where* the mind may make

A. M. 1. B. C. 4004. fruit thereof, [h] and did eat; and
gave also unto her husband with
her, [i] and he did eat.
7 And [k] the eyes of them both were opened, [l] and they knew that they
were naked; and they sewed
fig-leaves together, and made themselves
[m] aprons.

Ecclus xxv. 24; 1 Tim. ii. 14; 1 John ii. 16.——[i] Ver. 12, 17; Hos. vi. 7; Rom. v. 12–19.

[k] Verse 5.——[l] Chapter ii. 25.——[m] Or, *things to gird about.*

excursions and discoveries to its prejudice and ruin. There are doubtless many subjects which angels are capable of knowing, and which God chooses to conceal even from them, because *that* knowledge would tend neither to their perfection nor happiness. Of every attainment and object of pursuit it may be said, in the words of an ancient poet, who conceived correctly on the subject, and expressed his thoughts with perspicuity and energy:—

Est modus in rebus: sunt certi denique fines,
Quos ultra citraque nequit consistere rectum.
Hor. Sat., lib. i., Sat. 1., ver. 106.

"There is a rule for all things; there are in fine fixed and stated limits, on either side of which righteousness cannot be found." *On the line* of duty alone we must walk.

Such limits God certainly assigned from the beginning: Thou shalt *come up* to this; thou shalt not *pass* it. And as he assigned the *limits*, so he assigned the *means*. It is lawful for thee to acquire knowledge in *this way;* it is unlawful to seek it in *that*. And had he not a right to do so? And would his creation have been perfect without it?

Verse 7. *The eyes of them both were opened*] They now had a sufficient discovery of their sin and folly in disobeying the command of God; they could discern between good and evil; and what was the consequence? Confusion and shame were engendered, because innocence was lost and guilt contracted

Let us review the whole of this melancholy business, the *fall* and its *effects*.

1. From the New Testament we learn that Satan associated himself with the creature which we term the *serpent*, and the original the *nachash*, in order to seduce and ruin mankind; 2 Cor. xi. 3; Rev. xii. 9; xx. 2. 2. That this creature was the most suitable to his purpose, as being the most subtle, the *most intelligent* and *cunning* of all beasts of the field, endued with the gift of speech and reason, and consequently one in which he could best conceal himself. 3. As he knew that while they *depended on God* they could not be ruined, he therefore endeavoured to seduce them from this dependence. 4. He does this by working on that propensity of the mind to desire an increase of knowledge, with which God, for the most gracious purposes, had endued it. 5. In order to succeed, he insinuates that God, through motives of envy, had given the prohibition—*God doth know that in the day ye eat of it, ye shall be like himself*, &c. 6. As their present state of blessedness must be inexpressibly dear to them, he endeavours to persuade them that they could not fall from this state: *Ye shall* not *surely die*—ye shall not only retain your present blessedness, but it shall be greatly increased; a temptation by which he has ever since fatally succeeded in the ruin of multitudes of souls, whom he persuaded that being once *right* they could never *finally* go wrong. 7. As he kept the unlawfulness of the means proposed out of sight, persuaded them that they could not fall from their steadfastness, assured them that they should resemble God himself, and consequently be self-sufficient, and totally independent of him; they listened, and fixing their eye only on the promised good, neglecting the positive command, and determining to become wise and independent at all events, *they took of the fruit and did eat*.

Let us now examine the *effects*.

1. *Their eyes were opened*, and they saw they were naked. They saw what they never saw before, that they were stripped of their excellence; that they had lost their innocence; and that they had fallen into a state of indigence and danger. 2. Though their eyes were opened to see their nakedness, yet their mind was clouded, and their judgment confused. They seem to have lost all just notions of honour and dishonour, of what was shameful and what was praiseworthy. It was dishonourable and shameful to break the commandment of God; but it was neither to go *naked*, when clothing was not necessary. 3. They seem in a moment, not only to have lost sound judgment, but also *reflection:* a short time before Adam was so wise that he could name all the creatures brought before him, according to their respective natures and qualities; *now* he does not know the first principle concerning the Divine nature, that *it knows all things*, and that it is omnipresent, therefore he endeavours to hide himself among the trees from the eye of the *all-seeing* God! How astonishing is this! When the creatures were brought to him he could *name* them, because he could discern their respective natures and properties; when Eve was brought to him he could immediately tell *what* she was, *who* she was, and for *what end* made, though he was in *a deep sleep* when God formed her; and this seems to be particularly noted, merely to show the depth of his wisdom, and the perfection of his discernment. But alas! how are the mighty fallen! Compare his present with his past state, his state *before* the transgression with his state *after* it; and say, is this the same creature? the creature of whom God said, as he said of all his works, *He is very good*—just what he should be, a living image of the living God; but now lower than the beasts of the field? 4. This account could never have been credited had not the indisputable proofs and evidences of it been continued by uninterrupted succession to the present time. All the descendants of this first guilty pair resemble their degenerate ancestors, and copy their conduct. The original *mode* of transgression is still continued, and the *original sin* in consequence. Here are the proofs. 1. Every human being is endeavouring to obtain knowledge by unlawful

A. M. 1.
B. C. 4004.

8 And they heard [n] the voice of
the LORD God walking in the garden in the [o] cool of the day: and Adam and his wife [p] hid themselves from the presence of the LORD God amongst the trees of the garden.
9 And the LORD God called unto Adam, and said unto him, Where *art* thou?
10 And he said, I heard thy voice in the garden, [q] and I was afraid, because I *was* naked; and I hid myself.
11 And he said, Who told thee that thou *wast* naked? Hast thou eaten of the tree, whereof I commanded thee that thou shouldest not eat?
12 And the man said, [r] The woman whom thou gavest *to be* with me, she gave me of the tree, and I did eat.

A. M. 1.
B. C. 4004.

13 And the LORD God said unto the woman, What *is* this *that* thou hast done? And the woman said, [s] The serpent beguiled me, and I did eat.
14 And the LORD God said [t] unto the serpent, Because thou hast done this, thou *art* cursed above all cattle, and above every beast of the field; upon thy belly shalt thou go, and [u] dust shalt thou eat all the days of thy life:

[n] Job xxxviii. 1.—[o] Heb. *wind;* Job xxxiv. 21, 22; Psa. cxxxix. 1-12.—[p] Job xxxi. 33; Prov. v. 3; Jer. xxiii. 24; Amos ix. 3; Jonah i. 3, 10; Heb. iv. 13; chap. iv. 9; Josh. vii. 17-19; Rev. xx. 12, 13.—[q] Chap. ii. 25; Exod. iii. 6; Psa. cxix. 120; Isa. xxxiii. 14; lvii. 11; 1 John iii. 20.—[r] Chap. ii. 18, 20; Job xxxi. 33; Prov. xxviii. 13; Luke x. 29; James i. 13, 15.—[s] Ver. 4; 2 Cor. xi. 3; 1 Tim. ii. 14.—[t] Exod. xxi. 29, 32.—[u] Isa. lxv. 25; Mic. vii. 17.

means, even while the lawful means and every available help are at hand. 2. They are endeavouring to be *independent*, and to live without God in the world; hence *prayer*, the language of dependence on God's providence and grace, is neglected, I might say detested, by the great majority of men. Had I no other proof than this that man is a *fallen creature*, my soul would bow to this evidence. 3. Being destitute of the true knowledge of God they seek privacy for their crimes, not considering that the eye of God is upon them, being only solicitous to hide them from the eye of man. These are all proofs in point; but we shall soon meet with additional ones. See on ver. 10 and 12.

Verse 8. *The voice of the Lord*] The *voice* is properly used here, for as God is an infinite Spirit, and cannot be confined to any *form*, so he can have no *personal* appearance. It is very likely that God used to converse with them in the garden, and that the usual time was the *decline* of the day, לרוח היום *leruach haiyom*, in the *evening breeze;* and probably this was the time that our first parents employed in the more solemn acts of their religious worship, at which God was ever present. The time for this solemn worship is again come, and God is in his place; but Adam and Eve have sinned, and therefore, instead of being found in the place of worship, are hidden among the trees! Reader, how often has this been *thy* case!

Verse 10. *I was afraid, because I* was *naked*] See the immediate consequences of sin. 1. SHAME, because of the ingratitude marked in the rebellion, and because that in aiming to be like God they were now sunk into a state of the greatest wretchedness. 2. FEAR, because they saw they had been deceived by Satan, and were exposed to that death and punishment from which he had promised them an exemption. How worthy is it of remark that *this* cause continues to produce the very same effects! *Shame* and *fear* were the first fruits of sin, and fruits which it has *invariably* produced, from the first transgression to the present time.

Verse 12. *And the man said, &c.*] We have here some farther proofs of the fallen state of man, and that the consequences of that state extend to his remotest posterity. 1. On the question, *Hast thou eaten of the tree?* Adam is obliged to acknowledge his transgression; but he does this in such a way as to shift off the blame from himself, and lay it upon *God* and upon the *woman!* *This* woman whom THOU didst give to be with me, עמדי *immadi*, to be my companion, (for so the word is repeatedly used,) *she* gave me, and I did eat. *I* have no farther blame in this transgression; *I* did not *pluck* the fruit; *she* took it and gave it to me.

2. When the woman is questioned she lays the blame upon God and the serpent, (*nachash,*) *The serpent beguiled me, and I did eat.* Thou didst make him much wiser than thou didst make me, and therefore my simplicity and ignorance were overcome by his superior wisdom and subtlety; *I* can have no fault here, the fault is *his*, and his who made him *so wise* and me *so ignorant.* Thus we find that, while the eyes of their body were opened to see their degraded state, the eyes of their understanding were closed, so that they could not see the sinfulness of sin; and at the same time their hearts were hardened through its deceitfulness. In this also their posterity copy their example. How few ingenuously confess their own sin! They see not their guilt. They are continually making excuses for their crimes; the strength and subtlety of the tempter, the natural weakness of their own minds, the unfavourable circumstances in which they were placed, &c., &c., are all pleaded as excuses for their sins, and thus the possibility of repentance is precluded; for till a man *take his sin to himself*, till he acknowledge that *he alone* is guilty, he cannot be humbled, and consequently cannot be saved. Reader, till thou accuse thyself, and *thyself only*, and feel that *thou* alone art responsible for all thy iniquities, there is no hope of thy salvation.

Verse 14. *And the Lord God said unto the serpent*] The *tempter* is not asked *why he deceived the woman;* he cannot roll the blame on any other; *self-tempted he fell*, and it is natural for him, such is his enmity, to deceive and destroy all he can. His fault

A. M. 1.
B. C. 4004.

15 And I will put enmity between
thee and the woman, and between
[v] thy seed and [w] her seed; [x] it shall bruise thy
head, and thou shalt bruise his heel.
16 Unto the woman he said, I will greatly
multiply thy sorrow and thy conception; [y] in
sorrow thou shalt bring forth children; [z] and thy desire *shall be* [a] to
thy husband, and he shall [b] rule over thee.
17 And unto Adam he said, [c] Because thou
hast hearkened unto the voice of thy wife,
[d] and hast eaten of the tree [e] of which I com

[v] Matt. iii. 7; xiii. 38; xxiii. 33; John viii. 44; Acts xiii. 10; 1 John iii. 8.——[w] Psa. cxxxii. 11; Isa. vii. 14; Mic. v. 3; Matt. i. 23, 25; Luke i. 31, 34, 35; Gal. iv. 4.——[x] Rom. xvi. 20; Col. ii. 15; Heb. ii. 14; 1 John v. 5; Rev. xii. 7, 17.

[y] Psa. xlviii. 6; Isa. xiii. 8; xxi. 3; John xvi. 21; 1 Tim. ii. 15 [z] Chap. iv. 7.——[a] Or, *subject to thy husband.*——[b] 1 Cor. xi. 3; xiv. 34; Eph. v. 22, 23, 24; 1 Tim. ii. 11, 12; Tit. ii. 5; 1 Pet. iii. 1, 5, 6.——[c] 1 Sam. xv. 23.——[d] Ver. 6.——[e] Chap. ii. 17.

admits of no excuse, and therefore God begins to pronounce sentence on *him* first. And here we must consider a twofold sentence, one on *Satan* and the other on the *agent* he employed. The *nachash*, whom I suppose to have been at the head of all the inferior animals, and in a sort of society and intimacy with man, is to be greatly degraded, entirely banished from human society, and deprived of the gift of speech. *Cursed art thou above all cattle, and above every beast of the field*—thou shalt be considered the most contemptible of animals; *upon thy belly shalt thou go*—thou shalt no longer walk erect, but mark the ground equally with thy hands and feet; *and dust shalt thou eat*—though formerly possessed of the faculty to distinguish, choose, and cleanse thy food, thou shalt feed henceforth like the most stupid and abject quadruped, *all the days of thy life*—through all the innumerable generations of thy species. God saw meet to manifest his displeasure against the agent employed in this melancholy business; and perhaps this is founded on the part which the intelligent and subtle *nachash* took in the seduction of our first parents. We see that he was capable of it, and have some reason to believe that he became a *willing* instrument.

Verse 15. *I will put enmity between thee and the woman*] This has been generally supposed to apply to a certain enmity subsisting between men and serpents; but this is rather a fancy than a reality. It is yet to be discovered that the serpentine race have any peculiar enmity against mankind, nor is there any proof that men hate serpents *more* than they do other noxious animals. Men have much more enmity to the common rat and magpie than they have to all the serpents in the land, because the former destroy the grain, &c., and serpents in general, far from seeking to do men mischief, flee his approach, and generally avoid his dwelling. If, however, we take the word *nachash* to mean any of the *simia* or *ape* species, we find a more consistent meaning, as there is scarcely an animal in the universe so detested by most *women* as these are; and indeed *men* look on them as continual caricatures of themselves. But we are not to look for merely *literal meanings* here: it is evident that Satan, who actuated this creature, is alone intended in this part of the prophetic declaration. God in his endless mercy has put enmity between men and him; so that, though all mankind love his *service*, yet all invariably hate *himself*. Were it otherwise, who could be saved? A great point gained towards the conversion of a sinner is to convince him that it is *Satan* he has been serving, that it is to *him* he has been giving up his soul, body, goods, &c.; he starts with horror when this conviction fastens on his mind, and shudders at the thought of being in league with the old murderer. But there is a deeper meaning in the text than even this, especially in these words, *it shall bruise thy head*, or rather, הוא *hu*, HE; who? the seed of the *woman;* the person is to come by the *woman*, and by her *alone*, *without the concurrence of man*. Therefore the address is not to Adam and Eve, but to *Eve alone;* and it was in consequence of this purpose of God that Jesus Christ was born of a *virgin;* this, and this alone, is what is implied in the promise of the *seed of the woman* bruising the head of the serpent. Jesus Christ died to put away sin by the sacrifice of himself, and to destroy *him* who had the power of death, that is, the devil. Thus he *bruises his head*—destroys his *power* and *lordship* over mankind, turning them from the *power* of Satan unto God; Acts xxvi. 18. And Satan *bruises his heel*—God so ordered it, that the salvation of man could only be brought about by the *death* of Christ; and even the spiritual seed of our blessed Lord have the heel often bruised, as they suffer persecution, temptation, &c., which may be all that is intended by this part of the prophecy.

Verse 16. *Unto the woman he said*] She being second in the transgression is brought up the *second* to receive her condemnation, and to hear her punishment: I will greatly multiply, or *multiplying I will multiply;* i. e., I will multiply thy sorrows, and multiply those sorrows by other sorrows, and this during conception and pregnancy, and particularly so in parturition or child-bearing. And this curse has fallen in a heavier degree on the *woman* than on any other *female*. Nothing is better attested than this, and yet there is certainly no *natural* reason why it should be so; it is a part of her punishment, and a part from which even God's mercy will not exempt her. It is added farther, *Thy desire shall be to thy husband*—thou shalt not be able to shun the great pain and peril of child-bearing, for thy desire, *thy appetite*, shall be to thy husband; *and he shall rule over thee*, though at their creation both were formed with equal rights, and the woman had probably as much right to *rule* as the man; but subjection to the will of her husband is one part of her curse; and so very capricious is this *will* often, that a sorer punishment no human being can well have, to be at all in a state of liberty, and under the protection of wise and equal laws.

Verse 17. *Unto Adam he said*] The man being the *last* in the transgression is brought up *last* to receive his sentence: *Because thou hast hearkened unto the voice of thy wife*—"thou wast not *deceived*, she only gave and counselled thee to eat; this thou shouldst

A. M. 1. B. C. 4004. manded thee, saying, Thou shalt not eat of it; [f] cursed *is* the ground for thy sake: [g] in sorrow shalt thou eat *of* it all the days of thy life;

18 [h] Thorns also and thistles shall
it [i] bring forth to thee; and [k] thou
shalt eat the herb of the field:
19 [l] In the sweat of thy face shalt thou eat

[f] Eccles. i. 2, 3; Isa. xxiv. 5, 6; Rom. viii. 20.——[g] Job v. 7; Eccles. ii. 23.——[h] Job xxxi. 40.

[i] Heb. *cause to bud.*——[k] Psa. civ. 14; Job i. 21; Psa. xc. 3; civ. 2.——[l] Eccles. i. 13; 2 Thess. iii. 10.

have resisted;" and that he did not is the reason of his condemnation. *Cursed* is *the ground for thy sake*—from henceforth its fertility shall be greatly impaired; *in sorrow shalt thou eat* of *it*—be in continual perplexity concerning the seed time and the harvest, the cold and the heat, the wet and the dry. How often are all the fruits of man's toil destroyed by blasting, by mildew, by insects, wet weather, land floods, &c.! Anxiety and carefulness are the labouring man's portion.

Verse 18. *Thorns also and thistles, &c.*] Instead of producing nourishing grain and useful vegetables, noxious weeds shall be peculiarly prolific, injure the ground, choke the good seed, and mock the hopes of the husbandman; *and thou shalt eat the herb of the field*—thou shalt no longer have the privilege of this garden of delights, but must go to the common champaign country, and feed on such herbs as thou canst find, till by labour and industry thou hast raised others more suitable to thee and more comfortable.

In the curse pronounced on the *ground* there is much more implied than generally appears. The amazing fertility of some of the most common *thistles* and *thorns* renders them the most proper instruments for the fulfilment of this sentence against man. *Thistles* multiply enormously; a species called the *Carolina sylvestris* bears ordinarily from 20 to 40 heads, each containing from 100 to 150 seeds.

Another species, called the *Acanthum vulgare*, produces above 100 heads, each containing from 3 to 400 seeds. Suppose we say that these *thistles* produce at a medium only 80 heads, and that each contains only 300 seeds; the first crop from these would amount to 24,000. Let *these* be sown, and their crop will amount to 576 *millions*. Sow these, and their produce will be 13,824,000,000,000, or *thirteen billions, eight hundred and twenty-four thousand millions;* and a single crop from these, which is only the *third* year's growth, would amount to 331,776,000,000,000,000, or *three hundred and thirty-one thousand seven hundred and seventy-six billions;* and the fourth year's growth will amount to 7,962,624,000,000,000,000,000, or *seven thousand nine hundred and sixty-two trillions, six hundred and twenty-four thousand billions.* A progeny more than sufficient to stock not only the surface of the whole world, but of all the planets of the solar system, so that no other plant or vegetable could possibly grow, allowing but the space of one square foot for each plant.

The *Carduus vulgatissimus viarum*, or common hedge thistle, besides the almost infinite swarms of winged seeds it sends forth, spreads its roots around many yards, and throws up suckers everywhere, which not only produce seeds in their turn, but extend their roots, propagate like the parent plant, and stifle and destroy all vegetation but their own.

As to THORNS, the bramble, which occurs so commonly, and is so mischievous, is a sufficient proof how well the *means* are calculated to secure the end. The *genista*, or *spinosa vulgaris*, called by some *furze*, by others *whins*, is allowed to be one of the most mischievous shrubs on the face of the earth. Scarcely any thing can grow near it, and it is so thick set with prickles that it is almost impossible to touch it without being wounded. It is very prolific; almost half the year it is covered with flowers which produce *pods* filled with seeds. Besides, it shoots out roots far and wide, from which suckers and young plants are continually springing up, which produce others in their turn. Where it is permitted to grow it soon overspreads whole tracts of ground, and it is extremely difficult to clear the ground of its roots where once it has got proper footing. Such provision has the just God made to fulfil the curse which he has pronounced on the earth, because of the crimes of its inhabitants. See *Hale's* Vegetable Statics.

Verse 19. *In the sweat of thy face*] Though the whole body may be thrown into a profuse sweat, if hard labour be long continued, yet the *face* or *forehead* is the first part whence this sweat begins to issue; this is occasioned by the blood being strongly propelled to the brain, partly through stooping, but principally by the strong action of the muscles; in consequence of this the blood vessels about the head become turgid through the great flux of blood, the fibres are relaxed, the pores enlarged, and the sweat or serum poured out. Thus then the very commencement of every man's labour may put him in mind of his sin and its consequences.

Dust thou art, *and unto dust shalt thou return.*] God had said that in the day they ate of the forbidden fruit, *dying they should die*—they should then become *mortal*, and continue under the influence of a great variety of unfriendly agencies in the atmosphere and in themselves, from heats, colds, drought, and damps in the one, and morbid *increased* and *decreased* action in the solids and fluids of the other, till the spirit, finding its earthly house no longer tenable, should return to God who gave it; and the body, being decomposed, should be reduced to its primitive dust. It is evident from this that man would have been immortal had he never transgressed, and that this state of continual life and health depended on his obedience to his Maker. The tree of life, as we have already seen, was intended to be the means of continual preservation. For as no being but God can exist independently of any supporting agency, so man could not have continued to live without a particular supporting agent; and this supporting agent under God appears to have been the *tree of life.*

Ολιγη δε κεισομεσθα
Κονις, οστεων λυθεντων. Anac. Od. 4., v. 9.

"We shall lie down as a small portion of dust car bones being dissolved"

A. M. I.
B. C. 4004.

bread, till thou return unto the
ground; for out of it wast thou
taken: for [m] dust thou *art*, and [n] unto dust
shalt thou return.
20 And Adam called his wife's name [o] Eve;
[p] because she was the mother of all living.
21 Unto Adam also and to his wife did the
LORD God make coats of skins,
and clothed them.
22 And the LORD God said, [q] Behold, the
man is become as one of us, to know good
and evil: and now, lest he put forth his hand,
[r] and take also of the tree of life, and eat, and
live for ever;

[m] Chap. ii. 7; Dan. xii. 2.——[n] Job xxi. 26; xxxiv. 15; Psa. civ. 29; Eccles. iii. 20; xii. 7; Dan. xii. 2; Rom. v. 12; Heb. ix. 27.

[o] Heb. *Chavah;* that is, *living*.——[p] Acts xvii. 26.——[q] Ver. 5; like Isa. xix. 12; xlvii. 12, 13; Jer. xxii. 23.——[r] Chap. ii. 9.

Verse 20. *And Adam called his wife's name Eve; because she was the mother of all living.*] A man who does not understand the original cannot possibly comprehend the reason of what is said here. What has the word *Eve* to do with being *the mother of all living?* Our translators often follow the *Septuagint;* it is a pity they had not done so here, as the Septuagint transation is literal and correct: Και εκαλεσεν Αδαμ το ονομα της γυναικος αυτου Ζωη, ὁτι μητηρ παντων των ζωντων· "And Adam called his wife's name *Life*, because she was the mother of all the *living*." This is a proper and faithful representation of the Hebrew text, for the חוה *Chavvah* of the original, which we have corrupted into *Eve*, a word destitute of all meaning, answers exactly to the Ζωη of the Septuagint, both signifying *life*; as does also the Hebrew חי *chai* to the Greek ζωντων, both of which signify *the living*. It is probable that God designed by this name to teach our first parents these two important truths: 1. That though they had merited immediate death, yet they should be respited, and the accomplishment of the sentence be long delayed; they should be spared to propagate a numerous progeny on the earth. 2. That though much misery would be entailed on his posterity, and death should have a long and universal empire, yet ONE should in the fulness of time spring from the woman, who should destroy *death*, and bring *life* and *immortality* to light, 2 Tim. i. 10. Therefore Adam called his wife's name *Life*, because she was to be the mother of all human beings, and because she was to be the mother of HIM who was to give *life* to a world dead in trespasses, and dead in sins, Eph. ii. 1, &c.

Verse 21. *God made coats of skins*] It is very likely that the *skins* out of which their *clothing* was made were taken off animals whose blood had been poured out as a *sin-offering* to God; for as we find Cain and Abel offering sacrifices to God, we may fairly presume that God had given them instructions on this head; nor is it likely that the notion of a sacrifice could have ever occurred to the mind of man without an express revelation from God. Hence we may safely infer, 1. That as Adam and Eve needed this clothing as soon as they fell, and death had not as yet made any ravages in the animal world, it is most likely that the skins were taken off victims offered under the direction of God himself, and in faith of HIM who, in the fulness of time, was to make an atonement by his death. And it seems reasonable also that this matter should be brought about in such a way that Satan and death should have no triumph, when the very *first death* that took place in the world was an emblem and type of that death which should conquer Satan, destroy his empire, reconcile God to man, convert man to God, sanctify human nature, and prepare it for heaven.

Verse 22. *Behold, the man is become as one of us*] On all hands this text is allowed to be difficult, and the difficulty is increased by our translation, which is opposed to the original Hebrew and the most authentic versions. The Hebrew has היה *hayah*, which is the third person preterite tense, and signifies *was*, not *is*. The *Samaritan text*, the *Samaritan version*, the *Syriac*, and the *Septuagint*, have the same tense. These lead us to a very different sense, and indicate that there is an ellipsis of some words which must be supplied in order to make the sense complete. A very learned man has ventured the following paraphrase, which should not be lightly regarded: "*And the Lord God said, The man who* WAS *like one of us* in purity and wisdom, is now fallen and robbed of his excellence; he has added לדעת *ladaath, to the knowledge of the good*, by his transgression *the knowledge of the evil;* and *now, lest he put forth his hand, and take also of the tree of life, and eat and live for ever* in this miserable state, I will remove him, and guard the place lest he should re-enter. *Therefore the Lord God sent him forth from the garden of Eden,*" *&c.* This seems to be the most natural sense of the place. Some suppose that his removal from the tree of life was in mercy, to prevent a *second* temptation. He before imagined that he could gain an increase of wisdom by eating of the *tree of knowledge*, and Satan would be disposed to tempt him to endeavour to elude the sentence of *death*, by eating of the *tree of life*. Others imagine that the words are spoken *ironically*, and that the Most High intended by a cutting taunt, to upbraid the poor culprit for his offence, because he broke the Divine command in the expectation of being *like God* to know good from evil; and now that he had lost *all the good* that God had designed for him, and got nothing but *evil* in its place, therefore God taunts him for the total miscarriage of his project. But God is ever consistent with himself; and surely his infinite pity prohibited the use of either *sarcasm* or *irony*, in speaking of so dreadful a catastrophe, that was in the end to occasion the agony and bloody sweat, the cross and passion, the death and burial, of Him in whom dwelt all the fulness of the Godhead bodily, Col. ii. 9.

In chap. i. 26, 27, we have seen man in the perfection of his nature, the dignity of his office, and the plenitude of his happiness. Here we find the same creature, but stripped of his glories and happiness, so

A. M. 1.
B. C. 4004.

23 Therefore the LORD God sent him forth from the garden of Eden, [a]to till the ground from whence he was taken.
24 So he drove out the man; and he placed [t]at the east of the garden of Eden [u]Cherubims, and a flaming sword which turned every way, to keep the way of the tree of life.

[a] Chapter ii. 5; iv. 2; ix. 20; Ecclesiastes v. 9.——[t] Chapter ii. 8.

[u] Exod. xxv. 2, 20; 1 Kings vi. 25-28; Josh. v. 13; Psa. civ. 4; Heb. i. 7.

that the word *man* no longer conveys the same ideas it did before. *Man* and *intellectual excellence* were before so intimately connected as to appear inseparable; *man* and *misery* are now equally so. In our nervous mother tongue, the Anglo-Saxon, we have found the word Ʒob *God* signifying, not only the Supreme Being, but also *good* or *goodness;* and it is worthy of especial note that the word man *man*, in the same language, is used to express, not only the *human being* so called, both male and female, but also *mischief, wickedness, fraud, deceit,* and *villany*. Thus a simple monosyllable, still in use among us in its *first sense*, conveyed at once to the minds of our ancestors the two following particulars: 1. *The human being* in his *excellence*, capable of knowing, loving, and glorifying his Maker. 2. The *human being* in his *fallen state*, capable of and committing all kinds of wickedness. "Obiter hic notandum," says old Mr. Somner in his Saxon Dictionary, "venit, Ʒob *Saxonibus* et DEUM significasse et BONUM: uti man et *hominem* et *nequitiam*. Here it is to be noted, that among the Saxons the term GOD signified both the *Divine Being* and *goodness*, as the word *man* signified both the *human being* and *wickedness*." This is an additional proof that our Saxon ancestors both *thought* and *spoke* at the *same time*, which, strange as it may appear, is not a common case: their words in general are not arbitrary signs; but as far as sounds can convey the ideal meaning of things, their words do it; and they are so formed and used as necessarily to bring to view the nature and properties of those things of which they are the signs. In this sense the *Anglo-Saxon* is inferior only to the *Hebrew*.

Verse 24. *So he drove out the man*] Three things are noted here: 1. God's *displeasure* against sinful man, evidenced by his expelling him from this place of blessedness; 2. Man's *unfitness* for the place, of which he had rendered himself unworthy by his ingratitude and transgression; and, 3. His *reluctance* to leave this place of happiness. He was, as we may naturally conclude, *unwilling* to depart, and God *drove* him out.

He placed at the east] מקדם *mikkedem*, or before *the garden of Eden*, before what may be conceived its gate or entrance; *Cherubims*, הכרבים *hakkerubim*, THE *cherubim*. Hebrew plurals in the masculine end in general in *im:* to add an *s* to this when we introduce such words into English, is very improper; therefore the word should be written *cherubim*, not *cherubims*. But what were these? They are utterly unknown. Conjectures and guesses relative to their nature and properties are endless. Several think them to have been emblematical representations of the sacred *Trinity*, and bring reasons and scriptures in support of their opinion; but as I am not satisfied that this opinion is correct, I will not trouble the reader with it. From the description in Exod. xxvi. 1, 31; 1 Kings vi. 29, 32; 2 Chron. iii. 14, it appears that the cherubs were sometimes represented with *two* faces, namely, those of a *lion* and of a *man;* but from Ezek. i. 5, &c.; x. 20, 21, we find that they had *four faces* and *four wings;* the faces were those of a *man*, a *lion*, an *ox*, and an *eagle;* but it seems there was but one *body* to these heads. The *two-faced* cherubs were such as were represented on the curtains and veil of the tabernacle, and on the wall, doors, and veil of the temple; those with *four* faces appeared only in the holy of holies.

The word כרב or כרוב *kerub* never appears as a *verb* in the Hebrew Bible, and therefore is justly supposed to be a word compounded of כ *ke* a particle of resemblance, *like to, like as,* and רב *rab*, he was *great, powerful, &c.* Hence it is very likely that the cherubs, to whatever order of beings they belonged, were emblems of the ALL-MIGHTY, and were those creatures by whom he produced the great effects of his power. The word רב *rab* is a character of the Most High, Prov. xxvi. 10: *The great God who formed all;* and again in Psa. xlviii. 2, where he is called the *Great King*, מלך רב *melech rab*. But though this is rarely applied as a character of the Supreme Being in the Hebrew Bible, yet it is a common appellative of the Deity in the Arabic language. رب *rab*, and رب العالمين *rab'ulalameen* Lord of both worlds, or, Lord of the universe, are expressions repeatedly used to point out the *almighty energy* and *supremacy of God*. On this ground, I suppose, the cherubim were emblematical representations of the eternal power and Godhead of the Almighty. These angelic beings were for a time employed in guarding the entrance to Paradise, and keeping the way of or road to the tree of life. This, I say, *for a time;* for it is very probable that God soon removed the tree of life, and abolished the garden, so that its situation could never after be positively ascertained.

By *the flaming sword turning every way*, or flame folding back upon itself, we may understand the formidable appearances which these cherubim assumed, in order to render the passage to the tree of life inaccessible.

Thus terminates this most awful tragedy; a tragedy in which all the actors are slain, in which the most awful murders are committed, and the whole universe ruined! The *serpent*, so called, is degraded; the *woman* cursed with pains, miseries, and a subjection to the will of her husband, which was never *originally* designed; the *man*, the lord of this lower world, doomed to incessant labour and toil; and the *earth* itself cursed with comparative barrenness! To complete all, the *garden of pleasure* is interdicted, and this man, who was made after the image of God, and who *would be like him*, shamefully expelled from a

place where pure spirits alone could dwell. Yet in the midst of wrath God remembers mercy, and a promise of redemption from this degraded and cursed state is made to them through HIM who, in the fulness of time, is to be made flesh, and who, by dying for the sin of the world, shall destroy the power of Satan, and deliver all who trust in the merit of his sacrifice from the power, guilt, and nature of sin, and thus prepare them for the celestial Paradise at the right hand of God. Reader, hast thou repented of *thy* sin? for often hast thou sinned after the similitude of thy ancestor's transgression. Hast thou sought and found redemption in the blood of the Lamb? Art thou saved from a disposition which led thy first parents to transgress? Art thou living a life of *dependence* on thy Creator, and of faith and loving obedience to him who died for thee? *Wilt* thou live under the curse, and die eternally? God forbid! Return to him with all thy soul, and receive this exhortation as a call from his mercy.

To what has already been said on the awful contents of this chapter, I can add little that can either set it in a clearer light, or make its solemn subject more impressive. We see here that by the subtlety and envy of the devil sin entered into the world, and death by sin; and we find that death reigned, not only from Adam to Moses, but from Moses to the present day. How abominable must sin be in the sight of God, when it has not only defaced his own image from the soul of man, but has also become a source of natural and moral evil throughout every part of the globe! Disruption and violence appear in every part of nature; vice, profligacy, and misery, through all the tribes of men and orders of society. It is true that where sin hath abounded, there grace doth much more abound; but men shut their eyes against the light, and harden their hearts against the truth. Sin, which becomes propagated into the world by natural generation, growing with the growth and strengthening with the strength of man, would be as endless in its duration, as unlimited in its influence, did not God check and restrain it by his *grace*, and cut off its extending influence in the incorrigibly wicked by means of *death*. How wonderful is the economy of God! That which entered into the world as one of the prime fruits and effects of sin, is now an instrument in his hands to prevent the extension of its contagion. If men, now so greatly multiplied on the earth, and fertile in mischievous inventions, were permitted to live nearly a thousand years, as in the ancient world, to mature and perfect their infectious and destructive counsels, what a sum of iniquity and ruin would the face of the earth present! Even while they are laying plans to extend the empire of death, God, by the very means of *death* itself, prevents the completion of their pernicious and diabolic designs. Thus what man, by his wilful obstinacy does not permit *grace* to correct and restrain, God, by his sovereign power, brings in *death* to control. It is on this ground that wicked and blood-thirsty men live not out half their days; and what a mercy to the world that it is so! They who will not submit to the sceptre of mercy shall be broken in pieces by the rod of iron. Reader, provoke not the Lord to displeasure; thou art not stronger than he. Grieve not his Spirit, provoke him not to destroy thee; why shouldst thou die *before thy time?* Thou hast sinned much, and needest every moment of thy short life to make thy calling and election sure. Shouldst thou provoke God, by thy perseverance in iniquity, to cut thee off by death before this great work is done, better for thee thou hadst never been born!

How vain are all attempts to attain immortality here! For some thousands of years men have been labouring to find out means to prevent death; and some have even boasted that they had found out a medicine capable of preserving life for ever, by resisting all the attacks of disease, and incessantly repairing all the wastes of the human machine. That is, the alchymistic philosophers would have the world to believe that they had found out a private passage to the tree of immortality; but their *own deaths*, in the common order of nature, as well as the deaths of the millions which make no such pretensions, are not only a sufficient confutation of their baseless systems, but also a continual proof that *the cherubim, with their flaming swords, are turning every way to keep the passage of the tree of life.* Life and immortality are, however, brought to light by the Gospel; and he only who keepeth the sayings of the Son of God shall live for ever. Though the body is dead—consigned to death, because of sin, yet the spirit is life because of righteousness; and on those who are influenced by this Spirit of righteousness, the second death shall have no power.

CHAPTER IV.

The birth, trade, and religion of Cain and Abel, 1–7. *Cain murders his brother Abel,* 8. *God calls him into judgment for it,* 9, 10. *He is cursed,* 11, 12. *He despairs,* 13, 14. *A promise given him of preservation, and a mark set on him to prevent his being killed,* 15. *He departs from God's presence,* 16. *Has a son whom he calls Enoch; and builds a city, which he calls after his name,* 17. *Cain has several children, among whom are Lamech, the first bigamist,* 18, 19. *Jabal, who taught the use of tents and feeding cattle,* 20. *Jubal, the inventor of musical instruments,* 21. *Tubal-cain, the inventor of smith-work,* 22. *Strange speech of Lamech to his wives,* 23, 24. *Seth born to Adam and Eve in the place of Abel,* 25. *Enoch born, and the worship of God restored,* 26.

A. M. 2. B. C. 4003.

AND Adam knew Eve his wife; and she conceived, and bare [a] Cain, and said, I have gotten a man from the LORD.

2 And she again bare his brother [b] Abel. And Abel was [c] a keeper of sheep, but Cain was [d] a tiller of the ground.

A. M. cir. 129. B. C. cir. 3875.

3 And [e] in process of time it came to pass, that Cain brought [f] of the fruit of the ground an offering unto the LORD.

4 And Abel, he also brought of [g] the firstlings of his [h] flock, and of the fat thereof. And the LORD had [i] respect unto Abel and to his offering;

That is, *gotten* or *acquired*.——[b] Heb. *Hebel*.——[c] Heb. *a feeder*, ver. 25, 29; 1 John iii. 10, 12, 15; Psa. cxxvii. 3; John viii. 44.

[d] Chap. iii. 23; ix. 20.——[e] Heb. *at the end of days*.——[f] Num. xviii. 12.——[g] Num. xviii. 17; Prov. iii. 9.——[h] Heb. *sheep or goats*.——[i] Heb. xi. 4.

NOTES ON CHAP. IV.

Verse 1. *I have gotten a man from the Lord.*] Cain, קַיִן, signifies *acquisition;* hence Eve says קניתי *kanithi*, I have gotten or *acquired* a man, את יהוה *eth Yehovah*, the Lord. It is extremely difficult to ascertain the sense in which Eve used these words, which have been as variously translated as understood. Most expositors think that Eve imagined Cain to be the *promised seed* that should bruise the head of the serpent. This exposition really seems too refined for that period. It is very likely that she meant no more than to acknowledge that it was through God's peculiar blessing that she was enabled to conceive and bring forth a son, and that she had now a well-grounded hope that the race of man should be continued on the earth. Unless she had been under Divine inspiration she could not have called her son (even supposing him to be the promised seed) *Jehovah;* and that she was not under such an influence her *mistake* sufficiently proves, *for Cain*, so far from being the Messiah, *was of the wicked one;* 1 John iii. 12. We may therefore suppose that את יהוה *eth Yehovah*, THE LORD, is an elliptical form of expression for מאת יהוה *meeth Yehovah*, FROM THE LORD, or *through the Divine blessing*.

Verse 2. *And she again bare his brother Abel.*] Literally, *She added to bear* (ותסף ללדת *vattoseph laledeth*) *his brother*. From the very face of this account it appears evident that Cain and Abel were *twins*. In most cases where a subject of this kind is introduced in the Holy Scriptures, and the successive births of children of the same parents are noted, the acts of conceiving and bringing forth are mentioned in reference to each child; here it is *not* said that she *conceived* and brought forth Abel, but simply *she added to bring forth Abel his brother;* that is, as I understand it, Cain was the first-born, Abel, his twin brother, came next.

Abel was a keeper of sheep] Adam was originally a *gardener*, Abel a *shepherd*, and Cain an *agriculturist* or *farmer*. These were the *three* primitive employments, and, I may add, the most rational, and consequently the best calculated to prevent strife and an immoderate love of the world.

Verse 3. *In process of time*] מקץ ימים *mikkets yamim*, at the end of days. Some think the anniversary of the creation to be here intended; it is more probable that it means the *Sabbath*, on which Adam and his family undoubtedly offered oblations to God, as the Divine worship was certainly instituted, and no doubt the Sabbath properly observed in that family. This worship was, in its original institution, very simple. It appears to have consisted of *two* parts: 1. *Thanksgiving* to God as the author and dispenser of all the bounties of nature, and *oblations* indicative of that gratitude. 2. *Piacular sacrifices* to his justice and holiness, implying a *conviction* of their own sinfulness, *confession* of transgression, and *faith* in the promised Deliverer. If we collate the passage here with the apostle's allusion to it, Heb. xi. 4, we shall see cause to form this conclusion.

Cain brought of the fruit of the ground an offering] מנחה *minchah*, unto the Lord. The word *minchah* is explained, Lev. ii. 1, &c., to be *an offering of fine flour, with oil and frankincense*. It was in general a eucharistic or gratitude offering, and is simply what is implied in the *fruits of the ground* brought by Cain to the Lord, by which he testified his belief in him as the Lord of the universe, and the dispenser of secular blessings.

Verse 4. *Abel, he also brought of the firstlings of his flock*] Dr. Kennicott contends that the words *he also brought*, הביא גם הוא *hebi gam hu*, should be translated, Abel *brought* IT *also*, i. e. a *minchah* or *gratitude offering;* and beside this he brought of the first-born (מבכרות *mibbechoroth*) of his flock, and it was by *this* alone that he acknowledged himself a *sinner*, and professed faith in the promised *Messiah*. To this circumstance the apostle seems evidently to allude, Heb. xi. 4: *By* FAITH *Abel offered* πλειονα θυσιαν, a MORE OR GREATER *sacrifice;* not a more *excellent*, (for this is no meaning of the word πλειων,) which leads us to infer, according to Dr. Kennicott, that Abel, besides his *minchah* or gratitude offering, brought also θυσια, *a victim*, to be slain for his sins; and this he chose out of the *first-born* of his flock, which, in the order of God, was a representation of the Lamb of God that was to take away the sin of the world; and what confirms this exposition more is the observation of the apostle: *God testifying* τοις δωροις, *of his* GIFTS, which certainly shows he brought more than *one*. According to this interpretation, Cain, the father of Deism, not acknowledging the necessity of a vicarious sacrifice, nor feeling his need of an atonement, according to the dictates of his *natural religion*, brought a *minchah* or *eucharistic* offering to the God of the universe. Abel, not less grateful for the produce of his fields and the increase of his flocks, brought a *similar* offering, and by adding a *sacrifice* to it paid a proper regard to the will of God as far as it had then been revealed, acknowledged himself a *sinner*, and thus, deprecating the Divine displeasure, showed forth the death of Christ till he came. Thus his offerings were accepted, while

A. M. cir. 129.
B. C. cir. 3875.

5 But unto Cain and to his offering he had not respect. And Cain was very wroth, [k] and his countenance fell.

6 And the LORD said unto Cain, Why art thou wroth? and why is thy countenance fallen?

7 If thou doest well, shalt thou [l] not be accepted? and if thou doest not well, sin lieth at the door. And [m] unto thee *shall be* his desire, and thou shalt rule over him.

8 And Cain talked with Abel his brother:

A. M. cir. 129.
B. C. cir. 3875.

[k] Chap. xxxi. 2; Num. xvi. 15; Isa. iii. 10, 11; Psalm xx. 3.

[l] Or, have *the excellency;* Heb. xi. 4; Prov. xxi. 27; Job xxix. 4. — [m] Or, *subject unto thee;* chap. iii. 16.

those of Cain were rejected; for this, as the apostle says, was done by FAITH, and therefore he obtained witness that he was righteous, or a justified person, God testifying with his gifts, the *thank-offering* and the *sin-offering*, by accepting them, that faith in the promised seed was the only way in which he could accept the services and offerings of mankind. Dr. Magee, in his Discourses on the Atonement, criticises the opinion of Dr. Kennicott, and contends that there is no ground for the distinction made by the latter on the words *he also brought;* and shows that though the minchah in general signifies an unbloody offering, yet it is also used to express both kinds, and that the minchah in question is to be understood of the *sacrifice* then offered by Abel. I do not see that we gain much by this counter-criticism. See ver. 7.

Verse 5. *Unto Cain*] As being unconscious of his sinfulness, and consequently unhumbled, *and to his offering*, as not being accompanied, as Abel's was, with *faith* and a sacrifice for sin, *he had not respect*—He could not, consistently with his holiness and justice, approve of the one or receive the other. Of the manner in which God testified his *approbation* we are not informed; it was probably, as in the case of Elijah, by sending down fire from heaven, and consuming the sacrifice.

Cain was very wroth] That displeasure which should have been turned against his own unhumbled heart was turned against his innocent brother, who, though not more highly privileged than he, made a much better use of the advantages which he shared in common with his ungodly and unnatural brother.

Verse 6. *Why art thou wroth?*] This was designed as a gracious warning, and a preventive of the meditated crime.

Verse 7. *If thou doest well*] That which is right in the sight of God, *shalt thou not be accepted?* Does God reject any man who serves him in simplicity and godly sincerity? *But if thou doest not well*, can wrath and indignation against thy righteous brother save thee from the displeasure under which thou art fallen? On the contrary, have recourse to thy Maker for mercy; לפתח חטאת רבץ *lappethach chattath robets*, a *sin-offering* lieth at thy door; an animal proper to be offered as an atonement for sin is now *couching* at the door of thy fold.

The words חטאת *chattath*, and חטאה *chattaah*, frequently signify *sin;* but I have observed more than a hundred places in the Old Testament where they are used for *sin-offering*, and translated ἁμαρτια by the Septuagint, which is the term the apostle uses, 2 Cor. v. 21: *He hath made him to be sin* (ἁμαρτιαν, A SIN-OFFERING) *for us, who knew no sin.* Cain's fault now was his not bringing a sin-offering when his brother brought one, and his neglect and contempt caused his other offering to be rejected. However, God now graciously informs him that, though he had miscarried, his case was not yet desperate, as the means of faith, from the promise, &c., were in his power, and a victim proper for a sin-offering was lying (רבץ *robets*, a word used to express the lying down of a quadruped) at the door of his fold. How many sinners perish, not because there is not a Saviour able and willing to save them, but because they will not use that which is within their power! Of such how true is that word of our Lord, *Ye will not come unto me that ye might have life!*

Unto thee shall be *his desire, &c.*] That is, Thou shalt ever have the right of primogeniture, and in all things shall thy brother be subject unto thee. These words are not spoken of *sin*, as many have understood them, but of *Abel's* submission to Cain as his superior, and the words are spoken to remove Cain's envy.

Verse 8. *Cain talked with Abel his brother*] ויאמר קין vaiyomer Kayin, *and Cain said, &c.;* not *talked*, for this construction the word cannot bear without great violence to analogy and grammatical accuracy. But why should it be thus translated? Because our translators could not find that any thing was *spoken* on the occasion; and therefore they ventured to intimate that there was a conversation, indefinitely. In the most correct editions of the Hebrew Bible there is a small space left here in the text, and a circular mark which refers to a note in the margin, intimating that there is a hiatus or deficiency in the verse. Now this deficiency is supplied in the principal ancient versions, and in the Samaritan text. In this the supplied words are, LET US WALK OUT INTO THE FIELD. The Syriac has, Let us go to the desert. The Vulgate *Egrediamur foras*, Let us walk out. The Septuagint, Διελθωμεν εις το πεδιον, Let us go out into the field. The two *Chaldee Targums* have the same reading; so has the *Coptic* version. This addition is completely lost from every MS. of the Pentateuch now known; and yet it is sufficiently evident from the Samaritan text, the Samaritan version, the Syriac, Septuagint, and Vulgate, that it was in the most authentic copies of the Hebrew before and some time since the Christian era. The words may therefore be safely considered as a part of the sacred text, and with them the whole passage reads clear and consistently: "And Cain said unto Abel his brother, Let us go out into the field: and it came to pass, when they were in the field, that Cain rose up," &c. The Jerusalem Targum, and the Targum of Jonathan ben Uzziel, pretend to give us the subject of their conversation: as the

A. M. cir. 129. B. C. cir. 3875.

and it came to pass, when they
were in the field, that Cain rose
up against Abel his brother, and [n] slew him.
9 And the LORD said unto Cain, [o] Where
is Abel thy brother? And he said, [p] I know
not: *Am* I my brother's keeper?
10 And he said, What hast thou done? the
voice of thy brother's [q] blood [r] crieth unto me
from the ground.
11 And now *art* thou cursed from the earth,
which hath opened her mouth to
receive thy brother's blood from
thy hand;
12 When thou tillest the ground, it shall not
henceforth yield unto thee her strength; a fugitive and a vagabond shalt thou be in the earth.
13 And Cain said unto the LORD, [s] My
punishment *is* greater than I can bear.
14 [t] Behold, thou hast driven me out this day
from the face of the earth; and [u] from thy

[n] Job xi. 15; Psa. xxiv. 3–6; lv. 21; cxxxix. 19; Wisd. x. 3; Matt. xxiii. 35; 1 John iii. 12; Jude 11.——[o] Chap. iii. 9, 11; Psa. ix. 12.——[p] Job xxii. 13, 14; Psa. x. 13, 14; John viii. 44. [q] Heb. *bloods*.

[r] Acts v. 3, 9; Heb. xii. 24; James v. 4; Rev. vi. 10.——[s] Or, *Mine iniquity* is *greater than* that it may *be forgiven*; Rev. xvi. 9. [t] Job xv. 20–24; Prov. xiv. 32; xxviii. 1; Psa. cxliii. 7; 2 Thess. i. 9.——[u] Psa. li. 11.

piece is curious, I shall insert the substance of it, for the sake of those who may not have access to the originals.

"And Cain said unto Hebel his brother, Let us go out into the field; and it came to pass, when they were in the field, Cain answered and said to Hebel his brother, I thought that the world was created in mercy, but it is not governed according to the merit of good works, nor is there any judgment, nor a Judge, nor shall there be any future state in which good rewards shall be given to the righteous, or punishment executed on the wicked; and *now* there is respect of persons in judgment. On what account is it that thy sacrifice has been accepted, and mine not received with complacency? And Hebel answered and said, The world was created in mercy, and it is governed according to the fruit of good works; there is a Judge, a future world, and a coming judgment, where good rewards shall be given to the righteous, and the impious punished; and there is no respect of persons in judgment; but because my works were better and more precious than thine, my oblation was received with complacency. And because of these things they contended on the face of the field, and Cain rose up against Hebel his brother, and struck a stone into his forehead, and killed him."

It is here supposed that the first murder committed in the world was the consequence of a religious dispute; however *this* may have been, millions since have been sacrificed to prejudice, bigotry, and intolerance. Here, certainly, originated the many-headed monster, *religious persecution*; the spirit of the wicked one in his followers impels them to afflict and destroy all those who are partakers of the Spirit of God. Every persecutor is a legitimate son of the *old murderer*. This is the first triumph of Satan; it is not merely *a death* that he has introduced, but a *violent* one, as the first-fruits of sin. It is not the death of an *ordinary* person, but of the most *holy man* then in being; it is not brought about by the *providence* of God, or by a gradual failure and destruction of the earthly fabric, but by a violent separation of body and soul; it is not done by a *common enemy*, from whom nothing better could be expected, but by the hand of a *brother*, and for no other reason but because the object of his envy was more righteous than himself. Alas! how exceeding sinful does sin appear in its first manifestation!

Verse 10. *The voice of thy brother's blood*] It is probable that Cain, having killed his brother, dug a hole and buried him in the earth, hoping thereby to prevent the murder from being known; and that this is what is designed in the words, *Thy brother's blood crieth unto me* FROM THE GROUND—*which hath opened her mouth to receive it from thy hand.* Some think that by *the voice of thy brother's blood* the cries of Abel's widow and children are to be understood, as it is very probable that he was *father of a family*; indeed his occupation and sacrifices seem to render this probable, and probability is all we can expect on such a subject. God represents these as calling aloud for the punishment of the murderer; and it is evident that Cain expected to fall by the hands of some person who, from his *consanguinity*, had the right of the avenger of blood; for now that the murder is found out, he expects to suffer death for it. See ver. 14.

Verse 12. *A fugitive and a vagabond shalt thou be*] Thou shalt be expelled from the presence of God, and from thy family connections, and shalt have no fixed *secure* residence in any place. The Septuagint render this στενων και τρεμων εσῃ, *thou shalt be groaning and trembling* upon the earth—the horror of thy crime shall ever haunt thee, and thou shalt never have any well-grounded hope that God will remit the punishment thou deservest. No state out of endless perdition can be considered more awful than this.

Verse 13. *My punishment* is *greater than I can bear.*] The margin reads, *Mine iniquity* is *greater than* that it may *be forgiven*. The original words, גדול עוני מנשוא *gadol avoni minneso*, may be translated, *Is my crime too great to be forgiven?* words which we may presume he uttered on the verge of black despair. It is most probable that עון *avon* signifies rather the *crime* than the *punishment*; in this sense it is used Lev. xxvi. 41, 43; 1 Sam. xxviii. 10; 2 Kings vii. 9; and נשא *nasa* signifies to remit or forgive. The *marginal* reading is, therefore, to be preferred to that in the text.

Verse 14. *Behold, thou hast driven me out*] In verses 11, 12, God states two parts of Cain's punishment: 1. The ground was cursed, so that it was not to yield any adequate recompense for his most careful tillage. 2. He was to be a fugitive and a vagabond, having no place in which he could dwell with comfort or security. To these Cain himself adds others.

A. M. cir. 129.
B. C. cir. 3875.

face shall I be hid; and I shall
be a fugitive and a vagabond in
the earth: and it shall come to pass, [v] *that*
every one that findeth me shall slay me.
15 And the LORD said unto him, Therefore whosoever slayeth Cain, vengeance shall
be taken on him [w] seven-fold.
And the LORD [x] set a mark upon
Cain, lest any finding him should kill him.
16 And Cain [y] went out from the presence
of the LORD, and dwelt in the land of Nod,
on the east of Eden.

A. M. cir. 129.
B. C. cir. 3875.

[v] Chap. ix. 6; Num. xxxv. 19, 21, 27.——[w] Psa. lxxix. 12.

[x] Ezek. ix. 4, 6.——[y] 2 Kings xiii. 23; xxiv. 20; Jer. xxiii. 39; lii. 3.

1. His being hidden from the face of God; which appears to signify his being expelled from that *particular place* where God had manifested his presence, in or contiguous to Paradise, whither our first parents resorted as to an oracle, and where they offered their daily adorations. So in verse 16, it is said, *Cain went out from the presence of the Lord*, and was not permitted any more to associate with the family in acts of religious worship. 2. The continual apprehension of being slain, as all the inhabitants of the earth were at that time of the *same family*, the parents themselves still alive, and each having a right to kill this murderer of his relative. Add to all this, 3. The terrors of a guilty conscience; his awful apprehension of God's judgments, and of being everlastingly banished from the beatific vision. To this part of the punishment of Cain St. Paul probably alludes, 2 Thess. i. 9: *Who shall be punished with everlasting destruction from the presence of the Lord, and from the glory of his power.* The words are so similar that we can scarcely doubt of the allusion.

Verse 15. *The Lord set a mark upon Cain*] What this mark was, has given rise to a number of frivolously curious conjectures. Dr. Shuckford collects the most remarkable. Some say he was *paralytic;* this seems to have arisen from the version of the Septuagint, Στενων και τρεμων εσῃ, *Groaning and trembling shalt thou be.* The Targum of Jonathan ben Uzziel says the sign was from the great and precious name, probably one of the letters of the word יהוה *Yehovah.* The author of an Arabic Catena in the Bodleian Library says, "A sword could not pierce him; fire could not burn him; water could not drown him; the air could not blast him; nor could thunder or lightning strike him." The author of Bereshith Rabba, a comment on Genesis, says the mark was a circle of the sun rising upon him. Abravanel says the sign was Abel's dog, which constantly accompanied him. Some of the doctors in the Talmud say that it was the letter ת *tau* marked on his forehead, which signified his contrition, as it is the first letter i. the word תשובה *teshubah*, repentance. Rabbi Joseph, wiser than all the rest, says it was a long horn growing out of his forehead!

Dr. Shuckford farther observes that the Hebrew word אות *oth*, which we translate *a mark*, signifies *a sign* or *token*. Thus, Gen. ix. 13, the bow was to be לאות *leoth, for a sign* or *token* that the world should not be destroyed; therefore the words, *And the Lord set a mark upon Cain*, should be translated, And the Lord appointed to Cain a *token* or *sign*, to convince him that no person should be permitted to slay him. To have *marked* him would have been the most likely way to have brought all the evils he dreaded upon him; therefore the Lord gave him some miraculous sign or token that he should not be slain, to the end that he should not despair, but, having time to repent, might return to a gracious God and find mercy. Notwithstanding the allusion which I suppose St. Paul to have made to the punishment of Cain, some think that he did repent and find mercy. I can only say *this was possible.* Most people who read this account wonder why Cain should dread being killed, when it does not appear to them that there were any inhabitants on the earth at that time besides himself and his parents. To correct this mistake, let it be observed that the death of Abel took place in the one hundred and twenty-eighth or one hundred and twenty-ninth year of the world. Now, "supposing Adam and Eve to have had no other sons than Cain and Abel in the year of the world one hundred and twenty-eight, yet as they had daughters married to these sons, their descendants would make a considerable figure on the earth. Supposing them to have been married in the *nineteenth* year of the world, they might easily have had each eight children, some males and some females, in the twenty-fifth year. In the fiftieth year there might proceed from them in a direct line sixty-four persons; in the seventy-fourth year there would be five hundred and twelve; in the ninety-eighth year, four thousand and ninety-six; in the one hundred and twenty-second they would amount to thirty-two thousand seven hundred and sixty-eight: if to these we add the other children descended from Cain and Abel, their children, and their children's children, we shall have, in the aforesaid one hundred and twenty-eight years *four hundred and twenty-one thousand one hundred and sixty-four* men capable of generation, without reckoning the women either old or young, or such as are under the age of seventeen." See Dodd.

But this calculation may be disputed, because there is no evidence that the antediluvian patriarchs began to have children before they were *sixty-five* years of age. Now, supposing that Adam at one hundred and thirty years of age had one hundred and thirty children, which is quite possible, and each of these a child at sixty-five years of age, and one in each successive year, the whole, in the *one hundred and thirtieth* year of the world, would amount to *one thousand two hundred and nineteen persons;* a number sufficient to found several villages, and to excite the apprehensions under which Cain appeared at this time to labour.

Verse 16. *The land of Nod*] As נוד *nod* signifies the same as נד *nad*, a *vagabond*, some think this verse should be rendered, *And Cain went out from the presence of the Lord, from the east of Eden, and dwelt a vagabond on the earth;* thus the curse pronounced on him, verse 12, was accomplished.

A. M. cir. 129.
B. C. cir. 3875.

17 And Cain knew his wife; and
she conceived, and bare [z] Enoch:
and he builded a city, [a] and called the name
of the city, after the name of his son, Enoch.

A. M. cir. 194.
B. C. cir. 3810.

18 And unto Enoch was born
Irad: and Irad begat Mehujael:
and Mehujael begat Methusael: and Methusael
begat [b] Lamech.
19 And Lamech took unto him two wives:
the name of the one *was* Adah, and the name
of the other Zillah.

A. M. cir. 194.
B. C. cir. 3810.

20 And Adah bare Jabal: he
was the father of such as [c] dwell
in tents, and *of such as have* cattle.

A. M. cir. 500.
B. C. cir. 3504.

21 And his brother's name *was*
Jubal: he was the father of all
such as handle the harp and organ.
22 And Zillah, she also bare Tubal-cain,
an [d] instructer of every artificer in brass and
iron: and the sister of Tubal-cain *was* Naamah.
23 And Lamech said unto his wives, Adah
and Zillah, hear my voice; ye wives of

[z] Heb. *Chanoch*; chap. v. 18, 22.——[a] Psa. xlix. 11; 2 Sam. xviii. 18.——[b] Heb. *Lemech*; chap. v. 21; xxxvi. 2; ii. 18, 24.

[c] Jer. xxxv. 9, 10; Heb. xi. 9; Rom. iv. 11, 12.——[d] Heb. *whetter*; Exod. xxv. 3; 2 Chron. ii. 17.

Verse 17. *She—bare Enoch*] As חנוך *Chanoch* signifies *instructed*, *dedicated*, or *initiated*, and especially in sacred things, it may be considered some proof of Cain's repentance, that he appears to have dedicated this son to God, who, in his father's stead, might minister in the sacerdotal office, from which Cain, by his crime, was for ever excluded.

Verse 19. *Lamech took—two wives*] He was the first who dared to reverse the order of God by introducing polygamy; and from him it has been *retained*, practised, and defended to the present day.

Verse 20. *Jabal—was the father*] The *inventor* or *teacher*, for so the word is understood, 1 Sam. x. 12. He was the first who invented tent-making, and the breeding and managing of cattle; or he was, in these respects, the most eminent in that time. Though Abel was a shepherd, it is not likely he was such on an extensive scale.

Verse 21. *Jubal—the father*] i. e. The *inventor* of musical instruments, such as the כנור *kinnor*, which we translate *harp*, and the עוגב *ugab*, which we render *organ*; it is very likely that both words are *generic*, the former including under it all *stringed* instruments, and the latter, all *wind* instruments.

Verse 22. *Tubal-cain*] The first *smith* on record, who taught how to make *warlike* instruments and *domestic* utensils out of brass and iron. Agricultural instruments must have been in use long before, for Cain was a *tiller of the ground*, and so was Adam, and they could not have cultivated the ground without *spades*, *hooks*, &c. Some of these arts were useless to man while innocent and upright, but after his fall they became necessary. Thus is the saying verified: *God made man upright, but they have sought out many inventions.* As the power to get wealth is from God, so also is the invention of useful arts.

M. De Lavaur, in his *Conference de la Fable avec l'Histoire Sainte*, supposes that the Greeks and Romans took their smith-god *Vulcan* from Tubal-cain, the son of Lamech. The probability of this will appear, 1. From the *name*, which, by the omission of the *Tu* and turning the *b* into *v*, a change frequently made among the Hebrews, Greeks, and Romans, makes *Vulcain* or *Vulcan*. 2. From his *occupation* he was an artificer, a master smith in brass and iron. 3. He thinks this farther probable from the *names* and *sounds* in this verse. The melting metals in the fire, and hammering them, bears a near resemblance to the *hissing* sound of צלה *tsillah*, the mother of Tubal-cain; and צלל *tsalal* signifies to *tinkle* or make a sound like a *bell*, 1 Sam. iii. 11; 2 Kings xxi. 12. 4. Vulcan is said to have been lame; M. De Lavaur thinks that this notion was taken from the noun צלע *tsela*, which signifies a *halting* or *lameness*. 5. Vulcan had to wife Venus, the goddess of *beauty*; *Naamah*, the sister of Tubal-cain, he thinks, may have given rise to this part of the fable, as her name in Hebrew signifies *beautiful* or *gracious*. 6. Vulcan is reported to have been jealous of his wife, and to have forged nets in which he took Mars and her, and exposed them to the view of the whole celestial court: this idea he thinks was derived from the literal import of the name *Tubal-cain*; תבל *tebel* signifies an incestuous mixture of relatives, Lev. xx. 12; and קנא *kana*, to burn with jealousy; from these and concomitant circumstances the case of the detected adultery of Mars and Venus might be easily deduced. He is of opinion that a tradition of this kind might have readily found its way from the Egyptians to the Greeks, as the former had frequent intercourse with the Hebrews.

Of *Naamah* nothing more is spoken in the Scriptures; but the Targum of Jonathan ben Uzziel makes her the inventress of funeral songs and lamentations. R. S. Jarchi says she was the wife of Noah, and quotes *Bereshith Rabba* in support of the opinion. Some of the Jewish doctors say her name is recorded in Scripture because she was an upright and chaste woman; but others affirm that the *whole world wandered after her*, and that of her evil spirits were born into the world. This latter opinion gives some countenance to that of M. De Lavaur.

Verse 23. *And Lamech said unto his wives*] The speech of Lamech to his wives is in hemistichs in the original, and consequently, as nothing of this kind occurs before this time, it is very probably the *oldest piece of poetry in the world*.

The following is, as nearly as possible, a literal translation:

"And Lamech said unto his wives,
Adah and Tsillah, hear ye my voice;
Wives of Lamech, hearken to my speech;
For I have slain a man for wounding me,
And a young man for having bruised me.
If Cain shall be avenged seven-fold,
Also Lamech seventy and seven."

A. M. cir. 500.
B. C. cir. 3504.

Lamech, hearken unto my speech: for [e] I have slain a man to my wounding, and a young man [f] to my hurt.

24 [g] If Cain shall be avenged seven-fold, truly Lamech seventy and seven-fold.

25 And Adam knew his wife again; and she bare a son, and [h] called his name [i] Seth [k]: For God, *said she*, hath appointed me another seed instead of Abel, whom Cain slew.

A. M. 130.
B. C. 3874.

26 And to Seth, [l] to him also there was born a son; and he called his name [m] Enos: then began men [n] to call upon the name of the [o] LORD.

A. M. 235
B. C. 3769.

[e] Or, *I would slay a man in my wound*, &c.; chap. xlix. 6.——[f] Or, *in my hurt.*——[g] Ver. 15.——[h] Chap. v. 3.——[i] Heb. *Sheth.*——[k] That is, *appointed* or *put.*——[l] Chap. v. 6.——[m] Heb. *Enosh.*

[n] Or, *to call* themselves *by the name of the LORD.*——[o] 1 Kings xviii. 24; Psa. cxvi. 17; Isa. xliv. 5; xlviii. 1; lxiii. 19; Joel ii. 32; Zeph. iii. 9; Acts xi. 26; Rom. x. 13; 1 Cor. i. 2; Eph. iii. 14, 15.

It is supposed that Lamech had slain a man in his own defence, and that his wives being alarmed lest the kindred of the deceased should seek his life in return, to quiet their fears he makes this speech, in which he endeavours to prove that there was no room for fear on this account; for if the slayer of the wilful murderer, Cain, should suffer a seven-fold punishment, surely he, who should kill Lamech for having slain a man in self-defence, might expect a seventy seven-fold punishment.

This speech is very dark, and has given rise to a great variety of very strange conjectures. Dr. Shuckford supposes there is an ellipsis of some preceding speech or circumstance which, if known, would cast a light on the subject. In the antediluvian times, the nearest of kin to a murdered person had a right to revenge his death by taking away the life of the murderer. This, as we have already seen, appears to have contributed not a little to Cain's horror, verse 14. Now we may suppose that the descendants of Cain were in continual alarms, lest some of the other family should attempt to avenge the death of Abel on *them*, as they were not permitted to do it on Cain; and that in order to dismiss those fears, Lamech, the seventh descendant from Adam, spoke to this effect to his wives: "Why should you render yourselves miserable by such ill-founded fears? We have slain no person; we have not done the least wrong to our brethren of the other family; surely then reason should dictate to you that they have no right to injure us. It is true that Cain, one of our ancestors, killed his brother Abel; but God, willing to pardon his sin, and give him space to repent, threatened to punish those with a seven-fold punishment who should dare to kill him. If this be so, then those who should have the boldness to kill any of us who are innocent, may expect a punishment still more rigorous. For if Cain should be avenged seven-fold on the person who should slay him, surely Lamech or any of his innocent family should be avenged seventy-seven-fold on those who should injure them." The Targums give nearly the same meaning, and it makes a good sense; but who can say it is the true sense? If the words be read interrogatively, as they certainly may, the sense will be much clearer, and some of the difficulties will be removed:

"Have I slain a man, that I should be wounded?
Or a young man, that I should be bruised?"

But even this still supposes some previous reason or conversation. I shall not trouble my readers with a ridiculous Jewish fable, followed by St. Jerome, of Lamech having killed Cain by accident, &c.; and after what I have already said, I must leave the passage, I fear, among those which are inscrutable.

Verse 25. *God—hath appointed me another seed instead of Abel*] Eve must have received on this occasion some Divine communication, else how could she have known that this son was appointed in the *place* of Abel, to continue that holy line by which the Messiah was to come? From this we see that the line of the Messiah was determined from the beginning, and that it was not first fixed in the days of Abraham; for the promise was then only *renewed*, and *that* branch of his family designated by which the sacred line was to be continued. And it is worthy of remark, that Seth's posterity *alone* continued after the flood, when all the other families of the earth were destroyed, Noah being the tenth descendant from Adam through Seth.

Though all these persons are mentioned in the following chapter, I shall produce them here in the order of their succession: 1. Adam; 2. Seth; 3. Enos; 4. Cainan; 5. Mahalaleel; 6. Jared; 7. Enoch; 8. Methuselah; 9. Lamech, (the second;) 10. Noah. In order to keep this line distinct, we find particular care was taken that, where there were two or more sons in a family, the one through whom God particularly designed to bring his Son into the world was, by some especial providence, pointed out. Thus in the family of Adam, Seth was chosen; in the family of Noah, Shem; in the family of Abraham, Isaac; and in that of David, Solomon and Nathan. All these things God watched over by an especial providence from the beginning, that when Jesus Christ should come it might be clearly seen that he came by the promise, through *grace*, and not by *nature*.

Verse 26. *Then began men to call upon the name of the Lord.*] The marginal reading is, *Then began men to call* themselves *by the name of the Lord;* which words are supposed to signify that in the time of Enos the true followers of God began to distinguish themselves, and to be distinguished by others, by the appellation of *sons of God;* those of the other branch of Adam's family, among whom the Divine worship was not observed, being distinguished by the name, *children of men*. It must not be dissembled that many eminent men have contended that הוחל *huchal*, which we translate *began*, should be rendered *began profanely*, or *then profanation began*, and from this time they date the origin of idolatry. Most of the Jewish doctors were of this opinion, and Maimonides has discussed it

at some length in his Treatise on Idolatry; as this piece is curious, and gives the most probable account of the origin and progress of idolatry, I shall insert it here.

"In the days of Enos the sons of Adam erred with great error, and the counsel of the wise men of that age became brutish, and Enos himself was (one) of them that erred; and their error was this: they said, Forasmuch as God hath created these stars and spheres to govern the world, and set them on high, and imparted honour unto them, and they are ministers that minister before him; it is meet that men should laud, and glorify, and give them honour. For this is the will of God, that we magnify and honour whomsoever he magnifieth and honoureth; even as a king would have them honoured that stand before him, and this is the honour of the king himself. When this thing was come up into their hearts they began to build temples unto the stars, and to offer sacrifice unto them, and to laud and glorify them with words, and to worship before them, that they might in their evil opinion obtain favour of the Creator; and this was *the root of idolatry*, &c. And in process of time there stood up false prophets among the sons of Adam, which said that God had commanded and said unto them, Worship such a star, or all the stars, and do sacrifice unto them thus and thus; and build a temple for it, and make an image of it, that all the people, women, and children may worship it. And the false prophet showed them the image which he had feigned out of his own heart, and said it was the image of such a star, which was made known unto him by prophecy. And they began after this manner to make images in temples, and under trees, and on tops of mountains and hills, and assembled together and worshipped them, &c. And this thing was spread through all the world, to serve images with services different one from another, and to sacrifice unto and worship them. So, in process of time, the glorious and fearful name (of God) was forgotten out of the mouth of all living, and out of their knowledge, and they acknowledged him not. And there was found no people on the earth that knew aught, save images of wood and stone, and temples of stone, which they had been trained up from their childhood to worship and serve, and to swear by their names. And the wise men that were among them, as the priests and such like, thought there was no God save the stars and spheres, for whose sake and in whose likeness they had made these images; but as for the Rock everlasting, there was no man that acknowledged him or knew him save a few persons in the world, as Enoch, Methuselah, Noah, Shem, and Heber. And in this way did the world walk and converse till that pillar of the world, Abraham our father, was born." *Maim.* in Mishn. and *Ainsworth* in loco.

1. We see here the vast importance of worshipping God according to his own mind; no sincerity, no uprightness of intention, can atone for the neglect of positive commands delivered in Divine revelation, when this revelation is known. He who will bring a eucharistic offering instead of a sacrifice, while a sin-offering lieth at the door, as he copies Cain's conduct, may expect to be treated in the same manner. Reader, remember that thou hast an entrance unto the holiest through the veil, that is to say *his flesh*; and those who come in this way, God will in nowise cast out.

2. We see the horrible nature of envy: its eye is evil merely because God is good; it easily begets hatred; hatred, deep-settled malice; and malice, murder! Watch against the first appearance of this most destructive passion, the prime characteristic of which is to seek the destruction of the object of its malevolence, and finally to ruin its possessor.

3. Be thankful to God that, as weakness increased and wants became multiplied, God enabled man to find out useful inventions, so as to lessen excessive labour, and provide every thing indispensably necessary for the support of life. He who carefully attends to the dictates of honest, sober industry, is never likely to perish for lack of the necessaries of life.

4. As the followers of God at this early period found it indispensably necessary to separate themselves from all those who were irreligious and profane, and to make a public profession of their attachment to the truth, so it should be now. There are still men of profane minds, whose spirit and conduct are destructive to godliness; and in reference to such the permanent order of God is, *Come out from among them, touch not the unclean thing, and I will receive you.* He who is not determined to be a Christian at all events, is not far from being an infidel. Those only who confess Christ among men shall be acknowledged before his Father and the angels of God.

CHAPTER V

A recapitulation of the account of the creation of man, 1, 2; *and of the birth of Seth,* 3. *Genealogy of the ten antediluvian patriarchs,* 3–31. *Enoch's extraordinary piety,* 22; *his translation to heaven without seeing death,* 24. *The birth of Noah, and the reason of his name,* 29; *his age at the birth of Japheth,* 32.

A. M. 1. B. C. 4004.

1 THIS *is* the [a] book of the generations of Adam. In the day that God created man, in [b] the likeness of God made he him;

[a] 1 Chron. i. 1; Matt. i. 1; Luke iii. 36, 38. — [b] Chap. i. 26; Wisd. ii. 23; Eph. iv. 24; Col. iii. 10.

NOTES ON CHAP. V.

Verse 1. *The book of the generations*] ספר *sepher*, in Hebrew, which we generally translate *book*, signifies a *register*, an *account*, any kind of writing, even a *letter*, such as the bill of divorce. Here it means the *account* or *register* of the *generations of Adam* or his descendants to the five hundredth year of the life of Noah.

A. M. 1. B. C. 4004. 2 [c] Male and female created he
them; and blessed them, and called
their name Adam, in the day when they were
created.
A. M. 130. B. C. 3874. 3 And Adam lived a hundred and
thirty years, and begat *a son* in his
own likeness, after his image; and [d] called
his name Seth:
4 [e] And the days of Adam after he had begotten Seth were eight hundred years; [f] and
he begat sons and daughters:
A. M. 930. B. C. 3074. 5 And all the days that Adam lived
were nine hundred and thirty years:
[g] and he died.
A. M. 235. B. C. 3769. 6 And Seth lived a hundred and
five years, and [h] begat Enos:

7 And Seth lived after he begat A. M. 235. B. C. 3769.
Enos eight hundred and seven years,
and begat sons and daughters:
8 And all the days of Seth were A. M. 1042. B. C. 2962.
nine hundred and twelve years:
and he died.
9 And Enos lived ninety years, A. M. 325. B. C. 3679.
and begat [i] Cainan:
10 And Enos lived after he begat Cainan
eight hundred and fifteen years, and begat
sons and daughters:
11 And all the days of Enos A. M. 1140. B. C. 2864.
were nine hundred and five years:
and he died.
12 And Cainan lived seventy A. M. 395. B. C. 3609.
years, and begat [k] Mahalaleel:

[c] Chap. i. 27.——[d] Chap. iv. 25.——[e] 1 Chron. i. 1, &c. [f] Chap. i. 28.

[g] Chap. iii. 19; Heb. ix. 27.——[h] Chap. iv. 26.——[i] Heb. *Kenan.* [k] Gr. *Maleleel.*

In the likeness of God made he him] This account is again introduced to keep man in remembrance of the heights of glory whence he had fallen; and to prove to him that the miseries and death consequent on his present state were produced by his transgression, and did not flow from his original state. For, as he was created in the image of God, he was created free from natural and moral evil. As the *deaths* of the patriarchs are now to be mentioned, it was necessary to introduce them by this observation, in order to justify the ways of God to man.

Verse 3. *And Adam lived a hundred and thirty years, &c.*] The Scripture chronology, especially in the ages of some of the *antediluvian* and *postdiluvian* patriarchs, has exceedingly puzzled chronologists, critics, and divines. The printed Hebrew text, the Samaritan, the Septuagint, and Josephus, are all different, and have their respective vouchers and defenders. The following tables of the genealogies of the patriarchs *before* and *after* the flood, according to the Hebrew, Samaritan, and Septuagint, will at once exhibit the discordances.

ANTEDILUVIAN PATRIARCHS LIVED BEFORE THEIR SONS' BIRTH.

		Heb.	Samar.	Sept.
Adam,	Gen. v. 3.	130	130	230
Seth,	—— 6.	105	105	205
Enos,	—— 9.	90	90	190
Cainan,	—— 12.	70	70	170
Mahalaleel,	—— 15.	65	65	165
Jared,	—— 18.	162	62	162
Enoch,	—— 21.	65	65	165
Methuselah,	—— 25.	187	67	167
Lamech,	—— 28.	182	53	188
Noah, at the flood,	Gen. vii. 6.	600	600	600
Total before the flood,		1656	1307	2242*

In this first period the sum in Josephus is 2256, which is also adopted by Dr. Hales in his *New Analysis of Chronology*.

POSTDILUVIAN PATRIARCHS LIVED BEFORE THEIR SONS' BIRTH.

		Heb.	Samar.	Sept.
Shem begot Arphaxad after the flood, Gen. xi. 10.		2	2	2
Arphaxad, Gen. xi. 12.		35	135	135
Cainan (2d) mentioned only by the LXX. and Luke iii. 36.		0	0	130
Salah,	Gen. xi. 14.	30	130	130
Eber,	—— 16.	34	134	134
Peleg,	—— 18.	30	130	130
Reu,	—— 20.	32	132	132
Serug,	—— 22.	30	130	130
Nahor,	—— 24.	29	79	179
Terah,	—— 26.	70	70	70
Total to the 70th year of Terah,		292	942	1172*

In this second period the sum in Josephus is 1002.

*The Septuagint account of the ages of the *antediluvian* and *postdiluvian* patriarchs in the above tables, is taken from the VATICAN copy; but if we follow the ALEXANDRIAN MS., we shall have in the *first* period the whole sum of 2262 instead of 2242; and in the *second* period, 1072 instead of 1172. On this subject the different MSS. of the Septuagint abound with *various readings*.

For much satisfactory information on this subject I must refer to *A New Analysis of Chronology*, by the Rev. *William Hales*, D. D., 3 vols. 4to., London, 1809.

And begat a son *in his own likeness, after his image*] Words nearly the same with those chap. i. 26: *Let us make man in our image, after our likeness.* What

A. M. 395. B. C. 3609. 13 And Cainan lived after he begat Mahalaleel eight hundred and forty years, and begat sons and daughters:

A. M. 1235. B. C. 2769. 14 And all the days of Cainan were nine hundred and ten years: and he died.

A. M. 460. B. C. 3544. 15 And Mahalaleel lived sixty and five years, and begat [l] Jared:

16 And Mahalaleel lived after he begat Jared eight hundred and thirty years, and begat sons and daughters:

A. M. 1290. B. C. 2714. 17 And all the days of Mahalaleel were eight hundred ninety and five years: and he died.

18 And Jared lived a hundred sixty and two years, and he begat [m] Enoch: A. M. 622. B. C. 3382.

19 And Jared lived after he begat Enoch eight hundred years, and begat sons and daughters:

20 And all the days of Jared were nine hundred sixty and two years: and he died. A. M. 1422. B. C. 2582.

21 And Enoch lived sixty and five years, and begat [n] Methuselah: A. M. 687. B. C. 3317.

22 And Enoch [o] walked with God after he begat Methuselah three hundred years, and begat sons and daughters:

[l] Hebrew, *Jered*.——[m] Jude 14, 15.——[n] Gr. *Mathusala*.

[o] Chap. vi. 9; xvii. 1; xxiv. 40; 2 Kings xx. 3; Psa. xvi. 8; cxvi. 9; cxxviii. 1; Mic. vi. 8; Mal. ii. 6.

this *image* and *likeness* of God were, we have already seen, and we may rest assured that the *same* image and likeness are not meant here. The *body* of Adam was created provisionally immortal, i. e. while he continued obedient he could not die; but his obedience was voluntary, and his state a probationary one. The *soul* of Adam was created in the moral image of God, in *knowledge, righteousness*, and *true holiness*. He had now sinned, and consequently had *lost* this moral resemblance to his Maker; he had also become *mortal* through his breach of the law. His image and likeness were therefore widely different at *this time* from what they were *before;* and his begetting children in this image and likeness plainly implies that they were imperfect like himself, mortal like himself, sinful and corrupt like himself. For it is impossible that he, being impure, fallen from the Divine image, could beget a pure and holy offspring, unless we could suppose it possible that a *bitter* fountain could send forth *sweet* waters, or that a *cause* could produce *effects* totally dissimilar from itself. What is said here of Seth might have been said of all the other children of Adam, as they were all begotten after his fall; but the sacred writer has thought proper to mark it only in this instance.

Verse 22. *And Enoch walked with God—three hundred years*] There are several things worthy of our most particular notice in this account:

1. The *name* of this patriarch; *Enoch*, from חנך *chanack*, which signifies to *instruct*, to *initiate*, to *dedicate*. From his subsequent conduct we are authorized to believe he was early *instructed* in the things of God, *initiated* into the worship of his Maker, and *dedicated* to his service. By these means, under the influence of the Divine Spirit, which will ever attend pious parental instructions, his mind got that sacred bias which led him to act a part so distinguished through the course of a long life.

2. His religious conduct. *He walked with God;* יתהלך *yithhallech*, he *set himself to walk*, he was *fixedly purposed* and *determined* to live to God. Those who are acquainted with the original will at once see that it has this force. A verb in the conjugation called *hithpael* signifies a reciprocal act, that which a man does upon himself: here we may consider Enoch receiving a pious education, and the Divine influence through it; in consequence of which he determines to be a worker with God, and therefore takes up the resolution to walk with his Maker, that he might not receive the grace of God in vain.

3. The *circumstances* in which he was placed. He was a patriarch; the king, the priest, and the prophet of a numerous family, to whom he was to administer justice, among whom he was to perform all the rites and ceremonies of religion, and teach, both by precept and example, the way of truth and righteousness. Add to this, he was a *married man*, he had a numerous family of his own, independently of the collateral branches over which he was obliged, as *patriarch*, to preside; *he walked three hundred years with God, and begat sons and daughters;* therefore *marriage* is no hinderance even to the perfection of piety; much less inconsistent with it, as some have injudiciously taught.

4. The astonishing *height of piety* to which he had arrived; being cleansed from all filthiness of the flesh and of the spirit, and having perfected holiness in the fear of God, we find not only his soul but his body purified, so that, without being obliged to visit the empire of death, he was capable of immediate translation to the paradise of God. There are few cases of this kind on record; but probably there might be more, many more, were the followers of God more faithful to the grace they receive.

5. Enoch attained this state of religious and spiritual excellence in a time when, comparatively speaking, there were few helps, and no *written revelation*. Here then we cannot but see and admire how mighty the grace of God is, and what wonders it works in the behalf of those who are faithful, who *set themselves to walk with God*. It is not the want of grace nor of the means of grace that is the cause of the decay of this primitive piety, but the want of faithfulness in those who have the light, and yet will not walk as children of the light.

6. If the grace of God could work such a mighty change in those primitive times, when life and immortality were not brought to light by the Gospel, what

A. M. 987. B. C. 3017. 23 And all the days of Enoch
were three hundred sixty and five
years:
24 And [p] Enoch walked with God: and he
was not; for God took him.
A. M. 874. B. C. 3130. 25 And Methuselah lived a
hundred eighty and seven years,
and begat [q] Lamech:
26 And Methuselah lived after he begat
Lamech seven hundred eighty and two years,
and begat sons and daughters:
A. M. 1656. B. C. 2348. 27 And all the days of Methuselah were nine hundred sixty and
nine years: and he died.
28 And Lamech lived a hundred eighty
and two years, and begat a son: A. M. 1056. B. C. 2948.
29 And he called his name [r] Noah, [s] saying,
This *same* shall comfort us concerning our
work and toil of our hands, because of the
ground [t] which the Lord hath cursed.
30 And Lamech lived after he begat Noah
five hundred ninety and five years, and begat
sons and daughters:
31 And all the days of Lamech A. M. 1651. B. C. 2353.
were seven hundred seventy and
seven years: and he died.
32 And Noah was five hundred A. M. 1556. B. C. 2448.
years old: and Noah begat [u] Shem,
Ham, [v] and Japheth.

---

[p] 2 Kings ii. 11; Ecclus. xliv. 16; xlix. 14; Heb. xi. 5; [q] Heb. *Lemech.*——[r] Gr. *Noe*; Luke iii. 36; Heb. xi. 7; 1 Pet. iii. 20.——[s] That is, *rest* or *comfort.*——[t] Chap. iii. 17; iv. 11 [u] Chap. vi. 10.——[v] Chap. x. 21.

---

may we not expect in *these* times, in which the Son of God tabernacles among men, in which God gives the Holy Spirit to them who ask him, in which all things are possible to him who believes? No man can prove that Enoch had greater spiritual advantages than any of the other patriarchs, though it seems pretty evident that he made a better use of those that were common to all than any of the rest did; and it would be absurd to say that *he* had greater spiritual helps and advantages than Christians can now expect, for he lived under a dispensation much less perfect than that of the LAW, and yet the law itself was only the *shadow* of the glorious *substance* of Gospel blessings and Gospel privileges.

7. It is said that Enoch not only *walked with God*, setting him always before his eyes, beginning, continuing, and ending every work to his glory, but also that *he pleased God*, and had the *testimony that he did please God*, Heb. xi. 5. Hence we learn that it was *then* possible to live so as not to offend God, consequently so as not to commit sin against him; and to have the continual evidence or testimony that all that a man did and purposed was pleasing in the sight of Him who searches the heart, and by whom devices are weighed: and if it was possible *then*, it is surely, through the same grace, possible *now*; for God, and Christ, and *faith*, are still the *same*.

Verse 27. *The days of Methuselah were nine hundred sixty and nine years*] This is the longest life mentioned in Scripture, and probably the longest ever lived; but we have not authority to say positively that it was the longest. Before the flood, and before artificial refinements were much known and cultivated, the life of man was greatly protracted, and yet of him who lived within thirty-one years of a *thousand* it is said he *died*; and the longest life is but as a moment when it is past. Though life is uncertain, precarious, and full of natural evils, yet it is a blessing in all its periods if devoted to the glory of God and the interest of the soul; for while it lasts we may more and more acquaint ourselves with God and be at peace, and thereby good shall come unto us; Job xxii. 21.

Verse 29. *This* same *shall comfort us*] This is an allusion, as some think, to the name of Noah, which they derive from נחם *nacham*, to comfort; but it is much more likely that it comes from נח *nach* or נוח *nuach*, to rest, to settle, &c. And what is more *comfortable* than *rest* after *toil* and *labour*? These words seem to have been spoken *prophetically* concerning Noah, who built the ark for the preservation of the human race, and who seems to have been a typical person; for when he offered his sacrifice after the drying up of the waters, it is said that God smelled a savour of REST, and said he would not curse the ground any more for man's sake, chap. viii. 21; and from that time the earth seems to have had upon an average the same degree of fertility; and the life of man, in a few generations after, was settled in the mean at threescore years and ten. See chap. ix. 3.

Verse 32. *Noah begat Shem, Ham, and Japheth.*] From chap. x. 21; 1 Chron. i. 5, &c., we learn that Japheth was the eldest son of Noah, but *Shem* is mentioned first, because it was from him, in a direct line, that the Messiah came. *Ham* was certainly the *youngest* of Noah's sons, and from what we read, chap. ix. 22, the *worst* of them; and how *he* comes to be mentioned out of his natural order is not easy to be accounted for. When the Scriptures design to mark *precedency*, though the subject be a younger son or brother, he is always mentioned *first*; so *Jacob* is named before *Esau*, his elder brother, and *Ephraim* before *Manasses*. See chap. xxviii. 5; xlviii. 20.

Among many important things presented to our view in this chapter, several of which have been already noticed, we may observe that, of all the antediluvian patriarchs, Enoch, who was probably the best man, was the shortest time upon earth; his years were exactly as the days in a solar revolution, viz., *three hundred and sixty-five*; and like the sun he fulfilled a glorious course, shining more and more unto the perfect day and was taken, when in his meridian splendour, to shine like the sun in the kingdom of his Father for ever.

From computation it appears, 1. That Adam lived

to see Lamech, the ninth generation, in the fifty-sixth year of whose life he died; and as he was the first who lived, and the first that sinned, so he was the first who tasted death in a natural way. Abel's was not a natural but a violent death. 2. That Enoch was taken away next after Adam, seven patriarchs remaining witness of his translation. 3. That all the *nine* first patriarchs were taken away before the flood came, which happened in the sixth hundredth year of Noah's life. 4. That Methuselah lived till the very year in which the flood came, of which his name is supposed to have been prophetical; מתו *methu*, "he dieth," and שלח *shalach*, "he *sendeth out*;" as if God had designed to teach men that as soon as Methuselah died the flood should be sent forth to drown an ungodly world. If this were then so understood, even the *name* of this patriarch contained in it a *gracious warning*. See the *genealogical plate* after chap. xi

CHAPTER VI.

The children of God, among whom the true religion was at first preserved, corrupt it by forming matrimonial connections with irreligious women, 1, 2. *God, displeased with these connections and their consequences, limits the continuance of the old world to one hundred and twenty years,* 3. *The issue of those improper connections termed giants,* 4. *An affecting description of the depravity of the world,* 5, 6. *God threatens the destruction of every living creature,* 7. *Noah and his family find grace in his sight,* 8. *The character and family of Noah,* 9, 10. *And a farther description of the corruption of man,* 11, 12. *Noah is forewarned of the approaching destruction of the human race,* 13; *and is ordered to build an ark for the safety of himself and household, the form and dimensions of which are particularly described,* 14–16. *The deluge threatened,* 17. *The covenant of God's mercy is to be established between him and the family of Noah,* 18. *A male and female of all kinds of animals that could not live in the waters to be brought into the ark,* 19, 20. *Noah is commanded to provide food for their sustenance,* 21; *and punctually follows all these directions,* 22.

A. M. 1536.
B. C. 2468.

AND it came to pass, [a] when men began to multiply on the face of the earth, and daughters were born unto them,

2 That the sons of God saw the daughters of men that they *were* fair; and they [b] took them wives of all which they chose.

3 And the LORD said, [c] My Spirit shall not always strive with man, [d] for that he also *is* flesh: yet his days shall be a hundred and twenty years.

4 There were giants in the earth in those days; and also after that, when the sons of God came in unto the daughters of men, and they bare *children* to them, the same *became* mighty men which *were* of old, men of renown.

[a] Chap. i. 28; 2 Esdr. iii. 7.——[b] Deut. vii. 3, 4. [c] Gal. v. 16, 17; 1 Pet. iii. 19, 20.——[d] Psa. lxxviii. 39.

NOTES ON CHAP. VI.

Verse 1. *When men began to multiply*] It was not at *this* time that men *began* to multiply, but the inspired penman speaks *now* of a fact which had taken place long before. As there is a distinction made here between *men* and those called the *sons of God*, it is generally supposed that the immediate posterity of Cain and that of Seth are intended. The first were *mere men*, such as fallen nature may produce, degenerate sons of a degenerate father, governed by the desire of the flesh, the desire of the eye, and the pride of life. The others were *sons of God*, not *angels*, as some have dreamed, but such as were, according to our Lord's doctrine, *born again*, *born from above*, John iii. 3, 5, 6, &c., and made children of God by the influence of the Holy Spirit, Gal. v. 6. The former were apostates from the true religion, the latter were those among whom it was preserved and cultivated.

Dr. Wall supposes the first verses of this chapter should be paraphrased thus: "When men began to multiply on the earth, the *chief men* took wives of all the handsome *poor women* they chose. There were tyrants in the earth in those days; and also after the antediluvian days *powerful* men had unlawful connections with the inferior women, and the children which sprang from this illicit commerce were the renowned heroes of antiquity, of whom the heathens made their gods."

Verse 3. *My spirit shall not always strive*] It is only by the influence of the Spirit of God that the carnal mind can be subdued and destroyed; but those who wilfully resist and grieve that Spirit must be ultimately left to the hardness and blindness of their own hearts, if they do not repent and turn to God. God delights in mercy, and therefore a gracious warning is given. Even at this time the earth was ripe for destruction; but God promised them one hundred and twenty years' respite: if they repented in that interim, well; if not, they should be destroyed by a flood. See on ver. 5.

Verse 4. *There were giants in the earth*] נפלים *nephilim*, from נפל *naphal*, "he fell." Those who had *apostatized* or *fallen* from the true religion. The Septuagint translate the original word by γιγαντες, which literally signifies *earth-born*, and which we, following them, term *giants*, without having any reference to the meaning of the word, which we generally conceive to signify persons of *enormous stature*. But the word

A. M. 1536. B. C. 2468.
5 And God saw that the wickedness of man *was* great in the earth,
and *that* [e] every [f] imagination of the thoughts
of his heart *was* only evil [g] continually.
6 And it [h] repented the LORD that he had
made man on the earth, and it [i] grieved him
at his heart.
7 And the LORD said, I will destroy man
whom I have created from the face of the
earth; [k] both man and beast, and the creeping thing, and the fowls of the air; for it re-
penteth me that I have made them. A. M. 1536. B. C. 2468.
8 But Noah [l] found grace in the eyes of the
LORD.
9 These *are* the generations of Noah:
[m] Noah was a just man, *and* [n] perfect in his
generations, *and* Noah [o] walked with God:
10 And Noah begat three sons, A. M. cir. 1556 B. C. cir. 2448.
[p] Shem, Ham, and Japheth.
11 The earth also was corrupt [q] before
God, and the earth was [r] filled with violence.

---

[e] Or, *the whole imagination.* The Hebrew word signifieth, not only *the imagination*, but also *the purposes and desires.*——[f] Chap. viii. 21; Deut. xxix. 19; Prov. vi. 18; 2 Esdr. iii. 8; Matt. xv. 19.——[g] Heb. *every day.*——[h] See Num. xxiii. 19; 1 Sam. xv. 11, 29; 2 Sam. xxiv. 16; Mal. iii. 6; James i. 17.——[i] Isa. lxiii. 10; Eph. iv. 30.——[k] Heb. *from man unto beast.*——[l] Chap. xix. 19; Exod. xxxiii. 12, 13, 16, 17; Luke i. 30; Acts vii. 46.——[m] Chap. vii. 1; Ezek. xiv. 14, 20; Ecclus. xliv. 17; Rom. i. 17, Heb. xi. 7; 2 Pet. ii. 5.——[n] Or, *upright.*——[o] Chap. v. 22.——[p] Chap. v. 32.——[q] Chap. vii. 1; x. 9; xiii. 13; 2 Chron. xxxiv 27; Luke i. 6; Rom. ii. 13; iii. 19.——[r] Ezek. viii. 17; xxviii 16; Hab. ii. 8, 17.

---

when properly understood makes a very just distinction between the sons of men and the sons of God; those were the nephilim, the *fallen earth-born* men, with the animal and devilish mind. These were the *sons of God*, who were born from above; children of the kingdom, because children of God. Hence we may suppose originated the different appellatives given to *sinners and saints;* the former were termed γιγαντες, earth-born, and the latter, ἁγιοι, i. e. saints, persons *not of the earth*, or *separated from the earth.*

The same became *mighty men—men of renown.*] גברים *gibborim*, which we render *mighty men*, signifies properly *conquerors, heroes*, from גבר *gabar*, "he prevailed, was victorious," and אנשי השם *anshey hashshem*, "men of the name," ανθρωποι ονομαστοι, Septuagint; the same as we render *men of renown*, renominati, *twice named*, as the word implies, having one name which they derived from their fathers, and another which they acquired by their daring exploits and enterprises.

It may be necessary to remark here that our translators have rendered seven different Hebrew words by the one term *giants*, viz., *nephilim, gibborim, enachim, rephaim, emim*, and *zamzummim;* by which appellatives are probably meant in general persons of great knowledge, piety, courage, wickedness, &c., and not men of enormous stature, as is generally conjectured.

Verse 5. *The wickedness of man* was *great*] What an awful character does God give of the inhabitants of the antediluvian world! 1. They were *flesh*, (ver. 3,) wholly sensual, the desires of the mind overwhelmed and lost in the desires of the flesh, their souls no longer discerning their high destiny, but ever minding earthly things, so that they were sensualized, brutalized, and become flesh; incarnated so as not to retain God in their knowledge, and they lived, seeking their portion in this life. 2. They were in a *state* of wickedness. All was corrupt within, and all unrighteous without; neither the science nor practice of religion existed. Piety was gone, and every form of sound words had disappeared. 3. This wickedness was *great* רבה *rabbah*, "was multiplied;" it was continually increasing, and multiplying increase by increase, so that the *whole earth* was corrupt before God, and was filled with violence, (ver. 11;) profligacy among the lower, and cruelty and oppression among the higher classes, being only predominant. 4. *All the imaginations of their thoughts were evil*—the very first *embryo* of every idea, the *figment* of every thought, the very *materials* out of which perception, conception, and ideas were formed, were all *evil;* the fountain which produced them, with every thought, purpose, wish, desire, and motive, was incurably poisoned. 5. All these were evil *without any mixture of good*—the Spirit of God which strove with them was continually resisted, so that evil had its sovereign sway. 6. They were evil *continually*—there was no interval of good, no moment allowed for serious reflection, no holy purpose, no righteous act. What a finished picture of a fallen soul! Such a picture as God alone, who searches the heart and tries the spirit, could possibly give. 7. To complete the whole, God represents himself as *repenting* because he had made them, and as *grieved at the heart* because of their iniquities! Had not these been *voluntary* transgressions, crimes which they *might have avoided*, had they not grieved and quenched the Spirit of God, could he speak of them in the manner he does here? 8. So incensed is the most holy and the most merciful God, that he is determined to destroy the work of his hands: *And the Lord said, I will destroy man whom I have created;* ver. 7. How great must the evil have been, and how provoking the transgressions, which obliged the most compassionate God, for the vindication of his own glory, to form this awful purpose! Fools make a mock at sin, but none except *fools.*

Verse 8. *Noah found grace in the eyes of the Lord.*] Why? Because he was, 1. *A just man*, איש צדיק *ish tsaddik*, a man who *gave to all their due;* for this is the ideal meaning of the original word. 2. He was *perfect in his generation*—he was in all things a consistent character, never departing from the truth in principle or practice. 3. *He walked with God*—he was not only *righteous* in his conduct, but he was *pious*, and had continual communion with God. The same word is used here as before in the case of Enoch. See chap. v. 22.

Verse 11. *The earth also was corrupt*] See on verse 5.

A. M. cir. 1556.
B. C. cir. 2448.

12 And God [s] looked upon
the earth, and, behold, it was
corrupt; for all flesh had corrupted his way
upon the earth.
13 And God said unto Noah, [t] The end of
all flesh is come before me; for the earth is
filled with violence through them: [u] and, behold, I will destroy them [v] with the earth.

A. M. 1536.
B. C. 2468.

14 Make thee an ark of gopher
wood; [w] rooms shalt thou make in
the ark, and shalt pitch it [x] within and without with pitch.
15 And this *is the fashion* which thou shalt
make it *of:* The length of the ark *shall be*
three hundred cubits, [y] the breadth of it fifty
cubits, and the height of it thirty cubits.

[s] Chap. xviii. 21; Psa. xiv. 2; xxxiii. 13, 14; liii. 2, 3.——[t] Jer. li. 13; Ezek. vii. 2, 3, 6; Amos viii. 2; 1 Pet. iv. 7.

[u] Ver. 17.——[v] Or, *from the earth.*——[w] Heb. *nests.*——[x] Exod. ii. 3.——[y] Chap. vii. 20; Deut. iii. 11.

Verse 13. *I will destroy them with the earth.*] Not only the human race was to be destroyed, but all terrestrial animals, i. e. those which could not live in the waters. These must necessarily be destroyed when the whole surface of the earth was drowned. But destroying the earth may probably mean the alteration of its constitution. Dr. Woodward, in his natural history of the earth, has rendered it exceedingly probable that the whole terrestrial substance was amalgamated with the waters, after which the different materials of its composition settled in beds or strata according to their respective gravities. This theory, however, is disputed by others.

Verse 14. *Make thee an ark*] תבה *tebath*, a word which is used only to express *this vessel*, and that in which Moses was preserved, Exod. ii. 3, 5. It signifies no more than our word *vessel* in its common acceptation—a hollow place capable of containing persons, goods, &c., without any particular reference to *shape* or *form*.

Gopher wood] Some think the *cedar* is meant; others, the *cypress*. Bochart renders this probable, 1. From the appellation, supposing the Greek word *κυπαρισσος*, *cypress*, was formed from the Hebrew גפר *gopher;* for take away the termination *ισσος*, and then *gopher* and *κυπαρ* will have a near resemblance. 2. Because the cypress is not liable to rot, nor to be injured by worms. 3. The cypress was anciently used for ship-building. 4. This wood abounded in Assyria, where it is probable Noah built the ark. After all, the word is of doubtful signification, and occurs nowhere else in the Scriptures. The Septuagint render the place, *εκ ξυλων τετραγωνων*, "of *square timber;*" and the Vulgate, *de lignis lævigatis*, "of planed timber;" so it is evident that these translators knew not what kind of wood was intended by the original. The Syriac and Arabic trifle with the passage, rendering it *wicker* work, as if the ark had been a great *basket!* Both the Targums render it *cedar;* and the Persian, *pine* or *fir*.

Verse 15. *Thou shalt make—the length of the ark—three hundred cubits, the breadth of it fifty cubits, and the height of it thirty cubits*] Allowing the cubit, which is the length from the elbow to the tip of the middle finger, to be *eighteen* inches, the ark must have been *four hundred and fifty* feet in length, *seventy-five* in breadth, and *forty-five* in height. But that the ancient cubit was more than *eighteen* inches has been demonstrated by Mr. Greaves, who travelled in Greece, Palestine, and Egypt, in order to be able to ascertain the *weights, moneys*, and *measures* of antiquity. He measured the pyramids in Egypt, and comparing the accounts which Herodotus, Strabo, and others, give of their size, he found the length of a cubit to be *twenty-one* inches and *eight hundred* and *eighty-eight* decimal parts out of a thousand, or nearly *twenty-two* inches. Hence the *cube* of a cubit is evidently *ten thousand four hundred* and *eighty-six* inches. And from this it will appear that the *three hundred* cubits of the ark's length make *five hundred* and *forty-seven* feet; the *fifty* for its breadth, *ninety-one* feet *two* inches; and the *thirty* for its height, *fifty-four* feet *eight* inches When these dimensions are examined, the ark will be found to be a vessel whose capacity was more than sufficient to contain all persons and animals said to have been in it, with sufficient food for each for more than *twelve* months. This vessel Dr. Arbuthnot computes to have been *eighty-one thousand* and *sixty-two* tons in burden.

As many have supposed the capacity of the ark to have been much *too small* for the things which were contained in it, it will be necessary to examine this subject thoroughly, that every difficulty may be removed. The things contained in the ark, besides the *eight persons* of Noah's family, were one pair of all *unclean* animals, and seven pairs of all *clean* animals, with provisions for all sufficient for *twelve* months.

At the first view the number of animals may appear so immense that no space but the forest could be thought sufficient to contain them. If, however, we come to a calculation, the number of the different *genera* or *kinds* of animals will be found much less than is generally imagined. It is a question whether in this account any but the different *genera* of animals necessary to be brought into the ark should be included. Naturalists have divided the whole system of zoology into CLASSES and ORDERS, containing *genera* and *species*. There are six classes thus denominated: 1. *Mammalia;* 2. *Aves;* 3. *Amphibia;* 4. *Pisces;* 5. *Insectæ;* and 6. *Vermes*. With the three last of these, viz., *fishes, insects*, and *worms*, the question can have little to do.

The *first* CLASS, *Mammalia*, or animals with *teats* contains *seven* orders, and only *forty-three genera* if we except the *seventh* order, *cete*, i. e. all the *whale* kind, which certainly need not come into this account. The different *species* in this class amount, the *cete* excluded, to *five hundred* and *forty-three.*

The *second* CLASS, *Aves*, birds, contains *six* orders, and only *seventy-four* genera, if we exclude the *third* order, *anseres*, or *web-footed* fowls, all of which could very well live in the water. The different species in

a.

A. M. 1536.
B. C. 2468.

16 A window [z] shalt thou make
to the ark, and in a cubit shalt thou
finish it above; and the door [a] of the ark shalt
thou set in the side thereof; *with* lower,
second, and third *stories* shalt thou make it.
17 [b] And behold, I, even I, do bring a flood
of waters upon the earth, to destroy all flesh,
wherein *is* the breath of life, [c] from
under heaven; *and* every thing
that *is* in the earth shall die.
18 But with thee will I [d] establish my covenant; and [e] thou shalt come into the ark,
thou, and thy sons, and thy wife, and thy
sons' wives with thee.

A. M. 1536.
B. C. 2468.

[z] Chap. viii. 6.——[a] Chap. vii. 16; Luke xiii. 25.——[b] Ver. 13; chap. vii. 4, 21, 22, 23; 2 Pet. ii. 5; Psa. xxix. 10; xciii. 3, 4; Amos ix. 6.——[c] Chap. ii. 7; chap. vii. 15.——[d] Chap. ix. 9.——[e] Chap. vii. 1, 7, 13; 1 Pet. iii. 20; 2 Pet. ii. 5.

this class, the *anseres* excepted, amount to *two thousand three hundred* and *seventy-two.*

The *third* CLASS, *Amphibia,* contains only *two* orders, *reptiles* and *serpents;* these comprehend *ten genera,* and *three hundred* and *sixty-six* species, but of the reptiles many could live in the water, such as the *tortoise, frog, &c.* Of the former there are *thirty-three* species, of the latter *seventeen,* which excluded reduce the number to *three hundred* and *sixteen.* The whole of these would occupy but little room in the ark, for a small portion of *earth, &c.,* in the *hold* would be sufficient for *their* accommodation.

Bishop Wilkins, who has written largely and with his usual accuracy on this subject, supposes that quadrupeds do not amount to *one hundred* different kinds, nor *birds* which could not live in the water to *two hundred.* Of quadrupeds he shows that only *seventy-two* species needed a place in the ark, and the *birds* he divides into *nine* classes, including in the whole *one hundred* and *ninety-five* kinds, from which all the *web-footed* should be deducted, as these could live in the water.

He computes all the *carnivorous* animals equivalent, as to the bulk of their bodies and food, *to twenty-seven* wolves; and all the rest to *one hundred* and *eighty* oxen. For the former he allows *one thousand eight hundred* and *twenty-five* sheep for their annual consumption; and for the latter, *one hundred* and *nine thousand five hundred* cubits of *hay:* these animals and their food will be easily contained in the two *first stories,* and much room to spare; as to the *third story,* no person can doubt its being sufficient for the *fowls,* with *Noah* and his *family.*

One sheep each day he judges will be sufficient for *six* wolves; and a square cubit of hay, which contains *forty-one* pounds, as ordinarily pressed in our *ricks,* will be amply sufficient for *one ox* in the day. When the quantum of *room* which these animals and their provender required for one year, is compared with the *capacity* of the ark, we shall be lead to conclude, with the learned bishop, "that of the two it is more difficult to assign a number and bulk of necessary things to answer to the capacity of the ark, than to find sufficient room for the several species of animals and their food already known to have been there." This he attributes to the imperfection of our lists of animals, especially those of the unknown parts of the earth; and adds, "that the most expert mathematicians at this day," and he was one of the first in Europe, "could not assign the proportion of a vessel better accommodated to the purpose than is here done;" and concludes thus: "The capacity of the ark, which has been made an objection against Scripture, ought to be esteemed a confirmation of its Divine authority; since, in those ruder ages men, being less versed in arts and philosophy, were more obnoxious to vulgar prejudices than now, so that had it been a human invention it would have been contrived, according to those wild apprehensions which arise from a confused and general view of things, as much *too big* as it has been represented *too little.*" See Bishop Wilkins's *Essay towards a Philosophical Character and Language.*

Verse 16. *A window shalt thou make*] What this was cannot be absolutely ascertained. The original word צהר *tsohar* signifies *clear* or *bright;* the Septuagint translate it by *επισυναγων,* "*collecting,* thou shalt make the ark," which plainly shows they did not understand the word as signifying any kind of *window* or *light.* Symmachus translates it *διαφανες, a transparency;* and Aquila, *μεσημβρινον, the noon.* Jonathan ben Uzziel supposes that it was a precious luminous stone which Noah, by Divine command, brought from the river Pison. It is probably a word which should be taken in a collective sense, signifying *apertures* for *air* and *light.*

In a cubit shalt thou finish it above] Probably meaning that the roof should be left a cubit broad at the apex or top, and that it should not terminate in a *sharp* ridge. But this place is variously understood.

Verse 17. *I—do bring a flood*] מבול; *mabbul;* a word used only to designate the *general deluge,* being never applied to signify any other kind of inundation; and does not the Holy Spirit intend to show by this that no other *flood* was ever like this, and that it should continue to be the sole one of the kind? There have been many partial inundations in various countries, but never more than ONE *general deluge;* and we have God's promise, chap. ix. 15, that there shall never be *another.*

Verse 18. *With thee will I establish my covenant*] The word ברית *berith,* from בר *bar,* to purify or cleanse, signifies properly a *purification* or *purifier,* (see on chap. xv.,) because in all covenants made between God and man, *sin* and *sinfulness* were ever supposed to be on man's side, and that God could not enter into any covenant or engagement with him without a *purifier;* hence, in all covenants, a sacrifice was offered for the removal of offences, and the reconciliation of God to the sinner; and hence the word ברית *berith* signifies not only a *covenant,* but also the *sacrifice* offered on the occasion, Exod. xxiv. 8; Psalm l. 5; and Jesus Christ, the great atonement and purifier, has the same word for his title, Isa. xlii. 6; xlix. 8; and Zech. ix. 11.

A. M. 1536. B. C. 2468. 19 And of every living thing of all flesh, [f] two of every *sort* shalt thou bring into the ark, to keep *them* alive with thee; they shall be male and female.

20 Of fowls after their kind, and of cattle after their kind, of every creeping thing of the earth after his kind, two of every *sort* [g] shall come unto thee, to keep *them* alive. A. M. 1536. B. C. 2468.

21 And take thou unto thee of all food that is eaten, and thou shalt gather *it* to thee; and it shall be for food for thee, and for them.

22 [h] Thus did Noah; [i] according to all that God commanded him, so did he.

[f] Chap. vii. 8, 9, 15, 16.——[g] Chap. vii. 9, 15; see chap. ii. 19.

[h] Heb. xi. 7; see Exod. xl. 16.——[i] Chap. vii. 5, 9, 16.

Almost all nations, in forming alliances, &c., made their covenants or contracts in the same way. A sacrifice was provided, its throat was cut, and its blood poured out before God; then the whole carcass was divided through the spinal marrow from the head to the rump, so as to make exactly two equal parts; these were placed opposite to each other, and the contracting parties passed between them, or entering at opposite ends met in the centre, and there took the covenant oath. This is particularly referred to by Jeremiah, chap. xxxiv. 18, 19, 20: "I will give the men (into the hands of their enemies, ver. 20) that have transgressed my covenant, which have not performed the words of the covenant which they made before me, *when they cut the calf in twain, and passed between the parts thereof*," *&c.* See also Deut. xxix. 12.

A covenant, says Mr. Ainsworth, is a disposition of good things faithfully declared, which God here calls *his*, as arising from his *grace* towards Noah (ver. 8) and all men; but implying also *conditions on man's part*, and therefore is called *our* covenant, Zech. ix. 11. The apostles call it διαθηκη, a *testament* or *disposition;* and it is mixed of the properties both of *covenant* and *testament*, as the apostle shows, Heb. ix. 16, &c., and of both may be named a *testamental covenant*, whereby the disposing of God's favours and good things to us is declared. The covenant made with Noah signified, on *God's* part, that he should save Noah and his family from death by the ark. On Noah's part, that he should in faith and obedience make and enter into the ark—*Thou shalt come into the ark, &c.*, so committing himself to God's preservation, Heb. xi. 7. And under this the covenant or testament of eternal salvation by Christ was also implied, the apostle testifying, 1 Pet. iii. 21, that the antitype, baptism, doth also now save us; for baptism is a seal of our salvation, Mark xvi. 16. To *provide* a Saviour, and the means of salvation, is GOD'S *part:* to *accept* this Saviour, laying hold on the hope set before us, is *ours*. Those who refuse the way and means of salvation must perish; those who accept of the great Covenant Sacrifice cannot perish, but shall have eternal life. See on chap. xv. 10, &c.

Verse 19. *To keep* them *alive*] God might have destroyed all the animal creation, and created others to occupy the new world, but he chose rather to *preserve* those already created. The Creator and Preserver of the universe does nothing but what is essentially necessary to be done. Nothing should be wantonly wasted; nor should *power* or *skill* be lavished where no necessity exists; and yet it required more means and economy to preserve the old than to have created new ones. Such respect has God to the work of his hands, that nothing but what is essential to the credit of his justice and holiness shall ever induce him to destroy any thing he has made.

Verse 21. *Of all food that is eaten*] That is, of the food proper for every species of animals.

Verse 22. *Thus did Noah*] He prepared the ark; and during one hundred and twenty years preached righteousness to that sinful generation, 2 Pet. ii. 5. And this we are informed, 1 Pet. iii. 18, 19, &c., he did by the *Spirit of Christ;* for it was only through *him* that the doctrine of repentance could ever be successfully preached. The people in Noah's time are represented as *shut up in prison*—arrested and condemned by God's justice, but graciously allowed the space of one hundred and twenty years to repent in. This respite was an act of great mercy; and no doubt thousands who died in the interim availed themselves of it, and believed to the saving of their souls. But the great majority of the people did not, else the *flood* had never come.

CHAPTER VII.

God informs Noah that within seven days he shall send a rain upon the earth, that shall continue for forty days and nights; and therefore commands him to take his family, with the different clean and unclean animals, and enter the ark, 1–4. *This command punctually obeyed,* 5–9. *In the seventeenth day of the second month, in the six hundredth year of Noah's life, the waters, from the opened windows of heaven, and the broken up fountains of the great deep, were poured out upon the earth,* 10–12. *The different quadrupeds, fowls, and reptiles come unto Noah, and the Lord shuts him and them in,* 13–16. *The waters increase, and the ark floats,* 17. *The whole earth is covered with water fifteen cubits above the highest mountains,* 18–20. *All terrestrial animals die,* 21–23. *And the waters prevail one hundred and fifty days,* 24.

A. M. 1656.
B. C. 2348.

AND the LORD said unto Noah,
[a] Come thou and all thy house
into the ark: for [b] thee have I seen righteous
before me in this generation.
2 Of every [c] clean beast thou shalt take to
thee by [d] sevens, the male and his female;
[e] and of beasts that *are* not clean by two, the
male and his female
3 Of fowls also of the air by sevens, the
male and the female; to keep seed alive upon
the face of all the earth.
4 For yet seven days, and I will cause it to
rain upon the earth [f] forty days and forty
nights; and every living substance that I
have made will I [g] destroy from off the face
of the earth.
5 [h] And Noah did according unto all that
the LORD commanded him.
6 And Noah *was* six hundred years old
when the flood of waters was upon
the earth.

A. M. 1656.
B. C. 2348.

7 [i] And Noah went in, and his sons, and
his wife, and his sons' wives with him, into
the ark, because of the waters of the flood.
8 Of clean beasts, and of beasts that *are*
not clean, and of fowls, and of every thing
that creepeth upon the earth,
9 There went in two and two unto Noah
into the ark, the male and the female, as God
had commanded Noah.
10 And it came to pass, [k] after seven days,
that the waters of the flood were upon the
earth.
11 In the six hundredth year of Noah's life,
in the second month, the seventeenth day of
the month, the same day were all [l] the fountains of the great deep broken up, and the
[m] windows of heaven were [n] opened.

[a] Ver. 7, 13; Matt. xxiv. 38; Luke xvii. 26; Heb. xi. 7; 1 Pet. iii. 20; 2 Pet. ii. 5.——[b] Chap. vi. 9; Psa. xxxiii. 18, 19; Prov. x. 9; 2 Pet. ii. 9.——[c] Ver. 8; Lev. xi.——[d] Heb. *seven seven.*——[e] Lev. x. 10; Ezek. xliv. 23.

[f] Ver. 12, 17.——[g] Heb. *blot out.*——[h] Chap. vi. 22.——[i] Ver. 1.——[k] Or, *on the seventh day.*——[l] Chap. viii. 2; Prov. viii. 28; Ezek. xxvi. 19.——[m] Or, *flood-gates.*——[n] Chap. i. 7; viii. 2; Psa. lxxviii. 23.

NOTES ON CHAP. VII.

Verse 1. *Thee have I seen righteous*] See on chap. vi. 9.

Verse 2. *Of every clean beast*] So we find the distinction between clean and unclean animals existed long before the Mosaic law. This distinction seems to have been originally designed to mark those animals which were proper for sacrifice and food, from those that were not. See Lev. xi.

Verse 4. *For yet seven days*] God spoke these words probably on the seventh or Sabbath day, and the days of the ensuing week were employed in entering the ark, in embarking the mighty troop, for whose reception ample provision had been already made.

Forty days] This period became afterwards sacred, and was considered a proper space for humiliation. *Moses* fasted forty days, Deut. ix. 9, 11; so did *Elijah*, 1 Kings xix. 8; so did our *Lord*, Matt. iv. 2. Forty days' respite were given to the Ninevites that they might repent, Jonah iii. 4; and *thrice forty* (one hundred and twenty) years were given to the old world for the same gracious purpose, Gen. vi. 3. The forty days of Lent, in commemoration of our Lord's fasting, have a reference to the same thing; as each of these seems to be deduced from this primitive judgment.

Verse 11. *In the six hundredth year, &c.*] This must have been in the beginning of the six hundredth year of his life; for he was a year in the ark, chap. viii. 13; and lived three hundred and fifty years after the flood, and died nine hundred and fifty years old, chap. ix. 29; so it is evident that, when the flood commenced, he had just entered on his six hundredth year.

Second month] The first month was *Tisri*, which answers to the latter half of *September*, and first half of *October;* and the second was *Marcheshvan*, which answers to part of *October* and part of *November*. After the deliverance from Egypt, the beginning of the year was changed from *Marcheshvan* to *Nisan*, which answers to a part of our *March* and *April*. But it is not likely that this reckoning obtained *before* the flood. Dr. *Lightfoot* very probably conjectures that Methuselah was alive in the first month of this year. And it appears, says he, how clearly the Spirit of prophecy foretold of things to come, when it directed his father Enoch almost a thousand years before to name him *Methuselah*, which signifies *they die by a dart; or, he dieth, and then is the dart;* or, *he dieth, and then it is sent*. And thus Adam and Methuselah had measured the whole time between the *creation* and the *flood*, and lived above two hundred and forty years together. See chap. v. at the end.

Were all the fountains of the great deep broken up, and the windows of heaven were opened.] It appears that an immense quantity of waters occupied the centre of the antediluvian earth; and as these burst forth, by the order of God, the circumambient strata must sink, in order to fill up the vacuum occasioned by the elevated waters. This is probably what is meant by *breaking up the fountains of the great deep.* These waters, with the seas on the earth's surface, might be deemed sufficient to drown the whole globe, as the waters now on its surface are nearly three-fourths of the whole, as has been accurately ascertained by Dr. *Long*. See note on chap. i. ver. 10.

By the *opening of the windows of heaven* is probably meant the precipitating all the aqueous vapours which were suspended in the whole atmosphere, so that, as Moses expresses it, chap. i. 7, the *waters that were above the firmament* were again united to the waters *which were below the firmament*, from which on the second day of creation they had been *separated*. A multitude of facts have proved that *water* itself is com-

A. M. 1656. B. C. 2348.

12 [o] And the rain was upon the earth forty days and forty nights.

13 In the self-same day [p] entered Noah, and Shem, and Ham, and Japheth, the sons of Noah, and Noah's wife, and the three wives of his sons with them, into the ark;

14 [q] They, and every beast after his kind, and all the cattle after their kind, and every creeping thing that creepeth upon the earth after his kind, and every fowl after his kind, every bird of every [r] sort.

15 And they [s] went in unto Noah into the ark, two and two of all flesh, wherein *is* the breath of life.

16 And they that went in, went in male and female of all flesh, [t] as God had commanded him: and the LORD shut him in.

17 [u] And the flood was forty days upon the earth; and the waters increased, and bare up the ark, and it was lift up above the earth.

18 And the waters prevailed, and were increased greatly upon the earth; [v] and the ark went upon the face of the waters.

[o] Ver. 4, 17.——[p] Ver. 1, 7; chap. vi. 18; Heb. xi. 7; 1 Pet. iii. 20; 2 Pet. ii. 5.——[q] Ver. 2, 3, 8, 9.

[r] Heb. *wing*.——[s] Chap. vi. 20.——[t] Ver. 2, 3.——[u] Ver. 4, 12 [v] Psa. civ. 26.

posed of two airs, *oxygen* and *hydrogen;* and that 85 parts of the first and 15 of the last, making 100 in the whole, will produce exactly 100 parts of water. And thus it is found that these two *airs* form the constituent parts of water in the above proportions. The electric spark, which is the same as lightning, passing through these airs, decomposes them and converts them to water. And to this cause we may probably attribute the *rain* which immediately follows the flash of lightning and peal of thunder. God therefore, by the means of lightning, might have converted the whole atmosphere into water, for the purpose of drowning the globe, had there not been a sufficiency of merely aqueous vapours suspended in the atmosphere on the second day of creation. And if the electric fluid were used on this occasion for the production of water, the incessant glare of lightning, and the continual peals of thunder, must have added indescribable horrors to the scene. See the note on chap. viii. 1. These two causes concurring were amply sufficient, not only to overflow the earth, but probably to *dissolve* the whole terrene fabric, as some judicious naturalists have supposed: indeed, this seems determined by the word מבול *mabbul*, translated *flood*, which is derived from בל *bal* or בלל *balal*, to *mix*, *mingle*, *confound*, *confuse*, because the *aqueous* and terrene parts of the globe were then mixed and confounded together; and when the supernatural cause that produced this mighty change suspended its operations, the different particles of matter would settle according to their specific gravities, and thus form the various *strata* or *beds* of which the earth appears to be internally constructed. Some naturalists have controverted this sentiment, because in some cases the internal structure of the earth does not appear to justify the opinion that the various portions of matter had settled according to their specific gravities; but these anomalies may easily be accounted for, from the great changes that have taken place in different parts of the earth *since* the *flood*, by volcanic eruptions, earthquakes, &c. Some very eminent philosophers are of the opinion "that, by the *breaking up of the fountains of the great deep*, we are to understand *an eruption of waters from the Southern Ocean*." Mr. Kirwan supposes "that this is pretty evident from such animals as the elephant and rhinoceros being found in great masses in Siberia, mixed with different *marine substances;* whereas no animals or other substances belonging to the *northern regions* have been ever found in *southern* climates. Had these animals died natural deaths in their proper climate, their bodies would not have been found in such masses. But that they were carried no farther northward than Siberia, is evident from there being no remains of any animals besides those of whales found in the mountains of Greenland. That this great *rush of waters* was from the *south* or *south-east* is farther evident, he thinks, from the south and south-east sides of almost all great mountains being much steeper than their north or north-west sides, as they necessarily would be if the force of a great body of water fell upon them in that direction." On a subject like this men may innocently differ. Many think the first opinion accords best with the Hebrew text and with the phenomena of nature, for mountains do not always present the above appearance.

Verse 12. *The rain was upon the earth*] Dr. *Lightfoot* supposes that the rain began on the 18th day of the second month, or *Marcheshvan*, and that it ceased on the 28th of the third month, *Cisleu*.

Verse 15. *And they went in, &c.*] It was physically impossible for Noah to have collected such a vast number of tame and ferocious animals, nor could they have been retained in their wards by mere natural means. How then were they brought from various distances to the ark and preserved there? Only by the power of God. He who first miraculously brought them to Adam that he might give them their names, now brings them to Noah that he may preserve their lives. And now we may reasonably suppose that their natural enmity was so far removed or suspended that the lion might dwell with the lamb, and the wolf lie down with the kid, though each might still require his peculiar aliment. This can be no difficulty to the power of God, without the immediate interposition of which neither the deluge nor the concomitant circumstances could have taken place.

Verse 16. *The Lord shut him in.*] This seems to imply that God took him under his especial protection, and as he shut HIM *in*, so he shut the OTHERS *out*. God had waited one hundred and twenty years upon that generation; they did not repent; they filled up the measure of their iniquities, and then wrath came upon them to the uttermost.

A. M. 1656.
B. C. 2348.

19 And the waters prevailed exceedingly upon the earth; [w] and all the high hills, that *were* under the whole heaven, were covered.

20 Fifteen cubits upward did the waters prevail; and the mountains were covered.

21 [x] And all flesh died that moved upon the earth, both of fowl, and of cattle, and of beast, and of every creeping thing that creepeth upon the earth, and every man:

22 All in [y] whose nostrils *was* [z] the breath of life, of all that *was* in the dry *land*, died.

23 And every living substance was destroyed which was upon the face of the ground, both man, and cattle, and the creeping things, and the fowl of the heaven; and they were destroyed from the earth: and [a] Noah only remained *alive*, and they that *were* with him in the ark.

24 [b] And the waters prevailed upon the earth a hundred and fifty days.

[w] Psa. civ. 6; Jer. iii. 23.——[x] Chap. vi. 13, 17; ver. 4; Job xxii. 16; 2 Esdr. iii. 9, 10; Wisd. x. 4; Matt. xxiv. 39; Luke xvii. 27; 2 Pet. iii. 6.——[y] Chap. ii. 7.——[z] Heb. *the breath of the spirit of life*; chap. ii. 7; vii. 17.——[a] Ezra xiv. 14, 20; Mal. iii. 18; Wisd. x. 4; 1 Pet. iii. 20; 2 Pet. ii. 5; iii. 6. [b] Chap. viii. 3, 4, compared with ver. 11 of this chapter.

Verse 20. *Fifteen cubits upward*] Should any person object to the *universality* of the deluge because he may imagine there is not water sufficient to drown the whole globe in the manner here related, he may find a most satisfactory answer to all the objections he can raise on this ground in Mr. Ray's *Physico-theological Discourses*, 2d edit., 8vo., 1693.

Verse 22. *Of all that* was *in the dry* land] From this we may conclude that such animals only as *could not live in the water* were preserved in the ark.

Verse 24. *And the waters prevailed upon the earth a hundred and fifty days.*] The breaking up of the fountains of the great deep, and the raining forty days and nights, had raised the waters fifteen cubits above the highest mountains; after which forty days it appears to have continued at this height for one hundred and fifty days more. "So," says Dr. *Lightfoot*, "these two sums are to be reckoned distinct, and not the forty days included in the one hundred and fifty; so that when the one hundred and fifty days were ended, there were six months and ten days of the flood past." For an improvement of this awful judgment, see the conclusion of the following chapter.

CHAPTER VIII.

At the end of one hundred and fifty days the waters begin to subside, 1–3. *The ark rests on Mount Ararat,* 4. *On the first of the tenth month the tops of the hills appear,* 5. *The window opened and the raven sent out,* 6, 7. *The dove sent forth, and returns,* 8, 9. *The dove sent forth a second time, and returns with an olive leaf,* 10, 11. *The dove sent out the third time, and returns no more,* 12. *On the twentieth day of the second month the earth is completely dried,* 13, 14. *God orders* Noah, *his family, and all the* creatures *to come out of the ark,* 15–19. *Noah builds an altar, and offers sacrifices to the Lord,* 20. *They are accepted; and God promises that the earth shall not be cursed thus any more, notwitstanding the iniquity of man,* 21, 22.

A. M. 1656.
B. C. 2348.

AND God [a] remembered Noah, and every living thing, and all the cattle that *was* with him in the ark: [b] and God made a wind to pass over the earth, and the waters assuaged;

2 [c] The fountains also of the deep and the windows of heaven were stopped, and [d] the rain from heaven was restrained;

3 And the waters returned from off the earth [e] continually: and after the end [f] of the hundred and fifty days, the waters were abated.

[a] Chap. xix. 29; Exod. ii. 24; 1 Sam. i. 19.——[b] Exod. xiv. 21.——[c] Chap. xi. 7; Prov. viii. 28. [d] Job xxxviii. 37.——[e] Heb. *in going and returning.*——[f] Chap. vii. 24.

NOTES ON CHAP. VIII.

Verse 1. *And God made a wind to pass over the earth*] Such a wind as produced a strong and sudden evaporation. The effects of these winds, which are frequent in the east, are truly astonishing. A friend of mine, who had been bathing in the Tigris, not far from the ancient city of *Ctesiphon*, and within five days' journey of *Bagdad*, having on a pair of Turkish drawers, one of these hot winds, called by the natives *samiel*, passing rapidly across the river just as he had got out of the water, so effectually dried him in *a moment*, that not one particle of moisture was left either on his body or in his bathing dress! With such an electrified wind as this, how soon could God dry the whole of the earth's surface! An operation something similar to the conversion of water into its two constituent *airs, oxygen* and *hydrogen*, by means of the *galvanic* fluid, as these airs themselves may be

A. M. 1656.
B. C. 2348.

4 And the ark rested in the seventh
month, on the seventeenth day of
the month, upon the mountains of Ararat.
5 And the waters [g] decreased continually
until the tenth month: in the tenth *month,* on
the first *day* of the month, were the tops of
the mountains seen.
6 And it came to pass, at the end of forty
days, that Noah opened [h] the window of the
ark which he had made:
7 And he sent forth a raven, which went
forth [i] to and fro, until the waters were dried
up from off the earth.
8 Also he sent forth a dove from him, to
see if the waters were abated from off the face
of the ground;
9 But the dove found no rest for the sole of
her foot, and she returned unto him into the
ark, for the waters *were* on the face of the
whole earth; then he put forth his
hand, and took her, and [k] pulled
her in unto him into the ark.
10 And he stayed yet other seven days; and
again he sent forth the dove out of the ark;
11 And the dove came in to him in the
evening; and, lo, in her mouth *was* an olive
leaf pluckt off. So Noah knew that the
waters were abated from off the earth.
12 And he stayed yet other seven days, and
sent forth the dove; which returned not again
unto him any more.

A. M. 1657.
B. C. 2347.

13 And it came to pass in the
six hundredth [l] and first year, in
the first *month,* the first *day* of the month, the
waters were dried up from off the earth: and
Noah removed the covering of the ark, and
looked, and, behold, the face of the ground
was dry.

[g] Heb. *were in going and decreasing.*——[h] Chap. vi. 16.——[i] Heb. *in going forth and returning.*——[k] Heb. *caused her to come.*——[l] Chap. vii. 11.

reconverted into water by means of the *electric* spark. See the note on chap. vii. 11. And probably this was the agent that restored to the atmosphere the quantity of water which *it* had contributed to this vast inundation. The other portion of waters, which had proceeded from the breaking up of the fountains of the great deep, would of course subside more slowly, as openings were made for them to run off from the higher lands, and form seas. By the first cause, the hot wind, the *waters were assuaged,* and the atmosphere having its due proportion of vapours restored, the quantity below must be greatly lessened. By the second, the earth was gradually dried, the waters, as they found passage, lessening by degrees till the seas and gulfs were formed, and the earth completely drained. This appears to be what is intended in the third and fifth verses by *the waters decreasing continually,* or, according to the margin, they were *in going and decreasing,* ver. 5.

Verse 4. *The mountains of Ararat.*] That Ararat was a mountain of *Armenia* is almost universally agreed. What is commonly thought to be the Ararat of the Scriptures, has been visited by many travellers, and on it there are several monasteries. For a long time the world has been amused with reports that the *remains* of the ark were still visible there; but Mr. Tourne*fort,* a famous French naturalist, who was on the spot, assures us that nothing of the kind is there to be seen. As there is a great chain of mountains which are called by this name, it is impossible to determine on what part of them the ark rested; but the highest part, called by some the *finger mountain,* has been fixed on as the most likely place. These things we must leave, and they are certainly of very little consequence.

From the circumstance of the resting of the ark on the 17th of the seventh month, Dr. *Lightfoot* draws this curious conclusion: That the ark drew exactly *eleven cubits* of water. On the first day of the month *Ab* the mountain tops were first seen, and then the waters had fallen *fifteen cubits;* for so high had they prevailed above the tops of the mountains. This decrease in the waters took up *sixty* days, namely, from the first of *Sivan;* so that they appear to have abated in the proportion of *one cubit* in *four days.* On the 16th of *Sivan* they had abated but *four cubits;* and yet on the next day the ark rested on one of the hills, when the waters must have been as yet *eleven cubits* above it. Thus it appears that the ark drew *eleven cubits* of water.

Verse 7. *He sent forth a raven, which went forth to and fro*] It is generally supposed that the raven *flew off,* and was seen no more, but this meaning the Hebrew text will not bear; ויצא יצוא ושוב *vaiyetse yatso vashob,* and it went forth, going forth and returning. From which it is evident that she did *return,* but *was not taken into the ark.* She made frequent excursions, and continued on the wing as long as she could, having picked up such aliment as she found floating on the waters; and then, to rest herself, regained the ark, where she might perch, though she was not admitted. Indeed this must be allowed, as it is impossible she could have continued *twenty-one* days upon the wing, which she must have done had she not returned. But the text itself is sufficiently determinate.

Verse 8. *He sent forth a dove*] The dove was sent forth *thrice;* the *first* time she *speedily* returned, having, in all probability, gone but a little way from the ark, as she must naturally be terrified at the appearance of the waters. After seven days, being sent out a *second time,* she returned with an *olive leaf pluckt off,* ver. 11, an emblem of the restoration of peace between God and the earth; and from this circumstance the *olive* has been the *emblem of peace* among all civilized

a

A. M. 1657.
B. C. 2347.

14 And in the second month, on the seven and twentieth day of the month, was the earth dried.

15 And God spake unto Noah, saying,

16 Go forth of the ark, [m] thou, and thy wife, and thy sons, and thy sons' wives with thee.

17 Bring forth with thee [n] every living thing that *is* with thee, of all flesh, *both* of fowl, and of cattle, and of every creeping thing that creepeth upon the earth; that they may breed abundantly in the earth, and [o] be fruitful, and multiply upon the earth.

18 And Noah went forth, and his sons, and his wife, and his sons' wives with him:

A. M. 1657.
B. C. 2347.

19 Every beast, every creeping thing, and every fowl, *and* whatsoever creepeth upon the earth, after their [p] kinds, went forth out of the ark.

20 And Noah builded an altar unto the Lord; and took of [q] every clean beast, and of every clean fowl, and offered burnt-offerings on the altar.

21 And the Lord smelled [r] a [s] sweet savour. and the Lord said in his heart, I will not again [t] curse the ground any more for man's sake; [u] for the [v] imagination of man's heart *is* evil from his youth; [w] neither will I again smite any more every thing living, as I have done.

[m] Chap. vii. 13.——[n] Chap. vii. 15.——[o] Chap. i. 22.——[p] Heb. *families*.——[q] Lev. xi.——[r] Lev. i. 9; Ezek. xx. 41; 2 Cor. ii. 15; Eph. v. 2.——[s] Heb. *a savour of rest*.——[t] Chap. iii. 17; vi. 17.——[u] Or, *though*.——[v] Chap. vi. 5; Job xiv. 4; xv. 14; Psa. li. 5; Jer. xvii. 9; Matt. xv. 19; Rom. i. 21; iii. 23.——[w] Chap. ix. 11, 15.

nations. At the end of the other *seven* days the dove, being sent out the *third* time, returned no more, from which Noah conjectured that the earth was now sufficiently drained, and therefore removed the covering of the ark, which probably gave liberty to many of the fowls to fly off, which circumstance would afford him the greater facility in making arrangements for disembarking the beasts and reptiles, and heavy-bodied domestic fowls, which might yet remain. See verse 17.

Verse 14. *And in the second month, on the seven and twentieth day*] From this it appears that Noah was in the ark a *complete solar year*, or *three hundred and sixty-five* days; for he entered the ark the 17th day of the second month, in the *six hundredth* year of his life, chap. vii. 11, 13, and continued in it till the 27th day of the second month, in the *six hundredth and first* year of his life, as we see above. The months of the ancient Hebrews were lunar; the first *six* consisted of *thirty* days each, the latter *six* of *twenty-nine;* the whole twelve months making *three hundred and fifty-four* days: add to this *eleven days*, (for though he entered the ark the preceding year on the *seventeenth* day of the second month, he did not come out till the *twenty-seventh* of the same month in the following year,) which make exactly *three hundred and sixty-five days*, the period of a complete solar revolution; the odd hours and minutes, as being fractions of time, noncomputed, though very likely all included in the account. This year, according to the Hebrew computation, was the *one thousand six hundred and fifty-seventh* year from the creation; but according to the reckoning of the Septuagint it was the *two thousand two hundred and forty-second*, and according to Dr. Hales, the *two thousand two hundred and fifty-sixth*. See on chap. xi. 12.

Verse 20. *Noah builded an altar*] As we have already seen that Adam, Cain, and Abel, offered sacrifices, there can be no doubt that they had *altars* on which they offered them; but this, builded by Noah, is certainly the *first* on record. It is worthy of remark that, as the old world began with sacrifice, so also did the new. *Religion*, or the proper mode of worshipping the Divine Being, is the invention or institution of God himself; and *sacrifice*, in the *act* and *design*, is the *essence* of religion. Without sacrifice, actually offered or implied, there never was, there never can be, any religion. Even in the *heavens*, a lamb is represented before the throne of God as newly slain, Rev. v. 6, 12, 13. The design of sacrificing is two-fold: the *slaying* and *burning* of the victim point out, 1st, that the *life* of the sinner is forfeited to Divine justice; 2dly, that his *soul* deserves the *fire* of perdition.

The Jews have a tradition that the *place* where Noah built his altar was the same in which the altar stood which was built by Adam, and used by Cain and Abel, and the same spot on which Abraham afterwards offered up his son Isaac.

The word מזבח *mizbach*, which we render *altar*, signifies properly a *place for sacrifice*, as the root זבח *zabach* signifies simply to *slay*. *Altar* comes from the Latin *altus*, high or elevated, because places for sacrifice were generally either raised *very high* or built on the tops of *hills* and *mountains;* hence they are called *high places* in the Scriptures; but such were chiefly used for idolatrous purposes.

Burnt-offerings] See the meaning of every kind of offering and sacrifice largely explained on Lev. vii.

Verse 21. *The Lord smelled a sweet savour*] That is, he was well pleased with this religious act, performed in obedience to his own appointment, and in faith of the promised Saviour. That this sacrifice prefigured that which was offered by our blessed Redeemer in behalf of the world, is sufficiently evident from the words of St. Paul, Eph. v. 2: *Christ hath loved us, and given himself for us an offering and a sacrifice to God for a* SWEET-SMELLING SAVOUR; where the words οσμην ευωδιας of the apostle are the very words used by the Septuagint in this place.

I will not again curse the ground] לא אכף *lo osiph*, I *will not add* to curse the ground—there shall not be *another* deluge to destroy the whole earth; *for the imagination of man's heart*, כי *ki*, ALTHOUGH the imagination of man's heart *should be evil*, i. e. should they

A. M. 1657.
B. C. 2347.

22 [x] While the earth [y] remaineth, seed-time and harvest, and cold and heat, and summer and winter, and [z] day and night, shall not cease.

A. M. 1657.
B. C. 2347.

[x] Isa. liv. 8.——[y] Heb. *as yet all the days of the earth.*

[z] Jer. xxxiii. 20, 25.

become afterwards as evil as they have been before, I will not destroy the earth by a FLOOD. God has other means of destruction; and the next time he visits by a general judgment, FIRE is to be the agent. 2 Pet. iii. 7.

Verse 22. *While the earth remaineth, seed-time and harvest, &c.*] There is something very expressive in the original, עד כל ימי הארץ *od col yemey haarets*, until all the DAYS of the earth; for God does not reckon its duration by centu*ries*, and the words themselves afford a strong presumption that the earth shall not have an end*less* duration.

Seed-time and harvest.—It is very probable that the *seasons*, which were distinctly marked immediately after the deluge, are mentioned in this place; but it is difficult to ascertain them. Most European nations divide the year into four distinct parts, called *quarters* or *seasons;* but there are *six* divisions in the text, and probably all intended to describe the seasons in one of these postdiluvian years, particularly in that part of the globe, *Armenia*, where Noah was when God gave him, and mankind through him, this gracious promise. From the *Targum* of Jonathan on this verse we learn that in *Palestine* their *seed-time* was in September, at the autumnal equinox; their *harvest* in March, at the vernal equinox; that their *winter* began in December, at the solstice; and their *summer* at the solstice in June.

The *Copts* begin their autumn on the 15th of September, and extend it to the 15th of December. Their *winter* on the 15th of December, and extend it to the 15th of March. Their *spring* on the 15th of March, and extend it to the 15th of June. Their *summer* on the 15th of June, and extend it to the 15th of September, assigning to each season three complete months. *Calmet.*

There are certainly regions of the earth to which neither this nor our own mode of division can apply: there are some where *summer* and *winter* appear to divide the whole year, and others where, besides *summer*, *winter*, *autumn*, and *spring*, there are distinct seasons that may be denominated the *hot season*, the *cold season*, the *rainy season*, &c., &c.

This is a very merciful promise to the inhabitants of the earth. There may be a variety *in* the seasons, but no season essentially necessary to vegetation shall utterly fail. The times which are of greatest consequence to the preservation of man are distinctly noted; there shall be both *seed-time* and *harvest*—a proper time to deposit the different grain in the earth, and a proper time to *reap* the produce of this seed.

Thus ends the account of the general deluge, its cause, circumstances, and consequences. An account that seems to say to us, Behold the goodness and severity of God! Both his *justice* and *long-suffering* are particularly marked in this astonishing event. His *justice*, in the punishment of the incorrigibly wicked; and his *mercy*, in giving them so fair and full a warning, and in waiting so long to extend his grace to all who might seek him. Such a convincing proof has the destruction of the world by water given of the Divine justice, such convincing testimony of the truth of the sacred writings, that not only every part of the earth gives testimony of this extraordinary revolution, but also every nation of the universe has preserved records or traditions of this awful display of the justice of God.

A multitude of testimonies, collected from the most authentic sources in the heathen world, I had intended for insertion in this place, but want of room obliges me to lay them aside. But the state of the earth itself is a sufficient proof. Every part of it bears unequivocal evidence of disruption and violence. From the hand of the God of order it never could have proceeded in its present state. In every part we see marks of the crimes of men, and of the justice of God. And shall not the living lay this to heart? Surely God is not mocked; that which a man soweth he shall reap. He who soweth to the flesh shall of it reap destruction; and though the plague of water shall no more destroy the earth, yet an equal if not sorer punishment awaits the world of the ungodly, in the threatened destruction by fire.

In ancient times almost every thing was typical, and no doubt the *ark* among the rest; but *of what* and in *what way* farther than revelation guides, it is both difficult and unsafe to say. It has been considered a type of our blessed *Lord*; and hence it has been observed, that "as all those who were *out of the ark* perished by the flood, so those who take not refuge in the meritorious atonement of Christ Jesus must perish everlastingly." Of all those who, having the opportunity of hearing the Gospel, refuse to accept of the sacrifice it offers them, this saying is true; but the parallel is not good. Myriads of those who perished during the flood probably repented, implored mercy, and found forgiveness; for God ever delights to save, and Jesus was the *Lamb* slain from the foundation of the world. And though, generally, the people continned in carnal security and sensual gratifications till the flood came, there is much reason to believe that those who during the *forty days'* rain would naturally flee to the high lands and tops of the highest mountains, would earnestly implore that mercy which has never been denied, even to the most profligate, when under deep humiliation of heart they have returned to God. And who can say that this was not done by multitudes while they beheld the increasing flood; or that God, in this last extremity, had rendered it impossible?

St. Peter, 1st Epist. iii. 21, makes the ark a figure of baptism, and intimates that we are saved by this, as the eight souls were saved by the ark. But let us not mistake the apostle by supposing that the mere *ceremony* itself saves any person; he tells us that the salvation conveyed through this sacred rite *is not the putting away the filth of the flesh, but the answer of a good conscience toward God;* i. e. remission of sins and regeneration by the Holy Spirit, which are signi-

a

fied by this baptism A *good conscience* never existed where remission of sins had not taken place; and every person knows that it is God's prerogative to forgive sins, and that no ordinance can confer it, though ordinances may be the *means* to convey it when piously and believingly used.

CHAPTER IX.

God blesses Noah and his sons, 1. *The brute creation to be subject to them through fear,* 2. *The first grant of animal food,* 3. *Eating of blood forbidden,* 4. *Cruelty to animals forbidden,* 5. *A man-slayer to forfeit his life,* 6. *The covenant of God established between him and Noah and the whole brute creation,* 8–11. *The rainbow given as the sign and pledge of this covenant,* 12–17. *The three sons of Noah people the whole earth,* 18, 19. *Noah plants a vineyard, drinks of the wine, is intoxicated, and lies exposed in his tent,* 20, 21. *The reprehensible conduct of Ham,* 22. *The laudable carriage of Shem and Japheth,* 23. *Noah prophetically declares the servitude of the posterity of Ham,* 24, 25; *and the dignity and increase of Shem and Japheth,* 26, 27. *The age and death of Noah,* 28, 29.

A. M. 1657. B. C. 2347.

AND God blessed Noah and his sons, and said unto them, [a] Be fruitful, and multiply, and replenish the earth.
2 [b] And the fear of you and the dread of you shall be upon every beast of the earth, and upon every fowl of the air, upon all that moveth *upon* the earth, and upon all the fishes of the sea; into your hand are they delivered.
3 [c] Every moving thing that liveth shall be meat for you; even as the [d] green herb have I given you [e] all things:
4 [f] But flesh with the life thereof, *which is* the blood thereof, shall ye not eat.

[a] Chap. i. 28; ver. 7, 19; chap. x. 32.——[b] Chap. i. 28; Hos. ii. 18.——[c] Deut. xii. 15; xiv. 3, 9, 11; Acts x. 12, 13. [d] Chap. i. 29.

[e] Rom. xiv. 14, 20; 1 Cor. x. 23, 26; Col. ii. 16; 1 Tim. iv. 3, 4.——[f] Lev. xvii. 10, 11, 14; xix. 26; Deut. xii. 23; 1 Sam. xiv. 34; Acts xv. 20, 29.

NOTES ON CHAP. IX.

Verse 1. *God blessed Noah*] Even the increase of families, which appears to depend on merely natural means, and sometimes fortuitous circumstances, is all of God. It is by his power and wisdom that the human being is formed, and it is by his providence alone that man is supported and preserved.

Verse 2. *The fear of you and the dread, &c.*] Prior to the fall, man ruled the inferior animals by *love* and *kindness*, for then *gentleness* and *docility* were *their* principal characteristics. After the fall, untractableness, with savage ferocity, prevailed among almost all orders of the brute creation; enmity to man seems particularly to prevail; and had not God in his mercy impressed their minds with the *fear* and *terror* of man, so that some *submit* to his will while others *flee* from his residence, the human race would long ere this have been totally destroyed by the beasts of the field. Did the horse know his own strength, and the weakness of the miserable wretch who unmercifully *rides, drives, whips, goads,* and *oppresses* him, would he not with one stroke of his hoof destroy his tyrant possessor? But while God hides these things from him he impresses his mind with the *fear* of his owner, so that either by *cheerful* or *sullen submission* he is trained up for, and employed in, the most useful and important purposes; and even willingly submits, when tortured for the sport and amusement of his more bruitish oppressor. Tigers, wolves, lions, and hyænas, the determinate foes of man, incapable of being tamed or domesticated, flee, through the principle of *terror*, from the dwelling of man, and thus he is providentially safe. Hence, by *fear* and by *dread* man rules every beast of the earth, every fowl of the air, and every fish of the sea. How wise and gracious is this order of the Divine providence! and with what thankfulness should it be considered by every human being!

Verse 3. *Every moving thing—shall be meat*] There is no positive evidence that *animal* food was ever used *before* the flood. Noah had the first grant of this kind, and it has been continued to all his posterity ever since. It is not likely that this grant would have been now made if some extraordinary alteration had not taken place in the vegetable world, so as to render its productions less nutritive than they were before; and probably such a change in the constitution of man as to render a grosser and higher diet necessary. We may therefore safely infer that the earth was less productive *after* the flood than it was before, and that the human constitution was greatly impaired by the alterations which had taken place through the whole economy of nature. Morbid debility, induced by an often unfriendly state of the atmosphere, with sore and long-continued labour, would necessarily require a higher nutriment than vegetables could supply. That this was the case appears sufficiently clear from the grant of animal food, which, had it not been indispensably necessary, had not been made. That the constitution of man was then much altered appears in the greatly contracted lives of the postdiluvians; yet from the deluge to the days of Abraham the lives of several of the patriarchs amounted to some hundreds of years, but this was the effect of a *peculiar providence*, that the new world might be the more speedily repeopled.

Verse 4. *But flesh with the life thereof, which is the blood*] Though animal food was granted, yet the *blood* was most solemnly forbidden, because it was the *life of the beast*, and this *life* was to be offered to God

A. M. 1657. B. C. 2347.

5 And surely your blood of your lives will I require; [g] at the hand of every beast will I require it, and [h] at the hand of man; at the hand of every [i] man's brother will I require the life of man

6 [k] Whoso sheddeth man's blood, by man shall his blood be shed; [l] for in the image of God made he man.

7 And you, [m] be ye fruitful, and multiply: bring forth abundantly in the earth, and multiply therein.

8 And God spake unto Noah, and to his sons with him, saying,

9 And I, [n] behold, I establish [o] my covenant with you, and with your seed after you;

A. M. 1657. B. C. 2347.

10 [p] And with every living creature that *is* with you, of the fowl, of the cattle, and of every beast of the earth with you; from all that go out of the ark, to every beast of the earth.

11 And [q] I will establish my covenant with you: neither shall all flesh be cut off any more by the waters of a flood; neither shall there any more be a flood to destroy the earth.

[g] Exod. xxi. 28.——[h] Chap. iv. 9, 10; Psa. ix. 12.——[i] Acts xvii. 26.——[k] Exod. xxi. 12, 14; Lev. xxiv. 17; Matt. xxvi. 52; Rev. xiii. 10.——[l] Chap. i. 27.——[m] Ver. 1, 19; chap. i. 28——[n] Chap. vi. 18.——[o] Isa. liv. 9.——[p] Psa. cxlv. 9.——[q] Isa. liv. 9

as an atonement for sin. *Hence* the blood was ever held sacred, because it was the grand instrument of expiation, and because it was typical of that blood by which we enter into the holiest. 1. *Before* the deluge it was not eaten, because animal food was not in use. 2 *After* the deluge it was prohibited, as we find above; and, being one of the *seven* Noahic precepts, it was not eaten previously to the publication of the Mosaic law. 3. At the giving of the law, and at several times during the ministry of Moses, the prohibition was most solemnly, and with awful penalties renewed. Hence we may rest assured that no blood was eaten previously to the Christian era, nor indeed ever since by the *Jewish* people. 4. That the prohibition has been renewed under the Christian dispensation, can admit of little doubt by any man who *dispassionately* reads Acts xv. 20, 29; xxi. 25, where even the *Gentile converts* are charged to abstain from it on the authority, not only of the *apostles*, but of the *Holy Ghost*, who gave them *there* and *then* especial direction concerning *this* point; see Acts xv. 28; not *for fear of stumbling the* converted *Jews*, the gloss of theologians, but because it was one *των επαναγκες τουτων*, of *those* necessary *points*, from the *burden* (*βαρος*) of obedience to which they could not be excused. 5. This command is still scrupulously obeyed by the oriental Christians, and by the whole Greek Church; and why? because the reasons still subsist. No blood was eaten *under the law*, because it pointed out the blood that *was to be shed* for the sin of the world; and *under the Gospel* it should not be eaten, because it should ever be considered as representing the blood *which has been shed* for the remission of sins. If the eaters of blood in general knew that it affords a very crude, almost indigestible, and unwholesome aliment, they certainly would not on these *physical* reasons, leaving *moral* considerations out of the question, be so much attached to the consumption of that from which they could expect no wholesome nutriment, and which, to render it even pleasing to the palate, requires all the skill of the cook. See Lev. xvii. 2.

Verse 5. *Surely your blood—will I require; at the hand of every beast*] This is very obscure, but if taken *literally* it seems to be an awful warning against *cruelty* to the brute creation; and from it we may conclude that *horse-racers, hare-hunters, bull-baiters*, and *cock-fighters* shall be obliged to give an account to God for every creature they have *wantonly* destroyed. Instead of חיה *chaiyah*, "beast," the Samaritan reads ࠇࠉ *chai*, "living," any "living creature or person;" this makes a very good sense, and equally forbids cruelty either to men or brutes.

Verse 6. *Whoso sheddeth man's blood, by man shall his blood*] Hence it appears that whoever kills a man, unless *unwittingly*, as the Scripture expresses it, shall forfeit his own life.

A man is accused of the crime of murder; of this crime he is guilty or he is not: if he be guilty of murder he should die; if not, let him be punished according to the demerit of his crime; but for no offence *but murder* should he lose his life. Taking away the life of another is the highest offence that can be committed against the individual, and against society; and the highest punishment that a man can suffer for such a crime is the loss of his own life. As punishment should be ever proportioned to crimes, so the *highest punishment* due to the *highest crime* should not be inflicted for a *minor offence*. The law of God and the eternal dictates of reason say, that if a man kill another, the loss of his own life is at once the highest penalty he can pay, and an equivalent for his offence as far as civil society is concerned. If the death of the murderer be the highest penalty he can pay for the murder he has committed, then the infliction of this punishment for *any minor offence* is *injustice* and *cruelty*; and serves only to *confound* the claims of justice, the different degrees of moral turpitude and vice, and to render the profligate desperate: hence the adage so frequent among almost every order of delinquents, "It is as good to be hanged for a *sheep* as a *lamb*;" which at once marks their desperation, and the injustice of those penal laws which inflict the highest punishment for almost every species of crime. When shall a wise and judicious legislature see the absurdity and injustice of inflicting the punishment of *death* for stealing a *sheep* or a *horse*, forging a twenty *shillings'* note, and MURDERING A MAN; when the latter, in its moral turpitude and ruinous consequences, infinitely exceeds the others?*

* On this head the doctor's pious wish has been realized since this paragraph was written.—PUBLISHERS.

a

A. M. 1657.
B. C. 2347.

12 And God said, [r] This *is* the
token of the covenant which I make
between me and you and every living creature
that *is* with you, for perpetual generations:
13 I do set [s] my bow in the cloud, and it
shall be for a token of a covenant between
me and the earth.
14 [t] And it shall come to pass, when I bring
a cloud over the earth, that the bow shall be
seen in the cloud:
15 And [u] I will remember my covenant which
is between me and you and every living creature of all flesh; and the waters
shall no more become a flood to
destroy all flesh.
16 And the bow shall be in the cloud; and
I will look upon it, that I may remember [v] the
everlasting covenant between God and every
living creature of all flesh that *is* upon the
earth.
17 And God said unto Noah, This *is* the
token of the covenant which I have established
between me and all flesh that *is* upon the
earth.

[r] Chapter xvii. 11.——[s] Revelation iv. 3.——[t] Ecclus. xliii. 11, 12.

[u] Exod. xxviii. 12; Lev. xxvi. 42, 45; Ezek. xvi. 60.——[v] Chap. xvii. 13, 19.

Verse 13. *I do set my bow in the cloud*] On the origin and nature of the rainbow there had been a great variety of conjectures, till *Anthony de Dominis*, bishop of Spalatro, in a treatise of his published by *Bartholus* in 1611, partly suggested the true cause of this phenomenon, which was afterwards fully explained and demonstrated by *Sir Isaac Newton*. To enter into this subject here in detail would be improper; and therefore the less informed reader must have recourse to treatises on *Optics* for its full explanation. To readers in general it may be sufficient to say that the rainbow is a mere *natural effect of a natural cause:* 1. It is never seen but in showery weather. 2. Nor then unless the sun shines. 3. It never appears in any part of the heavens but in that *opposite* to the sun. 4. It never appears greater than a semicircle, but often much less. 5. It is always *double*, there being what is called the *superior* and *inferior*, or *primary* and *secondary* rainbow. 6. These bows exhibit the *seven* prismatic colours, *red*, *orange*, *yellow*, *green*, *blue*, *indigo*, and *violet*. 7. The whole of this phenomenon depends on the rays of the sun falling on spherical drops of water, and being in their passage through them, *refracted* and *reflected*.

The formation of the primary and secondary rainbow depends on the *two* following *propositions;* 1. When the sun shines on the drops of rain as they are falling, the rays that come from those drops to the eye of the spectator, after ONE *reflection* and TWO *refractions*, produce the *primary* rainbow. 2. When the sun shines on the drops of rain as they are falling, the rays that come from those drops to the eye of the spectator, after TWO *reflections* and TWO *refractions*, produce the *secondary* rainbow. The illustration of these propositions must be sought in treatises on *Optics*, assisted by *plates*.

From the well-known cause of this phenomenon it cannot be rationally supposed that there was no rainbow in the heavens *before* the time mentioned in the text, for as the rainbow is the natural effect of the sun's rays falling on drops of water, and of their being refracted and reflected by them, it must have appeared at different times from the creation of the sun and the atmosphere. Nor does the text intimate that the bow was *now* created for a *sign* to Noah and his posterity; but that what was *formerly* created, or rather that which was the necessary effect, in certain cases, of the creation of the sun and atmosphere, should *now* be considered by them as an unfailing token of their continual preservation from the waters of a deluge; therefore the text speaks of what *had already been done*, and not of what was *now* done, קשתי נתתי *kashti nathatti*, "My bow I *have* given, or put in the cloud;" as if he said: As surely as the rainbow is a necessary effect of sunshine in rain, and must continue such as long as the sun and atmosphere endure, so surely shall this earth be preserved from destruction by water; and its preservation shall be as necessary an effect of my promise as the rainbow is of the shining of the sun during a shower of rain.

Verse 17. *This is the token*] אות *oth*, The Divine sign or portent: *The bow shall be in the cloud*. For the reasons above specified it *must* be there, when the circumstances already mentioned occur; if therefore it cannot fail because of the reasons before assigned, no more shall my promise; and the bow shall be the proof of its perpetuity.

Both the *Greeks* and *Latins*, as well as the *Hebrews*, have ever considered the rainbow as a Divine token or portent; and both of these nations have even deified it, and made it a messenger of the gods.

Homer, Il. xi., ver. 27, speaking of the figures on Agamemnon's breastplate, says there were three dragons, whose colours were

——ιρισσιν εοικοτες, ἁς τε Κρονων.
Εν νεφεϊ στηριξε, τερας μεροπων ανθρωπων.

"like to the rainbow which the son of Saturn has placed in the cloud as a SIGN to mankind," or to *men of various languages*, for so the *μεροπων ανθρωπων* of the poet has been understood. Some have thought that the ancient Greek writers give this epithet to man from some tradition of the confusion and multiplication of tongues at Babel; hence in this place the words may be understood as implying mankind at large, the whole human race; God having given the rainbow for a sign to all the descendants of Noah, by whom the whole earth was peopled after the flood. Thus the celestial bow speaks a *universal language*, understood by all the sons and daughters of Adam. Virgil, from

A. M. 1657. B. C. 2347.

18 And the sons of Noah, that went forth of the ark, were Shem, and Ham, and Japheth: [w] and Ham *is* the father of [x] Canaan.

19 [y] These *are* the three sons of Noah: [z] and of them was the whole earth overspread.

20 And Noah began *to be* [a] a husbandman, and he planted a vineyard:

21 And he drank of the wine, [b] and was drunken; and he was uncovered within his tent.

22 And Ham, the father of Canaan, saw the nakedness of his father, and told his two brethren without.

23 [c] And Shem and Japheth took a garment, and laid *it* upon both their shoulders, and went

[w] Chap. x. 6.——[x] Heb. *Chenaan.*——[y] Chap. v. 32.——[z] Chap. viii. 17; x. 32; 1 Chron. i. 4, &c.——[a] Chap. iii. 19, 23; iv. 2; v. 29; Prov. x. 11; xii. 11; Ecclus. v. 9.——[b] Prov. xx. 1; 1 Cor. x. 12.——[c] Exod. xx. 12; Gal. vi. 1.

some disguised traditionary figure of the truth, considers the rainbow as a messenger of the gods. Æn. v., ver. 606:—

IRIM *de cœlo misit Saturnia Juno.*

"Juno, the daughter of Saturn, sent down the rainbow from heaven;" and again, Æn. ix., ver. 803:—

——*aeriam cœlo nam Jupiter* IRIM
Demisit.

"For Jupiter sent down the ethereal rainbow from heaven."

It is worthy of remark that both these poets understood the rainbow to be a *sign*, *warning*, or *portent* from heaven.

As I believe the rainbow to have been intended solely for the purpose mentioned in the text, I forbear to make spiritual uses and illustrations of it. Many have done this, and their observations may be very edifying, but they certainly have no foundation in the text.

Verse 20. *Noah began* to be *a husbandman*] איש האדמה *ish haadamah*, A man of the ground, a farmer; by his *beginning* to be a husbandman we are to understand his recommencing his agricultural operations, which undoubtedly he had carried on for six hundred years before, but this had been interrupted by the flood. And the transaction here mentioned might have occurred many years posterior to the deluge, even after Canaan was born and grown up, for the date of it is not fixed in the text.

The word *husband* first occurs here, and scarcely appears proper, because it is always applied to man in his *married state*, as *wife* is to the woman. The etymology of the term will at once show its propriety when applied to the *head* of a family. *Husband*, huſbanð, is Anglo-Saxon, and simply signifies the *bond* of the *house* or *family*; as by him the family is formed, *united*, and *bound* together, which, on his death, is *disunited* and *scattered*. It is on this etymology of the word that we can account for the *farmers* and *petty landholders* being called so early as the twelfth century, *husbandi*, as appears in a statute of David II., king of Scotland: we may therefore safely derive the word from huſ, *a house*, and bonð, from binðen, *to bind* or *tie*; and this etymology appears plainer in the orthography which prevailed in the thirteenth and fourteenth centuries, in which I have often found the word written *house-bond*; so it is in a MS. Bible before me, written in the fourteenth century. *Junius* disputes this etymology, but I think on no just ground.

Verse 21. *He drank of the wine, &c.*] It is very probable that this was the first time the vine was cultivated; and it is as probable that the strength or intoxicating power of the expressed juice was never before known. Noah, therefore, might have drunk it at this time without the least blame, as he knew not till this trial the effects it would produce. I once knew a case which I believe to be perfectly parallel. A person who had scarcely ever heard of *cider*, and whose beverage through his whole life had been only *milk* or *water*, coming wet and very much fatigued to a farmer's house in Somersetshire, begged for a little *water* or *milk*. The good woman of the house, seeing him very much exhausted, kindly said, "I will give you a little cider, which will do you more good." The honest man, understanding no more of cider than merely that it was the *simple juice of apples*, after some hesitation drank about a half a pint of it; the consequence was, that in less than half an hour he was perfectly intoxicated, and could neither speak plain nor walk! This case I myself witnessed. A stranger to the circumstances, seeing this person, would pronounce him *drunk*; and perhaps at a third hand he might be represented as a *drunkard*, and thus his character be blasted; while of the crime of drunkenness he was as innocent as an infant. This I presume to have been precisely the case with Noah; and no person without an absolute breach of every rule of charity and candour, can attach any blame to the character of Noah on this ground, unless from a *subsequent* account they were well assured that, knowing the power and effects of the liquor, he had repeated the act. Some expositors seem to be glad to fix on a fact like this, which by *their distortion* becomes a *crime*; and then, in a strain of sympathetic tenderness, affect to deplore "the failings and imperfections of the *best of men*;" when, from the interpretation that *should be* given of the place, neither *failing* nor *imperfection* can possibly appear.

Verse 22–24. *And Ham, the father of Canaan, &c.*] There is no occasion to enter into any detail here; the sacred text is circumstantial enough. Ham, and very probably his son Canaan, had treated their father on this occasion with contempt or reprehensible levity. Had Noah not been innocent, as my exposition supposes him, God would not have endued him with the spirit of prophecy on this occasion, and testified such marked disapprobation of *their* conduct. The conduct of Shem and Japheth was such as became pious and affectionate children, who appear to have been in the habit of treating their father with decency, reve-

A. M. cir. 1657. B. C. cir. 2347. backward, and covered the nakedness of their father; and their faces *were* backward, and they saw not their father's nakedness.

24 And Noah awoke from his wine, and knew what his younger son had done unto him.

25 And he said, [d] Cursed *be* Canaan; [e] a servant of servants shall he be unto his brethren.

26 And he said, [f] Blessed *be* the LORD God of Shem; and Canaan shall be [g] his servant. A. M. cir. 1657. B. C. cir. 2347.

27 God shall [h] enlarge Japheth, [i] and he shall dwell in the tents of Shem; and [k] Canaan shall be his servant.

28 And Noah lived after the flood three hundred and fifty years.

29 And all the days of Noah were nine hundred and fifty years: and he died. A. M. 2006. B. C. 1998.

[d] Deut. xxvii. 16.——[e] Josh. ix. 23; 1 Kings ix. 20, 21.——[f] Psa. cxliv. 15; Heb. xi. 16.——[g] Or, *servant to them.*——[h] Or, *persuade.*——[i] Eph. ii. 13, 14; iii. 6.——[k] Ver. 25, 26.

rence, and obedient respect. On the one the spirit of prophecy (not the incensed father) pronounces a curse: on the others the same spirit (not parental tenderness) pronounces a blessing. These things had been just as they afterwards occurred had Noah never spoken. God had wise and powerful reasons to induce him to sentence the one to perpetual servitude, and to allot to the others prosperity and dominion. Besides, the curse pronounced on Canaan neither fell immediately upon himself nor on his worthless father, but upon the Canaanites; and from the history we have of this people, in Lev. xviii., xx.; and Deut. ix. 4; xii. 31, we may ask, Could the curse of God fall more deservedly on any people than on these? Their profligacy was great, but *it was not the effect of the curse;* but, being foreseen by the *Lord*, the curse was the effect of their conduct. But even this curse does not exclude them from the possibility of obtaining salvation; it extends not to the *soul* and to *eternity*, but merely to their bodies and to time; though, if they continued to abuse their liberty, resist the Holy Ghost, and refuse to be saved on God's terms, then the wrath of Divine justice must come upon them to the uttermost. How many, even of these, repented, we cannot tell.

Verse 25. *Cursed* be *Canaan*] See on the preceding verses. In the 25th, 26th, and 27th verses, instead of Canaan simply, the Arabic version has *Ham the father of Canaan;* but this is acknowledged by none of the other versions, and seems to be merely a gloss.

Verse 29. *The days of Noah were nine hundred and fifty years*] The oldest patriarch on record, Methuselah only excepted. This, according to the common reckoning, was A. M. 2006, but according to Dr. Hales, 3505.

"HAM," says Dr. Hales, "signifies *burnt* or *black*, and this name was peculiarly significant of the regions allotted to his family. To the *Cushites*, or children of his eldest son *Cush*, were allotted the hot southern regions of *Asia*, along the coasts of the *Persian* Gulf, *Susiana* or *Chusistan*, *Arabia*, *&c.*; to the sons of Canaan, Palestine and Syria; to the sons of Misraim, Egypt and Libya, in Africa.

"The *Hamites* in general, like the Canaanites of old, were a seafaring race, and sooner arrived at civilization and the luxuries of life than their simpler pastoral and agricultural brethren of the other two families. The first great empires of *Assyria* and *Egypt* were founded by them, and the republics of *Sidon*, Tyre, and *Carthage* were early distinguished for their commerce, but they sooner also fell to decay; and Egypt, which was one of the first, became the last *and basest of the kingdoms*, Ezek. xxix. 15, and has been successively in subjection to the *Shemites* and *Japhethites*, as have also the settlements of the other branches of the *Hamites*.

"SHEM signifies *name* or *renown;* and his indeed was great in a temporal and spiritual sense. The finest regions of Upper and Middle *Asia* were allotted to his family, Armenia, Mesopotamia, Assyria, Media, Persia, &c., to the *Indus* and *Ganges*, and perhaps to *China* eastward.

"The chief renown of Shem was of a spiritual nature: he was destined to be the lineal ancestor of the blessed seed of the woman; and to this glorious privilege Noah, to whom it was probably revealed, might have alluded in that devout ejaculation, Blessed be the *LORD*, the GOD of *Shem!* The pastoral life of the *Shemites* is strongly marked in the prophecy by *the tents of Shem;* and such it remains to the present day, throughout their midland settlements in *Asia*.

"JAPHETH signifies *enlargement;* and how wonderfully did Providence *enlarge the boundaries of Japheth!* His posterity diverged eastward and westward throughout the whole extent of *Asia*, north of the great range of Taurus, as far as the Eastern Ocean, whence they probably crossed over to *America* by *Behring's* Straits from *Kamtschatka*, and in the opposite direction throughout *Europe* to the *Mediterranean* Sea and the *Atlantic* Ocean; from whence also they might have crossed over to *America* by *Newfoundland*, where traces of early settlements remain in parts now desert. Thus did they gradually *enlarge* themselves till they literally encompassed the earth, within the precincts of the northern temperate zone, to which their roving *hunter's* life contributed not a little. Their progress northwards was checked by the much greater extent of the *Black Sea* in ancient times, and the increasing rigour of the climates: but their hardy race, and enterprising, warlike genius, made them frequently encroach southwards on the settlements of *Shem*, whose pastoral and agricultural occupations rendered them more inactive, peaceable, and unwarlike; and so *they dwelt in the tents of Shem* when the Scythians invaded *Media*, and subdued western *Asia* southwards as far as *Egypt*, in the days of *Cyaxares;* when the Greeks, and after

wards the Romans, overran and subdued the Assyrians, Medes, and Persians in the east, and the Syrians and Jews in the south; as foretold by the Syrian prophet Balaam, Num. xxiv. 24:—

Ships shall come from *Chittim*,
And shall afflict the *Assyrians*, and afflict the *Hebrews;*
But he (the invader) shall perish himself at last.

"And by Moses: And the *Lord* shall bring thee (the Jews) into *Egypt* (or bondage) again with ships, &c., Deut. xxviii. 68. And by Daniel: For the ships of *Chittim* shall come against him, viz., Antiochus, king of Syria, Dan. xi. 30. In these passages *Chittim* denotes the southern coasts of Europe, bounding the *Mediterranean*, called the *isles of the Gentiles* or *Nations;* see Gen. x. 5. And the *isles of Chittim* are mentioned Jer. ii. 10. And in after times the *Tartars* in the east have repeatedly invaded and subdued the *Hindoos* and the *Chinese;* while the warlike and enterprising genius of the greatest of the isles of the Gentiles, GREAT BRITAIN and IRELAND, have spread their colonies, their arms, their language, their arts, and in some measure their religion, from the rising to the setting sun." See Dr. Hales's *Analysis of Chronology*, vol. i., p. 352, &c.

Though what is left undone should not cause us to lose sight of what *is done*, yet we have reason to lament that the inhabitants of the British isles, who of all nations under heaven have the purest light of Divine revelation, and the best means of diffusing it, have been much more intent on spreading their conquests and extending their commerce, than in propagating the Gospel of the Son of God. But the nation, by getting the Bible translated into every *living language*, and sending it to *all parts* of the habitable globe, and, by its various *missionary societies*, sending men of God to explain and enforce the doctrines and precepts of this sacred book, is rapidly redeeming its character, and becoming great in goodness and benevolence over the whole earth!

CHAPTER X.

The generations of the sons of Noah, 1. JAPHETH *and his descendants*, 2–4. *The isles of the Gentiles, or Europe, peopled by the Japhethites*, 5. HAM *and his posterity*, 6–20. *Nimrod, one of his descendants, a mighty hunter*, 8, 9, *founds the first kingdom*, 10. *Nineveh and other cities founded*, 11, 12. *The Canaanites in their nine grand branches or families*, 15–18. *Their territories*, 19. SHEM *and his posterity* 21–31. *The earth divided in the days of Peleg*, 25. *The territories of the Shemites*, 30. *The whole earth peopled by the descendants of Noah's three sons*, 32.

A. M. 1556. B. C. 2448.

1 NOW these *are* the generations of the sons of Noah; Shem, Ham, and Japheth: [a] and unto them were sons born after the flood.

[a] Genesis, chap. ix. 1, 7, 19.

NOTES ON CHAP. X.

Verse 1. *Now these* are *the generations*] It is extremely difficult to say what particular nations and people sprang from the three grand divisions of the family of Noah, because the names of many of those ancient people have become changed in the vast lapse of time from the deluge to the Christian era; yet some are so very distinctly marked that they can be easily ascertained, while a few still retain their original names.

Moses does not always give the name of the *first settler* in a country, but rather that of the *people* from whom the country *afterwards* derived its name. Thus *Mizraim* is the dual of *Mezer*, and could never be the name of an *individual*. The like may be said of *Kittim, Dodanim, Ludim, Ananim, Lehabim, Naphtuhim, Pathrusim, Casluhim, Philistim*, and *Caphtorim*, which are all *plurals*, and evidently not the names of *individuals*, but of *families* or *tribes*. See verses 4, 6, 13, 14.

In the posterity of Canaan we find whole nations reckoned in the genealogy, instead of the individuals from whom they sprang; thus the *Jebusite, Amorite, Girgasite, Hivite, Arkite, Sinite, Arvadite, Zemarite*, and *Hamathite*, ver. 16–18, were evidently whole nations or tribes which inhabited the promised land, and were called *Canaanites* from *Canaan*, the son of *Ham*, who settled there.

Moses also, in this genealogy, seems to have introduced even the name of some *places* that were remarkable in the sacred history, instead of the original *settlers*. Such as *Hazarmaveth*, ver. 26; and probably *Ophir* and *Havilah*, ver. 29. But this is not infrequent in the sacred writings, as may be seen 1 Chron. ii. 51, where *Salma* is called *the father of Bethlehem*, which certainly never was the name of a *man*, but of a *place* sufficiently celebrated in the sacred history; and in chap. iv. 14, where Joab is called *the father of the valley of Charashim*, which no person could ever suppose was intended to designate an *individual*, but the society of *craftsmen* or artificers who lived there.

Eusebius and others state (from what authority we know not) that Noah was commanded of God to *make a will* and bequeath the whole of the earth to his three sons and their descendants in the following manner:—To *Shem*, all the *East;* to *Ham*, all *Africa;* to *Japheth*, the *Continent of Europe* with its *isles*, and the *northern parts of Asia*. See the notes at the end of the preceding chapter.

A. M. 1556. B. C. 2448.
2 [b] The sons of Japheth; Gomer, and Magog, and Madai, and Javan, and Tubal, and Meshech, and Tiras.

A. M. cir. 1666. B. C. cir. 2338.
3 And the sons of Gomer; Ashkenaz, and Riphath, and Togarmah.

4 And the sons of Javan; Elishah, and Tarshish, Kittim, and [c] Dodanim.

5 By these were [d] the isles of the Gentiles divided in their lands; every one after his tongue, after their families, in their nations. A. M. 1757 B. C. 2247.

6 [e] And the sons of Ham; Cush, and Mizraim, and Phut, and Canaan. A. M. cir. 1676. B. C. cir. 2328.

7 And the Sons of Cush; Seba, and Ha-

[b] 1 Chron. i. 5, &c.——[c] Or, as some read it, *Rodanim.*——[d] Psa. lxxii. 10; Jer. ii. 10; xxv. 22; Zeph. ii. 11.——[e] 1 Chron. i. 8, &c.

Verse 2. *The sons of Japheth*] Japheth is supposed to be the same with the *Japetus* of the Greeks, from whom, in an extremely remote antiquity, that people were supposed to have derived their origin.

Gomer] Supposed by some to have peopled Galatia; so Josephus, who says that the *Galatians* were anciently named *Gomerites.* From him the *Cimmerians* or *Cimbrians* are supposed to have derived their origin. *Bochart* has no doubt that the *Phrygians* sprang from this person, and some of our principal commentators are of the same opinion.

Magog] Supposed by many to be the father of the *Scythians* and *Tartars*, or *Tatars*, as the word should be written; and in great Tartary many names are still found which bear such a striking resemblance to the *Gog* and *Magog* of the Scriptures, as to leave little doubt of their identity.

Madai] Generally supposed to be the progenitor of the *Medes;* but *Joseph Mede* makes it probable that he was rather the founder of a people in Macedonia called *Mædi*, and that Macedonia was formerly called *Emathia*, a name formed from *Ei*, an *island*, and *Madai*, because he and his descendants inhabited the maritime coast on the borders of the Ionian Sea. On this subject nothing certain can be advanced.

Javan] It is almost universally agreed that from him sprang the *Ionians*, of Asia Minor; but this name seems to have been anciently given to the *Macedonians*, *Achaians*, and *Bœotians.*

Tubal] Some think he was the father of the *Iberians*, and that a part at least of *Spain* was peopled by him and his descendants; and that *Meshech*, who is generally in Scripture joined with him, was the founder of the *Cappadocians*, from whom proceeded the *Muscovites.*

Tiras.] From this person, according to general consent, the *Thracians* derived their origin.

Verse 3. *Ashkenaz*] Probably gave his name to *Sacagena*, a very excellent province of Armenia. Pliny mentions a people called *Ascanitici*, who dwelt about the *Tanaïs* and the *Palus Mæotis;* and some suppose that from Ashkenaz the *Euxine Sea* derived its name, but others suppose that from him the Germans derived their origin.

Riphath] Or *Diphath*, the founder of the *Paphlagonians*, which were anciently called *Riphatæi.*

Togarmah.] The *Sauromates*, or inhabitants of Turcomania. See the reasons in *Calmet.*

Verse 4. *Elishah*] As *Javan* peopled a considerable part of Greece, it is in that region that we must seek for the settlements of his descendants; *Elishah* probably was the first who settled at *Elis*, in Peloponnesus.

Tarshish] He first inhabited *Cilicia*, whose capital anciently was the city of *Tarsus*, where the Apostle Paul was born.

Kittim] We have already seen that this name was rather the name of a *people* than of an *individual:* some think by *Kittim* Cyprus is meant: others, the isle of Chios; and others, the *Romans;* and others, the *Macedonians.*

Dodanim.] Or *Rodanim*, for the ד and ר may be easily mistaken for each other, because of their great similarity. Some suppose that this family settled at *Dodona* in Epirus; others at the isle of *Rhodes;* others, at the *Rhone* in France, the ancient name of which was *Rhodanus*, from the Scripture *Rodanim.*

Verse 5. *Isles of the Gentiles*] EUROPE, of which this is allowed to be a general epithet. Calmet supposes that it comprehends all those countries to which the Hebrews were obliged to go by sea, such as Spain, Gaul, Italy, Greece, and Asia Minor.

Every one after his tongue] This refers to the time posterior to the confusion of tongues and dispersion from *Babel.*

Verse 6. *Cush*] Who peopled the Arabic *nome* near the *Red Sea* in Lower Egypt. Some think the *Ethiopians* descended from him.

Mizraim] This family certainly peopled *Egypt;* and both in the East and in the West, Egypt is called *Mezr* and *Mezraim.*

Phut] Who first peopled an Egyptian *nome* or district, bordering on *Libya.*

Canaan.] He who first peopled the land so called, known also by the name of the *Promised Land.*

Verse 7. *Seba*] The founder of the Sabæans. There seem to be three different people of this name mentioned in this chapter, and a fourth in chap. xxv. 3.

Havilah] Supposed by some to mean the inhabitants of the country included within that branch of the river Pison which ran out of the Euphrates into the bay of Persia, and bounded Arabia Felix on the east.

Sabtah] Supposed by some to have first peopled an isle or peninsula called *Saphta*, in the Persian Gulf.

Raamah] Or *Ragmah*, for the word is pronounced both ways, because of the ע *ain*, which some make a vowel, and some a consonant. Ptolemy mentions a city called *Regma* near the Persian Gulf; it probably received its name from the person in the text.

Sabtechah] From the river called *Samidochus*, in Caramania; Bochart conjectures that the person in the text fixed his residence in that part.

A. M. cir. 1676. B. C. cir. 2328. vilah, and Sabtah, and Raamah,
and Sabtechah: and the sons
of Raamah; Sheba, and Dedan.
A. M. cir. 1715. B. C. cir. 2289. 8 And Cush begat Nimrod;
he began to be a mighty one in
the earth.
9 He was a mighty [f] hunter [g] before the
LORD: wherefore it is said, Even as Nimrod,
the mighty hunter before the LORD.
10 [h] And the beginning of his kingdom was
[i] Babel, and Erech, and Accad, A. M. cir. 1745. B. C. cir. 2259.
and Calneh, in the land of Shinar.
11 Out of that land [k] went A. M. cir. 1700. B. C. cir. 2304.
forth Asshur, and builded Nine-
veh, and [l] the city Rehoboth, and Calah,
12 And Resen between Nineveh and Calah:
the same *is* a great city.
13 And Mizraim begat Ludim, and Anamim,
and Lehabim, and Naphtuhim,
14 And Pathrusim, and Casluhim, ([m] out of

[f] Jer. xvi. 16; Mic. vii. 2.——[g] Chap. vi. 11.——[h] Mic. v. 6. [i] Gr. *Babylon.*

[k] Or, *he went out* into *Assyria.*——[l] Or, *the streets of the city.* [m] 1 Chron. i. 12.

Sheba] Supposed to have had his residence beyond the Euphrates, in the environs of Charran, Eden, &c.

Dedan.] Supposed to have peopled a part of Arabia, on the confines of Idumea.

Verse 8. *Nimrod*] Of this person little is known, as he is not mentioned except here and in 1 Chron. i. 10, which is evidently a copy of the text in Genesis. He is called a *mighty hunter before the Lord;* and from ver. 10, we learn that he founded a *kingdom* which included the cities *Babel, Erech, Accad, and Calneh, in the land of Shinar.* Though the words are not definite, it is very likely he was a very *bad man.* His name Nimrod comes from מרד *marad, he rebelled;* and the Targum, on 1 Chron. i. 10, says: *Nimrod began to be a mighty man in sin, a murderer of innocent men, and a rebel before the Lord.* The Jerusalem Targum says: "He was mighty in hunting (or in prey) and in sin before God, for he was a hunter of the children of men in their languages; and he said unto them, *Depart from the religion of Shem, and cleave to the institutes of Nimrod.*" The Targum of Jonathan ben Uzziel says: "From the foundation of the world none was ever found like Nimrod, powerful in hunting, and in rebellions against the *Lord.*" The Syriac calls him *a warlike giant.* The word ציד *tsayid,* which we render *hunter,* signifies *prey;* and is applied in the Scriptures to the *hunting of men* by persecution, oppression, and tyranny. Hence it is likely that Nimrod, having acquired power, used it in tyranny and oppression; and by rapine and violence founded that domination which was the first distinguished by the name of a *kingdom* on the face of the earth. How many kingdoms have been founded in the same way, in various ages and nations from that time to the present! From the Nimrods of the earth, God deliver the world!

Mr. Bryant, in his Mythology, considers Nimrod as the principal instrument of the *idolatry* that afterwards prevailed in the family of Cush, and treats him as an *arch rebel and apostate.* Mr. Richardson, who was the determined foe of Mr. Bryant's whole system, asks, *Dissertation,* p. 405, "Where is the authority for these aspersions? They are nowhere to be discovered in the originals, in the *versions,* nor in the *paraphrases* of the sacred writings." If they are *not* to be found either in *versions* or *paraphrases* of the sacred writings, the above quotations are all *false.*

Verse 10. *The beginning of his kingdom was Babel*] בבל *babel* signifies *confusion;* and it seems to have been a very proper name for the commencement of a kingdom that appears to have been founded in *apostasy* from God, and to have been supported by *tyranny, rapine,* and *oppression.*

In the land of Shinar.] The same as mentioned chap. xi. 2. It appears that, as Babylon was built on the river Euphrates, and the tower of Babel was in the land of *Shinar,* consequently Shinar itself must have been in the southern part of Mesopotamia.

Verse 11. *Out of that land went forth Asshur*] The *marginal* reading is to be preferred here. *He*—Nimrod, *went out* into *Assyria and built Nineveh;* and hence Assyria is called the *land of Nimrod,* Mic. v. 6. Thus did this mighty hunter extend his dominions in every possible way. The city of Nineveh, the capital of Assyria, is supposed to have had its name from *Ninus,* the son of Nimrod; but probably Ninus and Nimrod are the same person. This city, which made so conspicuous a figure in the history of the world, is now called *Mossul;* it is an inconsiderable place, built out of the ruins of the ancient Nineveh.

Rehoboth, and Calah, &c.] Nothing certain is known concerning the situation of these places; conjecture is endless, and it has been amply indulged by learned men in seeking for *Rehoboth* in the *Birtha* of Ptolemy, *Calah* in *Calachine, Resen* in *Larissa, &c., &c.*

Verse 13. *Mizraim begat Ludim*] Supposed to mean the inhabitants of the *Mareotis,* a canton in Egypt, for the name *Ludim* is evidently the name of a people.

Anamim] According to Bochart, the people who inhabited the district about the temple of Jupiter Ammon.

Lehabim] The *Libyans,* or a people who dwelt on the west of the Thebaïd, and were called *Libyo-Egyptians.*

Naphtuhim] Even the conjecturers can scarcely fix a place for these people. Bochart seems inclined to place them in *Marmarica,* or among the Troglodytæ.

Verse 14. *Pathrusim*] The inhabitants of the *Delta,* in Egypt, according to the Chaldee paraphrase; but, according to Bochart, the people who inhabited the Thebaïd, called *Pathros* in Scripture.

Casluhim] The inhabitants of *Colchis;* for almost all authors allow that Colchis was peopled from Egypt.

Philistim] The people called *Philistines,* the con-

A. M. cir. 1700. B. C. cir. 2304. whom came Philistim,) and Caphtorim.

15 And Canaan begat [n] Sidon his first-born, and Heth,

16 And the Jebusite, and the Amorite, and the Girgasite,

A. M. unknown. B. C. unknown. 17 And the Hivite, and the Arkite, and the Sinite,

18 And the Arvadite, and the Zemarite, and the Hamathite: and afterward were the families of the Canaanites spread abroad.

19 [o] And the border of the Canaanites was from Sidon, as thou comest to Gerar, unto [p] Gaza; as thou goest unto Sodom, and Gomorrah, and Admah, and Zeboim, even unto Lasha.

20 These *are* the sons of Ham, after their families, after their tongues, in their countries, *and* in their nations.

21 Unto Shem also, the father of all the children of Eber, the brother of Japheth the elder, even to him were *children* born. A. M. unknown. B. C. unknown.

22 The [q] children of Shem; Elam, and Asshur, and [r] Arphaxad, and Lud, and Aram. A. M. cir. 1660. B. C. cir. 2344.

23 And the children of Aram; Uz, and Hul, and Gether, and Mash.

24 And Arphaxad begat [s] Salah [t]; and Salah begat Eber.

25 [u] And unto Eber were born two sons: the name of one *was* [v] Peleg, for in his days was the earth divided; and his brother's name *was* Joktan. A. M. 1757. B. C. 2247.

26 And Joktan begat Almodad, and Sheleph, and Hazarmaveth, and Jerah,

27 And Hadoram, and Uzal, and Diklah,

[n] Heb. *Tzidon.*——[o] Chap. xiii. 12, 14, 15, 17; xv. 18–21; Num. xxxiv. 2–12; Josh. xii. 7, 8.——[p] Heb. *Azzah.*

[q] 1 Chron. i. 17, &c.——[r] Heb. *Arpachshad.*——[s] Heb. *Shelah.* [t] Chap. xi. 12.——[u] 1 Chron. i. 19.——[v] That is, *division.*

stant plagues and frequent oppressors of the Israelites, whose history may be seen at large in the books of Samuel, Kings, &c.

Caphtorim.] Inhabitants of *Cyprus* according to Calmet.

Verse 15. *Sidon*] Who probably built the city of this name, and was the father of the *Sidonians.*

Heth] From whom came the Hittites, so remarkable among the Canaanitish nations.

Verse 16. *The Jebusite—Amorite, &c.*] Are well known as being the ancient inhabitants of Canaan, expelled by the children of Israel.

Verse 20. *These are the sons of Ham after their families*] No doubt all these were well known in the days of Moses, and for a long time after; but at this distance, when it is considered that the political state of the world has been undergoing almost incessant revolutions through all the intermediate portions of time, the impossibility of fixing their residences or marking their descendants must be evident, as both the *names* of the people and the *places* of their residences have been changed beyond the possibility of being recognized.

Verse 21. *Shem also, the father of all the children of Eber*] It is generally supposed that the *Hebrews* derived their name from *Eber* or *Heber*, son of Shem; but it appears much more likely that they had it from the circumstance of Abraham *passing over* (for so the word עבר *abar* signifies) the river Euphrates to come into the land of Canaan. See the history of Abraham, chap. xiv. 13.

Verse 22. *Elam*] From whom came the *Elamites,* near to the Medes, and whose chief city was *Elymais.*

Asshur] Who gave his name to a vast province (afterwards a mighty empire) called *Assyria.*

Arphaxad] From whom *Arrapachitis* in Assyria was named, according to some; or *Artaxata* in Armenia, on the frontiers of Media, according to others.

Lud] The founder of the *Lydians,* in Asia Minor; or of the *Ludim,* who dwelt at the confluence of the Euphrates and Tigris, according to *Arias Montanus.*

Aram.] The father of the *Arameans,* afterwards called *Syrians.*

Verse 23. *Uz*] Who peopled *Cœlosyria,* and is supposed to have been the founder of *Damascus.*

Hul] Who peopled a part of *Armenia.*

Gether] Supposed by Calmet to have been the founder of the *Itureans,* who dwelt beyond the Jordan, having Arabia Deserta on the east, and the Jordan on the west.

Mash.] Who inhabited mount *Masius* in Mesopotamia, and from whom the river *Mazeca,* which has its source in that mountain, takes its name.

Verse 24. *Salah*] The founder of the people of *Susiana.*

Eber.] See ver. 21. The Septuagint add *Cainan* here, with *one hundred and thirty* to the chronology.

Verse 25. *Peleg*] From פלג *palag,* to divide, because *in his days,* which is supposed to be about *one hundred* years after the flood, *the earth was divided* among the sons of Noah. Though some are of opinion that a *physical* division, and not a *political* one, is what is intended here, viz., a separation of continents and islands from the main land; the earthy parts having been united into one great continent previously to the days of Peleg. This opinion appears to me the most likely, for what is said, ver. 5, is spoken by way of *anticipation.*

Verses 26–30. *Joktan*] He had *thirteen* sons who *had their dwelling from Mesha unto Sephar, a mount of the east,* which places Calmet supposes to be mount *Masius,* on the west in *Mesopotamia,* and the mountains of the *Saphirs* on the east in Armenia, or of the *Tapyrs* farther on in Media.

In confirmation that all men have been derived from one family, let it be observed that there are many

A. M. cir. 1797. B. C. cir. 2207. 28 And Obal, and Abimael, and Sheba,

29 And Ophir, and Havilah, and Jobab: all these *were* the sons of Joktan.

30 And their dwelling was from Mesha, as thou goest unto Sephar, a mount of the east.

31 These *are* the sons of Shem, after their families, after their tongues, in their lands, after their nations. A. M. cir. 1797. B. C. cir. 2207.

32 [w] These *are* the families of the sons of Noah, after their generations, in their nations, [x] and by these were the nations divided in the earth, after the flood.

[w] Verse 1. — [x] Chap. ix. 19.

customs and usages, both sacred and civil, which have prevailed in all parts of the world; and that these could owe their origin to nothing but a general institution, which could never have existed, had not mankind been originally of the same blood, and instructed in the same common notions before they were dispersed. Among these usages may be reckoned, 1. The numbering by *tens*. 2. Their computing time by a cycle of *seven* days. 3. Their setting apart the *seventh* day for religious purposes. 4. Their use of *sacrifices, propitiatory* and *eucharistical*. 5. The consecration of *temples* and *altars*. 6. The institution of *sanctuaries* or places of refuge, and their privileges. 7. Their giving a *tenth* part of the produce of their fields, &c., for the use of the altar. 8. The custom of worshipping the Deity *bare-footed*. 9. Abstinence of the men from all sensual gratifications previously to their offering sacrifice. 10. The order of *priesthood* and its support. 11. The notion of legal pollutions, defilements, &c. 12. The universal tradition of a general deluge. 13. The universal opinion that the *rainbow* was a Divine *sign*, or *portent*, &c., &c. See *Dodd*.

The wisdom and goodness of God are particularly manifested in repeopling the earth by means of *three persons*, all of the same family, and who had witnessed that awful display of Divine justice in the destruction of the world by the flood, while themselves were preserved in the ark. By this very means the true religion was propagated over the earth; for the sons of Noah would certainly teach their children, not only the precepts delivered to their father by God himself, but also how in his justice he had brought the flood on the world of the ungodly, and by his merciful providence preserved *them* from the general ruin. It is on this ground alone that we can account for the uniformity and universality of the above traditions, and for the grand outlines of religious truth which are found in every quarter of the world. God has so done his marvellous works that they may be had in everlasting remembrance.

CHAPTER XI.

All the inhabitants of the earth, speaking one language and dwelling in one place, 1, 2, *purpose to build a city and a tower to prevent their dispersion,* 3, 4. *God confounds their language, and scatters them over the whole earth,* 5–9. *Account of the lives and families of the postdiluvian patriarchs. Shem,* 10, 11. *Arphaxad,* 12, 13. *Salah,* 14, 15. *Eber,* 16, 17. *Peleg,* 18, 19. *Ragau or Reu,* 20, 21. *Serug,* 22, 23. *Nahor,* 24, 25. *Terah and his three sons, Haran, Nahor, and Abram,* 26, 27. *The death of Haran,* 28. *Abram marries Sarai, and Nahor marries Milcah,* 29. *Sarai is barren,* 30. *Terah, Abram, Sarai, and Lot, leave Ur of the Chaldees, and go to Haran,* 31. *Terah dies in Haran, aged two hundred and five years,* 32.

A. M. cir. 1757. B. C. cir. 2247. AND the whole earth was of one [a] language, and of one [b] speech.

2 And it came to pass, as they journeyed [c] from the east, that they found a plain in the land of Shinar; and they dwelt there. A. M. cir. 1757. B. C. cir. 2247.

3 And [d] they said one to another, Go to, let

[a] Heb. *lip*.—[b] Heb. *words*.—[c] Or, *eastward*, as ch. xiii. 11; 2 Sam. vi. 2, with 1 Chron. xiii. 6.—[d] Heb. *a man said to his neighbour*.

NOTES ON CHAP. XI.

Verse 1. *The whole earth was of one language*] *The whole earth*—all mankind *was of one language*, in all likelihood the HEBREW; *and of one speech*—articulating the same words in the same way. It is generally supposed, that after the confusion mentioned in this chapter, the Hebrew language remained in the family of *Heber*. The proper names, and their significations given in the Scripture, seem incontestable evidences that the Hebrew language was the original language of the earth—the language in which God spake to man, and in which he gave the revelation of his will to Moses and the prophets. "It was used," says Mr. Ainsworth, "in all the world for *one thousand seven hundred and fifty-seven* years, till Phaleg, the son of Heber, was born, and the tower of Babel was in building *one hundred* years after the flood, Gen. x. 25; xi. 9. After this, it was used among the Hebrews or Jews, called therefore the *Jews' language*, Isa. xxxvi. 11, until they were carried captive into Baby-

a

A. M. cir. 1757. B. C. cir. 2247. us make brick, and [e] burn them throughly. And they had brick for stone, and slime had they for mortar.
4 And they said, Go to, let us build us a city, and a tower [f] whose top *may reach* unto heaven; and let us make us a name, lest we be scattered abroad upon the face of the whole earth. A. M. cir. 1757 B. C. cir. 2247

[e] Heb. *burn them to a burning.* [f] Deut. i. 28.

lon, where the holy tongue ceased from being commouly used, and the *mixed* Hebrew (or Chaldee) came in its place."

It cannot be reasonably imagined that the Jews lost the Hebrew tongue entirely in the seventy years of their captivity in Babylon; yet, as they were mixed with the Chaldeans, their children would of course learn that dialect, and to *them* the pure Hebrew would be unintelligible; and this probably gave rise to the necessity of explaining the *Hebrew* Scriptures in the *Chaldee* tongue, that the children might understand as well as their fathers. As we may safely presume the parents could not have forgotten the Hebrew, so we may conclude the children in general could not have learned it, as they did not live in an insulated state, but were mixed with the Babylonians. This conjecture removes the difficulty with which many have been embarrassed; one party supposing that the knowledge of the Hebrew language was lost during the Babylonish captivity, and hence the necessity of the Chaldee Targums to explain the Scriptures; another party insisting that this was impossible in so short a period as seventy years.

Verse 2. *As they journeyed from the east*] Assyria, Mesopotamia, and the country on the borders and beyond the Euphrates, are called the *east* in the sacred writings. Balaam said that the king of Moab had brought him *from the mountains of the east*, Num. xxiii. 7. Now it appears, from chap. xxii. 5, that Balaam dwelt at Pethor, on the river Euphrates. And it is very probable that it was from this country that the wise men came to adore Christ; for it is said they came *from the east* to Jerusalem, Matt. ii. 1. Abraham is said to have come *from the east* to Canaan, Isa. xli. 2; but it is well known that he came from *Mesopotamia* and *Chaldea*. Isaiah, xlvi. 11, represents Cyrus as coming *from the east* against Babylon. And the same prophet represents the Syrians as dwelling *eastward* of Jerusalem, chap. ix. 12: *The Syrians before*, מקדם *mikkedem*, *from the east*, the same word which Moses uses here. Daniel ix. 44, represents Antiochus as troubled at news received *from the east;* i. e. of a revolt in the eastern provinces, *beyond the Euphrates.*

Noah and his family, landing after the flood on one of the mountains of Armenia, would doubtless descend and cultivate the valleys: as they increased, they appear to have passed along the banks of the Euphrates, till, at the time specified here, they came to the plains of *Shinar*, allowed to be the most fertile country in the east. See *Calmet.* That *Babel* was built in the land of Shinar we have the authority of the sacred text to prove; and that *Babylon* was built in the same country we have the testimony of Eusebius, Præp. Evang. lib. ix., c. 15; and Josephus, Antiq., lib. i., c. 5.

Verse 3. *Let us make brick*] It appears they were obliged to make use of *brick*, as there was an utter scarcity of *stones* in that district; and on the same account they were obliged to use *slime*, that is, bitumen, (*Vulg.*) ασφαλτος, (*Septuagint*,) for *mortar:* so it appears they had neither common stone nor *lime-stone;* hence they had *brick* for stone, and *asphaltus* or *bitumen* instead of mortar.

Verse 4. *Let us build us a city and a tower*] On this subject there have been various conjectures. Mr. Hutchinson supposed that the design of the builders was to erect a *temple to the host of heaven*—the sun, moon, planets, &c.; and, to support this interpretation, he says וראשו בשמים *verosho bashshamayim* should be translated, not, *whose top* may reach *unto heaven*, for there is nothing for *may reach* in the Hebrew, but *its head* or summit *to the heavens*, i. e. to the heavenly bodies: and, to make this interpretation the more probable, he says that previously to this time the descendants of Noah were all agreed in *one form of religious worship*, (for so he understands ושפה אחת *vesaphah achath, and of one lip*,) i. e. according to him, they had *one litany;* and as God confounded their litany, they began to disagree in their religious opinions, and branched out into sects and parties, each associating with those of his own sentiment; and thus their tower or temple was left unfinished.

It is probable that their being *of one language and of one speech* implies, not only a *sameness* of language, but also a *unity* of sentiment and design, as seems pretty clearly intimated in ver. 6. Being therefore strictly united in all things, coming to the fertile plains of Shinar they proposed to settle themselves there, instead of spreading themselves over all the countries of the earth, according to the design of God; and in reference to this purpose they encouraged one another to build a *city* and a *tower*, probably a *temple*, to prevent their separation, "lest," say they, "we be scattered abroad upon the face of the whole earth:" but God, miraculously interposing, confounded or frustrated their rebellious design, which was inconsistent with his will; see Deut. xxxii. 8; Acts xvii. 26; and, partly by confounding their language, and disturbing their counsels, they could no longer keep in a united state; so that agreeing in nothing but the *necessity of separating*, they went off in different directions, and thus became scattered abroad upon the face of the earth. The Targums, both of *Jonathan ben Uzziel* and of *Jerusalem*, assert that the *tower* was for idolatrous worship; and that they intended to place an image on the top of the tower with a sword in its hand, probably to act as a talisman against their enemies. Whatever *their* design might have been, it is certain that this temple or tower was afterwards devoted to idolatrous purposes. Nebuchadnezzar repaired and beautified this tower, and it was dedicated to *Bel*, or the sun.

An account of this tower, and of the confusion of tongues, is given by several ancient authors. *Herodo-*

A. M. cir. 1757.
B. C. cir. 2247.

5 [g] And the LORD came down to see the city and the tower,
which the children of men builded.
6 And the LORD said, Behold, [h] the people is one, and they have all [i] one language; and this they begin to do: and now nothing will be restrained from them, which they have [k] imagined to do.

A. M. cir. 1757.
B. C. cir. 2247.

[g] Chap. xviii. 21.——[h] Chap. ix. 19; Acts xvii. 26.

[i] Ver. 1.——[k] Psa. ii. 1.

tus saw the tower and described it. A *sybil*, whose oracle is yet extant, spoke both of it and of the confusion of tongues; so did *Eupolemus* and *Abydenus*. See *Bochart* Geogr. Sacr., lib. i., c. 13, edit. 1692. On this point Bochart observes that these things are taken from the Chaldeans, who preserve many remains of ancient facts; and though they often *add* circumstances, yet they are, in general, in some sort dependent on the text. 1. They say Babel was built by the *giants*, because Nimrod, one of the builders, is called in the Hebrew text נבור *gibbor*, a *mighty man;* or, as the Septuagint, γιγας, a *giant*. 2. These giants, they say, sprang from the earth, because, in Gen. x. 11, it is said, *He went*, מן הארץ ההוא *min haarets hahiv, out of that earth;* but this is rather spoken of *Asshur*, who was another of the Babel builders. 3. These giants are said to have waged war with the gods, because it is said of Nimrod, Gen. x. 9, *He was a mighty hunter before the Lord;* or, as others have rendered it, a *warrior and a rebel against the Lord*. See *Jarchi* in loco. 4. These giants are said to have raised a tower up to heaven, as if they had intended to have ascended thither. This appears to have been founded on "*whose top* may reach *to heaven*," which has been already explained. 5. It is said that the gods sent *strong winds* against them, which dispersed both them and their work. This appears to have been taken from the Chaldean history, in which it is said their dispersion was made *to the four winds of heaven*, בארבע רוחי שמיא *bearba ruchey shemaiya*, i. e. to the four quarters of the world. 6. And because the verb פוץ *phuts*, or נפץ *naphats*, used by Moses, signifies, not only to *scatter*, but also to *break to pieces;* whence *thunder*, Isa. xxx. 30, is called נפץ *nephets*, a breaking to pieces; hence they supposed the whole work was *broken to pieces* and overturned. It was probably from this disguised representation of the Hebrew text that the Greek and Roman poets took their fable of the giants waging war with the gods, and piling mountain upon mountain in order to scale heaven. See *Bochart* as above.

Verse 5. *And the Lord came down*] A lesson, says an ancient Jewish commentator, to magistrates to examine every evidence before they decree judgment and execute justice.

Verse 6. *The people is one, &c.*] From this, as before observed, we may infer, that as the people had the same language, so they had a unity of design and sentiment. It is very likely that the original language was composed of monosyllables, that each had a distinct *ideal* meaning, and only *one* meaning; as different acceptations of the same word would undoubtedly arise, either from compounding terms, or, when there were but few words in a language, using them by a different mode of pronunciation to express a variety of things. Where this simple monosyllabic language prevailed (and it must have prevailed in the first ages of the world) men would necessarily have *simple ideas*, and a corresponding *simplicity of manners*. The Chinese language is exactly such as this; and the Hebrew, if stripped of its vowel points, and its prefixes, suffixes, and postfixes separated from their combinations, so that they might stand by themselves, it would nearly answer to this character even in its present state. In order therefore to remove this unity of sentiment and design, which I suppose to be the necessary consequence of such a language, God confounded their language—caused them to articulate the same word differently, to affix different ideas to the same term, and perhaps, by transposing syllables and interchanging letters, form new terms and compounds, so that the mind of the speaker was apprehended by the hearer in a contrary sense to what was intended. This idea is not ill expressed by an ancient French poet, *Du Bartas;* and not badly, though rather *quaintly*, metaphrased by our countryman, Mr. Sylvester.

Some speak *between the teeth*, some in the *nose*,
Some in the *throat* their words do ill dispose . . .

"Bring me," quoth one, "a *trowel*, quickly, quick!"
One brings him up a *hammer*. "*Hew this brick*,"
Another bids; and then they *cleave a tree;*
"*Make fast this rope*," and then they *let it flee*
One calls for *planks*, another *mortar* lacks;
They bear the first a *stone*, the last an *axe*.
One would have *spikes*, and him a *spade* they give;
Another asks a *saw*, and gets a *sieve*.
Thus crossly crost, they *prate* and *point* in vain;
What one hath *made* another *mars* again.

. . . .

These masons then, seeing the storm arrived
Of God's just wrath, all weak and heart-deprived,
Forsake their purpose, and, like frantic fools,
Scatter their stuff and tumble down their tools.
DU BARTAS.—*Babylon*.

I shall not examine how the different languages of the earth were formed. It certainly was not the work of a *moment;* different climates must have a considerable share in the formation of tongues, by their influence on the organs of speech. The invention of new arts and trades must give birth to a variety of terms and expressions. Merchandise, commerce, and the cultivation of the sciences, would produce their share; and different forms of government, modes of life, and means of instruction, also contribute their quota. The *Arabic*, *Chaldee*, *Syriac*, and *Æthiopic*, still bear the most striking resemblance to their parent, the Hebrew. Many others might be reduced to a common source, yet everywhere there is sufficient evidence of this confusion. The anomalies even in the most regular languages sufficiently prove this

A TABLE

SHOWING THE

GENEALOGY OF THE PATRIARCHS,

FROM

ADAM TO JACOB,

(A Period of 2108 Years,)

AND ALSO,

OF [illegible] PATRIARCHS WERE CONTEMPORARY WITH EACH OTHER.

Presented to Dr. Adam Clarke, for his Commentary, by William Blair, Esq.

ADAM was contemporary with	Years	NOAH was contemporary with	Years	SHEM was contemporary with	Years
LAMECH	[illegible]	LAMECH	[illegible]	LAMECH	93
[illegible]	[illegible]	METHUSELAH	[illegible]	METHUSELAH	98
JARED	470		[illegible]	NOAH	448
MAHALALEEL	[illegible]	MAHALALEEL	[illegible]	after the Flood,	
CAINAN	[illegible]	CAINAN	[illegible]	ABRAHAM	150
ENOS	[illegible]	ENOS	84	ISAAC	50

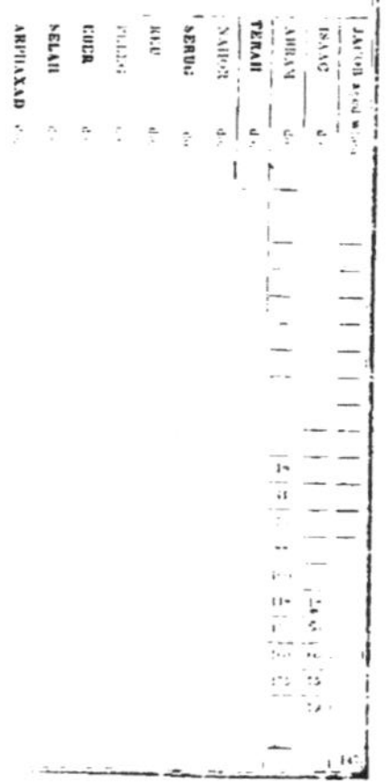

A. M. cir. 1757. B. C. cir. 2247.
7 Go to, [l] let us go down, and there confound their language, that they may [m] not understand one another's speech.

8 So [n] the Lord scattered them abroad from thence [o] upon the face of all the earth: and they left off to build the city.

9 Therefore is the name of it called [p] Babel; [q] because the Lord did there confound the language of all the earth: and from thence did the Lord scatter them abroad upon the face of all the earth.

A. M. 1658. B. C. 2346.
10 [r] These *are* the generations of Shem: Shem *was* a hundred years old, and begat Arphaxad two years after the flood:

A. M. 2158. B. C. 1846.
11 And Shem lived after he begat Arphaxad five hundred years, and begat sons and daughters.

A. M. 1693. B. C. 2311.
12 And Arphaxad lived five and thirty years, [s] and begat Salah:

A. M. 2096. B. C. 1908.
13 And Arphaxad lived after he begat Salah four hundred and three years, and begat sons and daughters.

A. M. 1723. B. C. 2281.
14 And Salah lived thirty years, and begat Eber:

A. M. 2126. B. C. 1878.
15 And Salah lived after he begat Eber four hundred and three years, and begat sons and daughters.

A. M. 1757. B. C. 2247.
16 [t] And Eber lived four and thirty years, and begat [u] Peleg:

17 And Eber lived after he begat Peleg four

[l] Chap. i. 26; Psa. ii. 4; Acts ii. 4, 5, 6.——[m] Chap. xlii. 23; Deut. xxviii. 49; Jer. v. 15; 1 Cor. xiv. 2, 11.——[n] Luke i. 51.——[o] Chap. x. 25, 32.

[p] That is, *confusion*.——[q] Wisd. x. 5; 1 Cor. xiv. 23.——[r] Chap. x. 22; 1 Chron. i. 17.——[s] See Luke iii. 36.——[t] 1 Chron. i. 19.——[u] Called, Luke iii. 35, *Phalec*.

Every language is co[illegible] [illegible] less or more but that eternal truth. This is ever the same; in all countries, climates, and ages, the language of truth, like the God from whom it sprang, is [illegible] [illegible]. It speaks in all tongues, to all nations, and in all hearts: "There is one God, the fountain of [illegible], justice, [illegible]. Man, thou art his [illegible], [illegible], weak, and dependent; but he is all-sufficient—hates nothing that he has made—loves *thee*—is able and willing to save *thee*; return to and depend on *him*, take his revealed will for thy law, submit to his authority, and accept eternal life on the terms proposed in his word, and thou shalt never perish nor be wretched." This language of truth all the ancient and modern Babel builders have not been able to confound, notwithstanding their repeated attempts. How have men laboured to make this language clothe their own ideas; and thus cause God to speak according to the pride, prejudice, and worst passions of men! But through the judgment of God, the language of all those who have attempted to do this has been confounded, and the word of the Lord abideth for ever.

Verse 7. *Go to*] A form of speech which, whatever it might have signified formerly, now means nothing. The Hebrew הבה *habah* signifies *come, make preparation*, as it were for a journey, the execution of a purpose, &c. Almost all the versions understand the word in this way; the Septuagint have δευτε, the Vulgate *venite*, both signifying *come*, or *come ye*. This makes a very good sense, *Come, let us go down, &c.* For the meaning of these latter words see chap. i. 26, and xviii. 21.

Verse 9. *Therefore is the name of it called Babel*] Babel, from בל *bal*, to *mingle, confound, destroy*; hence Babel, from the mingling together and confounding of the projects and language of these descendants of Noah; and this confounding did not so much imply the producing new languages, as giving them a different mode of pronouncing the same words, and leading them to affix different ideas to them.

Besides Mr. Hutchinson's opinion, (see on ver. 4,) there have been [illegible] [illegible] concerning the [illegible] for which this tower was built. Some suppose it was intended to prevent the effects of another flood, by affording an asylum to the builders and their families in case of another general deluge. Others think that it was designed to be a grand city, the seat of government, in order to prevent a general dispersion. This God would not permit, as he had purposed that men should be spread over the earth, and therefore used the means which they were using to prevent it to become the grand instrument of its accomplishment. Humanly speaking, the earth could not have been so speedily peopled, had it not been for this very [illegible] which the [illegible] of man had devised to prevent it. Some say that the families were divided into seventy-two nations, with seventy-two different languages; but this is an [illegible], [illegible] [illegible].

Verse 10. *These are the generations of Shem*] This may be called the *holy family*, as from it sprang *Abraham, Isaac, Jacob*, the [illegible] *patriarchs, David, Solomon*, and all the great progenitors of the Messiah.

We have already seen that the Scripture chronology, as it exists in the Hebrew text, the Samaritan, the Septuagint, Josephus, and some of the fathers, is greatly [illegible]; and it is yet much more so in the various systems of learned and [illegible] chronologists. For a full and [illegible] view of this subject, into which the nature of these notes forbids me farther to enter, I must refer my reader to Dr. Hales's laborious work, "A New Analysis of Sacred Chronology," vol. ii., part 1, &c., in which he enters into the subject with a cautious but firm step; and, if he has not been able to remove all its difficulties, has thrown very considerable light upon most parts of it.

Verse 12. *And Arphaxad lived*] The Septuagint bring in here a second Cainan, with an addition of one hundred and thirty years. St. Luke follows the Septuagint, and brings in the same person in the same way

A. M. cir. 1757. B. C. cir. 2247. 7 Go to, [l] let us go down, and
there confound their language,
that they may [m] not understand one another's
speech.
8 So [n] the LORD scattered them abroad from
thence [o] upon the face of all the earth: and
they left off to build the city.
9 Therefore is the name of it called [p] Babel;
[q] because the LORD did there confound the
language of all the earth: and from thence
did the LORD scatter them abroad upon the
face of all the earth.
A. M. 1658. B. C. 2346. 10 [r] These *are* the generations
of Shem: Shem *was* a hundred
years old, and begat Arphaxad two years after
the flood:
11 And Shem lived after he be- A. M. 2158. B. C. 1846.
gat Arphaxad five hundred years,
and begat sons and daughters.
12 And Arphaxad lived five and A. M. 1693. B. C. 2311.
thirty years, [s] and begat Salah:
13 And Arphaxad lived after he A. M. 2096 B. C. 1908.
begat Salah four hundred and three
years, and begat sons and daughters.
14 And Salah lived thirty years, A. M. 1723. B. C. 2281.
and begat Eber:
15 And Salah lived after he be- A. M. 2126. B. C. 1878.
gat Eber four hundred and three
years, and begat sons and daughters.
16 [t] And Eber lived four and A. M. 1757. B. C. 2247.
thirty years, and begat [u] Peleg:
17 And Eber lived after he begat Peleg four

[l] Chap. i. 26; Psa. ii. 4; Acts ii. 4, 5, 6.——[m] Chap. xlii. 23; Deut. xxviii. 49; Jer. v. 15; 1 Cor. xiv. 2, 11.——[n] Luke i. 51. [o] Chap. x. 25, 32.

[p] That is, *confusion*.——[q] Wisd. x. 5; 1 Cor. xiv. 23.——[r] Chap. x. 22; 1 Chron. i. 17.——[s] See Luke iii. 36.——[t] 1 Chron. i. 19. [u] Called, Luke iii. 35, *Phalec*.

Every language is confounded less or more but that of *eternal truth*. This is ever the same; in all countries, climates, and ages, the language of truth, like that God from whom it sprang, is unchangeable. It speaks in all tongues, to all nations, and in all hearts: "There is one GOD, the fountain of goodness, justice, and truth. MAN, thou art his creature, ignorant, weak, and dependent; but he is all-sufficient—hates nothing that he has made—loves *thee*—is able and willing to save *thee;* return to and depend on *him*, take his revealed will for thy law, submit to his authority, and accept eternal life on the terms proposed in his word, and thou shalt never perish nor be wretched." This language of truth all the ancient and modern Babel builders have not been able to confound, notwithstanding their repeated attempts. How have men toiled to make this language clothe their own ideas; and thus cause God to speak according to the pride, prejudice, and worst passions of men! But through a just judgment of God, the language of all those who have attempted to do this has been confounded, and the word of the Lord abideth for ever.

Verse 7. *Go to*] A form of speech which, whatever it might have signified formerly, now means nothing. The Hebrew הבה *habah* signifies *come, make preparation*, as it were for a journey, the execution of a purpose, &c. Almost all the versions understand the word in this way; the Septuagint have δευτε, the Vulgate *venite*, both signifying *come*, or *come ye*. This makes a very good sense, *Come, let us go down, &c.* For the meaning of these latter words see chap. i. 26, and xviii. 21.

Verse 9. *Therefore is the name of it called Babel*] בבל *babel*, from בל *bal*, to *mingle, confound, destroy;* hence *Babel*, from the mingling together and confounding of the projects and language of these descendants of Noah; and this confounding did not so much imply the producing new languages, as giving them a different method of pronouncing the same words, and leading them to affix different ideas to them.

Besides Mr. Hutchinson's opinion, (see on ver. 4,) there have been various conjectures concerning the purpose for which this tower was built. Some suppose it was intended to prevent the effects of another flood, by affording an asylum to the builders and their families in case of another general deluge. Others think that it was designed to be a grand city, the seat of government, in order to prevent a general dispersion. This God would not permit, as he had purposed that men should be dispersed over the earth, and therefore caused the means which they were using to prevent it to become the grand instrument of its accomplishment. Humanly speaking, the earth could not have been so speedily peopled, had it not been for this very circumstance which the counsel of man had devised to prevent it. Some say that these builders were divided into seventy-two nations, with seventy-two different languages; but this is an idle, unfounded tale.

Verse 10. *These* are *the generations of Shem*] This may be called the *holy family*, as from it sprang *Abraham, Isaac, Jacob*, the *twelve patriarchs, David, Solomon*, and all the great progenitors of the Messiah.

We have already seen that the Scripture chronology, as it exists in the Hebrew text, the Samaritan, the Septuagint, Josephus, and some of the fathers, is greatly embarrassed; and it is yet much more so in the various systems of learned and unlearned chronologists. For a full and rational view of this subject, into which the nature of these notes forbids me farther to enter, I must refer my reader to Dr. Hales's laborious work, "A New Analysis of Sacred Chronology," vol. ii., part I, &c., in which he enters into the subject with a cautious but firm step; and, if he has not been able to remove all its difficulties, has thrown very considerable light upon most parts of it.

Verse 12. *And Arphaxad lived*] The Septuagint bring in here a second Cainan, with an addition of one hundred and thirty years. St. Luke follows the Septuagint, and brings in the same person in the same way,

A. M. 2187. B. C. 1817. hundred and thirty years, and begat
sons and daughters.
A. M. 1787. B. C. 2217. 18 And Peleg lived thirty years,
and begat Reu:
A. M. 1996. B. C. 2008. 19 And Peleg lived after he begat Reu two hundred and nine
years, and begat sons and daughters.
A. M. 1819. B. C. 2185. 20 And Reu lived two and thirty
years, and begat [v] Serug:
A. M. 2026. B. C. 1978. 21 And Reu lived after he begat
Serug two hundred and seven years,
and begat sons and daughters.
A. M. 1849. B. C. 2155. 22 And Serug lived thirty years,
and begat Nahor:
A. M. 2049. B. C. 1955. 23 And Serug lived after he begat Nahor two hundred years, and
begat sons and daughters.
A. M. 1878. B. C. 2126. 24 And Nahor lived nine and
twenty years, and begat [w] Terah:
A. M. 1997. B. C. 2007. 25 And Nahor lived after he begat Terah a hundred and nineteen
years, and begat sons and daughters.
26 And Terah lived seventy years,
and [x] begat Abram, Nahor, and A. M. 1948. B. C. 2056.
Haran.
27 Now these *are* the generations A. M. 2008. B. C. 1996.
of Terah: Terah begat Abram,
Nahor, and Haran; and Haran begat Lot.
28 And Haran died before his father Terah in
the land of his nativity, in Ur of the Chaldees.
29 And Abram and Nahor took them wives:
the name of Abram's wife *was* [y] Sarai: and
the name of Nahor's [z] wife, Milcah, the
daughter of Haran, the father of Milcah, and
the father of Iscah.
30 But [a] Sarai was barren; she *had* no child.
31 And Terah [b] took Abram A. M. cir. 2078. B. C. cir. 1926.
his son, and Lot the son of
Haran his son's son, and Sarai his daughter-
in-law, his son Abram's wife; and they went
forth with them from [c] Ur of the Chaldees,
to go into [d] the land of Canaan; and they
came unto Haran, and dwelt there.
32 And the days of Terah A. M. 2083. B. C. 1921.
were two hundred and five years:
and Terah died in Haran.

---

[v] Luke iii. 35, *Saruch*.——[w] Luke iii. 34, *Thara*.——[x] Josh. xxiv. 2; 1 Chron. i. 26.——[y] Chap. xvii. 15; xx. 12.——[z] Chap. xxii. 20.

[a] Chap. xvi. 1, 2; xviii. 11, 12.——[b] Chap. xii. 1.——[c] Neh. ix. 7; Judith v. 7; Acts vii. 4; Heb. xi. 8.——[d] Chap. x. 19; xxiv. 10; xxix. 4.

But the Hebrew text, both here and in 1 Chron. i., is perfectly silent on this subject, and the best chronologists have agreed in rejecting this as a spurious generation.

Verse 26. *And Terah lived seventy years, and begat Abram, Nahor, and Haran.*] Haran was certainly the eldest son of Terah, and he appears to have been born when Terah was about seventy years of age, and his birth was followed in successive periods with those of *Nahor* his second, and *Abram* his *youngest* son. Many have been greatly puzzled with the account here, supposing because Abram is mentioned *first*, that therefore he was the *eldest* son of Terah: but he is only put first by way of *dignity*. An instance of this we have already seen, chap. v. 32, where Noah is represented as having *Shem, Ham*, and *Japheth* in this order of succession; whereas it is evident from other scriptures that *Shem* was the *youngest* son, who for dignity is named *first*, as Abram is here; and *Japheth* the *eldest*, named *last*, as *Haran* is here. Terah died two hundred and five years old, ver. 32; then Abram departed from Haran when seventy-five years old, chap. xii. 4; therefore Abram was born, not when his father Terah was seventy, but when he was one hundred and thirty.

When any case of dignity or pre-eminence is to be marked, then even the *youngest son* is set before all the rest, though contrary to the usage of the Scriptures in other cases. Hence we find *Shem*, the youngest son of Noah, always mentioned first; *Moses* is mentioned before his elder brother *Aaron;* and *Abram* before his two elder brethren *Haran* and *Nahor*. These observations are sufficient to remove all difficulty from this place.

Verse 29. *Milcah, the daughter of Haran*] Many suppose *Sarai* and *Iscah* are the same person under two different names; but this is improbable, as *Iscah* is expressly said to be the daughter of Haran, and *Sarai* was the daughter of Terah, and half sister of Abram.

Verse 31. *They went forth—from Ur of the Chaldees*] Chaldea is sometimes understood as comprising the whole of Babylonia; at other times, that province towards *Arabia Deserta*, called in Scripture *The land of the Chaldeans*. The capital of this place was *Babylon*, called in Scripture *The beauty of the Chaldees' excellency*, Isa. xiii. 19.

Ur appears to have been a city of some considerable consequence at that time in Chaldea; but *where* situated is not well known. It probably had its name *Ur* אור, which signifies *fire*, from the *worship* practised there. The learned are almost unanimously of opinion that the ancient inhabitants of this region were *ignicolists* or *worshippers of fire*, and in that place this sort of worship probably *originated;* and in honour of this element, the symbol of the Supreme Being, the whole *country*, or a particular *city* in it, might have had the name *Ur*. Bochart has observed that there is a place called *Ouri*, south of the Euphrates, in the way from Nisibis to the river Tigris. The Chaldees mentioned here had not this name in the time *of which* Moses *speaks*, but they were called so in the time *in which*

Moses *wrote*. *Chesed* was the son of Nahor, the son of Terah, chap. xxii. 22. From Chesed descended the *Chasdim*, whose language was the same as that of the *Amorites*, Dan. i. 4; ii. 4. These *Chasdim*, whence the Χαλδαιοι, *Chaldeans*, of the *Septuagint*, *Vulgate*, and all later versions, afterwards settled on the south of the Euphrates. Those who dwelt in *Ur* were either priests or astronomers, Dan. ii. 10, and also idolaters, Josh. xxiv. 2, 3, 14, 15. And because they were much addicted to astronomy, and probably to judicial astrology, hence all astrologers were, in process of time, called *Chaldeans*, Dan. ii. 2–5.

The building of Babel, the confusion of tongues, and the first call of Abram, are *three* remarkable particulars in this chapter; and these led to the accomplishment of *three* grand and important *designs:* 1. The peopling of the whole earth; 2. The preservation of the true religion by the means of one family; and 3. The preservation of the line uncorrupted by which the Messiah should come. When God makes a discovery of himself by a particular revelation, it must begin in some particular *time*, and be given to some particular *person*, and in some particular *place*. *Where*, *when*, and to *whom*, are comparatively matters of small importance. It is God's gift; and his own wisdom must determine the *time*, the *person*, and the *place*. But if this be the case, have not others cause to complain because not thus favoured? Not at all, unless the favouring of the one *for a time* should necessarily cut off the others *for ever*. But this is not the case. Abram was first favoured; that *time*, that *country*, and that *person* were chosen by infinite wisdom, for *there* and *then* God chose to commence these mighty operations of Divine goodness. Isaac and Jacob also received the promises, the twelve patriarchs through their father, and the whole Jewish people through them. Afterwards the designs of God's endless mercy were more particularly unfolded; and the word, which seemed to be confined for two thousand years to the descendants of a single family, bursts forth on all hands, salvation is preached to the Gentiles, and thus in Abram's seed all the nations of the earth are blessed. Hence none can find fault, and none can have cause to complain; as the salvation which for a time *appeared* to be restricted to a few, is now on the authority of God, liberally offered to the whole human race!

CHAPTER XII.

God calls Abram to leave Haran and go into Canaan, 1; *promises to bless him, and through him all the families of the earth*, 2, 3. *Abram, Sarai, Lot, and all their household, depart for Canaan*, 4, 5; *pass through Sichem*, 6. *God appears to him, and renews the promise*, 7. *His journey described*, 8, 9. *On account of a famine in the land he is obliged to go into Egypt*, 10. *Fearing lest, on account of the beauty of his wife, the Egyptians should kill him, he desires her not to acknowledge that she is his wife, but* only *his sister*, 11–13. *Sarai, because of her beauty, is taken into the palace of Pharaoh, king of Egypt, who is very liberal to Abram on her account*, 14–16. *God afflicts Pharaoh and his household with grievous plagues on account of Sarai*, 17. *Pharaoh, on finding that Sarai was Abram's wife, restores her honourably, and dismisses the patriarch with his family and their property*, 18–20.

A. M. 2083. B. C. 1921.

NOW the [a] LORD had said unto Abram, Get thee out of thy country, and from thy kindred, and from thy father's house, unto a land that I will show thee:

2 [b] And I will make of thee a great nation,

[a] Chap. xv. 7; Neh. ix. 7; Isa. xli. 2; Acts vii. 3; Heb. xi. 8. — [b] Chapter xvii. 6; xviii. 18; Deut. xxvi. 5; 1 Kings iii. 8.

NOTES ON CHAP. XII.

Verse 1. *Get thee out of thy country*] There is great dissension between commentators concerning the *call* of Abram; some supposing he had *two* distinct calls, others that he had but *one*. At the conclusion of the preceding chapter, ver. 31, we find Terah and all his family leaving Ur of the Chaldees, in order to go to Canaan. This was, no doubt, in consequence of some Divine admonition. While resting at Haran, on their road to Canaan, Terah died, chap. xi. 32; and then God repeats his call to Abram, and orders him to proceed to Canaan, chap. xii. 1.

Dr. Hales, in his Chronology, contends for *two* calls: "The first," says he, "is omitted in the Old Testament, but is particularly recorded in the New, Acts vii. 2–4: *The God of glory appeared to our father Abraham while he was* (at Ur of the Chaldees) *in Mesopotamia*, BEFORE HE DWELT IN CHARRAN; *and said unto him, Depart from thy land, and from thy kindred, and come into the land* (γην, *a land*) *which I will show thee.* Hence it is evident that God *had* called Abram *before* he came to Haran or Charran." The SECOND CALL is recorded only in this chapter: "The Lord said (not HAD said) unto Abram, Depart from *thy land*, and from *thy kindred*, and from *thy father's house*, unto THE LAND, הארץ HA-*arets*, (Septuagint, THN γην,) which I will show thee." "The difference of the two calls," says Dr. Hales, "more carefully translated from the originals, is obvious: in the former the *land* is *indefinite*, which was designed only for a *temporary* residence; in the latter it is *definite*, intimating his abode. A third condition is also annexed to the latter, that Abram shall now separate himself from *his father's house*, or leave his brother Nahor's family behind at Charran. This call Abram obeyed, still *not knowing whither he was going*, but trusting implicitly to the Divine guidance."

Thy kindred] Nahor and the different branches

A. M. 2083. B. C. 1921. [c] and I will bless thee, and make thy name great; [d] and thou shalt be a blessing:

3 [e] And I will bless them that bless thee, and curse him that curseth thee: [f] and in thee shall all families of the earth be blessed.

4 So Abram departed, as the LORD had spoken unto him; and Lot went with him: and Abram *was* seventy and five years old when he departed out of Haran.

5 And Abram took Sarai his wife, and Lot his brother's son, and all their substance that they had gathered, and [g] the souls that they had gotten [h] in Haran; and they went forth to go into the land of Canaan; and into the land of Canaan they came. A. M. 2083. B. C. 1921.

6 And Abram [i] passed through the land unto the place of Sichem, [k] unto the plain of Moreh. [l] And the Canaanite *was* then in the land.

7 [m] And the LORD appeared unto Abram, and said, [n] Unto thy seed will I give this land: and there builded he an [o] altar unto the LORD, who appeared unto him.

[c] Chap. xxiv. 35.——[d] Chap. xxviii. 4; Gal. iii. 14.——[e] Chap. xxvii. 29; Exod. xxiii. 22; Num. xxiv. 9.——[f] Chap. xviii. 18; xxii. 18; xxvi. 4; Psa. lxxii. 17; Acts iii. 25; Gal. iii. 8

[g] Chap. xiv. 14.——[h] Chap. xi. 31.——[i] Heb. xi. 9.——[k] Deut. xi. 30; Judg. vii. 1.——[l] Chap. x. 18, 19; xiii. 7.——[m] Chap. xvii. 1.——[n] Chap. xiii. 15; xvii. 8; Psa. cv. 9, 11.——[o] Chap. xiii. 4.

of the family of Terah, Abram and Lot excepted. That Nahor went with Terah and Abram as far as Padan-Aram, in Mesopotamia, and settled there, so that it was afterwards called *Nahor's city*, is sufficiently evident from the ensuing history, see chap. xxv. 20; xxiv. 10, 15; and that the same land was *Haran*, see chap. xxviii. 2, 10, and *there* were Abram's *kindred* and *country* here spoken of, chap. xxiv. 4.

Thy father's house] Terah being now dead, it is very probable that the family were determined to go no farther, but to settle at Charran; and as Abram might have felt inclined to stop with them in this place, hence the ground and necessity of the *second call* recorded here, and which is introduced in a very remarkable manner; לך לך *lech lecha*, GO FOR THYSELF. If none of the family will accompany thee, yet go for thyself unto THAT LAND *which I will show thee.* God does not tell him *what* land it is, that he may still cause him to walk by faith and not by sight. This seems to be particularly alluded to by Isaiah, chap. xli. 2: *Who raised up the righteous man* (Abram) *from the east, and called him to his foot;* that is, to *follow implicitly* the Divine direction. The apostle assures us that in all this Abram had spiritual views; he looked for a better country, and considered the land of promise only as typical of the heavenly inheritance.

Verse 2. *I will make of thee a great nation*] i. e., The Jewish people; *and make thy name great,* alluding to the change of his name from *Abram*, a high father, to *Abraham*, the father of a multitude.

Verse 3. *In thee*] In thy posterity, in the *Messiah*, who shall spring from thee, shall all families of the earth be blessed; for as he shall take on him human nature from the posterity of Abraham, he shall taste death for every man, his Gospel shall be preached throughout the world, and innumerable blessings be derived on all mankind through his *death* and *intercession.*

Verse 4. *And Abram was seventy and five years old*] As Abram was now seventy-five years old, and his father Terah had just died, at the age of two hundred and five, consequently Terah must have been one hundred and thirty when Abram was born; and the seventieth year of his age mentioned Gen. xi. 26, was the period at which *Haran*, not *Abram*, was born. See on the preceding chapter.

Verse 5. *The souls that they had gotten in Haran*] This may apply either to the persons who were employed in the service of Abram, or to the persons he had been the instrument of converting to the knowledge of the true God; and in this latter sense the Chaldee paraphrasts understood the passage, translating it, *The souls of those whom they proselyted in Haran.*

They went forth to go into the land of Canaan] A good land, possessed by a bad people, who for their iniquities were to be expelled, see Lev. xviii. 25. And this land was made a type of the kingdom of God. Probably the whole of this transaction may have a farther meaning than that which appears in the letter. As Abram left his own country, father's house, and kindred, took at the command of God a journey to this promised land, nor ceased till he arrived in it; so should we cast aside every weight, come out from among the workers of iniquity, set out for the kingdom of God, nor ever rest till we reach the heavenly country. How many set out for the kingdom of heaven, make good progress for a time in their journey, but halt before the race is finished! Not so Abram; *he went forth to go into the land of Canaan, and into the land of Canaan he came.* Reader, go thou and do likewise.

Verse 6. *The plain of Moreh.*] אלון *elon* should be translated *oak*, not *plain*; the Septuagint translate την δρυν την ὑψηλην, *the lofty oak*; and it is likely the place was remarkable for a grove of those trees, or for one of a stupendous height and bulk.

The Canaanite was *then in the land.*] This is thought to be an interpolation, because it is supposed that these words must have been written *after* the Canaanites were expelled from the land by the Israelites under Joshua; but this by no means follows. All that Moses states is simply that, at the time in which Abram passed through Sichem, the land was inhabited by the descendants of Canaan, which was a perfectly possible case, and involves neither a contradiction nor absurdity. There is no rule of criticism by which these words can be produced as an evidence of interpolation or incorrectness in the statement of the sacred historian. See this mentioned again, chap. xiii. 7.

Verse 7. *The Lord appeared*] In what way this appearance was made we know not; it was probably by the great angel of the covenant, Jesus the Christ

A. M. 2083. B. C. 1921. 8 And he removed from thence
unto a mountain on the east of
Beth-el, and pitched his tent, *having* Beth-el
on the west, and Hai on the east: and there
he builded an altar unto the LORD, and [p] called
upon the name of the LORD.
9 And Abram journeyed, [q] going [r] on still
toward the south.
A. M. cir. 2084. B. C. cir. 1920. 10 And there was [s] a famine
in the land; and Abram [t] went
down into Egypt to sojourn there, for the
famine *was* [u] grievous in the land.
11 And it came to pass, when A. M. cir. 2084. B. C. cir. 1920.
he was come near to enter into
Egypt, that he said unto Sarai his wife, Behold now, I know that thou *art* [v] a fair woman to look upon:
12 Therefore it shall come to pass, when the
Egyptians shall see thee, that they shall say,
This *is* his wife: and they [w] will kill me, but
they will save thee alive.
13 [x] Say, I pray thee, thou *art* my sister:
that it may be well with me for thy sake; and
my soul shall live because of thee.

[p] Chap. xiii. 4.——[q] Heb. *in going and journeying.*——[r] Chap. xiii. 3.——[s] Chap. xxvi. 1.——[t] Psa. cv. 13.

[u] Chap. xliii. 1.——[v] Ver. 14; chap. xxvi. 7.——[w] Chap. xx. 11; xxvi. 7.——[x] Chap. xx. 5, 13; see chap. xxvi. 7.

The appearance, whatsoever it was, perfectly satisfied Abram, and proved itself to be supernatural and Divine. It is worthy of remark that Abram is the *first* man to whom God is said to have *shown* himself or *appeared:* 1. In *Ur* of the *Chaldees*, Acts vii. 2; and 2. At the *oak of Moreh*, as in this verse. As מורה *Moreh* signifies a *teacher*, probably this was called the *oak of Moreh* or *the teacher*, because God manifested himself here, and *instructed* Abram concerning the future possession of that land by his posterity, and the dispensation of the mercy of God to all the families of the earth through the promised Messiah. See on chap. xv. 7.

Verse 8. *Beth-el*] The place which was afterwards called *Beth-el* by Jacob, for its first name was *Luz*. See chap. xxviii. 19. בית אל *beith El* literally signifies *the house of God*.

And pitched his tent—and—builded an altar unto the Lord] Where Abram has a *tent*, there God must have an ALTAR, as he well knows there is no safety but under the Divine protection. How few who build houses ever think on the propriety and necessity of building an altar to their Maker! The house in which the worship of God is not established cannot be considered as under the Divine protection.

And called upon the name of the Lord.] Dr. Shuckford strongly contends that קרא בשם *kara beshem* does not signify to *call* ON *the name*, but to *invoke* IN *the name*. So Abram *invoked Jehovah in* or *by the name of Jehovah*, who had appeared to him. He was taught even in these early times to approach God through a Mediator; and that Mediator, since manifested in the flesh, was known by the name Jehovah. Does not our Lord allude to such a discovery as this when he says, *Abraham rejoiced to see my day; and he saw it, and was glad?* John viii. 56. Hence it is evident that he was informed that the Christ should be born of his seed, that the nations of the world should be blessed through him; and is it then to be wondered at if he invoked God in the name of this great Mediator?

Verse 10. *There was a famine in the land*] Of Canaan. This is the first famine on record, and it prevailed in the most fertile land then under the sun; and why? God made it desolate for the wickedness of those who dwelt in it.

Went down into Egypt] He felt himself a stranger and a pilgrim, and by his unsettled state was kept in mind of the city that hath foundations that are permanent and stable, whose builder is the living God. See Heb. xi. 8, 9.

Verse 11. *Thou* art *a fair woman to look upon*] Widely differing in her *complexion* from the swarthy Egyptians, and consequently more likely to be coveted by them. It appears that Abram supposed they would not scruple to take away the life of the husband in order to have the undisturbed possession of the wife. The age of Sarai at this time is not well agreed on by commentators, some making her *ninety*, while others make her only *sixty-five*. From chap. xvii. 17, we learn that Sarai was ten years younger than Abram, for she was but *ninety* when he was *one hundred*. And from ver. 4 of chap. xii. we find that Abram was *seventy-five* when he was called to leave Haran and go to Canaan, at which time Sarai could be only *sixty five;* and if the transactions recorded in the preceding verses took place in the course of that year, which I think possible, consequently Sarai was but *sixty-five;* and as in those times people lived much longer, and *disease* seems to have had but a very contracted influence, women and men would necessarily arrive more slowly at a state of perfection, and retain their vigour and complexion much longer, than in later times. We may add to these considerations that *strangers* and *foreigners* are more coveted by the licentious than those who are *natives*. This has been amply illustrated in the West Indies and in America, where the *jetty, monkey-faced* African women are preferred to the elegant and beautiful Europeans! To this subject a learned British traveller elegantly applied those words of Virgil, Ecl. ii., ver. 18:—

Alba ligustra cadunt, vaccinia nigra leguntur.

White lilies lie *neglected* on the plain,
While *dusky hyacinths* for *use* remain. DRYDEN.

Verse 13. *Say, I pray thee, thou* art *my sister*] Abram did not wish his wife to tell a *falsehood*, but he wished her to suppress a part of the *truth*. From chap. xx. 12, it is evident she was his *step-sister*, i. e., his sister by his *father*, but by a different *mother*. Some suppose Sarai was the daughter of Haran, and

A. M. cir. 2084.
B. C. cir. 1920.

14 And it came to pass that, when Abram was come into Egypt, the Egyptians [y] beheld the woman that she *was* very fair.

15 The princes also of Pharaoh saw her, and commended her before Pharaoh; and the woman was [z] taken into Pharaoh's house.

16 And he [a] entreated Abram well for her sake: and he had sheep, and oxen, and he-asses, and men-servants, and maid-servants, and she-asses, and camels.

17 And the LORD [b] plagued Pharaoh and his house with great plagues, because of Sarai, Abram's wife.

A. M. cir. 2084.
B. C. cir. 1920.

18 And Pharaoh called Abram, and said, [c] What *is* this *that* thou hast done unto me? why didst thou not tell me that she *was* thy wife?

19 Why saidst thou, She *is* my sister? so I might have taken her to me to wife: now therefore behold thy wife, take *her*, and go thy way.

20 [d] And Pharaoh commanded *his* men concerning him: and they sent him away, and his wife, and all that he had.

[y] Chap. xxxix. 7; Matt. v. 28.——[z] Chap. xx. 2.——[a] Chap. xx. 14.

[b] Chap. xx. 18; 1 Chron. xvi. 21; Psa. cv. 14; Heb. xiii.——[c] Chap. xx. 9; xxvi. 10.——[d] Prov. xxi. 1.

consequently the *grand-daughter* of *Terah:* this opinion seems to be founded on chap. xi. 29, where *Iscah* is thought to be the same with Sarai, but the supposition has not a sufficiency of probability to support it.

Verse 15. *The woman was taken into Pharaoh's house.*] *Pharaoh* appears to have been the common appellative of the Cuthite shepherd kings of Egypt, who had conquered this land, as is conjectured, about seventy-two years before this time. The word is supposed to signify *king* in the ancient Egyptian language. If the meaning be sought in the Hebrew, the root פרע *para* signifies *to be free* or *disengaged*, a name which such *freebooters* as the Cuthite shepherds might naturally assume. All the kings of Egypt bore this name till the commencement of the Grecian monarchy, after which they were called *Ptolemies*.

When a woman was brought into the seraglio or haram of the eastern princes, she underwent for a considerable time certain purifications before she was brought into the king's presence. It was in this *interim* that God *plagued Pharaoh and his house with plagues*, so that Sarai was restored before she could have been taken to the bed of the Egyptian king.

Verse 16. *He had sheep, and oxen, &c.*] As some of these terms are liable to be confounded, and as they frequently occur, especially in the Pentateuch, it may be necessary to consider and fix their meaning in this place.

SHEEP; צאן *tson*, from *tsaan*, to be *plentiful* or *abundant;* a proper term for the eastern sheep, which almost constantly bring forth *twins*, Cant. iv. 2, and sometimes *three* and even *four* at a birth. Hence their great fruitfulness is often alluded to in the Scripture. See Psa. lxv. 13; cxliv. 13. But under this same term, which almost invariably means a *flock*, both *sheep* and *goats* are included. So the Romans include *sheep, goats*, and *small cattle* in general, under the term PECUS *pecoris;* so likewise they do larger cattle under that of PECUS *pecudis*.

OXEN; בקר *bakar*, from the root, to *examine, look out*, because of the full, broad, steady, unmoved look of most animals of the *beeve* kind; and hence the *morning* is termed *boker*, because of the light springing out of the east, and *looking out* over the whole of the earth's surface.

HE-ASSES; חמרים *chamorim*, from חמר *chamar*, to be *disturbed, muddy;* probably from the dull, stupid appearance of this animal, as if it were always affected with melancholy. *Scheuchzer* thinks the *sandy-coloured* domestic Asiatic ass is particularly intended. The word is applied to *asses* in general, though most frequently restrained to those of the *male kind*.

SHE-ASSES; אתנת *athonoth*, from אתן *ethan*, strength, probably the *strong animal*, as being superior in muscular force to every other animal of its size. Under this term both the male and female are sometimes understood.

CAMELS; גמלים *gemallim*, from גמל *gamal*, to *recompense, return, repay;* so called from its resentment of injuries, and revengeful temper, for which it is proverbial in the countries of which it is a native. On the animals and natural history in general, of the Scriptures, I must refer to the *Hierozoicon* of BOCHART, and the *Physica Sacra* of SCHEUCHZER. The former is the most learned and accurate work, perhaps, ever produced by one man.

From this enumeration of the riches of Abram we may conclude that this patriarch led a pastoral and itinerant life; that his *meat* must have chiefly consisted in the flesh of clean animals, with a sufficiency of pulse for bread; that his chief *drink* was their *milk;* his clothing, their *skins;* and his beasts of burden, *asses* and *camels;* (for as yet we read of no *horses;*) and the ordinary employment of his servants, to take care of the flocks, and to serve their master. Where the patriarchs became resident for any considerable time, they undoubtedly cultivated the ground to produce grain.

Verse 17. *The Lord plagued Pharaoh*] What these plagues were we know not. In the parallel case, chap. xx. 18, all the females in the family of Abimelech, who had taken Sarah in nearly the same way, were made barren; possibly this might have been the case here; yet much more seems to be signified by the expression *great plagues*. Whatever these plagues were, it is evident they were understood by Pharaoh as proofs of the disapprobation of God; and, consequently, even at this time in Egypt there was some knowledge of the primitive and true religion.

Verse 20. *Commanded* his *men concerning him*] Gave particular and strict orders to afford Abram and his family every accommodation for their journey; for,

having received a great increase of cattle and servants, it was necessary that he should have the favour of the king, and his permission to remove from Egypt with so large a property; hence, a particular charge is given to the officers of Pharaoh to treat him with respect, and to assist him in his intended departure.

The weighty and important contents of this chapter demand our most attentive consideration. Abram is a *second time* called to leave his country, kindred, and father's house, and go to a place he knew not. Every thing was apparently against him but the voice of God. This to Abram was sufficient; he could trust his Maker, and knew he could not do wrong in following his command. He is therefore proposed to us in the Scriptures as a pattern of faith, patience, and loving obedience. When he received the call of God, he spent no time in useless reasonings about the call itself, his family circumstances, the difficulties in the way, &c., &c. He was *called*, and he *departed*, and this is all we hear on the subject. *Implicit faith* in the promise of God, and *prompt obedience* to his commands, become us, not only as HIS *creatures*, but as *sinners* called to separate from evil workers and wicked ways, and travel, by that faith which worketh by love, in the way that leads to the paradise of God.

How greatly must the faith of this blessed man have been tried, when, coming to the very land in which he is promised so much blessedness, he finds instead of plenty a *grievous famine!* Who in his circumstances would not have gone back to his own country, and kindred? Still he is not stumbled; prudence directs him to turn aside and go to Egypt, till God shall choose to remove this famine. Is it to be wondered at that, in this *tried* state, he should have serious apprehensions for the safety of his life? Sarai, his affectionate wife and faithful companion, he supposes he shall lose; her beauty, he suspects, will cause her to be desired by men of power, whose will he shall not be able to resist. If he appear to be her *husband*, his death he supposes to be certain; if she pass for his *sister*, he may be well used on her account; he will not *tell a lie*, but he is tempted to *prevaricate* by suppressing a *part* of the truth. Here is a weakness which, however we may be inclined to pity and excuse it, we should never imitate. It is recorded with its own condemnation. He should have risked all rather than have prevaricated. But how could he think of lightly giving up *such a wife?* Surely he who would not risk his life for the protection and safety of a good wife, is not worthy of one. Here his faith was deficient. He still credited the *general promise*, and acted on that faith in reference to *it;* but he did not use his faith in reference to *intervening circumstances*, to which it was equally applicable. Many trust God for their *souls* and *eternity*, who do not trust in him for their *bodies* and for *time*. To him who follows God fully in simplicity of heart, every thing must ultimately succeed. Had Abram and Sarai simply passed for *what they were*, they had incurred no danger; for God, who had obliged them to go to Egypt, had prepared the way before them. Neither Pharaoh nor his courtiers would have noticed the woman, had she appeared to be the *wife* of the *stranger* that came to sojourn in their land. The issue sufficiently proves this. Every ray of the light of truth is an emanation from the holiness of God, and awfully sacred in his eyes. Considering the subject thus, a pious ancient spoke the following words, which refiners in prevarication have deemed by much *too strong:* "I would not," said he, "tell a lie to save the souls of the whole world." Reader, be on thy guard; thou mayest fall by comparatively small matters, while resolutely and successfully resisting those which require a giant's strength to counteract them. In every concern God is necessary; seek him for the *body* and for the *soul;* and do not think that any thing is too small or insignificant to interest him that concerns thy present or eternal peace.

CHAPTER XIII.

Abram and his family return out of Egypt to Canaan, 1, 2. *He revisits Beth-el, and there invokes the Lord,* 3, 4. *In consequence of the great increase in the flocks of Abram and Lot, their herdmen disagree; which obliges the patriarch and his nephew to separate,* 5–9. *Lot being permitted to make his choice of the land, chooses the plains of Jordan,* 10, 11, *and pitches his tent near to Sodom, while Abram abides in Canaan,* 12 *Bad character of the people of Sodom,* 13. *The Lord renews his promise to Abram,* 14–17. *Abram removes to the plains of Mamre, near Hebron, and builds an altar to the Lord,* 18.

A. M. cir. 2086.
B. C. cir. 1918.

AND Abram went up out of Egypt, he, and his wife, and all that he had, and Lot with him, [a] into the south.

2 [b] And Abram *was* very rich in cattle, in silver, and in gold.

[a] Chap. xii. 9.

[b] Chap. xxiv. 35; Psa. cxii. 3; Prov. x. 22.

NOTES ON CHAP. XIII.

Verse 1. *Abram went up out of Egypt—into the south.*] Probably the south of *Canaan*, as in leaving Egypt he is said to come *from the south*, ver. 3, for the southern part of the promised land lay north-east of Egypt.

Verse 2. *Abram* was *very rich*] The property of these patriarchal times did not consist in *flocks* only, but also in *silver* and *gold;* and in all these respects Abram was כבד מאד *cabed meod*, exceeding rich. Josephus says that a part of this property was acquired by teaching the Egyptians arts and sciences. Thus

A. M. cir. 2086. B. C. cir. 1918.

3 And he went on his journeys
[c] from the south even to Beth-el,
unto the place where his tent had been at the
beginning, between Beth-el and Hai;
4 Unto the [d] place of the altar, which he
had made there at the first: and there Abram
[e] called on the name of the LORD.
5 And Lot also, which went with Abram,
had flocks, and herds, and tents.
6 And [f] the land was not able to bear them,
that they might dwell together: for their substance
was great, so that they could not dwell
together.
7 And there was [g] a strife between the herdmen
of Abram's cattle and the herdmen of
Lot's cattle: [h] and the Canaanite and the
Perizzite dwelled then in the land.
8 And Abram said unto Lot, [i] Let there be
no strife, I pray thee, between me and thee,
and between my herdmen and thy herdmen;
for we *be* [k] brethren.
9 [l] *Is* not the whole land before
thee? separate thyself, I pray
thee, from me: [m] if *thou wilt take* the left
hand, then I will go to the right; or if *thou
depart* to the right hand, then I will go to
the left.

A. M. cir. 2087. B. C. cir. 1917.

10 And Lot lifted up his eyes,
and beheld all [n] the plain of
Jordan, that it *was* well watered every where,
before the LORD [o] destroyed Sodom and
Gomorrah, [p] *even* as the garden of the LORD,
like the land of Egypt, as thou comest unto
[q] Zoar.
11 Then Lot chose him all the plain of
Jordan; and Lot journeyed east: and they
separated themselves the one from the other.
12 Abram dwelled in the land of Canaan,
and Lot [r] dwelled in the cities of the plain,
and [s] pitched *his* tent toward Sodom.
13 But the men of Sodom [t] *were* wicked and
[u] sinners before the LORD exceedingly.

---

[c] Chap. xii. 8, 9.—[d] Chap. xii. 7, 8.—[e] Psa. cxvi. 17.—[f] Chap. xxxvi. 7.—[g] Chap. xxvi. 20.—[h] Chap. xii. 6.—[i] 1 Cor. vi. 7.—[k] Heb. *men brethren*; see chap. xi. 27, 31; Exod. ii. 13; Psa. cxxxiii. 1; Acts vii. 26.—[l] Chap. xx. 15; xxxiv. 10.—[m] Rom. xii. 18; Heb. xii. 14; James iii. 17.

[n] Chap. xix. 17; Deut. xxxiv. 3; Psa. cvii. 34.—[o] Chapter xix. 24, 25.—[p] Chap. ii. 10; Isa. li. 3.—[q] Chap. xiv. 2, 8; xix. 22.—[r] Chap. xix. 29.—[s] Chap. xiv. 12; xix. 1; 2 Pet. ii. 7, 8.—[t] Chap. xviii. 20; Ezek. xvi. 49; 2 Pet. ii. 7, 8.—[u] Chap. vi. 11.

---

did God fulfil his promises to him, by protecting and giving him a great profusion of temporal blessings, which were to him signs and pledges of spiritual things.

Verse 3. *Beth-el*] See chap. 8.

Verse 6. *Their substance was great*] As their families increased, it was necessary their flocks should increase also, as from those flocks they derived their clothing, food, and drink. Many also were offered in sacrifice to God.

They could not dwell together] 1. Because their flocks were great. 2. Because the Canaanites and the Perizzites had already occupied a considerable part of the land. 3. Because there appears to have been *envy* between the herdmen of Abram and Lot. To prevent disputes among them, that might have ultimately disturbed the peace of the two families, it was necessary that a separation should take place.

Verse 7. *The Canaanite and the Perizzite dwelled then in the land.*] That is, they were *there* at the time Abram and Lot came to fix their tents in the land. See on chap. xii. 6.

Verse 8. *For we* be *brethren.*] We are of the same family, worship the same God in the same way, have the same promises, and look for the same end. Why then should there be strife? If it appear to be unavoidable from our present situation, let that situation be instantly changed, for no secular advantages can counterbalance the loss of peace.

Verse 9. Is *not the whole land before thee?*] As the patriarch or head of the family, Abram, by prescriptive right, might have *chosen* his own portion first, and *appointed* Lot his; but intent upon peace, and feeling pure and parental affection for his nephew, he permitted him to make his choice first.

Verse 10. *Like the land of Egypt, as thou comest unto Zoar.*] There is an obscurity in this verse which *Houbigant* has removed by the following translation: *Ea autem, priusquam Sodomam Gomorrhamque Dominus deleril, erat, qua itur Segor, tota irrigua, quasi hortus Domini, et quasi terra Ægypti.* "But before the Lord had destroyed Sodom and Gomorrah, it was, as thou goest to Zoar, well watered, like the garden of the Lord, and like the land of Egypt." As paradise was watered by the four neighbouring streams and as Egypt was watered by the annual overflowing of the Nile; so were the plains of the Jordan, and all the land on the way to Zoar, well watered and fertilized by the overflowing of the Jordan.

Verse 11. *Then Lot chose him all the plain*] A little civility or good breeding is of great importance in the concerns of life. Lot either had none, or did not profit by it. He certainly should have left the choice to the patriarch, and should have been guided by his counsel; but he took his *own* way, trusting to his own judgment, and guided only by the sight of his eyes: *he beheld all the plain of Jordan, that it* was *well watered*, &c.; so he chose the *land*, without considering the character of the *inhabitants*, or what advantages or disadvantages it might afford him in spiritual things. This choice, as we shall see in the sequel, had nearly proved the ruin of his body, soul, and family.

Verse 13. *The men of Sodom* were *wicked*] רעים *raim*, from רע *ra*, *to break in pieces, destroy*, and

a

A. M. cir. 2087.
B. C. cir. 1917.

14 And the LORD said unto
Abram, after that Lot [v] was separated from him, Lift up now thine eyes, and
look from the place where thou art [w] northward,
and southward, and eastward, and westward:
15 For all the land which thou seest, [x] to
thee will I give it, and [y] to thy seed for ever.
16 And [z] I will make thy seed as the dust
of the earth: so that if a man can number
the dust of the earth, *then* shall
thy seed also be numbered.

A. M. cir. 2087
B. C. cir. 1917

17 Arise, walk through the land in the
length of it, and in the breadth of it; for I
will give it unto thee.
18 Then Abram removed *his* tent, and came
and [a] dwelt in the [b] plain of Mamre, [c] which *is*
in Hebron, and built there an altar unto the
LORD.

[v] Ver. 11.——[w] Chap. xxviii. 14.——[x] Chap. xii. 7; xv. 18; xvii. 8; xxiv. 7; xxvi. 4; Num. xxxiv. 12; Deut. xxxiv. 4; Acts vii. 5.——[y] 2 Chron. xx. 7; Psa. xxxvii. 22, 29; cxii. 2. [z] Chap. xv. 5; xxii. 17; xxvi. 4; xxviii. 14; xxxii. 12; Exod. xxxii. 13; Num. xxiii. 10; Deut. i. 10; 1 Kings iv. 20; 1 Chron. xxvii. 23; Isa. xlviii. 19; Jer. xxxiii. 22; Rom. iv. 16, 17, 18; Heb. xi. 12.——[a] Chap. xiv. 13.——[b] Heb. *plains*.——[c] Chapter xxxv. 27; xxxvii. 14.

afflict; meaning persons who broke the established order of things, destroyed and confounded the distinctions between right and wrong, and who afflicted and tormented both themselves and others. *And sinners,* חטאים *chattaim*, from חטא *chata, to miss the mark, to step wrong, to miscarry;* the same as *ἁμαρτανω* in Greek, from *a, negative,* and *μαρπτω, to hit a mark;* so a *sinner* is one who is ever aiming at happiness and constantly missing his mark; because, being *wicked*—radically evil within, every affection and passion depraved and out of order, he seeks for happiness where it never can be found, in worldly honours and possessions, and in sensual gratifications, the end of which is disappointment, affliction, vexation, and ruin. Such were the companions Lot must have in the *fruitful land he had chosen.* This, however, amounts to no more than the common character of sinful man; but the people of Sodom were *exceedingly sinful and wicked before*, or against, *the Lord*—they were sinners of no common character; they excelled in unrighteousness, and soon filled up the measure of their iniquities. See chap. xix.

Verse 14. *The Lord said unto Abram*] It is very likely that the angel of the covenant appeared to Abram in *open day*, when he could take a distinct view of the length and the breadth of this good land. The revelation made chap. xv. 5, was evidently made in the *night;* for then he was called to number the *stars*, which could not be seen but in the night season: here he is called on to *number the dust of the earth*, ver. 16, which could not be seen but in the *day-light.*

Verse 15. *To thee will I give it, and to thy seed for ever.*] This land was given to Abram, that it might lineally and legally descend to his posterity; and though Abram himself cannot be said to have possessed it, Acts vii. 5, yet it was the gift of God to him in behalf of his seed; and this was always the design of God, not that Abram *himself* should possess it, but that his posterity should, till the manifestation of Christ in the flesh. And this is chiefly what is to be understood by the words *for ever*, אר עולם *ad olam*, to the end of the present dispensation, and the commencement of the new. עולם *olam* means either ETERNITY, which implies the *termination* of all *time* or *duration*, such as is measured by the celestial luminaries; or a *hidden, unknown period*, such as includes a *completion* or *final termination* of a particular *era, dispensation*, &c.; therefore the first is its *proper* meaning, the latter its *accommodated* meaning. See the note on chap. xvii. 7; xxi. 33.

Verse 18. *Abram removed* his *tent*] Continued to travel and pitch in different places, till at last he fixed his tent in the *plain*, or *by the oak, of Mamre*, see chap. xii. 6, *which is in Hebron;* i. e., the district in which Mamre was situated *was called Hebron*. Mamre was an Amorite then living, with whom Abram made a league, chap. xiv. 13; and the oak probably went by his name, because he was the possessor of the ground. *Hebron* is called *Kirjath-arba*, chap. xxiii. 2; but it is very likely that *Hebron* was its primitive name, and that it had the above appellation from being the residence of *four* gigantic or powerful Anakim, for *Kirjath-arba* literally signifies the *city of the four;* see the note on chap. xxiii. 2

Built there an altar unto the Lord.] On which he offered sacrifice, as the word מזבח *mizbach*, from זבח *zabach, to slay*, imports.

THE increase of riches in the family of Abram must, in the opinion of many, be a source of felicity to them. If earthly possessions could produce happiness, it must be granted that they had now a considerable share of it in their power. But *happiness* must have its seat in the *mind*, and, like *that*, be of a *spiritual* nature; consequently earthly goods cannot give it; so far are they from either producing or procuring it, that they always engender care and anxiety, and often strifes and contentions. The peace of this amiable family had nearly been destroyed by the largeness of their possessions. To prevent the most serious misunderstandings, Abram and his nephew were obliged to separate. He who has much in general wishes to have more, for the eye is not satisfied with seeing. Lot, for the better accommodation of his flocks and family, chooses the most fertile district in that country, and even sacrifices reverence and filial affection at the shrine of worldly advantage; but the issue proved that a pleasant worldly prospect may not be the most advantageous, even to our secular affairs. Abram prospered greatly in the comparatively barren part of the land, while Lot lost all his possessions, and nearly the lives of himself and family, in that land which appeared to him *like the garden of the Lord*, like a second paradise. Rich and fertile countries have generally luxurious, effeminate, and profligate inhabit-

ants; so it was in this case. The inhabitants of *Sodom* were *sinners*, and *exceedingly wicked*, and their profligacy was of that kind which luxury produces; they fed themselves *without fear*, and they acted *without shame*. Lot however was, through the mercy of God, preserved from this contagion: he retained his religion; and this supported his soul and saved his life, when his *goods* and his *wife* perished. Let us learn from this to be jealous over our own wills and wishes; to distrust flattering prospects, and seek and secure a heavenly inheritance. "Man wants but little; nor *that little* long." A man's life—the comfort and happiness of it—does not consist in the multitude of the things he possesses. "One house, one day's food, and one suit of raiment," says the Arabic proverb, "are sufficient for thee; and if thou die before noon, thou hast one half too much." The example of Abram, in constantly erecting an altar wherever he settled, is worthy of serious regard; he knew the path of duty was the way of safety, and that, if he acknowledged God in all his ways, he might expect him to direct all his steps: he felt his dependence on God, he invoked him through a Mediator, and offered sacrifices in faith of the coming Saviour; he found blessedness in this work—it was not an empty service; he rejoiced to see the day of Christ—he saw it, and was glad. See on chap. xii. 8. Reader, has God an altar in *thy* house? Dost thou *sacrifice* to him? Dost thou offer up daily by faith, in behalf of thy soul and the souls of thy family, the Lamb of God who taketh away the sin of the world? *No man cometh unto the* Father *but by me*, said Christ: this was true, not only from the incarnation, but from the foundation of the world. And to this another truth, not less comfortable, may be added: *Whosoever cometh unto me I will in nowise cast out.*

CHAPTER XIV.

The war of four confederate kings against the five kings of Canaan, 1–3. *The confederate kings overrun and pillage the whole country*, 4–7. *Battle between them and the kings of Canaan*, 8, 9. *The latter are defeated, and the principal part of the armies of the kings of Sodom and Gomorrah slain*, 10; *on which these two cities are plundered*, 11. *Lot, his goods, and his family, are also taken and carried away*, 12. *Abram, being informed of the disaster of his nephew*, 13, *arms three hundred and eighteen of his servants, and pursues them*, 14; *overtakes and routs them, and recovers Lot, and his family, and their goods*, 15, 16; *is met on his return by the king of Sodom, and by Melchizedek, king of Salem, with refreshments for himself and men*, 17, 18. *Melchizedek blesses Abram, and receives from him, as priest of the most high God the* tenth *of all the spoils*, 19, 20. *The king of Sodom offers to Abram all the goods he has taken from the enemy*, 21; *which Abram positively refuses, having vowed to God to receive no recompense for a victory of which he knew God to be the sole author*, 22, 23; *but desires that a proportion of the spoils be given to* Aner, Eshcol, *and* Mamre, *who had accompanied him on this expedition*, 24.

A. M. cir. 2091. B. C. cir. 1913. AND it came to pass, in the days of Amraphel king of [a] Shinar, Arioch king of Ellasar, Chedorlaomer king of [b] Elam, and Tidal king of nations;

2 *That these* made war with Bera king of Sodom, and with Birsha king of Gomorrah, Shinab king of [c] Admah, and Shemeber king of Zeboiim, and the king of Bela, which is [d] Zoar. A. M. cir. 2091. B. C. cir. 1913.

3 All these were joined together in the vale of Siddim, [e] which is the salt sea.

4 Twelve years [f] they served Chedorlaomer, and in the thirteenth year they rebelled.

[a] Chap. x. 10; xi. 2.—[b] Isa. xi. 11.—[c] Deut. xxix. 23. [d] Chap. xix. 22.

[e] Deut. iii. 17; Num. xxxiv. 12; Josh. iii. 16; Psa. cvii. 34. [f] Chap. ix. 26.

NOTES ON CHAP. XIV.

Verse 1. *In the days of Amraphel*] Who this king was is not known; and yet, from the manner in which he is spoken of in the text, it would seem that he was a person well known, even when Moses wrote this account. But the *Vulgate* gives a different turn to the place, by rendering the passage thus: *Factum est in illo tempore, ut Amraphel, &c.* "It came to pass in that time that Amraphel, &c." The Chaldee Targum of Onkelos makes Amraphel king of Babylon, others make him king of Assyria; some make him the same as Nimrod, and others, one of his descendants.

Arioch king of Ellasar] Some think *Syria* is meant; but conjecture is endless where facts cannot be ascertained.

Chedorlaomer king of Elam] Dr. Shuckford thinks that this was the same as *Ninyas*, the son of *Ninus* and *Semiramis*; and some think him to be the same with *Keeumras*, son of Doolaved, son of Arphaxad, son of Shem, son of Noah; and that *Elam* means Persia; see chap. x. 22. The Persian historians unanimously allow that *Keeumras*, whose name bears some affinity to *Chedorlaomer*, was the first king of the *Peeshdadian* dynasty.

Tidal king of nations] גוים *goyim*, different peoples or clans. Probably some adventurous person, whose subjects were composed of *refugees* from different countries.

Verse 2. These *made war with Bera, &c.*] It appears, from ver. 4, that these five Canaanitish kings had been subdued by Chedorlaomer, and were obliged

A. M. cir. 2091.
B. C. cir. 1913.

5 And on the fourteenth year
came Chedorlaomer, and the kings
that *were* with him, and smote [g] the Rephaims
[h] in Ashteroth Karnaim, and [i] the Zuzims in
Ham, [k] and the Emims in [l] Shaveh Kiria-
haim,
6 [m] And the Horites in their mount Seir,
unto [n] El-paran, which *is* by the wilderness.
7 And they returned, and came to En-mishpat, which *is* Kadesh, and smote all the country of the Amalekites, and also the Amorites
that dwelt [o] in Hazezon-tamar.
8 And there went out the king of Sodom,
and the king of Gomorrah, and the king of
Admah, and the king of Zeboiim, and the king
of Bela, (the same *is* Zoar,) and they joined
battle with them in the vale of Siddim;
9 With Chedorlaomer the king of Elam, and
with Tidal king of nations, and
Amraphel king of Shinar, and
Arioch king of Ellasar; four kings with five.
10 And the vale of Siddim *was full of*
[p] slime-pits; and the kings of Sodom and
Gomorrah fled, and fell there; and they that
remained fled [q] to the mountain.
11 And they took [r] all the goods of Sodom
and Gomorrah, and all their victuals, and went
their way.
12 And they took Lot, Abram's [s] brother's
son, [t] who dwelt in Sodom, and his goods, and
departed.
13 And there came one that had escaped,
and told Abram the Hebrew; for [u] he dwelt
in the plain of Mamre the Amorite, brother of
Eshcol, and brother of Aner: [v] and these
were confederate with Abram.

[g] Chap. xv. 20; Deut. iii. 11.—[h] Josh. xii. 4; xiii. 12. [i] Deut. ii. 20.—[k] Deut. ii. 10, 11.—[l] Or, *the plain of Kiriathaim.*—[m] Deut. ii. 12, 22.—[n] Or, *the plain of Paran;* chap. xxi. 21; Num. xii. 16; xiii. 3.—[o] 2 Chron. xx. 2.—[p] Chap. xi. 3.—[q] Chap. xix. 17, 30.—[r] Ver. 16, 21.—[s] Chap. xii. 5. [t] Chap. xiii. 12.—[u] Chap. xiii. 18.—[v] Ver. 24.

to pay him tribute; and that, having been enslaved by him twelve years, wishing to recover their liberty, they revolted in the thirteenth; in consequence of which Chedorlaomer, the following year, summoned to his assistance three of his vassals, invaded Canaan, fought with and discomfited the kings of the *Pentapolis* or five cities—Sodom, Gomorrah, Zeboiim, Zoar, and Admah, which were situated in the fruitful plain of Siddim, having previously overrun the whole land.

Verse 5. *Rephaims*] A people of Canaan: chap. xv. 20.

Ashteroth] A city of Basan, where *Og* afterwards reigned; Josh. xiii. 31.

Zuzims] Nowhere else spoken of, unless they were the same with the *Zamzummims*, Deut. ii. 20, as some imagine.

Emims] *A people great and many* in the days of Moses, and *tall as the Anakim*. They dwelt among the Moabites, by whom they were reputed *giants;* Deut. ii. 10, 11.

Shaveh Kiriathaim] Rather, as the *margin*, the *plain of Kiriathaim*, which was a city afterwards belonging to *Sihon* king of Heshbon; Josh. xiii. 19.

Verse 6. *The Horites*] A people that dwelt in Mount Seir, till Esau and his sons drove them thence; Deut. ii. 22.

El-paran] The *plain* or *oak of Paran*, which was a city in the wilderness of Paran; chap. xxi. 21.

Verse 7. *En-mishpat*] The *well of judgment;* probably so called from the judgment pronounced by God on Moses and Aaron for their rebellion at that place; Num. xx. 1–10.

Amalekites] So called *afterwards*, from Amalek, son of Esau; chap. xxxvi. 12.

Hazezon-tamar.] Called, in the Chaldee, Engaddi; a city in the land of Canaan, which fell to the lot of Judah; Josh. xv. 62. See also 2 Chron. xx. 2. It appears, from Cant. i. 13, to have been a very fruitful place.

Verse 8. *Bela, the same* is *Zoar*] That is, it was called *Zoar* after the destruction of Sodom, &c., mentioned in chap. xix.

Verse 10. *Slime-pits*] Places where *asphaltus* or *bitumen* sprang out of the ground; this substance abounded in that country.

Fell there] It either signifies they were defeated on this spot, and many of them slain, or that multitudes of them had perished in the bitumen-pits which abounded there; that the place was *full of pits* we learn from the Hebrew, which reads here בארת בארת *beeroth beeroth*, pits, pits, i. e., multitudes of pits. A bad place to maintain a fight on, or to be obliged to run through in order to escape.

Verse 11. *They took all the goods, &c.*] This was a predatory war, such as the Arabs carry on to the present day; they pillage a city, town, or caravan; and then escape with the booty to the wilderness, where it would ever be unsafe, and often impossible, to pursue them.

Verse 12. *They took Lot, &c.*] The people, being exceedingly wicked, had provoked God to afflict them by means of those marauding kings; and Lot also suffered, being found in company with the workers of iniquity. Every child remembers the fable of the Geese and Cranes; the former, being found feeding where the latter were destroying the grain, were all taken in the same net. Let him that readeth understand.

Verse 13. *Abram the Hebrew*] See on chap. x. 21. It is very likely that Abram had this appellation from his coming *from beyond* the river Euphrates to enter Canaan; for העברי *haibri*, which we render *the Hebrew*, comes from עבר *abar*, *to pass over*, or come *from beyond*. It is supposed by many that he got this name

A. M. cir. 2091.
B. C. cir. 1913.

14 And when Abram heard that [w] his brother was taken captive, he [x] armed his [y] trained *servants,* [z] born in his own house, three hundred and eighteen, and pursued *them* [a] unto Dan.

15 And he divided himself against them, he and his servants, by night, and [b] smote them, and pursued them unto Hobah, which *is* on the left hand of Damascus.

16 And he brought back [c] all the goods, and also brought again his brother Lot, and his goods, and the women also, and the people.

A. M. cir. 2091.
B. C. cir. 1913.

17 And the king of Sodom [d] went out to meet him [e] after his return from the slaughter of Chedorlaomer, and of the kings that *were* with him, at the valley of Shaveh, which *is* the [f] king's dale.

18 And [g] Melchizedek king of Salem brought forth bread and wine: and he *was* [h] the priest of [i] the most high God.

[w] Chap. xiii. 8.——[x] Or, *led forth.*——[y] Or, *instructed.*——[z] Ch. xv. 3; xvii. 12, 27; Eccles. ii. 7.——[a] Deut. xxxiv. 1; Judg. xviii. 29.——[b] Isa. xli. 2, 3.——[c] Ver. 11, 12.

[d] Judg. xi. 34; 1 Sam. xviii. 6.——[e] Heb. vii. 1.——[f] 2 Sam. xviii. 18.——[g] Heb. vii. 1.——[h] Psa. cx. 4; Heb. v. 6.——[i] Mic. vi. 6; Acts xvi. 17; Ruth iii. 10; 2 Sam. ii. 5.

from *Eber* or *Heber*, son of Salah; see chap. xi. 15. But why he should get a name from Heber, rather than from his own father, or some other of his progenitors, no person has yet been able to discover. We may, therefore, safely conclude that he bears the appellation of *Hebrew* or *Ibrite* from the above circumstance, and not from one of his progenitors, of whom we know nothing but the name, and who preceded Abram not less than six generations; and during the whole of that time till the time marked here, none of his descendants were ever called *Hebrews;* this is a demonstration that Abram was not called the *Hebrew* from *Heber;* see chap. xi. 15–27.

These were *confederate with Abram.*] It seems that a kind of convention was made between Abram and the three brothers, *Mamre, Eshcol,* and *Aner,* who were probably all chieftains in the vicinity of Abram's dwelling: all petty princes, similar to the nine kings before mentioned.

Verse 14. *He armed his trained* servants] These amounted to three hundred and eighteen in number: and how many were in the divisions of Mamre, Eshcol, and Aner, we know not; but they and their men certainly accompanied him in this expedition. See ver. 24.

Verse 15. *And he divided himself against them*] It required both considerable courage and address in Abram to lead him to attack the victorious armies of these four kings with so small a number of troops, and on this occasion both his skill and his courage are exercised. His affection for Lot appears to have been his chief motive; he cheerfully risks his life for that nephew who had lately chosen the best part of the land, and left his uncle to live as he might, on what he did not think worthy his own acceptance. But it is the property of a great and generous mind, not only to forgive, but to forget offences; and at all times to repay evil with good.

Verse 16. *And he brought back—the women also*] This is brought in by the sacred historian with peculiar interest and tenderness. All who read the account must be in pain for the fate of *wives* and *daughters* fallen into the hands of a ferocious, licentious, and victorious *soldiery.* Other spoils the routed confederates might have left behind; and yet on their swift asses, camels, and dromedaries, have carried off the female captives. However, Abram had disposed his attack so judiciously, and so promptly executed his measures, that not only all the baggage, but all the *females* also, were recovered.

Verse 17. *The king of Sodom went out to meet him*] This could not have been *Bera*, mentioned ver. 2, for it seems pretty evident, from ver. 10, that both he and *Birsha*, king of Gomorrah, were slain at the bitumen-pits in the vale of Siddim; but another person in the mean time might have succeeded to the government.

Verse 18. *And Melchizedek, king of Salem*] A thousand idle stories have been told about this man, and a thousand idle conjectures spent on the subject of his short history given here and in Heb. vii. At present it is only necessary to state that he appears to have been as real a personage as *Bera, Birsha,* or *Shinab,* though we have no more of *his* genealogy than we have of *theirs.*

Brought forth bread and wine] Certainly to *refresh* Abram and his men, exhausted with the late battle and fatigues of the journey; not in the way of *sacrifice,* &c.; this is an idle conjecture.

He was *the priest of the most high God.*] He had preserved in his family and among his subjects the worship of the true God, and the primitive patriarchal institutions; by these the father of every family was both *king* and *priest;* so Melchizedek, being a worshipper of the true God, was *priest* among the people, as well as *king* over them.

Melchizedek is called here *king of Salem,* and the most judicious interpreters allow that by Salem *Jerusalem* is meant. That it bore this name anciently is evident from Psa. lxxvi. 1, 2: "In *Judah* is God known; his name is great in *Israel.* In SALEM also is his *tabernacle,* and his dwelling place in *Zion.*" From the use made of this part of the sacred history by David, Psa. cx. 4, and by St. Paul, Heb. vii. 1–10, we learn that there was something very mysterious, and at the same time typical, in the *person, name, office, residence,* and government of this Canaanitish prince. 1. In his *person* he was a representative and type of Christ; see the scriptures above referred to. 2. His *name* מלכי צדק *malki tsedek,* signifies *my righteous king,* or *king of righteousness.* This name he probably had from the pure and righteous administration of his government; and this is one of the characters of our blessed

a

A. M. cir. 2091. B. C. cir. 1913.

19 And he blessed him, and said, Blessed *be* Abram of the most high God, [k] possessor of heaven and earth.

20 And [l] blessed *be* the most high God, which hath delivered thine enemies into thy hand. And he gave him tithes [m] of all.

21 And the king of Sodom said unto Abram, Give me the [n] persons, and take the goods to thyself.

22 And Abram said to the king of Sodom, I [o] have lift up mine hand unto the LORD, the most high God, [p] the possessor of heaven and earth,

A. M. cir. 2091. B. C. cir. 1913.

23 That [q] I will not *take* from a thread even to a shoe-latchet, and that I will not take any thing that *is* thine, lest thou shouldest say, I have made Abram rich:

24 Save only that which the young men have eaten, and the portion of the men [r] which went with me, Aner, Eshcol, and Mamre; let them take their portion.

[k] Ver. 22; Matt. xi. 25.——[l] Chap. xxiv. 27.——[m] Heb. vii. 4.——[n] Heb. *souls*.——[o] Exod. vi. 8; Dan. xii. 7; Rev. x. 5, 6.——[p] Ver. 19; chap. xxi. 33.——[q] So Esther ix. 15, 16.——[r] Ver. 13.

Lord, a character which can be applied to him only, as he alone is *essentially righteous*, and the *only Potentate;* but a holy man, such as Melchizedek, might bear this name as his *type* or *representative*. 3. *Office;* he was a *priest of the most high God*. The word כהן *cohen*, which signifies both *prince* and *priest*, because the patriarchs sustained this double office, has both its root and proper signification in the Arabic; كهن *kahana* signifies *to approach, draw near, have intimate access to;* and from hence *to officiate as priest bfeore* God, and thus have intimate access to the Divine presence: and by means of the sacrifices which he offered he received *counsel* and *information* relative to what was *yet to take place*, and hence another acceptation of the word, *to foretell, predict future events, unfold hidden things* or *mysteries;* so the lips of the priests preserved knowledge, and they were often the interpreters of the will of God to the people. Thus we find that Melchizedek, being a priest of the most high God, represented Christ in his *sacerdotal* character, the word *priest* being understood as before explained. 4. His *residence;* he was king of *Salem*. שלם *shalam* signifies *to make whole, complete*, or *perfect;* and hence it means *peace*, which implies the *making whole* the *breaches* made in the political and domestic union of kingdoms, states, families, &c., making an end of discord, and establishing friendship. Christ is called the *Prince of peace*, because, by his incarnation, sacrifice, and mediation, he procures and establishes peace between God and man; heals the breaches and dissensions between heaven and earth, reconciling both; and produces glory to God in the highest, and on earth peace and good will among men. His *residence* is *peace* and quietness and assurance for ever, in every believing upright heart. He governs as the Prince and Priest of the most high God, ruling in righteousness, mighty to save; and he ever lives to make intercession for, and save to the uttermost all who come unto the Father by him. See the notes on Heb. vii.

Verse 19. *And he blessed him*] This was a part of the priest's office, *to bless in the name of the Lord, for ever*. See the *form* of this blessing, Num. vi. 23–26; and for the meaning of the word *to bless*, see Gen. ii. 3.

Verse 20. *And he gave him tithes*] A tenth part *of all* the spoils he had taken from the confederate kings. These Abram gave as a *tribute* to the *most high God*, who, being *the possessor of heaven and earth*, dispenses all spiritual and temporal favours, and demands the gratitude, and submissive, loving obedience, of all his subjects. Almost all nations of the earth have agreed in giving a *tenth part* of their property to be employed in religious uses. The *tithes* were afterwards granted to the Levites for the use of the sanctuary, and the maintenance of themselves and their families, as they had no other inheritance in Israel.

Verse 22. *I have lift up mine hand*] The primitive mode of appealing to God, and calling him to witness a particular transaction; this no doubt generally obtained among the faithful till *circumcision*, the *sign* of the covenant, was established. After this, in swearing, the hand was often placed on the circumcised part; see chap. xxiv. 2 and 9.

Verse 23. *From a thread even to a shoe-latchet*] This was certainly a proverbial mode of expression, the full meaning of which is perhaps not known. Among the rabbinical writers חוט *chut*, or חוטי *chuti*, signifies a *fillet worn by young women to tie up their hair;* taken in this sense it will give a good meaning here. As Abram had rescued both the *men* and *women* carried off by the confederate kings, and the king of Sodom had offered him *all the goods*, claiming only the *persons*, he answers by protesting against the accepting any of their property: "I have vowed unto the Lord, the proprietor of heaven and earth, that I will not receive the smallest portion of the property either of the *women* or *men*, from a girl's fillet to a man's shoe-tie."

Verse 24. *Save only that which the young men have eaten*] His own servants had partaken of the *victuals* which the confederate kings had carried away; see ver. 11. This was unavoidable, and this is all he claims; but as he had no right to prescribe the same liberal conduct to his assistants, Aner, Eshcol, and Mamre, he left them to claim the *share* that by *right of conquest* belonged to them of the recaptured booty. Whether they were as generous as Abram we are not told.

THE great variety of striking incidents in this chapter the attentive reader has already carefully noted To *read* and *not understand* is the property of the *foolish* and the *inconsiderate*. 1. We have already

seen the danger to which Lot exposed himself in preferring a fertile region, though peopled with the workers of iniquity. His sorrows commence in the captivity of himself and family, and the loss of all his property, though by the good providence of God he and they were rescued. 2. Long observation has proved that the company a man keeps is not an indifferent thing; it will either be the means of his salvation or destruction. 3. A generous man cannot be contented with mere personal safety while others are in danger, nor with his own prosperity while others are in distress. Abram, hearing of the captivity of his nephew, determines to attempt his rescue; he puts himself at the head of his own servants, three hundred and eighteen in number, and the few assistants with which his neighbours, Mamre, Aner, and Eshcol, could furnish him; and, trusting in God and the goodness of his cause, marches off to attack four confederate kings! 4. Though it is not very likely that the armies of those petty kings could have amounted to *many thousands*, yet they were numerous enough to subdue almost the whole land of Canaan; and consequently, humanly speaking, Abram must know that by numbers *he* could not prevail, and that in this case particularly *the battle was the Lord's*. 5. While depending on the Divine blessing and succour he knew he must use the means he had in his power; he therefore divided his troops skilfully that he might attack the enemy at *different points* at the *same time*, and he chooses the *night season* to commence his attack, that the *smallness* of his force might not be discovered. God requires a man to use all the faculties he has given him in every lawful enterprise, and only in the conscientious use of them can he expect the Divine blessing; when this is done the event may be safely trusted in the hands of God. 6. Here is a war undertaken by Abram on motives the most honourable and conscientious; it was to repel aggression, and to rescue the innocent from the heaviest of sufferings and the worst of slavery, not for the purpose of plunder nor the extension of his territories; therefore he takes no spoils, and returns peaceably to *his own possessions*. How happy would the world be were every sovereign actuated by the same spirit! 7. We have already noticed the appearance, person, office, &c., of *Melchizedek;* and, without indulging in the wild theories of either ancient or modern visionaries, have considered him as the Scriptures do, *a type of Christ*. All that has been already spoken on this head may be recapitulated in a few words. 1. The Redeemer of the world is the *King of righteousness;* he creates it, maintains it, and rules by it. 2. His empire is the *empire of peace;* this he proclaims to them who are afar off, and to them that are nigh; to the Jew and to the Gentile. 3. He is *Priest* of the most high God, and has laid down his life for the sin of the world; and through this sacrifice the *blessing* of God is derived on them that believe. Reader, take him for thy *King* as well as thy *Priest;* he saves those only *who submit to his authority*, and take his *Spirit* for the *regulator* of their *heart*, and his *word* for the *director* of their *conduct*. How many do we find, among those who would be sorry to be rated so low as to rank only with *nominal* Christians, talking of Christ as their *Prophet, Priest*, and *King*, who are not *taught* by his word and Spirit, who apply not for *redemption in his blood*, and who *submit not* to his *authority!* Reader, learn this deep and important truth: "*Where I am* there also shall my *servant* be; and he that *serveth* me, him shall my Father honour."

CHAPTER XV.

God appears to Abram in a vision, and gives him great encouragement, 1. *Abram's request and complaint*, 2, 3. *God promises him a son*, 4; *and an exceedingly numerous posterity*, 5. *Abram credits the promise, and his faith is counted unto him for righteousness*, 6. *Jehovah proclaims himself, and renews the promise of Canaan to his posterity*, 7. *Abram requires a sign of its fulfilment*, 8. *Jehovah directs him to offer a sacrifice of five different animals*, 9; *which he accordingly does*, 10, 11. *God reveals to him the affliction of his posterity in Egypt, and the duration of that affliction*, 12, 13. *Promises to bring them back to the land of Canaan with great affluence*, 14–16. *Renews the covenant with Abram, and mentions the possessions which should be given to his posterity*, 18–21.

A. M. cir. 2093.
B. C. cir. 1911.

AFTER these things the word of the LORD came unto Abram [a] in a vision, saying, [b] Fear not, Abram; I *am* thy [c] shield, *and* thy exceeding [d] great reward.
2 And Abram said, Lord GOD, what wilt

[a] Dan. x. 1; Acts x. 10, 11.——[b] Chap. xxvi. 24; Dan. x. 12; Luke i. 13, 30.——[c] Psa. iii. 3; v. 12; lxxxiv. 11; xci. 4; cxix. 114.——[d] Psa. xvi. 5; lviii. 11; Prov. xi. 18.

NOTES ON CHAP. XV.

Verse 1. *The word of the Lord came unto Abram*] This is the *first* place where God is represented as revealing himself by his *word*. Some learned men suppose that the דבר יהוה *debar Yehovah*, translated here *word of the Lord*, means the same with the λογος του Θεου of St. John, chap. i. 1, and, by the Chaldee paraphrases in the next clause, called מימרי *meimeri*, "my word," and in other places מימרא דיי *meimera daiya*, the word of *Yeya*, a contraction for *Jehovah*, which they appear always to consider as a *person;* and which they distinguish from פתגמא *pithgama*, which signifies merely a *word* spoken, or any *part* of *speech*. There have been various conjectures concern-

A. M. cir. 2093. B. C. cir. 1911.

thou give me, [e] seeing I go childless, and the steward of my house *is* this Eliezer of Damascus?

3 And Abram said, Behold, to me thou hast given no seed: and lo, [f] one born in my house is mine heir.

4 And behold, the word of the LORD *came* unto him, saying, This shall not be thine heir; but he that [g] shall come forth out of thine own bowels shall be thine heir.

5 And he brought him forth abroad, and

[e] Acts vii. 5.——[f] Chap. xiv. 14.

[g] 2 Sam. vii. 12; xvi. 11; 2 Chron. xxxii. 21.

ing the manner in which God revealed his will, not only to the patriarchs, but also to the prophets, evangelists, and apostles. It seems to have been done in different ways. 1. By a *personal appearance* of him who was afterwards incarnated for the salvation of mankind. 2. By an *audible voice*, sometimes accompanied with emblematical appearances. 3. By *visions* which took place either in the night in ordinary sleep, or when the persons were cast into a temporary trance by daylight, or when about their ordinary business. 4. By the *ministry of angels* appearing in human bodies, and performing certain miracles to accredit their mission. 5. By the powerful agency of the *Spirit of God upon the mind*, giving it a strong conception and supernatural persuasion of the truth of the things perceived by the understanding. We shall see all these exemplified in the course of the work. It was probably in the third sense that the revelation in the text was given; for it is said, *God appeared to Abram in a vision*, מחזה *machazeh*, from חזה *chazah*, to *see*, or according to others, to *fix*, *fasten*, *settle*; hence *chozeh*, a SEER, the person who *sees Divine things*, to whom *alone* they are revealed, on whose mind they are *fastened*, and in whose memory and judgment they are *fixed* and *settled*. Hence the *vision* which was mentally perceived, and, by the evidence to the soul of its Divine origin, *fixed* and *settled* in the mind.

Fear not] The late Dr. Dodd has a good thought on this passage; "I would read," says he, "the second verse in a parenthesis, thus: *For Abram* HAD *said, Lord God, what wilt thou give me, seeing I go childless, &c.* *Abram had said this* in the *fear* of his heart, upon which the Lord vouchsafed to him this prophetical *view*, and this strong renovation of the covenant. In this light all follows very properly. Abram had said so and so in ver. 2, upon which God appears and says, *I am thy shield, and thy exceeding great reward.* The patriarch then, ver. 3, freely opens the anxious apprehension of his heart, *Behold, to me thou hast given no seed, &c.*, upon which God proceeds to assure him of posterity."

I am thy shield, &c.] Can it be supposed that Abram understood these words as promising him *temporal* advantages at all corresponding to the magnificence of these promises? If he did he was disappointed through the whole course of his life, for he never enjoyed *such* a state of worldly prosperity as could justify the strong language in the text. Shall we lose sight of Abram, and say that his posterity was intended, and Abram understood the promises as relating to them, and not to himself or immediately to his own family? Then the question recurs, Did the Israelites ever enjoy such a state of temporal affluence as seems to be intended by the above promise? To this every man acquainted with their history will, without hesitation, say, No. What then is intended? Just what the words state. GOD was *Abram's portion*, and he is the *portion* of every *righteous soul*; for to *Abram*, and the *children of his faith*, he gives not a *portion in this life*. Nothing, says Father Calmet, proves more invincibly the immortality of the soul, the truth of religion, and the eternity of another life, than to see that in this life the righteous seldom receive the reward of their virtue, and that in temporal things they are often less happy than the workers of iniquity.

I am, says the Almighty, *thy shield*—thy constant covering and protector, *and thy exceeding great reward*, שכרך הרבה מאד *sekarcha harbeh meod*, "THAT superlatively multiplied reward of thine." It is not the Canaan I promise, but the *salvation* that is to come through the promised seed. Hence it was that *Abram rejoiced to see his day*. And hence the Chaldee Targum translates this place, *My* WORD *shall be thy strength, &c.*

Verse 2. *What wilt thou give me, seeing I go childless*] The anxiety of the Asiatics to have offspring is intense and universal. Among the *Hindoos* the want of children renders all other blessings of no esteem. See *Ward*.

And the steward of my house] Abram, understanding the promise as relating to that person who was to spring from his family, in whom all the nations of the earth should be blessed, expresses his surprise that there should be such a promise, and yet he is about to die childless! How then can the promise be fulfilled, when, far from a *spiritual seed*, he has not even a person in his family that has a *natural* right to his property, and that a *stranger* is likely to be his heir? This seems to be the general sense of the passage; but who this *steward of his house*, this *Eliezer of Damascus*, was, commentators are not agreed. The translation of the Septuagint is at least curious: 'Οδε υἱος Μασεκ της οικογενους μου, οὑτος Δαμασκος Ελιεζερ· *The son of Masek my home-born maid, this Eliezer of Damascus*, is my heir; which intimates that they supposed משק *meshek*, which we translate *steward*, to have been the name of a *female slave*, *born* in the family of Abram, of whom was born this Eliezer, who on account of the country either of his father or mother, was called a *Damascene* or one of Damascus. It is extremely probable that our Lord has this passage in view in his parable of the rich man and Lazarus, Luke xvi. 19. From the name *Eliezer*, by leaving out the first letter, *Liezer* is formed, which makes *Lazarus* in the New Testament, the person who, from an abject and distressed state, was raised to lie in the bosom of Abraham in paradise.

Verse 5. *Look now toward heaven*] It appears that

A. M. cir. 2093.
B. C. cir. 1911.

said, Look now toward heaven,
and [h] tell the [i] stars, if thou be
able to number them: and he said unto him,
[k] So shall thy seed be.
6 And he [l] believed in the LORD; and he
[m] counted it to him for righteousness.
7 And he said unto him, I *am* the LORD
that [n] brought thee out of [o] Ur of the Chaldees, [p] to give thee this land to inherit it.

8 And he said, Lord GOD,
[q] whereby shall I know that I
shall inherit it?
9 And he said unto him, [r] Take me a heifer
of three years old, and a she-goat of three
years old, and a ram of three years old, and
a turtle-dove, and a young pigeon.
10 And he took unto him all these, and
[s] divided them in the midst, and laid each

A. M. cir. 2093.
B. C. cir. 1911.

---

[h] Psa. cxlvii. 4.——[i] Jer. xxxiii. 22.——[k] Chap. xxii. 17; Exod. xxxii. 13; Deut. i. 10; x. 22; 1 Chron. xxvii. 23; Rom. iv. 18; Heb. xi. 12; see chap. xiii. 16.——[l] Rom. iv. 3, 9, 22; Gal. iii. 6; James ii. 23.——[m] Psa. cvi. 31.——[n] Chap. xii. 1.

[o] Chap. xi. 28, 31.——[p] Psa. cv. 42, 44; Rom. iv. 13.——[q] See chap. xxiv. 13, 14; Judg. vi. 17, 37; 1 Sam. xiv. 9, 10; 2 Kings xx. 8; Luke i. 18.——[r] Lev. i. 3, 10, 14; xii. 8; xiv. 22, 30; Luke xi. 24; Isa. xv. 5.——[s] Jer. xxxiv. 18, 19.

---

this whole transaction took place in the *evening;* see on chap xiii. 14. Abram had either two visions, that recorded in ver. 1, and that in ver. 12, &c.; or what is mentioned in the beginning of this chapter is a part of the occurrences which took place after the sacrifice mentioned ver. 9, &c.: but it is more likely that there was a vision of that kind already described, and afterwards a *second,* in which he received the revelation mentioned ver. 13–16. After the first vision he is *brought forth abroad* to see if he can number the stars; and as he finds this impossible, he is assured that as they are to him innumerable, so shall his posterity be; and that all should spring from one who should proceed from his own bowels—*one* who should be his own legitimate child.

Verse 6. *And he believed in the Lord; and he counted it to him for righteousness.*] This I conceive to be one of the most important passages in the whole Old Testament. It properly contains and specifies that doctrine of *justification by faith* which engrosses so considerable a share of the epistles of St. Paul, and at the foundation of which is the *atonement* made by the Son of God: *And he* (Abram) *believed* (האמן *heemin,* he put faith) *in Jehovah,* ויחשבה לו *vaiyachshebeha lo,* and he counted *it*—the faith he put in Jehovah, to HIM for *righteousness,* צדקה *tsedakah,* or justification; though there was no *act* in the case but that of the mind and heart, no *work* of any kind. Hence the doctrine of *justification by faith, without any merit of works;* for in this case there could be none—no works of Abram which could *merit the salvation of the whole human race.* It was the *promise* of God which he credited, and in the blessedness of which he became a partaker through faith. See at the close of the chapter; see also on Rom. iv.

Verse 7. *Ur of the Chaldees*] See on chap. xi.

Verse 8. *And he said, Lord God*] אדני יהוה, *Adonai Yehovah, my Lord Jehovah.* Adonai is the word which the Jews in reading always substitute for *Jehovah,* as they count it impious to pronounce this name. *Adonai* signifies my *director, basis, supporter, prop,* or *stay;* and scarcely a more appropriate name can be given to that God who is the *framer* and *director* of every righteous word and action; the *basis* or *foundation* on which every rational hope rests; the *supporter* of the souls and bodies of men, as well as of the universe in general; the *prop* and *stay* of the weak and fainting, and the *buttress* that shores up the building, which otherwise must necessarily fall. This word often occurs in the Hebrew Bible, and is rendered in our translation *Lord;* the same term by which the word Jehovah is expressed: but to distinguish between the two, and to show the reader when the original is יהוה *Yehovah,* and when אדני *Adonai,* the first is always put in capitals, LORD, the latter in plain Roman *characters,* Lord. For the word Jehovah see on chap. ii. 4, and on Exod. xxxiv. 6.

Whereby shall I know] By what *sign* shall I be assured, that I shall inherit this land? It appears that he expected some sign, and that on such occasions one was ordinarily given.

Verse 9. *Take me a heifer*] עגלה *eglah,* a *she-calf;* a *she-goat,* עז *ez,* a goat, male or female, but distinguished here by the *feminine* adjective; משלשת *meshullesheth,* a *three-yearling;* a *ram,* איל *ayil;* a *turtle-dove,* תר *tor,* from which come *turtur* and *turtle; young pigeon,* גוזל *gozal,* a word signifying the young of *pigeons* and *eagles.* See Deut. xxxii. 11. It is worthy of remark, that every animal allowed or commanded to be sacrificed under the Mosaic law is to be found in this list. And is it not a proof that God was now giving to Abram an *epitome* of that law and its sacrifices which he intended more fully to reveal to Moses; the essence of which consisted in its *sacrifices,* which typified the Lamb of God that takes away the sin of the world?

On the several animals which God ordered Abram to take, Jarchi remarks: "The idolatrous nations are compared in the Scriptures to *bulls, rams,* and *goats;* for it is written, Psa. xxii. 13: *Many bulls have compassed me about.* Dan. viii. 20: *The ram which thou hast seen is the king of Persia.* Ver. 21: *The rough goat is the king of Greece.* But the Israelites are compared to *doves, &c.;* Cant. ii. 14: *O my dove, that art in the cleft of the rock.* The *division* of the above carcasses denotes the *division* and *extermination* of the idolatrous nations; but the birds not *being divided,* shows that the Israelites are to *abide for ever.*" See Jarchi on the place.

Verse 10. *Divided them in the midst*] The ancient method of making covenants, as well as the original word, have been already alluded to, and in a general way explained. See chap. vi. 18. The word *covenant,* from *con,* together, and *venio,* I come, signifies an agreement, association, or meeting between two or more parties; for it is impossible that a covenant can

A. M. cir. 2093. B. C. cir. 1911. piece one against another: but [t] the birds divided he not.

11 And when the fowls came down upon the carcasses, Abram drove them away.

12 And when the sun was going down, [u] a deep sleep fell upon Abram; and, lo, a horror of great darkness fell upon him. A. M. cir. 2093. B. C. cir. 1911.

13 And he said unto Abram, Know of a surety [v] that thy seed shall be a stranger in a land *that is* not theirs, and shall serve them; and [w] they shall afflict them four hundred years;

[t] Lev. i. 17.——[u] Chap. ii. 21; Job. iv. 13.——[v] Exod. xii. 40; Psa. cv. 23; Acts vii. 6.——[w] Exodus i. 11; Psalm cv. 25.

be made between an individual and himself, whether God or man. This is a theological absurdity into which many have run; there must be at least *two* parties to contract with each other. And often there was a *third* party to *mediate* the agreement, and to witness it when made. Rabbi Solomon Jarchi says, "It was a custom with those who entered into covenant with each other to take a heifer and cut it in two, and then the contracting parties passed between the pieces." See this and the scriptures to which it refers particularly explained, chap. vi. 18. A covenant always supposed one of these *four* things: 1. That the contracting parties had been hitherto *unknown* to each other, and were brought by the covenant into a state of *acquaintance*. 2. That they had been previously in a state of *hostility* or *enmity*, and were brought by the covenant into a state of *pacification* and *friendship*. 3. Or that, being known to each other, they now agree to unite their counsels, strength, property, &c., for the accomplishment of a particular purpose, mutually subservient to the interests of both. Or, 4. It implies an agreement to succour and defend a *third party* in cases of oppression and distress. For whatever purpose a covenant was made, it was ever ratified by a sacrifice offered to God; and the passing between the divided parts of the victim appears to have signified that each agreed, if they broke their engagements, to submit to the punishment of being *cut asunder;* which we find from Matt. xxiv. 51; Luke xii. 46, was an ancient mode of punishment. This is farther confirmed by Herodotus, who says that Sabacus, king of Ethiopia, had a vision, in which he was ordered *μεσους διατεμειν*, *to cut in two*, all the Egyptian priests; lib. ii. We find also from the same author, lib. vii., that Xerxes ordered one of the sons of Pythius *μεσον διατεμειν*, *to be cut in two*, and one half to be placed on each side of the way, that his army might pass through between them. That this kind of punishment was used among the Persians we have proof from Dan. ii. 5; iii. 29. Story of Susanna, verses 55, 59. See farther, 2 Sam. xii. 31, and 1 Chron. xx. 3. These authorities may be sufficient to show that the *passing between* the parts of the divided victims signified the punishment to which those exposed themselves who broke their covenant engagements. And that covenant sacrifices were thus *divided*, even from the remotest antiquity, we learn from Homer, Il. A., v. 460.

> *Μηρους τ' εξεταμον κατα τε κνισσῃ εκαλυψαν,*
> *Διπτυχα ποιησαντες, επ' αυτων δ' ωμοθετησαν.*

"They cut the quarters, and cover them with the fat; *dividing them into two*, they place the raw flesh upon them."

But this place may be differently understood.

St. Cyril, in his work against Julian, shows that *passing between the divided parts of a victim* was used also among the Chaldeans and other people. As the *sacrifice* was required to make an atonement to God, so the *death of the animal* was necessary to signify to the contracting parties the punishment to which they exposed themselves, should they prove unfaithful.

Livy preserves the *form* of the imprecation used on such occasions, in the account he gives of the league made between the Romans and Albans. When the Romans were about to enter into some solemn league or covenant, they sacrificed a hog; and, on the above occasion, the *priest*, or *pater patratus*, before he slew the animal, stood, and thus invoked Jupiter: *Audi, Jupiter! Si prior defecerit publico consilio dolo malo, tum illo die, Diespiter, Populum Romanum sic ferito, ut ego hunc porcum hic hodie feriam; tantoque magis ferito, quanto magis potes pollesque!* LIVII *Hist.*, lib. i., chap. 24. "Hear, O Jupiter! Should the Romans in public counsel, through any evil device, first transgress these laws, in that same day, O Jupiter, thus smite the Roman people, as I shall at this time smite this hog; and smite them with a severity proportioned to the greatness of thy power and might!"

But the birds divided he not.] According to the law, Lev. i. 17, fowls were not to be divided asunder, but only cloven for the purpose of taking out the intestines.

Verse 11. *And when the fowls*] העיט *haayit*, birds of prey, *came down upon the carcasses* to devour them, *Abram*, who stood by his sacrifice waiting for the manifestation of GOD, who had ordered him to prepare for the ratification of the covenant, *drove them away*, that they might neither *pollute* nor *devour* what had been thus consecrated to God.

Verse 12. *A deep sleep*] תרדמה *tardemah*, the same word which is used to express the sleep into which Adam was cast, previous to the formation of Eve; chap. ii. 21.

A horror of great darkness] Which God designed to be expressive of the affliction and misery into which his posterity should be brought during the *four hundred* years of their bondage in Egypt; as the next verse particularly states.

Verse 13. *Four hundred years*] "Which began," says Mr. Ainsworth, "when Ishmael, son of Hagar, mocked and persecuted Isaac, Gen. xxi. 9; Gal. iv. 29; which fell out *thirty* years after the promise, Gen. xii. 3; which promise was *four hundred and thirty* years before the law, Gal. iii. 17; and *four hundred and thirty* years after that promise came Israel out of Egypt, Exod. xii. 41."

A. M. cir. 2093.
B. C. cir. 1911.

14 And also that nation, whom
they shall serve, [x] will I judge:
and afterward [y] shall they come out with great
substance.
15 And [z] thou shalt go [a] to thy fathers in
peace; [b] thou shalt be buried in a good old
age.
16 But [c] in the fourth generation they shall
come hither again; for the iniquity [d] of the
Amorites [e] *is* not yet full.
17 And it came to pass, that, when the sun
went down, and it was dark, behold a smoking
furnace, and [f] a burning lamp that
[g] passed between those pieces.
18 In the same day the LORD [h] made a covenant with Abram, saying, [i] Unto thy seed
have I given this land, from the river of Egypt
unto the great river, the river [k] Euphrates:
19 The [l] Kenites, and the Kenizzites, and
the Kadmonites,
20 And the Hittites, and the Perizzites, and
the [m] Rephaims,
21 And the [n] Amorites, and the Canaanites,
and the Girgashites, and the Jebusites.

A. M. cir. 2093
B. C. cir. 1911

[x] Exod. vi. 6; Deut. vi. 22.——[y] Exod. xii. 36; Psa. cv. 37.
[z] Job v. 26.——[a] Acts xiii. 36.——[b] Chap. xxv. 8.——[c] Exod. xii. 40.——[d] 1 Kings xxi. 26.——[e] Dan. viii. 23; Matt. xxiii. 32; 1 Thess. ii. 16.——[f] Heb. *a lamp of fire.*——[g] Jer. xxxiv. 18, 19.
[h] Chap. xxiv. 7.——[i] Chap. xii. 7; xiii. 15; xxvi. 4; Exod. xxiii. 31; Num. xxxiv. 3; Deut. i. 7; xi. 24; xxxiv. 4; Josh. i. 4; 1 Kings iv. 21; 2 Chron. ix. 26; Neh. ix. 8; Psa. cv. 11; Isa. xxvii. 12.——[k] Chap. ii. 14; 2 Sam. viii. 3; 1 Chron. v. 9.
[l] Num. xxiv. 21, 22.——[m] Chap. xiv. 5; Isa. xvii. 5.——[n] Chap. x. 15–19; Exod. xxiii. 23–28; xxxiii. 2; xxxiv. 11.

Verse 14. *And also that nation, &c.*] How remarkably was this promise fulfilled, in the redemption of Israel from its bondage, in the plagues and destruction of the Egyptians, and in the immense wealth which the Israelites brought out of Egypt! Not a more circumstantial or literally fulfilled promise is to be found in the sacred writings.

Verse 15. *Thou shalt go to thy fathers in peace*] This verse strongly implies the immortality of the soul, and a state of separate existence. He was gathered to his fathers—introduced into the place where separate spirits are kept, waiting for the general resurrection. Two things seem to be distinctly marked here: 1. The soul of Abram should be introduced among the assembly of the first-born; *Thou shalt go to thy fathers in peace.* 2. His body should be buried after a long life, *one hundred and seventy-five* years, chap. xxv. 7. The body was buried; the soul went to the spiritual world, to dwell among the *fathers*—the patriarchs, who had lived and died in the Lord. See the note on chap. xxv. 8.

Verse 16. *In the fourth generation*] In former times most people counted by *generations*, to each of which was assigned a term of years amounting to 20, 25, 30, 33, 100, 108, or 110; for the *generation* was of various lengths among various people, at different times. It is probable that the *fourth generation* here means the *same as the four hundred years* in the preceding verse. Some think it refers to the time when *Eleazar*, the son of *Aaron*, the son of *Amram*, the son of *Kohath*, came out of Egypt, and divided the land of Canaan to Israel, Josh. xiv. 1. Others think the fourth generation of the Amorites is intended, because it is immediately added, *The iniquity of the Amorites is not yet full*; but in the fourth generation they should be expelled, and the descendants of Abram established in their place. From these words we learn that there is a certain pitch of iniquity to which nations may arrive before they are destroyed, and beyond which Divine justice does not permit them to pass.

Verse 17. *Smoking furnace and a burning lamp*] Probably the smoking furnace might be designed as an emblem of the sore afflictions of the Israelites in Egypt; but the *burning lamp* was certainly the *symbol of the Divine presence*, which, passing between the pieces, ratified the covenant with Abram, as the following verse immediately states.

Verse 18. *The Lord made a covenant*] כרת ברית *carath berith* signifies to *cut a covenant*, or rather the covenant *sacrifice*; for as no covenant was made without one, and the creature was *cut in two* that the contracting parties might pass between the pieces, hence *cutting the covenant* signified making the covenant. The same form of speech obtained among the Romans; and because, in making their covenants they always slew an animal, either by *cutting its throat*, or *knocking it down* with a stone or axe, after which they *divided* the parts as we have already seen, hence among the *percutere fœdus*, to *smite* a covenant, and *scindere fœdus*, to *cleave* a covenant, were terms which signified simply to *make* or *enter* into a covenant.

From the river of Egypt] Not the Nile, but the river called *Sichor*, which was *before* or on the *border* of Egypt, near to the isthmus of Suez; see Josh. xiii. 3; though some think that by this a branch of the Nile is meant. This promise was fully accomplished in the days of David and Solomon. See 2 Sam. viii. 3, &c., and 2 Chron. ix. 26.

Verse 19. *The Kenites, &c.*] Here are *ten* nations mentioned, though afterwards reckoned but *seven*; see Deut. vii. 1; Acts xiii. 19. Probably some of them which existed in Abram's time had been blended with others before the time of Moses, so that *seven* only out of the *ten* then remained; see part of these noticed Gen. x.

IN this chapter there are *three* subjects which must be particularly interesting to the pious reader. 1. The *condescension of* GOD in revealing himself to mankind in a variety of ways, so as to render it absolutely evident that *he had spoken*, that he loved mankind, and that he had made every provision for their eternal welfare. So unequivocal were the discoveries which God made of himself, that on the minds of those to whom they were made not one doubt was left, relative either to the truth of the subject, or that it was God himself

who made the discovery. The subject of the discovery also was such as sufficiently attested its truth to all future generations, for it concerned matters yet in futurity, so distinctly marked, so positively promised, and so highly interesting, as to make them objects of *attention*, *memory*, and *desire*, till they did come; and of *gratitude*, because of the permanent blessedness they communicated through all generations *after* the facts had taken place.

2. *The way of salvation by faith* in the promised Saviour, which now began to be explicitly declared. God gives the promise of salvation, and by means in which it was impossible, humanly speaking, that it should take place; teaching us, 1. That the whole work was spiritual, supernatural, and Divine; and, 2. That no human power could suffice to produce it. This Abram believed while he was yet uncircumcised, and this faith was accounted to him for righteousness or justification; God thereby teaching that he would pardon, accept, and receive into favour all who should believe on the Lord Jesus Christ. And this very case has ever since been the *standard of justification by faith*; and the experience of millions of men, built on this foundation, has sufficiently attested the truth and solidity of the ground on which it was built.

3. The foundation of the doctrine itself is laid in the covenant made between God and Abram in behalf of all the families of the earth, and this covenant is ratified by a sacrifice. By this covenant man is bound to God, and God graciously binds himself to man. As this covenant referred to the incarnation of Christ; and Abram, both as to himself and posterity, was to partake of the benefits of it by *faith*; hence *faith*, not *works*, is the only condition on which God, through Christ, forgives sins, and brings to the promised spiritual inheritance. This covenant still stands open; all the successive generations of men are parties on the one side, and Jesus is at once the sacrifice and Mediator of it. As therefore the covenant still stands open, and Jesus is still the Lamb slain before the throne, every human soul must ratify the covenant for himself; and no man does so but he who, conscious of his guilt, accepts the sacrifice which God has provided for him. Reader, hast *thou* done so? And with a heart unto *righteousness* dost thou *continue* to believe on the Son of God? How merciful is God, who has found out such a way of salvation by providing a Saviour every way suitable to miserable, fallen, sinful man! One who is holy, harmless, undefiled, and separate from sinners; and who, being higher than the heavens, raises up his faithful followers to the throne of his own eternal glory! Reader, give God the praise, and avail thyself of the sin-offering which lieth at the door.

CHAPTER XVI.

Sarai, having no child, gives Hagar her maid to Abram for wife, 1–3. *She conceives and despises her mistress*, 4. *Sarai is offended and upbraids Abram*, 5. *Abram vindicates himself; and Hagar, being hardly used by her mistress, runs away*, 6. *She is met by an angel, and counselled to return to her mistress*, 7–9. *God promises greatly to multiply her seed*, 10. *Gives the name of Ishmael to the child that should be born of her*, 11. *Shows his disposition and character*, 12. *Hagar calls the name of the Lord who spoke to her*, Thou God seest me, 13. *She calls the name of the well at which the angel met her*, Beer-lahai-roi, 14. *Ishmael is born in the 86th year of Abram's age*, 15, 16.

A. M. 2092.
B. C. 1912.

NOW Sarai, Abram's wife, [a] bare him no children: and she had a handmaid, [b] an Egyptian, whose name *was* [c] Hagar.

2 [d] And Sarai said unto Abram, Behold now, the LORD [e] hath restrained me from bearing: I pray [f] thee, go in unto my maid; it may be that I may [g] obtain children by her. And Abram [h] hearkened to the voice of Sarai.

[a] Chap. xv. 2, 3.——[b] Chap. xxi. 9.——[c] Gal. iv. 24.——[d] Chap. xxx. 3.——[e] Chap. xx. 18; xxx. 2; 1 Sam. i. 5, 6.

[f] So chap. xxx. 3, 9.——[g] Heb. *be builded by her*.——[h] Chap. iii. 17.

NOTES ON CHAP. XVI.

Verse 1. *She had a handmaid, an Egyptian*] As Hagar was an Egyptian, St. Chrysostom's conjecture is very probable, that she was one of those female slaves which Pharaoh gave to Abram when he sojourned in Egypt; see chap. xii. 16. Her name הגר *hagar* signifies a *stranger* or *sojourner*, and it is likely she got this name in the family of Abram, as the word is pure Hebrew.

Verse 2. *Go in unto my maid.*] It must not be forgotten that female slaves constituted a part of the private patrimony or possessions of a wife, and that she had a right, according to the usages of those times, to dispose of them as she pleased, the husband having no authority in the case.

I may obtain children by her.] The *slave* being the absolute property of the mistress, not only her person, but the fruits of her labour, with all her children, were her owner's property also. The children, therefore, which were born of the slave, were considered as the children of the mistress. It was on this ground that Sarai gave her slave to Abram; and we find, what must necessarily be the consequence in all cases of polygamy, that strifes and contentions took place.

A. M. 2093.
B. C. 1911.

3 And Sarai, Abram's wife, took
Hagar her maid, the Egyptian, after
Abram [i] had dwelt ten years in the land of
Canaan, and gave her to her husband Abram
to be his wife.
4 And he went in unto Hagar, and she conceived: and when she saw that she had conceived, her mistress was [k] despised in her
eyes.
5 And Sarai said unto Abram, My wrong *be*
upon thee: I have given my maid into thy
bosom; and when she saw that she had conceived, I was despised in her eyes: [l] the LORD
judge between me and thee.
6 [m] But Abram said unto Sarai, [n] Behold,
thy maid *is* in thy hand; do to her [o] as it
pleaseth thee. And when Sarai [p] dealt
hardly with her, [q] she fled from
her face.

A. M. 2093.
B. C. 1911.

7 And the angel of the LORD found her by
a fountain of water in the wilderness, [r] by the
fountain in the way to [s] Shur.
8 And he said, Hagar, Sarai's maid, whence
camest thou? and whither wilt thou go? And
she said, I flee from the face of my mistress
Sarai.
9 And the angel of the LORD said unto her,
Return to thy mistress, and [t] submit thyself
under her hands.
10 And the angel of the LORD said unto
her, [u] I will multiply thy seed exceedingly,
that it shall not be numbered for multitude.
11 And the angel of the LORD said unto
her, Behold, thou *art* with child, and shalt

[i] Chap. xii. 5.——[k] 2 Sam. vi. 16; Prov. xxx. 21, 23.——[l] Chap. xxxi. 53; 1 Sam. xxiv. 12.——[m] Prov. xv. 1; 1 Pet. iii. 7.——[n] Job ii. 6; Psa. cvi. 41, 42; Jer. xxxviii. 5.

[o] Heb. that which is *good in thine eyes*.——[p] Heb. *afflicted her*.——[q] Exod. ii. 15.——[r] Chap. xxv. 18.——[s] Exod. xv. 22.——[t] Tit. ii. 9; 1 Pet. ii. 18.——[u] Chap. xvii. 20; xxi. 18; xxv. 12.

Verse 3. *And Sarai, Abram's wife, took Hagar—and gave her to her husband—to be his wife.*] There are instances of Hindoo women, when barren, consenting to their husbands marrying a second wife for the sake of children; and second marriages on this account, without consent, are very common.—*Ward.*

Verse 5. *My wrong* be *upon thee*] This appears to be intended as a reproof to Abram, containing an insinuation that it was his fault that she herself had not been a mother, and that now he carried himself more affectionately towards Hagar than he did to her, in consequence of which conduct the slave became petulant. To remove all suspicion of this kind, Abram delivers up Hagar into her hand, who was certainly under his protection while his concubine or secondary wife; but this right *given to him by Sarai* he restores, to prevent her jealousy and uneasiness.

Verse 6. *Sarai dealt hardly with her*] תענה *teanneha, she afflicted her;* the term implying *stripes* and *hard usage,* to *bring down* the *body* and *humble* the *mind.* If the slave was to blame in this business the mistress is not less liable to censure. *She* alone had brought her into those circumstances, in which it was natural for her to value herself beyond her mistress.

Verse 7. *The angel of the Lord*] That Jesus Christ, in a body suited to the dignity of his nature, frequently appeared to the patriarchs, has been already intimated. That the person mentioned here was greater than any created being is sufficiently evident from the following particulars:—

1. From his promising to *perform* what God alone could *do,* and *foretelling* what God alone could *know;* "*I will multiply thy seed exceedingly,*" *&c.*, ver. 10; "*Thou* art *with child, and shalt bear a son,*" *&c.*, ver. 11; "*He will be a wild man,*" *&c.*, ver. 12. All this shows a *prescience* which is proper to God alone.

2. Hagar considers the person who spoke to her as *God,* calls him אל *El,* and addresses him in the way of *worship,* which, had he been a created angel, he would have refused. See Rev. xix. 10; xxii. 9.

3. Moses, who relates the transaction, calls this angel expressly JEHOVAH; for, says *he,* she called שם יהוה *shem Yehovah,* the NAME of the LORD that spake to her, ver. 13. Now this is a name never given to any created being.

4. This person, who is here called מלאך יהוה *malach Yehovah,* the Angel of the Lord, is the same who is called המלאך הגאל *hammalach haggoel,* the *redeeming Angel* or *the Angel the Redeemer,* Gen. xlviii. 16; מלאך פניו *malach panaiv,* the Angel of God's presence, Isa. lxiii. 9; and מלאך הברית *malach habberith,* the Angel of the Covenant, Mal. iii. 1: and is the same person which the Septuagint, Isa. ix. 6, term *μεγαλης βουλης αγγελος, the Angel of the Great Counsel* or *Design,* viz., of redeeming man, and filling the earth with righteousness.

5. These things cannot be spoken of any *human* or *created* being, for the *knowledge, works, &c.*, attributed to this person are such as belong to God; and as in all these cases there is a most evident *personal appearance,* Jesus Christ alone can be meant; for of God the Father it has been ever true that *no man hath at any time seen his shape,* nor has he ever limited himself to any definable *personal* appearance.

In the way to Shur.] As this was the road from Hebron to Egypt, it is probable she was now returning to her own country.

Verse 8. *Hagar, Sarai's maid*] This mode of address is used to show her that she was *known,* and to remind her that she was the *property* of *another.*

Verse 10. *I will multiply thy seed exceedingly*] Who says this? The person who is called the Angel of the Lord; and he certainly speaks with all the authority which is proper to God.

Verse 11. *And shalt call his name Ishmael*] ישמעאל *Yishmael,* from שמע *shama,* he heard, and אל *El,* God;

A. M. 2093. B. C. cir. 1911.

bear a son, [v] and shalt call his
name [w] Ishmael; because the LORD
hath heard thy affliction.
12 [x] And he will be a wild man; his hand
will be against every man, and every man's
hand against him; [y] and he shall dwell in the
presence of all his brethren.

[v] Chap. xvii. 19; Matt. i. 21; Luke i. 13, 31.——[w] That is, *God shall hear*.——[x] Chap. xxi. 20.——[y] Chap. xxv. 18.

13 And she called the name of
the LORD that spake unto her,
Thou God seest me: for she said, Have I
also here looked after him [z] that seeth me?
14 Wherefore the well was called [a] Beer-
lahai-roi; [b] behold, *it is* [c] between Kadesh
and Bered.

A. M. 2093. B. C. 1911.

[z] Chap. xxxi. 42.——[a] Chap. xxiv. 62; xxv. 11.——[b] That is, *the well of him that liveth and seeth me*.——[c] Num. xiii. 26.

for, says the Angel, THE LORD HATH HEARD *thy affliction*. Thus the name of the child must ever keep the mother in remembrance of God's merciful interposition in her behalf, and remind the *child* and the *man* that he was an object of God's gracious and providential goodness. Afflictions and distresses have a voice in the ears of God, even when prayer is restrained; but how much more powerfully do they speak when endured in meekness of spirit, with confidence in and supplication to the Lord!

Verse 12. *He will be a wild man*] פרא אדם *pere adam*. As the root of this word does not appear in the Hebrew Bible, it is probably found in the Arabic فر *farra*, to *run away*, to *run wild*; and hence the *wild ass*, from its *fleetness* and its *untamable* nature. What is said of the wild ass, Job xxxix. 5–8, affords the very best description that can be given of the *Ishmaelites*, (*the Bedouins* and *wandering Arabs*,) the descendants of Ishmael: "Who hath sent out the wild ass (פרא *pere*) free? or who hath loosed the bands (ערוד *arod*, of the brayer? Whose house I have made the wilderness, and the barren land his dwellings. He scorneth the multitude of the city, neither regardeth he the crying of the driver. The range of the mountains is his pasture, and he searcheth after every green thing." Nothing can be more descriptive of the *wandering, lawless, freebooting* life of the Arabs than this.

God himself has *sent them out free*—he has *loosed* them from all political restraint. *The wilderness is their habitation*; and in the *parched land*, where no other human beings could live, they *have their dwellings*. *They scorn the city*, and therefore have no *fixed* habitations; for their *multitude*, they are not afraid; for when they make depredations on cities and towns, they retire into the desert with so much precipitancy that all pursuit is eluded. In this respect *the crying of the driver is disregarded*. They may be said to have no lands, and yet *the range of the mountains is their pasture*—they pitch their *tents* and feed their *flocks* wherever they please; and they *search after every green thing*—are continually looking after *prey*, and seize on every kind of property that comes in their way.

It is farther said, *His hand will be against every man, and every man's hand against him*.—Many potentates among the Abyssinians, Persians, Egyptians, and Turks, have endeavoured to subjugate the wandering or wild Arabs; but, though they have had temporary triumphs, they have been ultimately unsuccessful. *Sesostris*, *Cyrus*, *Pompey*, and *Trajan*, all endeavoured to conquer Arabia, but in vain. From the beginning to the present day they have maintained their independency, and God preserves them as a lasting monument of his providential care, and an incontestable argument of *the truth of Divine Revelation*. Had the Pentateuch no other argument to evince its Divine origin, the account of *Ishmael* and the prophecy concerning his *descendants*, collated with their history and manner of life during a period of nearly *four thousand years*, would be sufficient. Indeed the argument is so absolutely demonstrative, that the man who would attempt its refutation, in the sight of reason and common sense would stand convicted of the most ridiculous presumption and folly.

The country which these free descendants of Ishmael may be properly said to possess, stretches from Aleppo to the Arabian Sea, and from Egypt to the Persian Gulf; a tract of land not less than 1800 miles in length, by 900 in breadth; see chap. xvii. 20.

Verse 13. *And she called the name of the Lord*] She *invoked* (ותקרא *vattikra*) *the name of Jehovah who spake unto her*, thus: *Thou God seest me!* She found that the eye of a merciful God had been upon her in all her wanderings and afflictions; and her words seem to intimate that *she had been seeking* the Divine help and protection, for she says, *Have I also* (or *have I not also*) *looked after him that seeth me?*

This last clause of the verse is very obscure, and is rendered differently by all the versions. The general sense taken out of it is this, that Hagar was now convinced that God himself had appeared unto her, and was surprised to find that, notwithstanding this, she was still permitted to live; for it is generally supposed that if God appeared to any, they must be consumed by his glories. This is frequently alluded to in the sacred writings. As the word אחרי *acharey*, which we render simply *after*, in other places signifies the *last days* or *after times*, (see on Exod. xxxiii. 23,) it may probably have a similar meaning here; and indeed this makes a consistent sense: *Have I here also seen the* LATTER PURPOSES OR DESIGNS *of him who seeth me?* An exclamation which may be referred to that discovery which God made in the preceding verse of the *future state* of her descendants.

Verse 14. *Wherefore the well was called Beer-lahai-roi*] It appears, from ver. 7, that Hagar had sat down by a fountain or well of water in the wilderness of Shur, at which the Angel of the Lord found her; and, to commemorate the wonderful discovery which God had made of himself, she called the name of the well באר לחי ראי *beer-lachai-roi*, "A well to the Living One who seeth me." Two things seem implied here: 1. A dedication of the well to Him who had appeared to her; and, 2. Faith in the promise; for he who is the Living One, existing in all generations, must have

a

A. M. 2094. B. C. 1910.

15 And [d] Hagar bare Abram a son; and Abram called his son's name, which Hagar bare, [e] Ishmael.

16 And Abram *was* fourscore and six years old when Hagar bare Ishmael to Abram.

A. M. 2094. B. C. 1910.

[d] Gal. iv. 22.

[e] Ver. 11.

it ever in his power to accomplish promises which are to be fulfilled through the whole lapse of time.

Verse 15. *And Hagar bare Abram a son, &c.*] It appears, therefore, that Hagar returned at the command of the angel, believing the promise that God had made to her.

Called his son's name—Ishmael.] Finding by the account of Hagar, that God had designed that he should be so called. "Ishmael," says Ainsworth, "is the first man in the world whose name was given him of God before he was born."

In the preceding chapter we have a very detailed account of the covenant which God made with Abram, which stated that his seed should possess Canaan; and this promise, on the Divine authority, he steadfastly believed, and in simplicity of heart waited for its accomplishment. Sarai was not like minded. As she had no child herself, and was now getting old, she thought it necessary to secure the inheritance by such means as were in *her power;* she therefore, as we have seen, gave her slave to Abram, that she might have children by her. We do not find Abram remonstrating on the subject; and why is he blamed? God had not *as yet* told him *how* he was to have an heir; the promise simply stated, *He that shall come forth out of thine own bowels shall be thine heir*, chap. xv. 4. Concubinage, under that dispensation, was perfectly lawful; therefore he could, with equal justice and innocence, when it was lawful in itself, and now urged by the *express desire of Sarai*, take Hagar to wife. And it is very likely that he might think that *his* posterity, whether by *wife* or *concubine*, as both were lawful, might be *that* intended by the promise.

It is very difficult to believe that a promise which refers to some *natural event* can possibly be fulfilled but through some *natural means*. And yet, what is nature but an instrument in God's hands? What we call natural effects are all performed by supernatural agency; for nature, that is, the whole system of inanimate things, is as inert as any of the particles of matter of the aggregate of which it is composed, and can be a *cause* to no *effect* but as it is excited by a sovereign power. This is a doctrine of sound philosophy, and should be carefully considered by all, that men may see that without an overruling and universally energetic providence, no effect whatever can be brought about. But besides these general influences of God in nature, which are all exhibited by what men call *general laws*, he chooses often to act *supernaturally*, i. e., independently of or against these general laws, that we may see that there is a God who does not confine himself to *one way* of working, but *with* means, *without* means, and even *against natural* means, accomplishes the gracious purposes of his mercy in the behalf of man. Where God *has* promised let him be implicitly credited, because *he* cannot lie; and let not hasty nature intermeddle with his work.

The omniscience of God is a subject on which we should often reflect, and we can never do it unfruitfully while we connect it, as we ever should, with infinite goodness and mercy. Every thing, person, and circumstance, is under its notice; and doth not the eye of God affect his heart? The poor *slave*, the *stranger*, the *Egyptian*, suffering under the severity of her hasty, unbelieving mistress, is seen by the all-wise and merciful God. He permits her to go to the desert, provides the spring to quench her thirst, and sends the Angel of the covenant to instruct and comfort her. How gracious is God! He permits us to get into distressing circumstances that he may give us effectual relief; and in such a way, too, that the excellence of the power may appear to be of him, and that we may learn to trust in him in all our distresses. God *delights* to do his creatures good.

In all transactions between God and man, mentioned in the sacred writings, we see one uniform agency; the great *Mediator in* all, and *through* all; God ever coming to man by him, and man having access to God through him. This *was*, *is*, and ever *will be* the economy of grace. "The Father hath sent me:—and no man cometh unto the Father but by me." God forbid that he should have cause to complain of us, "Ye will not come unto me, that ye might have life."

CHAPTER XVII.

In the ninety-ninth year of Abram's life God again appears to him, announces his name as God Almighty, *and commands him to walk perfectly before him,* 1; *proposes to renew the covenant,* 2. *Abram's prostration,* 3. *The covenant specified,* 4. *Abram's name changed to* Abraham, *and the reason given,* 5. *The privileges of the covenant enumerated,* 6–8. *The conditions of the covenant to be observed, not only by Abraham but all his posterity,* 9. *Circumcision appointed as a sign or token of the covenant,* 10, 11. *The age at which and the persons on whom this was to be performed,* 12, 13. *The danger of neglecting this rite,* 14. *Sarai's name changed to* Sarah, *and a particular promise made to her,* 15, 16. *Abraham's joy at the prospect of the performance of a matter which, in the course of nature, was impossible,* 17. *His request for the preservation and prosperity of Ishmael,* 18. *The birth and blessedness of Isaac foretold,* 19. *Great prosperity promised to Ishmael,* 20. *But the covenant to be established not in his, but in Isaac's posterity,* 21. *Abraham, Ishmael, and all the males in the family circumcised,* 23–27.

A. M. 2107.
B. C. 1897.

AND when Abram was ninety years old and nine, the LORD
[a] appeared to Abram, and said unto him, [b] I
am the Almighty God, [c] walk before me, and
be thou [d] perfect.[e]
2 And I will make my covenant between me
and thee, and [f] will multiply thee exceedingly.
3 And Abram [g] fell on his face:
and God talked with him, saying,
4 As for me, behold, my covenant *is* with
thee, and thou shalt be [h] a father of [i] many
nations.
5 Neither shall thy name any more be called
Abram, but [k] thy name shall be [l] Abraham;

A. M. 2107.
B. C. 1897.

---

[a] Chap. xii. 1.——[b] Chap. xxviii. 3; xxxv. 11; Exod. vi. 3; Deut. x. 17.——[c] Chap. v. 22; xlviii. 15; 1 Kings ii. 4; viii. 25; 2 Kings xx. 3.——[d] Or, *upright; or, sincere.*——[e] Ch. vi. 9; Deut. xviii. 13; Job i. 1; Matt. v. 48.——[f] Ch. xii. 2; xiii. 16; xxii. 17. [g] Ver. 17.——[h] Rom. iv. 11, 12, 16; Gal. iii. 29.——[i] Heb. *multitude of nations.*——[k] Neh. ix. 7.——[l] That is, *father of a great multitude.*

NOTES ON CHAP. XVII.

Verse 1. *The Lord appeared to Abram*] See on chap. xv. 1.

I am *the Amighty God*] אני אל שדי *ani El shaddai, I am God all-sufficient;* from שדה *shadah*, to *shed*, to *pour out.* I am that God who *pours* out *blessings*, who gives them *richly, abundantly, continually.*

Walk before me] התהלך לפני *hithhallech lephanai, set thyself to walk*—be firmly purposed, thoroughly determined to obey, *before me;* for my eye is ever on thee, therefore ever consider that God seeth thee. Who can imagine a stronger incitement to conscientious, persevering obedience?

Be thou perfect.] והיה תמים *vehyeh thamim, and thou shalt be perfections*, i. e., altogether perfect. Be just such as the *holy* God would have thee to be, as the *almighty* God can make thee; and live as the *all-sufficient* God shall support thee; for he alone who makes the soul holy can preserve it in holiness. Our blessed Lord appears to have had these words pointedly in view, Matt. v. 48: Εσεσθε ὑμεις τελειοι, ὡσπερ ὁ Πατηρ ὑμων ὁ εν τοις ουρανοις τελειος εστι· *Ye* SHALL BE *perfect, as your Father who is in heaven is perfect.* But what does this imply? Why, to be saved from all the power, the guilt, and the contamination of sin. This is only the *negative* part of salvation, but it has also a *positive* part; to be made *perfect*—to be perfect as our Father who is in heaven is perfect, to be filled with the fulness of God, to have Christ dwelling continually in the heart by faith, and to be rooted and grounded in love. This is the state *in* which man was created, for he was made in the image and likeness of God. This is the state *from* which man fell, for he broke the command of God. And this is the state *into* which every human soul must be raised, who would dwell with God in glory; for Christ was incarnated and died to put away sin by the sacrifice of himself. What a glorious privilege! And who can doubt the possibility of its attainment, who believes in the omnipotent love of God, the infinite merit of the blood of atonement, and the all-pervading and all-purifying energy of the Holy Ghost? How many miserable souls employ that time to dispute and cavil against the possibility of being saved *from* their sins, which they should devote to praying and believing that they might be saved out of the hands of their enemies! But some may say, "You overstrain the meaning of the term; it signifies only, *be sincere;* for as perfect obedience is impossible, God accepts of *sincere* obedience." If by *sincerity* the objection means *good desires*, and generally *good purposes*, with an *impure heart* and *spotted life*, then I assert that no such thing is implied in the text, nor in the original word; but if the word *sincerity* be taken in its proper and literal sense, I have no objection to it. *Sincere* is compounded of *sine cera*, "without wax;" and, applied to moral subjects, is a metaphor taken from clarified honey, from which every atom of the comb or wax is separated. Then let it be proclaimed from heaven, *Walk before me, and be* SINCERE! purge out the old leaven, that ye may be a new lump unto God; and thus ye shall be perfect, as your Father who is in heaven is perfect. This is *sincerity.* Reader, remember that the blood of Christ cleanseth from all sin. Ten thousand quibbles on insulated texts can never lessen, much less destroy, the merit and efficacy of the great Atonement.

Verse 3. *And Abram fell on his face*] The eastern method of prostration was thus: the person first went down on his knees, and then lowered his head to his knees, and touched the earth with his forehead. A very painful posture, but significative of great humiliation and reverence.

Verse 5. *Thy name shall be Abraham*] Ab-ram אברם literally signifies a *high* or *exalted father.* Ab-ra-ham אברהם differs from the preceding only in one letter; it has ה *he* before the last radical. Though this may appear very simple and easy, yet the true etymology and meaning of the word are very difficult to be assigned. The reason given for the change made in the patriarch's name is this: *For a father of many nations have I made thee*, אב המון גוים *ab-hamon-goyim*, "a father of a multitude of nations." This has led some to suppose that אברהם *Abraham*, is a contraction for אב רב המון *ab-rab-hamon*, "the father of a great multitude."

Aben Ezra says the name is derived from אביר המון *abir-hamon*, "a powerful multitude."

Rabbi Solomon Jarchi defines the name *cabalistically*, and says that its *numeral letters* amount to *two hundred* and *forty-eight*, which, says he, is the exact number of the *bones in the human body.* But before the ה *he* was added, which stands for *five*, it was five short of this perfection.

Rabbi Lipman says the ה *he* being added as the *fourth letter*, signifies that the Messiah should come in the fourth millenary of the world.

Clarius and others think that the ה *he*, which is one of the letters of the Tetragrammaton, (or word of four letters, יהוה YeHoVaH,) was added for the sake of *dignity*, God associating the patriarch more nearly

A. M. 2107. B. C. 1897. [m] for a father of many nations have I made thee.

6 And I will make thee exceeding fruitful, and I will make [n] nations of thee, and [o] kings shall come out of thee.

7 And I will [p] establish my covenant between me and thee, and thy seed after thee, in their generations, for an everlasting covenant, [q] to be a God unto thee, and to [r] thy seed after thee.

8 And [s] I will give unto thee, and to thy seed after thee, the land [t] wherein [u] thou art a stranger, all the land of Canaan, for an everlasting possession: and [v] I will be their God. A. M. 2107. B. C. 1897.

9 And God said unto Abraham, Thou shalt keep my covenant therefore, thou, and thy seed after thee, in their generations.

10 This *is* my covenant, which ye shall keep, between me and you, and thy seed after thee; [w] Every man-child among you shall be circumcised.

[m] Rom. iv. 17.——[n] Chap. xxxv. 11.——[o] Ver. 16; chap. xxxv. 11; Matt. i. 6, &c.——[p] Gal. iii. 17.——[q] Chap. xxvi. 24; xxviii. 13; Heb. xi. 16.——[r] Rom. ix. 8.——[s] Chap. xii. 7; xiii. 15; Psa. cv. 9, 11.——[t] Heb. *of thy sojournings.*——[u] Chap. xxiii. 4; xxviii. 4.——[v] Exod. vi. 7; Lev. xxvi. 12; Deut. iv. 37; xiv. 2; xxvi. 18; xxix. 13.——[w] Acts vii. 8.

to himself, by thus imparting to him a portion of his own name.

Having enumerated so many opinions, that of *William Alabaster*, in his *Apparatus to the Revelation*, should not be passed by. He most wisely says that *ab-ram* or *ab-rom* signifies *father of the Romans*, and consequently the *pope;* therefore Abraham was *pope the first!* This is just as likely as some of the preceding etymologies.

From all these learned as well as puerile conjectures we may see the extreme difficulty of ascertaining the true meaning of the word, though the *concordance makers, and proper name explainers* find no difficulty at all in the case; and pronounce on it as readily and authoritatively as if they had been in the Divine council when it was first imposed.

Hottinger, in his *Smegma Orientale*, supposes the word to be derived from the Arabic root رهم *rahama*, which signifies *to be very numerous*. Hence اب رهم *ab raham* would signify a *copious father* or *father of a multitude*. This makes a very good sense, and agrees well with the context. Either this etymology or that which supposes the inserted ה *he* to be an abbreviation of the word המון *hamon, multitude*, is the most likely to be the true one. But this last would require the word to be written, when full, אב רם המון *ab-ram-hamon*.

The same difficulty occurs, verse 15, on the word *Sarai* שרי, which signifies *my prince* or *princess*, and *Sarah* שרה, where the whole change is made by the substitution of a ה *he* for a י *yod*. This latter might be translated *princess* in general; and while the former seems to point out her government in her *own family alone*, the latter appears to indicate her government over the *nations* of which her husband is termed the *father* or *lord;* and hence the promise states that *she shall be a mother of nations*, and that *kings of people should spring from her*. See ver. 15, 16.

Now as the only change in each name is made by the insertion of a single letter, and that letter the same in *both* names, I cannot help concluding that some *mystery* was designed by its insertion; and therefore the opinion of *Clarius* and some others is not to be disregarded, which supposes that God shows he had conferred a peculiar *dignity* on both, by adding to their names one of the letters of his own; a name by which his eternal power and Godhead are peculiarly pointed out.

From the difficulty of settling the etymology of these two names, on which so much stress seems to be laid in the text, the reader will see with what caution he should receive the *lists of explanations* of the *proper names* in the Old and New Testaments, which he so frequently meets with, and which I can pronounce to be in general *false* or *absurd*.

Verse 7. *An everlasting covenant*] ברית עולם *berith olam*. See on chap. xiii. 15. Here the word *olam* is taken in its own proper meaning, as the words immediately following prove—*to be a God unto thee, and thy seed after thee;* for as the soul is to endure for ever, so it shall eternally stand in need of the supporting power and energy of God; and as the reign of the Gospel dispensation shall be as long as sun and moon endure, and its consequences *eternal*, so must the covenant be on which these are founded.

Verse 8. *Everlasting possession*] Here עולם *olam* appears to be used in its *accommodated* meaning, and signifies the completion of the Divine counsel in reference to a particular period or dispensation. And it is literally true that the Israelites possessed the land of Canaan till the Mosaic dispensation was terminated in the complete introduction of that of the Gospel. But as the spiritual and temporal covenants are both blended together, and the former was pointed out and typified by the latter, hence the word even here may be taken in its own *proper* meaning, that of *ever-during*, or *eternal;* because the spiritual blessings pointed out by the temporal covenant *shall have no end*. And hence it is immediately added, *I will be their God*, not for a *time*, certainly, but *for ever* and *ever*. See the notes on chap. xxi. 33.

Verse 10. *Every man-child—shall be circumcised.*] Those who wish to invalidate the evidence of the Divine origin of the Mosaic law, roundly assert that the Israelites received the rite of circumcision from the Egyptians. Their apostle in this business is Herodotus, who, lib. ii., p. 116, Edit. Steph. 1592, says: "The Colchians, Egyptians, and Ethiopians, are the only nations in the world who have used circumcision απ' αρχης, from the remotest period; and the Phœnicians and Syrians who inhabit Palestine acknowledge they received this from the Egyptians." Herodotus cannot mean *Jews* by Phœnicians and Syrians; if he does he is incorrect, for no Jew ever did or ever could

a

A. M. 2107.
B. C. 1897.

11 And ye shall circumcise the flesh of your foreskin; and it shall be [x] a token of the covenant betwixt me and you.

12 And [y] he that is eight days old [z] shall be circumcised among you, every man-child in your generations, he that is born in the house, or bought with money of any stranger, which *is* not of thy seed.

13 He that is born in thy house, and he that is bought with thy money, must needs be circumcised: and my covenant shall be in your flesh for an everlasting covenant.

14 And the uncircumcised man-child whose flesh of his foreskin is not circumcised, that soul [a] shall be cut off from his people; he hath broken my covenant.

15 And God said unto Abraham, As for Sarai thy wife, thou shalt not call her name Sarai, but [b] Sarah *shall* her name *be*.

16 And I will bless her, [c] and give thee a son also of her: yea, I will bless her, and [d] she shall be *a mother* [e] of nations; kings of people shall be of her.

17 Then Abraham fell upon his face, [f] and laughed, and said in his heart, Shall *a child* be born unto him that is a hundred years old? and shall Sarah, that is ninety years old, bear?

[x] Acts vii. 8; Rom. iv. 11.——[y] Heb. *a son of eight days.*——[z] Lev. xii. 3; Luke ii. 21; John vii. 22; Phil. iii. 5.——[a] Exod. iv. 24.——[b] That is, *princess.*——[c] Chap. xviii. 10.——[d] Heb. *she shall become nations.*——[e] Ch. xxxv. 11; Gal. iv. 31; 1 Pet. iii. 6.——[f] Chap. xviii. 12; xxi. 6.

acknowledge this, with the history of Abraham in his hand. If Herodotus had written before the days of Abraham, or at least before the sojourning of the children of Israel in Egypt, and informed us that circumcision had been practised among them απ' αρχης, *from the beginning*, there would then exist a possibility that the Israelites while sojourning among them had learned and adopted this rite. But when we know that Herodotus flourished only 484 years before the Christian era, and that Jacob and his family sojourned in Egypt more than 1800 years before Christ, and that all the descendants of Abraham most conscientiously observed circumcision, and do so to this day, then the presumption is that the Egyptians received it from the Israelites, but that it was impossible the latter could have received it from the former, as they had practised it so long before their ancestors had sojourned in Egypt.

Verse 11. *And it shall be a token*] לאות *leoth*, for a sign of spiritual things; for the circumcision made in the flesh was designed to signify the purification of the heart from all unrighteousness, as God particularly showed in the law itself. See Deut. x. 16; see also Rom. ii. 25–29; Col. ii. 11. And it was *a seal of* that *righteousness* or justification that comes by *faith*, Rom. iv. 11. That some of the Jews had a just notion of its *spiritual* intention, is plain from many passages in the Chaldee paraphrases and in the Jewish writers. I borrow one passage from the book *Zohar*, quoted by Ainsworth: "At what time a man is sealed with this holy seal, (of circumcision,) thenceforth he seeth the holy blessed God properly, and the holy soul is united to him. If he be not worthy, and keepeth not this sign, what is written? *By the breath of God they perish*, (Job iv. 9,) because this seal of the holy blessed God was not kept. But if he be worthy, and keep it, the Holy Ghost is not separated from him."

Verse 12. *He that is eight days old*] Because previously to this they were considered unclean, Lev. xii. 2, 3, and circumcision was ever understood as a *consecration of the person to God.* Neither calf, lamb, nor kid, was offered to God till it was eight days old for the same reason, Lev. xxii. 27.

Verse 13. *He that is born in thy house*] The son of a servant; *he that is bought with thy money*—a slave on his coming into the family. According to the Jewish writers the father was to circumcise his son; and the master, the servant born in his house, or the slave bought with money. If the father or master neglected to do this, then the magistrates were obliged to see it performed; if the neglect of this ordinance was unknown to the magistrates, then the person himself, when he came of age, was obliged to do it.

Verse 14. *The uncircumcised—shall be cut off from his people*] By being cut off some have imagined that a sudden temporal death was implied; but the simple meaning seems to be that such should have no right to nor share in the blessings of the covenant, which we have already seen were both of a temporal and spiritual kind; and if so, then eternal death was implied, for it was impossible for a person who had not received the *spiritual purification* to enter into eternal glory. The *spirit* of this law extends to all ages, dispensations, and people; he whose heart is not purified from sin cannot enter into the kingdom of God. Reader, on *what* is thy hope of heaven founded?

Verse 15. *Thou shalt not call her name Sarai, but Sarah*] See on ver. 5.

Verse 16. *I will bless her, &c.*] Sarah certainly stands at the head of all the women of the Old Testament, on account of her extraordinary privileges. I am quite of Calmet's opinion that Sarah was a type of the blessed *Virgin*. St. Paul considers her a type of the *New Testament* and heavenly Jerusalem; and as all *true believers* are considered as the *children of Abraham*, so all *faithful holy women* are considered *the daughters of Sarah*, Gal. iv. 22, 24, 26. See also 1 Pet. iii. 6.

Verse 17. *Then Abraham—laughed*] I am astonished to find learned and pious men considering this as a token of Abraham's *weakness of faith* or *unbelief*, when they have the most positive assurance from

A.M. 2107. B. C. 1897.

18 And Abraham said unto God,
O that Ishmael might live before
thee!
19 And God said, [g] Sarah thy wife shall
bear thee a son indeed; and thou shalt call
his name Isaac: and I will establish my covenant with him for an everlasting covenant,
and with his seed after him.
20 And as for Ishmael, I have heard thee:
Behold, I have blessed him, and will make
him fruitful, and [h] will multiply him exceedingly; [i] twelve princes shall he beget, [k] and I
will make him a great nation.
21 But my covenant will I establish with Isaac, [l] which Sarah
shall bear unto thee at this set time in the
next year.
22 And he left off talking with him, and
[m] God went up from Abraham.
23 And Abraham took Ishmael his son, and
all that were born in his house, and all that
were bought with his money, every male
among the men of Abraham's house, and
circumcised the flesh of their foreskin in
the [n] selfsame day, as God had said unto
him.

[g] Chap. xviii. 10; xxi. 2; Gal. iv. 28.——[h] Chap. xvi. 10.——[i] Chap. xxv. 12-16.——[k] Chap. xxi. 18.——[l] Chapter xxi. 2.——[m] Chap. xviii. 33; xxxv. 13.——[n] Chap. xxxiv. 24; Josh. v. 2-9; Acts xvi. 3; Rom. ii. 25-29; iv. 9-12; Gal. v. 6; vi. 15.

the Spirit of God himself that *Abraham was not weak but strong in* the *faith;* that *he staggered not at the promise through unbelief,* but gave *glory to God,* Rom. iv. 19, 20. It is true the same word is used, chap. xviii. 12, concerning Sarah, in whom it was certainly a sign of doubtfulness, though mixed with pleasure at the thought of the possibility of her becoming a mother; but we know how possible it is to express both *faith* and *unbelief* in the same way, and even pleasure and disdain have been expressed by a smile or laugh. By *laughing* Abraham undoubtedly expressed his *joy* at the prospect of the fulfilment of so glorious a promise; and from this very circumstance *Isaac* had his name. יצחק *yitschak,* which we change into *Isaac,* signifies *laughter;* and it is the same word which is used in the verse before us: *Abraham fell on his face,* ויצחק *vaiyitschak, and he laughed;* and to the *joy* which he felt on this occasion our Lord evidently alludes, John viii. 56: *Your father Abraham* REJOICED *to see my day; and he saw it, and was* GLAD. And to commemorate this joy he called his son's name *Isaac.* See the note on chap. xxi. 6.

Verse 18. *O that Ishmael might live before thee!*] Abraham, finding that the covenant was to be established in *another* branch of his family, felt solicitous for his son Ishmael, whom he considered as necessarily excluded; on which God delivers that most remarkable prophecy which follows in the 20th verse, and which contains an answer to the prayer and wish of Abraham: *And as for Ishmael I have heard thee;* so that the object of Abraham's prayer was, that his son Ishmael might be the head of a prosperous and potent people.

Verse 20. *Twelve princes shall he beget, &c.*] See the names of these *twelve princes,* chap. xxv. 12-16. From Ishmael proceeded the various tribes of the Arabs, called also *Saracens* by Christian writers. They were anciently, and still continue to be, a very numerous and powerful people. "It was somewhat wonderful, and not to be foreseen by human sagacity," says Bishop Newton, "that a man's whole posterity should so nearly resemble him, and retain the same inclinations, the same habits, and the same customs, throughout all ages! These are the only people besides the Jews who have subsisted as a distinct people from the beginning, and in some respects they very much resemble each other. 1. The Arabs, as well as the Jews, are descended from Abraham, and both boast of their descent from the father of the faithful. 2. The Arabs, as well as the Jews, are circumcised, and both profess to have derived this ceremony from Abraham. 3. The Arabs, as well as the Jews, had originally *twelve patriarchs,* who were their princes or governors. 4. The Arabs, as well as the Jews, marry among themselves, and in their own tribes. 5. The Arabs, as well as the Jews, are singular in several of their customs, and are standing monuments to all ages of the exactness of the Divine predictions, and of the veracity of Scripture history. We may with more confidence believe the particulars related of Abraham and Ishmael when we see them verified in their posterity at this day. This is having, as it were, ocular demonstration for our faith." See Bp. Newton's *Second Dissertation on the Prophecies,* and see the notes on chap. xvi. 12.

Verse 21. *My covenant will I establish with Isaac*] All *temporal* good things are promised to Ishmael and his posterity, but the establishment of the Lord's covenant is to be with Isaac. Hence it is fully evident that this covenant referred chiefly to *spiritual* things—to the Messiah, and the salvation which should be brought to both Jews and Gentiles by his incarnation, death, and glorification.

Verse 22. *God went up from Abraham.*] Ascended evidently before him, so that he had the fullest proof that it was no human being, no earthly angel or messenger, that talked with him; and the promise of a son in the course of a single year, *at this set time in the next year,* ver. 21, which had every human probability against it, was to be the sure token of the truth of all that had hitherto taken place, and the proof that all that was farther promised should be fulfilled in its due time. Was it not in nearly the same way in which the Lord went up from Abraham, that Jesus Christ ascended to heaven in the presence of his disciples? Luke xxiv. 51.

Verse 23. *And Abraham took Ishmael, &c.*] Had not Abraham, his son, (who was of age to judge for himself,) and all the family, been fully convinced that this thing was of God, they could not have submitted

A. M. 2107. B. C. 1897. 24 And Abraham *was* ninety years old and nine, [o] when he was circumcised in the flesh of his foreskin.

25 And Ishmael his son *was* thirteen years old when he was circumcised in the flesh of his foreskin.

26 In the selfsame day was Abraham circumcised, and Ishmael his son. A. M. 2107. B. C. 1897.

27 And [p] all the men of his house, born in the house, and bought with money of the stranger, were circumcised with him.

[o] See ver. 1, 17; Rom. iv. 19.

[p] Chap. xviii. 19.

to it. A rite so painful, so repugnant to every feeling of delicacy, and every way revolting to nature, could never have sprung up in the imagination of man. To this day the Jews practise it as a Divine ordinance; and all the Arabians do the same. As a distinction between *them* and *other people* it never could have been designed, because it was a *sign* that was never to *appear*. The individual alone knew that he bore in his flesh this sign of the covenant, and he bore it by the order of God, and he knew it was a *sign* and *seal* of spiritual blessings, and not the blessings themselves, though a proof that these blessings were promised, and that he had a *right* to them. Those who did not consider it in this spiritual reference are by the apostle denominated the *concision*, Phil. iii. 2, i. e., persons whose flesh was cut, but whose hearts were not purified.

The contents of this chapter may be summed up in a few propositions:—

1. God, in renewing his *covenant* with Abram, makes an important *change* in his and Sarai's name; a change which should ever act as a help to their faith, that the promises by which God had bound himself should be punctually fulfilled. However difficult it may be for us to ascertain the precise import of the change then made, we may rest assured that it was perfectly understood by both; and that, as they had received this name from God, they considered it as placing them in a new relation both to their *Maker* and to their posterity. From what we have already seen, the change made in Abram's name is *inscrutable* to us; there is something like this in Rev. ii. 17: *To him that overcometh will I give a white stone*, and a NEW NAME—*which no man knoweth, saving he that receiveth it.* The full import of the *change* made in a soul that enters into covenant with God through Christ, is only known to itself; a stranger intermeddleth not with its joy. Hence, even men of learning and the world at large have considered experimental religion as enthusiasm, merely because they have not understood its nature, and have permitted themselves to be carried away by prejudices which they have imbibed perhaps at first through the means of ignorant or hypocritical pretenders to deep piety; but while they have the sacred writings before them, their prejudices and opposition to that without which they cannot be saved are as unprincipled as they are absurd.

2. God gives Abraham a *precept*, which should be observed, not only by himself, but by all his posterity; for this was to be a permanent sign of that covenant which was to endure for ever. Though the sign is now changed from *circumcision* to *baptism*, each of them equally significant, yet the covenant is not changed in any part of its essential meaning. Faith in God through the great sacrifice, remission of sins, and sanctification of the heart, are required by the new covenant as well as by the old.

3. The rite of *circumcision* was *painful* and *humiliating*, to denote that *repentance*, *self-denial*, *&c.*, are absolutely necessary to all who wish for redemption in the blood of the covenant; and *the putting away this filth of the flesh* showed the necessity of a pure heart and a holy life.

4. As eternal life is the free gift of God, he has a right to give it in what way he pleases, and on what terms. He says to Abraham and his seed, *Ye shall circumcise the flesh of your foreskin*, and he that doth not so *shall be cut off from his people*. He says also to sinners in general, *Let the wicked forsake his way, and the unrighteous man his thoughts; Repent, and believe the Gospel*; and, *Except ye repent, ye shall perish*. These are the *terms* on which he will bestow the blessings of the old and new covenants. And let it be remembered that stretching out the hand to receive an alms can never be considered as *meriting* the *bounty* received, neither can repentance or faith *merit* salvation, although they are the conditions on which it is bestowed.

5. The *precepts* given under both covenants were accompanied with a *promise* of the *Messiah*. God well knows that no religious rite can be properly observed, and no precept obeyed, unless he impart strength from on high; and he teaches us that that strength must ever come through the promised seed. Hence with the utmost propriety, we ask every blessing *through him*, in whom God is well pleased.

6. The *precept*, the *promise*, and the *rite*, were prefaced with, "I am God all-sufficient; walk before me, and be thou perfect." God, who is the sole object of religious worship, has the sole authority to prescribe that worship, and the rites and ceremonies which shall be used in it; hence he prescribed *circumcision* and *sacrifices* under the old law, and *baptism* and the *eucharist* under the Gospel; and to render both effectual to the end of their institution, *faith* in God was indispensably necessary.

7. Those who profess to believe in him must not live as *they* list, but as *he* pleases. Though redeemed from the curse of the law, and from the rites and ceremonies of the *Jewish Church*, they are *under the law to Christ*, and *must walk before him*—be in all things obedient to that *moral* law which is an emanation from the righteousness of God, and of eternal obligation; and let it ever be remembered that Christ is "the author of eternal salvation to all that obey him." Without faith and obedience there can be no holiness, and without holiness none can see the Lord. Be all that

God would have thee to be, and God will be to thee all that thou canst possibly require. He never gives a precept but he offers sufficient grace to enable thee to perform it. Believe as he would have thee, and act as he shall strengthen thee, and thou wilt believe all things *savingly*, and do all things *well*.

CHAPTER XVIII.

The Lord appears unto Abraham in Mamre, 1. *Three angels, in human appearance, come towards his tent,* 2. *He invites them in to wash and refresh themselves,* 3–5; *prepares a calf, bread, butter, and milk, for their entertainment; and himself serves them,* 6–8. *They promise that within a year Sarah shall have a son,* 9, 10. *Sarah, knowing herself and husband to be superannuated, smiles at the promise,* 11, 12. *One of the* three, *who is called the* Lord *or Jehovah, chides her, and asserts the sufficiency of the Divine power to accomplish the promise,* 13, 14. *Sarah, through fear, denies that she had laughed or showed signs of unbelief,* 15. *Abraham accompanies these Divine persons on their way to Sodom,* 16; *and that one who is called Jehovah informs him of his purpose to destroy Sodom and Gomorrah, because of their great wickedness,* 17–21. *The two former proceed toward Sodom, while the latter (Jehovah) remains with Abraham,* 22. *Abraham intercedes for the inhabitants of those cities, entreating the Lord to spare them provided* fifty *righteous persons should be found in them,* 23–25. *The Lord grants this request,* 26. *He pleads for the same mercy should only* forty-five *be found there; which is also granted,* 27, 28. *He pleads the same for* forty, *which is also granted,* 29; *for* thirty, *with the same success,* 30; *for* twenty, *and receives the same gracious answer,* 31; *for* ten, *and the Lord assures him that should* ten *righteous persons be found there, he will not destroy the place,* 32. *Jehovah then departs, and Abraham returns to his tent,* 33.

A. M. 2107. B. C. 1897.

AND the Lord appeared unto
him in the [a] plains of Mamre:
and he sat in the tent door in the heat of the
day:
2 [b] And he lift up his eyes and looked, and,
lo, three men stood by him: [c] and when
he saw *them*, he ran to meet them from the
tent door, and bowed himself toward the
ground,
3 And said, My Lord, if now I have found
favour in thy sight, pass not away,
I pray thee, from thy servant:
4 Let [d] a little water, I pray you, be fetched,
and wash your feet, and rest yourselves under
the tree:
5 And [e] I will fetch a morsel of bread, and
[f] comfort ye your [g] hearts; after that ye shall
pass on: [h] for therefore [i] are ye come to your
servant. And they said, So do, as thou hast said.
6 And Abraham hastened into the tent unto

[a] Chap. xiii. 18; xiv. 13.——[b] Heb. xiii. 2.——[c] Chap. xix. 1; Pet. iv. 9.——[d] Chap. xix. 2; xliii. 24.——[e] Judg. vi. 18; xiii. 15. [f] Heb. *stay*.——[g] Judg. xix. 5; Psa. civ. 15.——[h] Chap. xix. 8; xxxiii. 10.——[i] Heb. *you have passed*.

NOTES ON CHAP. XVIII.

Verse 1. *And the Lord appeared*] See on chap. xv. 1.

Sat in the tent door] For the purpose of enjoying the refreshing air *in the heat of the day*, when the sun had most power. A custom still frequent among the Asiatics.

Verse 2. *Three men stood by him*] נצבים עליו *nitstsabim alaiv*, were *standing over against him*; for if they had been *standing by him*, as our translation says, he needed not to have "run from the tent door to meet them." To Abraham these appeared at first as *men*; but he *entertained angels unawares*, see Heb. xiii. 2.

Verse 3. *And said, My Lord, &c.*] The word is אדני *Adonai*, not יהוה *Yehovah*, for as yet Abraham did not know the quality of his guests. For an explanation of this word, see on chap. xv. 8.

Verse 4. *Let a little water—be fetched, and wash your feet, &c.*] In these verses we find a delightful picture of primitive hospitality. In those ancient times shoes such as ours were not in use; and the foot was protected only by *sandals* or *soles*, which fastened round the foot with straps. It was therefore a great refreshment in so hot a country to get the feet washed at the end of a day's journey; and this is the *first* thing that Abraham proposes.

Rest yourselves under the tree] We have already heard of the *oak grove* of Mamre, chap. xii. 6, and this was the *second* requisite for the refreshment of a weary traveller, viz., rest in the shade.

Verse 5. *I will fetch a morsel of bread*] This was the *third* requisite, and is introduced in its proper order; as eating immediately after exertion or fatigue is very unwholesome. The strong action of the lungs and heart should have time to diminish before any food is received into the stomach, as otherwise concoction is prevented, and fever in a less or greater degree produced.

For therefore are ye come] In those ancient days every traveller conceived he had a right to refreshment, when he needed it, at the first tent he met with on his journey.

So do as thou hast said.] How exceedingly simple was all this! On neither side is there any *compliment* but such as a generous heart and sound sense dictate.

Verse 6. *Three measures of fine meal*] The סאה *seah*, which is here translated *measure*, contained,

A. M. 2107.
B. C. 1897.

Sarah, and said, Make [k] ready quickly three measures of fine meal; knead *it*, and make cakes upon the hearth.

7 And Abraham ran unto the herd, and fetched a calf, tender and good, and gave *it* unto a young man; and he hasted to dress it.

8 And [l] he took butter, and milk, and the calf which he had dressed, and set *it* before them; and he stood by them under the tree, and they did eat.

9 And they said unto him, Where *is* Sarah thy wife? and he said, Behold, [m] in the tent.

10 And he said, I [n] will certainly return unto thee [o] according to the time of life; and, lo, [p] Sarah thy wife shall have a son. And Sarah heard *it* in the tent door, which *was* behind him.

11 Now [q] Abraham and Sarah *were* old *and* well stricken in age; *and* it ceased to be with Sarah [r] after the manner of women.

12 Therefore [s] Sarah laughed within herself, saying, [t] After I am waxed old shall I have pleasure, my [u] lord being old also?

13 And the Lord said unto Abraham, Wherefore did Sarah laugh, saying, Shall I of a surety bear a child, which am old?

[k] Heb. *hasten*.——[l] Chap. xix. 3.——[m] Ch. xxiv. 67.——[n] Ver. 14.——[o] 2 Kings iv. 16.——[p] Chap. xvii. 19, 21; xxi. 2; Rom. ix. 9.

[q] Chap. xvii. 17; Rom. iv. 19; Heb. xi. 11, 12, 19.——[r] Chap. xxxi. 35.——[s] Chap. xvii. 17.——[t] Luke i. 18.——[u] 1 Pet. iii. 6.

according to Bishop Cumberland, about two gallons and a half; and Mr. Ainsworth translates the word *peck*. On this circumstance the following observations of the judicious and pious Abbé Fleury cannot fail to be acceptable to the reader. Speaking of the frugality of the patriarchs he says: "We have an instance of a splendid entertainment in that which Abraham made for the three angels. He set a whole *calf* before them, *new bread*, but baked on the hearth, together with *butter* and *milk*. *Three* measures of meal were baked into bread on this occasion, which come to more than two of our bushels, and nearly to fifty-six pounds of our weight; hence we may conclude that men were great eaters in those days, used much exercise, were probably of a much larger stature as well as longer lives than we. Homer (Odyss. lib. xiv., ver. 74, &c.) makes his heroes great eaters. When *Eumæus* entertained Ulysses, he dressed *two pigs* for himself and his guest.

'So saying, he girded quick his tunic close,
And issuing sought the styes; thence bringing *two*,
Of the imprisoned herd, he slaughtered *both*,
Singed them and slash'd and spitted them, and placed
The *whole* well roasted, banquets, spits, and all,
Reeking before Ulysses.' Cowper.

On another occasion a *hog* of *five* years old was slaughtered and served up for *five* persons:—

'——His wood for fuel he prepared,
And dragging thither a *well-fatted brawn*
Of the *fifth* year:—
Next piercing him, and scorching close his hair,
The joints they parted,' &c.
Ibid. ver. 419. Cowper.

Homer's heroes wait upon themselves and guests in the common occasions of life; the patriarchs do the same. Abraham, who had so many servants, and was nearly a hundred years old, brought the water himself to wash the feet of his guests, ordered his wife to make the bread quickly, went himself to choose the calf from the herd, and came again to serve them *standing*. I will allow that he was animated on this occasion with a desire of showing hospitality, but the lives of all the rest of the patriarchs were similar to this."

Make cakes upon the hearth.] Or under the ashes. This mode is used in the east to the present day. When the hearth is strongly heated with the fire that has been kindled on it, they remove the coals, sweep off the ashes, lay on the bread, and then cover it with the hot cinders.

Verse 8. *And he stood by them under the tree, and they did eat.*] Nothing is more common in *Hindostan* than to see travellers and guests *eating under the shade of trees*. Feasts are scarcely ever held in *houses*. The house of a Hindoo serves for *sleeping* and *cooking*, and for *shutting* up the *women*; but is never considered as a *sitting* or *dining* room.—*Ward.*

Verse 10. *I will certainly return*] Abraham was now *ninety-nine* years of age, and this promise was fulfilled when he was a *hundred*; so that the phrase *according to the time of life* must mean either a *complete year*, or *nine months* from the present time, the ordinary time of pregnancy. Taken in this latter sense, Abraham was now in the ninety-ninth year of his age, and Isaac was born when he was in his hundredth year.

Verse 11. *It ceased to be with Sarah after the manner of women.*] And consequently, naturally speaking, conception could not take place; therefore if she have a son it must be in a *supernatural* or *miraculous* way.

Verse 12. *Sarah laughed*] Partly through pleasure at the bare idea of the *possibility* of the thing, and partly from a conviction that it was extremely *improbable*. She appears to have been in the same spirit, and to have had the same feelings of those who, unexpectedly hearing of something of great consequence to themselves, *smile* and say, "The news is too good to be true;" see chap. xxi. 6. There is a case very similar to this mentioned Psa. cxxvi. 1, 2 On Abraham's laughing, see the note on chap. xvii. 17.

Verse 13. *And the* Lord (Jehovah) *said, &c.*] So it appears that one of those three persons was *Jehovah*, and as this name is never given to any created

A. M. 2107.
B. C. 1897.

14 [v] Is any thing too hard for
the Lord? [w] At the time appointed
I will return unto thee, according to the time
of life, and Sarah shall have a son.
15 Then Sarah denied, saying, I laughed
not; for she was afraid. And he said, Nay;
but thou didst laugh.
16 And the men rose up from thence, and
looked toward Sodom: and Abraham went
with them [x] to bring them on the way.
17 And the LORD said, [y] Shall I hide from
Abraham that thing which I do;
18 Seeing that Abraham shall surely become a great and mighty nation, and all the
nations of the earth shall be [z] blessed in him?
19 For I know him, [a] that he will command
his children and his household after him, and
they shall keep the way of the LORD, to do
justice and judgment; that the LORD may
bring upon Abraham that which
he hath spoken of him.

A. M. 2107.
B. C. 1897.

20 And the LORD said, Because [b] the cry
of Sodom and Gomorrah is great, and because
their sin is very grievous;
21 [c] I will go down now, and see whether
they have done altogether according to the
cry of it, which is come unto me; and if not,
[d] I will know.
22 And the men turned their faces from
thence, [e] and went toward Sodom; but Abraham [f] stood yet before the LORD.
23 And Abraham [g] drew near, and said,
[h] Wilt thou also destroy the righteous with the
wicked?
24 [i] Peradventure there be fifty righteous
within the city: wilt thou also destroy and
not spare the place for the fifty righteous that
are therein?

[v] Jer. xxxii. 17; Zech. viii. 6; Matt. iii. 9; xix. 26; Luke i. 37.——[w] Chap. xvii. 21; ver. 10; 2 Kings iv. 16.——[x] Rom. xv. 24; 3 John 6.——[y] Psa. xxv. 14; Amos iii. 7; John xv. 15. [z] Chap. xii. 3; xxii. 18; Acts iii. 25; Gal. iii. 8.——[a] Deut. iv. 9, 10; vi. 7; Josh. xxiv. 15; Eph. vi. 4.

[b] Chap. iv. 10; xix. 13; James v. 4.——[c] Chap. xi. 5; Exodus iii. 8.——[d] Deut. viii. 2; xiii. 3; Josh. xxii. 22; Luke xvi. 15; 2 Cor. xi. 11.——[e] Chap. xix. 1.——[f] Ver. 1.——[g] Heb. x. 22.——[h] Numbers xvi. 22; 2 Sam. xxiv. 17 [i] Jer. v. .

being, consequently the ever-blessed God is intended; and as he was never seen in any bodily shape, consequently the great Angel of the covenant, Jesus Christ, must be meant. See on chap. xvi. 7.

Verse 14. *Is any thing too hard for the Lord?*] היפלא מיהוה דבר *hayippale meihovah dabar*, shall a word (or thing) be wonderful from the Lord? i. e., Can any thing be too great a miracle for *him* to effect? The Septuagint translate the passage, Μη αδυνατησει παρα τῳ Θεῳ ῥημα; which St. Luke adopts almost literatim, only making it an *affirmative* position instead of a *question:* Ουκ αδυνατησει παρα τῳ Θεῳ παν ῥημα, which we translate, "With God nothing shall be impossible," Luke i. 37. Many copies of the Septuagint insert the word παν before ῥημα, as in St. Luke; but it makes little difference in the sense. It was to correct Sarah's unbelief, and to strengthen her faith, that God spoke these most important words; words which state that where human wisdom, prudence, and energy fail, and where nature herself ceases to be an agent, through lack of energy to act, or laws to direct and regulate energy, *there* also God has *full sway*, and by his own omnific power works all things after the counsel of his own will. Is there an effect to be produced? God can produce it as well *without* as *with* means. He produced nature, the whole system of causes and effects, when in the whole compass of his own eternity there was neither *means* nor *being*. HE spake, and it was done; HE commanded, and it stood fast. How great and wonderful is God!

Verse 16. *Abraham went with them to bring them on the way.*] This was another piece of primitive hospitality—to direct strangers in the way. Public roads did not then exist, and guides were essentially necessary in countries where villages were seldom to be met with, and where solitary dwellings did not exist.

Verse 17. *Shall I hide from Abraham*] That is, I will not hide. A common mode of speech in Scripture—a question asked when an affirmative is designed. *Do men gather grapes of thorns?* Men do not gather grapes of thorns, &c.

Verse 18. *Shall surely become a great and mighty nation*] The revelation that I make to him shall be preserved among his posterity; and the exact fulfilment of my promises, made so long before, shall lead them to believe in my name and trust in my goodness.

Verse 19. *And they shall keep the way of the Lord*] The true religion; God's WAY; that in which God walks himself, and in which, of course, his *followers* walk also; *to do justice and judgment;* not only to preserve the truth in their *creed*, but maintain it in their *practice*.

Verse 20. *Because the cry of Sodom and Gomorrah*] See the notes on chap. xiii. 13.

Verse 21. *I will go down now, &c.*] A lesson to magistrates, teaching them not to judge according to report, but accurately to inquire into the facts themselves.—*Jarchi*.

Verse 22. *And the men turned their faces*] That is, the two angels who accompanied Jehovah were now sent towards Sodom; while the third, who is called the LORD or *Jehovah*, remained with Abraham for the purpose of teaching him the great usefulness and importance of faith and prayer.

Verse 23. *Wilt thou also destroy the righteous with the wicked?*] A form of speech similar to that in verse 17, an invariable principle of justice, that the righteous shall not be punished for the crimes of the impious. And this Abraham lays down as the *foun-*

A. M. 2107.
B. C. 1897.
25 That be far from thee to do
after this manner, to slay the righteous with the wicked: and [k] that the righteous
should be as the wicked, that be far from thee:
[l] Shall not the Judge of all the earth do
right?
26 And the LORD said, [m] If I find in Sodom
fifty righteous within the city, then I will
spare all the place for their sakes.
27 And Abraham answered and said, [n] Behold now, I have taken upon me to speak
unto the LORD, which *am* [o] *but* dust and
ashes:
28 Peradventure there shall lack five of the
fifty righteous: wilt thou destroy all the city
for *lack of* five? And he said, If I find
there forty and five, I will not destroy *it*.
29 And he spake unto him yet again, and
said, Peradventure there shall be
forty found there. And he said, I
will not do *it* for forty's sake.
A. M. 2107.
B. C. 1897.
30 And he said *unto him,* O let not the
LORD be angry, and I will speak: Peradven
ture there shall thirty be found there. And
he said, I will not do *it* if I find thirty there.
31 And he said, Behold now, I have taken
upon me to speak unto the LORD: Peradventure there shall be twenty found there. And
he said, I will not destroy *it* for twenty's sake.
32 And he said, [p] O let not the LORD be
angry, and I will speak yet but this once:
Peradventure ten shall be found there. [q] And
he said, I will not destroy *it* for ten's sake.
33 And the LORD went his way, as soon as
he had left communing with Abraham: and
Abraham returned unto his place.

[k] Job viii. 20; Isa. iii. 10, 11.——[l] Job viii. 3; xxxiv. 17; Psa. lviii. 11; xciv. 2; Rom. iii. 6.——[m] Jer. v. 1; Ezek. xxii. 30.

[n] Luke xviii. 1.——[o] Chap. iii. 19; Job iv. 19; Eccles. xii. 7; 1 Cor. xv. 47, 48; 2 Cor. v. 1.——[p] Judg. vi. 39.——[q] James v. 16.

dation of his supplications. Who can pray with any hope of success who cannot assign a *reason* to God and his *conscience* for the petitions he offers? The great sacrifice offered by Christ is an infinite reason why a penitent sinner should expect to find the mercy for which he pleads.

Verse 25. *Shall not the Judge of all the earth do right?*] God alone is the Judge of all men. Abraham, in thus addressing himself to the person in the text, considers him either as the Supreme Being or his representative.

Verse 27. *Which* am but *dust and ashes*] עפר ואפר *aphar vaepher,* words very similar in sound, as they refer to matters which so much resemble each other. *Dust*—the lightest particles of earth. *Ashes*—the residuum of consumed substances. By these expressions he shows how deeply his soul was humbled in the presence of God. He who has *high* thoughts of himself must have *low* thoughts of the dignity of the Divine nature, of the majesty of God, and the sinfulness of sin.

Verse 32. *Peradventure ten shall be found there*] Knowing that in the family of his nephew the true religion was professed and practised, he could not suppose there could be less than ten righteous persons in the city, he did not think it necessary to urge his supplication farther; he therefore left off his entreaties, and the Lord departed from him. It is highly worthy of observation, that while he continued to pray the presence of God was continued; and when Abraham ended, "the glory of the Lord was lifted up," as the Targum expresses it.

THIS chapter, though containing only the preliminaries to the awful catastrophe detailed in the next, affords us several lessons of useful and important information.

1. The hospitality and humanity of Abraham are worthy, not only of our most serious regard, but also of our *imitation*. He sat in the door of his tent in the heat of the day, not only to enjoy the current of refreshing air, but that if he saw any weary and exhausted travellers he might invite them to rest and refresh themselves. Hospitality is ever becoming in one human being towards another; for every destitute man is a *brother* in distress, and demands our most prompt and affectionate assistance, according to that heavenly precept, "What ye would that men should do unto you, do even so unto them." From this conduct of Abraham a Divine precept is formed: "Be not forgetful to entertain strangers, for thereby some have entertained angels unawares." Heb. xiii. 2.

2. Whatever is given on the ground of humanity and mercy is given unto God, and is sure to meet with his approbation and a suitable reward. While Abraham entertained his guests God discovers himself, and reveals to him the counsels of his will, and renews the promise of a numerous posterity. Sarah, though naturally speaking past child-bearing, shall have a son; natural obstacles cannot hinder the purpose of God: nature is his instrument; and as it works not only by general laws, but also by any particular will of God, so it may accomplish that will in any way he may choose to direct. It is always difficult to credit God's *promises* when they relate to *supernatural* things, and still more so when they have for their object events that are *contrary* to the course of nature; but *as nothing is too hard for God,* so "all things are possible to him that believeth." It is that faith alone which is of the operation of God's Spirit, that is capable of crediting supernatural things; he who does not pray to be enabled to believe, or, if he do, uses not the power when received, can never believe to the saving of the soul.

3. Abraham trusts much in God, and God reposes much confidence in Abraham. He knows that God is

faithful, and will fulfil his promises; and God knows that Abraham is faithful, and will command his children and his household after him, and they shall keep the way of the Lord to do justice and judgment; ver. 19. No man lives unto himself; and God gives us neither *spiritual* nor *temporal* blessings for ourselves alone; our bread we are to divide with the hungry, and to help the stranger in distress. He who understands the *way of God* should carefully instruct his household in that way; and he who is the father of a family should pray to God to teach him, that he may teach his household. His ignorance of God and salvation can be no excuse for his neglecting his family: it is his indispensable duty to teach them; and God will teach him, if he earnestly seek it, that he may be able to discharge this duty to his family. Reader, if thy children or servants perish through thy neglect, God will judge thee for it in the great day.

4. The sin of Sodom and the cities of the plain was great and grievous; the measure of their iniquity was full, and God determined to destroy them. Judgment is God's *strange work*, but though rarely done it must be done sometimes, lest men should suppose that right and wrong, vice and virtue, are alike in the eye of God. And these judgments must be dispensed in such a way as to show they are not the results of natural causes, but come immediately from the incensed justice of the Most High.

5. Every man who loves God loves his neighbour also; and he who loves his neighbour will do all in his power to promote the well-being both of his soul and his body. Abraham cannot prevent the men of Sodom from sinning against God; but he can make prayer and intercession for their souls, and plead, if not in arrest, yet in mitigation, of judgment. He therefore intercedes for the transgressors, and God is well pleased with his intercessions. These are the offspring of God's own love in the heart of his servant.

6. How true is that word, The energetic faithful prayer of a righteous man availeth much! Abraham *draws near to God* by affection and faith, and in the most devout and humble manner makes prayer and supplication; and every petition is answered on the spot. Nor does God cease to promise to show mercy till Abraham ceases to intercede! What encouragement does this hold out to them that fear God, to make prayer and intercession for their sinful neighbours and ungodly relatives! Faith in the Lord Jesus endues prayer with a species of omnipotence; whatsoever a man asks of the Father in his name, he will do it. Prayer has been termed the *gate* of heaven, but without *faith* that gate cannot be *opened*. He who *prays* as he *should*, and *believes* as he *ought*, shall have the fulness of the blessings of the Gospel of peace.

CHAPTER XIX.

The two angels mentioned in the preceding chapter, come in the evening to Sodom, 1. *Lot, who was sitting at the gate, invites them to enter his house, take some refreshment, and tarry all night; which they at first refuse,* 2; *but on being pressingly solicited, they at last comply,* 3. *The abominable conduct of the men of Sodom,* 4, 5. *Lot's deep concern for the honour and safety of his guests, which leads him to make a most exceptionable proposal to those wicked men,* 6–8. *The violent proceedings of the Sodomites,* 9. *Lot rescued from their barbarity by the angels, who smite them with blindness,* 10, 11. *The angels exhort Lot and his family to flee from that wicked place, as God was about to destroy it,* 12, 13. *Lot's fruitless exhortation to his sons-in-law,* 14. *The angels hasten Lot and his family to depart,* 15, 16. *Their exhortation,* 17. *Lot's request,* 18–20. *He is permitted to escape to Zoar,* 21–23. *Fire and brimstone are rained down from heaven upon all the cities of the plain, by which they are entirely destroyed,* 24, 25. *Lot's wife, looking behind, becomes a pillar of salt,* 26. *Abraham, early in the morning, discovers the desolation of those iniquitous cities,* 27–29. *Lot, fearing to continue in Zoar, went with his two daughters to the mountain, and dwelt in a cave,* 30. *The strange conduct of his daughters, and his unhappy deception,* 31–36. *Moab and Ammon born, from whom sprang the Moabites and Ammonites,* 37, 38.

A. M. 2107. B. C. 1897. AND there [a] came two angels
to Sodom at even; and Lot
sat in the gate of Sodom: and Lot [b] seeing
them rose up to meet them; and he bowed
himself with his face toward the A. M. 2107. B. C. 1897.
ground;
2 And he said, Behold now, my lords, [c] turn
in, I pray you, into your servant's house, and

[a] Chap. xviii. 22.——[b] Chap. xviii. 1, &c. — [c] Heb. xiii. 2.

NOTES ON CHAP. XIX.

Verse 1. *Two angels*] The two referred to chap. xviii. 22.

Sat in the gate] Probably, in order to prevent unwary travellers from being entrapped by his wicked townsmen, he waited at the gate of the city to bring the strangers he might meet with to his own house, as well as to transact his own business. Or, as the gate was the place of judgment, he might have been sitting there as *magistrate* to hear and determine disputes.

Bowed himself] Not through religious reverence, for he did not know the *quality* of his guests; but through the customary form of civility. See on verses 3–5 of the preceding chapter.

Verse 2. *Nay; but we will abide in the street*] Instead of לא *lo*, nay, some MSS. have לו *lo*, to him: "And they said *unto him*, for we lodge in the street;"

a

A. M. 2107. B. C. 1897. tarry all night, and [d] wash your feet,
and ye shall rise up early, and go
on your ways. And they said, [e] Nay; but
we will abide in the street all night.
3 And he pressed upon them greatly; and
they turned in unto him, and entered into his
house; [f] and he made them a feast, and did
bake unleavened bread, and they did eat.
4 But before they lay down, the men of the
city, *even* the men of Sodom, compassed the
house round, both old and young, all the
people from every quarter:
5 [g] And they called unto Lot, and said unto
him, Where *are* the men which came in to
thee this night? [h] bring them out unto us that
we [i] may know them.
6 And [k] Lot went out at the door unto them,
and shut the door after him,
7 And said, I pray you, brethren, do not so
wickedly:
8 [l] Behold now, I have two daughters which
have not known man; let me, I pray you,
bring them out unto you, and do A. M. 2107. B. C. 1897.
ye to them as *is* good in your
eyes: only unto these men do nothing; [m] for
therefore came they under the shadow of
my roof.
9 And they said, Stand back. And they
said *again*, This one *fellow* [n] came in to sojourn, [o] and he will needs be a judge: now
will we deal worse with thee than with them.
And they pressed sore upon the man, *even*
Lot, and came near to break the door.
10 But the men put forth their hand, and
pulled Lot into the house to them, and shut
to the door.
11 And they smote the men [p] that *were* at
the door of the house with blindness, both
small and great; so that they wearied themselves to find the door.
12 And the men said unto Lot, Hast thou
here any besides? son-in-law, and thy sons,
and thy daughters, and whatsoever thou hast
in the city, [q] bring *them* out of this place:

[d] Chap. xviii. 4.—[e] See Luke xxiv. 28.—[f] Chap. xviii. 8; [g] Isa. iii. 9.—[h] Judg. xix. 22.—[i] Chap. iv. 1; Rom. i. 24, 27; Jude 7.—[k] Judg. xix. 23.—[l] See Judg. xix. 24.

[m] See chap. xviii. 5.—[n] 2 Pet. ii. 7, 8.—[o] Exod. ii. 14 [p] Wisd. xix. 17; see 2 Kings vi. 18; Acts xiii. 11.—[q] Chap vii. 1; 2 Pet. ii. 7, 9.

where, nevertheless, the negation is understood. Knowing the disposition of the inhabitants, and appearing in the mere character of travellers, they preferred the open street to any house; but as Lot pressed them vehemently, and they knew him to be a righteous man, not yet willing to make themselves known, they consented to take shelter under his hospitable roof. Our Lord, willing for the time being to conceal his person from the knowledge of the disciples going to Emmaus, made as though he would go farther, Luke xxiv. 13; but at last, like the angels here, yielded to the importunity of his disciples, and went into their lodgings.

Verse 5. *Where* are *the men which came in to thee, &c.*] This account justifies the character given of this depraved people in the preceding chapter, ver. 20, and in chap. xiii. 13. As their crime was the deepest disgrace to human nature, so it is too bad to be described; in the sacred text it is sufficiently marked; and the iniquity which, from these most abominable wretches, has been called *Sodomy*, is punished in our country with death.

Verse 8. *Behold now, I have two daughters*] Nothing but that sacred light in which the rights of hospitality were regarded among the eastern nations, could either justify or palliate this proposal of Lot. A man who had taken a stranger under his care and protection, was bound to defend him even at the expense of his own life. In this light the rights of hospitality are still regarded in Asiatic countries; and on these high notions only, the influence of which an Asiatic mind alone can properly appreciate, Lot's conduct on this occasion can be at all excused: but even then, it was not only the language of anxious solicitude, but of unwarrantable haste.

Verse 9. *And he will needs be a judge*] So *his sitting in the gate* is perhaps a farther proof of his being there in a *magisterial* capacity, as some have supposed.

Verse 11. *And they smote the men—with blindness*] This has been understood two ways: 1. The angels, by the power which God had given them, deprived these wicked men of a proper and regular use of their sight, so as either totally to deprive them of it, or render it so confused that they could no longer distinguish objects; or, 2. They caused such a deep darkness to take place, that they could not find Lot's door. The author of the book of *Wisdom* was evidently of this latter opinion, for he says they *were compassed about with horrible great darkness*, chap. xix. 17. See a similar case of Elisha and the Syrians, 2 Kings vi. 18, &c.

Verse 12. *Hast thou here any besides? son-in-law*] Here there appears to be but *one* meant, as the word חתן *chathan* is in the *singular* number; but in ver. 14 the word is *plural*, חתניו *chathanaiv*, his sons-in-law. There were only *two* in number; as we do not hear that Lot had more than two daughters: and these seem not to have been *actually* married to those daughters, but only *betrothed*, as is evident from what Lot says, ver. 8; for they had *not known man*, but were the spouses *elect* of those who are here called his sons-in-law. But though these might be reputed as a part of Lot's family, and entitled on this account to God's protection, yet it is sufficiently plain that they did not

A. M. 2107. B. C. 1897.

13 For we will destroy this place, because the [r] cry of them is waxen great before the face of the LORD; and [s] the LORD hath sent us to destroy it.

14 And Lot went out and spake unto his sons-in-law, [t] which married his daughters, and said, [u] Up, get you out of this place; for the LORD will destroy this city. [v] But he seemed as one that mocked unto his sons-in-law.

15 And when the morning arose, then the angels hastened Lot, saying, [w] Arise, take thy wife, and thy two daughters, which [x] are here; lest thou be consumed in the [y] iniquity of the city.

16 And [z] while he lingered, the men laid hold upon his hand, and upon the hand of his wife, and upon the hand of his two daughters; [a] the LORD being merciful unto him: [b] and they brought him forth, and set him without the city.

17 And it came to pass, when they had brought them forth abroad, that he said, [c] Escape for thy life; [d] look not behind thee, neither stay thou in all the plain; escape to the mountain, lest thou be consumed.

18 And Lot said unto them, O, [e] not so, my Lord:

19 Behold now, thy servant hath found grace in thy sight, and thou hast magnified thy mercy, which thou hast showed unto me in saving my life; and I cannot escape to the mountain, lest some evil take me, and I die.

20 Behold now, this city *is* near to flee unto, and it *is* a little one: O, let me escape thither, (*is* it not a little one?) and my soul shall live.

21 And he said unto him, See, [f] I have accepted [g] thee concerning this thing also, that I will not overthrow this city, for the which thou hast spoken.

22 Haste thee, escape thither; for [h] I cannot do any thing till thou be come thither. Therefore [i] the name of the city was called [k] Zoar.

[r] Chapter xviii. 20.——[s] 1 Chron. xxi. 15.——[t] Matt. i. 18.——[u] Num. xvi. 21, 45.——[v] Exod. ix. 21; Luke xvii. 28; xxiv. 11.——[w] Num. xvi. 24, 26; Rev. xviii. 4.——[x] Heb. *are found.*——[y] Or, *punishment.*——[z] Wisd. x. 6.——[a] Luke xviii. 13; Rom. ix. 15, 16.——[b] Psa. xxxiv. 22.——[c] 1 Kings xix. 3.——[d] Ver. 26; Matt. xxiv. 16, 17, 18; Luke ix. 62; Phil. iii. 13, 24.——[e] Acts x. 14.——[f] Job xlii. 8, 9; Psa. cxlv. 19.——[g] Heb. *thy face.*——[h] See chap. xxxii. 25, 26; Exod. xxxii. 10; Deut. ix. 14; Mark vi. 5.——[i] Chap. xiii. 10; xiv. 2.——[k] That is, *little;* ver. 20.

escape the perdition of these wicked men; and the reason is given, ver. 14, they received the solemn warning as a ridiculous tale, the creature of Lot's invention, or the offspring of his fear. Therefore they made no provision for their escape, and doubtless perished, notwithstanding the sincerely offered grace, in the perdition that fell on this ungodly city.

Verse 16. *While he lingered*] Probably in affectionate though useless entreaties to prevail on the remaining parts of his family to escape from the destruction that was now descending; *laid hold upon his hand*—pulled them away by mere force, *the Lord being merciful;* else they had been left to perish in their *lingering*, as the others were in their *gainsaying*.

Verse 17. *When they had brought them forth, &c.*] Every word here is emphatic, *Escape for thy* LIFE; thou art in the most imminent danger of perishing; thy *life* and thy *soul* are both at stake. *Look not behind thee*—thou hast but barely time enough to escape from the judgment that is now descending; no lingering, or thou art lost! one *look back* may prove fatal to thee, and God commands thee to avoid it. *Neither stay thou in all the plain*, because God will destroy that as well as the city. *Escape to the mountain*, on which these judgments shall not light, and which God has appointed thee for a place of refuge; *lest thou be* CONSUMED. It is not an ordinary judgment that is coming; a fire from heaven shall burn up the cities, the plain, and all that remain in the cities and in the plain. Both the *beginning* and *end* of this exhortation are addressed to his *personal feelings*. "Skin for skin, yea, all that a man hath will he give for his life;" and *self-preservation is the first law of nature*, to which every other consideration is minor and unimportant.

Verse 19. *I cannot escape to the mountain*] He saw the destruction so near, that he imagined he should not have time sufficient to reach the mountain before it arrived. He did not consider that God could give no command to his creatures that it would be impossible for them to fulfil; but the hurry and perturbation of his mind will at once account for and excuse this gross oversight.

Verse 20. *It is a little one*] Probably Lot wished to have it for an inheritance, and therefore pleaded its being a *little one*, that his request might be the more readily granted. Or he might suppose, that being *a little city*, it was less depraved than Sodom and Gomorrah, and therefore not so ripe for punishment; which was probably the case.

Verse 21. *See, I have accepted thee*] How prevalent is prayer with God! Far from refusing to grant a reasonable petition, he shows himself as if under embarrassment to deny any.

Verse 22. *I cannot do any thing till thou be come thither.*] So these heavenly messengers had the strictest commission to take care of Lot and his family: and even the purposes of Divine justice could not be accomplished on the rebellious, till this righteous man and his family had escaped from the place. A proof

A. M. 2107.
B. C. 1897.
23 The sun was [l] risen upon the
earth when Lot entered into Zoar.
24 Then [m] the LORD rained upon Sodom
and upon Gomorrah brimstone and
fire from the LORD out of heaven;
25 And he overthrew those cities, and all

[l] Heb. *gone forth*.——[m] Deuteronomy xxix. 23; Isaiah xiii. 19; Jeremiah xx. 16; l. 40; Ezekiel xvi. 49, 50; Hos. xi. 8; Amos iv. 11; Zephaniah ii. 9; Luke xvii. 29; 2 Pet. ii. 6; Jude 7.

of Abraham's assertion, *The Judge of all the earth will do right.*

The name of the city was called Zoar.] צוער *Tsoar*, LITTLE, its former name being *Bela*.

Verse 24. *The Lord rained—brimstone and fire from the Lord*] As all judgment is committed to the Son of God, many of the primitive fathers and several modern divines have supposed that the words ויהוה *vaihovah* and מאת יהוה *meeth Yehovah* imply, *Jehovah the Son* raining brimstone and fire from *Jehovah the Father*; and that this place affords no mean proof of the proper Divinity of our blessed Redeemer. It may be so; but though the point is sufficiently established elsewhere, it does not appear to me to be *plainly* indicated here. And it is always better on a subject of this kind not to have recourse to *proofs* which require *proofs* to confirm them. It must however be granted that *two* persons mentioned as Jehovah in one verse, is both a strange and curious circumstance; and it will appear more remarkable when we consider that the person called Jehovah, who conversed with Abraham, (see chap. xviii.,) and sent those two angels to bring Lot and his family out of this devoted place, and seems himself after he left off talking with Abraham to have ascended to heaven, ver. 33, does not any more appear on this occasion till we hear that JEHOVAH *rained upon Sodom and Gomorrah brimstone and fire from* JEHOVAH *out of heaven*. This certainly gives much countenance to the opinion referred to above, though still it may fall short of positive proof.

Brimstone and fire.—The word גפרית *gophrith*, which we translate *brimstone*, is of very uncertain derivation. It is evidently used metaphorically, to point out the utmost degrees of punishment executed on the most flagitious criminals, in Deut. xxix. 23; Job xviii. 15; Psa. xi. 6; Isa. xxxiv. 9; Ezek. xxxviii. 22. And as *hell*, or an everlasting separation from God and the glory of his power, is the utmost punishment that can be inflicted on sinners, hence brimstone and fire are used in Scripture to signify the torments in that place of punishment. See Isa. xxx. 33; Rev. xiv. 10; xix. 20; xx. 10; xxi. 8. We may safely suppose that it was quite possible that a shower of *nitrous* particles might have been precipitated from the atmosphere, here, as in many other places, called *heaven*, which, by the action of *fire* or the *electric fluid*, would be immediately ignited, and so consume the cities; and, as we have already seen that the plains about Sodom and Gomorrah abounded with *asphaltus* or *bitumen* pits, (see chap. xiv. 10,) that what is particularly meant here in reference to the plain is the setting fire to this vast store of inflammable matter by the agency of lightning or the electric fluid; and this, in the most natural and literal manner, accounts for the whole plain being burnt up, as that plain abounded with this bituminous substance; and thus we find *three* agents employed in the total ruin of these cities, and all the circumjacent plain: 1. Innumerable *nitrous particles* precipitated from the atmosphere. 2. The vast quantity of *asphaltus* or *bitumen* which abounded in that country: and, 3. *Lightning* or the electric spark, which ignited the nitre and bitumen, and thus consumed both the cities and the plain or champaign country in which they were situated.

Verse 25. *And he overthrew those cities, and all the plain*] This forms what is called the lake *Asphaltites*, *Dead Sea*, or *Salt Sea*, which, according to the most authentic accounts, is about seventy miles in length, and eighteen in breadth.

The most strange and incredible tales are told by many of the ancients, and by many of the moderns, concerning the *place* where these cities stood. Common fame says that the waters of this sea are so *thick* that a stone will not sink in them, so tough and *clammy* that the most boisterous wind cannot ruffle them, so *deadly* that no fish can live in them, and that if a bird happen to fly over the lake, it is killed by the poisonous effluvia proceeding from the waters; that scarcely any verdure can grow near the place, and that in the vicinity where there are any trees they bear a most beautiful fruit, but when you come to open it you find nothing but *ashes!* and that the place was burning long after the apostles' times. These and all similar tales may be safely pronounced great exaggerations of facts, or fictions of ignorant, stupid, and superstitious monks, or impositions of unprincipled travellers, who, knowing that the common people are delighted with the *marvellous*, have stuffed their narratives with such accounts merely to procure a better sale for their books.

The truth is, the waters are exceedingly salt, far beyond the usual saltness of the sea, and hence it is called the *Salt Sea*. In consequence of this circumstance bodies will float in it that would sink in common salt water, and probably it is on this account that few fish can live in it. But the monks of St. Saba affirmed to Dr. Shaw, *that they had seen fish caught in it*; and as to the reports of any noxious quality in the air, or in the evaporations from its surface, the simple fact is, lumps of bitumen often rise from the bottom to its surface, and exhale a fœtid odour which does not appear to have any thing poisonous in it. Dr. Pococke swam in it for nearly a quarter of an hour, and felt no kind of inconvenience; the water, he says, is *very clear*, and having brought away a bottle of it, he "had it *analyzed*, and found it to contain no substances besides *salt* and a *little alum*." As there are frequent eruptions of a bituminous matter from the bottom of this lake, which seem to argue a subterraneous fire, hence the accounts that this place was burning even after the days of the apostles. And this phenomenon still continues, for "masses of bitumen," says Dr. Shaw, "in large hemispheres, are raised at certain times from the bottom, which, as soon as they touch the surface, and are thereby acted upon by the

A. M. 2107.
B. C. 1897.
the plain, and all the inhabitants of the cities, and [n] that which grew upon the ground.

26 But his wife looked back from behind him, and she became [o] a pillar of salt.
A. M. 2107.
B. C. 1897.

[n] Chap. xiv. 3; Psa. cvii. 34.——[o] Ver. 17; Num. xvi. 38; Prov. xiv. 14; Wisd. x. 7; Luke xvii. 32; Heb. x. 38.

external air, burst at once, with *great smoke* and *noise*, like the *pulvis fulminans* of the chemists, and disperse themselves in a thousand pieces. But this only happens near the shore, for in greater depths the eruptions are supposed to discover themselves in such *columns of smoke* as are now and then observed to arise from the lake. And perhaps to such eruptions as these we may attribute that variety of *pits* and *hollows*, not unlike the traces of many of our ancient lime-kilns, which are found in the neighbourhood of this lake. The *bitumen* is in all probability accompanied from the bottom with *sulphur*, as both of them are found promiscuously upon the shore, and the latter is precisely the same with common native sulphur; the other is friable, yielding upon friction, or by being put into the fire, a fœtid smell." The bitumen, after having been some time exposed to the air, becomes indurated like a stone. I have some portions of it before me, brought by a friend of mine from the spot; it is very black, hard, and on friction yields a fœtid odour.

For several curious particulars on this subject, see Dr. Pococke's Travels, vol. ii., part 1, chap. 9, and Dr. Shaw's Travels, 4to. edit., p. 346, &c.

Verse 26. *She became a pillar of salt*] The vast variety of opinions, both ancient and modern, on the crime of Lot's wife, her change, and the manner in which that change was effected, are in many cases as unsatisfactory as they are ridiculous. On this point the sacred Scripture says little. God had commanded Lot and his family not to look behind them; the wife of Lot disobeyed this command; *she looked back from behind him*—Lot, her husband, *and she became a pillar of salt*. This is all the information the inspired historian has thought proper to give us on this subject; it is true the account is short, but commentators and critics have made it long enough by their laborious glosses. The opinions which are the most probable are the following: 1. "Lot's wife, by the miraculous power of God, was changed into a mass of rock salt, probably retaining the human figure." 2. "Tarrying too long in the plain, she was struck with lightning and enveloped in the bituminous and sulphuric matter which abounded in that country, and which, not being exposed afterwards to the action of the fire, resisted the air and the wet, and was thus rendered permanent." 3. "She was struck dead and consumed in the burning up of the plain; and this judgment on her disobedience being recorded, is an imperishable memorial of the fact itself, and an everlasting warning to sinners in general, and to backsliders or apostates in particular." On these opinions it may be only necessary to state that the two first understand the text *literally*, and that the last considers it *metaphorically*. That God might in a moment convert this disobedient woman into a *pillar* or *mass of salt*, or any *other substance*, there can be no doubt. Or that, by continuing in the plain till the brimstone and fire descended from heaven, she might be *struck dead with lightning*, and *indurated* or *petrified* on the spot, is as possible. And that the account of her becoming a *pillar of salt* may be designed to be understood *metaphorically*, is also highly probable. It is certain that *salt* is frequently used in the Scriptures as an emblem of *incorruption*, *durability*, &c. Hence a *covenant of salt*, Num. xviii. 19, is a *perpetual* covenant, one that is ever to be in full force, and never broken; on this ground a *pillar of salt* may signify no more *in this case* than an *everlasting* monument against criminal curiosity, unbelief, and disobedience.

Could we depend upon the various accounts given by different persons who pretend to have seen the wife of Lot standing in her complete human form, with all her *distinctive marks about her*, the difficulty would be at an end. But we cannot depend on these accounts; they are discordant, improbable, ridiculous, and often grossly absurd. Some profess to have seen her as a *heap of salt*; others, as a *rock of salt*; others, as a *complete human being* as to shape, proportion of parts, &c., &c., but only petrified. This human form, according to others, has still resident in it a miraculous continual energy; break off a finger, a toe, an arm, &c., it is immediately *reproduced*, so that though multitudes of curious persons have gone to see this woman, and every one has brought away a part of her, yet still she is found by the next comer a complete human form! To crown this absurd description, the author of the poem *De Sodoma*, usually attributed to Tertullian, and annexed to his works, represents her as yet *instinct with a portion of animal life, which is unequivocally designated by certain signs which every month produces*. I shall transcribe the whole passage and refer to my author; and as I have given above the *sense* of the whole, my readers must excuse me from giving a more literal translation:—

——————et simul illic
In *fragilem* mutata *salem*, stetit ipsa sepulchrum,
Ipsaque imago sibi, formam sine corpore servans.
Durat adhuc etenim nuda statione sub æthra,
Nec *pluviis dilapsa situ*, nec *diruta ventis*.
Quinetiam, si quis mutilaverit advena formam,
Protinus ex sese suggestu vulnera complet.
Dicitur et vivens alio sub corpore *sexus*
Munificos solito dispungere *sanguine menses*.

TERTULLIANI *Opera*, vol. ii., p. 731. Edit. OBERTHUR

The sentiment in the last lines is supported by Irenæus, who assures us that, though still remaining as a *pillar of salt*, the statue, in form and other *natural accidents*, exhibits decisive proofs of its original: *Jam non caro corruptibilis, sed statua salis semper manens*, et, per naturalia, ea *quæ sunt* consuetudinis hominis *ostendens*, lib. iv., c. 51. To complete this absurdity, this father makes her an emblem of the true Church, which, though she suffers much, and often loses whole

a

A. M. cir. 2107.
B. C. cir. 1897.

27 And Abraham gat up [p] early
in the morning to the place
where [q] he stood before the LORD:
28 And he looked toward Sodom and
Gomorrah, and toward all the land of the
plain, and beheld, and lo, [r] the smoke of the
country went up as the smoke of a furnace.
29 And it came to pass, when God destroyed the cities of the plain, that God [s] remembered Abraham, and sent Lot out of the
midst of the overthrow, when he overthrew the
cities in the which Lot dwelt.
30 And Lot went up out of
Zoar, and [t] dwelt in the moun-
tain, and his two daughters with him; for he
feared to dwell in Zoar: and he dwelt in a
cave, he and his two daughters.
31 And the first-born said unto the younger,
Our father *is* old, and *there is* not a man in
the earth [u] to come in unto us after the manner of all the earth:
32 Come, let us make our father drink
wine, and we will lie with him, that we [v] may
preserve seed of our father.

[p] Psa. v. 3.——[q] Chap. xviii. 22; Ezek. xvi. 49, 50; Hab. ii. 1; Heb. ii. 1.——[r] 2 Pet. ii. 7; Rev. xviii. 9.——[s] Ch. viii. 1; xviii. 23; Hos. xi. 8.——[t] Ver. 17, 19.——[u] Ch. xvi. 2, 4; xxxviii. 8, 9; Deut. xxv. 5.——[v] Chap. ix. 21; Prov. xxiii. 31–33; Mark xii. 19.

members, yet preserves the *pillar of salt*, that is, *the foundation of the true faith, &c.* See *Calmet.*

Josephus says that this pillar was standing in his time, and that himself had seen it: *Εις στηλην ἁλων μετεβαλεν, ἱστορηκα δ' αυτην· ετι γαρ και νυν διαμενει.* Ant. lib. i., c. xi. 3, 4.

St. Clement, in his *First Epistle to the Corinthians*, chap. ii., follows Josephus, and asserts that Lot's wife was remaining even at that time as a pillar of salt.

Authors of respectability and credit who have since travelled into the Holy Land, and made it *their business* to inquire into this subject in the most particular and careful manner, have not been able to meet with *any remains of this pillar;* and all accounts begin now to be confounded in the pretty general concession, both of Jews and Gentiles, that either the statue does not now remain, or that some of the heaps of salt or blocks of salt rock which are to be met with in the vicinity of the Dead Sea, may be the remains of Lot's wife! All speculations on this subject are perfectly idle; and if the general prejudice in favour of the *continued existence* of this monument of God's justice had not been very strong, I should not have deemed myself justified in entering so much at length into the subject. Those who profess to have seen it, have in general sufficiently invalidated their own testimony by the monstrous absurdities with which they have encumbered their relations. Had Lot's wife been changed in the way that many have supposed, and had she been still preserved somewhere in the neighbourhood of the Dead Sea, surely we might expect some account of it in after parts of the Scripture history; but it is never more mentioned in the Bible, and occurs nowhere in the New Testament but in the simple reference of our Lord to the *judgment itself*, as a warning to the disobedient and backsliding, Luke xvii. 32: *Remember Lot's wife!*

Verse 27. *Abraham gat up early in the morning*] Anxious to know what was the effect of the prayers which he had offered to God the preceding day; what must have been his astonishment when he found that all these cities, with the plain which resembled the garden of the Lord, chap. xiii. 10, burnt up, and the smoke ascending like the *smoke of a furnace*, and was thereby assured that even God himself could not discover *ten righteous* persons in four whole cities!

Verse 29. *God remembered Abraham*] Though he did not descend lower than *ten* righteous persons, (see chap. xviii. 32,) yet the Lord had respect to the spirit of his petitions, and spared all those who could be called *righteous*, and for Abraham's sake offered salvation to all the family of Lot, though neither his sons-in-law elect nor his own wife ultimately profited by it. The former ridiculed the warning; and the latter, though led out by the hands of the angel, yet by breaking the command of God perished with the other gainsayers.

Verse 30. *Lot went up out of Zoar*] From seeing the universal desolation that had fallen upon the land, and that the fire was still continuing its depredations, *he feared to dwell in Zoar*, lest that also should be consumed, and then went to those very mountains to which God had ordered him at first to make his escape. Foolish man is ever preferring his own wisdom to that of his Maker. It was wrong at first not to betake himself to the mountain; it was wrong in the next place to go to it when God had given him the assurance that *Zoar* should be spared for his sake. Both these cases argue a strange want of faith, not only in the truth, but also in the providence, of God. Had he still dwelt at Zoar, the shameful transaction afterwards recorded had in all probability not taken place.

Verse 31. *Our father* is *old*] And consequently not likely to re-marry; *and* there is *not a man in the earth*—none left, according to their opinion in all *the land* of Canaan, of *their own family* and *kindred;* and they might think it unlawful to match with others, such as the inhabitants of Zoar, who they knew had been devoted to destruction as well as those of Sodom and Gomorrah, and were only saved at the earnest request of their father; and probably while they lived among them they found them ripe enough for punishment, and therefore would have thought it both dangerous and criminal to have formed any matrimonial connections with them.

Verse 32. *Come, let us make our father drink wine*] On their flight from *Zoar* it is probable they had brought with them certain provisions to serve them for the time being, and the *wine* here mentioned among the rest.

After considering all that has been said to criminate both Lot and his daughters in this business, I cannot help thinking that the transaction itself will bear a more favourable construction than that which has been

A. M. cir. 2107.
B. C. cir. 1897.

33 [w] And they made their father
drink wine that night: and the
first-born went in, and lay with her father;
and he perceived not when she lay down, nor
when she arose.
34 And it came to pass on the morrow, that
the first-born said unto the younger, Behold,
I lay yesternight with my father: let us make
him drink wine this night also; and go thou
in, *and* lie with him, that we may preserve
seed of our father.
35 And they made their father drink wine
that night also: and the younger arose, and
lay with him; and he perceived
not when she lay down, nor when
she arose.

A. M. cir. 2107.
B. C. cir. 1897.

36 Thus were both the daughters of Lot
with child by their father.

A. M. cir. 2108.
B. C. cir. 1896.

37 And the first-born bare a
son, and called his name Moab:
[x] the same *is* the father of the Moabites unto
this day.
38 And the younger, she also bare a son,
and called his name Ben-ammi: [y] the same
is the father of the children of Ammon unto
this day.

[w] Lev. xviii. 6, 7; Hab. ii. 15, 16.——[x] Num. xxii. 36; Deut. ii. 9; 2 Sam. viii. 2; 2 Kings iii. 4-27.——[y] Deut. ii. 19; Judg. x. 6-18

generally put on it. 1. It does not appear that it was through any base or sensual desires that the daughters of Lot wished to deceive their father. 2. They might have thought that it would have been criminal to have married into any other family, and they knew that their husbands elect, who were probably of the same kindred, had perished in the overthrow of Sodom. 3. They might have supposed that there was no other way left to preserve the family, and consequently that righteousness for which it had been remarkable, but the way which they now took. 4. They appear to have supposed that their father would not come into the measure, because he would have considered it as profane; yet, judging the measure to be expedient and necessary, they endeavoured to *sanctify the improper means* used, by the *goodness of the end* at which they aimed; a doctrine which, though resorted to by many, should be reprobated by all. Acting on this bad principle they caused their father to drink wine. See on ver. 38.

Verse 33. *And he perceived not when she lay down, nor when, &c.*] That is, he did not perceive *the time* she came to his bed, nor *the time* she quitted it; consequently did not know *who it was* that had lain with him. In this transaction Lot appears to me to be in many respects excusable. 1. He had no accurate knowledge of what took place either on the first or second night, therefore he cannot be supposed to have been drawn away by his own lust, and enticed. That he must have been sensible that some person had been in his bed, it would be ridiculous to deny; but he might have judged it to have been some of his female domestics, which it is reasonable to suppose he might have brought from Zoar. 2. It is very likely that he was *deceived* in the wine, as well as in the consequences; either he knew not the strength of the wine, or wine of a superior power had been given to him on this occasion. As he had in general followed the simple pastoral life, it is not to be wondered at if he did not know the intoxicating power of wine, and being an old man, and unused to it, a small portion would be sufficient to overcome him; sound sleep would soon, at his time of life, be the effect of taking the liquor to which he was unaccustomed, and cause him to forget the effects of his intoxication. Except in this case, his *moral* conduct stands unblemished in the sacred writings; and as the whole transaction, especially as it relates to him, is capable of an interpretation not wholly injurious to his piety, both reason and religion conjoin to recommend that explanation. As to his daughters, let their *ignorance* of the real state of the case plead for them, as far as that *can* go; and let it be remembered that their sin was of that very peculiar nature as never to be capable of becoming a *precedent*. For it is scarcely possible that any should ever be able to plead similar circumstances in vindication of a similar line of conduct.

Verse 37. *Called his name Moab*] This name is generally interpreted *of the father*, or, according to Calmet, מואב *Moab, the waters of the father.*

Verse 38. *Ben-ammi*] בן עמי *Ben-ammi, the son of my people.* Both these names seem to justify the view taken of this subject above, *viz.*, that it was merely to *preserve the family* that the daughters of Lot made use of the above expedient; and hence we do not find that they ever attempted to *repeat* it, which, had it been done for any other purpose, they certainly would not have failed to do. On this subject Origen, in his fifth homily on Genesis, has these remarkable words: *Ubi hic libidinis culpa, ubi incesti criminis arguitur? Quomodo dabitur in* VITIO QUOD NON ITERATUR IN FACTO? *Vereor proloqui quod sentio, vereor, inquam, ne castior fuerit harum incestus, quam pudicitia multarum.* "Where, in all this transaction, can the crime of lust or of incest be proved? How can this be proved to be a *vice* when the *fact* was *never repeated?* I am afraid to speak my whole mind on the subject, lest the incest of *these* should appear more laudable than the chastity of multitudes." There is a distinction made here by Origen which is worthy of notice; a single *bad act*, though a *sin*, does not necessarily argue a *vicious* heart, as in order to be *vicious* a man must be *habituated* to sinful acts.

The generation which proceeded from this incestuous connection, whatever may be said in extenuation of the transaction, (its peculiar circumstances being considered,) was certainly a *bad* one. The *Moabites* soon fell from the faith of God, and became *idolaters*, the people of *Chemosh*, and of *Baal-peor*, Num. xxi 29; xxv. 1-3; and were enemies to the children of

a

Abraham. See Num. xxii.; Judg. iii. 14, &c. And the *Ammonites*, who dwelt near to the Moabites, united with them in idolatry, and were also enemies to Israel. See Judg. xi. 4, 24; Deut. xxiii. 3, 4. As both these people made afterwards a considerable figure in the sacred history, the impartial inspired writer takes care to introduce at this early period an account of their *origin*. See what has been said on the case of Noah's drunkenness, Gen. ix. 20, &c.

This is an awful history, and the circumstances detailed in it are as distressing to piety as to humanity. It may, however, be profitable to review the particulars.

1. From the commencement of the chapter we find that the example and precepts of Abraham had not been lost on his nephew Lot. He also, like his uncle, watches for opportunities to call in the weary traveller. *This* Abraham had taught his household, and we see the effect of his blessed teaching. Lot was both *hospitable* and *pious*, though living in the midst of a crooked and perverse race. It must be granted that from several circumstances in his history he appears to have been a *weak* man, but his weakness was such as was not inconsistent with general uprightness and sincerity. He and his family were not forgetful to entertain strangers, and they alone were free from the pollutions of this accursed people. How powerful are the effects of a religious education, enforced by pious example! It is one of God's especial means of grace. Let a man only do justice to his family, by bringing them up in the fear of God, and he *will* crown it with his blessing. How many excuse the profligacy of their family, which is often entirely owing to their own neglect, by saying, "O, we cannot give them grace!" No, *you* cannot; but you can afford them the *means* of grace. *This* is *your* work, *that* is the Lord's. If, through your neglect of *precept* and *example*, they perish, what an awful account must you give to the Judge of quick and dead! It was the sentiment of a great man, that should the worst of times arrive, and magistracy and ministry were both to fail, yet, if parents would but be faithful to their trust, pure religion would be handed down to posterity, both in its form and in its power.

2. We have already heard of the wickedness of the inhabitants of the cities of the plain; the cup of their iniquity was full; their sin was of no common magnitude, and what a terrible judgment fell upon them! Brimstone and fire are rained down from heaven upon these *traders in iniquity;* and what a *correspondence* between the *crime* and the *punishment?* They burned in lust towards each other, and God burned them up with fire and brimstone. Their sin was *unnatural*, and God punished it by *supernatural* means. Divine justice not only observes a proportion between the crime and the degree of punishment, but also between the *species* of crime and the *kind* of punishment inflicted.

3. Disobedience to the command of God must ever meet with severe reprehension, especially in those who have already partaken of his grace, because these know his salvation, and are justly supposed to possess, by his grace, the power of resisting all solicitations to sin. The servant who knew his lord's will and did it not, was to be beaten with many stripes; see Luke xii. 47. Lot's wife stands as an everlasting monument of admonition and caution to all *backsliders*. She ran well, she permitted Satan to hinder, and she died in her provocation! While we lament her fate, we should profit by her example. To *begin* in the good way is *well;* to *continue* in the path is *better;* and to *persevere* unto the end, *best* of all. The exhortation of our blessed Lord on this subject should awaken our caution, and strongly excite our diligence: *Remember Lot's wife!* On the conduct of Lot and his daughters, see the notes on ver. 31.

CHAPTER XX.

Abraham leaves Mamre, and, after having sojourned at Kadesh and Shur, settles in Gerar, 1. *Abimelech takes Sarah, Abraham having acknowledged her* only *as his* sister, 2. *Abimelech is warned by God in a dream to restore Sarah,* 3. *He asserts his innocence,* 4, 5. *He is farther warned,* 6, 7. *Expostulates with Abraham,* 8–10. *Abraham vindicates his conduct,* 11–13. *Abimelech restores Sarah, makes Abraham a present of sheep, oxen, and male and female slaves,* 14; *offers him a residence in any part of the land,* 15; *and reproves Sarah,* 16. *At the intercession of Abraham, the curse of barrenness is removed from Abimelech and his household,* 17, 18.

A. M. cir. 2107. B. C. cir. 1897.

AND Abraham journeyed from [a] thence toward the south country, and dwelled between [b] Kadesh and Shur, and [c] sojourned in Gerar.

2 And Abraham said of Sarah his wife, [d] She *is* my sister: and Abimelech king of Gerar sent, and [e] took Sarah.

[a] Chap. xviii. 1.—[b] Chap. xvi. 7.—[c] Chap. xxvi. 6.

[d] Chap. xii. 13; xxvi. 7.—[e] Chap. xii. 15.

NOTES ON CHAP. XX.

Verse 1. *And Abraham journeyed*] It is very likely that this holy man was so deeply affected with the melancholy prospect of the ruined cities, and not knowing what was become of his nephew Lot and his family, that he could no longer bear to dwell within sight of the place. Having, therefore, struck his tents, and sojourned for a short time at *Kadesh* and *Shur*, he fixed his habitation in Gerar, which was a city of Arabia Petræa, under a king of the Philistines

A. M. cir. 2107.
B. C. cir. 1897.

3 But [f] God came to Abimelech
[g] in a dream by night, and said
to him, [h] Behold, thou *art but* a dead man,
for the woman which thou hast taken; for she
is [i] a man's wife.
4 But Abimelech had not come near her:
and he said, LORD, [k] wilt thou slay also a
righteous nation?
5 Said he not unto me, She *is* my sister?
and she, even she herself said, He *is* my
brother: [l] in the [m] integrity of
my heart and innocency of my
hands have I done this.
6 And God said unto him in a dream, Yea,
I know that thou didst this in the integrity
of thy heart; for [n] I also withheld thee from
sinning [o] against me: therefore suffered I thee
not to touch her.
7 Now therefore restore the man *his* wife;
[p] for he *is* a prophet, and he shall pray for

A. M. cir. 2107.
B. C. cir. 1897.

[f] Psa. cv. 14.——[g] Job xxxiii. 15.——[h] Ver. 7.——[i] Heb. *married to a husband.*——[k] Chap. xviii. 23; ver. 18.——[l] 2 Kings xx. 3; 2 Cor. i. 12.——[m] Or, *simplicity; or, sincerity.*——[n] Chap. xxxi. 7; xxxv. 5; Exod. xxxiv. 24; 1 Sam. xxv. 26, 34.——[o] Chap. xxxix. 9; Lev. vi. 2; Psa. li. 4.——[p] 1 Sam. vii. 5; 2 Kings v. 11; Job xlii. 8; James v. 14, 15; 1 John v. 16.

called Abimelech, *my father king*, who appears to have been not only the *father of his people*, but also a righteous man.

Verse 2. *She* is *my sister*] See the parallel account, chap. xii., and the notes there. Sarah was now about ninety years of age, and probably pregnant with Isaac. Her beauty, therefore, must have been considerably impaired since the time she was taken in a similar manner by Pharaoh, king of Egypt; but she was probably now chosen by Abimelech more on the account of forming an *alliance* with Abraham, who was very rich, than on account of any personal accomplishments. A petty king, such as Abimelech, would naturally be glad to form an alliance with such a powerful chief as Abraham was: we cannot but recollect his late defeat of the four confederate Canaanitish kings. See on chap. xiv. 14, &c. This circumstance was sufficient to establish his credit, and cause his friendship to be courted; and what more effectual means could Abimelech use in reference to this than the taking of Sarah, who he understood was Abraham's sister, to be his concubine or second wife, which in those times had no kind of disgrace attached to it?

Verse 3. *But God came to Abimelech*] Thus we find that persons who were not of the *family of Abraham* had the knowledge of the true God. Indeed, all the *Gerarites* are termed גוי צדיק *goi tsaddik*, a righteous nation, ver. 4.

Verse 5. *In the integrity of my heart, &c.*] Had Abimelech any other than honourable views in taking Sarah, he could not have justified himself thus to his Maker; and that these views were of the most honourable kind, God himself, to whom the appeal was made, asserts in the most direct manner, *Yea, I know that thou didst this in the integrity of thy heart.*

Verse 7. *He* is *a prophet, and he shall pray for thee*] The word prophet, which we have from the Greek προφητης, and which is compounded of προ, *before*, and φημι, *I speak*, means, in its general acceptation, one who *speaks of things before they happen*, i. e., one who *foretells* future events. But that this was not the *original* notion of the word, its use in this place sufficiently proves. Abraham certainly was not a prophet in the present general acceptation of the term, and for the Hebrew נביא *nabi*, we must seek some other meaning. I have, in a discourse entitled "The Christian Prophet and his Work," proved that he proper ideal meaning of the original word is to *pray, entreat, make supplication, &c.*, and this meaning of it I have justified at large both from its application in this place, and from its pointed use in the case of Saul, mentioned 1 Sam. x., and from the case of the priests of Baal, 1 Kings xviii., where *prophesying* most undoubtedly means *making prayer* and *supplication*. As those who were in habits of intimacy with God by *prayer* and *faith* were found the most proper persons to communicate his mind to man, both with respect to the *present* and the *future*, hence, נביא *nabi*, the *intercessor*, became in process of time the public *instructer* or *preacher*, and also the predicter of future events, because to such faithful praying men God revealed the secret of his will. Hence St. Paul, 1 Cor. xiv. 3, seems to restrain the word wholly to the interpreting the mind of God to the people, and their instruction in Divine things, for, says he, *he that prophesieth speaketh unto men to edification and exhortation and comfort.* See the discourse on this text referred to above. The title was also given to men eminent for eloquence and for literary abilities; hence Aaron, because he was the spokesman of Moses to the Egyptian king, was termed נביא *nabi*, prophet; Exod. iv. 16; vii. 1. And Epimenides, a heathen poet, is expressly styled προφητης, a *prophet*, by St. Paul, Tit. i. 12, just as poets in general were termed *vates* among the Romans, which properly signifies the persons who professed to *interpret the will of the gods* to their votaries, after *prayers* and *sacrifices* duly performed. In Arabic the word نبا *naba* has nearly the same meaning as in Hebrew, but in the first conjugation it has a meaning which may cast light upon the subject in general. It signifies to itinerate, *move from one place or country to another*, compelled thereto either by persecution or the command of God; *exivit de una regione in aliam.*— نبي *migrans de loco in locum.*—GOLIUS. Hence Mohammed was called النبي *an nabi*, because of his *sudden removal from Mecca to Medina*, when, pretending to a Divine commission, *his townsmen sought to take away his life: e Mecca exiens Medinam, unde Muhammed suis* نبى الله *Nabi Allah dictus fuit.*—GOLIUS. If this meaning belonged originally to the Hebrew word, it will apply with great force to the case of Abraham, whose migratory, itinerant kind of life, generally under the immediate direction of God, might have given him the title *nabi*. However this may be, the term was a title of the high-

a

A. M. cir. 2107. B. C. cir. 1897. thee, and thou shalt live: and if thou restore *her* not, [q] know thou that thou shalt surely die, thou, [r] and all that *are* thine.

8 Therefore Abimelech rose early in the morning, and called all his servants, and told all these things in their ears: and the men were sore afraid.

9 Then Abimelech called Abraham, and said unto him, What hast thou done unto us? and what have I offended thee, [s] that thou hast brought on me and on my kingdom a great sin? thou hast done deeds unto me [t] that ought not to be done.

10 And Abimelech said unto Abraham, What sawest thou, that thou hast done this thing?

11 And Abraham said, Because I thought, Surely, [u] the fear of God *is* not in this place; and [v] they will slay me for my wife's sake.

12 And yet indeed [w] *she is* my sister; she *is* the daughter of my father, but not the daughter of my mother; and she became my wife. A. M. cir. 2107 B. C. cir. 1897.

13 And it came to pass, when [x] God caused me to wander from my father's house, that I said unto her, This *is* thy kindness which thou shalt show unto me; at every place whither we shall come, [y] say of me, He *is* my brother.

14 And Abimelech [z] took sheep, and oxen, and men-servants, and women-servants, and gave *them* unto Abraham, and restored him Sarah his wife.

15 And Abimelech said, Behold, [a] my land *is* before thee: dwell [b] where it pleaseth thee.

16 And unto Sarah he said, Behold, I have given [c] thy brother a thousand *pieces* of silver: [d] behold, he *is* to thee [e] a covering of the eyes, unto all that *are* with thee, and with all *other*: [f] thus she was reproved.

[q] Chap. ii. 17.——[r] Num. xvi. 32, 33.——[s] Chap. xxvi. 10; Exod. xxxii. 21; Josh. vii. 25.——[t] Chap. xxxiv. 7.——[u] Chap. xlii. 18; Psa. xxxvi. 1; Prov. xvi. 6.——[v] Chap. xii. 12; xxvi. 7. [w] See chap. xi. 29.

[x] Chap. xii. 1, 9, 11, &c.; Heb. xi. 8.——[y] Chap. xii. 13. [z] Chap. xii. 16.——[a] Chap. xiii. 9.——[b] Heb. *as is good in thine eyes.*——[c] Ver. 5.——[d] Chap. xxvi. 11.——[e] Chapter xxiv. 65. [f] Prov. ix. 8, 9; xxv. 12; xxvii. 5; Matt. vii. 7.

est respectability and honour, both among the Hebrews and Arabs, and continues so to this day. And from the *Hebrews* the word, in all the importance and dignity of its meaning, was introduced among the *heathens* in the προφητης and *vates* of the Greeks and Romans. See on the word *seer*, Gen. xv. 1.

Verse 8. *Abimelech rose early, &c.*] God came to Abimelech in a dream by night, and we find as the day broke he arose, assembled his servants, (what we would call his *courtiers*,) and communicated to them what he had received from God. They were all struck with astonishment, and discerned the hand of God in this business. Abraham is then called, and in a most respectful and pious manner the king expostulates with him for bringing him and his people under the Divine displeasure, by withholding from him the information that Sarah was his wife; when, by taking her, he sought only an honourable alliance with his family.

Verse 11. *And Abraham said*] The best excuse he could make for his conduct, which in *this* instance is far from defensible.

Verse 12. She is *my sister*] I have not told a lie; I have suppressed only a part of the truth. In this place it may be proper to ask, *What is a lie?* It is any action done or word spoken, whether true or false in itself, which the doer or speaker wishes the observer or hearer to take in a *contrary* sense to that which he knows to be true. It is, in a word, any action done or speech delivered with *the intention to deceive*, though both may be absolutely true and right in themselves. See the note on chap. xii. 13.

The daughter of my father, but not—of my mother] *Ebn Batrick*, in his annals, among other ancient traditions has preserved the following: "Terah first married *Yona*, by whom he had Abraham; afterwards he married *Tehevita*, by whom he had Sarah." Thus she was the sister of Abraham, being the daughter of the same father by a different mother.

Verse 13. *When God caused me to wander*] Here the word אלה׳ם *Elohim* is used with a plural verb, (התעו *hithu*, caused me to wander,) which is not very usual in the Hebrew language, as this *plural noun* is generally joined with *verbs* in the *singular* number. Because there is a departure from the general mode in this instance, some have contended that the word *Elohim* signifies *princes* in this place, and suppose it to refer to those in Chaldea, who expelled Abraham because he would not worship the *fire*; but the best critics, and with them the *Jews*, allow that *Elohim* here signifies the *true God*. Abraham probably refers to his *first call*.

Verse 16. *And unto Sarah he said*] But *what* did he say? Here there is scarcely any agreement among interpreters; the Hebrew is exceedingly obscure, and every interpreter takes it in his own sense.

A thousand pieces *of silver*] SHEKELS are very probably meant here, and so the Targum understands it. The Septuagint has χιλια διδραχμα, a thousand didrachma, no doubt meaning *shekels*; for in chap. xxiii. 15, 16, this translation uses διδραχμα for the Hebrew שקל *shekel*. As *shakal* signifies literally *to weigh*, and the shekel was a coin of such a weight, Mr. Ainsworth and others think this to be the origin of our word *scale*, the instrument to *weigh* with.

The shekel of the sanctuary weighed *twenty* gerahs, Exod. xxx. 13. And according to the Jews, the

A. M. cir. 2107. B. C. cir. 1897.

17 So Abraham [g] prayed unto God: and God healed Abimelech, and his wife, and his maid-servants; and they bare *children*.

18 For the LORD [h] had fast closed up all the wombs of the house of Abimelech, because of Sarah, Abraham's wife.

[g] Chap. xxix. 31; 1 Sam. v. 11, 12; Job xlii. 8, 9, 10.

[h] Chap. xii. 17; xvi. 2.

gerah weighed *sixteen* grains of barley. *R. Maimon* observes, that after the captivity the *shekel* was increased to *three hundred and eighty-four* grains or barley-corns. On the subject of ancient weights and measures, very little that is satisfactory is known.

Behold, he is to thee a covering of the eyes] *It*—the *one thousand shekels*, (not *he*—Abraham,) is *to thee for a covering*—to procure thee a veil to conceal thy beauty (*unto all that* are *with thee, and with all* other) from all thy own kindred and *acquaintance*, and from all *strangers*, that none, seeing thou art another man's wife, may covet thee on account of thy comeliness.

Thus she was reproved] The original is ונכחת *venochachath*, but the word is probably the second person preterite, used for the imperative mood, from the root נכח *nachach*, to make *straight, direct, right*; or to *speak rightly, correctly*; and may, in connection with the rest of the text, be thus paraphrased: *Behold, I have given thy* BROTHER (Abraham, gently alluding to the equivocation, ver. 2, 5) *a thousand* shekels *of silver; behold*, IT *is* (that is, the silver is, or *may be*, or *let it be*) *to thee a covering of the eyes* (to procure a veil; see above) *with regard to all those who are with thee, and to all* (or *and in all*) *speak thou the truth*. Correctly translated by the Septuagint, *και παντα αληθευσον, and in all things speak the truth*—not only tell a *part* of the truth, but tell the *whole*; say not merely *he is my brother*, but say also, *he is my husband too*. Thus *in* ALL *things speak the truth*. I believe the above to be the *sense* of this difficult passage, and shall not puzzle my readers with criticisms. See *Kennicott*.

Verse 17. *So Abraham prayed*] This was the prime office of the נביא *nabi*; see ver. 7.

Verse 18. *For the Lord had fast closed up all the wombs*] Probably by means of some *disease* with which he had smitten them, hence it is said *they were healed* at Abraham's intercession; and this seems necessarily to imply that they had been afflicted by some disease that rendered it impossible for them to have children till it was removed. And possibly this disease, as Dr. Dodd conjectures, had afflicted Abimelech, and by this he was withheld, ver. 6, from defiling Abraham's bed.

1. ON the *prevarication* of Abraham and Sarah, see the notes and concluding observations on chap. xii.; and while we pity this *weakness*, let us take it as a *warning*.

2. The *cause* why the patriarch did not acknowledge Sarah as his wife, was a fear lest he should lose his life on her account, for he said, *Surely the fear*, i. e., the true worship, *of* the true *God is not in this place*. Such is the natural bigotry and narrowness of the human heart, that we can scarcely allow that any besides ourselves possess the true religion. To indulge a disposition of this kind is highly blamable. The true religion is neither confined to *one spot* nor to *one people*; it is spread in various forms over the whole earth. He who fills immensity has left a record of himself in every nation and among every people under heaven. Beware of the spirit of intolerance! for bigotry produces uncharitableness; and uncharitableness, harsh judging; and in such a spirit a man may think he does God service when he tortures, or makes a burnt-offering of the person whom his narrow mind and hard heart have dishonoured with the name of *heretic*. Such a spirit is not *confined* to any *one community*, though it has predominated in some more than in others. But these things are highly displeasing in the sight of God. HE, as the Father of the spirits of all flesh, loves every branch of his vastly extended family; and as far as we love one another, no matter of what sect or party, so far we resemble HIM. Had Abraham possessed more charity for man and confidence in God at this time, he had not fallen into that snare from which he barely escaped. A hasty judgment is generally both erroneous and harsh; and those who are the most apt to form it are generally the most difficult to be convinced of the truth.

CHAPTER XXI.

Isaac is born according to the promise, 1–3; *and is circumcised when eight days old*, 4. *Abraham's age, and Sarah's exultation at the birth of their son*, 5–7. *Isaac is weaned*, 8. *Ishmael mocking on the occasion, Sarah requires that both he and his mother Hagar shall be dismissed*, 9, 10. *Abraham, distressed on the account, is ordered by the Lord to comply*, 11, 12. *The promise renewed to Ishmael*, 13. *Abraham dismisses Hagar and her son, who go to the wilderness of Beer-sheba*, 14. *They are greatly distressed for want of water*, 15, 16. *An angel of God appears to and relieves them*, 17–19. *Ishmael prospers and is married*, 20, 21. *Abimelech, and Phichol his chief captain, make a covenant with Abraham, and surrender the well of Beer-sheba for seven ewe lambs*, 22–32. *Abraham plants a grove, and invokes the name of the everlasting God*, 33.

A. M. 2108. B. C. 1896.

AND the LORD [a] visited Sarah as he had said, and the LORD did unto Sarah [b] as he had spoken.

2 For Sarah [c] conceived, and bare Abraham a son in his old age, [d] at the set time of which God had spoken to him.

3 And Abraham called the name of his son that was born unto him, whom Sarah bare to him, [e] Isaac.

4 And Abraham [f] circumcised his son Isaac being eight days old, [g] as God had commanded him.

5 And [h] Abraham was a hundred years old, when his son Isaac was born unto him.

6 And Sarah said, [i] God hath made me to laugh, *so that* all that hear [k] will laugh with me.

7 And she said, Who would have said unto Abraham, that Sarah should have given children suck? [l] for I have borne *him* a son in his old age. A. M. 2108. B. C. 1896.

8 And the child grew and was weaned; and Abraham made a great feast the *same* day that Isaac was weaned.

9 And Sarah saw the son of Hagar [m] the Egyptian, [n] which she had borne unto Abraham, [o] mocking. A. M. cir. 2110. B. C. cir. 1894.

10 Wherefore she said unto Abraham, [p] Cast out this bond-woman and her son: for the son of this bond-woman shall not be heir with my son, *even* with Isaac.

11 And the thing was very grievous in Abraham's sight, [q] because of his son.

[a] 1 Sam. ii. 21.——[b] Chap. xvii. 19; xviii. 10, 14; Gal. iv. 23, 28.——[c] Acts vii. 8; Gal. iv. 22; Heb. xi. 11.——[d] Chap. xvii. 21.——[e] Chap. xvii. 19.——[f] Acts vii. 8.——[g] Chap. xvii. 10, 12.——[h] Chap. xvii. 1, 17.

[i] Psa. cxxvi. 2; Isa. liv. 1; Gal. iv. 27.——[k] Luke i. 58. [l] Chap. xviii. 11, 12.——[m] Chap. xvi. 1.——[n] Chap. xvi. 15. [o] Gal. iv. 22.——[p] Gal. iv. 30; see chap. xxv. 6; xxxvi. 6, 7 [q] Chap. xvii. 18.

NOTES ON CHAP. XXI.

Verse 1. *The Lord visited Sarah*] That is, God fulfilled his promise to Sarah by giving her, at the advanced age of *ninety*, power to conceive and bring forth a son.

Verse 3. *Isaac.*] See the reason and interpretation of this name in the note on chap. xvii. 7.

Verse 4. *And Abraham circumcised his son*] See on chap. xvii. 10, &c.

Verse 6. *God hath made me to laugh*] Sarah alludes here to the circumstance mentioned chap. xviii. 12; and as she seems to use the word *to laugh* in this place, not in the sense of being *incredulous*, but to express such *pleasure* or *happiness* as almost *suspends* the reasoning faculty for a time, it justifies the observation on the above-named verse. See a similar case in Luke xxiv. 41, where the disciples were so overcome with the good news of our Lord's resurrection, that it is said, *They believed not for joy.*

Verse 8. *The child grew and was weaned*] Dæt cild ꞅoꝺlice ꝩeox ⁊ ꝩæꞃꝺ ꝫeꝩeneꝺ.—*Anglo-Saxon* VERSION. *Now the child waxed and became weaned.* We have the verb *to wean* from the Anglo-Saxon aꝩenꝺan *awendan*, to *convert*, *transfer*, *turn from one thing to another*, which is the exact import of the Hebrew word גמל *gamal* in the text. Hence ꝩenan *wenan*, to *wean*, to turn the child from the breast to receive another kind of aliment. And hence, probably, the word WEAN, *a young child*, which is still in use in the northern parts of Great Britain and Ireland, and which from its etymology seems to signify *a child taken from the breast*; surely not from the Scotch *wee-ane*, *a little one*, much less from the German *wenig*, *little*, as Dr. Johnson and others would derive it. At what time children were weaned among the ancients, is a disputed point. St. Jerome says there were two opinions on this subject. Some hold that children were always weaned at *five* years of age; others, that they were not weaned till they were *twelve*. From the speech of the mother to her son, 2 Mac. vii. 27, it seems likely that among the Jews they were weaned when *three* years old: *O my son, have pity upon me that bare thee nine months in my womb, and gave thee* SUCK THREE YEARS, *and nourished thee and brought thee up.* And this is farther strengthened by 2 Chron. xxxi. 16, where Hezekiah, in making provision for the Levites and priests, includes the children from *three* years old and upwards; which is a presumptive proof that previously to this age they were wholly dependent on the *mother* for their nourishment. Samuel appears to have been brought to the sanctuary when he was just *weaned*, and then he was capable of ministering before the Lord, 1 Sam. i. 22–28; and this certainly could not be before he was *three* years of age. The term among the Mohammedans is fixed by the Koran, chap. xxxi. 14, at *two* years of age.

Verse 9. *Mocking.*] What was implied in this mocking is not known. St. Paul, Gal. iv. 29, calls it *persecuting*; but it is likely he meant no more than some species of *ridicule* used by Ishmael on the occasion, and probably with respect to the age of Sarah at Isaac's birth, and her previous barrenness. *Jonathan ben Uzziel* and the *Jerusalem Targum* represent Ishmael as performing some idolatrous rite on the occasion, and that this had given the offence to Sarah. Conjectures are as useless as they are endless. Whatever it was, it became the occasion of the expulsion of himself and mother. Several authors are of opinion that the Egyptian bondage of *four hundred* years, mentioned chap. xv. 13, commenced with this persecution of the righteous seed by the son of an *Egyptian* woman.

Verse 10. *Cast out this bond-woman and her son*] Both Sarah and Abraham have been accused of cruelty in this transaction, because every word reads harsh to us. *Cast out;* גרש *garash* signifies not only to *thrust out*, *drive away*, and *expel*, but also to *divorce;* (see Lev. xxi. 7;) and it is in this latter sense the

A. M. cir. 2110.
B. C. cir. 1894.

12 And God said unto Abraham, Let it not be grievous in
thy sight because of the lad, and because of
thy bond-woman; in all that Sarah hath said
unto thee, hearken unto her voice; for [r] in
Isaac shall thy seed be called.
13 And also of the son of the bond-woman
will I make [s] a nation, because he *is* thy seed.
14 And Abraham rose up early in the morning, and took bread, and a bottle of water,
and gave *it* unto Hagar, (putting *it* on her
shoulder,) and the child, and [t] sent her away:
and she departed, and wandered in the wilderness of Beer-sheba.
15 And the water was spent in the bottle,
and she cast the child under one of the
shrubs.

16 And she went, and sat her
down over against *him* a good
way off, as it were a bow-shot: for she said,
Let me not see the death of the child. And
she sat over against *him*, and lift up her
voice, and wept.
17 And [u] God heard the voice of the lad;
and the angel of God called to Hagar out of
heaven, and said unto her, What aileth thee,
Hagar? fear not; for God hath heard the
voice of the lad where he *is*.
18 Arise, lift up the lad, and hold him in
thine hand; for [v] I will make him a great nation.
19 And [w] God opened her eyes, and she saw
a well of water; and she went, and filled the
bottle with water, and gave the lad drink.
20 And God [x] was with the lad; and he

A. M. cir. 2110.
B. C. cir. 1894.

[r] Rom. ix. 7, 8; Heb. xi. 18.——[s] Ver. 18; chap. xvi. 10; xvii. 20.——[t] John viii. 35.——[u] Exod. iii. 7.——[v] Ver. 13.

[w] Num. xxii. 31; see 2 Kings vi. 17, 18, 20; Luke xxiv. 16, 31.——[x] Chap. xxviii. 15; xxxix. 2, 3, 21.

word should be understood here. The child of Abraham by Hagar might be considered as having a right at least to a part of the inheritance; and as it was sufficiently known to Sarah that God had designed that the succession should be established in the line of Isaac, she wished Abraham to *divorce* Hagar, or to perform some sort of *legal act* by which Ishmael might be excluded from all claim on the inheritance.

Verse 12. *In Isaac shall thy seed be called.*] Here God shows the propriety of attending to the counsel of Sarah; and lest Abraham, in whose eyes the thing was grievous, should feel distressed on the occasion, God renews his promises to Ishmael and his posterity.

Verse 14. *Took bread, and a bottle*] By the word *bread* we are to understand the food or provisions which were necessary for her and Ishmael, till they should come to the place of their destination; which, no doubt, Abraham particularly pointed out. The *bottle*, which was made of skin, ordinarily a goat's skin, contained water sufficient to last them till they should come to the next well; which, it is likely, Abraham particularly specified also. This well, it appears, Hagar missed, and therefore *wandered about in the wilderness* seeking more water, till all she had brought with her was expended. We may therefore safely presume that she and her son were sufficiently provided for their journey, had they not missed their way. Travellers in those countries take only, to the present day, provisions sufficient to carry them to the next village or encampment; and water to supply them till they shall meet with the next well. What adds to the *appearance* of cruelty in this case is, that our translation seems to represent Ishmael as being a *young child;* and that Hagar was obliged to carry him, the bread, and the bottle of water on her back or shoulder at the same time. But that Ishmael could not be carried on his mother's shoulder will be sufficiently evident when his *age* is considered; Ishmael was born when Abraham was eighty-six years of age, chap. xvi. 16; Isaac was born when he was one hundred years of age, chap. xxi. 5; hence Ishmael was fourteen years old at the birth of Isaac. Add to this the age of Isaac when he was *weaned*, which, from ver. 8 of this chapter, (see the note,) was probably *three*, and we shall find that Ishmael was at the time of his leaving Abraham not less than seventeen years old; an age at which, in those primitive times, a young man was able to gain his livelihood, either by his bow in the wilderness, or by keeping flocks as Jacob did.

Verse 15. *And she cast the child*] ותשלך את הילד *vattashlech eth haiyeled*, and she sent the lad under one of the shrubs, viz., to screen him from the intensity of the heat. Here Ishmael appears to be utterly helpless, and this circumstance seems farther to confirm the opinion that he was now in a state of *infancy;* but the preceding observations do this supposition entirely away, and his present helplessness will be easily accounted for on this ground: 1. Young persons can bear much less fatigue than those who are arrived at mature age. 2. They require much more fluid from the greater quantum of heat in their bodies, strongly marked by the impetuosity of the blood; because from them a much larger quantity of the fluids is thrown off by sweat and insensible perspiration, than from grown up or aged persons. 3. Their digestion is much more rapid, and hence they cannot bear hunger and thirst as well as the others. On these grounds Ishmael must be much more exhausted with fatigue than his mother.

Verse 19. *God opened her eyes*] These words appear to me to mean no more than that God directed her to a well, which probably was at no great distance from the place in which she then was; and therefore she is commanded, ver. 18, to *support the lad*, literally, to *make her hand strong in his behalf*—namely, that he might reach the well and quench his thirst.

Verse 20. *Became an archer.*] And by his skill in this art, under the continual superintendence of the

A. M. cir. 2110. B. C. cir. 1894. grew, and dwelt in the wilderness, [y] and became an archer.
21 And he dwelt in the wilderness of Paran:
and his mother [z] took him a wife out of the
land of Egypt.
A. M. cir. 2118. B. C. cir. 1886. 22 And it came to pass at that
time, that [a] Abimelech, and Phi-
chol the chief captain of his host, spake unto
Abraham, saying, [b] God *is* with thee in all
that thou doest:
23 Now therefore [c] swear unto me here by
God [d] that thou wilt not deal falsely with me,
nor with my son, nor with my son's son: *but*
according to the kindness that I have done
unto thee, thou shalt do unto me, and to the
land wherein thou hast sojourned.
24 And Abraham said, I will swear.
25 And Abraham reproved Abimelech because of a well of water, which Abimelech's
servants [e] had violently taken away.
26 And Abimelech said, I wot not who hath
done this thing: neither didst A. M. cir. 2118. B. C. cir. 1886.
thou tell me; neither yet heard
I *of it*, but to-day.
27 And Abraham took sheep and oxen, and
gave them unto Abimelech; and both of them
[f] made a covenant.
28 And Abraham set seven ewe lambs of
the flock by themselves.
29 And Abimelech said unto Abraham,
[g] What *mean* these seven ewe lambs which
thou hast set by themselves?
30 And he said, For *these* seven ewe lambs
shalt thou take of my hand, that [h] they may be
a witness unto me, that I have digged this well.
31 Wherefore he [i] called that place [k] Beer-
sheba; because there they sware both of them.
32 Thus they made a covenant at Beer-
sheba: then Abimelech rose up, and Phichol
the chief captain of his host, and they returned
into the land of the Philistines.
33 And *Abraham* planted a [l] grove in Beer-

[y] Chap. xvi. 12.——[z] Chap. xxiv. 4.——[a] Chap. xx. 2; xxvi. 26.——[b] Chap. xxvi. 28.——[c] Josh. ii. 12; 1 Sam. xxiv. 21. [d] Heb. *if thou shalt lie unto me.*

[e] See chap. xxvi. 15, 18, 20, 21, 22.——[f] Chap. xxvi. 31. [g] Chap. xxxiii. 8.——[h] Chap. xxxi. 48, 52.——[i] Chap. xxvi. 33. [k] That is, *the well of the oath.*——[l] Or, *tree;* Amos viii. 14.

Divine Providence, (for *God was with the lad,*) he was undoubtedly enabled to procure a sufficient supply for his own wants and those of his parent.

Verse 21. *He dwelt in the wilderness of Paran*] This is generally allowed to have been a part of the desert belonging to Arabia Petræa, in the vicinity of Mount Sinai; and this seems to be its uniform meaning in the sacred writings.

Verse 22. *At that time*] This may either refer to the transactions recorded in the preceding chapter, or to the time of Ishmael's marriage, but most probably to the former.

God is *with thee*] מימרא דיי *meimera daiya, the* WORD of Jehovah; see before, chap. xv. 1. That the Chaldee paraphrasts use this term, not for a *word spoken*, but in the same sense in which St. John uses the *λογος του Θεου*, the WORD of God, chap. i., must be evident to every unprejudiced reader. See on chap. xv 1.

Verse 23. *Now therefore swear unto me*] The oath on such occasions probably meant no more than the mutual promise of both the parties, when they slew an animal, poured out the blood as a sacrifice to God, and then passed between the pieces. See this ceremony, chap. v. 18, and on chap. xv.

According to the kindness that I have done] The simple claims of justice were alone set up among virtuous people in those ancient times, which constitute the basis of the famous *lex talionis*, or law of *like for like, kind office for kind office*, and *breach for breach*.

Verse 25. *Abraham reproved Abimelech*] Wells were of great consequence in those hot countries, and especially where the flocks were numerous, because the water was scarce, and digging to find it was accompanied with much expense of time and labour.

Verse 26. *I wot not who hath done this thing*] The servants of Abimelech had committed these depredations on Abraham without any authority from their master, who appears to have been a very amiable man, possessing the fear of God, and ever regulating the whole of his conduct by the principles of righteousness and strict justice.

Verse 27. *Took sheep and oxen*] Some think that these were the sacrifices which were offered on the occasion, and which Abraham furnished at his own cost, and, in order to do Abimelech the greater honour, gave them to him to offer before the Lord.

Verse 28. *Seven ewe lambs*] These were either given as a *present*, or they were intended as the *price* of the well; and being accepted by Abimelech, they served as a *witness* that he had acknowledged Abraham's right to the *well* in question.

Verse 31. *He called that place Beer-sheba*] באר שבע *Beer-shaba*, literally, the *well of swearing* or *of the oath*, because *they both sware there*—mutually confirmed the covenant.

Verse 33. Abraham *planted a grove*] The original word אשל *eshel* has been variously translated a *grove*, a *plantation*, an *orchard*, a *cultivated field*, and an *oak*. From this word, says Mr. Parkhurst, may be derived the name of the famous *asylum*, opened by Romulus, *between two groves of oaks* at Rome; (*μεθοριον δυοιν δρυμων*, *Dionys. Hal.*, lib. ii. c. 16;) and as Abraham, Gen. xxi. 33, agreeably, no doubt, to the institutes of the patriarchal religion, planted an oak in Beer-sheba,

A. M. cir. 2118. B. C. cir. 1886. sheba, and [m] called there on the name of the Lord, [n] the everlasting God.

34 And Abraham sojourned in the Philistines' land many days. A. M. cir. 2118. B. C. cir. 1886.

[m] Chap. iv. 26; xxvi. 23, 25, 33.——[n] Deut. xxxiii. 27; Isa. xl. 28; Rom. i. 20; xvi. 26; 1 Tim. i. 17; Jer. x. 10.

and called on the name of Jehovah, the everlasting God, (compare Gen. xii. 8; xviii. 1,) so we find that *oaks* were sacred among the idolaters also. *Ye shall be ashamed of the* OAKS *ye have chosen*, says Isaiah, chap. i. 29, to the idolatrous Israelites. And in *Greece* we meet in very early times with the oracle of Jupiter at the oaks of Dodona. Among the Greeks and *Romans* we have *sacra Jovi quercus*, the *oak* sacred to Jupiter, even to a proverb. And in *Gaul* and *Britain* we find the highest religious regard paid to the same tree and to its *misletoe*, under the direction of the *Druids*, that is, the *oak prophets* or *priests*, from the Celtic *deru*, and Greek *δρυς*, an oak. Few are ignorant that the *misletoe* is indeed a very extraordinary plant, not to *be cultivated in the earth*, but always growing on some other tree. "The druids," says *Pliny*, Nat. Hist., lib. xvii., c. 44, "hold nothing more sacred than the *misletoe*, and the tree on which it is produced, provided it be the *oak*. They make choice of *groves of oak* on this account, nor do they perform any of their sacred rites without the leaves of those trees; so that one may suppose that they are for this reason called, by a Greek etymology, *Druids*. And whatever *misletoe* grows on the oak they think is sent from heaven, and is a sign that God himself has chosen that tree. This however is very rarely found, but when discovered is treated with great ceremony. They call it by a name which signifies in their language *the curer of all ills;* and having duly prepared their feasts and sacrifices under the tree, they bring to it two white bulls, whose horns are then for the first time tied; the priest, dressed in a white robe, ascends the tree, and with a *golden pruning hook* cuts off the *misletoe*, which is received into a white *sagum* or sheet. Then they sacrifice the victims, praying that God would bless his own gift to those on whom he has bestowed it." It is impossible for a *Christian* to read this account without thinking of HIM who was *the desire of all nations*, of the man whose name was *the* BRANCH, who had indeed no *father upon earth*, but came down from heaven, was given *to heal all our ills*, and, after being *cut off* through the Divine counsel, was wrapped in *fine linen* and laid in the sepulchre for our sakes. I cannot forbear adding that the *misletoe* was a *sacred emblem* to other *Celtic* nations, as, for instance, to the ancient inhabitants of *Italy*. The *golden branch*, of which Virgil speaks so largely in the sixth book of the Æneis, and without which, he says, none could return *from the infernal regions*, (see line 126,) seems an allusion to the *misletoe*, as he himself plainly intimates by comparing it to that plant, line 205, &c. See *Parkhurst*, under the word אשל *eshel*.

In the first ages of the world the worship of God was exceedingly simple; there were no *temples* nor covered edifices of any kind; an *altar*, sometimes a *single stone*, sometimes consisting of several, and at other times merely of *turf*, was all that was necessary; on this the fire was lighted and the sacrifice offered. Any *place* was equally proper, as they knew that the object of their worship filled the heavens and the earth. In process of time when families increased, and many sacrifices were to be offered, *groves* or shady places were chosen, where the worshippers might enjoy the protection of the *shade*, as a considerable time must be employed in offering *many* sacrifices. These groves became afterwards abused to *impure* and *idolatrous* purposes, and were therefore strictly forbidden. See Exod. xxxiv. 13; Deut. xii. 3; xvi. 21.

And called there on the name of the Lord] On this important passage Dr. Shuckford speaks thus: "Our English translation very erroneously renders this place, *he called upon the name of Jehovah;* but the expression קרא בשם *kara beshem* never signifies *to call* upon *the name;* קרא שם *kara shem* would signify *to invoke* or *call* upon *the name*, or קרא אל שם *kara el shem* would signify *to cry unto the name;* but קרא בשם *kara beshem* signifies *to invoke* IN *the name*, and seems to be used where the true worshippers of God offered their prayers in the name of the true Mediator, or where the idolaters offered their prayers in the name of false ones, 1 Kings xviii. 26; for as the true worshippers had but *one God* and *one Lord*, so the false worshippers had *gods many* and *lords many*, 1 Cor. viii. 5. We have several instances of קרא *kara*, and a noun after it, sometimes *with* and sometimes *without* the particle אל *el*, and then it signifies *to call* upon the person there mentioned; thus, קרא יהוה *kara Yehovah* is *to call upon the Lord*, Psa. xiv. 4; xvii. 6; xxxi. 17; liii. 4; cxviii. 5, &c.; and קרא אל יהוה *kara el Yehovah* imports the same, 1 Sam. xii. 17; Jonah i. 6, &c.; but קרא בשם *kara beshem* is either *to name* BY *the name*, Gen. iv. 17; Num. xxxii. 42; Psa. xlix. 11; Isa. xliii. 7; or *to invoke* IN *the name*, when it is used as an expression of religious worship." CONNEX. vol. i., p. 293. I believe this to be a just view of the subject, and therefore I admit it without scruple.

The everlasting God.] יהוה אל עילם *Yehovah el olam*, JEHOVAH, *the* STRONG GOD, *the* ETERNAL ONE. This is the first place in Scripture in which עולם *olam* occurs as an *attribute* of God, and here it is evidently designed to point out his eternal duration; that it can mean no *limited time* is self-evident, because nothing of this kind can be attributed to God. The Septuagint render the words Θεος αιωνιος, *the ever-existing God;* and the Vulgate has *Invocavit ibi nomen Domini, Dei æterni*, There he invoked the name of the Lord, the eternal God. The Arabic is nearly the same. From this application of both the Hebrew and Greek words we learn that עולם *olam* and αιων *aion* originally signified ETERNAL, or *duration without end*. עלם *alam* signifies *he was hidden, concealed*, or *kept secret;* and αιων, according to Aristotle, (*De Cælo;* lib. i., chap. 9, and a higher authority need not be sought,) is compounded of αει, *always*, and ων, *being*, αιων εστιν, απο

a

του αει ειναι. The same author informs us that God was termed *Aisa*, because he was always existing, λεγεσθαι—*Αισαν δε, αει ουσαν. De Mundo*, chap. xi., *in fine.* Hence we see that no words can more forcibly express the grand characteristics of eternity than these. It is that duration which is *concealed, hidden*, or *kept secret* from all created beings; which is *always existing*, still *running* ON but never *running* OUT; an *interminable, incessant*, and *immeasurable duration*; it is THAT, in the *whole of which* God alone can be said to *exist*, and *that* which the *eternal mind* can alone comprehend.

In all languages words have, in process of time, deviated from their original acceptations, and have become accommodated to particular purposes, and limited to particular meanings. This has happened both to the Hebrew עלם *alam*, and the Greek *αιων*; they have been both used to express a *limited* time, but in general a time the limits of which are *unknown*; and thus a pointed reference to the *original ideal meaning* is still kept up. Those who bring any of these terms in an *accommodated* sense to favour a particular doctrine, &c., must depend on the good graces of their opponents for permission to use them in this way. For as the real grammatical meaning of both words is *eternal*, and all other meanings are only *accommodated* ones, sound criticism, in all matters of dispute concerning the import of a word or term, must have recourse to the grammatical meaning, and its use among the earliest and most correct writers in the language, and will determine all *accommodated* meanings by this alone. Now the first and best writers in both these languages apply *olam* and *αιων* to express *eternal*, in the proper meaning of that word; and this is their proper meaning in the Old and New Testaments when applied to God, his attributes, his operations taken in connection with the *ends* for which he performs them, for *whatsoever he doth, it shall be for ever*—יהיה לעולם *yihyeh leolam, it shall be for eternity*, Eccl. iii. 14; *forms* and *appearances* of created things may change, but the *counsels* and *purposes* of God relative to them are permanent and eternal, and none of them can be frustrated; hence the words, when applied to things which from their nature must have a *limited* duration, are properly to be understood in this sense, because those things, though *temporal* in themselves, *shadow forth* things that are *eternal.* Thus the Jewish dispensation, which in the whole and in its parts is frequently said to be לעולם *leolam*, for ever, and which has terminated in the Christian dispensation, has the word properly applied to it, because it typified and introduced that dispensation which is to *continue* not only *while time shall last*, but is to have its incessant accumulating consummation throughout *eternity.* The word is, with the same strict propriety, applied to the duration of the rewards and punishments in a future state. And the argument that pretends to prove (and it is only pretension) that in the future punishment of the wicked "the worm *shall die*," and "the fire *shall be quenched*," will apply as forcibly to the state of happy spirits, and as fully prove that a point in eternity shall arrive when the repose of the righteous shall be interrupted, and the glorification of the children of God have an eternal end! See the notes on chap. xvii. 7, 8.

1. FAITHFULNESS is one of the attributes of God, and none of his promises can fail. According to the promise to Abraham, Isaac is born; but according to the course of nature it fully appears that both Abraham and Sarah had passed that term of life in which it was possible for them to have children. Isaac is the child of the *promise*, and the promise is *supernatural.* Ishmael is born according to the ordinary course of *nature*, and cannot inherit, because the inheritance is *spiritual*, and cannot come by *natural birth;* hence we see that no man can expect to enter into the kingdom of God by birth, education, profession of the true faith, &c., &c. Those alone who are *born from above*, and are made *partakers of the Divine nature*, can be admitted into the family of God in heaven, and everlastingly enjoy that glorious inheritance. Reader, art *thou* born again? Hath God changed thy heart and thy life? If not, canst thou suppose that in thy present state thou canst possibly enter into the paradise of God? I leave thy conscience to answer.

2. The actions of good men may be misrepresented, and their motives suspected, because those motives are not known; and those who are prone to think evil are the last to take any trouble to inform their minds, so that they may judge righteous judgment. Abraham, in the dismissal of Hagar and Ishmael, has been accused of *cruelty.* Though objections of this kind have been answered already, yet it may not be amiss farther to observe that what he did he did in conformity to a Divine command, and a command so unequivocally given that he could not doubt its Divine origin; and this very command was accompanied with a promise that *both the child and his mother should be taken under the Divine protection.* And it was so; nor does it appear that they lacked any thing but *water*, and that only for a *short time*, after which it was miraculously supplied. God will work a miracle when necessary, and never till then; and at such a time the Divine interposition can be easily ascertained, and man is under no temptation to attribute to *second causes* what has so evidently flowed from the *first.* Thus, while he is promoting his creatures' good, he is securing his own glory; and he brings men into straits and difficulties, that he may have the fuller opportunity to convince his followers of his providential care, and to prove how much he loves them.

3. Did we acknowledge God in all our ways, he would direct our steps. Abimelech, king of Gerar, and Phichol, captain of his host, seeing Abraham a worshipper of the true God, made him swear by the object of his worship that there should be a lasting peace between them and him; for as they saw that God was with Abraham, they well knew that he could not expect the Divine blessing any longer than he walked in *integrity* before God; they therefore require him to swear by God that he would not *deal falsely* with *them* or their posterity. From this very circumstance we may see the original purpose, design, and spirit of an oath, viz., *Let God prosper or curse me in all that I do, as I prove true or false to my engagements!* This is still the *spirit* of all oaths where God is called to witness, whether the *form* be by the *water of the Ganges*, the *sign of the cross, kissing the Bible*, or *lifting up the hand to heaven.* Hence we

may learn that he who falsifies an *oath* or *promise*, made in the presence and name of God, thereby forfeits all right and title to the approbation and blessing of his Maker.

But it is highly criminal to make such appeals to God upon *trivial* occasions. Only the *most solemn* matters should be thus determined. Legislators who regard the morals of the people should take heed not to multiply oaths in matters of *commerce* and *revenue*, if they even use them at all. Who can take the oaths presented by the custom house or excise, and be guiltless? I have seen a person kiss his pen or thumb nail instead of the book, thinking that he avoided the condemnation thereby of the false oath he was then taking!

CHAPTER XXII.

The faith and obedience of Abraham put to a most extraordinary test, 1. *He is commanded to offer his beloved son Isaac for a burnt-offering,* 2. *He prepares, with the utmost promptitude, to accomplish the will of God,* 3–6. *Affecting speech of Isaac,* 7; *and Abraham's answer,* 8. *Having arrived at mount Moriah he prepares to sacrifice his son,* 9, 10; *and is prevented by an angel of the Lord,* 11, 12. *A ram is offered in the stead of Isaac,* 13; *and the place is named* Jehovah-jireh, 14. *The angel of the Lord calls to Abraham a second time,* 15; *and, in the most solemn manner, he is assured of innumerable blessings in the multiplication and prosperity of his seed,* 16–18. *Abraham returns and dwells at Beer-sheba,* 19; *hears that his brother Nahor has eight children by his wife Milcah,* 20; *their names,* 21–23; *and four by his concubine Reumah,* 24.

A. M. 2132. B. C. 1872. *Jos. Ant.*

AND it came to pass after these things, that [a] God did tempt Abraham, and said unto him, Abraham: and he said, [b] Behold, *here* I *am.*
2 And he said, Take now thy son, [c] thine only *son* Isaac, whom thou lovest, and get thee [d] into the land of Moriah; and offer him there for a burnt-offering, upon one of the mountains which I will tell thee of.

A. M. cir. 2132. B. C. cir. 1872.

[a] 1 Cor. x. 13; Heb. xi. 17; James i. 12; 1 Pet. i. 7.

[b] Heb. *Behold me.*——[c] Heb xi. 17.——[d] 2 Chron. iii. 1.

NOTES ON CHAP. XXII.

Verse 1. *God did tempt Abraham*] The original here is very emphatic: והאלהים נסה את אברהם *vehaelohim nissah eth Abraham,* "And the Elohim he tried this Abraham;" God brought him into such circumstances as *exercised* and *discovered* his faith, love, and obedience. Though the word *tempt*, from *tento*, signifies no more than to *prove* or *try*, yet as it is now generally used to imply a solicitation to evil, in which way God never tempts any man, it would be well to avoid it here. The Septuagint used the word *επειρασε*, which signifies *tried, pierced through;* and Symmachus translates the Hebrew נסה *nissah* by *εδοξαζεν*, God *glorified* Abraham, or rendered him *illustrious*, supposing the word to be the same with נס *nas*, which signifies to *glister with light*, whence נס *nes*, an *ensign* or *banner displayed*. Thus then, according to him, the words should be understood: "God put great honour on Abraham by giving him this opportunity of showing to all successive ages the nature and efficacy of an unshaken faith in the power, goodness, and truth of God." The *Targum* of *Jonathan ben Uzziel* paraphrases the place thus: "And it happened that Isaac and Ishmael contended, and Ishmael said, I ought to be my father's heir, because I am his first-born; but Isaac said, It is more proper that I should be my father's heir, because I am the son of Sarah his wife, and thou art only the son of Hagar, my mother's slave. Then Ishmael answered, I am more righteous than thou, because I was circumcised when I was *thirteen* years of age, and if I had chosen, I could have prevented my circumcision; but thou wert circumcised when thou wert but *eight days* old, and if thou hadst had knowledge, thou wouldst probably not have suffered thyself to be circumcised. Then Isaac answered and said, Behold, I am now thirty-six years old, and if the holy and blessed God should require all my members, I would freely surrender them. These words were immediately heard before the Lord of the universe, and מימרא דיי *meimera daiya*, the WORD of the LORD, did try Abraham." I wish once for all to remark, though the subject has been referred to before, that the Chaldee term מימרא *meimera*, which we translate *word*, is taken *personally* in some hundreds of places in the *Targums*. When the author, Jonathan, speaks of the Divine Being as doing or saying any thing, he generally represents him as performing the whole by his *meimera*, which he appears to consider, not as a *speech* or *word spoken*, but as a *person* quite distinct from the Most High. St. John uses the word *λογος* in precisely the same sense with the Targumists, chap. i. 1; see the notes there, and see before on chap. xxi. 22, and xv. 1.

Verse 2. *Take now thy son*] Bishop Warburton's observations on this passage are weighty and important. "The order in which the words are placed in the original gradually increases the sense, and raises the passions higher and higher: *Take now thy son,* (rather, take I *beseech* thee נא *na*,) *thine only son whom thou lovest, even Isaac.* Jarchi imagines this minuteness was to preclude any doubt in Abraham. Abraham desired earnestly to be let into the mystery of *redemption;* and God, to instruct him in the infinite extent of the Divine goodness to mankind, *who spared not his own Son, but delivered him up for us all,* let Abraham feel by experience what it was to lose a be-

A. M. cir. 2132.
B. C. cir. 1872.

3 And Abraham rose up [e] early
in the morning, and saddled his
ass, and took two of his young men with him,
and Isaac his son, and clave the wood for the
burnt-offering, and rose up, and went unto the
place of which God had told him.
4 Then on the third day Abraham lifted up
his eyes, and saw the place afar off.
5 And Abraham said unto his young men,
Abide ye here with the ass; and
I and the lad will go yonder
and worship, and come again to you.
6 And Abraham took the wood of the burnt-
offering, and [f] laid *it* upon Isaac his son; and
he took the fire in his hand, and a knife: and
they went both of them together.
7 And Isaac spake unto Abraham his father,
and said, My father: and he said, [g] Here *am*

e Psa. cxix. 60; Eccles. ix. 10; Isa. xxvi. 3, 4; Luke xiv. 26; Heb. xi. 17-19. — f Isa. liii. 6; Matt. viii. 17; John xix. 17; 1 Pet. ii. 24. — g Heb. *Behold me.*

loved son, the son born miraculously when Sarah was past child-bearing, as Jesus was miraculously born of a virgin. The *duration*, too, of the action, ver 4, was the same as that between Christ's death and resurrection, both which are designed to be represented in it; and still farther not only the final archetypical sacrifice of the Son of God was figured in the command to offer Isaac, but the *intermediate typical* sacrifice in the Mosaic economy was represented by the *permitted* sacrifice of the ram offered up, ver. 13, instead of Isaac." See *Dodd.*

Only son] All that he had by Sarah his legal wife.

The land of Moriah] This is supposed to mean all the mountains of Jerusalem, comprehending Mount Gihon or Calvary, the mount of Sion and of Acra. As Mount Calvary is the highest ground to the west, and the mount of the temple is the lowest of the mounts, Mr. Mann conjectures that it was upon this mount Abraham offered up Isaac, which is well known to be the same mount on which our blessed Lord was crucified. Beer-sheba, where Abraham dwelt, is about forty-two miles distant from Jerusalem, and it is not to be wondered at that Abraham, Isaac, the two servants, and the ass laden with wood for the burnt offering, did not reach this place till the *third* day; see ver. 4.

Verse 3. *Two of his young men*] Eliezer and Ishmael, according to the Targum.

Clave the wood] Small wood, *fig* and *palm*, proper for a burnt-offering.—*Targum.*

Verse 4. *The third day*] "As the number SEVEN," says Mr. Ainsworth, "is of especial use in Scripture because of the *Sabbath* day, Gen. ii. 2, so THREE is a mystical number because of Christ's rising from the dead the *third* day, Matt. xvii. 23; 1 Cor. xv. 4; as he was crucified the *third* hour after noon, Mark xv. 25: and Isaac, as he was a figure of Christ, in being the only son of his father, and not spared but offered for a sacrifice, Rom. viii. 32, so in sundry particulars he resembled our Lord: the *third* day Isaac was to be offered up, so it was the *third* day in which Christ also was to be *perfected,* Luke xiii. 32; Isaac carried the wood for the burnt-offering, ver. 6, so Christ carried the tree whereon he died, John xix. 17; the binding of Isaac, ver. 9, was also typical, so Christ was bound, Matt. xxvii. 2.

"In the following remarkable cases this number also occurs. Moses desired to go *three* days' journey in the wilderness to sacrifice, Exod. v. 3; and they travelled *three* days in it before they found water, Exod. xv. 22; and *three* days' journey the ark of the covenant went before them, to search out a resting place, Num. x. 33; by the *third* day the people were to be ready to receive God's law, Exod. xix. 11; and after *three* days to pass over Jordan into Canaan, Josh. i. 14; the *third* day Esther put on the apparel of the kingdom, Esth. v. 1; on the *third* day Hezekiah, being recovered from his illness, went up to the house of the Lord, 2 Kings xx. 5; on the *third* day, the prophet said, God will raise us up and we shall live before him, Hos. vi. 2; and on the *third* day, as well as on the *seventh,* the unclean person was to purify himself, Num. xix. 12: with many other memorable things which the Scripture speaks concerning the *third* day, and not without mystery. See Gen. xl. 12, 13; xlii. 17, 18; Jonah i. 17; Josh. ii. 16; unto which we may add a Jew's testimony in *Bereshith Rabba,* in a comment on this place: *There are many* THREE DAYS *mentioned in the Holy Scripture, of which one is the resurrection of the Messiah.*"—*Ainsworth.*

Saw the place afar off.] He knew the place by seeing the cloud of glory smoking on the top of the mountain.—*Targum.*

Verse 5. *I and the lad will go—and come again*] How could Abraham consistently with truth say this, when he knew he was going to make his son a *burnt-offering?* The apostle answers for him: *By faith Abraham, when he was tried, offered up Isaac—accounting that God was able to raise him up even from the dead, from whence also he received him in a figure,* Heb. xi. 17, 19. He knew that previously to the birth of Isaac both he and his wife were *dead* to all the purposes of procreation; that his birth was a kind of life from the dead; that the promise of God was most positive, *In Isaac shall thy seed be called,* chap. xxi. 12; that this promise could not fail; that it was his duty to obey the command of his Maker; and that it was as easy for God to restore him to life after he had been a burnt-offering, as it was for him to give him life in the beginning. Therefore he went fully purposed to offer his son, and yet confidently expecting to have him restored to life again. *We will go yonder and worship*—perform a solemn act of devotion which God requires, *and come again to you.*

Verse 6. *Took the wood—and laid* it *upon Isaac*] Probably the mountain-top to which they were going was too difficult to be ascended by the ass; therefore either the father or the son must carry the wood, and it was most becoming in the latter.

A. M. cir. 2132. B. C. cir. 1872. I, my son. And he said, Behold the fire and the wood: but where *is* the [h] lamb for a burnt-offering?

8 And Abraham said, My son, God will provide himself a lamb [i] for a burnt-offering: so they went both of them together.

9 And they came to the place which God had told him of; and Abraham built an altar there, and laid the wood in order, and bound Isaac his son, and [k] laid him on the altar upon the wood.

10 And Abraham stretched forth his hand, and took the knife to slay his son. A. M. cir. 2132. B. C. cir. 1872.

11 And the angel of the LORD called unto him out of heaven, and said, Abraham, Abraham! and he said, Here *am* I.

12 And he said, [l] Lay not thine hand upon the lad, neither do thou any thing unto him: for [m] now I know that thou fearest God, seeing thou hast not withheld thy son, thine only *son*, from me.

[h] Or, *kid*.——[i] John i. 29, 36; Rev. v. 6, 12; xiii. 8.——[k] Heb. xi. 17; James ii. 21.

[l] 1 Sam. xv. 22; Mic. vi. 7, 8.——[m] Chap. xxvi. 5; Rom. viii. 32; James ii. 22; 1 John iv. 9, 10.

Verse 7. *Behold the fire and the wood: but where is the lamb*] Nothing can be conceived more tender, affectionate, and affecting, than the question of the son and the reply of the father on this occasion. A paraphrase would spoil it; nothing can be added without injuring those expressions of affectionate submission on the one hand, and dignified tenderness and simplicity on the other.

Verse 8. *My son, God will provide himself a lamb*] Here we find the same obedient unshaken faith for which this pattern of practical piety was ever remarkable. But we must not suppose that this was the language merely of faith and obedience; the patriarch spoke prophetically, and referred to that Lamb of God which HE had provided for himself, who in the fulness of time should take away the sin of the world, and of whom Isaac was a most expressive type. All the other lambs which had been offered from the foundation of the world had been such as MEN *chose* and MEN *offered;* but THIS was the Lamb which GOD *had provided*—emphatically, THE LAMB OF GOD.

Verse 9. *And bound Isaac his son*] If the patriarch had not been upheld by the conviction that he was doing the *will* of God, and had he not felt the most perfect confidence that his son should be *restored* even *from the dead,* what agony must his heart have felt at every step of the journey, and through all the circumstances of this extraordinary business? What must his affectionate heart have felt at the questions asked by his innocent and amiable son? What must he have suffered while building the altar, laying on the wood, binding his lovely son, placing him on the wood, taking the knife, and stretching out his hand to slay the child of his hopes? Every view we take of the subject interests the heart, and exalts the character of this father of the faithful. But has the character of Isaac been duly considered? Is not the consideration of *his* excellence lost in the supposition that he was *too young* to enter particularly into a sense of his danger, and *too feeble* to have made any resistance, had he been unwilling to submit? Josephus supposes that Isaac was now *twenty-five,* (see the chronology on ver. 1;) some rabbins that he was *thirty-six;* but it is more probable that he was now about *thirty-three,* the age at which his great Antitype was offered up; and on this *medium* I have ventured to construct the chronology, of which I think it necessary to give this notice to the reader. Allowing him to be only *twenty-five,* he might have easily resisted; for can it be supposed that an old man of at least one hundred and twenty-five years of age could have bound, without his consent, a young man in the very prime and vigour of life? In this case we cannot say that the *superior strength* of the father *prevailed,* but the *piety, filial affection,* and *obedience* of the son *yielded.* All this was most illustriously typical of Christ. In both cases the father himself offers up his only-begotten son, and the father himself binds him on the wood or to the cross; in neither case is the son *forced* to yield, but yields of his own accord; in neither case is the life taken away by the hand of *violence;* Isaac *yields* himself to the knife, Jesus *lays down* his life for the sheep.

Verse 11. *The angel of the Lord*] The very person who was represented by this offering; the Lord Jesus, who calls himself Jehovah, ver. 16, and on his own authority renews the promises of the covenant. HE was ever the great Mediator between God and man. See this point proved, chap. xv. 7.

Verse 12. *Lay not thine hand upon the lad*] As Isaac was to be the *representative* of Jesus Christ's *real* sacrifice, it was sufficient for this purpose that in his *own will,* and the *will* of his *father,* the *purpose* of the immolation was complete. Isaac was now fully offered both by his father and by himself. The father yields up the son, the son gives up his life; on both sides, as far as *will* and *purpose* could go, the sacrifice was complete. God simply spares the father the torture of putting the knife to his son's throat. Now was the time when it might properly be said, "Sacrifice, and offering, and burnt-offering, and sacrifice for sin thou wouldest not, neither hadst pleasure in them: then said *the Angel of the Covenant,* Lo! I come to do thy will, O God." Lay not thy hand upon the *lad;* an *irrational* creature will serve for the purpose of a *representative* sacrifice, from this till the fulness of time But without this most expressive representation of *the father offering his beloved, only-begotten son,* what reference can such sacrifices be considered to have to the great event of the incarnation and crucifixion of Christ? Abraham, the most dignified, the most immaculate of all the patriarchs; Isaac, the true pattern of piety to God and filial obedience, may well represent God *the Father* so loving the world as to give *his only-begotten Son,* JESUS CHRIST, to die for the sin of man. But

A. M. cir. 2132.
B. C. cir. 1872.

13 And Abraham lifted up his eyes, and looked, and behold, behind *him* a ram caught in a thicket by his horns; and Abraham went and took the ram, and offered him up for a burnt-offering in the stead of his son.

14 And Abraham called the name of that place [n] Jehovah-jireh: as it is said *to* this day, In the mount of the LORD it shall be seen.

15 And the angel of the LORD called unto Abraham out of heaven the second time,

16 And said, [o] By myself have I sworn, saith the LORD, for because thou hast done this thing, and hast not withheld thy son, thine only *son;*

17 That in blessing I will bless thee, and in multiplying I will multiply thy seed [p] as the stars of the heaven, [q] and as the sand which *is* upon the sea-shore; [r] and [s] thy seed shall possess [t] the gate of his enemies;

18 [u] And in thy seed shall all the nations of the earth be blessed; [v] because thou hast obeyed my voice.

19 So Abraham returned unto his young men, and they rose up, and went together to [w] Beer-sheba; and Abraham dwelt at Beer-sheba.

A. M. cir. 2142.
B. C. cir. 1862.

20 And it came to pass after these things, that it was told Abraham, saying, Behold, [x] Milcah, she hath also borne children unto thy brother Nahor;

21 [y] Huz his first-born, and Buz his brother, and Kemuel the father [z] of Aram,

[n] That is, *the LORD will see*, or, *provide.*——[o] Psa. cv. 9; Ecclus. xliv. 21; Luke i. 73; Heb. vi. 13, 14.——[p] Chap. xv. 5; Jer. xxxiii. 22.——[q] Ch. xiii. 16.——[r] Heb. *lip.*——[s] Chap. xxiv. 60.——[t] Mic. i. 9.

[u] Chap. xii. 3; xviii. 18; xxvi. 4; Ecclus. xliv. 22; Acts iii. 25; Gal. iii. 8, 9, 16, 18.——[v] Ver. 3, 10; chap. xxvi. 5.——[w] Chap. xxi. 31.——[x] Chap. xi. 29.——[y] Job i. 1.——[z] Job xxxii. 2.

the grand *circumstances* necessary to prefigure these important points could not be exhibited through the means of *any* or of the *whole brute* creation. The whole sacrificial system of the Mosaic economy had a *retrospective* and *prospective* view, referring FROM *the sacrifice of Isaac* TO *the sacrifice of Christ;* in the *first* the *dawning* of the Sun of righteousness was seen; in the *latter*, his *meridian splendour* and *glory*. Taken in this light (and this is the only light in which it should be viewed) Abraham offering his son Isaac is one of the most important facts and most instructive histories in the whole Old Testament. See farther on this subject, chap. xxiii. 2.

Verse 14. *Jehovah-jireh*] יהוה יראה *Yehovah-yireh*, literally interpreted in the margin, *The Lord will see;* that is, God will take care that every thing shall be done that is necessary for the comfort and support of them who trust in him: hence the words are usually translated, *The Lord will provide;* so our translators, ver. 8, אלהים יראה *Elohim yireh*, God will provide; because his *eye* ever affects his *heart*, and the wants he *sees* his hand is ever ready to *supply*. But all this seems to have been done under a Divine impulse, and the words to have been spoken *prophetically;* hence Houbigant and some others render the words thus: *Dominus videbitur*, the Lord shall be seen; and this translation the following clause seems to require, *As it is said to this day*, בהר יהוה יראה *behar Yehovah yeraeh*, ON THIS MOUNT THE LORD SHALL BE SEEN. From this it appears that the sacrifice offered by Abraham was understood to be a *representative* one, and a tradition was kept up that Jehovah should be seen in a sacrificial way on this mount. And this renders the opinion stated on ver. 1 more than probable, viz., that Abraham offered Isaac on that *very mountain* on which, in the fulness of time, Jesus suffered. See Bishop Warburton.

Verse 16. *By myself have I sworn*] So we find that the person who was called the *angel of the Lord* is here called *Jehovah;* see on ver. 2. An oath or an appeal to God is, among men, an end to strife; *as God could swear by no greater, he sware by himself:* being *willing more abundantly*, says the apostle, *to show unto the heirs of promise the immutability of his counsel*, he *confirmed it by an oath, that by two immutable things*, (his PROMISE and his OATH,) *in which it was impossible for God to lie, we might have a strong consolation, who have fled for refuge to lay hold on the hope set before us.* See Heb. vi. 13–18.

Verse 17. *Shall possess the gate of his enemies*] Instead of *gate* the Septuagint have πολεις, *cities;* but as there is a very near resemblance between πολεις, *cities*, and πυλας, *gates*, the latter might have been the original reading in the Septuagint, though none of the MSS. now acknowledge it. By the gates may be meant all the strength, whether troops, counsels, or fortified cities of their enemies. So Matt. xvi. 18: *On this rock I will build my Church, and the gates of hell shall not prevail against it*—the counsels, stratagems, and powers of darkness shall not be able to prevail against or overthrow the true Church of Christ; and possibly our Lord had this promise to Abraham and his spiritual posterity in view, when he spoke these words.

Verse 18. *And in thy seed, &c.*] We have the authority of St. Paul, Gal. iii. 8, 16, 18, to restrain this to our blessed Lord, who was THE SEED through whom alone all God's blessings of providence, mercy, grace, and glory, should be conveyed to the nations of the earth.

Verse 20. *Behold, Milcah, she hath also borne children unto thy brother*] This short history seems introduced solely for the purpose of preparing the reader for the transactions related chap. xxiv., and to show that the providence of God was preparing, in one of the branches of the family of Abraham, a suitable spouse for his son Isaac.

Verse 21. *Huz*] He is supposed to have peopled

A. M. cir. 2142.
B. C. cir. 1862.

22 And Chesed, and Hazo, and
Pildash, and Jidlaph, and Bethuel.
23 And [a] Bethuel begat [b] Rebekah: these eight
Milcah did bear to Nahor, Abraham's brother.
24 And his concubine, [c] whose
name *was* Reumah, she bare
also Tebah, and Gaham, and Thahash, and
Maachah.

A. M. cir. 2142.
B. C. cir. 1862.

[a] Chap. xxiv. 15, 24, 47; xxv. 20; xxviii. 2–5. — [b] Called, Rom. ix. 10, *Rebecca.* — [c] Chap. xvi. 3; xxv. 6.

the land of *Uz* or *Ausitis*, in Arabia Deserta, the country of Job.

Buz his brother] From this person *Elihu* the *Buzite*, one of the friends of Job, is thought to have descended.

Kemuel the father of Aram] *Kamouel, πατερα Συρων, the father of the Syrians*, according to the Septuagint. Probably the *Kamiletes*, a Syrian tribe to the westward of the Euphrates are meant; they are mentioned by *Strabo*.

Verse 23. *Bethuel begat Rebekah*] Who afterward became the wife of Isaac.

Verse 24. *His concubine*] We borrow this word from the Latin compound *concubina*, from *con*, together, and *cubo*, to lie, and apply it solely to a woman cohabiting with a man without being *legally* married. The Hebrew word is פילגש *pilegesh*, which is also a compound term, contracted, according to Parkhurst, from פלג *palag*, to divide or share, and נגש *nagash*, to approach; because the husband, in the delicate phrase of the Hebrew tongue, *approaches* the concubine, and *shares* the bed, &c., of the real wife with her. The pilegesh or concubine, (from which comes the Greek παλλακη *pallake*, and also the Latin *pellex*,) in Scripture, is a kind of *secondary* wife, not unlawful in the patriarchal times; though the progeny of such could not inherit. The word is not used in the Scriptures in that disagreeable sense in which we commonly understand it. Hagar was properly the concubine or *pilegesh* of Abraham, and this *annuente Deo*, and with his wife's consent. Keturah, his second wife, is called a concubine, chap. xxvi. 15; 1 Chron. i. 32; and Bilhah and Zilhah were concubines to Jacob, chap. xxxv. 22. After the patriarchal times many eminent men had *concubines*, viz., *Caleb*, 1 Chron. ii. 46, 48; *Manasses*, 1 Chron. vii. 14; *Gideon*, Judg. viii. 31; *Saul*, 2 Sam. iii. 7; *David*, 2 Sam. v. 13; *Solomon*, 2 Kings xi. 3; and *Rehoboam*, 2 Chron. xi. 21. The pilegesh, therefore, differed widely from a prostitute; and however unlawful under the New Testament, was not so under the Old.

From this chapter a pious mind may collect much useful instruction. From the trial of Abraham we again see, 1. That God may bring his followers into severe straits and difficulties, that they may have the better opportunity of both knowing and showing their own faith and obedience; and that he may seize on those occasions to show them the abundance of his mercy, and thus confirm them in righteousness all their days. There is a foolish saying among some religious people, which cannot be too severely reprobated: *Untried grace is no grace.* On the contrary, there may be much grace, though God, for good reasons, does not think proper for a time to put it to any severe trial or proof. But grace is certainly not fully *known* but in being called to trials of severe and painful obedience. But as all the gifts of God should be *used*, (and they are increased and strengthened by exercise,) it would be unjust to deny trials and exercises to *grace*, as this would be to preclude it from the opportunities of being strengthened and increased. 2. The offering up of Isaac is used by several religious people in a sort of metaphorical way, to signify their *easily-besetting sins, beloved idols, &c.* But this is a most reprehensible abuse of the Scripture. It is both insolent and wicked to compare some abominable lust or unholy affection to the amiable and pious youth who, for his purity and excellence, was deemed worthy to prefigure the sacrifice of the Son of God. To call our vile passions and unlawful attachments by the name of *our Isaacs* is unpardonable; and to talk of *sacrificing* such to God is downright blasphemy. Such sayings as these appear to be legitimated by long use; but we should be deeply and scrupulously careful not to use any of the words of God in any sense in which he has not spoken them. If, in the course of God's providence, a parent is called to give up to death an amiable, *only son*, then there is a parallel in the case; and it may be justly said, if pious resignation fill the parent's mind, such a person, like Abraham, has been called *to give his Isaac back to God.*

Independently of the *typical* reference to this transaction, there are two points which seem to be recommended particularly to our notice. 1. The astonishing faith and prompt obedience of the father. 2. The innocence, filial respect, and passive submission of the son. Such a father and such a son were alone worthy of each other.

CHAPTER XXIII.

The age and death of Sarah, 1, 2. *Abraham mourns for her, and requests a burial-place from the sons of Heth,* 2–4. *They freely offer him the choice of all their sepulchres,* 5, 6. *Abraham refuses to receive any as a* free gift, *and requests to* buy *the cave of Machpelah from Ephron,* 7–9. *Ephron proffers the cave and the field in which it was situated as a free gift unto Abraham,* 10, 11. *Abraham insists on giving its value in money,* 12, 13. *Ephron at last consents, and names the sum of four hundred shekels,* 14, 15 *Abraham weighs him the money in the presence of the people; in consequence of which the cave, the whole field, trees, &c., are made sure to him and his family for a possession,* 16–18. *The transaction being completed, Sarah is buried in the cave,* 19. *The sons of Heth ratify the bargain,* 20.

A. M. 2145. B. C. 1859.

AND Sarah was a hundred and seven and twenty years old: *these were* the years of the life of Sarah.

2 And Sarah died in [a] Kirjath-arba; the same *is* [b] Hebron in the land of Canaan: and Abraham came to mourn for Sarah, and to weep for her.

3 And Abraham stood up from before his dead, and spake unto the sons of Heth, saying,

4 [c] I *am* a stranger and a sojourner with you: [d] give me a possession of a burying place with you, that I may bury my dead out of my sight.

5 And the children of Heth answered Abraham, saying unto him,

[a] Joshua xiv. 15; Judges i. 10.—[b] Chapter xiii. 18; ver. 19.

[c] Chap. xvii. 8; 1 Chron. xxix. 15; Psa. cv. 12; Hebrews xi. 9, 13.—[d] Acts vii. 5.

NOTES ON CHAP. XXIII.

Verse 1. *And Sarah was a hundred and seven and twenty years old*] It is worthy of remark that Sarah is the only woman in the sacred writings whose *age*, *death*, and *burial* are distinctly noted. And she has been deemed worthy of *higher* honour, for St. Paul, Gal. iv. 22, 23, makes her a type of the *Church of Christ;* and her faith in the accomplishment of God's promise, that she should have a son, when all natural probabilities were against it, is particularly celebrated in the Epistle to the Hebrews, chap. xi. 11. Sarah was about ninety-one years old when Isaac was born, and she lived thirty-six years after, and saw him grown up to man's estate. With SARAH the promise of the incarnation of Christ *commenced*, though a comparatively obscure prophecy of it had been delivered to Eve, chap. iii. 15; and with MARY it terminated, having had its exact completion. Thus God put more honour upon these two women than upon all the daughters of Eve besides. Sarah's conception of Isaac was *supernatural;* she had passed the age and circumstances in which it was possible, naturally speaking, to have a child; therefore she laughed when the promise was given, knowing that the thing was impossible, because it had ceased to be with her after the manner of women. God allows this natural impossibility, and grants that the thing must be the effect of Divine interposition; and therefore asks, *Is any thing too hard for God?* The physical impossibility was increased in the case of *Mary*, she having no connection with man; but the same power interposed as in the case of Sarah: and we find that when all aptitude for natural procreation was gone, *Sarah received strength to conceive seed*, and bore a son, from whom, in a direct line, the Messiah, the Saviour of the world, was to descend; and through this same power we find a *virgin* conceiving and bearing a son against all natural impossibilities. Every thing is *supernatural* in the births both of the type and antitype; can it be wondered at then, if the spiritual offspring of the Messiah must have a supernatural birth likewise? hence the propriety of that saying, *Unless a man be born again—born from above—born*, not only *of water*, but of the *Holy Ghost*, *he cannot see the kingdom of God.* These may appear hard sayings, and those who are little in the habit of considering spiritual things may exclaim, "*It is enthusiasm!* Who can bear it? Such things cannot possibly be." To such persons I have only to say, God hath spoken. This is sufficient for those who credit his being and his Bible; nor is there any thing *too hard* for him. He, by whose almighty power, Sarah had strength to conceive and bear a son in her old age, and by whose miraculous interference a virgin conceived, and the man Christ Jesus was born of her, can by the same power transform the sinful soul, and cause it to bear the image of the heavenly as it has borne the image of the earthly.

Verse 2. *Sarah died in Kirjath-arba*] Literally *in the city of the four.* Some suppose this place was called the *city of the four* because it was the burial place of *Adam*, *Abraham*, *Isaac*, and *Jacob;* others, because according to the opinion of the rabbins, *Eve* was buried there, with *Sarah*, *Rebekah*, and *Leah.* But it seems evidently to have had its name from a Canaanite, one of the Anakim, probably called *Arba*, (for the text, Josh. xiv. 14, does not actually say this was his name,) who was the chief of the *four* brothers who dwelt there; the names of the others being *Sheshai*, *Ahiman*, and *Talmai.* See Judges i. 10. These three were destroyed by the tribe of Judah; probably the other had been previously dead.

Abraham came to mourn for Sarah] From verse 19 of the preceding chapter it appears that Abraham had settled at *Beer-sheba;* and here we find that Sarah died at Hebron, which was about twenty-four miles distant from Beer-sheba. For the convenience of feeding his numerous flocks, Abraham had probably several places of temporary residence, and particularly one at Beer-sheba, and another at Hebron; and it is likely that while he sojourned at Beer-sheba, Sarah died at Hebron; and his *coming* to *mourn* and *weep for her* signifies his coming from the former to the latter place on the news of her death.

Verse 3. *Abraham stood up from before his dead*] He had probably sat on the ground some days in token of sorrow, as the custom then was, (see Tobit ii. 12, 13; Isa. xlvii. 1; and Gen. xxxvii. 35;) and when this time was finished he arose and began to treat about a burying place.

Verse 4. *I am a stranger and a sojourner*] It appears from Heb. xi. 13–16; 1 Pet. ii. 11, that these words refer more to the *state of his mind* than of his body. He felt that he had no certain dwelling place, and was seeking by faith a city that had foundations.

Give me a possession of a burying place] It has been remarked that in different nations it was deemed ignominious to be buried in another's ground; probably this prevailed in early times in the east, and it may be in reference to a sentiment of this kind that Abraham refuses to accept the offer of the children of Heth to bury in any of their sepulchres, and earnestly requests them to sell him one, that he might bury his wife in a place that he could claim as *his own.*

A. M. 2145.
B. C. 1859.

6 Hear us, my lord: thou *art* [e] a mighty prince among us: [f] in the choice of our sepulchres bury thy dead; none of us shall withhold from thee his sepulchre, but that thou mayest bury thy dead.

7 And Abraham stood up, and bowed himself to the people of the land, *even* to the children of Heth.

8 And he communed with them, saying, If it be your mind that I should bury my dead out of my sight; hear me, and entreat for me to Ephron the son of Zohar,

9 That he may give me the cave of Machpelah, which he hath, which *is* in the end of his field; for [g] as much money as it is worth he shall give it me for a possession of a burying place amongst you.

10 And Ephron dwelt among the children of Heth: and Ephron the Hittite answered Abraham in the [h] audience of the children of Heth, *even* of all that [i] went in at the gate of his city, saying,

11 [k] Nay, my lord, hear me: the field give I thee, and the cave that *is* therein, I give it thee; in the presence of the sons of my people give I it thee: bury thy dead.

12 And Abraham bowed down himself before the people of the land.

13 And he spake unto Ephron in the audience of the people of the land, saying, But if thou *wilt give it,* I pray thee, hear me: I will give thee money for the field; take *it* of me, and I will bury my dead there

A. M. 2145
B. C. 1859.

14 And Ephron answered Abraham, saying unto him,

15 My lord, hearken unto me: the land *is worth* four hundred [l] shekels of silver; what *is* that betwixt me and thee? bury therefore thy dead.

16 And Abraham hearkened unto Ephron; and Abraham [m] weighed to Ephron the silver, which he had named in the audience of the sons of Heth, four hundred shekels of silver, current *money* with the merchant.

17 And [n] the field of Ephron, which *was* in Machpelah, which *was* before Mamre, the field, and the cave which *was* therein, and all the trees that *were* in the field, that *were* in all the borders round about, were made sure

18 Unto Abraham for a possession in the presence of the children of Heth, before all that went in at the gate of his city.

19 And after this Abraham buried Sarah his wife in the cave of the field of Machpelah before Mamre: the same *is* Hebron in the land of Canaan.

---

[e] Heb. *a prince of God.*——[f] Chap. xiii. 2; xiv. 14; xxiv. 35.——[g] Heb. *full money.*——[h] Heb. *ears.*——[i] Chap. xxxiv. 20, 24; Ruth iv. 4.——[k] See 2 Sam. xxiv. 21-24.——[l] Exod. xxx. 15; Ezek. xlv. 12.——[m] Jer. xxxii. 9.——[n] Chap. xxv. 9; xlix. 30, 31, 32; l. 13; Acts vii. 16.

Verse 6. *Thou* art *a mighty prince*] נשיא אלהים *nesi Elohim, a prince of God*—a person whom we know to be Divinely favoured, and whom, in consequence, we deeply respect and reverence.

Verse 8. *Entreat for me to Ephron*] Abraham had already seen the cave and field, and finding to whom they belonged, and that they would answer his purpose, came to the gate of Hebron, where the elders of the people sat to administer justice, &c., and where bargains and sales were made and witnessed, and having addressed himself to the elders, among whom *Ephron* was, though it appears he was not personally known to Abraham, he begged them to use their influence with the owner of the cave and field to sell it to him, that it might serve him and his family for a place of sepulture.

Verse 10. *And Ephron dwelt among the children of Heth*] And Ephron ישב *yosheb*, was sitting among the children of Heth, but, as was before conjectured, was personally unknown to Abraham; he therefore answered for himself, making a free tender of the field, &c., to Abraham, in the presence of all the people, which amounted to a *legal conveyance* of the whole property to the patriarch.

Verse 13. *If thou* wilt *give it*] Instead of, If thou *wilt give it,* we should read, But if thou *wilt sell it I will give thee money for the field;* כסף *keseph*, silver, not *coined* money, for it is not probable that any such was then in use.

Verse 15. *The land* is worth *four hundred shekels of silver*] Though the words *is worth* are not in the text, yet they are necessarily expressed here to adapt the Hebrew to the idiom of our tongue. A shekel, according to the general opinion, was equal to two shillings and sixpence; but according to Dr. Prideaux, whose estimate I shall follow, three shillings English, four hundred of which are equal to sixty pounds sterling; but it is evident that a certain *weight* is intended, and not a *coin*, for in verse 16 it is said, And Abraham *weighed* וישקל *vaiyishkol*, the silver, and hence it appears that this *weight* itself passed *afterwards* as a current coin, for the word שקל is not only used to express a coin or piece of silver, but also to *weigh;* see the note on chap. xx. 16.

Verse 16. *Current with the merchant.*] עבר לסחר *ober lassocher, passing to* or *with the traveller*—such as was commonly used by those who *travelled about* with merchandise of any sort. The word signifies the same as *hawker* or *pedlar* among us.

Verse 17. *All the trees that* were *in the field*] It is possible that all these were specified in the agreement

A. M. 2145. B. C. 1859.

20 And the field, and the cave that *is* therein, ° were made sure unto Abraham for a possession of a burying place ᵖ by the sons of Heth.

A. M. 2145. B. C. 1859.

° See Ruth iv. 7, 8, 9, 10; Jer. xxxii. 10, 11. — ᵖ Chap. l. 13; 2 Kings xxi. 18.

Verse 20. *And the field, &c. were made sure*] ויקם *vaiyakom*, were *established*, *caused to stand*; the whole transaction having been regulated according to all the forms of law then in use.

1. In this transaction between Abraham and the sons of Heth concerning the cave and field of Machpelah, we have the earliest account on record of the *purchase of land*. The simplicity, openness, and candour on both sides cannot be too much admired.

2. Sarah being dead, Abraham being only a *sojourner* in that land, shifting from place to place for the mere purpose of pasturing his flocks, and having no *right* to any part of the land, wished to *purchase* a place in which he might have the continual right of sepulture. For this purpose, 1. He goes to the gate of the city, the place where, in all ancient times, justice was administered, and bargains and sales concluded, and where for these purposes the elders of the people sat. 2. He there proposes to buy the cave known by the name of the *Cave of Machpelah*, the cave of the *turning* or the *double cave*, for a burying place for his family. 3. To prevent him from going to any unnecessary expense, the people with one voice offer him the privilege of burying his wife in any of their sepulchres; this appearing to them to be no more than the common rights of hospitality and humanity required. 4. Abraham, intent on making a purchase, Ephron, the owner of the field and cave, values them at four hundred shekels, but at the same time wishes Abraham to receive the whole as a *gift*. 5. Abraham refuses the gift and weighs down the silver specified. 6. The people who enter in at the gate, i. e., the inhabitants coming from or going to their ordinary occupations in the country, witness the transaction, and thus the conveyance to Abraham is made sure without the intervention of those puzzlers of civil affairs by whose tricks and chicanery property often becomes insecure, and right and succession precarious and uncertain. But this censure does not fall on *lawyers* properly so called, who are men of honour, and whose office, in every well-regulated state, is as useful as it is respectable. But the accumulation and complex nature of almost all modern systems of law puzzle even justice herself, and often induce decisions by which truth falls in the streets and equity goes backwards In the first ages of mankind, suspicion, deceit, and guile seem to have had a very limited influence. Happy days of primitive simplicity! When shall they return?

3. We often hear of the *rudeness* and *barbarity* of the primitive ages, but on what evidence? Every rule of politeness that could be acted upon in such a case as that mentioned here, is brought into full practice. Is it possible to read the simple narration in this place without admiring the amiable, decent, and polite conduct displayed on both sides? Had even Lord Chesterfield read this account, his good sense would have led him to propose it as a model in all transactions between man and his fellows. There is neither awkward, stiff formality on the one hand, nor frippery or affectation on the other. Decent respect, good sense, good nature, and good breeding, are all prominently displayed. And how highly laudable and useful is all this! A *pedant* or a *boor* on either side might have destroyed the simplicity of the whole transaction; the one by engendering *caution* and *suspicion*, and the other by *exciting disgust*. In all such transactions the *beau* and the *boor* are equally to be avoided. From the *first* no *sincerity* can be expected, and the manners of the *latter* render him intolerable. The religion of the Bible recommends and inculcates orderly behaviour, as well as purity of heart and life. They who, under the sanction of religion, trample under foot the decent forms of civil respect, supposing that because they are religious they have a right to be rude, totally mistake the spirit of Christianity, for *love* or *charity* (the soul and essence of that religion) *behaveth not itself unseemly*. Every attentive reader of the thirteenth chapter of St. Paul's first epistle to the Corinthians, will clearly discern that the description of true religion given in that place applies as forcibly to *good breeding* as to inward and outward holiness. What lessons of honesty, decent respect, and good manners could a sensible man derive from *Abraham* treating with the sons of Heth for the cave of Machpelah, and *William* Penn treating with the American Indians for the tract of land now called Pennsylvania! I leave others to draw the parallel, and to show how exactly the conduct and spirit of patriarch the *first* were exemplified in the conduct and spirit of patriarch the *second*. Let the righteous be had in everlasting remembrance!

CHAPTER XXIV.

Abraham, being solicitous to get his son Isaac properly married, calls his confidential servant, probably Eliezer, and makes him swear that he will not take a wife for Isaac from among the Canaanites, 1–3, *but from among his own kindred,* 4. *The servant proposes certain difficulties,* 5, *which Abraham removes by giving him the strongest assurances of* God's *direction in the business,* 6, 7, *and then specifies the conditions of the oath,* 8. *The form of the oath itself,* 9. *The servant makes preparations for his journey, and sets out for Mesopotamia, the residence of Abraham's kindred,* 10. *Arrives at a well near to the place,* 11. *His prayer to God,* 12–14. *Rebekah, the daughter of Bethuel, son of Nahor, Abraham's brother, comes to the well to draw water,* 15. *She is described,* 16. *Conversation between her and Abraham's servant, in*

which every thing took place according to his prayer to God, 17–21. *He makes her presents, and learns whose daughter she is,* 22–24. *She invites him to her father's house,* 25. *He returns thanks to God for having thus far given him a prosperous journey,* 26, 27. *Rebekah runs home and informs her family,* 28; *on which her brother Laban comes out, and invites the servant home,* 29–31. *His reception,* 32, 33. *Tells his errand,* 34, *and how he had proceeded in executing the trust reposed in him,* 35–48. *Requests an answer,* 49. *The family of Rebekah consent that she should become the wife of Isaac,* 50, 51. *The servant worships God,* 52, *and gives presents to Milcah, Laban, and Rebekah,* 53. *He requests to be dismissed,* 54–56. *Rebekah, being consulted, consents to go,* 57, 58. *She is accompanied by her nurse,* 59, *and having received the blessing of her parents and relatives,* 60, *she departs with the servant of Abraham,* 61. *They are met by Isaac, who was on an evening walk for the purpose of meditation,* 62–65. *The servant relates to Isaac all that he had done,* 66. *Isaac and Rebekah are married,* 67.

A. M. 2148. B. C. 1856.

AND Abraham [a] was old *and* [b] well stricken in age: and the
LORD [c] had blessed Abraham in all things.
2 And Abraham said [d] unto his eldest servant
of his house, that [e] ruled over all that he
had, [f] Put, I pray thee, thy hand under my
thigh:
3 And I will make thee [g] swear by the LORD,
the God of heaven, and the God of the earth,
that [h] thou shalt not take a wife unto my son of
the daughters of the Canaanites, among whom
I dwell:
4 [i] But thou shalt go [k] unto my country, and
to my kindred, and take a wife unto my son
Isaac.
5 And the servant said unto him, Peradventure the woman will not be willing to follow
me unto this land: must I needs
bring thy son again unto the land
from whence thou camest?
6 And Abraham said unto him, Beware thou
that thou bring not my son thither again.
7 The LORD God of heaven, which [l] took
me from my father's house, and from the land
of my kindred, and which spake unto me, and
that sware unto me, saying, [m] Unto thy seed
will I give this land; [n] he shall send his angel
before thee, and thou shalt take a wife unto
my son from thence.
8 And if the woman will not be willing to
follow thee, then [o] thou shalt be clear from
this my oath: only bring not my son thither
again.
9 And the servant put his hand under the

[a] Chap. xviii. 11; xxi. 5.——[b] Heb. *gone into days.*——[c] Chap. xiii. 2; ver. 35; Psa. cxii. 3; Prov. x. 22.——[d] Chap. xv. 2. [e] Ver. 10; chap. xxxix. 4, 5, 6.——[f] Chap. xlvii. 29; 1 Chron. xxix. 24; Lam. v. 6.——[g] Chap. xiv. 22; Deut. vi. 13; Josh. ii. 12.——[h] Chap. xxvi. 35; xxvii. 46; xxviii. 2; Exod. xxxiv. 16; Deut. vii. 3.——[i] Chap. xxviii. 2.——[k] Chapter xii. 1. [l] Chap. xii. 1, 7.——[m] Chap. xii. 7; xiii. 15; xv. 18; xvii. 8; Exod. xxxii. 13; Deut. i. 8; xxxiv. 4; Acts vii. 5. [n] Exodus xxiii. 20, 23; xxxiii. 2; Hebrews i. 14.——[o] Josh. ii. 17, 20.

NOTES ON CHAP. XXIV.

Verse 1. *And Abraham was old*] He was now about one hundred and forty years of age, and consequently Isaac was forty, being born when his father was one hundred years old. See chap. xxi. 5; xxv. 20.

Verse 2. *Eldest servant*] As this eldest servant is stated to have been the *ruler over all that he had*, it is very likely that Eliezer is meant. See chap. xv. 2, 3.

Put, I pray thee, thy hand] See on ver. 9.

Verse 3. *I will make thee swear*] See on ver. 9.

Of the Canaanites] Because these had already been devoted to *slavery*, &c., and it would have been utterly inconsistent as well with prudence as with the design of God to have united the child and *heir* of the *promise* with one who was under a *curse*, though that curse might be considered to be only of a political nature. See the curse of Canaan, chap. ix. 25.

Verse 4. *My country*] Mesopotamia, called here Abraham's country, because it was the place where the family of Haran, his brother, had settled; and where himself had remained a considerable time with his father Terah. In this family, as well as in that of Nahor, the true religion had been in some sort preserved, though afterwards considerably corrupted; see chap. xxxi. 19.

And take a wife unto my son] A young man in Bengal is precisely in the same circumstances as Isaac; he has nothing to do in the choice of a wife; parents employ *others* to seek wives for their sons. Those who leave their homes in search of employment always marry their children in their own country, and among their acquaintance at home; never among the people with whom they *reside*. In Asiatic countries this custom has prevailed from the infancy of the human race. See Ward's *Hindoo Customs*.

Verse 5. *Peradventure the woman will not be willing*] We may see, says Calmet, by this and other passages of Scripture, Josh. ix. 18, what the sentiments of the ancients were relative to an *oath*. They believed they were bound precisely by *what was spoken*, and had no liberty to interpret the intentions of those to whom the oath was made.

Verse 7. *The Lord God, &c.*] He expresses the strongest confidence in God, that the great designs for which he had brought him from his own kindred to propagate the true religion in the earth would be accomplished; and that therefore, when earthly instruments failed, heavenly ones should be employed. *He shall send his angel*, probably meaning the Angel of the Covenant, of whom see chap. xv. 7.

Verse 9. *Put his hand under the thigh of Abraham*] This *form* of swearing has greatly puzzled the commentators; but it is useless to detail opinions which

A. M. 2148.
B. C. 1856.
thigh of Abraham his master, and
sware to him concerning that
matter.

10 And the servant took ten camels, of the
camels of his master, and departed; ([p] for
[q] all the goods of his master *were* in his
hand:) and he arose, and went to Mesopotamia, unto [r] the city of Nahor.

11 And he made his camels to
kneel down without the city by a
well of water at the time of the evening, *even*
the time [s] that women go out to draw *water*.
12 And he said, [u] O LORD God of my
master Abraham, I pray thee, [v] send me good
speed this day, and show kindness unto my
master Abraham.

[p] Ver. 2.——[q] Or, *and*.——[r] Chap. xxvii. 43.——[s] Heb. *that women which draw water go forth*.——[t] Exod. ii. 16; 1 Sam. ix. 11.——[u] Ver. 27; chap. xxvi. 24; xxviii. 13; xxxii. 9; Exod. iii. 6, 15.——[v] Neh. i. 11; Psa. xxxvii. 5.

I neither believe myself, nor would wish my readers to credit. I believe the true sense is given in the *Targum* of *Jonathan ben Uzziel*, and that called the *Jerusalem Targum*. In the former it is said, *Put now thy hand* בגזירת מהולתי *bigzirath mehulathi, in sectione circumcisionis meæ;* in the latter תחות ירך קימי *techoth yerech keyami, sub femore fœderis mei*. When we put the circumstances mentioned in this and the third verse together, we shall find that they fully express the ancient method of binding by oath in such transactions as had a religious tendency. 1. The *rite* or *ceremony* used on the occasion: the person binding himself put his hand under the thigh of the person to whom he was to be bound; *i. e.*, he put his hand on the *part* that bore the mark of *circumcision*, the sign of God's covenant, which is tantamount to our *kissing the book*, or laying the hand upon the *New Testament* or *covenant* of our Lord Jesus Christ. 2. The *form* of the *oath* itself: the person swore *by Jehovah, the God of heaven* and the *God of the earth*. Three essential attributes of God are here mentioned: 1. His *self-existence* and *eternity* in the name *Jehovah*. 2. His *dominion* of *glory* and blessedness in the kingdom of *heaven*. 3. His *providence* and *bounty* in the *earth*. The meaning of the oath seems to be this: "As God is unchangeable in his nature and purposes, so shall I be in this engagement, under the penalty of forfeiting all expectation of temporal prosperity, the benefits of the mystical covenant, and future glory." An oath of this kind, taken at such a time, and on such an occasion, can never be deemed irreligious or profane. *Thou shalt swear by his name*—shalt acknowledge and bind thyself unto the *true God*, as the just Judge of thy motives and actions, is a command of the Most High; and such an oath as the above is at once (on such an occasion) both proper and rational. The person binding himself proposes for a *pattern* the *unchangeable* and *just* God; and as HE is the avenger of wrong, and the punisher of falsehood, and has all power in the heavens and in the earth, so he can punish perjury by privation of spiritual and temporal blessings, by the loss of life, and by inflicting the perdition due to ungodly men, among whom liars and perjured persons occupy the most distinguished rank. Our ideas of delicacy may revolt from the *rite* used on this occasion; but when the nature of the covenant is considered, of which *circumcision* was the *sign*, we shall at once perceive that this rite could not be used without producing sentiments of reverence and godly fear, as the contracting party must know that the God of this covenant was a consuming fire.

Verse 10. *Took ten camels*] It appears that Abraham had left the whole management of this business to the discretion of his servant, to take with him what *retinue* and what *dowry* he pleased; for it is added, *All the goods of his master were in his hand;* and in those times it was customary to *give* a dowry *for* a wife, and not to receive one *with* her.

Verse 11. *He made his camels to kneel down*] To rest themselves, or lie down, as the Septuagint has very properly expressed it, Και εκοιμισε τας καμηλους.

The time that women go out to draw water.] In Bengal it is the universal practice for the women to go to *pools* and *rivers* to fetch water. Companies of four, six, ten, or more, may be seen in every town daily going to fetch water, with the pitchers resting upon their sides; and, on their return from bathing, women frequently bring water home.—WARD.

Verse 12. *And he said, O Lord God, &c.*] "The conduct of this servant," says Dr. Dodd, "appears no less pious than rational. By supplicating for a sign, he acknowledges God to be the great superintendent and director of the universe, and of that event in particular; and at the same time, by asking a *natural* sign, such as betokened humanity, condescension, and other qualities which promised a discreet and virtuous wife, he puts his prayer upon such a discreet, rational footing, as to be a proper example for all to imitate who would not tempt the providence of God, by expecting extraordinary signs to be given them for the determination of cases which they are capable of deciding by a proper use of their rational faculties." This is all very good; but certainly the case referred to here is such a one as required especial direction from God; a case which no use of the rational faculties, without Divine influence, could be sufficient to determine. It is easy to run into extremes, and it is very natural so to do. In all things the assistance and blessing of God are necessary, even where human strength and wisdom have the fullest and freest sphere of action; but there are numberless cases, of infinite consequence to man, where his strength and prudence can be of little or no avail, and where the God of all grace must work all things according to the counsel of his own will. To expect the accomplishment of any good end, without a proper use of the means, is the most reprehensible enthusiasm; and to suppose that any good can be done or procured without the blessing and mercy of God, merely because proper means are used, is not less reprehensible. Plan, scheme, and labour like Eliezer, and then, by earnest faith and prayer, commit the whole to the direction and blessing of God.

A. M. 2148.
B. C. 1856.

13 Behold, [w] I stand *here* by the well of water; and [x] the daughters of the men of the city come out to draw water:

14 And let it come to pass, that the damsel to whom I shall say, Let down thy pitcher, I pray thee, that I may drink; and she shall say, Drink, and I will give thy camels drink also; *let the same be* she *that* thou hast appointed for thy servant Isaac: and [y] thereby shall I know that thou hast showed kindness unto my master.

15 And it came to pass, before he had done speaking, that, behold, Rebekah came out, who was born to Bethuel, son of [z] Milcah, the wife of Nahor, Abraham's brother, with her pitcher upon her shoulder.

16 And the damsel [a] *was* [b] very fair to look upon, a virgin, neither had any man known her: and she went down to the well, and filled her pitcher, and came up.

17 And the servant ran to meet her, and said, Let me, I pray thee, drink a little water of thy pitcher.

18 [c] And she said, Drink, my lord: and she hasted, and let down her pitcher upon her hand, and gave him drink.

A. M. 2148.
B. C. 1856.

19 And when she had done giving him drink, she said, I will draw *water* for thy camels also, until they have done drinking.

20 And she hasted, and emptied her pitcher into the trough, and ran again unto the well to draw *water*, and drew for all his camels.

21 And the man, wondering at her, held his peace, to wit, whether [d] the LORD had made his journey prosperous or not.

22 And it came to pass, as the camels had done drinking, that the man took a golden [e] ear-ring [f] of half a shekel weight, and two bracelets for her hands of ten *shekels* weight of gold;

23 And said, Whose daughter *art* thou? tell me, I pray thee: is there room *in* thy father's house for us to lodge in?

24 And she said unto him, [g] I *am* the daughter of Bethuel the son of Milcah, which she bare unto Nahor.

25 She said moreover unto him, We have both straw and provender enough, and room to lodge in.

26 And the man [h] bowed down his head, and worshipped the LORD.

[w] Ver. 43.——[x] Chap. xxix. 9; Exod. ii. 16.——[y] See Judg. vi. 17, 37; 1 Sam. vi. 7; xiv. 8; xx. 7; 1 Mic. v. 40.——[z] Ch. xi. 29; xxii. 23.——[a] Chap. xxvi. 7.——[b] Heb. *good of countenance.*

[c] 1 Pet. iii. 8; iv. 9.——[d] Ver. 12, 56.——[e] Exod. xxxii. 2, 3; Isa. iii. 19, 20, 21; Ezek. xvi. 11, 12; 1 Pet. iii. 3.——[f] Or, *jewel for the forehead.*——[g] Chap. xxii. 23.——[h] Ver. 52; Exod. iv. 31.

Verse 15. *Behold, Rebekah came out*] How admirably had the providence of God adapted every circumstance to the necessity of the case, and so as in the most punctual manner to answer the prayer which his servant had offered up!

Verse 19. *I will draw* water *for thy camels also*] Had Rebekah done *no more* than Eliezer had prayed for, we might have supposed that she acted not as a free agent, but was *impelled* to it by the absolutely controlling power of God; but as she exceeds all that was requested, we see that it sprang from her native benevolence, and sets her conduct in the most amiable point of view.

Verse 21. *The man, wondering at her*] And he was so lost in wonder and astonishment at her simplicity, innocence, and benevolence, that he permitted this delicate female to draw water for *ten camels*, without ever attempting to afford her any kind of assistance! I know not which to admire most, the benevolence and condescension of Rebekah, or the cold and apparently stupid indifference of the servant of Abraham. Surely they are both of an uncommon cast.

Verse 22. *The man took a golden ear-ring*] נזם זהב *nezem zahab.* That this could not be an *ear-ring* is very probable from its being in the *singular* number. The margin calls it a *jewel for the forehead;* but it most likely means a *jewel for the nose*, or *nose-ring*, which is in universal use through all parts of Arabia and Persia, particularly among young women. They are generally worn in the left nostril. The word is very properly translated επιρρινιον, an *ornament for the nose*, by Symmachus.

Half a shekel] For the weight of a shekel, see chap. xx. 16.

And two bracelets] ושני צמידים *usheney tsemidim.* As *tsemidim* comes from צמד *tsamad*, to *join* or *couple together*, it may very properly mean *bracelets*, or whatever may clasp round the arms or legs; for rings and ornaments are worn round both by females in India and Persia. The small part of the leg is generally decorated in this way, and so is the whole arm from the shoulder to the wrist. As these *tsemidim* were given to Rebekah *for her hands*, it sufficiently distinguishes them from a similar ornament used for the *ankles*.

In different parts of the sacred writings there are allusions to ornaments of various kinds still in use in different Asiatic countries. They are of seven different sorts: 1. for the *forehead;* 2. for the *nose;* 3. for the *ears;* 4. for the *arms;* 5. for the *fingers;* 6. for the *neck* and *breast;* 7. for the *ankles*. See ver. 22, 47; also Ezek. xvi. 12; Prov. xi. 22; Isa. iii. 21; Gen. xxxv. 4; Exod. xxxii. 2, 3; Job xlii. 11; Judg. viii. 24. The principal female ornaments are enumerated in the third chapter of Isaiah, which are very nearly

A. M. 2148.
B. C. 1856.

27 And he said, [i] Blessed *be* the
LORD God of my master Abraham,
who hath not left destitute my master of
[k] his mercy and his truth: I *being* in the
way, the LORD [l] led me to the house of my
master's brethren.
28 And the damsel ran, and told *them of*
her mother's house these things.
29 And Rebekah had a brother, and his
name *was* [m] Laban: and Laban ran out unto
the man, unto the well.
30 And it came to pass, when he saw the
ear-ring and bracelets upon his sister's hands,
and when he heard the words of Rebekah
his sister, saying, Thus spake the man unto
me, that he came unto the man; and, behold,
he stood by the camels at the well.
31 And he said, Come in, [n] thou blessed of
the LORD; wherefore standest thou without?
for I have prepared the house, and room for
the camels.
32 And the man came into the house: and
he ungirded his camels, and [o] gave straw and
provender for the camels, and water to wash
his feet, and the men's feet that *were* with him.
33 And there was set *meat* before him to
eat: but he said, [p] I will not eat
until I have told mine errand.
And he said, Speak on.
34 And he said, I *am* Abraham's servant.
35 And the LORD [q] hath blessed my master
greatly; and he is become great: and he hath
given him flocks, and herds, and silver, and
gold, and men-servants, and maid-servants, and
camels, and asses.
36 And Sarah my master's wife [r] bare a son
to my master when she was old, and [s] unto
him hath he given all that he hath.
37 And my master [t] made me swear, saying,
Thou shalt not take a wife to my son of the
daughters of the Canaanites, in whose land I
dwell:
38 [u] But thou shalt go unto my father's
house, and to my kindred, and take a wife
unto my son.
39 [v] And I said unto my master, Peradven
ture the woman will not follow me.
40 [w] And he said unto me, The LORD, [x] before whom I walk, will send his angel with
thee, and prosper thy way; and thou shalt
take a wife for my son of my kindred, and of
my father's house.

[i] Exod. xviii. 10; Ruth iv. 14; 1 Sam. xxv. 32, 39; 2 Sam. xviii. 28; Luke i. 68.——[k] Chapter xxxii. 10; Psa. xcviii. 3. [l] Ver. 48.——[m] Chap. xxix. 5.——[n] Chap. xxvi. 29; Judg. xvii. 2; Ruth iii. 10; Psa. cxv. 15.

[o] Chap. xliii. 24; Judg. xix. 21.——[p] Job xxiii. 12; John iv. 34; Eph. vi. 5, 6, 7.——[q] Ver. 1; chap. xiii. 2.——[r] Chap. xxi. 2.——[s] Ch. xxi. 10; xxv. 5.——[t] Ver. 3.——[u] Ver. 4.——[v] Ver. 5.——[w] Ver. 7.——[x] Chap. xvii. 1.

the same that are in use in Persia and India to the present time.

Verse 26. *Bowed down his head, and worshipped*] Two acts of adoration are mentioned here; 1. Bowing the head, יקד *yikkod;* and, 2. *Prostration* upon the earth, וישתחו *vaiyishtachu.* The *bowing of the head* was to *Rebekah,* to return her thanks for her kind invitation. The *prostration* was to *Jehovah,* in gratitude for the success with which he had favoured him.

Verse 27. *The Lord led me*] By desire of his master he went out on this journey; and as he acknowledged God in all his ways, the Lord directed all his steps.

Verse 28. *Her mother's house*] Some have conjectured from this that her father *Bethuel* was dead; and the person called *Bethuel,* verse 50, was a younger *brother.* This is possible, but the mother's house might be mentioned were even the father alive; for in Asiatic countries the women have apartments entirely separate from those of the men, in which their little children and grown-up daughters reside with them. This was probably the case here, though it is very likely that Bethuel was dead, as the whole business appears to be conducted by Rebekah's brothers.

Verse 31. *Thou blessed of the Lord*] Probably a usual mode of wishing prosperity, as he that is blessed of the Lord is worthy of all respect; for, enjoying the Divine favour, he is in possession of the sum of happiness.

Verse 32. *Provender for the camels*] These were the first objects of his care; for a good man is merciful to his beast.

Water to wash his feet] Thus it thus appears that he had servants with him; and as the fatigues of the journey must have fallen as heavily upon them as upon himself, so we find no distinction made, but water is provided to wash their feet also.

Verse 33. *I will not eat until I have told*] In Hindoostan it is not unusual for a Brahmin to enter a house and sit down, and when meat is offered, refuse to eat till he has obtained the object of his errand. Here is a servant who had his master's interest more at heart than his own. He refuses to take even necessary refreshment till he knows whether he is likely to accomplish the object of his journey. Did not our blessed Lord allude to the conduct of Abraham's servant, John iv. 34: *My meat is to do the will of him that sent me, and to finish his work?*

Verse 36. *Unto him hath he given all that he hath.*] He has made Isaac his sole heir. These things appear to be spoken to show the relatives of Rebekah that his master's son was a proper match for her; for even in those primitive times there was regard had to the suitableness of station and rank in life, as well as of education, in order to render a match

A. M. 2148. B. C. 1856.

41 [y] Then shalt thou be clear from *this* my oath, when thou comest to my kindred; and if they give not thee *one*, thou shalt be clear from my oath.

42 And I came this day unto the well, and said, [z] O LORD God of my master Abraham, if now thou do prosper my way which I go;

43 [a] Behold, I stand by the well of water; and it shall come to pass, that when the virgin cometh forth to draw *water*, and I say to her, Give me, I pray thee, a little water of thy pitcher to drink;

44 And she say to me, Both drink thou, and I will also draw for thy camels; *let* the same *be* the woman whom the LORD hath appointed out for my master's son.

45 [b] And before I had done [c] speaking in mine heart, behold, Rebekah came forth, with her pitcher on her shoulder; and she went down unto the well, and drew *water*: and I said unto her, Let me drink, I pray thee.

46 And she made haste, and let down her pitcher from her *shoulder*, and said, Drink, and I will give thy camels drink also: so I drank, and she made the camels drink also.

47 And I asked her, and said, Whose daughter *art* thou? And she said, The daughter of Bethuel, Nahor's son, whom Milcah bare unto him: and I [d] put the earring upon her face, and the bracelets upon her hands.

A. M. 2148. B. C. 1856.

48 [e] And I bowed down my head, and worshipped the LORD; and blessed the LORD God of my master Abraham, which had led me in the right way, to take [f] my master's brother's daughter unto his son.

49 And now if ye will [g] deal kindly and truly with my master, tell me; and if not, tell me; that I may turn to the right hand, or to the left.

50 Then Laban and Bethuel answered and said, [h] The thing proceedeth from the LORD: we cannot [i] speak unto thee bad or good.

51 Behold, Rebekah [k] *is* before thee, take *her*, and go, and let her be thy master's son's wife, as the LORD hath spoken.

52 And it came to pass, that, when Abraham's servant heard their words, he [l] worshipped the LORD, *bowing himself* to the earth.

53 And the servant brought forth [m] jewels of silver, [n] and jewels of gold, and raiment, and gave *them* to Rebekah: he gave also to her brother and to her mother [o] precious things.

[y] Ver. 8.——[z] Ver. 12.——[a] Ver. 13.——[b] Ver. 15, &c. [c] 1 Sam. i. 13.——[d] Ezek. xvi. 11, 12.——[e] Ver. 26.——[f] Chap. xxii. 23.——[g] Chap. xlvii. 29; Josh. ii. 14.——[h] Psa. cxviii. 23; Matt. xxi. 42; Mark xii. 11.——[i] Chap. xxxi. 24.——[k] Chap. xx. 15.——[l] Ver. 26.——[m] Heb. *vessels*.——[n] Exod. iii. 22; xi. 2; xii. 35.——[o] 2 Chron. xxi. 3; Ezra i. 6.

comfortable. Persons of dissimilar habits, as well as of dissimilar religious principles, are never likely to be very happy in a married life. Even the *poor* and the *rich* may better meet together in matrimonial alliances than the *religious* and the *profane*, the *well-bred* and the *vulgar*. A person may be unequally yoked in a great variety of ways: *Bear ye one another's burdens* is the command of God; but where there is unsuitableness in the dispositions, education, mental capacity, &c., of the persons, then *one side* is obliged to bear the whole burden, and endless dissatisfaction is the result. See at the end.

Verse 42. O *Lord God of my master*] As Abraham was the friend of God, Eliezer makes use of this to give weight and consequence to his petitions.

Verse 43. *When the virgin*] העלמה *haalmah*, from עלם *alam*, to hide, cover, or conceal; a pure virgin, a woman not *uncovered*, and in this respect still concealed from man. The same as בתולה *bethulah*, ver. 16, which, from the explanation there given, incontestably means a *virgin* in the proper sense of the word—a young woman, not that is *covered* or *kept at home*, the common gloss, but who was not *uncovered* in the *delicate sense* in which the Scripture uses this word. See this interpretation vindicated on Isa. vii. 14.

Verse 45. *Before I had done speaking in mine heart*] So we find that the whole of this prayer, so circumstantially related verses 12–14, and again 42–44, was mental, and heard only by that God to whom it was directed. It would have been improper to have used *public* prayer on the occasion, as his servants could have felt no particular interest in the accomplishment of his petitions, because they were not concerned in them, having none of the responsibility of this mission.

Verse 49. *That I may turn to the right hand or to the left.*] That is, That I may go elsewhere and seek a proper match for the son of my master. Some have imagined that Eliezer intimated by these expressions that if he did not succeed in obtaining Rebekah, he would go and seek for a wife either among the descendants of Ishmael or the descendants of Lot. This interpretation is fanciful.

Verse 50. *Laban and Bethuel*] These seem both to be *brothers*, of whom Laban was the eldest and chief; for the opinion of Josephus appears to be very correct, *viz.*, that Bethuel, the father, had been some time dead. See ver. 28.

Bad or good.] We can neither speak *for* nor *against*; it seems to be entirely the work of God, and we cordially submit: consult Rebekah; if she be willing, take her and go. See ver. 58.

Verse 53. *Jewels of silver, and jewels of gold*] The word כלי *keley*, which we here translate *jewels*

A. M. 2148.
B. C. 1856.

54 And they did eat and drink,
he and the men that *were* with him,
and tarried all night; and they rose up in the
morning, and he said, [p] Send me away unto
my master.
55 And her brother and her mother said,
Let the damsel abide with us [q] *a few* days, at
the least ten; after that she shall go.
56 And he said unto them, Hinder me not,
seeing the LORD hath prospered my way;
send me away that I may go to my master.
57 And they said, We will call the damsel,
and inquire at her mouth.
58 And they called Rebekah, and said unto
her, Wilt thou go with this man? And she
said, I will go.
59 And they sent away Rebekah their sister,
and [r] her nurse, and Abraham's servant, and
his men.
60 And they blessed Rebekah,
and said unto her, Thou *art* our
sister, be thou [s] *the mother* of thousands of
millions, and [t] let thy seed possess the gate
of those which hate them.
61 And Rebekah arose, and her damsels,
and they rode upon the camels, and followed
the man: and the servant took Rebekah, and
went his way.
62 And Isaac came from the way of the
[u] well Lahai-roi; for he dwelt in the south
country.
63 And Isaac went out [v] to meditate in the
field at the [w] eventide: and he lifted up his
eyes, and saw, and behold, the camels *were*
coming.
64 And Rebekah lifted up her eyes,
and when she saw Isaac, [x] she lighted off the
camel.

[p] Ver. 56, 59.——[q] Or, *a full year,* or, *ten* months; Judg. xiv. 8. ——[r] Chap. xxxv. 8.——[s] Chap. xvii. 16.——[t] Chap. xxii. 17.

[u] Chap. xvi. 14; xxv. 11.——[v] Or, *to pray.*——[w] Josh. i. 8; Psa. i. 2; lxxvii. 12; cxix. 15; cxliii. 5.——[x] Josh. xv. 18.

signifies properly *vessels* or *instruments;* and those presented by Eliezer might have been of various kinds. What he had given before, ver. 22, was in token of *respect,* what he gave now appears to have been in the way of *dowry.*

Precious things.] מגדנת *migdanoth.* This word is used to express *exquisite fruits* or *delicacies,* Deut. xxxiii. 13–16; *precious plants* or *flowers,* Cant. iv. 16; vii. 13. But it may mean *gifts* in general, though rather of an *inferior* kind to those mentioned above.

Verse 54. *And they did eat and drink*] When Eliezer had got a favourable answer, then he and his servants sat down to meat; this he had refused to do till he had told his message, ver. 33.

Verse 55. *Let the damsel abide with us* a few *days, at the least ten*] The original is very abrupt and obscure, because we are not acquainted with the precise meaning of the *form of speech* which is here used; ימים או עשור *yamim or asor* DAYS or TEN, probably meaning a *year* or *ten months,* as the margin reads it, or a *week* or *ten days.* This latter is the most likely sense, as there would be no propriety after having given their consent that she should go, in detaining her for a *year* or *ten months.* In matters of simple phraseology, or in those which concern peculiar customs, the *Septuagint* translation, especially in the Pentateuch, where it is most accurate and pure, may be considered a legitimate judge; this translation renders the words ἡμέρας ὡσεὶ δέκα, *about ten days.* Houbigant contends strongly that instead of the words ימים או עשור *yamim o asor,* days or ten, we should read חדש ימים *chodesh yamim,* a month of days, i. e., a full month; without which emendation he asserts, *locus explicari non possit,* "the passage cannot be explained." This emendation is supported by the *Syriac* version, which reads here ܝܪܚ ܝܘܡܝܢ *yerach yomin,* a month of days, or a full month. The reader may adopt the *Syriac* or the *Septuagint,* as he judges best.

Verse 58. *Wilt thou go with this man?*] So it appears it was left *ultimately* to the choice of Rebekah whether she would accept the proposals now made to her, unless we suppose that the question meant, *Wilt thou go immediately,* or *stay with us a month longer?*

She said, I will go.] It fully appears to be the will of God that it should be so, and I consent. This at once determined the whole business.

Verse 59. *And her nurse*] Whose name, we learn from chap. xxxv. 8, was *Deborah,* and who, as a second mother, was deemed proper to accompany Rebekah. This was a measure dictated by good sense and prudence. Rebekah had other female attendants. See ver. 61.

Verse 60. *Be thou* the mother *of thousands of millions*] לאלפי רבבה *lealphey rebabah,* for thousands ten thousand, or *for myriads of thousands,* a large family being ever considered, in ancient times, as a proof of the peculiar blessing and favour of God. Similar addresses to a daughter, when she is going from her father's house to live with her husband, are very common among the *Hindoos;* such as, "Be thou the mother of a son," "Be thou the wife of a king," &c. See *Ward.*

Verse 62. *And Isaac came*] Concerning this *well* see chap. xvi. 13, &c. As it appears from chap. xxv. 11, that Isaac dwelt at the well *Lahai-roi,* it has been conjectured that he had now come on a visit to his aged father at Beer-sheba, where he waited in expectation of his bride.

For he dwelt in the south country.] The southern part of the land of Canaan. See chap. xii. 9.

Verse 63. *Isaac went out to meditate*] לשוח *lasuach,* to bend down the body, or the mind, or both. He was probably in deep thought, with his eyes fixed upon

A. M. 2148. B. C. 1856.

65 For she *had* said unto the servant, What man *is* this that walketh in the field to meet us? And the servant *had* said, It *is* my master: therefore she took [y] a veil, and covered herself.

66 And the servant told Isaac all things that he had done.

67 And Isaac brought her into his mother [z] Sarah's tent, and took Rebekah, and she became his wife; and he loved her: and Isaac [a] was comforted after his mother's *death*.

y Chap. xx. 16; 1 Cor. xi. 1, 6, 10. — z Chap. xviii. 6, 9, 10.—a Chap. xxxviii. 12; 1 Thess. iv. 15.

the ground. What the subject of his meditation was it is useless to inquire; he was a pious man, and could not be *triflingly* employed.

Verse 65. *She took a veil*] הצעיף *hatstsaaif.* This is the first time this word occurs, and it is of doubtful signification; but most agree to render it a *veil* or a *cloak*. The former is the most likely, as it was generally used by women in the east as a sign of *chastity*, *modesty*, and *subjection*.

Verse 67. *Sarah's tent*] Sarah being dead, her tent became now appropriated to the use of Rebekah.

And took Rebekah, &c.] After what *form* this was done we are not told; or whether there was any form used on the occasion, more than solemnly receiving her as the person whom God had chosen to be his wife; for it appears from ver. 66 that the servant told him all the especial providential circumstances which had marked his journey. The primitive *form* of marriage we have already seen, chap. ii. 23, 24, which, it is likely, as far as *form* was attended to, was that which was commonly used in all the patriarchal times.

In this chapter we have an affecting and edifying display of that *providence* by which God disposes and governs the affairs of the universe, descending to the minutest particulars, and managing the great *whole* by directing and influencing all its *parts*. This *particular* or *especial* providence we see is not confined to work by *general laws;* it is wise and intelligent, for it is the mind, the will, and energy of God; it steps out of common ways, and takes particular directions, as endlessly varied human necessities may need, or the establishment and maintenance of godliness in the earth may require. What a history of providential occurrences, coming all in answer to the prayer and faith of a simple, humble individual, does this chapter exhibit!

As Abraham's servant has God's glory only in view in the errand on which he is going, he may well expect the Divine direction. See with what simplicity and confidence he prays to God! He even prescribes the way in which the Divine choice and approbation shall be made known; and God honours the purity of his motives and his pious faith, by giving him precisely the answer he wished. How honourable in the sight of God is *simplicity* of heart! It has nothing to fear, and all good to hope for; whereas a spirit warped by *self-interest* and *worldly views* is always *uncertain* and *agitated*, as it is ever seeking that from its *own counsels*, *projects*, and *schemes*, which should be sought in God alone. In every place the upright man meets with his God; his heart acknowledges his Maker, and his Maker acknowledges him; for such a one the whole economy of providence and grace is ever at work.

Abraham's solicitude to get a suitable wife for his son is worthy of the most serious regard. He was well aware that if Isaac formed a matrimonial alliance with the *Canaanites* it might be ruinous to his piety, and prevent the dissemination of the true religion; therefore he binds his most trusty servant by a solemn oath not to take a wife for his son from the daughters of Canaan, but from his own kindred, among whom the knowledge of the true God was best preserved. Others had different rays of the light of truth, but Abraham's family alone had THE *truth;* and to the descendants of this family were the promises made.

How careful should parents be to procure alliances for their children with those who fear God, as so much of the peace and comfort of the children, and the happiness of *their* posterity, depend on this circumstance! But alas! how many sacrifice the comfort and salvation of their offspring at the shrine of Mammon! If they can procure *rich husbands* and *wives* for their daughters and sons, then all, in their apprehension, is well. Marriages of this kind may be considered as mere *bargain* and *sale;* for there is scarcely ever any reference to God or eternity in them. The Divine institution of marriage is left out of sight; and the persons are united, not properly to *each other*, in the love, fear, and according to the ordinance of God, but they are wedded to so many *thousand pounds* sterling, and to so many *houses*, *fields*, &c. Thus like goes to like, *metal* to *metal*, *earth* to *earth*. Marriages formed on such principles are mere *licensed adulteries.* Let such *contractors* hear these awful words of God "Ye adulterers and adulteresses, know ye not that the friendship of the world is enmity with God?" James iv. 4. See on ver. 36.

Although under the patriarchal dispensation parents had a kind of absolute authority over their children, and might dispose of them as they pleased in general cases, yet it appears that in matrimonial connections they were under no compulsion. The suitable person was pointed out and recommended; but it does not appear that children were *forced*, against the whole tide of their affections, to take those persons who were the objects of the parent's choice. *Wilt thou go with this man?* was, in all likelihood, deemed essential to the completion of the contract; and by the answer, *I will go*, was the contract fully ratified. Thus the persons were ultimately left to their own choice, though the most prudent and proper means were no doubt used in order to direct and fix it. Whether this was precisely the plan followed in primitive times we cannot *absolutely* say: they were times of great *simplicity;* and probably connections on the mere principle

of *affection*, independently of all other considerations, seldom existed. And it must be allowed that matches formed on the sole principle of *conveniency* might as well be formed by the parents as by any others; and in Asiatic countries it was generally so, for *there* the female seldom presumes to have a choice of her own.

In all cases of this kind the child should invariably consult the *experience* and *wisdom* of the parents; and the parents should ever pay much respect to the *feelings* of the child, nor oppose an alliance which may be in all other respects suitable, because there may be a lack of *property* on *one side* of the intended match. If parents would proceed in this way, God would pour his blessing on their seed, and his Spirit upon their offspring.

CHAPTER XXV.

Abraham marries Keturah, 1. *Their issue*, 2–4. *Makes Isaac his heir*, 5; *but gives portions to the sons of his concubines, and sends them eastward from Isaac, to find settlements*, 6. *Abraham's age*, 7, *and death*, 8. *Is buried by his sons Isaac and Ishmael in the cave of Machpelah*, 9, 10. *God's blessing upon Isaac*, 11. *The generations of Ishmael*, 12–16. *His age*, 17, *and death*, 18. *Of the generations of Isaac*, 19, *who was married in his* fortieth *year*, 20. *Rebekah his wife being barren, on his prayer to God she conceives*, 21. *She inquires of the Lord concerning her state*, 22. *The Lord's answer*, 23. *She is delivered of twins*, 24. *Peculiarities in the birth of her sons Esau and Jacob, from which they had their names*, 25, 26. *Their different manner of life*, 27, 28. *Esau, returning from the field faint, begs pottage from his brother*, 29, 30. *Jacob refuses to grant him any but on condition of his selling him his birthright*, 31. *Esau, ready to die, parts with his birthright to save his life*, 32. *Jacob causes him to confirm the sale with an oath*, 33. *He receives bread and pottage of lentiles, and departs*, 34.

A. M. cir. 2154. B. C. cir. 1850.

THEN again [a] Abraham took a wife, and her name *was* Keturah.

A. M. cir. 2155 B. C. cir. 1849

2 And [b] she bare him Zimran, and Jokshan, and Medan, and [c] Midian, and Ishbak, and Shuah.

[a] Chap. xxiii. 1, 2.——[b] 1 Chron. i. 32, 33.——[c] Chap. xxxvii. 28; Exod. ii. 15, 16; xviii. 1-4; Num. xxii. 4; Judg. vi., vii., viii.

NOTES ON CHAP. XXV.

Verse 1. *Then again Abraham took a wife*] When Abraham took Keturah we are not informed; it might have been in the lifetime of Sarah; and the original ויסף *vaiyoseph, and he added, &c.*, seems to give some countenance to this opinion. Indeed it is not very likely that he had the children mentioned here *after* the death of Sarah; and from the circumstances of his age, feebleness, &c., at the birth of Isaac, it is still more improbable. Even at that age, forty years before the marriage of Isaac, the birth of his son is considered as not less miraculous on his part than on the part of Sarah; for the apostle expressly says, Rom. iv. 19, that Abraham *considered not his own body* NOW DEAD, *when he was about a hundred years old, nor the* DEADNESS *of Sarah's womb*; hence we learn that they were both past the procreation of children, insomuch that the birth of Isaac is ever represented as *supernatural*. It is therefore very improbable that he had any child after the birth of Isaac; and therefore we may well suppose that Moses had related this transaction out of its *chronological* order, which is not unfrequent in the sacred writings, when a variety of important facts relative to the accomplishment of some grand design are thought necessary to be produced in a connected series. On this account *intervening* matters of a different complexion are referred to a future time. Perhaps we may be justified in reading the verse: "And Abraham *had* added, and *had* taken a wife (besides Hagar) whose name was Keturah," &c. The chronology in the margin dates this marriage with Keturah A. M. 2154, nine years after the death of Sarah, A. M. 2145. *Jonathan ben Uzziel* and the *Jerusalem Targum* both assert that Keturah was the same as *Hagar*. Some rabbins, and with them Dr. Hammond, are of the same opinion; but both Hagar and Keturah are so distinguished in the Scriptures, that the opinion seems destitute of probability.

Verse 2. *Zimran*] Stephanus Byzantinus mentions a city in *Arabia Felix* called *Zadram*, which some suppose to have been named from this son of Keturah; but it is more likely, as Calmet observes, that all these sons of Abraham resided in *Arabia Deserta*; and Pliny, Hist. Nat., lib. vi., c. 28, mentions a people in that country called *Zamarenians*, who were probably the descendants of this person.

Jokshan] Several learned men have been of opinion that this Jokshan was the same as *Kachtan*, the father of the Arabs. The testimonies in favour of this opinion see in Dr. Hunt's Oration, *De Antiquitate*, &c., *Linguæ Arabicæ*, p. 4. Calmet supposes that the Cataneans, who inhabited a part of Arabia Deserta, sprang from this Jokshan.

Medan, and Midian] Probably those who peopled that part of Arabia Petræa contiguous to the land of Moab eastward of the Dead Sea. St. Jerome terms the people of this country *Madinæans*; and Ptolemy mentions a people called *Madianites*, who dwelt in the same place.

Ishbak] From this person Calmet supposes the brook *Jabbok*, which has its source in the mountains of Gilead, and falls into the sea of Tiberias, took its name.

Shuah.] Or *Shuach*. From this man the *Sacceans*, near to Batania, at the extremity of Arabia Deserta,

A. M. cir. 2180. B. C. cir. 1824.
3 And Jokshan begat Sheba,
and Dedan. And the sons of
A. M. cir. 2200. B. C. cir. 1804.
Dedan were Asshurim, and Letushim, and Leummim.
4 And the sons of Midian; Ephah, and
Epher, and Hanoch, and Abidah, and Eldaah.
All these *were* the children of Keturah.
A. M. cir. 2175. B. C. cir. 1829.
5 And [d] Abraham gave all that
he had unto Isaac.
6 But unto the sons of the concubines, which
Abraham had, Abraham gave
A. M. cir. 2175. B. C. cir. 1829.
gifts, and [e] sent them away from
Isaac his son, while he yet lived, eastward,
unto [f] the east country.
7 And these *are* the days of
A. M. cir. 2183. B. C. cir. 1821.
the years of Abraham's life
which he lived, a hundred threescore and
fifteen years.
8 Then Abraham gave up the ghost, and
[g] died in a good old age, an old man, and full

[d] Chap. xxiv. 36.——[e] Chap. xxi. 14.

[f] Judg. vi. 3.——[g] Chap. xv. 15; xlix. 29.

towards Syria, are supposed to have sprung. *Bildad* the *Shuhite*, one of Job's friends, is supposed to have descended from this son of Abraham.

Verse 3. *Sheba*] From whom sprang the Sabeans, who robbed Job of his cattle. See *Bochart* and *Calmet.*

Asshurim, and Letushim, and Leummim.] We know not who these were, but as each name is *plural* they must have been *tribes* or *families*, and not *individuals.* Onkelos interprets these words of persons dwelling in *camps, tents,* and *islands;* and Jonathan ben Uzziel calls them *merchants, artificers,* and *heads* or *chiefs of people.*

Verse 4. *Ephah, and Epher, &c.*] Of these we know no more than of the preceding; an abundance of conjectures is already furnished by the commentators.

Verse 5. *Gave all that he had unto Isaac.*] His principal flocks, and especially his right to the land of Canaan, including a confirmation to him and his posterity of whatever was contained in the promises of God.

Verse 6. *Unto the sons of the concubines*] Viz., Hagar and Keturah, Abraham gave gifts. Cattle for breed, seed to sow the land, and implements for husbandry, may be what is here intended.

And sent them away—while he yet lived] Lest after his death they should dispute a settlement in the Land of Promise with Isaac; therefore he very prudently sent them to procure settlements during his lifetime, that they might be under no temptation to dispute the settlement with Isaac in Canaan. From this circumstance arose that law which has prevailed in almost all countries, of *giving the estates to the eldest son* by a lawful wife; for though concubines, or wives of the second rank, were perfectly legitimate in those ancient times, yet their children did not inherit, except in case of the failure of *legal* issue, and with the consent of the lawful wife; and it is very properly observed by Calmet, that it was in consequence of the consent of Leah and Rachel that the children of their slaves by Jacob had a common and equal lot with the rest. By a law of Solon all natural children were excluded from the paternal inheritance, but their fathers were permitted to give them any sum not beyond a thousand drachma by way of *present.*

Eastward, unto the east country.] Arabia Deserta, which was eastward of Beer-sheba, where Abraham lived.

Verse 7. *The days of the years, &c.*] There is a beauty in this expression which is not sufficiently regarded. Good men do not live by *centuries*, though many such have lived several hundred years, nor do they count their lives even by *years*, but by *days*, living as if they were the creatures only of A DAY; having no more time than they can with any propriety call their own, and living that day in reference to *eternity.*

Verse 8. *Then Abraham gave up the ghost*] Highly as I value our translation for general accuracy, fidelity, and elegance, I must beg leave to dissent from this version. The original word יגוע *yigva*, from the root גוע *gava*, signifies *to pant for breath, to expire, to cease from breathing*, or *to breathe one's last;* and here, and wherever the original word is used, the simple term *expired* would be the proper expression. In our translation this expression occurs Gen. xxv. 8, 17; xxxv. 29; xlix. 33; Job iii. 11; x. 18; xi. 20; xiii. 19; xiv. 10; Lam. i. 19; in all of which places the original is גוע *gava.* It occurs also in our translation, Jer. xv. 9, but there the original is נפחה נפשה *naphecah naphshah, she breathed out her soul;* the verb גוע *gava* not being used. Now as our English word *ghost*, from the Anglo-Saxon ᵹaꞅꞇ *gast*, an *inmate, inhabitant, guest*, (a casual visitant,) also a *spirit*, is now restricted among us to the latter meaning, always signifying the *immortal spirit* or *soul* of man, the *guest* of the body; and as *giving up the spirit, ghost,* or *soul*, is an act not proper to man, though *commending it to God*, in our last moments, is both an act of faith and piety; and as *giving up the ghost*, i. e., *dismissing his spirit* from his body, is attributed to Jesus Christ, to whom alone it is proper, I therefore object against its use in *every other case.*

Every man since the fall has not only been *liable* to death, but has *deserved* it, as all have forfeited their lives because of sin. Jesus Christ, as born immaculate, and having never sinned, had not *forfeited* his life, and therefore may be considered as naturally and properly immortal. *No man*, says he, *taketh it*—my life, *from me, but I lay it down of myself; I have power to lay it down, and I have power to take it again: therefore doth the Father love me, because I lay down my life that I might take it again*, John x. 17, 18. Hence we rightly translate Matt. xxvii. 50, *αφηκε το πνευμα, he gave up the ghost;* i. e., he *dismissed his spirit* that he *might die for the sin of the world.* The Evangelist St. John, xix. 30, makes use of an expression to the same import, which we translate in the same way, *παρεδωκε το πνευμα, he delivered up his spirit.* We translate Mark xv. 37, and Luke xxiii. 46, *he gave up the ghost*, but not correctly, because the word in both these places is very different, *εξεπνευσε*, *he*

A. M. cir. 2183. B. C. cir. 1821.

of years; and [h] was gathered to his people.

9 And [i] his sons Isaac and Ishmael buried him in the cave of Machpelah, in the field of Ephron the son of Zohar the Hittite, which *is* before Mamre;

A. M. cir. 2183. B. C. cir. 1821.

[h] Chap. xxxv. 29; xlix. 33. — [i] Chap. xxxv. 29; l. 13.

breathed his last, or *expired,* though in the latter place (Luke xxiii. 46) there is an equivalent expression, *O Father, into thy hands* παρατιθεμαι το πνευμα μου, *I commit my spirit,* i. e., I place my soul in thy hand; proving that the act was *his own,* that no man could take his life away from him, that he did not die by the *perfidy* of his disciple, or the *malice* of the Jews, but by his *own free act.* Thus HE LAID DOWN *his life for the sheep.* Of Ananias and Sapphira, Acts v. 5, 10, and of Herod, Acts xii. 23, our translation says they *gave up the ghost;* but the word in both places is εξεψυξε, which simply means to *breathe out,* to *expire,* or *die;* but in no case, either by the *Septuagint* in the *Old* or any of the sacred writers in the *New Testament,* is αφηκε το πνευμα or παρεδωκε το πνευμα, *he dismissed his spirit* or *delivered up his spirit,* spoken of any person but Christ. Abraham, Isaac, Ishmael, Jacob, &c., *breathed their last;* Ananias, Sapphira, and Herod *expired;* but none, Jesus Christ excepted, *gave up the ghost, dismissed,* or *delivered up his own spirit,* and was consequently *free among the dead.* Of the patriarchs, &c., the *Septuagint* uses the word εκλειπων, *failing,* or κατεπαυσε, he *ceased* or *rested.*

An old man] Viz., one hundred and seventy-five, the youngest of all the patriarchs; *and full* of years. The word *years* is not in the text; but as our translators saw that some word was necessary to fill up the text, they added this in *Italics.* It is probable that the true word is ימים *yamim, days,* as in Gen. xxxv. 29; and this reading is found in several of *Kennicott's* and *De Rossi's* MSS., in the *Samaritan* text, *Septuagint, Vulgate, Syriac, Arabic, Persic,* and *Chaldee.* On these authorities it might be safely admitted into the text.

Being full of days, or *full of years.*—To be *satiated* with days or life, has been in use among different nations to express the termination of life, and especially life ended *without reluctance.* It seems to be a metaphor taken from a guest regaled by a plentiful banquet, and is thus used by the Roman poets.

Lucretius, lib. iii., ver. 947, ridiculing those who were unreasonably attached to life, and grievously afflicted at the prospect of death, addresses them in the following manner:—

———Quid mortem congemis, ac fles?
Nam si grata fuit tibi vita anteacta, priorque,
Et non omnia pertusum congesta quasi in vas
Commoda perfluxere, atque ingrata interiere:
Cur non, ut PLENUS VITÆ CONVIVA, RECEDIS?

Fond mortal, what 's the matter, thou dost sigh?
Why all these fears because thou once must die?
For if the race thou hast already run
Was pleasant, if with joy thou saw'st the sun,
If all thy pleasures did not pass thy mind
As through a sieve, but left some sweets behind,
Why dost thou not then, like a THANKFUL GUEST,
Rise cheerfully from life's ABUNDANT FEAST?

CREECH.

Et nec opinanti mors ad caput astitit ante,
Quam SATUR, ac PLENUS possis discedere rerum.

Ib. ver. 972.

And unexpected hasty death destroys,
Before thy *greedy* mind is FULL of JOYS. *Idem.*

Horace makes use of the same figure:—

Inde fit, ut raro, qui se vixisse beatum
Dicat, et exacto CONTENTUS tempore vitæ
Cedat, ut CONVIVA SATUR, reperire queamus.

Sat. l. i. *Sat.* i. ver. 117.

From hence how few, like SATED GUESTS, depart
From life's FULL BANQUET with a cheerful heart!

FRANCIS.

The same image is expressed with strong ridicule in his last EPISTLE—

Lusisti satis, edisti satis, atque bibisti;
Tempus ABIRE tibi est. Epist. l. ii., ver. 216.

Thou hast eaten, drunk, and play'd ENOUGH; then why
So stark reluctant to leave off, and DIE?

The poet Statius uses *abire paratum,* PLENUM *vita,* "prepared to depart, being FULL of LIFE," in exactly the same sense:—

———Dubio quem non in turbine rerum
Deprendet suprema dies; sed *abire* paratum,
Ac PLENUM VITA.

Sylv. l. ii., *Villa Surrentina,* ver. 128.

The man whose mighty soul is not immersed
In dubious whirl of secular concerns,
His final hour ne'er takes him by surprise,
But, FULL OF LIFE, he stands PREPARED to DIE.

It was the opinion of Aristotle that *a man should depart from life as he should rise from a banquet.* Thus Abraham died FULL *of days,* and SATISFIED *with life,* but in a widely different spirit from that recommended by the above writers—HE left life with a hope *full of immortality,* which they could never boast; for HE *saw the day of Christ, and was glad;* and his hope was crowned, for here it is expressly said, *He was gathered to his fathers;* surely not to the *bodies* of his sleeping ancestors, who were buried in Chaldea and not in Canaan, nor with his *fathers* in any sense, for he was deposited in the cave where his WIFE *alone* slept; but he was gathered to the *spirits of just men made perfect,* and *to the Church of the first-born, whose names are written in heaven;* Heb. xii. 23.

Verse 9. *His sons Isaac and Ishmael buried him*] Though Ishmael and his mother had been expelled from Abraham's family on the account of Isaac, yet, as he was under the same obligation to a most loving affectionate father as his brother Isaac, if any personal feuds remained, they agreed to bury them on this occasion, that both might dutifully join in doing the last offices to a parent who was an honour to them and to human nature: and, considering the rejection of Ishmael from

A. M. cir. 2183. B. C. cir. 1821.

10 [k] The field which Abraham
purchased of the sons of Heth:
[l] there was Abraham buried, and Sarah his
wife.
11 And it came to pass after the death of
Abraham, that God blessed his son Isaac;
and Isaac dwelt by the [m] well Lahai-roi.
12 Now these *are* the generations of Ishmael,
Abraham's son, [n] whom Hagar the Egyptian,
Sarah's handmaid, bare unto Abraham:
13 And [o] these *are* the names of the sons
of Ishmael, by their names, according to their
generations; the first-born of Ishmael, Nebajoth;
and Kedar, and Adbeel, and Mibsam,
14 And Mishma, and Duma, and Massa,
15 [p] Hadar, and Tema, Jetur, A. M. cir. 2183. B. C. cir. 1821.
Naphish, and Kedemah:
16 These *are* the sons of Ishmael, and these
are their names, by their towns, and by their
castles; [q] twelve princes according to their
nations.
17 And these *are* the years of A. M. 2231 B. C. 1773.
the life of Ishmael, a hundred and
thirty and seven years: and [r] he gave up the
ghost and died; and was gathered unto his
people.
18 [s] And they dwelt from Havilah unto Shur,
that *is* before Egypt, as thou goest toward
Assyria: *and* he [t] died [u] in the presence of
all his brethren.

[k] Chap. xxiii. 16.—[l] Chap. xlix. 31.—[m] Chap. xvi. 14; xxiv. 62.—[n] Ch. xvi. 15.—[o] 1 Chron. i. 29.—[p] Or, *Hadad*; 1 Chron. i. 30.—[q] Chap. xvii. 20.—[r] Ver. 8.—[s] 1 Sam. xv. 7.—[t] Heb. *fell*; Psa. lxxviii. 64.—[u] Chap. xv. 12.

the inheritance, this transaction shows his character in an amiable point of view; for though he was *a wild man*, (see chap. xvi. 12,) yet this appellation appears to be more characteristic of his *habits of life* than of his *disposition*.

For the character of Abraham see the conclusion of this chapter.

Verse 11. *God blessed his son Isaac*] The peculiar blessings and influences by which Abraham had been distinguished now rested upon Isaac; but how little do we hear in him of the work of faith, the patience of hope, and the labour of love! Only one Abraham and one Christ ever appeared among men; there have been some successful *imitators*, there should have been many.

Verse 12. *These* are *the generations of Ishmael*] The object of the inspired writer seems to be to show how the promises of God were fulfilled to both the branches of Abraham's family. *Isaac* has been already referred to; God blessed him according to the promise. He had also promised to multiply *Ishmael*, and an account of his generation is introduced to show how exactly the promise had also been fulfilled to him.

Verse 13. *Nebajoth*] From whom came the Nabatheans, whose capital was *Petra*, or, according to Strabo, *Nabathea*. They dwelt in Arabia Petræa, and extended themselves on the east towards Arabia Deserta.

Kedar] The founder of the *Cedreans*, who dwelt near to the *Nabatheans*. The descendants of Kedar form a part of the Saracens.

Adbeel, and Mibsam] Where these were situated is not known.

Verse 14. *Mishma, and Dumah, and Massa*] Where the first and last of these settled is not known; but it is probable that *Dumah* gave his name to a place called *Dumah* in Arabia. See a prophecy concerning this place, Isa. xxi. 11, from which we find that it was in the vicinity of *Mount Seir*.

These three names have passed into a proverb among the Hebrews, because of their signification. משמע *mishma* signifies HEARING; דומה *dumah*, SILENCE; and משא *massa*, PATIENCE. Hence, "Hear much, say little, and bear much," tantamount to the famous maxim of the Stoics, Ανεχου και απεχου, "*Sustain* and *abstain*," is supposed to be the spirit of the original words.

Verse 15. *Hadar*] This name should be read *Hadad* as in 1 Chron. i. 30. This reading is supported by more than three hundred MSS., versions, and printed editions. See ver. 18.

Tema] Supposed to be a place in Arabia Deserta, the same of which Job speaks, chap. vi. 19.

Jetur] From whom came the *Itureans*, who occupied a small tract of country beyond Jordan, which was afterwards possessed by the half-tribe of Manasseh.

Naphish] These are evidently the same people mentioned 1 Chron. v. 19, who, with the Itureans and the people of Nadab, assisted the Hagarenes against the Israelites, but were overcome by the two tribes of Reuben and Gad, and the half-tribe of Manasseh.

Kedemah] Probably the descendants of this person dwelt at *Kedemoth*, a place mentioned Deut. ii. 26. I wish the reader to observe, that concerning those ancient tribes mentioned here or elsewhere in the Pentateuch little is known; nor of their *places* of settlement have we more certain information. On this subject many learned men have toiled hard with but little fruit of their labour. Those who wish to enter into discussions of this nature must consult *Bochart's* Geographia Sacra, *Calmet*, &c.

Verse 16. *These* are *their names*] By which their *descendants* were called. *Their towns*—places of encampment in the wilderness, such as have been used by the Arabs from the remotest times. *Their castles*, טירתם *tirotham*, *their towers*, probably mountain tops, fortified rocks, and fastnesses of various kinds in woods and hilly countries.

Verse 18. *They dwelt from Havilah unto Shur*] The descendants of Ishmael possessed all that country which extends from east to west, from *Havilah* on the Euphrates, near its junction with the Tigris, to the desert of *Shur* eastward of Egypt; and which extends along the isthmus of Suez, which separates the *Red Sea* from the *Mediterranean*.

As thou goest toward Assyria] "These words," says Calmet, "may refer either to *Egypt*, to *Shur*, or to

a

A. M. 2108. B. C. 1896.
19 And these *are* the generations of Isaac, Abraham's son: Abraham begat Isaac;
A. M. 2148. B. C. 1856.
20 And Isaac was forty years old when he took Rebekah to wife, [w] the daughter of Bethuel the Syrian, of Padan-aram, [x] the sister to Laban the Syrian.
A. M. cir. 2167. B. C. cir. 1837.
21 And Isaac entreated the LORD for his wife, because she *was* barren: [y] and the LORD was entreated of him, and [z] Rebekah his wife conceived. A. M. cir. 2167. B. C. cir. 1837.
22 And the children struggled together within her; and she said, If *it be* so, why *am* I thus? [a] And she went to inquire of the LORD. A. M. 2168. B. C. 1836.
23 And the LORD said unto her, [b] Two nations *are* in thy womb, and two manner of

[v] Matt. i. 2.——[w] Chapter xxii. 23.——[x] Chapter xxiv. 29. [y] 1 Chron. v. 20; 2 Chron. xxxiii. 13; Ezra. viii. 23.

[z] Rom. ix. 10.——[a] 1 Samuel ix. 9; x. 22.——[b] Chap. xvii. 16; xxiv. 60.

Havilah. The desert of Shur is on the road from Egypt to Assyria in traversing Arabia Petræa, and in passing by the country of Havilah. I know not," adds he, " whether *Ashshurah* in the text may not mark out rather the *Asshurim* descended from *Keturah*, than the *Assyrians*, who were the descendants of *Asshur* the son of *Shem*."

He died in the presence of all his brethren.] The original will not well bear this translation. In ver. 17 it is said, *He gave up the ghost and died, and was gathered to his people.* Then follows the account of the *district* occupied by the Ishmaelites, at the conclusion of which it is added, על פני כל אחיו נפל *al peney col echaiv naphal*, " IT (the lot or district) FELL (or was divided to him) in the presence of all his brethren :" and this was exactly agreeable to the promise of God, chap. xvi. 12, *He shall dwell in the presence of all his brethren;* and to show that this promise had been strictly fulfilled, it is here remarked that his lot or inheritance was assigned him by Divine Providence, contiguous to that of the other branches of the family. The same word, נפל *naphal*, is used Josh. xxiii. 4, for *to divide by lot.*

On the subject of writing the same proper *name variously* in our common Bibles, the following observations and tables will not be unacceptable to the reader.

" Men who have read their Bible with care," says Dr. Kennicott, " must have remarked that the name of the same person is often expressed differently in different places. Indeed the variation is sometimes so great that we can scarcely persuade ourselves that *one and the same* person is really meant. A uniform expression of proper names is diligently attended to in other books: perhaps in every other book, except the Old Testament. But here we find strange variety in the expression, and consequently great confusion : and indeed there is scarcely any one general source of error which calls for more careful correction than the same proper names now wrongly expressed. I shall add here, from the *Pentateuch*, some proper names which are strangely varied: first, *twenty-three* names expressed differently in the *Hebrew* text itself, and *seventeen* of them in our English translation; and then *thirty-one* names expressed uniformly in the *Hebrew* yet differently in the *English*.

SAME NAMES DIFFERING IN THE *HEBREW*.

1	Gen. iv. 18.	Mehujael	Mehijael	in the same verse.
2	—— x. 3.	Riphath	Diphath	1 Chron. i. 6.
3	—— x. 4.	Tarshish	Tarshishah	—— i. 7.
4	—— x. 4.	Dodanim	Rodanim	—— i. 7.
5	—— x. 23.	Mash	Meshech	—— i. 17.
6	—— x. 28.	Obal	Ebal	—— i. 22.
7	—— xxxii. 30, 31.	Peniel	Penuel	in the next verse.
8	—— xxxvi. 11.	Zepho	Zephi	1 Chron. i. 36.
9	—— xxxvi. 23.	Shepho	Shephi	—— i. 40.
10	—— xxxvi. 39.	Pau	Pai	—— i. 50.
11	—— xxxvi. 40.	Alvah	Aliah	—— i. 51.
12	—— xlvi. 10.	Jemuel	Nemuel	Num. xxvi. 12.
13	—— xlvi. 10.	Jachin	Jarib	1 Chron. iv. 24.
14	—— xlvi. 10.	Zohar	Zerah	Num. xxvi. 13, and 1 Chron. iv. 24.
15	—— xlvi. 11.	Gershon	Gershom	1 Chron. vi. 1, 16.
16	—— xlvi. 13.	Job	Jashub	Num. xxvi. 24.
17	—— xlvi. 16.	Ezbon	Ozni	—— xxvi. 16.
18	—— xlvi. 21.	Huppim	Huram	1 Chron. viii. 5.
19	—— xlvi. 21.	Ard	Addar	—— viii. 3.
20	—— xlvi. 23.	Hushim	Shuham	Num. xxvi. 42.
21	Exod. iv. 18.	Jether	Jethro	in the same verse.
22	Num. i. 14.	Deuel	Reuel	Num. ii. 14.
23	Deut. xxxii. 44.	Hoshea	Joshua	Deut. xxxiv. 9.

A. M. 2168. B. C. 1836.

people shall be separated from thy bowels; and [c] *the one* people shall be stronger than *the other* people; and [d] the elder shall serve the younger.

A. M. 2168. B. C. 1836.

[c] 2 Sam. viii. 14.

[d] Chap. xxvii. 29; Mal. i. 3; Rom. ix. 12.

NAMES SAME IN *HEBREW* YET DIFFERENT IN *ENGLISH.*

1	Gen. v. 3.	Seth	Sheth	1 Chron. i. 1.
2	—— v. 6.	Enos	Enosh	—— i. 1.
3	—— v. 9.	Cainan	Kenan	—— i. 2.
4	—— v. 15.	Jared	Jered	—— i. 2.
5	—— v. 18.	Enoch	Henoch	—— i. 3.
6	—— v. 21.	Methuselah	Mathushelah	—— i. 3.
7	—— x. 6.	Phut	Put	—— i. 8.
8	—— x. 14.	Philistim	The Philistines	—— i. 12.
9	—— x. 14.	Caphtorim	Caphthorim	—— i. 12.
10	—— x. 16.	Emorite	Amorites	Gen. xv. 16, 21.
11	—— x. 16.	Girgasite	Girgashites	—— xv. 21.
12	—— x. 19, and Jer. xlvii. 5.	Gaza	Azzah	Deut. ii. 23, and Jer. xxv. 20.
13	Gen. x. 22.	Ashur	Asshur	1 Chron. i. 17.
14	—— x. 24.	Salah	Shelah	—— i. 18.
15	—— xiv. 2, 8.	Zeboiim	Zeboim	Deut. xxix. 23.
16	—— xiv. 5; xv. 20.	Rephaims	Giants	—— ii. 20; iii. 11, 13.
17	—— xxv. 15.	Naphish	Nephish	1 Chron. v. 19.
18	—— xxix. 6.	Rachel	Rahel	Jer. xxxi. 15.
19	—— xxxvi. 34.	Temani	The Temanites	1 Chron. i. 45.
20	—— xxxvi. 37.	Saul	Shaul	—— i. 48.
21	—— xxxvii. 25, 28.	Ishmeelites	Ishmaelites	Judg. viii. 24.
22	Exod. i. 11.	Raamses	Rameses	Exod. xii. 37.
23	—— vi. 18.	Izhar	Izehar	Num. iii. 19.
24	—— vi. 19.	Mahali	Mahli	1 Chron. vi. 19.
25	Lev. xviii. 21.	Molech	Moloch	Amos v. 26.
26	Num. xiii. 8, 16.	Oshea	Hoshea	Deut. xxxii. 44.
27	—— xiii. 16.	Jehoshua	Joshua	Num. xiv. 6.
28	—— xxi. 12.	Zared	Zered	Deut. ii. 13.
29	—— xxxii. 3.	Jazer	Jaazar	Num. xxxii. 35.
30	—— xxxiii. 31.	Bene-Jaakan	Children of Jaakan	Deut. x. 6.
31	Deut. iii. 17.	Ashdoth-pisgah	Springs of Pisgah	—— iv. 49.

"Nothing can be more clear than that these *fifty-four* proper names (at least the far greater part of them) should be expressed with the very same letters, in the places where they are now different. In the second list, instances 6, 10, and 13, have been corrected and expressed uniformly in the English Bible printed at Oxford in 1769. And surely the same justice in the translation should be done to the rest of these proper names, and to all others through the Bible; at least, where the original words are now properly the same. Who would not wonder at seeing the same persons named both *Simon* and *Shimon*, *Richard* and *Ricard?* And can we then admit here both *Seth* and *Sheth*, *Rachel* and *Rahel?* Again: whoever could admit (as above) both *Gaza* and *Azzah*, with *Rameses* and *Raamses*, should not object to *London* and *Ondon*, with *Amsterdam* and *Amstradam*. In short, in a history far more interesting than any other, the names of *persons* and *places* should be distinguished accurately, and defined with exact uniformity. And no true critic will think lightly of this advice of Origen, *Contemnenda non est accurata circa* NOMINA *diligentia ei, qui voluerit probe intelligere sanctas literas?* No person who desires thoroughly to understand the sacred writings, should undervalue a scrupulous attention to the proper names."—*Kennicott's* Remarks.

Verse 19. *These* are *the generations of Isaac*] This is the history of Isaac and his family. Here the *sixth* section of the law begins, called תולדת יצחק *toledoth yitschak;* as the *fifth*, called חיי שרה *chaiye Sarah*, which begins with chap. xxiii., ends at the preceding verse.

Verse 21. *Isaac entreated the Lord for his wife*] Isaac and Rebekah had now lived *nineteen* years together without having a child; for he was *forty* years old when he married Rebekah, ver. 20, and he was *threescore* years of age when Jacob and Esau were born, ver. 26. Hence it is evident they had lived *nineteen* years together without having a child.

The form of the original in this place is worthy of notice: Isaac entreated Jehovah, לנכח אשתו *lenochach ishto*, directly, purposely, especially, for his wife. Ainsworth thinks the words imply their *praying together* for this thing; and the rabbins say that "Isaac and Rebekah went on purpose to Mount Moriah, where he had been bound, and prayed together there that they

A. M. 2168.
B. C. 1836.

24 And when her days to be delivered were fulfilled, behold, *there were* twins in her womb.

might have a son." God was pleased to exercise the faith of Isaac previous to the birth of Jacob, as he had exercised that of Abraham previous to his own birth.

Verse 22. *The children struggled together*] יתרצצו *yithrotsatsu, they dashed against* or *bruised each other*, there was a violent agitation, so that the mother was apprehensive both of her own and her children's safety; and, supposing this was an uncommon case, she went to inquire of the Lord, as the good women in the present day would go to consult a surgeon or physician; for intercourse with God is not so common *now*, as it was in those times of great primitive simplicity. There are different opinions concerning the *manner* in which Rebekah *inquired of the Lord*. Some think it was by *faith* and *prayer* simply; others, that she went to *Shem* or *Melchizedek;* but Shem is supposed to have been dead ten years before this time; but as Abraham was yet alive, she might have gone to him, and consulted the Lord through his means. It is most likely that a *prophet* or *priest* was applied to on this occasion. It appears she was in considerable perplexity, hence that imperfect speech, *If so, why am I thus?* the simple meaning of which is probably this; If I must suffer such things, why did I ever wish to have a child? A speech not uncommon to mothers in their first pregnancy.

Verse 23. *Two nations are in thy womb*] "We have," says Bishop Newton, "in the prophecies delivered respecting the sons of Isaac, ample proof that these prophecies were not meant so much of *single persons* as of *whole nations* descended from them; for what was predicted concerning *Esau* and *Jacob* was not verified in *themselves*, but in their *posterity*. The *Edomites* were the offspring of *Esau*, the *Israelites* were of *Jacob;* and who but the Author and Giver of life could foresee that *two children in the womb* would multiply into *two nations?* Jacob had *twelve* sons, and their descendants were all united and incorporated into one nation; and what an overruling providence was it that two nations should arise from the two sons only of Isaac! and that they should be two such *different* nations! The *Edomites* and *Israelites* have been from the beginning two such *different people* in their manners, customs, and religion, as to be at perpetual variance among themselves. The *children struggled together in the womb*, which was an omen of their future disagreement; and when they grew up to manhood, they manifested very different inclinations. Esau was *a cunning hunter*, and delighted in the sports of the field; Jacob was *a plain man, dwelling in tents*—minding his sheep and his cattle. The religion of the Jews is well known; but whatever the Edomites were at first, in process of time they became *idolaters*. When Amaziah king of Judah overthrew them, he brought their gods, and set them up to be his gods. The king of Edom having refused a passage to the Israelites through his territories on their return from Egypt, the history of the Edomites afterwards is little more than the history of their wars with the Jews.

The one *people shall be stronger than* the other *people*] The same author continues to observe, that "for some time the family of Esau was the more powerful of the two, there having been *dukes* and *kings* in Edom before there was any king in Israel; but David and his captains made an entire conquest of the *Edomites*, slew several thousands of them, and compelled the rest to become tributaries, and planted garrisons among them to secure their obedience. In this state of *servitude* they continued about *one hundred and fifty* years, without a king of their own, being governed by deputies or viceroys appointed by the kings of Judah; but in the days of Jehoram they revolted, recovered their liberties, and set up a king of their own. Afterwards Amaziah, king of Judah, gave them a total overthrow in the valley of Salt; and Azariah took *Elath*, a commodious harbour on the Red Sea, from them. Judas Maccabeus also attacked and defeated them with a loss of more than *twenty thousand* at two different times, and took their chief city *Hebron*. At last *Hyrcanus* his nephew took other cities from them, and reduced them to the necessity of leaving their country or embracing the Jewish religion; on which they submitted to be *circumcised*, and become proselytes to the Jewish religion, and were ever afterwards incorporated into the Jewish Church and nation."

The elder shall serve the younger.] "This passage," says Dr. Dodd, "serves for a key to explain the *ninth* chapter of the Epistle to the Romans, where the words are quoted; for it proves to a demonstration that this cannot be meant of God's arbitrary predestination of particular persons to eternal happiness or misery, without any regard to their merit or demerit—a doctrine which some have most impiously fathered on God, who is the best of beings, and who cannot possibly hate, far less absolutely doom to misery, any creature that he has made: but that it means only his bestowing greater external favours, or, if you please, higher opportunities for knowing and doing their duty, upon some men, than he does upon others; and that merely according to his own wise purpose, without any regard to their merits or demerits, as having a right to confer greater or smaller degrees or perfection on whom he pleases."

The doctrine of *unconditional* predestination to eternal life and eternal death cannot be supported by the example of God's dealings with *Esau* and *Jacob*, or with the *Edomites* and *Israelites*. After long reprobation the *Edomites* were incorporated among the Jews, and have ever since been undistinguishable members in the Jewish Church. The *Jews*, on the contrary, the *elect of God*, have been cut off and reprobated, and continue so to this day. If a time should ever come when the *Jews* shall *all* believe in Christ Jesus, which is a general opinion, then the *Edomites*, which are now absorbed among them, shall also become the *elect*. And even now Isaac finds *both his children* within the pale of the Jewish Church, equally entitled to the promises of salvation by Christ Jesus, of whom he was the most expressive and the most illustrious *type*. See the account of Abraham's offering, chap. xxii.

Verse 24. There were *twins*] תומם *thomim*, from which comes *Thomas*, properly interpreted by the word

A. M. 2168.
B. C. 1836.

25 And the first came out red,
[e] all over like a hairy garment;
and they called his name Esau.
26 And after that came his brother out, and
[f] his hand took hold on Esau's heel; and [g] his
name was called Jacob: and Isaac *was* threescore years old when she bare them.
27 And the boys grew: and Esau was [h] a
cunning hunter, a man of the field; and Jacob
was [i] a plain man, [k] dwelling in tents.
28 And Isaac loved Esau, because [l] he did
[m] eat of *his* venison: [n] but Rebekah loved
Jacob.

A. M. cir. 2199.
B. C. cir. 1805.

29 And Jacob sod pottage:
and Esau came from the field,
and he *was* faint.
30 And Esau said to Jacob, Feed me, I
pray thee, [o] with that same red *pottage*; for
I *am* faint: therefore was his name called
[p] Edom.
31 And Jacob said, Sell me this day thy
birthright.
32 And Esau said, Behold, I *am* [q] at the
point to die; and what profit shall this birthright do to me?
33 And Jacob said, Swear to me this day;

[e] Chap. xxvii. 11, 16, 23.——[f] Hos. xii. 3.——[g] Chap. xxvii. 36.——[h] Chap. xxvii. 3, 5.——[i] Job i. 1, 8; ii. 3; Psa. xxxvii. 37. [k] Heb. xi. 9.

[l] Heb. *venison* was *in his mouth*.——[m] Chap. xxvii. 19, 25, 31. [n] Chap. xxvii. 6.——[o] Heb. *with that red*, with that *red* pottage. [p] That is, *red*.——[q] Heb. *going to die*.

Διδυμος, *Didymus*, which signifies a *twin;* so the first person who was called Thomas or Didymus, we may take for granted, had this name from the circumstance of his being a *twin*.

Verse 25. *Red, all over like a hairy garment*] This simply means that he was covered all over with red hair or down; and that this must be intended here is sufficiently evident from another part of his history, where Rebekah, in order to make her favourite son Jacob pass for his brother Esau, was obliged to take the skins of kids, and put them upon his hands and on the smooth part of his neck.

They called his name Esau.] It is difficult to assign the proper meaning of the original עשו *esau* or *esav;* if we derive it from עשה *asah* it must signify *made*, *performed*, and, according to some, *perfected;* عسا *esa* in Arabic signifies to *make firm* or *hard*, and also to *come to man's estate*, to *grow old*. Probably he had this name from his appearing to be more *perfect*, *robust*, &c., than his brother.

Verse 26. *His name was called Jacob*] יעקב *Yaacob*, from עקב *akab*, to *defraud*, *deceive*, to *supplant*, i. e., to overthrow a person by *tripping up his heels*. Hence this name was given to Jacob, because it was found he had laid hold on his brother's heel, which was emblematical of his supplanting Esau, and defrauding him of his birthright.

Verse 27. *A man of the field*] איש שדה *ish sadeh*, one who supported himself and family by *hunting* and by *agriculture*.

Jacob was *a plain man*] איש תם *ish tam*, a perfect or upright man; *dwelling in tents*—subsisting by breeding and tending cattle, which was considered in those early times the most *perfect* employment; and in this sense the word תם *tam*, should be here understood, as in its *moral* meaning it certainly could not be applied to Jacob till after his name was changed, after which time only his character stands fair and unblemished. See chap. xxxii. 26–30.

Verse 28. *Isaac loved Esau—but Rebekah loved Jacob.*] This is an early proof of unwarrantable parental attachment to one child in preference to another. *Isaac loved Esau*, and *Rebekah loved Jacob;* and in consequence of this the interests of the family were divided, and the house set in opposition to itself. The fruits of this unreasonable and foolish attachment were afterwards seen in a long catalogue of both *natural* and *moral* evils among the descendants of both families.

Verse 29. *Sod pottage*] זיד נזיד *yazed nazid*, he boiled a boiling; and this we are informed, ver. 34, was of עדשים *adashim*, what the Septuagint render φακος, and we, following them and the Vulgate *lens*, translate *lentiles*, a sort of pulse. Dr. Shaw casts some light on this passage, speaking of the inhabitants of Barbary. "Beans, lentiles, kidney beans, and *garvancos*," says he, "are the chiefest of their pulse kind: beans, when boiled and stewed with oil and garlic, are the principal food of persons of all distinctions; lentiles are dressed in the same manner with beans, dissolving easily into a mass, and making a pottage of a *chocolate colour*. This we find was the *red pottage* which Esau, from thence called *Edom*, exchanged for his *birthright*." *Shaw's* Travels, p. 140, 4to. edit.

Verse 30. *I am faint*] It appears from the whole of this transaction, that Esau was so completely exhausted by fatigue that he must have perished had he not obtained some immediate refreshment. He had been either hunting or labouring in the field, and was now returning for the purpose of getting some food, but had been so exhausted that his strength utterly failed before he had time to make the necessary preparations.

Verse 31. *Sell me this day thy birthright.*] What the בכרה *bechorah* or birthright was, has greatly divided both ancient and modern commentators. It is generally supposed that the following rights were attached to the primogeniture: 1. Authority and superiority over the rest of the family. 2. A double portion of the paternal inheritance. 3. The peculiar benediction of the father. 4. The priesthood, previous to its establishment in the family of Aaron. *Calmet* controverts most of these rights, and with apparent reason, and seems to think that the double portion of the paternal inheritance was the only incontestable right which the first-born possessed; the others were such as were rather *conceded* to the first-born, than fixed by any law in the family. However this may be, it appears, 1. That the first-born were peculiarly consecrated to God, Exod. xxii. 29. 2. Were next in

a

A. M. cir. 2199. B. C. cir. 1805.

and he sware unto him: and [r] he
sold his birthright unto Jacob.
34 Then Jacob gave Esau bread and pottage
of lentiles; and [s] he did eat and
drink, and rose up, and went his
way: thus Esau despised *his* birthright.

[r] Heb. xii. 16.

[s] Eccles. viii. 15; Isa. xxii. 13; 1 Cor. xv. 32.

honour to their parents, Gen. xlix. 3. 3. Had a double portion of their father's goods, Deut. xxi. 17. 4. Succeeded him in the government of the family or kingdom, 2 Chron. xxi. 3. 5. Had the sole right of conducting the service of God, both at the tabernacle and temple; and hence the tribe of Levi, which was taken in lieu of the *first-born*, had the sole right of administration in the service of God, Num. viii. 14–18; and hence we may presume, had originally a right to the *priesthood* previous to the giving of the law; but however this might have been, afterwards the priesthood is never reckoned among the privileges of the first-born.

That the birthright was a matter of very great importance, there can be no room to doubt; and that it was a *transferable* property, the transaction here sufficiently proves.

Verse 34. *Pottage of lentiles*] See on ver. 29.

Thus Esau despised his *birthright.*] On this account the apostle, Heb. xii. 16, calls Esau a *profane person*, because he had, by this act, alienated from himself and family those spiritual offices connected with the rights of primogeniture. While we condemn Esau for this bad action, (for he should rather have perished than have alienated this right,) and while we consider it as a proof that his mind was little affected with Divine or spiritual things, what shall we say of his most unnatural brother Jacob, who refused to let him have a morsel of food to preserve him from death, unless he gave him up his birthright? Surely he who *bought* it, in such circumstances, was as *bad* as he who *sold* it. Thus Jacob verified his right to the name of *supplanter*, a name which in its first imposition appears to have had no other object in view than the circumstance of his *catching his brother by the heel*; but all his subsequent conduct proved that it was truly descriptive of the qualities of his mind, as his whole life, till the time his name was changed, (and then he had a *change of nature*,) was a tissue of cunning and deception, the principles of which had been very early instilled into him by a mother whose regard for truth and righteousness appears to have been very superficial. See on chap. xxvii.

The death of Abraham, recorded in this chapter, naturally calls to mind the virtues and excellences of this extraordinary man. His *obedience* to the call of God, and *faith* in his promises, stand supereminent. No *wonders*, *signs*, or *miraculous displays* of the great and terrible God, as Israel required in Egypt, were used or were necessary to cause Abraham to believe and obey. He left his own land, not knowing *where* he was going, or for what purpose God had called him to remove. Exposed to various hardships, in danger of losing his life, and of witnessing the violation of his wife, he still obeyed and went on; courageous, humane, and disinterested, he cheerfully risked his life for the welfare of others; and, contented with having rescued the captives and avenged the oppressed, he refused to accept even the spoils he had taken from the enemy whom his skill and valour had vanquished. At the same time he considers the excellency of the power to be of God, and acknowledges this by giving to *him* the tenth of those spoils of which he would reserve nothing for his private use. His *obedience* to God, *in offering up his son Isaac*, we have already seen and admired; together with the *generosity* of his temper, and that *respectful decency* of *conduct* towards superiors and inferiors for which he was so peculiarly remarkable; see on chap. xxiii. Without *disputing* with his Maker, or *doubting* in his heart, he credited every thing that God had spoken; *hence he always walked in a plain way*. The *authority of God* was always sufficient for Abraham; he did not weary himself to find reasons for any line of conduct which he knew God had prescribed; it was his duty to obey; the success and the event he left with God. His obedience was as *prompt* as it was *complete*. As soon as he hears the voice of God, he girds himself to his work! *Not a moment is lost!* How rare is such conduct! But should not *we* do likewise? The present moment and its duties are ours; every past moment was once present; every future will be present; and, while we are thinking on the subject, the present is *past*, for life is made up of the *past* and the *present*. Are our past moments the cause of deep regret and humiliation? Then let us use the present so as *not* to increase this lamentable cause of our distresses. In other words, let us now *believe—love—obey*. Regardless of all consequences, let us, like Abraham, follow the *directions* of God's *word*, and the *openings* of his *providence*, and leave all events to Him who *doth all things well*.

See to what a state of moral excellence the grace of God can exalt a character, when there is simple, implicit faith, and prompt obedience! Abraham *walked before God*, and *Abraham was perfect*. Perhaps no human being ever exhibited a fairer, fuller portrait of the *perfect man* than Abraham. The more I consider the character of this most amiable patriarch, the more I think the saying of Calmet justifiable: "In the life of Abraham," says he, "we find an epitome of the whole *law of nature*, of the *written law*, and of the *Gospel of Christ*. He has manifested in his own person those virtues, for which reason and philosophy could scarcely find out names, when striving to sketch the character of their *sophist*—wise or perfect man. St. Ambrose very properly observes that 'philosophy itself could not equal, in its descriptions and wishes, what was exemplified by this great man in the whole of his conduct.' *Magnus plane vir, quem votis suis philosophia non potuit æquare; denique minus est quod illa finxit quam quod ille gessit.* The LAW which God gave to Moses, and in which he has proposed the great duties of the law of nature, seems to be a copy of the life of Abraham. This patriarch, without being under the law, has performed the most essential duties it

requires; and as to the GOSPEL, its grand *object* was that on which he had fixed his eye—that JESUS whose day he rejoiced to see; and as to its *spirit* and *design*, they were wondrously exemplified in that faith which was imputed to him for righteousness, receiving that grace which conformed his whole heart and life to the will of his Maker, and enabled him to persevere unto death. 'Abraham,' says the writer of Ecclesiasticus, xliv. 20, &c., 'was a great father of many people: in glory was there none like unto him, who kept the law of the Most High, and was in covenant with him. He established the covenant in his flesh, and when he was tried he was found faithful.'" See *Calmet*.

As a son, as a husband, as a father, as a neighbour, as a sovereign, and above all as a *man of God*, he stands unrivalled; so that under the most exalted and perfect of all dispensations, the Gospel of Jesus Christ, he is proposed and recommended as the *model* and *pattern* according to which the faith, obedience, and perseverance of the followers of the Messiah are to be formed. Reader, while you admire the *man*, do not forget the *God* that made him so great, so good, and so useful. Even Abraham had nothing but what he had received; from the free unmerited mercy of God proceeded all *his* excellences; but he was a *worker together with God*, and therefore *did not receive the grace of God in vain*. Go thou, believe, love, obey, and persevere in like manner.

CHAPTER XXVI.

A famine in the land obliges Isaac to leave Beer-sheba and go to Gerar, 1. *God appears to him, and warns him not to go to Egypt,* 2. *Renews the promises to him which he had made to his father Abraham,* 3–5. *Isaac dwells at Gerar,* 6. *Being questioned concerning Rebekah, and fearing to lose his life on her account, he calls her his* sister, 7. *Abimelech the king, discovers by certain familiarities which he had noticed between Isaac and Rebekah, that she was his wife,* 8. *Calls Isaac and reproaches him for his insincerity,* 9, 10. *He gives a strict command to all his people not to molest either Isaac or his wife,* 11. *Isaac applies himself to husbandry and breeding of cattle, and has a great increase,* 12–14. *Is envied by the Philistines, who stop up the wells he had digged,* 15. *Is desired by Abimelech to remove,* 16. *He obeys, and fixes his tent in the valley of Gerar,* 17. *Opens the wells dug in the days of Abraham, which the Philistines had stopped up,* 18. *Digs the well,* Ezek. 19, 20; *and the well* Sitnah, 21; *and the well* Rehoboth, 22. *Returns to Beer-sheba,* 23. *God appears to him, and renews his promises,* 24. *He builds an altar there, pitches his tent, and digs a well,* 25. *Abimelech, Ahuzzath, and Phichol, visit him,* 26. *Isaac accuses them of unkindness,* 27. *They beg him to make a covenant with them,* 28, 29. *He makes them a feast, and they bind themselves to each other by an oath,* 30, 31. *The well dug by Isaac's servants* (ver. 25) *called* Shebah, 33. *Esau, at forty years of age, marries two wives of the Hittites,* 34; *at which Isaac and Rebekah are grieved,* 35.

A. M. cir. 2200. B. C. cir. 1804.

AND there was a famine in
the land, beside [a] the first
famine that was in the days of Abraham.
And Isaac went unto [b] Abimelech, king of the
Philistines, unto Gerar.
2 And the LORD appeared unto him, and
said, Go not down into Egypt; dwell in
[c] the land which I shall tell
thee of:
3 [d] Sojourn in this land, and [e] I will be with
thee, and [f] will bless thee; for unto thee, and
unto thy seed, [g] I will give all these countries;
and I will perform [h] the oath which I sware
unto Abraham thy father:

[a] Chap. xii. 10.——[b] Chap. xx. 2.——[c] Chap. xii. 1.——[d] Chap. xx. 1; Psa. xxxix. 12; Heb. xi. 9.——[e] Chap. xxviii. 15.——[f] Chap. xii. 1.——[g] Chap. xiii. 15; xv. 18.——[h] Chap. xxii. 16; Psa. cv. 9.

NOTES ON CHAP. XXVI.

Verse 1. *There was a famine*] *When* this happened we cannot tell; it appears to have been after the death of Abraham. Concerning the *first famine*, see chap. xii. 10.

Abimelech] As we know not the time when the famine happened, so we cannot tell whether this was the same Abimelech, Phichol, &c., which are mentioned chap. xx. 1, &c., or the sons or other descendants of these persons.

Verse 2. *Go not down into Egypt*] As Abraham had taken refuge in that country, it is probable that Isaac was preparing to go thither also; and God, foreseeing that he would there meet with trials, &c., which might prove fatal to his peace or to his piety, warns him not to fulfil his intention.

Verse 3. *Sojourn in this land*] In Gerar, whither he had gone, ver. 1, and where we find he settled, ver. 6, though the *land of Canaan* in general might be here intended. That there were serious and important reasons why Isaac should not go to Egypt, we may be fully assured, though they be not assigned here; it is probable that even Isaac himself was not informed why he should not go down to Egypt. I have already supposed that God saw trials in his way which he might not have been able to bear. While a man acknowledges God in all his ways, he will direct all his steps, though he may not choose to give him the reasons of the workings of his providence. Abraham might go safely to Egypt, Isaac might not; in firmness and decision of character there was a wide difference between the two men.

A. M. cir. 2200.
B. C. cir. 1804.

4 And [i] I will make thy seed to
multiply as the stars of heaven,
and will give unto thy seed all these countries;
[k] and in thy seed shall all the nations of the
earth be blessed;
5 [l] Because that Abraham obeyed my voice,
and kept my charge, my commandments, my
statutes, and my laws.
6 And Isaac dwelt in Gerar.
7 And the men of the place asked *him* of
his wife; and [m] he said, She *is* my sister: for
[n] he feared to say, *She is* my wife; lest, *said*
he, the men of the place should kill me for
Rebekah; because she [o] *was* fair to look upon.
8 And it came to pass, when he had been
there a long time, that Abimelech king of the
Philistines looked out at a window, and saw,
and behold, Isaac *was* sporting
with Rebekah his wife.
9 And Abimelech called Isaac, and said,
Behold, of a surety she *is* thy wife; and how
saidst thou, She *is* my sister? And Isaac
said unto him, Because I said, Lest I die
for her.
10 And Abimelech said, What *is* this thou
hast done unto us? one of the people might
lightly have lien with thy wife, and [p] thou
shouldest have brought guiltiness upon us.
11 And Abimelech charged all *his* people,
saying, He that [q] toucheth this man or his
wife shall surely be put to death.
12 Then Isaac sowed in that land, and [r] received in the same year [s] a hundred-fold: and
the LORD [t] blessed him:

A. M. cir. 2200.
B. C. cir. 1804.

[i] Chap. xv. 5; xxii. 17.——[k] Chap. xii. 3; xxii. 18.——[l] Chap. xxii. 16, 18.——[m] Chap. xii. 13; xx. 2, 13.——[n] Proverbs xxix. 25.

[o] Chap. xxiv. 16.——[p] Chap. xx. 9.——[q] Psa. cv. 15.——[r] Heb. *found*.——[s] Matt. xiii. 8; Mark iv. 8.——[t] Ver. 3; chap. xxiv. 1, 35; Job xlii. 12.

Verse 4. *I will make thy seed—as the stars of heaven*]. A promise often repeated to Abraham, and which has been most amply fulfilled both in its *literal* and *spiritual* sense.

Verse 5. *Abraham obeyed my voice*] מימרי *meimeri*, my WORD. See chap. xv. 1.

My charge] משמרתי *mishmarti*, from שמר *shamar*, he kept, observed, &c., the *ordinances* or *appointments* of God. These were always of two kinds: 1. Such as tended to promote *moral improvement*, the increase of piety, the improvement of the age, &c. And 2. Such as were *typical* of the promised seed, and the salvation which was to come by him. For *commandments, statutes*, &c., the reader is particularly desired to refer to Lev. xvi. 15, &c., where these things are all explained in the alphabetical order of the Hebrew words.

Verse 7. *He said, She* is *my sister*] It is very strange that in the same place, and in similar circumstances, Isaac should have denied *his wife*, precisely as his father had done before him! It is natural to ask, Did Abraham never mention this circumstance to his son? Probably he did *not*, as he was justly ashamed of his weakness on the occasion—the only blot in his character; the son, therefore, not being forewarned, was not armed against the temptation. It may not be well in general for parents to tell their children of their former failings or vices, as this might lessen their authority or respect, and the children might make a bad use of it in extenuation of their own sins. But there are certain cases, which, from the nature of their circumstances, may often occur, where a candid acknowledgment, with suitable advice, may prevent those children from repeating the evil; but this should be done with great delicacy and caution, lest even the advice itself should serve as an incentive to the evil. I had not known lust, says St. Paul, if the law had not said, *Thou shalt not covet*. Isaac could not say of Rebekah, as Abraham had done of Sarah, *She is my sister*; in the case of Abraham this was *literally true*; it was not so in the case of Isaac, for Rebekah was only his *cousin*. Besides, though relatives, in the Jewish forms of speaking, are often called *brothers* and *sisters*, and the thing may be perfectly proper when this use of the terms is generally known and allowed, yet nothing of this kind can be pleaded *here* in behalf of Isaac; for he intended that the *Gerarites* should understand him in the proper sense of the term, and consequently have no suspicion that she was his *wife*. We have already seen that the proper definition of a lie is *any word spoken with the intention to deceive*. See chap. xx. 12.

Verse 8. *Isaac was sporting with Rebekah his wife.*] Whatever may be the precise meaning of the word, it evidently implies that there were liberties taken and freedoms used on the occasion, which were not lawful but between man and wife.

Verse 10. *Thou shouldest have brought guiltiness upon us.*] It is likely that Abimelech might have had some knowledge of God's intentions concerning the family of Abraham, and that it must be kept free from all impure and alien mixtures; and that consequently, had he or any of his people taken Rebekah, the Divine judgments might have fallen upon the land. Abimelech was a good and holy man; and he appears to have considered adultery as a grievous and destructive crime.

Verse 11. *He that toucheth*] He who injures Isaac or defiles Rebekah shall certainly die for it. Death was the punishment for adultery among the Canaanites, Philistines, and Hebrews. See chap. xxxviii. 24.

Verse 12. *Isaac sowed in that land*] Being now perfectly free from the fear of evil, he betakes himself to agricultural and pastoral pursuits, in which he has the especial blessing of God, so that his property becomes greatly increased.

A hundred-fold] מאה שערים *meah shearim*, literally, "A hundred-fold of barley;" and so the Septuagint, ἑκατοστευουσαν κριθην. Perhaps such a crop of this grain was a *rare* occurrence in Gerar. The words,

A. M. cir. 2200.
B. C. cir. 1804.

13 And the man [u] waxed great,
and [v] went forward, and grew
until he became very great;
14 For he had possession of flocks, and
possession of herds, and great store of [w] servants: and the Philistines [x] envied him.
15 For all the wells [y] which his father's
servants had digged in the days of Abraham
his father, the Philistines had stopped them,
and filled them with earth.
16 And Abimelech said unto Isaac, Go from
us; for [z] thou art much mightier than we.
17 And Isaac departed thence, and pitched
his tent in the valley of Gerar, and dwelt there.
18 And Isaac digged again the wells of
water, which they had digged in the days of
Abraham his father; for the Philistines had
stopped them after the death of Abraham:
[a] and he called their names after the names
by which his father had called
them.
19 And Isaac's servants digged in the
valley, and found there a well of [b] springing
water.
20 And the herdmen of Gerar [c] did strive
with Isaac's herdmen, saying, The water *is*
ours: and he called the name of the well
[d] Esek; because they strove with him.
21 And they digged another well, and strove
for that also: and he called the name of it
[e] Sitnah.
22 And he removed from thence, and digged
another well; and for that they strove not:
and he called the name of it [f] Rehoboth; and
he said, For now the LORD hath made room
for us, and we shall [g] be fruitful in the land.
23 And he went up from thence to Beer-
sheba.

[u] Chap. xxiv. 35; Psa. cxii. 3; Prov. x. 22.——[v] Heb. *went going*.——[w] Or, *husbandry*.——[x] Chap. xxxvii. 11; Eccles. iv. 4.——[y] Chap. xxi. 30.——[z] Exod. i. 9.——[a] Chap. xxi. 31.

[b] Heb. *living*.——[c] Chap. xxi. 25.——[d] That is, *Contention*.——[e] That is, *Hatred*.——[f] That is, *Room*.——[g] Chap. xvii. 6; xxviii. 3; xli. 52; Exod. i. 7.

however, may be taken in a general way, as signifying *a very great increase;* so they are used by our Lord in the parable of the sower.

Verse 13. *The man waxed great*] There is a strange and observable recurrence of the *same term* in the original: ויגדל האיש וילך הלוך וגדל עד כי גדל מאד *vaiyigdal haish vaiyelech haloch vegadel ad ki gadal meod, And the man was* GREAT; *and he went, going on, and was* GREAT, *until that he was exceeding* GREAT. How *simple* is this language, and yet how forcible!

Verse 14. *He had possession of flocks*] He who blessed him in the increase of his *fields* blessed him also in the increase of his *flocks;* and as he had extensive possessions, so he must have many *hands* to manage such concerns: therefore it is added, *he had great store of servants*—he had many domestics, some born in his house, and others purchased by his money.

Verse 15. *For all the wells—the Philistines had stopped them*] In such countries a good well was a great acquisition; and hence in predatory wars it was usual for either party to fill the wells with earth or sand, in order to distress the enemy. The filling up the wells in this case was a most unprincipled transaction, as they had pledged themselves to Abraham, by a solemn oath, not to injure each other in this or any other respect. See chap. xxi. 25–31.

Verse 16. *Go from us; for thou art much mightier than we.*] This is the first instance on record of what was termed among the Greeks *ostracism;* i. e., the banishment of a person from the state, of whose power, influence, or riches, the people were jealous. There is a remarkable saying of Bacon on this subject, which seems to intimate that he had this very circumstance under his eye: "Public *envy* is an *ostracism* that eclipseth men when they grow *too great*." On this same principle Pharaoh oppressed the Israelites. The Philistines appear to have been jealous of Isaac's growing prosperity, and to have considered it, not as a due reward of his industry and holiness, but as their individual loss, as though his gain was at their expense; therefore they resolved to drive him out, and take his well-cultivated ground, &c., to themselves, and compelled Abimelech to dismiss him, who gave this reason for it, עצמת ממנו *atsamta mimmennu, Thou hast obtained much wealth among us,* and my people are envious of thee. Is not this the better translation? for it can hardly be supposed that Isaac was "*mightier*" than the king of whole tribes.

Verse 18. *In the days of Abraham*] Instead of בימי *bimey,* in the days, Houbigant contends we should read עבדי *abdey,* servants. Isaac digged again the wells which the *servants* of Abraham his father had digged. This reading is supported by the *Samaritan, Septuagint, Syriac,* and *Vulgate;* and it is probably the true one.

Verse 19. *A well of springing water.*] באר מים חיים *beer mayim chaiyim, A well of living waters.* This is the oriental phrase for a *spring,* and this is its meaning both in the Old and New Testaments: Lev. xiv. 5, 50; xv. 30; Num. xix. 17; Cant. iv. 15. See also John iv. 10–14; vii. 38; Rev. xxi. 6; xxii. 1. And by these scriptures we find that an *unfailing spring* was an emblem of the *graces* and *influences* of the *Spirit of God.*

Verse 21. *They digged another well*] Never did any man more implicitly follow the Divine command, *Resist not evil,* than Isaac; whenever he found that his work was likely to be a subject of strife and contention, he gave place, and rather chose to suffer wrong than to have his own peace of mind disturbed. Thus he overcame *evil* with *good.*

A. M. cir. 2200. B. C. cir. 1804.

24 And the LORD appeared unto him the same night, and said, [h] I *am* the God of Abraham thy father: [i] fear not, for [k] I *am* with thee, and will bless thee, and multiply thy seed for my servant Abraham's sake.

25 And he [l] builded an altar there, and [m] called upon the name of the LORD, and pitched his tent there: and there Isaac's servants digged a well.

26 Then Abimelech went to him from Gerar, and Ahuzzath one of his friends, [n] and Phichol the chief captain of his army.

27 And Isaac said unto them, Wherefore come ye to me, seeing [o] ye hate me, and have [p] sent me away from you?

28 And they said, [q] We saw certainly that the LORD [r] was with thee: and we said, Let there be now an oath betwixt us, *even* betwixt us and thee, and let us make a covenant with thee;

29 [s] That thou wilt do us no hurt, as we have not touched thee, and as we have done unto thee nothing but good, and have sent thee away in peace: [t] thou *art* now the blessed of the LORD.

30 [u] And he made them a feast, and they did eat and drink.

31 And they rose up betimes in the morning, and [v] sware one to another: and Isaac sent them away, and they departed from him in peace.

32 And it came to pass the same day, that Isaac's servants came, and told him concerning the well which they had digged, and said unto him, We have found water.

33 And he called it [w] Shebah: [x] therefore the name of the city *is* [y] Beer-sheba unto this day.

34 [z] And Esau was forty years old when he took to wife Judith the daughter of Beeri the

[h] Chap. xvii. 7; xxiv. 12; xxviii. 13; Exod. iii. 6; Acts vii. 32.——[i] Chap. xv. 1.——[k] Ver. 3, 4.——[l] Chap. xii. 7; xiii. 18.——[m] Psa. cxvi. 17.——[n] Chap. xxi. 22.——[o] Judg. xi. 7.——[p] Ver. 16.——[q] Heb. *seeing we saw.*

[r] Chap. xxi. 22, 23.——[s] Heb. *if thou shalt,* &c.——[t] Chapter xxiv. 31; Psa. cxv. 15.——[u] Chap. xix. 3.——[v] Chap. xxi. 31.——[w] That is, *an oath.*——[x] Chap. xxi. 31.——[y] That is, *the well of the oath.*——[z] Chap. xxxvi. 2.

Verse 24. *The Lord appeared unto him*] He needed especial encouragement when insulted and outraged by the Philistines; for having returned to the place where his noble father had lately died, the remembrance of his *wrongs*, and the remembrance of his *loss*, could not fail to afflict his mind; and God immediately appears to comfort and support him in his trials, by a renewal of all his promises.

Verse 25. *Builded an altar there*] That he might have a *place* for God's worship, as well as a *place* for himself and family to dwell in.

And called upon the name of the Lord] And invoked in the name of Jehovah. See on chap. xii. 8; xiii. 15.

Verse 26. *Abimelech went to him*] When a man's ways please God, he makes even his enemies to be at peace with him; so Isaac experienced on this occasion. Whether this was the same Abimelech and Phichol mentioned chap. xxi. 22, we cannot tell; it is possible both might have been now alive, provided we suppose them *young* in the days of Abraham; but it is more likely that *Abimelech* was a general name of the Gerarite kings, and that *Phichol* was a name of *office*.

Ahuzzath] The *Targum* translates this word *a company*, not considering it as a proper name: "Abimelech and Phichol came with a *company* of their friends." The *Septuagint* calls him Οχοζαθ ὁ νυμφαγωγος, *Ochozath, the paranymph*, he who conducts the bride to the bridegroom's house. Could we depend on the correctness of this version, we might draw the following curious conclusions from it: 1. That this was the *son* of that Abimelech the friend of Abraham. 2. That he had been *lately married*, and on this journey brings with him his confidential friend, to whom he had lately intrusted the care of his spouse.

Verse 27. *Seeing ye hate me*] He was justified in thinking thus, because if *they* did not injure him, they had connived at their servants doing it.

Verse 28. *Let there be now an oath betwixt us*] Let us make a covenant by which we shall be mutually bound, and let it be ratified in the most solemn manner.

Verse 30. *He made them a feast*] Probably on the *sacrifice* that was offered on the occasion of making this covenant. This was a common custom.

Verse 31. *They rose up betimes*] Early rising was general among the primitive inhabitants of the world, and this was one cause which contributed greatly to their *health* and *longevity*.

Verse 33. *He called it Shebah*] This was probably the *same well* which was called *Beer-sheba* in the time of Abraham, which the Philistines had filled up, and which the servants of Isaac had reopened. The same name is therefore given to it which it had before, with the addition of the *emphatic* letter ה *he*, by which its signification became *extended*, so that now it signified not merely an *oath* or *full*, but *satisfaction* and *abundance*.

The name of the city is *Beer-sheba*] This name was given to it a hundred years before this time; but as the *well* from which it had this name originally was closed up by the Philistines, probably the name of the place was *abolished* with the well; when therefore Isaac reopened the well, he restored the ancient name of the place.

Verse 34. *He took to wife—the daughter &c.*] It

A. M. cir. 2200. B. C. cir. 1801. Hittite, and Bashemath the daughter of Elon the Hittite:

35 Which [a] were [b] a grief of mind unto Isaac and to Rebekah. A. M. cir. 2200. B. C. cir. 1801.

[a] Chap. xxvii. 46; xxviii. 1, 8.

[b] Heb. *bitterness of spirit.*

is very likely that the wives taken by Esau were daughters of *chiefs* among the Hittites, and by this union he sought to increase and strengthen his secular power and influence.

Verse 35. *Which were a grief of mind*] Not the *marriage*, though that was improper, but the *persons;* they, by their perverse and evil ways, brought bitterness into the hearts of Isaac and Rebekah. The Targum of *Jonathan ben Uzziel*, and that of *Jerusalem*, say they were addicted to idol worship, and rebelled against and would not hearken to the instructions either of Isaac or Rebekah. From *Canaanites* a different conduct could not be reasonably expected. Esau was far from being *spiritual*, and his wives were wholly *carnal*.

The same reflections which were suggested by Abraham's conduct in denying his wife in Egypt and Gerar, will apply to that of Isaac; but the case of Isaac was much less excusable than that of Abraham. The latter told no *falsity;* he only through fear *suppressed a part of the truth*.

1. A good man has a right to expect God's blessing on his honest industry. Isaac sowed, and received a hundred-fold, and he had possession of flocks, &c., for the Lord blessed him. *Worldly men*, if they pray at all, ask for *temporal* things: "What shall we eat? what shall we drink? and wherewithal shall we be clothed?" Most of the truly religious people go into another extreme; they forget the *body*, and ask only for the *soul!* and yet there are "things requisite and necessary as well for the body as the soul," and things which are only at God's disposal. The body lives for the soul's sake; its life and comfort are in many respects essentially requisite to the salvation of the soul; and therefore the things necessary for its support should be earnestly asked from the God of all grace, the Father of bounty and providence. *Ye have not because ye ask not*, may be said to many poor, afflicted religious people; and they are afraid to ask lest it should appear mercenary, or that they sought their portion in this life. They should be better taught. Surely to none of these will God give a *stone* if they ask *bread:* he who is so liberal of his heavenly blessings will not withhold earthly ones, which are of infinitely less consequence. Reader, expect God's blessing on thy honest industry; pray for it, and believe that God does not love *thee* less, who hast taken refuge in the same hope, than he loved Isaac. Plead not only his promises, but plead on the precedents he has set before thee. "Lord, thou didst so and so to Abraham, to Isaac, to Jacob, and to others who trusted in thee; bless *my* field, bless *my* flocks, prosper *my* labour, that I may be able to provide *things honest* in the sight of all men, and have something to dispense to those who are in want." And will not God hear such prayers? Yea, and answer them too, for he does not willingly afflict the children of men. And we may rest assured that there is more affliction and poverty in the world than either the justice or providence of God requires. There are, however, many who owe their poverty to their want of diligence and economy; they sink down into indolence, and forget that word, *Whatsoever thy hand findeth to do, do it with thy might;* nor do they consider that by idleness a man is clothed with rags. Be diligent in business and fervent in spirit, and God will withhold from thee no manner of thing that is good.

2. From many examples we find that the wealth of the primitive inhabitants of the world did not consist in *gold*, *silver*, or *precious stones*, but principally in *flocks* of useful cattle, and the produce of the field. With *precious metals* and *precious stones* they were not *unacquainted*, and the former were sometimes used in purchases, as we have already seen in the case of Abraham buying a field from the children of Heth. But the blessings which God promises are such as spring from the soil. *Isaac sowed in the land, and had possessions of flocks and herds, and great store of servants*, ver. 12–14. *Commerce*, by which nations and individuals so *suddenly* rise and as suddenly fall, had not been then invented; every man was obliged to acquire property by honest and persevering labour, or be destitute. *Lucky hits*, fortunate *speculations*, and adventurous *risks*, could then have no place; the *field* must be *tilled*, the *herds watched* and *fed*, and the proper *seasons* for *ploughing*, *sowing*, *reaping*, and *laying up*, be carefully *regarded* and *improved*. No man, therefore, could grow rich by *accident*. *Isaac waxed great, and went forward, and grew until he became very great*, ver. 13. *Speculation* was of no use, for it could have no object; and consequently many incitements to *knavery* and to *idleness*, that bane of the physical and moral health of the body and soul of man, could not show themselves. Happy times! when every man wrought with his hands, and God particularly blessed his honest industry. As he had no *luxuries*, he had no *unnatural* and *factitious wants*, few diseases, and a *long life*.

O fortunatos nimium, sua si bona norint,
Agricolas!————

O thrice happy husbandmen! did they but know their own mercies.

But has not what is termed *commerce* produced the reverse of all this? A *few* are *speculators*, and the *many* are comparatively *slaves;* and slaves, not to enrich themselves, (this is impossible,) but to enrich the speculators and adventurers by whom they are employed. Even the *farmers* become, at least partially, *commercial* men; and the *soil*, the fruitful parent of natural wealth, is comparatively disregarded: the consequence is, that the *misery* of the *many*, and the *luxury* of the *few*, increase; and from both these spring, on the one hand, pride, insolence, contempt of the poor, contempt of God's holy word and commandments, with the long catalogue of crimes which proceed from pampered appetites and unsubdued passions: and on the other, murmuring, repining, discon-

tent, and often *insubordination* and *revolt*, the most fell and most destructive of all the evils that can degrade and curse civil society. Hence wars, fightings, and revolutions of states, and public calamities of all kinds. Bad as the world and the times are, men have made them much worse by their unnatural methods of providing for the support of life. When shall men learn that even this is but a subordinate pursuit; and that the cultivation of the soul in the knowledge, love, and obedience of God, is essentially necessary, not only to future glory, but to present happiness?

CHAPTER XXVII.

Isaac, grown old and feeble, and apprehending the approach of death, desires his son Esau to provide some savoury meat for him, that having eaten of it he might convey to him the blessing *connected with the right of* primogeniture, 1–4. *Rebekah hearing of it, relates the matter to Jacob, and directs him how to personate his brother, and by deceiving his father, obtain the blessing*, 5–10. *Jacob hesitates*, 11, 12; *but being counselled and encouraged by his mother, he at last consents to use the means she prescribes*, 13, 14. *Rebekah disguises Jacob, and sends him to personate his brother*, 15–17. *Jacob comes to his father, and professes himself to be Esau*, 18, 19. *Isaac doubts, questions, and examines him closely, but does not discover the deception*, 20–24. *He eats of the savoury meat, and confers the blessing upon Jacob*, 25–27. *In what the blessing consisted*, 28, 29. *Esau arrives from the field with the meat he had gone to provide, and presents himself before his father*, 30, 31. *Isaac discovers the fraud of Jacob, and is much affected*, 32, 33. *Esau is greatly distressed on hearing that the blessing had been received by another*, 34. *Isaac accuses Jacob of deceit*, 35. *Esau expostulates, and prays for a blessing*, 36. *Isaac describes the blessing which he has already conveyed*, 37. *Esau weeps, and earnestly implores a blessing*, 38. *Isaac pronounces a blessing on Esau, and prophecies that his posterity should, in process of time, cease to be tributary to the posterity of Jacob*, 39, 40. *Esau purposes to kill his brother*, 41. *Rebekah hears of it, and counsels Jacob to take refuge with her brother Laban in Padan-aram*, 42–45. *She professes to be greatly alarmed, lest Jacob should take any of the Canaanites to wife*, 46.

A. M. cir. 2225.
B. C. cir. 1779.
Kennicott.

AND it came to pass, that
when Isaac was old, and
[a] his eyes were dim, so that he
could not see, he called Esau his eldest son,
and said unto him, My son: and he said unto
him, Behold, *here am* I.
2 And he said, Behold now, I am old, I
[b] know not the day of my
death:

A. M. cir. 2225.
B. C. cir. 1779.

3 [c] Now therefore take, I pray thee, thy
weapons, thy quiver and thy bow, and go out
to the field, and [d] take me *some* venison;
4 And make me savoury meat, such as I
love, and bring *it* to me, that I may eat; that

[a] Chap. xlviii. 10; 1 Sam. iii. 2.——[b] Prov. xxvii. 1; James iv. 14.——[c] Chap. xxv. 27, 28.——[d] Heb. *hunt.*

NOTES ON CHAP. XXVII.

Verse 1. *Isaac was old*] It is conjectured, on good grounds, that Isaac was now about one hundred and seventeen years of age, and Jacob about fifty-seven; though the commonly received opinion makes Isaac one hundred and thirty-seven, and Jacob seventy-seven; but see the notes on chap. xxxi. 38, &c.

And his eyes were dim] This was probably the effect of *that* affliction, of what kind we know not, under which Isaac now laboured; and from which, as well as from the affliction, he probably recovered, as it is certain he lived forty if not forty-three years after this time, for he lived till the return of Jacob from Padan-aram; chap. xxxv. 27–29.

Verse 2. *I know not the day of my death*] From his present weakness he had reason to suppose that his death could not be at any great distance, and therefore would leave no act undone which he believed it his duty to perform. He who lives not in reference to eternity, lives not at all.

Verse 3. *Thy weapons*] The original word כלי *keley* signifies *vessels* and *instruments* of any kind; and is probably used here for a *hunting spear, javelin, sword, &c.*

Quiver] תלי *teli*, from תלה *talah*, to *hang* or *suspend*. Had not the *Septuagint* translated the word φαρετραν, and the *Vulgate pharetram*, a quiver, I should rather have supposed some kind of *shield* was meant; but either can be *suspended* on the arm or from the shoulder. Some think a *sword* is meant; and because the original signifies to *hang* or *suspend*, hence they think is derived our word *hanger*, so called because it is generally worn in a *pendent* posture; but the word *hanger* did not exist in our language previously to the Crusades, and we have evidently derived it from the Persian خنجر *khanjar*, a poniard or dagger, the use of which, not only in battles, but in private assassinations, was well known.

Verse 4. *Savoury meat*] מטעמים *matammim*, from טעם *taam*, to *taste* or *relish*; how dressed we know not, but its name declares its nature.

That I may eat] The blessing which Isaac was to confer on his son was a species of Divine right, and must be communicated with appropriate ceremonies. As eating and drinking were used among the Asiatics on almost all religious occasions, and especially in making and confirming covenants, it is reasonable to suppose that something of this kind was essentially necessary on this occasion, and that Isaac could not

A. M. cir. 2225. B. C. cir. 1779. my soul [e] may bless thee before
I die.
5 And Rebekah heard when Isaac spake to
Esau his son. And Esau went to the field
to hunt *for* venison, *and* to bring *it*.
6 And Rebekah spake unto Jacob her son,
saying, Behold, I heard thy father speak unto
Esau thy brother, saying,
7 Bring me venison, and make me savoury
meat, that I may eat, and bless thee before the
LORD, before my death.
8 Now therefore, my son, [f] obey my voice
according to that which I command thee.
9 Go now to the flock, and fetch me from
thence two good kids of the goats; and I will
make them [g] savoury meat for thy father, such
as he loveth:
10 And thou shalt bring *it* to thy father,
that he may eat, and that he [h] may bless thee
before his death.
11 And Jacob said to Rebekah his mother,
Behold, [i] Esau my brother *is* a hairy man, and
I *am* a smooth man.
12 My father peradventure will
[k] feel me, and I shall seem to A. M. cir. 2225 B. C. cir. 1779.
him as a deceiver; and I shall bring [l] a curse
upon me, and not a blessing.
13 And his mother said unto him, [m] Upon
me *be* thy curse, my son: only obey my
voice, and go fetch me *them*.
14 And he went, and fetched, and brought
them to his mother: and his mother [n] made
savoury meat, such as his father loved.
15 And Rebekah took [o] goodly raiment of
her eldest son Esau,[p] which *were* with her in
the house, and put them upon Jacob her
younger son:
16 And she put the skins of the kids of the
goats upon his hands, and upon the smooth
of his neck:
17 And she gave the savoury meat and the
bread, which she had prepared, into the hand
of her son Jacob.
18 And he came unto his father, and said,
My father: and he said, Here *am* I; who *art*
thou, my son?

[e] Ver. 27; chapter xlviii. 9, 15; xlix. 28; Deut. xxxiii. 1. — [f] Ver. 13. — [g] Verse 4. — [h] Verse 4. — [i] Chapter xxv. 25. — [k] Ver. 22.

[l] Chap. ix. 25; Deut. xxvii. 18. — [m] Chap. xliii. 9; 1 Sam. xxv. 24; 2 Sam. xiv. 9; Matt. xxvii. 25. — [n] Verse 4, 9. — [o] Heb. *desirable*. — [p] Ver. 27.

convey the *right* till he had eaten of the meat provided for the purpose by *him* who was to receive the blessing. As Isaac was now old, and in a feeble and languishing condition, it was necessary that the flesh used on this occasion should be prepared so as to invite the appetite, that a *sufficiency* of it might be taken to revive and recruit his drooping strength, that he might be the better able to go through the whole of this ceremony.

This seems to be the sole reason why *savoury* meat is so particularly mentioned in the text. When we consider, 1. That no covenant was deemed *binding* unless the parties had *eaten* together; 2. That to convey this blessing some rite of this kind was necessary; and, 3. That Isaac's strength was now greatly exhausted, insomuch that he supposed himself to be dying; we shall at once see why *meat* was required on this occasion, and why that meat was to be prepared so as to deserve the epithet of *savoury*. As I believe this to be the true sense of the place, I do not trouble my readers with interpretations which I suppose to be either exceptionable or false.

Verse 5. *And Rebekah heard*] And was determined, if possible, to frustrate the design of Isaac, and procure the blessing for her favourite son. Some pretend that she received a *Divine inspiration* to the purpose; but if she had she needed not to have recourse to *deceit*, to help forward the accomplishment. Isaac, on being informed, would have had too much piety not to prefer the will of his Maker to his own partiality for his eldest son; but Rebekah had nothing of the kind to plead, and therefore had recourse to the most exceptionable means to accomplish her ends.

Verse 12. *I shall bring a curse upon me*] For even in those early times the *spirit* of that law was understood, Deut. xxvii. 18: *Cursed is he that maketh the blind to wander out of the way;* and Jacob seems to have possessed at this time a more tender conscience than his mother.

Verse 13. *Upon me* be *thy curse, my son*] Onkelos gives this a curious turn: *It has been revealed to me by prophecy that the curses will not come upon thee, my son.* What a dreadful responsibility did this woman take upon her at this time! The sacred writer states the facts as they were, and we may depend on the truth of the statement; but he nowhere says that God would have any man to copy this conduct. He often relates facts and sayings which he never recommends.

Verse 15. *Goodly raiment*] Mr. Ainsworth has a sensible note on this place. "The priest in the law had *holy garments* to minister in, Exod. xxviii. 2–4, which the Septuagint there and in this place term την στολην, THE *robe*, and στολην ἁγιαν, *the holy robe.* Whether the first-born, before the law, had such to minister in is not certain, but it is probable by this example; for had they been *common* garments, why did not Esau himself, or his wives, keep them? But being, in all likelihood, holy robes, received from their ancestors, the mother of the family kept them in sweet chests from moths and the like, whereupon it is said, ver. 27, *Isaac smelled the smell of his garments.*" The opinion of Ainsworth is followed by many critics.

A. M. cir. 2225. B. C. cir. 1779. 19 And Jacob said unto his
father, I *am* Esau thy first-born;
I have done according as thou badest me:
arise, I pray thee, sit and eat of my venison,
[q] that thy soul may bless me.
20 And Isaac said unto his son, How *is it*
that thou hast found *it* so quickly, my son?
And he said, Because the LORD thy God
brought *it* [r] to me.
21 And Isaac said unto Jacob, Come near,
I pray thee, that I [s] may feel thee, my son,
whether thou *be* my very son Esau or not.
22 And Jacob went near unto Isaac his
father; and he felt him, and said, The voice
is Jacob's voice, but the hands *are* the hands
of Esau.
23 And he discerned him not, because [t] his
hands were hairy, as his brother A. M. cir. 2225. B. C. cir. 1779.
Esau's hands: so he blessed him.
24 And he said, *Art* thou my very son Esau?
And he said, I *am*.
25 And he said, Bring *it* near to me, and I
will eat of my son's venison, [u] that my soul
may bless thee. And he brought *it* near to
him, and he did eat: and he brought him
wine, and he drank.
26 And his father Isaac said unto him,
Come near now, and kiss me, my son.
27 And he came near, and kissed him: and
he smelled the smell of his raiment, and blessed him, and said, See, [v] the smell of my son
is as the smell of a field which the LORD hath
blessed:
28 Therefore [w] God give thee of [x] the dew

[q] Verse 4.——[r] Heb. *before me.*——[s] Verse 12.——[t] Verse 16.——[u] Verse 4.

[v] Hosea xiv. 6.——[w] Hebrews xi. 20.——[x] Deut. xxxiii. 13, 28. 2 Sam. i. 21.

Verse 19. *I am Esau thy first-born*] Here are many palpable falsehoods, and such as should neither be imitated nor excused. "Jacob," says Calmet, "imposes on his father in three different ways. I. By his *words: I am thy first-born Esau.* 2. By his *actions;* he gives him *kids' flesh* for *venison*, and says he had executed his orders, and *got it by hunting.* 3. By his *clothing;* he puts on Esau's garments, and the kids' skins upon his hands and the smooth of his neck. In short, he made use of every species of deception that could be practised on the occasion, in order to accomplish his ends." To attempt to palliate or find excuses for such conduct, instead of *serving, disserves* the cause of religion and truth. Men have laboured, not only to excuse all this conduct of Rebekah and Jacob, but even to show that it was *consistent*, and that the whole was according to the *mind* and *will of God!*

Non tali auxilio, non defensoribus istis—

The cause of God and truth is under no obligation to such defenders; their hands are more unhallowed than those of Uzzah; and however the bearers may stumble, the ark of God requires not *their* support. It was the design of God that *the elder should serve the younger*, and he would have brought it about in the way of his own wise and just providence; but means such as here used he could neither sanction nor recommend.

Verse 23. *And he discerned him not, because his hands were hairy*] From this circumstance we may learn that Isaac's *sense of feeling* was much impaired by his present malady. When he could not discern the *skin of a kid* from the *flesh of his son*, we see that he was, through his infirmity, in a fit state to be imposed on by the deceit of his wife, and the cunning of his younger son.

Verse 27. *The smell of my son is as the smell of a field*] The smell of these garments, the *goodly raiment which had been laid up in the house*, was probably occasioned by some aromatic herbs, which we may naturally suppose were laid up with the clothes; a custom which prevails in many countries to the present day. *Thyme, lavender*, &c., are often deposited in wardrobes, to communicate an agreeable scent, and under the supposition that the moths are thereby prevented from fretting the garments. I have often seen the leaves of aromatic plants, and sometimes whole sprigs, put in eastern MSS., to communicate a pleasant smell, and to prevent the worms from destroying them. Persons going from Europe to the East Indies put pieces of Russia leather among their clothes for the same purpose. Such a smell would lead Isaac's recollection to the fields where aromatic plants grew in abundance, and where he had often been regaled by the scent.

Verse 28. *God give thee of the dew of heaven*] Bp. Newton's view of these predictions is so correct and appropriate, as to leave no wish for any thing farther on the subject.

"It is here foretold, and in ver. 39, of these two brethren, that as to situation, and other temporal advantages, they should be much alike. It was said to Jacob: *God give thee of the dew of heaven, and the fatness of the earth, and plenty of corn and wine;* and much the same is said to Esau, ver. 39: *Behold, thy dwelling shall be the fatness of the earth, and of the dew of heaven from above.* The spiritual blessing, or the promise of the blessed seed, could be given only to ONE; but temporal good things might be imparted to *both.* Mount Seir, and the adjacent country, was at first in the possession of the Edomites; they afterwards extended themselves farther into Arabia, and into the southern parts of Judea. But wherever they were situated, we find in fact that the Edomites, in temporal advantages, were little inferior to the Israelites. Esau had *cattle* and *beasts* and *substance* in abundance, and he went to dwell in Seir of his own accord; but he would hardly have removed thither with so many cattle, had it been such a barren and desolate country as some would represent it. The Edom-

A. M. cir. 2225. B. C. cir. 1779.

of heaven, and [y] the fatness of the earth, and [z] plenty of corn and wine:

29 [a] Let people serve thee, and nations bow down to thee; be lord over thy brethren, and [b] let thy mother's sons bow down to thee: [c] cursed *be* every one that curseth thee, and blessed *be* he that blesseth thee.

30 And it came to pass as soon as Isaac had made an end of blessing Jacob, and Jacob was yet scarce gone out from the presence of Isaac his father, that Esau his brother came in from his hunting.

A. M. cir. 2225. B. C. cir. 1779.

31 And he also had made savoury meat, and brought it unto his father, and said unto his father, Let my father arise, and [d] eat of his son's venison, that thy soul may bless me.

32 And Isaac his father said unto him, Who *art* thou? And he said, I *am* thy son, thy first-born, Esau.

33 And Isaac [e] trembled very exceedingly, and said, Who? where *is* he that hath [f] taken

[y] Chap. xlv. 18.——[z] Deut. xxxiii. 28.——[a] Chap. ix. 25; xxv. 23.——[b] Chap. xlix. 8.

[c] Chap. xii. 3.——[d] Ver. 4.——[e] Heb. *trembled with a great trembling greatly.*——[f] Heb. *hunted.*

ites had *dukes* and *kings* reigning over them, while the Israelites were *slaves* in Egypt. When the Israelites, on their return, desired leave to pass through the territories of Edom, it appears that the country abounded with FRUITFUL FIELDS and VINEYARDS: *Let us pass, I pray thee, through thy country; we will not pass through the fields, or through the vineyards, neither will we drink of the water of the wells;* Num. xx. 17. And the prophecy of Malachi, which is generally alleged as a proof of the *barrenness* of the country, is rather a proof of the contrary: *I hated Esau, and laid his mountains and his heritage waste for the dragons of the wilderness,* Mal. i. 3; for this implies that the country was fruitful before, and that its present unfruitfulness was rather an effect of war, than any natural defect in the soil. If the country is unfruitful now, neither is *Judea* what it was formerly." As there was but little rain in Judea, except what was termed the *early rain,* which fell about the beginning of spring, and the *latter rain,* which fell about September, the lack of this was supplied by the *copious dews* which fell both morning and evening, or rather through the whole of the night. And we may judge, says Calmet, of the *abundance* of these dews by what fell on Gideon's fleece, Judges vi. 38, which being wrung *filled a bowl.* And Hushai compares an army ready to fall upon its enemies to *a dew falling on the ground,* 2 Sam. xvii. 12, which gives us the idea that this fluid fell in great profusion, so as to saturate every thing. Travellers in these countries assure us that the *dews* fall there in an extraordinary abundance.

The fatness of the earth] What Homer calls ουθαρ αρουρης, Ilias ix., 141, and Virgil *uber glebæ,* Æneis i., 531, both signifying a soil *naturally fertile.* Under this, therefore, and the former expressions, Isaac wishes his son all the blessings which a plentiful country can produce; for, as *Le Clerc* rightly observes, if the dews and seasonable rains of heaven fall upon a fruitful soil, nothing but human industry is wanting to the plentiful enjoyment of all temporal good things. Hence they are represented in the Scripture as emblems of prosperity, of plenty, and of the blessing of God, Deut. xxxiii. 13, 28; Micah v. 7; Zech. viii. 12; and, on the other hand, the withholding of these denotes *barrenness, distress,* and the *curse of God;* 2 Sam. i. 21. See *Dodd.*

Verse 29. *Let people serve thee*] "However alike their temporal advantages were to each other," says Bp. Newton, "in all spiritual gifts and graces the younger brother was to have the superiority, was to be the happy instrument of conveying the blessing to all nations: *In thee and in thy seed shall all the families of the earth be blessed;* and to this are to be referred, in their full force, those expressions: *Let people serve thee, and nations bow down to thee. Cursed be every one that curseth thee, and blessed be he that blesseth thee.* The same promise was made to Abraham in the name of God: *I will bless them that bless thee, and curse him that curseth thee,* chap. xii. 3; and it is here repeated to Jacob, and thus paraphrased in the Jerusalem Targum: 'He who curseth thee shall be cursed as Balaam the son of Beor; and he who blesseth thee shall be blessed as Moses the prophet, the lawgiver of Israel.' It appears that Jacob was, on the whole, a man of more religion, and believed the Divine promises more, than Esau. The posterity of Jacob likewise preserved the true religion, and the worship of one God, while the Edomites were sunk in idolatry; and of the seed of Jacob was born at last the Saviour of the world. This was the peculiar privilege and advantage of Jacob, to be the happy instrument of conveying these blessings to all nations. This was his greatest superiority over Esau; and in this sense St. Paul understood and applied the prophecy: *The elder shall serve the younger,* Rom. ix. 12. The Christ, the Saviour of the world, was to be born of *some one family;* and Jacob's was preferred to Esau's, out of the good pleasure of Almighty God, who is certainly the best judge of fitness and expedience, and has undoubted right to dispense his favours as he shall see proper; for he says to Moses, as the apostle proceeds to argue, ver. 15: 'I will have mercy on whom I will have mercy, and I will have compassion on whom I will have compassion.' And when the Gentiles were converted to Christianity, the prophecy was fulfilled literally: *Let people serve thee, and let nations bow down to thee;* and will be more amply fulfilled when *the fulness of the Gentiles shall come in, and all Israel shall be saved.*"

Verse 33. *And Isaac trembled*] The marginal reading is very literal and proper, *And Isaac trembled with a great trembling greatly.* And this shows the deep concern he felt for his own deception, and the iniquity of the means by which it had been brought about.

A. M. cir. 2225. B. C. cir. 1779. venison, and b ought *it* me, and I have eaten of all before thou camest, and have blessed him? yea, [g] *and* he shall be blessed.

34 And when Esau heard the words of his father, [h] he cried with a great and exceeding bitter cry, and said unto his father, Bless me, *even* me also, O my father.

35 And he said, Thy brother came with subtilty, and hath taken away thy blessing.

36 And he said, [i] Is not he rightly named [k] Jacob? for he hath supplanted me these two times; [l] he took away my birthright; and behold, now he hath taken away my blessing. And he said, Hast thou not reserved a blessing for me?

37 And Isaac answered and said unto Esau, [m] Behold, I have made him thy lord, and all his brethren have I given to him for servants; and [n] with corn and wine have I [o] sustained him: and what shall I do now unto thee, my son? A. M. cir. 2225 B. C. cir. 1779

38 And Esau said unto his father, Hast thou but one blessing, my father? bless me, *even* me also, O my father. And Esau lifted up his voice, [p] and wept.

39 And Isaac his father answered and said unto him, Behold, [q] thy dwelling shall be [r] the fatness of the earth, and of the dew of heaven from above;

40 And by thy sword shalt thou live, and [s] shalt serve thy brother; and [t] it shall come

[g] Chap. xxviii. 3, 4; Rom. xi. 29.——[h] Heb. xii. 17.——[i] Chap. xxv. 26.——[k] That is, *a supplanter.*——[l] Chap. xxv. 33.——[m] Fulfilled, 2 Sam. viii. 14; ver. 29.——[n] Ver. 28.

[o] Or, *supported.*——[p] Heb. xii. 17.——[q] Ver. 28; Heb. xi. 20 [r] Or, *of the fatness.*——[s] Ch. xxv. 23; Obad. 18, 19, 20; 2 Sam. viii. 14.——[t] 2 Kings viii. 20.

Though Isaac must have heard of that which God had spoken to Rebekah, *The elder shall serve the younger*, and could never have wished to reverse this Divine purpose; yet he might certainly think that the spiritual blessing might be conveyed to Esau, and by him to all the nations of the earth, notwithstanding the superiority of secular dominion on the other side.

Yea, and he shall be blessed.] From what is said in this verse, collated with Heb. xii. 17, we see how *binding* the conveyance of the birthright was when communicated with the *rites* already mentioned. When Isaac found that he had been deceived by Jacob, he certainly would have reversed the blessing if he could; but as it had been conveyed in the *sacramental* way this was impossible. *I have blessed him*, says he, *yea, and he must*, or *will, be blessed.* Hence it is said by the apostle, Esau *found no place for repentance*, *μετανοιας γαρ τοπον ουχ εὑρε, no place* for *change of mind* or *purpose* in his father, *though he sought it carefully with tears.* The father could not reverse it because the *grant* had already been made and confirmed. But this had nothing to do with the final salvation of poor outwitted Esau, nor indeed with that of his unnatural brother.

Verse 35. *Hath taken away thy blessing.*] This blessing, which was a different thing from the birthright, seems to consist of *two parts:* 1. The dominion, generally and finally, over the other part of the family; and, 2. Being the progenitor of the Messiah. But the former is more explicitly declared than the latter. See the notes on chap. xxv. 31.

Verse 36. *Is not he rightly named Jacob?*] See on chap. xxv. 26.

He took away my birthright] So he might say with considerable propriety; for though he *sold* it to Jacob, yet as Jacob had taken advantage of his perishing situation, he considered the act as a species of robbery.

Verse 37. *I have made him thy lord*] See on ver. 28.

Verse 40. *By thy sword shalt thou live*] This does not absolutely mean that the Edomites should have constant wars; but that they should be of a fierce and warlike disposition, gaining their sustenance by *hunting*, and by predatory excursions upon the possessions of others. Bishop Newton speaks on this subject with his usual good sense and judgment: "The elder branch, it is here foretold, should delight more in war and violence, but yet should be subdued by the younger. *By thy sword shalt thou live, and shalt serve thy brother* Esau might be said to live much by the sword; for he was a cunning hunter, a man of the field. He and his children got possession of Mount Seir by force and violence, expelling from thence the *Horites*, the former inhabitants. By what means they spread themselves farther among the Arabians is not known; but it appears that upon a sedition and separation several of the Edomites came and siezed upon the south-west parts of Judea, during the Babylonish captivity, and settled there ever after. Before and after this they were almost continually at war with the Jews; upon every occasion they were ready to join with their enemies; and when Nebuchadnezzar besieged Jerusalem, they encouraged him utterly to destroy the city, saying, *Rase it, rase it, even to the foundations thereof.* Psa. cxxxvii. 7. And even long after they were subdued by the Jews, they retained the same martial spirit; for Josephus in his time gives them the character of 'a turbulent and disorderly nation, always erect to commotions, and rejoicing in changes; at the least adulation of those who beseech them, beginning war, and hasting to battles as to a feast.' And a little before the last siege of Jerusalem they came, at the entreaty of the *Zealots*, to assist them against the priests and people; and there, together with the Zealots, committed unheard-of cruelties, and barbarously murdered *Annas*, the high priest, from whose death Josephus dates the destruction of the city." See Dr. Dodd.

And—when thou shalt have the dominion] It is here foretold that there was to be a time when the elder was to have dominion and shake off the yoke of the younger. The word תריד *tarid*, which we translate

A. M. cir. 2225. B. C. cir. 1779.

to pass, when thou shalt have
the dominion, that thou shalt
break his yoke from off thy neck.
41 And Esau [u] hated Jacob because of the
blessing wherewith his father blessed him:
and Esau said in his heart, [v] The days of
mourning for my father are at hand; [w] then
will I slay my brother Jacob.
42 And these words of Esau her elder son
were told to Rebekah: and she sent and called
Jacob her younger son, and said
unto him, Behold, thy brother
Esau, as touching thee, doth [x] comfort himself, *purposing* to kill thee.
43 Now therefore, my son, obey my voice;
and arise, flee thou to Laban my brother [y] to
Haran;
44 And tarry with him a few days, until
thy brother's fury turn away;
45 Until thy brother's anger turn away from

A. M. cir. 2225. B. C. cir. 1779.

[u] Chap. iv. 2–8; xxxvii. 4, 8; Ezek. xxv. 12–15; 1 John iii. 12–15.——[v] Chap. xxv. 29; l. 3, 4, 10.

[w] Eccles. vii. 9; Obad. 10; Eph. iv. 26, 27.——[x] Psa. lxiv. 5. Prov. ii 14; iv. 16, 17.——[y] Chap. xi. 31.

have dominion, is rather of doubtful meaning, as it may be deduced from three different roots, ירד *yarad*, to *descend*, to *be brought down* or *brought low*; רדה *radah*, to *obtain rule* or *have dominion*; and רוד *rud*, to *complain*; meaning either that when reduced *very low* God would magnify his power in their behalf, and deliver them from the yoke of their brethren; or when they should be increased so as to venture to *set up a king over them*, or when they *mourned* for their transgressions, God would turn their captivity. The Jerusalem Targum gives the words the following turn: "When the sons of Jacob attend to the law and observe the precepts, they shall impose the yoke of servitude upon thy neck; but when they shall turn away themselves from studying the law and neglect the precepts, thou shalt break off the yoke of servitude from thy neck."

"It was David who imposed the yoke, and at that time the Jewish people observed the law; but the yoke was very galling to the Edomites from the first; and towards the end of Solomon's reign Hadad, the Edomite, of the blood royal, who had been carried into Egypt from his childhood, returned into his own country, and raised some disturbances, but was not able to recover his throne, his subjects being overawed by the garrisons which David had placed among them; but in the reign of Jehoram, the son of Jehoshaphat king of Judah, *the Edomites revolted from under the dominion of Judah, and made themselves a king*. Jehoram made some attempts to subdue them again, but could not prevail; *so the Edomites revolted from under the hand of Judah unto this day*, 2 Chron. xxi. 8, 10, and hereby this part of the prophecy was fulfilled about nine hundred years after it was delivered." See Bishop Newton.

"Thus," says Bishop Newton, "have we traced, in our notes on this and the xxvth chapter, the accomplishment of this prophecy from the beginning; and we find that the nation of the Edomites has at several times been conquered by and made tributary to the Jews, but never the nation of the Jews to the Edomites; and the Jews have been the more considerable people, more known in the world, and more famous in history. We know indeed little more of the history of the Edomites than as it is connected with that of the Jews; and where is the *name* or *nation* now? They were swallowed up and lost, partly among the Nabathean Arabs, and partly among the Jews; and the very name, as Dr. Prideaux has observed, was abolished and disused about the end of the first century of the Christian era. Thus were they rewarded for insulting and oppressing their brethren the Jews; and hereby other prophecies were fulfilled, viz., Jer. xlix. 7, &c.; Ezek. xxv. 12, &c.; Joel iii. 19; Amos i. 11, &c.; and particularly Obadiah; for at this day we see the Jews subsisting as a distinct people, while Edom is no more, agreeably to the words of Obadiah, ver. 10: *For thy violence against thy brother Jacob*, in the return of his posterity from Egypt, *shame shall cover thee, and thou shalt be cut off for ever*. And again, ver. 18: *There shall not be any remaining of the house of Esau, for the Lord hath spoken it*. In what a most extensive and circumstantial manner has God fulfilled all these predictions! and what a proof is this of the Divine inspiration of the Pentateuch, and the omniscience of God!"

Verse 41. *The days of mourning for my father are at hand*] Such was the state of Isaac's health at that time, though he lived more than forty years afterwards, that his death was expected by all; and Esau thought that would be a favourable time for him to avenge himself on his brother Jacob, as, according to the custom of the times, the sons were always present at the burial of the father. Ishmael came from his own country to assist Isaac to bury Abraham; and both Jacob and Esau assisted in burying their father Isaac, but the enmity between them had happily subsided long before that time.

Verse 42. *Doth comfort himself, purposing to kill thee*.] מתנחם לך *mithnachem lecha*, which Houbigant renders *cogitat super te*, he thinks or meditates to kill thee. This sense is natural enough here, but it does not appear to be the meaning of the original; nor does Houbigant himself give it this sense, in his *Racines Hebraiques*. There is no doubt that Esau, in his hatred to his brother, felt himself pleased with the thought that he should soon have the opportunity of avenging his wrongs.

Verse 44. *Tarry with him a few days*] It was probably forty years before he returned, and it is likely Rebekah saw him no more; for it is the general opinion of the Jewish rabbins that she died before Jacob's return from Padan-aram, whether the period of his stay be considered *twenty* or *forty* years. See on chap. xxxi. 38, &c.

Verse 45. *Why should I be deprived also of you both*] If Esau should kill Jacob, then the nearest akin

a

A. M. cir. 2225. B. C. cir. 1779.
thee, and he forget *that* which
thou hast done to him: then I will
send, and fetch thee from thence: why should
I be deprived also of you both in one day?
46 And Rebekah said to Isaac, [a] I am weary
of my life because of the daugh-
ters of Heth: [b] if Jacob take a
wife of the daughters of Heth, such as these
which are of the daughters of the land, what
good shall my life do me?

[a] Chap. xxvi. 35; xxviii. 8; Num. xi. 15; 1 Kings xix. 4; Job iii. 20-22.——[b] Chap. xxiv. 3.

to Jacob, who was by the patriarchial law, Gen. ix. 6, the avenger of blood, would kill Esau; and both these deaths might possibly take place in the same day. This appears to be the meaning of Rebekah. Those who are ever endeavouring to sanctify the *means* by the *end*, are full of perplexity and distress. God will not give his blessing to even a Divine service, if not done in his own way, on principles of truth and righteousness. Rebekah and her son would take the means out of God's hands; they compassed themselves with their own sparks, and warmed themselves with their own fire; and this had they at the hand of God, they lay down in sorrow. God would have brought about his designs in a way consistent with his own perfections; for he had fully determined that *the elder should serve the younger*, and that the Messiah should spring not from the family of Esau, but from that of Jacob; and needed not the cunning craftiness or deceits of men to accomplish his purposes. Yet in his mercy he overruled all these circumstances, and produced good, where things, if left to their own operations and issues, would have produced nothing but evil. However, after this reprehensible transaction, we hear no more of Rebekah. The Holy Spirit mentions her *no more*, her burial excepted, chap. xlix. 31. See on chap. xxxv. 8.

Verse 46. *I am weary of my life*] It is very likely that Rebekah kept many of the circumstances related above from the knowledge of *I*saac; but as Jacob could not go to Padan-aram without his knowledge, she appears here quite *in her own character*, framing an *excuse* for his departure, and *concealing* the true cause. Abraham had been solicitous to get a wife for his son *I*saac from a branch of his own family; hence *she* was brought from Syria. She is now afraid, or pretends to be afraid, that her son Jacob will marry among the *Hittites*, as Esau had done; and therefore makes this to *I*saac the *ostensible reason* why Jacob should immediately go to Padan-aram, that he might get a wife there. *I*saac, not knowing the true cause of sending him away, readily falls in with Rebekah's proposal, and immediately calls Jacob, gives him suitable directions and his blessing, and sends him away. This view of the subject makes all consistent and natural; and we see at once the reason of the abrupt speech contained in this verse, which should be placed at the beginning of the following chapter.

1. In the preceding notes I have endeavoured to represent things simply as they were. I have not copied the manner of many commentators, who have laboured to vindicate the character of Jacob and his mother in the transactions here recorded. As *I* fear God, and wish to follow him, *I* dare not bless what he hath not blessed, nor curse what he hath not cursed. *I* consider the whole of the conduct both of Rebekah and Jacob in some respects deeply criminal, and in all highly exceptionable. And the impartial relation of the facts contained in this and the xxvth chapter, gives me the fullest evidence of the truth and authenticity of the sacred original. How *impartial* is the history that God writes! We may see, from several commentators, what *man* would have done, had *he* had the same facts to relate. The history given by God details as well the *vices* as the *virtues* of those who are its subjects. How widely different from that in the Bible is the *biography* of the present day! Virtuous acts that were never performed, voluntary privations which were never borne, piety which was never felt, and in a word *lives* which were never *lived*, are the principal subjects of *our* biographical relations. These may be well termed the *Lives of the Saints*, for to these are attributed all the virtues which can adorn the human character, with scarcely a failing or a blemish; while on the other hand, those in general mentioned in the sacred writings stand marked with deep shades. What is the inference which a reflecting mind, acquainted with human nature, draws from a comparison of the biography of the *Scriptures* with that of *uninspired* writers? The inference is this—the Scripture history is natural, is probable, bears all the characteristics of veracity, narrates circumstances which seem to make against its own honour, yet *dwells* on them, and often seeks occasion to REPEAT them. It is true! infallibly true! *I*n this conclusion common sense, reason, and criticism join. On the other hand, of biography in general we must say that it is often unnatural, improbable; is destitute of many of the essential characteristics of truth; studiously avoids mentioning those circumstances which are dishonourable to its subject; ardently endeavours either to cast those which it cannot wholly hide into deep shades, or sublime them into virtues. This is notorious, and we need not go far for numerous examples. From these facts a reflecting mind will draw this general conclusion—an *impartial* history, in every respect true, can be expected only from God himself.

2. These should be only preliminary observations to an extended examination of the characters and conduct of Rebekah and her two sons; but this in detail would be an ungracious task, and *I* wish only to draw the reader's attention to what may, under the blessing of God, promote his moral good. No pious man can read the chapter before him without emotions of grief and pain. A mother teaches her favourite son to cheat and defraud his brother, deceive his father, and tell the most execrable lies! And God, the just, the impartial God relates all the circumstances in the most ample and minute detail! *I* have already hinted that this is a strong proof of the authenticity of the sacred

book. Had the Bible been the work of an impostor, a single trait of this history had never appeared. God, it is true, had purposed that *the elder should serve the younger;* but never designed that the supremacy should be brought about in this way. Had Jacob's unprincipled mother left the matter in the hands of God's providence, her favourite son would have had the precedency in such a way as would not only have manifested the justice and holiness of God, but would have been both *honourable* and *lasting* to HIMSELF. He got the *birthright*, and he got the *blessing;* and how little benefit did he personally derive from either! What was his life from this time till his return from Padan-aram? A mere tissue of vexations, disappointments, and calamities. Men may endeavour to palliate the iniquity of these transactions; but this must proceed either from weakness or mistaken zeal. God has sufficiently marked the whole with his disapprobation.

3. The enmity which Esau felt against his brother Jacob seems to have been transmitted to all his posterity; and doubtless the matters of the *birthright* and the *blessing* were the grounds on which that perpetual enmity was kept up between the descendants of both families, the *Edomites* and the *Israelites*. So unfortunate is an ancient family grudge, founded on the opinion that an injury has been done by one of the branches of the family, in a period no matter how remote, provided its operation still continues, and certain secular privations to one side be the result. How possible it is to keep feuds of this kind alive to any assignable period, the state of a neighbouring island sufficiently proves; and on the subject in question, the bloody contentions of the two *houses* of YORK and LANCASTER in this nation are no contemptible comment. The facts, however, relative to this point, may be summed up in a few words. 1. The descendants of Jacob were peculiarly favoured by God. 2. They generally had the dominion, and were ever reputed superior in every respect to the Edomites. 3. The Edomites were generally tributary to the Israelites. 4. They often revolted, and sometimes succeeded so far in their revolts as to become an *independent* people. 5. The Jews were never subjected to the Edomites. 6. As in the case between Esau and Jacob, who after long enmity were reconciled, so were the Edomites and the Jews, and at length they became one people. 7. The Edomites, as a nation, are now totally extinct; and the Jews still continue as a distinct people from all the inhabitants of the earth! So exactly have all the words of God, which he has spoken by his prophets, been fulfilled!

4. On the blessings pronounced on Jacob and Esau, these questions may naturally be asked. 1. Was there any thing in these blessings of such a spiritual nature as to affect the *eternal interests* of either? Certainly there was not, at least as far as might *absolutely* involve the salvation of the one, or the perdition of the other. 2. Was not the blessing pronounced on Esau as good as that pronounced on Jacob, the *mere temporary lordship*, and being the *progenitor* of the *Messiah*, excepted? So it evidently appears. 3. *If* the blessings had referred to their eternal states, had not Esau as fair a prospect for endless glory as his unfeeling brother? Justice and mercy both say—*Yes*. The truth is, it was their *posterity*, and not themselves, that were the objects of these blessings. Jacob, personally, gained no benefit; Esau, personally, sustained no loss.

CHAPTER XXVIII.

Isaac directs Jacob to take a wife from the family of Laban, 1, 2; *blesses and sends him away*, 3, 4. *Jacob begins his journey*, 5. *Esau, perceiving that the daughters of Canaan were not pleasing to his parents, and that Jacob obeyed them in going to get a wife of his own kindred*, 6–8, *went and took to wife* Mahalath, *the daughter of Ishmael his father's brother*, 9. *Jacob, in his journey towards Haran, came to a certain place*, (Luz, ver. 19,) *where he lodged all night*, 10, 11. *He sees in a dream a ladder reaching from earth to heaven, on which he beholds the angels of God ascending and descending*, 12. *God appears above this ladder, and renews those promises which he had made to Abraham and to Isaac*, 13, 14; *promises Jacob personal protection and a safe return to his own country*, 15. *Jacob awakes, and makes reflections upon his dream*, 16, 17. *Sets up one of the stones he had for his pillow, and pours oil on it, and calls the place* Beth-el, 18, 19. *Makes a vow that if God will preserve him in his journey, and bring him back in safety, the stone should be God's house, and that he would give him the tenths of all that he should have*, 20—22.

A. M. cir. 2225.
B. C. cir. 1779.

AND Isaac called Jacob, and [a]blessed him, and charged
him, and said unto him, [b]Thou shalt not
take a wife of the daughters of
Canaan.
2 [c]Arise, go to [d]Padan-aram, to the house

[a] Chap. xxvii. 33.——[b] Chap. xxiv. 3.

[c] Hos. xii. 11.——[d] Chap. xxv. 20.

NOTES ON CHAP. XXVIII.

Verse 1. *And Isaac called Jacob*] See the note on ver. 46 of the preceding chapter.

And blessed him] Now voluntarily and cheerfully confirmed to him the blessing, which he had before obtained through subtlety. It was necessary that he should have this confirmation previously to his departure; else, considering the way in which he had obtained both the *birthright* and the *blessing*, he might be doubtful, according to his own words, whether he might not

A. M. cir. 2225.
B. C. cir. 1779.

of [e] Bethuel thy mother's father; and take thee a wife from thence of the daughters of [f] Laban thy mother's brother.

3 [g] And God Almighty bless thee, and make thee fruitful, and multiply thee, that thou mayest be [h] a multitude of people:

4 And give thee [i] the blessing of Abraham, to thee, and to thy seed with thee: that thou mayest inherit the land [k] wherein [l] thou art a stranger, which God gave unto Abraham.

5 And Isaac sent away Jacob: and he went to Padan-aram unto Laban, son of Bethuel the Syrian, the brother of Rebekah, Jacob's and Esau's mother.

6 When Esau saw that Isaac had blessed Jacob, and sent him away to Padan-aram, to take him a wife from thence; and that as he blessed him, he gave him a charge, saying, Thou shalt not take a wife of the daughters of Canaan;

A. M. cir. 2225
B. C. cir. 1779.

7 And that Jacob obeyed his father, and his mother, and was gone to Padan-aram;

8 And Esau seeing [m] that the daughters of Canaan [n] pleased not Isaac his father;

9 Then went Esau unto Ishmael, and took unto the wives which he had, [o] Mahalath the daughter of Ishmael, Abraham's son, [p] the sister of Nebajoth, to be his wife.

10 And Jacob [q] went out from Beer-sheba, and went toward [r] Haran.

[e] Chap. xxii. 23.——[f] Chap. xxiv. 29.——[g] Chap. xvii. 1, 6. [h] Heb. *an assembly of people.*——[i] Chap. xii. 2.——[k] Heb. *of thy sojournings.*——[l] Chap. xvii. 8.

[m] Chap. xxiv. 3; xxvi. 35.——[n] Heb. were *evil in the eyes,* &c. [o] Chap. xxxvi. 3, she is called *Bashemath.*——[p] Chap. xxv. 13. [q] Hos. xii. 12.——[r] Called, Acts vii. 2, *Charran.*

have got a curse instead of a blessing. As the blessing now pronounced on Jacob was obtained without any deception on his part, it is likely that it produced a salutary effect upon his mind, might have led him to confession of his sin, and prepared his heart for those discoveries of God's goodness with which he was favoured at Luz.

Verse 2. *Go to Padan-aram*] This mission, in its spirit and design, is nearly the same as that in chap. xxiv., which see. There have been several ingenious conjectures concerning the *retinue* which Jacob had, or might have had, for his journey; and by some he has been supposed to have been *well attended.* Of this nothing is mentioned here, and the reverse seems to be intimated elsewhere. It appears, from ver. 11, that he lodged in the open air, with a stone for his pillow; and from chap. xxxii. 10, that he went *on foot* with his staff in his hand; nor is there even the most indirect mention of any attendants, nor is it probable there were any. He no doubt took *provisions* with him sufficient to carry him to the nearest encampment or village on the way, where he would naturally recruit his bread and water to carry him to the next stage, and so on. The *oil* that he poured on the pillar might be a little of that which he had brought for his own use, and can be no rational argument of his having a stock of provisions, servants, camels, &c., for which it has been gravely brought. He had God alone with him.

Verse 3. *That thou mayest be a multitude of people*] לקהל עמים *likhal ammim.* There is something very remarkable in the original words: they signify literally *for an assembly, congregation,* or *church* of *peoples;* referring no doubt to the Jewish Church in the wilderness, but more particularly to the *Christian Church,* composed of every kindred, and nation, and people, and tongue. This is one essential part of the blessing of Abraham. See ver. 4.

Verse 4. *Give thee the blessing of Abraham*] May he confirm the inheritance with all its attendant blessings to thee, to the exclusion of Esau; as he did to *me,* to the exclusion of *I*shmael. But, according to St. Paul, much more than this is certainly intended here, for it appears, from Gal. iii. 6–14, that *the blessing of Abraham,* which is *to come upon the Gentiles through Jesus Christ,* comprises the whole doctrine of justification by faith, and its attendant privileges, viz., redemption from the curse of the law, remission of sins, and the promise of the Holy Spirit, including the constitution and establishment of the Christian Church.

Verse 5. *Bethuel the Syrian*] *L*iterally the *Aramean,* so called, not because he was of the race of *Aram* the son of Shem, but because he dwelt in that country which had been formerly possessed by the descendants of Aram.

Verse 9. *Then went Esau unto Ishmael*] Those who are apt to take every thing by the wrong handle, and who think it was utterly impossible for Esau to do any right action, have classed his taking a daughter of *I*shmael among his crimes; whereas there is nothing more plain than that he did this with a sincere desire to *obey and please his parents.* Having heard the pious advice which *I*saac gave to Jacob, he therefore went and took a wife from the family of his grandfather Abraham, as Jacob was desired to do out of the family of his maternal uncle *L*aban. *Mahalath,* whom he took to wife, stood in the same degree of relationship to *I*saac his father as *Rachel* did to his mother Rebekah. Esau married his father's niece; Jacob married his mother's niece. It was therefore most obviously to please his parents that Esau took this additional wife. It is supposed that *I*shmael must have been dead thirteen or fourteen years before this time, and that *going to Ishmael* signifies only going to the *family* of *I*shmael. *I*f we follow the common computation, and allow that *I*saac was now about one hundred and thirty-six or one hundred and thirty-seven years of age, and Jacob seventy-seven, and as *I*shmael died in the one hundred and thirty-seventh year of his age, which according to the common computation was the one hundred and twenty-third of *I*saac, then Ish-

A. M. cir. 2225.
B. C. cir. 1779.

11 And he lighted upon a
certain place, and tarried there
all night, because the sun was set; and he
took of the stones of that place, and put *them*
for his pillows, and lay down in that place
to sleep.
12 And he [s] dreamed, and behold a ladder
set up on the earth, and the top of it reached
to heaven: and behold [t] the angels of God ascending and descending on it.
13 [u] And, behold, the LORD stood above it,
and said, [v] I *am* the LORD God of Abraham
thy father, and the God of Isaac: [w] the land
whereon thou liest, to thee will
I give it, and to thy seed;
14 And [x] thy seed shall be as the dust of
the earth, and thou shalt [y] spread abroad [z] to
the west, and to the east, and to the north,
and to the south: and in thee and [a] in thy
seed shall all the families of the earth be
blessed.
15 And, behold, [b] I *am* with thee, and will
[c] keep thee in all *places* whither thou goest,
and will [d] bring thee again into this land; for
[e] I will not leave thee, [f] until I have done *that*
which I have spoken to thee of.

[s] Chapter xli. 1; Job xxxiii. 15.——[t] John i. 51; Heb. i. 14.——[u] Chap. xxxv. 1; xlviii. 3.——[v] Chap. xxvi. 24.——[w] Chap. xiii. 15; xxxv. 12.——[x] Chapter xiii. 16.——[y] Heb. *break forth.*——[z] Chap. xiii. 14; Deut. xii. 20.

[a] Chap. xii. 3; xviii. 18; xxii. 18; xxvi. 4.——[b] See ver. 20, 21; chap. xxvi. 24; xxxi. 3.——[c] Chap. xlviii. 16; Psa. cxxi. 5, 7, 8.——[d] Chap. xxxv. 6.——[e] Deut. xxxviii. 6; Josh. i. 5; 1 Kings viii. 57; Heb. xiii. 5.——[f] Num. xxiii. 19.

mael must have been dead about *fourteen* years. But if we allow the ingenious reasoning of Mr. *Skinner* and Dr. *Kennicott*, that Jacob was at this time only *fifty-seven* years of age, and *I*saac consequently only *one hundred and seventeen*, it will appear that *I*shmael did not die till *six* years after this period; and hence with propriety it might be said, Esau went unto *Ishmael*, and took Mahalath the daughter of *I*shmael to be his wife. See the notes on chap. xxxi. 38, &c.

Verse 11. *A certain place, and tarried there*] From ver. 19 we find this *certain place* was *Luz*, or some part of its vicinity. Jacob had probably intended to reach Luz; but the sun being set, and night coming on, he either could not reach the city, or he might suspect the inhabitants, and rather prefer the open field, as he must have heard of the character and conduct of the men of Sodom and Gomorrah. Or the gates might be shut by the time he reached it, which would prevent his admission; for it frequently happens, to the present day, that travellers not reaching a city in the eastern countries previously to the shutting of the gates, are obliged to lodge under the walls all night, as when once shut they refuse to open them till the next day. This was probably Jacob's case.

He took of the stones] He took one of the stones that were in that place: from ver. 18 we find it was *one stone* only which he had for his pillow. Luz was about forty-eight miles distant from Beer-sheba; too great a journey for one day, through what we may conceive very unready roads.

Verse 12. *He dreamed, and behold a ladder*] A multitude of fanciful things have been spoken of Jacob's vision of the ladder, and its signification. It might have several designs, as God chooses to accomplish the greatest number of ends by the fewest and simplest means possible. 1. It is very likely that its primary design was to point out the *providence* of God, by which he watches over and regulates all terrestrial things; for nothing is left to merely natural causes; a heavenly agency pervades, actuates, and directs all. In his present circumstances it was highly necessary that Jacob should have a clear and distinct view of this subject, that he might be the better prepared to meet all occurrences with the conviction that all was working together for his good. 2. It might be intended also to point out the *intercourse between heaven and earth*, and the connection of both worlds by the means of *angelic ministry*. That this is fact we learn from many histories in the Old Testament; and it is a doctrine that is unequivocally taught in the New: *Are they not all ministering spirits, sent forth to minister for them who shall be heirs of salvation?* 3. It was probably a *type* of CHRIST, in whom both worlds meet, and in whom the Divine and human nature are conjoined. The LADDER *was set up on the* EARTH, *and the* TOP *of it reached to* HEAVEN; for GOD was manifested in the FLESH, and in him dwelt all the fulness of the Godhead bodily. Nothing could be a more expressive emblem of the incarnation and its effects; Jesus Christ is the grand connecting medium between heaven and earth, and between God and man. *By* him God comes down to man; *through* him man ascends to God. It appears that our *Lord* applies the vision in this way *himself*, 1st, In that remarkable speech to Nathanael, *Hereafter ye shall see the heaven opened, and the angels of God ascending and descending on the Son of man*, John i. 51. 2dly, *In* his speech to Thomas, John xiv. 6: *I am the* WAY, *and the truth, and the life; no man cometh unto the Father but by me.*

Verse 13. *I am the Lord God of Abraham*] Here God confirms to him the blessing of Abraham, for which *I*saac had prayed, ver. 3, 4.

Verse 14. *Thy seed shall be as the dust*] The people that shall descend from thee shall be extremely numerous, *and in thee and thy seed*—the *Lord* Jesus descending from thee, according to the *flesh, shall all the families of the earth*—not only all of *thy race*, but all the other *families* or *tribes* of mankind which have not proceeded from any branch of the Abrahamic family, *be blessed;* for *Jesus Christ by the grace of God tasted death* FOR EVERY MAN, Heb. ii. 9.

Verse 15. *And, behold, I am with thee*] For *I* fill the heavens and the earth. "My WORD *shall be thy help.*"—Targum. *And will keep thee in all places*, εν τῃ ὁδῳ πασῃ, *in all this way.—Septuagint.* I shall direct, help, and support thee in a peculiar manner, in thy

A. M. cir. 2225.
B. C. cir. 1779.

16 And Jacob awaked out
of his sleep, and he said, Surely
the LORD is in [g] this place; and I knew
it not.
17 And he was afraid, and said, How dreadful *is* this place! this *is* none other but the
house of God, and this *is* the gate of heaven.
18 And Jacob rose up early in the morning,
and took the stone that he had put *for* his pillows, and [h] set it up *for* a pillar, [i] and poured oil upon the top of it.

[g] Exod. iii. 5; Josh. v. 15.——[h] Chap. xxxi. 13, 45; xxxv. 14.——[i] Lev. viii. 10, 11, 12; Num. vii. 1.

present journey, be with thee while thou sojournest with thy uncle, *and will bring thee again into this land;* so that in all thy concerns thou mayest consider thyself under my especial providence, *for I will not leave thee.* Thy descendants also shall be my peculiar people, whom I shall continue to preserve as such *until I have done* that *which I have spoken to thee of*—until the Messiah shall be born of thy race, and *all the families of the earth*—the Gentiles, *be blessed through thee;* the Gospel being preached to them, and they, with the believing Jews, made ONE FOLD under ONE SHEPHERD, and one *Bishop* or *Overseer* of *souls.* And this circumstantial promise has been literally and punctually fulfilled.

Verse 16. *The Lord is in this place; and I knew it not.*] That is, God has made this place his peculiar residence; it is a place in which he meets with and reveals himself to his followers. Jacob might have supposed that this place had been consecrated to God. And it has already been supposed that, his mind having been brought into a humble frame, he was prepared to hold communion with his Maker.

Verse 17. *How dreadful* is *this place!*] The appearance of the *ladder*, the *angels*, and the *Divine glory* at the top of the ladder, must have left deep, solemn, and even awful impressions on the mind of Jacob; and hence the exclamation in the text, *How dreadful* is *this place!*

This is none other but the house of God] The *Chaldee* gives this place a curious turn: "This is not a common place, but a place in which God delights; and opposite to this place is the gate of heaven." *Onkelos* seems to suppose that the gate or entrance into heaven was actually *above* this spot, and that when the angels of God descended to earth, they came through that opening into this place, and returned by the same way. And it really appears that Jacob himself had a similar notion.

Verse 18. *And Jacob—took the stone—and set it up for a pillar*] He placed the stone in an erect posture, that it might stand as a monument of the extraordinary vision which he had in this place; *and he poured oil upon it,* thereby consecrating it to God, so that it might be considered an *altar* on which libations might be poured, and sacrifices offered unto God. See chap. xxxv. 14. The Brahmins anoint their *stone images* with *oil* before bathing; and some anoint them with sweet-scented oil. This is a practice which arises more from the *customs* of the Hindoos than from their *idolatry*. Anointing *persons* as an act of homage has been transferred to their *idols*.

There is a foolish tradition that the stone set up by Jacob was afterwards brought to Jerusalem, from which, after a long lapse of time, it was brought to Spain, from Spain to Ireland, from Ireland to Scotland, and on it the kings of Scotland sat to be crowned; and concerning which the following leonine verses were made:—

Ni fallat fatum,—Scoti quocunque locatum
Invenient lapidem,—regnare tenentur ibidem.

Or fate is blind—or Scots shall find
Where'er this stone—the royal throne.
Camden's Perthshire.

Edward *I.* had it brought to Westminster; and there this stone, called *Jacob's pillar*, and *Jacob's pillow*, is now placed under the chair on which the king sits when crowned! It would be as ridiculous to attempt to disprove the truth of this tradition, as to prove that the stone under the old chair in Westminster was the identical stone which served the patriarch for a bolster.

And poured oil upon the top of it.] Stones, images, and altars, dedicated to Divine worship, were always anointed with oil. This appears to have been considered as a consecration of them to the object of the worship, and a means of inducing the god or goddess to take up their residence there, and answer the petitions of their votaries. Anointing stones, images, &c., is used in idolatrous countries to the present day, and the whole idol is generally smeared over with oil. Sometimes, besides the anointing, a crown or garland was placed on the stone or altar to honour the divinity, who was supposed, in consequence of the *anointing*, to have set up his residence in that place. It appears to have been on this ground that the seats of polished stone, on which the kings sat in the front of their palaces to administer justice, were *anointed*, merely to invite the deity to reside there, that true judgment might be given, and a righteous sentence always be pronounced. Of this we have an instance in HOMER, *Odyss.* lib. v., ver. 406–410:—

Εκ δ' ελθων, κατ' αρ' ἑζετ' επι ξεστοισι λιθοισιν,
Οἱ οἱ εσαν προπαροιθε θυραων ὑψηλαων,
Λευκοι, αποστιλβοντες αλειφατος· οἱς επι μεν πριν
Νηλευς ἱζεσκεν, θεοφιν μηστωρ αταλαντος.

The old man early rose, walk'd forth, and sate
On *polish'd stone* before his palace gate;
With *unguent smooth* the lucid marble shone,
Where ancient Neleus sate, a rustic throne. POPE.

This gives a *part* of the sense of the passage; but the last line, on which much stress should be laid, is very inadequately rendered by the English poet. It should be translated,—

Where Neleus sat, equal *in counsel to the gods;*

because inspired by their wisdom, and which inspiration he and his successor took pains to secure by consecrating with the *anointing oil* the seat of judgment

A. M. cir. 2225. B. C. cir. 1779.

19 And he called the name of
[k]that place [l]Beth-el: but the
name of that city *was called* Luz at the first.
20 [m]And Jacob vowed a vow, saying, If
[n]God will be with me, and will
keep me in this way that I go,
and will give me [o]bread to eat, and raiment
to put on,

A. M. cir. 2225. B. C. cir. 1779.

[k]Judges i. 23, 26; Hosea iv. 15.——[l]That is, *the house of God.*——[m]Chap. xxxi. 13; Judg. xi. 30; 2 Sam. xv. 8.——[n]Ver. 15.——[o]1 Tim. vi. 8.

on which they were accustomed to sit. Some of the ancient commentators on Homer mistook the meaning of this place by not understanding the nature of the custom; and these *Cowper* unfortunately follows, translating "resplendent *as* with oil;" which *as* destroys the whole sense, and obliterates the allusion. This sort of anointing was a common custom in all antiquity, and was probably derived from this circumstance. *Arnobius* tells us that it was customary with himself while a heathen, "when he saw a smooth polished stone that had been smeared with oils, to kiss and adore it, as if possessing a Divine virtue." *Si quando conspexeram lubricatum lapidem, et ex olivi unguine sordidatum (ordinatum I) tanquam inesset vis præsens, adulabar, affabar.* And *Theodoret*, in his eighty-fourth question on Genesis, asserts that many pious women in his time were accustomed to *anoint* the coffins of the martyrs, &c. And in Catholic countries when a church is consecrated they *anoint* the door-posts, pillars, altars, &c. So under the law there was a *holy anointing oil* to sanctify the tabernacle, laver, and all other things used in God's service, Exod. xl. 9, &c.

Verse 19. *He called the name of that place Beth-el*] That is, the *house of God;* for in consequence of his having *anointed* the stone, and thus *consecrated* it to God, he considered it as becoming henceforth his peculiar residence; see on the preceding verse. This word should be always pronounced as two distinct syllables, each strongly accented, Beth-El.

Was called *Luz at the first.*] The Hebrew has אולם לוז *Ulam Luz*, which the Roman edition of the Septuagint translates Ουλαμλουζ *Oulamlouz;* the Alexandrian MS., Ουλαμμαυς *Oulammaus;* the Aldine, Ουλαμμαους *Oulammaous;* Symmachus, Λαμμαους *Lammaous;* and some others, Ουλαμ *Oulam*. The Hebrew אולם *ulam* is sometimes a particle signifying *as, just as;* hence it may signify that the place was called Beth-El, *as it was* formerly called Luz. As Luz signifies an *almond, almond* or *hazel tree*, this place probably had its name from a number of such trees growing in that region. Many of the ancients confounded this city with *Jerusalem*, to which they attribute the *eight* following names, which are all expressed in this verse:—

> *Solyma, Luza, Bethel, Hierosolyma, Jebus, Ælia,*
> Urbs sacra, *Hierusalem* dicitur atque *Salem.*

> Solyma, Luz, Beth-El, Hierosolyma, Jebus, Ælia,
> The holy city is call'd, as also Jerusalem and Salem.

From Beth-El came the *Baetylia, Bethyllia*, Βαιτυλια, or *animated stones*, so celebrated in antiquity, and to which Divine honours were paid. The tradition of Jacob anointing this stone, and calling the place *Beth-El*, gave rise to all the superstitious accounts of the *Baetylia* or *consecrated stones*, which we find in *Sanchoniathon* and others. These became abused to idolatrous purposes, and hence God strongly prohibits them, Lev. xxvi. 1; and it is very likely that stones of this kind were the most ancient objects of idolatrous worship: these were afterwards formed into beautiful human figures, male and female, when the art of *sculpture* became tolerably perfected, and hence the *origin of idolatry* as far as it refers to the worshipping of *images*, for these, being consecrated by anointing, &c., were supposed immediately to become *instinct* with the power and energy of some divinity. Hence, then, the *Baetylia* or *living stones* of the ancient Phœnicians, &c. As *oil* is an emblem of the gifts and graces of the Holy Spirit, so those who receive this anointing are considered as being *alive* unto God, and are expressly called by St. Peter *living stones*, 1 Pet ii. 4, 5. May not the apostle have reference to those living stones or *Baetyllia* of antiquity, and thus correct the notion by showing that these rather represented the true worshippers of God, who were consecrated to his service and made partakers of the Holy Ghost, and that these alone could be properly called the *living stones* out of which the true spiritual temple is composed?

Verse 20. *Vowed a vow*] A vow is a solemn, holy promise, by which a man bound himself to do certain things in a particular way, time, &c., and for power to accomplish which he depended on God; hence all vows were made with prayer.

If God will be with me, &c.] Jacob seems to make this vow rather for his *posterity* than for *himself*; as we may learn from ver. 13–15; for he particularly refers to the promises which God had made to him, which concerned the *multiplication of his offspring*, and *their establishment* in *that* land. *If*, then, God shall fulfil these promises, he binds his *posterity* to build God a house, and to devote for the maintenance of his worship the *tenth* of all their earthly goods. This mode of interpretation removes that appearance of *self-interest* which almost any other view of the subject presents. Jacob had certainly, long ere this, taken Jehovah for his God; and so thoroughly had he been instructed in the knowledge of Jehovah, that we may rest satisfied no reverses of fortune could have induced him to apostatize: but as his taking refuge with Laban was probably typical of the sojourning of his descendants in Egypt, his persecution, so as to be obliged to depart from Laban, the bad treatment of his posterity by the Egyptians, his rescue from death, preservation on his journey, re-establishment in his own country, &c., were all typical of the exodus of his descendants, their travels in the desert, and establishment in the promised land, where they built a house to God, and where, for the support and maintenance of the pure worship of God, they gave to the priests and Levites the *tenth of all their worldly produce*. *If* all this be understood as referring to Jacob *only*, the Scripture gives us no information how he performed his vow.

A. M. cir. 2225. B. C. cir. 1779.

21 So that [p] I come again to my
father's house in peace; [q] then
shall the LORD be my God:
22 And this stone, which I have set *for*
a pillar, [r] shall be God's house:
[s] and of all that thou shalt
give me I will surely give the tenth unto
thee.

[p] Judg. xi. 31; 2 Samuel xix. 24, 30.——[q] Exodus xv. 2; Deut. xxvi. 17; 2 Sam. xv. 8; 2 Kings v. 17.——[r] Ver. 17; chap. xiv. 20; xxxv. 7, 14.——[s] Lev. xxvii. 30-33; Deut. xiv. 22, 23.

Verse 22. *This stone—shall be God's house*] That is, (as far as this matter refers to Jacob alone,) should I be preserved to return in safety, I shall worship God in this place. And this purpose he fulfilled, for there he built an altar, anointed it with oil, and *poured a drink-offering thereon.*

For a practical use of Jacob's vision, see note on verse 12.

ON the doctrine of *tithes*, or an adequate support for the ministers of the Gospel, I shall here register my opinion. Perhaps a word may be borne from one who never received any, and has none in prospect. *Tithes* in their origin appear to have been a sort of *eucharistic offering* made unto God, and probably were something similar to the *minchah*, which we learn from Gen. iv. was in use almost from the foundation of the world. When God established a regular, and we may add an expensive worship, it was necessary that proper provision should be made for the support of those who were obliged to devote their whole time to it, and consequently were deprived of the opportunity of providing for themselves in any secular way. It was soon found that a *tenth* part of the produce of the whole land was necessary for this purpose, as a whole *tribe*, that of *Levi*, was devoted to the public service of God; and when the land was divided, this tribe received no inheritance among their brethren. Hence, for their support, the *law of tithes* was enacted; and by these the priests and Levites were not only supported as the ministers of God, but as the *teachers* and *intercessors* of the people, performing a great variety of religious duties *for them* which otherwise they themselves were bound to perform. As this mode of supporting the ministers of God was instituted by himself, so we may rest assured it was rational and just. Nothing can be more reasonable than to devote a portion of the earthly good which we receive from the free mercy of God, to his own service; especially when by doing it we are essentially serving ourselves. *If* the ministers of God give up their whole time, talents, and strength, to watch over, labour for, and instruct the people in spiritual things, justice requires that they shall receive their support from the work. How worthless and wicked must that man be, who is continually receiving good from the Lord's hands without restoring any part for the support of true religion, and for charitable purposes! To such God says, *Their table shall become a snare to them*, and that he *will curse their blessings.* God expects returns of gratitude in this way from every man; he that has much should give plenteously, he that has little should do his diligence to give of that little.

It is not the business of these notes to dispute on the article of *tithes;* certainly it would be well could a proper *substitute* be found for them, and the clergy paid by some other method, as this appears in the present state of things to be very objectionable; and the mode of *levying* them is vexatious in the extreme, and serves to sow dissensions between the clergyman and his parishioners, by which *many* are not only alienated from the Church, but also from the *power* as well as the *form* of godliness. But still the *labourer* is worthy of his hire; and the maintenance of the *public ministry* of the word of God should not be left to the caprices of men. He who is only supported *for his work*, will be probably abandoned when he is no longer capable of public service. I have seen many aged and worn-out ministers reduced to great necessity, and almost literally obliged to beg their bread among those whose opulence and salvation were, under God, the fruits of their ministry! Such persons may think they do God service by disputing against "*tithes*, as legal institutions long since abrogated," while they permit their worn-out ministers to starve:—but how shall they appear in that day when Jesus shall say, *I was hungry, and ye gave me no meat; thirsty, and ye gave me no drink; naked, and ye clothed me not?* It is true, that where a provision is *established* on a certain order of priesthood by the law, it may be sometimes claimed and consumed by the worthless and the profane; but this is no necessary consequence of such establishment, as there are laws which, if put in action, have sufficient energy to expel every wicked and slothful servant from the vineyard of Christ. This however is seldom done. At all events, this is no reason why those who have served God and their generation should not be comfortably supported during that service; and when incapable of it, be furnished at least with the *necessaries* of life. Though many ministers have reason to complain of this neglect, who have no claims on a legal ecclesiastical establishment, yet none have cause for louder complaint than the generality of those called *curates*, or unbeneficed ministers, in the Church of England: their employers clothe themselves with the wool, and feed themselves with the fat; they tend not the flock, and their substitutes that perform the labour and do the drudgery of the office, are permitted at least to *half starve* on an inadequate remuneration. Let a national worship be supported, but let the support be derived from a less objectionable source than *tithes;* for as the law now stands relative to them, no one purpose of moral instruction or piety can be promoted by the *system*. On their present plan tithes are oppressive and unjust; the clergyman has a right by law to the *tenth* of the produce of the *soil*, and to the *tenth* of all that is *supported by it*. He claims even the *tenth egg*, as well as the *tenth apple;* the *tenth* of all *grain*, of all *hay*, and even of all the produce of the *kitchen garden;* but he contributes nothing to the cultivation of the soil. A comparatively poor man rents a farm; it is entirely *out of heart*, for it

has been exhausted; it yields very little, and the *tenth* is not much; at the expense of all he has, he dresses and manures this ungrateful soil; to repay him and *keep up the cultivation* would require three years' produce. It begins to yield well, and the clergyman takes the *tenth* which is now in *quantity* and *quality* more in value than a *pound*, where before it was not a *shilling*. But the whole crop would not repay the farmer's expenses. *In* proportion to the farmer's improvement is the clergyman's tithe, who has never contributed one shilling to aid in this extra produce! Here then not only the *soil* pays *tithes*, but the man's *property* brought *upon the soil* pays *tithes:* his *skill* and *industry* also are *tithed;* or if he have been obliged to *borrow cash*, he not only has to pay *tithes* on the produce of this borrowed money, but five per cent. interest for the money itself. All this is oppressive and cruelly unjust. I say again, let there be a national religion, and a national clergy supported by the state; but let them be supported by a *tax*, not by *tithes*, or rather let them be paid out of the general taxation; or, if the *tithe* system must be continued, let the *poor-rates* be abolished, and the clergy, out of the tithes, support the poor in their respective parishes, as was the original custom

---

CHAPTER XXIX.

Jacob proceeds on his journey, 1. *Comes to a well where the flocks of his uncle Laban, as well as those of several others, were usually watered,* 2, 3. *Inquires from the shepherds concerning Laban and his family,* 4–6. *While they are conversing about watering the sheep,* 7, 8, *Rachel arrives,* 9. *He assists her to water her flock,* 10; *makes himself known unto her,* 11, 12. *She hastens home and communicates the tidings of Jacob's arrival to her father,* 12. *Laban hastens to the well, embraces Jacob, and brings him home,* 13. *After a month's stay, Laban proposes to give Jacob wages,* 14, 15. *Leah and Rachel described,* 16, 17. *Jacob proposes to serve seven years for Rachel,* 18. *Laban consents,* 19. *When the seven years were fulfilled, Jacob demands his wife,* 20, 21. *Laban makes a marriage feast,* 22; *and in the evening substitutes Leah for Rachel, to whom he gives Zilpah for handmaid,* 23, 24. *Jacob discovers the fraud, and upbraids Laban;* 25. *He excuses himself,* 26; *and promises to give him Rachel for another seven years of service,* 27. *After abiding a week with Leah, he receives Rachel for wife, to whom Laban gives Bilhah for handmaid,* 28, 29. *Jacob loves Rachel more than Leah, and serves seven years for her,* 30. *Leah being despised, the Lord makes her fruitful, while Rachel continues barren,* 31. *Leah bears* Reuben, 32, *and* Simeon, 33, *and* Levi, 34, *and* Judah; *after which she leaves off bearing,* 35.

A. M. cir. 2225. B. C. cir. 1779.

THEN Jacob [a] went on his journey, [b] and came into the land of the [c] people of the east.

2 And he looked, and behold a well in the field, and, lo, there *were* three flocks of sheep lying by it; for out of that well they watered the flocks: and a great stone *was* upon the well's mouth.

3 And thither were all the flocks gathered: and they rolled the stone from the well's mouth, and watered the sheep, and put the stone again upon the well's mouth in his place.

4 And Jacob said unto them, My brethren, whence *be* ye? And they said, [d] Of Haran *are* we.

[a] Heb. *lift up his feet.*——[b] Chap. xxviii. 5–7; Num. xxiii. 7; Judg. vi. 3, 33; Hos. xii. 12.——[c] Hebrews, *children.*——[d] Chapter xxvii. 43; xxviii. 10.

NOTES ON CHAP. XXIX.

Verse 1. *Then Jacob went on his journey*] The original is very remarkable: *And Jacob lifted up his feet, and he travelled unto the land of the children of the east.* There is a certain *cheerfulness* marked in the original which comports well with the state of mind into which he had been brought by the vision of the ladder and the promises of God. He now saw that having God for his protector he had nothing to fear, and therefore he went on his way rejoicing.

People of the east.] The inhabitants of Mesopotamia and the whole country beyond the Euphrates are called קדם *kedem*, or *easterns*, in the sacred writings.

Verse 2. *Three flocks of sheep*] צאן *tson*, small cattle, such as *sheep*, *goats*, &c.; see on chap. xii. 16. Sheep, in a healthy state, seldom drink in cold and comparatively cold countries: but it was probably different in hot climates. The *three flocks*, if *flocks* and not *shepherds* be meant, which were lying now at the well, did not belong to *Laban*, but to three other chiefs; for *Laban's* flock was yet to come, under the care of Rachel, ver. 6.

Verse 3. *All the flocks*] Instead of העדרים *hadarim*, *flocks*, the Samaritan reads ࠄࠓࠏࠉࠌ *haroim*, *shepherds*; for which reading *Houbigant* strongly contends, as well in this verse as in verse 8. *It* certainly cannot be said that *all the flocks rolled the stone from the well's mouth, and watered the sheep:* and yet so it appears to read if we prefer the common Hebrew text to the Samaritan. *It* is probable that the same reading was originally that of the second verse also.

And put the stone again upon the well's mouth] It is very likely that the stone was a *large one*, which was necessary to prevent ill-minded individuals from either disturbing the water, or filling up the well; hence a great stone was provided, which required the joint exertions of several shepherds to remove it; and hence those who arrived first waited till all the others were come up, that they might water their respective flocks in concert.

Verse 4. *My brethren, whence be ye?*] The lan-

A. M. cir. 2225.
B. C. cir. 1779.

5 And he said unto them, Know ye Laban the son of Nahor? And they said, We know *him*.

6 And he said unto them, [e] *Is* he well? [f] And they said, *He is* well: and behold, Rachel his daughter cometh with the sheep.

7 And he said, Lo, [g] *it is* yet high day: neither *is it* time that the cattle should be gathered together: water ye the sheep, and go *and* feed *them*.

8 And they said, We cannot, until all the flocks be gathered together, and *till* they roll the stone from the well's mouth; then we water the sheep.

9 And while he yet spake with them, [h] Rachel came with her father's sheep: for she kept them.

10 And it came to pass, when Jacob saw Rachel the daughter of Laban his mother's brother, and the sheep of Laban his mother's brother, that Jacob went near, and rolled [i] the stone from the well's mouth, and watered the flock of Laban his mother's brother.

A. M. cir. 2225.
B. C. cir. 1779.

11 And Jacob [k] kissed Rachel, and lifted up his voice, and wept.

12 And Jacob told Rachel that he *was* [l] her father's brother, and that he *was* Rebekah's son: [m] and she ran and told her father.

13 And it came to pass, when Laban heard the [n] tidings of Jacob his sister's son, that [o] he ran to meet him, and embraced him, and kissed him, and brought him to his house. And he told Laban all these things.

14 And Laban said to him, [p] Surely thou

[e] Heb. Is there *peace to him?*——[f] Chap. xliii. 27.——[g] Heb. *yet the day* is *great*.——[h] Exod. ii. 16.——[i] Exod. ii. 17.——[k] Ch. xxxiii. 4; xlv. 14, 15.

[l] Chap. xiii. 8; xiv. 14, 16.——[m] Chapter xxiv. 28.——[n] Heb. *hearing*.——[o] Chap. xxiv. 29.——[p] Chapter ii. 23; Judg. ix. 2; 2 Sam. v. 1; xix. 12, 13.

guage of Laban and his family was *Chaldee* and not Hebrew; (see chap. xxxi. 47;) but from the *names* which Leah gave to her children we see that the two languages had many words in common, and therefore Jacob and the shepherds might understand each other with little difficulty. It is possible also that Jacob might have learned the Chaldee or Aramitish language from his mother, as this was his *mother's tongue*.

Verse 5. *Laban the son of Nahor*] *Son* is here put for *grandson*, for Laban was the son of Bethuel the son of Nahor.

Verse 6. Is *he well?*] השלום לו *hashalom lo?* Is there peace to him? *Peace* among the Hebrews signified *all kinds of prosperity*. Is he a prosperous man in his family and in his property? And they said, He is *well*, שלום *shalom*, he prospers.

Rachel—cometh with the sheep.] רחל *rachel* (the *ch* sounded strongly guttural) signifies a *sheep* or *ewe;* and she probably had her name from her fondness for these animals.

Verse 7. It is *yet high day*] The day is but about half run; *neither* is it *time that the cattle should be gathered together*—it is surely not time yet to put them into the folds; give them therefore water, and take them again to pasture.

Verse 8. *We cannot, until all the flocks be gathered together*] It is a rule that the stone shall not be removed till all the shepherds and the flocks which have a right to this well be gathered together; then, and not before, we may water the sheep. See on ver. 3.

Verse 9. *Rachel came with her father's sheep*] So we find that young women were not *kept concealed in the house* till the time they were married, which is the common gloss put on עלמה *almah, a virgin, one concealed.* Nor was it beneath the dignity of the daughters of the most opulent chiefs to carry water from the well, as in the case of Rebekah; or tend sheep, as in the case of Rachel. The chief *property* in those times consisted in *flocks:* and who so proper to take care of them as those who were interested in their safety and increase? Honest labour, far from being a discredit, is an honour both to *high* and *low*. The *king* himself is served by the field; and without it, and the labour necessary for its cultivation, all ranks must perish. Let every son, let every daughter, learn that it is no discredit to be employed, whenever it may be necessary, in the meanest offices, by which the interests of the family may be *honestly* promoted.

Verse 10. *Jacob went near, and rolled the stone*] Probably the flock of Laban was the last of those which had a right to the well; that flock being now come, Jacob assisted the shepherds to roll off the stone, (for it is not likely he did it by himself,) and so assisted his cousin, to whom he was as yet unknown, to water her flock.

Verse 11. *Jacob kissed Rachel*] A simple and pure method by which the primitive inhabitants of the earth testified their friendship to each other, first abused by *hypocrites*, who pretended affection while their vile hearts meditated terror, (see the case of Joab,) and afterwards disgraced by refiners on morals, who, while they pretended to stumble at those innocent expressions of affection and friendship, were capable of committing the grossest acts of impurity.

And lifted up his voice] It may be, in thanksgiving to God for the favour he had shown him, in conducting him thus far in peace and safety.

And wept.] From a sense of the goodness of his heavenly Father, and his own unworthiness of the success with which he had been favoured. The same expressions of kindness and pure affection are repeated on the part of Laban, ver. 13.

Verse 14. *My bone and my flesh.*] One of my nearest relatives.

A. M. cir. 2225.
B. C. cir. 1779.

art my bone and my flesh. And he abode with him [q] the space of a month.

15 And Laban said unto Jacob, Because thou *art* my brother, shouldest thou therefore serve me for naught? tell me, what *shall* thy wages *be?*

16 And Laban had two daughters: the name of the elder *was* Leah, and the name of the younger *was* Rachel.

17 Leah *was* tender-eyed; but Rachel was [r] beautiful and well favoured.

18 And Jacob loved Rachel; and said, [s] I will serve thee seven years for Rachel thy younger daughter.

19 And Laban said, [t] *It is* better that I give her to thee, than that I should give her to another man: abide with me.

20 And Jacob [u] served seven years for

[q] Heb. *a month of days.*—[r] Chap. xii. 11; xxiv. 16; xxxix. 6; Prov. xxxi. 30.—[s] Chap. xxxi. 41; xxxiv. 12.

[t] Psa. xii. 2.—[u] Chap. xxx. 26; Hos. xii. 12; Cant. viii. 6, 7; 1 Cor. xiii. 7.

Verse 15. *Because thou* art *my brother, &c.*] Though thou art my nearest relative, yet I have no right to thy services without giving thee an adequate recompense. Jacob had passed a whole month in the family of Laban, in which he had undoubtedly rendered himself of considerable service. As Laban, who was of a very *saving* if not *covetous* disposition, saw that he was likely to be of great use to him in his secular concerns, he wished to secure his services, and therefore asks him what wages he wished to have.

Verse 17. *Leah* was *tender-eyed*] רכות *raccoth, soft, delicate, lovely.* I believe the word means just the *reverse* of the signification generally given to it. The design of the inspired writer is to *compare* both the sisters together, that the balance may appear to be greatly in favour of Rachel. The chief recommendation of Leah was her *soft* and *beautiful eyes;* but Rachel was יפת תאר *yephath toar,* beautiful in her *shape, person, mien,* and *gait,* and יפת מראה *yephath mareh,* beautiful in her *countenance.* The words plainly signify *a fine shape* and *fine features,* all that can be considered as essential to personal beauty. Therefore Jacob loved her, and was willing to become a *bond servant* for seven years, that he might get her to wife; for in his destitute state he could produce no dowry, and it was the custom of those times for the father to receive a portion *for* his daughter, and not to give one *with* her. One of the Hindoo lawgivers says, "A person may become a *slave* on account of love, or to obtain a wife." The bad system of education by which women are spoiled and rendered in general good for nothing, makes it necessary for the husband to get a dowry with his wife to enable him to maintain her; whereas in former times they were well educated and extremely useful, hence he who got a *wife* almost invariably got a *prize,* or as Solomon says, got a good thing.

Verse 20. *And Jacob served seven years for Rachel*] In ancient times it appears to have been a custom among all nations that men should give *dowries* for their wives; and in many countries this custom still prevails. When Shechem asked Dinah for wife, he said, *Ask me never so much dowry and gift, and I will give according as ye shall say unto me.* When Eliezer went to get Rebekah for Isaac, he took a profusion of riches with him, in *silver, gold, jewels,* and *raiment,* with other *costly things,* which, when the contract was made, he gave to Rebekah, her mother, and her brothers. David, in order to be Saul's son-in-law, must, instead of a *dowry,* kill Goliath; and when this was done, he was not permitted to espouse Michal till he had killed one hundred Philistines. The Prophet Hosea bought his wife for *fifteen pieces of silver, and a homer and a half of barley.* The same custom prevailed among the ancient *Greeks, Indians,* and *Germans.* The *Romans* also had a sort of marriage entitled *per coemptionem,* "by purchase." The *Tartars* and *Turks* still buy their wives; but among the latter they are bought as a sort of *slaves.*

Herodotus mentions a very singular custom among the *Babylonians,* which may serve to throw light on Laban's conduct towards Jacob. "In every district they annually assemble all the marriageable virgins on a certain day; and when the men are come together and stand round the place, the crier rising up sells one after another, always bringing forward the *most beautiful* first; and having sold her for a great sum of gold, he puts up her who is esteemed second in beauty. On this occasion the richest of the Babylonians used to contend for the fairest wife, and to outbid one another. But the vulgar are content to take the ugly and lame *with* money; for when all the beautiful virgins are sold, the crier orders the *most deformed* to stand up; and after he has openly demanded who will mary her *with a small sum,* she is at length given to the man that is contented to marry her with the *least.* And in this manner the money arising from the sale of the *handsome* served for a portion to those whose look was disagreeable, or who had any bodily imperfection. A father was not permitted to indulge his own fancy in the choice of a husband for his daughter; neither might the purchaser carry off the woman which he had bought without giving sufficient security that he would live with her as his own wife. Those also who received a sum of money with such as could bring no price in this market, were obliged also to give sufficient security that they would live with them, and if they did not they were obliged to refund the money." Thus Laban made use of the *beauty of Rachel* to dispose of his daughter *Leah,* in the *spirit* of the Babylonian custom, though not in the letter.

And they seemed unto him but *a few days*] If Jacob had been obliged to wait *seven years* before he married Rachel, could it possibly be said that they could appear to him *as a few days?* Though the *letter* of the text seems to say the contrary, yet there are emi

A. M. cir. 2225. B. C. cir. 1779. Rachel; and they seemed unto him *but* a few days, for the love he had to her.

A. M. cir. 2232. B. C. cir. 1772.
21 And Jacob said unto Laban, Give *me* my wife, for my days are fulfilled, that I may [v] go in unto her.
22 And Laban gathered together all the men of the place, and [w] made a feast.
23 And it came to pass in the evening, that he took Leah his daughter, and brought her to him; and he went in unto her.
24 And Laban gave unto his daughter Leah Zilpah his maid *for* a handmaid.
25 And it came to pass, that in the morning, behold, it *was* Leah: and he said to Laban, What *is* this thou hast done unto me? did not I serve with thee for Rachel? wherefore then hast thou beguiled me?
26 And Laban said, It must not be so done in our country, [x] to give the younger before the first-born.
27 [y] Fulfil her week, and we will give thee this also, for the service which thou shalt serve with me, yet seven other years.
28 And Jacob did so, and fulfilled her week:

[v] Judges xv. 1.—[w] Judges xiv. 10; Matthew xxii. 2-10; John ii. 1, 2.

[x] Heb. *place*.—[y] Judg. xiv. 12; Lev. xviii. 18; Mal. ii. 15; chap. xxix. 20.

nent men who strongly contend that he received Rachel soon after the month was finished, (see ver. 14,) and then served seven years for her, which might really appear but a few days to him, because of his increasing love to her; but others think this quite incompatible with all the circumstances marked down in the text, and on the supposition that Jacob was not now seventy-seven years of age, as most chronologers make him, but only fifty-seven, (see on chap. xxxi.,) there will be time sufficient to allow for all the transactions which are recorded in his history, during his stay with Laban. As to the incredibility of a *passionate lover*, as some have termed him, waiting patiently for *seven years* before he could possess the object of his wishes, and those seven years appearing to him as only a few days, it may be satisfactorily accounted for, they think, two ways: 1. He had the continual company of his elect spouse, and this certainly would take away all tedium in the case. 2. Love affairs were not carried to such a pitch of insanity among the patriarchs as they have been in modern times; *they* were much more sober and sedate, and scarcely ever married before they were forty years of age, and then more for *conveniency*, and the desire of having an *offspring*, than for any other purpose. At the very lowest computation Jacob was now fifty-seven, and consequently must have passed those days in which *passion* runs away with *reason*. Still, however, the obvious construction of the text shows that he got Rachel the week after he had married Leah.

Verse 21. *My days are fulfilled*] My seven years are now completed, let me have my wife, for whom I have given this service as a *dowry*.

Verse 22. *Laban—made a feast.*] משתה *mishteh* signifies a feast of *drinking*. As marriage was a very solemn contract, there is much reason to believe that *sacrifices* were offered on the occasion, and *libations* poured out; and we know that on festival occasions a cup of *wine* was offered to every guest; and as this was drunk with particular ceremonies, the feast might derive its name from this circumstance, which was the most prominent and observable on such occasions.

Verse 23. *In the evening—he took Leah his daughter*] As the bride was always *veiled*, and the bride chamber generally *dark*, or nearly so, and as Leah was brought to Jacob in the *evening*, the imposition here practised might easily pass undetected by Jacob, till the ensuing day discovered the fraud.

Verse 24. *And Laban gave—Zilpah his maid*] Slaves given in this way to a daughter on her marriage, were the peculiar property of the daughter; and over them the husband had neither right nor power.

Verse 26. *It must not be so done in our country*] It was an early custom to give daughters in marriage according to their *seniority*; and it is worthy of remark that the oldest people now existing, next to the Jews, I mean the *Hindoos*, have this not merely as a *custom*, but as a *positive law*; and they deem it criminal to give a *younger* daughter in marriage while an elder daughter remains unmarried. Among them it is a high offence, equal to adultery, "for a man to marry while his *elder brother* remains *unmarried*, or for a man to give his daughter to such a person, or to give his youngest daughter in marriage while the eldest sister remains unmarried."—Code of Gentoo Laws, chap. xv., sec. 1, p. 204. This was a custom at Mesopotamia; but Laban took care to conceal it from Jacob till after he had given him Leah. The words of Laban are literally what a Hindoo would say on such a subject.

Verse 27. *Fulfil her week*] The marriage feast, it appears, lasted *seven days*; it would not therefore have been proper to break off the solemnities to which all the men of the place had been invited, ver. 22, and probably Laban wished to keep his *fraud* from the public eye; therefore he informs Jacob that if he will fulfil the marriage *week* for Leah, he will give him Rachel at the end of it, on condition of his serving seven other years. To this the necessity of the case caused Jacob to agree; and thus Laban had *fourteen* years' service instead of *seven*; for it is not likely that Jacob would have served even seven *days* for Leah, as his affection was wholly set on Rachel, the wife of his own choice. By this stratagem Laban gained a settlement for both his daughters. What a man soweth, that shall he reap. Jacob had before practised deceit, and is now deceived; and Laban, the instrument of it, was afterwards deceived himself.

Verse 28. *And Jacob did so—and he gave him Rachel*] It is perfectly plain that Jacob did not serve

A. M. cir. 2232. B. C. cir. 1772. and he gave him Rachel his daughter to wife also.

29 And Laban gave to Rachel his daughter [a] Bilhah his handmaid to be her maid.

30 And he went in also unto Rachel, and he [a] loved also Rachel more than Leah, and served with him [b] yet seven other years.

31 And when the LORD [c] saw that Leah *was* hated, he [d] opened her womb: but Rachel *was* barren.

A. M. cir. 2233. B. C. cir. 1771. 32 And Leah conceived, and bare a son, and she called his name [e] Reuben: for she said, Surely the LORD hath [f] looked upon my affliction; now therefore my husband will love me.

33 And she conceived again, and bare a son; and said, Because the LORD hath heard that I *was* hated he hath therefore given me this *son* also: and she called his name [g] Simeon. A. M. cir. 2234 B. C. cir. 1770

34 And she conceived again, and bare a son; and said, Now this time will my husband be joined unto me, because I have borne him three sons: therefore was his name called [h] Levi. A. M. cir. 2235. B. C. cir. 1769.

35 And she conceived again, and bare a son; and she said, Now will I praise the LORD: therefore she called his name [i] Judah; [k] and [l] left bearing. A. M. cir. 2236 B. C. cir. 1768

[z] Verse 24; chapter xxx. 3–8.——[a] Verse 20; Deut. xxi. 15. [b] Chap. xxx. 26; xxxi. 41; Hosea xii. 12.——[c] Psa. cxxvii. 3. [d] Chap. xxx. 1.——[e] That is, *see a son.*

[f] Exod. iii. 7; iv. 31; Deut. xxvi. 7; Psa. xxv. 18; cvi. 44. [g] That is, *hearing.*——[h] That is, *joined;* see Num. xviii. 2, 4. [i] Matt. i. 2.——[k] That is, *praise.*——[l] Heb. *stood from bearing.*

seven years more *before* he got Rachel to wife; but having spent a week with Leah, and in keeping the marriage feast, he then got Rachel, and served afterwards seven years for *her*. Connections of this kind are now called *incestuous;* but it appears they were allowable in those ancient times. In taking both sisters, it does not appear that any blame attached to Jacob, though in consequence of it he was vexed by their jealousies. It was probably because of this that the law was made, *Thou shalt not take a wife to her sister, to vex her, besides the other in her life-time.* After this, all such marriages were strictly forbidden.

Verse 31. *The Lord saw that Leah* was *hated*] From this and the preceding verse we get the genuine meaning of the word שנא *sane, to hate,* in certain disputed places in the Scriptures. The word simply signifies *a less degree of love;* so it is said, ver. 30: "Jacob loved Rachel *more* than Leah," *i. e.,* he loved Leah *less* than Rachel; and *this* is called *hating* in ver. 31: *When the Lord saw that Leah was hated*—that she had *less affection* shown to her than was her due, as one of the legitimate wives of Jacob, *he opened her womb*—he blessed her with children. Now the frequent intercourse of Jacob with Leah (see the following verses) sufficiently proves that he did not *hate* her in the sense in which this term is used among us; but he felt and showed *less affection* for her than for her sister. So *Jacob have I loved, but Esau have I hated,* simply means, I have shown a greater degree of affection for Jacob and his posterity than I have done for Esau and his descendants, by giving the former a better earthly portion than I have given to the latter, and by choosing the family of Jacob to be the progenitors of the Messiah. But not one word of all this relates to the *eternal* states of either of the two nations. Those who endeavour to support certain peculiarities of their creed by such scriptures as these, do greatly err, not knowing the Scripture, and not properly considering either the *sovereignty* or the *mercy* of God.

Verse 32. *She called his name Reuben*] ראובן *reuben,* literally, *see ye* or *behold a son; for Jehovah hath looked upon,* ראה *raah, beheld,* my affliction; *behold* then the consequence, I have got a son!

Verse 33. *She called his name Simeon.*] שמעון *shimon, hearing;* i. e., God had blessed her with another son, *because* he had *heard that she was hated*—loved less than Rachel was.

Verse 34. *Therefore was his name called Levi.*] לוי *levi, joined;* because she supposed that, in consequence of all these children, Jacob would become *joined* to her in as strong affection, at least, as he was to Rachel. From Levi sprang the tribe of *Levites,* who instead of the *first-born,* were *joined* unto the priests in the service of the sanctuary. See Num. xviii. 2, 4.

Verse 35. *She called his name Judah*] יהודה *yehudah,* a *confessor;* one who *acknowledges* God, and acknowledges that all good comes from his hands, and gives him the praise due to his grace and mercy. From this patriarch the *Jews* have their name, and could it be now rightly applied to them, it would intimate that they were a people that *confess* God, *acknowledge* his bounty, and *praise* him for his grace.

Left bearing.] That is, *for a time;* for she had several children afterwards. Literally translated, the original תעמד מלדת *taamod milledeth—she stood still from bearing,* certainly does not convey the same meaning as that in our translation; the one appearing to signify that she *ceased entirely* from having children; the other, that she only *desisted for a time,* which was probably occasioned by a temporary suspension of Jacob's company, who appears to have deserted the tent of Leah through the jealous management of Rachel.

The intelligent and pious care of the original inhabitants of the world to call their children by those names which were descriptive of some *remarkable event* in *providence, circumstance* of their *birth,* or *domestic occurrence,* is worthy, not only of *respect,* but of *imitation.* As the *name* itself continually called to the mind, both of the parents and the child, the circumstance from which it originated, it could not fail to

be a lasting blessing to both. How widely different is our custom! Unthinking and ungodly, we impose names upon our offspring as we do upon our cattle; and often the dog, the horse, the monkey, and the parrot, share in common with our children the names which are called *Christian!* Some of our Christian names, so called, are *absurd*, others are *ridiculous*, and a third class *impious;* these last being taken from the demon gods and goddesses of heathenism. May we hope that the rational and pious custom recommended in the Scriptures shall ever be restored, even among those who profess to *believe* in, *fear*, and *love* God!

CHAPTER XXX.

Rachel *envies her sister, and chides Jacob,* 1. *He reproves her and vindicates himself,* 2. *She gives him her maid* Bilhah, 3, 4. *She conceives, and bears* Dan, 5, 6; *and afterwards* Naphtali, 7, 8. Leah *gives* Zilpah *her maid to Jacob,* 9. *She conceives and bears* Gad, 10, 11, *and also* Asher, 12, 13. Reuben *finds mandrakes, of which* Rachel *requests a part,* 14. *The bargain made between her and Leah,* 15. *Jacob in consequence lodges with Leah instead of Rachel,* 16. *She conceives, and bears* Issachar, 17, 18, *and* Zebulun, 19, 20, *and* Dinah, 21. *Rachel conceives, and bears* Joseph, 22–24. *Jacob requests permission from Laban to go to his own country,* 25, 26. *Laban entreats him to tarry, and offers to give him what wages he shall choose to name,* 27, 28. *Jacob details the importance of his services to Laban,* 29, 30, *and offers to continue those services for the* speckled *and* spotted *among the goats, and the* brown *among the sheep,* 31–33. *Laban consents,* 34, *and divides all the* ring-streaked *and* spotted *among the* he-goats, *the* speckled *and* spotted *among the* she-goats, *and the* brown *among the* sheep, *and puts them under the care of his sons, and sets three days' journey between himself and Jacob,* 35, 36. *Jacob's stratagem of the* pilled rods, *to cause the cattle to bring forth the* ring-streaked, speckled, *and* spotted, 37–39. *In consequence of which he increased his flock greatly, getting all that was strong and healthy in the flock of Laban,* 40–43.

A. M. cir. 2236. B. C. cir. 1768.

AND when Rachel saw that [a] she bare Jacob no children, Rachel [b] envied her sister; and said unto Jacob, Give me children, [c] or else I die.

2 And Jacob's anger was kindled against Rachel: and he said, [d] *Am* I in God's stead, who hath withheld from thee the fruit of the womb?

3 And she said, Behold, [e] my maid Bilhah, go in unto her; [f] and she shall bear upon my knees, [g] that I may also [h] have children by her.

4 And she gave him Bilhah her handmaid [i] to wife: and Jacob went in unto her.

5 And Bilhah conceived, and bare Jacob a son. A. M. cir. 2237. B. C. cir. 1767.

6 And Rachel said, God hath [k] judged me, and hath also heard my voice, and hath given me a son: therefore called she his name [l] Dan.

7 And Bilhah Rachel's maid conceived again, and bare Jacob a second son. A. M. cir. 2239. B. C. cir. 1765.

8 And Rachel said, With [m] great wrestlings have I wrestled with my sister, and I have prevailed: and she called his name [n] Naphtali.[o]

[a] Chapter xxix. 31.—[b] Chapter xxxvii. 11.—[c] Job v. 2. [d] Chap. xvi. 2; 1 Sam. i. 5.—[e] Chap. xvi. 2.—[f] Chap. l. 23; Job iii. 12.—[g] Chap. xvi. 2.—[h] Heb. *be built by her.*—[i] Ch. xvi. 3; xxxv. 22.—[k] Psalm xxxv. 24; xliii. 1; Lam. iii. 59. [l] That is, *judging.*—[m] Heb. *wrestlings of God;* chap. xxiii. 6. [n] That is, *my wrestling.*—[o] Called, Matt. iv. 13, *Nephthalim.*

NOTES ON CHAP. XXX.

Verse 1. *Give me children, or else I die.*] This is a most reprehensible speech, and argues not only *envy* and *jealousy*, but also a total want of dependence on God. She had the greatest share of her husband's affection, and yet was not satisfied unless she could engross all the privileges which her sister enjoyed! How true are those sayings, *Envy is as rottenness of the bones!* and, *Jealousy is as cruel as the grave!*

Verse 2. Am *I in God's stead*] Am I greater than God, to give thee what *he* has refused?

Verse 3. *She shall bear upon my knees*] The handmaid was the sole property of the mistress, as has already been remarked in the case of Hagar; and therefore not only all her labour, but even the children borne by her, were the property of the mistress. These female slaves, therefore, bore children *vicariously* for their mistresses; and this appears to be the import of the term, *she shall bear upon my knees.*

That I may also have children by her.] ואבנה מכנה *veibbaneh mimmennah, and I shall be built up by her.* Hence בן *ben, a son* or *child*, from בנה *banah, to build;* because, as a house is formed of the stones, &c., that enter into its composition, so is a family by children.

Verse 6. *Called she his name Dan.*] Because she found God had *judged* for her, and *decided* she should have a son by her handmaid; hence she called his name דן *dan, judging.*

Verse 8. *She called his name Naphtali.*] נפתלי *naphtali, my wrestling*, according to the common mode of interpretation; but it is more likely that the root פתל *pathal* signifies to *twist* or *entwine.* Hence Mr. Parkhurst translates the verse, "*By the twistings*—agency or operation, *of God, I am entwisted with my*

A. M. cir. 2239. B. C. cir. 1765.

9 When Leah saw that she
had left bearing, she took Zilpah
her maid, and [p] gave her Jacob to wife.

A. M. cir. 2240. B. C. cir. 1764.

10 And Zilpah Leah's maid
bare Jacob a son.

11 And Leah said, A troop cometh: and she
called his name [q] Gad.

A. M. cir. 2242. B. C. cir. 1762.

12 And Zilpah Leah's maid
bare Jacob a second son.

13 And Leah said, [r] Happy am I, for the
daughters [s] will call me blessed: and she
called his name [t] Asher.

A. M. cir. 2246. B. C. cir. 1758.

14 And Reuben went in the
days of wheat harvest, and found
[u] mandrakes in the field, and brought them
unto his mother Leah. Then Rachel said to
Leah, [v] Give me, I pray thee, of thy son's
mandrakes.

15 And she said unto her, A. M. cir. 2246 B. C. cir. 1758
[w] *Is it* a small matter that thou
hast taken my husband? and wouldest thou
take away my son's mandrakes also? And
Rachel said, Therefore he shall lie with thee
to-night for thy son's mandrakes.

16 And Jacob came out of the field in the
evening, and Leah went out to meet him, and
said, Thou must come in unto me; for surely
I have hired thee with my son's mandrakes.
And he lay with her that night.

17 And God hearkened unto A. M. cir. 2247. B. C. cir. 1757.
Leah, and she conceived, and
bare Jacob the fifth son.

18 And Leah said, God hath given me
my hire, because I have given my maiden
to my husband: and she called his name
[x] Issachar.

[p] Ver. 4.——[q] That is, *a troop* or *company*; chap. xlix. 19; Deut. xxxiii. 20, 21; Isa. lxv. 11.——[r] Heb. *in my happiness.* [s] Prov. xxxi. 28; Cant. vi. 9; Luke i. 48.

[t] That is, *happy*; chapter xlix. 20; Deut. xxxiii. 24, 25. [u] Cant. vii. 13.——[v] Chapter xxv. 30.——[w] Num. xvi. 9, 13. [x] That is, *a hire.*

sister; that is, my family is now *entwined* or *interwoven* with my sister's family, and has a chance of producing the promised Seed." The *Septuagint*, *Aquila*, and the *Vulgate*, have nearly the same meaning. It is, however, difficult to fix the true meaning of the original.

Verse 11. *She called his name Gad.*] This has been variously translated. גד *gad*, may signify a *troop*, an *army*, a *soldier*, a *false god*, supposed to be the same as *Jupiter* or *Mars*; for as Laban appears to have been, if not an idolater, yet a dealer in a sort of judicial astrology, (see chap xxxi. 19,) Leah, in saying בגד *bagad*, which we translate *a troop cometh*, might mean, *By* or *with the assistance of Gad*—a particular *planet* or *star*, *Jupiter* possibly, I have gotten this son; therefore she called him after the name of that planet or star from which she supposed the succour came. See the note on chap. xxxi. 19. The Septuagint translate it *εν τυχῃ*, *with good fortune*; the Vulgate, *feliciter*, happily; but in all this diversity our own translation may appear as probable as any, if not the genuine one, בא גד *ba gad*, for the *keri*, or marginal reading, has it in *two* words, *a troop cometh*; whereas the *textual* reading has it only in one, בגד *bagad*, *with a troop*. In the Bible published by *Becke*, 1549, the word is translated as an exclamation, *Good luck!*

Verse 13. *And Leah said, Happy am I*] באשרי *beoshri*, *in my happiness*, therefore she called his name אשר *asher*, that is, *blessedness* or *happiness*.

Verse 14. *Reuben—found mandrakes*] דודאים *dudaim*. What these were is utterly unknown, and learned men have wasted much time and pains in endeavouring to guess out a probable meaning. Some translate the word *lilies*, others *jessamine*, others *citrons*, others *mushrooms*, others *figs*, and some think the word means *flowers*, or *fine flowers* in general. *Hasselquist*, the intimate friend and pupil of *Linné*, who travelled into the Holy Land to make discoveries in natural history, imagines that the plant commonly called *mandrake* is intended; speaking of Nazareth in Galilee he says: "What I found most remarkable at this village was a great number of *mandrakes* which grew in a vale below it. I had not the pleasure to see this plant in blossom, the *fruit now* (May 5th, O. S.) *hanging ripe to the stem*, which lay withered on the ground. From the season in which *this mandrake* blossoms and ripens fruit, one might form a conjecture that it was Rachel's *dudaim*. These were brought her in *the wheat harvest*, which in Galilee is in *the month of May*, about this time, and the mandrake was now in fruit." Both among the Greeks and orientals this plant was held in high repute, as being of a prolific virtue, and helping conception; and from it *philtres* were made, and this is favoured by the meaning of the original, *loves*, i. e., incentives to matrimonial connections: and it was probably on this account that Rachel desired them. The whole account however is very obscure.

Verse 15. *Thou hast taken my husband*] It appears probable that Rachel had found means to engross the whole of Jacob's affection and company, and that she now agreed to let him visit the tent of Leah, on account of receiving some of the fruits or plants which Reuben had found.

Verse 16. *I have hired thee*] We may remark among the Jewish women an intense desire of having children; and it seems to have been produced, not from any peculiar affection for children, but through the hope of having a share in the blessing of Abraham, by bringing forth *Him* in whom all the nations of the earth were to be blessed.

Verse 18. *God hath given me my hire*] שכרי *sechari*. *And she called his name Issachar*, יששכר. This word is compounded of יש *yesh*, IS, and שכר *sachar*, WAGES, from שכר *sachar*, to *content*, *satisfy*, *saturate*; hence a satisfaction or compensation for work done, &c.

A. M. cir. 2249.
B. C. cir. 1755.

19 And Leah conceived again,
and bare Jacob the sixth son.
20 And Leah said, God hath endued me
with a good dowry; now will my husband
dwell with me, because I have borne him six
sons: and she called his name [y] Zebulun.[z]

A. M. cir. 2250.
B. C. cir. 1754.

21 And afterwards she bare a
daughter, and called her name
[a] Dinah.

A. M. cir. 2258.
B. C. cir. 1746.

22 And God [b] remembered
Rachel, and God hearkened to
her, and [c] opened her womb.

A. M. 2259.
B. C. 1745.

23 And she conceived, and bare
a son; and said, God hath taken
away [d] my reproach:
24 And she called his name [e] Joseph; and
said, [f] The LORD shall add to me another son.
25 And it came to pass, when Rachel had
borne Joseph, that Jacob said unto Laban,
[g] Send me away, that I may go unto [h] mine
own place, and to my country.
26 Give *me* my wives and my children, [i] for
whom I have served thee, and let me go: for
thou knowest my service which I
have done thee.

A. M. 2259.
B. C. 1745.

27 And Laban said unto him, I pray thee,
if I have found favour in thine eyes, *tarry*:
for [k] I have learned by experience that the
LORD hath blessed me [l] for thy sake.
28 And he said, [m] Appoint me thy wages,
and I will give *it*.
29 And he said unto him, [n] Thou knowest
how I have served thee, and how thy cattle
was with me.
30 For *it was* little which thou hadst before
I *came*, and it is *now* [o] increased unto a multitude; and the LORD hath blessed thee [p] since
my coming: and now, when shall I [q] provide
for mine own house also?
31 And he said, What shall I give thee?
And Jacob said, Thou shalt not give me any
thing; if thou wilt do this thing for me, I will
again feed *and* keep thy flock:
32 I will pass through all thy flock to-day
removing from thence all the speckled and
spotted cattle, and all the brown cattle among

[y] That is, *dwelling*.——[z] Called, Matthew iv. 13, *Zabulon*. [a] That is, *judgment*.——[b] Chap. viii. 1; 1 Sam. i. 19.——[c] Chap. xxix. 31.——[d] 1 Sam. i. 6; Isa. iv. 1; Luke i. 25.——[e] That is, *adding*.——[f] Chap. xxxv. 17.——[g] Chap. xxiv. 54, 56.——[h] Chap. xviii. 33; xxxi. 55.——[i] Chap. xxix. 20, 30.——[k] Chapter xxxix. 3, 5.——[l] See chap. xxvi. 24.——[m] Chap. xxix. 15.——[n] Chapter xxxi. 6, 38, 39, 40; Matt. xxiv. 45; Tit. ii. 10.——[o] Heb. *broken forth*; ver. 43.——[p] Heb. *at my foot*.——[q] 1 Tim. v. 8.

Verse 20. *Now will my husband dwell with me*] יזבלני *yizbeleni*; and she called his name *Zebulun*, זבלון, *a dwelling* or *cohabitation*, as she now expected that Jacob would *dwell* with *her*, as he had before dwelt with *Rachel*.

Verse 21. *And called her name Dinah.*] דינה *dinah*, *judgment*. As Rachel had called her son by Bilhah DAN, ver. 6, so Leah calls her daughter DINAH, God having *judged* and determined for her, as well as for her sister in the preceding instance.

Verse 22. *And God hearkened to her*] After the severe reproof which Rachel had received from her husband, ver. 2, it appears that she sought God by prayer, and that he heard her; so that her prayer and faith obtained what her impatience and unbelief had prevented.

Verse 24. *She called his name Joseph*] יוסף *Yoseph*, *adding*, or *he who adds*; thereby prophetically declaring that God would *add unto her another son*, which was accomplished in the birth of *Benjamin*, chap. xxxv. 18.

Verse 25. *Jacob said unto Laban, Send me away*] Having now, as is generally conjectured, fulfilled the *fourteen* years which he had engaged to serve for Leah and Rachel. See ver. 26, and conclusion of chap. xxxi.

Verse 27. *I have learned by experience*] נחשתי *nichashti*, from נחש *nachash*, *to view attentively*, to *observe*, to *pry into*. I have diligently considered the whole of thy conduct, and marked the increase of my property, and find that the Lord hath blessed me for thy sake. For the meaning of the word נחש *nachash*, see on chap. iii. 1, &c.

Verse 30. *For it was little which thou hadst before I came*] Jacob takes advantage of the concession made by his father-in-law, and asserts that it was for his sake that the Lord had blessed him: *Since my coming*, לרגלי *leragli*, *according to my footsteps*—every step I took in thy service, God prospered to the multiplication of thy flocks and property.

When shall I provide for mine own house] Jacob had already laid his plan; and, from what is afterwards mentioned, we find him using all his *skill* and *experience* to provide for his family by a rapid increase of his flocks.

Verse 32. *I will pass through all thy flock*] צאן *tson*, implying, as we have before seen, all *smaller cattle*, such as *sheep*, *goats*, &c.

All the speckled and spotted cattle] שה *seh*, which we translate *cattle*, signifies the *young* either of *sheep* or *goats*, what we call a *lamb* or a *kid*. *Speckled*, נקד *nakod*, signifies interspersed with *variously coloured spots*.

Spotted] טלוא *talu*, spotted with large spots, either of the same or different colours, from טלא *tala*, to *patch*, to *make party-coloured* or *patch-work*; see Ezek. xvi. 16. I have never seen such sheep as are here described but in the islands of Zetland. There I have seen the most beautiful *brown*, or fine *chocolate* colour among the sheep; and several of the *ring-streaked*, *spotted*, *speckled*, and *piebald* among the same; and some of the latter description I have brought over, and can exhibit a specimen of Jacob's flock brought from the North Seas, feeding in Middlesex.

And all the brown] חום *chum*. I should rather suppose this to signify a lively *brown*, as the root signifies to be *warm* or *hot*.

A. M. 2259. B. C. 1745. the sheep, and the spotted and speckled among the goats: and
[r] *of such* shall be my hire.
33 So shall my [s] righteousness answer for me [t] in time to come, when it shall come for my hire before thy face: every one that *is* not speckled and spotted among the goats, and brown among the sheep, that shall be counted stolen with me.
34 And Laban said, Behold, I would it might be according to thy word.
35 And he removed that day the he-goats that were ring-streaked and spotted, and all the she-goats that were speckled and spotted, *and* every one that had *some* white in it, and all the brown among the sheep, and gave *them* into the [u] hand of his sons.
36 And he set three days' journey betwixt himself and Jacob: and Jacob fed the rest of Laban's flocks.
37 And [v] Jacob took him rods of green poplar, and of the hazel and chestnut tree; and pilled white streaks in them, and made the white appear which *was* in the rods.

[r] Chap. xxxi. 8.——[s] Psa. xxxvii. 6.——[t] Heb. *to-morrow*; Exod. xiii. 14.——[u] Chap. xxxi. 9.——[v] See chap. xxxi. 9–12.

Verse 35. *The he-goats that were ring-streaked*] התישים העקדים *hatteyashim haakuddim*, the *he-goats* that had *rings* of *black* or *other coloured hair* around their *feet* or *legs*.

It is extremely difficult to find out, from the 32d and 35th verses, in *what* the bargain of Jacob with his father-in-law properly consisted. It appears from verse 32, that Jacob was to have for his wages all the *speckled, spotted,* and *brown* among the sheep and the goats; and of course that all those which were not party-coloured should be considered as the property of Laban. But in verse 35 it appears that Laban separated all the *party-coloured* cattle, and delivered them into the hands of *his own sons;* which seems as if he had taken these for his own property, and left the others to Jacob. It has been conjectured that Laban, for the greater security, when he had separated the party-coloured, which by the agreement belonged to Jacob, see verse 32, put them under the care of his own sons, while Jacob fed the flock of Laban, verse 36, three days' journey being between the two flocks. If therefore the flocks under the care of Laban's sons brought forth young that were all of *one colour,* these were put to the flocks of Laban under the care of Jacob; and if any of the flocks under Jacob's care brought forth *party-coloured* young, they were put to the flocks belonging to Jacob under the care of Laban's sons. This conjecture is not satisfactory, and the true meaning appears to be this: Jacob had agreed to take all the party-coloured for his wages. As he was now only *beginning* to act upon this agreement, consequently none of the cattle as yet belonged to him; therefore Laban separated from the flock, verse 35, all such cattle as Jacob might afterwards claim in consequence of his bargain, (for as yet he had no right;) therefore Jacob commenced his service to Laban with a flock that did not contain a single animal of the description of those to which he might be entitled; and the others were sent away under the care of Laban's sons, three days' journey from those of which Jacob had the care. The bargain, therefore, seemed to be wholly in favour of Laban; and to turn it to his own advantage, Jacob made use of the stratagems afterwards mentioned. This mode of interpretation removes all the apparent contradiction between the 32d and 35th verses, with which commentators in general have been grievously perplexed. From the whole account we learn that Laban acted with great *prudence* and *caution,* and Jacob with great *judgment.* Jacob had already served fourteen years; and had got no patrimony whatever, though he had now a family of *twelve* children, *eleven sons* and *one daughter,* besides his two wives, and their two maids, and several servants. See ver. 43. It was high time that he should get some property for these; and as his father-in-law was excessively parsimonious, and would scarcely allow him to live, he was in some sort obliged to make use of stratagem to get an equivalent for his services. But did he not push this so far as to ruin his father-in-law's flocks, leaving him nothing but the refuse? See ver. 42.

Verse 37. *Rods of green poplar*] לבנה לח *libneh lach.* The *libneh* is generally understood to mean the *white poplar;* and the word *lach,* which is here joined to it, does not so much imply *greenness* of *colour* as being *fresh,* in opposition to *witheredness.* Had they not been *fresh*—just cut off, he could not have pilled the bark from them.

And of the hazel] לוז *luz,* the *nut* or *filbert tree,* translated by others the *almond tree;* which of the two is here intended is not known.

And chestnut tree] ערמון *armon,* the *plane tree,* from ערם *aram,* he was *naked.* The plane tree is properly called by this name, because of the outer bark *naturally peeling off,* and leaving the tree *bare* in various places, having *smooth* places where it has fallen off. A portion of this bark the *plane tree* loses every year. The Septuagint translate it in the same way, *πλατανος·* and its name is supposed to be derived from *πλατυς, broad,* on account of its *broad spreading branches,* for which the *plane tree* is remarkable. So we find the Grecian army in Homer, *Il.* ii., ver. 307, sacrificing *καλῃ ὑπο πλατανιστῳ,* under a beautiful plane tree.

Virgil, *Geor.* iv. 146, mentions,

> ——*ministrantem platanum potantibus umbras.*
> The *plane tree* yielding the convivial shade.

And Petronius Arbiter in *Satyr.:—*

> *Nobilis æstivas* platanus *diffuderat umbras.*
> "The noble *plane* had spread its summer shade."

See more in *Parkhurst.* Such a tree would be peculiarly acceptable in *hot* countries, because of its *shade.*

A. M. 2259.
B. C. 1745.

38 And he set the rods which he had pilled before the flocks in the gutters in the watering troughs when the flocks came to drink, that they should conceive when they came to drink.
39 And the flocks conceived before the rods, and brought [w] forth cattle ring-streaked, speckled, and spotted.
40 And Jacob did separate the lambs, and set the faces of the flocks toward the ring-streaked, and all the brown in the flock of Laban; and he put his own flocks by themselves, and put them not unto Laban's cattle.
41 And it came to pass, whensoever the stronger cattle did conceive, that Jacob laid the rods before the eyes of the cattle in the gutters, that they might conceive among the rods.
42 But when the cattle were feeble, he put *them* not in: so the feebler were Laban's, and the stronger Jacob's.
43 And the man [x] increased exceedingly, and [y] had much cattle, and maid-servants, and men-servants, and camels, and asses.

[w] Jer. xxvii. 5.——[x] Ver. 30.——[y] Chap. xiii. 2; xxiv. 35; xxvi. 13, 14.

Pilled white streaks in them] Probably cutting the bark through in a *spiral line*, and taking it off in a certain breadth all round the rods, so that the rods would appear party-coloured, the *white* of the wood showing itself where the bark was stripped off.

Verse 38. *And he set the rods which he had pilled before the flocks*] It has long been an opinion that whatever makes a strong impression on the mind of a female in the time of conception and gestation, will have a corresponding influence on the mind or body of the fetus. This opinion is not yet rationally accounted for. It is not necessary to look for a miracle here; for though the fact has not been accounted for, it is nevertheless sufficiently plain that the effect does not exceed the powers of nature; and I have no doubt that the same modes of trial used by Jacob would produce the same results in similar cases. The finger of God works in nature myriads of ways unknown to us; we see effects without end, of which no rational cause can be assigned: it has pleased God to work thus and thus, and this is all that we know; and God mercifully hides the operations of his power from man in a variety of cases, that he may hide pride from him. Even with the little we know, how apt are we to be puffed up! We must adore God in a reverential silence on such subjects as these, confess our ignorance, and acknowledge that *nature* is the *instrument* by which he chooses to work, and that he performs all things according to the counsel of his own will, which is always infinitely *wise* and infinitely *good*.

Verse 40. *Jacob did separate the lambs, &c.*] When Jacob undertook the care of Laban's flock, according to the agreement already mentioned, there were no party-coloured sheep or goats among them, therefore the *ring-streaked*, &c., mentioned in this verse, must have been born *since* the agreement was made; and Jacob makes use of them precisely as he used the *pilled rods*, that, having these *before their eyes* during conception, the impression might be made upon their imagination which would lead to the results already mentioned.

Verse 41. *Whensoever the stronger cattle did conceive*] The word מקשרות *mekushsharoth*, which we translate *stronger*, is understood by several of the ancient interpreters as signifying the *early*, *first-born*, or *early spring* cattle; and hence it is opposed to עטפים *atuphim*, which we translate *feeble*, and which *Symmachus* properly renders δευτερογονοι, cattle of the *second birth*, as he renders the word *mekushsharoth* by πρωτογονοι, cattle of the *first* or *earliest birth*. Now this does not apply merely to *two births* from the same female in one year, which actually did take place according to the rabbins, the first in *Nisan*, about our *March*, and the second in *Tisri*, about our *September*; but it more particularly refers to *early* and *late lambs*, &c., in the *same year*; as those that are born just at the termination of winter, and in the very commencement of spring, are every way more valuable than those which were born later in the same spring. Jacob therefore took good heed not to try his experiments with those *late produced cattle*, because he knew these would produce a degenerate breed, but with the early cattle, which were *strong* and *vigorous*, by which his breed must be improved. Hence the whole flock of Laban must be necessarily injured, while Jacob's flock was preserved in a state of increasing perfection. All this proves a consummate knowledge in Jacob of his pastoral office. If extensive breeders in this country were to attend to the same plan, our breed would be improved in a most eminent degree. What a fund of instruction upon almost every subject is to be found in the sacred writings!

Verse 43. *And the man increased exceedingly*] No wonder, when he used such means as the above. And had *maid-servants*, and *men-servants*—he was obliged to increase *these* as his cattle multiplied. And *camels* and *asses*, to transport his tents, baggage, and family, from place to place, being obliged often to *remove* for the benefit of pasturage.

We have already seen many difficulties in this chapter, and strange incidents, for which we are not able to account. 1. The vicarious bearing of children; 2. The nature and properties of the mandrakes; 3. The bargain of Jacob and Laban; and 4. The business of the party-coloured flocks produced by means of the females looking at the variegated rods. These, especially the *three* last, may be ranked among the most difficult things in this book. Without encumbering the page with quotations and opinions, I have given the best sense I could; and think it much better and safer to confess *ignorance*, than, under the semblance of *wisdom* and *learning*, to multiply conjectures. Jacob certainly manifested much address in the whole of his conduct with Laban, but though nothing can excuse

overreaching or *insincerity*, yet no doubt Jacob supposed himself justified in taking these advantages of a man who had greatly injured and defrauded him. Had Jacob got Rachel at first, for whom he had honestly and faithfully served seven years, there is no evidence whatever that he would have taken a second wife. Laban, by having imposed his eldest daughter upon him, and by obliging him to serve seven years for her who never was an object of his affection, acted a part wholly foreign to every dictate of justice and honesty; (for though it was a custom in that country not to give the younger daughter in marriage before the elder, yet, as he did not mention this to Jacob, it cannot plead in his excuse;) therefore, speaking after the manner of men, he had reason to expect that Jacob should repay him in his own coin, and right himself by whatever means came into his power; and many think that he did not transgress the bounds of justice, even in the business of the party-coloured cattle.

The *talent* possessed by Jacob was a most dangerous one: he was what may be truly called *a scheming* man; his wits were still at work, and as he *devised* so he executed, being as fruitful in *expedients* as he was in *plans*. This was the principal and the most prominent characteristic of his life; and whatever was excessive here was owing to his mother's tuition; she was evidently a woman who paid little respect to what is called *moral principle*, and sanctified *all kinds of means* by the goodness of the *end* at which she aimed; which in social, civil, and religious life, is the most dangerous principle on which a person can possibly act. In this art she appears to have instructed her son; and, unfortunately for himself, he was in some instances but too apt a proficient. Early habits are not easily rooted out, especially those of a bad kind. Next to the influence and grace of the Spirit of God is a good and religious education. Parents should teach their children to despise and abhor low cunning, to fear a lie, and tremble at an oath; and in order to be sucesssful, they should illustrate their *precepts* by their own regular and conscientious *example*. How far God approved of the whole of Jacob's conduct I shall not inquire; it is certain that he attributes his success to Divine interposition, and God himself censures Laban's conduct towards him; see chap. xxxi. 7–12. But still he appears to have proceeded *farther* than this interposition authorized him to go, especially in the means he used to improve his own breed, which necessarily led to the deterioration of Laban's cattle; for, after the transactions referred to above, these cattle could be of but little worth. The whole account, with all its *lights* and *shades*, I consider as another proof of the impartiality of the Divine historian, and a strong evidence of the authenticity of the Pentateuch. Neither the spirit of *deceit*, nor the *partiality* of *friendship*, could ever pen such an account.

CHAPTER XXXI.

Laban and his sons envy Jacob, 1, 2; *on which he is commanded by the Lord to return to his own country*, 3. *Having called his wives together, he lays before them a detailed statement of his situation in reference to their father*, 4–5; *the services he had rendered him*, 6; *the various attempts made by Laban to defraud him of his hire*, 7; *how, by God's providence, his evil designs had been counteracted*, 8–12; *and then informs them that he is now called to return to his own country*, 13. *To the proposal of an immediate departure, Leah and Rachel agree; and strengthen the propriety of the measure by additional reasons*, 14–16; *on which Jacob collects all his family, his flocks and his goods, and prepares for his departure*, 17, 18. *Laban having gone to shear his sheep, Rachel secretes his images*, 19. *Jacob and his family, unknown to Laban, take their departure*, 20, 21. *On the third day Laban is informed of their flight*, 22; *and pursues them to Mount Gilead*, 23. *God appears to Laban in a dream, and warns him not to molest Jacob*, 24. *He comes up with Jacob at Mount Gilead*, 25; *reproaches him with his clandestine departure*, 26–29; *and charges him with having stolen his gods*, 30. *Jacob vindicates himself, and protests his innocence in the matter of the theft*, 31, 32. *Laban makes a general search for his images in Jacob's, Leah's, Bilhah's, and Zilpah's tents; and not finding them, proceeds to examine Rachel's*, 33. *Rachel, having hidden them among the camel's furniture, sat upon them*, 34; *and making a delicate excuse for not rising up, Laban desists from farther search*, 35. *Jacob, ignorant of Rachel's theft, reproaches Laban for his suspicions*, 36, 37; *enumerates his long and faithful services, his fatigues, and Laban's injustice*, 38–41; *and shows that it was owing to God's goodness alone that he had any property*, 42. *Laban is moderated, and proposes a covenant*, 43, 44. *Jacob sets up a stone, and the rest bring stones and make a heap, which Laban calls* Jegar-Sahadutha, *and Jacob* Galeed, 45–47. *They make a covenant, and confirm it by an oath*, 48–53. *Jacob offers a sacrifice; they eat together; and Laban and his companions, having lodged in the mount all night, take a friendly leave of Jacob and his family next morning, and depart*, 54, 55.

A. M. 2265. B. C. 1739.

AND he heard the words of Laban's sons, saying, Jacob hath taken away all that *was* our father's; and of *that* which *was* our father's hath he gotten all this [a] glory.

2 And Jacob beheld [b] the countenance of

[a] Psa. xlix. 16. — [b] Chap. iv. 5.

NOTES ON CHAP. XXXI.

Verse 1. *And he heard the words of Laban's sons*] The multiplication of Jacob's cattle, and the decrease and degeneracy of those of Laban, were sufficient to rouse the jealousy of Laban's sons. This, with Laban's unfair treatment, and the direction he re-

A. M. 2265.
B. C. 1739.
Laban, and, behold, it *was* not ᶜ toward him ᵈ as before.

3 And the LORD said unto Jacob, ᵉ Return unto the land of thy fathers, and to thy kindred and I will be with thee.

4 And Jacob sent and called Rachel and Leah to the field unto his flock,

5 And said unto them, ᶠ I see your father's countenance, that it *is* not toward me as before ; but the God of my father ᵍ hath been with me.

6 And ʰ ye know that with all my power I have served your father.

7 And your father hath deceived me, and

ⁱ changed my wages ᵏ ten times ; but God ˡ suffered him not to hurt me.

A. M. 2265.
B. C. 1739.

8 If he said thus, ᵐ The speckled shall be thy wages ; then all the cattle bare speckled and if he said thus, The ring-streaked shall be thy hire ; then bare all the cattle ring-streaked.

9 Thus God hath ⁿ taken away the cattle of your father, and given *them* to me.

10 And it came to pass at the time that the cattle conceived, that I lifted up mine eyes, and saw in a dream, and, behold, the ᵒ rams which leaped upon the cattle *were* ring-streaked, speckled, and grisled.

11 And ᵖ the angel of God spake unto me

ᶜ Deut. xxviii. 54.——ᵈ Heb. *as yesterday and the day before ;* 1 Sam. xix. 7.——ᵉ Chap. xxviii. 15, 20, 21 ; xxxii. 9.——ᶠ Ver. 2.——ᵍ Ver. 3.——ʰ Ver. 38, 39, 40, 41 ; chap. xxx. 29.

ⁱ Ver. 41.——ᵏ Num. xiv. 22 ; Neh. iv. 12 ; Job xix. 3 ; Zech. viii. 23.——ˡ Chap. xx. 6 ; Psa. cv. 14.——ᵐ Chapter xxx. 32 ⁿ Ver. 1, 16.——ᵒ Or, *he-goats.*——ᵖ Chap. xlviii. 16.

ceived from God, determined him to return to his own country.

Hath he gotten all this glory.] All these riches, this wealth, or property. The original word כבד signifies both to be *rich* and to be *heavy* ; and perhaps for this simple reason, that riches ever bring with them *heavy weight* and *burden* of cares and anxieties.

Verse 3. And the Lord said unto Jacob, Return— and I will be with thee.] I will take the same care of thee in thy *return*, as I took of thee on thy way to this place. The Targum reads, *My* WORD *shall be for thy help*, see chap. xv. 1. A promise of this kind was essentially necessary for the encouragement of Jacob, especially at this time ; and no doubt it was a powerful means of support to him through the whole journey ; and it was particularly so when he heard that his brother was coming to meet him, with four hundred men in his retinue, chap. xxxii. 6. At that time he went and pleaded the very words of this promise with God, chap. xxxii. 9.

Verse 4. Jacob sent and called Rachel and Leah] He had probably been at some considerable distance with the flocks ; and for the greater secrecy, he rather sends for them to the field, to consult them on this most momentous affair, than visit them in their tents, where probably some of the family of Laban might overhear their conversation, though Laban himself was at the time three days' journey off. It is possible that Jacob shore his sheep at the same time ; and that he sent for his wives and household furniture to erect tents on the spot, that they might partake of the festivities usual on such occasions. Thus they might all depart without being suspected.

Verse 7. Changed my wages ten times] There is a strange diversity among the ancient versions, and ancient and modern interpreters, on the meaning of these words. The Hebrew is עשרת מנים *asereth monim*, which Aquila translates δεκα αριθμους, *ten numbers ;* Symmachus, δεκακις αριθμω, *ten times in number ;* the Septuagint δεκα αμνων, *ten lambs*, with which Origen appears to agree. St. Augustine thinks that by *ten lambs* five years' wages is meant : that Laban had with-

held from him all the party-coloured lambs which had been brought forth for *five* years, and because the ewes brought forth lambs *twice* in the year, *bis gravidæ pecudes*, therefore the number *ten* is used, Jacob having been defrauded of his part of the produce of *ten* births. It is supposed that the Septuagint use *lambs* for *years*, as Virgil does *aristas.*

> *En unquam patrios longo post tempore fines,*
> *Pauperis et tuguri congestum cespite culmen,*
> *Post aliquot mea regna videns mirabor aristas !*
> VIRG. *Ec.* i., ver. 68.

Thus inadequately translated by DRYDEN :—

> O must the wretched exiles ever mourn ;
> Nor, after length of rolling years, return ?
> Are we condemn'd by Fate's unjust decree,
> No more our *harvests* and our homes to see ?
> Or shall we mount again the rural throng,
> And rule the country, kingdoms once our own !

Here *aristas*, which signifies *ears of corn*, is put for *harvest*, harvest for *autumn*, and autumn for *years.* After all, it is most natural to suppose that Jacob uses the word *ten times* for an indefinite number, which we might safely translate *frequently ;* and that it means an indefinite number in other parts of the sacred writings, is evident from Lev. xxvi. 26 : TEN *women shall bake your bread in one oven.* Eccles. vii. 19 : *Wisdom strengtheneth the wise more than* TEN *mighty men the city.* Num. xiv. 22 : *Because all these men have tempted me now these* TEN *times.* Job xix. 3 : *These* TEN *times have ye reproached me.* Zech. viii. 23 : *In those days—*TEN *men shall take hold of the skirt of him that is a Jew.* Rev. ii. 10 : *Ye shall have tribulation* TEN *days.*

Verse 11. The angel of God spake unto me in a dream] It is strange that we had not heard of this dream *before ;* and yet it seems to have taken place before the cattle brought forth, immediately after the bargain between him and Laban. If we follow the *Samaritan* the difficulty is at once removed, for it gives us the whole of this dream after verse 36 of the preceding chapter.

A. M. 2265.
B. C. 1739.

in a dream, *saying*, Jacob : and I said, Here *am* I.

12 And he said, Lift up now thine eyes, and see, all the rams which leap upon the cattle *are* ring-streaked, speckled, and grisled : for [q] I have seen all that Laban doeth unto thee.

13 I *am* the God of Beth-el, [r] where thou anointedst the pillar, *and* where thou vowedst a vow unto me : now [s] arise, get thee out from this land, and return unto the land of thy kindred.

14 And Rachel and Leah answered and said unto him, [t] *Is there* yet any portion or inheritance for us in our father's house ?

15 Are we not counted of him strangers ? for [u] he hath sold us, and hath quite devoured also our money.

16 For all the riches which God hath taken from our father, that *is* ours, and our children's: now then, whatsoever God hath said unto thee, do.

A. M. 2265.
B. C. 1739.

17 Then Jacob rose up, and set his sons and his wives upon camels ;

18 And he carried away all his cattle, and all his goods which he had gotten, (the cattle of his getting, which he had gotten in Padan aram,) for to go to Isaac his father in the land of Canaan.

19 And Laban went to shear his sheep : and Rachel had stolen the [v] images [w] that *were* her father's.

20 And Jacob stole away, [x] unawares to Laban the Syrian, in that he told him not that he fled.

[q] Exod. iii. 7.——[r] Chap. xxviii. 18, 19, 20.——[s] Ver. 3 ; chap. xxxii. 9.——[t] Chap. ii. 24.——[u] Chap. xxix. 15, 27.

[v] Heb. *teraphim* ; Judg. xvii. 5 ; 1 Sam. xix. 13 ; Hosea iii. 4. [w] Chap. xxxv. 2.——[x] Heb. *the heart of Laban.*

Verse 12. *Grisled*] ברדים *beruddim* ; ברד *barad* signifies *hail*, and the meaning must be, they had white spots on them similar to *hail*. Our word *grisléd* comes from the old French, *greslé, hail*, now written *grêle* ; hence *greslé*, grisled, spotted with white upon a dark ground.

Verse 15. *Are we not counted of him strangers ?*] Rachel and Leah, who well knew the disposition of their father, gave him here his true character. He has treated us as *strangers*—as *slaves* whom he had a right to dispose of as he pleased ; in consequence, he hath *sold us*—disposed of us on the mere principle of gaining by the sale.

And hath quite devoured also our money.] Has applied to his own use the profits of the sale, and has allowed us neither portion nor inheritance.

Verse 19. *Laban went to shear his sheep*] Laban *had gone* ; and this was a favourable time not only to take his images, but to return to Canaan without being perceived.

Rachel had stolen the images] תרפים *teraphim.* What the teraphim were is utterly unknown. In ver. 30 they are termed אלהי *elohai, gods* ; and to some it appears very likely that they were a sort of images devoted to superstitious purposes, not considered as gods, but as representatives of certain Divine attributes. Dr. Shuckford supposes them to be a sort of *tiles*, on which the names or figures of their ancestors were engraven. *Theodoret*, in his 89th question, calls them *idols* ; and says that Rachel, who was a *type* of the true Church, stole them from her father that he might be delivered from idolatry. *R. S. Jarchi* gives nearly the same reason.

The *Targum* of Jonathan ben Uzziel gives a strange turn to the whole passage. "And Rachel stole the images of her father : for they had murdered a man, who was a first-born *son* ; and having cut off his head, they embalmed it with salt and spices, and they wrote divinations upon a plate of gold, and put it under his tongue ; and placed it against the wall, and it conversed with them, and Laban worshipped it. And Jacob stole the science of Laban the Syrian, that it might not discover his departure."

If the word be derived from רפא *rapha*, to *heal* or *restore*, then the teraphim may be considered as a sort of *talismans*, kept for the purpose of averting and curing diseases ; and probably were kept by Laban for the same purpose that the Romans kept their *lares and penates.* It is however possible that תרפים *teraphim* is the same as שרפים *seraphim*, the ת *tau* and ש *sin* being changed, which is very frequent in the *Syrian* or *Chaldee* language ; and we know that Laban was an *Aramean* or *Syrian.* Fire has been considered from the earliest ages as a symbol of the Deity ; and as the word *seraphim* comes from שרף *saraph, to burn*, it has been conjectured that the teraphim of Laban were luminous forms, prepared of burnished brass, &c., which he might imagine a proper medium of communication between God and his worshippers. Mr. *Parkhurst* has observed that the teraphim were in use among believers and unbelievers. Among the *former*, see this chapter ; for he denies that Laban was an idolater. See also Judg. xvii. 5 ; xviii. 14, 18, 20 ; 1 Sam. xix. 13, 16. Among the latter, see 2 Kings xxiii. 24 ; Ezek. xxi. 21 ; Zech. x. 2. Compare 1 Sam. xv. 23, and Hos. iii. 4. These are all the places in which the original word is found.

The Persian translator seems to have considered these *teraphim* as *tables* or *instruments* that served for purposes of judicial astrology, and hence translates the word اسطرلابها *asterlabha, astrolabes.* As the astrolabe was an instrument with which they took the altitude of the pole-star, the sun, &c., it might, in the notion of the Persian translator, imply *tables*, &c., by which the culminating of particular stars might be determined, and the whole serve for purposes of *judicial astrology.* Now as many who have professed themselves to be believers in Christianity, have nevertheless addicted themselves to judicial astrology, we might suppose such a thing in this case, and still con-

A. M. 2265.
B. C. 1739.

21 So he fled with all that he
had; and[x] he rose up, and passed
over the river, and [y] set his face *toward* the
mount Gilead.
22 And it was told Laban on the third day
that Jacob was fled.
23 And he took [z] his brethren with him, and
pursued after him seven days' journey; and
they overtook him in the mount Gilead.
24 And God [a] came to Laban the Syrian in
a dream by night, and said unto him, Take
heed that thou [b] speak not to Jacob [c] either
good or bad.
25 Then Laban overtook Jacob. Now Jacob had pitched his tent in the mount: and
Laban with his brethren pitched in the mount
of Gilead.
26 And Laban said to Jacob, What hast
thou done, that thou hast stolen away unawares to me, and [d] carried away
my daughters, as captives *taken*
with the sword?
27 Wherefore didst thou flee away secretly,
and [e] steal away from me; and didst not tell
me, that I might have sent thee away with
mirth, and with songs, with tabret, and with
harp?
28 And hast not suffered me [f] to kiss my
sons and my daughters? [g] thou hast now done
foolishly in *so* doing.
29 It is in the power of my hand to do you
hurt: but the [h] God of your father spake unto
me [i] yesternight, saying, Take thou heed that
thou speak not to Jacob either good or bad.
30 And now, *though* thou wouldest needs be
gone, because thou sore longedst after thy
father's house, *yet* wherefore hast thou [k] stolen
my gods?

---

[y] Chap. xlvi. 28; 2 Kings xii. 17; Luke ix. 51, 53.——[z] Chap. xiii. 8.——[a] Chap. xx. 3; Job xxxiii. 15; Matt. i. 20.——[b] Ch. xxiv. 50.——[c] Heb. *from good to bad.*——[d] 1 Sam. xxx. 2.

[e] Heb. *hast stolen me.*——[f] Ver. 55; Ruth i. 9, 14; 1 Kings xix. 20; Acts xx. 37.——[g] 1 Sam. xiii. 13; 2 Chron. xvi. 9.——[h] Ver. 53; chap. xxviii. 13.——[i] Ver. 24.——[k] Ver. 19; Judg. xviii. 24.

---

sider Laban as no idolater. If the Persian translator has not hit on the true meaning, he has formed the most likely conjecture.

Verse 21. *Passed over the river*] The *Euphrates*, as the Targum properly notices. But how could he pass such a *river* with his flocks, &c.? This difficulty does not seem to have struck critics in general. The rabbins felt it, and assert that God wrought a miracle for Jacob on this occasion, and that he passed over dry shod. As we know not in what other way he could pass, it is prudent to refer it to the power of God, which accompanied him through the whole of his journey. There might, however, have been *fords* well known to both Jacob and Laban, by which they might readily pass.

The mount Gilead.] What the ancient name of this mountain was, we know not; but it is likely that it had not the name of *Gilead* till after the transaction mentioned ver. 47. The mountains of Gilead were eastward of the country possessed by the tribes of Reuben and Gad; and extended from Mount Hermon to the mountains of Moab.—*Calmet.* It is joined to Mount Libanus, and includes the mountainous region called in the New Testament Trachonitis.—*Dodd.*

Verse 24. *And God came to Laban*] God's caution to Laban was of high importance to Jacob—*Take heed that thou speak not to Jacob either good or bad;* or rather, as is the literal meaning of the Hebrew, מטוב עד רע *mittob ad ra*, from *good* to *evil;* for had he neither spoken *good nor evil* to Jacob, they could have had no intercourse at all. The original is, therefore, peculiarly appropriate; for when people meet, the language at first is the language of *friendship;* the command therefore implies, "Do not begin with *Peace be unto thee*, and then proceed to *injurious language* and *acts of violence.*" If this Divine direction were attended to, how many of those *affairs of honour*, so termed, which commence with, "I hope you are well"—"I am infinitely glad to see you"—"I am happy to see you well," &c., and end with *small swords* and *pistol bullets*, would be prevented! Where God and true religion act, all is fair, kind, honest, and upright; but where *these* are not consulted, all is hollow, deceitful, or malicious. Beware of *unmeaning* compliments, and particularly of saying what thy heart feels not. God hates a hypocrite and a deceiver.

Verse 27. *I might have sent thee away with mirth*] בשמחה *besimchah*, with *rejoicing*, making a *feast* or *entertainment* on the occasion; *and with songs*, בשירים *beshirim*, odes either in the praise of God, or to commemorate the splendid acts of their ancestors; *with tabret*, בתף *bethoph*, the *tympanum* used in the east to the present day, and there called دف *diff*, a thin broad wooden hoop, with parchment extended over one end of it, to which are attached small pieces of brass, tin, &c., which make a jingling noise; it is held in the air with one hand, and beat on with the fingers of the other. It appears to have been precisely the same with that which is called the *tambourine*, and which is frequently to be met with in our streets. *And with harp*, בכנור *bekinnor*, a sort of stringed instrument, a lute or harp; probably the same as the Greek κινυρα *kinura*, a harp; the name being evidently borrowed from the Hebrew. These four things seem to include all that was used in those primitive times, as expressive of gladness and satisfaction on the most joyous occasions.

Verse 29. *It is in the power of my hand to do you hurt*] Literally, *My hand is unto God to do you evil*, i. e., I have vowed to God that I will punish thee for thy flight, and the stealing of my teraphim; but the *God of* YOUR *father* has prevented me from doing it.

a

A. M. 2265.
B. C. 1739.

31 And Jacob answered and said
to Laban, Because I was afraid:
for I said, Peradventure thou wouldest take
by force thy daughters from me.
32 With whomsoever thou findest thy gods,
[l] let him not live: before our brethren discern
thou what *is* thine with me, and take *it* to
thee. For Jacob knew not that Rachel had
stolen them.
33 And Laban went into Jacob's tent, and
into Leah's tent, and into the two maid-servants' tents; but he found *them* not. Then
went he out of Leah's tent, and entered into
Rachel's tent.
34 Now Rachel had taken the images, and
put them in the camel's furniture, and sat
upon them. And Laban [m] searched all the
tent, but found *them* not.
35 And she said to her father, Let it not
displease my lord that I cannot [n] rise up before thee; for the custom of women
is upon me. And he searched, but
found not the images.

A. M. 2265.
B. C. 1739.

36 And Jacob was wroth, and chode with
Laban: and Jacob answered and said to
Laban, What *is* my trespass? what *is* my sin,
that thou hast so hotly pursued after me?
37 Whereas thou hast searched all my stuff,
what hast thou found of all thy household stuff?
set *it* here before my brethren and thy bre
thren, that they may judge betwixt us both.
38 This twenty years *have* I *been* with thee;
thy ewes and thy she-goats have not cast
their young, and the rams of thy flock have I
not eaten.
39 [o] That which was torn *of beasts* I brought
not unto thee; I bare the loss of it; of [p] my
hand didst thou require it, *whether* stolen by
day, or stolen by night.
40 *Thus* I was; in the day the drought

[l] See chap. xliv. 9.—[m] Heb. *felt*.—[n] Exod. xx. 12; Lev. xix. 32.—[o] Exod. xxii. 10, &c.—[p] Exod. xxii. 12.

It is a singular instance that the *plural* pronoun, when addressing an *individual*, should be twice used in this place—the God of *your* father, אביכם *abichem*, for אביך *abicha, thy* father.

Verse 32. *Let him not live*] It appears that anciently *theft* was punished by death; and we know that the patriarchs had the power of life and death in their hands. But previously to the law, the punishment of death was scarcely ever inflicted but for murder. The rabbins consider that this was an *imprecation* used by Jacob, as if he had said, Let God take away the life of the person who has stolen them! And that this was answered shortly after in the death of Rachel, chap. xxxv.

Verse 35. *The custom of women* is *upon me.*] This she knew must be a satisfactory reason to her father; for if the teraphim were used to any religious purpose, and they seem to have been used in this way, as Laban calls them his *gods*, he therefore could not suspect that a woman in such a situation, whose touch was considered as defiling, would have sat upon articles that were either the objects of his adoration, or used for any sacred purpose. The stratagem succeeded to her wish, and Laban departed without suspicion. It seems very natural to suppose that Rachel did believe that by the use of these teraphim Laban could find out their flight, and the direction they took, and therefore she stole them; and having stolen them she was afraid to acknowledge the theft, and probably might think that they might be of some use to herself. Therefore, for these reasons, she brought them away.

Verse 36. *And Jacob was wroth, and chode with Laban*] The expostulation of Jacob with Laban, and their consequent agreement, are told in this place with great spirit and dignity. Jacob was conscious that though he had made use of cunning to increase his flocks, yet Laban had been on the whole a great gainer by his services. He had served him at least twenty years, *fourteen* for Rachel and Leah, and *six* for the cattle; and some suppose he had served him twenty years besides the above, which is not unlikely: see the *remarks* at the conclusion of this chapter. *Forty* or even *twenty* years of a man's life, devoted to incessant labour and constantly exposed to all the inclemencies of the weather, (see ver. 40,) deserve more than an ordinary reward. Laban's constitutional sin was *covetousness*, and it was an *easily besetting sin;* for it appears to have governed all his conduct, and to have rendered him regardless of the interests of his children, so long as he could secure his own. That he had frequently falsified his agreement with Jacob, though the particulars are not specified, we have already had reason to conjecture from ver. 7, and with this Jacob charges his father-in-law, in the most positive manner, ver. 41. Perhaps some previous unfair transactions of this kind were the cause why Jacob was led to adopt the expedient of *outwitting* Laban in the case of the *spotted, spangled, ring-streaked,* and *grisled cattle.* This if it did take place, though it cannot justify the measure, is some palliation of it; and almost the whole of Jacob's conduct, as far as relates to Laban, can be better excused than his injuring Laban's breed, by leaving him none but the weak, unhealthy, and degenerated cattle.

Verse 39. *That which was torn—of my hand didst thou require it*] This more particularly marks the covetous and rigorous disposition of Laban; for the law of God required that what had been torn by beasts the shepherd should not be obliged to make good, Exod. xxii. 10, 13. And it is very likely that this law was in force from the earliest times.

Verse 40. *In the day the drought consumed me, and the frost by night*] The being exposed to the *heat* by *day*, and *frost* by *night*, is made part of the heaviest punishment of Prometheus by *Æschylus*.

A. M. 2265. B. C. 1739.

consumed me, and the frost by
night; and my sleep departed from
mine eyes.
41 Thus have I been twenty years in thy
house; I [q] served thee fourteen years for thy
two daughters, and six years for thy cattle:
and [r] thou hast changed my wages ten times.
42 [s] Except the God of my father, the God
of Abraham, and [t] the fear of Isaac, had been
with me, surely thou hadst sent me away now
empty. [u] God hath seen mine affliction and
the labour of my hands, and [v] rebuked *thee*
yesternight.
43 And Laban answered and said unto Jacob,
These daughters *are* my daughters, and
these children *are* my children, and *these* cattle
are my cattle, and all that thou seest *is*
mine: and what can I do this day unto these
my daughters, or unto their children which
they have born?
44 Now therefore, come thou, [w] let
us make a covenant, I and thou;
[x] and let it be for a witness between me and thee
45 And Jacob [y] took a stone, and set it up
for a pillar.
46 And Jacob said unto his brethren, Gather
stones; and they took stones, and made a
heap: and they did eat there upon the heap.
47 And Laban called it [z] Jegar-sahadutha·
but Jacob called it [a] Galeed.
48 And Laban said, [b] This heap *is* a witness
between me and thee this day. Therefore
was the name of it called Galeed,
49 And [c] Mizpah; [d] for he said, The LORD
watch between me and thee, when we are absent
one from another.
50 If thou shalt afflict my daughters, or if
thou shalt take *other* wives beside my daughters,
(no man *is* with us;) see, God *is* witness
betwixt me and thee.

A. M. 2265. B. C. 1739.

[q] Chap. xxix. 27, 28.——[r] Ver. 7.——[s] Psa. cxxiv. 1, 2.——[t] Verse 53; Isa. viii. 13.——[u] Chap. xxix. 32; Exodus iii. 7.——[v] 1 Chron. xii. 17; Jude 9.——[w] Chapter xxvi. 28.——[x] Josh. xxiv. 27.

[y] Chap. xxviii. 18.——[z] That is, *the heap of witness*; Chald.——[a] That is, *the heap of witness*; Heb.——[b] Josh. xxiv. 27.——[c] Judges xi. 29; 1 Sam. vii. 5.——[d] That is, *a beacon* or *watch tower*.

———*Σταθευτος δ' ἡλιου φοιβῃ φλογι,*
Χροιας αμειψεις ανθος· ασμενῳ δε σοι
Ἡ ποικιλειμων νυξ αποκρυψει φαος·
Παχνην θ' ἑῳαν ἡλιος σκεδᾳ παλιν.

Æschyl. Prom. Vinc., v. 22.

Opposed to the sun's most fervid beam,
The hue of beauty changed; till parch'd by heat
The night with spangled stole shall hide its light
From thee rejoicing, but again the sun
Chases the hoar frost from thy harass'd form.

J. B. B. C.

Verse 41. *Twenty years*] See the remarks at the end.

Verse 42. *The fear of Isaac*] It is strange that Jacob should say, the GOD *of Abraham* and the FEAR *of Isaac*, when both words are meant of the same *Being*. The reason perhaps was this; Abraham was long since dead, and God was *his unalienable* portion for ever. Isaac was yet alive in a state of *probation*, living in the fear of God, not exempt from the danger of *falling*; therefore God is said to be his *fear*—not only the object of his religious worship in a general way, but that holy and just God before whom he was still working out his salvation with fear and trembling—fear lest he should fall, and trembling lest he should offend.

Verse 46. *Made a heap*] גל *gal*, translated *heap*, signifies properly a *round* heap; and this heap was probably made for the double purpose of an *altar* and a *table*, and Jacob's stone or pillar was set on it for the purpose of a *memorial*.

Verse 47. *Laban called it Jegar-sahadutha*] יגר שהדותא *yegar sahadutha*, the *heap* or *round heap of witness; but Jacob called it* גלעד *galed*, which signifies the same thing. The first is pure *Chaldee*, the second pure *Hebrew*. אגר *agar* signifies to *collect*, hence יגר *yegar* and אוגר *ogar*, a *collection* or *heap* made up of gathered stones; and hence also אגורא *egora*, an *altar*, used frequently by the *Chaldee* paraphrast. See 1 Kings xii. 33; Judg. vi. 31; 2 Kings xxi. 3; Jer. xvii. 1. See *Castel's* Lexicon. From this example we may infer that the Chaldee language was nearly coeval with the Hebrew. A gloss made by St. Jerome, and which was probably only entered by him in his margin as a note, has crept into the text of the *Vulgate*. It is found in every copy of this version, and is as follows: *Uterque juxta proprietatem linguæ suæ*, Each according to the idiom of his own tongue.

Verses 48, 49. I think these two verses are badly divided, and should be read thus:—

Verse 48. *And Laban said, This heap* is *a witness between me and thee this day.*

Verse 49. *Therefore was the name of it called Galeed and Mizpah; for he said, The Lord watch between me and thee, when we are absent one from another.*

Mizpah] מצפה *mitspah* signifies a *watch-tower*; and Laban supposes that in consequence of the consecration of the place, and the covenant now solemnly made and ratified, that God would take possession of this heap, and stand on it as on a watch-tower, to prevent either of them from trenching on the conditions of their covenant.

Verse 50. *No man* is *with us*] Though all were present at the sacrifice offered, yet it appears that in making the contract Jacob and Laban withdrew, and transacted the business in private, calling on God to witness it.

Jacob had already four wives; but Laban feared that

A. M. 2265.
B. C. 1739.

51 And Laban said to Jacob,
Behold this heap, and behold *this*
pillar, which I have cast betwixt me and
thee;
52 This heap *be* witness, and *this* pillar *be*
witness, that I will not pass over this heap to
thee, and that thou shalt not pass over this
heap and this pillar unto me, for harm.
53 The God of Abraham, and the God of
Nahor, the God of their father, [e] judge betwixt us. And Jacob [f] sware by
[g] the fear of his father Isaac.
54 Then Jacob [h] offered sacrifice upon the
mount, and called his brethren to eat bread:
and they did eat bread, and tarried all night
in the mount.
55 And early in the morning Laban rose up,
and kissed his sons and his daughters, and
[i] blessed them: and Laban departed, and [k] returned unto his place.

A. M. 2265.
B. C. 1739.

[e] Chap. xvi. 5.——[f] Chap. xxi. 23.——[g] Ver. 42.——[h] Or, *killed beasts*.——[i] Chap. xxviii. 1.——[k] Chap. xviii. 33; xxx. 25.

he might take others, whose children would naturally come in for a share of the inheritance to the prejudice of his daughters and grandchildren. Though the Koran allows a man to have *four wives* if he can maintain them, yet we learn that in many cases where a man takes a wife, the parents or relatives of the woman stipulate that the man is not to take another during the lifetime of that one whom he now espouses; and notwithstanding the permission of the Koran, he is obliged to fulfil this agreement.

Verse 51. *And Laban said to Jacob—behold* this *pillar, which I have cast betwixt me and thee*] But this pillar, not *cast* but *set up*, was certainly *set up by Jacob;* for in ver. 45 we read, *And Jacob took a stone, and set it up for a pillar:* it is therefore for the honour of one Hebrew and one Samaritan MS. that they have preserved the true reading in ver. 51, ירית *yaritha*, THOU *hast set up.—Kennicott.* Instead of either of the above readings the Samaritan text has ࠉࠓࠀࠕ *yarata, The pillar which thou* SEEST *betwixt me and thee.*

Verse 53. *The God of their father*] As Laban certainly speaks of the *true God* here, with what propriety can he say that this God was the God of *Terah*, the father of Abraham and Nahor? It is certain that Terah was an idolater; of this we have the most positive proof, Josh. xxiv. 2. Because the clause is not in the Septuagint, and is besides wanting in some MSS., Dr. Kennicott considers it an interpolation. But there is no need of having recourse to this expedient if we adopt the reading אביכם *abichem*, YOUR *father*, for אביהם *abihem*, THEIR *father*, which is supported by several of Kennicott's and De Rossi's MSS., and is precisely the same form made use of by Laban, ver. 29, when addressing Jacob, and appears to me to be used here in the same way; for he there most manifestly uses the *plural pronoun*, when speaking only to Jacob himself. It is therefore to be considered as a *form of speech* peculiar to Laban; at least we have *two* instances of his use of it in this chapter.

Jacob sware by the fear of his father Isaac.] See on ver. 42.

Verse 54. *Offered sacrifice upon the mount*] It is very likely that Laban joined in this solemn religious rite, and that, having offered the blood and fat to God, they feasted upon the sacrifice.

Verse 55. *Kissed his sons and his daughters*] That is, his *grandchildren*, Jacob's *eleven* sons with Dinah their sister, and their mothers *Leah* and *Rachel*. All these he calls his *children*, ver. 43. *And blessed them*—prayed heartily for their prosperity, though we find from ver. 29 that he came having bound himself by a vow to God to do them some *injury*. Thus God turned his intended curse into a blessing.

THE most important topics in this chapter have already been considered in the notes, and to those the reader is referred. Jacob's character we have already seen, and hitherto have met in it little to admire; but we shall soon find a blessed change both in his mind and in his conduct. Laban's character appears in almost every instance to disadvantage; he does not seem to be what we commonly term a *wicked* man, but he was certainly both *weak* and *covetous;* and covetousness extinguished in him, as it does in all its votaries, the principles of righteousness and benevolence, and the very *charities of human life*. Provided he could get an increase of property, he regarded not who was wronged or who suffered. In this case he hid himself even from his own bowels, and cared not that his own children should lack even the necessaries of life, provided he could increase his own store! How watchful should we be against this destructive, *unnatural*, and degrading vice! It is impossible for a man who *loves money* to love either God or man; and consequently he must be in the broad way that leads to destruction.

For the difficulties in the chronology of Jacob's sojourning in Padan-aram, I beg leave to refer to the following remarks.

Remarks upon Gen. xxxi. 38, &c., relative to the time spent by Jacob in the service of his father-in-law Laban, in Mesopotamia; from Dr. Kennicott.

"If every reading which introduces but a single difficulty demands our attention, much greater must that demand be when several difficulties are caused by any one mistake, or any one mistranslation. Of this nature is the passage before us, which therefore shall be here considered more fully, especially as I have not already submitted to the learned any remarks upon this subject. Jacob's age, at the time of his going to Laban, has (till very lately) been fixed, perhaps universally, at *seventy-seven* years. But I think it has been shown by the learned Mr. *Skinner*, in an excellent dissertation, (4to. 1765,) that the number *seventy-seven* cannot here be right.

"Jacob was *one hundred and thirty* when he went down (with *sixty-six* persons) into Egypt. Joseph

had then been governor *ten* years; and when made governor was *thirty;* therefore Jacob could not be more than *ninety* at the birth of Joseph. Now, upon supposition that Jacob was *seventy-seven* at going to Laban, and that he had no son till he was *eighty-five*, and that he, with *eleven* sons, left Laban at *ninety-seven*, there will follow these amongst other strange consequences which are enumerated by Mr. *Skinner*, page 11, &c.: 1. Though Isaac and Esau married at *forty*, Jacob goes at *seventy-seven* to look for a wife, and agrees to marry her *seven* years after. 2. Issachar is born after the affair of the mandrakes, which Reuben finds and brings home when he (Reuben) was about *four* years old; that is, if Issachar was born before Joseph, agreeably to Gen. xxx. 18, 25. 3. Judah begets Er at *thirteen;* for in the first of the following tables Judah is born in Jacob's year *eighty-eight*, and Er in *one hundred and two.* 4. Er marries at *nine*, and is destroyed for profligacy. Er, born *one hundred and two*, marries in *one hundred and eleven.* See also Gen. xxxviii. 7. 5. Onan marries at *eight;* for Onan, born in *one hundred and three*, marries in *one hundred and eleven.* 6. Shelah, being grown at *ten*, ought to be married; for Shelah, born in *one hundred and four*, is marriageable, but not married to Tamar in *one hundred and fourteen.* See Gen. xxxviii. 14. 7. Pharez kept from marrying while young, yet has a son at *thirteen;* for Pharez, born in *one hundred and fifteen*, had two sons at going to Egypt in *one hundred and thirty.* 8. Esau goes to Ishmael and marries his daughter, after Jacob went to Laban at *seventy-seven;* though Ishmael died when Jacob was *sixty-three.* 9. If Jacob had no son till he was *eighty-five*, and if Joseph was born when his father was *ninety*, then the *eleven* sons and Dinah were born in *five* years. Lastly, if Jacob had no son till *eighty-five*, and he went to *Egypt* at *one hundred and thirty*, with sixty-six persons, only *forty-five* years are allowed for his family; whereas the larger sum of *sixty-five* years seems necessary for the births of so many children and grandchildren. On this subject Le Clerc has pronounced, Hisce in rebus occurrunt nodi, quos nemo hactenus solvit; neque porro, ut opinor, solvet. *There are difficulties here which have never been explained, and in my opinion never can be explained.* But upon the single principle of Mr. Skinner, that Jacob went to Laban at *fifty-seven*, (instead of *seventy-seven*,) these difficulties are solved. And it only remains to wish that some authority may be found to support this conjecture, thus strongly founded on the *exigentia loci.* The common opinion is formed by reckoning back from the age of Joseph, when governor of Egypt, to the time of his birth, and from the *twenty* years which Jacob was with Laban. This number, Mr. Skinner thinks, was originally *forty;* and I think that the Hebrew text as it now stands confirms the conjecture, and furnishes the very authority which is so much wanted.

"After Jacob had served Laban *fourteen* years for his two wives, where was Jacob to reside? Esau was still living; and Jacob might well be afraid of returning to him, till more years of absence had disarmed his resentment; and had the death of Esau happened, Jacob would then have been secure. But let us also remember that Isaac was still alive, and that Esau had determined to kill Jacob whenever their father should die. It would therefore be no wonder if Jacob should have desired to continue longer in Haran. And to carry this point more effectually, he might offer to take care of Laban's cattle, and to live in his neighbourhood, upon such terms of advantage to Laban as could not easily be withstood. Lastly, when the good effects to Laban from this connection had been experienced, without profit, nay with some losses, to Jacob, for *twenty* years, Jacob might naturally grow tired of thus assisting Laban without providing for his own growing family. Accordingly we find that Jacob covenants with Laban for *six* years of more close attendance and service in Laban's own house, for which the wages were expressly settled. Agreeable to the preceding possibilities seems to have been the fact, Jacob living in Haran *forty* years, and in this manner:—

14 years in Laban's house, a *covenant servant* for his wives.
20 —— in Laban's neighbourhood, as a *friend.*
6 —— in Laban's house, a *covenant servant* for cattle.
—
40

"Now the *twenty* concurrent years of *neighbourly assistance*, and the disjointed *twenty* of *covenant service*, seem both of them distinguished in the history itself. For upon Laban's pursuit of Jacob he mentions *twenty* years twice; which two sets of *twenty*, if really different, make *forty.* Each mention of the *twenty* years is introduced with the word זה *zeh*, which word, when repeated, is used by way of distinction; as when we say, this and that, the one or the other. Thus, Exod. xiv. 20: *So that the one came not near the other.* Eccles. vi. 5: *This hath more rest than the other.* And with the two words at a great distance, Job xxi. 23: *One* dieth; ver. 25; and *another* dieth, &c. So here, in Gen. xxxi. 38, Jacob says to Laban, זה עשרים שנה אנכי עמך *zeh esrim shanah anochi immach, during the* ONE *set of twenty years I was with thee, &c.;* meaning the time in which he lived, not in Laban's house, but in *his neighbourhood;* not as a *servant*, but a *friend;* after he had served in Laban's house *fourteen* years for his daughters, and before he served *six* years for his cattle. But then, as to the other *twenty*, he tells Laban, at verse 41, varying the phrase very remarkably, זה לי עשרים שנה בביתך עבדתיך *zeh li esrim shanah bebeithecha abadticha, during the other twenty years* (לי *li*) FOR MYSELF (for my own benefit) IN THY HOUSE; *I served thee fourteen years and six years, &c.* And during this last period, though only *six* years, he charges Laban with changing his wages *ten* times. So that Jacob insists upon having well earned his wages through the *twenty* years when he served for hire; but he makes a far greater merit of having, for *another twenty years*, assisted him without wages, and even with some losses; and therefore, with particular propriety, he reminds Laban of *that set of twenty years* in the first place.

The following Tables, taken chiefly from Mr. Skinner, will greatly elucidate the true chronology of Jacob.

TABLE I.—On Jacob's being at Haran only *twenty* years.

0	Jacob (and Esau) born.	
40	Esau marries two wives, Hittites	Gen. xxvi. 34.
63	Ishmael dies, aged 137	Gen. xxv. 17.
77	Jacob goes to Haran.	
84	—— marries Leah and Rachel	Gen. xxix. 20, 21, 27, 28.
85	REUBEN born of Leah	Gen. xxix. 32–35 (85–88)
86	SIMEON do.	
87	LEVI do.	
88	JUDAH do.	
89	*Dan* born of Bilhah	Gen. xxx. 6–24 (89–91)
	Naphtali do.	
	Gad born of Zilpah	
	Asher do.	
	ISSACHAR born of Leah	
	ZEBULUN and Dinah do.	
91	JOSEPH born of Rachel	
97	Jacob returns from Haran.	
98	—— dwells in Succoth.	
99	—— comes to Shalem, and continues there eight years.	
101	Judah marries Shuah's daughter.	
102	Er born,—103 Onan,—104 Shelah.	
106	Shechemites destroyed by Simeon and Levi.	
107	BENJAMIN is born, and Rachel dies.	
108	Joseph sold when seventeen	Gen. xxxvii. 2.
111	Tamar married to Er, and immediately afterwards to Onan.	
114	Tamar's incest with Judah.	
115	Pharez and Zarah born to Judah.	
120	Isaac dies, aged 180	Gen. xxxv. 28.
121	Joseph is made governor of Egypt	Gen. xli. 46.
130	Jacob goes into Egypt	Gen. xlvii. 9.
147	—— and dies	do. 28; and xlix. 33.

TABLE II.—On Jacob's being at Haran *forty* years.

	0	Jacob (and Esau) born.	
	40	Esau marries two wives, Hittites	Gen. xxvi. 34.
14 years' service	57	Jacob goes to Haran.	
	58	Esau goes to Ishmael, and marries his daughter	Gen. xxviii. 9.
	63	Ishmael dies, aged 137	Gen. xxv. 17.
	64	Jacob marries Leah and Rachel	Gen. xxix. 20, 21, 27, 28.
	65	Reuben born of Leah	Gen. xxix. 32–35. (65–68)
	66	Simeon do.	
	67	Levi do.	
	68	Judah do.	
		Rachel, not bearing, gives Bilhah	Gen. xxx. 6–24. (Rachel … Zebulun)
	69	Dan born of Bilhah	
	71	Naphtali do.	
		Leah, not bearing, gives Zilpah	
20 years' assist.	72	Gad born of Zilpah	
	74	Asher do.	
	78	Reuben at 13 finds the mandrakes	
	79	Issachar born of Leah	
	81	Zebulun do. 82 Dinah	
	86	Judah at 18 marries Shuah's daughter.*	
	87	Er born,—88 Onan,—89 Shelah.	
	91	Joseph born of Rachel.	
6	- - -	years' service for cattle.	
	97	Jacob comes from Haran to Succoth and Shalem.	
		Dinah defiled, and the Shechemites destroyed.	
	98	Benjamin is born, and Rachel dies.	
	103	Beriah, fourth son of Asher, born.	

* Not placed in order of time, Gen. xxxviii.

105	Tamar married to Er—106 to Onan.	
108	Joseph, at seventeen, is carried into Egypt . . .	Gen. xxxvii. 2.
109	Shelah, at twenty, not given to Tamar.	
110	Pharez and Zarah born of Tamar, by Judah.	
120	Isaac dies, aged 180	Gen. xxxv. 28.
121	Joseph, at thirty, governor of Egypt	Gen. xli. 46.
123	Beriah, at twenty, marries.	
125	Heber—127 Malchiel—born to Beriah.	
128	Pharez, at eighteen, marries.	
129	Hezron—130 Hamul—born to Pharez.	
130	Benjamin, at thirty-two, has ten sons.	
	Jacob goes to Egypt	Gen. xlvii. 9.
147	—— and dies	do. 28; and xlix. 33.

"Our translation now is, xxxi. 38: THIS TWENTY YEARS HAVE I BEEN WITH THEE; *thy ewes and thy she-goats have not cast their young, and the rams of thy flock have I not eaten.* 39. *That which was torn of beasts I brought not unto thee; I bare the loss of it; of my hand didst thou require it, whether stolen by day or stolen by night.* 40. *Thus I was; in the day the drought consumed me, and the frost by night; and my sleep departed from mine eyes.* 41. THUS HAVE I BEEN TWENTY YEARS IN THY HOUSE: *I served thee fourteen years for thy two daughters, and six years for thy cattle; and thou hast changed my wages ten times.*

"The alteration here recommended is this, chap. xxxi. 38: DURING THE ONE TWENTY YEARS I WAS WITH THEE; *thy ewes and thy she-goats have not cast their young, and the rams, &c., &c.* 41. DURING THE OTHER TWENTY YEARS FOR MYSELF, IN THY HOUSE, *I served, &c.* The same distinction is expressed in chap. xxx. 29: *Thou knowest how I have served thee, and how thy cattle was with me;* i. e., how I behaved during the time I was with thee as thy servant, and how thy cattle fared during the time they were with me as thy friend.

"It must not be omitted that Archbishop Usher and Bishop Lloyd ascribe sons to Jacob very soon after his coming to Laban; nay, assert that he was married almost as soon as he came to Haran, instead of waiting seven years, as he most evidently did. And Mr. Jackson allows that some of the sons of Benjamin, who are expressly numbered as going into Egypt with Jacob, might be born in Egypt! From such distresses, and such contradictions, does the distinction of two sets of *twenty* years happily deliver us."

Hoc temporis intervallo nemo concipere poterit tot res contingere potuisse. SPINOSA.

In such a short space of time, it is impossible that so many transactions could have taken place.

I shall leave this subject with chronologers and critics, and shall not attempt to decide on either opinion. That of Dr. Kennicott I think the most likely, and to it I have adapted the chronology in those cases to which it relates; but there are difficulties in both cases. See the note on chap. xxxviii. 1.

CHAPTER XXXII.

Jacob, proceeding on his journey, is met by the angels of God, 1, 2. *Sends messengers before him to his brother Esau, requesting to be favourably received,* 3–5. *The messengers return without an answer, but with the intelligence that Esau, with four hundred men, was coming to meet Jacob,* 6. *He is greatly alarmed, and adopts prudent means for the safety of himself and family,* 7, 8. *His affecting prayer to God,* 9–12. *Prepares a present of five droves of different cattle for his brother,* 13–15. *Sends them forward before him, at a certain distance from each other, and instructs the drivers what to say when met by Esau,* 15–20. *Sends his wives, servants, children and baggage, over the brook Jabbok, by night,* 21–23. *Himself stays behind, and wrestles with an angel until the break of day,* 24. *He prevails and gets a* new name, 25–29. *Calls the name of the place* Peniel, 30. *Is lame in his thigh in consequence of his wrestling with the angel,* 31, 32.

A. M. 2265. B. C. 1739.

AND Jacob went on his way, and [a] the angels of God met him.

2 And when Jacob saw them, he said, This *is* God's [b] host: and he called the name of that place [c] Mahanaim.

A. M. 2265. B. C. 1739.

[a] Psa. xci. 11; Heb. i. 14.——[b] Josh. v. 14; Psa. ciii. 21; cxlviii. 2; Luke ii. 13.——[c] That is, *two hosts* or *camps.*

NOTES ON CHAP. XXXII.

Verse 1. *The angels of God met him.*] Our word *angel* comes from the Greek αγγελος, *angelos,* which literally signifies a messenger; or, as translated in some of our old Bibles, a *tidings-bringer.* The Hebrew word מלאך *malach,* from לאך *laach,* to *send, minister to, employ,* is nearly of the same import; and hence we may see the propriety of St. Augustine's remark: *Nomen non naturæ sed officii,* "It is a name, not of nature, but of office;" and hence it is applied indifferently to a *human agent* or *messenger,* 2 Sam. ii. 5; to a *prophet,* Hag. i. 13; to a *priest,* Mal.

A. M. 2265. B. C. 1739.

3 And Jacob sent messengers before him to Esau his brother, [d] unto the land of Seir, [e] the [f] country of Edom.

4 And he commanded them, saying, [g] Thus shall ye speak unto my lord Esau; Thy servant Jacob saith thus: I have sojourned with Laban, and stayed there until now:

5 And [h] I have oxen, and asses, flocks, and men-servants, and women-servants: and I have sent to tell my lord, that [i] I may find grace in thy sight.

6 And the messengers returned to Jacob, saying, We came to thy brother Esau, and also [k] he cometh to meet thee, and four hundred men with him.

[d] Chap. xxxiii. 14, 16.——[e] Chapter xxxvi. 6, 7, 8; Deut. ii. 5. Josh. xxiv. 4.——[f] Heb. *field*.

[g] Prov. xv. 1.——[h] Chapter xxx. 43.——[i] Chapter xxxiii. 8, 15. [k] Chap. xxxiii. 1.

ii. 7; to *celestial spirits*, Psa. ciii. 19, 20, 22; civ. 4.

"We often," says Mr. Parkhurst, "read of the מלאך יהוה *malach Yehovah*, or מלאכי אלהים *malakey Elohim*, the angel of Jehovah, or the angels of God, that is, his *agent, personator, mean of visibility* or *action*, what was employed by God to render himself visible and approachable by flesh and blood." This *angel* was evidently a human form, surrounded or accompanied by *light* or *glory*, with or in which Jehovah was present; see Gen. xix 1, 12, 16; Judg. xiii. 6, 21; Exod. iii. 2, 6. "By this vision," says Mr. Ainsworth, "God confirmed Jacob's faith in him who commanded his angels to keep his people in all their ways, Psa. xci. 11. Angels are here called *God's host, camp*, or *army*, as in wars; for angels are God's *soldiers*, Luke ii. 13; *horses* and *chariots of fire*, 2 Kings ii. 11; fighting for God's people against their enemies, Dan. x. 20; of them there are *thousand thousands*, and *ten thousand times ten thousand*, Dan. vii. 10; and they are all sent forth to minister for them that shall be heirs of salvation, Heb. i. 14; and they pitch a camp about them that fear God, Psa. xxxiv. 7." One of the oldest of the Greek poets had a tolerably correct notion of the angelic ministry:—

Αυταρ επεικεν τουτο γενος κατα γαια καλυψεν
Τοι μεν Δαιμονες εισι, Διος μεγαλου δια βουλας,
Εσθλοι, επιχθονιοι, φυλακες θνητων ανθρωπων· κ. τ. λ.

HESIOD. *Op. & Dies*, l. i., ver. 120.

When in the grave this race of men was laid,
Soon was a world of holy demons made,
Aerial spirits, by great Jove design'd
To be on earth the *guardians of mankind*.
Invisible to mortal eyes they go,
And mark our actions good or bad below;
The immortal spies *with watchful care preside*,
And *thrice ten thousand* round their charges glide:
They can reward with glory or with gold,
A power they by *Divine permission* hold. COOKE.

Verse 2. *Mahanaim*.] The *two hosts*, if read by the *points*, the angels forming one, and Jacob and his company forming another; or simply *hosts* or *camps* in the plural. There was a city built afterwards here, and inhabited by the priests of God, Josh. xxi. 38. For what purpose the angels of God met Jacob, does not appear from the text; probably it was intended to show him that he and his company were under the care of an especial providence, and consequently to confirm his trust and confidence in God.

The doctrine of the ministration of angels has been much abused, not only among the *heathens*, but also among *Jews* and *Christians*, and perhaps most among the latter. Angels with feigned *names, titles*, and *influences*, have been and still are invoked and worshipped by a certain class of men; because they have found that God has been pleased to employ them to minister to mankind; and hence they have made supplications to them to extend their protection, to shield, defend, instruct, &c. This is perfectly absurd. 1. They are God's *instruments*, not *self-determining* agents. 2. They can only do what they are *appointed* to perform, for there is no evidence that they have any *discretionary* power. 3. God helps man by *ten thousand means* and *instruments*; some *intellectual*, as angels; some *rational*, as men; some *irrational*, as brutes; and some merely *material*, as the sun, wind, rain, food, raiment, and the various productions of the earth. He therefore helps by whom he will help, and to *him* alone belongs all the glory; for should he be determined to destroy, all these instruments collectively could not save. Instead therefore of worshipping *them*, we should take their own advice: *See* thou do it *not—Worship God.*

Verse 3. *Jacob sent messengers*] מלאכים *malachim*, the same word which is before translated *angels*. It is very likely that these messengers had been sent some time before he had this vision at Mahanaim, for they appear to have returned while Jacob encamped at the brook Jabbok, where he had the vision of angels; see verses 6 and 23.

The land of Seir, the country of Edom.] This land, which was, according to Dr. Wells, situated on the south of the Dead Sea, extending from thence to the Arabian Gulf, 1 Kings ix. 26, was formerly possessed by the *Horites*, Gen. xiv. 6; but Esau with his children drove them out, destroyed them, and dwelt in their stead, Deut. ii. 22; and thither Esau went from the face of his brother Jacob, chap. xxxvi. 6, 7. Thus we find he verified the prediction, *By thy sword shalt thou live*, chap. xxvii. 40.

Verse 4. *Thus shall ye speak unto my lord Esau*] Jacob acknowledges the *superiority* of his brother, for the time was not yet come in which it could be said, *The elder shall serve the younger*.

Verse 6. *Esau—cometh—and four hundred men with him*.] Jacob, conscious that he had injured his brother, was now apprehensive that he was coming with *hostile* intentions, and that he had every evil to fear from his displeasure. *Conscience* is a terrible accuser. It was a fine saying of a heathen,—

—— Hic murus aheneus esto,
Nil conscire sibi, nulla pallescere culpa.

HOR. *Ep.*, l. i., E. i., v 60.

a

A. M. 2265.
B. C. 1739.

7 Then Jacob was greatly afraid
and [l] distressed: and he divided
the people that *was* with him, and the
flocks, and herds, and the camels into two
bands;
8 And said, If Esau come to the one company, and smite it, then the other company which is left shall escape.
9 [m] And Jacob said, [n] O God of my father Abraham, and God of my father Isaac, the Lord [o] which saidst unto me, Return unto thy country, and to thy kindred, and I will deal well with thee:
10 [p] I am not worthy of the least of all the
[q] mercies, and of all the truth, which thou hast
showed unto thy servant; for with
[r] my staff I passed over this Jordan;
and now I am become two bands.
11 [s] Deliver me, I pray thee, from the hand of my brother, from the hand of Esau: for I fear him, lest he will come and smite me, *and* [t] the mother [u] with the children.
12 And [v] thou saidst, I will surely do thee good, and make thy seed as the sand of the sea, which cannot be numbered for multitude.
13 And he lodged there that same night; and took of that which came to his hand [w] a present for Esau his brother;
14 Two hundred she-goats, and twenty he-goats, two hundred ewes, and twenty rams,

[l] Chap. xxxv. 3.——[m] Psalm l. 15.——[n] Chapter xxviii. 13.
[o] Chap. xxxi. 3, 13.——[p] Heb. *I am less than all*, &c.——[q] Chap. xxiv. 27.

[r] Job viii. 7.——[s] Psalm lix. 1, 2.——[t] Hos. x. 14.——[u] Heb. *upon*.——[v] Chapter xxviii. 13, 14, 15.——[w] Chapter xliii. 11; Prov. xviii. 16.

Be this thy brazen bulwark of defence,
Still to preserve thy conscious innocence,
Nor e'er turn pale with guilt. Francis.

In other words, *He that has a good conscience has a brazen wall for his defence; for a guilty conscience needs no accuser;* sooner or later it will tell the truth, and not only make the man *turn pale* who has it, but also cause him to tremble even while his guilt is known only to himself and God.

It does not appear that Esau in this meeting had any *hostile* intention, but was really coming with a part of his servants or tribe to do his brother *honour*. If he had had any contrary intention, God had removed it; and the angelic host which Jacob met with before might have inspired him with sufficient confidence in God's protection. But we find that when he needed faith most, he appears to have derived but little benefit from its influence, partly from the sense he had of the injury he had done to his brother, and partly from not attending sufficiently to the assurance which God had given him of his gracious protection.

Verse 7. *He divided the people, &c.*] His prudence and cunning were now turned into a right channel, for he took the most effectual method to appease his brother, had he been irritated, and save at least a part of his family. This dividing and arranging of his flocks, family, and domestics, has something in it highly *characteristic*. To such a man as Jacob such expedients would naturally present themselves.

Verse 9. *O God of my father Abraham, &c.*] This prayer is remarkable for its simplicity and energy; and it is a model too for prayer, of which it contains the essential constituents: 1. Deep self-abasement. 2. Magnification of God's mercy. 3. Deprecation of the evil to which he was exposed. 4. Pleading the promises that God had made to him. And, 5. Taking encouragement from what God had already wrought.

Verse 10. *I am not worthy of the least of all the mercies*] The marginal reading is more consistent with the original: קטנתי מכל החסרים ומכל האמת *katonti miccol hachasadim umiccol hæmeth, I am less than all the compassions, and than all the faithfulness, which thou hast showed unto thy servant.* Probably St. Paul had his eye on this passage when he wrote, *Unto me, who am less than the least of all saints.* A man who sees himself in the light of God will ever feel that he has no good but what he has received, and that he deserves nothing of all that he has. The archangels of God cannot use a different language, and even the spirits of just men consummated in their plenitude of bliss, cannot make a higher boast.

For with my staff] i. e., *myself alone*, without any attendants, as the *Chaldee* has properly rendered it.

Verse 11. And *the mother with the children.*] He must have had an awful opinion of his brother when he used this expression, which implies the *utmost cruelty*, proceeding in the work of slaughter to total extermination. See Hos. x. 14.

Verse 12. *Make thy seed as the sand*] Having come to the *promise* by which the *covenant* was ratified both to *Abraham* and *Isaac*, he ceased, his faith having gained strong confirmation in a promise which he knew could not fail, and which he found was made over to *him*, as it had been to his father and grandfather.

Verse 13. *And took of that which came to his hand*] הבא בידו *habba beyado*, which came under his hand, i. e., what, in the course of God's providence, came under *his power*.

Verse 14. *Two hundred she-goats, &c.*] This was a princely present, and such as was sufficient to have compensated Esau for any kind of *temporal loss* he might have sustained in being deprived of his birthright and blessing. The thirty *milch camels* were particularly valuable, for *milch camels* among the Arabs constitute a principal part of their riches, the creature being every way so serviceable that the providence of God appears peculiarly kind and wise in providing such a beast for those countries where no other animal could be of equal service. "The she-camel gives milk continually, not ceasing till great with young; the milk of which," as Pliny has remarked, "when mixed with three parts of water, affords the most pleasant and

A. M. 2265. B. C. 1739.

15 Thirty milch camels with their colts, forty kine, and ten bulls, twenty she-asses, and ten foals.

16 And he delivered *them* into the hand of his servants, every drove by themselves; and said unto his servants, Pass over before me, and put a space betwixt drove and drove.

17 And he commanded the foremost, saying, When Esau my brother meeteth thee, and asketh thee, saying, Whose *art* thou? and whither goest thou? and whose *are* these before thee?

18 Then thou shalt say, *They be* thy servant Jacob's; it *is* a present sent unto my lord Esau: and, behold, also he *is* behind us.

19 And so commanded he the second, and the third, and all that followed the droves, saying, On this manner shall ye speak unto Esau, when ye find him.

20 And say ye moreover, Behold, thy servant Jacob *is* behind us. For he said, I will [x] appease him with the present that goeth before me, and afterward I will see his face: peradventure he will accept [y] of me.

A. M. 2265. B. C. 1739.

21 So went the present over before him: and himself lodged that night in the company

22 And he rose up that night, and took his two wives, and his two women-servants, and his eleven sons, [z] and passed over the ford Jabbok.

23 And he took them, and [a] sent them over the brook, and sent over that he had.

24 And Jacob was left alone, and there [b] wrestled a man with him until the [c] breaking of the day.

25 And when he saw that he prevailed not against him, he touched the hollow of his thigh: and [d] the hollow of Jacob's thigh was out of joint, as he wrestled with him.

[x] Proverbs xxi. 14.——[y] Heb. *my face;* Job xlii. 8, 9.——[z] Deut. iii. 16.——[a] Heb. *caused to pass.*

[b] Hos. xii. 3, 4; Eph. vi. 12.——[c] Heb. *ascending of the morning.* [d] See Matt. xxvi. 44; 2 Cor. xii. 7.

wholesome beverage." *Cameli* lac habent, donec iterum gravescant, suavissimumque *hoc existimatur, ad unam mensuram tribus aquæ additis.*—Hist. Nat., lib. xi., chap. 41.

Verse 15. *Ten bulls*] The Syriac and Vulgate have *twenty;* but *ten* is a sufficient proportion to the *forty kine.* By all this we see that Jacob was led to make *restitution* for the injury he had done to his brother. Restitution for injuries done to man is essentially requisite if in our power. He who can and will not make restitution for the wrongs he has done, can have no claim even on the *mercy* of God.

Verse 22. *Passed over the ford Jabbok.*] This brook or rivulet rises in the mountains of Galaad, and falls into the Jordan at the south extremity of the lake of Gennesaret.

Verse 24. *And there wrestled a man with him*] This was doubtless the Lord Jesus Christ, who, among the patriarchs, assumed that human form, which in the fulness of time he really took of a woman, and in which he dwelt thirty-three years among men. He is here styled an angel, because he was *μεγαλης βουλης Αγγελος*, (see the *Septuagint*, Isa. ix. 7,) *the Messenger of the great counsel* or *design* to redeem fallen man from death, and bring him to eternal glory; see chap. xvi. 7.

But it may be asked, Had he here a real human body, or only its *form?* The latter, doubtless. How then could he wrestle with Jacob? It need not be supposed that this angel must have assumed a human body, or something analagous to it, in order to render himself *tangible* by Jacob; for as the soul operates on the body by the order of God, so could an angel operate on the body of Jacob during a whole night, and produce in his *imagination*, by the effect of his power, every requisite idea of *corporeity*, and in his *nerves* every sensation of *substance*, and yet no substantiality be in the case.

If angels, in appearing to men, *borrow* human bodies as is thought, how can it be supposed that with such gross substances they can disappear in a *moment?* Certainly they do not take these bodies into the invisible world with them, and the established laws of *matter* and *motion* require a *gradual* disappearing, however swiftly it may be effected. But this is not allowed to be the case, and yet they are reported to vanish *instantaneously.* Then they must render themselves invisible by a *cloud*, and this must be of a very *dense* nature in order to hide a human body. But this very expedient would make their departure still more *evident*, as the cloud must be more *dense* and *apparent* than the *body* in order to hide it. This does not remove the difficulty. But if they assume a quantity of *air* or *vapour* so condensed as to become visible, and modified into the appearance of a human body, they can in a moment *dilate* and *rarefy* it, and so disappear; for when the vehicle is rarefied beyond the power of natural vision, as their own substance is invisible they can instantly vanish.

From Hos. xii. 4, we may learn that the wrestling of Jacob, mentioned in this place, was not merely a corporeal exercise, but also a spiritual one; *He wept and made supplication unto him.* See the notes there.

Verse 25. *The hollow of Jacob's thigh was out of joint*] What this implies is difficult to find out; it is not likely that it was a complete luxation of the thigh bone. It may mean no more than he received *a stroke* on the groin, not a *touch;* for the Hebrew word נגע *naga* often signifies to *smite with violence*, which stroke, even if comparatively slight, would effectually disable him for a time, and cause him to halt for many hours, if not for several days. I might add that in this place

a

A. M. 2265. B. C. 1739.

26 And [e] he said, Let me go,
for the day breaketh: And he
said, [f] I will not let thee go, except thou
bless me.
27 And he said unto him, What *is* thy
name? And he said, Jacob.
28 And he said, [g] Thy name shall be called
no more Jacob, but [h] Israel: for as a prince
hast thou [i] power with God and [k] with men,
and hast prevailed.
29 And Jacob asked *him*, and said, Tell *me*,
I pray thee, thy name. And he said, [l] Wherefore *is* it *that* thou dost ask after my
name? And he blessed him there.
30 And Jacob called the name of the place
[m] Peniel: for [n] I have seen God face to face,
and my life is preserved.
31 And as he passed over Penuel the sun
[o] rose upon him, and he halted upon his thigh.
32 Therefore the children of Israel eat not
of the sinew which shrank, which *is* upon the
hollow of the thigh, [p] unto this day: because
he touched the hollow of Jacob's thigh in the
sinew that shrank.

A. M. 2265. B. C. 1739.

[e] See Luke xxiv. 28.——[f] Hos. xii. 4.——[g] Chapter xxxv. 10; 2 Kings xvii. 34.——[h] That is, *a prince of God.*——[i] Hos. xii. 3, 4.——[k] Chap. xxv. 31; xxvii. 33.——[l] Judg. xiii. 18.

[m] That is, *the face of God.*——[n] Ch. xvi. 13; Exod. xxiv. 11; xxxiii. 20; Deut. v. 25; Judg. vi. 22; xiii. 22; Isaiah vi. 5. [o] Mal. iv. 2.——[p] 1 Sam. v. 5.

—the groin, a blow might be of fatal consequence; but as the angel gave it only as a proof of his power, and to show that he *could not* prevail because he *would not*, hence the blow was only *disabling*, without being *dangerous;* and he was probably cured by the time the sun rose.

Verse 26. *Let me go, for the day breaketh*] Probably meaning, that as it was now morning, Jacob must rejoin his wives and children, and proceed on their journey. Though *phantoms* are supposed to disappear *when the sun rises*, that could be no reason in this case. Most of the angelic appearances mentioned in the Old and New Testaments took place in *open day*, which put their reality out of question.

Verse 28. *Thy name shall be called no more Jacob, but Israel*] ישראל *Yisrael*, from שר *sar*, a prince, or שרה *sarah*, he ruled as a prince, and אל *el*, God; or rather from איש *ish*, a man, (the א aleph being dropped,) and ראה *raah*, he saw, אל *el*, God; and this corresponds with the name which Jacob imposed on the place, calling it פניאל *peniel*, the *faces* of God, or of *Elohim*, which faces being manifested to him caused him to say, verse 30, ראיתי אלהים פנים אל פנים *raithi Elohim panim el panim*, i. e., "*I have seen the Elohim faces to faces*, (*i. e.*, fully and completely, without any medium,) ותנצל נפשי *vattinnatsel napshi*, and my soul is redeemed."

We may learn from this that *the redemption of the soul* will be the blessed consequence of wrestling by prayer and supplication with God: "The kingdom of heaven suffereth violence, and the violent *take* it by force." From this time Jacob became a *new* man; but it was not till after a severe struggle that he got his *name*, his *heart*, and his *character* changed. After this he was no more *Jacob* the *supplanter*, but *Israel*—the *man who prevails with God*, and *sees him face to face*.

And hast prevailed.] More literally, *Thou hast had power with God, and with man thou shalt also prevail.* עם אלהים *im Elohim*, with the strong God; עם אנשים *im anashim*, with *weak, feeble man*. There is a beautiful opposition here between the two words: Seeing thou hast been powerful with the *Almighty*, surely thou shalt prevail over perishing *mortals;* as thou hast prevailed with God, thou *shalt* also prevail with men: God calling the things that were not as though they had already taken place, because the prevalency of this people, the Israelites, by means of the *Messiah*, who should proceed from them, was already determined in the Divine counsel. He has never said to the seed of Jacob, Seek ye my face in vain. He who *wrestles* must *prevail*.

Verse 29. *Tell* me, *I pray thee, thy name.*] It is very likely that Jacob wished to know the name of this angel, that he might invoke him in his necessities: but this might have led him into idolatry, for the doctrine of the incarnation could be but little understood at this time; hence, he refuses to give himself any name, yet shows himself to be the true God, and so Jacob understood him; (see verse 28;) but he wished to have heard from his own lips that name by which he desired to be invoked and worshipped.

Wherefore is *it* that *thou dost ask after my name?*] Canst thou be ignorant *who* I am? *And he blessed him there*—gave him the *new heart* and the *new nature* which God alone can give to fallen man, and by the change he wrought in him, sufficiently showed *who* he was. After this clause the *Aldine* edition of the Septuagint, and several MSS., add *ὁ εστι θαυμαστον*, or *και τουτο εστι θαυμαστον, which is wonderful;* but this addition seems to have been taken from Judges xiii. 18.

Verse 31. *The sun rose upon him*] Did the Prophet Malachi refer to this, chap. iv. 2: *Unto you that fear my name shall the Sun of righteousness arise with healing in his wings?* Possibly with the rising of the sun, which may here be understood as emblematical of the *Sun of righteousness*—the *Lord Jesus*, the pain and weakness of his thigh passed away, and he felt both in soul and body that he was healed of his plagues.

Verse 32. *Therefore the children of Israel eat not of the sinew*] What this sinew was neither *Jew* nor *Christian* can tell; and it can add nothing either to science, or to a true understanding of the text, to multiply conjectures. I have already supposed that the part which the angel touched or *struck* was the groin; and if this be right, the *sinew, nerve*, or *muscle* that *shrank*, must be sought for in that place.

The serious reader must meet with much instruction in this chapter.

1. After his reconciliation with Laban, Jacob proceeds on his way to Canaan; and as God, who was continually watching for his welfare, saw the trials to which he would shortly be exposed, therefore he provided for him the instructive vision of angels, that he might see that those who were for him were more than those who could be against him. A proper consideration of God's omniscience is of the utmost advantage to every genuine Christian. He knows whereof we are made, he remembers that we are but dust, he sees our trials and difficulties, and his eye affects his heart. Hence he is ever devising means that his banished be not expelled from him.

2. Jacob's recollection of his *unkindness* and *injustice* to his brother, when he hears that he is coming to meet him, fills his soul with fear, and obliges him to betake himself to God by prayer and supplication. How important is the office of *conscience!* And how necessary are times of *trial* and *difficulty* when its voice is loudest, and the heart is best prepared to receive its reproofs! In how many cases has conscience *slumbered* till it pleased God to send some *trial* by which it has been powerfully awakened, and the salvation of the sinner was the result! *Before I was afflicted I went astray.*

3. Though salvation be the free gift of God, yet he gives it not to any who do not earnestly seek it. The deeper the conviction of guilt and helplessness is, the more earnest the application to God for mercy is likely to be. They whose salvation costs them strong crying and tears, are not likely (humanly speaking) to part with it lightly; they remember the vinegar and the gall, and they watch and pray that they *enter not* into temptation.

4. In the strife and agony requisite to enter in at the strait gate, it is highly necessary that we should know that the grace and salvation of God are not *purchased* by our tears, &c.; for those things which are only proofs and arguments that we have sinned, can never remove the iniquity of our transgressions. A sensible and pious man observes on this subject, "That prayer and wrestling with God should be made as though no other means were to be practised, and then the best means be adopted as though no prayer or wrestling had been used." God marks even this strife, though highly pleasing in his sight, with such proofs of its own utter insufficiency, that we may carry about with us the memorial of our own weakness, worthlessness, and slowness of heart to believe. God smote the thigh of Jacob, 1. That he might know he had not prevailed by his *own strength*, but by the power and mercy of his God. 2. That he might have the most sensible evidence of the reality of the Divine interposition in his behalf. 3. That he might see God's displeasure against his unbelief. And 4. That men in general might be taught that those who will be the disciples of Christ must deny themselves, take up their cross daily, and mortify their members which are upon the earth. Those who have not cut off a right hand or foot, or plucked out a right eye, for the kingdom of heaven's sake, are never likely to see God. The religion that *costs* us *nothing*, is to us *worth nothing*.

CHAPTER XXXIII.

Esau, with four hundred men, meets Jacob, 1. *He places his children under their respective mothers, passes over before them, and bows himself to his brother,* 2, 3. *Esau receives him with great affection,* 4. *Receives the homage of the handmaids,* Leah, Rachel, *and their children,* 5–7. *Jacob offers him the present of cattle, which he at first refuses, but after much entreaty accepts,* 8–11. *Invites Jacob to accompany him to Mount* Seir, 12. *Jacob excuses himself because of his flocks and his children, but promises to follow him,* 13, 14. *Esau offers to leave him some of his attendants, which Jacob declines,* 15. *Esau returns to* Seir, 16, *and Jacob journeys to* Succoth, 17, *and to* Shalem, *in the land of Canaan,* 18. *Buys a parcel of ground from the children of* Hamor, 19, *and erects an altar which he calls* El-elohe-Israel, 20.

A. M. 2265. B. C. 1739.

AND Jacob lifted up his eyes, and looked; and, behold, [a] Esau came, and with him four hundred men. And he divided the children unto Leah, and unto Rachel, and unto the two handmaids.

2 And he put the handmaids and their children foremost, and Leah and her children after,

[a] Genesis, chap. xxxii. 6.

NOTES ON CHAP. XXXIII.

Verse 1. *Behold, Esau came, and with him four hundred men.*] It has been generally supposed that Esau came with an intention to destroy his brother, and for that purpose brought with him four hundred *armed* men. But, 1. There is no kind of evidence of this pretended hostility. 2. There is no proof that the four hundred men that Esau brought with him were at all *armed*. 3. But there is every proof that he acted towards his brother Jacob with all openness and candour, and with such a forgetfulness of past injuries as none but a great mind could have been capable of. Why then should the character of this man be perpetually vilified? Here is the secret. With some people, on the most ungrounded assumption, Esau is a *reprobate*, and the type and figure of all reprobates, and therefore he *must be* every thing that is *bad*. This serves a *system*; but, whether true or false in itself, it has neither countenance nor support from the character or conduct of Esau.

Verse 2. *He put the handmaids and their children foremost*] There is something so *artificial* in this arrangement of Jacob's family, that it must have had some peculiar *design*. Was Jacob still apprehensive

A. M. 2265. B. C. 1739. and Rachel and Joseph hindermost.

3 And he passed over before them, and [b] bowed himself to the ground seven times, until he came near to his brother.

4 [c] And Esau ran to meet him, and embraced him, [d] and fell on his neck, and kissed him: and they wept.

5 And he lifted up his eyes, and saw the women and the children: and said, Who *are* those [e] with thee? And he said, The children [f] which God hath graciously given thy servant.

6 Then the handmaidens came near, they and their children, and they bowed themselves.

7 And Leah also with her children came near, and bowed themselves: and after came Joseph near, and Rachel, and they bowed themselves.

8 And he said, [g] What *meanest* thou by [h] all this drove which I met? And he said, *These are* [i] to find grace in the sight of my lord.

9 And Esau said, I have enough, my brother; [k] keep that thou hast unto thyself.

10 And Jacob said, Nay, I pray thee, if now I have found grace in thy sight, then receive my present at my hand; for therefore I [l] have seen thy face, as though I had seen the face of God, and thou wast pleased with me. A. M. 2265. B. C. 1739.

11 Take, I pray thee, [m] my blessing that is brought to thee; because God hath dealt graciously with me, and because I have [n] enough. [o] And he urged him; and he took *it*.

12 And he said, Let us take our journey, and let us go, and I will go before thee.

13 And he said unto him, My lord knoweth that the children *are* tender, and the flocks and herds with young *are* with me: and if men should overdrive them one day, all the flock will die.

14 Let my lord, I pray thee, pass over before his servant; and I will lead on softly, according [p] as the cattle that goeth before me and the children be able to endure, until I come unto my lord [q] unto Seir.

15 And Esau said, Let me now [r] leave with thee *some* of the folk that *are* with me: and he said, [s] What needeth it? [t] let me find grace in the sight of my lord.

16 So Esau returned that day on his way unto Seir.

17 And Jacob journeyed to [u] Succoth, and

---

[b] Chap. xviii. 2; xlii. 6; xliii. 26.——[c] Chap. xxxii. 28. [d] Chap. xlv. 14, 15.——[e] Heb. *to thee.*——[f] Chap. xlviii. 9; Psa. cxxvii. 3; Isa. viii. 18.——[g] Heb. *What* is *all this band to thee?* [h] Chap. xxxii. 16.——[i] Chap. xxxii. 5.——[k] Heb. *be that to thee that* is *thine.*——[l] Chap. xliii. 3; 2 Sam. iii. 13; xiv. 24, 28, 32; Matt. xviii. 10.

[m] Judges i. 15; 1 Sam. xxv. 27; xxx. 26; 2 Kings v. 15. [n] Heb. *all things*; Phil. iv. 18.——[o] 2 Kings v. 23.——[p] Heb. *according to the foot of the work*, &c., *and according to the foot of the children.*——[q] Ch. xxxii. 3.——[r] Heb. *set* or *place.*——[s] Heb. *Wherefore* is *this?*——[t] Chap. xxxiv. 11; xlvii. 25; Ruth ii. 13. [u] Josh. xiii. 27; Judg. viii. 5; Psa. lx. 6.

---

of danger, and put those foremost whom he least esteemed, that if the foremost met with any evil, those who were behind might escape on their swift beasts? chap. xxxii. 7, 8. Or did he intend to keep his choicest treasure to the last, and exhibit his beautiful *Rachel* and favourite *Joseph* after Esau had seen all the rest, in order to make the deeper impression on his mind?

Verse 4. *Esau ran to meet him*] How sincere and genuine is this conduct of Esau, and at the same time how magnanimous! He had buried all his resentment, and forgotten all his injuries; and receives his brother with the strongest demonstrations, not only of forgiveness, but of fraternal affection.

And kissed him] וישקהו *vaiyishshakehu*. In the Masoretic Bibles each letter of this word is noted with a *point* over it to make it *emphatic*. And by this kind of notation the rabbins wished to draw the attention of the reader to the *change* that had taken place in Esau, and the *sincerity* with which he received his brother Jacob. A *Hindoo* when he meets a friend after absence throws his arms round him, and his head across his shoulders, twice over the right shoulder and once over the left, with other ceremonies according to the rank of the parties.

Verse 10. *Receive my present at my hand*] Jacob could not be certain that he had found favour with Esau, unless the present had been received; for in accepting it Esau necessarily became his *friend*, according to the custom of those times, and in that country. In the eastern countries, if your present be received by your superior, you may rely on his friendship; if it be not received, you have every thing to fear. It is on this ground that Jacob was so urgent with Esau to receive his present, because he knew that after this he must treat him as a friend.

Verse 14. *Until I come unto my lord unto Seir.*] It is very likely that Jacob was perfectly sincere in his expressed purpose of visiting Esau at Seir, but it is as likely that circumstances afterwards occurred that rendered it either improper or impracticable; and we find that Esau afterwards removed to Canaan, and he and Jacob dwelt there together for several years. See chap. xxxvi. 6.

Verse 17. *Journeyed to Succoth*] So called from סכת *succoth*, the *booths* or *tents* which Jacob erected

A. M. 2265. B. C. 1739. built him a house, and made booths
for his cattle: therefore the name
of the place is called [v] Succoth.
18 And Jacob came to [w] Shalem, a city of
[x] Shechem, [y] which *is* in the land of Canaan,
when he came from Padan-aram; and pitched
his tent before the city.

19 And [z] he bought a parcel A. M. 2265. B. C. 1739.
of a field, where he had spread
his tent, at the hand of the children of
[a] Hamor, Shechem's father, for a hundred
[b] pieces of money.
20 And he erected there an altar; and
[c] called it [d] El-elohe-Israel.

[v] That is, *booths*.——[w] John iii. 23.——[x] Called, Acts vii. 16, *Sychem*.——[y] Josh. xxiv. 1; Judges ix. 1.——[z] Josh. xxiv. 32; John iv. 5.——[a] Called, Acts vii. 16, *Emmor*.——[b] Or, *lambs*.——[c] Chap. xxxv. 7.——[d] That is, *God, the God of Israel*.

there for the resting and convenience of his family, who in all probability continued there for some considerable time.

Verse 18. *And Jacob came to Shalem, a city of Shechem*] The word שלם *shalem*, in the Samaritan שלום *shalom*, should be translated here *in peace*, or *in safety*. After resting some time at Succoth, which was necessary for the safety of his flocks and the comfort of his family, he got safely to a city of Shechem, in health of body, without any loss of his cattle or servants, his wives and children being also in safety. *Coverdale* and *Matthews* translate this word as above, and with them agree the *Chaldee* and the *Arabic:* it is not likely to have been the name of a city, as it is nowhere else to be found. Shechem is called in Acts vii. 16, *Sychem*, and in John iv. 5, *Sychar;* in the Arabic it is called *Nablous*, and to the present day *Neapolis*. It was near to Samaria; and the place where the wretched remains of the sect of the Samaritans were lately found, from whom Dr. Huntington received a perfect copy of the Samaritan Pentateuch.

Verse 19. *For a hundred pieces of money*.] The original, במאה קשיטה *bemeah kesitah*, has been a matter of long and learned discussion among critics. As *kesitah* signifies a *lamb*, it may imply that Jacob gave the Hamorites *one hundred lambs* for the field; but if it be the same transaction that St. Stephen refers to in Acts vii. 16, it was *money*, *τιμης αργυριον*, a *sum* or *price of silver*, which was given on the occasion. It has been conjectured that the money had the figure of a lamb stamped on it, because it was on an average the value of a lamb; and hence it might be called a *kesitah* or *lamb* from the impression it bore. It is certain that in many countries the coin has had its name from the *image* it bore; so among our ancestors a coin was called an *angel* because it bore the image of an angel; hence also a *Jacobus*, a *Carolus*, a *Lewis*, (*Louis d' Or*,) a *Joe*, because certain coins in England, Spain, France, and Portugal, bore on one side the image of the kings of those countries, *James*, *Charles*, *Lewis*, *Joseph*, or *Johannes*. The Athenians had a coin called *βους*, an *ox*, because it was stamped with the figure of an ox. Hence the saying in *Æschylus*:—

> *Τα δ' αλλα σιγω, βους επι γλωττης μεγας*
> *Βεβηκεν* AGAM. v. 36.

"I must be silent concerning other matters, a great ox has come upon my tongue;" to signify a person who had received *a bribe* for secrecy, i. e., a sum of money, on each piece of which an ox was stamped, and hence called *βους*, an *ox*. The word *opes*, riches, is a corruption of the word *oves*, sheep, because these animals in ancient times constituted the principal riches of their owners; but when other cattle were added, the word *pecunia*, (from *pecus*, cattle,) which we translate *money*, and from which we still have our English term *pecuniary*, appears to have been substituted for *oves*, because *pecus*, *pecoris*, and *pecus*, *pecudis*, were used to signify *all kinds* of cattle *large* and *small*. Among our *British* and *Saxon* ancestors we find coins stamped with the figure of an *ox*, *horse*, *hog*, *goat*, *&c.*, and this custom arose in all probability, both among them and other nations, from this circumstance, that in primitive times the coin was the ordinary value of the animal whose image it bore. It is, all circumstances weighed, most likely that a piece of *money* is here intended, and *possibly* marked with the image of a *lamb;* but as the original word קשיטה *kesitah* occurs only *here*, and in Josh. xxiv. 32, and Job xlii. 11, this is not sufficiently evident, the word itself being of very doubtful signification. Mr. Parkhurst is of opinion that the *kesitah* bore the image of a *lamb;* and that these *lamb coins* of the ancient Hebrews typified the Lamb of God, who in the Divine purpose was considered as slain from the foundation of the world, and who *purchased* us unto God with his own blood. The conjecture is at least *pious*, and should lead to useful reflections. Those who wish to see more on this subject may consult the writers in the *Critici Sacri*, and Calmet.

Verse 20. *And he erected there an altar*] It appears that Jacob had a very correct notion of the *providence* and *mercy* of God; hence he says, ver. 5: *The children which God hath* GRACIOUSLY *given thy servant;* and in ver. 11 he attributes all his *substance* to the bounty of his Maker: *Take, I pray thee, my blessing—because God hath dealt* GRACIOUSLY *with me, and because I have enough*. Hence he viewed God as the *God of all grace*, and to him he erects an altar, dedicating it to *God, the God of Israel*, referring particularly to the *change* of his own name, and the *mercies* which he then received; and hence perhaps it would be best to translate the words, *The strong God* (is) *the God of Israel;* as by the power of his grace and goodness he had rescued, defended, blessed, and supported him from his youth up until now. The erecting altars with particular names appears in other places; so, Exod. xvii. 15, Moses calls his altar *Jehovah-nissi*, "the Lord is my banner."

1. WHEN a man's ways please God, he maketh even his enemies to be at peace with him. When Jacob had got reconciled to God, God reconciled his brother to him. The hearts of all men are in the hands of God, and he turns them howsoever he will.

2. Since the time in which Jacob wrestled with the Angel of the covenant, we see in him much dependence on God, accompanied with a spirit of deep humility and gratitude. God's grace alone can change the heart of man, and it is by that grace only that we get a sense of our obligations; this lays us in the dust, and the more we receive the lower we shall lie.

3. "The first thing," says good Bishop Wilson, "that pious men do, is to provide for the honour and worship of God." Jacob buys a piece of ground, and erects an altar on it in the land of a heathen, that he might acknowledge God among his enemies, and turn them to the true faith; and there is every reason to believe that this expedient would have been successful, had it not been for the base conduct of his sons. How true is the saying, One sinner spoileth much good! Reader, beware, lest thy conduct should become a stumbling block to any.

CHAPTER XXXIV.

Dinah, *the daughter of Jacob and Leah, going out to see the daughters of the land, is ravished by Shechem, the son of Hamor,* 1, 2. *He entreats his father to get her for him to wife,* 3. *Jacob and his sons hear of the indignity offered to Dinah,* 5–7. *Hamor proposes the suit of Shechem to Jacob and his sons, and offers them a variety of advantages,* 8–10. *Shechem himself comes forward, begs to have Dinah to wife, and offers dowry to any extent,* 11, 12. *The sons of Jacob pretend scruples of conscience to give their sister to one who was uncircumcised; and require, as a condition of this marriage, and of intermarriages in general, that all the Shechemites should be circumcised,* 13–17. *Hamor and Shechem consent,* 18, 19. *They lay the business before the elders of their city, dwell on the advantages of a connection with Jacob and his family, and propose to them the condition required by the sons of Jacob,* 20–23. *The elders consent, and all the males are circumcised,* 24. *While the Shechemites are incapable of defending themselves, on the third day after their circumcision,* Simeon *and* Levi, *the brothers of Dinah, came upon the city, slew all the males, sacked the city, took the women and children captives, and seized on all the cattle belonging to the Shechemites,* 25–29. *Jacob is greatly displeased and alarmed at this treachery and cruelty of his sons, and lays before them the probable consequences,* 30. *They endeavour to vindicate their conduct,* 31.

A. M. cir. 2266. B. C. cir. 1738.

AND [a] Dinah the daughter of Leah, which she bare unto Jacob, [b] went out to see the daughters of the land.

2 And when Shechem the son of Hamor the Hivite, prince of the country, [c] saw her, he [d] took her, and lay with her, and [e] defiled her.

3 And his soul clave unto Dinah the daughter of Jacob; and he loved the damsel, and spake [f] kindly unto the damsel.

4 And Shechem [g] spake unto his father Hamor, saying, Get me this damsel to wife.

5 And Jacob heard that he had defiled Dinah his daughter: now his sons were with his cattle in the field; and Jacob [h] held his peace until they were come.

6 And Hamor the father of Shechem went out unto Jacob to commune with him.

7 And the sons of Jacob came out of the field when they heard *it:* and the men were grieved, and they [i] were very wroth, because he [k] had wrought folly in Israel, in lying with Jacob's daughter; [l] which thing ought not to be done.

[a] Chap. xxx. 21.——[b] Tit. ii. 5.——[c] Chap. vi. 2; Judg. xiv. 1.——[d] Chap. xx. 2.——[e] Heb. *humbled her;* Deut. xxii. 29.——[f] Heb. *to the heart of the damsel;* see Isa. xl. 2; Hos. ii. 14.

[g] Judg. xiv. 2.——[h] 1 Sam. x. 27; 2 Sam. xiii. 22.——[i] Chap. xlix. 7; 2 Sam. xiii. 21.——[k] Josh. vii. 15; Judg. xx. 6.——[l] Deut. xxiii. 17; 2 Sam. xiii. 12.

NOTES ON CHAP. XXXIV.

Verse 1. *And Dinah—went out to see the daughters of the land.*] It is supposed that Jacob had been now about seven or eight years in the land, and that Dinah, who was about seven years of age when Jacob came to Canaan, was now about fourteen or fifteen. Why or on what occasion she went out we know not, but the reason given by Josephus is very probable, *viz.*, that it was on one of their *festivals.*

Verse 2. *Prince of the country*] i. e., Hamor was prince; Shechem was the son of the prince or chief. Our version appears to represent Shechem as *prince*, but his father was the chief of the country. See verses 6, 8, &c.

Verse 3. *Spake kindly unto the damsel.*] Literally, *he spake to the heart of the damsel*—endeavoured to gain her affections, and to reconcile her to her disgrace. It appears sufficiently evident from this and the preceding verse that there had been no *consent* on the part of Dinah, that the whole was an act of *violence*, and that she was now detained *by force* in the house of *Shechem.* Here she was found when Simeon and Levi sacked the city, verse 26.

Verse 7. *He had wrought folly in Israel*] The land, afterwards generally called *Israel*, was not as yet so named; and the sons of Jacob were neither called *Israel*, *Israelites* nor *Jews*, till long after this. How then can it be said that Shechem had *wrought folly in Israel?* The words are capable of a more literal translation: בישראל *beyisrael*, may be translated, *against Israel.* The angel had said, *Thy name shall be called no more Jacob*—not only Jacob, *but Israel.* It was this that aggravated the offence of Shechem; he wrought folly against *Israel*, the prince of God,

A. M. cir. 2266.
B. C. cir. 1738.

8 And Hamor communed with
them, saying, The soul of my son
Shechem longeth for your daughter: I pray
you give her him to wife.
9 And make ye marriages with us, *and* give
your daughters unto us, and take our daughters
unto you.
10 And ye shall dwell with us: and [m] the
land shall be before you; dwell and [n] trade ye
therein, and [o] get you possession therein.
11 And Shechem said unto her father and
unto her brethren, Let me find grace in your
eyes, and what ye shall say unto me I will
give.
12 Ask me never so much [p] dowry and gift,
and I will give according as ye shall say unto
me; but give me the damsel to wife.
13 And the sons of Jacob answered Shechem
and Hamor his father [q] deceitfully, (and said,
Because he had defiled Dinah their sister:)
14 And they said unto them, We cannot do
this thing, to give our sister to one that is
uncircumcised; for [r] that *were* a reproach
unto us:
15 But in this will we consent unto you: If
ye will be as we *be*, that every male of you be
circumcised;
16 Then will we give our daughters unto
you, and we will take your daughters to us;
and we will dwell with you, and
we will become one people.
17 But if ye will not hearken unto us, to be
circumcised; then will we take our daughter,
and we will be gone.
18 And their words pleased Hamor, and
Shechem Hamor's son.
19 And the young man deferred not to do
the thing, because he had delight in Jacob's
daughter: and he *was* [s] more honourable than
all the house of his father.
20 And Hamor and Shechem his son came
unto the gate of their city, and communed with
the men of their city, saying,
21 These men *are* peaceable with us; therefore let them dwell in the land, and trade
therein; for the land, behold, *it is* large
enough for them; let us take their daughters
to us for wives, and let us give them our
daughters.
22 Only herein will the men consent unto
us for to dwell with us, to be one people, if
every male among us be circumcised, as they
are circumcised.
23 *Shall* not their cattle and their substance
and every beast of theirs *be* ours? only let us
consent unto them, and they will dwell with us
24 And unto Hamor and unto Shechem his
son hearkened all that [t] went out of the gate

[m] Chapter xiii. 9; xx. 15.——[n] Chap. xlii. 34.——[o] Chapter xlvii. 27.——[p] Exodus xxii. 16, 17; Deut. xxii. 29; 1 Samuel xviii. 25.

[q] See 2 Sam. xiii. 24, &c.——[r] Josh. v. 9.——[s] Num. xxii 15; 2 Chron. iv. 9; Isa. iii. 3-5.——[t] Chap. xxiii. 10; Matt. vii. 6; Rom. ii. 28, 29.

in lying with the daughter of Jacob. Here both the names are given; *Jacob*, whose daughter was defiled, and *Israel*, the *prince of God*, against whom the offence was committed.

Verse 12. *Ask me never so much dowry*] See on chap. xxix. 20, &c. See the law relative to this, Exod. xxii. 16, 17.

Verse 13. *Answered—deceitfully*] Which nothing could excuse; yet, to show that they had had much provocation, it is immediately subjoined וידברו *vaidabberu*, *they spoke* thus *because he had defiled Dinah their sister*; for so this parenthesis should be read.

Verse 14. *That* were *a reproach unto us*] Because the uncircumcised were not in the covenant of God; and to have given an heiress of the promise to one who had no kind of right to its spiritual blessings, from whom might spring children who would naturally walk in the way of their father, would have been *absurd*, *reproachful*, and *wicked*. Thus far they were perfectly right; but to make this holy principle a cloak for their deceitful and murderous purposes, was the full sum of all wickedness.

Verse 17. *Then will we take our daughter, and we will be gone.*] It is natural to suppose that the tribe of Hamor was very inconsiderable, else they would not have sought an alliance with the family of Jacob, and have come so readily into a painful, disgraceful measure, without having either the sanction of *Divine authority* or *reason*; for it does not appear that the sons of Jacob urged either. And they are *threatened* here that if they do not agree to be circumcised, Dinah shall be taken from them, and restored to her family; and this is probably what the Shechemites saw they had not power at present to prevent.

Verse 23. Shall *not their cattle and their substance*—be *ours?*] This was a bait held out for the poor unsuspecting people of Hamor by their prince and his son, who were not much less deceived than the people themselves.

Verse 24. *Every male was circumcised*] These simple people must have had very great affection for their chief and his son, or have been under the influence of the most *passive obedience*, to have come so readily into this measure, and to have submitted to this rite. But the *petty* princes in Asiatic countries have ever been *absolute* and *despotic*, their subjects paying them the most prompt and blind obedience. I shall give a few examples from Mr. Richardson's Dissertations.—

A. M. cir. 2266. B. C. cir. 1738.

of his city: and every male was circumcised, all that went out of the gate of his city.

25 And it came to pass on the third day, when they were sore, that two of the sons of Jacob, [u] Simeon and Levi, Dinah's brethren, took each man his sword, and came upon the city boldly, and slew all the males.

26 And they slew Hamor and Shechem his son with the [v] edge of the sword, and took Dinah out of Shechem's house, and went out.

27 The sons of Jacob came upon the slain, and spoiled the city, because they had defiled their sister.

28 They took their sheep, and their oxen, and their asses, and that which *was* in the city, and that which *was* in the field,

29 And all their wealth, and all their little ones, and their wives took they captive; and spoiled even all that *was* in the house.

30 And Jacob said to Simeon and Levi, [w] Ye have [x] troubled me [y] to make me to stink among the inhabitants of the land, among the Canaanites and the Perizzites: [z] and I *being* few in number, they shall gather themselves together against me, and slay me; and I shall be destroyed, I and my house.

31 And they said, Should he deal with our sister as with a harlot?

[u] Chapter xlix. 5, 6, 7.——[v] Hebrew, *mouth;* Deut. xxxii. 42; 2 Sam. ii. 26; Isa. xxxi. 8.

[w] Chap. xlix. 6.——[x] Josh. vii. 25.——[y] Exod. v. 21; 1 Samuel xiii. 4.——[z] Deut. iv. 27; Psa. cv. 12.

"*Abu Thaher*, chief of the *Carmathians*, about the year nine hundred and thirty, ravaged the territory of *Mecca*, defiled the temple, and destroyed nearly 40,000 people. With only 500 horse he went to lay siege to Bagdad: the caliph's general, at the head of 30,000 men, marched out to seize him, but before he attacked him he sent an officer to summon him to surrender. 'How many men has the caliph's general?' said Abu Thaher. 'Thirty thousand,' replied the officer 'Among them all,' says the Carmathian chief, 'has he got three like mine?' Then, ordering his followers to approach, he commanded one to stab himself, another to throw himself from a precipice, and a third to plunge into the Tigris; all three instantly obeyed, and perished. Then turning to the officer, he said, 'He who has such troops needs not value the *number* of his enemies!'

"*Hassan Sabat*, one of those petty princes formerly known in Asia and Europe by the title *Sheekh-ul-jibel*, or *old man of the mountain*, being required by an ambassador to do homage to his master, the Sultan *Malekshah Jelaleddin*, without giving any answer, ordered one of his attendants to poniard himself, and another to leap from the battlements of the tower; and he was instantly obeyed! Then turning to the ambassador, he said, 'Seventy thousand are thus attentive to my commands. Let this be my answer.'" On a principle of this kind we may account for the *prompt obedience* of the people of Hamor.

Verse 25. *On the third day, when they were sore*] When the inflammation was at the height, and a fever ensued which rendered the person utterly helpless, and his state critical, *Simeon and Levi*, the half brothers of Dinah, *took each man his sword*, probably assisted by that portion of the servants which helped *them* to take care of the flock, *came on the city boldly*, בטח *betach, securely*—without being *suspected*, and being in no danger of meeting with resistance, *and slew all the males*. Great as the provocation was, and it certainly was very great, this was an act of unparalleled treachery and cruelty.

Verse 27. *The sons of Jacob*] The rest of Jacob's sons, the remaining brothers of Simeon and Levi, *spoiled the city*. Though the others could slay the defenceless males, it was not likely that they could have carried away all the booty, with the women, children, and cattle; it is therefore most natural to suppose that the rest of the sons of Jacob assisted at last in the business.

Verse 30. *Ye have troubled me*] Brought my mind into great distress, and endangered my personal safety; *to make me to stink*—to render me odious to the surrounding tribes, so that there is every reason to suspect that when this deed is come abroad they will join in a confederacy against me, and extirpate my whole family. And had he not been under the peculiar protection of God, this in all human probability would have been the case; but he had prevailed with God, and he was also to prevail with men. That Jacob's resentment was not dissembled we have the fullest proof in his depriving these two sons of the birthright, which otherwise they had doubtless enjoyed. See chap. xlix. 5, 7, where some additional circumstances are related.

Verse 31. *Should he deal with our sister as with a harlot?*] On this outrage alone they vindicated their flagitious conduct. The word *harlot* first occurs here: the original is not פילגש *pilegesh*, which we render *concubine*, (see its explanation chap. xxii. 24,) but זונה *zonah*, which ordinarily signifies *one who prostitutes herself to any person for hire*. Our word *harlot* is said to have been derived from a very odd circumstance: Robert, duke of Normandy, seeing a fine-looking country girl dancing with her companions on the green, took her to his bed. She was the daughter of a *skinner*, and her name was *Arlotta;* and of her *William*, surnamed *The Conqueror*, was born. Hence it is said all such women were from her called *harlots*, as William himself was usually termed *the Bastard*. But *horelet*, the diminutive of *whore*, is not a less likely derivation.

SOLOMON has very properly said, *My son, enter not into the path of the wicked, and go not in the way of evil men; avoid it, pass not by it, turn from it, and pass away*, Prov. iv. 14, 15. Had not Dinah gone

out to see the daughters of the land, and very possibly at one of their idolatrous festivals, she had not suffered the foul disgrace mentioned in this chapter. Not only prudence dictates that young women should keep at *home*, but God expressly commands it, Tit. ii. 5. Dinah got among idolaters, and thus partook of their iniquities; and this led to the most base and cruel transaction upon record. How true is the saying, *Those who wander out of the way of understanding shall abide in the congregation of the dead!* In the case before us blame seems to attach to all parties.

1. It was wrong in *Jacob* to suffer his daughter, alone and unprotected, to visit the daughters of the land.

2. It was excessively wicked in *Shechem* to take this advantage of the daughter of a respectable stranger, who had sought his friendship, and came to sojourn among his people, and whose righteous dealing they must have witnessed for at least *seven years* past. In his behalf we may say, and it would be unjust not to say it, that having done the mischief, and sinned deeply against the laws of hospitality, he wished to make all the reparation in his power; and therefore in the most frank and liberal manner he not only offered, but most pressingly entreated, permission to take Dinah *to wife*. This was the utmost he could do in such a case. And in this he is a saint of the first order when compared with the noble and ignoble profligates who, while blaspheming the *Christian* name by continuing to assume it, commit all kinds of breaches on the virtue of simple females, and the peace of respectable families, and not only make no reparation, but glory in their shame.

3. It was *diabolical* in *Jacob's sons* to slay a whole tribe for the offence of one man, and especially as that one had offered to make all the restitution in his power. They required that Hamor, Shechem, and all their subjects should be circumcised before they could conscientiously consent to give their sister to Shechem in marriage. This *required conformity* was made the cloak of the most base and infamous designs. The simple unsuspecting Shechemites agreed to the proposal; and when rendered by this religious rite incapable of defending themselves, they were basely murdered by Simeon and Levi, and their city destroyed. Jacob, to his great honour, remonstrated against this barbarous and bloody act, committed apparently under the sanction of religion; and God showed his abhorrence of it by directing the patriarch, in his dying moments, to *proscribe* them from the blessings of the covenant, so that they barely retained a name among the tribes of Israel, being in general small, and ever disreputable, except merely in the service of the sanctuary, in which Levi was employed. How often since, notwithstanding this solemn warning, has the pure and benevolent religion of God been made, by wicked and designing men, a political stalking-horse to serve the basest purposes, and a covert to the worst of crimes! But shall we find fault with the holy religion of the blessed God because wicked men have abused it? God forbid! Were it not so good as it really is, it would be incapable of such abuse. An *evil* cannot be *abused*, a *good* may; and the greater and the more acknowledged the good, the more liable to abuse. As every good is so capable of being abused, does he act wisely who argues against the *use* of the thing on this account? Shall we say that various kinds of grain, fruits, and aliments are a *curse*, because wicked men abuse them to the purposes of *drunkenness* and *gluttony?* This would argue an utter perversion of all reason: and is it not on such a pretext as this that many persons have ventured to call in question even the *truths* of Christianity?

Whatever *such* men may be *determined* to think on the subject of this chapter, with the unprejudiced reader the ample and detailed relation which we have here of this barbarous transaction will appear an additional proof of the veracity and impartiality of the sacred historian

---

CHAPTER XXXV.

Jacob is commanded of God to go to Beth-el, *and to build an altar there*, 1. *His exhortation to his family to put away all strange gods, &c.*, 2, 3. *They deliver them all up, and Jacob hides them in the earth*, 4. *They commence their journey*, 5; *come to* Luz, 6; *build there the altar* El-beth-el, 7. *Burial place of* Deborah, *Rebekah's nurse*, 8. *God appears again unto Jacob*, 9. *Blesses him and renews the promises*, 10–13. *To commemorate this manifestation of God, Jacob sets up a pillar, and calls the place* Beth-el. 14, 15. *They journey to* Ephrath, *where* Rachel, *after hard labour, is delivered of* Benjamin, *and dies*, 16–19. *Jacob sets up a pillar on her grave*, 20. *They journey to* Edar, 21. *While at this place*, Reuben *defiles his father's bed*, 22. *Account of the children of Jacob, according to the mothers*, 23–26. *Jacob comes to* Mamre *to his father Isaac, who was probably then in the one hundred and fifty-eighth year of his age*, 27. *Isaac dies, and is buried by his sons Esau and Jacob*, 29.

A. M. cir. 2266. B. C. cir. 1738.

AND God said unto Jacob, Arise, go up to [a] Beth-el, and dwell there: and make there an altar unto God, [b] that appeared unto thee [c] when thou fleddest from the face of Esau thy brother.

A. M. cir. 2266. B. C. cir. 1738.

[a] Chap. xxviii. 19.——[b] Chap. xxviii. 13.

[c] Chap. xxvii. 43.

NOTES ON CHAP. XXXV.

Verse 1. *Arise, go up to Beth-el*] The transaction that had lately taken place rendered it unsafe for Jacob to dwell any longer at the city of Shechem; and it seems that while he was reflecting on the horrible act of Simeon and Levi, and not knowing what to do, God graciously appeared to him, and commanded him to go up to Beth-el, build an altar there, and

A. M. cir. 2266.
B. C. cir. 1738.

2 Then Jacob said unto his [d] household, and to all that *were* with him, Put away [e] the strange gods that *are* among you, and [f] be clean, and change your garments:

3 And let us arise, and go up to Beth-el; and I will make there an altar unto God, [g] who answered me in the day of my distress, [h] and was with me in the way which I went.

4 And they gave unto Jacob all the strange gods which *were* in their hand, and *all their* [i] ear-rings which *were* in their ears; and Jacob hid them under [k] the oak which *was* by Shechem.

5 And they journeyed: and [l] the terror of God was upon the cities that *were* round about them, and they did not pursue after the sons of Jacob.

6 So Jacob came to [m] Luz, which *is* in the land of Canaan, (that *is*, Beth-el,) he and all the people that *were* with him.

7 And he [n] built there an altar, and called the place [o] El-beth-el: because [p] there God appeared unto him, when he fled from the face of his brother.

8 But [q] Deborah, Rebekah's nurse, died, and she was buried beneath Beth-el, under an oak and the name of it was called [r] Allon-bachuth.

[d] Chap. xviii. 19; Josh. xxiv. 15.—[e] Chap. xxxi. 19, 34; Josh. xxiv. 2, 23; 1 Sam. vii. 3.—[f] Exod. xix. 10.—[g] Chap. xxxii. 7, 24; Psa. cvii. 6.—[h] Chap. xxviii. 20; xxxi. 3, 42.—[i] Hos. ii. 13.—[k] Josh. xxiv. 26; Judg. ix. 6.—[l] Exod. xv. 16; xxiii. 27; xxxiv. 24; Deut. xi. 25; Josh. ii. 9; v. 1; 1 Sam. xiv 15; 2 Chron. xiv. 14.—[m] Chap. xxviii. 19, 22.—[n] Eccles v. 4.—[o] That is, *the God of Beth-el.*—[p] Chap. xxviii. 13.—[q] Chap. xxiv. 59.—[r] That is, *the oak of weeping.*

thus perform the vow he had made, chap. xxviii. 20, 22.

Verse 2. *Put away the strange gods*] אלהי הנכר *elohey hannechar*, the *gods of the foreigners*, which were among them. Jacob's servants were all *Syrians*, and no doubt were addicted less or more to idolatry and superstition. These gods might belong to *them*, or, as some have conjectured, they were the *teraphim* which Rachel stole; but these have already been supposed to be *astrological tables*, or something of this kind, called by Laban his *gods*, because by them he supposed he could predict future events, and that they referred to certain astral and planetary intelligences, by whose influences sublunary things were regulated. But it is more natural to suppose that these gods found now in Jacob's family were images of silver, gold, or curious workmanship, which were found among the spoils of the city of Shechem. Lest these should become incitements to idolatry, Jacob orders them to be put away.

Be clean, and change your garments] Personal or outward purification, as emblematical of the sanctification of the soul, has been in use among all the true worshippers of God from the beginning of the world. In many cases the law of Moses *more solemnly* enjoined rites and ceremonies which had been in use from the earliest ages. "A *Hindoo* considers those clothes defiled in which he has been employed in business, and always changes them before eating and worship."—WARD.

Verse 3. *Answered me in the day of my distress*] Not only when he fled from the face of his brother, but more particularly when he was in his greatest strait at the brook of Jabbok.

Verse 4. *And—ear-rings which* were *in their ears*] Whether these rings were in the ears of the gods, or in those of Jacob's family, we may rest assured that they were not mere ornaments, but served for superstitious purposes. *Ear-rings* were certainly worn as *amulets* and *charms*, first consecrated to some god, or formed under some constellation, on which magical characters and images were drawn. A very ancient and beautiful one of this kind brought from Egypt, cut out of a solid piece of cornelian, now lies before me. It was evidently intended for the *ear*, as the opening is too small for any human finger; and it is engraved all over with strange characters and images, which prove that it was intended for a *talisman* or *amulet* It seems to be such a one as St. Augustine describes *Epist.* 73, which was suspended from the tip of the ears both of men and women, not for the purpose of ornament, but through an execrable superstition, for the service of demons. "Execranda superstitio ligaturarum, in quibus etiam inaures virorum in summis ex una parte auriculis suspensæ deputantur, non ad placendum hominibus, sed ad serviendum dæmonibus." See the notes on chap. xxiv. 22.

Verse 5. *The terror of God*] A supernatural awe sent by the Almighty, *was upon the cities that* were *round about*, so that they were not molested in their departure. This could be owing to nothing less than the especial providence of God.

Verse 7. *El-beth-el*] אל בית אל, *the strong God, the house of the strong God.* But the first אל *el* is wanting in one of De Rossi's MSS., as it is also in the Septuagint, Vulgate, Syriac, and some copies of the Arabic. The sentence reads much better without it, and much more consistent with the parallel passages.

Verse 8. *But Deborah, Rebekah's nurse, died*] She was sent with Rebekah when taken by Abraham's servant to be wife to Isaac, chap. xxiv. 59. How she came to be in Jacob's family, expositors are greatly puzzled to find out; but the text does not state that *she was in Jacob's family*. Her death is mentioned merely because Jacob and his family had now arrived at the place where she was buried, and the name of that place was called *Allon-bachuth*, "the oak of weeping," as it is likely her death had been greatly regretted, and a general and extraordinary mourning had taken place on the occasion. Of *Rebekah's* death we know nothing. After her counsel to her son, chap. xxvii., we hear no more of her history from the sacred writings, except of her burial in chap. xlix. 31. Her name is written in the dust. And is not this designed as a mark of the disapprobation of God? It

A. M. cir. 2266.
B. C. cir. 1738.

9 And [s] God appeared unto Jacob again, when he came out of Padan-aram, and blessed him.

10 And God said unto him, Thy name *is* Jacob: [t] thy name shall not be called any more Jacob, [u] but Israel shall be thy name: and he called his name Israel.

11 And God said unto him, [v] I *am* God Almighty: be fruitful and multiply; [w] a nation and a company of nations shall be of thee, and kings shall come out of thy loins:

12 And the land [x] which I gave Abraham and Isaac, to thee I will give it, and to thy seed after thee will I give the land.

13 And God [y] went up from him in the place where he talked with him.

14 And Jacob [z] set up a pillar in the place where he talked with him, *even* a pillar of stone: and he poured a drink-offering thereon, and he poured oil thereon.

15 And Jacob called the name of the place where God spake with him, [a] Beth-el.

16 And they journeyed from Beth-el; and there was but [b] a little way to come to Ephrath: and Rachel travailed, and she had hard labour.

17 And it came to pass, when she was in hard labour, that the midwife said unto her, Fear not; [c] thou shalt have this son also.

18 And it came to pass, as her soul was in departing, (for she died,) that she called his name [d] Ben-oni: but his father called him [e] Benjamin.

19 And [f] Rachel died, and was buried in the way to [g] Ephrath, which *is* Beth-lehem.

---

[s] Hos. xii. 4.——[t] Chap. xvii. 5.——[u] Chapter xxxii. 28. [v] Chap. xvii. 1; xlviii. 3, 4; Exod. vi. 3.——[w] Chap. xvii. 5, 6, 16; xxviii. 3; xlviii. 4.——[x] Chap. xii. 7; xiii. 15; xxvi. 3, 4; xxviii. 13.——[y] Chap. xvii. 22.——[z] Chap. xxviii. 18.

[a] Chap. xxviii. 19.——[b] Heb. *a little piece of ground*; 2 Kings v. 19.——[c] Chap. xxx. 24; 1 Sam. iv. 20.——[d] That is, *the son of my sorrow*.——[e] That is, *the son of the right hand*.——[f] Chap. xlviii. 7.——[g] Ruth i. 2; iv. 11; Mic. v. 2; Matt. ii. 6.

---

seems strange that such an inconsiderable person as a *nurse* should be mentioned, when even the person she brought up is passed by unnoticed! It has been observed that the nurse of Æneas is mentioned nearly in the same way by the poet Virgil; and in the circumstances, in both cases, there is a striking resemblance.

"Tu quoque littoribus nostris, Æneia nutrix,
Æternam moriens famam, Caieta, dedisti:
Et nunc servat honos sedem tunus; ossaque nomen,
Hesperia in magna, (si qua est ea gloria,) signat.
At pius exequiis Æneas rite solutis,
Aggere composito tumuli, postquam alta quierunt
Æquora, tendit iter velis, portumque relinquit."
Æn., lib. vii., ver. 1, &c.

"Thou too, Cajeta, whose indulgent cares
Nursed the great chief, and form'd his tender years,
Expiring here (an ever-honour'd name!)
Adorn Hesperia with immortal fame:
Thy name survives, to please thy pensive ghost;
Thy sacred relics grace the Latian coast.
Soon as her funeral rites the prince had paid,
And *raised a tomb* in honour of the dead;
The sea subsiding, and the tempests o'er,
He spreads the flying sails, and leaves the shore."
PITT.

Verse 9. *God appeared unto Jacob again*] He appeared to him first at Shechem, when he commanded him to go to Beth-el, and now that he is arrived at the place, God appears to him the *second* time, and reconfirms to him the Abrahamic blessing. To Isaac and Jacob these frequent appearances of God were necessary, but they were not so to Abraham; for to *him* one word was sufficient—*Abraham believed God.*

Verse 13. *And God went up from him*] This was not a vision, nor a strong mental impression, but a real manifestation of God. Jacob *saw* and *heard* him speak, and before his eyes *he went up*—ascended to heaven. This was no doubt the future Saviour, the Angel of the covenant. See chap. xvi. 7.

Verse 14. *A drink-offering*] נסך *nesech*, a *libation* These were afterwards very common in all countries. At first they consisted probably of *water* only, afterwards *wine* was used; see on Lev. vii. 1, &c. The *pillar* which Jacob set up was to commemorate the appearance of God to him; the *drink-offering* and the *oil* were intended to express his *gratitude* and *devotion* to his preserver. It was probably the same pillar which he had set up before, which had since been thrown down, and which he had consecrated afresh to God.

Verse 16. *There was but a little way to come to Ephrath*] The word כברת *kibrath*, translated here *a little way*, has greatly perplexed commentators. It occurs only here, in chap. xlviii. 7, and 2 Kings v. 19; and it seems to have been some sort of *measure* applied to land, as we say a *mile*, an *acre*, a *rood*, a *perch*; but what the exact quantity of the *kibrath* was cannot be ascertained. *Ephrath*, called also *Bethlehem*, and *Bethlehem Ephrata*, was the birthplace of our blessed Redeemer. See its meaning Matt. ii. 6.

Verse 18. *As her soul was in departing*] Is not this a proof that there is an immortal spirit in man, which can exist *separate* from and independent of the body? Of Rachel's death it is said, בצאת נפשה *betseth naphshah, in the going away of her soul*; her *body* did not go away, therefore her soul and body must have been distinct. If her *breath* only had been intended, נשמה *neshamah* or רוח *ruach* would have rather been used, as the first means *breath*, the latter *breath* or *spirit* indifferently.

She called his name Ben-oni] בן אוני *the son of my sorrow* or *affliction*, because of the *hard labour* she had in bringing him into the world; *but his father called him Benjamin*, בנימין, *the son of my right hand*, i. e., the son peculiarly dear to me. So *man of the right*

A. M. cir. 2266.
B. C. cir. 1738.

20 And Jacob set a pillar upon her grave: that *is* the pillar of Rachel's grave [h] unto this day.

21 And Israel journeyed, and spread his tent beyond [i] the tower of Edar.

22 And it came to pass, when Israel dwelt in that land, that Reuben went and [k] lay with Bilhah his father's concubine: and Israel heard *it*. Now the sons of Jacob were twelve:

23 The sons of Leah; [l] Reuben, Jacob's first-born, and Simeon, and Levi, and Judah, and Issachar, and Zebulun.

24 The sons of Rachel; Joseph, and Benjamin.

25 And the sons of Bilhah, Rachel's handmaid; Dan, and Naphtali.

26 And the sons of Zilpah, Leah's handmaid; Gad, and Asher. These *are* the sons of Jacob, which were born to him in Padan-aram.

27 And Jacob came unto Isaac his father unto [m] Mamre, unto the [n] city of Arbah, (which *is* Hebron,) where Abraham and Isaac sojourned.

[h] 1 Sam. x. 2; 2 Sam. xviii. 18.——[i] Mic. iv. 8.——[k] Chap. xlix. 4; 1 Chron. v. 1; see 2 Sam. xvi. 22; xx. 3; 1 Cor. v. 1.——[l] Chap. xlvi. 8; Exod. i. 2.——[m] Chapter xiii. 18; xxiii. 2, 19 ——[n] Josh. xiv. 15; xv. 13.

hand, Psa. lxxx. 17, signifies one much loved and regarded of God. The Samaritan has *Benyamin*, the *son of days*; *i. e.*, the son of *his old age*, as Judah calls him, chap. xliv. 20; and Houbigant contends that this is the true reading, and that the Chaldee termination *in* for *im* is a corruption. If it be a corruption, it is as old as the days of St. Jerome, who translates the place *Benjamin, id est, filius dextræ; Benjamin, that is, the son of the right hand.*

Verse 20. *Jacob set a pillar upon her grave*] Was not this the origin of funeral monuments? In ancient times, and among rude nations, a heap of stones designated the burial place of the chief; many of these still remain in different countries. Afterwards a rude stone, with a simple inscription, was used, containing only the name of the deceased, and that of his father. But where arts and sciences flourished, superb monuments were erected highly decorated, and pompously inscribed. It is very likely from the circumstances of Jacob that a single stone constituted the *pillar* in this case, on which, if writing did then exist, the name, or rather some hieroglyphical device, was probably inscribed. That which is now called *Rachel's pillar* is allowed, by those who have examined it, to be a comparatively *modern* structure.

Verse 21. *Tower of Edar.*] Literally, *the tower of the flock*, and so translated Mic. iv. 8. It is supposed that this tower was about a mile from Bethlehem, and to have been the place where the angels appeared to the shepherds. The Targum of Jonathan expressly says: "It is the place in which the King Messiah shall be manifested in the end of days." By the *tower of the flock* we may understand a place built by the shepherds near to some *well*, for the convenience of watering their flocks, and keeping watch over them by night.

Verse 22. *Reuben went and lay with Bilhah his father's concubine*] Jonathan, in his Targum, says that Reuben only overthrew the bed of Bilhah, which was set up opposite to the bed of his mother Leah, and that this was reputed to him as if he had lain with her. The colouring given to the passage by the Targumist is, that Reuben was incensed, because he found Bilhah preferred after the death of Rachel to his own mother Leah; and therefore in his anger he overthrew her couch. The same sentiment is repeated by Jonathan, and glanced at by the Jerusalem Targum, chap. xlix. 4. Could this view of the subject be proved to be correct, both piety and candour would rejoice.

And Israel heard it.] Not one word is added farther in the Hebrew text; but a break is left in the verse, opposite to which there is a Masoretic note, which simply states that *there is a hiatus in the verse.* This hiatus the Septuagint has thus supplied: *και πονηρον εφανη εναντιον αυτου, and it appeared evil in his sight.*

Now the sons of Jacob were twelve] Called afterwards the *twelve patriarchs*, because they became heads or *chiefs* of numerous *families* or tribes, Acts vii. 8; and the people that descended from them are called the *twelve tribes*, Acts xxvi. 7; James i. 1. *Twelve princes* came from Ishmael, chap. xxv. 16, who were heads of families and tribes. And in reference to the *twelve patriarchs*, our Lord chose *twelve apostles.* Strictly speaking, there were *thirteen* tribes among the Hebrews, as *Ephraim* and *Manasses* were counted for tribes, chap. xlviii. 5, 6; but the Scripture in naming them, says Mr. Ainsworth, usually sets down but twelve, omitting the name now of one, then of another, as may in sundry places be observed, Deut. xxxiii.; Ezek. xlviii.; Rev. vii., &c.

Verse 23. *The sons of Leah*] The children are arranged under their respective mothers, and not in order of their birth.

Verse 26. *Born to him in Padan-aram.*] *i. e.*, all but Benjamin was born in Canaan, ver. 16, 17.

It is well known that Padan-aram is the same as *Mesopotamia*, and hence the Septuagint translate *Μεσοποταμια της Συριας, Mesopotamia of Syria.* The word signifies *between the two rivers*, from *μεσος, the midst*, and *ποταμος, a river.* It is situated between the *Euphrates* and *Tigris*, having Assyria on the *east*, Arabia Deserta, with Babylonia, on the *south*, Syria on the *west*, and Armenia on the *north.* It is now the province of *Diarbek*, in Asiatic Turkey, and is sometimes called *Maverannahar*, the country beyond the river; and *Aram Naharaim*, Aram or Syria of the two rivers.

Verse 27. *The city of Arbah*, (*which* is *Hebron*)] See chap. xxiii. 2. It has been conjectured that Jacob must have paid a visit to his father before this time, as previously to this he had been some years in

A. M. 2288.
B. C. 1716.
28 And the days of Isaac were a hundred and fourscore years.
29 And Isaac gave up the ghost and died, and [o] was gathered unto his people, *being* old and full of days: and [p] his sons Esau and Jacob buried him.

A. M. 2288.
B. C. 1716.

[o] Chap. xv. 15; xxv. 8.

[p] So chap. xxv. 9; xlix. 31.

Canaan; but now, as he was approaching to his end, Jacob is supposed to have gone to live with and comfort him in his declining days.

Verse 29. *Isaac gave up the ghost—and was gathered unto his people*] See on chap. xxv. 8.

Esau and Jacob buried him.] See chap. xxv. 9. Esau, as we have seen chap. xxxiii., was thoroughly reconciled to his brother Jacob, and now they both join in fraternal and filial affection to do the last kind office to their amiable father. It is generally allowed that the death of Isaac is mentioned here out of its chronological order, as several of the transactions mentioned in the succeeding chapters, especially xxxvii. and xxxviii., must have happened during his life; but that the *history of Joseph* might not be disturbed, his death is anticipated in this place. It is supposed that he lived at least twelve years after Joseph was sold into Egypt.

This chapter contains several subjects which are well worthy of the reader's most serious attention.

1. That such a family as that of Jacob should have had false gods in it, is a matter not less astonishing than real: and suppose that we allow, as is very probable, that their *images* and *rings* were got from strangers, the Syrians and the Shechemites, yet their being tolerated in the family, though it is probable this was for a very short time, cannot be easily accounted for. It is true the LAW was not then given, and the unity of God not so particularly taught as it was afterwards. Besides, we have already seen that certain superstitions were compatible in those early times with general sincerity and attachment to the truth; those times and acts of ignorance were winked at, till superior light shone upon the world. Between many of the practices of Laban's family and those of the surrounding heathenish tribes, there might have been but little difference; and this was probably the reason why Dinah could so readily mix with the daughters of the land, chap. xxxiv. 1, which led to the fatal consequences already reviewed. Sin is like the letting out of water—when once a breach is made in the dyke, the stream becomes determined to a wrong course, and its progress is soon irresistible. Had not Jacob put away these strange gods, the whole family might have been infected with idolatry. This saying of one of the ancients is good, *Vitia transmittit ad posteros, qui præsentibus culpis ignoscit.*—SENECA. "He who is indulgent to present offences, transmits sin to *posterity*." The first motions of it should be firmly resisted; after struggles are too often fruitless.

2. The doctrine of a *particular* and *especial providence* has another proof in this chapter. After the sanguinary conduct of Jacob's sons, is it not surprising that the neighbouring tribes did not join together and extirpate the whole family? And so they certainly would, had not the terror of God fallen upon them, ver. 5. Jacob and the major part of his family were innocent of this great transgression; and on the preservation of their lives, the accomplishment of great events depended: therefore God watches over them, and shields them from the hands of their enemies.

3. The *impatience* and *fate* of the amiable Rachel, who can read of without deploring? *Give me children*, said she, *or else I die*, chap. xxx. 1. Her desire was granted, and her *death* was the consequence! God's way is ever best. We know not what we ask, nor what we ought to ask, and therefore often ask amiss when we petition for such secular things as belong to the *dispensations* of God's *providence*. For things of this kind we have no revealed directory; and when we ask for them, it should be with the deepest submission to the Divine will, as God alone knows what is *best* for us. With respect to the *soul*, every thing is clearly revealed, so that we may ask and receive, and have a fulness of joy; but as to our *bodies*, there is much reason to fear that the *answer of our petitions* would be, in numerous cases, our inevitable destruction. How many prayers does God in mercy shut out!

4. The transgression of Reuben, of whatsoever kind, was marked, not only by the displeasure of his father, but by that of God also; see chap. xlix. 4. It brought a curse upon him, and he forfeited thereby the right of primogeniture and the priesthood: the first was given to Judah, the second to Levi. Is it not in reference to this that our Lord addresses these solemn words to the angel of the Church of Philadelphia: *Behold, I come quickly; hold that fast which thou hast, that* NO MAN TAKE THY CROWN? A man, by sowing a *grain* of forbidden sweets, may reap an abundant harvest of eternal wretchedness. Reader, let not *sin* rob *thee* of the kingdom of God.

5. Here we have the death of *Isaac* recorded: most that can can be said of his character has been already anticipated, see chap. xxii., &c. He appears to have been generally pious, deeply submissive and obedient. He was rather an *amiable* and *good*, than a *great* and *useful*, man. If compared with his son Jacob, in the early part of their lives, he appears to great advantage, as possessing more sincerity and more personal piety. But if compared with his father Abraham, O, what a falling off is here! Abraham is the most perfect character under the Old Testament, and even under the *New* he has no parallel but St. Paul. Isaac, though falling far short of his father's excellences, will ever remain a pattern of piety and filial obedience

CHAPTER XXXVI.

The genealogy of Esau, i. e., *his* sons, *by his Canaanitish wives* Adah, Aholibamah, *and* Bashemath, 1–3. *The children of* Adah *and* Bashemath, 4. *Of* Aholibamah, 5. *Esau departs from Canaan and goes to Mount* Seir, 6–8. *The generations of Esau,* i. e., *his* grandchildren, *while in Seir,* 9–19. *The generations of* Seir, *the Horite,* 20–30. Anah *finds mules* (Yemim) *in the wilderness,* 24. *The kings which reigned in Edom,* 31–39. *The dukes that succeeded them,* 40–43.

A. M. cir. 2225. B. C. cir. 1779.
NOW these *are* the generations of Esau, [a] who *is* Edom.
A. M. cir. 2288. B. C. cir. 1716.
2 [b] Esau took his wives of the
daughters of Canaan; Adah the
daughter of Elon the Hittite, and [c] Aholibamah
the daughter of Anah the daughter of Zibeon
the Hivite;
A. M. cir. 2225. B. C. cir. 1779.
3 And [d] Bashemath Ishmael's
daughter, sister of Nebajoth.
A. M. cir. 2230. B. C. cir. 1774.
4 And [e] Adah bare to Esau
Eliphaz; and Bashemath bare
Reuel.
A. M. cir. 2292. B. C. cir. 1712.
5 And Aholibamah bare Jeush,
and Jaalam, and Korah: these
are the sons of Esau, which were born unto
him in the land of Canaan.
A. M. cir. 2266. B. C. cir. 1738.
6 And Esau took his wives,
and his sons, and his daughters,
and all the [f] persons of his house, and his
cattle, and all his beasts, and all his substance,
which he had got in the land of Canaan; and
went into the country from the A. M. cir. 2266. B. C. cir. 1738.
face of his brother Jacob.
7 [g] For their riches were more than that
they might dwell together; and [h] the land
wherein they were strangers could not bear
them, because of their cattle.
8 Thus dwelt Esau in [i] mount Seir: [k] Esau
is Edom.
9 And these *are* the generations of Esau
the father of [l] the Edomites in mount Seir.
10 These *are* the names of A. M. cir. 2230. B. C. cir. 1774.
Esau's sons; [m] Eliphaz the son
of Adah the wife of Esau, Reuel the son of
Bashemath the wife of Esau.
11 And the sons of Eliphaz A. M. cir. 2270. B. C. cir. [illegible]
were Teman, Omar, [n] Zepho, and
Gatam, and Kenaz.
12 And Timna was concubine to Eliphaz
Esau's son; and she bare to Eliphaz [o] Amalek:
these *were* the sons of Adah Esau's
wife.

[a] Chap. xxv. 30.—[b] Chap. xxvi. 34.—[c] Ver. 25.—[d] Chap. xxviii. 9.—[e] 1 Chron. i. 35.—[f] Heb. *souls.*—[g] Chap. xiii. 6, 11.—[h] Chap. xvii. 8; xxviii. 4.—[i] Chap. xxxii. 3; Deut. ii. 5; Josh. xxiv. 4.—[k] Ver. 1.—[l] Heb. *Edom.*—[m] 1 Chron. i. 35, &c.—[n] Or, *Zephi;* 1 Chron. i. 36.—[o] Exodus xvii. 8, 14; Num. xxiv. 20; 1 Sam. xv. 2, 3, &c.

NOTES ON CHAP. XXXVI.

Verse 1. *These* are *the generations of Esau*] We have here the genealogy of Esau in his sons and grandsons, and also the genealogy of *Seir* the Horite. The genealogy of the *sons of* Esau, born in Canaan, is related ver. 1–8; those of his grandchildren born in Seir, 9–19; those of *Seir* the Horite, 20–30. The generations of Esau are particularly marked, to show how exactly God fulfilled the promises he made to him, chap. xxv. and xxvii.; and those of *Seir* the *Horite* are added, because his family became in some measure blended with that of Esau.

Verse 2. *His wives*] It appears that Esau's wives went by very different names. *Aholibamah* is named *Judith,* chap. xxvi. 34; *Adah* is called *Bashemath* in the same place; and she who is here called *Bashemath* is called *Mahalath,* chap. xxviii. 9. These are variations which cannot be easily accounted for; and they are not of sufficient importance to engross much time. It is well known that the same persons in Scripture are often called by different names. See the Table of variations, chap. xxv., where there are some slight examples.

Anah the daughter of Zibeon] But this same *Anah* is said to be the *son* of Zibeon, ver. 24, though in this and the fourteenth verse he is said to be the *daughter* of Zibeon. But the *Samaritan,* the *Septuagint,* (and the *Syriac,* in ver. 2,) read *son* instead of *daughter,* which *Houbigant* and *Kennicott* contend to be the true reading. Others say that *daughter* should be referred to Aholibamah, who was the daughter of Anah, and *granddaughter* of Zibeon. I should rather prefer the reading of the Samaritan, Septuagint, and Syriac, and read, both here and in ver. 14, "Aholibamah, the daughter of Anah the SON of Zibeon," and then the whole will agree with verse 24.

Verse 6. *Esau took his wives, &c.*] So it appears that Esau and Jacob dwelt together in Canaan, whither the former removed from Seir, probably soon after the return of Jacob. That they were on the most friendly footing this sufficiently proves; and Esau shows the same dignified conduct as on other occasions, in leaving Canaan to Jacob, and returning again to Mount Seir; certainly a much less fruitful region than that which he now in behalf of his brother voluntarily abandoned.

Verse 12. *Timna was concubine to Eliphaz*] As Timna was sister to *Lotan* the Horite, ver. 22, we see how the family of Esau and the Horites got intermixed. This might give the sons of Esau a pre-

A. M. cir. 2270. B. C. cir. 1734. 13 And these are the sons of Reuel; Nahath, and Zerah, Shammah, and Mizzah: these were the sons of Bashemath Esau's wife.

A. M. cir. 2292. B. C. cir. 1712. 14 And these were the sons of Aholibamah, the daughter of Anah the daughter of Zibeon, Esau's wife: and she bare to Esau Jeush, and Jaalam, and Korah.

First aristocracy of dukes. From A. M. cir. 2429 to A. M. cir. 2471. From B. C. cir. 1575 to B. C. cir. 1533. 15 These *were* dukes of the sons of Esau: the sons of Eliphaz the first-born *son* of Esau; duke Teman, duke Omar, duke Zepho, duke Kenaz,

16 Duke Korah, duke Gatam, *and* duke Amalek: these *are* the dukes *that came* of Eliphaz in the land of Edom: these *were* the sons of Adah.

17 And these *are* the sons of Reuel Esau's son; duke Nahath, duke Zerah, duke Shammah, duke Mizzah: these *are* the dukes *that came* of Reuel in the land of Edom: these *are* the sons of Bashemath Esau's wife.

18 And these are the sons of Aholibamah Esau's wife; duke Jeush, duke Jaalam, duke Korah: these *were* the dukes *that came* of Aholibamah the daughter of Anah, Esau's wife. From B. C. cir. 1575 to B. C. cir. 1533.

19 These *are* the sons of Esau, who *is* Edom, and these *are* their dukes.

A. M. cir. 2198. B. C. cir. 1806. 20 [p] These *are* the sons of Seir [q] the Horite, who inhabited the land; Lotan, and Shobal, and Zibeon, and Anah.

A. M. cir. 2204. B. C. cir. 1800. 21 And Dishon, and Ezer, and Dishan: these *are* the dukes of the Horites, the children of Seir in the land of Edom.

A. M. cir. 2248. B. C. cir. 1756. 22 And the children of Lotan were Hori, and [r] Hemam; and Lotan's sister *was* Timna.

23 And the children of Shobal *were* these; [s] Alvan, and Manahath, and Ebal, [t] Shepho, and Onam.

24 And these *are* the children of Zibeon, both Ajah, and Anah: this *was that* Anah that found [u] the mules in the wilderness, as he fed the asses of Zibeon his father.

[p] 1 Chron. i. 38.——[q] Chapter xiv. 6; Deut. ii. 12, 22.——[r] Or, *Homam*; 1 Chron. i. 39.

[s] Or, *Alian*; 1 Chron. i. 40.——[t] Or, *Shephi*; 1 Chron. i. 40. [u] See Lev. xix. 19.

text to seize the land, and expel the ancient inhabitants, as we find they did, Deut. ii. 12.

Amalek] The father of the Amalekites, afterwards bitter enemies to the Jews, and whom God commanded to be entirely exterminated, Deut. xxv. 17, 19.

Verse 15. *Dukes of the sons of Esau*] The word *duke* comes from the Latin *dux*, a *captain* or *leader*. The Hebrew אלוף *alluph* has the same signification; and as it is also the term for a *thousand*, which is a grand *capital* or *leading* number, probably the אלופי *alluphey* or *dukes* had this name from being *leaders* of or *captains* over a company of one *thousand* men; just as those among the Greeks called *chiliarchs*, which signifies the same; and as the Romans called those *centurions* who were captains over one hundred men, from the Latin word *centum*, which signifies a hundred. The ducal government was that which prevailed first among the *Idumeans*, or descendants of Esau. Here *fourteen* dukes are reckoned to Esau, *seven* that came of his wife Adah, *four* of Bashemath, and *three* of Aholibamah.

Verse 16. *Duke Korah*] This Dr. Kennicott pronounces to be an interpolation. "It is certain, from verse 4, that Eliphaz was Esau's son by Adah; and from verses 11, 12, that *Eliphaz* had but *six* sons, *Teman*, *Omar*, *Zepho*, *Gatam*, *Kenaz*, and *Amalek*. It is also certain, from verses 5 and 14, that *Korah* was the son of *Esau* (not of Eliphaz) by *Aholibamah*; and as such he is properly mentioned in ver. 18: These are the sons of Aholibamah, Esau's wife: duke Jeush, duke Jaalam, DUKE KORAH. It is clear, therefore, that some transcriber has improperly inserted *duke Korah* in the 16th verse; from which interpolation both the *Samaritan text* and the *Samaritan version* are free."—KENNICOTT'S *Remarks*. Every thing considered, I incline to the opinion that these words were not originally in the text.

Verse 20. *These are the sons of Seir the Horite*] These Horites were the original inhabitants of the country of *Seir*, called the land of the Horites, and afterwards the land of the Idumeans, when the descendants of Esau had driven them out. These people are first mentioned chap. xiv. 6.

Verse 21. *These* are *the dukes of the Horites*] It appears pretty evident that the Horites and the descendants of Esau were mixed together in the same land, as before observed; and Calmet has very properly remarked, that if we compare this verse with verse 30, there were princes of Seir in the country of Seir, and in that of Edom; and in comparing the generations of Seir and Esau, we are obliged to consider these princes as *contemporary*.

Verse 24. *This* was that *Anah that found the mules in the wilderness*] The words את הימם *eth haiyemim*, here translated *mules*, has given rise to a great variety of conjectures and discordant opinions. *St. Jerome*, who renders it *aquas calidas*, *warm springs*, or *hot baths*, says there are as many opinions concerning it as there are commentators.

The *Septuagint* has τον Ιαμειν, which seems to be the name of a *man*; but this is expressed in a great variety of ways in different MSS. of that version.

A. M. cir. 2248.
B. C. cir. 1756.

25 And the children of Anah *were* these; Dishon, and Aholibamah the daughter of Anah.

26 And these *are* the children of Dishon; [v] Hemdan, and Eshban, and Ithran, and Cheran.

27 The children of Ezer *are* these; Bilhan, and Zaavan, and [w] Akan.

28 The children of Dishan *are* these; Uz, and Aran.

29 These *are* the dukes *that came* of the Horites; duke Lotan, duke Shobal, duke Zibeon, duke Anah,

30 Duke Dishon, duke Ezer, duke Dishan: these *are* the dukes *that came* of Hori, among their dukes in the land of Seir.

from A. M. cir. 2093, B. C. cir. 1911, to A. M. cir. 2429, B. C. cir. 1575.

31 And [x] these *are* the kings that reigned in the land of Edom, before there reigned any king over the children of Israel.

A. M. cir. 2093.
B. C. cir. 1911.

32 And Bela the son of Beor reigned in Edom: and the name of his city *was* Dimhabah.

[v] Or, *Amram*; 1 Chron. i. 41.
[w] Or, *Jakan*; 1 Chron. i. 42.——[x] 1 Chron. i. 43.

The *Syriac* renders it ܡܝܐ *mayé, waters*; the author of this version having read in the Hebrew copy from which he translated, מים *mayim, waters*, for ימם *yemim*, the two first letters being *transposed*.

Onkelos translates the word גבריא *gibbaraiya, giants*, or *strong* or *powerful men*.

The *Samaritan text* has ࠄࠀࠉࠌࠉࠌ *haaimim*, and the *Samaritan version* ࠏࠌ ࠀࠉࠌࠉࠀ *am aimai*, the *Emim*, a warlike people, bordering upon the *Horites*.

The *Targum* of *Jonathan ben Uzziel* paraphrases the place thus: "This is the Anah who united the *onager* with the tame *ass*, and in process of time he found *mules* produced by them." *R. D. Kimchi* says, that "Zibeon was both the father and brother of Anah; and this Anah, intent on heterogeneous mixtures, caused asses and horses to copulate, and so produced mules." *R. S. Jarchi* is of the same opinion. See his comment on this place.

Bochart believes the *Emim* are meant; and argues forcibly, 1. That מצא *matsa, he found*, never signifies to *invent*, but rather the *meeting with* or *happening on* a thing which already exists. 2. That mules are never called ימם *yemim* in the Scriptures, but פרדים *peradim*. 3. That Anah fed ASSES *only*, not *horses*. And, 4. That there is no mention of *mules* in Palestine till the days of David. From the whole he concludes that the *Emim* are meant, with whom Anah *fought*; and he brings many places of Scripture where the same form of expression, *he* or *they found*, signifies the *onset to battle*, Judg. i. 5; 1 Sam. xxxi. 3; 1 Kings xiii. 24; 2 Chron. xxii. 8; Num. xxxv. 27; Gen. iv. 14; with many others. See the Hierozoicon, vol. i., cap. 21, p. 238., edit. 1692.

Gusset, in Comment. Heb. Ling., examines what Bochart has asserted, and supposes that *mules*, not the *Emim*, were found by Anah.

Wagenseil would credit what Bochart has asserted, did not stronger reasons lead him to believe that the word means a sort of *plant!*

From the above *opinions* and *versions* the reader may choose which he likes best, or invent one for himself. My own opinion is, that *mules* were not known before the time of Anah; and that he was probably the first who coupled the *mare* and *ass* together to produce this mongrel, or was the first who met with creatures of this race in some very secluded part of the wilderness. Is it not probable that from this Anah, or ענה *enah*, the *Enetæ* derived at least their fabulous origin, whom Homer mentions as famous for their race of *wild* mules?

Παφλαγονων δ' ἡγειτο Πυλαιμενεος λασιον κηρ,
Εξ Ενετων, ὁθεν ἡμιονων γενος αγροτεραων.
IL., lib. ii., v. 852.

The Paphlagonians Pylæmenes rules,
Where rich HENETIA *breeds her* SAVAGE MULES. POPE.

The *Enetæ* or *Henetæ*, who were a people contiguous to Paphlagonia, Cappadocia, and Galatia, might have derived their origin from this *Anah*, or *Henah*, out of which the Ενετοι of the ancient Greek writers might have been formed; and according to Theophrastus, Strabo, and Plutarch, the *first mules* were seen among these people. See *Ludov. De Dieu and Scheuchzer.*

Verse 31. *Before there reigned any king over—Israel.*] I suppose all the verses, from this to the 39th inclusive, have been transferred to this place from 1 Chron. i. 43–50, as it is not likely they could have been written by Moses; and it is quite possible they might have been, at a very early period, written in the margin of an authentic copy, to make out the regal succession in Edom, prior to the consecration of Saul; which words being afterwards found in the margin of a valuable copy, from which others were transcribed, were supposed by the copyist to be a part of the text, which having been omitted by the mistake of the original writer, had been since added to make up the deficiency; on this conviction he would not hesitate to transcribe them consecutively in his copy. In most MSS. sentences and paragraphs have been left out by the copyists, which, when perceived, have been added in the margin, either by the original writer, or by some later hand. Now, as the *margin* was the ordinary place where glosses or explanatory notes were written, it is easy to conceive how the *notes*, as well as the parts of the original text found in the margin, might be all incorporated with the text by a future transcriber; and his MSS., being often copied, would of course multiply the copies with such *additions*, as we have much reason to believe has been the case. This appears very frequently in the Vulgate and Septuagint; and an English Bible now before me, written some time in the fourteenth century, exhibits several proofs of this principle. See the *preface* to this work.

A. M. cir. 2135. B. C. cir. [illegible]. 33 And Bela died, and Jobab
the son of Zerah of Bozrah
reigned in his stead.
A. M. cir. 2177. B. C. cir. 1827. 34 And Jobab died, and Husham of the land of Temani
reigned in his stead.
A. M. cir. 2210. B. C. cir. 1785. 35 And Husham died, and
Hadad the son of Bedad, who
smote Midian in the field of Moab, reigned in
his stead: and the name of his city *was* Avith.
A. M. cir. 2261. B. C. cir. 1743. 36 And Hadad died, and
Samlah of Masrekah reigned
in his stead.
A. M. cir. 2303. B. C. cir. 1701. 37 And Samlah died, and Saul
of Rehoboth, *by* the river, reign-
ed in his stead.
A. M. cir. 2345. B. C. cir. 1659. 38 And Saul died, and Baal-
hanan the son of Achbor reigned
in his stead.

39 And Baal-hanan the son of A. M. cir. 2387. B. C. cir. 1617.
Achbor died, and [y] Hadar reign-
ed in his stead: and the name of his city
was Pau; and his wife's name *was* Mehetabel,
the daughter of Matred, the daughter of
Mezahab.
40 And these *are* the names of Second aristocracy of dukes. From A. M. cir. 2471, B. C. cir. 1533, to A. M. cir. 2513, B. C. cir. 1491.
[z] the dukes *that came* of Esau,
according to their families, after
their places, by their names;
duke Timnah, duke [a] Alvah, duke
Jetheth.
41 Duke Aholibamah, duke Elah, duke
Pinon,
42 Duke Kenaz, duke Teman, duke Mibzar,
43 Duke Magdiel, duke Iram: [b] these *be* the
dukes of Edom, according to their habitations
in the land of their [c] possession: he *is* Esau
the [d] father of the Edomites.

[y] 1 Chron. i. 50; *Hadad Pai*; after his death was an aristocracy; Exodus xv. 15.——[z] 1 Chron. i. 51.——[a] Or, *Aliah.*

[b] Ver. 31; Exod. xv. 15; Num. xx. 14.——[c] Ver. 7, 8; Deut. ii. 5——[d] Chap. xxv. 30; xlv. 8; xxxvi. 43; 1 Chron. iv. 14; Heb. *Edom.*

I know there is another way of accounting for those words on the ground of their being written originally by Moses; but to me it is not satisfactory. It is simply this: the word *king* should be considered as implying any kind of *regular government*, whether by *chiefs, dukes, judges, &c.*, and therefore when Moses says these are the *kings* which reigned in Edom, before there was any king in Israel, he may be only understood as saying that these kings reigned among the Edomites before the family of Jacob had acquired any considerable power, or before the time in which his twelve sons had become the fathers of those numerous tribes, at the head of which, as *king* himself *in Jeshurun*, he now stood.

Esau, after his *dukes*, had *eight kings*, who reigned successively over their people, while Israel were in affliction in Egypt.

Verse 33. *Jobab the son of Zerah*] Many have supposed that *Jobab* is the same as *Job*, so remarkable for his afflictions and patience; and that *Eliphaz*, mentioned verse 10, &c., was the same who in the book of Job is called one of his friends: but there is no proper proof of this, and there are many reasons against it.

Verse 35. *Smote Midian in the field of Moab*] Bishop Cumberland supposes that this was Midian, the son of Abraham by Keturah, and that he was killed by Hadad some time before he was one hundred and nine years of age; and that Moses recorded this, probably, because it was a calamity to the ancestor of Jethro, his father-in-law.—*Orig. of Nat.*, p. 14.

Verse 40. *These* are *the names of the dukes* that came *of Esau*] These dukes did not govern the whole nation of the Idumeans, but they were chiefs in their respective *families*, in *their places*—the districts they governed, and to which they gave *their names*. Calmet thinks that those mentioned above were dukes in Edom or Idúmea at the time of the exodus of Israel from Egypt.

Verse 43. *He* is *Esau the father of the Edomites.*] That is, The preceding list contains an account of the posterity of Esau, who was the father of Edom. *Thus ends Esau's history*; for after this there is no farther account of his life, actions, or death, in the Pentateuch.

1. As Esau is so considerable a person in polemic divinity, it may be necessary, in this place especially, to say something farther of his conduct and character. I have already, in several places, endeavoured, and I hope successfully, to wipe off the odium that has been thrown upon this man, (see the notes on chap. xxvii. and chap. xxxiii.,) without attempting to lessen his faults; and the unprejudiced reader must see that, previously to this last account we have of him, his character stands without a blot, except in the case of selling his birthright, and his purpose to destroy his brother. To the first he was led by his famishing situation and the unkindness of his brother, who refused to save his life *but on this condition*; and the latter, made in the heat of vexation and passion, he never attempted to execute, even when he had the most ample means and the fairest opportunity to do it.

Dr. Shuckford has drawn an impartial character of Esau, from which I extract the following particulars: "Esau was a plain, generous, and honest man, for we have no reason, from any thing that appears in his life or actions, to think him *wicked* beyond other men of his age or times; and his generous and good temper appears from all his behaviour towards his brother. When they first met he was all humanity and affection, and he had no uneasiness when he found that Jacob followed him not to Seir, but went to live near his father. And at Isaac's death we do not find that he made any difficulty of quitting Canaan, which was the very

a

point which, if he had harboured any latent (evil) intentions, would have revived all his resentments. He is indeed called in Scripture the profane Esau; and it is written, *Jacob have I loved, and Esau have I hated;* but there is, I think, no reason to infer, from any of those expressions, that Esau was a *very wicked man*, or that God hated or punished him for an immoral life. For, 1. The sentence here against him is said expressly to be founded, not upon his actions, for it was determined *before the children had done good or evil.* 2. God's hatred of Esau was not a hatred which induced him to punish him with any evil, for he was as happy in all the blessings of this life as either Abraham, Isaac, or Jacob; and his posterity had a land designed by God to be their possession, as well as the children of Jacob, and they were put in possession of it *much sooner* than the Israelites; and God was pleased to *protect them* in the enjoyment of it, and to caution the Israelites against invading them with a remarkable strictness, Deut. ii. 4, 5. And as God was pleased thus to bless Esau and his children in the blessings of this life, even as much as he blessed Abraham, Isaac, or Jacob, if not more, why may we not hope to find him with them at the last day, as well as *Lot* or *Job* or any other good and virtuous man, who was not designed to be a partaker of the *blessing* given to *Abraham?* 3. All the punishment inflicted on Esau was an exclusion from being heir to the blessing promised to *Abraham* and to *his seed*, which was a favour not granted to *Lot*, to *Job*, to several other very *virtuous* and *good men.* 4. St. Paul, in the passage before cited, only intends to show the Jews that God had all along given the favours that led to the Messiah where he pleased; to *Abraham*, not to *Lot;* to *Jacob*, not to *Esau;* as at the time St. Paul wrote the *Gentiles* were made the people of God, not the *Jews.* 5. Esau is indeed called *profane*, (βεβηλος,) but I think that word does not mean *wicked* or *immoral*, ασεβης or ἁμαρτωλος· he was called profane for not having that due value for the priest's office which he should have had; and therefore, though I think it does not appear that he was cut off from being the heir of the promises by any particular action in his life, yet his turn of mind and thoughts do appear to have been such as to evidence that God's purpose towards Jacob was founded on the truest wisdom."—SHUCKFORD's *Connections*, vol. ii., p. 174, &c.

The truth is, the Messiah must spring from *some* ONE *family*, and God chose *Abraham's* through *Isaac, Jacob, &c.*, rather than the same through *Ishmael, Esau*, and the others in that line; but from this choice it does not follow that the first were all *necessarily saved*, and the others *necessarily lost.*

2. To some the *genealogical lists* in this chapter will doubtless appear uninteresting, especially those which concern *Esau* and his descendants; but it was as necessary to register the generations of *Esau* as to register those of *Jacob*, in order to show that the Messiah *did not* spring from the *former*, but that he *did* spring from the *latter.* The genealogical tables, so frequently met with in the sacred writings, and so little regarded by Christians in general, are extremely useful. 1. As they are standing proofs of the truth of the prophecies, which stated that the Messiah should come from a particular family, which prophecies were clearly fulfilled in the birth of Christ. 2. As they testify, to the conviction of the Jews, that the Messiah thus promised is found in the person of Jesus of Nazareth, who incontestably sprang from the last, the only remaining branch of the family of David. These registers were religiously preserved among the Jews till the destruction of Jerusalem, after which they were all destroyed, insomuch that there is not a Jew in the universe who can trace himself to the family of David; consequently, all expectation of a Messiah *to come* is, even on their own principles, nugatory and absurd, as nothing remains to legitimate his birth. When Christ came all these registers were in existence. When St. Matthew and St. Luke wrote, all these registers were still in existence; and had *they* pretended what could not have been supported, an appeal to the registers would have convicted them of a falsehood. But no Jew attempted to do this, notwithstanding the excess of their malice against Christ and his followers; and because they did not do it, we may safely assert no Jew *could* do it. Thus the *foundation* standeth sure

---

CHAPTER XXXVII.

Jacob continues to sojourn in Canaan, 1. *Joseph, being seventeen years of age, is employed in feeding the flocks of his father,* 2. *Is loved by his father more than the rest of his brethren,* 3. *His brethren envy him,* 4. *His* dream *of the* sheaves, 5–7. *His brethren interpret it, and hate him on the account,* 8. *His* dream *of the* sun, moon, *and* eleven stars, 9–11. *Jacob sends him to visit his brethren, who were with the flock in* Shechem, 13, 14. *He wanders in the field, and is directed to go to* Dothan, *whither his brethren had removed the flocks,* 15–17. *Seeing him coming they conspire to destroy him,* 18–20. *Reuben, secretly intending to deliver him, counsels his brethren not to kill, but to put him into a pit,* 21, 22. *They strip Joseph of his coat of many colours, and put him into a pit,* 23, 24. *They afterwards draw him out, and sell him to a company of* Ishmaelite *merchants for twenty pieces of silver, who carry him into* Egypt, 25–28. *Reuben returns to the pit, and not finding Joseph, is greatly affected,* 29, 30. *Joseph's brethren dip his coat in goat's blood to persuade his father that he had been devoured by a wild beast,* 31–33. *Jacob is greatly distressed,* 34, 35. *Joseph is sold in Egypt to Potiphar, captain of Pharaoh's guard,* 36.

AND Jacob dwelt in the land [a] wherein
[b] his father was a stranger, in the land of
Canaan.
A. M. 2276. B. C. 1728.
2 These *are* the generations of
Jacob. Joseph, *being* seventeen
years old, was feeding the flock with his brethren; and the lad *was* with the sons of
Bilhah, and with the sons of Zilpah, his
father's wives: and Joseph brought unto his
father [c] their evil report.
3 Now Israel loved Joseph more than all
his children, because he *was* [d] the son of his
old age: and he made him a coat of *many*
[e] colours.
4 And when his brethren saw that their
father loved him more than all his
brethren, they [f] hated him, and could
not speak peaceably unto him.
A. M. 2276. B. C. 1728.
5 And Joseph dreamed a dream, and he told
it his brethren: and they hated him yet the
more.
6 And he said unto them, Hear, I pray you,
this dream which I have dreamed:
7 For, [g] behold, we *were* binding sheaves in
the field, and, lo, my sheaf arose, and also
stood upright; and, behold, your sheaves stood
round about, and made obeisance to my sheaf
8 And his brethren said to him, Shalt thou
indeed reign over us? or shalt thou indeed
have dominion over us? and they hated him

[a] Heb. *of his father's sojournings.*——[b] Chap. xvii. 8; xxiii. 4; xxviii. 4; xxxvi. 7; Heb. xi. 9.——[c] 1 Sam. ii. 22–24.——[d] Ch. xliv. 20.——[e] Or, *pieces*; Judg. v. 30; 2 Sam. xiii. 18.——[f] Ch. xxvii. 41; xlix. 23.——[g] Chap. xlii. 6, 9; xliii. 26; xliv. 14.

NOTES ON CHAP. XXXVII.

Verse 1. *Wherein his father was a stranger*] מגורי אביו *megurey abiv*, Jacob dwelt in the land *of his father's sojournings*, as the margin very properly reads it. The place was probably the *vale of Hebron*, see ver. 14.

Verse 2. *These* are *the generations*] תלדות *toledoth*, *the history of the lives and actions of Jacob and his sons;* for in this general sense the original must be taken, as in the whole of the ensuing history there is no particular account of any *genealogical* succession. Yet the words may be understood as referring to the tables or genealogical lists in the preceding chapter; and if so, the original must be understood in its common acceptation.

The lad was *with the sons of Bilhah*] It is supposed that our word *lad* comes from the Hebrew ילד *yeled*, a *child*, a *son;* and that *lass* is a contraction of *ladess*, the female of *lad*, a *girl*, *a young woman*. Some have supposed that *King James* desired the translators to insert this word; but this must be a mistake, as the word occurs in this place in *Edmund Becke's* Bible, printed in 1549; and still earlier in that of *Coverdale*, printed in 1535.

Brought unto his father their evil report.] *Conjecture* has been busily employed to find out what this evil report might be; but it is needless to inquire what it was, as on this head the sacred text is perfectly silent. All the use we can make of this information is, that it was one cause of increasing his brothers' hatred to him, which was first excited by his father's *partiality*, and secondly by his own *dreams*.

Verse 3. *A coat of* many *colours.*] כתנת פסים *kethoneth passim*, a coat made up of stripes of differently coloured cloth. Similar to this was the *toga prætexta* of the Roman youth, which was *white*, striped or fringed with *purple;* this they wore till they were *seventeen* years of age, when they changed it for the *toga virilis*, or *toga pura*, which was all *white*. Such vestures as clothing of *distinction* are worn all over Persia, India, and China to the present day. It is no wonder that his brethren should envy him, when his father had thus made him such a distinguished object of his partial love. We have already seen some of the evils produced by this unwarrantable conduct of parents in preferring one child to all the rest. The old fable of *the ape and her favourite cub*, which she *hugged to death through kindness*, was directed against such foolish parental fondnesses as these.

Verse 4. *And could not speak peaceably unto him.*] Does not this imply, in our use of the term, that they were continually *quarrelling* with him? but this is no meaning of the original: ולא יכלו דברו לשלם *ve.o yachelu dabbero leshalom*, *they could not speak peace to him*, i. e., they would not accost him in a *friendly* manner. They would not even *wish him well*. The eastern method of salutation is, *Peace be to thee!* שלום לך *shalom lecha*, among the Hebrews, and سلام *salam*, *peace*, or سلام حبيبي *salam hebibi*, *peace to thee my friend*, among the Arabs. Now as *peace* among those nations comprehends all kinds of blessings spiritual and temporal, so they are careful not to say it to those whom they do not cordially wish well. It is not an unusual thing for an Arab or a Turk to hesitate to return the *salam*, if given by a Christian, or by one of whom he has not a favourable opinion: and this, in their own country, may be ever considered as a mark of *hostility;* not only as a proof that they do not wish you well, but that if they have an opportunity they will do you an injury. This was precisely the case with respect to Joseph's brethren: they would not give him the *salam*, and therefore felt themselves at liberty to take the first opportunity to injure him.

Verse 7. *We* were *binding sheaves in the field*] Though in these early times we read little of *tillage*, yet it is evident from this circumstance that it was practised by Jacob and his sons. The whole of this dream is so very plain as to require no comment, unless we could suppose that the *sheaves of grain* might have some reference to the *plenty* in Egypt under Joseph's superintendence, and the scarcity in Canaan, which obliged the brethren to go down to Egypt for corn, where the dream was most literally fulfilled

A. M. 2276.
B. C. 1728.
yet the more for his dreams, and for
his words.
9 And he dreamed yet another dream, and
told it his brethren, and said, Behold, I have
dreamed a dream more; and, behold, [h] the
sun and the moon and the eleven stars made
obeisance to me.
10 And he told *it* to his father, and to his
brethren: and his father rebuked him, and
said unto him, What *is* this dream that thou
hast dreamed? Shall I and thy mother and
[i] thy brethren indeed come to bow down ourselves to thee to the earth?
11 And [k] his brethren envied him; but his
father [l] observed the saying.
12 And his brethren went to feed their
father's flock in Shechem.
13 And Israel said unto Joseph, Do not thy
brethren feed *the flock* in Shechem? come,
and I will send thee unto them. And he said
to him, Here *am* I.
14 And he said to him, Go, I pray thee,
[m] see whether it be well with thy brethren,
and well with the flocks; and bring me word
again. So he sent him out of the
vale of [n] Hebron, and he came to
Schehem.
15 And a certain man found him, and, behold, *he was* wandering in the field: and the
man asked him, saying, What seekest thou?
16 And he said, I seek my brethren: [o] tell
me, I pray thee, where they feed *their
flocks*.
17 And the man said, They are departed
hence; for I heard them say, Let us go to
Dothan. And Joseph went after his brethren,
and found them in [p] Dothan.
18 And when they saw him afar off, even
before he came near unto them, [q] they con
spired against him to slay him.
19 And they said one to another, Behold,
this [r] dreamer cometh.
20 [s] Come now therefore, and let us slay
him, and cast him into some pit, and we will
say, Some evil beast hath devoured him:
and we shall see what will become of his
dreams.
21 And [t] Reuben heard *it*, and he delivered

[h] Ch. xlvi. 29.——[i] Ch. xxvii. 29.——[k] Acts vii. 9.——[l] Dan. vii. 28; Luke ii. 19, 51.——[m] Heb. *see the peace of thy brethren,* &c.; chapter xxix. 6.——[n] Chapter xxxv. 27.——[o] Cant. i. 7. [p] 2 Kings vi. 13.

[q] 1 Sam. xix. 1; Psa. xxxi. 13; xxxvii. 12, 32; xciv. 21; Matt. xxvii. 1; Mark xiv. 1; John xi. 53; Acts xxiii. 12. [r] Heb. *master of dreams.*——[s] Proverbs i. 11, 16; vi. 17; xxvii. 4. [t] Chap. xlii. 22.

his brethren there *bowing* in the most abject manner before him.

Verse 9. *He dreamed yet another dream*] This is as clear as the preceding. But how could Jacob say, *Shall I and thy mother, &c.*, when Rachel his mother was *dead* some time before this? Perhaps Jacob might hint, by this explanation, the *impossibility* of such a dream being fulfilled, because one of the persons who should be a *chief actor in it* was already dead. But any one wife or concubine of Jacob was quite sufficient to fulfil this part of the dream. It is possible, some think, that Joseph may have had these dreams before his mother Rachel died; but were even this the case, she certainly did not live to fulfil the part which appears to refer to herself.

The sun and the moon and the eleven stars] Why *eleven* stars? Was it merely to signify that his brothers might be represented by stars? Or does he not rather there allude to the *Zodiac*, his eleven brethren answering to *eleven* of the celestial signs, and himself to the *twelfth?* This is certainly not an unnatural thought, as it is very likely that the heavens were thus measured in the days of Joseph; for the zodiacal constellations have been distinguished among the eastern nations from time immemorial. See the notes at the end of chap. xlix.

Verse 14. *Go—see whether it be well with thy brethren*] Literally, Go, I beseech thee, and see the peace of thy brethren, and the peace of the flock. Go and see whether they are all in *prosperity*. See on ver. 4. As Jacob's sons were now gone to feed the flock on the parcel of ground they had bought from the Shechemites, (see chap. xxxiii. 19,) and where they had committed such a horrible slaughter, their father might feel more solicitous about their welfare, lest the neighbouring tribes should rise against them, and revenge the murder of the Shechemites.

As Jacob appears to have been at this time in the *vale of Hebron*, it is supposed that Shechem was about *sixty* English miles distant from it, and that *Dothan* was about *eight* miles farther. But I must again advertise my readers that all these calculations are very dubious; for we do not even know that the *same place* is intended, as there are many proofs that different places went by the same names.

Verse 19. *Behold, this dreamer cometh.*] בעל החלמות *baal hachalomoth*, this *master of dreams*, this *master dreamer*. A form of speech which conveys great contempt.

Verse 20. *Come now—and let us slay him*] What unprincipled savages these must have been to talk thus coolly about imbruing their hands in an innocent brother's blood! How necessary is a Divine revelation, to show man what God *hates* and what he *loves!* Ferocious cruelty is the principal characteristic of the nations and tribes who receive not the law at his mouth.

Verse 21. *Reuben heard* it] Though Reuben appears to have been a transgressor of no ordinary magnitude, if we take chap. xxxv. 22 according to the letter, yet his bosom was not the habitation of *cruelty*

A. M. 2276. B. C. 1728.

him out of their hands; and said, Let us not kill him.

22 And Reuben said unto them, Shed no
blood, *but* cast him into this pit that *is* in the
wilderness, and lay no hand upon him; that
he might rid him out of their hands, to deliver him to his father again.

23 And it came to pass, when Joseph was
come unto his brethren, that they stripped Joseph
out of his coat, *his* coat of *many* [u] colours that
was on him;

24 And they took him, and cast him into a
pit: and the pit *was* empty, *there was* no
water in it.

25 [v] And they sat down to eat bread: and
they lifted up their eyes and looked, and, behold, a company of [w] Ishmaelites came from
Gilead, with their camels bearing spicery, and
[x] balm and myrrh, going to carry *it* down to
Egypt.

26 And Judah said unto his brethren, What
profit *is it* if we slay our brother, and [y] conceal his blood?

27 Come, and let us sell him to the Ishmaelites, and [z] let not our
hand be upon him; for he *is* [a] our brother *and*
[b] our flesh. And his brethren [c] were content.

28 Then there passed by [d] Midianites, mer
chantmen; and they drew and lifted up Joseph
out of the pit, [e] and sold Joseph to the Ishmaelites for [f] twenty *pieces* of silver; and they
brought Joseph into Egypt.

29 And Reuben returned unto the pit: and
behold, Joseph *was* not in the pit; and he
[g] rent his clothes.

30 And he returned unto his brethren, and
said, The child [h] *is* not; and I, whither shall
I go?

31 And they took [i] Joseph's coat, and killed
a kid of the goats, and dipped the coat in the
blood;

32 And they sent the coat of *many* colours,
and they brought *it* to their father; and said,
This have we found: know now whether it
be thy son's coat or no.

33 And he knew it, and said, *It is* my son's

A. M. 2276. B. C. 1728.

[u] Or, *pieces.*—[v] Prov. xxx. 20; Amos vi. 6.—[w] See verse 28, 36.—[x] Jer. viii. 22.—[y] Chap. iv. 10; ver. 20; Job xvi. 18.—[z] 1 Sam. xviii. 17.—[a] Chap. xlii. 21.—[b] Chap. xxix. 14.

[c] Heb. *hearkened.*—[d] Judg. vi. 3; ch. xlv. 4, 5.—[e] Psa. cv. 17; Wisd. x. 13; Acts vii. 9.—[f] See Matt. xxvii. 9.—[g] Job i. 20.—[h] Chap. xlii. 13, 36; Jer. xxxi. 15.—[i] Ver. 23.

He determined, if possible, to save his brother from death, and deliver him safely to his father, with whose fondness for him he was sufficiently acquainted. *Josephus*, in his usual way, puts a long flourishing speech in the mouth of Reuben on the occasion, spoken in order to dissuade his brethren from their barbarous purpose; but as it is *totally unfounded*, it is worthy of no regard.

Verse 23. *They stripped Joseph out of his coat*] This probably was done that, if ever found, he might not be discerned to be a *person of distinction*, and consequently, no inquiry made concerning him.

Verse 25. *They sat down to eat bread*] Every act is perfectly in character, and describes forcibly the *brutish* and *diabolic* nature of their ruthless souls.

A company of Ishmaelites] We may naturally suppose that this was a *caravan*, composed of different tribes that, for their greater safety, were travelling *together*, and of which *Ishmaelites* and *Midianites* made the chief. In the Chaldee they are called *Arabians*, which, from ערב *arab*, to *mingle*, was in all probability used by the *Targumist* as the word *Arabians* is used among us, which comprehends a vast number of *clans*, or *tribes* of people. The *Jerusalem* Targum calls them כרקין *Sarkin*, what we term *Saracens*. In the *Persian*, the clause stands thus: كاروانى اشمعاليم عربان ايا *karavanee ishmaaleem araban aya.* "A caravan of Ishmaelite Arabs came." This seems to give the true sense.

Verse 28. *For twenty* pieces *of silver*] In the *Anglo-Saxon* it is ꝥpıtıgum penegum, *thirty pence.* This, I .nink, is the first instance on record of selling a man for a slave; but the practice certainly did not commence now, it had doubtless been in use long before. Instead of *pieces*, which our translators supply, the Persian has مثقال *miskal*, which was probably intended to signify a *shekel*; and if *shekels* be intended, taking them at *three shillings* each, Joseph was sold for about *three pounds* sterling. I have known a whole cargo of slaves, amounting to *eight hundred and thirteen*, bought by a slave captain in Bonny river, in Africa, on an average, for *six pounds* each; and this payment was made in *guns*, *gunpowder*, and *trinkets!* As there were only *nine* of the brethren present, and they sold Joseph for *twenty* shekels, each had more than *two* shekels as *his* share in this most infamous transaction.

Verse 29. *Reuben returned unto the pit*] It appears he was absent when the caravan passed by, to whom the other brethren had sold Joseph.

Verse 30. *The child* is *not; and I, whither shall I go?*] The words in the original are very plaintive, הילד איננו ואני אנה אני בא *haiyeled einennu, vaani anah, ani ba!*

Verse 32. *Sent the coat of* many *colours—to their father*] What *deliberate cruelty* to torture the feelings of their aged father, and thus harrow up his soul!

Verse 33. *Joseph is without doubt rent in pieces!*] It is likely he inferred this from the *lacerated* state of the coat, which, in order the better to cover their wickedness, they had not only besmeared with the blood of the goat, but it is probable reduced to *tatters*. And what must a father's heart have felt in such a case! As this coat is rent, so is the body of my beloved son rent in pieces! and *Jacob rent his clothes.*

a

A. M. 2276. B. C. 1728.

coat; [k] an evil beast hath devoured
him; Joseph is without doubt rent
in pieces [l]
34 And Jacob rent his clothes, and put
sackcloth upon his loins, and mourned for his
son many days.
35 And all his sons and all his daughters
[m] rose up to comfort him; but he
refused to be comforted: and he
said, For [n] I will go down into the grave unto my
son mourning. Thus his father wept for him.
36 And [o] the Midianites sold him into Egypt,
unto Potiphar, an [p] officer of Pharoah's, *and*
[q] captain of the guard.[r]

[k] Ver. 20; chap. xliv. 28.——[l] Ver. 29; 2 Sam. iii. 31.——[m] 2 Sam. xii. 17.——[n] Chap. xlii. 38; xliv. 29, 31.——[o] Chapter xxxix. 1.——[p] Heb. *eunuch.* But the word doth signify not only *eunuchs,* but also *chamberlains, courtiers,* and *officers;* Esth. i. 10.——[q] Heb. *chief of the slaughtermen* or *executioners.*——[r] Or, *chief marshal.*

Verse 35. *All his sons and all his daughters*] He had only one daughter, *Dinah;* but his *sons' wives* may be here included. But what hypocrisy in his sons to attempt to comfort him concerning the death of a son who they knew was alive; and what cruelty to put their aged father to such torture, when, properly speaking, there was no ground for it!

Verse 36. *Potiphar, an officer of Pharaoh's*] The word סריס *saris,* translated *officer,* signifies a *eunuch;* and lest any person should imagine that because this Potiphar *had a wife,* therefore it is absurd to suppose him to have been a *eunuch,* let such persons know that it is not uncommon in the east for eunuchs to have *wives,* nay, some of them have even a *harem* or *seraglio,* where they keep many women, though it does not appear that they have any *progeny;* and probably discontent on *this ground* might have contributed as much to the unfaithfulness of Potiphar's wife, as that less principled motive through which it is commonly believed she acted.

Captain of the guard.] שר הטבחים *sar hattabbachim, chief of the butchers;* a most appropriate name for the guards of an eastern despot. If a person offend one of the despotic eastern princes, the order to one of the life-guards is, *Go and bring me his head;* and this command is instantly obeyed, without judge, jury, or any form of law. Potiphar, we may therefore suppose, was captain of those *guards* whose business it was to take care of the royal person, and execute his sovereign will on all the objects of his displeasure. Reader, if thou hast the happiness to live under the British constitution, be thankful to God. *Here,* the will, the power, and utmost influence of the king, were he even so disposed, cannot deprive the meanest subject of his property, his liberty, or his life. All the solemn legal forms of justice must be consulted; the culprit, however accused, be heard by himself and his *counsel;* and in the end twelve honest, impartial men, chosen from among his fellows, shall decide on the validity of the evidence produced by the accuser. For the *trial by jury,* as well as for innumerable political blessings, may God make the inhabitants of Great Britain thankful!

1. With this chapter the history of Joseph commences, and sets before our eyes such a scene of wonders wrought by Divine Providence in such a variety of surprising instances, as cannot fail to confirm our faith in God, show the propriety of resignation to his will, and confidence in his dispensations, and prove that all things work together for good to them that love him. Joseph has often been considered as a type of Christ, and this subject in the hands of different persons has assumed a great variety of colouring. The following parallels appear the most probable; but I shall not pledge myself for the propriety of any of them: "Jesus Christ, prefigured by Joseph, the beloved of his father, and by him sent to visit his brethren, is the innocent person whom his brethren sold for a few pieces of silver, the bargain proposed by his brother *Judah,* (Greek *Judas,*) the very namesake of that disciple and *brother* (for so Christ vouchsafes to call him) who sold his Lord and Master; and who by this means became their Lord and Saviour; nay, the Saviour of *strangers,* and of the whole world; which had not happened but for this plot of destroying him, the act of rejecting, and exposing him to sale. In both examples we find the same fortune and the same innocence: Joseph in the prison between two criminals; Jesus on the cross between two thieves. Joseph foretells deliverance to one of his companions and death to the other, from the same omens: of the two thieves, one reviles Christ, and perishes in his crimes; the other believes, and is assured of a speedy entrance into paradise. Joseph requests the person that should be delivered to be mindful of him in his glory; the person saved by Jesus Christ entreats his deliverer to remember him when he came into his kingdom."—See *Pascal's Thoughts.* Parallels and coincidences of this kind should always be received cautiously, for where the Spirit of God has not marked a direct resemblance, and obviously referred to it as such in some other part of his word, it is bold, if not dangerous, to say "such and such *things* and *persons* are types of Christ." We have instances sufficiently numerous, legitimately attested, without having recourse to those which are of dubious import and precarious application. See the observation on chap. xl.

2. Envy has been defined, "pain felt, and malignity conceived, at the sight of excellence or happiness in another." Under this detestable passion did the brethren of Joseph labour; and had not God particularly interposed, it would have destroyed both its subjects and its object. Perhaps there is no vice which so directly filiates itself on Satan, as this does. In opposition to the assertion that *we cannot envy that by which we profit,* it may be safely replied that we may envy our neighbour's *wisdom,* though he gives us good counsel: his *riches,* though he supplies our wants; and his *greatness,* though he employs it for our protection.

3. How ruinous are family distractions! A house

divided against itself cannot stand. Parents should take good heed that their own conduct be not the first and most powerful cause of such dissensions, by exciting *envy* in some of their children through undue *partiality* to others; but it is in vain to speak to most parents on the subject; they will give way to foolish predilections, till, in the prevailing distractions of their families, they meet with the punishment of their imprudence, when regrets are vain, and the evil past remedy.

CHAPTER XXXVIII.

Judah *marries the daughter of a Canaanite*, 1, 2; *and begets of her* Er, 3, Onan, 4, *and* Shelah, 5. *Er marries* Tamar, 6; *is slain for his wickedness*, 7. *Onan, required to raise up seed to his brother, refuses*, 8, 9. *He also is slain*, 10. *Judah promises his son* Shelah *to Tamar, when he should be of age; but performs not his promise*, 11. *Judah's wife dies*, 12. *Tamar in disguise receives her father-in-law, he leaves his signet, bracelets, and staff in her hand, and she conceives by him*, 13–23. *Judah is informed that his daughter in-law is with child; and, not knowing that himself was the father, condemns her to be burnt*, 24. *She produces the signet, bracelets, and staff, and convicts Judah*, 25, 26. *She is delivered of twins, who are called* Pharez *and* Zarah, 27–30.

A. M. cir. 2251. B. C. cir. 1753.

AND it came to pass at that
time, that Judah went down
from his brethren, and [a] turned in to a certain
[b] Adullamite, whose name *was* Hirah.
2 And Judah [c] saw there a daughter of a
certain Canaanite, whose name *was* [d] Shuah;
and he took her, and went in unto her.

A. M. cir. 2252. B. C. cir. 1752.

3 And she conceived, and
bare a son; and he called his
name [e] Er.

A. M. cir. 2253. B. C. cir. 1751.

4 And she conceived again,
and bare a son; and she called
his name [f] Onan.

A. M. cir. 2256. B. C. cir. 1748.

5 And she yet again con-
ceived, and bare a son; and
called his name [g] Shelah: and he was at
Chezib, when she bare him.

A. M. cir. 2273. B. C. cir. 1731.

6 And Judah [h] took a wife for
Er, his first-born, whose name
was Tamar.

[a] Chap. xix. 2, 3; Judg. iv. 18; 2 Kings iv. 8; Prov. xiii. 20. [b] Josh. xv. 35; 1 Sam. xxii. 1; 2 Sam. xxiii. 13; Mic. i. 15. [c] Chap. xxxiv. 2.

[d] 1 Chron. ii. 3.——[e] Chap. xlvi. 12; Num. xxvi. 19.——[f] Ch. xlvi. 12; Num. xxvi. 19.——[g] Chapter xlvi. 12; Num. xxvi. 20. [h] Chap. xxi. 21.

NOTES ON CHAP. XXXVIII.

Verse 1. *And it came to pass at that time*] The facts mentioned here could not have happened at the times mentioned in the preceding chapter, as those times are all unquestionably too recent, for the very earliest of the transactions here recorded must have occurred long before the selling of Joseph. Mr. Ainsworth remarks "that Judah and his sons must have married when very young, else the chronology will not agree. For Joseph was born *six* years before Jacob left Laban and came into Canaan; chap. xxx. 25, and xxxi. 41. Joseph was *seventeen* years old when he was sold into Egypt, chap. xxxvii. 2, 25; he was *thirty* years old when he interpreted Pharaoh's dream, chap. xli. 46. And *nine* years after, when there had been *seven* years of plenty and *two* years of famine, did Jacob with his family go down into Egypt, chap. xli. 53, 54, and xlv. 6, 11. And at their going down thither, Pharez, the son of Judah, whose birth is set down at the end of this chapter, had two sons, Hezron and Hamul, chap. xlvi. 8, 12. Seeing then from the selling of Joseph unto Israel's going down into Egypt there cannot be above *twenty-three* years, how is it possible that Judah should take a wife, and have by her three sons successively, and Shelah the youngest of the three be marriageable when Judah begat Pharez of Tamar, chap. xxxviii. 14, 24, and Pharez be grown up, married, and have *two* sons, all within so short a space? The *time* therefore here spoken of seems to have been soon after Jacob's coming to Shechem, chap. xxxiii. 18, before the history of Dinah, chap. xxxiv., though Moses for special cause relates it in this place." I should rather suppose that this chapter originally stood after chap. xxxiii., and that it got by accident into this place. Dr. Hales, observing that some of Jacob's sons must have married remarkably young, says that "Judah was about *forty-seven* years old when Jacob's family settled in Egypt. He could not therefore have been above *fifteen* at the birth of his eldest son *Er*; nor *Er* more than *fifteen* at his marriage with Tamar; nor could it have been more than *two* years after *Er's* death till the birth of Judah's twin sons by his daughter-in-law Tamar; nor could *Pharez*, one of them, be more than *fifteen* at the birth of his twin sons *Hezron* and *Hamul*, supposing they were twins, just born before the departure from Canaan. For the aggregate of these numbers, 15, 15, 2, 15, or 47 years, gives the age of Judah; compare chap. xxxviii. with chap. xlvi. 12." See the remarks of Dr. Kennicott, at the end of chap. xxxi.

Adullamite] An inhabitant of Adullam, a city of Canaan, afterwards given for a possession to the sons of Judah, Josh. xv. 1, 35. It appears as if this Adullamite had kept a kind of *lodging house*, for *Shuah* the Canaanite and his family lodged with him; and *there* Judah lodged also. As the woman was a Canaanitess, Judah had the example of his fathers to prove at least the impropriety of such a connection.

Verse 5. *And he was at Chezib when she bare him.*] This town is supposed to be the same with *Achzib*,

A. M. cir. 2273.
B. C. cir. 1731.

7 And [i] Er, Judah's first-born, was wicked in the sight of the LORD; [k] and the LORD slew him.

A. M. cir. 2274.
B. C. cir. 1730.

8 And Judah said unto Onan, Go in unto [l] thy brother's wife, and marry her, and raise up seed to thy brother.

9 And Onan knew that the seed should not be [m] his; and it came to pass, when he went in unto his brother's wife, that he spilled *it* on the ground, lest that he should give seed to his brother.

10 And the thing which he did [n] displeased the LORD: wherefore he slew [o] him also.

11 Then said Judah to Tamar his daughter-in-law, [p] Remain a widow at thy father's house, till Shelah my son be grown: (for he said, Lest peradventure he die also, as his brethren *did.*) And Tamar went and dwelt [q] in her father's house.

A. M. cir. 2277.
B. C. cir. 1727.

12 And [r] in process of time the daughter of Shuah Judah's wife died, and Judah [s] was comforted, and went up unto his sheep-shearers to Timnath, he and his friend Hirah the Adullamite.

A. M. cir. 2277.
B. C. cir. 1727.

13 And it was told Tamar, saying, Behold, thy father-in-law goeth up [t] to Timnath to shear his sheep.

14 And she [u] put her widow's garments off from her, and covered her with a veil, and wrapped herself, and [v] sat in [w] an open place, which *is* by the way to Timnath; for she saw [x] that Shelah was grown, and she was not given unto him to wife.

15 When Judah saw her, he thought her *to be* a harlot: because she had covered her face.

16 And he turned unto her by the way, and said, Go to, I pray thee, let me come in unto thee; (for he knew not that she *was* his daughter-in-law.) And she said, What wilt thou give me, that thou mayest come in unto me?

17 And he said, [y] I will send *thee* [z] a kid from the flock. And she said, [a] Wilt thou give *me* a pledge till thou send *it?*

[i] Chap. xlv. 12; Num. xxvi. 19.——[k] 1 Chron. ii. 3.——[l] Deut. xxv. 5; Matt. xxii. 24.——[m] Deut. xxv. 6.——[n] Heb. *was evil in the eyes of the LORD.*——[o] Chap. xlvi. 12; Num. xxvi. 19.——[p] Ruth i. 13.——[q] Lev. xxii. 13.——[r] Heb. *the days were multiplied.*

[s] 2 Samuel xiii. 39.——[t] Joshua xv. 10, 57; Judges xiv. 1.——[u] Judith x. 3.——[v] Prov. vii. 12.——[w] Heb. *the door of eyes* or *of Enajim.*——[x] Verse 11, 26.——[y] Ezek. xvi. 33.——[z] Heb. *a kid of the goats.*——[a] Ver. 20.

which fell to the tribe of Judah, Josh. xv. 44. "The name," says Ainsworth, "has in Hebrew the signification of *lying;* and to it the prophet alludes, saying *the houses of Achzib shall be* (*Achzab*) *a lie to the kings of Israel,* Mic. i. 14."

Verse 7. *Er—was wicked in the sight of the Lord*] What this wickedness consisted in we are not told; but the phrase *sight of the Lord* being added, proves that it was some very great evil. It is worthy of remark that the Hebrew word used to express *Er's* wickedness is *his own name,* the letters *reversed. Er* ער; wicked, רע *ra.* As if the inspired writer had said, "Er was altogether wicked, a completely abandoned character."

Verse 9. *Onan knew that the seed should not be his*] That is, that the child begotten of his brother's widow should be reckoned as the child of his deceased brother, and *his* name, though the real father of it, should not appear in the genealogical tables.

Verse 10. *Wherefore he slew him also.*] The sin of Onan has generally been supposed to be *self-pollution;* but this is certainly a mistake; his crime was *his refusal to raise up seed to his brother,* and rather than do it, by the act mentioned above, he rendered himself incapable of it. We find from this history that long before the Mosaic law it was an established custom, probably founded on a Divine precept, that if a man died childless his brother was to take his wife, and the children produced by this second marriage were considered as the children of the first husband, and in consequence inherited his possessions.

Verse 12. *In process of time*] This phrase, which is in general use in the Bible, needs explanation; the original is וירבו הימים *vaiyirbu haiyamim, and the days were multiplied.* Though it implies an indefinite time, yet it generally embraces a pretty long period, and in this place may mean *several years.*

Verse 15. *Thought her to be a harlot*] See the original of this term, chap. xxxiv. 31. The Hebrew is זונה *zonah,* and signifies generally a person who prostitutes herself to the public for hire, or one who lives by the public; and hence very likely applied to a *publican,* a *tavern-keeper,* or *hostess,* Josh. ii. 1; translated by the Septuagint, and in the New Testament, πορνη, from περναω, *to sell,* which certainly may as well apply to her *goods* as to her *person.*

It appears that in very ancient times there were public persons of this description; and they generally veiled themselves, sat in public places by the highway side, and received certain *hire.* Though *adultery* was reputed a very flagrant crime, yet this public prostitution was not; for persons whose characters were on the whole morally good had connections with them But what could be expected from an age in which there was no *written* Divine revelation, and consequently the bounds of right and wrong were not sufficiently ascertained? This defect was supplied in a considerable measure by the *law* and the *prophets,* and now completely by the *Gospel of Christ.*

Verse 17. Will *thou give* me *a pledge till thou send it?*] The word ערבון *erabon* signifies an *earnest* of something promised, a *part of the price* agreed for

A. M. cir. 2277.
B. C. cir. 1727.

18 And he said, What pledge shall I give thee? And she said, [b] Thy signet, and thy bracelets, and thy staff that *is* in thine hand. And he gave *it* her, and came in unto her, and she conceived by him.

19 And she arose, and went away, and [c] laid by her veil from her, and put on the garments of her widowhood.

20 And Judah sent the kid by the hand of his friend the Adullamite, to receive *his* pledge from the woman's hand: but he found her not.

21 Then he asked the men of that place, saying, Where *is* the harlot that *was* [d] openly by the wayside? And they said, There was no harlot in this *place*.

22 And he returned to Judah, and said, I cannot find her; and also the men of the place said, *that* there was no harlot in this *place*.

A. M. cir. 2277.
B. C. cir. 1727.

23 And Judah said, Let her take *it* to her, lest we [e] be shamed: behold, I sent this kid, and thou hast not found her.

24 And it came to pass about three months after, that it was told Judah, saying, Tamar thy daughter-in-law hath [f] played the harlot and also, behold, she *is* with child by whoredom. And Judah said, Bring her forth, [g] and let her be burnt.

25 When she *was* brought forth, she sent to her father-in-law, saying, By the man, whose these *are*, *am* I with child: and she said, [h] Discern, I pray thee, whose *are* these, [i] the signet, and bracelets, and staff.

26 And Judah [k] acknowledged *them*, and said, [l] She hath been more righteous than I;

[b] Ver. 25.——[c] Ver. 14.——[d] Or, *in Enajim*.——[e] Heb. *become a contempt*.——[f] Judg. xix. 2.——[g] Lev. xxi. 9; Deut. xxii. 21.

[h] Chapter xxxvii. 32.——[i] Verse 18.——[k] Chapter xxxvii. 33. [l] 1 Sam. xxiv. 17.

between a buyer and seller, by *giving* and *receiving* of which the bargain was ratified; or a *deposit*, which was to be restored when the thing promised should be given. St. Paul uses the same word in Greek letters, αρραβων, 2 Cor. i. 22; Eph. i. 14. From the use of the term in this history we may at once see what the apostle means by the *Holy Spirit being the* EARNEST, *αρραβων, of the promised inheritance;* viz., *a security given in hand* for the fulfilment of all God's *promises* relative to grace and eternal life. We may learn from this that eternal life will be given in the great day to all who can produce this *erabon* or *pledge*. He who has the *earnest of the Spirit* then in his heart shall not only be saved from *death*, but have that *eternal life* of which it is the *pledge* and the evidence. What the pledge given by Judah was, see on ver. 25.

Verse 21. *Where is the harlot that was openly by the wayside?*] Our translators often render different *Hebrew* words by the same term in *English*, and thus many important shades of meaning, which involve *traits* of character, are lost. In ver. 15, Tamar is called a *harlot*, זונה *zonah*, which, as we have already seen, signifies a person who prostitutes herself for *money*. In this verse she is called a *harlot* in our version; but the original is not זונה but קדשה *kedeshah*, a holy or *consecrated person*, from קדש *kadash*, to *make holy*, or to *consecrate to religious purposes*. And the word here must necessarily signify a person consecrated by prostitution to the worship of some impure goddess.

The public prostitutes in the temple of Venus are called *ιεροδουλοι γυναικες*, *holy* or *consecrated female servants*, by *Strabo;* and it appears from the words *zonah* and *kedeshah* above, that impure rites and public prostitution prevailed in the worship of the Canaanites in the time of Judah. And among these people we have much reason to believe that *Astarte* and *Asteroth* occupied the same place in their theology as *Venus* did among the Greeks and Romans, and were worshipped with the same impure rites.

Verse 23. *Lest we be ashamed*] Not of the *act*, for this he does not appear to have thought criminal; but lest he should fall under the raillery of his companions and neighbours, for having been tricked out of his signet, bracelets, and staff, by a prostitute.

Verse 24. *Bring her forth, and let her be burnt.*] As he had ordered Tamar to live as a widow in her own father's house till his son Shelah should be marriageable, he considers her therefore as the wife of his son; and as Shelah was not yet given to her, and she is found with child, she is reputed by him as an *adulteress*, and *burning*, it seems, was anciently the punishment of this crime. *Judah*, being a patriarch or head of a family, had, according to the custom of those times, the supreme magisterial authority over all the branches of his own family; therefore he only acts here in his juridical capacity. How strange that in the very place where *adultery* was punished by the most violent death, *prostitution* for *money* and for religious purposes should be considered as no crime!

Verse 25. *The signet*] חתמת *chothemeth*, properly a *seal*, or instrument with which *impressions* were made to ascertain property, &c. These exist in all countries.

Bracelets] פתילים *pethilim*, from פתל *pathal*, to twist, wreathe, twine, may signify a girdle or a collar by which precedency, &c., might be indicated; not the muslin, silk, or linen wreath of his turban, as Mr. Harmer has conjectured.

Staff.] מטה *matteh*, either what we would call a common walking stick, or the staff which was the ensign of his tribe.

Verse 26. *She hath been more righteous than I*] It is probable that Tamar was influenced by no other motive than that which was common to all the Israelitish women, *the desire to have children who might be heirs of the promise made to Abraham, &c.* And as Judah had obliged her to continue in her widowhood under the promise of giving her his son Shelah when he should be of age, consequently his refusing or delaying

A. M. cir. 2277.
B. C. cir. 1727.

because that [m] I gave her not to Shelah my son. And he knew her again [n] no more.

27 And it came to pass in the time of her travail, that, behold, twins *were* in her womb.

28 And it came to pass, when she travailed, that *the one* put out *his* hand: and the midwife took and bound upon his hand a scarlet thread, saying, This came out first.

29 And it came to pass, as he drew back his hand, that, behold, his brother came out: and she said, [o] How hast thou broken forth? *this* breach *be* upon thee: therefore his name was called [p] Pharez.[q]

A. M. cir. 2277
B. C. cir. 1727

30 And afterward came out his brother, that had the scarlet thread upon his hand: and his name was called Zarah.

[m] Ver. 14.——[n] Job xxxiv. 31, 32.——[o] Or, *Wherefore hast thou made this breach against thee?*

[p] That is, *a breach.*——[q] Chap. xlvi. 12; Num. xxvi. 20; 1 Chron. ii. 4; Matt. i. 3.

to accomplish this promise was a breach of truth, and an injury done to Tamar.

Verse 28. *The midwife—bound upon his hand a scarlet thread*] The binding of the scarlet thread about the wrist of the child whose arm appeared first in the birth, serves to show us how *solicitously* the privileges of the *birthright* were preserved. Had not this caution been taken by the midwife, *Pharez* would have had the right of *primogeniture* to the prejudice of his elder brother *Zarah*. And yet Pharez is usually reckoned in the genealogical tables before Zarah; and from him, not Zarah, does the line of our Lord proceed. See Matt. i. 3. Probably the two brothers, as being twins, were conjoined in the privileges belonging to the *birthright*.

Verse 29. *How hast thou broken forth?*] מה פרצת *mah paratsta*, this *breach* be *upon thee*, עליך פרץ *aleycha parets*; thou shalt bear the name of the *breach* thou hast made, *i. e.*, in coming first into the world. Therefore his name was called פרץ *Parets*, i. e., the person who made the *breach*. The *breach* here mentioned refers to a certain circumstance in parturition which it is unnecessary to explain.

Verse 30. *His name was called Zarah.*] זרח *Zarach*, risen or sprung up, applied to the sun, rising and diffusing his light. "He had this name," says Ainsworth, "because he should have risen, *i. e.*, have been born first, but for the breach which his brother made."

There are several subjects in this chapter on which it may not be unprofitable to spend a few additional moments.

1. The insertion of this chapter is a farther proof of the *impartiality* of the sacred writer. The facts detailed, considered in *themselves*, can reflect no credit on the patriarchal history; but *Judah, Tamar, Zarah,* and *Pharez*, were progenitors of the Messiah, and therefore their birth must be recorded; and as the *birth*, so also the *circumstances* of that birth, which, even had they not a higher end in view, would be valuable as casting light upon some very ancient *customs*, which it is interesting to understand. These are not forgotten in the preceding notes.

2. On what is generally reputed to be the *sin of Onan*, something very pointed should be spoken. But *who* dares and will do it, and in *such language* that it may neither pollute the ear by describing the evil *as it is*, nor fail of its effect by a language so refined and so laboriously delicate as to *cover the sin* which it professes to disclose? *Elaborate treatises* on the subject will never be read by those who need them most, and *anonymous pamphlets* are not likely to be regarded.

The sin of *self-pollution*, which is generally considered to be that of Onan, is one of the most destructive evils ever practised by fallen man. In many respects it is several degrees worse than common whoredom, and has in its train more awful consequences, though practised by numbers who would shudder at the thought of criminal connections with a prostitute. It excites the powers of nature to *undue action*, and produces *violent secretions*, which necessarily and speedily *exhaust the vital principle* and *energy*; hence the muscles become flaccid and feeble, the tone and natural action of the nerves relaxed and impeded, the understanding confused, the memory oblivious, the judgment perverted, the will indeterminate and wholly without energy to resist; the eyes appear languishing and without expression, and the countenance vacant; the *appetite ceases*, for the stomach is incapable of performing its proper office; *nutrition fails*, tremors, fears, and terrors are generated; and thus the wretched victim drags out a most miserable existence, till, *superannuated* even before he had time to arrive at *man's estate*, with a mind often debilitated even to a state of idiotism, his worthless body tumbles into the grave, and his guilty soul (guilty of self-murder) is hurried into the awful presence of its Judge! Reader, this is no caricature, nor are the colourings overcharged in this shocking picture. Worse woes than my pen can relate I have witnessed in those addicted to this fascinating, unnatural, and most destructive of crimes. If *thou* hast entered into this snare, flee from the destruction both of body and soul that awaits thee! God alone can save thee. Advice, warnings, threatenings, increasing debility of body, mental decay, checks of conscience, expostulations of judgment and medical assistance, will all be lost on thee: God, and God *alone*, can save thee from an evil which has in its issue the destruction of thy body, and the final perdition of thy soul! Whether this may have been the sin of *Onan* or not, is a matter at present of small moment; it may be *thy sin*; therefore take heed lest *God slay thee for it*. The intelligent reader will see that prudence forbids me to enter any farther into this business. See the remarks at the end of chap. xxxix.

CHAPTER XXXIX.

Joseph, being brought to Potiphar's house, prospers in all his undertakings, **1–3.** *Potiphar makes him his overseer,* **4.** *Is prospered in all his concerns for Joseph's sake, in whom he puts unlimited confidence,* **5, 6.** *The wife of Potiphar solicits him to criminal correspondence,* **7.** *He refuses, and makes a fine apology for his conduct,* **8, 9.** *She continues her solicitations, and he his refusals,* **10.** *She uses violence, and he escapes from her hand,* **11–13.** *She accuses him to the domestics,* **14, 15,** *and afterward to Potiphar,* **16–18.** *Potiphar is enraged, and Joseph is cast into prison,* **19, 20.** *The Lord prospers him, and gives him great favour in the sight of the keeper of the prison,* **21,** *who intrusts him with the care of the house and all the prisoners,* **22, 23.**

A. M. 2276.
B. C. 1728.

AND Joseph was brought down to Egypt; and [a] Potiphar, an officer of Pharaoh, captain of the guard, an Egyptian, [b] bought him of the hands of the Ishmaelites, which had brought him down thither.

2 And [c] the LORD was with Joseph, and he was a prosperous man; and he was in the house of his master the Egyptian.

3 And his master saw that the LORD *was* with him, and that the LORD [d] made all that he did to prosper in his hand.

4 And Joseph [e] found grace in his sight, and he served him: and he made him [f] overseer over his house, and all *that* he had he put into his hand.

A. M. 2276.
B. C. 1728.

5 And it came to pass from the time *that* he had made him overseer in his house, and over all that he had, that [g] the LORD blessed the Egyptian's house for Joseph's sake; and the blessing of the LORD was upon all that he had in the house and in the field.

6 And he left all that he had in Joseph's hand; and he knew not aught he had, save the bread which he did eat. And Joseph [h] was *a* goodly *person*, and well-favoured.

[a] Ch. xxxvii. 36; Psa. cv. 17.—[b] Ch. xxxvii. 28.—[c] Ver. 21; chap. xxi. 22; xxvi. 24, 28; xxviii. 15; 1 Sam. xvi. 18; xviii. 14, 28; Acts vii. 9.—[d] Psa. i. 3.—[e] Chap. xviii. 3; xix. 19; ver. 21.—[f] Gen. xxiv. 2.—[g] Ch. xxx. 27.—[h] 1 Sam. xvi. 12.

NOTES ON CHAP. XXXIX.

Verse 1. *An officer of Pharaoh, captain of the guard*] Mr. Ainsworth, supposing that his office merely consisted in having charge of the king's prisoners, calls Potiphar *provost marshal!* See on chap. xxxvii. 36, and xl. 3.

Verse 4. *He made him overseer*] הפקיד *hiphkid*, from פקד *pakad*, to *visit, take care of, superintend*; the same as επισκοπος, *overseer* or *bishop*, among the Greeks. This is the term by which the Septuagint often express the meaning of the original.

Verse 6. *Joseph was a goodly* person, *and well favoured.*] יפה תאר ויפה מראה *yepheh thoar, vipheh march, beautiful in his person*, and *beautiful in his countenance.* The same expressions are used relative to Rachel; see them explained chap. xxix. 17. The beauty of Joseph is celebrated over all the East, and the Persian poets vie with each other in descriptions of his comeliness. Mohammed spends the twelfth chapter of the Koran entirely on Joseph, and represents him as a perfect beauty, and the most accomplished of mortals. From his account, the passion of *Zuleekha* (for so the Asiatics call Potiphar's wife) being known to the ladies of the court, they cast the severest reflections upon her: in order to excuse herself, she invited forty of them to dine with her, put knives in their hands, and gave them oranges to cut, and caused Joseph to attend. When they saw him they were struck with admiration, and so confounded, that instead of cutting their oranges they cut and hacked their own hands, crying out,

حاش لله ما هذا بشرا ان هذا الا ملك كريم

hasha lillahi ma hadha bashara in hadha illa malakon kareemon. "O God! this is not a human being; this is none other than a glorious angel!"—Surat xii., verse 32.

Two of the finest poems in the Persian language were written by the poets *Jamy* and *Nizamy* on the subject of Joseph and his mistress; they are both entitled *Yusuf we Zuleekha.* These poems represent Joseph as the most beautiful and pious of men; and Zuleekha the most chaste, virtuous, and excellent of women, previous to her having seen Joseph; but they state that when she saw him she was so deeply affected by his beauty that she lost all self-government, and became a slave to her passion. Hafiz expresses this, and apologizes for her conduct in the following elegant couplet:—

من از آن حسن روز افزون که یوسف داشت دانستم
که عشق از پرده عصمت برون آرد زلیخارا

Men az an husn-i roz afzoon keh Yusuf dasht danistam
Keh ishk az pardah-i ismat beroon arad Zuleekhara.

"I understand, from the daily increasing beauty which Joseph possessed,
How love tore away the veil of chastity from Zuleekha."

The Persian poets and eastern historians, however, contrive to carry on a sort of guiltless passion between them till the death of *Potiphar*, when Zuleekha, grown old, is restored to youth and beauty by the power of God, and becomes the wife of Joseph. What *traditions* they had beside the Mosaic text for what they say on this subject, are now unknown; but the whole story, with innumerable embellishments, is so generally current in the East that I thought it not amiss to take

A. M. cir. 2285. B. C. cir. 1719.

7 And it came to pass after these things, that his master's wife cast her eyes upon Joseph; and she said, [i] Lie with me.

8 But he refused, and said unto his master's wife, Behold, my master wotteth not what *is* with me in the house, and he hath committed all that he hath to my hand;

9 *There is* none greater in this house than I; neither hath he kept back any thing from me but thee, because thou *art* his wife: [k] how then can I do this great wickedness, and [l] sin against God?

10 And it came to pass, as she spake to Joseph day by day, that he hearkened not unto her, to lie by her, *or* to be with her.

11 And it came to pass about this time, that *Joseph* went into the house to do his business; and *there was* none of the men of the house there within.

12 And [m] she caught him by his garment, saying, Lie with me: and he left his garment in her hand, and fled, and got him out.

13 And it came to pass, when she saw that he had left his garment in her hand, and was fled forth,

14 That she called unto the men of her house, and spake unto them, saying, See, he hath brought in a Hebrew unto us to mock us: he came in unto me to lie with me, and I cried with a [n] loud voice:

15 And it came to pass, when he heard that I lifted up my voice and cried, that he left his garment with me, and fled, and got him out.

16 And she laid up his garment by her, until his lord came home.

17 And she [o] spake unto him according to these words, saying, The Hebrew servant which thou hast brought unto us, came in unto me to mock me:

18 And it came to pass, as I lifted up my voice and cried, that he left his garment with me, and fled out.

19 And it came to pass, when his master heard the words of his wife, which she spake unto him, saying, After this manner did thy servant to me; that his [p] wrath was kindled.

20 And Joseph's master took him, and [q] put him into the [r] prison, a place where the king's prisoners *were* bound: and he was there in the prison.

21 But the LORD was with Joseph, and [s] showed him mercy, and [t] gave him favour in the sight of the keeper of the prison.

22 And the keeper of the prison [u] committed to Joseph's hand all the prisoners that *were* in the prison; and whatsoever they did there, he was the doer *of it*.

23 The keeper of the prison looked not to any thing *that was* under his hand; because [v] the LORD was with him, and *that* which he did, the LORD made *it* to prosper.

[i] 2 Sam. xiii. 11.——[k] Prov. vi. 29, 32.——[l] Chap. xx. 6; Lev. vi. 2; 2 Sam. xii. 13; Psalm li. 4.——[m] Prov. vii. 13, &c. [n] Heb. *great.*——[o] Exod. xxiii. 1; Psa. cxx. 3.——[p] Prov. vi. 34, 35.——[q] Psa. cv. 18; 1 Pet. ii. 19.

[r] Chap. xl. 3, 15; xli. 14.——[s] Heb. *extended kindness unto him.*——[t] Exod. iii. 21; xi. 3; xii, 36; Psa. cvi. 46; Proverbs xvi. 7; Daniel i. 9; Acts vii. 9, 10.——[u] Chapter xl. 3, 4. [v] Ver. 2, 3.

this notice of it. The twelfth chapter of the Koran, which celebrates the beauty, piety, and acts of this patriarch, is allowed to be one of the finest specimens of Arabic composition ever formed; and the history itself, as told by Moses, is one of the most simple, natural, affecting, and well-told narratives ever published. It is a master-piece of composition, and never fails of producing its intended effect on the mind of a careful reader. The Arab lawgiver saw and felt the beauties and excellences of his model; and he certainly put forth all the strength of his own language, and all the energy of his mind, in order to rival it.

Verse 8. *My master wotteth not*] Knoweth not, from the old Anglo-Saxon ꝩitan, *witan, to know;* hence ꝩit, *wit, intellect, understanding, wisdom, prudence.*

Verse 9. *How then*] ואיך *veeik, and how?* Joseph gives two most powerful reasons for his noncompliance with the wishes of his mistress: 1. *Gratitude* to his master, to whom he owed all that he had. 2. His *fear of God*, in whose sight it would be a heinous offence, and who would not fail to punish him for it. With the kindness of his master and the displeasure of God before his eyes, how could he be capable of committing an act of transgression, which would at once have distinguished him as the most *ungrateful* and the most *worthless* of men?

Verse 14. *He hath brought in a Hebrew unto us*] Potiphar's wife affects to throw great blame on her *husband*, whom we may reasonably suppose she did not greatly love. He *hath brought in*—he hath raised this person to all his dignity and eminence, to give him the greater opportunity to mock us. לצחק *letsachek*, here translated *to mock*, is the same word used in chap. xxvi. 8, relative to Isaac and Rebekah; and is certainly used by Potiphar's wife in ver. 17, to signify some kind of familiar intercourse not allowable but between man and wife.

Verse 20. *Put him into the prison*] בית כהר *beith sohar*, literally the *round house;* in such a *form* the prison was probably built.

Verse 21. *The Lord was with Joseph*] It is but of little consequence where the lot of a servant of God may be cast; like Joseph he is ever employed for his master, and God honours him and prospers his work.

1. He who acknowledges God in all his ways, has the promise that God shall direct all his steps. Joseph's captivity shall promote God's glory; and to this end God works *in* him, *for* him, and *by* him. Even the irreligious can see when the Most High distinguishes his followers. Joseph's master saw *that Jehovah was with him*; and from this we may learn that the knowledge of the *true God* was in Egypt, even before the time of Joseph, though his worship was neither established nor even tolerated there. Both *Abraham* and *Isaac* had been in Egypt, and they had left a savour of true godliness behind them.

2. Joseph's virtue in resisting the solicitations of his mistress was truly exemplary. Had he reasoned after the manner of men, he might have soon found that the proposed intrigue might be carried on with the utmost secrecy and greatly to his secular advantage. But he chose to risk all rather than injure a kind benefactor, defile his conscience, and sin against God. Such conduct is so exceedingly rare that his example has stood on the records of time as almost without a parallel, admired by all, applauded by most, and in similar circumstances, I am afraid, imitated by few. The fable of the brave and virtuous Bellerophon and Sthenobœa, wife of Prœtus, king of the Argives, was probably founded on this history.

3. *Joseph fled and got him out.* To know *when* to *fight* and *when* to *fly* are of great importance in the Christian life. Some temptations must be manfully met, resisted, and thus overcome; from others we must *fly*. He who stands to contend or reason, especially in such a case as that mentioned here, is infallibly ruined. *Principiis obsta*, "resist the first overtures of sin," is a good maxim. After-remedies come too late.

4. A woman of the spirit of Potiphar's wife is capable of any species of evil. When she could not get her wicked ends answered, she began to *accuse*. This is precisely Satan's custom: he first tempts men to sin, and then accuses them *as having committed it*, even where the temptation has been faithfully and perseveringly resisted! By this means he can trouble a tender conscience, and weaken faith by bringing confusion into the mind. Thus the inexperienced especially are often distracted and cast down; hence Satan is properly called *the accuser of the brethren*, Rev. xii. 10.

Very useful lessons may be drawn from every part of the relation in this chapter, but detailing the facts and reasoning upon them would be more likely to produce than prevent the evil. An account of this kind cannot be touched with *too gentle* a hand. Others have been *profuse* here; I chose to be *parsimonious*, for reasons which the intelligent reader will feel as well as myself. Let this remark be applied to what has been said on the sin of Onan, chap. xxxviii.

CHAPTER XL.

Pharaoh's chief butler *and his chief* baker, *having offended their lord, are put in prison*, 1–3. *The captain of the guard gives them into the care of Joseph*, 4. *Each of them has a dream*, 5. *Joseph, seeing them sad, questions them on the subject*, 6, 7. *Their answer*, 8. *The chief butler tells his dream*, 9–11. *Joseph interprets it*, 12, 13. *Gives a slight sketch of his history to the chief butler, and begs him to think upon him when restored to his office*, 14, 15. *The chief baker tells his dream*, 16, 17. *Joseph interprets this also*, 18, 19. *Both dreams are fulfilled according to the interpretation, the chief butler being restored to his office, and the chief baker hanged*, 20–22. *The chief butler makes no interest for Joseph*, 23.

A. M. cir. 2286. B. C. cir. 1718.

AND it came to pass after these things, *that* the [a] butler of the king of Egypt and *his* baker had offended their lord the king of Egypt.

2 And Pharaoh was [b] wroth against two *of* his officers, against the chief of the butlers, and against the chief of the bakers.

3 [c] And he put them in ward in the house of the captain of the guard, into the prison, the place where Joseph *was* bound.

4 And the captain of the guard charged Joseph with them, and he served them: and they continued a season in ward.

[a] Neh. i. 11.——[b] Prov. xvi. 14.——[c] Chap. xxxix. 20, 23.

NOTES ON CHAP. XL.

Verse 1. *The butler*] משקה *mashkeh*, the same as ساقي *saky* among the Arabians and Persians, and signifying a *cup-bearer*.

Baker] אפה *opheh*; rather *cook, confectioner*, or the like.

Had offended] They had probably been accused of attempting to take away the king's life, one by poisoning his drink, the other by poisoning his *bread* or *confectionaries*.

Verse 3. *Where Joseph was bound.*] The place in which Joseph was now *confined*; this is what is implied in being *bound*; for, without doubt, he had his *personal* liberty. As the butler and the baker were state criminals they were put in the same prison with Joseph, which we learn from the preceding chapter, verse 20, was the *king's prison*. All the officers in the employment of the ancient kings of Egypt were, according to *Diodorus Siculus*, taken from the most illustrious families of the priesthood in the country; no slave or common person being ever permitted to serve in the presence of the king. As these persons, therefore, were of the most noble families, it is natural to expect they would be put, when accused, into the *state prison*.

Verse 4. *They continued a season*] ימים *yamim*, literally *days*; *how long* we cannot tell. But many

A. M. cir. 2287.
B. C. cir. 1717.

5 And they dreamed a dream, both of them, each man his dream in one night, each man according to the interpretation of his dream; the butler and the baker of the king of Egypt, which *were* bound in the prison.

6 And Joseph came in unto them in the morning, and looked upon them, and, behold, they *were* sad.

7 And he asked Pharaoh's officers that *were* with him in the ward of his lord's house, saying, Wherefore [d] look ye *so* sadly to-day?

8 And they said unto him, [e] We have dreamed a dream, and *there is* no interpreter of it. And Joseph said unto them, [f] *Do* not interpretations *belong* to God? tell me *them,* I pray you.

9 And the chief butler told his dream to Joseph, and said to him, In my dream, behold, a vine *was* before me;

10 And in the vine *were* three branches: and it *was* as though it budded, *and* her blossoms shot forth; and the clusters thereof brought forth ripe grapes:

11 And Pharaoh's cup *was* in my hand: and I took the grapes, and pressed them into Pharaoh's cup, and I gave the cup into Pharaoh's hand.

12 And Joseph said unto him, [g] This *is* the interpretation of it: The three branches [h] *are* three days: A. M. cir. 2287. B. C. cir. 1717.

13 Yet within three days shall Pharaoh [i] lift [k] up thine head, and restore thee unto thy place: and thou shalt deliver Pharaoh's cup into his hand, after the former manner when thou wast his butler.

14 But [l] think [m] on me when it shall be well with thee, and [n] show kindness, I pray thee unto me, and make mention of me unto Pharaoh, and bring me out of this house:

15 For indeed I was stolen away out of the land of the Hebrews: [o] and here also have I done nothing that they should put me into the dungeon.

16 When the chief baker saw that the interpretation was good, he said unto Joseph, I also *was* in my dream, and, behold, *I had* three [p] white baskets on my head:

17 And in the uppermost basket *there was* of all manner of [q] bakemeats for Pharaoh; and the birds did eat them out of the basket upon my head.

18 And Joseph answered and said, [r] This *is* the interpretation thereof: The three baskets *are* three days:

19 [s] Yet within three days shall Pharaoh

[d] Heb. are *your faces evil?* Neh. ii. 2.——[e] Chap. xli. 15. [f] See chap. xli. 16; Dan. ii. 11, 28, 47.——[g] Ver. 18; chap. xli. 12, 25; Judg. vii. 14; Dan. ii. 36; iv. 19.——[h] Chap. xli. 26. [i] 2 Kings xxv. 27; Psa. iii. 3; Jer. lii. 31.——[k] Or, *reckon.*

[l] Heb. *remember me with thee.*——[m] Luke xxiii. 42.——[n] Josh. ii. 12; 1 Sam. xx. 14, 15; 2 Sam. ix. 1; 1 Kings ii. 7.——[o] Chap. xxxix. 20.——[p] Or, *full of holes.*——[q] Heb. *meat of Pharaoh, the work of a baker or cook.*——[r] Ver. 12.——[s] Ver. 13.

suppose the word signifies a *complete year;* and as Pharaoh called them to an account on his *birthday,* verse 20, Calmet supposes they had offended on the preceding *birthday,* and thus had been one whole year in prison.

Verse 5. *Each man according to the interpretation*] Not like dreams in general, the disordered workings of the mind, the consequence of disease or repletion; these were dreams that had an interpretation, that is, that were *prophetic.*

Verse 6. *They* were *sad.*] They concluded that their dreams portended something of great importance, but they could not tell *what.*

Verse 8. There is *no interpreter*] They either had access to none, or those to whom they applied could give them no consistent, satisfactory meaning.

Do *not interpretations* belong *to God?*] God alone, the Supreme Being, knows what is in futurity; and if he have sent a significant dream, he alone can give the solution.

Verse 11. *And I took the grapes and pressed them into Pharaoh's cup*] From this we find that *wine* anciently was the *mere expressed juice of the grape,* without *fermentation.* The *saky,* or cup-bearer, took the bunch, pressed the juice into the cup, and instantly delivered it into the hands of his master. This was anciently the יין *yayin* of the *Hebrews,* the *οινος* of the *Greeks,* and the *mustum* of the ancient *Latins.*

Verse 12. *The three branches* are *three days*] That is, The three branches signify three days; so, *this* IS *my body,* that is, this bread *signifies* or *represents* my body; *this cup* IS *my blood,* REPRESENTS my blood; a form of speech frequently used in the sacred writings, for the Hebrew has no proper word by which our terms *signifies, represents,* &c., are expressed; therefore it says such a thing IS, for *represents, points out,* &c. And because several of our ancestors would understand such words in their *true, genuine, critical,* and *sole meaning,* Queen Mary, Bishops Gardiner, Bonner, and the rest of that demoniacal crew, reduced them to ashes in Smithfield and elsewhere!

Verse 14. *Make mention of me unto Pharaoh*] One would have supposed that the very circumstance of his restoration, according to the prediction of Joseph, would have almost necessarily prevented him from forgetting so extraordinary a person. But what have mere *courtiers* to do either with *gratitude* or *kindness?*

Verse 15. *For indeed I was stolen*] גנב גנבתי *gunnob*

A. M. cir. 2287. B. C. cir. 1717. [t] lift up thy head from off thee, and shall hang thee on a tree; and the birds shall eat thy flesh from off thee.

20 And it came to pass the third day, *which was* Pharaoh's [u] birthday, that he [v] made a feast unto all his servants: and he [w] lifted [x] up the head of the chief butler and of the chief baker among his servants.

21 And he [y] restored the chief butler unto his butlership again; and [z] he gave the cup into Pharaoh's hand:

22 But he [a] hanged the chief baker, as Joseph had interpreted to them.

23 Yet did not the chief butler remember Joseph, but [b] forgat him.

[t] Or, *reckon thee*, and take thy office *from thee*.—[u] Matt. xiv. 6. [v] Mark vi. 21.—[w] Ver. 13, 19; Matt. xxv. 19.—[x] Or, *reckoned*.

[y] Ver. 13.—[z] Neh. ii. 1.—[a] Ver. 19.—[b] Job xix. 14; Psa. xxxi. 12; Eccles. ix. 15, 16; Amos vi. 6.

gunnabti, stolen, I have been stolen—most assuredly I was stolen; *and here also have I done nothing.* These were simple assertions, into the proof of which he was ready to enter if called on.

Verse 19. *Lift up thy head from off thee*] Thus we find that *beheading, hanging*, and *gibbeting*, were modes of punishment among the ancient Egyptians; but the criminal was beheaded before he was hanged, and then either hanged on hooks, or by the hands. See Lam. v. 12.

Verse 20. *Pharaoh's birthday*] The distinguishing a birthday by a feast appears from this place to have been a very ancient custom. It probably had its origin from a correct notion of the immortality of the soul, as the *commencement* of life must appear of great consequence to that person who believed he was to live for ever. St. Matthew, xiv. 6, mentions Herod's keeping his birthday; and examples of this kind are frequent to the present time in most nations.

Lifted up the head of the chief butler, &c.] By lifting up the head, probably no more is meant than bringing them to trial, tantamount to what was done by Jezebel and the nobles of Israel to Naboth: *Set Naboth on high among the people; and set two men, sons of Belial, to bear witness against him, &c.*; 1 Kings xxi. 9, &c. The issue of the trial was, the baker alone was found *guilty* and hanged; and the butler, being *acquitted*, was restored to his office.

Verse 23. *Yet did not the chief butler remember Joseph*] Had he mentioned the circumstance to Pharaoh, there is no doubt that Joseph's case would have been examined into, and he would in consequence have been restored to his liberty; but, owing to the ingratitude of the chief butler, he was left *two years* longer in prison.

MANY commentators have seen in *every circumstance* in the history of Joseph a parallel between him and our blessed Lord So, "Joseph in prison represents Christ in the custody of the Jews; the chief butler and the chief baker represent the two thieves which were crucified with our Lord; and as one thief was pardoned, and the other left to perish, so the chief butler was restored to his office, and the chief baker hanged." I believe GOD never designed such parallels; and I am astonished to find comparatively grave and judicious men trifling in this way, and forcing the features of *truth* into the most distorted anamorphosis, so that even her friends blush to acknowledge her. This is not a light matter; we should beware how we attribute designs to God that he never had, and employ the Holy Spirit in forming trifling and unimportant similitudes. Of plain, direct truth we shall find as much in the sacred writings as we can receive and comprehend; let us not therefore hew out unto ourselves broken cisterns that can hold no water. Interpretations of this kind only tend to render the sacred writings uncertain; to expose to ridicule all the solemn types and figures which it *really* contains; and to furnish pretexts to infidels and irreligious people to scoff at all spirituality, and lead them to reject the word of GOD entirely, as incapable of being interpreted on any fixed or rational plan. The mischief done by this system is really incalculable. See the observations on chap. xxxvii

CHAPTER XLI.

Pharaoh's dream of the seven well-favoured and seven ill-favoured kine, 1–4. *His dream of the seven full and seven thin ears of corn,* 5–7. *The magicians and wise men applied to for the interpretation of them, but could give no solution,* 8. *The chief butler recollects and recommends Joseph,* 9–13. *Pharaoh commands him to be brought out of prison,* 14. *Joseph appears before Pharaoh,* 15, 16 *Pharaoh repeats his dreams,* 17–24. *Joseph interprets them,* 25–32, *and gives Pharaoh directions how to provide against the approaching scarcity,* 33–36. *Pharaoh, pleased with the counsel, appoints Joseph to be superintendent of all his affairs,* 37–41. *Joseph receives the badges of his new office,* 42, 43, *and has his powers defined,* 44; *receives a new name, and marries* Asenath, *daughter of* Poti-Pherah, *priest of ON,* 45. *Joseph's age when brought before Pharaoh,* 46. *Great fertility of Egypt in the seven plenteous years,* 47. *Joseph hoards up the grain,* 48, 49. *Ephraim and Manasseh born,* 50–52. *The seven years of famine commence with great rigour,* 53–55. *Joseph opens the storehouses to the Egyptians,* 56. *People from the neighbouring countries come to Egypt to buy corn, the famine being in all those lands,* 57.

A. M. 2289. B. C. 1715.

AND it came to pass at the end
of two full years, that Pharaoh
[a] dreamed: and, behold, he stood by [b] the
river.
2 And, behold, there came up out of the
river seven well-favoured [c] kine and fat-fleshed; and they fed in a meadow
3 And, behold, seven other kine came up
after them out of the river, ill-favoured and
lean-fleshed; and stood by the *other* kine
upon the brink of the river.
4 And the ill-favoured and lean-fleshed kine
did eat up the seven well-favoured and fat
kine. So Pharaoh awoke.
5 And he slept and dreamed the second
time; and, behold, seven ears of
corn came up upon one stalk, [d] rank
and good.
6 And, behold, seven thin ears and blasted
with the east wind sprung up after them.
7 And the seven thin ears devoured the
seven rank and full ears. And Pharaoh
awoke, and, behold, *it was* a dream.
8 And it came to pass in the morning, [e] that
his spirit was troubled; and he sent and called
for all [f] the magicians of Egypt, and all the
[g] wise men thereof: and Pharaoh told them
his dreams; but *there was* none that could
interpret them unto Pharaoh.
9 Then spake the chief butler unto Pharaoh,

A. M. 2289. B. C. 1715.

[a] Chap. xxxvii. 5–10; xl. 5; Esth. vi. 1; Dan. ii. 1–3; iv. 5; Matt. xxvii. 19.——[b] Ezek. xxix. 3, 9.——[c] See ver. 17–27.

[d] Heb. *fat*.——[e] Dan. ii. 1; iv. 5, 19.——[f] Exodus vii. 11, 22; Isa. xxix. 14; Dan. i. 20; ii. 2; iv. 7.——[g] Matt. ii. 1.

NOTES ON CHAP. XLI.

Verse 1. *Two full years*] שנתים ימים *shenathayim yamim*, two years of days, two complete solar revolutions, after the events mentioned in the preceding chapter.

The river.] The Nile, the cause of the fertility of Egypt.

Verse 2. *There came up out of the river seven well-favoured kine*] This must certainly refer to the *hippopotamus* or river horse, as the circumstances of *coming up out of the river and feeding in the field* characterize that animal *alone*. The hippopotamus is the well-known inhabitant of the Nile, and frequently by night comes out of the river to feed in the fields, or in the sedge by the river side.

Verse 6. *Blasted with the east wind*] It has been very properly observed that all the mischief done to corn or fruit, by blasting, smutting, mildews, locusts, &c., is attributed to the *east wind*. See Exod. x. 13; xiv. 21; Psa. lxxviii. 26; Ezek. xvii. 10; Jonah iv. 8. In Egypt it is peculiarly destructive, because it comes through the parched deserts of Arabia, often destroying vast numbers of men and women. The destructive nature of the *simoom* or *smoom* is mentioned by almost all travellers. Mr. Bruce speaks of it in his Travels in Egypt. On their way to Syene, *Idris* their guide, seeing one of these destroying blasts coming, cried out with a loud voice to the company, "Fall upon your faces, for here is the *simoom*!" "I saw," says Mr. B., "from the *S. E.* a haze come, in colour like the purple part of the rainbow, but not so compressed or thick. It did not occupy *twenty* yards in breadth, and was about *twelve* feet high from the ground. It was a kind of blush upon the air, and it moved very rapidly, for I scarce could turn to fall upon the ground, with my head northward, when I felt the heat of its current plainly upon my face. We all lay flat upon the ground, as if dead, till *Idris* told us it was blown over. The meteor or purple haze which I saw, was indeed passed, but the light air that still blew was of a heat to threaten suffocation. For my part, I found distinctly in my breast that I had imbibed a part of it; nor was I free from an asthmatic sensation till I had been some months in Italy, at the baths of Poretta, near two years afterwards."—Travels, vol. vi. p. 462. On another occasion the whole company were made ill by one of these pestilential blasts, so that they had scarcely strength to load their camels.—Ibid. p. 484. The action of this destructive wind is referred to by the Prophet Hosea, chap. xiii. 15: *Though he be fruitful among his brethren, an* EAST WIND *shall come, the wind of the Lord shall come up* FROM THE WILDERNESS, *and his spring shall* BECOME DRY, *and his fountain shall be* DRIED *up: he shall spoil the treasure of all pleasant vessels*.

Verse 8. *Called for all the magicians*] חרטמים *chartummim*. The word here used may probably mean no more than *interpreters of abstruse and difficult subjects*; and especially of the Egyptian *hieroglyphics*, an art which is now entirely lost. It is most likely that the term is Egyptian, and consequently its etymology must remain unknown to us. If Hebrew, Mr. Parkhurst's definition may be as good as any: "חרט *cheret*, a *pen* or *instrument* to *write* or *draw* with, and תם *tam*, to *perfect* or *accomplish*; those who were perfect in drawing their sacred, astrological, and hieroglyphical figures or characters, and who, by means of them, pretended to extraordinary feats, among which was the interpretation of dreams. They seem to have been such persons as Josephus (Ant., lib. ii., c. 9, s. 2) calls Ἱερογραμματεις, *sacred scribes*, or professors of sacred learning."

Wise men] חכמיה *chacameyha*, the persons who, according to Porphyry, "addicted themselves to the worship of God and the study of wisdom, passing their whole life in the contemplation of Divine things. Contemplation of the stars, self-purification, arithmetic, and geometry, and singing hymns in honour of their gods, was their continual employment."—See *Dodd*. It was probably among these that Pythagoras conversed, and from whom he borrowed that modest name by which he wished his countrymen to distinguish him, *viz.*, φιλοσοφος, a *philosopher*, simply, a *lover of wisdom*.

Verse 9. *I do remember my faults*] It is not pos-

A. M. 2289. B. C. 1715. saying, I do remember my faults this day:

10 Pharaoh was [h] wroth with his servants, [i] and put me in ward in the captain of the guard's house, *both* me and the chief baker:

11 And [k] we dreamed a dream in one night, I and he; we dreamed each man according to the interpretation of his dream.

12 And *there was* there with us a young man, a Hebrew, [l] servant to the captain of the guard; and we told him, and he [m] interpreted to us our dreams; to each man, according to his dream, he did interpret.

13 And it came to pass, [n] as he interpreted to us, so it was; me he restored unto mine office, and him he hanged.

14 [o] Then Pharaoh sent and called Joseph, and they [p] brought [q] him hastily [r] out of the dungeon: and he shaved *himself*, and changed his raiment, and came in unto Pharaoh.

15 And Pharaoh said unto Joseph, I have dreamed a dream, and *there is* none that can interpret it: [s] and I have heard say of thee, *that* [t] thou canst understand a dream to interpret it.

16 And Joseph answered Pharaoh, saying, [u] *It is* not in me: [v] God shall give Pharaoh an answer of peace. A. M. 2289. B. C. 1715.

17 And Pharaoh said unto Joseph, [w] In my dream, behold, I stood upon the bank of the river.

18 And, behold, there came up out of the river seven kine, fat-fleshed, and well favoured; and they fed in a meadow:

19 And, behold, seven other kine came up after them, poor, and very ill-favoured and lean-fleshed, such as I never saw in all the land of Egypt for badness:

20 And the lean and the ill-favoured kine did eat up the first seven fat kine;

21 And when they had [x] eaten them up, it could not be known that they had eaten them; but they *were* still ill-favoured, as at the beginning. So I awoke.

22 And I saw in my dream, and, behold, seven ears came up in one stalk, full and good:

23 And, behold, seven ears, [y] withered, thin, *and* blasted with the east wind, sprung up after them:

[h] Chapter xl. 2, 3.——[i] Chapter xxxix. 20.——[k] Chapter xl. 5.——[l] Chap. xxxvii. 36.——[m] Chap. xl. 12, &c.——[n] Chapter xl. 22.——[o] Psa. cv. 20.——[p] Dan. ii. 25.——[q] Heb. *made him run.*——[r] 1 Sam. ii. 8; Psa. cxiii. 7, 8.——[s] Ver. 12; Psa. xxv. 14; Dan. v. 16.

[t] Or, when *thou hearest a dream, thou canst interpret it.*——[u] Dan. ii. 30; Acts iii. 12; 2 Cor. iii. 5.——[v] Chap. xl. 8; Dan. ii. 22, 28, 47; iv. 2.——[w] Ver. 1.——[x] Heb. *come to the inward parts of them.*——[y] Or, *small.*

sible he could have *forgotten* the circumstance to which he here alludes; it was too intimately connected with all that was dear to him, to permit him ever to forget it. But it was not *convenient* for him to remember this before; and probably he would not have remembered it now, had he not seen, that giving this information in such a case was likely to serve his own interest. We are justified in thinking evil of this man because of his scandalous neglect of a person who foretold the rescue of his life from imminent destruction, and who, being unjustly confined, prayed to have his case fairly represented to the king that justice might be done him; but this *courtier*, though then in the same circumstances himself, found it convenient to forget the *poor, friendless Hebrew slave!*

Verse 14. *They brought him hastily out of the dungeon*] Pharaoh was in perplexity on account of his dreams; and when he heard of Joseph, he sent *immediately* to get him brought before him. He *shaved* himself—having let his beard grow all the time he was in prison, he now *trimmed* it, for it is not likely that either the Egyptians or Hebrews *shaved themselves* in our sense of the word: the change of raiment was, no doubt, furnished out of the king's wardrobe; as Joseph, in his present circumstances, could not be supposed to have any changes of raiment.

Verse 16 It is *not in me, &c.*] בלעדי *biladai, without* or *independently of me*—I am not essential to thy comfort, God himself has thee under his care. And *he will send thee*, or answer thee, *peace;* thou shalt have *prosperity* (שלום *shelom*) howsoever ominous thy dreams may appear. By this answer he not only conciliated the mind of the king, but led him to expect his help from that God from whom alone all comfort, protection, and prosperity, must proceed.

Verse 18. *Seven kine, fat-fleshed*] See on ver. 2. And observe farther, that the seven fat and the seven lean kine coming out of the same river plainly show, at once, the *cause* both of the *plenty* and the *dearth.* It is well known that there is scarcely any *rain* in Egypt; and that the country depends for its fertility on the overflowing of the Nile; and that the fertility is in proportion to the *duration* and *quantity* of the overflow. We may therefore safely conclude that the seven years of plenty were owing to an *extraordinary overflowing* of the Nile; and that the seven years of dearth were occasioned by a very partial, or total want of this essentially necessary inundation. Thus then the *two sorts of cattle*, signifying years of *plenty* and *want*, might be said to *come out of the* same *river*, as the inundation was either complete, partial, or wholly restrained. See on ver. 31.

Verse 21. *And when they had eaten them up, &c.*] Nothing can more powerfully mark the excess and severity of the famine than creatures of the beeve or of the hippopotamus kind eating each other, and yet without any effect; remaining as lean and as wretched as they were before. A sense of want increases the

a

A. M. 2289.
B. C. 1715.

24 And the thin ears devoured the seven good ears: and [z] I told *this* unto the magicians; but *there was* none that could declare *it* to me.

25 And Joseph said unto Pharaoh, The dream of Pharaoh *is* one: [a] God hath showed Pharaoh what he *is* about to do.

26 The seven good kine *are* seven years; and the seven good ears *are* seven years: the dream *is* one.

27 And the seven thin and ill-favoured kine that came up after them, *are* seven years; and the seven empty ears, blasted with the east wind, shall be [b] seven years of famine.

28 [c] This *is* the thing which I have spoken unto Pharaoh: what God *is* about to do, he showeth unto Pharaoh.

29 Behold, there come [d] seven years of great plenty throughout all the land of Egypt:

30 And there shall [e] arise after them seven years of famine; and all the plenty shall be forgotten in the land of Egypt; and the famine [f] shall consume the land;

A. M. 2289.
B. C. 1715.

31 And the plenty shall not be known in the land by reason of that famine following; for it *shall be* very [g] grievous.

32 And for that the dream was doubled unto Pharaoh twice; *it is* because the [h] thing *is* [i] established by God, and God will shortly bring it to pass.

33 Now therefore let Pharaoh look out a man discreet and wise, and set him over the land of Egypt.

34 Let Pharaoh do *this*, and let him appoint [k] officers over the land, and [l] take up the fifth part of the land of Egypt in the seven plenteous years:

35 And [m] let them gather all the food of those good years that come, and lay up corn

[z] Ver. 8; Daniel iv. 7.——[a] Dan. ii. 28, 29, 45; Rev. iv. 1.——[b] 2 Kings viii. 1.——[c] Ver. 25.——[d] Verse 47.——[e] Ver. 54.——[f] Chap. xlvii. 13.——[g] Heb. *heavy*.——[h] Num. xxiii. 19; Isa. xlvi. 10, 11.——[i] Or, *prepared of God*.——[k] Or, *overseers*.——[l] Proverbs vi. 6, 7, 8.——[m] Ver. 48.

appetite, and stimulates the digestive powers to unusual action; hence the concoction of the food becomes very rapid, and it is hurried through the intestines before its nutritive particles can be sufficiently absorbed; and thus, though much is eaten, very little nourishment is derived from it. *And when they had eaten them up, it could not be known that they had eaten them; but they* were *still ill-favoured, as at the beginning*. A most nervous and physically correct description.

Verse 25. *God hath showed Pharaoh what he is about to do.*] Joseph thus shows the Egyptian king that though the ordinary cause of plenty or want is the river Nile, yet its inundations are under the direction of God: the dreams are sent by him, not only to signify beforehand the *plenty* and *want*, but to show also that all these circumstances, however fortuitous they may appear to man, are under the direction of an overruling Providence.

Verse 31. *The plenty shall not be known in the land by reason of that famine following*] As Egypt depends for its fertility on the flowing of the Nile, and this flowing is not always equal, there must be a point to which it must rise to saturate the land sufficiently, in order to produce grain sufficient for the support of its inhabitants. Pliny, Hist. Nat., lib. v., cap. 9, has given us a *scale* by which the plenty and dearth may be ascertained; and, from what I have been able to collect from modern travellers, this scale may be yet considered as perfectly correct. *Justum incrementum est cubitorum* xvi. *Minores aquæ non omnia rigant, ampliores detinent, tardius recedendo.* H*Æ serendi tempora absumunt, solo madente,* ILLÆ *non dant, sitiente. Utrumque reputat provincia. In* xii. *cubitis famem sentit. In* xiii. *etiamnum esurit;* xiv. *cubita hilaritatem afferunt;* xv. *securitatem;* xvi. *delicias.* "The ordinary height of the inundations is *sixteen* cubits. When the waters are lower than this standard they do not overflow the whole ground; when above this standard, they are too long in running off. In the first case the ground is not saturated; by the second. the waters are detained so long on the ground that seed-time is lost. The province marks both. If it rise only *twelve* cubits, a *famine* is the consequence. Even at *thirteen* cubits *hunger* prevails; *fourteen* cubits produces *general rejoicing*; *fifteen*, *perfect security*; and *sixteen*, all the *luxuries of life*."

When the Nile rises to *eighteen* cubits it prevents the sowing of the land in due season, and as necessarily produces a famine as when it does not overflow its banks.

Verse 33. *A man discreet and wise*] As it is impossible that Joseph could have foreseen his own elevation, consequently he gave this advice without any reference to himself. The counsel therefore was either immediately inspired by God, or was dictated by policy, prudence, and sound sense.

Verse 34. *Let him appoint officers*] פקדים *pekidim*, visiters, overseers: translated by Ainsworth, *bishops*; see chap. xxxix. 1.

Take up the fifth part of the land] What is still called the *meery*, or that part of the *produce* which is claimed by the king *by way of tax*. It is probable that in Joseph's time it was not so much as a *fifth* part, most likely a *tenth:* but as this was an extraordinary occasion, and the earth brought forth by handfuls, ver. 47, the king would be justified in requiring a *fifth*; and from the great *abundance*, the people could pay this increased tax without feeling it to be oppressive.

Verse 35. *Under the hand of Pharaoh*] To be completely at the disposal of the king.

A. M. 2289. B. C. 1715.

under the hand of Pharaoh, and let
them keep food in the cities.
36 And that food shall be for store to the
land against the seven years of famine, which
shall be in the land of Egypt; that the land
[n] perish [o] not through the famine.
37 And [p] the thing was good in the eyes of
Pharaoh, and in the eyes of all his servants.
38 And Pharaoh said unto his servants, Can
we find *such a one* as this *is*, a man [q] in whom
the Spirit of God *is?*
39 And Pharaoh said unto Joseph, Forasmuch as God hath showed thee all this, *there*
is none so discreet and wise as thou *art*:
40 [r] Thou shalt be over my house,
and according unto thy word shall
all my people [s] be ruled: only in the throne
will I be greater than thou.
41 And Pharaoh said unto Joseph, See, I
have [t] set thee over all the land of Egypt.
42 And Pharaoh [u] took off his ring from his
hand, and put it upon Joseph's hand, and
[v] arrayed him in vestures of [w] fine linen, [x] and
put a gold chain about his neck;
43 And he made him to ride in the second
chariot which he had; [y] and they cried before
him, [z] Bow the knee: [a] and he made him
ruler [b] over all the land of Egypt.

[n] Heb. *be not cut off.*——[o] Chap. xlvii. 15, 19.——[p] Psalm cv. 19; Acts vii. 10.——[q] Num. xxvii. 18; Job xxxii. 8; Prov. ii. 6; Dan. iv. 8, 18; v. 11, 14; vi. 3.——[r] Psa. cv. 21, 22; 1 Mac. ii. 53; Acts vii. 10.

[s] Heb. *be armed*, or, *kiss.*——[t] Dan. vi. 3.——[u] Esth. iii. 10; viii. 2, 8.——[v] Esth. viii. 15.——[w] Or, *silk.*——[x] Dan. v. 7, 29.——[y] Esth. vi. 9.——[z] Or, *tender father*; chap. xlv. 8.——[a] Heb. *Abrech.*——[b] Chap. xlii. 6; xlv. 8, 26; Acts vii. 10.

Verse 37. *The thing was good*] Pharaoh and his courtiers saw that the counsel was prudent, and should be carefully followed.

Verse 38. *In whom the Spirit of God* is?] רוח אלהים *ruach Elohim*, the identical words used chap. i. 2; and certainly to be understood *here* as in the preceding place. If the Egyptians were idolaters, they acknowledged Joseph's God; and it is not to be supposed that they only became acquainted with him on this occasion. The knowledge of the true God was in Egypt long before; but it is very likely that though they acknowledged his influence with respect to Joseph, as they saw most clearly that he acted under an influence far beyond that of their magicians, for *he* interpreted dreams which *they* could not; yet they might, notwithstanding, have their gods many and their lords many at this time, for we know that in religious matters they were exceedingly corrupt afterwards.

Verse 40. *According unto thy word shall all my people be ruled*] Literally, *At thy mouth shall all my people kiss.* In the eastern countries it is customary to kiss any thing that comes from a superior, and this is done by way of testifying respect and submission. In this sense the words in the text are to be understood: All the people shall pay the profoundest respect and obedience to all thy orders and commands.

Only in the throne will I be greater than thou.] This, in one word, is a perfect description of a *prime minister*. Thou shalt have the sole management, *under me*, of all state affairs.

Verse 42. *And Pharaoh took off his ring—and put it upon Joseph's hand*] In this ring was probably set the *king's signet*, by which the royal instruments were sealed; and thus Joseph was constituted what we would call Lord Chancellor, or Lord Keeper of the Privy Seal.

Vestures of fine linen] שש *shesh.* Whether this mean *linen* or *cotton* is not known. It seems to have been a term by which both were denominated; or it may be some other substance or cloth with which we are unacquainted. If the fine linen of Egypt was such as that which invests the bodies of the mummies, and these in general were persons of the first distinction, and consequently were enveloped in cloth of the finest quality, it was only *fine* comparatively speaking, Egypt being the only place at that time where such cloth was manufactured. I have often examined the cloth about the bodies of the most splendidly ornamented mummies, and found it sackcloth when compared with the fine *Irish* linens. As this *shesh* appears to have been a part of the royal clothing, it was probably both *scarce* and *costly.* "By comparing," says Parkhurst, "Exod. xxv. 4, xxvi. 1, with 2 Chron. ii. 14, and Exod. xxvi. 31, with 2 Chron. iii. 14, it appears that בוץ *buts*, cotton, is called שש *shesh*; and by comparing Exod. xxviii. 42, with Exod. xxxix. 28, that בד *bad*, linen, is also called שש *shesh*; so that *shesh* seems a name expressive of either of these, from their *cheerful vivid whiteness.*"

Put a gold chain about his neck] This was not merely a *badge* of office. The *chain* might be intended to point out the *union* which should subsist between all parts of the government—the king, his ministers, and the people; as also that *necessary dependence* which they had reciprocally on each other, as well as the *connection* which must be preserved between the different members of the body politic, and the laws and institutions by which they were to be governed. Its being of *gold* might be intended to show the excellence, utility, and permanence of a government constituted on wise, just, and equal laws. We are justified in drawing such inferences as these, because in ancient times, in all nations, every thing was made an *emblem* or *representation* of some spiritual or moral subject. It is strange that, probably without adverting to the reasons, the *chain of gold* worn about the neck is in different nations an emblem of *civil authority.*

Verse 43. *He made him to ride in the second chariot*] That which usually followed the king's chariot in public ceremonies.

Bow the knee] אברך *abrech*, which we translate *bow the knee*, and which we might as well translate any thing else, is probably an *Egyptian* word, the signification of which is utterly unknown. If we could suppose it to be a *Hebrew* word, it might be considered

a

A. M. 2289. B. C. 1715.
44 And Pharaoh said unto Joseph,
I *am* Pharaoh, and without thee
shall no man lift up his hand or foot in all the
land of Egypt.
45 And Pharaoh called Joseph's name
[c] Zaphnath-paaneah; and he gave him to wife
Asenath the daughter of Poti-pherah [d] priest
of On. And Joseph went out over *all* the
land of Egypt.
46 And Joseph *was* thirty years old when
he [e] stood before Pharaoh king of Egypt.
And Joseph went out from the presence of
Pharaoh, and went throughout all the land of
Egypt.
From A. M. 2289. B. C. 1715. to A. M. 2296. B. C. 1708.
47 And in the seven plenteous
years the earth brought forth by
handfuls.
48 And he gathered up all the
food of the seven years, which
were in the land of Egypt, and
laid up the food in the cities: the food of
the field, which *was* round about every city,
laid he up in the same.
49 And Joseph gathered [f] corn as the sand
of the sea, very much, until he left numbering; for *it was* without number.
50 [g] And unto Joseph were born two sons
before the years of famine came, which Ase
nath the daughter of Poti-pherah [h] priest of
On bare unto him.
A. M. cir. 2292. B. C. cir. 1712.
51 And Joseph called the
name of the first-born [i] Manas-
seh: for God, *said he*, hath made me forget
all my toil, and all my father's house.
A. M. cir. 2293. B. C. cir. 1711.
52 And the name of the second
called he [k] Ephraim: for God

[c] Which in the Coptic signifies *a revealer of secrets*, or, *the man to whom secrets are revealed.*——[d] Or, *prince*; Exod. ii. 16; 2 Sam. viii. 18; xx. 26.——[e] 1 Sam. xvi. 21; 1 Kings xii. 6, 8; Dan. i. 19.——[f] Chap. xxii. 17; Judg. vii. 12; 1 Sam. xiii. 5; Psa. lxxviii. 27.——[g] Ch. xlvi. 20; xlviii. 5.——[h] Or, *prince*; ver. 45; 2 Sam. viii. 18.——[i] That is, *forgetting*.——[k] That is, *fruitful*.

as compounded of אב *ab*, *father*, and רך *rach*, *tender*; for Joseph might be denominated a *father*, because of his *care* over the people, and the *provision* he was making for their preservation; and *tender* because of his *youth*. Or it may be compounded of אב *ab*, *father*, and ברך *barech*, *blessing*, the latter ב *beth* being easily lost in the preceding one; and Joseph might have this epithet as well as the other, on account of the care he was taking to turn aside the heavy curse of the seven years of famine, by accumulating the *blessings* of the seven years of plenty. Besides, *father* seems to have been a name of office, and probably *father of the king* or *father of Pharaoh* might signify the same as the *king's minister* among us; see on chap. xlv. 8. But if it be an Egyptian word, it is vain to look for its signification in Hebrew.

Verse 44. *I am Pharaoh*] The same as if he had said, *I am the king*; for *Pharaoh* was the common title of the sovereigns of Egypt.

Verse 45. *Zaphnath-paaneah*] The meaning of this title is as little known as that of *abrech* in the preceding verse. Some translate it, *The revealer of secrets*; others, *The treasury of glorious comfort*. St. *Jerome* translates the whole verse in the most arbitrary manner. *Vertitque nomen ejus, et vocavit eum, lingua Ægyptiaca, Salvatorem mundi.* "And he changed his name, and called him in the Egyptian language, *The saviour of the world*." None of the Asiatic versions acknowledge this extraordinary gloss, and it is certainly worthy of no regard. The Anglo-Saxon nearly copies the Vulgate: ⁊ nemde hine on Egiptisc middaneardes hælend. And named him in Egyptian, *The healer of the world*. All the etymologies hitherto given of this word are, to say the least of them, *doubtful*. *I* believe *it* also to be an Egyptian epithet, designating the office to which he was now raised; and similar to our compound terms, *Prime-Minister*, *Lord-Chancellor*, *High-Treasurer*, *Chief-Justice*, *&c.*

Asenath, the daughter of Poti-pherah] There is no likelihood that the *Poti-pherah* mentioned here is the same as the *Potiphar* who had purchased Joseph, and, on the false accusations of his wife, cast him into prison. 1. The Scripture gives no intimation that they were one and the same person. 2. *Poti-pherah* had children, and *Potiphar* was an *eunuch*; see on chap. xxxvii. 36; for though eunuchs often kept women, there is no proof that they had any issue by them.

Priest of On.] For the signification of the word כהן *cohen* or *priest*, see on chap. xiv. 18. On is rendered *Heliopolis* (the city of the sun, Sunnan burh) by the Septuagint and *Anglo-Saxon*; and it is very likely that this *Poti-pherah* was *intendant* of that *nome* or *province*, under Pharaoh.

Joseph went out over all *the land*] No doubt for the building of granaries, and appointing proper officers to receive the corn in every place, as Dr. *Dodd* has very properly conjectured.

Verse 46. *Joseph* was *thirty years old*] As he was *seventeen* years old when he was sold into Egypt, chap. xxxvii. 2, and was now *thirty*, he must have been *thirteen* years in slavery.

Stood before Pharaoh] This phrase always means admission to the immediate presence of the sovereign, and having the honour of his most unlimited confidence. Among the Asiatic princes, the privilege of *coming even to their seat*, of *standing before them*, *&c.*, was granted only to the highest *favourites*.

Verse 47. *The earth brought forth by handfuls.*] This probably refers principally to *rice*, as it grows in tufts, a great number of stalks proceeding from the same seed. In those years the Nile probably rose *sixteen* cubits; see on ver. 31.

Verse 50. *Two sons*] Whom he called by names expressive of God's particular and bountiful providence towards him. MANASSEH, מנשה *menashsheh*, signifies *forgetfulness*, from נשה *nashah*, *to forget* and

A. M. cir. 2293.
B. C. cir. 1711.
hath caused me to be [l] fruitful in the land of my affliction.

A. M. 2296.
B. C. 1708.
53 And the seven years of plenteousness, that was in the land of Egypt, were ended.
54 [m] And the seven years of dearth began to come, [n] according as Joseph had said: and the dearth was in all lands; but in all the land of Egypt there was bread.
55 And when all the land of Egypt was famished, the people cried to Pharaoh for bread: and Pharaoh said unto all the Egyptians, Go unto Joseph; what he saith to you, do.
56 And the famine was over all the face of the earth. And Joseph opened [o] all the store-houses, and [p] sold unto the Egyptians; and the famine waxed sore in the land of Egypt.
57 [q] And all countries came into Egypt, to Joseph, for to buy *corn;* because that the famine was *so* sore in all lands.

[l] Chapter xlix. 22.——[m] Psalm cv. 16; Acts vii. 11. [n] Ver. 30.

[o] Heb. *all wherein was.*——[p] Chap. xlii. 6; xlvii. 14, 24. [q] Deut. ix. 28.

EPHRAIM, אפרים *ephrayim, fruitfulness,* from פרה *parah,* to be *fruitful;* and he called his sons by these names, because God had enabled him to *forget* all his toil, disgrace, and affliction, and had made him *fruitful* in the very land in which he had suffered the greatest misfortune and indignities.

Verse 54. *The seven years of dearth began to come*] Owing in Egypt to the Nile not rising more than *twelve* or *thirteen* cubits; (see on ver. 31;) but there must have been other causes which affected other countries, not immediately dependent on the Nile, though remotely connected with Egypt and Canaan.

The dearth was in all lands] All the countries dependent on the Nile. And it appears that a general *drought* had taken place, at least through all Egypt and Canaan; for it is said, ver. 57, *that the famine was sore in all lands*—Egypt and Canaan, and their respective dependencies.

Verse 55. *When all the land of Egypt was famished*] As Pharaoh, by the advice of Joseph, had exacted a *fifth part* of all the grain during the seven years of plenty, it is very likely that no more was left than what was merely necessary to supply the ordinary demand both in the way of home consumption, and for the purpose of *barter* or *sale* to neighbouring countries.

Verse 56. *Over all the face of the earth*] The original, כל פני הארץ *col peney haarets,* should be translated, *all the face of* that land, viz., *Egypt,* as it is explained at the end of the verse.

Verse 57. *All countries came into Egypt—to buy*] As there had not been a sufficiency of rains, vapours, &c., to swell the Nile, to effect a proper inundation in Egypt, the same cause would produce drought, and consequently scarcity, in all the *neighbouring* countries; and this may be all that is intended in the text.

1. As the providence of God evidently led the *butler* and *baker* of Pharaoh, as well as the *king* himself, to dream the prophetic dreams mentioned in this and the preceding chapter, so his Spirit in Joseph led to the true interpretation of them. What a proof do all these things give us of a providence that is so *general* as to extend its influence to every part, and so *particular* as to notice, influence, and direct the most minute circumstances! Surely God "has way every where, and all things serve *his will.*"

2. *Dreams* have been on one hand superstitiously regarded, and on the other skeptically disregarded. That some are *prophetic* there can be no doubt; that others are *idle* none can hesitate to believe. Dreams may be divided into the *six* following kinds: 1. Those which are the mere nightly result of the mind's reflections and perplexities during the business of the day. 2. Those which spring from a diseased state of the body, occasioning startings, terrors, &c. 3. Those which spring from an impure state of the heart, mental repetitions of those acts or images of illicit pleasure, riot, and excess, which form the business of a profligate life. 4. Those which proceed from a diseased *mind,* occupied with schemes of pride, ambition, grandeur, &c. These, as forming the characteristic conduct of the life, are repeatedly reacted in the deep watches of the night, and strongly agitate the soul with illusive enjoyments and disappointments. 5. Those which come immediately from Satan, which instil thoughts and principles opposed to *truth* and *righteousness,* leaving strong impressions on the mind suited to its natural bent and turn, which, in the course of the day, by favouring circumstances, may be called into action. 6. Those which come from God, and which necessarily lead to him, whether prophetic of future good or evil, or impressing holy purposes and heavenly resolutions. Whatever leads away from God, truth, and righteousness, must be from the source of evil; whatever leads to obedience to God, and to acts of benevolence to man, must be from the source of goodness and truth. Reader, there is often as much *superstition* in *disregarding* as in *attending to dreams;* and he who fears God will escape it in both.

CHAPTER XLII.

Jacob sends his ten sons to Egypt to buy corn, 1–3; *but refuses to permit Benjamin to go,* 4. *They arrive in Egypt, and bow themselves before Joseph,* 5, 6. *He treats them roughly and calls them spies,* 7–10. *They defend themselves and give an account of their family,* 11–13. *He appears unmoved, and puts them all in prison for three days,* 14–17. *On the third day he releases them on condition of their bringing Benjamin,* 18–20. *Being convicted by their consciences, they reproach themselves with their cruelty to their brother Joseph, and consider themselves under the displeasure of God,* 21–23. *Joseph is greatly affected, detains Simeon as a pledge for Benjamin, orders their sacks to be filled with corn, and the purchase money to be put in each man's sack,* 24, 25. *When one of them is going to give his ass provender he discovers his money in the mouth of his sack, at which they are greatly alarmed,* 26–28. *They come to their father in Canaan, and relate what happened to them in their journey,* 29–34. *On emptying their sacks, each man's money is found in his sack's mouth, which causes alarm both to them and their father,* 35. *Jacob deplores the loss of Joseph and Simeon, and refuses to let Benjamin go, though Reuben offers his two sons as pledges for his safety,* 36–38.

A. M. 2297. B. C. 1707.

NOW when [a] Jacob saw that there was corn in Egypt, Jacob said unto his sons, Why do ye look one upon another?

2 And he said, Behold, I have heard that there is corn in Egypt: get you down thither, and buy for us from thence; that we may [b] live, and not die.

3 And Joseph's ten brethren went down to buy corn in Egypt.

4 But Benjamin, Joseph's brother, Jacob sent not with his brethren; for he said, [c] Lest peradventure mischief befall him.

5 And the sons of Israel came to buy *corn* among those that came: for the famine was [d] in the land of Canaan.

6 And Joseph *was* the governor [e] over the land, *and* he *it was* that sold to all the people of the land: and Joseph's brethren came, and [f] bowed down themselves before him *with* their faces to the earth.

A. M. 2297. B. C. 1707.

7 And Joseph saw his brethren, and he knew them, but made himself strange unto them, and spake [g] roughly unto them; and said unto them, Whence come ye? And they said, From the land of Canaan to buy food.

8 (And Joseph knew his brethren, but they knew not him.)

9 And Joseph [h] remembered the dreams which he dreamed of them, and said unto them, Ye *are* spies; to see the nakedness of the land ye are come.

10 And they said unto him, Nay, my lord, but to buy food are thy servants come.

11 We *are* all one man's sons; we *are* true *men*, thy servants are no spies.

[a] Acts vii. 12.—[b] Chap. xliii. 8; Psa. cxviii. 17; Isa. xxxviii. 1. [c] Ver. 38.—[d] Acts vii. 11.

[e] Chap. xli. 41.—[f] Chap. xxxvii. 7.—[g] Heb. *hard things with them.*—[h] Chap. xxxvii. 5, 9.

NOTES ON CHAP. XLII.

Verse 1. *Jacob saw that there was corn*] That is, Jacob *heard* from the report of others that there was plenty in Egypt. The operations of one *sense*, in Hebrew, are often put for those of another. Before agriculture was properly known and practised, famines were frequent; Canaan seems to have been peculiarly vexed by them. There was one in this land in the time of Abraham, chap. xii. 10; another in the days of Isaac, chap. xxvi. 1; and now a third in the time of Jacob. To this St. Stephen alludes, Acts vii. 11: there was *great affliction, and our* fathers *found no sustenance.*

Verse 6. *Joseph* was *the governor*] שליט *shallit*, an *intendant*, a *protector*, from שלט *shalat*, to be *over as a protector*: hence שלטים *shelatim*, *shields*, or *arms for protection* and *defence*, 2 Sam. viii. 7; and שלטון *shilton*, *power* and *authority*, Eccles. viii. 4, 8; and hence the Arabic سلطان *sultan*, a *lord*, *prince*, or *king*, from سلط *salata*, he *obtained* and *exercised dominion*, he *ruled*. Was it not from this very circumstance, Joseph being *shallit*, that all the Mohammedan governors of Egypt, &c., took the title of *sultan?*

Bowed down themselves before him] Thus fulfilling the prophetic dream, chap. xxxvii. 7, 8, which they had taken every precaution to render null and void. But there is neither might nor counsel against the Lord.

Verse 9. *Ye* are *spies*] מרגלים אתם *meraggelim attem*, *ye* are *footmen*, *trampers about*, *footpads*, *vagabonds*, lying in wait for the property of others; persons who, under the pretence of wishing to buy corn, desire only to find out whether the land be so defenceless that the *tribes* to which ye belong (see ver. 11) may attack it successfully, drive out the inhabitants, and settle in it themselves; or, having plundered it, retire to their deserts. This is a frequent custom among the Arabs to the present day. Thus Joseph spake *roughly* to them merely to cover that warmth of affection which he felt towards them; and that being thus brought, apparently, into straits and dangerous circumstances, their consciences might be awakened to reflect on and abhor their own wickedness.

Verse 11. *We* are *all one man's sons*] We do not

A. M. 2297.
B. C. 1707.

12 And he said unto them, Nay,
but to see the nakedness of the
land ye are come.
13 And they said, Thy servants *are* twelve
brethren, the sons of one man in the land of
Canaan; and, behold, the youngest *is* this day
with our father, and one [i] *is* not.
14 And Joseph said unto them, That *is it*
that I spake unto you, saying, Ye *are* spies:
15 Hereby ye shall be proved: [k] By the
life of Pharaoh ye shall not go forth hence,
except your youngest brother come hither.
16 Send one of you, and let him fetch your
brother, and ye shall be [l] kept in prison, that
your words may be proved, whether *there be
any* truth in you: or else by the life of Pharaoh surely ye *are* spies.
17 And he [m] put them all together into ward
three days.
18 And Joseph said unto them the third
day, This do, and live; [n] *for* I fear God:
19 If ye *be* true *men*, let one of your brethren be bound in the house of your
prison: go ye, carry corn for the
famine of your houses:

A. M. 2297.
B. C. 1707.

20 But [o] bring your youngest brother unto
me: so shall your words be verified, and ye
shall not die. And they did so.
21 And they said one to another, [p] We *are*
verily guilty concerning our brother, in that
we saw the anguish of his soul, when he
besought us, and we would not hear; [q] therefore is this distress come upon us.
22 And Reuben answered them, saying,
[r] Spake I not unto you, saying, Do not sin
against the child; and ye would not hear?
therefore, behold, also his blood is [s] required.
23 And they knew not that Joseph understood *them*; for [t] he spake unto them by an
interpreter.
24 And he turned himself about from them,
and wept; and returned to them again, and
communed with them, and took from them
Simeon, and bound him before their eyes.

[i] Chap. xxxvii. 30; Lam. v. 7; see chap. xliv. 20.——[k] See 1 Sam. i. 26; xvii. 55; Judith xi. 7.——[l] Heb. *bound*.——[m] Heb. *gathered*.——[n] Lev. xxv. 43; Neh. v. 15.——[o] Ver. 24; chapter xliii. 5; xliv. 23.

[p] Job xxxvi. 8, 9; Hos. v. 15.——[q] Prov. xxi. 13; Matt. vii. 2.——[r] Chap. xxxvii. 21.——[s] Chap. ix. 5; 1 Kings ii. 32; 2 Chron. xxiv. 22; Psa. ix. 12; Luke xi. 50, 51.——[t] Heb. *an interpreter was between them*.

belong to *different tribes*, and it is not likely that *one family* would make a hostile attempt upon a whole kingdom. This seems to be the very ground that Joseph took, *viz*., that they were persons belonging to different tribes. Against this particularly they set up their defence, asserting that they all belonged to one family; and it is on the *proof* of this that Joseph puts them, ver. 15, in obliging them to leave one as a hostage, and insisting on their bringing their remaining brother; so that he took exactly the same precautions to detect them as if he had had no acquaintance with them, and had every reason to be suspicious.

Verse 13. *One* is *not*.] An elliptical sentence, *One* is *not* alive.

Verse 15. *By the life of Pharaoh*] חי פרעה *chey Pharoh, Pharaoh liveth*. As if he had said, As surely as the king of Egypt lives, so surely shall ye not go hence unless your brother come hither. Here therefore is no *oath*; it is just what they themselves make it in their report to their father, chap. xliii. 3: *the man did solemnly protest unto us*; and our translators should not have put it in the *form* of an oath, especially as the original not only will bear another version, but is absolutely repugnant to this in our sense of the word.

Verse 18. *I fear God*] את האלהים אני ירא *eth ha-elohim ani yare*, literally translated the passage runs thus, *I also fear the gods*; but the emphatic ה *ha* is probably added by Joseph, both here and in his conversation with Pharaoh, the more particularly to point out the eminence and perfection of the Supreme Being as contradistinguished from the gods of Egypt. He seems to say to his brethren, *I am* a worshipper of the true God, and ye have nothing to fear.

Verse 21. *We are verily guilty*] How finely are the office and influence of conscience exemplified in these words! It was about *twenty-two* years since they had sold their brother, and probably their conscience had been lulled asleep to the present hour. God combines and brings about those favorable circumstances which produce *attention* and *reflection*, and give weight to the expostulations of conscience. How necessary to hear its voice in time, for *here* it may be the instrument of salvation; but if not heard in this world, it must be heard in the next; and *there*, in association with the *unquenchable fire*, it will be the *never-dying worm*. Reader, has not *thy* sin as yet found *thee* out? Pray to God to take away the *veil* from thy heart, and to give thee that deep sense of guilt which shall oblige thee to flee for refuge to the hope which is set before thee in the Gospel of Christ.

Verse 23. *For he spake unto them by an interpreter*.] Either there was a very great difference between the two languages as *then* spoken, or Joseph, to prevent all suspicion, might affect to be ignorant of both. We have many evidences in this book that the Egyptians, Hebrews, Canaanites, and Syrians, could understand each other in a general way, though there are also proofs that there was a considerable difference between their dialects.

Verse 24. *Took—Simeon and bound him before their eyes*.] This was *retaliation*, if, as the rabbins suppose, it was Simeon who bound Joseph, and put him

A. M. 2297.
B. C. 1707.

25 Then Joseph commanded to fill their sacks with corn, and to restore every man's money into his sack, and to give them provision for the way: and [u] thus did he unto them.

26 And they laded their asses with the corn, and departed thence.

27 And as [v] one of them opened his sack to give his ass provender in the inn, he espied his money; for, behold, it *was* in his sack's mouth.

28 And he said unto his brethren, My money is restored; and, lo, *it is* even in my sack: and their heart [w] failed *them,* and they were afraid, saying one to another, What *is* this *that* God hath done unto us?

29 And they came unto Jacob their father unto the land of Canaan, and told him all that befell unto them; saying,

30 The man, *who is* the lord of the land, spake [x] roughly to us, and took us for spies of the country.

31 And we said unto him, We *are* true *men;* we are no spies:

32 We *be* twelve brethren, sons of our father; one *is* not, and the youngest *is* this day with our father in the land of Canaan.

A. M. 2297.
B. C. 1707.

33 And the man, the lord of the country, said unto us, [y] Hereby shall I know that ye *are* true *men;* leave one of your brethren *here* with me, and take *food for* the famine of your households, and be gone:

34 And bring your youngest brother unto me: then shall I know that ye *are* no spies, but *that* ye *are* true *men: so* will I deliver you your brother, and ye shall [z] traffic in the land.

35 And it came to pass as they emptied their sacks, that, behold, [a] every man's bundle of money *was* in his sack: and when *both* they and their father saw the bundles of money, they were afraid.

36 And Jacob their father said unto them, Me have ye [b] bereaved *of my children:* Joseph *is* not, and Simeon *is* not, and ye will take Benjamin *away:* all these things are against me.

[u] Matt. v. 44; Rom. xii. 17, 20, 21.——[v] See chap. xliii. 21. [w] Heb. *went forth.*

[x] Heb. *with us hard things.*——[y] Ver. 15, 19, 20.——[z] Ch. xxxiv. 10.——[a] See chap. xliii. 21.——[b] Chap. xlii. 14.

into the pit. A recollection of this circumstance must exceedingly deepen the sense he had of his guilt.

Verse 25. *Commanded to fill their sacks*] כליהם *keleyhem, their vessels;* probably large woollen bags, or baskets lined with leather, which, as Sir John Chardin says, are still in use through all Asia, and are called *tambellet;* they are covered with leather, the better to resist the wet, and to prevent dirt and sand from mixing with the grain. These *vessels,* of whatever sort, must have been different from those called שק *sak* in the *twenty-seventh* and following verses, which was probably only a small *sack* or bag, in which each had reserved a sufficiency of corn for his ass during the journey; the larger vessels or bags serving to hold the *wheat* or *rice* they had brought, and their own packages. The reader will at once see that the English word *sack* is plainly derived from the Hebrew.

Verse 26. *They laded their asses*] Amounting, no doubt, to several *scores,* if not *hundreds,* else they could not have brought a sufficiency of corn for the support of so large a family as that of Jacob.

Verse 27. *One of them opened his sack*] From ver. 35 we learn that each of the ten brethren on emptying his sack when he returned found his money in it; can we suppose that this was not discovered by them all before? It seems not; and the reason was probably this: the money was put in the *mouth* of the sack of *one* only, in the sacks of the others it was placed *at* or *near to the bottom;* hence only one discovered it on the road, the rest found it when they came to empty their sacks at their father's house.

In the inn] במלון *bammalon,* from לן *lan,* to *lodge, stay, remain, &c.* The place at which they stopped to bait or rest themselves and their asses. Our word *inn* gives us a false idea here; there were no such places of entertainment at that time in the desert over which they had to pass, nor are there any to the present day. Travellers generally endeavour to reach a *well,* where they fill their *girbahs,* or leathern bottles, with fresh water, and having clogged their camels, asses, &c., permit them to crop any little verdure there may be in the place, keeping watch over them by turns. This is all we are to understand by the *malon* or *inn* in the text, for even *caravanseries* were not then in use, which are generally no more than *four walls* perfectly exposed, the place being open at the top.

Verse 28. *Their heart failed* them] ויצא לבם *vaiyelse libbam, their heart went out.* This refers to that spasmodic affection which is felt in the breast at any sudden alarm or fright. Among the common people in our own country we find an expression exactly similar, "My heart was ready to leap out at my mouth," used on similar occasions.

What is this that God hath done unto us?] Their guilty consciences, now thoroughly awakened, were in continual alarms; they felt that they deserved God's curse, and every occurrence served to confirm and increase their suspicions.

Verse 35. *As they emptied their sacks*] See on ver. 27.

Verse 36. *All these things are against me.*] עלי היו כלנה *alai hayu cullanah;* literally, *All these things are*

A. M. 2297.
B. C. 1707.

37 And Reuben spake unto his
father, saying, Slay my two sons,
if I bring him not to thee: deliver him into
my hand, and I will bring him to thee again.
38 And he said, My son shall not go down
with you; for [c] his brother is dead,
and he is left alone: [d] if mischief
befall him by the way in the which ye go,
then shall ye [e] bring down my gray hairs with
sorrow to the grave.

[c] Ver. 13; chap. xxxvii. 33; xliv. 28. — [d] Ver. 4; chap. xliv. 29. — [e] Chap. xxxvii. 35; xliv. 31.

upon me. Not badly translated by the Vulgate, *In me hæc omnia mala reciderunt,* "All these evils fall back upon me." They lie upon me as heavy loads, hastening my death; they are more than I can bear.

Verse 37. *Slay my two sons, if I bring him not to thee*] What a strange proposal made by a *son* to his *father*, concerning his *grandchildren!* But they show the honesty and affection of Reuben's heart; he felt deeply for his father's distress, and was determined to risk and hazard every thing in order to relieve and comfort him. There is scarcely a transaction in which Reuben is concerned that does not serve to set his character in an amiable point of view, except the single instance mentioned chap. xxxv. 22, and which for the sake of decency and piety we should wish to understand as the Targumists have explained it. See the notes.

Verse 38. *He is left alone*] That is, *Benjamin* is the only remaining son of Rachel; for he supposed *Joseph*, who was the other son, to be dead.

Shall ye bring down my gray hairs with sorrow] Here he keeps up the idea of the oppressive *burden* mentioned ver. 36, to which every occurrence was adding an additional weight, so that he felt it impossible to support it any longer.

The following observations of Dr. Dodd on this verse are very appropriate and judicious: "Nothing can be more tender and picturesque than the words of the venerable patriarch. Full of affection for his beloved Rachel, he cannot think of parting with Benjamin, the only remaining pledge of that love, now Joseph, as he supposes, is no more. We seem to behold the gray-headed, venerable father pleading with his sons, the beloved Benjamin standing by his side, impatient sorrow in *their* countenances, and in *his* all the bleeding anxiety of paternal love. It will be difficult to find in any author, ancient or modern, a more exquisite picture."

1. There is one doctrine relative to the economy of Divine Providence little heeded among men; I mean the doctrine of *restitution*. When a man has done wrong to his neighbour, though, on his repentance, and faith in our Lord Jesus, God forgives him his sin, yet he requires him to make *restitution* to the person injured, *if it lie in the compass of his power*. If he do not, God will take care to exact it in the course of his providence. Such respect has he for the dictates of infinite justice that nothing of this kind shall pass unnoticed. Several instances of this have already occurred in this history, and we shall see several more. No man should expect mercy at the hand of God who, having wronged his neighbour, refuses, when he has it in his power, to make *restitution*. Were he to weep tears of blood, both the justice and mercy of God would shut out his prayer, if he made not his neighbour amends for the injury he may have done him. The mercy of God, through the blood of the cross, can *alone* pardon his guilt; but no dishonest man can expect this; and he is a dishonest man who illegally holds the property of another in his hand. The unnatural brethren who sold their brother are now about to be captivated themselves; and the *binder* himself is *bound* in his turn: and though a kind Providence permits not the evil to fall upon them, yet, while apprehending it, they feel all its reality, conscience supplying the lack of *prison, jailer,* and *bonds*.

2. The ways of Providence are often to us dark and perplexed, so that we are ready to imagine that good can never result from what appears to us to be directly contrary to our interest; and we are often tempted to think that those very providential dealings of God, which have for their object our present and eternal welfare, are rather proofs of his displeasure, or evidences of his vindictive judgment. *All these things are against me,* said poor desponding Jacob; whereas, instead of being *against* him, all these things were *for* him; and by all these means was the merciful God working for the preservation of himself and his family, and the fulfilment of his ancient promise, that the posterity of Abraham *should be as the stars of heaven for multitude.* How strange is it that our faith, after so many evidences of his goodness, should still be so weak; and that our opinion of him should be so imperfect, that we can never trust in him but while he is under our own eye! If we see him producing good, we can believe that he is doing so, and this is all. If we believe not, he abides faithful; but our unbelief must make our own way extremely perplexing and difficult.

CHAPTER XLIII.

The famine continuing, Jacob desires his sons to go again to Egypt and buy some food, 1, 2. *Judah shows the necessity of Benjamin's accompanying them, without whom it would be useless to return to Egypt,* 3–5. *Jacob expostulates with him,* 6. *Judah replies, and offers to become surety for Benjamin,* 7–10. *Jacob at last consents, and desires them to take a present with them for the governor of Egypt; and double money, that which they had brought back in their sacks' mouth, and the price of the load they were now to bring; and, having prayed for them, sends them away,* 11–15. *They arrive in Egypt, and are brought*

to Joseph's house to dine with him, at which they are greatly alarmed, 16–18. *They speak to the steward of Joseph's house concerning the money returned in their sacks,* 19–22. *He gives them encouragement,* 23, 24. *Having made ready the present, they bring it to Joseph when he came home to dine,* 25, 26. *He speaks kindly to them, and inquires concerning their health, and that of their father,* 27, 28. *Joseph is greatly affected at seeing his brother* Benjamin, 29–31. *They dine with him, and are distinguished according to their seniority; but Benjamin receives marks of peculiar favour,* 32–34.

A. M. 2297. B. C. 1707. AND the famine *was* [a] sore in
the land.
2 And it came to pass, when they had eaten
up the corn which they had brought out of
Egypt, their father said unto them, Go again,
buy us a little food.
3 And Judah spake unto him, saying, The
man [b] did solemnly protest unto us, saying,
Ye shall not see my face, except your [c] brother *be* with you.
4 If thou wilt send our brother with us, we
will go down and buy thee food:
5 But if thou wilt not send *him*, we will not
go down: for the man said unto us, Ye shall
not see my face, except your brother *be* with
you.
6 And Israel said, Wherefore dealt ye *so* ill
with me, *as* to tell the man whether ye had
yet a brother?
7 And they said, The man [d] asked us straitly
of our state, and of our kindred, saying, *Is*
your father yet alive? have ye A. M. 2297. B. C. 1707.
another brother? and we told him
according to the [e] tenor of these words: [f] could
we certainly know that he would say, Bring
your brother down?
8 And Judah said unto Israel his father,
Send the lad with me, and we will arise and
go; that we may live, and not die, both we,
and thou, *and* also our little ones.
9 I will be surety for him; of my hand shalt
thou require him: [g] if I bring him not unto
thee, and set him before thee, then let me bear
the blame for ever:
10 For except we had lingered, surely now
we had returned [h] this second time.
11 And their father Israel said unto them,
If *it must be* so now, do this; take of the
best fruits in the land in your vessels, and
[i] carry down the man a present, a little [k] balm,
and a little honey, spices and myrrh, nuts and
almonds:

[a] Chap. xli. 54, 57.——[b] Heb. *protesting protested.*——[c] Chap. xlii. 20; xliv. 23.——[d] Heb. *asking asked us.*——[e] Heb. *mouth.* [f] Heb. *knowing could we know.*

[g] Chap. xliv. 32; Philem. 18, 19.——[h] Or, *twice by this.* [i] Chap. xxxii. 20; Prov. xviii. 16.——[k] Chap. xxxvii. 25; Jer. viii. 22.

NOTES ON CHAP. XLIII.

Verse 8. *Send the lad with me*] As the original is not ילד *yeled*, from which we have derived our word *lad*, but נער *naar*, it would have been better had our translators rendered it by some other term, such as *the youth*, or *the young man*, and thus the distinction in the Hebrew would have been better kept up. Benjamin was at this time at least twenty-four years of age, some think *thirty*, and had a family of his own. See chap. xlvi. 21.

That we may live, and not die] An argument drawn from self-preservation, what some have termed *the first law of nature*. By your keeping Benjamin we are prevented from going to Egypt; if we go not to Egypt we shall get no corn; if we get no corn we shall all perish by famine; and Benjamin himself, who otherwise might live, must, with thee and the whole family, infallibly die.

Verse 9. *Let me bear the blame for ever*] וחטאתי לך כל הימים *vechatathi lecha col haiyamim, then shall I sin against thee all* my *days*, and consequently be liable to punishment for violating my faith.

Verse 11. *Carry down the man a present*] From the very earliest times *presents* were used as means of introduction to great men. This is particularly noticed by Solomon: *A man's gift maketh room for him, and bringeth him before great men*, Prov. xviii. 16. But what was the present brought to Joseph on this occasion? After all the labour of commentators, we are obliged to be contented with probabilities and conjecture. According to our translation, the gifts were *balm, honey, spices, myrrh, nuts,* and *almonds*.

Balm] צרי *tsori* is supposed to signify *resin* in general, or some kind of gum issuing from trees.

Honey] דבש *debash* has been supposed to be the same as the *rob* of *grapes*, called in Egypt *dibs*. Others think that *honey*, in the common sense of the term, is to be understood here: we know that honey was plentiful in Palestine.

Spices] נכאת *necholh* is supposed to mean gum *storax*, which might be very valuable on account of its qualities *as a perfume*.

Myrrh] לט *lot*, supposed by some to mean *stacte*; by others to signify *an ointment made of myrrh*.

Nuts] בטנים *botnim*, by some rendered *pistachio nuts*, those produced in Syria being the finest in the world; by others, *dates*; others, *walnuts*; others, *pine apples*; others, the nuts of the *terebinth tree*.

Almonds] שקדים *shekedim*, correctly enough translated, and perhaps the only article in the collection of which we know any thing with certainty. It is generally allowed that the land of Canaan produces the best almonds in the east; and on this account they might be deemed a very acceptable present to the

A. M. 2297.
B. C. 1707.

12 And take double money in your hand; and the money [l] that was brought again in the mouth of your sacks, carry *it* again in your hand; peradventure it *was* an oversight:

13 Take also your brother, and arise, go again unto the man:

14 And God Almighty give you mercy before the man, that he may send away your other brother, and Benjamin. [m] If [n] I be bereaved *of my children*, I am bereaved.

15 And the men took that present, and they took double money in their hand, and Benjamin; and rose up, and went down to Egypt, and stood before Joseph.

16 And when Joseph saw Benjamin with hem, he said to the [o] ruler of his house, Bring *these* men home, and [p] slay, and make ready; for *these* men shall [q] dine with me at noon.

17 And the man did as Joseph bade; and the man brought the men into Joseph's house.

18 And the men were afraid, because they were brought into Joseph's house; and they said, Because of the money that was returned in our sacks at the first time are we brought in: that he may [r] seek occasion against us, and fall upon us, and take us for bondmen, and our asses.

A. M. 2297.
B. C. 1707.

19 And they came near to the steward of Joseph's house, and they communed with him at the door of the house,

20 And said, O sir, [s] we [t] came indeed down at the first time to buy food:

21 And [u] it came to pass, when we came to the inn, that we opened our sacks, and, behold, *every* man's money *was* in the mouth of his sack, our money in full weight: and we have brought it again in our hand.

22 And other money have we brought down in our hands to buy food: we cannot tell who put our money in our sacks.

23 And he said, Peace *be* to you, fear not your God, and the God of your father, hath given you treasure in your sacks: [v] I had your money. And he brought Simeon out unto them.

24 And the man brought the men into Joseph's house, and [w] gave *them* water, and

[l] Chap. xlii. 25, 35.——[m] Esth. iv. 16.——[n] Or, *and I, as I have been*, &c.——[o] Chap. xxiv. 2; xxxix. 4; xliv. 1.——[p] Heb. *kill a killing*; 1 Sam. xxv. 11.——[q] Heb. *eat*.

[r] Heb. *roll himself upon us*; Job xxx. 14.——[s] Ch. xlii. 3, 10.——[t] Heb. *coming down we came down*.——[u] Chap. xlii. 27, 35.——[v] Heb. *your money came to me*.——[w] Chap. xviii. 4: xxiv. 32.

governor of Egypt. Those who wish to see this subject exhausted must have recourse to the *Physica Sacra* of *Scheuchzer*.

Verse 12. *Double money*] What was returned in their sacks, and what was farther necessary to buy another load.

Verse 14. This verse may be literally translated thus: "And God, the all-sufficient, shall give you tender mercies before the man, and send to you your other brother, and Benjamin; and I, as I shall be childless, so I shall be childless." That is, I will submit to this privation, till God shall restore my children. It appears that this verse is spoken *prophetically*; and that God at this time gave Jacob a supernatural evidence that his children should be restored.

Verse 16. *Slay, and make ready*] טבח טבח *teboach tebach*, *slay a slaying*, or make a *great slaughter*—let preparations be made for a great feast or entertainment. See a similar form of speech, Prov. ix. 2; 1 Sam. xxv. 11; and Gen. xxxi. 54.

Verse 18. *And the men were afraid*] *A guilty conscience needs no accuser.* Every thing alarms them; they now feel that God is exacting *retribution*, and they know not what the degrees shall be, nor where it shall stop.

Fall upon us] התגלל עלינו *hithgolel alainu*, roll himself upon us. A metaphor taken from *wrestlers*; when a man has overthrown his antagonist, he rolls himself upon him, in order to keep him down.

And our asses.] Which they probably had in *great number* with them; and which, if captured, would have been a great loss to the family of Jacob, as such cattle must have constituted a principal part of its riches.

Verse 20. *O sir, we came indeed—to buy food*] There is a frankness now in the conduct of Joseph's brethren that did not exist before; they simply and honestly relate the whole circumstance of the money being found in their sacks on their return from their last journey. *Afflictions* from the hand of God, and under his direction, have a wonderful tendency to humble the soul. Did men know how gracious his designs are in sending such, no murmur would ever be heard against the dispensations of Divine Providence.

Verse 23. *And he said*] The address of the steward in this verse plainly proves that the knowledge of the true God was in Egypt. It is probable that the steward himself was a *Hebrew*, and that Joseph had given him intimation of the whole affair; and though he was not at liberty to reveal it, yet he gives them assurances that the whole business would issue happily.

I had your money.] כספכם בא אלי *caspechem ba elai*, *your money comes to me*. As I am the steward, the cash for the corn belongs to me. Ye have no reason to be apprehensive of any evil; the whole transaction is between myself and you: receive therefore the money as a present from *the God of your father*, no matter whose hands he makes use of to convey it. The *conduct* of the steward, as well as his *words*, had a great tendency to relieve their burdened minds.

Verse 24. *Brought the men into Joseph's house, &c.*]

A. M. 2297. B. C. 1707. they washed their feet; and he gave their asses provender.

25 And they made ready the present against Joseph came at noon: for they heard that they should eat bread there.

26 And when Joseph came home, they brought him the present which *was* in their hand into the house, and [x] bowed themselves to him to the earth.

27 And he asked them of *their* [y] welfare, and said, [z] *Is* your father well, the old man [a] of whom ye spake? *Is* he yet alive?

28 And they answered, Thy servant our father *is* in good health, he *is* yet alive. [b] And they bowed down their heads, and made obeisance.

29 And he lifted up his eyes, and saw his brother Benjamin, [c] his mother's son, and said, *Is* this your younger brother, [d] of whom ye spake unto me? And he said, God be gracious unto thee, my son!

30 And Joseph made haste; for [e] his bowels did yearn upon his brother: and he sought *where* to weep; and he entered into *his* chamber, and [f] wept there. A. M. 2297. B. C. 1707.

31 And he washed his face, and went out, and refrained himself, and said, Set on [g] bread.

32 And they set on for him by himself, and for them by themselves, and for the Egyptians which did eat with him, by themselves: because the Egyptians might not eat bread with the Hebrews; for that *is* [h] an abomination unto the Egyptians.

33 And they sat before him, the first-born according to his birthright, and the youngest according to his youth: and the men marvelled one at another.

34 And he took *and sent* messes unto them from before him: but Benjamin's mess was [i] five times so much as any of theirs. And they drank and [k] were merry with him.

[x] Chap. xxxvii. 7, 10.——[y] Heb. *peace*; chap. xxxvii. 14. [z] Heb. Is there *peace to your father*?——[a] Chap. xlii. 11, 13. [b] Chap. xxxvii. 7, 10.——[c] Chap. xxxv. 17, 18.

[d] Chap. xlii. 13.——[e] 1 Kings iii. 26.——[f] Chap. xlii. 24. [g] Ver. 25.——[h] Chap. xlvi. 34; Exod. viii. 26.——[i] Chap. xlv. 22. [k] Heb. *drank largely*; see Hag. i. 6; John ii. 10.

This is exactly the way in which a *Hindoo* receives a guest. As soon as he enters, one of the first civilities is the presenting of water to wash his feet. So indispensable is this, that water to wash the feet makes a part of the offerings to an image.

Verse 27. *And he asked them of* their *welfare*] This verse may be thus translated: "And he asked them concerning their prosperity; and he said, Is your father prosperous, the old man who ye told me was alive? And they said, Thy servant our father prospers; he is yet alive."

Verse 29. *He lifted up his eyes, and saw his brother Benjamin*] They were probably introduced to him *successively*; and as Benjamin was the youngest, he would of course be introduced last.

God be gracious unto thee, my son!] A usual salutation in the east from the aged and *superiors* to the *younger* and *inferiors*, which, though very emphatic and expressive in ancient times, in the present day means no more than "I am your humble servant," or "I am exceedingly glad to see you;" words which among us mean—just nothing. Even in David's time they seem to have been, not only devoid of meaning, but to be used as a *cloak* for the basest and most treacherous designs: *They bless with their mouths, but they curse inwardly*. Hence *Joab* salutes *Amasa*, kisses him with apparent affection, and stabs him in the same moment! The case of *Judas*, betraying the Son of man with a *kiss*, will not be forgotten.

Verse 32. *They set on for him by himself, &c.*] From the text it appears evident that there were *three tables*, one for Joseph, one for the Egyptians, and one for the eleven brethren.

The Egyptians might not eat bread with the Hebrews] There might have been some *political* reason for this, with which we are unacquainted; but independently of this, two may be assigned. 1. The Hebrews were *shepherds*; and Egypt had been almost ruined by hordes of lawless wandering banditti, under the name of *Hycsos*, or *King-shepherds*, who had but a short time before this been expelled from the land by *Amasis*, after they had held it in subjection for 259 years, according to *Manetho*, committing the most wanton cruelties. 2. The Hebrews sacrificed those animals which the Egyptians held sacred, and fed on their flesh. The Egyptians were in general very superstitious, and would have no social intercourse with people of any other nation; hence we are informed that they would not even use the *knife* of a Greek, because they might have reason to suspect it had *cut the flesh of some of those animals which they held sacred*. Among the *Hindoos* different castes will not eat food cooked in the same vessel. If a person of another caste touch a cooking vessel, it is thrown away. Some are of opinion that the Egyptian idolatry, especially their worship of *Apis* under the figure of an *ox*, was *posterior* to the time of Joseph; ancient monuments are rather against this opinion, but it is impossible to decide either way. The clause in the Alexandrian Septuagint stands thus, Βδελυγμα γαρ εστιν τοις Αιγυπτιοις [πας ποιμην προβατων,] "For [every shepherd] is an abomination to the Egyptians;" but this clause is probably borrowed from chap. xlvi. 34, where it stands in the Hebrew as well as in the Greek. See the note on chap. xlvi. 34.

Verse 33. *The first-born according to his birthright*] This must greatly astonish these brethren, to find themselves treated with so much *ceremony*, and

at the same time with so much *discernment* of their respective ages.

Verse 34. *Benjamin's mess was five times so much as any of theirs.*] Sir John Chardin observes that "in Persia, Arabia, and the Indies, there are several houses where they place several plates in large salvers, and set one of these before each person, or before two or three, according to the magnificence of each house. This is the method among the Hindoos; the dishes are not placed on the table, but messes are sent to each individual by the master of the feast or by his substitute. The great men of the state are always served by themselves, in the feasts that are made for them; and with *greater profusion, their part of each kind of provision being always* DOUBLE, TREBLE, *or a* LARGER *proportion of each kind of meat.*" The circumstance of Benjamin's having a mess FIVE times as large as any of his brethren, shows the peculiar honour which Joseph designed to confer upon him. See several useful observations on this subject in *Harmer's Observ.*, vol. ii., p. 101, &c., Edit. 1808.

1. THE scarcity in Canaan was not *absolute;* though they had no *corn,* they had *honey, nuts, almonds, &c.* In the midst of *judgment,* God remembers *mercy.* If there was *scarcity* in *Canaan,* there was *plenty* in *Egypt;* and though his providence had denied one country *corn,* and accumulated it in the *other,* his bounty had placed in the former *money* enough to procure it from the latter. How true is the saying, "It is never *ill* with any but it might be *worse!*" Let us be deeply thankful to God that we have *any thing,* seeing we deserve *no good* at his hands.

2. If we examine our circumstances closely, and call to remembrance the dealings of God's providence towards us, we shall find that we can sing much both of *mercy* and of *judgment.* For one day of absolute unavoidable want, we shall find we had three hundred and sixty-four, if not of *fulness,* yet of a *competency.* *Famines,* though rarely happening, are everywhere *recorded; innumerable years of abundance* are scarcely ever *registered!* Such is the perverseness and ingratitude of man!

CHAPTER XLIV.

Joseph commands his steward to put his cup *secretly into Benjamin's sack,* 1, 2. *The sons of Jacob depart with the corn they had purchased,* 3. *Joseph commands his steward to pursue them, and charge them with having stolen his cup,* 4–6. *The brethren excuse themselves, protest their innocence, and offer to submit to be* slaves *should the cup be found with any of them,* 7–9. *Search is made, and the cup is found in Benjamin's sack,* 10–12. *They are brought back and submit themselves to Joseph,* 13–16. *He determines that Benjamin alone, with whom the cup is found, shall remain in captivity,* 17. *Judah, in a most affecting speech, pleads for Benjamin's enlargement, and offers himself to be a bondman in his stead,* 18–34.

A. M. 2297.
B. C. 1707.

AND he commanded [a] the steward of his house, saying, Fill the men's sacks *with* food, as much as they can carry, and put every man's money in his sack's mouth;

2 And put my cup, the silver cup, in the sack's mouth of the youngest, and his corn money. And he did according to the word that Joseph had spoken.

3 As soon as the morning was light, the men were sent away, they and their asses.

4 *And* when they were gone out of the city, *and* not *yet* far off, Joseph said unto his steward, Up, follow after the men: and when thou dost overtake them, say unto them, Wherefore have ye rewarded evil for good?

5 *Is* not this *it* in which my lord drinketh, and whereby indeed he [b] divineth? ye have done evil in so doing.

6 And he overtook them, and he spake unto them these same words.

[a] Heb. him *that was over his house.*

[b] Or, *maketh trial.*

NOTES ON CHAP. XLIV.

Verse 2. *Put my cup—in the sack's mouth of the youngest*] The stratagem of the cup seems to have been designed to bring Joseph's brethren into the *highest state of perplexity and distress,* that their deliverance by the discovery that Joseph was their brother might have its *highest effect.*

Verse 5. *Whereby—he divineth?*] Divination by cups has been from time immemorial prevalent among the Asiatics; and for want of knowing this, commentators have spent a profusion of learned labour upon these words, in order to reduce them to that kind of meaning which would at once be consistent with the scope and design of the history, and save Joseph from the impeachment of *sorcery* and *divination.* I take the word נחש *nachash* here in its general acceptation of *to view attentively, to inquire.* Now there has been in the east a tradition, the commencement of which is lost in immemorial time, that there was a CUP, which had passed successively into the hands of different potentates, which possessed the strange property of representing in it the *whole world* and all the *things which were then doing in it.* The cup is called جام جمشيد *jami Jemsheed,* the cup of Jemsheed, a very ancient king of Persia, whom late historians and poets have confounded with *Bacchus, Solomon, Alexander the Great, &c.* This CUP, filled with the *elixir of immortality,* they say was discovered

A. M. 2297.
B. C. 1707.

7 And they said unto him, Wherefore saith my lord these words?
God forbid that thy servants should do according to this thing:
8 Behold, [c] the money, which we found in
our sacks' mouths, we brought again unto thee
out of the land of Canaan: how then should
we steal out of thy lord's house silver or gold?
9 With whomsoever of thy servants it be
found, [d] both let him die, and we also will be
my lord's bondmen.
10 And he said, Now also *let* it *be* according unto your words: he, with whom it is
found, shall be my servant; and ye shall be
blameless.
11 Then they speedily took down every
man his sack to the ground, and opened every
man his sack.
12 And he searched, *and* began at the eldest,
and left at the youngest; and the cup was
found in Benjamin's sack.
13 Then they [e] rent their clothes,
and laded every man his ass, and
returned to the city.

A. M. 2297.
B. C. 1707.

14 And Judah and his brethren came to
Joseph's house; for he *was* yet there: and
they [f] fell before him on the ground.
15 And Joseph said unto them, What deed
is this that ye have done? wot ye not that
such a man as I can certainly [g] divine?
16 And Judah said, What shall we say unto
my lord? what shall we speak? or how shall
we clear ourselves? God hath found out the
iniquity of thy servants: behold, [h] we *are* my
lord's servants, both we, and *he* also with
whom the cup is found.
17 And he said, [i] God forbid that I should
do so: *but* the man in whose hand the cup
is found, he shall be my servant; and as for
you, get you up in peace unto your father.
18 Then Judah came near unto him, and
said, O, my lord, let thy servant, I pray thee,

[c] Chap. xliii. 21.——[d] Chap. xxxi. 32.——[e] Chap. xxxvii. 29, 34; Num. xiv. 6; 2 Sam. i. 11.

[f] Chap. xxxvii. 7.——[g] Or, *make trial;* verse 5.——[h] Verse 9.——[i] Prov. xvii. 15.

when digging to lay the foundations of *Persepolis*. The Persian poets are full of allusions to this cup, which, from its property of representing the whole world and its transactions, is styled by them جام جهان نما *jam jehan nima*, "the cup showing the universe;" and to the intelligence received by means of it they attribute the great prosperity of their ancient monarchs, as by it they understood all events, past, present, and to come. Many of the Mohammedan princes and governors affect still to have information of futurity by means of a *cup*. When Mr. Norden was at *Derri* in the farthest part of Egypt, in a very dangerous situation, an ill-natured and powerful Arab, in a threatening way, told one of their people whom they sent to him that "he knew what sort of people they were, for he had *consulted his cup*, and found by it that they were those of whom one of their prophets had said, that *Franks* (Europeans) would come in disguise; and, passing everywhere, examine the state of the country; and afterwards bring over a great number of other Franks, conquer the country, and exterminate all." By this we see that the tradition of the *divining cup* still exists, and in the *very same country* too in which Joseph formerly ruled. Now though it is not at all likely that Joseph practised any kind of *divination*, yet probably, according to the superstition of those times, (for I suppose the tradition to be even older than the time of Joseph,) supernatural influence might be attributed to *his cup;* and as the whole transaction related here was merely intended to deceive his brethren for a *short time*, he might as well affect *divination by his cup*, as he affected to believe they had *stolen* it. The steward therefore uses the word נחש *nachash* in its proper meaning: *Is not this it out of which my lord drinketh, and in which he inspecteth accurately?* ver. 5. And hence Joseph says, ver. 15: *Wot ye not*—did ye not know, *that such a person as I* (having such a cup) *would accurately and attentively look into it?* As I consider this to be the true meaning, I shall not trouble the reader with other modes of interpretation.

Verse 16. *What shall we say, &c.*] No words can more strongly mark *confusion* and *perturbation* of mind. They, no doubt, all thought that Benjamin had actually stolen the cup; and the probability of this guilt might be heightened by the circumstance of his having that very cup to drink out of at dinner; for as he had the most honourable mess, so it is likely he had the most honourable cup to drink out of at the entertainment.

Verse 18. *Thou art even as Pharaoh.*] As wise, as powerful, and as much to be dreaded as he. In the Asiatic countries, the reigning monarch is always considered to be the *pattern of all perfection;* and the highest honour that can be conferred on any person, is to resemble him to the monarch; as the monarch himself is likened, in the same complimentary way, to *an angel of God*. See 2 Sam. xiv. 17, 18. Judah is the chief speaker here, because it was in consequence of his becoming surety for Benjamin that Jacob permitted him to accompany them to Egypt. See chap. xliii. 9.

"EVERY man who reads," says Dr. Dodd, "to the close of this chapter, must confess that Judah acts here the part both of the affectionate brother and of the dutiful son, who, rather than behold his father's misery in case of Benjamin's being left behind, submits to become a bondman in his stead: and indeed there is such an air of candour and generosity running through the whole strain of this speech, the sentiments are so tender and affecting, the expressions so passionate, and flow so much from artless nature, that it is no wonder if they

A. M. 2297. B. C. 1707.

speak a word in my lord's ears, and [k] let not thine anger burn against thy servant: for thou *art* even as Pharaoh.
19 My lord asked his servants, saying, Have ye a father, or a brother?
20 And we said unto my lord, We have a father, an old man, and [l] a child of his old age, a little one; and his brother is dead, and he alone is left of his mother, and his father loveth him.
21 And thou saidst unto thy servants, [m] Bring him down unto me, that I may set mine eyes upon him.
22 And we said unto my lord, The lad cannot leave his father: for *if* he should leave his father, *his father* would die.
23 And thou saidst unto thy servants, [n] Except your youngest brother come down with you, ye shall see my face no more.
24 And it came to pass when we came up unto thy servant my father, we told him the words of my lord.
25 And [o] our father said, Go again, *and* buy us a little food.
26 And we said, We cannot go down: if our youngest brother be with us, then will we go down: for we may not see the man's face, except our youngest brother *be* with us.
27 And thy servant my father said unto us, Ye know that [p] my wife bare me two *sons:*
28 And the one went out from me, and I said, [q] Surely he is torn in pieces: and I saw him not since:
29 And if ye [r] take this also from me, and mischief befall him, ye shall bring down my gray hairs with sorrow to the grave.
30 Now therefore, when I come to thy servant my father, and the lad *be* not with us; (seeing that [s] his life is bound up in the lad's life;)
31 It shall come to pass, when he seeth that the lad *is* not *with us*, that he will die; and thy servants shall bring down the gray hairs of thy servant our father with sorrow to the grave.
32 For thy servant became surety for the lad unto my father, saying, [t] If I bring him not unto thee, then I shall bear the blame to my father for ever.
33 Now therefore, I pray thee, [u] let thy servant abide instead of the lad, a bondman to my lord; and let the lad go up with his brethren.
34 For how shall I go up to my father, and the lad *be* not with me? lest peradventure I see the evil that shall [v] come on my father.

[k] Chap. xviii. 30, 32; Exod. xxxii. 22.——[l] Chap. xxxvii. 3. [m] Chap. xlii. 15, 20.——[n] Chapter xliii. 3, 5.——[o] Chap. xliii. 2. [p] Chap. xlvi. 19.——[q] Chap. xxxvii. 33.

[r] Chap. xlii. 36, 38.——[s] 1 Sam. xviii. 1.——[t] Chap. xliii. 9. [u] Exod. xxxii. 32.——[v] Heb. *find my father;* Exod. xviii. 8; Job xxxi. 29; Psa. cxvi. 3; cxix. 143.

came home to Joseph's heart, and forced him to throw off the mask." "When one sees," says Dr. Jackson, "such passages related by men who affect no art, and who lived long *after* the parties who first uttered them, we cannot conceive how all particulars could be so naturally and fully recorded, unless they had been suggested by *His* Spirit who gives mouths and speech unto men; who, being alike present to all successions, is able to communicate the secret thoughts of forefathers to their children, and put the very words of the deceased, never registered before, into the mouths or pens of their successors born many ages after; and that as exactly and distinctly as if they had been caught, in characters of *steel* or *brass*, as they issued out of their mouths. For it is plain that every circumstance is here related with such natural *specifications*, as if Moses had heard them talk; and therefore could not have been thus represented to us, unless they had been written by *His* direction who knows all things, fore-past, present, or to come."

To two such able and accurate testimonies I may be permitted to add my own. No paraphrase can heighten the effect of Judah's address to Joseph. To *add* would be to diminish its excellence; to attempt to *explain* would be to obscure its beauties; to clothe the ideas in other language than that of Judah, and his translators in our Bible, would ruin its energy, and destroy its influence. It is perhaps one of the most tender, affecting pieces of natural oratory ever spoken or penned; and we need not wonder to find that when Joseph heard it he could not refrain himself, but wept aloud. His soul must have been insensible beyond what is common to human nature, had he not immediately yielded to a speech so delicately tender, and so powerfully impressive. We cannot but deplore the unnatural and unscientific *division* of the narrative in our common Bibles, which obliges us to have recourse to *another chapter* in order to witness the effects which this speech produced on the heart of Joseph.

CHAPTER XLV.

Joseph, deeply affected with the speech of Judah, could no longer conceal himself, but discovers himself to his brethren, 1–4. *Excuses their conduct towards him, and attributes the whole to the providence of God,* 5–8. *Orders them to hasten to Canaan, and bring up their father and their own families, cattle, &c., because there were five years of the famine yet to come,* 9–13. *He embraces and converses with all his brethren,* 14, 15. *Pharaoh, hearing that Joseph's brethren were come to Egypt, and that Joseph had desired them to return to Canaan and bring back their families, not only confirms the order, but promises them the best part of the land of Egypt to dwell in; and provides them carriages to transport themselves and their households,* 16–20. *Joseph provides them with wagons according to the commandment of Pharaoh; and having given them various presents, sends them away with suitable advice,* 21–24. *They depart, arrive in Canaan, and announce the glad tidings to their father, who for a time believes not, but being assured of the truth of their relation, is greatly comforted, and resolves to visit Egypt,* 25–28.

A. M. 2297.
B. C. 1707.

THEN Joseph could not refrain himself before all them that stood by him; and he cried, Cause every man to go out from me. And there stood no man with him, while Joseph made himself known unto his brethren.
2 And he [a] wept aloud: and the Egyptians and the house of Pharaoh heard.
3 And Joseph said unto his brethren, [b] I *am* Joseph; doth my father yet live? And his brethren could not answer him; for they were [c] troubled at his presence.
4 And Joseph said unto his brethren, Come near to me, I pray you. And they came near. And he said, I *am* Joseph your brother, [d] whom ye sold into Egypt.
5 Now therefore [e] be not grieved, [f] nor angry with yourselves, that ye sold me hither: [g] for God did send me before you to preserve life.

[a] Heb. *gave forth his voice in weeping;* Num. xiv. 1.——[b] Acts vii. 13.——[c] Or, *terrified;* Job iv. 5; xxiii. 15; Matt. xiv. 26; Mark vi. 50.——[d] Chap. xxxvii. 28.

[e] Isa. xl. 2; 2 Cor. ii. 7.——[f] Heb. *neither let there be anger in your eyes.*——[g] Chap. l. 20; Psa. cv. 16, 17; see 2 Sam. xvi. 10, 11; Acts iv. 24.

NOTES ON CHAP. XLV.

Verse 1. *Joseph could not refrain himself*] The word התאפק *hithappek* is very emphatic; it signifies to *force one's self, to do something against nature, to do violence to one's self.* Joseph could no longer constrain himself to act a feigned part—all the *brother* and the *son* rose up in him at once, and overpowered all his resolutions; he felt for his *father,* he realized his disappointment and agony; and he felt for his *brethren,* "now at his feet submissive in distress;" and, that he might give free and full scope to his feelings, and the most ample play to the workings of his affectionate heart, he ordered all his attendants to go out, *while he made himself known to his brethren.* "The beauties of this chapter," says Dr. Dodd, "are so striking, that it would be an indignity to the reader's judgment to point them out; all who can read and feel must be sensible of them, as there is perhaps nothing in sacred or profane history more highly wrought up, more interesting or affecting."

Verse 2. *The Egyptians and the house of Pharaoh heard.*] It seems strange that Joseph should have wept so loud that his cries should be heard at some considerable distance, as we may suppose his dwelling was not very nigh to the palace! "But this," says Sir John Chardin, "is exactly the genius of the people of Asia—their sentiments of joy or grief are properly *transports,* and their transports are ungoverned, excessive, and truly outrageous. When any one returns from a long journey, or dies, his family burst *into cries that may be heard twenty doors off;* and this is renewed at different times, and continues many days, according to the vigour of the passion. Sometimes they cease all at once, and then begin as suddenly, with a greater shrillness and loudness than one could easily imagine." This circumstance Sir John brings to illustrate the verse in question. See Harmer, vol. iii. p. 17. But *the house of Pharaoh* may certainly signify *Pharaoh's servants,* or any of the members of his household, such as those whom Joseph had desired to withdraw, and who might still be within hearing of his voice. After all, the words may only mean that the *report* was brought to Pharaoh's house. See ver. 16.

Verse 3. *I am Joseph*] Mr. Pope supposed that the discovery of Ulysses to his son Telemachus bears some resemblance to Joseph's discovery of himself to his brethren. The passage may be seen in Homer, Odyss. l. xvi., ver. 186–218.

A few lines from *Cowper's* translation will show much of the spirit of the original, and also a considerable analogy between the two scenes:—

"I am thy father, for whose sake thou lead'st
A life of wo by violence oppress'd.
So saying, he kiss'd his son; while from his cheeks
Tears trickled, tears till then *perforce restrain'd.*
——Then threw Telemachus
His arms around his father's neck, and wept.
Pangs of soft sorrow, *not to be suppress'd,*
Seized both.——
So they, their cheeks with *big round drops* of wo
Bedewing, stood."

Verse 5. *Be not grieved, nor angry with yourselves*] This discovers a truly *noble mind:* he not only *forgives* and *forgets,* but he wishes even those who had wronged him to forget the injury they had done, that

A. M. 2297.
B. C. 1707.

6 For these two years *hath* the
famine *been* in the land: and yet
there are five years, in the which *there shall*
neither *be* earing nor harvest.
7 And God sent me before you [h] to preserve
you a posterity in the earth, and to save your
lives by a great deliverance.
8 So now *it was* not you *that* sent me hither,
but God: and he hath made me [i] a father to
Pharaoh, and lord of all his house, and a ruler
throughout all the land of Egypt.
9 Haste ye, and go up to my father, and
say unto him, Thus saith thy son Joseph, God
hath made me lord of all Egypt: come down
unto me, tarry not.
10 And [k] thou shalt dwell in the land of
Goshen, and thou shalt be near
unto me, thou, and thy children,
and thy children's children, and thy flocks,
and thy herds, and all that thou hast:
11 And there will I nourish thee; (for yet
there are five years of famine;) lest thou,
and thy household, and all that thou hast,
come to poverty.
12 And, behold, your eyes see, and the eyes
of my brother Benjamin, that *it is* [l] my mouth
that speaketh unto you.
13 And ye shall tell my father of all my
glory in Egypt, and of all that ye have seen;
and ye shall haste and [m] bring down my father hither.
14 And he fell upon his brother Benjamin's

A. M. 2297.
B. C. 1707.

[h] Heb. *to put for you a remnant.*——[i] Ch. xli. 43; Judg. xvii. 10; Job xxix. 16.——[k] Ch. xlvii. 1.——[l] Ch. xlii. 23.——[m] Acts vii. 14.

they might not suffer distress on the account; and with deep piety he attributes the whole to the providence of God; for, says he, God did *send* me *before* you to *preserve life*. On every word here a strong emphasis may be laid. It is not *you*, but *God;* it is not you that *sold* me, but God who *sent* me; Egypt and Canaan must both have perished, had not a merciful provision been made; *you* were to come down hither, and God sent me *before* you; death must have been the consequence of this famine, had not God sent me here to *preserve life*.

Verse 6. There shall *neither* be *earing nor harvest.*] Earing has been supposed to mean collecting the *ears* of corn, which would confound it with *harvest:* the word, however, means *ploughing* or *seed-time*, from the Anglo-Saxon erian *erian*, probably borrowed from the Latin *aro*, to *plough*, and plainly means that there should be no *seed-time*, and consequently no *harvest;* and why? Because there should be a total want of *rain* in other countries, and the *Nile* should not rise above *twelve cubits* in Egypt; see on chap. xli. 31. But the expressions here must be qualified a little, as we find from chap. xlvii. 19, that the Egyptians came to Joseph to buy *seed;* and it is probable that even during this famine they sowed some of the ground, particularly on the borders of the river, from which a crop, though not an abundant one, might be produced. The passage, however, in the above chapter may refer to the *last year* of the famine, when they came to procure seed for the *ensuing* year.

Verse 8. *He hath made me a father to Pharaoh*] It has already been conjectured that *father* was a name of *office* in Egypt, and that *father of Pharaoh* might among them signify the same as *prime minister* or the *king's minister* does among us. Calmet has remarked that among the Phœnicians, Persians, Arabians, and Romans, the title of *father* was given to certain officers of state. The Roman emperors gave the name of *father* to the prefects of the Prætorium, as appears by the letters of Constantine to Ablavius. The caliphs gave the same name to their *prime ministers*. In Judges xvii. 10, Micah says to the young Levite, *Dwell with me, and be unto me a* FATHER *and a priest*. And Diodorus Siculus remarks that the *teachers* and *counsellors* of the kings of Egypt were chosen out of the *priesthood*.

Verse 10. *Thou shalt dwell in the land of Goshen*] Probably this district had been allotted to Joseph by the king of Egypt, else we can scarcely think he could have promised it so positively, without first obtaining Pharaoh's consent. Goshen was the most easterly province of *Lower Egypt*, not far from the *Arabian Gulf*, lying next to Canaan, (for Jacob went directly thither when he came into Egypt,) from whence it is supposed to have been about fourscore miles distant, though *Hebron* was distant from the *Egyptian capital* about three hundred miles. At Goshen Jacob stayed till Joseph visited him, chap. xlvi. 28. It is also called the *land of Rameses*, chap. xlvii. 11, from a city of that name, which was the metropolis of the country. Josephus, Antiq., l. ii., c. 4, makes *Heliopolis*, the city of Joseph's father-in-law, the place of the Israelites' residence. As גשם *geshem* signifies *rain* in Hebrew, St. Jerome and some others have supposed that גשן *Goshen* comes from the same root, and that the land in question was called thus because it had *rain*, which was not the case with Egypt in general; and as it was on the confines of the Arabian Gulf, it is very probable that it was *watered from heaven*, and it might be owing to this circumstance that it was peculiarly fertile, for it is stated to be the *best* of the land of Egypt. See chap. xlvii. 6, 11. See also *Calmet* and *Dodd*

Verse 12. *That* it is *my mouth that speaketh unto you.*] The Targum of *Jonathan ben Uzziel* renders the place thus:—"Your eyes see, and the eyes of my brother Benjamin, that it is my own mouth that speaketh with you, in the language of the house of the sanctuary." Undoubtedly Joseph laid considerable stress on his speaking with them in the *Hebrew tongue*, without the assistance of an *interpreter*, as in the case mentioned chap. xlii. 23.

Verse 14. *He fell upon his brother Benjamin's neck*] Among the Asiatics *kissing* the *beard*, the *neck*, and the *shoulders*, is in use to the present day; and probably

A. M. 2297. B. C. 1707. neck, and wept; and Benjamin wept upon his neck.

15 Moreover he kissed all his brethren, and wept upon them: and after that his brethren talked with him.

16 And the fame thereof was heard in Pharaoh's house, saying, Joseph's brethren are come: and it [n] pleased Pharaoh well, and his servants.

17 And Pharaoh said unto Joseph, Say unto thy brethren, This do ye: lade your beasts, and go, get you unto the land of Canaan;

18 And take your father, and your households, and come unto me: and I will give you the good of the land of Egypt, and ye shall eat [o] the fat of the land.

19 Now thou art commanded, this do ye; take you wagons out of the land of Egypt for your little ones, and for your wives, and bring your father, and come.

20 Also [p] regard not your stuff; for the good of all the land of Egypt *is* yours.

21 And the children of Israel did so: and Joseph gave them wagons, according to the [q] commandment of Pharaoh, and gave them provision for the way. A. M. 2297. B. C. 1707.

22 To all of them he gave each man changes of raiment; but to Benjamin he gave three hundred *pieces* of silver, and [r] five changes of raiment.

23 And to his father he sent after this *manner;* ten asses [s] laden with the good things of Egypt, and ten she-asses laden with corn and bread and meat for his father by the way

24 So he sent his brethren away, and they departed: and he said unto them, See that ye fall not out by the way.

25 And they went up out of Egypt, and came into the land of Canaan unto Jacob their father,

26 And told him, saying, Joseph *is* yet alive, and he *is* governor over all the land of Egypt. [t] And [u] Jacob's heart fainted, for he believed them not.

27 And they told him all the words of Joseph, which he had said unto them: and

[n] Heb. *was good in the eyes of Pharaoh;* chap. xli. 37. [o] Chap. xxvii. 28; Num. xviii. 12, 29.——[p] Heb. *let not your eyes spare,* &c.

[q] Heb. *mouth;* Num. iii. 16.——[r] Chap. xliii. 34.——[s] Heb. *carrying.*——[t] Job xxix. 24; Psa. cxxvi. 1; Luke xxiv. 11, 41. [u] Heb. *his.*

falling on the neck signifies no more than *kissing the neck* or *shoulders,* with the arms around.

Verse 20. *Regard not your stuff*] Literally, *Let not your eye spare your instruments* or *vessels.* כליכם *keleychem,* a *general term,* in which may be included household furniture, agricultural utensils, or implements of any description. They were not to delay nor encumber themselves with articles which could be readily found in Egypt, and were not worth so long a carriage.

Verse 21. *Joseph gave them wagons*] עגלות *agaloth,* from עגל *agal,* which, though not used as a *verb* in the Hebrew Bible, evidently means to *turn round, roll round,* be *circular,* &c., and hence very properly applied to *wheel carriages.* It appears from this that such vehicles were very early in use, and that the road from Egypt to Canaan must have been very *open* and much *frequented,* else such carriages could not have passed by it.

Verse 22. *Changes of raiment*] It is a common custom with all the Asiatic sovereigns to give both *garments* and *money* to ambassadors and persons of distinction, whom they particularly wish to honour. Hence they keep in their wardrobes several hundred changes of raiment, ready made up for presents of this kind. That such were given by way of reward and honour, see Judges xiv. 12, 19; Rev. vi. 11. At the close of a feast the *Hindoos,* among other presents to the guests, commonly give *new garments.* A *Hindoo garment* is merely a piece of cloth, requiring no work of the tailor.—*Ward.*

Verse 23. *Meat for his father by the way.*] מזון *mazon,* from זן *zan,* to *prepare, provide,* &c. Hence *prepared meat,* some made-up dish, *delicacies, confectionaries,* &c. As the word is used, 2 Chron. xvi. 14, for *aromatic* preparations, it may be restrained in its meaning to something of that kind here. In Asiatic countries they have several curious methods of preserving flesh by *potting,* by which it may be kept for any reasonable length of time sweet and wholesome. Some delicacy, similar to the savoury food which Isaac loved, may be here intended; and this was sent to Jacob in consideration of his age, and to testify the respect of his son. Of other kinds of meat he could need none, as he had large herds, and could kill a *lamb, kid, sheep,* or *goat,* whenever he pleased.

Verse 24. *See that ye fall not out by the way.*] This prudent caution was given by Joseph, to prevent his brethren from accusing each other for having *sold* him; and to prevent them from envying Benjamin, for the superior favour shown him by his brother. It is strange, but so it is, that children of the same parents are apt to envy each other, fall out, and contend; and therefore the exhortation in this verse must be always seasonable in a large family. But a rational, religious education will, under God, prevent every thing of this sort.

Verse 26. *Jacob's heart fainted*] Probably the good news so overpowered him as to cast him into a swoon. *He believed them not*—he thought it was *too good news to be true;* and though it occasioned his swooning, yet on his recovery he could not fully credit it. See a similar case, Luke xxiv. 41.

Verse 27. *When he saw the wagons—the spirit of Jacob—revived*] The wagons were additional evi-

A. M. 2297. B. C. 1707. when he saw the wagons which Joseph had sent to carry him, the spirit of Jacob their father revived:

28 And Israel said, *It is* enough; Joseph my son *is* yet alive: I will go and see him before I die. A. M. 2297. B. C. 1707.

dences of the truth of what he had heard from his sons; and the consequence was, that he was restored to fresh vigour, he seemed as if he had gained *new life*, ותחי *vattechi, and he lived; revixit*, says the Vulgate, *he lived afresh.* The Septuagint translate the original word by *ανεζωπυρησε*, which signifies the *blowing* and *stirring up* of *almost extinguished embers* that had been buried under the ashes, which word St. Paul uses, 2 Tim. i. 6, for *stirring up the gift of God.* The passage at once shows the debilitated state of the venerable patriarch, and the wonderful effect the news of Joseph's preservation and glory had upon his mind.

Verse 28. It is *enough; Joseph my son* is *yet alive*] It was not the state of *dignity* to which Joseph had arisen that particularly affected Jacob, it was the consideration that he was *still alive.* It was *this* that caused him to exclaim רב *rab; "much! multiplied!* my son is yet alive! I will go and see him before I die." None can realize this scene; the words, the circumstances, all refer to indescribable feelings.

1. In Joseph's conduct to his brethren there are several things for which it is difficult to account. It is strange, knowing how much his father loved him, that he never took an opportunity, many of which must have offered, to acquaint him that he was alive; and that self-interest did not dictate the propriety of this to him is at first view surprising, as his father would undoubtedly have paid his ransom, and restored him to liberty: but a little reflection will show that prudence dictated *secrecy.* His brethren, jealous and envious in the extreme, would soon have found out other methods of destroying his life, had they again got him into their power. Therefore for his personal safety, he chose rather to be a *bond-slave* in Egypt than to *risk his life* by returning home. On this ground it is evident that he could not with any safety have discovered the place of his residence.

2. His carriage to his brethren, previously to his making himself known, appears inexcusably *harsh*, if not *vindictive;* but when the *men* are considered, it will appear sufficiently evident that no other means would have been adequate to awaken their torpid consciences, and bring them to a due sense of their guilt. A desperate disease requires a desperate remedy. The event justified all that he did, and God appears to have been the director of the whole.

3. His conduct in requiring Benjamin to be as it were torn away from the bleeding heart of an aged, desolate father, in whose affection he himself had long lived, is the most difficult to be satisfactorily accounted for. Unless the Spirit of prophecy had assured him that this experiment would terminate in the most *favourable manner*, his conduct in making it cannot well be vindicated. To such prophetic intimation this conduct has been attributed by learned men; and we may say that this consideration, if it does not *untie* the *knot*, at least *cuts* it. Perhaps it is best to say that in all these things Joseph acted as he was directed by a providence, under the influence of which he might have been led to do many things which he had not previously designed. The issue proves that the hand of God's wisdom and goodness directed, regulated, and governed every circumstance, and the result was glory to God in the highest, and on earth, peace and good will among men.

4. This chapter, which contains the unravelling of the plot, and wonderfully illustrates the mysteries of these particular providences, is one of the most interesting in the whole account: the speech of Joseph to his brethren, ver. 1–13, is inferior only to that of *Judah* in the preceding chapter. He saw that his brethren were confounded at his presence, that they were struck with his present power, and that they keenly remembered and deeply deplored their own guilt. It was necessary to comfort them, lest their hearts should have been overwhelmed with overmuch sorrow. How delicate and finely wrought is the apology he makes for them! the whole heart of the affectionate brother is at once seen in it—*art* is confounded and swallowed up by nature—" Be not grieved, nor angry with yourselves—it was not *you* that sent me hither, but *God.*" What he says also concerning his *father* shows the warmest feelings of a benevolent and filial heart. Indeed, the whole chapter is a master-piece of composition; and it is the more impressive because it is evidently *a simple relation of facts just as they occurred;* for no attempt is made to heighten the effect by rhetorical colouring or philosophical reflections; it is all simple, sheer nature, from beginning to end. It is a history that has no fellow, crowded with incidents as probable as they are true; where every passion is called into action, where every one acts up to his own character, and where nothing is *outre* in time, or extravagant in degree. Had not the history of Joseph formed a part of the sacred Scriptures, it would have been published in all the living languages of man, and read throughout the universe! But it contains *the things of God*, and to all such the *carnal mind* is *enmity.*

CHAPTER XLVI.

Jacob begins his journey to Egypt, comes to Beer-sheba, and offers sacrifices to God, 1. *God appears to him in a vision, gives him gracious promises, and assures him of his protection,* 2–4. *He proceeds, with his family and their cattle, on his journey towards Egypt,* 5–7. *A genealogical enumeration of the* seventy *persons who went down to Egypt,* 8, *&c. The posterity of* Jacob *by* Leah. Reuben *and his sons,* 9, Simeon *and his sons,* 10. Levi *and his sons,* 11. Judah *and his sons,* 12. Issachar *and his sons,* 13.

And Zebulun *and his sons*, 14. *All the posterity of* Jacob *by* Leah, thirty and three, 15. *The posterity of* Jacob *by* Zilpah. Gad *and his sons*, 16. Asher *and his sons*, 17. *All the posterity of* Jacob *by* Zilpah, sixteer, 18. *The posterity of* Jacob *by* Rachel. Joseph *and his sons*, 19, 20. Benjamin *and his sons*, 21. *All the posterity of* Jacob *by* Rachel, fourteen, 22. *The posterity of* Jacob *by* Bilhah. Dan *and his sons*, 23. Naphtali *and his sons*, 24. *All the posterity of* Jacob *by* Bilhah, seven, 25. *All the* immediate *descendants of Jacob by his* four *wives*, threescore and six, 26 ; *and all the descendants of the house of Jacob*, seventy *souls*, 27. *Judah is sent before to inform Joseph of his father's coming*, 28. *Joseph goes to* Goshen *to meet Jacob*, 29. *Their affecting interview*, 30. *Joseph proposes to return to Pharaoh, and inform him of the arrival of his family*, 31, *and of their occupation, as keepers of cattle*, 32. *Instructs them what to say when called before Pharaoh, and questioned by him, that they might be permitted to dwell unmolested in the land of* Goshen, 33, 34.

A. M. 2298.
B. C. 1706.

AND Israel took his journey
with all that he had, and came
to [a] Beer-sheba, and offered sacrifices [b] unto
the God of his father Isaac.
2 And God spake unto Israel [c] in the visions
of the night, and said, Jacob, Jacob. And
he said, Here *am* I.
3 And he said, I *am* God, [d] the God of thy
father: fear not to go down into Egypt; for
I will there [e] make of thee a great nation:
4 [f] I will go down with thee into Egypt,
and I will also surely [g] bring thee up *again*:
and [h] Joseph shall put his hand upon thine eyes.
5 And [i] Jacob rose up from Beer-sheba: and
the sons of Israel carried Jacob their father,
and their little ones, and their wives,
in the wagons [k] which Pharaoh had
sent to carry him.
6 And they took their cattle, and their goods,
which they had gotten in the land of Canaan,
and came into Egypt, [l] Jacob, and all his seed
with him:
7 His sons, and his sons' sons with him,
his daughters, and his sons' daughters, and all
his seed brought he with him into Egypt.
8 And [m] these *are* the names of the children
of Israel, which came into Egypt, Jacob and
his sons: [n] Reuben, Jacob's first-born.
9 And the sons of Reuben; Hanoch, and
Phallu, and Hezron, and Carmi.

A. M. 2298.
B. C. 1706.

[a] Chap. xxi. 31, 33; xxviii. 10.——[b] Chap. xxvi. 24, 25; xxviii. 13; xxxi. 42.——[c] Chap. xv. 1; Job xxxiii. 14, 15.——[d] Chap. xxviii. 13.——[e] Chap. xii. 2; Deut. xxvi. 5.——[f] Chap. xxviii. 15; xlviii. 21.

[g] Chap. xv. 16; l. 13, 24, 25; Exod. iii. 8.——[h] Chap. l. 1.——[i] Acts vii. 15.——[k] Chap. xlv. 19, 21.——[l] Deut. xxvi. 5; Josh. xxiv. 4; Psa. cv. 23; Isa. lii. 4.——[m] Exod. i. 1; vi. 14.——[n] Num. xxvi. 5; 1 Chron. v. 1.

NOTES ON CHAP. XLVI.

Verse 1. *And came to Beer-sheba*] This place appears to be mentioned, not only because it was the way from *Hebron*, where Jacob resided, to Egypt, whither he was going, but because it was a *consecrated* place, a place where God had appeared to Abraham, chap. xxi. 33, and to Isaac, chap. xxvi. 23, and where Jacob is encouraged to expect a manifestation of the same goodness: he chooses therefore to begin his journey with a visit to *God's house;* and as he was going into a strange land, he feels it right to *renew his covenant* with God by *sacrifice*. There is an old proverb which applies strongly to this case: "Prayers and provender never hinder any man's journey." He who would travel safely must take God with him.

Verse 3. *Fear not to go down into Egypt*] It appears that there had been some doubts in the patriarch's mind relative to the propriety of this journey; he found, from the confession of his own sons, how little they were to be trusted. But every doubt is dispelled by this Divine manifestation. 1. He may go down confidently, no evil shall befall him. 2. Even in Egypt the covenant shall be fulfilled, God will make of him *there a great nation*. 3. God himself will acompany him on his journey, be with him in the strange land, and even bring back his bones to rest with those of his fathers. 4. He shall see Joseph, and this same beloved son shall be with him in his last hours, and do the last kind office for him. *Joseph shall put his hand upon thine eyes*. It is not likely that Jacob would have at all attempted to go down to Egypt, had he not received these assurances from God; and it is very likely that he offered his sacrifice merely to obtain this information. It was now a time of famine in Egypt, and God had forbidden his father Isaac to go down to Egypt when there was a famine there, chap. xxvi. 1–3; besides, he may have had some general intimation of the prophecy delivered to his grandfather Abraham, that his seed should be *afflicted* in Egypt, chap. xv. 13, 14; and he also knew that Canaan, not Egypt, was to be the inheritance of his family, chap. xii., &c. On all these accounts it was necessary to have the most explicit directions from God, before he should take such a journey.

Verse 7. *All his seed brought he with him into Egypt.*] When Jacob went down into Egypt he was in the *one hundred and thirtieth* year of his age, *two hundred and fifteen* years after the promise was made to Abraham, chap. xii. 1–4, in the year of the world 2298, and before Christ 1706.

Verse 8. *These are the names of the children of Israel*] It may be necessary to observe here, *First*, that several of these names are expressed differently elsewhere, *Jemuel* for *Nemuel*, *Jachin* for *Jarib*, *Gershon* for *Gershom*, *&c.*; compare Num. xxvi. 12; 1 Chron. iv. 24. But it is no uncommon case for the same person to have different names, or the same name to be differently pronounced; see chap. xxv. 15.

A. M. 2298. B. C. 1706.

10 And [o] the sons of Simeon; [p] Jemuel, and Jamin, and Ohad, and [q] Jachin, and [r] Zohar, and Shaul the son of a Canaanitish woman.

11 And the sons of [s] Levi; [t] Gershon, Kohath, and Merari.

12 And the sons of [u] Judah; Er, and Onan, and Shelah, and Pharez, and Zarah: but [v] Er and Onan died in the land of Canaan. And [w] the sons of Pharez were Hezron and Hamul.

13 [x] And the sons of Issachar; Tola, and [y] Phuvah, and Job, and Shimron.

14 And the sons of Zebulun; Sered, and Elon, and Jahleel.

15 These *be* the sons of Leah, which she bare unto Jacob in Padan-aram, with his daughter Dinah: all the souls of his sons and his daughters *were* thirty and three.

A. M. 2298. B. C. 1706.

16 And the sons of Gad; [z] Ziphion, and Haggi, Shuni, and [a] Ezbon, Eri, and [b] Arodi, and Areli.

17 [c] And the sons of Asher; Jimnah, and Ishuah, and Isui, and Beriah, and Serah their sister: and the sons of Beriah; Heber, and Malchiel.

18 [d] These *are* the sons of Zilpah, [e] whom Laban gave to Leah, his daughter; and these she bare unto Jacob, *even* sixteen souls.

19 The sons of Rachel [f] Jacob's wife; Joseph and Benjamin.

20 [g] And unto Joseph in the land of Egypt were born Manasseh and Ephraim, which Asenath the daughter of Poti-pherah [h] priest of On bare unto him.

[o] Exod. vi. 15; 1 Chron. iv. 24.——[p] Or, *Nemuel.*——[q] Or, *Jarib.*——[r] Or, *Zerah*; 1 Chron. iv. 24.——[s] 1 Chron. vi. 1, 16.——[t] Or, *Gershom.*——[u] 1 Chron. ii. 3; iv. 21.——[v] Chap. xxxviii. 3, 7, 10.——[w] Chap. xxxviii. 29; 1 Chron. ii. 5.

[x] 1 Chron. vii. 1.——[y] Or, *Puah*, and *Jashub.*——[z] Num. xxvi. 15, &c., *Zephon.*——[a] Or, *Ozni.*——[b] Or, *Arod.*——[c] 1 Chron. vii 30.——[d] Chap. xxx. 10.——[e] Chap. xxix. 24.——[f] Chap. xliv. 27.——[g] Chap. xli. 50.——[h] Or, *prince.*

Secondly, that it is probable that some names in this list are brought in by *prolepsis* or *anticipation*, as the persons were born (probably) during the *seventeen* years which Jacob sojourned in Egypt, see ver. 12. *Thirdly*, that the families of some are entered more at large than others because of their peculiar respectability, as in the case of *Judah*, *Joseph*, and *Benjamin*; but see the tables under verse 20.

Verse 12. *The sons of Pharez were Hezron and Hamul.*] It is not likely that Pharez was more than *ten* years of age when he came into Egypt, and if so he could not have had children; therefore it is necessary to consider *Hezron* and *Hamul* as being born during the *seventeen* years that Jacob sojourned in Egypt, see on ver. 8: and it appears necessary, for several reasons, to take these *seventeen* years into the account, as it is very probable that what is called *the going down into Egypt* includes the *seventeen* years which Jacob spent there.

Verse 20. *Unto Joseph—were born Manasseh and Ephraim*] There is a remarkable addition here in the Septuagint, which must be noticed: *Εγενοντο δε υἱοι Μανασση, οὑς ετεκεν αυτῳ ἡ παλλακη ἡ Συρα, τον Μαχιρ· Μαχιρ δε εγεννησε τον Γαλααδ. Υἱοι δε Εφραιμ αδελφου Μανασση, Σουταλααμ και Τααμ. Υἱοι δε Σουταλααμ, Εδεμ·* *These were the sons of Manasseh whom his Syrian concubine bore unto him: Machir; and Machir begat Galaad. The sons of Ephraim, Manasseh's brother, were Sutalaam and Taam; and the sons of Sutalaam, Edem.* These add *five* persons to the list, and make out the number given by *Stephen*, Acts vii. 14, which it seems he had taken from the text of the *Septuagint*, unless we could suppose that the text of Stephen had been *altered* to make it correspond to the Septuagint, of which there is not the slightest evidence from ancient MSS. or versions. The addition in the Septuagint is not found in either the Hebrew or the Samaritan at present; and some suppose that it was taken either from Num. xxvi. 29, 35, or 1 Chron. vii. 14–20, but in none of these places does the addition appear *as it stands* in the Septuagint, though some of the names are found interspersed. Various means have been proposed to find the *seventy* persons in the text, and to reconcile the Hebrew with the Septuagint and the New Testament.

A table given by *Scheuchzer*, extracted from the *Memoires de Trevoux*, gives the following general view:

The *twelve* sons of JACOB with their *children* and *grandchildren*.

Reuben and his *four* sons	5	
Simeon and his *six* sons	7	
Levi and his *three* sons	4	
Judah and his *seven* sons and grandsons	8	
Issachar and his *four* sons	5	
Zebulun and his *three* sons	4	
Total sons of JACOB and LEAH	——	33
Gad and his *seven* sons	8	
Asher and his *seven* sons and grandsons	8	
Total sons of JACOB and ZILPAH	——	16
Joseph and his *two* sons	3	
Benjamin and his *ten* sons	11	
Total sons of JACOB and RACHEL	——	14
Dan and his son	2	
Naphtali and his *four* sons	5	
Total sons of JACOB and BILHAH	——	7
Total sons of *Jacob* and his *four wives*	——	70

"To harmonize this with the *Septuagint* and St. *Stephen*, Acts vii. 14, to the number *sixty-six* (all the souls that came out of Jacob's loins, ver. 26) add *nine* of the patriarchs' wives, Judah's wife being already dead in Canaan, (chap. xxxviii. 12,) Benjamin being

A. M. 2298. B. C. 1706.

21 [i] And the sons of Benjamin *were* Bela, and Becher, and Ashbel, Gera, and Naaman, [k] Ehi, and Rosh, [l] Muppim, and [m] Huppim, and Ard.

22 These *are* the sons of Rachel, which were born to Jacob: all the souls *were* fourteen.

23 [n] And the sons of Dan; [o] Hushim.

24 [p] And the sons of Naphtali; Jahzeel, and Guni, and Jezer, and Shillem.

25 [q] These *are* the sons of Bilhah, [r] which Laban gave unto Rachel his daughter, and she bare these unto Jacob: all the souls *were* seven.

26 [s] All the souls that came with Jacob into Egypt, which came out of his [t] loins, besides Jacob's sons' wives, all the souls *were* threescore and six;

27 And the sons of Joseph, which were born him in Egypt, *were* two souls: [u] all the souls of the house of Jacob, which came into Egypt, *were* threescore and ten.

28 And he sent Judah before him unto Joseph, [v] to direct his face unto Goshen; and they came [w] into the land of Goshen.

29 And Joseph made ready his chariot, and went up to meet Israel his father, to Goshen,

[i] 1 Chron. vii. 6; viii. 1.——[k] Num. xxvi. 38; *Ahiram.* [l] Numbers xxvi. 39; *Shupham*; 1 Chron. vii. 12; *Shuppim.* [m] *Hupham*, Num. xxvi. 39.——[n] 1 Chron. vii. 12.——[o] Or, *Shuham*; Num. xxvi. 42.——[p] 1 Chron. vii. 13.——[q] Chap. xxx. 5, 7. [r] Ch. xxix. 29.——[s] Exod. i. 5.——[t] Heb. *thigh*; chap. xxxv. 11. [u] Deut. x. 22; see Acts vii. 14.——[v] Ch. xxxi. 21.——[w] Ch. xlvii. 1.

supposed to be as yet unmarried, and the wife of Joseph being already in Egypt, and therefore out of the case: the number will amount to *seventy-five*, which is that found in the Acts."—*Universal History*.

Dr. Hales' method is more simple, and I think more satisfactory: "Moses states that all the souls that came with Jacob into Egypt, *which issued from his loins*, (except his sons' wives,) were *sixty-six* souls, Gen. xlvi. 26; and this number is thus collected:—

JACOB'S children, eleven sons and one daughter .	12
Reuben's sons	4
Simeon's sons	6
Levi's sons	3
Judah's three sons and two *grandsons*	5
Issachar's sons	4
Zebulun's sons	3
Gad's sons	7
Asher's four sons, one daughter, and two grandsons	7
Dan's son	1
Naphtali's sons	4
Benjamin's sons	10
	66

"If to these *sixty-six* children, and grandchildren, and great grandchildren, we add *Jacob* himself, *Joseph* and his *two sons*, the amount is *seventy*, the whole amount of Jacob's family which settled in Egypt.

"In this statement the wives of Jacob's sons, who formed part of the household, are omitted; but they amounted to *nine*, for of the *twelve* wives of the *twelve* sons of Jacob, Judah's wife was dead, chap. xxxviii. 12, and Simeon's also, as we may collect from his youngest son *Shaul* by a Canaanitess, ver. 10, and Joseph's wife was already in Egypt. These *nine* wives, therefore, added to the *sixty-six*, give *seventy-five* souls, the whole amount of Jacob's household that went down with him to Egypt; critically corresponding with the statement in the New Testament, that 'Joseph sent for his father *Jacob and all his kindred*, amounting to *seventy-five* souls.' The expression *all his kindred*, including the wives which were Joseph's kindred, not only by *affinity*, but also by consanguinity, being probably of the families of *Esau*, *Ishmael*, or *Keturah*. Thus does the New Testament furnish an admirable comment on the Old."—*Analysis*, vol., ii. p. 159.

It is necessary to observe that this statement, which appears on the whole the most consistent, supposes that *Judah* was married when about *fourteen* years of age, his son *Er* at the *same* age, *Pharez* at the *same*, *Asher* and his fourth son *Beriah* under *twenty*, *Benjamin* about *fifteen*, and *Joseph's* sons and grandsons about *twenty*. But this is not improbable, as the children of Israel must all have married at a very early age, to have produced in about *two hundred and fifteen* years no less than *six hundred thousand* persons above *twenty* years old, besides women and children.

Verse 28. *He sent Judah before him unto Joseph*] Judah was certainly a man of sense, and also an eloquent man; and of him Joseph must have had a very favourable opinion from the speech he delivered before him, chap. xliv. 18, &c.; he was therefore chosen as the most proper person to go before and announce Jacob's arrival to his son Joseph.

To direct his face unto Goshen] The land of Goshen is the same, according to the Septuagint, as the land of Rameses, and Goshen itself the same as Heroopolis, Ἡρωων πολις *Heroon-polis*, the *city of heroes*, a name by which it went in the days of the *Septuagint*, and which it still retained in the time of Josephus, for he makes use of the same term in speaking of this place. See on ver. 34.

Verse 29. *And Joseph made ready his chariot*] מרכבתו *mercabto*. In chap. xli. 43, we have the first mention of a chariot, and if the translation be correct, it is a proof that the arts were not in a rude state in Egypt even at this early time. When we find *wagons* used to transport *goods* from place to place, we need not wonder that these suggested the idea of forming *chariots* for carrying *persons*, and especially those of high rank and authority. *Necessity* produces arts, and *arts* and *science* produce not only an increase of the *conveniences* but also of the *refinements* and *luxuries* of life. It has been supposed that a *chariot* is not intended here; for as the word מרכבה *mercabah*, which we and most of the ancient versions translate *chariot*, comes from רכב *rachab*, *he rode*, saddling his horse may be all that is intended. But it is more

A. M. 2298.
B. C. 1706.

and presented himself unto him;
and he [x] fell on his neck, and wept
on his neck a good while.
30 And Israel said unto Joseph, [y] Now let
me die, since I have seen thy face, because
hou *art* yet alive.
31 And Joseph said unto his brethren, and
unto his father's house, [z] I will go up, and
show Pharaoh, and say unto him, My brethren, and my father's house, which *were* in
the land of Canaan, are come unto me.
32 And the men *are* shepherds, for [a] their
trade hath been to feed cattle; and
they have brought their flocks, and
their herds, and all that they have.
33 And it shall come to pass, when Pharaoh
shall call you, and shall say, [b] What *is* your
occupation?
34 That ye shall say, Thy servants' [c] trade
hath been about cattle [d] from our youth even
until now, both we, *and* also our fathers;
that ye may dwell in the land of Goshen; for
every shepherd *is* [e] an abomination unto the
Egyptians.

[x] So chap. xlv. 14.——[y] So Luke ii. 29, 30.——[z] Chap. xlvii. 1. [a] Heb. *they are men of cattle.*——[b] Chap. xlvii. 2, 3.

[c] Ver. 32.——[d] Chap. xxx. 35; xxxiv. 5; xxxvii. 12.——[e] Chap. xliii. 32; Exod. viii. 26.

likely to signify a chariot, as the verb אסר *asar*, which signifies to *bind*, *tie*, or *yoke*, is used; and not חבש *chabash*, which signifies to *saddle*.

Fell on his neck] See chap. xlv. 14.

Verse 30. *Now let me die, since I have seen thy face*] Perhaps old *Simeon* had this place in view when, seeing the salvation of Israel, he said, *Lord, now lettest thou thy servant depart in peace, &c.*, Luke ii. 29.

Verse 34. *Thy servants' trade hath been about cattle*] "The land of Goshen, called also the land of *Rameses*, lay east of the Nile, by which it was never overflowed, and was bounded by the mountains of the Thebaid on the south, by the Nile and Mediterranean on the west and north, and by the Red Sea and desert of Arabia on the east. It was the Heliopolitan nome or district, and its capital was called ON. Its proper name was *Geshen*, the country of *grass* or *pasturage*, or of the *shepherds*, in opposition to the rest of the land which was *sown* after having been overflowed by the Nile."—*Bruce*. As this land was both fruitful and pleasant, Joseph wished to fix his family in that part of Egypt; hence he advises them to tell Pharaoh that their trade had been in *cattle* from their youth: and because every shepherd is an abomination to the Egyptians, hence he concluded that there would be less difficulty to get them quiet settlement in *Goshen*, as they would then be separated from the Egyptians, and consequently have the free use of all their religious customs. This scheme succeeded, and the consequence was the preservation both of their religion and their lives, though some of their posterity did afterwards corrupt themselves; see Ezek. xx. 8; Amos v. 26. As it is well known that the Egyptians had *cattle* and *flocks* themselves, and that Pharaoh even requested that some of Joseph's brethren should *be made rulers over his cattle*, how could it be said, as in ver. 34, *Every shepherd is an abomination unto the Egyptians?* Three reasons may be assigned for this: 1. Shepherds and feeders of cattle were usually a sort of lawless, freebooting banditti, frequently making inroads on villages, &c., carrying off cattle, and whatever spoils they could find. This might probably have been the case formerly, for it is well known it has often been the case since. On this account such persons must have been universally detested. 2. They must have abhorred *shepherds* if *Manetho's* account of the *hycsos* or *king-shepherds* can be credited. Hordes of marauders under this name, from Arabia, Syria, and Ethiopia, (whose chief occupation, like the *Bedouin Arabs* of the present day, was to keep flocks,) made a powerful irruption into Egypt, which they subdued and ruled with great tyranny for 259 years. Now, though they had been expelled from that land some considerable time before this, yet their name, and all persons of a similar occupation, were execrated by the Egyptians, on account of the depredations and long-continued ravages they had committed in the country. 3. The last and probably the best reason why the Egyptians abhorred such shepherds as the Israelites were, was, they sacrificed *those very animals*, the ox particularly, and the SHEEP, which the Egyptians held sacred. Hence the Roman historian *Tacitus*, speaking of the Jews, says: "Cæso ARIETE velut in contumelia AMMONIS; Bos quoque immolatur, quem Ægyptii APIM colunt." "They sacrifice the *ram* in order to insult *Jupiter Ammon*, and they sacrifice the *ox*, which the Egyptians worship under the name of *Apis*." Though some contend that this idolatry was not as yet established in Egypt, and that the *king-shepherds* were either after the time of Joseph, or that *Manetho* by them intends the *Israelites* themselves; yet, as the arguments by which these conjectures are supported are not sufficient to overthrow those which are brought for the support of the contrary opinions, and as there was evidently an *established religion* and *priesthood* in Egypt before Joseph's time, (for we find the priests had a certain portion of the land of Egypt which was held so sacred that Joseph did not attempt to buy it in the time of the famine, when he bought all the land which belonged to the people, chap. xlvii. 20-22,) and as that established priesthood was in all likelihood idolatrous, and as the worship of *Apis* under the form of an *ox* was one of the most ancient forms of worship in Egypt, we may rest tolerably certain that it was chiefly on this account that the shepherds, or those who fed on and sacrificed these objects of their worship, were an abomination to the Egyptians. *Calmet* has entered into this subject at large, and to his notes I must refer those readers who wish for farther information. See on chap. xliii. 32.

ON the principal subject of this chapter, the going down of Jacob and his family into Egypt, Bishop War-

burton, in his Divine Legation of Moses, makes the following judicious reflections: "The promise God made to Abraham, to give his posterity the land of Canaan, could not be performed till that family was grown strong enough to take and keep possession of it. In the meantime, therefore, they were necessitated to reside among idolaters, and to reside unmixed; but whoever examines their history will see that the Israelites had ever a violent propensity to join themselves to Gentile nations, and practise their manners. God therefore, in his infinite wisdom, brought them into Egypt, and kept them there during this period, the only place where they could remain for so long a time safe and unconfounded with the natives, the ancient Egyptians being by numerous institutions forbidden all fellowship with strangers, and bearing besides a particular aversion to the profession of the Israelites, who were shepherds. Thus the natural dispositions of the Israelites, which in Egypt occasioned their superstitions, and in consequence the necessity of a burdensome ritual, would in any other country have absorbed them into *Gentilism*, and confounded them with idolaters. From the Israelites going into Egypt arises a new occasion to adore the footsteps of Eternal Wisdom in his dispensations to his chosen people."

CHAPTER XLVII.

Joseph informs Pharaoh that his father and brethren are arrived in Goshen, 1. *He presents five of his brethren before the king,* 2, *who questions them concerning their occupation; they inform him that they are* shepherds, *and request permission to dwell in the land of* Goshen, 3, 4. *Pharaoh consents, and desires that some of the most active of them should be made rulers over his cattle,* 5, 6. *Joseph presents his father to Pharaoh,* 7, *who questions him concerning his age,* 8, *to which Jacob returns an affecting answer, and blesses* Pharaoh, 9, 10. *Joseph places his father and family in the land of* Rameses, (Goshen,) *and furnishes them with provisions,* 11, 12. *The famine prevailing in the land, the Egyptians deliver up all their* money *to Joseph to get food,* 13–15. *The next year they bring their* cattle, 16, 17. *The third, their* lands *and their* persons, 18–21. *The land of the priests Joseph does not buy, as it was a royal grant to them from Pharaoh,* 22. *The people receive seed to sow the land on condition that they shall give a* fifth *part of the produce to the king,* 23, 24. *The people agree, and Joseph makes it a law all over Egypt,* 25, 26. *The Israelites multiply exceedingly,* 27. *Jacob, having lived seventeen years in Goshen, and being one hundred and forty-seven years old,* 28, *makes Joseph promise not to bury him in Egypt, but in Canaan,* 29, 30. *Joseph promises and confirms it with an oath,* 31.

A. M. 2298.
B. C. 1706.

THEN Joseph [a] came and told
Pharaoh, and said, My father
and my brethren, and their flocks, and their
herds, and all that they have, are come out of
the land of Canaan; and, behold, they *are* in
[b] the land of Goshen.
2 And he took some of his brethren, *even*
five men, and [c] presented them unto Pharaoh.
3 And Pharaoh said unto his brethren,
[d] What *is* your occupation? And they said
unto Pharaoh, [e] Thy servants *are*
shepherds, both we, *and* also our
fathers.
4 (They said moreover unto Pharaoh,) [f] For
to sojourn in the land are we come; for thy
servants have no pasture for their flocks; [g] for
the famine *is* sore in the land of Canaan: now
therefore, we pray thee, let thy servants [h] dwell
in the land of Goshen.
5 And Pharaoh spake unto Joseph, saying,

[a] Chap. xlvi. 31.——[b] Chap. xlv. 10; xlvi. 28.——[c] Acts vii. 13. [d] Chap. xlvi. 33.——[e] Chap. xlvi. 34.

[f] Chap. xv. 13; Deut. xxvi. 5.——[g] Chap. xli. 27, 30, 31, 50, 56; xliii. 1; Acts vii. 11.——[h] Chap. xlvi. 34.

NOTES ON CHAP. XLVII.

Verse 2. *He took some of his brethren*] There is something very strange in the original; literally translated it signifies "from the end or extremity (מקצה *miktseh*) of his brethren he took five men." This has been understood *six* different ways. 1. Joseph took five of his brethren that came *first to hand*—at *random, without design or choice*. 2. Joseph took five of the *meanest-looking* of his brethren to present before Pharaoh, fearing if he had taken the *sightliest* that Pharaoh would detain them for his service, whereby their religion and morals might be corrupted. 3. Joseph took five of the *best made* and *finest-looking* of his brethren, and presented them before Pharaoh, wishing to impress his mind with a favourable opinion of the family which he had just now brought into Egypt, and to do himself honour. 4. Joseph took five of the *youngest* of his brethren. 5. He took five of the *eldest* of his brethren. 6. He took five from the *extremity* or *end* of his brethren, i. e., *some* of the *eldest* and *some* of the *youngest*, viz., Reuben, Simeon, Levi, Issachar, and Benjamin.—*Rab. Solomon.* It is certain that in Judges xviii. 2, the word may be understood as implying *dignity, valour, excellence*, and *pre-eminence: And the children of Dan sent of their family* FIVE *men* מקצותם *miktsotham*, not *from their coasts*, but of the *most eminent* or *excellent* they had; and it is probable they might have had their eye on what Joseph did here when they made their choice, choosing the same number, *five*, and of their *principal* men, as

A. M. 2298. B. C. 1706. Thy father and thy brethren are come unto thee:

6 [i] The land of Egypt *is* before thee; in the best of the land make thy father and brethren to dwell; [k] in the land of Goshen let them dwell: and if thou knowest *any* men of activity among them, then make them rulers over my cattle.

7 And Joseph brought in Jacob his father, and set him before Pharaoh: and Jacob blessed Pharaoh.

8 And Pharaoh said unto Jacob, [l] How old *art* thou?

9 And Jacob said unto Pharaoh, [m] The days of the years of my pilgrimage *are* a hundred and thirty years: [n] few and evil have the days of the years of my life been, and [o] have not attained unto the days of the years of the life of my fathers, in the days of their pilgrimage.

10 And Jacob [p] blessed Pharaoh, and went out from before Pharaoh. A. M. 2298. B. C. 1706.

11 And Joseph placed his father and his brethren, and gave them a possession in the land of Egypt, in the best of the land, in the land of [q] Rameses, [r] as Pharaoh had commanded.

12 And Joseph nourished his father, and his brethren, and all his father's household, with bread, [s] according to *their* families.[t]

13 And *there was* no bread in all the land; for the famine *was* very sore, [u] so that the land of Egypt, and *all* the land of Canaan, fainted by reason of the famine.

14 [v] And Joseph gathered up all the money that was found in the land of Egypt, and in the land of Canaan, for the corn which they bought: and Joseph brought the money into Pharaoh's house. A. M. cir. 2300. B. C. cir. 1704.

[i] Chap. xx. 15.——[k] Ver. 4.——[l] Heb. *how many are the days of the years of thy life?*——[m] Heb. xi. 9, 13; Psa. xxxix. 12. [n] Job xiv. 1.——[o] Chap. xxv. 7; xxxv. 28.——[p] Ver. 7.

[q] Exod. i. 11; xii. 37.——[r] Ver. 6.——[s] Or, *as a little child is nourished.*——[t] Heb. *according to the little ones;* chap. l. 21. [u] Chap. xli. 30; Acts vii. 11.——[v] Chap. xli. 56.

did Joseph, because the mission was important, *to go and search out the land*. But the word may be understood simply as signifying *some;* out of the *whole* of his brethren he took *only* five men, &c.

Verse 6. *In the best of the land make thy father and brethren to dwell; in the land of Goshen let them dwell*] So it appears that the land of Goshen was the *best of the land of Egypt*.

Men of activity] אנשי חיל *anshey chayil, stout* or *robust men*—such as were capable of bearing fatigue, and of rendering their authority respectable.

Rulers over my cattle.] מקנה *mikneh* signifies not only *cattle*, but *possessions* or *property* of any kind; though most usually *cattle* are intended, because in ancient times they constituted the principal part of a man's property. The word may be taken here in a more extensive sense, and the circumstances of the case seem obviously to require it. If every *shepherd* was an abomination to the Egyptians, however we may understand or qualify the expression, is it to be supposed that Pharaoh should desire that the *brethren* of his *prime minister*, of his *chief favourite*, should be employed in some of the very meanest offices in the land! We may therefore safely understand Pharaoh as expressing his will, that the brethren of Joseph should be appointed as *overseers* or *superintendents* of his *domestic* concerns, while Joseph superintended those of the *state*.

Verse 7. *Jacob blessed Pharaoh.*] Saluted him on his entrance with *Peace be unto thee*, or some such expression of respect and good will. For the meaning of the term *to bless*, as applied to God and man, see on chap. ii. 3.

Verse 9. *The days of the years of my pilgrimage*] מגורי *megurai*, of my *sojourning* or *wandering*. Jacob had always lived a migratory or wandering life, in different parts of Canaan, Mesopotamia, and Egypt, scarcely ever at rest; and in the places where he lived longest, always exposed to the fatigues of the field and the desert. Our word *pilgrim* comes from the French *pelerin* and *pelegrin*, which are corrupted from the Latin *peregrinus*, an *alien*, *stranger*, or *foreigner*, from the adverb *peregre, abroad, not at home*. The pilgrim was a person who took a journey, long or short, on some *religious account*, submitting during the time to many hardships and privations. A more appropriate term could not be conceived to express the *life of Jacob*, and the *motive* which induced him to live such a life. His journey to Padan-aram or Mesopotamia excepted, the principal part of his journeys were properly *pilgrimages*, undertaken in the course of God's providence *on a religious account*.

Have not attained unto the—life of my fathers] Jacob lived in the whole *one hundred and forty-seven* years; Isaac his father lived *one hundred and eighty;* and Abraham his grandfather, *one hundred and seventy-five*. These were *days of years* in comparison of the lives of the preceding patriarchs, some of whom lived nearly *ten centuries!*

Verse 14. *Gathered up all the money*] *i. e.*, by selling corn out of the public stores to the people; and this he did till the money failed, ver. 15, till all the money was exchanged for corn, and brought into Pharaoh's treasury. Besides the *fifth* part of the produce of the seven plentiful years, Joseph had bought additional corn with *Pharaoh's money* to lay up against the famine that was to prevail in the seven years of *dearth;* and it is very likely that this was sold out at the price for which it was bought, and the *fifth part*, which belonged to Pharaoh, sold out at the same price. And as money

A. M. 2301. B. C. 1703.
15 And when money failed in
the land of Egypt, and in the land
of Canaan, all the Egyptians came unto Joseph,
and said, Give us bread: for [w] why should
we die in thy presence? for the money faileth.
16 And Joseph said, Give your cattle; and
I will give you for your cattle, if money fail.
17 And they brought their cattle unto Joseph: and Joseph gave them bread *in exchange* for horses, and for the flocks, and for
the cattle of the herds, and for the asses; and
he [x] fed them with bread for all their cattle,
for that year.
A. M. 2302. B. C. 1702.
18 When that year was ended,
they came unto him the second
year, and said unto him, We will not hide *it*
from my lord, how that our money is spent;
my lord also hath our herds of cattle; there
is not aught left in the sight of my lord, but
our bodies and our lands:
19 Wherefore shall we die before thine eyes,
both we and our land? buy us and
our land for bread, and we and
our land will be servants unto Pharaoh: and
give *us* seed, that we may live, and not die, that
the land be not desolate.
20 And Joseph bought all the land of Egypt
for Pharaoh; for the Egyptians sold every
man his field, because the famine prevailed
over them: so the land became Pharaoh's.
21 (And as for the people, he removed them
to cities, from *one* end of the borders of
Egypt even to the *other* end thereof.)
22 [y] Only the land of the [z] priests bought
he not; for the priests had a portion *assigned
them* of Pharaoh, and did eat their portion
which Pharaoh gave them: wherefore they
sold not their lands.
A. M. 2203. B. C. 1701.
23 Then Joseph said unto the
people, Behold, I have bought you
this day and your land for Pharaoh: lo, *here
is* seed for you, and ye shall sow the land.

[w] Ver. 19.——[x] Heb. *led them.*——[y] Ezra vii. 24.

[z] Or, *princes;* chap. xli. 45; 2 Sam. viii. 18.

at that time could not be plentiful, the cash of the whole nation was thus exhausted, as far as that had circulated among the common people.

Verse 16. *Give your cattle*] This was the wisest measure that could be adopted, both for the preservation of the *people* and of the *cattle* also. As the people had not grain for their own sustenance, consequently they could have none for their cattle; hence the cattle were in the most imminent danger of starving; and the people also were in equal danger, as they must have divided a portion of that bought for themselves with the cattle, which for the sake of tillage, &c., they wished of course to preserve till the seven years of famine should end. The cattle being bought by Joseph were supported at the royal expense, and very likely returned to the people at the end of the famine; for how else could they cultivate their ground, transport their merchandise, &c., &c.? For this part of Joseph's conduct he certainly deserves high praise and no censure.

Verse 18. *When that year was ended*] The sixth year of the famine, *they came unto him the second year*, which was the *last* or *seventh* year of the famine, in which it was necessary to sow the land that there might be a crop the succeeding year; for Joseph, on whose prediction they *relied*, had foretold that the famine should continue only *seven years*, and consequently they expected the *eighth* year to be a fruitful year provided the land was *sowed*, without which, though the inundation of the land by the Nile might amount to the sixteen requisite cubits, there could be no crop.

Verse 19. *Buy us and our land for bread*] In times of famine in *Hindostan*, thousands of children have been sold to prevent their perishing. In the Burman empire the sale of *whole families* to discharge debts is very common.—*Ward's Customs.*

Verse 21. *And as for the people, he removed them to cities*] It is very likely that Joseph was influenced by no *political* motive in removing the people to the cities, but merely by a motive of *humanity* and *prudence*. As the corn was laid up in the cities he found it more convenient to bring them to the place where they might be conveniently fed; each being within the reach of an easy distribution. Thus then the *country* which could afford no sustenance was abandoned for the time being, that the people might be fed in those places where the provision was deposited.

Verse 22. *The land of the priests bought he not*] From this verse it is natural to infer that whatever the religion of Egypt was, it *was established by law* and supported by the *state*. Hence when Joseph bought all the lands of the Egyptians for Pharaoh, he bought not the land of the priests, for that was a *portion* assigned *them by Pharaoh; and they did eat*—did live on, that *portion*. This is the earliest account we have of an *established religion supported by the state*.

Verse 23. *I have bought you this day and your land for Pharaoh*] It fully appears that the kingdom of Egypt was previously to the time of Joseph a very limited monarchy. The king had his estates; the priests had their lands; and the common people their partrimony independently of both. The land of Rameses or Goshen appears to have been the king's land, ver. 11. The priests had their lands, which they did not sell to Joseph, ver. 22, 26; and that the people had lands independent of the crown, is evident from the purchases Joseph made, ver. 19, 20; and we may conclude from those purchases that Pharaoh had no power to levy taxes upon his subjects to increase his own revenue until he had bought the original right which each individual had in his possessions. And when Joseph bought this for the king he raised the

A. M. 2303.
B. C. 1701.

24 And it shall come to pass in
the increase, that ye shall give the
fifth *part* unto Pharaoh, and four parts shall
be your own, for seed of the field, and for
your food, and for them of your households,
and for food for your little ones.
25 And they said, Thou hast saved our
lives: [a] let us find grace in the sight of my
lord, and we will be Pharaoh's servants.
26 And Joseph made it a law over the land
of Egypt unto this day, *that* Pharaoh should
have the fifth *part;* [b] except the land of the
[c] priests only, *which* became not Pharaoh's.
27 And Israel [d] dwelt in the land of Egypt,
in the country of Goshen; and they had possessions therein, and [e] grew, and multiplied
exceedingly.

28 And Jacob lived in the land
of Egypt seventeen years: so [f] the
whole age of Jacob was a hundred forty and
seven years.

A. M. 2315.
B. C. 1689.

29 And the time [g] drew nigh that Israel must
die; and he called his son Joseph, and said
unto him, If now I have found grace in thy
sight, [h] put, I pray thee, thy hand under my
thigh, and [i] deal kindly and truly with me;
[k] bury me not, I pray thee, in Egypt.
30 But [l] I will lie with my fathers, and thou
shalt carry me out of Egypt, and [m] bury me
in their burying-place. And he said, I will
do as thou hast said.
31 And he said, Swear unto me; and he
sware unto him. And [n] Israel bowed himself
upon the bed's head.

[a] Chap. xxxiii. 15.——[b] Verse 22.——[c] Or, *princes;* verse 22. [d] Ver. 11.——[e] Chap. xlvi. 3.——[f] Heb. *the days of the years of his life;* see ver. 9.——[g] So Deut. xxxi. 14; 1 Kings ii. 1.

[h] Chap. xxiv. 2.——[i] Chap. xxiv. 49.——[k] So chap. l. 25. [l] 2 Sam. xix. 37.——[m] Ch. xlix. 29; l. 5, 13.——[n] Chap. xlviii. 2; 1 Kings i. 47; Heb. xi. 21.

crown an ample revenue, though he restored the lands, by obliging each to pay *one fifth* of the product to the king, ver. 24. And it is worthy of remark that the people of Egypt well understood the distinction between *subjects* and *servants;* for when they came to sell their land, they offered to sell *themselves* also, and said: *Buy us and our land, and we and our land will be servants unto Pharaoh,* ver. 19.

Diodorus Siculus, lib. i., gives the same account of the ancient constitution of Egypt. "The land," says he, "was divided into *three* parts: 1. *One* belonged to the PRIESTS, with which they provided all sacrifices, and maintained all the ministers of religion. 2. A *second* part was the KING'S, to support his court and family, and to supply expenses for wars if they should happen. Hence there were no *taxes,* the king having so ample an estate. 3. The *remainder* of the land belonged to the SUBJECTS, who appear (from the account of Diodorus) to have been all soldiers, a kind of standing militia, liable, at the king's expense, to serve in all wars for the preservation of the state." This was a constitution something like the *British;* the government appears to have been *mixed,* and the monarchy properly *limited,* till Joseph, by buying the land of the people, made the king in some sort despotic. But it does not appear that any improper use was made of this, as in much later times we find it still a comparatively limited monarchy.

Verse 24. *Ye shall give the fifth* part *unto Pharaoh*] This is precisely the case in *Hindostan;* the king has the *fifth part* of all the crops.

Verse 26. *And Joseph made it a law*] That the people should hold their land from the king, and give him the *fifth* part of the produce as a yearly tax. Beyond this it appears the king had no farther demands. The whole of this conduct of Joseph has been as strongly *censured* by some as *applauded* by others. It is natural for men to run into extremes in attacking or defending any position. Sober and judicious men will consider *what* Joseph did by *Divine appointment* as a prophet of God, and what he did merely as a *statesman* from the circumstances of the case, the complexion of the times, and the character of the people over whom he presided. When this is dispassionately done, we shall see much reason to adore *God,* applaud the *man,* and perhaps in some cases censure the *minister.* Joseph is never held up to our view as *an unerring* prophet of God. He was an honoured instrument in the hands of God of saving two nations from utter ruin, and especially of preserving that family from which the *Messiah* was to spring, and of perpetuating the true religion among them. In this character he is represented in the sacred pages. His conduct as the *prime minister* of Pharaoh was powerfully indicative of a deep and consummate politician, who had high notions of prerogative, which led him to use every prudent means to aggrandize his master, and at the same time to do what he judged *best on the whole* for the people he governed. See the conclusion of the 50th chapter.

Verse 29. *Put—thy hand under my thigh*] See on chap. xxiv. 2.

Verse 30. *I will lie with my fathers*] As God had promised the land of Canaan to Abraham and his posterity, Jacob considered it as a consecrated place, under the particular superintendence and blessing of God: and as Sarah, Abraham, and Isaac were interred near to Hebron, he in all probability wished to lie, not only in the same place, but in the same grave; and it is not likely that he would have been solicitous about this, had he not considered that promised land as being a *type of the rest that remains for the people of God,* and a *pledge* of the *inheritance* among the saints in light.

Verse 31. *And Israel bowed himself upon the bed's head.*] Jacob was now both old and feeble, and we may suppose him reclined on his couch when Joseph came; that he afterwards sat up erect (see chap.

xlviii. 2) while conversing with his son, and receiving his oath and promise; and that when this was finished he *bowed himself upon the bed's head*—exhausted with the conversation, he again reclined himself on his bed as before. This seems to be the simple meaning, which the text, unconnected with any religious system or prejudice, naturally proposes. But because שחה *shachah*, signifies not only to *bow* but to *worship*, because acts of religious worship were performed by *bowing* or *prostration*, and because מטה *mittah*, *a bed*, by the change of the *points*, only becomes *matteh*, a staff, in which sense the Septuagint took it, translating the original words thus: *Και προσεκυνησεν Ισραηλ επι το ακρον της ραβδου αυτου, and Israel worshipped upon the top of his staff*, which the writer of the Epistle to the Hebrews, chap. xi. 21, quotes *literatim*; therefore some have supposed that Jacob certainly had a *carved image* on the head or top of his staff, to which he paid a species of adoration; or that he bowed himself to the staff or sceptre of Joseph, thus fulfilling the prophetic import of his son's dreams! The sense of the *Hebrew text* is given above. If the reader prefers the sense of the *Septuagint* and the Epistle to the Hebrews, the meaning is, that Jacob, through feebleness, supported himself with a staff, and that, when he got the requisite assurance from Joseph that his dead body should be carried to Canaan, leaning on his staff he bowed his head in adoration to God, who had supported him all his life long, and hitherto ful filled all his promises.

CHAPTER XLVIII.

Joseph, hearing that his father was near death, took his two sons Ephraim *and* Manasseh, *and went to* Goshen *to visit him*, 1. *Jacob strengthens himself to receive them*, 2. *Gives Joseph an account of* God's *appearing to him at Luz, and repeating the promise*, 3, 4. *Adopts* Ephraim *and* Manasseh *as his own sons*, 5, 6. *Mentions the death of Rachel at Ephrath*, 7. *He blesses Ephraim and Manasseh, preferring the former, who was the younger, to his elder brother*, 8–17. *Joseph, supposing his father had mistaken in giving the right of primogeniture to the youngest, endeavours to correct him*, 18. *Jacob shows that he did it* designedly, *prophecies much good concerning both; but sets Ephraim the youngest* before *Manasseh*, 19, 20. *Jacob speaks of his death, and predicts the return of his posterity from Egypt*, 21. *And gives Joseph a portion above his brethren, which he had taken from the Amorites*, 22.

A. M. 2315. B. C. 1689.

AND it came to pass after these things, that *one* told Joseph, Behold, thy father *is* sick: and he took with him his two sons, Manasseh and Ephraim.
2 And *one* told Jacob, and said, Behold, thy son Joseph cometh unto thee: and Israel strengthened himself, and sat upon the bed.
3 And Jacob said unto Joseph, God almighty appeared unto me at [a] Luz in the land of Canaan, and blessed me,
4 And said unto me, Behold, I will make thee fruitful, and multiply thee, and I will make of thee a multitude of people; and will give this land to thy seed after thee, [b] *for* an everlasting possession.
5 And now thy [c] two sons, Ephraim and Manasseh, which were born unto thee in the land of Egypt, before I came unto thee into Egypt, *are* mine; as Reuben and Simeon, they shall be mine.
6 And thy issue, which thou begettest after them, shall be thine, *and* shall be called after the name of their brethren in their inheritance.
7 And as for me, when I came from Padan, [d] Rachel died by me in the land of Canaan

[a] Ch. xxviii. 13, 19; xxxv. 6, 9, &c.—[b] Ch. xvii. 8.—[c] Ch. xli. 50; xlvi. 20; Josh. xiii. 7; xiv. 4.—[d] Ch. xxxv. 9, 16, 19.

NOTES ON CHAP. XLVIII.

Verse 1. One *told Joseph, Behold, thy father* is *sick*] He was ill before, and Joseph knew it; but it appears that a messenger had been now despatched to inform Joseph that his father was apparently at the point of death.

Verse 2. *Israel strengthened himself, and sat upon the bed.*] He had been confined to his bed before, (see chap. xlvii. 31,) and now, hearing that Joseph was come to see him, he made what efforts his little remaining strength would admit, to sit up in bed to receive his son. This verse proves that a *bed*, not a *staff*, is intended in the preceding chapter, ver. 31.

Verse 3. *God Almighty*] אל שדי *El Shaddai, the all-sufficient God*, the *Outpourer and Dispenser of mercies*, (see chap. xvii. 1,) *appeared to me at Luz*, afterwards called *Beth-El*; see chap. xxviii. 13; xxxv. 6, 9.

Verse 5. *And now thy two sons, Ephraim and Manasseh*—are *mine*] I now adopt them into my own family, and they shall have their place among my twelve sons, and be treated in every respect as those, and have an equal interest in all the spiritual and temporal blessings of the covenant.

Verse 7. *Rachel died by me, &c.*] Rachel was the wife of Jacob's choice, and the object of his unvarying affection; he loved her in life—he loves her in death: many waters cannot quench love, neither can the floods drown it. A match of a man's own making, when guided by reason and religion, will necessarily be a happy one. When fathers and mothers make

A. M. 2315. B. C. 1689.

in the way, when yet *there was* but a little way to come unto Ephrath: and I buried her there in the way of Ephrath; the same *is* Beth-lehem.

8 And Israel beheld Joseph's sons, and said, Who *are* these?

9 And Joseph said unto his father, [e] They *are* my sons, whom God hath given me in this *place*. And he said, Bring them, I pray thee, unto me, and [f] I will bless them.

10 (Now [g] the eyes of Israel were [h] dim for age, *so that* he could not see.) And he
brought them near unto him; and he
[i] kissed them, and embraced them.

A. M. 2315. B. C. 1689.

11 And Israel said unto Joseph, [k] I had not thought to see thy face: and lo, God hath showed me also thy seed.

12 And Joseph brought them out from between his knees, and he bowed himself with his face to the earth.

13 And Joseph took them both, Ephraim in his right hand toward Israel's left hand, and Manasseh in his left hand toward Israel's right hand, and brought *them* near unto him.

[e] So chapter xxxiii. 5.—[f] Chapter xxvii. 4.—[g] Chapter xxvii. 1.

[h] Heb. *heavy;* Isaiah vi. 10; lix. 1.—[i] Chap. xxvii. 27. [k] Chap. xlv. 26.

matches for their children, which are dictated by motives, not of affection, but merely of convenience, worldly gain, &c., &c., such matches are generally wretched; it is *Leah* in the place of *Rachel* to the end of life's pilgrimage.

Verse 8. *Who* are *these?*] At verse 10 it is said, that Jacob's eyes were dim for age, that he *could not see*—could not discern any object unless it were near him; therefore, though he saw Ephraim and Manasseh, yet he could not *distinguish* them till they were brought nigh unto him.

Verse 11. *I had not thought to see thy face*] There is much delicacy and much tenderness in these expressions. He feels himself now amply recompensed for his long grief and trouble on account of the supposed death of Joseph, in seeing not only himself but his two sons, whom God, by an especial act of favour, is about to add to the number of his own. Thus we find that as Reuben and Simeon were heads of two distinct tribes in Israel, so were Ephraim and Manasseh; because Jacob, in a sort of sacramental way, had adopted them with equal privileges to those of his own sons.

Verse 12. *Joseph—bowed himself with his face to the earth.*] This act of Joseph has been extravagantly extolled by Dr. *Delaney* and others. "When I consider him on his knees to God," says Dr. Delaney, "I regard him as a poor *mortal* in the discharge of his *duty* to his CREATOR. When I behold him bowing before *Pharaoh*, I consider him in the *dutiful posture of a subject to his prince*. But when I see him *bending to the earth* before a *poor, old, blind, decrepit father*, I behold him with admiration and delight. How doth that humiliation exalt him!" This is insufferable! for it in effect says that it is a wondrous condescension in a young man, who, in the course of God's providence, with scarcely any efforts of his own, was raised to affluence and worldly grandeur, to show respect to his *father!* And that respect was the more *gratuitous* and *condescending*, because that father was *poor, old, blind*, and *decrepit!* The maxim of this most exceptionable flight of admiration is, that "children who have risen to affluence are not *obliged* to reverence their parents when reduced in their circumstances, and brought down by the weight of years and infirmities to the sides of the grave; and should they acknowledge and reverence them, it would be a mark of singular goodness, and be highly meritorious." Should positions of this kind pass without *reprehension?* I trow not. By the law of God and nature Joseph was as much bound to pay his dying father this *filial respect*, as he was to *reverence* his *king*, or to *worship* his *God*. As to myself, I must freely confess that I see nothing *peculiarly amiable* in this part of Joseph's conduct; he simply acquitted himself of a *duty* which God, nature, decency, and common sense, imperiously demanded of him, and all such in his circumstances, to discharge. To the present day children in the east, next to *God*, pay the deepest reverence to their *parents*. Besides, before *whom* was Joseph bowing? Not merely his *father*, but a most eminent PATRIARCH; one highly distinguished by the Lord, and one of the *three* of whom the Supreme Being speaks in the most favourable and affectionate manner; the *three* who received and transmitted the *true faith*, and kept unbroken the Divine covenant; I AM *the* GOD *of* ABRAHAM, *the* GOD *of* ISAAC, *and the* GOD *of* JACOB. He has never said, I am the GOD of JOSEPH. And if we compare the *father* and the *son* as *men*, we shall find that the latter was exceeded by the former in almost endless degrees. Joseph owed his advancement and his eminence to what some would call *good fortune*, and what *we* know to have been the *especial providence of God* working in his behalf, wholly *independent* of his own industry, &c., every event of that providence issuing in his favour. Jacob owed his own support and preservation, and the support and preservation of his numerous family, under God, to the continual exercise of the vast powers of a strong and vigorous mind, to which the providence of God seemed *ever in opposition;* because God chose to try to the uttermost the great gifts which he had bestowed. If therefore the most humble and abject *inferior* should reverence dignity and eminence raised to no common height, so should *Joseph* bow down his face to the earth before JACOB.

Besides, Joseph, in thus reverencing his father, only followed the customs of the Egyptians among whom he lived, who, according to Herodotus, (*Euterpe*, c. 80,) were particularly remarkable for the reverence they paid to old age. "For if a young person meet his senior, he instantly turns aside to make way for him; if an aged person enter an apartment, the youth always

A. M. 2315.
B. C. 1689.

14 And Israel stretched out his
right hand, and laid *it* upon Ephraim's
head, who *was* the younger, and his left hand
upon Manasseh's head, [l] guiding his hands
wittingly; for Manasseh *was* the first-born.
15 And [m] he blessed Joseph, and said, God,
[n] before whom my fathers Abraham and Isaac
did walk, the God which fed me
all my life long unto this day,
16 The Angel [o] which redeemed me from all
evil, bless the lads; and let [p] my name be
named on them, and the name of my fathers
Abraham and Isaac; and let them [q] grow into
a multitude in the midst of the earth.

[l] Ver. 19.——[m] Heb. xi. 21.——[n] Chap. xvii. 1; xxiv. 40.——[o] Chap. xxviii. 15; xxxi. 11, 13, 24; Psa. xxxiv. 22; cxxi. 7.——[p] Amos ix. 12; Acts xv. 17.——[q] Heb. *as fishes do increase*; see Num. i. 46; xxvi. 34, 37.

rise from their seats;" and Mr. *Savary* observes that the reverence mentioned by Herodotus is yet paid to old age on every occasion in Egypt. In Mohammedan countries the children sit as if dumb in the presence of their parents, never attempting to speak unless spoken to. Among the ancient Romans it was considered a crime worthy of death not to rise up in the presence of an aged person, and acting a contrary part was deemed an awful mark of the deep degeneracy of the times. Thus the satirist:—

Credebant hoc grande nefas, et morte piandum,
Si Juvenis VETULO *non* assurrexerat; et si
Barbato *cuicumque* puer. JUV. Sat. xiii., v. 54.

And had not men the *hoary heads revered,*
Or *boys* paid reverence when a *man* appear'd,
Both must have died. DRYDEN.

Indeed, though Dr. Delaney is much struck with what he thinks to be great and meritorious condescension and humility on the part of Joseph; yet we find the thing itself, the deepest reverence to parents and old age, practised by all the civilized nations in the world, not as a matter of meritorious courtesy, but as a point of rational and absolute duty.

Verse 14. *Israel stretched out his right hand, &c.*] Laying hands on the head was always used among the Jews in giving blessings, designating men to any office, and in the consecration of solemn sacrifices. This is the first time we find it mentioned; but we often read of it afterwards. See Num. xxvii. 18, 23; Deut. xxxiv. 9; Matt. xix. 13, 15; Acts vi. 6; 1 Tim. iv. 14. Jacob laid his right hand on the head of the younger, which we are told he did *wittingly*—well knowing what he was about, *for* (or *although*) *Manasseh was the first-born*, knowing by the Spirit of prophecy that Ephraim's posterity would be more powerful than that of Manasseh. It is observable how God from the beginning has preferred the younger to the elder, as *Abel* before *Cain; Shem* before *Japheth; Isaac* before *Ishmael; Jacob* before *Esau; Judah* and *Joseph* before *Reuben; Ephraim* before *Manasseh; Moses* before *Aaron;* and *David* before his *brethren.* "This is to be resolved entirely into the wise and secret counsel of God, so far as it regards temporal blessings and national privileges, as the apostle tells us, Rom. ix. 11; see the notes on chap. xxv. 23. But this preference has no concern with God's conferring a greater measure of his love and approbation on one person more than another; compare Gen. iv. 7, with Heb. xi. 4, and you will see that a difference in moral character was the sole cause why God preferred Abel to Cain."—*Dodd.* The grace that converts the soul certainly comes from the mere mercy of God, without any merit on man's part; and a sufficiency of this is offered to *every man*, Tit. ii. 11, 12. But it is not less certain that God *loves those best* who are *most faithful* to this grace.

Verse 15. *He blessed Joseph*] The father first, and then the sons afterwards. And this is an additional proof to what has been adduced under ver. 12, of Jacob's *superiority;* for the *less* is always blessed of the *greater.*

The God which fed me all my life long] Jacob is now standing on the verge of eternity, with his faith strong in God. He sees his life to be a series of mercies; and as he had been affectionately attentive, provident, and kind to his most helpless child, so has God been unto him; he has fed him all his life long; he plainly perceives that he owes every morsel of food which he has received to the mere mercy and kindness of God.

Verse 16. *The Angel which redeemed me from all evil*] הכלאך הגאל *hammalac haggoel.* The Messenger, the Redeemer or *Kinsman;* for so גאל *goel* signifies; for this term, in the law of Moses, is applied to that person whose right it is, from his being nearest *akin*, to redeem or purchase back a forfeited inheritance. But of whom does Jacob speak? We have often seen, in the preceding chapters, an angel of God appearing to the patriarchs; (see particularly chap. xvi. 7, and the note there;) and we have full proof that this was no *created* angel, but the Messenger of the Divine Council, the Lord Jesus Christ. Who then was the angel that *redeemed* Jacob, and whom he invoked to bless *Ephraim* and *Manasseh?* Is it not JESUS? He alone can be called *Goel*, the *redeeming Kinsman;* for he alone took part of our flesh and blood that the *right of redemption* might be *his;* and that the forfeited possession of the favour and image of God might be *redeemed, brought back*, and *restored* to all those who believe in his name. To have invoked any *other angel* or *messenger* in such a business would have been *impiety.* Angels bless not; to GOD *alone* this prerogative belongs. With what confidence may a truly religious father use these words in behalf of his children: "JESUS, the CHRIST, who hath *redeemed* me, bless the lads, redeem them also, and save them unto eternal life!"

Let my name be named on them] "Let them be ever accounted as a part of my own family; let them be true *Israelites*—persons who shall prevail with God as I have done; and *the name of Abraham*—being partakers of his faith; and the *name of Isaac*—let them be as remarkable for submissive obedience as he

A. M. 2315.
B. C. 1689.

17 And when Joseph saw that his father [r] laid his right hand upon the head of Ephraim, it [s] displeased him: and he held up his father's hand, to remove it from Ephraim's head unto Manasseh's head.

18 And Joseph said unto his father, Not so, my father: for this *is* the first-born; put thy right hand upon his head.

19 And his father refused, and said, [t] I know *it*, my son, I know *it*: he also shall become a people, and he also shall be great: but truly [u] his younger brother shall be greater than he, and his seed shall become a [v] multitude of nations.

20 And he blessed them that day, saying, [w] In thee shall Israel bless, saying, God make thee as Ephraim and as Manasseh: and he set Ephraim before Manasseh.

21 And Israel said unto Joseph, Behold, I die: but [x] God shall be with you, and bring you again unto the land of your fathers.

22 Moreover [y] I have given to thee one portion above thy brethren, which I took out of the hand [z] of the Amorite, with my sword and with my bow.

[r] Ver. 14.——[s] *Was evil in his eyes*; chap. xxviii. 8.——[t] Ver. 14.——[u] Num. i. 33, 35; ii. 19, 21; Deut. xxxiii. 17; Rev. vii. 6, 8.——[v] Heb. *fulness*.

[w] So Ruth iv. 11, 12.——[x] Chap. xlvi. 4; l. 24.——[y] Josh. xxiv. 32; 1 Chron. v. 2; John iv. 5.——[z] Chap. xv. 16; xxxiv. 28; Josh. xvii. 14, &c.

was. Let the virtues of Abraham, Isaac, and Jacob be accumulated in them, and invariably displayed by them!" These are the very words of adoption; and by the *imposition of hands*, the *invocation* of the *Redeemer*, and the solemn *blessing* pronounced, the adoption was completed. From this moment Ephraim and Manasseh had the same rights and privileges as Jacob's sons, which as the sons of *Joseph* they could never have possessed.

And let them grow into a multitude] וידגו לרב *veyidgu larob*; *Let them increase like fishes into a multitude.* Fish are the most prolific of all animals; see the instances produced on chap. i. 20. This prophetic blessing was verified in a most remarkable manner; see Num. xxvi. 34, 37; Deut. xxxiii. 17; Josh. xvii. 17. At one time the tribe of Ephraim amounted to 40,500 effective men, and that of Manasseh to 52,700, amounting in the whole to 93,200.

Verse 18. *Joseph said—Not so, my father*] Joseph supposed that his father had made a mistake in laying his right hand on the head of the youngest, because the *right hand* was considered as the most *noble*, and the instrument of conveying the highest dignities, and thus it has ever been considered among all nations, though the reason of it is not particularly obvious. Even in the heavens the *right hand of God* is the place of the *most exalted dignity*. It has been observed that Joseph spoke here as he was moved by *natural* affection, and that Jacob acted as he was influenced by the *Holy Spirit*.

Verse 20. *In thee shall Israel bless*] That is, In future generations the Israelites shall take their form of wishing prosperity to any nation or family from the circumstance of the good which it shall be known that God has done to Ephraim and Manasseh: *May God make thee as fruitful as Ephraim, and multiply thee as Manasseh!* So, to their daughters when married, the Jewish women are accustomed to say, *God make thee as Sarah and Rebekah!* The forms are still in use.

Verse 21. *Behold, I die*] With what composure is this most awful word expressed! Surely of Jacob it might be now said, "He turns his sight undaunted on the tomb;" for though it is not said that he *was full of days*, as were Abraham and Isaac, yet he is perfectly willing to bid adieu to earthly things, and lay his body in the grave. Could any person act as the patriarchs did in their last moments, who had no hopes of *eternal life*, no belief in the *immortality of the soul*? Impossible! With such a conviction of the being of God, with such proofs of his tenderness and regard, with such experience of his providential and miraculous interference in their behalf, could they suppose that they were only *creatures of a day*, and that God had wasted so much care, attention, providence, grace, and goodness, on creatures who were to be ultimately like the beasts that perish? The supposition that they could have no correct notion of the immortality of the soul is as dishonourable to God as to themselves. But what shall we think of Christians who have formed this hypothesis into a *system* to prove—what? Why, that the patriarchs lived and died in the dark! That either the soul has no immortality, or that God has not thought proper to reveal it. Away with such an opinion! It cannot be said to merit serious refutation.

Verse 22. *Moreover I have given to thee one portion*] שכם אחד *shechem achad*, one shechem or one *shoulder*. We have already seen the transactions between Jacob and his family on one part, and *Shechem* and the sons of *Hamor* on the other. See chap. xxxiii. 18, 19, and chap. xxxiv. As he uses the word *shechem* here, I think it likely that he alludes to the purchase of the field or parcel of ground mentioned chap. xxxiii. 18, 19. It has been supposed that this parcel of ground, which Jacob bought from *Shechem*, had been taken from him by the Amorites, and that he afterwards had recovered it *by his sword and by his bow*, i. e., *by force of arms*. Shechem appears to have fallen to the lot of Joseph's sons; (see Josh. xvii. 1, and xx. 7;) and in our Lord's time there was a parcel of ground near to *Sychar* or *Shechem* which was still considered as that portion which Jacob gave to his son Joseph, John iv. 5; and on the whole it was probably the *same* that Jacob bought for a *hundred pieces of money*, chap. xxxiii. 18, 19. But how it could be said that he *took this out of the hand of the Amorite with his sword and his bow*, we cannot tell. Many attempts have been made to explain this abstruse verse, but they have all hitherto been fruitless. Jacob's words were

a

no doubt perfectly well understood by Joseph, and probably alluded to some transaction that is not now on record; and it is much safer for us to confess our ignorance, than to hazard conjecture after conjecture on a subject of which we can know nothing certainly.

1. On filial respect to aged and destitute parents we have already had occasion to speak; see ver. 11. The duty of children to their parents only ceases when the parents are laid in their graves, and this duty is the next in order and importance to the duty we owe to God. No circumstances can alter its nature or lessen its importance; *Honour thy father and thy mother* is the sovereign, everlasting command of God. While the relations of *parent* and *child* exist, this commandment will be in full force.

2. The *Redeeming Angel*, the *Messenger of the covenant*, in his preserving and saving influence, is invoked by dying Jacob to be the protector and Saviour of Ephraim and Manasseh, ver. 16. With what advantage and effect can a dying parent recommend the Lord Jesus to his children, who can testify with his last breath that this Jesus has redeemed *him* from *all evil!* Reader, canst thou call Christ *thy Redeemer?* Hast thou, through him, recovered the forfeited inheritance? Or dost thou expect redemption *from all evil* by any other means? Through *him*, and him *alone*, God will redeem thee from all thy sins; and as thou knowest not what a *moment* may bring forth, thou hast not a moment to lose. Thou hast sinned, and there is no name given under heaven among men whereby thou canst be saved but *Jesus Christ*. Acquaint thyself now with him, and be at peace, and thereby good shall come unto thee.

3. We find that the patriarchs ever held the promised land in the most sacred point of view. It was *God's gift* to them; it was confirmed by a *covenant* that spoke of and referred to better things. We believe that this land typified the *rest* which remains for the people of God, and can we be indifferent to the excellence of this *rest!* A patriarch could not die in peace, however distant from this land, without an assurance that his bones should be laid in it. How can *we* live, how can we *die* comfortably, without the assurance that our lives are hid with Christ in God, and that we shall dwell in his presence for ever? There remains a rest for the people of God, and only for the people of God; for those alone who love, serve, reverence, and obey him, in his Son Jesus Christ, shall ever enjoy it.

CHAPTER XLIX.

Jacob, about to die, calls his sons together that he may bless them, or give prophetic declarations concerning their posterity, 1, 2. *Prophetic declaration concerning*, Reuben, 3, 4. *Concerning* Simeon *and* Levi, 5–7; *concerning* Judah, 8–12; *concerning* Zebulun, 13; *concerning* Issachar, 14, 15; *concerning* Dan, 16–18; *concerning* Gad, 19; *concerning* Asher, 20; *concerning* Naphtali, 21; *concerning* Joseph, 22–26; *concerning* Benjamin, 27. *Summary concerning the twelve tribes*, 28. *Jacob gives directions concerning his being buried in the cave of Machpelah*, 29–32. *Jacob dies*, 33.

A. M. 2315. B. C. 1689.

AND Jacob called unto his sons,
and said, Gather yourselves
together, that I may [a] tell you *that* which shall
befall you [b] in the last days.
2 Gather yourselves together,
and hear, ye sons of Jacob; and
[c] hearken unto Israel your father.
3 Reuben, thou *art* [d] my first-born, my might,

[a] Deut. xxxiii. 1; Amos iii. 7.—[b] Deut. iv. 30; Numbers xxiv. 14; Isa. ii. 2; xxxix. 6; Jer. xxiii. 20; Dan. ii. 28, 29; Acts ii. 17; Heb. i. 2.—[c] Psa. xxxiv. 11.—[d] Chap. xxix. 32.

NOTES ON CHAP. XLIX.

Verse 1. That *which shall befall you in the last days.*] It is evident from this, and indeed from the whole complexion of these important prophecies, that the twelve sons of Jacob had very little concern in them, *personally* considered, as they were to be fulfilled in the last days, i. e., in times remote from that period, and consequently to their *posterity*, and not to *themselves*, or to their *immediate families*. The whole of these prophetic declarations, from ver. 2 to ver. 27 inclusive, is delivered in strongly *figurative* language, and in the poetic form, which, in every translation, should be preserved as nearly as possible, rendering the version line for line with the original. This order I shall pursue in the succeeding notes, always proposing the verse first, in as literal a translation as possible, line for line with the Hebrew after the *hemistich* form, from which the sense will more readily appear; but to the Hebrew text and the common version the reader is ultimately referred.

2. Come together and hear, O sons of Jacob!
And hearken unto Israel your father.

Bishop Newton has justly observed that Jacob had received a double blessing, *spiritual* and *temporal*; the promise of being *progenitor of the Messiah*, and the promise of the *land of Canaan*. The promised land he might *divide* among his children as he pleased, but the other must be confined to one of his sons; he therefore assigns to each son a portion in the land of Canaan, but limits the descent of the blessed seed to the tribe of *Judah*. Some have put themselves to a great deal of trouble and learned labour to show that it was a general opinion of the ancients that the soul, a short time previous to its departure from the body, becomes endued with a certain measure of the

A. M. 2315.
B. C. 1689.

[e] and the beginning of my strength, the excellency of dignity, and the excellency of power:

4 Unstable as water, [f] thou [g] shalt not excel; because thou [h] wentest up to thy father's bed; then defiledst thou *it:* [i] he went up to my couch.

5 [k] Simeon and Levi *are* [l] brethren; [m] instruments [n] of cruelty *are in* their habitations.

6 O my soul, [o] come not thou into their

[e] Deut. xxi. 17; Psa. lxxviii. 51.——[f] Heb. *do not thou excel.*——[g] 1 Chron. v. 1.——[h] Chap. xxxv. 22; 1 Chron. v. 1; Deut. xxvii. 20.

[i] Or, *my couch is gone.*——[k] Chap. xxix. 33, 34.——[l] Prov. xviii. 9.——[m] Or, *their swords* are *weapons of violence.*——[n] Ch. xxxiv. 25.——[o] Prov. i. 15, 16.

prophetic gift or *foresight;* and that this was probably the case with Jacob. But it would be derogatory to the dignity of the prophecies delivered in this chapter, to suppose that they came by any other means than *direct inspiration*, as to their main matter, though certain circumstances appear to be left to the patriarch himself, in which he might express his own feelings both as a *father* and as a judge. This is strikingly evident, 1. In the case of *Reuben*, from whom he had received the grossest insult, however the passage relative to him may be understood; and, 2. In the case of *Joseph*, the tenderly *beloved son* of his most *beloved wife Rachel*, in the prophecy concerning whom he gives full vent to all those tender and affectionate emotions which, as a *father* and a *husband*, do him endless credit.

3. Reuben, my first-born art thou!
   My might, and the prime of my strength,
   Excelling in eminence, and excelling in power:

4. Pouring out like the waters:—thou shalt not excel,
   For thou wentest up to the bed of thy father,—
   Then thou didst defile: to my couch he went up!

Verse 3. Reuben as the *first-born* had a right to a double portion of all that the father had; see Deut. xxi. 17.

The *eminence* or dignity mentioned here may refer to the *priesthood;* the *power*, to the *regal government* or *kingdom*. In this sense it has been understood by all the ancient Targumists. The Targum of Onkelos paraphrases it thus: "*Thou shouldst have received* three *portions, the* birthright, *the* priesthood, *and the* kingdom:" and to this the Targums of *Jonathan ben Uzziel* and *Jerusalem* add: "*But because thou hast sinned, the* birthright *is given to* Joseph, *the* kingdom *to* Judah, *and the* priesthood *to* Levi." That the birthright was given to the sons of *Joseph* we have the fullest proof from 1 Chron. v. 1.

Verse 4. *Pouring out like the waters*] This is an obscure sentence because *unfinished*. It evidently relates to the defilement of his father's couch; and the word פחז *pachaz*, here translated *pouring out*, and in our Version *unstable*, has a *bad* meaning in other places of the Scripture, being applied to *dissolute, debauched*, and *licentious* conduct. See Judg. ix. 4; Zeph. iii. 4; Jer. xxiii. 14, 32; xxix. 23.

Thou shalt not excel] This tribe never rose to any eminence in Israel; was not so numerous by one third as either Judah, Joseph, or Dan, when Moses took the sum of them in the wilderness, Num. i. 21; and was among the *first* that were carried into captivity, 1 Chron. v. 26.

Then thou didst defile] Another unfinished sentence, similar to the former, and upon the same subject, passing over a transaction covertly, which delicacy forbade Jacob to enlarge on. For the crime of Reuben, see the notes on chap. xxxv. 22.

5. Simeon and Levi, brethren:
   They have accomplished their fraudulent purposes.
6. Into their secret council my soul did not come;
   In their confederacy my honour was not united:
   For in their anger they slew a man, (איש ish, *a noble*,)
   And in their pleasure they murdered a prince.
7. Cursed was their anger, for it was fierce!
   And their excessive wrath, for it was inflexible!
   I will divide them out in Jacob,
   And I will disperse them in Israel.

Verse 5. *Simeon and Levi* are *brethren*] Not only springing from the same parents, but they have the same kind of disposition, *headstrong, deceitful, vindictive*, and *cruel*.

They have accomplished, &c.] Our margin has it, *Their swords* are *weapons of violence*, i. e. Their swords, which they should have used in defence of their persons or the honourable protection of their families, they have employed in the base and dastardly murder of an innocent people.

The *Septuagint* gives a different turn to this line from our translation, and confirms the translation given above: *Συνετελεσαν αδικιαν εξαιρεσεως αυτων·* *They have accomplished the iniquity of their purpose;* with which the *Samaritan Version* agrees. In the *Samaritan text* we read ࠊࠋࠅ *calu, they have accomplished*, instead of the Hebrew כלי *keley, weapons* or *instruments*, which reading most critics prefer: and as to מכרתיהם *mecherotheyhem*, translated above *their fraudulent purposes*, and which our translation on almost no authority renders *their habitations*, it must either come from the *Æthiopic* מכר *macar*, he *counselled, devised stratagems, &c.*, (see *Castel*,) or from the *Arabic* مكر *macara*, he *deceived, practised deceit, plotted*, &c., which is nearly of the same import. This gives not only a *consistent* but evidently the *true* sense.

Verse 6. *Into their secret council*, &c.] Jacob here exculpates himself from all participation in the guilt of Simeon and Levi in the murder of the Shechemites. He most solemnly declares that he knew nothing of the *confederacy* by which it was *executed*, nor of the *secret council* in which it was *plotted*.

If it should be said that the words תבא *tabo* and תחד *techad* should be translated in the *future tense* or in the *imperative*, as in our translation, I shall not contend; though it is well known that the *preterite* is often used for the *future* in Hebrew, and vice versa. Taken thus, the words mark the strong detestation which this holy man's soul felt for the villany of his sons: "My soul *shall not come* into their secret

a

A. M. 2315. B. C. 1689.

secret; [p] unto their assembly,
[q] mine honour, be not thou united:
for [r] in their anger they slew a man, and in
their self-will they [s] digged down a wall.
7 Cursed *be* their anger, for *it was* fierce;
and their wrath, for it was cruel: [t] I
will divide them in Jacob, and scatter them in Israel.
8 [u] Judah, thou *art he* whom thy brethren
shall praise; [v] thy hand *shall be* in the neck

[p] Psa. xxvi. 9; Eph. v. 11.——[q] Psa. xvi. 9; xxx. 12; lvii. 8.
[r] Chap. xxxiv. 26.——[s] Or, *houghed oxen.*——[t] Josh. xix. 1; xxi. 5, 6, 7; 1 Chron. iv. 24, 39.——[u] Chap. xxix. 35; Deut. xxxiii. 7.
[v] Psa. xviii. 40.

council. My honour *shall not be united* to their confederacy."

For in their anger they slew a man] איש *ish*, a noble, an *honourable* man, viz., *Shechem*.

And in their pleasure] This marks the highest degree of wickedness and *settled malice*, they were *delighted* with their deed. A similar spirit Saul of Tarsus possessed previously to his conversion; speaking of the martyrdom of St. Stephen, St. Luke says, Acts viii. 1: *Σαυλος δε ην συνευδοκων τη αναιρεσει αυτου· And Saul was gladly consenting to his death.* He was with the others *highly delighted* with it; and thus the prediction of our Lord was fulfilled, John xvi. 2: *Yea, the time cometh, that whosoever killeth you will think that he doeth God service.* And it is represented as the highest pitch of profligacy and wickedness, not only to sin, but to *delight in it;* see Rom. i. 32. As the original word רצון *ratson* signifies, in general, *pleasure, benevolence, delight,* &c., it should neither be translated *self-will* nor *wilfulness,* as some have done, but simply as above; and the reasons appear sufficiently obvious. *They murdered a prince*—*Hamor*, the father of *Shechem*. Instead of שור *shor*, which *we* have translated *a wall*, and others an *ox*, I read שר *sar*, a prince, which makes a consistent sense; (see Kennicott's first Dissertation, p. 56, &c.;) as there is no evidence whatever that Simeon and Levi either *dug down a wall* or *houghed the oxen*, as some have translated the passage; (see the *margin;*) on the contrary, the text, chap. xxxv. 28, 29, proves that they had taken for their own use the *sheep, oxen, asses,* all *their wealth,* their *wives,* and *their little ones.*

Verse 7. *Cursed was their anger*]. The first motions of their violence *were savage; and their excessive* or *overflowing wrath,* עברה *ebrah, for it was inflexible*—neither the supplications of the males, nor the entreaties, tears, cries, and shrieks of the helpless females, could deter them from their *murderous purpose;* for this, ver. 5, they are said to have *accomplished.*

I will divide them out, אחלקם *achallekem, I will make them into lots,* giving a portion of them to one tribe, and a portion to another; but they shall never attain to any *political* consequence. This appears to have been literally fulfilled. *Levi* had no inheritance except forty-eight cities, scattered through different parts of the land of Canaan: and as to the tribe of Simeon, it is generally believed among the Jews that they became *schoolmasters* to the other tribes; and when they entered Canaan they had only a small portion, a few towns and villages in the worst part of Judah's lot, Josh. xix. 1, which afterwards finding too little, they formed different colonies in districts which they conquered from the *Idumeans* and *Amalekites,* 1 Chron. iv. 39, &c. Thus these two tribes were not only *separated from each other,* but even *divided from themselves,* according to this prediction of Jacob.

8. Judah! thou! Thy brethren shall praise thee.
Thy hand, in the neck of thine enemies:
The sons of thy father shall bow themselves to thee.
9. A lion's whelp is Judah:
From the prey, my son, thou hast ascended.
He couched, lying down like a strong lion,
And like a lioness; who shall arouse him?
10. From Judah the sceptre shall not depart,
Nor a teacher from his offspring,
Until that SHILOH shall come,
And to him shall be assembled the peoples.
11. Binding his colt to the vine,
And to the choice vine the foals of his ass,
He washed his garments in wine,
His clothes in the blood of the grape.
12. With wine shall his eyes be red,
And his teeth shall be white with milk.

Verse 8. *Thy brethren shall praise thee.*] As the name *Judah* signifies *praise,* Jacob takes occasion from its meaning to show that this tribe should be so eminent and glorious, that the rest of the tribes should *praise* it; that is, they should acknowledge its superior dignity, as in its privileges it should be distinguished beyond all the others. On the prophecy relative to Judah, Dr. *Hales* has several judicious remarks, and has left very little to be farther desired on the subject. Every reader will be glad to meet with them here.

"The prophecy begins with his name JUDAH, signifying the *praise of the Lord,* which was given to him at his birth by his mother *Leah,* chap. xxix. 35. It then describes the warlike character of this tribe, to which, by the Divine appointment, was assigned the *first lot* of the promised land, which was conquered accordingly by the pious and heroic *Caleb;* the first who *laid hands on the necks of his enemies,* and routed and subdued them, Josh. xiv. 11; xv. 1; Judg. i. 1, 2; and led the way for their total subjugation under *David;* who, in allusion to this prediction, *praises God,* and says: Thou hast given me the *necks* of mine enemies, that I might destroy them that hate me, Psa. xviii. 40. In the different stages of its strength, this tribe is compared to a *lion's whelp,* to a *full grown lion,* and to a *nursing lioness,* the fiercest of all. Hence a *lion* was the standard of Judah; compare Num. ii. 3, Ezek. i. 10. The city of David, where he reposed himself after his conquests, secure in the terror of his name, 1 Chron. xiv. 17, was called *Ariel,* the *lion of God,* Isa. xxix. 1; and our Lord himself, his most illustrious descendant, *the Lion of the tribe of Judah,* Rev. v. 5.

A. M. 2315. B. C. 1689. of thine enemies; [w] thy father's children shall bow down before thee.
9 Judah *is* [x] a lion's whelp: from the prey,
my son, thou art gone up: [y] he stooped down, he couched as a lion, and as an old lion; who shall rouse him up? A. M. 2315. B. C. 1689.

[w] Chap. xxvii. 29; 1 Chron. v. 2.

[x] Hos. v. 4; Rev. v. 5.——[y] Num. xxiii. 24; xxiv. 9.

"The duration of the power of this famous tribe is next determined: 'the sceptre of dominion,' as it is understood Esth. viii. 4; Isa. xiv. 5, &c., or its *civil government*, was not to cease or depart from Judah until the birth or coming of SHILOH, signifying the *Apostle*, as Christ is styled, Heb. iii. 1; nor was the native lawgiver, or *expounder of the law*, *teacher*, or *scribe*, intimating their ecclesiastical polity, to cease, until Shiloh should have a congregation of peoples, or religious followers, attached to him. And how accurately was this fulfilled in both these respects!

"1. Shortly before the birth of Christ a decree was issued by Augustus Cæsar that all the land of Judea and Galilee should be *enrolled*, or a registry of persons taken, in which Christ was included, Luke ii. 1–7; whence Julian the apostate unwittingly objected to his *title* of CHRIST or KING, that 'he was born a subject of Cæsar!' About eleven years after Judea was made a Roman province, attached to Syria on the deposal and banishment of *Archelaus*, the son of *Herod the Great*, for maladministration; and an assessment of properties or *taxing* was carried into effect by *Cyrenius*, then governor of Syria, the same who before, as the emperor's procurator, had made the enrolment, Luke ii. 2; Acts v. 37; and thenceforth Judea was governed by a Roman deputy, and the judicial power of life and death taken away from the Jews, John xviii. 31.

"2. Their ecclesiastical polity ceased with the destruction of their city and temple by the Romans, A. D. 70; at which time the Gospel had been preached through the known world by the apostles, 'his witnesses in *Jerusalem*, and in all *Judea*, and in *Samaria*, and unto the *uttermost parts* of the earth;' Acts ii. 8; Rom. x. 18.

"Our Lord's triumphant entry into Jerusalem, before his crucifixion, 'riding on an *ass*, even a *colt* the *foal* of an ass,' which by his direction his disciples brought to him for this purpose,—'Go into the village over against you, and presently ye shall find an *ass tied*, and a *colt* with her; *loose* them, and bring them to me,' Matt. xxi. 2–5, remarkably fulfilling the prophecy of Zechariah, ix. 9, is no less a fulfilment of this prophecy of *Shiloh*, 'binding or tying his *foal* to the *vine*, even his *ass's colt* to the *choice vine*.' In ancient times to ride upon *white asses* or *ass-colts* was the privilege of persons of high rank, *princes*, *judges*, and *prophets*, Judg. v. 10; x. 4; Num. xxii. 22. And as the children of Israel were symbolized by the *vine*, Psa. lxxx. 8, Hos. x. 1, and the men of Judah by 'a (choice) *vine* of *Sorek*,' in the original, both here and in the beautiful allegory of Isaiah, v. 1–7, adopted by Jeremiah, ii. 21, and by our Lord, Matt. xxi. 31, who styled himself the *true vine*, John xv. 1; so the union of both these images signified our Lord's assumption, as the promised Shiloh, of the dignity of *the king of the Jews*, not in a temporal but in a spiritual sense, as he declared to Pilate, John xviii. 36, as a prelude to his second coming in glory 'to restore again the kingdom to *Israel*.'

"The *vengeance* to be then inflicted on all the enemies of his Church, or congregation of faithful *Christians*, is expressed by the symbolical imagery of 'washing his garments in *wine*, and his clothes in the *blood of grapes*;' which to understand literally, would be incongruous and unusual any where, while it aptly represents his garments *crimsoned* in the blood of his foes, and their immense slaughter; an imagery frequently adopted in the *prophetic* scriptures.

"The strength and wholesomeness of Shiloh's doctrine are next represented by having 'his eyes red with *wine*, and his teeth white with *milk*.' And thus the evangelical prophet, in similar strains, invites the world to embrace the GOSPEL:—

Ho, every one that thirsteth, *come to the waters*,
And he that hath no money; come, buy and eat:
Yea, come, buy wine *and* milk,
Without money and without price. Isa. lv. 1.

"On the last day of the feast of *tabernacles* it was customary among the Jews for the people to bring water from the fountain of *Siloah* or *Siloam*, which they poured on the altar, singing the words of Isaiah, xii. 3: *With joy shall ye draw water from the fountain of salvation;* which the Targum interprets, 'With joy shall ye receive a new doctrine from the ELECT of the JUST ONE;' and the feast itself was also called Hosannah, *Save, we beseech thee.* And Isaiah has also described the apostasy of the Jews from their tutelar God IMMANUEL, under the corresponding imagery of their 'rejecting the gently-flowing *waters* of *Siloah*,' Isa. viii. 6–8.

"Hence our Lord, on the last day of the feast, significantly invited the Jews to come unto him as the true and living Fountain of waters, Jer. ii. 13. 'If any man thirst, let him come to ME and drink;' John vii. 37. He also compared his doctrine to *new wine*, which required to be put into *new bottles*, made of skins strong enough to contain it, Matt. ix. 17; while the Gospel is repeatedly represented as affording *milk for babes*, or the first principles of the oracles of God for *novices* in the faith, as well as strong meat [and strong wine] for *masters in Christ* or *adepts*, Matt. xiii. 11; Heb. v. 12–14.

"And our Lord's most significant miracle was wrought at this fountain, when he gave sight to a man forty years old, who had been blind from his birth, by sending him, after he had anointed his eyes with moistened clay, to wash in the pool of *Siloam*, which is the Greek pronunciation of the Hebrew שלח *Siloah* or *Siloh*, Isa. viii. 6, where the *Septuagint* version reads Σιλωαμ, signifying, according to the evangelist, *απεσταλμενος*, *sent forth*, and consequently derived from שלח *shalach*, *to send*, John ix. 7. Our Lord thus assuming to himself his two leading titles of MESSIAH, signifying *anointed*, and SHILOH, *sent forth*

A. M. 2315.
B. C. 1689.

10 [z] The sceptre shall not depart
from Judah, nor [a] a lawgiver [b] from
between his feet, [c] until Shiloh come; [d] and
unto him *shall* the gathering of the people *be*.
11 [e] Binding his foal unto the vine, and his
ass's colt unto the choice vine; he washed
his garments in wine, and his clothes in the
blood of grapes:
12 His [f] eyes *shall be* red with
wine, and his teeth white with
milk.
13 [g] Zebulun shall dwell at the haven of the
sea; and he *shall be* for a haven of ships;
and his border *shall be* unto Zidon.
14 Issachar *is* a strong ass couching down
between two burdens:

[z] Num. xxiv. 17; Jer. xxx. 21; Zech. x. 11.——[a] Psa. lx. 7; cviii. 8, or Num. xxi. 18.——[b] Deut. xxviii. 57.——[c] Isa. xi. 1; lxii. 11; Ezek. xxi. 27; Dan. ix. 25; Matt. xxi. 9; Luke i. 32, 33.——[d] Isa. ii. 2; xi. 10; xlii. 1, 4; xlix. 6, 7, 22, 23; lv. 4, 5; lx. 1, 3, 4, 5; Hag. ii. 7; Luke ii. 30, 31, 32.——[e] 2 Kings xviii. 32. [f] Prov. xxiii. 29.——[g] Deut. xxxiii. 18, 19; Josh. xix. 10, 11.

or *delegated* from God; as he had done before at the opening of his mission: 'The Spirit of the Lord is upon me, because he hath *anointed* me to preach the Gospel to the poor; he hath *sent me forth* (απεσταλκε) to heal the broken-hearted,' &c.; Luke iv. 18.

"And in the course of it he declared, I was *not sent forth* (απεσταλην) but unto the *lost sheep* of the house of *Israel*, Matt. xv. 24, by a twofold reference to his character in *Jacob's* prophecy of SHILOH and SHEPHERD OF ISRAEL, Gen. xlix. 10–24. 'This is life eternal, to know thee the only true God, and Jesus Christ whom thou *sentest forth*,' (απεστειλας,) to instruct and save mankind, John xvii. 3; and he thus distinguishes his own superior *mission* from his *commission* to his apostles: 'AS THE FATHER hath sent ME, (απεσταλκε με,) so I send you,' πεμπω ὑμας, John xx. 21. Whence St. Paul expressly styles Jesus Christ 'the *Apostle* (Ὁ Αποστολος) and *High Priest* of our profession,' Heb. iii. 1; and by an elaborate argument shows the superiority of his *mission* above that of Moses, and of his priesthood above that of Aaron, in the sequel of the epistle. His priesthood was foretold by David to be a *royal priesthood*, after the order of *Melchizedek*, Psa. cx. 4. But where shall we find his mission or apostleship foretold, except in Jacob's prophecy of Shiloh? which was evidently so understood by Moses when God offered to *send* him as his ambassador to Pharaoh, and he declined at first the arduous mission: 'O my Lord, send I pray thee by the hand of *Him whom thou wilt send*,' or by the promised *Shiloh*, Exod. iii. 10; iv. 13; by whom in his last blessing to the Israelites, parallel to that of Jacob, he prayed that 'God would bring back Judah to his people' from captivity, Deut. xxxiii. 7.

"Here then we find the true meaning and derivation of the much disputed term *Shiloh* in this prophecy of Jacob, which is fortunately preserved by the *Vulgate*, rendering *qui mittendus est, he that is to be sent*, and also by a rabbinical comment on Deut. xxii. 7: 'If you keep this precept, you hasten the coming of the *Messiah*, who is called SENT.'

"This important prophecy concerning Judah intimates, 1. The warlike character and conquests of this tribe; 2. The cessation of their civil and religious polity at the first coming of *Shiloh*; 3. His meek and lowly inauguration at that time, as spiritual *King of the Jews*, riding on an *ass* like the ancient *judges* and *prophets*; 4. His second coming as a warrior to trample on all his foes; and, 5. To save and instruct his faithful people."—*Hales' Anal.*, vol. ii., p. 167, &c.

Verse 10. *From Judah the sceptre shall not depart*] The Jews have a quibble on the word שבט *shebet*, which we translate *sceptre;* they say it signifies a *staff* or *rod*, and that the meaning of it is, that "*afflictions* shall not depart from the Jews till the Messiah comes;" that they are still under affliction, and therefore the Messiah is not come. This is a miserable *shift* to save a *lost cause*. Their chief Targumist, *Onkelos*, understood and translated the word nearly as we do; and the same meaning is adopted by the *Jerusalem* Targum, and by all the ancient versions, the Arabic excepted, which has قضيب *kazeeb*, a rod; but in a very ancient MS. of the Pentateuch in my own possession the word سبط *sebet* is used, which signifies a *tribe*. Judah shall continue a distinct *tribe* till the Messiah shall come; and it did so; and after his coming it was confounded with the others, so that all *distinction* has been ever since lost.

Nor a teacher from his offspring] I am sufficiently aware that the *literal* meaning of the original מבין רגליו *mibbeyn raglaiv* is *from between his feet*, and I am as fully satisfied that it should never be *so translated; from between the feet* and *out of the thigh* simply mean *progeny, natural offspring*, for reasons which surely need not be mentioned. The Targum of *Jonathan ben Uzziel*, and the *Jerusalem* Targum, apply the whole of this prophecy, in a variety of very minute particulars, to the *Messiah*, and give no kind of countenance to the fictions of the modern Jews.

13. At the haven of the seas shall Zebulun dwell,
And he *shall be* a haven for ships.
And his border shall extend unto Sidon.

Verse 13. Zebulun's lot or portion in the division of the Promised Land extended from the Mediterranean Sea on the west, to the lake of Gennesareth on the east; see his division, Josh. xix. 10, &c. The *Targum* of *Jonathan ben Uzziel* paraphrases the passage thus: "Zebulun shall be on the coasts of the sea, and he shall rule over the *havens;* he shall subdue the provinces of the sea with his ships, and his border shall extend unto Sidon."

14. Issachar is a strong ass
Couching between two burdens.
15. And he saw the resting place that *it was* good,
And the land that it was pleasant;
And he inclined his shoulder to the load,
And became a servant unto tribute.

Verse 14. *Issachar is a strong ass*] חמור גרם *chamor garem* is properly a *strong-limbed ass; couching be-*

A. M. 2315.
B. C. 1689.

15 And he saw that rest *was* good, and the land that *it was* pleasant; and bowed [h] his shoulder to bear, and became a servant unto tribute.

16 [i] Dan shall judge his people, as one of the tribes of Israel.

17 [k] Dan shall be a serpent by the way, [l] an adder in the path, that biteth the horse

[h] 1 Sam. x. 9.——[i] Deut. xxxiii. 22; Judg. xviii. 1, 2. [k] Judg. xviii. 27.——[l] Heb. *an arrow-snake.*

tween two burdens—bearing patiently, as most understand it, the fatigues of *agriculture*, and submitting to *exorbitant taxes* rather that exert themselves to drive out the old inhabitants.

The *two burdens* literally mean the *two sacks* or *panniers*, one on each side of the animal's body; and *couching down between* these refers to the well-known propensity of the ass, whenever wearied or overloaded, to lie down even with its burden on its back.

Verse 15. *He saw that rest*] The *inland portion* that was assigned to him between the other tribes. *He inclined his shoulder to the load;* the Chaldee paraphrast gives this a widely different turn to that given it by most commentators: "He saw his portion that it was good, and the land that it was fruitful; and he shall subdue the provinces of the people, and drive out their inhabitants, and those who are left shall be his servants, and his tributaries." Grotius understands it nearly in the same way. The *pusillanimity* which is generally attributed to this tribe certainly does not agree with the view in which they are exhibited in Scripture. In the song of Deborah this tribe is praised for the *powerful assistance* which it then afforded, Judg. v. 15. And in 1 Chron. vii. 1–5, they are expressly said to have been *valiant men of might in all their families, and in all their generations;* i. e., through every period of their history. It appears they were a laborious, hardy, valiant tribe, patient in *labour*, and invincible in *war;* bearing both these burdens with great constancy whenever it was necessary. When *Tola* of this tribe judged Israel, the land had rest twenty-three years, Judg. x. 1.

16. Dan shall judge his people,
As one of the tribes of Israel.
17. Dan shall be a serpent on the way,
A cerastes upon the track,
Biting the heels of the horse,
And his rider shall fall backwards.

Verse 16. *Dan shall judge*] Dan, whose name signifies *judgment*, was the eldest of Jacob's sons by Bilhah, Rachel's maid, and he is here promised an equal rule with those tribes that sprang from either *Leah* or *Rachel*, the *legal* wives of Jacob.

Some Jewish and some Christian writers understand this prophecy of *Samson*, who sprang from this tribe, and *judged*, or as the word might be translated *avenged*, the people of Israel twenty years. See Judg. xiii. 2; xv. 20.

Verse 17. *Dan shall be a serpent*] The original word is נחש *nachash*, and we have seen on chap. iii. that this has a great variety of significations. It is probable that a *serpent* is here intended, but of what kind we know not; yet as the principal reference in the text is to *guile*, *cunning*, &c., the same creature may be intended as in chap. iii.

A cerastes upon the track] The word שפיפן *shephiphon*, which is nowhere else to be found in the Bible, is thus translated by the *Vulgate*, and *Bochart* approves of the translation. The *cerastes* has its name from two little *horns* upon its head, and is remarkable for the property here ascribed to the *shephiphon*. The word ארח *orach*, which we translate *path*, signifies the *track* or *rut* made in the ground by the wheel of a *cart*, *wagon*, &c. And the description that *Nicander* gives of this serpent in his *Theriaca* perfectly agrees with what is here said of the *shephiphon*

εν δ' αμαθοισιν
Η *και ἁματροχιησι παρα στιβον ενδυκες αυει.* v. 262.
It lies under the sand, or in some cart rut by the way.

It is intimated that this tribe should gain the principal part of its conquests more by *cunning* and *stratagem*, than by *valour;* and this is seen particularly in their conquest of *Laish*, Judges xviii., and even in some of the transactions of *Samson*, such as burning the corn of the *Philistines*, and at last pulling down their temple, and destroying three thousand at one time, see Judg. xvi. 26–30.

18. For thy salvation have I waited, O Lord!

This is a remarkable ejaculation, and seems to stand perfectly unconnected with all that went before and all that follows; though it is probable that certain prophetic views which Jacob now had, and which he does not explain, gave rise to it; and by this he at once expressed both his *faith* and *hope* in God. Both Jewish and Christian commentators have endeavoured to find out the connection in which these words existed in the mind of the patriarch. The Targum of Jonathan expresses the whole thus: "When Jacob saw Gideon the son of Joash, and Samson the son of Manoah, which were to be saviours in a future age, he said: I do not wait for the salvation of Gideon, I do not expect the salvation of Samson, because their salvation is a temporal salvation; but I wait for and expect thy salvation, O Lord, because thy salvation is eternal." And the Jerusalem Targum much to the same purpose: "Our father Jacob said: Wait not, my soul, for the redemption of Gideon the son of Joash which is *temporal*, nor the redemption of Samson which is a created salvation; but for the salvation which thou hast said by THY WORD should come to thy people the children of Israel: my soul waits for this thy salvation." Indeed these Targums understand almost the whole of these prophecies of the Messiah, and especially what is said about *Judah*, every word of which they refer to him. Thus the *ancient Jews* convict the *moderns* of both false interpretations and vain expectations. As the tribe of Dan was the first that appears to have been seduced from the true worship of God, (see Judg. xviii. 30,) some have thought that Jacob refers particularly to this, and sees the end of the general apostasy only in the redemption by Jesus

A. M. 2315.
B. C. 1689.

heels, so that his rider shall fall
backward.
18 [m] I have waited for thy salvation, O LORD!
19 [n] Gad, a troop shall overcome him: but
he shall overcome at the last.

20 [o] Out of Asher his bread *shall be*
fat, and he shall yield royal dainties.
21 [p] Naphtali *is* a hind let loose: he giveth
goodly words.
22 Joseph *is* a fruitful bough, *even* a fruit-

[m] Psa. xxv. 6; cxix. 166, 174; Isa. xxv. 9.——[n] Deut. xxxiii. 20; 1 Chron. v. 18.

[o] Deuteronomy xxxiii. 24; Joshua xix. 24.——[p] Deuteronomy xxxiii. 23.

Christ, considering the *nachash* above as the *seducer*, and the *Messiah* the promised *seed*.

19. Gad, an army shall attack him,
And he shall attack in return.

This is one of the most obscure prophecies in the whole chapter; and no two interpreters agree in the translation of the original words, which exhibit a most singular *alliteration*:—

גד גדוד יגודנו *gad gedud yegudennu*;
והוא יגד עקב *vehu yagud akeb*.

The prophecy seems to refer generally to the frequent disturbances to which this tribe should be exposed, and their hostile, warlike disposition, that would always lead them to repel every aggression. It is likely that the prophecy had an especial fulfilment when this tribe, in conjunction with that of Reuben and the half tribe of Manasseh, got a great victory over the Hagarites, taking captive *one hundred thousand* men, *two thousand* asses, *fifty thousand* camels, and *two hundred and fifty thousand* sheep; see 1 Chron. v. 18–22. Dr. Durell and others translate the last word עקב *akeb*, *rear*—"He shall invade their *rear*;" which contains *almost no meaning*, as it only seems to state that though the army that invaded Gad should be successful, yet the *Gadites* would harass their rear as they returned: but this could never be a subject of sufficient consequence for a *prophecy*. The word עקב *ekeb* is frequently used as a *particle*, signifying *in consequence, because of, on account of*. After the *Gadites* had obtained the victory above mentioned, they continued to possess the land of their enemies till they were carried away captive. The Chaldee paraphrasts apply this to the *Gadites* going armed over Jordan before their brethren, discomfiting their enemies, and *returning back* with much *spoil*. See Josh. iv. 12, 13, and xxii. 1, 2, 8.

20. From Asher his bread *shall be* fat,
And he shall produce royal dainties.

This refers to the great fertility of the lot that fell to Asher, and which appears to have corresponded with the *name*, which signifies *happy* or *blessed*. His great *prosperity* is described by Moses in this figurative way: "Let Asher be *blessed* with children, let him be *acceptable* to his brethren, and let him *dip his foot in oil*;" Deut. xxxiii. 24.

21. Naphtali is a spreading oak,
Producing beautiful branches.

This is *Bochart's* translation; and perhaps no man who understands the genius of the Hebrew language will attempt to dispute its propriety; it is as *literal* as it is *correct*. Our own translation scarcely gives any sense. The fruitfulness of this tribe in children may be here intended. From his four sons *Jahzeel, Guni, Jezer*, and *Shillem*, which he took down into Egypt, chap. xlvi. 24, in the course of two hundred and fifteen years there sprang of effective men 53,400: but as great increase in this way was not an *uncommon* case in the descendants of Jacob, this may refer particularly to the *fruitfulness of their soil*, and the especial providential care and blessing of the Almighty; to which indeed Moses seems particularly to refer, Deut. xxxiii. 23: *O Naphtali, satisfied with favour, and full with the blessing of the Lord*. So that he may be represented under the notion of a *tree planted in a rich soil*, growing to a prodigious size, extending its branches in all directions, and becoming a *shade* for *men* and *cattle*, and a *harbour* for the *fowls of heaven*.

22. The son of a fruitful (vine) is Joseph;
The son of a fruitful (vine) by the fountain:
The daughters (branches) shoot over the wall.
23. They sorely afflicted him and contended with him;
The chief archers had him in hatred.
24. But his bow remained in strength,
And the arms of his hands were made strong
By the hand of the Mighty One of Jacob:
By the name of the Shepherd, the Rock of Israel;
25. By the God of thy father, for he helped thee;
And God All-sufficient, he blessed thee.
The blessing of the heavens from above,
And the blessings lying in the deep beneath,
The blessings of the breasts and of the womb.
26. The blessings of thy father have prevailed
Over the blessings of the eternal mountains,
And the desirable things of the everlasting hills.
These shall be on the head of Joseph,
And on his crown who was separated from his brethren.

Verse 22. *The son of a fruitful* vine] This appears to me to refer to Jacob himself, who was blessed with such a numerous posterity that in two hundred and fifteen years after this his own descendants amounted to upwards of 600,000 effective men; and the figures here are intended to point out the continual growth and increase of his posterity. *Jacob was a fruitful tree* planted by a fountain, which because it was *good* would yield *good fruit*; and because it was planted near a *fountain*, from being continually watered, would be *perpetually fruitful*. The same is used and applied to Jacob, Deut. xxxiii. 28: *The* FOUNTAIN *of* JACOB *shall be upon a land of corn, and wine, &c.*

The daughters, בנות *banoth*, put here for *branches shoot over* or *run upon the wall*.] Alluding probably to the case of the *vine*, which requires to be supported by a wall, trees, &c. Some commentators have understood this literally, and have applied it to the Egyptian women, who were so struck with the beauty of

A. M. 2315. B. C. 1689.

ful bough by a well; *whose* [q] branches run over the wall:

23 The archers have [r] sorely grieved him, and shot *at him*, and hated him:

24 But his [s] bow abode in strength, and the arms of his hands were made strong by the hands of [t] the mighty *God* of Jacob; [u] (from thence [v] *is* the shepherd, [w] the stone of Israel:)

25 [x] *Even* by the God of thy father, who shall help thee: [y] and by the Almighty, [z] who shall bless thee with blessings of heaven above, blessings of the deep that lieth under, blessings of the breast and of the womb:

26 The blessings of thy father have prevailed above the blessings of thy progenitors, [a] unto the utmost bound of the everlasting hills: [b] they shall be on the head of Joseph, and on the crown of the head of him that was sepa rate from his brethren.

[q] Heb. *daughters*.——[r] Chap. xxxvii. 4, 24, 28; xxxix. 20; xlii. 21; Psa. cxviii. 13.——[s] Job xxix. 20; Psa. xxxvii. 15.——[t] Psa. cxxxii. 2, 5.——[u] Chap. xlv. 11; xlvii. 12; l. 21.

[v] Psa. lxxx. 1.——[w] Isa. xxviii. 16.——[x] Chap. xxviii. 13, 21; xxxv. 3; xliii. 23.——[y] Chap. xvii. 1; xxxv. 11.——[z] Deut. xxxiii. 13.——[a] Deut. xxxiii. 15; Hab. iii. 6.——[b] Deut. xxxiii. 16.

Joseph as to get upon walls, the tops of houses, &c., to see him as he passed by. This is agreeable to the view taken of the subject by the *Koran*. See the notes on chap. xxxix. 7.

Verse 23. *The chief archers*] בעלי חצים *baaley chitstsim*, the *masters of arrows*—Joseph's brethren, who either used such weapons, while feeding their flocks in the deserts, for the protection of themselves and cattle, or for the purpose of *hunting;* and who probably excelled in archery. It may however refer to the *bitter speeches* and *harsh words* that they spoke to and of him, for *they hated him, and could not speak peaceably to him*, chap. xxxvii. 4. Thus they sorely afflicted him, and were incessantly scolding or finding fault.

Verse 24. *But his bow remained in strength*] The more he was persecuted, either by his brethren or in Egypt, the more resplendent his uprightness and virtues shone: and *the arms*—his *extended power* and *influence, of his hands—plans, designs*, and *particular operations* of his *prudence, judgment, discretion, &c.*, were all rendered successful by the *hand*—the powerful succour and protection, *of the Mighty One of Jacob*—that God who blessed and prospered all the counsels and plans of Jacob, and protected and increased him also when he was in a strange land, and often under the power of those who sought opportunities to oppress and defraud him.

By the name of the Shepherd; the Rock of Israel] *Jehovah*, and *El-Elohey Israel;* see chap. xxxiii. 20. This appears to me to refer to the subject of the *thirty-second* chapter, where Jacob wrestled with God, had God's *name* revealed to him, and his own name *changed* from *Jacob* to *Israel*, in consequence of which he built an altar, and dedicated it to God, who had appeared to him under the name of *Elohey-Israel*, the *strong God of Israel;* which circumstance led him to use the term *Rock*, which, as an emblem of *power*, is frequently given to God in the sacred writings, and may here refer to the *stone* which Jacob set up. It is very probable that the word *shepherd* is intended to apply to our *blessed Lord*, who is the Shepherd of Israel, the good Shepherd, John x. 11–17; and who, beyond all controversy, was the person with whom Jacob wrestled. See the notes on chap. xvi. 7, and xxxii. 24.

Verse 25. *The God of thy father*] How frequently God is called the *God of Jacob* none needs be told who reads the Bible.

God All-sufficient] Instead of את שרי ETH *Shaddai*, THE *Almighty* or *All-sufficient;* I read אל שרי EL *Shaddai*, GOD *All-sufficient;* which is the reading of the *Samaritan, Septuagint, Syriac*, and *Coptic*, and of three reputable MSS. in the collections of *Kennicott* and *De Rossi*. The copies used by those ancient versions had evidently אל EL, *God*, and not את *eth*, THE, a mistake produced in later times. On the word אל שרי *El Shaddai*, see the note on chap. xvii. 1.

The blessing of the heavens from above] A generally pure, clear, serene sky, frequently dropping down fertilizing showers and dews, so as to make a very fruitful soil and salubrious atmosphere.

Blessings lying in the deep beneath] Whatever riches could be gained from the sea or rivers, from *mines* and *minerals* in the bowels of the earth, and from abundant *springs* in different parts of his inheritance. Our translation of this line is excessively obscure: *Blessings of the deep that lieth under.* What is it that lies *under the deep?* By connecting ברכת *bircoth, blessings*, with רבצת *robetseth, lying*, all ambiguity is avoided, and the text speaks a plain and consistent sense.

The blessings of the breasts and of the womb.] A numerous offspring, and an abundance of cattle. The progeny of Joseph, by Ephraim and Manasseh, amounted at the first *census* or enumeration (Num. i.) to 75,900 men, which exceeded the sum of any one tribe; *Judah*, the greatest of the others, amounting to no more than 74,600. Indeed, Ephraim and Manasseh had multiplied so greatly in the days of Joshua, that a common *lot* was not sufficient for them. See their complaint, Josh. xvii. 14.

Verse 26. *The blessing of thy father, &c.*] The blessings which thy father now prays for and pronounces are neither *temporal* nor *transitory;* they shall exceed in their *duration* the *eternal mountains*, and in their *value* and *spiritual* nature all the *conveniences, comforts*, and *delicacies* which the *everlasting hills* can produce. They shall last when the heavens and the earth are no more, and shall extend throughout eternity. They are the blessings which shall be communicated to the world by means of the Messiah.

The Jerusalem Targum paraphrases the place thus: "The blessing of this father shall be added unto the blessings wherewith thy fathers Abraham and Isaac, who are likened to *mountains*, have blessed thee; and they shall exceed the blessings of the *four mothers*, Sarah, Rebekah, Rachel, and Leah, who are likened to the *hills:* all these blessings shall be a crown of

A. M. 2315. B. C. 1689.

27 Benjamin shall [c] raven *as* a wolf: in the morning he shall devour the prey, [d] and at night he shall divide the spoil.

28 All these *are* the twelve tribes of Israel: and this *is it* that their father spake unto them, and blessed them; every one according to his blessing he blessed them.

29 And he charged them, and said unto them, I [e] am to be gathered unto my people: [f] bury me with my fathers [g] in the cave that *is* in the field of Ephron the Hittite.

30 In the cave that *is* in the field of Machpelah, (which *is* before Mamre in the land of Canaan,) [h] which Abraham bought with the field of Ephron the Hittite for a possession of a burying-place.

31 ([i] There they buried Abraham and Sarah his wife; [k] there they buried Isaac and Rebekah his wife; and there I buried Leah.)

32 The purchase of the field and of the cave that *is* therein *was* from the children of Heth.

33 And when Jacob had made an end of commanding his sons, he gathered up his feet into the bed, and yielded up the ghost, and [l] was gathered unto his people.

---

[c] Judg. xx. 21, 25; Ezek. xxii. 25, 27.——[d] Num. xxiii. 24; Esth. viii. 11; Ezek. xxxix. 10; Zech. xiv. 1, 7.——[e] Ch. xv. 15; xxv. 8. [f] Ch. xlvii. 30; 2 Sam. xix. 37.——[g] Ch. l. 13.——[h] Ch. xxiii. 16 [i] Chap. xxiii. 19; xxv. 9.——[k] Chap. xxxv. 29.——[l] Ver. 29.

---

magnificence on the head of Joseph, and on the crown of the head of him who was a prince and governor in the land of Egypt."

27. Benjamin is a ravenous wolf:
In the morning he shall devour the prey,
And in the evening he shall divide the spoil.

This tribe is very fitly compared to a ravenous *wolf*, because of the rude courage and ferocity which they have invariably displayed, particularly in their war with the other tribes, in which they killed more men than the whole of their own numbers amounted to.

"This last tribe," says Dr. Hales, "is compared to a *wolf* for its ferocious and martial disposition, such as was evinced by their contests with the other tribes, in which, after two victories, they were almost exterminated, Judg. xix., xx." Its union with the tribe of Judah seems to be intimated in their joint conquests, expressed nearly in the same terms: "Judah went up from the prey;" "Benjamin devoured the prey." Moses in his parallel prophecy, Deut. xxxiii. 12, confirms this by signifying that the *sanctuary* should be fixed in his lot, and that he should continue as long as the existence of the temple itself:—

THE BELOVED OF THE LORD shall dwell with him in safety,
And shall cover him *all the day long*,
And shall dwell between his shoulders.
Deut. xxxiii. 12.

In the morning, &c.] These expressions have been variously understood. The sense given above is that in which the principal interpreters agree; but *Houbigant* protests against the prophecy signifying the *continuance* of this tribe, as the words, "in the *morning* devouring the prey," and "in the *evening* dividing the spoil," are supposed to imply; "because," he observes, "after the return from the Babylonish captivity, this tribe is no more mentioned." But this may be accounted for from the circumstance of its being *associated* with that of *Judah*, (see 1 Kings xii. 21–24,) after which it is scarcely ever mentioned but in that union. Being thus absorbed in the tribe of Judah, it continued from the *morning* till the *evening* of the Jewish dispensation, and consequently till the Lion of the tribe of Judah was seen in the wilderness of Israel.

In the morning, according to Mr. Ainsworth, "signifies the *first times;* for Ehud of Benjamin was the *second* judge that saved the Israelites from the hands of the Moabites, Judg. iii. 15, &c. Saul of Benjamin was the *first king* of Israel; he and his son were great warriors, making a prey of many enemies 1 Sam. xi. 6, 7, 11; xiv. 13, 15, 47, 48. And *the evening*, the *latter times;* for Mordecai and Esther of Benjamin delivered the Jews from a great destruction, and slew their enemies, Esth. viii. 7, 9, 11; ix 5, 6, 15, 16."

Verse 28. *Every one according to his blessing*] That is, guided by the unerring Spirit of prophecy Jacob now foretold to each of his sons all the important events which should take place during their successive generations, and the predominant characteristic of each tribe; and, at the same time, made some comparatively obscure references to the advent of the Messiah, and the redemption of the world by him.

Verse 29. *Bury me with my fathers, &c.*] From this it appears that the cave at Machpelah was a *common burying-place for Hebrews of distinction;* and indeed the first *public burying-place* mentioned in history. From ver. 31 we find that Abraham, Sarah, Isaac, Rebekah, and Leah, had been already deposited there, and among them Jacob wished to have his bones laid; and he left his dying charge with his children to bury him in this place, and this they conscientiously performed. See chap. l. 13.

Verse 33. *He gathered up his feet into the bed*] It is very probable that while delivering these prophetic blessings Jacob sat upon the side of his bed, leaning upon his staff; and having finished, he lifted up his feet into the bed, stretched himself upon it, and *expired!*

And was gathered unto his people.] The testimony that this place bears to the immortality of the soul, and to its existence *separate* from the body, should not be lightly regarded. In the same moment in which Jacob is said to have *gathered up his feet into the bed*, and to have expired, it is added, *and was gathered unto his people*. It is certain that his body was not *then gathered to his people*, nor till *seven* weeks after; and it is not likely that a circumstance, so distant in point both of time and place, would

have been thus *anticipated*, and associated with facts that took place in *that moment*. I cannot help therefore considering this an additional evidence for the *immateriality of the soul*, and that it was intended by the Holy Spirit to convey this grand and consolatory sentiment, that when a holy man ceases to live among his fellows, his soul becomes an inhabitant of another world, and is joined to the spirits of just men made perfect.

1. It has been conjectured (see the note, chap. xxxvii. 9) that the eleven stars that bowed down to Joseph might probably refer to the *signs of the Zodiac*, which were very anciently known in Egypt, and are supposed to have had their origin in *Chaldea*. On this supposition Joseph's eleven brethren answered to *eleven* of these signs, and himself to the *twelfth*. General *Vallancy* has endeavoured, in his *Collectanea de Rebus Hibernicis*, vol. vi., part ii., p. 343, to trace out the analogy between the twelve sons of Jacob and the twelve signs of the Zodiac, which Dr. Hales (*Analysis*, vol. ii., p. 165) has altered a little, and placed in a form in which it becomes more generally applicable. As this scheme is curious, many readers who may not have the opportunity of consulting the above works will be pleased to find it here. That there is an allusion to the *twelve signs* of the Zodiac, and probably to their ancient *asterisms*, may be readily credited; but how far the peculiar characteristics of the sons of Jacob were expressed by the *animals* in the Zodiac, is a widely different question.

1. Reuben—"Unstable (rather *pouring out*) as *waters*"—the sign Aquarius, represented as a *man pouring out waters from an urn.*
2. Simeon and Levi—"The *united brethren*"—the sign Gemini or the *Twins.*
3. Judah—"The strong *lion*"—the sign Leo.
4. Asher—"*His bread shall be fat*"—the sign Virgo or the *Virgin*, generally represented as holding a *full ear of corn.*
5. Issachar—"A strong *ass*" or *ox*, both used in husbandry—the sign Taurus or the *Bull.*
6. and 7. Dan—"A serpent biting the horse's heels"—Scorpio, the *Scorpion*. On the celestial sphere the Scorpion is actually represented as *biting the heel of the horse* of the archer *Sagittarius*; and *Chelæ*, "his claws," originally occupied the space of *Libra*.
8. Joseph—"His *bow* remained in strength"—the sign Sagittarius, the *archer* or *bow-man*; commonly represented, even on the *Asiatic Zodiacs*, with his *bow bent*, and the *arrow drawn up to the head*—the bow in *full strength.*
9. Naphtali—by a play on his name, טלה *taleh*, the *ram*—the sign Aries, according to the rabbins.
10. Zebulun—"A haven for ships"—denoted by Cancer, the *crab.*
11. Gad—"A troop or army"—reversed, *dag*, a *fish*—the sign Pisces.
12. Benjamin—"A ravening wolf"—Capricorn, which on the Egyptian sphere was represented by a *goat* led by *Pan*, with a *wolf's* head.

What likelihood the reader may see in all this, I cannot pretend to say; but that the *twelve signs* were at that time known in Egypt and Chaldea, there can be little doubt.

2. We have now seen the life of Jacob brought to a close; and have carefully traced it through all its various fortunes, as the facts presented themselves in the preceding chapters. Isaac his father was what might properly be called a *good man*; but in strength of mind he appears to have fallen far short of his father Abraham, and his son Jacob. Having left the management of his domestic concerns to Rebekah his wife, who was an artful and comparatively irreligious woman, the education of his sons was either neglected or perverted. The unhappy influence which the precepts and example of his mother had on the mind of her son we have seen and deplored. Through the mercy of God Jacob outlived the *shady* part of his own character, and his last days were his brightest and his best. He had many troubles and difficulties in life, under which an inferior mind must have necessarily sunk; but being a worker together with the providence of God, his difficulties only served in general to whet his invention, and draw out the immense resources of his own mind. He had to do with an avaricious, procrastinating relative, as destitute of *humanity* as he was of *justice*. Let this plead something in his excuse. He certainly did *outwit* his father-in-law; and yet, probably, had no more than the just recompense of his faithful services in the successful issue of all his devices. From the time in which God favoured him with that wonderful manifestation of grace at *Peniel*, chap. xxxii., he became a *new man*. He had frequent discoveries of God *before*, to encourage him in journeys, secular affairs, &c.; but none in which the *heart-changing* power of Divine grace was so abundantly revealed. Happy he whose last days are his best! We can scarcely conceive a scene more noble or dignified than that exhibited at the deathbed of Jacob. This great man was now *one hundred and forty-seven* years of age; though his body, by the waste of time, was greatly enfeebled, yet with a mind in perfect vigour, and a hope full of immortality, he calls his numerous family together, all of them in their utmost state of prosperity, and gives them his last counsels, and his dying blessing. His declarations show that the secret of the Lord was with him, and that his candle shone bright upon his tabernacle. Having finished his work, with perfect possession of all his faculties, and being determined that while he was able to *help himself* none should be called in to assist, (which was one of the grand characteristics of his life,) he, with that dignity which became a great man and a man of God, stretched himself upon his bed, and rather appears to have *conquered* death than to have *suffered* it. Who, seeing the end of this illustrious patriarch, can help exclaiming, There is none like the God of Jeshurun! Let Jacob's God be my God! Let *me* die the death of the righteous, and let my last end be like his! Reader, God is still the *same*: and though he may not make thee as *great* as was Jacob, yet he is ready to make thee as *good*; and, whatever thy past life may have been, to crown thee with loving-kindness and tender mercies, that thy end also may be *peace*.

CHAPTER L.

Joseph bewails the death of his father, and commands the physicians to embalm him, 1, 2. *The Egyptians mourn for him* seventy days, 3. *Joseph begs permission from Pharaoh to accompany his father's corpse to Canaan,* 4, 5. *Pharaoh consents,* 6. *Pharaoh's domestics and elders, the elders of Egypt, Joseph and his brethren, with chariots, horsemen, &c., form the funeral procession,* 7–9. *They come to the* threshing-floor *of* Atad, *and mourn there* seven days, 10. *The Canaanites call the place* Abel-Mizraim, 11. *They bury Jacob in the cave of* Machpelah, 12, 13. *Joseph returns to Egypt,* 14. *His brethren, fearing his displeasure, send messengers to him to entreat his forgiveness of past wrongs,* 15–17. *They follow, and prostrate themselves before him, and offer to be his servants,* 18. *Joseph receives them affectionately, and assures them and theirs of his care and protection,* 19–21. *Joseph and his brethren dwell in Egypt, and he sees the third generation of his children,* 22, 23. *Being about to die, he prophecies the return of the children of Israel from Egypt,* 24, *and causes them to swear that they will carry his bones to Canaan,* 25. *Joseph dies, aged* one hundred and ten years; *is embalmed, and put in a coffin in Egypt,* 26.

A. M. 2315.
B. C. 1689.

AND Joseph [a] fell upon his father's face, and [b] wept upon him, and kissed him.

2 And Joseph commanded his servants the physicians to [c] embalm his father; and the physicians embalmed Israel

[a] Chapter xlvi. 4.——[b] 2 Kings xiii. 14.——[c] Ver. 26; 2 Chron. xvi. 14; Matt. xxvi. 12; Mark xiv. 8; xvi. 1; Luke xxiv. 1.

NOTES ON CHAP. L.

Verse 1. *Joseph fell upon his father's face*] Though this act appears to be suspended by the unnatural division of this verse from the preceding chapter, yet we may rest assured it was the *immediate* consequence of Jacob's death.

Verse 2. *The physicians*] רפאים *ropheim*, the *healers*, those whose business it was to *heal* or restore the body from sickness by the administration of proper *medicines;* and when death took place, to *heal* or preserve it from dissolution by *embalming*, and thus give it a sort of *immortality* or *everlasting duration.* The original word חנט *chanat*, which we translate *to embalm*, has undoubtedly the same meaning with the Arabic حنط *hanata*, which also signifies *to embalm*, or to preserve from putrefaction by the application of spices, &c., and hence حنّاط *hantat*, an *embalmer.* The word is used to express the *reddening* of leather; and probably the ideal meaning may be something analogous to our *tanning*, which consists in *removing* the *moisture*, and *closing up the pores* so as to render them impervious to wet. This probably is the grand *principle* in embalming; and whatever effects this, will preserve *flesh* as perfectly as *skin.* Who can doubt that a human *muscle*, undergoing the same process of *tanning* as the *hide* of an *ox*, would not become equally *incorruptible?* I have seen a part of the muscle of a human thigh, that, having come into contact with some *tanning matter*, either in the coffin or in the grave, was in a state of perfect *soundness*, when the rest of the body had been long reduced to earth; and it exhibited the appearance of a thick piece of *well tanned leather.*

In the art of embalming, the Egyptians excelled all nations in the world; with them it was a *common practice.* Instances of the perfection to which they carried this art may be seen in the numerous *mummies*, as they are called, which are found in different European cabinets, and which have been all brought from *Egypt.* This people not only embalmed *men* and *women*, and thus kept the bodies of their beloved relatives from the empire of corruption, but they embalmed useful *animals* also. I have seen the body of the *Ibris* thus preserved; and though the work had been done for *some thousands of years*, the very *feathers* were in complete preservation, and the *colour* of the plumage discernible. The account of this curious process, the articles used, and the manner of applying them, I subjoin from *Herodotus* and *Diodorus Siculus*, as also the manner of their mournings and funeral solemnities, which are highly illustrative of the subjects in this chapter.

"When any man of quality dies," says Herodotus, "all the *women* of that family besmear their heads and faces with dirt; then, leaving the body at home, they go lamenting up and down the city with all their relations; their apparel being girt about them, and their breasts left naked. On the other hand the *men*, having likewise their clothes girt about them, beat themselves. These things being done, they carry the dead body to be *embalmed;* for which there are certain persons appointed who profess this *art.* These, when the body is brought to them, show to those that bring it certain models of dead persons in wood, according to any of which the deceased may be painted. *One* of these they say is accurately made like to one whom, in such a matter, I do not think lawful to name; του ουκ ὁσιον ποιουμαι το ουνομα επι τοιουτῳ πρηγματι ουνομαζειν; (probably *Osiris*, one of the principal gods of Egypt, is here intended;) then they show a *second* inferior to it, and of an easier price; and next a *third*, cheaper than the former, and of a very small value; which being seen, they ask them after which model the deceased shall be represented. When they have agreed upon the *price* they depart; and those with whom the dead corpse is left proceed to *embalm* it after the following manner: First of all, they with a crooked iron draw the brain out of the head through the nostrils; next, with a sharp *Æthiopic stone* they cut up that part of the *abdomen* called the *ilia*, and that way draw out all the bowels, which, having cleansed and washed with palm wine, they again rinse and wash with wine perfumed with pounded odours: then filling up the belly with pure *myrrh* and *cassia* grossly powdered, and all other odours except *frankincense*, they sew it up again.

A. M. 2315.
B. C. 1689.
3 And forty days were fulfilled for him; (for so are fulfilled the days of those which are embalmed:) and the Egyptians [d] mourned [e] for him threescore and ten days.
A. M. 2315.
B. C. 1689.
4 And when the days of his mourning were

[d] Heb. *wept.*

[e] Num. xx. 29; Deut. xxxiv. 8.

Having so done, they *salt* it up close with *nitre seventy days*, for longer they may not salt it. After this number of days are over they wash the corpse again, and then roll it up with fine linen, all besmeared with a sort of *gum*, commonly used by the *Egyptians* instead of glue. Then is the body restored to its relations, who prepare a wooden coffin for it in the shape and likeness of a man, and then put the *embalmed* body into it, and thus enclosed, place it in a repository in the house, setting it upright against the wall. After this manner they, with great expense, preserve their dead; whereas those who to avoid too great a charge desire a *mediocrity*, thus *embalm* them: they neither cut the belly nor pluck out the entrails, but fill it with clysters of oil of *cedar* injected up the *anus*, and then salt it the aforesaid number of days. On the last of these they press out the *cedar* clyster by the same way they had injected it, which has such virtue and efficacy that it brings out along with it the bowels wasted, and the nitre consumes the flesh, leaving only the skin and bones: having thus done, they restore the dead body to the relations, doing nothing more. The *third* way of *embalming* is for those of yet meaner circumstances; they with lotions wash the belly, then dry it up with salt for *seventy* days, and afterwards deliver it to be carried away. Nevertheless, beautiful women and ladies of quality were not delivered to be *embalmed* till three or four days after they had been dead;" for which Herodotus assigns a sufficient reason, however degrading to human nature: *Τουτο δε ποιεουσι ούτω τουδε είνεκα, ίνα μη σφι οί ταριχευται μισγωνται τησι γυναιξι· λαμφθηναι γαρ τινα φασι μισγομενον νεκρῳ προσφατῳ γυναικος· κατειπαι δε τον ὁμοτεχνον.* [The original should not be put into a plainer language; the abomination to which it refers being too gross.] "But if any stranger or *Egyptian* was either killed by a crocodile or drowned in the river, the city where he was cast up was to *embalm* and bury him honourably in the sacred monuments, whom no one, no, not a relation or friend, but the priests of the *Nile* only, might touch; because they buried one who was something more than a dead man."—Herod. Euterpe, p. 120, ed. *Gale.*

Diodorus Siculus relates the funeral ceremonies of the *Egyptians* more distinctly and clearly, and with some very remarkable additional circumstances. "When any one among the *Egyptians* dies," says he, "all his relations and friends, putting dirt upon their heads, go lamenting about the city, till such time as the body shall be buried: in the meantime, they abstain from baths and wine, and all kinds of delicate meats; neither do they, during that time, wear any costly apparel. The manner of their burials is *threefold:* one very costly, a second sort less chargeable, and a third very mean. In the first, *they say*, there is spent a talent of silver; in the second, twenty *minæ;* but in the last there is very little expense. Those who have the care of ordering the body are such as have been taught that art by their ancestors. These, showing each kind of burial, ask them after what manner they will have the body prepared. When they have agreed upon the manner, they deliver the body to such as are usually appointed for this office. First, he who has the name of *scribe*, laying it upon the ground, marks about the flank on the left side how much is to be cut away; then he who is called *παρασχιστης, paraschistes*, the *cutter* or *dissector*, with an *Æthiopic stone*, cuts away as much of the flesh as the law commands, and presently runs away as fast as he can; those who are present, pursuing him, cast stones at him, and curse him, hereby turning all the execrations which they imagine due to his office upon him. For whosoever offers violence, wounds, or does any kind of injury to a body of the same nature with himself, they think him worthy of hatred: but those who are *ταριχευται, taricheutæ*, the *embalmers*, they esteem worthy of honour and respect; for they are familiar with their priests, and go into the temples as holy men, without any prohibition. As soon as they come to embalm the dissected body, one of them thrusts his hand through the wound into the *abdomen*, and draws forth all the bowels but the heart and kidneys, which another washes and cleanses with wine made of palms and aromatic odours. Lastly, having washed the body, they anoint it with oil of cedar and other things for about thirty days, and afterwards with myrrh, cinnamon, and other such like matters, which have not only a power to preserve it a long time, but also give it a sweet smell; after which they deliver it to the kindred in such manner that every member remains whole and entire, and no part of it changed, but the beauty and shape of the face seem just as they were before; and the person may be known, even the eyebrows and eyelids remaining as they were at first. By this means many of the *Egyptians*, keeping the dead bodies of their ancestors in magnificent houses, so perfectly see the true visage and countenance of those that died many ages before they themselves were born, that in viewing the proportions of every one of them, and the lineaments of their faces, they take as much delight as if they were still living among them. Moreover, the friends and nearest relations of the deceased, for the greater pomp of the solemnity, acquaint the judges and the rest of their friends with the time prefixed for the funeral or day of sepulture, declaring that such a one (calling the dead by his name) is such a day to pass the lake; at which time above forty judges appear, and sit together in a semicircle, in a place prepared on the hither side of the lake, where a ship, provided beforehand by such as have the care of the business, is haled up to the shore, and steered by a pilot whom the *Egyptians* in their language called *Charon*. Hence they say *Orpheus*, upon seeing this ceremony while he was in *Egypt*, invented the fable of hell, partly imitating therein the people of *Egypt*, and partly adding somewhat of his own. The ship being thus brought to the

A. M. 2315.
B. C. 1689.
past, Joseph spake unto [f] the house
of Pharaoh, saying, If now I have
found grace in your eyes, speak, I pray you,
in the ears of Pharaoh, saying,
5 [g] My father made me swear, saying, Lo,
I die: in my grave [h] which I have digged for
me, in the land of Canaan, there shalt thou
bury me. Now, therefore, let me go up, I
pray thee, and bury my father, and I will
come again.
6 And Pharaoh said, Go up, and bury thy
father, according as he made thee swear.
7 And Joseph went up to bury his
father; and with him went up all
the servants of Pharaoh, the elders of his house,
and all the elders of the land of Egypt,
8 And all the house of Joseph, and his
brethren, and his father's house: only their
little ones, and their flocks, and their herds,
they left in the land of Goshen.
9 And there went up with him both chariots
and horsemen: and it was a very great company.
10 And they came to the threshing-floor of

[f] Esth. iv. 2.——[g] Chap. xlvii. 29. [h] 2 Chron. xvi. 14; Isa. xxii. 16; Matt. xxvii. 60.

lake side, before the coffin is put on board every one is at liberty by the law to accuse the dead of what he thinks him guilty. If any one proves he was a bad man, the judges give sentence that the body shall be deprived of sepulture; but in case the informer be convicted of false accusation, then he is severely punished. If no accuser appear, or the information prove false, then all the kindred of the deceased leave off mourning, and begin to set forth his praises, yet say nothing of his birth, (as the custom is among the *Greeks*,) because the Egyptians all think themselves equally noble; but they recount how the deceased was educated from his youth and brought up to man's estate, exalting his *piety* towards the *gods*, and *justice* towards *men*, his *chastity*, and other virtues wherein he excelled; and lastly pray and call upon the infernal deities (τους κατω θεους, *the gods below*) to receive him into the societies of the *just*. The common people take this from the others, and consequently all is said in his praise by a loud shout, setting forth likewise his virtues in the highest strains of commendation, as one that is to live for ever with the infernal gods. Then those that have tombs of their own inter the corpse in places appointed for that purpose; and they that have none rear up the body in its coffin against some strong wall of their house. But such as are denied sepulture on account of some crime or debt, are laid up at home *without coffins*; yet when it shall afterwards happen that any of their posterity grows rich, he commonly pays off the deceased person's debts, and gets his crimes absolved, and so buries him honourably; for the *Egyptians* are wont to boast of their parents and ancestors that were honourably buried. It is a custom likewise among them to *pawn* the dead bodies of their parents to their creditors; but then those that do not redeem them fall under the greatest disgrace imaginable, and are denied burial themselves at their deaths."—*Diod. Sic.* Biblioth., lib. i., cap. 91–93., edit. Bipont. See also the *Necrokedia*, or *Art of Embalming*, by *Greenhill*, 4to., p. 241, who endeavoured in vain to recommend and restore the art. But he could not give his countrymen *Egyptian manners*; for a dead carcass is to the British an object of horror, and scarcely any, except a *surgeon* or an *undertaker*, cares to touch it.

Verse 3. *Forty days*] The body it appears required this number of days to complete the process of embalming; afterwards it lay in *natron* thirty days more, making in the whole seventy days, according to the preceding accounts, during which the mourning was continued.

Verse 4. *Speak, I pray you, in the ears of* Pharaoh] But why did not Joseph apply himself? Because he was now in his *mourning habits*, and in such none must appear in the presence of the eastern monarchs. See Esth. iv. 2.

Verse 7. *The elders of his house*] Persons who, by reason of their age, had acquired *much experience*; and who on this account were deemed the best qualified to conduct the affairs of the king's household. Similar to these were the Ealdormen, *Eldermen*, or *Aldermen*, among our Saxon ancestors, who were *senators* and *peers* of the realm.

The funeral procession of Jacob must have been truly grand. *Joseph, his brethren* and their *descendants*, the *servants of* Pharaoh, the *elders of his house*, and *all the elders*—all the principal men, *of the land of Egypt, with chariots* and *horsemen*, must have appeared a *very great company* indeed. We have seen LORDS, for their *greater honour*, buried at *the public expense*; and all the male branches of the *royal family*, as well as the most eminent *men* of the nation, join in the funeral procession, as in the case of the late *Lord Nelson*; but what was all this in comparison of the funeral solemnity now before us? *Here* was no *conqueror*, no *mighty man of valour*, no person of *proud descent*; here was only a *plain man*, who had dwelt almost *all his life long in tents*, without any other *subjects* than his *cattle*, and whose kingdom was *not of this world*. Behold this man honoured by a *national mourning*, and by a *national funeral!* It may be said indeed that "all this was done out of respect to Joseph." Be it so; *why* was *Joseph thus* respected? Was it because he had *conquered nations*, had made his sword drunk with blood, had triumphed over the enemies of Egypt? NO! But because he had *saved men alive*; because he was the *king's faithful servant*, the *rich man's counsellor*, and the *poor man's friend*. *He* was a national blessing; and the nation mourns in his affliction, and unites to do *him* honour.

Verse 10. *The threshing-floor of* Atad] As אטד *atad* signifies a *bramble* or *thorn*, it has been understood by the Arabic, not as a *man's* name, but as the name of a *place*; but all the other *versions* and the

A. M. 2315. B. C 1689.

Atad, which *is* beyond Jordan, and
there they [i] mourned with a great
and very sore lamentation: [k] and he made a
mourning for his father seven days.
11 And when the inhabitants of the land,
the Canaanites, saw the mourning in the floor
of Atad, they said, This *is* a grievous mourning to the Egyptians: wherefore the name of
it was called [l] Abel-mizraim, which *is* beyond
Jordan.
12 And his sons did unto him according as
he commanded them:
13 For [m] his sons carried him into the land
of Canaan, and buried him in the
cave of the field of Machpelah,
(which Abraham [n] bought the field, for a
possession of a burying-place, of Ephron the
Hittite,) before Mamre.
14 And Joseph returned into Egypt, he
and his brethren, and all that went up with
him to bury his father, after he had buried
his father.
15 And when Joseph's brethren saw that
their father was dead, [o] they said, Joseph will
peradventure hate us, and will certainly requite
us all the evil which we did unto him.

A. M. 2315. B. C. 1689.

[i] 2 Sam. i. 17; Acts viii. 2.——[k] 1 Sam. xxxi. 13; Job ii. 13.——[l] That is, *the mourning of the Egyptians*.——[m] Chapter xlix. 29, 30; Acts vii. 16.——[n] Chapter xxiii. 16.——[o] Job xv. 21, 22.

Targums consider it as the name of a *man*. Threshing-floors were always in a field, in the open air; and *Atad* was probably what we would call a *great farmer* or *chief* of some *clan* or *tribe* in that place. Jerome supposed the place to have been about *two leagues from Jericho*; but we have no certain information on this point. The funeral procession stopped here, probably as affording *pasturage* to their cattle while they observed the *seven days' mourning* which terminated the funeral solemnities, after which nothing remained but the interment of the corpse. The mourning of the ancient Hebrews was usually of *seven* days' continuance, Num. xix. 19; 1 Sam. xxxi. 13; though on certain occasions it was extended to *thirty* days, Num. xx. 29; Deut. xxi. 13; xxxiv. 8, but *never longer*. The seventy days' mourning mentioned above was that of the Egyptians, and was rendered necessary by the long process of *embalming*, which obliged them to keep the body out of the grave for *seventy days*' as we learn both from *Herodotus* and *Diodorus*. *Seven days* by the order of God a man was to mourn for his dead, because during that time he was considered as *unclean*; but when those were finished he was to purify himself, and consider the morning as *ended*; Num. xix. 11, 19. Thus God gave *seven days*, in some cases *thirty*, to mourn in: man, ever in his own estimation wiser than the word of God, has *added eleven whole months* to the term, which nature itself pronounces to be absurd, because it is incapable of supporting grief for such a time; and thus mourning is now, except in the first seven or thirty days, a mere solemn *ill-conducted* FARCE, a *grave mimicry*, a *vain show*, that convicts itself of its own *hypocrisy*. Who will rise up on the side of God and common sense, and restore becoming sorrow on the death of a relative to decency of garb and moderation in its continuance? Suppose the near relatives of the deceased were to be allowed seven days of seclusion from society, for the purpose of meditating on death and eternity, and after this to appear in a mourning habit for thirty days; every important end would be accomplished, and hypocrisy, the too common attendant of man, be banished, especially from that part of his life in which deep sincerity is not less becoming than in the most solemn act of his religious intercourse with God

In a kind of politico-religious institution formed by his late majesty Ferdinand IV., king of Naples and the Sicilies, I find the following rational institute relative to this point: "There shall be no mourning among you but only on the death of a *father, mother, husband*, or *wife*. To render to these the last duties of affection, *children, wives*, and *husbands* only shall be permitted to wear a *sign* or *emblem* of grief: a man may wear a *crape* tied round his *right arm*; a *woman*, a *black handkerchief* around her *neck*; and this in both cases for only two months at the most." Is there a purpose which religion, reason, or decency can demand that would not be answered by such *external mourning* as this? Only such relatives as the above, brothers and sisters being included, can mourn; all others make only a part of the dumb hypocritical *show*.

Verse 12. *And his sons did unto him*] This and the thirteenth verse have been supposed by Mr. *Locke* and others to belong to the conclusion of the preceding chapter, in which connection they certainly read more consistently than they do here.

Verse 15. *Saw that their father was dead*] This at once argues both a *sense of guilt* in their own consciences, and a *want of confidence* in their brother. They might have supposed that hitherto he had forborne to punish them merely on their father's account; but now that he was dead, and Joseph having them completely in his power, they imagined that he would take vengeance on them for their former conduct towards him.

Thus conscience records criminality; and, by giving birth to continual fears and doubtfulness, destroys all peace of mind, security, and confidence. On this subject an elegant poet has spoken with his usual point and discernment:—

Exemplo quodcumque malo committitur, ipsi
Displicet auctori. *Prima est hæc ultio, quod se*
Judice nemo nocens absolvitur, *improba quamvis*
Gratia fallaci Prætoris vicerit urna.
Juv. Sat. xiii. 1, &c.

Happily metaphrased by Mr. *Dryden*:—

He that commits a fault shall quickly find
The pressing guilt lie heavy on his mind.

s

A. M. 2315.
B. C. 1689.

16 And they [p] sent a messenger unto Joseph, saying, Thy father did command before he died, saying,

17 So shall ye say unto Joseph, Forgive, I pray thee now, the trespass of thy brethren, and their sin; [q] for they did unto thee evil: and now, we pray thee, forgive the trespass of the servants of [r] the God of thy father. And Joseph wept when they spake unto him.

18 And his brethren also went and [s] fell down before his face; and they said, Behold, we *be* thy servants.

19 And Joseph said unto them, [t] Fear not: [u] for *am* I in the place of God?

20 [v] But as for you, ye thought evil against me; *but* [w] God meant it unto good, to bring to pass, as *it is* this day, to save much people alive.

21 Now therefore fear ye not: [x] I will nourish you, and your little ones. And he comforted them, and spake [y] kindly unto them.

A. M. 2315.
B. C. 1689.

22 And Joseph dwelt in Egypt, he, and his father's house: and Joseph lived a hundred and ten years.

A. M. 2369.
B. C. 1635.

23 And Joseph saw Ephraim's children [z] of the third *generation:* [a] the children also of Machir, the son of Manasseh, [b] were [c] brought up upon Joseph's knees.

24 And Joseph said unto his brethren, I die: and [d] God will surely visit you, and bring you out of this land, unto the land [e] which he sware to Abraham, to Isaac, and to Jacob.

25 And [f] Joseph took an oath of the children of Israel, saying, God will surely visit you, and ye shall carry up my bones from hence.

[p] Heb. *charged.*——[q] Prov. xxviii. 13.——[r] Chap. xlix. 25. [s] Chap. xxxvii. 7, 10.——[t] Chap. xlv. 5.——[u] Deut. xxxii. 35; Job xxxiv. 29; Rom. xii. 19; Heb. x. 30; 2 Kings v. 7.——[v] Psa. lvi. 5; Isaiah x. 7.——[w] Chapter xlv. 5, 7; Acts iii. 13, 14, 15. [x] Chap. xlvii. 12; Matt. v. 44.

[y] Heb. *to their hearts;* chap. xxxiv. 3.——[z] Job xlii. 16. [a] Num. xxxii. 39.——[b] Chap. xxx. 3.——[c] Heb. *borne.*——[d] Ch. xv. 14; xlvi. 4; xlviii. 21; Exod. iii. 16, 17; Heb. xi. 22. [e] Chap. xv. 14; xxvi. 3; xxxv. 12; xlvi. 4.——[f] Exod. xiii. 19; Josh. xxiv. 32; Acts vii. 16.

Though *bribes* or *favour* shall assert his cause,
Pronounce him *guiltless*, and elude the laws,
None quits himself; his own impartial thought
Will damn, and conscience will record the fault.
This, first, the wicked feels.

We have seen this in the preceding history often exemplified in the case of Joseph's brethren.

Verse 16. *Thy father did command*] Whether he did or not we cannot tell. Some think they had feigned this story, but that is not so likely. Jacob might have had suspicions too, and might have thought that the best way to prevent evil was to humble themselves before their brother, and get a fresh assurance of his forgiveness.

Verse 17. *The servants of the God of thy father.*] These words were wonderfully well chosen, and spoken in the most forcible manner to Joseph's *piety* and *filial affection.* No wonder then that *he wept when they spake to him.*

Verse 19. Am *I in the place of God?*] These words may be understood either as a *question*, or an *affirmative proposition.* How should I take any farther notice of your transgression? I have passed it by, the matter lies now between God and you. Or, In the order of Divine providence I am now in God's place; he has furnished me with means, and made me a distributor of his bounty; I will therefore not only nourish you, but also your little ones, ver. 21: and therefore he spake comfortably unto them, as in chap. xlv. 8, telling them that he attributed the whole business to the *particular providence of God* rather than to any *ill will* or *malice* in them, and that, in permitting him to be brought into Egypt, God had graciously saved their lives, the life of their father, the lives of the people of Canaan, and of the Egyptians: as therefore God had honoured him by making him vicegerent in the dispensations of his especial bounty towards so many people, it was impossible he should be displeased with the *means* by which this was brought about.

Verse 22. *Joseph dwelt in Egypt*] Continued in Egypt after his return from Canaan till his death; *he, and his father's house*—all the *descendants* of Israel, till the *exodus* or departure under the direction of Moses and Aaron, which was one hundred and forty-four years after.

Verse 23. *Were brought up upon Joseph's knees.*] They were educated by him, or under his direction; his sons and their children continuing to acknowledge him as *patriarch*, or head of the family, as long as he lived.

Verse 24. *Joseph said—I die*] That is, I am dying; *and God will surely visit you*—he will yet again give you, in the time when it shall be essentially necessary, the most signal proof of his unbounded love towards the seed of Jacob.

And bring you out of this land] Though ye have here every thing that can render life comfortable, yet this is not the *typical land*, the *land given by covenant*, the land which represents the *rest* that remains for the people of God.

Verse 25. *Ye shall carry up my bones*] That I may finally rest with my ancestors in the land which God gave to Abraham, to Isaac, and to Jacob; and which is a *pledge* as it is a *type* of the *kingdom of heaven.* Thus says the author of the Epistle to the *Hebrews*, chap. xi. 22: "*By* FAITH Joseph, when he died, (τελευτων, when *dying*,) made mention of the departure (εξοδου, of the EXODUS) of the children of Israel; and gave commandment concerning his bones." From this it is evident that Joseph considered all these

A. M. 2369. B. C. 1635.

26 So Joseph died, *being* a hundred and ten years old: and they [g] embalmed him, and he was put in a coffin in Egypt.

A. M. 2369. B. C. 1635.

[g] Genesis, chap. l. 2.

things as *typical*, and by this very commandment expressed his faith in the immortality of the soul, and the general resurrection of the dead. This oath, by which Joseph then bound his brethren, their posterity considered as binding on themselves; and Moses took care, when he departed from Egypt, to carry up Joseph's body with him, Exod. xiii. 19; which was afterwards buried in *Shechem*, Josh. xxiv. 32, the very *portion* which Jacob had purchased from the Amorites, and which he gave to his son Joseph, Gen. xlviii. 22; Acts vii. 16. See the reason for this command as given by Chrysostom, vol. ii., p. 695, sec. D. E.

Verse 26. *Joseph died*, being *a hundred and ten years old*] בן מאה ועשר שנים *ben meah vaeser shanim;* literally, *the son of a hundred and ten years.* Here the *period* of time he lived is *personified*, all the years of which it was composed being represented as a *nurse* or *father*, feeding, nourishing, and supporting him to the end. This figure, which is termed by rhetoricians *prosopopœia*, is very frequent in Scripture; and by this *virtues, vices, forms, attributes*, and *qualities*, with every part of *inanimate nature*, are represented as endued with *reason* and *speech*, and performing all the actions of *intelligent* beings.

They embalmed him] See on ver. 2. The same precautions were taken to preserve his body as to preserve that of his father Jacob; and this was particularly necessary in his case, because his body was to be carried to Canaan a hundred and forty-four years after; which was the duration of the Israelites' bondage after the death of Joseph.

And he was put in a coffin in Egypt.] On this subject I shall subjoin some useful remarks from *Harmer's Observations*, which several have borrowed without acknowledgment. I quote my own edition of this Work, vol. iii., p. 69, &c. Lond. 1808.

"There were some methods of *honouring the dead* which demand our attention; the being put into a *coffin* has been in particular considered as a mark of distinction.

"With *us* the poorest people have their *coffins;* if the *relations* cannot afford them, the *parish* is at the expense. In the east, on the contrary, they are *not* always used, even in our times. The ancient Jews probably buried their dead in the same manner: neither was the body of our Lord put in a *coffin*, nor that of *Elisha*, whose bones were *touched* by the corpse that was let down a little after into his sepulchre, 2 Kings xiii. 21. That *coffins* were anciently used in Egypt, all agree; and antique coffins of *stone* and of *sycamore* wood are still to be seen in that country, not to mention those said to be made of a sort of *pasteboard*, formed by folding and gluing cloth together a great number of times, curiously plastered, and then painted with hieroglyphics.

"As it was an ancient Egyptian custom, and was not used in the neighbouring countries, on these accounts the sacred historian was doubtless led to observe of Joseph that he was not only *embalmed*, but was also put in a *coffin*, both being practices almost peculiar to the Egyptians.

"Mr. *Maillet* conjectures that *all* were not inclosed in *coffins* which were laid in the Egyptian repositories of the dead, but that it was an honour appropriated to persons of distinction; for after having given an account of several *niches* which are found in those chambers of death, he adds: 'But it must not be imagined that the bodies deposited in these gloomy apartments were all inclosed in *chests*, and placed in niches. The greater part were simply *embalmed* and swathed, after which they laid them one by the side of the other, without any ceremony. Some were even put into these tombs *without any embalming* at all, or with such a slight one that there remains nothing of them in the linen in which they were wrapped but the bones, and these half rotten. It is probable that each considerable family had one of these burial-places to themselves; that the *niches* were designed for the bodies of the heads of the family; and that those of their domestics and slaves had no other care taken of them than merely laying them in the ground after being slighty embalmed, and sometimes even without that; which was probably all that was done to heads of families of less distinction.'—*Lett.* 7, p. 281. The same author gives an account of a mode of burial anciently practised in that country, which has been but recently discovered: it consisted in placing the bodies, after they were swathed up, on a layer of charcoal, and covering them with a mat, under a bed of sand seven or eight feet deep.

"Hence it seems evident that *coffins* were not *universally* used in Egypt, and were only used for persons of eminence and distinction. It is also reasonable to believe that in times so remote as those of Joseph they might have been much less common than afterwards, and that consequently Joseph's being put in a coffin in Egypt might be mentioned with a design to express the *great honours* the Egyptians did him in death, as well as in life; being treated after the most sumptuous manner, *embalmed*, and put *into a coffin*."

It is no objection to this account that the widow of Nain's son is represented as carried forth to be buried in a σορος or *bier;* for the present inhabitants of the Levant, who are well known to lay their dead in the earth *uninclosed*, carry them frequently out to burial in a kind of *coffin*, which is not deposited in the grave, the body being *taken out of it*, and placed in the grave in a reclining posture. It is probable that the coffins used at Nain were of the same kind, being intended for no other purpose but to carry the body to the place of interment, the body itself being buried without them.

It is very probable that the chief difference was not in being *with* or *without* a coffin, but in the *expensiveness* of the coffin itself; some of the Egyptian coffins being made of granite, and covered all over

with hieroglyphics, the cutting of which must have been done at a prodigious expense, both of time and money; the stone being so hard that we have no tools by which we can make any impression on it. Two of these are now in the British Museum, that appear to have belonged to some of the *nobles* of Egypt. They are dug out of the solid stone, and adorned with almost innumerable hieroglyphics. One of these, vulgarly called Alexander's tomb, is ten feet three inches and a quarter long, ten inches thick in the sides, in breadth at top five feet three inches and a half, in breadth at bottom four feet two inches and a half, and three feet ten in depth, and weighs about ten tons. In such a coffin I suppose the body of Joseph was deposited; and such a one could not have been made and transported to Canaan at an expense that any private individual could bear. It was with incredible labour and at an extraordinary expense that the coffin in question was removed the distance of but a few miles, from the ship that brought it from Egypt, to its present residence in the British Museum. Judge, then, at what an expense such a coffin must have been digged, engraved, and transported over the desert from Egypt to Canaan, a distance of three hundred miles! We need not be surprised to hear of carriages and horsemen, a very great company, when such a coffin was to be carried so far, with a suitable company to attend it.

Joseph's life was the *shortest* of all the patriarchs, for which Bishop Patrick gives a sound *physical* reason—he was the son of his father's *old age.* It appears from Archbishop Usher's Chronology that Joseph governed Egypt under four kings, *Mephramuthosis, Thmosis, Amenophis,* and *Orus.* His government, we know, lasted *eighty* years; for when he stood before Pharaoh he was *thirty* years of age, chap. xli. 46, and he died when he was *one hundred* and *ten.*

On the *character* and *conduct* of Joseph many remarks have already been made in the preceding notes. On the subject of his *piety* there can be but one opinion. It was truly exemplary, and certainly was tried in cases in which few instances occur of *persevering fidelity.* His high sense of the holiness of God, the strong claims of justice, and the rights of hospitality and gratitude, led him, in the instance of the solicitations of his master's wife, to act a part which, though absolutely just and proper, can never be sufficiently praised. Heathen authors boast of some persons of such singular constancy; but the intelligent reader will recollect that these relations stand in general in their *fabulous histories,* and are destitute of those characteristics which truth essentially requires; such, I mean, as the story of *Hippolytus* and *Phædra, Bellerophon* and *Antea* or *Sthenobœa, Peleus* and *Astydamia,* and others of this complexion, which appear to be marred pictures, taken from this highly finished original which the inspired writer has fairly drawn from life.

His *fidelity* to his master is not less evident, and God's approbation of his conduct is strongly marked; for he caused whatsoever he did to prosper, whether a slave in the house of his master, a prisoner in the dungeon, or a prime minister by the throne, which is a full proof that his ways pleased him; and this is more clearly seen in the providential deliverances by which he was favoured.

On the *political conduct* of Joseph there are conflicting opinions. On the one hand it is asserted that "he found the Egyptians a *free people,* and that he availed himself of a most afflicting providence of God to reduce them all to a *state of slavery,* destroyed their political consequence, and made their king despotic." In all these respects his political measures have been strongly vindicated, not only as being directed by God, but as being *obviously* the best, every thing considered, for the safety, honour, and welfare of his sovereign and the kingdom. It is true he bought the lands of the people for the king, but he *farmed them* to the original occupiers again, at the moderate and fixed crown rent of *one-fifth part* of the produce. "Thus did he provide for the *liberty and independence of the people,* while he strengthened the *authority* of the *king* by making him sole proprietor of the lands. And to secure the people from farther exaction, Joseph made it a law over all the land of Egypt, that Pharaoh (i. e. the king) should have only the fifth part; which law subsisted to the time of Moses, chap. xlvii. 21–26. By this wise regulation,' continues Dr. Hales, "the people had four-fifths of the produce of the lands for their own use, and were exempted from any farther taxes, the king being bound to support his civil and military establishment out of the crown rents." By the original constitution of Egypt established by *Menes,* and *Thoth* or *Hermes* his prime minister, the lands were divided into *three portions,* between the *king,* the *priests,* and the *military,* each party being bound to support its respective establishment by the *produce.* See the quotations from Diodorus Siculus, in the note on chap. xlvii. 23. It is certain, therefore, that the constitution of Egypt was considerably altered by Joseph, and there can be no doubt that much additional power was, by this alteration, vested in the hands of the king; but as we do not find that any improper use was made of this power, we may rest assured that it was so *qualified* and *restricted* by wholesome *regulations,* though they are not here particularized, as completely to prevent all *abuse* of the regal power, and all tyrannical usurpation of popular rights. That the people were nothing but slaves to the *king,* the *military,* and the *priests* before, appears from the account given by Diodorus; each of the three estates probably allowing them a certain portion of land for their own use, while cultivating the rest for the use and emolument of their masters. Matters, however, became more *regular* under the administration of Joseph; and it is perhaps not too much to say, that, previously to this, Egypt was without a fixed regular constitution, and that it was not the least of the blessings that it owed to the wisdom and prudence of Joseph, that he reduced it to a *regular form of government,* giving the people such an interest in the safety of the state as was well calculated to insure their exertions to defend the nation, and render the *constitution* fixed and permanent.

It is well known that *Justin,* one of the Roman historians, has made particular and indeed honourable mention of *Joseph's* administration in Egypt, in the account he gives of Jewish affairs, lib. xxxvi. cap. 2.

How the relation may have stood in *Trogus Pompeius*, from whose voluminous works in forty-four books or volumes Justin abridged his history, we cannot tell, as the work of Trogus is irrecoverably lost; but it is evident that the account was taken in the main from the Mosaic history, and it is written with as much candour as can be expected from a *prejudiced* and *unprincipled heathen*.

Minimus ætate inter fratres Joseph fuit, &c. "Joseph was the youngest of his brethren, who, being envious of his excellent endowments, stole him and privately sold him to a company of foreign merchants, by whom he was carried into Egypt; where, having diligently cultivated *magic arts*, he became, in a short time, a prime favourite with the king himself. For he was the most sagacious of men in explaining prodigies; and he was the first who constructed the science of *interpreting dreams*. Nor was there any thing relative to laws human or Divine with which he seemed unacquainted; for he predicted a failure of the crops many years before it took place; and the inhabitants of Egypt must have been famished had not the king, through his counsel, made an edict to preserve the fruits for several years. And his experiments were so powerful, that the responses appear to have been given, not by man, but by God." *Tantaque* experimenta *ejus fuerunt, ut non ab homine, sed a Deo, responsa dari viderentur.* I believe Justin refers here, in the word *experimenta*, to his figment of *magical incantations* eliciting *oracular answers*. Others have translated the words: "So *excellent were his regulations* that they seemed rather to be *oracular responses*, not given by *man*, but by God."

I have already compared Joseph with his father Jacob, see chap. xlviii. 12, and shall make no apology for having given the latter a most decided superiority. Joseph was great; but his greatness came through the interposition of especial providences. Jacob was great, *mentally* and *practically* great, under the *ordinary* workings of Providence; and, towards the close of his life, not less distinguished for piety towards God than his son Joseph was in the holiest period of his life.

Thus terminates the Book of Genesis, the most ancient record in the world; including the history of two grand subjects, Creation and Providence, of each of which it gives a summary, but astonishingly minute, and detailed account. From *this book* almost all the ancient philosophers, astronomers, chronologists, and historians have taken their respective *data;* and all the modern improvements and accurate discoveries in different arts and sciences have only served to confirm the facts detailed by Moses; and to show that all the ancient writers on these subjects have *approached* to or *receded* from truth and the *phenomena* of *nature*, in proportion as they have *followed* the *Mosaic history*.

In this book the creative power and energy of God are first introduced to the reader's notice, and the mind is overwhelmed with those grand creative acts by which the *universe* was brought into being. When this account is completed, and the introduction of sin, and its awful consequences in the destruction of the earth by a *flood*, noticed, then the Almighty Creator is next introduced as the Restorer and Preserver of the world; and thus the history of *Providence* commences: a history in which the mind of man is alternately delighted and confounded with the infinitely varied plans of *wisdom* and *mercy* in preserving the human species, counteracting the evil propensities of men and devils by means of *gracious influences* conveyed through *religious institutions*, planting and watering the seeds of righteousness which himself had sowed in the hearts of men, and leading forward and maturing the grand purposes of his *grace* in the final salvation of the *human race*.

After giving a minutely detailed account of the *peopling of the earth*, ascertaining and settling the bounds of the different nations of mankind, the sacred writer proceeds with the history of *one family* only; but he chooses that one through which, as from an ever-during fountain, the streams of justice, grace, goodness, wisdom, and truth, should emanate. Here we see a pure well of living water, springing up unto eternal life, restrained in its *particular* influence to one people till, in the fulness of time, the fountain should be opened in the house of David for sin and for uncleanness in *general*, and the earth filled with the knowledge and salvation of God; thus by means of one family, as extensive a view of the economy of providence and grace is afforded as it is possible for the human mind to comprehend.

In this *epitome* how wonderful do the workings of Providence appear! An astonishing concatenated train of *stupendous* and *minute* events is laid before us; and every transaction is so distinctly marked as everywhere to exhibit the *finger*, the *hand*, or the *arm* of God! But did God lavish his providential cares and attention on this one family, exclusive of the rest of his intelligent offspring? No: for the same superintendence, providential direction, and influence, would be equally seen in all the concerns of human life, in the preservation of individuals, the rise and fall of kingdoms and states, and in all the mighty revolutions, *natural, moral*, and *political*, in the universe, were God, as in the preceding instances, to give us the *detailed* history; but what was done in the family of Abraham, was done in behalf of the whole human race. This specimen is intended to show us that God *does work*, and that against him and the operations of his hand, no *might*, no *counsel*, no *cunning* of men or devils, can prevail; that he who walks uprightly walks securely; and that all things work together for good to them who love God; that none is so *ignorant, low*, or *lost*, that God cannot *instruct, raise up*, and *save*. In a word, he shows himself by this history to be the invariable *friend of mankind*, embracing every opportunity to do them good, and, to speak after the manner of men, rejoicing in the frequent recurrence of such opportunities; that every man, considering the subject, may be led to exclaim in behalf of all his fellows, BEHOLD how HE loveth THEM!

On the character of Moses as a historian and philosopher (for in his *legislative* character he does not yet appear) much might be said, did the nature of this work admit. But as *brevity* has been everywhere studied, and minute details rarely admitted, and only

where absolutely necessary, the candid reader will excuse any deficiencies of this kind which he may have already noticed.

Of the *accuracy* and *impartiality* of Moses as a *historian*, many examples are given in the course of the notes, with such observations and reflections as the subjects themselves suggested; and the succeeding books will afford many opportunities for farther remarks on these topics.

The character of Moses as a *philosopher* and *chronologist*, has undergone the severest scrutiny. A class of philosophers, professedly infidels, have assailed the Mosaic account of the formation of the universe, and that of the general deluge, with such repeated attacks as sufficiently prove that, in their apprehension, the pillars of their system must be shaken into ruin if those accounts could not be proved to be false. *Traditions*, supporting accounts different from those in the sacred history, have been borrowed from the most barbarous as well as the most civilized nations, in order to bear on this argument. These, backed by various geologic observations made in extensive travels, experiments on the formation of different *strata* or beds of earth, either by inundations or volcanic eruption, have been all condensed into one apparently strong but strange argument, intended to overthrow the Mosaic account of the creation. The argument may be stated thus: "The account given by Moses of the time when God commenced his creative acts is *too recent;* for, according to his Genesis, *six thousand* years have not yet elapsed since the formation of the universe; whereas a variety of phenomena prove that the earth itself must have existed, if not from eternity, yet at least *fourteen* if not *twenty thousand* years." This I call a *strange* argument, because it is well known that all the ancient nations in the world, the *Jews* excepted, have, to secure their honour and respectability, assigned to themselves a *duration* of the most improbable *length;* and have multiplied *months, weeks,* and even *days,* into *years,* in order to support their pretensions to the most remote antiquity. The *millions* of years which have been assumed by the *Chinese* and the *Hindoos* have been ridiculed for their manifest absurdity, even by those philosophers who have brought the *contrary charge* against the Mosaic account! So notorious are the pretensions to remote ancestry and remote eras, in every *false* and *fabricated system* of family pedigree and national antiquity, as to produce doubt at the very first view of their subjects, and to cause the impartial inquirer after truth to take every step with the extreme of caution, knowing that in going over such accounts he everywhere treads on a kind of enchanted ground.

When in the midst of these a writer is found who, without saying a word of the systems of other nations, professes to give a simple account of the creation and peopling of the earth, and to show the very conspicuous part that his own people acted among the various nations of the world, and who assigns to the earth and to its inhabitants a duration comparatively but as of *yesterday*, he comes forward with such a variety of claims to be heard, read, and considered, as no other writer can pretend to. And as he departs from the universal custom of all writers on similar subjects, in assigning a comparatively recent date, not only to his own nation, but to the universe itself, he must have been actuated by motives essentially *different* from those which have governed all other ancient historians and chronologists.

The generally acknowledged extravagance and absurdity of all the chronological systems of ancient times, the great simplicity and harmony of that of Moses, its facts evidently borrowed by others, though disgraced by the fables they have intermixed with them, and the very late invention of arts and sciences, all tend to prove, at the very first view, that the Mosaic account, which assigns the shortest duration to the earth, is the most ancient and the most likely to be true. But all this reasoning has been supposed to be annihilated by an argument brought against the Mosaic account of the creation by Mr. Patrick Brydone, F. R. S., drawn from the evidence of different eruptions of Mount Ætna. The reader may find this in his "Tour through Sicily and Malta," letter vii., where, speaking of his acquaintance with the *Canonico Recupero* at Catania, who was then employed on writing a natural history of Mount Ætna, he says: "Near to a vault which is now *thirty* feet below ground, and has probably been a burying-place, there is a draw-well where there are several strata of *lavas*, (i. e., the liquid matter formed of stones, &c., which is discharged from the mountain in its eruptions,) with earth to a considerable thickness over each stratum. *Recupero* has made use of this as an argument to prove the great antiquity of the eruptions of this mountain. For if it requires *two thousand* years and upwards to form but a scanty soil on the surface of a *lava*, there must have been more than that space of time between each of the eruptions which have formed these strata. But what shall we say of a pit they sunk near to *Jaci*, of a great depth? They pierced through *seven* distinct *lavas*, one under the other, the surfaces of which were parallel, and most of them covered *with a thick bed of rich earth.* Now, says he, the eruption which formed the lowest of these lavas, if we may be allowed to reason from analogy, must have flowed from the mountain at least *fourteen thousand* years ago! *Recupero* tells me, he is exceedingly embarrassed by these discoveries, in writing the history of the mountain; that Moses hangs like a dead weight upon him, and blunts all his zeal for inquiry, for that he *really has not the conscience to make his mountain so young as that prophet makes the world.*

"The bishop, who is strenuously orthodox, (for it is an excellent see,) has already warned him to be upon his guard; and not to pretend to be a better natural historian than Moses, nor to presume to urge any thing that may in the smallest degree be deemed contradictory to *his* sacred authority."

Though Mr. Brydone produces this as a sneer against revelation, bishops, and orthodoxy, yet the sequel will prove that it was good advice, and that the bishop was much better instructed than either *Recupero* or *Brydone*, and that it would have been much to their credit had they taken his advice.

I have given, however, this argument at length; and even in the insidious dress of Mr. Brydone, whose

faith in Divine revelation appears to have been upon a par with that of *Signior Recupero*, both being built nearly on the same foundation; to show from the answer how slight the strongest arguments are, produced from insulated facts by prejudice and partiality, when brought to the test of sober, candid, philosophical investigation, aided by an increased knowledge of the phenomena of nature. "In answer to this argument," says Bishop Watson, (Letters to Gibbon,) "it might be urged that the time necessary for converting *lavas* into fertile fields must be very different, according to the different consistencies of the *lavas*, and their different situations with respect to *elevation* and *depression*, or their being exposed to *winds, rains*, and other circumstances; as for instance, the *quantity of ashes* deposited over them, after they had cooled, &c., &c., just as the time in which heaps of *iron slag*, which resembles lava, are covered with verdure, is different at different furnaces, according to the nature of the *slag* and situation of the furnace; and something of this kind is deducible from the account of the Canon (Recupero) himself, since the *crevices* in the strata are often full of rich good soil, and have pretty large trees growing upon them. But should not all this be thought sufficient to remove the objection, I will produce the canon an *analogy* in opposition to his analogy, and which is grounded on more certain facts.

"Ætna and Vesuvius resemble each other in the causes which produce their eruptions, in the nature of their *lavas*, and in the time necessary to mellow them into soil fit for vegetation; or, if there be any slight difference in this respect, it is probably not greater than what subsists between different lavas of the same mountain. This being admitted, which no philosopher will deny, the canon's (Recupero's) analogy will prove just nothing at all if we can produce an instance of *seven* different *lavas*, with *interjacent strata of vegetable earth*, which have flowed from Mount Vesuvius within the space, not of *fourteen thousand*, but of somewhat less than *one thousand seven hundred* years; for then, according to our analogy, *a stratum of lava may be covered with vegetable soil in about two hundred and fifty years*, instead of requiring *two thousand* for that purpose.

"The eruption of Vesuvius, which destroyed *Herculaneum* and *Pompeii*, is rendered still more famous by the death of *Pliny*, recorded by his nephew in his letter to *Tacitus*. This event happened A. D. 79; but we are informed by unquestionable authority, (*Remarks on the nature of the soil of Naples and its vicinity*, by Sir William Hamilton, *Philos. Transact.*, vol. lxi., p. 7,) that the matter which covers the ancient town of *Herculaneum* is not the produce of *one* eruption only, for there are evident marks that the matter of *six* eruptions has taken its course over that which lies immediately over the town, and was the cause of its destruction. The strata are either of *lava* or burnt matter with *veins of good soil between them*. You perceive," says the bishop, "with what ease a *little attention* and *increase of knowledge* may remove a great difficulty; but had we been able to say nothing in explanation of this phenomenon, we should not have acted a very rational part in making our *ignorance* the *foundation of our infidelity*, or suffering a minute philosopher to rob us of our religion." In this, as well as in all other cases, the foundation stands sure, being deeply and legibly impressed with God's seal See also Dr. *Greaves's* Lectures on the Pentateuch.

There is a very sensible paper written by *Don Joseph Gioeni** on the eruption of Ætna in 1781; in which, among many other valuable observations, I find the following note: "I was obliged to traverse the current of lava made by the eruption of 1766, the most *ancient* of any that took this direction, viz., *Bronte*. I saw several streams of lava which had *crossed others*, and which afforded me evident proofs of the fallacy of the conclusions of those who seek to estimate the period of the formation of the beds of lava from the *change* they have undergone. Some *lava* of *earlier* date than others *still resist the weather*, and present a *vitreous* and *unaltered surface*, while the *lava* of *later date* already begin to be covered with vegetation."—See Pinkerton on Rock, vol. ii., p. 395.

On the *geology* and *astronomy* of the book of Genesis, much has been written, both by the enemies and friends of revelation; but as Moses has said but very little on these subjects, and nothing in a *systematic* way, it is unfair to invent a system pretendedly collected out of his words, and thus make him accountable for what he never wrote. There are systems of this kind, the preconceived fictions of their authors, for which they have sought support and credit by tortured meanings extracted from a few *Hebrew roots*, and then dignified them with the title of *The Mosaic System of the Universe*. This has afforded infidelity a handle which it has been careful to turn to its own advantage. On the first chapter of Genesis, I have given a general view of the solar system, without pretending that I had found it there. I have also ventured to apply the comparatively recent doctrine of *caloric* to the Mosaic account of the creation of *light* previous to the formation of the *sun*, and have supported it with such arguments as appeared to me to render it at least probable: but I have not pledged Moses to any of my explanations, being fully convinced that it was necessarily foreign from his design to enter into philosophic *details* of any kind, as it was his grand object, as has been already remarked, to give a history of CREATION and PROVIDENCE in the most *abridged* form of which it was capable. And who, in so few words, ever spoke so much? By *Creation* I mean the production of every being, animate and inanimate, material and intellectual. And by *Providence*, not only the preservation and government of all being, but also the various and extraordinary provisions made by Divine justice and mercy for the comfort and final salvation of man. These subjects I have endeavoured to trace out through every chapter of this book, and to exhibit them in such a manner as appeared to me the best calculated to promote *glory* to GOD *in the highest, and upon earth* PEACE AND GOOD WILL AMONG MEN.

Observations on the Jewish manner of DIVIDING *and* READING *the* LAW *and the* PROPHETS.

The ancient Jews divided the whole law of Moses into *fifty-four* sections, which they read in their syna-

* The *Chevalier Gioeni* was an inhabitant of the first region of Ætna.

gogues in the course of the *fifty-two* Sabbaths in the year, joining *two* of the shortest twice together, that the whole might be finished in one year's space; but in their *intercalated* years, in which they added a *month*, they had *fifty-four* Sabbaths, and then they had a section for each Sabbath: and it was to meet the exigency of the *intercalated* years that they divided the law into fifty-four sections at first. When Antiochus Epiphanes forbade the Jews on pain of death to read their law, they divided the *prophets* into the same number of sections, and read *them* in their synagogues in place of the *law;* and when, under the Asmoneans, they recovered their liberty, and with it the free exercise of their religion, though the reading of the law was resumed, they continued the use of the *prophetic sections*, reading them conjointly with those in the law. To this *first division* and mode of reading the law there is a reference, Acts xv. 21: *For Moses of old time hath in every city them that preach him*, being READ IN THE SYNAGOGUES EVERY SABBATH DAY. To the second division and *conjoint* reading of the law and the prophets we also find a reference, Acts xiii. 15: *And after the reading of the* LAW AND THE PROPHETS, *the rulers of the synagogue sent unto them, saying, &c.* And that the *prophets* were read in this way in our *Lord's time*, we have a proof, Luke iv. 16, &c, where, *going into the synagogue to read on the Sabbath day, as was his custom, there was delivered unto him the book of the Prophet Isaiah:* and it appears that the *prophetical section* for that Sabbath was taken from the sixty-first chapter of his prophecies.

Of these *sections* the book of Genesis contains twelve:

The FIRST, called ברשית *bereshith*, begins chap. i. ver. 1, and ends chap. vi. ver. 8.

The SECOND, called נח *Noach*, begins chap. vi. ver. 9, and ends chap. xi.

The THIRD, called לך לך *lech lecha*, begins chap. xii., and ends chap. xviii.

The FOURTH, called וירא *vaiyera*, begins chap. xviii., and ends chap. xxii.

The FIFTH, called חיי שרה *chaiyey Sarah*, begins chap. xxiii., and ends chap. xxv. ver. 18.

The SIXTH, called תולדת *toledoth*, begins chap. xxv. ver. 19, and ends chap. xxviii. ver. 9.

The SEVENTH, called ויצא *vaiyetse*, begins chap. xxviii. ver. 10, and ends chap. xxxii. ver. 3.

The EIGHTH, called וישלח *vaiyishlach*, begins chap. xxxii. ver. 4, and ends chap. xxxvi.

The NINTH, called וישב *vaiyesheb*, begins chap. xxxvii., and ends chap. xl.

The TENTH, called מקץ *mikkets*, begins chap. xli., and ends chap. xliv. ver. 17.

The ELEVENTH, called ויגש *vaiyiggash*, begins chap. xliv. ver. 18, and ends chap. xlvii. ver. 27.

The TWELFTH, called ויחי *vayechi*, begins chap. xlvii. ver. 28, and ends chap. l.

These sections have their *technical* names, from the words with which they commence; and are marked in the Hebrew Bibles with three פפפ *pe's*, which are an abbreviation for פרשה *parashah*, a *section* or *division;* and sometimes with three ססס *samech's*, which are an abbreviation for the word סדר *seder*, or סדרא *sidra*, an *order*, a full and absolute division. The former are generally called פרשיות *parashioth*, *distinctions*, *divisions*, *sections;* the latter סדרים *sedarim*, *orders*, *arrangements;* as it is supposed that the sense is more full and complete in *these* than in the *parashioth*. See the Tables, &c., at the end of the Book of Deuteronomy, where all these matters, and others connected with them, are considered in great detail.

MASORETIC *Notes* on the Book of GENESIS.

At the end of all the books in the Hebrew Bible, the *Masoretes* have affixed certain *notes*, ascertaining the *number* of *greater* and *smaller sections*, *chapters*, *verses*, and *letters*. These they deemed of the greatest importance, in order to preserve the integrity of their law, and the purity of their prophets. And to this end they not only numbered every verse, word, and letter, but even went so far as to ascertain how often *each letter* of the *alphabet* occurred in the *whole Bible!* Thus sacredly did they watch over their records in order to prevent every species of corruption.

The *sum* of all the VERSES in *Bereshith* (Genesis) is 1534. And the memorial sign of this sum is אך לד—*aleph* א signifying 1000; *final caph* ך 500; *lamed* ל 30, and *daleth* ד 4.=1534.

The *middle* verse of Genesis is the fortieth of chap. xxvii.: *By thy sword shalt thou live.*

The PARASHIOTH, or greater sections, are twelve. The symbol of which is the word זה *zeh*, THIS, Exod. iii. 15: *And* THIS *is my memorial to all generations.* Where *zain* ז stands for 7, and *he* ה for 5.=12.

The SEDARIM, or *orders*, (see above) are forty-three. The symbol of which is the word גם *gam*. Gen. xxvii. 33: YEA (גם *gam*) *and he shall be blessed.* Where *gimel* ג stands for 3, and *mem* ם for 40.=43.

The PERAKIM, or modern division of chapters, are fifty; the symbol of which is לך *lecha*, Isa. xxxiii. 2: *We have waited* FOR THEE. Where *lamed* ל stands for 30, and *caph* ך for 20.=50.

The *open sections* are 43, the *close sections* 48, total 91: the numerical sign of which is צא *tse*, GET THEE OUT, Exod. xi. 8, where *tsaddi* צ stands for 90, and *aleph* א for 1.=91.

The *number* of letters is about 52,740; but this last is more a matter of conjecture and *computation* than of *certainty*, and on it no dependence can safely be placed, it being a mere multiplication by *twelve*, the number of sections, of 4395, the known number of letters in the last or *twelfth* section of the book. On this subject see Buxtorf's *Tiberias*, p. 181.

A CHRONOLOGICAL TABLE

OF THE PRINCIPAL TRANSACTIONS RELATED IN THE BOOK OF GENESIS, ACCORDING TO THE COMPUTATION OF ARCHBISHOP USHER, WHICH IS CHIEFLY FOLLOWED IN THE PRECEDING NOTES; SHOWING IN WHAT YEAR OF THE WORLD, AND WHAT YEAR BEFORE CHRIST, EACH EVENT HAPPENED.

The reader will observe, from the chronological notes in the *margin* of the preceding work, that in a few instances I have departed from the Usherian computation, for which he will find my reasons in the notes.

This table I have considerably enlarged by inserting the *Edomitish kings* and *dukes*, and a few other transactions of profane history contemporary with the facts mentioned by Moses, by which the reader will have a synopsis or general view of all the transactions of the first two thousand four hundred years of the world, which stand upon any authentic records.

The *first* year of the world, answering to the 710th year of the Julian period, and supposed to be 4004 before the vulgar era of the birth of Christ.

A. M.		B. C.
1	First day's work: Creation of the heavens and earth; of light, with the distinction of day and night, Gen. i. 1–5.	4004
	Second day: Creation of the firmament, and separation of the superior and inferior waters, i. 6–8.	
	Third day: The earth drained, the seas, lakes, &c., formed; trees, plants, and vegetables produced, i. 9–13.	
	Fourth day: The sun, moon, planets, and stars produced, i. 14–19.	
	Fifth day: All kinds of fowls and fishes created, i. 20–23.	
	Sixth day: Beasts wild and tame, reptiles, insects, and man, i. 24–28.	
	Seventh day: Set apart and hallowed to be a Sabbath, or day of rest for ever, ii. 2, 3.	
	Tenth day: The first woman sins, leads her husband into the transgression, is called Eve, iii. 1–20. They are both expelled from Paradise, iii. 22–24.	
	N. B. This opinion, though rendered respectable by great names, is very doubtful, and should be received with very great caution. I think it wholly inadmissible; and though I insert it as the generally received opinion, yet judge it best to form no guesses and indulge no conjectures on such an obscure point.	
2	Cain and Abel born, iv. 1, 2.	4002
129	Abel killed by his brother Cain, iv. 8.	3875
130	Birth of Seth, iv. 25.	3874
235	Enos son of Seth born, iv. 26. Hence followed the distinction between the descendants of Cain and those of Seth; the former being called *sons of men*, the latter *sons of God*, vi. 1–4.	3769
325	Birth of Cainan, son of Enos, v. 9.	3679
395	—— of Mahalaleel, son of Cainan, v. 12.	3609
460	—— of Jared, son of Mahalaleel, v. 15.	3544
622	—— of Enoch, son of Jared, v. 18.	3382
687	Birth of Methuselah, son of Enoch, v. 21.	3317
874	—— of Lamech, son of Methuselah, v. 25.	3130
930	Death of Adam, aged 930 years, v. 5.	3074
987	Enoch is translated in the 365th year of his age, v. 24.	3017
1042	Seth dies, aged 912 years, v. 8.	2962
1056	Birth of Noah, son of Lamech, v. 29.	2948
1140	Enos dies, aged 905 years, v. 11.	2864
1235	Cainan dies, aged 910 years, v. 14.	2769
1290	Mahalaleel dies, aged 895 years, v. 17.	2714
1422	Jared dies, aged 962 years, v. 20.	2582
1536	God commissions Noah to preach repentance to the guilty world, and to announce the deluge. He commands him also to build an ark for the safety of himself and his family. This commission was given 120 years before the flood came, 1 Pet. iii. 20; 2 Pet. ii. 5; Gen. vi. 17.	2468
1556	Birth of Japheth, son of Noah, v. 32, compared with x. 21.	2448
1558	—— of Shem.	2446
1560	—— of Ham.	2444
1651	Death of Lamech, aged 777 years, v. 31.	2353
1656	—— of Methuselah, aged 969 years, v. 27.	2348
——	The *general* DELUGE, vii.	——
——	Noah, his family, and the animals to be preserved, enter the ark the 17th day of the 2d month of this year, vii. 11. The rain commences, and continues 40 days and nights, and the waters continue without decreasing 150 days; they afterwards begin to abate, and the ark rests on Mount Ararat, viii. 4.	——
——	Noah sends out a raven, viii. 7.	——
——	Seven days after he sends out a dove, which returns the same day; after seven days he sends out the dove a second time, which returns no more, viii. 8–12.	——
1657	Noah, his family, &c., leave the ark. He offers sacrifices to God, viii. and ix.	2347

A. M.		B. C.
1658	Birth of Arphaxad, son of Shem, xi. 10, 11.	2346
1693	—— of Salah, son of Arphaxad, xi. 12.	2311
1723	—— of Eber, son of Salah, xi. 14.	2281
1757	—— of Peleg, son of Eber, xi. 16.	2247
——	Building of the Tower of Babel, xi. 1–9.	——
1771	About this time Babylon was built by the command of Nimrod.	2233
1787	Birth of Reu, son of Peleg, xi. 18.	2217
1816	Commencement of the regal government of Egypt, from Mizraim, son of Ham. Egypt continued an independent kingdom from this time to the reign of Cambyses, king of Persia, which was a period of 1663 years, according to Constantinus Manasses.	2188
1819	Birth of Serug, son of Reu xi. 20.	2185
1849	—— of Nahor, son of Serug, xi. 22.	2155
1878	—— of Terah, son of Nahor, xi. 24.	2126
1915	About this time, Ægialeus founds the kingdom of Sicyon, according to Eusebius.	2089
1948	Birth of Nahor and Haran, sons of Terah, xi. 26.	2056
1996	Peleg dies, aged 239 years, xi. 19.	2008
1997	Nahor dies, aged 148 years, xi. 25.	2007
2006	Noah dies, aged 950 years, 350 years after the flood, ix. 29.	1998
2008	Birth of ABRAM, son of Terah, xi. 26.	1996
2018	—— of SARAI, wife of Abram.	1986
2026	Reu dies, xi. 21.	1978
2049	Serug dies, xi. 23.	1955
2079	Chedorlaomer, king of Elam, subdues the kings of the *Pentapolis*, Sodom, Gomorrah, &c., to whom they continued in subjection 12 years, xiv. 4.	1925
2083	The calling of Abram out of UR of the Chaldees, where the family had been addicted to idolatry, Josh. xxiv. 2. He comes to Haran in Mesopotamia, with Lot his nephew, Sarai his wife, and his father Terah, who dies at Haran, aged 205 years, xi. 31, 32.	1921
——	Abram comes to Canaan, when 75 years of age, Gen. xii. 4. From this period the 430 years of the sojourning of the Israelites, mentioned Exod. xii. 40, 41, is generally dated.	——
2084	Abram goes into Egypt because of the famine, xii. 10; causes Sarai to pass for his sister. Pharaoh (*Apophis*) takes her to his house; but soon restores her, finding her to be Abram's wife, ver. 14–20.	1920
2086	Abram and Lot, having returned to the land of Canaan, separate; Lot goes to Sodom, and Abram to the valley of Mamre, near to Hebron, xiii.	1918
2090	The kings of the *Pentapolis* revolt from Chedorlaomer, xiv. 4.	1914
2091	Chedorlaomer and his allies make war with the kings of the *Pentapolis*; Lot is taken captive; Abram with his allies pursues Chedorlaomer, defeats him and the confederate kings delivers Lot and the other captives, and is blessed by Melchizedek, king of Salem, xiv.	1913
2093	God promises Abram a numerous posterity, xv. 1.	1911
——	About this time Bela, the first king of the Edomites, began to reign, xxxvi. 32.	——
2094	Sarai gives Hagar to Abram, xvi. 2.	1910
——	Of her Ishmael is born, xvi. 15, Abram being then 86 years old.	——
2096	Arphaxad dies, 403 years after the birth of Salah, xi. 13.	1908
2107	God makes a covenant with Abram; gives him the promise of a son; changes his name into *Abraham*, and Sarai's into *Sarah*, and enjoins circumcision, xvii. 1, 5, 6, &c. Abraham entertains three angels on their way to destroy Sodom, &c., xviii. He intercedes for the inhabitants; but as *ten* righteous persons could not be found in those cities, they are destroyed, xix. 23. Lot is delivered, and for his sake Zoar is preserved, ver. 19, &c.	1897
——	Abraham retires to Beer-sheba, afterwards sojourns at Gerar. Abimelech, king of Gerar, takes Sarah, in order to make her his wife, but is obliged to restore her, xx.	——
2108	Isaac is born, xxi. 2, 3.	1896
——	Moab and Ben-ammi, the sons of Lot, born, xix. 37, 38.	——
2110	Abraham sends away Ishmael, xxi. 13, 14.	1894
2118	Abimelech and Phichol his chief captain make an agreement with Abraham, and surrender the well of Beer-sheba for seven ewe lambs, xxi. 22, &c.	1886
2126	Salah dies 403 years after the birth of Eber, xi. 15.	1878
2135	About this time Jobab, the second king of the Edomites, began to reign, xxxvi. 33.	1869
2141	Abraham is called to sacrifice his son Isaac, xxii.	1863
2145	Sarah dies, aged 127 years, xxiii. 1.	1859
2148	Abraham sends Eliezer to Mesopotamia to get a wife for his son Isaac, xxxiv.	1856
2154	About this time Abraham marries Keturah, xxv. 1.	1850
2158	Shem, son of Noah, dies 500 years after the birth of Arphaxad, xi. 11.	1846
2168	Birth of Jacob and Esau, Isaac their father being 60 years old, xv. 22, &c.	1836
2177	About this time Husham, the third king of the Edomites, began to reign, xxxvi. 34.	1827
2183	Abraham dies, aged 175 years, xxv. 7, 8.	1821

A. M.		B. C.
2187	Eber dies, 430 years after the birth of Peleg, xi. 17.	1817
2200	God appears to Isaac, and gives him glorious promises, xxvi. 4. He stays at Gerar during the famine, xxvi. 6.	1804
2208	Esau marries two Canaanitish women, xxvi. 34.	1796
2219	About this time Hadad, the fourth king of the Edomites, began to reign, xxxvi. 35.	1785
——	*Deluge of Ogyges in Greece,* 1020 *years before the first Olympiad.*	——
2225	Jacob by subtlety obtains Esau's blessing, xxvii. He goes to Haran, and engages to serve Laban seven years for Rachel, xxviii., xxix.	1779
——	Esau marries Mahalath, the daughter of Ishmael, xxviii. 9.	——
2231	Ishmael dies, aged 137 years, xxv. 17.	1773
2232	Jacob espouses Rachel seven years after his engagement with Laban: Leah is put in the place of her sister; but seven days after he receives Rachel, xxix.	1772
2233	Reuben is born, xxix. 32.	1771
2234	Simeon is born, xxix. 33.	1770
2235	Levi is born, xxix. 34.	1769
2236	Judah is born, xxix. 35.	1768
2237	Dan is born, xxx. 5, 6.	1767
2239	Naphtali is born, xxx. 7, 8.	1765
2240	Gad is born, xxx. 10, 11.	1764
2242	Asher is born, xxx. 12, 13.	1762
——	*Evechous begins to reign over the Chaldeans* 224 *years before the Arabs reigned in that country* (Julius Africanus.) *Usher supposes him to have been the same with* Belus, *who was afterwards worshipped by the Chaldeans.*	——
2247	Issachar is born, xxx. 17, 18.	1757
2249	Zebulun is born, xxx. 19, 20.	1755
2250	Dinah is born, xxx. 21.	1754
2259	Joseph is born, xxx. 23, 24.	1745
2261	About this time Samlah, the fifth king of the Edomites, began to reign, xxxvi. 36.	1743
2265	Jacob and his family, unknown to Laban, set out for Canaan. Laban, hearing of his departure, pursues him; after seven days he comes up with him at the mountains of Gilead; they make a covenant, and gather a heap of stones, and set up a pillar as a memorial of the transaction, xxxi.	1739
——	Jacob wrestles with an Angel, and has his name changed to that of Israel, xxxii. 24–29.	——
——	Esau meets Jacob, xxxiii. 4.	——
——	Jacob arrives in Canaan, and settles among the Shechemites, xxxiii. 18.	——
2266	Benjamin born, and Rachel dies immediately after his birth, xxxv. 18.	1738
2266	Dinah defiled by Shechem, and the subsequent murder of the Shechemites by Simeon and Levi, xxxiv.	1738
2276	Joseph, aged seventeen years, falling under the displeasure of his brothers, they conspire to take away his life, but afterwards change their minds, and sell him for a slave to some Ishmaelite merchants, who bring him to Egypt and sell him to Potiphar, xxxvii.	1728
2278	Pharez and Zarah, the twin-sons of Judah, born about this time, xxxviii 27–30.	1726
2285	Joseph, through the false accusation of his mistress, is cast into prison, where, about two years after, he interprets the dreams of the chief butler and the chief baker, xxxix., xl.	1719
2288	Isaac dies, aged 180 years, xxxv. 28.	1716
2289	Joseph interprets the two prophetic dreams of Pharaoh, xli.	1715
——	Commencement of the seven years of plenty.	——
2290	About this time was born Manasseh, Joseph's first-born.	1714
2292	About this time was born Ephraim, Joseph's second son.	1712
2296	*Commencement of the seven years of famine.*	1708
2297	Jacob sends his sons to Egypt to buy corn, xlii. 1, &c.	1707
2298	He sends them a second time, and with them his son Benjamin, xliii. 11.	1706
——	Joseph makes himself known to his brethren, sends for his father, and allots him and his household the land of Goshen to dwell in; Jacob being then 130 years old, xlv., xlvi.	——
2300	Joseph sells corn to the Egyptians, and brings all the money in Egypt into the king's treasury, xlvii. 14.	1704
2301	He buys all the cattle, xlvii. 16.	1703
2302	All the Egyptians give themselves up to be Pharaoh's servants, in order to get corn to preserve their lives and sow their ground, xlvii. 18, &c.	1702
2303	*The seven years of famine ended.*	1701
——	About this time Saul, the sixth king of the Edomites, began to reign, xxxvi. 37.	——
2315	Jacob, having blessed his sons and the sons of Joseph, Ephraim, and Manasseh, dies, aged 147 years. He is embalmed and carried into Canaan, and buried in the cave of Machpelah, xlix. 1.	1689
2345	About this time Baal-hanan, the seventh king of the Edomites, began to reign, xxxvi. 38.	1659
2369	Joseph dies, aged 110, having governed Egypt fourscore years.	1635
2387	About this time Hadar or Hadad, the	1617

a

CHRONOLOGY TO GENESIS.

A. M.		B. C.
	eighth and last king of the Edomites, began to reign, xxxvi. 39.	
2429	About this time the regal government of the Edomites is abolished, and the first aristocracy of dukes begins, xxxvi. 15, 16.	1575
2471	About this time the second aristocracy of Edomitish dukes begins, xxxvi. 40–43.	1533
2474	Caleb, the son of Jephunneh, born forty years before he was sent by Moses to spy out the land of Canaan.	1530
2494	*Ramasses Miamun* died in the 67th year of his reign, under whom, and his son *Amenophis*, who succeeded him, the children of Israel endured the cruel bondage and oppression mentioned in Exodus i.	1510

Finished the correction of this Part, April 6th, 1827.—A. Clarke.

PREFACE TO THE BOOK

OF

EXODUS.

THE *name* by which this book is generally distinguished is borrowed from the *Septuagint*, in which it is called Ἔξοδος, Exodus, the *going out* or *departure;* and by the Codex Alexandrinus, Ἔξοδος Αἰγύπτου, *the departure from Egypt*, because the departure of the Israelites from Egypt is the most remarkable fact mentioned in the whole book. In the Hebrew Bibles it is called ואלה שמות ve-elleh shemoth, *these are the names*, which are the words with which it commences. It contains a history of the transactions of 145 years, beginning at the death of Joseph, where the book of Genesis ends, and coming down to the erection of the tabernacle in the wilderness at the foot of Mount Sinai.

In this book Moses details the causes and motives of the persecution raised up against the Israelites in Egypt, the orders given by Pharaoh to destroy all the Hebrew *male* children, and the prevention of the execution of those orders through the *humanity* and *piety* of the midwives appointed to deliver the Hebrew women. The marriage of Amram and Jochebed is next related; the birth of Moses; the manner in which he was exposed on the river Nile, and in which he was discovered by the daughter of Pharaoh; his being providentially put under the care of his own mother to be nursed, and educated as the son of the Egyptian princess; how, when forty years of age, he left the court, visited and defended his brethren; the danger to which he was in consequence exposed; his flight to Arabia; his contract with Jethro, priest or prince of Midian, whose daughter Zipporah he afterwards espoused. While employed in keeping the flocks of his father-in-law, God appeared to him in a burning bush, and commissioned him to go and deliver his countrymen from the oppression under which they groaned. Having given him the most positive assurances of protection and power to work miracles, and having associated with him his brother Aaron, he sent them first to the Israelites to declare the purpose of Jehovah, and afterwards to Pharaoh to require him, in the name of the Most High, to set the Israelites at liberty. Pharaoh, far from submitting, made their yoke more grievous; and Moses, on a second interview with him, to convince him by whose authority he made the demand, wrought a miracle before him and his courtiers. This being in a certain way *imitated* by Pharaoh's magicians, he hardened his heart, and refused to let the people go, till God, by ten extraordinary plagues, convinced him of his omnipotence, and obliged him to consent to dismiss a people over whose persons and properties he had claimed and exercised a right founded only on the most tyrannical principles. The plagues by which God afflicted the whole land of Egypt, Goshen excepted, where the Israelites dwelt, were the following:—

1. He turned all the waters of Egypt into *blood.* 2. He caused innumerable *frogs* to come over the whole land. 3. He afflicted both man and beast with immense *swarms of vermin.* 4. Afterwards with a multitude of *different* kinds of *insects.* 5. He sent a grievous *pestilence* among their cattle. 6. Smote both man and beast with *boils.* 7. Destroyed their

crops with grievous storms of *hail*, accompanied with the most terrible *thunder* and *lightning*. 8. Desolated the whole land by innumerable swarms of *locusts*. 9. He spread a *palpable darkness* all over Egypt; and, 10. In one night *slew* all the *first-born*, both of man and beast, through the whole of the Egyptian territories. What proved the miraculous nature of all these plagues most particularly was, 1st, Their coming exactly according to the prediction and at the command of Moses and Aaron. 2dly, Their extending only to the Egyptians, and leaving the land of Goshen, the Israelites, their cattle and substance, entirely untouched.

After relating all these things in detail, with their attendant circumstances, Moses describes the institution, reason, and celebration of the *passover*; the preparation of the Israelites for their departure; their leaving Goshen and beginning their journey to the promised land, by the way of *Rameses*, *Succoth*, and *Etham*. How Pharaoh, repenting of the permission he had given them to depart, began to pursue them with an immense army of horse and foot, and overtook them at their encampment at *Baal-zephon*, on the borders of the Red Sea. Their destruction appearing then to be inevitable, Moses farther relates that having called earnestly upon God, and stretched his rod over the waters, they became divided, and the Israelites entered into the bed of the sea, and passed over to the opposite shore. Pharaoh and his host madly pursuing in the same track, the rear of their army being fairly entered by the time the last of the Israelites had made good their landing on the opposite coast, Moses stretching his rod again over the waters, they returned to their former channel and overwhelmed the Egyptian army, so that every soul perished.

Moses next gives a circumstantial account of the different encampments of the Israelites in the wilderness, during the space of nearly forty years: the *miracles* wrought in their behalf; the chief of which were the pillar of cloud by day, and the pillar of fire by night, to direct and protect them in the wilderness; the bringing water out of a rock for them and their cattle; feeding them with manna from heaven; bringing innumerable flocks of quails to their camp; giving them a complete victory over the Amalekites at the intercession of Moses; and particularly God's astonishing manifestation of himself on Mount Sinai, when he delivered to Moses an epitome of his whole law, in what was called the TEN WORDS or TEN COMMANDMENTS.

Moses proceeds to give a circumstantial detail of the different *laws*, *statutes*, and *ordinances* which he received from God, and particularly the giving of the *Ten Commandments* on Mount Sinai, and the awful display of the Divine Majesty on that solemn occasion; the formation of the ARK, holy *Table* and *Candlestick*; the TABERNACLE, with its furniture, covering, courts, &c., the *brazen Altar*, *golden Altar*, *brazen Laver*, *anointing oil*, *perfume*, *sacerdotal garments* for Aaron and his sons, and the artificers employed on the work of the Tabernacle, &c. He then gives an account of Israel's idolatry in the matter of the *golden calf*, made under the direction of Aaron; God's displeasure, and the death of the principal idolaters; the erection and consecration of the Tabernacle, and its being filled and encompassed with the Divine glory, with the order and manner of their marches by direction of the miraculous pillar; with which the book concludes.

THE SECOND BOOK OF MOSES,

CALLED

EXODUS.

Year before the common Year of Christ, 1706.—Julian Period, 3008.—Cycle of the Sun, 7.—Dominical Letter, F.—Cycle of the Moon, 2.—Indiction, 15.—Creation from Tisri or September, 2298

CHAPTER I.

The names and number of the children of Israel that went down into Egypt, 1–5. *Joseph and all his brethren of that generation die,* 6. *The great increase of their posterity,* 7. *The cruel policy of the king of Egypt to destroy them,* 8–11. *They increase greatly, notwithstanding their affliction,* 12. *Account of their hard bondage,* 13, 14. *Pharaoh's command to the Hebrew midwives to kill all the male children,* 15, 16. *The midwives disobey the king's commandment, and, on being questioned, vindicate themselves,* 17–19. *God is pleased with their conduct, blesses them, and increases the people,* 20, 21. *Pharaoh gives a general command to the Egyptians to drown all the male children of the Hebrews,* 22.

A. M. 2298. B. C. 1706.

NOW [a] these *are* the names of
the children of Israel, which
came into Egypt; every man and his household came with Jacob.
2 Reuben, Simeon, Levi, and Judah,
3 Issachar, Zebulun, and Benjamin,
4 Dan, and Naphtali, Gad, and Asher.
5 And all the souls that came out of the
[b] loins of Jacob were [c] seventy souls:
for Joseph was in Egypt *already*.

A. M. 2369. B. C. 1635.

6 And [d] Joseph died, and all his
brethren, and all that generation.
7 [e] And the children of Israel were fruitful,
and increased abundantly, and multiplied, and
waxed exceeding mighty; and the land was
filled with them.

[a] Gen. xlvi. 8; chap. vi. 14.—[b] Heb. *thigh*.—[c] Gen. xlvi. 26, 27; ver. 20; Deut. x. 22.

[d] Gen. l. 26; Acts vii. 15.—[e] Gen. xlvi. 3; Deut. xxvi. 5; Psa. cv. 24; Acts vii. 17.

NOTES ON CHAP. I.

Verse 1. *These* are *the names*] Though this book is a continuation of the book of Genesis, with which probably it was in former times conjoined, Moses thought it necessary to introduce it with an account of the names and number of the family of Jacob when they came to Egypt, to show that though they were then very few, yet in a short time, under the especial blessing of God, they had multiplied exceedingly; and thus the promise to Abraham had been literally fulfilled. See the notes on Gen. xlvi.

Verse 6. *Joseph died, and all his brethren*] That is, Joseph had now been some time dead, as also all his brethren, and all the Egyptians who had known Jacob and his twelve sons; and this is a sort of reason why the important services performed by Joseph were forgotten.

Verse 7. *The children of Israel were fruitful*] פרו *paru*, a general term, signifying that they were like *healthy trees*, bringing forth an *abundance of fruit*.

And increased] ישרצ *yishretsu*, they increased *like fishes*, as the original word implies. See Gen. i. 20, and the note there.

Abundantly] ירבו *yirbu*, they *multiplied;* this is a separate term, and should not have been used as an adverb by our translators.

And waxed exceeding mighty] ויעצמו במאד מאד *vaiyaatsmu bimod meod*, and they became strong beyond measure—*superlatively*, *superlatively*—so that *the land* (Goshen) *was filled with them*. This astonishing increase was, under the providence of God, chiefly owing to two causes: 1. The Hebrew women were exceedingly fruitful, suffered very little in parturition, and probably often brought forth *twins*. 2. There appear to have been no *premature* deaths among them. Thus in about two hundred and fifteen years they were

A. M. cir. 2400.
B. C. cir. 1604.

8 Now there [f] arose up a new
king over Egypt, which knew
not Joseph.
9 And he said unto his people, Behold,
[g] the people of the children of Israel *are* more
and mightier than we:
10 [h] Come on, let us [i] deal wisely with
them; lest they multiply, and it come to
pass, that, when there falleth out any war,
they join also unto our enemies, and fight
against us, and *so* get them up
out of the land.
11 Therefore they did set over them task-
masters [k] to afflict them with their [l] burdens.
And they built for Pharaoh treasure cities,
Pithom [m] and Raamses.
12 [n] But the more they afflicted them,
the more they multiplied and grew. And
they were grieved because of the children
of Israel.

[f] Acts vii. 18.——[g] Psa. cv. 24.——[h] Psa. x. 2; lxxxiii. 3, 4.——[i] Job v. 13; Psa. cv. 25; Prov. xvi. 25; xxi. 30; Acts vii. 19.

[k] Gen. xv. 13; chap. iii. 7; Deut. xxvi. 6.——[l] Chap. ii. 11; v. 4, 5; Psa. lxxxi. 6.——[m] Gen. xlvii. 11.——[n] Heb. *and as they afflicted them, so they multiplied,* &c.

multiplied to upwards of 600,000, independently of *old men, women,* and *children.*

Verse 8. *There arose up a new king*] Who this was it is difficult to say. It was probably *Ramesses Miamun,* or his son *Amenophis,* who succeeded him in the government of Egypt about A. M. 2400, before Christ 1604.

Which knew not Joseph.] The verb ידע *yada,* which we translate *to know,* often signifies to *acknowledge* or *approve.* See Judges ii. 10; Psa. i. 6; xxxi. 7; Hos. ii. 8; Amos iii. 2. The Greek verbs *ειδω* and *γινωσκω* are used precisely in the same sense in the New Testament. See Matt. xxv. 12, and 1 John iii. 1. We may therefore understand by the *new king's* not *knowing Joseph,* his *disapproving* of that system of government which Joseph had established, as well as his haughtily refusing to *acknowledge* the obligations under which the whole land of Egypt was laid to this eminent prime minister of one of his predecessors.

Verse 9. *He said unto his people*] He probably summoned a council of his nobles and elders to consider the subject; and the result was to persecute and destroy them, as is afterwards stated.

Verse 10. *They join also unto our enemies*] It has been conjectured that Pharaoh had probably his eye on the oppressions which Egypt had suffered under the *shepherd-kings,* who for a long series of years had, according to Manetho, governed the land with extreme cruelty. As the Israelites were of the same occupation, (viz., *shepherds,*) the jealous, cruel king found it easy to attribute to them the same motives; taking it for granted that they were only waiting for a favourable opportunity to join the enemies of Egypt, and so overrun the whole land.

Verse 11. *Set over them task-masters*] שרי מסים *sarey missim, chiefs* or *princes* of *burdens, works,* or *tribute; επιστατας των εργων,* Sept. *overseers of the works.* The persons who appointed them their work, and exacted the performance of it. The *work* itself being oppressive, and the *manner* in which it was exacted still more so, there is some room to think that they not only worked them unmercifully, but also obliged them to pay an exorbitant tribute at the same time.

Treasure cities] ערי מסכנות *arey miscenoth, store cities—public granaries.* Calmet supposes this to be the name of a city, and translates the verse thus: "They built cities, viz., Miscenoth, Pithom, and Rameses." *Pithom* is supposed to be that which Herodotus calls *Patumos. Raamses,* or rather *Rameses,* (for it is the same Hebrew word as in Gen. xlvii. 11, and should be written the same way here as there,) is supposed to have been the capital of the land of Goshen, mentioned in the book of Genesis by *anticipation;* for it was probably not erected till after the days of Joseph, when the Israelites were brought under that severe oppression described in the book of Exodus. The Septuagint add here, *και Ων, ἡ εστιν Ἡλιουπολις· and* ON, *which is Heliopolis;* i. e., the city of the Sun. The same reading is found also in the *Coptic* version.

Some writers suppose that beside these cities the Israelites built the *pyramids.* If this conjecture be well founded, perhaps they are intended in the word מסכנות *miscenoth,* which, from סכן *sachan,* to *lay up in store,* might be intended to signify places where Pharaoh laid up his treasures; and from their structure they appear to have been designed for something of this kind. If the history of the pyramids be not found in the book of Exodus, it is nowhere else extant; their origin, if not alluded to here, being lost in their very remote antiquity. Diodorus Siculus, who has given the best traditions he could find relative to them, says that there was no agreement either among the inhabitants or the historians concerning the building of the pyramids.—Bib. Hist., lib. i., cap. lxiv

Josephus expressly says that one part of the oppression suffered by the Israelites in Egypt was occasioned by *building pyramids.* See on ver. 14.

In the book of Genesis, and in this book, the word *Pharaoh* frequently occurs, which, though many suppose it to be a *proper name* peculiar to one person, and by this supposition confound the acts of several Egyptian kings, yet is to be understood only as a name of *office.*

It may be necessary to observe that all the Egyptian kings, whatever their *own* name was, took the surname of *Pharaoh* when they came to the throne; a name which, in its general acceptation signified the same as *king* or *monarch,* but in its *literal* meaning, as Bochart has amply proved, it signifies a *crocodile,* which being a *sacred animal* among the Egyptians, the word might be added to their *kings* in order to procure them the greater reverence and respect.

Verse 12. *But the more they afflicted them*] The margin has pretty nearly preserved the import of the original: *And as they afflicted them, so they multiplied*

A. M. cir. 2400.
B. C. cir. 1604.

13 And the Egyptians made
the children of Israel to serve
with rigour :
14 And they [o] made their lives bitter with
hard bondage, [p] in mortar, and in brick, and
in all manner of service in the field : all their
service, wherein they made them serve, *was*
with rigour.
15 And the king of Egypt spake to the
Hebrew midwives, of which the name of the
one *was* Shiphrah, and the name of the other
Puah :
16 And he said, When ye do the office of
a midwife to the Hebrew women,
and see *them* upon the stools ;
if it *be* a son, then ye shall kill him : but if
it *be* a daughter, then she shall live.
17 But the midwives [q] feared God, and did
not [r] as the king of Egypt commanded them,
but saved the men children alive.
18 And the king of Egypt called for the
midwives, and said unto them, Why have ye
done this thing, and have saved the men
children alive?
19 And [s] the midwives said unto Pharaoh,
Because the Hebrew women *are* not as the

A. M. cir. 2400.
B. C. cir. 1604.

[o] Chapter ii. 23; vi. 9; Num. xx. 15; Acts vii. 19, 34. — [p] Psa. lxxxi. 6. — [q] Prov. xvi. 6. — [r] Dan. iii. 16, 18; vi. 13; Acts v. 29. — [s] See Josh. ii. 4, &c.; 2 Sam. xvii. 19, 20.

and so they grew. That is, in proportion to their afflictions was their prosperity ; and had their sufferings been greater, their increase would have been still more abundant.

Verse 13. *To serve with rigour*] בפרך *bepharech*, with *cruelty, great oppression ;* being *ferocious* with them. The word *fierce* is supposed by some to be derived from the Hebrew, as well as the Latin *ferox*, from which we more immediately bring our English term. This kind of cruelty to slaves, and ferociousness, unfeelingness, and hard-heartedness, were particularly forbidden to the children of Israel. See Lev. xxv. 43, 46, where the same word is used : *Thou shalt not rule over him with* RIGOUR, *but shalt fear thy God.*

Verse 14. *They made their lives bitter*] So that they became weary of life, through the severity of their servitude.

With hard bondage] בעבדה קשה *baabodah kashah, with grievous servitude.* This was the general character of their life in Egypt ; it was a life of the most painful servitude, oppressive enough in itself, but made much more so by the cruel manner of their treatment while performing their tasks.

In mortar, and in brick] First, in digging the clay, kneading, and preparing it, and secondly, forming it into *bricks*, drying them in the sun, &c.

Service in the field] Carrying these materials to the places where they were to be formed into buildings, and serving the builders while employed in those public works. Josephus says "The Egyptians contrived a variety of ways to afflict the Israelites ; for they enjoined them to cut a great number of channels for the river, and to build walls for their cities and ramparts, that they might restrain the river, and hinder its waters from stagnating upon its overrunning its own banks ; they set them also to build pyramids, (πυραμιδας τε ανοικοδομουντες,) and wore them out, and forced them to learn all sorts of mechanic arts, and to accustom themselves to hard labour."—Antiq., lib. ii., cap. ix., sec. 1. Philo bears nearly the same testimony, p. 86, Edit. Mangey.

Verse 15. *Hebrew midwives*] *Shiphrah* and *Puah*, who are here mentioned, were probably certain *chiefs*, under whom all the rest acted, and by whom they were instructed in the *obstetric* art. *Aben Ezra* supposes there could not have been fewer than five hundred midwives among the Hebrew women at this time ; but that very few were requisite see proved on verse 19.

Verse 16. *Upon the stools*] על האבנים *al haobnayim.* This is a difficult word, and occurs nowhere else in the Hebrew Bible but in Jer. xviii. 3, where we translate it the *potter's wheels.* As אבן signifies a *stone*, the *obnayim* has been supposed to signify a *stone trough*, in which they received and washed the infant as soon as born. *Jarchi*, in his book of *Hebrew roots*, gives a very different interpretation of it ; he derives it from בן *ben*, a *son*, or בנים *banim, children ;* his words must not be literally translated, but this is the sense : "When ye do the office of a midwife to the Hebrew women, and ye see that the birth is broken forth, if it be a son, then ye shall kill him." Jonathan ben Uzziel gives us a curious reason for the command given by Pharaoh to the Egyptian women : "Pharaoh slept, and saw in his sleep a balance, and behold the whole land of Egypt stood in one scale, and a lamb in the other ; and the scale in which the lamb was outweighed that in which was the land of Egypt. Immediately he sent and called all the chief magicians, and told them his dream. And *Janes* and *Jimbres*, (see 2 Tim. iii. 8,) who were chief of the magicians, opened their mouths and said to Pharaoh, 'A child is shortly to be born in the congregation of the Israelites, whose hand shall destroy the whole land of Egypt.' *Therefore Pharaoh spake to the midwives, &c.*"

Verse 17. *The midwives feared God*] Because they knew that God had forbidden murder of every kind ; for though the law was not yet given, Exod. xx. 13, being Hebrews they must have known that God had from the beginning declared, *Whosoever sheddeth man's blood, by man shall his blood be shed*, Gen. ix. 6. Therefore they saved the male children of all to whose assistance they were called. See ver. 19.

Verse 19. *The Hebrew women* are *not as the Egyptian women*] This is a simple statement of what general experience shows to be a fact, viz., that women, who during the whole of their pregnancy are accustomed to hard labour, especially in the open air, have comparatively little pain in *parturition.* At this time the whole Hebrew nation, *men* and *women*, were

A. M. cir. 2400. B. C. cir. 1604.

Egyptian women; for they *are* lively, and are delivered ere the midwives come in unto them.
20 [t] Therefore God dealt well with the midwives: and the people multiplied, and waxed very mighty.
21 And it came to pass, because the midwives feared God, [u] that he made them houses.

[t] Proverbs xi. 18; Eccles. viii. 12; Isaiah iii. 10; Heb. vi. 10.

[u] 1 Samuel ii. 35; 2 Samuel vii. 11, 13, 27, 29; 1 Kings ii. 24; xi. 38; Psa. cxxvii. 1.

in a state of *slavery*, and were obliged to work *in mortar and brick, and all manner of service* IN THE FIELD, ver. 14, and this at once accounts for the ease and speediness of their travail. With the strictest truth the midwives might say, *The Hebrew women are not as the Egyptian women:* the *latter* fare delicately, are not inured to labour, and are kept shut up at home, therefore they have hard, difficult, and dangerous labours; but the Hebrew women are *lively*, חיות *chayoth*, are *strong, hale*, and *vigorous*, and therefore *are delivered ere the midwives come in unto them.* In such cases we may naturally conclude that the midwives were very *seldom even sent for.* And this is probably the reason why we find but *two* mentioned; as in such a state of society there could be but very little employment for persons of that profession, as a *mother*, an *aunt*, or any female acquaintance or neighbour, could readily afford all the assistance necessary in such cases. Commentators, pressed with imaginary difficulties, have sought for examples of easy parturition in Æthiopia, Persia, and India, as parallels to the case before us; but they might have spared themselves the trouble, because the case is *common in all parts of the globe* where the women labour hard, and especially *in the open air*. I have known several instances of the kind myself among the labouring poor. I shall mention one: I saw a poor woman in the open field at hard labour; she stayed away in the afternoon, but she returned the next morning to her work with her infant child, having in the interim been safely delivered! She *continued* at her daily work, having apparently suffered no inconvenience!

I have entered more particularly into this subject because, through want of proper information, (perhaps from a worse motive,) certain persons have spoken very unguardedly against this inspired record: "The Hebrew midwives told palpable lies, and God commends them for it; thus we may do evil that good may come of it, and sanctify the *means* by the *end*." Now I contend that there was neither *lie direct* nor even *prevarication* in the case. The midwives *boldly* state to Pharaoh a *fact*, (had it not been so, he had a thousand means of ascertaining the truth,) and they tate it in such a way as to bring conviction to his mind on the subject of his oppressive cruelty on the one hand, and the mercy of Jehovah on the other. As if they had said, "The very oppression under which, through thy cruelty, the Israelites groan, their God has turned to their advantage; they are not only *fruitful*, but they bring forth with comparatively *no trouble*; *we* have scarcely any employment among them." Here then is a *fact*, boldly announced in the face of danger; and we see that God was pleased with this frankness of the midwives, and he blessed them for it.

Verse 20. *Therefore God dealt well with the midwives: and the people multiplied, and waxed very mighty.*] This shows an especial providence and blessing of God; for though in all cases where females are kept to hard labour they have comparatively easy and safe travail, yet in a state of slavery the increase is generally very small, as the children die for want of proper nursing, the women, through their labour, being obliged to neglect their offspring; so that in the slave countries the *stock* is obliged to be recruited by foreign imports: yet in the case above it was not so; there was not one barren among their tribes, and even their women, though constantly obliged to perform their *daily tasks*, were neither rendered unfruitful by it, nor taken off by premature death through the violence and continuance of their labour, when even in the delicate situation mentioned above.

Verse 21. *He made them houses.*] Dr. Shuckford thinks that there is something wrong both in the punctuation and translation of this place, and reads the passage thus, adding the 21st to the 20th verse: "And they multiplied and waxed mighty; and this happened (ויהי *vayehi*) because the midwives feared God; and he (*Pharaoh*) made (להם *lahem*, masc.) them (*the Israelites*) houses; and commanded all his people, saying, Every son that is born, &c." The doctor supposes that previously to this time the Israelites had no fixed dwellings, but lived in tents, and therefore had a better opportunity of concealing their children; but now Pharaoh built them houses, and obliged them to dwell in them, and caused the Egyptians to watch over them, that all the male children might be destroyed, which could not have been easily effected had the Israelites continued to live in their usual scattered manner in tents. That the *houses* in question were not made for the *midwives*, but for the *Israelites* in general, the Hebrew text seems pretty plainly to indicate, for the pronoun להם *lahem, to them*, is the *masculine* gender; had the *midwives* been meant, the feminine pronoun להן *lahen* would have been used. Others contend that by *making them houses*, not only the *midwives* are intended, but also that the words mark an increase of their families, and that the objection taken from the masculine pronoun is of no weight, because these pronouns are often interchanged; see 1 Kings xxii. 17, where להם *lahem* is written, and in the parallel place, 2 Chron. xviii. 6, להן *lahen* is used. So בהם *bahem*, in 1 Chron. x. 7, is written בהן *bahen*, 1 Sam. xxxi. 7, and in several other places. There is no doubt that God did bless the midwives, his approbation of their conduct is strictly marked; and there can be no doubt of his prospering the Israelites, for it is particularly said that the people multiplied and waxed very mighty. But the words most probably refer to the Israelites, whose *houses* or *families* were built up by an extraordinary increase of children, notwithstanding the cruel policy of the Egyptian king. Vain is the counsel of man when opposed to the de

A. M. cir. 2431.
B. C. cir. 1573.

22 And Pharaoh charged all his people, saying, [y] Every son that is born ye shall cast into the river, and every daughter ye shall save alive.

A. M. cir. 2431.
B. C. cir. 1573.

[y] Acts vii. 19; chap. vii. 19–21; Rev. xvi. 4–6.

terminations of God! All the means used for the destruction of this people became in his hand instruments of their prosperity and increase. How true is the saying, If God be *for* us, who can be *against* us?

Verse 22. *Ye shall cast into the river*] As the *Nile*, which is here intended, was a sacred river among the Egyptians, it is not unlikely that Pharaoh intended the young Hebrews as an offering to his god, having two objects in view: 1. To increase the fertility of the country by thus procuring, as he might suppose, a proper and sufficient annual inundation; and 2. To prevent an increase of population among the Israelites, and in process of time procure their entire extermination.

It is conjectured, with a great show of probability, that the edict mentioned in this verse was not made till after the birth of Aaron, and that it was revoked soon after the birth of Moses; as, if it had subsisted in its rigour during the *eighty-six* years which elapsed between this and the deliverance of the Israelites, it is not at all likely that their males would have amounted to *six hundred thousand*, and those all *effective* men.

In the general preface to this work reference has been made to ORIGEN's *method of interpreting the Scriptures*, and some specimens promised. On the plain account of a simple matter of fact, related in the preceding chapter, this very eminent man, in his 2d Homily on Exodus, imposes an interpretation of which the following is the *substance*.

"*Pharaoh, king of Egypt*, represents the *devil;* the *male* and *female* children of the Hebrews represent the *animal* and *rational* faculties of the soul. *Pharaoh*, the *devil*, wishes to destroy all the *males*, i. e., the seeds of *rationality* and *spiritual science* through which the soul *tends to* and seeks *heavenly things;* but he wishes to preserve the *females* alive, i. e., all those *animal propensities* of man, through which he becomes *carnal* and *devilish*. Hence," says he, "when you see a man living in luxury, banquetings, pleasures, and sensual gratifications, know that there the *king of Egypt* has slain all the males, and preserved all the *females* alive. The *midwives* represent the *Old* and *New Testaments:* the one is called *Sephora*, which signifies a *sparrow*, and means that sort of *instruction* by which the soul is led to *soar aloft*, and contemplate heavenly things; the other is called *Phua*, which signifies *ruddy* or *bashful*, and points out the *Gospel*, which is ruddy with the blood of Christ, spreading the doctrine of his passion over the earth. By these, as midwives, the souls that are born into the Church are *healed*, for the *reading of the Scriptures corrects* and *heals* what is amiss in the mind. *Pharaoh*, the *devil*, wishes to *corrupt* those *midwives*, that all the *males*—the *spiritual propensities*, may be destroyed; and this he endeavours to do by bringing in *heresies* and *corrupt opinions*. But the foundation of God standeth sure. *The midwives feared God, therefore he builded them houses*. If this be taken *literally*, it has little or no meaning, and is of no importance; but it points out that the *midwives*—the *law* and the *Gospel*, by *teaching the fear of God*, build the *houses of the Church*, and fill the whole earth with *houses of prayer*. Therefore these midwives, because they *feared God*, and taught the fear of God, did not fulfil the command of the king of Egypt—they did *not kill the males*, and I dare confidently affirm that they did not preserve the *females alive;* for they do not teach vicious doctrines in the Church, nor preach up luxury, nor foster sin, which are what *Pharaoh* wishes in keeping the *females alive;* for by these virtue alone is cultivated and nourished. By *Pharaoh's daughter* I suppose the Church to be intended, which is gathered from among the Gentiles; and although she has an impious and iniquitous father, yet the prophet says unto her, *Hearken, O daughter, and consider, incline thine ear; forget also thine own people, and thy father's house, so shall the king greatly desire thy beauty*, Psa. xlv. 10, 11. This therefore is she who is come to the *waters to bathe*, i. e., to the *baptismal font*, that she may be washed from the sins which she has contracted in her *father's house*. Immediately she receives bowels of commiseration, and pities the infant; that is, the *Church*, coming from among the Gentiles, finds *Moses*—the *law*, lying in the *pool, cast out*, and *exposed by his own people* in an *ark of bulrushes, daubed over with pitch*—deformed and obscured by the carnal and absurd glosses of the Jews, who are ignorant of its spiritual sense; and while it continues with them is as a helpless and destitute infant; but as soon as it enters the doors of the Christian Church it becomes strong and vigorous; and thus *Moses*—the *law, grows up*, and becomes, through means of the Christian Church, more respectable even in the eyes of the Jews themselves, according to his own prophecy: *I will move them to jealousy with those which are not a people; I will provoke them to anger with a foolish nation*, Deut. xxxii. 21. Thus taught by the Christian Church, the *synagogue* forsakes *idolatry;* for when it sees the *Gentiles* worshipping the true God, it is ashamed of its *idols*, and worships them no more. In like manner, though we have had *Pharaoh for our father*—though the prince of this world has begotten us by wicked works, yet when we come unto the *waters of baptism* we take unto us *Moses*—the *law of God*, in its true and spiritual meaning; what is low or weak in it we leave, what is strong and perfect we take and place in the *royal palace* of our *heart*. Then we have Moses *grown up*—we no longer consider the law as *little* or *mean;* all is magnificent, excellent, elegant, for all is spiritually understood. Let us beseech the Lord Jesus Christ that he may reveal himself to us more and more, and show us how great and sublime Moses is; for he by his Holy Spirit reveals these things to whomsoever he will. To him be glory and dominion for ever and ever! Amen."

Neither the praise of piety nor the merit of *ingenuity* can be denied to this eminent man in such interpretations as these. But who at the same time does not see that if such a mode of exposition were to be

a

allowed, the trumpet could no longer give a *certain* sound? Every passage and fact might then be obliged to say *something, any thing, every thing,* or *nothing,* according to the *fancy,* peculiar *creed,* or *caprice* of the interpreter.

I have given this large specimen from one of the *ancients,* merely to save the *moderns,* from whose works on the sacred writings I could produce many specimens *equally singular* and *more absurd.* Reader, it is possible to *trifle* with the testimonies of God, and all the while speak *serious things;* but if all be not done according to the pattern shown in the mount, much evil may be produced, and many stumbling blocks thrown in the way of others, which may turn them totally out of the way of understanding; and then what a dreadful account must such interpreters have to give to that God who has pronounced a curse, not only on those who *take away* from his word, but also on those who *add* to it.

CHAPTER II.

Amram and Jochebed marry, 1. *Moses is born, and is hidden by his mother three months,* 2. *Is exposed in an ark of bulrushes on the river Nile, and watched by his sister,* 3, 4. *He is found by the daughter of Pharaoh, who commits him to the care of his own mother, and has him educated as her own son,* 5–9. *When grown up, he is brought to Pharaoh's daughter, who receives him as her own child, and calls him* Moses, 10. *Finding an Egyptian smiting a Hebrew, he kills the Egyptian, and hides him in the sand,* 11, 12. *Reproves two Hebrews that were contending together, one of whom charges him with killing the Egyptian,* 13, 14. *Pharaoh, hearing of the death of the Egyptian, sought to slay Moses, who, being alarmed, escapes to the land of Midian,* 15. *Meets with the seven daughters of Reuel, priest or prince of Midian, who came to water their flocks, and assists them,* 16, 17. *On their return they inform their father* Reuel, *who invites Moses to his house,* 18–20. *Moses dwells with him, and receives Zipporah his daughter to wife,* 21. *She bears him a son whom he calls* Gershom, 22. *The children of Israel, grievously oppressed in Egypt, cry for deliverance,* 23. *God remembers his covenant with Abraham, Isaac, and Jacob, and hears their prayer,* 24, 25.

A. M. cir. 2432. B. C. cir. 1572.

AND there went [a] a man of the house of Levi, and took *to wife* a daughter of Levi.

A. M. 2433. B. C. 1571.

2 And the woman conceived, and bare a son: and [b] when she saw him that he *was a* goodly *child,* she hid him three months.

A. M. 2433. B. C. 1571.

3 And when she could not longer hide him, she took for him an ark of bulrushes, and daubed it with slime and with pitch, and put the child therein; and she laid *it* in the flags by the river's brink.

4 [c] And his sister stood afar off, to wit what would be done to him.

[a] Chap. vi. 20; Num. xxvi. 59; 1 Chron. xxiii. 14. [b] Acts vii. 20; Heb. xi. 23.—[c] Ch. xv. 20; Num. xxvi. 59.

NOTES ON CHAP. II.

Verse 1. *There went a man*] *Amram,* son of Kohath, son of Levi, chap. vi. 16–20. *A daughter of Levi, Jochebed,* sister to Kohath, and consequently both the wife and aunt of her husband Amram, chap. vi. 20; Num. xxvi. 59. Such marriages were at this time lawful, though they were afterwards forbidden, Lev. xviii. 12. But it is possible that *daughter of Levi* means no more than a descendant of that family, and that probably Amram and Jochebed were only *cousin germans.* As a *new law* was to be given and a *new priesthood* formed, God chose a *religious family* out of which the *lawgiver* and the *high priest* were both to spring.

Verse 2. *Bare a son*] This certainly was not her first child, for Aaron was *fourscore and three* years old when Moses was but *fourscore,* see chap. vii. 7: and there was a sister, probably Miriam, who was older than either; see below, ver. 4, and see Num. xxvi. 59. Miriam and Aaron had no doubt been both born before the decree was passed for the destruction of the Hebrew male children, mentioned in the preceding chapter.

Goodly child] The text simply says כי טוב הוא *ki tob hu, that he was good,* which signifies that he was not only a perfect, well-formed child, but that he was very *beautiful;* hence the Septuagint translate the place, Ιδοντες δε αυτο αστειον, *Seeing him to be beautiful,* which St. Stephen interprets, Ην αστειος τῳ Θεῳ, *He was comely to God,* or *divinely beautiful.* This very circumstance was wisely ordained by the kind providence of God to be one means of his preservation. Scarcely any thing interests the heart more than the sight of a lovely babe in distress. His beauty would induce even his parents to double their exertions to save him, and was probably the sole motive which led the Egyptian princess to take such particular care of him, and to educate him as her own son, which in all likelihood she would not have done had he been only an ordinary child.

Verse 3. *An ark of bulrushes*] תבת גמא *tebath gome,* a small boat or basket made of the Egyptian reed called *papyrus,* so famous in all antiquity. This plant grows on the banks of the Nile, and in marshy grounds; the stalk rises to the height of *six* or *seven cubits* above the water, is triangular, and terminates in a crown of small filaments resembling hair, which the ancients used to compare to a thyrsus. This reed was of the greatest use to the inhabitants of Egypt, the pith contained in the stalk serving them for food, and the woody part to build vessels with; which ves-

A. M. 2433.
B. C. 1571.

5 And the [d] daughter of Pharaoh came down to wash *herself* at the river; and her maidens walked along by the river's side; and when she saw the ark among the flags, she sent her maid to fetch it.

[d] Acts, chap. vii. 21.

sels frequently appear on engraved stones and other monuments of Egyptian antiquity. For this purpose they made it up like rushes into bundles, and by tying them together gave their vessels the necessary figure and solidity. "The vessels of bulrushes or papyrus," says Dr. Shaw, "were no other than large fabrics of the same kind with that of Moses, Exod. ii. 3, which from the late introduction of planks and stronger materials are now laid aside." Thus *Pliny*, lib. vi., cap. 16, takes notice of the *naves papyraceas armamentaque Nili*, "ships made of papyrus and the equipments of the Nile:" and lib. xiii., cap. 11, he observes, *Ex ipsa quidem papyro navigia texunt:* "Of the papyrus itself they construct sailing vessels." *Herodotus* and *Diodorus* have recorded the same fact; and among the poets, *Lucan*, lib. iv., ver. 136: *Conseritur bibula Memphitis cymba papyro*, "The Memphian or Egyptian boat is constructed from the soaking papyrus." The epithet *bibula* is particularly remarkable, as corresponding with great exactness to the nature of the plant, and to its Hebrew name גמא *gome*, which signifies to *soak*, to *drink up*. See *Parkhurst* sub voce.

She laid it in the flags] Not willing to trust it in the *stream* for fear of a disaster; and probably choosing the place to which the Egyptian princess was accustomed to come for the purposes specified in the note on the following verse.

Verse 5. *And the daughter of Pharaoh*] Josephus calls her *Thermuthis*, and says that "the ark was borne along by the current, and that she sent one that could swim after it; that she was struck with the figure and uncommon beauty of the child; that she inquired for a nurse, but that he having refused the breasts of several, and his sister proposing to bring a Hebrew nurse, his own mother was procured." But all this is in Josephus's *manner*, as well as the long circumstantial *dream* that he gives to Amram concerning the future greatness of Moses, which cannot be considered in any other light than that of a *fable*, and not even a cunningly *devised* one.

To wash herself at the river] Whether the daughter of Pharaoh went to bathe in the river through motives of pleasure, health, or religion, or whether she bathed at all, the text does not specify. It is merely stated by the sacred writer that she *went down to the river to* WASH; for the word *herself* is not in the original. Mr. Harmer, Observat., vol. iii., p. 529, is of opinion that the time referred to above was that in which the Nile begins to *rise;* and as the dancing girls in Egypt are accustomed now to plunge themselves into the river at its rising, by which act they testify their gratitude for the inestimable blessing of its inundations, so it might have been formerly; and that Pharaoh's daughter was now coming down to the river on a similar account. I see no likelihood in all this. If she washed herself at all, it *might* have been a religious ablution, and yet extended no farther than to the *hands* and *face;* for the word רחץ *rachats*, to *wash*, is repeatedly used in the Pentateuch to signify *religious ablutions* of different kinds. Jonathan in his Targum says that God had smitten all Egypt with *ulcers*, and that the daughter of Pharaoh came to wash in the river in order to find relief; and that as soon as she touched the ark where Moses was, her ulcers were healed. This is all fable. I believe there was no *bathing* in the case, but simply what the text states, *washing*, not of her *person*, but of her *clothes*, which was an employment that even kings' daughters did not think beneath them in those primitive times. Homer, Odyss. vi., represents *Nausicaa, daughter* of *Alcinous, king of the Phæacians*, in company with her maidens, employed at the seaside in washing her own clothes and those of her *five* brothers! While thus employed they find Ulysses just driven ashore after having been shipwrecked, utterly helpless, naked, and destitute of every necessary of life. The whole scene is so perfectly like that before us that they appear to me to be almost parallels. I shall subjoin a few lines. The princess, having piled her clothes on a carriage drawn by several mules, and driven to the place of washing, commences her work, which the poet describes thus:—

Ται δ' απ' απηνης
Ειματα χερσιν ἑλοντο, και εσφορεον μελαν ὑδωρ.
Στειβον δ' εν βοθροισι θοως, εριδα προφερουσαι.
Αυταρ επει πλυναν τε, καθηραν τε ῥυπα παντα,
Εξειης πετασαν παρα θιν' ἁλος, ἡχι μαλιστα
Λαϊγγας ποτι χερσον αποπλυνεσκε θαλασσα.
ODYSS., lib. vi., ver. 90.

"Light'ning the carriage, next they bore in hand
The *garments down to the unsullied wave,*
And *thrust them heap'd into the pools;* their task
Despatching brisk, and with an emulous haste.
When *all were purified*, and neither *spot*
Could be perceived or *blemish* more, they *spread*
The raiment orderly along the beach,
Where dashing tides had cleansed the pebbles most."
COWPER.

When this task was finished we find the Phæacian princess and her ladies (*Κουρη δ' εκ θαλαμοιο—αμφιπολοι αλλαι*) employed in *amusing* themselves upon the beach, till the garments they had washed should *be dry* and fit to be folded up, that they might reload their carriage and return.

In the text of Moses the Egyptian princess, accompanied by *her maids*, נערתיה *naarotheyha*, comes down to the river, not to bathe *herself*, for this is not intimated, but merely to *wash*, לרחץ *lirchots;* at the time in which the ark is perceived we may suppose that she and her companions had finished their task, and, like the daughter of Alcinous and her maidens, were amusing themselves *walking along by the river's side*, as the others did by *tossing a ball*, *σφαιρῃ ται τ' αρ επαιζον*, when they as suddenly and as unexpectedly discovered *Moses adrift* on the flood, as *Nausicaa*

A. M. 2433. B. C. 1571. 6 And when she had opened *it*, she saw the child: and, behold, the babe wept. And she had compassion on him, and said, This *is one* of the Hebrews' children.

7 Then said his sister to Pharaoh's daughter, Shall I go and call to thee a nurse of the Hebrew women, that she may nurse the child for thee?

8 And Pharaoh's daughter said to her, Go. And the maid went, and called the child's mother.

9 And Pharaoh's daughter said unto her, Take this child away, and nurse it for me, and I will give *thee* thy wages. And the woman took the child, and nursed it.

10 And the child grew, and she brought him unto Pharaoh's daughter, and he became [e] her son. And she called his name [f] Moses: and she said, Because I drew him out of the water. A. M. 2433. B. C. 1571.

11 And it came to pass in those days, [g] when Moses was grown, that he went out unto his brethren, and looked on their [h] burdens: and he spied an Egyptian smiting a Hebrew, one of his brethren. A. M. 2473. B. C. 1531.

12 And he looked this way and that way, and when he saw that *there was* no man, he [i] slew the Egyptian, and hid him in the sand.

[e] Acts vii. 21.——[f] That is, *drawn out*.——[g] Acts vii. 23, 24; Heb. xi. 24, 25, 26.——[h] Chapter i. 11.——[i] Acts vii. 24

and her companions discovered Ulysses just escaped naked from shipwreck. In both the histories, that of the *poet* and this of the *prophet*, both the strangers, the shipwrecked Greek and the almost drowned Hebrew, were rescued by the princesses, nourished and preserved alive! Were it lawful to suppose that Homer had ever seen the Hebrew story, it would be reasonable to conclude that he had made it the basis of the 6th book of the Odyssey.

Verse 6. *She had compassion on him*] The sight of a beautiful babe in distress could not fail to make the impression here mentioned; see on ver. 2. It has already been conjectured that the cruel edict of the Egyptian king did not continue long in force; see chap. i. 22. And it will not appear unreasonable to suppose that the circumstance related here might have brought about its abolition. The daughter of Pharaoh, struck with the distressed state of the Hebrew children from what she had seen in the case of Moses, would probably implore her father to abolish this sanguinary edict.

Verse 7. *Shall I go and call—a nurse*] Had not the different circumstances marked here been placed under the superintendence of an especial providence, there is no human probability that they could have had such a happy issue. The parents had done every thing to save their child that piety, affection, and prudence could dictate, and having done so, they left the event to God. *By faith*, says the apostle, Heb. xi. 23, *Moses, when he was born, was hid three months of his parents, because they saw he was a proper child; and they were not afraid of the king's commandment.* Because of the king's commandment they were obliged to make use of the most prudent caution to save the child's life; and their faith in God enabled them to risk *their own safety*, for *they* were not afraid of the king's commandment—they feared God, and they had no other fear.

Verse 10. *And he became her son.*] From this time of his being brought home by his nurse his education commenced, and *he was learned in all the wisdom of the Egyptians*, Acts vii. 22, who in the knowledge of nature probably exceeded all the nations then on the face of the earth.

And she called his name] משה *mosheh*, because מן המים *min hammayim*, *out of the waters* משיתהו *meshithihu*, *have I drawn him*. משה *mashah* signifies *to draw out*; and *mosheh* is the person *drawn out*; the word is used in the same sense Psa. xviii. 17, and 2 Sam. xxii. 17. What name he had from his parents we know not; but whatever it might be it was ever after lost in the name given to him by the princess of Egypt. Abul Farajius says that Thermuthis delivered him to the wise men *Janees* and *Jimbrees* to be instructed in wisdom.

Verse 11. *When Moses was grown*] Being full *forty* years of age, as St. Stephen says, Acts vii. 23, *it came into his heart to visit his brethren*, i. e., he was excited to it by a Divine inspiration; *and seeing one of them suffer wrong*, by an Egyptian smiting him, probably one of the *task-masters*, *he avenged him and smote*—slew, *the Egyptian, supposing that God* who had given him commission, had given also *his brethren* to understand that they were to be delivered *by his hand*; see Acts vii. 23–25. Probably the Egyptian *killed* the Hebrew, and therefore on the *Noahic precept* Moses was justified in killing him; and he was authorized so to do by the commission which he had received from God, as all succeeding events amply prove. Previously to the mission of Moses to deliver the Israelites, Josephus says, "The Æthiopians having made an irruption into Egypt, and subdued a great part of it, a Divine oracle advised them to employ Moses the Hebrew. On this the king of Egypt made him general of the Egyptian forces; with these he attacked the Æthiopians, defeated and drove them back into their own land, and forced them to take refuge in the city of *Saba*, where he besieged them. Tharbis, daughter of the Æthiopian king, seeing him, fell desperately in love with him, and promised to give up the city to him on condition that he would take her to wife, to which Moses agreed, and the city was put into the hands of the Egyptians."—Jos. Ant. lib. ii., chap. 9. St. Stephen probably alluded to something

A. M. 2473.
B. C. 1531.

13 And [k] when he went out the second day, behold, two men of the Hebrews strove together: and he said to him that did the wrong, Wherefore smitest thou thy fellow?

14 And he said, [l] Who made thee [m] a prince and a judge over us? intendest thou to kill me, as thou killedst the Egyptian? And Moses feared, and said, Surely this thing is known.

15 Now when Pharaoh heard this thing, he sought to slay Moses. But [n] Moses fled from the face of Pharaoh, and dwelt in the land of Midian: and he sat down by [o] a well.

16 [p] Now [q] the priest of Midian had seven daughters: and [r] they came and drew *water*, and filled the troughs to water their father's flock.

17 And the shepherds came and drove them away: but Moses stood up and helped them, and [s] watered their flock.

18 And when they came to [t] Reuel, their father, he said, How *is it that* ye are come so soon to-day?

19 And they said, An Egyptian delivered us out of the hand of the shepherds, and also drew *water* enough for us, and watered the flock.

[k] Acts vii. 26.——[l] Acts vii. 27, 28.——[m] Heb. *a man, a prince*; Gen. xiii. 8.——[n] Acts vii. 29; Heb. xi. 27.——[o] Gen. xxiv. 11; xxix. 2.——[p] Chap. iii. 1.

[q] Or, *prince*, as Gen. xli. 45.——[r] Genesis xxiv. 11; xxix. 10; 1 Sam. ix. 11.——[s] Gen. xxix. 10.——[t] Num. x. 29; called also *Jethro* or *Jether*; chap. iii. 1; iv. 18; xviii. 1, &c.

of this kind when he said Moses was *mighty in deeds* as well as *words*.

Verse 13. *Two men of the Hebrews strove together*] How strange that in the very place where they were suffering a heavy persecution because they were *Hebrews*, the very persons themselves who suffered it should be found persecuting each other! It has been often seen that in those times in which the ungodly oppressed the Church of Christ, its own members have been separated from each other by disputes concerning comparatively unessential points of doctrine and discipline, in consequence of which both they and the truth have become an easy prey to those whose desire was to waste the heritage of the Lord. The Targum of Jonathan says that the two persons who strove were *Dathan* and *Abiram*.

Verse 14. *And Moses feared*] He saw that the Israelites were not as yet prepared to leave their bondage; and that though God had called him to be their leader, yet his providence had not yet sufficiently opened the way; and had he stayed in Egypt he must have endangered his life. Prudence therefore dictated an escape for the present to the land of Midian.

Verse 15. *Pharaoh—sought to slay Moses. But Moses fled from the face of Pharaoh*] How can this be reconciled with Heb. xi. 27: *By faith he* (Moses) *forsook Egypt, not fearing the wrath of the king?* Very easily. The apostle speaks not of *this* forsaking of Egypt, but of his and the Israelites' final departure from it, and of the bold and courageous manner in which Moses treated Pharaoh and the Egyptians, disregarding his threatenings and the multitudes of them that pursued after the people whom, in the name and strength of God, he led in the face of their enemies out of Egypt.

Dwelt in the land of Midian] A country generally supposed to have been in Arabia Petræa, on the eastern coast of the Red Sea, not far from Mount Sinai. This place is still called by the Arabs the *land of Midian* or the *land of Jethro*. *Abul Farajius* calls it the *land of the Arabs*. It is supposed that the Midianites derived their origin from Midian, the fourth son of Abraham by Keturah, thus:—Abraham, Zimran, Jokshan, Medan and Midian, Raguel, Jethro; see Gen. xxv. 1. But Calmet contends that if Jethro had been of the family of Abraham, either by *Jokshan*, or *Midian*, Aaron and Miriam could not have reproached Moses with marrying a *Cushite*, Zipporah, the daughter of Reuel. He thinks therefore that the Midianites were of the progeny of *Cush*, the son of *Ham*; see Gen. x. 6.

Verse 16. *The priest of Midian*] Or *prince*, or both; for the original כהן *cohen* has both meanings. See it explained at large, Gen. xv. 18. The transaction here very nearly resembles that mentioned Gen. xxix. concerning Jacob and Rachel; see the notes there.

Verse 17. *The shepherds—drove them*] The verb יגרשום *yegareshum*, being in the *masculine* gender, seems to imply that the shepherds drove away the *flocks* of Reuel's daughters, and not the *daughters* themselves. The fact seems to be, that, as the daughters of Reuel filled the troughs and brought their flocks to drink, the shepherds drove those away, and, profiting by the young women's labour, watered their own cattle. Moses resisted this insolence, and assisted them to water their flocks, in consequence of which they were enabled to return much sooner than they were wont to do, ver. 18.

Verse 18. *Reuel, their father*] In Num. x. 29 this person is called *Raguel*, but the Hebrew is the same in both places. The reason of this difference is that the ע *ain* in רעואל is sometimes used merely as *vowel*, sometimes as *g*, *ng*, and *gn*, and this is occasioned by the difficulty of the sound, which scarcely any European organs can enunciate. As pronounced by the Arabs it strongly resembles the first effort made by the throat in *gargling*, or as Meninski says, *Est vox vituli matrem vocantis*, "It is like the sound made by a calf in seeking its dam." *Raguel* is the worst method of pronouncing it; Re-u-el, the first syllable strongly accented, is nearer to the true sound. A proper uniformity in pronouncing the same word wherever it may occur, either in the Old or New Testament, is greatly to be desired. The person in question appears to have several names. Here he is called *Reuel*; in Num. x. 29, *Raguel*; in Exod. iii. 1, *Jethor*;

A. M. 2473. B. C. 1531.
20 And he said unto his daughters, And where *is* he? why *is* it
that ye have left the man? call him, that he
may [u] eat bread.
21 And Moses was content to dwell with
the man: and he gave Moses [v] Zipporah his
daughter.
22 And she bare *him* a son, and he called
his name [w] Gershom: [x] for he said, I have
been [y] a stranger in a strange land.
23 And it came to pass [z] in process of
time, that the king of Egypt A. M. cir. 2504. B. C. cir. 1500.
died: and the children of Israel
[a] sighed by reason of the bondage, and they
cried, and [b] their cry came up unto God by
reason of the bondage.
24 And God [c] heard their groaning, and God
[d] remembered his [e] covenant with Abraham,
with Isaac, and with Jacob.
25 And God [f] looked upon the children
of Israel, and God [g] had respect unto
them.[h]

[u] Gen. xxxi. 54; xliii. 25.——[v] Chapter iv. 25; xviii. 2.——[w] That is, *a stranger here*.——[x] Chap. xviii. 3.——[y] Acts vii. 29; Heb. xi. 13, 14.——[z] Chap. vii. 7; Acts vii. 30.——[a] Num. xx. 16; Deut. xxvi. 7; Psa. xii. 5.

[b] Gen. xviii. 20; chap. iii. 9; xxii. 23, 27; Deut. xxiv. 15; James v. 4.——[c] Chap. vi. 5.——[d] Chap. vi. 5; Psa. cv. 8, 42; cvi. 45.——[e] Gen. xv. 14; xlvi. 4.——[f] Ch. iv. 31; 1 Sam. i. 11; 2 Sam. xvi. 12; Luke i. 25.——[g] Heb. *knew*.——[h] Chap. iii. 7.

in Judges iv. 11, *Hobab;* and in Judges i. 16 he is called קיני *Keyni*, which in chap. iv. we translate *Kenite.* Some suppose that *Re-u-el* was father to *Hobab*, who was also called *Jethro.* This is the most likely; see the note on chap. iii. 1.

Verse 20. *That he may eat bread.*] That he may be entertained, and receive refreshment to proceed on his journey. *Bread*, among the Hebrews, was used to signify *all kinds of food* commonly used for the support of man's life.

Verse 21. *Zipporah his daughter.*] Abul Farajius calls her "*Saphura the black*, daughter of *Rewel* the Midianite, the son of Dedan, the son of Abraham by his wife Keturah." The Targum calls her the *grand-daughter* of Reuel. It appears that Moses obtained Zipporah something in the same way that Jacob obtained Rachel; namely, for the performance of certain services, probably keeping of sheep; see chap. iii. 1.

Verse 22. *Called his name Gershom*] Literally, *a stranger;* the reason of which Moses immediately adds, *for I have been an* ALIEN *in a strange land.*

The *Vulgate*, the *Septuagint*, as it stands in the *Complutensian Polyglot*, and in several MSS., the *Syriac*, the *Coptic*, and the *Arabic*, add the following words to this verse: *And the name of the second he called Eliezer, for the God of my father has been my help, and delivered me from the hand of Pharaoh.* These words are found in chap. xviii. 4, but they are certainly necessary here, for it is very likely that these two sons were born within a short space of each other; for in chap. iv. 20 it is said, Moses took his wife and his SONS, by which it is plain that he had both *Gershom* and *Eliezer* at that time. *Houbigant* introduces this addition in his Latin version, and contends that this is its most proper place. Notwithstanding the authority of the above versions, the clause is found in no copy, printed or MS., of the *Hebrew* text.

Verse 23. *In process of time—the king of Egypt died*] According to St. Stephen, (Acts vii. 30, compared with Exod. vii. 7,) the death of the Egyptian king happened about *forty* years after the escape of Moses to Midian. The words ויהי בימים הרבים ההם *vayehi baiyamim harabbim hahem*, which we translate *And it came to pass in process of time*, signify, *And it was in many days from these* that the king, &c. It has already been remarked that Archbishop Usher supposes this king to have been *Ramesses Miamun*, who was succeeded by his son Amenophis, who was drowned in the Red Sea when pursuing the Israelites, but *Abul Farajius* says it was *Amunfathis*, (Amenophis,) he who made the cruel edict against the Hebrew children.

Some suppose that Moses wrote the book of Job during the time he sojourned in Midian, and also the book of Genesis. See the preface to the book of Job, where this subject is considered.

Sighed by reason of the bondage] For the nature of their bondage, see on chap. i. 14.

Verse 24. *God remembered his covenant*] God's covenant is God's engagement; he had promised to Abraham, to Isaac, and to Jacob, to give their posterity a land flowing with milk and honey, &c. They are now under the most oppressive bondage, and this was the most proper time for God to show them his mercy and power in fulfilling his promise. This is all that is meant by God's *remembering* his covenant, for it was *now* that he began to give it its effect.

Verse 25. *And God had respect unto* them.] וידע אלהים *vaiyeda Elohim*, God *knew* them, i. e., he *approved* of them, and therefore it is said that *their cry came up before God, and he heard their groaning.* The word ידע *yada, to know*, in the Hebrew Bible, as well as γινωσκω in the Greek Testament, is frequently used in the sense of *approving;* and because God *knew*—had *respect* for and *approved* of, them, therefore he was determined to deliver them. For אלהים *Elohim*, GOD, in the last clause of this verse, Houbigant reads אליהם *aleyhem*, UPON THEM, which is countenanced by the *Vulgate, Septuagint, Chaldee, Coptic*, and *Arabic*, and appears to have been the original reading. The difference in the original consists in the interchange of two letters, the י *yod* and ה *he*. Our translators insert *unto them*, in order to make up that sense which this various reading gives without trouble.

THE farther we proceed in the sacred writings, the more the history both of the *grace* and *providence* of God opens to our view. He ever cares for his creatures, and is mindful of his promise. The very means

made use of to destroy his work are, in his hands, the instruments of its accomplishment. Pharaoh orders the male children of the Hebrews to be thrown into the river; Moses, who was thus exposed, is found by his own daughter, brought up as her own son, and from his Egyptian education becomes much better qualified for the great work to which God had called him; and his being obliged to leave Egypt was undoubtedly a powerful means to wean his heart from a land in which he had at his command all the advantages and luxuries of life. His sojourning also in a strange land, where he was obliged to earn his bread by a very painful employment, fitted him for the perilous journey he was obliged to take in the wilderness, and enabled him to bear the better the privations to which he was in consequence exposed.

The *bondage* of the Israelites was also wisely permitted, that they might with less reluctance leave a country where they had suffered the greatest oppression and indignities. Had they not suffered severely previously to their departure, there is much reason to believe that no inducements could have been sufficient to have prevailed on them to leave it. And yet their leaving it was of infinite consequence, in the order both of grace and providence, as it was indispensably necessary that they should be a people separated from all the rest of the world, that they might see the promises of God fulfilled under their own eyes, and thus have the fullest persuasion that their law was Divine, their prophets inspired by the Most High, and that the Messiah came according to the prophecies before delivered concerning him.

From the example of Pharaoh's daughter, (see note ver. 4,) and the seven daughters of Jethro, (ver. 16,) we learn that in the days of primitive simplicity, and in this respect the best days, the children, particularly the daughters of persons in the highest ranks in life, were employed in the most laborious offices. Kings' daughters performed the office of the *laundress* to their own families; and the daughters of princes tended and watered the flocks. We have seen similar instances in the case of *Rebekah* and *Rachel;* and we cannot be too pointed in calling the attention of modern delicate females, who are not only above serving their own parents and family, but even their own selves: the consequence of which is, they have neither vigour nor health; their growth, for want of healthy exercise, is generally cramped; their natural powers are prematurely developed, and their whole course is rather an apology for living, than a state of effective life. Many of these live not out half their days, and their offspring, when they have any, is more feeble than themselves; so that the race of man where such preposterous conduct is followed (and where is it not followed?) is in a state of gradual deterioration. Parents who wish to fulfil the intention of God and nature, will doubtless see it their duty to bring up their children on a different plan. A worse than the present can scarcely be found out.

Afflictions, under the direction of God's providence and the influence of his grace, are often the means of leading men to pray to and acknowledge God, who in the time of their prosperity hardened their necks from his fear. When the Israelites were sorely oppressed, they began to pray. If the cry of oppression had not been among them, probably the cry for mercy had not been heard. Though afflictions, considered in themselves, can neither atone for sin nor improve the moral state of the soul, yet God often uses them as means to bring sinners to himself, and to quicken those who, having already escaped the pollutions of the world, were falling again under the influence of an earthly mind. Of many millions besides David it may truly be said, Before they were afflicted they went astray.

CHAPTER III.

Moses *keeping the flock of* Jethro *at* Mount Horeb, *the angel of the Lord appears to him in a burning bush,* 1, 2. *Astonished at the sight, he turns aside to examine it,* 3, *when God speaks to him out of the fire, and declares himself to be the God of Abraham, Isaac, and Jacob,* 4–6; *announces his purpose of delivering the Israelites from their oppression, and of bringing them into the promised land,* 7–9; *commissions him to go to Pharaoh, and to be leader of the children of Israel from Egypt,* 10. *Moses excuses himself,* 11; *and God, to encourage him, promises him his protection,* 12. *Moses doubts whether the Israelites will credit him,* 13, *and God reveals to him his* NAME, *and informs him what he is to say to the people,* 14–17, *and instructs him and the elders of Israel to apply unto Pharaoh for permission to go three days' journey into the wilderness, to sacrifice unto the Lord,* 18; *foretells the obstinacy of the Egyptian king, and the miracles which he himself should work in the sight of the Egyptians,* 19, 20; *and promises that, on the departure of the Israelites, the Egyptians should be induced to furnish them with all necessaries for their journey,* 21, 22.

A. M. 2513. B. C. 1491.

NOW Moses kept the flock of Jethro his father-in-law, [a] the priest of Midian: and he led the flock to the backside of the desert, and came to [b] the mountain of God, *even* to Horeb.

A. M. 2513. B. C. 1491.

[a] Chap. ii. 16.

[b] Chap. xviii. 5; 1 Kings xix. 8.

NOTES ON CHAP. III.

Verse 1. *Jethro his father-in-law*] Concerning *Jethro*, see the note on chap. ii. 18. Learned men are not agreed on the signification of the word חתן *chothen*, which we translate *father-in-law*, and which in Gen. xix. 14, we translate *son-in-law*. It seems to

A. M. 2513. B. C. 1491.

2 And [c] the angel of the Lord appeared unto him in a flame of fire,
out of the midst of a bush: and he looked,
and, behold, the bush burned with fire, and
the bush *was* not consumed.
3 And Moses said, I will now turn aside,
and see this [d] great sight, why the
bush is not burned.
4 And when the Lord saw that he turned
aside to see, God called [e] unto him out of the
midst of the bush, and said, Moses, Moses
And he said, Here *am* I.

A. M. 2513. B. C. 1491.

[c] Deut. xxxiii. 16; Isa. lxiii. 9; Acts vii. 30.

[d] Psa. ·xi. 2; Acts vii. 31.——[e] Deut. xxxiii. 16.

be a general term for a *relative by marriage*, and the connection only in which it stands can determine its precise meaning. It is very possible that *Reuel* was now dead, it being forty years since Moses came to Midian; that Jethro was his son, and had succeeded him in his office of prince and priest of Midian; that Zipporah was the sister of Jethro; and that consequently the word חתן *chothen* should be translated *brother-in-law* in this place: as we learn from Gen. xxxiv. 9, Deut. vii. 3, Josh. xxiii. 12, and other places, that it simply signifies *to contract affinity by marriage*. If this conjecture be right, we may well suppose that, Reuel being dead, Moses was continued by his brother-in-law Jethro in the same employment he had under his father.

Mountain of God] Sometimes named *Horeb*, at other times *Sinai*. The mountain itself had two *peaks*; one was called *Horeb*, the other *Sinai*. Horeb was probably the primitive name of the mountain, which was afterwards called the *mountain of God*, because God appeared upon it to Moses; and Mount Sinai, סיני, from סנה *seneh*, a *bush*, because it was in a *bush* or *bramble*, in a flame of fire, that this appearance was made.

Verse 2. *The angel of the Lord*] Not a created angel certainly; for he is called יהוה *Jehovah*, ver. 4, &c., and has the most expressive attributes of the Godhead applied to him, ver. 14, &c. Yet he is an *angel*, מלאך *malach*, a *messenger*, in whom was the name of God, chap. xxiii. 21; and in whom dwelt all the fulness of the Godhead bodily, Col. ii. 9; and who, in all these primitive times, was the Messenger of the covenant, Mal. iii. 1. And who was this but Jesus, the Leader, Redeemer, and Saviour of mankind? See the note on Gen. xvi. 7.

A flame of fire, out of the midst of a bush] Fire was, not only among the Hebrews but also among many other ancient nations, a very significant emblem of the Deity. God accompanied the Israelites in all their journeyings through the wilderness as a pillar of fire by night; and probably a fire or flame in the holy of holies, between the cherubim, was the general symbol of his presence; and traditions of these things, which must have been current in the east, have probably given birth, not only to the pretty general opinion that God appears in the likeness of fire, but to the whole of the *Zoroastrian system of fire-worship*. It has been reported of Zoroaster, or *Zeradusht*, that having retired to a mountain for the study of wisdom, and the benefit of solitude, the whole mountain was one day enveloped with flame, out of the midst of which he came without receiving any injury; on which he offered sacrifices to God, who, he was persuaded, had then appeared to him. M. Anquetil du Perron gives much curious information on this subject in his *Zend Avesta*. The modern Parsees call fire the offspring of Ormusd, and worship it with a vast variety of ceremonies.

Among the fragments attributed to Æschylus, and collected by Stanley in his invaluable edition of this poet, p. 647, col. 1, we find the following beautiful verses:—

Χωριζε θνητων τον Θεον, και μη δοκει
'Ομοιον αυτῳ σαρκινον καθεσταναι.
Ουκ οισθα δ' αυτον· ποτε μεν ὡς πυρ φαινεται
Απλαστον ὁρμῃ· ποτε δ' ὑδωρ, ποτε δε γνοφος.

"Distinguish God from mortal men; and do not suppose that any thing fleshly is like unto him. Thou knowest him not: sometimes indeed he appears as a *formless* and *impetuous* FIRE, sometimes as *water*, sometimes as *thick darkness*." The poet proceeds:—

Τρεμει δ' ορη, και γαια, και πελωριος
Βυθος θαλασσης, κωρεων ὑψος μεγα,
'Οταν επιβλεψῃ γοργον ομμα δεσποτου.

"The mountains, the earth, the deep and extensive sea, and the summits of the highest mountains tremble whenever the terrible eye of the Supreme Lord looks down upon them."

These are very remarkable fragments, and seem all to be collected from traditions relative to the different manifestations of God to the Israelites in Egypt, and in the wilderness. Moses wished to see God, but he could behold nothing but an *indescribable glory*: nothing like *mortals*, nothing like a *human body*, appeared at any time to his eye, or to those of the Israelites. "Ye saw no manner of similitude," said Moses, "on the day that the Lord spake unto you in Horeb, out of the midst of the FIRE," Deut. iv. 15. But sometimes the Divine power and justice were manifested by the *indescribable, formless, impetuous, consuming flame*; at other times he appeared by the *water* which he brought out of the flinty rock; and in the *thick darkness* on Horeb, when the *fiery law* proceeded from his right hand, then the *earth quaked* and the *mountain trembled*: and when his *terrible eye* looked out upon the Egyptians through the pillar of cloud and fire, their chariot wheels were struck off, and confusion and dismay were spread through all the hosts of Pharaoh; Exod. xiv. 24, 25.

And the bush was not consumed.] 1. An emblem of the state of Israel in its various distresses and persecutions: it was in the fire of adversity, but was not consumed. 2. An emblem also of the state of the Church of God in the wilderness, in persecutions often, in the midst of its enemies, in the region of the shadow of death—yet not consumed. 3. An emblem also of the state of every follower of Christ: cast down, but not forsaken; grievously tempted, but not destroyed;

A. M. 2513. B. C. 1491.

5 And he said, Draw not nigh
hither: [f] put off thy shoes from
off thy feet, for the place whereon thou standest
is holy ground.
6 Moreover he said, [g] I *am* the God of thy
father, the God of Abraham, the God of Isaac,
and the God of Jacob. And Moses hid his
face; for [h] he was afraid to look upon God.
7 And the LORD said, I have surely seen
the affliction of my people which *are* in Egypt,
and [i] have heard their cry [k] by reason of their task-masters; for [l] I
know their sorrows;
8 And [m] I am come down to [n] deliver them
out of the hand of the Egyptians, and to bring
them up out of that land [o] unto a good land
and a large, unto a land [p] flowing with milk
and honey; unto the place of [q] the Canaanites,
and the Hittites, and the Amorites, and the
Perizzites, and the Hivites, and the Jebusites.

A. M. 2513. B. C. 1491.

[f] Chap. xix. 12; Josh. v. 15; Acts vii. 33.——[g] Gen. xxviii. 13; ver. 15; chap. iv. 5; Matt. xxii. 32; Mark xii. 26; Luke xx. 37; Acts vii. 32.——[h] So 1 Kings xix. 13; Isa. vi. 1, 5; Neh. ix. 9; Psa. cvi. 44; Acts vii. 34.——[i] Ch. ii. 23, 24.——[k] Chap. i. 11.

[l] Gen. xviii. 21; ch. ii. 25.——[m] Gen. xi. 5, 7; xviii. 21; l. 24.——[n] Ch. vi. 6, 8; xii. 51.——[o] Deut. i. 25; viii. 7, 8, 9.——[p] Ver. 17; chap. xiii. 5; xxxiii. 3; Num. xiii. 27; Deut. xxvi. 9, 15; Jer. xi. 5; xxxii. 22; Ezek. xx. 6.——[q] Gen. xv. 18.

walking through the fire, but still unconsumed! Why are all these preserved in the midst of those things which have a natural tendency to destroy them? Because GOD IS IN THE MIDST OF THEM; it was this that preserved the bush from destruction; and it was this that preserved the Israelites; and it is this, and this alone, that preserves the Church, and holds the soul of every genuine believer in the spiritual life. He in whose heart Christ dwells not by faith, will soon be consumed by the world, the flesh, and the devil.

Verse 5. *Put off thy shoes*] "It is likely that from this circumstance all the eastern nations have agreed to perform all the acts of their religious worship *barefooted*. All the Mohammedans, Brahmins, and Parsees do so still. The Jews were remarked for this in the time of Juvenal; hence he speaks of their performing their sacred rites *barefooted*; *Sat.* vi., ver. 158:

Observant ubi festa *mero pede* sabbata reges.

The ancient Greeks did the same. Jamblichus, in the life of Pythagoras, tells us that this was one of his maxims, Ανυποδητος θυε και προσκυνει, *Offer sacrifice and worship with your shoes off*. And Solinus asserts that no person was permitted to enter into the temple of Diana, in Crete, till he had taken off his shoes. "*Ædem Numinis* (*Dianæ*) *præterquam* nudus vestigio *nullus licito ingreditur*." Tertullian observes, *de jejunio*, that in a time of drought the worshippers of Jupiter deprecated his wrath, and prayed for rain, walking barefooted. "Cum stupet cœlum, et aret annus, *nudipedalia*, denunciantur." It is probable that נעלים *nealim*, in the text, signifies *sandals*, translated by the Chaldee סנדל *sandal*, and סנדלא *sandala*, (see Gen. xiv. 23,) which was the same as the Roman *solea*, a *sole* alone, strapped about the foot. As this sole must let in dust, gravel, and sand about the foot in travelling, and render it very uneasy, hence the custom of frequently *washing* the feet in those countries where these sandals were worn. *Pulling off the shoes* was, therefore, an emblem of laying aside the *pollutions* contracted by *walking* in the *way of sin*. Let those who name the Lord Jesus Christ depart from iniquity. In our western countries reverence is expressed by pulling off the hat; but how much more significant is the eastern custom! "The natives of Bengal never go into their own houses with their shoes on, nor into the houses of others, but always leave their shoes at the door. It would be a great affront not to attend to this mark of respect when visiting; and to enter a temple without pulling off the shoes would be an unpardonable offence."—*Ward.*

The place whereon thou standest is *holy ground.*] It was now particularly sanctified by the Divine presence; but if we may credit Josephus, a general opinion had prevailed that *God dwelt on that mountain;* and hence the shepherds, considering it as sacred ground, did not dare to feed their flocks there. Moses, however, finding the soil to be rich and the pasturage good, boldly drove his flock thither to feed on it.—Antiq., b. ii., c. xii., s. 1.

Verse 6. *I* am *the God of thy father*] Though the word אבי *abi, father*, is here used in the singular, St. Stephen, quoting this place, Acts vii. 32, uses the plural, Ὁ Θεος των πατερων σου, *The God of thy* FATHERS; and that this is the meaning the following words prove: The God of Abraham, the God of Isaac, and the God of Jacob. These were the fathers of Moses in a direct line. This reading is confirmed by the *Samaritan* and by the *Coptic*. ABRAHAM was the father of the *Ishmaelites*, and with him was the covenant first *made*. ISAAC was the father of the *Edomites* as well as the *Israelites*, and with him was the covenant *renewed*. JACOB was the father of the twelve patriarchs, who were founders of the *Jewish* nation, and to him were the promises *particularly confirmed*. Hence we see that the *Arabs* and *Turks* in general, who are descendants of *Ishmael;* the *Edomites*, now absorbed among the Jews, (see the note on Gen. xxv. 23,) who are the descendants of *Esau;* and the *Jewish people*, wheresoever scattered, who are the descendants of *Jacob*, are all heirs of the promises included in this primitive covenant; and their gathering in with the fulness of the Gentiles may be confidently expected.

And Moses hid his face] For similar acts, see the passages referred to in the margin. *He was afraid to look*—he was overawed by God's presence, and dazzled with the splendour of the appearance.

Verse 7. *I have surely seen*] ראה ראיתי *raoh raithi, seeing, I have seen*—I have not only seen the afflictions of this people because I am omniscient, but I have considered their sorrows, and my eye affects my heart.

Verse 8. *And I am come down to deliver them*] This is the very purpose for which I am now come

a

A. M. 2513.
B. C. 1491.

9 Now therefore, behold, [r] the cry of the children of Israel is come unto me: and I have also seen the [s] oppression wherewith the Egyptians oppress them.

10 [t] Come now therefore, and I will send thee unto Pharaoh, that thou mayest bring forth my people the children of Israel out of Egypt.

11 And Moses said unto God, [u] Who *am* I, that I should go unto Pharaoh, and that I should bring forth the children of Israel out of Egypt?

12 And he said, [v] Certainly I will be with thee; and this *shall be* a token unto thee that I have sent thee: When thou hast brought forth the people out of Egypt, ye shall serve God upon this mountain.

13 And Moses said unto God, Behold, *when* I come unto the children of Israel, and shall say unto them, The God of your fathers hath sent me unto you; and they shall say to me,

[r] Chap. ii. 23.——[s] Chap. i. 11, 13, 14, 22.——[t] Psa. cv. 26; Mic. vi. 4.——[u] See chap. vi. 12; 1 Sam. xviii. 18; Isa. vi. 5, 8; Jer. i. 6.——[v] Genesis xxxi. 3; Deut. xxxi. 23; Josh. i. 5; Rom. viii. 31.

down upon this mountain, and for which I manifest myself to thee.

Large—land] Canaan, when compared with the small tract of Goshen, in which they were now situated, and where, we learn, from chap. i. 7, they were straitened for room, might be well called a *large land*. See a fine description of this land Deut. viii. 7.

A land flowing with milk and honey] Excellent for pasturage, because abounding in the most wholesome herbage and flowers; and from the latter an abundance of wild honey was collected by the bees. Though cultivation is now almost entirely neglected in this land, because of the badness of the government and the scantiness of the inhabitants, yet it is still good for *pasturage*, and yields an abundance of *honey*. The terms used in the text to express the fertility of this land, are commonly used by ancient authors on similar subjects. It is a metaphor taken from a *breast* producing copious streams of milk. Homer calls Argos *ουθαρ αρουρης*, the *breast of the country*, as affording *streams* of milk and honey, Il. ix., ver. 141. So Virgil:—

Prima tulit tellus, eadem vos *ubere* læto
Accipiet. *Æn.*, lib. iii., ver. 95.

"The land that first produced you shall receive you again into its joyous *bosom*."

The poets feign that Bacchus, the fable of whom they have taken from the history of Moses, produced rivers of milk and honey, of water and wine:—

Ῥει δε γαλακτι πεδον,
Ῥει δ' οινῳ, ῥει δε μελισσαν
Νεκταρι. EURIP. *Bacch.*, Εποδ., ver. 8.

"The land flows with milk; it flows also with wine; it flows also with the nectar of bees, (honey.)" This seems to be a mere poetical copy from the Pentateuch, where the sameness of the metaphor and the correspondence of the descriptions are obvious.

Place of the Canaanites, &c.] See Gen. xv. 18, &c.

Verse 11. *Who am I—that I should bring*] He was so satisfied that this was beyond *his* power, and all the means that he possessed, that he is astonished that even God himself should appoint him to this work! Such indeed was the bondage of the children of Israel, and the power of the people by whom they were enslaved, that had not their deliverance come through supernatural means, their escape had been utterly impossible.

Verse 12. *Certainly I will be with thee*] This great event shall not be left to thy wisdom and to thy power; my counsel shall direct thee, and my power shall bring all these mighty things to pass.

And this shall be *a token*] Literally, *And* THIS *to thee for a sign*, i. e., this miraculous manifestation of the *burning bush* shall be a proof that I have sent thee; or, My being *with thee*, to encourage thy heart, strengthen thy hands, and enable thee to work miracles, shall be to thyself and to others the evidence of thy Divine mission.

Ye shall serve God upon this mountain.] This was not the *sign*; but God shows him, that in their return from Egypt they should take this mountain in their way, and should worship him in this place. There may be a prophetic allusion here to the giving of the law on Mount Sinai. As Moses received his commands *here*, so likewise should the Israelites receive theirs in the same place. After all, the Divine Being seems to testify a partial predilection for this mountain, for reasons that are not expressed. See the note on ver. 5.

Verse 13. *They shall say—What is his name?*] Does not this suppose that the Israelites had an idolatrous notion even of the Supreme Being? They had probably drank deep into the Egyptian superstitions, and had gods many and lords many; and Moses conjectured that, hearing of a supernatural deliverance, they would inquire who that God was by whom it was to be effected. The reasons given here by the rabbins are too refined for the Israelites at this time. "When God," say they, "*judgeth* his creatures, he is called אלהים *Elohim*; when he *warreth* against the wicked, he is called צבאות *Tsebaoth*; but when he showeth *mercy* unto the world, he is called יהוה *Yehovah*." It is not likely that the Israelites had much knowledge of God or of his ways at the time to which the sacred text refers; it is certain they had no *written* word. The book of Genesis, if even written, (for some suppose it had been composed by Moses during his residence in Midian,) had not yet been communicated to the people; and being so long without any revelation, and perhaps without even the *form* of Divine worship, their minds being degraded by the state of bondage in which they had been so long held, and seeing and hearing little in religion but the superstitions of those among whom they sojourned, they could

A. M. 2513. B. C. 1491.

What *is* his name? what shall I
say unto them?
14 And God said unto Moses, I AM THAT
I AM: and he said, Thus shalt thou say unto
the children of Israel, [w] I AM hath sent me
unto you.
15 And God said moreover unto Moses,
Thus shalt thou say unto the children of Israel,
The LORD God of your fathers, the God of
Abraham, the God of Isaac, and the God of
Jacob, hath sent me unto you: this *is* [x] my
name for ever, and this *is* my memorial unto
all generations.
16 Go, and [y] gather the elders of Israel
together, and say unto them, The LORD God
of your fathers, the God of Abraham, of Isaac, and of Jacob, ap-
peared unto me, saying, [z] I have surely visited
you, and *seen* that which is done to you in
Egypt:
17 And I have said, [a] I will bring you up
out of the affliction of Egypt unto the land
of the Canaanites, and the Hittites, and the
Amorites, and the Perizzites, and the Hivites,
and the Jebusites, unto a land flowing with
milk and honey.
18 And [b] they shall hearken to thy voice: and
[c] thou shalt come, thou and the elders of Israel,
unto the king of Egypt, and ye shall say unto
him, The LORD God of the Hebrews hath [d] met

A. M. 2513. B. C. 1491.

[w] Chap. vi. 3; John viii. 58; 2 Cor. i. 20; Heb. xiii. 8; Rev. i. 4.——[x] Psa. cxxxv. 13; Hos. xii. 5.——[y] Ch. iv. 29.——[z] Gen. l. 24; ch. ii. 25; iv. 31; Luke i. 68.——[a] Gen. xv. 14, 16; ver 8. [b] Ch. iv. 31.——[c] Ch. v. 1, 3.——[d] Num. xxiii. 3, 4, 15, 16.

have no distinct notion of the Divine Being. Moses himself might have been in doubt at first on this subject, and he seems to have been greatly on his guard against illusion; hence he asks a variety of questions, and endeavours, by all prudent means, to assure himself of the truth and certainty of the present appearance and commission. He well knew the power of the Egyptian magicians, and he could not tell from these first views whether there might not have been some delusion in this case. God therefore gives him the fullest proof, not only for the satisfaction of the people to whom he was to be sent, but for his own full conviction, that it was the supreme God who now spoke to him.

Verse 14. I AM THAT I AM] אהיה אשר אהיה EHEYEH *asher* EHEYEH. These words have been variously understood. The *Vulgate* translates EGO SUM QUI SUM, *I am who am.* The *Septuagint*, Εγω ειμι ὁ Ων, *I am he who exists.* The *Syriac*, the *Persic*, and the *Chaldee* preserve the original words without any gloss. The *Arabic* paraphrases them, *The Eternal, who passes not away;* which is the same interpretation given by *Abul Farajius*, who also preserves the original words, and gives the above as their interpretation. The *Targum* of *Jonathan*, and the *Jerusalem Targum* paraphrase the words thus: "He who spake, and the world was; who spake, and all things existed." As the original words literally signify, *I will be what I will be*, some have supposed that God simply designed to inform Moses, that what he *had been* to his fathers Abraham, Isaac, and Jacob, he *would be* to him and the Israelites; and that he would perform the promises he had made to his fathers, by giving their descendants the promised land. It is difficult to put a meaning on the words; they seem intended to point out the *eternity* and *self-existence* of God. Plato, in his *Parmenides*, where he treats sublimely of the nature of God, says, Ουδ' αρα ονομα εστιν αυτῳ, nothing can express his nature; *therefore no name can be attributed to him.* See the conclusion of this chapter, and on the word *Jehovah*, chap. xxxiv. 6, 7.

Verse 15. *This is my name for ever*] The name here referred to is that which immediately precedes, יהוה אלהים *Yehovah Elohim*, which we translate the LORD GOD, the name by which God *had* been known from the creation of the world, (see Gen. ii. 4,) and the name by which he is known among the same people to the present day. Even the heathens knew this name of the true God; and hence out of our יהוה *Yehovah* they formed their *Jao*, *Jeve*, and *Jove;* so that the word has been literally fulfilled, *This is my memorial unto all generations.* See the note on the word *Elohim*, Gen. i. 1. As to be self-existent and eternal must be attributes of God for ever, does it not follow that the לעלם *leolam, for ever*, in the text signifies *eternity?* "This is my name to eternity—and my memorial," לדר דר *ledor dor*, "to all succeeding generations." While human generations continue he shall be called the God of Abraham, the God of Isaac, and the God of Jacob; but when time shall be no more, he shall be Jehovah Elohim. Hence the first expression refers to his eternal existence, the latter to the discovery he should make of himself as long as time should last. See Gen. xxi. 33. Diodorus Siculus says, that "among the Jews, Moses is reported to have received his laws from the God named *Jao*," Ιαω, i. e., *Jeue, Jove*, or *Jeve;* for in all these ways the word יהוה *Yehovah* may be pronounced; and in this way I have seen it on Egyptian monuments. See Diod., lib. I., c. xciv.

Verse 16. *Elders of Israel*] Though it is not likely the Hebrews were permitted to have any regular government at this time, yet there can be no doubt of their having such a government in the time of Joseph, and for some considerable time after; the elders of each tribe forming a kind of court of magistrates, by which all actions were tried, and legal decisions made, in the Israelitish community.

I have surely visited you] An exact fulfilment of the prediction of Joseph, Gen. l. 24, *God will surely visit you*, and in the same words too.

Verse 18. *They shall hearken to thy voice*] This assurance was necessary to encourage him in an enterprise so dangerous and important.

A. M. 2513. B. C. 1491.

with us: and now let us go, we
beseech thee, three days' journey
into the wilderness, that we may sacrifice to
the LORD our God.
19 And I am sure that the king of Egypt
[e] will not let you go, [f] no, not by a mighty hand.
20 And I will [g] stretch out my hand, and
smite Egypt with [h] all my wonders which I
will do in the midst thereof: and [i] after that
he will let you go.
21 And [k] I will give this people
favour in the sight of the Egyptians:
and it shall come to pass, that, when ye go,
ye shall not go empty.
22 [l] But every woman shall borrow of her
neighbour, and of her that sojourneth in her
house, jewels of silver, and jewels of gold,
and raiment: and ye shall put *them* upon
your sons, and upon your daughters; and [m] ye
shall spoil [n] the Egyptians.

[e] Chap. v. 2; vii. 4.——[f] Or, *but by strong hand.*——[g] Ch. vi. 6; vii. 5; ix. 15.——[h] Chap. vii. 3; xi. 9; Deut. vi. 22; Neh. ix. 10; Psa. cv. 27; cxxxv. 9; Jer. xxxii. 20; Acts vii. 36; see chap. vii. to xiii.——[i] Chap. xii. 31.——[k] Chap. xi. 3; xii. 36; Psa. cvi. 46; Prov. xvi. 7.——[l] Gen. xv. 14; ch. xi. 2; xii. 35, 36. [m] Job xxvii. 17; Prov. xiii. 22; Ezek. xxxix. 10.——[n] Or, *Egypt.*

Three days' journey into the wilderness] Evidently intending *Mount Sinai*, which is reputed to be about three days' journey, the shortest way, from the land of Goshen. In ancient times, distances were computed by the *time* required to pass over them. Thus, instead of *miles*, *furlongs*, &c., it was said, the distance from one place to another was so many *days'*, so many *hours'* journey; and it continues the same in all countries where there are no regular roads or highways.

Verse 19. *I am sure that the king of Egypt will not let you go, no, not by a mighty hand*] When the facts detailed in this history have been considered in connection with the assertion as it stands in our Bibles, the most palpable contradiction has appeared. That the king of Egypt *did* let them go, and that *by a mighty hand*, the book itself amply declares. We should therefore seek for another meaning of the original word. ולא *velo*, which generally means *and not*, has sometimes the meaning of *if not*, *unless*, *except*, &c.; and in *Becke's* Bible, 1549, it is thus translated: *I am sure that the kyng of Egypt wyl not let you go*, EXCEPT *wyth a myghty hand.* This import of the negative particle, which is noticed by Noldius, *Heb. Part.*, p. 328, was perfectly understood by the *Vulgate*, where it is translated *nisi*, *unless;* and the *Septuagint* in their εαν μη, which is of the same import; and so also the *Coptic*. The meaning therefore is very plain: The king of Egypt, who now profits much by your servitude, will not let you go till he sees my hand stretched out, and he and his nation be smitten with *ten* plagues. Hence God immediately adds, ver. 20: *I will stretch out my hand, and smite Egypt with all my wonders—and after that, he will let you go.*

Verse 22. *Every woman shall borrow*]. This is certainly not a very correct translation: the original word שאל *shaal* signifies simply to *ask*, *request*, *demand*, *require*, *inquire*, &c.; but it does not signify to *borrow* in the proper sense of that word, though in a very few places of Scripture it is thus used. In this and the parallel place, chap. xii. 35, the word signifies to *ask* or *demand*, and not to *borrow*, which is a *gross mistake* into which scarcely any of the *versions*, ancient or modern, have fallen, except our own. The SEPTUAGINT has αιτησει, *she shall ask;* the VULGATE, *postulabit*, *she shall demand;* the SYRIAC, CHALDEE, SAMARITAN, SAMARITAN *Version*, COPTIC, and PERSIAN, are the same as the *Hebrew*. The *European* versions are generally correct on this point; and our *common* English version is almost the sole transgressor: I say, the *common* version, which, copying the Bible published by Becke in 1549, gives us the exceptionable term *borrow*, for the original שאל *shaal*, which in the *Geneva* Bible, and *Barker's* Bible of 1615, and some others, is rightly translated *aske*. God commanded the Israelites to *ask* or *demand* a certain recompense for their past services, and he inclined the hearts of the Egyptians to *give* liberally; and this, far from being a matter of *oppression*, *wrong*, or even *charity*, was no more than a very *partial recompense* for the long and painful services which we may say *six hundred thousand* Israelites had rendered to Egypt, during a considerable number of years. And there can be no doubt that while their heaviest oppression lasted, they were permitted to accumulate no kind of property, as all their gains went to their oppressors.

Our exceptionable *translation* of the original has given some countenance to the desperate cause of infidelity; its abettors have exultingly said: "Moses represents the *just* God as ordering the Israelites to *borrow* the goods of the Egyptians under the pretence of *returning* them, whereas he intended that they should march off with the booty." Let these men know that there was no *borrowing* in the case; and that if accounts were fairly balanced, *Egypt* would be found still in considerable arrears to *Israel*. Let it also be considered that the Egyptians had never *any right* to the services of the Hebrews. Egypt owed its policy, its opulence, and even its political existence, to the Israelites. What had *Joseph* for his important services? NOTHING! He had neither district, nor city, nor lordship in Egypt; *nor did he reserve any to his children.* All his services were *gratuitous;* and being animated with a better hope than any earthly possession could inspire, he desired that even his *bones* should be carried up out of Egypt. Jacob and his family, it is true, were permitted to sojourn in Goshen, but they were not provided for in that place; for they brought their *cattle*, their *goods*, *and all that they had into Egypt*, Gen. xlvi. 1, 6; so that they had nothing but the bare land to feed on; and had built *treasure cities* or *fortresses*, we know not how many; and two whole cities, *Pithom* and *Raamses*, besides; and for all these services *they had no compensation whatever*, but were

besides cruelly abused, and obliged to witness, as the sum of their calamities, the daily murder of their male infants. These particulars considered, will infidelity ever dare to produce this case again in support of its worthless pretensions?

Jewels of silver, &c.] The word כלי *keley* we have already seen signifies *vessels*, *instruments*, *weapons*, &c., and may be very well translated by our English term, *articles* or *goods*. The Israelites got both gold and silver, probably both in *coin* and in *plate* of different kinds; and such *raiment* as was necessary for the journey which they were about to undertake.

Ye shall spoil the Egyptians.] The verb נצל *natsal* signifies, not only to *spoil*, *snatch away*, but also to *get away*, to *escape*, to *deliver*, to *regain*, or *recover*. SPOIL signifies what is *taken* by *rapine* or *violence;* but this cannot be the meaning of the original word here, as the Israelites only *asked*, and the Egyptians without *fear*, *terror*, or *constraint*, freely gave. It is worthy of remark that the original word is used, 1 Sam. xxx. 22, to signify the *recovery of property that had been taken away by violence:* "Then answered all the wicked men, and men of Belial, of those that went with David, Because they went not with us we will not give them aught of the SPOIL (מהשלל *mehashSHALAL*) that we have RECOVERED, אשר הצלנו *asher HITSTSALNU*. In this sense we should understand the word here. The Israelites *recovered* a part of *their property*—their wages, of which they had been most unjustly deprived by the Egyptians.

IN this chapter we have much curious and important information; but what is most interesting is the *name* by which God was pleased to make himself known to Moses and to the Israelites, a name by which the Supreme Being was afterwards known among the wisest inhabitants of the earth. HE who IS and who WILL BE what he IS. This is a proper characteristic of the Divine Being, who is, properly speaking, the only BEING, because he is *independent* and *eternal;* whereas all other beings, in whatsoever forms they may appear, are derived, finite, changeable, and liable to destruction, decay, and even to *annihilation*. When God, therefore, announced himself to Moses by this name, he proclaimed his own *eternity* and *immateriality;* and the very name itself precludes the possibility of *idolatry*, because it was impossible for the mind, in considering it, to represent the Divine Being in any assignable shape; for who could represent BEING or *Existence* by any *limited form?* And who can have any idea of a form that is *unlimited?* Thus, then, we find that the first discovery which God made of himself was intended to show the people the *simplicity* and *spirituality* of his nature; that while they considered him as BEING, and the Cause of all BEING, they might be preserved from all *idolatry* for ever. The very name itself is a proof of a Divine revelation; for it is not possible that such an idea could have ever entered into the mind of man, unless it had been communicated from above. It could not have been produced by *reasoning*, for there were no *premises* on which it could be built, nor any *analogies* by which it could have been formed. We can as easily comprehend *eternity* as we can *being*, simply considered in and of itself, when nothing of assignable forms, colours, or qualities existed, besides its infinite and illimitable self.

To this Divine discovery the ancient Greeks owed the inscription which they placed above the door of the temple of *Apollo* at *Delphi:* the whole of the inscription consisted in the simple monosyllable EI, THOU ART, the second person of the Greek substantive verb *ειμι*, *I am*. On this inscription Plutarch, one of the most intelligent of all the Gentile philosophers, made an express treatise, *περι του ΕΙ εν Δελφοις*, having received the true interpretation in his travels in Egypt, whither he had gone for the express purpose of inquiring into their ancient learning, and where he had doubtless seen these words of God to Moses in the Greek version of the Septuagint, which had been current among the Egyptians (*for whose sake it was first made*) about four hundred years previously to the death of Plutarch. This philosopher observes that "this title is not only *proper*, but *peculiar to God*, because HE alone is *being;* for mortals have no participation of *true being*, because that which *begins* and *ends*, and is continually *changing*, is never *one* nor the *same*, nor in the *same state*. The deity on whose temple this word was inscribed was called *Apollo*, Απολλων, from *α*, *negative*, and *πολυς*, *many*, because God is ONE, his nature *simple*, his essence *uncompounded*." Hence he informs us the ancient mode of addressing God was, "ΕΙ ἝΝ, *Thou art One*, *ου γαρ πολλα το θειον εστιν*, for *many* cannot be attributed to the Divine nature: *και οὐ προτερον ουδεν εστιν, ουδ' ὑστερον, ουδε μελλον, ουδε παρωχημενον, ουδε πρεσβυτερον, ουδε νεωτερον*, in which there is neither *first* nor *last*, *future* nor *past*, *old* nor *young;* *αλλ' εἱς ων ενι τῳ νυν το αει πεπληρωκε*, but as being one, fills up in one NOW an eternal duration." And he concludes with observing that "this word corresponds to certain others on the same temple, viz., ΓΝΩΘΙ ΣΕΑΥΤΟΝ, *Know thyself;* as if, under the name EI, THOU ART, the Deity designed to excite men to venerate HIM as *eternally existing*, *ὡς οντα διαπαντος*, and to put them in mind of the frailty and mortality of their own nature."

What beautiful things have the ancient Greek philosophers stolen from the testimonies of God to enrich their own works, without any kind of acknowledgment! And, strange perversity of man! these are the very things which we so highly applaud in the *heathen copies*, while we neglect or pass them by in the *Divine originals!*

CHAPTER IV.

Moses continuing to express his fear that the Israelites would not credit his Divine mission, 1, *God, to strengthen his faith, and to assure him that his countrymen would believe him, changed his rod into a serpent, and the serpent into a rod,* 2–5; *made his hand* leprous, *and afterwards restored it,* 6, 7; *intimating that he had now endued him with power to work such miracles, and that the Israelites would believe,* 8; *and farther assures him that he should have power to turn the water into blood,* 9. *Moses excuses himself on the ground of his not being eloquent,* 10, *and God reproves him for his unbelief, and promises to give him supernatural assistance,* 11, 12. *Moses expressing his utter unwillingness to go on any account, God is angry, and then promises to give him his brother Aaron to be his spokesman,* 13–16, *and appoints his* rod *to be the instrument of working miracles,* 17. *Moses returns to his relative* Jethro, *and requests liberty to visit his brethren in Egypt, and is permitted,* 18. *God appears to him in Midian, and assures him that the Egyptians who sought his life were dead,* 19. *Moses, with his wife and children, set out on their journey to Egypt,* 20. *God instructs him what he shall say to Pharaoh,* 21–23. *He is in danger of losing his life, because he had not circumcised his son,* 24. *Zipporah immediately circumcising the child, Moses escapes unhurt,* 25, 26. *Aaron is commanded to go and meet his brother Moses; he goes and meets him at Horeb,* 27. *Moses informs him of the commission he had received from God,* 28. *They both go to their brethren, deliver their message, and work miracles,* 29, 30. *The people believe and adore God,* 31.

A. M. 2513. B. C. 1491.

AND Moses answered and said,
But, behold, they will not believe me, nor hearken unto my voice: for
they will say, The LORD hath not appeared
unto thee.
2 And the LORD said unto him, What *is*
that in thine hand? And he said, [a] A rod.
3 And he said, Cast it on the ground. And
he cast it on the ground, and it became a
serpent; and Moses fled from before it.
4 And the LORD said unto Moses, Put forth
thine hand, and take it by the tail. And he
put forth his hand, and caught
it, and it became a rod in his
hand:
5 That they may [b] believe that [c] the LORD
God of their fathers, the God of Abraham, the
God of Isaac, and the God of Jacob, hath
appeared unto thee.
6 And the Lord said furthermore unto him,
Put now thine hand into thy bosom. And
he put his hand into his bosom: and when
he took it out, behold, his hand *was* leprous
[d] as snow.

A. M. 2513. B. C. 1491.

[a] Ver. 17, 20.—[b] Chap. xix. 9.—[c] Chap. iii. 15.

[d] Num. xii. 10; 2 Kings v. 27.

NOTES ON CHAP. IV.

Verse 1. *They will not believe me*] As if he had said, Unless I be enabled to work miracles, and give them proofs by extraordinary *works* as well as by *words*, they will not believe that thou hast sent me.

Verse 2. *A rod.*] מטה *matteh*, a *staff*, probably his shepherd's crook; see Lev. xxvii. 32. As it was made the instrument of working many miracles, it was afterwards called the *rod of God;* see ver. 20.

Verse 3. *A serpent*] Of what sort we know not, as the word נחש *nachash* is a general name for serpents, and also means several other things, see Gen. iii. 1: but it was either of a kind that he had not seen before, or one that he knew to be dangerous; for it is said, *he fled from before it* Some suppose the staff was changed into a *crocodile;* see on chap. vii. 7.

Verse 4. *He put forth his hand, and caught it*] Considering the light in which Moses had viewed this serpent, it required considerable faith to induce him thus implicitly to obey the command of God; but he obeyed, and the noxious serpent became instantly the miraculous rod in his hand! Implicit faith and obedience conquer all difficulties; and he who believes in God, and obeys him in all things, has really nothing to fear.

Verse 5. *That they may believe*] This is an example of what is called an imperfect or unfinished speech, several of which occur in the sacred writings. It may be thus supplied: *Do this before them*, that they may believe that the Lord—hath appeared unto thee.

Verse 6. *His hand* was *leprous as snow.*] That is, the leprosy spread itself over the whole body in thin *white scales;* and from this appearance it has its Greek name λεπρα, from λεπις, *a scale.* Dr. Mead says, "I have seen a remarkable case of this in a countryman, whose whole body was so miserably seized with it, that his skin *was shining as if covered with snow;* and as the furfuraceous scales were daily rubbed off, the flesh appeared *quick* or *raw* underneath." The leprosy, at least among the Jews, was a most inveterate and contagious disorder, and deemed by them incurable. Among the heathens it was considered as inflicted by their gods, and it was supposed that they alone could remove it. It is certain that a similar belief prevailed among the Israelites; hence, when the king of Syria sent his general, Naaman, to the king of Israel to cure him of his leprosy, he rent his clothes, saying, *Am I God, to kill and to make alive, that this man doth send unto me to recover a man of his leprosy?* 2 Kings v. 7. This appears, therefore, to be the reason why God chose this sign, as the instantaneous infliction and removal of this disease were demonstrations which all would allow of

A. M. 2513.
B. C. 1491.

7 And he said, Put thine hand into thy bosom again. And he put his hand into his bosom again; and plucked it out of his bosom, and, behold, [e] it was turned again as his *other* flesh.

8 And it shall come to pass, if they will not believe thee, neither hearken to the voice of the first sign, that they will believe the voice of the latter sign.

9 And it shall come to pass, if they will not believe also these two signs, neither hearken unto thy voice, that thou shalt take of the water of the river, and pour *it* upon the dry *land:* and [f] the water which thou takest out of the river [g] shall become blood upon the dry *land.*

A. M. 2513.
B. C. 1491.

10 And Moses said unto the LORD, O my Lord, I *am* not [h] eloquent, neither [i] heretofore nor since thou hast spoken unto thy servant; but [k] I *am* slow of speech, and of a slow tongue.

11 And the LORD said unto him, [l] Who hath made man's mouth? or who maketh the dumb, or deaf, or the seeing, or the blind? have not I the LORD?

12 Now therefore go, and I will be [m] with thy mouth, and teach thee what thou shalt say.

13 And he said, O my Lord, [n] send, I pray thee, by the hand *of him whom* thou [o] wilt send.

[e] Deut. xxxii. 39; Num. xii. 13, 14; 2 Kings v. 14; Matt. viii. 3. —[f] Chap. vii. 19.—[g] Heb. *shall be and shall be.*—[h] Heb. *a man of words.*—[i] Heb. *since yesterday, nor since the third day.*

[k] Chap. vi. 12; Jer. i. 6.—[l] Psa. xciv. 9.—[m] Isa. l. 4; Jer. i. 9; Matt. x. 19; Mark xiii. 11; Luke xii. 11, 12; xxi. 14, 15 —[n] See Jonah i. 3.—[o] Or, *shouldest.*

the sovereign power of God. We need, therefore, seek for no other reasons for this miracle: the *sole* reason is sufficiently obvious.

Verse 8. *If they will not believe—the voice of the first sign, &c.*] Probably intimating that some would be more difficult to be persuaded than others: some would yield to the evidence of the *first* miracle; others would hesitate till they had seen the *second;* and others would not believe till they had seen the water of the Nile turned into blood, when poured upon the dry land; ver. 9.

Verse 10. *I* am *not eloquent*] לא איש דברים *lo ish debarim, I am not a man of words;* a periphrasis common in the Scriptures. So Job xi. 2, איש שפתים *ish sephathayim, a man of lips,* signifies one that is *talkative.* Psa. cxl. 12, איש לשון *ish lashon,* a *man of tongue,* signifies a *prattler.* But how could it be said that Moses was *not eloquent,* when St. Stephen asserts, Acts vii. 22, that he was *mighty in words* as well as in *deeds?* There are *three* ways of solving this difficulty: 1. Moses might have had some natural infirmity, of a late standing, which at that time rendered it impossible for him to speak readily, and which he afterwards overcame; so that though he was not *then* a *man of words,* yet he might afterwards have been *mighty in words* as well as *deeds.* 2. It is possible he was not intimately acquainted with the Hebrew tongue, so as to speak *clearly* and *distinctly* in it. The first *forty* years of his life he had spent in Egypt, chiefly at *court;* and though it is very probable there was an affinity between the two languages, yet they certainly were not the same. The last *forty* he had spent in Midian, and it is not likely that the pure Hebrew tongue prevailed there, though it is probable that a dialect of it was there spoken. On these accounts Moses might find it difficult to express himself with that readiness and persuasive flow of language, which he might deem essentially necessary on such a momentous occasion; as he would frequently be obliged to consult his memory for proper expressions, which would necessarily produce frequent hesitation, and general slowness of utterance, which he might think would ill suit an ambassador of God. 3. Though Moses was slow of speech, yet when acting as the messenger of God *his word was with power,* for at his command the plagues came and the plagues were stayed; thus was he *mighty in words* as well as in *deeds:* and this is probably the meaning of St. Stephen.

By the expression, *neither heretofore, nor since thou hast spoken unto thy servant,* he might possibly mean, that the natural inaptitude to speak readily, which he *had* felt, he *continued* to feel, even since God had begun to discover himself; for though he had wrought several miracles for him, yet he had not healed this infirmity. See on chap. vi. 12.

Verse 11. *Who hath made man's mouth? &c.*] Cannot he who formed the mouth, the whole organs of speech, and hath given the gift of speech also, cannot he give utterance? God can take away those gifts and restore them again. Do not provoke him: he who created the *eye,* the *ear,* and the *mouth,* hath also made the *blind,* the *deaf,* and the *dumb.*

Verse 12. *I will be with thy mouth*] The Chaldee translates, *My* WORD, *meimeri, shall be with thy mouth.* And Jonathan ben Uzziel paraphrases, *I and my* WORD *will be with the speech of thy mouth.* See on Gen. xv. 1, and Lev. xxv. 10.

Verse 13. *Send—by the hand* of him whom *thou wilt send.*] Many commentators, both ancient and modern, have thought that Moses prays here for the *immediate* mission of the *Messiah;* as if he had said: "Lord, thou hast purposed to send this glorious person at some time or other, I beseech thee send him *now,* for who can be sufficient to deliver and rule this people but himself alone?" The Hebrew שלח נא ביד תשלח *shelach na beyad tishlach* literally translated is, Send now (or, *I beseech thee*) by the hand thou wilt send; which seems to intimate, Send a person more fit for the work than I am. So the Septuagint: Προχειρισαι δυναμενον αλλον, ὀν αποστελεις· *Elect another powerful person, whom thou wilt send.* It is right to find out the Messiah wherever he is mentioned in the Old Testament; but to press scriptures into this service which have not an obvious tendency that way, is both impro-

A. M. 2513.
B. C. 1491.

14 And the anger of the LORD
was kindled against Moses, and he
said, *Is* not Aaron the Levite thy brother? I
know that he can speak well. And also, behold, [p] he cometh forth to meet thee; and
when he seeth thee, he will be glad in his
heart.
15 And [q] thou shalt speak unto him, and
[r] put words in his mouth: and I will be with
thy mouth, and with his mouth,
and [s] will teach you what ye
shall do.
16 And he shall be thy spokesman unto
the people: and he shall be, *even* he shall be
to thee instead of a mouth, and [t] thou shalt
be to him instead of God.
17 And thou shalt take [u] this rod in thine
hand, wherewith thou shalt do signs.

---

[p] Ver. 27; 1 Sam. x. 2, 3, 5.——[q] Chapter vii. 1, 2.——[r] Num. xxii. 38; xxiii. 5, 12, 16; Deut. xviii. 18; Isa. li. 16; Jer. i. 9.——[s] Deuteronomy v. 31.——[t] Chap. vii. 1; xviii. 19.——[u] Ver. 2.

---

per and dangerous. I am firmly of opinion that Moses had no reference to the Messiah when he spoke these words.

Verse 14. *And the anger of the Lord was kindled against Moses*] Surely this would not have been the case had he only in *modesty*, and from a deep sense of his own unfitness, desired that the *Messiah* should be preferred before him. But the whole connection shows that this interpretation is unfounded.

Is *not Aaron the Levite thy brother?*] Houbigant endeavours to prove from this that Moses, in ver. 13, did pray for the immediate mission of the Messiah, and that God gives him here a reason why this could not be, because the *Levitical* priesthood was to precede the priesthood of our Lord. Is *not Aaron the Levite*, &c. Must not the ministry of Aaron be first established, before the other can take place? Why then ask for that which is contrary to the Divine counsel? From the opinion of so great a critic as Houbigant no man would wish to dissent, except through necessity: however, I must say that it does appear to me that his view of these verses is fanciful, and the arguments by which he supports it are insufficient to establish his point.

I know that he can speak well.] ידעתי כי דבר ידבר הוא *yadati ki dabber yedabber hu, I know that in speaking he will speak.* That is, he is *apt to talk*, and has a ready utterance.

He cometh forth to meet thee] He shall meet thee at my mount, (ver. 27,) shall rejoice in thy mission, and most heartily co-operate with thee in all things. A necessary assurance, to prevent Moses from suspecting that Aaron, who was his elder brother, would *envy* his superior call and office.

Verse 15. *I will be with thy mouth, and with his mouth*] Ye shall be both, in all things which I appoint you to do in this business, under the continual *inspiration* of the Most High.

Verse 16. *He shall be thy spokesman*] Literally, *He shall speak for thee* (or in thy stead) *to the people.*

He shall be to thee instead of a mouth] He shall convey every message to the people; *and thou shalt be to him instead of God*—thou shalt deliver to him what I communicate to thee.

Verse 17. *Thou shalt take this rod*] From the story of Moses's rod the heathens have invented the fables of the *thyrsus* of Bacchus, and the *caduceus* of Mercury. Cicero reckons five *Bacchuses*, one of which, according to Orpheus, was born of the river *Nile*; but, according to the common opinion, he was born on the banks of that river. Bacchus is expressly said to have been *exposed on the river Nile*, hence he is called Nilus, both by *Diodorus* and *Macrobius*; and in the hymns of Orpheus he is named *Myses*, because he was *drawn out of the water*. He is represented by the poets as being *very beautiful*, and an *illustrious warrior*; they report him to have overrun *all Arabia* with a *numerous army both of men and women*. He is said also to have been an eminent *lawgiver*, and to have written his laws on *two tables*. He always carried in his hand the *thyrsus*, a *rod* wreathed with *serpents*, and by which he is reported to have wrought *many miracles*. Any person acquainted with the birth and exploits of the poetic Bacchus will at once perceive them to be all borrowed from the life and acts of Moses, as recorded in the Pentateuch; and it would be losing time to show the parallel, by quoting passages from the book of Exodus.

The *caduceus* or *rod* of Mercury is well known in poetic fables. It is another copy of the rod of Moses. *He* also is reported to have wrought a multitude of *miracles by this rod*; and particularly he is said to *kill* and *make alive*, to send souls to the invisible world and bring them back from thence. *Homer* represents Mercury taking his rod to work miracles precisely in the same way as God commands Moses to take his.

'Ερμης δε ψυχας Κυλληνιος εξεκαλειτο
Ανδρων μνηστηρων· εχε δε 'ΡΑΒΔΟΝ *μετα χερσιν*
Καλην, χρυσειην, τη τ' ανδρων ομματα θελγει,
'Ων εθελει, τους δ' αυτε και ὑπνωοντας εγειρει.

Odyss., lib. xxiv., ver. 1.

Cyllenian Hermes now call'd forth the souls
Of all the suitors; with his golden WAND
Of *power, to seal in balmy sleep whose eyes*
Soe'er he will, and open them again. COWPER.

Virgil copies Homer, but carries the parallel farther, tradition having probably furnished him with more particulars; but in both we may see a disguised copy of the sacred history, from which indeed the Greek and Roman poets borrowed most of their beauties.

Tum VIRGAM CAPIT: hac animas ille evocat Orco
Pallentes, alias sub tristia Tartara mittit;
Dat somnos, adimitque, et lumina morte resignat.
ILLA *fretus agit ventos*, et turbida tranat.

Æneid., lib. iv., ver. 242.

A. M. 2513. B. C. cir. 1490. 18 And Moses went and returned
to [v] Jethro his father-in-law, and
said unto him, Let me go, I pray thee, and
return unto my brethren which *are* in Egypt,
and see whether they be yet alive. And Jethro
said to Moses, Go in peace.
19 And the LORD said unto Moses in Midian,
Go, return into Egypt: for [w] all the men are
dead which sought thy life.
20 And Moses took his wife and A. M. 2513. B. C. 1491.
his sons, and set them upon an ass,
and he returned to the land of Egypt: and
Moses took [x] the rod of God in his hand.
21 And the LORD said unto Moses, When
thou goest to return into Egypt, see that thou
do all those [y] wonders before Pharaoh which
I have put in thine hand: but [z] I will harden
his heart, that he shall not let the people go.

[v] Heb. *Jether.*——[w] Chap. ii. 15, 23; Matt. ii. 20.——[x] Chapter xvii. 9; Num. xx. 8, 9.——[y] Chap. iii. 20.

[z] Chap. vii. 3, 13; ix. 12, 35; x. 1; xiv. 8; Deut. ii. 30; Josh. xi. 20; Isa. lxiii. 17; John xii. 40; Rom. ix. 18.

But first he grasps within his awful hand
The *mark of sovereign power*, the *magic wand;*
With this he draws the ghosts from hollow graves,
With this he *drives them down the Stygian waves;*
With this he *seals in sleep* the wakeful sight,
And eyes, though *closed in death, restores to light.*
Thus arm'd, the god begins his airy race,
And *drives the racking clouds* along the liquid space.
DRYDEN.

Many other resemblances between the *rod* of the *poets* and that of Moses, the learned reader will readily recollect. These specimens may be deemed sufficient.

Verse 18. *Let me go, I pray thee, and return unto my brethren*] Moses, having received his commission from God, and directions how to execute it, returned to his father-in-law, and asked permission to visit his family and brethren in Egypt, without giving him any intimation of the great errand on which he was going. His keeping this secret has been attributed to his *singular modesty:* but however true it might be that Moses was a truly humble and modest man, yet his *prudence* alone was sufficient to have induced him to observe silence on this subject; for, if once imparted to the family of his father-in-law, the news might have reached Egypt before he could get thither, and a general alarm among the Egyptians would in all probability have been the consequence; as *fame* would not fail to represent Moses as coming to stir up sedition and rebellion, and the whole nation would have been armed against them. It was therefore essentially necessary that the business should be kept secret.

In the Septuagint and Coptic the following addition is made to this verse: *Μετα δε τας ἡμερας τας πολλας εκεινας ετελευτησεν ὁ βασιλευς Αιγυπτου· After these many days, the king of Egypt died.* This was probably an ancient gloss or side note, which in process of time crept into the text, as it appeared to throw light on the following verse.

Verse 19. *In Midian*] This was a new revelation, and appears to have taken place *after* Moses returned to his father-in-law previous to his departure for Egypt.

Verse 20. *His wife and his sons*] Both Gershom and Eliezer, though the birth of the latter has not yet been mentioned in the Hebrew text. See the note on chap. ii. 22.

Set them upon an ass] The Septuagint reads the word in the plural, *επι τα ὑποζυγια, upon asses*, as it certainly required more than one to carry Zipporah, Gershom, and Eliezer.

The rod of God] The sign of sovereign power, by which he was to perform all his miracles; once the badge of his *shepherd's office*, and now that by which he is to *feed, rule*, and *protect* his *people Israel.*

Verse 21. *But I will harden his heart*] The case of Pharaoh has given rise to many fierce controversies, and to several strange and conflicting opinions. Would men but look at the whole account without the medium of their respective creeds, they would find little difficulty to apprehend the truth. If we take up the subject in a *theological* point of view, all sober Christians will allow the truth of this proposition of St. Augustine, when the subject in question is a person who has hardened his own heart by frequently resisting the grace and Spirit of God: *Non obdurat Deus impertiendo malitiam, sed non impertiendo misericordiam;* Epist. 194, ad Sixtum, "God does not harden men by infusing malice into them, but by not imparting mercy to them." And this other will be as readily credited: *Non operatur Deus in homine ipsam duritiam cordis; sed indurare eum dicitur quem mollire noluerit, sic etiam excæcare quem illuminare noluerit, et repellere eum quem noluerit vocare.* "God does not work this hardness of heart in man; but he may be said to harden him whom he refuses to soften, to blind him whom he refuses to enlighten, and to repel him whom he refuses to call." It is but just and right that he should withhold those graces which he had repeatedly offered, and which the sinner had despised and rejected. Thus much for the general principle. The verb חזק *chazak*, which we translate *harden*, literally signifies to *strengthen, confirm, make bold* or *courageous;* and is often used in the sacred writings to excite *to duty, perseverance*, &c., and is placed by the Jews at the end of most books in the Bible as an exhortation to the reader to *take courage*, and *proceed* with his *reading* and with the *obedience* it requires. It constitutes an essential part of the exhortation of God to Joshua, chap. i. 7: *Only be thou* STRONG, רק חזק *rak chazak*. And of Joshua's dying exhortation to the people, chap. xxiii. 6: *Be ye therefore* VERY COURAGEOUS, וחזקתם *vachazaktem, to keep and to do all that is written in the book of the law.* Now it would be very strange in these places to translate the word *harden: Only be thou hard, Be ye therefore very hard;* and yet if we use the word *hardy*, it would suit the sense and context perfectly

A. M. 2513.
B. C. 1491.

22 And thou shalt say unto Pharaoh, Thus saith the LORD, [a] Israel
is my son, [b] *even* my first-born:
23 And I say unto thee, Let my son go,
that he may serve me: and if thou refuse to
let him go, behold, [c] I will slay thy son, *even*
thy first-born.

24 And it came to pass by the
way in the inn, that the LORD [d] met
him, and sought to [e] kill him.
25 Then Zipporah took [f] a sharp [g] stone,
and cut off the foreskin of her son, and [h] cast
it at his feet, and said, Surely a bloody husband *art* thou to me.

A. M. 2513
B. C. 1491

[a] Hos. xi. 1; Rom. ix. 4; 2 Cor. vi. 18.——[b] Jer. xxxi. 9; James i. 18.——[c] Chap. xi. 5; xii. 29.

[d] Num. xxii. 22.——[e] Gen. xvii. 14.——[f] Josh. v. 2, 3.——[g] Or, *knife*.——[h] Heb. *made it touch*.

well: *Only be thou* HARDY; *Be ye therefore very* HARDY. Now suppose we apply the word in this way to Pharaoh, the sense would be good, and the justice of God equally conspicuous. I will make his heart hardy, bold, daring, presumptuous; for the same principle acting *against* God's order is *presumption*, which when acting *according* to it is *undaunted courage*. It is true that the verb קשה *kashah* is used, chap. vii. 3, which signifies to render stiff, tough, or stubborn, but it amounts to nearly the same meaning with the above.

All those who have read the Scriptures with care and attention, know well that God is frequently represented in them as *doing* what he only *permits* to be done. So because a man has grieved his Spirit and resisted his grace he withdraws that Spirit and grace from him, and thus he becomes bold and presumptuous in sin. Pharaoh made his own heart stubborn against God, chap. ix. 34; and God gave him up to judicial blindness, so that he rushed on stubbornly to his own destruction. From the whole of Pharaoh's conduct we learn that he was *bold*, *haughty*, and *cruel*; and God chose to *permit* these dispositions to have their full sway in his heart without check or restraint from Divine influence: the consequence was what God intended, he did not *immediately* comply with the requisition to let the people go; and this was done that God might have the fuller opportunity of manifesting his power by multiplying signs and miracles, and thus impress the hearts both of the Egyptians and Israelites with a due sense of his omnipotence and justice. The whole procedure was graciously calculated to do endless good to both nations. The *Israelites* must be satisfied that they had the true God for their protector; and thus their *faith* was strengthened. The *Egyptians* must see that *their gods* could do nothing against the God of *Israel*; and thus their dependence on *them* was necessarily shaken. These great ends could not have been answered had Pharaoh at once consented to let the people go. This consideration alone unravels the mystery, and explains every thing. Let it be observed that there is nothing spoken here of the *eternal state* of the Egyptian king; nor does any thing in the whole of the subsequent account authorize us to believe that God *hardened his heart against the influences of his own grace*, that he might occasion him so to sin that his justice might consign him to hell. This would be such an act of flagrant injustice as we could scarcely attribute to the worst of men. He who leads another into an offence that he may have a fairer pretence to punish him for it, or brings him into such circumstances that he cannot avoid committing a capital crime, and then hangs him for it, is surely the most execrable of mortals. What then should we make of the God of justice and mercy should we attribute to him a decree, the date of which is lost in eternity, by which he has determined to cut off from the possibility of salvation millions of millions of unborn souls, and leave them under a necessity of sinning, by actually hardening their hearts against the influences of his own grace and Spirit, that he may, on the pretext of *justice*, consign them to endless perdition? Whatever may be pretended in behalf of such *unqualified* opinions, it must be evident to all who are not deeply prejudiced, that neither the *justice* nor the *sovereignty* of God can be magnified by them. See farther on chap. ix. 16.

Verse 22. *Israel* is *my son*, even *my first-born*] That is, The Hebrew people are unutterably dear to me.

Verse 23. *Let my son go, that he may serve me*] Which they could not do in Goshen, consistently with the policy and religious worship of the Egyptians; because the most essential part of an Israelite's worship consisted in *sacrifice*, and the animals which they offered to God were sacred among the Egyptians. Moses gives Pharaoh this reason chap. viii. 26.

I will slay thy son, even *thy first-born*.] Which, on Pharaoh's utter refusal to let the people go, was accordingly done; see chap. xii. 29.

Verse 24. *By the way in the inn*] See the note on Gen. xlii 27. The account in this and the following verse is very obscure. Some suppose that the 23d verse is not a part of the message to Pharaoh, but was spoken by the Lord to Moses; and that the whole may be thus paraphrased: "*And I have said unto thee*, (Moses,) *Send forth* (שלח *shallach*) *my son*, (Gershom, by circumcising him,) *that he may serve me*, (which he cannot do till entered into the covenant by circumcision,) but thou hast refused to send him forth; *behold*, (therefore,) *I will slay thy son, thy first-born. And it came to pass by the way in the inn*, (when he was on his journey to Egypt,) *that Jehovah met him, and sought* (threatened) *to kill him* (Gershom.) *Then Zipporah took a sharp stone, and cut away the foreskin of her son, and caused it to touch his feet*, (Jehovah's, who probably appeared in a bodily shape; the Septuagint call him the *Angel of the Lord*,) *and said unto him, A spouse by blood* art *thou unto me. Then he* (Jehovah) *ceased from him* (Gershom.) *Then she said, A spouse by blood* art *thou unto me, because of this circumcision*." That is, I who am an *alien* have entered as fully into covenant with thee by *doing* this act, as my son has *on whom* this act has been *performed*.
The meaning of the whole passage seems to be this:—

A. M. 2513.
B. C. 1491.
26 So he let him go: then she
said, A bloody husband *thou art*,
because of the circumcision.
27 And the LORD said to Aaron, Go into the
wilderness [i] to meet Moses. And he went, and
met him in [k] the mount of God, and kissed him.
28 And Moses [l] told Aaron all the words
of the LORD who had sent him, and all the
[m] signs which he had commanded him.
29 And Moses and Aaron [n] went and ga
thered together all the elders of
the children of Israel:
30 [o] And Aaron spake all the words which
the LORD had spoken unto Moses, and did
the signs in the sight of the people.
31 And the people [p] believed: and when
they heard that the LORD had [q] visited the
children of Israel, and that he [r] had looked upon
their affliction, then [s] they bowed their heads
and worshipped.

A. M. 2513.
B. C. 1491.

Ver. 14.——[k] Chap. iii. 1.——[l] Verses 15, 16.——[m] Verses 8, 9. [n] Chap. iii. 16.——[o] Ver. 16.——[p] Chap. iii. 18; ver. 8, 9. [q] Chapter iii. 16.——[r] Chap. ii. 25; iii. 7.——[s] Gen. xxiv. 26; chap. xii. 27; 1 Chron. xxix. 20.

The son of Moses, *Gershom* or *Eliezer*, (for it does not appear which,) had not been circumcised, though it would seem that God had ordered the father to do it; but as he had neglected this, therefore Jehovah was about to have slain the child, because not in covenant with him by circumcision, and thus he intended to have punished the disobedience of the father by the natural death of his son. Zipporah, getting acquainted with the nature of the case and the danger to which her first-born was exposed, took a sharp stone and cut off the foreskin of her son. By this act the displeasure of the Lord was turned aside, and Zipporah considered herself as now allied to God because of this circumcision. According to the law, (Gen. xvii. 14,) *the uncircumcised child was to be cut off from his people*, so that there should be no inheritance for that branch of the family in Israel. Moses therefore, for neglecting to circumcise the child, exposed him to this *cutting off*, and it was but barely prevented by the prompt obedience of Zipporah. As *circumcision* was the *seal* of that justification by faith which comes through Christ, Moses by neglecting it gave a very bad example, and God was about to proceed against him with that severity which the law required.

The sharp stone mentioned ver. 25 was probably a knife made of *flint*, for such were anciently used, even where knives of metal might be had, for every kind of operation about the human body, such as embowelling for the purpose of embalming, circumcision, &c. Ancient authors are full of proofs of these facts. See the note on Gen. l. 2.

It is probable that Zipporah, being alarmed by this circumstance, and fearing worse evils, took the resolution to return to her father's house with her two sons. See chap. xviii. 1, &c.

Verse 27. *The Lord said to Aaron*] See ver. 14. By some secret but powerful movement on Aaron's mind, or by some voice or angelic ministry, he was now directed to go and meet his brother Moses; and so correctly was the information given to both, that they arrived at the *same time* on the sacred mountain.

Verse 30. *Aaron spake all the words*] It is likely that Aaron was better acquainted with the Hebrew tongue than his brother, and on this account he became the spokesman. See on ver. 8.

Did the signs] Turned the *rod into a serpent*, made the *hand leprous*, and *changed* the *water into blood*. See on ver. 8 and 9.

Verse 31. *The people believed*] They credited the account given of the Divine appointment of Moses and Aaron to be their deliverers out of their bondage, the miracles wrought on the occasion confirming the testimony delivered by Aaron.

They bowed their heads and worshipped.] See a similar act mentioned, and in the same words, Gen. xxiv. 26. The bowing the head, &c., here, may probably refer to the eastern custom of bowing the head down to the knees, then kneeling down and touching the earth with the forehead. This was a very painful posture and the most humble in which the body could possibly be placed. Those who pretend to worship God, either by prayer or thanksgiving, and keep themselves during the performance of those solemn acts in a state of perfect ease, either *carelessly standing* or *stupidly sitting*, surely cannot have a due sense of the majesty of God, and their own sinfulness and unworthiness. Let the *feelings* of the body put the soul in remembrance of its sin against God. Let a man put himself in such a position (*kneeling* for instance) as it is generally acknowledged a criminal should assume, when coming to his sovereign and judge to bewail his sins, and solicit forgiveness.

The Jewish custom, as we learn from Rabbi Maymon, was to bend the body so that every joint of the backbone became incurvated, and the head was bent towards the knees, so that the body resembled a *bow;* and *prostration* implied laying the body flat upon the earth, the arms and legs extended to the uttermost, the mouth and forehead touching the ground. In Matt. viii. 2 the leper is said to *worship* our Lord, προσεκυνει αυτῳ· but in Luke v. 12 he is said to have *fallen on his face*, πεσων επι προσωπον. These two accounts show that he first kneeled down, probably putting his face down to his knees, and touching the earth with his forehead; and then prostrated himself, his legs and arms being both extended. See on Gen. xvii. 3.

THE *backwardness* of Moses to receive and execute the commission to deliver the children of Israel, has something very instructive in it. He felt the importance of the charge, his own insufficiency, and the awful responsibility under which he should be laid if he received it. Who then can blame him for *hesitating?* If he miscarried (and how difficult in such a case not to miscarry!) he must account to a jealous

God, whose justice required him to punish every delinquency. What should ministers of the Gospel feel on such subjects? Is not their charge more important and more awful than that of Moses? How few consider this! It is *respectable*, it is *honourable*, to be in the Gospel ministry, but who is sufficient to *guide* and *feed* the flock of God? If through the pastor's *unfitness* or *neglect* any soul should go *astray*, or perish through want of proper spiritual nourishment, or through not getting his portion in *due season*, in what a dreadful state is the pastor! That soul, says God, shall die in his iniquities, but his blood will I require at the watchman's hands! Were these things duly considered by those who are candidates for the Gospel ministry, who could be found to undertake it? We should then indeed have the utmost occasion to *pray the Lord of the harvest*, εκβαλλειν, *to* THRUST OUT *labourers into the harvest*, as no one, duly considering those things would *go*, unless *thrust out* by God himself. O ye ministers of the sanctuary! tremble for your own souls, and the souls of those committed to your care, and go not into this work unless God go with you. Without his presence, unction, and approbation, ye can do nothing.

CHAPTER V.

Moses and Aaron open their commission to Pharaoh, 1. *He insultingly asks who* Jehovah *is, in whose name they require him to dismiss the people*, 2. *They explain*, 3. *He charges them with making the people disaffected*, 4, 5; *and commands the task-masters to increase their work, and lessen their means of performing it*, 6–9. *The task-masters do as commanded, and refuse to give the people* straw *to assist them in making brick, and yet require the fulfilment of their daily tasks as formerly, when furnished with all the necessary means*, 10–13. *The Israelites failing to produce the ordinary quantity of brick, their own officers, set over them by the task-masters, are cruelly insulted and beaten*, 14. *The officers complain to Pharaoh*, 15, 16; *but find no redress*, 17, 18. *The officers, finding their case desperate, bitterly reproach Moses and Aaron for bringing them into their present circumstances*, 19–21. *Moses retires, and lays the matter before the Lord, and pleads with him*, 22, 23.

A. M. 2513.
B. C. 1491.

AND afterward Moses and Aaron went in, and told Pharaoh, Thus saith the LORD God of Israel, Let my people go, that they may hold [a] a feast unto me in the wilderness.
2 And Pharaoh said, [b] Who *is* the LORD, that I should obey his voice to let Israel go? I know not the LORD, [c] neither will I let Israel go.
3 And they said, [d] The God of the Hebrews hath met with us: let us go, we pray thee, three days' journey into the desert, and sacrifice unto the LORD our God; lest he fall upon us with pestilence, or with the sword.

[a] Chap. x. 9.—[b] 2 Kings xviii. 35; Job xxi. 15.—[c] Chap. iii. 19.—[d] Chap. iii. 18.

NOTES ON CHAP. V.

Verse 1. *And afterward Moses and Aaron went*] This chapter is properly a continuation of the preceding, as the succeeding is a continuation of this; and to preserve the connection of the facts they should be read together.

How *simply*, and yet with what *authority*, does Moses deliver his message to the Egyptian king! *Thus saith* JEHOVAH, GOD *of* ISRAEL, *Let my people go.* It is well in this, as in almost every other case where יהוה *Jehovah* occurs, to preserve the original word: our using the word LORD is not sufficiently expressive, and often leaves the sense indistinct.

Verse 2. *Who is the Lord*] Who is *Jehovah*, that I should obey his voice? What claims has *he* on *me?* I am under no obligation to *him.* Pharaoh spoke here under the common persuasion that every *place* and *people* had a tutelary deity, and he supposed that this Jehovah might be the tutelary deity of the Israelites, to whom he, as an Egyptian, could be under no kind of obligation. It is not judicious to bring this question as a proof that Pharaoh was an *atheist:* of this the text affords no evidence.

Verse 3. *Three days' journey*] The distance from Goshen to Sinai; see chap. iii. 18.

And sacrifice unto the Lord] Great stress is laid on this circumstance. God required *sacrifice;* no religious acts which they performed could be acceptable to him without this. He had now showed them that it was their indispensable duty thus to worship him, and that if they did not they might expect him to send the *pestilence*—some plague or death proceeding immediately from himself, or the *sword*—extermination by the hands of an enemy. The original word דבר *deber*, from דבר *dabar*, to *drive off, draw under, &c.*, which we translate *pestilence* from the Latin *pestis, the plague*, signifies any kind of disease by which an extraordinary mortality is occasioned, and which appears from the circumstances of the case to come immediately from God. The Israelites could not sacrifice in the land of Egypt, because the animals they were to offer to God were held sacred by the Egyptians; and they could not omit this duty, because it was essential to religion even before the giving of the law. Thus we find that Divine justice required the life of the animal for the life of the transgressor, and the people were conscious, if this were not done, that God would consume them with the pestilence or the sword. From the foundation of the world the true religion required *sacrifice. Before, under*, and *after* the law, this was

A. M. 2513.
B. C. 1491.

4 And the king of Egypt said unto them, Wherefore do ye, Moses and Aaron, let the people from their works? get you unto your [e] burdens.

5 And Pharaoh said, Behold, the people of the land now *are* [f] many, and ye make them rest from their burdens.

6 And Pharaoh commanded the same day the [g] task-masters of the people, and their officers, saying,

7 Ye shall no more give the people straw to make brick, as heretofore: let them go and gather straw for themselves.

8 And the tale of the bricks, which they did make heretofore, ye shall lay upon them; ye shall not diminish *aught* thereof: for they *be* idle; therefore they cry, saying, Let us go *and* sacrifice to our God.

9 [h] Let there more work be laid upon the men, that they may labour therein; and let them not regard vain words.

10 And the task-masters of the people went out, and their officers, and they spake to the people, saying, Thus saith Pharaoh, I will not give you straw.

11 Go ye, get you straw where ye can find it: yet not aught of your work shall be diminished.

[e] Chap. i. 11.——[f] Chap. i. 7, 9.——[g] Chap. i. 11.

[h] Heb. *Let the work be heavy upon the men.*

deemed essential to salvation. Under the Christian dispensation Jesus is the lamb of God that taketh away the sin of the world; and being still the Lamb newly slain before the throne, no man cometh unto the Father but by him.

"In this first application to Pharaoh, we observe," says Dr. Dodd, "that proper respectful submission which is due from subjects to their sovereign. They represent to him the danger they should be in by disobeying their God, but do not so much as hint at any punishment that would follow to Pharaoh."

Verse 4. *Wherefore do ye, Moses and Aaron*] He hints that the Hebrews are in a state of *revolt*, and charges Moses and Aaron as being ringleaders of the sedition. This unprincipled charge has been, in nearly similar circumstances, often repeated since. Men who have laboured to bring the mass of the common people from ignorance, irreligion, and general profligacy of manners, to an acquaintance with themselves and God, and to a proper knowledge of their duty to him and to each other, have been often branded as being disaffected to the state, and as movers of sedition among the people! See on ver. 17.

Let the people] תפריעו *taphriu*, from פרע *para*, to *loose* or *disengage*, which we translate to *let*, from the Anglo-Saxon lettan *lettan*, to *hinder*. Ye hinder the people from working. *Get ye to your burdens.* "Let religion alone, and mind your work." The language not only of tyranny, but of the basest irreligion also.

Verse 5. *The people of the land now* are *many*] The sanguinary edict had no doubt been long before repealed, or they could not have multiplied so greatly.

Verse 6. *The task-masters of the people and their officers*] The task-masters were Egyptians, (see on chap. i. 11,) the *officers* were Hebrews; see below, ver. 14. But it is probable that the task-masters, chap. i. 11, who are called שרי מסים *sarey missim*, *princes of the burdens* or *taxes*, were different from those termed *task-masters* here, as the words are different; נגשים *nogesim* signifies *exactors* or *oppressors*—persons who exacted from them an unreasonable proportion either of labour or money.

Officers.—שטרים *shoterim*; those seem to have been an inferior sort of officers, who attended on superior officers or magistrates to execute their orders. They are supposed to have been something like our *sheriffs*.

Verse 7. *Straw to make brick*] There have been many conjectures concerning the use of straw in making bricks. Some suppose it was used merely for burning them, but this is unfounded. The eastern bricks are often made of *clay* and *straw* kneaded together, and then not burned, but thoroughly dried in the sun. This is expressly mentioned by Philo in his life of Moses, who says, describing the oppression of the Israelites in Egypt, that some were obliged to work in clay for the formation of bricks, and others to gather straw for the same purpose, *because straw is the bond by which the brick is held together*, *πλινθου γαρ αχυρα δεσμος*.—PHIL. *Oper.*, *edit.* MANG., vol. ii., p. 86. And Philo's account is confirmed by the most intelligent travellers. Dr. Shaw says that the straw in the bricks still preserves its original colour, which is a proof that the bricks were never *burned*. Some of these are still to be seen in the cabinets of the curious; and there are several from ancient Babylon now before me, where the straw which was amalgamated with the clay is still perfectly visible. From this we may see the reason of the complaint made to Pharaoh, ver. 16: the Egyptians refused to give the necessary portion of straw for kneading the bricks, and yet they required that the full tale or number of bricks should be produced each day as they did when all the necessary materials were brought to hand; so the people were obliged to go over all the cornfields, and pluck up the stubble, which they were obliged to substitute for *straw*. See ver. 12.

Verse 8. *And the tale of the bricks*] *Tale* signifies the *number*, from the Anglo-Saxon tellan, to *number*, to *count*, &c.

For they be *idle; therefore they cry—Let us go* and *sacrifice*] Thus their desire to worship the true God in a proper manner was attributed to their unwillingness to work; a reflection which the Egyptians (in principle) of the present day cast on those who, while they are fervent in spirit serving the Lord, are not slothful in business. See below, ver. 17.

A. M. 2513.
B. C. 1491.

12 So the people were scattered
abroad throughout all the land of
Egypt, to gather stubble instead of straw.
13 And the task-masters hasted *them*, saying, Fulfil your works, *your* [i] daily tasks, as
when there was straw.
14 And the officers of the children of Israel,
which Pharaoh's task-masters had set over
them, were beaten, *and* demanded, Wherefore
have ye not fulfilled your task, in making
brick both yesterday and to-day, as heretofore?
15 Then the officers of the children of Israel
came and cried unto Pharaoh, saying, Wherefore dealest thou thus with thy servants?
16 There is no straw given unto thy servants, and they say to us, Make brick: and,
behold, thy servants *are* beaten; but the fault
is in thine own people.
17 But he said, Ye *are* idle, *ye are* idle:
therefore ye say, Let us go *and* do sacrifice
to the LORD.
18 Go therefore now, *and* work; for there
shall no straw be given you, yet
shall ye deliver the tale of bricks.

A. M. 2513.
B. C. 1491.

19 And the officers of the children of Israel
did see *that* they *were* in evil *case*, after it
was said, Ye shall not diminish *aught* from
your bricks of your daily task.
20 And they met Moses and Aaron, who
stood in the way, as they came forth from
Pharaoh:
21 [k] And they said unto them, The LORD
look upon you, and judge; because ye have
made our savour [l] to be abhorred in the eyes
of Pharaoh, and in the eyes of his servants,
to put a sword in their hand to slay us.
22 And Moses returned unto the LORD, and
said, Lord, wherefore hast thou *so* evil entreated this people? why *is* it *that* thou hast
sent me?
23 For since I came to Pharaoh to speak
in thy name, he hath done evil to this people; [m] neither hast thou delivered thy people
at all.

[i] Heb. *a matter of a day in his day.*——[k] Chap. vi. 9.——[l] Heb. *to stink;* Gen. xxxiv. 30; 1 Sam. xiii. 4, xxvii. 12; 2 Samuel x. 6; 1 Chron. xix. 6.——[m] Hebrew, *delivering thou hast not delivered.*

Verse 14. *And the officers—were beaten*] Probably *bastinadoed;* for this is the common punishment in Egypt to the present day for minor offences. The manner of it is this: the culprit lies on his belly, his legs being turned up behind erect, and the executioner gives him so many blows on the soles of the feet with a stick. This is a very severe punishment, the sufferer not being able to walk for many weeks after, and some are lamed by it through the whole of their lives.

Verse 16. *The fault* is *in thine own people.*] חטאת *chatath*, the SIN, is in thy own people. 1st. Because they require impossibilities; and, 2dly, because they punish us for not doing what cannot be performed.

Verse 17. *Ye* are *idle—therefore ye say, Let us go* and *do sacrifice*] It is common for those who feel unconcerned about their own souls to attribute the religious earnestness of others, who feel the importance of eternal things, to idleness or a disregard of their secular concerns. Strange that they cannot see there is a medium! He who has commanded them to be *diligent in business*, has also commanded them to be *fervent in spirit, serving the Lord.* He whose diligence in business is not connected with a true religious fervour of spirit, is a lover of the world; and whatever *form* he may have he has not the *power* of godliness, and therefore is completely out of the road to salvation.

Verse 19. *Did see* that *they* were *in evil* case] They saw that they could neither expect justice nor mercy; that their deliverance was very doubtful, and their case almost hopeless.

Verse 21. *The Lord look upon you, and judge*] These were hasty and unkind expressions; but the afflicted must be allowed the privilege of complaining; it is all the solace that such sorrow can find; and if in such distress words are spoken which should not be justified, yet the considerate and benevolent will hear them with indulgence. God is merciful; and the stroke of this people was heavier even than their groaning.

Put a sword in their hand] Given them a pretence which they had not before, to oppress us even unto death.

Verse 22. *And Moses returned unto the Lord*] This may imply, either that there was a particular *place* into which Moses ordinarily went to commune with Jehovah; or it may mean that kind of turning of heart and affection to God, which every pious mind feels itself disposed to practise in any time or place. The old adage will apply here: "A praying *heart* never lacks a praying *place.*"

Lord, wherefore hast thou so *evil entreated this people?*] It is certain that in this address Moses uses *great plainness of speech.* Whether the offspring of a testy impatience and undue familiarity, or of strong faith which gave him more than ordinary access to the throne of his gracious Sovereign, it would be difficult to say. The latter appears to be the most probable, as we do not find, from the succeeding chapter, that God was displeased with his freedom; we may therefore suppose that it was kept within due bounds, and that the principles and motives were all pure and good. However, it should be noted, that such freedom of speech with the Most High should never be used but on very special occasions, and then only by his *extraordinary* messengers.

Verse 23. *He hath done evil to this people*] Their misery is increased instead of being diminished.

Neither hast thou delivered thy people at all.] The marginal reading is both literal and correct: *And delivering thou hast not delivered.* Thou hast *begun* the work by giving us counsels and a commission, but thou hast not brought the people from under their bondage. Thou hast signified thy pleasure relative to their deliverance, but thou hast not brought them out of the hands of their enemies.

1. IT is no certain proof of the displeasure of God that a whole people, or an individual, may be found in a state of great oppression and distress; nor are affluence and prosperity any certain signs of his approbation. God certainly loved the Israelites better than he did the Egyptians; yet the former were in the deepest adversity, while the latter were in the height of prosperity. Luther once observed, that if secular prosperity were to be considered as a criterion of the Divine approbation, then the grand Turk must be the highest in the favour of God, as he was at that time the most prosperous sovereign on the earth. An observation of this kind, on a case so obvious, was really well calculated to repress hasty conclusions drawn from these external states, and to lay down a correct rule of judgment for all such occasions.

2. In all our addresses to God we should ever remember that we have *sinned* against him, and deserve nothing but punishment from his hand. We should therefore bow before him with the deepest humiliation of soul, and take that caution of the wise man, "Be not rash with thy mouth, and let not thine heart be hasty to utter any thing before God; for God is in heaven, and thou upon earth; therefore let thy words be few," Eccles. v. 2. There is the more need to attend to this caution, because many ignorant though well-meaning people use very improper, not to say indecent, freedoms in their addresses to the throne of grace. With such proceedings God cannot be well pleased; and he who has not a proper impression of the dignity and excellence of the Divine Nature, is not in such a disposition as it is essentially necessary to feel, in order to receive help from God. He who knows he has sinned, and feels that he is less than the least of all God's mercies, will pray with the deepest humility, and even rejoice before God with trembling. A *solemn* AWE of the Divine Majesty is not less requisite to successful praying, than *faith* in our Lord Jesus Christ. When *we* have such a commission as that of Moses, we may make use of his freedom of speech; but till then, the publican's prayer will best suit the generality of those who are even dignified by the name of Christian—LORD, be *merciful* to ME, A SINNER!

CHAPTER VI.

God encourages Moses, and promises to show wonders upon Pharaoh, and to bring out his people with a strong hand, 1. *He confirms this promise by his essential name JEHOVAH,* 2, 3; *by the covenant he had made with their fathers,* 4, 5. *Sends Moses with a fresh message to the Hebrews, full of the most gracious promises, and confirms the whole by appealing to the name in which his unchangeable existence is implied,* 6–8. *Moses delivers the message to the Israelites, but through anguish of spirit they do not believe,* 9. *He receives a new commission to go to Pharaoh,* 10, 11. *He excuses himself on account of his unreadiness of speech,* 12. *The Lord gives him and Aaron a charge both to Pharaoh and to the children of Israel,* 13. *The genealogy of* Reuben, 14; *of* Simeon, 15; *of* Levi, *from whom descended* Gershon, Kohath, *and* Merari, 16. *The sons of* Gershon, 17; *of* Kohath, 18; *of* Merari, 19. *The marriage of* Amram *and* Jochebed, 20. *The sons of* Izhar *and* Uzziel, *the brothers of Amram,* 21, 22. *Marriage of* Aaron *and* Elisheba, *and the birth of their sons,* Nadab, Abihu, Eleazar, *and* Ithamar, 23. *The sons of* Korah, *the nephew of Aaron,* 24. *The marriage of* Eleazar *to one of the daughters of* Putiel, *and the birth of* Phinehas, 25. *These genealogical accounts introduced for the sake of showing the line of descent of Moses and Aaron,* 26, 27. *A recapitulation of the commission delivered to Moses and Aaron,* 29, *and a repetition of the excuse formerly made by Moses,* 30.

A. M. 2513. B. C. 1491.

THEN the LORD said unto Moses,
Now shalt thou see what I will
do to Pharaoh: for [a] with a strong hand shall
he let them go, and with a strong hand [b] shall
he drive them out of his land.

2 And God spake unto Moses,
and said unto him, I *am* the
[c] LORD:

3 And I appeared unto Abraham, unto Isaac,
and unto Jacob, by *the name of* [d] God Almighty,

[a] Chap. iii. 19.—[b] Chap. xi. 1; xii. 31, 33, 39.

[c] Or, *JEHOVAH.*—[d] Gen. xvii. 1; xxxv. 11; xlviii. 3.

NOTES ON CHAP. VI.

Verse 1. *With a strong hand*] יד חזקה *yad chazakah*, the same verb which we translate *to harden*; see on chap. iv. 21. The *strong hand* here means sovereign power, suddenly and forcibly applied. God purposed to manifest his sovereign power in the sight of Pharaoh and the Egyptians; in consequence of which Pharaoh would manifest his power and authority as sovereign of Egypt, in dismissing and *thrusting out* the people. See chap. xii. 31–33.

Verse 2. *I am the* LORD] It should be, *I am* JEHOVAH, and without this the reason of what is said in the 3d verse is not sufficiently obvious.

Verse 3. *By* the name of *God Almighty*] אל שדי EL-SHADDAI, God All-sufficient; God the dispenser or pourer-out of gifts. See on Gen xvii. 1.

A. M. 2513.
B. C. 1491.

but by my name [e] JEHOVAH was I not known to them.

4 [f] And I have also established my covenant with them, [g] to give them the land of Canaan, the land of their pilgrimage, wherein they were strangers.

5 And [h] I have also heard the groaning of the children of Israel, whom the Egyptians keep in bondage; and I have remembered my covenant.

6 Wherefore say unto the children of Israel, [i] I *am* the LORD, and [k] I will bring you out from under the burdens of the Egyptians, and I will rid you out of their bondage, and I will [l] redeem you with a stretched-out arm, and with great judgments:

[e] Chap. iii. 14; Psa. lxviii. 4; lxxxiii. 18; John viii. 58; Rev. i. 4.—[f] Gen. xv. 18; xvii. 4, 7.—[g] Gen. xvii. 8; xxviii. 4. [h] Chap. ii. 24.

[i] Ver. 2, 8, 29.—[k] Chap. iii. 17; vii. 4; Deut. xxvi. 8; Psa. lxxxi. 6; cxxxvi. 11, 12.—[l] Chap. xv. 13; Deut. vii. 8; 1 Chron. xvii. 21; Neh. i. 10.

But by my name JEHOVAH *was I not known to them.*] This passage has been a sort of *crux criticorum*, and has been variously explained. It is certain that the name Jehovah was in use long before the days of Abraham, see Gen. ii. 4, where the words יהוה אלהים *Jehovah Elohim* occur, as they do frequently afterwards; and see Gen. xv. 2, where Abraham expressly addresses him by the name *Adonai* JEHOVAH; and see the 7th verse, where God reveals himself to Abraham by this very name: *And he said unto him, I am* JEHOVAH, *that brought thee out of Ur of the Chaldees.* How then can it be said that by his name JEHOVAH *he was not known unto them?* Several answers have been given to this question; the following are the chief:—1. The words should be read *interrogatively*, for the negative particle לא *lo, not*, has this power often in Hebrew. "I appeared unto Abraham, Isaac, and Jacob by the name of God Almighty, and by my name Jehovah was I not also made known unto them?" 2. The name JEHOVAH was not revealed before the time mentioned here, for though it occurs so frequently in the book of Genesis, as that book was written *long after* the name had come into common use, as a principal characteristic of God, Moses employs it in his history because of this circumstance; so that whenever it appears *previously* to this, it is by the figure called *prolepsis* or anticipation. 3. As the name יהוה JEHOVAH signifies *existence*, it may be understood in the text in question thus: "I appeared unto Abraham, Isaac, and Jacob by my name God Almighty, or God *All-sufficient*, i. e., having all power to do all good; in this character I made a covenant with them, supported by great and glorious promises; but as those promises had respect unto their *posterity*, they could not be fulfilled to those fathers: but now, as JEHOVAH, I am about to give *existence* to all those promises relative to your support, deliverance from bondage, and your consequent settlement in the promised land." 4. The words may be considered as used *comparatively:* though God did appear to those patriarchs *as* JEHOVAH, and they acknowledged him by this name, yet it was but *comparatively known* unto them; they knew nothing of the power and goodness of God, in comparison of what the Israelites were now about to experience.

I believe the simple meaning is this, that though from the beginning the name JEHOVAH was known as one of the names of the Supreme Being, yet what it really *implied* they did not know. אל שדי *El-Shaddai, God All-sufficient*, they knew well by the *continual provision* he made for them, and the *constant protection* he afforded them: but the name יהוה JEHOVAH is particularly to be referred to the *accomplishment* of promises already made; to the giving them a *being*, and thus bringing them into *existence*, which could not have been done in the order of his providence sooner than here specified: this name therefore in its *power* and significancy *was not* known unto *them;* nor fully known unto their *descendants* till the *deliverance* from *Egypt* and the *settlement* in the *promised land.* It is surely possible for a man to bear the *name* of a certain *office* or *dignity* before he *fulfils* any of its functions. *King, mayor, alderman, magistrate, constable*, may be borne by the several persons to whom they legally belong, *before* any of the acts peculiar to those offices are performed. The KING, *acknowledged* as such on his coronation, is *known* to be such by his *legislative acts;* the *civil magistrate*, by his distribution of justice, and issuing warrants for the apprehending of culprits; and the *constable*, by *executing* those warrants. All these were *known* to have their respective *names*, but the *exercise of their powers* alone shows what is implied in being *king, magistrate*, and *constable.* The following is a case in point, which fell within my own knowledge.

A case of dispute between certain litigious neighbours being heard in court before a weekly sitting of the magistrates, a woman who came as an *evidence* in behalf of her *bad neighbour*, finding the magistrates inclining to give judgment against her mischievous companion, took her by the arm and said, "Come away! I told you you would get neither law nor justice in this place." A magistrate, who was as much an honour to his function as he was to human nature, immediately said, "Here, constable! take that woman and lodge her in Bridewell, that she may know there is some law and justice in this place."

Thus the worthy magistrate *proved* he had the *power* implied in the *name* by *executing* the duties of his office. And God who *was known as* JEHOVAH, the being who *makes* and *gives effect* to *promises*, was known to the descendants of the twelve tribes to be THAT JEHOVAH, by giving *effect* and *being* to the *promises* which he *had made* to their *fathers.*

Verse 4. *I have also established my covenant*] I have now fully purposed to give present effect to all my engagements with your fathers, in behalf of their posterity.

Verse 6. *Say unto the children of Israel, I* am *the* LORD, *and I will bring you out, &c.*] This confirms the explanation given of ver. 3, which see.

A. M. 2513.
B. C. 1491.

7 And I will [m] take you to me for
a people, and [n] I will be to you a
God: and ye shall know that I *am* the LORD
your God, which bringeth you out [o] from
under the burdens of the Egyptians.
8 And I will bring you in unto the land,
concerning the which I did [p] swear [q] to give
it to Abraham, to Isaac, and to Jacob; and I
will give it you for a heritage: I *am* the
LORD.
9 And Moses spake so unto the children of
Israel: [r] but they hearkened not unto Moses
for [s] anguish of spirit, and for cruel bondage.
10 And the LORD spake unto Moses, saying,
11 Go in, speak unto Pharaoh king of
Egypt, that he let the children of Israel go
out of his land.
12 And Moses spake before the LORD,
saying, Behold, the children of Israel have
[t] not hearkened unto me; how then shall
Pharaoh hear me, [u] who *am* of uncircumcised lips?

A. M. 2513.
B. C. 1491.

13 And the LORD spake unto Moses and
unto Aaron, and gave them a charge unto the
children of Israel, and unto Pharaoh king of
Egypt, to bring the children of Israel out of
the land of Egypt.
14 These *be* the heads of their fathers'
houses: [v] The sons of Reuben, the first-born
of Israel; Hanoch, and Pallu, Hezron, and
Carmi: these *be* the families of Reuben.
15 [w] And the sons of Simeon; Jemuel, and
Jamin, and Ohad, and Jachin, and Zohar, and
Shaul the son of a Canaanitish woman: these
are the families of Simeon.
16 And these *are* the names of [x] the sons
of Levi according to their generations; Gershon, and Kohath, and Merari; and the years
of the life of Levi *were* a hundred thirty and
seven years.

[m] Deut. iv. 20; vii. 6; xiv. 2; xxvi. 18; 2 Sam. vii. 24. — [n] Gen. xvii. 7, 8; chap. xxix. 45, 46; Deut. xxix. 13; Rev. xxi. 7. — [o] Chap. v. 4, 5; Psa. lxxxi. 6. — [p] Heb. *lift up my hand*; see Gen. xiv. 22; Deut. xxxii. 40. — [q] Gen. xv. 18; xxvi. 3; xxviii. 13; xxxv. 12. — [r] Chapter v. 21. — [s] Heb. *shortness*, or, *straitness*. — [t] Ver. 9. — [u] Ver. 30; chap. iv. 10; Jer. i. 6. [v] Gen. xlvi. 9; 1 Chron. v. 3. — [w] 1 Chron. iv. 24; Gen. xlvi. 10. — [x] Gen. xlvi. 11; Num. iii. 17; 1 Chron. vi. 1, 16.

Verse 7. *I will take you to me for a people, &c.*] This was precisely the covenant that he had made with Abraham. See Gen. xvii. 7, and the notes there.

And ye shall know that I am the LORD *your God*] By thus fulfilling my promises ye shall know what is implied in my name. See on ver. 3.

But why should God take such a most stupid, refractory, and totally worthless people for his people? 1. Because he had promised to do so to their noble ancestors Abraham, Isaac, Jacob, Joseph, Judah, &c., men worthy of all praise, because in general friends of God, devoted to his will and to the good of mankind.

2. "That (as Bishop Warburton properly observes) the extraordinary providence by which they were protected, might become the more visible and illustrious; for had they been endowed with the shining qualities of the more polished nations, the effects of that providence might have been ascribed to their own wisdom."

3. That God might show to all succeeding generations that he delights to instruct the ignorant, help the weak, and save the lost; for if he bore long with Israel, showed them especial mercy, and graciously received them whenever they implored his protection, none need despair. God seems to have chosen the worst people in the universe, to give by them unto mankind the highest and most expressive proofs, that he wills not the death of a sinner, but rather that he may turn from his iniquity and live.

Verse 8. *Which I did swear*] נשאתי את ידי *nasathi eth yadi, I have lifted up my hand.* The usual mode of making an appeal to God, and hence considered to be a *form of swearing.* It is thus that Isa. lxii. 8 is to be understood: *The Lord hath sworn by his right hand, and by the arm of his strength.*

Verse 9. *But they hearkened not*] Their bondage was become so extremely oppressive that they had lost all hope of ever being redeemed from it. After this verse the Samaritan adds, *Let us alone, that we may serve the Egyptians: for it is better for us to serve the Egyptians than that we should die in the wilderness.* This appears to be borrowed from chap. xiv. 12.

Anguish of spirit] קצר רוח *kotzer ruach, shortness of spirit* or *breath.* The words signify that their labour was so continual, and their bondage so cruel and oppressive, that they had scarcely time to breathe.

Verse 12. *Uncircumcised lips?*] The word ערל *aral,* which we translate *uncircumcised,* seems to signify any thing exuberant or superfluous. Had not Moses been remarkable for his excellent beauty, I should have thought the passage might be rendered *protuberant lips;* but as this sense cannot be admitted for the above reason, the word must refer to some natural impediment in his speech; and probably means a want of distinct and ready utterance, either occasioned by some defect in the organs of speech, or impaired knowledge of the Egyptian language after an absence of *forty* years. See the note on chap. iv. 10.

Verse 14. *These* be *the heads*] ראשי *rashey,* the *chiefs* or *captains.* The following genealogy was simply intended to show that Moses and Aaron came in a direct line from Abraham, and to ascertain the *time* of Israel's deliverance. The whole account from this verse to ver. 26 is a sort of parenthesis, and does not belong to the narration; and what follows from ver. 28 is a recapitulation of what was spoken in the preceding chapters.

Verse 16. *The years of the life of Levi*] "Bishop Patrick observes that Levi is thought to have lived the longest of all Jacob's sons, none of whose ages are recorded in Scripture but his and Joseph's, whom Levi

a

A. M. 2513. B. C. 1491.

17 [y] The sons of Gershon; Libni, and Shimi, according to their families.

18 And [z] the sons of Kohath; Amram, and Izhar, and Hebron, and Uzziel: and the years of the life of Kohath *were* a hundred thirty and three years.

19 And [a] the sons of Merari; Mahali and Mushi: these *are* the families of Levi according to their generations.

20 And [b] Amram took him Jochebed his father's sister to wife; and she bare him Aaron and Moses: and the years of the life of Amram *were* a hundred and thirty and seven years.

21 And [c] the sons of Izhar; Korah, and Nepheg, and Zichri.

22 And [d] the sons of Uzziel; Mishael, and Elzaphan, and Sithri.

23 And Aaron took him Elisheba, daughter of [e] Amminadab, sister of Naashon, to wife; and she bare him [f] Nadab, and Abihu, Eleazar, and Ithamar.

A. M. 2513. B. C. 1491.

24 And the [g] sons of Korah; Assir, and Elkanah, and Abiasaph: these *are* the families of the Korhites.

25 And Eleazar, Aaron's son, took him *one* of the daughters of Putiel to wife; and [h] she bare him Phinehas: these *are* the heads of the fathers of the Levites according to their families.

26 These *are* that Aaron and Moses, [i] to whom the LORD said, Bring out the children of Israel from the land of Egypt according to their [k] armies.

27 These *are* they which [l] spake to Pharaoh, king of Egypt, [m] to bring out the children of Israel from Egypt: these *are* that Moses and Aaron.

28 And it came to pass on the day *when* the LORD spake unto Moses in the land of Egypt,

[y] 1 Chron. vi. 17; xxiii. 7.——[z] Num. xxvi. 57; 1 Chron. vi. 2, 18.——[a] 1 Chron. vi. 19; xxiii. 21.——[b] Chap. ii. 1, 2; Num. xxvi. 59.——[c] Num. xvi. 1; 1 Chron. vi. 37, 38.——[d] Lev. x. 4; Num. iii. 30.——[e] Ruth iv. 19, 20; 1 Chron. ii. 10; Matt. i. 4.

[f] Lev. x. 1; Num. iii. 2; xxvi. 60; 1 Chron. vi. 3; xxiv. 1.——[g] Num. xxvi. 11.——[h] Num. xxv. 7, 11; Josh. xxiv. 33.——[i] Ver. 13.——[k] Chap. vii. 4; xii. 17, 51; Num. xxxiii. 1.——[l] Chap. v. 1, 3; vii. 10.——[m] Ver. 13; ch. xxxii. 7; xxxiii. 1; Psa. lxxvii. 20.

survived *twenty-seven* years, though he was much the elder brother. By the common computation this would be twenty-three years: by Kennicott's computation at the end of Gen. xxxi., Levi's birth is placed twenty-four years before that of Joseph; his death, therefore, would be only three years later. But this is not the only difficulty in ancient chronologies. Kohath, the *second* son of Levi, according to Archbishop Usher was *thirty* years old when Jacob came into Egypt, and lived there *one hundred and three* years. He attained to nearly the same age with Levi, to *one hundred and thirty-three* years; and his son Amram, the father of Moses, lived to the same age with Levi. We may observe here how the Divine promise, Gen. xv. 16, of delivering the Israelites out of Egypt in the *fourth* generation was verified; for Moses was the son of *Amram*, the son of *Kohath*, the son of *Levi*, the son of *Jacob*."—DODD.

Verse 20. *His father's sister*] דודתו *dodatho*. The true meaning of this word is uncertain. Parkhurst observes that דוד *dod* signifies an *uncle* in 1 Sam. x. 14; Lev. x. 4, and frequently elsewhere. It signifies also an *uncle's son*, a *cousin-german:* compare Jer. xxxii. 8 with ver. 12, where the Vulgate renders דדי *dodi* by *patruelis mei, my paternal cousin;* and in Amos vi. 10, for דודו *dodo*, the Targum has קריביה *karibiah, his near relation*. So the Vulgate, *propinquus ejus, his relative*, and the Septuagint, *οἱ οικειοι αυτων, those of their household*. The best critics suppose that Jochebed was the *cousin-german* of Amram, and not his *aunt*. See chap. ii. 1.

Bare him Aaron and Moses] The Samaritan, Septuagint, Syriac, and one Hebrew MS. add, *And Miriam their sister*. Some of the best critics suppose these words to have been originally in the Hebrew text.

Verse 21. *Korah*] Though he became a rebel against God and Moses, (see Num. xvi. 1, &c.,) yet Moses, in his great impartiality, inserts his name among those of his other progenitors.

Verse 22. *Uzziel*] He is called Aaron's *uncle*, Lev. x. 4.

Verse 23. *Elisheba*] The oath of the Lord. It is the same name as *Elizabeth*, so very common among Christians. She was of the royal tribe of Judah, and was sister to Nahshon, one of the princes; see Num. ii. 3.

Eleazar] He succeeded to the high priesthood on the death of his father Aaron, Num. xx. 25, &c.

Verse 25. *Phinehas*] Of the celebrated act of this person, and the most honourable grant made to him and his posterity, see Num. xxv. 7–13.

Verse 26. *According to their armies.*] צבאתם *tsibotham*, their *battalions—regularly arranged troops*. As God had these particularly under his care and direction, he had the name of יהוה צבאות *Yehovah tsebaoth, Lord of hosts* or *armies*.

"The plain and disinterested manner," says Dr. Dodd, "in which Moses speaks here of his relations, and the impartiality wherewith he inserts in the list of them such as were afterwards severely punished by the Lord, are striking proofs of his modesty and sincerity. He inserts the genealogy of Reuben and Simeon, because they were of the same mother with Levi; and though he says nothing of himself, yet he relates particularly what concerns Aaron, ver. 23, who married into an honourable family, the sister of a prince of the tribe of Judah."

Verse 28. *And it came to pass*] Here the *seventh* chapter should commence, as there is a complete ending of the *sixth* with ver. 27, and the 30th verse of

A. M. 2513.
B. C. 1491.

29 That the LORD spake unto Moses, saying, [n] I *am* the LORD: [o] speak thou unto Pharaoh, king of Egypt, all that I say unto thee.

30 And Moses said before the LORD, Behold, [p] I *am* of uncircumcised lips, and how shall Pharaoh hearken unto me?

[n] Ver. 2.——[o] Ver. 11; chap. vii. 2.

[p] Ver. 12; chap. iv. 10.

this chapter is intimately connected with the 1st verse of the succeeding.

THE principal subjects in this chapter have been so amply considered in the notes, that little of importance remains to be done. On the nature of a *covenant* (see ver. 4) ample information may be obtained by referring to Gen. vi. 18, and xv. 9–18, which places the reader will do well to consult.

Supposing Moses to have really laboured under some defect in speech, we may consider it as wisely designed to be a sort of counterbalance to his other excellences: at least this is an ordinary procedure of Divine Providence; personal accomplishments are counterbalanced by mental defects, and mental imperfections often by personal accomplishments. Thus the head cannot say to the foot, I have no need of thee. And God does all this in great wisdom, to hide pride from man, and that no flesh may glory in his presence. To be contented with our formation, endowments, and external circumstances, requires not only much submission to the providence of God, but also much of the mind of Christ. On the other hand, should we feel vanity because of some personal or mental accomplishment, we have only to take a view of *our whole* to find sufficient cause of humiliation; and after all, the meek and gentle spirit only is, in the sight of God, of great price.

CHAPTER VII.

The dignified mission of Moses and Aaron to Pharaoh—the one to be as God, the other as a prophet of the Most High, 1, 2. *The prediction that Pharaoh's heart should be hardened, that God might multiply his signs and wonders in Egypt, that the inhabitants might know he alone was the true God*, 3–6. *The age of Moses and Aaron*, 7. *God gives them directions how they should act before Pharaoh*, 8, 9. *Moses turns his rod into a serpent*, 10. *The magicians imitate this miracle, and Pharaoh's heart is hardened*, 11–13. *Moses is commanded to wait upon Pharaoh next morning when he should come to the river, and threaten to turn the waters into blood if he did not let the people go*, 14–18. *The waters in all the land of Egypt are turned into blood*, 19, 20. *The fish die*, 21. *The magicians imitate this, and Pharaoh's heart is again hardened*, 22, 23. *The Egyptians sorely distressed because of the bloody waters*, 24. *This plague endures seven days*, 25.

A. M. 2513.
B. C. 1491.

AND the LORD said unto Moses, See, I have made thee [a] a god to Pharaoh: and Aaron thy brother shall be [b] thy prophet.

2 Thou [c] shalt speak all that I command thee: and Aaron thy brother shall speak unto Pharaoh, that he send the children of Israel out of his land.

3 And [d] I will harden Pharaoh's heart, and [e] multiply my [f] signs and my wonders in the land of Egypt.

4 But Pharaoh shall not hearken unto you, [g] that I may lay my hand upon Egypt, and bring forth mine armies, *and* my people the children of Israel, out of the land of Egypt, [h] by great judgments.

5 And the Egyptians [i] shall know that I *am* the LORD, when I [k] stretch forth mine hand upon Egypt, and bring out the children of Israel from among them.

6 And Moses and Aaron [l] did as the LORD commanded them, so did they.

[a] Chap. iv. 16; Jer. i. 10.——[b] Chap. iv. 16.——[c] Chap. iv. 15.——[d] Chap. iv. 21.——[e] Chap. xi. 9.——[f] Chap. iv. 7.

[g] Chap. x. 1; xi. 9.——[h] Chap. vi. 6.——[i] Ver. 17; chap. viii. 22; xiv. 4, 18; Psa. ix. 16.——[k] Chap. iii. 20.——[l] Ver. 2.

NOTES ON CHAP. VII.

Verse 1. *I have made thee a god*] At thy word every plague shall come, and at thy command each shall be removed. Thus Moses must have appeared as a god to Pharaoh.

Shall be thy prophet.] Shall receive the word from thy mouth, and communicate it to the Egyptian king, ver. 2.

Verse 3. *I will harden Pharaoh's heart*] I will permit his stubbornness and obstinacy still to remain, that I may have the greater opportunity to multiply my wonders in the land, that the Egyptians may know that I only am Jehovah, the self-existent God. See on chap. iv. 21.

Verse 5. *And bring out the children of Israel*] Pharaoh's obstinacy was either caused or permitted in mercy to the Egyptians, that he and his magicians being suffered to oppose Moses and Aaron to the uttermost of their power, the Israelites might be brought out of Egypt in so signal a manner, in spite of al.

A. M. 2513.
B. C. 1491.

7 And Moses *was* [m] fourscore years old, and Aaron fourscore and three years old, when they spake unto Pharaoh.

8 And the LORD spake unto Moses and unto Aaron, saying,

9 When Pharaoh shall speak unto you, saying, [n] Show a miracle for you: then thou shalt say unto Aaron, [o] Take thy rod, and cast *it* before Pharaoh, *and* it shall become a serpent.

10 And Moses and Aaron went in unto Pharaoh, and they did so [p] as the LORD had commanded: and Aaron cast down his rod before Pharaoh, and before his servants, and it [q] became a serpent.

11 Then Pharaoh also [r] called the wise men and [s] the sorcerers: now the magicians of Egypt, they also [t] did in like manner with their enchantments.

[m] Deut. xxix. 5; xxxi. 2; xxxiv. 7; Acts vii. 23, 30.——[n] Isa. vii. 11; John ii. 18; vi. 30.——[o] Chap. iv. 2, 17.

[p] Verse 9.——[q] Chap. iv. 3.——[r] Gen. xli. 8.——[s] 2 Tim. iii. 8. [t] Ver. 22; chap. viii. 7, 18.

the opposition of the Egyptians, their king, and their gods, that Jehovah might appear to be *All-mighty* and *All-sufficient.*

Verse 7. *Moses* was *fourscore years old*] He was *forty* years old when he went to Midian, and he had tarried *forty* years in Midian; (see chap. ii. 11, and Acts vii. 30;) and from this verse it appears that Aaron was three years older than Moses. We have already seen that Miriam their sister was older than either, chap. ii. 4.

Verse 9. *Show a miracle for you*] A miracle, מופת *mopheth*, signifies an effect produced in nature which is opposed to its laws, or such as its powers are inadequate to produce. As Moses and Aaron professed to have a Divine mission, and to come to Pharaoh on the most extraordinary occasion, making a most singular and unprecedented demand, it was natural to suppose, if Pharaoh should even give them an audience, that he would require them to give him some proof by an extraordinary sign that their pretensions to such a Divine mission were well founded and incontestable. For it appears to have ever been the sense of mankind, that he who has a Divine mission to effect some extraordinary purpose can give a supernatural proof that he has got this extraordinary commission.

Take thy rod] This rod, whether a common staff, an ensign of office, or a shepherd's crook, was now consecrated for the purpose of working miracles; and is indifferently called the rod of God, the rod of Moses, and the rod of Aaron. God gave it the miraculous power, and Moses and Aaron used it indifferently.

Verse 10. *It became a serpent.*] תנין *tannin.* What kind of a serpent is here intended, learned men are not agreed. From the manner in which the original word is used in Psa. lxxiv. 13; Isa. xxvii. 1; li. 9; Job vii. 12; some very large creature, either aquatic or amphibious, is probably meant; some have thought that the *crocodile,* a well-known Egyptian animal, is here intended. In chap. iv. 3 it is said that this rod was changed into a *serpent,* but the original word there is נחש *nachash,* and here תנין *tannin,* the same word which we translate *whale,* Gen. i. 21.

As נחש *nachash* seems to be a term restricted to no one particular meaning, as has already been shown on Gen. iii.; so the words תנין *tannin,* תנינים *tanninim,* תנים *tannim,* and תנות *tannoth,* are used to signify different kinds of animals in the Scriptures. The word is supposed to signify the *jackal* in Job xxx. 29; Psa. xliv. 19; Isa. xiii. 22; xxxiv. 13; xxxv. 7; xliii. 20; Jer. ix. 11, &c., &c.; and also a *dragon, serpent,* or *whale,* Job vii. 12; Psa. xci. 13; Isa. xxvii. 1; li. 9; Jer. li. 34; Ezek. xxix. 3; xxxii. 2; and is termed, in our translation, a *sea-monster,* Lam. iv. 3. As it was a *rod* or *staff* that was changed into the *tannim* in the cases mentioned here, it has been supposed that an ordinary *serpent* is what is intended by the word, because the size of both might be then pretty nearly equal: but as a miracle was wrought on the occasion, this circumstance is of no weight; it was as easy for God to change the rod into a crocodile, or any other creature, as to change it into an adder or common snake.

Verse 11. *Pharaoh—called the wise men*] חכמים *chacamim,* the men of learning. *Sorcerers,* כשפים *cashshephim,* those who *reveal* hidden things; probably from the Arabic root كشف *kashafa, to reveal, uncover,* &c., signifying *diviners,* or those who pretended to *reveal* what was in futurity, to *discover* things lost, to *find* hidden treasures, &c. *Magicians,* חרטמי *chartummey, decypherers* of abstruse writings. See the note on Gen. xli. 8.

They also did in like manner with their enchantments.] The word להטים *lahatim,* comes from להט *lahat,* to *burn,* to *set on fire;* and probably signifies such incantations as required *lustral fires, sacrifices, fumigations, burning of incense, aromatic* and *odoriferous drugs,* &c., as the means of evoking departed spirits or assistant demons, by whose ministry, it is probable, the magicians in question wrought some of their deceptive miracles: for as the term *miracle* signifies properly something which exceeds the powers of nature or art to produce, (see ver. 9,) hence there could be no miracle in this case but those wrought, through the power of God, by the ministry of Moses and Aaron. There can be no doubt that real serpents were produced by the magicians. On this subject there are two opinions: 1st, That the serpents were such as they, either by juggling or sleight of hand, had brought to the place, and had secreted till the time of exhibition, as our common conjurers do in the public fairs, &c. 2dly, That the serpents were brought by the ministry of a familiar spirit, which, by the magic flames already referred to, they had evoked for the purpose. Both these opinions admit the serpents to be *real,* and no illusion of the sight, as some have supposed.

The first opinion appears to me insufficient to ac-

A. M. 2513.
B. C. 1491.

12 For they cast down every man
his rod, and they became serpents:
but Aaron's rod swallowed up their rods.
13 And he hardened Pharaoh's heart, that he
hearkened not unto them; [u] as the LORD
had said.
14 And the LORD said unto Moses, [v] Pharaoh's
heart *is* hardened, he refuseth to let
the people go.
15 Get thee unto Pharaoh in the morning;
lo, he goeth out unto the water; and thou
shalt stand by the river's brink against he
come; and [w] the rod which was turned to a
serpent shalt thou take in thine hand.
16 And thou shalt say unto him,
[x] The LORD God of the Hebrews
hath sent me unto thee, saying, Let my people
go, [y] that they may serve me in the wilderness:
and, behold, hitherto thou wouldest
not hear.
17 Thus saith the LORD, In this [z] thou shalt
know that I *am* the LORD: behold, I will
smite with the rod that *is* in mine hand upon
the waters which *are* in the river, and [a] they
shall be turned [b] to blood.
18 And the fish that *is* in the river shall die,
and the river shall stink; and the Egyptians
shall [c] loathe to drink of the water of the river.

[u] Chap. iv. 21; ver. 4.——[v] Chap. viii. 15; x. 1, 20, 27.——[w] Ch. iv. 2, 3; ver. 10.——[x] Chap. iii. 18.

[y] Chap. iii. 12, 18; v. 1, 3.——[z] Chap. v. 2; ver. 5.——[a] Chap. iv. 9.——[b] Rev. xvi. 4, 6.——[c] Ver. 24.

count for the phenomena of the case referred to. If the magicians *threw down their rods, and they became serpents* after they were thrown down, as the text expressly says, ver. 12, *juggling* or *sleight of hand* had nothing farther to do in the business, as the rods were then *out* of their hands. If Aaron's rod *swallowed up their rods*, their sleight of hand was no longer concerned. A man, by dexterity of hand, may so far impose on his spectators as to *appear* to eat a rod; but for rods lying on the ground to become serpents, and one of these to devour all the rest so that it alone remained, required something more than *juggling*. How much more rational at once to allow that these magicians had familiar spirits who could assume all shapes, change the appearances of the subjects on which they operated, or suddenly convey one thing away and substitute another in its place! Nature has no such power, and art no such influence as to produce the effects attributed here and in the succeeding chapters to the Egyptian magicians.

Verse 12. *Aaron's rod swallowed up their rods.*] As Egypt was remarkably addicted to magic, sorcery, &c., it was necessary that God should permit Pharaoh's wise men to act to the utmost of their skill in order to imitate the work of God, that his superiority might be clearly seen, and his powerful working incontestably ascertained; and this was fully done when *Aaron's rod swallowed up their rods.* We have already seen that the names of two of the chief of these magicians were *Jannes* and *Jambres*; see chap. ii. 10, and 2 Tim. iii. 8. Many traditions and fables concerning these may be seen in the eastern writers.

Verse 13. *And he hardened Pharaoh's heart*] ויחזק לב פרעה *vaiyechezak leb Paroh*, "And the heart of Pharaoh was hardened," the identical words which in ver. 22 are thus translated, and which should have been rendered in the same way here, lest the *hardening*, which was evidently the effect of his own obstinate shutting of his eyes against the truth, should be attributed to God. See on chap. iv. 21.

Verse 14. *Pharaoh's heart* is *hardened*] כבד *cabed*, is become *heavy* or *stupid*; he receives no conviction, notwithstanding the clearness of the light which shines upon him. We well know the power of *prejudice*: where persons are determined to think and act after a predetermined plan, arguments, demonstrations, and even miracles themselves, are lost on them, as in the case of Pharaoh here, and that of the obstinate Jews in the days of our Lord and his apostles.

Verse 15. *Lo, he goeth out unto the water*] Probably for the purpose of bathing, or of performing some religious ablution. Some suppose he went out to pay adoration to the river Nile, which was an object of religious worship among the ancient Egyptians. "For," says Plutarch, De Iside., *ουδεν ούτω τιμη Αιγυπτιοις ώς ὁ Νειλος·* "nothing is in greater honour among the Egyptians than the river Nile." Some of the ancient Jews supposed that Pharaoh himself was a magician, and that he walked by the river early each morning for the purpose of preparing magical rites, &c.

Verse 17. *Behold, I will smite*] Here commences the account of the TEN *plagues* which were inflicted on the Egyptians by Moses and Aaron, by the command and through the power of God. According to Archbishop Usher these ten plagues took place in the course of one month, and in the following order:—

The *first*, the WATERS *turned into* BLOOD, took place, he supposes, the 18th day of the sixth month; ver. 20.

The *second*, the plague of FROGS, on the 25th day of the sixth month; chap. viii. 1.

The *third*, the plague of LICE, on the 27th day of the sixth month; chap. viii. 16.

The *fourth*, grievous SWARMS of FLIES, on the 29th day of the sixth month; chap. viii. 24.

The *fifth*, the grievous MURRAIN, on the 2d day of the seventh month; chap. ix. 3.

The *sixth*, the plague of BOILS *and* BLAINS, on the 3d day of the seventh month; chap. ix. 10.

The *seventh*, the grievous HAIL, on the 5th day of the seventh month; chap. ix. 18.

The *eighth*, the plague of LOCUSTS, on the 8th day of the seventh month; chap. x. 12.

The *ninth*, the THICK DARKNESS, on the 10th day of Abib, (April 30,) now become the first month of the Jewish year; chap. x. 22. But see the note on chap. xii. 2.

The *tenth*, the SLAYING the FIRST-BORN, on the 15th of Abib; chap. xii. 29. But most of these dates are destitute of proof.

A. M. 2513.
B. C. 1491.

19 And the Lord spake unto
Moses, Say unto Aaron, Take thy
rod, and [d] stretch out thine hand upon the
waters of Egypt, upon their streams, upon
their rivers, and upon their ponds, and upon
all their [e] pools of water, that they may become blood; and *that* there may be blood
throughout all the land of Egypt, both in
vessels of wood, and in *vessels of* stone.
20 And Moses and Aaron did so, as the Lord
commanded; and he [f] lifted up the rod, and
smote the waters that *were* in the river, in the
sight of Pharaoh, and in the sight
of his servants; and all the [g] waters
that *were* in the river were turned to blood.
21 And the fish that *was* in the river died;
and the river stank, and the Egyptians [h] could
not drink of the water of the river; and
there was blood throughout all the land of
Egypt.
22 [i] And the magicians of Egypt did so with
their enchantments: and Pharaoh's heart was
hardened, neither did he hearken unto them;
[k] as the Lord had said.

[d] Chap. viii. 5, 6, 16; ix. 22; x. 12, 21; xiv. 21, 26.——[e] Heb. *gathering of their waters.*——[f] Chap. xvii. 5.——[g] Psa. lxxviii. 44; cv. 29; Rev. viii. 9.——[h] Ver. 18.——[i] Ver. 11; chap. viii. 7, 8; Wisd. xvii. 7.——[k] Prov. xxix. 1; Isa. xxvi. 11; Jer. v. 3; xxxvi. 24.

Verse 18. *The Egyptians shall loathe to drink of the water*] The force of this expression cannot be well felt without taking into consideration the peculiar pleasantness and great salubrity of the waters of the Nile. "The water of Egypt," says the Abbe Mascrier, "is so delicious, that one would not wish the heat to be less, or to be delivered from the sensation of thirst. The Turks find it so exquisite that they excite themselves to drink of it by eating *salt.* It is a common saying among them, that if Mohammed had drank of it he would have besought God that he might never die, in order to have had this continual gratification. When the Egyptians undertake the pilgrimage of Mecca, or go out of their country on any other account, they speak of nothing but the pleasure they shall have at their return in drinking of the waters of the Nile. There is no gratification to be compared to this; it surpasses, in their esteem, that of seeing their relations and families. All those who have tasted of this water allow that they never met with the like in any other place. When a person drinks of it for the first time he can scarcely be persuaded that it is not a water prepared by art; for it has something in it inexpressibly agreeable and pleasing to the taste; and it should have the same rank among *waters* that *champaign* has among *wines.* But its most valuable quality is, that it is exceedingly salutary. It never incommodes, let it be drank in what quantity it may: this is so true that it is no uncommon thing to see some persons drink three buckets of it in a day without the least inconvenience! When I pass such encomiums on the water of Egypt it is right to observe that I speak only of that of the *Nile,* which indeed is the only water drinkable, for their *well water* is detestable and unwholesome. *Fountains* are so rare that they are a kind of prodigy in that country; and as to *rain water,* that is out of the question, as scarcely any falls in Egypt."

"A person," says Mr. Harmer, "who never before heard of the deliciousness of the Nile water, and of the large quantities which on that account are drank of it, will, I am sure, find an energy in those words of Moses to Pharaoh, *The Egyptians shall loathe to drink of the water of the river,* which he never observed before. They will loathe to drink of that water which they used to prefer to all the waters of the universe; loathe to drink of that for which they had been accustomed to long, and will rather choose to drink of well water, which in their country is detestable!"—*Observations,* vol. iii., p. 564.

Verse 19. That *there may be blood—both in* vessels of *wood, and in* vessels of *stone.*] Not only the Nile itself was to be thus changed into blood in all its branches, and the canals issuing from it, but all the water of *lakes, ponds,* and *reservoirs,* was to undergo a similar change. And this was to extend even to *the water already brought into their houses for culinary and other domestic purposes.* As the water of the Nile is known to be very thick and muddy, and the Egyptians are obliged to filter it through pots of a kind of white earth, and sometimes through a paste made of almonds, Mr. Harmer supposes that the *vessels* of *wood* and *stone* mentioned above may refer to the process of filtration, which no doubt has been practised among them from the remotest period. The meaning given above I think to be more natural.

The first *plague. The* waters *turned into* blood.

Verse 20. *All the waters—were turned to blood.*] Not merely in appearance, but in reality; for these changed waters became corrupt and insalubrious, so that even the fish that were in the river died; and the smell became highly offensive, so that the waters could not be drank; ver. 21.

Verse 22. *And the magicians—did so*] But if all the water in Egypt was turned into blood by Moses, where did the magicians get the water which *they* changed into blood? This question is answered in verse 24. The Egyptians digged round about the river for water to drink, and it seems that the water obtained by this means was not bloody like that in the river: on *this* water therefore the magicians might operate. Again, though a general commission was given to Moses, not only to turn the waters of the river (Nile) into blood, but also those of their streams, rivers, ponds, and pools; yet it seems pretty clear from verse 20 that he did not proceed thus far, at least in the first instance; for it is there stated that only the waters of the river were turned into blood. Afterwards the plague doubtless became general. At the commencement therefore of this plague, the magicians might obtain other water to imitate the miracle; and it would not

A. M. 2513. B. C. 1491.

23 And Pharaoh turned and went into his house, [l] neither did he set his heart to this also.

24 And all the Egyptians digged round about the river for water to drink; [m] for they could not drink of the water of the river.

A. M. 2513. B. C. 1491.

25 And [n] seven days were fulfilled, after that the LORD had smitten the river.

[l] Ver. 3.—[m] Ver. 18, 21.

[n] 2 Sam. xxiv. 13.

be difficult for them, by *juggling tricks* or the *assistance of a familiar spirit*, (for we must not abandon the possibility of this use,) to give it a bloody appearance, a fetid smell, and a bad taste. On either of these grounds there is no contradiction in the Mosaic account, though some have been very studious to find one.

The plague of the bloody waters may be considered as a display of retributive justice against the Egyptians, for the murderous decree which enacted that all the male children of the Israelites should be drowned in *that* river, the waters of which, so necessary to their support and life, were now rendered not only insalubrious but *deadly*, by being turned into blood. As it is well known that the Nile was a chief object of Egyptian idolatry, (see on ver. 15,) and that annually they sacrificed a *girl*, or as others say, both a *boy* and a *girl*, to this river, in gratitude for the benefits received from it, (*Universal Hist.*, vol. i., p. 178, fol. edit.,) God might have designed this plague as a punishment for such cruelty: and the contempt poured upon this object of their adoration, by turning its waters into blood, and rendering them fetid and corrupt, must have had a direct tendency to correct their idolatrous notions, and lead them to acknowledge the power and authority of the true God.

Verse 25. *And seven days were fulfilled*] So we learn that this plague continued at least a whole week.

THE contention between Moses and Aaron and the magicians of Egypt has become famous throughout the world. Tradition in various countries has preserved, not only the account, but also the names of the chief persons concerned in the opposition made by the Egyptians to these messengers of God. Though their names are not mentioned in the sacred *text*, yet tradition had preserved them in the *Jewish records*, from which St. Paul undoubtedly quotes 2 Tim. iii. 8, where, speaking of the enemies of the Gospel, he compares them to *Jannes and Jambres, who withstood Moses*. That these names existed in the ancient Jewish records, their own writings show. In the *Targum* of Jonathan ben Uzziel on this place they are called יניס וימבריס *Janis* and *Jambris*; and in the Babylonian *Talmud* they are named *Joanne* and *Mambre*, and are represented as chiefs of the sorcerers of Egypt, and as having ridiculed Moses and Aaron for pretending to equal them in magical arts. And Rab. *Tanchum*, in his Commentary, names them *Jonos* and *Jombrus*. If we allow the readings of the ancient editions of Pliny to be correct, he refers, in *Hist. Nat.*, l. xxx., c. 2, to the same persons, the names being a little changed: *Est et alia magices factio, a Mose et Jamne et Jotape Judæis pendens, sed multis millibus annorum post Zoroastrem*; "There is also another faction of magicians which took its origin from the Jews, Moses, Jamnes, and Jotapes, many thousands of years after Zoroaster;" where he confounds Moses with the Egyptian magicians; for the heathens, having no just notion of the power of God, attributed all miracles to the influence of *magic*. *Pliny* also calls the Egyptian magicians *Jews*; but this is not the only mistake in his history; and as he adds, *sed multis millibus annorum post Zoroastrem*, he is supposed by some to refer to the *Christians*, and particularly the *apostles* who wrought many miracles, and whom he considers to be a magical sect derived from Moses and the Jews, because they were Jews by nation, and quoted Moses and the prophets in proof of the truth of the doctrines of Christianity, and of the Divine mission of Christ

Numenius, a Pythagorean philosopher, mentioned by Eusebius, names these magicians, *Jamnes* and *Jambres*, and mentions their opposition to Moses; and we have already seen that there was a tradition among the Asiatics that Pharaoh's daughter had Moses instructed by the wise men *Jannes* and *Jambres*; see *Abul Faraje*, edit. Pococ., p. 26. Here then is a very remarkable fact, the principal circumstances of which, and the chief actors in them, have been preserved by a sort of universal tradition. See *Ainsworth*.

When all the circumstances of the preceding case are considered, it seems strange that God should enter into any contest with such persons as the Egyptian magicians; but a little reflection will show the absolute necessity of this. Mr. *Psalmanazar*, who wrote the *Account of the Jews* in the first volume of the *Universal History*, gives the following judicious reasons for this: "If it be asked," says he, "why God did suffer the Egyptian magicians to borrow power from the devil to invalidate, if possible, those miracles which his servant wrought by his Divine power, the following reasons may be given for it: 1. It was necessary that these magicians should be suffered to exert the utmost of their power against Moses, in order to clear him from the imputation of *magic* or *sorcery*; for as the notion of such an extraordinary art was very rife, not only among the Egyptians, but all other nations, if they had not entered into this strenuous competition with him, and been at length overcome by him, both the Hebrews and the Egyptians would have been apter to have attributed all his miracles to his skill in magic, than to the Divine power.

"2. It was necessary, in order to confirm the faith of the wavering and desponding Israelites, by making them see the difference between Moses acting by the power of God, and the sorcerers by that of Satan.

"3. It was necessary, in order to preserve them afterwards from being seduced by any false miracles from the true worship of God."

To these a *fourth* reason may be added: God permitted this in mercy to the Egyptians, that they might see that the gods in whom they trusted were utterly incapable of saving them; that they could not *undo* or *counteract* one of the plagues sent on them by the power of Jehovah; the whole of their influence ex-

tending only to some superficial imitations of the genuine miracles wrought by Moses in the name of the true God. By these means it is natural to conclude that many of the Egyptians, and perhaps several of the servants of Pharaoh, were cured of their idolatry; though the king himself hardened his heart against the evidences which God brought before his eyes. Thus God is *known* by his judgments: for in every operation of his hand his design is to enlighten the minds of men, to bring them from false dependences to trust in himself alone; that, being saved from error and sin, they may become wise, holy, and happy. When his judgments are abroad in the earth, the inhabitants learn righteousness. See the note on chap. iv. 21.

CHAPTER VIII.

The plague of frogs *threatened,* 1, 2. *The extent of this plague,* 3, 4. *Aaron commanded to stretch ou. his hand, with the rod, over the river and waters of Egypt, in consequence of which the frogs came,* 5, 6. *The magicians imitate this miracle,* 7. *Pharaoh entreats Moses to remove the frogs, and promises to let the people go,* 8. *Moses promises that they shall be removed from every part of Egypt, the river excepted,* 9–11. *Moses prays to God, and the frogs die throughout the land of Egypt,* 12–14. *Pharaoh, finding himself respited, hardens his heart,* 15. *The plague of* lice *on man and beast,* 16, 17. *The magicians attempt to imitate this miracle, but in vain,* 18. *They confess it to be the* finger of God, *and yet Pharaoh continues obstinate,* 19. *Moses is sent again to him to command him to let the people go, and in case of disobedience he is threatened with* swarms of flies, 20, 21. *A promise made that the land of Goshen, where the Israelites dwelt, should be exempted from this plague,* 22, 23. *The* flies *are sent,* 24. *Pharaoh sends for Moses and Aaron, and offers to permit them to sacrifice in the land,* 25. *They refuse, and desire to go three days' journey into the wilderness,* 26, 27. *Pharaoh consents to let them go a* little way, *provided they would entreat the Lord to remove the flies,* 28. *Moses consents, prays to God, and the flies are removed,* 29–31. *After which Pharaoh yet hardened his heart, and refused to let the people go,* 32.

A. M. 2513. B. C. 1491. AND the LORD spake unto Moses, Go unto Pharaoh, and say unto him, Thus saith the LORD, Let my people go, [a] that they may serve me.

2 And if thou [b] refuse to let *them* go, behold, I will smite all thy borders with [c] frogs: A. M. 2513. B. C. 1491

3 And the river shall bring forth frogs

[a] Chap. iii. 12, 18.

[b] Chap. vii. 14; ix. 2.—[c] Rev. xvi. 13.

NOTES ON CHAP. VIII.

The SECOND *plague*—FROGS.

Verse 1. *Let my people go*] God, in great mercy to Pharaoh and the Egyptians, gives them notice of the evils he intended to bring upon them if they continued in their obstinacy. Having had therefore such warning, the evil might have been prevented by a timely humiliation and return to God.

Verse 2. *If thou refuse*] Nothing can be plainer than that Pharaoh had it still in his power to have dismissed the people, and that his refusal was the mere effect of his own wilful obstinacy.

With frogs] צפרדעים *tsepardeim.* This word is of doubtful etymology: almost all interpreters, both ancient and modern, agree to render it as we do, though some mentioned by Aben Ezra think the *crocodile* is meant; but these can never weigh against the conjoint testimony of the ancient versions. Parkhurst derives the word from צפר *tsaphar,* denoting the *brisk action,* or *motion of the light,* and ידע *yada,* to *feel,* as they seem to *feel* or *rejoice* in the *light,* croaking all the summer months, yet hiding themselves in the winter. The Arabic name for this animal is very nearly the same with the Hebrew ضفدع *zafda,* where the letters are the same, the ר *resch* being omitted. It is used as a quadriliteral root in the Arabic language, to signify *froggy,* or *containing frogs:* see *Golius.* But the true etymology seems to be given by Bochart, who says the word is compounded of ضفة *zifa,* a *bank,* and ردغ *rada, mud,* because the frog delights in muddy or marshy places; and that from these two words the noun ضفدع *zafda* is formed, the ر *re* being dropped. In the *Batrochomyomachia* of Homer, the frog has many of its epithets from this very circumstance. Hence Λιμνοχαρις, *delighting in the lake;* Βορβοροκοιτης, *lying* or *engendering in the mud;* Πηλευς and Πηλοβατης, *belonging to the mud, walking in the mud, &c., &c.*

A *frog* is in itself a very harmless animal; but to most people who use it not as an article of food, exceedingly loathsome. God, with equal ease, could have brought *crocodiles, bears, lions,* or *tigers* to have punished these people and their impious king, instead of *frogs, lice, flies, &c.* But had he used any of those formidable animals, the effect would have appeared so commensurate to the cause, that the hand of God might have been forgotten in the punishment; and the people would have been exasperated without being humbled. In the present instance he shows the greatness of his power by making an animal, devoid of every evil quality, the means of a terrible affliction to his enemies. How easy is it, both to the justice and mercy of God, to destroy or save by means of the most despicable and insignificant of instruments! Though he is the Lord of hosts he has no need of powerful armies, the ministry of angels, or the thunderbolts of justice, to punish a sinner or a sinful nation; the *frog* or the

A. M. 2513. B. C. 1491. abundantly, which shall go up and
come into thine house, and into
[d] thy bed-chamber, and upon thy bed, and
into the house of thy servants, and upon thy
people, and into thine ovens, and into thy
[e] kneading-troughs:
4 And the frogs shall come up both on thee,
and upon thy people, and upon all thy servants.
5 And the LORD spake unto Moses, Say
unto Aaron, [f] Stretch forth thine hand with
thy rod over the streams, over the rivers, and
over the ponds, and cause frogs to come up
upon the land of Egypt.
6 And Aaron stretched out his hand over
the waters of Egypt; and [g] the frogs came
up, and covered the land of Egypt. A. M. 2513. B. C. 1491.
7 [h] And the magicians did so with their
enchantments, and brought up frogs upon the
land of Egypt.
8 Then Pharaoh called for Moses and Aaron,
and said, [i] Entreat the LORD that he may take
away the frogs from me, and from my people;
and I will let the people go, that they may
do sacrifice unto the LORD.
9 And Moses said unto Pharaoh, [k] Glory
over me: [l] when shall I entreat for thee, and
for thy servants, and for thy people, [m] to destroy the frogs from thee and thy houses,
that they may remain in the river only?

[d] Psa. cv. 30.—[e] Or, *dough*.—[f] Ch. vii. 19.—[g] Psa. lxxviii. 45; cv. 30.—[h] Ch. vii. 11; Wisd. xvii. 7.—[i] Ch. ix. 28; x. 17; Num. xxi. 7; 1 Kings xiii. 6; Acts viii. 24.—[k] Or, *have this honour over me*, &c.—[l] Or, *against when*.—[m] Heb. *to cut off*.

fly in his hands is a sufficient instrument of vengeance.

Verse 3. *The river shall bring forth frogs abundantly*] The river Nile, which was an object of their adoration, was here one of the instruments of their punishment. The expression, *bring forth abundantly*, not only shows the *vast numbers* of those animals, which should now infest the land, but it seems also to imply that all the *spawn* or *ova* of those animals which were already in the river and marshes, should be brought miraculously to a state of perfection. We may suppose that the animals were already in an embryo existence, but multitudes of them would not have come to a state of perfection had it not been for this miraculous interference. This supposition will appear the more natural when it is considered that the Nile was remarkable for breeding frogs, and such other animals as are principally engendered in such marshy places as must be left in the vicinity of the Nile after its annual inundations.

Into thine ovens] In various parts of the east, instead of what we call *ovens* they dig a hole in the ground, in which they insert a kind of earthen pot, which having sufficiently heated, they stick their cakes to the inside, and when baked remove them and supply their places with others, and so on. To find such places *full of frogs* when they came to heat them, in order to make their bread, must be both disgusting and distressing in the extreme.

Verse 5. *Stretch forth thine hand—over the streams, over the rivers*] The streams and rivers here may refer to the *grand divisions* of the Nile in the Lower Egypt, which were at least *seven*, and to the *canals* by which these were connected; as there were no other streams, &c., but what proceeded from this great river.

Verse 6. *The frogs came up, and covered the land of Egypt.*] In some ancient writers we have examples of a similar plague. The Abderites, according to *Orosius*, and the inhabitants of Pæonia and Dardania, according to *Athenæus*, were obliged to abandon their country on account of the great numbers of frogs by which their land was infested.

Verse 7. *The magicians did so*] A little juggling or dexterity of hand might have been quite sufficient for the imitation of this miracle, because frogs in abundance had already been produced; and some of these kept in readiness might have been brought forward by the magicians, as proofs of their pretended power and equality in influence to Moses and Aaron.

Verse 9. *Glory over me*] התפאר עלי *hithpaer alai.* These words have greatly puzzled commentators in general; and it is not easy to assign their true meaning. The *Septuagint* render the words thus: Ταξαι προς με ποτε, &c., *Appoint unto me when I shall pray, &c.* The *constitue mihi quando* of the *Vulgate* is exactly the same; and in this sense almost all the *versions* understood this place. This countenances the conjectural emendation of *Le Clerc*, who, by the change of a single letter, reading התבאר *hithbaer* for התפאר *hithpaer*, gives the same sense as that in the ancient versions. *Houbigant*, supposing a corruption in the original, amends the reading thus: אתה באר עלי *attah baar-alai—Dic mihi quo tempore, &c.*, "*Tell me* when thou wishest me to pray for thee," &c., which amounts to the same in sense with that proposed by *Le Clerc*. Several of our English versions preserve the same meaning; so in the Saxon Heptateuch, Ƿeƿeтte me anne an dægan; so in Becke's Bible, 1549, "*And Moses sayed unto Pharaoh*, Appoint thou the time unto me." This appears to be the genuine import of the words, and the sense taken in this way is strong and good. We may conceive Moses addressing Pharaoh in this way: "That thou mayest be persuaded that Jehovah alone is the inflicter of these plagues, appoint the time when thou wouldst have the present calamity removed, and I will pray unto God, and thou shalt plainly see from his answer that this is no *casual* affliction, and that in continuing to harden thy heart and resist thou art sinning against God." Nothing could be a fuller proof that this plague was supernatural than the circumstance of Pharaoh's being permitted to assign *himself* the time of its being removed, and its removal at the intercession of Moses according to that appointment. And this is the very

a

A. M. 2513. B. C. 1491.

10 And he said, [n] To-morrow. And he said, *Be it* according to thy word: that thou mayest know that [o] *there is* none like unto the LORD our God.

11 And the frogs shall depart from thee, and from thy houses, and from thy servants, and from thy people; they shall remain in the river only.

12 And Moses and Aaron went out from Pharaoh, and Moses [p] cried unto the LORD, because of the frogs which he had brought against Pharaoh.

13 And the LORD did according to the word of Moses; and the frogs died out of the houses, out of the villages, and out of the fields.

14 And they gathered them together upon heaps: and the land stank.

15 But when Pharaoh saw that there was [q] respite, [r] he hardened his heart, and hearkened not unto them; as the LORD had said.

16 And the LORD said unto Moses, Say unto Aaron, Stretch out thy rod, and smite the dust of the land, that it may become lice throughout all the land of Egypt.

17 And they did so; for Aaron stretched out his hand with his rod, and smote the dust of the earth, and [s] it became lice in man, and in beast; all the dust of the land became lice, throughout all the land of Egypt.

[n] Or, *against to-morrow.*——[o] Chap. ix. 14; Deut. xxxiii. 26; 2 Sam. vii. 22; 1 Chron. xvii. 20; Psa. lxxxvi. 8; Isa. xlvi. 9; Jer. x. 6, 7.——[p] Ver. 40; ch. ix. 33; x. 18; xxxii. 11; James v. 16, 17, 18.——[q] Eccles. viii. 11.——[r] Chap. vii. 14.——[s] Psa. cv. 31.

use made of it by Moses himself, ver. 10, when he says, Be it *according to thy word: that thou mayest know that* there is *none like unto the Lord our God;* and that, consequently, he might no longer trust in his magicians, or in his false gods.

Verse 14. *They gathered them together upon heaps*] The killing of the frogs was a mitigation of the punishment; but the leaving them to rot in the land was a continual proof that such a plague *had* taken place, and that the displeasure of the Lord still continued.

The conjecture of *Calmet* is at least rational: he supposes that the plague of *flies* originated from the plague of *frogs;* that the former deposited their *ova* in the putrid masses, and that from these the innumerable swarms afterwards mentioned were hatched. In vindication of this supposition it may be observed, that God never works a miracle when the end can be accomplished by merely natural means; and in the operations of Divine providence we always find that the *greatest number* of *effects* possible are accomplished by the *fewest causes.* As therefore the natural means for this fourth *plague* had been miraculously provided by the second, the Divine Being had a right to use the instruments which he had already prepared.

The THIRD *plague*—LICE.

Verse 16. *Smite the dust of the land, that it may become lice*] If the vermin commonly designed by this name be intended, it must have been a very dreadful and afflicting plague to the Egyptians, and especially to their priests, who were obliged to shave the hair off every part of their bodies, and to wear a single tunic, that no vermin of this kind might be permitted to harbour about them. See *Herod. in Euterp.*, c. xxxvii., p. 104, edit. *Gale.* Of the nature of these insects it is not necessary to say much. The common louse is very prolific. In the space of twelve days a full-grown female lays one hundred eggs, from which, in the space of six days, about fifty males and as many females are produced. In eighteen days these young females are at their full growth, each of which may lay one hundred eggs, which will be all hatched in six days more. Thus, in the course of six weeks, the parent female may see 5,000 of its own descendants! So mightily does this scourge of *indolence* and *filthiness* increase!

But learned men are not agreed on the signification of the original word כנים *kinnim,* which different copies of the Septuagint render *σκνιφες, σκνιπες,* and *σκνηπες, gnats;* and the Vulgate renders *sciniphes,* which signifies the same.

Mr. Harmer supposes he has found out the true meaning in the word *tarrentes,* mentioned by *Vinisauf,* one of our ancient English writers; who, speaking of the expedition of King Richard I. to the Holy Land, says, that "while the army were marching from Cayphas to Cæsarea, they were greatly distressed every night by certain worms called *tarrentes,* which crept on the ground, and occasioned a very burning heat by most painful punctures; for, being armed with stings, they conveyed a poison which quickly occasioned those who were wounded by them to swell, and was attended with the most acute pain." All this is far fetched. Bochart has endeavoured to prove that the כנים *kinnim* of the text may mean *lice* in the common acceptation of the term, and not *gnats.* 1. Because those in question sprang from the *dust* of the earth, and not from the *waters.* 2. Because they were both on men and cattle, which cannot be spoken of *gnats.* 3. Because their name comes from the radix כון *kun,* which signifies to make *firm, fix, establish,* which can never agree to *gnats, flies,* &c., which are ever *changing their place,* and are almost constantly *on the wing.* 4. Because כנה *kinnah* is the term by which the Talmudists express the *louse,* &c. See his *Hierozoicon,* vol. ii., c. xviii., col. 571. The circumstance of their being *in* man and *in* beast agrees so well with the nature of the *acarus sanguisugus,* commonly called the *tick,* belonging to the seventh order of insects called APTERA, that I am ready to conclude this is the insect meant. This animal buries both its sucker and head equally in man or beast; and can with very great difficulty be extracted before it is grown to its proper size, and filled with the blood and juices of the animal on which

A. M. 2513. B. C. 1491.

18 And [t] the magicians did so
with their enchantments, to bring
forth lice, but they [u] could not: so there were
lice upon man and upon beast.
19 Then the magicians said unto Pharaoh,
This *is* [v] the finger of God: and Pharaoh's
[w] heart was hardened, and he hearkened not
unto them; as the LORD had said.
20 And the LORD said unto Moses, [x] Rise
up early in the morning, and stand before
Pharaoh; (lo, he cometh forth to the water;)
and say unto him, Thus saith the LORD, [y] Let
my people go, that they may
serve me.
21 Else, if thou wilt not let my people go,
behold, I will send [z] swarms *of flies* upon thee,
and upon thy servants, and upon thy people,
and into thy houses: and the houses of the
Egyptians shall be full of swarms *of flies*, and
also the ground whereon they *are*.
22 And [a] I will sever in that day the
land of Goshen, in which my people dwell,
that no swarms *of flies* shall be there; to
the end thou mayest know that I *am*

[t] Ch. vii. 11.——[u] Luke x. 18; Wisd. xvii. 7; 2 Tim. iii. 8, 9.——[v] 1 Sam. vi. 3, 9; Psa. viii. 3; Matt. xii. 28; Luke xi. 20.——[w] Ver. 15.——[x] Chap. vii. 15.——[y] Ver. 1.——[z] Or, *a mixture of* noisome beasts, &c.——[a] Chap. ix. 4, 6, 26; x. 23; xi. 6, 7; xii. 13.

it preys. When fully grown, it has a glossy black oval body: not only horses, cows, and sheep, are infested with it in certain countries, but even the *common people*, especially those who labour in the field, in woods, &c. I know no insect to which the Hebrew term so properly applies. This is the *fixed, established* insect, which will permit itself to be pulled in pieces rather than let go its hold; and this is literally באדם ובבהמה *baadam ubabbehemah*, IN *man and* IN *beast*, burying its trunk and head in the flesh of both. In woodland countries I have seen many *persons* as well as *cattle* grievously infested with these insects.

Verse 18. *The magicians did so*] That is, They tried the utmost of their skill, either to *produce* these insects or to *remove* this plague; *but they could not*, no *juggling* could avail here, because insects must be produced which would *stick to* and *infix* themselves in man and beast, which no kind of *trick* could possibly imitate; and to *remove* them, as some would translate the passage, was to their power equally impossible. If the magicians even acted by spiritual agents, we find from this case that these agents had assigned limits, beyond which they could not go; for every agent in the universe is acting under the *direction* or *control* of the Almighty.

Verse 19. *This* is *the finger of God*] That is, The power and skill of God are here evident. Probably before this the magicians supposed Moses and Aaron to be *conjurers*, like themselves; but now they are convinced that no man could do these miracles which these holy men did, unless God were with him. God permits evil spirits to manifest themselves in a certain way, that men may see that there is a spiritual world, and be on their guard against seduction. He at the same time shows that all these agents are under his control, that men may have confidence in his goodness and power.

The FOURTH *plague*—FLIES.

Verse 21. *Swarms* of flies *upon thee*] It is not easy to ascertain the precise meaning of the original word הערב *hearob*; as the word comes from ערב *arab*, he *mingled*, it may be supposed to express a multitude of various sorts of insects. And if the conjecture be admitted that the putrid frogs became the occasion of this plague, (*different insects* laying their eggs in the bodies of those dead animals, which would soon be hatched, see on verse 14,) then the supposition that a multitude of *different kinds of insects* is meant, will seem the more probable. Though the plague of the locusts was miraculous, yet God both brought it and removed it by natural means; see chap. x. 13–19.

Bochart, who has treated this subject with his usual learning and ability, follows the Septuagint, explaining the original by κυνομυια, the *dog-fly*; which must be particularly hateful to the Egyptians, because they held *dogs* in the highest veneration, and worshipped *Anubis* under the form of a dog. In a case of this kind the authority of the Septuagint is very high, as they translated the Pentateuch in the very place where these plagues happened. But as the Egyptians are well known to have paid religious veneration to all kinds of animals and monsters, whence the poet:—

Omnigenumque deum monstra, et latrator Anubis,

I am inclined to favour the literal construction of the word: for as ערב *ereb*, chap. xii. 38, expresses that *mixed multitude* of different kinds of people who accompanied the Israelites in their departure from Egypt; so here the same term being used, it may have been designed to express a *multitude* of *different kinds of insects*, such as *flies, wasps, hornets*, &c., &c. The ancient Jewish interpreters suppose that all kinds of *beasts* and *reptiles* are intended, such as *wolves, lions, bears, serpents*, &c. Mr. Bate thinks the *raven* is meant, because the original is so understood in other places; and thus he translates it in his literal version of the Pentateuch: but the meaning already given is the most likely. As to the objection against this opinion drawn from ver. 31, *there remained not one*, it can have very little weight, when it is considered that this may as well be spoken of *one* of any of the *different* kinds, as of an *individual* of *one species*.

Verse 22. *I will sever in that day*] הפליתי *hiphleythi*, has been translated by some good critics, *I will miraculously separate*; so the Vulgate: *Faciam mirabilem*, "I will do a marvellous thing." And the Septuagint, παραδοξασω, *I will render illustrious* the land of Goshen in that day; and this he did, by exempting that land, and its inhabitants the Israelites, from the plagues by which he afflicted the land of Egypt

A. M. 2513.
B. C. 1491.

the Lord in the midst of the earth.
23 And I will put [b] a division between my
people and thy people: [c] to-morrow shall this
sign be.
24 And the Lord did so: and [d] there came
a grievous swarm *of flies* into the house of
Pharaoh, and *into* his servants' houses, and
into all the land of Egypt: the land was
[e] corrupted by reason of the swarm *of flies.*
25 And Pharaoh called for Moses and for
Aaron, and said, Go ye, sacrifice to your God in the land.
26 And Moses said, It is not meet so to do,
for we shall sacrifice [f] the abomination of the
Egyptians to the Lord our God: lo, shall
we sacrifice the abomination of the Egyptians
before their eyes, and will they not stone us?
27 We will go [g] three days' journey into
the wilderness, and sacrifice to the Lord our
God, as [h] he shall command us.
28 And Pharaoh said, I will let you go,

[b] Heb. *a redemption.*——[c] Or, *by to-morrow.*——[d] Psa. lxxviii. 45; cv. 31; Wisd. xvi. 9.——[e] Or, *destroyed.*

[f] Gen. xliii. 32; xlvi. 34; Deut. vii. 25, 26; xii. 31.——[g] Chap. iii. 18.——[h] Chap. iii. 12.

Verse 23. *And I will put a division*] פדת *peduth, a redemption,* between my people and thy people; God hereby showing that he had redeemed them from those plagues to which he had abandoned the others.

Verse 24. *The land was corrupted*] Every thing was spoiled, and many of the inhabitants destroyed, being probably stung to death by these venomous insects. This seems to be intimated by the psalmist, "He sent divers sorts of flies among them, which DEVOURED them," Psa. lxxviii. 45.

In ancient times, when political, domestic, and personal cleanliness was but little attended to, and offal of different kinds permitted to corrupt in the streets and breed vermin, flies multiplied exceedingly, so that we read in ancient authors of whole districts being laid waste by them; hence different people had deities, whose office it was to defend them against flies. Among these we may reckon *Baalzebub*, the *fly-god* of Ekron; *Hercules, muscarum abactor*, Hercules, the expeller of flies, of the Romans; the *Muagrus* of the *Eleans*, whom they invoked against pestilential swarms of flies; and hence *Jupiter*, the supreme god of the heathens, had the epithets of Απομυιος and Μυωδης, because he was supposed to *expel flies*, and *defend* his worshippers against them. See *Dodd.*

Verse 25. *Sacrifice to your God in the land.*] That is, Ye shall not leave Egypt, but I shall cause your worship to be tolerated here.

Verse 26. *We shall sacrifice the abomination of the Egyptians*] That is, The animals which they hold sacred, and will not permit to be slain, are those which our customs require us to sacrifice to our God; and should we do this in Egypt the people would rise in a mass, and stone us to death. Perhaps few people were more superstitious than the Egyptians. Almost every production of nature was an object of their religious worship: the sun, moon, planets, stars, the river Nile, animals of all sorts, from the human being to the monkey, dog, cat, and ibis, and even the onions and leeks which grew in their gardens. Jupiter was adored by them under the form of a *ram*, Apollo under the form of a *crow*, Bacchus under that of a *goat*, and Juno under that of a *heifer*. The reason why the Egyptians worshipped those animals is given by Eusebius, viz., that when the giants made war on the gods, they were obliged to take refuge in Egypt, and assume the shapes or disguise themselves under different kinds of animals in order to escape. Jupiter hid himself in the body of a ram, Apollo in that of a crow, Bacchus in a goat, Diana in a cat, Juno in a white heifer, Venus in a fish, and Mercury in the bird ibis; all which are summed up by Ovid in the following lines:—

Duxque gregis fit Jupiter ———
Delius in corvo, proles Semeleïa capro,
Fele soror Phœbi, nivea Saturnia vacca,
Pisce Venus latuit, Cyllenius ibidis alis.
METAM., I. v., fab. v., I. 326.

How the gods fled to Egypt's slimy soil,
And hid their heads beneath the banks of Nile;
How *Typhon* from the conquer'd skies pursued
Their routed godheads to the seven-mouth'd flood;
Forced every god, his fury to escape,
Some beastly form to take, or earthly shape.
Jove, so she sung, was changed into a *ram*,
From whence the horns of Libyan *Ammon* came;
Bacchus a *goat*, *Apollo* was a *crow*,
Phœbe a *cat*, the wife of *Jove* a *cow*,
Whose hue was whiter than the falling snow;
Mercury, to a nasty *ibis* turn'd,
The change obscene, afraid of *Typhon* mourn'd
While *Venus* from a *fish* protection craves,
And once more plunges in her native waves
MAYNWARING.

These animals therefore became sacred to them on account of the deities, who, as the fable reports, had taken refuge in them. Others suppose that the reason why the Egyptians would not sacrifice or kill those creatures was their belief in the doctrine of the metempsychosis, or transmigration of souls; for they feared lest in killing an animal they should kill a relative or a friend. This doctrine is still held by the Hindoos.

Verse 27. *And sacrifice to the Lord—as he shall command us.*] It is very likely that neither Moses nor Aaron knew as yet in what manner God would be worshipped; and they expected to receive a direct revelation from him relative to this subject, when they should come into the wilderness.

Verse 28. *I will let you go—only ye shall not go very far away*] Pharaoh relented because the hand of God was heavy upon him; but he was not willing to give up his *gain*. The Israelites were very *profit-*

A. M. 2513.
B. C. 1491.

that ye may sacrifice to the LORD
your God in the wilderness; only
ye shall not go very far away: [i] entreat for me.
29 And Moses said, Behold, I go out from
thee, and I will entreat the LORD that the
swarms *of flies* may depart from Pharaoh,
from his servants, and from his people, to-
morrow: but let not Pharaoh [k] deal deceitfully
any more in not letting the people go to sacrifice to the LORD.

[i] Ver. 8; chap. ix. 28; 1 Kings xiii. 6.

30 And Moses went out from
Pharaoh, and [l] entreated the LORD.

A. M. 2513.
B. C. 1491.

31 And the LORD did according to the word
of Moses; and he removed the swarms
of flies from Pharaoh, from his servants,
and from his people; there remained not
one.
32 And Pharaoh [m] hardened his heart
at this time also, neither would he let the
people go.

[k] Ver. 15.—[l] Ver. 12.—[m] Ver. 15; chap. iv. 21.

able to him; they were *slaves* of the state, and their hard labour was very productive: hence he professed a willingness, first to *tolerate* their religion in the land, (ver. 25;) or to permit them to go into the wilderness, so that they went not far away, and would soon return. How ready is foolish man, when the hand of God presses him sore, to compound with his Maker! He will consent to give up some sins, provided God will permit him to keep others.

Entreat for me.] Exactly similar to the case of Simon Magus, who, like Pharaoh, fearing the Divine judgments, begged an interest in the prayers of Peter, Acts viii. 24.

Verse 31. *The Lord did according to the word of Moses*] How powerful is prayer! God permits his servant to prescribe even the manner and time in which he shall work.

He removed the swarms] Probably by means of a strong wind, which swept them into the sea.

Verse 32. *Pharaoh hardened his heart at this time also*] See ver. 15. This hardening was the mere effect of his self-determining obstinacy. He preferred his *gain* to the will and command of Jehovah, and God made his obstinacy the means of showing forth his own power and providence in a supereminent degree.

1. As every false religion proves there is a true one, as a *copy*, however marred or imperfect, shows there was an *original* from which it was taken, so false miracles prove that there were genuine miracles, and that God chooses at particular times, for the most important purposes, to invert the established order of nature, and thus prove his omnipotence and universal agency. That the miracles wrought at this time were *real* we have the fullest proof. The waters, for instance, were not *turned into blood* in appearance merely, but were really thus changed. Hence the people could not drink of them; and as blood in a very short time, when exposed to the air, becomes putrid, so did the bloody waters; therefore all the fish that were in the river died.

2. No human power or ingenuity could produce such *frogs* as annoyed the land of Egypt. This also was a real, not an imaginary, plague. Innumerable multitudes of these animals were produced for the purpose; and the heaps of their dead carcasses, which putrefied and infected the land, at once demonstrated the reality of the miracle.

3. The *lice* both on man and beast through the whole land, and the innumerable *swarms of flies*, gave such proofs of their reality as to put the truth of these miracles out of question for ever. It was necessary that this point should be fully proved, that both the Egyptians and Israelites might see the finger of God in these awful works.

4. To superficial observers only do "Moses and the magicians appear to be nearly matched." The power of God was shown in producing and removing the plagues. In certain cases the magicians imitated the production of a plague, but they had no power to remove any. They could not seem to *remove* the bloody colour, nor the putrescency from the waters through which the fish were destroyed, though they could imitate the colour itself; they could not *remove* the frogs, the lice, or swarms of flies, though they could imitate the former and latter; they could by dexterity of hand or diabolic influence produce serpents, but they could not bring one forward that could swallow up the rod of Aaron. In every respect they fall infinitely short of the power and wonderful energy evidenced in the miracles of Moses and Aaron. The opposition therefore of those men served only as a foil to set off the excellence of that power by which these messengers of God acted.

5. The courage, constancy, and faith of Moses, are worthy of the most serious consideration. Had he not been fully satisfied of the truth and certainty of his Divine mission, he could not have encountered such a host of difficulties; had he not been certain of the issue, he could not have persevered amidst so many discouraging circumstances; and had he not had a deep acquaintance with God, his faith in every trial must have necessarily failed. So strong was this grace in him that he could even pledge his Maker to the performance of works concerning which he had not as yet consulted him! He therefore let Pharaoh fix the very time on which he would wish to have the plague removed; and when this was done, he went to God by faith and prayer to obtain this new miracle; and God in the most exact and circumstantial manner fulfilled the word of his servant.

6. From all this let us learn that there is a God who worketh in the earth; that universal nature is under his control; that he can alter, suspend, counteract, or invert its general laws whensoever he pleases; and that he can save or destroy by the most feeble and most contemptible instruments. We should therefore

deeply reverence his eternal power and Godhead, and look with respect on every creature he has made, as the meanest of them may, in his hand, become the instrument of our salvation or our ruin.

7. Let us not imagine that God has so bound himself to work by general laws, that those destructions cannot take place which designate a particular providence. Pharaoh and the Egyptians are confounded, afflicted, routed, and ruined, while the land of Goshen and the Israelites are free from every plague! No blood appears in their streams; no frogs, lice, nor flies, in all their borders! They trusted in the true God, and could not be confounded. Reader, how secure mayest thou rest if thou hast this God for thy friend! He was the Protector and Friend of the Israelites through the blood of *that covenant* which is the very charter of *thy* salvation: trust in and pray to him as Moses did, and then Satan and his angels shall be bruised under thy feet, and thou shalt not only be preserved from every plague, but be crowned with his loving kindness and tender mercy. He is the same to-day that he was yesterday, and shall continue the same for ever. Hallelujah, the Lord God omnipotent reigneth!

CHAPTER IX.

The Lord sends Moses to Pharaoh to inform him that, if he did not let the Israelites depart, a destructive pestilence *should be sent among his cattle,* 1–3; *while the cattle of the Israelites should be preserved,* 4. *The next day this pestilence, which was the* fifth *plague, is sent, and all the cattle of the Egyptians die,* 5, 6. *Though Pharaoh finds that not one of the cattle of the Israelites had died, yet, through hardness of heart, he refuses to let the people go,* 7. *Moses and Aaron are commanded to sprinkle handfuls of ashes from the furnace, that the* sixth *plague, that of* boils *and* blains, *might come on man and beast,* 8, 9; *which having done, the plague takes place,* 10. *The magicians cannot stand before this plague, which they can neither imitate nor remove,* 11. *Pharaoh's heart is again hardened,* 12. *God's awful message to Pharaoh, with the threat of more severe plagues than before,* 13–17. *The* seventh *plague of* rain, hail, *and* fire *threatened,* 18. *The Egyptians commanded to house their cattle that they might not be destroyed,* 19. *Those who feared the word of the Lord brought home their servants and cattle, and those who did not regard that word left their cattle and servants in the fields,* 20, 21. *The storm of hail, thunder, and lightning takes place,* 22–24. *It nearly desolates the whole land of Egypt,* 25, *while the land of Goshen escapes,* 26. *Pharaoh confesses his sin, and begs an interest in the prayers of Moses and Aaron,* 27, 28. *Moses promises to intercede for him, and while he promises that the storm shall cease, he foretells the continuing obstinacy of both himself and his servants,* 29, 30. *The flax and barley, being in a state of maturity, are destroyed by the tempest,* 31; *while the wheat and the rye, not being grown up, are preserved,* 32. *Moses obtains a cessation of the storm,* 33. *Pharaoh and his servants, seeing this, harden their hearts, and refuse to let the people go,* 34, 35.

A. M. 2513.
B. C. 1491.

THEN the LORD said unto Moses, [a] Go in unto Pharaoh, and tell him, Thus saith the LORD God of the Hebrews, Let my people go, that they may serve me.

2 For if thou [b] refuse to let *them* go, and wilt hold them still,

3 Behold, the [c] hand of the LORD is upon thy cattle which *is* in the field, upon the horses, upon the asses, upon the camels, upon

A. M. 2513.
B. C. 1491.

[a] Chap. viii. 1.—[b] Chap. viii. 2.

[c] Chap. vii. 4.

NOTES ON CHAP. IX.

Verse 1. *The* LORD *God of the Hebrews*] It is very likely that the term Lord, יהוה *Yehovah*, is used here to point out particularly his eternal power and Godhead; and that the term God, אלהי *Elohey*, is intended to be understood in the sense of Supporter, Defender, Protector, &c. Thus saith the self-existent, omnipotent, and eternal Being, the Supporter and Defender of the Hebrews, "Let my people go, that they may worship me."

The FIFTH *plague—the* MURRAIN.

Verse 3. *The hand of the Lord*] The power of God manifested in judgment.

Upon the horses] סוסים *susim.* This is the first place the *horse* is mentioned; a creature for which Egypt and Arabia were always famous. סס *sus* is supposed to have the same meaning with שש *sas*, which signifies to be *active, brisk,* or *lively,* all which are proper appellatives of the horse, especially in Arabia and Egypt. Because of their activity and swiftness they were sacrificed and dedicated to the sun, and perhaps it was principally on this account that God prohibited the use of them among the Israelites.

A very grievous murrain.] The murrain is a very contagious disease among cattle, the symptoms of which are a hanging down and swelling of the head, abundance of gum in the eyes, rattling in the throat, difficulty of breathing, palpitation of the heart, staggering, a hot breath, and a shining tongue; which symptoms prove that a general inflammation has taken place. The original word דבר *deber* is variously translated. The *Septuagint* have θανατος, *death;* the *Vulgate* has *pestis,* a *plague* or *pestilence;* the old Saxon version, cpealme, from cpealan, to *die,* any *fatal disease.* Our English word *murrain* comes either from the French

A. M. 2513. B. C. 1491.

the oxen, and upon the sheep:
there shall be a very grievous
murrain.
4 And [d] the LORD shall sever between the
cattle of Israel, and the cattle of Egypt: and
there shall nothing die of all *that is* the children's of Israel.
5 And the LORD appointed a set time, saying, To-morrow the LORD shall do this thing
in the land.
6 And the LORD did that thing on the morrow, and [e] all the cattle of Egypt died: but
of the cattle of the children of Israel died not
one.
7 And Pharaoh sent, and, behold, there was
not one of the cattle of the Israelites dead.
And [f] the heart of Pharaoh was hardened,
and he did not let the people go.
8 And the LORD said unto Moses
and unto Aaron, Take to you handfuls of ashes of the furnace, and let Moses
sprinkle it toward the heaven in the sight of
Pharaoh.
9 And it shall become small dust in all the
land of Egypt, and shall be [g] a boil breaking
forth *with* blains upon man, and upon beast,
throughout all the land of Egypt.
10 And they took ashes of the furnace, and
stood before Pharaoh; and Moses sprinkled
it up toward heaven; and it became [h] a boil
breaking forth *with* blains upon man and
upon beast.
11 And the [i] magicians could not stand
before Moses, because of the boils; for the
boil was upon the magicians, and upon all the
Egyptians.

[d] Chapter viii. 22.——[e] Psa. lxxviii. 50.——[f] Chapter vii. 14; viii. 32.——[g] Rev. xvi. 2.——[h] Deuteronomy xxviii. 27.——[i] Chapter viii. 18, 19; 2 Tim. iii. 9.

mourir, to *die*, or from the Greek *μαραινω maraino*, to *grow lean, waste away*. The term *mortality* would be the nearest in sense to the original, as no particular disorder is specified by the Hebrew word.

Verse 4. *The Lord shall sever*] See on chap. viii. 22.

Verse 5. *To-morrow the Lord shall do this*] By thus foretelling the evil, he showed his prescience and power; and from this both the Egyptians and Hebrews must see that the mortality that ensued was no casualty, but the effect of a predetermined purpose in the Divine justice.

Verse 6. *All the cattle of Egypt died*] That is, All the cattle that did die belonged to the Egyptians, but not one died that belonged to the Israelites, ver. 4 and 6. That the whole stock of cattle belonging to the Egyptians did not die we have the fullest proof, because there were cattle both to be killed and saved alive in the ensuing plague, ver. 19–25. By this judgment the Egyptians must see the vanity of the whole of their national worship, when they found the animals which they not only held sacred but deified, slain without distinction among the common herd, by a pestilence sent from the hand of Jehovah. One might naturally suppose that after this the animal worship of the Egyptians could never more maintain its ground.

Verse 7. *And Pharaoh sent, &c.*] Finding so many of his own cattle and those of his subjects slain, he sent to see whether the mortality had reached to the cattle of the Israelites, that he might know whether this were a judgment inflicted by their God, and probably designing to replace the lost cattle of the Egyptians with those of the Israelites.

The SIXTH *plague—the* BOILS *and* BLAINS.

Verse 8. *Handfuls of ashes of the furnace*] As one part of the oppression of the Israelites consisted in their labour in the brick-kilns, some have observed a congruity between the *crime* and the *punishment*. The *furnaces*, in the labour of which they oppressed the Hebrews, now yielded the instruments of their punishment; for every particle of those *ashes*, formed by unjust and oppressive labour, seemed to be a boil or a blain on the tyrannic king and his cruel and hard-hearted people.

Verse 9. *Shall be a boil*] שחין *shechin*. This word is generally expounded, *an inflammatory swelling*, a *burning boil*; one of the most poignant afflictions, not immediately mortal, that can well affect the surface of the human body. If a single boil on any part of the body throws the whole system into a fever, what anguish must a multitude of them on the body at the same time occasion!

Breaking forth with *blains*] אבעבעת *ababuoth*, supposed to come from בעה *baah*, to *swell, bulge out*; any *inflammatory swelling, node*, or *pustule*, in any part of the body, but more especially in the more glandular parts, the neck, arm-pits, groin, &c. The Septuagint translate it thus: Και εσται ἑλκη φλυκτιδες αναζεουσαι· *And it shall be an ulcer with burning pustules.* It seems to have been a disorder of an *uncommon* kind, and hence it is called by way of distinction, *the botch of Egypt*, Deut. xxviii. 27, perhaps never known before in that or any other country. *Orosius* says that in the sixth plague "all the people were blistered, that the blisters burst with tormenting pain, and that worms issued out of them." Ðæt eall folc wæs on blædran, ⁊ ða wæron swiðe hreoplice berstende, and ða worms utfionde.—*Alfred's Oros.*, lib. i., c. vii.

Verse 11. *The boil was upon the magicians*] They could not produce a similar malady by throwing ashes in the air; and they could neither remove the plague from the people, nor from their own tormented flesh. Whether they perished in this plague we know not but they are no more mentioned. If they were not destroyed by this awful judgment, they at least left the field, and no longer contended with these messengers of God. The triumph of God's power was now complete, and both the Hebrews and Egyptians must see

A. M. 2513.
B. C. 1491.

12 And the LORD hardened the heart of Pharaoh, and he hearkened not unto them; [k] as the LORD had spoken unto Moses.

13 And the LORD said unto Moses, [l] Rise up early in the morning, and stand before Pharaoh, and say unto him, Thus saith the LORD God of the Hebrews, Let my people go, that they may serve me.

14 For I will at this time send all my plagues upon thine heart, and upon thy servants, and upon thy people; [m] that thou mayest know that *there is* none like me in all the earth.

15 For now I will [n] stretch out my hand, that I may smite thee and thy people with pestilence: and thou shalt be cut off from the earth.

16 And in very deed for [o] this *cause* have I [p] raised thee up, for to show *in* thee my power, and that my name may be declared throughout all the earth.

17 As yet exaltest thou thyself against my people, that thou wilt not let them go?

18 Behold, to-morrow about this time I will cause it to rain a very grievous hail, such as hath not been in Egypt since the foundation thereof even until now.

[k] Chap. iv. 21.—[l] Chapter viii. 20.—[m] Chapter viii. 10. [n] Chap. iii. 20.

[o] Rom. ix. 17; see chap. xiv. 17; Prov. xvi. 4; 1 Peter ii. 9. [p] *Heb. made thee stand.*

that there was neither might, nor wisdom, nor counsel against the Lord; and that, as universal nature acknowledged his power, devils and men must fail before him.

Verse 15. *For now I will stretch out my hand*] In the Hebrew the verbs are in the *past* tense, and not in the *future*, as our translation improperly expresses them, by which means a contradiction appears in the text; for neither Pharaoh nor his people *were smitten by a pestilence*, nor was he by any kind of mortality *cut off from the earth*. It is true the *first-born* were slain by a destroying angel, and Pharaoh himself was drowned in the Red Sea; but these judgments do not appear to be referred to in *this* place. If the words be translated, as they ought, in the subjunctive mood, or in the *past* instead of the *future*, this seeming contradiction to facts, as well as all ambiguity, will be avoided: *For if now* I HAD STRETCHED OUT (שלחתי *shalachti, had set forth*) *my hand, and had smitten thee* (ואך אותך *vaach otheca*) *and thy people with the pestilence, thou* SHOULDST HAVE BEEN *cut off* (תכחד *ticcached*) *from the earth*. 16. *But truly, on this very account, have I caused thee to* SUBSIST, (העמדתיך *heemadticha*,) *that I* MIGHT *cause thee to see my power*, (הראתך את כחי *harotheca eth cochi*,) *and that my name* MIGHT *be declared throughout all the earth*, (or, בכל הארץ *becol haarets, in all* THIS LAND.) See *Ainsworth* and *Houbigant*.

Thus God gave this impious king to know that it was in consequence of his especial providence that both he and his people had not been already destroyed by means of the *past* plagues; but God had preserved him for this very purpose, that he might have a farther opportunity of manifesting that he, Jehovah, was the only true God, for the full conviction both of the Hebrews and Egyptians, that the former might follow and the latter fear before him. Judicious critics of almost all creeds have agreed to translate the original as above, a translation which it not only can bear but requires, and which is in strict conformity to both the Septuagint and Targum. Neither the Hebrew העמדתיך *heemadticha, I have caused thee to stand*; nor the apostle's translation of it, Rom. ix. 17, εξηγειρα σε, *I have raised thee*; nor that of the Septuagint, ἑνεκεν τουτου διετηρηθης, *on this account art thou preserved*, viz., in the past plagues; can countenance that most exceptionable meaning put on the words by certain commentators, viz., "That God ordained or appointed Pharaoh *from all eternity*, by certain means, to *this end*; that he made him to exist in time; that he raised him to the throne; promoted him to that high honour and dignity; that he preserved him, and did not cut him off *as yet*; that he *strengthened* and *hardened* his heart; *irritated, provoked*, and *stirred him up against his people* Israel, and suffered him to go all the lengths he did go in his obstinacy and rebellion; all which was done *to show in him his power* in destroying him in the Red Sea. The sum of which is, that this man was raised up by God *in every sense* for God to show his power in his destruction." So *man* speaks; thus GOD hath not spoken. See *Henry* on the place.

Verse 17. *As yet exaltest thou thyself against my people*] So it appears that at this time he might have submitted, and thus prevented his own destruction.

The SEVENTH *plague—the* HAIL.

Verse 18. *To-morrow about this time*] The time of this plague is marked thus circumstantially to show Pharaoh that Jehovah was Lord of heaven and earth, and that the *water*, the *fire*, the *earth*, and the *air*, which were all objects of Egyptian idolatry, were the creatures of his power; and subservient to his will; and that, far from being able to help them, they were now, in the hands of God, instruments of their destruction.

To rain a very grievous hail] *To rain hail* may appear to some superficial observers as an unphilosophical mode of expression, but nothing can be more correct. "Drops of rain falling through a cold region of the atmosphere are frozen and converted into hail;" and thus the *hail* is produced by *rain*. When it begins to fall it is *rain*; when it is falling it is converted into *hail*; thus it is literally true that *it rains hail*. The farther a hail-stone falls the larger it generally is, because in its descent it meets with innumerable particles of water, which, becoming attached to it, are

A. M. 2513. B. C. 1491.

19 Send therefore now, *and* gather thy cattle, and all that thou hast in the field; *for upon* every man and beast which shall be found in the field, and shall not be brought home, the hail shall come down upon them, and they shall die.

20 He that feared the word of the LORD among the servants of Pharaoh made his servants and his cattle flee into the houses:

21 And he that [q] regarded not the word of the LORD left his servants and his cattle in the field.

22 And the LORD said unto Moses, Stretch forth thine hand toward heaven, that there may be [r] hail in all the land of Egypt, upon man, and upon beast, and upon every herb of the field, throughout the land of Egypt.

23 And Moses stretched forth his rod toward heaven: and [s] the LORD sent thunder and hail, and the fire ran along upon the ground; and the LORD rained hail upon the land of Egypt.

A. M. 2513. B. C. 1491.

24 So there was hail, and fire mingled with the hail, very grievous, such as there was none like it in all the land of Egypt since it became a nation.

25 And the hail smote throughout all the land of Egypt all that *was* in the field, both man and beast; and the hail [t] smote every herb of the field, and brake every tree of the field.

26 [u] Only in the land of Goshen, where the children of Israel *were*, was there no hail.

27 And Pharaoh sent and called for Moses and Aaron, and said unto them, [v] I have sinned this time: [w] the LORD *is* righteous, and I and my people *are* wicked.

28 [x] Entreat the LORD (for *it is* enough) that there be no *more* [y] mighty thunderings

[q] Heb. *set not his heart unto;* chap. vii. 23.——[r] Rev. xvi. 21. [s] Josh. x. 11; Psa. xviii. 13; lxxviii. 47; cv. 32; cxlviii. 8; Isa. xxx. 30; Ezek. xxxviii. 22; Rev. viii. 7.——[t] Psa. cv. 33. [u] Chap. viii. 22; ix. 4, 6; x. 23; xi. 7; xii. 13; Isa. xxxii. 18, 19.——[v] Chap. x. 16.——[w] 2 Chron. xii. 6; Psa. cxxix. 4; cxlv. 17; Lam. i. 18; Dan. ix. 14.——[x] Ch. viii. 8, 28; x. 17; Acts viii. 24.——[y] Heb. *voices of God;* Psa. xxix. 3, 4.

also frozen, and thus its bulk is continually increasing till it reaches the earth. In the case in question, if natural means were at all used, we may suppose a highly electrified state of an atmosphere loaded with vapours, which, becoming condensed and frozen, and having a considerable space to fall through, were of an unusually large size. Though this was a supernatural storm, there have been many of a natural kind, that have been exceedingly dreadful. A storm of hail fell near Liverpool, in Lancashire, in the year 1795, which greatly damaged the vegetation, broke windows, &c., &c. Many of the stones measured five inches in circumference. Dr. Halley mentions a similar storm of hail in Lancashire, Cheshire, &c., in 1697, April 29, that for *sixty* miles in length and *two* miles in breadth did immense damage, by splitting trees, killing fowls and all small animals, knocking down men and horses, &c., &c. Mezeray, in his History of France, says "that in Italy, in 1510, there was for some time a horrible darkness, thicker than that of night, after which the clouds broke into thunder and lightning, and there fell a shower of hail-stones which destroyed all the beasts, birds, and even fish of the country. It was attended with a strong smell of sulphur, and the stones were of a bluish colour, some of them weighing one hundred pounds' weight." The Almighty says to Job: "Hast thou seen the treasures of the hail, which I have reserved against the time of trouble, against the day of battle and war?" Job, chap. xxxviii. 22, 23. While God has such artillery at his command, how soon may he desolate a country or a world! See the account of a remarkable hail-storm in Josh. x. 11.

Verse 19. *Send—now,* and *gather thy cattle*] So in the midst of judgment, God remembered mercy. The miracle should be wrought that they might know he was the Lord; but all the lives both of men and beasts might have been saved, had Pharaoh and his servants taken the warning so mercifully given them. While some regarded not the word of the Lord, others feared it, and their cattle and their servants were saved. See ver. 20, 21.

Verse 23. *The Lord sent thunder*] קלת *koloth, voices;* but loud, repeated peals of thunder are meant.

And the fire ran along upon the ground] ותהלך אש ארצה *vattihalac esh aretsah, and the fire walked upon the earth.* It was not a sudden flash of lightning, but a devouring fire, *walking* through every part, destroying both animals and vegetables; and its progress was irresistible.

Verse 24. *Hail, and fire mingled with the hail*] It is generally allowed that the electric fluid is essential to the formation of hail. On this occasion it was supplied in a supernatural abundance; for streams of fire seem to have accompanied the descending hail, so that herbs and trees, beasts and men, were all destroyed by them.

Verse 26. *Only in the land of Goshen—was there no hail.*] What a signal proof of a most particular providence! Surely both the Hebrews and Egyptians profited by this display of the *goodness* and *severity* of God.

Verse 27. *The Lord* is *righteous, and I and my people* are *wicked.*] The original is very emphatic: *The Lord is* THE RIGHTEOUS ONE, (הצדיק *hatstsaddik,*) *and I and my people are* THE SINNERS, (הרשעים *hareshaim;*) i. e., He is *alone* righteous, and we *alone* are transgressors. Who could have imagined that after such an acknowledgment and confession, Pharaoh should have again hardened his heart?

Verse 28. It is *enough*] There is no need of any farther plague; I submit to the authority of Jehovah, and will rebel no more.

A. M. 2513.
B. C. 1491.
and hail; and I will let you go, and ye shall stay no longer.

29 And Moses said unto him, As soon as I am gone out of the city, I will [z] spread abroad my hands unto the LORD; *and* the thunder shall cease, neither shall there be any more hail; that thou mayest know how that the [a] earth *is* the LORD's.

[z] 1 Kings viii. 22, 38; Psa. cxliii. 6; Isa. i. 15. — [a] Psa. xxiv. 1; 1 Cor. x. 26, 28.

Mighty thunderings] קלת אלהים *koloth Elohim*, *voices of God*;—that is, superlatively loud thunder. So *mountains of God* (Psa. xxxvi. 6) means exceeding high mountains. So *a prince of God* (Gen. xxiii. 6) means a mighty prince. See a description of *thunder*, Psa. xxix. 3–8: "The VOICE OF THE LORD is upon the waters: the God of glory *thundereth*; the Lord is upon many waters. The *voice of the Lord* is powerful; the *voice of the Lord* is full of majesty. The *voice of the Lord* breaketh the cedars. The *voice of the Lord* divideth the flames of fire. The *voice of the Lord* shaketh the wilderness," &c. The production of rain by the electric spark is alluded to in a very beautiful manner, Jer. x. 13: *When he uttereth his voice, there is a multitude of waters in the heavens.* See the note on Gen. vii. 11, and viii. 1.

Verse 29. *I will spread abroad my hands*] That is, I will make *supplication* to God that he may remove this plague. This may not be an improper place to make some observations on the ancient manner of approaching the Divine Being in prayer. *Kneeling down, stretching out of the hands,* and *lifting them up* to heaven, were in frequent use among the Hebrews in their religious worship. SOLOMON *kneeled down* on his knees, and *spread forth his hands to heaven*; 2 Chron. vi. 13. So DAVID, Psa. cxliii. 6: *I stretch forth my hands unto thee.* So EZRA: *I fell upon my knees, and spread out my hands unto the Lord my God*; chap. ix. 5. See also JOB xi. 13: *If thou prepare thine heart, and stretch out thy hands towards him.* Most nations who pretended to any kind of worship made use of the same means in approaching the objects of their adoration, viz., *kneeling down* and *stretching out their hands*; which custom it is very likely they borrowed from the people of God. *Kneeling* was ever considered to be the proper posture of supplication, as it expresses *humility, contrition,* and *subjection.* If the person to whom the supplication was addressed was within reach, the supplicant caught him by the knees; for as among the ancients the *forehead* was consecrated to *genius*, the *ear* to *memory*, and the *right hand* to *faith*, so the *knees* were consecrated to *mercy*. Hence those who entreated favour fell at and caught hold of the knees of the person whose kindness they supplicated. This mode of supplication is particularly referred to in the following passages in Homer:—

Των νυν μιν μνησασα παρεζεο, και λαβε γουνων.
Iliad i., ver. 407.

Now therefore, of these things reminding Jove,
Embrace his knees. COWPER.

To which the following answer is made:—

Και τοτ' επειτα τοι ειμι Διος ποτι χαλκοβατες δω,
Και μιν γουνασομαι, και μιν πεισεσθαι οϊω.
Iliad i., ver. 426.

Then will I to Jove's brazen-floor'd abode,
That I may *clasp his knees*; and much misdeem
Of my endeavour, or my prayer shall speed. Id.

See the issue of thus addressing Jove, Ibid., ver. 500–502, and ver. 511, &c.

In the same manner we find our Lord accosted, Matt. xvii. 14: *There came to him a certain man, kneeling down to him, γονυπετων αυτον, falling down at his knees.*

As to the *lifting up* or *stretching out of the hands*, (often joined to kneeling,) of which we have seen already several instances, and of which we have a very remarkable one in this book, chap. xvii. 11, where the *lifting up* or *stretching out* of the hands of Moses was the means of Israel's prevailing over Amalek; we find many examples of both in ancient authors Thus HOMER:—

Εσθλον γαρ Διι χειρας ανασχεμεν, αι κ' ελεηση.
Iliad xxiv., ver. 301.

For right it is to *spread abroad* the hands
To Jove for mercy.

Also VIRGIL:—

Corripio e stratis corpus, TENDOQUE SUPINAS
AD CŒLUM *cum voce* MANUS, *et munera libo.*
Æneid iii., ver. 176.

I started from my bed, and *raised on high*
My hands and voice in rapture to the sky;
And pour libations. PITT.

Dixerat: et GENUA AMPLEXUS, *genibusque volutans*
Hærebat. Ibid., ver. 607.

Then *kneel'd* the wretch, and *suppliant clung around*
My knees with tears, and grovell'd on the ground. Id.

——— *media inter numina divum*
Multa Jovem MANIBUS SUPPLEX *orasse* SUPINIS.
Ibid. iv., ver. 204.

Amidst the statues of the gods he stands,
And spreading forth to Jove *his lifted hands.* Id.

Et DUPLICES *cum voce* MANUS *ad sidera* TENDIT.
Ibid. x., ver. 667.

And *lifted both his hands* and voice *to heaven.*

In some cases the person petitioning came forward, and either sat in the dust or kneeled on the ground, placing his *left hand on the knee* of him from whom he expected the favour, while he *touched the person's chin* with his *right.* We have an instance of this also in HOMER:—

Και ρα παροιθ' αυτοιο καθεζετο, και λαβε γουνων
Σκαιη· δεξιτερη δ' αρ' ὑπ' ανθερεωνος ἑλουσα.
Iliad i., ver. 500.

Suppliant the goddess stood: *one hand she placed*
Beneath his chin, and *one his knee embraced.* POPE.

A. M. 2513.
B. C. 1491.
30 But as for thee and thy servants, [b] I know that ye will not yet
fear the LORD God.
31 And the flax and the barley was smitten:
[c] for the barley *was* in the ear, and A. M. 2513 B. C. 1491.
the flax *was* bolled.
32 But the wheat and the rye were not
smitten: for they *were* [d] not grown up.

[b] Isa. xxvi. 10.——[c] Ruth i. 22; ii. 23.——[d] Heb. *hidden*, or *dark*.

When the supplicant could not approach the person to whom he prayed, as where a *deity* was the object of the prayer, he washed his hands, made an offering, and kneeling down, either *stretched out both his hands to heaven*, or *laid them upon the offering* or *sacrifice*, or *upon the altar*. Thus *Homer* represents the priest of Apollo praying :—

> *Χερνιψαντο δ' επειτα, και ουλοχυτας ανελοντο.*
> *Τοισιν δε Χρυσης μεγαλ' ευχετο, χειρας ανασχων.*
>
> Iliad i., ver. 449.

With *water purify their hands*, and take
The *sacred offering* of the salted cake,
While thus, with *arms* devoutly *raised in air*,
And solemn voice, the priest *directs his prayer*.

POPE.

How necessary ablutions of the whole body, and of the hands particularly, accompanied with offerings and sacrifices were, under the law, every reader of the Bible knows: see especially chap. xxix. 1–4, where Aaron and his sons were commanded to be washed, previously to their performing the priest's office; and chap. xxx. 19–21, where it is said: "Aaron and his sons shall *wash their hands*—that they die not." See also Lev. xvii. 15. When the high priest among the Jews blessed the people, *he lifted up his hands*, Lev. ix. 22. And the Israelites, when they presented a sacrifice to God, *lifted up their hands* and *placed them on the head of the victim*: "If any man of you bring an offering unto the Lord—of the cattle of the herd, and of the flock—he shall *put his hand upon the head of the burnt-offering*, and it shall be accepted for him, to make atonement for him;" Lev. i. 2–4. To these circumstances the apostle alludes, 1 Tim. ii. 8: "I will therefore that men pray everywhere, *lifting up holy hands*, without wrath and doubting." In the apostle's word *επαιροντας*, *lifting up*, there is a manifest reference to *stretching out the hands* to *place them* either *on the altar* or *on* the *head of the victim*. Four things were signified by this lifting up of the hands. 1. It was the posture of supplication, and expressed a strong invitation—*Come to my help*; 2. It expressed the earnest desire of the person to lay hold on the help he required, by bringing him who was the object of his prayer to his assistance; 3. It showed the ardour of the person to receive the blessings he expected; and 4. By this act he *designated* and *consecrated* his offering or sacrifice to his God.

From a great number of evidences and coincidences it is not unreasonable to conclude that the heathens borrowed all that was pure and rational, even in their *mode of worship*, from the ancient people of God; and that the preceding quotations are proofs of this.

Verse 31. *The flax and the barley was smitten*] The word פשתה *pishtah*, *flax*, Mr. Parkhurst thinks, is derived from the root פשט *pashat*, *to strip*, because the substance which we term *flax* is properly the *bark* or *rind* of the vegetable, pilled or stripped off the stalks. From time immemorial Egypt was celebrated for the production and manufacture of flax: hence the linen and fine linen of Egypt, so often spoken of in ancient authors.

Barley] שערה *seorah*, from שער *saar*, *to stand on end*, *to be rough*, *bristly*, &c.; hence שער *sear*, *the hair of the head*, *and* שעיר *sair*, *a he-goat*, because of its *shaggy hair*; and hence also *barley*, because of the *rough* and *prickly beard* with which the ears are covered and defended.

Dr. Pocock has observed that there is a double seed-time and harvest in Egypt: *Rice*, *India wheat*, and a grain called the *corn of Damascus*, and in Italian *surgo rosso*, are sown and reaped at a very different time from *wheat*, *barley* and *flax*. The first are sown in *March*, before the overflowing of the Nile, and reaped about *October*; whereas the *wheat* and *barley* are sown in *November* and *December*, as soon as the Nile is gone off, and are reaped before *May*.

Pliny observes, *Hist. Nat.*, lib. xviii., cap. 10, that in Egypt the barley is ready for reaping in *six* months after it is sown, and *wheat* in *seven*. *In Ægypto* HORDEUM *sexto a satu mense*, FRUMENTA *septimo*, *metuntur*.

The flax was *bolled*.] Meaning, I suppose, was grown up into a stalk: the original is גבעל *gibol*, *podded* or was *in the pod*. The word well expresses that globous pod on the top of the stalk of flax which succeeds the flower and contains the seed, very properly expressed by the Septuagint, *το δε λινον σπερματιζον*, *but the flax was in seed* or *was seeding*.

Verse 32. *But the wheat and the rye were not smitten*] *Wheat*, חטה *chittah*, which Mr. Parkhurst thinks should be derived from the Chaldee and Samaritan חטי *chati*, which signifies *tender*, *delicious*, *delicate*, because of the superiority of its *flavour*, &c., to every other kind of grain. But this term in Scripture appears to mean any kind of *bread-corn*. *Rye*, כסמת *cussemeth*, from כסם *casam*, *to have long hair* and hence, though the particular species is not known, the word must mean some *bearded* grain. The Septuagint call it *ολυρα*, the Vulgate *far*, and Aquila *ζεα*, which signify the grain called *spelt*; and some suppose that *rice* is meant.

Mr. Harmer, referring to the double harvest in Egypt mentioned by Dr. Pocock, says that the circumstance of the wheat and the rye being אפילת *aphiloth*, *dark* or *hidden*, as the margin renders it, (i. e., they were sown, but not grown up,) shows that it was the *Indian wheat* or *surgo rosso* mentioned ver. 31, which, with the *rye*, escaped, while the *barley* and *flax* were smitten because they were at or nearly at a state of maturity. See Harmer's Obs vol. iv., p. 11, edit. 1808. But what is intended by the words in the Hebrew text we cannot positively say, as there is a great variety of opinions on this

a

A. M. 2513. B. C. 1491.

33 And Moses went out of the
city from Pharaoh, and [e] spread
abroad his hands unto the LORD: and the
thunders and hail ceased, and the rain was
not poured upon the earth.
34 And when Pharaoh saw that the rain
and the hail and the thunders were
ceased, he sinned yet more, and
hardened his heart, he and his servants.
35 And [f] the heart of Pharaoh was hardened,
neither would he let the children of Israel go;
as the LORD had spoken [g] by Moses.

[e] Ver. 29; chap. viii. 12.——[f] Chap. iv. 21.

[g] Heb. *by the hand of Moses*; chap. iv. 13.

subject, both among the *versions* and the commentators. The *Anglo-Saxon* translator, probably from not knowing the meaning of the words, omits the whole verse.

Verse 33. *Spread abroad his hands*] Probably with the rod of God in them. See what has been said on the *spreading out of the hands* in prayer, ver. 29.

Verse 34. *He sinned yet more, and hardened his heart*] These were merely acts of his own; "for who can deny," says Mr. Psalmanazar, "that what God did on Pharaoh was much more proper to *soften* than to *harden* his heart; especially when it is observable that it was not till after seeing each miracle, and after the ceasing of each plague, that his heart is said to have been hardened? The verbs here used are in the conjugations *pihel* and *hiphil*, and often signify a bare *permission*, from which it is plain that the words should have been read, *God suffered the heart of Pharaoh to be hardened*."—Universal Hist., vol. i., p. 494. Note D.

Verse 35. *And the heart of Pharaoh was hardened*] In consequence of his *sinning yet more, and hardening his* own *heart* against both the judgments and mercies of God, we need not be surprised that, after God had given him the means of softening and repentance, and he had in every instance resisted and abused them, he should at last have been left to tho hardness and darkness of his own obstinate heart, so as to fill up the measure of his iniquity, and rush headlong to his own destruction.

IN the *fifth*, *sixth*, and *seventh* plagues described in this chapter, we have additional proofs of the *justice* and *mercy* of God, as well as of the *stupidity*, *rebellion*, and *wickedness* of Pharaoh and his courtiers. As these continued to contradict and resist, it was just that God should continue to inflict those punishments which their iniquities deserved. Yet in the midst of judgment he remembers mercy; and therefore Moses and Aaron are sent to inform the Egyptians that such plagues would come if they continued obstinate. Here is mercy; the cattle only are destroyed, and the people saved! Is it not evident from all these messages, and the repeated expostulations of Moses and Aaron in the name and on the authority of God, that Pharaoh was bound by no fatal necessity to continue his obstinacy; that he might have humbled himself before God, and thus prevented the disasters that fell on the land, and saved himself and his people from destruction? But he *would* sin, and therefore he must be punished.

In the *sixth* plague Pharaoh had advantages which he had not before. The magicians, by their successful imitations of the miracles wrought by Moses, made it doubtful to the Egyptians whether Moses himself was not a *magician* acting without any Divine authority; but the plague of the boils, which they could not imitate, by which they were themselves afflicted, and which they confessed to be the *finger of God*, decided the business. Pharaoh had no longer any excuse, and must know that he had now to contend, not with Moses and Aaron, mortals like himself, but with the living God. How strange, then, that he should continue to resist! Many affect to be astonished at this, and think it must be attributed only to a sovereign controlling influence of God, which rendered it impossible for him to repent or take warning. But the whole conduct of God shows the improbability of this opinion: and is not the conduct of Pharaoh and his courtiers copied and reacted by thousands who are never suspected to be under any such necessitating decree? Every sinner under heaven, who has the Bible in his hand, is acting the same part. God says to the swearer and the profane, *Thou shalt not take the name of the Lord thy God in vain;* and yet common swearing and profaneness are most scandalously common among multitudes who bear the *Christian* name, and who presume on the mercy of God to get at last to the kingdom of heaven! He says also, *Remember the Sabbath day to keep it holy; thou shalt not kill; thou shalt not commit adultery; thou shalt not steal; thou shalt not bear false witness; thou shalt not covet;* and sanctions all these commandments with the most awful penalties: and yet, with all these things before them, and the professed belief that they came from God, Sabbath-breakers, men-slayers, adulterers, fornicators, thieves, dishonest men, false witnesses, liars, slanderers, backbiters, covetous men, lovers of the world more than lovers of God, are found by hundreds and thousands! What were the crimes of the poor half-blind Egyptian king when compared with these! He sinned against a comparatively *unknown* God; these sin against the God of their fathers—against the God and Father of Him whom they call their Lord and Saviour, Jesus Christ! They sin with the Bible in their hand, and a conviction of its Divine authority in their hearts. They sin against light and knowledge; against the checks of their consciences, the reproofs of their friends, the admonitions of the messengers of God; against Moses and Aaron in the law; against the testimony of all the prophets; against the evangelists, the apostles, the Maker of heaven and earth, the Judge of all men, and the Saviour of the world! What were Pharaoh's crimes to the crimes of these? On comparison, his atom of moral turpitude is lost in their world of iniquity. And yet who supposes these to be under any *necessitating* decree to sin on, and go to perdition? Nor are they

nor was Pharaoh. In all things God has proved both his justice and mercy to be clear in this point. Pharaoh, through a principle of *covetousness*, refused to dismiss the Israelites, whose services he found profitable to the state: *these* are absorbed in the love of the world, the love of pleasure, and the love of gain; nor will they let one lust go, even in the presence of the thunders of Sinai, or in sight of the agony, bloody sweat, crucifixion, and death of Jesus Christ! Alas! how many are in the habit of considering Pharaoh the worst of human beings, inevitably cut off from the possibility of being saved because of his iniquities, who outdo him so far in the viciousness of their lives, that Pharaoh, hardening his heart against ten plagues, appears a saint when compared with those who are hardening their hearts against ten millions of mercies. Reader, art *thou* of this number? Proceed no farther! God's judgments linger not. Desperate as thy state is, thou mayest return; and thou, even *thou*, find mercy through the blood of the Lamb.

See the observations at the conclusion of the next chapter.

CHAPTER X.

Moses is again sent to Pharaoh, and expostulates with him on his refusal to let the Hebrews go, 1–3. *The* eighth *plague, viz., of* locusts, *is threatened,* 4. *The extent and oppressive nature of this plague,* 5, 6. *Pharaoh's servants counsel him to dismiss the Hebrews,* 7. *He calls for Moses and Aaron, and inquires who they are of the Hebrews who wish to go,* 8. *Moses having answered that the whole people, with their flocks and herds must go and hold a feast to the Lord,* 9, *Pharaoh is enraged, and having granted permission only to the* men, *drives Moses and Aaron from his presence,* 10, 11. *Moses is commanded to stretch out his hand and bring the locusts,* 12. *He does so, and an east wind is sent, which, blowing all that day and night, brings the locusts the next morning,* 13. *The devastation occasioned by these insects,* 14, 15. *Pharaoh is humbled, acknowledges his sin, and begs Moses to intercede with Jehovah for him,* 16, 17. *Moses does so, and at his request a strong west wind is sent, which carries all the locusts to the Red Sea,* 18, 19. *Pharaoh's heart is again hardened,* 20. *Moses is commanded to bring the* ninth *plague—an extraordinary* darkness *over all the land of Egypt,* 21. *The nature, duration, and effects of this,* 22, 23. *Pharaoh, again humbled, consents to let the people go, provided they leave their cattle behind,* 24. *Moses insists on having all their cattle, because of the sacrifices which they must make to the Lord,* 25, 26. *Pharaoh, again hardened, refuses,* 27. *Orders Moses from his presence, and threatens him with death should he ever return,* 28. *Moses departs with the promise of returning no more,* 29.

A. M. 2513. B. C. 1491.

AND the LORD said unto Moses,
Go in unto Pharaoh: [a] for I
have hardened his heart, and the heart of his
servants, [b] that I might show these my signs
before him:
2 And that [c] thou mayest tell in the ears of
thy son, and of thy son's son,
what things I have wrought in
Egypt, and my signs which I have done among
them; that ye may know how that I *am*
the LORD.
3 And Moses and Aaron came in unto Pha-

[a] Chap. iv. 21; vii. 14.——[b] Chap. vii. 4.

[c] Deut. iv. 9; Psa. xliv. 1; lxxi. 18; lxxviii. 5, &c.; Joel i. 3.

NOTES ON CHAP. X.

Verse 1. *Hardened his heart*] God suffered his natural obstinacy to prevail, that he might have farther opportunities of showing forth his eternal power and Godhead.

Verse 2. *That thou mayest tell in the ears of thy son*] That the miracles wrought at this time might be a record for the instruction of the latest posterity, that Jehovah alone, the God of the Hebrews, was the sole Maker, Governor, and Supporter of the heavens and the earth. Thus we find God *so did his marvellous works, that they might be had in everlasting remembrance*. It was not to crush the poor worm, Pharaoh, that he wrought such mighty wonders, but to convince his enemies, to the end of the world, that no cunning or power can prevail against him; and to show his followers that whosoever trusted in him should never be confounded.

Verse 3. *How long wilt thou refuse to humble thyself*] Had it been *impossible* for Pharaoh, in all the preceding plagues, to have humbled himself and repented, can we suppose that God could have addressed him in such language as the preceding? We may rest assured that there was always a time in which he might have relented, and that it was because he hardened his heart at such times that God is said to harden him, i. e., to give him up to his own stubborn and obstinate heart; in consequence of which he refused to let the people go, so that God had a fresh opportunity to work another miracle, for the very gracious purposes mentioned in ver. 2. Had Pharaoh relented *before*, the same gracious ends would have been accomplished by other means.

The EIGHTH *plague—the* LOCUSTS.

Verse 4. *To-morrow will I bring the locusts*] The word ארבה *arbeh*, a *locust*, is probably from the root רבה *rabah*, he *multiplied*, *became great*, *mighty*, &c., because of the immense swarms of these animals by which different countries, especially the east, are infested. The locust, in *entomology*, belongs to a genus of insects known among naturalists by the term GRYLLI;

A. M. 2513. B. C. 1491.

raoh, and said unto him, Thus saith the LORD God of the Hebrews, How long wilt thou refuse to [d] humble thyself before me? let my people go, that they may serve me;

4 Else, if thou refuse to let my people go, behold, to-morrow will I bring the [e] locusts into thy coast:

5 And they shall cover the [f] face of the earth, that one cannot be able to see the earth: and [g] they shall eat the residue of that which is escaped, which remaineth unto you from the hail, and shall eat every tree which groweth for you out of the field:

6 And they [h] shall fill thy houses, and the houses of all thy servants, and the houses of all the Egyptians; which neither thy fathers, nor thy fathers' fathers have seen, since the day that they were upon the earth unto this day. And he turned himself, and went out from Pharaoh.

7 And Pharaoh's servants said unto him, How long shall this man be [i] a snare unto us?

[d] 1 Kings xxi. 29; 2 Chron. vii. 14; xxxiv. 27; Job xiii. 6; Jer. xiii. 18; James iv. 10; 1 Pet. v. 6.——[e] Proverbs xxx. 27; Wisd. xvi. 9; Rev. ix. 3.

[f] Heb. *eye*; ver. 15.——[g] Chapter ix. 32; Joel i. 4; ii. 25. [h] Chap. viii. 3, 21.——[i] Chap. xxiii. 33; Josh. xxiii. 13; 1 Sam. xviii. 21; Eccles. vii. 26; 1 Cor. vii. 35.

and includes three species, crickets, grasshoppers, and those commonly called locusts; and as they multiply faster than any other animal in creation, they are properly entitled to the name ארבה *arbeh*, which might be translated the *numerous* or *multiplied insect*. See this circumstance referred to, Judg. vi. 5; vii. 12; Psa. cv. 34; Jer. xlvi. 23; li. 14; Joel i. 6; Nahum iii. 15; Judith ii. 19, 20; where the most numerous armies are compared to the *arbeh* or *locust*. The locust has a large open mouth; and in its two jaws it has four incisive teeth, which traverse each other like scissors, being calculated, from their mechanism, to gripe or cut. Mr. Volney, in his Travels in Syria, gives a striking account of this most awful *scourge* of God:—

"Syria partakes together with Egypt and Persia, and almost all the whole middle part of Asia, in that *terrible scourge*, I mean those clouds of locusts of which travellers have spoken; the quantity of which is incredible to any person who has not himself seen them, the earth being covered by them for several leagues round. The noise they make in browsing the plants and trees may be heard at a distance, like an army plundering in secret. Fire seems to follow their tracks. Wherever their legions march the verdure disappears from the country, like a curtain drawn aside; the trees and plants, despoiled of their leaves, make the hideous appearance of winter instantly succeed to the bright scenes of spring. When these clouds of locusts take their flight, in order to surmount some obstacle, or the more rapidly to cross some desert, one may literally say that *the sun is darkened by them*."

Baron de Tott gives a similar account: "Clouds of locusts frequently alight on the plains of the Noguais, (the Tartars,) and giving preference to their fields of millet, ravage them in an instant. Their approach darkens the horizon, and so enormous is their multitude, *it hides the light of the sun*. They alight on the fields, and there form a bed of *six or seven inches thick*. To the noise of their flight succeeds that of their devouring actively, which resembles the *rattling of hailstones*; but its consequences are infinitely more destructive. Fire itself eats not so fast; nor is there any appearance of vegetation to be found when they again take their flight, and go elsewhere to produce new disasters."

Dr. Shaw, who witnessed most formidable swarms of these in Barbary in the years 1724 and 1725, gives the following account of them: "They were much larger than our grasshoppers, and had brown-spotted wings, with legs and bodies of a bright yellow. Their first appearance was towards the latter end of March. In the middle of April their numerous swarms, like a succession of clouds, *darkened the sun*. In the month of May they retired to the adjacent plains to deposit their eggs: these were no sooner hatched in June than the young brood first produced, while in their caterpillar or worm-like state, formed themselves into a compact body of more than a furlong square, and, marching directly forward, climbed over trees, walls, and houses, devouring every plant in their way. Within a day or two another brood was hatched, and advancing in the same manner, gnawed off the young branches and bark of the trees left by the former, making a complete desolation. The inhabitants, to stop their progress, made a variety of pits and trenches all over their fields and gardens, which they filled with water, or else heaped up therein heath, stubble, &c., which they set on fire; but to no purpose: for the trenches were quickly filled up and the fires extinguished, by infinite swarms succeeding one another; while the front seemed regardless of danger, and the rear pressed on so close that a retreat was altogether impossible. In a month's time they threw off their worm-like state; and in a new form, with wings and legs, and additional powers, returned to their former voracity."—*Shaw's Travels*, 187, 188, 4to edition.

The descriptions given by these travellers show that *God's army*, described by the Prophet Joel, chap. ii., was innumerable swarms of locusts, to which the accounts given by Dr. Shaw and others exactly agree.

Verse 5. *They shall cover the face of the earth*] They sometimes cover the whole ground to the depth of *six* or *eight inches*. See the preceding accounts.

Verse 6. *They shall fill thy houses*] Dr. Shaw mentions this circumstance; "they entered," says he, "into our very houses and bed-chambers, like so many thieves."—Ibid. p. 187.

Verse 7. *How long shall this man be a snare unto us?*] As there is no noun in the text, the pronoun זה *zeh* may either refer to the Israelites, to the plague by

A. M. 2513. B. C. 1491. let the men go, that they may serve
the Lord their God: knowest thou
not yet that Egypt is destroyed?
8 And Moses and Aaron were brought again
unto Pharaoh; and he said unto them, Go,
serve the Lord your God: *but* [k] who *are* they
that shall go?
9 And Moses said, We will go with our
young and with our old, with our sons and
with our daughters, with our flocks and with
our herds will we go; for [l] we *must hold* a
feast unto the Lord.
10 And he said unto them, Let the Lord
be so with you, as I will let you go, and your little ones: look *to it*; for evil *is* before you. A. M. 2513. B. C. 1491.
11 Not so: go now ye *that are* men, and
serve the Lord; for that ye did desire. And
they were driven out from Pharaoh's presence.
12 And the Lord said unto Moses, [m] Stretch
out thine hand over the land of Egypt for the
locusts, that they may come up upon the land
of Egypt, and [n] eat every herb of the land,
even all that the hail hath left.
13 And Moses stretched forth his rod over
the land of Egypt, and the Lord brought an

[k] Heb. *who, and who, &c.*——[l] Chap. v. 1.

[m] Chap. vii. 19.——[n] Ver. 4, 5.

which they were then afflicted, or to Moses and Aaron, the instruments used by the Most High in their chastisement. The Vulgate translates, *Usquequo patiemur hoc scandalum?* "How long shall we suffer this scandal or reproach!"

Let the men go, that they may serve the Lord their God] Much of the energy of several passages is lost in translating יהוה *Yehovah* by the term *Lord*. The Egyptians had their gods, and they supposed that the Hebrews had *a god* like unto their own; that this Jehovah required their services, and would continue to afflict Egypt till his people were permitted to worship him in his own way.

Egypt is destroyed?] This last plague had nearly ruined the whole land

Verse 8. *Who* are *they that shall go?*] Though the Egyptians, about fourscore years before, wished to destroy the Hebrews, yet they found them now so profitable to the *state* that they were unwilling to part with them.

Verse 9. *We will go with our young and with our old, &c.*] As a feast was to be celebrated to the honour of Jehovah, all who were partakers of his bounty and providential kindness must go and perform their part in the solemnity. The *men* and the *women* must make the feast, the *children* must witness it, and the *cattle* must be taken along with them to furnish the sacrifices necessary on this occasion. This must have appeared reasonable to the Egyptians, because it was their *own custom* in their religious assemblies. Men, women, and children attended them, often to the amount of several hundred thousand. *Herodotus* informs us, in speaking of the six annual feasts celebrated by the Egyptians in honour of their deities, that they hold their chief one at the city of *Bubastis* in honour of *Neith* or Diana; that they go thither by water in boats —men, women, and children; that during their voyage some of the women play on castanets, and some of the men upon flutes, while the rest are employed in singing and clapping their hands; and that, when they arrive at Bubastis, they sacrifice a vast number of victims, and drink much wine; and that at one such festival, the inhabitants assured him, that there were not assembled fewer than 700,000 men and women, without reckoning the children.—*Euterpe*, chap. lix., lx. I find that the ancient Egyptians called Diana *Neith*; this comes as near as possible to the *Gaile* of the Isle of Man. The moon is called *yn neith* or *neath*; and also *ke-sollus*, from *ke*, *smooth* or *even*, and *sollus*, *light*, the SMOOTH LIGHT; perhaps to distinguish her from the sun, *grian*, from *gri-tien* or *cri-tien*, i. e., TREMBLING FIRE; *yn neith—easga*, as *Macpherson* has it, signifies *wan complexion*. I should rather incline to think it may come from *aise*. The Celtic nations thought that the heavenly luminaries were the residences of spirits which they distinguished by the name of *aise*, thus *grian-ais* signifies the spirit of the sun.

Moses and Aaron, requesting liberty for the Hebrews to go three days' journey into the wilderness, and with them all their wives, little ones, and cattle, in order to hold a feast unto Jehovah their God, must have at least appeared as reasonable to the Egyptians as their going to the city of Bubastis with their wives, little ones, and cattle, to hold a feast to *Neith* or Diana, who was there worshipped. The *parallel* in these two cases is too striking to pass unnoticed.

Verse 10. *Let the Lord be so with you*] This is an obscure sentence. Some suppose that Pharaoh meant it as a curse, as if he had said, "May your God be as surely with you, as I shall let you go!" For as he purposed not to permit them to go, so he wished them as much of the Divine help as they should have of his permission.

Look—for evil is *before you.*] ראו כי רעה נגד פניכם *reu ki raah neged peneychem, See ye that evil is before your faces*—if you attempt to go, ye shall meet with the punishment ye deserve. Probably Pharaoh intended to insinuate that they had some sinister designs, and that they wished to go in a body that they might the better accomplish their purpose; but if they had no such designs they would be contented for the males to go, and leave their wives and children behind: for he well knew if the *men* went and left their *families* they would infallibly return, but that if he permitted them to take their families with them, they would undoubtedly make their escape; therefore he says, ver. 11, *Go now ye* that are *men, and serve the Lord.*

Verse 13. *The Lord brought an east wind*] As locusts abounded in those countries, and particularly in Æthiopia, and more especially at this time of the year,

A. M. 2513.
B. C. 1491.

east wind upon the land all that day, and all *that* night; *and* when it was morning, the east wind brought the locusts.
14 And [o] the locusts went up over all the land of Egypt, and rested in all the coasts of Egypt: very grievous *were they;* [p] before them there were no such locusts as they, neither after them shall be such.
15 For they [q] covered the face of the whole earth, so that the land was darkened; and they [r] did eat every herb of the land, and all the fruit of the trees which the hail had left: and there remained not any green thing in the trees, or in the herbs of the field, through all the land of Egypt.
16 Then Pharaoh [s] called for Moses and Aaron in haste: and he said, [t] I have sinned against the LORD your God, and against you.
17 Now therefore forgive, I pray thee, my sin only this once, and [u] entreat the LORD your God, that he may take away from me this death only.
18 And he [v] went out from Pharaoh, and entreated the LORD.
19 And the LORD turned a mighty strong west wind, which took away the locusts, and [w] cast them [x] into the Red Sea; there remained not one locust in all the coasts of Egypt.
20 But the LORD [y] hardened Pharaoh's heart, so that he would not let the children of Israel go.
21 And the LORD said unto Moses, [z] Stretch out thine hand toward heaven, that there may be darkness over the land of Egypt, [a] even darkness *which* may be felt.
22 And Moses stretched forth his hand toward heaven; and there was a [b] thick darkness in all the land of Egypt three days:

[o] Psa. lxxviii. 46; cv. 34.——[p] Joel ii. 2.——[q] Ver. 5.——[r] Psa. cv. 35.——[s] Heb. *hastened to call.*——[t] Chap. ix. 27.——[u] Chap. ix. 28; 1 Kings xiii. 6.——[v] Chap. viii. 30.

[w] Heb. *fastened.*——[x] Joel ii. 20.——[y] Chapter iv. 21; xi. 10. [z] Ch. ix. 22.——[a] Heb. *that one may feel darkness.*——[b] Psa. cv. 28; Wisd. xvii. 2, &c.

God had no need to create new swarms for this purpose; all that was requisite was to cause such a wind to blow as would bring those which already existed over the land of Egypt. The miracle in this business was he bringing the locusts at the appointed time, and causing the proper wind to blow for that purpose; and then taking them away after a similar manner.

Verse 14. *Before them there were no such locusts, &c.*] They exceeded all that went before, or were since, in *number*, and in the *devastations* they produced. Probably both these things are intended in the passage. See ver. 15.

Ver. 15. *There remained not any green thing*] See the note on ver. 4.

Verse 17. *Forgive, I pray thee, my sin only this once*] What a strange case! And what a series of softening and hardening, of sinning and repenting! Had he not now another opportunity of returning to God? But the love of gain, and the gratification of his own self-will and obstinacy, finally prevailed.

Verse 19. *A mighty strong west wind*] רוח ים *ruach yam*, literally the *wind of the sea;* the wind that blew from the Mediterranean Sea, which lay north-west of Egypt, which had the Red Sea on the east. Here again God works by natural means; he brought the locusts by the east wind, and took them away by the west or *north-west* wind, which carried them to the Red Sea where they were drowned.

The Red Sea] ים סוף *yam suph*, the *weedy sea;* so called, as some suppose, from the great quantity of *alga* or sea-weed which grows in it and about its shores. But Mr. Bruce, who has sailed the whole extent of it, declares that he never saw in it a weed of any kind; and supposes it has its name *suph* from the vast quantity of coral which grows in it, as trees and plants do on land. "One of these," he observes, "from a root nearly central, threw out ramifications in a nearly circular form measuring *twenty-six* feet diameter every way."—Travels, vol. ii., p. 138. In the Septuagint it is called θαλασσα ερυθρα, the *Red Sea*, from which version we have borrowed the name; and Mr. Bruce supposes that it had this name from *Edom* or Esau, whose territories extended to its coasts; for it is well known that the word אדם *Edom* in Hebrew signifies *red* or *ruddy*. The *Red Sea*, called also the *Arabic Gulf*, separates Arabia from Upper Æthiopia and part of Egypt. It is computed to be *three hundred and fifty* leagues in length from Suez to the Straits of Babelmandel, and is about *forty* leagues in breadth. It is not very tempestuous, and the winds usually blow from *north to south*, and from *south to north*, six months in the year; and, like the monsoons of India, invariably determine the seasons of sailing into or out of this sea It is divided into two gulfs: that to the east called the *Elanitic Gulf*, from the city of Elana to the north end of it; and that to the west called the *Heroopolitan Gulf*, from the city of *Heroopolis;* the former of which belongs to Arabia, the latter to Egypt. The Heroopolitan Gulf is called by the Arabians *Bahr el Kolzum*, the *sea of destruction*, or of *Clysmæ*, an ancient town in that quarter; and the Elanitic Gulf *Bahr el Akaba*, the *sea of Akaba*, a town situated on its most inland point.

The NINTH *plague*—THICK DARKNESS.

Verse 21. *Darkness* which *may be felt.*] Probably this was occasioned by a superabundance of aqueous vapours floating in the atmosphere, which were so thick as to prevent the rays of the sun from penetrating through them; an extraordinarily thick mist supernaturally, i. e., miraculously, brought on. An awful emblem of the darkened state of the Egyptians and their king.

A. M. 2513. B. C. 1491. 23 They saw not one another,
neither rose any from his place for
three days: [c] but all the children of Israel
had light in their dwellings.
24 And Pharaoh called unto Moses, and
[d] said, Go ye, serve the LORD; only let your
flocks and your herds be stayed: let your
[e] little ones also go with you.
25 And Moses said, Thou must give [f] us
also sacrifices and burnt-offerings, that we may
sacrifice unto the LORD our God.
26 Our cattle also shall go with us; there
shall not a hoof be left behind; for A. M. 2513. B. C. 1491.
thereof must we take to serve the
LORD our God; and we know not with what we
must serve the LORD until we come thither.
27 But the LORD [g] hardened Pharaoh's
heart, and he would not let them go.
28 And Pharaoh said unto him, Get thee
from me, take heed to thyself, see my face
no more; for in *that* day thou seest my face
thou shalt die.
29 And Moses said, Thou hast spoken well,
[h] I will see thy face again no more.

[c] Chapter viii. 22; Wisdom xviii. 1.——[d] Verse 8. [e] Ver. 10.

[f] Heb. *into our hands*.——[g] Ver. 20; chapter iv. 21; xiv. 4, 8. [h] Heb. xi. 27.

Verse 23. *They saw not one another*] So deep was the obscurity, and probably such was its nature, that no artificial light could be procured; as the thick clammy vapours would prevent lamps, &c., from burning, or if they even could be ignited, the light through the palpable obscurity, could diffuse itself to no distance from the burning body. The author of the book of Wisdom, chap. xvii. 2–19, gives a fearful description of this plague. He says, "The Egyptians were shut up in their houses, the prisoners of darkness: and *were* fettered with the bonds of a long night. They were scattered under a dark veil of forgetfulness, being horribly astonished and troubled with *strange* apparitions; for neither might the corner that held them keep them from fear; but noises as *of waters* falling down sounded about them; and sad visions appeared unto them with heavy countenances. No power of the fire could give them light—only there appeared unto them a fire kindled of itself very dreadful; for being much terrified, they thought the things which they saw to be worse than the sight they saw not. For though no terrible thing did scare them, yet being scared with beasts that passed by, and hissing of serpents, they died for fear: for whether he were husbandman, or shepherd, or a labourer in the field, he was overtaken; for they were all bound with one chain of darkness. Whether it were a whistling wind, or a terrible sound of stones cast down, or a running that could not be seen of tripping beasts, or a roaring voice of most savage wild beasts, or a rebounding echo from the hollow mountains, these things made them to swoon for fear." See Psalm lxxviii. 49.

To this description nothing need be added except this circumstance, that the darkness, with its attendant horrors, lasted for *three days*.

All the children of Israel had light] By thus distinguishing the Israelites, God showed the Egyptians that the darkness was produced by his power; that he sent it in judgment against them for their cruelty to his people; that because they trusted in him they were exempted from these plagues; that in the displeasure of such a Being his enemies had every thing to fear, and in his approbation his followers had every thing to hope.

Verse 24. *Only let your flocks and your herds be stayed*] Pharaoh cannot get all he wishes; and as he sees it impossible to contend with Jehovah, he now consents to give up the Israelites, their wives and their children, provided he may keep their *flocks* and their *herds*. The *cruelty* of this demand is not more evident than its *avarice*. Had *six hundred thousand* men, besides women and children, gone three days' journey into the *wilderness* without their cattle, they must have inevitably perished, being without milk for their little ones, and animal food for their own sustenance, in a place where little as a substitute could possibly be found. It is evident from this that Pharaoh intended the total destruction of the whole Israelitish host.

Verse 26. *We know not with what we must serve the Lord, &c.*] The *law* was not yet given; the ordinances concerning the different kinds of sacrifices and offerings not known. What *kind* and what *number* of animals God should require to be sacrificed, even Moses himself could not as yet tell. He therefore very properly insists on taking the whole of their herds with them, and not leaving even *one hoof behind*.

Verse 27. *The Lord hardened Pharaoh's heart*] He had yet another miracle to work for the complete conviction of the Egyptians and triumph of his people; and till that was wrought he permitted the natural obstinacy of Pharaoh's haughty heart to have its full sway, after each resistance of the gracious influence which was intended to soften and bring him to repentance.

Verse 28. *See my face no more*] Hitherto Pharaoh had left the way open for negotiation; but now, in wrath against Jehovah, he dismisses his ambassador, and threatens him with death if he should attempt any more to come into his presence.

Verse 29. *I will see thy face again no more.*] It is very likely that this was the last interview that Moses had with Pharaoh, for what is related, chap. xi. 4–8, might have been spoken on this very occasion, as it is very possible that God gave Moses to understand his purpose to slay the first-born, while before Pharaoh at this time; so, in all probability, the interview mentioned here was the last which Moses had with the Egyptian king. It is true that in ver. 31 of chap. xii. it is stated that Pharaoh *called for Moses and Aaron by night*, and ordered them to leave Egypt, and to take all their substance with them, which seems to imply that there was another interview, but the words may imply no more than that Moses and Aaron *received such a message* from Pharaoh. If, however, this mode

of interpreting these passages should not seem satisfactory to any, he may understand the words of Moses thus: *I will see thy face*—seek thy favour, *no more* in behalf of my people, which was literally true; for if Moses did appear any more before Pharaoh, it was not as a *supplicant*, but merely as the ambassador of God, to denounce his judgments by giving him the final determination of Jehovah relative to the destruction of the first-born.

1. To the observations at the conclusion of the preceding chapter, we may add that at first view it seems exceedingly strange that, after all the proofs Pharaoh had of the power of God, he should have acted in the manner related in this and the preceding chapters, alternately sinning and repenting; but it is really a *common* case, and multitudes who condemn the conduct of this miserable Egyptian king, act in a similar manner. They relent when smarting under God's judgments, but harden their hearts when these judgments are removed. Of this kind I have witnessed numerous cases. To such God says by his prophet, *Why should ye be stricken any more? ye will revolt more and more.* Reader, are not the vows of God upon *thee?* Often when afflicted in thyself or family hast thou not said like Pharaoh, (ver. 17,) *Now therefore forgive, I pray thee, my sin only* THIS ONCE, and *take away from me this death* ONLY! And yet when thou hadst respite, didst thou not harden thy heart, and with returning health and strength didst thou not return unto iniquity? And art thou not still in the broad road of transgression? Be not deceived; God is not mocked; he warns thee, but he will not be mocked by thee. *What* thou *sowest*, that thou must *reap*. Think then what a most dreadful harvest thou mayest expect from the seeds of vice which thou hast already sown!

2. Even in the face of God's judgments the spirit of avarice will make its requisitions. *Only let your flocks and your herds be stayed*, says Pharaoh. The *love of gain* was the ruling principle of this man's soul, and he chooses desperately to contend with the justice of his Maker, rather than give up his bosom sin! Reader, is this not thy own case? And art thou not ready, with Pharaoh, to say to the messenger of God, who rebukes thee for thy worldly mindedness, &c., *Get thee gone from me. Take heed to thyself, and see my face no more.* Esau and Pharaoh have both got a very bad name, and many persons who are repeating their crimes are the foremost to cover them with obloquy! When shall we learn to look *at home?* to take warning by the miscarriages of others, and thus shun the pit into which we have seen so many fall? If God were to give the history of every man who hardens himself from his fear, how many Pharaoh-like cases should we have on record! But a day is coming in which the secrets of every heart shall be revealed, and the history of every man's life laid open to an assembled world.

CHAPTER XI.

God purposes to bring another plague upon Pharaoh, after which he should let the Israelites go, 1. They are commanded to ask gold and silver from the Egyptians, 2. The estimation in which Moses was held among the Egyptians, 3. Moses predicts the destruction of the first-born of the Egyptians, 4–6, and Israel's protection, 7. On seeing which, Pharaoh and his servants should entreat the Hebrews to depart, 8. The prediction of his previous obstinacy, 9, 10.

A. M. 2513. B. C. 1491.

AND the LORD said unto Moses,
Yet will I bring one plague
more upon Pharaoh, and upon Egypt; afterwards he will let you go hence: [a] when he
shall let *you* go, he shall surely thrust you
out hence altogether.
2 Speak now in the ears of the people, and
let every man borrow of his neighbour, and
every woman of her neighbour,
[b] jewels of silver, and jewels of gold.
3 [c] And the LORD gave the people favour in
the sight of the Egyptians. Moreover the man
[d] Moses *was* very great in the land of Egypt,
in the sight of Pharaoh's servants, and in the
sight of the people.
4 And Moses said, Thus saith the LORD,

[a] Ch. xii. 31, 33, 39.—[b] Ch. iii. 22; xii. 35.—[c] Ch. iii. 21; xii. 36; Psa. cvi. 46.—[d] 2 Sam. vii. 9; Esth. ix. 4; Eccles. xlv. 1.

NOTES ON CHAP. XI.

Verse 1. *The Lord said unto Moses*] Calmet contends that this should be read in the *preterpluperfect* tense, *for the Lord* HAD *said to Moses*, as the fourth, fifth, sixth, seventh, and eighth verses appear to have been spoken when Moses had the interview with Pharaoh mentioned in the preceding chapter; see the note there on verse 29. If therefore this chapter be connected with the preceding, as it should be, and the first three verses not only read in the *past* tense but also in a parenthesis, the sense will be much more distinct and clear than it now appears.

Verse 2. *Let every man borrow*] For a proper correction of the strange mistranslation of the word שאל *shaal* in this verse, see the note on chap. iii. 22.

Verse 3. *The man Moses was very great*] The miracles which Pharaoh and his servants had already seen him work had doubtless impressed them with a high opinion of his wisdom and power. Had he not appeared in their sight as a very extraordinary person, whom it would have been very dangerous to molest, we may naturally conclude that some violence would long ere this have been offered to his person.

Verse 4. *About midnight will I go out*] Whether

A. M. 2513. B. C. 1491.

[e] About midnight will I go out into
the midst of Egypt:
5 And [f] all the first-born in the land of
Egypt shall die, from the first-born of Pharaoh that sitteth upon his throne, even unto
the first-born of the maid-servant that *is* behind the mill; and all the first-born of beasts.
6 [g] And there shall be a great cry throughout
all the land of Egypt, such as
there was none like it, nor shall be
like it any more.
7 [h] But against any of the children of Israel
[i] shall not a dog move his tongue, against man
or beast: that ye may know how that the
Lord doth put a difference between the Egyptians and Israel.

[e] Chapter xii. 12, 23, 29; Amos v. 17.——[f] Chapter xii. 12, 29; Amos iv. 10.

[g] Chap. xii. 30; Amos v. 17; Wisd. xviii. 10.——[h] Chap. viii. 22.——[i] Josh. x. 21.

God did this by the ministry of a *good* or of an *evil* angel is a matter of little importance, though some commentators have greatly magnified it. Both kinds of angels are under his power and jurisdiction, and he may employ them as he pleases. Such a work of destruction as the slaying of the first-born is supposed to be more proper for a bad than for a good angel. But the works of God's justice are not less holy and pure than the works of his mercy; and the highest archangel may, with the utmost propriety, be employed in either.

Verse 5. *The first-born of Pharaoh, &c.*] From the heir to the Egyptian throne to the son of the most abject slave, or the principal person in each family. See the note on chap. xii. 29.

The maid-servant that is behind the mill] The meanest slaves were employed in this work. In many parts of the east they still grind all their corn with a kind of portable mill-stones, the upper one of which is turned round by a sort of *lever* fixed in the rim. A drawing of one of these machines as used in China is now before me, and the person who grinds is represented as pushing the *lever before* him, and thus running round with the stone. Perhaps something like this is intended by the expression BEHIND *the mill* in the text. On this passage Dr. Shaw has the following observation:—"Most families grind their wheat and barley at home, having *two portable mill-stones* for that purpose, the uppermost of which is turned round by a small handle of wood or iron that is placed in the rim. When this stone is large, or expedition required, a second person is called in to assist; and as it is usual for *women* alone to be concerned in this employment, who seat themselves over against each other with the mill-stone between them, we may see, not only the propriety of the expression (Exod. xi. 5) of *sitting behind the mill*, but the force of another, (Matt. xxiv. 40,) that *two women shall be grinding at the mill; the one shall be taken, and the other left.*"—Travels, p. 231, 4to edit. These portable mills, under the name of *querns*, were used among our ancestors in this and the sister kingdoms, and some of them are in use to the present day. Both the instrument and its name our forefathers seem to have borrowed from the continent. They have long existed among the inhabitants of Shetland, Iceland, Norway, Denmark, &c.

Verse 6. *There shall be a great cry*] Of the dying and for the dead. See more on this subject, chap. xii. 30.

Verse 7. *Not a dog move his tongue*] This passage has been generally understood as a *proverbial expression*, intimating that the Israelites should not only be free from this death, but that they should depart without any kind of molestation. For though there must be much bustle and comparative confusion in the sudden removal of *six hundred thousand* persons with their wives, children, goods, cattle, &c., yet this should produce so little alarm that even the dogs should not bark at them, which it would be natural to expect, as the principal stir was to be about midnight.

After giving this general explanation from others, I may be permitted to hazard a conjecture of my own. And, 1. Is it not probable that the allusion is here made to a well-known custom of dogs howling when any mortality is in a village, street, or even house, where such animals are? There are innumerable instances of the faithful house-dog howling when a death happens in a family, as if distressed on the account, feeling for the loss of his benefactor; but their apparent *presaging* such an event by their cries, as some will have it, may be attributed, not to any prescience, but to the exquisite keenness of their scent. If the words may be understood in this way, then the *great cry* through the whole land of Egypt may refer to this very circumstance: as dogs were sacred among them, and consequently religiously preserved, they must have existed in great multitudes. 2. We know that one of their principal deities was Osiris, whose son, worshipped under the form of a dog, or a man with a dog's head, was called *Anubis latrator*, the *barking Anubis*. May he not be represented as deploring a calamity which he had no power to prevent among his worshippers, nor influence to inflict punishment upon those who set his deity at naught? Hence while there was a great cry, צעקה גדלה *tseakah gedolah*, throughout all the land of Egypt, because of the mortality in every house, yet among the Israelites there was no death, consequently no dog moved his tongue to howl for their calamity; nor could the object of the Egyptians' worship inflict any similar punishment on the worshippers of Jehovah.

In honour of this dog-god there was a city called Anubis in Egypt, by the Greeks called *Cynopolis*, the city of the dog, the same that is now called *Menich*; in this he had a temple, and dogs, which were sacred to him, were here fed with consecrated victuals.

Thus, as in the first plagues their *magicians* were confounded, so in this last their *gods* were put to flight. And may not this be referred to in chap. xii. 12, when Jehovah says: *Against all the gods of Egypt I will execute judgment?* Should it be objected, that to consider the passage in this light would be to acknowledge the *being* and *deity* of the fictitious Anubis, it may be answered, that in the sacred writings it is not an un-

a

A. M. 2513.
B. C. 1491.

8 And [k] all these thy servants shall come down unto me, and bow down themselves unto me, saying, Get thee out, and all the people [l] that follow thee: and after that I will go out. And he went out from Pharaoh in [m] a great anger.

9 And the LORD said unto Moses, [n] Pharaoh shall not hearken unto you; that [o] my wonders may be multiplied in the land of Egypt.

A. M. 2513.
B. C. 1491.

10 And Moses and Aaron did all these wonders before Pharaoh: [p] and the LORD hardened Pharaoh's heart, so that he would not let the children of Israel go out of his land.

[k] Chap. xii. 33.——[l] Heb. *that is at thy feet;* so Judg. iv. 10; viii. 5; 1 Kings xx. 10; 2 Kings iii. 9.——[m] Heb. *heat of anger.*——[n] Chap. iii. 19; vii. 4; x. 1.——[o] Ch. vii. 3.——[p] Chap. x. 20, 27; Rom. ii. 5; ix. 22.

common thing to see the idol acknowledged in order to show its nullity, and the more forcibly to express contempt for it, for its worshippers, and for its worship. Thus Isaiah represents the Babylonish idols as being endued with sense, bowing down under the judgments of God, utterly unable to help themselves or their worshippers, and being a burden to the beasts that carried them: BEL *boweth down,* NEBO *stoopeth; their idols were upon the beasts and upon the cattle: your carriages were heavy laden;* they are *a burden to the weary* beast. THEY *stoop, they bow down together; they could not deliver the burden, but themselves are gone into captivity;* chap. xlvi. 1, 2. The case of Elijah and the prophets of Baal should not be forgotten here; this prophet, by seeming to acknowledge the reality of *Baal's* being, though by a strong *irony,* poured the most sovereign contempt upon him, his worshippers, and his worship: *And Elijah mocked them, and said, Cry aloud;* FOR HE IS A GOD: *either he is talking, or he is pursuing, or he is in a journey, or peradventure he sleepeth and must be awaked;* 1 Kings xviii. 27. See the observations at the end of chap. xii.

The Lord doth put a difference] See on chap. viii. 22. And for the variations between the Hebrew and Samaritan Pentateuch in this place, see at the end of the chapter.

Verse 8. *And all these thy servants shall come*] A prediction of what actually took place. See chap. xii. 31–33.

Verse 9. *Pharaoh shall not hearken unto you*] Though *shall* and *will* are both reputed signs of the future tense, and by many indiscriminately used, yet they make a most essential difference in composition in a variety of cases. For instance, if we translate לא ישמע *lo yishma,* Pharaoh SHALL *not hearken,* as in our text, the word *shall* strongly intimates that it was *impossible* for Pharaoh to hearken, and that *God had placed him under that impossibility:* but if we translate as we should do, Pharaoh WILL *not* hearken, it alters the case most essentially, and agrees with the many passages in the preceding chapters, where he is said to *have hardened his own heart;* as this proves that he, without any impulsive necessity, obstinately refused to attend to what Moses said or threatened; and that God took the advantage of this obstinacy to work another miracle, and thus multiply his wonders in the land.

Pharaoh WILL *not hearken unto you;* and because he *would* not God hardened his heart—left him to his own obstinacy.

To most critics it is well known that there are in several parts of the Pentateuch considerable differences between the Hebrew and Samaritan copies of this work. In this chapter the variations are of considerable importance, and competent critics have allowed that the Samaritan text, especially in this chapter, is fuller and better connected than that of the Hebrew. 1. It is evident that the eighth verse in the present Hebrew text has no natural connection with the seventh. For in the seventh verse Moses delivers to the Israelites what God had commanded him to say; and in the eighth he appears to *continue* a direct discourse unto Pharaoh, though it does not appear when this discourse was *begun.* This is quite contrary to the custom of Moses, who always particularly notes the commencement of his discourses.

2. It is not likely that the Samaritans have *added* these portions, as they could have no private interest to serve by so doing; and therefore it is likely that these additions were originally parts of the sacred text, and might have been omitted, because an ancient copyist found the substance of them in other places. It must however be granted, that the principal additions in the Samaritan are repetitions of speeches which exist in the Hebrew text.

3. The principal part of these additions do not appear to have been borrowed from any other quarter. Interpolations in general are easily discerned from the confusion they introduce; but instead of deranging the sense, the additions *here* make it much more apparent; for should these not be admitted it is evident that something is wanting, without which the connection is incomplete.—See *Calmet.* But the reader is still requested to observe, that the supplementary matter in the Samaritan is collected from other parts of the Hebrew text; and that the principal merit of the Samaritan is, that it preserves the words in a better arrangement.

Dr. *Kennicott* has entered into this subject at large, and by printing the two texts in parallel columns, the supplementary matter in the Samaritan and the hiatus in the Hebrew text will be at once perceived. It is well known that he preferred the Samaritan to the Hebrew Pentateuch; and his reasons for that preference *in this case* I shall subjoin. As the work is extremely scarce from which I select them, one class of readers especially will be glad to meet with them in this place.

"Within these *five* chapters, vii., viii., ix., x., and xi., are *seven* very great differences between the *Hebrew* and *Samaritan* Pentateuchs, relating to the *speeches* which denounced *seven* out of the *ten* judgments upon the Egyptians, viz., *waters* into *blood, frogs, flies, murrain, hail, locusts,* and *destruction of the first-born.* The *Hebrew* text gives the speeches concerning these judgments *only once* at each; but the *Samaritan* gives

each speech TWICE. In the Hebrew we have the speeches concerning the *five* first as in command from GOD to Moses, *without reading that Moses delivered them;* and concerning the two last, as delivered by Moses to Pharaoh, *without reading that* GOD *had commanded them.* Whereas in the *Samaritan* we find every speech TWICE: GOD *commands Moses to go and speak thus or thus before Pharaoh; Moses goes and denounces the judgment; Pharaoh disobeys, and the judgment takes place.* All this is perfectly regular, and exactly agreeable to the *double* speeches of *Homer* in very ancient times. I have not the least doubt that the Hebrew text now wants many words in each of the seven following places: chap. vii., between verses 18 and 19; end of chap. vii.; chap. viii., between 19 and 20; chap. x., between 2 and 3; chap. xi., at verses 3 and 4. The reader will permit me to refer him (for all the words thus omitted) to *my own edition of the Hebrew Bible,* (Oxford 1780, 2 vols. fol.,) where the whole differences are most clearly described. As this is a matter of very extensive consequence, I cannot but observe here, that the present Hebrew text of Exod. xi. did formerly, and does still appear to me to furnish a *demonstration* against itself, in proof of the *double* speech being formerly recorded there, as it is now in the *Samaritan.* And some very learned men have confessed the impossibility of explaining this chapter without the assistance of the *Samaritan Pentateuch.* I shall now give this important chapter as I presume it stood originally, distinguishing by *italics* all such words as are added to or differ from our present translation. And before this chapter must be placed the two last verses of the chapter preceding, Exod. x. 28: *And Pharaoh said unto him, Get thee from me, take heed to thyself, see my face no more; for in that day thou seest my face thou shalt die.* 29: *And Moses said, Thou hast well spoken, I will see thy face again no more.*

EXODUS XI.

HEBREW TEXT AND PRESENT VERSION.	SAMARITAN TEXT AND NEW VERSION.
1. And the Lord said unto Moses, Yet will I bring one plague more upon Pharaoh and upon Egypt, afterwards he will let you go hence: when he shall let you go, he shall surely thrust you out hence altogether.	1. Then Jehovah said unto Moses, Yet will I bring one plague more upon Pharaoh and upon Egypt, *and* afterwards he will send you out hence: when he will send you away, he will surely drive you hence altogether.
2. Speak now in the ears of the people; and let every man BORROW of his neighbour, and every woman of her neighbour, *jewels* of silver, and *jewels* of gold.	2. Speak now in the ears of the people; and let every man ASK of his neighbour, and every woman of her neighbour, *vessels* of silver, and *vessels* of gold *and raiment.*
3. *And* the LORD GAVE *the* people favour in the sight of the Egyptians.	3. *And* I will give *this* people favour in the sight of the Egyptians, *so that they shall give them what they ask.*

EXODUS XI.

HEBREW.	SAMARITAN.
	4. *For about midnight I will go forth into the midst of the land of Egypt.*
	5. *And every first-born in the land of Egypt shall die, from the first-born of Pharaoh who sitteth upon his throne, unto the first-born of the maid-servant that is behind the mill, and even unto the first-born of every beast.*
	6. *And there shall be a great cry through all the land of Egypt, such as there was none like it, nor shall be like it any more.*
	7. *But against any of the children of Israel shall not a dog move his tongue, against man or even against beast; that thou mayest know that Jehovah doth put a difference between the Egyptians and Israel.*
Moreover the man Moses was very great in the land of Egypt, in the sight of Pharaoh's servants, and in the sight of the people.	8. And thou also shalt be greatly honoured in the land of Egypt, in the sight of Pharaoh's servants, and in the sight of the people.
	9. THEN *Moses said unto Pharaoh,* Thus *saith Jehovah, Israel is my son, my first-born; and I said unto thee, Let my son go that he may serve me.*
	10. *But thou hast refused to let him go; behold, Jehovah slayeth thy son, thy first-born.*
4. And Moses said, Thus saith the Lord, About midnight will I go out into the midst of Egypt.	11. And Moses said, Thus saith Jehovah, About midnight will I go forth into the midst *of the land* of Egypt.
5. And all the first-born in the land of Egypt shall die, from the first-born of Pharaoh that sitteth upon his throne, even unto the first-born of the maid-servant that is behind the mill; and all the first-born of beasts.	12. And every first-born in the land of Egypt shall die, from the first-born of Pharaoh that sitteth upon his throne, unto the first born of the maid-servant that is behind the mill; and even unto the first-born of every beast.
6. And there shall be a great cry through all the land of Egypt, such as there was none like it, nor shall be like it any more.	13. And there shall be a great cry through all the land of Egypt, such as there was none like it, nor shall be like it any more.
7. But against any of	14. But against any of

EXODUS XI.

HEBREW.	SAMARITAN.
the children of Israel shall not a dog move his tongue, against man or beast; that ye may know how that the Lord doth put a difference between the Egyptians and Israel.	the children of Israel shall not a dog move his tongue, against man or *even against* beast: that thou mayest know that the Lord doth put a difference between the Egyptians and Israel.
8. And all these thy servants shall come down unto me, and bow down themselves unto me, saying, Get thee out and all the people that follow thee; and after that I will go out. And he went out from Pharaoh in great anger.	15. And all these thy servants shall come down to me, and bow down themselves to me, saying, Go forth, thou and all the people that follow thee; and then I will go forth. 16. Then went he forth from before Pharaoh in great indignation.
9. And the Lord said unto Moses, Pharaoh *shall* not hearken unto you, that my wonders may be multiplied in the land of Egypt.	17. And Jehovah said unto Moses, Pharaoh *doth* not hearken unto you, that my wonders may be multiplied in the land of Egypt.

EXODUS XI.

HEBREW.	SAMARITAN.
10. And Moses and Aaron did all these wonders before Pharaoh: and the Lord hardened Pharaoh's heart, so that he would not let the children of Israel go out of his land.	18. And Moses and Aaron performed all these wonders before Pharaoh: but Jehovah hardened Pharaoh's heart, so that he would not let the children of Israel go out of his land.

"The reader has now the whole of this chapter before him. When, therefore, he has first read the 28th and 29th verses of the preceding chapter, and has then observed with due surprise the confusion of the *Hebrew* text in chap. xi., he will be prepared to acknowledge with due gratitude the regularity and truth of the *Samaritan* text, through these many and very considerable differences."—REMARKS *on select passages in the Old Testament*, 8vo., Oxford, 1787.

The reader will pass his own judgment on the weight of this reasoning, and the importance of the additions preserved in the Samaritan text; a conviction of their utility has induced me to insert them

CHAPTER XII.

The month Abib *is to be considered as the commencement of the year*, 1, 2. *The* PASSOVER *instituted; the* lamb *or* kid *to be used on the occasion to be taken from the flock the* tenth *day of the month, and each family to provide one*, 3, 4. *The lamb or kid to be a male of the first year without blemish*, 5. *To be killed on the* fourteenth *day*, 6, *and the blood to be sprinkled on the side posts and lintels of the doors*, 7. *The flesh to be prepared by* roasting, *and not to be eaten either* sodden *or* raw, 8, 9; *and no part of it to be left till the morning*, 10. *The people to eat it with their loins girded, &c., as persons prepared for a journey*, 11. *Why called the* PASSOVER, 12. *The blood sprinkled on the door posts, &c., to be a token to them of preservation from the destroying angel*, 13. *The* fourteenth *day of the month* Abib *to be a feast for ever*, 14. *Unleavened bread to be eaten seven days*, 15. *This also to be observed in all their generations for ever*, 17–20. *Moses instructs the elders of Israel how they are to offer the lamb and sprinkle his blood, and for what purpose*, 21–23. *He binds them to instruct their children in the nature of this rite*, 24–27. *The children of Israel act as commanded*, 28. *All the first-born of Egypt slain*, 29, 30. *Pharaoh and the Egyptians urge Moses, Aaron, and the Israelites to depart*, 31–33. *They prepare for their departure, and get* gold, silver, *and* raiment *from the Egyptians*, 34–36. *They journey from* Rameses *to* Succoth, *in number* six hundred thousand *men, besides women and children, and a mixed multitude*, 37, 38. *They bake unleavened cakes of the dough they brought with them out of Egypt*, 39. *The time in which they sojourned in Egypt*, 40–42. *Different ordinances concerning the* PASSOVER, 43–49; *which are all punctually observed by the people, who are brought out of Egypt the same day*, 50, 51.

A. M. 2513. B. C. 1491. An. Exod. Isr. 1. Abib or Nisan.

AND the LORD spake unto Moses and Aaron in the land of Egypt, saying,

2 [a] This month *shall be* unto you the beginning of months: it *shall be* the first month of the year to you.

3 Speak ye unto all the congregation of

[a] Chap. xiii. 4; Deut. xvi. 1; xxiii. 15; xxxiv. 18; Lev. xiii. 5; Num. xxviii. 16; Esth. iii. 7.

NOTES ON CHAP. XII.

Verse 2. *This month* shall be *unto you the beginning of months*] It is supposed that God now changed the commencement of the Jewish year. The month to which this verse refers, the month *Abib*, answers to a part of our *March* and *April*; whereas it is supposed that previously to this the year began with *Tisri*, which answers to a part of our *September*; for in this month the Jews suppose God created the world, when the earth appeared at once with all its fruits in perfection. From this circumstance the Jews have formed a twofold commencement of the year, which has given rise to a twofold denomination of the year itself, to which they afterwards attended in all their reckonings: that which began with *Tisri* or *September* was called their *civil* year; that which began with *Abib* or *March* was called the *sacred* or *ecclesiastical* year.

As the *exodus of the Israelites* formed a particular

A. M. 2513. B. C. 1491. An. Exod. Isr. 1. Abib or Nisan.

Israel, saying, In the tenth *day*
of this month they shall take to
them every man a [b] lamb, ac-
cording to the house of *their* fathers, a lamb
for a house:
4 And if the household be too little for the
lamb, let him and his neighbour next unto his
house take *it*, according to the number of the
souls; every man, according to
his eating, shall make your count
for the lamb.
5 Your lamb shall be [c] without blemish, a
male [d] of the first year: ye shall take *it* out
from the sheep, or from the goats:
6 And ye shall keep it up until the [e] fourteenth day of the same month: and the whole

[b] Or, *kid*.——[c] Lev. xxii. 19, 20, 21; Mal. i. 8, 14; Heb. ix. 14; 1 Pet. i. 19.

[d] Heb. *son of a year*; Lev. xxiii. 12.——[e] Lev. xxiii. 5; Num. ix. 3; xxviii. 16; Deut. xvi. 1, 6.

era, which is referred to in Jewish reckonings down to the building of the temple, I have marked it as such in the chronology in the margin; and shall carry it down to the time in which it ceased to be acknowledged.

Some very eminently learned men dispute this; and especially Houbigant, who contends with great plausibility of argument that no new commencement of the year is noted in this place; for that the year had always begun in this month, and that the words *shall be*, which are inserted by different versions, have nothing answering to them in the Hebrew, which he renders literally thus: *Hic mensis vobis est caput mensium; hic vobis primus est anni mensis*. "This month is to you the head or chief of the months; it is to you the first month of the year." And he observes farther that God only marks it thus, as is evident from the context, to show the people that this month, which was the beginning of their year, should be so designated as to point out to their posterity on *what* month and on what day of the month they were to celebrate the passover and the feast of unleavened bread. His words are these: "Ergo superest, et Hebr. ipso ex contextu efficitur, non hic novi ordinis annum constitui, sed eum anni mensem, qui esset primus, ideo commemorari, ut posteris constaret, quo mense, et quo die mensis pascha et azyma celebranda essent."

Verse 3. *In the tenth* day *of this month*] In after times they began their preparation on the *thirteenth* day or day before the PASSOVER, which was not celebrated till the *fourteenth* day, see ver. 6: but on the present occasion, as this was their first *passover*, they probably required more time to get ready in; as a state of very great confusion must have prevailed at this time. Mr. Ainsworth remarks that on this day the Israelites did afterwards go through Jordan into the land of Canaan; Josh. iv. 19. And Christ, our Paschal Lamb, on this day entered Jerusalem, riding on an ass; the people bearing palm branches, and crying, Hosanna, John xii. 1, 12, 13, &c.: and in him this type was truly fulfilled.

A lamb] The original word שה *seh* signifies the young of sheep and of goats, and may be indifferently translated either *lamb* or *kid*. See ver. 5.

A lamb for a house] The whole *host* of Israel was divided into *twelve tribes*, these tribes into *families*, the families into *houses*, and the houses into *particular persons*; Num. i., Josh. vii. 14.—*Ainsworth*.

Verse 4. *If the household be too little*] That is, If there be not persons enough in one family to eat a whole lamb, then two families must join together. The rabbins allow that there should be at least *ten* persons to one paschal lamb, and not more than *twenty*.

Take it, *according to the number of the souls*] The persons who were to eat of it were to be first ascertained, and then the lamb was to be slain and dressed for *that number*.

Verse 5. *Without blemish*] Having no natural imperfection, no disease, no *deficiency* or *redundancy* of parts. On this point the rabbins have trifled most egregiously, reckoning *fifty* blemishes that render a lamb or a kid, or any animal, improper to be sacrificed: *five* in the *ear*, *three* in the *eyelid*, *eight* in the *eye*, *three* in the *nose*, *six* in the *mouth*, &c., &c.

A male of the first year] That is, any age in the *first* year between *eight days* and *twelve months*.

From the sheep, or from the goats] The שה *seh* means either; and either was equally proper if without blemish. The Hebrews however in general preferred the *lamb* to the *kid*.

Verse 6. *Ye shall keep it up until the fourteenth day*] The lamb or kid was to be taken from the flock on the *tenth* day, and kept up and fed by itself till the *fourteenth* day, when it was to be sacrificed. This was never commanded nor practised afterwards. The rabbins mark *four* things that were required in the first passover that were never required afterwards: I. The eating of the lamb in their houses dispersed through Goshen. 2. The taking the lamb on the tenth day. 3. The striking of its blood on the door posts and lintels of their houses. And, 4. Their eating it in haste. These things were not required of the succeeding generations.

The whole assembly—shall kill it] Any person might kill it, the sacrificial act in this case not being confined to the *priests*.

In the evening.] בין הערבים *beyn haarbayim*, "between the two evenings." The Jews divided the day into *morning* and *evening*: till the sun passed the *meridian* all was *morning* or *forenoon*; after that, all was *afternoon* or *evening*. Their *first evening* began just after *twelve o'clock*, and continued till *sunset*; their *second evening* began at *sunset* and continued till *night*, i. e., during the whole time of *twilight*; between twelve o'clock, therefore, and the termination of *twilight*, the passover was to be offered.

"The day among the Jews had *twelve* hours, John xi. 9. Their *first* hour was about six o'clock in the morning with us. Their *sixth* hour was our noon. Their *ninth* hour answered to our three o'clock in the afternoon. By this we may understand that the time

A. M. 2513. B. C. 1491. An. Exod. Isr. 1. Abib or Nisan.

assembly of the congregation of Israel shall kill it [f] in the evening.

7 And they shall take of the blood, and strike *it* on the two side posts, and on the upper door post of the houses, wherein they shall eat it.

8 And they shall eat the flesh in that night, roast with fire, and [g] unleavened bread; *and* with bitter *herbs* they shall eat it.

A. M. 2513. B. C. 1491. An. Exod. Isr. 1. Abib or Nisan.

9 Eat not of it raw, nor sodden at all with water, but [h] roast *with* fire; his head with his legs, and with the purtenance thereof.

10 [i] And ye shall let nothing of it remain until the morning; and that which remaineth

[f] Heb. *between the two evenings*; chap. xvi. 12.——[g] Ch. xxxiv. 25; Deut. xvi. 3; Num. ix. 11; 1 Cor. iv. 8.

[h] Deuteronomy xvi. 7.——[i] Chapter xxiii. 18; xxxiv. 25.

in which Christ was crucified began at the *third* hour, that is, at nine o'clock in the morning, the ordinary time for the *daily morning sacrifice*, and ended at the *ninth* hour, that is, three o'clock in the afternoon, the time of the evening sacrifice, Mark xv. 25, 33, 34, 37. Wherefore their *ninth* hour was their *hour of prayer*, when they used to go into the temple at the daily evening sacrifice, Acts iii. 1; and this was the ordinary time for the passover. It is worthy of remark that God sets no particular *hour* for the killing of the passover: any time between the two evenings, i. e., between twelve o'clock in the day and the termination of twilight, was lawful. The daily sacrifice (see Exod. xxix. 38, 39) was killed at *half past the eighth hour*, that is, *half an hour* BEFORE *three* in the afternoon; and it was offered up at *half past the ninth hour*, that is, *half an hour* AFTER *three*. In the evening of the passover it was killed at *half past the seventh hour*, and offered at *half past the eighth*, that is, *half an hour* BEFORE *three:* and if the evening of the passover fell on the evening of the Sabbath, it was killed at *half past the* SIXTH *hour*, and offered at *half past the* SEVENTH, that is, *half an hour* BEFORE *two* in the afternoon. The reason of this was, they were first obliged to kill the daily sacrifice, and then to kill and roast the paschal lamb, and also to rest the evening before the passover. Agreeably to this *Maimonides* says 'the killing of the passover is after mid-day, and if they kill it before it is not lawful; and they do not kill it till after the daily evening sacrifice, and burning of incense: and after they have trimmed the lamps they begin to kill the paschal lambs until the end of the day.' By this time of the day God foreshowed the sufferings of Christ in the evening of times or in the last days, Heb. i. 2; 1 Pet. i. 19, 20: and about the same time of the day, when the paschal lamb ordinarily died, HE died also, viz., at the *ninth* hour; Matt. xxvii. 46–50." See *Ainsworth.*

Verse 7. *Take of the blood, and strike* it *on the two side posts*] This was to be done by dipping a bunch of hyssop into the blood, and thus sprinkling it upon the posts, &c.; see ver. 22. That this sprinkling of the blood of the paschal lamb was an emblem of the sacrifice and atonement made by the death of Jesus Christ, is most clearly intimated in the sacred writings, 1 Pet. i. 2; Heb. ix. 13, 14; viii. 10. It is remarkable that no blood was to be sprinkled on the *threshold*, to teach, as Mr. Ainsworth properly observes, a reverent regard for the blood of Christ, that men should not *tread under foot the Son of GOD*, nor *count the blood of the covenant* wherewith they were sanctified *an unholy thing*; Heb. x. 29.

Verse 8. *They shall eat the flesh—roast with fire*] As it was the ordinary custom of the Jews to *boil* their flesh, some think that the command given here was in opposition to the custom of the Egyptians, who ate *raw* flesh in honour of Osiris. The Æthiopians are to this day remarkable for eating *raw flesh*, as is the case with most savage nations.

Unleavened bread] מצות *matstsoth*, from מצה *matsah*, to *squeeze* or *compress*, because the bread prepared without *leaven* or *yeast* was generally compressed, *sad* or *heavy*, as we term it. The word here properly signifies unleavened *cakes*; the word for leaven in Hebrew is חמץ *chamets*, which simply signifies to *ferment*. It is supposed that *leaven* was forbidden on this and other occasions, that the bread being less agreeable to the taste, it might be emblematical of their bondage and *bitter* servitude, as this seems to have been one design of the *bitter* herbs which were commanded to be used on this occasion; but this certainly was not the sole design of the prohibition: *leaven* itself is a species of *corruption*, being produced by *fermentation*, which in such cases tends to *putrefaction*. In this very light St. Paul considers the subject in this place; hence, alluding to the passover as a type of Christ, he says: *Purge out therefore the old leaven—for Christ our passover is sacrificed for us: therefore let us keep the feast, not with old leaven, neither with the leaven of malice and wickedness, but with the unleavened* bread *of sincerity and truth*; 1 Cor. v. 6–8.

Bitter herbs] What kind of herbs or salad is intended by the word מררים *merorim*, which literally signifies *bitters*, is not well known. The Jews think *cichory, wild lettuce, horehound*, and the like are intended. Whatever may be implied under the term, whether *bitter herbs* or *bitter ingredients* in general, it was designed to put them in mind of their bitter and severe bondage in the land of Egypt, from which God was now about to deliver them.

Verse 9. *With the purtenance thereof.*] All the intestines, for these were abused by the heathens to purposes of divination; and when roasted in the manner here directed they could not be thus used. The command also implies that the lamb was to be roasted whole; neither the *head* or *legs* were to be separated, nor the intestines removed. I suppose that these last simply included the *heart, lungs, liver, kidneys*, &c., and not the intestinal canal.

Verse 10. *Ye shall let nothing of it remain until the*

A. M. 2513. B. C. 1491. An. Exod. Isr. 1. Abib or Nisan.

of it until the morning ye shall
burn with fire.
11 And thus shall ye eat it;
with your loins girded, your shoes on your feet,
and your staff in your hand; and ye shall
eat it in haste: [k] it *is* the LORD's passover.
12 For I [l] will pass through
the land of Egypt this night, and
will smite all the first-born in the
land of Egypt, both man and beast; and
[m] against all the [n] gods of Egypt I will execute
judgment: [o] I *am* the LORD.

[k] Deut. xvi. 5.——[l] Chap. xi. 4, 5; Amos v. 17.——[m] Numbers xxxiii. 4.

[n] Or, *princes*; chap. xxi. 6; xxii. 28; Psa. lxxxii. 1, 6; John x. 34, 35.——[o] Chap. vi. 2.

morning] Merely to prevent *putrefaction;* for it was not meet that a thing offered to God should be subjected to corruption, which in such hot countries it must speedily undergo. Thus the body of our blessed Lord *saw no corruption*, Psalm xvi. 10; Acts ii. 27, because, like the paschal lamb, it was a *sacrifice* offered to God.

It appears that from the Jewish passover the heathens borrowed their sacrifice termed PROPTER VIAM. It was their custom previously to their undertaking a journey, to offer a sacrifice to their gods, and to eat the *whole* if possible, but if any part was left they burned it with fire; and this was called *propter viam*, because it was made to procure a *prosperous journey.* It was in reference to this that Cato is said to have rallied a person called *Q. Albidius*, who, having eaten up all his goods, set fire to his house, his only remaining property. "He has offered his sacrifice *propter viam*," says Cato, "because he has burned what he could not eat." This account is given by *Macrobius*, Saturn., lib. ii., 2, edit. Bipont., vol. i., p. 333; and is a remarkable instance how closely some of the religious observances of the people of God have been copied by the heathen nations.

Verse 11. *And thus shall ye eat it;* with *your loins girded*] As in the eastern countries they wear long loose garments, whenever they travel they tuck up the fore parts of their garments in the girdle which they wear round their loins.

Your shoes on your feet] This seems particularly mentioned because not customary. "The easterns throw off their shoes when they eat, because it would be troublesome," says Sir J. Chardin, "to keep their shoes upon their feet, they sitting cross-legged on the floor, and having no hinder quarters to their shoes, which are made like *slippers;* and as they do not use *tables* and *chairs* as we do in Europe, but have their floors covered with carpets, they throw off their shoes when they enter their apartments, lest they should soil those beautiful pieces of furniture." On the contrary the Israelites were to have their *shoes on*, because now about to commence their journey. It was customary among the Romans to lay aside their shoes when they went to a banquet. The servants took them off them when they entered the house, and returned them when they departed to their own habitations.

Your staff in your hand] The same writer observes that the eastern people universally make use of a *staff* when they travel on foot.

Ye shall eat it in haste] Because they were suddenly to take their departure: the destroying angel was at hand, their enemies were coming against them, and they had not a moment to lose.

It is the Lord's passover.] That is, Jehovah is now about to *pass over* the land, and the houses only where the blood is sprinkled shall be safe from the stroke of death. The Hebrew word פסח *pesach*, which we very properly translate PASSOVER, and which should always be pronounced as *two words*, has its name from the angel of God *passing by* or *over* the houses of the Israelites, on the posts and lintels of which the blood of the lamb was sprinkled, while he *stopped* at the houses of the Egyptians to slay their first-born.

Verse 12. *Against all the gods of Egypt, &c.*] As different animals were sacred among the Egyptians, the slaying of the *first-born* of all the beasts might be called executing judgment upon the *gods* of Egypt. As this however does not appear very clear and satisfactory, some have imagined that the word אלהי *elohey* should be translated *princes*, which is the rendering in our *margin;* for as these princes, who were rulers of the kingdom under Pharaoh, were equally hostile to the Hebrews with Pharaoh himself, therefore these judgments fell equally heavy on them also. But we may ask, Did not these judgments fall equally on all the families of Egypt, though multitudes of them had no particular part either in the evil counsel against the Israelites or in their oppression? Why then distinguish those in calamities in which all equally shared? None of these interpretations therefore appear satisfactory. *Houbigant*, by a very simple and natural emendation, has, he thinks, restored the whole passage to sense and reason. He supposes that אלהי *elohey*, GODS, is a mistake for אהלי *ahley*, TENTS or *habitations*, the ה *he* and the ל *lamed* being merely *interchanged.* This certainly gives a very consistent sense, and points out the universality of the desolation to which the whole context continually refers. He therefore contends that the text should be read thus: *And on all the* TENTS (or HABITATIONS) *of Egypt I will execute judgment;* by which words the Lord signified that not *one dwelling* in the whole land of Egypt should be exempted from the judgment here threatened. It is but justice to say that however probable this criticism may appear, it is not supported by any of the ancient versions, nor by any of the MSS. collated by *Kennicott* and *De Rossi.* The parallel place also Num. xxxiii. 4, is rather against Houbigant's interpretation: *For the Egyptians buried all their first-born, which the Lord had smitten among them: upon their gods also* [ובאלהיהם *ubeloheyhem*] *the Lord executed judgments.* But Houbigant amends the word in this place in the same way as he does that in Exodus. There appears also to be an allusion to this former judgment in Isa. xix. 1: *Behold, the Lord— shall come into Egypt, and the idols* [אלילי *eliley*] *of*

A. M. 2513. B. C. 1491. An. Exod. Isr. 1. Abib or Nisan.

13 And the blood shall be to
you for a token upon the houses
where ye *are:* and when I see
the blood, I will pass over you, and the plague
shall not be upon you [p] to destroy *you*, when
I smite the land of Egypt.
14 And this day shall be unto you [q] for a
memorial, and ye shall keep it a [r] feast to the
LORD throughout your generations; ye shall
keep it a feast [s] by an ordinance for ever.
15 [t] Seven days shall ye eat unleavened
bread; even the first day ye shall put away
leaven out of your houses: for
whosoever eateth leavened bread
from the first day until the seventh
day, [u] that soul shall be cut off from Israel
16 And in the first day *there shall be* [v] a
holy convocation, and in the seventh day there
shall be a holy convocation to you; no man
ner of work shall be done in them, save *that*
which every [w] man must eat, that only may
be done of you.
17 And ye shall observe *the feast of* unleavened bread; for [x] in this self-same day have

[p] Heb. *for a destruction.*——[q] Chap. xiii. 9.——[r] Lev. xxiii. 4, 5; 2 Kings xxiii. 21.——[s] Ver. 24, 43; chap. xiii. 10.——[t] Chap. xiii. 6, 7; xxiii. 15; xxxiv. 18, 25; Lev. xxiii. 5, 6; Num. xxviii. 17; Deut. xvi. 3, 8; 1 Cor. v. 7.——[u] Gen. xvii. 14; Num. ix. 13.——[v] Lev. xxiii. 7, 8; Num. xxviii. 18, 25.——[w] Heb. *soul.* [x] Chap. xiii. 3.

Egypt shall be moved at his presence. And in Jer. xliii. 13: *The houses of the gods* [בתי אלהי *bottey elohey*] *of the Egyptians shall he burn with fire.* The rabbins say that "when Israel came out of Egypt, the holy blessed God threw down all the images of their abominations, and they were broken to pieces." When a nation was conquered, it was always supposed that their gods had either abandoned them or were overcome. Thus Egypt was ruined, and their gods confounded and destroyed by Jehovah. See the note on chap. xi. 7.

Verse 13. *The blood shall be to you for a token*] It shall be the *sign* to the destroying angel, that the house on which he sees this blood sprinkled is under the protection of God, and that no person in it is to be injured. See on ver. 11.

Verse 14. *A memorial*] To keep up a remembrance of the severity and goodness, or justice and mercy, of God. *Ye shall keep it a feast*—it shall be annually observed, and shall be celebrated with solemn religious joy, *throughout your generations*—as long as ye continue to be a distinct people; an *ordinance*—a Divine appointment, an institution of God himself, neither to be altered nor set aside by any human authority.

For ever] חקת עולם *chukkath olam*, an everlasting or endless statute, because representative of the Lamb of God who taketh away the sin of the world; whose mediation, in consequence of his sacrifice, shall endure while *time itself lasts;* and to whose merits and efficacy the salvation of the soul shall be ascribable throughout *eternity*. This, therefore, is a statute and ordinance that can have no end, either in this world or in the world to come. It is remarkable that though the Jews have ceased from the whole of their sacrificial system, so that sacrifices are no longer offered by them in any part of the world, yet they all, in all their generations and in all countries, keep up the remembrance of the passover, and observe the feast of unleavened bread. But no lamb is sacrificed. Their sacrifices have all totally ceased, ever since the destruction of Jerusalem by the Romans. Even the flesh that is used on this occasion is partly *roasted* and partly *boiled*, that it may not even resemble the primitive sacrifice; for they deem it *unlawful* to sacrifice out of Jerusalem. The truth is, the true Lamb of God that taketh away the sin of the world *has been* offered, and they have no power to restore the ancient type. See on ver. 27.

Verse 15. *Seven days shall ye eat unleavened bread*] This has been considered as a distinct ordinance, and not essentially connected with the passover. The passover was to be observed on the fourteenth day of the first month; the feast of unleavened bread began on the *fifteenth* and lasted seven days, the first and last of which were holy convocations.

That soul shall be cut off] There are *thirty-six* places in which this *excision* or *cutting off* is threatened against the Jews for neglect of some particular duty; and what is implied in the thing itself is not well known. Some think it means a violent death, some a premature death, and some an eternal death. It is very likely that it means no more than a separation from the rights and privileges of an Israelite; so that after this excision the person was considered as a mere stranger, who had neither lot nor part in Israel, nor any right to the blessings of the covenant. This is probably what St. Paul means, Rom. ix. 3. But we naturally suppose this punishment was not inflicted but on those who had showed a *marked* and *obstinate* contempt for the Divine authority. This punishment appears to have been nearly the same with *excommunication* among the Christians; and from this general notion of the *cutting off*, the Christian excommunication seems to have been borrowed.

Verse 16. *In the first day—and in the seventh day there shall be a holy convocation*] This is the first place where we meet with the account of an *assembly* collected for the mere purpose of religious worship. Such assemblies are called *holy convocations*, which is a very appropriate appellation for a religious assembly; they were *called* together by the express command of God, and were to be employed in a work of *holiness*. מקרא *mikra*, *convocation*, is a word of similar import with the Greek *εκκλησια*, which we commonly translate *Church*, and which properly signifies an assembly convened by public *call*.

Verse 17. *Self-same day*] בעצם *beetsem*, in the body of this day, or in the strength of this day; probably they began their march about day-break, called here

A. M. 2513.
B. C. 1491.
An. Exod. Isr. 1.
Abib or Nisan.

I brought your armies out of the
land of Egypt: therefore shall ye
observe this day in your generations by an ordinance for ever.
18 [y] In the first *month*, on the fourteenth
day of the month at even, ye shall eat unleavened bread, until the one and twentieth day
of the month at even.
19 [z] Seven days shall there be no leaven
found in your houses: for whosoever eateth
that which is leavened, [a] even that soul shall
be cut off from the congregation of Israel,
whether he be a stranger, or born in the land.
20 Ye shall eat nothing leavened; in all
your habitations shall ye eat unleavened
bread.
21 Then Moses called for all the elders of
Israel, and said unto them, [b] Draw out and
take you a [c] lamb according to your families,
and kill the passover.
22 [d] And ye shall take a bunch of hyssop,
and dip *it* in the blood that *is* in
the basin, and [e] strike the lintel
and the two side posts with the
blood that *is* in the basin; and none of you
shall go out at the door of his house until
the morning.
23 [f] For the LORD will pass through to
smite the Egyptians; and when he seeth the
blood upon the lintel, and on the two side
posts, the LORD will pass over the door, and
[g] will not suffer [h] the destroyer to come in
unto your houses to smite *you*.
24 And ye shall observe this thing for an
ordinance to thee and to thy sons for ever.
25 And it shall come to pass, when ye be
come to the land which the LORD will give
you, [i] according as he hath promised, that ye
shall keep this service.
26 [k] And it shall come to pass, when your
children shall say unto you, What mean ye
by this service?

[y] Lev. xxiii. 5; Num. xxviii. 16.——[z] Exod. xxiii. 15; xxxiv. 18; Deut. xvi. 3; 1 Cor. v. 7, 8.——[a] Num. ix. 13.——[b] Ver. 3; Num. ix. 4; Josh. v. 10; 2 Kings xxiii. 21; Ezra vi. 20; Matt. xxvi. 18, 19; Mark xiv. 12–16; Luke xxii. 7, &c.

[c] Or, *kid*.——[d] Heb. xi. 28.——[e] Verse 7.——[f] Verse 12, 13.——[g] Ezek. ix. 6; Rev. vii. 3; ix. 4.——[h] 2 Sam. xxiv. 16; 1 Cor. x. 10; Heb. xi. 28.——[i] Chap. iii. 8, 17.——[k] Chap. xiii. 8, 14; Deut. xxxii. 7; Josh. iv. 6; Psa. lxxviii. 6.

the *body* or *strength* of the day, and in Deut. xvi. 1, *by night*—some time before the sun rose.

Verse 19. *No leaven found in your houses*] To meet the letter of this precept in the fullest manner possible, the Jews, on the eve of this festival, institute the most rigorous search through every part of their houses, not only removing all leavened bread, but sweeping every part clean, that no crumb of bread shall be left that had any leaven in it. And so strict were they in the observance of the letter of this law, that if even a mouse was seen to run across the floor with a crumb of bread in its mouth, they considered the whole house as polluted, and began their purification afresh. We have already seen that *leaven* was an emblem of sin, because it proceeded from corruption; and the putting away of this implied the turning to God with simplicity and uprightness of heart. See on ver. 8, and the note on ver. 27.

Verse 21. *Kill the passover.*] That is, the *lamb*, which was called the *paschal* or *passover* lamb. The *animal* that was to be sacrificed on this occasion got the name of the *institution* itself: thus the word *covenant* is often put for the sacrifice offered in making the covenant; so the *rock* was *Christ*, 1 Cor. x. 4; *bread* and *wine* the *body* and *blood* of *Christ*, Mark xiv. 22, 24. St. Paul copies the expression, 1 Cor. v. 7: *Christ our passover* (that is, our paschal lamb) *is sacrificed for us*.

Verse 22. *A bunch of hyssop*] The original word אזוב *ezob* has been variously translated *musk*, *rosemary*, *polypody of the wall*, *mint*, *origanum*, *marjoram*, and HYSSOP: the latter seems to be the most proper. Parkhurst says it is named from its detersive and cleansing qualities, whence it was used in sprinkling the blood of the paschal lamb, in cleansing the leprosy, Lev. xiv 4, 6, 51, 52; in composing the water of purification, Num. xix. 6, and sprinkling it, ver. 18. It was a type of the *purifying* virtue of the bitter sufferings of Christ. And it is plain, from Psa. li. 7, that the psalmist understood its meaning. Among botanists hyssop is described as "a genus of the *gymnospermia* (naked-seeded) order, belonging to the *didynamia* class of plants. It has under-shrubby, low, bushy stalks, growing a foot and a half high, small, spear-shaped, close-sitting, opposite leaves, with several smaller ones rising from the same joint; and all the stalks and branches terminated by erect whorled spikes of flowers of different colours, in the varieties of the plant. The leaves have an aromatic smell, and a warm pungent taste. The leaves of this plant are particularly recommended in humoral asthmas, and other disorders of the breast and lungs, and greatly promote expectoration." Its medicinal qualities were probably the reason why this plant was so particularly recommended in the Scriptures.

Verse 26. *What mean ye by this service?*] The establishment of this service annually was a very wise provision to keep up in remembrance this wonderful deliverance. From the remotest antiquity the institution of feasts, games, &c., has been used to keep up the memory of past grand events. Hence God instituted the *Sabbath*, to keep up the remembrance of the *creation*; and the *passover*, to keep up the remembrance of the *deliverance from Egypt*. All the other feasts were instituted on similar reasons. The Jews never took their sons to the tabernacle or temple till they

A. M. 2513.
B. C. 1491.
An. Exod. Isr. 1.
Abib or Nisan.

27 That ye shall say, [l] It *is*
the sacrifice of the LORD's passover, who passed over the houses
of the children of Israel in Egypt, when he
smote the Egyptians, and delivered our houses.
And the people [m] bowed the head
and worshipped.
28 And the children of Israel
went away, and [n] did as the LORD had commanded Moses and Aaron, so did they.

A. M. 2513.
B. C. 1491.
An. Exod. Isr.
Abib or Nisan.

[l] Ver. 11.——[m] Chap. iv. 31.——[n] Heb. xi. 28.

were *twelve years of age*, nor suffered them to eat of the flesh of any victim till they had themselves offered a sacrifice at the temple, which they were not permitted to do before the twelfth year of their age. It was at this age that Joseph and Mary took our blessed Lord to the temple, probably for the first time, to offer his sacrifice. See *Calmet*.

Verse 27. *It is the sacrifice of the Lord's passover*] We have already intimated that the paschal lamb was an illustrious type of Christ; and we shall find that every thing in this account is *typical* or representative. The bondage and affliction of the people of Israel may be considered as emblems of the hard slavery and wretchedness consequent on a state of sinfulness. Satan reigns over both body and soul, bringing the whole into subjection to the law of sin and death; while various evil tempers, passions, lusts, and irregular appetites, act as subordinate tormentors, making the lives of the vassals of sin bitter, because of the rigour by which they are obliged to serve. Reader, is this thy case? The mercy of God projects the redemption of man from this cruel bondage and oppression; and a *sacrifice* is appointed for the occasion by God himself, to be offered with particular and significant rites and ceremonies, all of which represent the *passion* and *death* of our blessed Lord, and the great *end* for which he became a *sacrifice*, viz., the redemption of a lost world from the power, the guilt, and the pollution of sin, &c. And it is worthy of remark, 1. That the *anniversary* or annual commemoration of the passover was strictly and religiously kept by the Jews on the *day*, and *hour* of the day, on which the original transaction took place, throughout all their succeeding generations. 2. That on one of these anniversaries, and, as many suppose, on the very day and hour on which the paschal lamb was originally offered, our blessed Lord expired on the cross for the salvation of the world. 3. That after the destruction of Jerusalem the paschal lamb ceased to be offered by the Jews throughout the world, though they continue to hold the anniversary of the passover, but *without any sacrifice*, notwithstanding their deep-rooted, inveterate antipathy against the author and grace of the Gospel. 4. That the *sacrament* of the Lord's Supper was instituted to keep this true paschal sacrifice in commemoration, and that this has been religiously observed by the whole Christian world (one very small class of Christians excepted) from the foundation of Christianity to the present day! 5. That the Jews were commanded to eat the paschal lamb; and our Lord, commemorating the passover, commanded his disciples, saying, Take, eat, THIS is my body, which is given for *you*; do this in *remembrance* of ME. In the communion service of the Church of England, the spirit and design both of the type and antitype are most expressly condensed into one point of view, in the address to the communicant: "Take and eat this in remembrance that Christ died for THEE; and FEED upon HIM, in thy *heart*, by FAITH with THANKSGIVING." Thus God continues the memorial of that grand transaction which he has said should be an ordinance *for ever*; evidently meaning thereby, that the *paschal lamb* should be the significator *till* the passion and death of Christ; and that afterwards *bread* and *wine* taken sacramentally, in commemoration of his crucifixion, should be the *continual representatives* of that sacrifice till the end of the world. Thus the passover in *itself*, and in its *reference*, is an *ordinance for ever*; and thus the words of the Lord are literally fulfilled. Reader, learn from this, 1. That if thou art not rescued from the thraldom of sin, thou must perish for ever. 2. That nothing less than the power and mercy of God can set thee free. 3. That God will save thee in no other way than by bringing thee out of thy sinful state, and from thy wicked practices and companions. 4. That in order to thy redemption it was absolutely necessary that the Son of God should take thy nature upon him, and *die in thy stead*. 5. That unless the blood of this sacrifice be sprinkled, in its atoning efficacy and merits, on thy heart and conscience, the guilt and power of thy sin cannot be taken away. 6. That as the blood of the paschal lamb must be sprinkled on *every house*, in order to the preservation of its inhabitants, so there must be a *personal* application of the blood of the cross to thy conscience, to take away thy sins. 7. As it was not enough that the passover was *instituted*, but the blood must be *sprinkled* on the lintels and door posts of every house to make the rite effectual to the salvation of each individual, so it is not enough that Christ should have taken human nature upon him, and died for the sin of the world; for no man who has the opportunity of hearing the Gospel is saved by that death, who does not, by faith, get a personal application of it to his own heart. 8. That those who wish for an application of the atoning blood, must receive this spiritual passover with a perfect readiness to depart from the land of their captivity, and travel to the rest that remains for the people of God; it being impossible, not only to a *gross sinner*, continuing such, to be finally saved, (however he may presume upon the *mercy* of God,) but also to a *worldly-minded* man, to get to the kingdom of God; for Christ died to save us *from the present evil world, according to the will of God*. 9. That in order to commemorate aright, in the sacrament of the Lord's Supper, the great atonement made for the sin of the world, *all leaven* of malice, bitterness, and insincerity, must be put away; as God will have no man to partake of this mystery who does not fully enter into its spirit and meaning. See 1 Cor. v. 7, 8.

A. M. 2513. B. C. 1491. An. Exod. Isr. 1. Abib or Nisan.

29 [o] And it came to pass, that
at midnight [p] the LORD smote all
the first-born in the land of Egypt,
[q] from the first-born of Pharaoh that sat on his
throne, unto the first-born of the captive that
was in the [r] dungeon; and all the
first-born of cattle.
30 And Pharaoh rose up in
the night, he, and all his servants, and all
the Egyptians; and there was a [s] great cry

[o] Chap. xi. 4.——[p] Num. viii. 17; xxxiii. 4; Psa. lxxviii. 51; cv. 36; cxxxv. 8; cxxxvi. 10.——[q] Chap. iv. 23; xi. 5; Wisd. xviii. 11.——[r] Heb. *house of the pit.*——[s] Chap. xi. 6; Prov. xxi. 13; Amos v. 17; James ii. 13.

Verse 29. *Smote all the first-born*] If we take the term *first-born* in its literal sense *only*, we shall be led to conclude that in a vast number of the houses of the Egyptians there could have been no death, as it is not at all likely that every first-born child of every Egyptian family was still alive, and that all the first-born of their cattle still remained. And yet it is said, ver. 30, that there was *not a house where* there was *not one dead.* The word therefore must not be taken in its literal sense only. From its use in a great variety of places in the Scriptures it is evident that it means the *chief, most excellent, best beloved, most distinguished,* &c. In this sense our blessed Lord is called *the* FIRST-BORN *of every creature*, Col. i. 15, and *the* FIRST-BORN *among many brethren*, Rom. viii. 29; that is, he is *more excellent* than all creatures, and *greater* than all the children of men. In the same sense we may understand Rev. i. 5, where CHRIST is called *the* FIRST-BEGOTTEN *from the dead*, i. e., the *chief* of all that have ever visited the empire of death, and on whom death has had any power; and the *only one* who by his own might quickened himself. In the same sense *wisdom* is represented as being *brought forth before all the creatures*, and being *possessed by the Lord in the beginning of his ways*, Prov. viii. 22–30; that is, the *wisdom* of God is *peculiarly conspicuous* in the production, arrangement, and government of every part of the creation. So *Ephraim* is called the Lord's FIRST-BORN, Jer. xxxi. 9. And the people of Israel are often called by the same name, see Exod. iv. 22: *Israel is my son, my* FIRST-BORN; that is, the people in whom I particularly delight, and whom I will especially support and defend. And because the *first-born* are in general peculiarly dear to their parents, and because among the Jews they had especial and peculiar privileges, whatever was most dear, most valuable, and most prized, was thus denominated. So Micah vi. 7: *Shall I give my* FIRST-BORN *for my transgression, the fruit of my body for the sin of my soul?* Shall I give up the *most beloved* child I have, he that is *most dear* and *most necessary* to me, in order to make an atonement for my sins! In like manner the Prophet Zechariah, speaking of the conversion of the Jews to the Gospel of Christ, represents them as looking on him *whom they have pierced*, and being as one that is *in bitterness for his* FIRST-BORN; that is, they shall feel distress and anguish as those who had lost their *most beloved* child. So the Church triumphant in the kingdom of God are called, Heb. xii. 23, *the general assembly and Church of the* FIRST-BORN, i. e., the *most noble* and *excellent* of all *human* if not *created* beings. So Homer, Il. iv., ver. 102: Αρνων πρωτογονων ρεξειν κλειτην ἑκατομβην· "A hecatomb of lambs all *firstlings* of the flock." That is, the *most excellent* of their kind.

In a *contrary* sense, when the word *first-born* is joined to another that signifies any kind of *misery* or *disgrace*, it then signifies the *depth* of misery, the *utmost* disgrace. So the FIRST-BORN *of the poor*, Isa. xiv. 30, signifies the most abject, destitute, and impoverished. *The* FIRST-BORN *of death*, Job. xviii. 13, means the *most horrible* kind of death. So in the threatening against Pharaoh, chap. xi. 5, where he informs him that he will slay all the first-born, *from the first-born of Pharaoh that sitteth upon the throne, to the first-born of the maid-servant that is behind the mill*, he takes in the very highest and lowest conditions of life. As there was no state in Egypt superior to the *throne*, so there was none inferior to that of the *female slave* that ground at the mill. The Prophet Habakkuk seems to fix this as the sense in which the word is used here; for speaking of the plagues of Egypt in general, and the salvation which God afforded his people, he says, chap. iii. 13: *Thou wentest forth for the salvation of thy people—thou woundedst the* HEAD (ראש *rosh*, the *chief*, the *most excellent*) *of the house of the wicked*—of Pharaoh and the Egyptians. And the author of the book of *Wisdom* understood it in the same way: *The master and the servant were punished after one manner; and like as the king, so suffered the common people—for in one moment the* NOBLEST OFFSPRING *of them was destroyed;* chap. xviii. 11, 12. And in no other sense can we understand the word in Psa. lxxxix. 27, where, among the promises of God to David, we find the following: *Also I will make him my* FIRST-BORN, *higher than the kings of the earth;* in which passage the latter clause explains the former; David, as *king*, should be the FIRST-BORN of God, i. e., he should be *higher than the kings of the earth*—the MOST EMINENT potentate in the universe. In this sense, therefore, we should understand the passage in question; the most eminent person in every family in Egypt, as well as those who were literally the *first-born*, being slain in this plague. Calmet and some other critics particularly contend for this sense.

Verse 30. *There was a great cry*] No people in the universe were more remarkable for their mournings than the Egyptians, especially in matters of religion; they whipped, beat, tore themselves, and howled in all the excess of grief. When a relative died, the people left the house, ran into the streets, and howled in the most lamentable and frantic manner. See Diod. Sicul., lib. i., and Herod., lib. ii., c. 85, 86. And this latter author happening to be in Egypt on one of their solemnities, saw myriads of people whipping and beating themselves in this manner, lib. ii., c. 60; and see Mr. Bryant on the Plagues of Egypt, where many examples are given, p. 162, &c. How dreadful then must the scene of horror and distress appear, when there was not one house or *family* in Egypt

A. M. 2513.
B. C. 1491.
An. Exod. Isr. 1.
Abib or Nisan.

in Egypt; for *there was* not a house where *there was* not one dead.

31 And [t] he called for Moses and Aaron by night, and said, Rise up, *and* get you forth from among my people, [u] both ye and the children of Israel; and go, serve the LORD, as ye have said.

32 [v] Also take your flocks and your herds, as ye have said, and be gone; and [w] bless me also.

33 [x] And the Egyptians were urgent upon the people, that they might send them out of the land in haste; for they said, [y] We *be* all dead *men*.

A. M. 2513.
B. C. 1491.
An. Exod. Isr. 1.
Abib or Nisan

34 And the people took their dough before it was leavened, their [z] kneading-troughs being bound up in their clothes upon their shoulders.

35 And the children of Israel did according to the word of Moses: and they borrowed of the Egyptians [a] jewels of silver, and jewels of gold, and raiment:

36 [b] And the LORD gave the people favour in the sight of the Egyptians, so that they lent unto them *such things as they required*. And [d] they spoiled the Egyptians.

37 And [d] the children of Israel journeyed from [e] Rameses to Succoth, about [f] six hun-

[t] Chap. xi. 1; Psa. cv. 38.——[u] Chap. x. 9.——[y] Chap. x. 26. [w] Gen. xxvii. 34.——[x] Chap. xi. 8; Psa. cv. 38.——[y] Gen. xx. 3. [z] Or, *dough*; chap. viii. 3.——[a] Chap. iii. 22; xi. 2.

[b] Chap. iii. 21; xi. 3.——[c] Gen. xv. 14; chap. iii. 22; Psa. cv. 37.——[d] Num. xxxiii. 3, 5.——[e] Gen. xlvii. 11.——[f] Gen. xii. 2; xlvi. 3; chap. xxxviii. 26; Num. i. 46; xi. 21.

where there was not one dead; and according to their custom, all the family running out into the streets bewailing this calamity!

Verse 31. *Called for Moses and Aaron*] That is, he sent the message here mentioned to them; for it does not appear that he had any farther interview with Moses and Aaron, after what is mentioned chap. x. 28, 29, and xi. 8. See the notes there.

Verse 33. *The Egyptians were urgent upon the people*] They felt much, they feared more; and therefore wished to get immediately rid of a people on whose account they found they were smitten with so many and such dreadful plagues.

Verse 34. *The people took their dough before it was leavened, &c.*] There was no time now to make any regular preparation for their departure, such was the universal hurry and confusion. The Israelites could carry but little of their household utensils with them; but some, such as they kneaded their bread and kept their meal in, they were obliged to carry with them. The *kneading troughs* of the Arabs are comparatively small wooden bowls, which, after kneading their bread in, serve them as dishes out of which they eat their victuals. And as to these being bound up in their clothes, no more may be intended than their wrapping them up in their long, loose garments, or in what is still used among the Arabs, and called *hykes*, which is a long kind of blanket, something resembling a highland plaid, in which they often carry their provision, wrap themselves by day, and sleep at night. Dr. Shaw has been particular in his description of this almost entire wardrobe of an Arab. He says they are of different sizes and of different qualities, but generally about six yards in length, and five or six feet broad. He supposes that what we call Ruth's veil, Ruth iii. 15, was a *hyke*, and that the same is to be understood of the clothes of the Israelites mentioned in this verse. See his Travels, p. 224, 4to edition.

Verse 35. *They borrowed of the Egyptians*] See the note on chap. iii. 22, where the very exceptionable term *borrow* is largely explained.

Verse 37. *From Rameses to Succoth*] Rameses appears to have been another name for *Goshen*, though it is probable that there might have been a chief city or village in that land, where the children of Israel rendezvoused previously to their departure, called Rameses. As the term Succoth signifies *booths* or *tents*, it is probable that this place was so named from its being the place of the first *encampment* of the Israelites.

Six hundred thousand] That is, There was this number of effective men, twenty years old and upwards, who were able to go out to war. But this was not the whole number, and therefore the sacred writer says they were *about* 600,000; for when the numbers were taken about thirteen months after this they were found to be *six hundred and three thousand five hundred and fifty*, without reckoning those under *twenty* years of age, or any of the tribe of Levi; see Num. i. 45, 46. But besides those *on foot*, or footmen, there were no doubt many *old* and comparatively *infirm persons*, who rode on camels, horses, or asses, besides the immense number of women and children, which must have been at least three to one of the others; and the mixed multitude, ver. 38, probably of refugees in Egypt, who came to sojourn there, because of the dearth which had obliged them to emigrate from their own countries; and who now, seeing that the hand of Jehovah was *against* the Egyptians and *with* the Israelites, availed themselves of the general consternation, and took their leave of Egypt, choosing Israel's God for their portion, and his people for their companions. Such a company moving at once, and emigrating from their own country, the world never before nor since witnessed; no doubt upwards of two millions of souls, besides their *flocks and herds*, even *very much cattle*; and what but the mere providence of God could support such a multitude, and in the wilderness, too, where to this day the necessaries of life are not to be found?

Suppose we take them at a rough calculation thus, two millions will be found too small a number.

A. M. 2513.
B. C. 1491.
An. Exod. Isr. 1.
Abib or Nisan.

dred thousand on foot *that were* men, besides children.

38 And [g] a mixed multitude went up also with them; and flocks, and herds, *even* very much cattle.

39 And they baked unleavened cakes of the dough which they brought forth out of Egypt, for it was not leavened; because [h] they were thrust out of Egypt, and could not tarry, neither had they prepared for themselves any victual.

40 Now the sojourning of the children of Israel, who dwelt in Egypt, *was* [i] four hundred and thirty years.

41 And it came to pass at the end of the four hundred and thirty years, even the selfsame day it came to pass, that all [k] the hosts of the LORD went out from the land of Egypt.

[g] Heb. *a great mixture;* Numbers xi. 4.——[h] Chapter vi. 1; xi. 1; ver. 33.——[i] Gen. xv. 13; Acts vii. 6; Gal. iii. 17.——[k] Chapter vii. 4; ver. 51.

Effective men, 20 years old and upward	600,000
Two-thirds of whom we may suppose were married, in which case their wives would amount to	400,000
These, on an average, might have 5 children under 20 years of age, an estimate which falls considerably short of the number of children each family must have averaged in order to produce from 75 persons, in A. M. 2298, upwards of 600,000 effective men in A. M. 2494, a period of only 196 years	2,000,000
The Levites, who probably were not included among the effective men . .	45,000
Their wives	33,000
Their children	165,000
The mixed multitude probably not less than	20,000
Total . .	3,263,000

Besides a multitude of *old* and *infirm* persons who would be obliged to ride on camels and asses, &c., and who must, from the proportion that such bear to the young and healthy, amount to many thousands more! Exclude even the Levites and their families, and upwards of three millions will be left.

"In Num. iii. 39 the male Levites, aged one month and upwards, are reckoned 22,000, perhaps the females did not much exceed this number, say 23,000, and 500 children, under one month, will make 45,500."—Anon.

Had not Moses the fullest proof of his Divine mission, he never could have put himself at the head of such an immense concourse of people, who, without the most especial and effective providence, must all have perished for lack of food. This single circumstance, unconnected with all others, is an ample demonstration of the Divine mission of Moses, and of the authenticity and Divine inspiration of the Pentateuch. To suppose that an impostor, or one pretending only to a Divine call, could have ventured to place himself at the head of such an immense body of people, to lead them through a trackless wilderness, utterly unprovided for such a journey, to a land as yet in the possession of several powerful nations whom they must expel before they could possess the country, would have implied such an extreme of madness and folly as has never been witnessed in an individual, and such a blind credulity in the multitude as is unparalleled in the annals of mankind! The succeeding stupendous events proved that Moses had the authority of God to do what he did; and the people had at least such a *general* conviction that he had this authority, that they implicitly followed his directions, and received their law from his mouth.

Verse 40. *Now the sojourning of the children of Israel, &c.*] The statement in this verse is allowed on all hands to be extremely difficult, and therefore the passage stands in especial need of illustration. "That the descendants of Israel did not dwell 430 years in *Egypt*," says Dr. Kennicott, "may be easily proved, and has often been demonstrated. Some therefore imagine that by *Egypt* here both *it* and *Canaan* are to be understood. But this greater latitude of place will not solve the difficulty, since the Israelites, including Israel their father, did not sojourn 430 years in both countries previous to their departure from Egypt. Others, sensible of the still remaining deficiency, would not only have Egypt in the text to signify *it* and *Canaan*, but by a figure more comprehensive would have the *children of Israel* to mean *Israel's children*, and *Israel* their father, and *Isaac* the father of Israel, and *part of the life of Abraham*, the father of Isaac.

"Thus indeed," says Dr. Kennicott, "we arrive at the exact sum, and by this method of reckoning we might arrive at any thing but *truth*, which we may presume was never thus conveyed by an inspired writer." But can the difficulty be removed without having recourse to such absurd shifts? Certainly it can. The *Samaritan* Pentateuch, in all its manuscripts and printed copies, reads the place thus:—

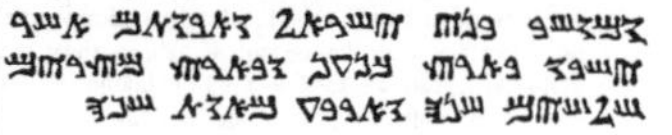

Umoshab beney Yishrael veabotham asher yashebu baarets Cenaan, ubaarets mitsraim sheloshim shanah vearba meoth shanah.

"*Now the sojourning of the children of Israel*, and of their fathers, *which they sojourned* in the land of Canaan and *in the land of Egypt, was* 430 *years.*" This same sum is given by St. Paul, Gal. iii. 17, who reckons from the promise made to Abraham, when God commanded him to go to Canaan, to the giving of the law, which soon followed the departure from Egypt; and this chronology of the apostle is concordant with the Samaritan Pentateuch, which, by preserving the two passages, *they and their fathers*, and *in the land of Canaan*, which are lost out of the present copies of the Hebrew text, has rescued this passage from all obscurity and contradiction. It may be

A. M. 2513. B. C. 1491. An. Exod. Isr. 1. Abib or Nisan.

42 It *is* [l] a night [m] to be much
observed unto the LORD for
bringing them out from the land
of Egypt: this *is* that night of the LORD to
be observed of all the children of Israel in
their generations.
43 And the LORD said unto Moses and
Aaron, This *is* [n] the ordinance of the passover: there shall no stranger
eat thereof:
44 But every man's servant
that is bought for money, when thou hast
[o] circumcised him, then shall he eat thereof.
45 [p] A foreigner and a hired servant shall
not eat thereof.
46 In one house shall it be eaten; thou

[l] Heb. *a night of observation.*——[m] See Deut. xvi. 6. [n] Num. ix. 14.——[o] Gen. xvii. 12, 13.——[p] Lev. xxii. 10.

necessary to observe that the Alexandrian copy of the Septuagint has the same reading as that in the Samaritan. The Samaritan Pentateuch is allowed by many learned men to exhibit the most correct copy of the five books of Moses; and the Alexandrian copy of the Septuagint must also be allowed to be one of the most authentic as well as most ancient copies of this version which we possess. As to St. Paul, no man will dispute the authenticity of his statement; and thus in the mouth of these three most respectable witnesses the whole account is indubitably established. That these three witnesses have the truth, the chronology itself proves: for from Abraham's entry into Canaan to the birth of Isaac was 25 years, Gen. xii. 4, xvii. 1–21; Isaac was 60 years old at the birth of Jacob, Gen. xxv. 26; and Jacob was 130 at his going down into Egypt, Gen. xlvii. 9; which three sums make 215 years. And then Jacob and his children having continued in Egypt 215 years more, the whole sum of 430 years is regularly completed. See *Kennicott's* Dissertation on the Hebrew Text.

Verse 42. *A night to be much observed*] A night to be held in everlasting remembrance, because of the peculiar display of the power and goodness of God, the observance of which annually was to be considered a religious precept while the Jewish nation should continue.

Verse 43. *This is the ordinance of the passover*] From the last verse of this chapter it appears pretty evident that this, to the 50th verse inclusive, constituted a part of the directions given to Moses relative to the proper observance of the first passover, and should be read conjointly with the preceding account beginning at verse 21. It may be supposed that these latter parts contain such particular directions as God gave to Moses after he had given those general ones mentioned in the preceding verses, but they seem all to belong to this first passover.

There shall no stranger eat thereof] בן נכר *ben nechar*, the *son of a stranger* or *foreigner*, i. e., one who was not of the genuine Hebrew stock, or one who had not received circumcision; for any *circumcised* person might eat the passover, as the total exclusion extends only to the *uncircumcised*, see ver. 48. As there are two sorts of *strangers* mentioned in the sacred writings; one who was admitted to all the Jewish ordinances, and another who, though he dwelt among the Jews, was not permitted to eat the passover or partake of any of their solemn feasts; it may be necessary to show what was the essential point of distinction through which the one was admitted and the other excluded.

In treatises on the religious customs of the Jews we frequently meet with the term *proselyte*, from the Greek προσηλυτος, a *stranger* or *foreigner*; one who *is come from his own people* and country to sojourn *with another*. All who were not descendants of some one of the twelve sons of Jacob, or of Ephraim and Manasseh, the two sons of Joseph, were reputed *strangers* or *proselytes* among the Jews. But of those strangers or proselytes there were two kinds, called among them *proselytes of the gate*, and *proselytes of justice* or of *the covenant*. The *former* were such as wished to dwell among the Jews, but would not submit to be circumcised; they, however, acknowledged the true God, avoided all idolatry, and observed the seven precepts of Noah, but were not obliged to observe any of the Mosaic institutions. The *latter* submitted to be circumcised, obliged themselves to observe all the rites and ceremonies of the law, and were in nothing different from the Jews but merely in their having once been *heathens*. The former, or *proselytes of the gate*, might not eat the passover or partake of any of the sacred festivals; but the latter, the *proselytes of the covenant*, had the same rights, spiritual and secular, as the Jews themselves. See ver. 48.

Verse 45. *A foreigner*] תושב *toshab*, from ישב *yashab*, to *sit down* or *dwell*; one who is a mere *sojourner*, for the purpose of traffic, merchandise, &c., but who is neither a proselyte of the *gate* nor of the *covenant*.

And a hired servant] Who, though he be bought with money, or has indented himself for a certain term to serve a Jew, yet has not become either a *proselyte of the gate* or of the *covenant*. None of these shall eat of it, because *not circumcised*—not brought under the *bond* of the covenant; and not being under obligation to observe the Mosaic law, had no right to its privileges and blessings. Even under the Gospel of our Lord Jesus Christ, he is *the author of eternal salvation* only *to them who* OBEY *him*, Heb. v. 9; and those who become Christians are *chosen to salvation through* SANCTIFICATION *of the Spirit, and belief of the truth*, 2 Thess. ii. 13; *for the grace of God, that bringeth salvation to all men, hath appeared, teaching us that*, DENYING UNGODLINESS *and* WORLDLY LUSTS, *we should live* SOBERLY, RIGHTEOUSLY, *and* GODLY, *in this present world*; Tit. ii. 11, 12. Such persons only walk worthy of the vocation wherewith they are called.

Verse 46. *In one house shall it be eaten*] In one family, if that be large enough; if not, a neighbouring family might be invited, ver. 4.

Thou shalt not carry forth aught of the flesh] Every family must abide *within doors* because of the destroy-

A. M. 2513.
B. C. 1491.
An. Exod. Isr. 1.
Abib or Nisan.

shalt not carry forth aught of the
flesh abroad out of the house;
[q] neither shall ye break a bone
thereof.
47 [r] All the congregation of Israel shall
[s] keep it.
48 And [t] when a stranger shall sojourn with
thee, and will keep the passover to the LORD,
let all his males be circumcised,
and then let him come near and
keep it; and he shall be as one
that is born in the land: for no uncircumcised
person shall eat thereof.
49 [u] One law shall be to him that is home-
born, and unto the stranger that sojourneth
among you.

[q] Num. ix. 12; John xix. 33, 36.——[r] Ver. 6; Num. ix. 13.——[s] Heb. *do it.*——[t] Numbers ix. 14.——[u] Numbers ix. 14; xv. 15, 16; Gal. iii. 28.

ing angel, none being permitted to go out of his house till the next day, ver. 22.

Neither shall ye break a bone thereof.] As it was to be *eaten in haste*, (ver. 11,) there was no time either to separate the bones, or to break them in order to extract the marrow; and lest they should be tempted to consume time in this way, therefore this ordinance was given. It is very likely that, when the whole lamb was brought to table, they cut off the flesh without even separating any of the large joints, leaving the skeleton, with whatever flesh they could not eat, to be *consumed with fire*, ver. 10. This precept was also given to point out a most remarkable circumstance which 1500 years after was to take place in the crucifixion of the Saviour of mankind, who was the true Paschal Lamb, that Lamb of God that takes away the sin of the world; who, though he was crucified as a common malefactor, and it was a universal custom to break the legs of such on the cross, yet so did the providence of God order it that a bone of HIM was not broken. See the fulfilment of this wondrously expressive type, John xix. 33, 36.

Verse 48. *And when a stranger—will keep the passover, &c.*] Let all who sojourn among you, and who desire to partake of this sacred ordinance, not only be circumcised themselves, but all the males of their families likewise, that they may all have an equal right to the blessings of the covenant.

Verse 49. *One law shall be to him that is home-born, &c.*] As this is the first place that the term תורה *torah* or LAW occurs, a term of the greatest importance in Divine revelation, and on the proper understanding of which much depends, I judge it best to give its genuine explanation once for all.

The word תורה *torah* comes from the root ירה *yarah*, which signifies to *aim at, teach, point out, direct, lead, guide, make straight*, or *even*; and from these significations of the word (and in all these senses it is used in the Bible) we may see at once the nature, properties, and design of the law of God. It is a system of INSTRUCTION *in righteousness*; it *teaches* the difference between moral good and evil; ascertains what is *right* and *fit* to be *done*, and what should be left *undone*, because *improper* to be performed. It continually *aims* at the glory of God, and the happiness of his creatures; *teaches* the true knowledge of the true God, and the destructive nature of sin; *points* out the absolute necessity of an atonement as the only means by which God can be reconciled to transgressors; and in its very significant rites and ceremonies *points* out the Son of God, till he should come to put away iniquity by the sacrifice of himself. It is a revelation of God's wisdom and goodness, wonderfully well calculated to *direct* the hearts of men into the truth, to *guide* their feet into the path of life, and to *make straight, even*, and *plain* that way which leads to God, and in which the soul must walk in order to arrive at eternal life. It is the fountain whence every correct notion relative to God—his perfections, providence, grace, justice, holiness, omniscience, and omnipotence, has been derived. And it has been the origin whence all the true principles of *law* and *justice* have been deduced. The pious study of it was the grand means of producing the greatest kings, the most enlightened statesmen, the most accomplished poets, and the most holy and useful men, that ever adorned the world. It is exceeded only by the Gospel of Jesus Christ, which is at once the accomplishment of its rites and predictions, and the fulfilment of its grand plan and outline. As a system of teaching or instruction, it is the most sovereign and most effectual; as by it is the knowledge of sin, and it alone is the schoolmaster, παιδαγωγος, that *leads* men to Christ, that they may be justified through faith, Gal. iii. 24. Who can absolutely ascertain the exact quantum of *obliquity* in a *crooked line*, without the application of a *straight* one? And could *sin*, in all its twistings, windings, and varied involutions, have ever been truly ascertained, had not God given to man this *perfect rule* to judge by? The nations who acknowledge this revelation of God have, as far as they attained to its dictates, the wisest, purest, most equal, and most beneficial laws. The nations that do not receive it have laws at once extravagantly severe and extravagantly indulgent. The proper distinctions between moral good and evil, in such states, are not known: hence the penal sanctions are not founded on the principles of justice, weighing the exact proportion of moral turpitude; but on the most arbitrary caprices, which in many cases show the utmost indulgence to first-rate crimes, while they punish minor offences with rigour and cruelty. What is the consequence? Just what might be reasonably expected: the will and caprice of a man being put in the place of the wisdom of God, the government is oppressive, and the people, frequently goaded to distraction, rise up in a mass and overturn it; so that the monarch, however powerful for a time, seldom lives out half his days. This *was* the case in *Greece*, in *Rome*, in the major part of the *Asiatic governments*, and *is* the case in all nations of the world to the present day, where the governor is *despotic*, and the laws not formed according to the *revelation of God.*

A. M. 2513.
B. C. 1491.
An. Exod. Isr. 1.
Abib or Nisan.

50 Thus did all the children of Israel; as the LORD commanded Moses and Aaron, so did they.

51 [v] And it came to pass the self-same day, *that* the LORD did bring the children of Israel out of the land of Egypt [w] by their armies.

A. M. 2513.
B. C. 1491.
An. Exod. Isr. 1.
Abib or Nisan.

[v] Ver. 41. — [w] Chap. vi. 26.

The word *lex, law,* among the Romans, has been derived from *lego, I read;* because when a law or statute was made, it was hung up in the most public places, that it might be *seen, read,* and *known* by all men, that those who were to obey the laws might not break them through ignorance, and thus incur the penalty. This was called *promulgatio legis,* q. *provulgatio, the promulgation of the law,* i. e., the laying it *before the common people.* Or from *ligo, I bind,* because the law *binds* men to the strict observance of its precepts. The Greeks call a law νομος *nomos,* from νεμω, to *divide, distribute, minister to,* or *serve,* because the law *divides* to all their just rights, *appoints* or *distributes* to each his proper duty, and thus *serves* or *ministers* to the welfare of the *individual* and the support of *society.* Hence where there are either no laws, or unequal and unjust ones, all is distraction, violence, rapine, oppression, anarchy, and ruin.

Verse 51. *By their armies.*] צבאתם *tsibotham,* from צבא *tsaba,* to *assemble, meet together,* in an *orderly* or *regulated* manner, and hence to *war,* to act together as troops in battle; whence צבאות *tsebaoth, troops, armies, hosts.* It is from this that the Divine Being calls himself יהוה צבאות *Yehovah tsebaoth, the* LORD *of* HOSTS or *armies,* because the Israelites were brought out of Egypt under his direction, marshalled and ordered by himself, guided by his wisdom, supported by his providence, and protected by his might. This is the true and simple reason why God is so frequently styled in Scripture the *Lord of hosts; for the* LORD *did bring the children of Israel out of the land of Egypt by their* ARMIES.

ON this chapter the notes have been so full and so explicit, that little can be added to set the subject before the reader in a clearer light. On the ordinance of the PASSOVER, the reader is requested to consult the notes on verses 7, 14, and 27. For the display of God's power and providence in *supporting* so great a multitude where, humanly speaking, there was no provision, and the *proof* that the exodus of the Israelites gives of the *truth* of the Mosaic history, he is referred to ver. 37. And for the meaning of the term LAW, to ver. 49.

On the ten plagues it may be but just necessary, after what has been said in the notes, to make a few general reflections. When the nature of the Egyptian idolatry is considered, and the plagues which were sent upon them, we may see at once the peculiarity of the judgment, and the great propriety of its being inflicted in the way related by Moses. The plagues were either inflicted on the *objects* of their idolatry, or by their *means.*

1. That the river *Nile* was an object of their worship, and one of their greatest gods, we have already seen. As the FIRST *plague,* its *waters* were therefore turned into *blood;* and the *fish,* many of which were objects also of their adoration, died. *Blood* was particularly offensive to them, and the touch of any dead animal rendered them unclean. When then their great god, the river, was turned into blood, and its waters became putrid, so that all the fish, minor objects of their devotion, died, we see a judgment at once calculated to punish, correct, and reform them. Could they ever more trust in gods who could neither save themselves nor their deluded worshippers?

2. Mr. Bryant has endeavoured to prove that *frogs,* the SECOND *plague,* were *sacred animals* in Egypt, and were dedicated to Osiris: they certainly appear on many ancient Egyptian monuments, and in such *circumstances* and *connections* as to show that they were held in religious veneration. *These* therefore became an awful scourge; first, by their *numbers,* and their intrusion into every place; and, secondly, by their *death,* and the infection of the atmosphere which took place in consequence.

3. We have seen also that the Egyptians, especially the priests, affected great *cleanliness,* and would not wear woollen garments lest any kind of vermin should harbour about them. The THIRD *plague,* by means of *lice* or such like vermin, was wisely calculated both to humble and confound them. In this they immediately saw a power superior to any that could be exerted by their gods or their magicians; and the latter were obliged to confess, *This is the finger of God!*

4. That *flies* were held sacred among the Egyptians and among various other nations, admits of the strongest proof. It is very probable that *Baal-zebub* himself was worshipped under the form of a *fly* or great *cantharid.* These, therefore, or some kind of winged noxious insects, became the prime agents in the FOURTH *plague;* and if the *cynomyia* or *dog-fly* be intended, we have already seen in the notes with what propriety and effect this judgment was inflicted.

5. The *murrain* or mortality among the cattle was the FIFTH *plague,* and the most decisive mark of the power and indignation of Jehovah. That *dogs, cats, monkeys, rams, heifers,* and *bulls,* were all objects of their most religious veneration, all the world knows. *These* were smitten in a most singular manner by the hand of God; and the Egyptians saw themselves deprived at once of all their imaginary helpers. Even *Apis,* their ox-god, in whom they particularly trusted, now suffers, groans, and dies under the hand of Jehovah. Thus does he execute judgment against all the gods of Egypt. See ver. 12.

6. The SIXTH *plague,* viz., of *boils* and *blains,* was as appropriate as any of the preceding; and the *sprinkling of the ashes,* the means by which it was produced, peculiarly significant. Pharmacy, Mr. Bryant has observed, was in high repute among the Egyptians; and *Isis,* their most celebrated goddess, was considered as the preventer or healer of all diseases. "For this

goddess," says Diodorus, Hist., lib. i., "used to reveal nerself to people in their sleep when they laboured under any disorder, and afford them relief. Many who placed their confidence in her influence *παραδοξως ὑγιαινεσθαι*, were miraculously restored. Many likewise who had been despaired of and given over by the physicians on account of the obstinacy of the distemper, were saved by this goddess. Numbers who had been deprived of their eyes, and of other parts of their bodies, were all restored on their application to Isis." By this disorder, therefore, which no application to their gods could cure, and which was upon the *magicians* also, who were supposed to possess most power and influence, God confounded their pride, showed the folly of their worship, and the vanity of their dependence. The *means* by which these boils and blains were inflicted, viz., the *sprinkling of ashes from the furnace*, was peculiarly appropriate. Plutarch assures us, De Iside et Osiride, that in several cities of Egypt they were accustomed to sacrifice human beings to Typhon, which they burned alive upon a high altar; and at the close of the sacrifice the priests gathered the ashes of these victims, and scattered them in the air: "I presume," says Mr. Bryant, "with this view, that where an atom of their dust was wafted, a blessing might be entailed. The like was done by Moses with the ashes of the furnace, that wherever any, the smallest portion, alighted, it might prove a plague and a curse to this cruel, ungrateful, and infatuated people. Thus there was a designed contrast in these workings of Providence, an apparent opposition to the superstition of the times."

7. The *grievous hail*, the SEVENTH *plague*, attended with *rain, thunder*, and *lightning*, in a country where these scarcely ever occur, and according to an express *prediction* of Moses, must in the most signal manner point out the power and justice of God. *Fire* and *water* were some of the principal objects of Egyptian idolatry; and fire, as Porphyry says, they considered *μεγαν ειναι θεον, to be a great god*. To find, therefore, that these very elements, the objects of their adoration, were, at the command of a *servant* of Jehovah, brought as a curse and scourge on the whole land, and upon men also and cattle, must have shaken their belief in these imaginary deities, while it proved to the Israelites that *there was none like the God of Jeshurun*.

8. In the EIGHTH *plague* we see by what insignificant creatures God can bring about a general destruction. A *caterpillar* is beyond all animals the most contemptible, and, taken singly, the least to be dreaded in the whole empire of nature; but in the hand of Divine justice it becomes one of the most formidable foes of the human race. From the examples in the notes we see how little human power, industry, or art, can avail against this most awful scourge. Not even the most contemptible animal should be considered with disrespect, as in the hand of God it may become the most terrible instrument for the punishment of a criminal individual or a guilty land.

9. The NINTH *plague*, the total and horrible *darkness* that lasted for *three days*, afforded both Israelites and Egyptians the most illustrious proof of the power and universal dominion of God; and was particularly to the latter a most awful yet instructive lesson against a species of idolatry which had been long prevalent in that and other countries, viz., the worship of the celestial *luminaries*. The *sun* and *moon* were both adored as supreme deities, as the sole dispensers of light and life; and the sun was invoked as the giver of immortality and eternal blessedness. *Porphyry*, De Abstin., l. 4, preserves the very *form* used by the Egyptian priests in addressing the sun on behalf of a deceased person, that he might be admitted into the society of the gods: *Ω δεσποτα Ἡλιε, και Θεοι παντες, οἱ την ζωην τοις ανθρωποις δοντες, προσδεξασθε με, και παραδοτε τοις αΐδιοις Θεοις συνοικον.* "O sovereign lord the sun, and all ye other deities who bestow life on mankind! receive me, and grant that I may be admitted as a companion with the immortal gods!" These objects of their superstitious worship Jehovah showed by this plague to be his *creatures*, dispensing or withholding their light merely at his will and pleasure; and that the people might be convinced that all this came by his appointment alone, he *predicted* this awful darkness; and that their *astronomers* might have the fullest proof that this was no natural occurrence, and could not be the effect of any kind of eclipse, which even when *total* could endure only about *four minutes*, (and this case could happen only once in a thousand years,) he caused this palpable darkness to continue for *three days!*

10. The TENTH and last *plague*, the slaying of the *first-born* or *chief* person in each family, may be considered in the light of a Divine *retribution:* for after that their nation had been preserved by one of the Israelitish family, "they had," says Mr. Bryant, "contrary to all right, and in defiance of original stipulation, enslaved the people to whom they had been so much indebted; and not contented with this, they had proceeded to murder their offspring, and to render the people's bondage intolerable by a wanton exertion of power. It had been told them that the family of the Israelites were esteemed as God's *first-born*, chap. iv. 22; therefore God said: Let my son go, that he may serve me; and if thou refuse—behold, I will slay thy son, even thy FIRST-BORN, ver. 23. But they heeded not this admonition, and hence those judgments came upon them that terminated in the death of the eldest in each family; a just retaliation for their disobedience and cruelty." See several curious and important remarks on this subject in a work entitled, *Observations upon the Plagues inflicted on the Egyptians*, by Jacob Bryant, 8vo., 1810.

On the whole we may say, Behold the goodness and severity of God! *Severity* mixed with *goodness* even to the same people. He *punished* and *corrected* them at the same time; for there was not one of these judgments that had not, from its peculiar nature and circumstances, some emendatory influence. Nor could a more effectual mode be adopted to demonstrate to that people the absurdity of their idolatry, and the inefficacy of their dependence, than that made use of on this occasion by the wise, just, and merciful God. At the same time the Israelites themselves must have received a lesson of the most impressive instruction on the vanity and wickedness of idolatry, to which they were at all times most deplorably prone, and of which they would no doubt have given many more examples,

had they not had the Egyptian plagues continually before their eyes. It was probably these signal displays of God's power and justice, and *these alone*, that induced them to leave Egypt at his command by Moses and Aaron; otherwise, with the dreadful wilderness before them, totally unprovided for such a journey, in which humanly speaking it was impossible for them and their households to subsist, they would have rather preferred the ills they then suffered, than have run the risk of greater by an attempt to escape from their present bondage. This is proved by their murmurings, chap. xvi., from which it is evident that they preferred Egypt with all its curses to their situation in the wilderness, and never could have been induced to leave it had they not had the fullest evidence that it was the will of God; which will they were obliged, on pain of utter destruction, to obey.

CHAPTER XIII.

God establishes the law concerning the first-born, *and commands that all such, both of man and beast, should be sanctified unto him,* 1, 2. *Orders them to remember the day in which they were brought out of Egypt, when they should be brought to the land of Canaan; and to keep this service in the month Abib,* 3–5. *Repeats the command concerning the* leavened bread, 6, 7, *and orders them to teach their children the cause of it,* 8, *and to keep strictly in remembrance that it was by the might of God alone they had been delivered from Egypt,* 9. *Shows that the consecration of the first-born, both of man and beast, should take place when they should be settled in Canaan,* 10–12. *The first-born of man and beast to be redeemed,* 13. *The reason of this also to be shown to their children,* 14, 15. Frontlets *or* phylacteries *for the hands and forehead commanded,* 16. *And the people are not led* directly *to the promised land, but about through the wilderness; and the reason assigned,* 17, 18. *Moses takes the bones of Joseph with him,* 19. *They journey from* Succoth *and come to* Etham, 20. *And the Lord goes before them by day in a* pillar of cloud, *and by night in a* pillar of fire, 21, *which miracle is regularly continued both by day and night,* 22.

A. M. 2513. B. C. 1491. An. Exod. Isr. 1. Abib or Nisan.

AND the LORD spake unto
Moses, saying,
2 [a] Sanctify unto me all the
first-born, whatsoever openeth the womb among
the children of Israel, *both* of man and of
beast: it *is* mine.
3 And Moses said unto the people, [b] Remember this day, in which ye came out from
Egypt, out of the house of [c] bondage; for [d] by
strength of hand the LORD brought you out
from this *place*: [e] there shall no leavened
bread be eaten.
4 [f] This day came ye out, in
the month Abib.
5 And it shall be, when the
LORD shall [g] bring thee into the land of the
Canaanites, and the Hittites, and the Amorites,
and the Hivites, and the Jebusites, which he
[h] sware unto thy fathers to give thee, a land
flowing with milk and honey, [i] that thou shalt
keep this service in this month.
6 [k] Seven days thou shalt eat unleavened
bread, and in the seventh day *shall be* a feast
to the LORD.

[a] Ver. 12, 13, 15; chap. xxii. 29, 30; xxxiv. 19; Lev. xxvii. 26; Num. iii. 13; viii. 16, 17; xviii. 15; Deut. xv. 19; Luke ii. 23.——[b] Chap. xii. 42; Deut. xvi. 3.

[c] Heb. *servants.*——[d] Chap. vi. 1.——[e] Chap. xii. 8.——[f] Chap. xxiii. 15; xxxiv. 18; Deut. xvi. 1.——[g] Chap. iii. 8.——[h] Chap. vi. 8.——[i] Chap. xii. 25, 26.——[k] Chap. xii. 15, 16.

NOTES ON CHAP. XIII.

Verse 1. *The Lord spake unto Moses*] The commands in this chapter appear to have been given at Succoth, on the same day in which they left Egypt.

Verse 2. *Sanctify unto me all the first-born*] To sanctify, קדש *kadash*, signifies to *consecrate, separate*, and *set apart* a thing or person from all secular purposes to some religious use; and exactly answers to the import of the Greek ἁγιαζω, from α, *privative*, and γη, *the earth*, because every thing offered or consecrated to God was *separated from all earthly uses.* Hence a *holy person* or *saint* is termed ἁγιος, i. e., a person separated from the earth; one who lives a holy life, entirely devoted to the service of God. Thus the persons and animals sanctified to God were employed in the *service of the tabernacle* and *temple*; and the animals, such as were proper, were offered in sacrifice.

The Hindoos frequenly make a vow, and devote to an idol the first-born of a *goat* and of a *man*. The *goat* is permitted to run wild, as a consecrated animal. A child thus devoted has a lock of hair separated, which at the time appointed is cut off and placed near the idol. Hindoo women sometimes pray to *Gunga* (the Ganges) for children, and promise to devote the first-born to *her*. Children thus devoted are cast into the Ganges, but are generally saved by the friendly hand of some stranger.—*Ward's Customs.*

Whatsoever openeth the womb] That is, the *first-born*, if a male; for females were not offered, nor the first male, if a female had been born previously. Again, if a man had several wives, the first-born of each, if a male, was to be offered to God. And all this was done to commemorate the preservation of the first-born of the Israelites, when those of the Egyptians were destroyed.

Verse 5. *When the Lord shall bring thee into the land*] Hence it is pretty evident that the Israelites were not obliged to celebrate the passover, or keep

A. M. 2513.
B. C. 1491.
An. Exod. Isr. 1.
Abib or Nisan.

7 Unleavened bread shall be
eaten seven days; and there
shall [l] no leavened bread be seen
with thee, neither shall there be leaven seen
with thee in all thy quarters.
8 And thou shalt [m] show thy son in that day,
saying, *This is done,* because of that *which*
the LORD did unto me, when I came forth out
of Egypt.
9 And it shall be for [n] a sign unto thee upon
thine hand, and for a memorial between thine
eyes, that the LORD's law may be
in thy mouth: for with a strong
hand hath the LORD brought thee
out of Egypt.
10 [o] Thou shalt therefore keep this ordinance in his season, from year to year.
11 And it shall be, when the LORD shall
bring thee into the land of the Canaanites, as
he sware unto thee and to thy fathers, and
shall give it thee,
12 [p] That thou shalt [q] set apart unto the LORD

[l] Chap. xii. 19.——[m] Ver. 14; chap. xii. 26.——[n] See ver. 16; chap. xii. 14; Num. xv. 39; Deut. vi. 8; xi. 18; Prov. i. 9; Isa. xlix. 16; Jer. xxii. 24; Matt. xxiii. 5.——[o] Chap. xii. 14, 24.

[p] Ver. 2; chapter xxii. 29; xxxiv. 19; Lev. xxvii. 26; Num. viii. 17; xviii. 15; Deut. xv. 19; Ezek. xliv. 30.——[q] Hebrew *cause to pass over.*

the feast of unleavened bread, till they were brought into the promised land.

Verse 6. *Unleavened bread*] See on chap. xii. 15, 16.

Verse 9. *And it shall be for a sign—upon thine hand*] This direction, repeated and enlarged ver. 16, gave rise to *phylacteries* or *tephillin*, and this is one of the passages which the Jews write upon them to the present day. The manner in which the Jews understood and kept these commands may appear in their practice. They wrote the following four portions of the law upon slips of parchment or vellum: *Sanctify unto me the first-born*, Exod. xiii., from verse 2 to 10 inclusive. *And it shall be, when the Lord shall bring thee into the land*, Exod. xiii., from verse 11 to 16 inclusive. *Hear, O Israel, the Lord our God is one Lord*, Deut. vi., from verse 4 to 9 inclusive. *And it shall come to pass, if ye shall hearken diligently*, Deut. xi., from verse 13 to 21 inclusive. These four portions, making in all 30 verses, written as mentioned above, and covered with leather, they tied to the *forehead* and to the *hand* or *arm*.

Those which were for the HEAD (the *frontlets*) they wrote on four slips of parchment, and rolled up each by itself, and placed them in four compartments, joined together in one piece of skin or leather. Those which were designed for the *hand* were formed of one piece of parchment, the four portions being written upon it in four columns, and rolled up from one end to the other. These were all correct transcripts from the Mosaic text, without one redundant or deficient letter, otherwise they were not lawful to be worn. Those for the *head* were tied on so as to rest on the forehead. Those for the hand or arm were usually tied on the left arm, a little above the elbow, on the inside, that they might be near the heart, according to the command, Deut. vi. 6: *And these words which I command thee this day shall be in thine heart.* These phylacteries formed no inconsiderable part of a Jew's religion; they wore them as a sign of their obligation to God, and as representing some future blessedness. Hence they did not wear them on feast days nor on the Sabbath, because these things were in themselves *signs;* but they wore them always when they read the law, or when they prayed, and hence they called them תפלין *tephillin, prayer, ornaments, oratories,* or *incitements to prayer.* In process of time the spirit of this law was lost in the letter, and when the word was not in their *mouth*, nor the law in their *heart*, they had their phylacteries on their *heads* and on their *hands.* And the Pharisees, who in our Lord's time affected extraordinary piety, made their phylacteries very broad, that they might have many sentences written upon them, or the ordinary portions in very large and observable letters.

It appears that the Jews wore these for *three* different purposes:—

1. As signs or *remembrancers.* This was the original design, as the institution itself sufficiently proves.

2. To *procure reverence* and *respect* in the sight of the heathen. This reason is given in the *Gemara*, Berachoth, chap. i.: "Whence is it proved that the phylacteries or tephillin are the strength of Israel? *Ans.* From what is written, Deut. xxviii. 10: All the people of the earth shall see that thou art called by the name of the LORD (יהוה *Yehovah*) and they shall be afraid of thee."

3. They used them as *amulets* or *charms*, to drive away evil spirits. This appears from the Targum on Canticles viii. 3: *His left hand is under my head, &c.* "The congregation of Israel hath said, I am elect above all people, because I bind my phylacteries on my left hand and on my head, and the scroll is fixed to the right side of my gate, the third part of which looks to my bed-chamber, that demons may not be permitted to injure me."

One of the original phylacteries or תפלין *tephillin* now lies before me; it is a piece of fine vellum, about *eighteen inches* long, and an *inch* and *quarter* broad. It is divided into four unequal compartments; the letters are very well formed, but written with many *apices*, after the manner of the German Jews. In the first compartment is written the portion taken from Exod. xiii. 2–10; in the second, Exod. xiii. 11–16; in the third, Deut. vi. 4–9; in the fourth, Deut. xi. 13–21, as before related. This had originally served for the hand or arm.

These passages seem to be chosen in vindication of the use of the phylactery itself, as the reader may see on consulting them at large. Bind them for a SIGN upon thy HAND; and for FRONTLETS between thy EYES; write them upon the POSTS of thy HOUSE and upon thy GATES; all which commands the Jews take in the most literal sense. To acquire the reputation of extraordinary sanctity they wore the *fringes* of their garments of an uncommon length. Moses had com-

A. M. 2513. B. C. 1491. An. Exod. Isr. 1. Abib or Nisan.

all that openeth the matrix, and
every firstling that cometh of a
beast which thou hast; the males
shall be the LORD'S.
13 And [r] every firstling of an ass thou shalt
redeem with a [s] lamb; and if thou wilt not
redeem it, then thou shalt break his neck:
and all the first-born of man among thy children [t] shalt thou redeem.
14 [u] And it shall be when thy son asketh
thee [v] in time to come, saying, What *is* this?
that thou shalt say unto him, [w] By strength
of hand the LORD brought us out from Egypt,
from the house of bondage:
15 And it came to pass, when Pharaoh
would hardly let us go, that [x] the LORD slew all
the first-born in the land of Egypt, both the
first-born of man, and the first-
born of beasts: therefore I sacrifice to the LORD all that openeth
the matrix, being males; but all the first-
born of my children I redeem.
16 And it shall be for [y] a token upon thine
hand, and for frontlets between thine eyes:
for by strength of hand the LORD brought us
forth out of Egypt.
17 And it came to pass, when Pharaoh had
let the people go, that God led them not
through the way of the land of the Philistines,
although that *was* near; for God said, Lest
peradventure the people [z] repent when they
see war, and [a] they return to Egypt:
18 But God [b] led the people about, *through*
the way of the wilderness of the Red Sea:

A. M. 2513. B. C. 1491. An. Exod. Isr. 1. Abib or Nisan.

[r] Chap. xxxiv. 20; Num. xviii. 15, 16.——[s] Or, *kid*.——[t] Num. iii. 46, 47; xviii. 15, 16.——[u] Chap. xii. 26; Deut. vi. 20; Josh. iv. 6, 21.——[v] Heb. *to-morrow*.

[w] Ver. 3.——[x] Chap. xii. 29.——[y] Ver. 9.——[z] Chap. xiv. 11, 12; Num. xiv. 1-4.——[a] Deut. xvii. 16.——[b] Ch. xiv. 2; Num. xxxiii. 6, &c.

manded them, Num. xv. 38, 39, to put fringes to the borders of their garments, that when they looked upon even these distinct threads they might remember, not only the law in general but also the very minutiæ or smaller parts of all the *precepts*, *rites*, and *ceremonies* belonging to it. As those hypocrites (for such our Lord proves them to be) were destitute of all the life and power of religion *within*, they endeavoured to supply its place with phylacteries and fringes *without*. The same principles distinguish hypocrites every where, and multitudes of them may be found among those termed *Christians* as well as among the *Jews*. It is probably to this institution relative to the phylactery that the words, Rev. xiv. 1, allude: And I looked, and, lo, a hundred and forty-four thousand having his Father's name *written on their foreheads*. "That is," says Mr. Ainsworth, "as a *sign* of the profession of God's law; for that which in the Gospel is called his NAME, (Matt. xii. 21,) in the prophets is called his LAW, (Isa. xlii. 4)." So again antichrist exacts the obedience to his precepts by a mark on men's *right hands* or on their *foreheads*, Rev. xiii. 16.

Verse 13. *Every firstling of an ass thou shalt redeem with a lamb*] Or a *kid*, as in the margin. In Num. xviii. 15, it is said: "The first-born of man shalt thou surely redeem; and the firstling of an unclean beast shalt thou redeem." Hence we may infer that *ass* is put here for any *unclean beast*, or for unclean beasts in general. The *lamb* was to be given to the Lord, that is, to his priest, Num. xviii. 8, 15. And then the owner of the ass might use it for his own service, which without this redemption he could not do; see Deut. xv. 19.

The first-born of man—shalt thou redeem.] This was done by giving to the priests *five standard shekels*, or shekels of the sanctuary, every shekel weighing *twenty gerahs*. What the gerah was, see on Gen. xx. 16. And for the shekel, see Gen. xxiii. 15.

It may be necessary to observe here that the Hebrew doctors teach, that if a father had neglected or refused thus to redeem his first-born, the son himself was obliged to do it when he came of age. As this redeeming of the first-born was instituted in consequence of sparing the first-born of the Israelites, when the first-born both of man and beast among the Egyptians was destroyed, on this ground all the first-born were the Lord's, and should have been employed in his service; but he permitted the first-born of a useful unclean animal to be *redeemed* by a *clean animal* of much less value. And he chose the tribe of Levi in place of all the first-born of the tribes in general; and the five shekels were ordered to be paid in lieu of such first-born sons as were liable to serve in the sanctuary, and the money was applied to the support of the priests and Levites. See this subject at large in Num. iii. 12, 13, 41, 43, 45, 47-51.

Verse 16. *It shall be for a token, &c.*] See the note on ver. 9.

Verse 17. *God led them not* through *the way of the land of the Philistines, &c.*] Had the Israelites been obliged to commence their journey to the promised land by a *military campaign*, there is little room to doubt that they would have been discouraged, have rebelled against Moses and Aaron, and have returned back to Egypt. Their long slavery had so degraded their minds that they were incapable of any great or noble exertions; and it is only on the ground of this mental degradation, the infallible consequence of *slavery*, that we can account for their many dastardly acts, murmurings, and repinings after their escape from Egypt. The reader is requested to bear this in mind, as it will serve to elucidate several circumstances in the ensuing history. Besides, the Israelites were in all probability *unarmed*, and totally unequipped for battle, encumbered with their flocks, and certain culinary utensils, which they were obliged to carry with them in the wilderness to provide them with bread, &c.

Verse 18. *But God led the people about*] Dr. Shaw

A. M. 2513.
B. C. 1491.
An. Exod. Isr. 1.
Abib or Nisan.

and the children of Israel went up [c] harnessed out of the land of Egypt.

19 And Moses took the bones of Joseph with him: for he had straitly sworn the children of Israel, saying, [d] God will surely visit you; and ye shall carry up my bones away hence with you.

20 And [e] they took their journey from Succoth, and encamped in Etham, in the edge of the wilderness.

21 And [f] the LORD went before them by day in a pillar of a cloud, to lead them the way; and by night in a pillar of fire, to give

[c] Or, *by five in a rank.*——[d] Gen. l. 25; Josh. xxiv. 32; Acts vii. 16.——[e] Num. xxxiii. 6.——[f] Chap. xiv. 19, 24; xl. 38; Num. ix. 15; x. 34; xiv. 14; Deut. i. 33; Neh. ix. 12, 19; Psa lxxviii. 14; xcix. 7; cv. 39; Isa. iv. 5; 1 Cor. x. 1.

has shown that there were two roads from Egypt to Canaan, one through the valleys of Jendilly, Rumeleah, and Baideah, bounded on each side by the mountains of the lower *Thebais;* the other lies higher, having the northern range of the mountains of Mocatee running parallel with it on the right hand, and the desert of the Egyptian Arabia, which lies all the way open to the land of the Philistines, to the left. See his account of these encampments at the end of Exodus.

Went up harnessed] חמשים *chamushim.* It is truly astonishing what a great variety of opinions are entertained relative to the meaning of this word. After having maturely considered all that I have met with on the subject, I think it probable that the word refers simply to that *orderly* or *well arranged* manner in which the Israelites commenced their journey from Egypt. For to *arrange, array,* or *set in order,* seems to be the ideal meaning of the word חמש *chamash.* As it was natural to expect that in such circumstances there must have been much hurry and confusion, the inspired writer particularly marks the contrary, to show that God had so disposed matters that the utmost regularity and order prevailed; and had it been otherwise, thousands of men, women, and children must have been trodden to death. Our margin has it *by five in a rank;* but had they marched only five abreast, supposing only one yard for each rank to move in, it would have required not less than sixty-eight miles for even the 600,000 to proceed on regularly in this way; for 600,000 divided by *five* gives 120,000 ranks of five each; and there being only 1760 yards in a mile, the dividing 120,000 by 1760 will give the number of miles such a column of people would take up, which by such an operation will be found to be something more than sixty-eight miles. But this the circumstances of the history will by no means admit.—*Harmer.* The simple meaning therefore appears to be that given above; and if the note on the concluding verse of the preceding chapter be considered, it may serve to place this explanation in a still clearer point of view.

Verse 19. *Moses took the bones of Joseph*] See the note on Gen. l. 25. It is supposed that the Israelites carried with them the bones or remains of *all the twelve sons of Jacob,* each tribe taking care of the bones of its own patriarch, while Moses took care of the bones of Joseph. St. Stephen expressly says, Acts vii. 15, 16, that not only Jacob, but the *fathers* were carried from Egypt into Sychem; and this, as Calmet remarks, was the only opportunity that seems to have presented itself for doing this: and certainly the reason that rendered it proper to remove the bones of Joseph to the promised land, had equal weight in reference to those of the other patriarchs. See the notes on Gen. xlix. 29.

Verse 20. *Encamped in Etham*] As for the reasons assigned on ver. 17, God would not lead the Israelites by the way of the Philistines' country, he directed them towards the wilderness of *Shur,* chap. xv. 22, upon the edge or extremity of which, next to Egypt, at the bottom of the Arabian Gulf, lay *Etham,* which is the second place of encampment mentioned. See the extracts from Dr. Shaw at the end of Exodus.

Verse 21. *The Lord went before them*] That by *the* LORD here is meant the Lord Jesus, we have the authority of St. Paul to believe, 1 Cor. x. 9: it was he whose Spirit they tempted in the wilderness, for it was he who led them through the desert to the promised rest.

Pillar of a cloud] This *pillar* or *column,* which appeared as a *cloud* by day, and a *fire* by night, was the symbol of the Divine presence. This was the *Shechinah* or Divine dwelling place, and was the continual proof of the presence and protection of GOD. It was necessary that they should have a guide to direct them through the wilderness, even had they taken the most direct road; and how much more so when they took a *circuitous* route not usually travelled, and of which they knew nothing but just as the luminous pillar pointed out the way! Besides, it is very likely that even Moses himself did not know the route which God had determined on, nor the places of encampment, till the pillar that went before them became stationary, and thus pointed out, not only the road, but the different places of rest. Whether there was more than *one* pillar is not clearly determined by the text. If there was but *one* it certainly assumed *three different appearances,* for the performance of THREE very important offices. 1. In the *day-time,* for the purpose of *pointing out the way,* a *column* or *pillar of a cloud* was all that was requisite. 2. At *night,* to prevent that confusion which must otherwise have taken place, the pillar of *cloud* became a *pillar of fire,* not to direct their journeyings, for they seldom travelled by night, but to *give light* to every part of the Israelitish camp. 3. In such a scorching, barren, thirsty desert, something farther was necessary than a *light* and a *guide.* Women, children, and comparatively infirm persons, exposed to the rays of such a burning sun, must have been destroyed if without a *covering;* hence we find that a *cloud overshadowed them:* and from what St. Paul observes, 1 Cor. x. 1, 2, we are led to conclude that this covering cloud was composed of *aqueous particles* for the cooling of the atmosphere and refreshment of themselves and their cattle; for he represents

A. M. 2513. B. C. 1491. An. Exod. Isr. 1. Abib or Nisan.

them light; to go by day and night:
22 He took not away the pillar of the cloud by day, nor the pillar of fire by night, *from* before the people.

A. M. 2513. B. C. 1491. An. Exod. Isr. 1 Abib or Nisan.

---

the whole camp as being *sprinkled* or *immersed* in the humidity of its vapours, and expressly calls it a being *under the cloud* and being *baptized in the cloud.* To the circumstance of the cloud *covering* them, there are several references in Scripture. Thus: *He spread a* CLOUD *for their* COVERING; Psa. cv. 39. And *the Lord will create upon every dwelling place of Mount Zion, and upon her assemblies,* A CLOUD *and* SMOKE BY DAY, *and the shining of a* FLAMING FIRE *by night; for upon all the glory shall be a* DEFENCE, (or COVERING,) Isa. iv. 5; which words contain the most manifest allusion to the *threefold* office of the cloud in the wilderness. See Num. ix. 16, 17, 18, &c.

Verse 22. *He took not away the pillar of the cloud*] Neither Jews nor Gentiles are agreed how long the cloud continued with the Israelites. It is very probable that it first visited them at *Succoth,* if it did not accompany them from Rameses; and that it continued with them till they came to the river Jordan, to pass over opposite to Jericho, for after that it appears that the *ark alone was their guide,* as it always marched at their head. See Josh. iii. 10, &c. But others think that it went no farther with them than Mount Hor, and never appeared after the death of Aaron. We may safely assert that while it was indispensably necessary it continued with them, when it was not so it was removed. But it is worthy of remark that the ark of the covenant became its substitute. While a miracle was necessary, a miracle was granted; when that was no longer necessary, then the *testimony* of the Lord deposited in the ark was deemed sufficient by Him who cannot err. So, under the Gospel dispensation, miracles were necessary at its first promulgation; but after that the canon of Scripture was completed, the new covenant having been made, ratified by the blood of the Lamb, and published by the Holy Spirit, then God withdrew generally those outward signs, leaving his *word* for a continual *testimony,* and sealing it on the souls of believers by the Spirit of truth.

It is also worthy of remark that the ancient heathen writers represent their gods, in their pretended manifestations to men, as always *encompassed with a cloud;* Homer and Virgil abound with examples of this kind: and is it not very probable that they borrowed this, as they did many other things in their mythologic theology, from the tradition of Jehovah guiding his people through the desert by means of the cloud, in and by which he repeatedly manifested himself?

1. EXTRAORDINARY manifestations and interpositions of providence and grace should be held in continual remembrance. We are liable to forget the hole of the pit whence we were digged, and the rock whence we were hewn. *Prudence* and *piety* will institute their *anniversaries,* that the merciful dealings of the Lord may never be forgotten. The *passover* and the *feast of unleavened bread,* by an annual commemoration, became standing proofs to the children of Israel of the Divine origin of their religion; and are supporting pillars of it to the present day. For when a fact is reported to have taken place, and certain rites or ceremonies have been instituted in order to commemorate it, which rites or ceremonies continue to be observed through succeeding ages, then the fact itself, no matter how remote the period of its occurrence may have been, has the utmost proofs of authenticity that it is possible for any fact to have; and such as every person pretending to reason and judgment is obliged to receive. On this ground the Mosaic religion, and the facts recorded in it, are indubitably proved; and the Christian religion and its facts, being commemorated in the same way, particularly by *baptism* and the *Lord's Supper,* stand on such a foundation of moral certainty as no other records in the universe can possibly boast. Reader, praise God for his *ordinances;* they are not only means of grace to thy soul, but standing irrefragable proofs of the truth of that religion which thou hast received as from HIM.

2. A serious *public profession* of the religion of Christ has in all ages of the Church been considered not only highly becoming, but indispensably necessary to salvation. He who consistently confesses Christ before men shall be confessed by him before God and his angels. A *Jew* wore his phylacteries on his *forehead,* on his *hands,* and round his *garments,* that he might have reverence in the sight of the heathen; he gloried in his law, and he exulted that Abraham was his father. *Christian!* with a zeal not less becoming, and more consistently supported, let the words of thy mouth, the acts of thy hands, and all thy goings, show that thou belongest unto God; that thou hast taken his Spirit for the guide of thy heart, his word for the rule of thy life, his people for thy companions, his heaven for thy inheritance, and himself for the portion of thy soul. And see that thou hold fast the truth, and that thou hold it in righteousness.

3. How merciful is God in the dispensations of his providence! He permits none to be tried above what he is able to bear, and he proportions the burden to the back that is to bear it. He led not the Israelites by the way of the Philistines, lest, *seeing war,* they should repent and be discouraged. Young converts are generally saved from severe spiritual conflicts and heavy temptations till they have acquired a habit of believing, are disciplined in the school of Christ, and instructed in the nature of the path in which they go, and the difficulties they may expect to find in it. They are informed that such things may take place, they are thus armed for the battle, and when trials do come they are not taken by surprise. God, the most merciful and kind God, "tempers even the blast to the shorn lamb." Trust in him therefore with all thy heart, and never lean to thy own understanding.

4. The *providence* and *goodness of God* are equally observable in the pillar of cloud and the pillar of fire. The former was the proof of his providential kindness by *day;* the latter, by *night.* Thus he adjusts the assistances of his grace and Spirit to the exigencies

of his creatures, giving at some times, when peculiar trials require it, more particular manifestations of his mercy and goodness; but at *all* times, such evidences of his approbation as are sufficient to satisfy a pious faithful heart. It is true the *pillar of fire* was more observable in the *night*, because of the general darkness, than the *pillar of cloud* was by *day;* yet the latter was as convincing and as evident a proof of his presence, approbation, and protection as the former. It is the duty and interest of every sound believer in Christ to have the witness of God's Spirit in his soul at all times, that his spirit and ways please his Maker; but in seasons of peculiar difficulty he may expect the more sensible manifestations of God's goodness. A good man is a temple of the Holy Spirit; but he who has an unholy heart, and who lives an unrighteous life, though he may have an orthodox creed, is a *hold* of unclean spirits, and an abomination in the sight of the Lord. Reader, let not these observations be fruitless to thee. God gives thee his word and his Spirit, obey this word that thou grieve not this Spirit. The following figurative saying of a Jewish rabbin is worthy of regard: "God addresses Israel and says, My son, I give thee my lamp, give me thy lamp. If thou keep my lamp, I will keep thy lamp; but if thou quench my lamp, I will extinguish thy lamp:" *i. e.*, I give thee my *word* and *Spirit*, give me thy *heart* and *soul*. If thou carefully attend to my word, and grieve not my Spirit, I will preserve thy soul alive; but if thou rebel against my word, and quench my Spirit, then thy light shall be put out, and thy soul's blessedness extinguished in everlasting darkness.

CHAPTER XIV.

The Israelites are commanded to encamp before Pi-hahiroth, 1, 2. *God predicts the pursuit of Pharaoh,* 3, 4. *Pharaoh is informed that the Israelites are fled, and regrets that he suffered them to depart,* 5. *He musters his troops and pursues them,* 6–8. *Overtakes them in their encampment by the* Red Sea, 9. *The Israelites are terrified at his approach,* 10. *They murmur against Moses for leading them out,* 11, 12. *Moses encourages them, and assures them of deliverance,* 13, 14. *God commands the Israelites to advance, and Moses to stretch out his rod over the sea that it might be divided,* 15, 16; *and promises utterly to discomfit the Egyptians,* 17, 18. *The angel of God places himself between the Israelites and the Egyptians,* 19. *The* pillar *of the* cloud *becomes darkness to the Egyptians, while it gives light to the Israelites,* 20. *Moses stretches out his rod, and a strong* east wind *blows, and the waters are divided,* 21. *The Israelites enter and walk on dry ground,* 22. *The Egyptians enter also in pursuit of the Israelites,* 23. *The Lord looks out of the pillar of cloud on the Egyptians, terrifies them, and disjoints their chariots,* 24, 25. *Moses is commanded to stretch forth his rod over the waters, that they may return to their former bed,* 26. *He does so, and the whole Egyptian army is overwhelmed,* 27, 28, *while every Israelite escapes,* 29. *Being thus saved from the hand of their adversaries, they acknowledge the power of God, and credit the mission of Moses,* 30, 31.

A. M. 2513.
B. C. 1491.
An. Exod. Isr. 1.
Abib or Nisan.

AND the LORD spake unto Moses, saying,
2 Speak unto the children of Israel, [a] that they turn and encamp before [b] Pi-hahiroth, between [c] Migdol and the sea, over against Baal-zephon; before it shall ye encamp by the sea.
3 For Pharaoh will say of the children of Israel, [d] They *are* entangled in the land, the wilderness hath shut them in.
4 And [e] I will harden Pharaoh's heart, that he shall follow after them; and I [f] will be honoured upon Pharaoh, and upon all his host;

[a] Chapter xiii. 18.—[b] Numbers xxxiii. 7.—[c] Jer. xliv. 1. [d] Psa. lxxi. 11.

[e] Chap. iv. 21; vii. 3.—[f] Chap. ix. 16; ver. 17, 18; Romans ix. 17, 22, 23.

NOTES ON CHAP. XIV.

Verse 2. *Encamp before Pi-hahiroth*] פי החירת *pi hachiroth*, the *mouth*, *strait*, or *bay of Chiroth*. *Between Migdol,* מגדל *migdol*, the *tower*, probably a fortress that served to defend the bay. *Over against Baal-zephon,* בעל צפן *baal tsephon*, the *lord* or *master of the watch*, probably an idol temple, where a continual guard, watch, or light was kept up for the defence of one part of the haven, or as a guide to ships. Dr. Shaw thinks that *chiroth* may denote the valley which extended itself from the wilderness of Etham to the Red Sea, and that the part in which the Israelites encamped was called *Pi-hachiroth*, i. e., the *mouth* or *bay of Chiroth*. See his Travels, p. 310, and his account at the end of Exodus.

Verse 3. *They* are *entangled in the land*] God himself brought them into straits from which no human power or art could extricate them. Consider their situation when once brought out of the open country, where alone they had room either to fight or fly. Now they had the Red Sea before them, Pharaoh and his host behind them, and on their right and left hand *fortresses* of the Egyptians to prevent their escape; nor had they one boat or transport prepared for their passage! If they be now saved, the arm of the Lord *must* be seen, and the vanity and nullity of the Egyptian idols be demonstrated. By bringing them into such a situation he took from them all hope of human help, and gave their adversaries every advantage against them, so that they themselves said, *They are entangled in the land, the wilderness hath shut them in.*

Verse 4. *I will harden Pharaoh's heart*] After re-

A. M. 2513. B. C. 1491. An. Exod. Isr. 1. Abib or Nisan.

[g] that the Egyptians may know that I *am* the LORD. And they did so.

5 And it was told the king of Egypt that the people fled: and [h] the heart of Pharaoh and of his servants was turned against the people, and they said, Why have we done this, that we have let Israel go from serving us?

6 And he made ready his chariot, and took his people with him:

7 And he took [i] six hundred chosen chariots, and all the chariots of Egypt, and captains over every one of them.

8 And the LORD [k] hardened the heart of Pharaoh king of Egypt, and he pursued after the children of Israel: and [l] the children of Israel went out with a high hand.

9 But the [m] Egyptians pursued after them, (all the horses *and* chariots of Pharaoh, and his horsemen, and his army,) and overtook them encamping by the sea, beside Pi-hahiroth, before Baal-zephon.

A. M. 2513. B. C. 1491. An. Exod. Isr. 1. Abib or Nisan.

10 And when Pharaoh drew nigh, the children of Israel lifted up their eyes, and, behold, the Egyptians marched after them; and they were sore afraid: and the children of Israel [n] cried out unto the LORD.

11 [o] And they said unto Moses, Because *there were* no graves in Egypt, hast thou taken us away to die in the wilderness? wherefore hast thou dealt thus with us, to carry us forth out of Egypt?

12 [p] *Is* not this the word that we did tell thee in Egypt, saying, Let us alone, that we may serve the Egyptians? For *it had been* better for us to serve the Egyptians, than that we should die in the wilderness.

13 And Moses said unto the people, [q] Fear ye not, stand still, and see the salvation of the LORD, which he will show to you to-day: [r] for the Egyptians whom ye have seen to-day, ye shall see them again no more for ever.

14 [s] The LORD shall fight for you, and ye shall [t] hold your peace.

[g] Chap. vii. 5.—[h] Psa. cv. 25.—[i] Chap. xv. 4.—[k] Ver. 4. Chap. vi. 1; xiii. 9; Num. xxxiii. 3.—[m] Chap. xv. 9; Josh. xxiv. 6; 1 Mac. iv. 9.—[n] Josh. xxiv. 7; Neh. ix. 9; Psa. xxxiv. 17; cvii. 6.—[o] Psa. cvi. 7, 8.—[p] Chap. v. 21; vi. 9.

[q] 2 Chron. xx. 15, 17; Isa. xli. 10, 13, 14.—[r] Or, *for whereas ye have seen the Egyptians to-day*, &c.—[s] Ver. 25; Deut. i. 30; iii. 22; xx. 4; Josh. x. 14, 42; xxiii. 3; 2 Chron. xx. 29; Neh. iv. 20; Isa. xxxi. 4.—[t] Isa. xxx. 15.

lenting and giving them permission to depart, he now changes his mind and determines to prevent them; and without any farther restraining grace, God permits him to rush on to his final ruin, for the *cup* of his iniquity was now *full*.

Verse 5. *And it was told the king—that the people fled*] Of their departure he could not be ignorant, because himself had given them liberty to depart: but the word *fled* here may be understood as implying that they had utterly left Egypt without any intention to return, which is probably what he did not expect, for he had only given them permission to go three days' journey into the wilderness, in order to sacrifice to Jehovah; but from the circumstances of their departure, and the property they had got from the Egyptians, it was taken for granted that they had no design to return; and this was in all likelihood the consideration that weighed most with this *avaricious* king, and determined him to pursue, and either recover the spoil or bring them back, or both. Thus *the heart of Pharaoh and his servants was turned against the people, and they said, Why have we let Israel go from serving us?* Here was the grand incentive to pursuit; their *service* was profitable to the state, and they were determined not to give it up.

Verse 7 *Six hundred chosen chariots, &c.*] According to the most authentic accounts we have of *war-chariots*, they were frequently drawn by *two* or by *four* horses, and carried three persons: one was charioteer, whose business it was to guide the horses, but he seldom fought; the second chiefly defended the charioteer; and the third alone was properly the combatant. It appears that in this case Pharaoh had collected all the cavalry of Egypt; (see ver. 17;) and though these might not have been very numerous, yet, humanly speaking, they might easily overcome the unarmed and encumbered Israelites, who could not be supposed to be able to make any resistance against *cavalry* and *war-chariots*.

Verse 10. *The children of Israel cried out unto the Lord.*] Had their prayer been accompanied with faith, we should not have found them in the next verses murmuring against Moses, or rather against the Lord, through whose goodness they were now brought from under that bondage from which they had often cried for deliverance. Calmet thinks that the most pious and judicious cried unto God, while the unthinking and irreligious murmured against Moses.

Verse 13. *Moses said—Fear ye not*] This exhortation was not given to excite them to resist, for of that there was no hope; they were unarmed, they had no courage, and their minds were deplorably degraded.

Stand still] Ye shall not be even workers together with God; only be quiet, and do not render yourselves wretched by your fears and your confusion.

See the salvation of the Lord] Behold the deliverance which God will work, independently of all human help and means.

Ye shall see them again no more] Here was strong faith, but this was accompanied by the spirit of pro

A. M. 2513.
B. C. 1491.
An. Exod. Isr. 1.
Abib or Nisan.

15 And the LORD said unto
Moses, Wherefore criest thou
unto me? speak unto the children of Israel, that they go forward:
16 But [u] lift thou up thy rod, and stretch
out thine hand over the sea, and divide it:
and the children of Israel shall go on dry
ground through the midst of the sea.
17 And I, behold, I will [v] harden the hearts
of the Egyptians, and they shall follow them:
and I will [w] get me honour upon Pharaoh,
and upon all his host, upon his chariots, and
upon his horsemen.
18 And the Egyptians [x] shall know that I *am*
the LORD, when I have gotten me honour
upon Pharaoh, upon his chariots,
and upon his horsemen.
19 And the angel of God,
[y] which went before the camp of Israel, removed and went behind them; and the pillar
of the cloud went from before their face, and
stood behind them:
20 And it came between the camp of the
Egyptians, and the camp of Israel; and [z] it
was a cloud and darkness *to them*, but it gave
light by night *to these*: so that the one came
not near the other all the night.
21 And Moses [a] stretched out his hand over
the sea; and the LORD caused the sea to go
back by a strong east wind all that night, and

[u] Verse 21, 26; chapter vii. 19.——[v] Verse 8; chapter vii. 3.——[w] Ver. 4.——[x] Ver. 4.

[y] Ch. xiii. 21; xxiii. 20; xxxii. 34; Num. xx. 16; Isa. lxiii. 9.——[z] See Isa. viii. 14; 2 Cor. iv. 3.——[a] Ver. 16.

phecy. God showed Moses what he would do, he believed, and therefore he spoke in the encouraging manner related above.

Verse 14. *The Lord shall fight for you*] Ye shall have no part in the honour of the day; God alone shall bring you off, and defeat your foes.

Ye shall hold your peace.] Your unbelieving fears and clamours shall be confounded, and ye shall see that by *might* none shall be able to prevail against the Lord, and that the feeblest shall take the prey when the power of Jehovah is exerted.

Verse 15. *Wherefore criest thou unto me?*] We hear not one word of Moses' praying, and yet here the Lord asks him why he cries unto him? From which we may learn that the *heart* of Moses was deeply engaged with God, though it is probable he did not *articulate* one word; but the language of *sighs, tears,* and *desires* is equally intelligible to God with that of *words.* This consideration should be a strong encouragement to every feeble, discouraged mind: *Thou* canst not *pray*, but thou canst *weep*; if even *tears* are denied thee, (for there may be deep and genuine repentance, where the distress is so great as to stop up those channels of relief,) then thou canst *sigh*; and God, whose Spirit has thus convinced thee of sin, righteousness, and judgment, knows thy unutterable groanings, and reads the inexpressible wish of thy burdened soul, a wish of which himself is the author, and which he has breathed into thy heart with the purpose to satisfy it.

Verse 16. *Lift thou up thy rod*] Neither Moses nor his rod could be any effective instrument in a work which could be accomplished only by the omnipotence of God; but it was necessary that he should appear in it, in order that he might have credit in the sight of the Israelites, and that they might see that God had chosen him to be the instrument of their deliverance.

Verse 18. *Shall know that I* am *the Lord*] Pharaoh had just recovered from the consternation and confusion with which the late plagues had overwhelmed him, and now he is *emboldened* to pursue after Israel; and God is determined to make his overthrow so signal by such an exertion of omnipotence, that he shall get himself honour by this miraculous act, and that the Egyptians shall know, i. e., *acknowledge*, that he is Jehovah, the omnipotent, self-existing, eternal God.

Verse 19. *The angel of God*] It has been thought by some that the *angel*, i. e., *messenger*, of the Lord, and the pillar of cloud, mean here the same thing. An angel might assume the appearance of a cloud; and even a material cloud thus particularly appointed might be called an *angel* or *messenger* of the Lord, for such is the literal import of the word מלאך *malach, an angel.* It is however most probable that the Angel of the covenant, the Lord Jesus, appeared on this occasion in behalf of the people; for as this deliverance was to be an illustrious type of the deliverance of man from the power and guilt of sin by his incarnation and death, it might have been deemed necessary, in the judgment of Divine wisdom, that *he* should appear *chief agent* in this most important and momentous crisis. On the word angel, and Angel of the covenant, see the notes on Gen. xvi. 7; xviii. 13; and Exod. iii. 2.

Verse 20. *It was a cloud and darkness* to them, *&c.*] That the Israelites might not be dismayed at the *appearance* of their enemies, and that these might not be able to discern the object of their pursuit, the pillar of cloud moved from the front to the rear of the Israelitish camp, so as perfectly to separate between them and the Egyptians. It appears also that this cloud had *two sides*, one *dark* and the other *luminous*: the luminous side gave light to the whole camp of Israel during the night of passage; and the dark side, turned towards the pursuing Egyptians, prevented them from receiving any benefit from that light. How easily can God make the *same* thing an instrument of destruction or salvation, as seems best to his godly wisdom! He alone can work by all agents, and produce any kind of effect even by the same instrument; for all things serve the purposes of his will.

Verse 21. *The Lord caused the sea to go* back] That part of the sea over which the Israelites passed was, according to Mr. Bruce and other travellers, about *four leagues* across, and therefore might easily be crossed in one night. In the dividing of the sea *two* agents

A. M. 2513.
B. C. 1491.
An. Exod. Isr. 1.
Abib or Nisan.

[b] made the sea dry *land,* and the
waters were [c] divided.
22 And [d] the children of Israel
went into the midst of the sea, upon the dry
ground: and the waters *were* [e] a wall unto
them on their right hand and on their left.
23 And the Egyptians pursued, and went
in after them to the midst of the sea, *even* all
Pharaoh's horses, his chariots,
and his horsemen.
24 And it came to pass, that in
the morning watch [f] the LORD looked unto the
host of the Egyptians, through the pillar of
fire and of the cloud, and troubled the host
of the Egyptians,
25 And took off their chariot wheels, [g] that

[b] Psalm lxvi. 6.——[c] Chap. xv. 8; Josh. iii. 16; iv. 23; Neh. ix. 11; Psa. lxxiv. 13; cvi. 9; cxiv. 3; Isa. lxiii. 12.——[d] Ver. 29; chap. xv. 19; Numbers xxxiii. 8; Psa. lxvi. 6; lxxviii. 13; Isaiah lxiii. 13; 1 Cor. x. 1; Hebrews xi. 29.——[e] Hab. iii. 10. [f] See Psalm lxxvii. 17, &c.——[g] Or, *and made them to go heavily.*

appear to be employed, though the effect produced can be attributed to neither. By stretching out the rod the waters were *divided;* by the blowing of the vehement, ardent, east wind, the *bed* of the sea was dried. It has been observed, that in the place where the Israelites are supposed to have passed, the water is about *fourteen fathoms* or *twenty-eight yards* deep: had the wind mentioned here been strong enough, naturally speaking, to have divided the waters, it must have blown in one narrow track, and continued blowing in the direction in which the Israelites passed; and a wind sufficient to have raised a mass of water *twenty-eight* yards deep and *twelve* miles in length, out of its bed, would necessarily have blown the whole *six hundred thousand* men away, and utterly destroyed them and their cattle. I therefore conclude that the east wind, which was ever remarked as a *parching,* burning wind, was used *after* the division of the waters, merely to *dry the bottom,* and render it passable. For an account of the hot drying winds in the east, see the note on Gen. viii. 1. God ever puts the highest honour on his instrument, *Nature;* and where *it* can act, he ever employs it. No natural agent could divide these waters, and cause them to stand as a *wall* upon the right hand and upon the left; therefore God did it by his own sovereign power. When the waters were thus divided, there was no need of a miracle to dry the bed of the sea and make it passable; therefore the strong desiccating east wind was brought, which soon accomplished this object. In this light I suppose the text should be understood.

Verse 22. *And the waters* were *a wall unto them on their right hand and on their left.*] This verse demonstrates that the passage was miraculous. Some have supposed that the Israelites had passed through, favoured by an extraordinary *ebb,* which *happened* at that time to be produced by a strong wind, which *happened* just then to blow! Had this been the case, there could not have been waters *standing on the right hand and on the left;* much less could those waters, contrary to every law of fluids, have stood as *a wall* on either side while the Israelites passed through, and then *happen* to become obedient to the laws of gravitation when the Egyptians entered in! An infidel may deny the revelation in toto, and from such we expect nothing better; but to hear those who profess to believe this to be a Divine revelation endeavouring to prove that the passage of the Red Sea *had nothing miraculous in it,* is really intolerable. Such a mode of interpretation requires a miracle to make itself credible. Poor infidelity! how miserable and despicable are thy *shifts!*

Verse 24. *The morning watch*] A *watch* was the fourth part of the time from sun-setting to sun-rising; so called from soldiers keeping guard by night, who being changed four times during the night, the periods came to be called *watches.—Dodd.*

As here and in 1 Sam. xi. 11 is mentioned the *morning watch;* so in Lam. ii. 19, the *beginning of the watches;* and in Judg. vii. 19, the *middle watch* is spoken of; in Luke xii. 38, the *second* and *third watch;* and in Matt. xiv 25, the *fourth watch of the night;* which in Mark xiii. 35 are named *evening, midnight, cock-crowing,* and *day-dawning.—Ainsworth.*

As the Israelites went out of Egypt at the vernal equinox, the morning watch, or, according to the Hebrew, באשמרת הבקר *beashmoreth habboker,* the *watch of day-break,* would answer to our *four o'clock* in the morning.—*Calmet.*

The Lord looked unto] This probably means that the cloud suddenly assumed a fiery appearance where it had been dark before; or they were appalled by violent *thunders* and *lightning,* which we are assured by the psalmist did actually take place, together with great *inundations of rain,* &c.: *The clouds* POURED OUT WATER; *the skies sent out a* SOUND: *thine* ARROWS *also went abroad. The* VOICE *of thy* THUNDER *was in the heaven; the* LIGHTNINGS LIGHTENED *the world; the earth* TREMBLED *and* SHOOK. *Thy way is in the sea, and thy path in the great waters. Thou leddest thy people like a flock, by the hand of Moses and Aaron;* Psa. lxxvii. 17–20. Such tempests as these would necessarily terrify the Egyptian horses, and produce general confusion. By their dashing hither and thither the wheels must be destroyed, and the chariots broken; and foot and horse must be mingled together in one universal ruin; see ver. 25. During the time that this state of horror and confusion was at its summit the Israelites had safely passed over; and then Moses, at the command of God, (ver. 26,) having stretched out his rod over the waters, the *sea returned to its strength;* (ver. 27;) i. e., the waters by their natural gravity resumed their *level,* and the whole Egyptian host were completely overwhelmed, ver. 28. But as to the Israelites, the waters had been a wall unto them on the *right* hand and on the *left,* ver. 29. This the waters could not have been, unless they had been supernaturally supported; as their own gravity would necessarily have occasioned them to have kept their level, or, if raised beyond it, to have regained it if left to their natural

A. M. 2513.
B. C. 1491.
An. Exod. Isr. 1.
Abib or Nisan.

they drave them heavily: so that
the Egyptians said, Let us flee
from the face of Israel; for the
LORD [h] fighteth for them against the Egyptians.
26 And the LORD said unto Moses, [i] Stretch
out thine hand over the sea, that the waters
may come again upon the Egyptians, upon
their chariots, and upon their horsemen.
27 And Moses stretched forth his hand over
the sea, and the sea [k] returned to his strength
when the morning appeared; and the Egyptians
fled against it; and the LORD [l] overthrew [m]
the Egyptians in the midst of the sea.
28 And [n] the waters returned, and [o] covered
the chariots, and the horsemen, *and* all the
host of Pharaoh, that came into
the sea after them; there remained
not so much as one of
them.
29 But [p] the children of Israel walked upon
dry *land*, in the midst of the sea; and the
waters *were* a wall unto them, on their right
hand, and on their left.
30 Thus the LORD [q] saved Israel that day
out of the hand of the Egyptians; and Israel
[r] saw the Egyptians dead upon the seashore.
31 And Israel saw that great [s] work which
the LORD did upon the Egyptians: and the
people feared the LORD, and [t] believed the
LORD, and his servant Moses.

A. M. 2513.
B. C. 1491.
An. Exod. Isr. 1.
Abib or Nisan.

---

[h] Ver. 14.——[i] Ver. 16.——[k] Josh. iv. 18.——[l] Chap. xv. 1, 7.——[m] Heb. *shook off*; Deut. xi. 4; Psa. lxxviii. 53; Neh. ix. 11; Heb. xi. 29.——[n] Hab. iii. 8, 13.——[o] Psa. cvi. 11.

[p] Ver. 22; Psa. lxxvii. 20; lxxviii. 52, 53.——[q] Psalm cvi. 8, 10.——[r] Psa. lviii. 10; lix. 10.——[s] Heb. *hand*.——[t] Chap. iv. 31; xix. 9; Psa. cvi. 12; John ii. 11; xi. 45.

---

law, to which they are ever subject, unless in cases of miraculous interference. Thus the enemies of the Lord perished; and that people who decreed that the male children of the Hebrews should be *drowned*, were themselves destroyed in the pit which they had destined for others. God's ways are all equal; and he renders to every man *according to his works*.

Verse 28. *There remained not so much as one of them.*] Josephus says that the army of Pharaoh consisted of *fifty thousand* horse, and *two hundred thousand* foot, of whom not one remained to carry tidings of this most extraordinary catastrophe.

Verse 30. *Israel saw the Egyptians dead upon the seashore.*] By the extraordinary agitation of the waters, no doubt multitudes of the dead Egyptians were cast on the shore, and by their spoils the Israelites were probably furnished with *considerable riches*, and especially *clothing* and *arms*; which latter were essentially necessary to them in their wars with the *Amalekites*, *Basanites*, and *Amorites*, &c., on their way to the promised land. If they did not get their arms in this way, we know not how they got them, as there is not the slightest reason to believe that they brought any with them out of Egypt.

Verse 31. *The people feared the Lord*] They were convinced by the interference of Jehovah that his power was unlimited, and that he could do whatsoever he pleased, both in the way of *judgment* and in the way of *mercy*.

And believed the Lord, and his servant Moses.] They now clearly discerned that God had fulfilled all his promises; and that not one thing had failed of all the good which he had spoken concerning Israel. And *they believed his servant Moses*—they had now the fullest proof that he was Divinely appointed to work all these miracles, and to bring them out of Egypt into the promised land.

Thus God got himself honour upon Pharaoh and the Egyptians, and credit in the sight of Israel. After this overthrow of their king and his host, the Egyptians interrupted them no more in their journeyings, convinced of the omnipotence of their Protector: and how strange, that after such displays of the justice and mercy of Jehovah, the Israelites should ever have been deficient in faith, or have given place to murmuring!

1. THE events recorded in this chapter are truly astonishing; and they strongly mark what God *can* do, and what he *will* do, both against his enemies and in behalf of his followers. In vain are all the forces of Egypt united to destroy the Israelites: at the breath of God's mouth they perish; and his feeble, discouraged, unarmed followers take the prey! With such a history before their eyes, is it not strange that sinners should run on frowardly in the path of transgression; and that those who are redeemed from the world, should ever doubt of the all-sufficiency and goodness of their God! Had we not already known the sequel of the Israelitish history, we should have been led to conclude that this people would have gone on their way rejoicing, trusting in God with their whole heart, and never leaning to their own understanding; but alas! we find that as soon as any new difficulty occurred, they murmured against God and their leaders, despised the pleasant land, and gave no credence to his word.

2. Their case is not a solitary one: most of those who are called *Christians* are not more remarkable for faith and patience. Every reverse will necessarily pain and discompose the people who are seeking their portion in this life. And it is a sure mark of a worldly mind, when we trust the God of Providence and grace no farther than we see the operations of his hand in our immediate supply; and murmur and repine when the hand of his bounty seems closed, and the influences of his Spirit restrained, though our unthankful and unholy carriage has been the *cause* of this change. Those alone who humble themselves under the mighty hand of God, shall be lifted up in due season. Reader, thou canst never be deceived in trusting thy all, the concerns of thy body and soul, to Him who divided the sea, saved the Hebrews, and destroyed the Egyptians.

CHAPTER XV.

Moses and the Israelites sing a song of praise to God for their late deliverance, in which they celebrate the power of God, gloriously manifested in the destruction of Pharaoh and his host, 1; *express their confidence in him as their strength and protector,* 2, 3; *detail the chief circumstances in the overthrow of the Egyptians,* 4–8; *and relate the purposes they had formed for the destruction of God's people,* 9, *and how he destroyed them in the imaginations of their hearts,* 10. *Jehovah is celebrated for the perfections of his nature and his wondrous works,* 11–13. *A prediction of the effect which the account of the destruction of the Egyptians should have on the Edomites, Moabites, and Canaanites,* 14–16. *A prediction of the establishment of Israel in the promised land,* 17. *The full chorus of praise,* 18. *Recapitulation of the destruction of the Egyptians, and the deliverance of Israel,* 19. Miriam *and the* women *join in and prolong the chorus,* 20, 21. *The people travel three days in the wilderness of* Shur, *and find no water,* 22. *Coming to* Marah, *and finding* bitter waters, *they murmur against Moses,* 23, 24. *In answer to the prayer of Moses, God shows him a tree by which the waters are sweetened,* 25. *God gives them statutes and gracious promises,* 26. *They come to* Elim, *where they find* twelve wells *of water and* seventy palm trees, *and there they encamp,* 27.

A. M. 2513. B. C. 1491. An. Exod. Isr. 1. Abib or Nisan.

THEN sang [a] Moses and the children of Israel this song unto the LORD; and spake, saying, I will [b] sing unto the LORD, for he hath triumphed gloriously: the horse and his

[a] Judg. v. 1; 2 Sam. xxii. 1; Psa. cvi. 12; Wisd. x. 20.——[b] Ver. 21.

NOTES ON CHAP. XV.

Verse 1. *Then sang Moses and the children of Israel this song*] POETRY has been cultivated in all ages and among all people, from the most refined to the most barbarous; and to it principally, under the kind providence of God, we are indebted for most of the *original accounts* we have of the ancient nations of the universe. Equally measured lines, with a harmonious collocation of expressive, sonorous, and sometimes highly metaphorical terms, the alternate lines either answering to each other in *sense*, or ending with similar *sounds*, were easily committed to *memory*, and easily *retained*. As these were often accompanied with a pleasing *air* or *tune*, the subject being a concatenation of striking and interesting events, histories formed thus became the amusement of youth, the softeners of the tedium of labour, and even the solace of age. In such a way the histories of most nations have been preserved. The interesting *events* celebrated, the *rhythm* or *metre*, and the accompanying *tune* or *recitativo air*, rendered them easily transmissible to posterity; and by means of *tradition* they passed safely from father to son through the times of comparative *darkness*, till they arrived at those ages in which the *pen* and the *press* have given them a sort of deathless duration and permanent stability, by multiplying the copies. Many of the ancient historic and heroic British tales are continued by tradition among the aboriginal inhabitants of Ireland to the present day; and the repetition of them constitutes the chief amusement of the winter evenings. Even the *prose* histories, which were written on the ground of the *poetic*, copied closely their exemplars, and the historians themselves were obliged to study all the *beauties* and *ornaments of style*, that their works might become *popular;* and to this circumstance we owe not a small measure of what is termed *refinement of language*. How observable is this in the history of *Herodotus*, who appears to have closely copied the ancient *poetic records* in his inimitable and harmonious prose; and, that his books might bear as near a resemblance as possible to the ancient and popular originals, he divided them into *nine*, and dedicated each to one of the *muses!* His work therefore seems to occupy the same place between the ancient *poetic compositions* and mere *prosaic histories*, as the *polype* does between *plants* and *animals*. Much even of our *sacred records* is written in *poetry*, which God has thus consecrated to be the faithful transmitter of remote and important events; and of this the *song* before the reader is a proof in point. Though this is not the first specimen of poetry we have met with in the Pentateuch, (see Lamech's speech to his wives, Gen. iv. 23, 24; Noah's prophecy concerning his sons, chap. ix. 25–27; and Jacob's blessing to the twelve patriarchs, chap. xlix. 2–27, and the notes there,) yet it is the first regular ode of any considerable length, having but *one* subject; and it is all written in *hemistichs*, or half lines, the usual form in Hebrew poetry; and though this form frequently occurs, it is not attended to in our common printed Hebrew Bibles, except in *this* and *three* other places, (Deut. xxxii., Judg. v., and 2 Sam. xxii.,) all of which shall be noticed as they occur. But in Dr. Kennicott's edition of the Hebrew Bible, all the poetry, wheresoever it occurs, is printed in its own *hemistich* form.

After what has been said it is perhaps scarcely necessary to observe, that as such ancient poetic histories commemorated great and extraordinary displays of *providence, courage, strength, fidelity, heroism*, and *piety;* hence the origin of EPIC *poems*, of which the song in this chapter is the *earliest* specimen. And on the principle of preserving the memory of such events, most nations have had their *epic poets*, who have *generally* taken for their subject the most splendid or most remote events of their country's history, which either referred to the *formation* or *extension* of their *empire*, the *exploits* of their *ancestors*, or the *establishment* of their *religion*. Hence the ancient HEBREWS had their *Shir Mosheh*, the piece in question; the GREEKS, their

A. M. 2513.
B. C. 1491.
An. Exod. Isr. 1.
Abib or Nisan.

rider hath he thrown into the sea.

2 The LORD *is* my strength and [c] song, and he is become my salvation: he *is* my God, and I will prepare him [d] a habitation; my [e] father's God, and I [f] will exalt him.

[c] Deut. x. 21; Psa. xviii. 2; xxii. 3; lix. 17; lxii. 6; cix. 1; cxviii. 14; cxl. 7; Isa. xii. 2; Hab. iii. 18, 19.——[d] Gen. xxviii. 21, 22; 2 Sam. vii. 5; Psa. cxxxii. 5.——[e] Chap. iii. 15, 16.——[f] 2 Sam. xxii. 47; Psa. xcix. 5; cxviii. 28; Isa. xxv. 1.

Ilias; the HINDOOS, their *Mahabarat;* the ROMANS, their *Æneis;* the NORWEGIANS, their *Edda;* the IRISH and SCOTCH, their *Fingal* and *Chronological poems;* the WELSH, their *Taliessin* and his *Triads;* the ARABS, their *Nebiun-Nameh* (exploits of Mohammed) and *Hamleh Heedry,* (exploits of Aly;) the PERSIANS, their SHAH *Nameh,* (book of kings;) the ITALIANS, their *Gerusalemme Liberata;* the PORTUGUESE, their *Lusiad;* the ENGLISH, their *Paradise Lost;* and, in humble imitation of all the rest, (*etsi non passibus æquis,*) the FRENCH, their *Henriade.*

The song of Moses has been in the highest repute in the Church of God from the beginning; the author of the *Book of Wisdom* attributes it in a particular manner to the wisdom of God, and says that on this occasion *God opened the mouth of the dumb, and made the tongues of infants eloquent;* chap. x. 21. As if he had said, Every person felt an interest in the great events which had taken place, and all laboured to give Jehovah that praise which was due to his name. "With this song of victory over Pharaoh," says Mr. Ainsworth, "the Holy Ghost compares the song of those who have gotten the victory over the spiritual Pharaoh, the *beast,* (Antichrist,) when they stand by the *sea of glass mingled with fire,* (as Israel stood here by the Red Sea,) *having the harps of God,* (as the women here had timbrels, ver. 20,) *and they sing the song of Moses the servant of God, and the song of the Lamb,* the Son of God;" Rev. xv. 2–4.

I will sing unto the Lord] Moses begins the song, and in the two first hemistichs states the *subject* of it; and these two first lines became the *grand chorus* of the piece, as we may learn from ver. 21. See Dr. Kennicott's arrangement and translation of this piece at the end of this chapter.

Triumphed gloriously] כי גאה גאה *ki gaoh gaah, he is exceedingly exalted,* rendered by the Septuagint, Ενδοξως γαρ δεδοξασται, *He is gloriously glorified;* and surely this was one of the most signal displays of the glorious majesty of God ever exhibited since the *creation* of the world. And when it is considered that the whole of this transaction shadowed out the *redemption of the human race* from the *thraldom* and *power* of *sin* and *iniquity* by the *Lord Jesus,* and the *final triumph* of the *Church* of God over all its *enemies,* we may also join in the song, and celebrate Him who has triumphed so gloriously, having conquered death, and opened the kingdom of heaven to all believers.

Verse 2. *The Lord* is *my strength and song*] How judiciously are the members of this sentence arranged! He who has God for his *strength,* will have him for his *song;* and he to whom Jehovah is become *salvation,* will *exalt his name.* Miserably and untunably, in the ears of God, does that man sing praises, who is not *saved* by the grace of Christ, nor *strengthened* by the *power* of his *might.*

It is worthy of observation that the word which we translate LORD here, is not יהוה JEHOVAH in the original, but יה JAH; "as if by abbreviation," says Mr. Parkhurst, "for יהיה *yeheieh* or יהי *yehi.* It signifies the Essence 'Ο ΩΝ, He who IS, simply, absolutely, and independently. The relation between יה *Jah* and the verb היה, to *subsist, exist, be,* is intimated to us the first time יה *Jah* is used in Scripture, (Exod. xv. 2:) 'My strength and my song *is* יה JAH, *and he is become* (ויהי *vajehi*) to me salvation.'" See Psa. lxviii. 5; lxxxix. 6; xciv. 7; cxv. 17, 18; cxviii. 17.

JAH יה is several times joined with the name Jehovah יהוה, so that we may be sure that it is not, as some have supposed, a mere abbreviation of that word. See Isa. xii. 2; xxvi. 4. Our blessed Lord solemnly claims to himself what is intended in this Divine name יה JAH, John viii. 58: "Before Abraham was, (*γενεσθαι, was born,*) *εγω ειμι,* I AM," not *I was,* but *I am,* plainly intimating his *Divine eternal existence.* Compare Isa. xliii. 13. And the Jews appear to have well understood him, *for then took they up stones to cast at him* as a blasphemer. Compare Col. i. 16, 17, where the Apostle Paul, after asserting that all things that are in heaven and that are in earth, visible and invisible, were created, *εκτισται,* by and for Christ, adds, *And* HE IS (*αυτος εστι,* not *ην, was*) *before all things, and by him all things συνεστηκε, have subsisted, and still subsist.* See *Parkhurst.*

From this Divine name יה *Jah* the ancient Greeks had their Ιη, Ιη, in their invocations of the gods, particularly of *Apollo* (the *uncompounded* ONE) the light, and hence ΕΙ, written after the oriental manner from right to left, afterwards ΙΕ, was inscribed over the great door of the temple at Delphi! See the note on chap. iii. 14, and the concluding observations there.

I will prepare him a habitation] ואנוהו *veanvehu.* It has been supposed that Moses, by this expression, intended the *building of the tabernacle;* but it seems to come in very strangely in this place. Most of the ancient versions understood the original in a very different sense. The *Vulgate* has *et glorificabo eum;* the *Septuagint δοξασω αυτον, I will* GLORIFY *him;* with which the *Syriac, Coptic,* the *Targum* of *Jonathan,* and the *Jerusalem Targum,* agree. From the *Targum* of *Onkelos* the present translation seems to have been originally derived; he has translated the place ואבני לה מקדש *veebnei leh makdash,* "And I will build him a sanctuary," which not one of the other versions, the *Persian* excepted, acknowledges. Our own old translations are generally different from the present: *Coverdale,* "This my God, I will magnify him;" *Matthew's, Cranmer's,* and the *Bishops' Bible,* render it *glorify,* and the sense of the place seems to require it. Calmet, Houbigant, Kennicott, and other critics, contend for this translation.

My father's God] I believe *Houbigant* to be right,

A. M. 2513.
B. C. 1491.
An. Exod. Isr. 1.
Abib or Nisan.

3 The LORD *is* a man of [g] war:
the LORD *is* his [h] name.
4 [i] Pharaoh's chariots and his
host hath he cast into the sea: [k] his chosen
captains also are drowned in the Red Sea.
5 [l] The depths have covered them: [m] they
sank into the bottom as a stone.
6 [n] Thy right hand, O LORD, is become
glorious in power: thy right hand, O LORD,
hath dashed in pieces the enemy.
7 And in the greatness of thine [o] excellency
thou hast overthrown them that rose up against
thee: thou sentest forth thy wrath, *which* [p] consumed them [q] as stubble.
8 And [r] with the blast of thy
nostrils the waters were gathered
together, [s] the floods stood upright as a heap, *and* the depths were congealed
in the heart of the sea.
9 [t] The enemy said, I will pursue, I will
overtake, I will [u] divide the spoil; my lust
shall be satisfied upon them; I will draw my
sword, my hand shall [v] destroy them.
10 Thou didst [w] blow with thy wind, [x] the
sea covered them: they sank as lead in the
mighty waters.
11 [y] Who *is* like unto thee, O LORD, among
the [z] gods? who *is* like thee, [a] glorious in

[g] Psa. xxiv. 8; Rev. xix. 11.——[h] Chap. vi. 3; Psa. lxxxiii. 18.——[i] Chap. xiv. 28.——[k] Chapter xiv. 7.——[l] Chap. xiv. 28. [m] Neh. ix. 11.——[n] Psalm cxviii. 15, 26.——[o] Deut. xxxiii. 26. [p] Psa. lix. 13.——[q] Isaiah v. 24; xlvii. 14.——[r] Chapter xiv. 21; 2 Sam. xxii. 16; Job iv. 9; 2 Thess. ii. 8.

[s] Psa. lxxviii. 13; Hab. iii. 10.——[t] Judg. v. 30.——[u] Gen. xlix. 27; Isa. liii. 12; Luke xi. 22.——[v] Or, *repossess.*——[w] Chap. xiv. 21; Psa. cxlvii. 18.——[x] Ver. 5; chap. xiv. 28.——[y] 2 Sam. vii. 22; 1 Kings viii. 23; Psa. lxxi. 19; lxxxvi. 8; lxxxix. 6, 8; Jer. x. 6; xlix. 19.——[z] Or, *mighty ones.*——[a] Isa. vi. 3.

who translates the original, אלהי אבי *Elohey abi, Deus meus, pater meus est,* "My God is my Father." Every man may call the Divine Being *his* GOD; but only those who are his *children* by adoption through grace can call him their FATHER. This is a privilege which God has given to none but his *children*. See Gal. iv. 6.

Verse 3. *The Lord* is *a man of war*] Perhaps it would be better to translate the words, *Jehovah is the man* or *hero of the battle.* As we scarcely ever apply the term to any thing but first-rate armed vessels, the change of the translation seems indispensable, though the common rendering is literal enough. Besides, the object of Moses was to show that *man* had no part in this victory, but that the whole was wrought by the miraculous power of God, and that therefore *he* alone should have all the glory.

The LORD is *his name.*] That is, JEHOVAH. He has now, as the name implies, given complete *existence* to all his promises. See the notes on Gen. ii. 4, and Exod. vi. 3.

Verse 4. *Pharaoh's chariots—his host—his chosen captains*] On such an expedition it is likely that the principal Egyptian nobility accompanied their king, and that the overthrow they met with here had reduced Egypt to the lowest extremity. Had the Israelites been intent on plunder, or had Moses been influenced by a spirit of ambition, how easily might both have gratified themselves, as, had they returned, they might have soon overrun and subjugated the whole land.

Verse 6. *Thy right hand*] Thy omnipotence, manifested in a most extraordinary way.

Verse 7. *In the greatness of thine excellency*] To this wonderful deliverance the Prophet Isaiah refers, chap. lxiii. 11–14: "Then he remembered the days of old, Moses *and* his people, *saying,* Where *is* he that brought them up out of the sea with the shepherd of his flock? Where *is* he that put his Holy Spirit within him? That led *them* by the right hand of Moses with his glorious arm, dividing the water before them, to make himself an everlasting name? That led them through the deep, as a horse in the wilderness, *that* they should not stumble? As a beast goeth down into the valley, the Spirit of the LORD caused him to rest; so didst thou lead thy people, to make thyself a glorious name."

Verse 8. *The depths were congealed*] The strong east wind (chap. xiv. 21) employed to dry the bottom of the sea, is here represented as the blast of God's nostrils that had *congealed* or *frozen* the waters, so that they stood in heaps like a wall on the right hand and on the left.

Verse 9. *The enemy said*] As this song was composed by Divine inspiration, we may rest assured that these words were spoken by Pharaoh and his captains, and the passions they describe felt, in their utmost sway, in their hearts; but how soon was their boasting confounded? "Thou didst blow with thy wind, and the sea covered them: they sank as lead in the mighty waters!"

Verse 11. *Who is like unto thee, O Lord, among the gods?*] We have already seen that all the Egyptian gods, or the objects of the Egyptians' idolatry, were confounded, and rendered completely despicable, by the *ten plagues,* which appear to have been directed principally against *them.* Here the people of God exult over them afresh: Who among *these gods* is like unto THEE? *They* can neither *save* nor *destroy;* THOU dost both in the most signal manner.

As the original words כי כמכה באלם יהוה *mi chamochah baelim Yehovah* are supposed to have constituted the *motto* on the ensign of the *Asmoneans,* and to have furnished the name of *Maccabeus* to *Judas,* their grand captain, from whom they were afterwards called *Maccabeans,* it may be necessary to say a few words on this subject. It is possible that Judas Maccabeus might have had this motto on his ensign, or at least the *initial* letters of it, for such a practice was not uncommon. For instance, on the Roman standard the letters S. P. Q. R. stood for *Senatus Populus Que Romanus,* i. e. the Senate and Roman People; and מ כ ב י M. C. B. I. might have stood for *Mi Chamochah Baelim Jehovah,* "Who among the gods (or *strong*

A. M. 2513. B. C. 1491. An. Exod. Isr. 1. Abib or Nisan.

holiness, fearful *in* praises, [b] doing wonders ?
12 Thou stretchedst out [c] thy
right hand, the earth swallowed them.
13 Thou in thy mercy hast [d] led forth the
people *which* thou hast redeemed : thou hast
guided *them* in thy strength unto [e] thy holy
habitation.
14 [f] The people shall hear, *and* be afraid :
[g] sorrow shall take hold on the inhabitants of
Palestina.
15 [h] Then [i] the dukes of Edom shall be
amazed ; [k] the mighty men of Moab, trembling
shall take hold upon them ; [l] all the inhabitants of Canaan shall melt away.
16 [m] Fear and dread shall fall
upon them ; by the greatness of
thine arm, they shall be *as* still
[n] as a stone ; till thy people pass over, O
LORD, till the people pass over, [o] *which* thou
hast purchased.
17 Thou shalt bring them in ; and [p] plant
them in the mountain of thine inheritance, *in*
the place, O LORD, *which* thou hast made for
thee to dwell in, *in* the [q] sanctuary, O LORD,
which thy hands have established.
18 [r] The LORD shall reign for ever and
ever.
19 For the [s] horse of Pharaoh went in with
his chariots and with his horsemen into the

[b] Psa. lxxvii. 14.——[c] Ver. 6.——[d] Psa. lxxvii. 15, 20 ; lxxviii. 52 ; lxxx. 1 ; cvi. 9 ; Isa. lxiii. 12, 13 ; Jer. ii. 6.——[e] Psa. lxxviii. 54.——[f] Num. xiv. 14 ; Deut. ii. 25 ; Josh. ii. 9, 10.——[g] Psalm xlviii. 6.——[h] Gen. xxxvi. 40.——[i] Deut. ii. 4.——[k] Num. xxii. 3 ; Hab. iii. 7.——[l] Josh. v. 1.——[m] Deut. ii. 25 ; xi. 25 ; Josh. ii. 9.

[n] 1 Sam. xxv. 37.——[o] Chap. xix. 5 ; Deut. xxxii. 9 ; 2 Sam. vii. 23 ; Psalm lxxiv. 2 ; Isaiah xliii. 1, 3 ; li. 10 ; Jer. xxxi. 11 ; Tit. ii. 14 ; 1 Pet. ii. 9 ; 2 Pet. ii. 1.——[p] Psa. xliv. 2 ; lxxx. 8. [q] Psa. lxxviii. 54.——[r] Psa. x. 16 ; xxix. 10 ; cxlvi. 10 ; Isa. lvii. 15.——[s] Chap. xiv. 23 ; Prov. xxi. 31.

ones) is like unto thee, O Jehovah !" But it appears from the Greek Μακκαβαιος, and also the Syriac ܡܩܒܝ *makabi*, that the name was written originally with ק *koph*, not כ *caph*. It is most likely, as Michaelis has observed, that the name must have been derived from מקב *makkab*, a *hammer* or *mallet ;* hence Judas, because of his bravery and success, might have been denominated the *hammer* or *mallet* by which the enemies of God had been *beaten*, *pounded*, and *broken* to *pieces*. Judas, the hammer of the Lord.

Glorious in holiness] Infinitely resplendent in this attribute, essential to the perfection of the Divine nature.

Fearful in praises] Such glorious holiness cannot be approached without the deepest reverence and fear, even by angels, who veil their faces before the majesty of God. How then should *man*, who is only *sin* and *dust*, approach the presence of his Maker !

Doing wonders ?] Every part of the work of God is wonderful ; not only *miracles*, which imply an inversion or suspension of the laws of nature, but every part of nature itself. Who can conceive how a single blade of grass is formed ; or how earth, air, and water become consolidated in the body of the oak ? And who can comprehend how the different tribes of plants and animals are preserved, in all the distinctive characteristics of their respective natures ? And who can conceive how the human being is formed, nourished, and its different parts developed ? What is the true cause of the circulation of the blood ? or, how different aliments produce the solids and fluids of the animal machine ? What is life, sleep, death ? And how an impure and unholy soul is *regenerated, purified, refined*, and made like unto its great Creator ? These are wonders which God alone works, and to himself only are they fully known.

Verse 12. *The earth swallowed them.*] It is very likely there was also an earthquake on this occasion, and that chasms were made in the bottom of the sea, by which many of them were swallowed up, though multitudes were overwhelmed by the waters, whose dead bodies were afterward thrown ashore. The psalmist strongly intimates that there was an *earthquake* on this occasion : *The voice of thy thunder was in the heaven ; the lightnings lightened the world ; the* EARTH TREMBLED *and* SHOOK ; Psa. lxxvii. 18.

Verse 13. *Thou hast guided* them *in thy strength unto thy holy habitation.*] As this ode was dictated by the Spirit of God, it is most natural to understand this and the following verses, to the end of the 18th, as containing a prediction of what God would do for this people which he had so miraculously redeemed. On this mode of interpretation it would be better to read several of the verbs in the *future* tense.

Verse 15. *The dukes of Edom*] Idumea was governed at this time by those called אלפים *alluphim*, *heads, chiefs*, or *captains*. See the note on Gen. xxxvi. 15.

Verse 16. *Till thy people pass over*] Not over the Red Sea, for that event had been already celebrated ; but over the desert and Jordan, in order to be brought into the promised land.

Verse 17. *Thou shalt bring them in*] By thy strength and mercy alone shall they get the promised inheritance.

And plant them] Give them a *fixed* habitation in Canaan, after their unsettled wandering life in the wilderness.

In the mountain] Meaning Canaan, which was a very *mountainous* country, Deut. xi. 11 ; or probably Mount Zion, on which the temple was built. Where the pure worship of God was *established*, there the people might expect both *rest* and *safety*. Wherever the purity of religion is established and preserved, and the high and the low endeavour to regulate their lives according to its precepts, the government of that country is likely to be permanent.

Verse 18. *The Lord shall reign for ever and ever.*] This is properly the grand chorus in which all the people joined. The words are expressive of God's

A. M. 2513.
B. C. 1491.
An. Exod. Isr. 1.
Abib or Nisan.

sea, and [t] the LORD brought again
the waters of the sea upon them;
but the children of Israel went
on dry *land*, in the midst of the sea.
20 And Miriam [u] the prophetess, [v] the sister
of Aaron, [w] took a timbrel in her hand; and
all the women went out after her [x] with timbrels and with dances.
21 And Miriam [y] answered
them, [z] Sing ye to the LORD, for he
hath triumphed gloriously: the
horse and his rider hath he thrown into the sea.
22 So Moses brought Israel from the Red
Sea, and they went out into the wilderness
of [a] Shur; and they went three days in the
wilderness, and found no water.

[t] Chap. xiv. 28, 29.——[u] Judg. iv. 4; 1 Sam. x. 5.——[v] Num. xxvi. 59.——[w] 1 Sam. xviii. 6.——[x] Judg. xi. 34; xxi. 21; 2 Sam. vi. 16; Psa. lxviii. 11, 25; cxlix. 3; cl. 4.——[y] 1 Sam. xviii. 7. [z] Ver. 1.——[a] Gen. xvi. 7; xxv. 18.

everlasting dominion, not only in the *world*, but in the *Church;* not only under the *law*, but also under the *Gospel;* not only in *time*, but through *eternity*. The original לעלם ועד *leolam vaed* may be translated, *for ever and onward;* or, by our very expressive compound term, *for* EVERMORE, i. e. *for ever and more*—not only through *time*, but also through all duration. His dominion shall be ever the same, active and infinitely extending. With this verse the song seems to end, as with it the hemistichs or poetic lines terminate. The 20th and beginning of the 21st are in plain prose, but the latter part of the 21st is in hemistichs, as it contains the *response* made by Miriam and the Israelitish women at different intervals during the song. See Dr. Kennicott's arrangement of the parts at the end of this chapter.

Verse 20. *And Miriam the prophetess*] We have already seen that Miriam was *older* than either Moses or Aaron: for when Moses was exposed on the Nile, she was a young girl capable of managing the stratagem used for the preservation of his life; and then Aaron was only three years and three months old, for he was *fourscore and three* years old when Moses was but *fourscore*, (see chap. vii. 7;) so that Aaron was older than Moses, and Miriam considerably older than either, not less probably than *nine* or *ten* years of age. See on chap. ii. 2.

There is great diversity of opinion on the origin of the name of *Miriam*, which is the same with the Greek Μαριαμ, the Latin *Maria*, and the English *Mary*. Some suppose it to be compounded of מר *mar*, a *drop*, (Isa. xl. 15,) and ים *yam*, the *sea*, and that from this etymology the heathens formed their Venus, whom they feign to have sprung from the sea. St. Jerome gives several etymologies for the name, which at once show how difficult it is to ascertain it: *she who enlightens me*, or *she who enlightens them*, or *the star of the sea*. Others, *the lady of the sea*, *the bitterness of the sea, &c.* It is probable that the first or the last is the true one, but it is a matter of little importance, as we have not the circumstance marked, as in the case of Moses and many others, that gave rise to the name.

The prophetess] הנביאה *hannebiah*. For the meaning of the word prophet, נביא *nabi*, see the note on Gen. xx. 7. It is very likely that Miriam was inspired by the Spirit of God to instruct the Hebrew women, as Moses and Aaron were to instruct the men; and when she and her brother Aaron sought to share in the government of the people with Moses, we find her laying claim to the prophetic influence, Num. xii. 2: *Hath the Lord indeed spoken only by Moses? Hath he not* SPOKEN ALSO BY US? And that she was constituted joint leader of the people with her two brothers, we have the express word of God by the Prophet Micah, chap. vi. 4: *For I brought thee up out of the land of Egypt—and I sent before thee Moses, Aaron, and Miriam.* Hence it is very likely that she was the instructress of the women, and regulated the times, places, &c., of their devotional acts; for it appears that from the beginning to the present day the Jewish women all worshipped *apart*.

A timbrel] תף *toph*, the same word which is translated *tabret*, Gen. xxxi. 27, on which the reader is desired to consult the note.

And with dances.] מחלת *mecholoth*. Many learned men suppose that this word means some instruments of wind music, because the word comes from the root חלל *chalal*, the ideal meaning of which is to *perforate, penetrate, pierce, stab,* and hence *to wound*. *Pipes* or *hollow tubes*, such as *flutes, hautboys,* and the like, may be intended. Both the Arabic and Persian understand it as meaning instruments of music of the pipe, drum, or sistrum kind; and this seems to comport better with the scope and design of the place than the term *dances*. It must however be allowed that religious dances have been in use from the remotest times; and yet in most of the places where the term occurs in our translation, an *instrument of music* bids as fair to be its meaning as a *dance* of any kind. Miriam is the first *prophetess* on record, and by this we find that God not only poured out his Spirit upon *men*, but upon *women* also; and we learn also that Miriam was not only a *prophetess*, but a *poetess* also, and must have had considerable skill in *music* to have been able to conduct her part of these solemnities. It may appear strange that during so long an oppression in Egypt, the Israelites were able to cultivate the fine arts; but that they did so there is the utmost evidence from the Pentateuch. Not only architecture, weaving, and such necessary arts, were well known among them, but also the arts that are called *ornamental*, such as those of the goldsmith, lapidary, embroiderer, furrier, &c., of which we have ample proof in the construction of the tabernacle and its utensils. However ungrateful, rebellious, &c., the Jews may have been, the praise of industry and economy can never be denied them. In former ages, and in all places even of their dispersions, they appear to have been frugal and industrious, and capable of great proficiency in the most elegant and curious arts; but they are now greatly degenerated.

Verse 22. *The wilderness of Shur*] This was on

A. M. 2513.
B. C. 1491.
An. Exod. Isr. 1.
Abib or Nisan.

23 And when they came to [b] Marah, they could not drink of the waters of Marah, for they *were* bitter: therefore the name of it was called [c] Marah.

24 And the people [d] murmured against Moses, saying, What shall we drink?

25 And he [e] cried unto the LORD; and the LORD showed him a [f] tree, [g] *which* when he had cast into the waters, the waters were made sweet. There he [h] made for them a statute and an ordinance, and there [i] he proved them

26 And said, [k] If thou wilt diligently hearken to the voice of the LORD thy God, and wilt do that which is right in his sight, and wilt give ear to his commandments, and keep all

[b] Numbers xxxiii. 8.——[c] That is, *bitterness*; Ruth i. 20. [d] Chap. xvi. 2; xvii. 3.——[e] Chap. xiv. 10; xvii. 4; Psa. l. 15. [f] Eccles. xxxviii. 5.

[g] See 2 Kings ii. 21; iv. 41.——[h] See Josh. xxiv. 25.——[i] Ch. xvi. 4; Deut. viii. 2, 16; Judg. ii. 22; iii. 1, 4; Psa. lxvi. 10; lxxxi. 7.——[k] Deut. vii. 12, 15.

the coast of the Red Sea on their road to Mount Sinai. See the map.

Verse 23. *Marah*] So called from the *bitter waters* found there. Dr. Shaw conjectures that this place is the same as that now called *Corondel*, where there is still a small rill which, if not diluted with dews or rain, continues brackish. See his account at the end of Exodus.

Verse 24. *The people murmured*] They were in a state of great mental degradation, owing to their long and oppressive vassalage, and had no firmness of character. See the note on chap. xiii. 17.

Verse 25. *He cried unto the Lord*] Moses was not only their leader, but also their *mediator*. Of prayer and dependence on the Almighty, the great mass of the Israelites appear to have had little knowledge at this time. Moses, therefore, had much to bear from their weakness, and the merciful Lord was long-suffering.

The Lord showed him a tree] What this tree was we know not: some think that the tree was extremely bitter itself, such as the *quassia*; and that God acted in this as he generally does, correcting contraries by contraries, which, among the ancient physicians, was a favourite maxim, *Clavus clavo expellitur*. The Targums of Jonathan and Jerusalem say that, when Moses prayed, "the WORD of the Lord showed him the tree ארדפני *ardiphney*, on which he wrote the great and precious name of (JEHOVAH,) and then threw it into the waters, and the waters thereby became sweet." But what the tree *ardiphney* was we are not informed.

Many suppose that this tree which healed the bitter waters was symbolical of the cross of our blessed Redeemer, that has been the means of healing infected nature, and through the virtue of which the *evils* and *bitters* of life are sweetened, and rendered subservient to the best interests of God's followers. Whatever may be in the metaphor, this is true in fact; and hence the greatest of apostles gloried in the *cross* of our Lord Jesus Christ, by which the world was crucified to him and he unto the world.

It appears that these waters were sweetened only for that occasion, as Dr. Shaw reports them to be still *brackish*, which appears to be occasioned by the abundance of *natron* which prevails in the surrounding soil. Thus we may infer that the natural cause of their bitterness or brackishness was permitted to resume its operations, when the occasion that rendered the change necessary had ceased to exist. Thus Christ simply changed that water into wine which was to be *drawn out* to be carried to the master of the feast; the rest of the water in the pots remaining as before. As the water of the Nile was so peculiarly excellent, to which they had been long accustomed, they could not easily put up with what was indifferent. See the note on chap. vii. 18.

There he made for them] Though it is probable that the Israelites are here intended, yet the word לו *lo* should not be translated *for them*, but *to him*, for these statutes were given to Moses that he might deliver them to the people.

There he proved them.] נסהו *nissahu, he proved* HIM. By this murmuring of the people he proved Moses, to see, speaking after the manner of men, whether he would be faithful, and, in the midst of the trials to which he was likely to be exposed, whether he would continue to trust in the Lord, and seek all his help from him.

Verse 26. *If thou wilt diligently hearken*] What is contained in this verse appears to be what is intended by the *statute* and *ordinance* mentioned in the preceding: *If thou wilt diligently hearken unto the voice of the Lord thy God, and wilt do that which is right in his sight, and wilt give ear to his commandments, and keep all his statutes, I will put none of these diseases upon thee, &c.* This statute and ordinance implied the three following particulars: 1. That they should acknowledge Jehovah for their God, and thus avoid all idolatry. 2. That they should receive his word and testimony as a Divine revelation, binding on their hearts and lives, and thus be saved from profligacy of every kind, and from acknowledging the maxims or adopting the customs of the neighbouring nations. 3. That they should continue to do so, and adorn their profession with a holy life. These things being attended to, then the promise of God was, that they should have none of the diseases of the Egyptians put on them; that they should be kept in a state of health of body and peace of mind; and if at any time they should be afflicted, on application to God the evil should be removed, because he was their *healer* or *physician*—*I am the Lord that healeth thee.* That the Israelites had in general a very good state of health, their history warrants us to believe; and when they were afflicted, as in the case of the fiery serpents, on application to God they were all healed. The Targum of Jonathan ben Uzziel states that the statutes which Moses received at this time were commandments con-

A. M. 2513.
B. C. 1491.
An. Exod. Isr. 1.
Abib or Nisan.

his statutes, I will put none of these [l]diseases upon thee, which I have brought upon the Egyptians: for I *am* the LORD [m]that healeth thee.

27 [n]And they came to Elim, where *were* twelve wells of water, and threescore and ten palm trees: and they encamped there by the waters.

A. M. 2513.
B. C. 1491.
An. Exod. Isr. 1.
Abib or Nisan.

[l] Deut. xxviii. 27, 60.——[m] Chap. xxiii. 25; Psa. xli. 3, 4; ciii. 3; cxlvii. 3.——[n] Num. xxxiii. 9.

cerning the observance of the Sabbath, duty to parents, the ordinances concerning wounds and bruises, and the penalties which sinners should incur by transgressing them. But it appears that the *general* ordinances already mentioned are those which are intended here, and this seems to be proved beyond dispute by Jer. vii. 22, 23: "For I spake not unto your fathers, nor commanded them in the day that I brought them out of the land of Egypt, concerning burnt-offerings or sacrifices: but this thing commanded I them, saying, Obey my voice, and I will be your God, and ye shall be my people; and walk ye in all the ways that I have commanded you, that it may be well unto you."

Verse 27. *They came to Elim*] This was in the desert of *Sin*, and, according to Dr. Shaw, about two leagues from *Tor*, and thirty from *Marah* or *Corondel*.

Twelve wells of water] One for each of the tribes of Israel, say the Targums of *Jonathan* and *Jerusalem*.

And threescore and ten palm trees] One for each of the seventy elders.—*Ibid.*

Dr. Shaw found *nine* of the twelve wells, the other *three* having been choked up with sand; and the seventy palm trees multiplied into more than 2000, the dates of which bring a considerable revenue to the Greek monks at Tor. See his account at the end of this book, and see also the map. Thus sufficient evidence of the authenticity of this part of the sacred history remains, after the lapse of more than 3000 years.

IN the preceding notes the reader has been referred to Dr. Kennicott's translation and arrangement of the song of Moses. To this translation he prefixes the following observations:—

"This triumphant ode was sung by Moses and the sons of Israel: and the women, headed by Miriam, answered the men by repeating the two first lines of the song, altering only the first word, which two lines were probably sung more than once *as a chorus*.

"*The conclusion* of this ode seems very manifest; and yet, though the ancient Jews had sense enough to write this song differently from prose; and though their authority has prevailed even to this day in *this* and three other poems in the Old Testament, (Deut. xxii.; Judg. v.; and 2 Sam. xxii.,) still expressed by them as poetry; yet have these critics carried their ideas of the song here to the end of verse 19. The reason why the same has been done by others probably is, they thought that the particle כי *for*, which begins verse 19, necessarily connected it with the preceding poetry. But this difficulty is removed by translating כי *when*, especially if we take verses 19–21 as being a *prose* explanation of the *manner* in which this song of triumph was performed. For these three verses say that the *men singers* were *answered* in the chorus by *Miriam and the women*, accompanying their words with musical instruments. '*When* the horse of Pharaoh *had gone* into the sea, and the Lord *had brought* the sea upon them; *and* Israel *had passed*, on dry land, in the midst of the sea; *then* Miriam took a timbrel, and all the women went out after her with timbrels and dances; and Miriam (with the women) *answered them* (להם *lahem*, the *men*, by way of chorus) in the words, *O sing ye, &c.*' That this chorus was sung *more than once* is thus stated by Bishop Lowth: *Maria, cum mulieribus, virorum choro* IDENTIDEM *succinebat.*—Prælect. 19.

"I shall now give what appears to me to be an exact translaton of this whole song:—

MOSES. *Part* I.

1. I will sing to JEHOVAH, for he hath triumphed gloriously;
   The horse and his rider hath he thrown into the sea.
2. My strength and my song is JEHOVAH;
   And he is become to me for salvation:
   This is my God, and I will celebrate him;
   The God of my father, and I will exalt him.
3. Jehovah is mighty in battle! } Perhaps a chorus sung by *the men*.
   Jehovah is his name! }

Chorus, by *Miriam and the women.*
Perhaps sung first in this place.

O sing ye to Jehovah, for he hath triumphed gloriously!
The horse and his rider hath he thrown into the sea

MOSES. *Part* II.

4. Pharaoh's chariots and his host hath he cast into the sea;
   And his chosen captains are drowned in the Red Sea.
5. The depths have covered them, they went down;
   (They sank) to the bottom as a stone.
6. Thy right hand, *Jehovah*, is become glorious in power;
   Thy right hand, *Jehovah*, dasheth in pieces the enemy.
7. And in the greatness of thine excellence thou overthrowest them that rise against thee.
   Thou sendest forth thy wrath, which consumeth them as stubble.
8. Even at the blast of thy displeasure the waters are gathered together;
   The floods stand upright as a heap,
   Congealed are the depths in the very heart of the sea.

O sing ye to JEHOVAH, &c. Chorus by *the women.*

MOSES. *Part* III.

9. The enemy said: '*I will pursue, I shall overtake; I shall divide the spoil, my soul shall be satiated with them;*
   I will draw my sword, my hand shall destroy them.'
10. Thou didst blow with thy wind, the sea covered them;
    They sank as lead in the mighty waters.
11. Who is like thee among the gods, O JEHOVAH?
    Who is like thee, glorious in holiness!

12. Fearful in praises; performing wonders!
Thou stretchest out thy right hand, the earth swalloweth them!
13. Thou in thy mercy leadest the people whom thou hast redeemed;
Thou in thy strength guidest to the habitation of thy holiness!
O sing ye to JEHOVAH, &c. Chorus by *the women.*

MOSES. *Part* IV.

14. The nations have heard, and are afraid;
Sorrow hath seized the inhabitants of Palestine.
15. Already are the dukes of Edom in consternation,
And the mighty men of Moab, trembling hath seized them;
All the inhabitants of Canaan do faint.
16. Fear and dread shall fall upon them;
Through the greatness of thine arm they shall be still as a stone:
17. Till thy people, JEHOVAH, pass over [Jordan;]
Till the people pass over whom thou hast redeemed.
18. Thou shalt bring them and plant them in the mount of thine inheritance:
The place for thy rest which thou, JEHOVAH, hast made;
The sanctuary, JEHOVAH, which thy hands have established.

Grand chorus by ALL.

JEHOVAH FOR EVER AND EVER SHALL REIGN."

1. When poetry is consecrated to the service of God, and employed as above to commemorate his marvellous acts, it then becomes a very useful handmaid to piety, and God is honoured by his gifts. God inspired the song of Moses, and perhaps from this very circumstance it has passed for current among the most polished of the heathen nations, that a poet is a person *Divinely inspired;* and hence the epithet of *προφητης, prophet*, and *vates*, of the same import, was given them among the Greeks and Romans.

2. The song of Moses is a proof of the miraculous passage of the Israelites through the Red Sea. There has been no period since the Hebrew nation left Egypt in which this song was not found among them, *as composed on that occasion, and to commemorate that event.* It may be therefore considered as completely authentic as any living witness could be who had himself passed through the Red Sea, and whose life had been protracted through all the intervening ages to the present day

3. We have already seen that it is a song of triumph for the deliverance of the people of God, and that it was intended to point out the final salvation and triumph of the whole Church of Christ; so that in the heaven of heavens the redeemed of the Lord, both among the Jews and the Gentiles, shall unite together to sing the *song of Moses* and the *song of the Lamb.* See Rev. xv. 2–4. Reader, implore the mercy of God to enable thee to make thy calling and election sure, that thou mayest bear thy part in this glorious and eternal triumph.

CHAPTER XVI.

The Israelites journey from Elim, *and come to the wilderness of* Sin, 1. *They murmur for lack of bread,* 2, 3. *God promises to rain bread from heaven for them,* 4, *of which they were to collect a double portion on the sixth day,* 5. *A miraculous supply of* flesh *in the* evening *and* bread *in the* morning, *promised,* 6–9. *The glory of the Lord appears in the cloud,* 10. *Flesh and bread promised as a proof of God's care over them,* 11, 12. Quails *come and cover the whole camp,* 13. *And a* dew *fell which left a small round substance on the ground, which Moses tells them was the bread which God had sent,* 14, 15. *Directions for gathering it,* 16. *The Israelites gather each an* omer, 17, 18. *They are directed to leave none of it till the next day,* 19; *which some neglecting, it became putrid,* 20. *They gather it every morning, because it melted when the sun waxed hot,* 21. *Each person gathers two omers on the* sixth *day,* 22. *Moses commands them to keep the* seventh *as a Sabbath to the Lord,* 23. *What was laid up for the Sabbath did not putrefy,* 24. *Nothing of it fell on that day, hence the strict observance of the Sabbath was enjoined,* 25–30. *The Israelites name the substance that fell with the dew* manna; *its appearance and taste described,* 31. *An omer of the manna is commanded to be laid up for a memorial of Jehovah's kindness,* 32–34. *The manna now sent continued daily for the space of* forty years, 35. *How much an omer contained,* 36.

A. M. 2513. B. C. 1491. An. Exod. Isr. 1. Ijar or Zif.

AND they [a] took their journey from Elim, and all the congregation of the children of Israel came unto the wilderness of [b] Sin, which *is* between Elim and Sinai, on the fifteenth day of the second month after their departing out of the land of Egypt.

[a] Num. xxxiii. 10, 11. — [b] Ezek. xxx. 15.

NOTES ON CHAP. XVI.

Verse 1. *The wilderness of Sin*] This desert lies between Elim and Sinai, and from Elim, Dr. Shaw says, Mount Sinai can be seen distinctly. Mr. Ainsworth supposes that this wilderness had its name from a strong city of Egypt called *Sin*, near which it lay. See Ezek. xxx. 15, 16. Before they came to the wilderness of *Sin*, they had a previous encampment by the

a

A. M. 2513. B. C. 1491. An. Exod. Isr. 1. Ijar or Zif.

2 And the whole congregation of the children of Israel [c] murmured against Moses and Aaron, in the wilderness:

3 And the children of Israel said unto them, [d] Would to God we had died by the hand of the LORD, in the land of Egypt, [e] when we sat by the flesh pots, *and* when we did eat bread to the full; for ye have brought us forth into this wilderness, to kill this whole assembly with hunger.

4 Then said the LORD unto Moses, Behold, I will rain [f] bread from heaven for you; and the people shall go out, and gather [g] a certain rate every day, that I may [h] prove them, whether they will walk in my law, or no.

5 And it shall come to pass, that on the sixth day they shall prepare *that* which they bring in; and [i] it shall be twice as much as they gather daily.

6 And Moses and Aaron said unto all the children of Israel, [k] At even, then ye shall know that the LORD hath brought you out from the land of Egypt:

A. M. 2513. B. C. 1491. An. Exod. Isr. 1. Ijar or Zif.

7 And in the morning, then ye shall see [l] the glory of the LORD; for that he heareth your murmurings against the LORD: and [m] what *are* we, that ye murmur against us?

8 And Moses said, *This shall be* when the LORD shall give you in the evening flesh to eat, and in the morning bread to the full; for that the LORD heareth your murmuring which ye murmur against him: and what *are* we? your murmurings *are* not against us, but [n] against the LORD.

9 And Moses spake unto Aaron, Say unto all the congregation of the children of Israel, [o] Come near before the LORD: for he hath heard your murmurings.

[c] Chap. xv. 24; Psa. cvi. 25; 1 Cor. x. 10.——[d] Lam. iv. 9. [e] Num. xi. 4, 5.——[f] Psa. lxxviii. 24, 25; cv. 40; John vi. 31, 32. 1 Cor. x. 3.——[g] Heb. *the portion of a day in his day;* Prov. xxx. 8; Matt. vi. 11.——[h] Chap. xv. 25; Deut. viii. 2, 16.

[i] See ver. 22; Lev. xxv. 21.——[k] See ver. 12, 13; chapter vi. 7; Num. xvi. 28, 29, 30.——[l] See ver. 10; Isa. xxxv. 2; xl. 15; John xi. 4, 40.——[m] Numbers xvi. 11.——[n] See 1 Sam. viii. 7; Luke x. 16; Rom. xiii. 2.——[o] Num. xvi. 16.

Red Sea after they left Elim, of which Moses makes distinct mention Num. xxxiii. 10, 11.

The fifteenth day of the second month] This was afterwards called *Ijar*, and they had now left Egypt *one month*, during which it is probable they lived on the provisions they brought with them from Rameses, though it is possible they might have had a supply from the sea-coast. Concerning Mount Sinai, see the note on chap. xix. 1.

Verse 2. *The whole congregation—murmured*] This is an additional proof of the degraded state of the minds of this people; see the note on chap. xiii. 17. And this very circumstance affords a convincing argument that a people so stupidly carnal could not have been induced to leave Egypt had they not been persuaded so to do by the most evident and striking miracles. Human nature can never be reduced to a more abject state in this world than that in which the body is enthralled by *political slavery*, and the soul debased by the influence of *sin*. These poor Hebrews were both *slaves* and *sinners*, and were therefore capable of the meanest and most disgraceful acts.

Verse 3. *The flesh pots*] As the Hebrews were in a state of slavery in Egypt, they were doubtless fed in various companies by their task masters in particular places, where large *pots* or *boilers* were fixed for the purpose of cooking their victuals. To these there may be a reference in this place, and the whole speech only goes to prove that they preferred their bondage in Egypt to their present state in the wilderness; for they could not have been in a state of *absolute want*, as they had brought an abundance of flocks and herds with them out of Egypt.

Verse 4. *I will rain bread*] Therefore this substance was not a production of the desert: nor was the dew that was the instrument of producing it *common* there, else they must have had this bread for a month before.

Verse 6. *Ye shall know that the Lord hath brought you out*] After all the miracles they had seen they appear still to suppose that their being brought out of Egypt was the work of Moses and Aaron; for though the miracles they had already seen were convincing for the time, yet as soon as they had passed by they relapsed into their former infidelity. God therefore saw it necessary to give them a daily miracle in the fall of the manna, that they might have the proof of his Divine interposition constantly before their eyes. Thus they knew that *Jehovah* had brought them out, and that it was not the act of Moses and Aaron.

Verse 7. *Ye shall see the glory of the Lord*] Does it not appear that the *glory of the Lord* is here spoken of as something distinct from the Lord? for it is said HE (the glory) *heareth your murmurings against the Lord;* though *the Lord* may be here put for *himself*, the *antecedent* instead of the *relative*. This passage may receive some light from Heb. i. 3: *Who being the brightness of his glory, and the express image of his person*, &c. And as St. Paul's words are spoken of the Lord Jesus, is it not likely that the words of Moses refer to *him* also? "No man hath seen God at any time;" hence we may infer that Christ was the *visible* agent in all the extraordinary and miraculous interferences which took place both in the patriarchal times and under the law.

Verse 8. *In the evening flesh to eat*] Viz., the *quails; and in the morning bread to the full*, viz., the *manna*.

And what are *we?*] Only his servants, obeying his commands.

A. M. 2513.
B. C. 1491.
An. Exod. Isr. 1.
Ijar or Zif.

10 And it came to pass, as Aaron spake unto the whole congregation of the children of Israel, that they looked toward the wilderness, and behold, the glory of the LORD [p] appeared in the cloud.

11 And the LORD spake unto Moses, saying,

12 [q] I have heard the murmurings of the children of Israel: speak unto them, saying, [r] At even ye shall eat flesh, and [s] in the morning ye shall be filled with bread; and ye shall know that I *am* the LORD your God.

13 And it came to pass, that at even [t] the quails came up, and covered the camp: and in the morning [u] the dew lay round about the host.

p Ver. 7; chapter xiii. 21; Num. xvi. 19; 1 Kings viii. 10, 11. — q Ver. 8. — r Ver. 6. — s Verse 7. — t Numbers xi. 31; Psalm lxxviii. 27, 28; cv. 40. — u Num. xi. 9.

Your murmurings are *not against us*] For *we* have not brought you up from Egypt; *but against the Lord*, who, by his own miraculous power and goodness, has brought you out of your slavery.

Verse 9. *Come near before the Lord*] This has been supposed to refer to some particular *place*, where the Lord manifested his presence. The great tabernacle was not yet built, but there appears to have been a small *tabernacle* or *tent* called the *Tabernacle of the Congregation*, which, after the sin of the golden calf, was always placed without the camp; see chap. xxxiii. 7: *And Moses took the Tabernacle and pitched it without the camp, afar off from the camp, and called it The Tabernacle of the Congregation; and it came to pass that every one that sought the Lord went out unto the Tabernacle of the Congregation, which was without the camp.* This could not be that portable temple which is described chap. xxvi., &c., and which was not set up till the first day of the first month of the second year, after their departure from Egypt, (chap. xl.,) which was upwards of *ten* months after the time mentioned in this chapter; and notwithstanding this, the Israelites are commanded (ver. 34) to lay up an *omer* of the manna *before the testimony*, which certainly refers to an ark, tabernacle, or some such portable shrine, already in existence. If the great tabernacle be intended, the whole account of laying up the manna must be introduced here by *anticipation*, Moses finishing the account of what was afterwards done, because the commencement of those circumstances which comprehended the reasons of the fact itself took place now. See the note on ver. 34.

But from the reasonings in the preceding verses it appears that much infidelity still reigned in the hearts of the people; and in order to convince them that it was God and not Moses that had brought them out of Egypt, he (Moses) desired them to *come near*, or pay particular attention to some extraordinary manifestation of the Lord. And we are told in the *tenth* verse, that "as Aaron spake unto them, *they looked toward the wilderness, and behold the glory of the Lord appeared*, and the Lord spake unto Moses," &c. Is not this passage explained by chap. xix. 9, "And the Lord said unto Moses, Lo, I come unto thee in a thick cloud, *that the people may hear*, when I speak with thee, and *believe thee for ever?*" May we not conclude that Moses invited them to *come near before the Lord*, and so witness his *glory*, that they might be convinced it was *God* and not *he* that led them out of Egypt, and that they ought to submit to *him*, and cease from their murmurings? It is said, chap. xix. 17, that Moses brought forth the people out of the camp *to meet with God.* And in this instance there might have been a similar though less awful manifestation of the Divine presence.

Verse 10. *As Aaron spake*] So he now became the spokesman or minister of Moses to the Hebrews, as he had been before unto Pharaoh; according to what is written, chap. vii. 1, &c.

Verse 13. *At even the quails came*] שלו *selav*, from שלה *salah*, to be *quiet*, *easy*, or *secure*; and hence the *quail*, from their remarkably living at *ease* and *plenty* among the corn. "An amazing number of these birds," says Hasselquist, Travels, p. 209, "come to Egypt at this time, (March,) for in this month the wheat ripens. They conceal themselves among the corn, but the Egyptians know that they are thieves, and when they imagine the field to be full of them they spread a net over the corn and make a noise, by which the birds, being frightened, and endeavouring to rise, are caught in the net in great numbers, and make a most delicate and agreeable dish." The *Abbé Pluche* tells us, in his *Histoire du Ciel*, that the quail was among the ancient Egyptians the emblem of *safety* and *security*.

"Several learned men, particularly the famous *Ludolf*, Bishop *Patrick*, and *Scheuchzer*, have supposed that the שלוים *selavim* eaten by the Israelites were *locusts*. But not to insist on other arguments against this interpretation, they are expressly called שאר *sheer*, *flesh*, Psalm lxxviii. 27, which surely locusts are not; and the Hebrew word is constantly rendered by the Septuagint *ορτυγομητρα*, *a large kind of quail*, and by the Vulgate *coturnices*, *quails*. Compare Wisd. xvi. 2, xix. 12; Num. xi. 31, 32; Psa. cv. 40; and on Num. xi. observe that כאמתים *keamathayim* should be rendered, not *two cubits high*, but as Mr. Bate translates it, '*two cubits distant*, (i. e., one from the other,) for *quails* do not settle like the *locusts* one upon another, but at small distances.' And had the quails lain for a day's journey round the camp, to the great height of *two cubits*, upwards of three feet, the people could not have been employed two days and a night in gathering them. The spreading them round the camp was in order to dry them in the burning sands for use, which is still practised in Egypt." See *Parkhurst*, sub voce שלה *salah*.

The difficulties which encumber the text, supposing these to be *quails*, led Bishop *Patrick* to imagine them to be *locusts*. The difficulties are *three:* "1. Their coming by a wind. 2. Their immense quantities, covering a circle of thirty or forty miles, two cubits

A. M. 2513.
B. C. 1491.
An. Exod. Isr. 1.
Ijar or Zif.

14 And when the dew that lay was gone up, behold, upon the face of the wilderness *there* *lay* [v] a small round thing, *as* small as the hoar frost on the ground.

A. M. 2513.
B. C. 1491.
An. Exod. Isr. 1.
Ijar or Zif.

[v] Num. xi. 7; Deut. viii. 3; Neh. ix. 15; Psa. lxxviii. 24; cv. 40; Wisd. xvi. 20.

thick. 3. Their being spread in the sun for drying, which would have been preposterous had they been *quails*, for it would have made them corrupt the sooner; but this is the principal way of preparing *locusts* to keep for a month or more, when they are boiled or otherwise dressed." This difficulty he thinks interpreters pass over, who suppose *quails* to be intended in the text. Mr. Harmer takes up the subject, removes the bishop's difficulties, and vindicates the common version.

"These difficulties appear pressing, or at least the two last; nevertheless, I have met with several passages in books of travels, which I shall here give an account of, that they may soften them; perhaps my reader may think they do more.

"No interpreters, the bishop complains, supposing they were quails, account for the spreading them out in the sun. Perhaps they have not. Let me then translate a passage of Maillet, which relates to a little island which covers one of the ports of Alexandria: 'It is on this island, which lies farther into the sea than the main land of Egypt, that the birds annually alight which come hither for refuge in autumn, in order to avoid the severity of the cold of our winters in Europe. There is so large a quantity of all sorts taken there, that after these little birds have been stripped of their feathers, and buried in the burning sands for about half a quarter of an hour, they are worth but two sols the pound. The crews of those vessels which in that season lie in the harbour of Alexandria, have no other meat allowed them.' Among other refugees of that time, Maillet elsewhere expressly mentions quails, which are, therefore, I suppose, treated after this manner. This passage then does what, according to the bishop, no commentator has done; it explains the design of spreading these creatures, supposing they were quails, round about the camp; it was to dry them in the burning sands in order to preserve them for use. So Maillet tells us of their drying fish in the sun of Egypt, as well as of their preserving others by means of pickle. Other authors speak of the Arabs drying camel's flesh in the sun and wind, which, though it be not at all salted, will if kept dry remain good a long while, and which oftentimes, to save themselves the trouble of dressing, they will eat raw. This is what St. Jerome may be supposed to refer to, when he calls the food of the Arabs *carnes semicrudæ*. This drying then of flesh in the sun is not so preposterous as the bishop imagined. On the other hand, none of the authors that speak of their way of preserving locusts in the east, so far as I at present recollect, give any account of drying them in the sun. They are, according to Pellow, first purged with water and salt, boiled in new pickle, and then laid up in dry salt. So, Dr. Russel says, the Arabs eat these insects when fresh, and also salt them up as a delicacy. Their immense quantities also forbid the bishop's believing they were quails; and in truth he represents this difficulty in all its force, perhaps too forcibly. A circle of forty miles in diameter, all covered with quails to the depth of more than forty-three inches, without doubt is a startling representation of this matter: and I would beg leave to add that the like quantity of locusts would have been very extraordinary: but then this is not the representation of Scripture; it does not even agree with it; for such a quantity of either quails or locusts would have made the clearing of places for spreading them out, and the passing of Israel up and down in the neighbourhood of the camp, very fatiguing, which is not supposed.

"Josephus supposed they were quails, which he says are in greater numbers thereabouts than any other kinds of birds; and that, having crossed the sea to the camp of Israel, they who in common fly nearer the ground than most other birds, flew so low through the fatigue of their passage as to be within reach of the Israelites. This explains what he thought was meant by *the two cubits from the face of the earth*—their flying within three or four feet of the ground.

"And when I read Dr. Shaw's account of the way in which the Arabs frequently catch birds that they have tired, that is, by running in upon them and knocking them down with their *zerwattys*, or bludgeons, as we should call them, I think I almost see the Israelites before me pursuing the poor, fatigued, and languid quails.

"This is indeed a laborious method of catching these birds, and not that which is now used in Egypt; for Egmont and Heyman tell us, that in a walk on the shore of Egypt they saw a sandy plain several leagues in extent, and covered with reeds without the least verdure; between which reeds they saw many nets laid for catching quails, which come over in large flights from Europe during the month of September. If the ancient Egyptians made use of the same method of catching quails that they now practise on those shores, yet Israel in the wilderness, without these conveniences, must of course make use of that more inartificial and laborious way of catching them. The Arabs of Barbary, who have not many conveniences, do the same thing still.

"Bishop Patrick supposes a day's journey to be sixteen or twenty miles, and thence draws his circle with a radius of that length; but Dr. Shaw, on another occasion, makes a day's journey but ten miles, which would make a circle but of twenty miles in diameter. and as the text evidently designs to express it very indeterminately, *as it were a day's journey*, it might be much less.

"But it does not appear to me at all necessary to suppose the text intended their covering a circular or nearly a circular spot of ground, but only that these creatures appeared on both sides of the camp of Israel, about a day's journey. The same word is used Exod. vii. 24, where *round about* can mean only on each side of the Nile. And so it may be a little illustrated by

A. M. 2513.
B. C. 1491.
An. Exod. Isr. 1.
Ijar or Zif.

15 And when the children of Israel saw *it*, they said one to another, w It *is* manna: for they wist not what it *was*. And Moses said unto them, x This *is* the bread which the

A. M. 2513.
B. C. 1491.
An. Exod. Isr. 1.
Ijar or Zif.

w Or, *What is this?* or, *it is a portion*.

x John vi. 31, 49, 58; 1 Cor. x. 3.

what Dr. Shaw tells us of the three flights of storks which he saw, when at anchor under the Mount Carmel, some of which were more scattered, others more compact and close, each of which took up more than three hours in passing, and extended itself more than half a mile in breadth. Had this flight of quails been no greater than these, it might have been thought, like them, to have been accidental; but so unusual a flock as to extend fifteen or twenty miles in breadth, and to be two days and one night in passing, and this, in consequence of the declaration of Moses, plainly determined that the finger of God was there.

"A third thing which was a difficulty with the bishop was their being brought with the wind. A hot southerly wind, it is supposed, brings the locusts; and why quails might not be brought by the instrumentality of a like wind, or what difficulty there is in that supposition, I cannot imagine. As soon as the cold is felt in Europe, Maillet tells us, turtles, quails, and other birds come to Egypt in great numbers; but he observed that their numbers were not so large in those years in which the winters were favourable in Europe; from whence he conjectured that it is rather necessity than habit which causes them to change their climate: if so, it appears that it is the increasing heat that causes their return, and consequently that the hot sultry winds from the south must have a great effect upon them, to direct their flight northwards.

"It is certain that it is about the time that the south wind begins to blow in Egypt, which is in April, that many of these migratory birds return. Maillet, who joins quails and turtles together, and says that they appear in Egypt when the cold begins to be felt in Europe, does not indeed tell us when they return: but Thevenot may be said to do it; for after he had told his reader that they catch snipes in Egypt from January to March, he adds that in May they catch turtles, and that the turtles return again in September; now as they go together southward in September, we may believe they return again northward much about the same time. Agreeably to which, Russel tells us that quails appear in abundance about Aleppo in spring and autumn.

"If natural history were more perfect we might speak to this point with great distinctness; at present, however, it is so far from being an objection to their being quails that their coming was caused by a wind, that nothing is more natural. The same wind would in course occasion sickness and mortality among the Israelites, at least it does so in Egypt. The miraculousness then in this story does not lie in their dying, but the prophet's foretelling with exactness the coming of that wind, and in the prodigious numbers of the quails that came with it, together with the unusualness of the place, perhaps, where they alighted.

"Nothing more remains to be considered but the gathering so large a quantity as ten omers by those that gathered fewest. But till that quantity is more precisely ascertained, it is sufficient to remark that this is only affirmed of those expert sportsmen among the people, who pursued the game two whole days and a whole night without intermission; and of them, and of them only, I presume it is to be understood that he that gathered fewest gathered ten omers. Hasselquist, who frequently expresses himself in the most dubious manner in relation to these animals, at other times is very positive that, if they were birds at all, they were a species of the quail different from ours, which he describes as very much resembling the 'red partridge, but as not being larger than the turtle-dove.' To this he adds, that 'the Arabians carry thousands of them to Jerusalem about Whitsuntide, to sell there,' p. 442. In another place he tells us 'it is found in Judea as well as in Arabia Petræa, and that he found it between Jordan and Jericho,' p. 203. One would imagine that Hasselquist means the *scata*, which is described by Dr. Russel, vol. ii., p. 194, and which he represents as brought to market at Aleppo in great numbers in May and June, though they are to be met with in all seasons.

"A whole ass-load of them, he informs us, has often been taken at once shutting a clasping net, in the above-mentioned months, they are in such plenty."—*Harmer*, vol iv., p. 367.

Verse 14. *Behold, upon the face of the wilderness* there lay *a small round thing*] It appears that this small round thing fell with the dew, or rather the dew fell first, and this substance fell *on it*. The dew might have been intended to cool the ground, that the manna on its fall might not be dissolved; for we find from ver. 21, that the heat of the sun melted it. The ground therefore being sufficiently cooled by the dew, the manna lay unmelted long enough for the Israelites to collect a sufficient quantity for their daily use.

Verse 15. *They said one to another, It* is *manna: for they wist not what it* was.] This is a most unfortunate translation, because it not only gives no sense, but it contradicts itself. The Hebrew מן הוא *man hu*, literally signifies, *What is this? for*, says the text, *they wist not what it was*, and therefore they could not give it a name. Moses immediately answers the question, and says, *This* is *the bread which the Lord hath given you to eat*. From ver. 31 we learn that this substance was afterwards called מן *man*, probably in commemoration of the question they had asked on its first appearance. Almost all our own ancient versions translate the words, *What is this?*

What this substance was we know not. It was nothing that was common to the wilderness. It is evident the Israelites never saw it before, for Moses says, Deut. viii. 3, 16: *He fed thee with manna which thou knewest not, neither did thy fathers know;* and it is very likely that nothing of the kind had ever been seen *before;* and by a pot of it being laid up in the ark, it is as likely that nothing of the kind ever appeared more, after the miraculous supply in the wilderness had ceased. It seems to have been *created* for the present occasion, and, like Him whom it typified,

a

A. M. 2513. B. C. 1491. An. Exod. Isr. 1. Ijar or Zif.

LORD hath given you to eat.
16 This *is* the thing which
the LORD hath commanded,
Gather of it every man according to his eating, [y] an omer [z] for every man, *according to* the number of your [a] persons; take ye every man for *them* which *are* in his tents.
17 And the children of Israel did so, and gathered, some more, some less.
18 And when they did mete *it* with an omer, [b] he that gathered much had nothing over, and he that gathered little had no lack; they gathered every man according to his eating.
19 And Moses said, Let no man leave of it till the morning.
20 Notwithstanding they hearkened not unto Moses; but some of them left of it until the morning, and it bred worms, and stank: and Moses was wroth with them

[y] Ver. 36.——[z] Heb. *by the poll,* or *head.*——[a] Heb. *souls.*——[b] 2 Cor. viii. 15.

to have been the *only thing of the kind,* the only bread from heaven, which God ever gave to preserve the life of man, as Christ is the true bread that came down from heaven, and was given for the life of the world. See John vi. 31–58.

Verse 16. *An omer for every man*] I shall here once for all give a short account of the measures of capacity among the Hebrews.

OMER, עמר, from the root *amar,* to *press, squeeze, collect, and bind together;* hence a *sheaf of corn*—a multitude of stalks *pressed together.* It is supposed that the *omer,* which contained about *three quarts* English, had its name from this circumstance; that it was the most *contracted* or the *smallest* measure of things *dry* known to the *ancient* Hebrews; for the קב *kab,* which was less, was not known till the reign of Jehoram, king of Israel, 2 Kings vi. 25.—*Parkhurst.*

The EPHAH, אפה or איפה *eiphah,* from אפה *aphah, to bake,* because this was probably the quantity which was baked at one time. According to Bishop Cumberland the *ephah* contained *seven gallons, two quarts, and about half a pint,* wine measure; and as the *omer* was the *tenth part of the ephah,* ver. 36, it must have contained about *six pints* English.

The KAB, קב, is said to have contained about the *sixth* part of a *seah,* or *three pints and one third* English.

The HOMER, חמר *chomer,* mentioned Lev. xxvii. 16, was quite a different measure from that above, and is a different word in the Hebrew. The *chomer* was the *largest* measure of capacity among the Hebrews, being equal to *ten baths* or *ephahs,* amounting to about *seventy-five gallons, three pints,* English. See Ezek. xlv. 11, 13, 14. Goodwin supposes that this measure derived its name from חמר *chamor,* an *ass,* being the ordinary load of that animal.

The BATH, בת, was the largest measure of capacity next to the *homer,* of which it was the *tenth part.* It was the same as the *ephah,* and consequently contained about *seven gallons, two quarts, and half a pint,* and is always used in Scripture as a measure of *liquids.*

The SEAH, סאה, was a measure of capacity for things dry, equal to about *two gallons and a half* English. See 2 Kings vii. 1, 16, 18.

The HIN, הין, according to Bishop Cumberland, was the one-sixth part of an *ephah,* and contained a little more than *one gallon and two pints.* See Exod. xxix. 40.

The LOG, לג, was the smallest measure of capacity for *liquids* among the Hebrews: it contained about *three quarters of a pint.* See Lev. xiv. 10, 12.

Take ye—for them *which* are *in his tents.*] Some might have been confined in their tents through sickness or infirmity, and charity required that those who were in health should gather a portion for them. For though the psalmist says, Psa. cv. 37, *There was not one feeble* person *among their tribes,* this must refer principally to their healthy state when brought out of Egypt; for it appears that there were many infirm among them when attacked by the Amalekites. See the note on chap. xvii. 8.

Verse 17. *Some more, some less.*] According to their respective families, an *omer* for a man; and according to the number of infirm persons, whose wants they undertook to supply.

Verse 18. *He that gathered much had nothing over*] Because his gathering was in proportion to the number of persons for whom he had to provide. And some having fewer, others more in family, and the gathering being in proportion to the persons who were to eat of it, therefore *he that gathered much had nothing over, and he that gathered little had no lack.* Probably every man gathered as much as he could; and then when brought home and measured by an omer, if he had a surplus, it went to supply the wants of some other family, that had not been able to collect a sufficiency, the family being large, and the time in which the manna might be gathered, before the heat of the day, not being sufficient to collect enough for so numerous a household, several of whom might be so confined as not to be able to collect for themselves. Thus there was an *equality,* and in this light the words of St. Paul, 2 Cor. viii. 15, lead us to view the passage. Here the 36th verse should come in: *Now an omer is the tenth part of an ephah.*

Verse 19. *Let no man leave of it till the morning.*] For God would have them to take no thought for the morrow, and constantly to depend on him for their daily bread. And is not that petition in our Lord's prayer founded on this very circumstance, *Give us day by day our daily bread?*

Verse 20. *It bred worms*] Their sinful curiosity and covetousness led them to make the trial; and they had a mass of the most loathsome putrefaction for their pains. How gracious is God! He is continually rendering disobedience and sin irksome to the transgressor; that finding his evil ways to be unprofitable, he may return to his Maker, and trust in God alone

A. M. 2513.
B. C. 1491.
An. Exod. Isr. 1.
Ijar or Zif.

21 And they gathered it every morning, every man according to his eating: and when the sun waxed hot, it melted.

22 And it came to pass, *that* on the sixth day they gathered twice as much bread, two omers for one *man:* and all the rulers of the congregation came and told Moses.

23 And he said unto them, This *is that* which the LORD hath said, To-morrow *is* [c] the rest of the holy Sabbath unto the LORD: bake *that* which ye will bake *to-day,* and seethe that ye will seethe; and that which remaineth over, lay up for you to be kept until the morning.

24 And they laid it up till the morning, as Moses bade; and it did not [d] stink, neither was there any worm therein.

25 And Moses said, Eat that to-day; for to-day *is* a Sabbath unto the LORD: to-day ye shall not find it in the field.

26 [e] Six days ye shall gather it; but on the seventh day, *which is* the Sabbath, in it there shall be none.

27 And it came to pass, *that* there went out *some* of the people on the seventh day for to gather, and they found none.

28 And the LORD said unto Moses, How long [f] refuse ye to keep my commandments and my laws?

29 See, for that the LORD hath given you the Sabbath, therefore he giveth you on the sixth day the bread of two days; abide ye every man in his place; let no man go out of his place on the seventh day.

[c] Gen. ii. 3; chapter xx. 8; xxxi. 15; xxxv. 3; Lev. xxiii. 3. — [d] Ver. 20.

[e] Chapter xx. 9, 10. — [f] 2 Kings xvii. 14; Psalm lxxviii. 10, 22; cvi. 13.

Verse 22. *On the sixth day they gathered twice as much*] This they did that they might have a provision for the Sabbath, for on that day no manna fell, ver. 26, 27. What a convincing miracle was this! No manna fell on the Sabbath! Had it been a *natural* production it would have fallen on the *Sabbath* as at other times; and had there not been a supernatural influence to keep it sweet and pure, it would have been corrupted on the Sabbath as well as on other days. By this series of miracles God showed his own power, presence, and goodness, 1. In sending the *manna* on each of the six days; 2. In sending *none* on the seventh, or Sabbath; 3. In preserving it from putrefaction when laid up for the use of *that day,* though it infallibly corrupted if kept over night on any other day.

Verse 23. *To-morrow* is *the rest of the holy Sabbath*] There is nothing either in the text or context that seems to intimate that the Sabbath was now *first* given to the Israelites, as some have supposed: on the contrary, it is here spoken of as being perfectly well known, from its having been generally observed. The commandment, it is true, may be considered as being now *renewed;* because they might have supposed that in their unsettled state in the wilderness they might have been exempted from the observance of it. Thus we find, 1. That when God finished his creation, he instituted the Sabbath; 2. When he brought the people out of Egypt, he insisted on the strict observance of it; 3. When he gave the LAW, he made it a *tenth* part of the whole, such importance has this institution in the eyes of the Supreme Being! On the supposed *change* of the Sabbath from what we call *Sunday* to *Saturday,* effected on this occasion, see the note on Deut. v. 15.

Verse 29. *Abide ye every man in his place*] Neither go out to seek manna nor for any other purpose; rest at home and devote your time to religious exercises. Several of the Jews understood by *place* in the text, the *camp,* and have generally supposed that no man should go out of the place, i. e., the city, town, or village in which he resides, any farther than one thousand cubits, about an English mile, which also is called a *Sabbath day's journey,* Acts i. 12; and so many cubits they consider the space round the city that constitutes its *suburbs,* which they draw from Num. xxxv. 3, 4. Some of the Jews have carried the rigorous observance of the letter of this law to such a length, that in whatever posture they find themselves on the Sabbath morning when they awake, they continue in the same during the day; or should they be up and happen to fall, they refuse even to rise till the Sabbath be ended! Mr. Stapleton tells a story of one Rabbi Solomon, who fell into a slough on the Jewish Sabbath, Saturday, and refused to be pulled out, giving his reason in the following Leonine couplet:—

Sabbatha sancta colo, De stercore surgere nolo.

"Out of this slough I will not rise,
For holy Sabbath day I prize."

The Christians, finding him thus disposed, determined he should honour their Sabbath in the same place, and actually kept the poor man in the slough all *Sunday,* giving their reasons in nearly the same way:—

Sabbatha nostra quidem, Solomon, celebrabis ibidem.

"In the same slough, thou stubborn Jew,
Our Sabbath day thou shalt spend too."

This might have served to convince him of his folly, but certainly was not the likeliest way to convert him to Christianity.

FABYAN, in his *Chronicles,* tells the following story of a case of this kind. "In this yere also (1259) fell that happe of the Iewe of Tewkysbury, which fell into a gonge upon the Satyrday, and wolde not for reverence of his sabbot day be pluckyd out; whereof heryng the Erle of Gloucetyr, that the Iewe

A. M. 2513.
B. C. 1491.
An. Exod. Isr. 1.
Ijar or Zif.

30 So the people rested on the
seventh day.
31 And the house of Israel
called the name thereof Manna: and [g] it *was*
like coriander seed, white; and the taste of it
was like wafers *made* with honey.
32 And Moses said, This *is* the thing which
the LORD commandeth, Fill an omer of it to
be kept for your generations; that they may
see the bread wherewith I have fed you in
the wilderness, when I brought you forth from
the land of Egypt.
33 And Moses said unto Aaron,
[h] Take a pot, and put an omer
full of manna therein, and lay it
up before the LORD, to be kept for your
generations.
34 As the LORD commanded Moses, so Aaron
laid it up [i] before the testimony, to be kept.
35 And the children of Israel did eat manna
[k] forty years, [l] until they came to a land in
habited; they did eat manna, until they came
unto the borders of the land of Canaan.
36 Now an omer *is* the tenth *part* of an ephah.

[g] Num. xi. 7, 8.——[h] Heb. ix. 4.——[i] Chap. xxv. 16, 21; xl. 20; Num. xvii. 10; Deut. x. 5; 1 Kings viii. 9.

[k] Num. xxxiii. 38; Deut. viii. 2, 3; Neh. ix. 20, 21; John vi. 31, 49.——[l] Josh. v. 12; Neh. ix. 15.

dyd so great reverence to his sabbot daye, thought he wolde doo as moche unto his holy day, which was Sonday, and so kepte hym there tyll Monday, at whiche season he was foundyn dede." Then the earl of Gloucester *murdered* the poor man.

Verse 31. *Called the name thereof Manna*] See note on ver. 15.

Verse 32. *To be kept for your generations*] See note on ver. 9.

Verse 34. *Laid it up before the testimony*] The עדות *eduth* or *testimony* belonged properly to the tabernacle, but that was not yet built. Some are of opinion that the tabernacle, built under the direction of Moses, was only a renewal of one that had existed in the patriarchal times. See the note on ver. 9. The word signifies *reference to something beyond itself;* thus the tabernacle, the manna, the tables of stone, Aaron's rod, &c., all bore reference and testimony to that spiritual good which was yet to come, viz., JESUS CHRIST and *his salvation.*

Verse 35. *The children of Israel did eat manna forty years*] From this verse it has been supposed that the book of Exodus was not written till *after* the miracle of the manna had ceased. But these words might have been added by Ezra, who under the direction of the Divine Spirit collected and digested the different inspired books, adding such *supplementary, explanatory,* and *connecting* sentences, as were deemed proper to complete and arrange the whole of the sacred canon. For previously to his time, according to the universal testimony of the Jews, all the books of the Old Testament were found in an unconnected and dispersed state.

Verse 36. *Now an omer* is *the tenth* part *of an ephah.*] About *six pints,* English. See the note on ver. 16. The true place of this verse seems to be immediately after ver. 18, for *here* it has no connection.

1. ON the miracle of the manna, which is the chief subject in this chapter, a good deal has already been said in the preceding notes. The sacred historian has given us the most circumstantial proofs that it was a supernatural and miraculous supply; that nothing of the kind had ever been seen before, and probably nothing like it had ever afterwards appeared. That it was a type of our blessed Redeemer, and of the salvation which he has provided for man, there can be no doubt, for in this way it is applied by Christ himself; and from it we may gather this general conclusion, that *salvation is of the Lord.* The Israelites must have perished in the wilderness, had not God fed them with bread from heaven; and every human soul must have perished, had not Jesus Christ come down from heaven, and given himself for the life of the world.

2. God would have the Israelites continually dependent on himself for all their supplies; but he would make them, in a certain way, workers with him. He provided the manna; they gathered and ate it. The first was God's work; the latter, their own. They could not *produce* the manna, and God would not *gather* it for them. Thus the providence of God appears in such a way as to secure the *co-operation* of man. Though man should *plant* and *water,* yet it is God who giveth the *increase.* But if man neither plant nor water, God will give *no* increase. We cannot do God's work, and he will not do ours. Let us, therefore, both in things spiritual and temporal, be *workers together with* HIM.

3. This *daily* supply of the manna probably gave rise to that petition, *Give us to-day our daily bread.* It is worthy of remark, 1. That what was left over night contrary to the command of God bred worms and stank; 2. That a *double* portion was gathered on the day preceding the Sabbath; 3. That this alone continued wholesome on the following day; and, 4. That none fell on the Sabbath! Hence we find that the Sabbath was considered a Divine institution previously to the giving of the Mosaic law; and that God continued to honour that day by permitting no manna to fall during its course. Whatever is earned on the Sabbath is a curse in a man's property. *They who* WILL *be rich, fall into temptation and into a snare, &c.;* for, using illicit means to acquire lawful things, they bring God's curse upon themselves, and are drowned in destruction and perdition. Reader, dost thou work on the Sabbath to increase thy property? See thou do it not! Property acquired in this way will be a curse both to thee and to thy posterity.

4. To show their children and children's children what God had done for their fathers, a pot of manna was laid up before the testimony. We should remember our providential and gracious deliverances in such

a way as to give God the praise of his own grace. An *ungrateful* heart is always associated with an unbelieving mind and an unholy life. Like Israel, we should consider with what bread God has fed our fathers, and see that we have the *same;* the same Christ —the bread of life, the same doctrines, the same ordinances, and the same religious experience. How little are we benefitted by being *Protestants,* if we be not partakers of the Protestant faith! And how useless will even that faith be to us, if we hold the truth in unrighteousness! Our fathers had religion enough to enable them to burn gloriously for the truth of God! Reader, hast thou so much of the life of God in thy soul, that thou couldst burn to ashes at the stake rather than lose it? In a word, couldst thou be a *martyr?* Or hast thou so little grace to lose, that thy life would be more than an equivalent for thy loss? Where is the manna on which thy fathers fed?

CHAPTER XVII.

The Israelites journey from the wilderness of Sin *to* Rephidim, 1, *where they murmur for lack of water,* 2, 3. *Moses asks counsel of God,* 4, *who commands him to take his rod and smite the rock,* 5, *and promises that water should proceed from it for the people to drink,* 6. *The place is called* Massah *and* Meribah, 7. *The* Amalekites *attack Israel in* Rephidim, 8. Joshua *is commanded to fight with them,* 9. Moses, Aaron, *and* Hur, *go to the top of a hill, and while Moses holds up his hands, the Israelites prevail; when he lets them down, Amalek prevails,* 10, 11. *Moses, being weary, sits down, and Aaron and Hur hold up his hands,* 12. *The Amalekites are totally routed,* 13, *and the event commanded to be recorded,* 14. *Moses builds an altar, and calls it* JEHOVAH-NISSI, 15. *Amalek is threatened with continual wars,* 16.

A. M. 2513. B. C. 1491. An. Exod. Isr. 1. Ijar or Zif.

AND [a] all the congregation of
the children of Israel journeyed from the wilderness of Sin,
after their journeys, according to the commandment of the LORD, and pitched in Rephidim:
and *there was* no water for the people to drink.
2 [b] Wherefore the people did chide with
Moses, and said, Give us water that we may
drink. And Moses said unto them, Why
chide ye with me? wherefore do ye [c] tempt
the LORD?
3 And the people thirsted there for water;
and the people [d] murmured against Moses,
and said, Wherefore *is* this *that*
thou hast brought us up out of
Egypt, to kill us and our children and our cattle with thirst?
4 And Moses [e] cried unto the LORD, saying,
What shall I do unto this people? they be
almost ready to [f] stone me.
5 And the LORD said unto Moses, [g] Go on
before the people, and take with thee of the
elders of Israel; and thy rod, wherewith [h] thou
smotest the river, take in thine hand, and go.
6 [i] Behold, I will stand before thee there,
upon the rock in Horeb; and thou shalt smite

A. M. 2513. B. C. 1491. An. Exod. Isr. 1. Ijar or Zif.

[a] Chapter xvi. 1; Num. xxxiii. 12, 14.——[b] Numbers xx. 3, 4. Deut. vi. 16; Psa. lxxviii. 18, 41; Isa. vii. 12; Matt. iv. 7; 1 Cor. x. 9.——[d] Chap. xvi. 2.——[e] Chap. xiv. 15.

[f] 1 Samuel xxx. 6; John viii. 59; x. 31.——[g] Ezekiel ii. 6. [h] Chap. vii. 20; Num. xx. 8.——[i] Num. xx. 10, 11; Psa. lxxviii. 15, 20; cv. 41; cxiv. 8; Wisd. xi. 4; 1 Cor. x. 4.

NOTES ON CHAP. XVII.

Verse 1. *Pitched in Rephidim*] In Num. xxxiii. 12–14 it is said, that when the Israelites came from *Sin* they encamped in *Dophkah,* and next in *Alush,* after which they came to *Rephidim.* Here, therefore, *two stations* are omitted, probably because nothing of moment took place at either. See the notes on Num. xxxiii.

Verse 2. *Why chide ye with me?*] God is your leader, complain to him; *Wherefore do ye tempt the Lord?* As he is your leader, all your murmurings against *me* he considers as directed against *himself;* why therefore do ye tempt *him?* Has he not given you sufficient proofs that he can destroy his enemies and support his friends? And is he not among you to do you good? ver. 7. Why therefore do ye doubt his power and goodness, and thus provoke him to treat you as his enemies?

Verse 3. *And the people murmured*] The reader must not forget what has so often been noted relating to the degraded state of the minds of the Israelites. A strong argument however may be drawn from this in favour of their supernatural escape from Egypt. Had it been a scheme concerted by the *heads* of the people, provision would necessarily have been made for such exigencies as these. But as God chose to keep them constantly dependent upon himself for every necessary of life, and as they had Moses alone as their mediator to look to, they murmured against him when brought into straits and difficulties, regretted their having left Egypt, and expressed the strongest desire to return. This shows that they had left Egypt reluctantly; and as Moses and Aaron never appear to have any *resources* but those which came most evidently in a *supernatural* way, therefore the whole exodus or departure from Egypt proves itself to have been no human contrivance, but a measure concerted by God himself.

Verse 6. *I will stand before thee there, upon the rock in Horeb*] THE *rock,* הצור *hatstsur.* It seems as if God had directed the attention of Moses to a *particular* rock, with which he was well acquainted; for every part of the mount and its vicinity must have been well

A. M. 2513.
B. C. 1491.
An. Exod. Isr. 1.
Ijar or Zif.

the rock, and there shall come
water out of it, that the people
may drink. And Moses did so
in the sight of the elders of Israel.
7 And he called the name of the place
[k] Massah,[1] and [m] Meribah, because of the
chiding of the children of Israel, and because
they tempted the LORD, saying,
Is the LORD among us, or not?
8 [n] Then came Amalek, and
fought with Israel in Rephidim.
9 And Moses said unto [o] Joshua, Choose us
out men, and go out, fight with Amalek: to
morrow I will stand on the top of the hill,

[k] Num. xx. 13; Psa. lxxxi. 7; xcv. 8; Heb. iii. 8.——[1] That is, *temptation.*——[m] That is, *chiding* or *strife.*

[n] Gen. xxxvi. 12; Num. xxiv. 20; Deut. xxv. 17; 1 Sam. xv. 2; Wisd. xi. 3.——[o] Called *Jesus*, Acts vii. 45; Heb. iv. 8.

known to Moses during the time he kept Jethro's flocks in those quarters. Dr. Priestley has left the following sensible observations upon this miracle:—

"The luminous cloud, the symbol of the Divine presence, would appear on the rock, and Horeb was probably a part of the same mountain with Sinai. This supply of water, on Moses only striking the rock, where no water had been before nor has been since, was a most wonderful display of the Divine power. The water must have been in great abundance to supply *two millions* of persons, which excluded all possibility of artifice or imposture in the case. The miracle must also have been of some *continuance*, no doubt so long as they continued in that neighbourhood, which was more than a year. There are sufficient traces of this extraordinary miracle remaining at this day. This rock has been visited, drawn, and described by Dr. Shaw, Dr. Pocock, and others; and holes and channels appear in the stone, which could only have been formed by the bursting out and running of the water. No *art* of man could have done it, if any motive could be supposed for the undertaking in such a place as this."

This miracle has not escaped the notice of the ancient Greek poets. *Callimachus* represents *Rhea* bringing forth water from a rock in the same way, after the birth of *Jupiter*.

Πληξεν ορος σκηπτρῳ, τε δε οἱ διχα πουλυ διεστη.
Εκ δ' εχεεν μεγα χευμα. Hymn *ad* Jov., ver. 31.

With her sceptre struck
The yawning cliff; from its disparted height
Adown the mount the gushing torrent ran. PRIOR.

The rock mentioned above has been seen and described by *Norden*, p. 144, 8vo.; Dr. *Shaw*, p. 314, 4to., where there is an accurate drawing of it; Dr. *Pocock*, vol. i., p. 143, &c., where the reader may find some fine plates of Mount Horeb and Sinai, and four different views of the wonderful rock of Meribah. It is a vast block of red granite, fifteen feet long, ten broad, and twelve high. See Dr. Shaw's account at the end of Exodus. My nephew, who visited this rock in 1823, confirms the account of the preceding travellers, and has brought a piece of this wonderful stone. The *granite* is fine, and the *quartz*, *mica*, and *feldspar* equally mixed in it. This rock or block of *granite* is the only type of Christ now existing.

Verse 7. *He called the name of the place Massah, and Meribah*] מסה *Massah* signifies *temptation* or *trial*; and מריבה *Meribah*, *contention* or *litigation*. From 1 Cor. x. 4, we learn that this rock was a type of Christ, and their drinking of it is represented as their being made partakers of the grace and mercy of God through Christ Jesus; and yet many who drank fell and perished in the wilderness in the very act of disobedience! Reader, be not high minded, but fear!

On the *smiting* of the rock by the *rod* of *Moses*, Mr. Ainsworth has the following pious note: "This rock signified *Christ*, and is therefore called a *spiritual Rock*, 1 Cor. x. 4. He being *smitten* with *Moses's rod*, and bearing the *curse* of the *law* for our sins, and by the preaching of the Gospel crucified among his people, Gal. iii. 1, from him floweth the spiritual drink wherewith all believing hearts are refreshed." John vii. 37, and Isa. liii. 1–3.

Verse 8. *Then came Amalek, and fought with Israel*] The Amalekites seem to have attacked the Israelites in the same way and through the same motives that the wandering Arabs attack the caravans which annually pass through the same desert. It does not appear that the Israelites gave them any kind of provocation, they seem to have attacked them merely through the hopes of plunder. The Amalekites were the posterity of Amalek, one of the dukes of Eliphaz, the son of Esau, and consequently Israel's brother, Gen. xxxvi. 15, 16.

Fought with Israel] In the most treacherous and dastardly manner; for they came at the rear of the camp, *smote the hindmost of the people, even all that were feeble behind, when they were faint and weary*; see Deut. xxv. 18. The baggage, no doubt, was the object of their avarice; but finding the women, children, aged and infirm persons, behind with the baggage, they smote them and took away their spoils.

Verse 9. *Moses said unto Joshua*] This is the first place in which Joshua the son of Nun is mentioned: the illustrious part which he took in Jewish affairs, till the settlement of his countrymen in the promised land, is well known. He was captain-general of the Hebrews under Moses; and on this great man's death he became his successor in the government. Joshua was at first called *Hoshea*, Num. xiii. 16, and afterwards called *Joshua* by Moses. Both in the Septuagint and Greek Testament he is called *Jesus:* the name signifies *Saviour;* and he is allowed to have been a very expressive type of our blessed Lord. He fought with and conquered the enemies of his people, brought them into the promised land, and divided it to them by lot. The parallel between him and the Saviour of the world is too evident to require pointing out.

Top of the hill] Probably some part of Horeb or Sinai, to which they were then near.

A. M. 2513. B. C. 1491. An. Exod. Isr. 1. Ijar or Zif.

with p the rod of God in mine
hand.
10 So Joshua did as Moses
had said to him, and fought with Amalek: and
Moses, Aaron, and Hur went up to the top of
the hill.
11 And it came to pass, when Moses q held
up his hand, that Israel prevailed; and when
he let down his hand, Amalek prevailed.
12 But Moses' hands *were* r heavy; and
they took a stone, and put *it* under him, and
he sat thereon; and Aaron and Hur stayed
up his hands, the one on the one
side, and the other on the other
side; and his hands were steady
until the going down of the sun.
13 And Joshua discomfited Amalek and his
people with the edge of the sword.
14 And the LORD said unto Moses, s Write
this *for* a memorial in a book, and rehearse *it*
in the ears of Joshua; for t I will utterly put
out the remembrance of Amalek from under
heaven.
15 And Moses built an altar, and called

p Chap. iv. 20.—q James v. 16.—r Psa. xxxv. 3; James i. 6; Heb. xii. 12.—s Chap. xxxiv. 27.

t Num. xxiv. 20; Deut. xxv. 19; 1 Sam. xv. 3, 7; xxx. 1, 17; 2 Sam. viii. 12; Ezra ix. 14.

Verse 10. *Moses, Aaron, and Hur went up*] It is very likely that the *Hur* mentioned here is the same with that *Hur* mentioned 1 Chron. ii. 19, who appears from the chronology in that chapter to have been the son of Caleb, the son of *Ezron*, the son of *Pharez*, the son of *Judah*. The rabbins and Josephus say he was the *brother-in-law* of Moses, having married his sister *Miriam*. He was a person in whom Moses put much confidence; for he left him conjoint governor of the people with Aaron, when he went to confer with God on the mount, chap. xxiv. 14. His grandson *Bezaleel* was the chief director in the work of the tabernacle; see chap. xxxi. 2–5.

Verse 11. *When Moses held up his hand*] We cannot understand this transaction in any *literal* way; for the lifting up or letting down the hands of Moses could not, humanly speaking, influence the battle. It is likely that he held up the rod of God in his hand, ver. 9, as an ensign to the people. We have already seen that in prayer the hands were generally *lifted up* and *spread out*, (see the note on chap. ix. 29,) and therefore it is likely that by this act *prayer* and *supplication* are intended. The Jerusalem Targum says, "When Moses held up his hands *in prayer*, the house of Israel prevailed; and when he let down his hands *from prayer*, the house of Amalek prevailed." We may therefore conclude, that by holding up the hands in this case these two things were intended: 1. That hereby a reference was made to God, as the source whence all help and protection must come, and that on him alone they must depend. 2. That prayer and supplication to God are essentially necessary to their prevalence over all their enemies. It is indisputably true that, while the hands are stretched out, that is, while the soul exerts itself in prayer and supplication to God, we are sure to conquer our spiritual adversaries; but if our hands become heavy—if we restrain prayer before God, Amalek will prevail—every spiritual foe, every internal corruption, will gain ground. Several of the fathers consider Moses, with his stretched-out hands, as a figure of Christ on the cross, suffering for mankind, and getting a complete victory over sin and Satan.

Verse 13. *Joshua discomfited Amalek and his people*] *Amalek* might have been the name of the ruler of this people continued down from their ancestor, (see on ver. 8,) as *Pharaoh* was the name of all succeeding kings in Egypt. If this were the case, then *Amalek and his people* mean the *prince* and the *army* that fought under him. But if *Amalek* stand here for the *Amalekites*, then *his people* must mean the confederates he had employed on this occasion.

Verse 14. *Write this* for *a memorial in a book*] This is the first mention of *writing* on record: what it signified, or how it was done, we cannot tell. But it is evident that either this passage is introduced here instead of Deut. xxv. 17, by way of *anticipation*, or that by the words כתב ספר *kethob* and *sepher* was intended only a *monumental declaration* of the defeat of *Amalek* by *Joshua*, by some *action* or *symbolical* representation; for it is immediately subjoined, "And Moses built an altar, and called the name of it *Jehovah-nissi*." See Dr. *A. Bayley*, and see the note on chap. xxx. It is very likely that the first *regular alphabetical* writing in the world was that written by the finger of God himself on the two tables of stone. What is said here was probably by way of *anticipation*, or means some other method of registering events than by *alphabetical* characters, if we allow that God gave the first specimen of regular writing on the tables of stone, which did not take place till some time after this.

Rehearse it *in the ears of Joshua*] Thus showing that Joshua was to succeed Moses, and that this charge should be given to every succeeding governor.

I will utterly put out the remembrance of Amalek] This threatening was accomplished by SAUL, 1 Sam. xv. 3, &c., four hundred and twelve years after. Judgment is God's *strange* work; but it must take place when the sins which incensed it are neither repented of nor forsaken. This people, by their continued transgressions, proved themselves totally unworthy of a political existence; and therefore said God to Saul, *Go, and utterly destroy the* SINNERS *the Amalekites;* 1 Sam. xv. 18. So their *continuance* in *sin* was the cause of their final destruction.

Verse 15. *Jehovah-nissi*] *Jehovah is my ensign* or *banner*. The hands and rod of Moses were held up as soldiers are wont to hold up their *standards* in the time of battle; and as these standards bear the arms of the country, the soldiers are said *to fight under that banner*, i. e., under the direction and in the defence of that government. Thus the Israelites fought under

A. M. 2513. B. C. 1491. An. Exod. Isr. 1. Ijar or Zif.

the name of it [u] JEHOVAH-
nissi:
16 For he said, [v] Because
[w] the LORD hath sworn *that* the
LORD *will have* war with Amalek,
from generation to generation.

A. M. 2513. B. C. 1491. An. Exod. Isr. 1. Ijar or Zif.

[u] That is, *the LORD my banner*; see Judg. vi. 24.——[v] Or, *because the hand* of Amalek is *against the throne of the LORD*, therefore, &c.——[w] Heb. *the hand upon the throne of the LORD.*

the direction of God, and in the defence of his truth; and therefore the name of JEHOVAH became the *armorial bearing* of the whole congregation. By his direction they fought, and in his name and strength they conquered; each one feeling himself, not his own, but the Lord's soldier.

Verse 16. *The Lord hath sworn* that *the Lord* will have *war with Amalek, &c.*] This is no translation of the words כי יד על כס יה מלחמה *ki yad al kes yah milchamah*, which have been variously rendered by different translators and critics; the most rational version of which is the following: *Because the hand of Amalek is against the throne of God, therefore will I have war with Amalek from generation to generation.* This gives a tolerably consistent sense, yet still there is considerable obscurity in the passage. *Houbigant*, a most judicious though bold critic, supposes that, as יהוה נסי *Jehovah-nissi, Jehovah my ensign*, was spoken of immediately before, כס *kes, a throne*, in this verse, is an error of some transcriber for נס *nes, an ensign*, which might be readily occasioned by the great similarity between the כ *caph* and the נ *nun*. He thinks farther that the two letters יה *yah*, which are supposed to be here a contraction of the word יהוה *Yehovah*, are separated, the י *yod* from the נס *nes*, which should be written נסי *nissi*, and the ה *he*, from מלחמה *milchamah*, which should be written המלחמה *hammilchamah*, and then the whole verse will run thus: *For the hand shall be upon the ensigns of war unto the Lord, against Amalek for ever*, i. e., God makes now a declaration of war against the Amalekites, which shall continue till their final destruction. The conjecture of Mr. *Julius Bate*, in his *Literal Translation of the Pentateuch*, deserves attention. He supposes that, as כס *cos* signifies a *cup*, and a *cup* is emblematically used for *wrath*, on one of the stones of the altar, mentioned in the preceding verse, a *hand holding a cup* was sculptured, this being a memorial, according to the custom of hieroglyphical writing, that the Lord would continue the cup of wrath, portending continual war, against Amalek for ever. I prefer *Houbigant's* exposition.

1. THIS first victory of Israel must have inspired them with a considerable measure of confidence in God, and in his servant Moses. Though God alone could give them the victory, yet it was necessary to show them that it was by the influence of Moses they got it. Moses could not deliver Amalek into their hands; yet if Moses did not continue to hold up his hands, i. e., to pray, Amalek must prevail. God, therefore, wrought this work in such a way as to instruct the people, promote his own glory, and secure the true honour of his servant. The Divine Being always performs the *greatest number* possible of ends, by the *fewest* and *simplest means.* In every work of God there is as much of *wisdom* and *economy*, as there is of *sovereign* uncontrolled power.

2. It is not probable that the people whom Joshua chose out to lead against Amalek were *unarmed;* and we have already seen that it is not at all likely that they came armed out of Egypt. And as the whole circumstances of this case show that those who *fought* against the Amalekites were properly equipped for the fight, we may then safely presume that they got their arms from the Egyptians, whose bodies were thrown on the shore after having been overwhelmed in the Red Sea. Thus, what was a judgment in the one case, was a most gracious providence in the other. *Judgment* on God's *foes* is *mercy* to his *friends.*

3. Of the efficacy of prayer we have already had the most striking examples. He who has the spirit of prayer, has the highest interest in the court of heaven; and the only way to retain it, is to keep it in constant employment. *Apostasy begins in the closet:* no man ever backslid from the life and power of Christianity who continued constant and fervent, especially in private prayer. He who *prays without ceasing* is likely to *rejoice evermore.*

CHAPTER XVIII.

Jethro, *called the father-in-law of Moses, hearing of the deliverance which God had granted to Israel,* 1, *took Zipporah and her two sons, Gershom and Eliezer, and brought them to Moses, when the Israelites were encamped near Horeb,* 2–5. *He sends to Moses, announcing his arrival,* 6. *Moses goes out to meet him,* 7, *and gives him a history of God's dealings with the Israelites,* 8. *Jethro greatly rejoices, and makes striking observations on the power and goodness of God,* 9–11. *He offers burnt-offerings and sacrifices to Jehovah, and Aaron and all the elders of Israel feast with him,* 12. *The next day Jethro, observing how much Moses was fatigued by being obliged to sit as judge and hear causes from morning to evening,* 13, *inquires why he did so,* 14. *Moses answers, and shows that he is obliged to determine causes between man and man, and to teach them the statutes and laws of God,* 15, 16. *Jethro finds fault, and counsels him to appoint men who fear God, love truth, and hate covetousness, to be judges over* thousands, hundreds, fifties, *and* tens, *to judge and determine in all smaller matters, and refer only the greater and most important to himself,* 17–22; *and shows that this plan will be advantageous both to himself and to the people,* 23. *Moses hearkens to the counsel of Jethro, and appoints proper officers over the people, who enter upon their functions, determine all minor causes, and refer only the most difficult to Moses,* 24–26. *Moses dismisses Jethro, who returns to his own country,* 27.

A. M. 2514.
B. C. 1490.
An. Exod. Isr. 2.
Ijar or Zif.

WHEN [a] Jethro, the priest of
Midian, Moses' father-in-
law, heard of all that [b] God had
done for Moses, and for Israel his people, *and*
that the LORD had brought Israel out of Egypt;
2 Then Jethro, Moses' father-in-law, took
Zipporah, Moses' wife, [c] after he had sent
her back,
3 And her [d] two sons; of which the [e] name
of the one *was* [f] Gershom; for he said,
I have been an alien in a
strange land:
4 And the name of the other
was [g] Eliezer; for the God of my father,
said he, was mine help, and delivered me
from the sword of Pharaoh:
5 And Jethro, Moses' father-in-law, came
with his sons and his wife unto Moses into
the wilderness, where he encamped at [h] the
mount of God:

[a] Chap. ii. 16; iii. 1.——[b] Psa. xliv. 1; lxxvii. 14, 15; lxxviii. 4; cv. 5, 43; cvi. 2, 8.——[c] Chap. iv. 26.——[d] Acts vii. 29.——[e] Chap. ii. 22.——[f] That is, *a stranger there*.——[g] That is, *my God is a help*.——[h] Chap. iii. 1, 12.

NOTES ON CHAP. XVIII.

Verse 1. *When Jethro, the priest of Midian, &c.*] Concerning this person and his several names, see the notes on chap. ii. 15, 16, 18; iii. 1; and iv. 20, 24. Jethro was probably the son of Reuel, the father-in-law of Moses, and consequently the brother-in-law of Moses; for the word חתן *chothen*, which we translate *father-in-law*, in this chapter means simply a *relative by marriage*. See the note on chap. iii. 1.

Verse 2. *After he had sent her back*] Why Zipporah and her two sons returned to Midian, is not certainly known. From the transaction recorded chap. iv. 20, 24, it seems as if she had been alarmed at the danger to which the life of one of her sons had been exposed, and fearing worse evils, left her husband and returned to her father. It is however possible that Moses, foreseeing the troubles to which his wife and children were likely to be exposed had he taken them down to Egypt, sent them back to his father-in-law till it should please God to deliver his people. Jethro, now finding that God had delivered them, and totally discomfited the Egyptians, their enemies, thought it proper to bring Zipporah and her sons to Moses, while he was in the vicinity of Horeb.

Verse 3. *The name of the one* was *Gershom*] See the note on chap. ii. 22.

Verse 5. *Jethro—came with his sons*] There are several reasons to induce us to believe that the fact related here is out of its due chronological order, and that Jethro did not come to Moses till the beginning of the second year of the exodus, (see Num. x. 11,) some time after the tabernacle had been erected, and the Hebrew commonwealth established, both in things *civil* and *ecclesiastical*. This opinion is founded on the following reasons:—

1. On this verse, where it is said that Jethro came to Moses *while he was encamped at the mount of God*. Now it appears, from chap. xix. 1, 2, that they were not yet come to Horeb, the mount of God, and that they did not arrive there till the *third* month after their departure from Egypt; and the transactions with which this account is connected certainly took place in the *second* month; see chap. xvi. 1.

2. Moses, in Deut. i. 6, 9, 10, 12-15, relates that when they were about to *depart from Horeb*, which was on the 20th day of the second month of the second year from their leaving Egypt, that he then complained that he was not able to bear the burden alone of the government of a people so numerous; and that it was at that time that he established judges and captains over *thousands* and *hundreds* and *fifties* and *tens*, which appears to be the very transaction recorded in *this place;* the measure itself being recommended by Jethro, and done in consequence of his advice.

3. From Num. x. 11, 29, &c., we find that when the cloud was taken up, and the Israelites were about to depart from Horeb, that Moses addressed *Hobab*, who is supposed to have been the same as *Jethro*, and who then was about to return to Midian, his own country, entreating him to stay with them as a guide while they travelled through the wilderness. It therefore seems necessary that the transaction recorded in this chapter should be inserted Num. x., between the 10th and 11th verses.

4. It has been remarked, that shortly after they had departed from Sinai the dispute took place between Miriam, Aaron, and Moses, concerning the Æthiopian woman Zipporah whom he had married, (see Num. xii. 1, &c.;) and this is supposed to have taken place shortly after she had been brought back by Jethro.

5. In the discourse between Moses and Jethro, mentioned in this chapter, we find that Moses speaks of *the statutes and laws of the Lord* as things already revealed and acknowledged, which necessarily implies that these laws had already been given, (ver. 16,) which we know did not take place till several months after the transactions mentioned in the preceding chapters.

6. Jethro offers *burnt-offerings* and *sacrifices to God* apparently in that way in which they were commanded in the law. Now the *law* respecting *burnt-offerings* was not given till *after* the transactions mentioned here, unless we refer this chapter to a time *posterior* to that in which it appears in this place. See the note on ver. 12.

From all these reasons, but particularly from the *two first* and the *two last*, it seems most likely that this chapter stands out of its due chronological order, and therefore I have adjusted the chronology in the margin to the time in which, from the reasons above alleged, I suppose these transactions to have taken place; but the matter is not of much importance, and the reader is at liberty to follow the common opinion. As Moses had in the preceding chapter related the war with Amalek and the curse under which they were

a

A. M. 2514.
B. C. 1490.
An. Exod. Isr. 2.
Ijar or Zif.

6 And he said unto Moses, I
thy father-in-law Jethro am come
unto thee, and thy wife, and her
two sons with her.
7 And Moses [i] went out to meet his father-
in-law, and did obeisance, and [k] kissed him;
and they asked each other of *their* [l] welfare;
and they came into the tent.
8 And Moses told his father-in-law all that
the LORD had done unto Pharaoh and to the
Egyptians for Israel's sake, *and* all the travail
that had [m] come upon them by the way, and
how the LORD [n] delivered them.
9 And Jethro rejoiced for all the goodness
which the LORD had done to Israel, whom he
had delivered out of the hand
of the Egyptians.

A. M. 2514.
B. C. 1490.
An. Exod. Isr. 2.
Ijar or Zif.

10 And Jethro said, [o] Blessed
be the LORD, who hath delivered you out of
the hand of the Egyptians, and out of the
hand of Pharaoh, who hath delivered the people from under the hand of the Egyptians.
11 Now I know that the LORD *is* [p] greater
than all gods: [q] for in the thing wherein they
dealt [r] proudly *he was* above them.
12 And Jethro, Moses' father-in-law, took
a burnt-offering and sacrifices for God: and
Aaron came, and all the elders of Israel, to
eat bread with Moses' father-in-law, [s] before
God.

[i] Gen. xiv. 17; xviii. 2; xix. 1; 1 Kings ii. 19.——[k] Gen. xxix. 13; xxxiii. 4.——[l] Heb. *peace;* Gen. xliii. 27; 2 Samuel xi. 7.——[m] Heb. *found them;* Gen. xliv. 34; Numbers xx. 14.——[n] Psalm lxxviii. 42; lxxxi. 7; cvi. 10; cvii. 2.——[o] Gen. xiv. 20; 2 Sam. xviii. 28; Luke i. 68.——[p] 2 Chron. ii. 5; Psa. xcv. 3; xcvii. 9; cxxxv. 5.——[q] Ch. i. 10, 16, 22; v. 2, 7; xiv. 8, 18.——[r] 1 Sam. ii. 3; Neh. ix. 10, 16, 29; Job xl. 11, 12; Psa. xxxi. 23; cxix. 21; Luke i. 51.——[s] Deut. xii. 7; 1 Chron. xxix. 22; 1 Cor. x. 18, 21, 31.

laid, he may be supposed to have introduced here the account concerning Jethro the Midianite, to show that he was free from that curse, although the Midianites and the Kenites, the family of Jethro, were as one people, dwelling with the Amalekites. See Judg. i. 16; 1 Chron. ii. 55; 1 Sam. xv. 6. For although the *Kenites* were some of those people whose lands God had promised to the descendants of Abraham, (see Gen. xv. 18, 19,) yet, in consideration of Jethro, the relative of Moses, all of them who submitted to the Hebrews were suffered to live in their own country; the rest are supposed to have taken refuge among the *Edomites* and *Amalekites*. See *Calmet, Locke, &c.*

Verse 6. *And he said unto Moses*] That is, by a messenger; in consequence of which Moses went out to meet him, as is stated in the next verse, for an interview had not yet taken place. This is supported by reading הנה *hinneh, behold,* for אני *ani, I,* which is the reading of the Septuagint and Syriac, and several Samaritan MSS.; instead therefore of *I, thy father*, we should read, *Behold thy father*, &c.—*Kennicott's* Remarks.

Verse 7. *And did obeisance*] וישתחו *vaiyishtachu, he bowed himself down,* (see on Gen. xvii. 3, and Exod. iv. 31;) this was the general token of respect. *And kissed him;* the token of friendship. *And they asked each other of* their *welfare;* literally, *and they inquired, each man of his neighbour, concerning peace* or *prosperity;* the proof of affectionate intercourse. These three things constitute *good breeding* and *politeness*, accompanied with *sincerity*.

And they came into the tent.] Some think that the *tabernacle* is meant, which it is likely had been erected before this time; see the note on ver. 5. Moses might have thought proper to take his relative first to the house of God, before he brought him to his own tent.

Verse 9. *And Jethro rejoiced for all the goodness*] Every part of Jethro's conduct proves him to have been a religious man and a true believer. His thanksgiving to Jehovah (ver. 10) is a striking proof of it; he first blesses God for the preservation of Moses, and next for the deliverance of the people from their bondage.

Verse 11. *Now I know that the Lord* is *greater than all gods*] Some think that Jethro was *now* converted to the true God; but it is very probable that he enjoyed this blessing before he knew any thing of Moses, for it is not likely that Moses would have entered into an alliance with this family had they been heathens. Jethro no doubt had the true patriarchal religion.

Wherein they dealt proudly] Acting as tyrants over the people of God; enslaving them in the most unprincipled manner, and still purposing more tyrannical acts. He was *above them*—he showed himself to be infinitely superior to all their gods, by the miracles which he wrought. Various translations have been given of this clause; the above I believe to be the sense.

Verse 12. *Jethro—took a burnt-offering*] עלה *olah.* Though it be true that in the patriarchal times we read of a *burnt-offering*, (see Gen. xxii. 2, &c.,) yet we only read of one in the case of *Isaac*, and therefore, though this offering made by Jethro is not a decisive proof that the law relative to burnt-offerings, &c., had already been given, yet, taken with other *circumstances* in this account, it is a presumptive evidence that the meeting between Moses and Jethro took place *after* the erection of the tabernacle. See the note on ver. 5.

Sacrifices for God] זבחים *zebachim, slain beasts,* as the word generally signifies. We have already seen that sacrifices were instituted by God himself as soon as sin entered into our world; and we see that they were continued and regularly practised among all the people who had the knowledge of the only true God, from that time until they became a legal establishment. Jethro, who was a *priest*, (chap. ii. 16,) had a right to offer these sacrifices; nor can there be a doubt of his being a worshipper of the true God, for those *Kenites*, from whom the *Rechabites* came, were descended from him; 1 Chron. ii. 55. See also Jer. xxxv.

And Aaron came, and all the elders of Israel, to eat bread] The *burnt-offering* was wholly consumed; every part was considered as the Lord's portion, and

A. M. 2514.
B. C. 1490.
An. Exod. Isr. 2.
Ijar or Zif.

13 And it came to pass on
the morrow, that Moses sat to
judge the people: and the people
stood by Moses from the morning unto the
evening.
14 And when Moses' father-in-law saw all
that he did to the people, he said, What *is*
this thing that thou doest to the people? why
sittest thou thyself alone, and all the people
stand by thee, from morning unto even?
15 And Moses said unto his father-in-law,
Because [t] the people come unto me to inquire
of God:
16 When they have [u] a matter, they come
unto me; and I judge between [v] one and
another; and I do [w] make *them*
know the statutes of God, and
his laws.
17 And Moses' father-in-law said unto him,
The thing that thou doest *is* not good.
18 [x] Thou wilt surely wear away, both thou,
and this people that *is* with thee: for this
thing *is* too heavy for thee; [y] thou art not
able to perform it thyself alone.
19 Hearken now unto my voice, I will
give thee counsel, and [z] God shall be with
thee: Be thou [a] for the people to God-ward,
that thou mayest [b] bring the cause unto God:
20 And thou shalt [c] teach them ordinances
and laws, and shalt show them [d] the way

[t] Lev. xxiv. 12; Num. xv. 34.——[u] Chap. xxiii. 7; xxiv. 14; Deut. xvii. 8; 2 Sam. xv. 3; Job xxxi. 13; Acts xviii. 15; 1 Cor. vi. 1.——[v] Heb. *a man and his fellow.*——[w] Lev. xxiv. 15; Num. xv. 35; xxvii. 6, &c.; xxxvi. 6, 7, 8, 9.

[x] Heb. *fading thou wilt fade.*——[y] Num. xi. 14, 17; Deut. i. 9, 12.——[z] Chap. iii. 12.——[a] Chap. iv. 16; xx. 19; Deut. v. 5. [b] Num. xxvii. 5.——[c] Deut. iv. 1, 5; v. 1; vi. 1, 2; vii. 11. [d] Psa. cxliii. 8.

therefore it was entirely burnt up. The other sacrifices mentioned here were such that, after the blood had been poured out before God, the officers and assistants might feed on the flesh. Thus, in ancient times, contracts were made and covenants sealed; see the notes on Gen. xv. 13, &c. It is very likely, therefore, that the sacrifices offered on this occasion, were those on the flesh of which Aaron and the elders of Israel feasted with Jethro.

Before God.] Before the *tabernacle*, where God dwelt; for it is supposed that the tabernacle was now erected. See on ver. 5; and see Deut. xii. 5–7, and 1 Chron. xxix. 21, 22, where the same form of speech, *before the Lord*, is used, and plainly refers to his manifested presence in the tabernacle.

Verse 13. *To judge the people*] To hear and determine controversies between man and man, and to give them instruction in things appertaining to God.

From the morning unto the evening.] Moses was obliged to sit all day, and the people were continually coming and going.

Verse 15. *The people come unto me to inquire of God*] To know the mind and will of God on the subject of their inquiries. Moses was the *mediator* between God and the people; and as they believed that all justice and judgment must come from him, therefore they came to Moses to know what God had spoken.

Verse 16. *I do make* them *know the statutes of God, and his laws.*] These words are so very particular that they leave little room for doubt that the law had been given. Such words would scarcely have been used had not the *statutes* and *laws* been then in existence. And this is one of the proofs that the transaction mentioned here stands out of its due chronological order; see on ver. 5.

Verse 18. *Thou wilt surely wear away*] נבל תבל *nabol tibbol, in wearing away, thou wilt wear away*—by being thus *continually* employed, thou wilt soon become *finally exhausted. And this people that* is *with thee;* as if he had said, "Many of them are obliged to wait so long for the determination of their suit that their patience must be soon necessarily worn out, as there is no one to hear every cause but thyself."

Verse 19. *I will give thee counsel, and God shall be with thee*] Jethro seems to have been a man of great *understanding* and prudence. His advice to Moses was most appropriate and excellent; and it was probably given under the immediate inspiration of God, for after such sacrificial rites, and public acknowledgment of God, the prophetic spirit might be well expected to descend and rest upon him. God could have showed Moses the propriety and necessity of adopting such measures before, but he chose in this case to help man by man, and in the present instance a permanent basis was laid to consolidate the union of the two families, and prevent all future misunderstandings.

Verse 20. *Thou shalt teach them ordinances*] חקים *chukkim*, all such *precepts* as relate to the *ceremonies of religion* and *political economy. And laws*, התורת, *hattoroth*, the instructions relative to the whole system of *morality*.

And shalt show them the way] את הדרך *eth hadderech*, THAT *very* WAY, that *only* way, which God himself has revealed, and in which they should walk in order to please him, and get their souls everlastingly saved.

And the work that they must do.] For it was not sufficient that they should *know* their duty both to God and man, but they must DO it too; יעשון *yaasun*, they must do it *diligently, fervently, effectually;* for the *paragogic* ן *nun deepens* and *extends* the meaning of the verb.

What a very comprehensive form of a preacher's duty does this verse exhibit! 1. He must *instruct* the people in the nature, use, and importance of the *ordinances* of religion. 2. He must lay before them the whole *moral law*, and their obligations to fulfil all its precepts. 3. He must point out to each his particular duty, and what is expected of him in his situation, connections, &c. And, 4. He must set them all *their work*, and see that they do it. On such a plan as this he will have full opportunity to show the people, 1. Their *sin, ignorance*, and *folly;* 2. The

A. M. 2514. B. C. 1490. An. Exod. Isr. 2. Ijar or Zif.

wherein they must walk, and
[e] the work that they must do.
21 Moreover thou shalt provide
out of all the people [f] able men, such as [g] fear
God, [h] men of truth, [i] hating covetousness;
and place *such* over them, *to be* rulers of
thousands, *and* rulers of hundreds, rulers of
fifties, and rulers of tens:
22 And let them judge the people [k] at all
seasons: [l] and it shall be, *that* every great
matter they shall bring unto thee, but every
small matter they shall judge: so shall it be
easier for thyself, and [m] they shall bear *the*
burden with thee.
23 If thou shalt do this thing, and God
command thee *so*, then thou shalt be [n] able
to endure, and all this people
shall also go to [o] their place in
peace.
24 So Moses hearkened to the voice of
his father-in-law, and did all that he had
said.
25 And [p] Moses chose able men out of all
Israel, and made them heads over the people,
rulers of thousands, rulers of hundreds, rulers
of fifties, and rulers of tens.
26 And they [q] judged the people at all seasons: the [r] hard causes they brought unto
Moses, but every small matter they judged
themselves.
27 And Moses let his father-in-law depart;
and [s] he went his way into his own land.

[e] Deut. i. 18.—[f] Ver. 25; Deut. i. 15, 16; xvi. 18; 2 Chron. xix. 5–10; Acts vi. 3.—[g] Genesis xlii. 18; 2 Sam. xxiii. 3; 2 Chron. xix. 9.—[h] Ezek. xviii. 8.—[i] Deut. xvi. 19.—[k] Ver. 26.—[l] Ver. 26; Lev. xxiv. 11; Num. xv. 33; xxvii. 2; xxxvi. 1; Deut. i. 17; xvii. 8.—[m] Numbers xi. 17.—[n] Verse 18. [o] Gen. xviii. 33; xxx. 25; chapter xvi. 29; 2 Samuel xix. 39. [p] Deut. i. 15; Acts vi. 5.—[q] Verse 22.—[r] Job xxix. 16. [s] Num. x. 29, 30.

pure and *holy law* which they have broken, and by which they are condemned; 3. The *grace of God* that bringeth salvation, by which they are to be *justified* and finally saved; and, 4. The necessity of showing their *faith* by their *works;* not only denying ungodliness and worldly lusts, but living soberly, righteously, and godly in this present world, looking for that blessed hope, and the glorious appearing of the great God and our Saviour, Jesus Christ.

Verse 21. *Able men*] Persons of wisdom, discernment, judgment, prudence, and fortitude; for who can be a *ruler* without these qualifications?

Such as fear God] Who are truly religious, without which they will feel little concerned either for the bodies or souls of the people.

Men of truth] Honest and true in their own hearts and lives; speaking the truth, and judging according to the truth.

Hating covetousness] Doing all for God's sake, and love to man; labouring to promote the general good; never perverting judgment, or suppressing the testimonies of God, for the love of money or through a base, man-pleasing spirit, but expecting their reward from the *mercy* of God in the resurrection of the just.

Rulers of thousands, &c.] *Millenaries, centurions, quinquagenaries,* and *decurions;* each of these, in all probability, dependent on that officer immediately above himself. So the *decurion*, or ruler over *ten*, if he found a matter too hard for him, brought it to the *quinquagenary*, or ruler of *fifty;* if, in the course of the exercise of *his* functions, *he* found a cause too complicated for him to decide on, he brought it to the *centurion*, or ruler over a *hundred*. In like manner the *centurion* brought his difficult case to the *millenary*, or ruler over a *thousand;* the case that was too hard for *him* to judge, he brought to *Moses;* and the case that was too hard for *Moses*, he brought immediately to God. It is likely that each of these classes had a court composed of its own members, in which causes were heard and tried. Some of the rabbins have supposed that there were 600 rulers of *thousands*, 6000 rulers of *hundreds*, 12,000 rulers of *fifties* and 60,000 rulers of *tens;* making in the whole 78,600 officers. But Josephus says (Antiq., lib. iii., chap. 4) that Moses, by the advice of Jethro, appointed rulers over *myriads*, and then over *thousands;* these he divided into *five hundreds*, and again into *hundreds*, and into *fifties;* and appointed rulers over each of these, who divided them into *thirties*, and at last into *twenties* and *tens;* that each of these companies had a chief, who took his name from the number of persons who were under his direction and government. Allowing what Josephus states to be correct, some have supposed that there could not have been less than 129,860 officers in the Israelitish camp. But such computations are either fanciful or absurd. That the people were divided into *thousands, hundreds, fifties* and *tens*, we know, for the text states it; but we cannot tell precisely how many of such divisions there were, nor, consequently, the number of officers.

Verse 23. *If thou shalt do this thing, and God command thee*] Though the measure was obviously of the utmost importance, and plainly recommended itself by its expediency and necessity; yet Jethro very modestly leaves it to the wisdom of Moses to choose or reject it; and, knowing that in all things his relative was now acting under the immediate direction of God, intimates that no measure can be safely adopted without a positive injunction from God himself. As the counsel was doubtless inspired by the Divine Spirit, we find that it was sanctioned by the same, for Moses acted in every respect according to the advice he had received.

Verse 27. *And Moses let his father-in-law depart*] But if this be the same transaction with that mentioned Num. x. 29, &c., we find that it was with *great reluctance* that Moses permitted so able a counsellor to leave him; for, having the highest opinion of his judgment, experience, and discretion, he pressed him to stay with them, that he might be *instead of eyes to*

them in the desert. But Jethro chose rather to return to his own country, where probably his family were so settled and circumstanced that they could not be conveniently removed, and it was more his duty to stay with *them*, to assist them with his counsel and advice, than to travel with the Israelites. Many others might be found that could be eyes to the Hebrews in the desert, but no man could be found capable of being a father to his family, but himself. It is well to labour for the public good, but our own families are the first claimants on our care, attention, and time. He who neglects his own household on pretence of labouring even for the good of the public, has surely denied the faith, and is worse than an infidel.

It is strange that after this we hear no more of Zipporah! Why is she forgotten? Merely because she was the *wife of Moses;* for he chose to conduct himself so that to the remotest ages there should be the utmost proofs of his *disinterestedness.* While multitudes of the families of Israel are *celebrated* and *dignified,* his own he writes in the dust. He had no interest but that of God and his people; to promote this, he employed his whole time and his uncommon talents. His body, his soul, his whole life, were a continual offering to God. They were always on the Divine altar; and God had from his creature all the praise, glory, and honour that a creature could possibly give. Like his great antitype, he went about doing good; and God was with him. The zeal of God's house consumed him, for in that *house, in all* its concerns, we have the testimony of God himself that *he was faithful*, Heb. iii. 2; and a higher character was never given, nor can be given of any governor, sacred or civil. He made no provision even for his own sons, Gershom and Eliezer; they and their families were incorporated with the Levites, 1 Chron. xxiii. 14, and had no higher employment than that of taking care of the tabernacle and the tent, Num. iii. 21–26, and merely to *serve* at the tabernacle and to *carry burdens*, Num. iv. 24–28. No history, sacred or profane, has been able to produce a complete parallel to the disinterestedness of Moses. This one consideration is sufficient to refute every charge of imposture brought against him and his laws. There never was an imposture in the world (says Dr. Prideaux, *Letter to the Deists*) that had not the following characters:—

1. It must always have for its end some *carnal interest.*
2. It can have none but *wicked men* for its authors.
3. Both of these must necessarily *appear* in the very *contexture* of the *imposture* itself.
4. That it can never be so framed, that it will not contain some *palpable falsities,* which will discover the falsity of all the rest.
5. That wherever it is first propagated, it must be done by *craft* and *fraud.*
6. That when intrusted to *many persons*, it cannot be *long concealed.*

1. The keenest-eyed adversary of Moses has never been able to fix on him any *carnal* interest. No gratification of sensual passions, no accumulation of wealth, no aggrandizement of his family or relatives, no pursuit of worldly honour, has ever been laid to his charge.

2. His life was *unspotted,* and all his actions the offspring of the purest benevolence.

3. As his own hands were pure, so were the *hands of those* whom he *associated* with himself in the work.

4. No *palpable falsity* has ever been detected in his writings, though they have for their subject the most complicate, abstruse, and difficult topics that ever came under the pen of man.

5. No *craft,* no *fraud,* not even what one of his own countrymen thought he might lawfully use, *innocent guile,* because he had to do with a people greatly degraded and grossly stupid, can be laid to his charge. His conduct was as open as the day; and though continually watched by a people who were ever ready to murmur and rebel, and industrious to find an excuse for their repeated seditious conduct, yet none could be found either in his spirit, private life, or public conduct.

6. None ever came after to say, "We have joined with Moses in a *plot,* we have feigned a Divine authority and mission, we have succeeded in our innocent imposture, and now the mask may be laid aside." The whole work proved itself so fully to be of God, that even the person who might wish to discredit Moses and his mission, could find no ground of this kind to stand on. The ten plagues of Egypt, the passage of the Red Sea, the destruction of the king of Egypt and his immense host, the quails, the rock of Horeb, the supernatural supply by the forty years' manna, the continual miracle of the Sabbath, on which the preceding day's manna kept good, though, if thus kept, it became putrid on any other day, together with the constantly attending supernatural cloud, in its threefold office of a *guide* by day, a *light* by night, and a *covering* from the ardours of the sun, all, all invincibly proclaim that God brought out this people from Egypt; that Moses was *the man of God,* chosen by him, and fully accredited in his mission; and that the laws and statutes which he gave were the offspring of the wisdom and goodness of Him who is the Father of Lights, the fountain of truth and justice, and the continual and unbounded benefactor of the human race.

CHAPTER XIX.

The children of Israel, having departed from Rephidim, *come to the wilderness of* Sinai *in the third month,* 1, 2. *Moses goes up into the mount to God, and receives a message which he is to deliver to the people,* 3–6. *He returns and delivers it to the people before the elders,* 7. *The people promise obedience,* 8. *The Lord proposes to meet Moses in the cloud,* 9. *He commands him to sanctify the people, and promises to come down visibly on Mount Sinai on the third day,* 10, 11. *He commands him also to set bounds, to prevent the people or any of the cattle from touching the mount, on pain of being stoned or shot through*

with a dart, 12, 13. *Moses goes down and delivers this message,* 14, 15. *The third day is ushered in with the appearance of the* thick cloud *upon the mount, and with* thunders, lightning, *and the sound of a* trumpet; *at which the people are greatly terrified,* 16. *Moses brings forth the people out of the camp to meet with God,* 17. *Mount Sinai is enveloped with smoke and fire,* 18. *After the trumpet had sounded long and loud, Moses spoke, and God answered him by a voice,* 19. *God calls Moses up to the mount,* 20, *and gives him a charge to the people and to the priests, that they do not attempt to come near to the mount,* 21, 22. *Moses, alleging that it was impossible for them to touch it because of the bounds,* 23, *is sent down to bring up Aaron, and to warn the people again not to break through the bounds,* 24. *Moses goes down and delivers this message,* 25; *after which we may suppose that he and Aaron went up to meet God in the mount.*

A. M. 2513.
B. C. 1491.
An. Exod. Isr. 1.
Sivan.

IN the third month, when the
children of Israel were gone
forth out of the land of Egypt,
the same day [a] came they *into* the wilderness
of Sinai.
2 For they were departed from [b] Rephidim,
and were come *to* the desert of Sinai, and
had pitched in the wilderness; and there
Israel encamped before [c] the mount.
3 And [d] Moses went up unto
God, and the LORD [e] called unto
him out of the mountain, saying,
Thus shalt thou say to the house of Jacob
and tell the children of Israel;
4 [f] Ye have seen what I did unto the Egyp
tians, and *how* [g] I bare you on eagles' wings,
and brought you unto myself.
5 Now [h] therefore, if ye will obey my voice

[a] Num. xxxiii. 15.——[b] Chap. xvii. 1, 8.——[c] Chapter iii. 1, 12. [d] Chap. xx. 21; Acts vii. 38.——[e] Chap. iii. 4.

[f] Deut. xxix. 2.——[g] Deut. xxxii. 11; Isa. lxiii. 9; Rev. xii. 14. [h] Deut. v. 2.

NOTES ON CHAP. XIX.

Verse 1. *In the third month*] This was called *Sivan,* and answers to our *May.* For the Jewish months, years, &c., see the tables at the end of Deuteronomy.

The same day] There are *three* opinions concerning the meaning of this place, which are supported by respectable arguments. 1. The *same day* means the same day of the third month with that, viz., the 15th, on which the Israelites had left Egypt. 2. The *same day* signifies here a day of the same number with the month to which it is applied, viz., the *third* day of the *third* month. 3. By the *same day,* the *first* day of the month is intended. The Jews celebrate the feast of pentecost *fifty* days after the *passover:* from the departure out of Egypt to the coming to Sinai were *forty-five* days; for they came out the *fifteenth* day of the first month, from which day to the *first* of the third month *forty-five* days are numbered. On the 2d day of this third month Moses went up into the mountain, when *three* days were given to the people to purify themselves; this gives the *fourth* day of the *third* month, or the *forty-ninth* from the departure out of Egypt. On the *next day,* which was the *fiftieth* from the celebration of the passover, the glory of God appeared on the mount; in commemoration of which the Jews celebrate the feast of *pentecost.* This is the opinion of St. Augustine and of several moderns, and is defended at large by Houbigant. As the word חדש *chodesh, month,* is put for new moon, which is with the Jews the *first* day of the month, this may be considered an additional confirmation of the above opinion.

The wilderness of Sinai.] Mount Sinai is called by the Arabs *Jibel Mousa* or the Mount of Moses, or, by way of eminence, *El Tor,* THE *Mount.* It is one hill, with two peaks or summits; one is called *Horeb,* the other *Sinai.* Horeb was probably its most ancient name, and might designate the whole mountain; but as the Lord had appeared to Moses on this mountain in a *bush,* סנה *seneh,* chap. iii. 2, from this circumstance it might have received the name of *Sinai* or הר סיני *har Sinai,* the *mount of the bush* or the mount of *bushes;* for it is possible that it was not in a *single bush,* but in a *thicket of bushes,* that the Angel of God made his appearance. The word *bush* is often used for *woods* or *forests.*

Verse 3. *Moses went up unto God*] It is likely that the cloud which had conducted the Israelitish camp had now removed to the top of Sinai; and as this was the symbol of the Divine presence, Moses went up to the place, there to meet the Lord.

The Lord called unto him] This, according to St. Stephen, was the *Angel of the Lord,* Acts vii. 38. And from several scriptures we have seen that the *Lord Jesus* was the person intended; see the notes on Gen. xvi. 7; xviii. 13; Exod. iii. 2.

Verse 4. How *I bare you on eagles' wings*] Mr. Bruce contends that the word נשר *nesher* does not mean the bird we term *eagle;* but a bird which the Arabs, from its *kind* and *merciful* disposition, call *rachama,* which is noted for its care of its young, and its carrying them upon its back. See his Travels, vol. vii., pl. 33. It is not unlikely that from this part of the sacred history the heathens borrowed their fable of the *eagle being a bird sacred to Jupiter,* and which was employed to carry the souls of departed heroes, kings, &c., into the celestial regions. The Romans have struck several medals with this device, which may be seen in different cabinets, among which are the following: one of *Faustina,* daughter of *Antoninus Pius,* on the reverse of which she is represented ascending to heaven on the *back of an eagle;* and another of *Salonia,* daughter of the Emperor *Galienus,* on the reverse of which she is represented on the *back of an eagle,* with a sceptre in her hand, ascending to heaven. *Jupiter* himself is sometimes represented on the *back of an eagle* also, with his *thunder* in his hand, as on a medal of *Licinus.* This brings us nearer to the letter of the text, where it appears that the heathens con-

A. M. 2513. B. C. 1491. An. Exod. Isr. 1. Sivan.

indeed, and keep my covenant, then [i] ye shall be a peculiar treasure unto me above all people: for [k] all the earth *is* mine:

6 And ye shall be unto me a [l] kingdom of priests, and a [m] holy nation. These *are* the words which thou shalt speak unto the children of Israel.

7 And Moses came and called for the elders of the people, and laid before their faces all these words which the LORD commanded him.

8 And [n] all the people answered together, and said, All that the LORD hath spoken we will do. And Moses returned the words of the people unto the LORD.

9 And the LORD said unto Moses, Lo, I come unto thee [o] in a thick cloud, [p] that the people may hear when I speak with thee, and [q] believe thee for ever. And Moses told the words of the people unto the LORD.

---

[i] Deut. iv. 20; vii. 6; xiv. 2, 21; xxvi. 18; xxxii. 8, 9; 1 Kings viii. 53; Psa. cxxxv. 4; Cant. viii. 12; Isa. xli. 8; xliii. 1; Jer. x. 16; Mal. iii. 17; Tit. ii. 14.——[k] Chap. ix. 29; Deut. x. 14; Job xli. 11; Psa. xxiv. 1; l. 12; 1 Cor. x. 26, 28. [l] Deut. xxxiii. 2, 3, 4; 1 Pet. ii. 5, 9; Rev. i. 6; v. 10; xx. 6.

[m] Lev. xx. 24, 26; Deut. vii. 6; xxvi. 19; xxviii. 9; Isaiah lxii. 12; 1 Cor. iii. 17; 1 Thess. v. 27.——[n] Chap. xxiv. 3, 7; Deut. v. 27; xxvi. 17.——[o] Ver. 16; chap. xx. 21; xxiv. 15, 16; Deut iv. 11; Psa. xviii. 11, 12; xcvii. 2; Matt. xvii. 5.——[p] Deut. iv. 12, 36; John xii. 29, 30.——[q] Chap. xiv. 31.

---

founded the figure made use of by the sacred penman, *I bare you on eagles' wings*, with the manifestation of God in *thunder* and *lightning* on Mount Sinai. And it might be in reference to all this that the Romans took the *eagle* for their ensign. See *Scheuchzer, Musellius*, &c.

Brought you unto myself.] In this and the two following verses, we see the design of God in selecting a people for himself. 1. They were *to obey his voice*, ver. 5, to receive a *revelation* from him, and to act according to that revelation, and not according to their reason or fancy, in opposition to his declarations. 2. They were to obey his voice *indeed*, שמוע תשמעו *shamoa tishmeu, in hearing they should hear*; they should consult his testimonies, *hear* them whenever read or proclaimed, and obey them as soon as heard, affectionately and steadily. 3. They must *keep his covenant*—not only copy in their lives the *ten commandments*, but they must receive and preserve the grand *agreement* made between God and man by *sacrifice*, in reference to the incarnation and death of Christ; for from the foundation of the world the covenant of God ratified by sacrifices referred to this, and now the sacrificial system was to be more fully opened by the giving of the law. 4. They should then be God's peculiar treasure, סגלה *segullah*, his own *patrimony*, a people in whom he should have all right, and over whom he should have exclusive authority above all the people of the earth; for though all the inhabitants of the world were his by his right of creation and providence, yet these should be peculiarly his, as receiving his revelation and entering into his covenant. 5. They should be a *kingdom of priests*, ver. 6. Their *state* should be a *theocracy*; and as God should be the sole governor, being *king in Jeshurun*, so all his subjects should be *priests*, all *worshippers*, all *sacrificers*, every individual offering up *the victim for himself*. A beautiful representation of the Gospel dispensation, to which the Apostles Peter and John apply it, 1 Pet. ii. 5, 9; Rev. i. 6; v. 10, and xx. 6; under which dispensation every believing soul offers up for himself that Lamb of God which was slain for and which takes away the sin of the world, and through which alone a man can have access to God.

Verse 6. *And a holy nation.*] They should be a *nation*, one people; firmly united among themselves, living under their own laws; and powerful, because united, and acting under the direction and blessing of God. They should be a *holy* nation, saved from their sins, righteous in their conduct, holy in their hearts; every external rite being not only a significant ceremony, but also a means of conveying light and life, grace and peace, to every person who conscientiously used it. Thus they should be both a *kingdom*, having God for their governor; and a *nation*, a multitude of peoples connected together; not a scattered, disordered, and disorganized people, but a *royal nation*, using their own rites, living under their own laws, subject in *religious* matters only to God, and in things *civil*, to every ordinance of man for God's sake.

This was the spirit and design of this wonderful institution, which could not receive its perfection but under the Gospel, and has its full accomplishment in every member of the mystical body of Christ.

Verse 7. *The elders of the people*] The head of each tribe, and the chief of each family, by whose ministry this gracious purpose of God was speedily communicated to the whole camp.

Verse 8. *And all the people answered, &c.*] The people, having such gracious advantages laid before them, most cheerfully consented to take God for their *portion*; as he had graciously promised to take them for his *people*. Thus a covenant was made, the parties being mutually bound to each other.

Moses returned the words] When the people had on their part consented to the covenant, Moses appears to have gone immediately up to the mountain and related to God the success of his mission; for he was now on the mount, as appears from ver. 14.

Verse 9. *A thick cloud*] This is interpreted by ver. 18: *And Mount Sinai was altogether on a* SMOKE *—and the* SMOKE *thereof ascended as the* SMOKE *of a furnace*; his usual appearance was in the cloudy pillar, which we may suppose was generally *clear* and *luminous*.

That the people may hear] See the note on chap. xv. 9. The Jews consider this as the fullest evidence their fathers had of the Divine mission of Moses; themselves were permitted to see this awfully glorious sight, and to hear God himself speak out of the thick dark-

A. M. 2513. B. C. 1491. An. Exod. Isr. 1. Sivan.

10 And the LORD said unto
Moses, Go unto the people, and
[r] sanctify them to-day and to-
morrow, and let them [s] wash their clothes,
11 And be ready against the third day: for
the third day the LORD [t] will come down in
the sight of all the people, upon Mount Sinai.
12 And thou shalt set bounds unto the
people round about, saying, Take heed to
yourselves, *that ye* go *not* up into the mount,
or touch the border of it: [u] whosoever
toucheth the mount shall be surely put to
death;
13 There shall not a hand touch it, but he
shall surely be stoned, or shot through; whether *it be* beast or man, it shall not live:
when the [v] trumpet [w] soundeth
long, they shall come up to the
mount.
14 And Moses went down from the mount
unto the people, and [x] sanctified the people;
and they washed their clothes.
15 And he said unto the people, [y] Be ready
against the third day: [z] come not at *your*
wives.
16 And it came to pass on the third day in
the morning, that there were [a] thunders and
lightnings, and a [b] thick cloud upon the mount,
and the [c] voice of the trumpet exceeding loud;
so that all the people that *was* in the camp
[d] trembled.
17 And [e] Moses brought forth the people

A. M. 2513. B. C. 1491. An. Exod. Isr. 1. Sivan.

[r] Lev. xi. 44, 45; Heb. x. 22.——[s] Ver. 14; Genesis xxxv. 2; Lev. xv. 5.——[t] Ver. 16, 18; chap. xxxiv. 5; Deut. xxxiii. 2. [u] Heb. xii. 20.——[v] Or, *cornet*.——[w] Ver. 16, 19.——[x] Ver. 10. [y] Ver. 11.

[z] 1 Sam. xxi. 4, 5; Zech. vii. 3; 1 Cor. vii. 5.——[a] Psa. lxxvii. 18; Heb. xii. 18, 19; Rev. iv. 5; viii. 5; xi. 19.——[b] Ver. 9; chap. xl. 34; 2 Chron. v. 14.——[c] Rev. i. 10; iv. 1.——[d] Heb. xii. 21.——[e] Deut. iv. 10.

ness: for before this, as Rabbi *Maymon* remarks, they might have thought that Moses wrought his miracles by *sorcery* or *enchantment;* but now, hearing the voice of God himself, they could no longer disbelieve nor even doubt.

Verse 10. *Sanctify them*] See the meaning of this term, chap. xiii. 2.

Let them wash their clothes] And consequently bathe their bodies; for, according to the testimony of the Jews, these always went together. It was necessary that, as they were about to appear in the presence of God, every thing should be clean and pure about them; that they might be admonished by this of the necessity of inward purity, of which the outward washing was the emblem.

From these institutions the heathens appear to have borrowed their precepts relative to *washings* and *purifications* previously to their offering sacrifice to their gods, examples of which abound in the Greek and Latin writers. They washed their hands and clothes, and bathed their bodies in pure water, before they performed any act of religious worship; and in a variety of cases, abstinence from all matrimonial connections was positively required, before a person was permitted to perform any religious rite, or assist at the performance.

Verse 12. *Thou shalt set bounds*] Whether this was a *line* marked out on the ground, beyond which they were not to go, or whether a *fence* was actually made to keep them off, we cannot tell; or whether this fence was made all round the mountain, or only at that part to which one wing of the camp extended, is not evident.

This verse strictly forbids the people from coming near and touching Mount Sinai, which was burning with FIRE. The words therefore in ver. 15, אל תגשו אל אשה *al tiggeshu el ishshah*, come not at your wives, seem rather to mean, *come not near unto the* FIRE; especially as the other phrase is not at all probable: but the *fire* is, on this occasion, spoken of so emphatically (see Deut. v. 4, 5, 22–25) that we are naturally led to consider אשה *ishshah* here as האש *ha-esh* transposed, or to say, with Simon in his Lexicon, אשה *fæm.* idem quod *masc.* אש *ignis.* So, among other instances, we have אבר and אברה a *wing;* אור and אורה *light;* אמץ and אמצה *strength;* and אמר and אמרה a *speech.* —*Buxt.* See KENNICOTT's *Remarks.*

Whosoever toucheth the mount shall be surely put to death] The place was awfully sacred, because the dreadful majesty of God was displayed on it. And this taught them that God is a consuming fire, and that it is a fearful thing to fall into the hands of the living God.

Verse 13. *There shall not a hand touch it*] בו *bo*, HIM, not the *mountain*, but the *man* who had presumed to touch the mountain. He should be considered altogether as an unclean and accursed thing, not to be touched for fear of conveying defilement; but should be immediately stoned or pierced through with a dart, Heb. xii. 20.

Verse 16. *Thunders and lightnings, and a thick cloud—and the voice of the trumpet*] The *thunders, lightnings,* &c., announced the coming, as they proclaimed the majesty, of God. Of the thunders and lightnings, and the *deep, dark, dismal, electric cloud,* from which the thunders and lightnings proceeded, we can form a tolerable apprehension; but of the *loud, long-sounding trumpet,* we can scarcely form a conjecture. Such were the appearances and the noise that all the people in the camp trembled, and Moses himself was constrained to say, "I exceedingly fear and quake," Heb. xii. 21. Probably the sound of the *trumpet* was something similar to that which shall be blown by the angel when he sweareth, by Him that liveth for ever, *There shall be time no longer!*

Verse 17. *And Moses brought forth the people—to meet with God*] For though they might not touch the mount till they had permission, yet when the trumpet sounded long, it appears they might come up to *the nether part of the mount,* (see ver. 13, and Deut. iv. 11;) and when the trumpet had ceased to sound, they

A. M. 2513. B. C. 1491. An. Exod. Isr. 1. Sivan.

out of the camp to meet with
God; and they stood at the
nether part of the mount.
18 And [f] Mount Sinai was altogether on a
smoke, because the Lord descended upon it
[g] in fire: [h] and the smoke thereof ascended
as the smoke of a furnace, and [i] the whole
mount quaked greatly.
19 And [k] when the voice of the trumpet
sounded long, and waxed louder and louder,
[l] Moses spake, and [m] God answered him by a
voice.
20 And the Lord came down
upon Mount Sinai, on the top of
the mount: and the Lord called
Moses *up* to the top of the mount; and Moses
went up.
21 And the Lord said unto Moses, Go
down, [n] charge the people, lest they break
through unto the Lord [o] to gaze, and many
of them perish.
22 And let the priests also, which come
near to the Lord, [p] sanctify themselves, lest
the Lord [q] break forth upon them.

[f] Deut. iv. 11; xxxiii. 2; Judg. v. 5; Psa. lxviii. 7, 8; Isa. vi. 4; Hab. iii. 3.——[g] Chap. iii. 2; xxiv. 17; 2 Chron. vii. 1, 2, 3.——[h] Gen. xv. 17; Psa. cxliv. 5; Rev. xv. 8.——[i] Psa. lxviii. 8; lxxvii. 18; cxiv. 7; Jer. iv. 24; Heb. xii. 26.——[k] Ver. 13.——[l] Heb. xii. 21.——[m] Neh. ix. 13; Psa. lxxxi. 7.——[n] Heb. *contest.*——[o] See chap. iii. 5; 1 Sam. vi. 19.——[p] Lev. x. 3.——[q] 2 Sam. vi. 7, 8.

might then go up unto the mountain, as to any other place.

It was absolutely necessary that God should give the people at large some particular evidence of his *being* and *power*, that they might be saved from idolatry, to which they were most deplorably prone; and that they might the more readily credit Moses, who was to be the constant mediator between God and them. God, therefore, in his indescribable majesty, descended on the mount; and, by the *thick dark cloud*, the *violent thunders*, the *vivid lightnings*, the *long and loud blasts of the trumpet*, the *smoke* encompassing the whole mountain, and the excessive *earthquake*, proclaimed his *power*, his *glory*, and his *holiness;* so that the people, however unfaithful and disobedient afterwards, never once doubted the Divine interference, or suspected Moses of any cheat or imposture. Indeed, so absolute and unequivocal were the proofs of supernatural agency, that it was impossible these appearances could be attributed to any cause but the unlimited power of the author of Nature.

It is worthy of remark that the people were informed *three days* before, ver. 9–11, that such an appearance was to take place; and this answered two excellent purposes: 1. They had time to *sanctify* and prepare themselves for this solemn transaction; and, 2. Those who might be *skeptical* had sufficient opportunity to make use of every precaution to prevent and detect an *imposture;* so this previous warning strongly serves the cause of Divine revelation.

Their being at first prohibited from touching the mount on the most awful penalties, and secondly, being permitted to see manifestations of the Divine majesty, and hear the words of God, subserved the same great purposes. Their being prohibited in the first instance would naturally whet their curiosity, make them cautious of being deceived, and ultimately impress them with a due sense of God's justice and their own sinfulness; and their being permitted afterwards to go up to the mount, must have deepened the conviction that all was fair and real, that there could be no imposture in the case, and that though the justice and purity of God forbade them to draw nigh for a time, yet his mercy, which had prescribed the means of purification, had permitted an access to his presence. The directions given from ver. 10 to 15 inclusive show, not only the *holiness* of God, but the *purity* he requires in his worshippers.

Besides, the whole scope and design of the chapter prove that no soul can possibly approach this holy and terrible Being but through a *mediator;* and this is the use made of this whole transaction by the author of the Epistle to the Hebrews, chap. xii. 18–24.

Verse 20. *The Lord came down*] This was undoubtedly done in a *visible* manner, that the people might witness the awful appearance. We may suppose that every thing was arranged thus: the *glory of the Lord* occupied the *top* of the mountain, and near to this *Moses* was permitted to approach. *Aaron* and the *seventy elders* were permitted to advance *some way up the mountain*, while the *people* were only permitted to come up to its *base*. Moses, as the lawgiver, was to receive the statutes and judgments from God's mouth; Aaron and the elders were to receive them from Moses, and deliver them to the people; and the people were to act according to the direction received. Nothing can be imagined more glorious, terrible, majestic, and impressive, than the whole of this transaction; but it was chiefly calculated to impress *deep reverence, religious fear,* and *sacred awe;* and he who attempts to worship God uninfluenced by these, has neither a proper sense of the Divine majesty, nor of the sinfulness of sin. It seems in reference to this that the apostle says, *Let us have grace whereby we may serve God acceptably with* REVERENCE *and* GODLY FEAR: *for our God is a* CONSUMING FIRE; Heb. xii. 28, 29. Who then shall dare to approach him in his *own* name, and without a *mediator?*

Verse 22. *Let the priests also—sanctify themselves*] That there were *priests* among the Hebrews *before* the consecration of Aaron and his sons, cannot be doubted; though their functions might be in a considerable measure suspended while under persecution in Egypt, yet the persons existed whose right and duty it was to offer sacrifices to God. Moses requested liberty from Pharaoh to go into the wilderness to *sacrifice;* and had there not been among the people both *sacrifices* and *priests*, the request itself must have appeared nugatory and absurd. *Sacrifices* from the *beginning* had constituted an essential part of the

A. M. 2513. B. C. 1491. An. Exod. Isr. 1. Sivan.

23 And Moses said unto the LORD, The people cannot come up to Mount Sinai: for thou chargedst us, saying, [r] Set bounds about the mount, and sanctify it.
24 And the LORD said unto him, Away, get thee down, and thou shalt come up, thou, and Aaron with thee; but let not the priests and the people break through, to come up unto the LORD, lest he break forth upon them.

A. M. 2513. B. C. 1491. An. Exod. Isr. 1. Sivan.

25 So Moses went down unto the people, and spake unto them.

---

[r] Ver. 12; Josh. iii. 4.

---

worship of God, and there certainly were *priests* whose business it was to offer them to God before the giving of the law; though this, for especial reasons, was restricted to Aaron and his sons after the law had been given. As sacrifices had not been offered for a considerable time, the priests themselves were considered in a state of impurity; and therefore God requires that they also should be purified for the purpose of approaching the mountain, and hearing their Maker promulgate his laws. See the note on chap. xxviii. 1.

Verse 23. *The people cannot come up*] Either because they had been so solemnly forbidden that they would not dare, with the penalty of instant death before their eyes, to transgress the Divine command; or the *bounds* which were set about the mount were such as rendered their passing them physically impossible.

And sanctify it.] וקדשתו *vekiddashto.* Here the word קדש *kadash* is taken in its proper literal sense, signifying the *separating* of a *thing, person,* or *place,* from all profane or common uses, and devoting it to sacred purposes.

Verse 24. *Let not the priests and the people break through*] God knew that they were heedless, criminally curious, and stupidly obstinate; and therefore his mercy saw it right to give them line upon line, that they might not transgress to their own destruction.

FROM the very solemn and awful manner in which the LAW was introduced, we may behold it as the ministration of terror and death, 2 Cor. iii. 7, appearing rather to exclude men from God than to bring them nigh; and from this we may learn that an approach to God would have been for ever impossible, had not infinite mercy found out the Gospel scheme of salvation. By this, and this alone, we draw nigh to God; *for we have an entrance into the holiest by the blood of Jesus,* Heb. x. 19. "For," says the apostle, "ye are not come unto the mount that might be touched, and that burned with fire; nor unto blackness, and darkness, and tempest, and to the sound of a trumpet, and the voice of words; which voice they that heard entreated that the word should not be spoken to them any more, (for they could not endure that which was commanded, And if so much as a beast touch the mountain it shall be stoned, or thrust through with a dart: and so terrible was the sight that Moses said, I exceedingly fear and quake:) but ye are come unto Mount Sion, and unto the city of the living God, the heavenly Jerusalem, and to an innumerable company of angels, to the general assembly and Church of the first-born, which are written in heaven; and to God, the Judge of all; and to the spirits of just men made perfect; and to Jesus the MEDIATOR of the NEW COVENANT; and to the blood of sprinkling, that speaketh better things than that of Abel;" Heb. xii. 18–24.

Reader, art thou still under the influence and condemning power of that fiery law which proceeded from his right hand? Art thou yet *afar off?* Remember, thou canst only *come nigh* by the blood of sprinkling; and till justified by his blood, thou art under the *curse.* Consider the terrible majesty of God. If thou have his *favour* thou hast *life;* if his *frown, death.* Be instantly reconciled to God, for though thou hast deeply *sinned,* and he is *just,* yet he is the justifier of him that believeth in Christ Jesus. Believe on him, receive his salvation, OBEY *his voice indeed,* and KEEP his *covenant,* and THEN *shalt thou be a king and a priest unto God and the Lamb,* and be finally saved with all the power of an endless life. *Amen.*

CHAPTER XX.

The preface to the ten commandments, 1, 2. *The* FIRST *commandment, against* mental *or* theoretic idolatry, 3. *The* SECOND, *against* making *and* worshipping images, *or* practical idolatry, 4–6. *The* THIRD, *against* false swearing, blasphemy, *and* irreverent use *of the* name *of* God, 7. *The* FOURTH, *against* profanation *of the* Sabbath, *and* idleness *on the* other days *of the* week, 8–11. *The* FIFTH, *against* disrespect *and* disobedience *to* parents, 12. *The* SIXTH, *against* murder *and* cruelty, 13. *The* SEVENTH, *against* adultery *and* uncleanness, 14. *The* EIGHTH, *against* stealing *and* dishonesty, 15. *The* NINTH, *against* false testimony, perjury, &c., 16. *The* TENTH, *against* covetousness, 17. *The people are alarmed at the awful appearance of God on the mount, and stand afar off,* 18. *They pray that Moses may be mediator between God and them,* 19. *Moses encourages them,* 20. *He draws near to the thick darkness, and God communes with him,* 21, 22. *Farther directions against idolatry,* 23. *Directions concerning making an altar of* earth 24; *and an altar of hewn stone,* 25. *None of these to be ascended by steps, and the reason given,* 26.

A. M. 2513.
B. C. 1491.
An. Exod. Isr. 1.
Sivan.

AND God spake [a] all these
words, saying,
2 [b] I *am* the LORD thy God,
which have brought thee out of the land of
Egypt, [c] out of the house of
[d] bondage.
3 [e] Thou shalt have no other
gods before me.

[a] Deut. v. 22.——[b] Lev. xxvi. 1, 13; Deut. v. 6; Psa. lxxxi. 10; Hos. xiii. 4.——[c] Chap. xiii. 3.

[d] Heb. *servants*.——[e] Deut. v. 7; vi. 14; 2 Kings xvii. 35; Jer. xxv. 6; xxxv. 15.

NOTES ON CHAP. XX.

Verse 1. *All these words*] Houbigant supposes, and with great plausibility of reason, that the clause את כל הדברים האלה *eth col haddebarim haelleh*, "all these words," belong to the latter part of the concluding verse of chap. xix., which he thinks should be read thus: *And Moses went down unto the people, and spake unto them* ALL THESE WORDS; i. e., delivered the solemn charge relative to their not attempting to come up to that part of the mountain on which God manifested himself in his glorious majesty, lest he should break forth upon them and consume them. For how could Divine justice and purity suffer a people so defiled to stand in his immediate presence? When Moses, therefore, had gone down and spoken *all these words*, and he and Aaron had reascended the mount, then the Divine Being, as supreme legislator, is majestically introduced thus: *And God spake, saying.* This gives a dignity to the commencement of this chapter of which the clause above mentioned, if not referred to the speech of Moses, deprives it. The *Anglo-Saxon* favours this emendation: Ᵹod ſpræc þuſ, *God spoke* THUS, which is the whole of the first verse as it stands in that version.

Some learned men are of opinion that the TEN COMMANDMENTS were delivered on May 30, being then the day of *pentecost*.

THE TEN COMMANDMENTS.

The laws delivered on Mount Sinai have been variously named. In Deut. iv. 13, they are called עשרת הדברים *asereth haddebarim*, THE TEN WORDS. In the preceding chapter, ver. 5, God calls them את בריתי *eth berithi*, *my* COVENANT, i. e., the agreement he entered into with the people of Israel to take them for his peculiar people, if they took him for their God and portion. IF *ye will obey my voice indeed*, and KEEP my COVENANT, THEN *shall ye be a peculiar treasure unto me.* And the word *covenant* here evidently refers to the *laws* given in this chapter, as is evident from Deut. iv. 13: *And he declared unto you his* COVENANT, *which he commanded you to perform*, even TEN COMMANDMENTS. They have been also termed the *moral law*, because they contain and lay down rules for the regulation of the *manners* or *conduct* of men. Sometimes they have been termed *the* LAW, התורה *hattorah*, by way of eminence, as containing the grand system of spiritual *instruction*, *direction*, *guidance*, &c. See on the word LAW, chap. xii. 49. And frequently the DECALOGUE, Δεκαλογος, which is a literal translation into Greek of the עשרת הדברים *asereth haddebarim*, or TEN WORDS, of Moses.

Among divines they are generally divided into what they term the *first* and *second* tables. The FIRST *table* containing the *first*, *second*, *third*, and *fourth* commandments, and comprehending the whole system of *theology*, the true notions we should form of the Divine nature, the reverence we owe and the religious service we should render to him. The SECOND, containing the *six* last commandments, and comprehending a complete system of *ethics*, or *moral duties* which man owes to his fellows, and on the due performance of which the order, peace, and happiness of society depend. By this division, the FIRST table contains our *duty* to GOD; the SECOND our *duty* to our NEIGHBOUR. This division, which is natural enough, refers us to the grand principle, love to God and love to man, through which both tables are observed. 1. Thou shalt love the Lord thy God with all thy heart, soul, mind, and strength. 2. Thou shalt love thy neighbour as thyself. On these two hang all the law and the prophets. See Matt. xxii. 37–40.

THE FIRST COMMANDMENT.

Against *mental* or *theoretic idolatry*.

Verse 2. *I* am *the* LORD *thy God*] יהוה אלהיך *Yehovah eloheycha*. On the word JEHOVAH, which we here translate LORD, see the notes on Gen. ii. 4, and Exod. vi. 3. And on the word *Elohim*, here translated GOD, see on Gen. i. 1. It is worthy of remark that each *individual* is addressed here, and not the *people collectively*, though they are all necessarily included; that each might feel that he was bound for *himself* to hear and do all these words. Moses laboured to impress this *personal interest* on the people's minds, when he said, Deut. v. 3, 4: "The Lord made this covenant with *us*, even *us*, who are all of *us* here alive this day."

Brought thee out of the land of Egypt, &c.] And by this very thing have proved myself to be superior to all gods, unlimited in power, and most gracious as well as fearful in operation. This is the preface or introduction, but should not be separated from the commandment. Therefore,—

Verse 3. *Thou shalt have no other gods before me.*] אלהים אחרים *elohim acherim*, no *strange* gods—none that thou art not *acquainted* with, none who has not *given thee* such *proofs* of his power and godhead as I have done in delivering thee from the Egyptians, dividing the Red Sea, bringing water out of the rock, quails into the desert, manna from heaven to feed thee, and the pillar of cloud to direct, enlighten, and shield thee. By these miracles God had rendered himself *familiar* to them, they were intimately *acquainted* with the operation of his hands; and therefore with great propriety he says, Thou shalt have no *strange gods* before me; על פני *al panai*, *before* or in *the place* of those *manifestations* which I have made of myself.

This commandment prohibits every species of *mental* idolatry, and all inordinate attachment to *earthly* and *sensible* things. As God is the *fountain of happiness*, and no intelligent creature can be happy but through him, whoever seeks happiness in the *creature*

A. M. 2513. B. C. 1491. An. Exod. Isr. 1. Sivan.

4 [f] Thou shalt not make unto thee any graven image, or any likeness *of any thing* that *is* in heaven above, or that *is* in the earth beneath, or that *is* in the water under the earth:

5 [g] Thou shalt not bow down thyself to them, nor serve them: for I the LORD thy God *am* [h] a jealous God, [i] visiting the iniquity of the fathers upon the children, unto the third and

[f] Lev. xxvi. 1; Deut. iv. 16; v. 8; xxvii. 15; Psa. xcvii. 7. — [g] Chap. xxiii. 24; Josh. xxiii. 7; 2 Kings xvii. 35; Isa. xliv. 15, 19. — [h] Chap. xxxiv. 14; Deut. iv. 24; vi. 15; Josh. xxiv. 19; Neh. i. 2. — [i] Chap. xxxiv. 7; Lev. xx. 5; xxvi. 39, 40; Num. xiv. 18, 33; 1 Kings xxi. 29; Job v. 4; xxi. 19; Psa. lxxix. 8; cix. 4; Isa. xiv. 20, 21; lxv. 6, 7; Jer. ii. 9; xxxii. 18.

is necessarily an *idolater;* as he puts the *creature* in the place of the *Creator,* expecting that from the gratification of his passions, in the use or abuse of earthly things, which is to be found in God alone. The very first commandment of the whole series is divinely calculated to prevent man's misery and promote his happiness, by taking him off from all false dependence, and leading him to God himself, the *fountain of all good.*

THE SECOND COMMANDMENT.

Against *making* and *worshipping images.*

Verse 4. *Thou shalt not make unto thee any graven image*] As the word פסל *pasal* signifies to *hew, carve, grave,* &c., פסל *pesel* may here signify any kind of image, either of *wood, stone,* or *metal,* on which the *axe,* the *chisel,* or the *graving tool* has been employed. This commandment includes in its prohibitions *every species of idolatry* known to have been practised among the Egyptians. The reader will see this the more plainly by consulting the notes on the *ten plagues,* particularly those on chap. xii.

Or any likeness, &c.] To know the full spirit and extent of this commandment, this place must be collated with Deut. iv. 15, &c.: *Take ye therefore good heed unto yourselves—lest ye corrupt yourselves—and make you a graven image, the similitude of any figure, the likeness of* MALE *or* FEMALE. All who have even the slightest acquaintance with the ancient history of Egypt, know that *Osiris* and his wife *Isis* were supreme divinities among that people.

The likeness of any beast.—בהמה *behemah,* such as the *ox* and the *heifer.* Among the Egyptians the ox was not only sacred but *adored,* because they supposed that in one of these animals *Osiris* took up his residence: hence they always had a *living ox,* which they supposed to be the habitation of this deity; and they imagined that on the death of one he entered into the body of another, and so on successively. This famous *ox-god* they called *Apis* and *Mnevis.*

The likeness of any winged fowl.—The *ibis,* or *stork,* or *crane,* and *hawk,* may be here intended, for all these were objects of Egyptian idolatry.

The likeness of any thing that CREEPETH.—The *crocodile, serpents,* the *scarabeus* or *beetle,* were all objects of their adoration; and Mr. Bryant has rendered it very probable that even the *frog* itself was a sacred animal, as from its *inflation* it was emblematic of the prophetic influence, for they supposed that the god *inflated* or *distended* the body of the person by whom he gave oracular answers.

The likeness of any FISH.—All *fish* were esteemed sacred animals among the Egyptians. One called *Oxurunchus* had, according to Strabo, lib. xvii., a temple, and divine honours paid to it. Another fish, called *Phagrus,* was worshipped at *Syene,* according to *Clemens Alexandrinus* in his *Cohortatio.* And the *Lepidotus* and *eel* were objects of their adoration, as we find from *Herodotus,* lib. ii., cap. 72. In short, *oxen, heifers, sheep, goats, lions, dogs, monkeys,* and *cats;* the *ibis,* the *crane,* and the *hawk;* the *crocodile, serpents, frogs, flies,* and the *scarabeus* or *beetle;* the *Nile* and its *fish;* the *sun, moon, planets,* and *stars; fire, light, air, darkness,* and *night,* were all objects of Egyptian idolatry, and all included in this very *circumstantial* prohibition as detailed in Deuteronomy, and very forcibly in the *general* terms of the text: *Thou shalt not make unto thee any graven image, or any likeness of any thing that is in the* HEAVENS *above, or that is in the* EARTH *beneath, or that is in the* WATER *under the earth.* And the reason of this becomes self evident, when the various objects of Egyptian idolatry are considered.

To countenance its *image worship,* the *Roman Catholic Church* has left the whole of this second commandment out of the decalogue, and thus lost one whole commandment out of the *ten;* but to keep up the *number* they have divided the *tenth* into *two.* This is totally contrary to the faith of God's elect and to the acknowledgment of that truth which is according to godliness. The verse is found in every MS. of the *Hebrew Pentateuch* that has ever yet been discovered. It is in all the *ancient versions,* Samaritan, Chaldee, Syriac, Septuagint, Vulgate, Coptic, and Arabic; also in the Persian, and in all modern versions. There is not one word of the whole verse wanting in the many hundreds of MSS. collected by *Kennicott* and *De Rossi.* This corruption of the word of God by the Roman Catholic Church stamps it, as a *false* and *heretical Church,* with the deepest brand of ever-during infamy!

This commandment also prohibits every species of *external* idolatry, as the *first* does all idolatry that may be called *internal* or *mental.* All *false worship* may be considered of this kind, together with all *image worship,* and all other superstitious rites and ceremonies. See the note on ver. 23.

Verse 5. *Jealous God*] This shows in a most expressive manner the love of God to this people. He felt for them as the most affectionate husband could do for his spouse; and was *jealous* for their fidelity, because he willed their invariable happiness.

Visiting the iniquity of the fathers upon the children] This necessarily implies—IF *the children walk in the steps of their fathers;* for no man can be condemned by Divine justice for a crime of which he was never guilty; see Ezek. xviii. *Idolatry* is however particularly intended, and *visiting* sins of this kind refers principally to *national judgments.* By withdrawing

A. M. 2513.
B. C. 1491.
An. Exod. Isr. 1.
Sivan.

fourth *generation* of them that
hate me;
6 And [k] showing mercy unto
thousands of them that love me, and keep my
commandments.
7 [l] Thou shalt not take the name of the
LORD thy God in vain; for
the LORD [m] will not hold him
guiltless that taketh his name
in vain.
8 [n] Remember the Sabbath day, to keep it
holy.

A. M. 2513.
B. C. 1491.
An. Exod. Isr. 1.
Sivan.

[k] Chap. xxxiv. 7; Deut. vii. 9; Psa. lxxxix. 34; Rom. xi. 28. — [l] Chap. xxiii. 1; Lev. xix. 12; Deut. v. 11; Psa. xv. 4; Matt. v. 33. — [m] Mic. vi. 11. — [n] Chap. xxxi. 13, 14; Lev. xix. 3, 30; xxvi. 2; Deut. v. 12.

the Divine protection the idolatrous Israelites were delivered up into the hands of their enemies, from whom the gods in whom they had trusted could not deliver them. This God did to the *third and fourth generations*, i. e., *successively;* as may be seen in every part of the Jewish history, and particularly in the book of *Judges*. And this, at last, became the grand and the only effectual and lasting means in his hand of their final deliverance from idolatry; for it is well known that after the Babylonish captivity the Israelites were so completely saved from idolatry, as never more to have disgraced themselves by it as they had formerly done. These national judgments, thus continued from generation to generation, appear to be what are designed by the words in the text, *Visiting the sins of the fathers upon the children*, &c.

Verse 6. *And showing mercy unto thousands*] Mark; even those who love God and keep his commandments *merit* nothing from him, and therefore the salvation and blessedness which these enjoy come from the *mercy* of God: *Showing mercy*, &c. What a disproportion between the works of *justice* and *mercy!* *Justice* works to the *third* or *fourth*, *mercy* to *thousands* of generations!

The heathen had maxims like these. Theocritus also teaches that the children of the good shall be blessed because of their parents' piety, and that evil shall come upon the offspring of the wicked:—

Ευσεβεων παιδεσσι τα λωια, δυσσεβεων δ' ου.
Idyll. 26, v. 32.

Upon the children of the righteous fall
The choicest blessings; on the wicked, wo.

That love me, and keep my commandments.] It was this that caused Christ to comprise the fulfilment of the whole law in *love* to God and man; see the note on ver. 1. And as love is the grand principle of obedience, and the only incentive to it, so there can be no *obedience* without it. It would be more easy even in Egyptian bondage to make brick without straw, than to do the will of God unless his love be shed abroad in the heart by the Holy Spirit. *Love*, says the apostle, *is the fulfilling of the law;* Rom. xiii. 10.

THE THIRD COMMANDMENT.

Against *false swearing, blasphemy*, and *irreverent use of the name of God.*

Verse 7. *Thou shalt not take the name of the Lord thy God in vain*] This precept not only forbids all *false oaths*, but all *common swearing* where the name of God is used, or where he is appealed to as a witness of the truth. It also necessarily forbids all *light* and *irreverent* mention of God, or any of his attributes; and this the original word לשוא *lashshav* particularly imports: and we may safely add to all these, that every *prayer, ejaculation*, &c., that is not accompanied with *deep reverence* and the *genuine spirit of piety*, is here condemned also. In how many thousands of instances is this commandment broken in the *prayers*, whether *read* or *extempore*, of inconsiderate, bold, and presumptuous worshippers! And how few are there who do not break it, both in their public and private devotions! How low is piety when we are obliged, in order to escape damnation, to pray to God to "pardon the *sins* of our *holy things!*"

Even heathens thought that the names of their gods should be treated with reverence.

Παντως μεν δη καλον επιτηδευμα, θεων ονοματα μη χραινειν ῥᾳδιως, εχοντα ὡς εχουσιν ἡμων ἑκαστοτε τα πολλα οἱ πλειστοι καθαροτητος τε και ἁγνειας τα περι τους θεους.

"It is most undoubtedly right not easily to pollute the names of the gods, using them as we do common names; but to watch with purity and holiness all things belonging to the gods."

The Lord will not hold him guiltless, &c.] Whatever the person himself may think or hope, however he may plead in his own behalf, and say he intends no evil, &c.; if he in any of the above ways, or in any other way, *takes the name of God in vain*, God will *not hold him guiltless*—he will account him *guilty* and punish him for it. Is it necessary to say to any truly spiritual mind, that all such interjections as *O God! my God! good God! good Heavens!* &c., &c., are formal positive breaches of this law? How many who pass for *Christians* are highly criminal here!

THE FOURTH COMMANDMENT.

Against *profanation* of the *Sabbath*, and *idleness* on the *other days* of the *week*.

Verse 8. *Remember the Sabbath day, to keep it holy.*] See what has been already said on this precept, Gen. ii. 2, and elsewhere. As this was the most ancient institution, God calls them to *remember* it; as if he had said, Do not *forget* that when I had finished my creation I instituted the Sabbath, and *remember* why I did so, and for what purposes. The word שבת *shabbath* signifies *rest* or *cessation* from *labour;* and the sanctification of the seventh day is commanded, as having something *representative* in it; and so indeed it has, for it typifies the *rest which remains for the people of God*, and in this light it evidently appears to have been understood by the apostle, Heb. iv. Because this commandment has not been particularly mentioned in the New Testament as a moral precept binding on all, therefore some have presumptuously

A. M. 2513.
B. C. 1491.
An. Exod. Isr. 1.
Sivan.

9 [o] Six days shalt thou labour,
and do all thy work:
10 But the [p] seventh day *is* the
Sabbath of the LORD thy God: *in it* thou shalt
not do any work, thou, nor thy son, nor thy
daughter, thy man-servant, nor thy maid-servant, nor thy cattle, [q] nor thy stranger that *is*
within thy gates:
11 For [r] *in* six days the LORD made heaven and earth, the sea, and all
that in them *is*, and rested the
seventh day; wherefore the
LORD blessed the Sabbath day, and hal
lowed it.
12 [s] Honour thy father and thy mother;
that thy days may be long upon the land
which the LORD thy God giveth thee.
13 [t] Thou shalt not kill.

A. M. 2513.
B. C. 1491.
An. Exod. Isr. 1.
Sivan.

[o] Chap. xxiii. 12; xxxi. 15; xxxiv. 21; Lev. xxiii. 3; Ezek. xx. 12; Luke xiii. 14.——[p] Gen. ii. 2, 3; chap. xvi. 26; xxxi. 15.——[q] Neh. xiii. 16, 17, 18, 19.——[r] Gen. ii. 2.

[s] Chap. xxiii. 26; Lev. xix. 3; Deut. v. 16; Jer. xxxv. 7, 18, 19; Matt. xv. 4; xix. 19; Mark vii. 10; x. 19; Luke xviii. 20; Eph. vi. 2.——[t] Deut. v. 17; Matt. v. 21; Rom. xiii. 9.

inferred that there is *no Sabbath* under the Christian dispensation. The truth is, the Sabbath is considered as a *type*: all types are of full force till the thing signified by them takes place; but the thing signified by the Sabbath is that *rest in glory* which *remains* for the people of God, therefore the moral obligation of the Sabbath must continue till *time* be swallowed up in eternity.

Verse 9. *Six days shalt thou labour*] Therefore he who idles away time on any of the six days, is as guilty before God as he who works on the Sabbath. No work should be done on the Sabbath that can be done on the preceding days, or can be deferred to the succeeding ones. Works of absolute *necessity* and *mercy* are alone excepted. He who works by his *servants* or *cattle* is equally guilty as if he worked himself. *Hiring out horses*, &c., for *pleasure* or *business*, *going on journeys*, *paying worldly visits*, or *taking jaunts* on the Lord's day, are breaches of this law. The whole of it should be devoted to the *rest of the body* and the improvement of the mind. God says *he has hallowed it*—he has made it *sacred* and set it apart for the above purposes. It is therefore the most proper day for public religious worship.

THE FIFTH COMMANDMENT.

Against *disrespect* and *disobedience* to *parents*.

Verse 12. *Honour thy father and thy mother*] There is a degree of affectionate respect which is owing to parents, that no person else can properly claim. For a considerable time parents stand as it were in the place of God to their children, and therefore rebellion against their lawful commands has been considered as rebellion against God. This precept therefore prohibits, not only all injurious acts, irreverent and unkind speeches to parents, but enjoins all necessary acts of kindness, filial respect, and obedience. We can scarcely suppose that a man *honours* his parents who, when they fall weak, blind, or sick, does not exert himself to the uttermost in their support. In such cases God as truly requires the children to *provide* for their parents, as he required the parents to feed, nourish, support, instruct, and defend the children when they were in the lowest state of helpless infancy. See the note on Gen. xlviii. 12. The rabbins say, *Honour the Lord with thy substance*, Prov. iii. 9; and, *Honour thy father and mother*. The LORD is to be honoured thus if thou have it; thy father and mother, whether thou have it or not; for if thou have nothing, thou art bound to *beg* for them. See *Ainsworth*.

That thy days may be long] This, as the apostle observes, Eph. vi. 2, is the *first commandment to which* God has annexed a promise; and therefore we may learn in some measure how important the duty is in the sight of God. In Deut. v. 16 it is said, *And that it may go well with thee*; we may therefore conclude that it will go *ill* with the disobedient; and there is no doubt that the untimely deaths of many young persons are the judicial consequence of their disobedience to their parents. Most who come to an untimely end are obliged to confess that *this*, with the *breach of the Sabbath*, was the principal cause of their ruin. Reader, art thou guilty? Humble thyself therefore before God, and repent. 1. As *children* are bound to succour their parents, so *parents* are bound to educate and instruct their children in all useful and necessary knowledge, and not to bring them up either in *ignorance* or *idleness*. 2. They should teach their children the fear and knowledge of God, for how can they expect affection or dutiful respect from those who have not the fear of God before their eyes? Those who are *best educated* are generally the *most dutiful*. Heathens also inculcated respect to parents.

Ουδεν προς θεων τιμιωτερον αγαλμα αν κτησαιμεθα πατρος και προπατορος παρειμενων γηρᾳ, και μητερων την αυτην δυναμιν εχουσων· οὑς ὁταν αγαλλῃ τις, τιμαις γεγηθεν ὁ θεος.——Πας δη νουν εχων φοβειται και τιμᾳ, γονεων ευχας ειδως πολλοις και πολλακις επιτελεις γενομενας. Plato de Leg., lib. xi., vol. ix, p. 160. Ed. Bipont.

"We can obtain no more honourable possession from the gods than fathers and forefathers worn down with age, and mothers who have undergone the same change, whom when we delight, God is pleased with the honour; and every one that is governed by right understanding fears and reverences them, well knowing that the prayers of parents oftentimes, and in many particulars, have received full accomplishment."

THE SIXTH COMMANDMENT.

Against *murder* and *cruelty*.

Verse 13. *Thou shalt not kill.*] This commandment, which is general, prohibits *murder* of every kind. 1. All *actions* by which the lives of our fellow creatures may be *abridged*. 2. All *wars* for extending empire, commerce, &c. 3. All *sanguinary laws*, by the operation of which the lives of men may be taken away for offences of comparatively trifling demerit

A. M. 2513.
B. C. 1491.
An. Exod. Isr. 1.
Sivan.

14 [u] Thou shalt not commit adultery.

15 [v] Thou shalt not steal.

16 [w] Thou shalt not bear false witness against thy neighbour.

17 [x] Thou shalt not covet thy neighbour's house, [y] thou shalt not covet thy neighbour's wife, nor his man-servant, nor his maid-servant, nor his ox, nor his ass, nor any thing that *is* thy neighbour's.

[u] Deut. v. 18; Matt. v. 27.——[v] Lev. xix. 11; Deut. v. 19; Matt. xix. 18; Rom. xiii. 9; 1 Thess. iv. 6.——[w] Chap. xxiii. 1; Deut. v. 20; xix. 16; Matt. xix. 18.

[x] Deut. v. 21; Mic. ii. 2; Hab. ii. 9; Luke xii. 15; Acts xx. 33; Rom. vii. 7; xiii. 9; Eph. v. 3, 5; Heb. xiii. 5.——[y] Job xxxi. 9; Prov. vi. 29; Jer. v. 8; Matt. v. 28.

4. All *bad dispositions* which lead men to wish evil to, or meditate mischief against, one another; for, says the Scripture, *He that hateth his brother* in his heart *is a murderer*. 5. All *want of charity* to the helpless and distressed; for he who has it in his power to save the life of another by a timely application of succour, food, raiment, &c., and does not do it, and the life of the person either *falls* or is *abridged* on this account, is in the sight of God *a murderer*. He who neglects to save life is, according to an incontrovertible maxim in *law*, the SAME as he who takes it away. 6. All *riot* and *excess*, all *drunkenness* and *gluttony*, all *inactivity* and *slothfulness*, and all *superstitious mortifications* and *self-denials*, by which life may be destroyed or shortened; all these are point-blank sins against the *sixth* commandment.

THE SEVENTH COMMANDMENT.

Against *adultery* and *uncleanness*.

Verse 14. *Thou shalt not commit adultery.*] Adultery, as defined by our laws, is of *two* kinds; *double*, when between two married persons; *single*, when *one* of the parties is married, the other single. One principal part of the *criminality* of adultery consists in its *injustice*. 1. It robs a man of his *right* by taking from him the *affection* of his wife. 2. It does him a *wrong* by fathering on him and obliging him to maintain *as his own* a spurious offspring—a child which is *not* his. The *act* itself, and every thing leading to the act, is prohibited by this commandment; for our Lord says, Even *he who looks on a woman to lust after her, has already committed adultery with her in his heart*. And not only *adultery* (the unlawful commerce between two married persons) is forbidden here, but also *fornication* and all kinds of mental and sensual uncleanness. All impure *books, songs, paintings*, &c., which tend to inflame and debauch the mind, are against this law, as well as another species of impurity, for the account of which the reader is referred to the notes on Gen. xxxviii. at the *end*. That *fornication* was included under this command we may gather from St. Matthew, xv. 19, where our Saviour expresses the sense of the different commandments by a *word for each*, and mentions them *in the order* in which they stand; but when he comes to the seventh he uses two words, μοιχειαι, πορνειαι, to express its meaning, and then goes on to the eighth, &c.; thus evidently showing that fornication was understood to be comprehended under the command, "Thou shalt not commit adultery." As to the word adultery, *adulterium*, it has probably been derived from the words *ad alterius torum, to another's bed*; for it is *going to the bed of another man* that constitutes the *act* and the *crime*. *Adultery* often means idolatry in the worship of God.

THE EIGHTH COMMANDMENT.

Against *stealing* and *dishonesty*.

Verse 15. *Thou shalt not steal.*] All *rapine* and *theft* are forbidden by this precept; as well *national* and *commercial* wrongs as petty larceny, highway robberies, and private stealing: even the taking advantage of a seller's or buyer's ignorance, to give the one *less* and make the other pay *more* for a commodity than its worth, is a breach of this sacred law. All *withholding of rights* and *doing of wrongs* are against the spirit of it. But the word is principally applicable to *clandestine stealing*, though it may undoubtedly include all *political injustice* and *private wrongs*. And consequently all *kidnapping, crimping*, and *slave-dealing* are prohibited here, whether practised by *individuals* or by the *state*. Crimes are not lessened in their demerit by the *number*, or *political importance* of those who commit them. A *state* that enacts *bad laws* is as criminal before God as the *individual* who breaks *good* ones.

It has been supposed that under the *eighth* commandment, injuries done to *character*, the depriving a man of his *reputation* or *good name*, are included; hence those words of one of our poets:—

Good *name* in man or woman
Is the immediate jewel of their souls.
Who *steals* my purse steals trash;—
But he that *filches from* me my good name,
Robs me of that which not enriches him,
And makes me *poor* indeed.

THE NINTH COMMANDMENT.

Against *false testimony, perjury*, &c.

Verse 16. *Thou shalt not bear false witness, &c.*] Not only false oaths, to deprive a man of his *life* or of his *right*, are here prohibited, but all *whispering, tale-bearing, slander*, and *calumny*; in a word, whatever is deposed as a truth, which is false in fact, and tends to injure another in his goods, person, or character, is against the *spirit* and *letter* of this law. *Suppressing the truth* when known, by which a person may be defrauded of his *property* or his *good name*, or lie under injuries or disabilities which a discovery of the truth would have prevented, is also a crime against this law. He who bears a *false* testimony against or belies even the devil himself, comes under the curse of this law, because his testimony is *false*. By the term *neighbour* any *human* being is intended, whether he rank among our *enemies* or *friends*.

THE TENTH COMMANDMENT.

Against *covetousness*.

Verse 17. Thou *shalt not covet thy neighbour's house—wife, &c.*] *Covet* signifies to desire or long after, in order to enjoy as a *property* the person or

a

A. M. 2513. B. C. 1491. An. Exod. Isr. 1. Sivan.

18 And [z] all the people [a] saw the thunderings, and the lightnings, and the noise of the trumpet, and the mountain [b] smoking: and when the people saw *it*, they removed, and stood afar off:

19 And they said unto Moses, [c] Speak thou with us, and we will hear: but [d] let not God speak with us, lest we die.

20 And Moses said unto the people, [e] Fear not: [f] for God is come to prove you, and [g] that his fear may be before your faces, that ye sin not.

21 And the people stood afar off, and Moses drew near unto [h] the thick darkness, where God *was*.

A. M. 2513. B. C. 1491. An. Exod. Isr. 1. Sivan.

22 And the LORD said unto Moses, Thus thou shalt say unto the children of Israel, Ye have seen that I have talked with you [i] from heaven.

23 Ye shall not make [k] with me gods of silver, neither shall ye make unto you gods of gold.

24 An altar of earth thou shalt make unto me, and shalt sacrifice thereon thy burnt offerings, and thy peace-offerings, [l] thy sheep and

[z] Heb. xii. 18.——[a] Rev. i. 10, 12.——[b] Ch. xix. 18.——[c] Deut. v. 27; xviii. 16; Gal. iii. 19, 20; Heb. xii. 19.——[d] Deut. v. 25. [e] 1 Sam. xii. 20; Isa. xli. 10, 13.——[f] Gen. xxii. 1; Deut. xiii. 3.——[g] Deut. iv. 10; vi. 2; x. 12; xvii. 13, 19; xix. 20; xxviii. 58; Prov. iii. 7; xvi. 6; Isa. viii. 13.——[h] Chap. xix. 16; Deut v. 5; 1 Kings viii. 12.——[i] Deut. iv. 36; Neh. ix. 13.——[k] Chap. xxxii. 1, 2, 4; 1 Sam. v. 4, 5; 2 Kings xvii. 33; Ezek. xx. 39, xliii. 8; Dan. v. 4, 23; Zeph. i. 5; 2 Cor. vi. 14, 15, 16.——[l] Lev. i. 2.

thing coveted. He breaks this command who by any means endeavours to deprive a man of his *house* or *farm* by taking them *over his head*, as it is expressed in some countries; who lusts after his neighbour's wife, and endeavours to ingratiate himself into her affections, and to lessen her husband in her esteem; and who endeavours to possess himself of the *servants, cattle*, &c., of another in any clandestine or unjustifiable manner. "This is a most excellent moral precept, the observance of which will prevent all public crimes; for he who feels the force of the law that prohibits the inordinate desire of any thing that is the property of another, can never make a breach in the peace of society by an act of wrong to any of even its feeblest members."

Verse 18. *And all the people saw the thunderings, &c.*] They had witnessed all these awful things before, (see chap. xix. 16,) but *here* they seem to have been repeated; probably at the end of each command, there was a peal of thunder, a blast of the trumpet, and a gleam of lightning, to impress their hearts the more deeply with a due sense of the Divine Majesty, of the holiness of the law which was now delivered, and of the fearful consequences of disobedience. This had the desired effect; the people were impressed with a deep religious fear and a terror of God's judgments; acknowledged themselves perfectly satisfied with the discoveries God had made of himself; and requested that Moses might be constituted the *mediator* between God and them, as they were not able to bear these tremendous discoveries of the *Divine Majesty*. "*Speak thou with us, and we will hear; but let not God speak with us, lest we die;*" ver. 19. This teaches us the absolute necessity of that great Mediator between God and man, Christ Jesus, as no man can come unto the Father but *by him*.

Verse 20. *And Moses said—Fear not: for God is come to prove you, and that his fear may be before your faces*] The maxim contained in this verse is, *Fear not, that ye may fear*—do not fear with such a fear as brings *consternation* into the soul, and produces nothing but terror and confusion; but fear with that *fear* which *reverence* and *filial affection* inspire, *that ye sin not*—that, through the love and reverence ye feel to your Maker and Sovereign, ye may abstain from every appearance of evil, lest you should forfeit that love which is to you better than life. He who fears in the *first* sense can neither *love* nor *obey*; he who *fears not* in the *latter* sense is sure to fall under the first temptation that may occur. *Blessed is the man who thus feareth always.*

Verse 22. *I have talked with you from heaven.*] Though God manifested himself by the *fire*, the *lightning*, the *earthquake*, the *thick darkness*, &c., yet the *ten words*, or *commandments* were probably uttered from the *higher regions of the air*, which would be an additional proof to the people that there was no *imposture* in this case; for though strange appearances and voices might be counterfeited on earth, as was often, no doubt, done by the magicians of Egypt; yet it would be utterly impossible to represent a voice, in a long continued series of instruction, as proceeding from heaven itself, or the higher regions of the atmosphere. This, with the earthquake and repeated thunders, (see on verse 18,) would put the *reality* of this whole procedure beyond all doubt; and this enabled Moses, Deut. v. 26, to make such an appeal to the people on a fact incontrovertible and of infinite importance, that God had indeed talked with them face to face.

Verse 23. *Ye shall not make with me gods of silver*] The expressions here are very remarkable. Before it was said, Ye shall have no other gods BEFORE *me*, על פני *al panai*, ver. 3. Here they are commanded, ye shall not make gods of *silver* or *gold* אתי *itti* WITH *me*, as *emblems* or *representatives* of God, in order, as might be pretended, to keep these displays of his magnificence in memory; on the contrary, he would have only an *altar of earth*—of *plain turf*, on which they should offer those sacrifices by which they should commemorate their own guilt and the necessity of an atonement to reconcile themselves to God. See the note on verse 4.

Verse 24. *Thy burnt-offerings, and thy peace-offerings*] The *law* concerning which was shortly to be given, though sacrifices of this kind were in use from the days of Abel.

A. M. 2513. B. C. 1491. An. Exod. Isr. 1. Sivan.

thine oxen: in all [m] places where
I record my name, I will come
unto thee, and I will [n] bless thee.
25 And [o] if thou wilt make me an altar of
stone, thou shalt not [p] build it of hewn stone;
for if thou lift up thy tool upon
it, thou hast polluted it.
26 Neither shalt thou go up
by steps unto mine altar, [q] that thy nakedness
be not discovered thereon.

[m] Deut. xii. 5, 11, 21; xiv. 23; xvi. 6, 11; xxvi. 2; 1 Kings viii. 43; ix. 3; 2 Chron. vi. 6; vii. 16; xii. 13; Ezra vi. 12; Neh. i. 9; Psa. lxxiv. 7; Jer. vii. 10, 12.

[n] Gen. xii. 2; Deut. vii. 13.——[o] Deut. xxvii. 5; Josh. viii. 31; 1 Mac. iv. 47.——[p] Heb. *build them with hewing;* Deut. xxvii. 5, 6.——[q] Lev. x. 3; Psa. lxxxix. 7; Heb. xii. 28, 29.

In all places where I record my name] Wherever I am worshipped, whether in the open wilderness, at the tabernacle, in the temple, the synagogues, or elsewhere, *I will come unto thee and bless thee.* These words are precisely the same in signification with those of our Lord, Matt. xviii. 20: *For where two or three are gathered together in my name, there am I in the midst of them.* And as it was JESUS who was the angel that spoke to them in the wilderness, Acts vii. 38, from the same mouth *this* promise in the *law* and *that* in the *Gospel* proceeded.

Verse 25. *Thou shalt not build it of hewn stone*] Because they were now in a wandering state, and had as yet no fixed residence; and therefore no time should be wasted to rear costly altars, which could not be transported with them, and which they must soon leave. Besides, they must not lavish skill or expense on the construction of an altar; the altar of itself, whether costly or mean, was nothing in the worship; it was only the *place* on which the victim should be laid, and their mind must be attentively fixed on that God to whom the sacrifice was offered, and on the sacrifice itself, as that appointed by the Lord to make an atonement for their sins.

Verse 26. *Neither shalt thou go up by steps unto mine altar*] The word *altar* comes from *altus, high* or *elevated,* though the Hebrew word מזבח *mizbach,* from זבח *zabach,* to *slay, kill,* &c., signifies merely a *place for sacrifice;* see Gen. viii. 20. But the heathens, who imitated the rites of the true God in their idolatrous worship, made their altars very high; whence they derived their name *altaria, altars,* i. e., very high or elevated places; which they built thus, partly through pride and vain glory, and partly that their gods might the better hear them. Hence also the *high places* or idolatrous altars so often and so severely condemned in the Holy Scriptures. The heathens made some of their altars excessively high; and some imagine that the pyramids were *altars* of this kind, and that the inspired writer refers to those in these prohibitions. God therefore ordered *his* altars to be made, 1. either of simple turf, that there might be no unnecessary expense, which, in their present circumstances, the people could not well afford; and that they might be no incentives to idolatry from their costly or curious structure; or 2. of *unhewn* stone, that no images of animals or of the celestial bodies might be sculptured on them, as was the case among the idolaters, and especially among the Egyptians, as several of their ancient altars which remain to the present day amply testify; which altars themselves, and the images carved on them, became in process of time incentives to idolatry, and even objects of worship. In short, God formed every part of his worship so that every thing belonging to it might be as dissimilar as possible from that of the surrounding heathenish nations, and especially the Egyptians, from whose land they had just now departed. This seems to have been the whole design of those statutes on which many commentators have written so largely and learnedly, imagining difficulties where probably there are none. The *altars* of the tabernacle were of a different kind.

IN this and the preceding chapter we have met with some of the most awful displays of the Divine Majesty; manifestations of justice and holiness which have no parallel, and can have none till that day arrive in which he shall appear in his glory, to judge the quick and the dead. The glory was truly terrible, and to the children of Israel insufferable; and yet how highly privileged to have God himself speaking to them from the midst of the fire, giving them statutes and judgments so righteous, so pure, so holy, and so truly excellent in their operation and their end, that they have been the admiration of all the wise and upright in all countries and ages of the world, where their voice has been heard! Mohammed defied all the poets and literati of Arabia to match the *language* of the *Koran;* and for purity, elegance, and dignity it bore away the palm, and remained unrivalled. This indeed was the only advantage which the work derived from its author; for its other excellences it was indebted to *Moses* and the *prophets,* to *Christ* and the *apostles;* as there is scarcely a pure, consistent, theologic notion in it, that has not been borrowed from our sacred books. Moses calls the attention of the people, not to the *language* in which these Divine laws were given, though that is all that it should be, and every way worthy of its author; compressed yet perspicuous; simple yet dignified; in short, such as God should speak if he wished his creatures to comprehend; but he calls their attention to the purity, righteousness, and usefulness of the grand revelation which they had just received. *For what nation,* says he, *is there so great, who hath God so nigh unto them, as Jehovah our God is, in all things that we call upon him for? And what nation hath statutes and judgments so righteous as all this law which I set before you this day?* And that which was the sum of all excellence in the present case was this, that the GOD who gave these laws dwelt among his people; to him they had continual access, and from him received that power without which obedience so extensive and so holy would have been impossible; and yet not one of these laws exacted more than eternal reason, the nature and fitness of things, the prosperity of the community, and the peace and happiness of the individual, required. *The* LAW *is holy, and the* COMMANDMENT *is* HOLY, JUST, *and* GOOD.

To show still more clearly the excellence and great utility of the ten commandments, and to correct some mistaken notions concerning them, it may be necessary to make a few additional observations. And 1. It is worthy of remark that there is none of these commandments, nor any part of one, which can fairly be considered as merely *ceremonial*. All are *moral*, and consequently of everlasting obligation. 2. When considered merely as to the *letter*, there is certainly no difficulty in the moral obedience required to them. Let every reader take them up one by one, and ask his conscience before God, which of them he is under a *fatal* and *uncontrollable necessity* to break? 3. Though by the incarnation and death of Christ all the *ceremonial* law which referred to him and his sacrifice is necessarily abrogated, yet, as none of these ten commandments refer to any thing properly *ceremonial*, therefore *they* are not abrogated. 4. Though Christ came into the world to redeem them who believe from the curse of the law, he did not redeem them from the necessity of *walking in that newness of life* which these commandments so strongly inculcate. 5. Though Christ is *said* to have *fulfilled the law* for us, yet it is nowhere intimated in the *Scripture* that he has so fulfilled these TEN LAWS, as to exempt us from the necessity and *privilege* of being *no* idolaters, swearers, Sabbath-breakers, disobedient and cruel children, murderers, adulterers, thieves, and corrupt witnesses. All these commandments, it is true, he punctually fulfilled himself; and all these he writes on the heart of every soul redeemed by his blood. 6. Do not those who scruple not to insinuate that the proper observation of these laws is *impossible in this life*, and that *every man since the fall does daily break them in thought, word*, and *deed*, bear false witness against God and his truth? and do they not greatly err, *not knowing the Scripture*, which teaches the necessity of such obedience, nor the *power of God*, by which the evil principle of the heart is destroyed, and the law of purity written on the soul? If even the *regenerate* man, as some have unwarily asserted, does *daily* break *these commands*, these ten words, in *thought, word*, and *deed*, he may be as bad as *Satan* for aught we know; for Satan himself cannot transgress in more *forms* than these, for sin can be committed in no other way, either by bodied or disembodied spirits, than by *thought*, or *word*, or *deed*. Such sayings as these tend to destroy the distinction between good and evil, and leave the infidel and the believer on a par as to their moral state. The people of God should be careful how they use them. 7. It must be granted, and indeed has sufficiently appeared from the preceding exposition of these commandments, that they are not only to be understood in the *letter* but also in the *spirit*, and that therefore they may be *broken* in the *heart* while *outwardly* kept *inviolate;* yet this does not prove that a soul influenced by the grace and spirit of Christ cannot most conscientiously observe them; for the grace of the Gospel not only saves a man from *outward* but also from *inward* sin; for, says the heavenly messenger, *his name shall be called* JESUS, (i. e., *Saviour*,) *because he shall save*, (i. e., DELIVER) *his people* FROM *their sins.* Therefore the weakness or corruption of human nature forms no argument here, because the blood of Christ cleanses from all unrighteousness; and *he* saves to the uttermost all who come unto the Father through him. It is therefore readily granted that no man *unassisted* and *uninfluenced* by the *grace* of Christ can keep these commandments, either in the *letter* or in the *spirit;* but he who is truly converted to God, and has Christ dwelling in his heart by faith, can, in the *letter* and in the *spirit*, do all these things, BECAUSE CHRIST STRENGTHENS *him.*—Reader, the following is a good prayer, and oftentimes thou hast *said* it; now learn to *pray* it: "Lord, have mercy upon us, and *incline* our hearts to keep these laws! Lord, have mercy upon us, and write all these thy laws *in our hearts*, we beseech thee!"—*Com Service*

CHAPTER XXI.

Laws concerning servants. *They shall serve for only seven years*, 1, 2. *If a servant brought a wife to servitude with him, both should go out free on the* seventh *year*, 3. *If his master had given him a wife, and she bore him children, he might go out free on the seventh year, but his wife and children must remain, as the property of the master*, 4. *If, through love to his master, wife, and children, he did not choose to avail himself of the privilege granted by the law, of going out free on the seventh year, his ear was to be bored to the door post with an awl, as an emblem of his being attached to the family for ever*, 5, 6. *Laws concerning* maid-servants, *betrothed to their masters or to the sons of their masters*, 7–11. *Laws concerning* battery *and* murder, 12–15. *Concerning* men-stealing, 16. *Concerning him that* curses his parents, 17. *Of* strife *between man and man*, 18, 19; *between a* master *and his* servants, 20, 21. *Of* injuries *done to women in pregnancy*, 22. *The* LEX TALIONIS, *or law of* like for like, 23–25. *Of injuries done to servants, by which they gain the right of freedom*, 26, 27. *Laws concerning the* ox *which has gored men*, 28–32. *Of the* pit *left uncovered, into which a man or a beast has fallen*, 33, 34. *Laws concerning the* ox *that kills another*, 35, 36.

A. M. 2513.
B. C. 1491.
An. Exod. Isr. 1.
Sivan.

NOW these *are* the judgments which thou shalt [a] set before them.

2 [b] If thou buy a Hebrew servant, six years he shall serve: and in the seventh he shall go out free for nothing.

3 If he came in [c] by himself, he shall go out by himself: if he were married, then his wife shall go out with him.

4 If his master have given him a wife, and she have borne him sons or daughters; the wife and her children shall be her master's, and he shall go out by himself.

A. M. 2513.
B. C. 1491.
An. Exod. Isr. 1.
Sivan.

5 [d] And if the servant [e] shall plainly say, I love my master, my wife, and my children; I will not go out free:

6 Then his master shall bring him unto the [f] judges; he shall also bring him to the door, or unto the door post; and his master shall [g] bore his ear through with an awl; and he shall serve him for ever.

[a] Chap. xxiv. 3, 4; Deut. iv. 14; vi. 1.——[b] Lev. xxv. 39, 40, 41; Deut. xv. 12; Jer. xxxiv. 14.——[c] Heb. *with his body*.

[d] Deut. xv. 16, 17.——[e] Heb. *saying shalt say*.——[f] Chap. xii. 12; xxii. 8, 28.——[g] Psa. xl. 6.

NOTES ON CHAP. XXI.

Verse 1. *Now these* are *the judgments*] There is so much good sense, feeling, humanity, equity, and justice in the following laws, that they cannot but be admired by every intelligent reader; and they are so very plain as to require very little comment. The laws in this chapter are termed *political*, those in the succeeding chapter *judicial*, laws; and are supposed to have been delivered to Moses *alone*, in consequence of the request of the people, chap. xx. 19, that God should communicate his will to Moses, and that Moses should, as mediator, convey it to them.

Verse 2. *If thou buy a Hebrew servant*] Calmet enumerates *six* different ways in which a Hebrew might lose his liberty: 1. In extreme *poverty* they might sell their liberty. Lev. xxv. 39: *If thy brother be waxen poor, and be sold unto thee*, &c. 2. A *father* might *sell his children*. *If a man sell his daughter to be a maid-servant*; see ver. 7. 3. *Insolvent debtors* became the slaves of their creditors. *My husband is dead—and the creditor is come to take unto him my two sons to be bondmen*, 2 Kings iv. 1. 4. A *thief*, if he had not money to pay the fine laid on him by the law, was to be sold for his profit whom he had robbed. *If he have nothing, then he shall be sold for his theft*; chap. xxii. 3, 4. 5. A *Hebrew* was liable to be taken *prisoner* in war, and so sold for a slave. 6. A Hebrew slave who had been ransomed from a Gentile by a Hebrew might be *sold* by him who ransomed him, to one of his *own nation*.

Six years he shall serve] It was an excellent provision in these laws, that no man could finally injure himself by any rash, foolish, or precipitate act. No man could make himself a servant or slave for more than *seven* years; and if he mortgaged the family inheritance, it must return to the family at the *jubilee*, which returned every *fiftieth* year.

It is supposed that the term *six years* is to be understood as referring to the *sabbatical* years; for let a man come into servitude at whatever part of the interim between two sabbatical years, he could not be detained in bondage beyond a sabbatical year; so that if he fell into bondage the *third* year after a sabbatical year, he had but *three* years to serve; if the *fifth*, but *one*. See on chap. xxiii. 11, &c. Others suppose that this privilege belonged only to the year of *jubilee*, beyond which no man could be detained in bondage, though he had been sold only one year before.

Verse 3. *If he came in by himself*] If he and his wife came in together, they were to go out together: in all respects as he entered, so should he go out. This consideration seems to have induced St. Jerome to translate the passage thus: *Cum quali veste intraverat, cum tali exeat.* "He shall have the same coat in going out, as he had when he came in;" i. e., if he came in with a new one, he shall go out with a new one, which was perfectly just, as the former coat must have been worn out in his master's service, and not his own.

Verse 4. *The wife and her children shall be her master's*] It was a law among the Hebrews, that if a Hebrew had children by a Canaanitish woman, those children must be considered as Canaanitish only, and might be sold and bought, and serve for ever. The law here refers to such a case only.

Verse 6. *Shall bring him unto the judges*] אל האלהים *el haelohim*, literally, *to God*; or, as the Septuagint have it, *προς το κριτηριον Θεου*, *to the judgment of God*; who condescended to dwell among his people; who determined all their differences till he had given them laws for all cases, and who, by his omniscience, brought to light the hidden things of dishonesty. See chap. xxii. 8.

Bore his ear through with an awl] This was a ceremony sufficiently significant, as it implied, 1. That he was closely *attached* to that house and family. 2. That he was bound to *hear* all his master's orders, and to *obey* them punctually. Boring of the ear was an ancient custom in the east. It is referred to by *Juvenal*:—

Prior, inquit, ego adsum.
Cur timeam, dubitemve locum defendere? quamvis
Natus *ad* Euphraten, MOLLES *quod in* AURE FENESTRÆ
Arguerint, *licet ipse negem.* *Sat.* i. 102.

"First come, first served, he cries; and I, in spite
Of your great lordships, will maintain my right:
Though *born a slave*, though my *torn* EARS are BORED,
'Tis not the birth, 'tis money makes the lord." DRYDEN.

Calmet quotes a saying from *Petronius* as attesting the same thing; and one from Cicero, in which he rallies a Libyan who pretended he did not hear him: "It is not," said he, "because your *ears* are not *sufficiently bored*;" alluding to his having been a *slave*

a

A. M. 2513.
B. C. 1491.
An. Exod. Isr. 1.
Sivan.

7 And if a man [h] sell his
daughter to be a maid-servant,
she shall not go out [i] as the
men-servants do.
8 If she [k] please not her master, who hath
betrothed her to himself, then shall he let her
be redeemed: to sell her unto a strange nation
he shall have no power, seeing he hath dealt
deceitfully with her.
9 And if he have betrothed her unto his son,
he shall deal with her after the manner of
daughters.
10 If he take him another *wife;* her food,
her raiment, [l] and her duty of marriage, shall
he not diminish.
11 And if he do not these three unto her,
then shall she go out free, without money.
12 [m] He that smiteth a man, so that he die,
shall be surely put to death.
13 And [n] if a man lie not in wait, but God
[o] deliver *him* into his hand; then [p] I will appoint thee a place whither he shall flee.
14 But if a man come [q] presumptuously
upon his neighbour, to slay him
with guile; [r] thou shalt take
him from mine altar, that he
may die.

A. M. 2513.
B. C. 1491.
An. Exod. Isr. 1.
Sivan.

15 And he that smiteth his father, or his
mother, shall be surely put to death.
16 And [s] he that stealeth a man, and [t] selleth
him, or if he be [u] found in his hand, he shall
surely be put to death.
17 And [v] he that [w] curseth his father, or his
mother, shall surely be put to death.
18 And if men strive together, and one
smite [x] another with a stone, or with *his* fist,
and he die not, but keepeth *his* bed:
19 If he rise again, and walk abroad [y] upon
his staff, then shall he that smote *him* be
quit: only he shall pay *for* [z] the loss of his
time, and shall cause *him* to be thoroughly
healed.
20 And if a man smite his servant, or his
maid, with a rod, and he die under his hand;
he shall be surely [a] punished.
21 Notwithstanding, if he continue a day or

[h] Neh. v. 5.——[i] Ver. 2, 3.——[k] Heb. *be evil in the eyes of,* &c. [l] 1 Cor. vii. 3.——[m] Gen. ix. 6; Lev. xxiv. 17; Num. xxxv. 30, 31; Matthew xxvi. 52.——[n] Numbers xxxv. 22; Deut. xix. 4, 5. [o] 1 Sam. xxiv. 4, 10, 18.——[p] Num. xxxv. 11; Deut. xix. 3; Josh. xx. 2.——[q] Num. xv. 30; xxxv. 20; Deut. xix. 11, 12; Heb. x. 26.——[r] 1 Kings ii. 28-34; 2 Kings xi. 15.——[s] Deut. xxiv. 7. [t] Gen. xxxvii. 28.——[u] Chap. xxii. 4.——[v] Lev. xx. 9; Prov. xx. 20; Matt. xv. 4; Mark vii. 10.——[w] Or, *revileth.*——[x] Or, *his neighbour.*——[y] 2 Sam. iii. 29.——[z] Heb. *his ceasing.*——[a] Heb. *avenged;* Gen. iv. 15, 24; Rom. xiii. 4.

Verse 7. *If a man sell his daughter*] This the Jews allowed no man to do but in extreme distress—when he had no goods, either movable or immovable left, even to the clothes on his back; and he had this permission only while she was *unmarriageable.* It may appear at first view strange that such a law should have been given; but let it be remembered, that this servitude could extend, at the utmost, only to *six* years; and that it was nearly the same as in some cases of *apprenticeship* among us, where the parents *bind* the child for *seven years,* and have from the master so much per week during that period.

Verse 9. *Betrothed her unto his son, he shall deal with her*] He shall give her the same dowry he would give to one of his own daughters. From these laws we learn, that if a man's son married his servant, by his father's consent, the father was obliged to treat her in every respect as a *daughter;* and if the son married another woman, as it appears he might do, ver. 10, he was obliged to make no abatement in the privileges of the *first* wife, either in her *food, raiment,* or *duty of marriage.* The word עונתה *onathah,* here, is the same with St. Paul's *οφειλομενην ευνοιαν, the marriage debt,* and with the ὁμιλιαν of the Septuagint, which signifies the *cohabitation of man and wife.*

Verse 11. *These three*] 1. Her *food,* שארה *sheerah,* her *flesh,* for she must not, like a common slave, be fed merely on *vegetables.* 2. Her *raiment*—her private wardrobe, with all occasional necessary additions. And, 3. The *marriage debt*—a due proportion of the husband's time and company.

Verse 13. *I will appoint thee a place whither he shall flee.*] From the earliest times the nearest akin had a right to revenge the murder of his relation, and as this right was universally acknowledged, no law was ever made on the subject; but as this might be abused, and a person who had killed another *accidentally,* having had no previous malice against him, might be put to death by the *avenger of blood,* as the nearest kinsman was termed, therefore God provided the cities of refuge to which the accidental manslayer might flee till the affair was inquired into, and settled by the civil magistrate.

Verse 14. *Thou shalt take him from mine altar*] Before the cities of refuge were assigned, the altar of God was the common *asylum.*

Verse 15. *That smiteth his father, or his mother*] As such a case argued peculiar depravity, therefore no mercy was to be shown to the culprit.

Verse 16. *He that stealeth a man*] By this law every man-stealer, and every receiver of the stolen person, should lose his life; no matter whether the latter stole the man himself, or gave money to a *slave captain* or *negro-dealer* to steal him for him.

Verse 19. *Shall pay for the loss of his time, and shall cause* him *to be thoroughly healed.*] This was a wise and excellent institution, and most courts of justice still regulate their decisions on such cases by this Mosaic precept.

Verse 21. If the slave who had been beaten by his master died under his hand, the master was punished with death; see Gen. ix. 5, 6. But if he survived

A. M. 2513. B. C. 1491. An. Exod. Isr. 1. Sivan.

two, he shall not be punished: for [b] he *is* his money.

22 If men strive, and hurt a woman with child, so that her fruit depart *from her*, and yet no mischief follow: he shall be surely punished, according as the woman's husband will lay upon him; and he shall [c] pay as the judges *determine*.

23 And if *any* mischief follow, then thou shalt give life for life,

24 [d] Eye for eye, tooth for tooth, hand for hand, foot for foot,

25 Burning for burning, wound for wound, stripe for stripe.

26 And if a man smite the eye of his servant, or the eye of his maid, that it perish; he shall let him go free for his eye's sake.

27 And if he smite out his man-servant's tooth, or his maid-servant's tooth; he shall let him go free for his tooth's sake.

28 If an ox gore a man or a woman, that they die: then [e] the ox shall be surely stoned, and his flesh shall not be eaten; but the owner of the ox *shall be* quit.

A. M. 2513. B. C. 1491. An. Exod. Isr. 1. Sivan.

29 But if the ox were wont to push with his horn in time past, and it hath been testified to his owner, and he hath not kept him in, but that he hath killed a man or a woman; the ox shall be stoned, and his owner also shall be put to death.

30 If there be laid on him a sum of money, then shall he give for [f] the ransom of his life whatsoever is laid upon him.

31 Whether he have gored a son, or have gored a daughter, according to this judgment shall it be done unto him.

32 If the ox shall push a man-servant or a maid-servant; he shall give unto their master [g] thirty shekels of silver, and the [h] ox shall be stoned.

[b] Lev. xxv. 45, 46.——[c] Ver. 30; Deut. xxii. 18, 19.——[d] Lev. xxiv. 20; Deut. xix. 21; Matt. v. 38.

[e] Gen. ix. 5.——[f] Ver. 22; Num. xxxv. 31.——[g] See Zech. xi 12, 13; Matt. xxvi. 15; Phil. ii. 7.——[h] Ver. 28.

the beating a *day* or *two* the master was not punished, because it might be presumed that the man died through some other cause. And all penal laws should be construed as favourably as possible to the accused.

Verse 22. *And hurt a woman with child*] As a *posterity* among the Jews was among the peculiar promises of their covenant, and as every man had some reason to think that the Messiah should spring from *his* family, therefore any injury done to a woman with child, by which the fruit of her womb might be destroyed, was considered a very heavy offence; and as the crime was committed principally against the husband, the degree of punishment was left to *his* discretion. But *if mischief followed*, that is, if the child had been fully formed, and was killed by this means, or the woman lost her life in consequence, then the punishment was as in other cases of murder—the person was put to death; ver. 23.

Verse 24. *Eye for eye*] This is the earliest account we have of the *lex talionis*, or law of *like for like*, which afterwards prevailed among the Greeks and Romans. Among the latter, it constituted a part of the *twelve tables*, so famous in antiquity; but the punishment was afterwards changed to a *pecuniary* fine, to be levied at the discretion of the prætor. It prevails less or more in most civilized countries, and is fully acted upon in the canon *law*, in reference to all calumniators: *Calumniator, si in accusatione defecerit, talionem recipiat.* "If the calumniator fail in the proof of his accusation, let him suffer the same punishment which he wished to have inflicted upon the man whom he falsely accused." Nothing, however, of this kind was left to *private revenge;* the magistrate awarded the punishment when the fact was proved, otherwise the *lex talionis* would have utterly destroyed the peace of society, and have sown the seeds of hatred, revenge, and all uncharitableness.

Verse 26. *If a man smite the eye, &c.*] See the following verse.

Verse 27. *If he smite out his—tooth*] It was a noble law that obliged the unmerciful slave-holder to set the slave at liberty whose eye or tooth he had knocked out. If this did not teach them *humanity*, it taught them *caution*, as one rash blow might have deprived them of all right to the future services of the slave; and thus self-interest obliged them to be cautious and circumspect.

Verse 28. *If an ox gore a man*] It is more likely that a *bull* is here intended, as the word signifies *both*, see chap. xxii. 1; and the Septuagint translate the שור *shor* of the original by ταυρος, *a bull*. Mischief of this kind was provided against by most nations. It appears that the Romans *twisted hay about the horns* of their dangerous cattle, that people seeing it might shun them; hence that saying of Horace, Sat., lib. i., sat. 4, ver. 34: *Fœnum habet in cornu, longe fuge.* "He has hay on his horns; fly for life!" The laws of the *twelve tables* ordered, *That the owner of the beast should pay for what damages he committed, or deliver him to the person injured.* See on chap. xxii. 1.

His flesh shall not be eaten] This served to keep up a due detestation of murder, whether committed by man or beast; and at the same time punished the man as far as possible, by the total loss of the beast.

Verse 30. *If there be laid on him a sum of money—the ransom of his life*] So it appears that, though by the law He forfeited his *life*, yet this might be commuted for a *pecuniary* mulct, at which the life of the deceased might be valued by the magistrates.

Verse 32. *Thirty shekels*] Each worth about three shillings English; see Gen. xx. 16; xxiii. 15. So, counting the shekel at its ut*most* value, the life of a slave was valued at *four pounds ten shillings*. And at this price these same vile people valued the life of our blessed

A. M. 2513.
B. C. 1491.
An. Exod. Isr. 1.
Sivan.

33 And if a man shall open a pit, or if a man shall dig a pit, and not cover it, and an ox or an ass fall therein;

34 The owner of the pit shall make *it* good, *and* give money unto the owner of them; and the dead *beast* shall be his.

35 And if one man's ox hurt another's, that he die; then they shall sell the live ox, and divide the money of it; and the dead *ox* also they shall divide.

36 Or if it be known that the ox hath used to push in time past, and his owner hath not kept him in; he shall surely pay ox for ox; and the dead shall be his own.

Lord; see Zech. xi. 12, 13; Matt. xxvi. 15. And in return, the justice of God has ordered it so, that *they have been sold for slaves* into every country of the universe. And yet, strange to tell, they see not the hand of God in so visible a retribution!

Verse 33. *And if a man shall open a pit, or—dig a pit*] That is, if a man shall open a *well* or *cistern* that had been before closed up, or dig a new one; for these two cases are plainly intimated: and if he did this in some public place where there was danger that men or cattle might fall into it; for a man might do as he pleased in his *own grounds*, as those were his private right. In the above case, if he had neglected to cover the pit, and his neighbour's ox or ass was killed by falling into it, he was to pay its value in money. The 33d and 34th verses seem to be out of their places. They probably should conclude the chapter, as, where they are, they interrupt the statutes concerning the *goring ox*, which begin at verse 28.

These different regulations are as remarkable for their justice and prudence as for their humanity. Their great tendency is to show the valuableness of human life, and the necessity of having peace and good understanding in every neighbourhood; and they possess that quality which should be the object of all good and wholesome laws—the *prevention of crimes*. Most criminal codes of jurisprudence seem more intent on the punishment of crimes than on *preventing* the commission of them. The law of God always *teaches* and *warns*, that his creatures may not fall into condemnation; for judgment is his strange work, i. e., one reluctantly and seldom executed, as this text is frequently understood.

CHAPTER XXII.

Laws concerning theft, 1–4; *concerning* trespass, 5; *concerning* casualties, 6. *Laws concerning* deposits, *or goods left in custody of others, which may have been* lost, stolen, *or* damaged, 7–13. *Laws concerning things* borrowed *or let out on* hire, 14, 15. *Laws concerning* seduction, 16, 17. *Laws concerning* witchcraft, 18; bestiality, 19; idolatry, 20. *Laws concerning* strangers, 21; *concerning* widows, 22–24; lending *money to the* poor, 25; *concerning* pledges, 26; *concerning* respect *to* magistrates, 28; *concerning the* first ripe fruits, *and the* first-born *of* man *and* beast, 29, 30. *Directions concerning* carcasses *found* torn *in the field*, 31.

A. M. 2513.
B. C. 1491.
An. Exod. Isr. 1.
Sivan.

IF a man shall steal an ox, or a [a] sheep, and kill it, or sell it; he shall restore five oxen for an ox, and [b] four sheep for a sheep.

2 If a thief be found [c] break-

[a] Or, *goat*.——[b] 2 Sam. xii. 6; Luke xix. 8; see Prov. vi. 31. [c] Matt. xxiv. 43.

NOTES ON CHAP. XXII.

Verse 1. *If a man shall steal*] This chapter consists chiefly of *judicial* laws, as the preceding chapter does of *political*; and in it the same good sense, and well-marked attention to the welfare of the community and the moral improvement of each individual, are equally evident.

In our translation of this verse, by rendering different Hebrew words by the same term in English, we have greatly obscured the sense. I shall produce the verse with the original words which I think improperly translated, because *one English* term is used for *two Hebrew* words, which in this place certainly do not mean the same thing. *If a man shall steal an ox* (שור *shor*) *or a sheep*, (שה *seh*,) *and kill it, or sell it; he shall restore five oxen* (בקר *bakar*) *for an ox*, (שור *shor*,) *and four sheep* (צאן *tson*) *for a sheep* (שה *seh*.) I think it must appear evident that the sacred writer did not intend that these words should be understood as above. A *shor* certainly is different from a *bakar*, and a *seh* from a *tson*. Where the difference in every case lies, wherever these words occur, it is difficult to say. The *shor* and the *bakar* are doubtless creatures of the *beeve* kind, and are used in different parts of the sacred writings to signify the *bull*, the *ox*, the *heifer*, the *steer*, and the *calf*. The *seh* and the *tson* are used to signify the *ram*, the *wether*, the *ewe*, the *lamb*, the *he-goat*, the *she-goat*, and the *kid*. And the latter word צאן *tson* seems frequently to signify the *flock*, composed of either of these lesser cattle, or both sorts conjoined.

As שור *shor* is used, Job xxi. 10, for a *bull*, probably it may mean so here. *If a man steal a* BULL *he shall give five* OXEN *for him*, which we may presume was

A. M. 2513. B. C. 1491. An. Exod. Isr. 1. Sivan.

ing up, and be smitten that he die, *there shall* [d] no blood *be shed* for him.

3 If the sun be risen upon him, *there shall be* blood *shed* for him; *for* he should make full restitution; if he have nothing, then he shall be [e] sold for his theft.

4 If the theft be certainly [f] found in his hand alive, whether it be ox, or ass, or sheep; he shall [g] restore double.

5 If a man shall cause a field or vineyard to be eaten, and shall put in his beast, and shall feed in another man's field; of the best of his own field, and of the best of his own vineyard, shall he make restitution.

6 If fire break out, and catch in thorns, so that the stacks of corn, or the standing corn, or the field, be consumed *therewith;* he that kindled the fire shall surely make restitution.

A. M. 2513. B. C. 1491. An. Exod. Isr. 1. Sivan.

7 If a man shall deliver unto his neighbour money or stuff to keep, and it be stolen out of the man's house; [h] if the thief be found, let him pay double.

8 If the thief be not found, then the master of the house shall be brought unto the [i] judges, *to see* whether he have put his hand unto his neighbour's goods.

9 For all manner of trespass, *whether it be* for ox, for ass, for sheep, for raiment, *or* for

[d] Num. xxxv. 27.——[e] Ch. xxi. 2.——[f] Chap. xxi. 16.——[g] See ver. 1, 7; Prov. vi. 31.——[h] Ver. 4.——[i] Chap. xxi. 6; ver. 28.

no more than his real value, as very few *bulls* could be kept in a country destitute of *horses*, where *oxen* were so necessary to till the ground. For though some have imagined that there were no castrated cattle among the Jews, yet this cannot be admitted on the above reason; for as they had no horses, and bulls would have been unmanageable and dangerous, they must have had *oxen* for the purposes of agriculture. *Tson* צאן is used for a flock either of *sheep* or *goats*, and *seh* שה for an individual of either species. For every *seh*, four, taken indifferently from the *tson* or flock, must be given; i. e., a sheep stolen might be recompensed with four out of the *flock*, whether of sheep or goats: so that a *goat* might be compensated with four *sheep*, or a *sheep* with four *goats*.

Verse 2. *If a thief be found*] If a thief was found breaking into a house in the night season, he might be killed; but not if the sun had risen, for then he might be known and taken, and the restitution made which is mentioned in the succeeding verse. So by the law of England it is a burglary to break and enter a house by night; and "anciently the *day* was accounted to begin only from sunrising, and to end immediately upon sunset: but it is now generally agreed that if there be daylight enough begun or left, either by the *light of the sun* or *twilight*, whereby the countenance of a person may reasonably be discerned, it is no burglary; but that this does not extend to *moonlight*, for then many *midnight* burglaries would go unpunished. And besides, the *malignity* of the offence does not so properly arise, as Mr. Justice *Blackstone* observes, from its being done in the dark, as at the *dead of night*, when all the creation except beasts of prey are at rest; when sleep has disarmed the owner, and rendered his castle defenceless."—*East's Pleas of the Crown*, vol. ii., p. 509.

Verse 4. *He shall restore double.*] In no case of theft was the life of the offender taken away; the utmost that the law says on this point is, that, if when *found breaking into a house, he should be smitten so as to die*, no *blood should be shed for him;* ver. 2. If he had *stolen* and *sold* the property, then he was to restore *four* or *fivefold*, ver. 1; but if the animal was found *alive* in his possession, he was to restore *double*.

Verse 6. *If fire break out*] Mr. Harmer observes that it is a common custom in the east to set the dry herbage on fire before the autumnal rains, which fires, for want of care, often do great damage: and in countries where great drought prevails, and the herbage is generally parched, great caution was peculiarly necessary; and a law to guard against such evils, and to punish inattention and neglect, was highly expedient. See *Harmer's* Observat., vol. iii., p. 310, &c.

Verse 7. *Deliver unto his neighbour*] This is called *pledging* in the law of *bailments;* it is a deposit of goods by a debtor to his creditor, to be kept till the debt be discharged. Whatever goods were thus left in the hands of another person, that person, according to the Mosaic law, became responsible for them; if they were stolen, and the thief was found, *he* was to pay double; if he could not be found, the *oath* of the person who had them in keeping, made before the magistrates, that he knew nothing of them, was considered a full acquittance. Among the Romans, if goods were lost which a man had intrusted to his neighbour, the depositary was obliged to pay their full value. But if a man had been driven by necessity, as in case of fire, to lodge his goods with one of his neighbours, and the goods were lost, the depositary was obliged to pay double their value, because of his unfaithfulness in a case of such distress, where his dishonesty, connected with the destruction by the *fire*, had completed the ruin of the sufferer. To this case the following law is applicable: *Cum quis fidem elegit, nec depositum redditur, contentus esse debet simplo: cum vero extante necessitate deponat, crescit perfidiæ crimen*, &c.—Digest., lib. xvi., tit. 3, l. 1.

Verse 8. *Unto the judges*] See the note on chap. xxi. 6.

Verse 9. *Challengeth to be his*] It was necessary that such a matter should come before the judges, because the person in whose possession the goods were found might have had them by a fair and honest purchase; and, by sifting the business, the thief might be

A. M. 2513.
B. C. 1491.
An. Exod. Isr. 1.
Sivan.

any manner of lost thing, which
another challengeth to be his, the
[k] cause of both parties shall
come before the judges; *and* whom the judges
shall condemn, he shall pay double unto his
neighbour.
10 If a man deliver unto his neighbour an
ass, or an ox, or a sheep, or any beast, to keep;
and it die, or be hurt, or driven away, no man
seeing *it:*
11 *Then* shall an [l] oath of the LORD be between them both, that he hath not put his
hand unto his neighbour's goods; and the
owner of it shall accept *thereof,* and he shall
not make *it* good.
12 And [m] if it be stolen from him, he shall
make restitution unto the owner thereof.
13 If it be torn in pieces, *then*
let him bring it *for* witness, *and*
he shall not make good that
which was torn.

A. M. 2513.
B. C. 1491.
An. Exod. Isr. 1.
Sivan.

14 And if a man borrow *aught* of his
neighbour, and it be hurt, or die, the owner thereof *being* not with it, he shall surely make *it* good.
15 *But* if the owner thereof *be* with it, he
shall not make *it* good: if it *be* a hired *thing,*
it came for his hire.
16 And [n] if a man entice a maid that is not
betrothed, and lie with her, he shall surely
endow her to be his wife.
17 If her father utterly refuse to give her
unto him, he shall [o] pay money, according to
the [p] dowry of virgins.
18 [q] Thou shalt not suffer a witch to live.

[k] Deut. xxv. 1; 2 Chron. xix. 10.——[l] Heb. vi. 16.——[m] Gen. xxxi. 39.——[n] Deut. xxii. 28, 29.——[o] Heb. *weigh*; Gen. xxiii. 16.

[p] Gen. xxxiv. 12; Deut. xxii. 29; 1 Sam. xviii. 25.——[q] Lev. xix. 26, 31; xx. 27; Deut. xviii. 10, 11; 1 Sam. xxviii. 3, 9.

found out, and if found, be obliged to pay *double* to his neighbour.

Verse 11. *An oath of the Lord be between them*] So solemn and awful were all appeals to God considered in those ancient times, that it was taken for granted that the man was innocent who could by an oath appeal to the omniscient God that he had not put his hand to his neighbour's goods. Since oaths have become *multiplied,* and since they have been administered on the most *trifling occasions,* their solemnity is gone, and their importance little regarded. Should the oath ever reacquire its weight and importance, it must be when administered only in cases of peculiar delicacy and difficulty, and as sparingly as in the days of Moses.

Verse 13. *If it be torn in pieces—let him bring it for witness*] Rather, *Let him bring* עד הטרפה *ed hat-terephah, a testimony* or *evidence of the torn thing,* such as the *horns, hoofs,* &c. This is still a law in some countries among graziers: if a horse, cow, sheep, or goat, intrusted to them, be lost, and the keeper asserts it was devoured by dogs, &c., the law obliges him to produce the *horns* and *hoofs,* because on these the owner's mark is generally found. If these can be produced, the keeper is acquitted by the law. The *ear* is often the place marked, but this is not absolutely required, because a ravenous beast may eat the *ear* as well as any other part, but he cannot eat the *horns* or the *hoofs.* It seems however that in after times *two* of the *legs* and the *ear* were required as evidences to acquit the shepherd of all guilt. See Amos iii. 12.

Verse 16. *If a man entice a maid*] This was an exceedingly wise and humane law, and must have operated powerfully against seduction and fornication; because the person who might feel inclined to take the advantage of a young woman knew that he must marry her, and give her a dowry, if her parents consented; and if they did not consent that their daughter should wed her seducer, in this case he was obliged to give her the full dowry which could have been demanded had she been still a virgin. According to the *Targumist* here, and to Deut. xxii. 29, the dowry was *fifty shekels* of silver, which the seducer was to pay to her father, and he was obliged to take her to wife; nor had he authority, according to the Jewish canons, *ever to put her away by a bill of divorce.* This one consideration was a powerful curb on disorderly passions, and must tend greatly to render marriages respectable, and prevent all crimes of this nature.

Verse 18. *Thou shalt not suffer a witch to live.*] If there had been no *witches,* such a law as this had never been made. The existence of the *law,* given under the direction of the Spirit of God, proves the existence of the *thing.* It has been doubted whether מכשפה *mecashshephah,* which we translate *witch,* really means a person who practised divination or sorcery by spiritual or infernal agency. Whether the persons thus denominated only *pretended* to have an art which had no existence, or whether they *really* possessed the power commonly attributed to them, are questions which it would be improper to discuss at length in a work of this kind; but that *witches, wizards,* those *who dealt with familiar spirits,* &c., are represented in the sacred writings as actually possessing a power to evoke the dead, to perform supernatural operations, and to discover hidden or secret things by spells, charms, incantations, &c., is evident to every unprejudiced reader of the Bible. Of Manasseh it is said: *He caused his children to pass through the fire in the valley of the son of Hinnom: also he observed times* [ועונן *veonen, he used divination by clouds*] *and used enchantments, and used witchcraft,* [וכשף *vechishsheph,*] *and dealt with a familiar spirit,* [ועשה אוב *veasah ob,* performed a variety of operations by means of what was afterwards called the *πνευμα πυθωνος,* the *spirit of Python,*] *and with wizards,* [ידעוני *yiddeoni,* the *wise* or *knowing ones;*] *and he wrought much evil in the sight of the Lord,* 2 Chron. xxxiii. 6. It is very likely that the Hebrew כשף *cashaph,* and the Arabic كشف *cashafa,* had originally the same meaning, to

A. M. 2513. B. C. 1491. An. Exod. Isr. 1. Sivan.

19 [r] Whosoever lieth with a
beast shall surely be put to
death.
20 [s] He that sacrificeth unto *any* god, save
unto the LORD only, he shall be utterly destroyed.
21 [t] Thou shalt neither vex a stranger, nor
oppress him: for ye were strangers in the land
of Egypt.
22 [u] Ye shall not afflict any widow, or fatherless child.
23 If thou afflict them in any
wise, and they [v] cry at all unto
me, I will surely [w] hear their cry;
24 And my [x] wrath shall wax hot, and I
will kill you with the sword; and [y] your
wives shall be widows, and your children
fatherless.
25 [z] If thou lend money to *any of* my peo
ple *that is* poor by thee, thou shalt not be to
him as a usurer, neither shalt thou lay upon
him usury.

A. M. 2513. B. C. 1491. An. Exod. Isr. 1. Sivan.

[r] Lev. xviii. 23; xx. 15.——[s] Num. xxv. 2, 7, 8; Deut. xiii. 1, 2, 5, 6, 9, 13, 14, 15; xvii. 2, 3, 5; 1 Mac. ii. 24.——[t] Chapter xxiii. 9; Lev. xix. 33; xxv. 35; Deut. x. 19; Jer. vii. 6; Zech. vii. 10; Mal. iii. 5.——[u] Deut. x. 18; xxiv. 17; xxvii. 19; Psa. xciv. 6; Isa. i. 17, 23; x. 2; Ezek. xxii. 7; Zech. vii. 10; James i. 27.——[v] Deut. xv. 9; xxiv. 15; Job xxxv. 9; Luke xviii. 7. [w] Ver. 23; Job xxxiv. 28; Psa. xviii. 6; cxlv. 19; James v. 4. [x] Job xxxi. 23; Psa. lxix. 24.——[y] Psalm cix. 9; Lam. v. 3 [z] Lev. xxv. 35, 36, 37; Deut. xxiii. 19, 20; Neh. v. 7; Psa. xv 5; Ezek. xviii. 8, 17.

uncover, to *remove a veil*, to *manifest*, *reveal*, *make bare* or *naked;* and مكاشفات *mecashefat* is used to signify *commerce with God*. See *Wilmet* and *Giggeius*. . The *mecashshephah* or *witch*, therefore, was probably a person who professed to *reveal hidden mysteries*, by *commerce with God*, or the *invisible world*.

From the severity of this law against witches, &c., we may see in what light these were viewed by Divine justice. They were seducers of the people from their allegiance to God, on whose judgment alone they should depend; and by impiously prying into futurity, assumed an attribute of God, *the foretelling of future events*, which implied in itself the grossest blasphemy, and tended to corrupt the minds of the people, by leading them away from God and the revelation he had made of himself. Many of the Israelites had, no doubt, learned these curious arts from their long residence with the Egyptians; and so much were the Israelites attached to them, that we find such arts in repute among them, and various practices of this kind prevailed through the whole of the Jewish history, notwithstanding the offence was capital, and in all cases punished with *death*.

Verse 19. *Lieth with a beast*] If this most abominable crime had not been common, it never would have been mentioned in a sacred code of laws. It is very likely that it was an *Egyptian* practice; and it is certain, from an account in Sonnini's Travels, that it is practised in Egypt to the present day.

Verse 20. *Utterly destroyed.*] The word חרם *cherem* denotes a thing utterly and finally separated from God and devoted to destruction, without the possibility of redemption.

Verse 21. *Thou shalt neither vex a stranger*, nor *oppress him*] This was not only a very *humane* law, but it was also the offspring of a sound policy: "Do *not vex a stranger;* remember ye were strangers. Do not *oppress* a stranger; remember ye were *oppressed*. Therefore do unto all men as ye would they should do to you." It was the produce of a sound policy: "Let strangers be well treated among you, and many will come to take refuge among you, and thus the strength of your country will be increased. If refugees of this kind be treated well, they will become proselytes to your religion, and thus their souls may be saved." In every point of view, therefore, justice, humanity, sound policy, and religion, say, *Neither vex nor oppress a stranger.*

Verse 22. *Ye shall not afflict any widow, or fatherless child.*] It is remarkable that offences against this law are not left to the discretion of the *judges* to be punished; God reserves the punishment to himself, and by this he strongly shows his abhorrence of the crime. It is no common crime, and shall not be punished in a common way; the *wrath of God shall wax hot* against him who *in any wise* afflicts or wrongs a *widow* or a *fatherless child:* and we may rest assured that he who *helps* either does a service highly acceptable in the sight of God.

Verse 25. *Neither shalt thou lay upon him usury.*] נשך *neshech*, from *nashach*, to *bite*, *cut*, or *pierce* with the *teeth; biting usury*. So the Latins call it *usura vorax*, *devouring usury*. "The increase of usury is called נשך *neshech*, because it resembles the biting of a serpent; for as this is so small as scarcely to be perceptible at first, but the venom soon spreads and diffuses itself till it reaches the vitals, so the *increase of usury*, which at first is not perceived nor felt, at length grows so much as by degrees to devour another's substance."—*Leigh*.

It is evident that what is here said must be understood of accumulated usury, or what we call *compound interest* only; and accordingly נשך *neshech* is mentioned with and distinguished from תרבית *tarbith* and מרבית *marbith*, *interest* or *simple interest*, Lev. xxv. 36, 37; Prov. xxviii. 8; Ezek. xviii. 8, 13, 17, and xxii. 12.—*Parkhurst*.

Perhaps *usury* may be more properly defined *unlawful interest*, receiving more for the loan of money than it is really worth, and more than the law allows. It *is* a wise regulation in the laws of England, that if a man be convicted of *usury*—taking unlawful interest, the *bond* or *security* is rendered void, and he forfeits *treble the sum* borrowed. Against such an oppressive practice the wisdom of God saw it essentially necessary to make a law to prevent a people, who were naturally what our Lord calls the Pharisees, φιλαργυροι, *lovers of money*, (Luke xvi. 14,) from oppressing each other; and who, notwithstanding the

A. M. 2513.
B. C. 1491.
An. Exod. Isr. 1.
Sivan.

26 [a] If thou at all take thy neighbour's raiment to pledge, thou shalt deliver it unto him by that the sun goeth down :

27 For that *is* his covering only, it *is* his raiment for his skin : wherein shall he sleep ? and it shall come to pass, when he [b] crieth

unto me, that I will hear ; for I am [c] gracious.

A. M. 2513.
B. C. 1491.
An. Exod. Isr. L
Sivan.

28 [d] Thou shalt not revile the [e] gods, nor curse the ruler of thy people.

29 Thou shalt not delay *to offer* [f] the [g] first of thy ripe fruits, and of thy [h] liquors : [i] the first-born of thy sons shalt thou give unto me

[a] Deut. xxiv. 6, 10, 13, 17 ; Job xxii. 6 ; xxiv. 3, 9 ; Proverbs xx. 16 ; xxii. 27 ; Ezek. xviii. 7, 16 ; Amos ii. 8.——[b] Verse 23. [c] Chap. xxxiv. 6 ; 2 Chron. xxx. 9 ; Psa. lxxxvi. 15.

[d] Eccles. x. 20 ; Acts xxiii. 5 ; Jude 8.——[e] Or, *Judges* ; ver. 8, 9 ; Psa. lxxxii. 6.——[f] Heb. *thy fulness.*——[g] Chap. xxiii. 16 19 ; Prov. iii. 9.——[h] Heb. *tear.*——[i] Ch. xiii. 2, 12 ; xxxiv. 19.

law in the text, practise usury in all places of their dispersion to the present day.

Verse 26. *If thou—take thy neighbour's raiment to pledge*] It seems strange that any pledge should be taken which must be so *speedily* restored ; but it is very likely that the pledge was restored by *night* only, and that he who pledged it brought it back to his creditor next morning. The opinion of the rabbins is, that whatever a man needed for the support of life, he had the use of it when absolutely necessary, though it was pledged. Thus he had the use of his working tools by day, but he brought them to his creditor in the evening. His *hyke*, which serves an Arab as a *plaid* does a Highlander, (see it described chap. xii. 34,) was probably the *raiment* here referred to : it is a sort of coarse blanket, about six yards long, and five or six feet broad, which an Arab always carries with him, and on which he sleeps at night, it being his only substitute for a bed. As the fashions in the east scarcely ever change, it is very likely that the raiment of the Israelites was precisely the same with that of the modern Arabs, who live in the very same desert in which the Hebrews were when this law was given. How necessary it was to restore the *hyke* to a poor man before the going down of the sun, that he might have something to repose on, will appear evident from the above considerations. At the same time, the returning it *daily* to the creditor was a continual acknowledgment of the debt, and served instead of a written acknowledgment or *bond*; as we may rest assured that writing, if practised at all before the giving of the law, was not common : but it is most likely that it did not exist.

Verse 28. *Thou shalt not revile the gods*] Most commentators believe that the word *gods* here means *magistrates*. The original is אלהים *Elohim*, and should be understood of the true God only : *Thou shalt not blaspheme* or *make light of* [תקלל *tekallel*] *God*, the fountain of justice and power, *nor curse the ruler of thy people*, who derives his authority from God. We shall ever find that he who despises a good civil government, and is disaffected to that under which he lives, is one who has little fear of God before his eyes. The spirit of disaffection and sedition is ever opposed to the religion of the Bible. When those who have been pious get under the spirit of misrule, they infal- libly get shorn of their spiritual strength, and become like salt that has lost its savour. He who can indulge himself in speaking evil of the civil ruler, will soon learn to blaspheme God. The highest authority says, *Fear God : honour the king.*

Verse 29. *The first of thy ripe fruits*] This offer- ing was a public acknowledgment of the bounty and goodness of God, who had given them their proper *seed time*, the *first* and the *latter rain*, and the *appoint- ed weeks of harvest*.

From the practice of the people of God the heathens borrowed a similar one, founded on the same reason. The following passage from *Censorinus*, *De Die Na- tali*, is beautiful, and worthy of the deepest attention :—

Illi enim (majores nostri) qui alimenta, patriam, lucem, se denique ipsos deorum dono habebant, ex omni- bus aliquid diis sacrabant, magis adeo, ut se gratos approbarent, quam quod deos arbitrarentur hoc indi- gere. Itaque cum perceperant fruges, antequam vesce- rentur, Diis libare instituerunt : et cum agros atque urbes, deorum munera, possiderent, partem quandam templis sacellisque, ubi eos celerent, dicavere.

" Our ancestors, who held their food, their country the light, and all that they possessed, from the bounty of the gods, consecrated to them a part of all their property, rather as a token of their gratitude, than from a conviction that the gods needed any thing. Therefore as soon as the harvest was got in, *before they had tasted of the fruits*, they appointed libations to be made to the gods. And as they held their fields and cities as gifts from their gods, they consecrated a certain part for temples and shrines, where they migh worship them."

Pliny is express on the same point, who attests that the Romans never tasted either their new corn or wine, till the priests had offered the FIRST-FRUITS to the gods. *Ac ne degustabant quidem, novas fruges aut vina, antequam sacerdotes* PRIMITIAS LIBASSENT.— Hist. Nat., lib. xviii., c. 2.

Horace bears the same testimony, and shows that his countrymen offered, not only their *first-fruits*, but the *choicest* of all their fruits, to the Lares or house- hold gods ; and he shows also the wickedness of those who sent these as presents to the *rich*, before the gods had been thus honoured :—

Dulcia poma,
Et quoscumque feret cultus tibi fundus honores
Ante Larem gustet venerabilior Lare dives.
Sat., lib. ii., s. v., ver. 12

" What your garden yields,
The choicest honours of your cultured fields,
To him be sacrificed, and let him taste,
Before your gods, the vegetable feast." DUNKIN.

And to the same purpose Tibullus, in one of the most beautiful of his elegies :—

A. M. 2513.
B. C. 1491.
An. Exod. Isr. 1.
Sivan.

30 [k] Likewise shalt thou do
with thine oxen, *and* with thy
sheep: [l] seven days it shall be
with his dam; on the eighth day thou shalt
give it me.

31 And ye shall be [m] holy
men unto me: [n] neither shall
ye eat *any* flesh *that is* torn of
beasts in the field; ye shall cast it to the
dogs.

[k] Deut. xv. 19.——[l] Lev. xxii. 27.——[m] Chap. xix. 6; Lev. xix. 2; Deut. xiv. 21.——[n] Lev. xxii. 8; Ezek. iv. 14; xliv. 31.

Et quodcumque mihi pomum novus educat annus,
Libatum agricolæ ponitur ante deo.
Flava Ceres, tibi sit nostro de rure corona
Spicea, quæ templi pendeat ante fores.
Eleg., lib. i., eleg. i. ver. 13.

"My grateful *fruits*, the *earliest* of the year,
Before the *rural god* shall daily wait.
From Ceres' gifts I'll cull each *browner ear*,
And hang a *wheaten wreath* before her gate."
GRAINGER.

The same subject he touches again in the fifth elegy of the same book, where he specifies the different offerings made for the produce of the *fields*, of the *flocks*, and of the *vine*, ver. 27 :—

Illa deo sciet agricolæ pro vitibus uvam,
Pro segete spicas, pro grege ferre dopem.

"With pious care will load each rural shrine,
For *ripen'd* crops a *golden sheaf* assign,
Cates for my *fold*, *rich clusters* for my *wine*."
Id.—See *Culmet.*

These quotations will naturally recall to our memory the offerings of Cain and Abel, mentioned Gen. iv. 3, 4.

The rejoicings at our *harvest-home* are distorted remains of that gratitude which our ancestors, with all the primitive inhabitants of the earth, expressed to God with appropriate signs and ceremonies. Is it not possible to restore, in some goodly form, a custom so pure, so edifying, and so becoming? There is a laudable custom, observed by some pious people, of dedicating a new house to God by prayer, &c., which cannot be too highly commended.

Verse 30. *Seven days it shall be with his dam*] For the *mother's health* it was necessary that the young one should suck so long; and prior to this time the process of nutrition in a young animal can scarcely be considered as completely formed. Among the Romans *lambs* were not considered as pure or clean before the *eighth day*; nor *calves* before the *thirtieth: Pecoris fœtus die octavo purus est, bovis trigesimo.*—Plin. Hist. Nat., lib. viii.

Verse 31. *Neither shall ye eat—flesh—torn of beasts in the field*] This has been supposed to be an ordinance against eating flesh cut off the animal while alive, and so the Syriac seems to have understood it. If we can credit Mr. Bruce, this is a frequent custom in Abyssinia; but human nature revolts from it. The *reason* of the prohibition against eating the flesh of animals that had been *torn*, or as we term it *worried* in *the field*, appears to have been simply this: That the people might not eat the *blood*, which in this case must be coagulated in the flesh; and the *blood*, being *the life of the beast*, and emblematical of the *blood of the covenant*, was ever to be held sacred, and was prohibited from the days of Noah. See on Gen. ix. 4.

IN the conclusion of this chapter we see the grand reason of all the ordinances and laws which it contains. No command was issued merely from the *sovereignty* of God. He gave them to the people as restraints on disorderly passions, and incentives to holiness; and hence he says, *Ye shall be holy men unto me.* Mere outward services could neither *please him* nor *profit them*; for from the very beginning of the world the end of the commandment was love out of a pure heart and good conscience, and faith unfeigned, 1 Tim. i. 5. And without these accompaniments no set of religious duties, however punctually performed, could be pleasing in the sight of that God who seeks truth in the inward parts, and in whose eyes the faith that worketh by love is alone valuable. A *holy heart* and a *holy, useful life* God invariably requires in all his worshippers. Reader, how standest *thou* in his sight?

CHAPTER XXIII.

Laws against evil-speaking, 1. *Against* bad company, 2. *Against* partiality, 3. *Laws commanding acts of* kindness *and* humanity, 4, 5. *Against* oppression, 6. *Against* unrighteous decisions, 7. *Against* bribery *and* corruption, 8. *Against* unkindness to strangers, 9. *The* ordinance *concerning the* Sabbatical year, 10, 11. *The* Sabbath *a day of rest*, 12. *General directions concerning circumcision, &c.*, 13. *The three annual festivals*, 14. *The feast of* unleavened bread, 15. *The feast of* harvest, *and the feast of* ingathering, 16. *All the males to appear before God thrice in a year*, 17. *Different* ordinances—no blood *to be offered with leavened bread—no* fat *to be left till the next day—the* first fruits *to be brought to the house of God—and a kid not to be seethed in its mother's milk*, 18, 19. *Description of the Angel of God, who was to lead the people into the promised land, and drive out the Amorites, &c.*, 20–23. Idolatry *to be avoided, and the images of idols destroyed*, 24. *Different promises to* obedience, 25–27. Hornets *shall be sent to drive out the Canaanites, &c.*, 28. *The ancient inhabitants to be driven out by little and little, and the* reason *why*, 29, 30. *The boundaries of the promised land*, 31. *No league or covenant to be made with the ancient inhabitants, who are all to be utterly expelled*, 32, 33.

A. M. 2513. B. C. 1491. An. Exod. Isr. 1. Sivan.

THOU [a] shalt not [b] raise a
false report: put not thine
hand with the wicked to be an
[c] unrighteous witness.
2 [d] Thou shalt not follow a multitude to *do*
evil; [e] neither shalt thou [f] speak in a cause
to decline after many to wrest *judgment:*
3 Neither shalt thou countenance a poor
man in his cause.
4 [g] If thou meet thine enemy's ox or his ass
going astray, thou shalt surely bring it back
to him again.
5 [h] If thou see the ass of him that hateth
thee lying under his burden, [i] and wouldest forbear to help him, thou shalt surely
help with him.
6 [k] Thou shalt not wrest the
judgment of thy poor in his cause.
7 [l] Keep thee far from a false matter; [m] and
the innocent and righteous slay thou not: for
[n] I will not justify the wicked.
8 And [o] thou shalt take no gift: for the gift
blindeth [p] the wise, and perverteth the words
of the righteous.
9 Also [q] thou shalt not oppress a stranger:
for ye know the [r] heart of a stranger, seeing
ye were strangers in the land of Egypt.
10 And [s] six years thou shalt sow thy land,

A. M. 2513. B. C. 1491. An. Exod. Isr. 1. Sivan.

[a] Verse 7; Lev. xix. 16; Psalm. xv. 3; ci. 5; Prov. x. 18; see 2 Sam. xix. 27, with xvi. 3.——[b] Or, *receive.*——[c] Chap. xx. 16; Deut. xix. 16, 17, 18; Psa. xxxv. 11; Prov. xix. 5, 9, 28; xxiv. 28; see 1 Kings xxi. 10, 13; Matt. xxvi. 59, 60, 61; Acts vi. 11, 13.——[d] Genesis vii. 1; xix. 4, 7; chapter xxxii. 1, 2; Josh. xxiv. 15; 1 Samuel xv. 9; 1 Kings xix. 10; Job xxxi. 34; Prov. i. 10, 11, 15; iv. 14; Matt. xxvii. 24, 26; Mark. xv. 15; Luke xxiii. 23; Acts xxiv. 27; xxv. 9.——[e] Ver. 6, 7; Lev. xix. 15; Deut. i. 17; Psa. lxxii. 2.——[f] Heb. *answer.*——[g] Deut. xxii. 1; Job xxxi. 29; Prov. xxiv. 17; xxv. 21; Matt. v. 44; Rom. xii. 20; 1 Thessalonians v. 15.——[h] Deut. xxii. 4.——[i] Or, *wilt thou cease to help him?* or, *and wouldest cease to leave* thy business *for him; thou shalt surely leave* it to join *with him.*——[k] Verse 2; Deut. xxvii. 19; Job xxxi. 13, 21; Eccles. v. 8; Isaiah x. 1, 2; Jer. v. 28; vii. 6; Amos v. 12; Mal. iii. 5.——[l] Verse 1; Lev. xix. 11; Luke iii. 14; Eph. iv. 25.——[m] Deut. xxvii. 25; Psa. xciv. 21; Prov. xvii. 15, 26; Jer. vii. 6; Matt. xxvii. 4.——[n] Ch. xxxiv. 7; Rom. i. 18.——[o] Deut. xvi. 19; 1 Sam. viii. 3; xii. 3; 2 Chron. xix. 7; Psalm xxvi. 10; Prov. xv. 27; xvii. 8, 23; xxix. 4; Isaiah i. 23; v. 23; xxxiii. 15; Ezek. xxii. 12; Amos v. 12; Eccles. xx. 29; Acts xxiv. 26.——[p] Hebrew, *the seeing.* [q] Chapter xxii. 21; Deuteronomy x. 19; xxiv. 14, 17; xxvii. 19; Psa. xciv. 6; Ezek. xxii. 7; Mal. iii. 5.——[r] Hebrew, *soul.* [s] Lev. xxv. 3, 4.

NOTES ON CHAP. XXIII.

Verse 1. *Thou shalt not raise a false report*] Acting contrary to this precept is a sin against the *ninth* commandment. And the *inventor* and *receiver* of false and slanderous reports, are almost equally criminal. The word seems to refer to *either*, and our translators have very properly retained both senses, putting *raise* in the *text*, and *receive* in the margin. The original לא תשא *lo tissa* has been translated, thou shalt not *publish*. Were there no *publishers* of slander and calumny, there would be no *receivers;* and were there none to receive them, there would be none to raise them; and were there no *raisers, receivers*, nor *propagators* of calumny, lies, &c., society would be in *peace*.

Verse 2. *Thou shalt not follow a multitude to* do *evil*] Be *singular*, Singularity, if in the right, can never be criminal. So completely disgraceful is the way of sin, that if there were not a multitude walking in that way, who help to keep each other in countenance, every *solitary* sinner would be obliged to hide his head. But רבים *rabbim*, which we translate *multitude*, sometimes signifies the *great, chiefs*, or *mighty ones;* and is so understood by some eminent critics in this place: "Thou shalt not follow the example of the great or rich, who may so far disgrace their own character as to live without God in the world, and trample under foot his laws." It is supposed that these directions refer principally to matters which come under the eye of the civil magistrate; as if he had said, "Do not join with great men in condemning an innocent or righteous person, against whom they have conceived a prejudice on the account of his religion," &c.

Verse 3. *Neither shalt thou countenance a poor man in his cause.*] The word דל *dal*, which we translate *poor man*, is probably put here in opposition to רבים *rabbim*, the great, or noblemen, in the preceding verse: if so, the meaning is, Thou shalt neither be influenced by the *great* to make an unrighteous decision, nor by the poverty or distress of the poor to give thy voice against the dictates of justice and truth. Hence the ancient maxim, FIAT JUSTITIA, RUAT CŒLUM. "Let justice be done, though the heavens should be dissolved."

Verse 4. *If thou meet thine enemy's ox—going astray*] From the humane and heavenly maxim in this and the following verse, our blessed Lord has formed the following precept: "Love your *enemies, bless* them that *curse* you, do *good* to them that *hate* you, and *pray* for them which *despitefully* use you and *persecute* you;" Matt. v. 44. A precept so plain, wise, benevolent, and useful, can receive no other comment than that which its influence on the heart of a kind and merciful man produces in his life.

Verse 6. *Thou shalt not wrest the judgment of thy poor*] Thou shalt neither countenance him in his crimes, nor condemn him in his righteousness. See verses 5 and 7.

Verse 8. *Thou shalt take no gift*] A strong ordinance against *selling* justice, which has been the disgrace and ruin of every state where it has been practised. In the excellent charter of British liberties called *Magna Charta*, there is one article expressly on this head: *Nulli vendemus, nulli negabimus aut differemus, rectum aut justitiam.*—Art. xxxiii. "To none will we sell, to none will we deny or defer, right or justice." This was the more necessary in those early and corrupt times, as he who had *most money*, and gave the largest presents (called then *oblata*) to the king or queen, was sure to gain his cause in the king's court, whether he had right and justice on his side or not.

Verse 9. *Ye know the heart of a stranger*] Having

A. M. 2513.
B. C. 1491.
An. Exod. Isr. 1.
Sivan.

and shall gather in the fruits
thereof:
11 But the seventh *year* thou
shalt let it rest and lie still; that the poor of
thy people may eat: and what they leave, the
beasts of the field shall eat. In like manner
thou shalt deal with thy vineyard, *and* with thy [t] olive-yard.
12 [u] Six days thou shalt do thy
work, and on the seventh day thou shalt rest; that
thine ox and thine ass may rest, and the son of thy
handmaid, and the stranger, may be refreshed.

[t] Or, *olive-trees*.

[u] Chap. xx. 8, 9; Deut. v. 13; Luke xiii. 14.

been strangers yourselves, under severe, long continued, and cruel oppression, ye know the fears, cares, anxieties, and dismal forebodings which the heart of a stranger feels. What a forcible appeal to humanity and compassion!

Verse 11. *The seventh* year *thou shalt let it rest*] As every *seventh day* was a *Sabbath day*, so every *seventh year* was to be a *Sabbath year*. The reasons for this ordinance Oulmet gives thus:—

"1. To maintain as far as possible an equality of condition among the people, in setting the slaves at liberty, and in permitting all, as children of one family, to have the free and indiscriminate use of whatever the earth produced.

"2. To inspire the people with sentiments of humanity, by making it their duty to give rest, and proper and sufficient nourishment, to the *poor*, the *slave*, and the *stranger*, and even to the *cattle*.

"3. To accustom the people to submit to and depend on the Divine providence, and expect their support from that in the *seventh* year, by an extraordinary provision on the *sixth*.

"4. To detach their affections from earthly and perishable things, and to make them disinterested and heavenly-minded.

"5. To show them God's dominion over the country, and that HE, not *they*, was lord of the soil; and that they held it merely from his bounty." See this ordinance at length, Lev. xxv.

That God intended to teach them the doctrine of *providence* by this ordinance, there can be no doubt; and this is marked very distinctly, Lev. xxv. 20, 21: "And if ye shall say, What shall we eat the seventh year? behold, we shall not sow, nor gather in our increase: then I will command my blessing upon you in the sixth year, and it shall bring forth fruit for three years." That is, There shall be, not *three* crops in *one* year, but *one* crop equal in its abundance to *three*, because it must supply the wants of three years. 1. For the *sixth* year, supplying fruit for its own consumption; 2. For the *seventh* year, in which they were neither to sow nor reap; and 3. For the *eighth* year, for though they ploughed, sowed, &c., that year, yet a whole course of its seasons was requisite to bring all these fruits to perfection, so that they could not have the fruits of the *eighth* year till the ninth, (see ver. 22,) till which time God promised that they should *eat of the old store*. What an astonishing proof did this give of the being, power, providence, mercy, and goodness of God! Could there be an infidel in such a land, or a sinner against God and his own soul, with such proofs before his eyes of God and his attributes as one sabbatical year afforded?

It is very remarkable that the observance of this ordinance is nowhere expressly mentioned in the sacred writings; though some suppose, but without sufficient reason, that there is a reference to it in Jer. xxxiv. 8, 9. Perhaps the major part of the people could not trust God, and therefore continued to sow and reap on the seventh year, as on the preceding. This greatly displeased the Lord, and therefore he sent them into captivity; so that the land enjoyed those *Sabbaths*, through lack of inhabitants, of which their ungodliness had deprived it. See Lev. xviii. 24, 25, 28; xxvi. 34, 35, 43; 2 Chron. xxxvi. 20, 21. Commentators have been much puzzled to ascertain the *time* in which the sabbatical year *began*; because, if it began in *Abib* or March, they must have lost two harvests; for they could neither reap nor plant that year, and of course they could have no crop the year following; but if it began with what was called the civil year, or in *Tisri* or *Marcheshvan*, which answers to the beginning of our *autumn*, they would then have had that year's produce reaped and gathered in.

Verse 12. *Six days thou shalt do thy work*] Though they were thus bound to keep the sabbatical year, yet they must not neglect the seventh day's rest or weekly Sabbath; for that was of perpetual obligation, and was paramount to all others. That the sanctification of the Sabbath was of great consequence in the sight of God, we may learn from the various repetitions of this law; and we may observe that it has still for its object, not only the benefit of the soul, but the health and comfort of the body also. Doth *God care for oxen?* Yes; and he mentions them with tenderness, *that thine ox and thine ass may rest*. How criminal to employ the labouring cattle on the Sabbath, as well as upon the other days of the week! More cattle are destroyed in England than in any other part of the world, in proportion, by excessive and continued labour. The noble horse in general has no Sabbath! Does God look on this with an indifferent eye? Surely he does not. "England," said a foreigner, "is the *paradise* of *women*, the *purgatory* of *servants*, and the *hell* of *horses*."

The son of thy handmaid, and the stranger—be refreshed.] ינפש *yinnaphesh* may be *re-spirited* or *new-souled*; have a complete renewal both of bodily and spiritual strength. The expression used by Moses here is very like that used by St. Paul, Acts iii. 19: "Repent ye therefore, and be converted, that your sins may be blotted out, when the times of refreshing (*καιροι αναψυξεως*, the times of *re-souling*) shall come from the presence of the Lord;" alluding, probably, to those times of refreshing and rest for body and soul originally instituted under the law.

A. M. 2513.
B. C. 1491.
An. Exod. Isr. 1.
Sivan.

13 And in all *things* that I
have said unto you, [v] be circumspect: and [w] make no mention
of the name of other gods, neither let it be
heard out of thy mouth.
14 [x] Three times thou shalt keep a feast
unto me in the year.
15 [y] Thou shalt keep the feast of unleavened
bread: (thou shalt eat unleavened bread seven
days, as I commanded thee, in the time appointed of the month Abib; for in it thou
camest out from Egypt: [z] and none shall
appear before me empty:)
16 [a] And the feast of harvest, the first-fruits
of thy labours, which thou hast
sown in thy field: and [b] the feast
of ingathering, *which is* in the
end of the year, when thou hast gathered in thy
labours out of the field.

A. M. 2513.
B. C. 1491.
An. Exod. Isr. 1
Sivan.

17 [c] Three times in the year all thy males
shall appear before the LORD God.
18 [d] Thou shalt not offer the blood of my
sacrifice with leavened bread; neither shall the
fat of my [e] sacrifice remain until the morning.
19 [f] The first of the first-fruits of thy land
thou shalt bring into the house of the LORD
thy God. [g] Thou shalt not seethe a kid in
his mother's milk.

[v] Deut. iv. 9; Josh. xxii. 5; Psa. xxxix. 1; Eph. v. 15; 1 Tim. iv. 16.——[w] Num. xxxii. 38; Deut. xii. 3; Josh. xxiii. 7; Psa. xvi. 4; Hos. ii. 17; Zech. xiii. 2.——[x] Chap. xxxiv. 23; Lev. xxiii. 4; Deut. xvi. 16.——[y] Chap. xii. 15; xiii. 6; xxxiv. 18; Lev. xxiii. 6; Deut. xvi. 8.——[z] Chap. xxxiv. 20; Deut. xvi. 16; Ecclus. xxxv. 4.——[a] Ch. xxxiv. 22; Lev. xxiii. 10.——[b] Deut. xvi. 13.——[c] Chap. xxxiv. 23; Deut. xvi. 16.——[d] Chap. xii. 8; xxxiv. 25; Lev. ii. 11; Deut. xvi. 4.——[e] Or, *feast*.——[f] Chap. xxii. 29; xxxiv. 26; Lev. xxiii. 10, 17; Numbers xviii. 12, 13; Deut. xxvi. 10; Neh. x. 35.——[g] Ch. xxxiv. 26; Deut. xiv. 21.

Verse 14. *Three times thou shalt keep a feast unto me in the year.*] The three feasts here referred to were, 1. The feast of the PASSOVER; 2. The feast of PENTECOST; 3. The feast of TABERNACLES.

1. The feast of the *Passover* was celebrated to keep in remembrance the wonderful deliverance of the Hebrews from Egypt. 2. The feast of *Pentecost*, called also the *feast of harvest* and the *feast of weeks*, chap. xxxiv. 22, was celebrated *fifty* days after the Passover to commemorate the giving of the law on Mount Sinai, which took place fifty days after, and hence called by the Greeks *Pentecost*. 3. The feast of *Tabernacles*, called also *the feast of the ingathering*, was celebrated about the 15th of the month *Tisri* to commemorate the Israelites' dwelling in tents for forty years, during their stay in the wilderness. See on Lev. xxiii.

"God, out of his great wisdom," says Calmet, "appointed several festivals among the Jews for many reasons: 1. To perpetuate the memory of those great events, and the wonders he had wrought for the people; for example, the *Sabbath* brought to remembrance the creation of the world; the *Passover*, the departure out of Egypt; the *Pentecost*, the giving of the law; the feast of *Tabernacles*, the sojourning of their fathers in the wilderness, &c. 2. To keep them faithful to their religion by appropriate ceremonies, and the splendour of Divine service. 3. To procure them lawful pleasures, and necessary rest. 4. To give them instruction; for in their religious assemblies the law of God was always read and explained. 5. To consolidate their social union, by renewing the acquaintance of their tribes and families; for on these occasions they come together from different parts of the land to the holy city."

Besides the feasts mentioned above, the Jews had,

1. The feast of the *Sabbath*, which was a *weekly* feast.

2. The feast of the *Sabbatical Year*, which was a *septennial* feast.

3. The feast of *Trumpets*, which was celebrated on the first day of what was called their civil year, which was ushered in by the blowing of a trumpet; Lev. xxiii. 23, &c.

4. The feast of the *New Moon*, which was celebrated on the first day the moon appeared after her change.

5. The feast of *Expiation*, which was celebrated annually on the tenth day of Tisri or September, on which a general atonement was made for all the sins, negligences, and ignorances, throughout the year.

6. The feast of *Lots* or *Purim*, to commemorate the preservation of the Jews from the general massacre projected by Haman. See the book of *Esther*.

7. The feast of the *Dedication*, or rather the *Restoration* of the temple, which had been profaned by *Antiochus Epiphanes*. This was also called the feast of *Lights*.

Besides these, the Jews have had several other feasts, such as the feast of *Branches*, to commemorate the taking of Jericho.

The feast of *Collections*, on the 10th of September, on which they make contributions for the service of the temple and synagogue.

The feast for the death of *Nicanor*, 1 Mac. vii. 48, &c.

The feast for the *discovery of the sacred fire*, 2 Mac. i. 18, &c.

The feast of the *carrying of wood* to the temple, called *Xylophoria*, mentioned by Josephus.—WAR, b. ii. c. 17.

Verse 17. *All thy males*] *Old* men, *sick* men, *male idiots*, and *male children* under *thirteen* years of age, excepted; for so the Jewish doctors understand this command.

Verse 18. *The blood of my sacrifice with leavened bread*] The sacrifice here mentioned is undoubtedly the *Passover*; (see chap. xxxiv. 25;) this is called by way of eminence MY *sacrifice*, because God had instituted it for that especial purpose, the redemption of Israel from the Egyptian bondage, and because it typified THE LAMB of GOD, who taketh away the sin of the world. We have already seen how strict the prohibition against *leaven* was during this festival, and what was signified by it. See on chap. xii.

Verse 19. *Thou shalt not seethe a kid in his mother's milk.*] This passage has greatly perplexed commen-

A. M. 2513.
B. C. 1491.
An. Exod. Isr. 1.
Sivan.

20 [h] Behold, I send an angel before thee, to keep thee in the way, and to bring thee into the place which I have prepared.

21 Beware of him, and obey his voice, [i] provoke him not; for he will [k] not pardon your transgressions: for [l] my name *is* in him.

22 But if thou shalt indeed obey his voice, and do all that I speak; then [m] I will be an enemy unto thine enemies, and [n] an adversary unto thine adversaries.

A. M. 2513.
B. C. 1491.
An. Exod. Isr. 1.
Sivan.

23 [o] For mine Angel shall go before thee, and [p] bring thee in unto the Amorites, and the Hittites, and the Perizzites, and the Canaanites, the Hivites, and the Jebusites: and I will cut them off.

24 Thou shalt not [q] bow down to their gods, nor serve them, [r] nor do after their works: [s] but thou shalt utterly overthrow them, and quite break down their images.

25 And ye shall [t] serve the LORD your God,

[h] Chap. xiv. 19; xxxii. 34; xxxiii. 2, 14; Num. xx. 16; Josh. v. 13; vi. 2; Psa. xci. 11; Isa. lxiii. 9.——[i] Num. xiv. 11; Psa. lxxviii. 40, 56; Eph. iv. 30; Heb. iii. 10, 16.——[k] Chap. xxxii. 34; Num. xiv. 35; Deut. xviii. 19; Josh. xxiv. 19; Jer. v. 7; Heb. iii. 11; 1 John v. 16.——[l] Isa. ix. 6; Jer. xxiii. 6; John x. 30, 38.

[m] Gen. xii. 3; Deut. xxx. 7; Jer. xxx. 20.——[n] Or, *I will afflict them that afflict thee.*——[o] Ver. 20; chap. xxxiii. 2.——[p] Josh. xxiv. 8, 11.——[q] Ch. xx. 5.——[r] Lev. xviii. 3; Deut. xii. 30, 31.——[s] Chap. xxxiv. 13; Numbers xxxiii. 52; Deut. vii. 5, 25; xii. 3.——[t] Deut. vi. 13; x. 12, 20; xi. 13, 14; xiii. 4; Joshua xxii. 5; xxiv. 14, 15, 21, 24; 1 Sam. vii. 3; xii. 20, 24; Matt. iv. 10.

tators; but Dr. Cudworth is supposed to have given it its true meaning by quoting a MS. comment of a *Karaite* Jew, which he met with, on this passage. "It was a custom of the ancient heathens, when they had gathered in all their fruits, to take a kid and boil it in the milk of its dam; and then, in a magical way, to go about and besprinkle with it all their trees and fields, gardens and orchards; thinking by these means to make them fruitful, that they might bring forth more abundantly in the following year."—*Cudworth* on *the Lord's Supper*, 4to.

I give this comment as I find it, and add that *Spenser* has shown that the *Zabii* used this kind of magical milk to sprinkle their trees and fields, in order to make them fruitful. Others understand it of eating flesh and milk together; others of a lamb or a kid *while it is sucking its mother*, and that the paschal lamb is here intended, which it was not lawful to offer while sucking.

After all the learned labour which critics have bestowed on this passage, and by which the obscurity in some cases is become more intense, the simple object of the precept seems to be this: "Thou shalt do nothing that may have any tendency to blunt thy moral feelings, or teach thee hardness of heart." Even *human* nature shudders at the thought of causing the mother to lend her milk to seethe the flesh of her young one! We need go no farther for the delicate, tender, humane, and impressive meaning of this precept.

Verse 20. *Behold, I send an Angel before thee*] Some have thought that this was *Moses*, others *Joshua*, because the word כלאך *malach* signifies an *angel* or *messenger*; but as it is said, ver. 21, *My name is in him*, (בקרבו *bekirbo*, *intimately*, *essentially in him*,) it is more likely that the great Angel of the Covenant, the Lord Jesus Christ, is meant, in whom *dwelt* all the fulness of the Godhead bodily. We have had already much reason to believe that this glorious personage often appeared in a human form to the patriarchs, &c.; and of him Joshua was a very expressive type, the names *Joshua* and *Jesus*, in Hebrew and Greek, being of exactly the same signification, because radically the same, from ישע *yasha*, he *saved*, *delivered*, *preserved*, or *kept safe*. Nor does it appear that the description given of the Angel in the text can belong to any other person.

Calmet has referred to a very wonderful comment on these words given by Philo Judæus *De Agricultura*, which I shall produce here at full length as it stands in Dr. *Mangey's* edition, vol. i., p. 308: Ὡς *ποιμην και βασιλευς ὁ Θεος αγει κατα δικην και νομον, προστησαμενος τον ορθον αυτου λογον πρωτογονον υἱον, ὁς την επιμελειαν της ἱερας ταυτης αγελης, οἱα τις μεγαλου βασιλεως ὑπαρχος, διαδεξεται.* Και γαρ ειρηται *που· Ιδου εγω ειμι, αποστελω αγγελον μου εις προσωπον σου, του φυλαξαι σε εν τῃ ὁδῳ.* "God, as the Shepherd and King, conducts all things according to law and righteousness, having established over them his *right* WORD, his ONLY-BEGOTTEN SON, who, as the Viceroy of the Great King, takes care of and ministers to this sacred flock. For it is somewhere said, (chap. xxiii. 20,) *Behold,* I AM, *and I will send my* ANGEL *before thy face, to keep thee* in *the way.*"

This is a testimony liable to no suspicion, coming from a person who cannot be supposed to be even friendly to Christianity, nor at all acquainted with that *particular doctrine* to which his words seem so pointedly to refer.

Verse 21. *He will not pardon your transgressions*] He is not like a man, with whom ye may think that ye may trifle; were he either man or *angel*, in the common acceptation of the term, it need not be said, *He will not pardon your transgressions*, for neither man nor angel could do it.

My name is in him.] The *Jehovah* dwells in him; in him dwelt all the fulness of the Godhead bodily; and because of this he could either pardon or punish. *All power is given unto me in heaven and earth*, Matt. xxviii. 18.

Verse 23. *Unto the Amorites*] There are only *six* of the *seven* nations mentioned here, but the Septuagint, Samaritan, Coptic, and one Hebrew MS., add *Girgashite*, thus making the *seven* nations.

Verse 24. *Break down their images.*] כצבתיהם *matstsebotheyhem*, from נצב *natsab*, to *stand up; pillars, anointed stones*, &c., such as the *baitulia*. See on Gen. xxviii. 18.

Verse 25. *Shall bless thy bread and thy water*] That is, all thy provisions, no matter of what sort; the meanest fare shall be sufficiently nutritive when God's blessing is in it.

A. M. 2513. B. C. 1491. An. Exod. Isr. 1. Sivan.

and [u] he shall bless thy bread and
thy water; and [v] I will take sickness away from the midst of thee.
26 [w] There shall nothing cast their young,
nor be barren, in thy land: the number of thy
days I will [x] fulfil.
27 I will send [y] my fear before thee, and
will [z] destroy all the people to whom thou
shalt come, and I will make all thine enemies
turn their [a] backs unto thee.
28 And [b] I will send hornets before thee,
which shall drive out the Hivite, the Canaanite,
and the Hittite, from before thee.
29 [c] I will not drive them out from before thee
in one year; lest the land become desolate,
and the beast of the field multiply against thee.
30 By little and little I will
drive them out from before thee,
until thou be increased, and inherit the land.

A. M. 2513. B. C. 1491. An. Exod. Isr. 1. Sivan.

31 And [d] I will set thy bounds from the
Red Sea even unto the sea of the Philistines,
and from the desert unto the river: for I will
[e] deliver the inhabitants of the land into your
hand; and thou shalt drive them out before
thee.
32 [f] Thou shalt make no covenant with
them, nor with their gods.
33 They shall not dwell in thy land, lest
they make thee sin against me: for if thou
serve their gods, [g] it will surely be a snare
unto thee.

[u] Deut. vii. 13; xxviii. 5, 8.——[v] Chap. xv. 26; Deut. vii. 15.——[w] Deut. vii. 14; xxviii. 4; Job xxi. 10; Mal. iii. 10, 11.——[x] Gen. xxv. 8; xxxv. 29; 1 Chron. xxiii. 1; Job v. 26; xlii. 17; Psa. lv. 23; xc. 10.——[y] Gen. xxxv. 5; chap. xv. 14, 16; Deut. ii. 25; xi. 25; Josh. ii. 9, 11; 1 Sam. xiv. 15; 2 Chron. xiv. 14.——[z] Deut. vii. 23.——[a] Heb. *neck*; Psa. xviii. 40.

[b] Deut. vii. 20; Josh. xxiv. 12; Wisd. xii. 8.——[c] Deut. vii. 22.——[d] Gen. xv. 18; Num. xxxiv. 3; Deut. xi. 24; Josh. i. 4; 1 Kings iv. 21, 24; Psa. lxxii. 8.——[e] Josh. xxi. 44; Judg. i. 4 xi. 21.——[f] Chap. xxxiv. 12, 15; Deut. vii. 2.——[g] Chap. xxxiv. 12; Deut. vii. 16; xii. 30; Josh. xxiii. 13; Judg. ii. 3; 1 Sam. xviii. 21; Psa. cvi. 36.

Verse 26. *There shall nothing cast their young, nor be barren*] Hence there must be a very great increase both of *men* and *cattle*.

The number of thy days I will fulfil.] Ye shall all live to a good old age, and none die *before his time*. This is the blessing of the righteous, for wicked men *live not out half their days*; Psa. lv. 23.

Verse 28. *I will send hornets before thee*] הצרעה *hatstsirah*. The root is not found in Hebrew, but it may be the same with the Arabic صرع *saraa*, to *lay prostrate*, to *strike down*; the *hornet*, probably so called from the destruction occasioned by the violence of its sting. The *hornet*, in natural history, belongs to the species *crabro*, of the genus *vespa* or *wasp*; it is a most voracious insect, and is exceedingly strong for its size, which is generally an inch in length, though I have seen some an inch and a half long, and so strong that, having caught one in a small pair of forceps, it repeatedly escaped by using violent contortions, so that at last I was obliged to abandon all hopes of securing it alive, which I wished to have done. How distressing and destructive a multitude of these might be, any person may conjecture; even the bees of one hive would be sufficient to sting a thousand men to madness, but how much worse must wasps and hornets be! No armour, no weapons, could avail against these. A few thousands of them would be quite sufficient to throw the best disciplined army into confusion and rout. From Josh. xxiv. 12, we find that two kings of the Amorites were actually driven out of the land by these hornets, so that the Israelites were not obliged to use either sword or bow in the conquest.

Verse 31. *I will set thy bounds from the Red Sea*] On the south-east, *even* unto *the sea of the Philistines*—the Mediterranean, on the north-west; *and from the desert*—of Arabia, or the wilderness of Shur, on the west, *to the river*—the Euphrates, on the north-east. Or in general terms, from the Euphrates on the east, to the Mediterranean Sea on the west; and from Mount Libanus on the north, to the Red Sea and the Nile on the south. This promise was not completely fulfilled till the days of David and Solomon. The general disobedience of the people *before* this time prevented a more speedy accomplishment; and their disobedience *afterwards* caused them to lose the possession. So, though *all the promises of God are* YEA *and* AMEN, yet they are fulfilled but to a few, because men are *slow of heart to believe*; and the blessings of providence and grace are taken away from several because of their *unfaithfulness*.

Verse 32. *Thou shalt make* no *covenant with them*] They were incurable idolaters, and the cup of their iniquity was full. And had the Israelites contracted any alliance with them, either sacred or civil, they would have enticed them into their idolatries, to which the Jews were at all times most unhappily prone; and as God intended that they should be the preservers of the true religion till the coming of the Messiah, hence he strictly forbade them to tolerate idolatry.

Verse 33. *They shall not dwell in thy land*] They must be utterly expelled. The land was the Lord's, and he had given it to the progenitors of this people, to Abraham, Isaac, and Jacob. The latter being obliged to leave it because of a famine, God is now conducting back his posterity, who alone had a *Divine* and *natural right* to it, and therefore their seeking to possess the inheritance of their fathers can be only criminal in the sight of those who are systematically opposed to the thing, because it is a part of *Divine revelation*.

WHAT a pity that the Mosaic Law should be so little studied! What a number of just and equal laws, pious and humane institutions, useful and instructive ordinances, does it contain! Everywhere we see the purity and benevolence of God always working to prevent crimes and make the people happy! But what

else can be expected from that God who is love, whose tender mercies are over all his works, and who hateth nothing that he has made? Reader, thou art not straitened in him, be not straitened in thy own bowels. Learn from him to be just, humane, kind, and merciful. Love thy enemy, and do good to him that hates thee. Jesus is with thee; hear and obey his voice; provoke him not, and he will be an enemy to thine enemies, and an adversary to thine adversaries. *Believe, love, obey;* and the road to the kingdom of God is plain before thee. Thou shalt inherit the good land, and be established in it for ever and ever.

CHAPTER XXIV.

Moses and Aaron, Nadab and Abihu, and the seventy elders, are commanded to go to the mount to meet the Lord, 1. *Moses alone to come near to the Divine presence,* 2. *He informs the people, and they promise obedience,* 3. *He writes the words of the Lord, erects an altar at the foot of the hill, and sets up twelve pillars for the twelve tribes,* 4. *The young priests offer burnt-offerings and peace-offerings,* 5. *Moses reads the book of the covenant, sprinkles the people with the blood, and they promise obedience,* 6–8. *Moses, Aaron, Nadab, Abihu, and the seventy elders of Israel, go up to the mount, and get a striking display of the majesty of God,* 9–11. *Moses alone is called up into the mount, in order to receive the tables of stone, written by the hand of God,* 12. *Moses and his servant Joshua go up, and Aaron and Hur are left regents of the people during his absence,* 13, 14. *The glory of the Lord rests on the mount, and the cloud covers it for six days, and on the seventh God speaks to Moses out of the cloud,* 15, 16. *The terrible appearance of God's glory on the mount,* 17. *Moses continues with God on the mount forty days,* 18.

A. M. 2513.
B. C. 1491.
An. Exod. Isr. 1.
Sivan.

AND he said unto Moses, Come up unto the LORD, thou, and Aaron, [a] Nadab, and Abihu, [b] and seventy of the elders of Israel; and worship ye afar off.

2 And Moses [c] alone shall come near the LORD: but they shall not come nigh; neither shall the people go up with him.

3 And Moses came and told the people all the words of the LORD, and all the judgments: and all the people answered with one voice, and said, [d] All the words which the LORD hath said will we do.

4 And Moses [e] wrote all the words of the LORD, and rose up early in the morning, and

[a] Chap. xxviii. 1; Lev. x. 1, 2.——[b] Chapter i. 5; Num. xi. 16.——[c] Ver. 13, 15, 18.——[d] Verse 7; chapter xix. 8; Deut. v. 27; Galatians iii. 19, 20.——[e] Deut. xxxi. 9.

NOTES ON CHAP. XXIV.

Verse 1. *Come up unto the Lord*] Moses and Aaron were already on the mount, or at least some way up, (chap. xix. 24,) where they had heard the voice of the Lord distinctly speaking to them: and the people also saw and heard, but in a less distinct manner, probably like the hoarse grumbling sound of distant thunder; see chap. xx. 18. Calmet, who complains of the apparent want of order in the facts laid down here, thinks the whole should be understood thus:—"After God had laid before Moses and Aaron all the laws mentioned from the beginning of the 20th chapter to the end of the 23d, before they went down from the mount to lay them before the people, he told them that, when they had proposed the conditions of the covenant to the Israelites, and they had ratified them, they were to come up again unto the mountain accompanied with Nadab and Abihu the sons of Aaron, and seventy of the principal elders of Israel. Moses accordingly went down, spoke to the people, ratified the covenant, and then, according to the command of God mentioned here, he and the others reascended the mountain. *Tout cela est raconté ici avec assez peu d'ordre.*"

Verse 2. *Moses alone shall come near*] The people stood at the foot of the mountain. Aaron and his two sons and the seventy elders went up, probably about half way, and Moses alone went to the summit.

Verse 3. *Moses—told the people all the words of the Lord*] That is, the *ten commandments*, and the various *laws* and *ordinances* mentioned from the beginning of the 20th to the end of the 23d chapter.

Verse 4. *Moses wrote all the words of the Lord*] After the people had promised obedience, (ver. 3,) and so entered into the bonds of the covenant, "it was necessary," says Calmet, "to draw up an *act* by which the memory of these transactions might be preserved, and confirm the covenant by authentic and solemn ceremonies." And this Moses does. 1. As *legislator*, he reduces to writing all the articles and conditions of the agreement, with the people's act of consent. 2. As their *mediator* and the *deputy* of the Lord, he accepts on his part the resolution of the people; and Jehovah on his part engages himself to Israel, to be their God, their King, and Protector, and to fulfil to them all the promises he had made to their fathers. 3. To make this the more solemn and affecting, and to ratify the covenant, which could not be done without sacrifice, shedding and sprinkling of blood, Moses builds an *altar*, probably of turf, as was commanded, chap. xx. 24, and erects twelve pillars, no doubt of unhewn stone, and probably set round about the altar. The *altar* itself represented the *throne of God;* the *twelve stones*, the *twelve tribes of Israel*. These were the *two parties*, who were to contract, or enter into covenant, on this occasion.

A. M. 2513. B. C. 1491. An. Exod. Isr. 1. Sivan.

builded an altar under the hill,
and twelve [f] pillars, according to
the twelve tribes of Israel.
5 And he sent young men of the children
of Israel, which offered burnt-offerings, and
sacrificed peace-offerings of oxen unto the
LORD.
6 And Moses [g] took half of the blood, and
put *it* in basins; and half of the blood he
sprinkled on the altar.
7 And he [h] took the book of the covenant,
and read in the audience of the
people: and they said, [i] All that
the LORD hath said will we do,
and be obedient.
8 And Moses took the blood, and sprinkled
it on the people, and said, Behold [k] the blood
of the covenant, which the LORD hath made
with you concerning all these words.
9 Then [l] went up Moses, and Aaron, Nadab,
and Abihu, and seventy of the elders of Israel:
10 And they [m] saw the God of Israel: and

[f] Gen. xxviii. 18; xxxi. 45.——[g] Heb. ix. 18.——[h] Heb. ix. 19. [i] Ver. 3.——[k] Heb. ix. 20; xiii. 20; 1 Pet. i. 2.——[l] Ver. 1.
[m] See Gen. xxxii. 30; ch. iii. 6; Judg. xiii. 22; Isa. vi. 1, 5, with ch. xxxiii. 20, 23; John i. 18; 1 Tim. vi. 16; 1 John iv. 12.

Verse 5. *He sent young men*] Stout, able, reputable young men, chosen out of the different tribes, for the purpose of killing, flaying, and offering the oxen mentioned here.

Burnt-offerings] They generally consisted of sheep and goats, Lev. i. 10. These were wholly consumed by fire.

Peace-offerings] Bullocks or goats; see Heb. ix. 19. The blood of these was poured out before the Lord, and then the priests and people might feast on the flesh.

Verse 7. *The book of the covenant*] The writing containing the laws mentioned in the three preceding chapters. As this writing contained the agreement made between God and them, it was called the *book of the covenant;* but as no covenant was considered to be ratified and *binding* till a sacrifice had been offered on the occasion, hence the necessity of the sacrifices mentioned here.

Half of the blood being sprinkled on the ALTAR, and *half of it sprinkled on the* PEOPLE, showed that both GOD and THEY were mutually bound by this covenant. GOD was bound to the PEOPLE to support, defend, and save them; the PEOPLE were bound to GOD to fear, love, and serve him. On the ancient method of making covenants, see on Gen. vi. 18; xv. 18. Thus the blood of the *new* covenant was necessary to propitiate the throne of justice on the one hand, and to reconcile men to God on the other. On the nature and various kinds of the Jewish offerings, see the note on Lev. vii. 1, &c.

Verse 10. *They saw the God of Israel*] The seventy elders, who were representatives of the whole congregation, were chosen to witness the manifestation of God, that they might be satisfied of the truth of the revelation which he had made of *himself* and of his *will;* and on this occasion it was necessary that the people also should be favoured with a sight of the glory of God; see chap. xx. 18. Thus the certainty of the revelation was established by many witnesses, and by those especially of the most *competent* kind.

A paved work of a sapphire stone] Or *sapphire brick-work.* I suppose that something of the *Musive* or *Mosaic pavement* is here intended; floors most curiously inlaid with variously coloured stones or small square tiles, disposed in a great variety of ornamental forms. Many of these remain in different countries to the present day. The Romans were particularly fond of them, and left monuments of their taste and ingenuity in pavements of this kind, in most countries where they established their dominion. Some very fine specimens are found in different parts of Britain.

Sapphire is a precious stone of a fine *blue* colour, next in hardness to the diamond. The *ruby* is considered by most mineralogists of the same genus; so is also the *topaz:* hence we cannot say that the sapphire is only of a *blue* colour; it is *blue, red,* or *yellow,* as it may be called *sapphire, ruby,* or *topaz;* and some of them are *blue* or *green,* according to the light in which they are held; and some *white.* A very large specimen of such a one is now before me. The ancient oriental sapphire is supposed to have been the same with the *lapis lazuli.* Supposing that these different kinds of sapphires are here intended, how glorious must a pavement be, constituted of polished stones of this sort, perfectly transparent, with an effulgence of heavenly splendour poured out upon them! The *red,* the *blue,* the *green,* and the *yellow,* arranged by the wisdom of God, into the most beautiful emblematic representations, and the whole *body of heaven in its clearness* shining upon them, must have made a most glorious appearance. As the Divine glory appeared *above* the mount, it is reasonable to suppose that the Israelites saw the sapphire pavement over their heads, as it might have occupied a space in the atmosphere equal in extent to the base of the mountain; and being *transparent,* the intense brightness shining upon it must have greatly heightened the effect.

It is necessary farther to observe that all this must have been only an appearance, unconnected with any *personal* similitude; for this Moses expressly asserts, Deut. iv. 15. And though the *feet* are here mentioned, this can only be understood of the sapphirine *basis* or pavement, on which this celestial and indescribable glory of the Lord appeared. There is a similar description of the glory of the Lord in the Book of Revelation, chap. iv. 3: "And he who sat [upon the throne] was to look upon like a *jasper* and a *sardine* stone; and there was a rainbow round about the throne, in sight like unto an *emerald.*" In neither of these appearances was there any similitude or likeness of any thing in heaven, earth, or sea. Thus God took care to preserve them from all incentives to *idolatry,* while he gave them the fullest proofs of his *being.*

A. M. 2513.
B. C. 1491.
An. Exod. Isr. 1.
Sivan.

there was under his feet as it
were a paved work of a [n] sapphire
stone, and as it were the [o] body
of heaven in *his* clearness.
11 And upon the nobles of the children of
Israel he [p] laid not his hand: also [q] they saw
God, and did [r] eat and drink.
12 And the LORD said unto Moses, [s] Come
up to me into the mount, and be there: and I
will give thee [t] tables of stone, and a law,
and commandments which I have written;
that thou mayest teach them.
13 And Moses rose up, and [u] his minister
Joshua: and Moses [v] went up into the mount
of God.
14 And he said unto the elders, Tarry ye
here for us, until we come again unto you:
and, behold, Aaron and Hur *are*
with you: if any man have any
matters to do, let him come unto
them.

A. M. 2513.
B. C. 1491.
An. Exod. Isr. 1.
Sivan.

15 And Moses went up into the mount, and
[w] a cloud covered the mount.
16 And [x] the glory of the LORD abode upon
Mount Sinai, and the cloud covered it six
days: and the seventh day he called unto
Moses, out of the midst of the cloud.
17 And the sight of the glory of the LORD
was like [y] devouring fire, on the top of the
mount, in the eyes of the children of Israel.
18 And Moses went into the midst of the
cloud, and gat him up into the mount: and
[z] Moses was in the mount forty days and
forty nights.

---

[n] Ezek. i. 26; x. 1; Rev. iv. 3.——[o] Matt. xvii. 2.——[p] Chap. xix. 21.——[q] Ver. 10; chap. xxxiii. 20; Gen. xvi. 13; xxxii. 30; Deut. iv. 33; Judg. xiii. 22.——[r] Gen. xxxi. 54; chap. xviii. 12; 1 Cor. x. 18.——[s] Ver. 2, 15, 18.——[t] Chap. xxxi. 18; xxxii. 15, 16; Deut. v. 22.——[u] Chap. xxxii. 17; xxxiii. 11.——[v] Ver. 2.
[w] Chap. xix. 9, 16; Matt. xvii. 5.——[x] Chap. xvi. 10; Num. xiv. 10.——[y] Chapter iii. 2; xix. 18; Deut. iv. 36; Heb. xii. 18, 29.
[z] Chap. xxxiv. 28; Deut. ix. 9.

In Scheuchzer's *Physica Sacra*, among his numerous fine engravings, there is one of this glorious manifestation, which cannot be too severely reprehended. The Supreme Being is represented as an old man, sitting on a throne, encompassed with glory, having a crown on his head, and a sceptre in his hand, the people prostrate in adoration at the foot of the piece. A print of this kind should be considered as utterly improper, if not *blasphemous*.

Verse 11. *Upon the nobles of—Israel he laid not his hand*] This laying on of the hand has been variously explained. 1. He did not conceal himself from the nobles of Israel by covering them with his hand, as he did Moses, chap. xxxiii. 22. 2. He did not endue any of the nobles, i. e., the *seventy elders*, with the gift of prophecy; for so laying on of the hand has been understood. 3. He did not slay any of them; none of them received any injury; which is certainly one meaning of the phrase: see Neh. xiii. 21; Psa. lv. 20. *Also they saw God*, i. e., although they had this discovery of his majesty, yet they *did eat and drink*, i. e., were preserved alive and unhurt. Perhaps the *eating and drinking* here may refer to the peace-offerings on which they feasted, and the libations that were then offered on the ratification of the covenant. But they rejoiced the more because they had been so highly favoured, and were still permitted to live; for it was generally apprehended that God never showed his glory in this signal manner but for the purpose of manifesting his *justice;* and therefore it appeared a strange thing that these should have seen God as it were face to face, and yet live. See Gen. xvi. 13; xxxiii. 30; and Judg. xiii. 22, 23.

Verse 12. *Come up to me into the mount, and be there*] We may suppose Moses to have been, with Aaron, Nadab, Abihu, and the seventy elders, about midway up the mount; for it plainly appears that there are several *stations* on it.

Verse 13. *Moses rose up*] In verse 16 it is said that *the glory of the Lord abode on the mount, and the cloud covered it.* The glory was probably above the cloud, and it was to the cloud that Moses and his servant Joshua ascended at this time, leaving Aaron and the elders below. After they had been in this region, viz., where the cloud encompassed the mountain, for six days, God appears to have called Moses up higher: compare the 16th and 18th verses. Moses then ascended to the *glory*, leaving Joshua in the cloud, with whom he had, no doubt, frequent conferences during the forty days he continued with God on the mount.

Verse 14. *Tarry ye here for us*] Probably Moses did not know that he was to continue so long on the mount, nor is it likely that the elders tarried the whole forty days where they were: they doubtless, after waiting some considerable time, returned to the camp; and their return is supposed to have been the grand cause why the Israelites made the golden calf, as they probably reported that Moses was lost.

Aaron and Hur are with you] Not knowing how long he might be detained on the mount, and knowing that many cases might occur which would require the interference of the chief magistrate, Moses constituted them regents of the people during the time he should be absent.

Verse 16. *And the seventh day he called*] It is very likely that Moses went up into the mount on the *first* day of the week; and having with Joshua remained in the *region of the cloud* during *six days*, on the *seventh*, which was the Sabbath, God spake to him, and delivered successively to him, during forty days and forty nights, the different statutes and ordinances which are afterwards mentioned.

Verse 17. *The glory of the* Lord *was like devouring fire*] This appearance was well calculated to inspire the people with the deepest reverence and godly fear; and this is the use the apostle makes of it, Heb. xii.

a

28, 29, where he evidently refers to this place, saying, *Let us have grace whereby we may serve God acceptably with reverence and godly fear; for our God is a* CONSUMING FIRE. Seeing the glory of the Lord upon the mount like a devouring fire, Moses having tarried long, the Israelites probably supposed that he had been devoured or consumed by it, and therefore the more easily fell into idolatry. But how could they do this, with this tremendous sight of God's glory before their eyes?

Verse 18. *Forty days and forty nights.*] During the whole of this time he neither ate bread nor drank water; see chap. xxxiv. 28; Deut. ix. 9. Both his body and soul were so sustained by the invigorating presence of God, that he needed no earthly support, and this may be the simple reason why he took none. Elijah fasted *forty* days and *forty* nights, sustained by the same influence, 1 Kings xix. 8; as did likewise our blessed Lord, when he was about to commence the public ministry of his own Gospel, Matt. iv. 2.

1. MOSES, who was the mediator of the Old Covenant, is alone permitted to draw nigh to God; none of the people are suffered to come up to the Divine glory, not even Aaron, nor his sons, nor the nobles of Israel. Moses was a type of Christ, who is the mediator of the *New Covenant;* and he alone has access to God in behalf of the human race, as Moses had in behalf of Israel.

2. The law can inspire nothing but terror, when viewed unconnected with its sacrifices, and those sacrifices are nothing but as they refer to Jesus Christ, the Lamb of God, who alone by the sacrifice of himself, bears away the sin of the world.

3. The blood of the victims was sprinkled both on the *altar* and on the *people,* to show that the death of Christ gave to Divine *justice* what it demanded, and to *men* what they needed. The people were sanctified by it unto God, and God was propitiated by it unto the people. By this sacrifice the law was magnified and made honourable, so Divine justice received its due; and those who believe are justified from all guilt, and sanctified from all sin, so they receive all that they need. Thus God is well pleased, and believers eternally saved. This is a glorious economy, highly worthy of God its author.

CHAPTER XXV.

The Lord addresses Moses out of the Divine glory, and commands him to speak unto the Israelites, that they may give him free-will *offerings,* 1, 2. *The different kinds of offerings,* gold, silver, *and* brass, 3. Purple, scarlet, fine linen, *and* goats' hair, 4. Rams' skins, badgers' skins, (*rather* violet-coloured *skins,*) *and* shittim wood, 5. Oil *and* spices, 6. Onyx stones, *and* stones *for the* ephod *and* breastplate, 7. *A* sanctuary *is to be made after the pattern of the tabernacle,* 8, [illegible] *The* ark *and its dimensions,* 10. *Its* crown *of* gold, 11. *Its* rings, 12. *Its* staves, *and their use,* 13–[illegible]e testimony *to be laid up in the ark,* 16. *The* mercy-seat *and its dimensions,* 17. *The* cherubi[illegible] *made and placed,* 18–20. *The mercy seat to be placed on the ark, and the testimony to be put within it,* 21. *The Lord promises to commune with the people from the mercy-seat,* 22. *The* table *of* shew-bread, *and its dimensions,* 23. *Its crown and border of gold,* 24, 25. *Its rings,* 26, 27. *Staves,* 28. *Dishes, spoons, and bowls,* 29. *Its use,* 30. *The* golden candlestick; *its branches, bowls, knops, and flowers,* 31–36. *Its* seven lamps, 37. *Tongs and snuffers,* 38. *The weight of the candlestick and its utensils, one talent of gold,* 39. *All to be made according to the pattern showed to Moses on the mount,* 40.

A. M. 2513. B. C. 1491. An. Exod. Isr. 1. Sivan.

AND the LORD spake unto Moses, saying,
2 Speak unto the children of Israel, that they [a] bring me an [b] offering: [c] of every man that giveth it willingly with his heart, ye shall take my offering.
3 And this *is* the offering which ye shall

[a] Hebrew, *take for me.*——[b] Or, *heave-offering.*

[c] Chap. xxxv. 5, 21; 1 Chron. xxix. 3, 5, 9, 14; Ezra ii. 68; iii. 5; vii. 16; Neh. xi. 2; 2 Cor. viii. 12; ix. 7.

NOTES ON CHAP. XXV.

Verse 2. *That they bring me an offering*] The offering here mentioned is the תרומה *terumah,* a kind of free-will offering, consisting of any thing that was necessary for the occasion. It signifies properly any thing that was *lifted up,* the *heave-offering,* because in presenting it to God it was *lifted up* to be laid on his altar; but see on chap. xxix. 26. God requires that they should build him a tent, suited in some sort to his dignity and eminence, because he was to act as their king, and to dwell among them; and they were to consider themselves as his subjects, and in this character to bring him presents, which was considered to be the duty of every subject appearing before his prince. See chap. xxiii. 15.

Verse 3. *This is the offering*] There were three kinds of metals: 1. GOLD, זהב *zahab,* which may properly signify *wrought gold;* what was *bright* and *resplendent,* as the word implies. In Job xxviii. 15, 16, 17, 19, gold is mentioned *five* times, and *four* of the words are different in the original. 1. סגור SEGOR, from סגר *sagar,* to *shut up; gold* in the *mine,* or *shut up* in its *ore.* 2. כתם KETHEM, from כתם *catham,* to *sign, seal,* or *stamp;* gold made current by being coined; standard or sterling gold, exhibiting the stamp expressive of its value. 3. זהב ZAHAB, *wrought gold, pure, highly polished gold;* probably what was used for *overlaying* or *gilding.* 4. פז PAZ, denoting *solidity, compactness,* and *strength;* probably *gold* formed into different kinds of *plate,* as it is joined in ver. 17 of

A. M. 2513.
B. C. 1491.
An. Exod. Isr. 1.
Sivan.

take of them; gold, and silver, and brass,
4 And blue, and purple, and scarlet, and [d] fine linen, and goats' *hair*;
5 And rams' skins dyed red,

[d] Or, *silk*; Gen. xli. 42.

the above chapter with כלי *keley, vessels.* The *zahab*, or *pure gold*, is here mentioned, because it was in a state that rendered it capable of being variously manufactured for the service of the sanctuary.

2. Silver, כסף *keseph*, from *casaph*, to be *pale, wan*, or *white;* so called from its well-known colour.

3. Brass, נחשת *nechosheth, copper;* unless we suppose that the factitious metal commonly called brass is intended: this is formed by a combination of the oxide or ore of zinc, called *lapis calaminaris*, with copper. Brass seems to have been very anciently in use, as we find it mentioned Gen. iv. 22; and the preparation of copper, to transform it into this factitious metal, seems to be very pointedly referred to Job xxviii. 2: *Iron is taken out of the earth, and brass* is *molten* out of *the stone;* אבן יצוק נחושה *eben yatsuk nechushah*, translated by the Vulgate, *Lapis, solutus calore, in æs vertitur*, "The stone, liquefied by heat, is turned into brass." Is it going too far to say that the stone here may refer to the *lapis calaminaris*, which was used to turn the copper into brass? Because brass was capable of so fine a polish as to become exceedingly bright, and keep its lustre a considerable time, hence it was used for all weapons of war and defensive armour among ancient nations; and *copper* seems to have been in no repute, but for its use in making *brass*.

Verse 4. *Blue*] תכלת *techeleth*, generally supposed to mean an *azure* or *sky colour;* rendered by the Septuagint ὑακινθον, and by the Vulgate *hyacinthum*, a *sky-blue* or *deep violet*.

Purple] ארגמן *argaman*, a very precious colour, extracted from the *purpura* or *murex*, a species of shell-fish, from which it is supposed the famous *Tyrian purple* came, so costly, and so much celebrated in antiquity. See this largely described, and the manner of dying it, in Pliny, Hist. Nat., lib. ix., c. 60–65, edit. Bipont.

Scarlet] תולעת *tolaath*, signifies a *worm*, of which this colouring matter was made; and, joined with שני *shani*, which signifies to *repeat* or *double*, implies that to strike this colour the wool or cloth was twice dipped: hence the Vulgate renders the original *coccum bis tinctum*, "scarlet twice dyed;" and to this Horace refers, *Odar.*, lib. ii., od. 16, v. 35:—

——*Te* bis *Afro*
Murice tinctæ
Vestiunt lanæ.——

"Thy robes the *twice dyed* purple stains."

It is the same colour which the Arabs call *al kermez*, whence the French *cramoisi*, and the English *crimson*. On this subject much may be seen in *Bochart, Calmet*, and *Scheuchzer*.

Fine linen] שש *shesh;* whether this means *linen, cotton*, or *silk*, is not agreed on among interpreters. Because שש *shesh* signifies *six*, the rabbins suppose that it always signifies the fine linen of Egypt, in which *six folds* constituted one thread; and that when a *single fold* was meant, בד *bad* is the term used. See the note on Gen. xli. 42.

Goats' hair] עזים *izzim, goats*, but used here elliptically for goats' hair. In different parts of Asia Minor, Syria, Cilicia, and Phrygia, the goats have long, fine, and beautiful hair, in some cases almost as fine as silk, which they shear at proper times, and manufacture into garments. From Virgil, Georg. iii., v. 305–311, we learn that goats' hair manufactured into cloth was nearly of equal value with that formed from *wool*.

Hæ quoque non cura nobis *leviore tuendæ;*
Nec minor usus erit: quamvis Milesia magno
Vellera mutentur, Tyrios incocta rubores.—
Nec minus interea barbas incanaque menta
Cinyphii tondent hirci, setasque comantes,
Usum in castrorum, et miseris velamina nautis.

"For hairy goats of equal profit are
With woolly sheep, and ask an equal care.
'Tis true the *fleece* when drunk with Tyrian juice
Is dearly sold, but not for needful use:
Meanwhile the pastor shears their *hoary beards*
And eases of their *hair* the loaden herds.
Their camelots, warm in tents, the soldier hold,
And shield the shivering mariner from the cold."
Dryden.

Verse 5. *Rams' skins dyed red*] ערת אילם מאדמים *oroth eylim meoddamim*, literally, *the skins of red rams*. It is a fact attested by many respectable travellers, that in the Levant sheep are often to be met with that have *red* or *violet*-coloured fleeces. And almost all ancient writers speak of the same thing. Homer describes the rams of Polyphemus as having a violet-coloured fleece.

Αρσενες οἰες ησαν εὐτρεφεες, δασυμαλλοι,
Καλοι τε, μεγαλοι τε, ιοδνεφες ειρος εχοντες.
Odyss., lib. ix., ver. 425.

"Strong were the rams, with native *purple* fair,
Well fed, and largest of the fleecy care." Pope.

Pliny, Aristotle, and others mention the same. And from facts of this kind it is very probable that the fable of the *golden fleece* had its origin. In the Zetland Isles I have seen sheep with variously coloured fleeces, some *white*, some *black*, some *black* and *white*, some of a very fine *chocolate colour*. Beholding those animals brought to my recollection those words of Virgil:—

Ipse sed in pratis Aries jam suave rubenti
Murice, jam croceo mutabit vellera luto.
Eclog. iv., ver. 43.

"No wool shall in *dissembled colours* shine;
But the luxurious father of the fold,
With native *purple* or unborrow'd *gold*,
Beneath his pompous fleece shall proudly sweat,
And under *Tyrian* robes the lamb shall bleat."
Dryden.

A. M. 2513.
B. C. 1491.
An. Exod. Isr. 1.
Sivan.

and badgers' skins, and shittim
wood;
6 [e] Oil for the light, [f] spices
for anointing oil, and for [g] sweet incense;
7 Onyx stones, and stones to
be set in the [h] ephod, and in the
[i] breastplate.
8 And let them make me a [k] sanctuary;

[e] Chapter xxvii. 20.——[f] Chapter xxx. 23.——[g] Chapter xxx. 34.——[h] Chap. xxviii. 4, 6.——[i] Chap. xxviii. 15.——[k] Chap. xxxvi. 1, 3, 4; Lev. iv. 6; x. 4; xxi. 12; Heb. ix. 1, 2.

Badgers' skins] ערת תחשים *oroth techashim.* Few terms have afforded greater perplexity to critics and commentators than this. Bochart has exhausted the subject, and seems to have proved that no kind of *animal* is here intended, but a *colour.* None of the ancient versions acknowledge an animal of any kind except the Chaldee, which seems to think the *badger* is intended, and from it we have borrowed our translation of the word. The Septuagint and Vulgate have skins dyed a *violet* colour; the Syriac, *azure;* the Arabic, *black;* the Coptic, *violet;* the modern Persic, *ram-skins,* &c. The colour contended for by Bochart is the *hysginus,* which is a very deep blue. So Pliny, *Coccoque tinctum Tyrio tingere, ut fieret hysginum.* "They dip crimson in purple to make the colour called *hysginus.*"—Hist. Nat., lib. ix., c. 65, edit. Bipont.

Shittim wood] By some supposed to be the finest species of the cedar; by others, the *acacia Nilotica,* a species of *thorn,* solid, light, and very beautiful. This acacia is known to have been plentiful in Egypt, and it abounds in Arabia Deserta, the very place in which Moses was when he built the tabernacle; and hence it is reasonable to suppose that he built it of that wood, which was every way proper for his purpose.

Verse 6. *Oil for the light*] This they must have brought with them from Egypt, for they could not get any in the wilderness where there were no olives; but it is likely that this and some other directions refer more to what was to be done when in their fixed and settled residence, than while wandering in the wilderness.

Spices] To make a confection for *sweet* incense, abounded in different parts of these countries.

Verse 7. *Onyx stones*] We have already met with the stone called שהם *shoham,* Gen. ii. 12, and acknowledged the difficulty of ascertaining what is meant by it. Some think the *onyx,* some the *sardine,* and some the *emerald,* is meant. We cannot say precisely what it was; possibly it might have been that fine pale pebble, called the *Egyptian pebble,* several specimens of which now lie before me, which were brought from the coast of the *Red Sea,* and other parts in Egypt, by a particular friend of mine, on purpose to add to my collection of minerals.

Stones to be set in the ephod] אבני מלאים *abney milluim, stones of filling up.* Stones so cut as to be proper to be set in the gold work of the breastplate.

The אפד *ephod.*—It is very difficult to tell what this was, or in what form it was made. It was a garment of some kind peculiar to the priests, and ever considered essential to all the parts of Divine worship, for without it no person attempted to inquire of God. As the word itself comes from the root אפד *aphad,* he *tied* or *bound close,* Calmet supposes that it was a kind of *girdle,* which, brought from behind the neck and over the shoulders, and so hanging down before, was put cross upon the stomach, and then carried round the waist, and thus made a girdle to the tunic. Where the ephod crossed on the breast there was a square ornament called חשן *choshen,* the *breastplate,* in which twelve precious stones were set, each bearing one of the names of the twelve sons of Jacob engraven on it There were two sorts of ephods, one of plain linen for the priests, the other very much embroidered for the high priest. As there was nothing singular in this common sort, no particular description is given; but that of the high priest is described very much in detail chap. xxviii. 6–8. It was distinguished from the common ephod by being composed of *gold, blue, purple, scarlet, fine twisted linen,* and *cunning work,* i. e., superbly ornamented and embroidered. This ephod was fastened on the shoulders with two precious stones, on which the twelve names of the twelve tribes of Israel were engraved, six names on each stone. These two stones, thus engraved, were different from those on the breastplate, with which they have been confounded. From Calmet's description the ephod seems to have been a series of belts, fastened to a collar, which were intended to keep the garments of the priest closely attached to his body: but there is some reason to believe that it was a sort of garment like that worn by our heralds; it covered the back, breast, and belly, and was open at the sides. A piece of the same kind of stuff with itself united it on the shoulders, where the two stones, already mentioned, were placed, and it was probably without sleeves. See on chap. xxviii. 2, &c.

Verse 8. *Let them make me a sanctuary*] מקדש *mikdash,* a *holy place,* such as God might dwell in; this was that part of the tabernacle that was called the most holy place, into which the high priest entered only once a year, on the great day of atonement.

That I may dwell among them.] "This," says Mr. Ainsworth, "was the main end of all; and to this all the particulars are to be referred, and by this they are to be opened. For this sanctuary, as Solomon's temple afterwards, was the place of prayer, and of the public service of God, Lev. xvii. 4–6; Matt. xxi. 13; and it signified the *Church* which is the habitation of God through the Spirit, 2 Cor. vi. 16; Eph. ii. 19–22; Rev. xxi. 2, 3; and was a visible sign of God's *presence* and *protection,* Lev. xxvi. 11, 12; Ezek. xxxvii. 27, 28; 1 Kings vi. 12, 13; and of his leading them to his heavenly glory. For as the high priest entered into the tabernacle, and through the veil into the most holy place where God dwelt; so Christ entered into the holy of holies, and we also enter through the veil, that is to say his flesh. See the use made of this by the apostle, Heb. ix. and x. Thus the *sanctuary* is to be applied as a type, 1. To *Christ's* person, Heb. viii. 2; ix. 11, 12; John ii. 19–21. 2. To every *Christian,* 1 Cor. vi. 19. 3. To the

A. M. 2513.
B. C. 1491.
An. Exod. Isr. 1.
Sivan.

that [l] I may dwell among
them.
9 [m] According to all that I
show thee, *after* the pattern of the tabernacle,
and the pattern of all the instruments thereof,
even so shall ye make *it*.
10 [n] And they shall make an ark *of* shittim
wood: two cubits and a half *shall be* the
length thereof, and a cubit and a half the
breadth thereof, and a cubit and a half the
height thereof.
11 And thou shalt overlay it with pure gold,
within and without shalt thou overlay it, and
shalt make upon it a crown of gold round about.
12 And thou shalt cast four
rings of gold for it, and put *them*
in the four corners thereof; and
two rings *shall be* in the one side of it, and
two rings in the other side of it.
13 And thou shalt make staves *of* shittim
wood, and overlay them with gold.
14 And thou shalt put the staves into the
rings by the sides of the ark, that the ark may
be borne with them.
15 [o] The staves shall be in the rings of the
ark; they shall not be taken from it.
16 And thou shalt put into the ark [p] the
testimony which I shall give thee.

[l] Chap. xxix. 45; 1 Kings vi. 13; 2 Cor. vi. 16; Heb. iii. 6; Rev. xxi. 3.——[m] Ver. 40.——[n] Chapter xxxvii. 1; Deut. x. 3; Heb. ix. 4.

[o] 1 Kings viii. 8.——[p] Chapter xvi. 34; xxxi. 18; Deut. x. 2, 5; xxxi. 26; 1 Kings viii. 9; 2 Kings xi. 12; Hebrews ix. 4.

Church; both *particular*, Heb. iii. 6; 1 Tim. iii. 15; and *universal*, Heb. x. 21: and it was because of the very extensive signification of this building, that the different things concerning this sanctuary are particularly set down by Moses, and so variously applied by the prophets and by the apostles."—*See Ainsworth.* As the *dwelling* in this tabernacle was the highest proof of God's grace and mercy towards the Israelites, so it typified Christ's dwelling by faith in the hearts of believers, and thus giving them the highest and surest proof of their reconciliation to God, and of his love and favour to them; see Eph. i. 22, iii. 17.

Verse 9. After *the pattern of the tabernacle*] It has been supposed that there had been a tabernacle before that erected by Moses, though it probably did not now exist; but the tabernacle which Moses is ordered to make was to be formed exactly on the model of this ancient one, the pattern of which God showed him in the mount, ver. 40. The word משכן *mishcan* signifies literally the *dwelling* or *habitation;* and this was so called because it was the dwelling place of God; and the *only* place on the earth in which he made himself manifest. See the note on ver. 40, and on chapter xxxiii. 7–10.

Verse 10. *They shall make an ark*] ארון *aron* signifies an *ark, chest, coffer*, or *coffin*. It is used particularly to designate that chest or coffer in which the *testimony* or two *tables of the covenant* was laid up, on the top of which was the *propitiatory* or *mercy-seat*, (see on ver. 17,) and at the end of which were the *cherubim* of gold, (ver. 18–20,) between whom the visible sign of the presence of the supreme God appeared as seated upon his throne. The ark was the most excellent of all the holy things which belonged to the Mosaic economy, and for its sake the tabernacle and the temple were built, chap. xxvi. 33; xl. 18, 21. It was considered as conferring a sanctity wherever it was fixed, 2 Chron. viii. 11; 2 Sam. vi. 12.

Two cubits and a half shall be *the length, &c.*] About *four* feet *five* inches in length, taking the cubit at *twenty-one* inches, and *two* feet *six* inches in breadth and in depth. As this ark was chiefly intended to deposit the two tables of stone in, which had been written by the finger of God, we may very reasonably conjecture that the length of those tables was not less than *four feet* and their breadth not less than *two*. As to their thickness we can say nothing, as the depth of the ark was intended for other matters besides the two tables, such as Aaron's rod, the pot of manna, &c., &c., though probably these were laid up *beside*, not *in*, the ark.

Verse 11. *A crown of gold round about.*] A border, or, as the Septuagint have it, *κυματια χρυσα στρεπτα κυκλω*, *waves of gold wreathed round about.*

Verse 15. *The staves—shall not be taken from it.*] Because it should ever be considered as in readiness to be removed, God not having told them at what hour he should command them to strike their tents. If the staves were never to be taken out, how can it be said, as in Num. iv. 6, that when the camp should set forward, they should *put in the staves thereof*, which intimates that when they encamped they *took out the staves*, which appears to be contrary to what is here said? To reconcile these two places, it has been supposed, with great show of probability, that besides the staves which passed through the rings of the ark, and by which it was carried, there were two other staves or poles in the form of a *bier* or *hand-barrow*, on which the ark was laid in order to be transported in their journeyings, when it and its own staves, still in their rings, had been wrapped up in the covering of what is called *badgers' skins* and *blue cloth*. The staves of the ark itself, which might be considered as its *handles* simply to lift it by, were never taken out of their rings; but the staves or poles which served as a bier were taken from under it when they encamped.

Verse 16. *The testimony*] The two tables of stone, which were not yet given; these tables were called עדות *eduth*, from עד *forward, onward, to bear witness to or of a person or thing.* Not only the tables of stone, but all the contents of the ark, Aaron's rod, the pot of manna, the holy anointing oil, &c., bore *testimony* to the Messiah in his *prophetic, sacerdotal*, and *regal* offices.

A. M. 2513.
B. C. 1491.
An. Exod. Isr. 1.
Sivan.

17 And [q] thou shalt make a mercy-seat *of* pure gold: two cubits and a half *shall be* the length thereof, and a cubit and a half the breadth thereof.

18 And thou shalt make two cherubims *of* gold, *of* beaten work shalt thou make them, in the two ends of the mercy-seat.

19 And make one cherub on the one end, and the other cherub on the other end; *even* [r] of the mercy-seat shall ye make the cherubims on the two ends thereof.

20 And [s] the cherubims shall stretch forth *their* wings on high, covering the mercy-seat with their wings, and their faces *shall look* one to another; toward the mercy-seat shall the faces of the cherubims be.

21 [t] And thou shalt put the mercy-seat above upon the ark; and [u] in the ark thou shalt put the testimony that I shall give thee.

22 And [v] there I will meet with thee, and I will commune with thee from above the mercy-seat, from [w] between the two cherubims which *are* upon the ark of the testimony, of all *things* which I will give thee in commandment unto the children of Israel.

23 [x] Thou shalt also make a table *of* shittim

[q] Chap. xxxvii. 6; Rom. iii. 25; Heb. ix. 5.——[r] Or, *of the* matter *of the mercy-seat.*——[s] 1 Kings viii. 7; 1 Chron. xxviii. 18; Heb. ix. 5.——[t] Chap. xxvi. 34.——[u] Ver. 16.——[v] Chapter xxix. 42, 43; xxx. 6, 36; Lev. xvi. 2; Num. xvii. 4.——[w] Num. vii. 89; 1 Samuel iv. 4; 2 Samuel vi. 2; 2 Kings xix. 15; Psalm lxxx. 1; xc. 1; Isaiah xxxvii. 16.——[x] Chap. xxxvii. 10; 1 Kings vii. 48; 2 Chron. iv. 8; Hebrews ix. 2.

Verse 17. *A mercy-seat*] כפרת *capporeth*, from כפר *caphar*, to *cover* or *overspread;* because by an act of pardon sins are represented as being *covered*, so that they no longer appear in the eye of Divine justice to displease, irritate, and call for punishment; and the person of the offender is *covered* or protected from the stroke of the broken law. In the Greek version of the Septuagint the word ἱλαστηριον, *hilasterion*, is used, which signifies a *propitiatory*, and is the name used by the apostle, Heb. ix. 5. This *mercy-seat* or *propitiatory* was made of pure gold; it was properly the lid or covering of that vessel so well known by the name of the *ark* and *ark of the covenant*. On and before this, the high priest was to sprinkle the blood of the *expiatory* sacrifices on the great day of *atonement:* and it was in this place that God promised to meet the people, (see ver. 22;) for *there* he dwelt, and *there* was the symbol of the Divine presence. At each end of this propitiatory was a cherub, between whom this glory was manifested; hence in Scripture it is so often said that *he dwelleth between the cherubim*. As the word ἱλαστηριον, *propitiatory* or *mercy-seat*, is applied to Christ, Rom. iii. 25, *whom God hath set forth to be a* PROPITIATION (ἱλαστηριον) *through faith in his blood—for the remission of sins that are past;* hence we learn that Christ was the true mercy-seat, the thing signified by the *capporeth*, to the ancient believers. And we learn farther that it was by *his blood* that an atonement was to be made for the sins of the world. And as God showed himself between the cherubim over this propitiatory or mercy-seat, so it is said, *God was in Christ reconciling the world unto himself;* 2 Cor. v. 19, &c. See on Lev. vii.

Verse 18. *Thou shall make two cherubims*] What these were we cannot distinctly say. It is generally supposed that a cherub was a creature with four heads and one body: and the animals, of which these emblematical forms consisted, were the noblest of their kinds; the *lion* among the *wild beasts*, the *bull* among the *tame* ones, the *eagle* among the *birds*, and *man* at the head of all; so that they might be, says Dr. Priestley, the representatives of *all nature*. Concerning their *forms* and design there is much difference of opinion among divines. It is probable that the term often means a *figure* of any kind, such as was ordinarily *sculptured* on *stone*, *engraved* on *metal*, *carved* on *wood*, or *embroidered* on *cloth*. See on chap. xxxv. 8. It may be only necessary to add, that cherub is the singular number; *cherubim*, not cherubims, the plural. See what has been said on this subject in the note on Gen. iii. 24.

Verse 22. *And there I will meet with thee*] That is, over the mercy-seat, between the cherubim. In this place God chose to give the most especial manifestations of himself; here the Divine glory was to be seen; and here Moses was to come in order to consult Jehovah, relative to the management of the people.

Ainsworth has remarked that the rabbins say, "The heart of man may be likened to God's sanctuary; for as, in the sanctuary, the *shechinah* or *Divine glory* dwelt, because *there* were the ark, the tables, and the cherubim; so, in the heart of man, it is meet that a place be made for the Divine Majesty to dwell in, and that it be the holy of holies." This is a doctrine most implicitly taught by the apostles; and the absolute necessity of having the heart made a habitation of God through the Spirit, is strongly and frequently insisted on through the whole of the New Testament. See the note on the following verse.

Verse 23. *Thou shalt also make a table* of *shittim wood*] The same wood, the *acacia*, of which the ark-staves, &c., were made. On the subject of the ark, table of shew-bread, &c., Dr. *Cudworth*, in his very learned and excellent treatise on the Lord's Supper, has the following remarks:—

"When God had brought the children of Israel out of Egypt, resolving to manifest himself in a peculiar manner present among them, he thought good to dwell amongst them in a visible and external manner; and therefore, while they were in the wilderness, and sojourned in tents, he would have a tent or tabernacle built to sojourn with them also. This mystery of the tabernacle was fully understood by the learned Nachmanides, who, in few words, but pregnant, expresseth

A. M. 2513.
B. C. 1491.
An. Exod. Isr. 1.
Sivan.

wood: two cubits *shall be* the length thereof, and a cubit the breadth thereof, and a cubit and a half the height thereof.

24 And thou shalt overlay it with pure gold, and make thereto a crown of gold round about.

25 And thou shalt make unto it a border of a hand-breadth round about, and thou shalt make a golden crown to the border thereof round about.

26 And thou shalt make for it four rings of gold, and put the rings in the four corners that *are* on the four feet thereof.

27 Over against the border shall the rings be for places of the staves to bear the table.

28 And thou shalt make the staves *of* shittim wood, and overlay them with gold, that the table may be borne with them.

29 And thou shalt make [y] the dishes thereof, and spoons thereof, and covers thereof, and bowls thereof, [z] to cover withal: *of* pure gold shalt thou make them.

30 And thou shalt set upon the table [a] shewbread before me alway.

[y] Chap. xxxvii. 16; Num. iv. 7. — [z] Or, *to pour out withal.* — [a] Lev. xxiv. 5, 6.

himself to this purpose: 'The mystery of the tabernacle was this, that it was to be a place for the shechinah, or habitation of Divinity, to be fixed in;' and this, no doubt, as a special type of God's future dwelling in Christ's human nature, which was the TRUE SHECHINAH: but when the Jews were come into their land, and had there built them houses, God intended to have a fixed dwelling-house also; and therefore his movable tabernacle was to be turned into a standing temple. Now the tabernacle or temple, being thus as a house for God to dwell in visibly, to make up the notion of dwelling or habitation complete there must be all things suitable to a house belonging to it; hence, in the holy place, there must be a table, and a candlestick, because this was the ordinary furniture of a room, as the fore-commended Nachmanides observes. The table must have its dishes, and spoons, and bowls, and covers belonging to it, though they were never used; and always be furnished with bread upon it. The candlestick must have its lamps continually burning. Hence also there must be a continual fire kept in this house of God upon the altar, as the *focus* of it; to which notion I conceive the Prophet Isaiah doth allude, chap. xxxi. 9: *Whose fire is in Zion, and his furnace in Jerusalem;* and besides all this, to carry the notion still farther, there must be some constant meat and provision brought into this house; which was done in the sacrifices that were partly consumed by fire upon God's own altar, and partly eaten by the priests, who were God's family, and therefore to be maintained by him. That which was consumed upon God's altar was accounted *God's mess*, as appeareth from Mal. i. 12, where the altar is called *God's table*, and the sacrifice upon it, *God's meat: Ye say, The table of the* LORD *is polluted; and the fruit thereof, even* HIS MEAT, *is contemptible.* And often, in the law, the sacrifice is called God's לחם *lechem*, i. e., his *bread* or *food*. Wherefore it is farther observable, that besides the flesh of the beast offered up in sacrifice, there was a *minchah*, i. e., a *meat-offering*, or rather *bread-offering*, made of flour and oil; and a *libamen* or *drink-offering*, which was always joined with the daily sacrifice, as the *bread* and *drink* which was to go along with God's meat. It was also strictly commanded that there should be salt in every sacrifice and oblation, because all meat is unsavoury without salt, as Nachmanides hath here also well observed; 'because it was not honourable that God's meat should be unsavoury, without salt.' Lastly, all these things were to be consumed on the altar only by the holy fire which came down from heaven, because they were God's portion, and therefore to be eaten or consumed by himself in an extraordinary manner." See on ver. 22.

Verse 29. *The dishes thereof*] קערתיו *kearothaiv*, probably the deep bowls in which they kneaded the mass out of which they made the *shew-bread.*

And spoons thereof] כפתיו *cappothaiv*, probably *censers*, on which they put up the incense; as seems pretty evident from Num. vii. 14, 20, 26, 32, 38, 44, 50, 56, 62, 68, 74, 80, 86, where the same word is used, and the instrument, whatever it was, is always represented as being filled with incense.

Covers thereof] קשותיו *kesothaiv*, supposed to be a *large cup* or *tankard*, in which pure wine was kept on the table along with the shew-bread for *libations*, which were poured out before the Lord every Sabbath, when the old bread was removed, and the new bread laid on the table.

Bowls thereof] מנקיתיו *menakkiyothaiv*, from נקה *nakah*, to *clear away*, *remove*, *empty*, &c.; supposed by Calmet to mean, either the *sieves* by which the Levites cleansed the wheat they made into bread, (for it is asserted that the grain, out of which the shew-bread was made, was sowed, reaped, ground, sifted, kneaded, baked, &c., by the Levites themselves,) or the *ovens* in which the bread was baked. Others suppose they were vessels which they dipped into the *kesoth*, to take out the wine for libations.

Verse 30. *Shew-bread*] לחם פנים *lechem panim*, literally, *bread of faces;* so called, either because they were placed *before the presence* or *face of God* in the sanctuary, or because they were made *square*, as the Jews will have it. It is probable that they were in the form of *cubes* or *hexaedrons*, each side presenting the same appearance; and hence the Jews might suppose they were called the *bread* or *loaves of faces:* but the Hebrew text seems to intimate that they were called the *bread of faces*, פנים *panim*, because, as the Lord says, they were set לפני *lephanai*, *before my* FACE. These loaves or cakes were *twelve*, representing, as is

A. M. 2513.
B. C. 1491.
An. Exod. Isr. 1.
Sivan.

31 [b] And thou shalt make a candlestick *of* pure gold; *of* beaten work shall the candlestick be made: his shaft, and his branches, his bowls, his knops, and his flowers, shall be of the same.

32 And six branches shall come out of the sides of it; three branches of the candlestick out of the one side, and three branches of the candlestick out of the other side:

33 Three bowls made like unto almonds, *with* a knop and a flower in one branch; and three bowls made like almonds in the other branch, *with* a knop and a flower: so in the six branches that come out of the candlestick.

34 And in the candlestick *shall be* four bowls, made like unto almonds, *with* their knops and their flowers.

35 And *there shall be* a knop under two branches of the same, and a knop under two branches of the same, and a knop under two branches of the same, according to the six branches that proceed out of the candlestick

36 Their knops and their branches shall be of the same: all of it *shall be* one beaten work *of* pure gold.

37 And thou shalt make the seven lamps

[b] Chap. xxxvii. 17; 1 Kings vii. 49; Zech. iv. 2; Heb. ix. 2; Rev. i. 12; iv. 5.

---

generally supposed, the twelve tribes of Israel. They were in two rows of six each. On the top of each row there was a golden dish with frankincense, which was burned before the Lord, as a memorial, at the end of the week, when the old loaves were removed and replaced by new ones, the priests taking the former for their domestic use.

It is more difficult to ascertain the use of these, or what they represented, than almost any other emblem in the whole Jewish economy. Many have *conjectured* their meaning, and I feel no disposition to increase their number by any addition of my own. The note on ver. 23, from Dr. Cudworth, appears to me more rational than any thing else I have met with. The tabernacle was God's house, and in it he had his *table*, his *bread*, his *wine*, *candlestick*, &c., to show them that he had *taken up his dwelling* among them. See the note on ver. 23.

Verse 31. *A candlestick of pure gold*] This *candlestick* or *chandelier* is generally described as having one *shaft* or *stock*, with *six branches* proceeding from it, adorned at equal distances with six flowers like lilies, with as many *bowls* and *knops* placed alternately. On each of the branches there was a lamp, and one on the top of the shaft which occupied the centre; thus there were *seven* lamps in all, ver. 37. These *seven lamps* were lighted every evening and extinguished every morning.

We are not so certain of the precise *form* of any instrument or utensil of the tabernacle or temple, as we are of this, the golden table, and the two silver trumpets.

Titus, after the overthrow of Jerusalem, A. D. 70, had the golden *candlestick* and the golden *table* of the shew-bread, the *silver trumpets*, and the book of the *law*, taken out of the temple and carried in triumph to Rome; and Vespasian lodged them in the temple which he had consecrated to the goddess of *Peace*. Some plants also of the balm of *Jericho* are said to have been carried in the procession. At the foot of Mount Palatine there are the ruins of an arch, on which the triumph of Titus for his conquest of the Jews is represented, and on which the several monuments which were carried in the procession are sculptured, and particularly the *golden candlestick*, the *table* of the *shew-bread* and the two *silver trumpets*. A *correct* MODEL of this arch, taken on the spot, now stands before me; and the spoils of the temple, the *candlestick*, the *golden table*, and the two *trumpets*, are represented on the panel on the left hand, in the inside of the arch, in *basso-relievo*. The *candlestick* is not so ornamented as it appears in many prints; at the same time it looks much better than it does in the engraving of this arch given by Montfaucon, *Antiq. Expliq.*, vol. iv., pl. 32. It is likely that on the real arch this candlestick is less in size than the *original*, as it scarcely measures three feet in height. See the *Diarium Italicum*, p. 129. To see these sacred articles given up by that God who ordered them to be made according to a pattern exhibited by himself, gracing the triumph of a *heathen* emperor, and at last consecrated to an *idol*, affords melancholy reflections to a pious mind. But these things had accomplished the end for which they were instituted, and were now of *no farther use*. The glorious personage typified by all this ancient apparatus, had about *seventy* years before this made his appearance. The true *light* was come, and the *Holy Spirit* poured out from on high; and therefore the *golden candlestick*, by which they were typified, was given up. The ever-during bread had been sent from heaven; and therefore the *golden table*, which bore its *representative*, the *shew-bread*, was now no longer needful. The *joyful sound* of the *everlasting Gospel* was then published in the world; and therefore the *silver trumpets* that typified this were carried into captivity, and their sound was no more to be heard. Strange providence but unutterable mercy of God! The Jews lost both the *sign* and the *thing signified;* and that very *people*, who destroyed the holy city, carried away the spoils of the temple, and dedicated them to the objects of their idolatry, were the first in the universe to receive the *preaching* of the Gospel, the *light* of salvation, and the *bread of life!* There is a sort of *coincidence* or *association* here, which is worthy of the most serious observation. The Jews had these significant *emblems* to lead them to, and prepare them for, the things *signified*. They trusted in the *former*, and rejected the *latter!* God therefore deprived them of *both*, and gave up their temple to the spoilers, their land to desolation,

A. M. 2513. B. C. 1491. An. Exod. Isr. 1. Sivan.

thereof: and [c] they shall [d] light the lamps thereof, that they may [e] give light over against [f] it.

38 And the tongs thereof, and the snuff-dishes thereof, *shall be of* pure gold.

39 *Of* a talent of pure gold shall he make it, with all these vessels.

A. M. 2513. B. C. 1491. An. Exod. Isr. 1. Sivan.

40 And [g] look that thou make *them* after their pattern, [h] which was showed thee in the mount.

[c] Chap. xxvii. 21; xxx. 8; Lev. xxiv. 3, 4; 2 Chron. xiii. 11. [d] Or, *cause to ascend*.——[e] Num. viii. 2.——[f] Heb. *the face of it.*

[g] Chap. xxvi. 30; Num. viii. 4; 1 Chron. xxviii. 11, 19; Acts vii. 44; Heb. viii. 5.——[h] Heb. *which thou wast caused to see.*

and themselves to captivity and to the sword. The *heathens* then carried away the *emblems of their salvation*, and God shortly gave unto those heathens that very salvation of which these things were the emblems! Thus, because of their unbelief and rebellion, *the kingdom of heaven*, according to the prediction of our blessed Lord, *was taken from the Jews, and given to a nation* (the Gentiles) *that brought forth the fruits thereof*; Matt. xxi. 43. Behold the GOODNESS and SEVERITY of God!

Verse 39. Of *a talent of pure gold shall he make it, with all these vessels.*] That is, a talent of gold in weight was used in making the candlestick, and the different vessels and instruments which belonged to it. According to Bishop Cumberland, a talent was *three thousand* shekels. As the Israelites brought each *half a shekel*, chap. xxxviii. 26, so that *one hundred talents, one thousand seven hundred and seventy-five shekels*, were contributed by *six hundred and three thousand five hundred and fifty* persons; by halving the number of the Israelites, he finds they contributed *three hundred and one thousand seven hundred and seventy-five* shekels in all. Now, as we find that this number of shekels made *one hundred* talents, and *one thousand seven hundred and seventy-five* shekels over, if we subtract *one thousand seven hundred and seventy-five*, the odd shekels, from *three hundred and one thousand seven hundred and seventy-five*, we shall have for a remainder *three hundred thousand*, the number of shekels in *one hundred* talents: and if this remainder be divided by *one hundred*, the number of talents, it quotes *three thousand*, the number of shekels in each talent. A silver shekel of the sanctuary, being equal, according to Dr. Prideaux, to *three shillings* English, *three thousand* such shekels will amount to *four hundred and fifty pounds* sterling; and, reckoning gold to silver as fifteen to one, a talent of gold will amount to *six thousand seven hundred and fifty pounds* sterling: to which add *two hundred and sixty-three pounds* for the *one thousand seven hundred and seventy-five* shekels, at *three shillings* each, and it makes a total of *seven thousand and thirteen pounds*, which immense sum was expended on the *candlestick* and its *furniture*. It is no wonder, then, (if the candlestick in the second temple was equal in value to that in the ancient tabernacle,) that *Titus* should think it of sufficient consequence to be one of the articles, with the *golden table*, and *silver trumpets*, that should be employed to grace his triumph. Their *intrinsic* worth was a matter of no consequence to Him whose are the silver and gold, the earth and its fulness; they had accomplished their design, and were of no farther use, either in the kingdom of providence, or the kingdom of grace. See the note on ver. 31, and see that on chap. xxxviii. 24.

Verse 40. *And look that thou make, &c.*] This verse should be understood as an order to Moses after the tabernacle, &c., had been described to him; as if he had said: "When thou comest to make all the things that I have already described to thee, with the other matters of which I shall afterwards treat, see that thou make every thing according to the pattern which thou didst see in the mount." The Septuagint have it, *κατα τον τυπον τον δεδειγμενον σοι· according to the* TYPE—*form* or *fashion, which was shown thee.* It appears to me that St. Paul had this command particularly in view when he gave that to his son Timothy which we find in the second epistle, chap. i. 13: *Ὑποτυπωσιν εχε ὑγιαινοντων λογων, ὡν παρ' εμου ηκουσας.* "*Hold fast* the FORM of *sound words* which thou hast heard *of me*." The tabernacle was a *type* of the Church of God; that Church is built upon the foundation of the prophets and apostles, Jesus Christ being the chief corner-stone, Eph. ii. 20–22: the *doctrines*, therefore, delivered by the prophets, Jesus Christ, and his apostles, are essential to the constitution of this Church. As God, therefore, gave the *plan* or *form* according to which the tabernacle must be constructed, so he gives the *doctrines* according to which the Christian Church is to be modelled; and apostles, and subordinate builders, are to have and hold fast that FORM of sound words, and construct this heavenly building according to that *form* or *pattern* which has come through the express revelation of God.

IN different parts of this work we have had occasion to remark that the heathens borrowed their best things from Divine revelation, both as it refers to what was *pure* in their *doctrines*, and *significant* in their *religious rites*. Indeed, they seem in many cases to have studied the closest imitation possible, consistent with the adaptation of all to their preposterous and idolatrous worship. They had their IAO or JOVE, in imitation of the true JEHOVAH; and from different *attributes* of the Divine Nature they formed an innumerable group of gods and goddesses. They had also their temples in imitation of the temple of God; and in these they had their holy and more holy places, in imitation of the courts of the Lord's house. The heathen temples consisted of several parts or divisions: 1. The *area* or porch; 2. The *ναος* or *temple*, similar to the *nave* of our churches; 3. The *adytum* or holy place, called also *penetrale* and *sacrarium*; and, 4. The *οπισθοδομος* or the *inner temple*, the most secret recess, where they had their *mysteria*, and which answered to the *holy* of *holies* in the tabernacle. And as there is no evidence whatever that there was any temple among the heathens prior to the tabernacle, it is reasonable to conclude that it served as a model for all that they afterwards built. They had even their *portable*

a

temples, to imitate the tabernacle; and the shrines for Diana, mentioned Acts xix. 24, were of this kind. They had even their *arks* or sacred *coffers*, where they kept their most holy things, and the mysterious emblems of their religion; together with *candlesticks* or *lamps*, to illuminate their temples, which had few windows, to imitate the golden candlestick in the Mosaic tabernacle. They had even their *processions*, in imitation of the carrying about of the ark in the wilderness; accompanied by such ceremonies as sufficiently show, to an unprejudiced mind, that they borrowed them from this sacred original. Dr. Dodd has a good note on this subject, which I shall take the liberty to extract.

Speaking of the ark, he says, "We meet with imitations of this Divinely instituted emblem among several heathen nations. Thus *Tacitus*, *De Moribus Germanorum*, cap. 40, informs us that the inhabitants of the north of Germany, our Saxon ancestors, in general worshipped *Herthum* or *Hertham*, i. e. the *mother earth: Hertham* being plainly derived from ארץ *arets*, *earth*, and אם *am*, *mother:* and they believed her to interpose in the affairs of men, and to visit nations: that to her, in a sacred grove in a certain island of the ocean, a *vehicle* covered with a *vestment* was consecrated, and allowed to be touched by the *priests only*, (compare 2 Sam. vi. 6, 7; 1 Chron. xiii. 9, 10,) who perceived when the goddess entered into her secret place, *penetrale*, and with profound veneration attended her *vehicle*, which was drawn by *cows;* see 1 Sam. vi. 7–10. While the goddess was on her progress, days of rejoicing were kept in every place which she vouchsafed to visit; they engaged in no war, they handled no weapons; peace and quietness were then only known, only relished, till the same priest reconducted the goddess to her temple. Then the *vehicle* and *vestment*, and, if you can believe it, the *goddess herself*, were washed in a sacred lake."

Apuleius, *De Aur. Asin.*, lib. ii., describing a solemn idolatrous procession, after the Egyptian mode, says, "A *chest*, or *ark*, was carried by another, containing their secret things, entirely concealing the mysteries of religion."

And *Plutarch*, in his treatise *De Iside*, &c., describing the rites of *Osiris*, says, "On the tenth day of the month, at night, they go down to the sea; and the stolists, together with the priest, carry forth the sacred *chest*, in which is a small boat or *vessel* of gold."

Pausanius likewise testifies, lib. vii., c. 19, that the ancient Trojans had a *sacred ark*, wherein was the image of BACCHUS, made by Vulcan, which had been given to Dardanus by Jupiter. As the ark was deposited in the *holy* of *holies*, so the heathens had in the inmost part of their temples an *adytum* or *penetrale*, to which *none had access but the priests*. And it is remarkable that, among the Mexicans, *Vitzliputzli*, their supreme god, was represented under a human shape, sitting on a throne, supported by an *azure globe* which they called heaven; *four poles* or *sticks came out* from two sides of this globe, at the end of which serpents' heads were carved, the whole making a *litter* which the priests carried on their shoulders whenever the idol was shown in public.—*Religious Ceremonies*, vol. iii., p. 146.

Calmet remarks that the ancients used to dedicate candlesticks in the temples of their gods, bearing a great number of lamps.

Pliny, *Hist. Nat.*, lib. xxxiv, c. 3, mentions one made in the form of a tree, with lamps in the likeness of apples, which Alexander the Great consecrated in the temple of Apollo.

And *Athenæus*, lib. xv., c. 19, 20, mentions one that supported *three hundred and sixty-five* lamps, which *Dionysius* the younger, king of Syracuse, dedicated in the *Prytaneum* at Athens. As the Egyptians, according to the testimony of *Clemens Alexandrinus*, *Strom.*, lib. i., were the first who used lamps in their temples, they probably borrowed the use from the golden candlestick in the tabernacle and temple.

From the solemn and very particular charge, *Look that thou make* them *after their pattern, which was showed thee in the mount*, it appears plainly that God showed Moses a *model* of the tabernacle and all its furniture; and to receive instructions relative to this was one part of his employment while on the mount forty days with God. As God designed that this building, and all that belonged to it, should be patterns or representations of good things to come, it was indispensably necessary that Moses should receive a model and specification of the whole, according to which he might direct the different artificers in their constructing the work. 1. We may observe that the whole tabernacle and its furniture resembled a dwelling-house and its furniture. 2. That this tabernacle was the house of God, not merely for the performance of his worship, but for his residence. 3. That God had promised to dwell among this people, and this was the habitation which he appointed for his glory. 4. That the tabernacle, as well as the temple, was a type of the incarnation of Jesus Christ. See John i. 14, and ii. 19, 21. 5. That as the glory of God was manifested between the cherubim, above the mercy-seat, in this tabernacle, so *God was in Christ, and in him dwelt all the fulness of the Godhead bodily.* 6. As in the tabernacle were found bread, light, &c., probably all these were emblematical of the ample provision made in Christ for the direction, support, and salvation of the soul of man. Of these, and many other things in the law and the prophets, we shall know more when mortality is swallowed up of life.

CHAPTER XXVI.

The ten curtains *of the tabernacle, and of what composed,* 1. *Their* length, 2, 3; *their* loops, 4, 5; *their* taches, 6. *The* curtains *of* goats' hair *for a covering,* 7; *their* length *and* breadth, 8. *Coupled with* loops, 9, 10, *and* taches, 11. *The remnant of the curtains, how to be employed,* 12, 13. *The* covering *of* rams' skins, 14. *The* boards *of the tabernacle for the south side,* 15; *their length,* 16, *tenons,* 17, *number,* 18, *sockets,* 19. *Boards, &c., for the north side,* 20, 21. *Boards, &c., for the west side,* 22; *for the corners,* 23; *their rings and sockets,* 24, 25. *The* bars *of the tabernacle,* 26–30. *The* veil, *its pillars, hooks, and taches,* 31–33. *How to place the* mercy-seat, 34. *The* table *and the* candlestick, 35. *The* hanging *for the door of the tent,* 36; *and the* hangings *for the pillars,* 37.

A. M. 2513. B. C. 1491. An. Exod. Isr. 1. Sivan.

MOREOVER [a] thou shalt make the tabernacle *with* ten curtains *of* fine twined linen, and blue, and purple, and scarlet: *with* cherubims [b] of cunning work shalt thou make them.

2 The length of one curtain *shall be* eight and twenty cubits, and the breadth of one curtain four cubits: and every one of the curtains shall have one measure.

3 The five curtains shall be coupled together one to another; and *other* five curtains *shall be* coupled one to another.

4 And thou shalt make loops of blue, upon the edge of the one curtain, from the selvage in the coupling; and likewise shalt thou make in the uttermost edge of *another* curtain, in the coupling of the second.

5 Fifty loops shalt thou make in the one curtain, and fifty loops shalt thou make in the edge of the curtain that *is* in the coupling of the second; that the loops may take hold one of another.

A. M. 2513. B. C. 1491. An. Exod. Isr. 1. Sivan.

6 And thou shalt make fifty taches of gold, and couple the curtains together with the taches; and it shall be one tabernacle.

7 And [c] thou shalt make curtains *of* goats' *hair,* to be a covering upon the tabernacle: eleven curtains shalt thou make.

8 The length of one curtain *shall be* thirty cubits, and the breadth of one curtain four cubits: and the eleven curtains *shall be all* of one measure.

9 And thou shalt couple five curtains by themselves, and six curtains by themselves, and shalt double the sixth curtain in the forefront of the tabernacle.

10 And thou shalt make fifty loops on the edge of the one curtain *that is* outmost in the coupling, and fifty loops in the edge of the curtain which coupleth the second.

[a] Chap. xxxvi. 8.——[b] Heb. *the work of a cunning workman* or *embroiderer.*——[c] Chap. xxxvi. 14.

NOTES ON CHAP. XXVI.

Verse 1. *Thou shalt make the tabernacle*] משכן *mischan,* from שכן *shachan,* to *dwell,* means simply a dwelling place or habitation of any kind, but here it means the dwelling place of Jehovah, who, as a king in his camp, had his *dwelling* or pavilion among his people, his *table* always spread, his *lamps* lighted, and the *priests,* &c., *his attendants,* always in waiting. From the minute and accurate description here given, a good workman, had he the same materials, might make a perfect *fac simile* of the ancient Jewish tabernacle. It was a movable building, and so constructed that it might be easily taken to pieces, for the greater convenience of carriage, as they were often obliged to transport it from place to place, in their various journeyings. For the *twined linen, blue, purple,* and *scarlet,* see the notes on chap. xxv. 4, &c.

Cherubims] See the note on chap. xxv. 18.

Cunning work] חשב *choshcb* probably means a sort of *diaper,* in which the figures appear equally perfect on both sides; this was probably formed in the loom. Another kind of curious work is mentioned, ver. 36, רקם *rokem,* which we term *needle-work;* this was probably similar to our *embroidery, tapestry,* or *cloth of arras.* It has been thought unlikely that these curious works were *all* manufactured in the wilderness: what was done in the loom, they might have brought with them from Egypt; what could be done by hand, without the use of complex machinery, the Israelitish women could readily perform with their needles, during their stay in the wilderness. But still it seems probable that they brought even their looms with them. The whole of this account shows that not only *necessary* but *ornamental* arts had been carried to a considerable pitch of perfection, both among the Israelites and Egyptians.

The inner curtains of the tabernacle were *ten* in number, and each in length *twenty-eight cubits,* and *four* in breadth; about *sixteen* yards *twelve* inches long, and *two* yards *twelve* inches broad. The curtains were to be coupled together, five and five of a side, by fifty loops, ver. 5, and as many golden clasps, ver. 6, so that each might look like one curtain, and the whole make one entire covering, which was the *first.*

Verse 7. *Curtains* of *goats'* hair] Stuff made of goats' hair. See the note on chap. xxv. 4. This was the *second* covering.

A. M. 2513.
B. C. 1491.
An. Exod. Isr. 1.
Sivan.

11 And thou shalt make fifty taches of brass, and put the taches into the loops, and couple the [d] tent together, that it may be one.

12 And the remnant that remaineth of the curtains of the tent, the half curtain that remaineth, shall hang over the backside of the tabernacle.

13 And a cubit on the one side, and a cubit on the other side, [e] of that which remaineth in the length of the curtains of the tent, it shall hang over the sides of the tabernacle, on this side and on that side, to cover it.

14 And [f] thou shalt make a covering for the tent *of* rams' skins dyed red, and a covering above *of* badgers' skins.

15 And thou shalt make boards for the tabernacle *of* shittim wood standing up.

16 Ten cubits *shall be* the length of a board, and a cubit and a half *shall be* the breadth of one board.

17 Two [g] tenons *shall there be* in one board, set in order one against another: thus shalt thou make for all the boards of the tabernacle.

18 And thou shalt make the boards for the tabernacle, twenty boards on the south side southward.

19 And thou shalt make forty sockets of silver under the twenty boards; two sockets under one board for his two tenons, and two sockets under another board for his two tenons.

20 And for the second side of the tabernacle, on the north side, *there shall be* twenty boards:

A. M. 2513.
B. C. 1491.
An. Exod. Isr. 1
Sivan.

21 And their forty sockets *of* silver; two sockets under one board, and two sockets under another board.

22 And for the sides of the tabernacle westward, thou shalt make six boards.

23 And two boards shalt thou make for the corners of the tabernacle in the two sides.

24 And they shall be [h] coupled together beneath, and they shall be coupled together above the head of it unto one ring: thus shall it be for them both; they shall be for the two corners.

25 And they shall be eight boards, and their sockets *of* silver, sixteen sockets; two sockets under one board, and two sockets under another board.

26 And thou shalt make bars *of* shittim wood; five for the boards of the one side of the tabernacle,

27 And five bars for the boards of the other side of the tabernacle, and five bars for the boards of the side of the tabernacle, for the two sides westward.

28 And the middle bar, in the midst of the boards, shall reach from end to end.

29 And thou shalt overlay the boards with gold, and make their rings *of* gold *for* places for the bars: and thou shalt overlay the bars with gold.

30 And thou shalt rear up the tabernacle, [i] according to the fashion thereof, which was showed thee in the mount.

[d] Or, *covering*.——[e] Hebrew, *in the remainder* or *surplusage*. [f] Chap. xxxvi. 19.——[g] Heb. *hands*.

[h] Hebrew, *twined*.——[i] Chapter xxv. 9, 40; xxvii. 8; Acts vii. 44; Heb. viii. 5.

Verse 14. *Rams' skins dyed red*] See on chap. xxv. 5. This was the *third* covering; and what is called the *badgers' skins* was the *fourth*. See the note on chap. xxv. 5. Why there should have been *four* coverings does not appear. They might have been designed partly for respect; and partly to keep off dust and dirt, and the extremely fine sand which in that desert rises as it were on every breeze; and partly to keep off the intense *heat* of the sun, which would otherwise have destroyed the poles, bars, boards, and the whole of the wood work. As to the conjecture of some that "the four coverings were intended the better to keep off the *rain*," it must appear unfounded to those who know that in that desert rain was rarely ever seen.

Verse 15. *Thou shalt make boards*] These formed what might be called the walls of the tabernacle, and were made of shittim wood, the *acacia Nilotica*, which Dr. Shaw says grows here in abundance. To have worked the acacia into these *boards* or *planks*, the Israelites must have had *sawyers*, *joiners*, &c., among them; but how they got the tools is a question. But as the Israelites were the *general workmen* of Egypt, and were brought up to every kind of trade for the service of their oppressors, we may naturally suppose that every artificer brought off some of his tools with him. For though it is not at all likely that they had any armour or defensive weapons in their power, yet for the reason above assigned they must have had the implements which were requisite for their respective trades.

Verse 16. *Ten cubits* shall be *the length of a board*] Each of these boards or planks was about *five* yards and *two* feet and a half long, and *thirty-two* inches broad; and as they are said to be *standing up*, this was the HEIGHT of the tabernacle. The length being *thirty* cubits, *twenty* boards, *one* cubit and a *half* broad each, make about *seventeen* yards and a *half*, and the BREADTH was about *five* yards.

Verse 29. *Thou shalt overlay the boards with gold*] It is not said how thick the gold was by which these boards, &c., were overlaid; it was no doubt done with *gold plates*, but these must have been very *thin*, else the boards, &c., must have been insupportably heavy. The gold was probably something like our *gold leaf*, but not brought to so great a degree of tenuity.

A. M. 2513.
B. C. 1491.
An. Exod. Isr. 1.
Sivan.

31 And [k] thou shalt make a veil *of* blue, and purple, and scarlet, and fine twined linen of cunning work: with cherubims shall it be made.

32 And thou shalt hang it upon four pillars of shittim *wood*, overlaid with gold: their hooks *shall be of* gold, upon the four sockets of silver.

33 And thou shalt hang up the veil under the taches, that thou mayest bring in thither within the veil [l] the ark of the testimony: and the veil shall divide unto you between [m] the holy *place* and the most holy.

A. M. 2513.
B. C. 1491.
An. Exod. Isr. I.
Sivan.

34 And [n] thou shalt put the mercy-seat upon the ark of the testimony, in the most holy *place*.

35 And [o] thou shalt set the table without the veil, and [p] the candlestick over against the table on the side of the tabernacle toward the south: and thou shalt put the table on the north side.

36 And [q] thou shalt make a hanging for the

[k] Chap. xxxvi. 35; Lev. xvi. 2; 2 Chron. iii. 14; Matt. xxvii. 51; Heb. ix. 3.——[l] Chapter xxv. 16; xl. 21.——[m] Lev. xvi. 2; Heb. ix. 2, 3.——[n] Chap. xxv. 21; xl. 20; Heb. ix. 5.——[o] Chap. xl. 22; Heb. ix. 2.——[p] Chap. xl. 24.——[q] Chap. xxxvi. 37.

Verse 31. *Thou shalt make a veil.*] פרכת *parocheth*, from פרך *parach*, to *break* or *rend*; the *inner veil* of the tabernacle or temple, (2 Chron. iii. 14,) which *broke*, *interrupted*, or *divided* between the *holy place* and the *most holy*; *the Holy Ghost this signifying, that the way into the holiest of all was not yet made manifest, while as the first tabernacle was standing.* Compare Heb. ix. 8. The Septuagint constantly render it by *καταπετασμα*. Does not the Hebrew name פרכת *parocheth* moreover intimate the *typical* correspondence of this *veil* to the *body* or *flesh* of Christ? For this *καταπετασμα* or *veil* was his *flesh*, (Heb. x. 20,) which, being *rent*, affords us *a new and living way into the holiest of all*, i. e., into heaven itself. Compare Heb. x. 19, 20; ix. 24. And accordingly when his blessed body was *rent* upon the cross, this *veil* also (*το καταπετασμα του ιερου*) *εσχισθη*, *was* RENT *in twain from the top to the bottom*; Matt. xxvii. 51.—See *Parkhurst*, under the word פרך.

The veil in the tabernacle was exceedingly costly; it was made of the same materials with the inner covering, blue, purple, scarlet, fine twined linen, embroidered with cherubim, &c. It served to divide the tabernacle into two parts: one, the outermost, called the *holy place*; the other, or innermost, called the *holy of holies*, or the most holy place. In this was deposited the ark of the covenant, and the other things that were laid up by way of memorial. Into this the high priest alone was permitted to enter, and that only once in the year, on the great day of atonement. It was in this inner place that Jehovah manifested himself between the cherubim. The Jews say that this veil was four fingers' breadth in thickness, in order to prevent any person from *seeing through it*; but for this, as Calmet observes, there was no necessity, as there was no window or place for light in the tabernacle, and consequently the most simple veil would have been sufficient to obstruct the discovery of any thing behind it, which could only be discerned by the light that came in at the door, or by that afforded by the golden candlestick which stood on the outside of this veil.

Verse 32. *Their hooks* shall be of *gold*] וויהם *vaveyhem*, which we translate *their hooks*, is rendered *κεφαλιδες*, *capitals*, by the *Septuagint*, and *capita* by the *Vulgate*. As the word וו *vau* or *vau*, plural ווים *vavim*, occurs only in this book, chap. xxvi. 32, 37; xxvii. 10, 11, 17; xxxvi. 36, 38; xxxviii. 10, 11, 12, 17, 19, 28; and is used in these places in reference to the same subject, it is very difficult to ascertain its precise meaning. Most commentators and lexicographers think that the ideal meaning of the word is to *connect*, *attach*, *join to*, *hook*; and that the letter ו *vau* has its name from its *hook-like* form, and its *use* as a particle in the Hebrew language, because it serves to *connect* the words and members of a sentence, and the sentences of a discourse *together*, and that therefore *hook* must be the obvious meaning of the word in all the above texts. Calmet thinks this reason of no weight, because the ו *vau* of the present Hebrew alphabet is widely dissimilar from the *vau* of the primitive Hebrew alphabet, as may be seen on the ancient shekels; on these the characters appear as in the word JEHOVAH, chap. xxviii. 36. This form bears no resemblance to a hook; nor does the Samaritan ࠅ *vau*, which appears to have been copied from this ancient character.

Calmet therefore contends, 1. That if Moses does not mean the *capitals* of the pillars by the ווים *vavim* of the text, he mentions *them nowhere*; and it would be strange that while he describes the pillars, their *sockets*, *bases*, *fillets*, &c., &c., with so much exactness, as will appear on consulting the preceding places, that he should make no mention of the *capitals*; or that pillars, every way so correctly formed, should have been destitute of this very necessary *ornament*.

2. As Moses was commanded to make the *hooks*, ווים *vavim*, of the pillars and their *fillets* of silver, chap. xxvii. 10, 11, and the hooks, *vavim*, of the pillars of the veil of gold, chap. xxxvi. 36; and as *one thousand seven hundred and seventy-five* shekels were employed in making these hooks, *vavim*, overlaying their chapiters, ראשיהם *rasheyhem*, their *heads*, and filleting them, chap. xxxviii. 28; it is more reasonable to suppose that all this is spoken of the *capitals* of the *pillars* than of any kind of *hooks*, especially as hooks are mentioned under the word *taches* or *clasps* in other places. On the whole it appears much more reasonable to translate the original by *capitals* than by *hooks*.

After this verse the Samaritan Pentateuch introduces the ten first verses of chap. xxx., and this appears to be their proper place. Those ten verses are not repeated in the thirtieth chapter in the Samaritan, the chapter beginning with the 11th verse.

Verse 36. *A hanging for the door of the tent*] This

a

A. M. 2513. B. C. 1491. An. Exod. Isr. 1. Sivan.

door of the tent, *of* blue, and purple, and scarlet, and fine twined linen, wrought with needlework.

37 And thou shalt make for the hanging [r] five pillars *of* shittim *wood,* and overlay them with gold, *and* their hooks *shall be of* gold: and thou shalt cast five sockets of brass for them.

[r] Exodus, chap. xxxvi. 38.

may be called the *first* veil, as it occupied the door or entrance to the tabernacle; the veil that separated the holy place from the holy of holies is called the *second* veil, Heb. ix. 3. These two veils and the inner covering of the tabernacle were all of the same materials, and of the same workmanship. See chap. xxvii. 16.

1. For the meaning and design of the tabernacle see the note on chap. xxv. 40: and while the reader is struck with the curious and costly nature of this building, as described by Moses, let him consider how pure and holy that Church should be of which it was a very expressive type; and what manner of person *he* should be in all holy conversation and godliness, who professes to be a member of that Church for which, it is written, Christ has given himself, that he might sanctify and cleanse it; that he might present it unto himself a glorious Church, not having spot, or wrinkle, or any such thing; but that it should be holy and without blemish. See Eph. v. 25–27.

2. In the Jewish tabernacle almost every thing was placed *out of the sight of the people.* The holy of holies was *inaccessible,* the testimony was comparatively *hidden,* as were also the *mercy-seat* and the *Divine glory.* Under the Gospel all these things are laid open, the way to the holiest is made manifest, the *veil* is *rent,* and *we have an entrance to the holiest by the blood of Jesus, by a new and living way, which he hath consecrated for us, through the veil, that is to say, his flesh;* Heb. x. 19, 20. How abundantly has God brought life and immortality to light by the Gospel! The awful distance is abolished, the ministry of reconciliation is proclaimed, the kingdom of heaven is opened to all believers, and the Lord is in his holy temple. Sinner, weary of thyself and thy transgressions, fainting under the load of thy iniquities, look to Jesus; he died for thee, and will save thee. Believer, stand fast in the liberty wherewith God has made thee free, and be not entangled again in the yoke of bondage.

CHAPTER XXVII.

The altar *of* burnt-offerings, *and its dimensions,* 1; *its* horns, 2; pans, shovels, *&c.,* 3; *its* grate *and* net-work, 4, 5; *its* staves, 6, 7. Court *of the tabernacle, with its* pillars *and* hangings, 9–15. Gate *of the court, its pillars, hangings, length, breadth, and height,* 16–18. *All the vessels used in the court of the tabernacle to be of* brass, 19. *The Israelites to provide* pure olive oil *for the light,* 20. *Every thing to be ordered by Aaron and his sons,* 21.

A. M. 2513. B. C. 1491. An. Exod. Isr. 1. Sivan.

AND thou shalt make [a] an altar *of* shittim wood, five cubits long, and five cubits broad: the altar shall be four-square; and the height thereof *shall be* three cubits.

2 And thou shalt make the horns of it upon the four corners thereof.

[a] Chap. xxxviii. 1; Ezek. xliii. 13.

NOTES ON CHAP. XXVII.

Verse 1. *Thou shalt make an altar*] מזבח *mizbeach,* from זבח *zabach,* to *slay:* Septuagint, θυσιαστηριον, from θυσιαζω, to *sacrifice,* or from θυω, to *kill,* &c. See the note on Gen viii. 20.

Four-square] As this altar was five cubits long and five broad, and the cubit is reckoned to be *twenty-one* inches, hence it must have been *eight feet nine inches* square, and about *five feet three inches* in height, the amount of *three cubits,* taken at the same ratio.

Verse 2. *Thou shalt make the horns of it*] The horns might have three uses: 1. For ornament. 2. To prevent carcasses, &c., from falling off. 3. To tie the victim to, previously to its being sacrificed. So David: *Bind the sacrifice with cords to the horns of the altar;* Psa. cxviii. 27. *Horns* were much used in all ancient altars among the heathen, and some of them were entirely constructed of the horns of the beasts that had been offered in sacrifice; but such altars appear to be erected rather as *trophies* in honour of their gods. On the *reverses* of several medals we find *altars* represented with *horns* at the corners. There is a medal of *Antoninus* on the reverse of which is an altar, on which a fire burns, consecrated *Divo Pio,* where the *horns* appear on each of the corners.

There is one of *Faustina,* on which the *altar* and its *horns* are very distinct, the legend *Pietas Augusta.* All the following have *altars* with *horns.* One of *Valerian,* legend *Consecratio;* one of *Claudius Gothicus,* same legend; one of *Quintillus,* same legend; one of *Crispina,* with the legend *Diis Genitalibus;* and several others. See *Numismatica Antiq.,* a Musellio, under *Consecratio,* in the index.

Callimachus, in his Hymn to Apollo, line 60, introduces him constructing an altar of the *horns* of the animals slain by Diana:—

—— πηξε δε βωμον
Εκ κεραων κ. τ. λ.

A. M. 2513. B. C. 1491. An. Exod. Isr. 1. Sivan.

his horns shall be of the same; and [b] thou shalt overlay it with brass.

3 And thou shalt make his pans to receive his ashes, and his shovels, and his basins, and his flesh-hooks, and his fire-pans: all the vessels thereof thou shalt make *of* brass.

4 And thou shalt make for it a grate of net-work *of* brass; and upon the net shalt thou make four brazen rings in the four corners thereof.

5 And thou shalt put it under the compass of the altar beneath, that the net may be even to the midst of the altar.

6 And thou shalt make staves for the altar, staves *of* shittim wood, and overlay them with brass.

7 And the staves shall be put into the rings, and the staves shall be upon the two sides of the altar, to bear it.

8 Hollow with boards shalt thou make it: [c] as [d] it was showed thee in the mount, so shall they make *it*.

9 And [e] thou shalt make the court of the tabernacle: for the south side southward, *there shall be* hangings for the court *of* fine twined linen of a hundred cubits long for one side:

A. M. 2513. B. C. 1491. An. Exod. Isr. 1. Sivan.

10 And the twenty pillars thereof and their twenty sockets *shall be of* brass; the hooks of the pillars and their fillets *shall be of* silver.

11 And likewise for the north side, in length *there shall be* hangings of a hundred *cubits* long, and his twenty pillars and their twenty sockets *of* brass; the hooks of the pillars and their fillets *of* silver.

12 And *for* the breadth of the court on the west side *shall be* hangings of fifty cubits: their pillars ten, and their sockets ten.

13 And the breadth of the court on the east side eastward *shall be* fifty cubits.

14 The hangings of one side *of the gate shall be* fifteen cubits; their pillars three, and their sockets three.

15 And on the other side *shall be* hangings fifteen *cubits*: their pillars three, and their sockets three.

16 And for the gate of the court *shall be* a hanging of twenty cubits, *of* blue, and purple, and scarlet, and fine twined linen, wrought

[b] See Num. xvi. 38.——[c] Chap. xxv. 40; xxvi. 30.

[d] Heb. *be showed*.——[e] Chap. xxxviii. 9.

Martial has these words: *Cornibus ara frequens.*

Verse 3. *Thou shalt make his pans*] סירתיו *sirothaiv*, a sort of large brazen dishes, which stood under the altar to receive the ashes that fell through the grating.

His shovels] יעיו *yaaiv*. Some render this *besoms;* but as these were brazen instruments, it is more natural to suppose that some kind of fire-shovels are intended, or scuttles, which were used to carry off the ashes that fell through the grating into the large pan or *siroth*.

His basins] מזרקתיו *mizrekothaiv*, from זרק *zarak*, to *sprinkle* or *disperse;* bowls or basins to receive the blood of the sacrifices, in order that it might be sprinkled on the people before the altar, &c.

His flesh-hooks] מזלגתיו *mizlegothaiv*. That this word is rightly translated *flesh-hooks* is fully evident from 1 Sam. ii. 13, where the same word is used in such a connection as demonstrates its meaning: *And the priest's custom with the people* was, that *when any man offered sacrifice, the priest's servant came, while the flesh was in the seething, with* a FLESH-HOOK (מזלג *mazleg*) *of three teeth* (prongs) *in his hand, and he struck it into the pan*, &c.; *all that the* FLESH-HOOK (מזלג *mazleg*) *brought up, the priest took for himself.* It was probably a kind of *trident*, or *fork* with *three* prongs, and these bent to a right angle at the middle, as the ideal meaning of the Hebrew seems to imply *crookedness* or *curvature* in general.

His fire-pans] מחתתיו *machtothaiv*. Bishop Patrick and others suppose that "this was a larger sort of vessel, wherein, probably, the *sacred fire* which came down from heaven (Lev. ix. 24) was kept burning, whilst they cleansed the altar and the grate from the coals and the ashes; and while the altar was carried from one place to another, as it often was in the wilderness."

Verse 4. *Thou shalt make for it a grate*] Calmet supposes this altar to have been a sort of box, covered with brass plates, on the top of which was a grating to supply the fire with air, and permit the ashes to fall through into the *siroth* or pan that was placed below. At the four corners of the grating were four rings and four chains, by which it was attached to the four horns; and at the sides were rings for the poles of shittim wood with which it was carried. Even on this there is a great variety of opinions.

Verse 8. *Hollow with boards*] It seems to have been a kind of *frame-work*, and to have had nothing solid in the inside, and only covered with the grating at the top. This rendered it more light and portable.

Verse 9. *The court of the tabernacle*] The tabernacle stood in an enclosure or court, open at the top. This court was made with pillars or posts, and hangings. It was *one hundred cubits*, or about *fifty-eight* yards and a half, in length; the breadth we learn from verses 12 and 18; and *five cubits*, or nearly *three yards*, high, ver. 18. And as this was but half the height of the tabernacle, chap. xxvi. 16, that sacred building might easily be seen by the people from without.

Verse 16. *And for the gate of the court*] It appears a

A. M. 2513.
B. C. 1491.
An. Exod. Isr. 1.
Sivan.

with needlework: *and* their pillars *shall be* four, and their sockets four.
17 All the pillars round about the court *shall be* filleted with silver; their hooks *shall be of* silver, and their sockets *of* brass.
18 The length of the court *shall be* a hundred cubits, and the breadth [f] fifty every where, and the height five cubits *of* fine twined linen, and their sockets *of* brass.
19 All the vessels of the tabernacle in all the service thereof, and all the pins thereof, and all the pins of the court, *shall be of* brass.
20 And [g] thou shalt command the children of Israel, that they bring thee pure oil olive beaten for the light, to cause the lamp [h] to burn always,
21 In the tabernacle of the congregation, [i] without the veil, which *is* before the testimony: [k] Aaron and his sons shall order it from evening to morning before the LORD: [l] *it shall be* a statute for ever unto their generations, on the behalf of the children of Israel.

[f] Heb. *fifty by fifty.*——[g] Lev. xxiv. 2.——[h] Heb. *to ascend up.* [i] Chap. xxvi. 31, 33.——[k] Chap. xxx. 8; 1 Sam. iii. 3; 2 Chron. xiii. 11.——[l] Chapter xxviii. 43, xxix. 9, 28; Lev. iii. 17; xvi. 34; xxiv. 9; Num. xviii. 23; xix. 21; 1 Sam. xxx. 25.

that the hangings of this gate were of the same materials and workmanship with that of the inner covering of the tabernacle, and the outer and inner veil. See chap. xxvi. 36.

Verse 19. *All the vessels*—shall be of *brass.*] It would have been improper to have used instruments made of the more precious metals about this altar, as they must have been soon worn out by the severity of the service.

Verse 20. *Pure oil olive beaten*] That is, such oil as could easily be expressed from the olives after they had been bruised in a mortar; the *mother drop*, as it is called, which drops out of itself as soon as the olives are a little broken, and which is much purer than that which is obtained after the olives are put under the *press*.

Columella, who is a legitimate evidence in all such matters, says that the oil which flowed out of the fruit either spontaneously, or with little application of the force of the press, was of a much finer flavour than that which was obtained otherwise. *Quoniam longe melioris saporis est, quod minore vi preli, quasi luxurians, defluxerit.*—COLUM., lib. xii., c. 50.

To cause the lamp to burn always] They were to be kept burning through the whole of the night, and some think all the day besides; but there is a difference of sentiment upon this subject. See the note on the following verse.

This oil and continual flame were not only emblematical of the unction and influences of the Holy Ghost, but also of that pure spirit of devotion which ever animates the hearts and minds of the genuine worshippers of the true God. The temple of VESTA, where a fire was kept perpetually burning, seems to have been formed on the model of the tabernacle; and from this the followers of Zeratusht, commonly called *Zoroaster*, appear to have derived their doctrine of the *perpetual fire*, which they still worship as an emblem of the Deity.

Verse 21. *The tabernacle of the congregation*] The place where all the assembly of the people were to worship, where the God of that assembly was pleased to reside, and to which, as the habitation of their king and protector, they were ever to turn their faces in all their adorations.

Before the testimony] That is, the ark where the tables of the covenant were deposited. See chap. xxv. 16.

Aaron and his sons] These and their descendants being the only legitimate priests, God having established the priesthood in this family.

Shall order it from evening to morning] Josephus says the whole of the seven lamps burned all the night; in the morning *four* were extinguished, and *three* kept burning through the whole day. Others assert that the whole seven were kept lighted both day and night continually; but it appears sufficiently evident, from 1 Sam. iii. 3, that these lamps were extinguished in the morning: *And ere the lamp of God went out in the temple of the Lord, where the ark of God was, and Samuel was laid down to sleep, &c.* See also chap. xxx. 8: *And when Aaron* LIGHTETH THE LAMPS AT EVEN. It appears therefore that the business of the priests was to light the lamps in the evening; and either to extinguish them in the morning, or permit them to burn out, having put in the night before as much oil as was necessary to last till day-light.

A statute for ever] This ordering of the lamps night and morning, and attendance on the service of the tabernacle, was a statute that was to be in full force while the tabernacle and temple stood, and should have its spiritual accomplishment in the Christian Church to the end of time. Reader, the tabernacle and temple are both destroyed; the Church of Christ is established in their place. The *seven golden candlesticks* were typical of this Church and the glorious light it possesses, Rev. i. 12–20; and Jesus Christ, the Fountain and Dispenser of this true light, walks in the midst of them. Reader, hast thou that celestial flame to enlighten and animate thy heart in all those acts of devotion which thou professest to pay to him as thy Maker, Redeemer, and Preserver? What is thy profession, and what thy religious acts and services, without this? A sounding brass, a tinkling cymbal.

TERTULLIAN asserts that all the ancient heathens borrowed their best notions from the sacred writings: "Which," says he, "of your poets, which of your sophists, have not drunk from the fountain of the prophets? It is from those sacred springs that your philosophers have refreshed their thirsty spirits; and if they found any thing in the Holy Scriptures which hit

their fancy, or which served their hypothesis, they took and turned it to a compliance with their own curiosity, not considering those writings to be sacred and unalterable, nor understanding their true sense, every one altering them according to his own fancy."—*Apologet.*

The reader's attention has already been called to this point several times in the preceding parts of this work, and the subject will frequently recur. At the conclusion of chap. xxv. we had occasion to observe that the heathens had imitated many things in that Divine worship prescribed by Moses; but in application to their own corrupt system every thing was in a certain measure falsified and distorted, yet not so far as to prevent the grand *outlines* of primitive truth from being discerned One of the most complete imitations of the tabernacle and its whole service is found in the very ancient temple of Hercules, founded probably by the Phœnicians, at *Gades*, now Cadiz, in Spain, so minutely described by Silius Italicus from actual observation. He observes that though the temple was at that time very ancient, yet the *beams* were the same that had been placed there by the founders, and that they were generally supposed to be *incorruptible*; a quality ascribed to the shittim wood, termed *ξυλον ασηπτον*, *incorruptible wood*, by the Septuagint. That *women were not permitted to enter this temple*, and that *no swine* were ever suffered to come near it. That the priests did not wear *party-coloured* vestments, but were always clothed in *fine linen*, and their *bonnets* made of the *same*. That they *offered incense* to their god, their clothes being *ungirded*; for the same reason doubtless given chap. xx. 26, that in going up to the altar nothing unseemly might appear, and therefore they permitted their long robes to fall down to their feet. He adds, that by the *laws of their forefathers* they bore on their *sacerdotal vestments* the *latus clavus*, which was a round knob or stud of *purple* with which the robes of the Roman knights and senators were adorned, which these priests seem to have copied from the *breastplate of judgment* made of cunning work, embroidered with *purple*, *blue*, &c. See chap. xxviii. 15. They also ministered *barefooted*, their hair was trimmed or cut off, and they observed the *strictest continency*, and kept a *perpetual fire* burning on their *altars*. And he farther adds that there was no *image* or *similitude* of the gods to be seen in that sacred place. This is the substance of his description; but as some of my readers may wish to see the original, I shall here subjoin it.

Vulgatum (nec cassa fides) ab origine fani
Impositas durare trabes, *solasque per ævum*
Condentum *novisse manus: hic credere gaudent*
Consedisse Deum, seniumque repellere templis.
Tum, queis fas et honos adyti penetralia nosse,
Fœmineos prohibent gressus, *ac limine curant*
Setigeros arcere sues: *nec* discolor ulli
Ante aras cultus: velantur *corpora* lino,
Et Pelusiaco *præfulget* stamine vertex.
Discinctis *mos* thura dare, *atque e lege parentum*
Sacrificam LATO vestem *distinguere* CLAVO.
Pes nudus, tonsæque comæ, castumque cubile,
Irrestincta *focis servant altaria* flammæ.
Sed nulla effigies, simulacrave *nota Deorum*
Majestate locum, et sacro implevere timore.
Punicor., lib. iii., ver. 17–31.

This is such a remarkable case that I think myself justified in quoting it at length, as an extraordinary monument, though corrupted, of the tabernacle and its service. It is probable that the original founders had consecrated this temple to the *true God*, under the name of אל EL, the *strong God*, or אל גבור EL GIBBOR, the *strong*, *prevailing*, and *victorious God*, Isa. ix. 6, out of whom the Greeks and Romans made their *Hercules*, or *god of strength*; and, to make it agree with this appropriation, the *labours of Hercules* were sculptured on the doors of this temple at Gades.

In foribus labor Alcidæ Lernæa recisis
Anguibus Hydra jacet, &c., &c.

CHAPTER XXVIII.

Aaron *and his* sons *are set apart for the priest's office*, 1. Garments *to be provided for them*, 2, 3. *What these garments were*, 4, *and of what made*, 5. *The* ephod, *its shoulder-pieces and girdle*, 6–8. *The two* onyx stones, *on which the names of the twelve tribes were to be engraven*, 9–14. *The* breastplate *of judgment; its twelve precious stones, engraving, rings, chains, and its use*, 15–29. *The* Urim *and* Thummim, 30. *The* robe *of the* ephod, *its border, bells, pomegranates, &c., and their use*, 31–35. *The* plate *of pure gold and its* motto, 36, *to be placed on Aaron's mitre*, 37, 38. *The* embroidered coat *for Aaron*, 39. *Coats, girdles, and bonnets*, 40. *Aaron and his sons to be anointed for the priest's office*, 41. *Other articles of clothing and their use*, 42, 43.

A. M. 2513.
B. C. 1491.
An. Exod. Isr. 1.
Sivan.

AND take thou unto thee [a] Aaron thy brother, and his sons with him, from among the children of Israel, that he may minister unto me in the priest's office, *even* Aaron, Nadab, and Abihu, Eleazar, and Ithamar, Aaron's sons.

[a] Num. xviii. 7; Ecclus. xlv. 6; Heb. v. 1, 4.

NOTES ON CHAP. XXVIII.

Verse 1. *Aaron—and his sons*] The priesthood was to be restrained to this family because the public worship was to be confined to *one* place; and previously to this the eldest in every family officiated as priest, there being no settled place of worship. It has been

A. M. 2513. B. C. 1491. An. Exod. Isr. 1. Sivan.

2 And [b] thou shalt make holy
garments for Aaron thy brother,
for glory and for beauty.

3 And [c] thou shalt speak unto all *that are*
wise-hearted, [d] whom I have
filled with the spirit of wisdom,
that they may make Aaron's
garments to consecrate him, that he may

[b] Chap. xxix. 5, 29; xxxi. 10; xxxix. 1, 2; Lev. viii. 7, 30; Num. xx. 26, 28; Ecclus. xlv. 7, 8.——[c] Chap. xxxi. 6; xxxv. 31–35; xxxvi. 1, 2; Isa. xxviii. 24–29.——[d] Chap. xxxi. 3 xxxv. 30, 31; Deut. xxxiv. 9; James i. 17.

very properly observed that, if Moses had not acted by the Divine appointment, he would not have passed by his own family, which continued in the condition of ordinary Levites, and established the *priesthood*, the only dignity in the nation, in the family of his brother Aaron. "The priests, however, had no power of a *secular* nature, nor does it appear from history that they ever arrived at any till the time of the Asmoneans or Maccabees." See the note on chap. xix. 22.

Verse 2. *For glory and for beauty.*] Four articles of dress were prescribed for the priests in ordinary, and four more for the high-priest. Those for the priests in general were a *coat, drawers*, a *girdle*, and a *bonnet.* Besides these the high-priest had a *robe*, an *ephod*, a *breastplate*, and a *plate* or *diadem of gold on his forehead.* The garments, says the sacred historian, were for *honour* and for *beauty*. They were emblematical of the office in which they ministered. 1. It was *honourable.* They were the ministers of the Most High, and employed by him in transacting the most important concerns between God and his people, concerns in which all the attributes of the Divine Being were interested, as well as those which referred to the present and eternal happiness of his creatures. 2. They were for *beauty*. They were emblematical of that holiness and purity which ever characterize the Divine nature and the worship which is worthy of him, and which are essentially necessary to all those who wish to serve him in the beauty of holiness here below, and without which none can ever see his face in the realms of glory. Should not the garments of all those who minister in holy things still be emblematical of the things in which they minister? Should they not be for *glory* and *beauty*, expressive of the dignity of the Gospel ministry, and that beauty of holiness without which none can see the Lord? As the high-priest's vestments, under the law, were emblematical of what *was to come*, should not the vestments of the ministers of the Gospel bear some resemblance of what *is come?* Is then the dismal *black*, now worn by almost all kinds of priests and ministers, *for glory and for beauty?* Is it emblematical of any thing that is good, glorious, or excellent? How unbecoming the *glad tidings* announced by Christian ministers is a colour emblematical of nothing but *mourning* and *wo, sin, desolation*, and *death!* How inconsistent the *habit* and *office* of these men! Should it be said, "These are only *shadows*, and are useless because the *substance* is come." I ask, Why then is *black* almost universally worn? why is *a* particular colour preferred, if there be no signification in *any?* Is there not a danger that in our zeal against *shadows*, we shall destroy or essentially change the *substance* itself? Would not the same sort of argumentation exclude *water* in baptism, and *bread* and *wine* in the sacrament of the Lord's Supper? The *white surplice* in the service of the Church is almost the only thing that remains of those ancient and *becoming* vestments which God commanded to be made for *glory* and *beauty.* Clothing, emblematical of *office*, is of more consequence than is generally imagined. Were the great officers of the crown, and the great officers of justice, to clothe themselves like the common people when they appear in their public capacity, both their *persons* and their *decisions* would be soon held in little estimation.

Verse 3. *Whom I have filled with the spirit of wisdom*] So we find that *ingenuity* in arts and sciences, even those of the *ornamental* kind, comes from God. It is not intimated here that these persons were filled with the spirit of wisdom for *this purpose only*; for the direction to Moses is, to select those whom he found to be *expert artists*, and those who were such, God shows by these words, had derived their knowledge from himself. Every man should be permitted as far as possible to follow the *bent* or *direction* of his own genius, when it evidently leads him to *new inventions*, and *improvements on old plans.* How much has both the labour of men and cattle been lessened by improvements in machinery! And can we say that the *wisdom* which found out these improvements did not come from God? No man, by course of *reading* or *study*, ever acquired a *genius* of this kind: *we* call it *natural*, and say it was *born with the man.* Moses teaches us to consider it as *Divine.* Who taught NEWTON to ascertain the laws by which God governs the universe, through which discovery a new source of profit and pleasure has been opened to mankind through every part of the civilized world? No reading, no study, no example, formed his *genius.* God, who made him, gave him that compass and bent of mind by which he made those discoveries, and for which his name is celebrated in the earth. When I see NAPIER inventing the logarithms; COPERNICUS, DES CARTES, and KEPLER contributing to pull down the false systems of the universe, and NEWTON *demonstrating the true one;* and when I see the long list of PATENTEES of *useful* inventions, by whose industry and skill long and tedious processes in the necessary arts of life have been shortened, labour greatly lessened, and much time and expense saved; I then see, with Moses, men who are *wise-hearted, whom God has filled with the spirit of wisdom* for these very purposes; that he might help man by man, and that, as time rolls on, he might give to his intelligent creatures such proofs of his *Being, infinitely varied wisdom*, and *gracious providence*, as should cause them to depend on him, and give him that glory which is due to his name.

How pointedly does the Prophet *Isaiah* refer to this sort of teaching as coming from God, even in the most common and less difficult arts of life! The whole passage is worthy of the reader's most serious attention.

"Doth the ploughman plough all day to sow? doth he

A. M. 2513. B. C. 1491. An. Exod. Isr. 1. Sivan.

minister unto me in the priest's
office.
4 And these *are* the garments
which they shall make; [e] a breastplate, and
[f] an ephod, and [g] a robe, and
[h] a broidered coat, a mitre, and
a girdle: and they shall make
holy garments for Aaron thy brother, and his

A. M. 2513. B. C. 1491. An. Exod. Isr. 1. Sivan.

[e] Ver. 15.——[f] Ver. 6.——[g] Ver. 31. [h] Ver. 39; Exod. xxxix. 2–21.

open and break the clods of his ground? When he hath made plain the face thereof, doth he not cast abroad the fitches, and scatter the cummin, and cast in the principal wheat, and the appointed barley, and the rye, in their place? For HIS GOD DOTH INSTRUCT HIM to discretion, *and* doth teach him. For the fitches are not threshed with a threshing-instrument, neither is a cart-wheel turned about upon the cummin; but the fitches are beaten out with a staff, and the cummin with a rod. Bread *corn* is bruised; because he will not ever be threshing it, nor break *it with* the wheel of his cart, nor bruise it *with* his horsemen. This also cometh forth from the LORD of hosts, *who* is wonderful in counsel, *and* excellent in working," Isa. xxviii. 24–29.

But let us take heed not to run into extremes here; *machinery* is to *help* man, not to render him *useless*. The *human hand* is the great and most perfect machine, let it not be laid aside. In our zeal for machinery we are rendering all the lower classes useless; filling the land with beggary and vice, and the workhouses with paupers; and ruining the husbandman with oppressive poor-rates. Keep machinery as a *help* to the human hand, and to lighten the labour, but never let it supersede either.

This principle, that *God is the author of all arts and sciences*, is too little regarded: *Every good gift, and every perfect gift*, says St. James, *comes from above, from the* FATHER *of* LIGHTS. Why has God constructed every part of nature with such a profusion of economy and skill, if he intended this skill should never be discovered by man, or that man should not attempt to examine his works in order to find them out? From the *works of* CREATION what proofs, astonishing and overwhelming proofs, both to believers and infidels, have been drawn both of the nature, being, attributes, and providence of God! What *demonstrations* of all these have the Archbishop of Cambray, Dr. Nieuwentyt, Dr. Derham, and Mr. Charles Bonnet, given in their philosophical works! And who gave those men this wisdom? GOD, from whom alone MIND, and all its attributes, proceed. While we see Count de *Buffon* and *Swammerdam* examining and tracing out all the curious relations, connections, and laws of the ANIMAL kingdom;—*Tournefort, Ray*, and *Linne*, those of the VEGETABLE;—*Theophrastus, Werner, Klaproth, Cronstedt, Morveau, Reamur, Kirwan*, and a host of philosophical chemists, *Boerhaave, Boylé, Stahl, Priestley, Lavoisier, Fourcroy, Black*, and *Davy*, those of the MINERAL; the discoveries they have made, the latent and important properties of vegetables and minerals which they have developed, the powerful machines which, through their discoveries, have been constructed, by the operations of which the *human slave* is restored to his own place in society, he *brute* saved from his destructive toil in our manufactories, and *inanimate, unfeeling* NATURE caused to perform the work of all these better, more expeditiously, and to much more profit; shall we not say that the *hand of GOD* is in all this? Only I again say, let *machinery* aid man, and not render him useless. The nations of Europe are pushing mechanical power to a destructive extreme. He alone *girded* those eminent men, though many of them *knew him not;* he inspired them with wisdom and understanding; by his all-pervading and all-informing spirit he opened to them the entrance of the paths of the depths of science, guided them in their researches, opened to them *successively* more and more of his astonishing treasures, crowned their persevering industry with his blessing, and made them his ministers for good to mankind. The *antiquary* and the *medalist* are also his agents; their discernment and penetration come from *him* alone. By them, how many dark ages of the world have been brought to light; how many names of men and places, how many customs and arts, that were lost, restored! And by their means a few *busts, images, stones, bricks, coins, rings*, and *culinary utensils*, the remaining wrecks of long-past numerous centuries, have supplied the place of *written documents*, and cast a profusion of light on the history of man, and the history of providence. And let me add, that the providence which preserved these materials, and raised up men to decipher and explain them, is itself gloriously illustrated by them.

Of all those men (and the noble list might be greatly swelled) we may say the same that Moses said of *Bezaleel* and *Aholiab:* "*GOD* hath filled them with the Spirit of God, in wisdom, and in understanding, and in knowledge; and in all manner of workmanship, to devise cunning works; to work in *gold* and in *silver*, and in *brass*, in *cutting* of *stones*, *carving* of *timber*, and in *all manner* of *workmanship;*" chap. xxxi. 3–6. "The *works* of the Lord are great, sought out of all them that have pleasure therein;" Psa. cxi. 2.

Verse 4. *Breastplate*] חשן *choshen*. See on chap. xxv. 7.

Ephod] אפד. See the note on chap. xxv. 7.

Robe] מעיל *meil*, from עלה *alah, to go up, go upon;* hence the *meil* may be considered as an upper coat, a *surtout*. It is described by Josephus as a garment that reaches down to the feet, not made of two distinct pieces, but was one entire long garment, woven throughout. This was immediately under the ephod. See on ver. 31, &c.

Broidered coat] כתנת תשבץ *kethoneth, tashbets*, what Parkhurst translates *a close, strait coat* or *garment;* according to Josephus, "a tunic circumscribing or *closely encompassing* the body, and having tight sleeves for the arms." This was immediately under the *meil* or robe, and answered the same purpose to the priests that our *shirts* do to us. See on ver. 13.

A. M. 2513.
B. C. 1491.
An. Exod. Isr. 1.
Sivan.

sons, that he may minister unto
me in the priest's office.
5 And they shall take gold, and
blue, and purple, and scarlet, and fine linen:
6 [i] And they shall make the ephod *of* gold,
of blue, and *of* purple, *of* scarlet, and fine
twined linen, with cunning work.
7 It shall have the two shoulder-pieces
thereof joined at the two edges thereof; and
so it shall be joined together.
8 And the [k] curious girdle of the ephod,
which *is* upon it, shall be of the same, according
to the work thereof; *even of* gold, *of* blue,
and purple, and scarlet, and fine twined linen.
9 And thou shalt take two onyx stones, and
grave on them the names of the children of
Israel:
10 Six of their names on one stone, and
the other six names of the rest
on the other stone, according to
their birth.

A. M. 2513.
B. C. 1491.
An. Exod. Isr. 1.
Sivan.

11 [l] With the work of an engraver in stone,
like the engravings of a signet, shalt thou engrave
the two stones with the names of the
children of Israel: thou shalt make them to
be set in ouches of gold.
12 And thou shalt put the two stones upon
the shoulders of the ephod *for* stones of memorial
unto the children of Israel: and [m] Aaron
shall bear their names before the LORD, upon
his two shoulders, [n] for a memorial.
13 And thou shalt make ouches *of* gold;
14 And two chains *of* pure gold at the ends;
of wreathen work shalt thou make them, and
fasten the wreathen chains to the ouches.
15 And [o] thou shalt make the breastplate

[i] Chap. xxxix. 2, 4, 27, 29.——[k] Or, *embroidered*; ch. xxxix. 20; Isa. xi. 5; Rev. i. 13.

[l] Wisd. xviii. 24.——[m] Ver. 29; chap. xxxix. 7.——[n] See Josh. iv. 7; Zech. vi. 14.——[o] Chap. xxxix. 8.

Mitre] מצנפת *mitsnepheth.* As this word comes from the root צנף *tsunaph, to roll* or *wrap round,* it evidently means that covering of the head so universal in the eastern countries which we call *turban* or *turband,* corrupted from the Persian دولبند *doolbend,* which signifies what *encompasses* and *binds* the head or body; and hence is applied, not only to this *covering of the head,* but to a *sash* in general. As the Persian word is compounded of دول *dool* or *dawal, a revolution, vicissitude, wheel,* &c., and بندن *binden, to bind;* it is very likely that the Hebrew words דור *dur, to go round,* and בנט *benet, a band,* may have been the original of *doolbend* and *turband.* It is sometimes called سربند *serbend,* from سر *ser, the head,* and بندن *binden, to bind.* The turban consists generally of two parts: the *cap,* which goes on the head; and the long *sash* of muslin, linen, or silk, that is wrapped round the head. These sashes are generally several yards in length.

A girdle] אבנט *abnet, a belt* or *girdle;* see before. This seems to have been the same kind of *sash* or *girdle,* so common in the eastern countries, that confined the loose garments about the waist; and in which their long skirts were tucked up when they were employed in work, or on a journey. After being tied round the waist, the two ends of it fell down before, to the skirts of their robes.

Verse 8. *The curious girdle of the ephod*] The word חשב *chesheb,* rendered here *curious girdle,* signifies merely a kind of *diaper,* or *embroidered* work; (see the note on chap. xxvi. 1;) and it is widely different from אבנט *abnet,* which is properly translated *girdle* ver. 4. The meaning therefore of the text, according to some, is this, that the two pieces, ver. 7, which connected the parts of the ephod at the shoulders where the onyx stones were set, should be of the same texture with the ephod itself, i. e., of *gold, blue, purple, scarlet,* and *fine twined linen,* embroidered together. But others suppose that some kind of a girdle is meant, different from the *abnet,* ver. 39, being only of *plain* workmanship.

Verse 9. *Two onyx stones*] See on chap. xxv. 7.

Verse 11. Like *the engravings of a signet*] So *signets* or *seals* were in use at this time, and *engraving on precious stones* was then an art, and this art, which was one of the most elegant and ornamental, was carried in ancient times to a very high pitch of perfection, and particularly among the ancient Greeks; such a pitch of perfection as has never been *rivalled,* and cannot now be even well *imitated.* And it is very likely that the Greeks themselves borrowed this art from the ancient *Hebrews,* as we know it flourished in Egypt and Palestine long before it was known in Greece.

Verse 12. *Aaron shall bear their names before the Lord*] He was to consider that he was the *representative* of the children of Israel; and the stones on the ephod and the stones on the breastplate were for a memorial to put Aaron in remembrance that he was the priest and mediator of the twelve tribes; and, speaking after the manner of men, God was to be put in mind of the children of Israel, their wants, &c., as frequently as the high priest appeared before him with the breastplate and the ephod. See ver. 29.

Verse 13. *Ouches of gold*] משבצת *mishbetsoth, strait places,* sockets to insert the stones in, from שבץ *shabats, to close, inclose, straiten. Socket,* in this place, would be a more proper translation, as *ouch* cannot be traced up to any legitimate authority. It appears sometimes to signify a *hook,* or some mode of *attaching* things together.

Verse 15. *The breastplate of judgment*] חשן משפט *choshen mishpat,* the same as the חשן *choshen,* see chap. xxv. 7, but here called the *breastplate of judgment,* because the high priest wore it upon his breast when he went to ask counsel of the Lord, to give judg-

A. M. 2513. B. C. 1491. An. Exod. Isr. 1. Sivan.

of judgment with cunning work; after the work of the ephod thou shalt make it; *of* gold, *of* blue, and *of* purple, and *of* scarlet, and *of* fine twined linen, shalt thou make it.

16 Four-square it shall be, *being* doubled; a span *shall be* the length thereof, and a span *shall be* the breadth thereof.

17 [p] And thou shalt [q] set in it settings of stones, *even* four rows of stones: *the first* row *shall be* a [r] sardius, a topaz, and a carbuncle: *this shall be* the first row.

18 And the second row *shall be* an emerald, a sapphire, and a diamond.

19 And the third row a ligure, an agate, and an amethyst.

20 And the fourth row a beryl, and an onyx, and a jasper: they shall be set in gold in their [s] enclosings.

21 And the stones shall be with the names of the children of Israel, twelve, according to their names, *like* the engravings of a signet; every one with his name shall they be according to the twelve tribes.

22 And thou shalt make upon the breast plate chains at the ends *of* wreathen work, *of* pure gold.

23 And thou shalt make upon the breast-

[p] Chap. xxxix. 10, &c.——[q] Heb. *fill it in fillings of stone.*

[r] Or, *ruby.*——[s] Heb. *fillings.*

ment in any particular case; as also when he sat as judge to teach the law, and to determine controversies. See Lev. x. 11; Deut. xvii. 8, 9.

Verse 16. *Four-square it shall be*] Here we have the exact dimensions of this breastplate, or more properly *breast-piece* or *stomacher*. It was a *span* in length and breadth when *doubled*, and consequently two spans long one way before it was doubled. Between these doublings, it is supposed, the *Urim* and *Thummim* were placed. See on ver. 30.

Verse 17. *Four rows of stones*] With a name on each stone, making in all the twelve names of the twelve tribes. And as these were disposed according to their birth, ver. 10, we may suppose they stood in this order, the stones being placed also in the order in which they are produced, ver. 17–20:—

		FIRST	ROW.		
Upon a	Sardius or *Ruby*	was engraven	Reuben	ראובן	Sons of Leah.
———	Topaz	—————	Simeon	שמעון	
———	Carbuncle	—————	Levi	לוי	
		SECOND	ROW.		
Upon an	Emerald	was engraven	Judah	יהודה	
——a	Sapphire	—————	Issachar	יששכר	
———	Diamond	—————	Zebulun	זבולן	
		THIRD	ROW.		
Upon a	Ligure or *Jacinth*	was engraven	Dan	דן	Sons of Bilhah, Rachel's maid.
———	Agate	—————	Naphtali	נפתלי	
———	Amethyst	—————	Gad	גד	Sons of Zilpah, Leah's maid
		FOURTH	ROW.		
Upon a	Beryl, or *Chrysolite*	was engraven	Asher	אשר	
———	Onyx, or *Sardonyx*	—————	Joseph	יוסף	Sons of Rachel.
———	Jasper	—————	Benjamin	בנימין	

In this order the Jews in general agree to place them. See the *Jerusalem Targum* on this place, and the *Targum* upon Canticles v. 14; and see also *Ainsworth*. The *Targum* of *Jonathan* says, "These four rows were placed opposite to the four quarters of the world; but this could only be when laid down horizontally, for when it hung on the breast of the high priest it could have had no such position. As it is difficult to ascertain in every case what these precious stones were, it may be necessary to consider this subject more at large.

1. A Sardius, אדם *odem*, from the root *adam*, he was *ruddy;* the *ruby*, a beautiful gem of a fine deep *red* colour. The *sardius*, or *sardie* stone, is defined to be a precious stone of a *blood-red colour*, the best of which come from Babylon.

2. A Topaz, פטדה *pitdah*, a precious stone of a *pale dead green*, with a mixture of *yellow*, sometimes of a fine yellow; and hence it was called *chrysolite* by the ancients, from its *gold* colour. It is now considered by mineralogists as a *variety* of the *sapphire*.

3. Carbuncle, ברקת *bareketh*, from ברק *barak*, to *lighten*, *glitter*, or *glister;* a very elegant gem of a *deep red* colour, with an admixture of *scarlet*. From its bright lively colour it had the name *carbunculus*, which signifies a *little coal;* and among the Greeks *ανθραξ anthrax*, a *coal*, because when held before the sun it appears like a piece of bright burning charcoal. It is found only in the East Indies, and there but rarely.

4. Emerald, נפך *nophech*, the same with the ancient *smaragdus;* it is one of the most beautiful of all the gems, and is of a bright green colour, without any other mixture. The true oriental *emerald* is very scarce, and is only found at present in the kingdom of *Cambay*.

5. Sapphire, ספיר *sappir*. See this described, chap. xxiv. 10.

A. M. 2513. B. C. 1491. An. Exod. Isr. 1. Sivan.

plate [t] two rings of gold, and shalt put the two rings on the two ends of the breastplate.

24 And thou shalt put the two wreathen *chains* of gold in the two rings, *which are* on the ends of the breastplate.

25 And *the other* two ends of the two [u] wreathen *chains*, thou shalt fasten in the two ouches, and put *them* on the shoulder-pieces[v] of the ephod before it.

26 And thou shalt make two rings of gold, and thou shalt put them upon the two ends of the breastplate, in the border thereof, which *is* in the side of the ephod inward.

27 And two *other* rings of gold thou shalt make, and shalt put them on the two sides of the ephod underneath, toward the forepart thereof, over against the *other* coupling thereof, above the curious girdle of the ephod.

A. M. 2513. B. C. 1491. An. Exod. Isr. 1. Sivan.

28 And they shall bind the breastplate by the rings thereof, unto the rings of the ephod with a lace of blue, that *it* may be above the curious girdle of the ephod, and that the breastplate be not loosed from the ephod.

29 And Aaron shall bear the names of the children of Israel in the breastplate of judgment upon his heart, when he goeth in unto the holy *place*, [w] for a memorial before the LORD continually.

[t] Chap. xxv. 11-15.——[u] Chap. xxviii. 14; xxxix. 15.——[v] Chap. xxviii. 7, 25; xxxix. 4.——[w] Ver. 12.

6. DIAMOND, יהלם *yahalom*, from הלם *halam*, to *beat* or *smite upon*. The diamond is supposed to have this name from its *resistance to a blow*, for the ancients have assured us that if it be struck with a hammer, upon an anvil, *it will not break*, but either *break them* or *sink* into the surface of that which is *softest*. This is a complete *fable*, as it is well known that the diamond can be easily broken, and is capable of being *entirely* volatilized or consumed by the action of fire. It is, however, the hardest, as it is the most valuable, of all the precious stones hitherto discovered, and one of the most combustible substances in nature.

7. LIGURE, לשם *leshem*, the same as the *jacinth* or *hyacinth*; a precious stone of a *dead red* or *cinnamon* colour, with a considerable mixture of *yellow*.

8. AGATE, שבו *shebo*. This is a stone that assumes such a variety of hues and appearances, that Mr. Parkhurst thinks it derives its name from the root שב *shab*, to *turn*, to *change*, "as from the circumstance of the agate changing its appearance without end, it might be called the *varier*." Agates are met with so variously figured in their substance, that they seem to represent the sky, the stars, clouds, earth, water, rocks, villages, fortifications, birds, trees, flowers, men, and animals of different kinds. Agates have a *white*, *reddish*, *yellowish*, or *greenish* ground. They are only varieties of the *flint*, and the lowest in value of all the precious stones.

9. AMETHYST, אחלמה *achlamah*, a gem generally of a *purple* colour, composed of a strong *blue* and *deep red*. The oriental *amethyst* is sometimes of a *dove* colour, though some are *purple*, and others *white* like *diamonds*. The name *amethyst* is Greek, αμεθυστος, and it was so called because it was supposed that it prevented *inebriation*.

10. The BERYL, תרשיש *tarshish*. Mr. Parkhurst derives this name from תר *tar*, to *go round*, and שש *shash*, to be *vivid* or *bright* in colour. If the *beryl* be intended, it is a pellucid gem of a *bluish green* colour, found in the East Indies, and about the gold mines of Peru. But some of the most learned mineralogists and critics suppose the *chrysolite* to be meant. This is a gem of a *yellowish green* colour, and ranks at present among the *topazes*. Its name in Greek, *chrysolite*, χρυσολιθος, literally signifies the *golden stone*.

11. The ONYX, שהם *shoham*. See the notes on Gen. ii. 12; Exod. xxv. 7. There are a great number of different sentiments on the meaning of the original; it has been translated *beryl*, *emerald*, *prasius*, *sapphire*, *sardius*, *ruby*, *cornelian*, *onyx*, and *sardonyx*. It is likely that the name may signify both the *onyx* and *sardonyx*. This latter stone is a mixture of the *chalcedony* and *cornelian*, sometimes in strata, at other times blended together, and is found striped with *white* and *red* strata or layers. It is generally allowed that there is no real difference, except in the degree of *hardness*, between the *onyx*, *cornelian*, *chalcedony*, *sardonyx*, and *agate*. It is well known that the *onyx* is of a *darkish horny* colour, resembling the *hoof* or *nail*, from which circumstance it has its name. It has often a plate of a *bluish white* or *red* in it, and when on one or both sides of this white there appears a plate of a *reddish* colour, the jewellers, says *Woodward*, call the stone a *sardonyx*.

12. JASPER, ישפה *yashepheh*. The similarity of the Hebrew name has determined most critics and mineralogists to adopt the *jasper* as intended by the original word. The *jasper* is usually defined a hard stone, of a beautiful *bright green* colour, sometimes *clouded* with *white*, and *spotted* with *red* or *yellow*. Mineralogists reckon not less than *fifteen* varieties of this stone: 1. *green*; 2. *red*; 3. *yellow*; 4. *brown*; 5. *violet*; 6. *black*; 7. *bluish grey*; 8. *milky white*; 9. *variegated* with *green*, *red*, and *yellow clouds*; 10. *green* with *red specks*; 11. *veined* with *various colours*, apparently in the form of *letters*; 12. with *variously coloured zones*; 13. with *various colours* mixed *without any order*; 14. with *many colours together*; 15. mixed with particles of *agate*. It can scarcely be called a precious stone; it is rather a dull opaque rock.

In examining what has been said on these different precious stones by the best critics, I have adopted such explanations as appeared to me to be best justified by the meaning and use of the original words; but I cannot say that the *stones* which I have described are

A. M. 2513.
B. C. 1491.
An. Exod. Isr. 1.
Sivan.

30 And [x] thou shalt put in the breastplate of judgment the Urim and the Thummim; and they shall be upon Aaron's heart when he goeth in before the LORD: [y] and Aaron shall bear the judgment of the children of Israel upon his heart before the LORD continually.

[x] Lev. viii. 8; Num. xxvii. 21; Deut. xxxiii. 8; 1 Sam. xxviii. 6; Ezra ii. 63; Neh. vii. 65; Ecclus. xlv. 10.

[y] Zech. vi. 13; 2 Cor. vii. 3; Heb. ii. 17.

precisely those intended by the terms in the Hebrew text, nor can I take upon me to assert that the *tribes* are arranged exactly in the manner intended by Moses; for as these things are not *laid down* in the *text* in such a way as to preclude all mistake, some things must be left to *conjecture*. Of several of these stones many fabulous accounts are given by the ancients, and indeed by the moderns also: these I have in general omitted because they are *fabulous;* as also all *spiritual* meanings which others have found so plentifully in each stone, because I consider some of them *puerile*, all *futile*, and not a few *dangerous*.

Verse 30. *Thou shalt put in the breastplate—the Urim and the Thummim*] What these were has, I believe, never yet been discovered. 1. They are nowhere described. 2. There is no direction given to Moses or any other *how to make them*. 3. Whatever they were, they do not appear to have been *made* on *this* occasion. 4. If they were the work of man at all, they must have been the articles in the *ancient* tabernacle, matters used by the *patriarchs*, and not here particularly described, because well known. 5. It is probable that nothing *material* is designed. This is the opinion of some of the Jewish doctors. Rabbi Menachem on this chapter says, "The *Urim* and *Thummim* were not the work of the artificer; neither had the artificers or the congregation of Israel in them any work or any voluntary offering; but they were a *mystery* delivered to Moses from the mouth of God, or they were the work of God himself, or a measure of the Holy Spirit." 6. That God was often consulted by *Urim* and *Thummim*, is sufficiently evident from *several* scriptures; but *how* or in *what manner* he was thus consulted appears in *none*. 7. This mode of consultation, whatever it was, does not appear to have been in use from the consecration of Solomon's temple to the time of its destruction; and after its destruction it is never once mentioned. Hence the Jews say that the *five* following things, which were in the first temple, were wanting in the second: "1. The *ark* with the *mercy-seat* and *cherubim;* 2. The *fire* which came down from heaven; 3. The *shechinah* or Divine presence; 4. The *Holy Spirit*, i. e., the gift of prophecy; and, 5. The *Urim* and *Thummim*."

8. As the word אורים *urim* signifies LIGHTS, and the word תמים *tummim*, PERFECTIONS, they were probably designed to point out the *light*—the *abundant information*, in spiritual things, afforded by the wonderful revelation which God made of himself by and under the LAW; and the *perfection—entire holiness* and *strict conformity to himself*, which this dispensation required, and which are *introduced* and *accomplished* by that dispensation of *light* and *truth*, the GOSPEL, which was prefigured and pointed out by the *law* and its *sacrifices*, &c.; and in this light the subject has been viewed by the Vulgate, where the words are translated *doctrina et veritas, doctrine and truth*—a system of teaching proceeding from *truth* itself. The Septuagint translate the original by *δηλωσις και αληθεια, the manifestation and the truth;* meaning probably the *manifestation* which God made of himself to Moses and the Israelites, and the *truth* which he had revealed to them, of which this breastplate should be a continual memorial.

All the other *versions* express nearly the same things, and all refer to intellectual and spiritual subjects, such as *light*, *truth*, *manifestation*, *doctrine*, *perfection*, &c., &c., not one of them supposing that any thing *material* is intended. The Samaritan text is however different; it adds here a whole clause not found in the Hebrew: ࠅࠏࠔࠉࠕ ࠀࠕ ࠄࠀࠅࠓࠉࠌ ࠅࠀࠕ ࠄࠕࠌࠉࠌ *veasitha eth haurim veeth hattummim, Thou shalt make the Urim and the Thummim*. If this reading be admitted, the Urim and Thummim were manufactured on this occasion as well as the other articles. However it be, they are indescribable and unknown.

The *manner* in which the Jews suppose that the inquiry was made by *Urim* and *Thummim* is the following: "When they inquired the priest stood with his face before the ark, and he that inquired stood behind him with his face to the back of the priest; and the inquirer said, *Shall I go up?* or, *Shall I not go up?* And forthwith the Holy Ghost came upon the priest, and he beheld the breastplate, and saw therein by the vision of prophecy, *Go up*, or, *Go not up*, in the *letters* which showed forth themselves upon the breastplate before his face." See Num. xxvii. 18, 21; Judg. i. 1; xx. 18, 28; 1 Sam. xxiii. 9–12; xxviii. 6; and see *Ainsworth*.

It was the letters that formed the names of the *twelve* tribes upon the breastplate, which the Jews suppose were used in a miraculous way to give answers to the inquirers. Thus when David consulted the Lord whether he should go into a city of Judea, three letters which constituted the word עלה *aloh*, GO, rose up or became prominent in the names on the breastplate; ע *ain*, from the name of *Simeon*, ל *lamed* from the name of *Levi*, and ה *he* from the name of *Judah*, But this supposition is without proof.

Among the Egyptians, a breastplate something like that of the Jewish high-priest was worn by the president of the courts of justice. *Diodorus Siculus* has these words: *Εφορει δ' οὑτος περι τον τραχηλον εκ χρυσης ἁλυσεως ηρτημενον ζωδιον των πολυτελων λιθων, ὁ προσηγορευον* ΑΛΗΘΕΙΑΝ. "He bore about his neck a golden chain, at which hung an image set about with or composed of precious stones, which was called TRUTH."—Bib. Hist., lib. i., chap. lxxv., p. 225. And he farther adds, "that as soon as the president put this gold chain about his neck, the legal proceedings commenced, but not before. And that when the

A. M. 2513.
B. C. 1491.
An. Exod. Isr. 1.
Sivan.

31 And [z] thou shalt make the
robe of the ephod all *of* blue.
32 And there shall be a hole
in the top of it, in the midst thereof: it shall
have a binding of woven work round about the
hole of it, as it were the hole of a [a] habergeon, that it be not rent.
33 And *beneath*, upon the [b] hem of it, thou
shalt make pomegranates *of* blue, and *of* purple, and *of* scarlet, round about the hem
thereof; and bells of gold between them round
about:
34 A golden bell and a pomegranate, a
golden bell and a pomegranate,
upon the hem of the robe round
about.

A. M. 2513.
B. C. 1491.
An. Exod. Isr. 1.
Sivan.

35 [c] And it shall be upon Aaron to minis
ter: and his sound shall be heard when he
goeth in unto the holy *place* before the LORD
and when he cometh out, that he die not.
36 And [d] thou shalt make a plate *of* pure
gold, and grave upon it, *like* the engravings
of a signet, HOLINESS TO THE LORD.
37 And thou shalt put it on a blue lace,
that it may be upon the mitre; upon the fore
front of the mitre it shall be.

[z] Chap. xxxix. 22; Lev. viii. 7.——[a] Chap. xxxix. 23.——[b] Or, *skirts*; chap. xxxix. 24–26.

[c] Ecclus. xlv. 9.——[d] Chapter xxxix. 30; Zech. xiv. 20, Ecclus. xlv. 12.

case of the plaintiff and defendant had been fully and fairly heard, the president turned the *image of truth*, which was hung to the golden chain round his neck, toward the person whose cause was found to be just," by which he seemed to intimate that truth was on *his* side.

Ælian, in his *Hist. Var.*, lib. xxxiv., gives the same account. "The chief justice or president," he says, "was always a priest, of a venerable age and acknowledged probity. *Ειχε δε και αγαλμα περι τον αυχενα εκ σαπφειρου λιθου, και εκαλειτο αγαλμα* ΑΛΗΘΕΙΑ. And he had an image which was called TRUTH engraved on a *sapphire*, and hung about his neck with a gold chain."

Peter du Val mentions a *mummy* which he saw at Cairo, in Egypt, round the neck of which was a chain, having a *golden plate* suspended, which lay on the breast of the person, and on which was engraved the figure of a *bird*. This person was supposed to have been one of the supreme judges; and in all likelihood the bird, of what kind he does not mention, was the emblem of *truth, justice*, or *innocence*.

I have now before me paintings, taken on the spot by a native Chinese, of the *different courts* in China where criminal causes were tried. In these the judge always appears with a piece of embroidery on his breast, on which a *white bird* of the *ardea* or *heron* kind is represented, with expanded wings. All these seem to have been derived from the same source, both among the *Hebrews*, the *Egyptians*, and the *Chinese*. And it is certainly not impossible that the two latter might have borrowed the notion and use of the *breastplate of judgment* from the Hebrews, as it was in use among *them* long before we have any account of its use either among the *Egyptians* or *Chinese*. The different *mandarins* have a *breast-piece* of this kind.

Verse 31. *The robe of the ephod*] See on ver. 4. From this description, and from what Josephus says, who must have been well acquainted with its form, we find that this *meil*, or robe, was one long straight piece of blue cloth, with a hole or opening in the centre for the head to pass through; which hole or opening was bound about, that it might not be rent in putting it on or taking it off, ver. 32.

Verse 35. *His sound shall be heard*] The bells were doubtless intended to keep up the people's attention to the very solemn and important office which the priest was then performing, that they might all have their hearts engaged in the work; and at the same time to keep Aaron himself in remembrance that he ministered *before Jehovah*, and should not come into his presence without due reverence.

That he die not.] This seems an allusion to certain ceremonies which still prevail in the eastern countries. Jehovah appeared among his people in the tabernacle as an *emperor in his tent* among his troops. At the doors of the tents or palaces of grandees was generally placed some sonorous body, either of metal or wood, which was struck to advertise those within that a person prayed for admittance to the presence of the king, &c. As the tabernacle had no door, but a *veil*, and consequently nothing to prevent any person from going in, Aaron was commanded to put the bells on his robe, *that his sound might be heard when he went into the holy place before the Lord*.

Verse 36. *Thou shalt make a plate of pure gold*] The word ציץ *tsits*, which we render *plate*, means a *flower*, or any appearance of this kind. The Septuagint translate it by *πεταλον*, a *leaf*; hence we might be led to infer that this plate resembled a wreath of *flowers* or *leaves*; and as it is called, chap. xxix. 6, נזר *nezer*, a *crown*, and the author of the book of *Wisdom*, chap. xviii. 24, who was a Jew, and may be supposed to know well what it was, calls it *διαδημα*, it was probably of the form, not of the ancient diadem, but rather of the *radiated* crown worn by the ancient Roman emperors, which was a gold band that went round the head from the vertex to the occiput; but the position of the Jewish sacerdotal crown was different, as that went round the *forehead*, under which there was a *blue lace* or *fillet*, ver. 37, which was probably attached to the *mitre* or *turban*, and formed its lowest part or border.

HOLINESS TO THE LORD.] This we may consider as the grand *badge* of the sacerdotal office. 1. The priest was to minister in *holy things*. 2. He was the representative of a *holy God*. 3. He was to offer *sacrifices* to make an *atonement* for and to *put away* SIN. 4. He was to *teach* the people the way of *righteousness* and *true holiness*. 5. As mediator, he was to obtain for them those Divine influences by which

A. M. 2513.
B. C. 1491.
An. Exod. Isr. 1.
Sivan.

38 And it shall be upon Aaron's forehead, that Aaron may [e] bear the iniquity of the holy things, which the children of Israel shall hallow in all their holy gifts; and it shall be always upon his forehead, that they may be [f] accepted before the LORD.

39 And thou shalt embroider the coat of fine linen, and thou shalt make the mitre *of* fine linen, and thou shalt make the girdle *of* needle-work.

40 [g] And for Aaron's sons thou shalt make coats, and thou shalt make for them girdles, and bonnets shalt thou make for them, for glory and for beauty.

41 And thou shalt put them upon Aaron thy brother, and his sons with him; and shalt [h] anoint them, and [i] consecrate [k] them, and sanctify them, that they may minister unto me in the priest's office.

A. M. 2513.
B. C. 1491.
An. Exod. Isr. 1.
Sivan.

42 And thou shalt make them [l] linen breeches to cover [m] their nakedness; from the loins even unto the thighs they shall [n] reach:

43 And they shall be upon Aaron, and upon his sons, when they come in unto the tabernacle of the congregation, or when they come near [o] unto the altar, to minister in the holy *place;* that they [p] bear not iniquity, and die: [q] *it shall be* a statute for ever unto him, and his seed after him.

[e] Ver. 43; Lev. x. 17; xxii. 9; Num. xviii. 1; Isa. liii. 11; Ezek. iv. 4, 5, 6; John i. 29; Heb. ix. 28; 1 Pet. ii. 24.——[f] Lev. i. 4; xxii. 27; xxiii. 11; Isa. lvi. 7.——[g] Ver. 4; ch. xxxix. 27, 28, 29, 41; Ezek. xliv. 17, 18.——[h] Chap. xxix. 7; xxx. 30; xl. 15; Lev. x. 7.——[i] Heb. *fill their hand.*

[k] Chap. xxix. 9, &c.; Lev. viii.; Heb. vii. 28.——[l] Ch. xxxix. 28; Lev. vi. 10; xvi. 4; Ezek. xliv. 18.——[m] Heb. *flesh of their nakedness.*——[n] Heb. *be.*——[o] Chap. xx. 26.——[p] Lev. v. 1, 17; xx. 19, 20; xxii. 9; Num. ix. 13; xviii. 22.——[q] Chapter xxvii. 21; Lev. xvii. 7.

they should be made *holy*, and be prepared to *dwell* with *holy spirits* in the kingdom of glory. 6. In the sacerdotal office he was the type of that *holy* and *just* ONE who, in the fulness of time, was to come and *put away sin* by the *sacrifice* of *himself*.

It is allowed on all hands that this inscription was, in the primitive *Hebrew* character, such as appears upon ancient *shekels*, and such as was used before the Babylonish captivity, and probably from the giving of the law on Mount Sinai. The קרש ליהוה *Kodesh Laihovah*, of the present Hebrew text, would in those ancient characters appear thus:—

which, in the modern Samaritan character, evidently derived from that above, is as follows: [illegible] And the word [illegible] in this ancient and original character is the famous *Tetragrammaton*, or word of *four letters*, which, to the present day, the Jews will neither *write* nor *pronounce*. The Jews teach that these letters were *embossed* on the gold, and not *engraven* in it, and that the plate on which they were embossed was about two fingers broad, and that it occupied a space on the forehead between the *hair* and the *eyebrows*. But it is most likely that it was attached to the lower part of the *mitre*.

Verse 38. *May bear the iniquity of the holy things*] ונשא אהרן את עון הקרשים *venasa Aharon eth avon hakkodashim. And Aaron shall bear* (in a vicarious and typical manner) *the sin of the holy* or *separated things —offerings* or *sacrifices*. Aaron was, as the high priest of the Jews, the type or representative of our blessed Redeemer; and as he offered the sacrifices prescribed by the law to make an atonement for sin, and was thereby represented as *bearing their sins* because he was *bound* to make an atonement for them; so Christ is represented as *bearing their sins*, i. e., the *punishment* due to the sins of the world, in his becoming a sacrifice for the human race. See Isa. liii. 4, 12, where the same *verb*, נשא *nasa*, is used; and see 1. Pet. ii. 24. By the inscription on the plate on his forehead Aaron was acknowledged as the holy minister of the holy God. To the people's services and their offerings much imperfection was attached, and therefore Aaron was represented, not only as *making an atonement* in general for the sins of the people by the sacrifices they brought, but also as making an atonement for the *imperfection* of the *atonement* itself, and the *manner* in which it was brought.

It shall be always upon his forehead] The plate inscribed with *Holiness to the Lord* should be always on his forehead, to teach that the law required *holiness;* that this was its aim, design, and end: and the same is required by the Gospel; for under this dispensation it is expressly said, *Without holiness no man shall see the Lord;* Heb. xii. 14.

Verse 40. *For glory and for beauty.*] See the note on ver. 2.

Verse 42. *Linen breeches*] This command had in view the necessity of *purity* and *decency* in every part of the Divine worship, in opposition to the shocking indecency of the pagan worship in general, in which the priests often ministered *naked*, as in the sacrifices to Bacchus, &c.

ON the garments of the high priest some general reflections have already been made; see ver. 2: and to what is there said it may be just necessary to add, that there can be no doubt of their being all emblematical of spiritual things; but of which, and in what way, no man can positively say. Many commentators have entered largely into this subject, and have made many edifying and useful remarks; but where no clue is given to guide us through a labyrinth in which the possibility of mistake is every moment occurring, it is much better not to attempt to be wise above what is written; for however edifying the reflections may be which are made on these subjects, yet, as they are not

clearly deducible from the text itself, they can give little satisfaction to a sincere inquirer after truth. These garments were all made for *glory* and for *beauty*, and this is the general account that it has pleased God to give of their nature and design: in a general sense, they represented, 1. The necessity of purity in every part of the Divine worship; 2. The necessity of an atonement for sin; 3. The purity and justice of the Divine Majesty; and, 4. The absolute necessity of that holiness without which none can see the Lord. And these subjects should be diligently kept in view by all those who wish to profit by the curious and interesting details given in this chapter. In the notes these topics are frequently introduced.

CHAPTER XXIX.

Ceremonies to be used in consecrating Aaron and his sons, 1–3. *They are to be washed,* 4. *Aaron is to be* clothed *with the holy vestments,* 5, 6; *to be* anointed, 7. *His sons to be clothed and girded,* 8, 9. *They are to offer a* bullock *for a* sin-offering, 10–14; *and a* ram *for a* burnt-offering, 15–18; *and a second* ram *for a* consecration-offering, 19–22. *A* loaf, *a* cake, *and a* wafer *or thin* cake, *for a* wave-offering, 23–25. *The* breast *of the wave-offering and the* shoulder *of the heave-offering to be sanctified,* 26–28. *Aaron's vestments to descend to his son, who shall succeed him,* 29, 30. *Aaron and his sons to eat the flesh of the ram of* consecration, 31, 32. *No* stranger *to eat of it,* 33. *Nothing of it to be left till the morning, but to be burnt with fire,* 34. Seven days *to be employed in consecrating Aaron and his sons,* 35–37. Two lambs, *one for the* morning *and the other for the* evening *sacrifice, to be offered continually,* 38–42. *God promises to sanctify Israel with his glory, and to dwell among them,* 43–46.

A. M. 2513.
B. C. 1491.
An. Exod. Isr. 1.
cir. Thammuz.

AND this *is* the thing that thou
shalt do unto them, to hallow
them, to minister unto me in the
priest's office: [a] Take one young bullock, and
two rams without blemish,

2 And [b] unleavened bread, and cakes unleavened tempered with oil, and wafers unleavened anointed with oil; *of* wheaten flour shalt thou make them.

3 And thou shalt put them into one basket, and bring them in the basket, with the bullock and the two rams.

4 And Aaron and his sons thou shalt bring unto the door of the tabernacle of the congregation, [c] and shalt wash them with water.

5 [d] And thou shalt take the garments, and put upon Aaron the coat, and the robe of the ephod, and the ephod, and the breastplate, and gird him with [e] the curious girdle of the ephod:

6 [f] And thou shalt put the mitre upon his head, and put the holy crown upon the mitre.

7 Then shalt thou take the anointing [g] oil, and pour *it* upon his head, and anoint him.

[a] Lev. viii. 2.——[b] Lev. ii. 4; vi. 20, 21, 22.——[c] Chapter xl. 12; Lev. viii. 6; Heb. x. 22.——[d] Chap. xxviii. 2; Lev. viii. 7.

[e] Chap. xxviii. 8.——[f] Lev. viii. 9.——[g] Chap. xxviii. 41; xxx. 25; Lev. viii. 12; x. 7; xxi. 10; Num. xxxv. 25.

NOTES ON CHAP. XXIX.

Verse 1. *Take one young bullock*] This consecration did not take place till after the erection of the tabernacle. See Lev. viii. 9, 10.

Verse 2. *Unleavened bread*] *Three* kinds of bread as to its *form* are mentioned here, but all unleavened: 1. מצות *matstsoth, unleavened bread,* no matter in what shape. See chap. xii. 9. 2. חלת *challoth, cakes, pricked* or *perforated,* as the root implies. 3. רקיקי *rekikey,* an exceeding thin *cake,* from רק *rak,* to be *attenuated,* properly enough translated *wafer.* The manner in which these were prepared is sufficiently plain from the text, and probably these were the principal *forms* in which flour was prepared for household use during their stay in the wilderness. These were all *waved* before the Lord, ver. 24, as an acknowledgment that the bread that sustains the body, as well as the mercy which saves the soul, comes from God alone.

Verse 4. *Thou—shalt wash them*] This was done emblematically, to signify that they were to put away all filthiness of the flesh and spirit, and perfect holiness in the fear of God; 2 Cor. vii. 1.

Verse 5. *Thou shalt take the garments*] As most offices of spiritual and secular dignity had appropriate habits and *insignia,* hence, when a person was appointed to an office and habited for the purpose, he was said to be *invested* with that office, from *in,* used intensively, and *vestio, I clothe,* because he was then *clothed* with the vestments peculiar to that office.

Verse 7. *Then shalt thou take the anointing oil*] It appears, from Isa. lxi. 1, that *anointing with oil,* in consecrating a person to any important office, whether *civil* or *religious,* was considered as an emblem of the communication of the gifts and graces of the *Holy Spirit.* This ceremony was used on *three* occasions, viz., the installation of *prophets, priests,* and *kings,* into their respective offices. But why should such an anointing be deemed necessary? Because the common sense of men taught them that all good, whether spiritual or secular, must come from God, its origin and cause. Hence it was taken for granted, 1. That no man could *foretell events* unless inspired by the Spirit of God. And therefore the *prophet* was anointed, to signify the communication of the Spirit of wisdom and knowledge. 2. That no person could offer an acceptable *sacrifice* to God for the sins of men, or profitably minister in holy things, unless enlightened,

A. M. 2513.
B. C. 1491.
An. Exod. Isr. 1.
cir. Thammuz.

8 And [h] thou shalt bring his sons, and put coats upon them.
9 And thou shalt gird them with girdles, Aaron and his sons, and [i] put the bonnets on them: and [k] the priest's office shall be theirs for a perpetual statute: and thou shalt [l] consecrate [m] Aaron and his sons.
10 And thou shalt cause a bullock to be brought before the tabernacle of the congregation: and [n] Aaron and his sons shall put their hands upon the head of the bullock.
11 And thou shalt kill the bullock before the LORD, *by* the door of the tabernacle of the congregation.
12 And thou [o] shalt take of the blood of the bullock, and put *it* upon [p] the horns of the altar with thy finger, and pour all the blood beside the bottom of the altar.
13 And [q] thou shalt take all the fat that covereth the inwards, and [r] the caul *that is* above the liver, and the two kidneys, and the fat that *is* upon them, and burn *them* upon the altar.
14 But [s] the flesh of the bullock, and his skin, and his dung, shalt thou burn with fire without the camp: it *is* a sin-offering.
15 [t] Thou shalt also take one ram; and Aaron and his sons shall [u] put their hands upon the head of the ram.
16 And thou shalt slay the ram, and thou shalt take his blood, and sprinkle *it* round about upon the altar.
17 And thou shalt cut the ram in pieces, and wash the inwards of him, and his legs, and put *them* unto his pieces, and [v] unto his head.
18 And thou shalt burn the whole ram upon the altar: it *is* a burnt-offering unto the LORD: it *is* a [w] sweet savour, an offering made by fire unto the LORD.
19 [x] And thou shalt take the other ram; and Aaron and his sons shall put their hands upon the head of the ram:

[h] Lev. viii. 13.—[i] Heb. *bind.*—[k] Num. xviii. 7.—[l] Heb. *fill the hand of.*—[m] Chap. xxviii. 41; Lev. viii. 22; Heb. vii. 28.—[n] Lev. i. 4; viii. 14.—[o] Lev. viii. 15.—[p] Chap. xxvii. 2; xxx. 2.—[q] Lev. iii. 3.

[r] It seemeth by anatomy and the Hebrew doctors, to be *the midriff.*—[s] Lev. iv. 11, 12, 21; Heb. xiii. 11.—[t] Lev. viii. 18.—[u] Lev. i. 4-9.—[v] Or, *upon.*—[w] Gen. viii. 21.—[x] Ver. 3; Lev. viii. 22.

influenced, and directed by the Spirit of grace and holiness. Hence the *priest* was anointed, to signify his being Divinely qualified for the due performance of his sacred functions. 3. That no man could enact just and equitable laws, which should have the prosperity of the community and the welfare of the individual continually in view, or could use the power confided to him only for the suppression of vice and the encouragement of virtue, but that man who was ever under the inspiration of the Almighty. Hence *kings* were inaugurated by anointing with oil. *Two* of these offices only exist in all civilized nations, the *sacerdotal* and *regal;* and in some countries the *priest* and *king* are still consecrated by *anointing.* In the Hebrew language משח *mashach* signifies *to anoint,* and משיח *mashiach,* the *anointed person.* But as no man was ever dignified by holding the *three offices,* so no person ever had the title *mashiach,* the *anointed one,* but Jesus the Christ. He alone is *King* of kings and Lord of lords: the king who *governs* the universe, and *rules* in the hearts of his followers; the *prophet,* to instruct men in the way wherein they should go; and the great *high priest,* to make atonement for their sins. Hence he is called the *Messias,* a corruption of the word המשיח *hammashiach,* THE *anointed* ONE, in Hebrew; which gave birth to ὁ Χριστος, *ho Christos,* which has precisely the same signification in Greek. Of him, Melchizedek, Abraham, Aaron, David, and others were illustrious types. But none of these had the title of THE MESSIAH, or THE ANOINTED of GOD. This does, and ever will, belong exclusively to JESUS *the* CHRIST.

Verse 10. *Shall put their hands upon the head of the bullock.*] By this rite the animal was *consecrated to God,* and was then proper to be offered in sacrifice. *Imposition of hands* also signified that they offered the life of this animal as an atonement for their sins, and to redeem their lives from that death which, through their sinfulness, they had deserved. In the case of the sin-offering and trespass-offering, the person who brought the sacrifice placed his hands on the head of the animal between the horns, and confessed his sin over the sin-offering, and his trespass over the trespass-offering, saying, "I have sinned, I have done iniquity; I have trespassed, and have done thus and thus; and do return by repentance before thee, and with *this* I make atonement." Then the animal was considered as vicariously bearing the sins of the person who brought it.

Verse 14. *It is a sin-offering.*] See the notes on Gen. iv. 7; xiii. 13; Lev. vii. 1, &c.

Verse 18. *It is a burnt-offering*] See the note on Lev. vii. 1, &c.

Verse 19. *The other ram*] There were two rams brought on this occasion: one was for a *burnt-offering,* and was to be entirely consumed; the other was the *ram of consecration,* ver. 22, איל מלאים *eil milluim,* the *ram of filling up,* because when a person was dedicated or consecrated to God, his hands were filled with some particular offering proper for the occasion, which he presented to God. Hence the word *consecration* signifies the *filling up* or *filling the hands,* some part of the sacrifice being put into the hands of such persons, denoting thereby that they had now a right to offer sacrifices and oblations to God. It seems in reference to this ancient mode of consecration, that in the Church of England, when a person is ordained priest, a Bible is put into his hands with these words,

A. M. 2513. B. C. 1491. An. Exod. Isr. 1. cir. Thammuz.

20 Then shalt thou kill the ram, and take of his blood, and put *it* upon the tip of the right ear of Aaron, and upon the tip of the right ear of his sons, and upon the thumb of their right hand, and upon the great toe of their right foot, and sprinkle the blood upon the altar round about.

21 And thou shalt take of the blood that *is* upon the altar, and of [y] the anointing oil, and sprinkle *it* upon Aaron, and upon his garments, and upon his sons, and upon the garments of his sons with him: and [z] he shall be hallowed, and his garments, and his sons, and his sons' garments with him.

22 Also thou shalt take of the ram the fat and the rump, and the fat that covereth the inwards, and the caul *above* the liver, and the two kidneys, and the fat that *is* upon them, and the right shoulder; for it *is* a ram of consecration:

A. M. 2513. B. C. 1491. An. Exod. Isr. 1. cir. Thammuz.

23 [a] And one loaf of bread, and one cake of oiled bread, and one wafer out of the basket of the unleavened bread, that *is* before the LORD:

24 And thou shalt put all in the hands of Aaron, and in the hands of his sons: and shalt [b] wave [c] them *for* a wave-offering before the LORD.

25 [d] And thou shalt receive them of their hands, and burn *them* upon the altar for a burnt-offering, for a sweet savour before the LORD: it *is* an offering made by fire unto the LORD.

26 And thou shalt take [e] the breast of the ram of Aaron's consecration, and wave it *for* a wave-offering before the LORD: and [f] it shall be thy part.

27 And thou shalt sanctify [g] the breast of the wave-offering, and the shoulder of the heave-offering, which is waved, and which is heaved

[y] Chap. xxx. 25, 31; Lev. viii. 30.——[z] Ver. 1; Heb. ix. 22. [a] Lev. viii. 26.——[b] Heb. *shake to and fro.*——[c] Lev. vii. 30.

[d] Lev. viii. 28.——[e] Lev. viii. 29.——[f] Psa. xcix. 6.——[g] Lev. vii. 31, 34; Num. xviii. 11, 18; Deut. xviii. 3.

"Take thou authority to preach the word of God," &c. The *filling the hands* refers also to the *presents* which, in the eastern countries, every inferior was obliged to bring when brought into the presence of a superior. Thus the sacrifice was considered, not only as an atonement for sin, but also as a means of approach and as a *present* to Jehovah.

Verse 20. *Take of his blood*] The putting the blood of the sacrifice on the *tip* of the *right ear*, the *thumb* of the *right hand*, and the *great toe* of the *right foot*, was doubtless intended to signify that they should *dedicate all their faculties and powers to the service of God;* their *ears* to the *hearing* and *study* of his *law*, their *hands* to *diligence* in the *sacred ministry* and to all *acts of obedience*, and their *feet* to *walking* in the *way of God's precepts*. And this *sprinkling* appears to have been used to teach them that they could neither *hear*, *work*, nor *walk* profitably, uprightly, and well-pleasing in the sight of God, without this application of the blood of the sacrifice. And as the blood of *rams*, *bulls*, and *goats*, could never take away sin, does not this prove to us that something infinitely *better* is shadowed out, and that *we* can do nothing holy and pure in the sight of a just and holy God, but through the blood of *atonement?* See on chap. xxx. 20.

Verse 22. *The fat and the rump*] The *rump* or *tail* of some of the eastern sheep is the best part of the animal, and is counted a great delicacy. They are also very large, some of them weighing from *twelve* to *forty pounds*' weight; "so that the owners," says Mr. *Ludolf*, in his *History of Ethiopia*, "are obliged to tie a little cart behind them, whereon they put the tail of the sheep, as well for the convenience of carriage, and to ease the poor creature, as to preserve the wool from dirt, and the tail from being torn among the bushes and stones." An engraving of this kind of sheep, his tail, cart, &c., may be seen at p. 53 of the above work.

Verse 23. *And one loaf of bread*] The bread of different kinds, (see on ver. 2,) in this offering, seems to have been intended as a *minchah*, or offering of *grateful* acknowledgment for providential blessings. The essence of worship consisted in acknowledging God, 1. As the Creator, Governor, and Preserver of all things, and the Dispenser of every good and perfect gift. 2. As the Judge of men, the Punisher of sin, and he who alone could pardon it. The minchahs, heave-offerings, wave-offerings, and thank-offerings, referred to the *first* point. The burnt-offerings, sin-offerings, and sacrifices in general, referred to the *second*.

Verse 24. For *a wave-offering*] See the notes on Lev. vii., where an ample account of *all the offerings*, *sacrifices*, &c., under the Mosaic dispensation, and the reference they bore to the great sacrifice offered by Christ, is given in detail.

Verse 25. *Thou shalt receive them of their hands*] Aaron and his sons are here considered merely as any common persons bringing an offering to God, and not having, as yet, any authority to present it themselves, but through the *medium* of a *priest*. Moses, therefore, was now to Aaron and his sons what they were afterwards to the children of Israel; and as the minister of God he now *consecrates* them to the sacred office, and presents their offerings to Jehovah.

Verse 27. *The breast of the wave-offering, and the shoulder of the heave-offering*] As the *wave-offering* was agitated *to* and *fro*, and the *heave-offering up* and *down*, some have conceived that this twofold action represented the *figure of the cross*, on which the great *Peace-offering* between God and man was offered in the personal sacrifice of our blessed Redeemer. Had we authority for this conjecture, it would certainly

A. M. 2513. B. C. 1491. An. Exod. Isr. 1. cir. Thammuz.

up, of the ram of the consecration, *even* of *that* which *is* for Aaron, and of *that* which is for his sons:

28 And it shall be Aaron's and his sons' [h] by a statute for ever, from the children of Israel: for it *is* a heave-offering. and [i] it shall be a heave-offering from the children of Israel, of the sacrifice of their peace-offerings, *even* their heave-offering unto the LORD.

29 And the holy garments of Aaron [k] shall be his sons' after him, [l] to be anointed therein, and to be consecrated in them.

A. M. 2513. B. C. 1491. An. Exod. Isr. 1. cir. Thammuz.

30 *And* [m] that [n] son that is priest in his stead shall put them on [o] seven days, when he cometh into the tabernacle of the congregation to minister in the holy *place*.

31 And thou shalt take the ram of the consecration, and [p] seethe his flesh in the holy place.

[h] Lev. x. 15.——[i] Lev. vii. 34.——[k] Num. xx. 26, 28.——[l] Num. xviii. 8; xxxv. 25.

[m] Heb. he *of his sons*.——[n] Num. xx. 28.——[o] Lev. viii. 35; ix 1, 8.——[p] Lev. viii. 31.

cast much light on the meaning and intention of these offerings; and when the intelligent reader is informed that one of the most judicious critics in the whole republic of letters is the author of this conjecture, viz., *Houbigant*, he will treat it with respect. I shall here produce his own words on this verse: Hic distinguuntur, תנופה et תרומה, ut ejusdem oblationis cæremoniæ duæ. In תנופה significatur, moveri oblatam victimam *huc* et *illuc*, ad *dextram* et ad *sinistram*. In תרומה *sursum* tolli, et *sublatam* rursus *deprimi*; nam pluribus vicibus id fiebat. Rem sic interpretantur Judæi; et Christianos docent, quanquam id non agentes, sic *adumbrari eam crucem, in quam generis humani victima illa pacifica sublata est*, quam veteres victimæ omnes prænunciabant. "The *heave-offering* and *wave-offering*, as two ceremonies in the same oblation, are here distinguished. The *wave-offering* implies that the victim was moved hither and thither, to the right hand and to the left; the *heave-offering* was lifted *up* and *down*, and this was done several times. In this way the Jews explain these things, and teach the Christians, that by these acts the *cross* was adumbrated, upon which that Peace-offering of the human race was lifted up which was prefigured by all the ancient victims."

The breast and the shoulder, thus *waved* and *heaved*, were by this consecration appointed to be the priests' portion for ever; and this, as Mr. Ainsworth piously remarks, "taught the priests how, with all their *heart* and all their *strength*, they should give themselves unto the service of the Lord in his Church." Moses, as *priest*, received on this occasion the *breast* and the *shoulder*, which became afterwards the portion of the priests; see ver. 28, and Lev. vii. 34. It is worthy of remark, that although Moses himself had no consecration to the sacerdotal office, yet he acts here as high priest, consecrates a high priest, and receives the *breast* and the *shoulder*, which were the priests' portion! But Moses was an *extraordinary* messenger, and derived his authority, without the medium of rites or ceremonies, immediately from God himself. It does not appear that Christ either baptized the *twelve apostles*, or ordained them by imposition of hands; yet, from his own infinite sufficiency, he gave them authority both to baptize, and to lay on hands, in appointing others to the work of the sacred ministry.

Verse 29. *The holy garments—shall be his sons' after him*] These garments were to descend from father to son, and no *new* garments were to be made.

Verse 30. *Seven days*] The priest in his consecration was to abide seven days and nights at the door of the tabernacle, keeping the Lord's watch. See Lev. viii. 33, &c. The number *seven* is what is called among the Hebrews a number of *perfection*; and it is often used to denote the *completion*, *accomplishment*, *fulness*, or *perfection* of a thing, as this period contained the whole course of that time in which God created the world, and appointed the day of rest. As this act of consecration lasted seven days, it signified a *perfect* consecration; and intimated to the priest that his whole body and soul, his time and talents, should be devoted to the service of God and his people.

The number *seven*, which was a sacred number among the *Hebrews*, was conveyed from them down to the Greeks by means of the Egyptian philosophy, from which they borrowed most of their mysteries; and it is most likely that the opinion which the Greeks give is the same that the original framers of the idea had. That there was some *mystical idea* attached to it, is evident from its being made the number of *perfection* among the Hebrews. *Philo* and *Josephus* say that the *Essenes*, an ancient sect of the Jews, held it sacred "because it results from the side of a *square* added to those of a *triangle*." But what meaning does this convey? A *triangle*, or *triad*, according to the *Pythagoreans*, who borrowed their systems from the *Egyptians*, who borrowed from the *Jews*, was the emblem of *wisdom*, as consisting of *beginning* (Monad,) *middle* (Duad,) and *end* (Triad itself;) so *wisdom* consists of *three* parts—*experience* of the *past*, *attention* to the *present*, and *judgment* of the *future*. It is also the most penetrating of all forms, as being the shape of the *wedge*; and indestructibility is essential to it, as a *triangle* can never be destroyed. From those *three properties* it was the emblem of *spirit*. The *square*, *solid*, and *tetrad*, by the same system were interchangeable signs. Now a *square* is the representation of a *solid* or *matter*, and thus the number *seven* contains within itself the properties of both the *triangle* or *solid*, and the *square* or *tetrad*, i. e., is an emblem of body and spirit; comprehends both the *intellectual* and *natural* world; embraces the idea of GOD, the chief of spirits or essences; and all *nature*, the result of his power; thus a very fit emblem of perfection. It is perhaps in this way that we must explain what CICERO, Tusc. Quest., lib. i., cap. 10, says of the number *seven*, where he calls it the *knot and cement of all things; as being that by which the natural and spiritual world are comprehended in one*

A. M. 2513.
B. C. 1491.
An. Exod. Isr. 1.
cir. Thammuz.

32 And Aaron and his sons
shall eat the flesh of the ram,
and the [q] bread that *is* in the
basket, *by* the door of the tabernacle of the
congregation.
33 And [r] they shall eat those things wherewith the atonement was made, to consecrate
and to sanctify them: [s] but a stranger shall
not eat *thereof*, because they *are* holy.
34 And if aught of the flesh of the consecrations, or of the bread, remain unto the
morning, then [t] thou shalt burn the remainder
with fire. it shall not be eaten, because it
is holy.
35 And thus shalt thou do unto Aaron, and
to his sons, according to all *things* which I
have commanded thee: [u] seven days shalt thou
consecrate them.
36 And thou shalt [v] offer every day a bullock *for* a sin-offering, for atonement: and
thou shalt cleanse the altar, when thou hast
made an atonement for it, [w] and thou shalt
anoint it, to sanctify it.
37 Seven days thou shalt make an atonement for the altar, and sanctify it; [x] and
it shall be an altar most holy:
[y] whatsoever toucheth the altar
shall be holy.

A. M. 2513.
B. C. 1491.
An. Exod. Isr. 1.
cir. Thammuz.

38 Now this *is that* which thou shalt offer
upon the altar; [z] two lambs of the first year
[a] day by day continually.
39 The one lamb thou shalt offer [b] in the
morning; and the other lamb thou shalt offer
at even:
40 And with the one lamb a tenth deal of
flour, mingled with the fourth part of a hin of
beaten oil; and the fourth part of a hin of
wine *for* a drink-offering.
41 And the other lamb thou shalt [c] offer
at even, and shalt do thereto according to
the meat-offering of the morning, and according to the drink-offering thereof, for a
sweet savour, an offering made by fire unto
the LORD.
42 *This shall be* [d] a continual burnt-offering
throughout your generations, *at* the door of
the tabernacle of the congregation, before
the LORD: [e] where I will meet you, to speak
there unto thee.
43 And there I will meet with the children

[q] Matthew xii. 4.—[r] Lev. x. 14, 15, 17.—[s] Lev. xxii. 10. [t] Lev. viii. 32.—[u] Exod. xl. 12; Lev. viii. 33, 34, 35.—[v] Heb. x. 11.—[w] Chap. xxx. 26, 28, 29; xl. 10.—[x] Chapter xl. 10. [y] Chap. xxx. 29; Matt. xxiii. 19.—[z] Num. xxviii. 3; 1 Chron. xvi. 40; 2 Chron. ii. 4; xiii. 11; xxxi. 3; Ezra iii. 3.

[a] See Dan. ix. 27; xii. 11.—[b] 2 Kings xvi. 15; Ezek. xlvi. 13, 14, 15.—[c] 1 Kings xviii. 29, 36; 2 Kings xvi. 15; Ezra ix. 4, 5; Psa. cxli. 2; Dan. ix. 21.—[d] Ver. 38; chap. xxx. 8; Num. xxviii. 6; Dan. viii. 11, 12, 13.—[e] Chap. xxv. 22; xxx. 6, 36; Num. xvii. 4.

idea. Thus the ancient philosophers spoke of *numbers*, themselves being the best judges of their own meaning.

Verse 33. *But a stranger shall not eat* thereof] That is, no person who was not of the *family* of *Aaron*—no *Israelite*, and not even a *Levite*.

Verse 34. *Burn the remainder with fire*] Common, voluntary, and peace-offerings, might be eaten even on the second day; see Lev. vii. 16; xix. 5, 6. But this being a *peculiar* consecration, in order to qualify a person to offer sacrifices for sin, like that great sacrifice, the paschal lamb, that typified the atonement made by Christ, none of *it* was to be left till the morning lest *putrefaction* should commence, which would be utterly improper in a sacrifice that was to make expiation for sin, and bring the soul into a state of *holiness* and *perfection* with God. See the note on Exod. xii. 10.

Verse 36. *Thou shalt cleanse the altar*] The altar was to be sanctified for seven days; and it is likely that on each day, previously to the consecration service, the altar was wiped clean, and the former day's ashes, &c., removed.

Verse 37. *Whatsoever touches the altar shall be holy.*] To this our Lord refers Matt. xxiii. 19, where he says the altar sanctifies the gift; and this may be understood as implying that whatever was laid on the altar became the *Lord's property*, and must be wholly devoted to sacred uses, for in no other sense could such things be *sanctified* by *touching the altar*.

Verse 39. *One lamb thou shalt offer in the morning*] These two lambs, one in the morning, and the other in the evening, were generally termed the *morning* and *evening daily sacrifices*, and were offered from the time of their settlement in the promised land to the destruction of Jerusalem by the Romans. The use of these sacrifices according to the Jews was this: "The morning sacrifice made atonement for the sins committed in the night, and the evening sacrifice expiated the sins committed during the day."

Verse 40. *A tenth deal of flour*] *Deal* signifies a *part*, from the Anglo-Saxon dælan, to *divide*; hence dæl, a *part*, a *portion* taken from the whole. From Num. xxviii. 5 we learn that this *tenth deal* was the *tenth part* of an *ephah*, which constituted what is called an *omer*. See chap. xvi. 36; and see the note on ver. 16 of the same chapter, where an account is given of different measures of capacity among the Hebrews. The *omer* contained about *three quarts* English.

The fourth part of a hin] The *hin* contained *one gallon* and *two pints*. The *fourth* part of this was about *one quart* and a *half of a pint*.

Drink-offering.] A libation poured out before the Lord. See its meaning, Lev. vii. 1, &c.

Verse 43. *There I will meet with the children of Israel*] See the note on chap. xxv. 22.

A. M. 2513.
B. C. 1491.
An. Exod. Isr. 1.
cir. Thammuz.

of Israel, and [f] *the tabernacle* [g] shall be sanctified by my glory.

44 And I will sanctify the tabernacle of the congregation, and the altar: I will [h] sanctify also both Aaron and his sons, to minister to me in the priest's office.

45 And [i] I will dwell among the children of Israel, and will be their God.

46 And they shall know that [k] I *am* the LORD their God, that brought them forth out of the land of Egypt, that I may dwell among them: I *am* the LORD their God.

[f] Or, Israel.——[g] Chap. xl. 34; 1 Kings viii. 11; 2 Chron. v. 14; vii. 1, 2, 3; Ezek. xliii. 5; Hag. ii. 7, 9; Mal. iii. 1.

[h] Lev. xxi. 15; xxii. 9, 16.——[i] Exod. xxv. 8; Lev. xxvi. 12; Zech. ii. 10; John xiv. 17, 23; 2 Cor. vi. 16; Rev. xxi. 3.——[k] Chap. xx. 2

Verse 44. *I will sanctify—both Aaron and his sons*] So we find the sanctification by Moses according to the Divine institution was only *symbolical;* and that Aaron and his sons must be sanctified, i. e., made holy, by God himself before they could officiate in holy things. From this, as well as from many other things mentioned in the sacred writings, we may safely infer that no designation by *man* only is sufficient to qualify any person to fill the office of a minister of the sanctuary. The approbation and consecration of man have both their propriety and use, but must never be made *substitutes* for the *unction* and *inspiration* of the Almighty. Let holy men *ordain*, but let God *sanctify;* then we may expect that his Church shall be built up on its most holy faith.

Verse 45. *I will dwell among the children of Israel*] This is the *great charter* of the people of God, both under the Old and New Testaments; see chap. xxv. 8; Lev. xxvi. 11, 12; 2 Cor. vi. 16; Rev. xxi. 3. God dwells AMONG them: he is ever to be found in his Church to enlighten, quicken, comfort, and support it; to dispense the light of life by the preaching of his word, and the influences of his Spirit for the conviction and conversion of sinners. And he dwells IN those who believe; and this is the very tenor of the New Covenant which God promised to make with the house of Israel; see Jer. xxxi. 31–34; Ezek. xxxvii. 24–28; Heb. viii. 7–12; and 2 Cor. vi. 16. And because God had promised to *dwell in all* his genuine followers, hence the frequent reference to this covenant and its privileges in the New Testament. And hence it is so frequently and strongly asserted that every believer is a habitation of God through the Spirit, Eph. ii. 22. That the Spirit of God witnesses with their spirits that they are the children of God, Rom. viii. 16. That the Spirit of Christ in their hearts enables them to call God their Father, Gal. iv. 6. And that if any man have not this Spirit, he is none of his, Rom. viii. 9, &c. And hence St. Paul states this to be the sum and substance of apostolical preaching, and the *riches of the glory of the mystery* of the Gospel *among the Gentiles*, viz., *Christ* IN *you the hope of glory; whom*, says he, *we preach, warning every man, and teaching every man in all wisdom; that we may present every man perfect* IN *Christ Jesus;* Col. i. 27, 28.

Verse 46. *And they shall know that I am the Lord their God*] That is, They shall *acknowledge* God, and their infinite obligations to him. In a multitude of places in Scripture the word *know* should be thus understood.

That I may dwell among them] For without this *acknowledgment* and consequent dependence on and gratitude and obedience to God, they could not expect him to *dwell* among them.

BY *dwelling among the people* God shows that he would be a continual resident in their *houses* and in their *hearts; that he would be their God*—the sole object of their religious worship, to whom they should turn and on whom they should trust in all difficulties and distresses; and that he would be to them all that the *Creator* could be to his *creatures*. That in consequence they should have a *full conviction* of his presence and blessing, and a *consciousness* that HE was *their* God, and that they were *his* people. Thus then God dwells among men that they may *know* him; and they must know him that he may continue to dwell among them. He who does not experimentally know God, cannot have him as an indwelling *Saviour;* and he who does not *continue* to know—to acknowledge, love, and obey him, cannot retain him as his *Preserver* and *Sanctifier*. From the beginning of the world, the salvation of the souls of men necessarily implied the *indwelling* influences of God. Reader, hast thou *this* salvation? This alone will support thee in all thy travels in this wilderness, comfort thee in death, and give thee boldness in the day of judgment. "He," says an old writer, "who has pardon may look his judge in the face."

CHAPTER XXX.

The altar *of* burnt incense, 1. *Dimensions*, 2. *Golden crown*, 3. *Rings and staves*, 4, 5. *Where placed*, 6, 7. *Use*, 8–10. *The* ransom price *of half a shekel*, 11–13. *Who were to pay it*, 14. *The rich and the poor to pay alike*, 15. *The use to which it was applied*, 16. *The* brazen laver, *and its use*, 17–21. *The* holy anointing oil, *and its component parts*, 22–25. *To be applied to the tabernacle, ark, golden table, candlestick, altar of burnt-offerings, and the laver*, 26–29. *And to Aaron and his sons*, 30. *Never to be applied to any other uses, and none like it ever to be made*, 31–33. *The* perfume, *and how made*, 34, 35. *Its use*, 36. *Nothing similar to it ever to be made*, 37, 38.

A. M. 2513.
B. C. 1491.
An. Exod. Isr. 1.
cir. Thammuz.

AND thou shalt make [a] an altar [b] to burn incense upon; *of* shittim wood shalt thou make it.

2 A cubit *shall be* the length thereof, and a cubit the breadth thereof; four-square shall it be: and two cubits *shall be* the height thereof: the horns thereof *shall be* of the same.

3 And thou shalt overlay it with pure gold, the [c] top thereof, and the [d] sides thereof round about, and the horns thereof; and thou shalt make unto it a crown of gold round about.

4 And two golden rings shalt thou make to it under the crown of it, by the two [e] corners thereof; upon the two sides of it shalt thou make *it;* and they shall be for places for the staves to bear it withal.

5 And thou shalt make the staves *of* shittim wood, and overlay them with gold.

6 And thou shalt put it before the veil that *is* by the ark of the testimony, before the [f] mercy-seat that *is* over the testimony, where I will meet with thee.

7 And Aaron shall burn thereon [g] sweet [h] incense every morning: when [i] he dresseth the lamps, he shall burn incense upon it.

A. M. 2513.
B. C. 1491.
An. Exod. Isr. 1.
cir. Thammu.

8 And when Aaron [k] lighteth [l] the lamps [m] at even, he shall burn incense upon it, a perpetual incense before the LORD throughout your generations.

9 Ye shall offer no [n] strange incense thereon, nor burnt-sacrifice, nor meat-offering; neither shall ye pour drink-offering thereon.

10 And [o] Aaron shall make an atonement upon the horns of it once in a year, with the blood of the sin-offering of atonements: once in the year shall he make atonement upon it throughout your generations: it *is* most holy unto the LORD.

11 And the LORD spake unto Moses, saying,

12 [p] When thou takest the sum of the children of Israel after [q] their number, then shall they give every man [r] a ransom for his soul unto the LORD, when thou numberest them; that there be no [s] plague among them when *thou* numberest them.

13 [t] This they shall give, every one that passeth among them that are numbered, half

Chap. xxxvii. 25; xl. 5.——[b] See ver. 7, 8, 10; Lev. iv. 7, 18, Rev. viii. 3.——[c] Heb. *roof.*——[d] Heb. *walls.*——[e] Heb. *ribs.* [f] Chap. xxv. 21, 22.——[g] Heb. *incense of spices.*——[h] Verse 34; 1 Sam. ii. 28; 1 Chron. xxiii. 13; Luke i. 9.——[i] Chap. xxvii. 21.——[k] Or, *setteth up.*——[l] Heb. *causeth to ascend.*——[m] Heb. *between the two evens;* chap. xii. 6.

[n] Lev. x. 1.——[o] Lev. xvi. 18; xxiii. 27.——[p] Chap. xxxviii. 25; Num. i. 2, 5; xxvi. 2; 2 Sam. xxiv. 2.——[q] Heb. *them that are to be numbered;* see Numbers xxxi. 50.——[r] Job xxxiii. 24; xxxvi. 18; Psa. xlix. 7; Matt. xx. 28; Mark x. 45; 1 Timothy ii. 6; 1 Peter i. 18, 19.——[s] 2 Samuel xxiv. 15.——[t] Matthew xvii. 24.

NOTES ON CHAP. XXX.

Verse 1. *Altar to burn incense*] The Samaritan omits the ten first verses of this chapter, because it inserts them after the 32d verse of chap. xxvi. See the note there.

Shittim wood] The same of which the preceding articles were made, because it was *abundant* in those parts, and because it was very *durable;* hence everywhere the Septuagint translation, which was made in Egypt, renders the original by *ξυλον ασηπτον, incorruptible wood.*

Verse 2. *Four-square*] That is, on the upper or under surface, as it showed four equal sides; but it was twice as *high* as it was *broad,* being *twenty-one* inches broad, and *three feet six inches* high. It was called, not only the *altar of incense,* but also the *golden altar,* Num. iv. 11. For the *crown, horns, staves,* &c., see on the altar of burnt-offering, chap. xxvi.

Verse 6. *Before the mercy-seat that* is *over the testimony*] These words in the original are supposed to be a repetition, by mistake, of the preceding clause; the word הפרכת *happarocheth,* the *veil,* being corrupted by interchanging two letters into הכפרת *haccapporeth,* the *mercy-seat;* and this, as Dr. Kennicott observes, places the altar of incense *before the mercy-seat,* and consequently IN the *holy of holies!* Now this could not be, as the altar of incense was attended *every day,* and the *holy of holies* entered only *once in the year.* The five words which appear to be a repetition are wanting in *twenty-six* of Kennicott's and De Rossi's MSS., and in the *Samaritan.* The verse reads better without them, and is more consistent with the rest of the account.

Verse 7. *When he dresseth the lamps*] Prepares the *wicks,* and puts in *fresh oil* for the evening.

Shall burn incense upon it.] Where so many sacrifices were offered it was essentially necessary to have some pleasing perfume to counteract the disagreeable smells that must have arisen from the slaughter of so many animals, the sprinkling of so much blood, and the burning of so much flesh, &c. The *perfume* that was to be burnt on this altar is described ver. 34. No blood was ever sprinkled on *this* altar, except on the day of general expiation, which happened only once in the year, ver. 10. But the *perfume* was necessary in every part of the tabernacle and its environs.

Verse 9. *No strange incense*] None made in any other way.

Nor burnt-sacrifice] It should be an altar for *incense,* and for no other use.

Verse 10. *An atonement—once in a year*] On the *tenth* day of the *seventh* month. See Lev. xvi. 18, &c., and the notes there.

Verse 12. *Then shall they give every man a ransom for his soul*] This was a very important ordinance, and should be seriously considered. See the following verse.

Verse 13. *Half a shekel*] Each of the Israelites

A. M. 2513.
B. C. 1491.
An. Exod. Isr. 1.
cir. Thammuz.

a shekel after the shekel of the
sanctuary: ([u] a shekel *is* twenty
gerahs:) [v] a half shekel *shall be*
the offering of the LORD.
14 Every one that passeth among them that
are numbered, from twenty years old and
above, shall give an offering unto the LORD.
15 The [w] rich shall not [x] give more, and
the poor shall not [y] give less than half a shekel,
when *they* give an offering unto the LORD,
to make an [z] atonement for your souls.
16 And thou shalt take the atonement money
of the children of Israel, and [a] shalt appoint
it for the service of the tabernacle of the
congregation; that it may be [b] a memorial
unto the children of Israel before the LORD, to
make an atonement for your souls.

[u] Lev. xxvii. 25; Num. iii. 47; Ezekiel xlv. 12.——[v] Chapter xxxviii. 26.——[w] Job xxxiv. 19; Prov. xxii. 2; Eph. vi. 9; Col. iii. 25.——[x] Heb. *multiply.*——[y] Heb. *diminish.*——[z] Ver. 12.

17 And the LORD spake unto
Moses, saying,
18 [c] Thou shalt also make a

A. M. 2513.
B. C. 1491.
An. Exod. Isr. 1.
cir. Thammuz.

laver *of* brass, and his foot *also of* brass, to
wash *withal:* and thou shalt [d] put it between
the tabernacle of the congregation and the altar
and thou shall put water therein.
19 For Aaron and his sons [e] shall wash their
hands and their feet thereat:
20 When they go into the tabernacle of the
congregation, they shall wash with water, that
they die not; or when they come near to the
altar to minister, to burn offering made by fire
unto the LORD:
21 So they shall wash their hands and their
feet, that they die not: and [f] it shall be a
statute for ever to them, *even* to him and to

[a] Chap. xxxviii. 25.——[b] Num. xvi. 40.——[c] Chap. xxxviii. 8; 1 Kings vii. 38.——[d] Chap. xl. 7, 30.——[e] Chap. xl. 31, 32; Psa. xxvi. 6; Isa. lii. 11; John xiii. 10; Heb. x. 22.——[f] Ch. xxviii. 43.

was ordered to give as a ransom for his soul (i. e., for his life) half a shekel, according to the shekel of the sanctuary. From this we may learn, 1. That the life of every man was considered as being forfeited to Divine justice. 2. That the redemption money given, which was doubtless used in the service of the sanctuary, was ultimately devoted to the use and profit of those who gave it. 3. That the *standard* by which the value of coin was ascertained, was kept in the sanctuary; for this appears to be the meaning of the words, *after the shekel of the sanctuary.* 4. The shekel is here said to be *twenty gerahs.* A gerah, according to Maimonides, weighed *sixteen* barleycorns, a shekel *three hundred and twenty* of *pure silver.* The shekel is generally considered to be equal in value to *three shillings* English; the redemption money, therefore, must be about *one shilling and sixpence.* 5. The *rich* were not to give *more,* the *poor* not to give *less;* to signify that all souls were equally precious in the sight of God, and that no difference of *outward* circumstances could affect the state of the soul; all had sinned, and all must be redeemed by the same price. 6. This atonement must be made that *there might be no plague among them,* intimating that a plague or curse from God must light on those souls for whom the atonement was *not* made. 7. This was to be a *memorial unto the children of Israel,* ver. 16, to bring to their remembrance their *past deliverance,* and to keep in view their *future redemption.* 8. St. Peter seems to allude to this, and to intimate that this mode of atonement was ineffectual in itself, and only pointed out the great sacrifice which, in the fulness of time, should be made for the sin of the world. "Ye know," says he, "that ye were not redeemed with corruptible things, as silver and gold, from your vain conversation received by tradition from your fathers; but with the precious blood of Christ, as of a lamb without blemish and without spot: who verily was foreordained before the foundation of the world," &c.; 1 Pet. i. 18, 19, 20. 9. Therefore all these things seem to refer to Christ alone, and to the atonement made by his blood; and upon him who is not interested in this atonement, God's plagues must be expected to fall. Reader, acquaint now thyself with God and be at peace, and thereby good shall come unto *thee.*

Verse 18. *A laver* of *brass*] כיור *kiyor* sometimes signifies a *caldron,* 1 Sam. ii. 14; but it seems to signify any large round vessel or basin used for washing the hands and feet. There were doubtless *cocks* or *spigots* in it to draw off the water, as it is not likely the feet were put into it in order to be washed. The *foot* of the laver must mean the *pedestal* on which it stood.

Verse 20. *They shall wash with water, that they die not*] This was certainly an emblematical washing; and as the *hands* and the *feet* are particularly mentioned, it must refer to the purity of their whole conduct. Their *hands*—all their works, their *feet*—all their goings, must be *washed*—must be holiness unto the Lord. And this washing must be *repeated* every time they entered *into the tabernacle,* or when they *came near to the altar to minister.* This washing was needful because the priests all ministered *barefoot;* but it was equally so because of the *guilt* they might have contracted, for the washing was emblematical of the putting away of sin, or what St. Paul calls the *laver* of *regeneration* and the *renewing* of the Holy Ghost, (Tit. iii. 5,) as the influences of the Spirit must be *repeated* for the purification of the soul, as frequently as any moral defilement has been contracted.

Verse 21. *And it shall be a statute for ever*] To continue, in its literal meaning, as long as the Jewish economy lasted, and, in its spiritual meaning, to the end of time. What an important lesson does this teach the ministers of the Gospel of Christ! Each time they minister in public, whether in *dispensing* the WORD or the SACRAMENTS, they should take heed that they have a fresh application of the grace and spirit of

A. M. 2513.
B. C. 1491.
An. Exod. Isr. 1.
cir. Thammuz.

his seed throughout their generations.

22 Moreover the LORD spake unto Moses, saying,

23 Take thou also unto thee [g] principal spices, of pure [h] myrrh five hundred *shekels*, and of sweet cinnamon half so much, *even* two hundred and fifty *shekels*, and of sweet [i] calamus two hundred and fifty *shekels*.

24 And of [k] cassia five hundred *shekels*, after the shekel of the sanctuary, and of oil olive a [l] hin.

25 And thou shalt make it an oil of holy ointment, an ointment compound after the art of the [m] apothecary: it shall be [n] a holy anointing oil.

26 [o] And thou shalt anoint the tabernacle of the congregation therewith, and the ark of the testimony,

27 And the table and all his vessels, and the candlestick and his vessels, and the altar of incense,

28 And the altar of burnt-offering with all his vessels, and the laver and his foot.

A. M. 2513.
B. C. 1491.
An. Exod. Isr. 1.
cir. Thammuz.

29 And thou shalt sanctify them, that they may be most holy: [p] whatsoever toucheth them shall be holy.

30 [q] And thou shalt anoint Aaron and his sons, and consecrate them, that *they* may minister unto me in the priest's office.

31 And thou shalt speak unto the children of Israel, saying, This shall be a holy anointing oil unto me throughout your generations.

32 Upon man's flesh shall it not be poured, neither shall ye make *any other* like it, after the composition of it: [r] it *is* holy, *and* it shall be holy unto you.

33 [s] Whosoever compoundeth *any* like it, or whosoever putteth *any* of it upon a stranger, [t] shall even be cut off from his people.

34 And the LORD said unto Moses, [u] Take unto thee sweet spices, stacte, and onycha, and galbanum; *these* sweet spices with pure frank-

[g] Cant. iv. 14; Ezek. xxvii. 22.——[h] Psa. xlv. 8; Prov. vii. 17.
[i] Cant. iv. 14; Jer. vi. 20.——[k] Psa. xlv. 8.——[l] Chap. xxix. 40.
[m] Or, *perfumer*.——[n] Chap. xxxvii. 29; Num. xxxv. 25; Psalm lxxxix. 20; cxxxiii. 2.

[o] Chap. xl. 9; Lev. viii. 10; Num. vii. 1.——[p] Chapter xxix. 37.——[q] Chap. xxix. 7, &c.; Lev. viii. 12, 30.——[r] Ver. 25, 37.
[s] Ver. 38.——[t] Gen. xvii. 14; chapter xii. 15; Lev. vii. 20, 21.
[u] Chap. xxv. 6; xxxvii. 29.

Christ, to do away past transgressions or unfaithfulness, and to enable them to minister with the greater effect, as being in the Divine favour, and consequently entitled to expect all the necessary assistances of the Divine unction, to make their ministrations spirit and life to the people. See on chap. xxix. 20.

Verse 23. *Take—unto thee principal spices*] From this and the following verse we learn that the holy anointing oil was compounded of the following ingredients:—

Pure myrh, מר דרור *mar deror* . . .	500 shekels.—Myrrh is the produce of an oriental tree not well known, and is collected by making an incision in the tree. What is now called by this name is precisely the same with that of the ancients.
Sweet cinnamon, קנמן בשם *kinnemon besem*, (probably from Arabia) . . .	250 shekels.
Sweet calamus, קנה בשם *keneh bosem*, or sweet cane, Jer. vi. 20.—*Calamus aromaticus* . . .	250 shekels.
Cassia, קדה *kiddah*, (*cassia lignea*,) brought also from Arabia	500 shekels.
Olive oil, שמן זית *shemen zayith*, one hin, about	5 *quarts*.

	lbs.	oz.	dwts.	grs.
500 shekels of the first and last, make	48	4	12	$21\frac{21}{31}$
250 of the cinnanon and calamus . .	24	2	6	$10\frac{26}{31}$

Olive oil is supposed to be the best preservative of *odours*. As the gifts and graces of the Holy Spirit are termed the *anointing* of the Holy Ghost, therefore this holy ointment appears to have been designed as emblematical of those gifts and graces. See Acts i. 5; x. 38; 2 Cor. i. 21; 1 John ii. 20, 27.

Verse 25. *After the art of the apothecary*] The original, רקח *rokeach*, signifies a *compounder* or *confectioner*; any person who compounds *drugs*, *aromatics*, &c.

Verse 30. *Thou shalt anoint Aaron and his sons*] For the reason of this anointing, see the note on chap. xxix. 7. It seems that this anointing oil was an emblem of Divine teaching, and especially of those influences by which the Church of Christ was, in the beginning, guided into all truth; as is evident from the allusion to it by St. John: "*Ye have an* unction *from the* HOLY ONE, *and ye know all things. The* anointing *which ye have received from him abideth in you, and ye need not that any man teach you; but as the same* anointing *teacheth you of all things, and is* truth, *and is no lie, and even as it hath taught you, ye shall abide in* HIM; I John ii. 20, 27.

Verse 34. *Take unto thee sweet spices*] The holy *perfume* was compounded of the following ingredients:

Stacte] נטף *nataph*, supposed to be the same with what was afterwards called the *balm of Jericho*. *Stacte* is the gum which spontaneously flows from the tree which produces *myrrh*. See the note on ver. 23

A. M. 2513.
B. C. 1491.
An. Exod. Isr. 1.
cir. Thammuz.

incense: of each shall there be a like *weight:*
35 And thou shalt make it a perfume, a confection [v] after the art of the apothecary, [w] tempered together, pure *and* holy:
36 And thou shalt beat *some* of it very small, and put of it before the testimony in the tabernacle of the congregation, [x] where I will meet with thee: [y] it shall be unto you most holy.
37 And *as for* the perfume which thou shalt make, [z] ye shall not make to yourselves according to the composition there of: it shall be unto thee holy for the LORD.
38 [a] Whosoever shall make like unto that, to smell thereto, shall even be cut off from his people.

[v] Ver. 25.——[w] Heb. *salted*; Lev. ii. 13.——[x] Chapter xxix. 42; Lev. xvi. 2.

[y] Verse 32; chapter xxix. 37; Lev. ii. 3.——[z] Verse 32. [a] Ver. 33.

Onycha] שחלת *shecheleth*, allowed by the best critics to be the *unguis odoriferans* described by *Rumph*, which is the external crust of the shell-fish *purpura* or *murex*, and is the basis of the principal perfumes made in the East Indies.

Galbanum] חלבנה *chelbenah*, the *bubon gummiferum* or African *ferula;* it rises with a ligneous stalk from *eight* to *ten* feet, and is garnished with leaves at each joint. The top of the stock is terminated by an umbel of *yellow flowers*, which are succeeded by oblong channelled seeds, which have a thin membrane or wing on their border. When any part of the plant is broken, there issues out a little thin milk of a cream colour. The gummy resinous juice which proceeds from this plant is what is commonly called *galbanum*, from the *chelbenah* of the Hebrews.

Pure frankincense] לבנה זכה *lebonah zaccah*. *Frankincense* is supposed to derive its name from *frank*, *free*, because of its *liberal* or ready distribution of its odours. It is a dry resinous substance, in pieces or drops of a pale yellowish white colour, has a strong smell, and bitter acrid taste. The tree which produces it is not well known. *Dioscorides* mentions it as gotten in India. What is called here *pure frankincense* is no doubt the same with the *mascula thura* of Virgil, and signifies what is *first obtained* from the tree—that which is strongest and most free from all adventitious mixtures. See the note on ver. 7.

THE Israelites were most strictly prohibited, on the most awful penalties, from making *any anointing oil* or *perfume* similar to those described in this chapter. He that should compound such, or apply any of this to any common purpose, even *to smell to*, verse 38, should *be cut off*, that is, excommunicated from his people, and so lose all right, title, and interest in the promises of God and the redemption of Israel. From all this we may learn how careful the Divine Being is to preserve his own worship and his own truth, so as to prevent them from being adulterated by human inventions; for he will save men in *his own way*, and upon *his own terms*. What are called *human inventions* in matters of religion, are not only of no worth, but are in general deceptive and ruinous. Arts and sciences in a certain way may be called inventions of men, for the *spirit of a man knoweth the things of a man*—can comprehend, plan, and execute, under the general influence of God, every thing in which human life is immediately concerned; but *religion*, as it is the *gift*, so it is the invention, of God: its doctrines and its ceremonies proceed from his wisdom and goodness, for he alone could devise the plan by which the human race may be restored to his favour and image, and taught to worship him in spirit and in truth. And that worship which himself has prescribed, we may rest assured, will be most pleasing in his sight. Nadab and Abihu offered *strange fire* before the Lord; and their destruction by the fire of Jehovah is recorded as a lasting warning to all presumptuous worshippers, and to all who attempt to model his religion, according to their own caprice, and to minister in sacred things without that authority which proceeds from himself alone. The imposition of hands whether of pope, cardinal, or bishop, can avail nothing here. The call and unction of God alone can *qualify* the minister of the Gospel of Jesus Christ

CHAPTER XXXI.

Bezaleel *appointed for the work of the tabernacle*, 1–5. Aholiab *appointed for the same*, 6. *The particular things on which they were to be employed, the* ark and mercy-seat, 7. Table, candlestick, *and* altar *of* incense, 8. Altar *of* burnt-offering *and the* laver, 9. Priest's garments, 10. Anointing oil *and* sweet incense, 11. *God renews the command relative to the sanctification of the Sabbath*, 12–17. *Delivers to Moses the two tables of stone*, 18.

A. M. 2513.
B. C. 1491.
An. Exod. Isr. 1.
cir. Thammuz.

AND the LORD spake unto Moses, saying,
2 [a] See, I have called by name Bezaleel the [b] son of Uri, the son of Hur, of the tribe of Judah:

[a] Chap. xxxv. 30; xxxvi. 1.

[b] 1 Chron. ii. 20.

NOTES ON CHAP. XXXI.

Verse 2. *I have called by name Bezaleel*] That is, I have particularly appointed this person to be the chief superintendent of the whole work. His name is significant, בצלאל *betsal-el*, *in* or *under the shadow of God*, meaning, under the especial protection of the

A. M. 2513.
B. C. 1491.
An. Exod. Isr. 1.
cir. Thammuz.

3 And I have [c] filled him with
the spirit of God, in wisdom, and
in understanding, and in knowledge, and in all manner of workmanship.
4 To devise cunning works, to work in gold,
and in silver, and in brass,
5 And in cutting of stones, to set *them*,
and in carving of timber, to work in all manner of workmanship.
6 And I, behold, I have given with him
[d] Aholiab, the son of Ahisamach, of the tribe
of Dan: and in the hearts of all that are
[e] wise-hearted I have put wisdom, that they
may make all that I have commanded thee;
7 [f] The tabernacle of the congregation, and
[g] the ark of the testimony, and [h] the mercy-
seat that *is* thereupon, and all the [i] furniture
of the tabernacle,
8 And [k] the table and his furniture, and [l] the pure candlestick
with all his furniture, and the
altar of incense;

A. M. 2513.
B. C. 1491.
An. Exod. Isr. 1.
cir. Thammuz.

9 And [m] the altar of burnt-offering with all
his furniture, and [n] the laver and his foot,
10 And [o] the clothes of service, and the
holy garments for Aaron the priest, and the
garments of his sons, to minister in the priest's
office;
11 [p] And the anointing oil, and [q] sweet incense for the holy *place:* according to all that
I have commanded thee, shall they do.
12 And the LORD spake unto Moses, saying,
13 Speak thou also unto the children of
Israel, saying, [r] Verily my Sabbaths ye shall
keep: for it *is* a sign between me and you
throughout your generations; that *ye* may

[c] Chapter xxxv. 31; 1 Kings vii. 14.—[d] Chapter xxxv. 34. [e] Chap. xxviii. 3; xxxv. 10, 35; xxxvi. 1.—[f] Chapter xxxvi. 8. [g] Chap. xxxvii. 1.—[h] Chapter xxxvii. 6.—[i] Hebrew, *vessels*. [k] Chap. xxxvii. 10.—[l] Chap. xxxvii. 17.

[m] Chap. xxxviii. 1.—[n] Chap. xxxviii. 8.—[o] Chap. xxxix. 1, 41; Num. iv. 5, 6, &c.—[p] Chap. xxx. 25, 31; xxxvii. 29. [q] Chap. xxx. 34; xxxvii. 29.—[r] Lev. xix. 3, 30; xxvi. 2; Ezek. xx. 12, 20; xliv. 24.

Most High. He was the son of *Uri*, the son of *Hur*, the son of *Caleb* or *Chelubai*, the son of *Esron*, the son of *Pharez*, the son of *Judah*. See 1 Chron. ii. 5, 9, 18, 19, 20, and the note on chap. xvii. 10.

Verse 3. *I have filled him with the spirit of God*] See the note on chap. xxviii. 3.

In wisdom] חכמה *chochmah*, from חכם *chacham*, to be *wise*, *skilful*, or *prudent*, denoting the compass of mind and strength of capacity necessary to form a *wise man:* hence our word *wisdom*, the power of *judging* what is *wise* or best to be done; from the Saxon, ƿiſan, *to teach*, *to advise*, and ꝺeman, *to judge;* hence ƿiſeꝺom, the *doom* or *judgment* of the *well taught*, *wise*, or *prudent man*.

Understanding] תבונה *tebunah*, from בן *ban* or *bun*, to *separate*, *distinguish*, *discern;* capacity to comprehend the different parts of a work, how to connect, arrange, &c., in order to make a complete *whole*.

Knowledge] דעת *daath*, denoting particular *acquaintance* with a person or thing; *practical*, *experimental* knowledge.

Verse 4. *Cunning works*] מחשבת *machashaboth*, works of *invention* or *genius*, in the goldsmith and silversmith line.

Verse 5. *In cutting of stones, &c.*] Every thing that concerned the *lapidary's*, *jeweller's*, and *carver's* art.

Verse 6. *In the hearts of all that are wise-hearted I have put wisdom*] So every man that had a *natural genius*, as we term it, had an increase of wisdom by immediate inspiration from God, so that he knew how to execute the different works which Divine wisdom designed for the tabernacle and its furniture. Dark as were the heathens, yet they acknowledged that all talents, and the seeds of all arts, came from God. Hence Seneca: *Insita nobis omnium artium semina, magisterque ex occulto Deus producit ingenia.*

In the same way Homer attributes such curious arts to *Minerva*, the *goddess* of *wisdom*, and *Vulcan*, the *god* of *handicrafts*.

> Ὡς δ' ὁτε τις χρυσον περιχευεται αργυρῳ ανηρ
> Ιδρις, ὁν Ἡφαιστος δεδαεν και Παλλας Αθηνη
> Τεχνην παντοιην, χαριεντα δε ἐργα τελειει.
>
> Odyss., l. vi., ver. 232.

> As by some artist, to whom VULCAN gives
> His *skill divine*, a breathing statue lives;
> By PALLAS *taught*, he frames the wondrous mould,
> And o'er the silver pours the fusile gold.—POPE.

And all this the wisest of men long before them declared; when speaking of the wisdom of God he says, *I, Wisdom, dwell with Prudence, and find out knowledge of witty inventions;* Prov. viii. 12. See the note on chap. xxviii. 3, to which the reader is particularly desired to refer. There is something remarkable in the name of this second superintendent, אהליאב *Aholiab, the tabernacle of the father*, or, *the father is my tabernacle;* a name nearly similar in its meaning to that of *Bezaleel*, see the note on ver. 1.

Verse 8. *The pure candlestick*] Called so either because of the *pure gold* of which it was made, or the *brightness* and *splendour* of its *workmanship*, or of the *light* which it imparted in the tabernacle, as the *purest*, *finest* oil was always burnt in it.

Verse 9. *The altar of burnt-offering*] See on chap. xxvii. 1.

The laver and his foot] The pedestal on which it stood.

Verse 10. *Clothes of service*] Vestments for the ordinary work of their ministry; *the holy garments*—those which were peculiar to the high priest.

Verse 11. *The anointing oil*] See on chap. xxx. 23.

Sweet incense] See on chap. xxx. 34.

Verse 13. *My Sabbaths ye shall keep*] See the notes on Gen. ii. 3; Exod. xx. 8.

A. M. 2513.
B. C. 1491.
An. Exod. Isr. 1.
cir. Thammuz.

know that I *am* the LORD that
doth sanctify you.
14 [s] Ye shall keep the Sab-
bath therefore; for it *is* holy unto you: every
one that defileth it shall surely be put to death:
for [t] whosoever doeth *any* work therein, that
soul shall be cut off from among his people.
15 [u] Six days may work be done; but in the
[v] seventh *is* the Sabbath of rest, [w] holy to the
LORD: whosoever doeth *any* work in the
Sabbath day, he shall surely be put to death.
16 Wherefore the children of Israel shall
keep the Sabbath, to observe
the Sabbath throughout their
generations, *for* a perpetual
covenant.
17 It *is* a [x] sign between me and the children
of Israel for ever: for [y] *in* six days the LORD
made heaven and earth, and on the seventh
day he rested, and was refreshed.
18 And he gave unto Moses, when he had
made an end of communing with him upon
Mount Sinai, [z] two tables of testimony, tables
of stone, written with the finger of God.

A. M. 2513.
B. C. 1491.
An. Exod. Isr. 1.
cir. Thammuz.

[s] Chap. xx. 8; Deut. v. 12; Ezek. xx. 12.——[t] Chapter xxxv. 2; Num. xv. 35.——[u] Chap. xx. 9.——[v] Gen. ii. 2; chapter xvi. 23; xx. 10.——[w] Heb. *holiness*.

[x] Ver. 13; Ezek. xx. 12, 20.——[y] Gen. i. 31; ii. 2.——[z] Ch. xxiv. 12; xxxii. 15, 16; xxxiv. 28, 29; Deut. iv. 13; v. 22; ix. 10, 11; 2 Cor. iii. 3.

Verse 14. *Every one that defileth it*] By any kind of idolatrous or profane worship.

Shall surely be put to death] The magistrates shall examine into the business, and if the accused be found guilty, he shall be stoned to death.

Shall be cut off] Because that person who could so far contemn the Sabbath, which was a *sign* to them of the *rest* which remained for the people of God, was of course an *infidel*, and should be cut off from all the privileges and expectations of an Israelite.

Verse 16. *A perpetual covenant.*] Because it is a sign of this *future* rest and blessedness, therefore the religious observance of it must be perpetually kept up. The type must continue in force till the antitype come.

Verse 17. *Rested, and was refreshed.*] God, in condescension to human weakness, applies to himself here what belongs to man. If a man *religiously* rests on the Sabbath, both his body and soul shall be refreshed; he shall acquire new *light* and *life*.

Verse 18. *When he had made an end of communing*] When the forty days and forty nights were ended.

Two tables of testimony] See on chap. xxxiv. 1.

Tables of stone] That the record might be *lasting*, because it was a testimony that referred to *future* generations, and therefore the materials should be durable.

Written with the finger of God.] All the letters cut by God himself. Dr. Winder, in his History of Knowledge, thinks it probable that this was the first writing in *alphabetical* characters ever exhibited to the world, though there might have been *marks* or *hieroglyphics* cut on wood, stone, &c., before this time; see chap. xvii. 14. That these tables were written, not by the *commandment* but by the power of God himself, the following passages seem to prove: "And the Lord said unto Moses, Come up to me into the mountain, and be thou there; and I will give thee tables of stone WHICH I HAVE WRITTEN, that thou mayest teach them;" Exod. xxiv. 12. "And he gave unto Moses, upon Mount Sinai, two tables of testimony, tables of stone, WRITTEN WITH THE FINGER OF GOD;" chap. xxxi. 18. "And Moses went down from the mount, and the two tables of testimony were in his hand; the tables were written on both their sides. And the tables were THE WORK OF GOD, and the WRITING WAS THE WRITING OF GOD, graven upon the tables;" chap. xxxii. 15, 16. "These words [the ten commandments] the Lord spake in the mount, out of the midst of the fire, of the cloud, and of the thick darkness, with a great voice; and he added no more, BUT HE WROTE THEM on two tables of stone;" Deut. v. 22. It is evident therefore that this writing was properly and literally the writing of God himself. God wrote now on tables of *stone* what he had originally written on the *heart* of man, and in mercy he placed that before his eyes which by sin had been obliterated from his soul; and by this he shows us what, by the Spirit of Christ, must be rewritten in the mind, 2 Cor. iii. 3; and this is according to the covenant which God long before promised to make with mankind, Jer. xxxi. 33. See also what is said on this subject, chap. xx. 1, and see chap. xxxiv. 1. See the note on chap. xvii. 14.

"No time," says Dr. A. Bayley, "seems so proper from whence to date the introduction of *letters* among the Hebrews as this, for *after* this period we find continual mention of *letters*, *reading*, and *writing*, in the now proper sense of those words. See Deut. xxvii. 8; xxxi. 9. Moses, it is said, επαιδευθη, *was educated in all the wisdom of the Egyptians*—in all the learning they possessed; but it is manifest that he had not learned of *them* any method of writing, otherwise there had been no want of God's act and assistance in writing the two tables of the law, no need of a miraculous writing. Had Moses known this art, the Lord might have said to him, as he does often afterwards, *Write thou these words*; Exod. xxxiv. 27. *Write on the stones the words of this law*; Deut. xxvii. 3. *Write you this song for you*; xxxi. 19. Perhaps it may be said, God's writing the law gave it a *sanction*. True; but why might it not also teach the first use of letters, unless it can be proved that they were in use prior to this transaction? It might be thought too much to *assert* that *letters* no more than *language* were a *natural discovery*; that it was impossible for man to have invented *writing*, and that he did not invent it: yet this may appear *really the case* from the following reflections:—1. *Reason* may show us how near to an impossibility it was that a *just* and *proper number* of *convenient* characters for the *sounds in language* should

naturally be hit upon by any man, for whom it was easy to *imitate* and *vary*, but not to *invent*. 2. From *evidence* of the Mosaic history, it appears that the introduction of writing among the Hebrews was not from *man*, but GOD. 3. There are no evident vestiges of letters subsisting among other nations till after the delivery of the law at Mount Sinai; nor then, among some, till very late."

CHAPTER XXXII.

The Israelites, finding that Moses delayed his return, desire Aaron to make them gods to go before them, 1. *Aaron consents, and requires their ornaments,* 2. *They deliver them to him, and he makes a* molten calf, 3, 4. *He builds an altar before it,* 5; *and the people offer burnt-offerings and peace-offerings,* 6. *The Lord commands Moses to go down, telling him that the people had corrupted themselves,* 7, 8. *The Lord is angry, and threatens to destroy them,* 9, 10. *Moses intercedes for them,* 11–13; *and the Lord promises to spare them,* 14. *Moses goes down with the tables in his hands,* 15, 16. *Joshua, hearing the noise they made at their festival, makes some remarks on it,* 17, 18. *Moses, coming to the camp, and seeing their idolatrous worship, is greatly distressed, throws down and breaks the two tables,* 19. *Takes the calf, reduces it to powder, strews it upon the water, and causes them to drink it,* 20. *Moses expostulates with Aaron,* 21. *Aaron vindicates himself,* 22–24. *Moses orders the Levites to slay the transgressors,* 25–27. *They do so, and* 3000 *fall,* 28, 29. *Moses returns to the Lord on the mount, and makes supplication for the people,* 30–32. *God threatens and yet spares,* 33. *Commands Moses to lead the people, and promises him the direction of an angel,* 34. *The people are plagued because of their sin,* 35.

A. M. 2513. B. C. 1491. An. Exod. Isr. 1. Ab.

AND when the people saw that
Moses [a] delayed to come
down out of the mount, the peo-
ple gathered themselves together unto Aaron,
and said unto him, [b] Up, make us gods, which
shall [c] go before us; for *as for* this Moses,
the man that brought us up out of the land of
Egypt, we wot not what is become of him.
2 And Aaron said unto them, Break off the
[d] golden ear-rings, which *are* in
the ears of your wives, of your
sons, and of your daughters, and
bring *them* unto me.
3 And all the people brake off the golden
ear-rings which *were* in their ears, and brought
them unto Aaron.
4 [e] And he received *them* at their hand, and
fashioned it with a graving tool, after he had

[a] Chap. xxiv. 18; Deut. ix. 9.—[b] Acts vii. 40.—[c] Chap. xiii. 21.—[d] Judg. viii. 24, 25, 26, 27.—[e] Chap. xx. 23; Deut. ix. 16; Judg. xvii. 3, 4; 1 Kings xii. 28; Neh. ix. 18; Psa. cvi. 19; Isa. xlvi. 6; Acts vii. 41; Rom. i. 23.

NOTES ON CHAP. XXXII.

Verse 1. *When the people saw that Moses delayed*] How long this was before the expiration of the *forty* days, we cannot tell; but it certainly must have been some considerable time, as the ornaments must be collected, and the calf or ox, after having been *founded*, must require a considerable time to fashion it with the graving tool; and certainly not more than two or three persons could work on it at once. This work, therefore, must have required several days.

The people gathered themselves together] They came in a tumultuous and seditious manner, insisting on having an object of religious worship made for them, as they intended under its direction to return to Egypt. See Acts vii. 39, 40.

As for *this Moses, the man that brought us up*] This seems to be the language of great contempt, and by it we may see the truth of the character given them by Aaron, verse 22, *they were set on mischief*. It is likely they might have supposed that Moses had perished in the fire, which they saw had invested the top of the mountain into which he went.

Verse 2. *Golden ear-rings*] Both men and women wore these ornaments, and we may suppose that these were a part of the spoils which they brought out of Egypt. How strange, that the very things which were granted them by an especial influence and providence of God, should be now abused to the basest idolatrous purposes! But it is frequently the case that the gifts of God become desecrated by being employed in the service of sin; *I will curse your blessings, saith the Lord*, Mal. ii. 2.

Verse 3. *And all the people brake off the golden earrings*] The human being is naturally *fond of dress*, though this has been improperly attributed to the female sex alone, and those are most fond of it who have the shallowest capacities; but on this occasion the *bent* of the people to idolatry was greater than even their love of dress, so that they readily stripped themselves of their ornaments in order to get a molten god. They made some compensation for this afterwards; see chap. xxxv., and the note on chap. xxxviii. 9.

Verse 4. *Fashioned it with a graving tool*] There has been much controversy about the meaning of the word חרט *cheret* in the text: some make it a *mould*, others a *garment*, *cloth*, or *apron*; some a *purse* or *bag*, and others a *graver*. It is likely that some *mould* was made on this occasion, that the gold when fused was cast into it, and that afterwards it was brought into form and symmetry by the action of the *chisel* and *graver*.

These be thy gods, O Israel] The whole of this is a most strange and unaccountable transaction. Was it possible that the people could have so soon lost sight of the wonderful manifestations of God upon the mount?

A. M. 2513. B. C. 1491. An. Exod. Isr. 1. Ab.

made it a molten calf: and they said, These *be* thy gods, O Israel, which brought thee up out of the land of Egypt.

5 And when Aaron saw *it*, he built an altar before it; and Aaron made [f] proclamation and said, To-morrow *is* a feast to the LORD.

6 And they rose up early on the morrow, and offered burnt-offerings, and brought peace-offerings; and the [g] people sat down to eat and to drink, and rose up to play.

7 And the LORD said unto Moses, [h] Go, get thee down; for thy people, which thou broughtest out of the land of Egypt, [i] have corrupted *themselves:*

8 They have turned aside quickly out of the way which [k] I commanded them: they have made them a molten calf, and have worshipped it, and have sacrificed thereunto, and said, [l] These *be* thy gods, O Israel, which have brought thee up out of the land of Egypt.

A. M. 2513. B. C. 1491. An. Exod. Isr. 1. Ab.

9 And the LORD said unto Moses, [m] I have seen this people, and, behold, it is a stiff-necked people:

10 Now therefore [n] let me alone that [o] my wrath may wax hot against them, and that I may consume them: and [p] I will make of thee a great nation.

11 [q] And Moses besought [r] the LORD his God, and said, LORD, why doth thy wrath wax hot against thy people, which thou hast brought forth out of the land of Egypt with great power, and with a mighty hand?

12 [s] Wherefore should the Egyptians speak, and say, For mischief did he bring them out,

[f] Lev. xxiii. 2, 4, 21, 37; 2 Kings x. 20; 2 Chron. xxx. 5. — [g] 1 Cor. x. 7. — [h] Deut. ix. 12; ver. 1; chap. xxxiii. 1; Dan. ix. 24. — [i] Gen. vi. 11, 12; Deut. iv. 16; xxxii. 5; Judg. ii. 19; Hos. ix. 9. — [k] Chap. xx. 3, 4, 23; Deut. ix. 16. — [l] 1 Kings xii. 28.

[m] Chapter xxxiii. 3, 5; xxxiv. 9; Deut. ix. 6, 13; xxxi. 27; 2 Chron. xxx. 8; Isa. xlviii. 4; Acts vii. 51. — [n] Deut. ix. 14, 19. — [o] Chap. xxii. 24. — [p] Num. xiv. 12. — [q] Deut. ix. 18, 26, 27, 28, 29; Psa. lxxiv. 1, 2; cvi. 23. — [r] Heb. *the face of the LORD.* — [s] Num. xiv. 13; Deut. ix. 28; xxxii. 27.

Was it possible that Aaron could have imagined that he could make any god that could help them? And yet it does not appear that he ever remonstrated with the people! Possibly he only intended to make them some *symbolical* representation of the Divine power and energy, that might be as evident to them as the pillar of cloud and fire had been, and to which God might attach an always present energy and influence; or in requiring them to sacrifice their *ornaments*, he might have supposed they would have desisted from urging their request: but all this is mere conjecture, with very little probability to support it. It must however be granted that Aaron does not appear to have even designed a worship that should *supersede* the worship of the Most High; hence we find him making proclamation, *To-morrow* is *a feast to the* LORD, (יהוה;) and we find farther that some of the proper rites of the true worship were observed on this occasion, for they brought *burnt-offerings* and *peace-offerings*, ver. 6, 7: hence it is evident he intended that the true God should be the *object* of their worship, though he permitted and even encouraged them to offer this worship through an idolatrous medium, *the molten calf.* It has been supposed that this was an exact resemblance of the famous Egyptian god *Apis* who was worshipped under the form of an *ox*, which worship the Israelites no doubt saw often practised in Egypt. Some however think that this worship of *Apis* was not then established; but we have already had sufficient proof that different animals were sacred among the Egyptians, nor have we any account of any worship in Egypt earlier than that offered to *Apis*, under the figure of an OX.

Verse 5. *To-morrow* is *a feast to the Lord*] In Bengal the officiating *Brahmin*, or an appointed person proclaims, "To-morrow, or on —— day of ——, such a ceremony will be performed!"

Verse 6. *The people sat down to eat and to drink*] The burnt-offerings were wholly consumed; the peace-offerings, when the blood had been poured out, became the food of the priests, &c. When therefore the strictly religious part of these ceremonies was finished, the *people sat down to eat* of the *peace-offerings*, and this they did merely as the *idolaters*, eating and drinking to excess. And it appears they went much farther, for it is said *they rose up to play*, לצחק *letsachek*, a word of ominous import, which seems to imply here fornicating and adulterous intercourse; and in some countries the verb *to play* is still used precisely in this sense. In this sense the original is evidently used, Gen. xxxix. 14.

Verse 7. *Thy people—have corrupted* themselves] They had not only got into the spirit of idolatry, but they had become abominable in their conduct, so that God *disowns* them to be his: THY *people* have broken the covenant, and are no longer entitled to *my* protection and love.

This is one pretence that the Roman Catholics have for the idolatry in their image worship. Their high priest, the pope, collects the ornaments of the people, and makes an image, a crucifix, a madona, &c. The people worship it; but the pope says it is only to keep God in remembrance. But of the whole God says, *Thy people have corrupted themselves;* and thus, as they continue in their idolatry, they have forfeited the blessings of the Lord's covenant. They are not God's people, they are the pope's people, and he is called "our holy father the pope."

Verse 9. *A stiff-necked people*] Probably an allusion to the stiff-necked ox, the object of their worship.

Verse 10. *Now therefore let me alone*] Moses had already begun to plead with God in the behalf of this rebellious and ungrateful people; and so powerful was

A. M. 2513. B. C. 1491. An. Exod. Isr. 1. Ab.

to slay them in the mountains,
and to comsume them from the
face of the earth? Turn from thy
fierce wrath, and [t] repent of this evil against
thy people.
13 Remember Abraham, Isaac, and Israel,
thy servants, to whom thou [u] swarest by thine
own self, and saidst unto them, [v] I will multiply your seed as the stars of heaven, and all
this land that I have spoken of will I give
unto your seed, and they shall inherit *it* for
ever.
14 And the LORD [w] repented of the evil
which he thought to do unto his people.
15 And [x] Moses turned, and went down
from the mount, and the two tables of the testimony *were* in his hand: the tables *were*
written on both their sides; on
the one side and on the other
were they written.
16 And the [y] tables *were* the work of God,
and the writing *was* the writing of God, graven
upon the tables.
17 And when Joshua heard the noise of the
people as they shouted, he said unto Moses,
There is a noise of war in the camp.
18 And he said, *It is* not the voice of *them*
that shout for mastery, neither *is it* the voice
of *them that* cry for [z] being overcome: *but*
the noise of *them that* sing do I hear.
19 And it came to pass, as soon as he came
nigh unto the camp, that [a] he saw the calf,
and the dancing: and Moses' anger waxed
hot, and he cast the tables out of his hands,

[t] Ver. 14.——[u] Gen. xxii. 16; Heb. vi. 13.——[v] Gen. xii. 7; xiii. 15; xv. 7, 18; xxvi. 4; xxviii. 13; xxxv. 11, 12.——[w] Deut. xxxii. 26; 2 Sam. xxiv. 16; 1 Chron. xxi. 15; Psa. cvi. 45; Jeremiah xviii. 8; xxvi. 13, 19; Joel ii. 13; Jonah iii. 10; iv. 2. [x] Deut. ix. 15.——[y] Chapter xxxi. 18.——[z] Hebrew, *weakness* [a] Deut. ix. 16, 17.

his intercession that even the Omnipotent represents himself as incapable of doing any thing in the way of judgment, unless his creature desisted from praying for mercy! See an instance of the prevalence of fervent intercession in the case of Abraham, Gen. xviii. 23–33, from the model of which the intercession of Moses seems to have been formed.

Verse 14. *And the Lord repented of the evil*] This is spoken merely after the manner of men who, having formed a purpose, permit themselves to be diverted from it by strong and forcible reasons, and so change their minds relative to their former intentions.

Verse 15. *The tables* were *written on both their sides*] If we take this literally, it was certainly a very unusual thing; for in ancient times the two sides of the same substance were never written over. However, some rabbins suppose that by the *writing on both sides* is meant the letters were *cut through* the tables, so that they might be read on both sides, though on one side they would appear reversed. Supposing this to be correct, if the letters were the same with those called *Hebrew* now in common use, the ס *samech*, which occurs twice, and the final ם *mem* which occurs *twenty-three* times in the ten commandments, both of these being *close* letters, could not be cut through on both sides without falling out, unless, as some of the Jews have imagined, they were held in by miracle; but if this ancient character were the same with the Samaritan, this *thorough cutting* might have been quite practicable, as there is not one *close* letter in the whole Samaritan alphabet. On this transaction there are the three following opinions: 1. We may conceive the tables of stone to have been *thin slabs* or a kind of *slate*, and the writing on the back side to have been a *continuation* of that on the front, the first not being sufficient to contain the whole. 2. Or the writing on the back side was probably the *precepts* that *accompanied* the ten commandments; the latter were written by the Lord, the former by Moses; see the note on chap. xxxiv. 1, 27. 3. Or the same words were written on *both sides*, so that when held up, two parties might read at the same time.

Verse 16. *The tables* were *the work of God*] Because *such* a law could proceed from none but himself; God alone is the fountain and author of LAW, of what is *right, just, holy*, and *good*. See the meaning of the word LAW, Exod. xii. 49.

The writing was *the writing of God*] For as he is the sole author of *law* and *justice*, so he alone can write them on the heart of man. This is agreeable to the spirit of the *new* covenant which God had promised to make with men in the latter days: *I will make a new covenant with the house of Israel—I will* PUT MY LAWS IN THEIR MINDS, AND WRITE THEM IN THEIR HEARTS, Jer. xxxi. 33; Heb. viii. 10; 2 Cor. iii. 3. That the writing of these tables was the *writing* of God, see proved at the conclusion of the last chapter.

Verse 17. *Joshua—said—*There *is a noise of war in the camp.*] How natural was this thought to the mind of a military man! Hearing a confused noise he supposed that the Israelitish camp had been attacked by some of the neighbouring tribes.

Verse 18. *And he said*] That is, Moses returned this answer to the observations of Joshua.

Verse 19. *He saw the calf, and the dancing*] Dancing before the idol takes place in almost every Hindoo idolatrous feast.—*Ward.*

He cast the tables out of his hands, and brake them] He might have done this through distress and anguish of spirit, on beholding their abominable idolatry and dissolute conduct; or he probably did it *emblematically*, intimating thereby that, as by this act of his the tables were broken in pieces, on which the law of God was written; so they, by their present conduct, had made a *breach* in the covenant, and broken the laws of their Maker. But we must not excuse this act; it

A. M. 2513.
B. C. 1491.
An. Exod. Isr. 1.
Ab.

and brake them beneath the
mount.
20 [b]And he took the calf
which they had made, and burnt *it* in the fire,
and ground *it* to powder, and strawed *it* upon
the water, and made the children of Israel
drink *of it*.
21 And Moses said unto Aaron, [c]What did
this people unto thee, that thou hast brought
so great a sin upon them?
22 And Aaron said, Let not the anger of my
lord wax hot: [d]thou knowest the people, that
they *are set* on mischief.
23 For they said unto me, [e]Make us gods,
which shall go before us: for *as for* this Moses,
the man that brought us up out of the land of
Egypt, we wot not what has become of him.
24 And I said unto them, Whosoever hath
any gold, let them break *it* off. So they gave
it me: then I cast it into the
fire, and there [f]came out this
calf.

A. M. 2513.
B. C. 1491.
An. Exod. Isr. 1.
Ab.

25 And when Moses saw that the people
were [g]naked, (for Aaron [h]had made them
naked, unto *their* shame, among [i]their enemies:)
26 Then Moses stood in the gate of the
camp, and said, Who *is* on the LORD's side?
let him come unto me. And all the sons of
Levi gathered themselves together unto him.
27 And he said unto them, Thus saith the
LORD God of Israel, Put every man his sword
by his side, *and* go in and out from gate to
gate throughout the camp, and [k]slay every
man his brother, and every man his companion, and every man his neighbour.
28 And the children of Levi did according
to the word of Moses: and there fell of the

[b] Deut. ix. 21.——[c] Gen. xx. 9; xxvi. 10.——[d] Chap. xiv. 11; xv. 24; xvi. 2, 20, 28; xvii. 2, 4.——[e] Ver. 1.——[f] Ver. 4.

[g] Chap. xxxiii. 4, 5.——[h] 2 Chron. xxviii. 19.——[i] Heb. *those that rose up against them*.——[k] Num. xxv. 5; Deut. xxxiii. 9.

was rash and irreverent; God's writing should not have been treated in this way.

Verse 20. *He took the calf—and burnt—and ground* it *to powder, &c.*] How truly contemptible must the object of their idolatry appear when they were obliged to drink their god, reduced to powder and strewed on the water! "But," says an objector, "how could *gold*, the most *ductile* of all metals, and the most *ponderous*, be *stamped* into *dust*, and *strewed* on *water?*" In Deut. ix. 21 this matter is fully explained: *I took*, says Moses, *your sin, the calf which ye had made, and burnt it with fire*, that is, melted it down, probably into ingots, or gross plates, *and stamped it*, that is, beat into *thin laminæ*, something like our gold leaf, *and ground* it *very small*, even *until it was as small as dust*, which might be very easily done by the action of the hands, when *beat* into *thin plates* or *leaves*, as the original words אכת *eccoth* and דק *dak* imply. *And I cast the dust thereof into the brook*, and being thus *lighter* than the water, it would readily *float*, so that they could easily see, in this reduced and useless state, the idol to which they had been lately offering Divine honours, and from which they were vainly expecting *protection* and *defence*. No mode of *argumentation* could have served so forcibly to demonstrate the folly of their conduct, as this method pursued by Moses.

Verse 21. *What did this people unto thee.*] It seems if Aaron had been *firm*, this evil might have been prevented.

Verse 22. *Thou knowest the people*] He excuses himself by the *wicked* and *seditious* spirit of the people, intimating that he was *obliged* to accede to their desires.

Verse 24. *I cast it into the fire and there came out this calf.*] What a silly and ridiculous subterfuge! He seems to insinuate that he only threw the metal into the fire, and that the calf came unexpectedly out by mere accident. The Targum of Jonathan ben Uzziel makes a similar excuse for him: "And I said unto them, Whosoever hath gold, let him break it off and give it to me; and I cast it into the fire, and *Satan entered into it*, and it came out in the form of this calf!" Just like the popish legend of the *falling* of the *shrine of our Lady of Loretta out of heaven!* These legends come from the same quarter. Satan can provide more when necessary for his purpose.

Verse 25. *Moses saw that the people* were *naked*] They were stripped, says the Targum, of the holy crown that was upon their heads, on which the great and precious name 𐤄𐤅𐤄𐤉 JEHOVAH was engraved. But it is more likely that the word פרע *parua* implies that they were reduced to the most *helpless and wretched* state, being abandoned by God in the midst of their enemies. This is exactly similar to that expression, 2 Chron. xxviii. 19: *For the Lord brought Judah low, because of Ahaz king of Israel: for he made Judah* NAKED, הפריע *hiphria, and transgressed sore against the Lord.* Their *nakedness*, therefore, though in the *first* sense it may imply that several of them were despoiled of their ornaments, yet it may also express their defenceless and abandoned state, in consequence of their sin. That they could not *literally* have *all* been despoiled of their ornaments, appears evident from their offerings. See chap. xxxv. 21, &c.

Verse 26. *Who is on the Lord's side?*] That is, Who among you is free from this transgression?

And all the sons of Levi, &c.] It seems they had no part in this idolatrous business.

Verse 27. *From gate to gate*] It is probable that there was an enclosed or intrenched camp, in which the chief rulers and heads of the people were, and that this camp had *two gates* or *outlets*; and the Levites were commanded to pass from one to the other, slaying as many of the transgressors as they could find.

Verse 28. *There fell—about three thousand men.*] These were no doubt the chief transgressors; having

a

A. M. 2513. B. C. 1491. An. Exod. Isr. 1. Ab. people that day, about three
thousand men.
29 [l] For [m] Moses had said,
[n] Consecrate yourselves to-day to the LORD,
even every man upon his son, and upon his
brother; that he may bestow upon you a
blessing this day.
30 And it came to pass on the morrow, that
Moses said unto the people, [o] Ye have sinned
a great sin: and now I will go
up unto the LORD; [p] peradventure I shall [q] make an atonement
for your sin.
31 And Moses [r] returned unto the LORD,
and said, O, this people have sinned a great
sin, and have [s] made them gods of gold;
32 Yet now, if thou wilt, forgive their sin
——; and if not, [t] blot me, I pray thee,

[l] Num. xxv. 11, 12, 13; Deut. xiii. 6–11; xxxiii. 9, 10; 1 Sam. xv. 18, 22; Prov. xxi. 3; Zech. xiii. 3; Matt. x. 37.——[m] Or, *And Moses said, Consecrate yourselves to-day to the LORD, because every man* hath been *against his son, and against his brother,* &c.——[n] Heb. *fill your hands.*——[o] 1 Samuel xii. 20, 23; Luke xv. 18.——[p] 2 Samuel xvi. 12; Amos v. 15.——[q] Numbers xxv. 13.——[r] Deut. ix. 18.——[s] Chap. xx. 23.——[t] Psa. lxix. 28; Rom. ix. 3.

broken the covenant by having *other gods besides Jehovah,* they lost the Divine protection, and then the justice of God laid hold on and slew them. Moses doubtless had positive orders from God for this act of justice, (see ver. 27;) for though, through his intercession, the people were spared so as not to be exterminated as a nation, yet the principal transgressors, those who were *set on mischief,* ver. 22, were to be put to death.

Verse 29. *For Moses had said, Consecrate yourselves*] *Fill your hands* to the Lord. See the reason of this form of speech in the note on chap. xxix. 19.

Verse 31. *Moses returned unto the Lord*] Before he went down from the mountain God had acquainted him with the general defection of the people, whereupon he immediately, without knowing the extent of their crime, began to make intercession for them; and God, having given him a *general* assurance that they should not be cut off, hastened him to go down, and bring them off from their idolatry. Having descended, he finds matters much worse than he expected, and ordered three thousand of the principal delinquents to be slain; but knowing that an evil so extensive must be highly provoking in the sight of the just and holy God, he finds it highly expedient that an *atonement* be made for the sin: for although he had the promise of God that as a *nation* they should not be *exterminated,* yet he had reason to believe that Divine justice must continue to contend with them, and prevent them from ever entering the promised land. That he was apprehensive that this would be the case, we may see plainly from the following verse.

Verse 32. *Forgive their sin ——; and if not, blot me—out of thy book*] It is probable that one part of Moses' work during the forty days of his residence on the mount with God, was his regulating the *muster-roll* of all the tribes and families of Israel, in reference to the parts they were respectively to act in the different transactions in the wilderness, promised land, &c.; and this, being done under the immediate direction of God, is termed *God's book which he had written,* (such muster-rolls or registers, called also genealogies, the Jews have had from the remotest period of their history;) and it is probable that God had told him, that those who should break the covenant which he had then made with them should be *blotted out of that list,* and never enter into the promised land. All this Moses appears to have particularly in view, and, without entering into any detail, immediately comes to the point which he knew was fixed when this *list* or *muster-roll* was made, namely, that those who should break the covenant should be *blotted out,* and never have any inheritance in the promised land: therefore he says, *This people have sinned a great sin, and have made them gods of gold;* thus they had *broken the covenant,* (see the first and second commandments,) and by this had forfeited their right to Canaan. *Yet now,* he adds, *if thou wilt forgive their sin,* that they may yet attain the promised inheritance ——; *and if not, blot me, I pray thee, out of thy book which thou hast written*—if thou wilt blot out their names from this register, and never suffer them to enter Canaan, blot me out also; for I cannot bear the thought of enjoying that blessedness, while my people and their posterity shall be for ever excluded. And God, in kindness to Moses, spared him the mortification of going into Canaan without taking the people with him. They had forfeited their lives, and were sentenced to die in the wilderness; and Moses' prayer was answered in mercy to him, while the people suffered under the hand of justice. But the promise of God did not fail; for, although those who sinned were blotted out of the book, yet their posterity enjoyed the inheritance.

This seems to be the simple and pure light in which this place should be viewed; and in this sense St. Paul is to be understood, Rom. ix. 3, where he says: *For I could wish that myself were* ACCURSED *from Christ for my brethren, my kinsmen according to the flesh; who are* ISRAELITES, *to whom pertaineth the* ADOPTION, *and the* GLORY, *and the* COVENANTS. Moses could not survive the destruction of his people by the neighbouring nations, nor their exclusion from the promised land; and St. Paul, seeing the Jews about to be cut off by the Roman sword for their rejection of the Gospel, was willing to be deprived of every earthly blessing, and even to become a *sacrifice* for them, if this might contribute to the preservation and salvation of the Jewish state. Both those eminent men, engaged in the same work, influenced by a spirit of unparalleled patriotism, were willing to forfeit every blessing of a secular kind, and even die for the welfare of the people. But certainly, neither of them could wish to go to eternal perdition, to save their countrymen from being cut off, the one by the sword of the *Philistines,* the other by that of the *Romans.* Even the supposition is monstrous.

On this mode of interpretation we may at once see

A. M. 2513. B. C. 1491. An. Exod. Isr. 1. Ab.

[u] out of thy book which thou
hast written.
33 And the LORD said unto
Moses, [v] Whosoever hath sinned against me,
him will I blot out of my book.
34 Therefore now go, lead the people unto
the place of which I have spoken unto thee :
[w] behold, mine angel shall go
before thee : nevertheless, [x] in
the day when I visit, I will visit
their sin upon them.
35 And the LORD plagued the people, because
[y] they made the calf, which Aaron
made.

[u] Psa. lvi. 8; cxxxix. 16; Dan. xii. 1; Phil. iv. 3; Rev. iii. 5; xiii. 8; xvii. 8; xx. 12, 15; xxi. 27; xxii. 19.——[v] Lev. xxiii. 30; Ezek. xviii. 4.

[w] Chapter xxxiii. 2, 14, &c.; Numbers xx. 16.——[x] Deut. xxxii. 35; Amos iii. 14; Romans ii. 5, 6.——[y] 2 Samuel xii. 9; Acts vii. 41.

what is implied in the *book of life*, and being *written in* or *blotted out* of such a book. In the public registers, all that were born of a particular tribe were entered in the list of their respective families under that tribe. This was the *book of life;* but when any of those died, his name might be considered as blotted out from this list. Our *baptismal registers*, which record the *births* of all the inhabitants of a particular *parish* or *district*, and which are properly our *books of life ;* and our *bills of mortality*, which are properly our *books of death*, or the lists of those who are thus *blotted out* from our *baptismal registers* or *books of life ;* are very significant and illustrative remains of the ancient registers, or *books of life* and *death* among the *Jews*, the *Greeks*, the *Romans*, and most ancient nations. It is worthy of remark, that in China the names of the persons who have been tried on criminal processes are written in *two distinct books*, which are called the *book of life* and the *book of death :* those who have been *acquitted*, or who have not been *capitally* convicted, are written in the *former ;* those who have been found *guilty*, in the *latter*. These two books are presented to the emperor by his ministers, who, as sovereign, has a right to *erase* any name from either : to place the *living* among the *dead*, that he may die ; or the *dead*, that is, the person condemned to death, among the *living*, that he may be preserved. Thus he *blots out* of the *book of life* or the *book of death* according to his sovereign pleasure, on the representation of his ministers, or the intercession of friends, &c. An ancient and extremely rich picture, in my own possession, representing this circumstance, painted in China, was thus interpreted to me by a native Chinese.

Verse 33. *Whosoever hath sinned against me, him will I blot out*] As if the Divine Being had said : "All my conduct is regulated by infinite justice and righteousness : in no case shall the *innocent* ever suffer for the guilty. That no man may transgress through ignorance, I have given you my law, and thus published my covenant ; the people themselves have acknowledged its justice and equity, and have voluntarily ratified it. He then that sins against me, (for sin is the tranrgression of the law, 1 John iii. 4, and the law must be published and known that it may be binding,) him will I blot out of my book." And is it not remarkable that to these conditions of the covenant God strictly adhered, so that not one soul of these transgressors ever entered into the promised rest ? Here was *justice*. And yet, though they deserved death, they were spared ! Here was *mercy*. Thus, as far as *justice* would permit, *mercy* extended ; and as far as *mercy* would permit, *justice* proceeded. Behold, O reader, the GOODNESS and SEVERITY of GOD ! MERCY saves all that JUSTICE *can* spare ; and JUSTICE destroys all that MERCY *should not* save.

Verse 34. *Lead the people unto* the place] The word *place* is not in the text, and is with great propriety omitted. For Moses never led this people into that place, they all died in the wilderness except Joshua and Caleb ; but Moses led them *towards* the place, and thus the particle אל *el* here should be understood, unless we suppose that God designed to lead them *to* the borders of the land, but not to take them *into* it.

I will visit their sin] I will not destroy them, but they shall not enter into the promised land. They shall wander in the wilderness till the present generation become extinct.

Verse 35. *The Lord plagued the people*] Every time they transgressed afterwards Divine justice seems to have remembered this transgression against them. The Jews have a metaphorical saying, apparently founded on this text : "No affliction has ever happened to Israel in which there was not some particle of the dust of the golden calf."

1. THE attentive reader has seen enough in this chapter to induce him to exclaim, How soon a clear sky may be overcast ! How soon may the brightest prospects be obscured ! Israel had just ratified its covenant with Jehovah, and had received the most encouraging and unequivocal pledges of his protection and love. But they sinned, and provoked the Lord to depart from them, and to destroy the work of his hands. A little more faith, patience, and perseverance, and they should have been safely brought into the promised land. For want of a little more dependence upon God, how often does an excellent beginning come to an unhappy conclusion ! Many who were just on the borders of the promised land, and about to cross Jordan, have, through an act of unfaithfulness, been turned back to wander many a dreary year in the wilderness. Reader, be on thy guard. Trust in Christ, and watch unto prayer.

2. Many people have been greatly distressed on losing their *baptismal register*, and have been reduced in consequence to great *political* inconvenience. But still they had their *lives*, and should a living man complain ? But a man may so sin as to provoke God to cut him off ; or, like a fruitless tree, be cut down, because he encumbers the ground. Or he may have sinned a *sin unto death*, 1 John v. 16, 17, that is, a sin which God will punish with *temporal* death, while he extends mercy to the soul.

3. With respect to the *blotting out of God's book*, on which there has been so much controversy, is it not evident that a soul could not be *blotted out of a book* in which it had *never been written?* And is it not farther evident from ver. 32, 33, that, although a man *be written in* God's book, if he *sins* he may be *blotted out?* Let him that readeth understand; and let him that standeth take heed lest he fall. Reader, be not high-minded, but fear. See the notes on verses 32 and 33.

CHAPTER XXXIII.

Moses is commanded to depart from the mount, and lead up the people towards the promised land, 1. *An angel is promised to be their guide,* 2. *The land is described, and the Lord refuses to go with them,* 3. *The people mourn, and strip themselves of their ornaments,* 4–6. *The tabernacle or tent is pitched without the camp,* 7. *Moses goes to it to consult the Lord, and the cloudy pillar descends on it,* 8, 9. *The people, standing at their tent doors witness this,* 10. *The Lord speaks familiarly with Moses; he returns to the camp, and leaves Joshua in the tabernacle,* 11. *Moses pleads with God, and desires to know whom he will send to be their guide, and to be informed of the way of the Lord,* 12, 13. *The Lord promises that his* presence *shall go with them,* 14. *Moses pleads that the people may be taken under the Divine protection,* 15, 16. *The Lord promises to do so,* 17. *Moses requests to see the Divine glory,* 18. *And God promises to make his goodness pass before him, and to proclaim his name,* 19. *Shows that no man can see his glory and live,* 20; *but promises to put him in the cleft of a rock, and to cover him with his hand while his glory passed by, and then to remove his hand and let him see his back parts,* 21–23.

A. M. 2513. B. C. 1491. An. Exod. Isr. 1. Ab.

AND the LORD said unto Moses,
Depart, *and* go up hence,
thou [a] and the people which thou
hast brought up out of the land of Egypt,
unto the land which I sware unto Abraham,
to Isaac, and to Jacob, saying, [b] Unto thy
seed will I give it:
2 [c] And I will send an angel before thee;
[d] and I will drive out the Canaanite, the Amorite,
and the Hittite, and the Perizzite, the
Hivite, and the Jebusite:
3 [e] Unto a land flowing with
milk and honey: [f] for I will not
go up in the midst of thee, for
thou *art* a [g] stiff-necked people, lest [h] I consume
thee in the way.
4 And when the people heard these evil
tidings, [i] they mourned; [k] and no man did put
on him his ornaments.
5 For the LORD had said unto Moses, Say
unto the children of Israel, [l] Ye *are* a stiff-necked
people: I will come up [m] into the

A. M. 2513. B. C. 1491. An. Exod. Isr. 1. Ab.

[a] Chap. xxxii. 7.—[b] Gen. xii. 7; chap. xxxii. 13.—[c] Chap. xxxii. 34; xxxiv. 11.—[d] Deut. vii. 22; Joshua xxiv. 11.—[e] Chap. iii. 8.—[f] Ver. 15, 17.—[g] Chap. xxxii. 9; xxxiv. 9. Deut. ix. 6, 13.—[h] Chap. xxiii. 21; xxxii. 10; Numbers xvi. 21, 45.—[i] Num. xiv. 1, 39.—[k] Lev. x. 6; 2 Sam. xix. 24; 1 Kings xxi. 27; 2 Kings xix. 1; Esther iv. 1, 4; Ezra ix. 3; Job i. 20; ii. 12; Isa. xxxii. 11; Ezek. xxiv. 17, 23; xxvi. 16.—[l] Ver. 3.—[m] See Num. xvi. 45, 46.

NOTES ON CHAP. XXXIII.

Verse 1. *Unto the land*] That is, towards it, or to the *borders* of it. See chap. xxxii. 34.

Verse 2. *I will send an angel*] In chap. xxiii. 20 God promises to send an angel to conduct them into the good land, in whom the name of God should be; that is, in whom God should dwell. See the note there. Here he promises that an angel shall be their conductor; but as there is nothing particularly specified of him, it has been thought that an ordinary angel is intended, and not that Angel of the Covenant promised before. And this sentiment seems to be confirmed by the following verse.

Verse 3. *I will not go up in the midst of thee*] Consequently, the angel here promised to be their guide was not that angel in whom Jehovah's name was: and so the people understood it; hence the mourning which is afterwards mentioned.

Verse 5. *Now put off thy ornaments from thee*] "The Septuagint, in their translation, suppose that the children of Israel not only laid aside their ear-rings, and such like ornaments, in a time of professed deep humiliation before God, but their upper or more beautiful garments too. Moses says nothing of this last circumstance; but as it is a modern practice, so it appears by their version to have been as ancient as their time, and probably took place long before that. The Septuagint gives us this as the translation of the passage: 'The people, having heard this sad declaration, mourned with lamentations. And the Lord said unto the children of Israel, Now, therefore, put off your robes of glory, and your ornaments, and I will show you the things I will do unto you. And the children of Israel put off their *ornaments* and robes by the mount, by Horeb.'

"If it had not been the custom to put off their upper garments in times of deep mourning, in the days that the Septuagint translation was made, they would not have inserted this circumstance in the account Moses gives of their mourning, and concerning which he was silent. They must have supposed too that this practice might be in use in those elder times.

"That it is now practised in the east, appears from the account Pitts gives of the ceremonies of the Mohammedan pilgrimage to Mecca. 'A few days after this we came to a place called Rabbock, about four

A. M. 2513.
B. C. 1491.
An. Exod. Isr. 1.
Ab.

midst of thee in a moment, and
consume thee; therefore now put
off thy ornaments from thee, that
I may [n] know what to do unto thee.
6 And the children of Israel stripped themselves of their ornaments by the mount Horeb.
7 And Moses took the tabernacle, and pitched it without the camp, afar off from the camp,
[o] and called it the tabernacle of the congregation. And it came to pass, *that* every one
which [p] sought the LORD went out unto the
tabernacle of the congregation,
which *was* without the camp.
8 And it came to pass, when
Moses went out unto the tabernacle, *that* all
the people rose up, and stood every man [q] *at*
his tent door, and looked after Moses, until he
was gone into the tabernacle.
9 And it came to pass, as Moses entered
into the tabernacle, the cloudy pillar descended, and stood *at* the door of the tabernacle,
and *the LORD* [r] talked with Moses.

[n] Deut. viii. 2; Psalm cxxxix. 23.——[o] Chapter xxix. 42, 43. [p] Deut. iv. 29; 2 Sam. xxi. 1.——[q] Numbers xvi. 27.——[r] Chapter xxv. 22; xxxi. 18; Psalm xcix. 7.

days' sail on this side of Mecca, where all the hagges or pilgrims, (excepting those of the female sex) do enter into *hirrawem* or *ihram*, i. e., they take off all their clothes, covering themselves with two hirrawems, or large white cotton wrappers; one they put about their middle, which reaches down to their ancles; with the other they cover the upper part of their body, except the head; and they wear no other thing on their bodies but these wrappers, only a pair of grimgameca, that is *thin-soled shoes* like sandals, the over-leather of which covers only the toes, the insteps being all naked. In this manner, like humble penitents, they go from Rabbock until they come to Mecca, to approach the temple, many times enduring the scorching heat of the sun until the very skin is burnt off their backs and arms, and their heads swollen to a very great degree.'—pp. 115, 116. Presently after he informs us 'that the time of their wearing this mortifying habit is about the space of seven days.' Again, (p 138:) 'It was a sight, indeed, able to pierce one's heart, to behold so many thousands in their garments of humility and mortification, with their naked heads, and cheeks watered with tears; and to hear their grievous sighs and sobs, begging earnestly for the remission of their sins, promising newness of life, using a form of penitential expressions, and thus continuing for the space of four or five hours.'

"The Septuagint suppose the Israelites made much the same appearance as these Mohammedan pilgrims, when Israel stood in anguish of soul at the foot of Mount Horeb, though Moses says nothing of putting off any of their vestments.

"Some passages of the Jewish prophets seem to confirm the notion of their stripping themselves of some of their clothes in times of deep humiliation, particularly Micah i. 8: *Therefore I will wail and howl; I will go stripped and naked; I will make a wailing like the dragons, and mourning as the owls.*

"Saul's stripping himself, mentioned 1 Sam. xix. 24, is perhaps to be understood of his assuming the appearance of those that were deeply engaged in devotional exercises, into which he was unintentionally brought by the prophetic influences that came upon him, and in which he saw others engaged."—*Harmer's Observat.*, vol. iv., p. 172.

The ancient Jewish commentators were of opinion that the Israelites had the name יהוה *Jehovah* inscribed on them in such a way as to ensure them the Divine protection; and that this, inscribed probably on a plate of gold, was considered their choicest ornament; and that when they gave their ornaments to make the golden calf, *this* was given by many, in consequence of which they were considered as *naked* and *defenceless.* All the *remaining* parts of their ornaments, which it is likely were all *emblematical* of spiritual things, God commands them here to lay off; for they could not with propriety bear the symbols of the Divine protection, who had forfeited that protection for their transgression.

That I may know what to do unto thee.] For it seems that while they had these emblematic ornaments on them, they were still considered as under the Divine protection. These were a *shield* to them, which God commands them to throw aside. Though many had parted with their choicest ornaments, yet not all, only a few comparatively, of the wives, daughters, and sons of 600,000 men, could have been thus stripped to make *one* golden calf. The major part still had these ornaments, and *they* are now commanded to lay them aside.

Verse 7. *Moses took the tabernacle*] את האהל *eth haohel, the* TENT; not את המשכן *eth hammishcan, the tabernacle*, the dwelling-place of Jehovah, see chap. xxxv. 11, for this was not as yet erected; but probably the *tent* of Moses, which was before in the midst of the camp, and to which the congregation came for judgment, and where, no doubt, God frequently met with his servant. This is now removed to a considerable distance from the camp, (*two thousand* cubits, according to the Talmudists,) as God refuses to dwell any longer *among* this rebellious people. And as this was the place to which all the people came for justice and judgment, hence it was probably called the *tabernacle*, more properly the *tent, of the congregation.*

Verse 9. *The cloudy pillar descended*] This very circumstance precluded the possibility of deception. The cloud descending at these times, and at none others, was a full proof that it was *miraculous*, and a pledge of the Divine presence. It was beyond the power of human art to counterfeit such an appearance; and let it be observed that all the people *saw* this, ver. 10. How many indubitable and irrefragable proofs of its own authenticity and Divine origin does the Pentateuch contain!

A. M. 2513. B. C. 1491. An. Exod. Isr. 1. Ab.

10 And all the people saw the cloudy pillar stand *at* the tabernacle door: and all the people rose up and [s] worshipped, every man *in* his tent door.

11 And [t] the LORD spake unto Moses face to face, as a man speaketh unto his friend. And he turned again into the camp: but [u] his servant Joshua, the son of Nun, a young man, departed not out of the tabernacle.

12 And Moses said unto the LORD, See, [v] thou sayest unto me, Bring up this people: and thou hast not let me know whom thou wilt send with me. Yet thou hast said, [w] I know thee by name, and thou hast also found grace in my sight.

13 Now therefore, I pray thee [x] if I have found grace in thy sight, [y] show me now thy way, that I may know thee, that I may find grace in thy sight: and consider that this nation *is* [z] thy people.

A. M. 2513. B. C. 1491. An. Exod. Isr. 1. Ab.

14 And he said, [a] My presence shall go *with thee*, and I will give thee [b] rest.

15 And he said unto him, [c] If thy presence go not *with me*, carry us not up hence.

16 For wherein shall it be known here that I and thy people have found grace in thy sight? [d] *is it* not in that thou goest with us? so [e] shall we be separated, I and thy people, from all the people that *are* upon the face of the earth.

17 And the LORD said unto Moses, [f] I will do this thing also that thou hast spoken: for

[s] Chap. iv. 31.——[t] Gen. xxxii. 30; Num. xii. 8; Deut. xxxiv. 10.——[u] Chap. xxiv. 13.——[v] Chap. xxxii. 34.——[w] Verse 17; Gen. xviii. 19; Psa. i. 6; Jer. i. 5 John x. 14, 15; 2 Tim. ii. 19.——[x] Ch. xxxiv. 9.——[y] Psa. xxv. 4; xxvii. 11; lxxxvi. 11; cxix. 33.——[z] Deut. ix. 26, 29; Joel ii. 17.

[a] Chapter xiii. 21; xl. 34-38; Isa. lxiii. 9.——[b] Deut. iii. 20; Josh. xxi. 44; xxii. 4; xxiii. 1; Psa. xcv. 11.——[c] Ver. 3; chap. xxxiv. 9.——[d] Num. xiv. 14.——[e] Chap. xxxiv. 10; Deut. iv. 7, 34; 2 Sam. vii. 23; 1 Kings viii. 53; Psa. cxlvii. 20.——[f] Gen. xix. 21; James v. 16.

Verse 11. *The Lord spake unto Moses face to face*] That there was no personal appearance here we may readily conceive; and that the communications made by God to Moses were not by *visions, ecstacies, dreams, inward inspirations*, or the *mediation of angels*, is sufficiently evident: we may therefore consider the passage as implying that *familiarity* and *confidence* with which the Divine Being treated his servant, and that he spake with him by articulate sounds in his own language, though no *shape* or *similitude* was then to be seen.

Joshua, the son of Nun, a young man] There is a difficulty here. Joshua certainly was not a young man in the *literal* sense of the word; "but he was called so," says Mr. Ainsworth, "in respect of his *service*, not of his *years*; for he was now above *fifty* years old, as may be gathered from Josh. xxiv. 29. But because *ministry* and *service* are usually by the younger sort, all *servants* are called *young men*, Gen. xiv. 24." See also Gen. xxii. 3, and xli. 12. Perhaps the word נער *naar*, here translated *young man*, means a *single person*, one *unmarried*.

Verse 12. *Moses said unto the Lord*] We may suppose that after Moses had quitted the tabernacle he went to the camp, and gave the people some general information relative to the conversation he lately had with the Lord; after which he returned to the tabernacle or tent, and began to plead with God, as we find in this and the following verses.

Thou hast not let me know, &c.] As God had said *he* would not go up with this people, Moses wished to know *whom* he would send with him, as he had only said, in general terms, that he would send an angel.

Verse 13. *Show me now thy way*] Let me know the manner in which thou wouldst have this people led up and governed, because this nation is *thy people*, and should be governed and guided *in thy own way*.

Verse 14. *My presence shall go* with thee] פני ילכו *panai yelechu, my faces shall go.* I shall give thee *manifestations* of my grace and goodness through the whole of thy journey. I shall vary my *appearances* for thee, as thy necessities shall require.

Verse 15. *If thy presence go not*] אם אין פניך הלכים *im ein paneycha holechim, if thy faces do not go*—if we have not *manifestations* of thy peculiar providence and grace, *carry us not up hence.* Without *supernatural* assistance, and a most *particular* providence, he knew that it would be impossible either to *govern* such a people, or *support* them in the desert; and therefore he wishes to be well assured on this head, that he may lead them up with confidence, and be able to give them the most explicit assurances of support and protection. But by what means should these manifestations take place? This question seems to be answered by the Prophet Isaiah, chap. lxiii. 9: *In all their affliction he was afflicted, and the Angel of his presence* (פניו *panaiv, of his faces*) *saved them.* So we find that the goodness and mercy of God were to be manifested by the *Angel of the Covenant*, the Lord Jesus, the Messiah; and this is the interpretation which the Jews themselves give of this place. Can any person lead men to the typical Canaan, who is not himself influenced and directed by the Lord? And of what use are all the means of grace, if not crowned with the *presence* and *blessing* of the God of Israel? It is on this ground that Jesus Christ hath said, *Where two or three are gathered together in my name, I am in the midst of them*, Matt. xviii. 20; without which, what would *preachings, prayers*, and even SACRAMENTS avail?

Verse 16. *So shall we be separated*] By having this Divine protection we shall be saved from idolatry, and be preserved in thy truth and in the true worshipping of thee; and thus shall we be separated from all the people that are upon the face of the earth: as all the nations of the world, the Jews only excepted, were at this time *idolaters*.

Verse 17. *I will do this thing also*] My presence

A. M. 2513. B. C. 1491. An. Exod. Isr. 1. Ab.

[g] thou hast found grace in my
sight, and I know thee by
name.
18 And he said, I beseech thee, show me
[h] thy glory.
19 And he said, [i] I will make all my goodness pass before thee, and I will proclaim the
name of the LORD before thee, [k] and will
be [l] gracious to whom I will be gracious, and
will show mercy on whom I will show
mercy.
20 And he said, Thou canst not see my
face: for [m] there shall no man
see me, and live.
21 And the LORD said, Behold,
there is a place by me, and thou shalt stand
upon a rock:
22 And it shall come to pass, while my
glory passeth by, that I will put thee [n] in a
cleft of the rock, and will [o] cover thee with my
hand while I pass by:
23 And I will take away mine hand, and
thou shalt see my back parts: but my face
shall [p] not be seen.

[g] Ver. 12.——[h] Ver. 20; 1 Timothy vi. 16.——[i] Chap. xxxiv. 5, 6, 7; Jer. xxxi. 14.——[k] Romans ix. 15, 16, 18.——[l] Romans iv. 4, 16.

[m] Gen. xxxii. 30; Deut. v. 24; Judg. vi. 22; xiii. 22; Isa. vi. 5; Rev. i. 16, 17; see chap. xxiv. 10.——[n] Isa. ii. 21.——[o] Psa. xci. 1, 4.——[p] Ver. 20; John i. 18.

shall go with thee, and I will keep thee *separate* from all the people of the earth. Both these promises have been remarkably fulfilled. God continued miraculously with them till he brought them into the promised land; and from the day in which he brought them out of Egypt to the present day, he has kept them a *distinct, unmixed* people! Who can account for this on any principle but that of a continual especial providence, and a constant Divine interference? The Jews have ever been a people *fond of money*; had they been mingled with the people of the earth among whom they have been scattered, their secular interests would have been greatly promoted by it; and they who have *sacrificed* every thing besides to their *love of money*, on this point have been incorruptible! They chose in every part of their dispersions rather to be a poor, despised, persecuted people, and continue *separate from all the people of the earth*, than to enjoy ease and affluence by becoming mixed with the nations. For what great purposes must God be preserving this people! for it does not appear that any moral principle binds them together—they seem lost to this; and yet in opposition to their interests, for which in other respects they would sacrifice every thing, they are still kept distinct from all the people of the earth: for this an especial providence alone can account.

Verse 18. *Show me thy glory*] Moses probably desired to see that which constitutes the peculiar glory or excellence of the Divine nature as it stands in reference to man. By many this is thought to signify his eternal mercy in sending Christ Jesus into the world. Moses perceived that what God was *now* doing had the most important and gracious designs which at present he could not distinctly discover; therefore he desires God to show him his glory. God graciously promises to indulge him in this request as far as possible, by *proclaiming his name, and making all his goodness pass before him*, ver. 19. But at the same time he assures him that he *could not see his face*—the fulness of his perfections and the grandeur of his designs, *and live*, as no human being could bear, in the present state, this full discovery. But he adds, *Thou shalt see my back parts*, את אחרי *eth achorai*, probably meaning *that appearance which he should assume in after times*, when it should be said, *God is manifest in the flesh*. This appearance *did* take place, for we find God putting him into a cleft of the rock, covering him with his hand, and passing by in such a way as to exhibit a *human similitude*. John may have had this in view when he said, *The Word was made flesh, and dwelt* AMONG US, *full of grace and truth, and* WE BEHELD HIS GLORY. What this glory was, and what was implied by this grace and truth, we shall see in the succeeding chapter.

Verse 19. *I will make all my goodness pass before thee*] Thou shalt not have a sight of my *justice*, for thou couldst not bear the infinite splendour of my purity: but I shall show myself to thee as the fountain of inexhaustible *compassion*, the sovereign *Dispenser* of my own mercy in my own way, being gracious to whom I will be gracious, and showing mercy on whom I will show mercy.

I will proclaim the name of the Lord.] See the note, chap. xxxiv. 6.

Verse 20. *No man see me, and live.*] The splendour would be insufferable to *man*; he only, whose mortality is swallowed up of life, can see God *as he is*. See 1 John iii. 2. From some disguised relation of the circumstances mentioned here, the fable of *Jupiter* and *Semele* was formed; she is reported to have entreated Jupiter to *show her his glory*, who was at first very reluctant, knowing that it would be fatal to her; but at last, yielding to her importunity, he discovered his divine majesty, and she was consumed by his presence. This story is told by Ovid in his Metamorphoses, book iii., fable iii., 5.

Verse 21. *Behold*, there is *a place by me*] There seems to be a reference here to a well-known place on the mount where God was accustomed to meet with Moses. This was a *rock*; and it appears there was a cleft or cave in it, in which Moses was to stand while the Divine Majesty was pleased to show him all that human nature was capable of bearing: but this appears to have referred more to the counsels of his mercy and goodness, relative to his purpose of redeeming the human race, than to any visible appearance of the Divine Majesty itself. See on ver. 18.

1. THE conclusion of this chapter is very obscure: we can scarcely pretend to say, in any precise man-

ner, what it means; and it is very probable that the whole concerned Moses *alone*. He was in great perplexity and doubt; he was afraid that God was about to abandon this people; and he well knew that if he did so, their destruction must be the consequence. He had received general directions to decamp, and lead the people towards the promised land; but this was accompanied with a threat that Jehovah would not go with them. The prospect that was before him was exceedingly gloomy and discouraging; and it was rendered the more so because God predicted their persevering stiff-neckedness, and gave this as one reason why he would not go up among them, for their provocations would be so great and so frequent that his justice would be so provoked as to break through in a moment and consume them. Moses, well knowing that God must have some great and important designs in delivering them and bringing them thus far, earnestly entreated him to give him some discovery of it, that his own mind might be satisfied. God mercifully condescends to meet his wishes in such a way as no doubt gave him full satisfaction; but as this referred to *himself alone*, the *circumstances* are not related, as probably they could be of no farther use to us than the mere gratifying of a principle of curiosity.

2. On some occasions to be kept in the dark is as instructive as to be brought into the light. In many cases those words of the prophet are strictly applicable. *Verily, thou art a God who* HIDEST THYSELF, *O God of Israel, the Saviour!* One point we see here very plainly, that while the people continued obstinate and rebellious, that presence of God by which his *approbation* was signified could not be manifested among them; and yet, without his presence to guide, protect, and provide for them, they could neither go up nor be saved. This presence is promised, and on the fulfilment of the promise the safety of Israel depended. The Church of God is often now in such a state that the approbation of God cannot be manifested in it; and yet if his presence were wholly withdrawn, truth would fall in the streets, equity go backward, and the Church must become extinct. How have the seeds of *light* and *life* been *preserved* during the long, dark, and cold periods when error was triumphant, and the pure worship of God adulterated by the impurities of idolatry and the thick darkness of superstition, by the presence of his endless mercy, preserving his own truth in circumstances in which he could not show his *approbation!* He was with the Church in the wilderness, and preserved the living oracles, kept alive the heavenly seeds, and is now showing forth the glory of those designs which before he concealed from mankind. He cannot *err* because he is infinitely *wise;* he can do nothing that is *unkind*, because he delighteth in mercy. We, as yet, see only through a glass darkly; by and by we shall see face to face. The Lord's presence is with his people; and those who trust in him have confident rest in his mercy.

CHAPTER XXXIV.

Moses is commanded to hew two tables similar to the first, and bring them up to the mount, to get the covenant renewed, 1–3. *He prepares the tables and goes up to meet the Lord*, 4. *The Lord descends, and proclaims his name JEHOVAH*, 5. *What this name signifies*, 6, 7. *Moses worships and intercedes*, 8, 9. *The Lord promises to renew the covenant, work miracles among the people, and drive out the Canaanites, &c.*, 10, 11. *No covenant to be made with the idolatrous nations, but their altars and images to be destroyed*, 12–15. *No matrimonial alliances to be contracted with them*, 16. *The Israelites must have no molten gods*, 17. *The commandment of the feast of unleavened bread, and of the sanctification of the first-born, renewed*, 18–20; *as also that of the Sabbath, and the three great annual feasts*, 21–23. *The promise that the surrounding nations shall not invade their territories, while all the males were at Jerusalem celebrating the annual feasts*, 24. *Directions concerning the passover*, 25; *and the first-fruits*, 26. *Moses is commanded to write all these words, as containing the covenant which God had now renewed with the Israelites*, 27. *Moses, being forty days with God without eating or drinking, writes the words of the covenant; and the Lord writes the ten commandments upon the tables of stone*, 28. *Moses descends with the tables; his face shines*, 29. *Aaron and the people are afraid to approach him, because of his glorious appearance*, 30. *Moses delivers to them the covenant and commandments of the Lord; and puts a veil over his face while he is speaking*, 31–33, *but takes it off when he goes to minister before the Lord*, 34, 35.

A. M. 2513. B. C. 1491. An. Exod. Isr. 1. Ab.

AND the Lord said unto Moses, [a] Hew thee two tables of stone like unto the first: [b] and I will write upon *these* tables the words that were in the first tables, which thou brakest.

[a] Chap. xxxii. 16, 19; Deut. x. 1.

[b] Ver. 28; Deut. x. 2, 4.

NOTES ON CHAP. XXXIV.

Verse 1. *Hew thee two tables of stone like unto the first*] In chap. xxxii. 16 we are told that the two first *tables were the work of God, and the writing was the writing of God;* but here Moses is commanded to provide tables of his own workmanship, and God promises to write on them the words which were on the first. That God wrote the first tables himself, see proved by different passages of Scripture at the end of chap. xxxii. But here, in ver. 27, it seems as if *Moses* was commanded *to write these words*, and in ver. 28 it is said, *And he wrote upon the tables;* but in Deut. x. 1–4 it is expressly said that God wrote the *second* tables as well as the *first*.

A. M. 2513.
B. C. 1491.
An. Exod. Isr. 1.
Ab.

2 And be ready in the morning, and come up in the morning
unto Mount Sinai, and present
thyself there to me [c] in the top of the mount.
3 And no man shall [d] come up with thee,
neither let any man be seen throughout all the
mount, neither let the flocks nor herds feed
before that mount.
4 And he hewed two tables of stone like
unto the first; and Moses rose
up early in the morning, and
went up unto Mount Sinai, as the
Lord had commanded him, and took in his
hand the two tables of stone.
5 And the Lord descended in the cloud,
and stood with him there, and [e] proclaimed
the name of the Lord.
6 And the Lord passed by before him, and

A. M. 2513.
B. C. 1491.
An. Exod. Isr. 1.
Ab.

[c] Chap. xix. 20; xxiv. 12.——[d] Chap. xix. 12, 13, 21.

[e] Chap. xxxiii. 19; Num. xiv. 17.

In order to reconcile these accounts let us suppose that the *ten words*, or ten commandments, were written on both tables by the hand of God himself, and that what Moses wrote, ver. 27, was a *copy* of these to be delivered to the people, while the tables themselves were laid up in the ark before the testimony, whither the people could not go to consult them, and therefore a copy was necessary for the use of the congregation; this copy, being taken off under the direction of God, was authenticated equally with the original, and the original itself was laid up as a record to which all succeeding copies might be continually referred, in order to prevent corruption. This supposition removes the apparent contradiction; and thus both God and Moses may be said to have written the covenant and the ten commandments: the former, the original; the latter, the copy. This supposition is rendered still more probable by the 27th verse itself: "And the Lord said unto Moses, *Write thou these words* (that is, as I understand it, a *copy* of the words which God had already written;) *for* AFTER THE TENOR (על פי *al pi*, ACCORDING TO THE MOUTH) *of these words I have made a covenant with thee and with Israel.*" Here the original writing is represented by an elegant prosopopœia, or personification, as *speaking* and giving out *from its own mouth* a copy of itself. It may be supposed that this mode of interpretation is contradicted by the 28th verse: AND HE *wrote upon the tables the words of the covenant;* but that the pronoun HE refers to the Lord, and not to Moses, is sufficiently proved by the *parallel* place, Deut. x. 1–4: *At that time the Lord said unto me, Hew thee two tables of stone like unto the first—and I will write on the tables the words that were in the first tables—and I hewed two tables of stone as at the first—And* HE *wrote on the tables according to the first writing.* This determines the business, and *proves* that God wrote the second as well as the first tables, and that the pronoun in the 28th verse of this chapter refers to the Lord, and not to *Moses*. By this mode of interpretation all contradiction is removed. Houbigant imagines that the difficulty may be removed by supposing that God wrote the ten commandments, and that Moses wrote the other parts of the covenant from ver. 11 to ver. 26, and thus it might be said that both God and Moses wrote on the same tables. This is not an improbable case, and is left to the reader's consideration. See on ver. 27.

There still remains a controversy whether what are called the *ten commandments* were at all written on the *first tables*, those tables containing, according to some, only the terms of the covenant without the *ten words*, which are supposed to be added here for the first time. "The following is a general view of this subject. In chap. xx. the ten commandments are given; and at the same time various *political* and *ecclesiastical statutes*, which are detailed in chapters xxi., xxii., and xxiii. To receive these, Moses had *drawn near unto the thick darkness where God was*, chap. xx. 21, and having received them he came again with them to the people, according to their request before expressed, ver. 19: *Speak thou with us—but let not the Lord speak with us, lest we die*, for they had been terrified by the manner in which God had uttered the ten commandments; see ver. 18. After this Moses, with Aaron, Nadab, and Abihu, and the seventy elders, went up to the mountain; and on his return he announced all these laws unto the people, chap. xxiv. 1, &c., and they promised obedience. Still there is no word of the *tables of stone*. Then he wrote all in a book, chap. xxiv. 4, which was called the book of the covenant, ver. 7. After this there was a second going up of Moses, Aaron, Nadab, Abihu, and the seventy elders, chap. xxiv. 9, when that glorious discovery of God mentioned in verses 10 and 11 of the same chapter took place. After their coming down Moses is again commanded to go up, and God promises to give him tables of stone, containing a *law* and *precepts*, ver. 12. This is the first place these tables of stone are mentioned; and thus it appears that the *ten commandments*, and several other precepts, were given to and accepted by the people, and the covenant sacrifice offered, chap. xxiv. 5, before the *tables of stone* were either written or mentioned." It is very likely that the commandments, laws, &c., were first published by the Lord in the hearing of the people; repeated afterwards by Moses; and the *ten words* or *commandments*, containing the sum and substance of the whole, afterwards written on the first tables of stone, to be kept for a record in the ark. These being broken, as is related chap. xxxii. 19, Moses is commanded to hew out two tables like to the first, and bring them up to the mountain, that God might write upon them what he had written on the former, chap. xxxiv. 1. And that this was accordingly done, see the preceding part of this note.

Verse 6. *And the Lord passed by—and proclaimed, The Lord, &c.*] It would be much better to read this verse thus: "And the Lord passed by before him, and proclaimed JEHOVAH," that is, showed Moses fully what was implied in this august name. Moses had requested God *to show him his glory*, (see the preced

A. M. 2513. B. C. 1491. An. Exod. Isr. 1. Ab.

proclaimed, The LORD, The LORD
[f] God, merciful and gracious,
long-suffering, and abundant in
[g] goodness and [h] truth,
7 [i] Keeping mercy for thousands, [k] forgiving
iniquity and transgression and sin, and [l] that
will by no means clear *the guilty;* visiting
the iniquity of the fathers upon the children,
and upon the children's children, unto the
third and to the fourth *generation.*
8 And Moses made haste, and
[m] bowed his head toward the earth, and worshipped.
9 And he said, If now I have found grace
in thy sight, O LORD, [n] let my Lord, I pray
thee, go among us; for [o] it *is* a stiff-necked
people; and pardon our iniquity and our

[f] Num. xiv. 18; 2 Chron. xxx. 9; Neh. ix. 17; Psa. lxxxvi. 15; ciii. 8; cxi. 4; cxii. 4; cxvi. 5; cxlv. 8; Joel ii. 13. — [g] Psalm xxxi. 19; Romans ii. 4. — [h] Psalm lvii. 10; cviii. 4. — [i] Chapter xx. 6; Deut. v. 10; Psalm lxxxvi. 15; Jer. xxxii. 18; Dan. ix. 4. — [k] Psa. ciii. 3; cxxx. 4; Dan. ix. 9; Eph. iv. 32; 1 John i. 9. — [l] Chap. xxiii. 7, 21; Josh. xxiv. 19; Job x. 14; Mic. vi. 11; Neh. i. 3. — [m] Chap. iv. 31. — [n] Chap. xxxiii. 15, 16. — [o] Chap. xxxiii. 3.

ing chapter, 18th verse,) and God promised to proclaim or fully declare the *name* JEHOVAH, (verse 19;) by which proclamation or interpretation Moses should see *how* God would "be gracious to whom he would be gracious," and *how* he would "be merciful to those to whom he would show mercy." Here therefore God fulfils that promise by proclaiming this name. It has long been a question, what is the meaning of the word יהוה JEHOVAH, *Yehovah, Yehue, Yehveh,* or *Yeve, Jeue, Jao, Iao, Jhueh,* and *Jove;* for it has been as variously pronounced as it has been differently interpreted. Some have maintained that it is utterly inexplicable; these of course have offered no mode of interpretation. Others say that it implies the essence of the Divine nature. Others, that it expresses the doctrine of the Trinity connected with the incarnation; the letter י *yod* standing for the Father, ה *he* for the Son, and ו *vau* (the connecting particle) for the Holy Spirit: and they add that the ה *he* being *repeated* in the word, signifies the *human* nature united to the *Divine* in the incarnation. These speculations are calculated to give very little satisfaction. How strange is it that none of these learned men have discovered that God himself interprets this name in verses 6 and 7 of this chapter! "*And the Lord passed by before him, and proclaimed* יהוה YEHOVAH *the* LORD GOD, *merciful and gracious, long-suffering, and abundant in goodness and truth, keeping mercy for thousands, forgiving iniquity and transgression and sin, and that will by no means clear the guilty.*" *These words* contain the proper interpretation of the venerable and glorious name JEHOVAH. But it will be necessary to consider them in detail.

The different names in this and the following verse have been considered as so many attributes of the Divine nature. Commentators divide them into *eleven,* thus:—1. יהוה JEHOVAH. 2. אל EL, the *strong* or *mighty* God. 3. רחום RACHUM, *the merciful Being,* who is full of tenderness and compassion. 4. חנון CHANNUN, the *gracious One;* he whose nature is *goodness* itself; the *loving God.* 5. ארך אפים ERECH APPAYIM, *long-suffering;* the Being who, because of his goodness and tenderness, is not easily irritated, but suffers long and is kind. 6. רב RAB, the *great* or *mighty One.* 7. חסד CHESED, the *bountiful Being;* he who is *exuberant* in his beneficence. 8. אמת EMETH, the *truth* or *true One;* he alone who can neither *deceive* nor be *deceived,* who is the *fountain of truth,* and from whom all *wisdom* and *knowledge* must be derived. 9. נצר חסד NOTSER CHESED, the *preserver of bountifulness;* he whose beneficence never ends, *keeping mercy for thousands* of generations, showing compassion and mercy while the world endures. 10. נשא עון ופשע וחטאה NOSE *avon vaphesha vechattaah,* he who *bears away iniquity* and *transgression* and *sin:* properly, the REDEEMER, the *Pardoner,* the *Forgiver;* the Being whose prerogative alone it is to forgive sin and save the soul. נקה לא (לו) ינקה NAKKEH *lo yenakkeh,* the *righteous Judge,* who distributes justice with an impartial hand, with whom no *innocent* person can ever be condemned. And, 11. פקד עון POKED *avon,* &c.; he who *visits* iniquity, who punishes transgressors, and from whose justice no sinner can escape. The God of *retributive* and *vindictive justice.*

These eleven attributes, as they have been termed, are all included in the name JEHOVAH, and are, as we have before seen, the proper interpretation of it; but the meaning of several of these words has been variously understood.

Verse 7. *That will by no means clear* the guilty] This last clause is rather difficult; literally translated it signifies, *in clearing he will not clear.* But the Samaritan, reading לו *lo, to him,* instead of the negative לא *lo, not,* renders the clause thus: *With whom the innocent shall be innocent;* i. e., an innocent or holy person shall never be treated as if he were a transgressor, by this just and holy God. The Arabic version has it, *He justifies and is not justified;* and the Septuagint is nearly as our *English* text, *και ου καθαριει τον ενοχον, and he doth not purify the guilty.* The Alexandrian copy of the Septuagint, edited by Dr. Grabe, has *και τον ενοχον καθαρισμῳ ου καθαριει, and the guilty he will not cleanse with a purification-offering.* The *Coptic* is to the same purpose. The *Vulgate* is a paraphrase: *nullusque apud te per se innocens est,* "and no person is innocent *by* or *of himself* before thee." This gives a *sound* theologic sense, stating a great truth, *That no man can make an atonement for his own sins, or purify his own heart; and that all have sinned and come short of the glory of God.*

Verse 9. *O Lord, let my Lord, I pray thee, go among us*] The original is not יהוה *Jehovah,* but אדני *Adonai* in both these places, and seems to refer particularly to the Angel of the Covenant, the Messiah See the note on Gen. xv. 8.

A. M. 2513.
B. C. 1491.
An. Exod. Isr. 1.
Ab.

sin, and take us for [p] thine
inheritance.
10 And he said, Behold, [q] I
make a covenant: before all thy people I will
[r] do marvels, such as have not been done in
all the earth, nor in any nation: and all the
people among which thou *art* shall see the
work of the LORD; for it *is* [s] a terrible thing
that I will do with thee.
11 [t] Observe thou that which I command
thee this day; behold, [u] I drive out before
thee the Amorite, and the Canaanite, and the
Hittite, and the Perizzite, and the Hivite, and
the Jebusite.
12 [v] Take heed to thyself, lest thou make
a covenant with the inhabitants of the land
whither thou goest, lest it be for [w] a snare in
the midst of thee:
13 But ye shall [x] destroy their altars, break
their [y] images, and [z] cut down their groves:
14 For thou shalt worship [a] no other god:
for the LORD, whose [b] name *is* Jealous, *is* a
[c] jealous God:
15 [d] Lest thou make a covenant with the
inhabitants of the land, and they [e] go a whoring
after their gods, and do sacrifice unto their
gods, and *one* [f] call thee, and thou [g] eat of his
sacrifice;
16 And thou take of [h] their daughters unto
thy sons, and their daughters [i] go
a whoring after their gods, and
make thy sons go a whoring after
their gods.

A. M. 2513.
B. C. 1491.
An. Exod. Isr. 1.
Ab.

17 [k] Thou shalt make thee no molten gods.
18 The feast of [l] unleavened bread shalt
thou keep. Seven days thou shalt eat unleavened bread, as I commanded thee, in the
time of the month Abib: for in the [m] month
Abib thou camest out from Egypt.
19 [n] All that openeth the matrix *is* mine;
and every firstling among thy cattle, *whether*
ox or sheep, *that is male*.
20 But [o] the firstling of an ass thou shalt
redeem with a [p] lamb: and if thou redeem
him not, then shalt thou break his neck. All
the first-born of thy sons thou shalt redeem.
And none shall appear before me [q] empty.
21 [r] Six days thou shalt work, but on the
seventh day thou shalt rest: in earing time
and in harvest thou shalt rest.
22 [s] And thou shalt observe the feast of
weeks, of the first-fruits of wheat harvest, and
the feast of ingathering at the [t] year's end.
23 [u] Thrice in the year shall all your men
children appear before the LORD God, the
God of Israel.
24 For I will [v] cast out the nations before
thee, and [w] enlarge thy borders: [x] neither shall

[p] Deut. xxxii. 9; Psa. xxviii. 9; xxxiii. 12; lxxviii. 62; xciv. 14; Jer. x. 16; Zech. ii. 12.——[q] Deut. v. 2; xxix. 12, 14.
[r] Deut. iv. 32; 2 Sam. vii. 23; Psa. lxxvii. 14; lxxviii. 12; cxlvii. 20.——[s] Deut. x. 21; Psa. cxlv. 6; Isa. lxiv. 3.——[t] Deut. v. 32; vi. 3, 25; xii. 28, 32; xxviii. 1.——[u] Chap. xxxiii. 2.
[v] Chap. xxiii. 32; Deut. vii. 2; Judg. ii. 2.——[w] Chap. xxiii. 33.
[x] Chap. xxiii. 24; Deut. xii. 3; Judg. ii. 2.——[y] Heb. *statues*.
[z] Deut. vii. 5; xii. 2; Judg. vi. 25; 2 Kings xviii. 4; xxiii. 14; 2 Chron. xxxi. 1; xxxiv. 3, 4.——[a] Chap. xx. 3, 5.——[b] So Isa. ix. 6; lvii. 15.——[c] Chap. xx. 5.——[d] Ver. 12.——[e] Deut. xxxi. 16; Judg. ii. 17; Jer. iii. 9; Ezek. vi. 9.——[f] Num. xxv. 2; 1 Cor. x. 27.——[g] Psa. cvi. 28; 1 Cor. viii. 4, 7, 10.

[h] Deut. vii. 3; 1 Kings xi. 2; Ezra ix. 2; Neh. xiii. 25.
[i] Num. xxv. 1, 2; 1 Kings xi. 4.——[k] Chap. xxxii. 8; Lev. xix. 4.——[l] Chap. xii. 15; xxiii. 15.——[m] Chap. xiii. 4.——[n] Chap. xiii. 2, 12; xxii. 29; Ezek. xliv. 30; Luke ii. 23.——[o] Chap. xiii. 13; Num. xviii. 15.——[p] Or, *kid*.——[q] Chap. xxiii. 15, Deut. xvi. 16; 1 Sam. ix. 7, 8; 2 Sam. xxiv. 24.——[r] Chap. xx. 9; xxiii. 12; xxxv. 2; Deut. v. 12, 13; Luke xiii. 14.——[s] Ch. xxiii. 16; Deut. xvi. 10, 13.——[t] Heb. *revolution of the year*.
[u] Chap. xxiii. 14, 17; Deut. xvi. 16.——[v] Chap. xxxiii. 2; Lev. xviii. 24; Deut. vii. 1; Psa. lxxviii. 55; lxxx. 8.——[w] Deut. xii. 20; xix. 8.——[x] See Gen. xxxv. 5; 2 Chron. xvii. 10; Prov. xvi. 7; Acts xviii. 10.

Verse 10. *I will do marvels*] This seems to refer to what God did in putting them in possession of the land of Canaan, causing the walls of Jericho to fall down; making the sun and moon to stand still, &c. And thus God made his covenant with them; binding *himself* to put them in possession of the promised land, and binding *them* to observe the precepts laid down in the following verses, from the 11th to the 26th inclusive.

Verse 13. *Ye shall destroy their—images*] See the subjects of this and all the following verses, to the 28th, treated at large in the notes on chap. xxiii.

Verse 21. *In earing time and in harvest thou shalt rest.*] This commandment is worthy of especial note; many break the Sabbath on the pretence of absolute necessity, because, if in harvest time the weather happens to be what is called *bad*, and the Sabbath day be *fair* and *fine*, they judge it perfectly lawful to employ that day in endeavouring to save the fruits of the field, and think that the goodness of the day beyond the preceding, is an indication from Providence that it should be thus employed. But is not the above command pointed directly against this? I have known this law often broken on this pretence, and have never been able to discover a single instance where the persons who acted thus succeeded one whit better than their more conscientious neighbours, who availed themselves of no such favourable circumstances, being determined to keep God's law, even to the prejudice of their secular interests; but no man ever yet ultimately suffered loss by a conscientious attachment to his duty to God. He who is willing and obedient, shall eat the good of the land; but God will ever distinguish those in his providence who respect his commandments.

Verse 24. *Neither shall any man desire thy land*]

A. M. 2513. B. C. 1491. An. Exod. Isr. 1. Ab.

any man desire thy land, when
thou shalt go up to appear before
the LORD thy God thrice in
the year.
25 [y] Thou shalt not offer the blood of my
sacrifice with leaven; [z] neither shall the sacrifice of the feast of the passover be left unto
the morning.
26 [a] The feast of the first-fruits of thy land
thou shalt bring unto the house of the LORD
thy God. [b] Thou shalt not seethe a kid in
his mother's milk.
27 And the LORD said unto Moses, Write
thou [c] these words: for after the tenor of
these words I have made a covenant with thee
and with Israel.
28 [d] And he was there with the LORD forty
days and forty nights; he did neither eat
bread, nor drink water. And [e] he wrote upon
the tables the words of the
covenant, the ten [f] commandments.

A. M. 2513. B. C. 1491. An. Exod. Isr. 1. Elul.

29 And it came to pass, when
Moses came dawn from Mount
Sinai with the [g] two tables of testimony in Moses' hand, when he came down
from the mount, that Moses wist not that [h] the
skin of his face shone while he talked with
him.
30 And when Aaron and all the children of
Israel saw Moses, behold, the skin of his face
shone; and they were afraid to come nigh
him.
31 And Moses called unto them; and Aaron
and all the rulers of the congregation returned unto him: and Moses talked with them.
32 And afterward all the children of Israel
came nigh: [i] and he gave them in command-

[y] Chapter xxiii. 18.——[z] Chap. xii. 10.——[a] Chap. xxiii. 19; Deut. xxvi. 2, 10.——[b] Chap. xxiii. 19; Deut. xiv. 21.——[c] Ver. 10; Deut. iv. 13; xxxi. 9.

[d] Chap. xxiv. 18; Deut. ix. 9, 18.——[e] Ver. 1; chap. xxxi. 18; xxxii. 16; Deut. iv. 13; x. 2, 4.——[f] Heb. *words*.——[g] Ch. xxxii. 15.——[h] Matt. xvii. 2; 2 Cor. iii. 7, 13.——[i] Chap. xxiv. 3.

What a manifest proof was this of the power and particular providence of God! How easy would it have been for the surrounding nations to have taken possession of the whole Israelitish land, with all their fenced cities, when there were none left to protect them but women and children! Was not this a standing proof of the Divine origin of their religion, and *a barrier* which no deistical mind could possibly surmount? Thrice every year did God work an especial miracle for the protection of his people; controlling even the very *desires* of their enemies, that they might not so much as meditate evil against them. They who have God for their protector have a sure refuge; and how true is the proverb, *The path of duty is the way of safety!* While these people went up to Jerusalem to keep the Lord's ordinances, he kept their families in peace, and their land in safety.

Verse 25. *The blood of my sacrifice*] That is, the paschal lamb. See on chap. xxiii. 18.

Verse 26. *Thou shalt not seethe a kid in his mother's milk.*] See this amply considered chap. xxiii. 19.

Verse 27. *Write thou these words*] Either a *transcript* of the whole law now delivered, or the words included from verse 11 to 26. God certainly wrote the *ten words* on both sets of tables. Moses either wrote a *transcript* of these and the accompanying precepts for the use of the people, or he wrote the precepts themselves in *addition* to the ten commandments which were written by the finger of God. See on ver. 1. Allowing this mode of interpretation, the accompanying precepts were, probably, what was written on the *back side* of the tables by Moses; the *ten commandments*, what were written on the *front* by the finger of Jehovah: for we must pay but little attention to the supposition of the rabbins, that the letters on each table were cut through the stone, so as to be legible on each side. See chap. xxxii. 15.

Verse 28. *Forty days and forty nights*] See the note on chap. xxiv. 18.

Verse 29. *The skin of his face shone*] קרן *karan, was horned:* having been long in familiar intercourse with his Maker, his *flesh*, as well as his *soul*, was penetrated with the effulgence of the Divine glory, and his looks expressed the light and life which dwelt within. Probably Moses appeared now as he did when, in our Lord's transfiguration, he was seen with Elijah on the mount, Matt. xvii. As the original word קרן *karan* signifies to *shine out*, to *dart forth*, as *horns* on the head of an animal, or *rays of light* reflected from a polished surface, we may suppose that the heavenly glory which filled the soul of this holy man darted out from his face in coruscations, in that manner in which light is generally represented. The *Vulgate* renders the passage, *et ignorabat quod cornuta esset facies sua*, "and he did not know that his face was horned;" which version, *misunderstood*, has induced painters in general to represent Moses with *two very large horns*, one proceeding from each temple! But we might naturally ask, while they were indulging themselves in such fancies, why only *two* horns? for it is very likely that there were *hundreds* of these radiations, proceeding at once from the face of Moses. It was no doubt from this very circumstance that almost all the nations of the world who have heard of this transaction, have agreed in representing those men to whom they attributed extraordinary *sanctity*, and whom they supposed to have had familiar intercourse with the Deity, with a *lucid nimbus* or *glory* round their heads. This has prevailed both in the east and in the west; not only the *Greek* and *Roman* saints, or eminent persons, are thus represented, but those also among the *Mohammedans*, *Hindoos*, and *Chinese*.

Verse 30. *They were afraid to come nigh him.*] A sight of his face alarmed them; their consciences were

A. M. 2513. B. C. 1491. An. Exod. Isr. 1. Elul.

ment all that the Lord had
spoken with him in Mount Sinai.
33 And *till* Moses had done
speaking with them, he put [k] a veil on his face.
34 But [l] when Moses went in before the
Lord to speak with him, he took the veil off
until he came out. And he came out, and
spake unto the children of
Israel *that* which he was commanded.
35 And the children of Israel saw the face
of Moses, that the skin of Moses' face shone:
and Moses put the veil upon his face again,
until he went in to speak with him.

A. M. 2513. B. C. 1491. An. Exod. Isr. 1. Elul.

[k] 2 Cor. iii. 13.

[l] 2 Cor. iii. 16.

still guilty from their late transgression, and they had not yet received the atonement. The very appearance of superior sanctity often awes the guilty into respect.

Verse 33. *And* till *Moses had done speaking*] The meaning of the verse appears to be this: As often as Moses spoke in public to the people, he put the veil on his face, because they could not bear to look on the brightness of his countenance; but when he entered into the tabernacle to converse with the Lord, he removed this veil, ver. 34. St. Paul, 2 Cor. iii. 7, &c., makes a very important use of the transactions recorded in this place. He represents the brightness of the face of Moses as emblematical of the *glory* or *excellence* of that *dispensation;* but he shows that however glorious or excellent that was, it had no glory when compared with the *superior excellence of the Gospel.* As Moses was glorious in the eyes of the Israelites, but that glory was absorbed and lost in the splendour of God when he entered into the tabernacle, or went to meet the Lord upon the mount; so the brightness and excellence of the Mosaic dispensation are eclipsed and absorbed in the transcendent brightness or excellence of the Gospel of Christ. One was the *shadow,* the other is the *substance.* One showed SIN in its exceeding sinfulness, together with the *justice* and *immaculate purity* of God; but, in and of itself, made no provision for pardon or sanctification. The other exhibits Jesus, the Lamb of God, typified by all the sacrifices under the law, putting away sin by the sacrifice of himself, reconciling God to man and man to God, diffusing his Spirit through the souls of believers, and cleansing the very thoughts of their hearts by his inspiration, and causing them to perfect holiness in the fear of God. The *one* seems to shut heaven against mankind, because by the law was the *knowledge,* not the *cure,* of SIN; the *other* opens the kingdom of heaven to all believers. The former was a ministration of *death,* the latter a dispensation of *life.* The former ministered *terror,* so that even the high priest was afraid to approach, the people withdrew and stood afar off, and even Moses, the mediator of it, exceedingly feared and trembled; by the latter we have *boldness* to enter into the holiest through the blood of Jesus, who is the end of the law for righteousness—justification, to every one that believeth. The former gives a partial view of the Divine nature; the latter shows God as he is,

"Full orbed, in his whole round of rays complete."

The apostle farther considers the veil on the face of Moses, as being emblematical of the metaphorical nature of the different rites and ceremonies of the Mosaic dispensation, each *covering* some spiritual meaning or a spiritual subject; and that the Jews did not lift the veil to penetrate the spiritual sense, and did not look to *the end of the commandment,* which was to be *abolished,* but rested in the *letter* or literal meaning, which conferred neither light nor life.

He considers the veil also as being emblematical of that state of intellectual darkness into which the Jewish people, by their rejection of the Gospel, were plunged, and from which they have never yet been recovered. When a Jew, even at the present day, reads the law in the synagogue, he puts over his head an oblong woollen veil, with four tassels at the four corners, which is called the *taled* or *thaled.* This is a very remarkable circumstance, as it appears to be an emblem of the intellectual veil referred to by the apostle, which is still upon their hearts when Moses is read, and which prevents them from looking to the end of that which God designed should be abrogated, and which has been abolished by the introduction of the Gospel. The veil is upon their hearts, and prevents the light of the glory of God from shining into them; *but we all,* says the apostle, speaking of believers in Christ, *with open face,* without any veil, *beholding as in a glass the glory of God, are changed into the same image, from glory to glory, as by the Spirit of the Lord;* 2 Cor. iii. 18. Reader, dost thou know this excellence of the religion of Christ? Once thou wert darkness; art thou now light in the Lord? Art thou still under the letter that killeth, or under the Spirit that giveth life? Art thou a slave to sin or a servant of Christ? Is the veil on thy heart, or hast thou found redemption in his blood, the remission of sins? Knowest thou not these things? Then may God pity, enlighten, and save thee!

CHAPTER XXXV.

Moses assembles the congregation to deliver to them the commandments of God, 1. *Directions concerning the Sabbath,* 2, 3. Free-will offerings *of* gold, silver, brass, *&c., for the tabernacle,* 4–7. *Of* oil *and* spices, 8. *Of* precious stones, 9. *Proper* artists *to be employed,* 10. *The* tabernacle *and its* tent, 11. *The* ark, 12. Table *of the* shew-bread, 13. Candlestick, 14. Altar of incense, 15. Altar of burnt-offering, 16. Hangings, pins, *&c.,* 17, 18. Clothes *of* service, *and* holy vestments, 19. *The people cheer-*

fully bring their ornaments *as offerings to the Lord,* 20–22; *together with blue, purple, scarlet, &c., &c.,* 23, 24. *The* women *spin, and bring the produce of their skill and industry,* 25, 26. *The* rulers *bring precious stones, &c.,* 27, 28. *All the people offer willingly,* 29. Bezaleel *and* Aholiab *appointed to conduct and superintend all the work of the tabernacle, for which they are qualified by the spirit of wisdom,* 30–35.

A. M. 2513. B. C. 1491. An. Exod. Isr. 1. Elul.

AND Moses gathered all the congregation of the children of Israel together, and said unto them, [a] These *are* the words which the LORD hath commanded, that *ye* should do them.

2 [b] Six days shall work be done, but on the seventh day there shall be to you [c] a holy day, a Sabbath of rest to the LORD: whosoever doeth work therein shall be put to death.

3 [d] Ye shall kindle no fire throughout your habitations upon the Sabbath day.

4 And Moses spake unto all the congregation of the children of Israel, saying, [e] This *is* the thing which the LORD commanded, saying,

5 Take ye from among you an offering unto the LORD: [f] whosoever *is* of a willing heart, let him bring it, an offering of the LORD; gold, and silver, and brass,

6 And blue, and purple, and scarlet, and fine linen, and goats' *hair,*

7 And rams' skins dyed red, and badgers' skins, and shittim wood,

8 And oil for the light, [g] and spices for anointing oil, and for the sweet incense,

9 And onyx stones, and stones to be set for the ephod, and for the breastplate.

10 And [h] every wise-hearted man among you shall come, and make all that the LORD hath commanded;

11 [i] The tabernacle, his tent, and his covering, his taches, and his boards, his bars, his pillars, and his sockets;

A. M. 2513. B. C. 1491. An. Exod. Isr. 1. Elul.

12 [k] The ark, and the staves thereof, *with* the mercy-seat, and the veil of the covering;

13 The [l] table, and his staves, and all his vessels, [m] and the shew-bread;

14 [n] The candlestick also for the light, and his furniture, and his lamps, with the oil for the light;

15 [o] And the incense altar and his staves, [p] and the anointing oil, and [q] the sweet incense, and the hanging for the door at the entering in of the tabernacle;

16 [r] The altar of burnt-offering, with his brazen gate, his staves, and all his vessels, the laver, and his foot;

17 [s] The hangings of the court, his pillars, and their sockets, and the hanging for the door of the court;

18 The pins of the tabernacle, and the pins of the court, and their cords;

19 [t] The clothes of service, to do service in the holy *place,* the holy garments for Aaron the priest, and the garments of his sons, to minister in the priest's office.

20 And all the congregation of the children of Israel departed from the presence of Moses.

[a] Chap. xxxiv. 32.——[b] Chap. xx. 9; xxxi. 14, 15; Lev. xxiii. 3; Num. xv. 32, &c.; Deut. v. 12; Luke xiii. 14.——[c] Heb. *holiness.*——[d] Chap. xvi. 23.——[e] Chap. xxv. 1, 2.——[f] Chapter xxv. 2.——[g] Chapter xxv. 6.——[h] Chap. xxxi. 6.——[i] Chapter xxvi. 1, 2, &c.

[k] Chapter xxv. 10, &c.——[l] Chapter xxv. 23.——[m] Chap. xxv. 30; Lev. xxiv. 5, 6.——[n] Chapter xxv. 31, &c.——[o] Chap. xxx. 1.——[p] Chap. xxx. 23.——[q] Chap. xxx. 34.——[r] Chap. xxvii. 1.——[s] Chap. xxvii. 9.——[t] Chap. xxxi. 10; xxxix. 1, 41; Numbers iv. 5, 6, &c.

NOTES ON CHAP. XXXV.

Verse 1. *And Moses gathered*] The principal subjects in this chapter have been already largely considered in the notes on chapters xxv., xxvi., xxvii., xxviii., xxix., xxx., and xxxi., and to those the reader is particularly desired to refer, together with the parallel texts in the margin.

Verse 3. *Ye shall kindle no fire*] The Jews understand this precept as forbidding the kindling of fire *only* for the purpose of *doing work* or *dressing victuals;* but to give them *light* and *heat,* they judge it lawful to light a fire on the Sabbath day, though themselves rarely kindle it—they get *Christians* to do this work for them.

Verse 5. *An offering*] A *terumah* or heave-offering; see Lev. vii. 1, &c.

Verses 5 and 6. See, on these *metals* and *colours,* chap. xxv. 3, 4, &c.

Verse 7. *Rams' skins, &c.*] See chap. xxv. 5.

Verse 8. *Oil for the light*] See chap. xxv. 6.

Verse 9. *Onyx stones*] See chap. xxv. 7.

Verse 11. *The tabernacle*] See chap. xxv. 8.

Verse 12. *The ark*] See chap. xxv. 10–17.

Verse 13. *The table*] See chap. xxv. 23–28.

Verse 14. *The candlestick*] See chap. xxv. 31–39.

Verse 15. *The incense altar*] The golden altar, see chap. xxx. 1–10.

Verse 16. *The altar of burnt-offering*] The brazen altar, see chap. xxvii. 1–8.

Verse 17. *The hangings of the court*] See chap. xxvii. 9.

Verse 19. *The clothes of service*] Probably *aprons,*

A. M. 2513.
B. C. 1491.
An. Exod. Isr. 1.
Elul.

21 And they came, every one [u] whose heart stirred him up, and every one whom his spirit made willing, *and* they brought the LORD's offering to the work of the tabernacle of the congregation, and for all his service, and for the holy garments.

22 And they came, both men and women, as many as were willing-hearted, *and* brought bracelets, and ear-rings, and rings, and tablets, all jewels of gold: and every man that offered, *offered* an offering of gold unto the LORD.

23 And [v] every man, with whom was found blue, and purple, and scarlet, and fine linen, and goats' *hair*, and red skins of rams, and badgers' skins, brought *them*.

24 Every one that did offer an offering of silver and brass, brought the LORD's offering: and every man, with whom was found shittim wood for any work of the service, brought *it*.

25 And all the women that were [w] wise-hearted did spin with their hands, and brought that which they had spun, *both* of blue, and of purple, *and* of scarlet, and of fine linen.

26 And all the women whose heart stirred them up in wisdom, spun goats' *hair*.

27 And [x] the rulers brought onyx stones, and stones to be set, for the ephod, and for the breastplate;

28 And [y] spice, and oil for the light, and for the anointing oil, and for the sweet incense.

A. M. 2513.
B. C. 1491.
An. Exod. Isr. 1.
Elul.

29 The children of Israel brought a [z] willing offering unto the LORD, every man and woman, whose heart made them willing to bring for all manner of work, which the LORD had commanded to be made by the hand of Moses.

30 And Moses said unto the children of Israel, See, [a] The LORD hath called by name Bezaleel the son of Uri, the son of Hur, of the tribe of Judah;

31 And he hath filled him with the Spirit of God, in wisdom, in understanding, and in knowledge, and in all manner of workmanship;

32 And to devise curious works, to work in gold, and in silver, and in brass,

33 And in the cutting of stones, to set *them*, and in carving of wood, to make any manner of cunning work.

34 And he hath put in his heart that he may teach, *both* he, and [b] Aholiab, the son of Ahisamach, of the tribe of Dan:

35 Them hath he [c] filled with wisdom of heart, to work all manner of work, of the engraver, and of the cunning workman, and of the embroiderer, in blue, and in purple, in scarlet, and in fine linen, and of the weaver, *even* of them that do any work, and of those that devise cunning work.

---

[u] Ver. 5, 22, 26, 29; chap. xxv. 2; xxxvi. 2; 1 Chron. xxviii. 2, 9; xxix. 9; Ezra vii. 27; 2 Cor. viii. 12; ix. 7.——[v] 1 Chron. xxix. 8.——[w] Chap. xxviii. 3; xxxi. 6; xxxvi. 1; 2 Kings xxiii. 7; Prov. xxxi. 19, 22, 24.

[x] 1 Chron. xxix. 6; Ezra ii. 68.——[y] Chap. xxx. 23.——[z] Ver. 21; 1 Chron. xxix. 9.——[a] Chap. xxxi. 2, &c.——[b] Chap. xxxi. 6; Isa. xxviii. 24–29.——[c] Ver. 31; chap. xxxi. 3, 6; 1 Kings vii. 14; 2 Chron. ii. 14; Isa. xxviii. 26.

---

towels, and such like, used in the common service, and different from the *vestments* for Aaron and his sons. See these latter described chap. xxviii. 1, &c.

Verse 21. *Every one whose heart stirred him up*] Literally, *whose heart was lifted up*—whose affections were set on the work, being cordially engaged in the service of God.

Verse 22. *As many as were willing-hearted*] For no one was *forced* to lend his help in this sacred work; all was a *free-will* offering to the Lord.

Bracelets] חח *chach*, whatever *hooks together*; ornaments for the wrists, arms, legs, or neck.

Ear-rings] נזם *nezem*, see this explained Gen. xxiv. 22.

Rings] טבעת *tabbaath*, from טבע *taba*, to *penetrate*, *enter into*; probably rings for the fingers.

Tablets] כומז *cumaz*, a word only used here and in Num. xxxi. 50, supposed to be a *girdle* to *support the breasts*.

Verse 25. *All the women that were wise-hearted did spin*] They had before learned this art, they were wise-hearted; and now they practise it, and God condescends to require and accept their services. In building this house of God, all were ambitious to do something by which they might testify their piety to God, and their love for his worship. The spinning practised at this time was simple, and required little *apparatus*. It was the plain *distaff* or twirling pin, which might be easily made out of any wood they met with in the wilderness.

Verse 27. *The rulers brought onyx stones*] These, being persons of consequence, might be naturally expected to furnish the more scarce and costly articles. See how all join in this service! The men *worked* and brought offerings, the women spun and brought their ornaments, the rulers united with them and delivered up their jewels! and all the children of Israel brought a willing offering unto the Lord, ver. 29.

Verse 30. *The Lord hath called by name Bezaleel*] See this subject discussed at large in the note on chap. xxxi. 3, where the subject of superseding the work of the hand by the extra use of machinery is particularly considered.

1. From the nature of the offerings made for the service of the tabernacle, we see of what sort the spoils were which the Israelites brought out of Egypt: *gold, silver, brass, blue, purple, scarlet, fine linen, rams' skins dyed red,* what we call *badgers' skins, oil, spices, incense, onyx stones,* and other stones, the names of which are not here mentioned. They must also have brought *looms, spinning wheels,* instruments for *cutting precious stones, anvils, hammers, furnaces, melting-pots* with a vast variety of *tools* for the different artists employed on the work of the tabernacle, viz., smiths, joiners, carvers, gilders, &c.

2. God could have erected his tabernacle without the help or skill of man; but he condescended to employ him. As all are interested in the worship of God, so all should bear a part in it; here God employs the whole *congregation:* every male and female, with even their *sons* and their *daughters,* and the very ornaments of their persons, are given to raise and adorn the house of God. The women who had not ornaments, and could neither give gold nor silver, could spin goat's hair, and the Lord graciously employs them in this work, and accepts what they can give and what they can do, for they did it with a willing mind; they were *wise of heart*—had learned a useful business, their hearts were *lifted up* in the work, ver. 21, and all felt it a high privilege to be able to put only a nail in the holy place. By the free-will offerings of the people the tabernacle was erected, and all the costly utensils belonging to it provided. This was the primitive mode of providing proper places for Divine worship; and as it was the primitive, so it is the most *rational* mode. Taxes levied by law for building or repairing churches were not known in the ancient times of religious simplicity. It is an honour to be permitted to do any thing for the support of public worship; and he must have a strange, unfeeling, and ungodly heart, who does not esteem it a high privilege to have a stone of his own laying or procuring in the house of God. How easily might all the buildings necessary for the purpose of public worship be raised, if the money that is spent in needless self-indulgence by ourselves, our sons, and our daughters, were devoted to this purpose! By sacrifices of this kind the house of the Lord would be soon built, and the top-stone brought on with shouting, Grace, grace unto it!

CHAPTER XXXVI.

Moses appoints Bezaleel, Aholiab, and their associates, to the work, and delivers to them the free-will offerings of the people, 1–3. *The people bring offerings more than are needed for the work, and are only restrained by the proclamation of Moses,* 4–7. *The curtains, their loops, taches, &c., for the tabernacle,* 8–18. *The covering for the tent,* 19. *The boards,* 20–30. *The bars,* 31–34. *The veil and its pillars,* 35, 36. *The hangings and their pillars,* 37, 38.

A. M. 2514.
B. C. 1490.
An. Exod. Isr. 1.
Tisri to Adar.

THEN wrought Bezaleel and Aholiab, and every [a] wise-hearted man, in whom the Lord put wisdom and understanding, to know how to work all manner of work for the service of the [b] sanctuary, according to all that the Lord had commanded.

2 And Moses called Bezaleel and Aholiab, and every wise-hearted man, in whose heart the Lord had put wisdom, *even* every one [c] whose heart stirred him up to come unto the work to do it:

3 And they received of Moses all the offering which the children of Israel [d] had brought for the work of the service of the sanctuary, to make it *withal.* And they brought yet unto him free offerings every morning.

4 And all the wise men, that wrought all the work of the sanctuary, came every man from his work which they made;

5 And they spake unto Moses, saying, [e] The people bring much more than enough for the

[a] Chapter xxviii. 3; xxxi. 6; xxxv. 10, 35.——[b] Chapter xxv. 8.

[c] Chapter xxxv. 2, 26; 1 Chron. xxix. 5.——[d] Chapter xxxv. 27. [e] 2 Cor. viii. 2, 3.

NOTES ON CHAP. XXXVI.

Verse 1. *Then wrought, &c.*] The *first* verse of this chapter should end the preceding chapter, and this should begin with verse the *second;* as it now stands, it does not make a very consistent sense. By reading the first word ויעשה *veasah, then wrought,* in the *future tense* instead of the *past,* the proper connection will be preserved: for all grammarians know that the conjunction ו *vau* is often *conversive,* i. e., it turns the *preterite* tense of those verbs to which it is prefixed into the *future,* and the *future* into the *preterite:* this power it evidently has here; and joined with the last verse of the preceding chapter the connection will appear thus, chap. xxxv. ver. 30, &c.: *The Lord hath called by name Bezaleel and Aholiab;* them hath *he filled with wisdom of heart to* work all manner of work. Chap. xxxvi. 1.: *And Bezaleel and Aholiab* SHALL WORK, *and every wise-hearted man, in whom the Lord put wisdom.*

Verse 5. *The people bring much more than enough*] With what a liberal spirit do these people bring their free-will offerings unto the Lord! Moses is obliged to make a proclamation to prevent them from bringing any more, as there was at present more than enough!

A. M. 2514.
B. C. 1490.
An. Exod. Isr. 1.
Tisri to Adar.

service of the work, which the LORD commanded to make.

6 And Moses gave commandment, and they caused it to be proclaimed throughout the camp, saying, Let neither man nor woman make any more work for the offering of the sanctuary. So the people were restrained from bringing.

7 For the stuff they had was sufficient for all the work to make it, and too much.

8 [f] And every wise-hearted man among them that wrought the work of the tabernacle, made ten curtains *of* fine twined linen, and blue, and purple, and scarlet: *with* cherubims of cunning work made he them.

9 The length of one curtain *was* twenty and eight cubits, and the breadth of one curtain four cubits: the curtains *were* all of one size.

10 And he coupled the five curtains one unto another: and *the other* five curtains he coupled one unto another.

11 And he made loops of blue on the edge of one curtain from the selvage in the coupling: likewise he made in the uttermost side of *another* curtain in the coupling of the second.

12 [g] Fifty loops made he in one curtain, and fifty loops made he in the edge of the curtain which *was* in the coupling of the second: the loops held one *curtain* to another.

13 And he made fifty taches of gold, and coupled the curtains one unto another with the taches: so it became one tabernacle.

14 [h] And he made curtains *of* goats' *hair* for the tent over the tabernacle: eleven curtains he made them.

15 The length of one curtain *was* thirty cubits, and four cubits *was* the breadth of one curtain: the eleven curtains *were* of one size.

A. M. 2514.
B. C. 1490.
An. Exod. Isr. 1.
Tisri to Adar.

16 And he coupled five curtains by themselves, and six curtains by themselves.

17 And he made fifty loops upon the uttermost edge of the curtain in the coupling, and fifty loops made he upon the edge of the curtain which coupleth the second.

18 And he made fifty taches *of* brass, to couple the tent together, that it might be one.

19 [i] And he made a covering for the tent *of* rams' skins dyed red, and a covering *of* badgers' skins above *that*.

20 [k] And he made boards for the tabernacle *of* shittim wood, standing up.

21 The length of a board *was* ten cubits, and the breadth of a board one cubit and a half.

22 One board had two tenons, equally distant one from another: thus did he make for all the boards of the tabernacle.

23 And he made boards for the tabernacle; twenty boards for the south side southward:

24 And forty sockets of silver he made under the twenty boards; two sockets under one board for his two tenons, and two sockets under another board for his two tenons.

25 And for the other side of the tabernacle, *which is* toward the north corner, he made twenty boards,

26 And their forty sockets of silver; two sockets under one board, and two sockets under another board.

[f] Chap. xxvi. 1.——[g] Chap. xxvi. 5.——[h] Chap. xxvi. 7.

[i] Chap. xxvi. 14.——[k] Chap. xxvi. 15.

Had Moses been intent upon gain, and had he not been perfectly disinterested, he would have encouraged them to continue their contributions, as thereby he might have multiplied to himself gold, silver, and precious stones. But he was doing the Lord's work, under the inspiration of the Divine Spirit, and therefore he sought no secular gain. Indeed, this one circumstance is an ample proof of it. Every thing necessary for the worship of God will be cheerfully provided by a people whose hearts are in that worship. In a state where all forms of religion and modes of worship are tolerated by the laws, it would be well to find out some less exceptionable way of providing for the national clergy than by *tithes*. Let them by all means have the provision allowed them by the law; but let them not be needlessly exposed to the resentment of the people by the *mode* in which this provision is made, as this often alienates the affections of their flocks from them, and exceedingly injures their usefulness. See the note on Gen. xxviii. *in fine*, where the subject is viewed on all sides.

Verse 8. *Cherubims of cunning work*] See on chap. xxvi. 18. Probably the word means no more than *figures* of any kind wrought in the *diaper* fashion in the *loom*, or by the *needle* in *embroidery*, or by the *chisel* or *graving tool* in *wood, stone*, or *metal*; see on chap. xxv. 18. This meaning Houbigant and other excellent critics contend for. In some places the word seems to be restricted to express a particular figure then well known; but in many other places it seems to imply any kind of figure commonly formed by sculpture on stone, by carving on wood, by engraving upon brass, and by weaving in the loom, &c.

Verse 9. *The length of one curtain*] Concerning these curtains, see chap. xxvi. 1, &c.

Verse 20. *And he made boards*] See the notes on chap. xxvi. 15, &c.

A. M. 2514. B. C. 1490. An. Exod. Isr. 1. Tisri to Adar.

27 And for the sides of the tabernacle westward he made six boards.

28 And two boards made he for the corners of the tabernacle in the two sides.

29 And they were [l] coupled beneath, and coupled together at the head thereof, to one ring: thus he did to both of them, in both the corners.

30 And there were eight boards; and their sockets *were* sixteen sockets of silver, [m] under every board two sockets.

31 And he made [n] bars of shittim wood; five for the boards of the one side of the tabernacle,

32 And five bars for the boards of the other side of the tabernacle, and five bars for the boards of the tabernacle for the sides westward.

33 And he made the middle bar to shoot through the boards from the one end to the other.

A. M. 2514. B. C. 1490. An. Exod. Isr. 1. Tisri to Adar.

34 And he overlaid the boards with gold, and made their rings *of* gold *to be* places for the bars, and overlaid the bars with gold.

35 And he made [o] a veil *of* blue, and purple, and scarlet, and fine twined linen: *with* cherubims made he it of cunning work.

36 And he made thereunto four pillars *of* shittim *wood*, and overlaid them with gold: their hooks *were of* gold; and he cast for them four sockets of silver.

37 And he made a [p] hanging for the tabernacle door, *of* blue, and purple, and scarlet, and fine twined linen, [q] of needle-work;

38 And the five pillars of it with their hooks; and he overlaid their chapiters and their fillets with gold; but their five sockets *were of* brass.

[l] Heb. *twined*.——[m] Heb. *two sockets, two sockets under one board*. [n] Chap. xxvi. 26. [o] Chap. xxvi. 31.——[p] Chap. xxvi. 36.——[q] Heb. *the work of a needle-worker* or *embroiderer*.

Verse 31. *He made bars*] See on chap. xxvi. 26, &c.

Verse 35. *He made a veil*] See on chap. xxvi. 31, &c.

Verse 37. *Hanging for the—door*] See on ch. xxvi. 36.

Verse 38. *The five pillars of it with their hooks*] Their capitals. See the note on chap. xxvi. 32.

There is scarcely any thing particular in this chapter that has not been touched on before; both it and the following to the end of the book being in general a repetition of what we have already met in detail in the preceding chapters from chap. xxv. to xxxi. inclusive, and to those the reader is requested to refer. God had before commanded this work to be done, and it was necessary to record the execution of it to show that all was done according to the pattern shown to Moses; without this detailed account we should not have known whether the work had ever been *executed* according to the directions given.

At the commencement of this chapter the reader will observe that I have *advanced* the dates A. M. and B. C. one year, without altering the year of the exodus, which at first view may appear an error; the reason is, that the above dates commence at *Tisri*, but the years of the exodus are dated from *Abib*.

CHAPTER XXXVII.

Bezaleel and Aholiab make the ark, 1–5. *The mercy-seat*, 6. *The two cherubim*, 7–9. *The table of the shew-bread, and its vessels*, 10–16. *The candlestick*, 17–24. *The golden altar of incense*, 25–28. *The holy anointing oil and perfume*, 29.

A. M. 2514. B. C. 1490. An. Exod. Isr. 1. Tisri to Adar.

AND Bezaleel made [a] the ark *of* shittim wood: two cubits and a half *was* the length of it, and a cubit and a half the height of it:

2 And he overlaid it with pure gold within and without, and made a crown of gold to it round about.

3 And he cast for it four rings of gold, *to be set* by the four corners of it; even two rings upon the one side of it, and two rings upon the other side of it.

A. M. 2514. B. C. 1490. An. Exod. Isr. 1. Tisri to Adar.

4 And he made staves *of* shittim wood, and overlaid them with gold.

5 And he put the staves into the rings by the sides of the ark, to bear the ark.

6 And he made the [b] mercy-seat *of* pure gold: two cubits and a half *was* the length thereof, and one cubit and a half the breadth thereof.

[a] Chap. xxv. 10. [b] Chap. xxv. 17.

NOTES ON CHAP. XXXVII.

Verse 1. *And Bezaleel made the ark, &c.*] For a description of the ark, see chap. xxv. 10, &c.

Verse 6. *He made the mercy-seat*] See this described chap. xxv. 17.

Verse 10. *He made the table*] See chap. xxv. 23.

A. M. 2514.
B. C. 1490.
An. Exod. Isr. 1.
Tisri to Adar.

7 And he made two cherubims *of* gold, beaten out of one piece made he them, on the two ends of the mercy-seat.

8 One cherub ᶜ on the end on this side, and another cherub ᵈ on the *other* end on that side: out of the mercy-seat made he the cherubims, on the two ends thereof.

9 And the cherubims spread out *their* wings on high, *and* covered with their wings over the mercy-seat, with their faces one to another; *even* to the mercy-seatward were the faces of the cherubims.

10 And he made ᵉ the table *of* shittim wood: two cubits *was* the length thereof, and a cubit the breadth thereof, and a cubit and a half the height thereof:

11 And he overlaid it with pure gold, and made thereunto a crown of gold round about.

12 Also he made thereunto a border of a hand breadth round about; and made a crown of gold for the border thereof round about.

13 And he cast for it four rings of gold, and put the rings upon the four corners that *were* in the four feet thereof.

14 Over against the border were the rings, the places for the staves to bear the table.

15 And he made the staves *of* shittim wood, and overlaid them with gold, to bear the table.

16 And he made the vessels which *were* upon the table, his ᶠ dishes, and his spoons, and his bowls, and his covers ᵍ to cover withal, *of* pure gold.

17 And he made the ʰ candlestick *of* pure gold: of beaten work made he the candlestick; his shaft, and his branch, his bowls, his knops, and his flowers, were of the same:

18 And six branches going out of the sides thereof; three branches of the candlestick out of the one side thereof, and three branches of the candlestick out of the other side thereof:

A. M. 2514.
B. C. 1490.
An. Exod. Isr. 1.
Tisri to Adar.

19 Three bowls made after the fashion of almonds in one branch, a knop and a flower; and three bowls made like almonds in another branch, a knop and a flower: so throughout the six branches going out of the candlestick.

20 And in the candlestick *were* four bowls made like almonds, his knops, and his flowers:

21 And a knop under two branches of the same, and a knop under two branches of the same, and a knop under two branches of the same, according to the six branches going out of it.

22 Their knops and their branches were of the same: all of it *was* one beaten work *of* pure gold.

23 And he made his seven lamps, and his snuffers, and his snuff dishes, *of* pure gold.

24 *Of* a talent of pure gold made he it, and all the vessels thereof.

25 ⁱ And he made the incense altar *of* shittim wood: the length of it *was* a cubit, and the breadth of it a cubit; *it was* four-square; and two cubits *was* the height of it; the horns thereof were of the same.

26 And he overlaid it with pure gold, *both* the top of it, and the sides thereof round about, and the horns of it; also he made unto it a crown of gold round about.

27 And he made two rings of gold for it under the crown thereof, by the two corners of it, upon the two sides thereof, to be places for the staves to bear it withal.

28 And he made the staves *of* shittim wood, and overlaid them with gold.

29 And he made ᵏ the holy anointing oil, and the pure incense of sweet spices, according to the work of the apothecary.

ᶜ Or, *out of*, &c.——ᵈ Or, *out of*, &c.——ᵉ Chap. xxv. 23.
ᶠ Chap. xxv. 29.——ᵍ Or, *to pour out withal.*

ʰ Chap. xxv. 31.——ⁱ Chap. xxx. 1.——ᵏ Chap. xxx. 23, 34; Isa. lxi. 1; 1 John ii. 20, 27; Psa. cxli. 2.

Verse 16. *He made the vessels*] See all these particularly described in the notes on chap. xxv. 29.

Verse 17. *He made the candlestick*] See this described in the note on chap. xxv. 31.

Verse 25. *He made the incense altar*] See this described chap. xxx. 1.

Verse 29. *He made the holy anointing oil*] See this and the *perfume*, and the materials out of which they were made, described at large in the notes on chap. xxx. 23–25 and 34–38. As this chapter also is a repetition of what has been mentioned in preceding chapters, the reader is desired to refer to them

CHAPTER XXXVIII.

Bezaleel makes the altar of burnt-offering, 1–7. *He makes the laver and its foot out of the mirrors given by the women,* 8. *The court, its pillars, hangings, &c.,* 9–20. *The whole tabernacle and its work finished by Bezaleel, Aholiab, and their assistants,* 21–23. *The amount of the* gold *contributed,* 24. *The amount of the* silver, *and how it was expended,* 25–28. *The amount of the* brass, *and how this was used,* 29–31.

A. M. 2514. B. C. 1490. An. Exod. Isr. 1. Tisri to Adar.

AND [a] he made the altar
of burnt-offering *of* shittim
wood: five cubits *was* the length
thereof, and five cubits the breadth thereof; *it*
was four-square; and three cubits the height
thereof.

2 And he made the horns thereof on the four
corners of it; the horns thereof were of the
same: and he overlaid it with brass.

3 And he made all the vessels of the altar,
the pots, and the shovels, and the basins, *and*
the flesh hooks, and the firepans: all the vessels
thereof made he *of* brass.

4 And he made for the altar a brazen grate
of network, under the compass
thereof beneath, unto the midst
of it.

5 And he cast four rings for the four ends of
the grate of brass, *to be* places for the staves.

6 And he made the staves *of* shittim wood,
and overlaid them with brass.

7 And he put the staves into the rings on
the sides of the altar, to bear it withal; he
made the altar hollow with boards.

8 And he made [b] the laver *of* brass, and the
foot of it *of* brass, of the [c] looking-glasses of
the women [d] assembling, which assembled *at*
the door of the tabernacle of the congregation.

[a] Chap. xxvii. 1–8; chap. xl. 6, 20.——[b] Chap. xxx. 18.——[c] Or, *brazen glasses.*——[d] Heb. *assembling by troops,* as 1 Sam. ii. 22.

NOTES ON CHAP. XXXVIII.

Verse 1. *The altar of burnt-offering*] See the notes on chap. xxvii. 1; and for its horns, pots, shovels, basins, &c., see the meaning of the Hebrew terms explained, chap. xxvii. 3–5.

Verse 8. *He made the laver*] See the notes on chap. xxx. 18, &c.

The looking-glasses] The word מראת *maroth*, from ראה *raah, he saw*, signifies *reflectors* or *mirrors* of any kind. Here *metal*, highly polished, must certainly be meant, as glass was not yet in use; and had it even been in use, we are sure that *looking*-GLASSES could not make a BRAZEN *laver*. The word therefore should be rendered *mirrors*, not *looking-glasses*, which in the above verse is perfectly absurd, because from those *maroth* the *brazen laver* was made.. The first *mirrors* known among men were the clear, still *fountain*, and unruffled *lake*; and probably the mineral called *mica*, which is a very general substance through all parts of the *earth*. Plates of it have been found of three feet square, and it is so extremely divisible into laminæ, that it has been divided into plates so thin as to be only the *three hundred thousandth part of an inch*. A plate of this forms an excellent mirror when any thing *black* is attached to the opposite side. A plate of this mineral, nine inches by eight, now lies before me; a piece of *black cloth*, or any other *black* substance, at the back, converts it into a *good mirror*; or it would serve as it is for a *square of glass*, as every object is clearly perceivable through it. It is used in Russian ships of war, instead of glass, for windows. The first artificial mirrors were apparently made of *brass*, afterwards of polished *steel*, and when luxury increased they were made of *silver*; but they were made at a very early period of mixed metal, particularly of *tin* and *copper*, the best of which, as Pliny tells us, were formerly manufactured at Brundusium: *Optima apud majores fuerant Brundisina*, stanno *et*ære *mixtis*.—Hist. Nat. lib. xxxiii., cap. 9. But, according to him, the most esteemed were those made of *tin*; and he says that *silver mirrors* became so common that even the *servant girls* used them: *Specula* (ex stanno) *laudatissima Brundisii temperabantur; donec argenteis uti cœpere et ancillæ;* lib. xxxiv., cap. 17. When the Egyptian women went to the temples, they always carried their mirrors with them. The Israelitish women probably did the same, and Dr. Shaw states that the Arabian women carry them constantly hung at their breasts. It is worthy of remark, that at *first* these women freely gave up their ornaments for this important service, and now give their very *mirrors*, probably as being of little farther service, seeing they had already given up the principal decorations of their persons. Woman has been invidiously defined by Aristotle, *an animal fond of dress*, (though this belongs to the whole *human race*, and not exclusively to woman.) Had this been true of the Israelitish women, in the present case we must say they nobly sacrificed their incentives to pride to the service of their God. Woman, go *thou* and do likewise.

Of the women—*which assembled* at *the door*] What the employment of these women was at the door of the tabernacle, is not easily known. Some think they assembled there for purposes of devotion. Others, that they kept watch there during the night; and this is the most probable opinion, for they appear to have been in the same employment as those who assembled at the door of the tabernacle of the congregation in the days of Samuel, who were abused by the sons of the high priest Eli, 1 Sam. ii. 22. Among the ancients women were generally employed in the office of *porters* or *doorkeepers*. Such were employed about the house of the high priest in our Lord's time; for a woman is actually represented as keeping the door of

A. M. 2514.
B. C. 1490.
An. Exod. Isr. 1.
Tisri to Adar.

9 And he made [e] the court: on the south side southward the hangings of the court *were of* fine twined linen, a hundred cubits:

10 Their pillars *were* twenty, and their brazen sockets twenty; the hooks of the pillars and their fillets *were of* silver.

11 And for the north side *the hangings were* a hundred cubits, their pillars *were* twenty, and their sockets of brass twenty; the hooks of the pillars and their fillets *of* silver.

12 And for the west side *were* hangings of fifty cubits, their pillars ten, and their sockets ten; the hooks of the pillars and their fillets *of* silver.

13 And for the east side eastward, fifty cubits.

14 The hangings of the one side *of the gate were* fifteen cubits; their pillars three, and their sockets three.

15 And for the other side of the court gate, on this hand and that hand, *were* hangings of fifteen cubits; their pillars three, and their sockets three.

16 All the hangings of the court round about *were* of fine twined linen.

17 And the sockets for the pillars *were of* brass; the hooks of the pillars and their fillets *of* silver; and the overlaying of their chapiters *of* silver; and all the pillars of the court *were* filleted with silver.

A. M. 2514.
B. C. 1490.
An. Exod. Isr. 1.
Tisri to Adar.

18 And the hanging for the gate of the court *was* needlework, *of* blue, and purple, and scarlet, and fine twined linen: and twenty cubits *was* the length, and the height in the breadth *was* five cubits, answerable to the hangings of the court.

19 And their pillars *were* four, and their sockets *of* brass four; their hooks *of* silver, and the overlaying of their chapiters and their fillets *of* silver.

20 And all the [f] pins of the tabernacle, and of the court round about, *were of* brass.

21 This is the sum of the tabernacle, *even* of [g] the tabernacle of testimony, as it was counted, according to the commandment of Moses, *for* the service of the Levites, [h] by the hand of Ithamar, son to Aaron the priest.

22 And [i] Bezaleel the son of Uri, the son of Hur, of the tribe of Judah, made all that the Lord commanded Moses.

23 And with him *was* Aholiab, son of Ahisamach, of the tribe of Dan, an engraver, and a cunning workman, and an embroiderer in blue, and in purple, and in scarlet, and fine linen

24 All the gold that was occupied for the

[e] Chap. xxvii. 9.——[f] Chap. xxvii. 19.——[g] Num. i. 50, 53; ix. 15; x. 11; xvii. 7, 8; xviii. 2; 2 Chron. xxiv. 6; Acts vii. 44.

[h] Num. iv. 28, 33.——[i] Chap. xxxi. 2, 6.

the palace of the high priest, John xviii. 17: *Then saith the* DAMSEL *that* KEPT THE DOOR *unto Peter;* see also Matt. xxvi. 69. In 2 Sam. iv. 6, both the *Septuagint* and *Vulgate* make a woman *porter* or *doorkeeper* to Ishbosheth. *Aristophanes* mentions them in the same office, and calls them Σηκις, *Sekis*, which seems to signify a common maid-servant. *Aristoph.* in Vespis, ver. 768:—

Ὁτι την θυραν ανεῳξεν ἡ Σηκις λαθρα.

Homer, Odyss., Ψ, ver. 225–229, mentions Actoris, Penelope's maid, whose office it was to keep the door of her chamber:—

Ακτορις——————
Ἡ νῶϊν ειρυτο θυρας πυκινου θαλαμοιο.

And *Euripides, in Troad.*, ver. 197, brings in *Hecuba*, complaining that she who was wont to sit upon a throne is now reduced to the miserable necessity of becoming a *doorkeeper* or a *nurse*, in order to get a morsel of bread.

——————*η ταν*
Παρα προθυροις φυλακαν κατεχουσα,
Η παιδων θρεπτειρα.

Sir *John Chardin* observes, that women are employed to keep the gate of the palace of the Persian kings. *Plautus, Curcul.*, act i., scene 1, mentions an *old woman* who was keeper of the gate.

Anus hic solet cubitare, custos janitrix.

Many other examples might be produced. It is therefore very likely that the persons mentioned here, and in 1 Sam. ii. 22, were the women who guarded the tabernacle; and that they regularly relieved each other, a *troop* or *company* regularly keeping watch: and indeed this seems to be implied in the original, צבאו *tsabeu*, they *came by troops;* and these troops successively consecrated their mirrors to the service of the tabernacle. See *Calmet* on John xviii. 16.

Verse 9. *The court*] See on chap. xxvii. 9.

Verse 17. *The hooks—and their fillets*] The capitals, and the silver bands that went round them; see the note on chap. xxvi. 32.

Verse 21. *This is the sum of the tabernacle.*] That is, The foregoing account contains a detail of all the articles which Bezaleel and Aholiab were commanded to make; and which were reckoned up by the Levites, over whom *Ithamar*, the son of Aaron, presided.

Verse 24. *All the gold that was occupied for the work, &c.*] To be able to ascertain the quantum and value of the gold, silver, and brass, which were employed in the tabernacle, and its different utensils,

a

A. M. 2514. B. C. 1490. An. Exod. Isr. 1. Tisri to Adar.

work, in all the work of the holy *place*, even the gold of the offering, was twenty and nine talents, and seven hundred and thirty shekels, after [k] the shekel of the sanctuary.

A. M. 2514. B. C. 1490. An. Exod. Isr. 1. Tisri to Adar.

[k] Chap. xxx. 13, 24; Lev. v. 15; xxvii. 3, 25; Num. iii. 47; xviii. 16.

altars, &c., it will be necessary to enter into the subject in considerable detail.

In the course of my notes on this and the preceding book, I have had frequent occasion to speak of the *shekel* in use among the ancient Hebrews, which, following Dean Prideaux, I have always computed at 3*s.* English. As some value it at 2*s.* 6*d.*, and others at 2*s.* 4*d.*, I think it necessary to lay before the reader the learned dean's mode of computation as a proper introduction to the calculations which immediately follow.

"Among the ancients, the way of reckoning their money was by *talents.* So the *Hebrews*, so the *Babylonians*, and so the *Romans* did reckon. And of these talents they had subdivisions which were usually in *minas* and *drachms;* i. e., of their *talents* into *minas*, and their *minas* into *drachms.* The *Hebrews* had, besides these, their *shekels* and *half-shekels* or *bekas;* and the *Romans* their *denarii*, which last were very nearly of the same value with the *drachms* of the *Greeks.* What was the value of a *Hebrew talent* appears from Exod. xxxviii. 25, 26, for there 603,550 persons being taxed at half a shekel a head, they must have paid in the whole 301,775 *shekels;* and that sum is there said to amount to *one hundred talents*, and 1775 *shekels* over: if therefore we deduct the 1775 *shekels* from the number 301,775, and divide the remaining sum, i. e., 300,000, by *a hundred*, this will prove each of those *talents* to contain *three thousand shekels.* Each of these *shekels* weighed about *three shillings* of our money; and sixty of them, Ezekiel tells us, chap. xlv. 12, made a mina; and therefore *fifty* of those *minas* made a *talent.* And as to their *drachms*, it appears by the Gospel of St. Matthew that it was the *fouth part of a shekel*, that is, nine-pence of our money. For there (chap. xvii. 24) the tribute money annually paid to the temple, by every *Jew*, (*Talmud* in shekalim,) which was *half a shekel*, is called Διδραχμον, (i. e., the *two drachm piece;*) and therefore, if *half a shekel* contained *two drachms*, a *drachm* must have been the *quarter part of a shekel*, and every *shekel* must have contained *four* of them: and so *Josephus* tells us it did; for he says, Antiq., lib. iii., c. 9, that a *shekel* contained *four Attic drachms*, which is not exactly to be understood according to the *weight*, but according to the *valuation* in the currency of common payments. For according to the *weight*, the heaviest *Attic* drachms did not exceed *eight-pence farthing half-farthing*, of our money; and a *Hebrew* drachm, as I have said, was *nine-pence;* but what the *Attic* drachm fell short of the *Hebrew* in *weight* might be made up in the *fineness*, and its ready currency in all countries, (which last the Hebrew drachm could not have,) and so might be made equivalent in common estimation among the *Jews.* Allowing therefore a *drachm*, as well *Attic* as *Jewish*, as valued in *Judea*, to be equivalent to *nine-pence* of our money, a BEKA or *half-shekel* will be *one shilling and six-pence;* a SHEKEL, *three shillings;* a MINA, *nine pounds;* and a TALENT, *four hundred and fifty pounds.* So it was in the time of *Moses* and *Ezekiel;* and so was it in the time of *Josephus* among that people, for he tells us, Antiq., lib. xiv., c. 12, that a *Hebrew* mina contained *two* LITRAS and a *half*, which comes exactly to *nine pounds* of our money: for a *litra*, being the same with a *Roman libra*, contained *twelve ounces* troy weight, that is, *ninety-six drachms;* and therefore *two litras* and a *half* must contain *two hundred and forty drachms*, which being estimated at *nine-pence* a *drachm*, according to the *Jewish* valuation, comes exactly to *sixty shekels*, or *nine pounds* of our money. And this account agrees exactly with that of *Alexandria.* For the *Alexandrian* talent contained 12,000 *Attic* drachms; and 12,000 *Attic* drachms, according to the *Jewish* valuation, being 12,000 of our *nine-pences*, they amount to 450 *pounds* of sterling money which is the same in value as the *Mosaic* talent. But here it is to be observed, that though the *Alexandrian* talent amounted to 12,000 *Attic* drachms, yet they themselves reckoned it but at 6000 drachms, because every *Alexandrian* drachm contained two *Attic* drachms; and therefore the *Septuagint* version being made by the *Alexandrian* Jews, they there render the *Hebrew* word shekel, by the *Greek* διδραχμον, which signifies *two drachms*, because two *Alexandrian* drachms make a *shekel*, two of them amounting to as much as four *Attic* drachms. And therefore, computing the *Alexandrian* money according to the same method in which we have computed the *Jewish*, it will be as follows: *One drachm* of *Alexandria* will be of our money *eighteen pence;* one *didrachm* or shekel, consisting of two drachms of *Alexandria*, or four of *Attica*, will be *three shillings;* one *mina*, consisting of *sixty didrachms* or *shekels*, will be *nine pounds;* and one *talent*, consisting of *fifty minas*, will be *four hundrea and fifty pounds*, which is the talent of *Moses*, Exod. xxxviii. 25, 26: and so also is it the talent of *Josephus*, Antiq., lib. iii., c. 7; for he tells us that a *Hebrew talent* contained one hundred *Greek* (i. e., Attic) minas. For those *fifty minas*, which here make an *Alexandrian* talent, would be one hundred *Attic* minas in the like method of valuation; the *Alexandrian* talent containing double as much as the *Attic* talent, both in the *whole*, and also in all its *parts*, in whatever method both shall be equally distributed. Among the Greeks the established rule was, *Jul. Polluc.* Onomast., lib. x., c. 6, that one *hundred drachms* made a *mina*, and *sixty minas* a *talent.* But in some different states their drachms being different, accordingly their minas and talents were within the same proportion different also. But the money of *Attica* was the *standard* by which all the rest were valued, according as they more or less differed from it. And therefore, it being of most note, wherever any *Greek* historian speaks of talents, minas, or drachms, if they be simply mentioned, it is to be always understood of

A. M. 2514.
B. C. 1490.
An. Exod. Isr. 1.
Tisri to Adar.

25 And the silver of them that
were numbered of the congregation *was* a hundred talents, and a
thousand seven hundred and threescore and fifteen shekels, after the
shekel of the sanctuary:

A. M. 2514.
B. C. 1490.
An. Exod. Isr. 1.
Tisri to Adar.

talents, minas, or drachms of *Attica*, and never of the talents, minas, or drachms of any other place, unless it be expressed. Mr. *Brerewood*, going by the goldsmith's weights, reckons an *Attic drachm* to be the same with a *drachm* now in use in their shops, that is, the *eighth part* of an *ounce;* and therefore lays it at the value of *seven-pence halfpenny* of our money, or the eighth part of a *crown*, which is or ought to be an *ounce* weight. But Dr. *Bernard*, going more accurately to work, lays the middle sort of *Attic* drachms at *eight-pence farthing* of our money, and the *minas* and *talents* accordingly, in the proportions above mentioned. The *Babylonish* talent, according to *Pollux*, Onomast., lib. x., c. 6, contained *seven thousand* of those drachms. The *Roman* talent (see *Festus Pompeius*) contained seventy-two *Italic* minas, which were the same with the *Roman libras;* and ninety-six Roman *denariuses*, each being of the value of *seven-pence halfpenny* of our money, made a Roman *libra*. But all the valuations I have hitherto mentioned must be understood only of *silver money*, and not of *gold;* for that was much higher. The proportion of gold to silver was among the ancients commonly as *ten* to *one;* sometimes it was raised to be as *eleven* to *one*, sometimes as *twelve*, and sometimes as *thirteen* to *one*. In the time of King *Edward* the *First* it was here, in England, at the value of *ten* to *one;* but it is now gotten at *sixteen* to *one*, and so I value it in all the reductions which I make in this history of ancient sums to the present value. But to make the whole of this matter the easier to the reader, I will lay all of it before him for his clear view in this following table of valuations:—

Hebrew *money*.	£	s.	d.
A Hebrew *drachm* - - - - - -			9
Two *drachms* made a *beka* or *half-shekel*, which was the tribute money paid by every *Jew* to the temple -		1	6
Two *bekas* made a *shekel* - - - -		3	0
Sixty *shekels* made a *mina* - - -	9	0	0
Fifty *minas* made a *talent* - - -	450	0	0
A *talent of gold*, sixteen to one - -	7200	0	0

Attic *money*, according to Mr. Brerewood.			
An Attic *drachm* - - - - - -			$7\frac{1}{2}$
A hundred *drachms* made a *mina* -	3	2	6
Sixty *minas* made a *talent* - - - -	187	10	0
A *talent of gold*, sixteen to one - -	3000	0	0

Attic *money*, according to Dr. Bernard.			
An Attic *drachm* - - - - - -			$8\frac{1}{4}$
A hundred *drachms* made a *mina* - -	3	8	9
Sixty *minas* made a *talent* - - -	206	5	0
A *talent of gold*, sixteen to one - -	3300	0	0

Babylonish *money*, according to Mr. Brerewood.			
A Babylonish talent of silver containing seven thousand Attic *drachms*	218	15	0
A Babylonish *talent* in gold, sixteen to one - - - - - - - - -	3500	0	0

Babylonish *money*, according to Dr. Bernard.			
A Babylonish *talent* in silver - - -	£240	12	6
A Babylonish talent in gold, sixteen to one - - - - - - - - -	3850	0	0

Alexandrian *money*.			
A *drachm* of Alexandria, containing two Attic *drachms*, as valued by the Jews		1	6
A *didrachm* of Alexandria, containing two Alexandrian *drachms*, which was a *Hebrew shekel* - - - -		3	0
Sixty *didrachms* or *Hebrew shekels* made a *mina* - - - - - - -	9	0	0
Fifty *minas* made a *talent* - - - -	450	0	0
A *talent of gold*, sixteen to one - -	7200	0	0

Roman *money*.			
Four *sesterciuses* made a Roman *denarius* - - - - - - - - -			$7\frac{1}{2}$
Ninety-six *Roman denariuses* made an *Italic mina*, which was the same with a Roman *libra* - - - -	3	0	0
Seventy-two Roman *libras* made a *talent*	216	0	0"

See the *Old and New Testament* connected, &c. Vol. i., preface, pp. xx–xxvii.

There were *twenty-nine* talents *seven hundred and thirty* shekels of GOLD; *one hundred* talents *one thousand seven hundred and seventy-five* shekels of SILVER; and *seventy* talents *two thousand four hundred* shekels of BRASS.

If with Dean Prideaux we estimate the value of the *silver* shekel at *three shillings* English, we shall obtain the weight of the shekel by making use of the following proportion. As *sixty-two shillings*, the value of a pound weight of silver as settled by the British laws, is to *two hundred and forty*, the number of *pennyweights* in a pound *troy*, so is *three shillings*, the value of a *shekel* of silver, to 11 dwts. $14\frac{22}{31}$ grains, the *weight* of the *shekel* required.

In the next place, to find the value of a shekel of *gold* we must make use of the proportion following: As *one ounce* troy is to 3*l*. 17*s*. $10\frac{1}{2}$*d*., the legal value of an ounce of gold, so is 11 dwts. $14\frac{22}{31}$ grains, the weight of the shekel as found by the last proportion, to 2*l*. 5*s*. $2\frac{1}{2}$ $\frac{42}{93}$*d*., the value of the *shekel of gold* required. From this *datum* we shall soon be able to ascertain the value of all the gold employed in the work of this holy place, by the following arithmetical process: Reduce 2*l*. 5*s*. $2\frac{1}{2}$ $\frac{42}{93}$*d*. to the lowest term mentioned, which is 201,852 ninety-third parts of a *farthing*. Multiply this last number by 3000, the number of shekels in a talent, and the product by 29, the number of talents; and add in 730 times 201,852, on account of the 730 shekels which were above the 29 talents employed in the work, and we shall have for the last product 17,708,475,960, which, divided successively by 93, 4, 12, and 20, will give 198,347*l*. 12*s*. 6*d*. for the *total value of the gold* employed in the tabernacle, &c.

The value of the silver contributed by 603,550 Israelites, at half a shekel or *eighteen pence* per man,

A. M. 2514. B. C. 1490. An. Exod. Isr. 1. Tisri to Adar.

26 [l] A bekah for [m] every man,
that is, half a shekel, after the
shekel of the sanctuary, for every
one that went to be numbered, from twenty
years old and upward, for [n] six hundred thou
sand, and three thousand, and five hundred and
fifty *men.*
27 And of the hundred talents of silver were
cast [o] the sockets of the sanctuary, and the
sockets of the veil; a hundred sockets of the
hundred talents, a talent for a socket.
28 And of the thousand seven hundred
seventy and five *shekels* he made hooks for
the pillars, and overlaid their chapiters, and filleted them.
29 And the brass of the offering
was seventy talents, and two thousand and
four hundred shekels.
30 And therewith he made the sockets to
the door of the tabernacle of the congregation,
and the brazen altar, and the brazen grate for
it, and all the vessels of the altar.
31 And the [p] sockets of the court round about,
and the sockets of the court gate, and all the
pins of the tabernacle, and all the pins of the
court round about.

[l] Chap. xxx. 13, 15.——[m] Heb. *a poll.*——[n] Num. i. 46.——[o] Chap. xxvi. 19, 21, 25, 32.——[p] Chap. xxvi. 37; chap. xxvii. 10, 17.

may be found by an easy arithmetical calculation to amount to 45,266*l.* 5*s.*

The value of the brass at 1*s.* per pound will amount to 513*l.* 17*s.*

The GOLD of the holy place weighed 4245 pounds.

The SILVER of the tabernacle 14,602 pounds.

The BRASS 10,277 pounds troy weight.

The total value of all the *gold, silver,* and *brass* of the tabernacle will consequently amount to 244,127*l.* 14*s.* 6*d.* And the total *weight* of all these three metals amounts to 29,124 pounds *troy,* which, reduced to *avoirdupois* weight, is nearly *ten tons and a half.* When all this is considered, besides the quantity of gold which was employed in the golden calf, and which was all destroyed, it is no wonder that the sacred text should say the Hebrews spoiled the Egyptians, particularly as in those early times the precious metals were probably not very plentiful in Egypt.

Verse 26. *A bekah for every man*] The Hebrew word בקע *beka,* from בקע *baka,* to *divide, separate into two,* seems to signify, not a particular coin, but a shekel *broken* or *cut in two;* so, anciently, our *farthing* was a penny divided in the midst and then subdivided, so that each division contained the *fourth part* of the *penny;* hence its name *fourthing* or *fourthling,* since corrupted into *farthing.*

THERE appear to be *three* particular reasons why much riches should be employed in the construction of the tabernacle, &c. 1. To impress the people's minds with the glory and dignity of the Divine Majesty, and the importance of his service. 2. To take out of their hands the occasion of covetousness; for as they brought much spoils out of Egypt, and could have little if any use for gold and silver in the wilderness, where it does not appear that they had much intercourse with any other people, and were miraculously supported, so that they did not need their riches, it was right to employ that in the worship of God which otherwise might have engendered that love which is the root of all evil. 3. To prevent pride and vain-glory, by leading them to give up to the Divine service even the ornaments of their persons, which would have had too direct a tendency to divert their minds from better things. Thus God's worship was rendered august and respectable, incitements to sin and low desires removed, and the people instructed to consider nothing valuable, but as far as it might be employed to the glory and in the service of God.

CHAPTER XXXIX.

Bezaleel makes the clothes of service *for the holy place, and the* holy garments, 1. *The* ephod, 2. Gold *is beaten into* plates, *and cut into* wires *for embroidery,* 3. *He makes the* shoulder-pieces *of the ephod,* 4. *The* curious girdle, 5. *Cuts the* onyx stones *for the shoulder-pieces,* 6. *Makes the* breastplate, *its chains, ouches, rings, &c.,* 7–21. *The* robe *of the* ephod, 22–26. Coats *of fine linen,* 27. *The* mitre, 28. *The* girdle, 29. *The* plate *of the* holy crown, 30, 31. *The completion of the work of the tabernacle,* 32. *All the work is brought unto Moses,* 33–41. *Moses, having examined the whole, finds every thing done as the Lord had commanded, in consequence of which he blesses the people,* 42, 43.

A. M. 2514. B. C. 1490. An. Exod. Isr. 1. Tisri to Adar.

AND of [a] the blue, and purple, and scarlet, they made
[b] clothes of service, to do service
in the holy *place,* and made the
holy garments for Aaron; [c] as the
LORD commanded Moses.

[a] Chap. xxxv. 23.——[b] Chap. xxxi. 10; xxxv. 19.——[c] Chap. xxviii. 4.

NOTES ON CHAP. XXXIX.

Verse 1. *Blue, and purple, and scarlet*] See this subject largely explained in the notes on chap. xxv. 4.

Verse 2. *Ephod*] See this described, chap. xxv. 7.

Verse 3. *They did beat the gold into thin plates*] For the purpose, as it is supposed, of cutting it into

A. M. 2514. B. C. 1490. An. Exod. Isr. 1. Tisri to Adar.

2 [d] And he made the ephod *of* gold, blue, and purple, and scarlet, and fine twined linen.

3 And they did beat the gold into thin plates, and cut *it into* wires, to work *it* in the blue, and in the purple, and in the scarlet, and in the fine linen, *with* cunning work.

4 They made shoulder-pieces for it, to couple *it* together: by the two edges was it coupled together.

5 And the curious girdle of his ephod, that *was* upon it, *was* of the same, according to the work thereof; *of* gold, blue, and purple, and scarlet, and fine twined linen; as the LORD commanded Moses.

6 [e] And they wrought onyx stones inclosed in ouches of gold, graven, as signets are graven, with the names of the children of Israel.

7 And he put them on the shoulders of the ephod, *that they should be* stones for a [f] memorial to the children of Israel; as the LORD commanded Moses.

8 [g] And he made the breastplate *of* cunning work, like the work of the ephod; *of* gold, blue, and purple, and scarlet, and fine twined linen.

9 It was four-square; they made the breastplate double: a span *was* the length thereof, and a span the breadth thereof, *being* doubled.

10 [h] And they set in it four rows of stones; *the first* row *was* a [i] sardius, a topaz, and a carbuncle: this *was* the first row.

11 And the second row, an emerald, a sapphire, and a diamond.

12 And the third row, a ligure, an agate, and an amethyst.

13 And the fourth row, a beryl, an onyx, and a jasper: *they were* inclosed in ouches of gold in their inclosings.

14 And the stones *were* according to the names of the children of Israel, twelve, according to their names, *like* the engravings of a signet, every one with his name, according to the twelve tribes.

A. M. 2514. B. C. 1490. An. Exod. Isr. 1. Tisri to Adar.

15 And they made upon the breastplate chains at the ends, *of* wreathen work *of* pure gold.

16 And they made two ouches *of* gold, and two gold rings, and put the two rings in the two ends of the breastplate.

17 And they put the two wreathen chains of gold in the two rings on the ends of the breastplate.

18 And the two ends of the two wreathen chains they fastened in the two ouches, and put them on the shoulder-pieces of the ephod before it.

19 And they made two rings of gold, and put them on the two ends of the breastplate, upon the border of it, which *was* on the side of the ephod inward.

20 And they made two *other* golden rings, and put them on the two sides of the ephod underneath, toward the forepart of it, over against the *other* coupling thereof, above the curious girdle of the ephod.

21 And they did bind the breastplate by his rings unto the rings of the ephod with a lace of blue, that it might be above the curious girdle of the ephod, and that the breastplate might not be loosed from the ephod; as the LORD commanded Moses.

22 [k] And he made the robe of the ephod *of* woven work, all *of* blue.

23 And *there was* a hole in the midst of the robe, as the hole of a habergeon, *with* a band round about the hole, that it should not rend.

24 And they made upon the hems of the robe pomegranates *of* blue, and purple, and scarlet, *and* twined *linen.*

25 And they made [l] bells *of* pure gold, and

[d] Chap. xxviii. 6.——[e] Chap. xxviii. 9.——[f] Chap. xxviii. 12. [g] Chap. xxviii. 15.

[h] Chap. xxviii. 17, &c.——[i] Or, *ruby*.——[k] Chap. xxviii. 31. [l] Chap. xxviii. 33.

wires (פתילם) or *threads;* for to *twist* or *twine* is the common acceptation of the root פתל *pathal.* I cannot suppose that the Israelites had not then the art of making *gold thread,* as they possessed several ornamental arts much more difficult: but in the present instance, figures made in a more solid form than that which could have been effected by *gold thread,* might have been required.

Verse 6. *Onyx stones*] Possibly the *Egyptian pebble.* See chap. xxv. 7, and xxviii. 17, &c.

Verse 8. *Breastplate*] See on chap. xxviii. 18.

Verse 10. *And they set in it four rows of stones*] See all these precious stones particularly explained in the notes on chap. xxviii. 17, &c.

Verse 23. *As the hole of a habergeon*] The *habergeon* or *hauberk* was a small coat of mail, something in form of a half shirt, made of small iron rings curiously united together. It covered the neck and breast, was very light, and resisted the stroke of a sword. Sometimes it went over the whole head as well as over the breast. This kind of defensive armour was used among the Asiatics, particularly the

A. M. 2514. B. C. 1490. An. Exod. Isr. 1. Tisri to Adar.

put the bells between the pomegranates upon the hem of the robe, round about between the pomegranates;
26 A bell and a pomegranate, a bell and a pomegranate, round about the hem of the robe to minister *in*, as the LORD commanded Moses.
27 [m] And they made coats *of* fine linen *of* woven work for Aaron, and for his sons,
28 [n] And a mitre *of* fine linen, and goodly bonnets *of* fine linen, and [o] linen breeches *of* fine twined linen,
29 [p] And a girdle *of* fine twined linen, and blue, and purple, and scarlet, *of* needle-work; as the LORD commanded Moses.
30 [q] And they made the plate of the holy crown *of* pure gold, and wrote upon it a writing, *like to* the engravings of a signet, HOLINESS TO THE LORD.
31 And they tied unto it a lace of blue, to fasten *it* on high upon the mitre; as the LORD commanded Moses.
32 Thus was all the work of the tabernacle of the tent of the congregation finished: and the children of Israel did [r] according to all that the LORD commanded Moses, so did they.
33 And they brought the tabernacle unto Moses, the tent, and all his furniture, his taches, his boards, his bars, and his pillars, and his sockets,
34 And the covering of rams' skins dyed red, and the covering of badgers' skins, and the veil of the covering,

A. M. 2514. B. C. 1490. An. Exod. Isr. 1. Tisri to Adar.

35 The ark of the testimony, and the staves thereof, and the mercy-seat,
36 The table, *and* all the vessels thereof, and the shew-bread,
37 The pure candlestick, *with* the lamps thereof, *even with* the lamps to be set in order, and all the vessels thereof, and the oil for light,
38 And the golden altar, and the anointing oil, and the [s] sweet incense, and the hanging for the tabernacle door,
39 The brazen altar, and his grate of brass, his staves, and all his vessels, the laver and his foot,
40 The hangings of the court, his pillars, and his sockets, and the hanging for the court gate, his cords, and his pins, and all the vessels of the service of the tabernacle, for the tent of the congregation,
41 The clothes of service, to do service in the holy *place*, and the holy garments for Aaron the priest, and his sons' garments, to minister in the priest's office.
42 According to all that the LORD commanded Moses, so the children of Israel [t] made all the work.
43 And Moses did look upon all the work, and, behold, they had done it as the LORD had commanded, even so had they done it: and Moses [u] blessed them.

[m] Chap. xxviii. 39, 40.——[n] Chap. xxviii. 4, 39; Ezek. xliv. 18.——[o] Chapter xxviii. 42.——[p] Chap. xxviii. 39.——[q] Chapter xxviii. 36, 37.——[r] Ver. 42, 43; chap. xxv. 40.

[s] Heb. *the incense of sweet spices.*——[t] Chap. xxxv. 10.——[u] Lev. ix. 22, 23; Num. vi. 23; Josh. xxii. 6; 2 Sam. vi. 18; 1 Kings viii. 14; 2 Chron. xxx. 27.

ancient Persians, among whom it is still worn. It seems to have been borrowed from the Asiatics by the Norman crusaders.

Verse 30. *The holy crown* of *pure gold*] On Asiatic monuments, particularly those that appear in the ruins of Persepolis and on many Egyptian monuments, the priests are represented as wearing *crowns* or *tiaras*, and sometimes their heads are crowned with laurel. *Cuper* observes, that the priests and priestesses, among the ancient Greeks, were styled *στεφανοφοροι*, or *crown-bearers*, because they officiated having sometimes *crowns of gold*, at others, *crowns of laurel*, upon their heads.

Verse 32. *Did according to all that the Lord commanded Moses*] This refers to the command given chap. xxv. 40; and Moses has taken care to *repeat* every thing in the most circumstantial detail, to show that he had conscientiously observed all the directions he had received.

Verse 37. *The pure candlestick*] See the note on chap. xxv. 31.

The lamps to be set in order] To be trimmed and fresh oiled every day, for the purpose of being lighted in the evening. See the note on chap. xxvii. 21.

Verse 43. *And Moses did look upon all the work*] As being the general superintendent of the whole, under whom Bezaleel and Aholiab were employed, as the other workmen were under them.

They had done it as the Lord had commanded] Exactly according to the pattern which Moses received from the Lord, and which he laid before the workmen to work by.

And Moses blessed them.] Gave them that praise which was due to their skill, diligence, and fidelity. See this meaning of the original word in the note on Gen. ii. 3. See also a fine instance of ancient courtesy between masters and their servants, in the case of Boaz and his reapers, Ruth ii. 4. Boaz came from Bethlehem, and said to the reapers, *The Lord be with* YOU! And they answered him, *The Lord bless* THEE! It is, however, very probable that Moses prayed to God in their behalf, that they might be prospered in all their undertakings, saved from every evil, and be brought at last to the inheritance that fadeth not away. This

blessing seems to have been given, not only to the workmen, but to all the people. The people contributed liberally, and the workmen wrought faithfully, and the blessing of God was pronounced upon ALL.

THE promptitude, cordiality, and despatch used in this business cannot be too highly commended, and are worthy of the imitation of all who are employed in any way in the service of God. The prospect of having God to *dwell among them* inflamed every heart, because they well knew that on this depended their prosperity and salvation. They therefore hastened to build him a house, and they spared no expense or skill to make it, as far as a house made with hands could be, worthy of that Divine Majesty who had promised to take up his residence in it. This tabernacle, like the temple, was a type of the human nature of the Lord Jesus; that was a shrine not made with hands, formed by God himself, and worthy of that fulness of the Deity that dwelt in it.

It is scarcely possible to form an adequate opinion of the riches, costly workmanship, and splendour of the tabernacle; and who can adequately conceive the glory and excellence of that human nature in which the fulness of the Godhead bodily dwelt? That this *tabernacle* typified the *human nature* of Christ, and the *Divine shechinah* that dwelt in it the *Deity* that dwelt in the man Christ Jesus, these words of St. John sufficiently prove: *In the beginning was the* WORD, *and the* WORD *was with God, and the* WORD *was* GOD. *And the* WORD *was made flesh, and dwelt among us,* (εσκηνωσεν εν ἡμιν, *made his* TABERNACLE *among us,*) *full of grace and truth*—possessing the true *Urim* and *Thummim;* all the *lights* and *perfections,* the *truth* and the *grace,* typified by the Mosaic economy. John i. 1, 14. And hence the evangelist adds, *And we beheld his glory;* as the Israelites beheld the glory of God resting on the tabernacle, so did the disciples of Christ see the Divine glory resting on him, and showing itself forth in all his *words, spirit,* and *works.* And for what purpose was the tabernacle erected? That God might dwell in it among the children of Israel. And for what purpose was the human nature of Christ so miraculously produced? That the Godhead might dwell in *it;* and that God and man might be reconciled through this wonderful economy of Divine grace, God being in Christ reconciling the world unto himself, 2 Cor. v. 19. And what was implied by this reconciliation? The union of the soul with God, and the indwelling of God in the soul. Reader, has God yet filled *thy tabernacle* with his glory? Does Christ dwell in thy heart by faith; and dost thou abide in him, bringing forth fruit unto holiness? Then thy end shall be eternal life. Why shouldst thou not go on thy way rejoicing with Christ in thy heart, heaven in thine eye, and the world, the devil, and the flesh, under thy feet?

CHAPTER XL.

Moses is commanded to set up the tabernacle, the first day of the first month of the second year of their departure from Egypt, 1, 2. *The ark to be put into it,* 3. *The table and candlestick to be brought in also with the golden altar,* 4, 5. *The altar of burnt-offering to be set up before the door, and the laver between the tent and the altar,* 6, 7. *The court to be set up,* 8. *The tabernacle and its utensils to be anointed,* 9–11. *Aaron and his sons to be washed, clothed, and anointed,* 12–15. *All these things are done accordingly,* 16. *The tabernacle is erected; and all its utensils, &c., placed in it on the first of the first month of the second year,* 17–33. *The cloud covers the tent, and the glory of the Lord fills the tabernacle, so that even Moses is not able to enter,* 34, 35. *When they were to journey, the cloud was taken up; when to encamp, the cloud rested on the tabernacle,* 36, 37. *A cloud by day and a fire by night was upon the tabernacle, in the sight of all the Israelites, through the whole course of the journeyings,* 38.

A. M. 2514. B. C. 1490. An. Exod. Isr. 1. Tisri to Adar.

AND the LORD spake unto
Moses, saying,
2 On the first day of the [a] first
month shalt thou set up [b] the tabernacle of
the tent of the congregation.
3 And [c] thou shalt put therein the ark of
the testimony, and cover the ark
with the veil.
4 And [d] thou shalt bring in the
table, and [e] set in order [f] the things that are to
be set in order upon it; [g] and thou shalt bring
in the candlestick, and light the lamps thereof.

A. M. 2514. B. C. 1490. An. Exod. Isr. 1 Tisri to Adar.

[a] Chap. xii. 2; xiii. 4.——[b] Ver. 17; ch. xxvi. 1, 30.——[c] Ver. 21; chap. xxvi. 33; Num. iv. 5.——[d] Ver. 22; ch. xxvi. 35.

[e] Ver. 23; chapter xxv. 30; Lev. xxiv. 5, 6.——[f] Heb. *the order thereof.*——[g] Ver. 24, 25.

NOTES ON CHAP. XL.

Verse 2. *The first day of the first month*] It is generally supposed that the Israelites began the work of the tabernacle about the *sixth month* after they had left Egypt; and as the work was finished about the end of the first year of their exodus, (for it was set up the *first day* of the *second year,*) that therefore they had spent about *six* months in making it: so that the tabernacle was erected one year all but *fifteen* days after they had left Egypt. Such a building, with such a profusion of *curious* and *costly* workmanship, was never got up in so short a time. But it was the work of the Lord, and the people did service as unto the Lord; for the people had a mind to work.

Verse 4. *Thou shalt bring in the table, and set in order the things, &c.*] That is, Thou shalt place the twelve loaves upon the table in the order before mentioned. See the note on chap. xxv. 30.

a

A. M. 2514.
B. C. 1490.
An. Exod. Isr. 1.
Tisri to Adar.

5 [h] And thou shalt set the altar of gold for the incense before the ark of the testimony, and put the hanging of the door to the tabernacle.

6 And thou shalt set the altar of the burnt-offering before the door of the tabernacle of the tent of the congregation.

7 And [i] thou shalt set the laver between the tent of the congregation and the altar, and shalt put water therein.

8 And thou shalt shut up the court round about, and hang up the hanging at the court gate.

9 And thou shalt take the anointing oil, and [k] anoint the tabernacle, and all that *is* therein, and shalt hallow it, and all the vessels thereof: and it shall be holy.

10 And thou shalt anoint the altar of the burnt-offering, and all his vessels, and sanctify the altar: and [l] it shall be an altar [m] most holy.

11 And thou shalt anoint the laver and his foot, and sanctify it.

12 [n] And thou shalt bring Aaron and his sons unto the door of the tabernacle of the congregation, and wash them with water.

13 And thou shalt put upon Aaron the holy garments, [o] and anoint him, and sanctify him; that he may minister unto me in the priest's office.

14 And thou shalt bring his sons, and clothe them with coats:

15 And thou shalt anoint them, as thou didst anoint their father, that they may minister unto me in the priest's office: for their anointing shall surely be [p] an everlasting priesthood throughout their generations.

16 Thus did Moses: according to all that the LORD commanded him, so did he.

A. M. 2514.
B. C. 1490.
An. Exod. Isr. 2.
Abib or Nisan.

17 And it came to pass in the first month in the second year, on the first *day* of the month, *that* the [q] tabernacle was reared up.

18 And Moses reared up the tabernacle, and fastened his sockets, and set up the boards thereof, and put in the bars thereof, and reared up his pillars.

19 And he spread abroad the tent over the tabernacle, and put the covering of the tent above upon it; as the LORD commanded Moses.

20 And he took and put [r] the testimony into the ark, and set the staves on the ark, and put the mercy-seat above upon the ark:

21 And he brought the ark into the tabernacle, and [s] set up the veil of the covering, and covered the ark of the testimony; as the LORD commanded Moses.

22 [t] And he put the table in the tent of the congregation, upon the side of the tabernacle northward without the veil.

23 [u] And he set the bread in order upon it

[h] Verse 26.——[i] Ver. 30; chap. xxx. 18.——[k] Chap. xxx. 26. [l] Chap. xxix. 36, 37.——[m] Heb. *holiness of holinesses.*——[n] Lev. viii. 1-13.

[o] Chap. xxviii. 41.——[p] Num. xxv. 13.——[q] Ver. 1; Num. vii. 1.——[r] Chap. xxv. 16.——[s] Chap. xxvi. 33; xxxv. 12.——[t] Chap. xxvi. 35.——[u] Ver. 4.

Verse 15. *For their anointing shall surely be an everlasting priesthood*] By this anointing a right was given to Aaron and his family to be high priests among the Jews for ever; so that all who should be born of this family should have a *right* to the priesthood without the repetition of this unction, as they should enjoy this honour in their father's right, who had it by a particular grant from God. But it appears that the high priest, on his consecration, did receive the *holy unction*; see Lev. iv. 3; vi. 22; xxi. 10. And this continued till the destruction of the first temple, and the Babylonish captivity; and according to Eusebius, Cyril of Jerusalem, and others, this custom continued among the Jews to the advent of our Lord, after which there is no evidence it was ever practised. See Calmet's note on chap. xxix. 7. The Jewish high priest was a type of Him who is called *the high priest over the house of God*, Heb. x. 21; and when he came, the functions of the *other* necessarily ceased. This case is worthy of observation. The Jewish sacrifices were never resumed after the destruction of their city and temple, *for they hold it unlawful to sacrifice anywhere out of Jerusalem*; and the unction of their high priests ceased from that period also: and why? Because the true priest and the true sacrifice were come, and the *types* of course were no longer necessary after the manifestation of the *antitype*.

Verse 19. *He spread abroad the tent over the tabernacle*] By the *tent*, in this and several other places, we are to understand the *coverings* made of rams' skins, goats' hair, &c., which were thrown over the building; for the tabernacle had no other kind of *roof*.

Verse 20. *And put the testimony into the ark*] That is, the two tables on which the ten commandments had been written. See chap. xxv. 16. The ark, the golden table with the shew-bread, the golden candlestick, and the golden altar of incense, were all *in* the tabernacle, *within the veil* or curtains, which served as a *door*, ver. 22, 24, 26. And the altar of burnt-offering was *by the door*, ver. 29. And the brazen laver, *between* the tent of the congregation and the brazen altar, ver. 30; still farther *outward*, that it might be the *first thing* the priests met with when entering into the court to minister, as their hands and feet must be washed before they could perform any part of the holy service, ver. 31, 32. When all these things were thus placed,

A. M. 2514. B. C. 1490. An. Exod. Isr. 2. Abib or Nisan.

before the LORD; as the LORD had commanded Moses.

24 [v] And he put the candlestick in the tent of the congregation, over against the table, on the side of the tabernacle southward.

25 And [w] he lighted the lamps before the LORD; as the LORD commanded Moses.

26 [x] And he put the golden altar in the tent of the congregation before the veil:

27 [y] And he burnt sweet incense thereon; as the LORD commanded Moses.

28 [z] And he set up the hanging *at* the door of the tabernacle.

29 [a] And he put the altar of burnt-offering *by* the door of the tabernacle of the tent of the congregation, and [b] offered upon it the burnt-offering and the meat-offering; as the LORD commanded Moses.

30 [c] And he set the laver between the tent of the congregation and the altar, and put water there, to wash *withal.*

31 And Moses, and Aaron, and his sons, washed their hands and their feet thereat:

32 When they went into the tent of the congregation, and when they came near unto the altar, they washed; [d] as the LORD commanded Moses.

A. M. 2514. B. C. 1490. An. Exod. Isr. 2. Abib or Nisan.

33 [e] And he reared up the court round about the tabernacle and the altar, and set up the hanging of the court gate. So Moses finished the work.

34 [f] Then a cloud covered the tent of the congregation, and the glory of the LORD filled the tabernacle.

35 And Moses [g] was not able to enter into the tent of the congregation, because the cloud abode thereon; and the glory of the LORD filled the tabernacle.

36 [h] And when the cloud was taken up from over the tabernacle, the children of Israel [i] went onward in all their journeys:

37 But [k] if the cloud were not taken up, then they journeyed not till the day that it was taken up.

38 For [l] the cloud of the LORD *was* upon the tabernacle by day, and fire was on it by night, in the sight of all the house of Israel, throughout all their journeys.

[v] Chap. xxvi. 35.——[w] Ver. 4; chap. xxv. 37.——[x] Verse 5; chap. xxx. 6.——[y] Chap. xxx. 7.——[z] Ver. 5; chapter xxvi. 36. [a] Ver. 6.——[b] Chap. xxix. 38, &c.——[c] Ver. 7; chapter xxx. 18. [d] Chap. xxx. 19, 20.——[e] Ver. 8; chap. xxvii. 9, 16.——[f] Chap. xxix. 43; Lev. xvi. 2; Numbers ix. 15; 1 Kings viii. 10, 11; 2 Chron. v. 13; vii. 2; Isa. vi. 4; Hag. ii. 7, 9; Rev. xv. 8. [g] Lev. xvi. 2; 1 Kings viii. 11; 2 Chron. v. 14.——[h] Num. ix. 17; x. 11; Neh. ix. 19.——[i] Heb. *journeyed.*——[k] Num. ix. 19-22. [l] Chap. xiii. 21; Num. ix. 15.

then the *court* that surrounded the tabernacle, which consisted of posts and hangings, was set up, ver. 33.

Verse 34. *Then a cloud covered the tent*] Thus God gave his approbation of the work; and as this was visible, so it was a sign to all the people that Jehovah was among them.

And the glory of the Lord filled the tabernacle.] How this was manifested we cannot tell; it was probably by some light or brightness which was insufferable to the sight, for Moses himself could not enter in because of the cloud and the glory, ver. 35. Precisely the same happened when Solomon had dedicated his temple; for it is said that *the cloud filled the house of the Lord, so that the priests could not stand to minister because of the cloud; for the glory of the Lord had filled the house of the Lord;* 1 Kings viii. 10, 11. Previously to this the cloud of the Divine glory had rested upon that *tent* or tabernacle which Moses had *pitched without the camp,* after the transgression in the matter of the molten calf; but now the cloud removed from that tabernacle and rested upon this one, which was made by the command and under the direction of God himself. And there is reason to believe that *this* tabernacle was pitched in the centre of the camp, all the twelve tribes pitching their different tents in a certain order around it.

Verse 36. *When the cloud was taken up*] The subject of these three last verses has been very largely explained in the notes on chap. xiii. 21, to which, as well as to the general remarks on that chapter, the reader is requested immediately to refer.

Verse 38. *For the cloud of the Lord* was *upon the tabernacle by day*] This daily and nightly appearance was at once both a merciful providence, and a demonstrative proof of the Divinity of their religion: and these tokens continued with them *throughout all their journeys;* for, notwithstanding their frequently repeated disobedience and rebellion, God never withdrew these tokens of his presence from them, till they were brought into the promised land. When, therefore, the tabernacle became *fixed,* because the Israelites had obtained their inheritance, this mark of the Divine presence was no longer visible in the sight of all Israel, but appears to have been confined to the holy of holies, where it had its fixed residence upon the mercy-seat between the cherubim; and in this place continued till the first temple was destroyed, after which it was no more seen in Israel till God was manifested in the flesh.

As in the book of GENESIS we have God's own account of the *commencement* of the WORLD, the origin of nations, and the peopling of the earth; so in the book of EXODUS we have an account, from the same source of infallible truth, of the *commencement* of the *Jewish* CHURCH, and the means used by

the endless mercy of God to propagate and continue his pure and undefiled religion in the earth, against which neither human nor diabolic power or policy have ever been able to prevail! The preservation of this religion, which has ever been opposed by the great mass of mankind, is a standing proof of its Divinity. As it has ever been in hostility against the corrupt passions of men, testifying against the world that its deeds were evil, these passions have ever been in hostility to it. Cunning and learned men have argued to render its authority dubious, and its tendency suspicious; whole states and empires have exerted themselves to the uttermost to oppress and destroy it; and its professed friends, by their conduct, have often betrayed it: yet *librata ponderibus suis*, supported by the arm of God and its own intrinsic excellence, it lives and flourishes; and the *river* that makes glad the city of God has run down with the tide of time 5800 years, and is running on with a more copious and diffusive current.

Labitur, et labetur in omne volubilis ævum.

"Still glides the river, and will ever glide."

We have seen how, by the miraculous cloud, all the movements of the Israelites were directed. They struck or pitched their tents, as it removed or became stationary. Every thing that concerned them was under the direction and management of God. But these things happened unto them for ensamples; and it is evident, from Isa. iv. 5, that all these things typified the presence and influence of God in his Church, and in the souls of his followers. His Church can possess no sanctifying knowledge, no quickening power but from the presence and influence of his Spirit. By this influence all his followers are taught, enlightened, led, quickened, purified, and built up on their most holy faith; and without the *indwelling* of his Spirit, light, life, and salvation are impossible. These Divine influences are necessary, not only for a time, but through *all our journeys*, ver. 38; through every changing scene of providence, and through every step in life. And these the followers of Christ are to possess, not by inference or inductive reasoning, but *consciously*. The influence is to be *felt*, and the fruits of it to appear as fully as the *cloud of the Lord by day*, and the *fire by night*, appeared in *the sight of all the house of Israel.* Reader, hast thou this Spirit? Are all thy goings and comings ordered by its continual guidance? Does Christ, who was *represented* by this tabernacle, and *in whom dwelt all the fulness of the Godhead bodily*, dwell in thy heart by faith? If not, call upon God for that blessing which, for the sake of his Son, he is ever disposed to impart; then shalt thou be glorious, *and on all thy glory there shall be a defence.* Amen, Amen.

On the ancient division of the law into *fifty-four* sections, see the notes at the end of Genesis. Of these *fifty-four* sections Genesis contains *twelve;* and the commencement and ending of each has been marked in the note already referred to. Of these sections Exodus contains *eleven*, all denominated, as in the former case, by the words in the original with which they commence. I shall point these out as in the former, carrying the enumeration from Genesis.

The THIRTEENTH section, called שמות *shemoth*, begins Exod. i. 1, and ends chap. vi. 1.

The FOURTEENTH, called וארא *vaera*, begins chap. vi. 2, and ends chap. ix. 35.

The FIFTEENTH, called בא *bo*, begins chap. x. 1, and ends chap. xiii. 16.

The SIXTEENTH, called בשלח *beshallach*, begins chap. xiii. 17, and ends chap. xvii. 16.

The SEVENTEENTH, called יתרו *yithro*, begins chap. xviii. 1, and ends chap. xx. 26.

The EIGHTEENTH, called משפטים *mishpatim*, begins chap. xxi. 1, and ends chap. xxiv. 18.

The NINETEENTH, called תרומה *terumah*, begins chap. xxv. 2, and ends chap. xxvii. 19.

The TWENTIETH, called תצוה *tetsavveh*, begins chap. xxvii. 20, and ends chap. xxx. 10.

The TWENTY-FIRST, called תשא *tissa*, begins chap. xxx. 11, and ends chap. xxxiv. 35.

The TWENTY-SECOND, called ויקהל *vaiyakhel*, begins chap. xxxv. 1, and ends chap. xxxviii. 20.

The TWENTY-THIRD, called פקודי *pekudey*, begins chap. xxxviii. 21, and ends chap. xl. 38.

It will at once appear to the reader that these sections have their technical names from some remarkable word, either in the first or second verse of their commencement.

MASORETIC *Notes* on EXODUS.

Number of VERSES in *Veelleh shemoth*, (Exodus,) 1209.

The symbol of this number is אר״ט; א׳ *aleph* denoting 1000, ר *resh* 200, and ט *teth* 9.

The *middle* verse is ver. 28 of chap. xxii.: *Thou shalt not revile God, nor curse the ruler of thy people.*

Its *parashioth*, or larger sections, are 11. The symbol of this is the word אי׳ *ei*, Isa. lxvi. 1: WHERE *is the house that ye will build unto me?* In which א *aleph* stands for 1, and י *yod* for 10.

Its *sedarim* are 29. The symbol of which is taken from Psa. xix. 3, יחוה *yechavveh: Night unto night* SHOWETH FORTH *knowledge.* In which word, י *yod* stands for 10, ח *cheth* for 8, ו *vau* for 6, and ה *he* for 5; amounting to 29.

Its *pirkey*, *perakim*, or present chapters, 40. The symbol of which is בלבו *belibbo*, taken from Psa. xxxvii. 31: *The law of God is* IN HIS HEART. In this word, ב *beth* stands for 2, ל *lamed* for 30, ב *beth* for 2, and ו *vau* for 6; amounting to 40.

The *open sections* are 69. The *close sections* are 95. Total 164. The symbol of which is יסעדך *yisadecha*, from Psa. xx. 2: STRENGTHEN THEE *out of* Zion. In which numerical word ע *ain* stands for 70, ס *samech* for 60, ך *caph* for 20, י *yod* for 10, and ד *daleth* for 4; making together 164.

Number of words, 16513; of letters, 63467.

But on these subjects, important to some, and trifling to others, see what is said in the concluding note on GENESIS.

ADDITIONAL OBSERVATIONS ON THE TRAVELS OF THE ISRAELITES THROUGH THE WILDERNESS.

In the preceding notes I have had frequent occasion to refer to Dr. Shaw's account of the different stations of the Israelites, of which I promised an abstract in this place. This will doubtless be acceptable to every reader who knows that Dr. Shaw travelled over the same ground, and carefully, in person, noted every spot to which reference is made in the preceding chapters.

After having endeavoured to prove that Goshen was that part of the Heliopolitan Nomos, or of the land of Rameses, which lay in the neighbourhood of *Kairo, Matta-reah*, and *Bishbesh*, and that Cairo might be Rameses, the capital of the district of that name, where the Israelites had their rendezvous before they departed out of Egypt, he takes up the text and proceeds thus:—

"*Now, lest peradventure* (chap. xiii. 17) *when the Hebrews saw war they should repent and return to Egypt, God did not lead them through the way of the land of the Philistines*, (viz., either by *Heroopolis* in the midland road, or by *Bishbesh, Tineh*, and so along the *seacoast* towards *Gaza* and *Ascalon*,) although that was the nearest, but he *led them* ABOUT *through the way of the wilderness of the Red Sea.* There are accordingly two roads through which the Israelites might have been conducted from *Kairo* to *Pihahhiroth*, on the banks of the Red Sea. One of them lies through the valleys, as they are now called, of Jendily, Rumeleah, and Baideah, bounded on each side by the mountains of the lower Thebais. The other lies higher, having the northern range of these mountains (the mountains of *Mocattee*) running parallel with it on the right hand, and the desert of the *Egyptian Arabia*, which lies all the way open to the *land of the Philistines*, on the left. About the middle of this range we may turn short upon our right hand into the valley of *Baideah* through a remarkable breach or discontinuation, in which we afterwards continued to the very bank of the *Red Sea. Suez*, a small city upon the northern point of it, at the distance of thirty hours or *ninety* Roman miles from Kairo, lies a little to the northward of the promontory that is formed by this same range of mountains, called at present *Attackah*, as that which bounds the valley of *Baideah* to the southward is called *Gewoubee*.

"This road then through the valley of Baideah, which is some hours longer than the other open road which leads us directly from *Kairo* to *Suez*, was, in all probability, the very road which the *Israelites* took to *Pihahhiroth*, on the banks of the Red Sea. Josephus then, and other authors who copy after him, seem to be too hasty in making the Israelites perform this journey of *ninety* or *one hundred Roman* miles in three days, by reckoning each of the stations that are recorded for one day. Whereas the Scriptures are altogether silent with regard to the time or distance, recording the stations only. The fatigue, likewise, would have been abundantly too great for a nation on foot, encumbered with their *dough*, their *kneading-troughs*, their *little children and cattle*, to walk at the rate of *thirty Roman* miles a day. Another instance of the same kind occurs chap. xxxiii. 9, where *Elim* is mentioned as the next station after *Marah*, though *Elim* and *Marah* are farther distant from each other than *Kairo* is from the *Red Sea*. Several intermediate stations, therefore, as well here as in other places, were omitted, the *holy penman* contenting himself with laying down such only as were the most remarkable, or attended with some notable transaction. *Succoth*, then, the first station from Rameses, signifying only *a place of tents*, may have no fixed situation, being probably nothing more than some considerable *Dou-war* of the *Ishmaelites* or *Arabs*, such as we still meet with at *fifteen* or *twenty* miles' distance from *Kairo*, in the road to the *Red Sea*. The *rendezvous* of the *caravan* which conducted us to *Suez* was at one of these *Douwars;* at the same time we saw another at about *six* miles' distance, under the mountains of *Mocattee*, or in the very same direction which the Israelites may be supposed to have taken in their marches from *Goshen* towards the *Red Sea*.

"That the *Israelites*, before they turned towards *Pihahhiroth*, had travelled in an open country, (the same way, perhaps, which their forefathers had taken in coming into Egypt,) appears to be farther illustrated from the following circumstance: that upon their being ordered to remove from the edge of the wilderness, and to *encamp* before *Pihahhiroth*, it immediately follows that *Pharaoh* should then say, *they are entangled in the land, the wilderness* (betwixt the mountains we may suppose of *Gewoubee* and *Attackah*) *hath shut them in*, chap. xiv. 3, or, as it is in the original, (סגר *sagar*,) *viam illis clausit*, as that word is explained by *Pagninus;* for in these circumstances the *Egyptians* might well imagine that the *Israelites* could have no possible way to escape, inasmuch as the mountains of *Gewoubee* would stop their flight or progress to the southward, as the mountains of *Attackah* would do the same towards the land of the *Philistines;* the *Red Sea* likewise lay before them to the east, whilst *Pharaoh* closed up the valley behind them with his *chariots* and *horsemen*. This valley ends at the sea, in a small bay made by the eastern extremities of the mountains which I have been describing, and is called *Tiah Beni Israel*, i. e., the road of the Israelites, by a tradition that is still kept up by the Arabs, of their having passed through it; so it is also called *Baideah*, from the *new* and unheard-of *miracle* that was wrought near it, by dividing the *Red Sea*, and destroying therein *Pharaoh, his chariots, and his horsemen*. The third notable encampment then of the Israelites was at this bay. It was to be *before* Pihahhiroth, *betwixt* Migdol and the sea, over against Baal-tsephon, chap. xiv. 2; and in Num. xxxiii. 7 it was to be *before* Migdol, where the word לפני *liphney*, (*before*, as we render it,) being applied to *Pihahhiroth* and *Migdol*, may signify no more than that they pitched within sight of, or at a small distance from, the one and the other of those places. Whether *Baal-tsephon* then may have relation to the northern situation of the place itself, or to some

watch tower or *idol temple* that was erected upon it, we may probably take it for the eastern extremity of the mountains of *Suez* or *Attackah*, the most conspicuous of these deserts, inasmuch as it overlooks a great part of the lower *Thebais*, as well as the wilderness that reaches towards, or which rather makes part of, the *land of the Philistines*. *Migdol* then might lie to the south, as Baal-tsephon did to the north, of *Pihahhiroth;* for the marches of the *Israelites* from the edge of the wilderness being to the seaward, that is, towards the south-east, their encampments *betwixt* Migdol *and the sea*, or *before* Migdol, as it is otherwise noted, could not well have another situation.

"*Pihahhiroth*, or *Hhiroth* rather, without regarding the *prefixed* part of it, may have a more general signification, and denote the valley or that whole space of ground which extended itself from the edge of the wilderness of *Etham* to the *Red Sea:* for that particular part only, where the Israelites were ordered to encamp, appears to have been called Pihahhiroth, i. e., *mouth of Hhiroth;* for when Pharaoh overtook them, it was in respect to his coming down upon them, chap. xiv. 9, על פי החירת i. e., *beside* or *at the mouth*, or the most advanced part, of *Hhiroth* to the eastward. Likewise in Num. xxxiii. 7, where the Israelites are related to have encamped before Migdol, it follows, ver. 8, that *they departed* מפני החירת *from before Hhiroth*, and not *from before Pihahhiroth*, as it is rendered in our translation.

"There are likewise other circumstances to prove that the *Israelites* took their departure from this valley in their passage through the *Red Sea*, for it could not have been to the northward of the mountains of Attackah, or in the higher road, which I have taken notice of; because as this lies for the most part upon a level, the *Israelites* could not have been here, as we find they were, shut in and entangled. Neither could it have been on the other side, viz., to the south of the mountains of Gewoubee, for then (besides the insuperable difficulties which the *Israelites* would have met with in climbing over them, the same likewise that the *Egyptians* would have had in pursuing them) the opposite shore could not have been the desert of *Shur* where the *Israelites* landed, chap. xv. 22, but it would have been the desert of *Marah*, that lay a great way beyond it. What is now called *Corondel* might probably be the southern portion of the desert of *Marah*, the shore of the *Red Sea*, from *Suez*, hitherto having continued to be low and sandy; but from *Corondel* to the port of *Tor*, the shore is for the most part rocky and mountainous, in the same manner with the *Egyptian* coast that lies opposite to it; neither the one nor the other of them affording any convenient place, either for the departure of a multitude from the one shore, or the reception of it upon the other. And besides, from *Corondel* to *Tor*, the channel of the Red Sea, which from *Suez* to *Sdur* is not above nine or ten miles broad, begins here to be so many leagues, too great a space certainly for the *Israelites*, in the manner they were encumbered, to pass over in one night. At *Tor* the *Arabian* shore begins to wind itself round about *Ptolemy's* promontory of *Paran*, towards the gulf of *Eloth*, whilst the *Egyptian* shore retires so far to the south-west that it can scarce be perceived. As the *Israelites* then, for these reasons, could not, according to the opinion of some authors, have landed either at *Corondel* or *Tor*, so neither could they have landed at *Ain Mousa*, according to the conjectures of others. For if the passage of the *Israelites* had been so near the extremity of the Red Sea, it may be presumed that the very encampments of six hundred thousand men, besides children and a mixed multitude, which would amount to as many more, would have spread themselves even to the farther or the Arabian side of this narrow *isthmus*, whereby the interposition of Providence would not have been at all necessary; because, in this case and in this situation, there could not have been room enough for *the waters*, after they were divided, to have *stood on a heap*, or to have *been a wall unto them*, particularly *on the left hand*. This, moreover, would not have been a division, but a *recess* only of the water to the southward. *Pharaoh* likewise, by overtaking them as they were encamped in this open situation by the sea, would have easily surrounded them on all sides. Whereas the contrary seems to be implied by the *pillar of the cloud*, chap. xiv. 19, 20, which (divided or) *came between the camp of the Egyptians and the camp of Israel*, and thereby left the *Israelites* (provided this cloud should have been removed) in a situation only of being molested in the rear. For the narrow valley which I have described, and which we may presume was already occupied and filled up *behind* by the host of *Egypt*, and *before* by the encampments of the *Israelites*, would not permit or leave room for the *Egyptians* to approach them, either on the right hand or on the left. Besides, if this passage was at *Ain Mousa*, how can we account for that remarkable circumstance, chap. xv. 22, where it is said that, *when Moses brought Israel from the Red Sea, they went out into* (or landed in) *the wilderness of Shur?* For *Shur*, a particular district of the wilderness of Etham, lies directly fronting the valley from which I suppose they departed, but a great many miles to the southward of *Ain Mousa*. If they landed likewise at *Ain Mousa*, where there are several fountains, there would have been no occasion for the sacred historian to have observed, at the same time, that the *Israelites* after *they went out* from the sea *into the wilderness of Shur, went three days in the wilderness*, always directing their marches toward *Mount Sinai, and found no water;* for which reason Marah is recorded, ver. 23, to be the first place where they found water, as their wandering so far before they found it seems to make Marah also their first station, after their passage through the *Red Sea*. Moreover, the channel over against Ain Mousa is not above three miles over, whereas that betwixt Shur or Sedur and Jibbel Gewoubee and Attackah, is nine or ten, and therefore capacious enough, as the other would have been too small, for *covering* or drowning therein, chap. xv. 28, *the chariots and horsemen, and all the host of Pharaoh*. And therefore, by impartially weighing all these arguments together, this important point in the *sacred geography* may with more authority be fixed at *Sedur*, over against the valley of *Baideah*, than at *Tor*, *Corondel*, *Ain Mousa*, or any other place.

"Over against *Jibbel Attackah* and the valley of *Baideah* is the desert, as it is called, of *Sdur*, (the same with *Shur*, chap. xv. 22,) where the *Israelites*

landed after they had passed through the interjacent gulf of the *Red Sea*. The situation of this gulf, which is the ים סוף *Jam suph, the weedy sea* or *the tongue of the Egyptian sea* in the Scripture language; the gulf of *Heroopolis* in the *Greek* and *Latin* geography; and the *Western arm*, as the *Arabian* geographers call it, of the sea of *Kolzum;* stretches itself nearly north and south, and therefore lies very properly situated to be traversed by that strong *east wind* which was sent to divide it, chap. xiv. 21. The division that was thus made in the channel, the *making the waters of it to stand on a heap*, (Psa. lxxviii. 13,) *their being a wall to the Israelites on the right hand and on the left*, (chap. xiv. 22,) besides the twenty miles' distance, at least, of this passage from the extremity of the gulf, are circumstances which sufficiently vouch for the *miraculousness* of it, and no less contradict all such idle suppositions as pretend to account for it from the nature and quality of tides, or from any such extraordinary recess of the sea as it seems to have been too rashly compared to by Josephus.

"In travelling from *Sdur* towards *Mount Sinai* we come into the desert, as it is still called, of *Marah*, here the *Israelites* met with those *bitter waters* or *waters of Marah*, chap. xv. 23. And as this circumstance did not happen till after they had wandered *three days in the wilderness*, we may probably fix these waters at *Corondel*, where there is still a small rill which, unless it be diluted by the dews and rain, still continues to be brackish. Near this place the sea forms itself into a large bay called *Berk el Corondel*, i. e., the lake of Corondel, which is remarkable from a strong current that sets into it from the northward, particularly at the recess of the tide. The *Arabs*, agreeably to the interpretation of Kolzum, (the name for this sea,) preserve a tradition, that a numerous host was formerly drowned at this place, occasioned no doubt by what is related chap. xiv. 30, that the Israelites saw the *Egyptians* dead upon the seashore, i. e., all along, as we may presume, from *Sdur* to *Corondel*, and at *Corondel* especially, from the assistance and termination of the current as it has been already mentioned.

"There is nothing farther remarkable till we see the *Israelites* encamped at *Elim*, chap. xv. 27, Num. xxxiii. 9, upon the northern skirts of the desert of *Sin*, two leagues from *Tor*, and near thirty from *Corondel*. I saw no more than nine of the *twelve wells* that are mentioned by Moses, the other three being filled up by those drifts of sand which are common in Arabia. Yet this loss is amply made up by the great increase of the *palm-trees*, the *seventy* having propagated themselves into more than two thousand. Under the shade of these trees is *the Hamman Mousa* or *bath of Moses*, particularly so called, which the inhabitants of *Tor* have in great esteem and veneration, acquainting us that it was here where the household of Moses was encamped.

"We have a distinct view of *Mount Sinai* from *Elim*, the wilderness, as it is still called, of סין *Sin* lying betwixt them. We traversed these plains in nine hours, being all the way diverted with the sight of a variety of *lizards* and *vipers* that are here in great numbers. We were afterwards near twelve hours in passing the many windings and difficult ways which lie betwixt these deserts and those of *Sinai*. The latter consists of a beautiful plain, more than a league in breadth, and nearly three in length, lying open towards the north-east, where we enter it, but is closed up to the southward by some of the lower eminences of *Mount Sinai*. In this direction likewise the higher parts of this mountain make such encroachments upon the plain that they divide it into two, each of them capacious enough to receive the whole encampment of the *Israelites*. That which lies to the eastward may be the desert of *Sinai*, properly so called, where *Moses saw the angel of the Lord in the burning bush, when hew as guarding the flocks of Jethro*, chap. iii. 2. *The convent of St. Catharine* is built over the place of this *Divine appearance*. It is near *three hundred* feet square, and more than *forty* in height, being built partly with stone, partly with mud and mortar mixed together. The more immediate place of the shechinah is honoured with a little chapel which this old fraternity of *St. Basil* has in such esteem and veneration that, in imitation of *Moses, they put off their shoes from off their feet* whenever they enter it. This, with several other chapels dedicated to particular *saints*, is included within the *church*, as they call it, of the *transfiguration*, which is a large beautiful structure covered with lead, and supported by two rows of marble columns. The floor is very elegantly laid out in a variety of devices in *Mosaic* work. Of the same tessellated workmanship likewise are both the floor and the walls of the *presbyterium*, upon the latter whereof are represented the *effigies* of the *Emperor Justinian*, together with the history of the *transfiguration*. Upon the partition which separates the *presbyterium* from the body of the *church*, there is placed a small *marble shrine*, wherein are preserved the skull and one of the hands of St. Catharine, the rest of the sacred body having been bestowed at different times upon such *Christian princes* as have contributed to the support of this convent.

"Mount *Sinai*, which hangs over this convent, is called by the *Arabs Jibbel Mousa*, i. e., *the mountain of Moses*, and sometimes only, by way of eminence, *El Tor*, i. e., *the mountain*. The summit of *Mount Sinai* is not very spacious, where the *Mohammedans*, the *Latins*, and the *Greeks*, have each of them a small chapel.

"After we had descended, with no small difficulty, down the other or western side of this *mount*, we come into the plain or wilderness of *Rephidim*, chap. xvii. 1, where we see that extraordinary antiquity, the *rock of Meribah*, chap. xvii. 6, which has continued down to this day without the least injury from time or accidents. This is rightly called, (Deut. viii. 15,) from its hardness, a *rock of flint*, צור החלמיש; though, from the purple or reddish colour of it, it may be rather rendered the rock of חלם or אחלמה *amethyst*, or the amethystine or granite rock. It is about six yards square, lying tottering as it were, and loose, near the middle of the valley; and seems to have been formerly a part or cliff of *Mount Sinai*, which hangs in a variety of precipices all over this plain. *The waters* which *gushed out and the stream* which *flowed withal*, Psa. lxxviii. 20, have hollowed, across one corner of this rock, a channel about two inches deep and twenty wide, all over incrustated like the inside of a tea-kettle

that has been long used. Besides several mossy productions that are still preserved by the dew, we see all over this channel a great number of holes, some of them four or five inches deep and one or two in diameter, the lively and demonstrative tokens of their having been formerly so many fountains. Neither could art or chance be concerned in the contrivance, inasmuch as every circumstance points out to us a miracle; and in the same manner, with the rent in the rock of *Mount Calvary* in *Jerusalem*, never fails to produce the greatest seriousness and devotion in all who see it.

"From *Mount Sinai* the *Israelites* directed their marches northward, toward the land of *Canaan*. The next remarkable encampments therefore were in the desert of *Paran*, which seems to have commenced immediately upon their departing from *Hazaroth*, three stations' or days' journey, i. e., *thirty* miles, as we will only compute them from *Sinai*, Num. x. 33, and xii. 16. And as tradition has continued down to us the names of *Shur*, *Marah*, and *Sin*, so it has also that of *Paran;* the ruins of the late convent of Paran, built upon the ruins of an ancient city *of that name*, (which might give denomination to the whole of that desert,) being about the half way betwixt *Sinai* and *Corondel*, which lie at forty leagues' distance. This situation of *Paran*, so far to the south of *Kadesh*, will illustrate Gen. xiv. 5, 6, where *Chedorlaomer, and the kings that were with him, are said to have smote the Horites in their Mount Seir unto El Paran*, (i. e., unto the city, as I take it, of that name,) *which is* in or *by the wilderness*. From the more advanced part of the wilderness of *Paran*, (the same that lay in the road betwixt *Midian* and *Egypt*, 1 Kings xi. 18,) *Moses sent a man out of every tribe to spy out the land of Canaan*, Num. xxiii. 3, *who returned to him after forty days, unto the same wilderness, to Kadesh Barnea*, Num. xxxii. 8; Deut. i. 10; ix. 23; Josh. xiv. 7. This place or city, which in Gen. xiv. 7 is called *Enmishpat*, (i. e., the fountain of *Mishpat*,) is in Num. xx. 1; xxvii. 14; xxxiii. 36, called *Tzin Kadesh*, or simply *Kadesh*, as in Gen. xvi. 14; xx. 1; and being equally ascribed to the desert of *Tzin*, (צין,) and to the desert of *Paran*, we may presume that the desert of *Tzin* and *Paran* were one and the same; צין or צנים may be so called from the plants of divers palm grounds upon it.

"A late ingenious author has situated *Kadesh Barnea*, a place of no small consequence in Scripture history, which we are now inquiring after, at eight hours' or twenty miles' distance only from *Mount Sinai*, which I presume cannot be admitted for various reasons, because several texts of Scripture insinuate that *Kadesh* lay at a much greater distance. Thus in Deut. i. 19, it is said, they *departed from Horeb through that great and terrible wilderness*, (which supposes by far a much greater extent both of time and space,) *and came to Kadesh Barnea;* and in ix. 23, *when the Lord sent you from Kadesh Barnea to possess the land;* which, Num. xx. 16, is described to be *a city in the uttermost parts of the border of Edom;* the border of the land of *Edom* and that of the *land of promise* being contiguous, and in fact the very same. And farther, Deut. i. 2, it is expressly said, *There are eleven days' journey from Horeb, by the way of Mount Seir, to Kadesh Barnea;* which, from the context, cannot be otherwise understood than of marching along the *direct road*. For Moses hereby intimates how soon the *Israelites* might have entered upon the borders of the *land of promise*, if they had not been a stubborn and rebellious people. Whereas the number of their stations betwixt *Sinai* and *Kadesh*, as they are particularly enumerated Num. xxxiii. (each of which must have been at least one day's journey,) appear to be near twice as many, or *twenty-one*, in which they are said with great truth and propriety, Psa. cvii. 4, *to have wandered in the wilderness out of the way;* and in Deut. ii. 1, *to have compassed Mount Seir*, rather than to have travelled directly through it. If then we allow *ten* miles for each of these eleven days' journey, (and fewer I presume cannot well be insisted upon,) the distance of *Kadesh* from *Mount Sinai* will be about *one hundred and ten* miles. That *ten* miles (I mean in a direct line, as laid down in the map, without considering the deviations which are everywhere, more or less) were equivalent to one day's journey, may be farther proved from the history of the *spies*, who searched the land (Num. xiii. 21) *from Kadesh to Rehob, as men come to Hamath*, and returned in forty days. *Rehob*, then, the farthest point of this expedition to the northward, may well be conceived to have been *twenty* days' journey from *Kadesh;* and therefore to know the true position of *Rehob* will be a material point in this disquisition. Now it appears from Josh. xix. 29, 30, and Judg. i. 31, that *Rehob* was one of the maritime cities of the tribe of Asher, and lay (in travelling, as we may suppose, by the common or nearest way along the seacoast) לבא חמת, Num. xiii. 21, (not as we render it, *as men come to Hamath*, but,) *as men go towards Hamath, in going to Hamath*, or *in the way* or *road to Hamath*. For to have searched the land as far as *Hamath*, and to have returned to *Kadesh* in forty days, would have been altogether impossible. Moreover, as the tribe of *Asher* did not reach beyond *Sidon*, (for that was its northern boundary, Josh. xix. 28,) Rehob must have been situated to the southward of *Sidon*, upon or (being a derivative perhaps from רחב, *latum esse*) below in the plain, under a long chain of mountains that runs east and west through the midst of that tribe. And as these mountains, called by some the mountains of *Saran*, are all along, except in the narrow road which I have mentioned, near the sea, very rugged and difficult to pass over, the *spies*, who could not well take another way, might imagine they would run too great a risk of being discovered in attempting to pass through it. For in these eastern countries a watchful eye was always, as it is still, kept upon strangers, as we may collect from the history of the two angels at *Sodom*, Gen. xix. 5, and of the spies at *Jericho*, Josh. ii. 2, and from other instances. If then we fix *Rehob* upon the skirts of the plains of *Acre*, a little to the south of this narrow road (the *Scala Tyriorum* as it was afterwards named) somewhere near *Egdippa*, the distance betwixt *Kadesh* and *Rehob* will be about *two hundred and ten* miles, whereas, by placing *Kadesh twenty* miles only from *Sinai* or *Horeb*, the distance will be *three hundred and thirty* miles And instead of *ten* miles a day,

according to the former computation, the *spies* must have travelled near *seventeen*, which for *forty* days successively seems to have been too difficult an expedition in this hot and consequently fatiguing climate, especially as they were on foot or *footpads*, as מרגלים (their appellation in the original) may probably import. These geographical circumstances therefore, thus corresponding with what is actually known of those countries at this time, should induce us to situate *Kadesh*, as I have already done, *one hundred and ten* miles to the northward of *Mount Sinai*, and *forty-two* miles to the westward of *Eloth*, near *Callah Nahur*, i. e., the castle of the river or fountain, (probably the Ain Mishpat,) a noted station of the *Mohammedans* in their pilgrimage to *Mecca*.

"From *Kadesh* the *Israelites* were ordered to turn into the *wilderness by the way of the Red Sea*, (Num. xiv. 25; Deut. i. 40,) i. e., they were at this time, in punishment of their murmurings, infidelity, and disobedience, to advance no farther northward towards the land of *Canaan*. Now, these marches are called *the compassing of Mount Seir*, Deut. ii. 1, and *the passing by from the children of Esau, which dwelt in Seir, through the way of the plain of Eloth and Ezion-gaber*, ver. 8. The wandering, therefore, of the children of *Israel*, during the space of thirty-eight years, (Deut. ii. 14,) was confined, in all probability to that neck of land only which lies bounded by the gulfs of *Eloth* and *Heroopolis*. If then we could adjust the true position of *Eloth*, we should gain one considerable point towards the better laying down and circumscribing this mountainous tract, where the *Israelites* wandered for so many years. Now, there is a universal consent among geographers that אילת *Eloth*, *Ailah*, or *Aelana*, as it is differently named, was situated upon the northern extremity of the gulf of that name. *Ptolemy*, indeed, places it *forty-five minutes* to the south of *Heroopolis*, and nearly *three degrees* to the east: whereas *Abulfeda*, whose later authority, and perhaps greater experience, should be more regarded, makes the extremities of the two gulfs to lie nearly in the same parallel, though without recording the distance between them. I have been often informed by the Mohammedan pilgrims, who, in their way to *Mecca*, pass by them both, that they direct their marches from Kairo eastward, till they arrive at *Callah Accaba*, or the castle (situated below the mountains) of *Accaba*, upon the *Elanitic* point of the *Red Sea*. Here they begin to travel betwixt the south and south-east, with their faces directly towards *Mecca*, which lay hitherto upon their right hand; having made in all, from *Adjeroute*, *ten* miles to the north north-west of *Suez*, to this castle, a journey of *seventy* hours. But as this whole tract is very mountainous, the road must consequently be attended with great variety of windings and turnings, which would hinder them from making any greater progress than at the rate, we will suppose, of about half a league an hour. *Eloth*, then, (which is the place of a *Turkish* garrison at present, as it was a *præsidium* of the *Romans* in former times,) will lie, according to this calculation, about *one hundred* and *forty* miles from *Adjeroute*, in an east by south direction; a position which will likewise *receive* farther confirmation from the distance that is assigned to it from *Gaza*, in the old geography. For, as this distance was *one hundred* and *fifty Roman* miles according to *Pliny*, or *one hundred* and *fifty-seven* according to other authors, *Eloth* could not have had a more southern situation than latitude *twenty-nine degrees, forty minutes*; neither could it have had a more northern latitude, insomuch as this would have so far invalidated a just observation of *Strabo's*, who makes *Heroopolis* and *Pelusium* to be much nearer each other than *Eloth* and *Gaza*. And, besides, as *Gaza* is well known to lie in latitude *thirty-one degrees, forty minutes*, (as we have placed *Eloth* in latitude *twenty-nine degrees, forty minutes*,) the difference of latitude betwixt them will be *two degrees* or one hundred and twenty geographical miles; which converted into Roman miles, (*seventy-five* and a *half* of which make one *degree*,) we have the very distance (especially as they lie nearly under the same meridian) that is ascribed to them above by *Strabo* and *Pliny*. Yet, notwithstanding this point may be gained, it would be too daring an attempt, even to pretend to trace out above two or three of the encampments mentioned Num. xxxiii., though the greatest part of them was in all probability confined to this tract of Arabia Petræa, which I have bounded to the east by the meridian of *Eloth*, and to the west by that of *Heroopolis*, Kadesh lying near or upon the skirts of it to the northward.

"However, one of their more southern stations, after they had left *Mount Sinai* and *Paran*, seems to have been at *Ezion-gaber*; which being the place from whence *Solomon's navy went for gold to Ophir* 1 Kings ix. 26, 2 Chron. viii. 17, we may be induced to take it for the present *Meenah el Dsahab*, i. e., *the port of gold*. According to the account I had of this place from the *monks of St. Catharine*, it lies in the gulf of *Eloth*, betwixt two and three days' journey from them,—enjoying a spacious harbour; from whence they are sometimes supplied, as I have already mentioned, with plenty of lobsters and shell fish. *Meenah el Dsahab* therefore, from this circumstance, may be nearly at the same distance from *Sinai* with *Tor*; from whence they are likewise furnished with the same provisions, which, unless they are brought with the utmost expedition, frequently corrupt and putrefy. I have already given the distance between the north-west part of the desert of *Sin* and *Mount Sinai*, to be *twenty-one* hours; and if we farther add *three* hours, (the distance betwixt the desert of *Sin* and the port of *Tor*, from whence these fish are obtained,) we shall have in all *twenty-four* hours; i. e., in round numbers, about *sixty* miles. *Ezion-gaber* consequently may lie a little more or less at that distance from *Sinai*; because the days' journeys which the monks speak of are not, perhaps, to be considered as ordinary and common ones; but such as are made in haste, that the fish may arrive in good condition.

"In the *description of the East*, p. 157, *Ezion-gaber* is placed to the south-east of *Eloth*, and at two or three miles only from it; which, I presume, cannot be admitted. For, as *Eloth* itself is situated upon the very point of the gulf, *Ezion-gaber*, by lying to the south-east of it would belong to the *land of Midian*; whereas *Ezion-gaber* was undoubtedly a sea-port in the *land of Edom*, as we learn from the authorities

above related, viz., where *King Solomon* is said to have *made a navy of ships in Ezion-gaber, which is* את אילות, *beside Eloth, on the shore of the Red Sea, in the land of Edom.* Here it may be observed that the word את which we render *beside Eloth,* should be rendered, *together with Eloth;* not denoting any vicinity between them, but that they were both of them *ports of the Red Sea, in the land of Edom.*

"From *Ezion-gaber* the *Israelites* turned back again to *Kadesh,* with an intent to direct their marches that way into the *land of Canaan.* But upon *Edom's* refusing to give *Israel passage through his border,* (Num. xx. 18,) *they turned away from him* to the right hand, as I suppose, toward *Mount Hor,* (Num. xx. 21,) which might lie to the eastward of *Kadesh,* in the road from thence to the *Red Sea;* and as *the soul of the children of Israel* is said to have been here *much discouraged because of the way,* it is very probable that *Mount Hor* was the same chain of mountains that are now called *Accaba* by the *Arabs,* and were the easternmost range, as we may take them to be, of Ptolemy's μελανα ορη above described. Here, from the badness of the road, and the many rugged passes that are to be surmounted, the *Mohammedan pilgrims* lose a number of camels, and are no less fatigued than the Israelites were formerly in getting over them. I have already hinted, that this chain of mountains, the μελανα ορη of Ptolemy, reached from *Paran* to *Judea. Petra,* therefore, according to its later name, the *metropolis* of this part of *Arabia,* may well be supposed to lie among them, and to have been left by the *Israelites* on their left hand, in journeying toward *Moab.* Yet it will be difficult to determine the situation of this city, for want of a sufficient number of geographical *data* to proceed upon. In the old geography, Petra is placed *one hundred and thirty-five miles* to the eastward of *Gaza,* and four days' journey from *Jericho,* to the southward. But neither of these distances can be any ways accounted for; the first being too great, the other too deficient. For, as we may well suppose Petra to lie near, or upon the borders of *Moab, seven days' journey* would be the least: the same that the three kings took hither, 2 Kings iii. 9, (by fetching a compass, as we may imagine,) from *Jerusalem,* which was nearer to that border than *Jericho.* However, at a *medium, Petra* lay in all probability about the half way between the south extremity of the *Asphaltic* lake, and the gulf of *Eloth,* and may be therefore fixed near the confines of the country of the *Midianites* and *Moabites* at *seventy* miles distance from *Kadesh,* towards the north-east; and *eighty-five* from *Gaza,* to the south. According to *Josephus,* it was formerly called *Arce,* which *Bochart* supposes to be a corruption of *Rekem,* the true and ancient name. The *Amalekites,* so frequently mentioned in Scripture, were once seated in the neighbourhood of this place, who were succeeded by the *Nabathæans,* a people no less famous in profane history. From Mount *Hor,* the direction of their marches through *Zalmona, Punon,* &c., seems to have been between the north and north-east. For it does not appear that they *wandered* any more *in the wilderness out of the direct way* that was to conduct them through the country of *Moab,* (Num. xxxiii. 35–49,) into the *land of promise.*"—SHAW'S *Travels,* chap. v., p. 304, &c.

A CHRONOLOGICAL TABLE

OF THE

PRINCIPAL EVENTS RECORDED IN THE BOOK OF EXODUS,

SHOWING IN WHAT YEAR OF THE WORLD, IN WHAT YEAR BEFORE CHRIST, IN WHAT YEAR FROM THE DELUGE, AND IN WHAT YEAR FROM THEIR DEPARTURE FROM EGYPT, EACH EVENT HAPPENED; INTERSPERSED WITH A FEW CONNECTING CIRCUMSTANCES FROM PROFANE HISTORY, ACCORDING TO THE PLAN OF ARCHBISHOP USHER.

A. M.	B. C.		An. Dil.
2365	1639	Levi, the third son of Jacob, dies in the 137th year of his age, chap. vi, 16.—N. B. *This event is placed twenty years later by most chronologists, but I have followed the computation of* Mr. Skinner *and* Dr. Kennicott. *See the note on* Gen. xxxi. 41.	709
2375	1629	*About this time* Acenchres, *son of* Orus, *began to reign in Egypt, and reigned* twelve years *and* one month.	719
2385	1619	*The* Ethiopians, *from the other side of the* Indus, *first settle in the middle of Egypt.*	729
2387	1617	Rathotis, *the brother of Acenchres, began about this time to reign over the Egyptians, and reigned* nine years.	731
2396	1608	Acencheres, *the son of* Rathotis, *succeeds his father and reigns* twelve years *and* six months.	740
2400	1604	About this time it is supposed the Egyptians began to be jealous of the Hebrews, on account of their prodigious multiplication.	744
2409	1595	Ancencheres *succeeds* Acencheres, *and reigns* twelve years *and* three months.	753
2421	1583	Armais *succeeds* Ancencheres, *and reigns* four years *and* one month.	765
——	——	About this time Kohath, the son of Levi, and grandfather of Moses, died in the 133d year of his age; chap. vi. 18.—N. B. *There are several years of uncertainty in the date of this event.*	——
2425	1579	Rameses *succeeds* Armais *in the government, and reigns* one year *and* four months.	769
2427	1577	Rameses Miamun *succeeds* Rameses, *and reigns* sixty-seven years.	771
2430	1574	Aaron, son of Amram, brother of Moses, born eighty-three years before the exodus of the Israelites; chap. vi. 20; vii. 7.	774
2431	1573	About this time Pharaoh (supposed to be the same with Rameses Miamun) published an edict, ordering all the male children of the Hebrews to be drowned in the Nile, chap. i. 22.	775
2433	1571	Moses, the Jewish lawgiver, born; chap. ii. 2.	777
2448	1556	*The kingdom of the Athenians founded about this time by Cecrops.*	792
2465	1539	*In this year, which was the eighteenth of Cecrops, the Chaldeans waged war with the Phœnicians.*	809
2466	1538	*About this time the Arabians subdued the Chaldeans, and took possession of their country.*	810
2473	1531	Moses, being forty years of age, kills an Egyptian, whom he found smiting a Hebrew; in consequence of which, being obliged to fly for his life, he escapes to the land of Midian, where becoming acquainted with the family of Jethro, he marries Zipporah; chap. ii. 11–22.	817
2474	1530	The birth of Caleb, the son of Jephunneh.	818
2494	1510	*Rameses Miamun, king of Egypt, dies about this time in the sixty-seventh year of his reign, and is succeeded by his son Amenophis, who reigns nineteen years and six months.*	838
2495	1509	The death of Amram, the father of Moses, is supposed to have taken place about this time.	839
2513	1491	While Moses keeps the flock of Jethro at Mount Horeb, the Angel of God appears to him in a burning bush, promises to deliver the Hebrews from their oppression in Egypt, and sends him to Pharaoh to command him to let Israel go; chap. iii.	857
		Aaron and Moses assemble the elders of Israel, inform them of the Divine purpose, and then go to Pharaoh and desire him, in the name of the God of the Hebrews, to let the people go three days' journey into the wilderness to hold a feast unto the Lord. Pharaoh is enraged, and increases the oppression of the Israelites; chap. v.	
		Aaron throws down his rod, which becomes a serpent. The Egyptian magicians imitate this miracle; chap. vii.	
		Pharaoh refusing to let the Israelites go, God sends his FIRST *plague* upon the Egyptians, and the *waters are turned into blood;* chap. vii. 19–25.	

A. M. B. C. An. Dil.

2513 1491 Pharaoh remaining impenitent, God sends immense numbers of *frogs*, which infest the whole land of Egypt. This was the SECOND *plague;* chap. viii. 1–7. 857

This plague not producing the desired effect, God sends the THIRD *plague*, the dust of the ground becoming *lice* on man and beast; chap. viii. 16–20.

Pharaoh's heart still remaining obdurate, God sends the FOURTH *plague* upon the nation, by causing great swarms of flies to cover the whole land; chap. viii. 20–32.

The Egyptian king still refusing to dismiss the Hebrews, God sends his FIFTH *plague*, which is a universal murrain or mortality among the cattle; chap. ix. 1–7.

This producing no good effect, the SIXTH *plague* of boils and blains is sent; chap. ix. 8–12.

Pharaoh still hardening his heart, God sends the SEVENTH *plague*, viz., a grievous hail which destroyed the whole produce of the field; chap. ix. 22–26.

This, through Pharaoh's obstinacy, proving ineffectual, the EIGHTH *plague* is sent, immense swarms of locusts, which devour the land; chap. x. 1–20.

Pharaoh refusing to submit to the Divine authority, the NINTH *plague*, a total darkness of three days' continuance, is spread over the whole land of Egypt; chap. x. 21–24.

Pharaoh continuing to refuse to let the people go, God institutes the rite of the passover, and sends the TENTH *plague* upon the Egyptians, and the first-born of man and beast died throughout the whole land. This was in the fourteenth night of the month *Abib*. The Israelites are driven out of Egypt, chap. xii. 1–36; and carry Joseph's bones with them; chap. xiii. 19.

An. Dil. An. Ex.

2513 1491 The Israelites march from Succoth to Etham; thence to Pi-hahiroth, the Lord guiding them by a miraculous pillar; chap. xiii. 20–22; xiv. 1, 2. 857 Isr. 1.

Towards the close of this month, Pharaoh and the Egyptians pursue the Israelites; God opens a passage for these through the Red Sea, and they pass over as on dry land, which the Egyptians essaying to do, are all drowned; chap. xiv; Heb. ix. 29. Abib.

The Israelites come to *Marah*, and murmur because of the bitter waters; Moses is directed to throw a certain tree into them, by which they are rendered sweet; chap. xv. 23–25.

About the beginning of this month the Israelites come to Elim; chap. xv. 27. Ijar or Zif.

On the fifteenth day of this month the Israelites come to the desert of *Sin*, where, murmuring for want of bread, quails are sent, and manna from heaven; chap. xvi.

Coming to Rephidim they murmur for want of water, and God supplies this want by miraculously bringing water out of a rock in Horeb, chap. xvii. 1–7.

The Amalekites attack the Israelites in Rephidim, and are discomfited; chap. xvii. 8–16.

The Israelites come to the wilderness of Sinai. God calls Moses up to the mount, where he receives the ten commandments and other precepts; chap. xix.–xxiv.: is instructed how to make the tabernacle; xxv.–xxviii Aaron and his sons are dedicated to the priest's office; chap. xxviii. Sivan.

Moses delaying to come down from the mount, the people make a molten calf, and worship it. Moses, coming down, sees their idolatry, is distressed, and breaks the tables; three thousand of the idolaters are slain; and, at the intercession of Moses, the rest of the people are saved from destruction; chap. xxxii. Ab.

Moses is again called up into the mount, where God renews the covenant, and writes the two tables afresh. Moses desires to see the Divine glory; his request is partially granted; chap. xxxiii. 18–23; xxxiv. 1–27.

Moses, after having been in the mount forty days and forty nights, during which time he ate nothing, comes down with the two tables of stone: his face shines so that he is obliged to cover it with a veil; chap. xxxiv. 29–35. Elul.

2514 1490 From this time to the month *Adar*, including *Marcheshvan, Cisleu, Thebet*, and *Sebat*, Bezaleel, Aholiab, and their assistants are employed in constructing the tabernacle, &c., according to the pattern delivered to Moses on the mount; chap. xxxvi.–xxxix. 858 Tisri

On the first of this month, being the first month of the second year after their

A. M. B. C. An. Dil. An. Ex.

departure from Egypt, the tabernacle is reared up, and Aaron and his sons set apart for the priest's office; chap. xl. 17–32.—N. B. *The ceremonies attending this consecration form the chief part of the following book,* Leviticus. 858 Isr. 2. Abib or Nisan

2514 1490 Jethro brings Zipporah and her two sons to Moses in the wilderness, and gives him wholesome directions concerning the best mode of governing the people, which Moses thankfully accepts, and God approves; chap. xviii., and see the notes there. Ijar or Zif

---

A TABLE of the THREE GREAT EPOCHS, A. M., B. C., and the JULIAN PERIOD, synchronized with the reigns of the sovereigns of the four principal monarchies; viz., Egypt, Sicyon, the Argivi, and the Athenians, from the death of Jacob, A. M. 2315, to the erection of the tabernacle, A. M. 2514, by which any event in the preceding *Chronological Table* may be referred to its corresponding year of the reign of any of the above sovereigns.

E. G. To find out the year of the birth of Moses, inspect the preceding table, by which it appears he was born A. M. 2433, B. C. 1571, and from the Deluge 777. Then look in the following table for A. M. 2433, where it appears that this event took place in the year of the *Julian Period* 3143—the 7th of *Rameses Miamun*, king of *Egypt*—the 46th of *Orthopolis*, king of *Sicyon*—the 17th of *Phorbas*, king of the *Argivi*—and the 15th *before* the reign of *Cecrops*, king of the *Athenians*.

A. M.	B. C.	Julian Period.	Kings of Egypt.	Kings of Sicyon.	Kings of the Argivi.	Kingdom of the Athenians.	A. M.	B. C.	Julian Period.	Kings of Egypt	Kings of Sicyon.	Kings of the Argivi.	Kingdom of the Athenians.
2315	1689	3025	6 Amenophis.	22 Prœtus.	23 Argus.	133 Before the foundation of this kingdom.	2356	1648	3066	17 Orus.	17 Plemnæus.	64 Argus.	92 Before the foundation of this kingdom.
2316	1688	3026	7	23	24	132	2357	1647	3067	18	18	65	91
2317	1687	3027	8	24	25	131	2358	1646	3068	19	19	66	90
2318	1686	3028	9	25	26	130	2359	1645	3069	20	20	67	89
2319	1685	3029	10	26	27	129	2360	1644	3070	21	21	68	88
2320	1684	3030	11	27	28	128	2361	1643	3071	22	22	69	87
2321	1683	3031	12	28	29	127	2362	1642	3072	23	23	70	86
2322	1682	3032	13	29	30	126	2363	1641	3073	24	24	1 Criasus.	85
2323	1681	3033	14	30	31	125	2364	1640	3074	25	25	2	84
2324	1680	3034	15	31	32	124	2365	1639	3075	26	26	3	83
2325	1679	3035	16	32	33	123	2366	1638	3076	27	27	4	82
2326	1678	3036	17	33	34	122	2367	1637	3077	28	28	5	81
2327	1677	3037	18	34	35	121	2368	1636	3078	29	29	6	80
2328	1676	3038	19	35	36	120	2369	1635	3079	30	30	7	79
2329	1675	3039	20	36	37	119	2370	1634	3080	31	31	8	78
2330	1674	3040	21	37	38	118	2371	1633	3081	32	32	9	77
2331	1673	3041	22	38	39	117	2372	1632	3082	33	33	10	76
2332	1672	3042	23	39	40	116	2373	1631	3083	34	34	11	75
2333	1671	3043	24	40	41	115	2374	1630	3084	35	35	12	74
2334	1670	3044	25	41	42	114	2375	1629	3085	36	36	13	73
2335	1669	3045	26	42	43	113	2376	1628	3086	1 Acenchres.	37	14	72
2336	1668	3046	27	43	44	112	2377	1627	3087	2	38	15	71
2337	1667	3047	28	44	45	111	2378	1626	3088	3	39	16	70
2338	1666	3048	29	45	46	110	2379	1625	3089	4	40	17	69
2339	1665	3049	30	46	47	109	2380	1624	3090	5	41	18	68
2340	1664	3050	1 Orus.	1 Plemnæus.	48	108	2381	1623	3091	6	42	19	67
2341	1663	3051	2	2	49	107	2382	1622	3092	7	43	20	66
2342	1662	3052	3	3	50	106	2383	1621	3093	8	44	21	65
2343	1661	3053	4	4	51	105	2384	1620	3094	9	45	22	64
2344	1660	3054	5	5	52	104	2385	1619	3095	10	46	23	63
2345	1659	3055	6	6	53	103	2386	1618	3096	11	47	24	62
2346	1658	3056	7	7	54	102	2387	1617	3097	12	48	25	61
2347	1657	3057	8	8	55	101	2388	1616	3098	1 Rathotis.	1 Orthopolis.	26	60
2348	1656	3058	9	9	56	100	2389	1615	3099	2	2	27	59
2349	1655	3059	10	10	57	99	2390	1614	3100	3	3	28	58
2350	1654	3060	11	11	58	98	2391	1613	3101	4	4	29	57
2351	1653	3061	12	12	59	97	2392	1612	3102	5	5	30	56
2352	1652	3062	13	13	60	96	2393	1611	3103	6	6	31	55
2353	1651	3063	14	14	61	95	2394	1610	3104	7	7	32	54
2354	1650	3064	15	15	62	94	2395	1609	3105	8	8	33	53
2355	1649	3065	16	16	63	93	2396	1608	3106	9	9	34	52

CHRONOLOGY OF ANCIENT KINGDOMS.

A. M.	B. C.	Julian Period.	Kings of Egypt.	Kings of Sicyon.	Kings of the Argivi.	Kingdom of the Athenians.	A. M.	B. C.	Julian Period.	Kings of Egypt.	Kings of Sicyon.	Kings of the Argivi.	Kingdom of the Athenians.
2397	1607	3107	1 Acencheres.	10 Orthopolis.	35 Criasus.	51 Before the foundation of this kingdom.	2456	1548	3166	30 Rameses Miamun.	7 Marathon.	5 Triopas.	9 Cecrops, the first monarch.
2398	1606	3108	2	11	36	50	2457	1547	3167	31	8	6	10
2399	1605	3109	3	12	37	49	2458	1546	3168	32	9	7	11
2400	1604	3110	4	13	38	48	2459	1545	3169	33	10	8	12
2401	1603	3111	5	14	39	47	2460	1544	3170	34	11	9	13
2402	1602	3112	6	15	40	46	2461	1543	3171	35	12	10	14
2403	1601	3113	7	16	41	45	2462	1542	3172	36	13	11	15
2404	1600	3114	8	17	42	44	2463	1541	3173	37	14	12	16
2405	1599	3115	9	18	43	43	2464	1540	3174	38	15	13	17
2406	1598	3116	10	19	44	42	2465	1539	3175	39	16	14	18
2407	1597	3117	11	20	45	41	2466	1538	3176	40	17	15	19
2408	1596	3118	12	21	46	40	2467	1537	3177	41	18	16	20
2409	1595	3119	1 Acencheres.	22	47	39	2468	1536	3178	42	19	17	21
2410	1594	3120	2	23	48	38	2469	1535	3179	43	20	18	22
2411	1593	3121	3	24	49	37	2470	1534	3180	44	21	19	23
2412	1592	3122	4	25	50	36	2471	1533	3181	45	22	20	24
2413	1591	3123	5	26	51	35	2472	1532	3182	46	23	21	25
2414	1590	3124	6	27	52	34	2473	1531	3183	47	24	22	26
2415	1589	3125	7	28	53	33	2474	1530	3184	48	25	23	27
2416	1588	3126	8	29	54	32	2475	1529	3185	49	26	24	28
2417	1587	3127	9	30	1 Phorbas.	31	2476	1528	3186	50	27	25	29
2418	1586	3128	10	31	2	30	2477	1527	3187	51	28	26	30
2419	1585	3129	11	32	3	29	2478	1526	3188	52	29	27	31
2420	1584	3130	12	33	4	28	2479	1525	3189	53	30	28	32
2421	1583	3131	1 Armais.	34	5	27	2480	1524	3190	54	1 Marathus.	29	33
2422	1582	3132	2	35	6	26	2481	1523	3191	55	2	30	34
2423	1581	3133	3	36	7	25	2482	1522	3192	56	3	31	35
2424	1580	3134	4	37	8	24	2483	1521	3193	57	4	32	36
2425	1579	3135	5	38	9	23	2484	1520	3194	58	5	33	37
2426	1578	3136	1 Rameses.	39	10	22	2485	1519	3195	59	6	34	38
2427	1577	3137	1 Rameses Miamun.	40	11	21	2486	1518	3196	60	7	35	39
2428	1576	3138	2	41	12	20	2487	1517	3197	61	8	36	40
2429	1575	3139	3	42	13	19	2488	1516	3198	62	9	37	41
2430	1574	3140	4	43	14	18	2489	1515	3199	63	10	38	42
2431	1573	3141	5	44	15	17	2490	1514	3200	64	11	39	43
2432	1572	3142	6	45	16	16	2491	1513	3201	65	12	40	44
2433	1571	3143	7	46	17	15	2492	1512	3202	66	13	41	45
2434	1570	3144	8	47	18	14	2493	1511	3203	67	14	42	46
2435	1569	3145	9	48	19	13	2494	1510	3204	1 Amenophis II.	15	43	47
2436	1568	3146	10	49	20	12	2495	1509	3205	2	16	44	48
2437	1567	3147	11	50	21	11	2496	1508	3206	3	17	45	49
2438	1566	3148	12	51	22	10	2497	1507	3207	4	18	46	50
2439	1565	3149	13	52	23	9	2498	1506	3208	5	19	1 Crotopus.	1 Cranaus.
2440	1564	3150	14	53	24	8	2499	1505	3209	6	20	2	2
2441	1563	3151	15	54	25	7	2500	1504	3210	7	1 Echyteus.	3	3
2442	1562	3152	16	55	26	6	2501	1503	3211	8	2	4	4
2443	1561	3153	17	56	27	5	2502	1502	3212	9	3	5	5
2444	1560	3154	18	57	28	4	2503	1501	3213	10	4	6	6
2445	1559	3155	19	58	29	3	2504	1500	3214	11	5	7	7
2446	1558	3156	20	59	30	2	2505	1499	3215	12	6	8	8
2447	1557	3157	21	60	31	1	2506	1498	3216	13	7	9	9
2448	1556	3158	22	61	32	1 Cecrops, the first monarch.	2507	1497	3217	14	8	10	10
2449	1555	3159	23	62	33	2	2508	1496	3218	15	9	11	1 Amphyction.
2450	1554	3160	24	1 Marathon.	34	3	2509	1495	3219	16	10	12	2
2451	1553	3161	25	2	35	4	2510	1494	3220	17	11	13	3
2452	1552	3162	26	3	1 Triopas.	5	2511	1493	3221	18	12	14	4
2453	1551	3163	27	4	2	6	2512	1492	3222	19	13	15	5
2454	1550	3164	28	5	3	7	2513	1491	3223	20	14	16	6
2455	1549	3165	29	6	4	8	2514	1490	3224		15	17	7

PREFACE TO THE BOOK

OF THE

LEVITICUS.

THE Greek version of the SEPTUAGINT, and the VULGATE *Latin*, have given the title of LEVITICUS to the third book of the Pentateuch, and the name has been retained in almost all the modern versions. The book was thus called because it treats principally of the laws and regulations of the *Levites* and priests in general. In Hebrew it is termed ויקרא *Vaiyikra,* "And he called," which is the *first* word in the book, and which, as in preceding cases, became the running title to the whole. It contains an account of the ceremonies to be observed in the offering of burnt-sacrifices; meat, peace, and sin-offerings; the consecration of priests, together with the institution of the three grand national festivals of the Jews, the PASSOVER, PENTECOST, and TABERNACLES, with a great variety of other ecclesiastical matters. It seems to contain little more than the history of what passed during the *eight days* of the consecration of Aaron and his sons, though Archbishop Usher supposes that it comprises the history of the transactions of a whole month, viz., from *April* 21 to *May* 21, of the year of the world 2514, which answers to the *first* month of the *second* year after the departure from Egypt. As there are no *data* by which any chronological arrangement of the facts mentioned in it can be made, it would be useless to encumber the page with conjectures which, because *uncertain,* can answer no end to the serious reader for doctrine, reproof, or edification in righteousness. As the *law was our schoolmaster unto Christ,* the whole sacrificial system was intended to point out that *Lamb of God,* Christ Jesus, *who takes away the sin of the world.* In reading over *this* book, *this* point should be kept particularly in view, as without *this* spiritual reference no interest can be excited by a perusal of the work.

The principal events recorded in this book may be thus deduced in the order of the chapters:

Moses having set up the tabernacle, as has been related in the conclusion of the preceding book; and the cloud of the Divine glory, the symbol of the presence of God, having rested upon it; God called to him out of this tabernacle, and delivered the laws and precepts contained in the seven first chapters.

In chap. i. he prescribes every thing relative to the nature and quality of *burnt offerings,* and the ceremonies which should be observed, as well by the person who brought the sacrifice as by the priest who offered it.

In chap. ii. he treats of *meat-offerings* of fine flour with oil and frankincense; of cakes, and the oblations of first-fruits.

Chap. iii. treats of *peace-offerings,* prescribes the ceremonies to be used in such offerings, and the parts which should be consumed by fire.

Chap. iv. treats of the offerings made for *sins of ignorance;* for the sins of the *priests, rulers,* and of the *common people.*

Chap. v. treats of the sin of him who, being adjured as a *witness,* conceals his knowledge of a fact; the case of him who touches an *unclean thing;* of him who binds himself by a *vow* or an *oath;* and of *trespass-offerings* in cases of *sacrilege,* and in *sins of ignorance.*

Chap. vi. treats of the *trespass-offerings* for sins *knowingly* committed; and of the offerings for the priests, the parts which should be consumed, and the parts which should be considered as the priests' portion. And in

Chap. vii. the same subject is continued.

Chap. viii. treats of the *consecration* of *Aaron and his sons;* their sin-offering; burnt-offering; ram of consecration; and the time during which these solemn rites should continue.

Chap. ix. After Aaron and his sons were consecrated, on the *eighth* day they were commanded to offer sin-offerings and burnt-offerings for *themselves* and for the *people*, which they accordingly did, and Aaron and Moses having blessed the people, a fire came forth from before the Lord, and consumed the offering that was laid upon the altar.

Chap. x. Nadab and Abihu, the sons of Aaron, having offered *strange fire* before the Lord, are consumed; and the priests are forbidden the use of wine and all inebriating liquors.

Chap. xi. treats of *clean* and *unclean* beasts, fishes, birds, and reptiles.

Chap. xii. treats of the purification of women after child-birth, and the offerings they should present before the Lord.

Chap. xiii. prescribes the manner of discerning the infection of the *leprosy* in persons, garments, and houses.

Chap. xiv. prescribes the sacrifices and ceremonies which should be offered by those who were cleansed from the leprosy.

Chap. xv. treats of certain uncleannesses in man and woman; and of their purifications.

Chap. xvi. treats of the solemn yearly expiation to be made for the sins of the priest and of the people, of the goat and bullock for a sacrifice, and of the *scape-goat;* all which should be offered annually on the *tenth* day of the *seventh* month.

Chap. xvii. The Israelites are commanded to offer all their sacrifices at the tabernacle; the eating of *blood* is prohibited, as also the flesh of those animals which die of themselves, and of those that are torn by dogs.

Chap. xviii. shows the different degrees within which *marriages* were not to be contracted, and prohibits various acts of impurity.

Chap. xix. recapitulates a variety of laws which had been mentioned in the preceding book, (Exodus,) and adds several new ones.

Chap. xx. prohibits the consecration of their children to *Molech*, forbids their consulting *wizards* and those which had *familiar spirits*, and also a variety of incestuous and unnatural mixtures.

Chap. xxi. gives different ordinances concerning the *mourning* and *marriages* of *priests*, and prohibits those from the sacerdotal office who have certain *personal defects*.

Chap. xxii. treats of those infirmities and uncleannesses which rendered the priests unfit to officiate in sacred things, and lays down directions for the perfection of the sacrifices which should be offered to the Lord.

Chap. xxiii. treats of the *Sabbath* and the great *annual festivals*—the *passover*, *pentecost*, *feast of trumpets*, *day of atonement*, and *feast of tabernacles*.

Chap. xxiv. treats of the *oil* for the *lamps*, and the *shew-bread;* the law concerning which had already been given, see Exod. xxv., &c.; mentions the case of the person who *blasphemed* God, and his punishment; lays down the law in cases of *blasphemy* and *murder;* and recapitulates the *lex talionis*, or law of *like for like*, prescribed Exod. xxi.

Chap. xxv. recapitulates the law, given Exod. xxiii., relative to the *Sabbatical year;* prescribes the year of *jubilee;* and lays down a variety of statutes relative to *mercy*, *kindness*, *benevolence*, *charity*, &c.

Chap. xxvi. prohibits idolatry, promises a great variety of blessings to the obedient, and threatens the disobedient with many and grievous curses.

Chap. xxvii. treats of *vows*, of things *devoted*, and of the *tithes* which should be given for the service of the tabernacle.

No *Chronological Table* can be affixed to this book, as the transactions of it seem to have been included within the space of *eight days*, or of a month at the utmost, as we have already seen. And even some of the facts related here seem to have taken place previously to the erection of the tabernacle; nor is the order in which the others occurred so distinguished as to enable us to lay down the *precise days* in which they took place.

THE THIRD BOOK OF MOSES,

CALLED

LEVITICUS.

Year before the common Year of Christ, 1490.—Julian Period, 3224.—Cycle of the Sun, 27.—Dominical Letter, D.—Cycle of the Moon, 9.—Indiction, 6.—Creation from Tisri or September, 2514.

CHAPTER I.

The Lord calls to Moses out of the tabernacle, and gives him directions concerning burnt-offerings *of the* beeve *kind*, 1, 2. *The burnt-offering to be a* male *without blemish*, 3. *The person bringing it to lay his hands upon its head, that it might be accepted for him*, 4. *He is to kill, flay, and cut it in pieces, and bring the blood to the priests, that they might sprinkle it round about the altar*, 5, 6. *All the pieces to be laid upon the altar and burnt*, 7–9. *Directions concerning offerings of the* SMALLER CATTLE, *such as* sheep *and* goats, 10–13. *Directions concerning offerings of* FOWLS, *such as* doves *and* pigeons, 14–17.

A. M. 2514. B. C. 1490. An. Exod. Isr. 2. Abib or Nisan.

AND the LORD [a] called unto
Moses, and spake unto him
[b] out of the tabernacle of the
congregation, saying,

2 Speak unto the children of
Israel, and say unto them, [c] If
any man of you bring an offer-
ing unto the LORD, ye shall bring your offer-

[a] Exod. xix. 3.—[b] Exod. xl. 34, 35; Num. xii. 4, 5.

[c] Chap. xxii. 18, 19.

NOTES ON CHAP. I.

Verse 1. *And the Lord called unto Moses*] From the manner in which this book commences, it appears plainly to be a continuation of the preceding; and indeed the whole is but *one law*, though divided into *five* portions, and why thus divided is not easy to be conjectured.

Previously to the erection of the tabernacle God had given no particular directions concerning the manner of offering the different kinds of sacrifices; but as soon as this Divine structure was established and consecrated, Jehovah took it as his dwelling place; described the rites and ceremonies which he would have observed in his worship, that his people might know what was best pleasing in his sight; and that, when thus worshipping him, they might have confidence that they pleased him, every thing being done according to his own directions. A consciousness of acting according to the revealed will of God gives strong confidence to an upright mind.

Verse 2. *Bring an offering*] The word קרבן *korban*, from קרב *karab*, to *approach* or *draw near*, signifies an *offering* or *gift* by which a person had access unto God: and this receives light from the universal custom that prevails in the east, no man being permitted to approach the presence of a superior without a *present* or *gift*; and the offering thus brought was called *korban*, which properly means the *introduction-offering*, or *offering* of *access*. This custom has been often referred to in the preceding books. See also chap. vii.

Of the cattle] הבהמה *habbehemah*, animals of the *beeve* kind, such as the *bull*, *heifer*, *bullock*, and *calf*; and restrained to these alone by the term *herd*, בקר *bakar*, which, from its general use in the Levitical writings, is known to refer to the *ox*, *heifer*, &c. And therefore other animals of the *beeve* kind were excluded.

Of the flock] צאן *tson*, SHEEP and GOATS; for we have already seen that this term implies both kinds; and we know, from its use, that no other animal of the *smaller* clean domestic quadrupeds is intended, as no other animal of this class, besides the *sheep* and *goat*, was ever offered in sacrifice to God. The animals mentioned in this chapter as proper for sacrifice are the very same which God commanded Abraham to offer; see Gen. xv. 9. And thus it is evident that God delivered to the patriarchs an epitome of that law which was afterwards given in detail to Moses, the essence of which consisted in its *sacrifices;* and those sacrifices were of clean animals, the most perfect, useful, and healthy, of all that are brought under the immediate government and influence of man. Gross-feeding and ferocious animals were all excluded, as were also all birds of *prey*. In the pagan worship it was widely different; for although the ox was esteemed among them, according to *Livy*, as the *major hostia;* and according to *Pliny*, the *victima optima, et laudatis-*

A. M. 2514.
B. C. 1490.
An. Exod. Isr. 2.
Abib or Nisan.

ing of the cattle, *even* of the
herd, and of the flock.
3 If his offering *be* a burnt-
sacrifice of the herd, let him offer a male
[d] without blemish: he shall offer it of his
own voluntary will at the door of the tabernacle
of the congregation before the LORD.
4 [e] And he shall put his hand upon the head
of the burnt-offering; and it shall be [f] accepted
for him [g] to make atonement for him.
5 And he shall kill the [h] bullock before the
LORD: [i] and the priests, Aaron's
sons, shall bring the blood, [k] and
sprinkle the blood round about
upon the altar that *is by* the door of the taber
nacle of the congregation.
6 And he shall flay the burnt-offering, and
cut it into his pieces.
7 And the sons of Aaron the priest shall
put fire upon the altar, and [l] lay the wood in
order upon the fire.
8 And the priests, Aaron's sons, shall lay

A. M. 2514.
B. C. 1490.
An. Exod. Isr. 2
Abib or Nisan.

[d] Exod. xii. 5; chap. iii. 1; xxii. 20, 21; Deut. xv. 21; Mal. i. 14; Eph. v. 27; Heb. ix. 14; 1 Pet. i. 19.——[e] Chap. iv. 15; iii. 2, 8, 13; viii. 14, 22; xvi. 21; Exodus xxix. 10, 15, 19. [f] Chap. xxii. 21, 27; Isa. lvi. 7; Rom. xii. 1; Phil. iv. 18.

[g] Chap. iv. 20, 26, 31, 35; ix. 7; xvi. 24; Num. xv. 25, 2 Chron. xxix. 23, 24; Rom. v. 11.——[h] Mic. vi. 6.——[i] 2 Chron xxxv. 11; Heb. x. 11.——[k] Chap. iii. 8; Heb. xii. 24; 1 Pet i. 2.——[l] Gen. xxii. 9.

sima deorum placatio, Plin. Hist. Nat., lib. viii., c. 45, "the chief sacrifice and the most availing offering which could be made to the gods;" yet obscene fowls and ravenous beasts, according to the nature of their deities, were frequently offered in sacrifice. Thus they sacrificed *horses* to the SUN, *wolves* to MARS, *asses* to PRIAPUS, *swine* to CERES, *dogs* to HECATE, &c., &c. But in the worship of God all these were declared *unclean*, and only the three following kinds of QUADRUPEDS were commanded to be sacrificed: 1. The *bull* or *ox*, the *cow* or *heifer*, and the *calf*. 2. The *he-goat*, *she-goat*, and the *kid*. 3. The *ram*, the *ewe*, and the *lamb*. Among FOWLS, only *pigeons* and *turtle-doves* were commanded to be offered, except in the case of cleansing the leper, mentioned chap. xiv. 4, where two clean birds, generally supposed to be *sparrows* or other small birds, though of what species is not well known, are specified. *Fish* were not offered, because they could not be readily brought to the tabernacle *alive*.

Verse 3. *Burnt-sacrifice*] The most important of all the sacrifices offered to God; called by the Septuagint ὁλοκαυτωμα, because it was *wholly consumed*, which was not the case in any other offering. See on chap. vii.

His own voluntary will] לרצנו *lirtsono, to gain himself acceptance* before the Lord: in this way all the versions appear to have understood the original words, and the connection in which they stand obviously requires this meaning.

Verse 4. *He shall put his hand upon the head of the burnt-offering*] By the imposition of hands the person bringing the victim acknowledged, 1. The sacrifice as his own. 2. That he offered it as an atonement for his sins. 3. That he was worthy of death because he *had* sinned, having forfeited his life by breaking the law. 4. That he entreated God to accept the *life* of the innocent animal in place of his own. 5. And all this, to be done profitably, must have respect to HIM whose life, in the fulness of time, should be made a sacrifice for sin. 6. The *blood* was to be *sprinkled round about upon the altar*, ver. 5, as by the sprinkling of blood the atonement was made; for the blood was the *life* of the beast, and it was always supposed that *life* went to redeem *life*. See note on Exod. xxix. 10. On the required perfection of the sacrifice see the note on Exod. xii. 5.

It has been sufficiently remarked by learned men that almost all the people of the earth had their *burnt-offerings*, on which also they placed the greatest dependence. It was a general maxim through the heathen world, that there was no other way to appease the incensed gods; and they sometimes even offered human sacrifices, from the supposition, as Cæsar expresses it, that life was necessary to redeem life, and that the gods would be satisfied with nothing less. "Quod pro vita hominis nisi vita hominis redditur, non posse aliter deorum immortalium numen placari arbitrantur."—Com. de Bell. Gal., lib. vi. But this was not the case only with the Gauls, for we see, by Ovid, *Fast.*, lib. vi., that it was a commonly received maxim among more polished people:—

"——Pro parvo victima parva cadit.
Cor pro corde, precor, pro fibris sumite fibras.
Hanc animam vobis pro meliore damus."

See the whole of this passage in the above work, from ver. 135 to 163.

Verse 6. *He shall flay*] Probably meaning the *person who brought the sacrifice*, who, according to some of the rabbins, killed, flayed, cut up, and washed the sacrifice, and then presented the parts and the blood to the priest, that he might burn the one, and sprinkle the other upon the altar. But it is certain that the priests also, and the Levites, flayed the victims, and the priest had the skin to himself; see chap. vii. 8, and 2 Chron. xxix. 34. The red heifer alone was not flayed, but the whole body, with the skin, &c., consumed with fire. See Num. xix. 5.

Verse 7. *Put fire*] The fire that came out of the tabernacle from before the Lord, and which was kept perpetually burning; see chap. ix. 24. Nor was it lawful to use any other fire in the service of God. See the case of Nadab and Abihu, chap. x.

Verse 8. *The priests—shall lay the parts*] The sacrifice was divided according to its larger joints. 1. After its blood was poured out, and the skin removed, the head was cut off. 2. They then opened it and took out the omentum, or caul, that invests the intestines. 3. They took out the intestines with the mesentery, and washed them well, as also the fat. 4. They then placed the four quarters upon the altar, covered them with the fat, laid the remains of the in-

A. M. 2514.
B. C. 1490.
An. Exod. Isr. 2.
Abib or Nisan.

the parts, the head, and the fat,
in order upon the wood that *is*
on the fire which *is* upon the altar.
9 But his inwards and his legs shall he
wash in water: and the priest shall burn all on
the altar, to *be* a burnt-sacrifice, an offering
made by fire, of a [m] sweet savour unto the
LORD.
10 And if his offering *be* of the flocks,
namely, of the sheep, or of the goats, for a
burnt-sacrifice; he shall bring it a male [n] without blemish.
11 [o] And he shall kill it on the side of the
altar northward before the LORD: and the
priests, Aaron's sons, shall sprinkle his blood
round about upon the altar:
12 And he shall cut it into his pieces, with
his head and his fat: and the priest shall lay
them in order on the wood that *is* on the fire
which *is* upon the altar.
13 But he shall wash the inwards and the
legs with water: and the priest
shall bring *it* all, and burn *it* upon
the altar: it *is* a burnt-sacrifice,
an offering made by fire, of a sweet savour
unto the LORD.

A. M. 2514.
B. C. 1490.
An. Exod. Isr. 2.
Abib or Nisan.

14 And if the burnt-sacrifice for his offering
to the LORD *be* of fowls, then he shall bring his
offering of [p] turtle-doves, or of young pigeons.
15 And the priests shall bring it unto the
altar, and [q] wring off his head, and burn *it* on
the altar; and the blood thereof shall be wrung
out at the side of the altar.
16 And he shall pluck away his crop with
[r] his feathers, and cast it [s] beside the altar on
the east part, by the place of the ashes.
17 And he shall cleave it with the wings
thereof, *but* [t] shall not divide *it* asunder: and
the priests shall burn it upon the altar, upon
the wood that *is* upon the fire: [u] it *is* a burnt-
sacrifice, an offering made by fire, of a sweet
savour unto the LORD.

[m] Gen. viii. 21; Ezek. xx. 28, 41; 2 Cor. ii. 15; Eph. v. 2; Phil. iv. 18.——[n] Ver. 3.——[o] Ver. 5.——[p] Chap. v. 7; xii. 8; Luke ii. 24.——[q] Or, *pinch off the head with the nail.*——[r] Or, the *filth thereof.*——[s] Chap. vi. 10.——[t] Gen. xv. 10.——[u] Ver. 9, 13.

testines upon them, and then laid the head above all. 5. The sacred fire was then applied, and the whole mass was consumed. This was the *holocaust*, or complete burnt-offering.

Verse 9. *An offering—of a sweet savour*] אשה ריח ניחוח *ishsheh reiach nichoach*, a *fire-offering*, an *odour of rest*, or, as the Septuagint express it, *θυσια οσμη ευωδιας*, "a sacrifice for a sweet-smelling savour;" which place St. Paul had evidently in view when he wrote Eph. v. 2: "Christ hath loved us, and hath given himself for us an *offering*, *και θυσιαν—εις οσμην ευωδιας*, *and a sacrifice, for a sweet-smelling savour*;" where he uses the same terms as the Septuagint. Hence we find that the *holocaust*, or *burnt-offering*, typified the sacrifice and death of Christ for the sins of the world.

Verse 10. *His offering* be *of the flocks*] See on ver. 2.

Verse 12. *Cut it into his pieces*] See the notes on Gen. xv.

Verse 16. *Pluck away his crop with his feathers*] In this sacrifice of fowls the head was violently wrung off, then the blood was poured out, then the feathers were plucked off, the breast was cut open, and the crop, stomach, and intestines taken out, and then the body was burnt. Though the bird was split up, yet it was not divided asunder. This circumstance is particularly remarked in Abram's sacrifice, Gen. xv. 10. See the notes there.—See *Ainsworth*.

WE have already seen, on ver. 2, that *four* kinds of animals might be made burnt-offerings to the Lord. 1. *Neat cattle*, such as bulls, oxen, cows, and calves. 2. He-goats, she-goats, and kids. 3. Rams, ewes, and lambs. 4. Pigeons and turtle-doves; and in one case, viz., the cleansing of the leper, *sparrows* or some small bird. All these must be without spot or blemish—the most perfect of their respective kinds, and be wholly consumed by fire. The RICH were to bring the most *costly*; the POOR, those of *least price*. Even in this requisition of *justice* how much *mercy* was mingled! If a man could not bring a *bullock* or a *heifer*, a *goat* or a *sheep*, let him bring a *calf*, a *kid*, or a *lamb*. If he could not bring any of these because of his *poverty*, let him bring a *turtle-dove*, or a *young pigeon*, (see chap. v. 7;) and it appears that in cases of extreme poverty, even a *little meal* or *fine flour* was accepted by the bountiful Lord as a sufficient oblation; see chap. v. 11. This brought down the benefits of the sacrificial service within the reach of the poorest of the poor; as we may take for granted that every person, however low in his circumstances, might be able to provide the tenth part of an ephah, about three quarts of meal, to make an offering for his soul unto the Lord. But every man must bring *something*; the law stooped to the lowest circumstances of the poorest of the people, but every man must *sacrifice*, because every man had *sinned*. Reader, what sort of a sacrifice dost thou bring to God? To Him thou owest thy whole body, soul, and substance; are all these consecrated to his service? Or has he the refuse of thy time, and the offal of thy estate? God requires thee to sacrifice as his providence has blessed thee. If thou have much, thou shouldst give *liberally* to God and the poor; if thou have but little, *do thy diligence to give of that little*. God's *justice* requires a measure of that which his *mercy* has bestowed. But remember that as thou hast *sinned*, thou needest a *Saviour*. Jesus is that lamb without spot which has been offered to God for the sin of the world, and which thou must offer to him for thy sin; and it is only

through Him that thou canst be accepted, even when thou dedicatest thy whole body, soul, and substance to thy Maker. Even when we present ourselves a living sacrifice to God, we are accepted for *his sake* who carried our sins, and bore our sorrows. Thanks be to God, the rich and the poor have equal access unto him through the Son of his love, and equal right to claim the benefits of the great sacrifice!

CHAPTER II.

The meat-offering *of* flour *with* oil *and* incense, 1–3. *The* oblation *of the meat-offering baked in the* oven *and in the* pan, 4–6. *The meat-offering baked in the* frying-pan, 7–10. *No* leaven *nor* honey *to be offered with the meat-offering*, 11. *The oblation of the* first-fruits, 12. Salt *to be offered with the meat-offering*, 13. Green ears *dried by the fire, and corn to be beaten out of full ears, with oil and frankincense, to be offered as a meat-offering of first-fruits*, 14–16.

A. M. 2514.
B. C. 1490.
An. Exod. Isr. 2.
Abib or Nisan.

AND when any will offer [a] a meat-offering unto the LORD, his offering shall be *of* fine flour; and he shall pour oil upon it, and put frankincense thereon:

[a] Chap. vi. 14; ix. 17; Num. xv. 4.

NOTES ON CHAP. II.

Verse 1. *Meat-offering*]. מנחה *minchah.* For an explanation of this word see the note on Gen. iv. 3, and Lev. vii. Calmet has remarked that there are *five* kinds of the *minchah* mentioned in this chapter. 1. סלת *soleth*, simple *flour* or *meal*, ver. 1. 2. *Cakes* and *wafers*, or whatever was baked in the *oven*, ver. 4. 3. *Cakes* baked in the *pan*, ver. 5. 4. *Cakes* baked on the *frying-pan*, or probably a *gridiron*, verse 7. 5. *Green ears* of corn parched, ver. 14. All these were offered without *honey* or *leaven*, but accompanied with *wine*, *oil*, and *frankincense*. It is very likely that the *minchah*, in some or all of the above forms, was the earliest oblation offered to the Supreme Being, and probably was in use *before* sin entered into the world, and consequently before *bloody sacrifices*, or *piacular victims*, had been ordained. The *minchah* of *green ears* of corn dried by the fire, &c., was properly the *gratitude-offering* for a good *seed time*, and the prospect of a plentiful *harvest*. This appears to have been the offering brought by Cain, Gen. iv. 3; see the note there. The *flour*, whether of wheat, rice, barley, rye, or any other grain used for aliment, was in all likelihood equally proper; for in Num. v. 15, we find the *flour of barley*, or *barley meal*, is called *minchah*. It is plain that in the institution of the *minchah* no *animal* was here included, though in other places it seems to include both kinds; but in general the *minchah* was not a *bloody offering*, nor used by way of *atonement* or *expiation*, but merely in a eucharistic way, expressing gratitude to God for the produce of the soil. It is such an offering as what is called *natural religion* might be reasonably expected to suggest: but alas! so far lost is man, that even *thankfulness* to God for the fruits of the earth must be taught by a Divine revelation; for in the heart of man even the *seeds of gratitude* are not found, till sown there by the hand of Divine *grace*.

Offerings of different kinds of *grain*, *flour*, *bread*, *fruits*, &c., are the most ancient among the heathen nations; and even the people of God have had them from the beginning of the world. See this subject largely discussed on Exod. xxiii. 29, where several examples are given. *Ovid* intimates that these gratitude-offerings originated with agriculture. "In the most ancient times men lived by rapine, hunting, &c., for the *sword* was considered to be more honourable than the *plough*; but when they sowed their fields, they dedicated the first-fruits of their harvest to *Ceres*, to whom the ancients attributed the art of agriculture, and to whom burnt-offerings of corn were made, according to immemorial usages." The passage to which I refer, and of which I have given the substance, is the following:—

"Non habuit tellus doctos antiqua colonos:
Lassabant agiles aspera bella viros.
Plus erat in *gladio* quam *curvo* laudis *aratro*.
Neglectus domino *pauca* ferebat *ager*.
Farra tamen veteres jaciebant, *farra* metebant:
Primitias Cereri farra resecta dabant.
Usibus admoniti *flammis torrenda* dedere:
Multaque peccato damna tulere suo."
FASTOR., lib. ii., ver. 515.

Pliny observes that "*Numa* taught the Romans to offer fruits to the gods, and to make supplications before them, bringing salt cakes and parched corn; as grain in this state was deemed most wholesome." *Numa instituit deos* FRUGE *colere, et* MOLA SALSA *supplicare*, atque (ut auctor est Hemina) *far torrere*, quoniam *tostum cibo salubrius esset*.—HIST. NAT., lib. xviii., c. 2. And it is worthy of remark, that the ancient Romans considered "no grain as pure or proper for divine service that had not been previously parched." *Id uno modo consecutum, statuendo non esse purum ad rem divinam nisi tostum.*—Ibid.

God, says *Calmet*, requires nothing here which was not in common use for nourishment; but he commands that these things should be offered with such articles as might give them the most exquisite relish, such as *salt*, *oil*, and *wine*, and that the flour should be of the finest and purest kind. The ancients, according to Suidas, seem to have made much use of meal formed into a paste with milk, and sometimes with water. (See Suidas in Μαζα.) The priests kept in the temples a certain mixture of flour mingled with oil and

A. M. 2514.
B. C. 1490.
An. Exod. Isr. 2.
Abib or Nisan.

2 And he shall bring it to Aaron's sons the priests: and he
shall take thereout his handful
of the flour thereof, and of the oil thereof, with
all the frankincense thereof; and the priest
shall burn [b] the memorial of it upon the altar,
to be an offering made by fire, of a sweet savour
unto the LORD:
3 And [c] the remnant of the meat-offering *shall
be* Aaron's and his sons': [d] *it is* a thing most
holy of the offerings of the LORD made by fire.
4 And if thou bring an oblation
of a meat-offering baken in the
oven, *it shall be* unleavened cakes
of fine flour mingled with oil, or unleavened
wafers [e] anointed with oil.
5 And if thy oblation *be* a meat-offering
baken [f] in a pan, it shall be *of* fine flour unleavened, mingled with oil.
6 Thou shalt part it in pieces, and pour oil
thereon: it *is* a meat-offering.
7 And if thy oblation *be* a meat-offering

A. M. 2514.
B. C. 1490.
An. Exod. Isr. 2.
Abib or Nisan.

[b] Ver. 9; chap. v. 12; vi. 15; xxiv. 7; Isa. lxvi. 3; Ecclus. xlv. 16; Acts x. 4.——[c] Chap. vii. 9; x. 12, 13; Ecclus. vii. 31.——[d] Exod. xxix. 37; Num. xviii. 9.——[e] Exod. xxix. 2.——[f] Or, *on a flat plate* or *slice.*

wine, which they called Ὑγιεια *Hugicia* or *health*, and which they used as a kind of *amulet* or charm against sickness; after they had finished their sacrifices, they generally threw some *flour* upon the fire, mingled with *oil* and *wine*, which they called θυλημata *thulemata*, and which, according to Theophrastus, was the ordinary sacrifice of the poor.

Verse 2. *His handful of the flour*] This was for a *memorial*, to put God in mind of his covenant with their fathers, and to recall to *their* mind his gracious conduct towards them and their ancestors. Mr. *Ainsworth* properly remarks, "that there was neither *oil* nor *incense* offered with the *sin* and *jealousy* offerings; because they were no offerings of *memorial*, but such as brought *iniquities* to remembrance, which were neither gracious nor sweet-smelling before the Lord." Num. v. 15; Lev. v. 11.

In this case a handful only was burnt, the rest was reserved for the priest's use; but *all* the *frankincense* was burnt, because from it the priest could derive no advantage.

Verse 4. *Baken in the oven*] תנור *tannur*, from נר *nar*, to *split, divide*, says Mr. Parkhurst; and hence the *oven*, because of its burning, dissolving, and melting heat.

Verse 5. Baken *in a pan*] מחבת *machabath*, supposed to be a *flat iron plate*, placed over the fire; such as is called a *griddle* in some countries.

Verse 7. *The frying-pan*] מרחשת *marchesheth*, supposed to be the same with that called by the Arabs a *ta-jen*, a shallow earthen vessel like a *frying-pan*, used not only to fry in, but for other purposes. On the different instruments, as well as the manner of *baking* in the east, Mr. Harmer, in his observations on select passages of Scripture, has collected the following curious information.

"Dr. Shaw informs us that in the cities and villages of Barbary, there are *public ovens*, but that among the *Bedouins*, who live in tents, and the *Kabyles*, who live in miserable hovels in the mountains, their bread, made into thin cakes, is baked either immediately upon the coals, or else in a *ta-jen*, which he tells us is a *shallow earthen vessel like a frying-pan:* and then cites the *Septuagint* to show that the supposed pan, mentioned chap. ii. 5, was the same thing as a *ta-jen*. The *ta-jen*, according to Dr. Russel, is exactly the same among the Bedouins as the τηγανον, a word of the same sound as well as meaning, was among the Greeks. So the Septuagint, chap. ii. 5: *If thy oblation be a meat-offering*, baken *in a pan*, (απο τηγανου,) *it shall be of fine flour unleavened, mingled with oil.*

"This account given by the doctor is curious; but as it does not give us all the eastern ways of baking, so neither does it furnish us, I am afraid, with a complete comment on that variety of methods of preparing the meat-offerings which is mentioned by Moses in chap. ii. So long ago as Queen Elizabeth's time, *Rauwolff* observed that travellers frequently baked bread in the deserts of Arabia on the ground, heated for that purpose by fire, covering their cakes of bread with *ashes* and *coals*, and turning them several times until they were baked enough; but that some of the Arabians had in their tents, *stones*, or *copper plates*, made on purpose for baking. Dr. *Pococke* very lately made a like observation, speaking of *iron hearths* used for baking their bread.

"Sir *John Chardin*, mentioning the several ways of baking their bread in the east, describes these *iron plates* as small and *convex*. These plates are most commonly used, he tells us, in Persia, and among the wandering people that dwell in tents, as being the easiest way of baking, and done with the least expense; the bread being as thin as a *skin*, and soon prepared. *Another* way (for he mentions four) is by baking on the *hearth*. That bread is about an inch thick; they make no other all along the Black Sea from the Palus Mæotis to the Caspian Sea, in Chaldea, and in Mesopotamia, except in towns. This, he supposes, is owing to their being *woody* countries. These people make a fire in the middle of a room, when the bread is ready for baking they sweep a corner of the hearth, lay the bread there, and cover it with *hot ashes and embers;* in a quarter of an hour they turn it: this bread is very good. The *third* way is that which is common among us. The *last* way, and that which is common through all Asia, is thus: they make an oven in the ground, four or five feet deep and three in diameter, well plastered with mortar. When it is hot, they place the bread (which is commonly long, and not thicker than a finger) against the sides, and it is baked in a moment.

"*D'Arvieux* mentions another way used by the Arabs about Mount Carmel, who sometimes bake in an oven, and at other time on the hearth; but have a third method, which is, to make a fire in a great *stone pitcher*,

A. M. 2514.
B. C. 1490.
An. Exod. Isr. 2.
Abib or Nisan.

baken in the frying-pan, it shall
be made *of* fine flour with oil.
8 And thou shalt bring the
meat-offering that is made of
these things unto the LORD:
and when it is presented unto

and when it is heated, they mix meal and water, as we do to make *paste* to glue things together, which they apply with the hollow of their hands to the outside of the pitcher, and this extremely soft paste spreading itself upon it is baked in an instant. The heat of the pitcher having dried up all the moisture, the bread comes off as thin as our *wafers;* and the operation is so speedily performed that in a very little time a sufficient quantity is made.

"*Maimonides* and the *Septuagint* differ in their explanation of ver. 5; for that Egyptian rabbi supposes this verse speaks of a flat plate, and these more ancient interpreters, of a *ta-jen*. But they both seem to agree that these were two of the methods of preparing the meat-offering; for Maimonides supposes the *seventh* verse speaks of a *frying-pan* or *ta-jen;* whereas the *Septuagint*, on the contrary, thought the word *there* meant a *hearth*, which term takes in an iron or copper plate, though it extends farther.

"The *meat-offerings* of the *fourth* verse answer as well to the Arab bread, baked by means of their *stone pitchers*, which are used by them for the baking of *wafers*, as to their cakes of bread mentioned by *D'Arvieux*, who, describing the way of baking among the modern Arabs, after mentioning some of their methods, says they bake their best sort of bread, either by heating an oven, or a large pitcher, half full of certain little smooth shining flints, upon which they lay the dough, spread out in form of a thin broad cake. The mention of *wafers* seems to fix the meaning of Moses to these *oven pitchers*, though perhaps it may be thought an objection that this meat-offering is said to have been baked in an oven; but it will be sufficient to observe that the Hebrew words only signify a meat-offering of the oven, and consequently may be understood as well of wafers baked on the *outside* of these oven pitchers, as of cakes of bread baked *in* them. *And if thou bring an oblation, a baked thing, of the oven, it shall be an unleavened cake of fine flour mingled with oil, or unleavened wafers anointed with oil.* Whoever then attends to these accounts of the stone pitcher, the ta-jen, and the copper plate or iron hearth, will enter into this second of Leviticus, I believe, much more perfectly than any commentator has done, and will find in these accounts what answers perfectly well to the description Moses gives us of the different ways of preparing the meat-offerings. A *ta-jen* indeed, according to Dr. Shaw, serves for a *frying-pan* as well as for a baking vessel; for he says, the *bagreah* of the people of Barbary differs not much from our pancakes, only that, instead of rubbing the ta-jen or pan in which they fry them with butter, they rub it with soap, to make them like a honeycomb.

"Moses possibly intended a meat-offering of that kind might be presented to the Lord; and our translators seem to prefer that supposition, since, though the margin mentions the opinion of Maimonides, the reading of the text in the sixth verse opposes a pan for baking to a pan for frying in the seventeenth verse. The thought, however, of Maimonides seems to be most just, as Moses appears to be speaking of different kinds of bread only, not of other farinaceous preparations.

"These oven pitchers mentioned by *D'Arvieux*, and used by the modern Arabs for baking cakes of bread in them, and wafers on their outsides, are not the only portable ovens of the east. St. Jerome, in his commentary on Lam. v. 10, describes an eastern oven as a round vessel of brass, blackened on the outside by the surrounding fire which heats it within. Such an oven I have seen used in England. Which of these the Mishnah refers to when it speaks of the women lending their ovens to one another, as well as their mills and their sieves, I do not know; but the foregoing observations may serve to remove a surprise that this circumstance may otherwise occasion in the reader of the Mishnah. Almost every body knows that little portable handmills are extremely common in the Levant; movable ovens are not so well known. Whether ovens of the kind which St. Jerome mentions be as ancient as the days of Moses, does not appear, unless the ta-jen be used after this manner; but the pitcher ovens of the Arabs are, without doubt, of that remote antiquity.

"Travellers agree that the eastern bread is made in small thin moist cakes, must be eaten new, and is good for nothing when kept longer than a day. This however, admits of exceptions. Dr. Russel of late and Rauwolff formerly, assure us that they have several sorts of bread and cakes: some, Rauwolff tells us, done with yolk of eggs; some mixed with several sorts of seed, as of *sesamum*, Romish *coriander*, and wild *garden saffron*, which are also strewed upon it; and he elsewhere supposes that they prepare biscuits for travelling. Russel, who mentions this strewing of seeds on their cakes says, they have a variety of *rusks* and *biscuits*. To these authors let me add Pitts, who tells us the biscuits they carry with them from Egypt will last them to Mecca and back again.

"The Scriptures suppose their loaves of bread were very small, *three* of them being requisite for the entertainment of a single person, Luke xi. 5. That they were generally eaten new, and baked as they wanted them, as appears from the case of Abraham. That sometimes, however, they were made so as to keep several days; so the *shew-bread* was fit food, after lying before the Lord a week. And that bread for travellers was wont to be made to keep some time, as appears from the pretences of the Gibeonites, Josh. ix. 12, and the preparations made for Jacob's journey into Egypt, Gen. xlv. 23. The bread or *rusks* for travelling is often made in the form of large rings, and is moistened or soaked in water before it is used. In like manner, too, they seem to have had there a variety of eatables of this kind as the Aleppines now have. In particular, some made like those on which seeds are strewed, as we may collect from that part of the presents of Jeroboam's wife to the Prophet Ahi-

A. M. 2514. B. C. 1490. An. Exod. Isr. 2. Abib or Nisan.

the priest, he shall bring it unto
the altar.
9 And the priest shall take from
the meat-offering [g] a memorial thereof, and
shall burn *it* upon the altar: *it is* an [h] offering
made by fire, of a sweet savour unto the
LORD.
10 And [i] that which is left of the meat-
offering *shall be* Aaron's and his sons': *it is* a
thing most holy of the offerings
of the LORD made by fire.
11 No meat-offering, which ye
shall bring unto the LORD, shall be made
with [k] leaven: for ye shall burn no leaven,
nor any honey, in any offering of the LORD
made by fire.
12 [l] As for the oblation of the first-fruits, ye
shall offer them unto the LORD: but they

g Verse 2.——h Exodus xxix. 18.——i Verse 3.——k Chapter vi. 17; see Matthew xvi. 12; Mark viii. 15; Luke xii. 1; 1 Corinthians v. 8; Gal. v. 9.——l Exod. xxii. 29; chap. xxiii. 10, 11.

jah, which our translators have rendered *cracknels*, 1 Kings xiv. 3. Buxtorf indeed supposes the original word נקדים *nikkuddim* signifies biscuits, called by this name, either because they were formed into little buttons like some of our gingerbread, or because they were pricked full of holes after a particular manner. The last of these two conjectures, I imagine, was embraced by our translators of this passage; for *cracknels*, if they are all over England of the same form, are full of holes, being formed into a kind of flourish of lattice-work. I have seen some of the unleavened bread of the English Jews made in like manner in a net form. Nevertheless I should think it more natural to understand the word of biscuit spotted with seeds; for it is used elsewhere to signify works of gold spotted with studs of silver; and, as it should seem, bread spotted with mould, Josh. ix. 5–12; how much more natural is it then to understand the word of cakes *spotted with seeds*, which are so common in the east! Is not לבבות *lebiboth*, in particular, the word that in general means rich *cakes?* a sort of which Tamar used to prepare that was not common, and furnished Amnon with a pretence for desiring her being sent to his house, that she might make some of that kind for him in the time of his indisposition, his fancy running upon them; see 2 Sam. xiii. 2–8. Parkhurst supposes the original word to signify *pancakes*, and translates the root לבב *labab* to *move* or *toss up and down:* 'And she took the dough, (ותלוש *vattalosh*,) and *kneaded* (ותלבב *vattelabbeb*, and *tossed*) it in his sight, ותבשל *vattebashshel*, and *dressed* the cakes.' In this passage, says Mr. Parkhurst, it is to be observed that לבב is distinguished from לש to *knead*, and from בשל to *dress*, which agrees with the interpretation here given.

"The account which Mr. Jackson gives of an Arab baking apparatus, and the manner of *kneading* and *tossing their cakes*, will at once, if I mistake not, fix the meaning of this passage, and cast much light on chap. xi. 35. 'I was much amused by observing the dexterity of the Arab women in baking their bread. They have a small place built with clay, between two and three feet high, having a hole in the bottom for the convenience of drawing out the ashes, somewhat similar to that of a lime-kiln. The oven, which I think is the most proper name for this place, is usually about fifteen inches wide at top, and gradually grows wider to the bottom. It is heated with wood, and when sufficiently hot, and perfectly clear from smoke, having nothing but clear embers at the bottom, which continue to reflect great heat, they prepare the dough in a large bowl, and mould the cakes to the desired size on a board or stone placed near the oven. After they have kneaded the cake to a proper consistence, they pat it a little, *then toss it about* with great dexterity in one hand till it is as thin as they choose to make it. They then wet one side of it with water, at the same time wetting the hand and arm with which they put it into the oven. The side of the cake adheres fast to the side of the oven till it is sufficiently baked, when, if not paid proper attention to, it would fall down among the embers. If they were not exceedingly quick at this work, the heat of the oven would burn their arms; but they perform it with such amazing dexterity that one woman will continue keeping three or four cakes in the oven at once, till she has done baking. This mode, let me add, does not require half the fuel that is made use of in Europe.'" See more in HARMER'S *Observat.*, vol. i., p. 414, &c., Edit. 1808.

Verse 8. *Thou shalt bring the meat offering*] It is likely that the person himself who offered the sacrifice brought it to the priest, and then the priest presented it before the Lord.

Verse 11. *No meat-offering—shall be made with leaven*] See the reason of this prohibition in the note on Exod. xii. 8.

Nor any honey] Because it was apt to produce *acidity*, as some think, when wrought up with flour paste; or rather because it was apt to *gripe* and prove *purgative*. On this latter account the College of Physicians have totally left it out of all medicinal preparations. This effect which it has in most constitutions was a sufficient reason why it should be prohibited here, as a principal part of all these offerings was used by the priests as a part of their ordinary diet; and these offerings, being those of the poorer sort, were in greater abundance than most others. On this account, the griping, and purgative quality of the honey must render it extremely improper. As *leaven* was forbidden because producing *fermentation*, it was considered a species of *corruption*, and was therefore used to signify *hypocrisy, malice*, &c., which corrupt the soul; it is possible that *honey* might have had a moral reference, also, and have signified, as St. Jerome thought, *carnal pleasures* and *sensual gratifications*. Some suppose that the honey mentioned here was a sort of saccharine matter extracted from *dates*. Leaven and honey might be offered with the *first-fruits*, as we learn from the next verse; but they were forbidden to be burnt on the altar.

A. M. 2514.
B. C. 1490.
An. Exod. Isr. 2.
Abib or Nisan.

shall not [m] be burnt on the altar
for a sweet savour.
13 And every oblation of thy
meat-offering [n] shalt thou season with salt:
neither shalt thou suffer [o] the salt of the covenant of thy God to be lacking from thy meat-
offering: [p] with all thine offerings thou shalt
offer salt.
14 And if thou offer a meat-offering of thy
first-fruits unto the LORD, [q] thou shalt offer,
for the meat-offering of thy first-
fruits, green ears of corn dried
by the fire, *even* corn beaten out
of [r] full ears.
15 And [s] thou shalt put oil upon it, and lay
frankincense thereon: it *is* a meat-offering.
16 And the priest shall burn [t] the memorial of
it, *part* of the beaten corn thereof, and *part* of
the oil thereof, with all the frankincense there
of: *it is* an offering made by fire unto the LORD

A. M. 2514.
B. C. 1490.
An. Exod. Isr. 2.
Abib or Nisan.

[m] Heb. *ascend*.—[n] Mark ix. 49; Col. iv. 6.—[o] Num. xviii. 19.—[p] Ezek. xliii. 24.

[q] Chapter xxiii. 10, 14.—[r] 2 Kings iv. 42.—[s] Verse 1. [t] Ver. 2.

Verse 13. *With all thine offerings thou shalt offer salt.*] SALT was the opposite to *leaven*, for it preserved from *putrefaction* and *corruption*, and signified the *purity* and *persevering fidelity* that were necessary in the worship of God. Every thing was seasoned with it, to signify the purity and perfection that should be extended through every part of the Divine service, and through the hearts and lives of God's worshippers. It was called the *salt of the covenant of God*, because as salt is incorruptible, so was the covenant made with Abram, Isaac, Jacob, and the patriarchs, relative to the redemption of the world by the incarnation and death of Jesus Christ. Among the heathens *salt* was a common ingredient in all their sacrificial offerings; and as it was considered essential to the comfort and preservation of life, and an emblem of the most perfect corporeal and mental endowments, so it was supposed to be one of the most acceptable presents they could make unto their gods, from whose sacrifices it was never absent. That inimitable and invaluable writer, Pliny, has left a long chapter on this subject, the *seventh* of the *thirty-first* book of his *Natural History*, a few extracts from which will not displease the intelligent reader. Ergo, hercule, vita humanior sine Sale nequit degere: adeòque necessarium elementum est. ut transierit intellectus ad voluptates animi quoque. Nam ita SALES appellantur omnisque vitæ lepos et summa hilaritas, laborumque requies non alio magis vocabulo constat. Honoribus etiam militiæque interponitur, SALARIIS inde dictis—Maxime tamen in sacris intelligitur auctoritas, quando nulla conficiuntur sine *mola salsa*. "So essentially necessary is salt that without it human life cannot be preserved: and even the pleasures and endowments of the mind are expressed by it; the delights of life, repose, and the highest mental serenity, are expressed by no other term than *sales* among the Latins. It has also been applied to designate the honourable rewards given to soldiers, which are called *salarii* or *salaries*. But its importance may be farther understood by its use in *sacred things*, as no sacrifice was offered to the gods without the *salt cake*."

So Virgil, Eclog. viii., ver. 82: *Sparge molam.*

"Crumble the sacred *mole* of *salt* and *corn*."

And again, Æneid., lib. iv., ver. 517:—

Ipsa mola, manibusque piis, altaria juxta.

"Now with the sacred *cake*, and lifted hands,
All bent on death, before her altar stands."
PITT.

In like manner Homer:—

Πασσε δ' ἁλος θειοιο, κρατευταων επαειρας.
Iliad, lib. ix., ver. 214

"And taking sacred *salt* from the hearth side,
Where it was treasured, pour'd it o'er the feast."
COWPER.

Quotations of this kind might be easily multiplied, but the above may be deemed sufficient.

Verse 14. *Green ears of corn dried by the fire*] Green or half-ripe ears of wheat parched with fire is a species of food in use among the poor people of Palestine and Egypt to the present day. As God is represented as *keeping a table* among his people, (for the tabernacle was his *house*, where he had the golden table, shew-bread, &c.,) so he represents himself as *partaking* with them of all the aliments that were in use, and even sitting down with the *poor* to a repast on *parched corn!* We have already seen that these green ears were presented as a sort of eucharistical offering for the blessings of seed time, and the prospect of a plentiful harvest. See the note on ver. 1; several other examples might be added here, but they are not necessary.

The command to offer salt with every oblation, and which was punctually observed by the Jews, will afford the pious reader some profitable reflections. It is well known that salt has two grand properties. 1. It seasons and renders palatable the principal aliments used for the support of life. 2. It prevents putrefaction and decay. The covenant of God, that is, his agreement with his people, is called a *covenant of salt*, to denote as we have seen above, its stable undecaying nature, as well as to point out its importance and utility in the preservation of the life of the soul. The *grace* of God by Christ Jesus is represented under the emblem of *salt*, (see Mark ix. 49; Eph. iv. 29; Col. iv. 6,) because of its relishing, nourishing, and preserving quality. Without it no offering, no sacrifice, no religious service, no work even of charity and mercy, can be acceptable in the sight of God. In all things we must come unto the Father THROUGH HIM. And from none of our sacrifices or services must this salt of the covenant of our God be lacking.

CHAPTER III.

***The law of the peace-offering in general,* 1–5. *That of the peace-offering taken from the flock,* 6–11; *and the same when the offering is a goat,* 12–17.**

A. M. 2514.
B. C. 1490.
An. Exod. Isr. 2.
Abib or Nisan.

AND if his oblation *be* a [a] sacrifice of peace-offering, if he offer *it* of the herd, whether *it be* a male or female, he shall offer it [b] without blemish before the LORD.

2 And [c] he shall lay his hand upon the head of his offering, and kill it *at* the door of the tabernacle of the congregation: and Aaron's sons the priests shall sprinkle the blood upon the altar round about.

3 And he shall offer of the sacrifice of the peace-offering an offering made by fire unto the LORD; [d] the [e] fat that covereth the inwards, and all the fat that *is* upon the inwards,

4 And the two kidneys, and the fat that *is* on them, which *is* by the flanks, and the [f] caul above the liver, with the kidneys, it shall he take away.

5 And Aaron's sons [g] shall burn it on the altar upon the burnt-sacrifice, which *is* upon the wood that *is* on the fire: *it is* an offering made by fire, of a sweet savour unto the LORD.

6 And if his offering for a sacrifice of peace-offering unto the LORD *be* of the flock, male or female, [h] he shall offer it without blemish.

A. M. 2514.
B. C. 1490.
An. Exod. Isr. 2.
Abib or Nisan.

7 If he offer a lamb for his offering, then shall he offer it before the LORD.

8 And he shall lay his hand upon the head of his offering, and kill it before the tabernacle of the congregation: and Aaron's sons shall sprinkle the blood thereof round about upon the altar.

9 And he shall offer of the sacrifice of the peace-offering, an offering made by fire unto the LORD; the fat thereof, *and* the whole rump, it shall he take off hard by the backbone; and the fat that covereth the inwards, and all the fat that *is* upon the inwards,

10 And the two kidneys, and the fat that *is* upon them, which *is* by the flanks, and the caul above the liver, with the kidneys, it shall he take away.

11 And the priest shall burn it upon the altar *it is* [i] the food of the offering made by fire unto the LORD.

[a] Chap. vii. 11, 29; xxii. 21.——[b] Chap. i. 3.——[c] Chap. i. 4, 5; Exodus xxix. 10.——[d] Exod. xxix. 13, 22; chapter iv. 8, 9. [e] Or, *suet.*

[f] Or, *midriff over the liver* and *over the kidneys.*——[g] Chap. vi. 12; Exod. xxix. 13.——[h] Ver. 1, &c.——[i] See chapter xxi. 6, 8, 17, 21, 22; xxii. 25; Ezek. xliv. 7; Mal. i. 7, 12.

NOTES ON CHAP. III.

Verse 1. *Peace-offering*] שלמים *shelamim*, an offering to make peace between God and man; see on chap. vii., and Gen. xiv. 18.

Verse 2. *Lay his hand upon the head of his offering*] See this rite explained on Exod. xxix. 10, and chap. i. 4. "As the *burnt-offering*, (chap. i.,)" says Mr. Ainsworth, "figured our reconciliation to God by the death of Christ, and the *meat-offering*, (chap ii.,) our sanctification in him before God, so this *peace-offering* signified both Christ's oblation of himself whereby he became our *peace* and salvation, (Eph. ii. 14–16; Acts xiii. 47; Heb. v. 9; ix. 28,) and our oblation of praise, thanksgiving, and prayer unto God."

Verse 3. *The fat that covereth the inwards*] The *omentum*, caul or *web*, as some term it. *The fat that* is *upon the inwards;* probably the *mesentery* or fatty part of the substance which connects the convolutions of the alimentary canal or small intestines.

Verse 5. *Aaron's sons shall burn it*] As the *fat* was deemed the most *valuable* part of the animal, it was offered in preference to all other parts; and the heathens probably borrowed this custom from the Jews, for they burnt the *omentum* or *caul* in honour of their gods.

Verse 9 *The whole rump, it shall he take off hard by the backbone*] To what has already been said on the *tails* of the eastern sheep, in the note on Exod. xxix. 22, we may add the following observation from Dr. Russel concerning the sheep at Aleppo. "Their *tails*," says he, "are of a substance between *fat* and *marrow*, and are not eaten separately, but mixed with the lean meat in many of their dishes, and also often used instead of butter." He states also that a common sheep of this kind, without the head, fat, skin, and entrails, weighs from *sixty* to *seventy* English pounds, of which the tail usually weighs *fifteen* pounds and upwards; but that those of the largest breed, when fattened, will weigh *one hundred and fifty* pounds, and their tails *fifty*, which corresponds with the account given by *Ludolf* in the note referred to above. The sheep about *Jerusalem* are the same with those in *Abyssinia* mentioned by *Ludolf*, and those of *Syria* mentioned by *Dr. Russel.*

Verse 11. It is *the food of the offering*] We have already remarked that God is frequently represented as *feasting with his people* on the sacrifices they offered; and because these sacrifices were consumed by that fire which was kindled from heaven, therefore they were considered as *the food of that fire*, or rather of the Divine Being who was represented by it. "In the same idiom of speech," says Dodd, "the gods of the heathens are said, Deut. xxxii. 38, to eat

A. M. 2514. B. C. 1490. An. Exod. Isr. 2. Abib or Nisan.

12 And if his offering *be* a goat, then [k] he shall offer it before the LORD.

13 And he shall lay his hand upon the head of it, and kill it before the tabernacle of the congregation: and the sons of Aaron shall sprinkle the blood thereof upon the altar round about.

14 And he shall offer thereof his offering, *even* an offering made by fire unto the LORD; the fat that covereth the inwards, and all the fat that *is* upon the inwards,

15 And the two kidneys, and the fat that *is* upon them, which *is* by the flanks, and the caul above the liver, with the kidneys, it shall he take away.

16 And the priest shall burn them upon the altar: *it is* the food of the offering made by fire for a sweet savour: [l] all the fat *is* the LORD'S.

17 *It shall be* a [m] perpetual statute for your generations throughout all your dwellings, that ye eat neither [n] fat nor [o] blood.

[k] Verses 1, 7, &c.——[l] Chapter vii. 23, 25; 1 Sam. ii. 15; 2 Chron. vii. 7.——[m] Chapter vi. 18; vii. 36; xvii. 7; xxiii. 14. [n] Verse 16; compare with Deuteronomy xxxii. 14; Nehemiah viii. 10.——[o] Gen. ix. 4; chap. vii. 23, 26; xvii. 10, 14; Deuteronomy xii. 16; 1 Samuel xiv. 33; Ezekiel xliv. 7, 15.

the fat and drink the wine which were consumed on their altars."

Verse 12. *A goat*] Implying the whole species, *he-goat*, *she-goat*, and *kid*, as we have already seen.

Verse 17. *That ye eat neither fat nor blood.*] It is not likely that the *fat* should be forbidden in the same manner and in the same latitude as the *blood*. The blood was the *life* of the beast, and that was offered to make an atonement for their souls; consequently, this was never eaten in all their generations: but it was impossible to separate the fat from the flesh, which in many parts is so intimately intermixed with the muscular fibres; but the blood, being contained in separate vessels, the *arteries* and *veins*, might with great ease be entirely removed by cutting the throat of the animal, which was the Jewish method. By the *fat* therefore mentioned here and in the preceding verse, we may understand any fat that exists in a *separate* or *unmixed* state, such as the *omentum* or *caul*, the fat of the *mesentery*, the fat on the *kidneys*, and whatever else of the internal fat was easily separable, together with the whole of the *tail* already described. And probably it was the fat of such animals only as were offered to God in sacrifice, that was unlawful to be eaten.

As all temporal as well as spiritual blessings come from God, he has a right to require that such of them should be dedicated to his service as he may think proper to demand. He required the most perfect of all the animals, and the best parts of these perfect animals. This he did, not that he needed any thing, but to show the perfection of his nature and the purity of his service. Had he condescended to receive the *meanest animals* and the *meanest parts* of animals as his offerings, what opinion could his worshippers have entertained of the perfection of his nature? If such imperfect offerings were worthy of this God, then his nature must be only worthy of such offerings. It is necessary that every thing employed in the worship of God should be the most perfect of its kind that the time and circumstances can afford. As sensible things are generally the medium through which spiritual impressions are made, and the impression usually partakes of the nature of the medium through which these impressions are communicated; hence every thing should not only be *decent*, but as far as circumstances will admit *dignified*, in the worship of God: the *object* of religious worship, the *place* in which he is worshipped, and the worship itself, should have the strongest and most impressive correspondence possible.

CHAPTER IV.

The law concerning the sin-offering for transgressions committed through ignorance, 1, 2. *For the* priest *thus sinning*, 3–12. *For the sins of ignorance of the whole* congregation, 13–21. *For the sins of ignorance of a* ruler, 22–26. *For the sins of ignorance of any of the* common people, 27–35.

A. M. 2514. B. C. 1490. An. Exod. Isr. 2. Abib or Nisan.

AND the LORD spake unto Moses, saying,

2 Speak unto the children of Israel, saying, [a] If a soul shall sin through ignorance against any of the commandments of the

[a] Chap. v. 15, 17; Num. xv. 22, &c.; 1 Sam. xiv. 27; Psa. xix. 12.

NOTES ON CHAP. IV.

Verse 2. *If a soul shall sin through ignorance*] That is, If any man shall do what God has forbidden, or leave undone what God has commanded, through ignorance of the law relative to these points; as soon as the transgression or omission comes to his knowledge, he shall offer the sacrifice here prescribed, and shall not suppose that his *ignorance* is an excuse for his sin. He who, when his iniquity comes to his knowledge, refuses to offer such a sacrifice, sins obstinately

A. M. 2514.
B. C. 1490.
An. Exod. Isr. 2.
Abib or Nisan.

LORD, *concerning things* which ought not to be done, and shall do against any of them:

3 [b] If the priest that is anointed do sin according to the sin of the people; then let him bring for his sin, which he hath sinned, [c] a young bullock without blemish, unto the LORD, for a sin-offering.

4 And he shall bring the bullock [d] unto the door of the tabernacle of the congregation, before the LORD; and shall lay his hand upon the bullock's head, and kill the bullock before the LORD.

5 And the priest that is anointed [e] shall take of the bullock's blood, and bring it to the tabernacle of the congregation.

6 And the priest shall dip his finger in the blood, and sprinkle of the blood seven times before the LORD, before the veil of the sanctuary.

7 And the priest shall [f] put *some* of the blood upon the horns of the altar of sweet incense before the LORD, which *is* in the tabernacle of the congregation; and shall pour [g] all the blood of the bullock at the bottom of the altar of the burnt-offering, which *is at* the door of the tabernacle of the congregation.

8 And he shall take off from it all the fat of the bullock for the sin-offering; the fat that covereth the inwards, and all the fat that *is* upon the inwards,

A. M. 2514.
B. C. 1490.
An. Exod. Isr. 2.
Abib or Nisan.

9 And the two kidneys, and the fat that *is* upon them, which *is* by the flanks, and the caul above the liver, with the kidneys, it shall he take away,

10 [h] As it was taken off from the bullock of the sacrifice of peace-offerings: and the priest shall burn them upon the altar of the burnt offering.

11 [i] And the skin of the bullock, and all his flesh, with his head, and with his legs, and his inwards, and his dung,

12 Even the whole bullock shall he carry forth [k] without the camp unto a clean place, [l] where the ashes are poured out, and [m] burn him on the wood with fire: [n] where the ashes are poured out shall he be burnt.

13 And [o] if the whole congregation of Israel sin through ignorance, [p] and the thing be hid from the eyes of the assembly, and they have done *somewhat against* any of the commandments of the LORD, *concerning things* which should not be done, and are guilty;

[b] Chap. viii. 12.—[c] Chap. ix. 2.—[d] Chap. i. 3, 4.—[e] Ch. xvi. 14; Numbers xix. 4.—[f] Chapter viii. 15; ix. 9; xvi. 18. [g] Ch. v. 9.—[h] Ch. iii. 3, 4, 5.—[i] Exod. xxix. 14; Num. xix. 5.

[k] Heb. *to without the camp.*—[l] Chap. vi. 11.—[m] Heb. xiii. 11.—[n] Heb. *at the pouring out of the ashes.*—[o] Num. xv. 24; Josh. vii. 11.—[p] Chap. v. 2, 3, 4, 17.

and *wilfully*, and to him there *remains no* other *sacrifice for sin*—no other mode by which he can be reconciled to God, *but he has a certain fearful looking for of judgment—which shall devour* such *adversaries*; and this seems the case to which the apostle alludes, Heb. x. 26, &c., in the words above quoted. There have been a great number of subtle questions started on this subject, both by Jews and Christians, but the above I believe to be the sense and spirit of the law.

Verse 3. *If the priest that is anointed*] Meaning, most probably, the high priest. *According to the sin of the people*; for although he had greater advantages than the people could have, in being more conversant with the law of God, and his lips should understand and preserve knowledge, yet it was possible even for him, in that time in which the word of God had not been fully revealed, to transgress through ignorance; and his transgression might have the very worst tendency, because the people might be thereby led into sin. Hence several critics understand this passage in this way, and translate it thus: *If the anointed priest shall lead the people to sin*; or, literally, *if the anointed priest shall sin to the sin of the people*; that is, so as to cause the people to transgress, the shepherd going astray, and the sheep following after him.

Verse 4. *Lay his hand upon the bullock's head*] See on chap. i. 4.

Verse 6. *Seven times*] See the note on Exod. xxix. 30. The blood of this sacrifice was applied in three different ways: 1. The priest put his finger in it, and sprinkled it seven times before the veil, ver. 6. 2. He put some of it on the horns of the altar of incense. 3. He poured the remaining part at the bottom of the altar of burnt-offerings, ver. 7.

Verse 12. *Without the camp*] This was intended figuratively to express the sinfulness of this sin, and the availableness of the atonement. The sacrifice, as having the sin of the priest transferred from himself to it by his confession and imposition of hands, was become unclean and abominable, and was carried, as it were, out of the Lord's sight; from the tabernacle and congregation it must be carried without the camp, and thus its own offensiveness was removed, and the sin of the person in whose behalf it was offered. The apostle (Heb. xiii. 11–13) applies this in the most pointed manner to Christ: "For the bodies of those beasts whose blood is brought into the sanctuary by the high priest for sin, are burned *without the camp.* Wherefore JESUS also, that he might sanctify the people with his own blood, suffered *without the gate.* Let us go forth therefore unto him *without the camp*, bearing his reproach."

Verse 13. *If the whole congregation of Israel sin*] This probably refers to some oversight in acts of re-

A. M. 2514.
B. C. 1490.
An. Exod. Isr. 2.
Abib or Nisan.

14 When the sin, which they have sinned against it, is known, then the congregation shall offer a young bullock for the sin, and bring him before the tabernacle of the congregation.

15 And the elders of the congregation [q] shall lay their hands upon the head of the bullock before the LORD: and the bullock shall be killed before the LORD.

16 [r] And the priest that is anointed shall bring of the bullock's blood to the tabernacle of the congregation.

17 And the priest shall dip his finger *in some* of the blood, and sprinkle *it* seven times before the LORD, *even* before the veil.

18 And he shall put *some* of the blood upon the horns of the altar which *is* before the LORD, that *is* in the tabernacle of the congregation, and shall pour out all the blood at the bottom of the altar of the burnt-offering, which *is at* the door of the tabernacle of the congregation.

19 And he shall take all his fat from him, and burn *it* upon the altar.

20 And he shall do with the bullock as he did [s] with the bullock for a sin-offering, so shall he do with this: [t] and the priest shall make an atonement for them, and it shall be forgiven them.

21 And he shall carry forth the bullock without the camp, and burn him as he burned the first bullock: it *is* a sin-offering for the congregation.

22 When a ruler hath sinned, and [u] done *somewhat* through ignorance *against* any of the commandments of the LORD his God, *concerning things* which should not be done, and is guilty;

23 Or [v] if his sin, wherein he hath sinned, come to his knowledge; he shall bring his offering, a kid of the goats, a male without blemish:

24 And [w] he shall lay his hand upon the head of the goat, and kill it in the place where they kill the burnt-offering before the LORD: it *is* a sin-offering.

25 [x] And the priest shall take of the blood of the sin-offering with his finger, and put *it* upon the horns of the altar of burnt-offering, and shall pour out his blood at the bottom of the altar of burnt-offering.

26 And he shall burn all his fat upon the altar, as [y] the fat of the sacrifice of peace-offerings: [z] and the priest shall make an atonement for him as concerning his sin, and it shall be forgiven him.

27 And [a] if [b] any one of the [c] common people sin through ignorance, while he doeth *somewhat against* any of the commandments of the

[q] Chap. i. 4.—[r] Ver. 5; Heb. ix. 12, 13, 14.—[s] Ver. 3. [t] Num. xv. 25; Dan. ix. 24; Rom. v. 11; Heb. ii. 17; x. 10, 11, 12; 1 John i. 7; ii. 2.—[u] Ver. 2, 13.

[v] Ver. 14.—[w] Ver. 4, &c.—[x] Ver. 30.—[y] Chap. iii. 5. [z] Ver. 20; Num. xv. 28.—[a] Ver. 2; Num. xv. 27.—[b] Heb. *any soul.*—[c] Heb. *people of the land.*

ligious worship, or to some transgression of the letter of the law, which arose out of the peculiar circumstances in which they were then found, such as the case mentioned 1 Sam. xiv. 32, &c., where the people, through their long and excessive fatigue in their combat with the Philistines, being faint, *flew on the spoil*, and *took sheep, oxen*, and *calves, and slew them on the ground, and did eat with the blood;* and this was partly occasioned by the rash adjuration of Saul, mentioned ver. 24: *Cursed be the man that eateth* any *food until evening.*

The sacrifices and rites in this case were the same as those prescribed in the preceding, only here the elders of the congregation, i. e., *three of the sanhedrim*, according to *Maimonides*, laid their hands on the head of the victim in the name of all the congregation.

Verse 22. *When a ruler hath sinned*] Under the term נשיא *nasi*, it is probable that any person is meant who held any kind of political dignity among the people, though the rabbins generally understand it of the *king*.

A kid of the goats was the sacrifice in this case, the rites nearly the same as in the preceding cases, only the *fat* was burnt as that of the *peace-offering*. See ver. 26, and chap. iii. 5.

Verse 27. *The common people*] עם הארץ *am haarets*, *the people of the land*, that is, any individual who was not a *priest, king*, or *ruler* among the people; any of the poor or ordinary sort. Any of these, having transgressed through ignorance, was obliged to bring a lamb or a kid, the ceremonies being nearly the same as in the preceding cases. The original may denote the very lowest of the people, the labouring or agricultural classes.

The law relative to the general cases of sins committed through ignorance, and the sacrifices to be offered on such occasions, so amply detailed in this chapter, may be thus recapitulated. For all sins and transgressions of this kind committed by the *people*, the *prince*, and the *priest*, they must offer expiatory offerings. The person so sinning must bring the sacrifice to the door of the tabernacle, and lay his hands upon its head, as in a case already referred to, acknowledging the sacrifice to be his, that he needed it for his transgression; and thus he was considered as confessing his sin, and the sin was considered as transferred to the animal, whose blood was then spilt

A. M. 2514.
B. C. 1490.
An. Exod. Isr. 2.
Abib or Nisan.

Lord, *concerning things* which
ought not to be done, and be guilty;
28 Or [d] if his sin, which he hath
sinned, come to his knowledge; then he shall
bring his offering, a kid of the goats, a female
without blemish, for his sin which he hath sinned.
29 [e] And he shall lay his hand upon the head
of the sin-offering, and slay the sin-offering in
the place of the burnt-offering.
30 And the priest shall take of the blood
thereof with his finger, and put *it* upon the horns
of the altar of burnt-offering, and shall pour out
all the blood thereof at the bottom of the altar.
31 And [f] he shall take away all the fat thereof,
[g] as the fat is taken away from off the sacrifice of peace-offering; and the priest shall
burn *it* upon the altar for a [h] sweet savour
unto the Lord; [i] and the priest shall make an
atonement for him, and it shall be forgiven him.
32 And if he bring a lamb for
a sin-offering, [k] he shall bring it
a female without blemish.
33 And he shall lay his hand upon the head of
the sin-offering, and slay it for a sin-offering,
in the place where they kill the burnt-offering.
34 And the priest shall take of the blood of
the sin-offering with his finger, and put *it* upon
the horns of the altar of burnt-offering, and
shall pour out all the blood thereof at the bot
tom of the altar:
35 And he shall take away all the fat thereof
as the fat of the lamb is taken away from the
sacrifice of the peace-offerings; and the priest
shall burn them upon the altar, [l] according to
the offerings make by fire unto the Lord:
[m] and the priest shall make an atonement for
his sin that he hath committed, and it shall be
forgiven him.

A. M. 2514.
B. C. 1490.
An. Exod. Isr. 2
Abib or Nisan.

[d] Verse 23.——[e] Ver. 4, 24.——[f] Chap. iii. 14.——[g] Chap. iii. 3. [h] Exod. xxix. 18; chap. i. 9.

[i] Verse 26.——[k] Verse 28.——[l] Chapter iii. 5.——[m] Verse 26, 31.

to make an atonement. See on chap. i. 4. Such institutions as these could not be considered as terminating in themselves, they necessarily had reference to something of infinitely higher moment; in a word, they typified Him whose soul was made an offering for sin, Isa. liii. 10. And taken out of this reference they seem both absurd and irrational. It is obviously in reference to these innocent creatures being brought as sin-offerings to God for the guilty that St. Paul alludes 2 Cor. v. 21, where he says, *He* (God) *made him to be sin* (ἁμαρτιαν, a sin-offering) *for us* WHO KNEW NO SIN, *that we might be made the righteousness of God*—holy and pure by the power and grace of God, *in* or *through him.* And it is worthy of remark, that the Greek word used by the apostle is the same by which the Septuagint, in more than fourscore places in the Pentateuch, translate the Hebrew word חטאה *chattaah, sin,* which in all those places our translation renders *sin-offering.* Even sins of *ignorance* cannot be unnoticed by a strict and holy law; these also need the great atonement: on which account we should often pray with David, *Cleanse thou me from secret faults!* Psa. xix. 12. How little attention is paid to this solemn subject! Sins of this kind—sins committed sometimes ignorantly, and more frequently *heedlessly,* are permitted to accumulate in their number, and consequently in their guilt; and from this very circumstance we may often account for those painful *desertions,* as they are called, under which many comparatively good people labour. They have committed sins of *ignorance* or *heedlessness,* and have not offered the sacrifice which can alone avail in their behalf. How necessary in ten thousand cases is the following excellent prayer! "That it may please thee to give us *true repentance;* to forgive us all our *sins, negligences,* and *ignorances;* and to endue us with the grace of thy Holy Spirit, to *amend our lives* according to thy Holy Word."—*Litany.*

CHAPTER V.

Concerning witnesses who, being adjured, refuse to tell the truth, 1. *Of those who contract defilement by touching unclean things or persons,* 2, 3. *Of those who bind themselves by vows or oaths, and do not fulfil them,* 4, 5. *The trespass-offering prescribed in such cases, a lamb or a kid,* 6; *a turtle-dove or two young pigeons,* 7–10; *or an ephah of fine flour with oil and frankincense,* 11–13. *Other laws relative to trespasses, through ignorance in holy things,* 14–16. *Of trespasses in things unknown,* 17–19.

A. M. 2514.
B. C. 1490.
An. Exod. Isr. 2.
Abib or Nisan.

AND if a soul sin, [a] and hear
the voice of swearing, and *is*
a witness, whether he hath seen
or known *of it;* if he do not
utter *it,* then he shall [b] bear his
iniquity.

A. M. 2514.
B. C. 1490.
An. Exod. Isr. 2.
Abib or Nisan.

[a] 1 Kings viii. 31; Matt. xxvi. 63.

[b] Ver. 17; chap. vii. 18; xvii. 16; xix. 8; xx. 17; Num. ix. 13.

NOTES ON CHAP. V.

Verse 1. *If a soul sin*] It is generally supposed that the case referred to here is that of a person who, being demanded by the civil magistrate to answer upon oath, refuses to tell what he knows concerning the subject; such a *one shall bear his iniquity*—shall

A. M. 2514.
B. C. 1490.
An. Exod. Isr. 2.
Abib or Nisan.

2 Or [c] if a soul touch any
unclean thing, whether *it be* a
carcass of an unclean beast, or
a carcass of unclean cattle, or the carcass of
unclean creeping things, and *if* it be hidden
from him; he also shall be unclean, and
[d] guilty.
3 Or if he touch [e] the uncleanness of man,
whatsoever uncleanness *it be* that a man shall
be defiled withal, and it be hid from him;
when he knoweth *of it*, then he shall be guilty.
4 Or if a soul swear, pronouncing with *his*
lips [f] to do evil, or [g] to do good, whatsoever *it*
be that a man shall pronounce with an oath,
and it be hid from him; when he knoweth *of*
it, then he shall be guilty in one of these.
5 And it shall be, when he shall be guilty in
one of these *things*, that he shall [h] confess
that he hath sinned in that *thing:*
6 And he shall bring his trespass-offering
unto the LORD, for his sin which he hath sinned, a female from the flock, a lamb or a kid
of the goats, for a sin-offering; and the priest
shall make an atonement for him concerning
his sin.
7 And [i] if [k] he be not able to bring a lamb,
then he shall bring for his trespass, which he
hath committed, two [l] turtle-doves, or two
young pigeons, unto the LORD; one for a sin-
offering, and the other for a burnt-offering.
8 And he shall bring them unto the priest,
who shall offer *that* which *is* for
the sin-offering first, and [m] wring
off his head from his neck, but
shall not divide *it* asunder:
9 And he shall sprinkle of the blood of the
sin-offering upon the side of the altar; and
[n] the rest of the blood shall be wrung out at
the bottom of the altar: it *is* a sin-offering
10 And he shall offer the second *for* a burnt-
offering, according to the [o] manner: [p] [q] and the
priest shall make an atonement for him for his
sin which he hath sinned, and it shall be forgiven him.
11 But if he be not able to bring two turtle-
doves, or two young pigeons, then he that
sinned shall bring for his offering the tenth
part of an ephah of fine flour for a sin-offering; [r] he shall put no oil upon it, neither shall
he put *any* frankincense thereon: for it *is* a
sin-offering.
12 Then shall he bring it to the priest, and
the priest shall take his handful of it, [s] *even* a
memorial thereof, and burn *it* on the altar, [t] according to the offerings made by fire unto the
LORD: it *is* a sin-offering.
13 [u] And the priest shall make an atonement
for him as touching his sin that he hath sinned
in one of these, and it shall be forgiven him:
and [v] *the remnant* shall be the priest's, as a
meat-offering.
14 And the LORD spake unto Moses, saying,

[c] Chap. xi. 24, 28, 31, 39; Num. xix. 11, 13, 16.——[d] Ver. 17. [e] Chap. xii., xiii., xv.——[f] See 1 Sam. xxv. 22; A s xxiii. 12. [g] See Mark vi. 23.——[h] Chap. xvi. 21; xxvi. 40; Num. v. 7; Ezra x. 11, 12.——[i] Chap. xii. 8; xiv. 21.——[k] Heb. *his hand cannot reach to the sufficiency of a lamb.*——[l] Chap. i. 14.——[m] Chap. i. 15.——[n] Chap. iv. 7, 18, 30, 34.——[o] Or, *ordinance.*——[p] Chap. i. 14.——[q] Chap. iv. 26.——[r] Num. v. 15. [s] Chap. ii. 2.——[t] Chap. iv. 35.——[u] Chap. iv. 26.——[v] Chap. ii. 3.

be considered as guilty in the sight of God, of the transgression which he has endeavoured to conceal, and must expect to be punished by him for hiding the iniquity to which he was privy, or suppressing the truth which, being discovered, would have led to the exculpation of the innocent, and the punishment of the guilty.

Verse 2. *Any unclean thing*] Either the *dead* body of a *clean* animal, or the *living* or *dead carcass* of any *unclean* creature. All such persons were to wash their clothes and themselves in clean water, and were considered as unclean till the evening, chap. xi. 24–31. But if this had been neglected, they were obliged to bring a *trespass-offering*. What this meant, see in the notes on chap. vii.

Verse 4. *To do evil, or to do good*] It is very likely that rash promises are here intended; for if a man vow to do an act that is evil, though it would be criminal to keep such an oath or vow, yet he is guilty because he made it, and therefore must offer the *trespass-offering*. If he neglect to do the *good* he has vowed, he is guilty, and must in both cases confess his iniquity, and bring his trespass-offering.

Verse 5. *He shall confess that he hath sinned*] Even *restitution* was not sufficient without this *confession*, because a man might make restitution without being much *humbled;* but the confession of sin has a direct tendency to humble the soul, and hence it is so frequently required in the Holy Scriptures, as without *humiliation* there can be no salvation.

Verse 7. *If he be not able to bring a lamb*] See the conclusion of chap. i.

Verse 8. *But shall not divide* it] See the note on chap. i. 16.

Verse 10. *He shall offer the second* for *a burnt-offering*] The pigeon for the burnt-offering was wholly consumed, it was the Lord's property; that for the sin-offering was the priest's property, and was to be eaten by him after its blood had been partly sprinkled on the side of the altar, and the rest poured out at the bottom of the altar. See also chap. vi. 26.

Verse 11. *Tenth part of an ephah*] About *three*

A. M. 2514. B. C. 1490. An. Exod. Isr. 2. Abib or Nisan.

15 [w]If a soul commit a trespass, and sin through ignorance, in the holy things of the LORD; then [x]he shall bring for his trespass unto the LORD a ram without blemish out of the flocks, with thy estimation by shekels of silver, after [y]the shekel of the sanctuary, for a trespass-offering:

16 And he shall make amends for the harm that he hath done in the holy thing, and [z]shall add the fifth part thereto, and give it unto the priest: [a]and the priest shall make an atonement for him with the ram of the trespass-offering, and it shall be forgiven him.

17 And if a [b]soul sin, and commit any of these things which are forbidden to be done by the commandments of the LORD; [c]though he wist *it* not, yet is he [d]guilty, and shall bear his iniquity.

A. M. 2514. B. C. 1490. An. Exod. Isr. 2. Abib or Nisan.

18 [e]And he shall bring a ram without blemish out of the flock, with thy estimation, for a trespass-offering, unto the priest: [f]and the priest shall make an atonement for him concerning his ignorance wherein he erred and wist *it* not, and it shall be forgiven him.

19 It *is* a trespass-offering: [g]he hath certainly trespassed against the LORD.

[w] Chap. xxii. 14.—[x] Ezra x. 19.—[y] Exod. xxx. 13; chap. xxvii. 25.—[z] Chap. vi. 5; xxii. 14; xxvii. 13, 15, 27, 31; Num. v. 7.—[a] Chap. iv. 26.

[b] Chap. iv. 2.—[c] Ver. 15; chap. iv. 2, 13, 22, 27; Psa. xix. 12; Luke xii. 48.—[d] Ver. 1, 2.—[e] Ver. 15.—[f] Ver. 16. [g] Ezra x. 2.

quarts. The ephah contained a little more than *seven* gallons and a *half.*

Verse 15. *In the holy things of the Lord*] This law seems to relate particularly to *sacrilege*, and *defrauds* in spiritual matters; such as the neglect to consecrate or redeem the first-born, the withholding of the first-fruits, tithes, and such like; and, according to the rabbins, making any secular gain of Divine things, keeping back any part of the price of things dedicated to God, or withholding what man had vowed to pay. See a long list of these things in *Ainsworth.*

With thy estimation] The wrong done or the defraud committed should be estimated at the number of shekels it was worth, or for which it would sell. These the defrauder was to pay down, to which he was to add a *fifth* part more, and bring a ram without blemish for a sin-offering besides. There is an obscurity in the text, but this seems to be its meaning.

Verse 16. *Shall make amends*] Make restitution for the wrong he had done according to what is laid down in the preceding verse.

Verse 19. *He hath certainly trespassed*] And because he hath sinned, therefore he must bring a sacrifice. On no other *ground* shall he be accepted by the Lord. Reader, how dost thou stand in the sight of thy Maker?

ON the subject of this chapter it may be proper to make the following reflections.

When the infinite purity and strict justice of God are considered, the exceeding breadth of his commandment, our slowness of heart to believe, and our comparatively cold performance of sacred duties, no wonder that there is sinfulness found in our *holy things;* and at what a low ebb must the Christian life be found when this is the case! This is a sore and degrading evil in the Church of God; but there is one even worse than this, that is, the strenuous endeavour of many religious people to reconcile their minds to this state of inexcusable imperfection, and *defend* it zealously, on the supposition that it is at once both *unavoidable* and *useful*—unavoidable, for they think they cannot live without it; and useful, because they suppose it tends to humble them! The more inward sin a man has, the more *pride* he will feel; the less, the more *humility.* A sense of God's infinite kindness to us, and our constant dependence on him, will ever keep the soul in the dust. Sin can never be necessary to the maintenance or extension of the Christian life, it is the thing which Jesus Christ came into the world to *destroy;* and his name is called JESUS or *Saviour* because he *saves his people from their sins.* But how little of the spirit and influence of his Gospel is known in the world! He saves, unto the uttermost, them who come unto the Father through him. But alas! how few are *thus* saved! for they will not come unto him that they might have life. Should any Christian refuse to offer up the following prayer to God? "Almighty God, unto whom all hearts be open, and from whom no secrets are hid, cleanse the thoughts of our hearts by the inspiration of thy Holy Spirit, that we may *perfectly love* thee, and *worthily magnify* thy holy name, through Christ our Lord. Amen."—*The Liturgy.*

CHAPTER VI.

Laws relative to detention of property intrusted to the care of another, to robbery, and deceit, 1, 2; *finding of goods lost, keeping them from their owner, and swearing falsely,* 3. *Such a person shall not only restore what he has thus unlawfully gotten, but shall add a* fifth part *of the value of the property besides,* 4, 5; *and bring a ram without blemish, for a trespass-offering to the Lord,* 6, 7. *Laws relative to the* burnt-offering *and the* perpetual fire. 8–13. *Law of the* meat-offering, *and who may lawfully eat of it,* 14–18. *Laws relative to the offerings of* Aaron *and his* sons *and their* successors, *on the day of their anointing,* 19–23. *Laws relative to the* sin-offering, *and those who might eat of it,* 24–30.

A. M. 2514.
B. C. 1490.
An. Exod. Isr. 2.
Abib or Nisan.

AND the LORD spake unto
Moses, saying,
2 If a soul sin, and [a] commit a
trespass against the LORD, and [b] lie unto his
neighbour in that [c] which was delivered him
to keep, or in [d] fellowship, [e] or in a thing
taken away by violence, or hath [f] deceived his
neighbour;
3 Or [g] have found that which was lost, and
lieth concerning it, and [h] sweareth falsely; in
any of all these that a man doeth, sinning
therein:
4 Then it shall be, because he hath sinned,
and is guilty, that he shall restore that which
he took violently away, or the thing which he
hath deceitfully gotten, or that which was delivered him to keep, or the lost thing which
he found,
5 Or all that about which he
hath sworn falsely; he shall even
[i] restore it in the principal, and
shall add the fifth part more thereto, *and* give
it unto him to whom it appertaineth, [k] in [l] the
day of his trespass-offering.
6 And he shall bring his trespass-offering
unto the LORD, [m] a ram without blemish out
of the flock, with thy estimation, for a trespass-offering unto the priest:
7 [n] And the priest shall make an atonement
for him before the LORD: and it shall be forgiven him for any thing of all that he hath
done in trespassing therein.
8 And the LORD spake unto Moses, saying,
9 Command Aaron and his sons, saying,
This *is* the law of the burnt-offering: It *is*
the burnt-offering, [o] because of the burning

A. M. 2514.
B. C. 1490.
An. Exod. Isr. 2.
Abib or Nisan.

[a] Num. v. 6.——[b] Chap. xix. 11; Acts v. 4; Col. iii. 9.——[c] Exod. xxii. 7, 10.——[d] Or, *in dealing.*——[e] Heb. *putting of the hand.*——[f] Prov. xxiv. 28; xxvi. 19.——[g] Deut. xxii. 1, 2, 3.——[h] Exod. xxii. 11; chap. xix. 12; Jer. vii. 9; Zech. v. 4.

[i] Chap. v. 16; Num. v. 7; 2 Sam. xii. 6; Luke xix. 8.——[k] Or, *in the day of his being found guilty.*——[l] Heb. *in the day of his trespass.*——[m] Chap. v. 15.——[n] Chap. iv. 26.——[o] Or, *for the burning.*

NOTES ON CHAP. VI.

Verse 2. *Lie unto his neighbour, &c.*] This must refer to a case in which a person delivered his property to his neighbour to be preserved for him, and took no witness to attest the delivery of the goods; such a person therefore might deny that he had ever received such goods, for he who had deposited them with him could bring no proof of the delivery. On the other hand, a man might accuse his neighbour of detaining property which had never been confided to him, or, after having been confided, had been restored again; hence the law here is very cautious on these points: and because in many cases it was impossible to come at the whole truth without a direct revelation from God, which should in no *common* case be expected, the penalties are very moderate; for in such cases, even when guilt was discovered, the man might not be so criminal as appearances might intimate. See the law concerning this laid down and explained on Exod. xxii. 7, &c.

Verse 3. *Have found that which was lost*] The Roman lawyers laid it down as a sound maxim of jurisprudence, "that he who found any property and applied it to his own use, should be considered as a thief whether he knew the owner or not; for in their view the crime was not lessened, supposing the finder was totally ignorant of the right owner." *Qui alienum quid jacens lucri faciendi causa sustulit, furti obstringitur, sive scit, cujus sit, sive ignoravit; nihil enim ad furtum minuendum facit, quod, cujus sit, ignoret.*—DIGESTOR, lib. xlvii., TIT. ii., *de furtis*, *Leg.* xliii., sec. 4. On this subject every honest man must say, that the man who finds any lost property, and does not make all due inquiry to find out the owner, should, in sound policy, be treated as a *thief*. It is said of the Dyrbæans, a people who inhabited the tract between Bactria and India, that if they met with any lost property, even on the public road, they never even touched it. This was actually the case in *this* kingdom in the time of Alfred the Great, about A. D. 888; so that golden bracelets hung up on the public roads were untouched by the finger of rapine. One of Solon's laws was, *Take not up what you laid not down.* How easy to act by this principle in case of finding lost property: "This is not mine, and it would be criminal to convert it to my use unless the owner be dead and his family extinct." When all due inquiry is made, if no owner can be found, the lost property may be legally considered to be the property of the finder.

Verse 5. *All that about which he hath sworn falsely*] This supposes the case of a man who, being convicted by his own conscience, comes forward and confesses his sin.

Restore it in the principal] The property itself if still remaining, or the full value of it, to which a *fifth* part more was to be added.

Verse 6. *With thy estimation*] See the note on chapter v. 15.

Verse 8. *And the Lord spake unto Moses*] At this verse the Jews begin the 25th section of the law; and here, undoubtedly, the 6th chapter should commence, as the writer enters upon a new subject, and the preceding verses belong to the *fifth* chapter. The best edited Hebrew Bibles begin the 6th chapter at this verse.

Verse 9. *This is the law of the burnt-offering*] This law properly refers to that burnt-offering which was daily made in what was termed the *morning* and *evening* sacrifice; and as he had explained the nature of this burnt-offering in general, with its necessary ceremonies, as far as the persons who brought them were concerned, he now takes up the same in relation to the priests who were to receive them from the hands of the offerer, and present them to the Lord on the altar of burnt-offerings.

A. M. 2514. B. C. 1490. An. Exod. Isr. 2. Abib or Nisan.

upon the altar all night unto the
morning; and the fire of the altar
shall be burning in it.
10 [p] And the priest shall put on his linen garment, and his linen breeches shall he put upon his flesh, and take up the ashes which the fire hath consumed with the burnt-offering on the altar, and he shall put them [q] beside the altar.
11 And [r] he shall put off his garments, and put on other garments, and carry forth the ashes without the camp [s] unto a clean place.
12 And the fire upon the altar shall be burning in it; it shall not be put out: and the priest shall burn wood on it every morning, and lay the burnt-offering in order upon it; and he shall burn thereon [t] the fat of the peace-offerings.
13 The fire shall ever be burning upon the altar, it shall never go out.
14 [u] And this *is* the law of the meat-offering: the sons of Aaron shall offer it before the LORD, before the altar.
15 And he shall take of it his handful of the flour of the meat-offering, and of the oil thereof, and all the frankincense which *is* upon
the meat-offering, and shall burn *it* upon the altar *for* a sweet savour, *even* the [v] memorial of it, unto the LORD.

A. M. 2514. B. C. 1490. An. Exod. Isr. 2. Abib or Nisan.

16 And [w] the remainder thereof shall Aaron and his sons eat: [x] with unleavened bread shall it be eaten in the holy place: in the court of the tabernacle of the congregation they shall eat it.
17 [y] It shall not be baken with leaven. [z] I have given it *unto them for* their portion of my offerings made by fire; [a] it *is* most holy, as *is* the sin-offering, and as the trespass-offering.
18 [b] All the males among the children of Aaron shall eat of it. [c] *It shall be* a statute for ever in your generations, concerning the offerings of the LORD made by fire: [d] every one that toucheth them shall be holy.
19 And the LORD spake unto Moses, saying,
20 [e] This *is* the offering of Aaron and of his sons, which they shall offer unto the LORD in the day when he is anointed: the tenth part of an [f] ephah of fine flour for a meat-offering perpetual, half of it in the morning, and half thereof at night.

[p] Chap. xvi. 4; Exod. xxviii. 39, 40, 41, 43; Ezek. xiv. 17, 18. — [q] Chap. i. 16. — [r] Ezek. xliv. 19. — [s] Chap. iv. 12. — [t] Chap. iii. 3, 9, 14. — [u] Chap. ii. 1; Num. xv. 4. — [v] Chap. ii. 2, 9. — [w] Chap. ii. 3; Ezek. xliv. 29. — [x] Ver. 26; chap. x. 12, 13; Numbers xviii. 10. — [y] Chap. ii. 11. — [z] Numbers xviii. 9, 10. — [a] Ver. 25; chap. ii. 3; vii. 1; Exod. xxix. 37. — [b] Ver. 29; Num. xviii. 10. — [c] Chap. iii. 17. — [d] Chap. xxii. 3, 4, 5, 6, 7; Exod. xxix. 37. — [e] Exod. xxix. 2. — [f] Exod. xvi. 36.

Because of the burning upon the altar all night] If the burnt-offering were put *all* upon the fire at once, it could not be burning *all night*. We may therefore reasonably conclude that the priests sat up by turns the whole night, and fed the fire with *portions* of this offering till the whole was consumed, which they would take care to lengthen out till the time of the morning sacrifice. The same we may suppose was done with the morning sacrifice; it was also consumed by *piecemeal* through the whole day, till the time of offering the evening sacrifice. Thus there was a *continual* offering by fire unto the Lord; and hence in ver. 13 it is said: *The fire shall ever be burning upon the altar, it shall never go out.* If at any time any extraordinary offerings were to be made, the daily sacrifice was consumed more speedily, in order to make room for such extra offerings. See more on this subject in the note on ver. 23.

The Hebrew doctors teach that no sacrifice was ever offered in the morning before the morning sacrifice; and none, the passover excepted, ever offered in the evening after the evening sacrifice; for all sacrifices were made by *day-light*. The fat seems to have been chiefly burned in the night season, for the greater light and conveniency of keeping the fire alive, which could not be so easily done in the night as in the day time.

Verse 11. *And put on other garments*] The priests approached the altar in their holiest garments; when carrying the ashes, &c., from the altar, they put on *other garments*, the holy garments being only used in the holy place.

Clean place.] A place where no dead carcasses, dung, or filth of any kind was laid; for the ashes were *holy*, as being the remains of the offerings made by fire unto the Lord.

Verse 13. *The fire shall ever be burning*] See on ver. 9 and ver. 20. In imitation of this perpetual fire, the ancient Persian Magi, and their descendants the *Parsees*, kept up a perpetual fire; the latter continue it to the present day. This is strictly enjoined in the *Zend Avesta*, which is a code of laws as sacred among them as the *Pentateuch* is among the Jews. A Sagnika Brahmin preserves the fire that was kindled at his investiture with the poita, and never suffers it to go out, using the same fire at his wedding and in all his burnt-offerings, till at length his body is burnt with it.—WARD's *Customs.*

Verse 14. *The meat-offering*] See on chap. ii. 1, &c.

Verse 15. *His handful of the flour*] An *omer* of flour, which was the *tenth part of an ephah*, and equal to about *three quarts* of our measure, was the least quantity that could be offered even by the poorest sort, and this was generally accompanied with a *log* of oil, which was a little more than *half a pint*. This quantity both of flour and oil might be *increased* at pleasure, but *no less* could be offered.

Verse 20. *In the day when he is anointed*] Not only *in* that day, but *from* that day forward, for this

A. M. 2514. B. C. 1490. An. Exod. Isr. 2. Abib or Nisan.

21 In a pan it shall be made
with oil; *and when it is* baken,
thou shalt bring it in: *and* the
baken pieces of the meat-offering shalt thou
offer *for* a sweet savour unto the LORD.
22 And the priest of his sons [g] that is
anointed in his stead shall offer it: *it is* a
statute for ever unto the LORD; [h] it shall be
wholly burnt.
23 For every meat-offering for the priest
shall be wholly burnt: it shall not be eaten.
24 And the LORD spake unto Moses, saying,
25 Speak unto Aaron and to his sons, saying,
[i] This *is* the law of the sin-offering: [k] In
the place where the burnt-offering is killed
shall the sin-offering be killed before the
LORD: [l] it *is* most holy.
26 [m] The priest that offereth it for sin shall
eat it: [n] in the holy place shall it
be eaten, in the court of the tabernacle of the congregation.
27 [o] Whatsoever shall touch the flesh thereof shall be holy: and when there is sprinkled of
the blood thereof upon any garment, thou shalt
wash that whereon it was sprinkled in the
holy place.
28 But the earthen vessel wherein it is
sodden [p] shall be broken: and if it be sodden
in a brazen pot, it shall be both scoured, and
rinsed in water.
29 [q] All the males among the priests shall
eat thereof: [r] it *is* most holy.
30 [s] And no sin-offering, whereof *any* of the
blood is brought into the tabernacle of the
congregation, to reconcile *withal* in the holy
place, shall be eaten: it shall be burnt in the fire.

[g] Chap. iv. 3.——[h] Exod. xxix. 25.——[i] Chap. iv. 2.——[k] Chap. i. 3, 5, 11, iv. 24, 29, 33.——[l] Ver. 17; chap. xxi. 22.——[m] Chap. x. 17, 18; Num. xviii. 9, 10; Ezek. xliv. 28, 29.

[n] Ver. 16.——[o] Exod. xxix. 37; xxx. 29.——[p] Chap. xi. 33; xv. 12.——[q] Ver. 18; Num. xviii. 10.——[r] Ver. 25.——[s] Chap. iv. 7, 11, 12, 18, 21; x. 18; xvi. 27; Heb. xiii. 11.

was to them and their successors a *statute for ever*. See verse 22.

Verse 23. *For every meat-offering for the priest shall be wholly burnt*] Whatever the priest offered was *wholly* the Lord's, and therefore must be entirely consumed: the sacrifices of the common people were offered to the Lord, but the priests partook of them; and thus they who ministered at the altar were fed by the altar. Had the priests been permitted to live on their own offerings as they did on those of the people, it would have been as if they had offered *nothing*, as they would have taken again to themselves what they appeared to give unto the Lord. Theodoret says that this marked "the high perfection which God required in the ministers of his sanctuary," as his not eating of his own sin-offering supposes him to stand free from all sin; but a better reason is given by Mr. Ainsworth: "The people's meat-offering was eaten by the priests that made atonement for them, ver. 15, 16, chap. vii. 7; but because no priest, being a sinner, could make atonement for himself, therefore his meat-offering might not be eaten, but all burnt on the altar, to teach him to expect salvation, not by his legal service or works, but by Christ; for the eating of the sin-offering figured the bearing of the sinner's iniquity;" chap. x. 17.

Verse 25. *In the place where the burnt-offering is killed, &c.*] The place here referred to was the north side of the altar. See chap. i. 11.

Verse 26. *The priest—shall eat it*] From the expostulation of Moses with Aaron, chap. x. 17, we learn that the priest, by eating the sin-offering of the people, was considered as bearing their sin, and typically removing it from them: and besides, this was a part of their maintenance, or what the Scripture calls their *inheritance*; see Ezek. xliv. 27–30. This was afterwards greatly abused; for improper persons endeavoured to get into the priest's office *merely* that they might get a *secular* provision, which is a horrible profanity in the sight of God. See 1 Sam. ii. 36; Jer. xxiii. 1, 2; Ezek. xxxiv. 2–4; and Hos. iv. 8.

Verse 27. *Whatsoever shall touch the flesh thereof shall be holy*] The following note of Mr. Ainsworth is not less judicious than it is pious:—

"All this rite was peculiar to the sin-offering, (whether it were that which was to be eaten, or that which was to be burnt,) above all the other most holy things. As the sin-offering in special sort figured Christ, who was made sin for us, (2 Cor. v. 21,) so this ordinance—for all that touched the flesh of the sin-offering to be holy, the garments sprinkled with the blood to be washed, the vessels wherein the flesh was boiled to be broken, or scoured and rinsed—taught a holy use of this mystery of our redemption, whereof they that are made partakers ought to be washed, cleansed, and sanctified by the Spirit of God; that we possess our vessels in holiness and honour, and yield not our members as instruments of unrighteousness unto sin," 1 Thess. iv. 4; Rom. vi. 13.

Verse 28. *The earthen vessel—shall be broken*] Calmet states that this should be considered as implying the vessels brought by individuals to the court of the temple or tabernacle, and not of the vessels that belonged to the priests for the ordinary service. That the people dressed their sacrifices sometimes in the court of the tabernacle, he gathers from 1 Sam. ii. 13, 14, to which the reader is desired to refer.

In addition to what has been already said on the different subjects in this chapter, it may be necessary to notice a few more particulars. The *perpetual meat-offering*, מנחה תמיד *minchah tamid*, ver. 20, the *perpetual fire*, אש תמיד *esh tamid*, ver. 13, and the *perpetual burnt-offering*, עלת תמיד *olath tamid*, Exod. xxix. 42, translated by the Septuagint θυσια διαπαντος, πυρ διαπαντος, and ὁλοκαυτωσις and ὁλοκαυτωμα διαπαντος, all cast much light on Heb. vii. 25, where it is said, Christ *is able to save them to the* uttermost (εις το

παντελες, perpetually, to all intents and purposes) *that come unto God by him; seeing he ever liveth (παντοτε ζων, he is perpetually living) to make intercession for them;* in which words there is a manifest allusion to the *perpetual minchah*, the *perpetual fire*, and the *perpetual burnt-offering*, mentioned here by Moses. As the *minchah*, or gratitude-offering should be perpetual, so our gratitude for the innumerable mercies of God should be perpetual. As the burnt-offering must be perpetual, so should the sacrifice of our blessed Lord be considered as a perpetual offering, that all men, *in all ages*, should come unto God through him who is ever living, in his sacrificial character, to make intercession for men; and who is therefore represented even in the heavens as the Lamb just slain, standing before the throne, Rev. v. 6; Heb. x. 19–22. And as the fire on the altar must be perpetual, so should the influences of the Holy Spirit in every member of the Church, and the flame of pure devotion in the hearts of believers, be ever energetic and permanent. A continual sacrifice for continual successive generations of sinners was essentially necessary. Continual

influences of the Holy Spirit on the souls of men were essentially necessary to apply and render effectual this atonement, to the salvation of the soul. And incessant gratitude for the ineffable love of God, manifested by his unspeakable gift, is surely required of all those who have tasted that the Lord is gracious. Reader, dost thou feel thy obligations to thy Maker? Does the perpetual fire burn on the altar of *thy* heart? Art *thou* ever looking unto Jesus, and beholding, by faith, the Lamb of God which taketh away the sin of the world? And dost thou feel the influences of his Spirit, at all times witnessing with thy spirit that thou art his child, and exciting thee to acts of *gratitude* and *obedience?* If not, of what benefit has the religion of Christ been to thee to the present day? Of a contrary state to that referred to above, it may be well said, This is not the way to heaven, for the way of life is above to the wise, that they may depart from the snares of death beneath. Arise, therefore, and shake thyself from the dust; and earnestly call upon the Lord thy God, that he may save thy soul, and that thou fall not into the bitter pains of an eternal death.

CHAPTER VII.

The law of the trespass-offering, and the priest's portion in it, 1–7. *As also in the sin-offerings and meat-offerings,* 8–10. *The law of the sacrifice of peace-offering,* 11, *whether it was a thanksgiving-offering,* 12–15 ; *or a vow or voluntary offering,* 16–18. *Concerning the flesh that touched any unclean thing,* 19. 20, *and the person who touched any thing unclean,* 21. *Laws concerning eating of fat,* 22–25, *and concerning eating of blood,* 26, 27. *Farther ordinances concerning the peace-offerings and the priest's portion in them,* 28–36. *Conclusion of the laws and ordinances relative to burnt-offerings, meat-offerings, sin-offerings, and peace-offerings, delivered in this and the preceding chapters,* 37, 38.

A. M. 2514.
B. C. 1490.
An. Exod. Isr. 2
Abib or Nisan.

LIKEWISE [a] this *is* the law of the trespass-offering : [b] it *is* most holy.

2 [c] In the place where they kill the burnt-offering, shall they kill the trespass-offering : and the blood thereof shall he sprinkle round about upon the altar.

3 And he shall offer of it [d] all the fat thereof ; the rump, and the fat that covereth the inwards,

4 And the two kidneys, and the fat that *is* on them, which *is* by the flanks, and the caul *that is* above the liver, with the kidneys, it shall he take away :

5 And the priest shall burn them upon the altar *for* an offering made by fire unto the LORD : it *is* a trespass-offering.

A. M. 2514.
B. C. 1490.
An. Exod. Isr. 2
Abib or Nisan.

6 [e] Every male among the priests shall eat thereof : it shall be eaten in the holy place : [f] it *is* most holy.

7 As the sin-offering *is*, so *is* [g] the trespass-offering : *there is* one law for them : the priest that maketh atonement therewith shall have *it*.

8 And the priest that offereth any man's burnt-offering, *even* the priest shall have to

[a] Chap. v., vi. 1-7.——[b] Chap. vi. 17, 25 ; xxi. 22.——[c] Chap. i. 3, 5, 11 ; iv. 24, 29, 33.——[d] Chap. iii. 4, 9, 10, 14, 15, 16 ;
iv. 8, 9 ; Exod. xxix. 13.——[e] Chap. vi. 16, 17, 18 ; Num. xviii. 9, 10.——[f] Chap. ii. 3.——[g] Chap. vi. 25, 26 ; xiv. 13.

NOTES ON CHAP. VII.

Verse 1. *Trespass-offering*] See end of the chapter.

Verse 2. *In the place where they kill the burnt-offering*] Viz., on the *north side of the altar*, chap. i. 11.

Verse 3. *The rump*] See the notes on chap. iii. 9, where the principal subjects in this chapter are explained, being nearly the same in both.

Verse 4. *The fat that is on them*] Chiefly the fat that was found in a *detached* state, not mixed with the muscles ; such as the *omentum* or *caul*, the fat of the

mesentery, the fat about the *kidneys*, &c. See the notes on chap. iii. 9, &c.

Verse 8. *The priest shall have to himself the skin*] Bishop Patrick supposes that this right of the priest to the *skin* commenced with the offering of Adam, " for it is probable," says he, " that Adam himself offered the first sacrifice, and had the skin given him by God to make garments for him and his wife ; in conformity to which the priests ever after had the skin of the whole burnt-offerings for their portion, which was a

A. M. 2514.
B. C. 1490.
An. Exod. Isr. 2.
Abib or Nisan.

himself the skin of the burnt-
offering which he hath offered.
9 And [h] all the meat-offering
that is baken in the oven, and all that is
dressed in the frying-pan, and [i] in the pan,
shall be the priest's that offereth it.
10 And every meat-offering, mingled with
oil, and dry, shall all the sons of Aaron have,
one *as much* as another.
11 And [k] this *is* the law of the sacrifice of
peace-offerings, which he shall offer unto the
LORD.
12 If he offer it for a thanksgiving, then he
shall offer with the sacrifice of
thanksgiving unleavened cakes
mingled with oil, and unleavened
wafers [l] anointed with oil, and cakes mingled
with oil, of fine flour, fried.
13 Besides the cakes, he shall offer *for* his
offering [m] leavened bread with the sacrifice of
thanksgiving of his peace-offerings.
14 And of it he shall offer one out of the
whole oblation *for* a heave-offering unto the
LORD, [n] *and* it shall be the priest's that sprinkleth the blood of the peace-offerings.
15 [o] And the flesh of the sacrifice of his

A. M. 2514.
B. C. 1490.
An. Exod. Isr. 2.
Abib or Nisan.

[h] Chap. ii. 3, 10; Num. xviii. 9; Ezek. xliv. 29.——[i] Or, *on the flat plate* or *slice*.——[k] Chap. iii. 1; xxii. 18, 21.

[l] Chap. ii. 4; Num. vi. 15.——[m] Amos iv. 5.——[n] Num. xviii. 8, 11, 19.——[o] Chap. xxii. 30.

custom among the Gentiles as well as the Jews, who gave the skins of their sacrifices to their priests, when they were not burnt with the sacrifices, as in some sin-offerings they were among the Jews, see chap. iv. 11. And they employed them to a superstitious use, by lying upon them in their temples, in hopes to have future things revealed to them in their dreams. Of this we have a proof in Virgil, Æn. lib. vii., ver. 86–95.

"————huc dona sacerdos
Cum tulit, et *cæsarum ovium* sub nocte silenti
Pellibus incubuit stratis, somnosque petivit;
Multa modus simulacra videt volitantia miris,
Et varias audit voces, fruiturque deorum
Colloquio, atque imis Acheronta affatur Avernis.
Hic et tum pater ipse petens responsa Latinus
Centum lanigeras mactabat rite bidentes,
Atque harum effultus tergo *stratisque jacebat*
Velleribus. Subita ex alto vox reddita luco est."

First, *on the fleeces* of the *slaughter'd sheep*
By night the *sacred priest dissolves in sleep*,
When in a train, before his slumbering eye,
Thin airy forms and wondrous visions fly.
He calls the powers who guard the infernal floods,
And talks, inspired, familiar with the gods.
To this dread oracle the prince withdrew,
And first a *hundred sheep the monarch slew;*
Then *on their fleeces lay;* and from the wood
He heard, distinct, these accents of the god.—PITT.

The same superstition, practised precisely in the same way and for the same purposes, prevails to the present day in the Highlands of Scotland, as the reader may see from the following note of Sir Walter Scott, in his *Lady of the Lake:*—

"The Highlanders of Scotland, like all rude people, had various superstitious modes of inquiring into futurity. One of the most noted was the *togharm*. A person was wrapped up in the *skin of a newly-slain bullock*, and deposited beside a water-fall, or at the bottom of a precipice, or in some other strange, wild, and unusual situation, where the scenery around him suggested nothing but objects of horror. In this situation he revolved in his mind the question proposed; and whatever was impressed upon him by his exalted imagination, passed for the inspiration of the disembodied spirits who haunt these desolate recesses. One way of consulting this oracle was by a party of men, who first retired to solitary places, remote from any house, and there they singled out one of their number, and *wrapt him in a big cow's hide*, which they folded about him; his whole body was covered with it except his head, and so left in this posture all night, until his invisible friends relieved him by giving a proper answer to the question in hand; which he received, as he fancied, from several persons that he found about him all that time. His consorts returned to him at day-break; and then he communicated his news to them, which often proved fatal to those concerned in such unwarrantable inquiries.

"Mr. Alexander Cooper, present minister of North Virt, told me that one *John Erach*, in the Isle of Lewis, assured him it was his fate to have been led by his curiosity with some who consulted this oracle, and that he was a night *within the hide above mentioned*, during which time he felt and heard such terrible things that he could not express them: the impression made on him was such as could never go off; and he said, for a thousand worlds he would never again be concerned in the like performance, for it had disordered him to a high degree. He confessed it ingenuously, and with an air of great remorse, and seemed to be very penitent under a just sense of so great a crime: he declared this about five years since, and is still living in the Isle of Lewis for any thing I know."—*Description of the Western Isles*, p. 110. See also Pennant's *Scottish Tour*, vol. ii., p. 301; and Sir W. Scott's *Lady of the Lake*.

Verse 9. *Baken in the oven*] See the notes on chap. ii. 5, &c.

Verse 12. *If he offer it for a thanksgiving*] See the notes at the end of this chapter.

Verse 15. *He shall not leave any of it until the morning.*] Because in such a hot country it was apt to putrefy, and as it was considered to be *holy*, it would have been very improper to expose that to putrefaction which had been consecrated to the Divine Being. Mr. Harmer supposes that the law here refers rather to the custom of *drying flesh* which had been devoted to religious purposes, which is practised among the Mohammedans to the present time. This,

A. M. 2514.
B. C. 1490.
An. Exod. Isr. 2.
Abib or Nisan.

peace-offerings for thanksgiving shall be eaten the same day that it is offered; he shall not leave any of it until the morning.

16 But [p] if the sacrifice of his offering *be* a vow, or a voluntary offering, it shall be eaten the same day that he offereth his sacrifice: and on the morrow also the remainder of it shall be eaten:

17 But the remainder of the flesh of the sacrifice on the third day shall be burnt with fire.

18 And if *any* of the flesh of the sacrifice of his peace-offerings be eaten at all on the third day, it shall not be accepted, neither shall it be [q] imputed unto him that offereth it: it shall be an [r] abomination, and the soul that eateth of it shall bear his iniquity.

19 And the flesh that toucheth any unclean *thing* shall not be eaten; it shall be burnt with fire: and as for the flesh, all that be clean shall eat thereof.

20 But the soul that eateth *of* the flesh of the sacrifice of peace-offerings that *pertain* unto the LORD, [s] having his uncleanness upon him, even that soul [t] shall be cut off from his people.

21 Moreover the soul that shall touch any unclean *thing, as* [u] the uncleanness of man, or *any* [v] unclean beast, or any [w] abominable unclean *thing*, and eat of the flesh of the sacrifice of peace-offerings, which *pertain* unto the LORD, even that soul [x] shall be cut off from his people.

A. M. 2514.
B. C. 1490.
An. Exod. Isr. 2.
Abib or Nisan.

22 And the LORD spake unto Moses, saying,

23 Speak unto the children of Israel, saying, [y] Ye shall eat no manner of fat, of ox, or of sheep, or of goat.

24 And the fat of the [z] beast that dieth of itself, and the fat of that which is torn with beasts, may be used in any other use: but ye shall in nowise eat of it.

25 For whosoever eateth the fat of the beast, of which men offer an offering made by fire unto the LORD, even the soul that eateth *it* shall be cut off from his people.

26 [a] Moreover ye shall eat no manner of blood, *whether it be* of fowl or of beast, in any of your dwellings.

27 Whatsoever soul *it be* that eateth any manner of blood, even that soul shall be cut off from his people.

28 And the LORD spake unto Moses, saying,

29 Speak unto the children of Israel, saying, [b] He that offereth the sacrifice of his peace offerings unto the LORD shall bring his oblation unto the LORD, of the sacrifice of his peace-offerings.

30 [c] His own hands shall bring the offerings of the LORD made by fire, the fat with the breast, it shall he bring, that [d] the breast may be waved *for* a wave-offering before the LORD.

[p] Chap. xix. 6, 7, 8.——[q] Num. xviii. 27.——[r] Chap. xi. 10, 11, 41; xix. 7.——[s] Chap. xv. 3.——[t] Gen. xvii. 14.——[u] Chap. xii., xiii., xv.——[v] Chap. xi. 24, 28.——[w] Ezek. iv. 14.——[x] Ver. 20. [y] Chap. iii. 17.

[z] Heb. *carcass;* chap. xvii. 15; Deut. xiv. 21; Ezek. iv. 14; xliv. 31.——[a] Gen. ix. 4; chap. iii. 17; xvii. 10–14.——[b] Chap. iii. 1.——[c] Chap. iii. 3, 4, 9, 14.——[d] Exod. xxix. 24, 27; chap viii. 27; ix. 21; Num. vi. 20.

he thinks, might have given rise to the prohibition, as the sacred flesh thus preserved might have been abused to superstitious purposes. Therefore God says, ver. 18, "If any of the flesh of the sacrifice—be eaten at all on the third day, it shall not be accepted, neither shall it be imputed unto him that offereth it; it is an abomination, and the soul that eateth of it shall bear his iniquity." That is, on Mr. Harmer's hypothesis, This sacred flesh shall avail nothing to him that eats it after the first or second day on which it is offered; however consecrated *before*, it shall not be considered sacred *after* that time. See *Harmer's Obs.*, vol. i., p. 394, edit. 1808.

Verse 20. *Having his uncleanness upon him*] Having touched any unclean thing by which he became legally defiled, and had not washed his clothes, and bathed his flesh.

Verse 21. *The uncleanness of man*] Any ulcer, sore, or leprosy; or any sort of cutaneous disorder, either *loathsome* or *infectious*.

Verse 23. *Fat, of ox, or of sheep, or of goat.*] Any *other* fat they might eat, but the fat of these was sacred, because they were the only animals which were offered in sacrifice, though many others ranked among the *clean* animals as well as these. But it is likely that this prohibition is to be understood of these animals *when* offered in sacrifice, and *then only* in reference to the *inward fat*, as mentioned on ver. 4. Of the fat in any other circumstances it cannot be intended, as it was one of the especial blessings which God gave to the people. *Butter of kine, and milk of sheep, with* FAT *of* LAMBS, *and* RAMS *of the breed of Bashan, and* GOATS, were the provision that he gave to his followers. See Deut. xxxii. 12–14.

Verse 27. *Whatsoever soul—that eateth any manner of blood*] See the note on Gen. ix. 4. *Shall be cut off*—excommunicated from the people of God, and so deprived of any part in their inheritance, and in their blessings. See the note on Gen. xvii. 14.

Verse 29. *Shall bring his oblation*] Meaning those things which were given out of the peace-offerings to the Lord and to the priest.—*Ainsworth*.

Verse 30. *Wave-offering*] See on Exod. xxix. 27,

A. M. 2514.
B. C. 1490.
An. Exod. Isr. 2.
Abib or Nisan.

31 [e]And the priest shall burn the fat upon the altar: [f] but the breast shall be Aaron's and his sons'.

32 And [g] the right shoulder shall ye give unto the priest *for* a heave-offering of the sacrifices of your peace-offerings.

33 He among the sons of Aaron, that offereth the blood of the peace-offerings, and the fat, shall have the right shoulder for *his* part.

34 For [h] the wave breast and the heave shoulder have I taken of the children of Israel from off the sacrifices of their peace-offerings, and have given them unto Aaron the priest, and unto his sons, by a statute for ever, from among the children of Israel.

35 This *is the portion* of the anointing of Aaron, and of the anointing of his sons, out of the offerings of the LORD made by fire, in the day *when* he presented them to minister unto the LORD in the priest's office,

A. M. 2514.
B. C. 1490.
An. Exod. Isr. 2.
Abib or Nisan.

36 Which the LORD commanded to be given them of the children of Israel, [i] in the day that he anointed them, *by* a statute for ever throughout their generations.

37 This *is* the law [k] of the burnt-offering, [l] of the meat-offering, [m] and of the sin-offering, [n] and of the trespass-offering, [o] and of the consecrations, and [p] of the sacrifice of the peace-offerings,

38 Which the LORD commanded Moses in Mount Sinai, in the day that he commanded the children of Israel [q] to offer their oblations unto the LORD, in the wilderness of Sinai.

[e] Chap. iii. 5, 11, 16.——[f] Ver. 34.——[g] Ver. 34; chap. ix. 21; Num. vi. 20.——[h] Exod. xxix. 28; chap. x. 14, 15; Num. xviii. 18, 19; Deut. xviii. 3.

[i] Chap. viii. 12, 30; Exod. xl. 13, 15.——[k] Chap. vi. 9. [l] Chap. vi. 14.——[m] Chap. vi. 25.——[n] Ver. 1.——[o] Chap. vi. 20; Exod. xxix. 1.——[p] Ver. 11.——[q] Chap. i. 2.

Verse 32. *The right shoulder*] See on Exod. xxix. 27.

Verse 36. *In the day that he anointed them*] See the note on Exod. xl. 15.

Verse 38. *In the wilderness of Sinai.*] These laws were probably given to Moses while he was on the mount with God; the time was quite sufficient, as he was there with God not less than fourscore days in all; forty days at the *giving*, and forty days at the *renewing*, of the law.

As in the course of this book the different kinds of sacrifices commanded to be offered are repeatedly occurring, I think it best, once for all, to give a general account of them, and a definition of the original terms, as well as of all others *relative* to this subject which are used in the Old Testament, and the reference in which they all stood to the great sacrifice offered by Christ.

1. אשם ASHAM, TRESPASS-*offering*, from אשם *asham*, to be *guilty*, or *liable to punishment;* for in this sacrifice the guilt was considered as being transferred to the animal offered up to God, and the offerer redeemed from the penalty of his sin, ver. 37. Christ is said to have made his soul an offering for sin, (אשם,) Isa. liii. 10.

2. אשה ISHSHEH, FIRE-*offering*, probably from אשש *ashash*, to be *grieved*, *angered*, *inflamed;* either pointing out the distressing nature of sin, or its property of incensing Divine justice against the offender, who, in consequence, deserving burning for his offence, made use of this sacrifice to be freed from the punishment due to his transgression. It occurs Exod. xxix. 18, and in many places of this book.

3. הבהבים HABHABIM, ITERATED OR REPEATED *offerings*, from יהב *yahab*, to *supply*. The word occurs only in Hos. viii. 13, and probably means no more than the continual *repetition* of the accustomed offerings, or continuation of each part of the sacred service.

4. זבח ZEBACH, a SACRIFICE, (in Chaldee, דבח *debach*, the ז *zain* being changed into ד *daleth*,) a creature slain in sacrifice, from זבח *zabach*, to *slay;* hence the altar on which such sacrifices were offered was termed מזבח *mizbeach*, the place of sacrifice. See the note on Gen. viii. 2. *Zebach* is a common name for sacrifices in general.

5. חג CHAG, a *festival*, especially such as had a periodical return, from חגג *chagag*, to *celebrate a festival*, to *dance round and round in circles*. See Exod. v. 1; xii. 24. The circular dance was probably intended to point out the revolution of the heavenly bodies, and the exact return of the different seasons. See *Parkhurst*.

6. חטאת CHATTATH and חטאה CHATTAAH, SIN-*offering*, from חטא *chata*, to *miss the mark*; it also signifies *sin* in general, and is a very apt term to express its nature by. A sinner is continually aiming at and seeking happiness; but as he does not seek it in God, hence the Scripture represents him as *missing his aim*, or *missing the mark*. This is precisely the meaning of the Greek word ἁμαρτια, translated *sin* and *sin-offering* in our version; and this is the term by which the Hebrew word is translated both by the Septuagint and the inspired writers of the New Testament. The sin-offering was at once an acknowledgment of guilt, in having forsaken the fountain of living waters, and hewed out cisterns that could hold none; and also of the firm purpose of the offerer to return to God, the true and pure fountain of blessedness. This word often occurs. See the note on Gen. iv. 7; xiii. 13.

7. כפר COPHER, the EXPIATION OR ATONEMENT, from כפר *caphar*, to *cover*, to *smear over*, or *obliterate*, or annul a contract. Used often to signify the atonement or expiation made for the pardon or cancelling of iniquity. See more in the note on Exod. xxv. 17.

8. מועד MOED, an APPOINTED *annual festival*, from יעד *yaad*, to *appoint* or *constitute*, signifying such feasts as were instituted in commemoration of some great event or deliverance, such as the deliverance from Egypt.

See Exod. xiii. 10, and thus differing from the *chag* mentioned above. See the note on Gen. i. 14.

9. מלאים MILLUIM, CONSECRATIONS or *consecration-offerings*, from מלא *mala*, to *fill;* those offerings made in consecrations, of which the priests *partook*, or, in the Hebrew phrase, had their *hands filled*, or which had filled the hands of them that offered them. See the note on Exod. xxix. 19; and see 2 Chron. xiii. 9.

10. מנחה MINCHAH, MEAT-*offering*, from נח *nach*, to *rest*, *settle* after toil. It generally consisted of things without life, such as green ears of corn, full ears of corn, flour, oil, and frankincense; (see on chap. ii. 1, &c.;) and may be considered as having its name from that *rest* from labour and toil which a man had when the fruits of the autumn were brought in, or when, in consequence of obtaining any *rest*, *ease*, &c., a significant offering or sacrifice was made to God. It often occurs. See the note on Gen. iv. 3. The jealousy-offering (Num. v. 15) was a simple *minchah*, consisting of *barley-meal* only.

11. מסך MESECH and ממסך MIMSACH, a MIXTURE-*offering*, or MIXED LIBATION, called a DRINK-*offering*, Isa. lv. 11, from מסך *masach*, to *mingle;* it seems in general to mean *old wine mixed with the less*, which made it extremely intoxicating. This offering does not appear to have had any place in the worship of the *true* God; but from Isa. lxv. 11, and Prov. xxiii. 30, it seems to have been used for idolatrous purposes, such as the Bacchanalia among the Greeks and Romans, "when all got drunk in honour of the god."

12. משאת MASSEETH, an OBLATION, things *carried* to the temple to be presented to God, from נשא *nasa*, to *bear* or *carry*, to bear sin; *typically*, Exod. xxviii. 38; chap. x. 17; xvi. 21; *really*, Isa. liii. 4, 12. The sufferings and death of Christ were the true *masseeth* or *vicarious bearing* of the sins of mankind, as the passage in Isaiah above referred to sufficiently proves. See this alluded to by the Evangelist John, chap. i. 29; and see the root in *Parkhurst*.

13. נדבה NEDABAH, FREE-WILL or *voluntary offering;* from נדב *nadab*, to be *free*, *liberal*, *princely*. An offering not commanded, but given as a particular proof of extraordinary gratitude to God for especial mercies, or on account of some vow or engagement *voluntarily* taken, ver. 16.

14. נסך NESECH, LIBATION, or DRINK-*offering*, from נסך *nasach*, to *diffuse* or *pour out*. Water or wine poured out at the conclusion or confirmation of a treaty or covenant. To this kind of offering there is frequent allusion and reference in the New Testament, as it typified the blood of Christ poured out for the sin of the world; and to this our Lord himself alludes in the institution of the holy eucharist. The whole Gospel economy is represented as a covenant or treaty between God and man, Jesus Christ being not only the *mediator*, but the *covenant sacrifice*, whose blood was poured out for the ratification and confirmation of this covenant or agreement between God and man.

15. עלה and עולה OLAH, BURNT-*offering*, from עלה *alah*, to *ascend*, because this offering, as being wholly consumed, *ascended* as it were to God in *smoke* and *vapour*. It was a very expressive type of the sacrifice of Christ, as nothing less than his complete and full sacrifice could make atonement for the sin of the world. In most other offerings the priest, and often the offerer, had a *share*, but in the whole burnt-offering *all* was given to God.

16. קטרת KETORETH, INCENSE or PERFUME-*offering*, from קטר *katar*, to *burn*, i. e. the *frankincense*, and other aromatics used as a perfume in different parts of the Divine service. To this St. Paul compares the agreeableness of the sacrifice of Christ to God, Eph. v. 2: *Christ hath given himself for us, an offering—to God for a* SWEET-SMELLING *savour*. From Rev. v. 8 we learn that it was intended also to represent the *prayers of the saints*, which, offered up on that altar, Christ Jesus, that sanctifies every gift, are highly pleasing in the sight of God.

17. קרבן KOREAN, the GIFT-*offering*, from קרב *karab*, to *draw nigh* or *approach*. See this explained on chap. i. 2. *Korban* was a general name for *any kind of offering*, because through these it was supposed a man had *access* to his Maker.

18. שלמים SHELAMIM, PEACE-*offering*, from שלם *shalam*, to *complete*, *make whole;* for by these offerings that which was *lacking* was considered as being now *made up*, and that which was *broken*, viz., the covenant of God, by his creatures' transgression, was supposed to be *made whole;* so that after such an offering, the sincere and conscientious mind had a right to consider that the breach was made up between God and it, and that it might lay confident hold on this covenant of peace. To this the apostle evidently alludes, Eph. ii. 14–19: *He is our peace*, (i. e. our *shalam* or peace-offering,) *who has made both one, and broken down the middle wall; having abolished in his flesh the enmity*, &c. See the whole passage, and see the note on Gen. xiv. 18.

19. תודה TODAH, THANK-*offering*, from ידה *yadah*, to *confess;* offerings made to God with public confession of his power, goodness, mercy, &c.

20. תנופה TENUPHAH, WAVE-*offering*, from נף *naph*, to *stretch out;* an offering of the first-fruits *stretched out before God*, in acknowledgment of his providential goodness. This offering was moved from the right hand to the left. See the note on Exod. xxix. 27.

21. תרומה TERUMAH, HEAVE-*offering*, from רם *ram*, to *lift up*, because the offering was *lifted up* towards heaven, as the *wave*-offering, in token of the kindness of God in granting rain and fruitful seasons, and filling the heart with food and gladness. As the wave offering was moved from *right* to *left*, so the heave offering was moved *up* and *down;* and in both cases this was done several times. These offerings had a blessed tendency to keep alive in the breasts of the people a due sense of their dependence on the Divine providence and bounty, and of their obligation to God for his continual and liberal supply of all their wants. See the note on Exod. xxix. 27.

In the above collection are comprised, as far as I can recollect, an explanation of all the terms used in the Hebrew Scriptures which signify sacrifice, oblation, atonement, offering, &c., &c., as well as the reference they bear to the great and only sufficient atonement, sacrifice, oblation, and satisfaction made by Christ Jesus for the sins of mankind. Larger accounts must be sought in authors who treat professedly on these subjects.

CHAPTER VIII.

Moses is commanded to consecrate Aaron and his sons, 1–3. *Moses convenes the congregation; washes, clothes, and anoints Aaron,* 4–12. *He also clothes Aaron's sons,* 13. *Offers a bullock for them as a sin-offering,* 14–17. *And a ram for a burnt-offering,* 18–21. *And another ram for a consecration-offering,* 22–24. *The fat, with cakes of unleavened bread, and the right shoulder of the ram, he offers as a wave-offering, and afterwards burns,* 25–28. *The breast, which was the part of Moses, he also waves,* 29. *And sprinkles oil and blood upon Aaron and his sons,* 30. *The flesh of the consecration ram is to be boiled and eaten at the door of the tabernacle,* 31, 32. *Moses commands Aaron and his sons to abide seven days at the door of the tabernacle of the congregation, which they do accordingly,* 33–36.

A. M. 2514.
B. C. 1490.
An. Exod. Isr. 2.
Abib or Nisan.

AND the LORD spake unto Moses, saying,

2 [a] Take Aaron, and his sons with him, and [b] the garments, and [c] the anointing oil, and a bullock for the sin-offering, and two rams, and a basket of unleavened bread;

3 And gather thou all the congregation together unto the door of the tabernacle of the congregation.

4 And Moses did as the LORD commanded him; and the assembly was gathered together unto the door of the tabernacle of the congregation.

5 And Moses said unto the congregation, [d] This *is* the thing which the LORD commanded to be done.

6 And Moses brought Aaron and his sons, [e] and washed them with water.

7 [f] And he put upon him the [g] coat, and girded him with the girdle, and clothed him with the robe, and put the ephod upon him, and he girded him with the curious girdle of the ephod, and bound *it* unto him therewith.

8 And he put the breastplate upon him: also he [h] put in the breastplate the Urim and the Thummim.

9 [i] And he put the mitre upon his head; also upon the mitre, *even* upon his forefront, did he put the golden plate, the holy crown; as the LORD [k] commanded Moses.

10 [l] And Moses took the anointing oil, and anointed the tabernacle and all that *was* therein, and sanctified them.

A. M. 2514.
B. C. 1490.
An. Exod. Isr. 2.
Abib or Nisan.

11 And he sprinkled thereof upon the altar seven times, and anointed the altar and all his vessels, both the laver and his foot, to sanctify them.

12 And he [m] poured of the anointing oil upon Aaron's head, and anointed him, to sanctify him.

13 [n] And Moses brought Aaron's sons, and put coats upon them, and girded them with girdles, and [o] put bonnets upon them; as the LORD commanded Moses.

14 [p] And he brought the bullock for the sin-offering: and Aaron and his sons [q] laid their hands upon the head of the bullock for the sin-offering.

15 And he slew *it;* [r] and Moses took the blood, and put *it* upon the horns of the altar round about with his finger, and purified the altar, and poured the blood at the bottom of the altar, and sanctified *it,* to make reconciliation upon it.

16 [s] And he took all the fat that *was* upon the inwards, and the caul *above* the liver, and the two kidneys, and their fat, and Moses burned *it* upon the altar.

17 But the bullock, and his hide, his flesh, and his dung, he burnt with fire without the camp; as the LORD [t] commanded Moses.

[a] Exod. xxix. 1, 2, 3.—[b] Exod. xxviii. 2, 4.—[c] Exod. xxx. 24, 25.—[d] Exod. xxix. 4.—[e] Exod. xxix. 4.—[f] Exod. xxix. 5.—[g] Exod. xxviii. 4.—[h] Exod. xxviii. 30.—[i] Exod. xxix. 6.—[k] Exod. xxviii. 37, &c.—[l] Exod. xxx. 26, 27, 28, 29.—[m] Chap. xxi. 10, 12; Exod. xxix. 7; xxx. 30; Psa. cxxxiii. 2; Ecclus. xlv. 15.—[n] Exod. xxix. 8, 9.—[o] Heb. *bound.* [p] Exod. xxix. 10; Ezek. xliii. 19.—[q] Chap. iv. 4.—[r] Exod. xxix. 12, 36; chap. iv. 7; Ezek. xliii. 20, 26; Heb. ix. 22. [s] Exod. xxix. 13; chap. iv. 8.—[t] Chap. iv. 11, 12; Exod. xxix. 14.

NOTES ON CHAP. VIII.

Verse 2. *Take Aaron and his sons*] The whole subject of this chapter has been anticipated in the notes on Exod. xxviii. 1, &c., and xxix. 1, &c., in which all the sacrifices, rites, and ceremonies have been explained in considerable detail; and to those notes the reader is referred. It is only necessary to observe that Aaron and his sons were not anointed until *now. Before,* the thing was *commanded; now,* first *performed.*

Verse 8. *He put in the breastplate the Urim and the Thummim.*] The Urim and Thummim are here supposed to be something different from the breastplate itself. See the notes on Exod. xxviii. 15, 16, 30.

Verse 9. *And he put the mitre*] See the note on Exod. xxviii. 37.

Verse 14. *The bullock for the sin-offering*] This was offered each day during the seven days of consecration. See Exod. xxix. 36.

A. M. 2514.
B. C. 1490.
An. Exod. Isr. 2.
Abib or Nisan.

18 [u] And he brought the ram for the burnt-offering: and Aaron and his sons laid their hands upon the head of the ram.

19 And he killed *it;* and Moses sprinkled the blood upon the altar round about.

20 And he cut the ram into pieces; and Moses burnt the head, and the pieces, and the fat.

21 And he washed the inwards and the legs in water; and Moses burnt the whole ram upon the altar: it *was* a burnt-sacrifice for a sweet savour, *and* an offering made by fire unto the LORD; [v] as the LORD commanded Moses.

22 And [w] he brought the other ram, the ram of consecration: and Aaron and his sons laid their hands upon the head of the ram.

23 And he slew *it;* and Moses took of the blood of it, and put *it* upon the tip of Aaron's right ear, and upon the thumb of his right hand, and upon the great toe of his right foot.

A. M. 2514.
B. C. 1490.
An. Exod. Isr. 2.
Abib or Nisan.

24 And he brought Aaron's sons, and Moses put of the blood upon the tip of their right ear, and upon the thumbs of their right hands, and upon the great toes of their right feet: and Moses sprinkled the blood upon the altar round about.

25 [x] And he took the fat, and the rump, and all the fat that *was* upon the inwards, and the caul *above* the liver, and the two kidneys, and their fat, and the right shoulder:

26 [y] And out of the basket of unleavened bread, that *was* before the LORD, he took one unleavened cake, and a cake of oiled bread, and one wafer, and put *them* on the fat, and upon the right shoulder:

[u] Exod. xxix. 15.——[v] Exod. xxix. 18.——[w] Exod. xxix. 19, 31.

[x] Exod. xxix. 22.——[y] Exod. xxix. 23.

Verse 23. *Put it upon the tip of Aaron's right ear, &c.*] See this significant ceremony explained in the note on Exod. xxix. 20. Calmet remarks that the consecration of the high priest among the Romans bore a considerable resemblance to the consecration of the Jewish high priest. "The Roman priest, clothed with a garment of silk, his head covered with a crown of gold adorned with sacred ribbons, was conducted into a subterranean place, over which there was a floor of planks pierced through with many holes. On this floor they sacrificed a bullock, whose blood was freely poured out on the planks or floor, which running through the holes fell upon the priest, who stood under to receive this sacred aspersion, and who, in order to be completely covered with the blood, took care to present the whole of his body, his clothes, face, eyes, nose, lips, and even his tongue, to receive the drops of blood falling through the pierced floor above. Being completely covered with this sanguineous shower, he ascended from his subterranean place, and was acknowledged and adored by the people as *Pontifex Maximus*, or supreme high priest." These rites, which bear a striking allusion to those used in the consecration of Aaron, and from which they were probably borrowed, and disguised by the introduction of their own superstitions, are particularly described by *Aurelius Prudentius*, in his poem entitled *Romani Martyris Supplicium*, from which I shall select those verses, the subject of which is given above, as the passage is curious, and the work not common.

"Summus sacerdos nempe sub terram scrobe
Acta in profundum consecrandus mergitur,
Mire infulatus, *festa vittis tempora*
Nectens, *corona* tum repexus *aurea*,
Cinctu Gabino *sericam* fultus *togam*.
Tabulis superne strata texunt pulpita,
Rimosa rari pegmatis compagibus,
Scindunt subinde vel terebrant aream,
Crebroque lignum *perforant* acumine,
Patcat *minutis* ut frequens *hiatibus*.—
Hic ut statuta est *immolanda bellua*,
Pectus sacrata dividunt venabulo,
Eructat amplum vulnus undam sanguinis—&c.
Tum per *frequentes mille rimarum vias*
Illapsus imber, tabidum rotem pluit,
Defossus intus quem sacerdos excipit,
Guttas ad omnes turpe subjectans *caput*,
Et *veste* et *omni* putrefactus *corpore:*
Quin *os* supinat, obvias offert *genas*
Supponit *aures, labra, nares* objicit,
Oculos et ipsos perluit liquoribus,
Nec jam *palato* parcit, et *linguam* rigat,
Donec cruorem totus atrum combibat.—
Procedit inde pontifex visu horridus—&c.
Omnes *salutant* atque *adorant* eminus,
Vilis quod illum sanguis, et *bos mortuus*
Fœdis latentem sub cavernis laverint."

Of these lines the reader will not be displeased to find the following poetical version:—

"For when, with sacred pomp and solemn state,
Their great high priest the Romans consecrate,
His silken vest in Gabine cincture bound,
A festal fillet twines his temples round:
And, while aloft the gorgeous mitre shines,
His awful brow a golden crown confines.
In a deep dyke, for mystic ritual made,
He stands, surrounded with terrific shade.
High o'er his holy head a stage they place,
Adorn with paintings, and with statues grace;
Then with keen piercers perforate the floor,
Till thronging apertures admit no more.
Thither the victim ox is now convey'd,
To glut the vengeance of the thirsty blade.
The sacred spear his sturdy throat divides,
Down, instant streaming, gush the gory tides.
Through countless crevices the gaping wood
Distils corrupted dew and smoking blood;

A. M. 2514.
B. C. 1490.
An. Exod. Isr. 2.
Abib or Nisan.

27 And he put all [z] upon Aarons' hands, and upon his son's hands, and waved them *for* a wave-offering before the LORD.

28 [a] And Moses took them from off their hands, and burnt *them* on the altar upon the burnt-offering: they *were* consecrations for a sweet savour: it *is* an offering made by fire unto the LORD.

29 And Moses took the breast, and waved it *for* a wave-offering before the LORD: *for* of the ram of consecration it was Moses' [b] part; as the LORD commanded Moses.

30 And [c] Moses took of the anointing oil, and of the blood which *was* upon the altar, and sprinkled *it* upon Aaron, *and* upon his garments, and upon his sons, and upon his sons' garments with him; and sanctified Aaron, *and* his garments, and his sons, and his sons' garments with him.

31 And Moses said unto Aaron and to his sons, [d] Boil the flesh *at* the door of the tabernacle of the congregation: and there eat it with the bread that *is* in the basket of consecrations, as I commanded, saying, Aaron and his sons shall eat it.

A. M. 2514.
B. C. 1490.
An. Exod. Isr. 2.
Abib or Nisan.

32 [e] And that which remaineth of the flesh and of the bread shall ye burn with fire.

33 And ye shall not go out of the door of the tabernacle of the congregation *in* seven days, until the days of your consecration be at an end: for [f] seven days shall he consecrate you.

34 [g] As he hath done this day, *so* the LORD hath commanded to do, to make an atonement for you.

35 Therefore shall ye abide *at* the door of the tabernacle of the congregation day and night seven days, and [h] keep the charge of the LORD, that ye die not: for so I am commanded.

36 So Aaron and his sons did all things which the LORD commanded by the hand of Moses.

[a] Exod. xxix. 24, &c.—[z] Exod. xxix. 25.—[b] Exod. xxix. 26.—[c] Exod. xxix. 21; xxx. 30; Num. iii. 3.—[d] Exod. xxix. 31, 32.—[e] Exod. xxix. 34.—[f] Exod. xxix. 30, 35; Ezek. xliii. 25 26.—[g] Heb. vii. 16.—[h] Num. iii. 7; ix. 19; Deut. xi. 1, 1 Kings ii. 3.

Drop after drop, in swift succession shed,
Falls on the holy pontiff's mitred head;
While, to imbibe the sanctifying power,
His outspread garments drink the crimson shower;
Then on his back in reeking streams he lies,
And laves in livid blood his lips and eyes;
Bares every limb, exposes every pore,
To catch the virtue of the streaming gore;
With open mouth expects the falling flood,
Moistens his palate and his tongue with blood;
Extends his ears to meet the sanguine rain,
Nor lets a single drop descend in vain.
Then from the gloomy cave comes forth to light,
Bathed in black blood, and horrible to sight!—
By the vile torrent, and the victim slain,
In the dark cavern cleansed from mortal stain,
Their priest, enveloped in atoning gore,
With trembling awe surrounding throngs adore."

Prudentius was born about the middle of the fourth century, and was no doubt intimately acquainted with the circumstances he describes.

Verse 27. *And waved them* for *a wave-offering*] See the nature of this and the *heave-offering* in the note on Exod. xxix. 27.

Verse 30. *And Moses took—the blood—and sprinkled* it *upon Aaron, &c.*] Thus we find that the high priest himself must be sprinkled with the blood of the sacrifice; and our blessed Lord, of whom Aaron was a type, was sprinkled with his own blood. 1. In his agony in the garden. 2. In his being crowned with thorns. 3. In the piercing of his hands and his feet. And, 4. In his side being pierced with the spear. All these were so many acts of atonement performed by the high priest.

Verse 33. *For seven days shall he consecrate you.*] This number was the number of *perfection* among the Hebrews; and the seven days' consecration implied a *perfect* and *full consecration* to the sacerdotal office. See the note on Exod. xxix. 30.

Verse 36. *So Aaron and his sons did*] This chapter shows the exact fulfilment of the commands delivered to Moses, Exod. xxix.; and consequently the complete preparation of Aaron and his sons to fill the awfully important office of priests and mediators between God and Israel, to offer sacrifices and make atonement for the sins of the people.

"Thus," says Mr. Ainsworth, "the covenant of the priesthood was confirmed unto the tribe of Levi in Aaron and his sons, which covenant was *life and peace*, Mal. ii. 5. But these are made priests *without an oath*; also, there were *many priests*, because they were not suffered to continue by reason of death; and they served unto the example and shadow of heavenly things, offering gifts and sacrifices which could not make him who did the service perfect as pertaining to the conscience; for they were carnal ordinances imposed upon them till the time of reformation, that is, until the time of Christ, who was made a priest of God *with an oath*, and made surety of a better covenant, established on better promises. And because he continueth for ever, he hath a priesthood which passeth not from one to another, and is a minister of the true tabernacle, which God pitched and not man. Not by the blood of bulls and of goats, but by his own blood, he entered once into the holy place, having found ever-

lasting redemption for us; and is therefore able to save to the uttermost them who come unto God through him, as he ever liveth to make intercession for them." Taken in reference to his priesthood and sacrifice, all these rites and ceremonies are significant and edifying; but taken out of this relation, they would be as absurd and nugatory as the consecration of the Roman Pontifex Maximus, mentioned above by Prudentius.

CHAPTER IX.

Aaron is commanded to offer, on the eighth day, a sin-offering and a burnt-offering, 1, 2. *The people are commanded also to offer a sin-offering, a burnt-offering, peace-offerings, and a meat-offering,* 3, 4. *They do as they were commanded; and Moses promises that God shall appear among them,* 5, 6. *Aaron is commanded to make an atonement for the people,* 7. *He and his sons prepare and offer the different sacrifices.* 8–21. *Aaron and Moses bless the congregation,* 22, 23. *And the fire of the Lord consumes the sacrifice,* 24.

A. M. 2514.
B. C. 1490.
An. Exod. Isr. 2.
Abib or Nisan.

AND [a] it came to pass on the
eighth day, *that* Moses called
Aaron and his sons, and the elders
of Israel;
2 And he said unto Aaron, [b] Take thee a
young calf for a sin-offering, [c] and a ram for
a burnt-offering, without blemish, and offer
them before the LORD.
3 And unto the children of Israel thou shalt
speak, saying, [d] Take ye a kid of the goats
for a sin-offering; and a calf and a lamb, *both*
of the first year, without blemish, for a burnt-
offering;
4 Also a bullock and a ram for peace-offerings, to sacrifice before the LORD; and [e] a
meat-offering mingled with oil: for [f] to-day
the LORD will appear unto you.
5 And they brought *that* which Moses commanded before the tabernacle of
the congregation: and all the congregation drew near and stood
before the LORD.
6 And Moses said, This *is* the thing which
the LORD commanded that ye should do; and
[g] the glory of the LORD shall appear unto you.
7 And Moses said unto Aaron, Go unto the
altar, and [h] offer thy sin-offering, and thy
burnt-offering, and make an atonement for
thyself, and for the people: and [i] offer the
offering of the people, and make an atonement
for them; as the LORD commanded.
8 Aaron therefore went unto the altar, and
slew the calf of the sin-offering, which *was* for
himself.
9 [k] And the sons of Aaron brought the blood
unto him: and he dipped his finger in the

A. M. 2514.
B. C. 1490.
An. Exod. Isr. 2
Abib or Nisan.

---

[a] Ezek. xliii. 27.—[b] Chap. iv. 3; viii. 14; Exod. xxix. 1.—[c] Chap. viii. 18.—[d] Chap. iv. 23; Ezra vi. 17; x. 19.—[e] Chap. ii. 4.—[f] Ver. 6, 23; Exod. xxix. 43.

[g] Ver. 23; Exod. xxiv. 16.—[h] Chap. iv. 3; 1 Sam. iii. 14; Heb. v. 3; vii. 27; ix. 7.—[i] Chap. iv. 16, 20; Heb. v. 1.—[k] Chap. viii. 15.

NOTES ON CHAP. IX.

Verse 1. *On the eighth day*] This was the first day after their consecration, before which they were deemed unfit to minister in holy things, being considered as in a state of imperfection. "All creatures," says Ainsworth, "for the most part were in their uncleanness and imperfection *seven days*, and perfected on the *eighth*; as *children* by circumcision, Lev. xii. 2, 3; young beasts for sacrifice, chap. xxii. 27; persons that were unclean by leprosies, issues, and the like, chap. xiv. 8–10; xv. 13, 14; Num. vi. 9, 10. So here, the priests, until the *eighth day*, were not admitted to minister in their office."

Verse 2. *Take thee a young calf, &c.*] As these sacrifices were for Aaron himself, they are furnished by himself and not by the people, for they were designed to make atonement for his own sin. See chap. iv. 3. And this is supposed by the Jews to have been intended to make an atonement for his sin in the matter of the *golden calf*. This is very probable, as no formal atonement for that transgression had yet been made.

Verse 3. *Take ye a kid*] In chap. iv. 14 a young bullock is commanded to be offered for the sin of the people; but here the offering is a *kid*, which was the sacrifice appointed for the sin of the *ruler*, chap. iv. 22, 23, and hence some think that the reading of the *Samaritan* and the *Septuagint* is to be preferred. *Speak unto the* ELDERS *of Israel*, these being the only *princes* or *rulers* of Israel at that time; and for them it is possible this sacrifice was designed. It is however supposed that the sacrifice appointed chap. iv. 14 was for a *particular* sin, but *this* for sin in *general;* and that it is on this account that the sacrifices differ.

Verse 6. *And the glory of the Lord shall appear*] God shall give the most sensible signs of his presence among you; this he did in general by the cloud on the tabernacle, but in this case the *particular* proof was the fire that came out from before the Lord, and consumed the burnt-offering; see ver. 23, 24.

Verse 7. *Make an atonement for thyself*] This showed the imperfection of the Levitical law; the high priest was obliged to make an expiation for his own sins before he could make one for the sins of the

A. M. 2514. B. C. 1490. An. Exod. Isr. 2. Abib or Nisan.

blood, and [l] put *it* upon the horns of the altar, and poured out the blood at the bottom of the altar:

10 [m] But the fat, and the kidneys, and the caul above the liver, of the sin-offering, he burnt upon the altar; [n] as the LORD commanded Moses.

11 [o] And the flesh and the hide he burnt with fire without the camp.

12 And he slew the burnt-offering; and Aaron's sons presented unto him the blood, [p] which he sprinkled round about upon the altar.

13 [q] And they presented the burnt-offering unto him, with the pieces thereof, and the head: and he burnt *them* upon the altar.

14 [r] And he did wash the inwards and the legs, and burnt *them* upon the burnt-offering on the altar.

15 [s] And he brought the people's offering, and took the goat, which *was* the sin-offering for the people, and slew it, and offered it for sin, as the first.

16 And he brought the burnt-offering, and offered it [t] according to the [u] manner.

17 And he brought [v] the meat-offering, and [w] took a handful thereof and burnt *it* upon the altar, [x] beside the burnt-sacrifice of the morning.

A. M. 2514. B. C. 1490. An. Exod. Isr. 2. Abib or Nisan.

18 He slew also the bullock and the ram *for* [y] a sacrifice of peace-offerings, which *was* for the people: and Aaron's sons presented unto him the blood, which he sprinkled upon the altar round about;

19 And the fat of the bullock and of the ram, the rump, and that which covereth *the inwards*, and the kidneys, and the caul *above* the liver:

20 And they put the fat upon the breasts, [z] and he burnt the fat upon the altar:

21 And the breasts and the right shoulder Aaron waved [a] *for* a wave-offering before the LORD; as Moses commanded.

22 And Aaron lifted up his hand toward the people, and [b] blessed them, and came down from offering of the sin-offering, and the burnt-offering, and peace-offerings.

23 And Moses and Aaron went into the tabernacle of the congregation, and came out, and blessed the people: [c] and the glory of

[l] See chap. iv. 7.——[m] Chap. viii. 16.——[n] Chap. iv. 8.——[o] Chap. iv. 11; viii. 17.——[p] Chap. i. 5; viii. 19.——[q] Chap. viii. 20.——[r] Chap. viii. 21.——[s] Ver. 3; Isa. liii. 10; Heb. ii. 17; v. 3.——[t] Chap. i. 3, 10.——[u] Or, *ordinance*.——[v] Ver. 4; chap. ii. 1, 2.——[w] Heb. *filled his hand out of it*.——[x] Exod. xxix. 38.——[y] Chap. iii. 1, &c.——[z] Chap. iii. 5, 16.——[a] Exod. xxix. 24, 26; chap. vii. 30, 31, 32, 33, 34.——[b] Num. vi. 23; Deut. xxi. 5; Luke xxiv. 50.——[c] Ver. 6; Num. xiv. 10; xvi. 19, 42.

people. See the use made of this by the apostle, Heb. v. 3; vii. 27; ix. 7.

Verse 22. *And Aaron lifted up his hand toward the people, and blessed them*] On lifting up the hands in prayer, see Exod. ix. 29. The *form* of the blessing we have in Num. vi. 23, &c.: "The LORD bless thee and keep thee! The LORD make his face shine upon thee, and be gracious unto thee! The LORD lift up his countenance upon thee, and give thee peace!" See the notes on these passages.

And came down from offering of the sin-offering, &c.] A sin-offering, a burnt-offering, a meat-offering, and peace-offerings, were made to God that his glory might appear to the whole congregation. This was the *end* of all sacrifice and religious service; not to confer any *obligation* on God, but to make an atonement for sin, and to engage him to dwell among and influence his worshippers.

Verse 23. *Moses and Aaron went into the tabernacle*] It is supposed that Moses accompanied Aaron into the tabernacle to show him how to offer the incense, prepare the lamps and the perfume, adjust the shew-bread, &c., &c.

And the glory of the Lord appeared] To show that every thing was done according to the Divine mind, 1. The glory of Jehovah appears unto all the people; 2. A fire came out from before the Lord, and consumed the burnt-offering. This was the proof which God gave upon extraordinary occasions of his acceptance of the sacrifice. This was done probably, 1. In the case of Abel, Gen. iv. 4. 2. In the case of Aaron; see above, ver. 24. 3. In the case of Gideon, Judg. vi. 21. 4. In the case of Manoah and his wife. Compare Judg. xiii. 19–23. 5. In the case of David dedicating the threshing-floor of Ornan, 1 Chron. xxi. 28. 6. In the case of Solomon dedicating the temple, 2 Chron. vii. 1. 7. In the case of Elijah, 1 Kings xviii. 38. Hence to express the *accepting* of an offering, sacrifice, &c., the verb דשן *dishshen* is used, which signifies *to reduce to ashes*, i. e., by fire from heaven. See Psa. xx. 3. In such a case as this, it was necessary that the fire should appear to be *divinely* sent, and should come in such a way as to preclude the supposition that any art or deceit had been practised on the occasion. Hence it is not intimated that Moses and Aaron brought it out of the tabernacle, professing that God had kindled it *there* for them, but the *fire* CAME OUT *from* BEFORE *the Lord*, and ALL *the* PEOPLE SAW *it*. The victims were consumed by a fire evidently of no *human kindling*. Josephus says that "a fire proceeded from the victims themselves of its own accord, which had the appearance of a flash of lightning;" *εξ αυτων πυρ ανηφθη αυτοματον, και ὁμοιον αστραπης λαμπηδονι δρωμενον τη φλογι·* "and consumed all that was upon the altar."—Antiq., lib. iii., c. 8, s. 6, edit. Haverc. And it is very likely that by the agency of the *ethereal* or *electric* spark, sent immediately from the Divine presence, the victims

A. M. 2514.
B. C. 1490.
An. Exod. Isr. 2.
Abib or Nisan.

the LORD appeared unto all the
people.
24 And [d] there came a fire out
from before the LORD, and consumed upon
the altar the burnt-offering and
the fat; *which* when all the people saw, [e] they shouted, and fell
on their faces.

[d] Gen. iv. 4; Judg. vi. 21; 1 Kings xviii. 38; 2 Chron. vii. 1; Psa. xx. 3; 2 Mac. ii. 10, 11.

[e] Exod. xxxii. 17; 1 Kings xviii. 39; 2 Chron. vii. 3; Ezra iii. 11.

were consumed. The heathens, in order to give credit to their worship, imitated this miracle, and pretended that Jupiter testified his approbation of the sacrifices offered to him by thunder and lightning: to this VIRGIL seems to allude, though the words have been understood differently.

Audiat hæc genitor, qui fœdera fulmine sancit.
Æn. xii., ver. 200.

"Let Jupiter hear, who sanctions covenants by his thunder."

On which words Servius makes this remarkable comment: Quia cum fiunt fœdera, si coruscatio fuerit, confirmantur. Vel certe quia apud majores aræ non incendebantur, sed ignem divinum precibus eliciebant qui incendebant altaria. "To sanction the covenant signifies to confirm it; for when a covenant was made, if there were a flash of lightning, it was considered to be thereby confirmed: or rather because our ANCESTORS lighted no fire upon the altars, but obtained by their supplications divine fire," &c. The expression *apud majores*, "among our *ancestors*," shows that they could boast of no such divine fire *then;* nor could they ever *before*, as the whole account was borrowed from the Jews. *Solinus Polyhistor* gives us an account to the same effect; for, speaking of the hill of Vulcan in Sicily, he says: In quo, qui divinæ rei operantur, ligna vitea super aras struunt, nec ignis apponitur in hanc congeriem: cum prosicias intulerunt, si adest deus, si sacrum probatur, sarmenta licet viridia sponte concipiunt, et nullo inflagrante halitu, ab ipso numine fit accendium, cap. v. *in fine.* "They who perform sacred rites in this place, put a bundle of vine-tree wood upon the altar, but put no fire to it; for when they lay the pieces of the victim upon it, if the deity be present, and he approve the sacrifice, the bundle, although of green wood, *takes fire of itself*, and without any other means the deity himself kindles the flame." These are remarkable instances, and show how exactly the heathen writers have borrowed from the sacred records. And in farther imitation of this miracle, they had their *perpetual fire* in the temple of *Vesta*, which they feigned to *have descended* at first *from heaven*, and which they kept with the most religious veneration.

Verse 24. *When all the people saw, they shouted, and fell on their faces.*] 1. The miracle was done in such a way as gave the fullest conviction to the people of its reality. 2. They exulted in the thought that the God of almighty power and energy had taken up his abode among them. 3. They prostrated themselves in his presence, thereby intimating the deep sense they had of HIS goodness, of *their* unworthiness, and of the obligation they were under to live in subjection to his authority, and obedience to his will.—This celestial fire was carefully preserved among the Israelites till the time of Solomon, when it was *renewed*, and continued among them till the Babylonish captivity. This Divine fire was the emblem of the Holy Spirit. And as no sacrifice could be acceptable to God which was not *salted*, i. e., seasoned and rendered pleasing, *by this fire*, as our Lord says, Mark ix. 49; so no soul can offer acceptable sacrifices to God, but through the influences of the Divine Spirit. Hence the *promise* of the Spirit under the emblem of fire, Matt. iii. 11, and its actual descent in this similitude on the day of pentecost, Acts ii. 3, 4.

THE most remarkable circumstance in this chapter is the manifestation of the presence of God, and the consuming of the victims by the miraculous fire. We have already seen that the chief design of these sacrificial rites was to obtain *reconciliation to God*, that the Divine Presence might dwell and be manifested among them. To encourage the people to make the necessary preparations, to offer the sacrifices in a proper spirit, and to expect especial mercies from the hand of God, Moses promises, ver. 4, that the *Lord would appear unto them on the morrow*, and that *his glory should appear*, ver. 6. In hope or expectation of this, the *priest*, the *elders*, and the *people* purified themselves by offering the different sacrifices which God had appointed; and when this was done God did appear, and gave the fullest proofs of his approbation, by miraculously consuming the sacrifices which were prepared on the occasion. Does not St. John evidently refer to these circumstances, 1st Epist., chap. iii. 2, 3: "Beloved, now are we the sons of God; and it doth not yet appear what we shall be; but we know that when he shall *appear*, we shall be like him, for we shall see him *as he is;* and every man that hath this *hope* in him, *purifieth* himself, even as he is pure." This manifestation of God in the tabernacle was a type of his presence, first, in the Church militant on earth; and secondly, in the Church triumphant in heaven. They who expect to have the presence of God here, must propitiate his throne of justice by the only available *sacrifice;* they who wish to enjoy everlasting felicity, must be purified from all unrighteousness, for without holiness none can see the Lord. If we *hope* to see him *as he is*, we must resemble him. How vain is the expectation of *glory*, where there is *no meetness for the place!* And how can we enter into the holiest but by the blood of Jesus? Heb. x. 19. And of what use can this sacrifice be to those who do not properly believe in it? And can any faith, even in that sacrifice, be effectual to salvation, that does not purify the heart? Reader! earnestly pray to God that thou hold not the *truth* in *unrighteousness.*

CHAPTER X.

Nadab and Abihu offer strange fire before the Lord, and are destroyed, 1–5. *Aaron and his family forbidden to mourn for them,* 6, 7. *He and his family are forbidden the use of wine,* 8–11. *Directions to Aaron and his sons concerning the eating of the meat-offerings, &c.,* 12–15. *Moses chides Aaron for not having eaten the sin-offering,* 16–18. *Aaron excuses himself, and Moses is satisfied,* 19, 20.

A. M. 2514.
B. C. 1490.
An. Exod. Isr. 2.
Abib or Nisan.

AND [a] Nadab and Abihu, the
sons of Aaron, [b] took either
of them his censer, and put fire
therein, and put incense thereon, and offered
[c] strange fire before the LORD, which he commanded them not.
2 And there [d] went out fire
from the LORD, and devoured
them, and they died before the
LORD.
3 Then Moses said unto Aaron, This *is it*
that the LORD spake, saying, I will be sancti-

[a] Chap. xvi. 1; xxii. 9; Num. iii. 3, 4; xxvi. 61; 1 Chron. xxiv. 2. — [b] Chap. xvi. 12; Num. xvi. 18. — [c] Exod. xxx. 9. — [d] Chap. ix. 24; Num. xvi. 35; 2 Samuel vi. 7.

NOTES ON CHAP. X.

Verse 1. *And Nadab and Abihu—took either of them his censer*] The manner of burning incense in the temple service was, according to the Jews, as follows:—"One went and gathered the ashes from off the altar into a golden vessel, a second brought a vessel full of incense, and a third brought a censer with fire, and put coals on the altar, and he whose office it was to burn the incense strewed it on the fire at the command of the governor. At the same time all the people went out of the temple from between the porch and the altar. Each day they burned the weight of a hundred denaries of incense, *fifty* in the morning, and *fifty* in the evening. The hundred denaries weighed *fifty* shekels of the sanctuary, each shekel weighing *three hundred and twenty* barleycorns; and when the priest had burned the incense, he bowed himself down and went his way out. See *Maimonides'* Treatise of the *Daily Service*, chap. iii. So when Zacharias, as his lot fell, burned incense in the temple, the whole multitude of the people were without at prayer while the incense was burning, Luke i. 9, 10. By this service God taught them that the prayers of his faithful people are pleasing to him, whilst our High Priest, Christ Jesus, by his mediation puts incense to their prayers; (see Psa. cxli. 2; Rom. viii. 34; Heb. viii. 1, 2; ix. 24; Rev. viii. 3, 4;) for the priests under the law served unto the example and shadow of heavenly things; Heb. viii. 5." See *Ainsworth* in loco.

In the preceding chapter we have seen how God intended that every part of his service should be conducted; and that every sacrifice might be acceptable to him, he sent his *own fire* as the emblem of his presence, and the means of consuming the sacrifice.—Here we find Aaron's sons neglecting the Divine ordinance, and offering incense with *strange*, that is, *common* fire,—fire not of a celestial origin; and therefore the fire of God consumed *them*. So that very fire which, if properly applied, would have sanctified and consumed their gift, become now the very instrument of their destruction! How true is the saying, *The Lord is a consuming fire!* He will either *hallow* or *destroy* us: he will purify our souls by the influence of his Spirit, or consume them with the breath of his mouth! The tree which is properly planted in a good soil is nourished by the genial influences of the sun: pluck it up from its roots, and the sun which was the cause of its vegetative life and perfection now dries up its juices, decomposes its parts, and causes it to moulder into dust. Thus must it be done to those who grieve and do despite to the Spirit of God. Reader, hast *thou* this heavenly fire? Hear then the voice of God, QUENCH *not the* SPIRIT.

Some critics are of opinion that the fire used by the sons of Aaron was the *sacred* fire, and that it is only called *strange* from the manner of placing the incense on it. I cannot see the force of this opinion.

Which he commanded them not.] Every part of the religion of God is Divine. He alone knew what he designed by its rites and ceremonies, for that which they prefigured—the whole economy of redemption by Christ—was conceived in his own mind, and was out of the reach of human wisdom and conjecture. He therefore who *altered* any part of this representative system, who *omitted* or *added* any thing, assumed a prerogative which belonged to God alone, and was certainly guilty of a very high offence against the wisdom, justice, and righteousness of his Maker. This appears to have been the sin of Nadab and Abihu, and this at once shows the reason why they were so severely punished. The most awful judgments are threatened against those who either add too, or take away from, the declarations of God. See Deut. iv. 2; Prov. xxx. 6; and Rev. xxii. 18, 19.

Verse 3. *And Aaron held his peace.*] וידם אהרן *vaiyiddom Aharon, and Aaron was dumb.* How elegantly expressive is this of his parental affection, his deep sense of the presumption of his sons, and his own submission to the justice of God! The flower and hope of his family was nipped in the bud and blasted; and while he exquisitely feels as a father, he submits without murmuring to this awful dispensation of Divine justice. It is an awful thing to introduce innovations either into the *rites* and *ceremonies*, or into the *truths*, of the religion of Christ: he who acts thus cannot stand guiltless before his God.

It has often been remarked that excessive grief stupifies the mind, so that amazement and deep anguish prevent at once both *tears* and *complaints*; hence that saying of Seneca, *Curæ leves loquantur; graviores silent.* "Slight sorrows are loquacious; deep anguish has no voice." See on ver. 19.

A. M. 2514.
B. C. 1490.
An. Exod. Isr. 2.
Abib or Nisan.

fied in them [e] that come nigh
me, and before all the people I
will be [f] glorified. [g] And Aaron
held his peace.
4 And Moses called Mishael and Elzaphan,
the sons of [h] Uzziel the uncle of Aaron,
and said unto them, Come near, [i] carry your
brethren from before the sanctuary out of the
camp.
5 So they went near, and carried them in
their coats out of the camp; as Moses had said.
6 And Moses said unto Aaron, and unto
Eleazar and unto Ithamar, his sons, [k] Uncover
not your heads, neither rend your clothes;
lest ye die, and lest [l] wrath come upon all the
people: but let your brethren, the whole house
of Israel, bewail the burning which the LORD
hath kindled.
7 [m] And ye shall not go out from the door of
the tabernacle of the congregation, lest ye die:
[n] for the anointing oil of the LORD *is* upon you.
And they did according to the word of Moses.
8 And the LORD spake unto Aaron, saying,
9 [o] Do not drink wine nor strong drink,
thou, nor thy sons with thee,
when ye go into the tabernacle
of the congregation, lest ye die:
it shall be a statute for ever throughout your
generations:

A. M. 2514.
B. C. 1490.
An. Exod. Isr. 2.
Abib or Nisan.

10 And that ye may [p] put difference between
holy and unholy, and between unclean and
clean;
11 [q] And that ye may teach the children of
Israel all the statutes which the LORD hath
spoken unto them, by the hand of Moses.
12 And Moses spake unto Aaron, and unto
Eleazar and unto Ithamar, his sons that were
left, Take [r] the meat-offering that remaineth
of the offerings of the LORD made by fire, and
eat it without leaven beside the altar: for [s] it
is most holy:
13 And ye shall eat it in the holy place,
because it *is* thy due, and thy sons' due, of
the sacrifices of the LORD made by fire: for
[t] so I am commanded.
14 And [u] the wave-breast and heave-shoulder
shall ye eat in a clean place; thou, and thy
sons, and thy daughters with thee: for *they*

[e] Exod. xix. 22; xxix. 43; chap. xxi. 6, 17, 21; Isa. lii. 11; Ezek. xx. 41; xlii. 13.——[f] Isa. xlix. 3; Ezek. xxviii. 22; John xiii. 31, 32; xiv. 13; 2 Thess. i. 10.——[g] Psalm xxxix. 9. [h] Exod. vi. 18, 22; Num. iii. 19, 30.——[i] Luke vii. 12; Acts v. 6, 9, 10; viii. 2.——[k] Exod. xxxiii. 5; chap. xiii. 45; xxi. 1, 10; Num. vi. 6, 7; Deut. xxxiii. 9; Ezek. xxiv. 16, 17.——[l] Num. xvi. 22, 46; Josh. vii. 1; xxii. 18, 20; 2 Sam. xxiv. 1.

[m] Chap. xxi. 12.——[n] Exod. xxviii. 41; chap. viii. 30. [o] Ezek. xliv. 21; Luke i. 15; 1 Tim. iii. 3; Tit. i. 7.——[p] Chap. xi. 47; xx. 25; Jer. xv. 19; Ezek. xxii. 26; xliv. 23.——[q] Deut. xxiv. 8; Neh. viii. 2, 8, 9, 13; Jer. xviii. 18; Mal. ii. 7. [r] Exod. xxix. 2; chap. vi. 16; Num. xviii. 9, 10.——[s] Chap. xxi. 22.——[t] Chap. ii. 3; vi. 16.——[u] Exod. xxix. 24, 26, 27; chap. vii. 31, 34; Num. xviii. 11.

Verse 4. *Uzziel the uncle of Aaron*] He was brother to Amram the father of Aaron; see Exod. vi. 18–22.

Verse 5. *Carried them in their coats out of the camp*] The modern impropriety of burying the dead within towns, cities, or places inhabited, had not yet been introduced; much less that *abomination*, at which both piety and common sense shudder, burying the dead *about* and even *within* places dedicated to the worship of God!

Verse 6. *Uncover not your heads, &c.*] They were to use no sign of *grief* or *mourning*, 1. Because those who were employed in the service of the sanctuary should avoid every thing that might incapacitate them for that service; and, 2. Because the crime of their brethren was so highly provoking to God, and so fully merited the punishment which *he* had inflicted, that their mourning might be considered as accusing the Divine justice of undue severity.

Verse 7. *The anointing oil of the Lord is upon you.*] They were consecrated to the Divine service, and this required their constant attendance, and most willing and cheerful service.

Verse 9. *Do not drink wine nor strong drink*] The cabalistical commentator, *Baal Hatturim*, and others, have supposed, from the introduction of this command here, that Aaron's sons had sinned through excess of wine, and that they had attempted to celebrate the Divine service in a state of inebriation.

Strong drink.—The word שכר *shechar*, from *shachar*, to *inebriate*, signifies any kind of *fermented* liquors This is exactly the same prohibition that was given in the case of *John Baptist*, Luke i. 15: Οινον και σικερα ου μη πιῃ· *Wine and sikera he shall not drink.* Any inebriating liquor, says St. Jerome, (*Epist. ad nepot.*,) is called *sicera*, whether made of *corn*, *apples*, *honey*, *dates*, or other *fruit*. One of the four prohibited drinks among the Mohammedans in India is called سكر *sakar*, (see the *Hedaya*, vol. iv., p. 158,) which signifies *inebriating drink* in general, but especially *date wine* or *arrack*. From the original word probably we have borrowed our term *cider* or *sider*, which among us exclusively signifies the fermented juice of apples. See on Luke i. 15.

Verse 10. *That ye may put difference between holy and unholy*] This is a strong reason why they should drink no inebriating liquor, that their understanding being clear, and their judgment correct, they might be always able to discern between the clean and the unclean, and ever pronounce righteous judgment. Injunctions similar to this were found among the Egyptians, Carthaginians, and Greeks. Indeed, common sense itself shows that neither a *drunkard* nor a *sot* should ever be suffered to minister in holy things.

Verse 14. *Wave-breast and heave-shoulder*] See chap. vii., and on Exod. xxix. 27.

a

A. M. 2514.
B. C. 1490.
An. Exod. Isr. 2.
Abib or Nisan.

be thy due, and thy sons' due,
which are given out of the sacrifices of peace-offerings of the
children of Israel.
15 [v] The heave-shoulder and the wave-breast
shall they bring with the offerings made by
fire of the fat, to wave *it for* a wave-offering
before the LORD; and it shall be thine, and
thy sons' with thee, by a statute for ever; as
the LORD hath commanded.
16 And Moses diligently sought [w] the goat
of the sin-offering, and, behold, it was burnt:
and he was angry with Eleazar and Ithamar,
the sons of Aaron *which were* left *alive*, saying,
17 [x] Wherefore have ye not eaten the sin-
offering in the holy place, seeing it *is* most
holy, and *God* hath given it you
to bear the iniquity of the congregation, to make atonement
for them before the LORD?

A. M. 2514.
B. C. 1490.
An. Exod. Isr. 2.
Abib or Nisan.

18 Behold, [y] the blood of it was not brought
in within the holy *place*: ye should indeed
have eaten it in the holy *place*, [z] as I commanded.
19 And Aaron said unto Moses, Behold,
[a] this day have they offered their sin-offering
and their burnt-offering before the LORD; and
such things have befallen me: and *if* I had
eaten the sin-offering to-day, [b] should it have
been accepted in the sight of the LORD?
20 And when Moses heard *that*, he was
content.

[v] Chap. vii. 29, 30, 34.—[w] Chap. ix. 3, 15.—[x] Chap. vi. 26, 29.—[y] Chap. vi. 30.—[z] Chap. vi. 26.—[a] Chap. ix. 8, 12.—[b] Jer. vi. 20; xiv. 13; Hos. ix. 4; Mal. i. 10, 13.

Verse 16. *Moses diligently sought the goat*] The goat which was offered the same day for the sins of the priests and the people, (see chap. ix. 15, 16,) and which, through the confusion that happened on account of the death of Nadab and Abihu, was *burnt* instead of being *eaten*. See ver. 18.

Verse 17. *To bear the iniquity of the congregation*] See on chap. vi. 26, &c.

Verse 19. *And such things have befallen me, &c.*] The excuse which Aaron makes for not feasting on the sin-offering according to the law is at once appropriate and dignified; as if he had said: "God certainly has commanded me to eat of the sin-offering; but when such things as these have happened unto me, could it be good in the sight of the Lord? Does he not expect that I should feel as a *father* under such afflicting circumstances?" With this spirited answer Moses was satisfied; and God, who knew his situation, took no notice of the *irregularity* which had taken place in the solemn service. To human nature God has given the privilege to weep in times of affliction and distress. In his infinite kindness he has ordained that *tears*, which are only external evidences of our grief, shall be the *outlets* to our sorrows, and tend to exhaust the cause from which they flow. See on ver. 3.

Verse 20. *When Moses heard* that, *he was content.*] The argument used by Aaron had in it both good sense and strong reason, and Moses, as a reasonable man, felt its force; and as God evidenced no kind of displeasure at this irregularity, which was, in a measure at least, justified by the present necessity, he thought proper to urge the matter no farther.

THOUGH the punishment of Nadab and Abihu may appear *severe*, because the sacred text does not specify clearly the nature and extent of their crime, we may rest assured that it was of such a nature as not only to justify but to demand such a punishment. God has here given us a full proof that he will not suffer *human institutions* to take the place of his own prescribed worship. It is true this is frequently done, for by many what is called *natural religion* is put in the place of *Divine revelation*; and God seems not to regard it: but though vengeance is not speedily executed on an evil work, and therefore the hearts of the children of men are set to do wickedness, yet God ceases not to be just; and those who have *taken from* or *added to* his words, or put their own inventions in their place, shall be reproved and found liars in the great day. His long-suffering leads to repentance; but if men *will harden* their hearts, and put their *own* ceremonies, rites, and creeds, in the place of Divine ordinances and eternal truths, they must expect to give an awful account to him who is shortly to judge the quick and the dead.

Were the religion of Christ stripped of all that state policy, fleshly interest, and gross superstition have added to it, how plain and simple, and may we not add, how amiable and glorious, would it appear! Well may we say of human inventions in Divine worship what one said of the *paintings* on old cathedral windows, *Their principal tendency is to prevent the light from coming in.* Nadab and Abihu would perform the worship of God, not according to *his command*, but in *their own way*;—and God not only would not receive the sacrifice from their hands, but, while encompassing themselves with their own sparks, and warming themselves with their own fire, this had they from the hand of the Lord—they lay down in sorrow, for *there went out a fire from the Lord, and devoured them.* What is written above is to be understood of persons who make a religion for themselves, leaving Divine revelation; for, being wilfully ignorant of God's righteousness, they go about to establish their own. This is a high offence in the sight of God. Reader, God is a Spirit, and they who worship him must worship him in spirit and truth. Such worshippers the Father seeketh.

CHAPTER XI.

Laws concerning clean *and* unclean *animals,* 1, 2. *Of* QUADRUPEDS, *those are* clean *which* divide the hoof *and* chew the cud, 3. *Those to be reputed* unclean *which do not divide the hoof, though they chew the cud.* 4–6. *Those to be reputed unclean also which, though they divide the hoof, do not chew the cud,* 7. *Whosoever eats their flesh, or touches their carcasses, shall be reputed unclean,* 8. *Of* FISH, *those are clean, and may be eaten which have* fins *and* scales, 9. *Those which have not fins and scales to be reputed unclean,* 10–12. *Of* FOWLS, *those which are unclean,* 13–21. *Of* INSECTS, *the following may be eaten: the* bald locust, beetle, *and* grasshopper, 22. *All others are unclean and abominable, their flesh not to be eaten, nor their bodies touched,* 23–25. *Farther directions relative to unclean beasts,* 26–28. *Of* REPTILES, *and some small* quadrupeds, *those which are unclean,* 29, 30. *All that touch them shall be unclean,* 31; *and the things touched by their dead carcasses are unclean also,* 32–35. *Large* fountains, *or* pits *of water, are not defiled by their carcasses, provided a part of the water be drawn out,* 36. *Nor do they defile* seed *by accidentally touching it, provided the water which has touched their flesh do not touch or moisten the seed* 37, 38. *A beast that dieth of itself is unclean, and may not be touched or eaten,* 39, 40. *All creeping things are abominable,* 41–44. *The reason given for these laws,* 45–47.

A. M. 2514.
B. C. 1490.
An. Exod. Isr. 2.
Abib or Nisan.

AND the LORD spake unto
Moses and to Aaron, say-
ing unto them,
2 Speak unto the children of Israel, saying,
[a] These *are* the beasts which ye shall eat
among all the beasts that *are*
on the earth.
3 Whatsoever parteth the hoof,
and is cloven-footed, *and* cheweth the cud,
among the beasts, that shall ye eat.

A. M. 2514.
B. C. 1490.
An. Exod. Isr. 2.
Abib or Nisan.

[a] Deut. xiv. 4; Acts x. 12, 14.

NOTES ON CHAP. XI.

Verse 1. *And the Lord spake unto Moses*] In the preceding chapter the priests are expressly forbidden to drink wine; and the reason for this law is given also, that they might be able at all times to *distinguish between clean and unclean,* and be qualified to teach the children of Israel all the statutes which the Lord had spoken, chap. x. 10, 11; for as inebriation unfits a person for the regular performance of every function of life, it must be especially sinful in those who minister in holy things, and to whom the teaching of the ignorant, and the cure of souls in general, are intrusted.

Scheuchzer has remarked that no Christian state has made any civil law against drunkenness, (he must only mean the *German* states, for we have several acts of parliament against it in England,) and that it is only punished by contempt. "Custom," says he, "that tyrant of the human race, not only permits it, but in some sort authorizes the practice, insomuch that we see *priests* and *ministers* of the Church ascend the pulpit in a state of intoxication, *judges* seat themselves upon the benches, *physicians* attend their patients, and others attempt to perform the different avocations of life, in the same disgraceful state."—*Physic. Sacr.*, vol. iii., p. 64.

This is a horrible picture of German manners; and while we deplore the extensive ravages made by this vice, and the disgrace with which its votaries are overwhelmed, we have reason to thank God that it very rarely has ever appeared in the *pulpit*, and perhaps was never once seen upon the *bench*, in our own country.

Having delivered the law against drinking wine, Moses proceeds to deliver a series of ordinances, all well calculated to prevent the Israelites from mixing with the surrounding nations, and consequently from being contaminated by their idolatry. In chap. xi. he treats of *unclean* MEATS. In chap. xii., xiii., xiv., and xv., he treats of *unclean* PERSONS, GARMENTS, and DWELLINGS. In chap. xvi. he treats of the *uncleanness* of the PRIESTS and the PEOPLE, and prescribes the proper *expiations* and *sacrifices* for *both*. In chap. xvii. he continues the subject, and gives particular directions concerning the *mode of offering*, &c. In chap. xviii. he treats of unclean *matrimonial connections*. In chap. xix. he repeats sundry laws relative to these subjects, and introduces some new ones. In chap. xx. he mentions certain *uncleannesses* practised among the idolatrous nations, and prohibits them on pain of death. In chap. xxi. he treats of the *mourning, marriages,* and *personal defects* of the *priests,* which rendered them unclean. And in chap. xxii. he speaks of *unclean sacrifices,* or such as should not be offered to the Lord. After this, to the close of the book, many important and excellent political and domestic regulations are enjoined, the whole forming an ecclesiastico-political system superior to any thing the world ever saw.

Bishop *Wilson* very properly observes that, "by these laws of clean and unclean animals, &c., God did keep this people separated from the idolatrous world: and this is a standing proof, even to the present day, of the Divine authority of these Scriptures; for no power or art of man could have obliged so great and turbulent a nation to submit to such troublesome precepts as the Jews always have submitted to, had they not been fully convinced, from the very first, that the command was from God, and that it was to be obeyed at the peril of their souls."

Verse 3. *Whatsoever parteth the hoof, and is cloven-footed*] These two words mean the same thing—a *divided hoof,* such as that of the ox, where the hoof is divided into two toes, and each toe is *cased* with *horn.*

Cheweth the cud] Ruminates; casts up the grass, &c., which had been taken into the stomach for the purpose of mastication. Animals which chew the cud, or ruminate, are provided with *two, three,* or *four stomachs.* The ox has four: in the *first* or largest, called the *ventriculus* or *paunch,* the food is collected without

A. M. 2514. B. C. 1490. An. Exod. Isr. 2. Abib or Nisan.

4 Nevertheless these shall ye
not eat of them that chew the
cud, or of them that divide the
hoof: *as* the camel, because he cheweth the
cud, but divideth not the hoof; he *is* unclean
unto you.
5 And the coney, because he cheweth the
cud, but divideth not the hoof; he *is* unclean
unto you.
6 And the hare, because he cheweth the
cud, but divideth not the hoof; he *is* unclean
unto you.
7 And [b] the swine, though he divide the
hoof, and be cloven-footed, yet he cheweth
not the cud; [c] he *is* unclean to you.
8 Of their flesh shall ye not eat, and their
carcass shall ye not touch; [d] they
are unclean to you.
9 [e] These shall ye eat of all
that *are* in the waters: whatsoever hath fins
and scales in the waters, in the seas, and in
the rivers, them shall ye eat.
10 And all that have not fins and scales in the
seas, and in the rivers, of all that move in the
waters, and of any living thing which *is* in the
waters, they *shall be* an [f] abomination unto you:
11 They shall be even an abomination unto
you; ye shall not eat of their flesh, but ye
shall have their carcasses in abomination.
12 Whatsoever hath no fins nor scales in the
waters, that *shall be* an abomination unto you.
13 [g] And these *are they which* ye shall have

A. M. 2514. B. C. 1490. An. Exod. Isr. 2 Abib or Nisan.

[b] 2 Mac. vi. 18; vii. 1.——[c] Isa. lxv. 4; lxvi. 3, 17.——[d] Isa. lii. 11; see Matt. xv. 11, 20; Mark vii. 2, 15, 18; Acts x. 14, 15; xv. 29; Rom. xiv. 14, 17; 1 Cor. viii. 8; Col. ii. 16, 21; Heb. ix. 10.——[e] Deut. xiv. 9.——[f] Chap. vii. 18; Deut. xiv. 3. [g] Deut. xiv. 12; Job xxxix. 27–30.

being masticated, the grass, &c., being received into it as the beast crops it from the earth. The food, by the force of the muscular coats of this stomach, and the liquors poured in, is sufficiently macerated; after which, formed into small balls, it is thrown up by the œsophagus into the mouth, where it is made very small by mastication or chewing, and then sent down into the second stomach, into which the œsophagus or gullet opens, as well as into the first, ending exactly where the two stomachs meet. This is what is termed *chewing the cud*. The second stomach, which is called the *reticulum, honey-comb, bonnet*, or *king's hood*, has a great number of small shallow cells on its inward surface, of a pentagonal or *five-sided* form, exactly like the cells in a honey-comb; in this the food is farther macerated, and then pushed onward into the *third stomach*, called the *omasum* or *manyplies*, because its inward surface is covered with a great number of thin membraneous partitions. From this the food passes into the *fourth stomach*, called the *abomasum*, or *reed*. In this stomach it is *digested*, and from the digested mass the *chyle* is formed, which, being absorbed by the *lacteal* vessels, is afterwards thrown into the mass of blood, and becomes the principle of nutrition to all the solids and fluids of the body. The intention of rumination, or *chewing the cud*, seems to be, that the food may be sufficiently comminuted, that, being more fully acted on by the stomachs, it may afford the greatest possible portion of nutritive juices.

The word *cud* is probably not originally *Saxon*, though found in that language in the same signification in which it is still used. *Junius*, with great show of probability, derives it from the Cambro-British *chwyd*, a *vomit*, as it is the ball of food *vomited*, or thrown up, from the *first stomach* or *paunch* through the œsophagus into the mouth, which is called by this name. Those who prefer a Saxon derivation may have it in the verb ceopan, whence our word *chew;* and so *cud* might be considered a contraction of *chewed*, but this is not so likely as the preceding.

Verse 5. *The coney*] שפן *shaphan*, not the *rabbit*, but rather a creature nearly resembling it, which abounds in Judea, Palestine, and Arabia, and is called by Dr. Shaw *daman Israel*, and by Mr. Bruce *ashkoko*. As this creature nearly resembles the *rabbit*, with which *Spain* anciently abounded, Bochart supposes that the Phœnicians might have given it the name of שפניה *spaniah*, from the multitude of שפנים *shephanim* (or *spanim*, as others pronounce it) which were found there. Hence the emblem of Spain is a woman sitting with a *rabbit* at her feet. See a coin of Hadrian in Scheuchzer.

Verse 6. *The hare*] ארנבת *arnebeth*, as Bochart and others suppose, from ארה *arah*, to *crop*, and ניב *nib*, the *produce of the ground*, these animals being remarkable for destroying the fruits of the earth. That they are notorious for destroying the tender blade of the young corn, is well known. It is very likely that different species of these animals are included under the general terms שפן *shaphan*, and ארנבת *arnebeth*, for some travellers have observed that there are *four* or *five* sorts of these animals, which are used for food in the present day in those countries. See *Harmer*, vol. iii., p. 331, edit. 1808. Some think the *mountain rat, marmot, squirrel*, and *hedgehog*, may be intended under the word *shaphan*.

Verse 7. *And the swine*] חזיר *chazir*, one of the most gluttonous, libidinous, and filthy quadrupeds in the universe; and, because of these qualities, sacred to the *Venus* of the Greeks and Romans, and the *Friga* of our Saxon ancestors; and perhaps on these accounts forbidden, as well as on account of its flesh being strong and difficult to digest, affording a very gross kind of aliment, apt to produce cutaneous, scorbutic, and scrofulous disorders, especially in hot climates.

Verse 9. *Whatsoever hath fins and scales*] Because these, of all the fish tribe, are the most nourishing; the others which are without *scales*, or whose bodies are covered with a thick glutinous matter, being in general very difficult of digestion.

Verse 13. *And these—among the fowls—the eagle*] נשר *nesher*, from *nashar*, to *lacerate, cut*, or *tear to*

A. M. 2514.
B. C. 1490.
An. Exod. Isr. 2.
Abib or Nisan.

in abomination among the fowls; they shall not be eaten, they *are* an abomination: the eagle, and the ossifrage, and the ospray,
14 And the vulture, and the kite after his kind;
15 Every raven after his kind;
16 And the owl, and the night hawk, and the cuckoo, and the hawk after his kind,
17 And the little [h] owl, and the cormorant, and the great owl,

A. M. 2514.
B. C. 1490.
An. Exod. Isr. 2.
Abib or Nisan.

[h] Isaiah, chap. xxxiv. 11.

pieces; hence the *eagle,* a most rapacious bird of prey, from its tearing the flesh of the animals it feeds on; and for this purpose birds of prey have, in general, strong, crooked talons and a hooked beak. The eagle is a cruel bird, exceedingly ravenous, and almost insatiable.

The ossifrage] Or bone-breaker, from *os,* a *bone,* and *frango, I break,* because it not only strips off the flesh, but *breaks* the *bone* in order to extract the *marrow.* In Hebrew it is called פרס *peres,* from *paras,* to *break* or *divide in two,* and probably signifies that species of the eagle anciently known by the name of *ossifraga,* and which we render *ossifrage.*

Ospray] עזניה *ozniyah,* from עזן *azan,* to be *strong, vigorous;* generally supposed to mean the *black eagle,* such as that described by *Homer,* Iliad. lib. xxi., ver 252.

Αιετου οιματ' εχων μελανος, του θηρητηρος,
'Ος θ' αμα καρτιστος τε και ωκιστος πετεηνων.

"Having the rapidity of the *black eagle,* that bird of prey, at once the swiftest and the strongest of the feathered race."

Among the Greeks and Romans the eagle was held sacred, and is represented as carrying the thunderbolts of Jupiter. This occurs so frequently, and is so well known, that references are almost needless. See *Scheuchzer.*

Verse 14. *The vulture*] ראה *daah,* from the root *to fly,* and therefore more probably the *kite* or *glede,* from its remarkable property of *gliding* or sailing with expanded wings through the air. The ראה *daah* is a different bird from the דיה *daiyah,* which signifies the vulture. See *Bochart,* vol. iii., col. 195.

The kite] איה *aiyah,* thought by some to be the *vulture,* by others the *merlin.* Parkhurst thinks it has its name from the root אוה *avah,* to *covet,* because of its rapaciousness; some contend that the *kite* is meant. That it is a species of the *hawk,* most learned men allow. See *Bochart,* vol. iii., col. 192.

Verse 15. *Every raven*] ערב *oreb,* a general term comprehending the raven, crow, rook, jackdaw, and magpie.

Verse 16. *The owl*] בת היענה *bath haiyaanah,* the *daughter of vociferation,* the *female ostrich,* probably so called from the noise they make. "In the lonesome part of the night," says Dr. Shaw, "the ostriches frequently make a very doleful and hideous noise, sometimes resembling the *roar* of the *lion;* at other times, the hoarser voice of the *bull* or *ox.*" He adds, "I have heard them *groan* as if in the deepest agonies."—Travels, 4to edition, p. 455. The ostrich is a very unclean animal, and eats its own ordure as soon as it voids it, and of this Dr. Shaw observes, (see above,) it is remarkably fond! This is a sufficient reason, were others wanting, why such a fowl should be reputed to be unclean, and its use as an article of diet prohibited.

The night hawk] תחמס *tachmas,* from חמס *chamas,* to *force away, act violently* and *unjustly;* supposed by *Bochart* and *Scheuchzer* to signify the *male ostrich,* from its cruelty towards its young; (see Job xxxix. 17–19;) but others, with more reason, suppose it to be the bird described by Hasselquist, which he calls the *strix Orientalis,* or Oriental owl. "It is of the size of the common owl, living in the ruins and old deserted houses of Egypt and Syria; and sometimes in inhabited houses. The Arabs in Egypt call it *Massasa,* the Syrians *Bana.* It is very ravenous in Syria, and in the evenings, if the windows be left open, it flies into the house *and kills infants,* unless they are carefully watched; wherefore the women are much afraid of it."—Travels, p. 196.

If this be the fowl intended, this is a sufficient reason why *it* should be considered an *abomination.*

The cuckoo] שחף *shachaph,* supposed rather to mean the *sea mew;* called *shachaph,* from שחפת *shachepheth,* a *wasting distemper,* or *atrophy,* (mentioned chap. xxvi. 16; Deut. xxviii. 22,) because its body is the *leanest,* in proportion to its bones and feathers, of most other birds, always appearing as if under the influence of a *wasting distemper.* A foul which, from its natural constitution or manner of life, is incapable of becoming *plump* or *fleshy,* must always be unwholesome; and this is reason sufficient why such should be prohibited.

And the hawk] נץ *nets,* from the root נצה *natsah,* to *shoot forth* or *spring forward,* because of the rapidity and length of its flight, the hawk being remarkable for both. As this is a bird of *prey,* it is forbidden, and all others of its kind.

Verse 17. *The little owl*] כוס *cos,* the *bittern, night-raven,* or *night-owl,* according to most interpreters. Some think the *onocrotalus* or *pelican* may be intended; for as the word כוס *cos* signifies a *cup* in Hebrew, and the *pelican* is remarkable for a *pouch* or *bag* under the lower jaw, it might have had its Hebrew name from this circumstance; but the *kaath* in the following verse is rather supposed to mean this fowl, and the *cos* some species of the *bubo* or *owl.* See Bochart, vol. iii., col. 272.

The cormorant] שלך *shalach,* from the root which signifies to *cast down;* hence the Septuagint *καταρρακτης,* the *cataract,* or bird which falls *precipitately down* upon its prey. It probably signifies the *plungeon* or *diver,* a sea fowl, which I have seen at sea *dart down* as swift as an arrow into the water, and seize the fish which it had discovered while even flying, or rather soaring, at a very great height.

A. M. 2514.
B. C. 1490.
An. Exod. Isr. 2.
Abib or Nisan.

18 And the [i] swan, and the
[k] pelican, and the gier eagle,
19 And the [l] stork, the heron
after her kind, and the lapwing, and the bat.
20 All fowls that creep, going upon *all* four,
shall be an abomination unto you.
21 Yet these may ye eat, of every flying
creeping thing that goeth upon *all*
four, which have legs above their
feet, to leap withal upon the earth;
22 *Even* these of them ye may eat; [m] the
locust after his kind, and the bald locust after
his kind, and the beetle after his kind, and
the grasshopper after his kind.

[i] Deut. xiv. 16.——[k] Psa. cii. 6; Deut. xiv. 17.——[l] Deut. xiv. 18. Psa. civ. 17; Jer. viii. 7; Zech. v. 9.——[m] Matt. iii. 4; Mark i. 6

The great owl] ינשוף *yanshuph*, according to the *Septuagint* and the *Vulgate*, signifies the *ibis*, a bird well known and held sacred in Egypt. Some critics, with our translation, think it means a species of *owl* or *night* bird, because the word may be derived from נשף *nesheph*, which signifies the *twilight*, the time in which *owls* chiefly fly about. See *Bochart*, vol. iii., col. 281.

Verse 18. *The swan*] תנשמת *tinshemeth*. The Septuagint translate the word by πορφυριωνα, the *porphyrion*, *purple* or *scarlet* bird. Could we depend on this translation, we might suppose the *flamingo* or some such bird to be intended. Some suppose the *goose* to be meant, but this is by no means likely, as it cannot be classed either among *ravenous* or *unclean* fowls. *Bochart* thinks the *owl* is meant. See on ver. 30.

The pelican] קאת *kaath*. As קאה *kaah* signifies to *vomit up*, the name is supposed to be very descriptive of the *pelican*, who receives its food into the *pouch* under its lower jaw, and, by pressing it on its breast with its bill, *throws* it up for the nourishment of its young. Hence the fable which represents the pelican wounding her breast with her bill, that she might feed her young with her own blood; a fiction which has no foundation but in the above circumstance. *Bochart* thinks the *bittern* is meant, vol iii. col. 292.

The gier eagle] רחם *racham*. As the root of this word signifies *tenderness* and *affection*, it is supposed to refer to some bird remarkable for its *attachment to its young;* hence some have thought that the *pelican* is to be understood. *Bochart* endeavours to prove that it means the *vulture*, probably that species called the *golden vulture*.—*Bochart*, vol. iii., col. 303.

Verse 19. *The stork*] חסידה *chasidah*, from חסד *chasad*, which signifies *to be abundant in kindness*, or *exuberant in acts of beneficence;* hence applied to the *stork*, because of its *affection to its young*, and its kindness in tending and feeding its parents when old; facts attested by the best informed and most judicious of the Greek and Latin natural historians. See *Bochart*, *Scheuchzer*, and *Parkhurst*, under the word חסד *chasad*. It is remarkable for destroying and eating serpents, and on this account might be reckoned by Moses among *unclean* birds.

The heron] אנפה *anaphah*. This word has been variously understood: some have rendered it the *kite*, others the *woodcock*, others the *curlew*, some the *peacock*, others the *parrot*, and others the *crane*. The root אנף *anaph*, signifies to *breathe short* through the nostrils, to *snuff*, as in *anger;* hence to be *angry:* and it is supposed that the word is sufficiently descriptive of the *heron*, from its very *irritable* disposition. It will attack even a man in defence of its nest; and I have known a case where a man was in danger of losing his life by the stroke of a heron's bill, near the eye, who had climbed up into a high tree to take its nest. Bochart supposes a species of the *eagle* to be meant, vol. iii., col. 335.

The lapwing] דוכיפת *duchiphath*, the *upupa*, *hoopoe*, or *hoop*, a crested bird, with beautiful plumage, but very unclean. See *Bochart* and *Scheuchzer*. Concerning the genuine meaning of the original, there is little agreement among interpreters.

The bat] עטלף *atalleph*, so called, according to Parkhurst, from עט *at*, to *fly*, and עלף *alaph*, *darkness* or *obscurity*, because it flies about in the *dusk of the evening*, and in the *night:* so the Septuagint νυκτεpις, from νυξ, the *night;* and the Vulgate *vespertilio*, from *vesper*, the *evening*. This being a sort of monster partaking of the nature of both a *bird* and *beast*, it might well be classed among *unclean* animals, or animals the use of which in food should be avoided.

Verse 20. *All fowls that creep*] Such as the *bat*, already mentioned, which has claws attached to its leathern wings, and which serve in place of feet to crawl by, the feet and legs not being distinct; but this may also include all the different kinds of *insects*, with the exceptions in the following verse.

Going upon all *four*] May signify no more than walking regularly or progressively, *foot after foot* as *quadrupeds* do; for it cannot be applied to *insects* literally, as they have in general *six feet*, many of them *more*, some reputed to have a *hundred*, hence called *centipedes;* and some a *thousand*, hence called *millipedes;* words which often signify no more than that such insects have a *great number of feet*.

Verse 21. *Which have legs above their feet*] This appears to refer to the different kinds of locusts and grasshoppers, which have very remarkable hind legs, long, and with high joints, projecting above their backs, by which they are enabled to spring up from the ground, and leap high and far.

Verse 22. *The locust*] ארבה *arbeh*, either from ארב *arab*, to *lie in wait* or in *ambush*, because often immense flights of them *suddenly alight* upon the fields, vineyards, &c., and destroy all the produce of the earth; or from רבה *rabah*, he *multiplied*, because of their prodigious swarms. See a particular account of these insects in the notes on Exod. x. 4.

The bald locust] סלעם *solam*, compounded, says Mr. Parkhurst, from סלע *sala*, to *cut*, *break*, and עם *am*, *contiguity;* a kind of locust, probably so called from its *rugged*, *craggy* form. See the first of *Scheuchzer's* plates, vol. iii., p. 100.

The beetle] חרגל *chargol*. "The Hebrew name seems a derivative from חרג *charag*, to *shake*, and רגל *regel*, the *foot;* and so to denote the nimbleness of its

A. M. 2514.
B. C. 1490.
An. Exod. Isr. 2.
Abib or Nisan.

23 But all *other* flying creeping things, which have four feet, *shall be* an abomination unto you.

24 And for these ye shall be unclean: whosoever toucheth the carcass of them shall be unclean until the even.

25 And whosoever beareth *aught* of the carcass of them, [n] shall wash his clothes, and be unclean until the even.

26 *The carcasses* of every beast which divideth the hoof, and *is* not cloven-footed, nor cheweth the cud, *are* unclean unto you: every one that toucheth them shall be unclean.

27 And whatsoever goeth upon his paws, among all manner of beasts that go on *all* four, those *are* unclean unto you: whoso toucheth their carcass shall be unclean until the even.

28 And he that beareth the carcass of them shall wash his clothes, and be unclean until the even: they *are* unclean unto you.

29 These also *shall be* unclean unto you among the creeping things that creep upon the earth; the weasel, and [o] the mouse, and the tortoise after his kind,

30 And the ferret, and the chameleon, and the lizard, and the [p] snail, and the mole.

31 These *are* unclean to you among all that creep: whosoever doth touch them, when they be dead, shall be unclean until the even.

32 And upon whatsoever *any* of them, when they are dead, doth fall, it shall be unclean

[n] Chap. xiv. 8; xv. 5; Num. xix. 10. 22; xxxi. 24. — [o] Isa. lvi. 17. — [p] Psa. lviii. 8.

motions. Thus in English we call an animal of the locust kind a *grasshopper;* the French name of which is *sauterelle,* from the verb *sauter,* to leap."—*Parkhurst.* This word occurs only in this place. The *beetle* never can be intended here, as that insect never was eaten by man, perhaps, in any country of the universe.

The grasshopper] חגב *chagab.* Bochart supposes that this species of locust has its name from the Arabic verb حجب *hajaba* to *veil;* because when they fly, as they often do, in great swarms, they *eclipse even the light of the sun.* See the notes on Exod. x. 4, and the description of *ten* kinds of locusts in *Bochart,* vol. iii., col. 441. And see the figures in *Scheuchzer,* in whose plates 20 different species are represented, vol. iii., p. 100. And see Dr. Shaw on the animals mentioned in this chapter, Travels, p. 419, &c., 4to. edition; and when all these are consulted, the reader will see how little dependence can be placed on the most learned conjectures relative to these and the other animals mentioned in Scripture. One thing however is fully evident, viz., that the *locust* was eaten, not only in those ancient times, in the time of John Baptist, Matt. iii. 4, but also in the present day. Dr. Shaw ate of them in Barbary "fried and salted," and tells us that "they tasted very like crayfish." They have been eaten in Africa, Greece, Syria, Persia, and throughout Asia; and whole tribes seem to have lived on them, and were hence called *acridophagoi,* or locust-eaters, by the Greeks. See *Strabo,* lib. xvi., and *Pliny,* Hist. Nat., l. xvii., c. 30.

Verse 27. *Whatsoever goeth upon his paws*] כפיו *cappaiv,* his *palms* or *hands,* probably referring to those animals whose feet resemble the hands and feet of the human being, such as *apes, monkeys,* and all creatures of that genus; together with *bears, frogs,* &c.

Verse 29. *The weasel*] חלד *choled,* from *chalad,* Syr., to *creep in.* Bochart conjectures, with great propriety, that the *mole,* not the *weasel,* is intended by the Hebrew word: its property of *digging into* the earth, and *creeping* or *burrowing under the surface,* is well known

The mouse] עכבר *achbar.* Probably the large field *rat,* or what is called by the Germans the *hamster,* though every species of the *mus* genus may be here prohibited.

The tortoise] צב *tsab.* Most critics allow that the tortoise is not intended here, but rather the *crocodile,* the *frog,* or the *toad.* The *frog* is most probably the animal meant, and all other creatures of its kind.

Verse 30. *The ferret*] אנקה *anakah,* from אנק *anak,* to *groan,* to *cry out:* a species of lizard, which derives its name from its piercing, doleful cry. See *Bochart,* vol. ii., col. 1066.

The chameleon] כח *coach.* Bochart contends that this is the ورل *waril* or *guaril,* another species of *lizard,* which derives its name from its remarkable *strength* and *vigour* in destroying serpents, the Hebrew כח *cach* signifying to be *strong, firm, vigorous;* it is probably the same with the *mongoose,* a creature still well known in India, where it is often domesticated in order to keep the houses free from snakes, rats, mice, &c.

The lizard] לטאה *letaah.* Bochart contends that this also is a species of *lizard,* called by the Arabs وحرة *wahara,* which *creeps close to the ground,* and is poisonous.

The snail] חמט *chomet,* another species of *lizard,* according to Bochart, called حلكا *huluka* by the Arabians, which lives chiefly in the *sand.*—Vol. ii., col. 1075.

The mole.] תנשמת *tinshameth,* from נשם *nasham,* to *breathe.* Bochart seems to have proved that this is the *chameleon,* which has its Hebrew name from its wide gaping mouth, very large lungs, and its deriving its nourishment from small animals which float in the *air,* so that it has been conjectured by some to feed on the air itself.—Vol. iii., col. 1078. A *bird* of the same name is mentioned ver. 13, which Bochart supposes to be the *night-owl.*—Vol. iii., col. 286.

Verse 32. *Any vessel of wood*] Such as the *wooden bowls* still in use among the Arabs. *Or raiment, or skin*—any *trunks* or *baskets* covered with *skins,* another part of the furniture of an Arab tent; the *goat-skins*

A. M. 2514. B. C. 1490. An. Exod. Isr. 2. Abib or Nisan.

whether *it be* any vessel of wood, or raiment, or skin, or sack, whatsoever vessel *it be*, wherein *any* work is done, [q] it must be put into water, and it shall be unclean until the even; so it shall be cleansed.

33 And every earthen vessel, whereinto *any* of them falleth, whatsoever *is* in it shall be unclean; and [r] ye shall break it.

34 Of all meat which may be eaten, *that* on which *such* water cometh shall be unclean: and all drink that may be drunk in every *such* vessel shall be unclean.

35 And every *thing* whereupon *any part* of their carcass falleth shall be unclean; *whether it be* oven, or ranges for pots, they shall be broken down: *for* they *are* unclean, and shall be unclean unto you.

36 Nevertheless a fountain or pit, [s] *wherein there is* plenty of water, shall be clean: but that which toucheth their carcass shall be unclean.

37 And if *any part* of their carcass fall upon any sowing seed, which is to be sown, it *shall be* clean.

38 But if *any* water be put upon the seed, and *any part* of their carcass fall thereon, it *shall be* unclean unto you.

A. M. 2514. B. C. 1490. An. Exod. Isr. 2. Abib or Nisan.

39 And if any beast, of which ye may eat, die; he that toucheth the carcass thereof shall be unclean until the even.

40 And [t] he that eateth of the carcass of it shall wash his clothes, and be unclean until the even: he also that beareth the carcass of it shall wash his clothes and be unclean until the even.

41 And every creeping thing, that creepeth upon the earth, *shall be* an abomination; it shall not be eaten.

42 Whatsoever goeth upon the belly, and whatsoever goeth upon *all* four, or whatsoever [u] hath more feet among all creeping things that creep upon the earth, them ye shall not eat; for they *are* an abomination.

43 [v] Ye shall not make [w] yourselves abominable with any creeping thing that creepeth, neither shall ye make yourselves unclean with them, that ye should be defiled thereby.

44 For I *am* the LORD your God: ye shall therefore sanctify yourselves, and [x] ye shall be holy; for I *am* holy: neither shall ye defile yourselves with any manner of creeping thing that creepeth upon the earth.

45 [y] For I *am* the LORD that bringeth you up out of the land of Egypt, to be your God: [z] ye shall therefore be holy; for I *am* holy.

[q] Chap. xv. 12.——[r] Chap. vi. 28; xv. 12.——[s] Heb. *a gathering together of waters.*——[t] Chap. xvii. 15; xxii. 8; Deut. xiv. 21; Ezek. iv. 14; xliv. 31.

[u] Heb. *doth multiply feet.*——[v] Chap. xx. 25.——[w] Heb. *souls.* [x] Exod. xix. 6; chap. xix. 2; xx. 7, 26; 1 Thess. iv. 7; 1 Pet. i. 15, 16.——[y] Exod. vi. 7.——[z] Ver. 44.

in which they churn their milk, may be also intended. *Or sack*—any *hair-cloth* used for the purpose of transporting goods from place to place.

Verse 33. *And every earthen vessel*] Such *pitchers* as are commonly used for drinking out of, and for holding liquids. M. *De la Roque* observes that *hair-sacks*, *trunks*, and *baskets*, covered with skin, are used among the travelling Arabs to carry their household utensils in, which are *kettles* or *pots*, great *wooden bowls*, *hand-mills*, and *pitchers*. It is very likely that these are nearly the same with those used by the Israelites in their journeyings in the wilderness, for the customs of these people do not change.

Verse 35. *Ranges for pots*] To understand this, we must observe that the Arabs dig a hole in their tent, about a foot and a half deep; three-fourths of this, says *Rauwolff*, they lay about with stones, and the fourth part is left open for the purpose of throwing in their fuel. This little temporary building is probably what is here designed by *ranges for pots;* and *this* was to be *broken down* when any unclean thing had fallen upon it. See *Harmer*, vol. i., p. 464.

Verse 36. *A fountain or pit, &c.*] This must either refer to running water, the stream of which soon carries off all impurities, or to large reservoirs where the water soon purifies itself; the water in either which touched the unclean thing, being considered as impure, the rest of the water being clean.

Verse 37. *Any sowing seed*] If any part of an impure carcass fall *accidentally* on seed about to be sown, it shall not on that account be deemed unclean; but if the water put to the seed to prepare it for being sown, shall be touched by such impure carcass, the seed shall be considered as unclean, ver. 38. Probably this may be the meaning of these passages.

Verse 42. *Whatsoever goeth upon the belly*] In the word גחון *gahOn*, the *vau holem*, in most Hebrew Bibles, is much larger than the other letters; and a *Masoretic* note is added in the margin, which states that this is the *middle letter* of the law; and consequently this verse is the *middle verse* of the Pentateuch.

Whatsoever hath more feet] Than *four;* that is, all many-footed reptiles, as well as those which *go upon the belly* having no feet, such as *serpents;* besides the *four-footed* smaller animals mentioned above.

Verse 44. *Ye shall—sanctify yourselves*] Ye shall keep yourselves *separate* from all the people of the earth, that *ye may be holy; for I am holy.* And this was the grand design of God in all these prohibitions and commands; for these external sanctifications were only the emblems of that internal purity which the holiness of God requires here, and without which none

A. M. 2514.
B. C. 1490.
An. Exod. Isr. 2.
Abib or Nisan.

46 This *is* the law of the beasts, and of the fowl, and of every living creature that moveth in the waters, and of every creature that creepeth upon the earth:

47 [a] To make a difference between the unclean and the clean, and between the beast that may be eaten, and the beast that may not be eaten.

[a] Leviticus, chap. x. 10.

can dwell with him in glory hereafter. See at the conclusion of this chapter.

The contents of this chapter must furnish many profitable reflections to a pious mind.

1. From the great difficulty of ascertaining what animals are meant in this part of the law, we may at once see that the law itself must be considered as abrogated; for there is not a Jew in the universe who knows what the animals are, a very few excepted, which are intended by these Hebrew words; and therefore he may be repeatedly breaking this law by touching and being touched either by the animals themselves or their produce, such as hair, wool, fur, skin, intestines, differently manufactured, &c., &c. It therefore appears that this people have as little *law* as they have *gospel*.

2. While God keeps the *eternal interests* of man steadily in view, he does not forget his *earthly comfort;* he is at once solicitous both for the health of his body and his soul. He has not forbidden certain aliments because he is a *Sovereign*, but because he knew they would be injurious to the health and morals of his people. The close connection that subsists between the body and the soul we cannot fully comprehend; and as little can we comprehend the influence they have on each other. Many moral alterations take place in the mind in consequence of the influence of the bodily organs; and these latter are greatly influenced by the kind of aliment which the body receives. God knows what is in man, and he knows what is in all creatures; he has therefore graciously forbidden what would injure both body and mind, and commanded what is best calculated to be useful to both. *Solid-footed* animals, such as the *horse*, and *many-toed* animals, such as the *cat*, &c., are here prohibited. Beasts which have *bifid* or cloven hoofs, such as the *ox* and *sheep*, are considered as proper for food, and therefore commanded. The former are *unclean*, i. e., unwholesome, affording a gross nutriment, often the parent of scorbutic and scrofulous disorders; the latter *clean*, i. e., affording a copious and wholesome nutriment, and not laying the foundation of any disease. *Ruminating* animals, i. e., those which *chew the cud*, concoct their food better than the others which swallow it with little mastication, and therefore their flesh contains more of the nutritious juices, and is more easy of digestion, and consequently of assimilation to the solids and fluids of the human body; on this account they are termed *clean*, i. e., peculiarly wholesome, and fit for food. The animals which do not *ruminate* do not concoct their food *so well*, and hence they abound with gross animal juices, which yield a comparatively unwholesome nutriment to the human system. Even the animals which have *bifid* hoofs but do not chew the cud, such as the *swine*, and those which chew the cud but are not *bifid*, such as the *hare* and *rabbit*, are by Him who knows all things forbidden, because he knew them to be comparatively innutritive. In all this God shows himself as the tender Father of a numerous family, pointing out to his inexperienced, froward, and ignorant children, those kinds of aliments which he knows will be injurious to their health and domestic happiness, and prohibiting them on pain of his highest displeasure. On the same ground he forbade all *fish* that have not both *fins* and *scales*, such as the *conger*, *eel*, &c., which abound in gross juices and fat which very few stomachs are able to digest. Who, for instance, that lives solely on *swine's* flesh, has pure blood and healthy juices? And is it not evident, in many cases, that the *man* partakes considerably of the nature of the *brute* on which he *exclusively* feeds? I could pursue this inquiry much farther, and bring many proofs founded on indisputable facts, but I forbear; for he who might stand most in need of *caution*, would be the first to take *offence*.

3. As the *body* exists only for the sake of the *soul*, and God feeds and nourishes it through the day of probation, that the soul may here be prepared for the kingdom of heaven; therefore he shows in the conclusion of these ordinances, that the grand scope and design of all was that they *might be a holy people*, and that they might resemble him who is a holy God.—God is holy; and this is the eternal reason why all his people should be holy—should be purified from all *filthiness* of the *flesh* and *spirit*, perfecting holiness in the fear of God. No faith in any particular *creed*, no religious *observance*, no *acts of benevolence and charity*, no *mortification*, *attrition*, or *contrition*, can be a *substitute* for this. We must be made partakers of the Divine nature. We must be saved from our sins—from the corruption that is in the world, and be made holy *within* and righteous *without*, or never see God. For this very purpose Jesus Christ lived, died, and revived, that he might purify us unto himself; that through faith in his blood our sins might be blotted out, and our souls restored to the image of God.—Reader, art thou hungering and thirsting after righteousness? Then blessed art thou, for thou shalt be filled.

CHAPTER XII

Ordinances concerning the purification of women after child-birth, 1; *after the birth of a* son, *who is to be circumcised the eighth day,* 2, 3. *The mother to be considered unclean for forty days,* 4. *After the birth of a* daughter, *fourscore days,* 5. *When the days of her purifying were ended, she was to bring a lamb for a burnt-offering, and a young pigeon or a turtle-dove for a sin-offering,* 6, 7. *If* poor, *and not able to bring a lamb, she was to bring either two turtle-doves or two young pigeons,* 8.

A. M. 2514.
B. C. 1490.
An. Exod. Isr. 2.
Abib or Nisan.

AND the LORD spake unto
Moses, saying,
2 Speak unto the children of
Israel, saying, If a [a] woman have conceived
seed, and borne a man child: then [b] she shall
be unclean seven days; [c] according to the days
of the separation for her infirmity, shall she
be unclean.
3 And in the [d] eighth day, the flesh of his
foreskin shall be circumcised.
4 And she shall then continue in the blood
of her purifying three and thirty days; she
shall touch no hallowed thing, nor come into
the sanctuary, until the days of
her purifying be fulfilled.
5 But if she bear a maid child,
then she shall be unclean two weeks, as in
her separation: and she shall continue in
the blood of her purifying threescore and
six days.
6 And [e] when the days of her purifying are
fulfilled, for a son, or for a daughter, she shall
bring a lamb [f] of the first year for a burnt-offering,
and a young pigeon, or a turtle-dove,
for a sin-offering, unto the door of the tabernacle
of the congregation, unto the priest:

[a] Chap. xv. 19.——[b] Luke ii. 22.——[c] Chap. xv. 19.——[d] Gen. xvii. 12; Luke i. 59; ii. 21; John vii. 22, 23.

[e] Luke ii. 22.——[f] Heb. *a son of his year.*

NOTES ON CHAP. XII.

Verse 2. *If a woman have conceived*] In the extent mentioned here the ordinances of this chapter have little relation to us; and to inquire into their physical reasons, as far as they related to the Jews, could afford but little edification; and to make such a subject sufficiently plain would require such minute examination and circumstantial detail as could scarcely be proper for general readers. All that is *necessary* to be said the reader will find on ver. 4.

Verse 3. *And in the eighth day*] Before this time the child could scarcely be considered as having strength sufficient to bear the operation; after this time it was not necessary to delay it, as the child was not considered to be in covenant with God, and consequently not under the especial protection of the Divine providence and grace, till this rite had been performed. On *circumcision* see the note on Gen. xvii. 10. Circumcision was to every man a *constant, evident* sign of the covenant into which he had entered with God, and of the moral obligations under which he was thereby laid. It was also a means of *purity,* and was especially necessary among a people naturally incontinent, and in a climate not peculiarly favourable to chastity. This is a light in which this subject should ever be viewed, and in which we see the reasonableness, propriety, expediency, and moral tendency of the ceremony.

Verse 4. *The blood of her purifying*] A few words will make this subject sufficiently plain. 1. God designs that the human female should bring forth children. 2. That children should derive, under his providence, their being, all their solids and all their fluids, in a word, the whole mass of their bodies, from the substance of the mother. 3. For this purpose he has given to the body of the female an extra quantity of blood and nutritious juices. 4. Before pregnancy this superabundance is evacuated at periodical times. 5. In pregnancy, that which was formerly evacuated is retained for the formation and growth of the fetus, or the general strengthening of the system during the time of pregnancy. 6. After the birth of the child, for *seven* or *fourteen* days, more or less according to certain circumstances, that superabundance, no longer necessary for the growth of the child as before, continues to be evacuated: this was called the time of the female's *purification* among the Jews. 7. When the lacerated vessels are rejoined, this superfluity of blood is returned into the general circulation, and, by a wise law of the Creator, becomes principally useful to the *breasts,* and helps in the production of *milk* for the nourishment of the new-born infant. 8. And thus it continues till the *weaning of the child,* or renewed pregnancy takes place. Here is a series of mercies and wise providential regulations which cannot be known without being admired, and which *should be known* that the great Creator and Preserver may have that praise from his creatures which his wonderful working demands.

The term *purifying* here does not imply that there is any thing *impure* in the blood at this or the other times referred to above; on the contrary, the blood is pure, perfectly so, as to its *quality,* but is excessive in *quantity* for the reasons above assigned. The idle tales found in certain works relative to the infectious nature of this fluid, and of the female in such times are as impious as they are irrational and absurd.

Verse 6. *When the days of her purifying*] It is not easy to account for the difference in the times of purification, after the birth of a male and female child. After the birth of a *boy* the mother was considered unclean for forty days; after the birth of a *girl,* fourscore days. There is probably no *physical* reason for this difference, and it is difficult to assign a *political* one. Some of the ancient physicians assert that a woman is in the order of nature much longer in com-

A. M. 2514.
B. C. 1490.
An. Exod. Isr. 2.
Abib or Nisan.

7 Who shall offer it before
the LORD, and make an atonement for her; and she shall be
cleansed from the issue of her blood. This *is*
the law for her that hath borne a male or a
female.
8 [g] And if [h] she be not able to
bring a lamb, then she shall bring
two turtles, or two young pigeons;
the one for the burnt-offering, and the other for
a sin-offering: [i] and the priest shall make an
atonement for her, and she shall be clean.

[g] Chap. v. 7; Luke ii. 24.

[h] Heb. *her hand find not sufficiency of.*——[i] Chap. iv. 26.

pletely recovering after the birth of a female than after the birth of a male child. This assertion is not justified either by observation or matter of fact. Others think that the difference in the time of purification after the birth of a male and female is intended to mark the *inferiority* of the *female* sex. This is a miserable reason, and pitifully supported.

She shall bring—a burnt-offering, and—a sin-offering] It is likely that all these ordinances were intended to show man's *natural* impurity and *original* defilement by sin, and the necessity of an *atonement* to cleanse the soul from unrighteousness.

Verse 8. *And if she be not able to bring a lamb, then she shall bring two turtles, or two young pigeons*] As the Virgin Mary brought only the latter, hence it is evident that she *was not able*, i. e., she was not *rich* enough to provide the former; for such a holy woman would not have brought the *less offering* had she been capable of bringing the *greater*. How astonishing is this! The only heir to the throne of David was not able to bring a *lamb* to offer in sacrifice to God! How abominable must SIN be when it required him who was in the form of God thus to empty and to humble himself, yea, even to the death of the cross, in order to make an atonement for it, and to purify the soul from all defilement!

The priest shall make an atonement for her] Every act of man is sinful, but such as proceed from the influence of the grace and mercy of God. Her sorrow in conception, and her pain in bringing forth children, reminded the woman of her original offence; an offence which deserved *death*, an offence which she could not expiate, and for which a sacrifice must be offered: and in reference to better things the life of an animal must be offered as a ransom for her life. And being saved in childbed, though she deserved to die, she is required, as soon as the days of her separation were ended, to bring a sacrifice according to her ability to the priest, that he might offer it to God as an atonement for her. Thus, wherever God keeps up the remembrance of *sin*, he keeps up also the memorial of *sacrifice*, to show that the state of a sinner, howsoever *deplorable*, is not *hopeless*, for that he himself has found out a ransom. Every where, in the *law* and in the *Gospel*, in every *ordinance* and in every *ceremony*, we may see both the *justice* and the *mercy* of God. Hence, while we have the knowledge of our *sin* we have also the knowledge of our *cure*.

Reader, whilst thou art confessing thy own *misery* do not forget the Lord's *mercy*; and remember, he saves to the uttermost all that come through Christ unto him.

CHAPTER XIII.

Laws relative to the leprosy. It is to be known by a rising in the flesh, *a* scab, *or a* bright spot, 1, 2. *When the priest sees these signs he shall pronounce the man unclean, infected with the leprosy, and unfit for society*, 3. *Dubious or equivocal signs of this disorder, and how the person is to be treated in whom they appear*, 4–8. *In what state of this disorder the priest may pronounce a man clean or unclean*, 9–13. *Of the* raw flesh, *the sign of the unclean leprosy*, 14, 15. *Of the* white flesh, *the sign of the leprosy called clean*, 16, 17. *Of the leprosy which succeeds a* boil, 18–20. *Equivocal marks relative to this kind of leprosy*, 21, 22. *Of the* burning boil, 23. *Of the leprosy arising out of the burning boil*, 24, 25. *Equivocal marks relative to this kind of leprosy*, 26–28. *Of the plague on the* head *or in the* beard, 29. *Of the* scall, *and how it is to be treated*, 30–37. *Of the plague of the* bright white spots, 38, 39. *Of the* bald head, 40, 41. *Of the* white reddish sore *in the bald head*, 42–44. *The leper shall rend his clothes, put a patch on his upper lip, and cry unclean*, 45. *He shall be obliged to avoid society, and live by himself without the camp*, 46. *Of the garments infected by the leprosy, and the signs of this infection*, 47–52. *Equivocal marks relative to this infection, and how the garment is to be treated, by* washing *or by* burning, 53–58. *Conclusion relative to the foregoing particulars*, 59.

A. M. 2514.
B. C. 1490.
An. Exod. Isr. 2.
Abib or Nisan.

AND the LORD spake unto
Moses and Aaron, saying,
2 When a man shall have in
the skin of his flesh a [a] rising,
[b] a scab, or bright spot, and it
be in the skin of his flesh *like*

[a] Or, *swelling*.

[b] Deut. xxviii. 27; Isa. iii. 17.

NOTES ON CHAP. XIII.

Verse 2. *The plague of leprosy*] This dreadful disorder has its name *leprosy*, from the Greek λεπρα, from λεπις, a *scale*, because in this disease the body was often covered with *thin white scales*, so as to give it the appearance of *snow*. Hence it is said of the

A. M. 2514. B. C. 1490. An. Exod. Isr. 2. Abib or Nisan.

the plague of leprosy; [c] then he shall be brought unto Aaron the priest, or unto one of his sons the priests:

3 And the priest shall look on the plague in the skin of the flesh: and *when* the hair in the plague is turned white, and the plague in sight *be* deeper than the skin of his flesh, it *is* a plague of leprosy: and the priest shall look on him, and pronounce him unclean.

4 If the bright spot *be* white in the skin of his flesh, and in sight *be* not deeper than the skin, and the hair thereof be not turned white; then the priest shall shut up *him that hath* the plague seven days:

5 And the priest shall look on him the seventh day: and, behold, *if* the plague in his sight be at a stay, *and* the plague spread not in the skin; then the priest shall shut him up seven days more:

6 And the priest shall look on him again the seventh day: and, behold, *if* the plague *be* somewhat dark, *and* the plague spread not in the skin, the priest shall pronounce him clean: it *is but* a scab: and he [d] shall wash his clothes, and be clean.

7 But if the scab spread much abroad in the skin, after that he hath been seen of the priest for his cleansing, he shall be seen of the priest again:

8 And *if* the priest see that, behold, the scab spreadeth in the skin, then the priest shall pronounce him unclean: it *is* a leprosy.

[c] Deut. xvii. 8, 9; xxiv. 8; Luke xvii. 14.

[d] Chap. xi. 25; xiv. 8.

hand of Moses, Exod. iv. 6, that it was *leprous as snow;* and of Miriam, Num. xii. 10, that she became *leprous,* as white *as snow;* and of Gehazi, 2 Kings v. 27, that, being judicially struck with the disease of Naaman, *he went out* from Elisha's *presence a leper* as white *as snow.* See the note on Exod. iv. 6.

In Hebrew this disease is termed צרעת *tsaraath,* from צרע *tsara,* to *smite* or *strike;* but the root in Arabic signifies to *cast down* or *prostrate,* and in Æthiopic, to *cause to cease,* because, says *Stockius,* "it *prostrates* the *strength* of man, and obliges him to *cease from all work* and *labour.*"

There were *three* signs by which the leprosy was known. 1. A *bright spot.* 2. A *rising* (enamelling) of the surface. 3. A *scab;* the enamelled place producing a variety of layers, or stratum super stratum, of these scales. The account given by Mr. Maundrell of the appearance of several persons whom he saw infected with this disorder in Palestine, will serve to show, in the clearest light, its horrible nature and tendency.

"When I was in the Holy Land," says he, in his letter to the Rev. Mr. Osborn, Fellow of Exeter College, "I saw several that laboured under Gehazi's distemper; particularly at *Sichem,* (now *Naplosu,*) there were no less than *ten* that came begging to us at one time. Their manner is to come with small buckets in their hands, to receive the alms of the charitable; their *touch* being still held infectious, or at least *unclean.* The distemper, as I saw it on *them,* was quite different from what I have seen it in England; for it not only defiles the whole surface of the body with a foul *scurf,* but also deforms the *joints* of the body, particularly those of the wrists and ankles, making them swell with a *gouty scrofulous substance,* very loathsome to look on. I thought their legs like those of old *battered horses,* such as are often seen in drays in England. The whole distemper, indeed, as it there appeared, was so noisome, that it might well pass for the utmost corruption of the human body on this side the grave. And certainly the inspired penman could not have found out a fitter emblem, whereby to express the uncleanness and odiousness of vice."—*Maundrell's Travels.* Letters at the end. The reader will do well to collate this account with that given from Dr. *Mead* in the note on Exod. iv. 6.

Verse 3. *The priest shall—pronounce him unclean.*] וטמא אתו *vetimme otho;* literally, *shall pollute him,* i. e., in the Hebrew idiom, shall *declare* or *pronounce* him *polluted;* and in ver. 23 it is said, *the priest shall pronounce him clean,* וטהרו הכהן *vetiharo haccohen,* the *priest shall cleanse him,* i. e., *declare* him *clean.* In this phrase we have the proper meaning of Matt. xvi. 19: *Whatsoever ye bind on earth shall be bound in heaven; and whatsoever ye loose on earth shall be loosed in heaven.* By which our Lord intimates that the disciples, from having the *keys,* i. e., the *true knowledge* of the doctrine, of the kingdom of heaven, should, from particular evidences, be at all times able to distinguish between the clean and the unclean, the sincere and the hypocrite; and pronounce a judgment as infallible as the priest did in the case of the leprosy, from the tokens already specified. And as this *binding* and *loosing,* or pronouncing *fit* or *unfit* for fellowship with the members of Christ, must in the case of the disciples be always according to the doctrine of the kingdom of heaven, the sentence should be considered as proceeding immediately from thence, and consequently as Divinely ratified. The priest *polluted* or *cleansed,* i. e., declared the man clean or unclean, according to signs well known and infallible. The disciples or ministers of Christ *bind* or *loose,* declare to be *fit* or *unfit* for Church fellowship, according to unequivocal evidences of *innocence* or *guilt.* In the former case, the priest declared the person fit or unfit for civil society; in the latter, the ministers of Christ declare the person against whom the suspicion of guilt is laid, *fit* or *unfit* for continued association with the Church of God. The office was the same in both, a *declaration of the truth,* not from any power that they possessed of *cleansing* or *polluting,* of *binding* or of *loosing,* but by the knowledge they gained from the infallible signs and evidences produced on the respective cases.

A. M. 2514.
B. C. 1490.
An. Exod. Isr. 2.
Abib or Nisan.

9 When the plague of leprosy
is in a man, then he shall be
brought unto the priest;
10 [e] And the priest shall see *him:* and,
behold, *if* the rising *be* white in the skin, and
it have turned the hair white, and *there be*
[f] quick raw flesh in the rising;
11 It *is* an old leprosy in the skin of his
flesh, and the priest shall pronounce him unclean, and shall not shut him up: for he *is*
unclean.
12 And if a leprosy break out abroad in the
skin, and the leprosy cover all the skin of *him*
that hath the plague, from his head even to
his foot, wheresoever the priest looketh;
13 Then the priest shall consider: and, behold, *if* the leprosy have covered all his flesh,
he shall pronounce *him* clean *that hath* the
plague: it is all turned white: he *is* clean.
14 But when raw flesh appeareth in him, he
shall be unclean.
15 And the priest shall see the raw flesh,
and pronounce him to be unclean: *for* the
raw flesh *is* unclean: it *is* a leprosy.
16 Or if the raw flesh turn again, and be
changed into white, he shall come unto the
priest;
17 And the priest shall see him: and, behold, *if* the plague be turned into white; then
the priest shall pronounce *him* clean *that hath*
the plague: he *is* clean.
18 The flesh also, in which, *even* in the
skin thereof, was a [g] boil, and is healed;
19 And in the place of the boil there be a
white rising, or a bright spot,
white, and somewhat reddish,
and it be showed to the priest;

A. M. 2514.
B. C. 1490.
An. Exod. Isr. 2.
Abib or Nisan.

20 And if, when the priest seeth it, behold,
it *be* in sight lower than the skin, and the hair
thereof be turned white; the priest shall pronounce him unclean; it *is* a plague of leprosy
broken out of the boil.
21 But if the priest look on it, and, behold,
there be no white hairs therein, and *if* it *be* not
lower than the skin, but *be* somewhat dark;
then the priest shall shut him up seven days:
22 And if it spread much abroad in the skin,
then the priest shall pronounce him unclean:
it *is* a plague.
23 But if the bright spot stay in his place,
and spread not, it *is* a burning boil: and the
priest shall pronounce him clean.
24 Or if there be *any* flesh, in the skin,
whereof *there is* [h] a hot burning, and the quick
flesh that burneth have a white bright spot,
somewhat reddish or white;
25 Then the priest shall look upon it: and,
behold, *if* the hair in the bright spot be turned
white, and it *be in* sight deeper than the skin;
it *is* a leprosy broken out of the burning:
wherefore the priest shall pronounce him unclean: it *is* the plague of leprosy.
26 But if the priest look on it, and, behold,
there be no white hair in the bright spot, and
it *be* no lower than the *other* skin, but *be*
somewhat dark; then the priest shall shut him
up seven days:
27 And the priest shall look upon him the

[e] Numbers xii. 10, 12; 2 Kings v. 27; 2 Chronicles xxvi. 20.

[f] Hebrew, *the quickening of living flesh.*——[g] Exodus ix. 9.——[h] Heb. *a burning of fire.*

Verse 13. If *the leprosy have covered all his flesh, he shall pronounce* him *clean*] Why is it that the *partial* leper was pronounced *unclean*, and the person *totally* covered with the disease *clean?* This was probably owing to a different *species* or *stage* of the disease; the *partial* disease was contagious, the *total* not contagious. That there are two different species or degrees of the same disease described here, is sufficiently evident. In one, the body was *all covered with a white enamelled scurf;* in the other, there was *a quick raw flesh in the risings.* On this account the one might be deemed unclean, i. e., *contagious*, the other not; for contact with the *quick raw flesh* would be more likely to communicate the disease than the touch of the *hard dry scurf.* The ichor proceeding from the former, when brought into *contact* with the flesh of another, would soon be taken into the constitution by means of the *absorbent vessels;* but where the whole surface was perfectly dry, the absorbent vessels of another person coming in contact with the diseased man could imbibe nothing, and therefore there was comparatively no danger of infection. Hence that *species* or *stage* of the disease that exhibited the *quick raw rising* was capable of conveying the infection for the reasons already assigned, when the other was not. Dr. Mead thus accounts for the circumstance mentioned in the text. See on ver. 18. As the leprosy infected *bodies, clothes*, and even the *walls* of houses, is it not rational to suppose that it was occasioned by a species of *animalcula* or *vermin* burrowing under the skin? Of this opinion there are some learned supporters.

Verse 18. *In the skin thereof, was a boil*] *Scheuchzer* supposes this and the following verse to speak of phlegmonic, erysipelatous, gangrenous, and phagedenic ulcers, all of which were subjected to the examination of the priest, to see whether they were infectious, or whether the leprosy might not take its origin from

A. M. 2514. B. C. 1490. An. Exod. Isr. 2. Abib or Nisan.

seventh day: *and* if it be spread much abroad in the skin, then the priest shall pronounce him unclean: it *is* the plague of leprosy.

28 And if the bright spot stay in his place, *and* spread not in the skin, but it *be* somewhat dark; it *is* a rising of the burning, and the priest shall pronounce him clean: for it is *an* inflammation of the burning.

29 If a man or a woman have a plague upon the head or the beard;

30 Then the priest shall see the plague: and, behold, if it *be* in sight deeper than the skin; *and there be* in it a yellow thin hair; then the priest shall pronounce him unclean: it *is* a dry scall, *even* a leprosy upon the head or beard.

31 And if the priest look on the plague of the scall, and, behold, it *be* not in sight deeper than the skin, and *that there is* no black hair in it: then the priest shall shut up *him that hath* the plague of the scall seven days:

32 And in the seventh day the priest shall look on the plague: and, behold, *if* the scall spread not, and there be in it no yellow hair, and the scall *be* not in sight deeper than the skin;

33 He shall be shaven, but the scall shall he not shave; and the priest shall shut up *him that hath* the scall seven days more;

34 And in the seventh day the priest shall look on the scall: and, behold, *if* the scall be not spread in the skin, nor *be* in sight deeper than the skin; then the priest shall pronounce him clean: and he shall wash his clothes, and be clean.

35 But if the scall spread much in the skin after his cleansing;

36 Then the priest shall look on him: and, behold, if the scall be spread in the skin, the priest shall not seek for yellow hair; he *is* unclean.

A. M. 2514. B. C. 1490. An. Exod. Isr. 2. Abib or Nisan.

37 But if the scall be in his sight, at a stay, and *that* there is black hair grown up therein; the scall his healed, he *is* clean: and the priest shall pronounce him clean.

38 If a man also or a woman have in the skin of their flesh bright spots, *even* white bright spots;

39 Then the priest shall look: and, behold, *if* the bright spots in the skin of their flesh *be* darkish white; it *is* a freckled spot *that* groweth in the skin; he *is* clean.

40 And the man whose [i] hair is fallen off his head, he *is* bald; *yet is* he clean.

41 And he that hath his hair fallen off from the part of his head toward his face, he *is* forehead bald; *yet is* he clean.

42 And if there be in the bald head, or bald forehead, a white reddish sore; it *is* a leprosy sprung up in his bald head, or his bald forehead.

43 Then the priest shall look upon it: and, behold, *if* the rising of the sore *be* white reddish in his bald head, or in his bald forehead, as the leprosy appeareth in the skin of the flesh;

44 He is a leprous man, he *is* unclean: the priest shall pronounce him utterly unclean; his plague *is* in his head.

45 And the leper in whom the plague *is*, his clothes shall be rent, and his head bare, and he shall [k] put a covering upon his upper lip, and shall cry, [l] Unclean, unclean.

46 All the days wherein the plague *shall be* in him he shall be defiled; he *is* unclean: he

[i] Heb. *head is pilled.*—[k] Ezek. xxiv. 17, 22; Mic. iii. 7.

[l] Lam. iv. 15.

them. A person with any *sore* or disposition to contagion was more likely to catch the infection by contact with the diseased person, than he was whose *skin* was *whole* and *sound*, and his *habit good.*

Verse 29. *A plague upon the head or the beard*] This refers to a disease in which, according to the Jews, the hair either on the head or the chin dropped out by the roots.

Verse 33. *The scall shall he not shave*] Lest the place should be irritated and inflamed, and assume in consequence other appearances besides those of a leprous infection; in which case the priest might not be able to form an accurate judgment.

Verse 45. *His clothes shall be rent, &c.*] The leprous person is required to be as one that mourned for the dead, or for some great and public calamity. He was to have his clothes rent in token of extreme sorrow; his head was to be made bare, the ordinary bonnet or turban being omitted; and he was to have a *covering upon his upper lip,* his jaws being tied up with a linen cloth, after the same manner in which the Jews bind up the dead, which custom is still observed among the Jews in Barbary on funeral occasions: a custom which, from Ezek. xxiv. 17, we learn had prevailed very anciently among the Jews in Palestine. He was also to cry, *Unclean, unclean,* in order to prevent any person from coming near him, lest the contagion might be thus communicated and diffused through

A. M. 2514.
B. C. 1490.
An. Exod. Isr. 2.
Abib or Nisan.

shall dwell alone; [m] without the camp *shall* his habitation *be.*

47 The garment also that the plague of leprosy is in, *whether it be* a woollen garment, or a linen garment;

48 Whether *it be* in the warp, or woof; of linen, or of woollen; whether in a skin, or in any [n] thing made of skin;

49 And if the plague be greenish or reddish in the garment, or in the skin, either in the warp or in the woof, or in any [o] thing of skin; it *is* a plague of leprosy, and shall be showed unto the priest:

50 And the priest shall look upon the plague, and shut up *it that hath* the plague seven days:

51 And he shall look on the plague on the seventh day: if the plague be spread in the garment, either in the warp or in the woof, or in a skin, *or* in any work that is made of skin; the plague *is* [p] a fretting leprosy; it *is* unclean.

52 He shall therefore burn that garment, whether warp or woof, in woollen or in linen, or any thing of skin, wherein the plague is: for it *is* a fretting leprosy; it shall be burnt in the fire.

53 And if the priest shall look, and, behold, the plague be not spread in the garment, either in the warp, or in the woof, or in any thing of skin;

54 Then the priest shall command that they wash *the thing* wherein the plague *is,* and he shall shut it up seven days more:

55 And the priest shall look on the plague, after that it is washed; and, behold, *if* the plague have not changed his colour, and the plague be not spread; it *is* unclean; thou shalt burn it in the fire; it *is* fret inward, [q] *whether* it *be* bare within or without.

56 And if the priest look, and, behold, the plague *be* somewhat dark after the washing of it; then he shall rend it out of the garment, or out of the skin, or out of the warp, or out of the woof:

57 And if it appear still in the garment, either in the warp, or in the woof, or in any thing of skin; it *is* a spreading *plague:* thou shalt burn that wherein the plague *is* with fire.

58 And the garment, either warp, or woof, or whatsoever thing of skin *it be,* which thou shalt wash, if the plague be departed from them, [r] then it shall be washed the second time, and shall be clean.

59 This *is* the law of the plague of leprosy in a garment of woollen or linen, either in the warp, or woof, or any thing of skins, to pronounce it clean, or to pronounce it unclean.

[m] Num. v. 2; xii. 14; 2 Kings vii. 3; xv. 5; 2 Chron. xxvi. 21; Luke xvii. 12.——[n] Heb. *work of.*——[o] Heb. *vessel,* or, *instrument.*——[p] Chap. xiv. 44.——[q] Heb. whether *it* be *bald in the head thereof,* or, *in the forehead thereof.*——[r] 2 Kings v. 10, 14; Psa. li. 2; 2 Cor. vii. 1; Rev. i. 5; vii. 14.

society; and hence the Targumist render it, *Be not ye made unclean! Be not ye made unclean!* A caution to others not to come near him.

Verse 47. *The garment also*] The whole account here seems to intimate that the garment was *fretted* by this contagion; and hence it is likely that it was occasioned by a species of small *animals,* which we know to be the cause of the *itch;* these, by breeding in the garments, must necessarily multiply their kind, and *fret* the garments, i. e., corrode a portion of the finer parts, after the manner of *moths,* for their nourishment. See ver. 52.

Verse 52. *He shall therefore burn that garment*] There being scarcely any means of *radically* curing the infection. It is well known that the garments infected by the *psora,* or itch animal, have been known to communicate the disease even six or seven years after the first infection. This has been also experienced by the sorters of *rags* at some paper mills.

Verse 54. *He shall shut it up seven days more*] To give time for the spreading of the contagion, if it did exist there; that there might be the most unequivocal marks and proofs that the garment *was* or was *not* infected.

Verse 58. *It shall be washed the second time*] According to the Jews the *first* washing was to put away the *plague,* the *second* to *cleanse* it.

Both among Jews and Gentiles the leprosy has been considered as a most expressive emblem of sin, the properties and circumstances of the one pointing out those of the other. The similitude or parallel has been usually run in the following manner:—

1. The leprosy began with a *spot,* a simple hidden infection being the cause.

2. This spot was very *conspicuous,* and argued the source whence it proceeded.

3. It was of a *diffusive* nature, soon spreading over the whole body.

4. It *communicated* its infectious nature, not only to the whole of the person's body, but also to his *clothes* and *habitation.*

5. It rendered the infected person *loathsome, unfit* for and *dangerous* to society, because of its infectious nature.

6. The person infected was obliged to be *separated from society,* both religious and civil; to dwell *by himself* without the camp or city, and hold commerce with none.

7. He was obliged to *proclaim his own uncleanness,* publicly acknowledge his defilement, and, sensible of his plague, continue humbled and abased before God and man.

How expressive all these are of the nature of sin and the state of a sinner, a spiritual mind will at once perceive.

1. The *original infection* or corruption of nature is the grand *hidden cause*, source, and spring of all transgression.

2. Iniquity is a *seed* that has its growth, gradual increase, and perfection. As the various powers of the mind are developed, so it diffuses itself, infecting every passion and appetite through their whole extent and operation.

3. As it *spreads* in the *mind*, so it *diffuses itself through the life;* every action partaking of its influence, till the whole conduct becomes a tissue of transgression, because every imagination of the thoughts of a sinner's heart is only evil continually, Gen. vi. This is the natural state of man.

4. As a sinner is *infected*, so is he *infectious;* by his precept and example he spreads the infernal contagion wherever he goes; joining with the multitude to do evil, strengthening and being strengthened in the ways of sin and death, and becoming especially a *snare* and a *curse* to his own *household*.

5. That a sinner is *abominable* in the sight of God and of all good men, that he is unfit for the society of the righteous, and that he cannot, as such, be admitted into the kingdom of God, needs no proof.

6. It is owing to the *universality* of the evil that sinners are not expelled from society as the most dangerous of all monsters, and obliged to live without having any commerce with their fellow creatures. *Ten lepers* could associate together, because partaking of the same infection: and civil society is generally maintained, because composed of a leprous community.

7. He that wishes to be saved from his sins must humble himself before God and man, sensible of his own sore and the plague of his heart; confess his transgressions; look to God for a cure, from whom alone it can be received; and bring that Sacrifice by which alone the guilt can be taken away, and his soul be purified from all unrighteousness. See the conclusion of the following chapter.

CHAPTER XIV.

Introduction to the sacrifices and ceremonies to be used in cleansing the leper, 1–3. *Two* living birds, cedar-wood, scarlet, *and* hyssop, *to be brought for him who was to be cleansed,* 4. *One of the birds to be killed,* 5; *and the living bird, with the cedar-wood, scarlet, and hyssop, to be dipped in the blood, and to be sprinkled on him who had been infected with the leprosy,* 6, 7; *after which he must wash his clothes, shave his head, eyebrows, beard, &c., bathe himself, tarry abroad* seven days, 8, 9; *on the* eighth day *he must bring two* he-lambs, *one* ewe-lamb, *a* tenth deal *of* flour, *and a* log *of* oil, 10; *which the priest was to present as a* trespass-offering, wave-offering, *and* sin-offering *before the Lord,* 11–13. *Afterwards he was to sprinkle both the blood and oil on the person to be cleansed,* 14–18. *The atonement made by these offerings,* 19, 20. *If the person were poor,* one lamb, *with the* flour *and* oil, two turtle-doves, *or* two young pigeons, *were only required,* 21, 22. *These to be presented, and the blood and oil applied as before,* 23–32. *Laws and ordinances relative to* houses *infected by the leprosy,* 33–48. *An atonement to be made in order to cleanse the house, similar to that made for the healed leper,* 49–53. *A summary of this and the preceding chapter, relative to leprous* persons, garments, *and* houses, 54–56. *The end for which these different laws were given,* 57.

A. M. 2514.
B. C. 1490.
An. Exod. Isr. 2.
Abib or Nisan.

AND the LORD spake unto
Moses, saying,
2 This shall be the law of the
leper in the day of his cleansing: He [a] shall
be brought unto the priest;
3 And the priest shall go forth
out of the camp; and the priest
shall look, and, behold, *if* the
plague of leprosy be healed in the leper;
4 Then shall the priest command to take for

A. M. 2514.
B. C. 1490.
An. Exod. Isr. 2.
Abib or Nisan.

[a] Matt. viii. 2–4; Mark i. 40, 44; Luke v. 12, 14; xvii. 14.

NOTES ON CHAP. XIV.

Verse 3. *The priest shall go forth out of the camp*] As the leper was separated from the people, and obliged, because of his uncleanness, to dwell without the camp, and could not be admitted till the priest had declared that he was clean; hence it was necessary that the priest should go out and inspect him, and, if healed, offer for him the sacrifices required, in order to his re-admission to the camp. As the priest alone had authority to declare a person *clean* or *unclean*, it was necessary that the healed person should show himself to the *priest*, that he might make a declaration that he was clean and fit for civil and religious society, without which, in no case, could he be admitted; hence, when Christ cleansed the lepers, Matt. viii. 2–4, he commanded them to *go and show themselves to the priest*, &c.

Verse 4. *Two birds alive* and *clean, &c.*] Whether these birds were *sparrows*, or *turtle-doves*, or *pigeons*, we know not; probably any kind of *clean* bird, or bird proper to be eaten, might be used on this occasion, though it is more likely that *turtle-doves* or *pigeons* were employed, because these appear to have been the only birds offered in sacrifice. Of the *cedar-wood, hyssop, clean bird*, and *scarlet wool* or *fillet*, were made an *aspergillum*, or instrument to *sprinkle* with. The *cedar-wood* served for the *handle*, the *hyssop* and *living bird* were attached to it by means of the *scarlet wool* or *crimson fillet*. The bird was so bound to this handle as that its tail should be downwards, in

A. M. 2514.
B. C. 1490.
An. Exod. Isr. 2.
Abib or Nisan.

him that is to be cleansed two [b] birds alive *and* clean, and [c] cedar-wood, and [d] scarlet, and [e] hyssop:

5 And the priest shall command that one of the birds be killed in an earthen vessel over running water.

6 As for the living bird, he shall take it, and the cedar-wood, and the scarlet, and the hyssop, and shall dip them and the living bird in the blood of the bird *that was* killed over the running water;

7 And he shall [f] sprinkle upon him that is to be cleansed from the leprosy [g] seven times, and shall pronounce him clean; and shall let the living bird loose [h] into the open field.

8 And he that is to be cleansed [i] shall wash his clothes, and shave off all his hair, [k] and wash himself in water, that he may be clean: and after that he shall come into the camp, and [l] shall tarry abroad out of his tent seven days.

9 But it shall be on the seventh day, that he shall shave all his hair off his head and his beard and his eyebrows, even all his hair he shall shave off: and he shall wash his clothes; also he shall wash his flesh in water, and he shall be clean.

A. M. 2514.
B. C. 1490.
An. Exod. Isr. 2.
Abib or Nisan.

10 And on the eighth day [m] he shall take two he-lambs without blemish, and one ewe-lamb [n] of the first year without blemish, and three tenth deals of fine flour *for* [o] a meat-offering, mingled with oil, and one log of oil.

11 And the priest that maketh *him* clean shall present the man that is to be made clean, and those things, before the LORD, *at* the door of the tabernacle of the congregation.

12 And the priest shall take one he-lamb, and [p] offer him for a trespass-offering, and the log of oil, and [q] wave them *for* a wave-offering before the LORD.

13 And he shall slay the lamb [r] in the place

[b] Or, *sparrows.*——[c] Numbers xix. 6.——[d] Hebrews ix. 19. [e] Psa. li. 7.——[f] Heb. ix. 13.——[g] 2 Kings v. 10, 14.——[h] Heb. *upon the face of the field.*——[i] Chap. xiii. 6.——[k] Chap. xi. 25. Num. xii. 15.

[m] Matt. viii. 4; Mark i. 44; Luke v. 14.——[n] Heb. *the daughter of her year.*——[o] Chap. ii. 1; Num. xv. 4, 15.——[p] Chap. v. 2, 18; vi. 6, 7.——[q] Exod. xxix. 24.——[r] Exod. xxix. 11; chap. i. 5, 11; iv. 4, 24.

order to be dipped into the blood of the bird that had been killed. The whole of this made an instrument for the sprinkling of this blood, and when this business was done, the living bird was let loose, and permitted to go whithersoever it would. In this ceremony, according to some rabbins, "the *living bird* signified that the *dead flesh* of the leper was restored to soundness; the *cedar-wood*, which is not easily corrupted, that he was healed of his *putrefaction;* the *scarlet thread, wool*, or *fillet*, that he was restored to his good complexion; and the *hyssop*, which was purgative and odoriferous, that the disease was completely removed, and the bad scent that accompanied it entirely gone." *Ainsworth, Dodd*, and others, have given many of these rabbinical conceits. Of all these purifications, and their accompanying circumstances, we may safely say, because authorized by the New Testament so to do, that they pointed out the purification of the soul through the atonement and Spirit of Christ; but to run analogies between the *type* and the *thing typified* is difficult and precarious. The *general meaning* and *design* we sufficiently understand; the particulars are not readily ascertainable, and consequently of little importance; had they been otherwise, they would have been pointed out.

Verse 5. *Over running water.*] Literally, *living*, that is, *spring* water. The meaning appears to be this: Some water (about a quarter of a log, an egg-shell and a half full, according to the rabbins) was taken from a *spring*, and put into a clean *earthen vessel*, and they killed the bird over this water, that the blood might drop into it; and in this blood and water mixed they dipped the instrument before described, and sprinkled it seven times upon the person who was to be cleansed. The *living* or *spring water* was chosen because it was *purer* than what was taken from pits or wells, the latter being often in a putrid or corrupt state; for in a ceremony of purifying or cleansing, every thing must be as pure and perfect as possible.

Verse 7. *Shall let the living bird loose*] The Jews teach that *wild* birds were employed on this occasion, no *tame* or *domestic* animal was used. Mr. Ainsworth piously conjectures that the *living* and *dead* birds were intended to represent the *death* and *resurrection* of Christ, by which an atonement was made to purify the soul from its spiritual leprosy. The bird let loose bears a near analogy to the *scape-goat*. See chap. xvi

Verse 8. *And shave off all his hair*] That the water by which he was to be washed should reach every part of his body, that he might be cleansed from whatever defilement might remain on any part of the surface of his body. The Egyptian priests shaved the whole body every third day, to prevent all manner of defilement.

Verse 10. *Two he-lambs*] One for a *trespass-offering*, ver. 12, the other for a *burnt-offering*, ver. 19, 20.

One ewe-lamb] This was for a *sin-offering*, ver. 19.

Three tenth deals] Three parts of an *ephah*, or three *omers;* see all these measures explained, Exod. xvi. 16. The three tenth deals of flour were for a *minchah, meat* or *gratitude-offering*, ver. 20. The *sin-offering* was for his *impurity;* the *trespass-offering* for his *transgression;* and the *gratitude-offering* for his gracious *cleansing*. These constituted the offering which each was ordered to bring to the priest; see Matt. viii. 4.

Verse 12. *Wave-offering*] See Exod. xxix. 27, and chap. vii., where the reader will find an ample

A. M. 2514.
B. C. 1490.
An. Exod. Isr. 2.
Abib or Nisan.

where he shall kill the sin-offering and the burnt-offering, in the holy place: for [s] as the sin-offering *is* the priest's, *so is* the trespass-offering; [t] it *is* most holy.

14 And the priest shall take *some* of the blood of the trespass-offering, and the priest shall put *it* [u] upon the tip of the right ear of him that is to be cleansed, and upon the thumb of his right hand, and upon the great toe of his right foot:

15 And the priest shall take *some* of the log of oil, and pour *it* into the palm of his own left hand:

16 And the priest shall dip his right finger in the oil that *is* in his left hand, and shall sprinkle of the oil with his finger seven times before the LORD:

17 And of the rest of the oil that *is* in his hand shall the priest put upon the tip of the right ear of him that is to be cleansed, and upon the thumb of his right hand, and upon the great toe of his right foot, upon the blood of the trespass-offering:

18 And the remnant of the oil that *is* in the priest's hand he shall pour upon the head of him that is to be cleansed: [v] and the priest shall make an atonement for him before the LORD.

19 And the priest shall offer [w] the sin-offering, and make an atonement for him that is to be cleansed from his uncleanness; and afterward he shall kill the burnt-offering:

20 And the priest shall offer the burnt-offering and the meat-offering upon the altar; and the priest shall make an atonement for him, and he shall be clean.

21 And [x] if he *be* poor, and [y] cannot get so much, then he shall take one lamb *for* a trespass-offering [z] to be waved, to make an atonement for him, and one tenth deal of fine flour mingled with oil for a meat-offering, and a log of oil;

22 [a] And two turtle-doves, or two young pigeons, such as he is able to get: and the one shall be a sin-offering, and the other a burnt-offering.

A. M. 2514.
B. C. 1490.
An. Exod. Isr. 2.
Abib or Nisan.

23 [b] And he shall bring them on the eighth day for his cleansing unto the priest, unto the door of the tabernacle of the congregation, before the LORD.

24 [c] And the priest shall take the lamb of the trespass-offering, and the log of oil, and the priest shall wave them *for* a wave-offering before the LORD:

25 And he shall kill the lamb of the trespass-offering, [d] and the priest shall take *some* of the blood of the trespass-offering, and put *it* upon the tip of the right ear of him that is to be cleansed, and upon the thumb of his right hand, and upon the great toe of his right foot:

26 And the priest shall pour of the oil into the palm of his own left hand;

27 And the priest shall sprinkle with his right finger *some* of the oil that *is* in his left hand, seven times before the LORD:

28 And the priest shall put of the oil that *is* in his hand upon the tip of the right ear of him that is to be cleansed, and upon the thumb of his right hand, and upon the great toe of his right foot, upon the place of the blood of the trespass-offering:

29 And the rest of the oil that *is* in the priest's hand he shall put upon the head of him that is to be cleansed, to make an atonement for him before the LORD.

30 And he shall offer the one of [e] the turtle-doves, or of the young pigeons, such as he can get;

31 *Even* such as he is able to get, the one *for* a sin-offering, and the other *for* a burnt-offering, with the meat-offering: and the priest shall make an atonement for him that is to be cleansed, before the LORD.

32 This *is* the law *of him* in whom *is* the plague of leprosy, whose hand is not able to

[s] Chap. vii. 7.——[t] Chap. ii. 3; vii. 6; xxi. 22.——[u] Exod. xxix. 20; chap. viii. 23.——[v] Chap. iv. 26.——[w] Chap. v. 1, 6; xii. 7.——[x] Chap. v. 7; xii. 8.

[y] Heb. *his hand reach not.*——[z] Heb. *for a waving.*——[a] Chap. xii. 8; xv. 14, 15.——[b] Ver. 11.——[c] Ver. 12.——[d] Ver. 14.——[e] Ver. 22; chap. xv. 15.

account of all the various offerings and sacrifices used among the Jews.

Verse 14. *Upon the tip of the right ear, &c.*] See the note on Exod. xxix. 20.

Verse 21. *And if he be poor—he shall take one lamb*] There could be no cleansing without a sacrifice. On this ground the apostle has properly observed that *all things under the law are purged with blood;* and that *without shedding of blood there is no remission.* Even if the person be poor, he must provide *one lamb;* this could not be dispensed with:—so every soul to whom the word of Divine revelation comes,

A. M. 2514.
B. C. 1490.
An. Exod. Isr. 2.
Abib or Nisan.

get [f] *that which pertaineth* to his
cleansing.
33 And the LORD spake unto
Moses and unto Aaron, saying,
34 [g] When ye be come into the land of
Canaan, which I give to you for a possession,
and I put the plague of leprosy in a house
of the land of your possession;
35 And he that owneth the house shall come
and tell the priest, saying, It seemeth to me
there is as it were [h] a plague in the house:
36 Then the priest shall command that they
[i] empty the house, before the priest go *into it*
to see the plague, that all that *is* in the house
be not made unclean: and afterward the
priest shall go in to see the house:
37 And he shall look on the plague, and,
behold, *if* the plague *be* in the walls of the
house with hollow streaks, greenish or reddish,
which in sight *are* lower than the wall;
38 Then the priest shall go out of the house
to the door of the house, and shut up the
house seven days:
39 And the priest shall come again the
seventh day, and shall look: and, behold, *if*
the plague be spread in the walls of the
house;
40 Then the priest shall command that they
take away the stones in which the plague *is*,
and they shall cast them into an unclean place
without the city:
41 And he shall cause the house to be
scraped within, round about, and they shall
pour out the dust that they scrape off, without the city, into an unclean place:
42 And they shall take other
stones, and put *them* in the place
of those stones; and he shall
take other mortar and shall plaster the house

A. M. 2514.
B. C. 1490.
An. Exod. Isr. 2.
Abib or Nisan.

43 And if the plague come again, and break
out in the house, after that he hath taken away
the stones, and after he hath scraped the house,
and after it is plastered:
44 Then the priest shall come and look, and,
behold, *if* the plague be spread in the house,
it *is* [k] a fretting leprosy in the house: it *is*
unclean.
45 And he shall break down the house, the
stones of it, and the timber thereof, and all
the mortar of the house; and he shall carry
them forth out of the city into an unclean place.
46 Moreover he that goeth into the house
all the while that it is shut up, shall be unclean until the even.
47 And he that lieth in the house shall wash
his clothes; and he that eateth in the house
shall wash his clothes.
48 And if the priest [l] shall come in, and
look *upon it*, and, behold, the plague hath not
spread in the house, after the house was plastered; then the priest shall pronounce the
house clean, because the plague is healed.
49 And [m] he shall take to cleanse the house
two birds, and cedar-wood, and scarlet, and
hyssop:
50 And he shall kill the one of the birds in
an earthen vessel, over running water:
51 And he shall take the cedar-wood, and
the hyssop, and the scarlet, and the living
bird, and dip them in the blood of the slain

[f] Ver. 10.——[g] Gen. xvii. 8; Num. xxxii. 22; Deut. vii. 1; xxxii. 49.——[h] Psa. xci. 10; Prov. iii. 33; Zech. v. 4.

[i] Or, *prepare*.——[k] Chap. xiii. 51; Zech. v. 4.——[l] Heb. *in coming in shall come in, &c.*——[m] Ver. 4.

must bring that Lamb of God which takes away the sin of the world. There is no redemption but in his blood.

Verse 34. *When ye be come into the land—and I put the plague of leprosy*] It was probably from this text that the leprosy has been generally considered to be a disease inflicted immediately by God himself; but it is well known that in Scripture God is frequently represented as *doing* what, in the course of his providence, he only *permits* or suffers to be done. It is supposed that the infection of the house, as well as of the person and the garments, proceeded from *animalcula*. See the notes on chap. xiii. 47, 52.

Verse 45. *He shall break down the house*] "On the suspicion of a house being infected, the priest examined it, and ordered it to be shut up seven days; if he found the plague, or signs of the plague, (hollow streaks, greenish or reddish,) were not spread, he commanded it to be shut up seven days more. On the *thirteenth* day he revisited it; and if he found the infected place *dim*, or gone away, he took out that part of the wall, carried it out to an unclean place, mended the wall, and caused the whole house to be new plastered. It was then shut up a third seven days, and he came on the *nineteenth*, and if he found that the plague was broken out anew, he ordered the house to be pulled down." See *Ainsworth*. From all this may we not learn a lesson of instruction? If the means made use of by God and his ministers for the conversion of a sinner be, through his wilful obstinacy, rendered of no avail; if by his evil practices he trample under foot the blood of the covenant wherewith he might have been sanctified, and do despite to the Spirit of God; then God will pull down his house—dislodge his soul from its earthly tabernacle, consign the house, the body, to corruption, and the spirit to the perdition of ungodly

A. M. 2514. B. C. 1490. An. Exod. Isr. 2. Abib or Nisan.

bird, and in the running water, and sprinkle the house seven times:

52 And he shall cleanse the house with the blood of the bird, and with the running water, and with the living bird, and with the cedar-wood, and with the hyssop, and with the scarlet:

53 But he shall let go the living bird out of the city into the open fields, and [n] make an atonement for the house: and it shall be clean.

54 This *is* the law for all manner of plague of leprosy, and [o] scall,

55 And for the [p] leprosy of a garment, [q] and of a house.

56 And [r] for a rising, and for a scab, and for a bright spot:

57 To [s] teach [t] when *it is* unclean, and when *it is* clean: this *is* the law of leprosy.

A. M. 2514. B. C. 1490. An. Exod. Isr. 2. Abib or Nisan.

[n] Ver. 20.——[o] Chap. xiii. 30.——[p] Chap. xiii. 47.——[q] Ver. 34. [r] Chap. xiii. 2.

[s] Deut. xxiv. 8; Ezek. xliv. 23.——[t] Heb. *in the day of the unclean, and in the day of the clean.*

men. Reader, see well how it stands with *thy* soul. God is not mocked: what a man soweth, that shall he reap.

Verse 53. *He shall let go the living bird*] This might as well be called the *scape-bird*; as the *goat*, in chap. xvi., is called the *scape-goat*. The rites are similar in both cases, and probably had nearly the same meaning.

We have already taken occasion to observe (see the end of the preceding chapter) that the *leprosy* was strongly emblematical of *sin;* to which we may add here,—

1. That the leprosy was a disease generally acknowledged to be incurable by any human means; and therefore the Jews did not attempt to cure it. What is directed to be done here was not in order to cure the leper, but to declare him cured and fit for society. In like manner the contagion of sin, its guilt and its power, can only be removed by the hand of God; all means, without his especial influence, can be of no avail.

2. The body must be sprinkled and washed, and a sacrifice offered for the sin of the soul, before the leper could be declared to be clean. To cleanse the spiritual leper, the Lamb of God must be slain, and the sprinkling of his blood be applied. Without the shedding of this blood there is no remission.

3. When the leper was cleansed, he was obliged to show himself to the priest, whose province it was to pronounce him clean, and declare him fit for intercourse with civil and religious society. When a sinner is converted from the error of his ways, it is the business, as it is the prerogative, of the *ministers* of Christ, after having duly acquainted themselves with every circumstance, to declare the person *converted* from sin to holiness, to unite him with the people of God, and admit him to all the ordinances which belong to the faithful.

4. When the leper was cleansed, he was obliged by the law to offer a *gift* unto the Lord for his healing, as a proof of his *gratitude*, and an evidence of his *obedience*. When a sinner is restored to the Divine favour, he should offer continually the sacrifice of a grateful heart, and, in willing obedience, show forth the virtues of Him who has called him from darkness and wretchedness to marvellous light and happiness.

Reader, such was the leprosy, its destructive nature and consequences, and the means of removing it; such is the spiritual evil represented by it, such *its* consequences, and such the means by which alone *it* can be removed. The disease of sin, inflicted by the devil, can only be cured by the power of God. 1. Art *thou* a leper? Do the *spots* of this spiritual infection begin to appear on *thee?* 2. Art thou *young*, and only entering into the ways of the world and sin? Stop! bad habits are more easily conquered to-day than they will be to-morrow. 3. Art thou *stricken in years*, and rooted in transgression? How kind is thy Maker to have preserved thee *alive* so long! Turn from thy transgressions, humble thy soul before Him, confess thine iniquity and implore forgiveness. Seek, and thou shalt find. Behold the Lamb of God, who taketh away the sin of the world! 4. Hast thou been *cleansed*, and hast not returned to give glory to God? hast not continued in the truth, serving thy Maker and Saviour with a loving and obedient heart? How cutting is that word, *Were there not* TEN *cleansed? but where are the* NINE? *Thou* art probably *one* of them. Be confounded at thy ingratitude, and distressed for thy backsliding; and apply a second time for the healing efficacy of the great Atonement. Turn, thou backslider; *for he is married unto thee, and will heal thy backslidings, and will love thee freely.* Amen. So be it, Lord Jesus!

CHAPTER XV.

Laws concerning uncleanness of men, 1–12. *Mode of cleansing*, 13–15. *Of uncleanness, accidental and casual*, 16–18. *Laws concerning the uncleanness of women*, 19–27. *Mode of cleansing*, 28–30. *Recapitulation of the ordinances relative to the preceding cases*, 31–33.

A. M. 2514.
B. C. 1490.
An. Exod. Isr. 2.
Abib or Nisan.

AND the LORD spake unto
Moses and to Aaron, saying,
2 Speak unto the children of
Israel, and say unto them, [a] When any man hath
a [b] running issue out of his flesh, *because of*
his issue he *is* unclean.
3 And this shall be his uncleanness in his
issue: whether his flesh run with his issue,
or his flesh be stopped from his issue, it *is*
his uncleanness.
4 Every bed, whereon he lieth that hath the
issue, is unclean: and every [c] thing whereon
he sitteth shall be unclean.
5 And whosoever toucheth his bed shall
wash his clothes, [d] and bathe *himself* in water,
and be unclean until the even.
6 And he that sitteth on *any* thing whereon
he sat that hath the issue shall wash his
clothes, and bathe *himself* in water, and be
unclean until even.
7 And he that toucheth the
flesh of him that hath the issue
shall wash his clothes, and bathe
himself in water, and be unclean until the
even.
8 And if he that hath the issue spit upon him
that is clean; then he shall wash his clothes,
and bathe *himself* in water, and be unclean
until the even.
9 And what saddle soever he rideth upon
that hath the issue shall be unclean.
10 And whosoever toucheth any thing that
was under him shall be unclean until the
even: and he that beareth *any of* those things
shall wash his clothes, and bathe *himself* in
water, and be unclean until the even.
11 And whomsoever he toucheth that hath
the issue, and hath not rinsed his hands in
water, he shall wash his clothes, and bathe
himself in water, and be unclean until the even.

[a] Chapter xxii. 4; Num. v. 2; 2 Samuel iii. 29; Matt. ix. 20; Mark v. 25; Luke viii. 43. — [b] Or, *running of the reins.* — [c] Heb. *vessel.* — [d] Chap. xi. 25; xvii. 15.

NOTES ON CHAP. XV.

Verse 2. *When any man hath a running issue*] The cases of natural uncleanness, both of men and women, mentioned in this chapter, taken in a theological point of view, are not of such importance to us as to render a particular description necessary, the letter of the text being, in general, plain enough. The disease mentioned in the former part of this chapter appears to *some* to have been either the consequence of a very bad infection, or of some criminal indulgence; for they find that it might be *communicated* in a variety of ways, which they imagine are here distinctly specified. On this ground the person was declared *unclean*, and all commerce and connection with him strictly forbidden. The Septuagint version renders הזב *hazzab*, the man with the *issue*, by ὁ γονοῤῥυης, the man with a *gonorrhœa*, no less than nine times in this chapter; and that it means what in the present day is commonly understood by that disorder, taken not only in its mild but in its worst sense, they think there is little room to doubt. Hence they infer that a disease which is supposed to be comparatively *recent* in Europe, has existed almost from time immemorial in the Asiatic countries; that it ever has been, in certain measures, what it is now; and that it ever must be the effect of sensual indulgence, and illicit and extravagant intercourse between the sexes. The disgraceful disorder referred to here is a foul blot which the justice of God in the course of providence has made in general the inseparable consequent of these criminal indulgences, and serves in some measure to correct and restrain the vice itself. In countries where public prostitution was permitted, where it was even a religious ceremony among those who were idolaters, this disease must necessarily have been frequent and prevalent. When the pollutions and libertinism of former times are considered, it seems rather strange that medical men should have adopted the opinion, and consumed so much time in endeavouring to prove it, viz., that the disease is *modern*. It must have existed, in certain measures, ever since prostitution prevailed in the world; and this has been in every nation of the earth from its earliest era. That the Israelites might have received it from the Egyptians, and that it must, through the *Baal-peor* and *Ashteroth* abominations which they learned and practised, have prevailed among the Moabites, &c., there can be little reason to doubt. Supposing this disease to be at all hinted at *here*, the laws and ordinances enjoined were at once wisely and graciously calculated to remove and prevent it. By contact, contagion of every kind is readily communicated; and to keep the *whole* from the *diseased* must be essential to the check and eradication of a contagious disorder. This was the wise and grand object of this most enlightened Legislator in the ordinances which he lays down in this chapter. I grant, however, that it was probably of a milder kind in ancient times; that it has gained strength and virulence by continuance; and that, associated with some foreign causes, it became greatly exacerbated in Europe about 1493, the time in which some have supposed it first began to exist, though there are strong evidences of it in *this* country ever since the eleventh century.

Verse 11. *And whomsoever he toucheth*] Here we find that the saliva, sitting on the same seat, lying on the same bed, riding on the same saddle, or simple contact, was sufficient to render the person *unclean*, meaning, *possibly*, in certain cases, to communicate the disorder; and it is well known that in all these ways the contagion of this disorder may be communicated. Is it not even possible that the effluvia from

A. M. 2514.
B. C. 1490.
An. Exod. Isr. 2.
Abib or Nisan.

12 And the [e] vessel of earth,
that he toucheth which hath the
issue, shall be broken: and every
vessel of wood shall be rinsed in water.
13 And when he that hath an issue is
cleansed of his issue; then [f] he shall number
to himself seven days for his cleansing, and
wash his clothes, and bathe his flesh in running
water, and shall be clean.
14 And on the eighth day he shall take to
him [g] two turtle-doves, or two young pigeons,
and come before the LORD unto the door of
the tabernacle of the congregation, and give
them unto the priest:
15 And the priest shall offer them, [h] the one
for a sin-offering, and the other *for* a burnt-offering;
[i] and the priest shall make an atonement
for him before the LORD, for his issue.
16 And [k] if any man's seed of copulation go
out from him, then he shall wash all his flesh
in water, and be unclean until the even.
17 And every garment, and every skin,
whereon is the seed of copulation, shall be
washed with water, and be unclean until the
even.
18 The woman also with whom man shall
lie *with* seed of copulation, they shall *both* bathe
themselves in water, and [l] be unclean until the
even.
19 And [m] if a woman have an issue, *and* her
issue in her flesh be blood, she shall be [n] put
apart seven days: and whosoever toucheth
her shall be unclean until the even.
20 And every thing that she lieth upon in
her separation shall be unclean: every thing
also that she sitteth upon shall
be unclean.
21 And whosoever toucheth
her bed shall wash his clothes, and bathe
himself in water, and be unclean until the
even.
22 And whosoever toucheth any thing that
she sat upon, shall wash his clothes, and
bathe *himself* in water, and be unclean until
the even.
23 And if it *be* on *her* bed, or on any thing
whereon she sitteth, when he toucheth it, he
shall be unclean until the even.
24 And [o] if any man lie with her at all, and
her flowers be upon him, he shall be unclean
seven days; and all the bed whereon he lieth
shall be unclean.
25 And if [p] a woman have an issue of her
blood many days, out of the time of her separation,
or if it run beyond the time of her
separation; all the days of the issue of her
uncleanness shall be as the days of her separation:
she *shall be* unclean.
26 Every bed whereon she lieth, all the days
of her issue, shall be unto her as the bed of
her separation: and whatsoever she sitteth
upon shall be unclean, as the uncleanness of
her separation.
27 And whosoever toucheth those things
shall be unclean, and shall wash his clothes,
and bathe *himself* in water, and be unclean
until the even.
28 But [q] if she be cleansed of her issue, then
she shall number to herself seven days, and
after that she shall be clean.

[e] Chap. vi. 28; xi. 32, 33.——[f] Ver. 28; chap. xiv. 8.——[g] Chap. xiv. 22, 23.——[h] Chap. xiv. 30, 31.——[i] Chap. xiv. 19, 31. [k] Chap. xxii. 4; Deut. xxiii. 10.——[l] 1 Sam. xxi. 4.——[m] Chap. xii. 2.——[n] Heb. *in her separation.* [o] See chap. xx. 18.——[p] Matt. ix. 20; Mark v. 25; Luke viii. 43.——[q] Ver. 13.

the body of an infected person may be the means of communicating the disease? Sydenham expressly says that it may be communicated by lactation, handling, the saliva, sweat, and by the breath itself, as well as by those grosser means of which there is no question. But the term *unclean*, in this and the following cases, is generally understood in a mere *legal* sense, the rendering a person *unfit for sacred ordinances.* And as there was a mild kind of gonorrhœa that was brought on by excessive fatigue and the like, it may be that kind only which the law has in view in the above ordinances.

Verse 18. *They shall* both *bathe* themselves] What a wonderful tendency had these ordinances to prevent all excesses! The *pains* which such persons must take, the *separations* which they must observe, and the *privations* which, in consequence, they must be exposed to in the way of commerce, traffic, &c., would prevent them from making an unlawful use of lawful things.

Verse 24. The common sense of all mankind has led them to avoid the gross impropriety referred to in this verse; and it has been a general opinion, that offspring obtained in this way has been infected with leprous, scrofulous, and other deeply radicated diseases, from which they and their posterity have been scarcely ever freed. In chap. xx. 18, persons guilty of this are condemned to death; *here* only to a *seven days' separation;* because, in the former case, Moses speaks of the act when both the man and woman were *acquainted* with the situation: in the latter, he speaks of a case where the circumstance was *not known* till afterwards; at least, so it appears these two places should be understood, so as to be reconciled.

A. M. 2514.
B. C. 1490.
An. Exod. Isr. 2.
Abib or Nisan.

29 And on the eighth day, she
shall take unto her two turtles,
or two young pigeons, and bring
them unto the priest, to the door of the tabernacle of the congregation.
30 And the priest shall offer the one *for* a
sin-offering, and the other *for* a burnt-offering; and the priest shall make an atonement
for her before the LORD, for the issue of her
uncleanness.
31 Thus shall ye [r] separate the children of
Israel from their uncleanness; that they die not in their uncleanness, when they [s] defile my
tabernacle that *is* among them.
32 [t] This *is* the law of him that hath an issue,
[u] and *of him* whose seed goeth from him, and
is defiled therewith;
33 [v] And of her that is sick of her flowers,
and of him that hath an issue, of the man,
[w] and of the woman; [x] and of him that lieth
with her that is unclean.

[r] Chap. xi. 47; Deut. xxiv. 8; Ezek. xliv. 23.——[s] Num. v. 3; xix. 13, 20; Ezek. v. 11; xxiii. 38.

[t] Verse 2.——[u] Verse 16.——[v] Verse 19.——[w] Verse 25. [x] Ver. 24.

Verse 29. *Two turtles, or two young pigeons*] In all these cases moral pollution was ever considered as being less or more present, as even such infirmities sprang from the original defection of man. On these accounts *sacrifices* must be offered; and in the case of the woman, one of the birds above mentioned must be sacrificed as a *sin-offering*, the other as a *burnt-offering*, ver. 30.

Verse 31. *Thus shall ye separate the children of Israel from their uncleanness*] By this *separation* the *cause* became less frequent, and the *contagion*, if it did exist, was prevented from spreading. So *pest-houses* and *fever-wards* are constructed for the purpose of separating the infected from the sound; and thus contagion is lessened, and its diffusion prevented.

That they die not] That life may be prolonged by these prudential cares; and that he who is morally and legally unclean, may not presume to enter into the tabernacle of God till purified, lest he provoke Divine justice to consume him, while attempting to worship with a polluted mind and impure hands.

1. How unpromising and how forbidding, at the first view, is this chapter! and yet how full of wise, humane, and moral regulations, manifesting at once the wisdom and kindness of the great Legislator! Every word of God is *pure* in itself, and of great importance to us. He who cannot derive instruction from the chapter before him, and be led by a proper consideration of its contents to adore the wisdom and goodness of God, must have either a very stupid or a very vitiated mind.

2. In all these ordinances we may plainly see that God has *purity of heart* continually in view—that the soul may be holy, he cuts off the *occasions* of sin; and that men may be obliged to keep within due bounds, and possess their vessels in sanctification and honour, he hedges up their way with briars and thorns, and renders transgression *painful, shameful*, and *expensive.*

3. *Preventing* grace is not less necessary than that which *saves* and which *preserves*. These three chapters, avoided and neglected by *most*, contain lessons of instruction for *all;* and though many things contained in them belong exclusively to the Jewish people as to the letter, yet in their spirit and gracious design they form a part of those *revealed* things which are for us and for our children; and although they cannot be made the subject of public oral instruction, yet they are highly necessary to be known, and hence the advantage of reading the Scriptures in regular order in private. May we *read* so as to *understand*, and *practise* what we *know*, that, being wise unto salvation, we may walk as children of the light and of the day, in whom there shall be no *occasion of stumbling!*

CHAPTER XVI.

The solemn yearly expiation for the high priest, who must not come at all times into the holy place, 1, 2. *He must take a bullock for a sin-offering, and a ram for a burnt-offering, bathe himself, and be dressed in his sacerdotal robes,* 3, 4. *He shall take two goats, one of which is to be determined by lot to be a sacrifice; the other to be a* scape-goat, 5–10. *He shall offer a bullock for himself and for his family,* 11–14. *And shall kill the goat as a sin-offering for the people, and sprinkle its blood upon the mercy-seat, and hallow the altar of burnt-offerings,* 15–19. *The* scape-goat *shall be then brought, on the head of which he shall lay his hands, and confess the iniquities of the children of Israel; after which the goat shall be permitted to escape to the wilderness.* 20–22. *After this Aaron shall bathe himself, and make a burnt offering for himself and for the people,* 23–28. *This is to be an everlasting statute, and the day on which the atonement is to be made shall be a* Sabbath, *or day of rest, through all their generations,* 29–34.

A. M. 2514.
B. C. 1490.
An. Exod. Isr. 2.
Abib or Nisan.

AND the LORD spake unto Moses after [a] the death of the two sons of Aaron, when they offered before the LORD, and died:

2 And the LORD said unto Moses, Speak unto Aaron thy brother, that he [b] come not at all times into the holy *place* within the veil before the mercy-seat, which *is* upon the ark; that he die not: for [c] I will appear in the cloud upon the mercy-seat.

3 Thus shall Aaron [d] come into the holy *place:* [e] with a young bullock for a sin-offering, and a ram for a burnt-offering.

4 He shall put on [f] the holy linen coat, and he shall have the linen breeches upon his flesh, and shall be girded with a linen girdle, and with the linen mitre shall he be attired: these *are* holy garments; therefore [g] shall he wash his flesh in water, and *so* put them on.

5 And he shall take of [h] the congregation of the children of Israel two kids of the goats for a sin-offering, and one ram for a burnt-offering.

6 And Aaron shall offer his bullock of the sin-offering, which *is* for himself, and [i] make an atonement for himself, and for his house.

7 And he shall take the two goats, and present them before the LORD *at* the door of the tabernacle of the congregation.

[a] Chap. x. 1, 2.——[b] Exod. xxx. 10; chap. xxiii. 27; Heb. ix. 7; x. 19.——[c] Exod. xxv. 22; xl. 34; 1 Kings viii. 10, 11, 12. [d] Heb. ix. 7, 12, 24, 25.——[e] Chap. iv. 3.——[f] Exod. xxviii. 39, 42, 43; chap. vi. 10; Ezek. xliv. 17, 18.

[g] Exodus xxx. 20; chapter viii. 6, 7.——[h] See chapter iv 14; Numbers xxix. 11; 2 Chronicles xxix. 21; Ezra vi. 17; Ezek. xlv. 22, 23.——[i] Chap. ix. 7; Hebrews v. 2; vii. 27, 28; ix. 7.

NOTES ON CHAP. XVI.

Verse 1. *After the death of the two sons of Aaron*] It appears from this verse that the natural place of this chapter is immediately after the *tenth*, where probably it originally stood; but the transposition, if it did take place, must be very *ancient*, as all the versions acknowledge this chapter in the place in which it now stands.

Verse 2. *That he come not at all times into the holy place*] By the holy place we are to understand here what is ordinarily called the *Holy of Holies*, or *most holy place;* that place within the veil where the ark of the covenant, &c., were laid up; and where God manifested his presence between the cherubim. In ordinary cases the high priest could enter this place only *once in the year*, that is, on the day of annual atonement; but in extraordinary cases he might enter more frequently, viz., while in the wilderness, in decamping and encamping, he must enter to take down or adjust the things; and on solemn pressing public occasions, he was obliged to enter in order to consult the Lord: but he never entered without the deepest reverence and due preparation.

That it may appear that the grand subject of this chapter, the ordinance of the *scape-goat*, typified the death and resurrection of Christ, and the atonement thereby made, I beg leave to refer to Heb. ix. 7–12, and 24–26, which I shall here transcribe, because it is a key to the whole of this chapter. "Into the second [tabernacle] *went* the high priest alone once every year, not without blood, which he offered for himself, and *for* the errors of the people. The Holy Ghost this signifying, that the way into the holiest of all was not yet made manifest, while as the first tabernacle was yet standing: which was a figure for the time then present, in which were offered both gifts and sacrifices that could not make him that did the service perfect, as pertaining to the conscience; *which stood* only in meats and drinks, and divers washings, and carnal ordinances, imposed *on them* until the time of reformation. But Christ being come, a high priest of good things to come, by a greater and more perfect tabernacle, not made with hands, that is to say, not of this building; neither by the BLOOD of GOATS and CALVES, but by his OWN BLOOD; he entered into the holy place, having obtained eternal redemption *for us*. For Christ is not entered into the holy places made with hands, *which are* the figures of the true; but into heaven itself, now to appear in the presence of God for us: nor yet that he should offer himself often, as the high priest entereth into the holy place every year with the blood of others; (for then must he often have suffered since the foundation of the world;) but now once in the end of the world, hath he appeared TO PUT AWAY SIN BY THE SACRIFICE OF HIMSELF."

Verse 3. *With a young bullock for a sin-offering*] The *bullock* was presented as a *sin-offering* for *himself*, his *family*, the whole *priesthood*, and probably the *Levites*. The *ram* was for a *burnt-offering*, to signify that he and his associates were *wholly consecrated*, and to be *wholly employed* in this work of the ministry. The ceremonies with which these two sacrifices were accompanied are detailed in the following verses.

Verse 4. *He shall put on the holy linen coat*] He was not to dress in his *pontifical* garments, but in the simple sacerdotal vestments, or those of the Levites, because it was a day of *humiliation;* and as he was to offer sacrifices for his *own sins*, it was necessary that he should appear in habits suited to the occasion. Hence he has neither the *robe*, the *ephod*, the *breastplate*, the *mitre*, &c.; these constituted his dress of *dignity* as the high priest of God, ministering for others and the representative of Christ: but now he appears, before God as a *sinner*, offering an atonement for his transgressions, and his garments are those of humiliation.

Verse 7. *And he shall take the two goats*] It is allowed on all hands that this ceremony, taken in all its parts, pointed out the Lord Jesus *dying* for our sins and *rising again* for our justification; being put to death in the flesh, but quickened by the Spirit. *Two goats* are brought, one to be *slain* as a *sacrifice*

A. M. 2514.
B. C. 1490.
An. Exod. Isr. 2.
Abib or Nisan.

8 And Aaron shall cast lots upon
the two goats; one lot for the
LORD, and the other lot for the
[k] scape-goat.
9 And Aaron shall bring the goat upon
which the LORD'S lot [l] fell, and
offer him *for* a sin-offering.
10 But the goat, on which the
lot fell to be the scape-goat, shall be presented
alive before the LORD, to make an [m] atonement

[k] Heb. *azazel*.——[l] Heb. *went up*.

[m] 1 John ii. 2.

for sin, the other to have the transgressions of the people confessed over his head, and then to be sent away into the wilderness. The animal by this act was represented as bearing away or carrying off the sins of the people. The two goats made only *one sacrifice*, yet only one of them was slain. *One* animal could not point out both the *Divine* and *human* nature of Christ, nor show both his *death* and *resurrection*, for the goat that was *killed* could not be made *alive*. The *Divine* and *human* natures in Christ were essential to the grand expiation: yet the *human* nature alone *suffered*, for the *Divine nature* could not *suffer*; but its *presence* in the human nature, while agonizing unto death, stamped those agonies, and the consequent death, with infinite *merit*. The goat therefore that was *slain* prefigured his human nature and its *death*; the goat that *escaped* pointed out his *resurrection*. The one shows the atonement for sin, as the ground of justification; the other Christ's victory, and the total removal of sin in the sanctification of the soul. Concerning these ceremonies we shall see farther particulars as we proceed.

According to Maimonides *fifteen* beasts were offered on this day. "The *daily*, or *morning* and *evening* sacrifice, was offered as usual: besides a *bullock*, a *ram*, and seven *lambs*, all burnt-offerings; and a *goat* for a sin-offering, which was eaten in the evening. Then a *bullock* for a sin-offering, and this they burnt; and a *ram* for a burnt-offering: these both for the high priest. Then the *ram* for the consecration, (see ver. 5,) which is called the *people's ram*. They brought also for the congregation *two he-goats*; the one for a sin-offering, the other for a *scape-goat*. Thus all the beasts offered on this great and solemn day were FIFTEEN: the *two* daily sacrifices, *one* bullock, *two* rams, and *seven* lambs: all of these burnt-offerings. *Two* goats for sin-offerings; one offered *without* and eaten on the evening, the other offered *within* and burnt; and *one* bullock for a sin-offering for the high priest. The service of all these *fifteen* beasts is performed on this day by the high priest only." See Maimonides and Ainsworth on the place.

Verse 8. *Aaron shall cast lots upon the two goats*] The Jews inform us that there were two *lots* made either of *wood*, *stone*, or any kind of *metal*. On one was written לשם LASHSHEM, *for the* NAME, *i. e.*, יהוה JEHOVAH, which the Jews will neither write nor pronounce; on the other was written לעזאזל LAAZAZEL, for the SCAPE-GOAT: then they put the two lots into a vessel which was called קלפי *kalpey*, the goats standing with their faces towards the west. Then the priest came, and the goats stood before him, one on the right hand and the other on the left; the *kalpey* was then shaken, and the priest put in both his hands and brought out a lot in each: that which was in his right hand he laid on he goat th:* was on his right, and that in his left hand he laid on the goat that was on his left; and according to what was written on the lots, the *scape-goat* and the *goat for sacrifice* were ascertained. See the Mishna, in Tract. *Yoma*.

The determining this solemn business by *lot*, the disposal of which is with the Lord, Prov. xvi. 33, shows that God alone was to select and point out the person by whom this great atonement was to be made; hence he says: *Behold I lay in Zion a stone, elect* (that is, *chosen* by himself) *and precious*—of infinite value.

Verse 10. *To be the scape-goat*] עזאזל *azazel*, from עז *az*, a *goat*, and אזל *azal*, to *dismiss*; the *dismissed* or *sent away* goat, to distinguish it from the *goat* that was to be offered in *sacrifice*. Most ancient nations had *vicarious* sacrifices, to which they transferred by certain rites and ceremonies the guilt of the community at large, in the same manner in which the scape-goat was used by the Jews. The *white bull* that was sacrificed by the Egyptians to their god *Apis* was of this kind; they cut off the head of the victim which they had sacrificed, and after having loaded it with execrations, "that if there be any evil hanging over them or the land of Egypt, it may be poured out upon that head," they either sold it to the Greeks or threw it into the Nile.—See HEROD. *Euterp.*, p. 104, edit. *Gale*.

Petronius Arbiter says that it was a custom among the ancient inhabitants of *Marseilles*, whenever they were afflicted by any pestilence, to take one of the poorer citizens who offered himself for the purpose, and having fed him a whole year with the purest and best food, they adorned him with vervain, and clothed him with sacred vestments: they then led him round their city, loading him with execrations; and having prayed that all the evils to which the city was exposed might fall upon *him*, they then precipitated him from the top of a rock.—*Satiricon*, in *fine*.

Suidas, under the word περιψημα, observes that it was a custom to devote a man annually to death for the safety of the people, with these words, Περιψημα ἡμων γενου, *Be thou our purifier*; and, having said so, to throw him into the sea as a sacrifice to Neptune. It was probably to this custom that *Virgil* alludes when speaking of the pilot *Palinurus*, who fell into the sea and was drowned, he says:—

Unum pro multis dabiter caput.—Æn., lib. v., ver. 815.
"One life is given for the preservation of many."

But the nearest resemblance to the *scape-goat* of the *Hebrews* is found in the *Ashummeed Jugg* of the *Hindoos*, where a *horse* is used instead of a *goat*, the description of which I shall here introduce from Mr Halhed's Code of Gentoo Laws; Introduction, p. xix.

"That the curious," says he, "may form some idea of this Gentoo sacrifice when reduced to a symbol, as well as from the subsequent plain account given of it in a chapter of the Code, sec. ix., p. 127, an expla-

a

A. M. 2514.
B. C. 1490.
An. Exod. Isr. 2.
Abib or Nisan.

with him, *and* to let him go for a scape-goat into the wilderness.

11 And Aaron shall bring the bullock of the sin offering, which *is* for himself, and shall make an atonement for himself and for his house, and shall kill the bullock of the sin-offering which is for himself:

12 And he shall take [n] a censer full of burning coals of fire, from off the altar before the LORD, and his hands full of [o] sweet incense beaten small, and bring *it* within the veil:

13 [p] And he shall put the incense upon the fire before the LORD, that the cloud of the incense may cover the [q] mercy-seat that *is* upon the testimony, that he die not:

14 And [r] he shall take of the blood of the bullock, and [s] sprinkle *it* with his finger upon the mercy-seat eastward; and before the mercy-seat shall he sprinkle of the blood with his finger seven times.

15 [t] Then shall he kill the goat of the sin-offering, that *is* for the people, and bring his blood [u] within the veil, and do with that blood as he did with the blood of the bullock, and sprinkle it upon the mercy-seat, and before the mercy-seat:

16 And he shall [v] make an atonement for the holy *place*, because of the uncleanness of the children of Israel, and because of their transgressions in all their sins: and so shall he do for the tabernacle of the congregation, that [w] remaineth among them in the midst of their uncleanness.

17 [x] And there shall be no man in the tabernacle of the congregation when he goeth in to make an atonement in the holy *place*, until he come out, and have made an atonement for himself, and for his household, and for all the congregation of Israel.

18 And he shall go out unto the altar that *is* before the LORD, and [y] make an atonement for it; and shall take of the blood of the bullock, and of the blood of the goat, and put *it* upon the horns of the altar round about.

[n] Chap. x. 1; Num. xvi. 18, 46; Rev. viii. 5.——[o] Exod. xxx. 34.——[p] Exod. xxx. 1, 7, 8; Num. xvi. 7, 18, 46; Rev. viii. 3, 4.——[q] Exod. xxv. 21.——[r] Chapter iv. 5; Hebrews ix. 13, 25; x. 4.——[s] Chap. iv. 6.——[t] Heb. ii. 17; v. 2; ix. 7, 28.

[u] Ver. 2; Heb. vi. 19; ix. 3, 7, 12.——[v] See Exod. xxix. 36; Ezek. xlv. 18; Heb. ix. 22, 23.——[w] Heb. *dwelleth.*——[x] See Exod. xxxiv. 3; Luke i. 10.——[y] Exod. xxx. 10; chapter iv. 7, 18; Heb. ix. 22, 23.

nation of it is here inserted from *Darul Shekúh's* famous Persian translation of some commentaries upon the four Beids, or original Scriptures of Hindostan. The work itself is extremely scarce, and it was by mere accident that this little specimen was procured:—

"The *Ashummeed Jugg* does not merely consist in the performance of that ceremony which is open to the inspection of the world, namely, in bringing a *horse* and sacrificing him; but *Ashummeed* is to be taken in a mystic signification, as implying, that the sacrificer must *look upon himself to be typified in that horse*, such as he shall be described; because the religious duty of the *Ashummeed Jugg* comprehends all those other religious duties to the performance of which the wise and holy direct all their actions, and by which all the sincere professors of every different faith aim at perfection. The mystic signification thereof is as follows: The *head* of that unblemished horse is the symbol of the *morning*; his *eyes* are the *sun*; his *breath*, the *wind*; his *wide-opening mouth* is the *bish-waner*, or that *innate warmth* which invigorates all the world; his *body* typifies one *entire year*; his *back*, *paradise*; his *belly*, the *plains*; his *hoof*, this *earth*; his *sides*, the *four quarters of the heavens*; the *bones* thereof, the *intermediate spaces between the four quarters*; the rest of his *limbs* represent all *distinct matter*; the *places* where those limbs meet, or his *joints*, imply the *months*, and *halves* of the *months*, which are called *peche*, (or fortnights;) his *feet* signify *night* and *day*; and night and day are of four kinds: 1. The night and day of *Brihma*; 2. The night and day of *angels*; 3. The night and day of the *world of the spirits of deceased ancestors*; 4. The night and day of *mortals*. These four kinds are typified in his four feet. The rest of his *bones* are the *constellations* of the fixed stars, which are the *twenty-eight stages of* the moon's course, called the *lunar year*; his *flesh* is the *clouds*; his *food*, the *sand*; his *tendons*, the *rivers*; his *spleen* and *liver*, the *mountains*; the *hair* of his body, the *vegetables*; and his *long hair*, the *trees*; the *forepart of his body* typifies the *first half of the day*, and the *hinder part*, the *latter half*; his *yawning* is the *flash* of the *lightning*, and his *turning* himself is the *thunder* of the *cloud*; his *urine* represents the *rain*, and his *mental reflection* is his only *speech*. The *golden vessels* which are prepared before the horse is let loose are the *light of the day*, and the *place* where those vessels are *kept* is a type of the *ocean* of the *east*; the *silver vessels* which are prepared after the horse is let loose are the *light of the night*, and the *place* where those vessels are *kept* is a type of the *ocean of the west*. These two sorts of vessels are always before and after the horse. The *Arabian* horse, which on account of his swiftness is called *Hy*, is the performer of the journeys of angels; the *Tajee*, which is of the race of *Persian* horses, is the performer of the journeys of the *Kundherps*, (or good spirits;) the *Wazba*, which is of the race of the deformed *Tazee* horses, is the performer of the journeys of the *Jins*, (or demons;) and the *Ashov*, which is of the race of *Turkish* horses, is the performer of the journeys of *mankind*: this one horse which performs these several services

A. M. 2514.
B. C. 1490.
An. Exod. Isr. 2.
Abib or Nisan.

19 And he shall sprinkle of the
blood upon it with his finger seven
times, and cleanse it, and [z] hallow
it from the uncleanness of the children of
Israel.
20 And when he hath made an end of [a] reconciling the holy *place*, and the tabernacle
of the congregation, and the altar, he shall
bring the live goat:
21 And Aaron shall lay both his hands upon
the head of the live goat, and confess over
him all the iniquities of the children of Israel,
and all their transgressions in all their sins,
[b] putting them upon the head of the goat, and
shall send *him* away by the hand
of [c] a fit man into the wilderness:
22 And the goat shall [d] bear upon him all
their iniquities, unto a land [e] not inhabited:
and he shall let go the goat in the wilderness.
23 And Aaron shall come into the tabernacle
of the congregation, [f] and shall put off the
linen garments which he put on when he went
into the holy *place*, and shall leave them there:
24 And he shall wash his flesh with water
in the holy place, and put on his garments,
and come forth, [g] and offer his burnt-offering,
and the burnt-offering of the people, and make

[z] Ezek. xliii. 20.——[a] Ver. 16; Ezek. xlv. 20.——[b] Isa. liii. 6.——[c] Heb. *a man of opportunity.*——[d] Isa. liii. 11, 12; John i. 29; Hebrews ix. 28; 1 Pet. ii. 24.——[e] Heb. *of separation.* [f] Ezek. xlii. 14; xliv. 19.——[g] Ver. 3, 5.

on account of his four different sorts of riders, obtains the four different appellations. The *place* where this horse remains is the great *ocean*, which signifies the great *spirit of* Perm-*Atma*, or the universal soul, which proceeds also from that Perm-*Atma*, and is comprehended in the same Perm-*Atma*. The intent of this sacrifice is, that a *man should consider himself to be in the place of that horse*, and look upon all these articles as typified in himself; and conceiving the *Atma* (or Divine soul) to be an ocean, should let all thought of self be absorbed in that Atma."

This sacrifice is explained, in sec. ix., p. 127, of the Code of Hindoo Laws, thus:—

"An *Ashummeed Jugg* is when a person, having commenced a *Jugg*, (i. e., religious ceremony,) writes various articles upon a scroll of paper on a horse's neck, and dismisses the horse, sending along with the horse a stout and valiant person, equipped with the best necessaries and accoutrements to accompany the horse day and night whithersoever he shall choose to go; and if any creature, either man, genius, or dragon, should seize the horse, that man opposes such attempt, and having gained the victory upon a battle, again gives the horse his freedom. If any one in this world, or in heaven, or beneath the earth, would seize this horse, and the horse of himself comes to the house of the celebrator of the *Jugg*, upon killing that horse he must throw the flesh of him upon the fire of the *Juk*, and utter the prayers of his deity; such a *Jugg* is called a *Jugg Ashummeed*, and the merit of it as a religious work is infinite."

This is a most curious circumstance; and the coincidence between the religious rites of two people who probably never had any intercourse with each other, is very remarkable. I would not however say that the Hindoo ceremony could not have been borrowed from the Jews; (though it is very unlikely;) no more than I should say, as some have done, that the Jewish rite was borrowed from the Egyptian sacrifice to Apis mentioned above, which is still more unlikely. See particularly the note on chap. i. 4.

Verse 21. *Aaron shall lay both his hands upon the head, &c.*] What this imposition of hands meant see in the notes on Exod. xxix. 10, and on chap. i. 4.

And confess over him all the iniquities—transgressions—sins] The three terms used here, INIQUITIES, עונת avonoth, from עוה *avah*, to *pervert*, *distort*, or *turn aside*; TRANSGRESSIONS, פשעים *peshaim*, from פשע *pasha*, to *transgress*, to *rebel*; and SINS, חטאת *chattaoth*, from חטא *chata*, to *miss the mark*, are supposed by the Jews to comprise every thing that implies a breach of the Divine law, or an offence against God. See the note on Gen. xii. 13. Maimonides gives us the confession in the following words:—

"O Lord, thy people, the house of Israel, have sinned and done iniquity, and trespassed before thee. O Lord, make atonement now for the iniquities and transgressions and sins that thy people, the house of Israel, have sinned and transgressed against thee; as it is written in the law of Moses thy servant, saying: That *in this day he shall make atonement for you, to cleanse you from all your sins before the Lord, and ye shall be clean.*"—See the *Mishna*, vol. ii., p. 239.

When this confession was finished, the goat was sent by a proper hand to the wilderness, and there let loose; and nothing farther was ever heard of it. Did not all this signify that Christ has so carried and borne away our sins, that against them who receive him as the only true atoning sacrifice they should never more be brought to remembrance?

On the head of the *scape-goat* a piece of scarlet cloth was tied, and the tradition of the Jews states that if God accepted the sacrifice, the scarlet cloth turned *white* while the goat was led to the desert; but if God had not accepted this expiation, the *redness* continued, and the rest of the year was spent in mourning.

From the foundation of the Church of God it was ever believed by his followers, that there were certain infallible tokens by which he discovered to genuine believers his acceptance of them and their services. This was sometimes done by a fire from heaven consuming the sacrifice; sometimes by an oracular communication to the priest or prophet; and at other times, according to the Jewish account, by changing the fillet or cloth on the head of the *scape-goat* from *scarlet* to *white*: but most commonly, and especially under the Gospel dispensation, he gives this assurance

A. M. 2514.
B. C. 1490.
An. Exod. Isr. 2.
Abib or Nisan.

an atonement for himself, and
for the people.
25 And [h] the fat of the sin-
offering shall he burn upon the altar.
26 And he that let go the goat for the
scape-goat shall wash his clothes, [i] and bathe
his flesh in water, and afterward come into
the camp.
27 [k] And the bullock *for* the sin-offering,
and the goat *for* the sin-offering, whose blood
was brought in to make atonement in the holy
place, shall *one* carry forth without the camp;
and they shall burn in the fire their skins, and
their flesh, and their dung.
28 And he that burneth them shall wash his
clothes, and bathe his flesh in water, and
afterward he shall come into the camp.
29 And *this* shall be a statute for ever unto
you: *that* [l] in the seventh month, on the tenth
day of the month, ye shall afflict your souls,
and do no work at all, *whether it be* one of
your own country, or a stranger that sojourneth among you:
30 For on that day shall *the
priest* make an atonement for
you, to [m] cleanse you, *that* ye
may be clean from all your sins before the
LORD.

A. M. 2514.
B. C. 1490.
An. Exod. Isr. 2.
Abib or Nisan.

31 [n] It *shall be* a Sabbath of rest unto you,
and ye shall afflict your souls, by a statute
for ever.
32 [o] And the priest, whom he shall anoint,
and whom he shall [p] consecrate [q] to minister
in the priest's office in his father's stead, shall
make the atonement, and [r] shall put on the
linen clothes, *even* the holy garments:
33 And [s] he shall make an atonement for the
holy sanctuary, and he shall make an atonement for the tabernacle of the congregation,
and for the altar, and he shall make an atonement for the priests, and for all the people of
the congregation.
34 [t] And this shall be an everlasting statute
unto you, to make an atonement for the children of Israel, for all their sins [u] once a year.
And he did as the LORD commanded Moses.

[h] Chap. iv. 10.——[i] Chap. xv. 5.——[k] Chap. iv. 12, 21; vi. 30; Heb. xiii. 11.——[l] Exod. xxx. 10; chap. xxiii. 27; Num. xxix. 7; Isa. lviii. 3-5; Daniel x. 3-12.——[m] Psa. li. 2; Jer. xxxiii. 8; Eph. v. 26; Hebrews ix. 13, 14; x. 1, 2; 1 John. i. 7-9.

[n] Chap. xxiii. 32.——[o] Chap. iv. 3, 5, 16.——[p] Heb. *fill his hand.*——[q] Exod. xxix. 29, 30; Num. xx. 26-28.——[r] Ver. 4. [s] Ver. 6, 16, 18, 19, 24.——[t] Chap. xxiii. 31; Numbers xxix. 7. [u] Exod. xxx. 10; Heb. ix. 7-25.

to true believers by the testimony of his Spirit in their consciences, that he has forgiven their iniquities, transgressions, and sins, for *his* sake who has carried their griefs, and borne their sorrows.

Verse 26. *He that let go the goat—shall wash, &c.*] Not only the person who led him away, but the priest who consecrated him, was reputed unclean, because the goat himself was unclean, being considered as bearing the sins of the whole congregation. On this account both the priest and the pèrson who led him to the wilderness were obliged to wash their clothes and bathe themselves, before they could come into the camp.

Verse 29. *The seventh month, on the tenth* day *of the month*] The commandment of fasting, and sanctifying this *tenth* day, is again repeated chapter xxiii. 27-32; but in the last verse it is called the *ninth day at even*, because the Jewish day began with the evening. The sacrifices which the day of atonement should have *more* than other days, are mentioned Num. xxix. 7-11; and the jubilee which was celebrated every fiftieth year was solemnly proclaimed by sound of trumpet on *this tenth day*, chap. xxv. 8, 9. A shadow, says Mr. Ainsworth, of that acceptable year of the Lord, the year of freedom, which Christ has proclaimed by the trumpet of his Gospel, Luke iv. 18-21; 2 Cor. vi. 2. This seventh month was *Tisri*, and answers to a part of our *September* and *October*. It was the *seventh* of the *sacred* and the *first* month of the *civil* year.

THE great day of atonement, and the sacrifices, rites, and ceremonies prescribed for it, were commanded to be solemnized by the Jews through the whole of their dispensation, and as long as God should acknowledge them for his people: yet in the present day scarcely a shadow of these things remains; there is no longer a *scape-goat*, nor a *goat for sacrifice*, provided by them in any place. They are *sinners*, and they are without an *atonement*. How strange it is that they do not see that the *essence* of their religion is *gone*, and that consequently God has thrown them entirely out of covenant with himself! The true expiation, the Christ crucified, they refuse to receive, and are consequently without temple, altar, scape-goat, atonement, or any *means* of salvation! The state of the Gentile world is bad, but that of the Jews is doubly deplorable. Their total excision excepted, wrath is come upon them to the uttermost. What a proof is this of the truth of the predictions in their own law, and of those in the Gospel of Christ! Who, with the *Jews* and the *Bible* before his eyes, can doubt the truth of that Bible as a Divine revelation? Had this people been extinct, we might have doubted whether there were ever a people on the earth that acknowledged such a law, or observed such ordinances; but the people, their law, and their prophets are still in being, and all proclaim what God *has* wrought, and that he has now ceased to work among *them*, because they have refused to receive and profit by the great atonement; and yet he preserves them alive, and in a state of complete separation from all the people of the earth in all places of their dispersion! How power-

fully does the preservation of the Jews as a distinct people bear testimony at once to the truth of their own *law* which they *acknowledge*, and the *Gospel of Christ* which they *reject !*

2. But while the Jews sit in thick darkness, because of the veil that is on their hearts, though the light of the glory of God is shining all *around* them, but not *into* them because of their unbelief; in what state are those who profess to see *their unbelief* and obstinacy, acknowledge the truth of the New Testament, and yet are living without an atonement applied to their souls for the removal of *their* iniquities, transgressions, and sins? These are also in the gall of bitterness, and bond of iniquity. An *all-sufficient Saviour* held out in the *New Testament* can do *them* no more good than a *scape-goat* and day of *atonement* described in the *law* can do the *Jews*. As well may a man imagine that the word *bread* can nourish his body, as that the *name* Christ can save his soul. Both must be *received* and *applied* in order that the man may live.

3. The Jews prepared themselves to get benefit from this most solemn ordinance by the deepest humiliations. According to their canons, they were obliged to abstain from all *meat* and *drink*—from the *bath*—from *anointing* themselves—to go *barefoot*—and to be in a state of perfect *continency*. He who is likely to get benefit for his soul through the redemption that is in Christ, must humble himself under the mighty hand of God, confess his iniquity, abstain from every appearance of evil, and believe on him who died for his offences, and rose again for his justification. The soul that *seeks not* shall not *find*, even under the Gospel of Christ.

CHAPTER XVII.

The people are commanded to bring all the cattle they intend to kill to the door of the tabernacle, where they are to be made an offering to the Lord; and those who disobey are to be cut off, 1–5. *The priest is to sprinkle the blood,* 6. *They are forbidden to offer sacrifices to devils,* 7. *The injunction to bring their offerings to the door of the tabernacle is repeated,* 8, 9. *The eating of blood is solemnly forbidden,* 10. *It is the life of the beast, and is given to make an atonement for their souls,* 11, 12. *If a bird or beast be taken in hunting, its blood must be poured out and covered with dust, for the reasons before assigned,* 13, 14. *None shall eat an animal that dies of itself, or is torn by beasts; if any act otherwise he must bathe his clothes and his flesh, or bear his iniquity,* 15, 16.

A. M. 2514.
B. C. 1490.
An. Exod. Isr. 2.
Abib or Nisan.

AND the LORD spake unto
Moses, saying,
2 Speak unto Aaron, and unto
his sons, and unto all the children of Israel,
and say unto them; This *is* the thing which
the LORD hath commanded, saying,
3 What man soever *there be* of the house of
Israel, [a] that killeth an ox, or lamb, or goat, in
the camp, or that killeth *it* out of the camp,
4 [b] And bringeth it not unto the door of the
tabernacle of the congregation, to offer an
offering unto the LORD before the
tabernacle of the LORD, blood shall
be [c] imputed unto that man; he
hath shed blood; and that man [d] shall be cut
off from among his people:
5 To the end that the children of Israel may
bring their sacrifices, [e] which they offer in the
open field, even that they may bring them unto
the LORD, unto the door of the tabernacle of
the congregation, unto the priest, and offer them
for peace-offerings unto the LORD.

A. M. 2514.
B. C. 1490.
An. Exod. Isr. 2.
Abib or Nisan.

[a] See Deut. xii. 5, 15, 21.—[b] Deut. xii. 5, 6, 13, 14.—[c] Rom. v. 13.—[d] Gen. xvii. 14.—[e] Gen. xxi. 33; xxii. 2; xxxi. 54; Deut. xii. 2; 1 Kings xiv. 23; 2 Kings xvi. 4; xvii. 10; 2 Chron. xxviii. 4; Ezek. xx. 28; xxii. 9.

NOTES ON CHAP. XVII.

Verse 4. *And bringeth it not unto the door*] As *sacrifice* was ever deemed essential to true religion, it was necessary that it should be performed in such a way as to secure the great purpose of its institution. God alone could show how this should be done so as to be pleasing in his sight, and therefore he has given the most plain and particular directions concerning it. The Israelites, from their long residence in Egypt, an idolatrous country, had doubtless adopted many of their usages; and many portions of the Pentateuch seem to have been written merely to correct and bring them back to the purity of the Divine worship.

That no blood should be offered to idols, God commands every animal used for food or sacrifice to be slain at the door of the tabernacle. While every animal was slain in this sacrificial way, even the daily food of the people must put them in mind of the necessity of a sacrifice for sin. Perhaps St. Paul had this circumstance in view when he said, *Whether therefore ye eat or drink, or whatsoever ye do, do all to the glory of God*, 1 Cor. x. 31; and, *Whatsoever ye do in word or deed, do all in the name of the Lord Jesus, giving thanks to God and the* Father *by him.*

While the Israelites were encamped in the wilderness, it was comparatively easy to prevent all abuses of this Divine institution; and therefore they were all commanded to bring the *oxen, sheep,* and *goats* to the door of the tabernacle of the congregation, that they might be slain there, and *their blood sprinkled upon the altar of the Lord.* But when they became settled in the promised land, and the distance, in many cases, rendered it impossible for them to bring the animals to be slain for domestic uses to the temple, they were

A. M. 2514.
B. C. 1490.
An. Exod. Isr. 2.
Abib or Nisan.

6 And the priest [f] shall sprinkle the blood upon the altar of the LORD *at* the door of the tabernacle of the congregation, and [g] burn the fat for a sweet savour unto the LORD.

7 And they shall no more offer their sacrifices [h] unto devils, after whom they [i] have gone a whoring. This shall be a statute for ever unto them throughout their generations.

8 And thou shalt say unto them, Whatsoever man *there be* of the house of Israel, or of the strangers which sojourn among you, [k] that offereth a burnt-offering or sacrifice,

9 And [l] bringeth it not unto the door of the tabernacle of the congregation, to offer it unto the LORD; even that man shall be cut off from among his people.

A. M. 2514.
B. C. 1490.
An. Exod. Isr. 2.
Abib or Nisan.

10 [m] And whatsoever man *there be* of the house of Israel, or of the strangers that sojourn among you, that eateth any manner of blood; [n] I will even set my face against that soul that eateth blood, and will cut him off from among his people.

11 [o] For the life of the flesh *is* in the blood: and I have given it to you upon the altar, [p] to make an atonement for your souls; for [q] it *is* the blood *that* maketh an atonement for the soul.

12 Therefore I said unto the children of Israel, No soul of you shall eat blood, neither

[f] Chap. iii. 2.——[g] Exod. xxix. 18; chap. iii. 5, 11, 16; iv. 31; Num. xviii. 17.——[h] Deut. xxxii. 17; 2 Chron. xi. 15; Psa. cvi. 37; 1 Cor. x. 20; Rev. ix. 20.——[i] Exod. xxxiv. 15; chap. xx. 5; Deut. xxxi. 16; Ezek. xxiii. 8.——[k] Chap. i. 2, 3.——[l] Ver. 4.——[m] Gen. ix. 4; chap. iii. 17; vii. 26, 27; xviii. 26; Deut. xii. 16, 23; xv. 23; 1 Sam. xiv. 33; Ezek. xliv. 7.——[n] Chap. xx. 3, 5, 6; xxvi. 17; Jer. xliv. 11; Ezek. xiv. 8; xv. 7.——[o] Ver. 14.——[p] Matt. xxvi. 28; Mark xiv. 24; Rom. iii. 25; v. 9; Eph. i. 7; Col. i. 14, 20; Heb. xiii. 12; 1 Pet. i. 2; 1 John i. 7; Rev. i. 5.——[q] Heb. ix. 22.

permitted to pour out the blood in a sacrificial way unto God at their respective dwellings, and to cover it with the dust; see ver. 13, and Deut. xii. 20, 21.

Blood shall be imputed unto that man] Having poured out the blood improperly, he shall be considered as guilty of *murder*, because that blood, had it been properly and *sacrificially* employed, might have made atonement for the *life* of a man.

Verse 7. *They shall no more offer their sacrifices unto devils*] They shall not sacrifice לשעירים *lasseirim*, to the *hairy ones*, to *goats*. The famous heathen god, *Pan*, was represented as having the posteriors, horns, and ears of a goat; and the *Mendesians*, a people of Egypt, had a deity which they worshipped under this form. Herodotus says that all goats were worshipped in Egypt, but the *he-goat* particularly. It appears also that the different ape and monkey species were objects of superstitious worship; and from these sprang, not only *Mendes* and *Jupiter Ammon*, who was worshipped under the figure of a *ram*, but also *Pan* and the *Sileni*, with the innumerable herd of those imaginary beings, *satyrs*, *dryads*, *hamadryads*, &c., &c., all *woodland* gods, and held in veneration among the Egyptians, Greeks, and Romans.

After whom they have gone a whoring.] Though this term is frequently used to express *idolatry*, yet we are not to suppose that it is not to be taken in a *literal* sense in many places in Scripture, even where it is used in connection with idolatrous acts of worship. It is well known that *Baal Peor* and *Ashtaroth* were worshipped with unclean rites; and that public prostitution formed a grand part of the worship of many deities among the Egyptians, Moabites, Canaanites, Greeks, and Romans. The great god of the two latter nations, *Jupiter*, was represented as the general corrupter of women; and of *Venus*, *Flora*, *Priapus*, and others, it is needless to speak. That there was public prostitution in the patriarchal times, see the note on Gen. xxxviii. 21. And that there was public prostitution of women to goats in Egypt, see Herodotus, lib. ii., c. 46, p. 108, edit. Gale, who gives a case of this abominable kind that took place in Egypt while he was in that country. See also many examples in *Bochart*, vol. ii., col. 641; and see the note on chap. xx. 16.

Verse 11. *For the life of the flesh is in the blood*] This sentence, which contains a most important truth, had existed in the Mosaic writings for 3600 years before the attention of any philosopher was drawn to the subject. This is the more surprising, as the nations in which philosophy flourished were those which especially enjoyed the Divine oracles in their respective languages. That the blood actually possesses a *living principle*, and that the life of the whole body is derived from it, is a doctrine of Divine revelation, and a doctrine which the observations and experiments of the most accurate anatomists have served strongly to confirm. The proper *circulation* of this important fluid through the *whole* human system was first taught by Solomon in figurative language, Eccles. xii. 6; and discovered, as it is called, and demonstrated by Dr. Harvey in 1628; though some Italian philosophers had the same notion a little before. This accurate anatomist was the first who fully revived the Mosaic notion of the *vitality* of the blood; which notion was afterward adopted by the justly celebrated Dr. John Hunter, professor of anatomy in London, and fully established by him by a great variety of strong reasoning and accurate experiments. To support this opinion Dr. Hunter proves,—

1. That the blood unites living parts in some circumstances as certainly as the yet recent juices of the branch of one tree unite with that of another; and he thinks that if either of these fluids were dead matter, they would act as *stimuli*, and no union would take place in the animal or vegetable kingdom; and he shows that in the nature of things there is not a more intimate connection between *life* and a *solid* than between *life* and a *fluid*.

2. He shows that the blood becomes *vascular*, like other living parts of the body; and he demonstrated

A. M. 2514. B. C. 1490. An. Exod. Isr. 2. Abib or Nisan.

shall any stranger that sojourneth
among you eat blood.
13 And whatsoever man *there*
be of the children of Israel, or of
the strangers that sojourn among
you, [r]which [s]hunteth and catch-

[r] Heb. *that hunteth any hunting*.

[s] Chap. vii. 26.

this by a preparation in which *vessels* were clearly seen to arise from what had been a *coagulum* of blood; for those vessels opened into the stream of the circulating blood, which was in contiguity with this coagulated mass.

3. He proved that if blood be taken from the arm in the most intense cold that the human body can suffer, it will raise the thermometer to the same height as blood taken in the most sultry heat. This is a very powerful argument for the *vitality* of the blood, as it is well known that living bodies alone have the power of resisting great degrees of heat and cold, and of maintaining in almost every situation while in health that temperature which we distinguish by the name of *animal heat*.

4. He proves that blood is capable of being acted upon by a stimulus, as it coagulates on exposure to the air, as certainly as the cavities of the abdomen and thorax become inflamed from the same cause. The more the blood is alive, i. e., the more the animal is in health, the sooner the blood coagulates on exposure; and the more it has lost of the living principle, as in cases of violent inflammation, the less sensible it is to the stimulus produced by being exposed, and coagulates more slowly.

5. He proves that the blood preserves life in different parts of the body. When the *nerves* going to any part are *tied* or *cut*, the part becomes paralytic, and loses all power of motion, but it does not mortify. But let the *artery* be cut, and then the part dies and *mortification* ensues. It must therefore be the *vital* principle of the *blood* that keeps the part *alive;* nor does it appear that this fact can be accounted for on any other principle.

6. He thinks this *vitality* farther proved from the case of a person who was brought to St. George's hospital for a simple fracture of the *os humeri*, and who died about a month after. As the bones had not united, he injected the arm, and thus found that the coagulated blood which filled the cavity between the extremities of the fractured bones was become *vascular*, and in some places very much so, which *vessels*, had it been dead matter, it never could have produced.

This system has been opposed, and arguments have been adduced to prove that the principle of *vitality* exists not in the *blood* but in the *nervous system*. But every argument on this ground appears to be done away by the simple consideration that the whole nervous system, as well as every other part of the body, is originally derived from the blood; for is it not from the blood of the mother that the fetus has its being and nourishment in the womb? Do not all the nerves, as well as the brain, &c., originate from that *alone?* And if it be not *vital* can it give the principle of *vitality* to something else, which then exclusively (though the effect of a cause) becomes the principle of vitality to all the solids and fluids of the body? This seems absurd. That the human being proceeded originally from the blood admits of no doubt; and it is natural and reasonable to suppose that as it was the cause under God which generated all the other parts of the body, so it still continues to be the principle of life, and by it alone all the wastes of the system are repaired. Two points relative to this subject are strongly asserted in Divine revelation, one by MOSES, the other by St. PAUL.

1. *Moses* says, *The* LIFE *of the flesh is in the* BLOOD, ver. 11. This has been proved by the most indisputable facts.

2. *St. Paul* says, *God hath made of* ONE BLOOD *all nations of men*, Acts xvii. 26. And this is demonstrated, not only from there being only one pair from whom all the nations of men have been derived, but also from the fact that every human being, from the first-born of Eve to the present hour, has been formed out of and supported by the mother's blood; and that from the agency of this fluid the human body, after being born into the world, has its increment and support. The reason given by God for the law against eating blood is perfectly conclusive: *I will set my face against that soul that eateth blood—for the* LIFE (נפש *nephesh*) *of the flesh is in the* BLOOD, *and I have given it to you upon the altar, to make an atonement for your souls* (נפשתיכם *naphshotheychem, your* LIVES:) *for it is the blood* (because it is the LIFE, נפש *nephesh*) *that maketh an atonement for the soul* (בנפש *bannephesh*, for the *life;* for the word is the same in all these cases.) By transgression a man forfeits his LIFE to Divine *justice*, and he must *die* did not *mercy* provide him a *substitute*. The *life* of a *beast* is appointed and accepted by God as a *substitute* for the sinner's *life* (in reference to the *life* of *Christ*, which was to be given for the *life* of the *world;*) but as this *life* is in the BLOOD, and as the *blood* is the grand principle of *vitality*, therefore the *blood* is to be poured out upon the altar: and thus the *life* of the *beast* becomes a substitute for the *life* of the *man*.

And it is well worthy of being remarked, that Christ not only *died* for sinners, but our redemption is every where attributed to his BLOOD, and the *shedding of that blood;* and that on the altar of the cross, this might make an atonement for the *lives* and *souls* of men, he not only *bowed his head, and gave up the ghost*, but his side was opened, the pericardium and the heart evidently pierced, that the *vital fluid* might be poured out from the *very seat of life*, and that thus the *blood*, which is the *life*, should be poured out to make an atonement for the *life* of the *soul*.

The doctrine of *Moses* and *Paul* proves the truth of the doctrine of *Harvey* and *Hunter;* and the reasonings and experiments of *Harvey* and *Hunter* illustrate and confirm the doctrine of *Moses* and *Paul*.—Here then is a farther proof of the truth and authority of Divine revelation. See the note on Gen. ix. 4; Dr. J. Corrie's *Essay on the Vitality of the Blood;* and the article *Blood*, in the *Encyclopædias*.

A. M. 2514.
B. C. 1490.
An. Exod. Isr. 2.
Abib or Nisan.

eth any beast or fowl that may be eaten; he shall even [t] pour out the blood thereof, and [u] cover it with dust.

14 [v] For *it is* the life of all flesh; the blood of it *is* for the life thereof: therefore I said unto the children of Israel, Ye shall eat the blood of no manner of flesh: for the life of all flesh *is* the blood thereof: whosoever eateth it shall be cut off.

15 [w] And every soul that eateth [x] that which died *of itself*, or that which was torn *with beasts*, *whether it be* one of your own country, or a stranger, [y] he shall both wash his clothes, [z] and bathe *himself* in water, and be unclean until the even: then shall he be clean.

A. M. 2514.
B. C. 1490.
An. Exod. Isr. 2.
Abib or Nisan.

16 But if he wash *them* not, nor bathe his flesh; then [a] he shall bear his iniquity.

[t] Deut. xii. 16, 24; xv. 23.—[u] Ezek. xxiv. 7.—[v] Ver. 11, 12; Gen. ix. 4; Deut. xii. 23.—[w] Exod. xxii. 31; ch. xxii. 8; Deut. xiv. 21; Ezek. iv. 14; xliv. 31.—[x] Heb. *a carcass.*—[y] Ch. xi. 25.—[z] Chap. xv. 5.—[a] Ch. v. 1; vii. 18; xix. 8; Num. xix. 20.

Verse 14. *Ye shall eat the blood of no manner of flesh*] Independently of the moral reasons given above, we may add, 1. That blood, being highly *alkalescent*, especially in hot climates, is subject to speedy putrefaction. 2. That it affords a gross nutriment, being very difficult of digestion, so much so that *bull's blood* was used in ancient times as poison, "its extreme viscidity rendering it totally indigestible by the powers of the human stomach." 3. It is allowed that when blood was used in this country in great quantities, the *scurvy* was more frequent than at other times. 4. It appears from history that those nations who lived most on it were very fierce, savage, and barbarous, such as the *Scythians*, *Tartars*, *Arabs* of the desert, the *Scandinavians*, &c., &c., some of whom drank the blood of their enemies, making cups of their sculls!

Verse 15. *That which died* of itself, *or that which was torn*] Because, in both cases, the blood was retained in the body; hence the council at Jerusalem forbade *things strangled* as well as *blood*, because in such beasts the blood was coagulated in the veins and arteries. See Acts xv. 28.

EVERY thing considered, surely there is as little *propriety* in eating of blood as there is *necessity* to do it. They who will do otherwise must bear their iniquity. If blood eating be no offence, then they have no sin to answer for. The principal subjects of this chapter have been already so amply handled in the notes, that there is no need to add any thing by way of reflection or improvement.

CHAPTER XVIII.

The people are commanded to avoid the doings of the Egyptians and Canaanites, 1–3. *They are to do God's judgments, and to keep his ordinances, that they may live,* 4, 5. Marriages *with those who are* near of kin *are prohibited,* 6. *None to marry with his* mother *or* step-mother, 7, 8; *with his* sister *or* step-sister, 9; *with his* grand-daughter, 10; *nor with the* daughter *of his* step-mother, 11; *nor with his* aunt, *by father or mother,* 12, 13; *nor with his* uncle's wife, 14; *nor with his* daughter-in-law, 15; *nor* sister-in-law, 16; *nor with a* woman *and her* daughter, son's daughter, *or* daughter's daughter, 17; *nor with* two sisters *at the same time,* 18. *Several abominations prohibited,* 19–23, *of which the Canaanites, &c., were guilty, and for which they were cast out of the land,* 24, 25. *The people are exhorted to avoid these abominations, lest they be treated as the ancient inhabitants of the land were treated, and so cast out,* 26–28 *Threatenings against the disobedient,* 29, *and promises to the obedient,* 30.

A. M. 2514.
B. C. 1490.
An. Exod. Isr. 2.
Abib or Nisan.

AND the LORD spake unto Moses, saying,

2 Speak unto the children of Israel, and say unto them, [a] I *am* the LORD your God.

3 [b] After the doings of the land of Egypt, wherein ye dwelt, shall ye not do: and [c] after the doings of the land of Canaan, whither I bring you, shall ye not do: neither shall ye walk in their ordinances.

A. M. 2514
B. C. 1490.
An. Exod. Isr. 2.
Abib or Nisan.

4 [d] Ye shall do my judgments, and keep mine ordinances, to walk therein: I *am* the LORD your God.

5 Ye shall therefore keep my statutes, and my judgments: [e] which if a man do, he

[a] Verse 4; Exodus vi. 7; chapter xi. 44; xix. 4, 10, 34; xx. 7; Ezekiel xx. 5, 7, 19, 20.—[b] Ezekiel xx. 7, 8; xxiii. 8.—[c] Exod. xxiii. 24; chap. xx. 23; Deut. xii. 4, 30, 31.—[d] Deut. iv. 1, 2; vi. 1; Ezek. xx. 19.—[e] Ezek. xx. 11, 13, 21; Luke x. 28; Rom. x. 5; Gal. iii. 12.

NOTES ON CHAP. XVIII.

Verse 3. *The doings of the land of Egypt—the land of Canaan*] The worshipping of demons, beasts, &c., as mentioned in the preceding chapter, verse 7, and the abominations mentioned in this chapter from verse 21 to 23.

A. M. 2514.
B. C. 1490.
An. Exod. Isr. 2.
Abib or Nisan.

shall live in them: [f] I *am* the LORD.

6 None of you shall approach to any that is [g] near of kin to him, to uncover *their* nakedness: I *am* the LORD.

7 [h] The nakedness of thy father, or the nakedness of thy mother, shalt thou not uncover: she *is* thy mother; thou shalt not uncover her nakedness.

8 [i] The nakedness of thy father's wife shalt thou not uncover: it *is* thy father's nakedness.

9 [k] The nakedness of thy sister, the daughter of thy father, or daughter of thy mother, *whether she be* born at home, or born abroad, *even* their nakedness thou shalt not uncover.

10 The nakedness of thy son's daughter, or of thy daughter's daughter, *even* their nakedness thou shalt not uncover: for theirs *is* thine own nakedness.

11 The nakedness of thy father's wife's daughter, begotten of thy father, she *is* thy sister, thou shalt not uncover her nakedness.

12 [l] Thou shalt not uncover the nakedness of thy father's sister: she *is* thy father's near kinswoman.

13 Thou shalt not uncover the nakedness of thy mother's sister: for she *is* thy mother's near kinswoman.

A. M. 2514.
B. C. 1490.
An. Exod. Isr. 2.
Abib or Nisan.

14 [m] Thou shalt not uncover the nakedness of thy father's brother, thou shalt not approach to his wife: she *is* thine aunt.

15 [n] Thou shalt not uncover the nakedness of thy daughter-in-law: she *is* thy son's wife; thou shalt not uncover her nakedness.

16 [o] Thou shalt not uncover the nakedness of thy brother's wife: it *is* thy brother's nakedness.

17 [p] Thou shalt not uncover the nakedness of a woman and her daughter, neither shalt thou take her son's daughter, or her daughter's daughter, to uncover her nakedness; *for* they *are* her near kinswomen: it *is* wickedness.

18 Neither shalt thou take [q] a wife to her sister, [r] to vex *her*, to uncover her nakedness, beside the other in her life *time*.

19 [s] Also thou shalt not approach unto a woman to uncover her nakedness, as long as she is put apart for her uncleanness.

20 Moreover [t] thou shalt not lie carnally with thy neighbour's wife, to defile thyself with her.

21 And thou shalt not let any of thy seed [u] pass through *the fire* to [v] Molech, neither

[f] Exod. vi. 2, 6, 29; Mal. iii. 6.——[g] Heb. *remainder of his flesh*.——[h] Chap. xx. 11.——[i] Gen. xlix. 4; chap. xx. 11; Deut. xxii. 30; xxvii. 20; Ezek. xxii. 10; Amos ii. 7; 1 Cor. v. 1.——[k] Chap. xx. 17; 2 Sam. xiii. 12; Ezek. xxii. 11.——[l] Chap. xx. 19.——[m] Chap. xx. 20.——[n] Gen. xxxviii. 18, 26; chap. xx. 12; Ezek. xxii. 11.——[o] Chap. xx. 21; Matt. xiv. 4; see Deut. xxv. 5; Matt. xxii. 24; Mark xii. 19.——[p] Chap. xx. 14.

[q] Or, one *wife to another*; Exod. xxvi. 3.——[r] 1 Sam. i. 6, 8.——[s] Chap. xx. 18; Ezek. xviii. 6; xxii. 10.——[t] Chap. xx. 10; Exod. xx. 14; Deut. v. 18; xxii. 22; Prov. vi. 29, 32; Mal. iii. 5; Matt. v. 27; Romans ii. 22; 1 Cor. vi. 9; Heb. xiii. 4.——[u] Chap. xx. 2; 2 Kings xvi. 3; xxi. 6; xxiii. 10; Jer. xix. 5; Ezek. xx. 31; xxiii. 37, 39.——[v] 1 Kings xi. 7, 33; called, Acts vii. 43, *Moloch*.

Verse 6. *Any that is near of kin*] כל שאר בשרו *col shear besaro*, *any remnant of his flesh*, i. e., to any particularly allied to his own family, the prohibited degrees in which are specified from the 7th to the 17th verse inclusive. Notwithstanding the prohibitions here, it must be evident that in the infancy of the world, persons very near of kin must have been joined in matrimonial alliances; and that even brothers must have matched with their own sisters. This must have been the case in the family of Adam. In these first instances necessity required this; when this necessity no longer existed, the thing became inexpedient and improper for two reasons: 1. That the duties owing by nature to *relatives* might not be *confounded* with those of a *social* or *political* kind; for could a man be a brother and a husband, a son and a husband, at the same time, and fulfil the duties of both? Impossible. 2. That by intermarrying with other families, the bonds of social compact might be strengthened and extended, so that the love of our neighbour, &c., might at once be felt to be not only a maxim of sound policy, but also a very practicable and easy duty; and thus feuds, divisions, and wars be prevented.

Verse 16. *Thy brother's wife*] This was an illegal marriage, unless the brother died *childless*. In that case it was not only lawful for her to marry her brother-in-law, but *he* was *obliged* by the law, Deut. xxv. 5, to take her to wife.

Verse 18. *A wife to her sister*] Thou shalt not marry two sisters at the same time, as Jacob did Rachel and Leah; but there is nothing in this law that rendered it illegal to marry a sister-in-law when her sister was dead; therefore the text says, *Thou shalt not take her in her life* time, *to vex her*, alluding probably to the case of the jealousies and vexations which subsisted between Leah and Rachel, and by which the family peace was so often disturbed. Some think that the text may be so understood as also to forbid *polygamy*.

Verse 19. *As long as she is put apart*] See the note on chap. xv. 24.

Verse 20. *Thy neighbour's wife*] See the note on Exod. xx. 14.

Verse 21. *Pass through* the fire *to Molech*] The name of this idol is mentioned for the first time in this place. As the word מלך *molech* or *melech* signifies *king* or *governor*, it is very likely that this idol represented the *sun*; and more particularly as the *fire* appears to have been so much employed in his wor-

A. M. 2514. B. C. 1490. An. Exod. Isr. 2. Abib or Nisan.

shalt thou [w] profane the name of
thy God: I *am* the LORD.
22 [x] Thou shalt not lie with mankind as with womankind: it *is* abomination.
23 [y] Neither shalt thou lie with any beast to
defile thyself therewith: neither shall any
woman stand before a beast to lie down
thereto: it *is* [z] confusion.
24 [a] Defile not ye yourselves in any of these
things: [b] for in all these the nations are defiled which I cast out before you:
25 And [c] the land is defiled: therefore I do
[d] visit the iniquity thereof upon it, and the
land itself [e] vomiteth out her inhabitants.
26 [f] Ye shall therefore keep my statutes and
my judgments, and shall not commit *any* of
these abominations: *neither* any of your own
nation, nor any stranger that sojourneth among you:
27 (For all these abominations
have the men of the land done, which *were*
before you, and the land is defiled;)
28 That [g] the land spue not you out also,
when ye defile it, as it spued out the nations
that *were* before you.
29 For whosoever shall commit any of
these abominations, even the souls that commit *them* shall be cut off from among their
people.
30 Therefore shall ye keep mine ordinance,
[h] that *ye* commit not *any one* of these abominable customs, which were committed before
you, and that ye [i] defile not yourselves therein:
[k] I *am* the LORD your God.

[w] Chap. xix. 12; xx. 3; xxi. 6; xxii. 2, 32; Ezek. xxxvi. 20, &c.; Mal. i. 12.——[x] Chap. xx. 13; Rom. i. 27; 1 Cor. vi. 9; 1 Tim. i. 10.——[y] Chap. xx. 15, 16; Exod. xxii. 19.——[z] Chap. xx. 12.——[a] Ver. 30; Matt. xv. 18, 19, 20; Mark vii. 21, 22, 23; 1 Cor. iii. 17.——[b] Chap. xx. 23; Deut. xviii. 12.——[c] Num. xxxv. 34; Jer. ii. 7; xvi. 18; Ezek. xxxvi. 17.——[d] Psa. lxxxix 32; Isa. xxvi. 21; Jer. v. 9, 29; ix. 9; xiv. 10; xxiii. 2; Hos ii. 13; viii. 13; ix. 9.——[e] Ver. 28.——[f] Ver. 5, 30; chap. xx. 22 23.——[g] Chap. xx. 22; Jer. ix. 19; Ezek. xxxvi. 13, 17.——[h] Ver 3, 26; chap. xx. 23; Deut. xviii. 9.——[i] Ver. 24.——[k] Ver. 2, 4

ship. There are several opinions concerning the meaning of *passing through the fire* to Molech. 1. Some think that the *semen humanum* was offered on the fire to this idol. 2. Others think that the children were actually made a *burnt-offering* to him. 3. But others suppose the children were not *burnt*, but only passed through the fire, or *between two fires*, by way of consecration to him. That some were *actually burnt alive* to this idol several scriptures, according to the opinion of commentators, seem strongly to intimate; see among others, Psa. cvi. 38; Jer. vii. 31, and Ezek. xxiii. 37–39. That others were only *consecrated* to his service by *passing between two fires* the rabbins strongly assert; and if Ahaz had but one son, *Hezekiah*, (though it is probable he had others, see 2 Chron. xxviii. 3,) he is said to have *passed through the fire to Molech*, 2 Kings xvi. 3, yet he succeeded his father in the kingdom, chapter xviii. 1, therefore this could only be a *consecration*, his idolatrous father intending thereby to initiate him early into the service of this demon. See the note on chapter xx. 2.

Verse 22. *With mankind*] This abominable crime, frequent among the Greeks and Romans as well as the Canaanites, may be punished with *death* in this country.

Verse 23. *With any beast*] This abomination is also punishable with *death* by the laws of this country.

Any woman stand before a beast] That this was often done in Egypt there can be no doubt; and we have already seen, from the testimony of *Herodotus*, that a fact of this kind actually took place while he was in Egypt. See the note on chap. xvii. 7, and xx. 16.

Verse 25. *The land itself vomiteth out her inhabitants.*] This is a very nervous *prosopopœia* or *personification*; a figure by which any part of inanimate nature may be represented as possessing the passions and reason of man. Here the *land* is represented as an intelligent being, with a deep and refined sense of moral good and evil: information concerning the abominations of the people is brought to this personified land, with which it is so deeply affected that a *nausea* is produced, and it vomits out its abominable and accursed inhabitants. It was natural for the inspired penman to make use of such a figure, as the description he was obliged to give of so many and enormous abominations must have affected him nearly in the same way in which he represents the land to be affected.

Verse 30. *Shall ye keep mine ordinance*] The only way to be preserved from all false worship is seriously to consider and devoutly to observe the ordinances of the true religion. He who in the things of God goes no farther than he can say, *Thus it is written, and thus it behoves me to do*, is never likely to receive a false creed, nor perform a superstitious act of worship.

1. How true is that word, *The law of the Lord is* PERFECT! In a small compass, and in a most minute detail, it comprises every thing that is calculated to *instruct, direct, convince, correct*, and *fortify* the mind of man. Whatever has a tendency to corrupt or injure man, that it *forbids*; whatever is calculated to comfort him, promote and secure his best interests, that it *commands*. It takes him in all possible *states*, views him in all *connections*, and provides for his present and eternal happiness.

2. As the human soul is polluted and tends to pollution, the great doctrine of the law is *holiness to the Lord*: this it keeps invariably in view in all its commands, precepts, ordinances, rites, and ceremonies. And how forcibly in all these does it say, *Thou shalt love the Lord thy God with all thy heart, and with all thy soul, and with all thy mind, and with all thy strength; and thy neighbour as thyself!* This is the prominent doctrine of the preceding chapter; and this shall be fulfilled in all them who *believe*, for *Christ is*

the end of the law for righteousness to them that believe. Reader, magnify God for his *law*, for by it is the *knowledge* of sin; and magnify him for his *Gospel*, for by this is the *cure* of sin. Let the *law* be thy schoolmaster to bring thee to Christ, that thou mayest be justified by faith; and that the righteousness of the law may be fulfilled in thee, and that thou mayest walk, not after the flesh, but after the Spirit.

CHAPTER XIX.

Exhortations to holiness, *and a repetition of various laws*, 1, 2. *Duty to* parents, *and observance of the* Sabbath, 3. *Against* idolatry, 4. *Concerning* peace-offerings, 5–8. *The* gleanings *of the* harvest *and* vintage *to be left for the poor*, 9, 10. *Against* stealing *and* lying, 11; false swearing, 12; defrauding *the* hireling, 13. *Laws in behalf of the* deaf *and the* blind, 14. *Against* respect of persons *in judgment*, 15; tale-bearing, 16; hatred *and* uncharitableness, 17; revenge, 18; unlawful mixtures *in* cattle, seed, *and* garments, 19. *Laws relative to the* bondmaid *that is betrothed*, 20–22. *The fruit of the trees of the land not to be eaten for the first three years*, 23; *but this is lawful in the* fourth *and* fifth *years*, 24, 25. *Against* eating *of* blood, *and using* incantations, 26; superstitious cutting *of the* hair, 27; *and* cutting *of the* flesh *in the times of mourning*, 28; prostitution, 29. Sabbaths *to be reverenced*, 30. *Against consulting those who are* wizards, *and have* familiar spirits, 31. *Respect must be shown to the* aged, 32. *The* stranger *shall not be oppressed*, 33, 34. *They shall keep just* measures, weights, *and* balances, 35, 36. *Conclusion*, 37.

A. M. 2514. B. C. 1490. An. Exod. Isr. 2. Abib or Nisan.

AND the Lord spake unto Moses, saying,
2 Speak unto all the congregation of the children of Israel, and say unto them, [a] Ye shall be holy: for I the Lord your God *am* holy.
3 [b] Ye shall fear every man his mother, and his father, and [c] keep my Sabbaths: I *am* the Lord your God.
4 [d] Turn ye not unto idols, [e] nor make to yourselves molten gods: I *am* the Lord your God.
5 And [f] if ye offer a sacrifice of peace-offerings unto the Lord, ye shall offer it at your own will.
6 It shall be eaten the same day ye offer it, and on the morrow: and if aught remain until the third day, it shall be burnt in the fire.
7 And if it be eaten at all on the third day, it *is* abominable; it shall not be accepted.
8 Therefore *every one* that eateth it shall bear his iniquity, because he hath profaned the hallowed thing of the Lord: and that soul shall be cut off from among his people.
9 And [g] when ye reap the harvest of your land, thou shalt not wholly reap the corners of thy field, neither shalt thou gather the gleanings of the harvest.
10 And thou shalt not glean thy vineyard, neither shalt thou gather *every* grape of thy vineyard; thou shalt leave them for the poor and stranger: I *am* the Lord your God.
11 [h] Ye shall not steal, neither deal falsely, [i] neither lie one to another.
12 And ye shall not [k] swear by my name falsely, [l] neither shalt thou profane the name of thy God: I *am* the Lord.
13 [m] Thou shalt not defraud thy neighbour,

[a] Chap. xi. 44; xx. 7, 26; 1 Pet. i. 16.——[b] Exod. xx. 12. [c] Exod. xx. 8; xxxi. 13.——[d] Exod. xx. 4; chap. xxvi. 1; 1 Cor. x. 14; 1 John v. 21.——[e] Exod. xxxiv. 17; Deut. xxvii. 15. [f] Chap. vii. 16.——[g] Chap. xxiii. 22; Deut. xxiv. 19, 20, 21; Ruth ii. 15, 16.——[h] Exod. xx. 15: xxii. 1, 7, 10; Deut. v. 19. [i] Chap. vi. 2; Eph. iv. 25; Col. iii. 9.——[k] Exod. xx. 7; chap. vi. 3; Deut. v. 11; Matt. v. 33; James v. 12.——[l] Chap. xviii. 21.——[m] Ecclus. x. 6; Mark x. 19; 1 Thess. iv. 6.

NOTES ON CHAP. XIX.

Verse 3. *Ye shall fear every man his mother, &c.*] Ye shall have the profoundest reverence and respect for them. See the notes on Gen. xlviii. 12, and on Exod. xx. 8, 12.

Verse 4. *Turn ye not unto idols*] אלילם *elilim*, literally *nothings*; and to this St. Paul seems to allude 1 Cor. viii. 4, where he says, *We know that an idol is* NOTHING *in the world*.

Verse 5. *Peace-offerings*] See the notes at the conclusion of chap. vii.

Verse 7. *If it be eaten—on the third day*] See the note on chap. vii. 15.

Verse 9. *When ye reap the harvest*] Liberty for the poor to glean both the corn-fields and vineyards was a Divine institution among the Jews; for the whole of the Mosaic dispensation, like the Christian, breathed love to God and benevolence to man. The poor in Judea were to live by gleanings from the corn-fields and vineyards. To the honour of the public and charitable spirit of the English, this merciful law is in general as much attended to as if it had been incorporated with the Gospel.

Verse 11. *Ye shall not steal, &c.*] See the notes on Exod. xx.

Verse 13. *The wages—shall not abide with thee all*

a

A. M. 2514.
B. C. 1490.
An. Exod. Isr. 2.
Abib or Nisan.

neither rob *him*: [n] the wages of
him that is hired shall not abide
with thee all night until the
morning.
14 Thou shalt not curse the deaf, [o] nor put a
stumbling-block before the blind, but shalt
[p] fear thy God: I *am* the LORD.
15 [q] Ye shall do no unrighteousness in
judgment: thou shalt not respect the person
of the poor, nor honour the person of the
mighty; *but* in righteousness shalt thou judge
thy neighbour.
16 [r] Thou shalt not go up and down *as* a
tale-bearer among thy people; neither shalt
thou [s] stand against the blood of
thy neighbour: I *am* the LORD.
17 [t] Thou shalt not hate thy
brother in thine heart: [u] thou shalt in any wise
rebuke thy neighbour, [v] and not suffer sin
upon him.
18 [w] Thou shalt not avenge, nor bear any
grudge against the children of thy people,
[x] but thou shalt love thy neighbour as thyself:
I *am* the LORD.
19 Ye shall keep my statutes. Thou shalt
not let thy cattle gender with a diverse kind:
[y] thou shalt not sow thy field with mingled
seed: [z] neither shall a garment mingled of

[n] Deut. xxiv. 14, 15; Mal. iii. 5; Tob. iv. 14; James v. 4. — [o] Deut. xxvii. 18; Rom. xiv. 13. — [p] Ver. 32; chap. xxv. 17; Gen. xlii. 18; Eccles. v. 7; 1 Pet. ii. 17. — [q] Exod. xxiii. 2, 3; Deut. i. 17; xvi. 19; xxvii. 19; Psa. lxxxii. 2; Prov. xxiv. 23; James ii. 9. — [r] Exod. xxiii. 1; Psa. xv. 3; l. 20; Prov. xi. 13; xx. 19; Ezek. xxii. 9. — [s] Exod. xxiii. 1, 7; 1 Kings xxi. 13; Matt. xxvi. 60, 61; xxvii. 4. — [t] 1 John ii. 9, 11; iii. 15. — [u] Ecclus. xix. 13; Matt. xviii. 15; Luke. xvii. 3; Gal. vi. 1; Eph. v. 11; 1 Tim. v. 20; 2 Tim. iv. 2; Tit. i. 13; ii. 15. — [v] Or, *that thou bear not sin for him;* see Rom. i. 32; 1 Cor. v. 2; 1 Tim. v. 22; 2 John 11. — [w] 2 Sam. xiii. 22; Prov. xx. 22; Rom. xii. 17, 19; Gal. v. 20; Eph. iv. 31; 1 Pet. ii. 1; James v. 9. — [x] Matt. v. 43; xxii. 39; Rom. xiii. 9; Gal. v. 14; James ii. 8. — [y] Deut. xxii. 9, 10. — [z] Deut. xxii. 11.

night] For this plain reason, it is the support of the man's life and family, and they need to expend it as fast as it is earned.

Verse 14. *Thou shalt not curse the deaf*] Or *speak evil* of him, because he cannot *hear*, and so cannot vindicate his own character.

Nor put a stumbling-block before the blind] He who is capable of doing this, must have a heart cased with cruelty. The spirit and design of these precepts are, that no man shall in any case take advantage of the ignorance, simplicity, or inexperience of his neighbour, but in all things do to his neighbour as he would, on a change of circumstances, that his neighbour should do to him.

Verse 16. *Thou shalt not go up and down* as *a talebearer*] רכיל *rachil* signifies a *trader*, a *pedlar*, and is here applied to the person who travels about dealing in scandal and calumny, getting the secrets of every person and family, and *retailing* them wherever he goes. A more despicable character exists not: such a person is a pest to society, and should be exiled from the habitations of men.

Neither shalt thou stand against the blood, &c.] Thou shalt not be a false witness, because by such testimony the *blood*—the *life* of an innocent man may be endangered.

Verse 17. *Thou shalt not hate thy brother*] Thou shalt not only not do him any kind of evil, but thou shalt harbour no hatred in thy heart towards him. On the contrary, *thou shalt love him as thyself*, ver. 18. Many persons suppose, from misunderstanding our Lord's words, John xiii. 34, *A new commandment give I unto you, that ye love one another*, &c., that loving our neighbour as ourselves was first instituted under the Gospel. This verse shows the opinion to be unfounded: but to love another *as* Christ has loved us, i. e., *to lay down our lives* for each other, is certainly a *new* commandment; we have it simply on the authority of Jesus Christ alone.

And not suffer sin upon him.] If thou see him sin, or know him to be addicted to any thing by which the safety of his soul is endangered, thou shalt mildly and affectionately reprove him, and by no means permit him to go on without counsel and advice in a way that is leading him to perdition. In a multitude of cases timely reproof has been the means of saving the soul. Speak to him *privately* if possible; if not, write to him in such a way that himself *alone* shall see it.

Verse 19. *Gender with a diverse kind*] These precepts taken literally seem to imply that they should not permit the *horse* and the *she-ass*, nor the *he-ass* and the *cow*, (as they do in the East,) to couple together; nor sow different kinds of *seeds* in the same *field* or *garden;* nor have *garments* of *silk* and *woollen*, *cotton* and *silk*, *linen* and *wool*, &c. And if all these were forbidden, there must have been some moral reason for the prohibitions, because domestic economy *required* several of these mixtures, especially those which relate to *seeds* and *clothing*. With respect to heterogeneous mixtures among *cattle*, there is something very unnatural in it, and it was probably forbidden to prevent excitements to such unnatural lusts as those condemned in the preceding chapter, ver. 22, 23. As to *seeds*, in many cases it would be very improper to sow different kinds in the same plot of ground. It would be improvident to sow *oats* and *wheat* together: the latter would be *injured*, the former *ruined*. The *turnip* and *carrot* would not succeed conjointly, where either of them separately would prosper and yield a good crop; so we may say of many other kinds of *seeds;* and if this be all that is intended, the counsels are prudential agricultural maxims. As to different kinds of *garments*, such as the *linsey woolsey*, the prohibition here might be intended as much against *pride* and *vanity* as any thing else; for it is certain that both these articles may be so manufactured in conjunction as to minister to pride, though in general the *linsey woolsey* or *drugget* is the clothing of the *poor*. But we really do not know what the original word שעטנז *shaatnez*, which we translate *linen* and *woollen*, means.

A. M. 2514.
B. C. 1490.
An. Exod. Isr. 2.
Abib or Nisan.

linen and woollen come upon
thee.
20 And whosoever lieth carnally
with a woman that *is* a bondmaid, [a] betrothed
to a husband, [b] and not at all redeemed, nor
freedom given her; [c] she shall be [d] scourged:
they shall not be put to death, because she
was not free.
21 And [e] he shall bring his trespass-offering
unto the LORD, unto the door of the tabernacle of the congregation, *even* a ram for a trespass-offering.
22 And the priest shall make an atonement
for him with the ram of the trespass-offering
before the LORD, for his sin which he hath
done; and the sin which he hath
done shall be forgiven him.

A. M. 2514.
B. C. 1490.
An. Exod. Isr. 2.
Abib or Nisan.

23 And when ye shall come into
the land, and shall have planted all manner of
trees for food, then ye shall count the fruit thereof as uncircumcised: three years shall it be as
uncircumcised unto you: it shall not be eaten of:
24 But in the fourth year all the fruit thereof
shall be [f] holy, [g] to praise the LORD *withal.*
25 And in the fifth year shall ye eat of the
fruit thereof, that it may yield unto you the
increase thereof: I *am* the LORD your God
26 [h] Ye shall not eat *any thing* with the
blood; [i] neither shall ye use enchantment, nor
observe times.

[a] Or, *abused by any.*—[b] Heb. *reproached by* or *for man.* [c] Or, *they.*—[d] Heb. *there shall be a scourging.*—[e] Chap. v. 15; vi. 6.—[f] Heb. *holiness of praises to the LORD.*

[g] Deut. xii. 17, 18; Prov. iii. 9.—[h] Chap. xvii. 10, &c.; Deut. xii. 23.—[i] Deut. xviii. 10, 11, 14; 1 Sam. xv. 23; 2 Kings xvii. 17; xxi. 6; 2 Chron. xxxiii. 6; Mal. iii. 5.

it is true that in Deut. xxii. 11, where it is again used, it seems to be explained by the words immediately following, *Thou shalt not wear a garment of divers sorts,* as *of linen and woollen together;* but this may as well refer to a garment *made up of a sort of patch-work differently coloured* and *arranged* for pride and for show. A folly of this kind prevailed anciently in this very land, and I shall give a proof of it, taken from a sermon *against luxury in dress,* composed in the *fourteenth* century.

"As to the first sinne in superfluitie of clothing, soche that maketh it so dere, to the harme of the peple, nat only the cost of enbraudering, the disguised endenting, or barring, ounding paling, winding or bending and semblable wast of clothe in vanite. But there is also the costlewe furring in their gounes, so moche pounsing of chesel, to make holes; so moche dagging with sheres foorth; with the superfluitie in length of the forsaied gounes,—to grete dammage of pore folke.—And more ouer—they shewe throughe disguising, in departing of ther hosen in *white and red,* semeth that halfe ther members were slain.—They departe ther hosen into other colours, as is *white and blewe,* or *white and blacke,* or *blacke and red,* and so forth; than semeth it as by variaunce of colour, that the halfe part of ther members ben corrupt by the fire of Saint Anthony, or by canker, or other suche mischaunce." The *Parson's Tale,* in Chaucer, p. 198. *Urry's* edit. The reader will pardon the antiquated spelling.

"What could exhibit," says Dr. Henry, "a more fantastical appearance than an English beau of the 14th century? He wore long pointed shoes, fastened to his knees by gold or silver chains; *hose of one colour* on the *one leg,* and of *another colour* on the *other;* short breeches which did reach to the middle of his thighs; a coat the *one half white,* the *other half black* or *blue;* a long beard; a silk hood buttoned under his chin, embroidered with grotesque figures of animals, dancing men, &c., and sometimes ornamented with gold and precious stones." This dress was the height of the mode in the reign of King Edward III.

Something of the same kind seems to have existed in the *patriarchal times;* witness the *coat of many colours* made by Jacob for his son Joseph. See the note on Gen. xxxvii. 3. Concerning these different mixtures much may be seen in the *Mishna,* Tract. *Kilaim,* and in *Ainsworth,* and *Calmet* on this place.

Verse 20. *A woman that is a bondmaid*] Had she been *free,* the law required that she should be put to death; (see Deut. xxii. 24;) but as she was a *slave,* she is supposed to have less self-command, and therefore less guilt: but as it is taken for granted she did not make resistance, or did consent, she is to be *scourged,* and the man is to bring a ram for a *trespass-offering.*

Verse 23. *Three years shall it be as uncircumcised*] I see no great reason to seek for mystical meanings in this prohibition. The fruit of a young tree cannot be good; for not having arrived at a state of maturity the juices cannot be sufficiently elaborated to produce fruit excellent in its kind. The Israelites are commanded not to eat of the fruit of a tree till the fifth year after its planting: in the three first years the fruit is unwholesome; in the *fourth* year the fruit is holy, it belongs to God, and should be consecrated to him, ver. 24; and in the *fifth* year and afterward the fruit may be employed for common use, ver. 25.

Verse 26. *Neither shall ye use enchantment*] לא תנחשו *lo thenachashu.* Conjecture itself can do little towards a proper explanation of the terms used in this verse. נחש *nachash* in Gen. iii. 1 we translate *serpent,* and with very little propriety; but though the word may not signify a serpent in that place, it has that signification in others. Possibly, therefore, the superstition here prohibited may be what the Greeks called *Ophiomanteia,* or *divination by serpents.*

Nor observe times.] ולא תעוננו *velo teonenu,* ye shall *not divine by clouds,* which was also a superstition much in practice among the heathens, as well as divination by the *flight of birds.* What these prohibitions may particularly refer to, we know not. See the notes on Gen. xli. 8.

A. M. 2514.
B. C. 1490.
An. Exod. Isr. 2.
Abib or Nisan.

27 [k] Ye shall not round the corners of your heads, neither shalt thou mar the corners of thy beard.

28 Ye shall not [l] make any cuttings in your flesh for the dead, nor print any marks upon you: I *am* the LORD.

[k] Chap. xxi. 5; Jer. ix. 26; xlviii. 37; Isa. xv. 2.

[l] Chap. xxi. 5; Deut. xiv. 1; Jer. xvi. 6; xlviii. 37.

Verse 27. *Ye shall not round the corners of your heads*] This and the following verse evidently refer to customs which must have existed among the Egyptians when the Israelites sojourned in Egypt; and what they were it is now difficult, even with any probability, to conjecture. *Herodotus* observes that the Arabs *shave* or *cut their hair round*, in honour of Bacchus, who, they say, had his hair cut in this way, lib. iii., cap. 8. He says also that the *Macians*, a people of Libya, *cut their hair round*, so as to leave a *tuft* on the top of the head, lib. iv., cap. 175. In this manner the Chinese cut their hair to the present day. This might have been in honour of some idol, and therefore forbidden to the Israelites.

The *hair* was much used in divination among the ancients, and for purposes of religious superstition among the Greeks; and particularly about the time of the giving of this law, as this is supposed to have been the era of the Trojan war. We learn from *Homer* that it was customary for parents to dedicate the hair of their children to some god; which, when they came to manhood, they cut off and consecrated to the deity. *Achilles*, at the funeral of Patroclus, cut off his golden locks which his father had dedicated to the river god *Sperchius*, and threw them into the flood:—

Στας απανευθε πυρης ξανθην απεκειρατο χαιτην,
Την ῥα Σπερχειῳ ποταμῳ τρεφε τηλεθοωσαν·
Οχθησας δ' αρα ειπεν, ιδων επι οινοπα ποντον·
Σπερχει', αλλως σοι γε πατηρ ηρησατο Πηλευς. κ. τ. λ.
Iliad, l. xxiii., ver. 142, &c.

But great Achilles stands apart in prayer,
And from *his head* divides the *yellow hair*,
Those curling locks *which from his youth he vowed*,
And sacred threw to Sperchius' honoured flood.
Then sighing, to the deep his looks he cast,
And rolled his eyes around the watery waste.
Sperchius! whose waves, in mazy errors lost,
Delightful roll along my native coast!
To whom we vainly *vowed*, at our return,
These locks to fall, and hecatombs to burn——
So *vowed* my *father*, but he *vowed* in vain,
No more Achilles sees his native plain;
In that vain hope *these hairs no longer grow;*
Patroclus *bears them to the shades below.* POPE.

From *Virgil* we learn that the *topmost lock* of hair was dedicated to the *infernal gods;* see his account of the death of Dido:—

"Nondum illi *flavum* Proserpina *vertice crinem*
Abstulerat, Stygioque caput damnaverat orco—
——————Hunc ego Diti
Sacrum jussa fero; teque isto corpore solvo.
Sic ait, et dextra *crinem secat*." Æn., l. iv., ver. 698.

The sisters had not *cut the topmost hair*,
Which Proserpine and they can only know,
Nor made her *sacred to the shades below*—
This offering to the *infernal gods* I bear;
Thus while she spoke, *she cut the fatal hair.*
DRYDEN.

If the hair was *rounded*, and dedicated for purposes of this kind, it will at once account for the prohibition in this verse.

The corners of thy beard.] Probably meaning the hair of the cheek that connects the hair of the head with the beard. This was no doubt cut in some peculiar manner for the superstitious purposes mentioned above. Several of our own countrymen wear this said hair in a curious form; for what purposes they know best: we cannot say precisely that it is the ancient Egyptian custom revived. From the images and paintings which remain of the ancient Egyptians, we find that they were accustomed to shave the whole hair off their face, except merely that upon the chin, which last they cut off only in times of *mourning*.

Verse 28. *Any cuttings in your flesh for the dead*] That the ancients were very violent in their grief, tearing the hair and face, beating the breast, &c., is well known. Virgil represents the sister of Dido "tearing her face with her nails, and beating her breast with her fists."

"Unguibus ora *soror* fœdans, *et* pectora pugnis."
Æn., l. iv., ver. 672.

Nor print any marks upon you] It was a very ancient and a very general custom to carry marks on the body in honour of the object of their worship. All the castes of the Hindoos bear on their foreheads or elsewhere what are called the *sectarian marks*, which distinguish them, not only in a civil but also in a religious point of view, from each other.

Most of the barbarous nations lately discovered have their faces, arms, breasts, &c., curiously carved or *tatooed*, probably for superstitious purposes. Ancient writers abound with accounts of marks made on the face, arms, &c., in honour of different idols; and to this the inspired penman alludes, Rev. xiii. 16, 17; xiv. 9, 11; xv. 2; xvi. 2; xix. 20; xx. 4, where false worshippers are represented as receiving in their hands and in their forehead the marks of the beast. These were called *στιγματα stigmata* among the Greeks, and to these St. Paul refers when he says, *I bear about in my body the* MARKS (*stigmata*) *of the Lord Jesus;* Gal vi. 17. I have seen several cases where persons have got the figure of the cross, the Virgin Mary, &c., made on their arms, breasts, &c., the skin being first punctured, and then a blue colouring matter rubbed in, which is never afterward effaced. All these were done for superstitious purposes, and to such things probably the prohibition in this verse refers. Calmet, on this verse, gives several examples. See also *Mariner's Tonga Islands*, vol. i., p. 311-313.

A. M. 2514. B. C. 1490. An. Exod. Isr. 2. Abib or Nisan.

29 [m] Do not [n] prostitute thy
daughter, to cause her to be a
whore; lest the land fall to whoredom, and the land become full of wickedness.
30 [o] Ye shall keep my Sabbaths, and [p] reverence my sanctuary: I *am* the LORD.
31 [q] Regard not them that have familiar
spirits, neither seek after wizards, to be defiled
by them: I *am* the LORD your God.
32 [r] Thou shalt rise up before the hoary
head, and honour the face of the old man,
and [s] fear thy God: I *am* the LORD.
33 And [t] if a stranger sojourn with thee in
your land, ye shall not [u] vex him.
34 [v] *But* the stranger that dwelleth with you
shall be unto you as one born
among you, and [w] thou shalt love
him as thyself; for ye were
strangers in the land of Egypt: I *am* the
LORD your God.
35 [x] Ye shall do no unrighteousness in
judgment, in mete-yard, in weight, or in
measure.
36 [y] Just balances, just [z] weights, a just
ephah, and a just hin, shall ye have: I *am*
the LORD your God, which brought you out
of the land of Egypt.
37 [a] Therefore shall ye observe all my statutes, and all my judgments, and do them: I
am the LORD.

[m] Deut. xxiii. 17.——[n] Heb. *profane.*——[o] Ver. 3; chap. xxvi. 2.——[p] Ecclus. v. 1.——[q] Exod. xxii. 18; chap. xx. 6, 27; Deut. xviii. 10; 1 Sam. xxviii. 7; 1 Chron. x. 13; Isa. viii. 19; Acts xvi. 16.——[r] Prov. xx. 29; 1 Tim. v. 1.——[s] Ver. 14.

[t] Exod. xxii. 21; xxiii. 9.——[u] Or, *oppress.*——[v] Exod. xii. 48, 49.——[w] Deut. x. 19.——[x] Ver. 15.——[y] Deut. xxv. 13, 15; Prov. xi. 1; xvi. 11; xx. 10.——[z] Heb. *stones.*——[a] Chap. xviii. 4, 5; Deut. iv. 5, 6; v. 1; vi. 25.

Verse 29. *Do not prostitute thy daughter*] This was a very frequent custom, and with examples of it writers of antiquity abound. The Cyprian women, according to Justin, gained that portion which their husbands received with them at marriage by previous public prostitution. And the *Phœnicians*, according to *Augustine*, made a gift to Venus of the gain acquired by the public prostitution of their daughters, previously to their marriage. "Veneri donum dabant, et prostitutiones filiarum, antequam jungerent eas viris."—De Civit. Dei, lib. xviii., c. 5; and see *Calmet*.

Verse 31. *Regard not them that have familiar spirits*] The Hebrew word אבות *oboth* probably signifies a kind of *engastromuthoi* or *ventriloquists*, or such as the Pythoness mentioned Acts xvi. 16, 18; persons who, while under the *influence of their demon*, became greatly *inflated*, as the Hebrew word implies, and gave answers in a sort of phrensy. See a case of this kind in Virgil, Æneid, l. vi., ver. 46, &c.:—

"——Deus ecce, Deus! cui talia fanti
Ante fores, subito non vultus, non color unus,
Non comptæ mansere comæ; sed *pectus anhelum*,
Et rabie fera *corda tument; majorque videri*,
Nec mortale sonans, *afflata* est *numine* quando
Jam *propiore Dei*."

——————Invoke the skies,
I feel the god, the rushing god, she cries.
While yet she spoke, enlarged her features grew,
Her colour changed, her locks dishevelled flew.
The *heavenly tumult* reigns in every part,
Pants in her breast, and *swells* her *rising heart*:
Still *swelling to the sight*, the priestess glowed,
And *heaved* impatient of the *incumbent* god. PITT.

Neither seek after wizards] ידענים *yiddeonim*, the *wise* or *knowing ones*, from ידע *yada*, to *know* or *understand*; called *wizard* in Scotland, *wise* or *cunning man* in England; and hence also the *wise woman*, the *white witch*. Not only all real dealers with familiar spirits, or necromantic or magical superstitions, are here forbidden, but also all *pretenders* to the knowledge of futurity, fortune-tellers, astrologers, &c., &c. To attempt to know what God has not thought proper to reveal, is a sin against his wisdom, providence, and goodness. In mercy, great mercy, God has hidden the knowledge of futurity from man, and given him *hope*—the *expectation of future good*, in its place. See the note on Exod. xxii. 18.

Verse 32. *Before the hoary head*] See the note on Gen. xlviii. 12.

Verse 33. *If a stranger sojourn*] This law to protect and comfort the stranger was at once humane and politic. None is so desolate as the stranger, and none needs the offices of benevolence and charity more: and we may add that he who is not affected by the desolate state of the stranger has neither benevolence nor charity. It was politic to encourage strangers, as in consequence many came, not only to sojourn, but to settle among the Jews, and thus their political strength became increased; and many of these settlers became at least *proselytes of the gate* if not *proselytes of the covenant*, and thus got their souls saved. Hence humanity, sound policy, and religion said, *Vex not the stranger; thou shalt love him as thyself.* The apostle makes use of a strong argument to induce men to hospitality towards strangers: *Be not forgetful to entertain strangers, for thereby some have entertained angels unawares*, Heb. xiii. 2. Moses also uses a powerful motive: *Ye were strangers in the land of Egypt.* The spirit of the precept here laid down, may be well expressed in our Lord's words: *Do unto all men as ye would they should do unto you.*

Verse 35. *Ye shall do no unrighteousness*] Ye shall not act contrary to the strictest justice in any case, and especially in the *four* following, which properly understood, comprise all that can occur between a man and his fellow. 1. JUDGMENT in all cases that come before the civil magistrate; he is to judge and decide according to the *law*. 2. METE-YARD, במדה *bammiddah*, in measures of *length* and *surface*, such as the *reed, cubit, foot, span, hand's breadth*, among the *Jews*; or *ell, yard, foot*, and *inch*, among us. 3. WEIGHT,

במשקל *bammishkal*, in any thing that is *weighed*, the weights being all according to the *standards* kept for the purpose of trying the rest in the sanctuary, as appears from Exod. xxx. 13; 1 Chron. xxiii. 29; these weights were the *talent*, *shekel*, *barleycorn*, &c. 4. MEASURE, במשורה *bammesurah*, from which we derive our term. This refers to all measures of *capacity*, such as the *homer*, *ephah*, *seah*, *hin*, *omer*, *kab*, and *log*. See all these explained Exod. xvi. 16.

Verse 36. *Just balances*] *Scales, steel-yard*, &c. *Weights*, אבנים *abanim*, *stones*, as the weights appear to have been originally formed out of stones. *Ephah*, *hin*, &c., see before.

Verse 37. *Shall ye observe all my statutes*] חקתי *chukkothi*, from חק *chak*, to *describe*, *mark*, or *trace out*; the righteousness which I have described, and the path of duty which I have traced out. *Judgments*, משפטי *mishpatai*, from שפט *shaphat*, to *discern*, *determine*, *direct*, &c.; that which Divine Wisdom has *discerned* to be best for man, has *determined* shall promote his best interest, and has *directed* him conscientiously to use. See the note on chap. xxvi. 15.

1 MANY difficulties occur in this very important chapter, but they are such only to *us*; for there can be no doubt of their having been perfectly well known to the Israelites, to whom the precepts contained in this chapter were given. Considerable pains however have been taken to make them plain, and no serious mind can read them without profit.

2. The precepts against injustice, fraud, slander, enmity, &c., &c., are well worth the notice of every Christian; and those against *superstitious* usages are not less so; and by these last we learn, that having recourse to *astrologers*, *fortune-tellers*, &c., to get intelligence of lost or stolen goods, or to know the future events of our own lives, or those of others, is highly criminal in the sight of God. Those who have recourse to such persons renounce their baptism, and in effect renounce the *providence* as well as the *word* of God.

3. The precepts of humanity and mercy relative to the *poor*, the *hireling*, and the *stranger*, are worthy of our most serious regard. Nor are those which concern *weights* and *measures*, traffic, and the whole system of commutative justice, less necessary to be observed for the benefit and comfort of the *individual*, and the safety and prosperity of the *state*

CHAPTER XX.

Of giving seed to Molech, *and the punishment of this crime*, 1–5. *Of consulting* wizards, *&c.*, 6–8. *Of* disrespect *to* parents, 9. *Of* adultery, 10. *Of* incestuous *mixtures*, 11, 12. Bestiality, 13–16. *Different cases of* incest *and* uncleanness, 17–21. *Exhortations and promises*, 22–24. *The difference between* clean *and* unclean *animals to be carefully observed*, 25. *The Israelites are separated from other nations, that they may be holy*, 26. *A repetition of the law against* wizards *and them that have* familiar spirits, 27.

A. M. 2514. B. C. 1490. An. Exod. Isr. 2. Abib or Nisan.

AND the LORD spake unto Moses, saying,

2 [a] Again thou shalt say to the children of Israel, [b] Whosoever *he be* of the children of Israel, or of the strangers that sojourn in Israel, that giveth *any* of his seed unto Molech; he shall surely be put to death: the people of the land shall stone him with stones.

3 And [c] I will set my face against that man, and will cut him off from among his people; because he hath given of his seed unto Molech, to [d] defile my sanctuary, and [e] to profane my holy name.

4 And if the people of the land do any ways hide their eyes from the man, when he giveth of his seed unto Molech, and [f] kill him not;

A. M. 2514. B. C. 1490. An. Exod. Isr. 2. Abib or Nisan.

[a] Chap. xviii. 21.——[b] Chap. xviii. 21; Deut. xii. 31; xviii. 10; 2 Kings xvii. 17; xxiii. 10; 2 Chron. xxxiii. 6; Jer. vii. 31; xxxii. 35; Ezek. xx. 26, 31.——[c] Chap. xvii. 10.——[d] Ezek. v. 11; xxiii. 38, 39.——[e] Chap. xviii. 21.——[f] Deut. xvii. 2, 3, 5.

NOTES ON CHAP. XX.

Verse 2. *That giveth* any *of his seed unto Molech*] To what has been said in the note on chap. xviii. 21, we may add, that the rabbins describe this idol, who was probably a representative or emblematical personification of the solar influence, as made of brass, in the form of a man, with the head of an ox; that a fire was kindled in the inside, and the child to be sacrificed to him was put in his arms, and roasted to death. Others say that the idol, which was hollow, was divided into *seven compartments* within; in one of which they put *flour*, in the second *turtle-doves*, in the third a *ewe*, in the fourth a *ram*, in the fifth a *calf*, in the sixth an *ox*, and in the seventh a *child*, which, by heating the statue on the outside, were all *burnt alive together*. I question the whole truth of these statements, whether from Jewish or Christian rabbins. There is no evidence of all this in the sacred writings. And there is but presumptive proof, and that not very strong, that *human* sacrifices were at all offered to Molech by the Jews. The *passing through the fire*, so frequently spoken of, might mean no more than a simple rite of *consecration* to the service of this idol. Probably a kind of *ordeal* was meant, the persons passing *suddenly* through the flame of a large fire, by which, though they might be *burnt* or *scorched*, yet they were neither *killed* nor *consumed*. Or they might have passed *between two large fires*, as a sort of purification. See the notes on ver. 14; and chap. xviii. 21.

Cæsar, in his history of the Gallic war, lib. vi., c. 16,

A. M. 2514.
B. C. 1490.
An. Exod. Isr. 2.
Abib or Nisan.

5 Then [g] I will set my face
against that man, and [h] against
his family, and will cut him off,
and all that [i] go a whoring after him, to commit whoredom with Molech, from among their
people.
6 And [k] the soul that turneth after such as
have familiar spirits, and after wizards, to go
a whoring after them, I will even set my face
against that soul, and will cut him off from
among *his* people.
7 [l] Sanctify yourselves therefore, and be ye
holy: for I *am* the LORD your God.
8 [m] And ye shall keep my statutes, and do
them: [n] I *am* the LORD which sanctify you.
9 [o] For every one that curseth his father or
his mother shall be surely put to death: he
hath cursed his father or his mother; [p] his
blood *shall be* upon him.
10 And [q] the man that committeth adultery
with *another* man's wife, *even he* that committeth adultery with his neighbour's wife,
the adulterer and the adulteress
shall surely be put to death.
11 [r] And the man that lieth with
his father's wife, hath uncovered his father's
nakedness: both of them shall surely be put
to death; their blood *shall be* upon them.
12 [s] And if a man lie with his daughter-in-
law, both of them shall surely be put to death:
[t] they have wrought confusion; their blood
shall be upon them.
13 [u] If a man also lie with mankind, as he
lieth with a woman, both of them have committed an abomination: they shall surely be
put to death; their blood *shall be* upon them.
14 [v] And if a man take a wife and her
mother, it *is* wickedness: they shall be burnt
with fire, both he and they; that there be no
wickedness among you.
15 [w] And if a man lie with a beast, he shall
surely be put to death: and ye shall slay the
beast.
16 And if a woman approach unto any beast,

[g] Chap. xvii. 10.——[h] Exod. xx. 5.——[i] Chap. xvii. 7.
[k] Chap. xix. 31.——[l] Chap. xi. 44; xix. 2; 1 Pet. i. 16.——[m] Chap. xix. 37.——[n] Exod. xxxi. 13; chap. xxi. 8; Ezek. xxxvii. 28.
[o] Exod. xxi. 17; Deut. xxvii. 16; Prov. xx. 20; Matt. xv. 4.
[p] Ver. 11, 12, 13, 16, 27; 2 Sam. i. 16.

[q] Chap. xviii. 20; Deut. xxii. 22; John viii. 4, 5.——[r] Chap. xviii. 8; Deut. xxvii. 23.——[s] Chap. xviii. 15.——[t] Chap. xviii. 23.——[u] Chap. xviii. 22; Deut. xxiii. 17; see Gen. xix. 5; Judg. xix. 22.——[v] Chap. xviii. 17; Deut. xxvii. 23.——[w] chap. xviii. 23; Deut. xxvii. 21.

mentions a custom of the Druids similar to this. They made an image of *wicker*-work, inclosed those in it whom they had adjudged to death, and, setting the whole on fire, all were consumed together.

Verse 6. *Familiar spirits*] See the notes on chap. xix. 31; and Exod. xxii. 18.

Verse 9. *Curseth his father or his mother*] See the notes on Gen. xlviii. 12, and Exod. xx. 12. He who conscientiously keeps the *fifth* commandment can be in no danger of this judgment. The term יקלל *yekallel* signifies, not only to *curse*, but to speak of a person *contemptuously* and *disrespectfully*, to *make light of*; so that all speeches which have a tendency to lessen our parents in the eyes of others, or to render their judgment, piety, &c., suspected and contemptible, may be here included; though the act of *cursing*, or of treating the parent with injurious and opprobrious language, is that which is particularly intended.

Verse 10. *Committeth adultery*] To what has been said in the note on Exod. xx. 14, we may add, that the word *adultery* comes from the Latin *adulterium*, which is compounded of *ad*, *to* or *with*, and *alter*, *another*, or, according to Minshieu, of *ad alterius torum*, he that approaches to *another man's bed*.

Verse 12. *They have wrought confusion*] See chap. xviii., and especially the note on ver. 6.

Verse 14. *They shall be burnt with fire*] As there are worse crimes mentioned here, (see verses 11 and 17,) where the delinquent is ordered simply to be *put to death*, or to be *cut off*, it is very likely that the crime mentioned in this verse was not punished by *burning alive*, but by some kind of *branding*, by which they were ever after rendered infamous. I need not add that the original, באש ישרפו *baesh yishrephu*, may, without violence to its grammatical meaning, be understood as above, though in other places it is certainly used to signify a consuming by fire. But the case in question requires some explanation; it is this: a man marries a wife, and afterward takes his mother-in-law or wife's mother to wife also; now for this offence the text says all three shall be *burnt with fire*, and this is understood as signifying that they shall be *burnt alive*. Now the first wife, we may safely presume, was completely *innocent*, and was legally married; for a man may take to wife the daughter if *single*, or the mother if a *widow*, and in neither of these cases can any blame attach to the man or the party he marries; the crime therefore lies in taking *both*. Either, therefore, they were all branded as *infamous* persons, and this certainly was severe enough in the case of the first wife; or the man and the woman taken last were *burnt*: but the text says, both *he* and *they*; therefore we should seek for another interpretation of *they shall be burnt with fire*, than that which is commonly given. *Branding* with a hot iron would certainly accomplish every desirable end both for punishment and prevention of the crime; and because the Mosaic laws are so generally distinguished by *humanity*, it seems to be necessary to limit the meaning of the words as above.

Verse 16. *If a woman approach unto any beast*] We have the authority of one of the most eminent

A. M. 2514.
B. C. 1490.
An. Exod. Isr. 2.
Abib or Nisan.

and lie down thereto, thou shalt
kill the woman and the beast:
they shall surely be put to death;
their blood *shall be* upon them.
17 [x] And if a man shall take his sister, his
father's daughter, or his mother's daughter, and
see her nakedness, and she see his nakedness,
it *is* a wicked thing; and they shall be cut off in
the sight of their people: he hath uncovered his
sister's nakedness; he shall bear his iniquity.
18 [y] And if a man shall lie with a woman
having her sickness, and shall uncover her
nakedness; he hath [z] discovered her fountain,
and she hath uncovered the fountain of her
blood: and both of them shall be cut off from
among their people.
19 [a] And thou shalt not uncover the nakedness of thy mother's sister, nor of thy father's
sister: [b] for he uncovereth his near kin: they
shall bear their iniquity.
20 [c] And if a man shall lie with his uncle's
wife, he hath uncovered his uncle's nakedness:
they shall bear their sin; they shall die childless.
21 [d] And if a man shall take his brother's wife,
it *is* [e] an unclean thing: he hath uncovered his
brother's nakedness; they shall be childless.
22 Ye shall therefore keep all my [f] statutes,
and all my judgments, and do
them: that the land, whither I
bring you to dwell therein, [g] spue
you not out.

A. M. 2514.
B. C. 1490.
An. Exod. Isr. 2.
Abib or Nisan.

23 [h] And ye shall not walk in the manners of
the nation, which I cast out before you: for
they committed all these things, and [i] therefore I abhorred them.
24 But [k] I have said unto you, Ye shall inherit their land, and I will give it unto you to
possess it, a land that floweth with milk and
honey: I *am* the Lord your God, [l] which
have separated you from *other* people.
25 [m] Ye shall therefore put difference between
clean beasts and unclean, and between unclean
fowls and clean: [n] and ye shall not make
your souls abominable by beast, or by fowl,
or by any manner of living thing that [o] creepeth
on the ground, which I have separated from
you as unclean.
26 And ye shall be holy unto me: [p] for I the
Lord *am* holy, and [q] have severed you from
other people, that ye should be mine.
27 [r] A man also or woman that hath a familiar spirit, or that is a wizard, shall surely be
put to death: they shall stone them with
stones: [s] their blood *shall be* upon them.

[x] Chap. xviii. 9; Deut. xxvii. 22; see Gen. xx. 12.——[y] Chap. xviii. 19; see chap. xv. 24.——[z] Heb. *made naked.*——[a] Chap. xviii. 12, 13.——[b] Chap. xviii. 6.——[c] Chap. xviii. 14.——[d] Chap. xviii. 16.——[e] Heb. *a separation.*——[f] Chap. xviii. 26; xix. 37. [g] Chap. xviii. 25, 28.——[h] Chap. xviii. 3, 24, 30.——[i] Chap. xviii. 27; Deut. ix. 5.

[k] Exod. iii. 17; vi. 8.——[l] Ver. 26; Exod. xix. 5; xxxiii. 16; Deut. vii. 6; xiv. 2; 1 Kings viii. 53.——[m] Chap. xi. 47; Deut. xiv. 4——[n] Chap. xi. 43.——[o] Or, *moveth.*——[p] Ver. 7; chap. xix. 2; 1 Pet. i. 16.——[q] Ver. 24; Tit. ii. 14.——[r] Chap. xix. 31; Exod. xxii. 18; Deut. xviii. 10, 11; 1 Sam. xxviii. 7, 8. [s] Ver. 9.

historians in the world, Herodotus, to say that this was a crime not unknown in Egypt; yea, that a case of this nature actually took place while he was there. *Εγενετο δ' εν τῳ νομῳ τουτῳ επ' εμευ τουτο το τερας, Γυναικι Τραγος εμισγετο αναφανδον. Τουτο ες επιδειξιν ανθρωπων απικετο.*—Herod. in Euterp., p. 108. Edit. Gale, Lond. 1679. "In this district, within my own recollection, this portentous business took place: a goat coupled so publicly with a woman that every person knew it, &c." After this, need we wonder that God should have made laws of this nature, when it appears these abominations were not only practised among the Egyptians, but were parts of a superstitious religious system? This one observation will account for many of those strange prohibitions which we find in the Mosaic law; others, the reasons of which are not so plain, we should see the propriety of equally, had we ampler historic records of the customs that existed in that country.

Verse 22. *The land, whither I bring you to dwell therein, spue you not out.*] See this energetic prosopopœia explained in the note on chap. xviii. 25. From this we learn that the cup of the iniquities of the Canaanitish nations was full; and that, consistently with Divine justice, they could be no longer spared.

Verse 24. *A land that floweth with milk and honey*] See this explained Exod. iii. 8.

Verse 25. *Between clean beasts and unclean*] See the notes on chap. xi.

Verse 27. *A familiar spirit*] A spirit or demon, which, by magical rites, is supposed to be bound to appear at the call of his employer. See the notes on Gen. xli. 8; Exod. vii. 11, 22, 25; and chap xix. 31.

From the accounts we have of the abominations both of Egypt and Canaan, we may blush for human nature; for wherever it is without cultivation, and without the revelation of God, it is every thing that is vile in *principle* and detestable in *practice*. Nor would any part of the habitable globe materially differ from Egypt and Canaan, had they not that rule of righteousness, the revealed law of God, and had not *life* and *immortality* been brought to light by the Gospel among them. From these accounts, for which we could easily find parallels in ancient Greece and Italy, we may see the absolute need of a Divine revelation, without which man, even in his best estate, differs little from the *brute*.

CHAPTER XXI.

The priests shall not mourn for the dead, except for near relatives, such as mother, father, son, daughter, *and* sister *if a virgin,* 1–4. *They shall not shave their heads nor beards, nor make any cuttings in the flesh, because they are holy unto God,* 5, 6. *A priest shall not marry a woman who is a whore, profane, or divorced from her husband,* 7, 8. *Of the priest's daughter who profanes herself,* 9. *The high priest shall not uncover his head, or rend his clothes,* 10; *nor go in unto a dead body,* 11; *nor go out of the sanctuary,* 12. *Of his marriage and offspring,* 13–15. *No person shall be made a priest that has any blemish, nor shall any person with any of the blemishes mentioned here be permitted to officiate in the worship of God,* 16–24.

A. M. 2514.
B. C. 1490.
An. Exod. Isr. 2.
Abib or Nisan.

AND the Lord said unto Moses, Speak unto the priests the sons of Aaron, and say unto them, [a] There shall none be defiled for the dead among his people:

2 But for his kin, that is near unto him, *that is,* for his mother, and for his father, and for his son, and for his daughter, and for his brother,

3 And for his sister a virgin, that is nigh unto him, which hath had no husband; for her may he be defiled.

4 *But* [b] he shall not defile himself, *being* a chief man among his people, to profane himself.

5 [c] They shall not make baldness upon their head, neither shall they shave off the corner of their beard, nor make any cuttings in their flesh.

6 They shall be holy unto their God, and [d] not profane the name of their God: for the offerings of the Lord made by fire, *and* [e] the bread of their God, they do offer; therefore they shall be holy.

A. M. 2514.
B. C. 1490.
An. Exod. Isr. 2.
Abib or Nisan.

7 [f] They shall not take a wife *that is* a whore, or profane; neither shall they take a woman [g] put away from her husband: for he *is* holy unto his God.

8 Thou shalt sanctify him therefore; for he offereth the bread of thy God: he shall be holy unto thee: [h] for I the Lord, which sanctify you, *am* holy.

9 [i] And the daughter of any priest, if she profane herself by playing the whore, she profaneth her father: she shall be burnt with fire.

10 [k] And *he that is* the high priest among his brethren, upon whose head the anointing oil was poured, and [l] that is consecrated to

[a] Chap. x. 6, 7; Ezek. xliv. 25; 1 Thess. iv. 13, 14, 15. [b] Or, *being a husband among his people, he shall not defile himself* for his wife, &c.; see Ezek. xxiv. 16, 17.——[c] Chap. xix. 27, 28; Deut. xiv. 1; Ezek. xliv. 20.

[d] Chap. xviii. 21; xix. 12.——[e] See chap. iii. 11.——[f] Ezek. xliv. 22.——[g] See Deut. xxiv. 1, 2.——[h] Chap. xx. 7, 8.——[i] Gen. xxxviii. 24.——[k] Exod. xxix. 29, 30; chap. viii. 12; xvi. 32; Num. xxxv. 25.——[l] Exod. xxviii. 2; chap. xvi. 32.

NOTES ON CHAP. XXI.

Verse 1. *There shall none be defiled for the dead*] No priest shall assist in laying out a dead body, or preparing it for interment. Any contact with the dead was supposed to be of a defiling nature, probably because putrefaction had then taken place; and animal putrefaction was ever held in detestation by all men.

Verse 4. *A chief man among his people*] The word בעל *baal* signifies a *master, chief, husband,* &c., and is as variously translated here. 1. He being a *chief* among the people, it would be improper to see him in such a state of humiliation as mourning for the dead necessarily implies. 2. Though a *husband* he shall not defile himself even for the death of a wife, because the anointing of his God is upon him. But the first sense appears to be the best.

Verse 5. *They shall not make baldness*] See the note on chap. xix. 27. It is supposed that these things were particularly prohibited, because used superstitiously by the Egyptian priests, who, according to *Herodotus,* shaved the whole body every third day, that there might be no uncleanness about them when they ministered in their temples. This appears to have been a general custom among the heathen. In the book of Baruch, chap. vi. 31, the priests of Babylon are represented *sitting in their temples, with their clothes rent, and their heads and beards shaven, and having nothing upon their heads.* Every person knows the *tonsure* of the Catholic priests. Should not this be avoided as an approach to a heathenish custom?

Verse 7. That is *a whore*] A prostitute, though even reclaimed.

Profane] A heathen, or one who is not a cordial believer in the true God.

Put away from her husband] Because this very circumstance might lead to suspicion that the priest and the divorced woman might have been improperly connected before.

Verse 9. *She shall be burnt with fire.*] Probably not burnt alive, but strangled first, and then burnt afterward. Though it is barely possible that some kind of *branding* may be intended.

Verse 10. He that is *the high priest*] This is the first place where this title is introduced; the title is very emphatic, הכהן הגדול *haccohen haggadol, that priest, the great one.* For the meaning of כהן *cohen,*

A. M. 2514.
B. C. 1490.
An. Exod. Isr. 2.
Abib or Nisan.

put on the garments, [m] shall not
uncover his head, nor rend his
clothes;
11 Neither shall he [n] go in to any dead
body, nor defile himself for his father, or for
his mother;
12 [o] Neither shall he go out of the sanctuary,
nor profane the sanctuary of his God; for
[p] the crown of the anointing oil of his God *is*
upon him: I *am* the LORD.
13 And [q] he shall take a wife in her virginity.
14 A widow, or a divorced woman, or profane, *or* a harlot, these shall he not take:
but he shall take a virgin of his own people
to wife.
15 Neither shall he profane his seed among
his people: for [r] I the LORD do sanctify him.
16 And the LORD spake unto
Moses, saying,
17 Speak unto Aaron, saying,
Whosoever *he be* of thy seed in their generations that hath *any* blemish, let him not [s] approach to offer the [t] bread of his God.
18 For whatsoever man *he be* that hath a
blemish, he shall not approach: a blind man,
or a lame, or he that hath a flat nose, or any
thing [u] superfluous;
19 Or a man that is broken-footed, or broken-
handed;
20 Or crook-backed, or [v] a dwarf, or that hath
a blemish in his eye, or be scurvy, or scabbed,
or [w] hath his stones broken:
21 No man that hath a blemish, of the seed
of Aaron the priest, shall come nigh to [x] offer

[m] Chap. x. 6.—[n] Num. xix. 14; see ver. 1, 2.—[o] Chap. x. 7.—[p] Exod. xxviii. 36; chap. viii. 9, 12, 30.—[q] Ver. 7; Ezek. xliv. 22.—[r] Ver. 8.

[s] Chap. x. 3; Num. xvi. 5; Psa. lxiv. 4.—[t] Or, *food;* chap. iii. 11.—[u] Chap. xxii. 23.—[v] Or, *too slender.*—[w] Deut. xxiii. 1.—[x] Ver. 6.

see the note on Gen. xiv. 18. As the chief or high priest was a representative of our blessed Lord, therefore *he* was required to be especially holy; and he is represented as God's *king* among the people.

Verse 12. *The crown of the anointing oil—is upon him*] By his *office* the priest represented Christ in his *sacrificial* character; by his *anointing*, the *prophetic* influence; and by the crown, the *regal dignity* of our Lord.

Verse 13. *He shall take a wife in her virginity.*] בתוליה *bethuleyha.* This is a full proof that בתולה *bethulah* is the proper Hebrew term for a *virgin;* from the emphatic root בתל *bathal*, to *separate;* because such a person was in her *separate* state, and had never been in any way *united* to man.

Verse 17. *Whosoever—hath* any *blemish, let him not approach to offer the bread of his God.*] Never was a wiser, a more rational, and a more expedient law enacted relative to sacred matters. The man who ministers in holy things, who professes to be the interpreter of the will of God, should have nothing in his *person* nor in his *manner* which cannot contribute to render him respectable in the eyes of those to whom he ministers. If, on the contrary, he has any *personal defect*, any thing that may render him contemptible or despicable, his usefulness will be greatly injured, if not entirely prevented. If however a man have received any damage in the work of God, by persecution or otherwise, his scars are honourable, and will add to his respectability. But if he be received into the ministry with any of the blemishes specified here, he never will and never can have that respect which is essentially necessary to secure his usefulness. Let no man say this is a part of the *Mosaic law*, and we are not bound by it. It is an eternal law, founded on *reason, propriety, common sense*, and *absolute necessity.* The priest, the prophet, the Christian minister, is the representative of *Jesus Christ;* let nothing in his *person, carriage*, or *doctrine*, be unworthy of the personage he represents. A *deformed person*, though consummate in diplomatic wisdom, would never be employed as an ambassador by any enlightened court, if any fit person, unblemished, could possibly be procured.

Verse 18. *A blind man*] That is, in *one* eye; for he that was utterly blind could not possibly be employed in such a service. A *flat nose*, like that of an *ape;* so the best versions. *Any thing superfluous*, such as six fingers, six toes, &c.

Verse 19. *Broken-footed, or broken-handed*] Club-footed, bandy-legged, &c.; or having the ankle, wrist, or fingers dislocated.

Verse 20. *Crook-backed*] Hunch-backed or gibbous. A *dwarf*, דק *dak*, a person too *short* or too *thin*, so as to be either particularly observable, or ridiculous in his appearance.

A blemish in his eye] A protuberance on the eye, observable spots or suffusions.

Scurvy, or scabbed] A bad habit of body, evidenced by scorbutic or scrofulous affections.

Stones broken] Is ruptured; an infirmity which would render him incapable of fulfilling the duties of his office, which might be often very fatiguing.

In the above list of blemishes we meet with some that might render the priest *contemptible* in the eyes of men, and be the means of leading them, not only to despise the man, but to despise the *ministry* itself; and we meet with others that would be a very great *impediment* in the discharge of his ministerial duties, and therefore any person thus blemished is by this law precluded from the ministry.

The blemishes here enumerated have been considered by some in an allegorical point of view, as if only referring to the necessity of moral purity; but although *holiness of heart* and *righteousness of life* be essentially necessary in a minister of God, yet an absence of the defects mentioned above is, I fully believe, what God intends here, and for the reasons too which have been already advanced. It must however be

A. M. 2514. B. C. 1490. An. Exod. Isr. 2. Abib or Nisan.

the offerings of the LORD made by fire: he hath a blemish; he shall not come nigh to offer the bread of his God.

22 He shall eat the bread of his God, *both* of the [y] most holy, and of the [z] holy.

23 Only he shall not go in unto the veil, nor come nigh unto the altar, because he hath a blemish; that [a] he profane not my sanctuaries: for I the LORD do sanctify them.

24 [b] And Moses told *it* unto Aaron, and to his sons, and unto all the children of Israel.

[y] Chap. ii. 3, 10; vi. 17, 29; vii. 1; xxiv. 9; Num. xviii. 9. — [z] Chap. xxii. 10, 11, 12; Num. xviii. 19.

[a] Ver. 12, chap. xv. 21; Ezek. xliv. 9-14. — [b] Mal. ii. 1 7; Col. iv. 17; 2 Tim. ii. 2.

granted, that there have been some eminent divines who have been deformed; and some with certain blemishes have been employed in the Christian ministry, and have been useful. The Mosaic rule, however, will admit of but few exceptions, when even examined according to the more extended interpretation of the Christian system.

"The Hebrews say there are in all 120 blemishes which disable the priest—eight in the *head*, two in the *neck*, nine in the *ears*, five in the *brows*, seven in the *eyelids*, nineteen in the *eyes*, nine in the *nose*, nine in the *mouth*, three in the *belly*, three in the *back*, seven in the *hands*, sixteen in the *secrets*, eight in *any part* of the *body*, eight in the *skin*, and seven in the *strength* and in the *breath*."—Ainsworth. In ancient times, even among heathens, persons of the most respectable appearance were appointed to the priesthood; and the emperor, both among the ancient Greeks and Romans, was both *king* and *priest*. It is reported of *Metellus*, that, having lost an eye in endeavouring to save the *Palladium* from the flames, when the temple of Vesta was on fire, he was denied the priesthood, though he had rendered such an excellent piece of service to the public; yet the public opinion was that a priest who was defective in any member was to be avoided as *ominous*.—See Dodd. "At Elis, in Greece, the judges chose the finest looking man to carry the sacred *vessels* of the deity; he that was next to him in beauty and elegance led the *ox;* and the third in personal beauty, &c., carried the *garlands, ribbons, wine,* and the other matters used for the sacrifice."—*Athen.* Deipnosoph., l. xiii., c. 2.

Formerly the Church of England was very cautious in admitting to her ministry those who had gross personal defects; but now we find the *hump-backed*, the *jolt-headed, bandy-legged, club-footed, one-eyed, &c.,* priests even of her *high* places. Why do our prelates ordain such?

Verse 23. *He shall not go in unto the veil*] The priest with a blemish was not permitted to enter into the holy of holies, nor to burn incense, nor to offer the shew-bread, nor to light the golden candlestick, &c. In short, he was not permitted to perform any essential function of the priesthood.

1. THE great perfection required in the Jewish high priest was intended principally to point out the perfection of that priesthood of which the Jewish was only the type. And yet, as the apostle assures us, that law made nothing perfect, but pointed out that most perfect priesthood and sacrifice by which we draw near to God.

2. As none who had a blemish could enter into the holy of holies, and this holy of holies was a type of the kingdom of God, so nothing that is defiled can enter into heaven; for he gave himself for his Church that he might purify it to himself, and present it at last before the presence of the Divine glory *having neither spot nor wrinkle, nor any such thing,* Eph. v. 27; a passage which evidently refers to the directions in the preceding verse. Reader, art thou become a *king* and *priest* unto God and the Lamb? and hast thou obtained, or art thou earnestly seeking, that holiness without which thou canst not see the kingdom of heaven?

CHAPTER XXII.

Of the uncleanness of the priests, by which they were prevented from ministering in holy things, 1–5. *How they should be cleansed,* 6, 7. *The priest must not eat of any animal that had died of itself, or was torn by wild beasts, but must keep God's ordinances,* 8, 9. *No stranger, sojourner, nor hired servant shall eat of the holy things,* 10. *A servant bought with money may eat of them,* 11. *Who of the priest's family may not eat of them,* 12, 13. *Of improper persons who partake of the holy things unknowingly,* 14–16. *Freewill-offerings, and sacrifices in general, must be without blemish,* 17–25. *The age at which different animals were to be offered to God,* 26, 27. *No animal and its young shall be offered on the same day,* 28. *How the sacrifice of thanksgiving was to be offered,* 29, 30. *All God's testimonies to be observed, and the reason,* 31–33.

A. M. 2514.
B. C. 1490.
An. Exod. Isr. 2.
Abib or Nisan.

AND the LORD spake unto
Moses, saying,
2 Speak unto Aaron and to his
sons, that they [a] separate themselves from the
holy things of the children of Israel, and that
they [b] profane not my holy name *in those things*
which they [c] hallow unto me: I *am* the LORD.
3 Say unto them, Whosoever *he be* of all your
seed, among your generations, that goeth unto
the holy things which the children of Israel
hallow unto the LORD, [d] having his uncleanness upon him, that soul shall be cut off from
my presence: I *am* the LORD.
4 What man soever of the seed of Aaron *is*
a leper, or hath [e] a [f] running issue; he shall
not eat of the holy things [g] until he be clean.
And [h] whoso toucheth any thing *that is* unclean
by the dead, or [i] a man whose seed goeth
from him;
5 Or [k] whosoever toucheth any creeping
thing, whereby he may be made unclean, or
[l] a man of whom he may take uncleanness,
whatsoever uncleanness he hath;
6 The soul which hath touched any such
shall be unclean until even, and shall not eat
of the holy things, unless he
[m] wash his flesh with water.
7 And when the sun is down,
he shall be clean, and shall afterward eat of
the holy things; because [n] it *is* his food.
8 [o] That which dieth of itself, or is torn *with
beasts*, he shall not eat to defile himself therewith: I *am* the LORD.
9 They shall therefore keep mine ordinance,
[p] lest they bear sin for it, and die therefore, if
they profane it: I the LORD do sanctify them.
10 [q] There shall no stranger eat *of* the holy
thing: a sojourner of the priest, or a hired
servant, shall not eat *of* the holy thing.
11 But if the priest buy *any* soul [r] with his
money, he shall eat of it, and he that is born
in his house; [s] they shall eat of his meat.
12 If the priest's daughter also be *married*
unto [t] a stranger, she may not eat of an offering of the holy things.
13 But if the priest's daughter be a widow,
or divorced, and have no child, and is [u] returned unto her father's house, [v] as in her
youth, she shall eat of her father's meat: but
there shall no stranger eat thereof.

A. M. 2514.
B. C. 1490.
An. Exod. Isr. 2.
Abib or Nisan.

---

[a] Num. vi. 3.——[b] Chap. xviii. 21.——[c] Exod. xxviii. 38; Num. xviii. 32; Deut. xv. 19.——[d] Chap. vii. 20.——[e] Chap. xv. 2.——[f] Heb. *running of the reins.*——[g] Chap. xiv. 2; xv. 13. [h] Num. xix. 11, 22.——[i] Chap. xv. 16.——[k] Chap. xi. 24, 43, 44. [l] Chap. xv. 7, 19.——[m] Chap. xv. 5; Heb. x. 22.——[n] Chap. xxi. 22; Num. xviii. 11, 13.——[o] Exod. xxii. 31; chap. xvii. 15; Ezek. xliv. 31.——[p] Exod. xxviii. 43; Num. xviii. 22, 32. [q] See 1 Sam. xxi. 6.——[r] Heb. *with the purchase of his money.* [s] Num. xviii. 11, 13.——[t] Heb. *a man a stranger.*——[u] Gen. xxxviii. 11.——[v] Chap. x. 14; Num. xviii. 11, 19.

NOTES ON CHAP. XXII.

Verse 2. *Speak unto Aaron and to his sons, that they separate themselves*] The same subject is continued in this chapter as in the preceding, with this addition, that besides the perfection of the priests, it was indispensably necessary that the sacrifices also should be *perfect*. In the service of God, according to the law, neither an imperfect *offering* nor an imperfect *offerer* could be admitted. What need then of a *mediator* between a *holy* God and *sinful* men! And can we expect that any of our services, however *sincere* and *well-intentioned*, can be accepted, unless offered on that living Altar that sanctifies the gift!

Verse 4. Is *a leper, or hath a running issue*] See the case of the leper treated at large in the notes on chapters xiii. and xiv.; and for other *uncleannesses*, see the notes on chap. xv.

Verse 10. *There shall no stranger eat* of *the holy thing*] For the meaning of the word *stranger*, see the note on Exod. xii. 43. The Jews suppose that *stranger* here means one who has had his ear pierced, (see the note on Exod. xxi. 6,) and that *sojourner* means a servant who is to go free on the Sabbatical year. Neither of these was permitted to eat of the holy things, because they were not properly members of the priest's family, and might go out and defile themselves even with the abominations of the heathen; but the servant or slave that was bought with money, ver. 10, might eat of these things, because he was the property of the master for ever.

We see that it was lawful, under the Mosaic economy, to have *slaves* under certain restrictions; but these were taken from among the heathen, and instructed in the true religion: hence we find, as in the above case, that they were reckoned as a *part of the priest's own family*, and *treated as such*. They certainly had privileges which did not extend either to *sojourners* or to *hired* servants; therefore their situation was incomparably better than the situation of the slaves under different European governments, of whose souls their pitiless possessors in general take no care, while they themselves venture to profess the Christian religion, and quote the Mosaic law in vindication of their system of slavery. How preposterous is such conduct! and how intolerable!

Verse 13. *But if the priest's daughter be a widow—and is returned unto her father's house*] A widow in Bengal not unfrequently returns to her father's house on the death of her husband: the union betwixt her and her own family is never so dissolved as among European nations. Thousands of widows in Bengal, whose husbands die before the consummation of marriage, never leave their parents.—WARD.

A. M. 2514.
B. C. 1490.
An. Exod. Isr. 2.
Abib or Nisan.

14 [w] And if a man eat *of* the
holy thing unwittingly, then he
shall put the fifth *part* thereof
unto it, and shall give *it* unto the priest with
the holy thing.
15 And [x] they shall not profane the holy
things of the children of Israel, which they
offer unto the LORD;
16 Or [y] suffer them [z] to bear the iniquity of
trespass, when they eat their holy things: for
I the LORD do sanctify them.
17 And the LORD spake unto Moses, saying,
18 Speak unto Aaron, and to his sons, and
unto all the children of Israel, and say unto
them, [a] Whatsoever *he be* of the house of
Israel, or of the strangers in Israel, that will
offer his oblation for all his vows, and for all
his freewill-offerings, which they will offer
unto the LORD for a burnt-offering;
19 [b] *Ye shall offer*, at your own will, a male
without blemish of the beeves, of the sheep,
or of the goats.
20 [c] *But* whatsoever hath a blemish, *that*
shall ye not offer: for it shall not be acceptable for you.
21 And [d] whosoever offereth a sacrifice of
peace-offerings unto the LORD [e] to accomplish
his vow, or a freewill-offering in
beeves or [f] sheep, it shall be
perfect to be accepted; there
shall be no blemish therein.
22 [g] Blind, or broken, or maimed, or having
a wen, or scurvy, or scabbed, ye shall not offer
these unto the LORD, nor make [h] an offering
by fire of them upon the altar unto the LORD.
23 Either a bullock or a [i] lamb that hath
any thing [k] superfluous or lacking in his parts,
that mayest thou offer *for* a freewill-offering;
but for a vow it shall not be accepted.
24 Ye shall not offer unto the LORD that
which is bruised, or crushed, or broken, or
cut; neither shall ye make *any offering thereof*
in your land.
25 Neither [l] from a stranger's hand shall ye
offer [m] the bread of your God of any of these;
because their [n] corruption *is* in them, *and*
blemishes *be* in them; they shall not be accepted for you.
26 And the LORD spake unto Moses, saying,
27 [o] When a bullock, or a sheep, or a goat,
is brought forth, then it shall be seven days
under the dam; and from the eighth day and
thenceforth it shall be accepted for an offering
made by fire unto the LORD.

A. M. 2514
B. C. 1490
An. Exod. Isr. 2
Abib or Nisan.

[w] Chap. v. 15, 16.—[x] Num. xviii. 32.—[y] Or, *lade themselves with the iniquity of trespass in their eating.*—[z] Ver. 9.—[a] Chap. i. 2, 3, 10; Num. xv. 14.—[b] Chap. i. 3.—[c] Deut. xv. 21; xvii. 1; Mal. i. 8, 14; Eph. v. 27; Heb. ix. 14; 1 Pet. i. 19. [d] Chap. iii. 1, 6.

[e] Chap. vii. 16; Num. xv. 3, 8; Deut. xxiii. 21, 23; Psa. lxi. 8; lxv. 1; Eccles. v. 4, 5.—[f] Or, *goats.*—[g] Ver. 20; Mal. i. 8.—[h] Chap. i. 9, 13; iii. 3, 5.—[i] Or, *kid.*—[k] Chap. xxi. 18. [l] Num. xv. 15, 16.—[m] Chap. xxi. 6, 17.—[n] Mal. i. 14. [o] Exod. xxii. 30.

Verse 14. *Then he shall put the fifth* part *thereof unto it*] The holy thing of which he has unknowingly eaten shall be fairly valued, and to this value he shall add one *fifth* more, and give the whole to the priest.

Verse 20. *Whatsoever hath a blemish*] The same perfection is required in the sacrifice that was required in the priest; see on ver. 2, and the notes on the preceding chapter.

Verse 23. *That hath any thing superfluous or lacking*] The term שרוע *sarua* signifies any thing *extended* beyond the usual size, and the term קלוט *kalut* signifies any thing unusually *contracted;* and both mean any monstrosity, whether in *redundance* or *defect.* Such things, it seems, might be offered for a *freewill-offering*, because that was *not* prescribed by the law; God left it to a man's piety and gratitude to offer such additional gifts as he *could:* what the law required was indispensably necessary, because it pointed out the Gospel economy; but he that made a *vow* to offer such a sacrifice as the law had not required, could of course bring an *imperfect* offering. Some contend that the last clause of this verse should be thus read: *If thou offer it either for a freewill-offering, or for a vow, it shall not be accepted.* It was the opinion of the Jews, and it appears to be correct, that none of these imperfect animals were ever offered on the altar; but the person who made the freewill-offering of *such things as he had*, sold the animal, and gave its *price* for the support of the sanctuary.

Verse 24. *Bruised, or crushed, or broken, or cut*] That is, no bullock or lamb that is injured in any of the above ways, shall be offered unto the Lord.

Verse 25. *Their corruption* is *in them*] Viz., they are *bruised, crushed, broken*, &c.

Verse 27. *When a bullock—is brought forth*] This is a most unfortunate as well as absurd translation. The creature called an *ox* is a bull *castrated;* surely then a *bullock* was never yet *brought forth!* The original word שור *shor* signifies a bull, a bullock, or indeed any thing of the *neat* kind: here, even common sense required that it should be translated *calf;* and did I not hold myself sacredly bound to print the text of the *common version* with scrupulous exactness, I should translate the former clause of this verse thus, and so enter it into the text: *When a* CALF, *or a* LAMB, *or a* KID *is brought forth*, instead of, *When a bullock, a sheep, or a goat is brought forth*, the absurdity of which is glaring.

Seven days under the dam] In vindication of the

A. M. 2514. B. C. 1490. An. Exod. Isr. 2. Abib or Nisan.

28 And *whether it be* cow or
[p] ewe, ye shall not kill it [q] and
her young both in one day.
29 And when ye will [r] offer a sacrifice of
thanksgiving unto the LORD, offer *it* at your
own will.
30 On the same day it shall be eaten up;
ye shall leave [s] none of it until the morrow: I
am the LORD.
31 [t] Therefore shall ye keep
my commandments, and do them:
I *am* the LORD.
32 [u] Neither shall ye profane my holy name;
but [v] I will be hallowed among the children
of Israel: I *am* the LORD which [w] hal
low you,
33 [x] That brought you out of the land of
Egypt, to be your God: I *am* the LORD.

[p] Or, *she-goat.*——[q] Deut. xxii. 6.——[r] Chap. vii. 12; Psalm cvii. 22; cxvi. 17; Amos iv. 5.——[s] Chap. vii. 15.——[t] Chapter xix. 37; Num. xv. 40; Deut. iv. 40.——[u] Chap. xviii. 21.——[v] Chap. x. 3; Matt. vi. 9; Luke xi. 2.——[w] Chap. xx. 8.——[x] Exod. vi. 7; chap. xi. 45; xix. 36; xxv. 38; Num. xv. 41.

propriety of this precept it may be justly asserted, that the flesh of *very young* animals is comparatively innutritive, and that animal food is not sufficiently nourishing and wholesome till the animal has arrived at a certain growth, or acquired the perfection of its nature. There is something *brutish* in eating the young of *beast* or *fowl* before the *hair* and *hoofs* are perfect in the one, and the *feathers* and *claws* in the other. Before this period their flesh is not good for food. See the note on chap. ix. 1.

Verse 28. *Ye shall not kill it and her young—in one day.*] This precept was certainly intended to inculcate *mercy* and *tenderness* of heart; and so the Jews understood it. When it is necessary to take away the lives of innocent animals for the support of our own, we should do it in such a way as not to blunt our moral feelings; and deplore the necessity, while we feel an express gratitude to God for permission, to do it.

Verse 30. *Leave none of it until the morrow*] See the note on chap. vii. 18.

Verse 32. *Neither shall ye profane my holy name*] God's name is profaned or rendered common when we treat his commands as we often do those of our fellows, when they do not appear to have *self-interest* to recommend them. He therefore profanes God's holy name who does not both *implicitly believe* and *conscientiously obey* all his *words* and all his *precepts*.

I will be hallowed among the children of Israel] The words *children of Israel*, בני ישראל *beney Yishrael*, which so frequently occur, should be translated either *the descendants* or *posterity of Israel*, or *the people of Israel*. The word *children* has a tendency to beget a false notion, especially in the minds of young people, and lead them to think that *children*, in the proper sense of the word, i. e., *little ones*, are meant.

Verse 33. *Brought you out of the land of Egypt*] By such a series of miraculous interferences, *to be your God*—to save you from all *idolatry*, *false* and *superstitious worship*, teach you the right way, lead and support you in it, and preserve you to my eternal kingdom and glory. God, infinite in his own perfections, has no need of his creatures; but they need him; and, as a source of endless felicity, he opens himself to all his intelligent offspring.

CHAPTER XXIII.

The feasts of the Lord, 1, 2. *The* Sabbath, 3. *The* passover *and unleavened bread*, 4–8. *The feast of* first-fruits, 9–14. *The feast of* pentecost, 15–21. *Gleanings to be left for the poor*, 22. *The feast of* trumpets, 23–25. *The great day of* atonement, 26–32. *The feast of* tabernacles, 33–44.

A. M. 2514. B. C. 1490. An. Exod. Isr. 2. Abib or Nisan.

AND the LORD spake unto
Moses, saying,
2 Speak unto the children of
Israel, and say unto them, *Concerning* [a] the
feasts of the LORD, which ye shall [b] proclaim
to be holy convocations, *even*
these *are* my feasts.
3 [c] Six days shall work be
done: but the seventh day *is* the Sabbath
of rest, a holy convocation; ye shall do no

[a] Verse 4, 37.——[b] Exodus xxxii. 5; 2 Kings x. 20; Psa. lxxxi. 3.——[c] Exod. xx. 9; xxiii. 12; xxxi. 15; xxxiv. 21; chap. xix. 3; Deut. v. 13; Luke xiii. 14.

NOTES ON CHAP. XXIII.

Verse 2. *These* are *my feasts.*] The original word מוער *moad* is properly applied to any solemn anniversary, by which great and important ecclesiastical, political, or providential facts were recorded; see on Gen. i. 14. Anniversaries of this kind were observed in all nations; and some of them, in consequence of scrupulously regular observation, became *chronological epochs* of the greatest importance in history: the *Olympiads*, for example.

Verse 3. *The seventh day* is *the Sabbath*] This, because the first and greatest solemnity, is first mentioned. He who kept not this, in the most religious manner, was not capable of keeping any of the others. The religious observance of the Sabbath stands at the very threshold of all religion. See the note on Gen. ii. 3.

A. M. 2514.
B. C. 1490.
An. Exod. Isr. 2.
Abib or Nisan.

work *therein*: it *is* the Sabbath
of the LORD in all your dwellings.
4 [d] These *are* the feasts of the LORD, *even*
holy convocations, which ye shall proclaim in
their seasons.
5 [e] In the fourteenth *day* of the first month
at even *is* the LORD's passover.
6 And on the fifteenth day of the same month
is the feast of unleavened bread unto the LORD:
seven days ye must eat unleavened bread.
7 [f] In the first day ye shall have a holy convocation: ye shall do no servile work therein.
8 But ye shall offer an offering made by fire
unto the LORD seven days: in the seventh
day *is* a holy convocation: ye shall do no
servile work *therein*.
9 And the LORD spake unto Moses, saying,
10 Speak unto the children of Israel, and
say unto them, [g] When ye be come into the
land which I give unto you, and shall reap
the harvest thereof, then ye shall bring a
[h] sheaf [i] of [k] the first-fruits of your harvest
unto the priest:
11 And he shall [l] wave the sheaf before the
LORD, to be accepted for you: on the morrow
after the Sabbath the priest shall wave it.
12 And ye shall offer that day, when ye wave
the sheaf, a he-lamb without blemish, of the
first year, for a burnt-offering unto the LORD.
13 [m] And the meat-offering thereof *shall be*
two tenth deals of fine flour mingled with oil,
an offering made by fire unto the LORD *for* a
sweet savour: and the drink-offering thereof
shall be of wine, the fourth *part* of a hin.
14 And ye shall eat neither bread, nor parched
corn, nor green ears, until the selfsame day
that ye have brought an offering
unto your God: *it shall be* a
statute for ever throughout your
generations, in all your dwellings.
15 And [n] ye shall count unto you from the
morrow after the Sabbath, from the day that ye
brought the sheaf of the wave-offering; seven
Sabbaths shall be complete:
16 Even unto the morrow after the seventh
Sabbath shall ye number [o] fifty days; and ye
shall offer [p] a new meat-offering unto the
LORD.
17 Ye shall bring out of your habitations
two wave loaves of two tenth deals: they
shall be of fine flour; they shall be baken with
leaven; *they are* [q] the first-fruits unto the
LORD.
18 And ye shall offer with the bread seven
lambs without blemish of the first year, and
one young bullock, and two rams: they shall
be *for* a burnt-offering unto the LORD, with
their meat-offering, and their drink-offerings,
even an offering made by fire, of sweet savour
unto the LORD.
19 Then ye shall sacrifice [r] one kid of the
goats for a sin-offering, and two lambs of the
first year for a sacrifice of [s] peace-offerings.
20 And the priest shall wave them with the
bread of the first-fruits, *for* a wave-offering before the LORD, with the two lambs: [t] they
shall be holy to the LORD for the priest.
21 And ye shall proclaim on the selfsame
day, *that* it may be a holy convocation unto
you: ye shall do no servile work *therein*: *it
shall be* a statute for ever in all your dwellings
throughout your generations.
22 And [u] when ye reap the harvest of your

[d] Ver. 2, 37; Exod. xxiii. 14.——[e] Exod. xii. 6, 14, 18; xiii. 3, 10; xxiii. 15; xxxiv. 18; Num. ix. 2, 3; xxviii. 16, 17; Deut. xvi. 1–8; Josh. v. 10.——[f] Exod. xii. 16; Num. xxviii. 18, 25.——[g] Exod. xxiii. 16, 19; xxxiv. 22, 26; Num. xv. 2, 18; xxviii. 26; Deut. xvi. 9; Josh. iii. 15.——[h] Or, *handful*.——[i] Heb. *omer*.——[k] Rom. xi. 16; 1 Cor. xv. 20; James i. 18; Rev. xiv. 4.

[l] Exod. xxix. 24.——[m] Chap. ii. 14, 15, 16.——[n] Chap. xxv. 8; Exod. xxxiv. 22; Deut. xvi. 9.——[o] Acts ii. 1.——[p] Num. xxviii. 26.——[q] Exod. xxiii. 16, 19; xxii. 29; xxxiv. 22, 26; Num. xv. 17; xxviii. 26; Deut. xxvi. 1.——[r] Ch. iv. 23, 28; Num. xxviii. 30.——[s] Chapter iii. 1.——[t] Numbers xviii. 12; Deut. xviii. 4.——[u] Chap. xix. 9.

Verse 5. *The Lord's passover.*] See this largely explained in the notes on Exod. xii. 21–27.

Verse 11. *He shall wave the sheaf*] He shall move it to and fro before the people, and thereby call their attention to the work of Divine Providence, and excite their gratitude to God for *preserving to them the kindly fruits of the earth*. See the notes on Exod. xxix. 27, and chap. vii. at the end.

Verse 14. *Ye shall eat neither bread, nor parched corn, nor green ears*] It is right that God, the dispenser of every blessing, should be acknowledged as such, and the *first-fruits* of the field, &c., dedicated to him. Concerning the dedication of the *first-fruits*, see the note on Exod. xxii. 29. *Parched ears* of corn and *green ears, fried*, still constitute a part, and not a disagreeable one, of the food of the Arabs now resident in the Holy Land. See *Hasselquist*.

Verse 15. *Ye shall count unto you—seven Sabbaths*] That is, from the *sixteenth* of the *first* month to the *sixth* of the *third* month. These *seven weeks*, called here *Sabbaths*, were to be complete, i. e., the forty-nine days must be finished, and the next day, the fiftieth, is what, from the Septuagint, we call *pentecost*. See the note on Luke vi. 1.

Verse 22. *Neither shalt thou gather any gleaning*] See the note on chap. xix. 9.

A. M. 2514. B. C. 1490. An. Exod. Isr. 2. Abib or Nisan.

land, thou shalt not make clean riddance of the corners of thy field when thou reapest, [v] neither shalt thou gather any gleaning of thy harvest: thou shalt leave them unto the poor, and to the stranger: I *am* the LORD your God.

23 And the LORD spake unto Moses, saying,

24 Speak unto the children of Israel, saying, In the [w] seventh month, in the first *day* of the month, shall ye have a Sabbath, [x] a memorial of blowing of trumpets, a holy convocation.

25 Ye shall do no servile work *therein:* but ye shall offer an offering made by fire unto the LORD.

26 And the LORD spake unto Moses, saying,

27 [y] Also on the tenth *day* of this seventh month *there shall be* a day of atonement: it shall be a holy convocation unto you; and ye shall afflict your souls, and offer an offering made by fire unto the LORD.

28 And ye shall do no work in that same day: for it *is* a day of atonement, to make an atonement for you before the LORD your God.

29 For whatsoever soul *it be* that shall not be afflicted in that same day, [z] he shall be cut off from among his people.

30 And whatsoever soul *it be* that doeth any work in that same day, [a] the same soul will I destroy from among his people.

31 Ye shall do no manner of work: *it shall be* a statute for ever throughout your generations, in all your dwellings.

32 It *shall be* unto you a Sabbath of rest, and ye shall afflict your souls: in the ninth *day* of the month at even, from even unto even, shall ye [b] celebrate your Sabbath.

A. M. 2514. B. C. 1490. An. Exod. Isr. 2. Abib or Nisan.

33 And the LORD spake unto Moses, saying,

34 Speak unto the children of Israel, saying, [c] The fifteenth day of this seventh month *shall be* the feast of tabernacles, *for* seven days unto the LORD.

35 On the first day *shall be* a holy convocation: ye shall do no servile work *therein.*

36 Seven days ye shall offer an offering made by fire unto the LORD: [d] on the eighth day shall be a holy convocation unto you; and ye shall offer an offering made by fire unto the LORD: it *is* [e] a solemn assembly; [f] *and* ye shall do no servile work *therein.*

37 [g] These *are* the feasts of the LORD, which ye shall proclaim *to be* holy convocations, to offer an offering made by fire unto the LORD, a burnt-offering, and a meat-offering, a sacrifice, and drink-offerings, every thing upon his day:

38 [h] Beside the Sabbaths of the LORD, and beside your gifts, and beside all your vows, and beside all your freewill-offerings, which ye give unto the LORD.

39 Also in the fifteenth day of the seventh month, when ye have [i] gathered in the fruit of the land, ye shall keep a feast unto the LORD seven days: on the first day *shall be* a Sabbath, and on the eighth day *shall be* a Sabbath.

[v] Deut. xxiv. 19.——[w] Num. xxix. 1.——[x] Chap. xxv. 9. [y] Chap. xvi. 30; Num. xxix. 7.——[z] Gen. xvii. 14.——[a] Chap. xx. 3, 5, 6.——[b] Heb. *rest.*——[c] Exod. xxiii. 16; Num. xxix. 12; Deut. xvi. 13; Ezra iii. 4; Neh. viii. 14; Zech. xiv. 16; 1 Esd. v. 51; John vii. 2.——[d] Num. xxix. 35; Neh. viii. 18; John vii. 37.——[e] Heb. day of *restraint.*——[f] Deut. xvi. 8; 2 Chron. vii. 9; Neh. viii. 18; Joel i. 14; ii. 15.——[g] Ver. 2, 4.——[h] Num. xxix. 39.——[i] Exod. xxiii. 16; Deut. xvi. 13.

Verse 24. *A memorial of blowing of trumpets*] This is generally called *the feast of trumpets;* and as it took place on the *first day* of the *seventh month, Tisri,* which answers to *September,* which month was the *commencement* of what was called the *civil year,* the feast probably had no other design than to celebrate the commencement of that year, if indeed such a distinction obtained among the *ancient* Jews. See the note on Exod. xii. 2. Some think *creation* began at this time.

Verse 28. *A day of atonement*] See the note on chapter xvi. 3, &c., where this subject is largely explained.

Verse 34. *The feast of tabernacles*] In this solemnity the people left their houses, and dwelt in *booths* or tents made of the branches of *goodly trees* and *thick trees,* (of what kind the text does not specify,) together with *palm-trees* and *willows of the brook,* ver. 40. And in these they dwelt *seven days,* in commemoration of their forty years' sojourning and dwelling in *tents* in the wilderness while destitute of any fixed habitations. In imitation of this feast among the people of God, the Gentiles had their *feasts of tents.* Plutarch speaks particularly of feasts of this kind in honour of Bacchus, and thinks from the custom of the Jews in celebrating the feast of tabernacles, that they worshipped the god Bacchus, "because he had a feast exactly of the same kind called the *feast of tabernacles,* Σκηνη, which they celebrated in the time of vintage, bringing tables out into the open air furnished with all kinds of fruit, and sitting under tents made of vine branches and ivy."—PLUT. *Symp.,* lib. iv., Q. 6. According to Ovid the feast of *Anna Perenna* was celebrated much in the same way. Some remained in the open air, others formed to themselves *tents* and *booths made of branches of trees,* over which they spread garments, and kept the festival with great rejoicings.

a

A. M. 2514.
B. C. 1490.
An. Exod. Isr. 2.
Abib or Nisan.

40 And ᵏ ye shall take you on the first day the ˡ boughs of goodly trees, branches of palm-trees, and the houghs of thick trees, and willows of the brook; ᵐ and ye shall rejoice before the LORD your God seven days.

41 ⁿ And ye shall keep it a feast unto the LORD seven days in the year. *It shall be a statute for ever in your generations:* ye shall celebrate it in the seventh month.

42 ᵒ Ye shall dwell in booths seven days; all that are Israelites born shall dwell in booths:

A. M. 2514.
B. C. 1490.
An. Exod. Isr. 2.
Abib or Nisan.

43 ᵖ That your generations may know that I made the children of Israel to dwell in booths, when I brought them out of the land of Egypt: I *am* the LORD your God.

44 And Moses ᑫ declared unto the children of Israel the feasts of the LORD.

ᵏ Neh. viii. 15.——ˡ Heb. *fruit.*——ᵐ Deut. xvi. 14, 15.
ⁿ Num. xxix. 12; Neh. viii. 18.

ᵒ Neh. viii. 14, 15, 16.——ᵖ Deut. xxxi. 13; Psa. lxxviii. 5, 6.
ᑫ Ver. 2.

"Sub Jove pars durat ; pauci tentoria ponunt ;
 Sunt, quibus e ramis frondea facta casa est.
Pars sibi pro rigidis calamos statuere columnis ;
 Desuper extentas imposuere togas."
 Ovid, Fast., lib. iii.

Concerning this feast of tabernacles, see the note on John vii. 37, 38 ; and for the various feasts among the Jews, see the note on Exod. xxiii. 14.

Verse 40. *Boughs of goodly trees*] The Jews and many critics imagine the *citron-tree* to be intended, and by *boughs of thick trees* the myrtle.

Verse 43. *That your generations may know, &c.*] By the institution of this feast God had two great objects in view : 1. To perpetuate the wonderful display of his providence and grace in bringing them out

of Egypt, and in preserving them in the wilderness. 2. To excite and maintain in them a spirit of gratitude and obedience, by leading them to consider deeply the greatness of the favours which they had received from his most merciful hands.

SIGNAL displays of the mercy, kindness, and providential care of God should be particularly remembered. When we recollect that we deserve nothing at his hands, and that the debt of gratitude is all the debt we can pay, in it we should be cheerful, fervent, and frequent. An ungrateful heart is an unfeeling, unloving, unbelieving, and disobedient heart. Reader, pray to God that he may deliver thee from its influence and its curse.

CHAPTER XXIV.

Pure olive oil must be provided for the lamps, 1, 2. Aaron is to take care that the lamps be lighted from evening to morning continually, 3, 4. How the shew-bread is to be made and ordered, 5–8. Aaron and his sons shall eat this bread in the holy place, 9. Of the son of Shelomith, an Israelitish woman, who blasphemed the name, 10, 11. He is imprisoned till the mind of the Lord should be known, 12. He is commanded to be stoned to death, 13, 14. The ordinance concerning cursing and blaspheming the Lord, 15, 16. The law against murder, 17. The lex talionis, or law of like for like, repeated, 18–21. This law to be equally binding both on themselves and on strangers, 22. The blasphemer is stoned, 23.

A. M. 2514.
B. C. 1490.
An. Exod. Isr. 2.
Abib or Nisan.

AND the LORD spake unto Moses, saying,

2 ᵃ Command the children of Israel, that they bring unto thee pure oil olive beaten for the light, ᵇ to cause the lamps to burn continually.

3 Without the veil of the testimony, in the tabernacle of the congregation, shall Aaron order it from the evening unto the morning, before the LORD continually : *it shall be a* statute for ever in your generations.

4 He shall order the lamps upon ᶜ the pure candlestick, before the LORD continually.

A. M. 2514.
B. C. 1490.
An. Exod. Isr. 2.
Abib or Nisan.

5 And thou shalt take fine flour, and bake twelve ᵈ cakes thereof : two tenth deals shall be in one cake.

6 And thou shalt set them in two rows, six on a row, ᵉ upon the pure table before the LORD.

7 And thou shalt put pure frankincense upon *each* row, that it may be on the bread for a

ᵃ Exod. xxvii. 20, 21.——ᵇ Heb. *to cause to ascend.*——ᶜ Exod. xxxi. 8; xxxix. 37.

ᵈ Exod. xxv. 30.——ᵉ 1 Kings vii. 48; 2 Chron. iv. 19; xiii. 11: Heb. ix. 2.

NOTES ON CHAP. XXIV.

Verse 2. *Pure oil olive*] See every thing relative to this ordinance explained on Exod. xxvii. 20, 21.

Verse 5. *Bake twelve cakes*] See the whole account

of the *shew-bread* in the notes on Exod. xxv. 30 ; and relative to the *table* on which they stood, the *golden candlestick* and *silver trumpets* carried in triumph to Rome, see the note on Exod. xxv. 31.

A. M. 2514.
B. C. 1490.
An. Exod. Isr. 2.
Abib or Nisan.

memorial, *even* an offering made
by fire unto the LORD.
8 [f] Every Sabbath he shall set
it in order before the LORD continually, *being*
taken from the children of Israel by an everlasting covenant.
9 And [g] it shall be Aaron's and his sons';
[h] and they shall eat it in the holy place: for
it *is* most holy unto him, of the offerings of
the LORD made by fire by a perpetual statute.
10 And the son of an Israelitish woman,
whose father *was* an Egyptian, went out among
the children of Israel: and this son of the
Israelitish *woman* and a man of Israel strove
together in the camp;
11 And the Israelitish woman's
son [i] blasphemed the name *of the*
LORD, and [k] cursed. And they
[l] brought him unto Moses: (and his mother's
name *was* Shelomith, the daughter of Dibri,
of the tribe of Dan:)
12 And they [m] put him in ward, [n] that [o] the
mind of the LORD might be showed them.
13 And the LORD spake unto Moses,
saying,
14 Bring forth him that hath cursed without
the camp; and let all that heard *him* [p] lay
their hands upon his head, and let all the con
gregation stone him.
15 And thou shalt speak unto the children

A. M. 2514.
B. C. 1490.
An. Exod. Isr. 2.
Abib or Nisan.

[f] Num. iv. 7; 1 Chron. ix. 32; 2 Chron. ii. 4.—[g] 1 Samuel xxi. 6; Matt. xii. 4; Mark ii. 26; Luke vi. 4.—[h] Exod. xxix. 33; chap. viii. 3; xxi. 22.—[i] Ver. 16.—[k] Job i. 5, 11, 22; ii. 5, 9, 10; Isa. viii. 21.

[l] Exod. xviii. 22, 26.—[m] Num. xv. 34.—[n] Heb. *to expound unto them according to the mouth of the LORD.*—[o] Exodus xviii. 15, 16; Numbers xxvii. 5; xxxvi. 5, 6.—[p] Deut. xiii. 9; xvii. 7.

Verse 10. *The son of an Israelitish woman, whose father* was *an Egyptian, &c.*] This is a very obscure account, and is encumbered with many difficulties. 1. It seems strange that a person proceeding from such an illegal mixture should have been *incorporated* with the Israelites. 2. What the *cause* of the strife between this mongrel person and the Israelitish man was is not even hinted at. The rabbins, it is true, supply in their way this deficiency; they say he was the son of the Egyptian whom Moses slew, and that attempting to pitch his tent among those of the *tribe of Dan*, to which he belonged by his mother's side, ver. 11, he was prevented by a person of that tribe as having no right to a station among them who were true Israelites both by father and mother. In consequence of this they say he blasphemed the name of the Lord. But, 3 The sacred text does not tell us *what name* he blasphemed; it is simply said ויקב את השם *vaiyikkob eth hashshem, he pierced through*, distinguished, explained, or *expressed the name*. (See below, article 10.) As the Jews hold it *impious* to pronounce the name יהוה *Yehovah*, they always put either אדני *Adonai, Lord*, or השם *hashshem*, THE NAME, in the place of it; but in this sense *hashshem* was never used prior to the days of rabbinical superstition, and therefore it cannot be put here for the word *Jehovah*. 4. Blaspheming the name of the Lord is mentioned in ver. 16, and there the proper Hebrew term is used שם יהוה *shem Yehovah*, and not the rabbinical השם *hashshem*, as in ver. 11. 5. Of all the manuscripts collated both by Kennicott and De Rossi, not one, either of the *Hebrew* or *Samaritan*, has the word *Jehovah* in this place. 6. Not one of the ancient VERSIONS, Targum of *Onkelos*, *Hebræo-Samaritan*, *Samaritan version*, *Syriac*, *Arabic*, *Septuagint*, or *Vulgate* Latin, has even attempted to supply the sacred name. 7. *Houbigant* supposes that the Egypto-Israelitish man did not use the name of the true God at all, but had been swearing by one of his country gods; and if this was the case the mention of the name of a *strange god* in the camp of Israel would constitute a very high crime, and certainly expose to the punishment mentioned in ver. 14. 8. Probably the word השם *hashshem* was the proper name of some Egyptian deity. 9. The fifteenth verse seems to countenance the supposition that the god whose name was produced on this occasion was not the true God, for it is there said, *whosoever curseth his god*, אלהיו *elohaiv, shall bear his sin*—shall have the punishment due to him as an *idolater*; but *he that blasphemeth the name* of the LORD, שם יהוה *shem Yehovah, shall surely be put to death—when he blasphemeth the name* (שם *shem*) *he shall die*, ver. 16. 10. The verb נקב *nakab*, which we translate *blaspheme*, signifies to pierce, bore, make hollow; also to EXPRESS or DISTINGUISH by NAME; see Isa. lxii. 2; Num. i. 17; 1 Chron. xii. 31; xvi. 41; xxviii. 15; or, as the Persian translator has it, شرح كرد مر ان نام *sherah kerd, mir an nam, he expounded or interpreted the name*. Hence all that we term *blasphemy* here may only signify the *particularizing some false god*, i. e., *naming* him by his name, or imploring his aid as a helper, and when spoken of the true God it may signify using that sacred name as the idolaters did the names of their idols. On *blaspheming God*, and the nature of *blasphemy*, see the notes on Matt. ix. 3.

In whatever point of view we consider the relation which has been the subject of this long note, one thing is sufficiently plain, that he who speaks irreverently of God, of his *works*, his *perfections*, his *providence*, &c., is destitute of every moral feeling and of every religious principle, and consequently so dangerous to society that it would be criminal to suffer him to be at large, though the longsuffering of God may lead him to repentance, and therefore it may be consistent with mercy to preserve his life.

Verse 14. *Lay their hands upon his head*] It was by this ceremony that the people who heard him curse bore their public testimony in order to his being fully convicted, for without this his punishment would not have been lawful. By this ceremony also they in effect said to the man, *Thy blood be upon thy own head.*

Verse 15. *Whosoever curseth his God*] יקלל אלהיו

A. M. 2514.
B. C. 1490.
An. Exod. Isr. 2.
Abib or Nisan.

of Israel, saying, Whosoever
curseth his God [q] shall bear
his sin.
16 And he that [r] blasphemeth the name of
the LORD, he shall surely be put to death, *and*
all the congregation shall certainly stone him:
as well the stranger as he that is born in the
land, when he blasphemeth the name *of the*
LORD, shall be put to death.
17 [s] And he that [t] killeth any man shall
surely be put to death.
18 [u] And he that killeth a beast shall make
it good; [v] beast for beast.
19 And if a man cause a blemish in his
neighbour: as [w] he hath done, so shall it be
done to him;
20 Breach for breach, eye for
eye, tooth for tooth: as he hath
caused a blemish in a man, so
shall it be done to him *again*.
21 [x] And he that killeth a beast, he shall
restore it: [y] and he that killeth a man, he
shall be put to death.
22 Ye shall have [z] one manner of law,
as well for the stranger as for one of your
own country: for I *am* the LORD your
God.
23 And Moses spake to the children of
Israel, [a] that they should bring forth him that
had cursed out of the camp, and stone him
with stones. And the children of Israel did
as the LORD commanded Moses.

A. M. 2514.
B. C. 1490.
An. Exod. Isr. 2.
Abib or Nisan.

[q] Chap. v. 1; xx. 17; Num. ix. 13.——[r] 1 Kings xxi. 10, 13; Psa. lxxiv. 10, 18; Matt. xii. 31; Mark iii. 28; James ii. 7. [s] Exod. xxi. 12; Num. xxxv. 31; Deut. xix. 11, 12.——[t] Heb. *smiteth the life of a man.*

[u] Ver. 21.——[v] Heb. *life for life.*——[w] Exod. xxi. 24; Deut. xix. 21; Matt. v. 38; vii. 2.——[x] Exod. xxi. 33; ver. 18. [y] Ver. 17.——[z] Exod. xii. 49; chap. xix. 34; Num. xv. 16. [a] Ver. 14.

yekallel Elohaiv, he who *makes light* of him, who does not treat him and sacred things with due reverence, *shall bear his sin*—shall have the guilt of this transgression imputed to him, and may expect the punishment.

Verse 16. *Blasphemeth the name of the Lord*] ונקב שם יהוה *venokeb shem Yehovah*, he who *pierces*, *transfixes*, or, as some translate it, *expounds*, the name of Jehovah; see the note on the tenth verse. This being the name by which especially the Divine Essence was pointed out, it should be held peculiarly sacred. We have already seen that the Jews never pronounce this name, and so long has it been disused among them that the true pronunciation is now totally lost; see on the word JEHOVAH, Exod. vi. 3.

Verse 17. *He that killeth any man*] Blasphemy against God, i. e., speaking *injuriously* of his name, his attributes, his government, and his revelation, together with murder, is to be punished with death: he that blasphemes God is a curse in society, and he who takes away, wilfully and by malicious intent, the life of any man, should certainly be put to death. In this respect God has absolutely required that life shall go for life.

Verse 20. *Breach for breach*] This is a repetition of the *lex talionis*, which see explained Exod. xxi. 24.

Verse 22. *Ye shall have one manner of law, as well for the stranger as for one of your own country*] Equal laws, where each individual receives the same protection and the same privileges, are the boast only of a *sound political constitution*. He who *respects* and *obeys* the laws has a *right* to *protection* and *support*, and his person and property are as sacred in the sight of justice as the person and property of the prince. He who *does not obey* the laws of his country forfeits all right and title to protection and privilege; his own actions condemn him, and justice takes him up on the evidence of his own transgressions. He who does what is right need not *fear the power* of the civil magistrate, for he holds the sword only to punish *transgressors*. Universal obedience to the laws is the duty of every citizen; none can do more, none should do less: therefore each individual in a well regulated state must have *equal rights* and *privileges* in every thing that relates to the safety of his person, and the security of his property. Reader, such *was* the *Mosaic code*; such IS the BRITISH CONSTITUTION.

Verse 23. *And stone him with stones.*] We are not to suppose that the culprit was exposed to the unbridled fury of the thousands of Israel; this would be *brutality*, not *justice*, for the very worst of tempers and passions might be produced and fostered by such a procedure. The Jews themselves tell us that their manner of stoning was this: they brought the condemned person without the camp, because his crime had rendered him *unclean*, and whatever was unclean must be put *without the camp*. When they came within four cubits of the place of execution, they stripped the criminal, if a man, leaving him nothing but a cloth about the waist. The place on which he was to be executed was elevated, and the witnesses went up with him to it, and laid their hands upon him, for the purposes mentioned ver. 14. Then one of the witnesses struck him with a stone upon the loins; if he was not killed with that blow, then the witnesses took up a great stone, as much as two men could lift, and threw it upon his breast. This was the *coup de grace*, and finished the tragedy. When a man was stoned by the *mob*, then brutal rage armed every man, justice was set aside, and the *will* and *fury* of the people were law, judge, jury, and executioner. Such disgraceful stonings as these were, no doubt, frequent among the Jews. See *Calmet's* Dict., article STONING, and *Ainsworth* on this place.

WHAT the crime of Shelomith's son was, we cannot distinctly say; doubtless it was some species of blasphemy: however, we find it was a new and unprecedented case; and as there was no law by which the quantum of guilt could be ascertained, nor consequently the degree of punishment, it was necessary to consult

the great Lawgiver on the occasion; the man was therefore secured till the mind of the Lord should be known. Moses, no doubt, had recourse to the tabernacle, and received the directions afterward mentioned from Him who dwelt between the cherubim. In what way the answer of the Lord was communicated we know not, (probably by *Urim* and *Thummim*,) but it came in such a manner as to preclude all doubt upon the subject: the man was declared to be guilty, and was sentenced to be stoned to death; and on this occasion a law is made relative to blasphemy in general. However sinful the *Jews* might have been at this time, we have reason to believe they did not take the name of the Lord in vain, and blasphemy was not known among them. But what shall we say of *Christians*, so called, whose mouths are full of cursing and bitterness? Were every blasphemer among us to be stoned to death, how many of the people would fall in every corner of the land! God is longsuffering; may this lead them to repentance! We have excellent laws against all profaneness, but, alas for our country! they are not enforced; and he who attempts to put the laws in force against profane swearers, Sabbath breakers, &c., is considered a litigious man, and a disturber of the peace of society. Will not God visit for these things? This is not only *contempt of God's holy word and commandments*, but rebellion against the *laws*.

CHAPTER XXV.

The law concerning the Sabbatical or seventh year repeated, 1–7. *The law relative to the jubilee, or fiftieth year, and the hallowing of the fiftieth*, 8–12. *In the year of jubilee every one to return unto his possessions*, 13. *None to oppress another in buying and selling*, 14. *Purchases to be rated from jubilee to jubilee, according to the number of years unexpired*, 15–17. *Promises to obedience*, 18, 19. *Promises relative to the Sabbatical year*, 20–22. *No inheritance must be finally alienated*, 23, 24. *No advantage to be taken of a man's poverty in buying his land*, 25–28. *Ordinances relative to the selling of a house in a walled city*, 29, 30; *in a village*, 31. *Houses of the Levites may be redeemed at any time*, 32, 33. *The fields of the Levites in the suburbs must not be sold*, 34. *No* usury *to be taken from a poor brother*, 35–38. *If an Israelite be sold to an Israelite, he must not be obliged to serve as a* slave, 39, *but be as a* hired servant *or as a* sojourner, *till the year of jubilee*, 40, *when he and his family shall have liberty to depart*, 41; *because God claims all* Israelites as his servants, *having redeemed them from bondage in Egypt*, 42, 43. *The Israelites are permitted to have* bond-men *and* bond-women *of the* heathens, *who, being bought with their money, shall be considered as their property*, 44–46. *If an Israelite, grown poor, be sold to a sojourner who has waxed rich, he may be redeemed by one of his relatives, an* uncle *or* uncle's son, 47–49. *In the interim between the jubilees, he may be redeemed; but if not redeemed, he shall go free in the jubilee*, 50–54. *Obedience enforced by God's right over them as his servants*, 55.

A. M. 2514. B. C. 1490. An. Exod. Isr. 2. Abib or Nisan.

AND the LORD spake unto Moses in Mount Sinai, saying,

2 Speak unto the children of Israel, and say unto them, When ye come into the land which I give you, then shall the land [a] keep [b] a Sabbath unto the LORD.

3 Six years thou shalt sow thy field, and six years thou shalt prune thy vineyard, and gather in the fruit thereof:

4 But in the seventh year shall be a Sabbath of rest unto the land, a Sabbath for the LORD: thou shalt neither sow thy field, nor prune thy vineyard.

A. M. 2514. B. C. 1490. An. Exod. Isr. 2. Abib or Nisan.

5 [c] That which groweth of its own accord of thy harvest, thou shalt not reap, neither gather the grapes [d] of thy vine undressed: *for* it is a year of rest unto the land.

6 And the Sabbath of the land shall be meat for you; for thee, and for thy servant, and for thy maid, and for thy hired servant, and for thy stranger that sojourneth with thee,

7 And for thy cattle, and for the beast that

[a] Heb. *rest*.—[b] Exod. xxiii. 10; see ch. xxvi. 34, 35; 2 Chron. xxxvi. 21.—[c] 2 Kings xix. 29.—[d] Heb. *of thy separation*.

NOTES ON CHAP. XXV.

Verse 2. *The land keep a Sabbath*] See this ordinance explained in the note on Exod. xxiii. 11. It may be asked here: If it required all the annual produce of the field to support the inhabitants, how could the people be nourished the seventh year, when no produce was received from the fields? To this it may be answered, that God sent his blessing in an especial manner on the *sixth* year, (see verses 21, 22,) and it brought forth fruit for *three* years. How astonishing and convincing was this miracle! Could there possibly be any deception here? NO! The miracle speaks for itself, proves the Divine authenticity of the law, and takes every prop and stay from the system that wishes to convict the Mosaic ordinances of imposture. See Exod. xxiii. 11. It is evident from this that the Mosaic law must have had a Divine origin, as no man in his senses, without God's authority, could have made such an ordinance as this; for the *sixth* year, from its promulgation, would have amply refuted his pretensions to a Divine mission.

A. M. 2514.
B. C. 1490.
An. Exod. Isr. 2.
Abib or Nisan.

are in thy land, shall all the
increase thereof be meat.
8 And thou shalt number seven
Sabbaths of years unto thee, seven times seven
years; and the space of the seven Sabbaths of
years shall be unto thee forty and nine years.
9 Then shalt thou cause the trumpet [e] of
the jubilee to sound, on the tenth *day* of the
seventh month, [f] in the day of atonement
shall ye make the trumpet sound throughout
all your land.
10 And ye shall hallow the fiftieth year, and
[g] proclaim liberty throughout *all* the land unto
all the inhabitants thereof: it shall be a jubilee unto you; [h] and ye shall return every man
unto his possession, and ye shall return every
man unto his family.

A. M. 2514.
B. C. 1490.
An. Exod. Isr. 2.
Abib or Nisan.

11 A jubilee shall that fiftieth
year be unto you: [i] ye shall not
sow, neither reap that which
groweth of itself in it, nor gather *the grapes*
in it of thy vine undressed.
12 For it *is* the jubilee; it shall be holy
unto you: [k] ye shall eat the increase thereof
out of the field.
13 [l] In the year of this jubilee ye shall return every man unto his possession.
14 And if thou sell aught unto thy neighbour, or buyest *aught* of thy neighbour's hand,
[m] ye shall not oppress one another:
15 [n] According to the number of years after
the jubilee, thou shalt buy of thy neighbour;
and according unto the number of years of the
fruits, he shall sell unto thee:

[e] Heb. *loud of sound.*——[f] Chap. xxiii. 24, 27.——[g] Isa. lxi. 2; lxiii. 4; Jer. xxxiv. 8, 15, 17; Luke iv. 19.——[h] Ver. 13; Num. xxxvi. 4.——[i] Ver. 5.

[k] Ver. 6, 7.——[l] Ver. 10; chap. xxvii. 24; Num. xxxvi. 4.——[m] Ver. 17; chap. xix. 13; 1 Sam. xii. 3, 4; Mic. ii. 2; 1 Cor vi. 8.——[n] Chap. xxvii. 18, 23.

Verse 8. *Thou shalt number seven Sabbaths of years*] This seems to state that the jubilee was to be celebrated on the *forty-ninth* year; but in ver. 10 and 11 it is said, *Ye shall hallow the fiftieth year*, and, *A jubilee shall this fiftieth year be.* Probably in this verse Moses either includes the preceding jubilee, and thus with the *forty-ninth* makes up the number *fifty*; or he speaks of *proclaiming* the jubilee on the *forty-ninth*, and celebrating it on the *fiftieth* year current. Some think it was celebrated on the *forty-ninth* year, as is stated in ver. 8; and this prevented the *Sabbatical* year, or seventh year of rest, from being confounded with the jubilee, which it must otherwise have been, had the celebration of this great solemnity taken place on the *fiftieth* year; but it is most likely that the *fiftieth* was the real jubilee.

Verse 11. *A jubilee shall that fiftieth year be*] The literal meaning of the word *jubilee*, יובל *yobel* in *Hebrew*, and יוביל *yobil* in the *Samaritan*, has not been well ascertained. *Josephus* and the *rabbins* have caused many to err; the former says the word signifies *liberty*; *Ελευθεριαν δε σημαινει τουνομα*, Antiq., l. 3, cap. 12, edit. Haverc., vol. i., p. 184; but the word *liberty* signifies rather the *intention* of the *institution*, than the *meaning* of the *Hebrew term*. The rabbins say it signifies a *ram's horn*, because the trumpets which were used in proclaiming this solemnity were made out of ram's horns. This meaning is adopted in a few places in our *translation*, but none of the ancient versions acknowledge this sense of the term, the *Chaldee* excepted. Some derive it from יבל *yabal*, *to bring, carry away*, because the Israelites at this time *carried away* the right of repossessing their inheritances which had been forfeited or alienated. The most natural derivation is from הוביל *hobil*, *to cause to bring back*, or *recall*, because estates, &c., which had been alienated, were then *brought back* to their primitive owners. This was a wise and excellent institution, but appears to have been little regarded by the Jews after the Babylonish captivity. Indeed, it is not mentioned under the second temple, and the observance must have ceased among the Jews when they were brought under a foreign yoke.

The jubilee seems to have been typical, 1. Of the great time of release, the Gospel dispensation, when all who believe in Christ Jesus are redeemed from the bondage of sin—repossess the favour and image of God, the only inheritance of the human soul, having all debts cancelled, and the *right* of inheritance restored. To this the prophet Isaiah seems to allude, chap. xxvi. 13, and particularly lxi. 1–3. 2. Of the general resurrection. "It is," says Mr. Parkhurst, "a lively prefiguration of the grand consummation of time, which will be introduced in like manner by the *trump of God*, 1 Cor. xv. 52, when the children and heirs of God shall be delivered from all their forfeitures, and restored to the eternal *inheritance* allotted to them by their Father; and thenceforth rest from their labours, and be supported in life and happiness by what the field of God shall supply."

It is worthy of remark that the jubilee was not proclaimed till the tenth day of the seventh month, *on the very day* when the great *annual atonement* was made for the sins of the people; and does not this prove that the great *liberty* or *redemption* from thraldom, published under the Gospel, could not take place till the great *Atonement*, the sacrifice of the Lord Jesus, had been offered up? See ver. 9.

Verse 14. *Ye shall not oppress one another*] Ye shall take no advantage of each other's *ignorance* either in *buying* or *selling*; for he that buys an article at *less* than it is worth, or sells one for *more* than it is worth, taking advantage in both cases of the *ignorance* of the *vender* or *buyer*, is no better than a *thief*, as he actually robs his neighbour of as much property as he has *bought* the article at *below* or *sold* it *above* its current value.

Verse 15. *According to the number of years*] The

A. M. 2514.
B. C. 1490.
An. Exod. Isr. 2.
Abib or Nisan.

16 According to the multitude
of years, thou shalt increase the
price thereof; and according to
the fewness of years, thou shalt diminish the
price of it: for *according* to the number *of the*
years of the fruits, doth he sell unto thee.
17 [o] Ye shall not therefore oppress one
another; [p] but thou shalt fear thy God: for I
am the LORD your God.
18 [q] Wherefore ye shall do my statutes, and
keep my judgments, and do them; [r] and ye
shall dwell in the land in safety.
19 And the land shall yield her fruit, and [s] ye
shall eat your fill, and dwell therein in safety.
20 And if ye shall say, [t] What shall we eat
the seventh year? behold, [u] we shall not sow,
nor gather in our increase:
21 Then I will [v] command my blessing upon
you in the sixth year, and it shall bring forth
fruit for three years.
22 [w] And ye shall sow the eighth year, and
eat *yet* of [x] old fruit until the ninth year; until
her fruits come in ye shall eat *of* the old *store*.
23 The land shall not be sold [y] for [z] ever:
for [a] the land *is* mine; for ye
are [b] strangers and sojourners
with me.

A. M. 2514.
B. C. 1490.
An. Exod. Isr. 2.
Abib or Nisan.

24 And in all the land of your possession
ye shall grant a redemption for the land.
25 [c] If thy brother be waxen poor, and hath
sold away *some* of his possession, and if [d] any
of his kin come to redeem it, then shall he
redeem that which his brother sold.
26 And if the man have none to redeem it
and [e] himself be able to redeem it;
27 Then [f] let him count the years of the sale
thereof, and restore the overplus unto the man
to whom he sold it; that he may return unto
his possession.
28 But if he be not able to restore *it* to him,
then that which is sold shall remain in the
hand of him that hath bought it, until the year
of jubilee: [g] and in the jubilee it shall go out,
and he shall return unto his possession.
29 And if a man sell a dwelling house in a
walled city, then he may redeem it within a
whole year after it is sold; *within* a full year
may he redeem it.

[o] Ver. 14.——[p] Ver. 43; chap. xix. 14, 32.——[q] Chap. xix. 37. [r] Chap. xxvi. 5; Deut. xii. 10; Psa. iv. 8; Prov. i. 33; Jer. xxiii. 6.——[s] Chap. xxvi. 5; Ezek. xxxiv. 25, 27, 28.——[t] Matt. vi. 25, 31.——[u] Ver. 4, 5.——[v] Deut. xxviii. 8; see Exod. xvi. 29.——[w] 2 Kings xix. 29.——[x] Josh. v. 11, 12.——[y] Or, *to be quite cut off*.

[z] Heb. *for cutting off*.——[a] Deut. xxxii. 43; 2 Chron. vii. 20; Psa. lxxxv. 1; Joel ii. 18; iii. 2.——[b] 1 Chron. xxix. 15; Psa. xxxix. 12; cxix. 19; 1 Peter ii. 11.——[c] Ruth ii. 20; iv. 4, 6. [d] See Ruth iii. 2, 9, 12; Jer. xxxii. 7, 8.——[e] Heb. *his hand hath attained, and found sufficiency*; chap. v. 7.——[f] Ver. 50, 51, 52.——[g] Ver. 13.

purchases that were to be made of lands were to be regulated by the number of years unelapsed of the current jubilee. This was something like buying the unexpired term of a lease among us; the purchase is always regulated by the *number of years* between the time of purchase and the expiration of the term.

Verse 20. *What shall we eat the seventh year?*] A very natural question, which could only be laid at rest by the sovereign promise in the next verse: *I will* COMMAND *my* BLESSING *upon you in the sixth year, and it shall bring forth fruit for* THREE YEARS. See on verse 2.

Verse 23. *The land shall not be sold for ever—the land* is *mine*] As God in a miraculous manner gave them possession of this land, they were therefore to consider themselves merely as *tenants* to him; and on this ground *he*, as the great landholder or lord of the soil, prescribes to them all the conditions on which they shall hold it. This one circumstance was peculiarly favourable to their advancement in religion, in righteousness, and true holiness; for feeling that they had nothing which they could call their *own* upon earth, they must frequently, by this, be put in mind of the necessity of having a permanent dwelling in the heavenly inheritance, and of that preparation without which it could not be possessed.

Verse 25. *Any of his kin come to redeem it*] The land that was sold might be redeemed, in the interim between jubilee and jubilee, by the *former owner* or by one of his *kinsmen* or *relatives*. This *kinsman* is called in the text גאל *goel* or *redeemer;* and was not this a lively emblem of the redemption of man by Christ Jesus? That *he* might have a *right* to redeem *man*, he took upon him *human nature*, and thus became a *kinsman* of the great family of the human race, and thereby *possessed the right of redeeming* that fallen nature of which he took part, and of *buying back* to man that *inheritance* which had been *forfeited* by transgression.

Verse 29. *Sell a dwelling house in a walled city*] A very proper difference is put between houses in a *city* and houses in the *country*. If a man sold his house in the *city*, he might redeem it any time in the course of a *year;* but if it were not redeemed within that time, it could no more be redeemed, nor did it go out even in the jubilee. It was not so with a house in the *country;* such a house might be redeemed during any part of the interim; and if not redeemed, must go out at the jubilee. The reason in both cases is sufficiently evident; the house in the city might be built for purposes of *trade* or *traffic* merely, the house in the country was built on or attached to the *inheritance* which God had divided to the respective families, and it was therefore absolutely necessary that the same law should apply to the *house* as to the *inheritance*. But the same necessity did not hold good with respect to

A. M. 2514.
B. C. 1490.
An. Exod. Isr. 2.
Abib or Nisan.

30 And if it be not redeemed within the space of a full year, then the house that *is* in the walled city shall be established for ever to him that bought it, throughout his generations: it shall not go out in the jubilee.
31 But the houses of the villages, which have no walls round about them, shall be counted as the fields of the country: [h] they may be redeemed, and they shall go out in the jubilee.
32 Notwithstanding [i] the cities of the Levites, *and* the houses of the cities of their possession, may the Levites redeem at any time.
33 And if [k] a man purchase of the Levites, then the house that was sold, and the city of his possession, [l] shall go out in *the year of* jubilee; for the houses of the cities of the Levites *are* their possession among the children of Israel.
34 But [m] the field of the suburbs of their cities may not be sold; for it *is* their perpetual possession.
35 And if thy brother be waxen poor, and [n] fallen in decay with thee; then thou shalt [o] relieve him: [p] *yea, though he be* a stranger, or a sojourner; that he may live with thee.
36 [q] Take thou no usury of him, or increase: but [r] fear thy God; that thy brother may live with thee.
37 Thou shalt not give him thy money upon usury, nor lend him thy victuals for increase.
38 [s] I *am* the LORD your God, which brought you forth out of the land of Egypt, to give you the land of Canaan, *and* to be your God.
39 And [t] if thy brother *that dwelleth* by thee be waxen poor, and be sold unto thee; thou shalt not [u] compel him to serve as a bondservant:
40 *But* as a hired servant, *and* as a sojourner, he shall be with thee, *and* shall serve thee unto the year of jubilee:
41 And *then* shall he depart from thee, *both* he and his children [v] with him, and shall return unto his own family, and [w] unto the possession of his fathers shall he return.
42 For they *are* [x] my servants, which I brought forth out of the land of Egypt: they shall not be sold [y] as bondmen.

[h] Heb. *redemption belongeth unto it.*—[i] See Num. xxxv. 2; Josh. xxi. 2, &c.—[k] Or, one *of the Levites redeem* them. [l] Ver. 28.—[m] See Acts iv. 36, 37.—[n] Heb. *his hand faileth.* [o] Heb. *strengthen.*—[p] Deut. xv. 7, 8; Psa. xxxvii. 26; xli. 1; cxii. 5, 9; Prov. xiv. 31; Luke. vi. 35; Acts xi. 29; Rom. xii. 18; 1 John iii. 17.—[q] Exod. xxii. 25; Deut. xxiii. 19; Neh. v. 7; Psa. xv. 5; Prov. xxviii. 8; Ezek. xviii. 8, 13, 17; xxii. 12.—[r] Ver. 17; Neh. v. 9.—[s] Chap. xxii. 32, 33.—[t] Exod. xxi. 2; Deut. xv. 12; 1 Kings ix. 22; 2 Kings iv. 1; Neh. v. 5; Jer. xxxiv. 14.—[u] Heb. *serve thyself with him with the service,* &c.; ver. 46; Exod. i. 14; Jer. xxv. 14; xxvii. 7; xxx. 8.—[v] Exod. xxi. 3.—[w] Ver. 28.—[x] Ver. 55; Rom. vi. 22; 1 Cor. vii. 23.—[y] Heb. *with the sale of a bondman.*

the house in the city: and as we may presume the house in the city was merely for the purpose of *trade,* when a man bought such a house, and got his business *established* there, it would have been very inconvenient for him to have removed; but as it was possible that the former owner might have sold the house *rashly,* or through the *pressure of some very urgent necessity,* a *year* was allowed him, that during that time he might have leisure to reconsider his rash act, or so to get through his pressing necessity as to be able to get back his dwelling. This time was sufficiently *long* in either of the above cases; and as such occurrences might have been the cause of his selling his house, it was necessary that he might have the opportunity of redeeming his pledge. Again, as the purchaser, having bought the house merely for the purpose of *trade, manufacture,* &c., must have been at great pains and expense to fit the place for his work, and establish his business, in which himself, his children, and his children's children, were to labour and get their bread; hence it was necessary that he should have some *certainty* of permanent possession, without which, we may naturally conjecture, no such purchases ever would be made. This seems to be the simple reason of the law in both cases.

Verse 32. *The cities of the Levites*] The law in this and the following verses was also a very wise one. A *Levite* could not ultimately sell his house: if sold he could redeem it at any time in the interim between the two jubilees; but if not redeemed, it must go out at the following jubilee. And why? "Because Moses framed his laws so much in favour of the *priesthood,* that they had *peculiar* privileges?" &c. Just the reverse: they were so far from being peculiarly favoured that they had no *inheritance* in Israel, only their *cities,* to dwell in: and because their *houses* in these cities were the whole that they could call their own, therefore these houses could not be ultimately alienated. All that they had to live on besides was from that most precarious source of support, the freewill-offerings of the people, which depended on the prevalence of pure religion in the land.

Verse 36. *Take thou no usury of him*] Usury, at present, signifies unlawful interest for money. Properly, it means the *reward* or *compensation* given for the use of a thing, but is principally spoken of *money.* See the definition of the original term in the note on Exod. xxii. 25.

Verse 42. *For they* are *my servants*] As God redeemed every Israelite out of Egyptian bondage, they were therefore to consider themselves as his property, and that consequently they should not alienate themselves from him. It was in being his *servants,* and devoted to his work, that both their religious and po-

A. M. 2514. B. C. 1490. An. Exod. Isr. 2. Abib or Nisan.

43 [z] Thou shalt not rule over him [a] with rigour; but [b] shalt fear thy God.

44 Both thy bondmen, and thy bondmaids, which thou shalt have, *shall be* of the heathen that are round about you; of them shall ye buy bondmen and bondmaids.

45 Moreover of [c] the children of the strangers that do sojourn among you, of them shall ye buy, and of their families that *are* with you, which they begat in your land: and they shall be your possession.

46 And [d] ye shall take them as an inheritance for your children after you, to inherit *them for* a possession; [e] they shall be your bondmen for ever: but over your brethren the children of Israel, [f] ye shall not rule one over another with rigour.

47 And if a sojourner or stranger [g] wax rich by thee, and [h] thy brother *that dwelleth* by him wax poor, and sell himself unto the stranger *or* sojourner by thee, or to the stock of the stranger's family:

48 After that he is sold he may be redeemed again; one of his brethren may [i] redeem him:

49 Either his uncle, or his uncle's son, may redeem him, or *any* that is nigh of kin unto him, of his family, may redeem him; or if [k] he be able, he may redeem himself.

50 And he shall reckon with him that bought him, from the year that he was sold to him unto the year of jubilee: and the price of his sale shall be according unto the number of years, [l] according to the time of a hired servant shall it be with him.

51 If *there be* yet many years *behind*, according unto them he shall give again the price of his redemption, out of the money that he was bought for.

52 And if there remain but few years unto the year of jubilee, then he shall count with him, *and* according unto his years shall he give him again the price of his redemption.

53 *And* as a yearly hired servant shall he be with him: *and the other* shall not rule with rigour over him in thy sight.

54 And if he be not redeemed [m] in these *years*, then [n] he shall go out in the year of jubilee, *both* he, and his children with him.

55 For [o] unto me the children of Israel *are* servants; they *are* my servants whom I brought forth out of the land of Egypt: I *am* the Lord your God.

[z] Eph. vi. 9; Col. iv. 1.——[a] Ver. 46; Exod. i. 13.——[b] Ver. 17; Exod. i. 17, 21; Deut. xxv. 18; Mal. iii. 5.——[c] Isa. lvi. 3, 6. [d] Isa. xiv. 2.——[e] Heb. *ye shall serve yourselves with them*; ver 39. [f] Ver. 43.——[g] Heb. *his hand obtain*, &c.; ver. 26.——[h] Ver. 25, 35. [i] Neh. v. 5.——[k] Ver. 26.——[l] Job vii. 1; Isa. xvi. 14; xxi. 16. [m] Or, *by these* means.——[n] Ver. 41; Exod. xxi. 2, 3.——[o] Ver. 42.

litical service consisted. And although their *political* liberty might be lost, they knew that their spiritual liberty never could be forfeited except by an utter alienation from God. God therefore claims the same right to their persons which he does to their lands; see the note on ver. 23.

Verse 43. *Thou shalt not rule over him with rigour*] What is rigorous service? "Service which is not *determined*, and service whereof *there is no need*." This is the definition given by the Jews; but much more is implied in this command than is expressed here. Labour beyond the person's strength, or labour too long continued, or in unhealthy or uncomfortable places and circumstances, or without sufficient food, &c., is *labour exacted with rigour*, and consequently inhuman; and this law is made, not for the Mosaic dispensation and the Jewish people, but for every dispensation and for every people under heaven.

Verse 50. *The price of his sale shall be, &c.*] This was a very equitable law, both for the sojourner to whom the man was sold, and to the Israelite who had been thus sold. The Israelite might redeem himself, or one of his kindred might redeem him; but this must not be done to the prejudice of his master, the sojourner. They were therefore to reckon the years he must have served from that time till the jubilee; and then, taking the current wages of a servant per year at that time, multiply the remaining years by that sum, and the aggregate was the sum to be given to his master for his redemption. The Jews hold that the kindred of such a person were bound, if in their power, to redeem him, lest he should be swallowed up among the heathen; and we find, from Neh. v. 8, that this was done by the Jews on their return from the Babylonish captivity: *We, after our ability, have redeemed our brethren the Jews, who were sold unto the heathen.*

Verse 55. *For unto me the children of Israel are servants*] The *reason* of this law we have already seen, (see on ver. 42,) but we must look farther to see the great *end* of it. The Israelites were a *typical* people; they represented those under the Gospel dispensation who are children of God by faith in Christ Jesus. But these last have a peculiarity of blessing: they are not merely *servants*, but they are SONS; though they also *serve God*, yet it is in the *newness of the spirit*, and not in the *oldness of the letter*. And to this difference of state the apostle seems evidently to allude, Gal. iv. 6, &c.: *And because ye are* SONS, *God hath sent forth the Spirit of his Son into your hearts, crying Abba, Father. Wherefore thou art no more a* SERVANT, *but a* SON; *and if a* SON, *then an* HEIR *of God through Christ*; genuine believers in Christ not being heirs of an *earthly* inheritance, nor merely of a *heavenly* one, for they are heirs of God.

God himself therefore is *their* portion, without whom even *heaven* itself would not be a state of consummate blessedness to an immortal spirit.

The jubilee was a wonderful institution, and was of very great service to the *religion*, *freedom*, and *independence* of the Jewish people. "The motive of this law," says Calmet, "was to prevent the rich from oppressing the poor, and reducing them to perpetual slavery; and that they should not get possession of all the lands by way of purchase, mortgage, or, lastly, usurpation. That *debts* should not be multiplied too much, lest thereby the poor should be entirely ruined; and that *slaves* should not continue always, they, their wives and children, in *servitude*. Besides, Moses intended to preserve, as much as possible, personal liberty, an equality of property, and the regular order of families, among the Hebrews. Lastly, he designed that the people should be strongly attached to their country, lands, and inheritances; that they should have an affection for them, and consider them as estates which descended to them from their ancestors which they were to leave to their posterity, without any fear of their going ultimately out of their families."

But this institution especially pointed out the redemption of man by Christ Jesus: 1. Through him, he who was in debt to God's justice had his debt discharged, and his sin forgiven. 2. He who sold himself for naught, who was a bond-slave of sin and Satan, regains his liberty and becomes a son of God through faith in his blood. 3. He who by transgression had forfeited all right and title to the kingdom of God, becomes an heir of God, and a joint heir with Christ. Heaven, his forfeited inheritance, is restored, for the kingdom of heaven is *opened to all believers*; and thus, redeemed from his debt, restored to his liberty, united to the heavenly family, and re-entitled to his inheritance, he goes on his way rejoicing, till he enters the paradise of his Maker, and is for ever with the Lord. Reader, hast thou applied for this redemption? Does not the trumpet of the jubilee, the glad tidings of salvation by Christ Jesus, sound in the land? Surely it does. Why then continue a *bond-slave of sin*, a child of wrath, and an heir of hell, when such a salvation is offered unto thee without money and without price? O suffer not this provision to be made ultimately in vain for *thee!* For what art thou advantaged if thou gain the whole *world* and lose thy *soul?*

CHAPTER XXVI.

Idolatry forbidden, 1. *The Sabbath to be sanctified*, 2, 3. Promises *to obedience, of fruitful fields, plentiful harvests, and vintage*, 4, 5. *Of peace and security*, 6. *Discomfiture of their enemies*, 7–9. *Of abundance*, 10. *Of the Divine presence*, 11–13. Threatenings *against the disobedient*, 14, 15. *Of terror and dismay*, 16. *Their enemies shall prevail against them*, 17, 18. *Of barrenness*, 19, 20. *Of desolation by wild beasts*, 21, 22. *And if not humbled and reformed, worse evils shall be inflicted upon them*, 23, 24. *Their enemies shall prevail, and they shall be wasted by the pestilence*, 25, 26. *If they should still continue refractory, they shall be yet more sorely punished*, 27, 28. *The famine shall so increase that they shall be obliged to* eat their own children, 29. *Their carcasses shall be cast upon the carcasses of their idols*, 30. *Their cities shall be wasted, and the sanctuary desolated*, 31; *the land destroyed*, 32, *themselves scattered among their enemies, and pursued with utter confusion and distress*, 33–39. *If under these judgments they confess their sin and return to God, he will remember them in mercy*, 40–43; *visit them even in the land of their enemies*, 44; *and remember his covenant with their fathers*, 45. *The conclusion, stating these to be the judgments and laws which the Lord made between himself and the children of Israel in Mount* Sinai, 46.

A. M. 2514. B. C. 1490. An. Exod. Isr. 2. Abib or Nisan.

YE shall make you [a] no idols,
nor graven image, neither
rear you up a [b] standing image,
neither shall ye set up *any* [c] image [d] of stone
in your land, to bow down unto it: for I *am*
the LORD your God.
2 [e] Ye shall keep my Sabbaths, and reverence my sanctuary: I *am* the
LORD.
3 [f] If ye walk in my statutes,
and keep my commandments, and do them;
4 [g] Then I will give you rain in due season,
[h] and the land shall yield her increase, and
the trees of the field shall yield their fruit.

[a] Exod. xx. 4, 5; Deut. v. 8; xvi. 22; xxvii. 15; Psa. xcvii. 7.——[b] Or, *pillar*.——[c] Or, *figured stone*.——[d] Heb. *a stone of picture*.——[e] Chap. xix. 30.

[f] Deut. xi. 13, 14, 15; xxviii. 1–14.——[g] Isa. xxx. 23; Ezek. xxxiv. 26; Joel ii. 23, 24.——[h] Psa. lxvii. 6; lxxxv. 12; Ezek. xxxiv. 27; xxxvi. 30; Zech. viii. 12.

NOTES ON CHAP. XXVI.

Verse 1. *Ye shall make you no idols*] See the note on Exod. xx. 4, and see the note on Gen. xxviii. 18, 19, concerning *consecrated stones*. Not only *idolatry* in general is forbidden here, but also the *superstitious use* of *innocent* and *lawful things*. Probably the *stones* or *pillars* which were first set up, and *anointed* by holy men in commemoration of signal interpositions of God in their behalf, were afterward abused to idolatrous and superstitious purposes, and therefore prohibited. This we know was the case with the brazen serpent, 2 Kings xviii. 4.

Verse 3. *If ye walk in my statutes*] For the meaning of this and similar words used in the law, see the note on ver. 15.

Verse 4. *Rain in due season*] What in Scripture

A. M. 2514.
B. C. 1490.
An. Exod. Isr. 2.
Abib or Nisan.

5 And [i] your threshing shall
reach unto the vintage, and the
vintage shall reach unto the sow-
ing time: and [k] ye shall eat your bread to the
full, and [l] dwell in your land safely.
6 And [m] I will give peace in the land, and
[n] ye shall lie down, and none shall make *you*
afraid: and I will [o] rid [p] evil beasts out of
the land, neither shall [q] the sword go through
your land.
7 And ye shall chase your enemies, and they
shall fall before you by the sword.
8 And [r] five of you shall chase a hundred,
and a hundred of you shall put ten thousand
to flight: and your enemies shall fall before
you by the sword.
9 For I will [s] have respect unto you, and
[t] make you fruitful, and multiply
you, and establish my covenant
with you.
10 And ye shall eat [u] old store, and bring
forth the old because of the new.
11 [v] And I will set my tabernacle among
you: and my soul shall not [w] abhor you.
12 [x] And I will walk among you, and [y] will
be your God, and ye shall be my people.
13 [z] I *am* the LORD your God, which brought
you forth out of the land of Egypt, that ye
should not be their bondmen; [a] and I have
broken the bands of your yoke, and made you
go upright.
14 [b] But if ye will not hearken unto me, and
will not do all these commandments;
15 And if ye shall [c] despise my statutes, or

[i] Amos ix. 13.——[k] Chap. xxv. 19; Deut. xi. 15; Joel ii. 19, 26.——[l] Chap. xxv. 18; Job xi. 18; Ezekiel xxxiv. 25, 27, 28.——[m] 1 Chron. xxii. 9; Psa. xxix. 11; cxlvii. 14; Isa. xlv. 7; Hag. ii. 9.——[n] Job xi. 19; Psa. iii. 5; iv. 8; Isa. xxxv. 9; Jer. xxx. 10; Ezek. xxxiv. 25; Hos. ii. 18; Zeph. iii. 13.——[o] Heb. *cause to cease.*——[p] 2 Kings xvii. 25; Ezek. v. 17; xiv. 15.——[q] Ezek. xiv. 17.——[r] Deut. xxxii. 30; Josh. xxiii. 10.——[s] Exod. ii. 25; 2 Kings xiii. 23.——[t] Gen. xvii. 6, 7; Neh. ix. 23; Psa. cvii. 38.——[u] Chap. xxv. 22.——[v] Exod. xxv. 8; xxix. 45; Josh. xxii. 19; Psa. lxxvi. 2; Ezek. xxxvii. 26, 27, 28; Rev. xxi. 3.——[w] Ch. xx. 23; Deut. xxxii. 19.——[x] 2 Cor. vi. 16.——[y] Exodus vi. 7; Jer. vii. 23; xi. 4; xxx. 22; Ezek. xi. 20; xxxvi. 28.——[z] Chap. xxv. 38, 42, 55.——[a] Jeremiah ii. 20; Ezek. xxxiv. 27.——[b] Deut. xxviii. 15; Lam. ii. 17; Mal. ii. 2.——[c] Ver. 43; 2 Kings xvii. 15.

is called the *early* and the *latter* rain. The first fell in Palestine at the commencement of *spring*, and the latter in *autumn.*—*Calmet.*

Verse 5. *Your threshing shall reach unto the vintage*] According to Pliny, *Hist. Nat.*, l. xviii., c. 18, the Egyptians reaped their barley six months, and their oats seven months, after seed time; for they sowed all their grain about the end of summer, when the overflowings of the Nile had ceased. It was nearly the same in Judea: they sowed their corn and barley towards the end of autumn, and about the month of October; and they began their barley-harvest after the *passover*, about the middle of March; and in one month or six weeks after, about *pentecost*, they began that of their wheat. After their wheat-harvest their vintage commenced. Moses here leads the Hebrews to hope, if they continued faithful to God, that between their harvest and vintage, and between their vintage and seed-time, there should be no interval, so great should the abundance be; and these promises would appear to them the more impressive, as they had just now come out of a country where the inhabitants were obliged to remain for nearly three months shut up within their cities, because the Nile had then inundated the whole country. See *Calmet.*

"This is a nervous and beautiful promise of such entire plenty of corn and wine, that before they could have *reaped* and *threshed* out their *corn*, the *vintage* should be ready, and before they could have *pressed out their wine* it would be time to *sow again.* The Prophet Amos, chap. ix. 13, expresses the same blessing in the same manner: *The ploughman shall overtake the reaper, and the treader of grapes him who soweth seed.*"—Dodd.

Verse 11. *I will set my tabernacle among you*] This and the following verse contain the grand promise of the *Gospel dispensation*, viz. the *presence*, *manifestation*, and *indwelling of God* in human nature, and his constant indwelling in the souls of his followers. So John i. 14: the WORD *was made flesh*, *και εσκηνωσεν εν ἡμιν, and* MADE HIS TABERNACLE *among us.* And to this promise of the law St. Paul evidently refers, 2 Cor. vi. 16–18, and vii. 1.

Verse 15. *If ye shall despise my statutes—abhor my judgments*] As these words, and others of a similar import, which point out different properties of the revelation of God, are frequently occurring, I judge it best to take a general view of them, once for all, in this place, and show how they differ among themselves, and what property of the Divine law each points out.

1. STATUTES. חקת *chukkoth*, from חק *chak*, to *mark out*, *define*, &c. This term seems to signify the things which God has *defined*, *marked*, and *traced out*, that men might have a perfect copy of pure conduct always before their eyes, to teach them how they might walk *so* as to please him in all things, which they could not do without such instruction as God gives in his word, and the help which he affords by his Spirit.

2. JUDGMENTS. שפטים *shephatim*, from שפט *shaphat*, to *distinguish*, *regulate*, and *determine;* meaning those things which God has *determined* that men shall pursue, by which their whole conduct shall be *regulated*, making the proper *distinction* between virtue and vice, good and evil, right and wrong, justice and injustice; in a word, between what is proper to be *done*, and what is proper to be left *undone*.

3. COMMANDMENTS. מצות *mitsvoth*, from צוה *tsavah*, to *command*, *ordain*, and *appoint*, *as a legislator.* This term is properly applied to those parts of the law which contain the *obligation* the people are under to

A. M. 2514.
B. C. 1490.
An. Exod. Isr. 2.
Abib or Nisan.

if your soul abhor my judgments,
so that ye will not do all my
commandments, *but* that ye break
my covenant:
16 I also will do this unto you; I will even
appoint [d] over you [e] terror, [f] consumption, and
the burning ague, that shall [g] consume the
eyes, and cause sorrow of heart;
and [h] ye shall sow your seed in
vain, for your enemies shall eat it.
17 And [i] I will set my face against you, and
[k] ye shall be slain before your enemies: [l] they
that hate you shall reign over you; and [m] ye
shall flee when none pursueth you.

[d] Heb. *upon you.*——[e] Deut. xxviii. 65, 66, 67; xxxii. 25; Jer. xv. 8.——[f] Deut. xxviii. 22.——[g] 1 Sam. ii. 33.——[h] Deut. xxviii. 33, 51; Job. xxxi. 8; Jer. v. 17; xii. 13; Mic. vi. 15.

[i] Chap. xvii. 10.——[k] Deut. xxviii. 25; Judg. ii. 14; Jer. xix. 7.——[l] Psa. cvi. 41.——[m] Ver. 36; Psa. liii. 5; Prov. xxviii. 1.

act according to the *statutes*, *judgments*, &c., already established, and which prohibit them by penal sanctions from acting contrary to the laws.

4. Covenant. ברית *berith*, from בר *bar*, to *clear*, *cleanse*, or *purify*; because the *covenant*, the whole system of revelation given to the Jews, was intended to *separate* them from all the people of the earth, and to make them *holy*. *Berith* also signifies the *covenant-sacrifice*, which *prefigured* the atonement made by Christ for the sin of the world, by which he *purifies* believers unto himself, and makes them a *peculiar people*, *zealous of good works*. Besides those *four*, we may add the following, from other places of Scripture.

5. Testimonies. עדות *edoth*, from עד *ad*, *beyond*, *farther*, *besides*; because the whole ritual law referred to something *farther on* or *beyond* the Jewish dispensation, even to that sacrifice which in the fulness of time was to be offered for the sins of men. Thus all the sacrifices, &c., of the Mosaic law *referred to Christ*, and bore *testimony* to him *who was to come*.

6. Ordinances. משמרות *mishmaroth*, from שמר *shamar*, to *guard*, *keep safe*, *watch over*; those parts of Divine revelation which exhorted men to *watch their ways*, *keep their hearts*, and promised them, in consequence, the continual *protection* and blessing of God their Maker.

7. Precepts. פקודים *pikkudim*, from פקד *pakad*, to *overlook*, *take care* or *notice of*, *to visit*; a very expressive character of the Divine testimonies, the *overseers* of a man's conduct, those who *stand by* and *look on* to see whether he acts according to the commands of his Master; also the *visiters*, because God's precepts are suited to all the circumstances of human life; some are applicable in adversity, others in prosperity; some in times of temptation and sadness, others in seasons of spiritual joy and exultation, &c., &c. Thus they may be said to *overlook* and *visit* man in all times, places, and circumstances.

8. Truth. אמת *emeth*, from אם *am*, to *support*, *sustain*, *confirm*; because God is *immutable* who has promised, threatened, commanded, and therefore all his promises, threatenings, commandments, &c., are *unalterable* and *eternal*. Error and falsity promise to *direct* and *sustain*, but they *fail*. God's word is *supported* by his own *faithfulness*, and it *supports* and *confirms* them who conscientiously believe it.

9. Righteousness. צדקה *tsedakah*, from צדק, which, though not used as a *verb* in the Hebrew Bible, seems to convey, from its use as a *noun*, the idea of *giving just weight* or *good measure*, see chap. xix. 36. This is one of the characters which is attributed to the revelation God makes of himself; (see Psa. cxix;) and by this the *impartiality* of the Divine testimonies is pointed out. God gives to all their *due*, and his word *distributes* to every man according to his state, circumstances, talents, graces, &c.; to none *too much*, to none *too little*, to all *enough*.

10. Word of Jehovah. דבר יהוה *debar Yehovah*, from דבר *dabar*, to *drive*, *lead*, *bring forward*, hence to *bring forward*, or *utter one's sentiments*; so the word of God is what God has *brought forth to man* from his own mind and counsel; it is a perfect *similitude* of his own *righteousness*, *holiness*, *goodness*, and *truth*. This Divine law is sometimes expressed by

11. אמרה *imrah*, *speech* or *word*, variously modified from אמר *amar*, to *branch out*, because of the interesting *details* into which the word of God enters in order to instruct man and make him wise unto salvation, or, as the apostle expresses it, "God, who at sundry times, and in divers manners, spake unto the fathers by the prophets," πολυμερως και πολυτροπως, in *many distinct parcels*, and by *various tropes* or *figures*; a curious and elegant description of Divine revelation; Heb. i. 1.

12. All these collectively are termed the law, תורה *torah*, or תורת יהוה *torath Yehovah*, the *law of the Lord*, from ירה *yarah*, to *direct*, *set straight and true*, *as stones in a building*, to *teach* and *instruct*, because this whole system of Divine revelation is calculated to *direct* men to the attainment of present and eternal felicity, to *set them right* in their notions concerning the supreme God, to *order* and *adjust them* in the several departments of civil and religious society, and thus to *teach* and *instruct* them in the knowledge of themselves, and in the true knowledge of God. Thus those who receive the truth become the *city of* the living God—the temple of the Most High, *built together* for a habitation of God through the Spirit. To complete this description of the word *law*, see the note on Exod. xii. 49, where other properties of the law of God are specified.

Verse 16. *I will even appoint over you terror, &c.*] How dreadful is this curse! A whole train of evils are here *personified* and appointed to be the governors of a disobedient people. *Terror* is to be one of their keepers. How awful a state! to be continually under the influence of dismay, feeling indescribable evils, and fearing worse! *Consumption*, שחפת *shachepheth*, generally allowed to be some kind of *atrophy* or *marasmus*, by which the flesh was consumed, and the whole body dried up by *raging fever* through lack of sustenance. See the note on chap. xi. 16. How cir-

A. M. 2514.
B. C. 1490.
An. Exod. Isr. 2.
Abib or Nisan.

18 And if ye will not yet for
all this hearken unto me, then I
will punish you [n] seven times
more for your sins.
19 And I will [o] break the pride of your
power; and I [p] will make your heaven as iron,
and your earth as brass:
20 And your [q] strength shall be spent in
vain: for [r] your land shall not yield her increase, neither shall the trees of the land yield
their fruits.
21 And if ye walk [s] contrary unto me, and
will not hearken unto me; I will bring seven
times more plagues upon you, according to
your sins.
22 [t] I will also send wild beasts among you,
which shall rob you of your children, and destroy your cattle, and make you few in number; and [u] your *high* ways shall be desolate.
23 And if ye [v] will not be reformed by me by
these things, but will walk contrary unto me;
24 [w] Then will I also walk contrary unto
you, and will punish you yet seven times for
your sins.
25 And [x] I will bring a sword upon you,
that shall avenge the quarrel of *my* covenant:
and when ye are gathered together within
your cities, [y] I will send the pestilence among
you; and ye shall be delivered
into the hand of the enemy.

A. M. 2514.
B. C. 1490.
An. Exod. Isr. 2.
Abib or Nisan.

26 [z] *And* when I have broken
the staff of your bread, ten women shall bake
your bread in one oven, and they shall deliver
you your bread again by weight: and [a] ye shall
eat, and not be satisfied.
27 And [b] if ye will not for all this hearken
unto me, but walk contrary unto me;
28 Then I will walk contrary unto you also
[c] in fury; and I, even I, will chastise you
seven times for your sins.
29 [d] And ye shall eat the flesh of your sons,
and the flesh of your daughters shall ye eat.
30 And [e] I will destroy your high places, and
cut down your images, and [f] cast your carcasses
upon the carcasses of your idols, and my soul
shall [g] abhor you.
31 [h] And I will make your cities waste,
and [i] bring your sanctuaries unto desolation,
and I will not smell the savour of your sweet
odours.
32 [k] And I will bring the land into desolation: and your enemies which dwell therein
shall be [l] astonished at it.
33 And [m] I will scatter you among the heathen, and will draw out a sword after you: and
your land shall be desolate, and your cities waste.

[n] 1 Sam. ii. 5; Psa. cxix. 164; Prov. xxiv. 16.——[o] Isa. xxv. 11; xxvi. 5; Ezek. vii. 24; xxx. 6.——[p] Deut. xxviii. 23.——[q] Psa. cxxvii. 1; Isa. xlix. 4.——[r] Deut. xi. 17; xxviii. 18; Hag. i. 10.——[s] Or, *at all adventures with me;* and so ver. 24.——[t] Deut. xxxii. 24; 2 Kings xvii. 25; Ezek. v. 17; xiv. 15.——[u] Judg. v. 6; 2 Chron. xv. 5; Isa. xxxiii. 8; Lam. i. 4; Zech. vii. 14.——[v] Jer. ii. 30; v. 3; Amos iv. 6–12.——[w] 2 Sam. xxii. 27; Psa. xviii. 26.——[x] Ezek. v. 17; vi. 3; xiv. 17; xxix. 8; xxxiii. 2.——[y] Num. xiv. 12; Deut. xxviii. 21; Jer. xiv. 12; xxiv. 10; xxix. 17, 18; Amos iv. 10.——[z] Psa. cv. 16; Isa. iii. 1; Ezek. iv. 16; v. 16; xiv. 13.

[a] Isa. ix. 20; Mic. vi. 14; Hag. i. 6.——[b] Ver. 21, 24.——[c] Isa. lix. 18; lxiii. 3; lxvi. 15; Jer. xxi. 5; Ezek. v. 13, 15; viii. 18.——[d] Deut. xxviii. 53; 2 Kings vi. 29; Ezek. v. 10; Lam. iv. 10; Bar. ii. 3.——[e] 2 Chron. xxxiv. 3, 4, 7; Isa. xxvii. 9; Ezek. vi. 3, 4, 5, 6, 13.——[f] 2 Kings xxiii. 20; 2 Chron. xxxiv. 5.——[g] Lev. xx. 23; Psa. lxxviii. 59; lxxxix. 38; Jer. xiv. 19.——[h] Neh. ii. 3; Jer. iv. 7; Ezek. vi. 6.——[i] Psa. lxxiv. 7; Lam. i. 10; Ezek. ix. 6; xxi. 7.——[k] Jer. ix. 11; xxv. 11, 18.——[l] Deut. xxviii. 37; 1 Kings. ix. 8; Jer. xviii. 16; xix. 8; Ezek. v. 15.——[m] Deut. iv. 27; xxviii. 64; Psa. xliv. 11; Jer. ix. 16; Ezek. xii. 15; xx. 23; xxii. 15; Zech. vii. 14.

cumstantially were all these threatenings fulfilled in this disobedient and rebellious people! Let a *deist* read over this chapter and compare it with the state of the Jews since the days of Vespasian, and then let him doubt the authenticity of this word if he can.

Verse 22. *I will also send wild beasts among you*] God fulfilled these threatenings at different times. He sent *fiery* SERPENTS among them, Num. xxi. 6; LIONS, 2 Kings xvii. 25; BEARS, 2 Kings ii. 24, and threatened them with total desolation, so that their land should be overrun with *wild beasts*, &c., see Ezek. v. 17. "Spiritually," says Mr. *Ainsworth*, "these are *wicked rulers* and *tyrants* that kill and spoil, Prov. xxviii. 15; Dan. vii. 3–6; Psa. lxxx. 13; and *false prophets* that devour souls, Matt. vii. 15; Rev. xiii. 1, &c. So the prophet, speaking of their punishment by *tyrants*, says: *A* LION *out of the forest shall slay them; a* WOLF *of the evening shall spoil them; a* LEOPARD *shall watch over their cities; every one that goeth out thence shall be torn to pieces, because their transgressions be many.* And of their *prophets* it is said: *O Israel, thy prophets are like* FOXES *in the deserts,* Ezek. xiii. 4; Jer. viii. 17; xv. 3."

Verse 26. *Ten women shall bake your bread in one oven*] Though in general every family in the East bakes its own bread, yet there are some *public bakehouses* where the bread of several families is baked at a certain price. Moses here foretells that the desolation should be so great and the want so pressing that there should be many *idle hands* to be employed, many mouths to be fed, and very little for each: *Ten women shall bake your bread in one oven*, &c.

Verse 29. *Ye shall eat the flesh of your sons, &c.*] This was literally fulfilled at the siege of Jerusalem. Josephus, WARS of the Jews, book vii., chap. ii., gives us a particular instance in dreadful detail of a woman named *Mary*, who, in the extremity of the famine during the siege, killed her sucking child, roasted, and had eaten part of it when discovered by the soldiers! See this threatened, Jer. xix. 9.

A. M. 2514.
B. C. 1490.
An. Exod. Isr. 2.
Abib or Nisan.

34 [n] Then shall the land enjoy her Sabbaths, as long as it lieth desolate, and ye *be* in your enemies' land; *even* then shall the land rest, and enjoy her Sabbaths.

35 As long as it lieth desolate it shall rest; because it did not rest in your [o] Sabbaths, when ye dwelt upon it.

36 And upon them that are left *alive* of you, [p] I will send a faintness into their hearts in the lands of their enemies; and [q] the sound of a [r] shaken leaf shall chase them; and they shall flee, as fleeing from a sword; and they shall fall when none pursueth.

37 And [s] they shall fall one upon another, as it were before a sword, when none pursueth: and [t] ye shall have no power to stand before your enemies.

38 And ye shall perish among the heathen, and the land of your enemies shall eat you up.

39 And they that are left of you [u] shall pine away in their iniquity, in your enemies' lands; and also in the iniquities of their fathers shall they pine away with them.

40 [v] If they shall confess their iniquity, and the iniquity of their fathers, with their trespass which they trespassed against me, and that also they have walked contrary unto me;

41 And *that* I also have walked contrary unto them, and have brought them into the land of their enemies; if then their [w] uncircumcised hearts be [x] humbled, and they then accept of the punishment of their iniquity;

A. M. 2514.
B. C. 1490.
An. Exod. Isr. 2.
Abib or Nisan.

42 Then will I [y] remember my covenant with Jacob, and also my covenant with Isaac, and also my covenant with Abraham will I remember; and I will [z] remember the land.

43 [a] The land also shall be left of them, and shall enjoy her Sabbaths, while she lieth desolate without them: and they shall accept of the punishment of their iniquity: because, even because they [b] despised my judgments, and because their soul abhorred my statutes.

44 And yet for all that, when they be in the land of their enemies, [c] I will not cast them away, neither will I abhor them, to destroy them utterly, and to break my covenant with them: for I *am* the LORD their God.

45 But I will [d] for their sakes remember the covenant of their ancestors, [e] whom I brought forth out of the land of Egypt, in the sight of [f] the heathen, that I might be their God: I *am* the LORD.

46 [g] These *are* the statutes, and judgments, and laws, which the LORD made between him and the children of Israel [h] in Mount Sinai, by the hand of Moses.

---

[n] 2 Chron. xxxvi. 21.—[o] Ch. xxv. 2.—[p] Ezek. xxi. 7, 12, 15.—[q] Ver. 17; Job xv. 21; Prov. xxviii. 1.—[r] Heb. *driven.* [s] Isa. x. 4; see Judg. vii. 22; 1 Sam. xiv. 15, 16.—[t] Josh. vii. 12, 13; Judg. ii. 14.—[u] Deut. iv. 27; xxviii. 64; Neh. i. 9; Jer. iii. 25; xxix. 12, 13; Ezek. iv. 17; vi. 9; xx. 43; xxiv. 23; xxxiii. 10; xxxvi. 31; Hos. v. 15; Zech. x. 9.—[v] Num. v. 7; 1 Kings viii. 33, 35, 47; Neh. ix. 2; Dan. ix. 3, 4; Prov. xxviii. 13; Luke xv. 18; 1 John i. 9.

[w] See Jer. vi. 10; ix. 25, 26; Ezek. xliv. 7; Acts vii. 51; Rom. ii. 29; Col. ii. 11.—[x] 1 Kings xxi. 29; 2 Chron. xii. 6, 7, 12; xxxii. 26; xxxiii. 12, 13.—[y] Exod. ii. 24; vi. 5; Psa. cvi. 45; Ezek. xvi. 60.—[z] Psa. cxxxvi. 23.—[a] Ver. 34, 35. [b] Verse 15.—[c] Deut. iv. 31; 2 Kings xiii. 23; Rom. xi. 2. [d] Rom. xi. 28.—[e] Chap. xxii. 33; xxv. 38.—[f] Psa. xcviii. 2; Ezek. xx. 9, 14, 22.—[g] Chapter xxvii. 34; Deut. vi. 1; xii. 1; xxxiii. 4; John i. 17.—[h] Chap. xxv. 1.

Verse 34. *Then shall the land enjoy her Sabbaths*] This Houbigant observes to be a historical truth.—"From Saul to the Babylonish captivity are numbered about *four hundred and ninety years*, during which period there were *seventy Sabbaths* of years; for 7, multiplied by 70, make 490. Now the Babylonish captivity lasted *seventy years*, and during that time the land of Israel *rested*. Therefore the land rested just *as many years* in the Babylonish captivity, as it *should have rested Sabbaths* if the Jews had observed the law relative to the Sabbaths of the land." This is a most remarkable fact, and deserves to be particularly noticed, as a most literal fulfilment of the prophetic declaration in this verse: *Then shall the land enjoy her Sabbaths as long as it lieth desolate, and ye be in your enemies' land.*

May it not be argued from this that the law concerning the Sabbatical year *was observed till Saul's time*, as it is only *after* this period the land enjoyed its rest in the seventy years' captivity? And if that breach of the law was thus punished, may it not be presumed it had been fulfilled till then, or else the captivity would have lasted longer, i. e., till the land had enjoyed *all* its rests, of which it had ever been thus deprived?

Verse 38. *The land of your enemies shall eat you up.*] Does this refer to the total loss of the *ten tribes?* These are so completely swallowed up in *some enemies'* land, that nothing concerning their existence or place of residence remains but mere conjecture.

Verse 44. *Neither will I abhor them to destroy them utterly*] Though God has literally fulfilled all his threatenings upon this people, in dispossessing them of their land, destroying their polity, overturning their city, demolishing their temple, and scattering themselves over the face of the whole earth; yet he has, in his providence, strangely preserved them as a *distinct* people, and in very considerable numbers also. He still remembers the *covenant of their ancestors*, and in his providence and grace he has some very important design in their favour. All Israel shall yet be saved, and, with the Gentiles, they shall all be re-

stored to his favour; and under Christ Jesus, the great Shepherd, become, with them, one grand everlasting fold.

Verse 46. *These* are *the statutes, and judgments, &c.*] See on ver. 15. This verse appears to be the proper concluding verse of the whole book; and I rather think that the 27th chapter originally followed the 25th. As the law was anciently written upon skins of parchment, sheep or goat skins, pasted or stitched together, and all rolled up in one roll, the matter being written in columns, one of those columns might have been very easily displaced, and thus whole chapters might have been readily interchanged.—It is likely that this might have been the case in the present instance. Others endeavour to solve this difficulty, by supposing that the 27th chapter was *added* after the book had been finished; and therefore there is apparently a double conclusion, one at the end of the 26th and the other at the end of the 27th chapter. However the above may have been, all the ancient versions agree in concluding both the chapters in nearly the same way; yet the 26th chapter must be allowed to be by far the most natural conclusion of the book.

The most important points in this chapter have already been particularly noticed in the notes; and to those on the 15th, 34th, and 44th verses, the reader is especially referred. How unwilling is God to cast off his people! and yet how sure is their rejection if they refuse to obey and live to him! No nation has ever been so signally *elected* as the Jews; and yet no nation has ever been so signally and so awfully *reprobated*. O Britain, be not high-minded, but fear! Behold here the goodness and severity of God!

CHAPTER XXVII.

Laws concerning vows, 1, 2. *Of males and females from twenty to sixty years of age, and their valuation,* 3, 4. *Of the same from five to twenty years,* 5. *Of the same from* a month *to five years of age,* 6. *Of males and females from sixty years old and upwards, and their valuation,* 7. *The priest shall value the poor according to his ability,* 8. *Concerning* beasts *that are vowed, and their valuation,* 9–13. *Concerning the sanctification of* a house, 14, 15. *Concerning the field that is sanctified or consecrated to the Lord, to the year of jubilee,* 16–24. *Every estimation shall be made in* shekels, *according to the shekel of the sanctuary,* 25. *The firstlings of clean beasts, being already the Lord's, cannot be vowed,* 26. *That of an unclean beast may be redeemed,* 27. *Every thing* devoted *to God shall be unalienable and unredeemable, and continue the Lord's property till death,* 28, 29. *All the tithe of the land is the Lord's,* 30; *but it may be redeemed by adding a fifth part,* 31. *The tithe of the* herd *and the* flock *is also his,* 32. *The tenth that passes under the rod shall not be changed,* 33. *The conclusion of the book,* 34.

A. M. 2514. B. C. 1490. An. Exod. Isr. 2. Abib or Nisan.

AND the Lord spake unto
Moses, saying,
2 Speak unto the children of
Israel, and say unto them, [a] When a man
shall make a singular vow, the persons *shall
be* for the Lord, by thy estimation.
3 And thy estimation shall be
of the male, from twenty years
old even unto sixty years old,
even thy estimation [b] shall be fifty shekels of
silver, [c] after the shekel of the sanctuary.
4 And if it *be* a female, then thy

[a] Num. vi. 2; see Judg. xi. 30, 31, 39; 1 Sam. i. 11, 28; Gen. xxviii. 20–22; Deut. xxiii. 21–23.——[b] Num. xviii. 16.——[c] Exod. xxx. 13.

NOTES ON CHAP. XXVII.

Verse 2. *When a man shall make a singular vow*] The verse is short and obscure, and may be translated thus: *A man who shall have separated a vow, according to thy estimation, of souls unto the Lord;* which may be paraphrased thus: He who shall have vowed or consecrated a soul, i. e., a living creature, whether *man* or *beast*, if he wish to redeem what he has thus vowed or consecrated, he shall ransom or redeem it according to the priest's estimation; for the priest shall judge of the properties, qualifications, and age of the person or beast, and the circumstances of the person who has vowed it, and shall regulate the value accordingly; and the money shall be put into his hands for the service of the sanctuary. A vow (says Mr. Ainsworth) is a religious promise made unto the Lord, and for the most part with prayer, and paid with thanksgiving, Num. xxi. 2, 3; Psa. lxvi. 13, 14. Vows were either of abstinence, such as are spoken of Num. xxx., and the vow of the Nazarite, Num. vi.; or they were to give something to the Lord, as sacrifices, Lev. vii. 16, or the value of persons, beasts, houses, or lands, concerning which the law is here given. A man might vow or devote *himself*, his *children*, (ver. 5, 6,) his *domestics*, his *cattle*, his *goods*, &c. And in this chapter rules are laid down for the redemption of all these things. But if, after consecrating these things, he refused to redeem them, then they became the Lord's property for ever. The *persons* continued all their lives devoted to the service of the sanctuary; the *goods* were sold for the profit of the temple or the priests; the *animals*, if clean, were offered in sacrifice; if not proper for sacrifice, were sold, and the price devoted to sacred uses. This is a general view of the different laws relative to *vows*, mentioned in this chapter.

Verse 3. *From twenty years old even unto sixty—fifty shekels*] A man from *twenty* to *sixty* years of age, if consecrated to the Lord by a vow, might be redeemed for *fifty shekels*, which, at 3*s*. each, amounted to 7*l*. 10*s*. sterling.

Verse 4. *And if it be a female*] The *woman*, at

A. M. 2514.
B. C. 1490.
An. Exod. Isr. 2.
Abib or Nisan.

estimation shall be thirty shekels.
5 And if *it be* from five years
old even unto twenty years old, then thy estimation shall be of the male twenty shekels,
and for the female ten shekels.
6 And if *it be* from a month old even unto
five years old, then thy estimation shall be of
the male five shekels of silver, and for the
female thy estimation *shall be* three shekels
of silver.
7 And if *it be* from sixty years old, and above;
if *it be* a male, then thy estimation shall be
fifteen shekels, and for the female ten shekels.
8 But if he be poorer than thy estimation,
then he shall present himself before the priest,
and the priest shall value him; according to
his ability that vowed shall the priest value him.
9 And if *it be* a beast, whereof men bring an
offering unto the LORD, all that *any man* giveth
of such unto the LORD, shall be holy.
10 He [d] shall not alter it, nor change it, a
good for a bad, or a bad for a
good: and if he shall at all
change beast for beast, then it
and the exchange thereof shall be holy.
11 And if *it be* any unclean beast, of which
they do not offer a sacrifice unto the LORD, then
he shall present the beast before the priest:
12 And the priest shall value it, whether it
be good or bad: [e] as thou valuest it, *who art*
the priest, so shall it be.
13 [f] But if he will at all redeem it, then he
shall add a fifth *part* thereof unto thy estimation.
14 And when a man shall sanctify his house
to be holy unto the LORD, then the priest shall
estimate it, whether it be good or bad: as the
priest shall estimate it, so shall it stand.
15 [g] And if he that sanctified it will redeem
his house, then he shall add the fifth *part* of
the money of thy estimation unto it, and it
shall be his.
16 And if a man shall sanctify unto the
LORD *some part* of a field of his possession,

[d] James i. 8.——[e] Heb. *according to thy estimation, O priest.*

[f] Ver. 15, 19.——[g] Ver. 13.

the same age, vowed unto the Lord, might be redeemed for *thirty shekels*, 4*l*. 10*s*. sterling, a little more than one half of the value of the man; for this obvious reason, that a *woman*, if employed, could not be of so much use in the service of the sanctuary as the *man*, and was therefore of much less value.

Verse 5. *From five years old*] The *boy* that was vowed might be redeemed for *twenty* shekels, 3*l*. sterling; the *girl*, for *ten* shekels, just one half, 1*l*. 10*s*.

Verse 6. *A month old*] The *male child*, *five* shekels, 15*s*., the *female*, *three* shekels, 9*s*. Being both in comparative infancy, they were nearly of an equal value. None were vowed under a *month* old: the first-born being always considered as the Lord's property, could not be vowed, see ver. 26.

Verse 7. *Sixty years old*] The *old man* and the *old woman*, being nearly past labour, were nearly of an *equal value;* hence the one was estimated at *fifteen* shekels, 2*l*. 5*s*., the other at *ten* shekels, 1*l*. 10*s*. This was about the same ratio as that of the children, ver. 5, and for the same reason.

Verse 10. *He shall not alter it, nor change it, a good for a bad, &c.*] Whatever was consecrated to God by a *vow*, or purpose of heart, was considered from that moment as the Lord's property; to *change* which was *impiety;* to *withhold* it, *sacrilege*. Reader, hast thou ever dedicated thyself, or any part of thy property, to the service of thy Maker? If so, hast thou paid thy vows? Or hast thou *altered* thy *purpose*, or *changed* thy *offering?* Has he received from thy hands a *bad* for a *good?* Wast *thou* not vowed and consecrated to God in thy baptism? Are his vows still upon thee? Hast thou "renounced the devil and all his works, the pomps and vanities of this wicked world, and all the sinful lusts of the flesh?" Dost thou feel thyself bound "to keep God's holy will and commandments, and walk in the same all the days of thy life?" Was not this thy baptismal covenant? And hast thou renounced IT? Take heed! God is not mocked: that which thou sowest, thou shalt also reap. If thou rob God of thy *heart*, he will deprive thee of his *heaven*.

Verse 11. *Any unclean beast*] See on ver. 2.

Verse 13. *Shall add a fifth* part] This was probably intended to prevent *rash* vows and covetous redemptions. The priest alone was to value the thing; and to whatever his valuation was, a *fifth part* must be added by him who wished to redeem the consecrated thing. Thus, if the priest valued it at *forty shekels*, if the former owner redeemed it he was obliged to give *forty-eight*.

Verse 14. *Shall sanctify his house*] The yearly rent of which, when thus consecrated, went towards the repairs of the tabernacle, which was the house of the Lord.

Verse 16. Some part *of a field*] Though the preceding words are not in the text, yet it is generally allowed they should be supplied here, as it was not lawful for a man to vow his *whole estate*, and thus make his family beggars, in order to enrich the Lord's sanctuary: this God would not permit. The rabbins teach that the land or field, whether good or bad, was valued at *forty-eight* shekels, for all the years of the jubilee, provided the field was large enough to sow a *homer* of barley. The חמר *chomer* was different from the עמר *omer:* the latter held about *three quarts*, the former, *seventy-five gallons three pints;* see the note on Exod. xvi. 16. Some suppose that the land was rated, not at *fifty shekels* for the whole of the years of the jubilee, for this would be but about 3*s*. per annum;

a

A. M. 2514. B. C. 1490. An. Exod. Isr. 2. Abib or Nisan.

then thy estimation shall be according to the seed thereof: [h] a homer of barley seed *shall be valued* at fifty shekels of silver.

17 If he sanctify his field from the year of jubilee, according to thy estimation it shall stand.

18 But if he sanctify his field after the jubilee, then the priest shall [i] reckon unto him the money according to the years that remain, even unto the year of the jubilee, and it shall be abated from thy estimation.

19 [k] And if he that sanctified the field will in any wise redeem it, then he shall add the fifth *part* of the money of thy estimation unto it, and it shall be assured to him.

20 And if he will not redeem the field, or if he have sold the field to another man, it shall not be redeemed any more.

21 But the field, [l] when it goeth out in the jubilee, shall be holy unto the LORD, as a field [m] devoted; [n] the possession thereof shall be the priest's.

22 And if *a man* sanctify unto the LORD a field which he hath bought, which *is* not of the fields of [o] his possession;

23 [p] Then the priest shall reckon unto him the worth of thy estimation, *even* unto the year of the jubilee: and he shall give thine estimation in that day, *as* a holy thing unto the LORD.

24 [q] In the year of the jubilee the field shall return unto him of whom it was bought, *even* to him to whom the possession of the land *did belong*.

25 And all thy estimation shall be according to the shekel of the sanctuary: [r] twenty gerahs shall be the shekel.

26 Only the [s] firstling [t] of the beasts, which should be the LORD's firstling, no man shall sanctify it; whether *it be* ox, or sheep: it *is* the LORD's.

27 And if *it be* of an unclean beast, then he shall redeem *it* according to thine estimation, [u] and shall add a fifth *part* of it thereto: or if it be not redeemed, then it shall be sold according to thy estimation.

28 [v] Notwithstanding no devoted thing, that a man shall devote unto the LORD of all that he hath, *both* of man and beast, and of the field of his possession, shall be sold or redeemed: every devoted thing *is* most holy unto the LORD.

29 [w] None devoted, which shall be devoted of men, shall be redeemed; *but* shall surely be put to death.

[h] Or, the land of a *homer*, &c.——[i] Chap. xxv. 15, 16. [k] Ver. 13.——[l] Chap. xxv. 10, 28, 31.——[m] Ver. 28.——[n] Num. xviii. 14; Ezek. xliv. 29.——[o] Chap. xxv. 10, 25.——[p] Ver. 18. [q] Chap. xxv. 28.

[r] Exod. xxx. 13; Num. iii. 47; xviii. 16; Ezek. xlv. 12. [s] Heb. *first-born*, &c.——[t] Exod. xiii. 2, 12; xxii. 30; Num. xviii. 17; Deut. xv. 19.——[u] Ver. 11, 12, 13.——[v] Ver. 21; Josh. vi. 17, 18, 19.——[w] Num. xxi. 2, 3.

but that it was rated *according to its produce*, *fifty* shekels for every *homer* of barley it produced.

Verse 21. *As a field devoted*] It is חרם *cherem*, a thing *so devoted to God* as never more to be capable of being redeemed. See on ver. 29.

Verse 25. *Shekel of the sanctuary*] A standard shekel; the standard being kept in the sanctuary to try and regulate all the weights in the land by. See Gen. xx. 16; xxiii. 15.

Verse 28. *No devoted thing—shall be sold or redeemed*] This is the חרם *cherem*, which always meant an absolute unredeemable grant to God.

Verse 29. *Which shall be devoted of men*] Every man who is devoted shall surely be put to death; or, as some understand it, be the Lord's property, or be employed in his service, till death. The law mentioned in these two verses has been appealed to by the enemies of Divine revelation as a proof, that under the Mosaic dispensation *human sacrifices* were offered to God; but this can never be conceded. Had there been such a law, it certainly would have been more explicitly revealed, and not left in the compass of a few words only, where the meaning is very difficult to be ascertained; and the words themselves differently translated by most interpreters. That there were *persons* devoted to destruction under the Mosaic dispensation, is sufficiently evident, for the whole Canaanitish nations were thus devoted by the Supreme Being himself, because the cup of their iniquity was full; but that they were not *sacrificed to God*, the whole history sufficiently declares. *Houbigant* understands the passage as speaking of these alone; and says, *Non alios licebat anathemate voveri, quam Chananæos, quos jusserat Deus ad internecionem deleri.* "It was not lawful to devote any persons to death but the Canaanites, whom God had commanded to be entirely extirpated." This is perfectly correct; but he might have added that it was because they were the most impure idolaters, and because the cup of their iniquity was full. These God commanded to be put to death; and who can doubt *his* right to do so, who is the Maker of man, and the Fountain of justice? But what has this to do with *human sacrifices?* Just nothing. No more than the execution of an ordinary criminal, or a *traitor*, in the common course of justice, has to do with a sacrifice to God. In the destruction of such idolaters, no religious formality whatever was observed; nor any thing that could give the transaction even the most distant semblance of a sacrifice. In this way Jericho was commanded to be destroyed, Josh. vi. 17;

A. M. 2514.
B. C. 1490.
An. Exod. Isr. 2.
Abib or Nisan.

30 And [x] all the tithe of the land, *whether* of the seed of the land, *or* of the fruit of the tree, *is* the LORD'S: *it is* holy unto the LORD.

31 [y] And if a man will at all redeem *aught* of his tithes, he shall add thereto the fifth *part* thereof.

32 And concerning the tithe of the herd, or of the flock, *even* of whatsoever [z] passeth under the rod, the tenth shall be holy unto the LORD.

33 He shall not search whether it be good or bad, [a] neither shall he change it: and if he change it at all, then both it and the change thereof shall be holy; it shall not be redeemed.

34 [b] These *are* the commandments which the LORD commanded Moses for the children of Israel, in Mount Sinai.

[x] Gen. xxviii. 22; Num. xviii. 21, 24; 2 Chron. xxxi. 5, 6, 12; Neh. xiii. 12; Mal. iii. 8, 10.
[y] Ver. 13.——[z] See Jer. xxxiii. 13; Ezek. xx. 37; Mic. vii. 14.
[a] Ver. 10.——[b] Chap. xxvi. 46.

and the Amalekites, Deut. xxv. 19; 1 Sam. xv. 3: but in all these cases the people commanded to be destroyed were such *sinners* as God's justice did not think proper to spare longer. And has not every system of law the same power? And do we not concede such power to the civil magistrate, for the welfare of the state? God, who is the sovereign arbiter of life and death, acts here in his juridical and legislative capacity; but these are victims to *justice*, not *religious sacrifices*.

It may be necessary just farther to note that two kinds of vows are mentioned in this chapter:—1. The נדר *neder*, (see on chap. vii.,) which comprehends all those things which, when once devoted, might be redeemed at a certain price, according to the valuation of the priest. 2. The חרם *cherem*, those things vowed to God of which there remained no power of redemption; they were *most holy*, i. e., so absolutely devoted to God that they could neither be changed, alienated, nor redeemed: probably because no mental reservation had been made, as in the above case may be supposed. On this ground the word was afterward applied to the most solemn and awful kind of *excommunication*, meaning a person so entirely devoted to the stroke of vindictive justice, as never to be capable of receiving pardon; and hence the word may be well applied in this sense to the *Canaanites*, the cup of whose iniquity was full, and who were consigned, without reprieve, to final *extermination*.

Verse 30. *All the tithe of the land*] This God claims as his own; and it is spoken of here as being a point perfectly settled, and concerning which there was neither doubt nor difficulty. See my view of this subject Gen. xxviii., after ver. 22, to which I do not see the necessity of adding any thing.

Verse 32. *Whatsoever passeth under the rod*] The signification of this verse is well given by the rabbins: "When a man was to give the tithe of his sheep or calves to God, he was to shut up the whole flock in one fold, in which there was one narrow door capable of letting out one at a time. The owner, about to give the tenth to the Lord, stood by the door with a rod in his hand, the end of which was dipped in vermilion or red ochre. The mothers of those lambs or calves stood without: the door being opened, the young ones ran out to join themselves to their dams; and as they passed out the owner stood with his rod over them, and counted one, two, three, four, five, &c., and when the *tenth* came, he touched it with the coloured rod, by which it was distinguished to be the tithe calf, sheep, &c., and whether poor or lean, perfect or blemished, that was received as the legitimate tithe." It seems to be in reference to this custom that the Prophet Ezekiel, speaking to Israel, says: *I will cause you to pass under the rod, and will bring you into the bond of the covenant*—you shall be once more claimed as the *Lord's property*, and be in all things devoted to his service, being *marked* or *ascertained*, by especial providences and manifestations of his kindness, to be his *peculiar people*.

Verse 34. *These are the commandments*] This conclusion is very similar to that at the end of the preceding chapter. I have already supposed that this chapter should have followed the 25th, and that the 26th originally terminated the book.

Mr. *Ainsworth*, the whole of whose writings are animated with the spirit of piety, concludes this book with the following excellent remarks:—

"The *tithes* in Israel being thus sanctified by the commandment of God to his *honour*, the maintenance of his *ministers*, and the relief of the *poor*, it taught them and teaches us to *honour the Lord with our substance*, (Prov. iii. 9,) acknowledging him to be the author of all our *increase and store;* (Deut. viii. 13–18; Hos. ii. 8;) to honour his MINISTERS, and *to communicate unto them in all good things*, (1 Tim. v. 17, 18; Gal. vi. 6,) that *they who sow unto us spiritual things should reap our carnal things*, (1 Cor. ix. 11,) and *to give* ALMS *of such things as we have, that all things may be clear unto us*, (Luke xi. 41,) yea, even *to sell that we have, and give alms; to provide ourselves bags that wax not old, a treasure in the heavens that faileth not*, Luke xii. 33." They who forget their *Maker*, his *ministers*, and the *poor*, are never likely to hear that blessed word in the great day: "Come, ye blessed of my Father, inherit the kingdom prepared for *you;* for I was hungry, and *ye* gave me meat; thirsty, and *ye* gave me drink; naked, and *ye* clothed me; sick and in prison, and *ye* came unto me."

READER, thou hast now gone through the whole of this most interesting book; a book whose subject is too little regarded by Christians in general. Here thou mayest discover the rigid requisitions of Divine justice, the sinfulness of sin, the exceeding breadth of the commandment, and the end of all human perfec-

tion. And now what thinkest thou of that word, "Whatsoever the law saith, it saith to them who are under the law?" Rom. iii. 19. But who are under the law—the condemning power of the pure, rigid, moral law of God? Not the *Jews* only, but every soul of man: all to whom it is sent, and who acknowledge it as a Divine revelation, and have not been redeemed from the guilt of sin by the grace of our Lord Jesus Christ; for "cursed is every one that continueth not in all things that are written in the book of the law to do them." By this law then is the *knowledge*, but not the *cure*, of sin. Hear then what God saith unto thee: "If therefore perfection were by the Levitical priesthood, (for under it the people received the law,) what farther need was there that another priest should rise after the order of Melchisedec, and not be called after the order of Aaron? For the priesthood being changed, there is made of necessity a change also of the law; Heb. vii. 11, 12. Now of the things which we have spoken, this is the sum: We have such a high priest, who is set on the right hand of the throne of the Majesty in the heavens; a minister of the sanctuary, and of the true tabernacle, which the Lord pitched, and not man; ibid. viii. 1, 2. For it is not possible that the blood of bulls and of goats should take away sins; ibid. x. 4. But Christ being come a high priest of good things to come,—neither by the blood of goats and calves, but by his own blood, he entered in once into the holy place, having obtained eternal redemption for us. And for this cause he is the Mediator of the New Testament, that, by means of death, they which are called might receive the promise of eternal inheritance. And without shedding of blood is no remission. So Christ was once offered to bear the sins of many, and unto them that look for him shall he appear the second time, without sin, unto salvation;" Heb. ix. 11, 12, 15, 22, 28. We see then that Christ was the END of the law for *righteousness* (for *justification*) to every one that believeth. "Unto him, therefore, who hath loved us, and washed us from our sins in his own blood, and hath made us kings and priests unto God and his Father; to him be glory and dominion for ever and ever. Amen." Rev. i. 5, 6.

SECTIONS in the Book of Leviticus, carried on from Exodus, which ends with the TWENTY-THIRD.

The TWENTY-FOURTH, called ויקרא *vaiyikra*, begins chap. i. 6, and ends chap. vi. 7.

The TWENTY-FIFTH, called צו *tsav*, begins chap. vi. 8, and ends chap. viii. 36.

The TWENTY-SIXTH, called שמיני *shemini*, begins chap. ix. 1, and ends chap. xi. 47.

The TWENTY-SEVENTH, called תזריע *tazria*, begins chap. xii. 1, and ends chap. xiii. 59.

The TWENTY-EIGHTH, called מצרע *metsora*, begins chap. xiv. 1, and ends chap. xv. 33.

The TWENTY-NINTH, called אחרי מות *acharey moth*, begins chap. xvi. 1, and ends chap. xviii. 30.

The THIRTIETH, called קדשים *kedoshim*, begins chap. xix. 1, and ends chap. xx. 27.

The THIRTY-FIRST, called אמר *emor*, begins chap. xxi. 1, and ends chap. xxiv. 23.

The THIRTY-SECOND, called בהר סיני *behar Sinai*, begins chap. xxv. 1, and ends chap. xxvi. 2.

The THIRTY-THIRD, called בחקתי *bechukkothai*, begins chap. xxvi. 3, and ends chap. xxvii. 34.

These sections, as was observed on Exodus, have their technical names from some remarkable word, either in the first or second verse of their commencement.

MASORETIC *Notes* on LEVITICUS.

The *number* of *verses* in *vaiyikra*, i. e., Leviticus, is 859. The symbol of which is נט"ף. ף *pe* final stands for 800, נ *nun* for 50, and ט *teth* for 9.

The *middle verse* is the 11th of chap. xv.: *And he that toucheth the flesh, &c.*

Its *pareshioth*, or larger sections, are 10, the memorial symbol of which is taken from Gen. xxx. 11; בא גד *ba gad, a troop cometh:* in which ב *beth* stands for 2, א *aleph* for 1, ג *gimel* for 3, and ד *daleth* for 4.

Its *sedarim*, or Masoretic sections, are 23. The symbol of which is taken from Psa. i, 2, יהגה *yehgeh: In thy law shall he* MEDITATE *day and night.*

Its *perakim*, or modern chapters, are 27. The memorial sign of which is ואהיה *veeyeheh*, Gen. xxvi. 3: AND I WILL BE *with thee, and will bless thee.*

The number of its *open divisions* is 52; of its *close divisions*, 46: total 98. The memorial sign of which is צח *tsach*, Cant. v. 10; *My beloved is* WHITE *and ruddy.* In this word צ *tsaddi* stands for 90, and ח *cheth* for 8.

VERSES 859. WORDS 11,902. LETTERS computed to be 44,989.

See the concluding note on GENESIS.

Finished the correction of Exodus and Leviticus, April 2, 1827.—A. Clarke.

PREFACE TO THE BOOK

OF

NUMBERS.

THIS, which is the fourth book in order of the Pentateuch, has been called NUMBERS, from its containing an account of the *numbering* and *marshalling* the Israelites in ther journey through the wilderness to the promised land. Its ENGLISH name is derived from the title it bears in the VULGATE Latin, *Numeri*, which is a literal translation of the Greek word Αριθμοι, its title in the SEPTUAGINT; and from both, our SAXON ancestors called it Ꝼetel, *numeration*, "because in this the children of Israel were numbered," ꝼoꞃ ꝥam ꝥe Iꞅꞃahela beaꞃn ꝥæꞃon on ꝥæꞃe ȝeteald. This title, however, does not properly apply to more than the *three* first chapters, and the 26th. This book, like the preceding, takes its name among the HEBREWS from a distinguishing word in the commencement. It is frequently called וידבר VAIDABBER, *and he spoke*, from its initial word; but in most Hebrew Bibles its running title is במדבר BEMIDBAR, *in the wilderness*, which is the *fifth* word in the *first* verse.

The contents of the book of Numbers are briefly the following: On the *first day* of the *first month* of the *second year* after the departure from Egypt, the tabernacle being erected, and it and the priests consecrated, Moses is commanded to make a *census* or enumeration of the people, the Levites excepted, who were appointed to watch over, guard, pitch, and carry the tabernacle and its holy furniture; chap. i.

To form the vast mass of the people into a regular camp, each tribe by itself under its own captain or chief, known by his proper standard, and occupying an assigned place in reference to the tabernacle; chap. ii.

Moses is commanded to separate the Levites to the service of the tabernacle, whom God chooses to take, instead of the first-born of every family, which he claimed as his own. When these were selected in their families, &c., the sum amounted to 22,273; chap. iii.

All this tribe is appointed to serve the tabernacle in a variety of offices, each person from the age of thirty till fifty, after which he was excused from farther service; chap. iv.

When these points were settled, God commands them to purify the camp by the expulsion of every unclean person, and establishes the trial of the suspected adulteress by the *waters of jealousy*; chap. v.

He next institutes the laws relative to *Nazarites*; and lays down the *form* according to which the people shall be blessed; chap. vi.

Then follows a particular account of the offerings made to the tabernacle by the princes, or chiefs of the twelve tribes, and the amount of those offerings; chap. vii.

When this work was finished, the Levites were consecrated to their respective services and the duration of the service of each ascertained; chap. viii.

The passover is commanded to be kept, and the first one is celebrated in the wilderness on the 14th of the first month of the second year after their departure from Egypt chap. ix.

Moses is commanded to make two silver trumpets; he is informed of their use, in what order the different tribes shall march, with the ceremonies at fixing and removing the tabernacle and the departure of the people from the wilderness of Sinai on the twentieth day of the second month of the second year of their exodus from Egypt; chap. x.

The people murmuring, the fire of the Lord consumes many of them; it ceases on the intercession of Moses: they murmur again, *quails* are sent, and they are smitten with a great plague; chap. xi.

Miriam and her brother Aaron rise up seditiously against Moses, having conceived some dislike against his *Cushite* wife, and supposing that he assumed too great an authority over the people: at this sedition the Lord is displeased, and smites Miriam with the leprosy; chap. xii.

Twelve spies are sent to examine the promised land; they pass through the whole, return at the end of forty days, and by bringing an evil report, dishearten the people; chap. xiii.

In consequence of this the whole congregation meditate a return to Egypt: God is displeased, and pronounces that all of them, from twenty years old and upwards, shall die in the wilderness. They repent, attack the Amalekites contrary to the commandment of God, and are discomfited; chap. xiv.

A number of ordinances and directions are given relative to the manner of conducting the worship of God in the promised land: different laws are repeated, and a Sabbath-breaker stoned to death; chap. xv.

Korah, Dathan, Abiram, and their associates, form an insurrection against Moses: they are swallowed up by an earthquake; the congregation murmur, and 14,700 of them are cut off; chap. xvi.

As a proof that God had called Aaron and his family to the priesthood, his *rod*, or *staff*, *buds*, and miraculously brings forth *blossoms* and *fruit*, and is commanded to be laid up before the testimony; chap. xvii.

The charges of the priests and Levites, and the portions they were to have of the Lord's offerings, for their support in the work; chap. xviii.

The ordinances of the *red heifer;* the *water of purification*, and its uses; chap. xix.

The death of Miriam; the waters of Meribah. The Lord tells Moses that, because he did not sanctify him in the eyes of the congregation, he shall not bring the people into the promised land. The king of *Edom* refuses the Israelites a passage through his territories. Aaron is stripped of his sacerdotal vestments on Mount Hor, and they are put on Eleazar, his son, who is to be a high priest in his stead. Aaron dies, and the people mourn for him thirty days; chap. xx.

Arad, one of the Canaanitish kings, attacks Israel, and he and his people are utterly destroyed. The people murmur for lack of bread and water; *fiery serpents* are sent among them, they repent; are healed by looking at a *brazen serpent*. They journey and come to *Beer*, where they find water; *Sihon*, king of the Amorites, attacks them, and is defeated; so is likewise *Og*, king of Bashan, and the people possess the lands of both; chap. xxi.

Balak, king of Moab, sends for *Balaam* to curse Israel; he departs, is opposed by an angel, and reproved by his ass, whom God, for the purpose, miraculously endued with the gift of speech. He comes to Balak, king of Moab, and shows him that Jehovah had limited his power; chap. xxii.

Balak offers sacrifices, and Balaam, under the influence of God, prophesies good concerning Israel; chap. xxiii.

Continuing to foretell the prosperity of Israel, and the destruction of their enemies, the king of Moab dismisses Balaam in great wrath; chap. xxiv.

The Israelites, seduced by the women of *Moab* and *Midian*, commit fornication and idolatry: the chiefs are hanged—bold act of Phinehas; chap. xxv.

A second *census* or enumeration of the people takes place, and the amount is 601,730, among whom not one of those of the first *census* was now found except *Joshua* and *Caleb;* chap. xxvi.

From the case of the daughters of *Zelophehad* a law is made to enable *daughters* to inherit. Moses ascends Mount Abarim, sees the promised land, and constitutes Joshua his successor; chap. xxvii.

A repetition of the laws relative to *burnt-offerings*, the *Sabbath*, the *passover*, *first-fruits*, &c.; chap. xxviii

The three solemnities of the seventh month are commanded to be held on the *first*, *tenth*, and *fourteenth* days of the month; chap. xxix.

Several laws and ordinances concerning *vows* of different kinds, made by various persons; when they should be confirmed, and in what cases annulled; chap. xxx.

Twelve thousand Israelites go against the people of Midian and slay them, their five kings, and Balaam their prophet; and the Israelites take immense booty in *persons*, *cattle*, *gold*, *silver*, and *precious stones*, of which they make a great offering to the Lord, because in this contest they lost not one man; chap. xxxi.

The children of *Reuben* and *Gad*, and the *half tribe* of *Manasseh*, request to receive for their inheritance the territories of *Sihon* and *Og* on the east side of Jordan; their desire is granted on the condition of their going over armed with their brethren, to assist them in conquering the land; chap. xxxii.

A circumstantial account of the forty-two journeys of the Israelites from their departure from *Rameses* till their arrival at *Jordan*. They are commanded to expel all the ancient inhabitants; chap. xxxiii.

The borders of the land are described, and the persons appointed by God, who should assist Joshua in dividing the land among the nine tribes and half; chap. xxxiv.

Forty-eight cities are to be assigned to the *Levites*, out of the twelve tribes, for their goods and for their cattle: and out of these they were to appoint six cities of refuge for the person who had unawares slain his neighbour; to one of which cities the manslayer was to escape, and tarry there till the death of the high priest; chap. xxxv.

A law established that the daughters to whom the paternal inheritance descends, shall not marry out of their own tribes, lest their inheritances should become alienated and lost by being blended with those of other tribes; chap. xxxvi. See the case of Zelophehad's daughters, chap. xxvii.

In this book, which comprehends the history of between thirty-eight and thirty-nine years, we have in one word a distinct account of the several stages of the Israelites' journey in the wilderness, the various occurrences on the way, their trials, rebellions, punishments, deliverances, conquests, &c., with several laws and ordinances not mentioned in the preceding books, together with a repetition and explanation of some others which had been previously delivered; the whole forming a most interesting history of the justice, mercy, and providence of God.

THE FOURTH BOOK OF MOSES,

CALLED

NUMBERS.

Year before the common Year of Christ, 1490.—Julian Period, 3224.—Cycle of the Sun, 27.—Dominical Letter, D.—Cycle of the Moon, 9.—Indiction, 6.—Creation from Tisri or September, 2514.

CHAPTER I.

On the first day *of the* second month *of the* second year *after Israel came out of Egypt, God commands Moses to number all the males of the people from* twenty years *and upward, who were effective men and able to go to war,* 1–3. *A chief of each tribe is associated with Moses and Aaron in this business,* 4; *the names of whom are given,* 5–16. *Moses assembles the people, who declare their pedigrees according to their families,* 17–19. *The descendants of* REUBEN *are numbered, and amount to* 46,500, *ver.* 20, 21. *Those of* SIMEON, 59,300, *ver.* 22, 23. *Those of* GAD, 45,650, *ver.* 24, 25. *Those of* JUDAH, 74,600, *ver.* 26, 27. *Those of* ISSACHAR, 54,400, *ver.* 28, 29. *Those of* ZEBULUN, 57,400, *ver.* 30, 31, *Those of* EPHRAIM, 40,500, *ver.* 32, 33. *Those of* MANASSEH, 32,200, *ver.* 34, 35. *Those of* BENJAMIN, 35,400, *ver.* 36, 37. *Those of* DAN, 62,700, *ver.* 38, 39. *Those of* ASHER, 41,500, *ver.* 40, 41. *Those of* NAPHTALI, 53,400, *ver.* 42, 43. *The amount of all the effective men in Israel, from* twenty *years old and upward, was* 603,550, *ver.* 44–46. *The* LEVITES *are not numbered with the tribes, because they were dedicated to the service of God. Their particular work is specified,* 47–54.

A. M. 2514.
B. C. 1490.
An. Exod. Isr. 2.
Ijar or Zif.

AND the LORD spake unto Moses [a] in the wilderness of Sinai, [b] in the tabernacle of the congregation, on the first *day* of the second month, in the second year after they were come out of the land of Egypt, saying,
2 [c] Take ye the sum of all the congregation of the children of Israel, after their families, by the house of their fathers, with the number of *their* names, every male by their polls;
3 From [d] twenty years old and upward, all that are able to go forth to war in Israel: thou and Aaron shall number them by their [e] armies.

[a] Exod. xix. 1; chap. x. 11, 12.——[b] Exod. xxv. 22.——[c] Exod. xxx. 12; xxxviii. 26; chap. xxvi. 2, 63, 64; 2 Sam. xxiv. 2; 1 Chron. xxi. 2.——[d] Exod. xxx. 14; Deut. iii. 18.——[e] Exod. xii. 17.

NOTES ON CHAP. I.

Verse 1. *The Lord spake unto Moses—on the first day of the second month*] As the tabernacle was erected upon the first day of the first month, in the second year after their coming out of Egypt, Exod. xl. 17; and this muster of the people was made on the first day of the second month, in the same year; it is evident that the transactions related in the preceding book must all have taken place in the space of *one month*, and during the time the Israelites were encamped at Mount Sinai, before they had begun their journey to the promised land.

Verse 2. *Take ye the sum, &c.*] God, having established the commonwealth of Israel by just and equitable laws, ordained every thing relative to the due performance of his own worship, erected his tabernacle, which was his throne, and the place of his residence among the people, and consecrated his priests who were to minister before him; he now orders his subjects to be mustered, 1. That they might see he had not forgotten his promise to Abraham, but was multiplying his posterity. 2. That they might observe due order in their march toward the promised land. 3. That the tribes and families might be properly distinguished; that all litigations concerning property, inheritance, &c., might, in all future times, be prevented. 4. That the promise concerning the Messiah might be known to have its due accomplishment, when in the fulness of time God should send him from the seed of Abraham through the house of David. And, 5. That they might know their strength for war; for although they should ever consider God as their protector and defence, yet it was necessary that they should be assured of their own fitness, naturally speaking, to cope with any ordinary enemy, or to surmount any common difficulties.

Verse 3. *From twenty years old and upward*] In this census no *women* were reckoned, nor *children*,

A. M. 2514.
B. C. 1490.
An. Exod. Isr. 2.
Ijar or Zif.

4 And with you there shall be a man of every tribe; every one head of the house of his fathers.

5 And these *are* the names of the men that shall stand with you: of *the tribe of* Reuben; Elizur the son of Shedeur.

6 Of Simeon; Shelumiel the son of Zurishaddai.

7 Of Judah; Nahshon the son of Amminadab.

8 Of Issachar; Nethaneel the son of Zuar.

9 Of Zebulun; Eliab the son of Helon.

10 Of the children of Joseph: of Ephraim; Elishama the son of Ammihud: of Manasseh; Gamaliel the son of Pedahzur.

11 Of Benjamin; Abidan the son of Gideoni.

12 Of Dan; Ahiezer the son of Ammishaddai.

13 Of Asher; Pagiel the son of Ocran.

14 Of Gad; Eliasaph the son of [f] Deuel.

15 Of Naphtali; Ahira the son of Enan.

16 [g] These *were* the renowned of the congregation, princes of the tribes of their fathers, [h] heads of thousands in Israel.

17 And Moses and Aaron took these men which are expressed by *their* names:

18 And they assembled all the congregation together on the first *day* of the second month, and they declared their pedigrees after their families, by the house of their fathers, according to the number of the names, from twenty years old and upward, by their polls.

19 As the LORD commanded Moses, so he numbered them in the wilderness of Sinai.

A. M. 2514.
B. C. 1490.
An. Exod. Isr. 2.
Ijar or Zif.

20 And the children of Reuben, Israel's eldest son, by their generations, after their families, by the house of their fathers, according to the number of the names, by their polls, every male from twenty years old and upward, all that were able to go forth to war;

21 Those that were numbered of them, *even* of the tribe of [i] Reuben, *were* forty and six thousand and five hundred.

22 Of the children of [k] Simeon, by their generations, after their families, by the house of their fathers, those that were numbered of them, according to the number of the names, by their polls, every male from twenty years old and upward, all that were able to go forth to war;

23 Those that were numbered of them, *even* of the tribe of Simeon, *were* fifty and nine thousand and three hundred.

24 Of the children of [l] Gad, by their generations, after their families, by the house of their fathers, according to the number of the names, from twenty years old and upward, all that were able to go forth to war;

25 Those that were numbered of them, *even* of the tribe of Gad, *were* forty and five thousand six hundred and fifty.

[f] Chap. vii. 48; chap. x. 22; chap. ii. 14, he is called *Reuel*. — [g] Chap. vii. 2; 1 Chron. xxvii. 16. — [h] Exod. xviii. 21, 25.

[i] Chap. ii. 10, 11; chap. xxvi. 7. — [k] Gen. xxix. 33; chap. xxxiv. 25–30. — [l] Gen. xxx. 10, 11.

nor *strangers*, nor the *Levites*, nor *old men*, which, collectively, must have formed an immense multitude; the Levites alone amounted to 22,300. True-born Israelites only are reckoned; such as were able to carry arms, and were expert for war.

Verse 14. *Eliasaph, the son of Deuel.*] This person is called *Reuel*, chap. ii. 14. As the ד *daleth* is very like the ר *resh*, it was easy to mistake the one for the other. The *Septuagint* and the *Syriac* have *Reuel* in this chapter; and in chap. ii. 14, the *Vulgate*, the *Samaritan*, and the *Arabic* have *Deuel* instead of *Reuel*, with which reading a vast number of MSS. concur; and this reading is supported by chap. x. 20; we may safely conclude therefore that דעואל *Deuel*, not רעואל *Reuel*, was the original reading. See *Kennicott*.

An ancient Jewish rabbin pretends to solve every difficulty by saying that "*Eliasaph* was a proselyte; that before he embraced the true faith he was called the son of *Reuel*, but that after his conversion he was called the son of *Deuel*." As *Reuel* may be translated the *breach of God*, and *Deuel* the *knowledge of God*, I suppose the rabbin grounded his supposition on the different meanings of the two words.

Verse 16. *These* were *the renowned*] Literally, *the called*, *of the congregation*—those who were summoned by *name* to attend. The order of the tribes in the above enumeration may be viewed thus:—

1. Reuben	Sons of Leah.
2. Simeon	
3. Judah	
4. Issachar	
5. Zebulun	
6. Ephraim	Sons of Rachel.
7. Manasseh	
8. Benjamin	
9. Dan . .	1st son of Bilhah, Rachel's maid.
10. Asher . .	2d son of Zilpah, Leah's maid.
11. Gad . .	1st son of Zilpah.
12. Naphtali .	2d son of Bilhah.

Verse 25. *Forty and five thousand six hundred and fifty.*] Mr. Ainsworth has remarked that Gad, the *handmaid's* son, is the only one of all the tribes whose number ends with *fifty*, all the others are by *thousands*, and end with *hundreds*; which shows God's admirable providence and blessing in multiplying them so, that no *odd* or *broken* number was among all the tribes. But see on ver. 46.

A. M. 2514.
B. C. 1490.
An. Exod. Isr. 2.
Ijar or Zif.

26 Of the children of [m] Judah, by their generations, after their families, by the house of their fathers, according to the number of the names, from twenty years old and upward, all that were able to go forth to war;

27 Those that were numbered of them, *even* of the tribe of Judah, *were* threescore and fourteen thousand and six hundred.

28 Of the children of [n] Issachar, by their generations, after their families, by the house of their fathers, according to the number of the names, from twenty years old and upward, all that were able to go forth to war;

29 Those that were numbered of them, *even* of the tribe of Issachar, *were* fifty and four thousand and four hundred.

30 Of the children of [o] Zebulun, by their generations, after their families, by the house of their fathers, according to the number of the names, from twenty years old and upward, all that were able to go forth to war;

31 Those that were numbered of them, *even* of the tribe of Zebulun, *were* fifty and seven thousand and four hundred.

32 Of the children of [p] Joseph, *namely*, of the children of [q] Ephraim, by their generations, after their families, by the house of their fathers, according to the number of the names, from twenty years old and upward, all that were able to go forth to war;

33 Those that were numbered of them, *even* of the tribe of Ephraim, *were* forty thousand and five hundred.

34 Of the children of [r] Manasseh, by their generations, after their families, by the house of their fathers, according to the number of the names, from twenty years old and upward, all that were able to go forth to war;

35 Those that were numbered of them, *even* of the tribe of Manasseh, *were* thirty and two thousand and two hundred.

A. M. 2514.
B. C. 1490.
An. Exod. Isr. 2.
Ijar or Zif.

36 Of the children of [s] Benjamin, by their generations, after their families, by the house of their fathers, according to the number of the names, from twenty years old and upward, all that were able to go forth to war;

37 Those that were numbered of them, *even* of the tribe of Benjamin, *were* thirty and five thousand and four hundred.

38 Of the children of [t] Dan, by their generations, after their families, by the house of their fathers, according to the number of the names, from twenty years old and upward, all that were able to go forth to war;

39 Those that were numbered of them, *even* of the tribe of Dan, *were* threescore and two thousand and seven hundred.

40 Of the children of Asher, by their generations, after their families, by the house of their fathers, according to the number of the names, from twenty years old and upward, all that were able to go forth to war;

41 Those that were numbered of them, *even* of the tribe of Asher, *were* forty and one thousand and five hundred.

42 Of the children of Naphtali, throughout their generations, after their families, by the house of their fathers, according to the number of the names, from twenty years old and upward, all that were able to go forth to war;

43 Those that were numbered of them, *even* of the tribe of Naphtali, *were* fifty and three thousand and four hundred.

44 [u] These *are* those that were numbered, which Moses and Aaron numbered, and the princes of Israel, *being* twelve men: each one was for the house of his fathers.

45 So were all those that were numbered of the children of Israel, by the house of their fathers, from twenty years old and upward, all that were able to go forth to war in Israel;

46 Even all they that were numbered were

[m] Gen. xxix. 35.——[n] Gen. xxx. 18.——[o] Gen. xxx. 20.——[p] Gen. xxx. 24.——[q] Gen. xlviii. 5, 6.

[r] Gen. xlviii. 12–20.——[s] Gen. xxxv. 16–18.——[t] Gen. xxx. 5, 6.
[u] Chap. xxvi. 64.

Verse 33. *The tribe of Ephraim—forty thousand and five hundred.*] Ephraim, as he was blessed beyond his eldest brother Manasseh, Gen. xlviii. 20, so here he is increased by thousands more than Manasseh, and more than the whole tribe of Benjamin, and his blessing continued above his brother, Deut. xxxiii. 17. And thus the prophecy, Gen. xlviii. 19, was fulfilled: *His younger brother* (Ephraim) *shall be greater than he*, (Manasseh.) No word of God can possibly fall to the ground: he alone sees the end from the beginning; his infinite wisdom embraces all occurrences, and it is his province alone to determine what is right, and to predict what himself has purposed to accomplish.

Verse 46. *All they that were numbered were six hundred thousand and three thousand and five hundred and fifty.*] What an astonishing increase from *seventy* souls that went down into Egypt, Gen. xlvi. 27, about 215 years before, where latterly they had endured the greatest hardships! But God's promise cannot fail,

A. M. 2514.
B. C. 1490.
An. Exod. Isr. 2.
Ijar or Zif.

[v] six hundred thousand and three
thousand and five hundred and
fifty.
47 But [w] the Levites after the tribe of their
fathers were not numbered among them.
48 For the LORD had spoken unto Moses,
saying,
49 [x] Only thou shalt not number the tribe
of Levi, neither take the sum of them among
the children of Israel:
50 [y] But thou shalt appoint the Levites over
the tabernacle of testimony, and over all the
vessels thereof, and over all things that *belong*
to it: they shall bear the tabernacle, and all the
vessels thereof; and they shall minister unto it,
[z] and shall encamp round about the tabernacle.
51 [a] And when the tabernacle setteth forward, the Levites shall take it
down: and when the tabernacle
is to be pitched, the Levites shall
set it up: [b] and the stranger that cometh nigh
shall be put to death.
52 And the children of Israel shall pitch
their tents, [c] every man by his own camp, and
every man by his own standard, throughout
their hosts.
53 [d] But the Levites shall pitch round about
the tabernacle of testimony, that there be no
[e] wrath upon the congregation of the children
of Israel: [f] and the Levites shall keep the
charge of the tabernacle of testimony.
54 And the children of Israel did according
to all that the LORD commanded Moses, so
did they.

[v] Exod. xxxviii. 26; see Exod. xii. 37; chap. ii. 32; xxvi. 51. — [w] Chap. ii. 33; see chap. iii., iv., xxvi. 57; 1 Chron. vi., xxi. 6. — [x] Chap. ii. 33; xxvi. 62. — [y] Exod. xxxviii. 21; chap. iii. 7, 8; iv. 15, 25, 26, 27, 33. — [z] Chap. iii. 23, 29, 35, 38.

[a] Chap. x. 17, 21. — [b] Chap. iii. 10, 38; xviii. 22. — [c] Chap. ii. 2, 34. — [d] Ver. 50. — [e] Lev. x. 6; chap. viii. 19; xvi. 46; xviii. 5; 1 Sam. vi. 19. — [f] Chap. iii. 7, 8; viii. 24, 25, 26; xviii 3, 4, 5; xxxi. 30, 47; 1 Chron. xxiii. 32; 2 Chron. xiii. 10.

(Gen. xvi. 5;) and who can resist his will, and bring to naught his counsel? That a comparative view may be easily taken of the state of the tribes, I shall produce them here from the first census mentioned in the first chapter of this book, in their *decreasing* proportion, beginning with the *greatest* and proceeding to the *least*; and in the second census, mentioned chap. xxvi., where the *increase* of some and the *decrease* of others may be seen in one point of view. It may be just remarked, that except in the case of *Gad* in this chapter, and *Reuben* in chap. xxvi., all the numbers are what may be called *whole* or *round* numbers, beginning with *thousands*, and ending with *hundreds*, *Gad* and *Reuben* alone ending with *tens*; but the Scripture generally uses *round* numbers, *units* and *fractions* being almost constantly disregarded.

	1st census, ch. i.	2d census, ch. xxvi.
1. Judah	74,600	76,500
2. Dan	62,700	64,400
3. Simeon	59,300	22,200
4. Zebulun	57,400	60,500
5. Issachar	54,400	64,300
6. Naphtali	53,400	45,400
7. Reuben	46,500	43,730
8. Gad	45,650	40,500
9. Asher	41,500	53,400
10. Ephraim	40,500	32,500
11. Benjamin	35,400	45,600
12. Manasseh	32,200	52,700
	Total 603,550	Total 601,730

Thus we find *Judah* the *most populous* tribe, and *Manasseh* the *least* so; the difference between them being so great as 42,400, for which no very satisfactory reason can be assigned.

In the second census, mentioned chap. xxvi. 34, *Judah* still has the pre-eminency; and *Simeon*, the third in number before, is become the least. Now we see also that the little tribe of *Manasseh* occupies the *seventh* place for number. *Seven* of the tribes had an *increase*; *five* a *decrease*. *Manasseh* had an increase of 20,500; *Judah*, 1,900; *Issachar*, 9,900; *Zebulun*, 3,100; *Benjamin*, 10,200; *Dan*, 1,700; *Asher*, 11,900.

On the contrary there was a *decrease* in *Reuben* of 2,770; in *Simeon*, 37,100; *Gad*, 5,150; *Ephraim*, 8,000; *Naphtali*, 8,000. Decrease in the whole, 61,020 effective men. See on chap. xxvi.; but balanced with the *increase*, the decrease was upon the whole only 1,820.

On the subject of these enumerations, and the manner in which this vast multitude sprang in about *four* generations from *seventy-five* persons, Scheuchzer has some valuable calculations, though liable to some objections, which I shall take the liberty to insert, as they tend to throw considerable light upon the subject.

"We find in the writings of Moses *three* enumerations of the Jewish people, that follow each other pretty closely:—

The first, which was made at their departure from Egypt, Exod. xii. 37, amounted to	600,000
One year after, to	603,550
On entering the land of Canaan, to .	601,730
If we add to the number . . . 603,550 } that of the *Levites* given us in chap. iii. 39, and which amounted to . .	22,000
We shall have for the sum total . .	625,550

"We find the same number, on adding that of each tribe given us in detail, which is the best proof of the exactness of the calculation.

"I think I shall afford the reader some degree of pleasure by presenting him, in this place, the number of each tribe *separately*, beginning at their earliest ancestors. We shall see, by this means, how faithfully God fulfilled the promise he had made to Abraham, as well as the great utility of the mathematics for the right understanding of the Holy Scriptures.

I shall begin with a Genealogical Table of that *family* which God so wonderfully blessed; and to it I shall afterward add each separate tribe, following the calculation of *Reyher*, (Math. Mos., p. 222.) And we shall see that the *fourth* generation, taken with the *third*, produces the very number mentioned in the text.

Children of JACOB by LEAH. Gen. xlvi. 15.

REUBEN	Hanoch Phallu Hezron Carmi	- -	46,500.	Num. i. 21.
SIMEON	Jemuel Jamin Ohad Jachin Zohar Shaul	- -	59,300.	Num. i. 23.
LEVI -	Gershon	Libni Shimei	7,500.	Num. iii. 22.
LEVI -	Kohath	Amram Izehar Hebron Uzziel	8,600.	Num. iii. 26.
	Merari	Mahli Mushi	6,200.	Num. iii. 34.
IUDAH	Shelah Pharez Zerah	Hezron Hamul	74,600.	Num. i. 27.
ISSACHAR	Tola Phuvah Job Shimron	- -	54,400.	Num. i. 29.
ZEBULUN	Sered Elon Jahleel	- -	57,400.	Num. i. 31.
DINAH				

Children of JACOB by ZILPAH. Gen. xlvi. 18.

GAD -	Ziphion Haggai Shuni Ezbon Eri Arodi Areli	- -	45,650.	Num. i. 25.
ASHER	Jimnah Ishuah Isui Beriah	Heber Malchiel	41,500.	Num. i. 41.

Children of JACOB by RACHEL. Gen. xlvi. 22.

JOSEPH	Manasseh	- - -	32,200.	
	Ephraim	- - -	40,500.	
BENJAMIN	Belah Becher Ashbel Gerah Naaman Ehi Rosh Muppim Huppim Ard	- -	35,400.	Num. i. 37.

Children of JACOB by BILHAH. Gen. xlvi. 25.

DAN -	Hushim	- -	62,700.	Num. i. 39.
NAPHTALI	Jahzeel Guni Jezer Shillem		53,400.	Num. i. 43.

I.—REUBEN 46,500.

"Let us now descend to the particular enumeration of each tribe. REUBEN had *four* sons: now if we suppose that one of these *four* sons had *seven*, and that each of the other *three* had *eight*, we shall find the number 31 for the *first* Egyptian generation. If we afterward suppose that each of these 31 sons had *five* sons, the *second* generation will amount to 155, which, multiplied by 15, will produce 2,325 for the *third* generation; and these, multiplied by 19, will make 44,175 for the *fourth;* so that the *third*, together with the *fourth*, will make 46,500. We shall have the same product if the given sum, 46,500, be divided by the most probable number of children, for example, by the number 19; we shall then have 2,447 for the *third* generation; which sum being deducted from the sum total, there will remain 44,053 for the *fourth* generation, which is exactly the number that is produced in multiplying 2,440 of the *third* generation by 18, and the other 7 by 19. If we wish to make the same calculation with respect to the preceding generations, i. e., divide them by the most probable number of children, we shall have the following sums:—

Sons of Reuben - - -	4
I. Generation - - -	31
II. Ditto - - - -	215
III. Ditto - - - -	2,583
IV. Ditto - - - -	43,917
Amount of generations III. and IV.	46,500

II.—SIMEON 59,300.

"SIMEON had *six* sons. Let us suppose that each of the three first had *six* children, and each of the three others *seven*, we shall have *thirty-nine* for the first generation. If we multiply 31 of this number by 9, and 8 by 10, we shall have for the second generation 359; of which number, if we multiply 355 by 11, and 4 by 12, the third generation will give us 3,953. Let us then multiply 3,948 of these by 14, and 5 of them by 15, and we shall have for the fourth 55,347. The *third* and *fourth*, added together, will make 59,300.

III.—LEVI 22,300.

"*Gershon*, Levi's eldest son, had *two* children: let us give to one of these 16 children, and to the other 17, and we shall have 33 for the *second* generation; 28 of which, multiplied by 15, and 5 by 16, will produce 500 for the *third*. Multiply each by 14, and these will produce 7,000; and the *third* and *fourth* together, 7,500.

"*Kohath*, Levi's second son, had *four* sons, which form the first line. Give to one of them 10 sons, and 11 to each of the other three, for the *second* generation there will be 43. Multiply them by 10, there will be 430 for the *third;* these, multiplied by 19 for the *fourth*, will produce the number of 8,170. The *third* and *fourth* added together make 8,600.

"*Merari*, the *third* son of Levi, had *two* sons. Give

10 children to each of them, there will then be 20 for the *second* generation. Now if we say that 10 of these 20 had each 15 sons, and each of the others 16, we shall have 310, which, multiplied by 19, will give us 5,890 for the *fourth;* and the *two* last together, 6,200. This may be seen by the following example :—

	Gershonites.	Kohathites.	Merarites.
I. Generation	2	4	2
II. Ditto	33	43	20
III. Ditto	500	430	310
IV. Ditto	7000	8170	5890

"Amount of generations III. and IV. : Gershonites, 7,500 ; Kohathites, 8,600 ; and Merarites, 6,200—total number of Levites, 22,300.

IV.—Judah 74,600.

"The sons of *Judah* were *Shelah, Pharez,* and *Zerah.* His grandsons by *Pharez* were *Hezron* and *Hamul. Hezron* had two sons. Suppose each of them had *six* children, which will make 12 for the first generation; to *eight* of whom allow *eight* children, and *nine* to each of the others, and there will be 100 for the *second* generation. To 92 of these then give 18 children, and 19 to the *eight* others; this will produce for the *third* generation 1,808. If we then suppose that 1,800 of these had each 18 children, and that each of the other *eight* had 19, the *fourth* generation will be 32,552, which, added to the product of the *third,* will make the descendants of *Hezron* amount to 34,360.

"*Hamul* had *two* sons, who, multiplied by 10, produce the number of 20 for the *second* generation: these, multiplied by 20, will make 400 for the *third,* and these again by 25 will produce 10,000 for the *fourth.* And thus the two last generations will amount together to the number of 10,400.

"If we allow *five* sons to Shelah, and *six* to Zerah, we shall have 11 for the first generation. To *three* of whom allow 10 children and 11 to the other *eight,* this will give us 118 for the second. To 113 of these give 14, and 15 to the other *five,* and 1657 will be produced for the *third.* Give 17 to 1643, and 18 to the 14 remaining, and for the *fourth* there will be 28,183. The *third* and *fourth* added together will produce the number of 29,840.

"According to this calculation, all these generations will amount to the following numbers :—

Hezronites - - -	34,360
Hamulites - - - -	10,400
Shelanites and Zarhites -	29,840
	74,600

V.—Issachar 54,400.

Issachar had *five* sons. Suppose that *three* of them had each *five* children, and the other *two, six,* we shall have 27 for the first generation. If we then imagine that of these 19 had each *nine* sons, and each of the other *eight* 10, the second generation will be 251. Now 241 of these, multiplied by 12, will produce 2,892, and the 10 others, multiplied by 13, will make 130; consequently the *third* generation will amount to 3,022. If 3,018 of these had each 17 sons, and each of the other *four* had 18, the *fourth* generation will be 51,378; the *third* and *fourth* generations, then, will produce a number of 54,400

VI.—Zebulun 57,400.

"*Zebulun* had *three* sons. If we suppose that *two* of them had in all fourteen children, and the *third, six,* here will be 20 for the *first* generation. The *second* will produce 143, on multiplying 17 by 7, and 3 by 8. If we multiply 135 by 16, and 8 by 17, the *third* will amount to 2,296. By multiplying the *third* by 24, the *fourth* will give us 55,104. The two last will produce, together, 57,400.

VII.—Gad 45,650.

"Gad had *seven* sons.

I. Generation: multiply 3 by 9, and 4 by 10, there will be - - - - -	67
II. Ditto multiply 61 by 7, and 6 by 8 -	475
III. Ditto multiply 471 by 8, and 4 by 9 -	3,804
IV. Ditto multiply 3,802 by 11, and 2 by 12	41,846
Amount of generations III. and IV.	45,650

VIII.—Asher 41,500.

"The sons of Asher, *Jimnah, Ishua,* and *Isui,* multiplied by 8, produce for the

I. Generation - - - - - -	24
II. Ditto multiply 24 by 8 - - -	192
III. Ditto multiply 182 by 11, and 10 by 12	2,122
IV. Ditto multiply 2,118 by 12, and 4 by 13	25,468
Amount of generations III. and IV.	27,590

"*Heber* and *Malchiel* were sons of *Beriah.* Now these *two* sons multiplied by 5, give us for

I. Generation - - - - -	10
II. Ditto multiply 10 by 11 - - -	110
III. Ditto multiply by 9 - - - -	990
IV. Ditto multiply by 12 - - -	11,880
Amount of generations III. and IV.	12,870

"Another son of *Beriah* had in the

I. Generation - - - - - -	1
II. Ditto multiply by 8 - - - - -	8
III. Ditto multiply by 10 - - -	80
IV. Ditto multiply by 12 - - -	960
Amount of generations III. and IV.	1,040

All these generations added together, amount to 41,500

IX.—Joseph.

Manasseh 32,200.

"I. Generation - - - - - -	10
II. Ditto multiply 6 by 13, and 4 by 14 -	134
III. Ditto multiply 132 by 12, and 2 by 13	1,610
IV. Ditto multiply by 19 - - -	30,590
Amount of generations III. and IV.	32,200

Ephraim 40,500.

"I. Generation - - - - - -	16
II. Ditto multiply by 10 - - - -	160
III. Ditto multiply 152 by 12, and 8 by 13	1,928
IV. Ditto multiply 1,916 by 20, and 12 by 21	38,572
Amount of generations III. and IV.	40,500

X.—Benjamin 35,400.

"He had 10 sons; two of whom, multiplied by 9, and the other 8 by 10, will give for the

I. Generation	- - - - - -	98
II. Ditto multiply 95 by 9, and 3 by 10	-	885
III. Ditto multiply by 5	- - - -	4,425
IV. Ditto multiply by 7	- - -	30,975
Amount of generations III. and IV.		35,400

XI.—Dan 62,700.

"I. Generation	- - - -	11
II. Ditto multiply by 12	- - -	132
III. Ditto multiply by 19	- - -	2,508
IV. Ditto multiply by 24	- - -	60,192
Amount of generations III. and IV.		62,700

XII.—Naphtali 53,400.

"He had 4 sons, the half of whom, multiplied by 7, and the other half by 6, give us for the

I. Generation	- - - - - -	26
II. Ditto multiply 16 by 11, and 10 by 12		296
III. Ditto multiply 288 by 12, and 8 by 13		3,560
IV. Ditto multiply by 14	- - -	49,840
Amount of generations III. and IV.		53,400

Total number of all the tribes.

I. Reuben	- - -	46,500
II. Simeon	- - -	59,300
III. Levi	- - -	22,300
IV. Judah	- - -	74,600
V. Issachar	- - -	54,400
VI. Zebulun	- - -	57,400
VII. Gad	- - -	45,650
VIII. Asher	- - -	41,500
IX. Manasseh	- - -	32,200
Ephraim	- - -	40,500
X. Benjamin	- - -	35,400
XI. Dan	- - -	62,700
XII. Naphtali	- - -	53,400
Total		625,850

"And indeed, without counting the Levites, the number of the Israelites (chap. i. 46) amounts to - -	603,550
The Levites (chap. iii. 39) amount to	22,300
The whole number together, as above -	625,850"

In the above calculations, *Scheuchzer* and *Reyher* take for granted, 1. That from the going down to Egypt to the exodus there were *four* generations. 2. That the first two generations had died in Egypt. 3. That the promise of God in multiplying them as the stars of heaven, had taken place particularly in the two last generations. 4. That these two last generations alone form the aggregate sums given in the sacred text. 5. That their method of accounting for this aggregate through the four generations, is not only perfectly natural and mathematical, but strictly accordant with the promises made by God to them, as the sum of each tribe sufficiently proves. 6. That the whole account shows the truth of the Divine promise, the great accuracy of the Jewish lawgiver, and a proof of the inspiration of the sacred writings. But even to these calculations and deductions there may be objections, e. g., "Scheuchzer gives to 2,508 families of Dan, 24 male children, each above the age of 20: we may fairly allow an equal number of females, and add 5 more under 20, as in the note under Exod. xii. 37, and we have 53 children on the average through all the families of a tribe; whilst to 4,425 families of Benjamin are allotted 7 males aged 20, and adding 7 females at 5 children, we have 19 children in each family; a tolerable number; but apparently more reasonable than the other."—Anon.

CHAPTER II.

Moses commanded to teach the Israelites how they are to pitch their tents, and erect the ensigns of their fathers' houses, 1, 2. Judah, Issachar, *and* Zebulun, *on the* EAST, *amounting to* 186,400 *men,* 3–9. Reuben, Simeon, *and* Gad, *on the* SOUTH, *with* 151,450 *men,* 10–16. *The* Levites *to be in the midst of the camp,* 17. Ephraim, Manasseh, *and* Benjamin, *on the* WEST, *with* 108,100 *men,* 18–24. Dan, Asher, *and* Naphtali, *on the* NORTH, *with* 157,600 *men,* 25–31. *The sum total of the whole,* 603,550 *men,* 32. *But the* Levites *are not included,* 33. *The people do as the Lord commands them,* 34.

A. M. 2514. B. C. 1490. An. Exod. Isr. 2. Ijar or Zif.

AND the Lord spake unto Moses and unto Aaron, saying,

2 [a] Every man of the children of Israel shall pitch by his own standard, with the ensign of their father's house: [b] far off about [c] the tabernacle of the congregation shall they pitch.

[a] Chap. i. 52.—[b] Heb. *over against.* [c] Josh. iii. 4.

NOTES ON CHAP. II.

Verse 2. *Every man—shall pitch by his own standard*] Commentators, critics, philosophers, and professional men, have taken a great deal of pains to illustrate this chapter by showing the best method of encampment for such a vast number of men, and the manner in which they conceive the Israelites formed their camp in the wilderness. As God gave them the plan, it was doubtless in every respect perfect; and fully answered the double purpose of convenience and security. *Scheuchzer* has entered into this subject with his usual ability, and in very considerable detail. Following the plan of *Reyher*, as in the preceding chapter, he endeavours to ascertain the precise order

A. M. 2514.
B. C. 1490.
An. Exod. Isr. 2.
Ijar or Zif.

3 And on the east side toward the rising of the sun, shall they of the standard of the camp of Judah pitch throughout their armies: and [d] Nahshon the son of Amminadab *shall be* captain of the children of Judah.

4 And his host, and those that were numbered of them, *were* threescore and fourteen thousand and six hundred.

5 And those that do pitch next unto him *shall be* the tribe of Issachar: and Nethaneel the son of Zuar *shall be* captain of the children of Issachar.

6 And his host, and those that were numbered thereof, *were* fifty and four thousand and four hundred.

7 *Then* the tribe of Zebulun: and Eliab the son of Helon *shall be* captain of the children of Zebulun.

8 And his host, and those that were numbered thereof, *were* fifty and seven thousand and four hundred.

9 All that were numbered in the camp of Judah *were* a hundred thousand and fourscore thousand and six thousand and four hundred, throughout their armies. [e] These shall first set forth.

10 On the south side *shall be* the standard of the camp of Reuben according to their armies: and the captain of the children of Reuben *shall be* Elizur the son of Shedeur.

11 And his host, and those that were numbered thereof, *were* forty and six thousand and five hundred.

12 And those which pitch by him *shall be* the tribe of Simeon: and the captain of the children of Simeon *shall be* Shelumiel the son of Zurishaddai.

13 And his host, and those that were numbered of them, *were* fifty and nine thousand and three hundred.

A. M. 2514.
B. C. 1490.
An. Exod. Isr. 2.
Ijar or Zif.

14 Then the tribe of Gad: and the captain of the sons of Gad *shall be* Eliasaph the son of [f] Reuel.

15 And his host, and those that were numbered of them, *were* forty and five thousand and six hundred and fifty.

16 All that were numbered in the camp of Reuben *were* a hundred thousand and fifty and one thousand and four hundred and fifty, throughout their armies [g] And they shall set forth in the second rank.

17 [h] Then the tabernacle of the congregation shall set forward with the camp of the Levites in the midst of the camp: as they encamp, so shall they set forward, every man in his place by their standards.

18 On the west side *shall be* the standard of the camp of Ephraim, according to their armies: and the captains of the sons of Ephraim *shall be* Elishama the son of Ammihud.

19 And his host, and those that were numbered of them, *were* forty thousand and five hundred.

20 And by him *shall be* the tribe of Manasseh: and the captain of the children of Manasseh *shall be* Gamaliel the son of Pedahzur.

21 And his host, and those that were numbered of them, *were* thirty and two thousand and two hundred.

22 Then the tribe of Benjamin: and the captain of the sons of Benjamin *shall be* Abidan the son of Gideoni.

23 And his host, and those that were num-

[d] Chap. x. 14; Ruth iv. 20; 1 Chron. ii. 10; Matt. i. 4; Luke iii. 32, 33.——[e] Chap. x. 14.

[f] *Deuel*; chapter i. 14; vii. 42, 47; x. 20.——[g] Chap. x. 18. [h] Chap. x. 17, 21.

in which the several tribes were disposed; and as his work is both scarce and dear, the reader will not be displeased to meet here with a translation of all that refers to the subject.

SCHEUCHZER'S DESCRIPTION AND PLAN OF THE ENCAMPMENTS OF THE ISRAELITES IN THE WILDERNESS.

"If we form a proper idea of God, of his essence and his attributes, we shall easily perceive that this infinite and supreme Being wills and executes what his Divine *wisdom* appoints; in a word, we shall see that he is the God of *order*. This order displays itself in the perfection, arrangement, and assemblage of all created beings; in the construction of the earth which we inhabit, where every thing is formed in order, number, weight, and measure; and in all bodies, great and small. It is certain that *Noah's ark* is a perfect model of *naval architecture*. The *temple of Solomon*, and that of *Ezekiel* were likewise masterpieces in their kind. But at present we are to consider the Divine arrangement of the Israelitish camp, and the manner in which it was formed.

"The Israelitish army was divided into three principal divisions. The *first*, which was the least in extent, but the strongest and the most powerful, occupied the centre of the army: this was the *throne of God*, i. e., the TABERNACLE. The *second*, which was composed of the *priests* and *Levites*, surrounded the

A. M. 2514.
B. C. 1490.
An. Exod. Isr. 2.
Ijar or Zif.

bered of them, *were* thirty and
five thousand and four hundred.
24 All that were numbered of
the camp of Ephraim *were* a hundred thousand and eight thousand and a hundred,
throughout their armies. [i] And they shall go
forward in the third rank.
25 The standard of the camp of Dan *shall*
be on the north side by their armies: and the
captain of the children of Dan *shall be* Ahiezer the son of Ammishaddai.
26 And his host, and those that were numbered of them, *were* threescore and two thousand and seven hundred.
27 And those that encamp by him *shall be*
the tribe of Asher: and the captain of the children of Asher *shall be* Pagiel the son of Ocran.
28 And his host, and those that were numbered of them, *were* forty and one thousand
and five hundred.
29 Then the tribe of Naphtali: and the
captain of the children of Naphtali *shall be*
Ahira the son of Enan.
30 And his host, and those that
were numbered of them, *were*
fifty and three thousand and four
hundred.

A. M. 2514.
B. C. 1490.
An. Exod. Isr. 2.
Ijar or Zif.

31 All they that were numbered in the
camp of Dan *were* a hundred thousand
and fifty and seven thousand and six hundred. [k] They shall go hindmost with their
standards.
32 These *are* those which were numbered
of the children of Israel by the house of their
fathers: [l] all those that were numbered of the
camps throughout their hosts *were* six hundred thousand and three thousand and five
hundred and fifty.
33 But [m] the Levites were not numbered
among the children of Israel; as the LORD
commanded Moses.
34 And the children of Israel did according
to all that the LORD commanded Moses: [n] so
they pitched by their standards, and so they
set forward, every one after their families, according to the house of their fathers.

[i] Chap. x. 22.—[k] Chap. x. 25.—[l] Exod. xxxviii. 26; chap. i. 46; xi. 21.—[m] Chap. i. 47.—[n] Chap. xxiv. 2, 5, 6.

first. The *third*, and the farthest from the centre, took in all the other tribes of Israel, who were at least about a mile from the tabernacle. For it appears from Josephus, iii. 4, that the nearest approach they dared make to the ark, except during the time of worship, was a distance of 2,000 cubits. The reverence due to the Divine Majesty, the numerous army of the Israelites, composed of 600,000 soldiers, with their families, which made about 3,000,000 souls, naturally demanded a considerable extent of ground. We are not to imagine that all these families pitched their tents pellmell, without order, like beasts, or as the troops of Tartary, and the eastern armies; on the contrary, their camp was divided according to the most exact rules. And we cannot even doubt that their camp was laid out, and the place of every division and tribe exactly assigned by some engineers, or geometricians, before the army stopped to encamp, in order that every person might at once find his own quarter, and the road he ought to take to reach the other tents.

"Four divisions, which faced the four quarters of the heavens, each with his own ensign, formed the centre of the army. JUDAH was placed on the east, and under him he had *Issachar* and *Zebulun;* on the south was REUBEN, and under him *Simeon* and *Gad:* on the west was EPHRAIM, and under him *Manasseh* and *Benjamin;* finally, DAN was on the north, and he had under him *Asher* and *Naphtali.* It has been pretended by some that these four principal divisions were not alone distinguished by their ensigns, but that each particular tribe had likewise its standard or ensign. On this subject we might refer to the Talmudists, who have gone so far as to define the *colours,* and the *figures* or *arms,* of the very ensigns. They pretend that on that of JUDAH a *lion* was painted, with this inscription: '*Rise, Lord, let thine enemies be dispersed, and let those that hate thee flee before thee;*' and they found this description of Judah's ensign in Gen. xlix. 9. They give to ISSACHAR an *ass,* Gen. xlix. 14; to ZEBULUN a *ship,* Gen. xlix. 13; to REUBEN a *river,* Gen. xlix. 4, (others give Reuben the *figure of a man;*) to SIMEON a *sword,* Gen. xlix. 5; to GAD a *lion,* Deut. xxxiii. 20; to EPHRAIM a *unicorn,* Deut. xxxiii. 17; an *ox* to MANASSEH, Deut. xxxiii. 17; a *wolf* to BENJAMIN, Gen. xlix. 27; and a *serpent* to DAN, Gen. xlix. 17, though others give him an *eagle.* In short, they pretend that the ensign of ASHER was a *handful of corn,* Gen. xlix. 20, and that of NAPHTALI a *stag,* Gen. xlix. 21.

"To prove that the sums here are correctly added, we have but to join together the detached numbers, and see if they agree with the total. The text will furnish us with an example of this: there was in the quarter of

Judah	186,400	ver. 9.
Reuben	151,450	ver. 16.
Ephraim	108,100	ver. 24.
Dan	157,600	ver. 31.

"Among other things we must remark that rule of military tactics which requires that the *advanced* and *rear guards* should be stronger than the centre.

"In a well-regulated camp, cleanliness is considered indispensably necessary; this is particularly remarkable in the Israelitish army, where the most exact order was maintained. Hence every person who had

any kind of disease, and those who were reputed *unclean*, were forbidden to enter it; Num. v. 2, 3; Deut. xxiii. 10.

"Those who have the health of men, and of a whole army confided to them, are not ignorant that diseases may be easily produced by putrid exhalations from excrementitious matter; and that such matter will produce in camps pestilential fevers and dysenteries. For this reason, care should be always taken that offices, at a distance from the camp, be provided for the soldiers, and also that those who are sick should be separated from the others, and sent to hospitals to be properly treated.

"In military tactics we find two distinct wings spoken of; the right and the left. The Israelitish army not only had them on one side, as is customary, but on all their four sides. On the *eastern* side, the tribe of Issachar formed the *right*, that of Zebulun the *left*, and that of Judah the *centre*. On the *south*, Simeon formed the *right wing*, Gad the *left*, and Reuben the *centre*. Towards the *west*, Manasseh composed the *right*, Benjamin the *left*, and Ephraim the *centre*. And on the *north*, Asher was on the *right wing*, Naphtali on the *left wing*, and Dan in the *centre*. Notwithstanding this, however, the army was not in danger of being easily broken; for every tribe being numerous, they were supported by several ranks, in such a manner that the first being broken, the second was capable of making resistance; and if the second gave way, or shared the same fate as the first, it found itself supported by the third, and so on with the rest. The square form in which the Jewish army was ordinarily placed, was the very best for security and defence. The use and importance of the *hollow square* in military tactics is well known.

"For so large a multitude of people, and for so numerous an army, it was needful that all the necessary articles of life should be prepared beforehand, or be found ready to purchase. In these respects nothing was wanting to the Israelites. Their bread came down to them from heaven, and they had besides an abundance of every thing that could contribute to magnificence. If we may credit Josephus, they had amongst them *public markets*, and a *variety of shops*. Ant., l. iii. c. 12, sec. 5. The tabernacle being erected, it was placed in the midst of the camp, each of the three tribes stretching themselves on the wings, and leaving between them a sufficient space to pass.

"It was, says Josephus, like a well appointed market where every thing was ready for sale in due order, and all sorts of artificers kept their shops; so that this camp might be considered a movable city.

"In Exod. xxxii. 27 we likewise find that mention is made of the *gates* of the camp: 'Put every man his sword by his side, and go in and out from gate to gate throughout the camp.' From whence we may certainly conclude that if the camp had *gates*, the Israelites had also *sentinels* to guard them. If this be true, we may also believe that they were *surrounded with entrenchments*, or that at least their gates were defended by some fortifications. *Sagittarius* (de Jan. Vet., c. 18. § 10) pretends that the tabernacle was not only guarded by the Levites, but that there were likewise sentinels at the gates, and at the entrance of the Israelitish camps. See the note on Exod. xxxii. 27.

"If we examine and compare the camp of Israel with that of our most numerous armies, which in these days are composed of 100,000 or of 150,000 men, we cannot but consider it of vast extent. The Jews say it was twelve miles in circumference; this is not at all improbable, and consequently the front of each wing must be three miles in extent. But taking in the tents, the soldiers and their numerous families, the beasts of burden, the cattle, and the goods, it certainly must have formed a very considerable inclosure, much more than twelve miles. See the notes on Exod. xii. 37, and xiii. 18. *Reyher* (Math. Mos., p. 568) assigns to the

Tribe of Judah,

A space of	$298\frac{2}{5}$	cubits in breadth
and	250	in length
Which makes	74,600	square cubits.

"We must observe that we are here merely speaking of the ground which the soldiers of this tribe occupied whilst remaining *close to each other* in their ranks, and that in this computation there is but one cubit square allowed for each man; wherefore, if we take in the arrangement of the soldiers, the tents, the necessary spaces, the families, the beasts of burden, and the movables, a much larger extent of ground is requisite. All those circumstances do not come into *Reyher's* calculation. He continues thus:—

For the tribe of Issachar,		
	$217\frac{3}{5}$	cubits in breadth
	250	in length
Total	54,400	
For the tribe of Gad,		
	$140\frac{6}{13}$	cubits in breadth
	325	in length
Total	45,650	
For the tribe of Zebulun,		
	$229\frac{3}{5}$	cubits in breadth
	250	in length
Total	57,400	
For the tribe of Ephraim,		
	$202\frac{1}{2}$	cubits in breadth
	200	in length
Total	40,500	
For the tribe of Reuben,		
	$143\frac{1}{5}$	cubits in breadth
	325	in length
Total	46,500	
For the tribe of Manasseh,		
	161	cubits in breadth
	200	in length
Total	32,200	

For the tribe of SIMEON,

$182\frac{6}{13}$	cubits in breadth
325	in length
Total 59,300	

For the tribe of BENJAMIN,

177	cubits in breadth
200	in length
Total 35,400	

For the tribe of DAN,

$156\frac{3}{4}$	cubits in breadth
400	in length
Total 62,700	

For the tribe of ASHER,

$103\frac{3}{4}$	cubits in breadth
400	in length
Total 41,500	

For the tribe of NAPHTALI,

$133\frac{1}{2}$	cubits in breadth
400	in length
Total 53,400	

"If we make the ichnography, or even the scenography, of the camp on this plan, in following it we must first, in the *centre*, form a *parallelogram* of 100 cubits long and 50 broad for the *court* of the tabernacle with an empty space all round of 50 cubits broad. We must then place the camp of the Levites in the following order :—

To the west, the *Gershonites*, chap. iii. 22, 23.

Breadth	30	cubits
Length	250	cubits
Total	7500	

To the south, the *Kohathites*, chap. iii. 28, 29.

Breadth	86	cubits
Length	100	cubits
Total	8600	

To the north, the *Merarites*, chap. iii. 34, 35.

Breadth	62	cubits
Length	100	cubits
Total	6200	

"On the east we must place tents for Moses, Aaron, and his sons, chap. iii. 38.

"At the place where the camp of the Levites ends, a space must be left of 2,000 square cubits, after which we must take the dimensions of the camp of the twelve tribes.

"This plan is in the main well imagined, but it does not afford an ichnography of sufficient extent. To come more accurately to a proper understanding of this subject, I shall examine the rules that are now in use for encampments, and compare them afterward with what is laid down in the Holy Scriptures, in order that we may hereby form to ourselves an idea of the camp of God. the grandeur and perfection of which surpassed every thing of the kind ever seen. I shall now mention what I am about to propose as the foundation upon which I shall proceed.

"In Exod. xviii. 21, Deut. i. 15, we find the advice given by Jethro to Moses respecting political government and military discipline: 'Thou shalt provide out of all the people able men, such as fear God, men of truth, hating covetousness; and place such over them, to be rulers of thousands, and rulers of hundreds, rulers of fifties, and rulers of tens.' [See the note on Exod. xviii. 21.] We may very well compare these *tribunes*, or rather these *chiliarchs*, to our *colonels*, the *centurions* or *hecatontarchs* to *commanders* or *captains*, the *quinquagenaries* or *pentecontarchs* to *lieutenants*, and the *decurions* or *decarchs* to our *sergeants*. These chiefs, whether they were named *magistrates* or *officers*, were each drawn from his own particular tribe, so that it was not permitted to place over one tribe an officer taken from another. Whatever matter the *decarchs* could not decide upon or terminate, went to the *pentecontarchs*, and from thence by degrees to the *hecatontarchs*, to the *chiliarchs*, to *Moses*, and at length to GOD himself, the sovereign head of the army. If we divide the whole army (such as it was at its departure from Egypt) by the numbers already laid down, we shall find 600 chiliarchs, 6,000 hecatontarchs, 12,000 pentecontarchs, 60,000 decarchs, which in all make 78,600 officers. Josephus regulates the number of them still more exactly by saying that there were chiefs set over 10,000, 1,000, 500, 50, 30, 20, and 10. We find this regulation in *Ant. Jud.*, b. iii., c. 4: 'Take a review of the army, and appoint chosen rulers over tens of thousands, and then over thousands, then divide them into five hundreds, and again into hundreds, and into fifties, and set rulers over each of them who may distinguish them into thirties, and keep them in order; and at last number them by twenties and by tens, and let there be one commander over each number, to be denominated from the number of those over whom they are rulers.'

"We ought not to pass over in silence this division by *tens*, for twice 10 make 20, three times 10, 30, five times 10, 50, ten times 10, 100, ten times 50, 500, ten times 1,000, 10,000. It was in this manner, as is pretended, that *Cangu*, the first of the great Khams, (as he is called,) and after him *Tamerlane*, drew out an army, i. e., by 10, 100, 1,000, 10,000, mentioned in *Alhazen*, c. v. Probably these Tartars borrowed from the very Hebrews themselves this manner of laying out a camp. At all events it is certain that nothing more ancient of the kind can be found than that mentioned in the books of Moses. To distinguish it from that of the Greeks and Romans we may with justice call it the Hebrew castrametation, or, if we judge it more proper, the Divine castrametation, and consequently the most perfect of all. For although Moses places the *pentecontarchs* in the middle, between the *hecatontarchs* and the *decarchs*, i. e., 50 between 100 and 10; and although Josephus afterward places 1,000 between 500 and 10,000, and 30 and 20 between 10 and 50, this does not at all derange the progression by *tens*, which is the foundation of arithmetic. These subaltern officers were equally useful aud necessary, as we now see that their

number, far from creating confusion, helps to maintain order, and that the more there are of them the better is order preserved. According to the modern method of carrying on war, the next in rank to the generals of the army (who have the supreme command) are *field marshals* and *brigadiers*, who command 5,000 men.

"There are then between the *chiliarchs* or *colonels* and the *hecatontarchs* or *captains*, *lieutenant-colonels;* and between the *hecatontarchs* and the *decarchs*, *lieutenant-captains;* and these have under them *lieutenants* and *ensigns*.

"It is certain that this method of distributing an army by *tens*, and of encamping, which is very concise, has far greater advantages even with respect to expense than the very best plans of the *Greeks*, *Romans*, or any other ancient nation. On this subject we have the testimony of *Simon Steven*, Castrametat. c. 1, art. 1, and c. 4, art. 3, *Oper. Math.*, p. 574 and 596, &c. According to this arrangement each soldier, or if more proper, each *father of a family*, being thus placed by *ten* and *ten* in a straight line one after the other, might very easily name themselves *first*, *second*, &c. Each troop in like manner might be distinguished by its *ensigns*, that of 100 might have them small, that of 1,000 larger, and that of 10,000 still larger. Every officer, from the lowest subaltern to the general officers of the camp, and even to the generalissimos themselves, had only an easy inspection of ten men each; the *decarch* had the inspection of 10 soldiers, the *hecatontarch* of 10 *decarchs*, and the *chiliarch* of 10 *hecatontarchs*. After the *chiliarchs*, which in no troop can amount to ten, there is the chief or head of each tribe. Each then exactly fulfilling the duty assigned him, we may suppose every thing to be in good order, even were the camp larger and more numerous. The same may be said respecting the contentions that might arise among the soldiers, as well as every thing relative to the general duty of the officers, as to the labours they were to undertake, whether for striking their tents for works of fortification or for making entrenchments. This arrangement might be easily retained in the memory, or a general list be kept of the names of both officers and soldiers to distribute to them their pay, and to keep exact accounts.

"It was possible in one moment to know the number of those who were either wanting or were out of their ranks, and to avoid this disorder in future by obliging each man to attend to his duty and keep in his rank. If by chance it happened that any one man wished to desert or had escaped, it was easy to notice him and inflict on him the punishment he merited. The *ensigns* being distinguished by their *marks*, and the *company* being known, it was easy to find any soldier whatever.

"The armies themselves might have certain marks to distinguish them, and by that means they might at once ascertain the person in question; for example: 8. 2. 7. 3. might signify the *eighth* soldier or *father* of a family, of the *second rank*, of the *seventh* company, in the third *chiliad;* 7. 3. 5. the *halberdier* of the *decurion* or *sergeant* of the *seventh* line, in the *third* company, of the *fifth chiliad* or thousand; 5. 8. the *hecatontarchs* or captains of the *fifth* company, in the eighth *chiliad;* 7. the *chiliarchs* or *colonels* of the *seventh* rank; 0. finally, the general of the whole army. Farther, by the same means the loss or misplacing of their arms might be prevented. Again, the soldiers might in a very short time be instructed and formed to the exercise of arms, each *decad* having its *sergeant* for its master; and the chariots or other carriages might easily be divided amongst several, 10 under the *decurion*, 100 under the *hecatontarch;* and by thus following the above method, every thing might be kept in good order.

A PLAN OF THE WHOLE ISRAELITISH CAMP.

"We shall finally, in one plate, represent the whole camp of the Israelites, in that order which appears the most proper. For this purpose we must extract the square roots of the preceding spaces, in order that we may be able to assign to each tribe square areas, or rectangular parallelograms. I therefore find for

Reuben	3049	square cubits.
Simeon	3443	
The Gershonites	1224	
The Kohathites	1311	
The Merarites	1113	
Judah	3862	
Issachar	3298	
Zebulun	3388	
Gad	3019	
Asher	2880	
Manasseh	2537	
Ephraim	2846	
Benjamin	2660	
Dan	3541	
Naphtali	3268	

"The tabernacle, which was 100 cubits long and 50 broad, I place in the centre of the camp, at the distance of 840 feet from the camp of the Levites, which is placed exactly in the same manner as described in the sacred writings. I find therefore that the whole space of the camp is 259,600,000 feet. Now, according to the manner we have just divided the camp for each tribe, the sum total being 125,210,000, it follows that the space between the tents contained 134,390,000. If, with *Eisenschmid*, we estimate the Roman mile at 766 French fathoms and two feet, (consequently 21,141,604 square feet to a Roman square mile,) the Israelitish camp will contain a little more than 12 such square miles."

The reader will have the goodness to observe that the preceding observations, as well as the following plate or diagram, which was made by Scheuchzer on the exactest *proportions*, could not be accurately copied here without an *engraved* plate; and after all, the common reader could have profited no more by the *plate* than he can by the diagram. It is not even hoped that disquisitions of this kind can give any thing more than a *general idea* how the thing probably was; for to pretend to minute exactness, in such cases, would be absurd. The sacred text informs us that such and such tribes occupied the *east*, such the *west*, &c., &c.; but how they were arranged individually we cannot pretend absolutely to say. Scheuchzer's plan is such as we may suppose judgment and skill would lay down; but still it is very probable that

the plan of the Israelites' castrametation was more perfect than any thing we can well imagine; for as it was the plan which probably God himself laid down, it must be in every respect what it ought to be, for the comfort and safety of this numerous multitude.

As there are some differences between the mode of distributing the command of a large army among the British, and that used on the continent, which is followed by Scheuchzer, I shall lay down the *descending* scale of British commanders, which some may think applies better to the preceding arrangement of the Israelitish army than the other.

The command of a large army in the British service is thus divided :—

1. The commander-in-chief.
2. Lieutenant-generals, who command divisions of the army: (these divisions consist of 2 or 3 brigades each, which, on an average, amount to 5,000 men.)
3. Major-generals, who command brigades: (these brigades consist of from 2 to 3,000 men [2,500 is perhaps the average] according to the strength of the respective regiments of which the brigade is composed.)
4. Colonels in the army, or lieutenant-colonels, who command single regiments; they are assisted in the command of these regiments by the *majors* of the regiments. [I mention the *major*, that there may be no break in the descending scale of gradation of ranks, as in the event of the absence of the above two officers, he is the next in command.]
5. Captains who command companies: these companies (on the war establishment) consist of 100 men each, and there are 10 companies in every regiment, consequently a colonel, or lieutenant-colonel, commands 1,000 men.
6. Lieutenants, of which there are 2 to every company.
7. Ensign; 1 to each company.

(6 and 7:) Subaltern officers, having no command, but assisting the captain.

1. Commander-in-chief.
2. Lieutenant-generals commanding divisions 5,000 each.
3. Major-generals, brigades 2,500.

(1–3:) These are called general officers.

4. Colonels, lieutenant-colonels, and majors; 3 officers belonging to each regiment in the service, and are solely employed in the disciplining and commanding the men; these are mounted on horseback, and termed field-officers.
5. 1 Captain
6. 2 Lieutenants
7. 1 Ensign

(5–7:) to each company.

Ascending scale of ranks which every officer must pass through.

Ensign,
Lieutenant,
Captain,
Major,
Lieutenant-colonel,
Colonel,

(Ensign to Colonel:) to every regiment.

Major-general, brigade-commander.
Lieutenant-general, division-commander.
General-in-chief, who commands the whole army.

DIAGRAM OF THE ISRAELITISH CAMP.

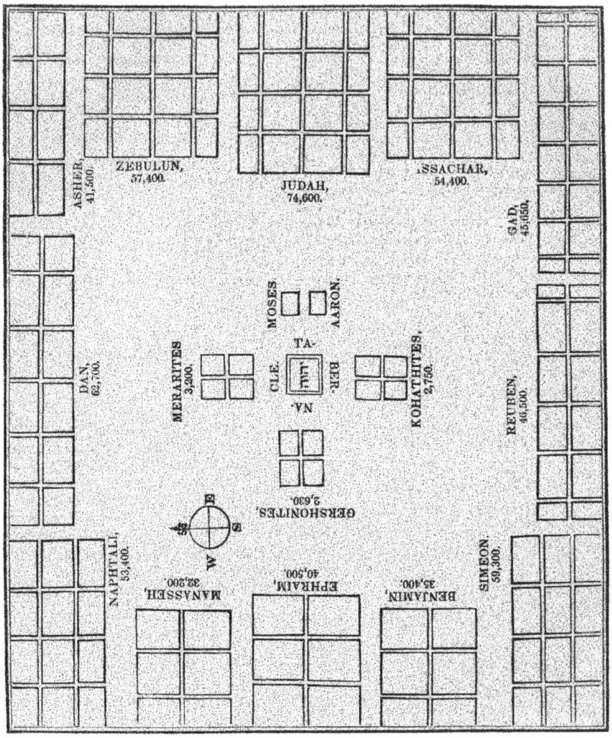

Though I particularly refer the reader to the above diagram of the Israelitish camp, taken from Scheuchzer's plate, which I have thought necessary to be subjoined to his description, yet I think it also proper to introduce that on the following page, as it gives a general and tolerably correct idea of this immense camp, in the description of which the inspired writer has been so very particular; but still I must say these things are to be considered as PROBABLE, not as *absolutely certain;* as comprising a *general view* of what may be supposed probable, likely, and practicable.

The whole may be said to consist of three camps, *viz.*, 1. The camp of the *Lord;* 2. The camp of the *Levites;* and, 3. The camp of the *people.* These in the grand camp in the wilderness, corresponded with the *holy of holies*, the *holy place*, and the *outward court* of the Temple at Jerusalem. See *Ainsworth.*

EAST.

186,400 Men,
FIRST GRAND DIVISION.

JUDAH,
74,600.
ISSACHAR, and ZEBULON,
54,400. 57,400.

MOSES, AARON,
AND
THE PRIESTS.

שכינה
TABERNACLE.

LEVITES
OF
MERARI,
3200.

LEVITES
OF
KOHTH,
2750.

DAN,
62,700.
ASHER, and NAPHTALI,
41,500. 53,400.

REUBEN,
46,500.
SIMEON, 3nd GAD,
59,300. 45,650.

NORTH.

FOURTH GRAND DIVISION.
157,600 Men.

SECOND GRAND DIVISION.
151,450 Men.

SOUTH.

GERSHON,
OF
LEVITES
2650.

EPHRAIM,
40,500.
MANASSEH, and BENJAMIN,
32,200. 35,400.

THIRD GRAND DIVISION.
108,100 Men.

WEST.

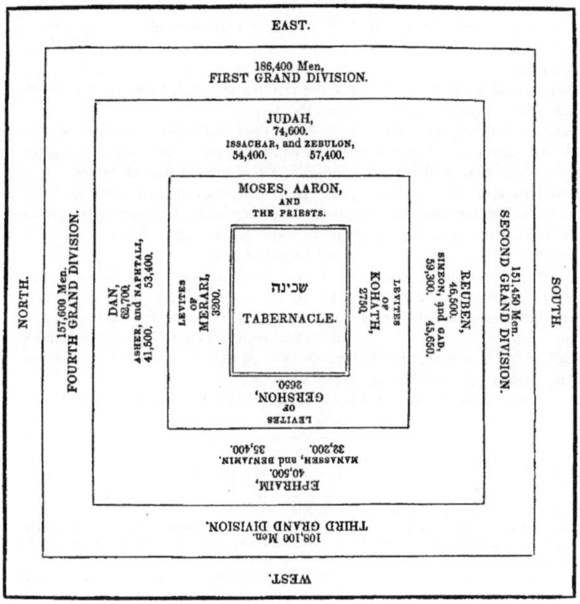

CHAPTER III.

The generations of Aaron and Moses, 1–4. The tribe of Levi to minister to the Lord under Aaron and his sons, 5–10. They are taken in the place of the first-born, 11–13. Moses is commanded to number them, 14–16. Gershon, Kohath, and Merari, the names of the three heads of families of the Levites, 17. Of Gershon and his family, 18–21. Their number, 7,500, ver. 22. Their place behind the tabernacle, westward, 23. Their chief, Eliasaph, 24. Their charge, 25, 26. Of Kohath and his family, 27. Their number, 8,600, ver. 28. Their place, beside the tabernacle, southward, 29. Their chief, Elizaphan, 30. Their charge, 31. The chief of the Levites, Eleazar, son of Aaron, 32. Of Merari and his family, 33, Their number, 6,200, ver. 34. Their chief, Zuriel, they shall pitch beside the tabernacle, northward, 35. Their charge, 35–37. Moses and Aaron to encamp before the tabernacle, eastward, 38. The amount of all the males among the Levites from a month old and upwards, 22,000, ver. 39. Moses is commanded to number the first-born, 40 ; and to take the Levites and their cattle, instead of the first-born of man and beast among the Israelites, 41. Moses numbers the first-born, who amount to 22,273, ver. 43. As the first-born were 273 more than the Levites, Moses is commanded to take from the people five shekels apiece for them, 44–47, which is to be given to Aaron and his sons, 48. Moses does accordingly, and finds the amount of the money to be 1,365 shekels, 49,50, which is given to Aaron and his sons, 51.

A. M. 2514.
B. C. 1490.
An. Exod. Isr. 2.
Ijar or Zif.

THESE also *are* the generations of Aaron and Moses
in the day *that* the LORD
spake with Moses in Mount
Sinai.

2 And these *are* the names of

A. M. 2514.
B. C. 1490.
An. Exod. Isr. 2.
Ijar or Zif.

NOTES ON CHAP. III.

Verse 1. *The generations of Aaron and Moses*]
Though Aaron and Moses are both mentioned here,
yet the family of Aaron alone appears in the list ;

hence some have thought that the word *Moses* was
not originally in the text. Others think that the words
ואלה תולדות *veelleh toledoth, these are the generations,*
should be rendered *these are the acts,* or *transactions,*

a

A. M. 2514.
B. C. 1490.
An. Exod. Isr. 2.
Ijar or Zif.

the sons of Aaron; Nadab the [a] first-born, and Abihu, Eleazar, and Ithamar.

3 These *are* the names of the sons of Aaron, [b] the priests which were anointed, [c] whom he consecrated to minister in the priest's office.

4 [d] And Nadab and Abihu died before the LORD, when they offered strange fire before the LORD, in the wilderness of Sinai, and they had no children: and Eleazar and Ithamar ministered in the priest's office, in the sight of Aaron their father.

5 And the LORD spake unto Moses, saying,

6 [e] Bring the tribe of Levi near, and present them before Aaron the priest, that they may minister unto him.

7 And they shall keep his charge, and the charge of the whole congregation before the tabernacle of the congregation, to do [f] the service of the tabernacle.

8 And they shall keep all the instruments of the tabernacle of the congregation, and the charge of the children of Israel, to do the service of the tabernacle.

9 And [g] thou shalt give the Levites unto Aaron and to his sons: they *are* wholly given unto him out of the children of Israel.

10 And thou shalt appoint Aaron and his sons, [h] and they shall wait on their priest's office: [i] and the stranger that cometh nigh shall be put to death.

11 And the LORD spake unto Moses, saying,

12 And I, behold, [k] I have taken the Levites from among the children of Israel instead of all the first-born that openeth the matrix among the children of Israel: therefore the Levites shall be mine:

13 Because [l] all the first-born *are* mine: [m] *for* on the day that I smote all the first-born

[a] Exod. vi. 23.——[b] Exod. xxviii. 41; Lev. viii.——[c] Hebrew *whose hand he filled.*——[d] Lev. x. 1; chap. xxvi. 61; 1 Chron. xxiv. 2.——[e] Chap. viii. 6; xviii. 2.——[f] See chap. i. 50; viii. 11, 15, 24, 26.

[g] Chap. viii. 19; xviii. 6.——[h] Chap. xviii. 7.——[i] Verse 38; chap. i. 51; xvi. 40.——[k] Verse 41; chapter viii. 16; xviii. 6. [l] Exod. xiii. 2; Lev. xxvii. 26; chapter viii. 16; Luke ii. 23. [m] Exod. xiii. 12, 15; chap. viii. 17.

or the *history of the lives*, as the same phrase may be understood in Gen. ii. 4; vi. 9. However this may be, it is evident that in this genealogy the family of Aaron are alone mentioned, probably because these belonged to the priesthood. Moses passes by his own family, or immediate descendants; he gave no rank or privilege to them during his life, and left nothing to them at his death. They became incorporated with the Levites, from or amongst whom they are never distinguished. What a strong proof is this of the celestial origin of his religion! Had it been of *man*, it must have had the gratification of some impure passion for its object; lust, ambition, or avarice: but none of these ever appear during the whole of his administration amongst the Israelites, though he had it constantly in his power to have gratified each. What an essential difference between the religion of the *Pentateuch* and that of the *Koran!* The former is God's workmanship; the latter is a motley mixture of all bad crafts, with here and there a portion of heavenly fire, stolen from the Divine altar in the Old and New Testaments, to give some vitality to the otherwise inert mass.

Verse 4. *Nadab and Abihu died*] See the notes on Lev. chap. x.

Verse 6. *Bring the tribe of Levi near*] The original word הקרב *hakreb* is properly a sacrificial word, and signifies the presenting of a sacrifice or offering to the Lord. As an offering, the tribe of *Levi* was given up entirely to the service of the sanctuary, to be no longer their own, but the Lord's property.

Verse 7. *The charge of the whole congregation*] They shall work *for* the whole congregation; and *instead* of the *first-born*.

Verse 8. *All the instruments*] The tabernacle itself and all its contents: see all described, ver. 25, 26, 31, 36, 37. The *Levites* were to perform the most common and laborious offices. It was their business to take down, put up, and carry the tabernacle and its utensils; for it was the object of their peculiar care. In a word, *they* were the servants of the *priests*.

Verse 10. *Aaron and his sons—shall wait on their priest's office*] It was the business of the *priests* to offer the different sacrifices to God; to consecrate the shewbread, pour out the libations, burn the incense, sprinkle the blood of the victims, and bless the people. In a word, *they* were the servants of God alone.

Verse 12. *I have taken the Levites—instead of all the first-born*] The Levites are taken for the service of the sanctuary in place of the first-born. The *first-born* were dedicated to God in commemoration of his slaying the *first-born* of the Egyptians, and preserving those of the Israelites. Even the *cattle* of the Levites were taken in place of the *first-born of the cattle* of the rest of the tribes. See ver. 45.

Several reasons have been assigned why God should give this honour to the tribe of Levi in preference to all the others, but they do not seem to me to be conclusive. Their zeal in destroying those who had corrupted the worship of God in the business of the golden calf, Exod. xxxii. 28, has been thought a sufficient reason. A better reason is, that this was the *smallest* tribe, and they were quite enough for the service. To have had a more *numerous* tribe at this time would have been very inconvenient.

Aaron, says Mr. Ainsworth, being in his priesthood a type of Christ, all these rites are fulfilled in him For unto Christ God gave *children*, Heb. ii. 13. And they are *a congregation of first-born, whose names*

A. M. 2514.
B. C. 1490.
An. Exod. Isr. 2.
Ijar or Zif.

in the land of Egypt, I hallowed unto me all the first-born in Israel, both man and beast: mine shall they be: I *am* the LORD.

14 And the LORD spake unto Moses in the wilderness of Sinai, saying,

15 Number the children of Levi after the house of their fathers, by their families: [n] every male, from a month old and upward, shalt thou number them.

16 And Moses numbered them according to the [o] word of the LORD, as he was commanded.

17 [p] And these were the sons of Levi by their names; Gershon, and Kohath, and Merari.

18 And these *are* the names of the sons of Gershon by their families; [q] Libni, and Shimei.

19 And the sons of Kohath by their families; [r] Amram, and Izehar, Hebron, and Uzziel.

20 [s] And the sons of Merari by their families; Mahli, and Mushi. These *are* the families of the Levites, according to the house of their fathers.

21 Of Gershon was the family of the Libnites, and the family of the Shimites: these *are* the families of the Gershonites.

22 Those that were numbered of them, according to the number of all the males, from a month old and upward, *even* those that were numbered of them *were* seven thousand and five hundred.

23 [t] The families of the Gershonites shall pitch behind the tabernacle westward.

A. M. 2514.
B. C. 1490.
An. Exod. Isr. 2.
Ijar or Zif.

24 And the chief of the house of the father of the Gershonites *shall be* Eliasaph the son of Lael.

25 And [u] the charge of the sons of Gershon in the tabernacle of the congregation *shall be* [v] the tabernacle, and [w] the tent, [x] the covering thereof, and [y] the hanging for the door of the tabernacle of the congregation,

26 And [z] the hangings of the court, and [a] the curtain for the door of the court, which *is* by the tabernacle, and by the altar round about, and [b] the cords of it for all the service thereof

27 [c] And of Kohath *was* the family of the Amramites, and the family of the Izeharites, and the family of the Hebronites, and the family of the Uzzielites: these *are* the families of the Kohathites.

28 In the number of all the males, from a month old and upward, *were* eight thousand and six hundred, keeping the charge of the sanctuary.

29 [d] The families of the sons of Kohath shall pitch on the side of the tabernacle southward.

30 And the chief of the house of the father of the families of the Kohathites *shall be* Elizaphan the son of Uzziel.

31 And [e] their charge *shall be* [f] the ark, and [g] the table, and [h] the candlestick, and [i] the altars, and the vessels of the sanctuary wherewith they minister, and [k] the hanging, and all the service thereof.

32 And Eleazar the son of Aaron the priest *shall be* chief over the chief of the Levites,

[n] Ver. 39; chap. xxvi. 62.——[o] Heb. *mouth*.——[p] Gen. xlvi. 11; Exod. vi. 16; chap. xxvi. 57; 1 Chron. vi. 1. 16; xxiii. 6. [q] Exod. vi. 17.——[r] Exod. vi. 18.——[s] Exod. vi. 19.——[t] Chap. i. 53.——[u] Chap. iv. 24, 25, 26.——[v] Exod. xxv. 9.——[w] Exod. xxvi. 1.

[x] Exod. xxvi. 7, 14.——[y] Exod. xxvi. 36.——[z] Exod. xxvii. 9 [a] Exod. xxvii. 16.——[b] Exod. xxxv. 18.——[c] 1 Chron. xxvi. 23. [d] Chap. i. 53.——[e] Chap. iv. 15.——[f] Exod. xxv. 10.——[g] Exod. xxv. 23.——[h] Exod. xxv. 31.——[i] Exod. xxvii. 1; xxx. 1. [k] Exod. xxvi. 32.

are written in heaven, Heb. xii. 23, being of God's own will *begotten by the word of truth*, that they should be *a kind of first-fruits of his creatures*, James i. 18, to whom he also gives the first-fruits of his Spirit, Rom. viii. 23. These *wait on* and *follow the Lamb*, being *first-fruits unto God and to the Lamb*, Rev. xiv. 4; and Christ *hath made us kings and priests unto God and his Father*, that we *may serve him day and night in his temple*, Rev. i. 6; vii. 15.

Verse 15. *A month old and upward*] The males of all the other tribes were numbered, from *twenty years and upward;* had the *Levites* been numbered in this way, they would not have been nearly equal in number to the first-born of the twelve tribes. Add to this, that as there must have been *first-born* of *all ages* in the other tribes, it was necessary that the *Levites*, who were to be their *substitutes*, should be also of *all ages;* and it appears to have been on this ground, at least partly, that the Levites were numbered from *four weeks* old and upward.

Verse 16. *Moses numbered them*] Though Moses and Aaron conjointly numbered the *twelve tribes*, yet Moses alone numbered the Levites; "for as the money with which the first-born of Israel, who exceeded the number of Levites, were redeemed, was to be paid to Aaron and his sons, ver. 48, it was decent that he, whose advantage it was that the number of the first-born of Israel should *exceed*, should not be authorized to take that number himself."—*Dodd*, from Bishop *Kidder*.

Verse 22. *Seven thousand and five hundred*] Perhaps originally ר *resh*, 200, instead of ך *caph*, 500; see the following note.

A. M. 2514.
B. C. 1490.
An. Exod. Isr. 2.
Ijar or Zif.

and have the oversight of them that keep the charge of the sanctuary.

33 Of Merari *was* the family of the Mahlites, and the family of the Mushites: these *are* the families of Merari.

34 And those that were numbered of them, according to the number of all the males, from a month old and upward, *were* six thousand and two hundred.

35 And the chief of the house of the father of the families of Merari, *was* Zuriel the son of Abihail: [l] *these* shall pitch on the side of the tabernacle northward.

36 And [m] *under* [n] the custody and charge of the sons of Merari *shall be* the boards of the tabernacle, and the bars thereof, and the pillars thereof, and the sockets thereof, and all the vessels thereof, and all that serveth thereto,

37 And the pillars of the court round about, and their sockets, and their pins, and their cords.

38 [o] But those that encamp before the tabernacle toward the east, *even* before the tabernacle of the congregation eastward, *shall be* Moses, and Aaron and his sons, [p] keeping the charge of the sanctuary [q] for the charge of the children of Israel; and [r] the stranger that cometh nigh shall be put to death.

39 [s] All that were numbered of the Levites, which Moses and Aaron numbered at the commandment of the LORD, throughout their families, all the males from a month old and upward, *were* twenty and two thousand.

40 And the LORD said unto Moses, [t] Number all the first-born of the males of the children of Israel, from a month old and upward, and take the number of their names.

A. M. 2514.
B. C. 1490.
An. Exod. Isr. 2.
Ijar or Zif.

41 [u] And thou shalt take the Levites for me (I *am* the LORD) instead of all the first-born among the children of Israel; and the cattle of the Levites instead of all the firstlings among the cattle of the children of Israel

42 And Moses numbered, as the LORD commanded him, all the first-born among the children of Israel.

43 And all the first-born males by the number of names, from a month old and upward, of those that were numbered of them, were twenty and two thousand two hundred and threescore and thirteen.

44 And the LORD spake unto Moses, saying,

45 [v] Take the Levites instead of all the first-born among the children of Israel, and the cattle of the Levites instead of their cattle; and the Levites shall be mine: I *am* the LORD.

46 And for those that are to be [w] redeemed of the two hundred and threescore and thirteen of the first-born of the children of Israel, [x] which are more than the Levites:

47 Thou shalt even take [y] five shekels apiece by the poll, after the shekel of the sanctuary shalt thou take *them*: ([z] the shekel *is* twenty gerahs:)

48 And thou shalt give the money, wherewith the odd number of them is to be redeemed, unto Aaron and to his sons.

49 And Moses took the redemption money of them that were over and above them that were redeemed by the Levites:

[l] Chap. i. 53.——[m] Heb. *the office of the charge.*——[n] Chap. iv. 31, 32.——[o] Chap. i. 53.——[p] Chap. xviii. 5.——[q] Ver. 7, 8.——[r] Ver. 10.——[s] See chap. xxvi. 62.——[t] Ver. 15.——[u] Ver. 12, 45.

[v] Ver. 12, 41.——[w] Exod. xiii. 13; chap. xviii. 15.——[x] Ver. 39, 43.——[y] Lev. xxvii. 6; chap. xviii. 16.——[z] Exod. xxx. 13; Lev. xxvii. 25; chap. xviii. 16; Ezek. xlv. 12.

Verse 39. *Which Moses and Aaron numbered*] The word ואהרן *veaharon*, "*and Aaron*," has a point over each of its letters, probably designed as a mark of *spuriousness*. The word is wanting in the *Samaritan*, *Syriac*, and *Coptic*; it is wanting also in *eight* of Dr. *Kennicott's* MSS., and in *four* of De *Rossi's*. Moses alone, as *Houbigant* observes, is commanded to take the number of the *Levites*; see ver. 5, 11, 40, 44, and 51.

All the males—were twenty and two thousand.] This total does not agree with the particulars; for the Gershonites were 7,500, the Kohathites 8,600, the Merarites 6,200, total 22,300. Several methods of solving this difficulty have been proposed by learned men; Dr. *Kennicott's* is the most simple Formerly the numbers in the Hebrew Bible were expressed by *letters*, and not by *words at full length*; and if two nearly similar letters were mistaken for each other, many errors in the numbers must be the consequence. Now it is probable that an error has crept into the number of the *Gershonites*, ver. 22, where, instead of 7,500, we should read 7,200, as ך *caph*, 500, might have been easily mistaken for ר *resh*, 200, especially if the down stroke of the *caph* had been a little shorter than ordinary, which is often the case in MSS. The extra 300 being taken off, the total is just 22,000, as mentioned in the 39th verse.

Verse 43. *All the first-born males—were twenty and two thousand two hundred and threescore and thirteen.*] Thus we find there were 273 *first-born*

A. M. 2514.
B. C. 1490.
An. Exod. Isr. 2.
Ijar or Zif.

50 Of the first-born of the children of Israel took he the money; [a] a thousand three hundred and threescore and five *shekels*, after the shekel of the sanctuary:

51 And Moses [b] gave the money of them that were redeemed unto Aaron and to his sons, according to the word of the LORD, as the LORD commanded Moses.

[a] Ver. 46, 47. — [b] Ver. 48.

beyond the number of the *Levites*. These are ordered, ver. 46, to be *redeemed;* and the redemption price is to be *five shekels* each, ver. 47, about 15*s*. And this money, amounting to 1,365 shekels, equal to £204. 15*s*. English, he took of the first-born of Israel, verse 50. But how was this collected among 22,273 persons? *Rabbi Solomon Jarchi* says, "to prevent contention, Moses took 22,000 slips of parchment, and wrote on each *a son of Levi*, and 273 others, on which he wrote *five shekels;* then he mixed them in a basket, and each man took out one; those who drew the slips on which *five shekels* were written, paid the money; the others went free." This is a most stupid and silly tale, for such a mode of settlement never could have been resorted to by an intelligent people. It would have been much more simple to have paid it out of a general fund; and it is very likely that in this way the expense was defrayed.

This species of redeeming of men is referred to by St. Peter, 1 Epist. i. 18, 19: "Ye know that ye were not redeemed with corruptible things, as silver *and* gold, from your vain conversation, received by tradition from your fathers; but with the precious (τιμιῳ αἱματι, *valuable*) blood of Christ, as of a lamb without blemish and without spot," &c. And it is not the *first-born* only which are thus redeemed, for he, by the grace of God, tasted death for EVERY man; Heb. ii. 9. Reader, give glory to God that such a ransom has been paid for thy soul, and see that, redeemed from thy vain conversation, thy empty, fruitless, and graceless observances, on which thou hast built thy hopes of salvation, thou walk in newness of life, giving thy whole soul with thankfulness unto the Father who hath translated thee from darkness, and placed thee in the kingdom of his beloved Son. To Him be glory and dominion for ever and ever! Amen.

CHAPTER IV.

Moses is commanded to take the sum of the sons of Kohath *from thirty years old and upward*, 1–4. *The service which they had to perform*, 5–15. *The office of* Eleazar, 16. *The family of* Kohath *to be continued among the Levites*, 17–19. *They are not to go into the holy of holies*, 20. *The sum of the sons of* Gershon, 21–23. *The service they had to perform*, 24–27. *They are to be under* Ithamar, 28. *The sum of the sons of* Merari, 29, 30. *The service they had to perform*, 31–33. *The sum of all the families of* Kohath, 2,750, *ver.* 34–37. *The sum of the families of* Gershon, 2,630, *ver.* 38–41. *The sum of the families of* Merari, 3,200, *ver.* 42–45. *The sum total of the families of* Gershon, Kohath, *and* Merari, 8,580, *ver.* 46–49.

A. M. 2514.
B. C. 1490.
An. Exod. Isr. 2.
Ijar or Zif.

AND the LORD spake unto Moses and unto Aaron, saying,

2 Take the sum of the sons of Kohath from among the sons of Levi, after their families, by the house of their fathers,

3 [a] From thirty years old and upward even

[a] See chap. viii. 24; 1 Chron. xxiii. 3, 24, 27.

NOTES ON CHAP. IV.

Verse 3. *From thirty years old*] In chap. viii. 24, the Levites are ordered to enter on the service of the tabernacle at the age of *twenty-five* years; and in 1 Chron. xxiii. 24, they were ordered to commence that work at *twenty* years of age. How can these different times be reconciled? 1. At the time of which Moses speaks here, the Levitical service was exceedingly *severe*, and consequently required men *full grown, strong*, and *stout*, to perform it; the age therefore of *thirty* years was appointed as the period for commencing this service, the *weightier* part of which is probably here intended. 2. In chap. viii. 24, Moses seems to speak of the service in a *general* way; the *severe*, which was to be performed by the full-grown Levites, and the less laborious work which younger men might assist in; hence the age of *twenty-five* is fixed. 3. In David's time and afterwards, in the *fixed* tabernacle and temple, the *laboriousness* of the service no longer existed, and hence *twenty* years was the age fixed on for all Levites to enter into the work of the sanctuary. The rabbins say that the Levites began to learn to do the service at *twenty-five*, and that having been instructed *five* years, they began the public service at *thirty*, and thus they reconcile the two periods referred to above. We may well suppose that the *sons of the prophets* continued a considerable time under instructions before they were called fully to exercise themselves in the prophetic office.

Until fifty years old] This was allowing *twenty* years for public severe service; a very considerate

A. M. 2514.
B. C. 1490.
An. Exod. Isr. 2.
Ijar or Zif.

until fifty years old, all that enter into the host, to do the work in the tabernacle of the congregation.

4 [b] This *shall be* the service of the sons of Kohath in the tabernacle of the congregation, *about* [c] the most holy things:

5 And when the camp setteth forward, Aaron shall come, and his sons, and they shall take down [d] the covering veil, and cover the [e] ark of testimony with it:

6 And shall put thereon the covering of badgers' skins, and shall spread over *it* a cloth wholly of blue, and shall put in [f] the staves thereof.

7 And upon the [g] table of shew-bread they shall spread a cloth of blue, and put thereon the dishes, and the spoons, and the bowls, and covers to [h] cover withal: and the continual bread shall be thereon:

8 And they shall spread upon them a cloth of scarlet, and cover the same with a covering of badgers' skins, and shall put in the staves thereof.

9 And they shall take a cloth of blue, and cover the [i] candlestick of the light, [k] and his lamps, and his tongs, and his snuff dishes, and all the oil vessels thereof, wherewith they minister unto it:

10 And they shall put it and all the vessels thereof within a covering of badgers' skins, and shall put *it* upon a bar.

11 And upon [l] the golden altar they shall spread a cloth of blue, and cover it with a covering of badgers' skins, and shall put to the staves thereof:

12 And they shall take all the instruments of ministry, wherewith they minister in the sanctuary, and put *them* in a cloth of blue, and cover them with a covering of badgers' skins, and shall put *them* on a bar:

A. M. 2514.
B. C. 1490.
An. Exod. Isr. 2
Ijar or Zif.

13 And they shall take away the ashes from the altar, and spread a purple cloth thereon:

14 And they shall put upon it all the vessels thereof, wherewith they minister about it, *even* the censers, the flesh hooks, and the shovels, and the [m] basons, all the vessels of the altar; and they shall spread upon it a covering of badgers' skins, and put to the staves of it.

15 And when Aaron and his sons have made an end of covering the sanctuary, and all the vessels of the sanctuary, as the camp is to set forward; after that, [n] the sons of Kohath shall come to bear *it*: [o] but they shall not touch *any* holy thing, lest they die. [p] These *things are* the burden of the sons of Kohath in the tabernacle of the congregation.

16 And to the office of Eleazar the son of Aaron the priest, *pertaineth* [q] the oil for the light, and the [r] sweet incense, and [s] the daily meat-offering, and the [t] anointing oil, *and* the oversight of all the tabernacle, and of all that therein *is*, in the sanctuary, and in the vessels thereof.

17 And the LORD spake unto Moses and unto Aaron, saying,

18 Cut ye not off the tribe of the families of the Kohathites from among the Levites:

19 But thus do unto them, that they may live, and not die, when they approach unto [u] the most holy things: Aaron and his sons shall go in, and appoint them every one to his service and to his burden:

20 [v] But they shall not go in to see when

[b] Ver. 15.——[c] Ver. 19.——[d] Exod. xxvi. 31.——[e] Exod. xxv. 10, 16.——[f] Exod. xxv. 13.——[g] Exod. xxv. 23, 29, 30; Lev. xxiv. 6, 8.——[h] Or, *pour out withal.*——[i] Exod. xxv. 31.——[k] Exod. xxv. 37, 38.——[l] Exod. xxx. 1, 3.——[m] Or, *bowls.*

[n] Chap. vii. 9; x. 21; Deut. xxxi. 9; 2 Sam. vi. 13; 1 Chron. xv. 2, 15.——[o] 2 Sam. vi. 6, 7; 1 Chron. xiii. 9, 10.——[p] Chap. iii. 31.——[q] Exod. xxv. 6; Lev. xxiv. 2.——[r] Exod. xxx. 34.——[s] Exod. xxix. 40.——[t] Exod. xxx. 23.——[u] Ver. 4.——[v] See Exod. xix. 21; 1 Sam. vi. 19.

and merciful ordinance. A preacher who devotes his whole time and strength to the service of the Church of God from twenty to fifty or sixty years of age, should be then excused from his *severer labour*, and maintained at the charge of the sanctuary. This would not only be a great comfort to a worn-out servant of God but also of great use to the work of the ministry, which, to be faithfully and effectually performed, requires all the powers of the body and mind of man. *Old faithful ministers* are to be highly respected for their work's sake, and to be supplied with all the necessaries and comforts of life; but how little can they do in the public ministry of the word, however willing to work, when their eye waxes dim and their bodily strength fails! See on chap. viii. 25. Both for their own sakes, and for the good of the Church, they should be excused from a labour to which they must be almost every way inadequate. But notwithstanding this comparative inactivity, their counsels, advice, and experience will always be considered as a treasure to the Church of Christ.

Verse 20. *When the holy things are covered*] Literally, כבלע *keballa*, when they are *swallowed down;* which shows the promptitude with which every thing belonging to the holy of holies was put out of sight, for these mysteries must ever be treated with the deep-

A. M. 2514. B. C. 1490. An. Exod. Isr. 2. Ijar or Zif.

the holy things are covered, lest
they die.
21 And the LORD spake unto
Moses, saying,
22 Take also the sum of the sons of Gershon, throughout the houses of their fathers,
by their families;
23 [w] From thirty years old and upward until
fifty years old shalt thou number them; all
that enter in [x] to perform the service, to do the
work in the tabernacle of the congregation.
24 This *is* the service of the families of the
Gershonites, to serve, and for [y] burdens:
25 And [z] they shall bear the curtains of the
tabernacle, and the tabernacle of the congregation, his covering, and the covering of the
badgers' skins that *is* above upon it, and the
hanging for the door of the tabernacle of the
congregation,
26 And the hangings of the court, and the
hanging for the door of the gate of the court,
which *is* by the tabernacle and by the altar
round about, and their cords, and all the instruments of their service, and all that is made for
them: so shall they serve.
27 At the [a] appointment of Aaron and his
sons shall be all the service of the sons of the
Gershonites, in all their burdens, and in all
their service: and ye shall appoint unto them
in charge all their burdens.
28 This *is* the service of the families of the
sons of Gershon in the tabernacle of the congregation: and their charge *shall be* under the
hand of Ithamar the son of Aaron
the priest.

A. M. 2514. B. C. 1490. An. Exod. Isr. 2. Ijar or Zif.

29 As for the sons of Merari,
thou shalt number them after their families, by
the house of their fathers;
30 [b] From thirty years old and upward even
unto fifty years old shalt thou number them,
every one that entereth into the [c] service, to do
the work of the tabernacle of the congregation.
31 And [d] this *is* the charge of their burden,
according to all their service in the tabernacle
of the congregation; [e] the boards of the tabernacle, and the bars thereof, and the pillars
thereof, and sockets thereof,
32 And the pillars of the court round about,
and their sockets, and their pins, and their
cords, with all their instruments, and with all
their service: and by name ye shall [f] reckon
the instruments of the charge of their burden.
33 This *is* the service of the families of the
sons of Merari, according to all their service,
in the tabernacle of the congregation, under
the hand of Ithamar the son of Aaron the
priest.
34 [g] And Moses and Aaron and the chief of
the congregation numbered the sons of the
Kohathites after their families, and after the
house of their fathers,
35 From thirty years old and upward even
unto fifty years old, every one that entereth
into the service, for the work in the tabernacle
of the congregation:
36 And those that were numbered of them

[w] Ver. 3.—[x] Heb. *to war the warfare.*—[y] Or, *carriage.*—[z] Chap. iii. 25, 26.—[a] Heb. *mouth.*

[b] Ver. 3.—[c] Heb. *warfare.*—[d] Chap. iii. 36, 37.—[e] Exod. xxvi. 15.—[f] Exod. xxxviii. 21.—[g] Ver. 2.

est reverence; and indeed without this they could not have been to them the representatives of heavenly realities. See the concluding note.

Verse 36. *Those that were numbered*] In chapter iii. 27, &c., we have an account of the whole number of the Levites, and here of those only who were *able to serve the Lord in the sanctuary.* By comparing the two places we find the numbers to stand thus:—

KOHATHITES	Able men	2750
	Unable	5850
	Total	8600
GERSHONITES	Able men	2630
	Unable	4870
	Total	7500
MERARITES	Able men	3200
	Unable	3000
	Total	6200

Thus we find that the whole number of the Levites amounted to 22,300, of whom 8,580 were fit for service, and 13,720 unfit, being either too old or too young. What an astonishing number of men, all properly ecclesiastics; all performing some service by which God was glorified, and the congregation at large benefited! See *Ainsworth.*

FROM this and the preceding chapter we see the very severe labour which the Levites were obliged to perform while the journeyings of the Israelites lasted. When we consider that there was not less than 10 *tons* 13 *cwt.* 24 *lb.* 14. *oz.*, i. e., almost *ten tons* and fourteen hundred pounds' weight of *metal* employed in the tabernacle, (see the notes on Exod. xxxviii.,) besides the immense weight of the *skins, hangings, cords, boards,* and *posts,* we shall find it was no very easy matter to transport this movable temple from place to place.

The *Gershonites,* who were 7,500 men in the ser-

A. M. 2514. B. C. 1490. An. Exod. Isr. 2. Ijar or Zif.

by their families were two thousand seven hundred and fifty.
37 These *were* they that were
numbered of the families of the Kohathites,
all that might do service in the tabernacle of
the congregation, which Moses and Aaron did
number according to the commandment of the
LORD by the hand of Moses.
38 And those that were numbered of the
sons of Gershon, throughout their families,
and by the house of their fathers,
39 From thirty years old and upward even
unto fifty years old, every one that entereth
into the service, for the work in the tabernacle
of the congregation,
40 Even those that were numbered of them,
throughout their families, by the house of their
fathers, were two thousand and six hundred
and thirty.
41 [h] These *are* they that were numbered of
the families of the sons of Gershon, of all that
might do service in the tabernacle of the congregation, whom Moses and Aaron did number
according to the commandment of the LORD.
42 And those that were numbered of the families of the sons of Merari, throughout their
families, by the house of their fathers,
43 From thirty years old and upward even
unto fifty years old, every one
that entereth into the service, for
the work in the tabernacle of the
congregation,
44 Even those that were numbered of them
after their families, were three thousand and
two hundred.
45 These *be* those that were numbered of
the families of the sons of Merari, whom
Moses and Aaron numbered [i] according to the
word of the LORD by the hand of Moses.
46 All those that were numbered of the Levites, whom Moses and Aaron and the chief
of Israel numbered, after their families, and
after the house of their fathers,
47 [k] From thirty years old and upward, even
unto fifty years old, every one that came to do
the service of the ministry, and the service of the
burden in the tabernacle of the congregation,
48 Even those that were numbered of them,
were eight thousand and five hundred and
fourscore.
49 According to the commandment of the
LORD they were numbered by the hand of
Moses, [l] every one according to his service,
and according to his burden: thus were they
numbered of him, [m] as the LORD commanded
Moses.

[h] Ver. 22.——[i] Ver. 29.——[k] Ver. 3, 23, 30.

[l] Ver. 15, 24, 31.——[m] Ver. 1, 21.

vice, had to carry the *tent, coverings, veils, hangings of the court, &c., &c.*, chap. iii. 25, 26.

The *Kohathites*, who were 8,600 men, had to carry the *ark, table, candlestick, altars*, and *instruments* of the *sanctuary*, chap. iii. 31.

The *Merarites*, who were 6,200 men, had to carry the *boards, bars, pillars, sockets*, and all *matters* connected with these belonging to the *tabernacle*, with the *pillars* of the *court*, their *sockets, pins*, and *cords*, chap. iii. 36, 37.

The tabernacle was an epitome of the temple: the *temple* and *tabernacle* were representatives of the Church of the living God, and of the *humanity* of our blessed Lord. As God dwelt in the tabernacle and temple, so his fulness dwelt in the *man* Christ Jesus. These again were types of the Christian Church, which is termed the body of Christ, Eph. i. 23, where he dwells in the plenitude of the graces of his Spirit.

Mr. Ainsworth has a very useful note on the 20th verse of this chapter, the most edifying part of which I shall here lay before the reader. He considers the *tabernacle* and *temple*, not only as pointing out the *old dispensation*, the *annulling* of which was typified by their *destruction*, but he considers also the former as emblematical of the *body* of man.

"The apostle," says he, "treating of the death of the saints, uses this similitude: 'If our earthly house of this tabernacle were dissolved, we have a building of God, a house not made with hands, eternal in the heavens. For we that are in THIS TABERNACLE do groan, being burdened, not for that we would be unclothed, but clothed upon, that mortality might be swallowed up of life;' 2 Cor. v. 1–4. So Peter calls his death the *putting off* of his TABERNACLE, 2 Pet. i. 14. And this similitude is very fit; for, as here, in the tabernacle of Moses, the holy things were first covered and taken away, (see ver. 20,) so the soul and its powers are first withdrawn from the body by death. 2. As the curtains and coverings were taken off and folded up, so the skin and flesh of our bodies are pulled off and consumed. 3. As the boards of the tabernacle were disjointed and pulled asunder, so shall our bones and sinews: compare Job's description of the formation of man, chap. x. 8–12; and Solomon's account of his dissolution, Eccles. xii. 3, 4. 4. As the disjointed and dissolved tabernacle was afterwards set up again, Num. x. 21, so shall our *bodies* in the day of the resurrection; see 1 Cor. xv. 51–54."

CHAPTER V.

The Israelites are commanded to purify the camp by excluding all lepers, and all diseased and unclean persons, 1–3. *They do so,* 4. *Law concerning him who has defrauded another—he shall confess his sin, restore the principal, and add besides one* fifth *of its value,* 5–7. *If he have* no kinsman *to whom the recompense can be made, it shall be given unto the Lord,* 8. *All the holy things offered to the Lord shall be the priest's portion,* 9, 10. *The law concerning jealousy,* 11–14. *The suspected woman's offering,* 15. *She is to be brought before the Lord,* 16. *The priest shall take holy water, and put it in dust from the floor of the tabernacle,* 17. *Shall put the offering in her hand, and adjure her,* 18–20. *The form of the oath,* 21, 22; *which is to be written on a book, blotted out in the bitter waters, and these the suspected person shall be obliged to drink,* 23, 24. *The jealousy-offering shall be waved before the Lord,* 25, 26. *The effect which shall be produced if the suspected person be* guilty, 27. *The effect if* not guilty, 28. *Recapitulation, with the purpose and design of the law,* 29, 30.

A. M. 2514.
B. C. 1490.
An. Exod. Isr. 2.
Ijar or Zif.

AND the LORD spake unto
Moses, saying,
2 Command the children of
Israel, that they put out of the camp every
[a] leper, and every one that hath an [b] issue, and
whosoever is defiled by the [c] dead:
3 Both male and female shall ye put out,
without the camp shall ye put them; that they
defile not their camps, [d] in the midst whereof
I dwell.
4 And the children of Israel
did so, and put them out without
the camp: as the LORD spake
unto Moses, so did the children of Israel.
5 And the LORD spake unto Moses, saying,
6 Speak unto the children of Israel, [e] When
a man or woman shall commit any sin that
men commit, to do a trespass against the
LORD, and that person be guilty;
7 [f] Then they shall confess their sin which

[a] Lev. xiii. 3, 46; chap. xii. 14.——[b] Lev. xv. 2.——[c] Lev. xxi. 1; chap. ix. 6, 10; xix. 11, 13; xxxi. 19.

[d] Lev. xxvi. 11, 12; 2 Cor. vi. 16.——[e] Lev. vi. 2, 3.——[f] Lev. v. 5; xxvi. 40; Josh. vii. 19.

NOTES ON CHAP. V.

Verse 2. *Put out of the camp every leper*] According to the preceding plan, it is sufficiently evident that each camp had a space behind it, and on one side, whither the infected might be removed, and where probably convenient places were erected for the accommodation of the infected; for we cannot suppose that they were driven out into the naked wilderness. But the expulsion mentioned here was founded, 1. On a purely *physical* reason, *viz.*, the diseases were *contagious*, and therefore there was a necessity of putting those afflicted by them apart, that the infection might not be communicated. 2. There was also a *spiritual* reason; the camp was the habitation of God, and nothing impure should be permitted to remain where he dwelt. 3. The camp was an emblem of the Church, where nothing that is defiled should enter, and in which nothing that is unholy should be tolerated. All *lepers*—all persevering impenitent sinners, should be driven from the sacred pale, nor should any such ever be permitted to enter.

Verse 4. *And the children of Israel—put them out*] This is the earliest account we have of such separations; and probably this ordinance gave the first idea of a *hospital*, where all those who are afflicted with contagious disorders are put into particular wards, under medical treatment. Though no mention be made of the situation, circumstances, &c., of those expelled persons, we may certainly infer that they were treated with that humanity which their distressed state required. Though sinners must be separated from the Church of God, yet they should be treated with affectionate regard, because *they may be reclaimed.* It is too often the case when a man backslides from the way of truth, he is abandoned by all; finding his case desperate, he plunges yet deeper into the mire of sin, and the man who, with tender treatment, might have been reclaimed, becomes incurably hardened. One class says, he cannot finally fall, and shall in due time be restored; another class says, he may finally fall and *utterly perish.* If the unfortunate person be restored, his recovery is taken as a proof of the first doctrine; if he be not, his wretched end is considered a proof of the second. In the first case the person himself may presume on his restoration as a point infallibly determined in the Divine counsel; or in the second, he may consider his case *hopeless*, and so abandon himself to profligacy and desperation. Thus both parties leave him, and both opinions (misunderstood certainly) render him *secure* or *desperate;* and in either case totally *inactive* in behalf of his own soul. Who is he that properly estimates the worth of one immortal spirit? He who does will at once feel that, in a state of *probation*, any man *may fall* through sin, and any sinner may be renewed again unto repentance, through the infinitely meritorious sacrifice, and all powerfully efficacious grace, of Christ. This truth properly felt equally precludes both presumption and despair, and will induce the followers of God to be active in *preserving* those who have escaped from the corruption that is in the world, and make them diligent to *recover* those who have turned back to earth and sin.

Verse 7. *Shall confess their sin*] Without *confession* or *acknowledgment* of sin, there was no hope of mercy held out.

He shall recompense] For without *restitution*, in every possible case, God will not forgive the iniquity

A. M. 2514. B. C. 1490. An. Exod. Isr. 2. Ijar or Zif.

they have done: and he shall recompense his trespass [g] with the principal thereof, and add unto it the fifth *part* thereof, and give *it* unto *him* against whom he hath trespassed.

8 But if the man have no kinsman to recompense the trespass unto, let the trespass be recompensed unto the LORD, *even* to the priest; beside [h] the ram of the atonement, whereby an atonement shall be made for him.

9 And every [i] offering [k] of all the holy things of the children of Israel, which they bring unto the priest, shall be his.

10 And every man's hallowed things shall be his: whatsoever any man giveth the priest, it shall be [l] his.

11 And the LORD spake unto Moses, saying,

12 Speak unto the children of Israel, and say unto them, If any man's wife go aside, and commit a trespass against him,

13 And a man [m] lie with her carnally, and it be hid from the eyes of her husband, and be kept close, and she be defiled, and *there be* no witness against her, neither she be taken *with the manner;*

14 And the spirit of jealousy come upon him, and he be jealous of his wife, and she be defiled: or if the spirit of jealousy come upon him, and he be jealous of his wife, and she be not defiled:

15 Then shall the man bring his wife unto the priest, and he shall bring her offering for her, the tenth *part* of an ephah of barley meal; he shall pour no oil upon it, nor put frankincense thereon; for it *is* an offering of jealousy, an offering of memorial, [n] bringing iniquity to remembrance.

A. M. 2514. B. C. 1490. An. Exod. Isr. 2. Ijar or Zif.

16 And the priest shall bring her near, and set her before the LORD:

17 And the priest shall take holy water in an earthen vessel; and of the dust that is in the floor of the tabernacle the priest shall take, and put *it* into the water:

18 And the priest shall set the woman before the LORD, and uncover the woman's head, and put the offering of memorial in her hands, which *is* the jealousy-offering: and the priest shall have in his hand the bitter water that causeth the curse:

19 And the priest shall charge her by an oath, and say unto the woman, If no man have lain with thee, and if thou hast not gone aside to uncleanness [o] *with another* [p] instead of thy husband, be thou free from this bitter water that causeth the curse:

20 But if thou hast gone aside *to another* instead of thy husband, and if thou be defiled, and some man have lain with thee beside thine husband:

21 Then the priest shall [q] charge the woman with an oath of cursing, and the priest shall say unto the woman, [r] The LORD make thee a curse and an oath among thy people, when the LORD doth make thy thigh to [s] rot, and thy belly to swell;

22 And this water that causeth the curse

[g] Lev. vi. 5.——[h] Lev. vi. 6, 7; vii. 7.——[i] Or, *heave-offering.* [k] Exod. xxix. 28; Lev. vi. 17, 18, 26; vii. 6, 7, 9, 10, 14; chap. xviii. 8, 9, 19; Deut. xviii. 3, 4; Ezek. xliv. 29, 30.——[l] Lev. x. 13.——[m] Lev. xviii. 20.

[n] 1 Kings xvii. 18; Ezek. xxix. 16.——[o] Or, *being in the power of thy husband;* Rom. vii. 2.——[p] Heb. *under thy husband.* [q] Josh. vi. 26; 1 Sam. xiv. 24; Neh. x. 29.——[r] Jer. xxix. 22. [s] Heb. *fall.*

of a man's sin. How can any person in a case of defraud, with his neighbour's property in his possession, expect to receive mercy from the hand of a just and holy God! See this subject considered in the notes on Gen. xlii. at the close.

Verse 8. *If the man have no kinsman*] The Jews think that this law respects the *stranger* and the *sojourner* only, because every Israelite is in a state of affinity to all the rest; but there might be a *stranger* in the camp who has no relative in any of the tribes of Israel.

Verse 14. *The spirit of jealousy*] רוח קנאה *ruach kinah*, either a supernatural diabolic influence, exciting him to jealousy, or the *passion* or *affection* of jealousy, for so the words may be understood.

Verse 17. *Holy water*] Water out of the laver, called *holy* because consecrated to sacred uses. This is the most ancient case of the trial by *ordeal*. See at the end of the chapter.

In an earthen vessel] Supposed by the Jews to be such as had never been previously used.

Dust that is in the floor] Probably intended to point out the baseness of the crime of which she was accused.

Verse 18. *Uncover the woman's head*] To take off a woman's veil, and expose her to the sight of men, would be considered a very great degradation in the East. To this St. Paul appears to allude, 1 Cor. xi. 5, 6, 10.

Verse 21. *The Lord make thee a curse and an oath*] Let thy name and punishment be remembered and mentioned as an example and terror to all others. Like that mentioned Jer. xxix. 22, 23: "The Lord make thee like Zedekiah, and like Ahab, whom the king of Babylon roasted in the fire, because they have committed villany in Israel, and have committed adultery with their neighbours' wives."—*Ainsworth.*

Verse 22. Thy *belly to swell, and* thy *thigh to rot*]

A. M. 2514.
B. C. 1490.
An. Exod. Isr. 2.
Ijar or Zif.

[t] shall go into thy bowels, to make *thy* belly to swell, and *thy* thigh to rot: [u] And the woman shall say, Amen, amen.

23 And the priest shall write these curses in a book, and he shall blot *them* out with the bitter water:

24 And he shall cause the woman to drink the bitter water that causeth the curse: and the water that causeth the curse shall enter into her, *and become* bitter.

25 Then the priest shall take the jealousy-offering out of the woman's hand, and shall [v] wave the offering before the LORD, and offer it upon the altar:

26 [w] And the priest shall take a handful of the offering, *even* the memorial thereof, and burn *it* upon the altar, and afterward shall cause the woman to drink the water.

27 And when he hath made her to drink the water, then it shall come to pass, *that*, if she be defiled, and have done trespass against her husband, that the water that causeth the curse shall enter into her, *and become* bitter, and her belly shall swell, and her thigh shall rot: and the woman [x] shall be a curse among her people.

28 And if the woman be not defiled, but be clean; then she shall be free, and shall conceive seed.

29 This *is* the law of jealousies, when a wife goeth aside *to another* [y] instead of her husband, and is defiled;

30 Or when the spirit of jealousy cometh upon him, and he be jealous over his wife, and shall set the woman before the LORD, and the priest shall execute upon her all this law.

31 Then shall the man be guiltless from iniquity, and this woman [z] shall bear her iniquity

[t] Psa. cix. 18.——[u] Deut. xxvii. 15.——[v] Lev. viii. 27. [w] Lev. ii. 2, 9.——[x] Deut. xxviii. 37; Psa. lxxxiii. 9, 11; Jer. xxiv. 9; xxix. 18, 22; xlii. 18; Zech. viii. 13.——[y] Ver. 19 [z] Lev. xx. 17, 19, 20.

What is meant by these expressions cannot be easily ascertained. לנפל ירך *lanpel yarech* signifies literally thy *thigh to fall*. As the *thigh, feet*, &c., were used among the Hebrews delicately to express the parts which nature conceals, (see Gen. xlvi. 26,) the expression here is probably to be understood in this sense; and the *falling down of the thigh* here must mean something similar to the *prolapsus uteri*, or falling down of the womb, which might be a natural effect of the preternatural distension of the abdomen. In 1 Cor. xi. 29, St. Paul seems to allude to the case of the guilty woman drinking the bitter cursed waters that caused her destruction: *He who eateth and drinketh unworthily, eateth and drinketh damnation* (κριμα, *condemnation* or *judgment*) *to himself;* and there is probably a reference to the same thing in Psalm cix. 18, and in Dan. ix. 11.

And the woman shall say, Amen, amen.] This is the first place where this word occurs in the common form of a concluding wish in prayer. The root אמן *aman* signifies to be *steady, true, permanent*. And in prayer it signifies *let it be so—make it steady—let it be ratified*. Some have supposed that it is composed of the initial letters of ארני מלך נאמן Adonai Melech Neeman, *My Lord the faithful King*, but this derivation is both far-fetched and unnecessary.

Verse 23. *The priest shall write these curses—and he shall blot* them *out*] It appears that the curses which were written down with a kind of ink prepared for the purpose, as some of the rabbins think, without any calx of iron or other material that could make a permanent dye, were washed off the parchment into the water which the woman was obliged to drink, so that she drank the very *words* of the execration. The ink used in the East is almost all of this kind—a wet sponge will completely efface the finest of their writings. The rabbins say that the trial by the waters of jealousy was omitted after the Babylonish captivity because adulteries were so frequent amongst them that they were afraid of having the name of the Lord profaned by being so frequently appealed to! This is a most humiliating confession. "Though," says pious Bishop Wilson, "this judgment is not executed now on adulteresses, yet they have reason from this to conclude that a more terrible vengeance will await them hereafter without a bitter repentance; these being only a shadow of heavenly things, i. e., of what the Gospel requires of its professors, *viz.*, a strict purity, or a severe repentance." The pious bishop would not preclude the necessity of pardon through the blood of the cross, for without this the *severest repentance* would be of no avail.

Verse 24. *The bitter water that causeth the curse*] Though the rabbins think that the priest put some bitter substance in the water, yet, as nothing of the kind is intimated by Moses, we may consider the word as used here metaphorically for *affliction, death*, &c. These waters were *afflicting* and *deadly* to her who drank them, being guilty. In this sense *afflictions* are said to be *bitter*, Isa. xxxviii. 17; so also is *death*, 1 Sam. xv. 32; Eccles. vii. 26.

Verse 29. *This* is *the law of jealousies*] And this is the most singular law in the whole Pentateuch: a law that seems to have been copied by almost all the nations of the earth, whether civilized or barbarian, as we find that similar modes of trial for suspected offences were used when complete evidence was wanting to convict; and where it was expected that the object of their worship would interfere for the sake of justice, in order that the *guilty* should be brought to punishment, and the *innocent* be cleared. For general information on this head see at the end of this chapter.

Verse 31. *This woman shall bear her iniquity*]

That is, her belly shall swell, and her thigh shall rot; see on ver. 22. But if not guilty after such a trial, she had great honour, and, according to the rabbins, became *strong, healthy*, and *fruitful;* for if she was before *barren*, she now began to *bear children;* if before she had only *daughters*, she now began to have *sons;* if before she had *hard travail*, she now had *easy;* in a word, she was blessed in her body, her soul, and her substance: so shall it be done unto the *holy* and *faithful* woman, for such the Lord delighteth to honour; see 1 Tim. ii. 15.

On the principal subject of this chapter, I shall here introduce a short account of the trial by *ordeal*, as practised in different parts of the world, and which is supposed to have taken its origin from the *waters of jealousy*.

The trial by what was afterwards called ORDEAL is certainly of very remote antiquity, and was evidently of Divine appointment. In this place we have an institution relative to a mode of *trial* precisely of that kind which among our ancestors was called *ordeal;* and from this all similar trials in *Asia, Africa*, and *Europe*, have very probably derived their origin.

Ordeal, Latin, *ordalium*, is, according to *Verstegan*, from the Saxon orðal, *ordal* and *ordel*, and is derived by some from or, great, and DÆL, judgment, signifying the *greatest*, most *solemn*, and *decisive* mode of *judgment*.—*Hickes*. Others derive it from the *Francic* or *Teutonic Urdela*, which signifies simply to *judge*. But *Lye*, in his Anglo-Saxon Dictionary, derives the term from or, which is often in Anglo-Saxon, a *privative* particle, and ðæl, *distinction* or *difference;* and hence applied to that kind of judgment in which there was *no respect of persons*, but every one had absolute justice done him, as the decision of the business was supposed to belong to GOD alone. It always signified an appeal to the *immediate interposition* of GOD, and was therefore called *Judicium Dei, God's Judgment;* and we may naturally suppose was never resorted to but in very important cases, where persons accused of great crimes protested their innocence, and there was no sufficient *evidence* by which they could be cleared from the accusation, or proved to be guilty of the crime laid to their charge. Such were the cases of jealousy referred to in this chapter.

The rabbins who have commented on this text give us the following information: When any man, prompted by the spirit of jealousy, suspected his wife to have committed adultery, he brought her first before the judges, and accused her of the crime; but as she asserted her innocency, and refused to acknowledge herself guilty, and as he had no witnesses to produce, he required that she should be sentenced to *drink the waters of bitterness* which the law had appointed; that God, by this means, might discover what she wished to conceal. After the judges had heard the *accusation* and the *denial*, the man and his wife were both sent to Jerusalem, to appear before the Sanhedrin, who were the sole judges in such matters. The rabbins say that the judges of the Sanhedrin, at first endeavoured with threatenings to confound the woman, and cause her to confess her crime; when she still persisted in her innocence, she was led to the eastern gate of the court of Israel, where she was stripped of the clothes she wore, and dressed in black before a number of persons of her own sex. The priest then told her that if she knew herself to be innocent she had no evil to apprehend; but if she were guilty, she might expect to suffer all that the law threatened; to which she answered, *Amen, amen.*

The priest then wrote the words of the law upon a piece of vellum, with ink that had no vitriol in it, tha it might be the more easily blotted out. The words written on the vellum were, according to the rabbins, the following:—

"If a strange man have not come near thee, and thou art not polluted by forsaking the bed of thy husband, these bitter waters which I have cursed will not hurt thee: but if thou have gone astray from thy husband, and have polluted thyself by coming near to another man, may thou be accursed of the Lord, and become an example for all his people; may thy thigh rot, and thy belly swell till it burst! may these cursed waters enter into thy belly, and, being swelled therewith, may thy thigh putrefy!"

After this the priest took a new pitcher, filled it with water out of the brazen bason that was near the altar of burnt-offering, cast some dust into it taken from the pavement of the temple, mingled something bitter, as *wormwood*, with it, and having read the curses above mentioned to the woman, and received her answer of *Amen*, he scraped off the curses from the vellum into the pitcher of water. During this time another priest tore her clothes as low as her bosom, made her head bare, untied the tresses of her hair, fastened her torn clothes with a girdle below her breasts, and presented her with the tenth part of an ephah, or about three pints of *barley-meal*, which was in a frying pan, without oil or incense.

The other priest, who had prepared the waters of jealousy, then gave them to be drank by the accused person, and as soon as she had swallowed them, he put the pan with the meal in it into her hand. This was waved before the Lord, and a part of it thrown into the fire of the altar. If the woman was innocent, she returned with her husband; and the waters, instead of incommoding her, made her more healthy and fruitful than ever: if on the contrary she were guilty, she was seen immediately to grow pale, her eyes started out of her head, and, lest the temple should be defiled with her death, she was carried out, and died instantly with all the ignominious circumstances related in the curses, which the rabbins say had the same effect on him with whom she had been criminal, though he were absent and at a distance. They add, however, that if the husband himself had been guilty with another woman, then the waters had no bad effect even on his criminal wife; as in that case the transgression on the one part was, in a certain sense, balanced by the transgression on the other.

There is no instance in the Scriptures of this kind of *ordeal* having ever been resorted to; and probably it never was during the purer times of the Hebrew republic. God had rendered himself so terrible by his judgments, that no person would dare to appeal to this mode of trial who was conscious of her guilt: and in case of simple adultery, where the matter was either

detected or confessed, the parties were ordered by the law to be put to death.

But other ancient nations have also had their trials by *ordeal.*

We learn from *Ferdusi*, a Persian poet, whose authority we have no reason to suspect, that the *fire ordeal* was in use at a very early period among the ancient Persians. In the famous epic poem called the *Shah Nameh* of this author, who is not improperly styled the *Homer* of *Persia*, under the title *Dastan Seeavesh ve Soodabeh, The account of* Seeavesh *and* Soodabeh, he gives a very remarkable and circumstantial account of a trial of this kind.

It is very probable that the *fire ordeal* originated among the ancient Persians, for by them *fire* was not only held sacred, but considered as a *god*, or rather as the *visible emblem* of the supreme Deity; and indeed this kind of trial continues in extensive use among the Hindoos to the present day. In the code of Gentoo laws it is several times referred to under the title of *Purrah Reh*, but in the *Shah Nameh*, the word سوگند *Soogend* is used, which signifies literally an *oath*, as the persons were obliged to declare their innocence by an *oath*, and then put their veracity to test by passing through the کوه اتش *kohi atesh*, or *fire pile;* see the *Shah Nameh* in the title *Dastan Seeavesh ve Soodabeh*, and Halhed's code of Gentoo laws; Preliminary Discourse, p. lviii., and chap. v., sec. iii., pp. 117, &c.

A circumstantial account of the different kinds of ordeal practised among the Hindoos, communicated by Warren Hastings, Esq., who received it from Ali Ibrahim Khan, chief magistrate at Benares, may be found in the Asiatic Researches, vol. i., p. 389.

This trial was conducted among this people *nine* different ways: first, by the *balance;* secondly, by *fire;* thirdly, by *water;* fourthly, by *poison;* fifthly, by the *cosha*, or water in which an idol has been washed; sixthly, by *rice;* seventhly, by *boiling oil;* eighthly, by *red hot iron;* ninthly, by *images.*

There is, perhaps, no mode of judiciary decision that has been in more common use in ancient times, than that of ordeal, in some form or other. We find that it was also used by the ancient *Greeks* 500 years before the Christian era; for in the *Antigone* of Sophocles, a person suspected by Creon of a misdemeanor, declares himself ready "to handle hot iron, and to walk over fire," in proof of his innocence, which the scholiast tells us was then a very usual purgation.

> Ημεν δ' ἑτοιμοι και μυδρους αιρειν χεροιν,
> Και πυρ διερπειν, και θεους ὁρκωμοτειν. Ver. 270.

The *scholiast* on this line informs us that the custom in binding themselves by the most solemn oath, was this: they took *red hot iron* in their hands, and throwing it into the sea, swore that the oath should be inviolate till that iron made its appearance again.

Virgil informs us that the priests of Apollo at *Soracte* were *accustomed to walk over burning coals unhurt.*

> ———*Et* medium. *freti pietate, per* ignem
> *Cultores* multa premimus vestigia pruna.
> Æn. xi. 787.

Grotius gives many instances of water ordeal in Bithynia, Sardinia, and other places. Different species of fire and water ordeal are said to have prevailed among the *Indians* on the coast of Malabar; the *negroes* of Loango, Mosambique, &c., &c., and the Calmuc *Tartars.*

The first formal mention I find of this trial in Europe is in the laws of King *Ina*, composed about A. D. 700. See L. 77, entitled, Dom be haten irene and water, *Decision by hot iron and water.* I find it also mentioned in the council of *Mentz*, A. D. 847; but *Agobard*, archbishop of Lyons, wrote against it sixty years before this time. It is afterwards mentioned in the council of *Trevers*, A. D. 895. It did not exist in Normandy till after the *Conquest*, and was probably first introduced into England in the time of *Ina*, in whose laws and those of *Athelstan* and *Ethelred*, it was afterwards inserted. The ordeal by *fire* was for noblemen and women, and such as were *free* born: the *water* ordeal was for *husbandmen*, and the *meaner classes* of the people, and was of two sorts; by *cold* water and by *hot.* See the proceedings in these trials declared particularly in the law of King *Ina;* WILKINS, *Leges Anglo-Saxonicæ*, p. 27.

Several popes published edicts against this species of trial. Henry III. abolished trials by ordeal in the third year of his reign, 1219. See the act in *Rymer*, vol. i., p. 228; and see *Dugdale's* Origines Juridicales, fol. 87; *Spelman's* Glossary, *Wilkins, Hickes, Lombard, Somner*, and *Du Cange*, art. *Ferrum.*

The ordeal or trial by *battle* or *combat* is supposed to have come to us from the *Lombards*, who, leaving Scandinavia, overran Europe: it is thought that this mode of trial was instituted by Frotha III., king of Denmark, about the time of the birth of Christ; for he ordained that every controversy should be determined by the *sword.* It continued in *Holsatia* till the time of Christian III., king of Denmark, who began his reign in 1535. From these northern nations the practice of duels was introduced into Great Britain.

I need scarcely add, that this detestable form of trial was the foundation of the no less detestable crime of duelling, which so much disgraces our age and nation, a practice that is defended only by ignorance, false honour, and injustice: it is a relic of barbarous superstition, and was absolutely unknown to those brave and generous nations, the Greeks and Romans, whom it is so much the fashion to admire; and who, in this particular, so well merit our admiration!

The *general* practice of duelling is supposed to have taken its rise in 1527, at the breaking up of a treaty between the Emperor Charles V. and Francis I. The former having sent a herald with an insulting message to Francis, the king of France sent back the herald with a cartel of defiance, in which he gave the emperor the lie, and challenged him to single combat: Charles accepted it; but after several messages concerning the arrangement of all the circumstances relative to the combat, the thoughts of it were entirely laid aside. The example of two personages so illustrious drew such general attention, and carried with it so much authority, that it had considerable influence in introducing an important change in manners all over Europe.

It was so much the custom in the middle ages of Christianity to respect the *cross*, even to superstition, that it would have been indeed wonderful if the same ignorant bigotry had not converted *it* into an *ordeal:* accordingly we find it used for this purpose in so many different ways as almost to preclude description.

Another trial of this kind was the *Corsned*, or the consecrated *bread* and *cheese:* this was the ordeal to which the clergy commonly appealed when they were accused of any crime. A few concluding observations from Dr. Henry may not be unacceptable to the reader:—

"If we suppose that few or none escaped conviction who exposed themselves to these fiery trials, we shall be very much mistaken. For the histories of those times contain innumerable examples of persons plunging their naked arms into boiling water, handling red hot balls of iron, and walking upon burning ploughshares, without receiving the least injury. Many learned men have been much puzzled to account for this, and disposed to think that Providence graciously interposed in a miraculous manner for the preservation of injured innocence.

"But if we examine every circumstance of these fiery ordeals with due attention, we shall see sufficient reason to suspect that the whole was a gross imposition on the credulity of mankind. The accused person was committed wholly to the priest who was to perform the ceremony three days before the trial, in which he had time enough to bargain with him for his deliverance, and give him instructions how to act his part. On the day of trial no person was permitted to enter the church but the priest and the accused till after the iron was heated, when twelve friends of the accuser, and twelve of the accused, and no more, were admitted and ranged along the wall on each side of the church, at a respectful distance. After the iron was taken out of the fire several prayers were said: the accused drank a cup of holy water, and sprinkled his hand with it, which might take a considerable time if the priest were indulgent. The space of nine feet was measured by the accused himself, with his own feet, and he would probably give but scanty measure. He was obliged only to touch one of the marks with the toe of his right foot, and allowed to stretch the other foot as far towards the other mark as he could, so that the conveyance was almost instantaneous. His hand was not immediately examined, but wrapped in a cloth prepared for that purpose three days. May we not then, from all these precautions, suspect that these priests were in possession of some secret that secured the hand from the impression of such a momentary touch of hot iron, or removed all appearances of these impressions in three days; and that they made use of this secret when they saw reason? Such readers as are curious in matters of this kind may find two different directions for making ointments that will have this effect, in the work here quoted. What greatly strengthens these suspicions is, that we meet with no example of any champion of the *Church* who suffered the least injury from the touch of hot iron in this ordeal: but where any one was so foolhardy as to appeal to *it*, or to that of *hot water*, with a view to deprive the Church of any of her possessions, he never failed to burn his fingers, and lose his cause." I have made the scanty extract above from a very extensive history of the trial by *ordeal*, which I wrote several years ago, but never published.

All the forms of adjuration for the various ordeals of hot water, cold water, red hot iron, bread and cheese, &c., may be seen in the *Codex Legum Antiquarum*, Lindenbrogii, fol. Franc. 1613, p. 1299, &c.

CHAPTER VI.

The vow of the Nazarite, 1, 2. *In what it consisted*, 3–8. *When accidentally defiled, how he is to be purified*, 9–12. *The sacrifices he is to bring, and the rites he is to perform, when the vow of his separation is fulfilled*, 13–21. *The manner in which the priests are to bless the people*, 22–26. *The name of the* LORD *is to be put on the children of Israel, whom He promises to bless*, 27.

A. M. 2514.
B. C. 1490.
An. Exod. Isr. 2.
Ijar or Zif.

AND the LORD spake unto Moses, saying,

2 Speak unto the children of Israel, and say unto them, When either man or woman shall [a] separate [b] *themselves* to vow a vow of a Nazarite, to separate *themselves* unto the LORD:

[a] Or, *make* themselves *Nazarites*.

[b] Lev. xxvii. 2; Judg. xiii. 5; Acts xxi. 23; Rom. i. 1.

NOTES ON CHAP. VI.

Verse 2. *When either man or woman shall separate, &c.*] The word נזיר *nazir*, from נזר *nazar*, to *separate*, signifies merely a *separated* person, i. e., one peculiarly devoted to the service of God by being separated from all servile employments. From the *Nazarites* sprang the *Rechabites*, from the *Rechabites* the *Essenes*, from the *Essenes* the *Anchorites* or *Hermits*, and in imitation of those, the different *monastic* orders. Some contend strongly that the Nazarite was a type of our Lord; but neither analogy nor proof can be produced. Our blessed Lord both drank wine and touched the dead, which no Nazarite would do: as to his either shaving his hair or letting it grow, we know nothing. His being called a Nazarene, Matt. ii. 23, is nothing to the purpose, as it can mean no more than either that he was an inhabitant of *Nazareth*, which was a place of no credit, and therefore used as a term of *reproach*; or that he was in a general sense *consecrated to the service of God*—so were *Samson*, *Samuel*, *Jeremiah*, and *John Baptist*; or rather, that he was the נצר *netser* or BRANCH, Isa. xi. 1, and צמח

a

A. M. 2514.
B. C. 1490.
An. Exod Isr. 2.
Ijar or Zif.

3 [c] He shall separate *himself* from wine and strong drink; and shall drink no vinegar of wine, or vinegar of strong drink, neither shall he drink any liquor of grapes, nor eat moist grapes, or dried.

4 All the days of his [d] separation shall he eat nothing that is made of the [e] vine-tree, from the kernels even to the husk.

5 All the days of the vow of his separation there shall no [f] razor come upon his head; until the days be fulfilled, in the which he separateth *himself* unto the LORD, he shall be holy, *and* shall let the locks of the hair of his head grow.

6 All the days that he separateth *himself* unto the LORD, [g] he shall come at no dead body.

7 [h] He shall not make himself unclean for his father, or for his mother, for his brother, or for his sister, when they die; because the [i] consecration of his God *is* upon his head.

8 All the days of his separation he *is* holy unto the LORD.

A. M. 2514.
B. C. 1490.
An. Exod. Isr. 2.
Ijar or Zif.

9 And if any man die very suddenly by him, and he hath defiled the head of his consecration; then he shall [k] shave his head in the day of his cleansing, on the seventh day shall he shave it.

10 And [l] on the eighth day he shall bring two turtles, or two young pigeons, to the priest, to the door of the tabernacle of the congregation:

11 And the priest shall offer the one for a sin offering, and the other for a burnt-offering, and make an atonement for him, for that he sinned by the dead, and shall hallow his head that same day.

12 And he shall consecrate unto the LORD the days of his separation, and shall bring a lamb of the first year [m] for a trespass-offering: but the days that were before shall [n] be lost, because his separation was defiled.

[c] Amos ii. 12; Luke i. 15.——[d] Or, *Nazariteship.*——[e] Heb. *vine of the wine.*——[f] Judg. xiii. 5; xvi. 17; 1 Sam. i. 11.——[g] Lev. xxi. 11; chap. xix. 11, 16.

[h] Lev. xxi. 1, 2, 11; ch. ix. 6.——[i] Heb. *separation.*——[k] Acts xviii. 18; xxi. 24.——[l] Lev. v. 7; xiv. 22; xv. 14, 29.——[m] Lev. v. 6.——[n] Heb. *fall.*

tsemach, Zech. iii. 8; vi. 12, which is quite a different word; but this title is expressly applied to our blessed Lord by the above prophets; but in no place do they or any other prophets call him a *Nazarite*, in the sense in which נזיר *nazir* is used. Indeed it could not in truth be applied to him, as the distinguishing marks of a Nazarite never belonged to him. He was, it is true, the נצר *netser* or *branch* out of the root of Jesse, the genuine heir to the throne of David, whose dominion should extend over the universe, who should be King of kings, and Lord of lords; but the word Ναζωραιος, Matt. ii. 23, signifies merely a *Nazoræan*, or inhabitant of Nazareth.

Verse 3. *No vinegar of wine, &c.*] חמץ *chomets* signifies *fermented* wine, and is probably used here to signify wine of a strong body, or any highly intoxicating liquor. Dr. Lightfoot supposes that the LEPER being the most defiled and loathsome of creatures, was an emblem of the wretched, miserable state of man *by the fall*; and that the NAZARITE was the emblem of man in his *state of innocence*. Wine and grapes are here particularly forbidden to the Nazarite because, as the doctor thinks, being an emblem of man in his paradisaical state, he was forbidden that *tree* and its fruits by eating of which Adam fell; for the doctor, as well as the Jewish rabbins, believed the tree of knowledge to have been none other than the *vine*.

Vinegar of strong drink] See the note on Lev. x. 9.

Verse 5. *There shall no razor come upon his head*] The vow of the Nazarite consisted in the following particulars:—1. He consecrated himself in a very especial and extraordinary manner to God. 2. This was to continue for a certain season, probably never less than a whole year, that he might have a full growth of hair to *burn in the fire which is under the sacrifice of the peace-offering*, ver. 18. 3. During the time of his separation, or *nazarate*, he drank no *wine* nor *strong drink*; nor used any *vinegar* formed from any inebriating liquor, nor ate flesh or dried *grapes*, nor tasted even the *kernels* or *husks* of any thing that had grown upon the vine. 4. He never *shaved his head*, but let his *hair grow*, as the proof of his being in this separated state, and under vows of peculiar austerity. 5. He never touched any dead body, nor did any of the last offices, even to his nearest kin; but was considered as the *priests*, who were wholly taken up with the service of God, and regarded nothing else. 6. *All the days of his separation he was holy*, ver. 8. During the whole time he was to be incessantly employed in religious acts.

Verse 7. *The consecration of his God* is *upon his head.*] Literally, *The separation of his God* is *upon his head;* meaning his *hair*, which was the proof and emblem of his separation. Now as the *hair* of the Nazarite was a token of his *subjection* to God through all the peculiarities of his nazarate, a woman, *who is married*, is considered as a Nazarite for life, i. e., *separated* from all others, and joined to one husband who is her lord; hence St. Paul, probably alluding to this circumstance, says, 1 Cor. xi. 10: *The woman ought to have power upon her head*, i. e., wear her hair and veil; for this hair is a proof of her nazarate, and of her being in subjection to her *husband*, as the Nazarite was under subjection to the LORD by the rule of his *order*.

Verse 10. *Two turtles, or two young pigeons*] The same kind of offering made by him who had an issue, Lev. xv. 14, &c.

A. M. 2514. B. C. 1490. An. Exod. Isr. 2. Ijar or Zif.

13 And this *is* the law of the
Nazarite, [o] when the days of his
separation are fulfilled: he shall
be brought unto the door of the tabernacle of
the congregation;
14 And he shall offer his offering unto the
LORD, one he-lamb of the first year without
blemish for a burnt-offering, and one ewe-lamb
of the first year without blemish [p] for a sin-
offering, and one ram without blemish [q] for
peace-offerings;
15 And a basket of unleavened bread, [r] cakes
of fine flour mingled with oil, and wafers of
unleavened bread [s] anointed with oil, and their
meat-offering, and their [t] drink-offerings.
16 And the priest shall bring *them* before
the LORD, and shall offer his sin-offering, and
his burnt-offering:
17 And he shall offer the ram *for* a sacrifice
of peace-offerings unto the LORD, with the
basket of unleavened bread: the priest shall
offer also his meat-offering, and his drink-
offering.
18 [u] And the Nazarite shall shave the head
of his separation *at* the door of the tabernacle
of the congregation, and shall
take the hair of the head of his
separation, and put *it* in the fire
which *is* under the sacrifice of the peace-
offerings.
19 And the priest shall take the [v] sodden
shoulder of the ram, and one unleavened cake
out of the basket, and one unleavened wafer,
and [w] shall put *them* upon the hands of the
Nazarite, after *the hair of* his separation is
shaven:
20 And the priest shall wave them *for* a
wave-offering before the LORD: [x] this *is* holy
for the priest, with the wave-breast and heave-
shoulder: and after that the Nazarite may
drink wine.
21 This *is* the law of the Nazarite who hath
vowed, *and of* his offering unto the LORD for
his separation, beside *that* that his hand shall
get: according to the vow which he vowed,
so he must do after the law of his separation.
22 And the LORD spake unto Moses, saying,
23 Speak unto Aaron and unto his sons, saying, On this wise [y] ye shall bless the children
of Israel, saying unto them,

[o] Acts xxi. 26.—[p] Lev. iv. 2, 27, 32.—[q] Lev. iii. 6.—[r] Lev. ii. 4.—[s] Exod. xxix. 2.—[t] Chap. xv. 5, 7, 10.—[u] Acts xxi. 24.—[v] 1 Sam. ii. 15.—[w] Exod. xxix. 23, 24.—[x] Exod. xxix. 27, 28.—[y] Lev. ix. 22; 1 Chron. xxiii. 13.

Verse 18. *Shall take the hair—and put* it *in the fire*] The hair was permitted to grow for this purpose; and as the Nazarite was a kind of sacrifice, offered to God through the whole term of his *nazarate* or *separation*, and no human flesh or blood could be offered on the altar of the Lord, he offered his *hair* at the conclusion of his separation, as a sacrifice—that hair which was the token of his complete subjection to the Lord, and which was now considered as the Lord's *property*.

The Hindoos, after a vow, do not cut their hair during the term of their vow; but at the expiration of it they shave it off at the place where the vow was made.

That the *hair of the head* was superstitiously used among different nations, we have already had occasion to remark; (see the notes on Lev. xix. 27;) and that the Gentiles might have learned this from the Jews is possible, though some learned men think that this consecration of the hair to a deity was in use among the heathens before the time of Moses, and in nations who had no intercourse or connection with the Jews.

Verse 21. *This* is *the law of the Nazarite*] We learn from Maimonides, in his Treatise of the Nazarite, that a man might become a Nazarite in *behalf of another;* that is, might assist him in bearing the expenses of the sacrifices, &c. "A son may fulfil the vow his deceased father hath made, but did not live to accomplish:—He that saith, upon me be the shaving of a Nazarite, he is bound to bring the offerings of shaving for cleanness, and may offer them by the hand of what Nazarite he will. If he say, Upon me be half the oblations of a Nazarite, then he bringeth half the offerings by what Nazarite he will, and that Nazarite payeth his offerings out of that which is his."

"By this," says Mr. Ainsworth, "we may see the reason of that which *James* said to *Paul*, though he had no Nazarite's vow upon him: 'We have four men who have a vow on them; them take and sanctify thyself with them, and BE AT CHARGES WITH THEM, that they may shave their heads, &c. Then Paul took the men, and the next day, sanctifying himself with them, entered into the temple to signify the accomplishment of the days of sanctification, (or Nazariteship,) until that an offering should be offered for every one of them;' see Acts xxi. 23–26. For though Paul had not vowed or fulfilled a Nazariteship himself, yet might he *contribute* with them, and partake of their *charges* about the sacrifices."

Verse 23. *On this wise ye shall bless the children of Israel*] The prayer which God makes for his followers, and puts into their mouth, we are sure must be right; and to it, when sincerely, faithfully, and fervently offered, we may confidently expect an answer. If he condescended to give us a *form of blessings* or a *form of prayer*, we may rest assured that he will accept what he himself has made. This consideration may produce great confidence in them who come with either prayer or praise to the throne of grace, both of which should be, as far as circumstances will admit,

A. M. 2514. B. C. 1490. An. Exod. Isr. 2. Ijar or Zif.

24 The LORD bless thee, and
[z] keep thee:
25 The LORD [a] make his face
shine upon thee, and [b] be gracious unto
thee:
26 [c] The LORD lift up his
countenance upon thee, and
[d] give thee peace.
27 [e] And they shall put my name upon the
children of Israel; and [f] I will bless them.

[z] Psa. cxxi. 7; John xvii. 11.——[a] Psa. xxxi. 16; lxvii. 1; lxxx. 3, 7, 19; cxix. 135; Dan. ix. 17.——[b] Gen. xliii. 29.——[c] Psa. iv. 6.——[d] John xiv. 27; 2 Thess. iii. 16.——[e] Deut. xxviii. 10; 2 Chron. vii. 14; Isa. xliii. 7; Dan. ix. 18, 19.——[f] Psa. cxv. 12.

in the very words of Scripture; for we can readily attach a consequence to the *words of God,* which we shall find difficult to attach to the best ordered words of men. *Take with you words, and turn unto the Lord.* What *words?* Why *those* which God immediately puts into their mouths. *Take away all iniquity, and receive us graciously; so will we render the calves of our lips;* we shall then give the *sacrifices* of which our *lips* have spoken, when we made our *vows* unto thee. See Hos. xiv. 2.

Verse 24. *The Lord bless thee*] There are *three* forms of blessing here, *any* or *all* of which the priests might use on any occasion. The following is a verbal translation:—

1. May Jehovah bless thee and preserve thee!
2. May Jehovah cause his faces to shine upon thee, and be gracious unto thee!
3. May Jehovah lift up his faces upon thee, and may he put prosperity unto thee!

This is a very comprehensive and excellent prayer, and may be paraphrased thus:—

1. May God *speak good unto thee,* by giving thee his excellent *promises!* (See the note on Gen. ii. 3.) May he *preserve* thee in the possession of all the *good* thou hast, and *from* all the *evil* with which thou art threatened!

2. May the Holy Trinity *illuminate thy heart,* giving thee the true knowledge of thyself and of thy Maker; and may he show thee his *graciousness* in pardoning thy sins, and supporting thy soul!

3. May God give thee communion with the Father, Son, and Spirit, with a constant sense of his *approbation;* and grant thee *prosperity* in thy *soul,* and in all thy *secular affairs!*

This I suppose to be the spirit and design of this form of benediction. Others will doubtless interpret it after their manner. Several wise and learned men believe that the mystery of the Holy Trinity is not obscurely hinted at in it. God the FATHER blesses and keeps his followers. God the SON is gracious unto sinners in remitting their offences, which he died to blot out. God the HOLY SPIRIT takes of the things which are Christ's, and shows them unto genuine Christians, and diffuses the *peace of God* in their hearts. In a word, Christ, the gift of the Father by the energy of the Holy Spirit, came to *bless* every one of us by turning us away from our iniquities.

1. EVERY genuine Christian is a true *Nazarite.* He is *separated* from the world, and dedicated solely to the service of God. 2. His life is a life of self-denial; he mortifies and keeps the flesh in obedience to the Spirit. 3. All this enters into the spirit of his baptismal *vow;* for in that he promises to renounce the devil and all his works, the pomps and vanities of this wicked world, and all the sinful lusts of the flesh—to keep God's holy word and commandments, and to walk in the same all the days of his life. 4. The person who is faithful has the *blessing of God* entailed upon him. *Thus shall ye bless the children of Israel,* &c., &c. See the notes on ver. 5 and 7.

CHAPTER VII.

When the tabernacle was fully set up, it appeared that the princes of the twelve tribes had prepared six covered wagons, drawn by two oxen each, one wagon for two tribes, for the service of the tabernacle, 1–3. *Moses is commanded to receive this offering, and distribute the whole to the Levites according to their service,* 4, 5. *Moses does so, and gives two wagons and four oxen to the sons of* Gershon, 6, 7; *and four wagons and eight oxen to the sons of* Merari, 8. *The sons of* Kohath *have none, because they were to bear the ark, &c., on their* shoulders, 9. *Each prince is to take a day for presenting his offerings,* 10, 11. *On the* first *day* Nahshon, *of the tribe of* JUDAH, *offers a* silver charger, *a* silver bowl, *a* golden spoon, *a* young bullock, *a* ram, *a* lamb, *and a* kid, *for a* SIN-OFFERING; two oxen, five rams, five he-goats, *and* five lambs, *for a* PEACE-OFFERING, 12–17. *On the* second *day* Nethaneel, *of the tribe of* ISSACHAR, *offers the like,* 18–23. *On the* third *day* Eliab, *of the tribe of* ZEBULUN, *offers the like,* 24–29. *On the* fourth *day* Elizur, *of the tribe of* REUBEN, *offers the like,* 30–35. *On the* fifth *day* Shelumiel, *of the tribe of* SIMEON, *made a similar offering,* 36–41. *On the* sixth *day* Eliasaph, *of the tribe of* GAD, *made his offering,* 42–47. *On the* seventh *day* Elishama, *of the tribe of* EPHRAIM, *made his offering,* 48–53. *On the* eighth *day* Gamaliel, *of the tribe of* MANASSEH, *made his offering,* 54–59. *On the* ninth *day* Abidan, *of the tribe of* BENJAMIN, *made his offering,* 60–65. *On the* tenth *day* Ahiezer, *of the tribe of* DAN, *made his offering,* 66–71. *On the* eleventh *day* Pagiel, *of the tribe of* ASHER, *made his offering,* 72–77. *On the* twelfth *day* Ahira, *of the tribe of* NAPHTALI, *made the same kind of offering,* 78–83. *The sum total of all vessels and cattle which were offered was* twelve *silver* chargers, *and* twelve *silver* bowls; twelve *golden* spoons; twelve bullocks, twelve rams, *and* twelve kids; twenty-four bullocks, sixty rams, sixty he-goats, *and* sixty lambs, 84–88. *The offerings being ended, Moses goes into the tabernacle, and hears the voice of the Lord from the mercy-seat,* 89.

A. M. 2514.
B. C. 1490.
An. Exod. Isr. 2.
Ijar or Zif.

AND it came to pass on the day that Moses had fully [a] set up the tabernacle, and had anointed it, and sanctified it, and all the instruments thereof, both the altar and all the vessels thereof, and had anointed them, and sanctified them;

2 That [b] the princes of Israel, heads of the house of their fathers, who *were* the princes of the tribes, [c] and were over them that were numbered, offered:

3 And they brought their offering before the LORD, six covered wagons, and twelve oxen; a wagon for two of the princes, and for each one an ox: and they brought them before the tabernacle.

4 And the LORD spake unto Moses, saying,

5 [d] Take *it* of them, that they may be to do the service of the tabernacle of the congregation; and thou shalt give them unto the Levites, to every man according to his service.

6 And Moses took the wagons and the oxen, and gave them unto the Levites.

7 Two wagons and four oxen [e] he gave unto the sons of Gershon, according to their service:

8 [f] And four wagons and eight oxen he gave unto the sons of Merari, according unto their service, [g] under the hand of Ithamar the son of Aaron the priest.

9 But unto the sons of Kohath he gave none; because [h] the service of the sanctuary belonging unto them [i] *was that* they should bear upon their shoulders.

A. M. 2514.
B. C. 1490.
An. Exod. Isr. 2.
Ijar or Zif.

10 And the princes offered for [k] dedicating of the altar in the day that it was anointed, even the princes offered their offering before the altar.

11 And the LORD said unto Moses, They shall offer their offering, each prince on his day, for the dedicating of the altar.

12 And he that offered his offering the first day was [l] Nahshon, the son of Amminadab, of the tribe of Judah:

13 And his offering *was* one silver charger, the weight thereof *was* a hundred and thirty *shekels*, one silver bowl of seventy shekels, after [m] the shekel of the sanctuary; both of them *were* full of fine flour mingled with oil for a [n] meat-offering:

14 One spoon of ten *shekels* of gold, full of [o] incense:

15 [p] One young bullock, one ram, one lamb of the first year, for a burnt-offering:

16 One kid of the goats for a [q] sin-offering:

17 And for [r] a sacrifice of peace-offerings, two oxen, five rams, five he-goats, five lambs of the first year: this *was* the offering of Nahshon the son of Amminadab.

18 On the second day Nethaneel, the son of

[a] Exod. xl. 18; Lev. viii. 10, 11.—[b] Chap. i. 4, &c.—[c] Heb. *who stood*.—[d] Exod. xxv. 2; xxxv. 5.—[e] Chap. iv. 25. [f] Chap. iv. 31.—[g] Chap. iv 28, 33.—[h] Chap. iv. 15.—[i] Chap. iv. 6, 8, 10, 12, 14; 2 Sam. vi. 13.

[k] See Deut. xx. 5; 1 Kings viii. 63; 2 Chron. vii. 5, 9; Ezra vi. 16; Neh. xii. 27; Psa. xxx. title.—[l] Chap. ii. 3.—[m] Exod. xxx. 13.—[n] Lev. ii. 1.—[o] Exod. xxx. 34.—[p] Lev. i. 2. [q] Lev. iv. 23.—[r] Lev. iii. 1.

NOTES ON CHAP. VII.

Verse 1. *On the day that Moses had fully set up the tabernacle*] The transactions mentioned in this chapter took place on the *second day* of the *second month* of the *second year* after their departure from Egypt; and the proper place of this account is immediately after the *tenth* chapter of *Leviticus*.

Verse 3. *Six covered wagons*] שש עגלת צב *shesh egloth tsab, six tilted wagons*, the Septuagint translate ἑξ ἁμαξας λαμπηνικας, with which the *Coptic* agrees; but what *lampenic chariots* were, no person pretends to know. *Covered* or *tilted* is probably the meaning of the original. The wagons were given for the more convenient exporting of the heavier parts of the tabernacle, which could not be conveniently carried on men's shoulders.

Verse 5. *According to his service.*] That is, distribute them among the Levites *as they may need them*, giving most to those who have the *heaviest burdens* to bear.

Verse 7. *Two wagons—unto the sons of Gershon*] The Gershonites carried only the *curtains*, *coverings*, and *hangings*, chap. iv. 25. And although this was a *cumbersome* carriage, and they needed the wagons, yet it was not a *heavy* one.

Verse 8. *Four wagons—unto the sons of Merari*] Because they had the *boards*, *bars*, *pillars*, and *sockets* of the tabernacle to carry, chap. iv. 31, 32, therefore they had as many more wagons as the *Gershonites*.

Verse 9. *Unto the sons of Kohath he gave none*] Because they had the charge of the *ark*, *table*, *candlestick*, *altars*, &c., chap. iv. 5–15, which were to be carried *upon their shoulders*; for those sacred things must not be drawn by *beasts*.

Verse 10. *And the princes offered*] Every *prince* or *chief* offered in the *behalf*, and doubtless at the *expense*, of his whole tribe.

Verse 13. *One silver charger*] קערת *kaarath*, a *dish*, or *deep bowl*, in which they kneaded the paste. See Exod. xxv. 29.

One silver bowl] מזרק *mizrak*, a *bason*, to receive the blood of the sacrifice in. See on Exod. xxvii. 3.

Verse 14. *One spoon*] כף *caph*, a *censer*, on which they put the incense. See Exod. xxv. 29.

a

A. M. 2514.
B. C. 1490.
An. Exod. Isr. 2.
Ijar or Zif.

Zuar, prince of Issachar, did offer:

19 He offered *for* his offering one silver charger, the weight whereof *was* a hundred and thirty *shekels*, one silver bowl of seventy shekels, after the shekel of the sanctuary; both of them full of fine flour mingled with oil for a meat-offering:

20 One spoon of gold of ten *shekels*, full of incense:

21 One young bullock, one ram, one lamb of the first year, for a burnt-offering:

22 One kid of the goats for a sin-offering:

23 And for a sacrifice of [s] peace-offerings, two oxen, five rams, five he-goats, five lambs of the first year: this *was* the offering of Nethaneel the son of Zuar.

24 On the third day [t] Eliab, the son of Helon, prince of the children of Zebulun, *did offer:*

25 His offering *was* one silver charger, the weight whereof *was* a hundred and thirty *shekels*, one silver bowl of seventy shekels, after the shekel of the sanctuary; both of them full of fine flour mingled with oil for a meat-offering:

26 One golden spoon of ten *shekels*, full of incense:

27 One young bullock, one ram, one lamb of the first year, for a burnt-offering:

28 One kid of the goats for a sin-offering:

29 And for a sacrifice of peace-offerings, two oxen, five rams, five he-goats, five lambs of the first year: this *was* the offering of Eliab the son of Helon.

A. M. 2514.
B. C. 1490.
An. Exod. Isr. 2.
Ijar or Zif.

30 On the fourth day [u] Elizur, the son of Shedeur, prince of the children of Reuben, *did offer:*

31 His offering *was* one silver charger of the weight of a hundred and thirty *shekels*, one silver bowl of seventy shekels, after the shekel of the sanctuary; both of them full of fine flour mingled with oil for a meat-offering:

32 One golden spoon of ten *shekels*, full of incense:

33 One young bullock, one ram, one lamb of the first year, for a burnt-offering:

34 One kid of the goats for a sin-offering

35 And for a sacrifice of peace-offerings, two oxen, five rams, five he-goats, five lambs of the first year: this *was* the offering of Elizur the son of Shedeur.

36 On the fifth day [v] Shelumiel, the son of Zurishaddai, prince of the children of Simeon, *did offer:*

37 His offering *was* one silver charger, the weight whereof *was* a hundred and thirty *shekels*, one silver bowl of seventy shekels, after the shekel of the sanctuary; both of them full of fine flour mingled with oil for a meat-offering:

38 One golden spoon of ten *shekels*, full of incense:

39 One young bullock, one ram, one lamb of the first year, for a burnt-offering:

40 One kid of the goats for a sin-offering:

41 And for a sacrifice of peace-offerings, two oxen, five rams, five he-goats, five lambs

[s] Lev. vii. 11-18; 1 Kings viii. 63.——[t] Chap. i. 9; ii. 7.

[u] Chap. i. 5; ii. 10.——[v] Chap. i. 16; ii. 12.

It is worthy of remark that the different tribes are represented here as bringing their offerings precisely in the same order in which they encamped about the tabernacle. See chap. ii. and chap. x.

1. JUDAH	the chief	*Nahshon*, ver.	12.	East.
2. ISSACHAR	. . .	*Nethaneel*,	18.	
3. ZEBULUN	. . .	*Eliab*,	24.	
4. REUBEN	. . .	*Elizur*,	30.	South.
5. SIMEON	. . .	*Shelumiel*,	36.	
6. GAD	. . .	*Eliasaph*,	42.	
7. EPHRAIM	. . .	*Elishama*,	48.	West.
8. MANASSEH	. . .	*Gamaliel*,	54.	
9. BENJAMIN	. . .	*Abidan*,	60.	
10. DAN	. . .	*Ahiezer*,	66.	North.
11. ASHER	. . .	*Pagiel*,	72.	
12. NAPHTALI	. . .	*Ahira*,	78.	

It is worthy of remark also, that every tribe offers the *same kind of offering*, and in the *same quantity*, to show, that as every tribe was equally indebted to God for its support, so each should testify an equal sense of obligation. Besides, the vessels were all sacrificial vessels, and the animals were all clean animals, such as were proper for sacrifices; and therefore every thing was intended to point out that the people were to be a holy people, fully dedicated to God, and that God was to dwell among them; hence there were *fine flour* and *oil*, for a *meat-offering*, ver. 13. A *bullock*, a *ram*, and a *lamb*, for a *burnt-offering*, ver. 15, 16. *Five oxen*, *five rams*, *five he-goats*, and *five lambs*, for a *peace-offering*, ver. 17. Thus, as the priests, altar, &c., were anointed, and the tabernacle dedicated, so the people, by this offering, became con secrated to God. Therefore every act here was religious act.

"Thus," says Mr. Ainsworth, "by sacrifices of all sorts, figuring the death of Christ, and the benefits that were to be received thereby, they reconciled and made themselves and theirs acceptable to God, and were made partakers of his grace, to remission of sins,

A. M. 2514.
B. C. 1490.
An. Exod. Isr. 2.
Ijar or Zif.

of the first year: this *was* the
offering of Shelumiel the son of
Zurishaddai.
42 On the sixth day [w] Eliasaph, the son
of Deuel, prince of the children of Gad,
offered:
43 His offering *was* one silver charger of the
weight of a hundred and thirty *shekels,* a silver
bowl of seventy shekels, after the shekel of
the sanctuary; both of them full of fine flour
mingled with oil for a meat-offering:
44 One golden spoon of ten *shekels,* full of
incense:
45 One young bullock, one ram, one lamb
of the first year, for a burnt-offering:
46 One kid of the goats for a sin-offering:
47 And for a sacrifice of peace-offerings,
two oxen, five rams, five he-goats, five lambs
of the first year: this *was* the offering of
Eliasaph the son of Deuel.
48 On the seventh day [x] Elishama, the
son of Ammihud, prince of the children of
Ephraim, *offered:*
49 His offering *was* one silver charger, the
weight whereof *was* a hundred and thirty
shekels, one silver bowl of seventy shekels,
after the shekel of the sanctuary; both of
them full of fine flour mingled with oil for a
meat-offering:
50 One golden spoon of ten *shekels,* full of
incense:
51 One young bullock, one ram, one lamb
of the first year, for a burnt-offering:
52 One kid of the goats for a sin-offering:
53 And for a sacrifice of peace-offerings,
two oxen, five rams, five he-goats, five lambs
of the first year: this *was* the offering of
Elishama the son of Ammihud.
54 On the eighth day *offered* [y] Gamaliel,
the son of Pedahzur, prince of the children
of Manasseh:
55 His offering *was* one silver charger of
the weight of a hundred and thirty *shekels,*
one silver bowl of seventy shekels, after the
shekel of the sanctuary; both of them full of
fine flour mingled with oil for a
meat-offering:
56 One golden spoon of ten
shekels, full of incense:
57 One young bullock, one ram, one lamb
of the first year, for a burnt-offering:
58 One kid of the goats for a sin-offering.
59 And for a sacrifice of peace-offerings, two
oxen, five rams, five he-goats, five lambs of
the first year: this *was* the offering of Gamaliel the son of Pedahzur.
60 On the ninth day [z] Abidan, the son of
Gideoni, prince of the children of Benjamin,
offered:
61 His offering *was* one silver charger, the
weight whereof *was* a hundred and thirty
shekels, one silver bowl of seventy shekels, after
the shekel of the sanctuary; both of them full
of fine flour mingled with oil for a meat-offering:
62 One golden spoon of ten *shekels,* full of
incense:
63 One young bullock, one ram, one lamb
of the first year, for a burnt-offering:
64 One kid of the goats for a sin-offering:
65 And for a sacrifice of peace-offerings,
two oxen, five rams, five he-goats, five lambs
of the first year: this *was* the offering of
Abidan the son of Gideoni.
66 On the tenth day [a] Ahiezer the son of
Ammishaddai, prince of the children of Dan,
offered:
67 His offering *was* one silver charger, the
weight whereof *was* a hundred and thirty
shekels, one silver bowl of seventy shekels, after
the shekel of the sanctuary; both of them full
of fine flour mingled with oil for a meat-offering:
68 One golden spoon of ten *shekels,* full of
incense:
69 One young bullock, one ram, one lamb
of the first year, for a burnt-offering:
70 One kid of the goats for a sin-offering:
71 And for a sacrifice of peace-offerings,
two oxen, five rams, five he-goats, five lambs
of the first year: this *was* the offering of
Ahiezer the son of Ammishaddai.

[w] Chap. i. 14; ii. 14.——[x] Chap. i. 10; ii. 18.——[y] Chap. i. 10; ii. 20.——[z] Chap. i. 11; ii. 22.——[a] Chap. i. 12; ii. 25.

and sanctification through faith, and in the work of the Holy Ghost, in the communion and feeling whereof they rejoiced before God."

Verse 48. *On the seventh day*] Both Jewish and Christian writers have been surprised that this work of offering went forward on the *seventh day,* which they suppose to have been a *Sabbath,* as well as on the other days. But 1. There is no absolute proof that this *seventh day* of offering was a *Sabbath.* 2. Were it even so, could the people be better employed than in thus consecrating themselves and their services to the Lord? We have already seen that every

a

A. M. 2514.
B. C. 1490.
An. Exod. Isr. 2.
Ijar or Zif.

72 On the eleventh day [b] Pagiel the son of Ocran, prince of the children of Asher, *offered:*

73 His offering *was* one silver charger, the weight whereof *was* a hundred and thirty *shekels*, one silver bowl of seventy shekels, after the shekel of the sanctuary; both of them full of fine flour mingled with oil for a meat-offering:

74 One golden spoon of ten *shekels*, full of incense:

75 One young bullock, one ram, one lamb of the first year, for a burnt-offering:

76 One kid of the goats for a sin-offering:

77 And for a sacrifice of peace-offerings, two oxen, five rams, five he-goats, five lambs of the first year: this *was* the offering of Pagiel the son of Ocran.

78 On the twelfth day [c] Ahira the son of Enan, prince of the children of Naphtali, *offered:*

79 His offering *was* one silver charger, the weight whereof *was* a hundred and thirty *shekels*, one silver bowl of seventy shekels, after the shekel of the sanctuary; both of them full of fine flour mingled with oil for a meat-offering:

80 One golden spoon of ten *shekels*, full of incense:

81 One young bullock, one ram, one lamb of the first year, for a burnt-offering:

82 One kid of the goats for a sin-offering:

83 And for a sacrifice of peace-offerings, two oxen, five rams, five he-goats, five lambs of the first year: this *was* the offering of Ahira the son of Enan.

A. M. 2514.
B. C. 1490.
An. Exod. Isr. 2.
Ijar or Zif.

84 This *was* the dedication of the altar, in the day when it was anointed, by the princes of Israel: twelve chargers of silver, twelve silver bowls, twelve spoons of gold:

85 Each charger of silver *weighing* a hundred and thirty *shekels*, each bowl seventy: all the silver vessels *weighed* two thousand and four hundred *shekels*, after the shekel of the sanctuary:

86 The golden spoons *were* twelve, full of incense, *weighing* ten *shekels* apiece, after the shekel of the sanctuary: all the gold of the spoons *was* a hundred and twenty *shekels*.

87 All the oxen for the burnt-offering *were* twelve bullocks, the rams twelve, the lambs of the first year twelve, with their meat-offering and the kids of the goats for sin-offering twelve.

88 And all the oxen for the sacrifice of the peace-offerings *were* twenty and four bullocks, the rams sixty, the he-goats sixty, the lambs of the first year sixty. This *was* the dedication of the altar, after that it was [d] anointed.

89 And when Moses was gone into the tabernacle of the congregation [e] to speak with [f] him, then he heard [g] the voice of one speaking unto him from off the mercy-seat, that *was* upon the ark of testimony, from [h] between the two cherubims: and he spake unto him.

[b] Chap. i. 18; ii. 27.—[c] Chap. i. 15; ii. 29.—[d] Ver. 1, 10–84.—[e] Chap. xii. 8; Exod. xxxiii. 9, 11.—[f] That is, *God.*—[g] Exod. xxv. 22.—[h] Exod. xxv. 18–21; 1 Sam. iv. 4.

act was a religious act; and we may rest assured that no day was *too holy* for the performance of such acts as are recorded here.

Verse 72. *On the eleventh day*] The Hebrew form of expression, here and in the 78th verse, has something curious in it. ביום עשתי עשר יום *beyom ashtey asar yom, In the day, the first and tenth day;* ביום שנים עשר יום *beyom sheneym asar yom, In the day, two and tenth day.* But this is the idiom of the language, and to an original Hebrew our almost anomalous words *eleventh* and *twelfth*, by which we translate the original, would appear as strange as his, literally translated, would appear to us. In reckoning after *twelve*, it is easy to find out the composition of the words *thirteen*, as *three* and *ten*, *fourteen*, *four* and *ten*, and so on; but *eleven* and *twelve* bear scarcely any analogy to *ten* and *one*, and *ten* and *two*, which nevertheless they intend. But this is a subject of philology rather than of Biblical criticism.

Verse 84. *This* was *the dedication of the altar, in the day, &c.*] Meaning here the *time* in which it was dedicated; for as each tribe had a whole day for its representative or prince to present the offerings it had provided, consequently the dedication, in which each had his day, must have lasted *twelve* days: the words therefore, in this text, refer to the last day or *twelfth*, in which this dedication was completed.

Verse 88. *After that it was anointed.*] By the anointing the altar was consecrated to God; by this dedication it was solemnly appointed to that service for which it had been erected.

Verse 89. *To speak with him*] To confer with God, and to receive farther discoveries of his will.

He heard the voice of one speaking unto him] Though Moses saw no similitude, but *only heard a voice*, yet he had the fullest proof of the *presence* as well as of the *being* of the Almighty. In this way God chose to manifest himself during that dispensation, till the fulness of the time came, in which the WORD *was made flesh, and* DWELT AMONG US. No man hath seen God at any time; the only-begotten Son, who is in the bosom of the Father, he hath declared him.

The mercy-seat] See the note on Exod. xxv. 17. As God gave oracular answers from this place, and *spoke* to Moses as it were *face to face*, hence the place was called the ORACLE, דביר *debir*, or *speaking place*,

from דבר *dabar*, he *spoke*, 1 Kings vi. 23. And as this *mercy-seat* represented our blessed Redeemer, so the apostle says that *God, who* had *at sundry times, and in divers manners,* SPOKEN *in time past to the fathers by the prophets, hath, in these last days,* SPOKEN *unto us by his Son,* Heb. i. 1, 2. Hence the *incarnated* Christ is the true דביר *debir* or *oracle*, in and by whom God *speaks* unto man.

On this occasion we find there were offered

12 silver *chargers* each weighing	130 shekels.
12 silver *bowls*, each	70 shekels.
Total amount of silver vessels	2,400 shekels.
12 golden *spoons*, each weighing	10 shekels.
Total amount of golden vessels	120 shekels.

	oz.	dwts.	gr.
A silver charger at 130 shekels, reduced to troy weight, makes -	75	9	$16\frac{8}{31}$
A silver bowl, at 70 shekels, amounts to	40	12	$21\frac{21}{31}$
Total weight of the 12 chargers	905	16	$3\frac{3}{31}$
Total weight of the 12 bowls	487	14	$20\frac{4}{31}$
Total	1393	10	$23\frac{7}{31}$
Which, at 5*s*. per oz., is equal to	£348	7*s*.	9*d*.

	oz.	dwts.	gr.
The 12 golden spoons, allowing each to be	5	16	$3\frac{3}{31}$
amount to	69	13	$13\frac{5}{31}$
Which, at £4 per ounce, is equal to	£278	14*s*.	$2\frac{1}{4}$*d*
And added to the amount of the silver,	£348	7*s*.	9*d*.
make a total of	£627	1*s*.	11*d*.

Besides the above there were

Bullocks	-	12
Rams	-	12
Lambs	-	12
Goats	-	24
Rams	-	60
He-goats	-	60
Lambs	-	60
Total		240 clean beasts for sacrifice.

By which we may at once see that though the *place* in which they now sojourned was a *wilderness*, as to *cities, villages,* and *regular inhabitants*, yet there was plenty of pasturage, else the Israelites could not have furnished these cattle, with all the sacrifices necessary for different occasions, and especially for the passover, which was celebrated during their sojourning in the desert, and which itself must have required an immense number of lambs, (see chap. ix.,) when each family of the 600,000 males was obliged to provide one for itself.

CHAPTER VIII.

Directions how the lamps are to be lighted, 1–3. *How the candlestick was formed,* 4. *The Levites to be consecrated to their service by being cleansed, sprinkled, shaved, purified, and their clothes washed,* 5–7. *To offer a meat-offering and a sin-offering,* 8. *The people to put their hands upon them,* 9, 10. *Aaron is to offer them before the Lord,* 11. *The Levites to lay their hands on the heads of the bullocks, &c.,* 12. *The Levites are taken to assist Aaron and his sons in the place of all the* first-born *of Israel,* 13–19. *Moses and Aaron do as they were commanded, the Levites are presented, purified, and commence their service,* 20–22. *They are to begin their service at twenty-five years of age, and leave off at fifty,* 23–25. *After this they shall have the general inspection of the service,* 26.

A. M. 2514. B. C. 1490. An. Exod. Isr. 2. Ijar or Zif.

AND the LORD spake unto
Moses, saying,
2 Speak unto Aaron, and say
unto him, When thou [a] lightest the lamps, the
seven lamps shall give light over against the
candlestick.
3 And Aaron did so; he lighted the lamps
thereof over against the candlestick, as the
LORD commanded Moses.
4 [b] And this work of the candlestick *was of* beaten gold, unto the
shaft thereof, unto the flowers
thereof, *was* [c] beaten work: [d] according unto
the pattern which the LORD had showed
Moses, so he made the candlestick.
5 And the LORD spake unto Moses, saying,
6 Take the Levites from among the children
of Israel, and cleanse them.

[a] Exod. xxv. 37; xl. 25.—[b] Exod. xxv. 31.

[c] Exod. xxv. 18.—[d] Exod. xxv. 40.

NOTES ON CHAP. VIII.

Verse 2. *The seven lamps shall give light*] The whole seven shall be lighted at one time, that seven may be ever burning.

Verse 4. *This work of the candlestick, &c.*] See many curious particulars relative to this candlestick in the notes on Exod. xxv. 31 and 39. The *candlestick* itself was an emblem of the *Church* of Christ; the *oil*, of the graces and gifts of the Spirit of God; and the *light*, of those gifts and graces in *action* among men. See Rev. i. 12–20. God builds his Church and sends forth his Spirit to dwell in it, to sanctify and cleanse it, that it may be shown unto the world as his *own* workmanship. The *seven* lights in the candlesticks point out the *seven Spirits of God*, the Holy Ghost being thus termed, Rev. iii. 1, from the *variety* and *abundance* of his gifts and influences; *seven* being used among the Hebrews to denote any thing *full, complete,* and *perfect.* A *candlestick* or *lamp* without *oil* is of no use; *oil* not burning is of no use. So a *Church* or *society of religious people* without the *influence* of the *Holy Ghost* are dead while they have a name to

A. M. 2514.
B. C. 1490.
An. Exod. Isr. 2.
Ijar or Zif.

7 And thus shalt thou do unto them, to cleanse them: Sprinkle [e] water of purifying upon them, and [f] let [g] them shave all their flesh, and let them wash their clothes, and *so* make themselves clean.

8 Then let them take a young bullock with [h] his meat-offering, *even* fine flour mingled with oil, and another young bullock shalt thou take for a sin-offering.

9 [i] And thou shalt bring the Levites before the tabernacle of the congregation: [k] and thou shalt gather the whole assembly of the children of Israel together:

10 And thou shalt bring the Levites before the LORD: and the children of Israel [l] shall put their hands upon the Levites:

11 And Aaron shall [m] offer the Levites before the LORD *for* an [n] offering of the children of Israel, that [o] they may execute the service of the LORD.

12 [p] And the Levites shall lay their hands upon the heads of the bullocks: and thou shalt offer the one *for* a sin-offering, and the other *for* a burnt-offering, unto the LORD, to make an atonement for the Levites.

A. M. 2514.
B. C. 1490.
An. Exod. Isr. 2.
Ijar or Zif.

13 And thou shalt set the Levites before Aaron, and before his sons, and offer them *for* an offering unto the LORD.

14 Thus shalt thou separate the Levites from among the children of Israel, and the Levites shall be [q] mine.

15 And after that shall the Levites go in to do the service of the tabernacle of the congregation: and thou shalt cleanse them, and [r] offer them *for* an offering.

16 For they *are* wholly given unto me from among the children of Israel; [s] instead of such as open every womb, *even instead of* the first-born of all the children of Israel, have I taken them unto me.

17 [t] For all the first-born of the children of Israel *are* mine, *both* man and beast: on the day that I smote every first-born in the land of Egypt I sanctified them for myself.

18 And I have taken the Levites for all the first-born of the children of Israel.

[e] Chap. xix. 9, 17, 18.——[f] Heb. *let them cause a razor to pass over*, &c.——[g] Lev. xiv. 8, 9.——[h] Lev. ii. 1.——[i] See Exod. xxix. 4; xl. 12.——[k] Lev. viii. 3.——[l] Lev. i. 4.——[m] Heb. *wave.*——[n] Heb. *wave-offering.*——[o] Heb. *they may be to execute*, &c. [p] Exod. xxix. 10.——[q] Chap. iii. 45; xvi. 9.——[r] Ver. 11, 13. [s] Chap. iii. 12, 45.——[t] Exod. xiii. 2, 12, 13, 15; chap. iii. 13; Luke ii. 23.

live; and if they have a measure of this light, and do not let it *shine* by purity of living and holy zeal before men, their religion is neither useful to *themselves* nor to *others*. Reader, it is possible to be *in* the Church of God and not be *of* that Church; it is possible to have a measure of the Spirit and neither profit nor be profited. Feel this dreadful possibility, and pray to God that thou be not a proof of it.

Verse 7. *Sprinkle water of purifying*] מי חטאת *mey chattath, water of sin*, or *water* of the *sin-offering*. As this purifying water was made by the *ashes of the red heifer, cedar-wood, hyssop*, and *scarlet*; and the heifer herself was sacrificed, and her blood sprinkled seven times before the tabernacle, Num. xix. 3–6; she may be considered as a proper *sacrifice for sin*, and consequently the water thus prepared be termed the *water of the sin-offering*. As the *ashes* were kept ready at hand for purifying from all legal pollutions, the preparation might be considered as a *concentration* of the essential properties of the sin-offering, and might be resorted to at all times with comparatively little expense or trouble, and no loss of time. As there were so many things by which legal pollution might be contracted, it was necessary to have always at hand, in all their dwellings, a mode of purifying at once convenient and unexpensive. As the *water* by which the Levites were here purified must have been the water prepared from the ashes of the red heifer, this ordinance was undoubtedly instituted *before* this time, though not described till chap. xix. 1–10 of this book; but that chapter might be in connection with any of the preceding ordinances, as well as where it is now found. We see from Heb. ix. 13, 14, that these ashes mingled with water, and sprinkled on the unclean, and which sanctified to the purification of the flesh, were intended to typify the *blood of Christ*, which purges the conscience from dead works to serve the living God, ver. 15; for as without this sprinkling with the *water* of the *sin-offering* the Levites were not fit to *serve God* in the wilderness, so without this sprinkling of the blood of Christ no *conscience can be purged from dead works to serve the living God*. See the notes on chap. xix. 1–10.

Verse 10. *Shall put their hands upon the Levites*] It has been argued from this that the congregation had a part in the appointment of their own ministers, and that this was done by the *imposition of hands*. However that may be, it appears that what was done on *this occasion* meant no more than that the people gave up this whole tribe to God in place of their *first-born*; and that by this act they bound themselves to *provide for them* who, because of their sacred service, could follow no *secular* work. And surely it was right, that they who served the altar should live by the altar. The ministers of God perform offices for the people which the people cannot perform for themselves; and nothing can be more reasonable than that the people should give them the necessaries and comforts of life while they are thus employed in their behalf.

Verse 17. *For all the first-born—are mine*] See

A. M. 2514.
B. C. 1490.
An. Exod. Isr. 2.
Ijar or Zif.

19 And [u] I have given the Levites *as* [v] a gift to Aaron and to his sons from among the children of Israel, to do the service of the children of Israel in the tabernacle of the congregation, and to make an atonement for the children of Israel: [w] that there be no plague among the children of Israel, when the children of Israel come nigh unto the sanctuary.

20 And Moses, and Aaron, and all the congregation of the children of Israel, did to the Levites according unto all that the LORD commanded Moses concerning the Levites, so did the children of Israel unto them.

21 [x] And the Levites were purified, and they washed their clothes; [y] and Aaron offered them *as* an offering before the LORD; and Aaron made an atonement for them to cleanse them.

22 [z] And after that went the Levites in to do their service in the tabernacle of the congregation before Aaron, and before his sons: [a] as the LORD had commanded Moses concerning the Levites, so did they unto them.

A. M. 2514.
B. C. 1490.
An. Exod. Isr. 2.
Ijar or Zif.

23 And the LORD spake unto Moses, saying,

24 This *is it* that *belongeth* unto the Levites: [b] from twenty and five years old and upward, they shall go in [c] to wait upon the service of the tabernacle of the congregation:

25 And from the age of fifty years they shall [d] cease waiting upon the service *thereof*, and shall serve no more:

26 But shall minister with their brethren in the tabernacle of the congregation, [e] to keep the charge, and shall do no service. Thus shalt thou do unto the Levites touching their charge.

[u] Chap. iii. 9.——[v] Heb. *given*.——[w] Chap. i. 53; xvi. 46; xviii. 5.——2 Chron. xxvi. 16.——[x] Ver. 7.——[y] Ver. 11, 12.——[z] Ver. 15.——[a] Ver. 5, &c.

[b] See. chap. iv. 3; 1 Chron. xxiii. 3, 24, 27.——[c] Heb. *to war the warfare of*, &c.; 1 Tim i. 18.——[d] Heb. *return from the warfare of the service*.——[e] Chap. i. 53.

the manner of redeeming the first-born, chap. xviii. 6.

Verse 21. *And Aaron made an atonement for them*] Though the Levites had been most solemnly consecrated to the Lord's service, and though all legal washings and purifications were duly performed on the occasion, yet they could not approach God till an *atonement* had been made for them. How strange is it, after all these significations, of the will and purpose of God relative to man, that any priest or any people will attempt to draw nigh to God without an atonement! As sure as God hath spoken it, there is no entrance into the holiest but through the blood of Jesus, Heb. x. 19, 20.

Verse 24. *From twenty and five years old*] See the note on chap. iv. 47, where the two terms of twenty-five and thirty years are reconciled.

Verse 26. *To keep the charge, and shall do no service.*] They shall no longer be obliged to perform any laborious service, but act as general directors and counsellors; therefore they were to be near the camp, sing praises to God, and see that no stranger or unclean person was permitted to enter. So the Jews and many other persons have understood this place.

1. IF it required so much legal purity to fit the Levites for their work in the tabernacle, can we suppose that it requires less spiritual purity to fit ministers of the Gospel to proclaim the righteousness of the Most High, and administer the sacred ordinances of Christianity to the flock of Christ? If these must be without *spot*, as the priests before without *blemish*, and these were only typical men, we may rest assured that a Christian minister requires no ordinary measures of holiness to prepare him for an acceptable and profitable discharge of his office.

2. If the Christian ministry be established to prepare men for the kingdom of God, of the holiness of which the purity of the camp was but a faint emblem, how can any man expect to enter that place of blessedness, who has not his heart sprinkled from an evil conscience, and his body washed with pure water; his life and conversation agreeable to the sacred precepts laid down in the Gospel of Christ? If the law of Moses were more read in reference to the Gospel, the Gospel itself and its requisitions would be much better understood. Reader, however it may be with thee, *Antinomianism* is more general among religious people than is usually imagined. What multitudes of all denominations are expecting to enter into the kingdom of God without any proper preparation for the place! Without holiness none shall see the Lord; and from this decision of the Divine justice there shall never be any appeal.

CHAPTER IX.

The Israelites are reminded of the law that required them to keep the passover *at its proper time, and with all its rites*, 1–3. *They kept the* passover *on the fourteenth day of the* first *month*, 4, 5. *The case of the men who, being unclean through touching a dead body, could not keep the* passover, 6, 7. *Moses inquires at the Lord concerning them*, 8; *and the Lord appoints the fourteenth day of the* second *month for all those who through any accidental uncleanness, or by being absent on a journey, could not keep it at the usual time*, 9–12. *Those who neglect to keep this solemn feast to be cut off from among his people*, 13.

The stranger who wishes to keep the passover is at liberty to do it, 14. *The cloud covers the tabernacle both by day and night, from the time of its dedication,* 15, 16. *This cloud regulates all the encampments and marchings of the Israelites through the wilderness,* 17–22. *Their journeyings and restings were all directed by the commandment of the Lord,* 23.

A. M. 2514.
B. C. 1490.
An. Exod. Isr. 2.
Abib or Nisan.

AND the LORD spake unto
Moses in the wilderness of
Sinai, in the first month of the
second year after they were come out of the
land of Egypt, saying,
2 Let the children of Israel also keep [a] the
passover at his appointed season.
3 In the fourteenth day of this month, [b] at
even, ye shall keep it in his appointed season:
according to all the rites of it, and according
to all the ceremonies thereof, shall ye keep it.
4 And Moses spake unto the children of
Israel, that they should keep the passover.
5 And [c] they kept the passover on the fourteenth day of the first month at even in the
wilderness of Sinai; according to all that the
LORD commanded Moses, so did the children
of Israel.
6 And there were certain men
who were [d] defiled by the dead
body of a man, that they could
not keep the passover on that day: [e] and they
came before Moses and before Aaron on
that day:
7 And those men said unto him, We *are*
defiled by the dead body of a man: wherefore are we kept back, that we may not offer
an offering of the LORD in his appointed season, among the children of Israel?
8 And Moses said unto them, Stand still, and
[f] I will hear what the LORD will command concerning you.
9 And the LORD spake unto Moses, saying,
10 Speak unto the children of Israel, saying,
If any man of you or of your posterity shall be
unclean by reason of a dead body, or *be* in a

A. M. 2514.
B. C. 1490.
An. Exod. Isr. 2.
Abib or Nisan.

[a] Exod. xii. 1, &c.; Lev. xxiii. 5; chap. xxviii. 16; Deut. xvi. 1, 2.——[b] Heb. *between the two evenings*; Exod. xii. 6.——[c] Josh. v. 10.——[d] Ch. v. 2; xix. 11, 16; see John xviii. 28.——[e] Exod. xviii. 15, 19, 26; chap. xxvii. 2.——[f] Chap. xxvii. 5.

NOTES ON CHAP. IX.

Verse 1. *The Lord spake unto Moses*] The fourteen first verses of this chapter certainly refer to transactions that took place at the time of those mentioned in the commencement of this book, before the numbering of the people, and several learned men are of opinion that these fourteen verses should be referred back to that place. We have already met with instances where *transpositions* have very probably taken place, and it is not difficult to account for them. As in very early times writing was generally on leaves of the Egyptian flag *papyrus*, or on thin *laminæ* of different substances, facts and transactions thus entered were very liable to be deranged; so that when afterwards a series was made up into a book, many transactions might be inserted in wrong places, and thus the exact *chronology* of the facts be greatly disturbed. MSS. written on leaves of trees, having a *hole* in each, through which a cord is passed to keep them all in their places, are frequently to be met with in the cabinets of the curious, and many such are now before me, especially in *Singalese*, *Pali*, and *Burman*. Should the cord break, or be accidentally unloosed, it would be exceedingly difficult to string them all in their proper places; accidents of this kind I have often met with to my very great perplexity, and in some cases found it almost impossible to restore each individual leaf to its own place; for it should be observed that these separate pieces of oriental writing are not always *paged* like the leaves of our printed books; nor are there frequently any catch-words or signatures at the bottom to connect the series. This one consideration will account for several *transpositions*, especially in the Pentateuch, where they occur more frequently than in any other part of the sacred writings. *Houbigant*, who grants the existence of such transpositions, thinks that this is no sufficient reason why the present order of narration should be changed: "It is enough," says he, *non ignorare libros eos Mosis esse acta rerum suo tempore gestarum, non historiam filo perpetuo elaboratam*, "to know that these books contain an account of things transacted in the days of Moses, though not in their regular or chronological order."

Verse 3. *According to all the rites of it*] See all those rites and ceremonies largely explained in the notes on Exod. xii.

Verse 7. *We are defiled by the dead body of a man*] It is probable that the defilement mentioned here was occasioned by assisting at the burial of some person—a work both of necessity and mercy. This circumstance however gave rise to the ordinance delivered in verses 10–14, so that on particular occasions the passover might be *twice* celebrated: 1. At its regular time, the 14th of the *first* month; 2. An extra time, the 14th of the *second* month. But the man who had no legal hinderance, and did not celebrate it on one or other of these times, was to be cut off from the people of God; and the reason given for this cutting off is, that *he brought not the offering of God in his appointed season*—therefore *that man shall bear his sin*, ver. 13. We have already seen, from the authority of St. Paul, that Christ, our Passover, is sacrificed for us; and that it was his sacrifice that was pointed out by the paschal lamb: on this, therefore, we may observe, that those who do not sooner or later eat the true Passover, and get the salvation procured by the sprinkling of his blood, shall be cut off from among those that shall enter into the rest prepared for the people of God;

A. M. 2514. B. C. 1490. An. Exod. Isr. 2. Abib or Nisan.

journey afar off, yet he shall keep the passover unto the LORD.

11 [g] The fourteenth day of the second month at even they shall keep it, *and* [h] eat it with unleavened bread and bitter *herbs*.

12 [i] They shall leave none of it unto the morning, [k] nor break any bone of it: [l] according to all the ordinances of the passover they shall keep it.

13 But the man that *is* clean, and is not in a journey, and forbeareth to keep the passover, even the same soul [m] shall be cut off from among his people: because he [n] brought not the offering of the LORD in his appointed season, that man shall [o] bear his sin.

14 And if a stranger shall sojourn among you, and will keep the passover unto the LORD; according to the ordinance of the passover, and according to the manner thereof, so shall he do: [p] ye shall have one ordinance, both for the stranger, and for him that was born in the land.

15 And [q] on the day that the tabernacle was reared up the cloud covered the tabernacle, *namely*, the tent of the testimony: and [r] at even there was upon the tabernacle as it were the appearance of fire, until the morning.

16 So it was alway: the cloud covered it *by day*, and the appearance of fire by night.

17 And when the cloud [s] was taken up from the tabernacle, then after that the children of Israel journeyed: and in the place where the cloud abode, there the children of Israel pitched their tents.

A. M. 2514. B. C. 1490. An. Exod. Isr. 2. Abib or Nisan.

18 At the commandment of the LORD the children of Israel journeyed, and at the commandment of the LORD they pitched: as long as the cloud abode upon the tabernacle they rested in their tents.

19 And when the cloud [u] tarried long upon the tabernacle many days, then the children of Israel [v] kept the charge of the LORD, and journeyed not.

20 And *so* it was, when the cloud was a few days upon the tabernacle; according to the commandment of the LORD they abode in their tents, and according to the commandment of the LORD they journeyed.

21 And *so* it was, when the cloud [w] abode from even unto the morning, and *that* the cloud was taken up in the morning, then they journeyed: whether *it was* by day or by night that the cloud was taken up, they journeyed.

22 Or *whether it were* two days, or a month, or a year, that the cloud tarried upon the tabernacle, remaining thereon, the children of Israel [x] abode in their tents, and journeyed not: but when it was taken up, they journeyed.

23 At the commandment of the LORD they rested in the tents, and at the commandment of the LORD they journeyed: they [y] kept the charge of the LORD, at the commandment of the LORD by the hand of Moses.

[g] 2 Chron. xxx. 2, 15.—[h] Exod. xii. 8.—[i] Exod. xii. 10. [k] Exod. xii. 46; John xix. 36.—[l] Exod. xii. 43.—[m] Gen. xvii. 14; Exod. xii. 15.—[n] Ver. 7.—[o] Chap. v. 31.—[p] Exod. xii. 49.

[q] Exod. xl. 34; Neh. ix. 12, 19; Psa. lxxviii. 14.—[r] Exod. xiii. 21; xl. 38.—[s] Exod. xl. 36; chap. x. 11, 33, 34; Psa. lxxx. 1.—[t] 1 Cor. x. 1.—[u] Heb. *prolonged*.—[v] Chap. i. 53; iii. 8.—[w] Heb. *was*.—[x] Exod. xl. 36, 37.—[y] Ver. 19.

and for the same reason too; *they bring not the offering of God in its appointed season*, and therefore *they shall bear their sin*.

Verse 15. *The cloud covered the tabernacle*] See the whole account of this supernatural cloud largely explained, Exod. xiii. 21; and xl. 34-38.

Calmet observes that the 15th verse, beginning a new subject, should begin a new chapter, as it has no connection with what goes before; and he thinks this chapter, begun with the 15th verse, should end with the 28th verse of the following.

Verse 21. *Whether—by day or by night*] As the heat of the day is very severe in that same desert, the *night season* is sometimes chosen for the performance of a journey; though it is very likely that in the case of the Israelites this was seldom resorted to.

Verse 22. *Two days—a month—a year*] It was by the Divine counsel alone that they were directed in all their peregrinations; and from the above words we see that their *times* of *tarrying* at different stations were very unequal.

Verse 23. *Kept the charge of the Lord*] When we consider the strong disposition which this people ever testified to follow their own will in all things, we may be well surprised to find them, in these journeyings, so implicitly following the direction of God. There could be no trick or imposture here. Moses, had he been the most cunning of men, never could have imitated the *appearances* referred to in this chapter. The cloud, and every thing in its motion, was so evidently *supernatural*, that the people had no doubt of its being the symbol of the Divine presence.

GOD chose to keep this people so dependent upon himself, and so submissive to the decisions of his own will, that he would not even give them regular times of marching or resting; they were to do both when and where God saw best. Thus they were ever kept ready for their march, though perfectly ignorant of the

time when they should commence it. But this was all well; they had the presence of God with them; the cloud by day and the fire by night demonstrated that God was amongst them. Reader, thou art here a tenant at will to God Almighty. How soon, in what place, or in what circumstances, he may call thee to march into the eternal world, thou knowest not. But this uncertainty cannot perplex *thee*, if thou be properly subject to the *will* of God, ever willing to lose thy own in it. But thou canst not be thus subject, unless thou have the testimony of the presence and approbation of God. How awful to be obliged to walk into the valley of the shadow of death without this! Reader, prepare to meet thy God.

CHAPTER X.

Moses is commanded to make two silver trumpets *for calling the assembly*, 1, 2. *On what occasions these trumpets should be sounded.* First, *for calling the assembly to the door of the tabernacle*, 3. Secondly, *to summon the princes and captains of the thousands of Israel*, 4. Thirdly, *to make the* eastern *camps strike their tents*, 5. Fourthly, *to make those on the* south *do the like*, 6. *No alarm to be sounded when the* congregation *only is to be assembled*, 7. *The sons of Aaron alone shall sound these trumpets, it shall be a perpetual ordinance*, 8. Fifthly, *the trumpets are to be sounded in the time of war*, 9. Sixthly, *on* festival *occasions*, 10. *On the* twentieth *day of the* second *month, in the* second *year, the Israelites began their journey from the wilderness of* Sinai, *and came to the wilderness of* Paran, 11, 12. *By the commandment of God to Moses the first division, at the head of which was the standard of* JUDAH, *marched*, first, 13, 14. *Under him followed the tribe of* ISSACHAR, 15; *and after them the tribe of* ZEBULUN, 16. *Then the* Gershonites *and* Merarites *followed with the tabernacle*, 17. *At the head of the second division was the standard and camp of* REUBEN, 18; *and under him were that of* SIMEON, 19; *and that of* GAD, 20. *Next followed the* Kohathites, *bearing the sanctuary*, 21. *Then followed the* third division, *at the head of which was the standard of the camp of* EPHRAIM, 22; *and under him* MANASSEH, 23; *and* BENJAMIN, 24. *At the head of the* fourth division *was the standard of the camp of* DAN, 25; *and under him* ASHER, 26; *and* NAPHTALI, 27. *This was their ordinary method of marching in the wilderness*, 28. *Moses entreats* Hobab *the Midianite to accompany them through the wilderness*, 29. *He refuses*, 30. *Moses continues and strengthens his entreaties with reasonings and promises*, 31, 32. *They depart from Sinai three days' journey*, 33. *The cloud accompanies them by day and night*, 34. *The words used by Moses when the ark set forward*, 35, *and when it rested*, 36.

A. M. 2514.
B. C. 1490.
An. Exod. Isr. 2.
Abib or Nisan.

AND the LORD spake unto Moses, saying,

2 Make thee two trumpets of silver; of a whole piece shalt thou make them: that thou mayest use them for the [a] calling of the assembly, and for the journeying of the camps.

3 And when [b] they shall blow with them, all the assembly shall assemble themselves to thee at the door of the tabernacle of the congregation.

4 And if they blow *but* with one *trumpet*, then the princes, *which are* [c] heads of the thousands of Israel, shall gather themselves unto thee.

5 When ye blow an alarm, then [d] the camps that lie on the east parts shall go forward.

[a] Isa. i. 13.——[b] Jer. iv. 5; Joel ii. 15. [c] Exod. xviii. 21; chap. i. 16; vii. 2.——[d] Chap. ii. 3.

NOTES ON CHAP. X.

Verse 2. *Make thee two trumpets of silver*] The necessity of such instruments will at once appear, when the amazing extent of this numerous army is considered; and how even the sound of two trumpets could reach them all is difficult to conceive; but we may suppose that, when they were sounded, the motion of those that were within reach of that sound taught the others in *succession* what they should do.

As the trumpets were to be blown by the *priests* only, the sons of Aaron, there were only *two*, because there were only two such persons to use them at this time, *Eleazar* and *Ithamar*. In the time of Joshua there were *seven* trumpets used by the priests, but these were made, according to our text, of *rams' horns*, Josh. vi. 4. In the time of Solomon, when the priests had greatly increased, there were 120 priests sounding with trumpets, 2 Chron. v. 12.

Josephus intimates that one of these trumpets was always used to call the *nobles* together, the other to assemble the *people*; see ver. 4. It is possible that these trumpets were made of different *lengths* and *wideness*, and consequently they would emit different tones. Thus the *sound* itself would at once show which was the summons for the *congregation*, and which for the *princes* only. These trumpets were allowed to be emblematical of the sound of the Gospel, and in this reference they appear to be frequently used. Of the *fate* of the trumpets of the sanctuary, see the note on Exod. xxv. 31.

Verse 5. *When ye blow an alarm*] תרועה *teruah*, probably meaning *short*, *broken*, *sharp* tones, terminating with *long* ones, blown with both the trumpets at once. From the similarity in the words some suppose that the Hebrew *teruah* was similar to the Roman *tara tantara*, or sound of their *clarion*.

A. M. 2514.
B. C. 1490.
An. Exod. Isr. 2.
Abib or Nisan.

6 When ye blow an alarm the second time, then the camps that lie on [e] the south side shall take their journey: they shall blow an alarm for their journeys.

7 But when the congregation is to be gathered together, [f] ye shall blow, but ye shall not [g] sound an alarm.

8 [h] And the sons of Aaron, the priests, shall blow with the trumpets; and they shall be to you for an ordinance for ever throughout your generations.

9 And [i] if ye go to war in your land against the enemy that [k] oppresseth you, then ye shall blow an alarm with the trumpets; and ye shall be [l] remembered before the LORD your God, and ye shall be saved from your enemies.

10 Also [m] in the day of your gladness, and in your solemn days, and in the beginnings of your months, ye shall blow with the trumpets over your burnt-offerings, and over the sacrifices of your peace-offerings; that they may be to you [n] for a memorial before your God: I *am* the LORD your God.

A. M. 2514.
B. C. 1490.
An. Exod. Isr. 2.
Ijar or Zif.

11 And it came to pass, on the twentieth *day* of the second month, in the second year, that the cloud [o] was taken up from off the tabernacle of the testimony.

12 And the children of Israel took [p] their journeys out of the [q] wilderness of Sinai; and the cloud rested in the [r] wilderness of Paran.

13 And they first took their journey [s] according to the commandment of the LORD by the hand of Moses.

14 [t] In the first *place* went the standard of the camp of the children of Judah, according

[e] Chap. ii. 10.——[f] Ver. 3.——[g] Joel ii. 1.——[h] Chap. xxxi. 6; Josh. vi. 4; 1 Chron. xv. 24; 2 Chron. xiii. 12; 1 Mac. xvi. 8.——[i] Chap. xxxi. 6; Josh. vi. 5; 2 Chron. xiii. 14.——[k] Judg. ii. 18; iv. 3; vi. 9; x. 8, 12; 1 Sam. x. 18; Psa. cvi. 42.——[l] Gen. viii. 1; Psa. cvi. 4.——[m] Chap. xxix. 1; Lev. xxiii. 24; 1 Chron. xv. 24; 2 Chron. v. 12; vii. 6; xxix. 26; Ezra iii. 10; Neh. xii. 35; Psa. lxxxi. 3.——[n] Ver. 9.——[o] Chap. ix. 17.——[p] Exod. xl. 36; chap. ii. 9, 16, 24, 31.——[q] Exod. xix. 1; chap. i. 1; ix. 5.——[r] Gen. xxi. 21; chap. xii. 16; xiii. 3, 26; Deut. i. 1.——[s] Ver. 5, 6; chap. ii. 34.——[t] Chap. ii. 3, 9.

Verse 6. *When ye blow an alarm the second time*] A *single* alarm, as above stated, was a signal for the *eastward* division to march; *two* such alarms, the signal for the *south* division; and probably *three* for the *west* division, and *four* for the *north*. It is more likely that this was the case, than that a single alarm served for each, with a small interval between them.

The camps, or grand divisions of this great army, always lay, as we have already seen, to the east, south, west, and north: and here the east and south camps alone are mentioned; the *first* containing *Judah, Issachar*, and *Zebulun*; the *second, Reuben, Simeon*, and *Gad*. The *west* and *north* divisions are not named, and yet we are sure they marched in consequence of express orders or signals, as well as the other two. There appears therefore a deficiency here in the Hebrew text, which is thus supplied by the Septuagint: *Και σαλπιειτε σημασιαν τριτην, και εξαρουσιν αἱ παρεμβολαι αἱ παρεμβαλλουσαι παρα θαλασσαν· και σαλπιειτε σημασιαν τεταρτην, και εξαρουσιν αἱ παρεμβολαι αἱ παρεμβαλλουσαι προς βορῤαν.* "And when ye blow a *third* alarm or signal, the camps on the *west* shall march: and when ye blow a *fourth* alarm or signal, the camps on the *north* shall march." This addition, however, is not acknowledged by the *Samaritan*, nor by any of the other versions but the *Coptic*. Nor are there any various readings in the collections of *Kennicott* and *De Rossi*, which countenance the *addition* in the above versions. Houbigant thinks this addition so evidently necessary, that he has inserted the Latin in his text, and in a note supplied the Hebrew words, and thinks that these words were originally in the Hebrew text, but happened to be omitted in consequence of so many *similar words* occurring so often in the same verse, which might dazzle and deceive the eye of a transcriber.

Verse 9. *If ye go to war*] These trumpets shall be sounded for the purpose of collecting the people together, to deliberate about the war, and to implore the protection of God against their enemies.

Ye shall be remembered before the Lord] When ye *decamp, encamp, make war*, and hold *religious festivals*, according to his appointment, which appointment shall be signified to you by the priests, who at the command of God, for such purposes, shall blow the trumpets, then ye may expect both the presence and blessing of Jehovah in all that ye undertake.

Verse 10. *In the day of your gladness*] On every festival the people shall be collected by the same means.

Verse 11. *The twentieth* day *of the second month*] The Israelites had lain encamped in the wilderness of Sinai about *eleven months* and *twenty days*; compare Exod. xix. 1 with this verse. They now received the order of God to decamp, and proceed towards the promised land; and therefore the Samaritan introduces at this place the words which we find in Deut. i. 6–8: "The Lord our God spake unto us *in Horeb*, saying: Ye have dwelt long enough in this mount, turn and take your journey," &c.

Verse 12. *The cloud rested in the wilderness of Paran*.] This was three days' journey from the wilderness of Sinai, (see ver. 33,) and the people had three stations; the first at *Kibroth-hattaavah*, the second at *Hazeroth*, chap. xi. 35, and the third in the wilderness of *Paran*, see chap. xii. 16. But it is extremely difficult to determine these journeyings with any degree of exactness; and we are often at a loss to know whether the place in question was in a *direct* or *retrograde* position from the place previously mentioned.

Verse 14. *The standard—of Judah*] See this order

A. M. 2514.
B. C. 1490.
An. Exod. Isr. 2.
Ijar or Zif.

to their armies: and over his host *was* [u] Nahshon the son of Amminadab.

15 And over the host of the tribe of the children of Issachar *was* Nethaneel the son of Zuar.

16 And over the host of the tribe of the children of Zebulun *was* Eliab the son of Helon.

17 And [v] the tabernacle was taken down; and the sons of Gershon, and the sons of Merari, set forward, [w] bearing the tabernacle.

18 And [x] the standard of the camp of Reuben set forward, according to their armies: and over his host *was* Elizur the son of Shedeur.

19 And over the host of the tribe of the children of Simeon *was* Shelumiel the son of Zurishaddai.

20 And over the host of the tribe of the children of Gad *was* Eliasaph the son of Deuel.

21 And the Kohathites set forward, bearing the [y] sanctuary: and [z] *the other* did set up the tabernacle against they came.

22 And [a] the standard of the camp of the children of Ephraim set forward, according to their armies: and over his host *was* Elishama the son of Ammihud.

23 And over the host of the tribe of the children of Manasseh *was* Gamaliel the son of Pedahzur.

A. M. 2514.
B. C. 1490.
An. Exod. Isr. 2.
Ijar or Zif.

24 And over the host of the tribe of the children of Benjamin *was* Abidan the son of Gideoni.

25 And [b] the standard of the camp of the children of Dan set forward, *which was* the rereward of all the camps throughout their hosts: and over his host *was* Ahiezer the son of Ammishaddai.

26 And over the host of the tribe of the children of Ashur *was* Pagiel the son of Ocran.

27 And over the host of the tribe of the children of Naphtali *was* Ahira the son of Enan.

28 [c] Thus [d] *were* the journeyings of the children of Israel, according to their armies, when they set forward.

29 And Moses said unto Hobab, the son of [e] Raguel, the Midianite, Moses' father-in-law, We are journeying unto the place of which the LORD said, [f] I will give it you: come thou with us, and [g] we will do thee good: for [h] the LORD hath spoken good concerning Israel.

30 And he said unto him, I will not go;

[u] Chap. i. 7.——[v] Chap. i. 51.——[w] Chap. iv. 24, 31; vii. 6, 7, 8.——[x] Chap. ii. 10, 16.——[y] Chap. iv. 4, 15; vii. 9.——[z] That is, *the Gershonites and the Merarites*; see ver. 17; chap. i. 51.

[a] Chap. ii. 18, 24.——[b] Chap. ii. 25, 31; Josh. vi. 9.——[c] Heb. *these.*——[d] Chap. ii. 34.——[e] Exod. ii. 18.——[f] Gen. xii. 7.——[g] Judg. i. 16; iv. 11.——[h] Gen. xxxii. 12; Exod. iii. 8; vi. 7, 8.

of marching explained at large on chap. ii. The following is the order in which this vast company proceeded in their march:—

JUDAH
Issachar
Zebulun
Gershonites, and
Merarites carrying the tabernacle.
REUBEN
Simeon
Gad
The Kohathites with the sanctuary.
EPHRAIM
Manasseh
Benjamin
DAN
Asher
Naphtali.

Verse 29. *Moses said unto Hobab*] For a circumstantial account of this person see the notes on Exod. ii. 15, 16, 18; iii. 1; iv. 20, 24; and for the transaction recorded here, and which is probably out of its place, see Exod. xviii. 5, where the subject is discussed at large.

We are journeying] God has brought us out of thraldom, and we are thus far on our way through the wilderness, travelling towards the place of rest which he has appointed us, trusting in his promise, guided by his presence, and supported by his power. *Come thou with us, and we will do thee good.* Those who wish to enjoy the heavenly inheritance must walk in the way towards it, and associate with the people who are going in that way. True religion is ever benevolent. They who know most of the goodness of God are the most forward to invite others to partake of that goodness. That religion which excludes all others from salvation, unless they believe a particular creed, and worship in a particular way, is not of God. Even *Hobab*, the Arab, according to the opinion of Moses, might receive the same blessings which God had promised to Israel, provided he accompanied them in the same way.

The Lord hath spoken good concerning Israel.] The name *Israel* is taken in a general sense to signify the *followers of God*, and to them all the promises in the Bible are made. God has spoken good *of* them, and he has spoken good *to* them; and not one word that he hath spoken shall fail. Reader, hast thou left thy unhallowed connections in life? Hast thou got into the camp of the Most High? Then continue to follow God with Israel, and thou shalt be incorporated in the heavenly family, and share in Israel's benedictions.

Verse 30. *I will not go; but I will depart to mine own land, and to my kindred.*] From the strong expostulations in verses 31 and 32, and from Judg. i. 16;

A. M. 2514. B. C. 1490. An. Exod. Isr. 2. Ijar or Zif.

but I will depart to mine own
land, and to my kindred.
31 And he said, Leave us not,
I pray thee; forasmuch as thou knowest how
we are to encamp in the wilderness, and thou
mayest be to us [i] instead of eyes.
32 And it shall be, if thou go with us,
yea, it shall be, that [k] what goodness the
LORD shall do unto us, the same will we do
unto thee.
33 And they departed from [l] the mount of
the LORD three days' journey: and the ark of
the covenant of the LORD [m] went
before them in the three days'
journey, to search out a resting
place for them.
34 And [n] the cloud of the LORD *was* upon
them by day, when they went out of the camp.
35 And it came to pass, when the ark set
forward, that Moses said, [o] Rise up, LORD, and
let thine enemies be scattered; and let them
that hate thee flee before thee.
36 And when it rested, he said, Return, O
LORD, unto the [p] many thousands of Israel.

A. M. 2514. B. C. 1490. An. Exod. Isr. 2. Ijar or Zif.

[i] Job xxix. 15.——[k] Judg. i. 16.——[l] See Exod. iii. 1.——[m] Deut. i. 33; Josh. iii. 3, 4, 6; Psa. cxxxii. 8; Jer. xxxi. 2; Ezek. xx. 6.——[n] Exod. xiii. 21; Neh. ix. 12, 19.——[o] Psa. lxviii. 1, 2; cxxxii. 8.——[p] Heb. *ten thousand thousands.*

iv. 11, and 1 Sam. xv. 6, it is likely that Hobab changed his mind; or that, if he did go back to Midian, he returned again to Israel, as the above scriptures show that his *posterity* dwelt among the Israelites in Canaan. Reader, after having been almost persuaded to become a Christian, to take Christ, his cross, his reproach, and his crown, for thy portion, art thou again purposing to go back to thy own land, and to thy kindred? Knowest thou not that this land is the place of destruction—that the children of this world, who are not taking God for their portion, are going to perdition? Up, get thee hence, for the Lord will destroy this place by fire; and all who are not of the kindred and family of Christ shall perish at the brightness of his appearing!

Verse 31. *Thou mayest be to us instead of eyes.*] But what need had they of Hobab, when they had the pillar and fire continually to point out their way? Answer: The cloud directed their *general* journeys, but not their *particular* excursions. Parties took several journeys while the grand army lay still. (See chap. xiii., xx., xxxi., xxxii., &c.) They therefore needed such a person as Hobab, who was well acquainted with the desert, to direct these particular excursions; to point them out watering places, and places where they might meet with fuel, &c., &c. What man cannot, under the direction of God's providence, do for himself, God will do in the way of especial mercy. He could have directed them to the fountains and to the places of fuel, but *Hobab* can do this, therefore let Hobab be employed; and let Hobab know for his encouragement that, while he is serving others in the way of God's providence, he is securing his own best interests. On these grounds Hobab should be invited, and for this reason Hobab should go. Man cannot do God's work; and God will not do the work which he has qualified and commanded man to perform. Thus then the Lord is ever seen, even while he is helping man by man. See some valuable observations on this subject in *Harmer*, vol. ii., 286. Instead of, *And thou mayest be to us instead of eyes*, the Septuagint translate the passage thus. *Και εσῃ εν ἡμιν πρεσβυτης*, *And thou shalt be an elder among us.* But Moses probably refers to Hobab's accurate knowledge of the wilderness, and to the assistance he could give them as a *guide*.

Verse 33. *The ark—went before them*] We find from ver. 21 that the ark was carried by the *Kohathites* in the centre of the army; but as the army never moved till the cloud was taken up, it is said to *go before them*, i. e., to be the first to move, as without this motion the Israelites continued in their encampments.

Verse 35. *Rise up, Lord, and let thine enemies be scattered*] If God did not arise in this way and scatter his enemies, there could be no hope that Israel could get safely through the wilderness. God must go first, if Israel would wish to follow in safety.

Verse 36. *Return, O Lord, unto the many thousands of Israel.*] These were the words spoken by Moses, at the moment the divisions halted in order to pitch their tents. In reference to this subject, and the history with which it is connected, the 68th Psalm seems to have been composed, though applied by David to the bringing the ark from Kirjath-jearim to Jerusalem. See the notes on Psa. lxviii. *Many thousands*, literally *the ten thousand thousands.* Unless the ark *went* with *them*, and the cloud of the Divine glory with *it*, they could have neither *direction* nor *safety*; unless the ark *rested* with them, and the cloud of glory with *it*, they could have neither *rest* nor *comfort.* How necessary are the *word of God* and the *Spirit of God* for the direction, comfort, and defence of every genuine follower of Christ! Reader, pray to God that thou mayest have both with thee through all the wilderness, through all the changes and chances of this mortal life: if thou be guided by *his* counsel, thou shalt be at last received into his glory.

CHAPTER XI.

The people complain, the Lord is displeased, and many of them are consumed by fire, 1. *Moses intercedes for them, and the fire is quenched,* 2. *The place is called* Taberah, 3. *The* mixed multitude *long for flesh, and murmur,* 4–6. *The manna described,* 7–9. *The people weep in their tents, and the Lord is displeased,* 10. *Moses deplores his lot in being obliged to hear and bear with all their murmurings,* 11–15.

He is commanded to bring seventy of the elders to God that he may endue them with the same spirit, and cause them to divide the burden with him, 16, 17. *He is also commanded to inform the people that they shall have flesh for a whole month,* 18–20. *Moses expresses his doubt of the possibility of this,* 21, 22. *The Lord confirms his promise,* 23. *The seventy men are brought to the tabernacle,* 24; *and the spirit of prophecy rests upon them,* 25. Eldad *and* Medad *stay in the camp and prophesy,* 26, 27. *Joshua beseeches Moses to forbid them,* 28. *Moses refuses,* 29, 30. *A wind from the Lord brings* quails *to the camp,* 31, 32. *While feeding on the flesh, a plague from the Lord falls upon them, and many of them die,* 33. *The place is called* Kibroth-hattaavah, *or the graves of lust,* 34. *They journey to* Hazeroth, 35

A. M. 2514. B. C. 1490. An. Exod. Isr. 2.

AND [a] *when* the people [b] complained, [c] it displeased the
LORD: and the LORD heard *it;*
[d] and his anger was kindled; and the [e] fire of
the LORD burnt among them, and consumed
them that were in the uttermost parts of the
camp.
2 And the people cried unto Moses; and
when Moses [f] prayed unto the LORD, the fire
[g] was quenched.
3 And he called the name of the place [h] Taberah: because the fire of the LORD burnt
among them.
4 And the [i] mixed multitude that *was* among
them [k] fell a lusting: and the children of Israel
also [l] wept again, and said, [m] Who shall give
us flesh to eat?
5 [n] We remember the fish,
which we did eat in Egypt freely;
the cucumbers, and the melons,
and the leeks, and the onions, and the garlic:
6 But now [o] our soul *is* dried away: *there
is* nothing at all, beside this manna, *before* ou
eyes.
7 And [p] the manna *was* as coriander seed, and
the [q] colour thereof as the colour of [r] bdellium.
8 *And* the people went about, and gathered
it, and ground *it* in mills, or beat *it* in a mortar, and baked *it* in pans, and made cakes of it:
and [s] the taste of it was as the taste of fresh oil.
9 And [t] when the dew fell upon the camp in
the night, the manna fell upon it.
10 Then Moses heard the people weep
throughout their families, every man in the

A. M. 2514. B. C. 1490. An. Exod. Isr. 2.

[a] Deut. ix. 22.——[b] Or, *were as it were complainers.*——[c] Heb. *it was evil in the ears of,* &c.——[d] Psa. lxxviii. 21.——[e] Lev. x. 2; chap. xvi. 35; 2 Kings i. 12; Psa. cvi. 18.——[f] James v. 16.——[g] Heb. *sunk.*——[h] That is, *a burning;* Deut. ix. 22.——[i] As Exod. xii. 38.——[k] Heb. *lusted a lust.*——[l] Heb. *returned and wept.*——[m] Psa. lxxviii. 18; cvi. 14; 1 Cor. x. 6.——[n] Exod. xvi. 3.——[o] Chap. xxi. 5.——[p] Exod. xvi. 14, 31.——[q] Heb. *eye of it as the eye of.*——[r] Gen. ii. 12.——[s] Exod. xvi. 31.——[t] Exod. xvi. 13, 14.

NOTES ON CHAP. XI.

Verse 1. *And* when *the people complained*] What the cause of this complaining was, we know not. The conjecture of St. Jerome is probable; they complained because of the *length of the way.* But surely no people had ever less cause for murmuring; they had God among them, and miracles of goodness were continually wrought in their behalf.

It displeased the Lord] For his extraordinary kindness was lost on such an ungrateful and rebellious people. *And his anger was kindled*—Divine justice was necessarily incensed against such inexcusable conduct.

And the fire of the Lord burnt among them] Either a supernatural fire was sent for this occasion, or the lightning was commissioned against them, or God smote them with one of those hot suffocating winds which are very common in those countries.

And consumed—in the uttermost parts of the camp.] It pervaded the whole camp, from the centre to the circumference, carrying death with it to all the murmurers; for we are not to suppose that it was confined to the uttermost parts of the camp, unless we could imagine that there were none culpable any where else. If this were the same with the case mentioned ver. 4, then, as it is possible that the mixed multitude occupied the outermost parts of the camp, consequently the burning might have been confined to them.

Verse 2. *The fire was quenched.*] Was *sunk,* or swallowed up, as in the margin. The plague, of whatever sort, ceased to act, and the people had respite.

Verse 4. *The mixed multitude*] האספסף *hasaphsuph,* the *collected* or *gathered people.* Such as came out of Egypt with the Israelites; and are mentioned Exod. xii. 38. This *mongrel* people, who had comparatively little of the knowledge of God, feeling the difficulties and fatigues of the journey, were the first to complain; and then we find the children of Israel joined them in their complainings, and made a common cause with these demi-infidels.

Verse 5. *We remember, &c.*] The choice aliments which those murmurers complained of having lost by their leaving Egypt, were the following: *fish, cucumbers, melons, leeks, onions,* and *garlic.* A European may smile at such *delicacies;* but *delicacies* they were in that country. Their *fish* is excellent; their *cucumbers* and *water melons* highly salubrious and refreshing; and their *onions, garlic,* &c., exquisitely flavoured, differing as much from vegetables of the same species in these northern climes as a *bad turnip* does from a *good apple.* In short, this enumeration takes in almost all the commonly attainable delicacies in those countries.

Verse 7. *The manna* was *as coriander seed*] Probably this short description is added to show the iniquity of the people in murmuring, while they had so adequate a provision. But the baseness of their minds appears in every part of their conduct.

About the *bdellium* of the ancients the learned are

A. M. 2514.
B. C. 1490.
An. Exod. Isr.
2.

door of his tent; and [u] the anger of the LORD was kindled greatly; Moses also was displeased.

11 [v] And Moses said unto the LORD, Wherefore hast thou afflicted thy servant? and wherefore have I not found favour in thy sight, that thou layest the burden of all this people upon me?

12 Have I conceived all this people? have I begotten them, that thou shouldest say unto me, [w] Carry them in thy bosom, as a [x] nursing father beareth the sucking child, unto the land which thou [y] swarest unto their fathers?

13 [z] Whence should I have flesh to give unto all this people? for they weep unto me, saying, Give us flesh, that we may eat.

14 [a] I am not able to bear all this people alone, because *it is* too heavy for me.

15 And if thou deal thus with me, [b] kill me, I pray thee, out of hand, if I have found favour in thy sight; and let me not [c] see my wretchedness.

16 And the LORD said unto Moses, Gather unto me [d] seventy men of the elders of Israel, whom thou knowest to be the elders of the people, and [e] officers over them; and bring them unto the tabernacle of the congregation, that they may stand there with thee.

17 And I will [f] come down and talk with thee there: and [g] I will take of the spirit which *is* upon thee, and will put *it* upon them; and they shall bear the burden of the people with thee, that thou bear *it* not thyself alone.

A. M. 2514.
B. C. 1490.
An. Exod. Isr.
2.

18 And say thou unto the people, [h] Sanctify yourselves against to-morrow, and ye shall eat flesh: for ye have wept [i] in the ears of the LORD, saying, Who shall give us flesh to eat? [k] for *it was* well with us in Egypt: therefore the LORD will give you flesh, and ye shall eat.

19 Ye shall not eat one day, nor two days, nor five days, neither ten days, nor twenty days;

20 [l] *But* even a [m] whole month, until it come out at your nostrils, and it be loathsome unto you: because that ye have despised the LORD which *is* among you, and have wept before him, saying, [n] Why came we forth out of Egypt?

21 And Moses said, [o] The people, among whom I *am, are* six hundred thousand footmen; and thou hast said, I will give them flesh, that they may eat a whole month.

22 [p] Shall the flocks and the herds be slain for them, to suffice them? or shall all the fish of the sea be gathered together for them, to suffice them?

[u] Psa. lxxviii. 21.——[v] Deut. i. 12.——[w] Isa. xl. 11.——[x] Isa. xlix. 23; 1 Thess. ii. 7.——[y] Gen. xxvi. 3; l. 24; Exod. xiii. 5.——[z] Matt. xv. 33; Mark viii. 4.——[a] Exod. xviii. 18.——[b] See 1 Kings. xix. 4; Jonah iv. 3.——[c] Zeph. iii. 15.——[d] See Exod. xxiv. 1, 9.——[e] Deut. xvi. 18.——[f] Ver. 25; Gen. xi. 5; xviii. 21; Exod. xix. 20.

[g] 1 Sam. x. 6; 2 Kings ii. 15; Neh. ix. 20; Isa. xliv. 3; Joel ii. 28.——[h] Exod. xix. 10.——[i] Exod. xvi. 7.——[k] Ver. 5; Acts vii. 39.——[l] Psa. lxxviii. 29; cvi. 15.——[m] Heb. *month of days.*——[n] Chap. xxi. 5.——[o] Gen. xii. 2; Exod. xii. 37; xxxviii. 26; chap. i. 46.——[p] See 2 Kings vii. 2; Matt. xv. 33; Mark viii. 4; John. vi. 7, 9.

not agreed; and I shall not trouble the reader with conjectures. See the note on Gen. ii. 12. Concerning the manna, see the notes on Exod. xvi.

Verses 11–15. The complaint and remonstrance of Moses in these verses serve at once to show the deeply distressed state of his mind, and the degradation of the minds of the people. We have already seen that the slavery they had so long endured had served to debase their minds, and to render them incapable of every high and dignified sentiment, and of every generous act.

Verse 17. *I will take of the spirit which* is *upon thee*] From this place Origen and Theodoret take occasion to compare Moses to a lamp, at which seventy others were lighted, without losing any of its brightness. To convince Moses that God had sufficiently qualified him for the work which he had given him to do, he tells him that of the gifts and graces which he has given him he will qualify seventy persons to bear the charge with him. This was probably intended as a gracious reproof. Query. Did not Moses lose a measure of his gifts in this business? And is it not right that he whom God has called to and qualified for some particular office, should lose those gifts which he either undervalues or refuses to employ for God in the way appointed? Is there not much reason to believe that many cases have occurred where the spiritual endowments of particular persons have been taken away and given to others who made a better use of them? Hence the propriety of that exhortation, Rev. iii. 11: *Hold that fast which thou hast, that no man take thy crown.*

The gracious God never called a man to perform a work without furnishing him with adequate strength; and to refuse to do it on the pretence of inability is little short of rebellion against God.

This institution of the seventy persons to help Moses the rabbins consider as the origin of their grand council called the *Sanhedrin.* But we find that a council of seventy men, elders of Israel, had existed among the people a year before this time. See Exod. xxiv. 9; see the advice given by Jethro to Moses, Exod. xviii. 17, &c., and the notes thero.

Verse 22. *Shall the flocks and the herds be slain*] There is certainly a considerable measure of *weakness* and *unbelief* manifested in the complaints and questions

3

A. M. 2514. B. C. 1490. An. Exod. Isr. 2.

23 And the LORD said unto
Moses, [q] Is the LORD's hand
waxed short? thou shalt see now
whether [r] my word shall come to pass unto
thee or not.
24 And Moses went out, and told the people
the words of the LORD, and [s] gathered the
seventy men of the elders of the people, and
set them round about the tabernacle.
25 And the LORD [t] came down in a cloud,
and spake unto him, and took of the spirit that
was upon him, and gave *it* unto the seventy
elders: and it came to pass, *that*, [u] when the
spirit rested upon them, [v] they prophesied, and
did not cease.
26 But there remained two *of*
the men in the camp, the name
of the one *was* Eldad, and the
name of the other Medad: and the spirit rested
upon them: and they *were* of them that were
written, but [w] went not out unto the tabernacle: and they prophesied in the camp.
27 And there ran a young man, and told
Moses, and said, Eldad and Medad do prophesy in the camp.
28 And Joshua the son of Nun, the servant
of Moses, *one* of his young men, answered and
said, My lord Moses, [x] forbid them.
29 And Moses said unto him, Enviest thou
for my sake? [y] would God that all the LORD's

[q] Isa. l. 2; lix. 1.——[r] Chap. xxiii. 19; Ezek. xii. 25; xxiv. 14. [s] Ver. 16.——[t] Ver. 17; chap. xii. 5.——[u] See 2 Kings ii. 15. [v] See 1 Sam. x. 5, 6, 10; xix. 20, 21, 23; Joel ii. 29; Acts ii. 17, 18; 1 Cor. xiv. 1, &c.——[w] See 1 Sam. xx. 26; Jer. xxxvi. 5. [x] See Mark ix. 38; Luke ix. 49; John iii. 26.——[y] 1 Cor. xiv. 5.

of Moses on this occasion; but his conduct appears at the same time so very *simple, honest*, and *affectionate*, that we cannot but admire it, while we wonder that he had not stronger confidence in that God whose miracles he had so often witnessed in Egypt.

Verse 23. *Is the Lord's hand waxed short?*] Hast thou forgotten the miracles which I have already performed? or thinkest thou that my power is decreased? The power that is *unlimited* can never be *diminished*.

Verse 25. *When the spirit rested upon them, they prophesied*] By *prophesying* here we are to understand their performing those civil and sacred functions for which they were qualified; exhorting the people to quiet and peaceable submission, to trust and confidence in the goodness and providence of God, would make no small part of the duties of their new office. The ideal meaning of the word נבא *naba* is to *pray, entreat*, &c. The prophet is called נביא *nabi*, because he prays, supplicates, in reference to *God;* exhorts, entreats, in reference to *man*. See on Gen. xx. 7.

Verse 27. *Eldad and Medad do prophesy*] These, it seems, made two of the seventy elders; they were written, though they went not out to the tabernacle; they were enrolled as of the elders, but went not to meet God at the tabernacle, probably at that time prevented by some legal hinderance, but they continued in the camp using their new function in exhorting the people.

Verse 28. *My lord Moses, forbid them.*] Joshua was afraid that the authority and influence of his master Moses might be lessened by the part Eldad and Medad were taking in the government of the people, which might ultimately excite sedition or insurrection among them.

Verse 29. *Enviest thou for my sake?*] Art thou jealous of their influence only on my account? I am not alarmed; on the contrary, I would to God that all his people were endued with the same influence, and actuated by the same motives.

Persons may be under the especial direction of grace and providence while apparently performing a work out of *regular* order. And if the act be good and the effects good, we have no right to question the motive nor to forbid the work. What are order and regularity in the sight of man may be disorder and confusion in the sight of God, and *vice versa*. John wished to prevent a man from casting out demons in the name of Jesus, because he did not follow Christ in company with the disciples. Our Lord's conduct in that case should regulate ours in all similar ones; see Luke ix. 49, 50.

A late eminent divine and poet has made a good use of this transaction to illustrate that species of Divine call to the ministry, so instrumental in the salvation of myriads, which some have decried, because it appeared to them irregular, and not authorized by the hierarchy of the nation. I shall give this piece, not for the *amusement* but the *instruction* of the reader:—

Verse 27. *Eldad and Medad do prophesy, &c.*]

ELDAD, they said, and MEDAD there,
Irregularly bold,
By *Moses* uncommission'd, dare
A separate meeting hold!
And still whom none but heaven will own,
Men whom the world decry,
Men *authorized* by GOD *alone*,
Presume to prophesy!

Verse 28. *My lord Moses, forbid them.*]

How often have I blindly done
What zealous *Joshua* did,
Impatient to the rulers run,
And cried, "My *lords*, forbid!
Silence the schismatics, constrain
Their *thoughts* with ours t' agree,
And sacrifice the souls of men
To *idol* UNITY!"

Verse 29. *Enviest thou for my sake?*]

MOSES, the minister of God,
Rebukes our partial love,
Who envy at the gifts bestow'd
On those *we* disapprove.

A. M. 2514. B. C. 1490. An. Exod. Isr. 2.

people were prophets, *and* that the LORD would put his Spirit upon them!

30 And Moses gat him into the camp, he and the elders of Israel.

31 And there went forth a [a] wind from the LORD, and brought quails from the sea, and let *them* fall by the camp, [a] as it were a day's journey on this side, and as it were a day's journey on the other side, round about the camp; and as it were two cubits *high* upon the face of the earth.

32 And the people stood up all that day, and all *that* night, and all the next day, and they gathered the quails: he that gathered least gathered ten [b] homers; and they spread *them* all abroad for themselves round about the camp.

33 And while the [c] flesh *was* yet between their teeth, ere it was chewed, the wrath of the LORD was kindled against the people, and the LORD smote the people with a very great plague.

34 And he called the name of that place [d] Kibroth-hattaavah: because there they buried the people that lusted.

35 [e] *And* the people journeyed from Kibroth hattaavah unto Hazeroth; and [f] abode at Hazeroth.

---

[a] Exod. xvi. 13; Psa. lxxviii. 26, 27, 28; cv. 40.——[a] Heb. *as it were the way of a day.*——[b] Exod. xvi. 36; Ezek. xlv. 11.

[c] Psa. lxxviii. 30, 31.——[d] That is, *the graves of lust;* Deut. ix. 22.——[e] Chap. xxxiii. 17.——[f] Heb. *they were in,* &c.

We do not our own spirit know,
Who wish to see suppress'd
The men that *Jesu's* spirit show,
The men whom God hath bless'd.

Would God that all the Lord's people were prophets]
SHALL *we* the Spirit's course restrain,
Or quench the heavenly fire?
Let God his messengers ordain,
And whom he will *inspire.*
Blow as he list, the Spirit's choice
Of instruments we bless;
We will, if *Christ* be preached, rejoice,
And wish the word success.
Can all be *prophets* then? are all
Commission'd from above?
No: but whome'er the Lord shall call
We joyfully approve.
O that the Church might all receive
The spirit of prophecy,
And all in *Christ* accepted live,
And all in *Jesus* die!

Short Hymns on Select Passages of the Holy Scriptures, by Charles Wesley, M. A., and Presbyter of the Church of England. Bristol, 1762. *2 vols. 12mo.*

These sentiments are the more particularly remarkable as they come from one who was sufficiently bigoted to what was called ecclesiastical *orders* and *regularity.*

Verse 31. *A wind from the Lord*] An extraordinary one, not the effect of a natural cause. *And brought quails,* a bird which in great companies visits Egypt about the time of the year, March or April, at which the circumstance marked here took place. Mr. *Hasselquist,* the friend and pupil of the famous Linnæus, saw many of them about this time of the year, when he was in Egypt. See his Travels, p. 209.

Two cubits high *upon the face of the earth.*] We may consider the quails as *flying within two cubits of the ground;* so that the Israelites could easily take as many of them as they wished, while flying within the reach of their hands or their clubs. The common notion is, that the quails were brought round about the camp, and fell there in such multitudes as to lie two feet thick upon the ground; but the Hebrew will not bear this version. The Vulgate has expressed the sense, *Volabantque in aere duobus cubitis altitudine super terram.* "And they flew in the air, two cubits high above the ground."

Verse 32. *The people stood up, &c.*] While these immense flocks were flying at this short distance from the ground, fatigued with the strong wind and the distance they had come, they were easily taken by the people; and as various flocks continued to succeed each other for two days and a night, enough for a month's provision might be collected in that time. If the quails had fallen about the tents, there was no need to have stood up two days and a night in gathering them; but if they were on the wing, as the text seems to suppose, it was necessary for them to use despatch, and avail themselves of the passing of these birds whilst it continued. See Harmer, and see the note on Exod. xvi. 13.

And they spread them *all abroad*] Maillet observes that birds of all kinds come to Egypt for refuge from the cold of a northern winter; and that the people catch them, pluck, and bury them in the burning sand for a few minutes, and thus prepare them for use. This is probably what is meant by *spreading them all abroad round the camp.*

Some authors think that the word שלוים *salvim,* rendered *quails* in our translation, should be rendered *locusts.* There is no need of this conjecture; all difficulties are easily resolved without it. The reader is particularly referred to the note on Exod. xvi. 13.

Verse 33. *The wrath of the Lord was kindled*] In what way, and with what effects, we cannot precisely determine. Some heavy judgment fell upon these murmurers and complainers, but of what kind the sacred writer says nothing.

Verse 34. *Kibroth-hattaavah*] *The graves of lust;* and thus their scandalous crime was perpetuated by the name of the place.

1. ST. JUDE speaks of persons who were murmurers and complainers, walking after their own lusts, ver. 16, and seems to have this people particularly in view.

whom the sacred text calls μεμψιμοιροι, *complainers of their lot.* They could never be satisfied; even God himself could not please them, because they were ever preferring their own wisdom to his. God will save us in his own way, or not at all; because that way, being the plan of infinite wisdom, it is impossible that we can be saved in any other. How often have we professed to pray, "Thy will be done!" And how seldom, very seldom, have our hearts and lips corresponded! How careful should we be in all our prayers to ask nothing but what is perfectly consistent with the will of God! Many times our prayers and desires are such that, were they answered, our ruin would be inevitable. "Thy will be done!" is the greatest of all prayers; and he who would pray *safely* and successfully, must at least have the spirit of these words in all his petitions. The Israelites asked flesh when they should not have asked for it; God yields to their murmuring, and the death of multitudes of these murmurers was the consequence! We hear of such punishments, and yet walk in the same way, presuming on God's *mercy*, while we continue to provoke his *justice.* Let us settle it in our minds as an indisputable truth, that God is better acquainted with our wants than we are ourselves; that he knows infinitely better what we need; and that he is ever more ready to hear than we are to pray, and is wont to give more than we can desire or deserve.

2. In no case has God at any time withheld from his meanest followers any of the spiritual or temporal mercies they needed. Were he to call *us* to travel through a *wilderness*, he would send us *bread from heaven*, or cause the wilderness to smile and blossom as the rose. How strange is it that we will neither believe that God has worked, or will work, unless we see him working!

CHAPTER XII.

Miriam and Aaron raise a sedition against Moses, because of the Ethiopian woman he had married, 1, *and through jealousy of his increasing power and authority,* 2. *The character of Moses,* 3. *Moses, Aaron, and Miriam, are suddenly called to the tabernacle,* 4. *The Lord appears in the pillar of the cloud, and converses with them,* 5. *Declares his purpose to communicate his will to Moses only,* 6–8. *His anger is kindled against Miriam, and she is smitten with the leprosy,* 9, 10. *Aaron deplores his transgression, and entreats for Miriam,* 11, 12. *Moses intercedes for her,* 13. *The Lord requires that she be shut out of the camp for* seven *days,* 14. *The people rest till she is restored,* 15, *and afterwards leave* Hazeroth, *and pitch in the wilderness of* Paran, 16.

A. M. 2514. B. C. 1490. An. Exod. Isr. 2.

AND Miriam and Aaron spake against Moses because of the [a] Ethiopian woman whom he had married: for [b] he had [c] married an Ethiopian woman.
2 And they said, Hath the Lord indeed spoken only by Moses? [d] hath he not spoken also by us? And the Lord [e] heard *it*.
3 (Now the man Moses *was* [f] very meek, above all the men which *were* upon the face of the earth.)
4 [g] And the Lord spake suddenly unto Moses, and unto Aaron, and unto Miriam, Come out ye three unto the tabernacle of the congregation. And they three came out.
5 [h] And the Lord came down in the pillar of the cloud, and stood *in* the door of the

A. M. 2514. B. C. 1490. An. Exod. Isr. 2.

[a] Or, *Cushite.*——[b] Exod. ii. 21.——[c] Heb. *taken.*——[d] Exod. xv. 20; Mic. vi. 4.——[e] Gen. xxix. 33; chap. xi. 1; 2 Kings xix. 4; Isa. xxxvii. 4; Ezek. xxxv. 12, 13.——[f] Ecclus. xlv. 4.——[g] Psa. lxxvi. 9.——[h] Chap. xi. 25; xvi. 19.

NOTES ON CHAP. XII.

Verse 1. *Miriam and Aaron spake against Moses*] It appears that jealousy of the power and influence of Moses was the real cause of their complaint, though his having married an Ethiopian woman—האשה הכשית *haishshah haccushith*—THAT WOMAN, *the Cushite*, probably meaning *Zipporah*, who was an *Arab* born in the land of *Midian*—was the *ostensible* cause.

Verse 2. *Hath the Lord indeed spoken only by Moses?*] It is certain that both Aaron and Miriam had received a portion of the prophetic spirit, (see Exod. iv. 15, and xv. 20, and therefore they thought they might have a share in the *government;* for though there was no kind of *gain* attached to this government, and no honour but such as came from God, yet the love of power is natural to the human mind; and in many instances men will sacrifice even *honour, pleasure*, and *profit* to the *lust* of *power.*

Verse 3. *Now the man Moses* was *very meek*] How could Moses, who certainly was as *humble* and *modest* as he was *meek*, write this encomium upon himself? I think the word is not rightly understood; ענו *anav*, which we translate *meek*, comes from ענה *anah*, to *act upon*, to *humble, depress, afflict*, and is translated so in many places in the Old Testament; and in this sense it should be understood here: "Now this man Moses was *depressed* or *afflicted* more than any man האדמה *haadamah, of that land.*" And why was he so? Because of the great burden he had to bear in the care and government of this people, and because of their ingratitude and rebellion both against God and himself: of this depression and affliction, see the fullest proof in the preceding chapter. The very power they envied was oppressive to its possessor, and was more than either of *their* shoulders could sustain.

Verse 4. *And the Lord spake suddenly*] The sud

A. M. 2514.
B. C. 1490.
An. Exod. Isr.
2.

tabernacle, and called Aaron and
Miriam: and they both came forth.
6 And he said, Hear now my
words: If there be a prophet among you, *I* the
LORD will make myself known unto him [i] in a
vision, *and* will speak unto him [k] in a dream.
7 [l] My servant Moses *is* not so, [m] who *is*
faithful in all [n] mine house.
8 With him will I speak [o] mouth to mouth,
even [p] apparently, and not in dark speeches;
and [q] the similitude of the LORD shall he behold: wherefore then [r] were ye not afraid to
speak against my servant Moses?
9 And the anger of the LORD was kindled
against them; and he departed.
10 And the cloud departed from off the tabernacle; and, [s] behold, Miriam *became* [t] leprous,
white as snow: and Aaron looked
upon Miriam, and, behold, *she*
was leprous.
11 And Aaron said unto Moses, Alas, my
lord, I beseech thee, [u] lay not the sin upon us,
wherein we have done foolishly, and wherein
we have sinned.
12 Let her not be [v] as one dead, of whom
the flesh is half consumed when he cometh
out of his mother's womb.
13 And Moses cried unto the LORD, saying,
Heal her now, O God, I beseech thee.
14 And the LORD said unto Moses, [w] If her
father had but spit in her face, should she not
be ashamed seven days? let her be [x] shut out
from the camp seven days, and after that let
her be received in *again*.

[i] Gen. xv. 1; xlvi. 2; Job xxxiii. 15; Ezek. i. 1; Dan. viii. 2; x. 8, 16, 17; Luke i. 11, 22; Acts x. 11, 17; xxii. 17, 18. — [k] Gen. xxxi. 10, 11; 1 Kings iii. 5; Matt. i. 20. — [l] Psa. cv. 26. — [m] Heb. iii. 2, 5. — [n] 1 Tim. iii. 15. — [o] Exod. xxxiii. 11; Deut. xxxiv. 10. — [p] 1 Cor. xiii. 12. — [q] Exod. xxxiii. 19. — [r] 2 Pet. ii. 10; Jude 8. — [s] Deut. xxiv. 9. — [t] 2 Kings v. 27; xv. 5; 2 Chron. xxvi. 19, 20. — [u] 2 Sam. xix. 19; xxiv. 10; Prov. xxx. 32. — [v] Psa. lxxxviii. 4. — [w] See Heb. xii. 9. — [x] Lev. xiii. 46; chap. v. 2, 3.

den interference of God in this business shows at once the importance of the case and his displeasure.

Verse 6. *If there be a prophet*] We see here the different ways in which God usually made himself known to the prophets, viz., by *visions*—emblematic appearances, and by *dreams*, in which the future was announced by *dark speeches*, בחידת *bechidoth*, by enigmas or figurative representations, ver. 8. But to Moses God had communicated himself in a different way—he spoke to him *face to face, apparently*, showing him his glory: not in dark or enigmatical speeches; this could not be admitted in the case in which Moses was engaged, for he was to receive *laws* by Divine inspiration, the *precepts* and *expressions* of which must all be *ad captum vulgi*, within the reach of the meanest capacity. As Moses, therefore, was chosen of God to be the *lawgiver*, so was he chosen to see these laws duly enforced for the benefit of the people among whom he presided.

Verse 7. *Moses—is faithful*] נאמן *neeman*, a *prefect* or *superintendent*. So Samuel is termed, 1 Sam. ii. 35; iii. 20; David is so called, 1 Sam. xviii. 27, *Neeman*, and son-in-law of the king. Job, xii. 20, speaks of the *Neemanim* as a name of dignity. It seems also to have been a title of *respect* given to ambassadors, Prov. xiii. 17; xxv. 13. Calmet well observes that the word *fidelity* is often used for an employ, office, or dignity, and refers to 1 Chron. ix. 22, 26, 31; 2 Chron. xxxi. 12, 15; xxxiv. 12, &c. Moses was a faithful, well-tried servant in the house of God, and therefore he uses him as a familiar, and puts confidence in him.

Verse 10. *Miriam* became *leprous*] It is likely Miriam was *chief* in this mutiny; and it is probable that it was on this ground she is mentioned *first*, (see ver. 1,) and punished here, while Aaron is spared. Had he been smitten with the leprosy, his sacred character must have greatly suffered, and perhaps the *priesthood* itself have fallen into contempt. How many priests and preachers who deserved to be exposed to reproach and infamy, have been spared for the sake of the holy character they bore, that the ministry might not be blamed! But the just God will visit their transgressions in some other way, if they do not deeply deplore them and find mercy through Christ. Nothing tends to discredit the work of God so much as the transgressions and miscarriages of those who minister in holy things.

Verse 14. *If her father had but spit in her face*] This appears to have been done only in cases of great provocation on the part of the child, and strong irritation on the side of the parent. *Spitting in the face* was a sign of the deepest contempt. See Job xxx. 10; Isa. l. 6; Mark xiv. 65. In a case where a parent was obliged by the disobedient conduct of his child to treat him in this way, it appears he was banished from the father's presence for *seven days*. If then this was an allowed and judged case in matters of high provocation on the part of a child, should not the punishment be equally severe where the creature has rebelled against the Creator? Therefore Miriam was shut out of the camp for seven days, and thus debarred from coming into the presence of God her father, who is represented as dwelling among the people. To a soul who knows the value and inexpressible blessedness of communion with God, how intolerable must seven days of spiritual darkness be! But how indescribably wretched must their case be who are cast out into *outer darkness*, where the light of God no more shines, and where his approbation can no more be felt for ever! Reader, God save thee from so great a curse!

Several of the fathers suppose there is a great mystery hidden in the quarrel of Miriam and Aaron with Moses and Zipporah. Origen (and after him several others) speaks of it in the following manner:—

a

A. M. 2514.
B. C. 1490.
An. Exod. Isr.
2.

15 [y] And Miriam was shut out from the camp seven days: and the people journeyed not till Miriam was brought in *again*

16 And afterward the people removed from [z] Hazeroth, and pitched in the wilderness of Paran.

[y] Deut. xxiv. 9; 2 Chron. xxvi. 20, 21.

[z] Chap. xi. 35; xxxiii. 18.

"1. Zipporah, a *Cushite* espoused by *Moses*, evidently points out the choice which Jesus Christ has made of the *Gentiles* for his spouse and Church. 2. The jealousy of Aaron and Miriam against Moses and Zipporah signifies the hatred and envy of the Jews against Christ and the apostles, when they saw that the mysteries of the kingdom of heaven had been opened to the Gentiles, of which they had rendered themselves unworthy. 3. The *leprosy* with which Miriam was smitten shows the gross ignorance of the Jews, and the ruinous, disordered state of their religion, in which there is neither a head, a temple, nor a sacrifice. 4. Of none but Jesus Christ can it be said that he was the *most meek* and patient of men; that *he saw God face to face;* that he had every thing clearly revealed without enigmatical representations; and that he *was faithful in all the house of God.*" This, and much more, Origen states in the sixth and seventh homilies on the book of Numbers, and yet all this he considers as little in comparison of the vast mysteries that lie hidden in these accounts; for the shortness of the time, and the magnitude of the mysteries, only permit him "to pluck a few flowers from those vast fields—not as many as the exuberance of those fields afford, but only such as by their odour he was led to select from the rest." *Licebat tamen ex ingentibus campis paucos flosculos legere, et non quantum ager exuberet, sed quantum odoratui sufficiat, carpere.*

Verse 16. *The wilderness of Paran.*] This could not be the same Paran with that mentioned Deut. i. 1, for that was on the borders of the promised land, see the note on Deut. i. 1, 2; they were long near the borders of Canaan, and might have speedily entered into it, had it not been for their provocations and iniquities. They spent thirty-eight years in a journey which might have been accomplished in a few weeks! How many through their unfaithfulness have been *many years* in gaining that for which, in the ordinary procedure of Divine grace, a *few days* had been sufficient! How much ground may a man lose in the Divine life by one act of unfaithfulness or transgression! Israel wandered in the wilderness because Israel despised the pleasant land, and did not give credence to the word of the Lord. They would have a golden calf, and they had nothing but tribulation and wo in return

CHAPTER XIII.

Twelve men, *one out of every tribe, are sent to examine the nature and state of the land of Canaan*, 1–3. *Their* names, 4–16. *Moses gives them particular directions*, 17–20. *They proceed on their journey*, 21, 22. *Come to* Eshcol, *and cut down a branch with a cluster of grapes, which they bear between two of them upon a staff*, 23, 24. *After forty days they return to* Paran, *from searching the land, and show to Moses and the people the fruit they had brought with them*, 25, 26. *Their report—they acknowledge that the land is good, but that the inhabitants are such as the Israelites cannot hope to conquer*, 27–29. *Caleb endeavours to do away the bad impression made, by the report of his fellows, upon the minds of the people*, 30. *But the others persist in their former statement*, 31; *and greatly amplify the difficulties of conquest*, 32, 33.

A. M. 2514.
B. C. 1490.
An. Exod. Isr.
2.

AND the LORD spake unto Moses, saying,

2 [a] Send thou men, that they may search the land of Canaan, which I give unto the children of Israel: of every tribe of their fathers shall ye send a man, every one a ruler among them.

3 And Moses by the commandment of the LORD sent them [b] from the wilderness of Paran: all those men *were* heads of the children of Israel.

4 And these *were* their names: of the tribe of Reuben, Shammua the son of Zaccur.

[a] Chap. xxxii. 8; Deut. i. 22.

[b] Chap. xii. 16; xxxii. 8; Deut. i. 19; ix. 23.

NOTES ON CHAP. XIII.

Verse 2. *Send thou men, that they may search*] It appears from Deut. i. 19–24 that this was done in consequence of the request of the people, after the following address of Moses: "And when we departed from Horeb, we went through all that great and terrible wilderness—and we came unto Kadesh-Barnea; and I said unto you, Ye are come unto the mountain of the Amorites, which the Lord our God doth give unto us. Behold the Lord thy God hath set the land before thee: go up *and* possess *it*, as the Lord God of thy fathers hath said unto thee; fear not, neither be discouraged. And ye came near unto me every one of you, and said: WE WILL SEND MEN BEFORE US, AND THEY SHALL SEARCH US OUT THE LAND, and bring us word again, by what way we must go up, and into

A. M. 2514.
B. C. 1490.
An. Exod. Isr.
2.

5 Of the tribe of Simeon, Shaphat the son of Hori.
6 [c] Of the tribe of Judah, [d] Caleb the son of Jephunneh.
7 Of the tribe of Issachar, Igal the son of Joseph.
8 Of the tribe of Ephraim, [e] Oshea the son of Nun.
9 Of the tribe of Benjamin, Palti the son of Raphu.
10 Of the tribe of Zebulun, Gaddiel the son of Sodi.
11 Of the tribe of Joseph, *namely*, of the tribe of Manasseh, Gaddi the son of Susi.
12 Of the tribe of Dan, Ammiel the son of Gemalli.
13 Of the tribe of Asher, Sethur the son of Michael.
14 Of the tribe of Naphtali, Nahbi the son of Vophsi.
15 Of the tribe of Gad, Geuel the son of Machi.
16 These *are* the names of the men which Moses sent to spy out the land.
And Moses called [f] Oshea the son of Nun, Jehoshua.

A. M. 2514.
B. C. 1490.
An. Exod. Isr.
2.

17 And Moses sent them to spy out the land of Canaan, and said unto them, Get you up this *way* [g] southward, and go up into [h] the mountain:
18 And see the land, what it *is*; and the people that dwelleth therein, whether they *be* strong or weak, few or many;
19 And what the land *is* that they dwell in, whether it *be* good or bad; and what cities *they be* that they dwell in, whether in tents, or in strong holds;
20 And what the land *is*, whether it *be* [i] fat or lean, whether there be wood therein or not. And [k] be ye of good courage, and bring of the fruit of the land. (Now the time *was* the time of the first-ripe grapes.)
21 So they went up, and searched the land [l] from the wilderness of Zin unto [m] Rehob, as men come to Hamath.
22 And they ascended by the south, and

[c] Chap. xxxiv. 19; 1 Chron. iv. 15.—[d] Ver. 30; chap. xiv. 6, 30; Josh. xiv. 6, 7, 13, 14; Judg. i. 12.—[e] Ver. 16.—[f] Ver. 8; Exod. xvii. 9; chap. xiv. 6, 30.—[g] Ver. 21.

[h] Gen. xiv. 10; Judg. i. 9, 19.—[i] Neh. ix. 25, 35; Ezek. xxxiv. 14.—[k] Deut. xxxi. 6, 7, 23.—[l] Chap. xxxiv. 3; Josh. xv. 1.—[m] Josh. xix. 28.

what cities we shall come. And the saying pleased me well, and I took twelve men of you, one of a tribe," &c., &c. Nearly the whole of these verses is added *here* by the *Samaritan*.

Every one a ruler] Not any of the *princes* of the people, (see chap. i.,) for these names are different from those; but these now sent were men of consideration and importance in their respective tribes.

Verse 13. *Sethur, the son of Michael.*] It would have been strange had the numerous searches after the explanation of the mystical number 666, Rev. xiii. 18; xvii. 5, met with nothing to their purpose in the *name* of this son of Michael. סתור *Sethur*, from סתר *sathar*, to *hide* or *conceal*, signifies *hidden* or *mysterious*, and includes in it the numerical letters of the No. 666: ס 60, + ת 400, + ו 6, + ר 200, = 666. But of what utility can such expositions be to any subject of history or theology?

Verse 16. *And Moses called Oshea—Jehoshua.*] *Oshea*, Heb. הושע, should be written *Hoshea*: the word signifies *saved*, or a *saviour*, or *salvation*; but יהושע, *he shall save*, or *the salvation of God*; a *letter*, says Calmet, of the incommunicable name of God, being *added* to his former name. This was not the first time in which he had the name *Joshua*; see Exod. xvii. 9, and the note there. Some suppose he had this change of name in consequence of his victory over Amalek; see Exod. xvii. 13, 14.

Verse 18. *See the land, what it is*] What sort of a COUNTRY it is; how situated; its natural advantages or disadvantages.

And the people—whether they be *strong or weak*] Healthy, robust, hardy men; or little, weak, and pusillanimous.

Verse 20. *The land—whether it* be *fat or lean*] Whether the SOIL be *rich* or *poor*; which might be known by its being well *wooded*, and by the *fruits* it produced; and therefore they were desired to examine it as to the *trees*, &c., and to bring some of the *fruits* with them.

Verse 21. *From the wilderness of Zin*] The place called צן *Tsin*, here, is different from that called סין *Sin* or *Seen*, Exod. xvi. 1; the latter was nigh to *Egypt*, but the former was near *Kadesh Barnea*, not far from the borders of the promised land.

"The spies having left Kadesh Barnea, which was in the desert of *Paran*, see ver. 26, they proceeded to the desert of *Tsin*, all along the land of Canaan, nearly following the course of the river Jordan, till they came to Rehob, a city situated near Mount Libanus, at the northern extremity of the Holy Land, towards the road that leads to *Hamath*. Thence they returned through the midst of the same land by the borders of the Sidonians and Philistines, and passing by Mount Hebron, rendered famous by the residence of Abraham formerly, and by the gigantic descendants of *Anak* at that time, they passed through the valley of the brook of *Eshcol*, where they cut down the bunch of grapes mentioned ver. 23, and returned to the Israelitish camp after an absence of forty days," ver. 25. See *Calmet* on this place.

Verse 22. ***Hebron was built seven years before Zoan***

A. M. 2514.
B. C. 1490.
An. Exod. Isr. 2.

came unto Hebron; where [n] Ahiman, Sheshai, and Talmai, [o] the
children of Anak, *were.* (Now
[p] Hebron was built seven years before [q] Zoan
in Egypt.)
23 [r] And they came unto the [s] brook of
Eshcol, and cut down from thence a branch
with one cluster of grapes, and they bare it
between two upon a staff; and *they brought*
of the pomegranates, and of the figs.
24 The place was called the [t] brook [u] Eshcol, because of the cluster of grapes which the
children of Israel cut down from thence.
25 And they returned from searching of the
land after forty days.
26 And they went and came to Moses, and
to Aaron, and to all the congregation of the
children of Israel, [v] unto the wilderness of
Paran, to [w] Kadesh; and brought back word
unto them, and unto all the congregation, and
showed them the fruit of the land.
27 And they told him, and said,
We came unto the land whither
thou sentest us, and surely it
floweth with [x] milk and honey; [y] and this *is*
the fruit of it.
28 Nevertheless [z] the people *be* strong that
dwell in the land, and the cities *are* walled,
and very great; and moreover we saw [a] the
children of Anak there.
29 [b] The Amalekites dwell in the land of
the south: and the Hittites, and the Jebusites,
and the Amorites, dwell in the mountains;
and the Canaanites dwell by the sea, and by
the coast of Jordan.
30 And [c] Caleb stilled the people before
Moses, and said, Let us go up at once, and
possess it; for we are well able to overcome it.
31 [d] But the men that went up with him said,
We be not able to go up against the people;
for they *are* stronger than we.

[n] Josh. xi. 21, 22; xv. 13, 14; Judg. i. 10.——[o] Ver. 33. [p] Josh. xxi. 11.——[q] Psa. lxxviii. 12; Isa. xix. 11; xxx. 4.——[r] Deut. i. 24, 25.——[s] Or, *valley;* chap. xxxii. 9; Judg. xvi. 4.——[t] Or, *valley.*——[u] That is, *a cluster of grapes.* [v] Ver. 3.

[w] Chap. xx. 1, 16; xxxii. 8; xxxiii. 36; Deut. i. 19; Josh. xiv. 6.——[x] Exod. iii. 8; xxxiii. 3.——[y] Deut. i. 25.——[z] Deut. i. 28; ix. 1, 2.——[a] Ver. 33.——[b] Exod. xvii. 8; chap. xiv. 43; Judg. vi. 3; 1 Sam. xiv. 48; xv. 3, &c.——[c] See chap. xiv. 6, 24; Josh. xiv. 7.——[d] Chap. xxxii. 9; Deut. i. 28; Josh. xiv. 8.

In Egypt.] The *Zoan* of the Scriptures is allowed to be the *Tanis* of the heathen historians, which was the capital of Lower Egypt. Some think it was to humble the pride of the Egyptians, who boasted the highest antiquity, that this note concerning the higher antiquity of Hebron was introduced by Moses. Some have supposed that it is more likely to have been originally a *marginal note*, which in process of time crept into the text; but all the versions and all the MSS. that have as yet been collated, acknowledge it.

Verse 23. *They bare it between two upon a staff*] It would be very easy to produce a great number of witnesses to prove that grapes in the promised land, and indeed in various other hot countries, grow to a prodigious size. By *Calmet, Scheuchzer*, and *Harmer*, this subject has been exhausted, and to these I may refer the reader. Pliny mentions bunches of grapes in Africa each of which was larger than an *infant.*—*Radzvil* saw at Rhodes bunches of grapes three quarters of an ell in length, each grape as large as a plum. *Dandini* saw grapes of this size at Mount Libanus; and *Paul Lucas* mentions some bunches which he saw at Damascus that weighed above forty-five pounds. From the most authentic accounts the Egyptian grape is very *small*, and this being the only one with which the Israelites were acquainted, the great size of the grapes of *Hebron* would appear still more extraordinary. I myself once cut down a bunch of grapes nearly twenty pounds in weight. Those who live in cold climates can scarcely have any conception to what perfection both grapes and other fruits grow in climates that are warm, and where the soil is suitable to them.

From what is mentioned ver. 20, *Now the time was the time of the first-ripe grapes*, it is very probable that the spies received their orders about the beginning of August, and returned about the middle of September, as in those countries grapes, pomegranates, and figs, are ripe about this time; see Harmer, vol. i., p. 108–110. At Sheeraz, in Persia, I find from a MS. journal, that the small *white grape, askerie*, came into season August 6; and *pomegranates* September 6; and the large *red grape, sahibi*, September 10.

The spies' carrying the bunch of grapes on a staff between two men was probably not rendered necessary by the *size* of the bunch or cluster; but to preserve it from being *bruised*, that the Israelites might have a fair specimen of the fruit. As Joshua and Caleb were the only persons who gave a favourable account of the land, it is most likely that they were the persons who had gathered these fruits, and who brought them to the Israelitish camp. And it is likely they were gathered as short a time as possible before their return, that they might not be injured by the length of the time they had been separated from their respective trees.

Verse 27. *We came unto the land, &c.*] It is astonishing that men so dastardly as these should have had courage enough to risk their persons in searching the land. But probably though destitute of valour they had a sufficiency of cunning, and this carried them through. The report they brought was exceedingly discouraging, and naturally tended to produce the effect mentioned in the next chapter. The conduct of Joshua and Caleb was alone magnanimous, and worthy of the cause in which they were embarked.

A. M. 2514.
B. C. 1490.
An. Exod. Isr. 2.

32 And they [e] brought up an
evil report of the land which
they had searched unto the chil-
dren of Israel, saying, The land through which
we have gone to search it *is* a land that eateth
up the inhabitants thereof: and [f] all the people
that we saw in it *are* [g] men of a
great stature.
33 And there we saw the giants,
[h] the sons of Anak, *which come* of the giants
and we were in our own sight as [i] grasshoppers, and so we were [k] in their sight.

A. M. 2514.
B. C. 1490.
An. Exod. Isr. 2.

[e] Chap. xiv. 36, 37.——[f] Amos ii. 9.——[g] Heb. *men of statures.* [h] Deut. i. 28; ii. 10; ix. 2.——[i] Isa. xl. 22.——[k] 1 Sam. xvii. 42.

Verse 32. *Men of a great stature*] אנשי מדות *anshey middoth*, men of measures—two men's height; i. e., exceedingly tall men.

Verse 33. *There we saw the giants*] נפלים *nephilim.* It is evident that they had seen a robust, sturdy, warlike race of men, and of great stature; for the asserted fact is not denied by Joshua or Caleb.

Tales of *gigantic men* are frequent in all countries, but they are generally of such as have lived in times very *remote* from those in which such tales are told. That there have been *giants* at different times, in various parts of the earth, there can be no doubt; but that there ever was a nation of men twelve and fourteen feet high, we cannot, should not believe. *Goliath* appears to have been at least nine feet high: this was very extraordinary. I knew three young men in my own neighbourhood, two of them brothers, each of whom was upwards of seven feet, the third was eight feet six inches, and these men were very well proportioned. Others I have seen of extraordinary stature, but they were generally disproportioned, especially in their limbs. These instances serve to prove the possibility of cases of this nature. The *Anakim* might appear to the Israelites as a very tall, robust nation; and in comparison of the latter it is very probable that they were so, as it is very likely that the growth of the Israelites had been greatly cramped with their long and severe servitude in Egypt. And this may in some measure account for their alarm. On this subject the reader is desired to turn back to the note on Gen. vi. 4.

CANAAN was a type of the kingdom of God; the wilderness through which the Israelites passed, of the difficulties and trials to be met with in the present world. The promise of the kingdom of God is given to every believer; but how many are discouraged by the difficulties in the way! A slothful heart sees dangers, lions, and giants, every where; and therefore refuses to proceed in the heavenly path. Many of the *spies* contribute to this by the bad reports they bring of the heavenly country. Certain preachers allow "that the land is good, that it flows with milk and honey," and go so far as to show some of its fruits; but they discourage the people by stating the impossibility of overcoming their enemies. "Sin," say they, "cannot be destroyed in this life—it will always dwell in you—the *Anakim* cannot be conquered—we are but as grasshoppers against the Anakim," &c., &c. Here and there a Joshua and a Caleb, trusting alone in the power of God, armed with faith in the infinite efficacy of that blood which cleanses from all unrighteousness, boldly stand forth and say: "Their defence is departed from them, and the Lord is with us; let us go up at once and possess the land, for we are well able to overcome." We can do all things through Christ strengthening us: he will purify us unto himself, and give us that rest from sin here which his death has procured and his word has promised. Reader, canst thou not take God at his word? He has never yet failed thee. Surely then thou hast no reason to doubt. Thou hast never yet tried him to the uttermost. Thou knowest not how far and how fully he can save. Do not be dispirited: the sons of Anak shall fall before thee, if thou meet them in the name of the LORD of HOSTS.

CHAPTER XIV.

The whole congregation weep at the account brought by the spies, 1. *They murmur,* 2, 3; *and propose to make themselves a captain, and go back to Egypt,* 4. *Moses and Aaron are greatly affected,* 5. *Joshua and Caleb endeavour to appease and encourage the people,* 6–9. *The congregation are about to stone them,* 10. *The glory of the Lord appears, and he is about to smite the rebels with the pestilence,* 11, 12. *Moses makes a long and pathetic intercession in their behalf,* 13–19. *The Lord hears and forbears to punish,* 20; *but purposes that not one of that generation shall enter into the promised land save Joshua and Caleb,* 21–24. *Moses is commanded to turn and get into the wilderness by way of the Red Sea,* 25. *The Lord repeats his purpose that none of that generation shall enter into the promised land—that their carcasses shall fall in the wilderness, and that their children alone, with Joshua and Caleb, shall possess the land of the Canaanites, &c.,* 26–32. *As many days as they have searched the land shall they wander* years *in the desert, until they shall be utterly consumed,* 33–35. *All the spies save Joshua and Caleb die by a plague,* 36–38. *Moses declares God's purpose to the people, at which they are greatly affected,* 39. *They acknowledge their sin, and purpose to go up at once and possess the land,* 40. *Moses cautions them against resisting the purpose of God,* 41–43. *They, notwithstanding, presume to go, but Moses and the ark abide in the camp,* 44. *The Amalekites and Canaanites come down from the mountains, and defeat them,* 45.

A. M. 2514.
B. C. 1490.
An. Exod. Isr. 2.

AND all the congregation lifted
up their voice, and cried; and
[a] the people wept that night.
2 [b] And all the children of Israel murmured
against Moses and against Aaron: and the
whole congregation said unto them, Would
God that we had died in the land of Egypt! or
[c] would God we had died in this wilderness!
3 And wherefore hath the LORD brought us
unto this land, to fall by the sword, that our
wives and our children should be a prey? were
it not better for us to return into Egypt?
4 And they said one to another, [d] Let us
make a captain, and [e] let us return into Egypt.
5 Then [f] Moses and Aaron fell on their faces
before all the assembly of the congregation of
the children of Israel.
6 [g] And Joshua the son of Nun, and Caleb
the son of Jephunneh, *which were* of them
that searched the land, rent their clothes:
7 And they spake unto all the company of
the children of Israel, saying, [h] The land, which
we passed through to search it,
is an exceeding good land.
8 If the LORD [i] delight in us,
then he will bring us into this land, and give it
us; [k] a land which floweth with milk and
honey.
9 Only [l] rebel not ye against the LORD,
[m] neither fear ye the people of the land: for
[n] they *are* bread for us; their [o] defence is departed from them, [p] and the LORD *is* with us:
fear them not.
10 [q] But all the congregation bade stone them
with stones. And [r] the glory of the LORD appeared in the tabernacle of the congregation
before all the children of Israel.
11 And the LORD said unto Moses, How
long will this people [s] provoke me? and how
long will it be ere they [t] believe me, for all
the signs which I have showed among them.
12 I will smite them with the pestilence, and
disinherit them, and [u] will make of thee a
greater nation and mightier than they.

A. M. 2514.
B. C. 1490.
An. Exod. Isr. 2.

[a] Chap. xi. 4.——[b] Exod. xvi. 2; xvii. 3; chap. xvi. 41; Psa. cvi. 25.——[c] See ver. 28, 29.——[d] Neh. ix. 17.——[e] See Deut. xvii. 16; Acts vii. 39.——[f] Chap. xvi. 4, 22.——[g] Ver. 24, 30, 38; chap. xiii. 6, 8.——[h] Chap. xiii. 27; Deut. i. 25.——[i] Deut. x. 15; 2 Sam. xv. 25, 26; xxii. 20; 1 Kings x. 9; Psa. xxii. 8; cxlvii. 10, 11; Isa. lxii. 4.——[k] Chap. xiii. 27.——[l] Deut. ix. 7, 23, 24.——[m] Deut. vii. 18; xx. 3.——[n] Chap. xxiv. 8.——[o] Heb. *shadow*; Psa. cxxi. 5; Isa. xxx. 2, 3; Jer. xlviii. 45.

[p] Gen. xlviii. 21; Exod. xxxiii. 16; Deut. xx. 1, 3, 4; xxxi. 6, 8; Josh. i. 5; Judg. i. 22; 2 Chron. xiii. 12; xv. 2; xx. 17; xxxii. 8; Psa. xlvi. 7, 11; Isa. xli. 10; Amos v. 14; Zech. viii. 23.——[q] Exod. xvii. 4.——[r] Exod. xvi. 10; xxiv. 16, 17; xl. 34; Lev. ix. 23; chap. xvi. 19, 42; xx. 6.——[s] Ver. 23; Deut. ix. 7, 8, 22. Psa. xcv. 8; Heb. iii. 8, 16.——[t] Deut. i. 32; ix. 23; Psa. lxxviii. 22, 32, 42; cvi. 24; John xii. 37; Heb. iii. 18.——[u] Exod. xxxii. 10.

NOTES ON CHAP. XIV.

Verse 1. *Cried; and—wept that night.*] In almost every case this people gave deplorable evidence of the degraded state of their minds. With scarcely any mental firmness, and with almost no religion, they could bear no reverses, and were ever at their wit's end. They were headstrong, presumptuous, pusillanimous, indecisive, and fickle. And because they were such, therefore the power and wisdom of God appeared the more conspicuously in the whole of their history.

Verse 4. *Let us make a captain*] Here was a formal renunciation of the authority of Moses, and flat rebellion against God. And it seems from Neh. ix. 17 that they had actually appointed *another leader*, under whose direction they were about to return to Egypt. How astonishing is this! Their lives were made bitter, because of the rigour with which they were made to serve in the land of Egypt; and yet they are willing, yea *eager*, to get back into the same circumstances again! Great evils, when once some time *past*, affect the mind less than *present* ills, though much inferior. They had partly forgot their Egyptian bondage, and now smart under a little discouragement, having totally lost sight of their high calling, and of the power and goodness of God.

Verse 6. *And Joshua, &c.*] See on the preceding chapter, ver. 33.

Verse 9. *Their defence*] צלם *tsillam, their shadow*, a metaphor highly expressive of *protection* and *support* in the sultry eastern countries. The *protection* of God is so called; see Psa. xci. 1; cxxi. 5; see also Isa. li. 16; xlix. 2; xxx. 2.

The Arabs and Persians have the same word to express the same thing. نمايند ظل دولت ممدود باد *nemayeed zulli doulet mamdood bad.* "May the *shadow* of thy prosperity be extended!" نمايند ظل دولت برمفارق خيرخواهي ممدود باد *nemayeed zulli doulet ber mufareki khayr khwahen mamdood bad.* "May the *shadow* of thy prosperity be spread over the heads of thy well-wishers!" They have also the following elegant distich:—

سايهات كم مباد از سرما
بسط الله ظلكم ابدا

Sayahat kem mubad az seri ma
Bast Allah zullikem abeda.

"May thy protection never be removed from my head!
May God extend thy *shadow* eternally!"

Here the Arabic ظل *zull* answers exactly to the Hebrew צל *tsel*, both signifying that which *overspreads* or *overshadows*. See the note on ver. 14.

Verse 10. *The glory of the Lord appeared*] This timely appearance of the Divine glory prevented these faithful servants of God from being stoned to death by this base and treacherous multitude. "Every man is immortal till his work is done," while in simplicity of heart he is following his God.

A. M. 2514.
B. C. 1490.
An. Exod. Isr.
2.

13 And [v] Moses said unto the
LORD, Then the Egyptians shall
hear *it*, (for thou broughtest up
this people in thy might from among them ;)
14 And they will tell *it* to the inhabitants of
this land; [w] *for* they have heard that thou
LORD *art* among this people, that thou LORD
art seen face to face, and *that* [x] thy cloud
standeth over them, and *that* thou goest before
them, by day-time in a pillar of a cloud, and
in a pillar of fire by night.
15 Now *if* thou shalt kill *all* this people as
one man, then the nations which have heard
the fame of thee will speak, saying,
16 Because the LORD was not [y] able to bring
this people into the land which he sware unto
them, therefore he hath slain them in the wilderness.
17 And now, I beseech thee, let the power
of my LORD be great, according as thou hast
spoken, saying,
18 The LORD *is* [z] longsuffering, and of great
mercy, forgiving iniquity and transgression, and
by no means clearing *the guilty*, [a] visiting the
iniquity of the fathers upon the
children unto the third and fourth
generation.

A. M. 2514.
B. C. 1490.
An. Exod. Isr.
2.

19 [b] Pardon, I beseech thee, the iniquity of
this people [c] according unto the greatness of
thy mercy, and [d] as thou hast forgiven this
people, from Egypt even [e] until now.
20 And the LORD said, I have pardoned [f] according to thy word :
21 But *as* truly *as* I live, [g] all the earth shall
be filled with the glory of the LORD.
22 [h] Because all those men which have seen
my glory, and my miracles, which I did in
Egypt and in the wilderness, have tempted me
now [i] these ten times, and have not hearkened
to my voice ;
23 [k] Surely [l] they shall not see the land
which I sware unto their fathers, neither shall
any of them that provoke me see it :
24 But my servant [m] Caleb, because he had
another spirit with him, and [n] hath followed
me fully, him will I bring into the land whereinto he went; and his seed shall possess it.
25 (Now the Amalekites and the Canaanites

[v] Exod. xxxii. 12 ; Psa. cvi. 23 ; Deut. ix. 26, 27, 28 ; xxxii. 27 ; Ezek. xx. 9, 14.——[w] Exod. xv. 14 ; Josh. ii. 9, 10 ; v. 1. Exod. xiii. 21 ; xl. 38 ; chap. x. 34 ; Neh. ix. 12 ; Psa. lxxviii. 14 ; cv. 39.——[y] Deut. ix. 28 ; Josh. vii. 9.——[z] Exod. xxxiv. 6, 7 ; Psa. ciii. 8 ; cxlv. 8 ; Jonah iv. 2.——[a] Exod. xx. 5 ; xxxiv. 7.——[b] Exod. xxxiv. 9.

[c] Psa. cvi. 45.——[d] Psa. lxxviii. 38.——[e] Or, *hitherto*.——[f] Psa. cvi. 23 ; James v. 16 ; 1 John v. 14, 15, 16.——[g] Psa. lxxii. 19.——[h] Deut. i. 35 ; Psa. xcv. 11 ; cvi. 26 ; Heb. iii. 17, 18.——[i] Gen. xxxi. 7.——[k] Chap. xxxii. 11 ; Ezek. xx. 15.——[l] Heb. *if they see the land*.——[m] Deut. i. 36 ; Josh. xiv. 6, 8, 9, 14.——[n] Chap. xxxii. 12.

Verse 14. That *thy cloud standeth over them*] This *cloud*, the symbol of the Divine glory, and proof of the Divine presence, appears to have assumed *three* different forms for three important purposes.

1. It appeared by day in the form of a *pillar* of a sufficient height to be seen by all the camp, and thus went before them to point out their way in the desert. Exod. xl. 38.

2. It appeared by night as a pillar of fire to give them light while travelling by night, which they probably *sometimes* did ; (see chap. ix. 21 ;) or to illuminate their tents in their encampments ; Exod. xiii. 21, 22.

3. It stood at certain times *above* the whole congregation, overshadowing them from the scorching rays of the sun ; and probably at other times condensed the vapours, and precipitated rain or dew for the refreshment of the people. *He spread a cloud for their covering ; and fire to give light in the night ;* Psa. cv. 39. It was probably from this circumstance that *the shadow of the Lord* was used to signify the Divine *protection*, not only by the Jews, but also by other Asiatic nations. See the note on ver. 9, and see particularly the note on Exod. xiii. 21.

Verse 18. *The Lord* is *longsuffering*] See the note on Exod. xxxiv. 6.

Verse 19. *Pardon, I beseech thee, the iniquity of this people*] From ver. 13 to ver. 19 inclusive we have the words of Moses's intercession ; they need no explanation, they are full of simplicity and energy ; his arguments with God (for he did reason and argue with his Maker) are pointed, cogent, and respectful ; and while they show a heart full of humanity, they evidence the deepest concern for the glory of God. The *argumentum ad hominem* is here used in the most unexceptionable manner, and with the fullest effect.

Verse 20. *I have pardoned*] That is, They shall not be cut off *as* they deserve, because thou hast interceded for their lives.

Verse 21. *All the earth shall be filled, &c.*] כל הארץ *kol haarets, all* THIS *land*, i. e., the land of Canaan ; which was only fulfilled to the letter when the preaching of Christ and his apostles was heard through all the cities and villages of Judea. It does not appear that the whole of the terraqueous globe is meant by this expression in any of the places where it occurs connected with this promise of the diffusion of the Divine light. See Psa. lxxii. 19 ; Isa. xl. 5 ; Hab. ii. 14.

Verse 24. *But my servant Caleb, &c.*] Caleb had *another spirit*—not only a bold, generous, courageous, noble, and heroic spirit ; but the Spirit and influence of the God of heaven thus raised him above human inquietudes and earthly fears, therefore he *followed God fully ;* וימלא אחרי *vaimalle acharai*, literally, *he filled after me :* God showed him the *way* he was to take, and the *line* of conduct he was to pursue, and he *filled*

A. M. 2514.
B. C. 1490.
An. Exod. Isr. 2.

dwelt in the valley.) To-morrow turn you, [o] and get you into the wilderness by the way of the Red Sea.

26 And the LORD spake unto Moses and unto Aaron, saying,

27 [p] How long *shall I bear with* this evil congregation, which murmur against me? [q] I have heard the murmurings of the children of Israel, which they murmur against me.

28 Say unto them, [r] *As truly as* I live, saith the LORD, [s] as ye have spoken in mine ears, so will I do to you:

29 Your carcasses shall fall in this wilderness; and [t] all that were numbered of you, according to your whole number, from twenty years old and upward, which have murmured against me,

30 Doubtless ye shall not come into the land, *concerning* which I [u] sware to make you dwell therein, [v] save Caleb the son of Jephunneh, and Joshua the son of Nun.

31 [w] But your little ones, which ye said should be a prey, them will I bring in, and they shall know the land which [x] ye have despised.

32 But *as for* you, [y] your carcasses, they shall fall in this wilderness.

33 And your children shall [z] wander [a] in the wilderness [b] forty years, and [c] bear your whoredoms, until your carcasses be wasted in the wilderness.

34 [d] After the number of the days in which ye searched the land, *even* [e] forty days, each day for a year, shall ye bear your iniquities, *even* forty years, [f] and ye shall know [g] my breach of promise.

35 [h] I the LORD have said, I will surely do it unto all [i] this evil congregation, that are gathered together against me: in this wilderness they shall be consumed, and there they shall die.

36 [k] And the men, which Moses sent to search the land, who returned, and made all the congregation to murmur against him, by bringing up a slander upon the land,

37 Even those men that did bring up the evil report upon the land, [l] died by the plague before the LORD.

38 [m] But Joshua the son of Nun, and Caleb

[o] Deut. i. 40.—[p] Ver. 11; Exod. xvi. 28; Matt. xvii. 7.—[q] Exod. xvi. 12.—[r] Ver. 23; chap. xxvi. 65; xxxii. 11; Deut. i. 35; Heb. iii. 17.—[s] See ver. 2.—[t] Chap. i. 45; xxvi. 64.—[u] Heb. *lifted up my hand;* Gen. xiv. 22.—[v] Ver. 38; chap. xxvi. 65; xxxii. 12; Deut. i. 36, 38.—[w] Deut. i. 39.—[x] Psa. cvi. 24.—[y] 1 Cor. x. 5; Heb. iii. 17.—[z] Or, *feed.*—[a] Chap. xxxii. 13; Psa. cvii. 40.—[b] See Deut. ii. 14.—[c] Ezek. xxiii. 35.—[d] Chap. xiii. 25.—[e] Psa. xcv. 10; Ezek. iv. 6.—[f] See 1 Kings viii. 56; Psa. lxxvii. 8; cv. 42; Heb. iv. 1.—[g] Or, *altering of my purpose.*—[h] Chap. xxiii. 19.—[i] Ver. 27, 29; chap. xxvi. 65; 1 Cor. x. 5.—[k] Chap. xiii. 31, 32.—[l] 1 Cor. x. 10; Heb iii. 17; Jude 5.—[m] Chap. xxvi. 65; Josh. xiv. 6, 10.

up this line, and in all things *followed* the will of his Maker. *He* therefore shall see the promised land, and *his* seed shall possess it. A *dastardly* spirit in the things of God is a heavy curse. How many are retarded in their course, and fall short of the blessings of the Gospel, through magnifying the *number* and *strength* of their adversaries, their own weakness and the difficulties of the way, with which we may connect their distrust of the power, faithfulness, and goodness of God! And how many are prevented from receiving the higher degrees of salvation by foolishly attributing insurmountable power, either to their inward corruptions or outward enemies! Only such men as Joshua and Caleb, who take God at his word, and who know that against his wisdom no cunning can stand, and against his might no strength can prevail, are likely to *follow God fully*, and receive the heights, lengths, breadths, and depths of the salvation of God.

Verse 34. *After the number of the days*] The spies were *forty days* in searching the land, and the people who rebelled on their evil report are condemned to wander *forty years* in the wilderness! Now let them make them a captain and go back to Egypt *if they can*. God had so hedged them about with his power and providence that they could neither go back to Egypt nor get forward to the promised land! God has provided innumerable *spiritual* blessings for mankind, but in the pursuit of *earthly* good they lose them, and often lose the others also! *If ye be willing and obedient, ye shall eat the fruit of the land*, but not *otherwise;* unless for your farther punishment God give you your portion *in* THIS *life*, and ye get none in the life to come. From so great a curse may God save *thee*, thou money-loving, honour-hunting, pleasure-taking, thoughtless, godless man!

And ye shall know my breach of promise.] This is certainly a most harsh expression; and most learned men agree that the words את תנואתי *eth tenuathi* should be translated *my vengeance*, which is the rendering of the *Septuagint, Vulgate, Coptic*, and *Anglo-Saxon;* and which is followed by almost all our ancient *English* translations. The meaning however appears to be this: As God had promised to bring them into the good land, provided they kept his statutes, ordinances, &c., and they had now broken their engagements, he was no longer held by his covenant; and therefore, by excluding them from the promised land, he showed them at once his *annulling of the covenant* which they had broken, and his *vengeance* because they had broken it.

Verse 37. *Those men that did bring up the evil report—died*] Thus *ten* of the twelve that searched out the land were struck dead, by the justice of God, on the spot! *Caleb*, of the tribe of Judah, and *Joshua*, of the tribe of Ephraim, alone escaped, because they had

A. M. 2514.
B. C. 1490.
An. Exod. Isr.
2.

the son of Jephunneh, *which were*
of the men that went to search
the land, lived *still.*
39 And Moses told those sayings unto all
the children of Israel: [n] and the people mourned greatly.
40 And they rose up early in the morning,
and gat them up into the top of the mountain,
saying, Lo, [o] we *be here,* and will go up unto
the place which the LORD hath promised: for
we have sinned.
41. And Moses said, Wherefore now do ye
transgress [p] the commandment of the LORD?
but it shall not prosper.
42 [q] Go not up, for the LORD *is* not among
you; that ye be not smitten
before your enemies.
43 For the Amalekites and the
Canaanites *are* there before you, and ye shall
fall by the sword: [r] because ye are turned
away from the LORD, therefore the LORD will
not be with you.
44 [s] But they presumed to go up unto the
hill top: nevertheless the ark of the covenant
of the LORD, and Moses, departed not out of
the camp.
45 [t] Then the Amalekites came down, and
the Canaanites which dwelt in that hill, and
smote them, and discomfited them, *even* unto
[u] Hormah.

[n] Exod. xxxiii. 4.——[o] Deut. i. 41.——[p] Ver. 25; 2 Chron. xxiv. 20.——[q] Deut. i. 42.——[r] 2 Chron. xxiv. 2.——[s] Deut. i. 43.——[t] Ver. 43; Deut. i. 44.——[u] Chap. xxi. 3; Judg. i. 17.

followed God fully. Let preachers of God's word take heed how they straiten the way of salvation, or render, by unjust description, that way perplexed and difficult which God has made plain and easy.

Verse 40. *We—will go up unto the place, &c.*] They found themselves on the very borders of the land, and they heard God say they should not enter it, but should be consumed by a forty years' wandering in the wilderness; notwithstanding, they are determined to render vain this purpose of God, probably supposing that the temporary sorrow they felt for their late rebellion would be accepted as a sufficient atonement for their crimes! They accordingly went up, and were cut down by their enemies; and why? God went not with them. How vain is the counsel of man against the wisdom of God! Nature, poor, fallen human nature, is ever running into extremes. This miserable people, a short time ago, thought that though they had Omnipotence with them they could not conquer and possess the land! Now they imagine that though God himself go not with them, yet they shall be sufficient to drive out the inhabitants, and take possession of their country! Man is ever supposing he can either do *all things* or *do nothing;* he is therefore sometimes *presumptuous,* and at other times in *despair.* Who but an apostle, or one under the influence of the *same* Spirit, can say, *I can do* ALL THINGS THROUGH CHRIST *who strengtheneth me?*

CHAPTER XV.

Directions concerning the different offerings they should bring unto the Lord when they should come to the land of Canaan, 1–3. *Directions relative to the* meat-offering, 4; *to the* drink-offering, 5. *Of the* burnt-offering, vow-offering, peace-offering, drink-offering, *&c.,* 6–12. *All born in the country must perform these rites,* 13, *and the strangers also,* 14–16. *They shall offer unto the Lord a* heave-offering *of the* first-fruits *of the land,* 17–21. *Concerning omissions through ignorance, and the sacrifices to be offered on such occasions,* 22–29. *He who sins* presumptuously *shall be cut off,* 30, 31. *History of the person who* gathered sticks on the Sabbath, 32. *He is brought to Moses and Aaron,* 33. *They put him in confinement till the mind of the Lord should be known on the case,* 34. *The Lord commands him to be* stoned, 35. *He is stoned to death,* 36. *The Israelites are commanded to make* fringes *to the borders of their garments,* 37, 38. *The end for which these fringes were to be made,* that *they might remember the commandments of the Lord, that they might be holy,* 39–41.

A. M. 2514.
B. C. 1490.
An. Exod. Isr.
2.

AND the LORD spake unto
Moses, saying,
2 [a] Speak unto the children of
Israel, and say unto them, When ye be come
into the land of your habitations,
which I give unto you,
3 And [b] will make an offering
by fire unto the LORD, a burnt-offering, or a

[a] Ver. 18; Lev. xxiii. 10; Deut. vii. 1.——[b] Lev. i. 2, 3.

NOTES ON CHAP. XV.

Verse 2. *When ye be come into the land*] Some learned men are of opinion that several offerings prescribed by the law were not intended to be made in the *wilderness,* but in the promised land; the former not affording those conveniences which were necessary to the complete observance of the Divine worship in this and several other respects.

Verse 3. *And will make an offering*] For the different kinds of offerings, sacrifices, &c., see Lev. i. 2, and vii.

A. M. 2514.
B. C. 1490.
An. Exod. Isr.
2.

sacrifice [c] in [d] performing a vow, or in a freewill-offering, or [e] in your solemn feasts, to make a [f] sweet savour unto the LORD, of the herd, or of the flock:

4 Then [g] shall he that offereth his offering unto the LORD bring [h] a meat-offering of a tenth deal of flour mingled [i] with the fourth *part* of a hin of oil.

5 [k] And the fourth *part* of a hin of wine for a drink-offering shalt thou prepare with the burnt-offering or sacrifice, for one lamb.

6 [l] Or for a ram, thou shalt prepare *for* a meat-offering, two tenth deals of flour mingled with the third *part* of a hin of oil.

7 And for a drink-offering thou shalt offer the third *part* of a hin of wine, *for* a sweet savour unto the LORD.

8 And when thou preparest a bullock *for* a burnt-offering, or *for* a sacrifice in performing a vow, or [m] peace-offerings unto the LORD:

9 Then shall he bring [n] with a bullock a meat-offering of three tenth deals of flour mingled with half a hin of oil.

10 And thou shalt bring for a drink-offering half a hin of wine, *for* an offering made by fire, [o] of a sweet savour unto the LORD.

11 [p] Thus shall it be done for one bullock, or for one ram, or for a lamb, or a kid.

12 According to the number that ye shall prepare, so shall ye do to every one according to their number.

13 All that are born of the country shall do these things after this manner, in offering an offering made by fire, of a sweet savour unto the LORD.

A. M. 2514.
B. C. 1490.
An. Exod. Isr.
2.

14 And if a stranger sojourn with you, or whosoever *be* among you in your generations, and will offer an offering made by fire, of a sweet savour unto the LORD; as ye do, so he shall do.

15 [q] One ordinance *shall be both* for you of the congregation, and also for the stranger that sojourneth *with you,* an ordinance for ever in your generations: as ye *are,* so shall the stranger be before the LORD.

16 One law and one manner shall be for you, and for the stranger that sojourneth with you.

17 And the LORD spake unto Moses, saying,

18 [r] Speak unto the children of Israel, and say unto them, When ye come into the land whither I bring you,

19 Then it shall be, that, when ye eat of [s] the bread of the land, ye shall offer up a heave-offering unto the LORD.

20 [t] Ye shall offer up a cake of the first of your dough *for* a heave-offering: as *ye do* [u] the heave-offering of the threshing-floor, so shall ye heave it.

21 Of the first of your dough ye shall give unto the LORD a heave-offering in your generations.

22 And [v] if ye have erred, and not observed all these commandments, which the LORD hath spoken unto Moses,

[c] Lev. vii. 16; xxii. 18, 21.——[d] Heb. *separating;* Lev. xxvii. 2.——[e] Lev. xxiii. 8, 12, 36; chap. xxviii. 19, 27; xxix. 2, 8, 13; Deut. xvi. 10.——[f] Gen. viii. 21; Exod. xxix. 18.——[g] Lev. ii. 1; vi. 14.——[h] Exod. xxix. 40; Lev. xxiii. 13.——[i] Lev. xiv. 10; chap. xxviii. 5.

[k] Chap. xxviii. 7, 14.——[l] Chap. xxviii. 12, 14.——[m] Lev. vii. 11.——[n] Chap. xxviii. 12, 14.——[o] Ecclus. l. 15.——[p] Chapter xxviii.——[q] Ver. 29; Exod. xii. 49; chap. ix. 14.——[r] Verse 2; Deut. xxvi. 1.——[s] Josh. v. 11, 12.——[t] Deut. xxvi. 2, 10; Prov. iii. 9, 10.——[u] Lev. ii. 14; xxiii. 10, 16.——[v] Lev. iv. 2.

Verse 5. *The fourth* part *of a hin*] The quantity of meal and flour was augmented in proportion to the *size* of the sacrifice with which it was offered. With a LAMB OR A KID were offered *one* tenth deal of flour, (the tenth part of an ephah, see on Exod. xxix. 40,) the *fourth* part of a hin of *oil*, and the *fourth* part of a hin of *wine*. With a RAM, *two* tenth deals of flour, a *third* part of a hin of *oil*, and a *third* part of a hin of *wine*. With a BULLOCK, *three* tenth deals of flour, *half* a hin of *oil*, and *half* a hin of *wine*. See ver. 4–11.

Verse 14. *If a stranger sojourn*] See the notes on Lev. xix. 33; xxii. 9. When the case of the Jewish people is fairly considered, and their situation with respect to the surrounding idolatrous nations, we shall see the absolute necessity of having but one *form* of *worship* in the land. That alone was genuine which was prescribed by the Almighty, and no others could be tolerated, because they were idolatrous. All *strangers*—all that came to *sojourn* in the land, were required to conform to it; and it was right that those who did conform to it should have equal rights and privileges with the Hebrews themselves, which we find was the case. But under the Christian dispensation, as no particular *form* of worship is prescribed, the types and ceremonies of the Mosaic institution being all fulfilled, unlimited toleration should be allowed; and while the sacred writings are made the basis of the worship offered to God, every man should be allowed to worship according to his own conscience, for in this respect every one is

"Lord of himself, accountable to none
But to his conscience and his God alone."

Verse 20. *Ye shall offer—the first of your dough*] Concerning the offerings of *first-fruits*, see the notes on Exod. xxii. 29.

A. M. 2514. B. C. 1490. An. Exod. Isr. 2.

23 *Even* all that the LORD hath commanded you by the hand of Moses, from the day that the LORD commanded *Moses*, and henceforward among your generations;

24 Then it shall be, [w] if *aught* be committed by ignorance, [x] without the knowledge of the congregation, that all the congregation shall offer one young bullock for a burnt-offering, for a sweet savour unto the LORD, [y] with his meat-offering, and his drink-offering, according to the [z] manner, and [a] one kid of the goats for a sin-offering.

25 [b] And the priest shall make an atonement for all the congregation of the children of Israel, and it shall be forgiven them; for it *is* ignorance: and they shall bring their offering, a sacrifice made by fire unto the LORD, and their sin-offering before the LORD, for their ignorance:

26 And it shall be forgiven all the congregation of the children of Israel, and the stranger that sojourneth among them; seeing all the people *were* in ignorance.

27 And [c] if any soul sin through ignorance, then he shall bring a she-goat of the first year for a sin-offering.

28 [d] And the priest shall make an atonement for the soul that sinneth ignorantly, when he sinneth by ignorance before the LORD, to make an atonement for him; and it shall be forgiven him.

29 [e] Ye shall have one law for him that [f] sinneth through ignorance, *both for* him that is born among the children of Israel, and for the stranger that sojourneth among them.

A. M. 2514. B. C. 1490. An. Exod. Isr. 2.

30 [g] But the soul that doeth *aught* [h] presumptuously, *whether he be* born in the land, or a stranger, the same reproacheth the LORD; and that soul shall be cut off from among his people.

31 Because he hath [i] despised the word of the LORD, and hath broken his commandment, that soul shall utterly be cut off; [k] his iniquity *shall be* upon him.

32 And while the children of Israel were in the wilderness, [l] they found a man that gathered sticks upon the Sabbath day.

33 And they that found him gathering sticks brought him unto Moses and Aaron, and unto all the congregation.

34 And they put him [m] in ward, because it was not declared what should be done to him.

35 And the LORD said unto Moses, [n] The man shall be surely put to death: all the congregation shall [o] stone him with stones without the camp.

36 And all the congregation brought him without the camp, and stoned him with stones, and he died; as the LORD commanded Moses.

37 And the LORD spake unto Moses, saying,

38 Speak unto the children of Israel, and bid [p] them that they make them fringes in the bor

[w] Lev. iv. 13.——[x] Heb. *from the eyes.*——[y] Ver. 8, 9, 10.——[z] Or, *ordinance.*——[a] See. Lev. iv. 23; chap. xxviii. 15; Ezra vi. 17; viii. 35.——[b] Lev. iv. 20.——[c] Lev. iv. 27, 28.——[d] Lev. iv. 35.——[e] Ver. 15.——[f] Heb. *doth.*——[g] Deut. xvii. 12; Psa. xix. 13; Heb. x. 26; 1 Pet. ii. 10.

[h] Heb. *with a high hand.*——[i] 2 Sam. xii. 9; Prov. xiii. 13.——[k] Lev. v. 1; Ezek. xviii. 20.——[l] Exod. xxxi. 14, 15; xxxv. 2, 3.——[m] Lev. xxiv. 12.——[n] Exod. xxxi. 14, 15.——[o] Lev. xxiv. 14; 1 Kings xxi. 13; Acts vii. 58.——[p] Deut. xxii. 12; Matt. xxiii. 5.

Verse 24. *If* aught *be committed by ignorance*] See the notes on Lev. iv. 2, and v. 17. The case here probably refers to the whole congregation; the cases above, to the sin of an individual.

Verse 25. *The priest shall make an atonement*] Even sins committed through ignorance required an atonement; and God in his mercy has provided one for them.

Verse 30. *But the soul that doeth* aught *presumptuously*] Bold daring acts of transgression against the fullest evidence, and in *despite* of the Divine authority, admitted of no atonement; the person was to be *cut off*—to be excluded from God's people, and from all their privileges and blessings.

Probably the presumption mentioned here implied an utter contempt of the word and authority of God, springing from an *idolatrous* or *atheistical* mind. In such a case all repentance was precluded, because of the denial of the *word* and *being* of God. It is probably a case similar to that mentioned Heb. vi. 4–8; x. 26–31; on which passages see the notes.

Verse 32. *They found a man that gathered sticks upon the Sabbath*] This was in all likelihood a case of that kind supposed above: the man despised the word of the Lord, and therefore broke his commandment; see ver. 31. On this ground he was punished with the utmost rigour of the law.

Verse 36. *Stoned him*] See the note on Lev. xxiv. 23.

Verse 38. *Bid them—make them fringes*] We learn from ver. 39 that these *fringes* were emblematical of the various *commands* of God. That there was any analogy between a *fringe* and a *precept*, it would be bold to assert; but when a thing is appointed to *represent* another, no matter how different, that first object becomes the regular representative or sign of the other. There is no analogy between the term *bread* and the *farinaceous* nutritive substance thereby signified; but

a

A. M. 2514. B. C. 1490. An. Exod. Isr. 2.

ders of their garments throughout their generations, and that they put upon the fringe of the borders a ribbon of blue:

39 And it shall be unto you for a fringe, that ye may look upon it, and remember all the commandments of the LORD, and do them; and that ye [q] seek not after your own heart and your own eyes, after which ye use [r] to go a whoring:

40 That ye may remember, and do all my commandments, and be [s] holy unto your God.

41 I *am* the LORD your God, which brought you out of the land of Egypt, to be your God: I *am* the LORD your God.

A. M. 2514. B. C. 1490. An. Exod. Isr. 2.

[q] See Deut. xxix. 19; Job xxxi. 7; Jer. ix. 14; Ezek. vi. 9. — [r] Psa. lxxiii. 27; cvi. 39; James iv. 4. — [s] Lev. xi. 44, 45; Rom. xii. 1; Col. i. 22; 1 Pet. i. 15, 16.

because this term is used to express and represent that thing, every person thus understands it; and when the word *bread* is seen or heard, a perfect knowledge, not of the *letters* which compose that word, but of the *thing* signified by it, is conveyed to the mind. So the *fringes*, being appointed by God to represent and bring to mind the *commandments* of God, ver. 39, the mention or sight of them conveyed the intelligence intended. All the Jews wore these, and so probably did our Lord; see Matt. ix. 20, where the word κρασπεδον is rather to be understood of the *fringe* than of the *hem* of his garment.

CHAPTER XVI.

The rebellion of Korah and his company against Moses, 1–3. *He directs them how to try, in the course of the next day, whom God had called to the priesthood,* 4–11. *Dathan and Abiram use the most seditious speeches,* 12–14. *Moses is wroth,* 15; *and orders Korah and his company to be ready on the morrow with their censers and incense,* 16–18. *Korah gathers his company together,* 19. *The glory of the Lord appears, and he threatens to consume them,* 20, 21. *Moses and Aaron intercede for them,* 22. *The people are commanded to leave the tents of the rebels,* 23–26. *They obey, and Korah and his company come out and stand before the door of their tents,* 27. *Moses in a solemn address puts the contention to issue,* 28–30. *As soon as he had done speaking, the earth clave and swallowed them, and all that appertained to them,* 31–34; *and the* 250 *men who offered incense are consumed by* fire, 35. *The Lord commands* Eleazar *to preserve the censers, because they were hallowed,* 36–39. *Eleazar makes of them a covering for the altar,* 39, 40. *The next day the people murmur anew, the glory of the Lord appears, and Moses and Aaron go to the tabernacle,* 41–43. *They are commanded to separate themselves from the congregation,* 44, 45. *Moses, perceiving that God had sent a plague among them, directs Aaron to hasten and make an atonement,* 46. *Aaron does so, and the plague is stayed,* 47, 48. *The number of those who died by the plague,* 14,700 *men,* 49, 50.

A. M. cir. 2533. B. C. cir. 1471. An. Exod. Isr. cir. 20.

NOW [a] Korah, the son of Izhar, the son of Kohath, the son of Levi, and Dathan and Abiram, the sons of Eliab, and On, the son of Peleth, sons of Reuben, took *men:*

2 And they rose up before Moses, with certain of the children of Israel, two hundred and fifty princes of the assembly, [b] famous in the congregation, men of renown:

3 And [c] they gathered themselves together against Moses and against Aaron, and said

A. M. cir. 2533. B. C. cir. 1471. An. Exod. Isr. cir. 20.

[a] Exod. vi. 21; chap. xxvi. 9; xxvii. 3; Ecclus. xlv. 18; Jude 11.—[b] Gen. vi. 4; chap. xxvi. 9.—[c] Psa. cvi. 16.

NOTES ON CHAP. XVI.

Verse 1. *Now Korah—took* men] Had not these been the most brutish of men, could they have possibly so soon forgotten the signal displeasure of God manifested against them so lately for their rebellion. The word *men* is not in the original; and the verb ויקח *vaiyikkach, and he took,* is not in the plural but the singular, hence it cannot be applied to the act of all these chiefs. In every part of the Scripture where this rebellion is referred to it is attributed to Korah, (see chap. xxvi. 3, and Jude, ver. 11,) therefore the verb here belongs to him, and the whole verse should be translated thus:—*Now Korah, son of Yitsar, son of Kohath, son of Levi,* HE TOOK *even Dathan and Abiram, the sons of Eliab, and On, son of Peleth,* SON OF REUBEN; *and they rose up,* &c. This makes a very regular and consistent sense, and spares all the learned labour of Father Houbigant, who translates יקח *yikkach,* by *rebellionem fecerunt, they rebelled,* which scarcely any rule of criticism can ever justify. Instead of בני ראובן *beney Reuben,* SONS *of Reuben,* some MSS. have בן *ben,* SON, in the singular; this reading, supported by the *Septuagint* and the *Samaritan* text, I have followed in the above translation. But as *Eliab* and *Peleth* were both *Reubenites,* the common reading, SONS, may be safely followed.

Verse 3. Ye take *too much upon you*] The original is simply רב לכם *rab lachem, too much for you.* The spirit of this saying appears to me to be the following:—"Holy offices are not equally distributed:

A. M. cir. 2533. B. C. cir. 1471. An. Exod. Isr. cir. 20.

unto them, [d] *Ye take* too much upon you, seeing [e] all the congregation *are* holy, every one of them, [f] and the LORD *is* among them: wherefore then lift ye up yourselves above the congregation of the LORD?

4 And when Moses heard *it,* [g] he fell upon his face:

5 And he spake unto Korah and unto all his company, saying, Even to-morrow the LORD will show who *are* his, and *who is* [h] holy; and will cause *him* to come near unto him: even *him* whom he hath [i] chosen will he cause to [k] come near unto him.

6 This do: Take you censers, Korah, and all his company;

7 And put fire therein, and put incense in them before the LORD to-morrow: and it shall be *that* the man whom the LORD doth choose, he *shall be* holy: *ye take* too much upon you, ye sons of Levi.

8 And Moses said unto Korah, Hear, I pray you, ye sons of Levi:

9 *Seemeth it but* [l] a small thing unto you, that the God of Israel hath [m] separated you from the congregation of Israel, to bring you near to himself, to do the service of the tabernacle of the LORD, and to stand before the congregation to minister unto them?

10 And he hath brought thee near *to him,* and all thy brethren the sons of Levi with thee: and seek ye the priesthood also?

11 For which cause *both* thou and all thy company *are* gathered together against the LORD: [n] and what *is* Aaron, that ye murmur against him?

A. M. cir. 2533. B. C. cir. 1471. An. Exod. Isr. cir. 20.

12 And Moses sent to call Dathan and Abiram, the sons of Eliab: which said, We will not come up:

13 [o] *Is it* a small thing that thou hast brought us up out of a land that floweth with milk and honey, to kill us in the wilderness, except thou [p] make thyself altogether a prince over us?

14 Moreover thou hast not brought us into [q] a land that floweth with milk and honey, or given us inheritance of fields and vineyards: wilt thou [r] put out the eyes of these men? we will not come up.

15 And Moses was very wroth, and said unto the LORD, [s] Respect not thou their offering: [t] I have not taken one ass from them, neither have I hurt one of them.

16 And Moses said unto Korah, [u] Be thou and all thy company [v] before the LORD, thou, and they, and Aaron, to-morrow:

17 And take every man his censer, and put incense in them, and bring ye before the LORD every man his censer, two hundred and fifty censers; thou also, and Aaron, each *of you* his censer.

18 And they took every man his censer, and put fire in them, and laid incense thereon, and stood in the door of the tabernacle of the congregation with Moses and Aaron.

19 And Korah gathered all the congregation against them unto the door of the tabernacle of the congregation: and [w] the glory of the LORD appeared unto all the congregation.

20 And the LORD spake unto Moses and unto Aaron, saying,

[d] Heb. it is *much for you.*——[e] Exod. xix. 6.——[f] Exod. xxix. 45; chap. xiv. 14; xxxv. 34.——[g] Chap. xiv. 5; xx. 6.——[h] Ver. 3; Lev. xxi. 6, 7, 8, 12, 15.——[i] Exod. xxviii. 1; chap. xvii. 5; 1 Sam. ii. 28; Psa. cv. 26.——[k] Chap. iii. 10; Lev. x. 3; xxi. 17, 18; Ezek. xl. 46; xliv. 15, 16.——[l] 1 Sam. xviii. 23; Isa. vii. 13.

[m] Chap. iii. 41, 45; viii. 14; Deut. x. 8.——[n] Exod. xvi. 8; 1 Cor. iii. 5.——[o] Ver. 9.——[p] Exod. ii. 14; Acts vii. 27, 35.——[q] Exod. iii. 8; Lev. xx. 24.——[r] Heb. *bore out.*——[s] Gen. iv. 4, 5.——[t] 1 Sam. xiii. 3; Acts xx. 33; 2 Cor. vii. 2.——[u] Ver. 6, 7.——[v] 1 Sam. xii. 3, 7.——[w] Ver. 42; Exod. xvi. 7, 10; Lev. ix. 6, 23; chap. xiv. 10.

you arrogate to yourselves the most important ones, as if *your* superior holiness entitled you *alone* to them; whereas all the congregation are *holy,* and have an equal right with you to be employed in the most holy services." Moses retorts this saying ver 7: *Ye take too much upon you,* רב לכם *rab lachem;* Ye have too much already, *ye sons of Levi;* i. e., by your present spirit and disposition you prove yourselves to be wholly unworthy of any *spiritual* employment.

Verse 5. *The Lord will show who* are *his*] It is supposed that St. Paul refers to this place, 2 Tim. ii. 19: *The foundation of God*—the whole sacrificial system, referring to Christ Jesus, the foundation of the salvation of men; *standeth sure,* notwithstanding the rebellions, intrusions, and false doctrines of men; *having this seal*—this stamp of its Divine authenticity, *The Lord knoweth them that are his;* εγνω Κυριος τους οντας αυτου, a literal translation of וירע יהוה את אשר לו *veyoda Yehovah eth asher lo;* and both signifying, The Lord approveth of his own; or, will own that which is of his own appointment. *And let every one that nameth the name of Christ depart from iniquity,* alluding to the exhortation of Moses, ver. 26: *Depart, I pray you, from the tents of these wicked men.*

Verse 15. *Respect not thou their offering*] There was no danger of this: they wished to set up a priesthood and a sacrificial system of their own; and God never has blessed, and never can bless, any scheme

A. M. cir. 2533. B. C. cir. 1471. An. Exod. Isr. cir. 20.

21 [x] Separate yourselves from among this congregation, that I may [y] consume them in a moment.

22 And they [z] fell upon their faces, and said, O God, [a] the God of the spirits of all flesh, shall one man sin, and wilt thou be wroth with all the congregation?

23 And the LORD spake unto Moses, saying,

24 Speak unto the congregation, saying, Get you up from about the tabernacle of Korah, Dathan, and Abiram.

25 And Moses rose up and went unto Dathan and Abiram; and the elders of Israel followed him.

26 And he spake unto the congregation, saying, [b] Depart, I pray you, from the tents of these wicked men, and touch nothing of theirs, lest ye be consumed in all their sins.

27 So they gat up from the tabernacle of Korah, Dathan, and Abiram, on every side: and Dathan and Abiram came out, and stood in the door of their tents, and their wives, and their sons, and their little children.

28 And Moses said, [c] Hereby ye shall know that the LORD hath sent me to do all these works; for *I have* not *done them* [d] of mine own mind.

29 If these men die [e] the common death of all men, or if they be [f] visited after the visitation of all men; *then* the LORD hath not sent me.

A. M. cir. 2533. B. C. cir. 1471. An. Exod. Isr. cir. 20.

30 But if the LORD [g] make [h] a new thing, and the earth open her mouth, and swallow them up, with all that *appertain* unto them, and they [i] go down quick into the pit; then ye shall understand that these men have provoked the LORD.

31 [k] And it came to pass, as he had made an end of speaking all these words, that the ground clave asunder that *was* under them:

32 And the earth opened her mouth, and swallowed them up, and their houses, and [l] all the men that *appertained* unto Korah, and all *their* goods.

33 They, and all that *appertained* to them, went down alive into the pit, and the earth closed upon them: and they perished from among the congregation.

34 And all Israel that *were* round about them fled at the cry of them: for they said, Lest the earth swallow us up *also*.

35 And there [m] came out a fire from the LORD, and consumed [n] the two hundred and fifty men that offered incense.

36 And the LORD spake unto Moses, saying,

37 Speak unto Eleazar the son of Aaron the priest, that he take up the censers out of the

[x] Ver. 45; see Gen. xix. 17, 22; Jer. li. 6; Acts ii. 40; Rev. xviii. 4.——[y] Ver. 45; Exod. xxxii. 10; xxxiii. 5.——[z] Ver. 45; chap. xiv. 5.——[a] Chap. xxvii. 16; Job xii. 10; Ecclus. xii. 7; Isa. lvii. 16; Zech. xii. 1; Heb. xii. 9.——[b] Gen. xix. 12, 14; Isa lii. 11; 2 Cor. vi. 17; Rev. xviii. 4.——[c] Exod. iii. 12; Deut. xviii. 22; Zech. ii. 9, 10; iv. 9; John v. 36.——[d] Chap. xxiv. 13; Jer. xxiii. 16; Ezek. xiii. 17; John v. 30; vi. 38.

[e] Heb. *as every man dieth.*——[f] Exod. xx. 5; xxxii. 34; Job xxxv. 15; Isa. x. 3; Jer. v. 9.——[g] Heb. *create a creature;* Isa. xlv. 7.——[h] Job xxxi. 3; Isa. xxviii. 21.——[i] Ver. 33; Psa. lv. 15.——[k] Chap. xxvi. 10; xxvii. 3; Deut. xi. 6; Psa. cvi. 17.——[l] See ver. 17; chap. xxvi. 11; 1 Chron. vi. 22, 37.——[m] Lev. x. 2; chap. xi. 1; Psa. cvi. 18.——[n] Ver. 17.

of salvation which is not of his own appointment. Man is ever supposing that he can mend his Maker's work, or that he can make one of his own that will do in its place.

Verse 22. *O God, the God of the spirits of all flesh*] אל אלהי הרוחת לכל בשר *El Elohey haruchoth lechol basar*. This address sufficiently proves that these holy men believed that man is a being compounded of flesh and spirit, and that these principles are perfectly distinct. Either the *materiality* of the human soul is a human fable, or, if it be a true doctrine, these men did not pray under the influence of the Divine Spirit. In chap. xxvii. 16 there is a similar form of expression: *Let the Lord, the God of the spirits of all flesh.* And in Job xii. 10: *In whose hand is the soul* (נפש *nephesh*) *of all living; and the spirit* (רוח *ruach*) *of all flesh of man.* Are not these decisive proofs that the Old Testament teaches that there is an immortal spirit in man? "But does not רוח *ruach* signify *wind* or *breath?*" Sometimes it does, but certainly not *here;* for how absurd would it be to say, O God, the God of the *breaths* of all flesh!

Verse 30. *If the Lord make a new thing*] ואם בריאה יברא יהוה *veim beriah yibra Yehovah, and if Jehovah should create a creation*, i. e., do such a thing as was never done before.

And they go down quick *into the pit*] שאלה *sheolah*, a proof, among many others, that שאל *sheol*, signifies here a *chasm* or *pit* of the earth, and not the place called *hell;* for it would be absurd to suppose that their *houses* had gone to hell; and it would be wicked to imagine that their little innocent children had gone thither, though God was pleased to destroy their lives with those of their iniquitous fathers.

Verse 33. *They, and all that* appertained *to them*] Korah, Dathan, and Abiram, and all that appertained to their respective families, went down into the pit caused by this supernatural earthquake; while the fire from the Lord consumed the 250 men that bare censers. Thus there were *two* distinct punishments, the *pit* and the *fire*, for the *two divisions* of these rebels.

Verse 37. *The censers—are hallowed.*] קדשו *kadeshu*, are *consecrated*, i. e., *to the service of God*, though in this instance improperly employed.

A. M. cir. 2533. B. C. cir. 1471. An. Exod. Isr. cir. 20.

burning, and scatter thou the fire yonder; for [o] they are hallowed.

38 The censers of these [p] sinners against their own souls, let them make them broad plates *for* a covering of the altar: for they offered them before the LORD, therefore they are hallowed: [q] and they shall be a sign unto the children of Israel.

39 And Eleazar the priest took the brazen censers, wherewith they that were burnt had offered; and they were made broad *plates for* a covering of the altar:

40 *To be* a memorial unto the children of Israel, [r] that no stranger, which *is* not of the seed of Aaron, come near to offer incense before the LORD; that he be not as Korah, and as his company: as the LORD said to him by the hand of Moses.

41 But on the morrow [s] all the congregation of the children of Israel murmured against Moses and against Aaron, saying, Ye have killed the people of the LORD.

42 And it came to pass, when the congregation was gathered against Moses and against Aaron, that they looked toward the tabernacle of the congregation: and, behold, [t] the cloud covered it, and [u] the glory of the LORD appeared.

A. M. cir. 2533. B. C. cir. 1471. An. Exod. Isr. cir. 20.

43 And Moses and Aaron came before the tabernacle of the congregation.

44 And the LORD spake unto Moses, saying,

45 [v] Get you up from among this congregation, that I may consume them as in a moment. And [w] they fell upon their faces.

46 And Moses said unto Aaron, Take a censer, and put fire therein from off the altar, and put on incense, and go quickly unto the congregation, and make an atonement for them: [x] for there is wrath gone out from the LORD; the plague is begun.

47 And Aaron took as Moses commanded, and ran into the midst of the congregation; and, behold, the plague was begun among the people: and he put on incense, and made an atonement for the people.

48 And he stood between the dead and the living; and the plague was stayed.

49 Now they that died in the plague were fourteen thousand and seven hundred, beside them that died about the matter of Korah.

50 And Aaron returned unto Moses unto the door of the tabernacle of the congregation: and the plague was stayed.

[o] See Lev. xxvii. 28.——[p] Prov. xx. 2; Hab. ii. 10.——[q] Chap. xvii. 10; xxvi. 10; Ezek. xiv. 8.——[r] Chap. iii. 10; 2 Chron. xxvi. 18.——[s] Chap. xiv. 2; Psa. cvi. 25.

[t] Exod. xl. 34.——[u] Ver. 19; chap. xx. 6.——[v] Ver. 21, 24.——[w] Ver. 22; chap. xx. 6.——[x] Lev. x. 6; chap. i. 53; viii. 19; xi. 33; xviii. 5; 1 Chron. xxvii. 24; Psa. cvi. 29.

Verse 41. *On the morrow all the congregation—murmured*] It is very likely that the people persuaded themselves that Moses and Aaron had used some *cunning* in this business, and that the *earthquake* and *fire* were artificial; else, had they discerned the hand of God in this punishment, could they have dared the anger of the Lord in the very face of justice?

Verse 46. *The plague is begun.*] God now punished them by a *secret blast*, so as to put the matter beyond all dispute; his hand, and his alone, was seen, not only in the plague, but in the *manner* in which the mortality was arrested. It was necessary that this should be done in *this way*, that the whole congregation might see that those men who had perished were not the *people of the Lord;* and that GOD, not *Moses* and *Aaron*, had destroyed them.

Verse 48. *He stood between the dead and the living; and the plague, &c.*] What the plague was we know not, but it seems to have begun at one part of the camp, and to have proceeded regularly onward; and Aaron went to the quarter where it was then *prevailing*, and stood with his atonement where it was now making its ravages, *and the plague was stayed;* but not before 14,700 had fallen victims to it, ver. 49.

If Aaron the high priest, with his censer and incense, could disarm the wrath of an insulted, angry Deity, so that a guilty people, who deserved nothing but destruction, should be spared; how much more effectual may we expect the great atonement to be which was made by the Lord Jesus Christ, of whom Aaron was only the *type!* The *sacrifices* of living animals pointed out the *death* of Christ on the cross; the *incense*, his *intercession*. Through his *death* salvation is purchased for the world; by his *intercession* the offending children of men are spared. Hence St. Paul, Rom. v. 10, says: *If, while we were enemies, we were reconciled to God by the death of his Son, much more, being reconciled, we shall be saved* THROUGH HIS LIFE, i. e., by the prevalence of his continual intercession. 2 Cor. v. 18, 19: "And all things *are* of God, who hath reconciled us to himself by Jesus Christ, and hath given to us the ministry of reconciliation; to wit, that God was in Christ, reconciling the world unto himself, not imputing their trespasses unto them; and hath committed unto us the word of reconciliation."

By the awful transactions recorded in this chapter, we may see how jealous God is of the sole right of appointing the *way* and *means* of salvation. Had any priesthood, and any kind of service, no matter how solemn and sincere, been equally available in the sight of Divine justice and mercy, God would not have resented in so awful a manner the attempts of Korah and

a

his company in their new service. The way of God's own appointment, the agony and death of Christ, is the only way in which souls can be saved. His is the *priesthood*, and *his* is the only available sacrifice. All other modes and schemes of salvation are the inventions of men or devils, and will in the end prove ruinous to all those who trust in them. Reader, forget not the Lord who bought thee.

CHAPTER XVII.

The twelve chiefs of the tribes are commanded to take their rods, and to write the name of each tribe upon the rod that belonged to its representative; but the name of Aaron *is to be written on the rod of the tribe of Levi,* 1–3. *The rods are to be laid up before the Lord, who promises that the man's rod whom he shall choose for priest shall blossom,* 4, 5. *The rods are produced and laid up before the tabernacle,* 6, 7. *Aaron's rod alone buds, blossoms, and bears fruit,* 8, 9. *It is laid up before the testimony as a token of the manner in which God had disposed of the priesthood,* 10, 11. *The people are greatly terrified, and are apprehensive of being destroyed,* 12, 13.

A. M. cir. 2533. B. C. cir. 1471. An. Exod. Isr. cir. 20.

AND the LORD spake unto
Moses, saying,
2 Speak unto the children of
Israel, and take of every one of them a rod
according to the house of *their* fathers, of all
their princes according to the house of their
fathers twelve rods: write thou every man's
name upon his rod.
3 And thou shalt write Aaron's name upon
the rod of Levi: for one rod *shall be* for the
head of the house of their fathers.
4 And thou shalt lay them up in the tabernacle of the congregation before the testimony,
[a] where I will meet with you.
5 And it shall come to pass, *that* the man's
rod, [b] whom I shall choose, shall blossom:
and I will make to cease from me the murmurings of the children of Israel, [c] whereby
they murmur against you.
6 And Moses spake unto the
children of Israel, and every one
of their princes gave him [d] a rod
apiece, for each prince one, according to their
fathers' houses, *even* twelve rods: and the rod
of Aaron *was* among their rods.
7 And Moses laid up the rods before the
LORD in [e] the tabernacle of witness.
8 And it came to pass, that on the morrow
Moses went into the tabernacle of witness;
and, behold, the rod of Aaron for the house
of Levi was budded, and brought forth
buds, and bloomed blossoms, and yielded
almonds.
9 And Moses brought out all the rods from
before the LORD unto all the children of
Israel: and they looked, and took every man
his rod.
10 And the LORD said unto Moses, Bring

A. M. cir. 2533. B. C. cir. 1471. An. Exod. Isr. cir. 20.

[a] Exodus xxv. 22; xxix. 42, 43; xxx. 36.——[b] Chapter xvi. 5. [c] Chap. xvi. 11.

[d] Hebrew *a rod for one prince, a rod for one prince.*——[e] Exod xxxviii. 21; Num. xviii. 2; Acts vii. 44.

NOTES ON CHAP. XVII.

Verse 2. *And take of every one of them a rod*] מטה *matteh*, the *staff* or *sceptre*, which the *prince* or *chief* of each tribe bore, and which was the sign of *office* or *royalty* among almost all the people of the earth.

Verse 5. *The man's rod, whom I shall choose, shall blossom*] It was necessary that something *farther* should be done to quiet the minds of the people, and for ever to settle the dispute, in what tribe the priesthood should be fixed. God therefore took the method described in the text, and it had the desired effect; the Aaronical priesthood was never after disputed.

Verse 8. *The rod of Aaron—was budded, &c.*] That is, on the same rod or staff were found *buds, blossoms,* and *ripe fruit.* This fact was so unquestionably miraculous, as to decide the business for ever; and probably this was intended to show that in the *priesthood*, represented by that of Aaron, the *beginning, middle,* and *end* of every good work must be found. The buds of good desires, the blossoms of holy resolutions and promising professions, and the ripe fruit of faith, love, and obedience, all spring from the priesthood of the Lord Jesus. It has been thought by some that Aaron's *staff* (and perhaps the *staves* of all the tribes) was made out of the *amygdala communis*, or common *almond tree.* In a favourable soil and climate it grows to twenty feet in height, is one of the most noble, flourishing trees in nature: its flowers are of a delicate red, and it puts them forth early in March, having begun to bud in January. It has its name שקד *shaked* from *shakad,* to *awake,* because it buds and flowers *sooner* than most other trees. And it is very likely that the staves of office, borne by the chiefs of all the tribes, were made of this tree, merely to signify that *watchfulness* and assiduous care which the chiefs should take of the persons committed, in the course of the Divine providence, to their keeping.

Every thing in this miracle is so far beyond the power of nature, that no doubt could remain on the minds of the people, or the envious chiefs, of the Divine appointment of Aaron, and of the especial interference of God in this case. To see a piece of *wood*

A. M. cir. 2533. B. C. cir. 1471. An. Exod. Isr. cir. 20.

[f] Aaron's rod again before the testimony, to be kept [g] for a token
against the [h] rebels; [i] and thou
shalt quite take away their murmurings from
me, that they die not.
11 And Moses did *so*: as the LORD commanded him, so did he.

A. M. cir. 2533. B. C. cir. 1471. An. Exod. Isr. cir. 20.

12 And the children of Israel
spake unto Moses, saying, Behold, we die, we perish, we all
perish.
13 [k] Whosoever cometh any thing near unto
the tabernacle of the LORD shall die: shall
we be consumed with dying?

[f] Heb. ix. 4.——[g] Chap. xvi. 38.——[h] Heb. *children of rebellion.*

[i] Ver. 5.——[k] Chap. i. 51, 53; xviii. 4, 7.

long *cut off* from the parent stock, without *bark* or *moisture* remaining, laid up in a *dry place* for a *single night*, with others in the same circumstances,—to see such a piece of wood resume and evince the perfection of vegetative life, *budding*, *blossoming*, and *bringing forth ripe fruit* at the same time, must be such a demonstration of the peculiar interference of God, as to silence every doubt and satisfy every scruple. It is worthy of remark that a *sceptre*, or *staff* of office, resuming its vegetative life, was considered an *absolute impossibility* among the ancients; and as they were accustomed to *swear by their sceptres*, this circumstance was added to establish and confirm the oath. A remarkable instance of this we have in HOMER, Iliad, lib. i., ver. 233, &c., where Achilles, in his rage against Agamemnon, thus speaks:—

Αλλ' εκ τοι ερεω, και επι μεγαν όρκον ομουμαι·
Ναι μα τοδε σκηπτρον, το μεν ουποτε φυλλα και οζους
Φυσει, επειδη πρωτα τομην εν ορεσσι λελοιπεν,
Ουδ' αναθηλησει· περι γαρ ῥα ἑ χαλκος ελεψε
Φυλλα τε και φλοιον· . . . .
. . . . *ὁ δε τοι μεγας εσσεται ὁρκος.*

But hearken: I shall swear a solemn oath:
By this same *sceptre* which *shall never bud*,
Nor boughs bring forth, as once; which, having left
Its parent on the mountain top, what time
The woodman's axe lopp'd off its *foliage green*,
And *stripp'd its bark*, *shall never grow again.*
COWPER.

VIRGIL represents King Latinus swearing in the same way, to confirm his covenant with Æneas:—

Ut SCEPTRUM hoc (dextra sceptrum nam forte gerebat)
Nunquam *fronde levi fundet virgulta* neque *umbras*,
Cum semel in silvis *imo de stirpe recisum*.
Matre caret, *posuitque comas et brachia ferro;*
Olim arbos, nunc artificis manus ære decoro
Inclusit, patribusque dedit gestare Latinis.
Talibus inter se firmabant fœdera dictis.
Æn., lib. xii., ver. 206-12.

Even as this royal SCEPTRE (for he bore
A sceptre in his hand) *shall never more*
Shoot out in branches, or *renew the birth;*
An orphan now, cut from the *mother earth*
By the keen axe, dishonour'd of its *hair*,
And cased in brass, for Latian kings to bear.
And thus in public view the peace was tied
With solemn vows, and sworn on either side.
DRYDEN.

When the circumstance of the *rod* or *sceptre* being used anciently in this way, and the absolute impossibility of its revivescence so strongly appealed to, is considered, it appears to have been a very proper instrument for the present occasion, for the change that passed on it must be acknowledged as an immediate and incontestable miracle.

Verse 12. *Behold, we die, we perish, we all perish.*] גוענו *gavaenu* signifies not so much to *die* simply, as *to feel an extreme difficulty of breathing*, which, producing *suffocation*, ends at last in death. See the folly and extravagance of this sinful people. At *first, every person* might *come near to God*, for *all*, they thought, were sufficiently *holy*, and every way qualified to minister in holy things. *Now, no one*, in their apprehension, can come near to the tabernacle without being *consumed*, ver. 13. In both cases they were wrong; *some* there were who might approach, *others* there were who might not. God had put the difference. His decision should have been final with them; but sinners are ever running into extremes.

CHAPTER XVIII.

The priests are to bear the iniquity of the sanctuary, 1. *The Levites to minister to the priests, and have charge of the tabernacle,* 2-4. *The priests alone to have the charge of the sanctuary, &c., no stranger to come nigh on pain of death,* 5-7. *The portion allowed for their maintenance,* 8. *They shall have every meat-offering; and they shall eat them in the holy place,* 9, 10. *The wave-offerings,* 11. *The first-fruits of the* oil, wine, *and* wheat, *and whatever is first ripe, and every devoted thing,* 12-14; *also, all the first-born of men and beasts,* 15-18; *and heave-offerings,* 19. *The priests shall have no inheritance,* 20. *The Levites shall have no inheritance, but shall have the tenth of the produce in Israel,* 21-24, *of which they are to give a tenth to the priests, taken from the best parts,* 25-30.

A. M. cir. 2533.
B. C. cir. 1471.
An. Exod. Isr. cir. 20.

AND the Lord said unto Aaron, [a] Thou and thy sons, and thy father's house with thee, shall [b] bear the iniquity of the sanctuary: and thou and thy sons with thee shall bear the iniquity of your priesthood.

2 And thy brethren also of the tribe of Levi, the tribe of thy father, bring thou with thee, that they may be [c] joined unto thee, and [d] minister unto thee: but [e] thou and thy sons with thee *shall minister* before the tabernacle of witness.

3 And they shall keep thy charge, and [f] the charge of all the tabernacle: [g] only they shall not come nigh the vessels of the sanctuary and the altar, [h] that neither they, nor ye also, die.

4 And they shall be joined unto thee, and keep the charge of the tabernacle of the congregation, for all the service of the tabernacle: [i] and a stranger shall not come nigh unto you.

5 And ye shall keep [k] the charge of the sanctuary, and the charge of the altar: [l] that there be no wrath any more upon the children of Israel.

6 And I, behold, I have [m] taken your brethren the Levites from among the children of Israel: [n] to you *they are* given *as* a gift for the Lord, to do the service of the tabernacle of the congregation.

7 Therefore [o] thou and thy sons with thee shall keep your priest's office for every thing of the altar, and [p] within the veil; and ye shall serve: I have given your priest's office *unto you as* a service of gift: and the stranger that cometh nigh shall be put to death.

8 And the Lord spake unto Aaron, Behold, [q] I also have given thee the charge of mine heave-offerings of all the hallowed things of the children of Israel; unto thee have I given them [r] by reason of the anointing, and to thy sons, by an ordinance for ever.

A. M. cir. 2533.
B. C. cir. 1471.
An. Exod. Isr. cir. 20.

9 This shall be thine of the most holy things, *reserved* from the fire: every oblation of theirs, every [s] meat-offering of theirs, and every [t] sin-offering of theirs, and every [u] trespass-offering of theirs, which they shall render unto me, *shall be* most holy for thee and for thy sons.

10 [v] In the most holy *place* shalt thou eat it; every male shall eat it: it shall be holy unto thee.

11 And this *is* thine; [w] the heave-offering of their gift, with all the wave-offerings of the children of Israel: I have given them unto [x] thee, and to thy sons and to thy daughters with thee, by a statute for ever: [y] every one that is clean in thy house shall eat of it.

12 [z] All the [a] best of the oil, and all the best of the wine, and of the wheat, [b] the first-fruits of them which they shall offer unto the Lord, them have I given thee.

13 *And* whatsoever is first ripe in the land, [c] which they shall bring unto the Lord, shall be thine; [d] every one that is clean in thine house shall eat *of* it.

14 [e] Every thing devoted in Israel shall be thine.

15 Every thing that openeth [f] the matrix in all flesh, which they bring unto the Lord, *whether it be* of men or beasts, shall be thine: nevertheless [g] the first-born of man shalt thou surely redeem, and the firstling of unclean beasts shalt thou redeem.

[a] Chap. xvii. 13.—[b] Exod. xxviii. 38.—[c] See Gen. xxix. 34.—[d] Chap. iii. 6, 7.—[e] Chap. iii. 10.—[f] Chap. iii. 25, 31, 36.—[g] Chap. xvi. 40.—[h] Chap. iv. 15.—[i] Chap. iii. 10. [k] Exodus xxvii. 21; xxx. 7; Leviticus xxiv. 3; chap. viii. 2. [l] Chap. xvi. 46.—[m] Chap. iii. 12, 45.—[n] Chap. iii. 9; viii. 19.—[o] Ver. 5; chap. iii. 10.—[p] Heb. ix. 3, 6.—[q] Lev. vi. 16, 18, 26; vii. 6, 32; chap. v. 9.—[r] Exod. xxix. 29; xl. 13, 15. [s] Lev. ii. 2, 3; x. 12, 13.—[t] Lev. iv. 22, 27; vi. 25, 26.

[u] Lev. v. 1; vii. 7; x. 12; xiv. 13.—[v] Lev. vi. 16, 18, 26, 29; vii. 6.—[w] Exod. xxix. 27, 28; Lev. vii. 30, 34.—[x] Lev. x. 14; Deut. xviii. 3.—[y] Lev. xxii. 2, 3, 11, 12, 13.—[z] Exod. xxiii. 19; Deut. xviii. 4; Neh. x. 35, 36.—[a] Heb. *fat*; ver. 29. [b] Exod. xxii. 29.—[c] Exod. xxii. 29; xxiii. 19; xxxiv. 26; Lev. ii. 14; chap. xv. 19; Deut. xxvi. 2.—[d] Ver. 11.—[e] Lev. xxvii. 28.—[f] Exod. xiii. 2; xxii. 29; Lev. xxii. 26; chap. iii. 13. [g] Exod. xiii. 13; xxxiv. 20.

NOTES ON CHAP. XVIII.

Verse 1. *Thou and thy sons—shall bear the iniquity of the sanctuary, &c.*] That is, They must be answerable for its legal pollutions, and must make the necessary *atonements* and *expiations*. By this they must feel that though they had got a high and important office confirmed to them by a miraculous interference, yet it was a place of the highest *responsibility*; and that they must not be high-minded, but fear.

Verse 2. *Thy brethren also of the tribe of Levi—may be joined unto thee*] There is a fine paronomasia, or play upon words, in the original. לוי *Levi* comes from the root לוה *lavah*, to *join to*, *couple*, *associate*: hence Moses says, the *Levites*, ילוו *yillavu*, shall be *joined*, or *associated* with the priests; they shall conjointly perform the whole of the sacred office, but the priests shall be *principal*, the Levites only their *associates* or *assistants*. For an explanation of many parts of this chapter, see the notes on several of the passages referred to in the *margin*.

Verse 15. *The first-born of man—and the firstling of unclean beasts*] Thus vain man is ranked with the beasts that perish; and with the *worst* kinds of them too, those deemed *unclean*.

A. M. cir. 2533. B. C. cir. 1471. An. Exod. Isr. cir. 20.

16 And those that are to be
redeemed from a month old shalt
thou redeem, [h] according to thine
estimation, for the money of five shekels, after
the shekel of the sanctuary, [i] which *is* twenty
gerahs.
17 [k] But the firstling of a cow, or the firstling of a sheep, or the firstling of a goat,
thou shalt not redeem; they *are* holy: [l] thou
shalt sprinkle their blood upon the altar, and
shalt burn their fat *for* an offering made by
fire, for a sweet savour unto the LORD.
18 And the flesh of them shall
be thine, as the [m] wave-breast,
and as the right shoulder are
thine.
19 [n] All the heave-offerings of the holy
things, which the children of Israel offer unto
the LORD, have I given thee, and thy sons
and thy daughters with thee, by a statute for
ever: [o] it *is* a covenant of salt for ever before
the LORD, unto thee and to thy seed with thee.
20 And the LORD spake unto Aaron, Thou
shalt have no inheritance in their land, neither

A. M. cir. 2533. B. C. cir. 1471. An. Exod. Isr. cir. 20.

[h] Lev. xxvii. 2, 6; chap. iii. 47.——[i] Exod. xxx. 13; Lev. xxvii. 25; chap. iii. 47; Ezek. xlv. 12.——[k] Deut. xv. 19.

[l] Lev. iii. 2, 5.——[m] Exod. xxix. 26, 28; Lev. vii. 31, 32, 34. [n] Ver. 11.——[o] Lev. ii. 13; 2 Chron. xiii. 5.

Verse 16. *Shalt thou redeem—for the money of five shekels*] Redemption of the first-born is one of the rites which is still practised among the Jews. According to Leo of Modena, it is performed in the following manner:—When the child is thirty days old, the father sends for one of the descendants of Aaron: several persons being assembled on the occasion, the father brings a cup containing several pieces of gold and silver coin. The priest then takes the child into his arms, and addressing himself to the mother, says: *Is this thy son?*—MOTHER. Yes.—PRIEST. *Hast thou never had another child, male or female, a miscarriage or untimely birth?*—MOTHER. No.—PRIEST. *This being the case, this child, as first-born, belongs to me.* Then, turning to the father, he says: *If it be thy desire to have this child, thou must redeem it.*—FATHER. I present thee with this gold and silver for this purpose.—PRIEST. *Thou dost wish, therefore, to redeem the child?*—FATHER. I do wish so to do.—The priest then, turning himself to the assembly, says: *Very well; this child, as first-born, is mine, as it is written in Bemidbar*, (Num. xviii. 16,) *Thou shalt redeem the first-born of a month old for five shekels, but I shall content myself with this in exchange.* He then takes two gold crowns, or thereabouts, and returns the child to his parents.

Verse 19. *It is a covenant of salt*] That is, an incorruptible, everlasting covenant. As *salt* was added to different kinds of viands, not only to give them a relish, but to preserve them from putrefaction and decay, it became the emblem of *incorruptibility* and *permanence*. Hence, a *covenant of salt* signified an *everlasting covenant*. We have already seen that, among the Asiatics, eating together was deemed a bond of perpetual friendship; and as *salt* was a common article in all their repasts, it may be in reference to this circumstance that a perpetual covenant is termed a *covenant of salt;* because the parties ate together of the sacrifice offered on the occasion, and the whole transaction was considered as a league of endless friendship. See the note on Lev. ii. 13.

Verse 20. *I am thy part and thine inheritance*] The principal part of what was offered to God was the portion of the priests, therefore they had no inheritance of *land* in Israel; independently of that they had a very ample provision for their support. The rabbins say *twenty-four* gifts were given to the priests, and they are all expressed in the law. *Eight* of those gifts the priests ate nowhere but in the sanctuary: these *eight* are the following:—

1. The flesh of the SIN-OFFERING, whether of beasts or fowls, Lev. vi. 25, 26.
2. The flesh of the TRESPASS-OFFERING, Lev. vii. 1, 6.
3. The PEACE-OFFERINGS of the congregation, Lev. xxiii. 19, 20.
4. The *remainder* of the OMER or SHEAF, Lev. xxiii. 10, &c.
5. The *remnants* of the MEAT-OFFERINGS of the Israelites, Lev. vi. 16.
6. The two LOAVES, Lev. xxiii. 17.
7. The SHEW-BREAD, Lev. xxiv. 9.
8. The LOG of OIL offered by the *leper*, Lev. xiv 10, &c.

Five of those gifts they ate only in Jerusalem:—

1. The *breast* and *shoulder* of the PEACE-OFFERINGS, Lev. vii. 31, 34.
2. The HEAVE-OFFERING of the sacrifice of *confession*, Lev. vii. 12–14.
3. The HEAVE-OFFERING of the Nazarite's *ram*, Lev. vi. 17–20.
4. The FIRSTLING of the *clean beast*, Num. xviii. 15; Deut. xv. 19, 20.
5. The FIRST-FRUITS, Num. xviii. 13.

FIVE gifts were not due unto them by the law, but in the land of Israel only:—

1. The *heave-offering* or FIRST-FRUITS, Num. xviii. 12.
2. The *heave-offering* of the TITHE, Num. xviii. 28.
3. The CAKE, Num. xv. 20. These three were *holy*.
4. The *first-fruits* of the FLEECE, Deut. xviii. 4.
5. The FIELD of POSSESSION, Num. xxxv. These two were *common*.

FIVE gifts were due unto them both *within* and *without* the land:—

1. The *gifts* of the BEASTS SLAIN, Deut. xviii. 3.
2. The redemption of the FIRST-BORN SON, Num. xviii. 15.
3. The LAMB for the *firstling* of an *ass*, Exod. iv 20; Num. xviii.
4. The restitution of that taken by violence from a stranger, Num. v. 8.
5. All DEVOTED *things*, Num. xviii. 14.

A. M. cir. 2533.
B. C. cir. 1471.
An. Exod. Isr. cir. 20.

shalt thou have any part among
them: [p] I *am* thy part and thine
inheritance among the children
of Israel.
21 And, behold, [q] I have given the children of
Levi all the tenth in Israel for an inheritance,
for their service which they serve, *even* [r] the
service of the tabernacle of the congregation.
22 [s] Neither must the children of Israel
henceforth come nigh the tabernacle of the
congregation, [t] lest they bear sin, [u] and die.
23 [v] But the Levites shall do the service of
the tabernacle of the congregation, and they
shall bear their iniquity: *it shall be* a statute
for ever throughout your generations, that
among the children of Israel they have no inheritance.
24 [w] But the tithes of the children of Israel,
which they offer *as* a heave-offering unto the
LORD, I have given to the Levites to inherit:
therefore I have said unto them, [x] Among
the children of Israel they shall have no inheritance.
25 And the LORD spake unto Moses, saying,
26 Thus speak unto the Levites, and say
unto them, When ye take of the children of
Israel the tithes which I have given you from
them for your inheritance, then ye shall offer
up a heave-offering of it for
the LORD, *even* [y] a tenth *part* of
the tithe.

A. M. cir. 2533.
B. C. cir. 1471
An. Exod. Isr. cir. 20.

27 [z] And *this* your heave-offering shall be
reckoned unto you, as though *it were* the
corn of the threshing-floor, and as the fulness
of the wine-press.
28 Thus ye also shall offer a heave-offering
unto the LORD of all your tithes, which ye receive of the children of Israel; and ye shall
give thereof the LORD'S heave-offering to
Aaron the priest.
29 Out of all your gifts ye shall offer every
heave-offering of the LORD, of all the [a] best
thereof, *even* the hallowed part thereof out of it.
30 Therefore thou shalt say unto them,
When ye have heaved the best thereof from
it, [b] then it shall be counted unto the Levites
as the increase of the threshing-floor, and as
the increase of the wine-press.
31 And ye shall eat it in every place, ye and
your households: for it *is* [c] your reward for
your service in the tabernacle of the congregation.
32 And ye shall [d] bear no sin by reason of
it, when ye have heaved from it the best of it:
neither shall ye [e] pollute the holy things of the
children of Israel, lest ye die.

[p] Deut. x. 9; xii. 12; xiv. 27, 29; xviii. 1, 2; Josh. xiii. 14, 33; xiv. 3; xviii. 7; Psa. xvi. 5; Ezek. xliv. 28.——[q] Ver. 24, 26; Lev. xxvii. 30, 32; Neh. x. 37; xii. 44; Heb. vii. 5, 8, 9.——[r] Chap. iii. 7, 8.——[s] Chap. i. 51.——[t] Lev. xxii. 9.——[u] Heb. *to die*.

[v] Chap. iii. 7.——[w] Ver. 21.——[x] Ver. 20; Deut. x. 9; xiv. 27, 29; xviii. 1.——[y] Neh. x. 38.——[z] Ver. 30.——[a] Heb. *fat*; ver. 12.——[b] Ver. 27.——[c] Matt. x. 10; Luke x. 7; 1 Cor. ix. 13; 1 Tim. v. 18.——[d] Lev. xix. 8; xxii. 16.——[e] Lev. xxii. 2, 15.

ONE gift was due unto them from the sanctuary:—

1. The *skins of the burnt-offering*, and all the skins of the other most holy things, Lev. vii. 8. In all 24. See *Ainsworth.*

The gifts which the females of the priests' families had a part in were these:—

1. The *heave-offering*, or *first-fruits*. 2. The heave-offering of the *tithe*. 3. The *cake*. 4. The gifts of the *beast*, Deut. xviii. 3. 5. The first of the *fleece*.—See Mishna, Tract. *Biccurim*, and Ainsworth on the Pentateuch.

Besides all this the priests had the tribute money mentioned Num. xxxi. 28, 29.

Verse 21. *Behold, I have given the children of Levi all the tenth*] First, the Levites had the tenth of all the productions of the land.

2. They had forty-eight cities, each forming a square of 4,000 cubits.

3. They had 2,000 cubits of ground round each city. Total of the land they possessed, 53,000 acres.

4. They had the first-fruits and certain parts of all the animals killed in the land.

Canaan contained about 11,264,000 acres; therefore the portion possessed by the Levites was rather less than as *one* to *two hundred and twelve;* for 11,264,000 divided by 53,000, quotes only $212\frac{28}{53}$.—See *Lowman, Dodd*, &c. But though this was a very small proportion for a *whole tribe* that had consented to annihilate its *political existence*, that it might wait upon the service of God, and labour for the people's souls; yet let it be considered that what they possessed was the *best of the land:* and while it was a slender remuneration for their services, yet their portion was such as rendered them independent, and kept them comfortable; so that they could wait on the Lord's work without distraction. This is a proper pattern for the maintenance of the ministers of God: let them have a *sufficiency* for *themselves* and *families*, that there may be no *distracting cares;* and let them not be encumbered with *riches* or *worldly possessions*, that they may not be prevented from taking *care of souls.*

Verse 28. *Thus ye also shall offer a heave-offering*] As the Levites had the tithe of the whole land, they themselves were obliged to give the *tithe* of this *tithe* to the priests, so that this considerably lessened their revenue. And this tithe or tenth they were obliged to select from the *best part* of the substance they had received, ver. 29, &c. A portion of all must be given to God, as an evidence of his goodness, and their dependence on him. See the end of chap. xx.

CHAPTER XIX.

The ordinance of the red heifer, 1, 2. *She shall be slain by Eleazar without the camp, and her blood sprinkled before the tabernacle,* 3, 4. *Her whole body and appurtenance shall be reduced to ashes, and while burning, cedar wood, scarlet, and hyssop, shall be thrown into the fire,* 5, 6. *The priest, and he that burns her, to bathe themselves and be reputed unclean till the evening,* 7, 8. *Her ashes to be laid up for a water of purification,* 9. *How, and in what cases it is to be applied,* 10–13. *The law concerning him who dies in a tent, or who is killed in the open field,* 14–16. *How the persons, tent, and vessels are to be purified by the application of these ashes,* 17–19. *The unclean person who does not apply them, to be cut off from the congregation,* 20. *This is to be a perpetual statute,* 21, 22.

A. M. cir. 2533.
B. C. cir. 1471.
An. Exod. Isr. cir. 20.

AND the LORD spake unto
Moses and unto Aaron, saying,
2 This *is* the ordinance of the law which the
LORD hath commanded, saying, Speak unto
the children of Israel, that they bring thee a
red heifer without spot, wherein *is* no blemish,
[a] *and* upon which never came yoke:
3 And ye shall give her unto Eleazar the
priest, that he may bring her [b] forth without
the camp, and *one* shall slay her before his
face:
4 And Eleazar the priest shall take of her
blood with his finger, and [c] sprinkle of her
blood directly before the taberna-
cle of the congregation seven
times:
5 And *one* shall burn the heifer in his sight;
[d] her skin, and her flesh, and her blood, with
her dung, shall he burn:
6 And the priest shall take [e] cedar wood,
and hyssop, and scarlet, and cast *it* into the
midst of the burning of the heifer.
7 [f] Then the priest shall wash his clothes,
and he shall bathe his flesh in water, and
afterward he shall come into the camp, and
the priest shall be unclean until the even.
8 And he that burneth her shall wash his

A. M. cir. 2533.
B. C. cir. 1471.
An. Exod. Isr. cir. 20.

[a] Deut. xxi. 3; 1 Sam. vi. 7.——[b] Lev. iv. 12, 21; xvi. 27; Heb. xiii. 11.——[c] Lev. iv. 6; xvi. 14, 19; Heb. ix. 13.

[d] Exodus xxix. 14; Lev. iv. 11, 12.——[e] Lev. xiv. 4, 6, 49. [f] Lev. xi. 25; xv. 5.

NOTES ON CHAP. XIX.

Verse 2. *Speak unto the children of Israel that they bring thee, &c.*] The ordinance of the *red heifer* was a sacrifice of general application. All the people were to have an interest in it, and therefore the people at large are to provide the sacrifice. This Jewish rite certainly had a reference to things done under the Gospel, as the author of the Epistle to the Hebrews has remarked: "For if," says he, "the blood of bulls and of goats," alluding, probably, to the sin-offerings and the scape-goat, "and the ashes of a *heifer*, sprinkling the unclean, sanctifieth to the purifying of the flesh; how much more shall the blood of Christ, who through the eternal Spirit offered himself without spot to God, purge your conscience from dead works to serve the living God!" Heb. ix. 13, 14. As the principal stress of the allusion here is to the ordinance of the *red heifer*, we may certainly conclude that it was designed to typify the sacrifice of our blessed Lord.

We may remark several curious particulars in this ordinance.

1. A *heifer* was appointed for a sacrifice, probably, in opposition to the Egyptian superstition which held these *sacred*, and actually worshipped their great goddess *Isis* under this form; and this appears the more likely because *males* in general were preferred for sacrifice, yet here the *female* is chosen.

2. It was to be a *red* heifer, because *red bulls* were sacrificed to appease the evil demon *Typhon*, worshipped among the Egyptians. See *Spencer*.

3. The heifer was to be *without spot*—having no mixture of any other colour. Plutarch remarks, *De Iside et de Osiride*, that if there was a *single hair* in the animal either *white* or *black*, it marred the sacrifice. See *Calmet*, and see the note on chap. viii. 7.

4. *Without blemish*—having no kind of imperfection in her body; the other, probably, applying to the *hair* or *colour*.

5. *On which never came yoke*, because any animal which had been used for any common purpose was deemed improper to be offered in sacrifice to God. The heathens, who appear to have borrowed much from the Hebrews, were very scrupulous in this particular. Neither the Greeks nor Romans, nor indeed the Egyptians, would offer an animal in sacrifice that had been employed for agricultural purposes. Of this we have the most positive evidence from *Homer*, *Porphyry*, *Virgil*, and *Macrobius*.

Just such a sacrifice as that prescribed here, does Diomede vow to offer to Pallas.—Iliad, lib. x., ver. 291.

Ὡς νυν μοι εθελουσα παριστασο, και με φυλασσε·
Σοι δ' αυ εγω ῥεξω βουν ηνιν ευρυμετωπον,
Αδμητην, ἡν ουπω ὑπο ζυγον ηγαγεν ανηρ·
Την τοι εγω ῥεξω, χρυσον κερασιν περιχευας.

"So now be present, O celestial maid;
So still continue to the race thine aid;
A *yearling heifer* falls beneath the stroke,
Untamed, unconscious *of the galling yoke*,
With ample forehead and with spreading horns,
Whose *tapering tops refulgent gold adorns*."
Altered from POPE

In the very same words Nestor, Odyss., lib. iii., ver 382, promises a similar sacrifice to Pallas.

a

A. M. cir. 2533.
B. C. cir. 1471.
An. Exod. Isr. cir. 20.

clothes in water, and bathe his flesh in water, and shall be unclean until the even.

9 And a man *that is* clean shall gather up [g] the ashes of the heifer, and lay *them* up without the camp in a clean place, and it shall be kept for the congregation of the children of Israel [h] for a water of separation: it *is* a purification for sin.

10 And he that gathereth the ashes of the heifer shall wash his clothes, and be unclean until the even: and it shall be unto the children of Israel, and unto the stranger that sojourneth among them, for a statute for ever.

11 [i] He that toucheth the dead body of any [k] man shall be unclean seven days.

12 [l] He shall purify himself with it on the third day, and on the seventh day he shall be clean: but if he purify not himself the third day, then the seventh day he shall not be clean.

13 Whosoever toucheth the dead body of any man that is dead, and purifieth not himself, [m] defileth the tabernacle of the LORD; and that soul shall be cut off from Israel: because [n] the water of separation was not sprinkled upon him, he shall be unclean; [o] his uncleanness *is* yet upon him.

14 This *is* the law, when a man dieth in a tent: all that come into the tent, and all that *is* in the tent, shall be unclean seven days.

15 And every [p] open vessel, which hath no covering bound upon it, *is* unclean.

16 And [q] whosoever toucheth one that is slain with a sword in the open fields, or a dead body, or a bone of a man, or a grave, shall be unclean seven days.

A. M. cir. 2533.
B. C. cir. 1471.
An. Exod. Isr. cir. 20.

17 And for an unclean *person* they shall take of the [r] ashes [s] of the burnt heifer of purification for sin, and [t] running water shall be put thereto in a vessel:

18 And a clean person shall take [u] hyssop, and dip *it* in the water, and sprinkle *it* upon the tent, and upon all the vessels, and upon the persons that were there, and upon him that touched a bone, or one slain, or one dead, or a grave:

19 And the clean *person* shall sprinkle upon the unclean on the third day, and on the seventh day: [v] and on the seventh day he shall purify himself, and wash his clothes, and bathe himself in water, and shall be clean at even.

20 But the man that shall be unclean, and shall not purify himself, that soul shall be cut off from among the congregation, because he hath [w] defiled the sanctuary of the LORD: the water of separation hath not been sprinkled upon him; he *is* unclean.

21 And it shall be a perpetual statute unto them, that he that sprinkleth the water of separation shall wash his clothes; and he that toucheth the water of separation shall be unclean until even.

22 And [x] whatsoever the unclean *person* toucheth shall be unclean; and [y] the soul that toucheth *it* shall be unclean until even.

[g] Heb. ix. 13.——[h] Ver. 13, 20, 21; chap. xxxi. 23.——[i] Ver. 16; Lev. xxi. 1; chap. v. 2; ix. 6, 10; xxxi. 19; Lam. iv. 14; Hag. ii. 13.——[k] Heb. *soul of man.*——[l] Chap. xxxi. 19.——[m] Lev. xv. 31.——[n] Ver. 9; chap. viii. 7.

[o] Lev. vii. 20; xxii. 3.——[p] Lev. xi. 32; chap. xxxi. 20.——[q] Ver. 11.——[r] Heb. *dust.*——[s] Ver. 9.——[t] Heb. *living waters shall be given*; Gen. xxvi. 19.——[u] Psa. li. 7.——[v] Lev. xiv. 9——[w] Ver. 13.——[x] Hag. ii. 13.——[y] Lev. xv. 5.

The Romans had the same religion with the Greeks, and consequently the same kind of sacrifices; so Virgil, Georg. iv., ver. 550.

> Quatuor eximios præstanti corpore tauros
> Ducit, et *intacta* totidem cervice *juvencas*.
>
> ——— "From his herd he culls
> For slaughter four the fairest of his bulls;
> Four *heifers* from his female stock he took,
> All *fair*, and all *unknowing of the yoke*."—DRYDEN.

It is very likely that the Gentiles learnt their first sacrificial rites from the patriarchs; and on this account we need not wonder to find so many coincidences in the sacrificial system of the patriarchs and Jews, and all the neighbouring nations.

Verse 9. *For a water of separation*] That is, the ashes were to be kept, in order to be mixed with water, ver. 17, and sprinkled on those who had contracted any legal defilement.

Verse 11. *He that toucheth the dead body of any man shall be unclean seven days.*] How low does this lay man! He who touched a dead *beast* was only unclean for *one day*, Lev. xi. 24, 27, 39; but he who touches a dead *man* is unclean for *seven days*. This was certainly designed to mark the peculiar impurity of man, and to show his sinfulness—*seven* times worse than the vilest animal! O thou son of the morning, how art thou fallen!

Verse 12. *He shall purify himself with it*] יתחטא בו *yithchatta bo*, literally, *he shall sin himself with it.* This Hebrew form of speech is common enough among us in other matters. Thus *to fleece, to bark*, and *to skin*, do not signify to *add* a *fleece*, another *bark*, or a *skin*, but to take one away; therefore, *to sin himself*, in the Hebrew idiom, is not to *add* sin, but to take it away, to *purify*. The verb חטא *chata* signifies to *miss the mark*, to *sin*, to *purify from sin*, and to *make a sin-offering*. See the note on Gen. xiii. 13.

The Hebrews generally sacrificed males, no matter of what colour; but here a heifer, and a heifer of a red colour, is ordered. The reason of these circumstances is not very well known.

"The rabbins, with all their boldness," says Calmet, "who stick at nothing when it is necessary to explain what they do not understand, declare that the cause of this law is entirely unknown; and that Solomon, with all his wisdom, could not find it out."

Several *fathers*, as well *modern* as *ancient*, profess to understand the whole clearly. 1. The *red* heifer with them signifies the *flesh of our Lord*, formed out of an earthly substance. 2. Being *without spot*, &c., the *infinite holiness* of Christ. 3. The *sex* of the animal, the *infirmity* of our flesh, with which he clothed himself. 4. The *red* colour, his *passion*. 5. Being *unyoked*, his being righteous in all his conduct, and never *under the yoke of sin*. 6. *Eleazar's* sacrificing the heifer instead of *Aaron*, ver. 3, signifies the *change of the priesthood* from the family of Aaron, in order that a new and more perfect priesthood might take place. 7. *The red heifer being taken without the camp* (ver. 3) to be slain, points out the *crucifixion* of our Lord *without the city*. 8. The complete *consuming* of the heifer by fire, the *complete offering* of the whole body and soul of Christ as a sacrifice to God for the sin of man: for as the heifer was *without blemish*, the whole might be offered to God; and as Christ was *immaculate*, his whole body and soul were made a sacrifice for sin. 9. As the fire of this sacrifice *ascended* up to God, so it points out the *resurrection* and *ascension* of our blessed Lord. 10. And as the *ashes* of this victim communicated a legal purity to those who were defiled, so true *repentance*, signified by those *ashes*, is necessary for the expiation of the offences committed after baptism. A great part of this is true in itself; but how little evidence is there that all these things were intended in the ordinance of the *red heifer?* See on chap. viii. 7.

CHAPTER XX.

The Israelites come to Zin, and Miriam dies, 1. *They murmur for want of water,* 2–5. *Moses and Aaron make supplication at the tabernacle, and the glory of the Lord appears,* 6. *He commands Moses to take his rod, gather the congregation together, and bring water out of the rock,* 7, 8. *Moses takes the rod, gathers the Israelites together, chides with them, and smites the rock twice, and the waters flow out plenteously,* 9–11. *The Lord is offended with Moses and Aaron because they did not sanctify him in the sight of the children of Israel,* 12. *The place is called* Meribah, 13. *Moses sends a friendly message to the king of Edom, begging liberty to pass through his territories,* 14–17. *The Edomites refuse,* 18. *The Israelites expostulate,* 19. *The Edomites still refuse, and prepare to attack them,* 20, 21. *The Israelites go to Mount Hor,* 22. *Aaron is commanded to prepare for his death,* 23, 24. *Aaron is stripped on Mount Hor, and his vestments put on Eleazar his son; Aaron dies,* 25–28. *The people mourn for him thirty days,* 29.

A. M. 2553. B. C. 1451. An. Exod. Isr. 40.

THEN [a] came the children of
Israel, *even* the whole congregation, into the desert of Zin,
in the first month: and the people abode in
Kadesh; and [b] Miriam died there,
and was buried there.
2 [c] And there was no water for
the congregation: [d] and they gathered them-

[a] Chap. xxxiii. 36. —— [b] Exod. xv. 20; chap. xxvi. 59.

[c] Exod. xvii. 1. —— [d] Chap. xvi. 19, 42.

NOTES ON CHAP. XX.

Verse 1. *Then came the children of Israel, &c.*] This was the first month of the *fortieth* year after their departure from Egypt. See chap. xxxiii. 38, compared with ver. 28 of this chapter, and Deut. i. 3. The transactions of *thirty-seven* years Moses passes by, because he writes not as a historian but as a legislator; and gives us particularly an account of the laws, ordinances, and other occurrences of the first and last years of their peregrinations. The year now spoken of was the last of their journeyings; for from the going out of the spies, chap. xiii., unto this time, was about *thirty-eight* years, Deut. i. 22, 23, ii. 14.

Desert of Zin] Calmet contends that this is not the same desert mentioned Exod. xvi. 1, where Israel had their *eighth* encampment; that in Exodus being called in the original סין *sin*, this here צין *tsin:* but this is no positive proof, as letters of the same organ are frequently interchanged in all languages, and particularly in Hebrew.

And Miriam died there] Miriam was certainly older than Moses. When he was an infant, exposed on the river Nile, she was intrusted by her parents to watch the conduct of Pharaoh's daughter, and to manage a most delicate business, that required much address and prudence. See Exod. ii. It is supposed that she was at the time of her death *one hundred and thirty* years of age, having been at least *ten* years old at her brother's birth. The Catholic writers represent her as a type of the Virgin Mary; as having preserved a perpetual virginity; as being legislatrix over the Israelitish women, as Moses was over the men; and as having a large portion of the spirit of prophecy. Eusebius says that her tomb was to be seen at *Kadesh*, near the city of Petra, in his time. She appears to have died about *four* months before her brother Aaron, chap. xxxiii. 38, and *eleven* before her brother Moses; so that these three, the most eminent of human beings, died in the space of one year!

Verse 2. *And there was no water for the congrega-*

A. M. 2553. B. C. 1451. An. Exod. Isr. 40.

selves together against Moses and against Aaron.

3 And the people [e] chode with Moses, and spake, saying, Would God that we had died [f] when our brethren died before the LORD!

4 And [g] why have ye brought up the congregation of the LORD into this wilderness, that we and our cattle should die there?

5 And wherefore have ye made us to come up out of Egypt, to bring us in unto this evil place? it *is* no place of seed, or of figs, or of vines, or of pomegranates; neither *is* there any water to drink.

6 And Moses and Aaron went from the presence of the assembly unto the door of the tabernacle of the congregation, and [h] they fell upon their faces: and [i] the glory of the LORD appeared unto them.

7 And the LORD spake unto Moses, saying,

8 [k] Take the rod, and gather thou the assembly together, thou and Aaron thy brother, and speak ye unto the rock before their eyes; and it shall give forth his water, and [l] thou shalt bring forth to them water out of the rock: so thou shalt give the congregation and their beasts drink.

9 And Moses took the rod [m] from before the LORD, as he commanded him.

10 And Moses and Aaron gathered the congregation together before the rock, and he said unto them, [n] Hear now, ye rebels; must we fetch you water out of this rock?

A. M. 2553. B. C. 1451. An. Exod. Isr. 40.

11 And Moses lifted up his hand, and with his rod he smote the rock twice: and [o] the water came out abundantly, and the congregation drank, and their beasts *also*.

12 And the LORD spake unto Moses and Aaron, Because [p] ye believed me not, to [q] sanctify me in the eyes of the children of Israel, therefore ye shall not bring this congregation into the land which I have given them.

13 [r] This *is* the water of [s] Meribah; because the children of Israel strove with the LORD, and he was sanctified in them.

14 [t] And Moses sent messengers from Kadesh unto the king of Edom, [u] Thus saith thy brother Israel, Thou knowest all the travel that hath [v] befallen us:

15 [w] How our fathers went down into Egypt, [x] and we have dwelt in Egypt a long time; [y] and the Egyptians vexed us, and our fathers:

16 And [z] when we cried unto the LORD, he heard our voice, and [a] sent an angel, and hath brought us forth out of Egypt: and, behold, we *are* in Kadesh, a city in the uttermost of thy border:

17 [b] Let us pass, I pray thee, through thy country: we will not pass through the fields,

[e] Exod. xvii. 2; chapter xiv. 2.——[f] Chap. xi. 1, 33; xiv. 37; xvi. 32, 35, 49.——[g] Exod. xvii. 3.——[h] Ch. xiv. 5; xvi. 4, 22, 45.——[i] Ch. xiv. 10.——[k] Exod. xvii. 5.——[l] Neh. ix. 15; Psa. lxxviii. 15, 16; cv. 41; cxiv. 8; Isaiah xliii. 20; xlviii. 21. [m] Chap. xvii. 10.——[n] Psa. cvi. 33.——[o] Exodus xvii. 6; Deut. viii. 15; 1 Cor. x. 4.——[p] Chap. xxvii. 14; Deut. i. 37; iii. 26; xxxii. 51.——[q] Lev. x. 3; Ezek. xx. 41; xxxvi. 23; xxxviii. 16; 1 Peter iii. 15.——[r] Deut. xxxiii. 8; Psa. xcv. 8; cvi. 32, &c. [s] That is, *strife*; see Exodus xvii. 7.——[t] Judg. xi. 16, 17. [u] Deut. ii. 4, &c.; xxiii. 7; Obad. x. 12.——[v] Heb. *found us*, Exod. xviii. 8.——[w] Gen. xlvi. 6; Acts vii. 15.——[x] Exod. xii. 40.——[y] Exod. i. 11, &c.; Deut. xxvi. 6; Acts vii. 19.——[z] Exod. ii. 23; iii. 7.——[a] Exod. iii. 2; xiv. 19; xxiii. 20; xxxiii. 2. [b] See chap. xxi. 22; Deut. ii. 27.

tion] The same occurrence took place to the children of Israel at *Kadesh*, as did formerly to their fathers at *Rephidim*, see Exod. xvii. 1; and as the *fathers* murmured, so also did the *children*.

Verse 12. *Because ye believed me not*] What was the offence for which Moses was excluded from the promised land? It appears to have consisted in some or all of the following particulars: 1. God had commanded him (ver. 8) *to take the rod in his hand, and go and* SPEAK TO THE ROCK, *and it should give forth water*. It seems Moses did not think *speaking* would be sufficient, therefore he *smote* the rock without any command so to do. 2. He did this *twice*, which certainly in this case indicated a great perturbation of spirit, and want of attention to the presence of God. 3. He permitted his *spirit* to be carried away by a sense of the people's disobedience, and thus, being *provoked*, he was led to *speak unadvisedly with his lips: Hear now, ye* REBELS, ver. 10. 4. He did not acknowledge GOD in the miracle which was about to be wrought, but took the honour to himself and Aaron: "*Must* WE *fetch you water out of this rock?*" Thus it plainly appears that they did not properly *believe* in God, and did not *honour* him in the sight of the people; for in their presence they seem to express a doubt whether the thing could be possibly done. As Aaron appears to have been consenting in the above particulars, therefore he is also excluded from the promised land.

Verse 14. *Sent messengers—unto the king of Edom*] Archbishop Usher supposes that the king now reigning in Edom was *Hadar*, mentioned Gen. xxxvi. 39.

Thus saith thy brother Israel] The Edomites were the descendants of Edom or Esau, the brother of Jacob or Israel, from whom the Israelites were descended.

Verse 17. *We will go by the king's high-way*] This is the first time this phrase occurs; it appears to have been a public road made by the king's authority at the expense of the state.

A. M. 2553.
B. C. 1451.
An. Exod. Isr.
40.

or through the vineyards, neither
will we drink *of* the water of the
wells: we will go by the king's
high-way, we will not turn to the right hand
nor to the left, until we have passed thy
borders.
18 And Edom said unto him, Thou shalt not
pass by me, lest I come out against thee with
the sword.
19 And the children of Israel said unto him,
We will go by the high-way: and if I and my
cattle drink of thy water, [c] then I will pay for
it: I will only, without *doing* any thing *else*,
go through on my feet.
20 And he said, [d] Thou shalt not go through.
And Edom came out against him with much
people, and with a strong hand.
21 Thus Edom [e] refused to give Israel passage through his border: wherefore Israel
[f] turned away from him.
22 And the children of Israel, *even* the
whole congregation, journeyed from [g] Kadesh,
[h] and came unto Mount Hor.
23 And the LORD spake unto Moses and
Aaron in Mount Hor, by the coast
of the land of Edom, saying,

A. M. 2553.
B. C. 1451.
An. Exod. Isr.
40.

24 Aaron shall be [i] gathered
unto his people: for he shall not enter into
the land which I have given unto the children
of Israel, because [k] ye rebelled against my
[l] word at the water of Meribah.
25 [m] Take Aaron and Eleazar his son, and
bring them up unto Mount Hor:
26 And strip Aaron of his garments, and
put them upon Eleazar his son: and Aaron
shall be gathered *unto his people*, and shall
die there.
27 And Moses did as the LORD commanded:
and they went up into Mount Hor, in the
sight of all the congregation.
28 [n] And Moses stripped Aaron of his garments, and put them upon Eleazar his son;
and [o] Aaron died there in the top of the mount:
and Moses and Eleazar came down from the
mount.
29 And when all the congregation saw that
Aaron was dead, they mourned for Aaron
[p] thirty days, *even* all the house of Israel.

---

[c] Deut. ii. 6, 28.—[d] Judg. xi. 17.—[e] See Deut. ii. 27, 29. [f] Deut. ii. 4, 5, 8; Judg. xi. 18.—[g] Chap. xxxiii. 37.—[h] Chap. xxi. 4.—[i] Gen. xxv. 8; chap. xxvii. 13; xxxi. 2; Deut. xxxii. 50.

[k] Ver. 12.—[l] Heb. *mouth*.—[m] Chap. xxxiii. 38; Deut. xxxii. 50.—[n] Exod. xxix. 29, 30.—[o] Chap. xxxiii. 38; Deut. x. 6; xxxii. 50.—[p] So Deut. xxxiv. 8.

Verse 21. *Thus Edom refused to give Israel passage through his border*] Though every king has a right to refuse passage through his territories to any strangers; yet in a case like this, and in a *time* also in which *emigrations* were frequent and universally allowed, it was both cruelty and oppression in Edom to refuse a passage to a comparatively unarmed and inoffensive multitude, who were all their own near *kinsmen*. It appears however that it was only the *Edomites of Kadesh* that were thus unfriendly and cruel; for from Deut. ii. 29 we learn that the *Edomites* who dwelt in *Mount Seir* treated them in a hospitable manner. This cruelty in the Edomites of Kadesh is strongly reprehended, and threatened by the Prophet Obadiah, ver. 10, &c.

Verse 26. *Strip Aaron of his garments*] This was, in effect, depriving him of his office; and putting the clothes on his son Eleazar implied a transfer of that office to him. A transfer of office, from this circumstance of *putting the clothes* of the late possessor on the person intended to succeed him, was called *investing* or *investment*, (*clothing*;) as removing a person from an office was termed *divesting* or *unclothing*. Among the Catholics, and in the Church of England, this same method is used in degrading ecclesiastics. Hence such a degradation is termed by the common people *stripping a man of his gown*.

Verse 28. *And Aaron died there*] Hence, as Dr. Lightfoot has justly observed, we have an "indisputable proof that the earthly Canaan was not the utmost felicity at which God's promises to the Israelites aimed, since the best men among them were excluded from it."

THE remark of some of the fathers here is worthy of attention: "Neither Moses the representative of the law, nor Miriam the representative of the prophets, nor Aaron the representative of the priesthood and its sacrificial rites, could bring the Israelites into possession of the promised land. This was reserved for *Joshua*, who was in name and conduct the lively type of our Lord and Saviour Jesus Christ." He alone can bring those who believe in his name into that rest which remains for the people of God.

There are some observations made by Dr. Lightfoot on this and some of the preceding chapters which should be more generally known.

"The *place* where the people murmured upon the return of the spies was *Kadesh-Barnea*, chap. xiii. 26; xxxii. 8; Deut. i. 19. This place was called *Rithmah* before, (chap. xxxiii. 18, compared with chap. xii. 16, and xiii. 26,) and was so called probably from the *juniper* trees that grew there; but is now named *Kadesh*, because the Lord was there *sanctified* upon the people, as chap. xx. 13; and *Barnea*, or the *wandering son*, because here was the decree made of their long *wandering* in the wilderness. They continued a good space at Kadesh before they removed; for so said Moses, *Ye abode in Kadesh many days;* or as the Hebrew, *According to the days that ye had made abode*, namely, at Sinai, ver. 6. And so they spent

one whole year there, for so they had done at Sinai. And whereas God commands them at their murmuring to turn back to the Red Sea, (Deut. i. 40,) his meaning was, that at their next march, whensoever it was, they should not go forward unto Canaan, but back again towards the Red Sea, whence they came; (but see on Deut. i. 1.) And they did so, for they wandered by many stations and marches from *Kadesh-Barnea* till they came to *Kadesh-Barnea* again, *seven* or *eight* and *thirty* years after they had first left it. These marches, mentioned in chap. xxxiii., were these: From *Kadesh* or *Rithmah* to *Rimmon Parez*, to *Libnah*, to *Rissah*, to *Kehelathah*, to Mount *Shapher*, to *Haradah*, to *Makheloth*, to *Tahath*, to *Tarah*, to *Mithcah*, to *Hashmonah*, to *Moseroth*, to *Benejaakan*, to *Horhagidgad*, to *Jotbathah*, to *Ebronah*, to *Ezion-Gaber*, to *Kadesh* again, in the fortieth year. And though it was only *eleven days'* journey from Horeb, by the way of Mount Seir to *Kadesh-Barnea*, (Deut. i. 2,) they made it above thrice *eleven years'* journey!" Had they trusted in God, and obeyed him, their enemies long ere this would have been discomfited, and themselves quietly established in possession of the promised inheritance. But they grieved the Spirit of God, and did not believe his promise; and it would have been inconsistent with the whole economy of grace to have introduced unbelievers into that rest which was a type of the kingdom of God.

CHAPTER XXI.

Arad, a king of the Canaanites, attacks Israel, and makes some prisoners, 1. *They devote him and his people to destruction*, 2; *which they afterwards accomplished*, 3. *They journey from* Hor, *and are greatly discouraged*, 4. *They murmur against God and Moses, and loathe the manna*, 5. *The Lord sends fiery serpents among them*, 6. *They repent, and beg Moses to intercede for them*, 7. *The Lord directs him to make a brazen serpent, and set it on a pole, that the people might look on it and be healed*, 8. *Moses does so, and the people who beheld the brazen serpent lived*, 9. *They journey to* Oboth, Ije-abarim, Zared, *and* Arnon, 10–13. *A quotation from the* book of the wars of the Lord, 14, 15. *From* Arnon *they come to* Beer, 16. *Their song of triumph*, 17–20. *Moses sends messengers to the Amorites for permission to pass through their land*, 21, 22. Sihon *their king refuses, attacks Israel, is defeated, and all his cities destroyed*, 23–26. *The poetic proverbs made on the occasion*, 27–30. *Israel possesses the land of the Amorites*, 31, 32. *They are attacked by* Og *king of Bashan*, 33. *They defeat him, destroy his troops and family, and possess his land*, 34, 35.

A. M. 2553. B. C. 1451. An. Exod. Isr. 40.

AND when [a] King Arad the
Canaanite, which dwelt in
the south, heard tell that Israel
came [b] by the way of the spies; then he
fought against Israel, and took *some* of them
prisoners.
2 [c] And Israel vowed a vow unto the LORD,
and said, If thou wilt indeed deliver this people
into my hand, then [d] I will utterly destroy
their cities.
3 And the LORD hearkened to the voice of
Israel, and delivered up the Canaanites: and
they utterly destroyed them and
their cities: and he called the
name of the place [e] Hormah.
4 And [f] they journeyed from Mount Hor by
the way of the Red Sea, to [g] compass the land
of Edom: and the soul of the people was
much [h] discouraged [i] because of the way.
5 And the people [k] spake against God, and
against Moses, [l] Wherefore have ye brought
us up out of Egypt to die in the wilderness?
for *there is* no bread, neither *is there any* water,
and [m] our soul loatheth this light bread.

A. M. 2553. B. C. 1451. An. Exod. Isr. 40.

[a] Chap. xxxiii. 40; see Judg. i. 16.——[b] Chap. xiii. 21. [c] Gen. xxviii. 20; Judg. xi. 30.——[d] Lev. xxvii. 28.——[e] That is, *utter destruction.*

[f] Chap. xx. 22; xxxiii. 41.——[g] Judg. xi. 18.——[h] Or, *grieved.* [i] Heb. *shortened*; Exod. vi. 9.——[k] Psa. lxxviii. 19.——[l] Exod. xvi. 3; xvii. 3.——[m] Chap. xi. 6.

NOTES ON CHAP. XXI.

Verse 1. *The way of the spies*] אתרים *atharim*. Some think that this signifies the way that the spies took when they went to search the land. But this is impossible, as Dr. Kennicott justly remarks, because Israel had now marched from *Meribah-Kadesh* to Mount *Hor*, beyond *Ezion-Gaber*, and were turning round *Edom* to the south-east; and therefore the word is to be understood here as the name of a *place*.

Verse 3. *The Lord hearkened to the voice of Israel*] The whole of this verse appears to me to have been added after the days of Joshua. It is certain the Canaanites were not utterly destroyed at the time here spoken of, for this did not take place till after the death of Moses. If, instead of *utterly destroyed them*, ויחרם *vaiyacharem*, we translate *they devoted them to utter destruction*, it will make a good sense, and not repugnant to the Hebrew; though some think it more probable that the verse was added afterwards by Joshua or Ezra, in testimony of the fulfilment of God's promise; for *Arad*, who is mentioned as being destroyed here, is mentioned among those destroyed by Joshua long after, (see Josh. xii. 14:) but this is quite consistent with their being *devoted to destruction*, as this might be fulfilled any time after. See the note on Lev. xxvii.

Verse 5. *This light bread.*] הקלקל *hakkelokel*, a

A. M. 2553.
B. C. 1451.
An. Exod. Isr.
40.

6 And [n] the LORD sent [o] fiery
serpents among the people, and
they bit the people; and much
people of Israel died.
7 [p] Therefore the people came to Moses, and
said, We have sinned, for [q] we have spoken
against the LORD, and against thee: [r] pray unto
the LORD, that he take away the serpents from
us. And Moses prayed for the
people.
8 And the LORD said unto
Moses, Make thee a fiery serpent, and set it
upon a pole: and it shall come to pass, that
every one that is bitten, when he looketh upon
it, shall live.
9 And [s] Moses made a serpent of brass, and

[n] Wisd. xvi. 1, 5; 1 Cor. x. 9.——[o] Deut. viii. 15.——[p] Psa. lxxviii. 34.——[q] Ver. 5.——[r] Exod. viii. 8, 28; 1 Sam. xii. 19; 1 Kings xiii. 6; Acts viii. 24.——[s] 2 Kings xviii. 4; John iii. 14, 15.

word of excessive scorn; as if they had said, This innutritive, unsubstantial, cheat-stomach stuff.

Verse 6. *Fiery serpents*] הנחשים השרפים *hannechashim hasseraphim.* I have observed before, on Gen. iii., that it is difficult to assign a name to the creature termed in Hebrew *nachash;* it has different significations, but its meaning here and in Gen. iii. is most difficult to be ascertained. *Seraphim* is one of the orders of angelic beings, Isa. vi. 2, 6; but as it comes from the root שרף *saraph*, which signifies to *burn*, it has been translated *fiery* in the text. It is likely that St. Paul alludes to the seraphim, Heb. i. 7: *Who maketh his angels spirits, and his ministers a* FLAME *of* FIRE. The animals mentioned here by Moses may have been called *fiery* because of the heat, violent inflammation, and thirst, occasioned by their bite; and consequently, if *serpents*, they were of the *prester* or *dipsas* species, whose bite, especially that of the former, occasioned a violent inflammation through the whole body, and a fiery appearance of the countenance. The poet Lucan has well expressed this terrible effect of the bite of the *prester*, and also of the *dipsas*, in the ninth book of his Pharsalia, which, for the sake of those who may not have the work at hand, I shall here insert.

Of the mortal effects of the bite of the *dipsas* in the deserts of Libya he gives the following description:—

"Signiferum juvenem Tyrrheni sanguinis Aulum
Torta caput retro *dipsas* calcata momordit.
Vix dolor aut sensus dentis fuit: ipsaque læti
Frons caret invidia: nec quidquam plaga minatur.
Ecce subit *virus* tacitum, *carpitque medullas*
Ignis edax, calidaque incendit viscera tabe.
Ebibit humorem circum vitalia fusum
Pestis, et in *sicco* linguam *torrere* palato
Cœpit: defessos iret qui sudor in artus
Non fuit, atque oculos lacrymarum vena refugit."

Aulus, a noble youth of Tyrrhene blood,
Who bore the standard, on a *dipsas* trod;
Backward the wrathful serpent bent her head,
And, fell with rage, the unheeded wrong repaid.
Scarce did some little mark of hurt remain,
And scarce he found some little sense of pain.
Nor could he yet the danger doubt, nor fear
That death with all its terrors threatened there.
When lo! unseen, the *secret venom* spreads,
And every nobler part at once invades;
Swift flames consume the *marrow* and the *brain*,
And the *scorched entrails* rage with *burning pain;*
Upon his heart the *thirsty* poisons prey,
And *drain the sacred juice of life away.*
No *kindly* floods of *moisture* bathe his tongue,
But cleaving to the *parched* roof it hung;
No trickling drops distil, no dewy sweat,
To ease his weary limbs, and *cool the raging heat.*
ROWE.

The effects of the bite of the *prester* are not less terrible:—

"Nasidium Marsi cultorem *torridus* agri
Percussit *prester:* illi *rubor igneus* ora
Succendit, tenditque cutem, pereunte figura,
Miscens cuncta tumor toto jam corpore major:
Humanumque egressa modum super omnia membra
Efflatur sanies, late tollente veneno."

A fate of different kind Nasidius found,
A *burning prester* gave the deadly wound;
And straight, a *sudden flame* began to spread,
And paint his visage with a *glowing red.*
With swift expansion swells the bloated skin,
Naught but an undistinguished mass is seen;
While the fair human form lies lost within.
The puffy poison spreads, and heaves around,
Till all the *man* is in the *monster* drowned.
ROWE.

Bochart supposes that the *hydrus* or *chersydrus* is meant; a serpent that lives in *marshy places*, the bite of which produces the most terrible inflammations, burning heat, fetid vomitings, and a putrid solution of the whole body. See his works, vol. iii., col. 421. It is more likely to have been a serpent of the *prester* or *dipsas* kind, as the *wilderness* through which the Israelites passed did neither afford *rivers* nor *marshes*, though *Bochart* endeavours to prove that there *might have been* marshes in that part; but his arguments have very little weight. Nor is there need of a *water serpent* as long as the *prester* or *dipsas*, which abound in the deserts of *Libya*, might have abounded in the deserts of *Arabia* also. But very probably the *serpents* themselves were immediately sent by God for the chastisement of this rebellious people. The *cure* was certainly preternatural; this no person doubts; and why might not the *agent* be so, that inflicted the disease?

Verse 8. *Make thee a fiery serpent*] Literally, make thee a seraph.

And put it upon a pole] על נס *al nes*, upon a *standard* or *ensign.*

Verse 9. *And Moses made a serpent of brass*] נחש נחשת *nechash nechosheth.* Hence we find that the word for *brass* or *copper* comes from the same root with *nachash*, which here signifies a serpent, probably on ac-

A. M. 2553. B. C. 1451. An. Exod. Isr. 40.

put it upon a pole, and it came to
pass, that if a serpent had bitten
any man, when he beheld the
serpent of brass, he lived.
10 And the children of Israel set forward,
and [t] pitched in Oboth.
11 And they journeyed from Oboth, and
[u] pitched at [v] Ije-abarim, in the wilderness
which *is* before Moab, toward the sunrising.
12 [w] From thence they removed, and pitched
in the valley of Zared.
13 From thence they removed, and pitched
on the other side of Arnon, which
is in the wilderness that cometh
out of the coasts of the Amorites:
for [x] Arnon *is* the border of Moab, between
Moab and the Amorites.
14 Wherefore it is said in the book of the
wars of the LORD, [y] What he did in the Red
Sea, and in the brooks of Arnon,
15 And at the stream of the brooks that
goeth down to the dwelling of Ar, [z] and [a] lieth
upon the border of Moab.
16 And from thence *they went* [b] to Beer: that

[t] Chap. xxxiii. 43.——[u] Chap. xxxiii. 43.——[v] Or, *heaps of Abarim.* [w] Deut. ii. 13.——[x] Chap. xxii. 36; Judg. xi. 18.

[y] Or, *Vaheb in Suphah.*——[z] Deut. ii. 18, 29.——[a] Heb. *leaneth.* [b] Judg. ix. 21.

count of the *colour;* as most serpents, especially those of the bright spotted kind, have a very glistening appearance, and those who have brown or yellow spots appear something like *burnished brass:* but the true meaning of the root cannot be easily ascertained.

On the subject of the cure of the serpent-bitten Israelites, by looking at the brazen serpent, there is a good comment in the book of Wisdom, chap. xvi. 4–12, in which are these remarkable words: "They were admonished, having a sign of salvation, (i. e., the brazen serpent,) to put them in remembrance of the commandments of thy law. For he that turned himself towards it was not saved by the THING that he saw, but by THEE, that art the Saviour of all." To the circumstance of looking at the brazen serpent in order to be healed, our Lord refers, John iii. 14, 15: "As Moses lifted up the serpent in the wilderness, even so must the Son of man be lifted up, that whosoever believeth in him should not perish, but have eternal life." The brazen serpent was certainly *no type* of Jesus Christ; but from our Lord's words we may learn, 1. That *as* the serpent was lifted up on the pole or *ensign, so* Jesus Christ was lifted up on the cross. 2. That *as* the Israelites were to look at the brazen serpent, *so* sinners must look to Christ for salvation. 3. That *as* God provided no other remedy than this *looking* for the wounded Israelites, *so* he has provided no other way of salvation than *faith* in the blood of his Son. 4. That *as* he who looked at the brazen serpent was *cured* and did *live, so* he that believeth on the Lord Jesus Christ shall *not perish,* but have *eternal life.* 5. That *as* neither the *serpent,* nor *looking at it,* but the invisible power of GOD healed the people, so neither the *cross* of Christ, nor his merely *being crucified,* but the *pardon* he has *bought by his blood,* communicated by the *powerful energy of his Spirit,* saves the souls of men. May not all these things be plainly seen in the *circumstances* of this transaction, without making the *serpent* a type of Jesus Christ, (the most exceptionable that could possibly be chosen,) and running the parallel, as some have done, through ten or a dozen particulars?

Verse 12. *They—pitched in the valley of Zared.*] נחל זרד *nachal zared.* This should be translated *the brook Zared,* as it is in Deut. ii. 13, 14. This *stream* has its origin in the mountains eastward of Moab, and runs from east to west, and discharges itself into the Dead Sea.

Verse 13. *Arnon*] Another river which takes its rise in the mountains of Moab, and, after having separated the ancient territories of the Moabites and Ammonites, falls into the Dead Sea, near the mouth of Jordan.

Verse 14. *The book of the wars of the Lord*] There are endless conjectures about this book, both among ancients and moderns. Dr. Lightfoot's opinion is the most simple, and to me bears the greatest appearance of being the true one. "This book seems to have been some book of *remembrances* and *directions,* written by Moses for Joshua's private instruction for the management of the wars after him. See Exod. xvii. 14–16. It may be that this was the same book which is called the *book of Jasher,* i. e., the *book of the upright,* or a directory for Joshua, from Moses, what to do and what to expect in his wars; and in this book it seems as if Moses directed the setting up of *archery,* see 2 Sam. i. 18, and warrants Joshua to command the sun, and expect its obedience, Josh. x. 13."

What he did in the Red Sea, and in the brooks of Arnon] This clause is impenetrably obscure. All the versions, all the translators, and all the commentators, have been puzzled with it. Scarcely any two agree. The original is את והב בסופה *eth vaheb besuphah,* which our translators render, *what he did in the Red Sea,* following here the Chaldee Targum; but not satisfied with this version, they have put the most difficult words in *English letters* in the margin, *Vaheb in Suphah. Calmet's* conjecture here is ingenious, and is adopted by *Houbigant;* instead of והב *vaheb,* he reads זרד *zared.* Now a ז *zain* may be easily mistaken for a ו *vau,* and vice versa; and a ה *he* for a ר *resh,* if the left limb happened to be a little obliterated, which frequently occurs, not only in MSS., but in *printed* books; the ב *beth* also might be mistaken for a ד *daleth,* if the *ruled line* on which it stood happened in that place to be a little *thicker* or blacker than usual. Thus then והב *vaheb* might be easily formed out of זרד *zared,* mentioned ver. 12; the whole might then be read, *They* encamped *at the brook Zared,* and they came to *Suphah,* and thence *to the brook Arnon.* Take the passage as we may, it is evidently defective. As I judge the whole clause to have been

A. M. 2553.
B. C. 1451.
An. Exod. Isr. 40.

is the well whereof the LORD
spake unto Moses, Gather the
people together, and I will give
them water.
17 [c] Then Israel sang this song, [d] Spring up,
O well; [e] sing ye unto it:
18 The princes digged the well, the nobles of
the people digged it, by *the direction of* [f] the
lawgiver, with their staves. And from the
wilderness *they went* to Mattanah:
19 And from Mattanah to Nahaliel: and from
Nahaliel to Bamoth:
20 And from Bamoth *in* the valley, that *is* in
the [g] country of Moab, to the top of [h] Pisgah,
which looketh [i] toward [k] Jeshimon.
21 And [l] Israel sent messengers unto Sihon
king of the Amorites, saying,
22 [m] Let me pass through thy land: we will
not turn into the fields, or into the vineyards;
we will not drink *of* the waters of the well:
but we will go along by the king's *high*-way,
until we be past thy borders.

23 [n] And Sihon would not suffer
Israel to pass through his border:
but Sihon gathered all his people
together, and went out against Israel into the
wilderness: [o] and he came to Jahaz, and
fought against Israel.
24 And [p] Israel smote him with the edge of
the sword, and possessed his land from Arnon
unto Jabbok, even unto the children of Ammon:
for the border of the children of Ammon
was strong.
25 And Israel took all these cities: and
Israel dwelt in all the cities of the Amorites,
in Heshbon, and in all the [q] villages thereof.
26 For Heshbon *was* the city of Sihon the
king of the Amorites, who had fought against
the former king of Moab, and taken all his
land out of his hand, even unto Arnon.
27 Wherefore they that speak in proverbs say,
Come into Heshbon, let the city of Sihon be
built and prepared:
28 For there is [r] a fire gone out of Heshbon,

[c] Exod. xv. 1; Psa. cv. 2; cvi. 12.——[d] Heb. *ascend.*——[e] Or, *answer.*——[f] Isa. xxxiii. 22.——[g] Heb. *field.*——[h] Or, *the hill.* [i] Chap. xxiii. 28.——[k] Or, *the wilderness.*——[l] Deut. ii. 26, 27; Judg. xi. 19.

[m] Chap. xx. 17.——[n] Deut. xxix. 7.——[o] Deut. ii. 32; Judg xi. 20.——[p] Deut. ii. 33; xxix. 7; Josh. xii. 1, 2; xxiv. 8; Neh ix. 22; Psa. cxxxv. 10, 11; cxxxvi. 19; Amos ii. 9.——[q] Heb *daughters.*——[r] Jer. xlviii. 45, 46.

a *common proverb* in those days, and *Vaheb* to be a proper name, I therefore propose the following translation, which I believe to be the best: *From Vaheb unto Suph, and unto the streams of Arnon.* If we allow it to have been a proverbial expression, used to point out extensive distance, then it was similar to that well known phrase, *From Dan even unto Beersheba.*

Verse 17. *Spring up, O well, &c.*] This is one of the most ancient war songs in the world, but is not easily understood, which is commonly the case with all very ancient compositions, especially the *poetic*. See the remarks Exod. xv. 1, &c.

Verse 18. *The princes digged the well—with their staves.*] This is not easily understood. Who can suppose that the princes dug this well with their *staves?* And is their any other idea conveyed by our translation? The word חפרו *chapharu*, which is translated *they digged*, should be rendered *they searched out*, which is a frequent meaning of the root; and במשענתם *bemishanotham*, which we render *with their staves*, should be translated *on their borders* or *confines*, from the root שען *shaan*, to *lie along*. With these corrections the whole song may be read thus:—

Spring up, O well! Answer ye to it. { i. e. Repeat the other part of the song.
The well, the princes searched it out. This is the answer.
The nobles of the people have digged it. { This was the
By a decree, upon their own borders. { chorus.

This is the whole of the quotation from what is called the book of the wars of the Lord. But see Dr. *Kennicott's* remarks at the end of this chapter.

Verse 26 *For Heshbon* was *the* city *of Sihon, &c.*] It appears therefore that the territory now taken from Sihon by the Israelites was taken from a former king of Moab, in commemoration of which an epikedion or war song was made, several verses of which, in their ancient poetic form, are here quoted by Moses.

Verse 27. *They that speak in proverbs*] המשלים *hammoshelim*, from משל *mashal*, to *rule*, to *exercise authority;* hence a *weighty proverbial saying*, because admitted as an *axiom* for the *government of life*. The *moshelim* of the ancient Asiatics were the same, in all probability, as the *Poetæ* among the Greeks and Latins, the شعرا *shaara* among the Arabs, who were esteemed as Divine persons, and who had their name from شعر *shaara*, he *knew, understood;* whose poems celebrated past transactions, and especially those which concerned the *military history* of their nation. These poets were also termed صاحب ديوان *sahebi deewan*, *companions* or *lords of the council of state*, because their *weighty* sayings and universal *knowledge* were held in the highest repute. Similar to these were the *bards* among the ancient *Druids*, and the *Sennachies* among the ancient Celtic inhabitants of these nations.

The ode from the 27th to the 30th verse is composed of three parts. The *first* takes in verses 27 and 28; the *second* ver. 29; and the *third* verse 30.

The *first* records with bitter irony the late insults of Sihon and his subjects over the conquered Moabites.

The *second* expresses the compassion of the Israelites over the desolations of Moab, with a bitter sarcasm against their god *Chemosh*, who had abandoned his votaries in their distress, or was not able to rescue them out of the hands of their enemies.

A. M. 2553. B. C. 1451. An. Exod. Isr. 40.

a flame from the city of Sihon:
it hath consumed [s] Ar of Moab,
and the lords of the high places
of Arnon.
29 Wo to thee, Moab! thou art undone, O
people of [t] Chemosh: he hath given his sons
that escaped, and his daughters, into captivity
unto Sihon king of the Amorites.
30 We have shot at them; Heshbon is perished even [u] unto Dibon, and we have laid
them waste even unto Nophah, which *reacheth* unto [v] Medeba.
31 Thus Israel dwelt in the land of the
Amorites.
32 And Moses sent to spy out [w] Jaazer, and
they took the villages thereof, and
drove out the Amorites that *were*
there.
33 [x] And they turned and went up by the
way of Bashan: and Og the king of Bashan
went out against them, he, and all his people,
to the battle [y] at Edrei.
34 And the LORD said unto Moses, [z] Fear
him not: for I have delivered him into thy
hand, and all his people, and his land; and
[a] thou shalt do to him as thou didst unto Sihon
king of the Amorites, which dwelt at Heshbon.
35 [b] So they smote him, and his sons, and
all his people, until there was none left him
alive: and they possessed his land.

A. M. 2553. B. C. 1451. An. Exod. Isr. 40.

[s] Deut. ii. 9, 18; Isa. xv. 1.——[t] Judg. xi. 24; 1 Kings xi. 7, 33; 2 Kings xxiii. 13; Jer. xlviii. 7, 13.——[u] Jer. xlviii. 18, 22. [v] Isa. xv. 2.

[w] Chap. xxxii. 1; Jer. xlviii. 32.——[x] Deut. iii. 1; xxix. 7. [y] Josh. xiii. 12.——[z] Deut. iii. 2.——[a] Ver. 24; Psa. cxxxv. 10, 11; cxxxvi. 20.——[b] Deut. iii. 3, 4, &c.

The *third* sets forth the revenge taken by Israel upon the whole country of Sihon, from *Heshbon* to *Dibon*, and from *Nophah* even to *Medeba*. See Isa. xv. 1, 2.

The whole poem, divided into its proper hemistichs, as it stands in Kennicott's Hebrew Bible, is as follows:—

VERSE 27. PART I.

Come ye to Heshbon, let it be rebuilt;
The city of Sihon, let it be established.

VERSE 28.

For from Heshbon the fire went out,
And a flame from the city of Sihon:
It hath consumed the city of Moab,
With the lords of the heights of Arnon.

VERSE 29. PART II.

Alas for thee, O Moab!
Thou hast perished, O people of *Chemosh!*
He hath given up his fugitive sons
And his daughters into captivity,
To the king of the Amorites, Sihon.

VERSE 30. PART III.

But on them have WE lifted destruction,
From Heshbon even to Dibon;
We have destroyed even to Nophah,
The fire did reach to Medebah.

See *Kennicott's* Remarks.

Verse 35. *So they smote him, and his sons*] There is a curious note of Dr. Lightfoot here, of which I should think it wrong to deprive the reader.

"Sihon and Og conquered, A. M. 2553. Of the life of Moses, 120. From the Exodus, 40. It is now *six* and *twenty* generations from the creation, or from Adam to Moses; and accordingly doth Psa. cxxxvi. rehearse the durableness of God's mercy *six* and *twenty* times over, beginning the story with the creation, and ending it in the conquest of Sihon and Og. The numerals of the name יהוה *Jehovah* amount to the sum of *six* and *twenty*."

ON some difficulties in this chapter Dr. Kennicott makes the following observations:—

"This one chapter has several very considerable difficulties; and some verses, as now translated, are remarkably unintelligible. A true state of this chapter is not, however, to be despaired of; and it has in it some circumstances which merit more than common attention. It contains the history of the last part of the travels of the Israelites in their way to the promised land; beginning with them at *Mount Hor*, the thirty-fourth encampment, and concluding with them, as in their forty-second and last encampment, near Jordan, in the country which they had acquired by conquest over Sihon, king of the Amorites.

"It begins with saying—that *King Arad, the Canaanite, who dwelt in the south,* (in the land of Canaan, chap. xxxiii. 40,) attacked Israel and was defeated, and that *Israel destroyed their cities;* and that, after destroying these *Canaanite cities*, and consequently after being in a part of Cannaan, a part of the very country they were going to, on the *west* of the *Dead* Sea, they returned towards the *Red* Sea, and near the *eastern* tongue or gulf of the Red Sea, on the *south of Edom*, marched round *Edom* to the *east* of the *Dead* Sea, in order to enter Canaan from the *east* side of Jordan!

"This surprising representation of so vast and dangerous a march, quite unnecessarily performed, is owing to two circumstances. The first is, (chapter xxi. 1,) the Canaanites heard that Israel was coming by *the way of the spies*, meaning, by the way *the spies* went *from Kadesh-Barnea* into *Canaan*. But this being impossible, because Israel had now marched from *Meribah-Kadesh* to *Mount Hor*, beyond *Ezion-gaber*, and were turning round *Edom*, to the south-east; it is happy that the word rendered *spies*, in our version, is in the Greek a proper name, (*Atharim*,) which removes that difficulty: and the other difficulty (verses 2, 3) is removed by the Greek version likewise, according to which, the vow made, with the facts subsequent, does not signify *destroying* the Canaanite cities, but *devoting them to destruction* at some future time. See *Wall's* Crit. Notes.

' It proceeds with saying, that after defeating the Canaanites at *Mount Hor*, they journeyed *from Mount Hor by the way of the Red Sea*, (in the road from *Ammon*, *Midian*, &c., to the *eastern* gulf of the Red Sea,) *to compass the land of Edom;* that on their murmuring for want both of bread and of water they were punished by fiery serpents, after which they marched to *Oboth*, and thence to *Ije-abarim* in the *wilderness*, *east of Moab*. The encampments of the Israelites, amounting to *forty-two*, are recorded all together, in historical succession, in chap. xxxiii., where *Ije-abarim* is the 38th; *Dibon-gad*, 39; *Almon-Diblathaim*, 40; *mountains of Abarim*, 41; and *the plains of Moab*, by *Jordan*, 42. This regular detail in chap. xxxiii. has occasioned great perplexity as to chap. xxi., where, after the stations at *Oboth* and *Ije-abarim*, in verses 10 and 11, we have, in verses 19 and 20, the words *Mattanah*, *Nahaliel*, and *Bamoth;* which are usually considered as the proper names of three places, but widely different from the three proper names after *Ije-abarim* in the catalogue at chap. xxxiii.

" But there is, in reality, no inconsistency here. In the plain and historical catalogue (chap. xxxiii.) the words are strictly *the proper names of the three places;* but here the words *Mattanah*, *Nahaliel*, and *Bamoth* follow some lines of poetry, and seem to form a continuation of the song. They evidently express figurative and poetical ideas. The verbs *journeyed from* and *pitched in* are not found here, though necessary to prose narration: see verses 10 and 11 here, and chap. xxxiii. Lastly, verse 20th, (in this 21st chapter,) usually supposed to express *the last encampment*, does not. *Pisgah* signifies *a hill;* and the Israelites could not encamp on the top of any single hill, such as this is described. Balak took Balaam to *the top of Peor*, which *looketh toward Jeshimon*, (chap. xxiii. 28,) which *Peor* undoubtedly was in *Moab*. He took him to another hill in *Moab*, when he took him (chap. xxiii. 14) to the top of *Pisgah*, in *the field of Zophim*. And if the Pisgah or hill in chap. xxi. 20, was in the country of *Balak*, it could not point out *the last encampment*, which was not in Balak's country, but *north of Arnon*.

" The word *Mattanah* probably alludes to a place distinguished by some *gift* or *blessing* from God. Fagius says: *Nomen loci, ab eventu aquarum quas Dominus ibi dedit, sic appellati;* כמתנה *nam significat donum* —' The name of the place was so called, from the circumstance of the waters which the Lord gave there; for *Mattanah* signifies a *gift*.' נחליאל *Nahaliel* is *torrentes Dei;* i. e., great streams, particularly seasonable or salutary. And במות *Bamoth* (ver. 28) may point out any high places of signal benefit in the country of *Moab*, or it may answer to *the last station but one*, which was *the mountains of Abarim*. If, therefore, these words were meant to express poetically some eminent blessing, what blessing was so likely to be then celebrated as *copious streams of water?* And after they had wandered nearly *forty* years through many a barren desert, and after (compare Deut. viii. 15) having passed through *that great and terrible wilderness*, wherein were *fiery serpents* and *drought*, where there was *no water*, it is no wonder they should shout for joy at finding *water in plenty*, and finding it almost on the banks of *Arnon*, the last river they were to pass, in their way to their last station, east of Jordan. No wonder they should sing in poetic rapture, that after *the wilderness* was (*Mattanah*) the GIFT of GOD; meaning *the great well* in Moab, dug by public authority; and no wonder that, after such a *gift*, there were (*Nahaliel*) *blessed streams*, by which they passed, till they came to (*Bamoth*) the high places from which, perhaps, these streams descended. And the thanksgiving ends, where the blessing was no longer wanted, on their coming down into *the valley*, along the banks of Arnon, which was then the north boundary of Moab.

" The Israelites had spent no less than *thirty-eight* years in coming from *Kadesh-Barnea* to their encampment north of *Zared*. Here, at this *fortieth* station, they were commanded to pass through Moab by ער *Ar*, the chief city; but were not to stop till they came to *the valley* on the south of Arnon. At this last station but one they probably continued no longer than was necessary for *sending messengers to Sihon*, king of the Amorites, at Heshbon, and receiving his answer. They then crossed the Arnon; and having vanquished *Sihon* and *Og*, took possession of the *forty-second* and last encampment.

" This one chapter has *three* pieces of poetry, either fragments or complete; and poetry, seldom found in a historical narrative, may be here accounted for from the exuberance of joy which must have affected these wearied travellers, when arriving thus happily near their journey's end. What occurs first is in ver. 14; and has often been called *the fragment of an old Amorite song*. But it may have been *Amorite* or *Moabite*, or *either* or *neither*, for the subject matter of it, as it is generally understood, if indeed it can be said to be understood at all. The words את והב בסופה ואת הנחלים ארנון usually supposed to contain this fragment, do not signify, as in our English version, *What he did in the Red Sea, and in the brooks of Arnon*. Without enumerating the many interpretations given by others, I shall offer a new one, which seems to make good sense, and a sense very pertinent.

" Observe first, that there must have been a *place* called *Suph*, near the conflux of the *Arnon* and *Jordan;* because Moses, whilst in that last station, begins *Deuteronomy* with saying, he was on *this* side (i. e., east) of Jordan, over against *Suph*. By this word is not here meant the *Red Sea;* partly, because that has every where else the word for *sea* before it, and partly, because of the great distance of the Red Sea now from Moses. The single word, therefore, signifies here some *place* in itself obscure, because no where mentioned but in these two passages. And yet we cannot wonder that Moses should mention it twice, as the word *Suph*, introduced in speaking of the two last encampments, recalled to mind the *Sea of Suph*, so glorious to Israel, near the beginning of their march towards Canaan.

" Moses had now led Israel *from the Red Sea* to the river Arnon, through many dreadful dangers, partly from hostile nations, partly from themselves; such dangers as no other people ever experienced, and such as no people could have surmounted, without the signal favour of *the Almighty*. And here, just before the battles with *Sihon* an *Og*, he reminds them of *Pha-*

raoh, &c.; and he asserts, that *in the history of the wars it shall be recorded* that JEHOVAH, who had triumphantly brought *Israel* through *the Sea of Suph*, near Egypt, at first, had now conducted him to *Suph*, near Arnon; that

JEHOVAH *went with him to* SUPH,
And he came to the streams of Arnon.

"This version removes the difficulties urged by *Hobbes*, page 266, fol. 1750; by *Spinoza*, page 108, 4to., 1670; and retailed in a deistical pamphlet called *The Doubts of the Infidels*, page 4, 8vo., 1781.

"The general meaning of the next piece of poetry seems to be this: that at some distance from the city of *Ar*, by which the Israelites were to pass, (Deut. ii. 18,) they came to A WELL of uncommon size and magnificence, which seems to have been *sought out, built up*, and *adorned* for the public, by *the rulers* of Moab. And it is no wonder that, on their arrival at *such a well*, they should look upon it as *a blessing from Heaven*, and speak of it as a new miracle in their favour.

17. *Then Israel sang this song:—*

Spring up, O WELL! Sing ye thereto!
18. THE WELL! princes searched it out;
The nobles of the people have digged it;
By their decree, by their act of government.
So, after the *wilderness*, was *Mattanah!*
19. And after *Mattanah* were *Nahaliel!*
And after *Nahaliel* were *Bamoth!*
20. And after *Bamoth* was the *valley;*
Where, in the country of *Moab*,
Appeareth the top of *Pisgah*,
Which is over against *Jeshimon*.

See Dr. KENNICOTT'S *Remarks upon Select Passages in the Old Testament.*

CHAPTER XXII.

The Israelites pitch in the plains of Moab, 1. *Balak, king of Moab, is greatly terrified*, 2–4; *and sends to Balaam, a diviner, to come and curse them*, 5, 6. *The elders of Moab take a reward and carry it to Balaam*, 7. *He inquires of the Lord, and is positively ordered not to go with them*, 8–12. *He communicates this to the elders of Moab*, 13. *They return to Balak with this information*, 14. *He sends some of his princes to Balaam with promises of great honour*, 15–17. *He consults God, and is permitted to go, on certain conditions*, 18–20. *Balaam sets off, is opposed by an angel of the Lord, and the Lord miraculously opens the mouth of his ass to reprove him*, 21–30. *Balaam sees the angel, and is reproved by him*, 31–33. *He humbles himself, and offers to go back*, 34; *but is ordered to proceed, on the same conditions as before*, 35. *The king of Moab goes out to meet him*, 36. *His address to him*, 37. *Balaam's firm answer*, 38. *Balak sacrifices, and takes Balaam to the high places of Baal, that he may see the whole of the Israelitish camp*, 39–41.

A. M. 2553. B. C. 1451. An. Exod. Isr. 40.

AND [a] the children of Israel set forward, and pitched in the plains of Moab, on this side Jordan *by* Jericho.
2 And [b] Balak the son of Zippor saw all that Israel had done to the Amorites.
3 And [c] Moab was sore afraid of the people, because they *were* many: and Moab was distressed because of the children of Israel.
4 And Moab said unto [d] the elders of Midian, Now shall this company lick up all *that are* round about us, as the ox licketh up the grass of the field. And Balak the son of Zippor *was* king of the Moabites at that time.
5 [e] He sent messengers therefore unto Balaam the son of Beor to [f] Pethor, which *is* by the river of the land of the children of his people, to call him, saying, Behold, there is a people come out from Egypt: behold, they cover the [g] face of the earth, and they abide over against me:

[a] Chap. xxxiii. 48.——[b] Judg. xi. 25.——[c] Exod. xv. 15.——[d] Chap. xxxi. 8; Josh. xiii. 21.——[e] Deut. xxiii. 4; Josh. xiii. 22; xxiv. 9; Neh. xiii. 1, 2; Mic. vi. 5; 2 Pet. ii. 15; Jude 11; Rev. ii. 14.——[f] See chap. xxiii. 7; Deut. xxiii. 4.——[g] Heb. *eye*.

NOTES ON CHAP. XXII.

Verse 1. *And pitched in the plains of Moab*] They had taken no part of the country that at *present* appertained to the Moabites; they had taken only that part which had formerly belonged to this people, but had been taken from them by Sihon, king of the Amorites.

On this side Jordan] On the east side. By *Jericho*, that is, over against it.

Verse 5. *To Pethor, which* is *by the river of the land of the children of his people*] Dr. Kennicott justly remarks, that "the description now given of Balaam's residence, instead of being particular, agrees with any place in any country where there is a *river;* for he lived by *Pethor, which is by the river of the land of the children of his people.* But was Pethor then near the *Nile* in *Egypt?* Or in *Canaan*, near *Jordan?* Or in *Mesopotamia*, near the *Euphrates*, and belonging to the *Ammonites?* This last was in fact the case; and therefore it is well that twelve Hebrew MSS. (with two of *De Rossi's*) confirm the *Samaritan* text here in reading, instead of עמו *ammo, his people*, עמון *Ammon*, with the Syriac and Vulgate versions." Houbigant properly contends for this reading; and necessity urges the propriety of adopting it.

A. M. 2553.
B. C. 1451.
An. Exod. Isr.
40.

6 Come now, therefore, I pray
thee, [h] curse me this people; for
they *are* too mighty for me:
peradventure I shall prevail, *that*
we may smite them, and *that* I
may drive them out of the land:

A. M. 2553.
B. C. 1451.
An. Exod. Isr.
40.

[h] Numbers, chap. xxiii. 7.

It should therefore stand thus: *by the river of the land of the children of Ammon;* and thus it agrees with Deut. xxiii. 4.

Verse 6. *Come now, therefore, I pray thee, curse me this people*] Balaam, once a prophet of the true God, appears to have been one of the *Moshelim*, (see chap. xxi. 27,) who had added to his poetic gift that of *sorcery* or *divination*. It was supposed that prophets and sorcerers had a power to *curse persons* and *places* so as to *confound* all their *designs*, *frustrate* their *counsels*, *enervate* their *strength*, and fill them with fear, terror, and dismay. See Gen. ix. 25; Psa. cix. 6, 20; Josh. vi. 26; Jer. xvii. 5, 6.

Macrobius has a whole chapter *De carmine quo evocari solebant dii tutelares, et aut urbes, aut exercitus devoveri.* "Of the incantations which were used to induce the tutelary gods to forsake the cities, &c., over which they presided, and to devote cities and whole armies to destruction." See *Saturnal.*, lib. iii., cap. ix. He gives us *two* of the ancient forms used in reference to the destruction of *Carthage;* the first, *to call over the protecting deities*, was pronounced by the dictator or general, and none other, when they began the siege. It is as follows, *literatim et punctatim:*—

Si. Deus. si. Dea. est. cui. popolus. civitas. que. Karthaginiensis. est. in. tutela. te. que. maxime. ille. qui. urbis. hujus. popoli. que. tutelam. recepisti. precor. veneror. que. veniam. que. a. vobis. peto. ut. vos. popolum. civitatem. que. Karthaginiensem. deseratis. loca. templa. sacra. urbem. que. eorum. relinquatis. absque. his. abeatis. ei. que. popolo. civitati. que. metum. formidinem. oblivionem. injiciatis. proditi. que. Romam. ad. me. meos. que. veniatis. nostra. que. vobis. loca. templa. sacra. urbs. acceptior. probatior. que. sit. mihi. que. popolo. que. Romano. militibus. que. meis. præpositi. sitis. ut. sciamus. intelligamus. que. Si. ita. feceritis. voveo. vobis. templa. ludos. que. facturum.

"Whether it be god or goddess, under whose protection the people and city of Carthage are placed; and thee, especially, who hast undertaken to defend this city and people; I pray, beseech, and earnestly entreat that you would forsake the people and city of Carthage, and leave their places, temples, sacred things, and city, and depart from them: and that you would inspire this people and city with fear, terror, and forgetfulness: and that, coming out from them, you would pass over to Rome, to me, and to mine: and that our places, temples, sacred things, and city may be more agreeable and more acceptable to you: and that you would preside over me, the Roman people, and my soldiers; that we may know and perceive it. If ye will do this, I promise to consecrate to your honour both temples and games."

The second, to devote the city to destruction, which it was supposed the tutelary gods had abandoned, is the following:—

Dis. Pater. Vejovis. Manes. sive. vos. quo. alio. nomine. fas. est. nominare. ut. omnes. illam. urbem. Karthaginem. exercitum. que. quem. ego. me. sentio. dicere. fuga. formidine. terrore. que. compleatis. qui. que. adversum. legiones. exercitum. que. nostrum. arma. tela. que. ferent. Uti. vos. eum. exercitum. eos. hostes. eos. que. homines. urbes. agros. que. eorum. et. qui. in. his. locis. regionibus. que. agris. urbibus. ve. habitant. abducatis. lumine. supero. privetis. exercitum. que. hostium. urbes. agros. que. eorum. quos. me. sentio. dicere. uti. vos. eas. urbes. agros. que. capita. ætates. que. eorum. devotas. consecratas. que. habeatis. illis. legibus. quibus. quando. quo. sunt. maxime. hostes. devoti. eos. que. ego. vicarios. pro. me. fide. magistratu. que. meo. pro. popolo. Romano. exercitibus. legionibus. que. nostris. do. devoveo. ut. me. meam. que. fidem. imperium. que. legiones. exercitum. que. nostrum. qui. in. his. rebus. gerundis. sunt. bene. salvos. siritis. esse. Si. hæc. ita. faxitis. ut. ego. sciam. sentiam. intelligam. que. tunc. quisquis. hoc. votum. faxit. ubi. ubi. faxit. recte. factum. esto. ovibus. atris. tribus. Tellus. mater. te. que. Juppiter. obtestor.

"Dis. Pater. Vejovis. Manes., or by whatsoever name you wish to be invoked, I pray you to fill this city of Carthage with fear and terror; and to put that army to flight which I mention, and which bears arms or darts against OUR legions and armies: and that ye may take away this army, those enemies, those men, their cities and their country, and all who dwell in those places, regions, countries, or cities; and deprive them of the light above: and let all their armies, cities, country, chiefs, and people be held by you consecrated and *devoted*, according to those laws by which, and at what time, enemies can be most effectually devoted. I also give and devote them as vicarious sacrifices for myself and my magistracy; for the Roman people, and for all our armies and legions; and for the whole empire, and that all the armies and legions which are employed in these countries may be preserved in safety. If therefore ye will do these things, as I know, conceive, and intend, then he who makes this vow wheresoever and whensoever he shall make it, I engage shall sacrifice *three black sheep* to thee, O mother Earth, and to thee, O Jupiter." "When the execrator mentions the *earth*, he stoops down and places both his hands on it; and when he names *Jupiter*, he lifts up both his hands to heaven; and when he mentions his *vow*, he places his hands upon his breast." Among the ancient records, Macrobius says he found many cities and people devoted in this way. The Romans held that no city could be taken till its *tutelary god* had forsaken it; or if it could be taken, it would be unlawful, as it would be sacrilegious to have the gods in captivity. They therefore endeavoured to persuade the gods of their enemies to come over to their party. *Virgil* intimates that Troy was destroyed, only because the tutelary gods had forsaken it:—

A. M. 2553.
B. C. 1451.
An. Exod. Isr.
40.

for I wot that he whom thou
blessest *is* blessed, and he whom
thou cursest is cursed.

7 And the elders of Moab and the elders of
Midian departed with [i] the rewards of divination in their hand; and they came unto Balaam,
and spake unto him the words of Balak.

8 And he said unto them, [k] Lodge here this
night, and I will bring you word again, as the
LORD shall speak unto me: and the princes
of Moab abode with Balaam.

9 [l] And God came unto Balaam, and said,
What men *are* these with thee?

10 And Balaam said unto God, Balak the
son of Zippor, king of Moab, hath sent unto
me, *saying*,

11 Behold, *there is* a people come out of
Egypt, which covereth the face of the earth:
come now, curse me them; peradventure [m] I
shall be able to overcome them, and drive
them out.

12 And God said unto Balaam, Thou shalt
not go with them; thou shalt
not curse the people: for [n] they
are blessed.

A. M. 2553.
B. C. 1451.
An. Exod. Isr.
40.

13 And Balaam rose up in the morning, and
said unto the princes of Balak, Get you into
your land: for the LORD refuseth to give me
leave to go with you.

14 And the princes of Moab rose up, and
they went unto Balak, and said, Balaam refuseth to come with us.

15 And Balak sent yet again princes, more,
and more honourable than they.

16 And they came to Balaam, and said to
him, Thus saith Balak the son of Zippor, [o] Let
nothing, I pray thee, hinder thee from coming
unto me:

17 For I will promote thee unto very great
honour, and I will do whatsoever thou sayest
unto me: [p] come therefore, I pray thee, curse
me this people.

18 And Balaam answered and said unto the
servants of Balak, [q] If Balak would give me

[i] 1 Sam. ix. 7, 8.——[k] Ver. 19.——[l] Gen. xx. 3; ver. 20.——[m] Heb. *I shall prevail in fighting against him.*

[n] Chap. xxiii. 20; Rom. xi. 29.——[o] Heb. *be not thou letted from, &c.*——[p] Ver. 6.——[q] Chap. xxiv. 13.

Excessere omnes, adytis arisque relictis,
Dii, quibus imperium hoc steterat.
ÆN., lib. ii., ver. 351.

"All the gods, by whose assistance the empire had hitherto been preserved, forsook their altars and their temples." And it was on this account that the Greeks employed all their artifice to steal away the *Palladium*, on which they believe the safety of Troy depended.

Tacitus observes that when *Suetonius Paulinus* prepared his army to cross over into *Mona*, (Anglesea,) where the *Britons* and *Druids* made their last stand, the *priestesses*, with dishevelled hair, white vestments, and torches in their hands, ran about like furies, *devoting their enemies to destruction;* and he farther adds that the *sight*, the *attitude*, and horrible *imprecations* of these priestesses had such effect on the Roman soldiers, that for a while they stood still and suffered themselves to be pierced with the darts of the Britons, without making any resistance. Tacit. Ann., l. xiv., c. 29. Many accounts are related in the Hindoo *Pooran* of kings employing sages to curse their enemies when too powerful for them.—WARD's *Customs.*

The Jews also had a most horrible form of execration, as may be seen in Buxtorf's Talmudical Lexicon under the word חרם. These observations and authorities, drawn out in so much detail, are necessary to cast light on the strange and curious history related in this and the two following chapters.

Verse 7. *The rewards of divination*] Whoever went to consult a prophet took with him a present, as it was on such gratuitous offerings the prophets lived; but here more than a mere present is intended, perhaps every thing necessary to provide materials for the *incantation.* The *drugs*, &c., used on such occasions were often very expensive. It appears that Balaam was very *covetous*, and that he loved the wages of unrighteousness, and probably lived by it; see 2 Pet. ii. 15.

Verse 8. *I will bring you word again, as the Lord shall speak*] So it appears he knew the true God, and had been in the habit of consulting him, and receiving oracles from his mouth.

Verse 12. *Thou shalt not go with them; thou shalt not curse the people*] That is, Thou shalt not go with them to curse the people. With them he *might go*, as we find he afterwards did by God's own command, but not to *curse* the people; this was wholly forbidden. Probably the command, *Thou shalt not go*, refers here to *that time*, viz., the first invitation: and in this sense it was most punctually obeyed by Balaam; see ver. 13.

Verse 14. *Balaam refuseth to come with us.*] "Observe," says Mr. Ainsworth, "Satan's practice against God's word, seeking to lessen the same, and that from *hand to hand*, till he bring it to naught. Balaam told the princes *less* than God told him, and they relate to Balak *less* than Balaam told them; so that when the answer came to the king of Moab, it was not *the word of God*, but the *word of man;* it was simply, *Balaam refuseth to come*, without ever intimating that God had forbidden him." But in this Balaam is not to blame; he told the messengers in the most positive manner, *Jehovah refuseth to give me leave to go with you*, ver. 13; and more explicit he could not be.

Verse 18. *I cannot go beyond the word of the Lord my God*] Balaam knew God too well to suppose he could reverse any of his purposes; and he respected

A. M. 2553.
B. C. 1451.
An. Exod. Isr.
40.

his house full of silver and gold,
[r] I cannot go beyond the word of
the LORD my God, to do less
or more.
19 Now therefore, I pray you, [s] tarry ye
also here this night, that I may know what
the LORD will say unto me more.
20 [t] And God came unto Balaam at night,
and said unto him, If the men come to call thee,
rise up, *and* go with them; but [u] yet the word
which I shall say unto thee, that shalt thou do.
21 And Balaam rose up in the morning, and
saddled his ass, and went with the princes of
Moab.
22 And God's anger was kindled because he
went: [v] and the angel of the LORD stood in
the way for an adversary against him. Now
he was riding upon his ass, and his two servants
were with him.
23 And [w] the ass saw the angel of the LORD
standing in the way, and his sword drawn in
his hand: and the ass turned aside out of the
way, and went into the field: and Balaam
smote the ass, to turn her into the way.
24 But the angel of the LORD stood in a
path of the vineyards, a wall
being on this side, and a wall on
that side.

A. M. 2553.
B. C. 1451.
An. Exod. Isr.
40.

25 And when the ass saw the angel of the
LORD, she thrust herself unto the wall, and
crushed Balaam's foot against the wall: and
he smote her again.
26 And the angel of the LORD went further,
and stood in a narrow place, where *was* no
way to turn either to the right hand or to the left.
27 And when the ass saw the angel of the
LORD, she fell down under Balaam: and Balaam's
anger was kindled, and he smote the
ass with a staff.
28 And the LORD [x] opened the mouth of the
ass, and she said unto Balaam, What have I
done unto thee, that thou hast smitten me these
three times?
29 And Balaam said unto the ass, Because
thou hast mocked me: I would there were a
sword in mine hand, [y] for now would I kill thee.
30 [z] And the ass said unto Balaam, *Am* not
I thine ass, [a] upon which thou hast ridden
[b] ever since *I was* thine unto this day? was I ever
wont to do so unto thee? And he said, Nay.

[r] 1 Kings xxii. 14; 2 Chron. xviii. 13.——[s] Ver. 8.——[t] Ver. 9.——[u] Verse 35; chapter xxiii. 12, 26; xxiv. 13.——[v] Exodus iv. 24.——[w] See 2 Kings vi. 17; Dan. x. 7; Acts xxii. 9; 2 Peter ii. 16; Jude 11.——[x] 2 Peter ii. 16.——[y] Prov. xii. 10.——[z] 2 Peter ii. 16.——[a] Heb. *who hast ridden upon me.*——[b] Or, *ever since thou wast, &c.*

him too much to attempt to do any thing without his permission. Though he was *covetous*, yet he dared not, even when strongly tempted both by *riches* and *honours*, to go contrary to the command of his God. Many make all the professions of Balaam, without justifying them by their conduct. "They pretend," says one, "they would not do any thing against the word of God for a *house full* of gold, and yet will do it for a *handful!*"

Verse 19. *What the Lord will say unto me more.*] He did not know but God might make a farther discovery of his will to him, and therefore he might very innocently seek farther information.

Verse 20. *If the men come—go with them*] This is a confirmation of what was observed on the twelfth verse; though we find his going was marked with the Divine displeasure, because he wished, for the sake of the *honours* and *rewards*, to fulfil as far as possible the will of the king of Moab. Mr. Shuckford observes that the pronoun הוא *hu* is sometimes used to denote a person's *doing a thing out of his own head*, without regard to the *directions* of another. Thus in the case of Balaam, when God had allowed him to go with the messengers of Balak, *if they came in the morning to call him*; because he was more hasty than he ought to have been, and went to *them* instead of staying till *they* should come to *him*, it was said of him, not כי הלך *ki halach, that he went*, but כי הולך הוא *ki holech hu*, i. e., *he went of his own head*—without being called; and in this, Mr. Shuckford supposes, his iniquity chiefly lay.—*Connex.*, vol. iii., p. 115. How many are restrained from sinning, merely through the *fear* of God! They would gladly do the evil, but it is forbidden on awful penalties; they wish the thing were not prohibited, for they have a strong desire to do it.

Verse 23. *And the ass saw the angel*] When God granted *visions*, those alone who were particularly interested saw them, while others in the same company saw nothing; see Dan. x. 7; Acts ix. 7.

Verse 26. *And the angel—stood in a narrow place*] In this carriage of the angel, says Mr. Ainsworth, the Lord shows us the proceedings of his judgments against sinners: *First*, he mildly *shakes* his *rod* at them, but lets them go untouched. *Secondly*, he comes *nearer*, and touches them with an easy correction, as it were wringing their foot against the wall. *Thirdly*, when all this is ineffectual, he brings them into such *straits*, that they can neither turn to the right hand nor to the left, but must fall before his judgments, if they do not fully turn to him.

Verse 28. *The Lord opened the mouth of the ass*] And where is the wonder of all this? If the *ass* had opened *her own mouth*, and reproved the rash prophet, we might well be astonished; but when *God opens the mouth*, an *ass* can speak as well as a *man*. It is worthy of remark here, that Balaam testifies no surprise at this miracle, because he saw it was the *Lord's* doing. Of animate and inanimate things receiving for a short

A. M. 2553.
B. C. 1451.
An. Exod. Isr. 40.

31 Then the LORD [c] opened
the eyes of Balaam, and he saw
the angel of the LORD standing
in the way, and his sword drawn in his hand:
and he [d] bowed down his head, and [e] fell flat
on his face.
32 And the angel of the LORD said unto him,
Wherefore hast thou smitten thine ass these
three times? behold, I went out [f] to withstand
thee, because *thy* way is [g] perverse before me:
33 And the ass saw me, and turned from
me these three times: unless she had turned
from me, surely now also I had slain thee,
and saved her alive.
34 And Balaam said unto the angel of the
LORD, [h] I have sinned; for I knew not that thou
stoodest in the way against me: now therefore,
if it [i] displease thee, I will get me back again.
35 And the angel of the LORD said unto Balaam,
Go with the men: [k] but only the word
that I shall speak unto thee, that thou shalt
speak. So Balaam went with the princes of
Balak.

A. M. 2553.
B. C. 1451.
An. Exod. Isr. 40.

36 And when Balak heard that
Balaam was come, [l] he went out
to meet him unto a city of Moab,
[m] which *is* in the border of Arnon, which *is*
in the utmost coast.
37 And Balak said unto Balaam, Did I
not earnestly send unto thee to call thee?
wherefore camest thou not unto me? am
I not able indeed [n] to promote thee to
honour?
38 And Balaam said unto Balak, Lo, I am
come unto thee: have I now any power at all
to say any thing? [o] the word that God putteth
in my mouth, that shall I speak.
39 And Balaam went with Balak, and they
came unto [p] Kirjath-huzoth.
40 And Balak offered oxen and sheep, and
sent to Balaam, and to the princes that *were*
with him.
41 And it came to pass on the morrow, that
Balak took Balaam, and brought him up into
the [q] high places of Baal, that thence he might
see the utmost *part* of the people.

[c] See Gen. xxi. 19; 2 Kings vi. 17; Luke xxiv. 16, 31. — [d] Exod. xxxiv. 8. — [e] Or, *bowed himself.* — [f] Heb. *to be an adversary unto thee.* — [g] 2 Pet. ii. 14, 15. — [h] 1 Sam. xv. 24, 30; xxvi. 21; 2 Sam. xii. 13; Job xxxiv. 31, 32.

[i] Heb. *be evil in thine eyes.* — [k] Verse 20. — [l] Gen. xiv. 17. — [m] Chap. xxi. 13. — [n] Ver. 17; chap. xxiv. 11. — [o] Chap. xxiii. 26; xxiv. 13; 1 Kings xxii. 14; 2 Chron. xviii. 13. — [p] Or, *a city of streets.* — [q] Chap. xxiii. 2, 14, 30; Deut. xii. 2.

time the gift of speech, the heathen mythology furnishes many fictitious examples, with which I do not deem it proper to occupy the reader's time.

Verse 33. *Surely now also I had slain thee*] How often are the meanest animals, and the most trivial occurrences, instruments of the preservation of our lives, and of the salvation of our souls! The messenger of justice would have killed Balaam, had not the mercy of God prevented the ass from proceeding.

Verse 34. *If it displease thee, I will get me back again.*] Here is a proof, that though he *loved the wages of unrighteousness*, yet he still feared God; and he is now willing to drop the enterprise if God be displeased with his proceeding. The piety of many called Christians does not extend thus far; they see that the thing displeases God, and yet they proceed. Reader, is this *thy* case?

Verse 38. *The word that God putteth in my mouth, that shall I speak.*] Here was a noble resolution, and he was certainly faithful to it: though he wished to please the king, and get wealth and honour, yet he would not displease God to realize even these bright prospects. Many who slander this poor semi-antinomian prophet, have not half his piety.

Verse 40. *And Balak offered oxen, &c.*] This was to gain the favour of his gods, and perhaps to propitiate Jehovah, that the end for which he had sent for Balaam might be accomplished.

Verse 41. *That—he might see the utmost* part *of the people.*] As he thought Balaam must have them all in his eye when he pronounced his curse, lest it might not extend to those who were not in sight. On this account he took him up into the high places of Baal.

CHAPTER XXIII.

Being arrived at the high places of Baal, (chap. xxii. 41,) *Balaam orders Balak to build seven altars, and prepare oxen and rams for sacrifice,* 1, 2. *Balaam inquires of the Lord, receives an answer, with which he returns to Balak,* 3–10. *Balak, finding that this was a prediction of the prosperity of the Israelites, is greatly troubled,* 11. *Balaam excuses himself,* 12. *He brings him to another place, where he might see only a part of Israel, and repeats his sacrifices,* 13, 14. *Balaam again consults the Lord,* 15–17. *Returns with his answer, and again predicts the glory of Israel,* 18–24. *Balak is angry,* 25; *and Balaam again excuses himself. Balak proposes another trial, takes him to another place, and repeats the ame sacrifices,* 26–30.

A. M. 2553. B. C. 1451. An. Exod. Isr. 40.

AND Balaam said unto Balak, [a] Build me here seven altars, and prepare me here seven oxen and seven rams.

2 And Balak did as Balaam had spoken; and Balak and Balaam [b] offered on *every* altar a bullock and a ram.

3 And Balaam said unto Balak, [c] Stand by thy burnt-offering, and I will go: peradventure the LORD will come [d] to meet me: and whatsoever he showeth me I will tell thee. And [e] he went to a high place.

4 [f] And God met Balaam: and he said unto him, I have prepared seven altars, and I have offered upon *every* altar a bullock and a ram.

5 And the LORD [g] put a word in Balaam's mouth, and said, Return unto Balak, and thus thou shalt speak.

6 And he returned unto him, and, lo, he stood by his burnt sacrifice, he, and all the princes of Moab.

A. M. 2553. B. C. 1451. An. Exod. Isr. 40.

7 And he [h] took up his parable, and said, Balak, the king of Moab, hath brought me from Aram, out of the mountains of the east, *saying,* [i] Come, curse me Jacob, and come, [k] defy Israel.

8 [l] How shall I curse, whom God hath not cursed? or how shall I defy, *whom* the LORD hath not defied?

9 For from the top of the rocks I see him, and from the hills I behold him: lo, [m] the people shall dwell alone, and [n] shall not be reckoned among the nations.

10 [o] Who can count the dust of Jacob, and the number of the fourth *part* of Israel? Let [p] me die [q] the death of the righteous, and let my last end be like his!

11 And Balak said unto Balaam, What hast thou done unto me? [r] I took thee to curse mine enemies, and, behold, thou hast blessed *them* altogether.

12 And he answered and said, [s] Must I not

[a] Ver. 29.——[b] Ver. 14, 30.——[c] Ver. 15.——[d] Chap. xxiv. 1.
[e] Or, *he went solitary.*——[f] Ver. 16.——[g] Ver. 16; ch. xxii. 35; Deut. xviii. 18; Jer. i. 9.——[h] Ver. 18; chap. xxiv. 3, 15, 23; Job xxvii. 1; xxix. 1; Psa. lxxviii. 2; Ezek. xvii. 2; Mic. ii. 4; Hab. ii. 6.

[i] Chap. xxii. 6, 11, 17.——[k] 1 Sam. xvii. 10.——[l] Isa. xlvii. 12, 13.——[m] Deut. xxxiii. 28.——[n] Exodus xxxiii. 16; Ezra ix. 2; Eph. ii. 14.——[o] Gen. xiii. 16; xxii. 17.——[p] Heb. *my soul*, or, *my life.*——[q] Psa. cxvi. 15.——[r] Chapter xxii. 11, 17; xxiv. 10.
[s] Chap. xxii. 38.

NOTES ON CHAP. XXIII.

Verse 1. *Build me here seven altars, &c.*] The *oxen* and the *rams* were such as the Mosaic law had ordered to be offered to God in sacrifice; the building of seven altars was not commanded. Some think that these seven altars were built to the *seven planets:* this is most gratuitously said; of it there is no proof whatever; it is mere trifling, even with conjecture. As *seven* was a number of perfection, Balaam chose it on this occasion, because he intended to offer a grand sacrifice, and to offer a bullock and a ram upon each of the altars; the whole to be made a burnt-offering at the *same time.* And as he intended to offer seven bullocks and seven rams at the same time, it could not be conveniently done on *one* altar, therefore he ordered seven to be built. We need go no farther to find out his reasons.

Verse 3. *Stand by thy burnt-offering*] We have already seen that blessing and cursing in this way were considered as religious *rites*, and therefore must be always preceded by sacrifice. See this exemplified in the case of *Isaac*, before he blessed Jacob and Esau, Gen. xxvii., and the notes there. The venison that was brought to Isaac, of which he did eat, was properly the preparatory sacrifice.

Verse 7. *And he took up his parable*] משלו *meshalo*, see on chap. xxi. 27. All these oracular speeches of Balaam are in *hemistich* metre in the original. They are highly dignified, and may be considered as immediate *poetic* productions of the Spirit of God; for it is expressly said, ver. 5, that God put the word in Balaam's mouth, and that *the Spirit of God came upon him*, chap. xxiv. 2.

Verse 8. *How shall I curse, whom God hath not cursed?*] It was granted on all hands that no *incantations* nor imprecations could avail, unless God concurred and ratified them. From God's communication to Balaam he saw that God was determined to bless and defend Israel, and therefore all endeavours to injure them must be in vain.

Verse 9. *From the top of the rocks I see him*] That is, from the high places of Baal where he went, chap. xxii. 41, that he might the more advantageously see the *whole* camp of Israel.

The people shall dwell alone] They shall ever be preserved as a *distinct* nation. This prophecy has been literally fulfilled through a period of 3300 years to the present day. This is truly astonishing.

Verse 10. *Let me die the death of the righteous*] Probably Balaam had some presentiment that he should be taken off by a premature death, and therefore he lodges this petition against it. The death of the righteous in those times implied *being gathered to one's fathers in a good old age*, having seen his children, and children's children; and to this, probably, the latter part of this petition applies: *And let my last end be like his,* (ותהי אחריתי כמהו *uthehi acharithi chamohu, And let my* POSTERITY *be like his.*) It has been generally supposed that Balaam is here praying for a happy death, such as true Christians die who die in the Lord; and in this way his words are generally applied; but I am satisfied this is not their meaning. The prayer, however, understood in the common way, is a good one, and may be offered to God profitably. A righteous man is one who is *saved from his sins*, who is *justified* and *sanctified* through the blood of the covenant

a

A. M. 2553.
B. C. 1451.
An. Exod. Isr.
40.

take heed to speak that which the
LORD hath put in my mouth?
13 And Balak said unto him,
Come, I pray thee, with me unto another
place, from whence thou mayest see them:
thou shalt see but the utmost part of them,
and shalt not see them all: and curse me
them from thence.
14 And he brought him into the field of
Zophim, to the top of [t] Pisgah, [u] and built
seven altars, and offered a bullock and a ram
on *every* altar.
15 And he said unto Balak, Stand here by
thy burnt-offering, while I meet *the LORD*
yonder.
16 And the LORD met Balaam, and [v] put a
word in his mouth, and said, Go again unto
Balak, and say thus.
17 And when he came to him, behold, he
stood by his burnt-offering, and
the princes of Moab with him.
And Balak said unto him, What
hath the LORD spoken?

A. M. 2553.
B. C. 1451.
An. Exod. Isr.
40.

18 And he took up his parable, and said,
[w] Rise up, Balak, and hear; hearken unto me,
thou son of Zippor:
19 [x] God *is* not a man, that he should lie;
neither the son of man, that he should repent:
hath he said, and shall he not do *it?* or hath
he spoken, and shall he not make it good?
20 Behold, I have received *commandment*
to bless: and [y] he hath blessed; and I cannot
reverse it.
21 [z] He hath not beheld iniquity in Jacob,
neither hath he seen perverseness in Israel:
[a] the LORD his God *is* with him, [b] and the
shout of a king *is* among them.
22 [c] God brought them out of Egypt; he

[t] Or, *the hill*.——[u] Verse 1, 2.——[v] Ver. 5; chapter xxii. 35.——[w] Judg. iii. 20.——[x] 1 Sam. xv. 29; Mal. iii. 6; Romans xi. 29; James i. 17; Tit. i. 2.

[y] Gen. xii. 2; xxii. 17; Num. xxii. 12.——[z] Rom. iv. 7, 8.——[a] Exod. xiii. 21; xxix. 45, 46; xxxiii. 14.——[b] Psa. lxxxix. 15.——[c] Chap. xxiv. 8.

and who lives, not only an *innocent*, but also a *holy* and *useful* life. He who would *die well* should *live well;* for a *bad death* must be the issue of a *bad life.*

Verse 13. *Thou shalt see but the utmost part of them*] Balak thought that the sight of such an immense camp had intimidated Balaam, and this he might gather from what he said in the tenth verse: *Who can count the dust of Jacob,* &c.; he thought therefore that he might get Balaam to curse them in *detached parties,* till the *whole camp* should be devoted to destruction by successive execrations.

Verse 17. *What hath the Lord spoken?*] Balak himself now understood that Balaam was wholly under the influence of *Jehovah,* and would say nothing but what God commanded him; but not knowing Jehovah as Balaam did, he hoped that he might be induced to change his mind, and curse a people whom he had hitherto determined to bless.

Verse 19. *God* is *not a man, that he should lie*] This seems to be spoken to correct the foregoing supposition of Balak that God could change his mind. Even the heathen would not allow that their supreme god could be caught in a falsity. Hence ÆSCHYLUS, in *Prometh. vinct.* 1068:—

> Ψευδηγορειν γαρ ουκ επισταται στομα
> Το Διον, αλλα παν επος τελει.

> "The mouth of Jove knows not to frame a lie;
> But every word finds full accomplishment."

Verse 21. *He hath not beheld iniquity in Jacob, neither hath he seen perverseness in Israel*] This is a difficult passage; for if we take the words as spoken of the *people* Israel, as their *iniquity* and their *perverseness* were almost unparalleled, such words cannot be spoken of *them* with strict truth. If we consider them as spoken of the patriarch *Jacob* and *Israel,* or of Jacob *after* he became *Israel,* they are most strictly true, as *after that time* a more unblemished and noble character (*Abraham* excepted) is not to be found in the page of history, whether sacred or profane; and for his sake, and for the sake of *his* father *Isaac,* and his grandfather *Abraham,* God is ever represented as favouring, blessing, and sparing a rebellious and undeserving people; see the concluding note, Gen. xlix. In this way, I think, this difficult text may be safely understood.

There is another way in which the words may be interpreted, which will give a good sense. און *aven* not only signifies *iniquity,* but most frequently *trouble, labour, distress,* and *affliction;* and these indeed are its *ideal* meanings, and *iniquity* is only an accommodated or metaphorical one, because of the *pain, distress,* &c., produced by sin. עמל *amal,* translated here *perverseness,* occurs often in Scripture, but is never translated *perverseness* except in this place. It signifies simply *labour,* especially that which is of an *afflictive* or *oppressive* kind. The words may therefore be considered as implying that God will not suffer the people either to be exterminated by the *sword,* or to be brought under a yoke of *slavery.* Either of these methods of interpretation gives a good sense, but our common version gives none.

Dr. Kennicott contends for the reading of the Samaritan, which, instead of לא הביט *lo hibbit, he hath not seen,* has לא אבט *lo abbit, I do not see,* I do not discover any thing among them on which I could ground my curse. But the sense above given is to be preferred.

Verse 22. *The strength of a unicorn.*] ראם *reem* and ראים *reim.* It is generally allowed that there is no such beast in nature as the *unicorn;* i. e., a creature of the horse kind, with one long rich curled horn in the forehead. The creature painted from fancy is represented as one of the supporters of the *royal arms* of Great Britain. It is difficult to say what kind of

A. M. 2553. B. C. 1451. An. Exod. Isr. 40.

hath as it were [d] the strength of
a unicorn.
23 Surely *there is* no enchant-
ment [e] against Jacob, neither *is there* any
divination against Israel: according to this
time it shall be said of Jacob and of Israel,
[f] What hath God wrought!
24 Behold, the people shall rise up [g] as a great
lion, and lift up himself as a young lion: [h] he
shall not lie down until he eat *of* the prey, and
drink the blood of the slain.
25 And Balak said unto Balaam, Neither
curse them at all, nor bless them at all.
26 But Balaam answered and said unto
Balak, Told not I thee, saying,
[i] All that the LORD speaketh, that
I must do?
27 And Balak said unto Balaam, [k] Come, I
pray thee, I will bring thee unto another place;
peradventure it will please God that thou mayest
curse me them from thence.
28 And Balak brought Balaam unto the top
of Peor, that looketh [l] toward Jeshimon.
29 And Balaam said unto Balak, [m] Build me
here seven altars, and prepare me here seven
bullocks and seven rams.
30 And Balak did as Balaam had said, and
offered a bullock and a ram on *every* altar.

A. M. 2553. B. C. 1451. An. Exod. Isr. 40.

[d] Deut. xxxiii. 17; Job xxxix. 10, 11.——[e] Or, *in*.——[f] Psa. xxxi. 19; xliv. 1.——[g] Gen. xlix. 9.——[h] Gen. xlix. 27.

[i] Verse 12; chapter xxii. 38; 1 Kings xxii. 14.——[k] Verse 13. [l] Chap. xxi. 20.——[m] Ver. 1.

beast is intended by the original word. The Septuagint translate the word *μονοκερως*, the *unicorn*, or *one-horned animal*; the Vulgate, sometimes, *unicornus*; and in the text *rhinocerotis*, by which the *rhinoceros*, a creature which has its name from the *horn* on its *nose*, is supposed to be meant. That no single-horned animal can be intended by the *reem* of Moses, is sufficiently evident from this, that Moses, speaking of Joseph, says, "he has the HORNS of A *unicorn*," or *reem*, where the *horns* are spoken of in the *plural*, the *animal* in the *singular*. The creature referred to is either the *rhinoceros*, some varieties of which have *two* horns on the nose, or the wild *bull*, *urus*, or *buffalo*; though some think the beast intended is a species of *goat*; but the *rhinoceros* seems the most likely. There is literally a *monoceros*, or *unicorn*, with *one large curled ivory horn* growing horizontally out of his *snout*; but this is not a *land animal*, it is the *modiodan* or *nurwal*, a marine animal of the *whale* kind, a horn of which is now before me, measuring seven feet four inches; but I believe the *rhinoceros* is that intended by the sacred writers.

Verse 23. There is *no enchantment, &c.*] Because God has determined to save them, therefore no enchantment can prevail against them.

According to this time, &c.] I think this clause should be read thus: "As at this time it shall be told to Jacob and to Israel what God worketh;" i. e., this people shall always have *prophetic information* of what God is about to work. And indeed, they are the only people under heaven who ever had this privilege. When God himself designed to punish them because of their sins, he always *forewarned* them by the prophets; and also took care to apprise them of all the plots of their enemies against them.

Verse 24. *Behold, the people shall rise up as a great lion*] לביא *labi*, the *great, mighty*, or *old lion*, the king of the forest, who is feared and respected by all the other beasts of the field; so shall Israel be the subduer and possessor of the whole land of Canaan. And *as a young lion*, ארי *ari* from ארה *arah, to tear off*, the *predatory lion*, or the lion in the act of *seizing* and *tearing* his prey;—the nations against whom the Israelites are now going shall be no more able to defend themselves against their attacks, than the feeblest beasts of the forest are against the attacks of the strong lion.

Verse 28. *Unto the top of Peor*] Probably the place where the famous Baal-peor had his chief temple. He appears to have been the Priapus of the Moabites, and to have been worshipped with the same obscene and abominable rites.

CHAPTER XXIV.

Balaam, finding that God was determined to bless Israel, seeks no longer for enchantments, 1. *The Spirit of God coming upon him, he delivers a most important prophetic parable,* 2–9. *Balak's anger is kindled against him, and he commands him to depart to his own country,* 10, 11. *Balaam vindicates his conduct,* 12, 13; *and delivers a prophecy relative to the future destruction of Moab by the Israelites,* 14–17; *also of Edom,* 18, 19; *of the Amalekites,* 20; *and of the Kenites,* 21, 22. *Predicts also the destruction of Asshur and Eber, by the naval power of Chittim, which should afterwards be itself destroyed,* 23, 24. *Balaam and Balak separate,* 25.

A. M. 2553. B. C. 1451. An. Exod. Isr. 40.

AND when Balaam saw that it
pleased the LORD to bless
Israel, he went not, as at [a] other
times, [b] to seek for enchantments,

A. M. 2553. B. C. 1451. An. Exod. Isr. 40.

[a] Chap. xxiii. 3, 15.

[b] Heb. *to the meeting of enchantments.*

NOTES ON CHAP. XXIV.

Verse 1. *He went not, as at other times, to seek for enchantments*] We have already had occasion to observe that the proper meaning of the word נחש *nachash* is not easily ascertained; see chap. xxi. 9, and see on Gen. iii. 1. Here the plural נחשים *nechashim*

A. M. 2553.
B. C. 1451.
An. Exod. Isr. 40.

but he set his face toward the
wilderness.
2 And Balaam lifted up his
eyes, and he saw Israel [c] abiding *in his tents*
according to their tribes; and [d] the Spirit of
God came upon him.
3 [e] And he took up his parable, and said, Balaam the son of Beor hath said, and the man
[f] whose eyes are open hath said:
4 He hath said, which heard the words of
God, which saw the vision of
the Almighty, [g] falling *into a*
trance, but having his eyes
open:
5 How goodly are thy tents, O Jacob, *and*
thy tabernacles, O Israel!
6 As the valleys are they spread forth, as
gardens by the river's side, [h] as the trees of lign
aloes [i] which the LORD hath planted, *and* as
cedar trees beside the waters.

[c] Chap. ii. 2, &c.——[d] Chap. xi. 25; 1 Sam. x. 10; xix. 20, 23; 2 Chron. xv. 1.——[e] Chap. xxiii. 7, 18.——[f] Heb. *who had his eyes shut*, but now opened.

[g] See 1 Sam. xix. 24; Ezek. i. 28; Dan. viii. 18; x. 15, 16; 2 Cor. xii. 2, 3, 4; Rev. i. 10, 17.——[h] Psalm i. 3; Jer. xvii. 8.——[i] Psa. civ. 16.

is rendered *enchantments;* but it probably means no more than the *knowledge of future events.* When Balaam saw that it pleased God to bless Israel, he therefore thought it unnecessary to apply for any farther *prophetic declarations* of God's will as he had done before, for he could safely infer every good to this people, from the evident disposition of God towards them.

Verse 2. *The Spirit of God came upon him.*] This Divine afflatus he had not expected on the present occasion, but God had not yet declared the whole of his will.

Verse 3. *He took up his parable*] His prophetic declaration couched in highly poetic terms, and in regular metre, as the preceding were.

The man whose eyes are open] I believe the original שתם *shethum*, should be translated *shut*, not *open;* for in the next verse, where the opening of his eyes is mentioned, a widely different word is used, גלה *galah*, which signifies to *open* or *reveal*. At first the eyes of Balaam were *shut*, and so closely too that he could not *see* the angel who withstood him, till God *opened* his eyes; nor could he see the gracious intentions of God towards Israel, till the *eyes of his understanding were opened* by the power of the Divine Spirit. This therefore he mentions, we may suppose, with humility and gratitude, and to the credit of the prophecy which he is now about to deliver, that the Moabites may receive it as the *word of God*, which must be fulfilled in due season. His words, in their meaning, are similar to those of the blind man in the Gospel: "Once I was *blind*, but now I *see*."

Verse 4. *Falling* into a trance] There is no indication in the Hebrew that he fell into a *trance;* these words are added by our translators, but they are not in the original. נפל *nophel* is the only word used, and simply signifies *falling*, or *falling down*, perhaps in this instance by way of religious prostration.

Verse 6. *Lign aloes which the Lord hath planted*] Or, as the tents which the Lord hath pitched; for it is the same word, אהלים *ohalim*, which is used in the 5th verse. But from other parts of Scripture we find that the word also signifies a species of *tree*, called by some the *sandal* tree, and by others the *lignum* or wood *aloes.* This tree is described as being *eight* or *ten* feet high, with very large leaves growing at the top; and it is supposed that a forest of those at some distance must bear some resemblance to a numerous encampment. As the word comes from the root אהל *ahal*, which signifies to *spread* or *branch out*, and therefore is applied to *tents*, because of their being *extended* or *spread out* on the ground; so when it is applied to *trees* it must necessarily mean such as were remarkable for their widely-extended branches; but what the particular species is, cannot be satisfactorily ascertained. By the *Lord's planting* are probably meant such trees as grow independently of the *cultivation of man.—Nullis hominum cogentibus;* or, as *Virgil* expresses it,—

Sponte sua quæ se tollunt in luminis oras.
VIRG., Geor. ii., ver. 47.

"Such as sprung up *spontaneously* into the regions of light."

As cedar trees] *Gabriel Sionita*, a very learned Syrian Maronite, who assisted in editing the Paris Polyglot, a man worthy of all credit, thus describes the cedars of Mount Lebanon, which he had examined on the spot:—

"The *cedar* grows on the most elevated part of the mountain, is taller than the *pine*, and so thick that five men together could scarcely fathom one. It shoots out its branches at ten or twelve feet from the ground; they are large, and distant from each other, and are perpetually green. The cedar distils a kind of gum, to which different effects are attributed. The wood of it is of a brown colour, very solid, and incorruptible if preserved from *wet*. It bears a small apple, like to that of the *pine*."

De la Roque relates some curious particulars concerning this tree, which he learned from the Maronites of Mount Libanus: "The branches grow in parallel rows round the tree, but lessen gradually from the bottom to the top, shooting out parallel to the horizon, so that the tree is, in appearance, similar to a *cone*. As the snows, which fall in vast quantities on this mountain, must necessarily, by their weight on such a vast surface, break down these branches, nature, or rather the God of nature, has so ordered it that at the approach of winter, and during the snowy season, the branches erect themselves, and cling close to the body of the tree, and thus prevent any quantity of snow from lodging on them."

Mr. *Maundrell*, who visited Mount Libanus in 1697, gives the following description of the *cedars* still growing there:—

A. M. 2553.
B. C. 1451.
An. Exod. Isr.
40.

7 He shall pour the water out
of his buckets, and his seed *shall*
be [k] in many waters, and his king
shall be higher than [l] Agag, and his [m] kingdom shall be exalted.
8 [n] God brought him forth out of Egypt; he
hath as it were the strength of a unicorn;
he shall [o] eat up the nations his enemies, and
shall [p] break their bones, and [q] pierce *them*
through with his arrows.
9 [r] He couched, he lay down as a lion, and
as a great lion: who shall stir him up?
[s] Blessed *is* he that blesseth thee, and cursed
is he that curseth thee.
10 And Balak's anger was kindled against
Balaam, and he [t] smote his hands together:
and Balak said unto Balaam, [u] I called thee
to curse mine enemies, and, behold, thou hast
altogether blessed *them* these three times.
11 Therefore now flee thou to thy place:
[v] I thought to promote thee unto
great honour; but, lo, the LORD
hath kept thee back from honour.

A. M. 2553.
B. C. 1451.
An. Exod. Isr.
40.

12 And Balaam said unto Balak, Spake I
not also to thy messengers which thou sentest
unto me, saying,
13 [w] If Balak would give me his house full
of silver and gold, I cannot go beyond the
commandment of the LORD, to do *either* good
or bad of mine own mind; *but* what the LORD
saith, that will I speak?
14 And now, behold, I go unto my people:
come *therefore, and* [x] I will advertise thee
what this people shall do to thy people [y] in the
latter days.
15 [z] And he took up his parable, and said,
Baalam the son of Beor hath said, and the
man whose eyes are open hath said:
16 He hath said, which heard the words of
God, and knew the knowledge of the Most

[k] Jer. li. 13; Rev. xvii. 1, 15.——[l] 1 Sam. xv. 9.——[m] 2 Sam. v. 12; 1 Chron. xiv. 2.——[n] Chap. xxiii. 22.——[o] Chap. xiv. 9; xxiii. 24.——[p] Psa. ii. 9; Isa. xxxviii. 13; Jer. l. 17.——[q] Psa. xlv. 5; Jer. l. 9.——[r] Gen. xlix. 9.

[s] Gen. xii. 3; xxvii. 29.——[t] Ezek. xxi. 14, 17; xxii. 13.——[u] Chap. xxiii. 11; Deut. xxiii. 4, 5; Josh. xxiv. 9, 10; Neh. xiii. 2.——[v] Chap. xxii. 17, 37.——[w] Chap. xxii. 18.——[x] Mic. vi. 5; Rev. ii. 14.——[y] Gen. xlix. 1; Dan. ii. 28; x. 14.——[z] Ver. 3, 4.

"These noble trees grow among the snow, near the highest part of Lebanon, and are remarkable, as well for their own age and largeness as for those frequent allusions to them in the word of God. Some of them are very old, and of a prodigious bulk; others younger, and of a smaller size. Of the former I could reckon only *sixteen*, but the latter are very numerous. I measured one of the largest, and found it *twelve* yards and *six* inches in girt, and yet *sound*, and *thirty-seven* yards in the spread of its branches. At about five or six yards from the ground it was divided into five limbs, each of which was equal to a great tree."—*Journey from Aleppo to Jerusalem*, p. 142.

Verse 7. *He shall pour the water out of his buckets, &c.*] Here is a very plain allusion to their method of raising water in different parts of the East. By the *well* a tall pole is erected, which serves as a fulcrum to a very long lever, to the smaller end of which a bucket is appended. On the opposite end, which is much larger, are many notches cut in the wood, which serve as steps for a man, whose business it is to climb up to the fulcrum, in order to lower the bucket into the well, which, when filled, he raises by walking back on the opposite arm, till his weight brings the bucket above the well's mouth: a person standing by the well empties the bucket into a trench, which communicates with the ground intended to be watered.

His seed shall be *in many waters*] Another simple allusion to the sowing of *rice*. The ground must not only be *well watered*, but *flooded*, in order to serve for the proper growth of this grain. The rice that was sown in *many waters* must be the most fruitful. By an elegant and chaste metaphor all this is applied to the *procreation of a numerous posterity*.

His king shall be higher than Agag] This name is supposed to have been as common to all the Amalekitish kings as *Pharaoh* was to those of Egypt. But several critics, with the Septuagint, suppose that a small change has taken place here in the original word, and that instead of מאגג *meagag, than Agag*, we should read מגוג *miggog, than Gog*. As *Gog* in Scripture seems to mean the enemies of God's people, then the promise here may imply that the true worshippers of the Most High shall ultimately have dominion over all their enemies.

Verse 8. *God brought him forth out of Egypt*] They were neither *expelled* thence, nor came *voluntarily* away. God alone, with a high hand and uplifted arm, brought them forth. Concerning the *unicorn*, see on chap. xxiii. 22.

Verse 9. *He couched, he lay down as a lion, &c.*] See the original terms explained chap. xxiii. 24.

These oracles, delivered by Balaam, are evident prophecies of the victories which the Israelites should gain over their enemies, and of their firm possession of the promised land. They may also refer to the great victories to be obtained by the Lord Jesus Christ, that Lion of the *tribe of Judah*, over sin, death, and Satan, the grand enemies of the human race; and to that most numerous posterity of *spiritual children* which should be begotten by the preaching of the Gospel.

Verse 11. *Lo, the Lord hath kept thee back from honour.*] A bitter and impious sarcasm. "Hadst thou cursed this people, I would have promoted thee to great honour; but thou hast chosen to follow the directions of Jehovah rather than mine, and what will *he* do for thee!"

Verse 15. *The man whose eyes are open*] See on ver. 3. It seems strange that our version should have fallen into such a mistake as to render שתם *shethum*,

A. M. 2553.
B. C. 1451.
An. Exod. Isr.
40.

High, *which* saw the vision of the Almighty, falling *into a trance*, but having his eyes open:

17 [a] I shall see him, but not now: I shall behold him, but not nigh: there shall come [b] a Star out of Jacob, and [c] a Sceptre shall rise out of Israel, and shall [d] smite the corners of Moab, and destroy all the children of Sheth.

A. M. 2553.
B. C. 1451.
An. Exod. Isr.
40.

18 And [e] Edom shall be a possession, Seir also shall be a possession for his enemies; and Israel shall do valiantly.

19 [f] Out of Jacob shall come he that shall have dominion, and shall destroy him that remaineth of the city.

---

[a] Rev. i. 7.——[b] Matt. ii. 2; Rev. xxii. 16.——[c] Gen. xlix. 10; Psa. cx. 2.——[d] Or, *smite through the princes of Moab;* 2 Sam. viii. 2; Jer. xlviii. 45.——[e] 2 Sam. viii. 14; Psa. lx. 8, 9, 12. [f] Gen. xlix. 10.

---

open, which it does not signify, when the very *sound* of the word expresses the *sense*. The Vulgate has very properly preserved the true meaning, by rendering the clause *cujus obturatus est oculus*, he whose eyes are shut. The Targum first paraphrased the passage *falsely*, and most of the versions followed it.

Verse 17. *I shall see him, but not now*] Or, *I shall see him, but he is not now. I shall behold him, but not nigh—I shall have a full view of him, but the time is yet distant.* That is, The person of whom I am now prophesying does not at present exist among these Israelites, nor shall he appear in this generation. *There shall come a Star out of Jacob, and a Sceptre shall rise out of Israel*—a person *eminent* for *wisdom*, and *formidable* for *strength* and *power*, shall arise as *king* among this people. *He shall smite the corners of Moab*—he shall bring the Moabites perfectly under subjection; (See 2 Sam. viii. 2;) *and destroy all the children of Sheth.* The original word קרקר *karkar*, from קרה *karah*, to *meet*, *associate*, *join*, *blend*, and the like, is variously translated: *vastabit, he shall waste*, VULGATE.—*προνομευσει, shall prey on*, SEPT.—ישלוט *yishlot, shall rule over*, TARGUM.—*Shall shake*, ARABIC. — بربند *barbend, shall put a yoke on*, PERS.—*Shall unwall*, AINSWORTH, &c., &c.

The *Targum* of *Onkelos* translates the whole passage thus: "I shall see him, but not now: I shall behold him, but he is not near. When a king shall arise from the house of Jacob, and the Messiah be anointed from the house of Israel, he shall slay the princes of Moab, and rule over all the children of men."

The *Jerusalem Targum* is a little different: "A king shall arise from the house of Jacob, a redeemer and governor from the house of Israel, who shall slay the chiefs of the Moabites, and empty out and destroy all the children of the East."

Rabbi Moses ben Maimon has, in my opinion, perfectly hit the meaning of the prophecy in the following paraphrase of the text: "*I shall see him, but not now.* This is DAVID.—*I shall behold him, but not nigh.* This is the king MESSIAH.—*A Star shall come out of Jacob.* This is DAVID.—*And a Sceptre shall rise out of Israel.* This is the king MESSIAH.—*And shall smite the corners of Moab.* This is DAVID, (as it is written, 2 Sam. viii. 2: *And he smote Moab, casting them down to the ground.*)—*And shall destroy all the children of Sheth.* This is the king MESSIAH, of whom it is written, (Psa. lxii. 8,) *He shall have dominion from sea to sea.*"

Verse 18. *And Edom shall be a possession*] That is, to DAVID; as it is said: "And all they of Edom became David's servants;" 2 Sam. viii. 14.

Seir also shall be a possession] That is, unto the king MESSIAH; as it is said: "And saviours shall come upon Mount Zion to judge the Mount of Esau; and the kingdom shall be the Lord's;" Obad., ver. 21. See *Ainsworth.*

Verse 19. *Out of Jacob shall come, &c.*] This is supposed to refer to Christ, because of what is said Gen. xlix. 10.

It is exceedingly difficult to fix the true sense of this prophecy in all its particulars. Probably the *star*, ver. 17, is only an emblem of *kingly* power. Among the Egyptians a *star* is said to have been the symbol of the Divine Being. The *sceptre* refers to the kingly power in *exercise*. The *corners* or outskirts may mean the petty Moabitish governments, as the Chaldee has understood the term. If *karkar*, which we translate *utterly destroy*, be not the name of a *place* here, as it is in Judg. viii. 10, (which is not very likely,) it may be taken in one of those senses assigned to it, (see on ver. 17,) and signify the *blending together* the *children of Sheth*, that is, all the inhabitants of the earth; for so the children of *Sheth* must necessarily be understood, unless we consider it here as meaning some king of the *Moabites*, according to *Grotius*, or a city on the borders of Moab, according to *Rabbi Nathan*. As neither Israel nor the Messiah ever destroyed all the children of men, we must (in order to leave the children of Sheth what they are generally understood to be, *all the inhabitants of the world*) understand the whole as a prophecy of the final universal sway of the sceptre of Christ, when the middle wall of partition shall be broken down, and the *Jews and Gentiles* become one *united*, *blended* fold, under one shepherd and bishop of their souls.

I cannot think that the *meteoric star* which guided the wise men of the east to Bethlehem can be intended here; nor do I think that Peter refers to this prophecy when he calls Christ *the day star*, 2 Epist. i. 19; nor that Rev. ii. 28, where Christ is called *the morning star*, nor Rev. xxii. 16, where he is called *the bright and morning star*, refers at all to this prophecy of Balaam. Nor do I think that the *false Christ* who rose in the time of *Adrian*, and who called himself *Barcochab*, which literally signifies the *son of a star*, did refer to this prophecy. If he had, he must have defeated his own intention, because the SON *of the star* is not THE STAR that should arise, but at the utmost a *descendant*; and then, to vindicate his right to the Jewish throne, he must show that the person who was called *the star*, and of whom he pretended to be the *son* or *descendant*, had actually reigned before him. As the *sun, moon, stars, planets, light, splendour, efful-*

A. M. 2553. B. C. 1451. An. Exod. Isr. 40.

20 And when he looked on Amalek, he took up his parable, and said, Amalek *was* [g] the first of the nations; but his latter end [h] *shall be* that he perish for ever.

21 And he looked on the Kenites, and took up his parable, and said, Strong is thy dwelling place, and thou puttest thy nest in a rock.

22 Nevertheless [i] the Kenite shall be wasted, [k] until Asshur shall carry thee away captive.

23 And he took up his parable, and said, Alas, who shall live when God doeth this!

A. M. 2553. B. C. 1451. An. Exod. Isr. 40.

24 And ships *shall come* from the coast of [l] Chittim, and shall afflict Asshur, and shall afflict [m] Eber, and he also shall perish for ever.

25 And Baalam rose up, and went and [n] returned to his place: and Balak also went his way.

[g] Or, *the first of the nations that warred against Israel*; Exod. xvii. 8.——[h] Or, shall be *even to destruction*; Exod. xvii. 14; 1 Sam. xv. 3, 8.

[i] Heb. *Kain*; Gen. xv. 19.——[k] Or, *how long* shall it be ere *Asshur carry thee away captive?*——[l] Gen. x. 4; Dan. xi. 30. [m] Gen. x. 21, 25.——[n] See chap. xxxi. 8.

gence, day, &c., were always considered among the Asiatics as emblems of *royalty, government*, &c., therefore many, both men and women, had these names given to them as titles, surnames, &c. So the queen of Alexander the Great, called Roxana by the Greeks, was a *Persian* princess, and in her native tongue her name was روشن *Roushen*, splendour. *Hadassah*, who became queen to *Ahasuerus*, in place of the repudiated *Vashti*, and is called *Esther* by Europeans in general, was called in the language of Persia ستاره *Sitareh*; from whence by corruption came both *Esther*, the Persian queen, and our word *star*. And to waive all farther examples, a Mohammedan prince, at first named *Eesouf* or *Joseph*, was called روشن اختر *Roushen Akhter* when he was raised to the throne, which signifies a *splendid or luminous star*. This prince, by a joyful reverse of fortune, was brought from a gloomy prison and exalted to the throne of Hindostan; on which account the following couplet was made. in which there is a paronomasia or play on the name *Roushen Akhter*; and the last line alludes to the history of the patriarch *Joseph*, who was brought out of *prison* and exalted to the highest honours in Egypt.

روشن اختر بود اکنون ماه شد
یوسف از زندان بر امد شاه شد

Roushen Akhter bood, aknoon mah shud:
Yousef az zendan ber amd shah shud.

"He was a *bright star*, but is now become a *moon*.
Joseph is brought out of *prison*, and is become *a glorious king*."

Verse 20. *Amalek* was *the first of the nations*] The most *ancient* and most powerful of all the nations or states then within the view of Balaam; *but his latter end shall be that he perish for ever*, or *his posterity* אחריתו *acharitho, shall be destroyed*, or *shall utterly fail*. This oracle began to be fulfilled by *Saul*, 1 Sam. xv. 7, 8, who overthrew the Amalekites, and took their king, Agag, prisoner. Afterwards they were nearly destroyed by *David*, 1 Sam. xxvii. 8, and they were finally exterminated by the sons of *Simeon* in the days of *Hezekiah*, 1 Chron. iv. 41–43; since that time they have ceased to exist as a people, and now no vestige of them remains on the face of the earth; so completely is their *posterity* cut off, according to this prophecy. The *marginal reading* does not appear to give the proper sense.

Verse 21. *He looked on the Kenites*] Commentators are not well agreed who the Kenites were. Dr. Dodd's opinion is, I think, nearest to the truth. *Jethro*, the father-in-law of Moses, is called a priest or prince of Midian, Exod. iii. 1, and in Judg. i. 16 he is called a *Kenite*; we may infer, therefore, says he, that the Kenites and the Midianites were the same, or at least that the Kenites and the Midianites were confederate tribes. Some of these we learn from Judg. i. followed the Israelites, others abode still among the Midianites and Amalekites. When Saul destroyed the latter, we find he had no commission against the Kenites, 1 Sam. xv. 6, for it appears that they were then a small and inconsiderable people; they had doubtless been *wasted*, as the text says, though by what means does not appear from history. On the other hand, it may be observed that the Midianites mentioned here lived close to the Dead Sea, at a great distance from the Midian where Jethro lived, which was near Horeb. Perhaps they were a colony or tribe that had migrated from the vicinity of Mount Sinai. It seems that at this time the *Kenites* occupied a very strong position: *Strong is thy dwelling place, and thou puttest thy nest in a rock;* where there is a play on the original word קן, which signifies both a *Kenite* and a *nest*. High rocks in these countries were generally used as their strong places.

Verse 22. *Until Asshur shall carry thee away captive.*] The Assyrians and Babylonians who carried away captive the ten tribes, 2 Kings xvii. 6, and the Jews into Babylon, 2 Kings xxv., probably carried away the Kenites also. Indeed this seems pretty evident, as we find some Kenites mentioned among the Jews after their return from the Babylonish captivity, 1 Chron. ii. 55.

Verse 23. *Who shall live when God doeth this!*] There are two senses in which these words may be taken:—1. That the event is so distant that none then alive could possibly live to see it. 2. That the times would be so distressing and desolating that scarcely any should be able to escape. The words are very similar to those of our Lord, and probably are to be taken in the same sense: "Wo to them that are with child, and to them that give suck in those days."

Verse 24. *Ships* shall come *from the coast of Chittim*] Some think by Chittim the Romans, others the Macedonians under Alexander the Great, are meant. It is certain that the Romans did conquer the Assy-

rians, including all the people of Syria, Mesopotamia, &c.; but Calmet strongly contends that by Chittim Macedonia is meant, and that the prophecy refers to the conquests of Alexander. Chittim was one of the sons of Javan, the son of Japheth, the son of Noah, Gen. x. 4; and his posterity, according to Josephus, Antiq., l. iii., c. 22, settled in Cilicia, Macedonia, Cyprus, and Italy also; and therefore, says Mr. Ainsworth, the prophecy may imply both the troubles that befell the Assyrians and Jews by the Greeks and Seleucidæ, in the troublous days of Antiochus.

And shall afflict Eber] Probably not the Hebrews, as some think, but the people on the other side the Euphrates, from עבר *abar, to pass over, go beyond;* all which people were discomfited, and their empire destroyed by Alexander the Great.

Verse 25. *And Balaam—returned to his place*] Intended to have gone to Mesopotamia, his native country, (see Deut. xxiii. 4,) but seems to have settled among the Midianites, where he was slain by the Israelites; see chap. xxxi. 8.

Though the notes in the preceding chapters have been extended to a considerable length, yet a few additional remarks may be necessary: the reader's attention is earnestly requested to the following propositions:—

1. It appears sufficiently evident from the preceding account that Balaam knew and worshipped the true God.

2. That he had been a true prophet, and appears to have been in the habit of receiving oracles from God.

3. That he practised some illicit branches of knowledge, or was reputed by the Moabites as a sorcerer, probably because of the high reputation he had for wisdom; and we know that even in our own country, in the fifteenth and sixteenth centuries, persons who excelled their contemporaries in wisdom were reputed as magicians.

4. That though he was a believer in the true God, yet he was covetous; he *loved the wages of unrighteousness.*

5. That it does not appear that in the case before us he *wished* to curse Israel when he found they were the servants of the true God.

6. That it is possible he did not know this at first. Balak told him that there was a numerous people come out of Egypt; and as marauders, wandering hordes, freebooters, &c., were frequent in those days, he might take them at first for such spoilers, and the more readily go at Balak's request to consult God concerning them.

7. That so conscientiously did he act in the whole business, that as soon as he found it displeased God he cheerfully offered to return; and did not advance till he had not only the permission, but the authority of God to proceed.

8. That when he came in view of the Israelitish camp he did not attempt to make use of any means of sorcery, evocation of spirits, necromantic spells, &c., to accomplish the wish of Balak.

9. That he did seek to find out the will of the true God, by using *those means* which God himself had prescribed, viz., supplication and prayer, and the sacrifice of clean beasts.

10. That though he knew it would greatly displease Balak, yet he most faithfully and firmly told him all that God said on every occasion.

11. That notwithstanding his allowed covetous disposition, yet he refused all promised honours and proffered rewards, even of the most extensive kind, to induce him to act in any respect contrary to the declared will of God.

12. That God on this occasion communicated to him some of the most extraordinary prophetic influences ever conferred on man.

13. That his prophecies are, upon the whole, clear and pointed, and have been fulfilled in the most remarkable manner, and furnish a very strong argument in proof of Divine revelation.

14. That notwithstanding the wicked counsel given to the Midianites, the effects of which are mentioned in the following chapter, on which account he probably lost his life, (chap. xxxi. 8,) the badness of this man's character has been very far overrated; and that it does not appear that he was either a *hypocrite, false prophet,* or a *sorcerer* in the common acceptation of the term, and that he risked even life itself in following and fulfilling the will of the Lord!

15. That though it is expressly asserted, chap. xxxi. 16, and Rev. ii. 14, that Israel's committing whoredom with the daughters of Moab was brought about by the evil counsel given by Balaam to cast this stumbling-block in their way, yet it does not appear from the text that he had those most criminal intentions which are generally attributed to him; for as we have already seen so much good in this man's character, and that this, and his love of money (and who thinks this a *sin?*) are almost the only blots in it, it must certainly be consistent with candour and charity to suggest a method of removing at least some part of this blame.

16. I would therefore simply say that the counsel given by Balaam to Balak might have been "to form *alliances* with this people, especially through the medium of *matrimonial connections;* and seeing they could not conquer them, to endeavour to make them their *friends.*" Now, though this might not be designed by Balaam to bring them into a snare, yet it was a bad doctrine, as it led to the corruption of the holy seed, and to an unequal yoking with unbelievers; which, though even in a *matrimonial* way, is as contrary to sound policy as to the word of God. See the notes on chap. xxv. 3, 6.

17. That it was the Moabitish women, not Balaam, that called the people to the sacrifice of their gods; and it argued great degeneracy and iniquity in the hearts of the people on so slight an invitation to join so suddenly so impure a worship, and so speedily to cast off the whole form of godliness, with every portion of the fear of the Almighty; therefore the high blame rests ultimately with themselves.

CHAPTER XXV.

While Israel abode in Shittim the people commit whoredom with the daughters of Moab, 1. *They become idolaters,* 2. *The anger of the Lord is kindled against them, and he commands the ringleaders to be hanged,* 3, 4. *Moses causes the judges to slay the transgressors,* 5. Zimri, *one of the Israelitish princes of the tribe of* Simeon, *brings a Midianitish princess, named* Cozbi, *into his tent, while the people are deploring their iniquity before the tabernacle,* 6. *Phinehas, the son of Eleazar, incensed by this insult to the laws and worship of God, runs after them and pierces them both with a javelin,* 7, 8. *Twenty-four thousand die of the plague, sent as a punishment for their iniquity,* 9. *The Lord grants to Phinehas a covenant of peace and an everlasting priesthood,* 10–13. *The name and quality of the Israelitish man and Midianitish woman,* 14, 15. *God commands the Israelites to vex and smite the Midianites, who had seduced them to the worship of Baal-peor,* 16–18.

A. M. 2553. B. C. 1451. An. Exod. Isr. 40.

AND Israel abode in [a] Shittim,
and [b] the people began to
commit whoredom with the
daughters of Moab.
2 And [c] they called the people unto [d] the
sacrifices of their gods: and the people did
eat, and [e] bowed down to their gods.
3 And Israel joined himself unto Baal-peor:
and [f] the anger of the LORD was kindled against
Israel.
4 And the LORD said unto Moses, [g] Take all
the heads of the people, and hang them up
before the LORD against the sun, [h] that the
fierce anger of the LORD may be turned away
from Israel.
5 And Moses said unto [i] the
judges of Israel, [k] Slay ye every
one his men that were joined unto
Baal-peor.
6 And, behold, one of the children of Israel
came and brought unto his brethren a Midianitish woman in the sight of Moses, and in the
sight of all the congregation of the children of
Israel, [l] who *were* weeping *before* the door of
the tabernacle of the congregation.
7 And [m] when Phinehas [n] the son of Eleazar,
the son of Aaron the priest, saw *it*, he rose up
from among the congregation, and took a jave
lin in his hand;
8 And he went after the man of Israel into

[a] Chap. xxxiii. 49; Josh. ii. 1; Mic. vi. 5.—[b] Chap. xxxi. 16; 1 Cor. x. 8.—[c] Joshua xxii. 17; Psa. cvi. 28; Hos. ix. 10.—[d] Exodus xxxiv. 15, 16; 1 Cor. x. 20.—[e] Exodus xx. 5.—[f] Psa. cvi. 29.

[g] Deut. iv. 3; Josh. xxii. 17.—[h] Ver. 11; Deut. xiii. 17.—[i] Exod. xviii. 21, 25.—[k] Exod. xxxii. 27; Deut. xiii. 6, 9, 13, 15.—[l] Joel ii. 17.—[m] Psa. cvi. 30; Ecclus. xlv. 23; 1 Mac. ii. 54.—[n] Exod. vi. 25.

NOTES ON CHAP. XXV.

Verse 3. *Israel joined himself unto Baal-peor*] The same as the Priapus of the Romans, and worshipped with the same obscene rites as we have frequently had occasion to remark.

The *joining to Baal-peor*, mentioned here, was probably what St. Paul had in view when he said, 2 Cor. vi. 14: *Be ye not unequally yoked together with unbelievers.* And this joining, though done even in a matrimonial way, was nevertheless *fornication*, (see Rev. ii. 14,) as no marriage between an Israelite and a Midianite could be legitimate, according to the law of God. See the propositions at the close of the preceding chapter.

Verse 4. *Take all the heads of the people, &c.*] Meaning the chiefs of those who had transgressed; as if he had said, "Assemble the chiefs and judges, institute an inquiry concerning the transgressors, and hang them who shall be found guilty *before the Lord*, as a matter required by his justice." *Against the sun*—in the most public manner, and in daylight.

Dr. Kennicott has remarked that the Samaritan and Hebrew texts must be both taken together, to make the sense here complete: And the Lord said unto Moses, SPEAK unto *all* the heads of the people; AND LET THEM SLAY THE MEN THAT WERE JOINED TO BAAL-PEOR; *and hang them up before the Lord against the sun,* &c.

Verse 5. *Slay ye every one his men*] In the different departments where you preside over *thousands, hundreds, fifties,* and *tens*, slay all the *culprits* that shall be found.

Verse 6. *One of the children of Israel*] *Zimri*, the son of *Salu*, a prince of a chief family in the tribe of *Simeon*, ver. 14, *brought a Midianitish woman, Cozbi*, daughter of *Zur*, head over a people of one of the chief families in Midian, ver. 15. The *condition* of these two persons plainly proves it to have been a *matrimonial* alliance, the one was a *prince*, the other a *princess*; therefore I must conclude that fornication or whoredom, in the common sense of the word, was not practised on this occasion. The matter was bad enough, as the marriage was in flat opposition to the law of God; and we need not make it worse by representing the woman as a common prostitute, as the *Vulgate* and several others have done. In such a case this is absolutely inadmissible. Josephus positively says that *Zimri* had married *Cozbi*, Antiq., l. iv., cap. 6; and if he had not said so, still the thing is nearly self-evident. See the conclusion of chap. xxiv.

The children of Israel, who were *weeping*] This aggravated the crime, because the people were then in a state of great humiliation, because of the late impure and illegal transactions.

Verse 8. *Thrust both of them through*] Inspired undoubtedly by the Spirit of the God of justice to do

A. M. 2553.
B. C. 1451.
An. Exod. Isr. 40.

the tent, and thrust both of them through, the man of Israel, and the woman through her belly. So [o] the plague was stayed from the children of Israel.

9 And [p] those that died in the plague were twenty and four thousand.

10 And the LORD spake unto Moses, saying,

11 [q] Phinehas the son of Eleazar, the son of Aaron the priest, hath turned my wrath away from the children of Israel, while he was zealous [r] for my sake among them, that I consumed not the children of Israel in [s] my jealousy.

12 Wherefore say, [t] Behold, I give unto him my covenant of peace:

13 And he shall have it, and [u] his seed after him, *even* the covenant of [v] an everlasting priesthood; because he was [w] zealous for his God, and [x] made an atonement for the children of Israel.

A. M. 2553.
B. C. 1451.
An. Exod. Isr. 40.

14 Now the name of the Israelite that was slain, *even* that was slain with the Midianitish woman, *was* Zimri, the son of Salu, a prince of [y] a chief house among the Simeonites.

15 And the name of the Midianitish woman that was slain *was* Cozbi, the daughter of [z] Zur; he *was* head over a people, *and* of a chief house in Midian.

16 And the LORD spake unto Moses, saying,

17 [a] Vex the Midianites, and smite them:

18 For they vex you with their [b] wiles, wherewith they have beguiled you in the matter of Peor, and in the matter of Cozbi, the daughter of a prince of Midian, their sister, which was slain in the day of the plague for Peor's sake.

[o] Psa. cvi. 30.——[p] Deut. iv. 3; 1 Cor. x. 8.——[q] Psa. cvi. 30; Ecclus. xlv. 23.——[r] Heb. *with my zeal*; see 2 Cor. xi. 2. [s] Exod. xx. 5; Deut. xxxii. 16, 21; 1 Kings xiv. 22; Psa. lxxviii. 58; Ezek. xvi. 38; Zeph. i. 18; iii. 8.——[t] Mal. ii. 4, 5; iii. 1; Ecclus. xlv. 24; 1 Mac. ii. 54.——[u] See 1 Chron. vi. 4, &c. [v] Exod. xl. 15; Ecclus. xlv. 24.——[w] Acts xxii. 3; Rom. x. 2. [x] Heb. ii. 17.——[y] Heb. *house of a father*.——[z] Chap. xxxi. 8; Josh. xiii. 21.——[a] Chap. xxxi. 2.——[b] Chap. xxxi. 16; Rev. ii. 14.

this act, which can never be a *precedent* on any common occasion. An act something similar occurs in our own history. In 1381, in the minority of Richard II., a most formidable insurrection took place in Kent and Essex; about 100,000 men, chiefly under the direction of *Wat Tyler*, seized on London, massacred multitudes of innocent people, and were proceeding to the greatest enormities, when the king requiring a conference in Smithfield with the rebel leader, Sir *William Walworth*, then mayor of London, provoked at the insolence with which *Tyler* behaved to his sovereign, knocked him off his horse with his mace, after which he was instantly despatched. While his partisans were bending their bows to revenge the death of their leader, Richard, then only *sixteen* years of age, rode up to them, and with great courage and presence of mind thus addressed them: "What, my people, will you kill your king! be not concerned for the death of your leader; follow me, and I will be your general." They were suddenly appeased, and the rebellion terminated. The action of Sir William Walworth was that of a *zealot*, of essential benefit at the time, and justified only by the pressing exigencies of the case.

Verse 9. *Those that died—were twenty and four thousand.*] St. Paul, 1 Cor. x. 8, reckons only *twenty-three* thousand; though some MSS. and versions, particularly the latter *Syriac* and the *Armenian*, have *twenty-four* thousand, with the Hebrew text. Allowing the 24,000 to be the genuine reading, and none of the Hebrew MSS. exhibit any various reading here, the two places may be reconciled thus: 1000 men were slain in consequence of the examination instituted ver. 4, and 23,000 in consequence of the orders given ver. 5; making 24,000 in the whole. St. Paul probably refers only to the latter number.

Verses 12, 13. *My covenant of peace—of an everlasting priesthood*] As the word *peace* implied all kinds of blessings, both spiritual and temporal, it may mean no more here than the promise of God, to grant him and his family the *utmost prosperity* in reference to *both worlds*. The *everlasting priesthood* refers properly to the *priesthood of Christ* which was shadowed out by the priesthood under the law; no matter in what family it was continued. Therefore the כהנת עולם *kehunnath olam*, or *eternal priesthood*, does not merely refer to any sacerdotal ministrations which should be continued in the family of Phinehas, during the Mosaic dispensation, but to that priesthood of Christ typified by that of Aaron and his successors. The priesthood alone is everlasting, and a covenant or grant of that was made to Phinehas, and his descendants. The Jews reckon twelve high priests of the race of Phinehas, from this time to the days of Solomon, nine more from that time to the captivity, (see 1 Chron. vi. 4, 15,) and fifteen from their return to the time of *Antiochus Eupator*, the last of whom was Onias, slain by Lysias. Ezra, the great priest and scribe, was of this line, Ezra vii. 1, 5. The family of Ithamar, uncle of Phinehas, had the priesthood for about 150 years; but it was restored to the family of Phinehas in the person of *Zadok* the priest, 1 Chron. vi. 50, in which it continued in the whole about 950 years. Probably the *Maccabees* were of the same family; but though this is not certain, there is no evidence against it. See *Calmet*. God therefore sufficiently fulfilled his promise; he gave to him and his descendants almost the utmost *temporal* length that could be given of *that* priesthood which is, in its own nature, *eternal*. Here then the word עולם *olam* means, not a limited time, but what is eternal in its duration. See the note on Gen. xxi. 33.

Verse 17. *Vex the Midianites, &c.*] See this order fulfilled, chap. xxxi. 1–20. Twelve thousand Israelites attacked the Midianites, destroyed all their cities, slew their five kings, every male, and every grown up woman, and took all their spoils.

CHAPTER XXVI.

Moses and Eleazar are commanded to take the sum of the Israelites, in the plains of Moab, 1–4. Reuben *and his posterity,* 43,730, *ver.* 5–11. Simeon *and his posterity,* 22,200, *ver.* 12–14. Gad *and his posterity,* 40,500, *ver.* 15–18. Judah *and his posterity,* 76,500, *ver.* 19–22. Issachar *and his posterity,* 64,300, *ver.* 23–25. Zebulun *and his posterity,* 60,500, *ver.* 26, 27. Manasseh *and his posterity,* 52,700, *ver.* 28–34. Ephraim *and his posterity,* 32,500, *ver.* 35–37. Benjamin *and his posterity,* 45,600, *ver.* 38–41. Dan *and his posterity,* 64,400, *ver.* 42, 43. Asher *and his posterity,* 53,400, *ver.* 44–47. Naphtali *and his posterity,* 45, 400, *ver.* 48–50. *Total amount of the twelve tribes,* 601,730, *ver.* 51. *The land is to be divided by lot, and how,* 52–56. *The Levites and their families,* 57, 58. *Their genealogy,* 59–61. *Their number,* 23,000, *ver.* 62. *In this census or enumeration not one man was found, save* Joshua *and* Caleb, *of all who had been reckoned* 38 *years before, the rest having died in the wilderness,* 63–65.

A. M. 2553.
B. C. 1451.
An. Exod. Isr. 40.

AND it came to pass after the plague, that the LORD spake unto Moses, and unto Eleazar the son of Aaron the priest, saying,

2 [a] Take the sum of all the congregation of the children of Israel, [b] from twenty years old and upward, throughout their fathers' house, all that are able to go to war in Israel.

3 And Moses and Eleazar the priest spake with them [c] in the plains of Moab by Jordan *near* Jericho, saying,

4 *Take the sum of the people,* from twenty years old and upward; as the LORD [d] commanded Moses and the children of Israel, which went forth out of the land of Egypt.

5 [e] Reuben, the eldest son of Israel: the children of Reuben; Hanoch, *of whom cometh* the family of the Hanochites: of Pallu, the family of the Palluites:

6 Of Hezron, the family of the Hezronites: of Carmi, the family of the Carmites.

7 These *are* the families of the Reubenites: and they that were numbered of them were forty and three thousand and seven hundred and thirty.

8 And the sons of Pallu; Eliab.

9 And the sons of Eliab; Nemuel, and Dathan, and Abiram. This *is that* Dathan and Abiram *which were* [f] famous in the congregation who strove against Moses and against Aaron in the company of Korah, when they strove against the LORD:

10 [g] And the earth opened her mouth, and swallowed them up together with Korah, when that company died, what time the fire devoured two hundred and fifty men: [h] and they became a sign.

11 Notwithstanding [i] the children of Korah died not.

12 The sons of Simeon after their families of [k] Nemuel, the family of the Nemuelites of Jamin, the family of the Jaminites: of [l] Jachin, the family of the Jachinites:

13 Of [m] Zerah, the family of the Zarhites. of Shaul, the family of the Shaulites.

14 These *are* the families of the Simeonites, twenty and two thousand and two hundred.

15 The children of Gad after their families: of [n] Zephon, the family of the Zephonites: of Haggi, the family of the Haggites: of Shuni, the family of the Shunites:

[a] Exod. xxx. 12; xxxviii. 25, 26; chap. i. 2.——[b] Chap. i 3. [c] Ver. 63; chap. xxii. 1; xxxi. 12; xxxiii. 48; xxxv. 1.——[d] Ch. i. 1.——[e] Gen. xlvi. 8; Exod. vi. 14; 1 Chron. v. 1.——[f] Chap. xvi. 1, 2.——[g] Chap. xvi. 32, 35.

[h] Chap. xvi. 38; see 1 Cor. x. 6; 2 Pet. ii. 6.——[i] Exod. vi. 24; 1 Chron. vi. 22.——[k] Gen. xlvi. 10; Exod. vi. 15, *Jemuel.* [l] 1 Chron. iv, 24, *Jarib.*——[m] Gen. xlvi. 10, *Zohar.*——[n] Gen. xlvi. 16, *Ziphion.*

NOTES ON CHAP XXVI.

Verse 2. *Take the sum of all the congregation*] After thirty-eight years God commands a *second census* of the Israelites to be made, to preserve the distinction in families, and to regulate the tribes previously to their entry into the promised land, and to ascertain the proportion of land which should be allowed to each tribe. For though the whole was divided by *lot,* yet the portions were so disposed that a numerous tribe did not draw where the lots assigned small inheritances. See verses 53–56, and also the note on chap. i. 1.

Verse 10. *Together with Korah*] The Samaritan text does not intimate that Korah was *swallowed up,* but that he was *burnt,* as appears in fact to have been the case. *And the earth swallowed them up, what time that company died; and the fire devoured Korah with the two hundred and fifty men, who became a sign.*

Verse 11. *The children of Korah died not.*] It is difficult to reconcile this place with chap. xvi. 27, 31–33, where it seems to be intimated that not only the *men,* but *the wives,* and *the sons, and the little ones* of Korah, Dathan, and Abiram, were swallowed up by the earthquake; see especially ver. 27, collated with ver. 33, of chap. xvi. But the text *here* expressly says, *The children of Korah died not;* and on a close in-

A. M. 2553. B. C. 1451. An. Exod. Isr. 40.

16 Of [o] Ozni, the family of the Oznites: of Eri, the family of the Erites:

17 Of [p] Arod, the family of the Arodites: of Areli, the family of the Arelites.

18 These *are* the families of the children of Gad according to those that were numbered of them, forty thousand and five hundred.

19 [q] The sons of Judah *were* Er and Onan: and Er and Onan died in the land of Canaan.

20 And [r] the sons of Judah after their families were; of Shelah, the family of the Shelanites: of Pharez, the family of the Pharezites: of Zerah, the family of the Zarhites.

21 And the sons of Pharez were; of Hezron, the family of the Hezronites: of Hamul, the family of the Hamulites.

22 These *are* the families of Judah according to those that were numbered of them, threescore and sixteen thousand and five hundred.

23 [s] *Of* the sons of Issachar after their families: *of* Tola, the family of the Tolaites: of Pua, the family of the Punites:

24 Of [u] Jashub, the family of the Jashubites: of Shimron, the family of the Shimronites.

25 These *are* the families of Issachar according to those that were numbered of them, threescore and four thousand and three hundred.

26 [v] *Of* the sons of Zebulun after their families: of Sered, the family of the Sardites: of Elon, the family of the Elonites: of Jahleel, the family of the Jahleelites.

27 These *are* the families of the Zebulunites according to those that were numbered of them, threescore thousand and five hundred.

28 [w] The sons of Joseph after their families *were* Manasseh and Ephraim.

29 Of the sons of Manasseh: of [x] Machir, the family of the Machirites: and Machir begat Gilead: of Gilead *come* the family of the Gileadites.

30 These *are* the sons of Gilead: *of* [y] Jeezer, the family of the Jeezerites: of Helek, the family of the Helekites:

31 And *of* Asriel, the family of the Asrielites: and *of* Shechem, the family of the Shechemites:

32 And *of* Shemida, the family of the Shemidaites: and *of* Hepher, the family of the Hepherites.

33 And [z] Zelophehad the son of Hepher had no sons, but daughters: and the names of the daughters of Zelophehad *were* Mahlah, and Noah, Hoglah, Milcah, and Tirzah.

34 These *are* the families of Manasseh, and those that were numbered of them, fifty and two thousand and seven hundred.

35 These *are* the sons of Ephraim after their families: of Shuthelah, the family of the Shuthalhites: of [a] Becher, the family of the Bachrites: of Tahan, the family of the Tahanites.

36 And these *are* the sons of Shuthelah: of Eran, the family of the Eranites

37 These *are* the families of the sons of Ephraim according to those that were numbered of them, thirty and two thousand and five hundred. These *are* the sons of Joseph after their families.

38 [b] The sons of Benjamin after their families: of Bela, the family of the Belaites: of Ashbel, the family of the Ashbelites: of [c] Ahiram, the family of the Ahiramites:

39 Of [d] Shupham, the family of the Shuphamites: of Hupham, the family of the Huphamites.

40 And the sons of Bela were [e] Ard and Naaman: *of Ard*, the family of the Ardites: *and* of Naaman, the family of the Naamites.

41 These *are* the sons of Benjamin after their families: and they that were numbered of them *were* forty and five thousand and six hundred.

42 [f] These *are* the sons of Dan after their families: of [g] Shuham, the family of the Shuhamites. These *are* the families of Dan after their families.

[o] Or, *Ezbon*, Gen. xlvi. 16.——[p] Gen. xlvi. 16, *Arodi*.——[q] Gen. xxxviii. 2, &c.; xlvi. 12.——[r] 1 Chron. ii. 3.——[s] Gen. xlvi. 13; 1 Chron. vii. 1.——[t] Or, *Phuvah*.——[u] Or, *Job*.——[v] Gen. xlvi. 14.——[w] Gen. xlvi. 20.——[x] Josh. xvii. 1; 1 Chron. vii. 14, 15. [y] Called *Abiezer*, Josh. xvii. 2; Judg. vi. 11, 24, 34.

[z] Chap. xxvii. 1; xxxvi. 11.——[a] 1 Chron. vii. 20, *Bered*. [b] Gen. xlvi. 21; 1 Chron. vii. 6.——[c] Gen. xlvi. 21, *Ehi*; 1 Chron. viii. 1, *Aharah*.——[d] Genesis xlvi. 21, *Muppim and Huppim*. [e] 1 Chron. viii. 3, *Addar*.——[f] Genesis xlvi. 23.——[g] Or, *Hushim*.

spection of ver. 27 of the above-mentioned chapter, we shall find that the *sons and the little ones* of Dathan and Abiram alone are mentioned. *So they gat up from the tabernacle of Korah, Dathan, and Abiram, on every side: and Dathan and Abiram came out—and their wives, and their sons, and their little ones.* Here is no mention of the *children of Korah*, they therefore escaped, while it appears those of Dathan and Abiram perished with their fathers. See the note on chap. xvi. 30.

A. M. 2553. B. C. 1451. An. Exod. Isr. 40.

43 All the families of the
Shuhamites, according to those
that were numbered of them,
were threescore and four thousand and four
hundred.
44 [h] *Of* the children of Asher after their
families: of Jimna, the family of the Jimnites:
of Jesui, the family of the Jesuites: of Beriah, the family of the Beriites.
45 Of the sons of Beriah: of Heber, the
family of the Heberites: of Malchiel, the family of the Malchielites.
46 And the name of the daughter of Asher
was Sarah.
47 These *are* the families of the sons of
Asher according to those that were numbered
of them; *who were* fifty and three thousand
and four hundred.
48 [i] *Of* the sons of Naphtali after their families: of Jahzeel, the family of the Jahzeel-
ites: of Guni, the family of the Gunites:
49 Of Jezer, the family of the Jezerites: of
[k] Shillem, the family of the Shil-
lemites.

A. M. 2553. B. C. 1451. An. Exod. Isr. 40.

50 These *are* the families of
Naphtali according to their families: and they
that were numbered of them *were* forty and
five thousand and four hundred.
51 [l] These *were* the numbered of the children of Israel, six hundred thousand and a
thousand seven hundred and thirty.
52 And the LORD spake unto Moses, saying,
53 [m] Unto these the land shall be divided for
an inheritance according to the number of
names.
54 [n] To many thou shalt [o] give the more in
heritance, and to few thou shalt [p] give the less
inheritance: to every one shall his inheritance
be given according to those that were numbered of him.
55 Notwithstanding the land shall be [q] divided
by lot: according to the names of the tribes of
their fathers they shall inherit.
56 According to the lot shall the possession

[h] Gen. xlvi. 17; 1 Chron. vii. 30.——[i] Gen. xlvi. 24; 1 Chron. vii. 13.——[k] 1 Chron. vii. 13, *Shallum*.——[l] See chapter i. 46. [m] Josh. xi. 23; xiv. 1.

[n] Chap. xxxiii. 54.——[o] Heb. *multiply his inheritance*.——[p] Heb. *diminish his inheritance*.——[q] Ch. xxxiii. 54; xxxiv. 13; Josh. xi. 23; xiv. 2.

Verse 51. *These* were *the numbered of the children of Israel, six hundred thousand and a thousand seven hundred and thirty.*] The following comparative statement will show how much some of the tribes had *increased*, and others had *diminished*, since the enumeration in chap. i.

	Now	Before	
Reuben	43,730	46,500	2,770 *decrease*
Simeon	22,200	59,300	37,100 *decrease*
Gad	40,500	45,650	5,150 *decrease*
Judah	76,500	74,600	1,900 increase
Issachar	64,300	54,400	9,900 increase
Zebulun	60,500	57,400	3,100 increase
Manasseh	52,700	32,200	20,500 increase
Ephraim	32,500	40,500	8,000 *decrease*
Benjamin	45,600	35,400	10,200 increase
Dan	64,400	62,700	1,700 increase
Asher	53,400	41,500	11,900 increase
Naphtali	45,400	53,400	8,000 *decrease*
Total	601,730	603,550	1,820 *decrease* on the *whole*, in 38 years.

Decrease in all, 61,020 Increase in all, 59,200.

Let it be observed, 1. That among these there was not a man of the former census, save Joshua and Caleb, see ver. 64, 65. 2. That though there was an *increase* in seven tribes of not less than 74,800 men, yet so great was the *decrease* in the other *five* tribes, that the balance against the present census is 1,820, as appears above: thus we find that there was an increase of 601,728 from 603,550 in the space of thirty-eight years.

Notwithstanding the amazing increase in some and decrease in other tribes, the same sort of proportion is preserved in the *east*, *west*, *north*, and *south* divisions, as before; so as to keep the division of *Judah*, which was always in the *front* or *van*, the largest; and the division of *Dan*, which was always in the *rear*, the next in number. But it is worthy of remark that as they are now, properly speaking, to commence their grand military operations, so their *front*, or *advanced division*, is increased from 186,400 to 201,300; and their *rear* from 157,600 to 163,200. The *first* division is strengthened 14,900 men, and the *last* division 5,600 men. The reasons for this are sufficiently obvious.

Mr. *Ainsworth* has a curious remark on the number of families in the 12 tribes. "Here are families,

1. Of Manasseh	8	7. Of Reuben	4
2. Of Benjamin	7	8. Of Issachar	4
3. Of Gad	7	9. Of Ephraim	4
4. Of Simeon	5	10. Of Naphtali	4
5. Of Judah	5	11. Of Zebulun	3
6. Of Asher	5	12. Of Dan	1

"In all 57; to whom if we add the 12 *patriarchs*, and *Jacob* their father, the whole number is 70, the exact number of the souls in Jacob's house that went down to Egypt, Gen. xlvi. 27." In a variety of things in this ancient economy there is a most surprising *proportion* kept up, which never could have been a fortuitous effect of general causes. But *proportion, harmony*, and *order* distinguish all the works of God, both in the *natural* and *moral* world.

Verse 55. *The land shall de divided by lot*] The

a

A. M. 2553.
B. C. 1451.
An. Exod. Isr. 40.

thereof be divided between many
and few.
57 [r] And these *are* they that
were numbered of the Levites after their families: of Gershon, the family of the Gershonites: of Kohath, the family of the Kohathites:
of Merari, the family of the Merarites.
58 These *are* the families of the Levites:
the family of the Libnites, the family of the
Hebronites, the family of the Mahlites, the
family of the Mushites, the family of the Ko-
rathites. And Kohath begat Amram.
59 And the name of Amram's wife *was*
[s] Jochebed, the daughter of Levi, whom *her
mother* bare to Levi in Egypt: and she bare
unto Amram Aaron and Moses, and Miriam
their sister.
60 [t] And unto Aaron was born Nadab, and
Abihu, Eleazar, and Ithamar.
61 And [u] Nadab and Abihu died, when they
offered strange fire before the
LORD.
62 [v] And those that were num-
bered of them were twenty and three thousand,
all males from a month old and upward; [w] for
they were not numbered among the children
of Israel, because there was [x] no inheritance
given them among the children of Israel.
63 These *are* they that were numbered by
Moses and Eleazar the priest, who numbered
the children of Israel [y] in the plains of Moab,
by Jordan *near* Jericho.
64 [z] But among these there was not a man
of them whom Moses and Aaron the priest
numbered, when they numbered the children
of Israel in the wilderness of Sinai.
65 For the LORD had said of them, They
[a] shall surely die in the wilderness. And there
was not left a man of them, [b] save Caleb the
son of Jephunneh, and Joshua the son of Nun.

A. M. 2553.
B. C. 1451.
An. Exod. Isr. 40.

[r] Gen. xlvi. 11; Exod. vi. 16–19; 1 Chron. vi. 1, 16.——[s] Exod. ii. 1, 2; vi. 20.——[t] Chap. iii. 2.——[u] Lev. x. 1, 2; chap. iii. 4; 1 Chron. xxiv. 2.——[v] See chap. iii. 39.

[w] Chap. i. 49.——[x] Chap. xviii. 20, 23, 24; Deut. x. 9; Josh. xiii. 14, 33; xiv. 3.——[y] Ver. 3.——[z] Chap. i; Deut. ii. 14, 15. [a] Chap. xiv. 28, 29; 1 Cor. x. 5, 6.——[b] Chap. xiv. 30.

word גורל *goral*, translated *lot*, is supposed by some to signify the *stone* or *pebble* formerly used for the purpose of what we term *casting lots*. The word hlot *hlot* is Anglo-Saxon, from hleotan, to *divide*, or *portion out*, i. e., fortuitously: it answers to the Greek *κληρος*, which some think comes from *κλαω*, *to break*; because the lot, being a sort of appeal to God, ("The lot is cast into the lap, but the whole disposing thereof is of the Lord," Prov. xvi. 33,) *broke* off all contentions and litigations relative to the matter in dispute. From this original division of the promised land by *lot* to the children of Israel, all *portions*, *appointments*, *offices*, *shares*, or *divisions* in spiritual and ecclesiastical matters, were termed *lots*. So in the New Testament, the word *κληρος*, *lot*, is used to signify a *portion of spiritual blessedness*, and *κληρονομια*, a *division by lot*, an *inheritance*; and *κληροι*, the *lotted* or *appointed persons* to different works, shares, &c.; hence our word *clergy*, *κληροι*, *persons appointed by lot* to a lot, portion, or inheritance; see the case of Matthias, Acts i. 26. Persons thus appointed were by accommodation termed *inheritors*, because originally, when there could be no *claims* of exclusive *right*, all lands where a wandering tribe chose to take up its residence were divided by lot, as the promised land in the case before us. So Judah says to Simeon his brother, Judg. i. 3: "Come up with me into my *lot*." And as God was ever supposed to be the whole disposer in such matters, whatever *fell out* in the course of *God's providence* was called a *lot*. "This is the *lot* of them that rob us;" Isa. xvii. 14. "Thou hast neither part nor *lot* in this matter;" Acts viii. 21. A *lot* in the promised *land* was evidently *typical* of a *place* in *eternal glory*. "That they may receive forgiveness of sins, and an inheritance (*κληρον*, a *lot*) among them that are sanctified;" Acts xxvi. 18. "Who hath made us meet to be partakers of the inheritance (*κληρον*, of the *lot*) of the saints in light;" Col. i. 12. "Which is the earnest of our inheritance, (*κληρονομιας*, of our *allotted portion*;") Eph. i. 14. "What is the riches of the glory of his inheritance," (*κληρονομιας*, *allotted portion*;) Eph. i. 18. As therefore the promised land was divided by lot to the believing Israelites, God determining the lot as he saw good, none of the people having any *claim* on or *right* to it; so the kingdom of heaven is a *lot* given by the mere good will of God to them that believe and obey him; for as unbelief and disobedience threw 600,000 people out of the inheritance of the promised land; so none who disbelieve God's word, and rebel against his authority, shall ever enter into the kingdom of heaven.—See *Ainsworth*. These things happened unto them for examples: see then, reader, that thou fall not after the same example of unbelief.

CHAPTER XXVII.

The daughters of Zelophehad claim their inheritance, 1–4. *Moses brings their case before the Lord*, 5. *He allows their claim*, 6, 7; *and a law is made to regulate the inheritance of daughters*, 8–11. *Moses is commanded to go up to Mount* Abarim, *and view the promised land*, 12; *is apprised of his death*, 13; *and because he did not sanctify God at the waters of* Meribah, *he shall not enter into it*, 14. *Moses*

***requests the Lord to appoint a person to supply his place as leader of the Israelites,* 15–17. *God appoints Joshua, commands Moses to lay his hands upon him, to set him before Eleazar the priest, and give him a charge in the sight of the people,* 18–20. *Eleazar shall ask counsel for him by* Urim, *and at his command shall the Israelites go out and come in,* 21. *Moses does as the Lord commanded him, and consecrates Joshua,* 22, 23.**

A. M. 2553.
B. C. 1451.
An. Exod. Isr. 40.

THEN came the daughters of [a] Zelophehad, the son of Hepher, the son of Gilead, the son of Machir, the son of Manasseh, of the families of Manasseh the son of Joseph: and these *are* the names of his daughters; Mahlah, Noah, and Hoglah, and Milcah, and Tirzah.

2 And they stood before Moses, and before Eleazar the priest, and before the princes and all the congregation, *by* the door of the tabernacle of the congregation, saying,

3 Our father [b] died in the wilderness, and he was not in the company of them that gathered themselves together against the LORD [c] in the company of Korah; but died in his own sin, and had no sons.

4 Why should the name of our father be [d] done away from among his family, because he hath no son? [e] Give unto us *therefore* a possession among the brethren of our father.

5 And Moses [f] brought their cause before the LORD.

A. M. 2553.
B. C. 1451.
An. Exod. Isr. 40.

6 And the LORD spake unto Moses, saying,

7 The daughters of Zelophehad speak right: [g] thou shalt surely give them a possession of an inheritance among their father's brethren; and thou shalt cause the inheritance of their father to pass unto them.

8 And thou shalt speak unto the children of Israel, saying, If a man die, and have no son, then ye shall cause his inheritance to pass unto his daughter.

9 And if he have no daughter, then ye shall give his inheritance unto his brethren.

10 And if he have no brethren, then ye shall give his inheritance unto his father's brethren.

11 And if his father have no brethren, then ye shall give his inheritance unto his kinsman that is next to him of his family, and he shall

[a] Chap. xxvi. 33; xxxvi. 1, 11; Josh. xvii. 3.——[b] Chap. xiv. 35; xxvi. 64, 65.——[c] Chap. xvi. 1, 2.

[d] Heb. *diminished.*——[e] Josh. xvii. 4.——[f] Exod. xviii. 15, 19. [g] Chap. xxxvi. 2; Jer. xlix. 11; Gal. iii. 28.

NOTES ON CHAP. XXVII.

Verse 1. *The daughters of Zelophehad*] The singular case of these women caused an additional law to be made to the civil code of Israel, which satisfactorily ascertained and amply secured the right of succession in cases of inheritance. The law, which is as reasonable as it is just, stands thus: 1. On the demise of the *father* the estate goes to the *sons;* 2. If there be no *son,* the *daughters* succeed; 3. If there be no *daughter,* the *brothers* of the deceased inherit; 4. If there be no *brethren* or paternal *uncles,* the estate goes to the *brothers* of his *father;* 5. If there be no *grand uncles* or *brothers* of the *father* of the deceased, then the *nearest akin* succeeds to the inheritance. Beyond this *fifth* degree the law does not proceed, because as the families of the Israelites were kept distinct in their respective tribes, there must always be some who could be called *kinsmen,* and were really such, having descended without interruption from the patriarch of the tribe.

Verse 7. *Thou shalt surely give them—an inheritance among their father's brethren*] There is a curious anomaly here in the Hebrew text which cannot be seen in our translation. In Hebrew *they, them,* and *their, you, ye,* and *your,* are both of the masculine and feminine genders, according as the nouns are to which they are affixed; but these words are of no gender in English. In this verse, speaking of the brethren of the father of those women, the *masculine* termination הם *hem,* THEIR, is used instead of the *feminine,* הן *hen,* governed by בנות *benoth, daughters.* So להם *lahem,* to THEM, and אביהם *abihem,* THEIR *fathers,* masculine, are found in the present text, instead of להן *lahen* and אביהן *abihen,* feminine. Interpreters have sought for a *hidden* meaning *here,* and they have found several, whether *hidden here* or not. One says, "the *masculine* gender is used because these daughters are treated as if they were *heirs male.*" Another, "that it is because of their *faith* and conscientious regard to the ancient customs, and to keep the memory of their father in being, which might well befit *men.*" Another, "that it signifies the free gift of God in Christ, where there is neither *male* nor *female, bond* or *free,* for all are one in Christ;" and so on, for where there is no rule there is no end to conjecture. Now the plain truth is, that the masculine is in the present printed text a mistake for the feminine. The *Samaritan,* which many think by far the most authentic copy of the Pentateuch, has the *feminine* gender in both places; so also have upwards of *fourscore* of the MSS. collated by *Kennicott* and *De Rossi.* Therefore all the curious reasons for this anomaly offered by interpreters are only serious trifling on the blunder of some heedless copyists.

While on the subject of mysterious reasons and meanings, some might think it unpardonable if I passed by the mystery of the *fall, recovery,* and *full salvation* of man, signified, as some will have it, by the *names* of Zelophehad and his daughters. "1. Zelophehad's daughters, claiming a portion in the promised land, may represent believers in Christ claiming an inheritance among the saints in light. 2. These five

A. M. 2553. B. C. 1451. An. Exod. Isr. 40.

possess it: and it shall be unto
the children of Israel [h] a statute
of judgment, as the LORD commanded Moses.
12 And the LORD said unto Moses, [i] Get thee
up into this Mount Abarim, and see the land
which I have given unto the children of Israel.
13 And when thou hast seen it, thou also
[k] shalt be gathered unto thy people, as Aaron
thy brother was gathered.
14 For ye [l] rebelled against my commandment in the desert of Zin, in the strife of the
congregation, to sanctify me at the water before their eyes: that *is* the [m] water of Meribah in Kadesh in the wilderness of Zin.
15 And Moses spake unto the LORD, saying,
16 Let the LORD, [n] the God of the spirits of
all flesh, set a man over the congregation,
17 [o] Which may go out before them, and
which may go in before them, and which may
lead them out, and which may
bring them in; that the congregation of the LORD be not [p] as sheep
which have no shepherd.
18 And the LORD said unto Moses, Take
thee Joshua the son of Nun, a man [q] in whom
is the spirit, and [r] lay thine hand upon him;
19 And set him before Eleazar the priest,
and before all the congregation, and [s] give
him a charge in their sight.
20 And [t] thou shalt put *some* of thine honour
upon him, that all the congregation of the
children of Israel [u] may be obedient.
21 [v] And he shall stand before Eleazar the
priest, who shall ask *counsel* for him [w] after
the judgment of Urim before the LORD: [x] at his
word shall they go out, and at his word they
shall come in, *both* he, and all the children of
Israel with him, even all the congregation.
22 And Moses did as the LORD commanded

A. M. 2553. B. C. 1451. An. Exod. Isr. 40.

[h] Chap. xxxv. 29.——[i] Chap. xxxiii. 47; Deut. iii. 27; xxxii. 49; xxxiv. 1.——[k] Chap. xx. 24, 28; xxxi. 2; Deut. x. 6.——[l] Chap. xx. 12, 24; Deut. i. 37; xxxii. 51; Psa. cvi. 32.——[m] Exod. xvii. 7.——[n] Chap. xvi. 22; Heb. xii. 9.——[o] Deut. xxxi. 2; 1 Sam. viii. 20; xviii. 13; 2 Chron. i. 10.——[p] 1 Kings xxii. 17; Zech. x. 2; Matt. ix. 36; Mark vi. 34.

[q] Gen. xli. 38; Judg. iii. 10; xi. 29; 1 Sam. xvi. 13, 18.——[r] Deut. xxxiv. 9.——[s] Deut. xxxi. 7.——[t] See chap. xi. 17, 28; 1 Sam. x. 6, 9; 2 Kings ii. 15.——[u] Josh. i. 16, 17.——[v] See Josh. ix. 14; Judg. i. 1; xx. 18, 23, 26; 1 Sam. xxiii. 9; xxx. 7.——[w] Exod. xxviii. 30.——[x] Joshua ix. 14; 1 Samuel xxii. 10, 13, 15.

virgins may be considered as the *five wise virgins*, (Matt. xxv. 1–10,) who took oil in their vessels with their lamps, and consequently are types of those who make a wise provision for their eternal state. 3. They are examples of encouragement to weak and *destitute* believers, who, though they are *orphans* in this world, shall not be deprived of their heavenly inheritance. 4. Their *names* are mysterious; for *Zelophehad*, צלפחד TSELOPHCHAD, signifies the *shadow of fear* or *dread*. His first daughter, מחלה MACHLAH, *infirmity;* the second, נעה NOAH, *wandering;* the third, חגלה CHOGLAH, *turning about* or *dancing* for joy; the fourth, מלכה MILCAH, a *queen;* the fifth, תרצה TIRTSAH, *well-pleasing* or *acceptable*. By these names we may observe our reviving by grace in Christ; for we are all born of the *shadow of fear*, (*Tselophchad*,) being brought forth in sin, and through fear of death being all our life time subject to bondage, Heb. ii. 15. This begets (*Machlah*) *infirmity* or *sickness*—grief of heart for our estate. After which (*Noah*) *wandering* about for help and comfort we find it in Christ, by whom our sorrow is turned into *joy* (*Choglah*.) He communicates of his *royalty* (*Milcah*) to us, making us *kings* and priests unto God and his Father, Rev. i. 6. So we shall at last be presented unto him glorious and without blemish, being (*Tirtsah*) *well-pleasing* and *acceptable* in his sight." This is a specimen of *pious* INGENUITY, which has been endeavouring to do *the work of an* EVANGELIST in the Church of God from the time of Origen to the present day.

Verse 12. *Get thee up into this Mount Abarim*] The mountain which Moses was commanded to ascend was certainly Mount *Nebo*, see Deut. xxxii. 49, &c., which was the same as *Pisgah*, see Deut. xxxiv. 1. The mountains of *Abarim*, according to Dr. Shaw, are a long ridge of frightful, rocky, precipitous hills, which are continued all along the eastern coast of the Dead Sea, as far as the eye can reach. As in Hebrew עבר *abar* signifies to *pass over*, *Abarim* here probably signifies *passages;* and the ridge in this place had its name in all likelihood from the *passage* of the Israelites, as it was opposite to these that they passed the Jordan into the promised land.

Verse 14. *Ye rebelled against my commandment*] See the notes on chap. xx. 8.

Verse 16. *The Lord, the God of the spirits of all flesh*] See the notes on chap. xvi. 22.

Verse 17. *That the congregation of the Lord be not as sheep which have no shepherd.*] This is a beautiful expression, and shows us in what light Moses viewed himself among his people. He was their *shepherd;* he sought no higher place; he *fed* and *guided* the flock of God under the direction of the Divine Spirit, and was faithful in all his Master's house. To this saying of Moses our Lord alludes, Matt. ix. 36.

Verse 18. *In whom is the spirit*] This must certainly mean the *Spirit of God;* and because he was endued with this Spirit, therefore he was capable of leading the people. How miserably qualified is that man for the work of God who is not guided and influenced by the Holy Ghost! God never chooses a man to accomplish his designs but that one whom he himself has qualified for the work.

Verse 20. *And thou shalt put, &c.*] מהודך *mehodecha*, of *thine honour* or *authority* upon him. Thou shalt show to the whole congregation that thou hast *associated* him with thyself in the government of the people.

Verse 21. *Eleazar the priest—shall ask* counsel *for*

A. M. 2553. B. C. 1451. An. Exod. Isr. 40.

him: and he took Joshua, and set him before Eleazar the priest, and before all the congregation:

23 And he laid his hands upon him, [y] and gave him a charge, as the LORD commanded by the hand of Moses.

A. M. 2553. B. C. 1451. An. Exod. Isr. 40.

[y] Deut. iii. 28; xxxi. 7.

him] Here was a remarkable difference between *him* and *Moses*. God talked with Moses face to face; but to Joshua only through the *medium* of the high priest.

Verse 23. *He laid his hands upon him*] As a proof of his being appointed to and qualified for the work. So at the word of Joshua they were to *go out*, and at his word to *come in*, ver. 21. And thus he was a type of our blessed Lord as to his mediatorial office, and Divine appointment as *man* to the work of our salvation; and to this circumstance of the appointment of Joshua to this work, and his receiving of Moses's honour and glory, St. Peter seems to refer in these words, 2 Epist. i. 16, 17: "We were eye-witnesses of his majesty; for he received from God the Father honour and glory, when there came such a voice to him from the excellent glory: This is my beloved Son, in whom I am well pleased; HEAR HIM." See Matt. xvii. 5. But one infinitely greater that either Moses or Joshua is here.

CHAPTER XXVIII.

All the offerings of God to be offered in their due season, 1, 2. *The continual burnt-offering for the morning*, 3–6; *and its drink-offering*, 7. *The continual burnt-offering for the evening*, 8. *The offerings for the Sabbath*, 9, 10. *The offerings for the beginning of each month*, 11–15. *Repetition of the ordinances concerning the passover*, 16–25. *Ordinances concerning the day of first-fruits or pentecost*, 26–31.

A. M. cir. 2553. B. C. cir. 1451. An. Exod. Isr. cir. 40.

AND the LORD spake unto Moses, saying,

2 Command the children of Israel, and say unto them, My offering, *and* [a] my bread for my sacrifices made by fire, *for* [b] a sweet savour unto me, shall ye observe to offer unto me in their due season.

3 And thou shalt say unto them, [c] This *is* the offering made by fire which ye shall offer unto the LORD; two lambs of the first year without spot [d] day by day, *for* a continual burnt-offering.

4 The one lamb shalt thou offer in the morning, and the other lamb shalt thou offer [e] at even;

A. M. cir. 2553. B. C. cir. 1451. An. Exod. Isr. cir. 40.

5 And [f] a tenth *part* of an ephah of flour for a [g] meat-offering, mingled with the fourth *part* of a [h] hin of beaten oil.

6 *It is* [i] a continual burnt-offering, which was ordained in Mount Sinai for a sweet savour, a sacrifice made by fire unto the LORD.

7 And the drink-offering thereof *shall be* the fourth *part* of a hin for the one lamb: [k] in the holy *place* shalt thou cause the strong wine to

[a] Lev. iii. 11; xxi. 6, 8; Mal. i. 7, 12.——[b] Heb. *a savour of my rest*.——[c] Exod. xxix. 38.——[d] Heb. *in a day*.——[e] Heb. *between the two evenings*; Exod. xii. 6.

[f] Exodus xvi. 36; chap. xv. 4.——[g] Lev. ii. 1.——[h] Exodus xxix. 40.——[i] Exodus xxix. 42; see Amos v. 25.——[k] Exod. xxix. 42.

NOTES ON CHAP. XXVIII.

Verse 2. *Command the children of Israel*, &c.] It is not easy to account for the reason of the introduction of these precepts here, which had been so circumstantially delivered before in different parts of the books of Exodus and Leviticus. It is possible that the *daily*, *weekly*, *monthly*, and *yearly* services had been considerably interrupted for several years, owing to the unsettled state of the people in the wilderness, and that it was necessary to *repeat* these laws for two reasons: 1. Because they were now about to enter into the promised land, where these services must be established and constant. 2. Because the former generations being all dead, multitudes of the present might be ignorant of these ordinances.

In their due season] Moses divides these offerings into

1. DAILY. The *morning* and *evening* sacrifices: *a lamb* each time, ver. 3, 4.

2. WEEKLY. The *Sabbath* offerings, *two lambs* of a year old, ver. 9, &c.

3. MONTHLY. At the beginning of each month *two young bullocks*, *one ram*, and *seven lambs* of a year old, and a *kid* for a sin-offering, ver. 11, &c.

4. ANNUAL. 1. The passover to last seven days; the offerings, *two* young *bullocks*, *one ram*, *seven lambs* of a year old, and a *he-goat* for a sin-offering, ver. 16, &c. 2. The day of FIRST-FRUITS. The sacrifices, the same as on the beginning of the month, ver. 26, &c. With these sacrifices were offered *libations*, or *drink-offerings of strong wine*, ver. 7, 14, and *minchahs*, or *meat-offerings*, composed of *fine flour* mingled with *oil*, ver. 8, 12, &c. For an ample account of all these offerings, see the notes on Lev. vii., and Exod. xii.

Verse 7. *Strong wine*] *Sikera*; see the note on chap. x. 9, where this is largely explained.

A. M. cir. 2553.
B. C. cir. 1451.
An. Exod. Isr.
cir. 40.

be poured unto the LORD *for* a drink-offering.

8 And the other lamb shalt thou offer at even: as the meat-offering of the morning, and as the drink-offering thereof, thou shalt offer *it*, a sacrifice made by fire, of a sweet savour unto the LORD.

9 And on the Sabbath day two lambs of the first year without spot, and two tenth deals of flour *for* a meat-offering, mingled with oil, and the drink-offering thereof:

10 *This is* [l] the burnt-offering of every Sabbath, beside the continual burnt-offering, and his drink-offering.

11 And [m] in the beginnings of your months ye shall offer a burnt-offering unto the LORD; two young bullocks, and one ram, seven lambs of the first year without spot;

12 And [n] three tenth deals of flour *for* a meat-offering, mingled with oil, for one bullock; and two tenth deals of flour *for* a meat-offering, mingled with oil, for one ram;

13 And a several tenth deal of flour mingled with oil *for* a meat-offering unto one lamb; *for* a burnt-offering of a sweet savour, a sacrifice made by fire unto the LORD.

14 And their drink-offering shall be half a hin of wine unto a bullock, and the third *part* of a hin unto a ram, and a fourth *part* of a hin unto a lamb: this *is* the burnt-offering of every month throughout the months of the year.

15 And [o] one kid of the goats for a sin-offering unto the LORD shall be offered, beside the continual burnt-offering, and his drink-offering.

16 [p] And in the fourteenth day of the first month *is* the passover of the LORD.

17 [q] And in the fifteenth day of this month *is* the feast: seven days shall unleavened bread be eaten.

18 In the [r] first day *shall be* a holy convocation; ye shall do no manner of servile work *therein:*

19 But ye shall offer a sacrifice made by fire *for* a burnt-offering unto the LORD; two young bullocks, and one ram, and seven lambs of the first year: [s] they shall be unto you without blemish:

A. M. cir. 2553.
B. C. cir. 1451.
An. Exod. Isr.
cir. 40.

20 And their meat-offering *shall be of* flour mingled with oil: three tenth deals shall ye offer for a bullock, and two tenth deals for a ram;

21 A several tenth deal shalt thou offer for every lamb, throughout the seven lambs:

22 And [t] one goat *for* a sin-offering, to make an atonement for you.

23 Ye shall offer these beside the burnt-offering in the morning, which *is* for a continual burnt-offering.

24 After this manner ye shall offer daily, throughout the seven days, the meat of the sacrifice made by fire, of a sweet savour unto the LORD: it shall be offered beside the continual burnt-offering, and his drink-offering.

25 And [u] on the seventh day ye shall have a holy convocation; ye shall do no servile work.

26 Also [v] in the day of the first-fruits, when ye bring a new meat-offering unto the LORD, after your weeks *be out*, ye shall have a holy convocation; ye shall do no servile work:

27 But ye shall offer the burnt-offering for a sweet savour unto the LORD; [w] two young bullocks, one ram, seven lambs of the first year;

28 And their meat-offering of flour mingled with oil, three tenth deals unto one bullock, two tenth deals unto one ram,

29 A several tenth deal unto one lamb, throughout the seven lambs;

30 *And* one kid of the goats, to make an atonement for you.

31 Ye shall offer *them* beside the continual burnt-offering, and his meat-offering, ([x] they shall be unto you without blemish,) and their drink-offerings.

---

[l] Ezek. xlvi. 4.——[m] Chap. x. 10; 1 Sam. xx. 5; 1 Chron. xxiii. 31; 2 Chron. ii. 4; Ezra iii. 5; Neh. x. 33; Isa. i. 13, 14; Ezek. xlv. 17; xlvi. 6; Hos. ii. 11; Col. ii. 16.——[n] Chap. xv. 4-12.——[o] Ver. 22; chap. xv. 24.——[p] Exod. xii. 6, 18; Lev. xxiii. 5; chap. ix. 3; Deut. xvi. 1; Ezek. xlv. 21.

[q] Lev. xxiii. 6.——[r] Exod. xii. 16; Lev. xxiii. 7.——[s] Ver. 31; Lev. xxii. 20; chap. xxix. 8; Deut. xv. 21.——[t] Ver. 15.——[u] Exod. xii. 16; xiii. 6; Lev. xxiii. 8.——[v] Exod. xxiii. 16; xxxiv. 22; Lev. xxiii. 10, 15; Deut. xvi. 10; Acts ii. 1.——[w] See Lev. xxiii. 18, 19.——[x] Ver. 19.

Verse 26. *Day of the first-fruits*] Called also the feast of weeks, and the feast of pentecost. See it explained Exod. xxiii. 14, and Lev. xxiii. 15.

Verse 31. *Without blemish*] This is to be understood as applying, not only to the animals, but also to the *flour*, *wine*, and *oil*; every thing must be *perfect* in its *kind*.

CHAPTER XXIX.

The feast of trumpets *on the* first *day of the seventh month, and its sacrifices,* 1–6. *The* feast of expiation, *or* annual atonement, *on the* tenth *day of the same month, with its sacrifices,* 7–11. *The* feast of tabernacles *held on the* fifteenth *day of the same month, with its* eight *days' offerings,* 12. *The offerings of the* first day, *thirteen* bullocks, *two* rams, *fourteen* lambs, *and one* kid, 13–16. *The offerings of the* second day, *twelve* bullocks, *two* rams, *fourteen* lambs, *and one* kid, 17–19. *The offerings of the* third day, *eleven* bullocks; *the rest as before,* 20–22. *The offerings of the* fourth day, *ten* bullocks; *the rest as before,* 23–25. *The offerings of the* fifth day, *nine* bullocks, *&c.,* 26–28. *The offerings of the* sixth day, *eight* bullocks, *&c.,* 29–31. *The offerings of the* seventh day, *seven* bullocks, *&c.,* 32–34. *The offerings of the* eighth day, *one* bullock, *one* ram, *seven* lambs, *and one* goat, 35–38. *These sacrifices to be offered, and feasts to be kept, besides* vows, freewill-offerings, *&c., &c.,* 39. *Moses announces all these things to the people,* 40.

A. M. cir. 2535. B. C. cir. 1451. An. Exod. Isr. cir. 40.

AND in the seventh month, on the first *day* of the month, ye shall have a holy convocation; ye shall do no servile work: [a] it is a day of blowing the trumpets unto you.

2 And ye shall offer a burnt-offering for a sweet savour unto the LORD; one young bullock, one ram, *and* seven lambs of the first year without blemish:

3 And their meat-offering *shall be of* flour mingled with oil, three tenth deals for a bullock, *and* two tenth deals for a ram,

4 And one tenth deal for one lamb, throughout the seven lambs:

5 And one kid of the goats *for* a sin-offering, to make an atonement for you:

6 Beside [b] the burnt-offering of the month, and his meat-offering, and [c] the daily burnt-offering, and his meat-offering, and their drink-offerings, [d] according unto their manner, for a sweet savour, a sacrifice made by fire unto the LORD.

7 And [e] ye shall have on the tenth *day* of this seventh month a holy convocation; and ye shall [f] afflict your souls: ye shall not do any work *therein:*

A. M. cir. 2553. B. C. cir. 1451. An. Exod. Isr. cir. 40.

8 But ye shall offer a burnt-offering unto the LORD *for* a sweet savour; one young bullock, one ram, *and* seven lambs of the first year; [g] they shall be unto you without blemish:

9 And their meat-offering *shall be of* flour mingled with oil, three tenth deals to a bullock, *and* two tenth deals to one ram,

10 A several tenth deal for one lamb, throughout the seven lambs:

11 One kid of the goats *for* a sin-offering; beside [h] the sin-offering of atonement, and the continual burnt-offering, and the meat-offering of it, and their drink-offerings.

12 And [i] on the fifteenth day of the seventh month ye shall have a holy convocation; ye shall do no servile work, and ye shall keep a feast unto the LORD seven days:

13 And [k] ye shall offer a burnt-offering, a sacrifice made by fire, of a sweet savour unto the LORD; thirteen young bullocks, two rams, *and* fourteen lambs of the first year; they shall be without blemish:

14 And their meat-offering *shall be of* flour mingled with oil, three tenth deals unto every bullock of the thirteen bullocks, two tenth

[a] Lev. xxiii. 24, 25; Ezra iii. 6; chap. x. 1–10; 1 Chron. xv. 28; Psa. lxxxi. 3; lxxxix. 15.——[b] Chap. xxviii. 11.——[c] Chap. xxviii. 3.——[d] Chap. xv. 11, 12.

[e] Lev. xvi. 29; xxiii. 27.——[f] Psa. xxxv. 13; Isa. lviii. 5. [g] Chap. xxviii. 19.——[h] Lev. xvi. 3, 5.——[i] Lev. xxiii. 33; Deut. xvi. 13; Ezek. xlv. 25.——[k] Ezra iii. 4.

NOTES ON CHAP. XXIX.

Verse 1. *And in the seventh month, &c.*] This was the beginning of their *civil* year, and was a time of great festivity, and was ushered in by the blowing of trumpets. It answers to a part of our September. In imitation of the Jews different nations began their new year with sacrifices and festivity. The ancient Egyptians did so; and the *Persians* still celebrate their نو روز *nawi rooz*, or *new year's day*, which they hold on the vernal equinox. The first day of the year is generally a time of festivity in all civilized nations. On this day the Israelites offered *one young bullock, one ram, seven lambs*, and a *kid*, for a sin-offering, besides *minchahs* or *meat-offerings*.

Verse 7. *On the tenth* day] See the notes on Lev. xvi. 29; xxiii. 24.

Verse 12. *On the fifteenth day of the seventh month*] On this day there was to be a solemn assembly, and for *seven* days sacrifices were to be offered; on the *first* day thirteen young bullocks, two rams, and fourteen lambs. On each succeeding day one bullock *less*, till on the seventh day there were only *seven*, making in all *seventy*. What an expensive service! How should we magnify God for being delivered from it! Yet these were all the taxes they had to pay. At the public charge there were annually offered to God, independently of trespass-offerings and voluntary vows, fifteen goats, twenty-one kids, seventy-two rams, one

a

A. M. cir. 2553. B. C. cir. 1451. An. Exod. Isr. cir. 40.

deals to each ram of the two rams,

15 And a several tenth deal to each lamb of the fourteen lambs:

16 And one kid of the goats *for* a sin-offering; beside the continual burnt-offering, his meat-offering, and his drink-offering.

17 And on the second day *ye shall offer* twelve young bullocks, two rams, fourteen lambs of the first year without spot:

18 And their meat-offering and their drink-offerings for the bullocks, for the rams, and for the lambs, *shall be* according to their number, [l] after the manner:

19 And one kid of the goats *for* a sin-offering; beside the continual burnt-offering, and the meat-offering thereof, and their drink-offerings.

20 And on the third day, eleven bullocks, two rams, fourteen lambs of the first year without blemish;

21 And their meat-offering and their drink-offerings for the bullocks, for the rams, and for the lambs, *shall be* according to their number, [m] after the manner:

22 And one goat *for* a sin-offering; beside the continual burnt-offering, and his meat-offering, and his drink-offering.

23 And on the fourth day ten bullocks, two rams, *and* fourteen lambs of the first year without blemish:

24 Their meat-offering and their drink-offerings for the bullocks, for the rams, and for the lambs, *shall be* according to their number, after the manner:

25 And one kid of the goats *for* a sin-offering; beside the continual burnt-offering, his meat-offering, and his drink-offering.

26 And on the fifth day nine bullocks, two rams, *and* fourteen lambs of the first year without spot:

27 And their meat-offering and their drink-offerings for the bullocks, for the rams, and for the lambs, *shall be* according to their number, after the manner:

28 And one goat *for* a sin-offering; beside the continual burnt-offering, and his meat-offering, and his drink-offering.

A. M. cir. 2553. B. C. cir. 1451 An. Exod. Isr. cir. 40.

29 And on the sixth day eight bullocks, two rams, *and* fourteen lambs of the first year without blemish:

30 And their meat-offering and their drink-offerings for the bullocks, for the rams, and for the lambs, *shall be* according to their number, after the manner:

31 And one goat *for* a sin-offering; beside the continual burnt-offering, his meat-offering, and his drink-offering.

32 And on the seventh day seven bullocks, two rams, *and* fourteen lambs of the first year without blemish:

33 And their meat-offering and their drink-offerings for the bullocks, for the rams, and for the lambs, *shall be* according to their number, after the manner:

34 And one goat *for* a sin-offering; beside the continual burnt-offering, his meat-offering, and his drink-offering.

35 On the eighth day ye shall have a [n] solemn assembly: ye shall do no servile work *therein*:

36 But ye shall offer a burnt-offering, a sacrifice made by fire, of a sweet savour unto the LORD: one bullock, one ram, seven lambs of the first year without blemish:

37 Their meat-offering and their drink-offerings for the bullock, for the ram, and for the lambs, *shall be* according to their number, after the manner:

38 And one goat *for* a sin-offering, beside the continual burnt-offering, and his meat-offering, and his drink-offering.

39 These *things* ye shall [o] do unto the LORD in your [p] set feasts, beside your [q] vows, and your freewill-offerings, for your burnt-offerings, and for your meat-offerings, and for your drink-offerings, and for your peace-offerings.

40 And Moses told the children of Israel according to all that the LORD commanded Moses.

[l] Ver. 3, 4, 9, 10; chap. xv. 12; xxviii. 7, 14.——[m] Ver. 18. [n] Lev. xxiii. 36.——[o] Or, *offer*.——[p] Lev. xxiii. 2; 1 Chron. xxiii. 31; 2 Chron. xxxi. 3; Ezra iii. 5; Neh. x. 33; Isa. i. 14. [q] Lev. vii. 11, 16; xxii. 21, 23.

hundred and thirty-two bullocks, and eleven hundred and one lambs! But how little is all this when compared with the lambs slain every year at the *passover*, which amounted in one year to the immense number of 255,600 slain in the temple itself, which was the answer that *Cestius*, the Roman general, received when he asked the priests *how many persons* had come to Jerusalem at their annual festivals; the priests, numbering the *people* by the *lambs* that had been slain, said, "twenty-five myriads, five thousand and six hundred."—For an account of the feast of tabernacles, see on Lev. xxiii. 34.

Verse 35. *On the eighth day ye shall have a solemn assembly*] This among the Jews was esteemed the

chief or high day of the feast, though fewer sacrifices were offered on it than on the others; the people seem to have finished the solemnity with a greater measure of spiritual devotion, and it was on this day of the feast that our blessed Lord called the Jews from the *letter* to the *spirit* of the law, proposing himself as the sole fountain whence they could derive the streams of salvation, John vii. 37. On the subject of this chapter see the notes on Lev. xii., xvi., and xxiii.

CHAPTER XXX.

The law concerning vows of men, 1, 2. *Of women under age, and in what cases the father may annul them,* 3–5. *The vows of a wife, and in what cases the husband may annul them,* 6–8. *The vows of a widow, or divorced woman, in what cases they may be considered either as confirmed or annulled,* 9–15. *Recapitulation of these ordinances,* 16.

A. M. cir. 2553. B. C. cir. 1451. An. Exod. Isr. cir. 40.

AND Moses spake unto [a] the heads of the tribes concerning the children of Israel, saying, This *is* the thing which the LORD hath commanded.

2 [b] If a man vow a vow unto the LORD, or [c] swear an oath to bind his soul with a bond; he shall not [d] break his word, he shall [e] do according to all that proceedeth out of his mouth.

3 If a woman also vow a vow unto the LORD, and bind *herself* by a bond, *being* in her father's house in her youth;

4 And her father hear her vow, and her bond wherewith she hath bound her soul, and her father shall hold his peace at her: then all her vows shall stand, and every bond wherewith she hath bound her soul shall stand.

5 But if her father disallow her in the day that he heareth; not any of her vows, or of her bonds wherewith she hath bound her soul, shall stand: and the LORD shall forgive her, because her father disallowed her.

6 And if she had at all a husband, when [f] she vowed, or uttered aught out of her lips, wherewith she bound her soul;

A. M. cir. 2553. B. C. cir. 1451. An. Exod. Isr. cir. 40.

7 And her husband heard *it*, and held his peace at her in the day that he heard *it*: then her vows shall stand, and her bonds wherewith she bound her soul shall stand.

8 But if her husband [g] disallowed her on the day that he heard *it*; then he shall make her vow which she vowed, and that which she uttered with her lips, wherewith she bound her soul, of none effect: and the LORD shall forgive her.

9 But every vow of a widow, and of her that is divorced, wherewith they have bound their souls, shall stand against her.

10 And if she vowed in her husband's house, or bound her soul by a bond with an oath;

11 And her husband heard *it*, and held his peace at her, *and* disallowed her not: then all her vows shall stand, and every bond wherewith she bound her soul shall stand.

12 But if her husband hath utterly made them

[a] Chapter i. 4, 16; vii. 2.——[b] Lev. xxvii. 2; Deut. xxiii. 21; Judg. xi. 30, 35; Eccles. v. 4.——[c] Lev. v. 4; Matt. xiv. 9; Acts xxiii. 14.——[d] Heb. *profane*; Psa. lv. 20.

[e] Job xxii. 27; Psa. xxii. 25; l. 14; lxvi. 13, 14; cxvi. 14. 18; Nah. i. 15.——[f] Heb. *her vows were upon her*; Psa. lvi. 12. [g] Gen. iii. 16.

NOTES ON CHAP. XXX.

Verse 2. *If a man vow a vow*] A *vow* is a religious promise made to God. Vows were of several kinds: 1. Of *abstinence* or *humiliation*, see ver. 13; 2. Of the *Nazarite*, see chap. vi.; 3. Of *giving certain things* or *sacrifices* to the Lord, Lev. vii. 16; 4. Of *alms* given to the *poor*, see Deut. xxiii. 21. The law in this chapter must have been very useful, as it both *prevented* and *annulled rash vows*, and provided a proper sanction for the support and performance of those that were rationally and piously made. Besides, this law must have acted as a great preventive of *lying* and *hypocrisy*. If a vow was properly made, a man or woman was bound, under penalty of the displeasure of God, to fulfil it.

Verse 3. *In her youth*] That is, say the rabbins, under *twelve* years of age; and under *thirteen* in case of a *young man*. Young persons of this age were considered to be under the authority of their parents, and had consequently no power to vow away the property of another. A *married woman* was in the same circumstances, because she was under the *authority* of her *husband*. If however the *parents* or the *husband* heard of the vow, and objected to it in the *same day in which they heard of it*, (ver. 5,) then the vow was annulled; or, if having heard of it, they held their peace, this was considered a ratification of the vow.

A *rash vow* was never to be kept; "for," says Philo, and common sense and justice say the same, "he who commits an unjust action because of his vow adds one crime to another, 1. By making an unlawful *vow*; 2. By doing an unlawful *action*."

Verse 12. *Concerning the bond of her soul*] Her

A. M. cir. 2553. B. C. cir. 1451. An. Exod. Isr. cir. 40.

void on the day he heard *them;* *then* whatsoever proceeded out of her lips concerning her vows, or concerning the bond of her soul, shall not stand: her husband hath made them void; and the LORD shall forgive her.

13 Every vow, and every binding oath to afflict the soul, her husband may establish it, or her husband may make it void.

14 But if her husband altogether hold his peace at her from day to day; then he establisheth all her vows, or all her bonds, which *are* upon her: he confirmeth them, because he held his peace at her in the day that he heard *them*.

15 But if he shall any ways make them void after that he hath heard *them;* then he shall bear her iniquity.

16 These *are* the statutes, which the LORD commanded Moses, between a man and his wife, between the father and his daughter, *being yet* in her youth in her father's house.

life is at stake if she fulfil not the obligation under which she has laid herself.

Verse 16. *These* are *the statutes*] It is very probable that this law, like that concerning the succession of *daughters*, (chap. xxvii.,) rose from the exigency of some particular case that had just then occurred.

Making vows, in almost any case, is a dangerous business; they seldom do any good, and often much evil. He who does not feel himself bound to do what is *fit*, *right*, and *just*, from the standing testimony of God's word, is not likely to do it from any obligation he may lay upon *his own* conscience. If *God's word* lack weight with him, his own will prove lighter than vanity. Every man who professes the Christian religion is under the most *solemn obligation* to devote body, soul, and spirit to God, not only to the utmost extent of his powers, but also as long as he exists. Being *baptized*, and receiving the *sacrament* of the Lord's Supper, are additional ratifications of the great, general, Christian vow; but every true follower of Christ should always remember, and frequently renew his covenant with God.

CHAPTER XXXI.

The command of the Lord to make war on the Midianites, 1, 2. *One thousand men are chosen out of each of the twelve tribes, and sent with Phinehas against the Midianites*, 3–6. *They slay all the males*, 7; *their five kings and Balaam*, 8. *They take all the women captives, with the flocks and goods*, 9; *burn their cities, and bring away the spoil*, 10, 11. *They bring the captives, &c., to Moses, who is wroth with the officers for sparing the women, who had formerly been the cause of their transgression and punishment*, 12–16. *He commands all the male children and all the grown up females to be slain*, 17, 18. *How the soldiers were to purify themselves*, 19, 20; *and the different articles taken in war*, 21–24. *They are commanded to take the sum of the prey, to divide it into two parts; one for the* 12,000 *warriors, and the other for the rest of the congregation*, 25–27. One *of* 500, *both of persons and cattle, of the share of the warriors, to be given to the Lord*, 28, 29; *and one part of* fifty, *of the people's share, to be given to the Levites*, 30. *The sum of the prey remaining after the above division; sheep* 675,000, *beeves* 72,000, *asses* 61,000, *young women* 32,000, *ver.* 31–35. *How the soldiers' part was divided*, 36–40. *How the part belonging to the congregation was divided*, 41–47. *The officers report that they had not lost a man in this war*, 48, 49. *They bring a voluntary oblation to God, of gold and ornaments*, 50, 51; *the amount of which was* 16,750 *shekels*, 52, 53. *Moses and Eleazar bring the gold into the tabernacle for a memorial*, 54.

A. M. 2553. B. C. 1451. An. Exod. Isr. 40.

AND the LORD spake unto Moses, saying,

2 [a] Avenge the children of Israel of the Midianites: afterward shalt thou [b] be gathered unto thy people.

3 And Moses spake unto the

[a] Chap. xxv. 17. [b] Chap. xxvii. 13.

NOTES ON CHAP. XXXI.

Verse 2. *Gathered unto thy people.*] When? Not in the *grave* surely. Moses was gathered with *none of them*, his burial-place no man ever knew. "But being gathered unto one's people means dying." It does *imply* dying, but it does not *mean* this only. The truth is, God considers all those who are *dead* to *men* in a state of *conscious existence* in another world. Therefore he calls himself the *God of Abraham, and of Isaac, and of Jacob; now God is not the God of the dead, but of the living;* because all LIVE to HIM, whether *dead* to *men* or not. Moses therefore was to *be gathered to his people*—to enter into that *republic of Israel* which, having died in the faith, fear, and love of God, were now living in a state of conscious blessedness beyond the confines of the grave. See the note on Gen. xxv. 8, and xlix. 33.

Verse 3. *Avenge the Lord of Midian.*] It was God's *quarrel*, not their *own*, that they were now to take up. These people were idolaters; idolatry is an offence against GOD; the *civil* power has no authority to meddle with what belongs to Him, without especial

A. M. 2553.
B. C. 1451.
An. Exod. Isr.
40.

people, saying, Arm some of
yourselves unto the war, and let
them go against the Midianites,
and avenge the Lord of Midian.
4 [c] Of every tribe a thousand, throughout all
the tribes of Israel, shall ye send to the war.
5 So there were delivered out of the thousands of Israel, a thousand of *every* tribe,
twelve thousand armed for war.
6 And Moses sent them to the war, a thousand of *every* tribe, them and Phinehas the
son of Eleazar the priest, to the war, with the
holy instruments, and [d] the trumpets to blow in
his hand.
7 And they warred against the Midianites,
as the Lord commanded Moses; and [e] they
slew all the [f] males.
8 And they slew the kings of Midian, beside
the rest of them that were slain; *namely,* [g] Evi,
and Rekem, and Zur, and Hur, and Reba, five
kings of Midian: [h] Balaam also the son of
Beor they slew with the sword.
9 And the children of Israel took *all* the
women of Midian captives, and their little ones,
and took the spoil of all their cattle, and all
their flocks, and all their goods.
10 And they burnt all their cities wherein
they dwelt, and all their goodly castles, with
fire.
11 And [i] they took all the spoil, and all the
prey, *both* of men and of beasts.

A. M. 2553.
B. C. 1451.
An. Exod. Isr.
40.

12 And they brought the captives, and the prey, and the spoil,
unto Moses, and Eleazar the
priest, and unto the congregation of the children of Israel, unto the camp at the plains of
Moab, which *are* by Jordan *near* Jericho.
13 And Moses, and Eleazar the priest, and
all the princes of the congregation, went forth
to meet them without the camp.
14 And Moses was wroth with the officers
of the host, *with* the captains over thousands,
and captains over hundreds, which came from
the [k] battle.
15 And Moses said unto them, Have ye
saved [l] all the women alive?
16 Behold, [m] these caused the children of
Israel, through the [n] counsel of Balaam, to
commit trespass against the Lord in the matter of Peor, and [o] there was a plague among
the congregation of the Lord.
17 Now therefore [p] kill every male among
the little ones, and kill every woman that hath
known man by lying with [q] him.
18 But all the women children, that have
not known a man by lying with him, keep
alive for yourselves.
19 And [r] do ye abide without the camp seven
days: whosoever hath killed any person, and
[s] whosoever hath touched any slain, purify
both yourselves and your captives on the third
day, and on the seventh day.

[c] Heb. *a thousand of a tribe, a thousand of a tribe.*——[d] Chap. x. 9.——[e] Deut. xx. 13; Judg. xxi. 11; 1 Sam. xxvii. 9; 1 Kings xi. 15, 16.——[f] See Judg. vi. 1, 2, 33.——[g] Josh. xiii. 21.——[h] Josh. xiii. 22.——[i] Deut. xx. 14.

[k] Heb. *host of war.*——[l] See Deut. xx. 13; 1 Samuel xv. 3.——[m] Chap. xxv. 2.——[n] Chap. xxiv. 14; 2 Pet. ii. 15; Rev. ii. 14.——[o] Chap. xxv. 9.——[p] Judg. xxi. 11.——[q] Heb. *a male.*——[r] Chap. v. 2.——[s] Chap. xix. 11, &c.

directions, certified in the most unequivocal way. Private revenge, extension of territory, love of plunder, were to have no place in this business; the Lord is to be avenged; and through Him the children of Israel, (ver. 2,) because their *souls* as well as their *bodies* had been well nigh ruined by their idolatry.

Verse 6. *A thousand of* every *tribe*] Twelve thousand men in the whole. *And Phinehas, the son of Eleazar;* some think he was made general in this expedition, but this is not likely. The ark and its contents must proceed to this battle, because the battle was the Lord's, and he dwelt between the cherubim over the ark; and *Phinehas,* who had before got a grant in the eternal priesthood, was chosen to accompany the ark in place of his father *Eleazar,* who was probably now too far advanced in years to undergo the fatigue. Who then was general? *Joshua,* without doubt, though not here mentioned, because the battle being the Lord's, he alone is to have the supreme direction, and all the glory. Besides, it was an extraordinary war, and not conducted on the common principle, for we do not find that peace was offered to the Midianites, and that they refused it; see Deut. xx. 10, &c. In such a case only hostilities could lawfully commence; but they were sinners against GOD; the cup of their iniquity was full, and God thought proper to destroy them. Though a leader there certainly was, and Joshua was probably that leader, yet because God, for the above reason, was considered as *commander-in-chief,* therefore no one else is mentioned; for it is evident that the sole business of Phinehas was to take care of the *holy instruments* and *to blow with the trumpet.*

Verse 8. *Balaam—they slew with the sword.*] This man had probably committed what St. John calls *the sin unto death*—a sin which God punishes with temporal death, while at the same time he extends mercy to the soul. See the remarks at the end of chap. xxiv.

Verse 17. *Kill every male among the little ones*] For this action I account simply on the principle that God, who is the author and supporter of life, has a right to

a

A. M. 2553.
B. C. 1451.
An. Exod. Isr.
40.

20 And purify all *your* raiment, and all [t] that is made of skins, and all work of goats' *hair*, and all things made of wood.

21 And Eleazar the priest said unto the men of war, which went to the battle, This *is* the ordinance of the law which the LORD commanded Moses;

22 Only the gold, and the silver, the brass, the iron, the tin, and the lead,

23 Every thing that may abide the fire, ye shall make *it* go through the fire, and it shall be clean: nevertheless it shall be purified [u] with the water of separation: and all that abideth not the fire ye shall make go through the water.

24 [v] And ye shall wash your clothes on the seventh day, and ye shall be clean, and afterward ye shall come into the camp.

25 And the LORD spake unto Moses, saying,

26 Take the sum of the prey [w] that was taken, *both* of man and of beast, thou, and Eleazar the priest, and the chief fathers of the congregation:

27 And [x] divide the prey into two parts; between them that took the war upon them, who went out to battle, and between all the congregation:

28 And levy a tribute unto the LORD of the men of war which went out to battle: [y] one soul of five hundred, *both* of the persons, and of the beeves, and of the asses, and of the sheep:

29 Take *it* of their half, and give *it* unto Eleazar the priest, *for* a heave-offering of the LORD.

A. M. 2553.
B. C. 1451.
An. Exod. Isr.
40.

30 And of the children of Israel's half, thou shalt take [z] one portion of fifty, of the persons, of the beeves, of the asses, and of the [a] flocks, of all manner of beasts, and give them unto the Levites, [b] which keep the charge of the tabernacle of the LORD.

31 And Moses and Eleazar the priest did as the LORD commanded Moses.

32 And the booty, *being* the rest of the prey which the men of war had caught, was six hundred thousand and seventy thousand and five thousand sheep,

33 And threescore and twelve thousand beeves,

34 And threescore and one thousand asses,

35 And thirty and two thousand persons in all, of women that had not known man by lying with him.

36 And the half, *which was* the portion of them that went out to war, was in number three hundred thousand and seven and thirty thousand and five hundred sheep:

37 And the LORD's tribute of the sheep was six hundred and threescore and fifteen.

38 And the beeves *were* thirty and six thousand: of which the LORD's tribute *was* threescore and twelve.

39 And the asses *were* thirty thousand and five hundred; of which the LORD's tribute *was* threescore and one.

40 And the persons *were* sixteen thousand:

[t] Heb. *instrument*, or *vessel of skins*.——[u] Chap. xix. 9, 17.——[v] Lev. xi. 25.——[w] Heb *of the captivity*.——[x] Josh. xxii. 8; 1 Sam. xxx. 4.——[y] See ver. 30, 47; chap. xviii. 26.——[z] See ver. 42-47.——[a] Or, *goats*.——[b] Chap. iii. 7, 8, 25, 31, 36; xviii. 3, 4.

dispose of it *when* and *how* he thinks proper; and the Judge of all the earth can do nothing but what is *right*. Of the *women* killed on this occasion it may be safely said, their lives were forfeited by their *personal* transgressions; and yet even in this case there can be little doubt that God showed mercy to their souls. The little ones were safely lodged; they were taken to heaven and saved from the evil to come.

Verse 23. *The water of separation*] The *water* in which the *ashes of the red heifer* were mingled; see on chap. viii. 7; xix. 2, &c. Garments, whether of cloth or skins, were to be *washed*. Gold, silver, brass, iron, tin, and lead, to pass through the *fire*, probably to be *melted* down.

Verse 28. *And levy a tribute unto the Lord—one soul of five hundred, &c.*] The *persons* to be employed in the Lord's service, under the Levites—the *cattle* either for sacrifice, or for the use of the Levites, ver. 30. Some monsters have supposed that *one* out of every *five hundred* of the captives was offered in sacrifice to the Lord! but this is abominable. When God chose to have the life of a man, he took it in the way of *justice*, as in the case of the Midianites above; but never in the way of *sacrifice*.

Verse 32. *The booty*] It appears from the enumeration here that the Israelites, in this war against the Midianites, took 32,000 female prisoners, 61,000 asses, 72,000 beeves, 675,000 sheep and small cattle; besides the immense number of *males* who fell in battle, and the *women* and *children* who were slain by the Divine command, ver. 17. And it does not appear that in this expedition, a single man of Israel fell! This was naturally to be expected, because the battle was the Lord's, ver. 49.

As the booty was divided into two equal parts, ver. 22, one for the *soldiers* employed in the expedition, and the other for *those* who, being equally willing to be employed, were ordered to stay in the camp; so each of the parties in this booty was to give a certain proportion to the Lord. The *soldiers* to give to the

A. M. 2553.
B. C. 1451.
An. Exod. Isr.
40.

of which the LORD's tribute *was* thirty and two persons.

41 And Moses gave the tribute, *which was* the LORD's heave-offering, unto Eleazar the priest, [c] as the LORD commanded Moses.

42 And of the children of Israel's half, which Moses divided from the men that warred,

43 (Now the half *that pertained unto* the congregation was three hundred thousand and thirty thousand *and* seven thousand and five hundred sheep,

44 And thirty and six thousand beeves,

45 And thirty thousand asses and five hundred,

46 And sixteen thousand persons;)

47 Even [d] of the children of Israel's half, Moses took one portion of fifty, *both* of man and of beast, and gave them unto the Levites, which kept the charge of the tabernacle of the LORD; as the LORD commanded Moses.

48 And the officers which *were* over thousands of the host, the captains of thousands, and captains of hundreds, came near unto Moses:

A. M. 2553.
B. C. 1451.
An. Exod. Isr.
40.

49 And they said unto Moses, Thy servants have taken the sum of the men of war which *are* under our [e] charge, and there lacketh not one man of us.

50 We have therefore brought an oblation for the LORD, that every man hath [f] gotten, of jewels of gold, chains, and bracelets, rings, earrings, and tablets, [g] to make an atonement for our souls before the LORD.

51 And Moses and Eleazar the priest took the gold of them, *even* all wrought jewels.

52 And all the gold of the [h] offering that they offered up to the LORD, of the captains of thousands, and of the captains of hundreds, was sixteen thousand seven hundred and fifty shekels.

53 (*For* [i] the men of war had taken spoil, every man for himself.)

54 And Moses and Eleazar the priest took the gold of the captains of thousands and of hundreds, and brought it into the tabernacle of the congregation, [k] *for* a memorial for the children of Israel before the LORD.

[c] See chapter xviii. 8, 19.——[d] Ver. 30.——[e] Heb. *hand.* [f] Heb. *found.*——[g] Exod. xxx. 12, 16.

[h] Hebrew, *heave-offering.*——[i] Deut. xx. 14.——[k] Exodus xxx. 16.

Lord *one* out of every *five hundred persons, beeves, asses,* and *sheep,* ver. 28. The *people,* who by staying at home risked nothing, and had no fatigue, were to give *one* out of *fifty* of the above, ver. 30. The booty, its divisions among the soldiers and people, the proportion given by each to the Lord and to the Levites, will be seen in one view by the following table, which I copy from *Houbigant.*

Total of sheep	675,000	To the soldiers	337,500	To the *Lord* from the *soldiers*	675
		To the people	337,500	To the *Levites* from the *people*	6,750
of beeves	72,000	To the soldiers	36,000	To the *Lord* from the *soldiers*	72
		To the people	36,000	To the *Levites* from the *people*	720
of asses	61,000	To the soldiers	30,500	To the *Lord* from the *soldiers*	61
		To the people	30,500	To the *Levites* from the *people*	610
of persons	32,000	To the soldiers	16,000	To the *Lord* from the *soldiers*	32
		To the people	16,000	To the *Levites* from the *people*	320

In this table the booty is equally divided between the people and the soldiers; a five-hundredth part being given to the Lord, and a fiftieth part to the Levites.

Verse 50. *We have—brought an oblation for the Lord*] So it appears there was a great deal of booty taken which did not come into the general account; and of this the soldiers, of their own will, made a very extensive offering to God, because he had preserved them from falling in battle. That not one man should have been slain is a most extraordinary circumstance, and powerfully marks the peculiar superintendence of God's especial providence. The Midianites must certainly have made some resistance; but that was ineffectual, because it was against the Lord. When any nation undertakes a *crusade* against those whom they are pleased to call *the Lord's enemies,* let them bring from the contest this proof of their Divine mission, viz., that not one man of them is either *lost* or *missing;* and then, and *not till then,* shall we believe that God hath sent them.

To make an atonement for our souls] That is, to make an acknowledgment to God for the preservation of their *lives.* The gold offered on this occasion amounted to 16,750 shekels, equal to £37,869. 16*s.* 5*d.* of our money. See the note on Exod. xxv. 39, where the true value of the shekel is given, and a rule laid down to reduce it to English money

CHAPTER XXXII.

The Reubenites and Gadites request Moses to give them their inheritance on this side of Jordan, 1–5. *Moses expostulates with and reproves them,* 6–15. *They explain themselves, and propose conditions, with which Moses is satisfied—they are to build cities for their wives and children, and folds for their cattle, and go over Jordan armed with the other tribes, and fight against their enemies till the land is subdued; after which they are to return,* 16–27. *Moses proposes the business to Eleazar, Joshua, and the elders,* 28–30. *The Gadites and Reubenites promise a faithful observance of the conditions,* 31, 32; *on which Moses assigns to them, and the half tribe of Manasseh, the kingdom of Sihon, king of the Amorites, and the kingdom of Og, king of Bashan,* 33. *The cities built by the Gadites,* 34–36. *The cities built by the Reubenites,* 37, 38. *The children of Machir, the son of Manasseh, expel the Amorites from Gilead,* 39, *which Moses grants to them,* 40. *Jair, the son of Manasseh, takes the small towns of Gilead,* 41. *And Nobah takes Kenath and its villages,* 42.

A. M. 2553.
B. C. 1451.
An. Exod. Isr.
40.

NOW the children of Reuben
and the children of Gad had
a very great multitude of cattle:
and when they saw the land of [a] Jazer, and the
land of Gilead, that, behold, the place *was* a
place for cattle;
2 The children of Gad and the children of
Reuben came and spake unto Moses, and to
Eleazar the priest, and unto the princes of the
congregation, saying,
3 Ataroth, and Dibon, and Jazer, and [b] Nimrah, and Heshbon, and Elealeh, and [c] Shebam,
and Nebo, and [d] Beon,
4 *Even* the country [e] which the LORD smote
before the congregation of Israel, *is* a land for
cattle, and thy servants have cattle:
5 Wherefore, said they, if we have found
grace in thy sight, let this land be given unto
thy servants for a possession, *and* bring us
not over Jordan.
6 And Moses said unto the children of Gad
and to the children of Reuben, Shall your
brethren go to war, and shall ye sit here?
7 And wherefore [f] discourage ye the heart of
the children of Israel from going over into the
land which the LORD hath given them?
8 Thus did your fathers, [g] when I sent them
from Kadesh-barnea [h] to see the land.
9 For [i] when they went up unto the valley
of Eshcol, and saw the land, they
discouraged the heart of the children of Israel, that they should not
go into the land which the LORD had given them.
10 [k] And the LORD's anger was kindled the
same time, and he sware, saying,
11 Surely none of the men that came up out
of Egypt, [l] from twenty years old and upward,
shall see the land which I sware unto Abraham, unto Isaac, and unto Jacob; because
[m] they have not [n] wholly followed me:
12 Save Caleb the son of Jephunneh the
Kenezite, and Joshua the son of Nun: [o] for
they have wholly followed the LORD.
13 And the LORD's anger was kindled against
Israel, and he made them [p] wander in the wilderness forty years, until [q] all the generation
that had done evil in the sight of the LORD,
was consumed.
14 And, behold, ye are risen up in your fathers' stead, an increase of sinful men, to augment yet the [r] fierce anger of the LORD toward Israel.
15 For if ye [s] turn away from after him, he
will yet again leave them in the wilderness;
and ye shall destroy all this people.
16 And they came near unto him, and said,
We will build sheepfolds here for our cattle,
and cities for our little ones:

A. M. 2553.
B. C. 1451.
An. Exod. Isr.
40.

[a] Chap. xxi. 32; Josh. xiii. 25; 2 Sam. xxiv. 5.—[b] Ver. 36, *Beth-nimrah.*—[c] Ver. 38, *Shibmah.*—[d] Ver. 38, *Baal-meon.*—[e] Chap. xxi. 24, 34.—[f] Heb. *break.*—[g] Chap. xiii. 3, 26.—[h] Deut. i. 22.—[i] Chap. xiii. 24, 31; Deut. i. 24, 28.—[k] Chap. xiv. 11, 21; Deut. i. 34.—[l] Chap. xiv. 28, 29; Deut. i. 35.—[m] Chap. xiv. 24, 30.—[n] Heb. *fulfilled after me.*—[o] Chap. xiv. 24; Deut. i. 36; Josh. xiv. 8, 9.—[p] Chap. xiv. 33, 34, 35.—[q] Chap. xxvi. 64, 65.—[r] Deut. i. 34.—[s] Deut. xxx. 17; Josh. xxii. 16, 18; 2 Chron. vii. 19; xv. 2.

NOTES ON CHAP. XXXII.

Verse 3. *Ataroth, and Dibon, &c.*] The places mentioned here belonged to Sihon, king of the Amorites, and Og, king of Bashan, which being conquered by the Israelites, constituted ever after a part of their territories, ver. 33.

Verse 5. *Let this land be given unto thy servants*] Because it was good for *pasturage*, and they had many *flocks*, ver. 1.

Verse 12. *Caleb the son of Jephunneh the Kenezite*] It was Jephunneh that was the Kenezite, and not Caleb. Kenaz was probably the *father* of Jephunneh.

Verse 16. *We will build—cities for our little ones*] It was impossible for these, numerous as they might be, to build cities and fortify them for the defence of their families in their absence. Calmet supposes they meant no more than *repairing* the cities of the Amorites which they had lately taken; which work might

A. M. 2553.
B. C. 1451.
An. Exod. Isr. 40.

17 But [t] we ourselves will go ready armed before the children of Israel, until we have brought them unto their place: and our little ones shall dwell in the fenced cities because of the inhabitants of the land.

18 [u] We will not return unto our houses, until the children of Israel have inherited every man his inheritance.

19 For we will not inherit with them on yonder side Jordan, or forward; [v] because our inheritance is fallen to us on this side Jordan eastward.

20 And [w] Moses said unto them, If ye will do this thing, if ye will go armed before the LORD to war,

21 And will go all of you armed over Jordan before the LORD, until he hath driven out his enemies from before him,

22 And [x] the land be subdued before the LORD: then afterward [y] ye shall return, and be guiltless before the LORD, and before Israel; and [z] this land shall be your possession before the LORD.

23 But if ye will not do so, behold, ye have sinned against the LORD: and be sure [a] your sin will find you out.

24 [b] Build you cities for your little ones, and folds for your sheep; and do that which hath proceeded out of your mouth.

25 And the children of Gad and the children of Reuben spake unto Moses, saying, Thy servants will do as my lord commandeth.

26 [c] Our little ones, our wives, our flocks, and all our cattle, shall be there in the cities of Gilead:

27 [d] But thy servants will pass over, every man armed for war, before the LORD to battle, as my lord saith.

A. M. 2553.
B. C. 1451.
An. Exod. Isr. 40.

28 So [e] concerning them Moses commanded Eleazar the priest, and Joshua the son of Nun, and the chief fathers of the tribes of the children of Israel:

29 And Moses said unto them, If the children of Gad and the children of Reuben will pass with you over Jordan, every man armed to battle, before the LORD, and the land shall be subdued before you; then ye shall give them the land of Gilead for a possession:

30 But if they will not pass over with you armed, they shall have possessions among you in the land of Canaan.

31 And the children of Gad and the children of Reuben answered, saying, As the LORD hath said unto thy servants, so will we do.

32 We will pass over armed before the LORD into the land of Canaan, that the possession of our inheritance on this side Jordan *may be* ours.

33 And [f] Moses gave unto them, *even* to the children of Gad, and to the children of Reuben, and unto half the tribe of Manasseh the son of Joseph, [g] the kingdom of Sihon king of the Amorites, and the kingdom of Og king of Bashan, the land, with the cities thereof in the coasts, *even* the cities of the country round about.

34 And the children of Gad built [h] Dibon, and Ataroth, and [i] Aroer,

35 And Atroth, Shophan, and [k] Jaazer, and Jogbehah,

[t] Josh. iv. 12, 13.——[u] Josh. xxii. 4.——[v] Ver. 33; Josh. xii. 1; xiii. 8.——[w] Deut. iii. 18; Josh. i. 14; iv. 12, 13.——[x] Deut. iii. 20; Josh. xi. 23; xviii. 1.——[y] Josh. xxii. 4.——[z] Deut. iii. 12, 15, 16, 18; Josh. i. 15; xiii. 8, 32; xxii. 4, 9.——[a] Gen. iv. 7; xliv. 16; Isa. lix. 12.——[b] Ver. 16, 34, &c.——[c] Josh. i. 14.——[d] Josh. iv. 12.——[e] Josh. i. 13.——[f] Deut. iii. 12-17; xxix. 8; Josh. xii. 6; xiii. 8; xxii. 4.——[g] Chap. xxi. 24, 33, 35.——[h] Chap. xxxiii. 45, 46.——[i] Deut. ii. 36.——[k] Ver. 1. 3, *Jazer*.

have been very easily accomplished in the time which they spent on this side of Jordan, before they went over with their brethren, to put them in possession of the land.

Verse 17. *Because of the inhabitants of the land.*] These were the Ammonites, Moabites, Idumeans, and the remains of the Midianites and Amorites. But could the women and children even keep the defenced cities, when placed in them? This certainly cannot be supposed possible. Many of the men of war must of course stay behind. In the last census, chap. xxvi., the tribe of Reuben consisted of 43,730 men; the tribe of Gad, 40,500; the tribe of Manasseh, 52,700; the half of which is 26,350. Add this to the sum of the other two tribes, and the amount is 110,580. Now from Joshua iv. 13 we learn that of the tribes of Reuben and Gad, and the half of the tribe of Manasseh, only 40,000 armed men passed over Jordan to assist their brethren in the reduction of the land: consequently the number of 70,580 men were left behind for the defence of the women, the children, and the flocks. This was more than sufficient to defend them against a people already panic struck by their late discomfitures and reverses.

Verse 34. *The children of Gad built—Aroer*] This was situated on the river Arnon, Deut. ii. 36; 2 Kings x. 33. It was formerly inhabited by the *Emim*, a warlike and perhaps gigantic people. They were expelled by the Moabites; the Moabites by the Amorites; and the Amorites by the Israelites. The Gadites then

A. M. 2553. B. C. 1451. An. Exod. Isr. 40.

36 And [l] Beth-nimrah, and Beth-haran, [m] fenced cities: and folds for sheep.

37 And the children of Reuben [n] built Heshbon, and Elealeh, and Kirjathaim,

38 And [o] Nebo, and [p] Baal-meon, ([q] their names being changed,) and Shibmah: and [r] gave other names unto the cities which they builded.

39 And the children of [s] Machir the son of Manasseh went to Gilead, and took it, and dispossessed the Amorite which *was* in it.

40 And Moses [t] gave Gilead unto Machir the son of Manasseh; and he dwelt therein.

41 And [u] Jair the son of Manasseh went and took the small towns thereof, and called them [v] Havoth-jair.

42 And Nobah went and took Kenath, and the villages thereof, and called it Nobah, after his own name.

[l] Ver. 3, *Nimrah.*——[m] Ver. 24.——[n] Chap. xxi. 27.——[o] Isa. xlvi. 1.——[p] Chap. xxii. 41.——[q] See ver. 3; Exod. xxiii. 13; Josh. xxiii. 7.——[r] Heb. *they called by names the names of the cities.*

[s] Gen. l. 23.——[t] Deut. iii. 12, 13, 15; Josh. xiii. 31; xvii. 1.——[u] Deut. iii. 14; Josh. xiii. 30; 1 Chron. ii. 21, 22, 23.——[v] Judg. x. 4; 1 Kings iv. 13.

possessed it till the captivity of their tribe, with that of Reuben and the half of the tribe of Manasseh, by the Assyrians, 2 Kings xv. 29, after which the *Moabites* appear to have repossessed it, as they seem to have occupied it in the days of Jeremiah, chap. xlviii. 15–20.

Verse 38. *And Nebo—their names being changed*] That is, Those who conquered the cities called them after their own names. Thus the city *Kenath*, being conquered by *Nobah*, was called after his name, ver. 42.

Verse 41. *Havoth-jair.*] That is, the *villages* or *habitations of Jair;* and thus they should have been translated. As these two tribes and a half were the *first*, says Ainsworth, who had their inheritance assigned to them in the promised land, so they were the first of all Israel that were carried captive out of their own land, because of their sins. "For they transgressed against the God of their fathers, and went a whoring after other gods. And God delivered them into the hands of *Pul* and *Tiglath-Pilneser*, kings of Assyria, and they brought them to *Halah*, *Habor*, *Hara*, and *Gozan*, unto this day." See 1 Chron. v. 25, 26

CHAPTER XXXIII.

The journeyings of the Israelites written out by Moses, according to the commandment of the Lord, 1, 2. *They depart from Rameses on the fifteenth day of the first month, on the day after the passover, the first-born of the Egyptians having been slain,* 3, 4. *Their* forty-two *stations enumerated,* 5–49. *They are authorized to expel all the former inhabitants, and destroy all remnants of idolatry,* 50–53. *The land is to be divided by lot,* 54. *Should they not drive out the former inhabitants, they shall be to them as pricks in their eyes and thorns in their sides,* 55. *And if not obedient, God will deal with them as he has purposed to do with the Canaanites,* 56.

A. M. 2553. B. C. 1451. An. Exod. Isr. 40.

THESE *are* the [a] journeys of the children of Israel, which went forth out of the land of Egypt with their armies, under the [b] hand of Moses and Aaron.

2 And Moses wrote their [c] goings out according to their journeys, by the commandment of the LORD: and these *are* their journeys according to their goings out.

[a] Exod. xii. 38, 51; xiii. 18.——[b] Josh. xxiv. 5.

[c] Chap. ix. 17–23; x. 6, 13; Deut. i. 2, 10, 11.

NOTES ON CHAP. XXXIII.

Verse 2. *And Moses wrote their goings out according to their journeys*] We may consider the whole book of Numbers as a *diary*, and indeed the first *book of travels* ever published. Dr. Shaw, Dr. Pococke, and several others, have endeavoured to mark out the route of the Israelites through this great, dreary, and trackless desert, and have ascertained many of the stages here described. Indeed there are sufficient evidences of this important journey still remaining, for the descriptions of many are so particular that the places are readily ascertained by them; but this is not the case with all. Israel was the Church of God in the wilderness, and its unsettled, wandering state under Moses may point out the unsettled state of religion under the law. Their being brought, after the death of Moses, into the promised rest by Joshua, may point out the establishment, fixedness, and certainty of that salvation provided by Jesus Christ, of whom Joshua, in *name* and conduct, was a remarkable type. Mr. Ainsworth imagines that the *forty-two* stations here enumerated, through which the Israelites were brought to the verge of the promised land, and afterwards taken over Jordan into the rest which God had promised, point out the *forty-two generations* from Abraham unto Christ, through whom the Saviour of the world came, by whose blood we have an entrance into the holiest, and enjoy the inheritance among the saints in light.

A. M. 2513.
B. C. 1491.
An. Exod. Isr. 1.
Abib or Nisan.

3 And they [d] departed from Rameses in [e] the first month, on the fifteenth day of the first month; on the morrow after the passover the children of Israel went out [f] with a high hand in the sight of all the Egyptians.

4 For the Egyptians buried all *their* first-born, [g] which the LORD had smitten among them: [h] upon their gods also the LORD executed judgments.

5 [i] And the children of Israel removed from Rameses, and pitched in Succoth.

6 And they departed from [k] Succoth, and pitched in Etham, which *is* in the edge of the wilderness.

7 And [l] they removed from Etham, and turned again unto Pi-hahiroth, which *is* before Baal-zephon: and they pitched before Migdol.

8 And they departed from before Pi-hahiroth, and [m] passed through the midst of the sea into the wilderness, and went three days' journey in the wilderness of Etham, and pitched in Marah.

9 And they removed from Marah, and [n] came unto Elim: and in Elim *were* twelve fountains of water, and three score and ten palm trees; and they pitched there.

10 And they removed from Elim, and encamped by the Red Sea.

A. M. 2513.
B. C. 1491.
An. Exod. Isr. 1.
Ijar or Zif.

11 And they removed from the Red Sea, and encamped in the [o] wilderness of Sin.

12 And they took their journey out of the wilderness of Sin, and encamped in Dophkah.

13 And they departed from Dophkah, and encamped in Alush.

14 And they removed from Alush, and encamped at [p] Rephidim, where was no water for the people to drink.

A. M. 2513.
B. C. 1491.
An. Exod. Isr. 1
Sivan.

15 And they departed from Rephidim, and pitched in the [q] wilderness of Sinai.

[d] Exod. xii. 37.——[e] Exod. xii. 2; xiii. 4.——[f] Exod. xiv. 8. [g] Exod. xii. 29.——[h] Exod. xii. 12; xviii. 11; Isa. xix. 1; Rev. xii. 8.——[i] Exod. xii. 37.——[k] Exod. xiii. 20.

[l] Exod. xiv. 2, 9.——[m] Exod. xiv. 22; xv. 22, 23.——[n] Exod xv. 27.——[o] Exod. xvi. 1.——[p] Exod. xvii. 1; xix. 2.——[q] Exod xvi. 1; xix. 1, 2.

And Mr. Bromley, in his *Way to the Sabbath of Rest*, considers each name and place as descriptive of the spiritual state through which a soul passes in its way to the kingdom of God. But in cases of this kind *fancy* has much more to do than *judgment*.

Verse 3. *From Rameses*] This appears to have been the metropolis of the land of Goshen, and the place of rendezvous whence the whole Israelitish nation set out on their journey to the promised land; and is supposed to be the same as *Cairo*. See the notes on Exod. xii. 37.

HERE FOLLOW THE FORTY-TWO STATIONS.

STATION I. Verse 5. *And pitched in* SUCCOTH.] This name signifies *booths* or *tents*, and probably refers to no *town* or *village*, but simply designates the *place* where they pitched their tents for the first time after their departure from *Rameses*.

STAT. II. Verse 6. ETHAM, *which* is *in the edge of the wilderness*.] This place is not well known; Dr. Shaw supposes it to have been *one* mile from *Cairo*. Calmet thinks it is the city of *Buthum* mentioned by Herodotus, which he places in Arabia, on the frontiers of Egypt.

STAT. III. Verse 7. PI-HAHIROTH] See on Exod. xiv. 1. *Baal-zephon* Calmet supposes to be the *Clysma* of the Greeks, and the *Kolzum* of the Arabians.

STAT. IV. Verse 8. *And went three days' journey in the wilderness of Etham*] Called the wilderness of *Shur*, Exod. xv. 22.

And pitched in MARAH.] Dr. Shaw supposes this place to be at *Sedur*, over against the valley of *Baideah*, on the opposite side of the Red Sea.

STAT. V. Verse 9. *And came unto* ELIM] A place on the skirts of the deserts of *Sin*, two leagues from *Tor*, and nearly thirty from *Corondel*, a large bay on the east side of the Red Sea. Dr. Shaw, when he visited this place, found but *nine* of the *twelve* wells mentioned in the text, and instead of 70 palm trees, he found upwards of 2,000. See on Exod. xv. 27.

STAT. VI. Verse 10. *Encamped by the* RED SEA.] It is difficult to assign the *place* of this encampment, as the Israelites were now on their way to *Mount Sinai*, which lay considerably to the east of *Elim*, and consequently farther from the sea than the former station. It might be called *by the Red Sea*, as the Israelites had *it*, as the principal object, still in view. This station however is mentioned nowhere else. By the *Red Sea* we are not to understand a sea, the waters of which are *red*, or the *sand* red, or any thing else *about* or *in* it *red;* for nothing of this kind appears. It is called in Hebrew ים סוף *yam suph*, which signifies the *weedy sea*. The *Septuagint* rendered the original by θαλασσα ερυθρα, and the *Vulgate* after it by *mare rubrum*, and the European versions followed these, and, in opposition to etymology and reason, translated it *the Red Sea*. See the note on Exod. x. 19.

STAT. VII. Verse 11. *The wilderness of* SIN.] This lies between *Elim* and *Mount Sinai*. Dr. Shaw and his companions traversed these plains in nine hours.

STAT. VIII. Verse 12. DOPHKAH.] This place is not mentioned in Exodus, and its situation is not known.

STAT. IX. Verse 13. ALUSH.] Neither is this mentioned in Exodus, and its situation is equally unknown.

STAT. X. Verse 14. REPHIDIM] Remarkable for the

a

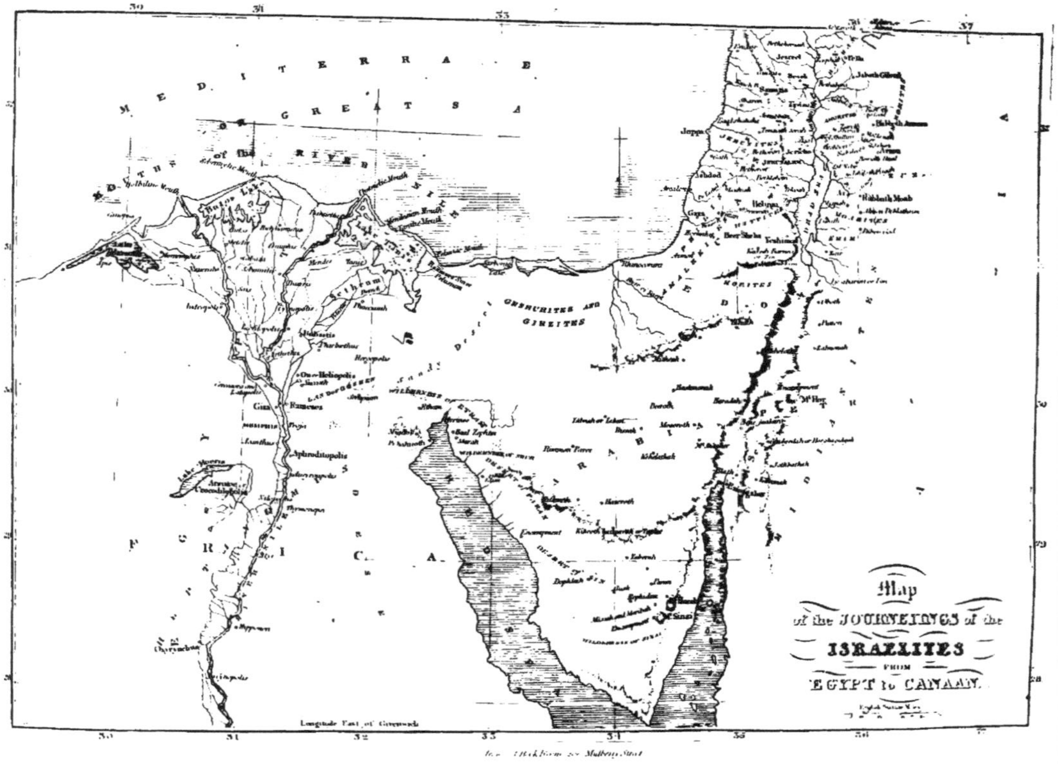

Map
of the JOURNEYINGS of the
ISRAELITES
FROM
EGYPT to CANAAN.
MEDITERRANEAN
GREAT SEA
MOUTHS of the RIVER NILE
GESHURITES AND GIRZITES
ARABIA
EDOM
MOABITES
AFRICA
Joppa
Gaza
Hebron
Beer Sheba
Rameses
On or Heliopolis
Mt. Sinai
Mt. Hor
Longitude East of Greenwich

A. M. 2514.
B. C. 1490.
An. Exod. Isr.
2.

Chronology very
uncertain after
they leave
Kibroth-hattaa-
vah, till they
come to the
desert of Zin.

16 And they removed from the desert of Sinai, and pitched *r* at *s* Kibroth-hattaavah.

17 And they departed from Kibroth-hattaavah, and *t* encamped at Hazeroth.

18 And they departed from Hazeroth, and pitched in *u* Rithmah.

19 And they departed from Rithmah, and pitched at Rimmon-parez.

20 And they departed from Rimmon-parez, and pitched in Libnah.

21 And they removed from Libnah, and pitched at Rissah.

22 And they journeyed from Rissah, and pitched in Kehelathah.

23 And they went from Kehelathah, and pitched in mount Shapher.

24 And they removed from Mount Shapher, and encamped in Haradah.

25 And they removed from Haradah, and pitched in Makheloth.

26 And they removed from Makheloth, and encamped at Tahath.

27 And they departed from Tahath, and pitched at Tarah.

28 And they removed from Tarah, and pitched in Mithcah.

29 And they went from Mithcah, and pitched in Hashmonah.

30 And they departed from Hashmonah, and *v* encamped at Moseroth.

31 And they departed from Moseroth, and pitched in Bene-jaakan.

32 And they removed from *w* Bene-jaakan, and *x* encamped at Hor-hagidgad.

33 And they went from Hor-hagidgad, and pitched in Jotbathah.

34 And they removed from Jotbathah, and encamped at Ebronah.

35 And they departed from Ebronah, *y* and encamped at Ezion-gaber.

Chronology very
uncertain after
they leave
Kibroth-hattaa-
vah, till they
come to the
desert of Zin.

r Chap. xi. 34.——*s* That is, *the graves of lust.*——*t* Chap. xi. 35. *u* Chap. xii. 16; 1 Mac. v. 9, *Lathema.*——*v* Deut. x. 6.

w 1 Mac. v. 4, *Bean* ; see Gen. xxxvi. 27 ; Deut. x. 6 ; 1 Chron. i. 42.——*x* Deut. x. 7.——*y* Deut. ii. 8 ; 1 Kings ix. 26 ; xxii. 48.

rebellion of the Israelites against Moses, because of the want of water, Exod. xvii.

STAT. XI. Verse 15. *The* WILDERNESS *of* SINAI.] Somewhere northward of Mount Sinai, on the straight road to the promised land, to which they now directed their course.

STAT. XII. Verse 16. KIBROTH-HATTAAVAH.] No city, village, &c., but a *place* in the open desert, which had its name from the plague that fell upon the Israelites, through their murmuring against God, and their inordinate desire of flesh. See on chap. xi. But it appears that the Israelites had travelled three days' journey in order to reach this place, chap. x. 33, and commentators suppose there must have been other stations which are not laid down here, probably because the places were not remarkable.

STAT. XIII. Verse 17. HAZEROTH.] This place Dr. Shaw computes to have been about thirty miles distant from Mount Sinai.

STAT. XIV. Verse 18. RITHMAH.] This place lay somewhere in the wilderness of *Paran*, through which the Israelites were now passing. See chap. xiii. 1. The name signifies the juniper tree ; and the place probably had its name from the great number of those trees growing in that district.

STAT. XV. Verse 19. RIMMON-PAREZ.] Unknown.

STAT. XVI. Verse 20. LIBNAH.] The situation of this place is uncertain. A city of this name is mentioned Josh. x. 29, as situated between Kadesh-barnea and Gaza.

STAT. XVII. Verse 21. RISSAH.] A place mentioned nowhere else in the sacred writings. Its situation utterly uncertain.

STAT. XVIII. Verse 22. KEHELATHAH.] Utterly

unknown ; though some conjecture that it might have been the place called Keilah, 1 Sam. xxiii. 1, &c., but this is unlikely.

STAT. XIX. Verse 23. SHAPHER.] Where this mountain lay cannot be determined.

STAT. XX. Verse 24. HARADAH.] Unknown. Calmet supposes that it may be the place called *Bered*, Gen. xvi. 14, which was in the vicinity of *Kadesh*.

STAT. XXI. Verse 25. MAKHELOTH.] A name found nowhere else in Scripture.

STAT. XXII. Verse 26. TAHATH.] Unknown.

STAT. XXIII. Verse 27. TARAH.] Also unknown.

STAT. XXIV. Verse 28. MITHCAH.] Calmet conjectures that this may be *Mocha*, a city in Arabia Petræa.

STAT. XXV. Verse 29. HASHMONAH.] Supposed by some to be the same as *Azmon*, chap. xxxiv. 4.

STAT. XXVI. Verse 30. MOSEROTH.] Situation unknown. In Deut. x. 6 it is said that the Israelites took their journey from Beeroth, the wells of the children of *Jaakan*, to Mosera, and there Aaron died. If so, Mosera, Moseroth, and Hor, must be different names of the same place ; or Moseroth, or Mosera, must have been some town or village near Mount Hor, for there Aaron died. See ver. 38.

STAT. XXVII. Verse 31. BENE-JAAKAN.] Unknown. The *sons of Jaakan.* See the preceding verse.

STAT. XXVIII. Verse 32. HOR-HAGIDGAD.] The *hole* or *pit of Gidgad.* Unknown. It was a place perhaps remarkable for some vast pit or cavern, from which it took its name.

STAT. XXIX. Verse 33. JOTBATHAH.] Situation unknown. It is said in Deut. x. 7 to be a *land of rivers of waters.*

A. M. cir. 2553. B. C. cir. 1451. An. Exod. Isr. cir. 40.

36 And they removed from Ezion-gaber, and pitched in the [z] wilderness of Zin, which *is* Kadesh.

37 And they removed from [a] Kadesh, and pitched in Mount Hor, in the edge of the land of Edom.

38 And [b] Aaron the priest went up into Mount Hor at the commandment of the LORD, and died there, in the fortieth year after the children of Israel were come out of the land of Egypt, in the first *day* of the fifth month.

39 And Aaron *was* a hundred and twenty and three years old when he died in Mount Hor.

40 And [c] King Arad, the Canaanite, which dwelt in the south in the land of Canaan, heard of the coming of the children of Israel.

41 And they departed from Mount [d] Hor, and pitched in Zalmonah.

42 And they departed from Zalmonah, and pitched in Punon.

43 And they departed from Punon, and [e] pitched in Oboth.

A. M. 2553. B. C. 1451. An. Exod. Isr. 40.

44 And [f] they departed from Oboth, and pitched in [g] Ije-abarim, [h] in the border of Moab.

45 And they departed from Iim, and pitched [i] in Dibon-gad.

46 And they removed from Dibon-gad, and encamped in Almon[k]-diblathaim.

47 And they removed from Almon-diblathaim, [l] and pitched in the mountains of Abarim, before Nebo.

48 And they departed from the mountains of Abarim, and [m] pitched in the plains of Moab by Jordan *near* Jericho.

49 And they pitched by Jordan, from Beth-jesimoth *even* unto [n] Abel-shittim [o] in the plains of Moab.

50 And the LORD spake unto Moses in the plains of Moab by Jordan *near* Jericho, saying,

51 Speak unto the children of Israel, and say unto them, [p] When ye are passed over Jordan into the land of Canaan;

52 [q] Then ye shall drive out all the inhabitants of the land from before you, and destroy

[z] Chap. xx. 1; xxvii. 14.——[a] Chap. xx. 22, 23; xxi. 4.——[b] Ch. xx. 25, 28; Deut. x. 6; xxxii. 50.——[c] Chap. xxi. 1, &c. [d] Chap. xxi. 4.——[e] Chap. xxi. 10.——[f] Chap. xxi. 11.——[g] Or, *heaps of Abarim.*——[h] Chap. xxi. 11.——[i] Chap. xxxii. 34.

[k] Jer. xlviii. 22; Ezek. vi. 14.——[l] Chap. xxi. 20; Deut. xxxii. 49. [m] Chap. xxii. 1.——[n] Or, *the plains of Shittim.*——[o] Chap. xxv. 1; Josh. ii. 1.——[p] Deut. vii. 1, 2; ix. 1; Josh. iii. 17.——[q] Exod. xxiii. 24, 33; xxxiv. 13; Deut. vii. 2, 5; xii. 3; Josh. xi. 12; Judg. ii. 2.

STAT. XXX. Verse 34. EBRONAH.] Nowhere else mentioned.

STAT. XXXI. Verse 35. EZION-GABER.] Dr. Shaw places this port on the western coast of the *Elanitic gulf* of the Red Sea. It is now called *Meenah el Dsahab*, or the *golden port*, by the Arabs; because it was from this place that Solomon sent his ships for gold to Ophir, 1 Kings ix. 26. He supposes it to be about sixty miles distant from Mount Sinai.—*Travels*, p. 322, 4to. edition.

STAT. XXXII. Verse 36. ZIN, *which* is KADESH.] A place remarkable for the death of Miriam the prophetess, and bringing water out of the rock. As this place was on the borders of *Edom*, the Israelites, being denied permission to pass through their land, which lay on the direct road to the promised land, were obliged to turn to the right to Mount Hor, now called *Accaba* by the Arabs.

STAT. XXXIII. Verse 37. HOR.] Famous for the death of Aaron. See on chap. xx. Perhaps Moseroth or Mosera, ver. 30, was a village near this mountain. See the note on ver. 30.

STAT. XXXIV. Verse 41. ZALMONAH.] Probably in the neighbourhood of the land of Edom. As צלם *tselem* signifies an *image*, this place probably had its name from the brazen serpent set up by Moses. See chap. xxi. 5, &c. From the same root the word *telesm*, corruptly called *talisman*, which signifies a consecrated *image*, is derived.

STAT. XXXV. Verse 42. PUNON.] A place in Idumea. Nowhere else mentioned.

STAT. XXXVI. Verse 43. OBOTH.] Mentioned before, chap. xxi. 10.

STAT. XXXVII. Verse 44. IJE-ABARIM.] The *heaps of Abarim*. See chap. xxi. 11. Situation uncertain. It is called *Iim* in the following verse. As the word signifies heaps or protuberances, it probably means tumuli or small hills near some of the *fords* of Jordan.

STAT. XXXVIII. Verse 45. DIBON-GAD.] Supposed to be the same as *Dibon*, chap. xxxii. 34, and to be situated on the brook *Arnon*.

STAT. XXXIX. Verse 46. ALMON-DIBLATHAIM.] Situation not known. It belonged to the Moabites in the time of the prophet Jeremiah. Jer. xlviii. 22.

STAT. XL. Verse 47. *Mountains of* ABARIM, *before* NEBO.] The mountain on which Moses died. They came to this place after the overthrow of the *Amorites*. See chap. xxi.

STAT. XLI. Verse 48. *The* PLAINS *of* MOAB.] This was the scene of the transactions between *Balaam* and *Balak*; see chapters xxiii., xxiv., xxv.

STAT. XLII. Verse 49. *From* BETH-JESIMOTH even *unto* ABEL-SHITTIM] The former of these places fell to the Reubenites, Josh. xiii. 15–20. The Israelites were now come to the edge of Jordan, over against Jericho, where they afterwards passed.

For farther information on the subject of these different encampments, the reader is requested to refer to the extract from Dr. Shaw at the end of the book of Exodus.

Verse 52. *Ye shall—destroy all their pictures*]

A. M. 2553.
B. C. 1451.
An. Exod. Isr. 40.

all their pictures, and destroy all their molten images, and quite pluck down all their high places.

53 And ye shall dispossess *the inhabitants of* the land, and dwell therein: for I have given you the land to possess it.

54 And [r] ye shall divide the land by lot for an inheritance among your families: *and* to the more ye shall [s] give the more inheritance, and to the fewer ye shall [t] give the less inheritance: every man's *inheritance* shall be in the place where his lot falleth; according to the tribes of your fathers ye shall inherit.

A. M. 2553.
B. C. 1451.
An. Exod. Isr. 40.

55 But if ye will not drive out the inhabitants of the land from before you; then it shall come to pass, that those which ye let remain of them *shall be* [u] pricks in your eyes, and thorns in your sides, and shall vex you in the land wherein ye dwell.

56 Moreover it shall come to pass, *that* I shall do unto you, as I thought to do unto them.

[r] Chap. xxvi. 53, 54, 55.——[s] Heb. *multiply his inheritance.* [t] Heb. *diminish his inheritance.*

[u] Josh. xxiii. 13; Judg. ii. 3; Psa. cvi. 34, 36; see Exod. xxiii. 33; Ezek. xxviii. 24.

משכיתם *maskiyotham*, from שכה *sachah*, to be *like*, or *resemble*, either *pictures, carved* work, or *embroidery*, as far as these things were employed to exhibit the abominations of idolatry. *Molten images,* צלמי מסכתם *tsalmey massechotham*, metallic *talismanical figures*, made under certain constellations, and supposed in consequence to be possessed of some extraordinary influences and virtues.

Verse 55. Shall be *pricks in your eyes*] Under these metaphors, the continual mischief that should be done to them, both in soul and body, by these idolaters, is set forth in a very expressive manner. What can be more vexatious than a continual goading of each side, so that the attempt to avoid the one throws the body more forcibly on the other? And what can be more distressing than a continual pricking in the eye, harassing the mind, tormenting the body, and *extinguishing the sight?*

1. It has been usual among pious men to consider these Canaanites *remaining* in the land, as emblems of *indwelling sin;* and it must be granted that what those remaining Canaanites were to the people of Israel, who were disobedient to God, *such* is *indwelling sin* to all those who will not have the blood of the covenant to cleanse them from all unrighteousness. For a time, while conscience is tender, such persons feel themselves straitened in all their goings, hindered in all their religious services, and distressed beyond measure because of the *law*—the *authority* and *power of sin*, which they find warring in their members: by and by the *eye* of their mind becomes obscured by the constant piercings of sin, till at last, fatally persuaded that *sin must dwell in them as long as they live*, they accommodate their minds to their situation, their consciences cease to be tender, and they content themselves with expecting redemption where and when it has never been promised, viz., *beyond the grave!* On the subject of the journeyings of the Israelites, the following observations from old Mr. *Ainsworth* cannot fail to interest the reader.

2. "The TRAVELS of Israel through that *great and terrible wilderness, wherein were fiery serpents, and scorpions, and drought, where there was no water,* Deut. viii. 15, which was *a land of deserts, and of pits, a land of drought, and of the shadow of death, a land that no man passed through, and where no man dwelt,* Jer. ii. 6, signified the many *troubles* and *afflictions* through which we must enter into the kingdom of God, Acts xiv. 22. The *helps, comforts,* and *deliverances* which God gave unto his people in their distresses, are examples of his love and mercy towards his followers; for he comforts them in all their tribulation, that as the sufferings of Christ abound in them, so their consolation also abounds in Christ, 2 Cor. i. 45. The *punishments* which God inflicted upon the disobedient, who perished in the wilderness for their sins, happened unto them for ensamples, and they are *written for our admonition, upon whom the ends of the world are come,* 1 Cor. x. 1, 11; Heb. iii. 17, 18, 19, and iv. 1, 2. By the *names* of their encamping places, and histories adjoined, it appears how Israel came sometimes into *straits* and *troublesome ways*, as at *Pi-hahiroth*, Exod. xiv. 2, 3, 10, &c.; and at *Zalmonah*, Num. ii. 1, 4, &c.; sometimes into *large* and ample *room*, as at the *plains of Moab:* sometimes to places of *hunger* and *thirst*, as at *Rephidim* and *Kadesh*, Exod. xvi., xvii.; Num. xx.; sometimes to places of *refreshing*, as at *Elim* and *Beer*, Exod. xv. 27; Num. xxi. 16; sometimes where they had *wars*, as at *Rephidim, Kadesh, Edrei*, Exod. xvii. 8; Num. xxi. 1, 33; sometimes where they had *rest*, as at *Mount Sinai:* sometimes they went *right forward*, as from *Sinai* to *Kadesh-barnea;* sometimes they *turned backward*, as from *Kadesh-barnea* to the *Red Sea:* sometimes they came to *mountains*, as *Sinai, Shapher, Hor-Gidgad;* sometimes to *valleys*, as *Tahath*, &c.: sometimes to places of *bitterness*, as *Marah;* sometimes, of *sweetness*, as *Mithcah*.

3. "The SINS which they committed in the wilderness were many and great: as open IDOLATRY by the calf, at Horeb, Exod. xxxii., and with *Baal-peor*, Num. xxv. UNBELIEF, at *Kadesh*, Num. xiv.; and afterwards PRESUMPTUOUS BOLDNESS in the same place; MURMURING against God sundry times, with tempting of Christ, (as the apostle speaks, 1 Cor. x.) CONTENTION and REBELLION against their governors often; *lusting for flesh* to fill their appetite, and *loathing manna*, the heavenly food; WHOREDOM with the daughters of Moab, and many other provocations; so that this complaint is after made of them, *How oft did they provoke him in the wilderness, and grieve him in the desert!* Psa. lxxviii. 40. *All sorts* of persons sinned against God; the *multitude* of people very often; the

mixed multitude of strangers among them, Num. xi. The *princes*, as the ten spies, *Dathan*, *Abiram*, &c. The *Levites*, as *Korah* and his company; *Miriam* the prophetess, Num. xii.; *Aaron* the priest with her, besides his sin at Horeb, Exod. xxxii.; and at the water of *Meribah*, Num. xx. Moses also himself at the same place, for which he was excluded from the land of Canaan.

4. "The PUNISHMENTS laid on them by the Lord for their disobedience were many. They died by the *sword of the enemy*, as of the *Amalekites*, Exod. xvii., and of the *Canaanites*, Num. xiv. 45; and some by the *sword of their brethren*, Exod. xxxii. Some were *burned with fire*, Num. xi., xvi.; some *died with surfeit*, Num. xi.; some were *swallowed up alive in the earth*, Num. xvi.; some were *killed with serpents*, Num. xxi.; many *died of the pestilence*, Num. xvi. 46, and chap. v. 25; and generally all that generation which were first mustered, after their coming out of Egypt, perished, Num. xxvi. 64, 65. God consumed their days in vanity, and their years in terror, Psa. lxxviii. 33.

5. "Nevertheless, for his name's sake, he magnified his MERCIES unto them and their posterity. *He had divided the sea*, and led them through on dry land, drowning their enemies, Exod. xiv. He led them with a *cloud by day*, and a *pillar of fire by night*, continually. He gave them *manna* from heaven daily. He *clave the rock*, and gave them water for their thirst. He fed them with *quails*, when they longed for flesh. He *sweetened* the *bitter waters*. He saved them from the sword of their enemies He delivered them from the fiery serpents and scorpions. Their raiment waxed not old upon them, neither did their foot swell for forty years, Deut. viii. 4. He delivered them from the intended curse of Balaam, and turned it into a blessing because he loved them, Num. xxii.; Deut. xxiii. 5. He came down from Mount Sinai, and spake with them from heaven, and gave them right judgments and true laws, good statutes and commandments, and gave also his good Spirit to instruct them, Neh. ix. 13, 20. In the times of his wrath he remembered mercy; his eye spared them from destroying them, neither did he make an end of them in the wilderness, Ezek. xx. 17, 22. He gave them kingdoms and nations, and they possessed the lands of their enemies; and he multiplied their children as the stars of heaven, and brought them into the land promised unto their forefathers, Neh. ix. 22, 23. Now whatsoever things were written aforetime were written for our learning, that we, through patience and comfort of the Scriptures, might have hope, Rom. xv. 4." Let him that readeth understand.

CHAPTER XXXIV.

The land of Canaan is described, 1, 2. *The* south *quarter*, 3–5. *The* western *border*, 6. *The* north *border*, 7–9. *The* east *border*, 10–12. *This land to be divided by lot among the* nine tribes and half, 13; *two tribes and half, Reuben and Gad, and the half of Manasseh, having already got their inheritance on the east side of Jordan*, 14, 15. *Eleazar the priest, and Joshua, to assist in dividing the land*, 16, 17; *and with them a chief out of every tribe*, 18. *The names of the twelve chiefs*, 19–29.

A. M. 2553.
B. C. 1451.
An. Exod. Isr. 40.

AND the Lord spake unto
Moses, saying,
2 Command the children of
Israel, and say unto them, When ye come
into [a] the land of Canaan; (this *is* the land
that shall fall unto you for an inheritance,
even the land of Canaan with the coasts
thereof:)
3 Then [b] your south quarter shall be from
the wilderness of Zin along by the coast of
Edom, and your south border shall be the
outmost coast of [c] the salt sea eastward:
4 And your border shall turn
from the south [d] to the ascent of
Akrabbim, and pass on to Zin:
and the going forth thereof shall be from the
south [e] to Kadesh-barnea, and shall go on to
[f] Hazar-addar, and pass on to Azmon:
5 And the border shall fetch a compass from
Azmon [g] unto the river of Egypt, and the
goings out of it shall be at the sea.
6 And *as for* the western border, ye shall
even have the great sea for a border: this
shall be your west border.

A. M. 2553.
B. C. 1451.
An. Exod. Isr. 40.

[a] Gen. xvii. 8; Deut. i. 7; Psa. lxxviii. 55; cv. 11; Ezek. xlvii. 14.——[b] Josh. xv. 1; see Ezek. xlvii. 13, &c.——[c] Gen. xiv. 3; Josh. xv. 2.

[d] Joshua xv. 3.——[e] Chap. xiii. 26; xxxii. 8.——[f] See Joshua xv. 3, 4.——[g] Gen. xv. 18; Josh. xv. 4–47; 1 Kings viii. 65; Isa. xxvii. 12.

NOTES ON CHAP. XXXIV.

Verse 2. *The land of Canaan with the coasts thereof*] All description here is useless. The situation and boundaries of the land of Canaan can only be known by actual survey, or by consulting a good map.

Verse 3. *The salt sea*] The Dead Sea, or lake Asphaltites. See the note on Gen. xix. 25.

Verse 5. *The river of Egypt*] The eastern branch of the river Nile; or, according to others, a river which is south of the land of the Philistines, and falls into the gulf or bay near *Calieh*.

Verse 6. *Ye shall even have the great sea for a border*] The *Mediterranean* Sea, called here the *Great Sea*, to distinguish it from the *Dead Sea*, the *Sea of Tiberias*, &c., which were only a sort of *lakes*.

A. M. 2553.
B. C. 1451.
An. Exod. Isr. 40.

7 And this shall be your north
border: from the great sea ye shall
point out for you [h] Mount Hor:
8 From Mount Hor ye shall point out *your*
border [i] unto the entrance of Hamath; and the
goings forth of the border shall be to [k] Zedad:
9 And the border shall go on to Ziphron,
and the goings out of it shall be at [l] Hazar-
enan: this shall be your north border.
10 And ye shall point out your east border
from Hazar-enan to Shepham:
11 And the coast shall go down from Shepham [m] to Riblah, on the east side of Ain; and
the border shall descend, and shall reach unto
the [n] side of the sea [o] of Chinnereth eastward:
12 And the border shall go down to Jordan,
and the goings out of it shall be at [p] the salt
sea: this shall be your land with the coasts
thereof round about.
13 And Moses commanded the children of
Israel, saying, [q] This *is* the land which ye
shall inherit by lot, which the LORD commanded to give unto the nine
tribes, and to the half tribe:

A. M. 2553.
B. C. 1451.
An. Exod. Isr. 40.

14 [r] For the tribe of the chil-
dren of Reuben according to the house of their
fathers, and the tribe of the children of Gad
according to the house of their fathers, have
received *their inheritance;* and half the tribe
of Manasseh have received their inheritance:
15 The two tribes and the half tribe have
received their inheritance on this side Jordan
near Jericho eastward, toward the sunrising.
16 And the LORD spake unto Moses, saying,
17 These *are* the names of the men which
shall divide the land unto you: [s] Eleazar the
priest, and Joshua the son of Nun.
18 And ye shall take one [t] prince of every
tribe, to divide the land by inheritance.
19 And the names of the men *are* these:
Of the tribe of Judah, [u] Caleb the son of
Jephunneh.
20 And of the tribe of the children of Simeon, Shemuel the son of Ammihud.

[h] Chap. xxxiii. 37.—[i] Chap. xiii. 21; 2 Kings xiv. 25.—[k] Ezek. xlvii. 15.—[l] Ezek. xlvii. 17.—[m] 2 Kings xxiii. 33; Jer. xxxix. 5, 6.—[n] Heb. *shoulder.*—[o] Deut. iii. 17; Josh. xi. 2; xix. 35; Matt. xiv. 34; Luke v. 1.—[p] Ver. 3.—[q] Ver. 1; Josh. xiv. 1, 2.—[r] Chap. xxxii. 33; Josh. xiv. 2, 3.—[s] Josh. xiv. 1; xix. 51.—[t] Chap. i. 4, 16.—[u] Chap. xiii. 30; xiv. 6, 24, 30, 38; xxvi. 65.

In Hebrew there is properly but one term, ים *yam*, which is applied to all *collections* of water apparently stagnant, and which is generally translated *sea*. The Greek of the New Testament follows the Hebrew, and employs, in general, the word *θαλασσα*, SEA, whether it speaks of the *Mediterranean*, or of the *sea* or *lake* of *Galilee*.

Verse 11. *The sea of Chinnereth*] The same as the *sea of Galilee, sea of Tiberias*, and *sea of Gennesareth*.

Verse 12. *The border shall go down to Jordan*] This river is famous both in the Old and New Testaments. It takes its rise at the foot of Mount Libanus, passes through the sea of *Chinnereth* or *Tiberias*, and empties itself into the lake *Asphaltites* or Dead Sea, from which it has no outlet. In and by it God wrought many miracles. God cut off the waters of this river as he did those of the Red Sea, so that they stood on a heap on each side, and the people passed over on dry ground. Both *Elijah* and *Elisha* separated its waters in a miraculous way, 2 Kings ii. 8–14. *Naaman*, the Syrian general, by washing in it at the command of the prophet, was miraculously cured of his leprosy, 2 Kings v. 10–14. In this river *John* baptized great multitudes of Jews; and in it was CHRIST himself baptized, and the Spirit of God descended upon him, and the voice from heaven proclaimed him the great and only Teacher and Saviour of men, Matt. iii. 16, 17; Mark i. 5–11.

Verse 13. *This is the land which ye shall inherit by lot*] Much of what is said concerning this land is peculiarly emphatic. It is a land that contains a multitude of advantages in its climate, its soil, situation, &c. It is bounded on the *south* by a *ridge of mountains*, which separate it from *Arabia*, and screen it from the burning and often pestiferous winds which blow over the desert from that quarter. On the *west* it is bounded by the *Mediterranean Sea;* on the *north*, by Mount *Libanus*, which defends it from the cold northern blasts; and on the *east* by the *river Jordan*, and its fertile, well-watered plains. It is described by God himself as "a good land, a land of brooks of water, of fountains, and depths that spring out of valleys and hills; a land of wheat, and barley, and vines, and fig trees, and pomegranates; a land of olive oil and honey; a land wherein there was no scarcity of bread, and where both iron and copper mines abounded," Deut. viii. 7–9: a land finely diversified with hills and valleys, and well watered by the rain of heaven, in this respect widely different from Egypt; a land which God cared for, on which his eyes were continually placed from the beginning to the end of the year; watched over by a most merciful Providence; in a word, a land which flowed with milk and honey, and was the most pleasant of all lands; Deut. xi. 11. 12; Ezek. xx. 6. Such was *the land*, and such were the advantages that this most favoured people were called to possess. They were called to possess it *by lot* that each might be satisfied with his possession, as considering it to be appointed to him by the especial providence of God; and its boundaries were ascertained on Divine authority, to prevent all covetousness after the territories of others.

Verse 19, &c. *And the names of the men* are *these*]

A. M. 2553.
B. C. 1451.
An. Exod. Isr.
40.

21 Of the tribe of Benjamin,
Elidad the son of Chislon.
22 And the prince of the tribe
of the children of Dan, Bukki the son of Jogli.
23 The prince of the children of Joseph, for
the tribe of the children of Manasseh, Hanniel
the son of Ephod.
24 And the prince of the tribe of the children
of Ephraim, Kemuel the son of Shiphtan.
25 And the prince of the tribe of the children of Zebulun, Elizaphan the son of Parnach.
26 And the prince of the tribe
of the children of Issachar, Paltiel
the son of Azzan.
27 And the prince of the tribe of the children of Asher, Ahihud the son of Shelomi.
28 And the prince of the tribe of the children of Naphtali, Pedahel the son of Ammihud.
29 These *are they* whom the LORD commanded to [v] divide the inheritance unto the
children of Israel in the land of Canaan.

A. M. 2553.
B. C. 1451.
An. Exod. Isr.
40.

[v] Josh. xiii. 32; xiv. 1; xix. 51.

It is worthy of remark that Moses does not follow any order hitherto used of placing the tribes, neither that in chap i., nor that in chap. vii., nor that in chap. xxvi., nor any other; but places them here exactly in that order in which they possessed the land. 1. Judah; 2. Simeon; 3. Benjamin; 4. Dan; 5. Manasseh; 6. Ephraim; 7. Zebulun; 8. Issachar; 9. Asher; 10. Naphtali. *Judah* is first, having the first lot; and he dwelt in the south part of the land, Josh. xv. 1, &c.; and next to him *Simeon*, because his inheritance was *within the inheritance of the children of Judah*, Josh. xix. 1. *Benjamin* was *third;* he had his inheritance by Judah, *between the children of Judah and the children of Joseph*, Josh. xviii. 11. *Dan* was the *fourth;* his lot fell westward of that of Benjamin, in the country of the Philistines, as may be seen in Josh. xix. 40, 41, &c. *Fifth, Manasseh;* and *sixth*, by him, his brother *Ephraim*, whose inheritances were behind that of Benjamin, Josh. xvi. 7. Next to these dwelt, *seventh, Zebulun;* and *eighth, Issachar;* concerning whose lots see Josh. xix. 10–17. *Ninth, Asher;* and *tenth, Naphtali;* see Josh. xix. 24, 32, &c. And as in encamping about the tabernacle they were arranged according to their *fraternal* relationship, (see chap. ii.,) so they were in the division and inheriting of the promised land. *Judah* and *Simeon*, both sons of *Leah*, dwelt abreast of each other. *Benjamin*, son of *Rachel*, and *Dan*, son of *Rachel's* maid, dwelt next abreast. *Manasseh* and *Ephraim*, both sons of *Joseph*, son of *Rachel*, had the next place abreast. *Zebulun* and *Issachar*, who dwelt next together, were both sons of *Leah;* and the last pair were *Asher*, of *Leah's maid*, and *Naphtali*, of *Rachel's maid.* Thus God, in nominating the princes that should divide the land, signified beforehand the manner of their possession, and that they should be so situated as to dwell together as brethren in unity, for the mutual help and comfort of each other. See *Ainsworth.* In this arrangement there is much skill, judgment, and kindness every where displayed.

CHAPTER XXXV.

The Israelites are commanded to give the Levites, out of their inheritances, cities and their suburbs for themselves and for their cattle, goods, &c., 1–3. *The suburbs to be* 3,000 *cubits round about from the wall of the city,* 4, 5. *The cities to be forty-two, to which six cities of refuge should be added, in all forty-eight cities,* 6, 7. *Each tribe shall give of these cities in proportion to its possessions,* 8. *These cities to be appointed for the person who might slay his neighbour unawares,* 9–12. *Of these six cities there shall be three on each side Jordan,* 13, 14. *The cities to be places of refuge for all who kill a person* unawares, *whether they be Israelites, strangers, or sojourners,* 15. *Cases of murder to which the benefit of the cities of refuge shall* not *extend,* 16–21. *Cases of manslaughter to which the benefits of the cities of refuge* shall *extend,* 22, 23. *How the congregation shall act between the manslayer and the avenger of blood,* 24, 25. *The manslayer shall abide in the city of refuge till the death of the high priest; he shall then return to the land of his possession,* 26–28. *Two witnesses must attest a murder before a murderer can be put to death,* 29, 30. *Every murderer to be put to death,* 31. *The manslayer is not to be permitted to come to the land of his inheritance till the death of the high priest,* 32. *The land must not be polluted with blood, for the Lord dwells in it,* 33, 34.

A. M. 2553.
B. C. 1451.
An. Exod. Isr.
40.

AND the LORD spake unto Mo-
ses in the plains of Moab by
Jordan *near* Jericho, saying,
2 [a] Command the children of
Israel, that they give unto the
Levites of the inheritance of

A. M. 2553.
B. C. 1451.
An. Exod. Isr.
40.

[a] Josh. xiv. 3, 4; xxi. 2; see Ezek. xlv. 1, &c.; xlviii. 8, &c.

NOTES ON CHAP. XXXV.

Verse 4. *And the suburbs of the cities*—shall reach *from the wall of the city and outward a thousand cubits round about.*

Verse 5. *And ye shall measure from without the city—two thousand cubits, &c.*] Commentators have been much puzzled with the accounts in these two verses. In ver. 4 the measure is said to be 1,000

A. M. 2553. B. C. 1451. An. Exod. Isr. 40.

their possession, cities to dwell in; and ye shall give *also* unto the Levites suburbs for the cities round about them.

3 And the cities shall they have to dwell in; and the suburbs of them shall be for their cattle, and for their goods, and for all their beasts.

4 And the suburbs of the cities, which ye shall give unto the Levites, *shall reach* from the wall of the city and outward a thousand cubits round about.

5 And ye shall measure from without the city on the east side two thousand cubits, and on the south side two thousand cubits, and on the west side two thousand cubits, and on the north side two thousand cubits; and the city *shall be* in the midst: this shall be to them the suburbs of the cities.

6 And among the cities which ye shall give unto the Levites *there shall be* [b] six cities for refuge, which ye shall appoint for the manslayer, that he may flee thither: and [c] to them ye shall add forty and two cities.

7 *So* all the cities which ye shall give to the Levites *shall be* [d] forty and eight cities: them *shall ye give* with their suburbs.

8 And the cities which ye shall give *shall be* [e] of the possession of the children of Israel: [f] from *them that have* many, ye shall give many; but from *them that have* few, ye shall give few: every one shall give of his cities unto the Levites, according to his inheritance which [g] he inheriteth.

A. M. 2553. B. C. 1451. An. Exod. Isr. 40.

9 And the LORD spake unto Moses, saying,

10 Speak unto the children of Israel, and say unto them, [h] When ye be come over Jordan into the land of Canaan;

11 Then [i] ye shall appoint you cities to be cities of refuge for you; that the slayer may flee thither, which killeth any person [k] at unawares.

12 [l] And they shall be unto you cities for refuge from the avenger; that the manslayer die not, until he stand before the congregation in judgment.

13 And of these cities which ye shall give, [m] six cities shall ye have for refuge.

14 [n] Ye shall give three cities on this side Jordan, and three cities shall ye give in the land of Canaan, *which* shall be cities of refuge.

15 These six cities shall be a refuge, *both* for the children of Israel, and [o] for the stranger, and for the sojourner among them; that every one that killeth any person unawares may flee thither.

16 [p] And if he smite him with an instrument of iron, so that he die, he *is* a murderer: the murderer shall surely be put to death.

[b] Ver. 13; Deut. iv. 41; Josh. xx. 2, 7, 8; xxi. 3, 13, 21, 27, 32, 36, 38.——[c] Heb. *above them ye shall give.*——[d] Josh. xxi. 41.——[e] Josh. xxi. 3.——[f] Chap. xxvi. 54.——[g] Heb. *they inherit.*——[h] Deut. xix. 2; Josh. xx. 2.

[i] Exod. xxi. 13.——[k] Heb. *by error.*——[l] Deut. xix. 6; Josh. xx. 3, 5, 6.——[m] Verse 6.——[n] Deut. iv. 41; Joshua xx. 8.——[o] Chap. xv. 16.——[p] Exod. xxi. 12, 14; Lev. xxiv. 17; Deut. xix. 11, 12.

cubits from the wall; in ver. 5 the measure is said to be 2,000 from without the city. It is likely these two measures mean the same thing; at least so it was understood by the Septuagint and Coptic, who have διαχιλιους πηχεις, 2,000 cubits, in the *fourth*, as well as in the *fifth* verse; but this reading of the Septuagint and Coptic is not acknowledged by any other of the ancient versions, nor by any of the MSS. collated by *Kennicott* and *De Rossi*. We must seek therefore for some other method of reconciling this apparently contradictory account. Sundry modes have been proposed by commentators, which appear to me, in general, to require full as much explanation as the text itself. Maimonides is the only one intelligible on the subject. "The suburbs," says he, "of the cities are expressed in the law to be 3,000 cubits on every side from the wall of the city and outwards. The first thousand cubits are the suburbs, and the 2,000, which they measured without the suburbs, were for fields and vineyards." The whole, therefore, of the city, suburbs, fields, and vineyards, may be represented by the following diagram:—

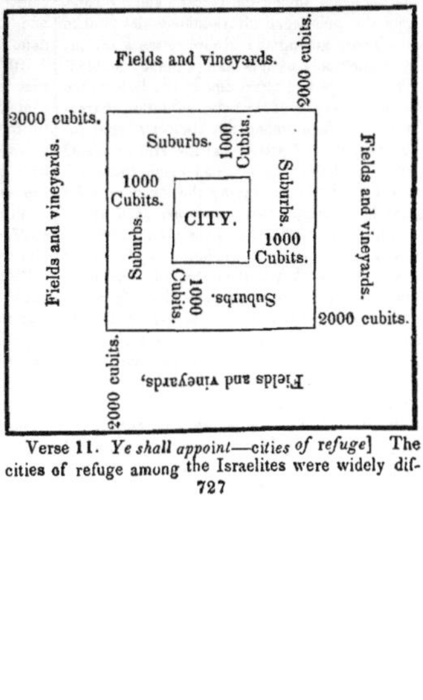

Verse 11. *Ye shall appoint—cities of refuge*] The cities of refuge among the Israelites were widely dif-

A. M. 2553.
B. C. 1451.
An. Exod. Isr.
40.

17 And if he smite him [q] with throwing a stone, wherewith he may die, and he die, he *is* a murderer: the murderer shall surely be put to death.

18 Or *if* he smite him with a hand weapon of wood, wherewith he may die, and he die, he *is* a murderer: the murderer shall surely be put to death.

19 [r] The revenger of blood himself shall slay the murderer: when he meeteth him, he shall slay him.

20 But [s] if he thrust him of hatred, or hurl at him [t] by laying of wait, that he die;

21 Or in enmity smite him with his hand, that he die: he that smote *him* shall surely be put to death; *for* he *is* a murderer: the revenger of blood shall slay the murderer, when he meeteth him.

22 But if he thrust him suddenly [u] without enmity, or have cast upon him any thing without laying of wait,

23 Or with any stone, wherewith a man may die, seeing *him* not, and cast *it* upon him, that he die, and *was* not his enemy, neither sought his harm:

24 Then [v] the congregation shall judge between the slayer and the revenger of blood according to these judgments:

25 And the congregation shall deliver the slayer out of the hand of the revenger of blood; and the congregation shall restore him to the city of his refuge, whither he was fled: and [w] he shall abide in it unto the death of the high priest, [x] which was anointed with the holy oil.

A. M. 2553.
B. C. 1451.
An. Exod. Isr.
40.

26 But if the slayer shall at any time come without the border of the city of his refuge, whither he was fled;

27 And the revenger of blood find him without the borders of the city of his refuge, and the revenger of blood kill the slayer; [y] he shall not be guilty of blood:

28 Because he should have remained in the city of his refuge until the death of the high priest: but after the death of the high priest the slayer shall return into the land of his possession.

29 So these *things* shall be for [z] a statute of judgment unto you throughout your generations in all your dwellings.

30 Whoso killeth any person, the murderer shall be put to death by the [a] mouth of witnesses: but one witness shall not testify against any person *to cause him* to die.

31 Moreover, ye shall take no satisfaction for the life of a murderer, which *is* [b] guilty of death; but he shall be surely put to death.

[q] Heb. *with a stone of the hand.*——[r] Ver. 21, 24, 27; Deut. xix. 6, 12; Josh. xx. 3, 5.——[s] Gen. iv. 8; 2 Sam. iii. 27; xx. 10; 1 Kings ii. 31, 32.——[t] Exod. xxi. 14; Deut. xix. 11. [u] Exod. xxi. 13.

[v] Ver. 12; Josh. xx. 6.——[w] Josh. xx. 6.——[x] Exod. xxix. 7; Lev. iv. 3; xxi. 10.——[y] Heb. *no blood* shall be *to him;* Exod. xxii. 2.——[z] Chap. xxvii. 11.——[a] Deut. xvii. 6; xix. 15; Matt. xviii. 16; 2 Cor. xiii. 1; Heb. x. 28.——[b] Heb. *faulty to die.*

ferent from the *asyla* among the Greeks and Romans, as also from the *privileged altars* among the Roman Catholics. Those among the Hebrews were for the protection of such only as had slain a person involuntarily. The temples and altars among the latter often served for the protection of the most profligate characters. Cities of refuge among the Hebrews were necessary, because the old patriarchal law still remained in force, viz., that the *nearest akin* had a right to avenge the death of his relation by slaying the murderer; for the original law enacted that *whosoever shed man's blood, by man should his blood be shed,* Gen. ix. 6, and none was judged so proper to execute this law as the man who was nearest akin to the deceased. As many rash executions of this law might take place, from the very nature of the thing, it was deemed necessary to qualify its claims, and prevent injustice; and the cities of refuge were judged proper for this purpose. Nor do we ever read that they were ever found inefficient, or that they were ever abused.

Verse 12. *Until he stand before the congregation in judgment.*] So one of these cities was not a perpetual asylum; it was only a *pro tempore* refuge, till the case could be fairly examined by the magistrates in the presence of the people, or the elders their representatives; and this was done in the city or place where he had done the murder, Josh. xx. 4, 6. If he was found worthy of death, they delivered him to the avenger that he might be slain, Deut. xix. 12; if not, they sent him back to the city of refuge, where he remained till the death of the high priest, ver. 25. Before the cities of refuge were appointed, the *altar* appears to have been a sanctuary for those who had killed a person unwittingly; see on Exod. xxi. 13, 14.

Verse 19. *The revenger of blood*] גאל הדם *goel haddam,* the *redeemer of blood;* the next in blood to him who was slain. See on the preceding verse.

Verse 30. *But one witness shall not testify against any*] This was a just and necessary provision. One man may be *mistaken,* or so violently *prejudiced* as to impose even on his own judgment, or so *wicked* as to endeavour through malice to compass the life of his neighbour: but it is not likely that *two* or *more* should be of this kind; and even were they, their separate examination would lead to a discovery of the truth, and to their conviction.

Verse 31. *Ye shall take no satisfaction for the life of a murderer*] No atonement could be made for *him,*

A. M. 2553. B. C. 1451. An. Exod. Isr. 40.

32 And ye shall take no satisfaction for him that is fled to the city of his refuge, that he should come again to dwell in the land, until the death of the priest.

33 So ye shall not pollute the land wherein ye *are:* for blood [c] it defileth the land: and [d] the land cannot be cleansed of the blood that is shed therein, but [e] by the blood of him that shed it.

34 [f] Defile not therefore the land which ye shall inhabit, wherein I dwell: for [g] I the LORD dwell among the children of Israel.

[c] Psa. cvi. 38; Mic. iv. 1.——[d] Heb. *there can be no expiation for the land.*

[e] Gen. ix. 6.——[f] Lev. xviii. 25; Deut. xxi. 23.——[g] Exod. xxix. 45, 46.

nor any *commutation*, so as to save him from death. All the laws of the civilized world have either adjudged the murderer to death, or to a punishment equivalent to it; such as perpetual imprisonment, in a dungeon, under ground, on a stone floor, without light, and to be fed on a small portion of bread and water. In such circumstances a man could live but a short time; and though it is not called the punishment of *death*, yet, from its inevitable consequences, it only differed from it by being a little longer respite than was usual where the punishment of death was awarded. See the note on Gen. ix. 6.

Verse 32. *Until the death of the priest.*] Probably intended to typify, that no sinner can be delivered from his banishment from God, or recover his forfeited inheritance, till Jesus Christ, the great high priest, had died for his offences, and risen again for his justification.

Verse 33. *For blood it defileth the land*] The very land was considered as guilty till the blood of the murderer was shed in it. No wonder God is so particularly strict in his laws against murderers, 1. Because he is the author of life, and none have any right to dispose of it but himself. 2. Because life is the time to prepare for the eternal world, and on it the salvation of the soul accordingly depends; therefore it is of infinite consequence to the man that his life be lengthened out to the utmost limits assigned by Divine Providence. As he who takes a man's life away before his time may be the murderer of his soul as well as of his body, the severest laws should be enacted against this, both to punish and prevent the crime.

THE Mosaic *cities of refuge* have in general been considered, not merely as civil institutions, but as types or representations of infinitely better things; and in this light St. Paul seems to have considered them and the *altar of God*, which was a place of *general refuge*, as it is pretty evident that he had them in view when writing the following words: "God, willing more abundantly to show unto the heirs of promise the immutability of his counsel, confirmed it by an oath; that by two immutable things, (his *oath* and *promise*,) in which it was impossible for God to lie, we might have a strong consolation who have FLED for REFUGE to lay HOLD upon the HOPE set before us," Heb. vi. 17, 18. Independently of this, it was a very wise political institute; and while the patriarchal law on this point continued in force, this law had a direct tendency to cool and moderate the spirit of *revenge*, to secure the proper accomplishment of the ends of *justice*, and to make way for every claim of *mercy* and *equity*. But this is not peculiar to the ordinance of the *cities of refuge*; every institution of God is distinguished in the same way, having his own glory, in the present and eternal welfare of man, immediately in view.

CHAPTER XXXVI.

The inconveniences which might be produced by daughters, inheritrixes, marrying out of their own tribe, remedied on the recommendation of certain chiefs of the tribe of Joseph, who stated the case of the daughters of Zelophehad, 1–4. The daughters of Zelophehad are commanded to marry in their own tribe, 5, 6; which is to be an ordinance in all similar circumstances, 7–9. The daughters of Zelophehad marry their father's brother's sons, and thus their inheritance is preserved in their own tribe, 10–12. The conclusion of the commandments given by the Lord to the Israelites in the plains of Moab, 13.

A. M. 2553. B. C. 1451. An. Exod. Isr. 40.

AND the chief fathers of the families of the [a] children of Gilead, the son of Machir, the son of Manasseh, of the families of the sons of Joseph, came near, and spake before Moses, and before the princes, the chief fathers of the children of Israel:

2 And they said, [b] The LORD commanded my lord to give the land for an inheritance by lot to the children of Israel:

[a] Chap. xxvi. 29.

[b] Chap. xxvi. 55; xxxiii. 54; Josh. xvii. 3.

NOTES ON CHAP. XXXVI.

Verse 2. *To give the inheritance of Zelophehad—unto his daughters.*] See this case spoken of at large on chap xxvii. Either the first *eleven* verses of chap. xxvii. should come in before this chapter, or this chapter should come in immediately after those eleven verses; they certainly both make parts of the same subject.

A. M. 2553.
B. C. 1451.
An. Exod. Isr. 40.

and [c] my lord was commanded by the LORD to give the inheritance of Zelophehad our brother unto his daughters.

3 And if they be married to any of the sons of the *other* tribes of the children of Israel, then shall their inheritance be taken from the inheritance of our fathers, and shall be put to the inheritance of the tribe [d] whereunto they are received; so shall it be taken from the lot of our inheritance.

4 And when [e] the jubilee of the children of Israel shall be, then shall their inheritance be put unto the inheritance of the tribe whereunto they are received: so shall their inheritance be taken away from the inheritance of the tribe of our fathers.

5 And Moses commanded the children of Israel according to the word of the LORD, saying, The tribe of the sons of Joseph [f] hath said well.

6 This *is* the thing which the LORD doth command concerning the daughters of Zelophehad, saying, Let them [g] marry to whom they think best; [h] only to the family of the tribe of their father shall they marry.

7 So shall not the inheritance of the children of Israel remove from tribe to tribe: for every one of the children of Israel shall [i] keep [k] himself to the inheritance of the tribe of his fathers.

8 And [l] every daughter, that possesseth an inheritance in any tribe of the children of Israel, shall be wife unto one of the family of the tribe of her father, that the children of Israel may enjoy every man the inheritance of his fathers.

9 Neither shall the inheritance remove from *one* tribe to another tribe; but every one of the tribes of the children of Israel shall keep himself to his own inheritance.

10 Even as the LORD commanded Moses, so did the daughters of Zelophehad:

11 [m] For Mahlah, Tirzah, and Hoglah, and Milcah, and Noah, the daughters of Zelophehad, were married unto their father's brother's sons:

12 *And* they were married [n] into the families of the sons of Manasseh the son of Joseph, and their inheritance remained in the tribe of the family of their father.

13 These *are* the [o] commandments and the judgments, which the LORD commanded by the hand of Moses unto the children of Israel [p] in the plains of Moab, by Jordan *near* Jericho.

[c] Chap. xxvii. 1, 7; Josh. xvii. 3, 4.——[d] Heb. *unto whom they shall be.*——[e] Lev. xxv. 10.——[f] Chap. xxvii. 7.——[g] Heb. *be wives.*——[h] Ver. 12; Tob. i. 9.——[i] Heb. *cleave to thee,* &c.

[k] 1 Kings xxi. 3.——[l] 1 Chron. xxiii. 22.——[m] Chap. xxvii. 1.——[n] Heb. to some that were *of the families.*——[o] Chap. xxxv. 29.——[p] Chap. xxvi. 3; xxxiii. 50.

Here Moses determines that heiresses should marry in their own tribe, that no part of the ancient inheritance might be alienated from the original family.

Verse 6. *Let them marry to whom they think best*] Here was latitude sufficient, and yet a salutary and reasonable restraint, which prevented a vexatious mixture of property and possession.

Verse 8. *Every daughter that possesseth an inheritance*] This law affected none but *heiresses;* all others were at liberty to marry into any of the other tribes. The priests and Levites, who could have no inheritance, were exempt from the operation of this law. Jehoiada had the king of Judah's daughter to wife, 2 Chron. xxii. 11. And another priest had for wife one of the daughters of *Barzillai* the *Gileadite,* Ezra ii. 61. "By reason of such marriages," says Mr. Ainsworth, "there might be kindred between Elizabeth, the mother of John the Baptist, who was of the daughters of Aaron, and Mary the virgin, the mother of our Lord, who was of the lineage of David, and tribe of Judah;" Luke i. 5, 36; iii. 23-31.

Verse 11. *Mahlah, Tirzah, &c.*] For a curious account of these names, see the notes on chap. xxvii. 7.

Verse 12. *And their inheritance remained in—the family*] "By this example, and the law of inheritances in the Holy Land, the people of God," says Ainsworth, "are taught to hold fast their inheritance in his promises, and their right in Christ, which they hold by faith; that as the Father hath made them meet to be partakers of the inheritance among the saints in light, Col. i. 12, so they may keep the faith and grace which they have received to the end."

Verse 13. *These are the commandments, &c.*] See these different terms analyzed and explained, Lev. xxv. 5.

THUS ends the book of Numbers, containing a series of astonishing providences and events. Scarcely any piece of history in the sacred writings is better calculated to impress the mind of a serious reader with a sense of the goodness and severity of God. In every transaction his holiness and justice appear in closest union with his benevolence and mercy. From such a *Being* what have the wicked not to fear! From such a *Father* and *Friend* what have the upright not to hope! His *justice* requires him to punish iniquity, but his *mercy* inclines him to pardon all who truly repent and believe in the Son of his love.

The journeyings of this people, from the time they left Egypt, exhibit a series of *providential wonders.* Every *where,* and in every *circumstance,* God appears: and yet there is no *circumstance* or *occasion* that does

not justify those signal displays of his GRACE and his JUSTICE. The genuine history of God's providence must be sought for in this book alone; and as every *occurrence* happened as an *example*, we have authority to conclude that in every case where his own glory and the salvation of man are interested, he will interfere and give the fullest proofs that he is the *same today* that he was *yesterday*, and will continue unchangeable for *ever* and *ever*. Reader, are these matters *ensamples* to *thee*? Art *thou*, like the Israelites, come into the plains of Moab, on the very verge of the promised land? Jordan alone separates thee from the promised inheritance. O, watch and pray, that thou come not short of the glory of God. The last enemy that shall be destroyed is *death*; see then that the sting of death, which is *sin*, be extracted from thy soul, that, being justified by Christ's blood, thou mayest be made an heir according to the hope of an eternal life. Amen, amen.

"I will bring you into the WILDERNESS of the people, and there will I plead with you face to face, like as I pleaded with your fathers in the WILDERNESS of the land of Egypt. And I will cause you to pass under the rod, and bring you into the bond of the covenant," Ezek. xx. 35-37.

"He (Christ) is the Mediator of the New Testament, that by means of death, for the redemption of the transgressions *that were* under the first testament, they which are called might receive the promise of eternal inheritance," Heb. ix. 15.

SECTIONS in the Book of Numbers, carried on from Leviticus, which ends with the THIRTY-THIRD.

The THIRTY-FOURTH, called במדבר *bemidbar*, begins chap. i. 1, and ends chap. iv. 20.

The THIRTY-FIFTH, called נשא *nasa*, begins chap. iv. 21, and ends chap. vii. 89.

The THIRTY-SIXTH, called, בהעלתך *behaalothecha*, begins chap. viii. 1, and ends chap. xii. 16.

The THIRTY-SEVENTH, called שלח *shelach*, begins chap. xiii. 1, and ends chap. xv. 41.

The THIRTY-EIGHTH, called קרח *korach*, begins chap. xvi. 1, and ends chap. xviii. 32.

The THIRTY-NINTH, called חקת *chukkath*, begins chap. xix. 1, and ends chap. xxii. 1.

The FORTIETH, called בלק *balak*, begins chap. xxii. 2, and ends chap. xxv. 9.

The FORTY-FIRST, called פינחס *pinechas*, begins chap. xxv. 10, and ends chap. xxx. 1.

The FORTY-SECOND, called מטות *mattoth*, begins chap. xxx. 2, and ends chap. xxxii. 42.

The FORTY-THIRD, called מסעי *masey*, begins chap. xxxiii. 1, and ends chap. xxxvi. 13.

MASORETIC *Notes* on NUMBERS.

The *number* of *verses* in this book is 1,288, of which ארפח is the symbol: for א *aleph* stands for 1000, ר *resh* for 200, פ *phe* for 80, and ח *cheth* for 8.

The *middle verse* is the 20th of chap. xvii. *And the man's rod whom I shall choose shall blossom.* (N. B. In our English Bibles this is ver. 5 of chap. xvii.)

Its *pareshioth*, or larger sections, are 10, expressed by the letters of the word בדד *badad*, *alone: The Lord* ALONE *did lead him*, Deut. xxxii. 12. ד *daleth* stands for 4, repeated here, 8, and ב *beth* for 2.

Its *sedarim*, or Masoretic sections, are 32, expressed by the word לב *leb*, *heart*, Psa. li. 12: *Create in me a clean* HEART, *O God;* in which word ב *beth* stands for 2, and ל *lamed* for 30.

Its *chapters* are 36, expressed by the word לו *lu*, *O!* Deut. xxxii. 29: *O that they were wise!* in which word ל *lamed* stands for 30, and ו *vau* for 6.

The number of its *open sections* is 92; its *close* or *shut sections*, 66; together 158; expressed in the memorial word חלקך *chelkecha: I am* THY PORTION; in which word ק *koph* stands for 100, ל *lamed* for 30, כ *caph* for 20, and ח *cheth* for 8.

Though this sort of notations may appear trifling to some, yet to an upright Jew they were of much consequence. The very technical words used in such cases put him always in mind of something in which the glory of God and the happiness and salvation of his own soul were concerned. See the note at the end of Genesis, and see the concluding notes on the Book of Deuteronomy.

***Revised and corrected for a new edition, Aug. 4th,* 1827.—A. CLARKE.**

PREFACE TO THE BOOK

OF

DEUTERONOMY.

WE have borrowed the name of this book, as in former cases, from the Vulgate Latin, *Deuteronomium*, as the Vulgate has done from the Greek version of the Septuagint, Δευτερονομιον, which is a compound term literally signifying the *second law*, because it seems to contain a *repetition* of the preceding laws, from which circumstance it has been termed by the rabbins משנה *mishneh*, the *iteration* or *doubling*.

It appears that both these names are borrowed from chap. xvii. 18, where the king is commanded to write him a copy of this law; the original is משנה התורה *mishneh hattorah*, a *repetition* or *doubling of the law*, which the Septuagint have translated *το δευτερονομιον*, *this second law*, which we, properly enough, translate a *copy of the law:* but in Hebrew, like the preceding books, it takes its name from its commencement, אלה הדברים ELLEH HADDEBARIM, *these are the words;* and in the best rabbinical Bibles its running title is ספר דברים SEPHER DEBARIM, *the book of debarim*, or *the book of the words*. Our Saxon ancestors termed it Ðeo æfter æ, *the after law*.

The Book of Deuteronomy contains an account of what passed in the wilderness from the *first day* of the *eleventh month* of the *fortieth year* after the departure of the Israelites from Egypt to the *seventh day* of the *twelfth month* of the same; making in the whole a history of the transactions of exactly *five weeks*, the months of the Jews being *lunar*. The history is continued about seven days after the death of Moses; for he began to deliver his first discourse to the people in the plains of Moab the *first day* of the *eleventh month* of the *fortieth year*, chap. i. 3, and died on the *first day* of the *twelfth month* of the same year, aged 120 years.

As the Israelites were now about to enter into the promised land, and many of them had not witnessed the different transactions in the wilderness, the former generation having been all destroyed except Joshua and Caleb; to impress their hearts with a deep sense of their obligation to God, and to prepare them for the inheritance which God had prepared for them, Moses here *repeats* the principal occurrences of the forty years, now almost elapsed; shows them the absolute necessity of fearing, loving, and obeying God; repeats the *ten commandments*, and particularly explains each, and the ordinances belonging to them, adding others which he had not delivered before; confirms the whole law in a most solemn manner, with exceeding great and precious promises to them that keep it, and a denunciation of the most awful judgments against those who should break it; renews the covenant between God and the people; prophesies of things which should come to pass in the latter days; blesses each of the tribes, prophetically, with the choicest spiritual and temporal blessings; and then, having viewed the whole extent of the land, from the top of Mount Nebo or Pisgah, he yielded up the ghost, and was privately buried by God, leaving Joshua the son of Nun for his successor.

The Book of Deuteronomy and the Epistle to the Hebrews contain the best comment on the nature, design, and use of the law; the former may be considered as an evangelical commentary on the four preceding books, in which the spiritual reference and signification of the different parts of the law are given, and given in such a manner as none could give who had not a clear discovery of the glory which was to be revealed. It may be safely asserted that very few parts of the Old Testament Scriptures can be read with greater profit by the genuine Christian than the Book of *Deuteronomy*.

PREFACE TO DEUTERONOMY.

The contents of the different chapters may be thus briefly summed up :—

On the first day of the eleventh month of the fortieth year, after the departure from Egypt, the Israelites being then on the east side of Jordan, in the land of the Moabites, Moses gives them a brief recapitulation of what took place in the wilderness, from their leaving Mount *Horeb* till they came to *Kadesh ;* chap. i.

Their travels from Kadesh till they come to the country of the Amorites, with the defeat of Sihon their king; chap. ii.

The war with Og, king of Bashan, with the dividing his land and that of Sihon among the tribes of Reuben and Gad, and the half tribe of Manasseh; chap. iii.

Moses exhorts them to observe the Divine precepts; threatens those who should violate them; and appoints Bezer, Ramoth, and Golan, to be the cities of refuge on the east side of Jordan; chap. iv.

Repeats the *decalogue,* and tells the people what effect the publication of it had on their fathers, when God spoke to them from the mount; chap. v.

Exhorts them to love God with all their heart, and promises them an abundance of good things; chap. vi.

Repeats the command to exterminate the Canaanites, and all vestiges of their idolatry, chap. vii.

Recites the many interpositions of God's kindness which they had received during their forty years' travel in the wilderness, and strongly exhorts them to remember those mercies, and not to forfeit a continuance of his favours by ingratitude and disobedience; chap. viii.

Shows them that they were to pass Jordan in a short time, and that God was about to bring them in, not on account of their goodness, but of his mercy; chap. ix.

Gives an account of the second tables of the law, which he made at the command of God· mentions their journey from Beeroth to Jotbath, the choosing of the Levites, and the neces sity of having the heart circumcised; chap. x.

Continues an account of God's mighty acts in their behalf, and shows the blessings which should come on them who kept his law, and the curse on those who were disobedient. The blessings to be pronounced on Mount *Gerizim,* and the curses on Mount *Ebal ;* chap. xi.

Commands them to destroy all monuments of idolatry in the land, to offer the different offerings and sacrifices, and to avoid eating of blood; chap. xii.

Ordinances against false prophets, idolatrous cities, &c.; chap. xiii.

Forbids their cutting themselves at funerals, recapitulates the law concerning clean and unclean animals, and exhorts them to remember the Levites; chap. xiv.

Every seventh year shall be a year of release for the poor of usury; first-born, &c.; chap. xv.

Concerning the annual feasts, passover, pentecost, and tabernacles; the establishment of judges and officers; no groves to be planted near the altar of God; chap. xvi.

Idolaters are to be put to death; difficult cases in equity to be referred to the superior judges; of a king and his duties; chap. xvii.

All divination is prohibited. The grand promise of an EXTRAORDINARY PROPHET. How false prophets are to be distinguished; chap. xviii.

The laws relative to the cities of refuge, and how the intentional murderer is to be treated: chap. xix.

Laws relative to the carrying on of war; who should be sent back from the army, how they are to treat the Canaanites, and how they are to commence sieges, chap. xx.

How to make expiation for an uncertain murder; marriages with captives; rights of the first-born, &c.; chap. xxi.

Things lost or strayed are to be restored to their right owners; men and women must not interchange apparel; improper mixtures to be avoided; of the tokens of virginity; adulterers and adulteresses to be put to death; chap. xxii.

Eunuchs, bastards, Moabites, and Ammonites, are not to be permitted to enter into the congregation of the Lord. Harlots not to be tolerated; chap. xxiii.

Laws relative to divorce; privileges of the newly-married man; concerning pledges, wages, gleanings, &c.; chap. xxiv.

More than forty stripes shall not be given. If a man die childless, his brother shall take his wife. Of weights, measures, &c.; chap. xxv.

Different ceremonies to be used in offering the first-fruits; tithes. Of full self-consecration to God; chap. xxvi.

The words of the law to be written on stones, and to be set up on Mount Ebal. The tribes which stand on Mount Gerizim to bless the obedient, and those which should stand on Mount Ebal to curse the disobedient. Who they are that are to be cursed; chap. xxvii.

The blessings of those who are faithful; curses against the disobedient; chap. xxviii.

A recital of the covenant of God, made not only with them, but for their posterity; chap. xxix.

Promises of pardon to the penitent; good and evil, life and death, are set before them; ch. xxx.

Moses, being now 120 years old, delivers a copy of the law which he had written into the hands of the priests, to be laid up in the ark, and to be publicly read every seventh year; a charge is given to Joshua; chap. xxxi.

The prophetical and historical song of Moses: he is commanded to go up to Mount Nebo that he may see the promised land; chap. xxxii.

The prophetical blessing of the twelve tribes. The indescribable happiness of Israel; chap. xxxi.

Moses views the promised land from the top of Mount Nebo, dies, and is privately buried by the Lord. The Israelites mourn for him thirty days. Joshua takes command of the people. The character of Moses; chap. xxxiv.

At the close of this book I have added a number of useful TABLES, such as no edition of the Bible ever could boast, viz.:

Table I. A *perpetual table*, showing through the course of 13 lunar cycles (which embrace every possible variation) *the day of the week* with which the Jewish *year* begins, and on which the *passover* is held; as also the lengths of the months *Marchesvan* and *Cisleu.*

Table II. Containing the *whole variations* in the reading of the *Pareshioth* or *sections of the law* for every year of the Jewish cycle of 247 years.

Table III. To find, with the help of Table IV., the *day of the week* upon which any Jewish *new moon* or festival happens.

Table IV. To determine upon *what day of the week any Jewish month commences* for any given year; as also *the day of the week* upon which the Jews celebrate their principal *fasts* and *festivals.*

Table V. Containing the *order of reading* the *Pareshioth* and *Haphtaroth* for 90 Jewish years, i. e., from A. M. 5572 to A. M. 5661, both inclusive, connected with the corresponding dates in the CHRISTIAN ERA, according to the *Gregorian* or *new style.*

Table VI. Containing the year of the *Jewish lunar cycle*, the *golden number*, the *first day of the Jewish passover*, *Easter Sunday*, and the *commencement* of each *Jewish year* according to the *Gregorian Calendar*, A. D. 1812 to A. D. 1900, both inclusive. All concluded with an *explanation of the preceding tables.* To them succeeds A Chronology of the Pentateuch, with the Book of Joshua; or a Systematic Arrangement of Events from the *creation* of ADAM, A. M. 1, to the *birth* of *Peleg*, A. M. 1757, and thence to the death of *Joshua*, A. M. 2561. This chronology includes *two tables*, viz.: Table I. The birth and death of all the patriarchs, from Adam, A. M. 1, to Rhea, son of Peleg, A. M. 1787. Table II. A chronology of *ancient kingdoms* synchronized with the sacred history, from A. M. 1757, B. C. 2247, to A. M. 2561, B. C. 1443. The whole so calculated as to prevent the necessity of having recourse to systems of chronology for historic facts in anywise connected with those mentioned in the SACRED WRITINGS.

The great utility of these tables will, I think, be at once evident to every Biblical critic, *chronologist*, and antiquary; and for the immense labour employed in their construction the editor, no doubt, will have their hearty thanks.

ADAM CLARKE.

THE FIFTH BOOK OF MOSES,

CALLED

DEUTERONOMY.

Year before the common Year of Christ, 1451.—Julian Period, 3263.—Cycle of the Sun, 10.—Dominical Letter, B.—Cycle of the Moon, 10.—Indiction, 15.—Creation from Tisri or September, 2553

CHAPTER I.

Introduction to the book, 1, 2. *Moses addresses the people in the fortieth year after the exodus from Egypt*, 3–5; *and shows how God had spoken to them in Horeb, and the directions he gave them*, 6–8. *How, at the commandment of the Lord, he had appointed officers, judges, &c., to share the government with him*, 9–18. *Of their travels in the terrible wilderness*, 19–21. *The people's request to have spies sent to search out the land*, 22–25. *Of their murmuring and rebellion when they heard the report of the spies*, 26–28. *How Moses encouraged them*, 29–33. *The displeasure of the Lord against them because of their murmurings, and his purpose to exclude them from the good land, and give it to their children only*, 34–40. *How they repented, and yet, without the authority of God, went against the Amorites, by whom they were defeated*, 41–44. *Their return to* Kadesh, *where they abode many days*, 45, 46.

A. M. 2553. B. C. 1451. An. Ex. Isr. 40. Sebat.

THESE *be* the words which Moses spake unto all Israel [a] on this side Jordan in the wilderness, in the plain over against [b] the Red *Sea*, between Paran, and Tophel, and Laban, and [c] Hazeroth, and Dizahab.

2 (*There are* eleven days' *journey* from Horeb by the way of Mount Seir [d] unto Kadesh-barnea.)

3 And it came to pass [e] in the fortieth year, in the eleventh month, on the first *day* of the

[a] Josh. ix. 1, 10; xxii. 4, 7.—[b] Or, *Zuph*.—[c] Num. xi. 35. xxxiii. 17, 18.—[d] Num. xiii. 26; ch. ix. 23.—[e] Num. xxxiii. 38.

NOTES ON CHAP. I.

Verse 1. *These* be *the words which Moses spake*] The *five* first verses of this chapter contain the introduction to the rest of the book: they do not appear to be the work of Moses, but were added probably either by Joshua or Ezra.

On this side Jordan] בעבר *beeber, at the passage* of Jordan, i. e., near or opposite to the place where the Israelites passed over after the death of Moses. Though עבר *eber* is used to signify both on *this side* and on *the other side*, and the connection in which it stands can only determine the meaning; yet here it signifies neither, but simply the *place* or *ford* where the Israelites *passed over* Jordan.

In the plain] That is, of Moab; *over against the Red* Sea—not the *Red Sea*, for they were now farther from it than they had yet been: the word *sea* is not in the text, and the word סוף *suph*, which we render *red*, does not signify the *Red Sea*, unless joined with ים *yam*, *sea*; here it must necessarily signify a *place* in or adjoining to the plains of Moab. Ptolemy mentions a people named *Sophonites*, that dwelt in *Arabia Petrœa*, and it is probable that they took their name from this place; but see the note from *Lightfoot*, Num. xx., at the end.

Paran] This could not have been the Paran which was contiguous to the Red Sea, and not far from Mount Horeb; for the place here mentioned lay on the very borders of the promised land, at a vast distance from the former.

Dizahab.] The word should be separated, as it is in the Hebrew, די זהב *Di Zahab*. As *Zahab* signifies *gold*, the Septuagint have translated it τα χρυσεια, the *gold mines;* and the Vulgate *ubi aurum est plurimum*, where there is much gold. It is more likely to be the name of a *place*.

Verse 2. There are *eleven days' journey*] The Israelites were eleven days in going from Horeb to Kadesh-barnea, where they were near the verge of the promised land; after which they were thirty-eight years wandering up and down in the vicinity of this place, not being permitted, because of their rebellions, to enter into the promised rest, though they were the whole of that time within a few miles of the land of Canaan!

Verse 3. *The fortieth year*] This was a melancholy

A. M. 2553. B. C. 1451. An. Ex. Isr. 40. Sebat.

month, *that* Moses spake unto
the children of Israel, according
unto all that the LORD had given
him in commandment unto them;
4 [f] After he had slain Sihon the king of the
Amorites, which dwelt in Heshbon, and Og
the king of Bashan, which dwelt at Astaroth
[g] in Edrei:
5 On this side Jordan, in the land of Moab,
began Moses to declare this law, saying,
6 The LORD our God spake unto us [h] in
Horeb, saying, Ye have dwelt long [i] enough
in this mount:
7 Turn you, and take your journey, and go
to the mount of the Amorites, and unto [k] all
the places nigh thereunto, in the plain, in the
hills, and in the vale, and in the south, and
by the sea-side, to the land of the Canaanites,
and unto Lebanon, unto the great river, the
river Euphrates.
8 Behold, I have [l] set the land
before you: go in and possess
the land which the LORD sware
unto your fathers, [m] Abraham, Isaac, and
Jacob, to give unto them and to their seed
after them.
9 And [n] I spake unto you at that time, say
ing, I am not able to bear you myself alone.
10 The LORD your God hath multiplied you,
and, behold, [o] ye *are* this day as the stars of
heaven for multitude.
11 ([p] The LORD God of your fathers make
you a thousand times so many more as ye *are*,
and bless you, [q] as he hath promised you!)
12 [r] How can I myself alone bear your cum-
brance, and your burden, and your strife!
13 [s] Take [t] you wise men, and understanding, and known among your tribes, and I will
make them rulers over you.
14 And ye answered me, and said, The thing

A. M. 2553. B. C. 1451. An. Ex. Isr. 40. Sebat.

[f] Numbers xxi. 24, 33.——[g] Num. xxi. 33; Joshua xiii. 12.——[h] Exod. iii. 1.——[i] See Exod. xix. 1; Num. x. 11.——[k] Heb. *all his neighbours*.——[l] Heb. *given*.——[m] Gen. xii. 7; xv. 18; xvii. 7, 8; xxvi. 4; xxviii. 13.

[n] Exod. xviii. 18; Num. xi. 14.——[o] Gen. xv. 5; chap. x. 22; xxviii. 62.——[p] 2 Sam. xxiv. 3.——[q] Gen. xv. 5; xxii. 17; xxvi. 4; Exod. xxxii. 13.——[r] 1 Kings iii. 8, 9.——[s] See Exod. xviii. 21; Num. xi. 16, 17.——[t] Heb. *give*.

year to the Hebrews in different respects; in the first month of this year Miriam died, Num. xx.; on the first day of the fifth month Aaron died, Num. xxxiii. 38; and about the conclusion of it, Moses himself died.

Verse 5. *Began Moses to declare this law*] Began, הואיל *hoil*, willingly undertook; to declare, באר *beer*, to make *bare, clear, &c., fully to explain*, this law. See the conclusion of the preface.

Verse 6. *Ye have dwelt long enough, &c.*] They came to Sinai in the third month after their departure from Egypt, Exod. xix. 1, 2; and left it the twentieth of the second month of the second year, so it appears they had continued there nearly a whole year.

Verse 7. *Go to the mount of the Amorites*] On the south of the land of Canaan, towards the Dead Sea.

Land of the Canaanites] That is, Phœnicia, the country of Sidon, and the coasts of the Mediterranean Sea from the country of the Philistines to Mount Libanus. The *Canaanites* and *Phœnicians* are often confounded.

The river Euphrates.] Thus Moses fixes the bounds of the land, to which on all quarters the territories of the Israelites might be extended, should the land of Canaan, properly so called, be found insufficient for them. Their SOUTH border might extend to the mount of the Amorites; their WEST to the borders of the Mediterranean Sea; their NORTH to Lebanon; and their EAST border to the river Euphrates: and to this extent Solomon reigned; see 1 Kings iv. 21. So that in his time, at least, the promise to Abraham was literally fulfilled; see below.

Vese 10. *Ye are this day as the stars of heaven for multitude.*] This was the promise God made to Abraham, Gen. xv. 5, 6; and Moses considers it now as amply fulfilled. But was it really so? Many suppose the expression to be hyperbolical; and others, no friends to revelation, think it a vain empty boast, because the stars, in their apprehension, amount to innumerable millions. Let us consider this subject. How many in number are the stars which appear to the naked eye? for it is by *what appears to the naked eye* we are to be governed in this business, for *God brought Abraham forth abroad*, i. e., out of doors, *and bade him look towards heaven*, not with a telescope, but with his naked eyes, Gen. xv. 5. Now I shall beg the objector to come forth abroad, and look up in the brightest and most favourable night, and count the stars—he need not be terrified at their abundance; the more they are, the more he can count; and I shall pledge myself to find a male Israelite in the very last census taken of this people, Num. xxvi., for every star he finds in the whole upper hemisphere of heaven. The truth is, only about 3,010 stars can be seen by the naked eye in both the northern and southern hemispheres; and the Israelites, independently of women and children, were at the above time more than 600,000. And suppose we even allow that, from the late discoveries of Dr. Herschel and others with telescopes which have magnified between 35 and 36,000 times, there may be 75 millions of stars visible by the help of such instruments, which is the highest calculation ever made, yet still the Divine word stands literally true: St. Matthew says, chap. i., that the generations from Abraham to Christ were 42; now we find at the second census that the fighting men among the Hebrews amounted to 603,000; and the Israelites, who have never ceased to be a distinct people, have so multiplied as far to exceed the number of all the fixed stars taken together.

Verse 13. *Take you wise men*] חכמים *chachamim*, such as had gained knowledge by great labour and study. *Understanding* נבנים *nebonim*, persons of dis-

A. M. 2553.
B. C. 1451.
An. Ex. Isr. 40.
Sebat.

which thou hast spoken *is* good *for us* to do.

15 So I took the chief of your tribes, wise men, and known, [u] and [v] made them heads over you, captains over thousands, and captains over hundreds, and captains over fifties, and captains over tens, and officers among your tribes.

16 And I charged your judges at that time, saying, Hear *the causes* between your brethren, and [w] judge righteously between *every* man and his [x] brother, and the stranger *that is* with him.

17 [y] Ye shall not [z] respect persons in judgment; *but* ye shall hear the small as well as the great; ye shall not be afraid of the face of man; for [a] the judgment *is* God's: and the cause that is too hard for you, [b] bring *it* unto me, and I will hear it.

18 And I commanded you at that time, all the things which ye should do.

19 And when we departed from Horeb, [c] we went through all that great and terrible wilderness, which ye saw by the way of the mountain of the Amorites, as the LORD our God commanded us; and [d] we came to Kadesh-barnea.

20 And I said unto you, Ye are come unto the mountain of the Amorites, which the LORD our God doth give unto us.

21 Behold, the LORD thy God hath set the land before thee: go up *and* possess *it*, as the LORD God of thy fathers hath said unto thee; [e] fear not, neither be discouraged.

A. M. 2553.
B. C. 1451.
An. Ex. Isr. 40.
Sebat.

22 And ye came near unto me every one of you, and said, We will send men before us, and they shall search us out the land, and bring us word again by what way we must go up, and into what cities we shall come.

23 And the saying pleased me well: and [f] I took twelve men of you, one of a tribe:

24 And [g] they turned and went up into the mountain, and came unto the valley of Eshcol, and searched it out.

25 And they took of the fruit of the land in their hands, and brought *it* down unto us, and brought us word again, and said, [h] *It is* a good land which the LORD our God doth give us.

26 [i] Notwithstanding ye would not go up, but rebelled against the commandment of the LORD your God:

27 And ye murmured in your tents, and said, Because the LORD [k] hated us, he hath brought us forth out of the land of Egypt, to deliver us into the hand of the Amorites, to destroy us.

28 Whither shall we go up? our brethren have [l] discouraged our heart, saying, [m] The people *is* greater and taller than we; the cities *are* great and walled up to heaven; and moreover we have seen the sons of the [n] Anakims there.

[u] Exod. xviii. 25.——[v] Heb. *gave.*——[w] Chap. xvi. 18; John vii. 24.——[x] Lev. xxiv. 22.——[y] Lev. xix. 15; chap. xvi. 19; 1 Sam. xvi. 7; Prov. xxiv. 23; James ii. 1.——[z] Heb. *acknowledge faces.*——[a] 2 Chron. xix. 6.——[b] Exod. xviii. 22, 26.——[c] Num. x. 12; chap. viii. 15; Jer. ii. 6.

[d] Num. xiii. 26.——[e] Josh. i. 9.——[f] Num. xiii. 3.——[g] Num. xiii. 22, 23, 24.——[h] Num. xiii. 27.——[i] Numbers xiv. 1, 2, 3, 4; Psa. cvi. 24, 25.——[k] Chapter ix. 28.——[l] Heb. *melted;* Josh. ii. 11.——[m] Num. xiii. 28, 31, 32, 33; chap. ix. 1, 2.——[n] Num. xiii. 28.

cernment, judicious men. *Known*, ידעים *yeduim*, persons practised in the operations of nature, capable of performing curious and important works.

Verse 15. *Captains over thousands, &c.*] What a curious and well-regulated economy was that of the Israelites! See its order and arrangement: 1. GOD, the KING and Supreme Judge; 2. *Moses*, God's prime minister; 3. The *priests*, consulting him by *Urim* and *Thummim;* 4. The *chiefs* or princes of the twelve tribes; 5. *Chiliarchs*, or captains over thousands; 6. *Centurions*, or captains over hundreds; 7. *Tribunes*, or captains over fifty men; 8. *Decurions*, or captains over ten men; and, 9. *Officers*, persons who might be employed by the different chiefs in executing particular commands. All these held their authority from God, and yet were subject and accountable to each other. See the notes on Num. ii.

Verse 17. *Ye shall not respect persons*] Heb. *faces.* Let not the bold, daring countenance of the rich or mighty induce you to give an unrighteous decision; and let not the abject look of the poor man induce you either to favour him in an unrighteous cause, or to give judgment against him at the demand of the oppressor. Be uncorrupt and incorruptible, for *the judgment is God's;* ye minister in the place of God, act like HIM.

Verse 22. *We will send men before us*] See on Num. xiii.

Verse 28. *Cities—walled up to heaven*] That is, with very high walls which could not be easily scaled. High walls around houses, &c., in these parts of Arabia are still deemed a sufficient defence against the Arabs, who scarcely ever attempt any thing in the way of plunder but on *horseback.* The monastery on Mount Sinai is surrounded with very high walls without any *gate;* in the upper part of the wall there is a sort of window, or opening, from which a basket is suspended by a pulley, by which both persons and goods are received into and sent from the place. It is the same with the convent of St. Anthony, in Egypt; and this sort of wall is deemed a sufficient defence against the Arabs, who, as we have already observed, scarcely ever like to alight from their horses.

A. M. 2553.
B. C. 1451.
An. Ex. Isr. 40.
Sebat.

29 Then I said unto you, Dread not, neither be afraid of them.

30 [o] The LORD your God which goeth before you, he shall fight for you, according to all that he did for you in Egypt before your eyes;

31 And in the wilderness, where thou hast seen how that the LORD thy God [p] bare thee, as a man doth bear his son, in all the way that ye went, until ye came into this place.

32 Yet in this thing [q] ye did not believe the LORD your God,

33 [r] Who went in the way before you, [s] to search you out a place to pitch your tents *in*, in fire by night, to show you by what way ye should go, and in a cloud by day.

34 And the LORD heard the voice of your words, and was wroth, [t] and sware, saying,

35 [u] Surely there shall not one of these men of this evil generation see that good land, which I sware to give unto your fathers,

36 [v] Save Caleb the son of Jephunneh; he shall see it, and to him will I give the land that he hath trodden upon, and to his children, because [w] he hath [x] wholly followed the LORD.

37 [y] Also the LORD was angry with me for your sakes, saying, Thou also shalt not go in thither.

38 [z] *But* Joshua the son of Nun, [a] which standeth before thee, he shall go in thither; [b] encourage him, for he shall cause Israel to inherit it.

A. M. 2553.
B. C. 1451.
An. Ex. Isr. 40.
Sebat.

39 [c] Moreover your little ones, which [d] ye said should be a prey, and your children, which in that day [e] had no knowledge between good and evil, they shall go in thither, and unto them will I give it, and they shall possess it.

40 [f] But *as for* you, turn you, and take your journey into the wilderness by the way of the Red Sea.

41 Then ye answered and said unto me, [g] We have sinned against the LORD, we will go up and fight, according to all that the LORD our God commanded us. And when ye had girded on every man his weapons of war, ye were ready to go up into the hill.

42 And the LORD said unto me, Say unto them, [h] Go not up, neither fight; for I *am* not among you; lest ye be smitten before your enemies.

43 So I spake unto you; and ye would not hear, but rebelled against the commandment of the LORD, and [i] went [k] presumptuously up into the hill.

44 And the Amorites, which dwelt in that mountain, came out against you and chased you, [l] as bees do, and destroyed you in Seir, *even* unto Hormah.

45 And ye returned and [m] wept before the LORD; but the LORD [n] would not hearken to your voice, nor give ear unto you.

46 [o] So ye abode in Kadesh many days, according unto the days that ye abode *there*.

[o] Exod. xiv. 14, 25; Neh. iv. 20.——[p] Exod. xix. 4; chap. xxxii. 11, 12; Isa. xlvi. 3, 4; lxiii. 9; Hos. xi. 3; see on Acts xiii. 18. [q] Psa. cvi. 24; Jude 5.——[r] Exod. xiii. 21; Psa. lxxviii. 14. [s] Num. x. 33; Ezek. xx. 6.——[t] Chap. ii. 14, 15.——[u] Num. xiv. 22, 23; Psa. xcv. 11.——[v] Num. xiv. 24, 30; Josh. xiv. 9. [w] Num. xiv. 24.——[x] Heb. *fulfilled* to go *after*.——[y] Num. xx. 12; xxvii. 14; chap. iii. 26; iv. 21; xxxiv. 4; Psa. cvi. 32.

[z] Num. xiv. 30.——[a] Exod. xxiv. 13; xxxiii. 11; see 1 Sam. xvi. 22.——[b] Num. xxvii. 18, 19; chap. xxxi. 7, 23.——[c] Num. xiv. 31.——[d] Num. xiv. 3.——[e] Isa. vii. 15, 16; Rom. ix. 11. [f] Num. xiv. 25.——[g] Num. xiv. 40.——[h] Num. xiv. 42.——[i] Heb. *ye were presumptuous and went up*.——[k] Num. xiv. 44, 45. [l] Psa. cxviii. 12.——[m] Psa. lxxviii. 34.——[n] Heb. xii. 17. [o] Num. xiii. 25; xx. 1, 22; Judg. xi. 17.

Verse 30. *The Lord—shall fight for you*] In the *Targum* of Onkelos, it is, the WORD of *the Lord shall fight for you.* In a great number of places the Targums or Chaldee paraphrases use the term מימרא דיי *meimera dayeya* or *Yehovah*, the Word of the Lord, exactly in the same way in which St. John uses the term Λογος *Logos* in the first chapter of his Gospel. Many instances of this have already occurred.

Verse 34. *The Lord—was wroth*] That is, his justice was incensed, and he evidenced his displeasure against you; and he could not have been a *just* God if he had not done so.

Verse 36. *Caleb—wholly followed the Lord.*] See on Num. xiv. 24.

Verse 37. *The Lord was angry with me*] See on Num. xx. 10, &c., where a particular account is given of the sin of Moses.

Verse 44. *The Amorites—chased you*] See the note on Num. xiv. 40; *as bees do*—by irresistible numbers.

Verse 46. *According unto the days that ye abode* there.] They had been a long time at this place, see Num. xiii. 27; xx. 1, 14, 21. And some think that the words mean, "Ye abode as long at Kadesh, when you came to it the second time, as ye did at the first." Or, according to others, "While ye were in that part of the desert, ye encamped at Kadesh."

1. As one grand object of the law of God was to instruct the people in those things which were calculated to *promote* their *peace* and *insure* their *prosperity*; and as they were apt to lose sight of their *spiritual* interests, without a due attention to which their *secular* interest could not be promoted; Moses, not only in this chapter, but through the whole book, calls upon them

to recollect their former miserable situation, in which they held neither *life* nor *property* but at the *will* of a *merciless tyrant*, and the great kindness and power of God manifested in their deliverance from a bondage that was as *degrading* as it was *oppressive*. These things properly remembered would lead them to prize their blessings, and duly appreciate the mercy of their Maker.

2. But it was not only this general display of God's kindness, in the grand act of their deliverance from Egypt, that he wished them to keep constantly in view, but also that gracious *providence* which was manifested in every step they took; which directed all their movements, provided for all their wants, continually showing *what* they should do, *how* they should do it, and also the most proper *time* and *place* for every act, whether *religious* or *civil*. By bringing before them in one point of view the history of almost *forty years*, in which the strangest and most stupendous occurrences had taken place that had ever been exhibited to the world, he took the readiest way to impress their minds, not only with their deep obligation to God, but also to show them that they were a people on whom their Maker had set his heart to do them good, and that if they feared him they should lack nothing that was good. He lays out also before them a history of their miscarriages and rebellion, and the privations and evils they had suffered in consequence, that this might act as a continual *warning*, and thus become, in the hands of God, a preventive of crimes.

3. If every *Christian* were thus to call his past life into review, he would see equal proofs of God's gracious regards to his body and soul; equal proofs of eternal mercy in providing for his deliverance from the galling yoke and oppressive tyranny of sin, as the Israelites had in their deliverance from Egypt; and equal displays of a most gracious providence, that had also been his incessant companion through all the changes and chances of this mortal life, guiding him by its counsel, that he might be at last received into glory. O reader, remember what God has done for *thee* during *thy* forty, fifty, &c., years! He has nourished, fed, clothed, protected, and saved *thee*. How often and how powerfully has his Spirit striven with thee! How often and how impressively thou hast heard his voice in his Gospel and in his providences! Remember the good resolutions thou hast made, the ingratitude and disobedience that have marked thy life; how his vows are *still* upon thee, and how his mercy still *spares* thee! And wilt thou live so as to perish for ever? God forbid! He *still* waits to be gracious, and rejoices over thee to do thee good. Learn from what is before thee how thou shouldst fear, love, believe in, and obey thy God. The Lamb of God, that taketh away the sin of the world, is still before the throne; and whosoever cometh unto God through him shall in nowise be cast out. He who believes these things with an upright heart will soon be enabled to live a sanctified life.

CHAPTER II.

Moses continues to relate how they compassed Mount Seir, 1. *And the commands they received not to meddle with the descendants of* Esau, 2–8; *nor to distress the* Moabites, 9. *Of the* Emims, 10, 11; *the* Horims, 12. *Their passage of the brook* Zered, 13. *The time they spent between* Kadesh-barnea *and* Zered, 14; *during which all the men of war that came out of Egypt were consumed*, 15, 16. *The command not to distress the* Ammonites, 17–19. *Of the* Zamzummims, 20, *the* Anakims, 21, *the* Horims, 22, *the* Avims *and* Caphtorims, *all destroyed by the* Ammonites, 23. *They are commanded to cross the river* Arnon, *and are promised the land of* Sihon, *king of the Amorites*, 24, 25. *Of the message sent to* Sihon, *to request a passage through his territories*, 26–29. *His refusal*, 30. *The consequent war*, 31, 32. *His total overthrow*, 33; *and extermination of his people*, 34. *The spoils that were taken*, 35. *And his land possessed from* Aroer *to* Arnon *by the Israelites*, 36; *who took care, according to the command of God, not to invade any part of the territories of the* Ammonites, 37.

A. M. 2553. B. C. 1451. An. Ex. Isr. 40. Sebat.

THEN we turned, and took our journey into the wilderness by the way of the Red Sea, [a] as the LORD spake unto me: and we compassed Mount Seir many days.

2 And the LORD spake unto me, saying,

3 Ye have compassed this mountain [b] long enough: turn you northward.

4 And command thou the people, saying, [c] Ye *are* to pass through the coast of your brethren the children of Esau, which dwell in Seir; and they shall be afraid of you: take ye good heed unto yourselves therefore:

5 Meddle not with them; for I will not give you of their land, [d] no, not so much as a foot breadth; [e] because I have given Mount Seir unto Esau *for* a possession.

[a] Num. xiv. 25; chap. i. 40.——[b] See ver. 7, 14.——[c] Num. xx. 14.——[d] Hebrew, *even to the treading of the sole of the foot*.——[e] Gen. xxxvi. 8; Josh. xxiv. 4.

NOTES ON CHAP. II.

Verse 3. *Turn you northward.*] From Mount Seir, in order to get to Canaan. This was not the way they went before, viz., by Kadesh-barnea, but they were to proceed between Edom on the one hand, and Moab and Ammon on the other, so as to enter into Canaan through the land of the Amorites.

Verse 5. *Meddle not with them*] That is, the Edomites. See on Num. xx. 14–21.

A. M. 2553.
B. C. 1451.
An. Ex. Isr. 40.
Sebat.

6 Ye shall buy meat of them for money, that ye may eat; and ye shall also buy water of them for money, that ye may drink.

7 For the LORD thy God hath blessed thee in all the works of thy hand: he knoweth thy walking through this great wilderness: [f] these forty years the LORD thy God *hath been* with thee; thou hast lacked nothing.

8 [g] And when we passed by from our brethren the children of Esau, which dwelt in Seir, through the way of the plain from [h] Elath, and from Ezion-gaber, we turned and passed by the way of the wilderness of Moab.

9 And the LORD said unto me, [i] Distress not the Moabites, neither contend with them in battle: for I will not give thee of their land *for* a possession; because I have given [k] Ar unto [l] the children of Lot *for* a possession.

10 [m] The Emims dwelt therein in times past, a people great, and many, and tall, as [n] the Anakims;

11 Which also were accounted giants, as the Anakims; but the Moabites call them Emims.

12 [o] The Horims also dwelt in Seir beforetime; but the children of Esau [p] succeeded them, when they had destroyed them from before them, and dwelt in their [q] stead; as Israel did unto the land of his possession, which the LORD gave unto them.

A. M. 2553.
B. C. 1451.
An. Ex. Isr. 40.
Sebat.

13 Now rise up, *said I,* and get you over [r] the [s] brook Zered. And we went over the brook Zered.

14 And the space in which we came [t] from Kadesh-barnea, until we were come over the brook Zered, *was* thirty and eight years; [u] until all the generation of the men of war were wasted out from among the host, [v] as the LORD sware unto them.

15 For indeed the [w] hand of the LORD was against them, to destroy them from among the host, until they were consumed.

16 So it came to pass, when all the men of war were consumed and dead from among the people,

17 That the LORD spake unto me, saying,

18 Thou art to pass over through Ar, the coast of Moab, this day:

19 And *when* thou comest nigh over against the children of Ammon, distress them not, nor meddle with them: for I will not give thee of the land of the children of Ammon *any* possession; because I have given it unto [x] the children of Lot *for* a possession.

20 (That also was accounted a land of giants: giants dwelt therein in old time; and the Ammonites call them [y] Zamzummims;

21 [z] A people great, and many, and tall, as the Anakims; but the LORD destroyed them

[f] Chap. viii. 2, 3, 4.——[g] Judg. xi. 18.——[h] 1 Kings ix. 26.——[i] Or, *Use no hostility against Moab.*——[k] Num. xxi. 28.——[l] Gen. xix. 36, 37.——[m] Gen. xiv. 5.——[n] Num. xiii. 22, 33; chap. ix. 2.——[o] Ver. 22; Gen. xiv. 6; xxxvi. 20.——[p] Heb. *inherited them.*——[q] Or, *room.*

[r] Num. xxi. 12.——[s] Or, *valley;* Num. xiii. 23.——[t] Numbers xiii. 26.——[u] Numbers xiv. 33; xxvi. 64.——[v] Numbers xiv. 35; chap. i. 34, 35; Ezek. xx. 15.——[w] Psa. lxxviii. 33; cvi. 26.——[x] Gen. xix. 38.——[y] Gen. xiv. 5, *Zuzims.*——[z] See verse 10.

Verse 7. *The Lord—hath blessed thee, &c.*] God had given them much property, and therefore they had no need of plunder; they had gold and silver to buy the provender they needed, and therefore God would not permit them to take any thing by violence.

Verse 10. *The Emims dwelt therein*] Calmet supposes that these people were destroyed in the war made against them by Chedorlaomer and his allies, Gen. xiv. 5. Lot possessed their country after the destruction of Sodom and Gomorrha. They are generally esteemed as *giants;* probably they were a hardy, fierce, and terrible people, who lived, like the wandering Arabs, on the plunder of others. This was sufficient to gain them the appellation of giants, or men of prodigious stature. See below.

Verse 11. *Which also were accounted giants*] This is not a fortunate version. The word is not *giants*, but רפאים *Rephaim*, the name of a *people*. It appears that the *Emim*, the *Anakim*, and the *Rephaim*, were probably the same people, called by different names in the different countries where they dwelt; for they appear originally to have been a kind of wandering freebooters, who lived by plunder. (See on the preceding verse.) It must be granted, however, that there were several men of this race of extraordinary stature. And hence all gigantic men have been called *Rephaim.* (See on Gen. vi. 4, and xiv. 5.) But we well know that *fear* and *public report* have often added whole cubits to men's height. It was under this influence that the spies acted, when they brought the disheartening report mentioned Num. xiii. 33.

Verse 12. *The Horims also dwelt in Seir*] The whole of this verse was probably added by Joshua or Ezra.

Verse 20. *That also was accounted a land of giants*] That was accounted the land or territory of the *Rephaim.*

Zamzummims] Supposed to be the same as the *Zuzim*, Gen. xiv. 5. Of these ancient people we know very little; they were probably inconsiderable tribes or clans, "pursuing and pursued, each other's prey," till at length a *stronger* totally destroyed or subdued them, and their name became either extinct or absorbed in that of their conquerors. From the 10th to the 12th, and from the 20th to the 23d verse inclusive, we have certain historical remarks introduced

A. M. 2553.
B. C. 1451.
An. Ex. Isr. 40.
Sebat.

before them; and they succeeded them, and dwelt in their stead:

22 As he did to the children of Esau, [a] which dwelt in Seir, when he destroyed [b] the Horims from before them; and they succeeded them, and dwelt in their stead even unto this day:

23 And [c] the Avims which dwelt in Hazerim, *even* unto [d] Azzah, [e] the Caphtorims, which came forth out of Caphtor, destroyed them, and dwelt in their stead.)

24 Rise ye up, take your journey, and [f] pass over the river Arnon: behold, I have given into thine hand Sihon the Amorite, king of Heshbon, and his land: [g] begin to possess *it*, and contend with him in battle.

25 [h] This day will I begin to put the dread of thee, and the fear of thee, upon the nations *that are* under the whole heaven, who shall hear report of thee, and shall tremble, and be in anguish because of thee.

26 And I sent messengers out of the wilderness of Kedemoth, unto Sihon king of Heshbon, [i] with words of peace, saying,

27 [k] Let me pass through thy land: I will go along by the high-way, I will neither turn unto the right hand nor to the left.

28 Thou shalt sell me meat for money, that I may eat; and give me water for money, that I may drink: [l] only I will pass through on my feet;

29 ([m] As the children of Esau which dwell in Seir, and the Moabites which dwell in Ar, did unto me;) until I shall pass over Jordan, into the land which the Lord our God giveth us.

A. M. 2553.
B. C. 1451.
An. Ex. Isr. 40
Sebat.

30 [n] But Sihon king of Heshbon would not let us pass by him: for [o] the Lord thy God [p] hardened his spirit, and made his heart obstinate, that he might deliver him into thy hand, as *appeareth* this day.

31 And the Lord said unto me, Behold, I have begun to [q] give Sihon and his land before thee: begin to possess, that thou mayest inherit his land.

32 [r] Then Sihon came out against us, he and all his people, to fight at Jahaz.

33 And [s] the Lord our God delivered him before us; and [t] we smote him, and his sons, and all his people.

34 And we took all his cities at that time, and [u] utterly destroyed [v] the men, and the women, and the little ones, of every city, we left none to remain:

35 Only the cattle we took for a prey unto ourselves, and the spoil of the cities which we took.

36 [w] From Aroer, which *is* by the brink of the river of Arnon, and *from* the city that *is* by the river, even unto Gilead, there was not one city too strong for us: [x] the Lord our God delivered all unto us:

37 Only unto the land of the children of Ammon thou camest not, *nor* unto any place of the river [y] Jabbok, nor unto the cities in the mountains, nor unto [z] whatsoever the Lord our God forbade us.

---

[a] Gex. xxxvi. 8.——[b] Gen. xiv. 6; xxxvi. 20–30; ver. 12.——[c] Josh. xiii. 3.——[d] Jer. xxv. 20.——[e] Gen. x. 14; Amos ix. 7.——[f] Num. xxi. 13, 14; Judg. xi. 18, 21.——[g] Heb. *begin, possess.*——[h] Exod. xv. 14, 15; chap. xi. 25; Josh. ii. 9, 10.——[i] Chap. xx. 10.——[k] Num. xxi. 21, 22; Judg. xi. 19.——[l] Num. xxi. 19.——[m] See Num. xx. 18; chap. xxiii. 3, 4; Judg. xi. 17, 18.

[n] Num. xxi. 23.——[o] Josh. xi. 20.——[p] Exod. iv. 21.——[q] Chap. i. 8.——[r] Num. xxi. 23.——[s] Chap. vii. 2; xx. 16.——[t] Num. xxi. 24; chap. xxix. 7.——[u] Lev. xxvii. 28; chap. vii. 2, 26.——[v] Heb. *every city of men, and women, and little ones.*——[w] Chap. iii. 12; iv. 48; Josh. xiii. 9.——[x] Psa. xliv. 3.——[y] Gen. xxxii. 22; Num. xxi. 24; chap. iii. 16.——[z] Ver. 5, 9, 19.

---

which do not seem to have been made by Moses, but rather by Joshua or Ezra. By the introduction of these verses the thread of the narrative suffers considerable interruption. Dr. Kennicott considers both these passages to be interpolations. That they could not have made a part of the speech of Moses originally, needs little proof.

Verse 29. *As the children of Esau which dwell in Seir*] See the note on Num. xx. 21.

Verse 30. *The Lord—hardened his spirit*] See the notes on Exod. iv. 21, and ix. 15, &c.

Verse 36. *From Aroer—by the brink of the river of Arnon*] See on Num. xxi. 13, &c.

Verse 37. *Only unto the land of the children of Ammon thou camest not*] God gave them their commission; and those only were to be cut off, the cup of whose iniquity was full. Though the Moabites and Ammonites were thus spared, they requited good with evil, for they fought against the Israelites, and cast them out of their possessions, Judg. xi. 4, 5; 2 Chron. xx. 1, &c., and committed the most shocking cruelties; see Amos i. 13. Hence God enacted a law, that none of these people should enter into the congregation of the Lord even to their tenth generation: see chap. xxiii. 3–6.

CHAPTER III.

The war with OG, *king of* Bashan, 1, 2. *He is defeated,* 3. *Sixty fortified* cities *with many unwalled towns taken,* 4, 5. *The utter destruction of the people,* 6. *The spoils,* 7; *and extent of the land taken,* 8–10. *Account of* OG's *iron bedstead,* 11. *The land given to the* Reubenites, Gadites, *and half tribe of* Manasseh, 12, 13. Jair *takes the country of* Argob, 14. Gilead *is given unto* Machir, 15. *And the rest of the land possessed by the* Reubenites *and* Gadites, 16, 17. *The directions given to those tribes,* 18–20. *The counsel given to Joshua,* 21, 22. *Moses's prayer to God for permission to go into the promised land,* 23–25; *and God's refusal,* 26. *He is commanded to go up to Mount* Pisgah *to see it,* 27; *and to encourage Joshua,* 28. *They continue in the valley opposite to* Beth-peor, 29.

A. M. 2553. B. C. 1451. An. Ex. Isr. 40. Sebat.

THEN we turned, and went up the way to Bashan: and [a] Og the king of Bashan came out against us, he and all his people, to battle [b] at Edrei.
2 And the LORD said unto me, Fear him not: for I will deliver him, and all his people, and his land, into thy hand; and thou shalt do unto him as thou didst unto [c] Sihon king of the Amorites, which dwelt at Heshbon.
3 So the LORD our God delivered into our hands Og also, the king of Bashan, and all his people: [d] and we smote him until none was left to him remaining.
4 And we took all his cities at that time, there was not a city which we took not from them, threescore cities, [e] all the region of Argob, the kingdom of Og in Bashan.
5 All these cities *were* fenced with high walls, gates, and bars; beside unwalled towns a great many.
6 And we utterly destroyed them, as we did unto Sihon, king of Heshbon, utterly destroying the men, women, and children, of every city.
7 But all the cattle, and the spoil of the cities, we took for a prey to ourselves.
8 And we took at that time out of the hand of the two kings of the Amorites the land that *was* on this side Jordan, from the river of Arnon unto Mount Hermon;
9 (*Which* [g] Hermon the Sidonians call Sirion; and the Amorites call it [h] Shenir;)
10 [i] All the cities of the plain, and all Gilead, and [k] all Bashan, unto Salchah and Edrei, cities of the kingdom of Og in Bashan.
11 [l] For only Og king of Bashan remained of the remnant of [m] giants: behold, his bedstead *was* a bedstead of iron; *is* it not in [n] Rabbath, of the children of Ammon? nine cubits *was* the length thereof, and four cubits the breadth of it, after the cubit of a man.
12 And this land, *which* we possessed at that time, [o] from Aroer, which *is* by the river Arnon, and half Mount Gilead, and [p] the cities thereof, gave I unto the Reubenites and to the Gadites.
13 [q] And the rest of Gilead, and all Bashan, *being* the kingdom of Og, gave I unto the half tribe of Manasseh; all the region of Argob, with all Bashan, which was called the land of giants.

[a] Num. xxi. 33, &c.; chap. xxix. 7.——[b] Chap. i. 4.——[c] Num. xxi. 24.——[d] Num. xxi. 35.——[e] 1 Kings iv. 13.——[f] Chap. ii. 24; Psa. cxxxv. 10, 11, 12; cxxxvi. 19, 20, 21.——[g] Chap. iv. 48; Psa. xxix. 6.——[h] 1 Chron. v. 23.——[i] Chap. iv. 49.

[k] Josh. xii. 5; xiii. 11.——[l] Amos ii. 9.——[m] Gen. xiv. 5.——[n] 2 Sam. xii. 26; Jer. xlix. 2; Ezek. xxi. 20.——[o] Chap. ii. 36; Josh. xii. 2.——[p] Num. xxxii. 33; Josh. xii. 6; xiii. 8, &c.——[q] Josh. xiii. 29.

NOTES ON CHAP. III.

Verse 4. *All the region of Argob*] כל חבל ארגב *col chebel Argob*, all the *cable* or cord of Argob; this expression, which is used in various other parts of Scripture,) see, in the original, Amos vii. 17; Mic. ii. 5; Deut. xxxii. 9; Psa. xv. 6,) shows that anciently land was measured by lines or cords of a certain length, in a similar way to that by the *chain* among us, and the *schœnus* or cord among the Egyptians. Some think that it was the region of Argob that was afterwards called the region of *Trachonitis*.

Verse 9. *Hermon the Sidonians call—Shenir*] I suppose this verse to have been a marginal remark, which afterwards got incorporated with the text, or an addition by Joshua or Ezra.

Verse 11. *Og king of Bashan remained*] Og was the last king of the Amorites; his kingdom appears to have taken its name from the hill of *Bashan;* the country has been since called *Batanæa*.

Remnant of giants] Of the *Rephaim*. See on chap. ii. 10, 11.

His bedstead was—*of iron*] Iron was probably used partly for its strength and durability, and partly to prevent noxious vermin from harbouring in it.

Is *it not in Rabbath, of the children of Ammon?*] The bedstead was probably taken in some battle between the Ammonites and Amorites, in which the former had gained the victory. The bedstead was carried a trophy and placed in Rabbath, which appears, from 2 Sam. xii. 26, to have been the *royal city* of the children of Ammon.

Nine cubits was *the length—four cubits the breadth*]

A. M. 2553.
B. C. 1451.
An. Ex. Isr. 40.
Sebat.

14 [r] Jair the son of Manasseh took all the country of Argob [s] unto the coasts of Geshuri and Maachathi; and [t] called them after his own name, Bashan-havoth-jair, unto this day.

15 [u] And I gave Gilead unto Machir.

16 And unto the Reubenites [v] and unto the Gadites I gave from Gilead even unto the river Arnon half the valley, and the border even unto the river Jabbok, [w] *which is* the border of the children of Ammon:

17 The plain also, and Jordan, and the coast *thereof*, from [x] Chinnereth [y] even unto the sea of the plain, [z] *even* the salt sea, [a] under Ashdoth-pisgah eastward.

18 And I commanded you at that time, saying, The LORD your God hath given you this land to possess it: [b] ye shall pass over armed before your brethren the children of Israel, all *that are* [c] meet for the war.

19 But your wives, and your little ones, and your cattle, (*for* I know that ye have much cattle,) shall abide in your cities which I have given you;

20 Until the LORD have given rest unto your brethren, as well as unto you, and *until* they also possess the land which the LORD your God hath given them beyond Jordan: and *then* shall ye [d] return every man unto his possession, which I have given you.

21 And [e] I commanded Joshua at that time, saying, Thine eyes have seen all that the LORD your God hath done unto these two kings: so shall the LORD do unto all the kingdoms whither thou passest.

22 Ye shall not fear them: for [f] the LORD your God he shall fight for you.

23 And [g] I besought the LORD at that time, saying,

24 O LORD God, thou hast begun to show thy servant [h] thy greatness, and thy mighty hand: for [i] what God *is there* in heaven or in earth that can do according to thy works, and according to thy might?

25 I pray thee, let me go over, and see [k] the good land that *is* beyond Jordan, that goodly mountain, and Lebanon.

26 But the LORD [l] was wroth with me for

[r] 1 Chron. ii. 22.——[s] Josh. xiii. 13; 2 Sam. iii. 3; x. 6.——[t] Num. xxxii. 41.——[u] Num. xxxii. 39.——[v] 2 Sam. xxiv. 5.——[w] Num. xxi. 24; Josh. xii. 2.——[x] Num. xxxiv. 11.——[y] Chap. iv. 49; Numbers xxxiv. 11; Joshua xii. 3.——[z] Genesis xiv. 3.——[a] Or, *under the springs of Pisgah*, or, *the hill*.——[b] Numbers xxxii. 20, &c.

[c] Heb. *sons of power*.——[d] Josh. xxii. 4.——[e] Num. xxvii. 18.——[f] Exod. xiv. 14; chap. i. 30; xx. 4.——[g] See. 2 Cor. xii. 8, 9.——[h] Chap. xi. 2.——[i] Exod. xv. 11; 2 Sam. vii. 22; Psa. lxxi. 19; lxxx. 8; lxxxix. 6, 8.——[k] Exod. iii. 8; chap. iv. 22.——[l] Num. xx. 12; xxvii. 14; chap. i. 37; xxxi. 2; xxxii. 51, 52; xxxiv. 4; Psa. cvi. 32.

Allowing the bedstead to have been one cubit longer than Og, which is certainly sufficient, and allowing the cubit to be about *eighteen* inches long, for this is perhaps the average of *the cubit of a man*, then Og was *twelve feet high*. This may be deemed extraordinary, and perhaps almost incredible, and therefore many commentators have, according to their fancy, *lengthened* the *bedstead* and *shortened* the *man*, making the former one-third longer than the person who lay on it, that they might reduce Og to *six* cubits; but even in this way they make him at least *nine feet high*.

On this subject the rabbins have trifled most sinfully. I shall give one specimen. In the Targum of Jonathan ben Uzziel on Num. xxi. 35, 36, it is said that "Og having observed that the camp of the Israelites extended six miles, he went and tore up a mountain six miles in its base, and put it on his head, and carried it towards the camp, that he might throw it on the Israelites and destroy them; but the *word of the Lord* prepared a *worm*, which bored a hole in the mountain over his head, so that it fell down upon his shoulders: at the same time his teeth, growing out in all directions, stuck into the mountain, so that he could not cast it off his head. Moses, (who was himself *ten* cubits high,) seeing Og thus entangled, took an axe *ten* cubits long, and having leaped *ten* cubits in height, struck Og on the ankle bone, so that he fell and was slain."

From this account the distance from the *sole* of Og's foot to his *ankle* was *thirty* cubits in length! I give this as a very slight specimen of rabbinical comment. I could quote places in the Talmud in which Og is stated to be several *miles* high! This relation about Og I suppose to be also an historical note added by a subsequent hand.

Verse 14. *Bashan-havoth-jair*] Bashan of the *cities of Jair*; see Num. xxxii. 41.

Verse 17. *From Chinnereth*] See on Num. xxxiv. 11.

Verses 24, 25. The prayer of Moses recorded in these two verses, and his own reflections on it, ver. 26, are very affecting. He had suffered much both in body and mind in bringing the people to the borders of the promised land; and it was natural enough for him to wish to see them established in it, and to enjoy a portion of that inheritance himself, which he knew was a type of the heavenly country. But notwithstanding his very earnest prayer, and God's especial favour towards him, he was not permitted to go over Jordan! He had grieved the Spirit of God, and he passed a sentence against him of exclusion from the promised land. Yet he permitted him to see it, and gave him the fullest assurances that the people whom he had brought out of Egypt should possess it. Thus God may choose to deprive those of earthly possessions to whom he is nevertheless determined to give a heavenly inheritance.

A. M. 2553.
B. C. 1451.
An. Ex. Isr. 40.
Sebat.

your sakes, and would not hear me : and the LORD said unto me, Let it suffice thee ; speak no more unto me of this matter.

27 ᵐ Get thee up into the top of ⁿ Pisgah, and lift up thine eyes westward, and northward, and southward, and eastward, and behold it with thine eyes : for thou shalt not go over this Jordan.

28 But ᵒ charge Joshua, and encourage him, and strengthen him : for he shall go over before this people, and he shall cause them to inherit the land which thou shalt see.

A. M. 2553.
B. C. 1451.
An. Ex. Isr. 40.
Sebat.

29 So we abode in ᵖ the valley over against Beth-peor.

ᵐ Num. xxvii. 12.——ⁿ Or, the hill.——ᵒ Num. xxvii. 18, 23 ; chap. i. 38 ; xxxi. 3, 7.——ᵖ Chap. iv. 46 ; xxxiv. 6.

Verse 26. *Let it suffice thee*] רב לך *rab lach, there is an abundance to thee*—thou hast had honour enough already, and may well dispense with going over Jordan. He surely has no reason to complain who is taken from earthly felicity to heavenly glory. In this act God showed to Moses both his goodness and severity.

Verse 28. *But charge Joshua, &c.*] Give him *authority* in the sight of the people, let them see that he has the same *commission* which I gave to thee. *Encourage him*; for he will meet with many difficulties in the work to which he is called. *And strengthen him*—show him my unfailing promises, and exhort him to put his trust in me alone ; *for he shall go over before this people, and shall cause them to inherit the land* ; of this let him rest perfectly assured.

Verse 29. *Beth-peor.*] This was a city in the kingdom of Sihon king of the Amorites ; and as בית *beth* signifies a *house*, the place probably had its name from a *temple* of the god Peor, who was worshipped there. *Peor* was nearly the same among the Moabites that *Priapus* was among the Romans—the obscene god of an obscene people. This we have already seen.

Ir is very likely that what God speaks here, both concerning *Moses* and *Joshua*, was designed to be typical of the procedure of his justice and grace in the salvation of man. 1. The land of Canaan was a type of the kingdom of heaven. 2. The law, which shows the holiness of God and the exceeding sinfulness of sin, could not bring the people to the possession of that kingdom. 3. Moses may probably be considered here as the emblem of that law by which is the knowledge of sin, but not redemption from it. 4. Joshua, the same as *Jesus*, the name signifying a *Saviour*, is appointed to bring the people into the rest which God had provided for them ; thus it is by *Jesus Christ* alone that the soul is *saved*—fitted for and brought into the possession of the heavenly inheritance, (see John i. 17 ; Gal. ii. 16 ; iii. 12, 13, 24 ;) for he is the *end of the law*—the great scope and design of the law, for *righteousness*—for justification, to them that believe ; Rom. x. 4. Such a use as this every pious reader may make of the circumstances recorded here, without the danger of pushing analogy or metaphor beyond their reasonable limits.

CHAPTER IV.

Exhortations to obedience, 1. Nothing to be added to or taken from the testimonies of God, 2. The people are exhorted to recollect how God had destroyed the ungodly among them, 3 ; and preserved those who were faithful, 4. The excellence of the Divine law, 5, 6. No nation in the world could boast of any such statutes, judgments, &c., 7, 8. They are exhorted to obedience by the wonderful manifestations of God in their behalf, 9–13. Moses exhorts them to beware of idolatry, and to make no likeness of any thing in heaven or earth as an object of adoration, 14–20. He informs them that he must die in that land, as God had refused to let him go into the promised land, being angry with him on their account, 21, 22. Repeats his exhortations to obedience, 23, 24. Predicts the judgments of God against them, should they turn to idolatry, 25–28. Promises of God's mercy to the penitent, 29–31. The grand and unparalleled privileges of the Israelites, 32–40. Moses severs three cities on the east side of Jordan for cities of refuge, 41, 42. Their names, 43. When and where Moses gave these statutes and judgments to Israel, 44–49.

A. M. 2553.
B. C. 1451.
An. Ex. Isr. 40.
Sebat.

ΝOW therefore hearken, O Israel, unto ᵃ the statutes and unto the judgments which I teach you, for to do *them*, that ye may live, and go

in and possess the land which the LORD God of your fathers giveth you.

A. M. 2553.
B. C. 1451.
An. Ex. Isr. 40.
Sebat.

2 ᵇ Ye shall not add unto the word which I

ᵃ Lev. xix. 37; xx. 8; xxii. 31; chap. v. 1; viii. 1 ; Ezek. xx. 11 ; Rom. x. 5. ᵇ Chap. xii. 32; Josh. i. 7; Prov. xxx. 6; Eccles. xii. 13; Rev. xxii. 18, 19.

NOTES ON CHAP. IV.

Verse 1. *Hearken—unto the statutes*] Every thing that concerned the rites and ceremonies of religion ; *judgments.—*all that concerned matters of civil right and wrong.

Verse 2. *Ye shall not add*] Any book, chapter, *verse, or word*, which I have not spoken ; nor give any comment that has any tendency to corrupt, weaken, or destroy any part of this revelation.

Neither shall ye diminish] Ye shall not only not

A. M. 2553. B. C. 1451. An. Ex. Isr. 40. Sebat.

command you, neither shall ye diminish *aught* from it, that ye may keep the commandments of the LORD your God which I command you.

3 Your eyes have seen what the LORD did because of [c] Baal-peor: for all the men that followed Baal-peor, the LORD thy God hath destroyed them from among you.

4 But ye that did cleave unto the LORD your God *are* alive every one of you this day.

5 Behold, I have taught you statutes and judgments, even as the LORD my God commanded me, that ye should do so in the land whither ye go to possess it.

6 Keep therefore and do *them;* for this *is* [d] your wisdom and your understanding in the sight of the nations, which shall hear all these statutes, and say, Surely this great nation *is* a wise and understanding people.

7 For [e] what nation *is there so* great, who *hath* [f] God *so* nigh unto them, as the LORD our God *is* in all *things that* we call upon him *for?*

8 And what nation *is there so* great, that hath statutes and judgments *so* righteous as all this law, which I set before you this day?

9 Only take heed to thyself, and [g] keep thy soul diligently, [h] lest thou forget the things which thine eyes have seen, and lest they depart from thy heart all the days of thy life: but [i] teach them thy sons, and thy sons' sons;

A. M. 2553. B. C. 1451. An. Ex. Isr. 40. Sebat.

10 *Specially* [k] the day that thou stoodest before the LORD thy God in Horeb, when the LORD said unto me, Gather me the people together, and I will make them hear my words, that they may learn to fear me all the days that they shall live upon the earth, and *that* they may teach their children.

11 And ye came near and stood under the mountain: and the [l] mountain burned with fire unto the [m] midst of heaven, with darkness, clouds, and thick darkness.

12 [n] And the LORD spake unto you out of the midst of the fire: [o] ye heard the voice of the words, but saw no similitude; [p] only [q] *ye heard* a voice.

13 [r] And he declared unto you his covenant, which he commanded you to perform, *even* [s] ten commandments; and [t] he wrote them upon two tables of stone.

14 And [u] the LORD commanded me at that

[c] Num. xxv. 4, &c.; Josh. xxii. 17; Psa. cvi. 28, 29.——[d] Job xxviii. 28; Psa. xix. 7; cxi. 10; Prov. i. 7.——[e] 2 Sam. vii. 23. [f] Psa. xlvi. 1; cxlv. 18; cxlviii. 14; Isa. lv. 6.——[g] Prov. iv. 23. [h] Prov. iii. 1, 3; iv. 21.——[i] Gen. xviii. 19; chap. vi. 7; xi. 19; Psa. lxxviii. 5, 6; Eph. vi. 4.——[k] Exod. xix. 9, 16; xx. 18; Heb. xii. 18, 19.——[l] Exod. xix. 18; chap. v. 23.——[m] Heb. *heart.*——[n] Chap v. 4, 22.——[o] Ver. 33, 36.——[p] Exod. xx. 22; 1 Kings xix. 12.——[q] Heb. *save a voice.*——[r] Chap. ix. 9, 11. [s] Exod. xxxiv. 28.——[t] Exod. xxiv. 12; xxxi. 18.——[u] Exodus xxi. 1; chap. xxii., xxiii.

take away any larger portion of this word, but ye shall not take one *jot* or *tittle* from the LAW; it is that word of God that *abideth for ever.*

Verse 6. *Keep—and do* them; *for this* is *your wisdom*] There was no mode of worship at this time on the face of the earth that was not wicked, obscene, puerile, foolish, or ridiculous, except that established by God himself among the Israelites. And every part of this, taken in its *connection* and *reference,* may be truly called a *wise* and *reasonable service.*

The nations—and say, Surely this great nation is *a wise and understanding people.*] Almost all the nations in the earth showed that they had formed this opinion of the Jews, by borrowing from them the principal part of their civil code. Take away what *Asia* and *Europe,* whether *ancient* or *modern,* have borrowed from the *Mosaic laws,* and you leave little behind that can be called excellent.

Verse 9. *Only take heed to thyself*] Be circumspect and watchful.

Keep thy soul diligently] Be mindful of thy eternal interests. Whatever becomes of the *body,* take care of the *soul.*

Lest thou forget] God does his works that they may be had in everlasting *remembrance;* and he that *forgets* them, forgets his own mercies. Besides, if a man forget the work of God on his soul, he loses that work.

Lest they depart from thy heart] It is not sufficient to lay up Divine things in the *memory,* they must be laid up in the *heart. Thy word have I hidden in my heart,* says David, *that I might not sin against thee.* The life of God in the soul of man can alone preserve the soul to life everlasting; and this grace must be retained *all the days of our life.* When Adam fell, his condition was not meliorated by the reflection that he had been *once in paradise;* nor does it avail Satan *now* that he was *once* an angel of light. Those who let the grace of God depart from their hearts, lose that grace; and those who lose the grace, fall from the grace; and as some have fallen and risen no more, so may others; therefore, *take heed to thyself,* &c. Were it impossible for men finally to fall from the grace of God, exhortations of this kind had never been given, because they would have been unnecessary, and God never does an unnecessary thing.

But teach them thy sons] If a man know the worth of his own soul, he will feel the importance of the salvation of the souls of his family. Those who neglect *family religion,* neglect *personal religion;* if more attention were paid to the former, even among those called religious people, we should soon have a better

A. M. 2553.
B. C. 1451.
An. Ex. Isr. 40.
Sebat.

time to teach you statutes and judgments, that ye might do them in the land whither ye go over to possess it.

15 [v] Take ye therefore good heed unto yourselves; for ye saw no manner of [w] similitude on the day *that* the LORD spake unto you in Horeb out of the midst of the fire:

16 Lest ye [x] corrupt *yourselves,* and [y] make you a graven image, the similitude of any figure, [z] the likeness of male or female,

17 The likeness of any beast that *is* on the earth, the likeness of any winged fowl that flieth in the air,

18 The likeness of any thing that creepeth on the ground, the likeness of any fish that *is* in the waters beneath the earth:

19 And lest thou [a] lift up thine eyes unto heaven, and when thou seest the sun, and the moon, and the stars, *even* [b] all the host of heaven, shouldest be driven to [c] worship them, and serve them, which the LORD thy God hath [d] divided unto all nations under the whole heaven.

20 But the LORD hath taken you, and [e] brought you forth out of the iron furnace, *even* out of Egypt, [f] to be unto him a people of inheritance, as *ye are* this day.

A. M. 2553.
B. C. 1451.
An. Ex. Isr. 40.
Sebat.

21 Furthermore [g] the LORD was angry with me for your sakes, and sware that I should not go over Jordan, and that I should not go in unto that good land, which the LORD thy God giveth thee *for* an inheritance:

22 But [h] I must die in this land, [i] I must not go over Jordan: but ye shall go over, and possess [k] that good land.

23 Take heed unto yourselves, [l] lest ye forget the covenant of the LORD your God, which he made with you, [m] and make you a graven image, *or* the likeness of any *thing,* which the LORD thy God hath forbidden thee.

24 For [n] the LORD thy God *is* a consuming fire, *even* [o] a jealous God.

25 When thou shalt beget children, and children's children, and ye shall have remained long in the land, and [p] shall corrupt *yourselves,* and make a graven image, *or* the

[v] Joshua xxiii. 11.—[w] Isa. xl. 18.—[x] Exodus xxxii. 7. [y] Exodus xx. 4, 5; ver. 23; chap. v. 8.—[z] Rom. i. 23. [a] Chap. xvii. 3; Job xxxi. 26, 27.—[b] Gen. ii. 1; 2 Kings xvii. 16; xxi. 3.—[c] Rom. i. 25.—[d] Or, *imparted.*—[e] 1 Kings viii. 51; Jer. xi. 4.—[f] Exod. xix. 5; chap. ix. 29; xxxii. 9.

[g] Num. xx. 12; chap. i. 37; iii. 26.—[h] See 2 Pet. i. 13, 14, 15.—[i] Chap. iii. 27.—[k] Chap. iii. 25.—[l] Ver. 9.—[m] Ver. 16; Exod. xx. 4, 5.—[n] Exod. xxiv. 17; chap. ix. 3; Isa. xxxiii. 14; Heb. xii. 29.—[o] Exod. xx. 5; chap. vi. 15; Isa. xlii. 8. [p] Ver. 16.

state of civil society. On *family religion* God lays much stress; and no head of a family can neglect it without endangering the final salvation of his own soul. See the note at the conclusion of Gen. xviii.; and that at the end of Gen. xix., and the note on chap. vi. 7.

Verse 15. *Ye saw no manner of similitude*] Howsoever God chose to appear or manifest himself, he took care never to assume any describable form. He would have no *image worship,* because he is a SPIRIT, and they who worship him *must worship him in Spirit and in truth.* These outward things tend to draw the mind out of itself, and diffuse it on sensible, if not sensual, objects; and thus spiritual worship is prevented, and the Holy Ghost grieved. Persons acting in this way can never know much of the religion of the heart.

Verse 16. *The likeness of male or female*] Such as *Baal-peor* and the Roman *Priapus, Ashtaroth* or *Astarte,* and the Greek and Roman *Venus;* after whom most nations of the world literally *went a whoring.*

Verse 17. *The likeness of any beast, &c.*] Such as the Egyptian god *Apis,* who was worshipped under the form of a white *bull;* the *ibis* and *hawk,* among the FOWLS, had also Divine honours paid to them; *serpents* and the *crocodile* among REPTILES; besides *monkeys, dogs, cats,* the *scarabæus, leeks,* and *onions!* See this explained at large, Exod. xx. 4.

Verse 19. *When thou seest the sun, and the moon, and the stars*] The worship of the heavenly bodies was the oldest species of idolatry. Those who had not the knowledge of the true God were led to consider the sun, moon, planets, and stars, as not only self-existing, but the authors of all the blessings possessed by mankind. The knowledge of a rational system of astronomy served to destroy this superstition; and very little of it remains now in the world, except among a few Christian and Mohammedan *astrologers;* those *miserable* sinners who endeavour, as much as possible, to revive the old idolatry, while vainly professing to believe in the true God! Nor is it to be doubted that God will proceed with them as he has done of old with the worshippers of the host of heaven. Sound philosophy is next in importance to sound divinity; and next to the study of the work of grace is that of the operations of God in nature; for these *visible* things make known his eternal power and Godhead.

Verse 20. *Out of the iron furnace*] From this mention of the word *iron furnace* there can be little doubt that the Israelites were employed in Egypt in the most laborious works of *metallurgy.* Digging, smelting, and forging of *iron,* in so hot a climate must have been oppressive works indeed.

Verse 21. *The Lord was angry with me*] And if with *me,* so as to debar me from entering into the promised land, can *you* think to escape if guilty of greater provocations?

Verse 24. *Thy God is a consuming fire*] They had seen him on the mount as an *unconsuming* fire, while

A. M. 2553.
B. C. 1451.
An. Ex. Isr. 40.
Sebat.

likeness of any *thing*, and [q] shall
do evil in the sight of the LORD
thy God, to provoke him to anger:
26 [r] I call heaven and earth to witness
against you this day, that ye shall soon utterly
perish from off the land whereunto ye
go over Jordan to possess it; ye shall not
prolong *your* days upon it, but shall utterly be
destroyed.
27 And the LORD [s] shall scatter you among
the nations, and ye shall be left few in number
among the heathen, whither the LORD
shall lead you.
28 And [t] there ye shall serve gods, the work
of men's hands, wood and stone, [u] which
neither see, nor hear, nor eat, nor smell.
29 [v] But if from thence thou shalt seek the
LORD thy God, thou shalt find *him*, if thou
seek him with all thy heart and
with all thy soul.
30 When thou art in tribulation,
and all these things [w] are come upon thee,
[x] *even* in the latter days, if thou [y] turn to the
LORD thy God, and shalt be obedient unto his
voice;
31 (For the LORD thy God *is* [z] a merciful
God;) he will not forsake thee, neither destroy
thee, nor forget the covenant of thy
fathers which he sware unto them.
32 For [a] ask now of the days that are past,
which were before thee, since the day that
God created man upon the earth, and *ask*
[b] from the one side of heaven unto the other,
whether there hath been *any such thing* as
this great thing *is*, or hath been heard like it?
33 [c] Did *ever* people hear the voice of God

[q] 2 Kings xvii. 17, &c.——[r] Ch. xxx. 18, 19; Isa. i. 2; Mic. vi. 2.——[s] Lev. xxvi. 33, chapter xxviii. 62, 64; Neh. i. 8. [t] Chap. xxviii. 64; 1 Sam. xxvi. 19; Jer. xvi. 13.——[u] Psa. cxv. 4, 5; cxxxv. 15, 16; Isa. xliv. 9; xlvi. 7.——[v] Lev. xxvi. 39, 40; chap. xxx. 1, 2, 3; 2 Chron. xv. 4; Neh. i. 9; Isa. lv. 6, 7; Jer. xxix. 12, 13, 14.——[w] Heb. *have found thee;* Exod. xviii. 8; chap. xxxi. 17.——[x] Gen. xlix. 1; chap. xxxi. 29; Jer. xxiii. 20; Hos. iii. 5.——[y] Joel ii. 12.——[z] 2 Chron. xxx. 9; Neh. ix. 31; Psa. cxvi. 5; Jonah iv. 2.——[a] Job viii. 8.——[b] Matt. xxiv. 31. [c] Exod. xxiv. 11; xxxiii. 20; chap. v. 24, 26.

appearing to Moses, and giving the law; and they had seen him as a *consuming* fire in the case of Korah, Dathan, Abiram, and their company. They had, therefore, every good to expect from his approbation, and every evil to dread from his displeasure.

Verse 26. *I call heaven and earth to witness against you*] A most solemn method of adjuration, in use among all nations in the world. So Virgil, Æn., lib. xii., ver. 176, &c.

Tum pius Æneas stricto sic ense precatur:
Esto nunc Sol testis et hæc mihi terra vocanti—
Fontesque fluviosque voco, quæque ætheris alti
Relligio, et quæ cæruleo sunt numina ponto, &c.

"Then the great Trojan prince unsheathed his sword,
And thus, with lifted hands, the gods adored:
Thou land for which I wage this war, and thou
Great *source of day*, be witness to my vow!—
Almighty *king of heaven* and *queen of air*,
Propitious now and reconciled by prayer,—
Ye *springs*, ye *floods*, ye *various powers* who lie
Beneath the deep, or *tread the golden sky*,—
HEAR and ATTEST!" PITT.

God and man being called upon to bear testimony to the truth of what was spoken, that if there was any flaw or insincerity, it might be detected; and if any crime, it might not go unpunished. Such appeals to God, for such purposes, show at once both the origin and use of *oaths*. See the note on chap. vi. 13.

Verse 27. *The Lord shall scatter you among the nations*] This was amply verified in their different captivities and dispersions.

Verse 28. *There ye shall serve gods—wood and stone*] This was also true of the Israelites, not only in their captivities, but also in their own land. And it may now be literally the case with the ten tribes who were carried away captive by the Assyrians, and of whose residence no man at present knows any thing with certainty. That they still exist there can be no doubt; but they are now, most probably, so completely incorporated with the idolaters among whom they dwell, as to be no longer distinguishable: yet God can gather them.

Verse 29. *But if from thence thou shalt seek the Lord*] God is longsuffering, and of tender mercy; and waits, ever ready, to receive a backsliding soul when it returns to him. Is not this promise left on record for the encouragement and salvation of *lost Israel*?

Verse 30. *When thou art in tribulation—in the latter days*] Are not *these* the times spoken of? And is there not still hope for Israel? Could we see them become zealous for their *own law* and religious observances—could we see them humble themselves before the God of Jacob—could we see them conduct their public worship with any tolerable decency and decorum—could we see them zealous to avoid every moral evil, inquiring the road to Zion, with their faces thitherward; then might we hope that the redemption of Israel was at hand: but alas! there is not the most distant evidence of any thing of the kind, except in a very few solitary instances. They are, perhaps, in the present day, more lost to every sacred principle of their own institutions than they have ever been since their return from the Babylonish captivity. *By whom shall Jacob arise? for* in this sense *he is small*—deeply fallen, and greatly degraded.

Verse 33. *Did* ever *people hear the voice of God*] It seems to have been a general belief that if God *appeared* to men, it was for the purpose of destroying them; and indeed most of the extraordinary manifestations of God were in the way of *judgment;* but

A. M. 2553.
B. C. 1451.
An. Ex. Isr. 40.
Sebat.

speaking out of the midst of
the fire, as thou hast heard, and
live?
34 Or hath God assayed to go *and* take
him a nation from the midst of *another* nation,
[d] by temptations, [e] by signs, and by wonders,
and by war, and [f] by a mighty hand, and [g] by
a stretched-out arm, [h] and by great terrors,
according to all that the LORD your God did
for you in Egypt before your eyes?
35 Unto thee it was showed, that thou
mightest know that the LORD he *is* God:
[i] *there is* none else beside him.
36 [k] Out of heaven he made thee to hear
his voice, that he might instruct thee: and
upon earth he showed thee his great fire; and
thou heardest his words out of
the midst of the fire.
37 And because [l] he loved thy
fathers, therefore he chose their seed after
them, and [m] brought thee out in his sight,
with his mighty power, out of Egypt;
38 [n] To drive out nations from before thee
greater and mightier than thou *art*, to bring
thee in, to give thee their land *for* an inheritance, as *it is* this day.
39 Know therefore this day, and consider *it*
in thine heart, that [o] the LORD he *is* God in
heaven above, and upon the earth beneath:
there is none else.
40 [p] Thou shalt keep therefore his statutes
and his commandments, which I command thee

[d] Chap. vii. 19; xxix. 3.——[e] Exod. vii. 3.——[f] Exod. xiii. 3. [g] Exod. vi. 6.——[h] Chap. xxvi. 8; xxxiv. 12.——[i] Chap. xxxii. 39; 1 Sam. ii. 2; Isa. xlv. 5, 18, 22; Mark xii. 29, 32.

[k] Exod. xix. 9, 19; xx. 18, 22; xxiv. 16; Heb. xii. 18. [l] Chap. x. 15.——[m] Exod. xiii. 3, 9, 14.——[n] Chap. vii. 1; ix. 1, 4, 5.——[o] Ver. 35; Josh. ii. 11.——[p] Lev. xxii. 31.

here it was different; God did appear in a sovereign and extraordinary manner; but it was for the deliverance and support of the people. 1. They heard his voice speaking with them in a distinct, articulate manner. 2. They saw the fire, the symbol of his presence, the appearances of which demonstrated it to be supernatural. 3. Notwithstanding God appeared so terrible, yet no person was destroyed, for he came, not to *destroy*, but to *save*.

Verse 34. *From the midst of* another *nation*] This was a most extraordinary thing, that a whole people, consisting of upwards of 600,000 effective men, besides women and children, should, without striking a blow, be brought out of the midst of a very powerful nation, to the political welfare of which their services were so essential; that they should be brought out in so open and public a manner; that the sea itself should be supernaturally divided to afford this mighty host a passage; and that, in a desert utterly unfriendly to human life, they should be sustained for forty years. These were such instances of the almighty power and goodness of God as never could be forgotten.

In this verse Moses enumerates *seven* different means used by the Almighty in effecting Israel's deliverance.

1. TEMPTATIONS, מסת *massoth*, from נסה *nasah*, to *try* or *prove;* the miracles which God wrought to try the faith and prove the obedience of the children of Israel.

2. SIGNS, אתת *othoth*, from אתה *athah*, to *come near;* such signs as God gave them of his continual presence and especial providence, particularly the pillar of cloud and pillar of fire, *keeping near* to them night and day, and always directing their journeys, showing them *when* and *where* to pitch their tents, &c., &c.

3. WONDERS, מופתים *mophethim*, from יפת *yaphath*, *to persuade;* persuasive facts and events, says Parkhurst, whether strictly miraculous, and exceeding the powers of nature, as Exod. vii. 9; xi. 9, 10; or not, as Isa. xx. 3; Ezek. xii. 6, 11. It probably means *typical* representations: in this signification the word is used, Zech. iii. 8. Joshua, the high priest, and his companions were אנשי מופת *anshey mopheth, typical men*, raised up by God as types of Christ, and proofs that God would bring his servant THE BRANCH. All the *dealings* of God with this people, and even the *people* themselves, were *types*—present significators of distant facts and future occurrences.

4. WAR, מלחמה *milchamah, hostile engagements;* such as those with the Amalekites, the Amorites, and the Bashanites, in which the *hand of God* was seen, rather than the *hand of man*.

5. A MIGHTY HAND, יד חזקה *yad chazakah;* one that is *strong* to deal its blows, *irresistible* in its operations, and *grasps* its enemies hard, so that they cannot escape, and protects its friends so powerfully that they cannot be injured. Neither stratagem nor policy was used in this business, but the openly displayed power of God.

6. A STRETCHED-OUT ARM, זרוע נטויה *zeroa netuyah;* a *series of almighty operations*, following each other in quick and astonishing succession. Let it be noted that in the Scriptures, 1. The *finger* of God denotes *any manifestation of the Divine power*, where effects are produced beyond the power of art or nature. 2. The *hand* of God signifies the same power, but put forth in a *more* signal manner. 3. The *arm* of God, the Divine omnipotence manifested in the most stupendous miracles. 4. The *arm* of God *stretched out*, this same omnipotence exerted in a *continuation* of stupendous miracles, both in the way of judgment and mercy. In this latter sense it appears to be taken in the text: the judgments were poured out on the Egyptians; the mercies wrought in favour of the Israelites.

7. GREAT TERRORS, מוראים גדלים *moraim gedolim;* such terror, dismay, and consternation as were produced by the ten plagues, to which probably the inspired penman here alludes: or, as the Septuagint has it, εν ὁραμασιν μεγαλοις, *with great* or *portentous sights;* such as that when God looked out of the cloud upon the Egyptians, and their chariot wheels

A. M. 2553. B. C. 1451. An. Ex. Isr. 40. Sebat.

this day, [q] that it may go well with thee, and with thy children after thee, and that thou mayest prolong *thy* days upon the earth, which the LORD thy God giveth thee, for ever.

41 Then Moses [r] severed three cities on this side Jordan, toward the sunrising;

42 [s] That the slayer might flee thither, which should kill his neighbour unawares, and hated him not in times past; and that fleeing unto one of these cities he might live:

43 *Namely,* [t] Bezer in the wilderness, in the plain country of the Reubenites; and Ramoth in Gilead, of the Gadites; and Golan in Bashan, of the Manassites.

44 And this *is* the law which Moses set before the children of Israel:

45 These *are* the testimonies, and the statutes, and the judgments, which Moses spake unto the children of Israel, after they came forth out of Egypt,

46 On this side Jordan, [u] in the valley over against Beth-peor, in the land of Sihon king of the Amorites, who dwelt at Heshbon, whom Moses and the children of Israel [v] smote, after they were come forth out of Egypt:

47 And they possessed his land, and the land [w] of Og king of Bashan, two kings of the Amorites, which *were* on this side Jordan, toward the sunrising;

48 [x] From Aroer, which *is* by the bank of the river Arnon, even unto Mount Sion, which *is* [y] Hermon.

49 And all the plain on this side Jordan, eastward, even unto the sea of the plain, under the [z] springs of Pisgah.

[q] Chap. v. 16; vi. 3, 18; xii. 25, 28; xxii. 7; Eph. vi. 3. — [r] Num. xxxv. 6, 14. — [s] Chap. xix. 4. — [t] Josh. xx. 8. — [u] Chap. iii. 29. — [v] Num. xxi. 24; chap. i. 4. — [w] Num. xxi. 35; chap. iii. 3, 4. — [x] Chap. ii. 36; iii. 12. — [y] Chap. iii. 9; Psa. cxxxiii. 3. — [z] Chap. iii. 17.

were taken off, Exod. xiv. 24, 25. More awful displays of God's judgments, power, and might, were never witnessed by man.

Verse 41. *Then Moses severed three cities*] See the law relative to the cities of refuge explained Num. xxxv. 9, &c.

Verse 43. *Bezer in the wilderness*] As the cities of refuge are generally understood to be types of the salvation provided by Christ for sinners; so their names have been thought to express some attribute of the Redeemer of mankind. See them explained Josh. xx. 7, 8.

I SUPPOSE the last nine verses of this chapter to have been added by either *Joshua* or *Ezra.*

CHAPTER V.

God's covenant with the people in Horeb, 1–4. *Moses the mediator of it,* 5. *A repetition of the ten commandments,* 6–21; *which God wrote on two tables of stone,* 22. *The people are filled with dread at the terrible majesty of God,* 23–26; *and beseech Moses to be their mediator,* 27. *The Lord admits of their request,* 28; *and deplores their ungodliness,* 29. *They are exhorted to obedience, that they may be preserved in the possession of the promised land,* 30–33.

A. M. 2553. B. C. 1451. An. Ex. Isr. 40. Sebat.

AND Moses called all Israel, and said unto them, Hear, O Israel, the statutes and judgments which I speak in your ears this day, that ye may learn them, and [a] keep, and do them.

2 [b] The LORD our God made a covenant with us in Horeb.

3 The LORD [c] made not this covenant with our fathers, but with us, *even* us, who *are* all of us here alive this day.

4 [d] The LORD talked with you face to face, in the mount, out of the midst of the fire,

5 ([e] I stood between the LORD and you at

[a] Heb. *keep to do them.* — [b] Exod. xix. 5; chap. iv. 23. — [c] See Matt. xiii. 17; Heb. viii. 9. — [d] Exod. xix. 9, 19; xx. 22; chap. iv. 33, 36; xxxiv. 10. — [e] Exod. xx. 21; Gal. iii. 19.

NOTES ON CHAP. V.

Verse 1. *And Moses called all Israel, and said—Hear, &c.*] 1. God speaks to the people. 2. The people are called to *hear* what God speaks. 3. To *learn* what they heard, that they may be thoroughly instructed in the will of God. 4. To *keep* God's testimonies ever in mind, and to treasure them up in a believing and upright heart. 5. That they might *do them*—obey the whole will of God, taking his word for the invariable rule of their conduct. Should not all these points be kept in view by every Christian assembly?

Verse 3. *The Lord made not this covenant with our fathers* (only) *but with us* (also.)

A. M. 2553.
B. C. 1451.
An. Ex. Isr. 40.
Sebat.

that time, to show you the word of the LORD: for [f] ye were afraid by reason of the fire, and went not up into the mount;) saying,

6 [g] I *am* the LORD thy God, which brought thee out of the land of Egypt, from the house of [h] bondage.

7 [i] Thou shalt have none other gods before me.

8 [k] Thou shalt not make thee *any* graven image, *or* any likeness *of any thing* that *is* in heaven above, or that *is* in the earth beneath, or that *is* in the waters beneath the earth:

9 Thou shalt not bow down thyself unto them, nor serve them: for I the LORD thy God *am* a jealous God, [l] visiting the iniquity of the fathers upon the children unto the third and fourth *generation* of them that hate me,

10 [m] And showing mercy unto thousands of them that love me, and keep my commandments.

11 [n] Thou shalt not take the name of the LORD thy God in vain: for the LORD will not hold *him* guiltless that taketh his name in vain.

12 [o] Keep the Sabbath day to sanctify it, as the LORD thy God hath commanded thee.

13 [p] Six days thou shalt labour, and do all thy work:

14 But the seventh day *is* the [q] Sabbath of the LORD thy God: *in it* thou shalt not do any work, thou, nor thy son, nor thy daughter, nor thy man-servant, nor thy maid-servant, nor thine ox, nor thine ass, nor any of thy cattle, nor thy stranger that *is* within thy gates; that thy man-servant and thy maid-servant may rest as well as thou.

A. M. 2553.
B. C. 1451.
An. Ex. Isr. 40.
Sebat.

15 [r] And remember that thou wast a servant in the land of Egypt, and *that* the LORD thy God brought thee out thence [s] through a mighty hand, and by a stretched-out arm: therefore the LORD thy God commanded thee to keep the Sabbath day.

16 [t] Honour thy father and thy mother, as the LORD thy God hath commanded thee; [u] that thy days may be prolonged, and that it may go well with thee, in the land which the LORD thy God giveth thee.

17 [v] Thou shalt not kill.

18 [w] Neither shalt thou commit adultery.

19 [x] Neither shalt thou steal.

20 [y] Neither shalt thou bear false witness against thy neighbour.

21 [z] Neither shalt thou desire thy neighbour's wife, neither shalt thou covet thy neighbour's house, his field, or his man-servant, or his maid-servant, his ox, or his ass, or any *thing* that *is* thy neighbour's.

22 These words the LORD spake unto all your assembly in the mount out of the midst of the fire, of the cloud, and of the thick darkness, with a great voice: and he added no more. And [a] he wrote them in two tables of stone, and delivered them unto me.

23 [b] And it came to pass, when ye heard

[f] Exod. xix. 16; xx. 18; xxiv. 2.——[g] Exod. xx. 2, &c.; Lev. xxvi. 1; ch. vi. 4; Psa. lxxxi. 10.——[h] Heb. *servants*.——[i] Exod. xx. 3.——[k] Exod. xx. 4.——[l] Exod. xxxiv. 7.——[m] Jer. xxxii. 18; Dan. ix. 4.——[n] Exodus xx. 7; Lev. xix. 12; Matthew v. 33.——[o] Exod. xx. 8.——[p] Exod. xxiii. 12; xxxv. 2; Ezek. xx. 12.——[q] Gen. ii. 2; Exod. xvi. 29, 30; Heb. iv. 4.——[r] Chap. xv. 15; xvi. 12; xxiv. 18, 22.

[s] Chap. iv. 34, 37.——[t] Exod. xx. 12; Lev. xix. 3; chap. xxvii. 16; Eph. vi. 2, 3; Col. iii. 20.——[u] Chap. iv. 40.——[v] Exod. xx. 13; Matt. v. 21.——[w] Exod. xx. 14; Luke xviii. 20; James ii. 11.——[x] Exod. xx. 15; Rom. xiii. 9.——[y] Exod. xx. 16.——[z] Exod. xx. 17; Mic. ii. 2; Hab. ii. 9; Luke xii. 15; Rom. vii. 7; xiii. 9.——[a] Exod. xxiv. 12; xxxi. 18; chap. iv. 13.——[b] Exod. xx. 18, 19.

Verse 6. *I* am *the Lord thy God*] See these commandments explained in the notes on Exod. xx.

Verse 15. *And remember that thou wast a servant*] In this and the latter clause of the preceding verse Moses adds another reason why one day in *seven* should be sanctified, viz., *that the servants might rest*, and this is urged upon them on the consideration of *their* having been servants in the land of Egypt. We see therefore that God had three grand ends in view by appointing a Sabbath. 1. To commemorate the creation. 2. To give a due proportion of rest to man and beast. When in Egypt they had no rest; their cruel task-masters caused them to labour without intermission: now God had given rest, and as he had showed them mercy, he teaches them to show mercy to their servants: *Remember that thou wast a servant.* 3. To afford peculiar spiritual advantages to the soul, that it might be kept in remembrance of the *rest* which remains at the right hand of God.

Therefore the Lord thy God commanded thee to keep the Sabbath day.] Here is a variation in the manner of expression, *Sabbath day* for *seventh*, owing, it is supposed, to a change of the day at the exodus from *Sunday* to *Saturday*, effected upon the gathering of the manna, Exod. xvi. 23. The Sabbath now became a *twofold* memorial of the *deliverance*, as well as of the *creation*; and this accounts for the new reason assigned for its observance: "Therefore the Lord thy God commanded thee to keep the Sabbath day." See Dr. A. BAYLEY's Heb. and Eng. Bible, and the note on Exod. xvi. 23.

Verse 21. *His field*] This clause is not in the tenth commandment as it stands in Exod. xx. 17.

Verse 23, &c. *And it came to pass, when*

A. M. 2553. B. C. 1451. An. Ex. Isr. 40. Sebat.

the voice out of the midst of the darkness, (for the mountain did burn with fire,) that ye came near unto me, *even* all the heads of your tribes, and your elders;

24 And ye said, Behold, the LORD our God hath showed us his glory and his greatness, and [c] we have heard his voice out of the midst of the fire: we have seen this day that God doth talk with man, and he [d] liveth.

25 Now therefore why should we die? for this great fire will consume us: [e] if we [f] hear the voice of the LORD our God any more, then we shall die.

26 [g] For who *is there of* all flesh, that hath heard the voice of the living God speaking out of the midst of the fire, as we *have,* and lived?

27 Go thou near, and hear all that the LORD our God shall say: and [h] speak thou unto us all that the LORD our God shall speak unto thee; and we will hear *it,* and do *it.*

28 And the LORD heard the voice of your words, when ye spake unto me; and the LORD said unto me, I have heard the voice of the words of this people, which they have spoken unto thee: [i] they have well said all that they have spoken.

A. M. 2553. B. C. 1451. An. Ex. Isr. 40. Sebat.

29 [k] O that there were such a heart in them, that they would fear me, and [l] keep all my commandments always, [m] that it might be well with them, and with their children for ever!

30 Go say to them, Get you into your tents again.

31 But as for thee, stand thou here by me, [n] and I will speak unto thee all the commandments, and the statutes, and the judgments, which thou shalt teach them, that they may do *them* in the land which I give them to possess it.

32 Ye shall observe to do therefore as the LORD your God hath commanded you: [o] ye shall not turn aside to the right hand or to the left.

33 Ye shall walk in [p] all the ways which the LORD your God hath commanded you, that ye may live, [q] and *that it may be* well with you, and *that* ye may prolong *your* days in the land which ye shall possess.

---

[c] Exod. xix. 19.—[d] Chap. iv. 33; Judg. xiii. 22.—[e] Chap. xviii. 16.—[f] Heb. *add to hear.*—[g] Chap. iv. 33.—[h] Exod. xx. 19; Heb. xii. 19.—[i] Chap. xviii. 17.—[k] Chap. xxxii. 29; Psa. lxxxi. 13; Isa. xlviii. 18; Matt. xxiii. 37; Luke xix. 42.

[l] Chap. xi. 1.—[m] Chap. iv. 40.—[n] Gal. iii. 19.—[o] Chap. xvii. 20; xxviii. 14; Joshua i. 7; xxiii. 6; Proverbs iv. 27.—[p] Chap. x. 12; Psa. cxix. 6; Jer. vii. 23; Luke i. 6.—[q] Chap. iv. 40; Exod. xx. 12.

---

ye heard the voice] See the notes on Exod. xx. 18, &c.

Verse 29. *O that there were such a heart in them*] Or rather, מי יתן והיה לבבם זה *mi yitten vehayah lebabam zeh, Who will give such a heart to them, that they may fear,* &c. They refuse to receive such a heart from *me;* who then can supply it? If they had not been such perfectly free agents as could either use or abuse their liberty, could God have made the complaint or expressed the earnest desire we find in this verse? He made the human will *free;* and in spite of all the influence of sin and Satan, he preserves its *liberty.* Had man no free will, he could neither be *punished* nor *rewarded,* because a *mere machine,* and consequently no more accountable for his actions than the fire for its consuming quality, or the stone for its *gravity;* the one having burned the house of the righteous, the other having crushed the innocent to death. See the note on chap. xxix. 4.

Verse 32. *Ye shall observe to do*] He who *marks* not the *word* of God is never likely to fulfil the *will* of God.

Ye shall not turn aside to the right hand or to the left.] The way of truth and righteousness is a *right line;* a man must walk straight forward who wishes to go to glory; no crooked or devious path ever led to God or happiness.

Verse 33. *Ye shall walk in all the ways, &c.*] God never gave a commandment to man which he did not design that he should obey. He who selects from the Divine testimonies such precepts as he feels but little inclination to transgress, and lives in the breach of others, sins against the grand legislative authority of God, and shall be treated as a rebel.

That ye may live] תחיון *ticheyun,* that ye *may enjoy life,* (for the paragogic ן *nun,* at the end of the word, deepens the sense,) *that it may be well with you,* וטוב לכם *vetob lachem,* and good shall be to you—God will prosper you in all things essential to the welfare of your bodies, and the salvation of your souls.

That *ye may prolong* your *days in the land*] That ye may arrive at a good old age, and grow more and more meet for the inheritance among the saints in light.

On this very important verse we may remark, a long life is a great blessing, if a man live to God, because it is in life, and in life alone, that a preparation for eternal glory may be acquired. Those who wish to die *soon,* have never yet learned to live, and know not the value of life or time. Many have a vain hope that they shall get either in death, or in the other world, a preparation for glory. This is a fatal error. *Here,* alone, we may acquaint ourselves with God, and receive that holiness without which none can see him. Reader, be thankful to him that thou art still in a state of probation; and pray that thou mayest live for eternity.

CHAPTER VI.

The great design of God in giving his laws is, that the people may fear and obey him, that they may continue in peace and prosperity, and be mightily increased, 1–3. *The great commandment of the law,* 4, 5, *which shall be laid up in their hearts,* 6 ; *taught to their children,* 7 ; *and affixed as a sign to their hands, heads, doors, and gates,* 8, 9. *How they are to act when they shall come into the promised land,* 10–19. *How they shall instruct their children, and relate the history to them of God's wonderful acts,* 20–25.

A. M. 2553.
B. C. 1451.
An. Ex. Isr. 40.
Sebat.

NOW these *are* [a] the commandments, the statutes, and the
judgments, which the LORD your
God commanded to teach you, that ye might
do *them* in the land whither ye [b] go to possess it:
2 [c] That thou mightest fear the LORD thy
God, to keep all his statutes and his commandments, which I command thee, thou, and
thy son, and thy son's son, all the days of thy
life ; [d] and that thy days may be
prolonged.
3 Hear therefore, O Israel,
and observe to do *it ;* that it may be well
with thee, and that ye may increase mightily,
[e] as the LORD God of thy fathers hath pro
mised thee, in [f] the land that floweth with milk
and honey.
4 [g] Hear, O Israel: The LORD our God *is*
one LORD:

A. M. 2553.
B. C. 1451.
An. Ex. Isr. 40.
Sebat.

[a] Chap. iv. 1; v. 31; xii. 1.——[b] Heb. *pass over.*——[c] Exod. xx. 20; chap. x. 12, 13; Psa. cxi. 10; cxxviii. 1; Eccles. xii. 13.

[d] Chap. iv. 40; Prov. iii. 1, 2.——[e] Genesis xv. 5; xxii. 17. [f] Exod. iii. 8.——[g] Isa. xlii. 8; Mark xii. 29, 32; John xvii. 3; 1 Cor. viii. 4, 6.

NOTES ON CHAP. VI.

Verse 1. *Now these* are *the commandments, &c.*] See the difference between commandments, statutes, judgments, &c., pointed out Lev. xxvi. 15.

Do them] That is, live in the continual practice of them; for by this they were to be distinguished from all the nations of the world, and all these were to be in force till the Son of God should come. *Whither ye go,* עברים *oberim,* whither *ye pass over,* referring to the river Jordan, across which they must pass to get into Canaan.

Verse 2. *That thou mightest fear the Lord*] Respect his sovereign authority as a lawgiver, and ever feel thyself bound to obey him. No man can walk either conscientiously or safely who has not the *fear of God* continually before his eyes. When this is gone, more than a guardian angel is fled.

Thou, and thy son, and thy son's son] Through all thy successive generations. Whoever fears God will endeavour to bring up his children in the way of righteousness, that they also may fear God, and that pure and undefiled religion may be preserved in his family through all its generations, not only in word, but in practice also.

Verse 3. *Hear therefore, O Israel, and observe to do* it] Literally, Ye shall hear, O Israel, and thou shalt keep to do *them.* 1. *God is to be heard;* no *obligation* without *law* to found it on, and no *law* in religion but from God. 2. The commandment must be *understood* in order to be obeyed. 3. It must be *observed*—attentively considered, in order to be understood. And, 4. It must be *performed,* that the *end* for which it was given may be accomplished, viz., that GOD may be *glorified,* and that it may *be well* with the *people.* What is here spoken applies powerfully to every part of the *moral* law; God has given IT as a *rule of life,* therefore obedience to it is indispensably necessary, not to the *purchase of salvation,* for no human merit can ever extend to that, but it is the *way* by which both the justice and mercy of God choose to conduct men to heaven. But let it be fully understood that no man can walk in the way of obedience but by and under the influence of the grace of God.

Verse 4. *Hear, O Israel*] שמע ישראל יהוה אלהינו יהוה אחד *shemA Yisrael, Yehovah Eloheinu, Yehovah achaD.* These words may be variously rendered into English; but almost all possible *verbal* varieties in the translation (and there can be none other) amount to the same sense: "Israel, hear! Jehovah, our God, is one Jehovah;" or, "Jehovah is our God, Jehovah is one;" or, "Jehovah is our God, Jehovah alone;" or, "Jehovah is our God, Jehovah who is one;" or, "Jehovah, who is our God, is the one Being." On this verse the Jews lay great stress; it is one of the four passages which they write on their phylacteries, and they write the last letter in the first and last words very large, for the purpose of exciting attention to the weighty truth it contains. It is perhaps in reference to this custom of the Jews that our blessed Lord alludes, Matt. xxii. 38; Mark xii. 29, 30, where he says, *This is the first and great commandment;* and this is nearly the comment that *Maimonides* gives on this place: "Hear, O Israel; because in these words the property, the love, and the doctrine of God are contained."

Many think that Moses teaches in these words the doctrine of the Trinity in Unity. It may be so; but if so, it is not more clearly done than in the first verse of Genesis, to which the reader is referred. When this passage occurs in the Sabbath readings in the synagogue, the whole congregation repeat the last word אחד *achad* for several minutes together with the loudest vociferations: this I suppose they do to vent a little of their spleen against the Christians, for they suppose the latter hold *three Gods,* because of their doctrine of the *Trinity;* but all their skill and cunning can never prove that there is not a *plurality* expressed in the word אלהינו *Eloheinu,* which is translated *our God;* and were the Christians, when reading this verse, to vociferate *Eloheinu* for several minutes as

A. M. 2553.
B. C. 1451.
An. Ex. Isr. 40.
Sebat.

5 And [h] thou shalt love the LORD thy God [i] with all thine heart, and with all thy soul, and with all thy might.

6 And [k] these words, which I command thee this day, shall be in thine heart:

7 And [l] thou shalt [m] teach them diligently unto thy children, and shalt talk of them when thou sittest in thine house, and when thou walkest by the way, and when thou liest down, and when thou risest up.

8 [n] And thou shalt bind them for a sign upon thine hand, and they shall be as frontlets between thine eyes.

9 [o] And thou shalt write them upon the posts of thy house, and on thy gates.

10 And it shall be, when the LORD thy God shall have brought thee into the land which he sware unto thy fathers, to Abraham, to Isaac, and to Jacob, to give thee great and goodly cities, [p] which thou buildedst not,

11 And houses full of all good *things*, which thou filledst not, and wells digged, which thou diggedst not, vineyards and olive-trees, which thou plantedst not; [q] when thou shalt have eaten and be full;

12 *Then* beware lest thou forget the LORD,

[h] Chap. x. 12; Matt. xxii. 37; Mark xii. 30; Luke x. 27. — [i] 2 Kings xxiii. 25. — [k] Chap. xi. 18; xxxii. 46; Psa. xxxvii. 31; xl. 8; cxix. 11, 98; Prov. iii. 3; Isa. li. 7. — [l] Ch. iv. 9; xi. 19; Psa. lxxviii. 4, 5, 6; Eph. vi. 4. — [m] Heb. *whet* or *sharpen*. — [n] Exod. xiii. 9, 16; ch. xi. 18; Prov. iii. 3; vi. 21; vii. 3. — [o] Ch. xi. 20; Isa. lvii. 8. — [p] Josh. xxiv. 13; Psa. cv. 44. — [q] Ch. viii. 10, &c.

the Jews do *achad*, it would apply more forcibly in the way of conviction to the Jews of the *plurality* of persons in the *Godhead*, than the word *achad*, of *one*, against any pretended false tenet of Christianity, as every Christian receives the doctrine of the *unity* of God in the most conscientious manner. It is because of their rejection of this doctrine that the wrath of God continues to rest on them; for the doctrine of the atonement cannot be received, unless the doctrine of the *Godhead of Christ* is received too. Some Christians have joined the Jews against this doctrine, and some have even outdone them, and have put themselves to extraordinary pains to prove that אלהים *Elohim* is a noun of the *singular* number! This has not yet been proved. It would be as easy to prove that there is no *plural* in language.

Verse 5. *Thou shalt love the Lord, &c.*] Here we see the truth of that word of the apostle, 1 Tim. i. 5: *Now the* END *of the* COMMANDMENT *is* LOVE *out of a pure heart*, &c. See the whole of the doctrine contained in this verse explained on Matt. xxii. 36–40.

Verse 6. *Shall be in thine heart*] For where else can *love* be? If it be not in the *heart*, it exists not. And if *these words* be not *in the heart*—if they are not esteemed, prized, and received as a high and most glorious privilege, what hope is there that this love shall ever reign there?

Verse 7. *Thou shalt teach them diligently*] שננתם *shinnantam*, from שנן *shanan*, *to repeat*, *iterate*, or do a thing *again* and *again;* hence to *whet* or *sharpen* any instrument, which is done by *reiterated friction* or *grinding*. We see here the spirit of this Divine injunction. God's testimonies must be taught to our children, and the utmost diligence must be used to make them understand them. This is a most difficult task; and it requires much patience, much prudence, much judgment, and much piety in the parents, to enable them to do this good, this most important work, in the best and most effectual manner. See at the end of this chapter.

And shalt talk of them when thou sittest in thine house] Thou shalt have religion at *home*, as well as in the *temple* and *tabernacle*.

And when thou walkest by the way] Thou shalt be religious *abroad* as well as at *home*, and not be ashamed to own God wheresoever thou art.

When thou liest down, and when thou risest up.] Thou shalt *begin* and *end* the day with God, and thus religion will be the great business of thy life. O how good are these sayings, but how little regarded!

Verse 8. *Thou shalt bind them for a sign upon thine hand*] Is not this an allusion to an ancient and general custom observed in almost every part of the world? When a person wishes to remember a thing of importance, and is afraid to trust to the common operations of memory, he *ties a knot* on some part of his clothes, or a *cord* on his hand or finger, or places something out of its *usual order*, and in *view*, that his memory may be whetted to recollection, and his eye affect his heart. God, who knows how slow of heart we are to understand, graciously orders us to make use of every help, and through the means of things *sensible*, to rise to things *spiritual*.

And they shall be as frontlets] טטפת *totaphoth* seems to have the same meaning as *phylacteries* has in the New Testament; and for the meaning and description of these appendages to a Jew's dress and to his religion, see the notes on Exod. xiii. 9, and on Matt. xxiii. 5, where a *phylactery* is particularly described.

Verse 9. *Write them upon the posts of thy house, and on thy gates.*] The *Jews*, forgetting the *spirit* and design of this precept, used these things as superstitious people do *amulets* and *charms*, and supposed, if they had these passages of Scripture written upon slips of pure parchment, wrapped round their foreheads, tied to their arm, or nailed to their door-posts, that they should then be delivered from every evil! And how much better are many *Christians*, who keep a Bible *in* their house merely that *it* may keep the devil *out;* and will have it in their rooms, or under their pillows, to ward off spirits and ghosts in the night? How ingenious is the heart of man to find out every wrong way, and to miss the right!

Verse 12. *Beware lest thou forget the Lord*] In *earthly* prosperity men are apt to forget *heavenly* things. While the *animal senses* have every thing

A. M. 2553. B. C. 1451. An. Ex. Isr. 40. Sebat.

which brought thee forth out of
the land of Egypt, from the
house of [r] bondage.
13 Thou shalt [s] fear the LORD thy God,
and serve him, and [t] shalt swear by his name.
14 Ye shall not [u] go after other gods, [v] of
the gods of the pepole which *are* round about
you;
15 (For [w] the LORD thy God *is* a jealous
God among you;) [x] lest the anger of the LORD
thy God be kindled against thee, and destroy
thee from off the face of the earth.

[r] Heb. *bondmen* or *servants*.——[s] Chap. x. 12, 20; xiii. 4; Matt. iv. 10; Luke iv. 8.——[t] Psa. lxiii. 11; Isa. xlv. 23; lxv. 16; Jer. iv. 2; v. 7; xii. 16.——[u] Chap. viii. 19; xi. 28; Jer. xxv. 6. [v] Chap. xiii. 7.

16 [y] Ye shall not tempt the
LORD your God, [z] as ye tempted
him in Massah.
17 Ye shall [a] diligently keep the commandments of the LORD your God, and his testimonies, and his statutes, which he hath commanded thee.
18 And thou [b] shalt do *that which is* right
and good in the sight of the LORD: that it
may be well with thee, and that thou mayest
go in and possess the good land which the
LORD sware unto thy fathers,

A. M. 2553. B. C. 1451. An. Ex. Isr. 40. Sebat.

[w] Exodus xx. 5; chap. iv. 24.——[x] Chap. vii. 4; xi. 17. [y] Matt. iv. 7; Luke iv. 12.——[z] Exod. xvii. 2, 7; Num. xx. 3, 4; xxi. 4, 5; 1 Cor. x. 9.——[a] Chap. xi. 13, 22; Psa. cxix. 4 [b] Exod. xv. 26; chap. xii. 28; xiii. 18.

they can wish, it is difficult for the soul to urge its way to heaven; the animal man is happy, and the desires of the soul are absorbed in those of the flesh. God knows this well; and therefore, in his love to man, makes comparative poverty and frequent affliction his general lot. Should not every soul therefore magnify God for this lot in life? "Before I was afflicted," says David, "I went astray;" and had it not been for poverty and affliction, as instruments in the hands of God's grace, multitudes of souls now happy in heaven would have been wretched in hell. It is not too much to speak thus far; because we ever see that the rich and the affluent are generally negligent of God and the interests of their souls. It must however be granted that extreme poverty is as injurious to religion as excessive affluence. Hence the wisdom as well as piety of Agur's prayer, Prov. xxx. 7–9: "Give me neither *poverty* nor *riches*, lest I be *full* and *deny* thee, or lest I be *poor* and *steal*," &c.

Verse 13. *Thou shalt fear the Lord thy God*] Thou shalt respect and reverence him as thy Lawgiver and Judge; as thy Creator, Preserver, and the sole object of thy religious adoration.

And serve him] Our blessed Lord, in Matt. iv. 10; Luke iv. 8, quotes these words thus: *And him* ONLY (αυτῳ μονῳ) *shalt thou serve*. It appears, therefore, that לבדו *lebaddo* was anciently in the Hebrew text, as it was and is in the SEPTUAGINT, (αυτῳ μονῳ,) from which our Lord quoted it. The COPTIC preserves the same reading; so do also the VULGATE, (*illi soli*,) and the ANGLO-SAXON, (peopa him anum.) Dr. Kennicott argues, that without the word *only* the text would not have been conclusive for the purpose for which our Lord advanced it; for as we learn from Scripture that some men worshipped false gods in conjunction with the true, the quotation here would not have been full to the point without this *exclusive* word. It may be proper to observe that the omitted word לבדו *lebaddo*, retained in the above *versions*, does not exist in the Hebrew printed text, nor in any MS. hitherto discovered.

Shalt swear by his name.] תשבע *tishshabea*, from שבע *shaba*, he was *full*, *satisfied*, or gave that which was *full* or *satisfactory*. Hence an *oath* and *swearing*, because appealing to God, and taking him for witness in any case of promise, &c., gave *full* and *sufficient security* for the performance; and if done in evidence, or to the truth of any particular fact, it gave *full security* for the truth of that evidence. An oath, therefore, is an *appeal to God*, who knows all things, of the truth of the matter in question: and when a religious man takes such an oath, he gives full and reasonable satisfaction that the thing is *so*, as stated; for it is ever to be presumed that no man, unless in a state of the deepest *degradation*, would make such an appeal falsely, for this would imply an attempt to *make God a party in the deception*.

Verse 14. *Ye shall not go after other gods*] The object of religious worship among every people, whether that object be true or false, is ever considered as the pattern or exemplar to his worshippers. Christians are termed the *followers* of God; they take God for their pattern, and *walk*—act, as he does. Hence we see the meaning of the terms in this verse: *Ye shall not go after*—ye shall not take false gods for your *patterns*. The Canaanites, Greeks, Romans, &c., were a most impure people, because the objects of their worship were impure, and they *went after* them, i. e., were like their gods. This serves to show us that such as our Redeemer is, such should we be; and indeed this is the uniform language of God to man: *Be ye holy, for I am holy*, Lev. xxi. 8; *Be ye perfect, as your Father who is in heaven is perfect*, Matt. v. 48.

Verse 15. *A jealous God*] Jehovah has *betrothed* you to himself as a bride is to her husband. Do not be unfaithful, else that *love* wherewith he has now distinguished you shall assume the form of *jealousy*, and so divorce and consume you.

Verse 16. *Ye shall not tempt the Lord*] Ye shall not provoke him by entertaining doubts of his mercy, goodness, providence, and truth.

As ye tempted him *in Massah.*] How did they tempt him in Massah? They said, *Is the Lord among us or not?* Exod. xvii. 1–7. After such proofs as they had of his presence and his kindness, this was exceedingly provoking. Doubting God's kindness where there are so many evidences of it, is highly insulting to God Almighty.

Verse 17. *Ye shall diligently keep, &c.*] On this and the following verse see the note on ver. 3

A. M. 2553. B. C. 1451. An. Ex. Isr. 40. Sebat.

19 [c] To cast out all thine enemies from before thee, as the LORD hath spoken.
20 *And* [d] when thy son asketh thee [e] in time to come, saying, What *mean* the testimonies, and the statutes, and the judgments, which the LORD our God hath commanded you?
21 Then thou shalt say unto thy son, We were Pharaoh's bondmen in Egypt; and the LORD brought us out of Egypt [f] with a mighty hand:
22 [g] And the LORD showed signs and wonders, great and [h] sore, upon Egypt, upon Pharaoh, and upon all his household, before our eyes:
23 And he brought us out from thence, that he might bring us in, to give us the land which he sware unto our fathers.
24 And the LORD commanded us to do all these statutes, [i] to fear the LORD our God, [k] for our good always, that [l] he might preserve us alive, as *it is* at this day.
25 And [m] it shall be our righteousness, if we observe to do all these commandments before the LORD our God, as he hath commanded us.

[c] Num. xxxiii. 52, 53.——[d] Exod. xiii. 14.——[e] Heb. *to-morrow.*——[f] Exod. iii. 19; xiii. 3.——[g] Exod. vii., viii., ix., x., xi., xii.; Psa. cxxxv. 9.——[h] Heb. *evil.*

[i] Ver. 2.——[k] Chap. x. 13; Job xxxv. 7, 8; Jer. xxxii. 39.——[l] Chap. iv. 1; viii. 1; Psa. xli. 2; Luke x. 28.——[m] Lev. xviii. 5; chap. xxiv. 13; Rom. x. 3, 5.

Verse 20. And *when thy son asketh thee, &c.*] "Here," as Mr. Ainsworth justly remarks, "followeth a brief *catechism*, containing the grounds of religion."

What mean *the testimonies, &c.*] The Hebrew language has no word to express to *mean* or *signify*, and therefore uses simply the substantive verb *what is*, i. e., what mean or signify, &c. *The seven thin ears* ARE, i. e., *signify*, seven years of famine. This form of speech frequently occurs.

Verse 25. *It shall be our righteousness*] The *evidence* that we are under the influence of the fear and love of God. Moses does not say that this righteousness could be wrought without the influence of God's mercy, nor does he say that they should purchase heaven by it; but, God required them to be conformed to his will in all things, that they might be holy in heart, and righteous in every part of their moral conduct.

1. ON a very important subject in this chapter, it may be necessary to make some farther observations.

A most injurious and destructive maxim has lately been advanced by a few individuals, which it is to be hoped is disowned by the class of Christians to which they belong, though the authors affect to be thought *Christians*, and *rational* ones too; the sum of the maxim is this: "Children ought not to be taught religion for fear of having their minds biassed to some particular creed, but they should be left to themselves till they are capable of making a *choice*, and *choose* to make one." This maxim is in flat opposition to the command of God, and those who teach it show how little they are affected by the religion they profess. If they felt it to be good for any thing, they would certainly wish their children to possess it; but they do not teach religion to their children, because they feel it to be of no use to themselves. Now the Christian religion properly applied saves the soul, and fills the heart with love to God and man; for the love of God is shed abroad in the heart of a genuine believer, by the Holy Ghost given to him. These persons have no such love, because they have not the religion that inspires it; and the spurious religion which admits of the maxim above mentioned, is not the religion of God, and consequently better untaught than taught. But what can be said to those parents who, possessing a better faith, equally neglect the instruction of their children in the things of God? They are highly criminal; and if their children perish through neglect, which is very probable, what a dreadful account must they give in the great day! PARENTS! hear what the Lord saith unto *you:* Ye shall diligently teach your children that there is one Lord, *Jehovah, Elohim;* the Father, the Son, and the Holy Ghost: and that they must love him with all their heart, with all their soul, and with all their might. And as children are heedless, apt to forget, liable to be carried away by sensible things, repeat and re-repeat the instruction, and add line upon line, precept upon precept, here a little and there a little, carefully studying *time, place,* and *circumstances*, that your labour be not in vain: show it in its amiableness, excite *attention* by exciting *interest;* show how good, how useful, how blessed, how ennobling, how glorious it is. *Whet* these things on their hearts till the keenest edge is raised on the strongest desire, till they can say, "Whom have I in heaven but thee? and there is none upon earth I desire besides thee!"

See the notes on chap. iv. 9, and on Gen. xviii. and xix. at the end.

2. Without offence to any, I hope, a few words more may be said on the nature of an *oath*, in addition to the note on ver. 13. The matter is important, and perhaps not well understood by many.

The making an *appeal* to the Supreme Being, and calling him to witness and record, constitutes the *spirit* and *essence* of an oath. It is no matter in what *form* this appeal is made, whether by putting the hand *under the thigh*, as among the *patriarchs;* by the *water of the Ganges*, as among the *Hindoos;* on a *surat* or *chapter of the Koran*, as among the *Mohammedans;* on a *Hebrew Pentateuch*, as among the *Jews;* on the *form of the cross*, as among the *Roman Catholics; kissing* the *New Testament*, as among *Protestants* in general; or *holding up the hand*, and making *affirmation*, as among the people called *Quakers;* still the

oath is the same, for the *appeal is made to God*. On this ground (and this is the true ground) *the holding up of the hand* in a court of justice, is as perfect, as substantial, and as formal an oath, as *kissing the New Testament*. Why then so many objections against taking an oath in a court of justice by any *one particular form*, when the same thing is done in spirit, essence, and substance, when God is called to witness and record, though the *form* be different? When God says, *Thou shalt fear the Lord thy God, and shalt swear by his name*, he says, in effect, Thou shalt have no god besides me; thou shalt consider me the fountain of truth, the rewarder of righteousness, and the punisher of perfidy and wickedness. *Swear by my name*—bind thyself to *me*; take *me* for witness to all thy actions; and act in all things as having *me* continually before thine eyes, and knowing that for every *act* and *word* thou shalt give account to *me* in the day of judgment. Our Lord's command, *Swear not at all*, can never relate to an oath in a civil cause, taken according to the definition above given: profane and common swearing, with all light, irreverent oaths and imprecations, and all such oaths as are not required by the civil magistrate, in cases where the Lord is supposed to be witness, are certainly intended in our blessed Lord's prohibition. See on chap. iv. 26

CHAPTER VII.

With the seven nations that God shall cast out, 1, *they shall make no covenant*, 2, *nor form any matrimonial alliances*, 3; *lest they should be enticed into idolatry*, 4. *All monuments of idolatry to be destroyed*, 5. *The Israelites are to consider themselves a holy people*, 6; *and that the Lord had made them such, not for their merits, but for his own mercies*, 7, 8. *They shall therefore love him, and keep his commandments*, 9–11. *The great privileges of the obedient*, 12–24. *All idolatry to be avoided*, 25, 26.

A. M. 2553.
B. C. 1451.
An. Ex. Isr. 40.
Sebat.

WHEN the [a] LORD thy God shall bring thee into the land whither thou goest to possess it, and hath cast out many nations before thee, [b] the Hittites, and the Girgashites, and the Amorites, and the Canaanites, and the Perizzites, and the Hivites, and the Jebuzites, seven nations [c] greater and mightier than thou;

2 And when the LORD thy God shall [d] deliver them before thee; thou shalt smite them, *and* [e] utterly destroy them; [f] thou shalt make no covenant with them, nor show mercy unto them.

3 [g] Neither shalt thou make marriages with them; thy daughter thou shalt not give unto his son, nor his daughters shalt thou take unto thy son.

A. M. 2553.
B. C. 1451.
An. Ex. Isr. 40.
Sebat.

4 For they will turn away thy son from following me, that they may serve other gods: [h] so will the anger of the LORD be kindled against you, and destroy thee suddenly.

5 But thus shall ye deal with them: ye shall [i] destroy their altars, and break down their [k] images, and cut down their groves, and burn their graven images with fire.

6 [l] For thou *art* a holy people unto the LORD thy God: [m] the LORD thy God hath chosen thee to be a special people unto himself, above all people that *are* upon the face of the earth.

7 The LORD did not set his love upon you, nor choose you, because ye were more in number than any people; for ye *were* [n] the fewest of all people.

[a] Chap. xxxi. 3; Psa. xliv. 2, 3.——[b] Gen. xv. 19, &c.; Exod. xxxiii. 2.——[c] Chap. iv. 38; ix. 1.——[d] Ver. 23; chap. xxiii. 14.——[e] Lev. xxvii. 28, 29; Num. xxxiii. 52; chap. xx. 16, 17; Josh. vi. 17; viii. 24; ix. 24; x. 28, 40; xi. 11, 12.——[f] Exod. xxiii. 32; xxxiv. 12, 15, 16; Judg. ii. 2; see chap. xx. 10, &c.; Josh. ii. 14; ix. 18; Judg. i. 24.——[g] Josh. xxiii. 12; 1 Kings xi. 2; Ezra ix. 2.——[h] Chap. vi. 15.——[i] Exod. xxiii. 24; xxxiv. 13; chap. xii. 2, 3.——[k] Heb. *statues* or *pillars*.——[l] Exod. xix. 6; chap. xiv. 2; xxvi. 19; Psa. l. 5; Jer. ii. 3.——[m] Exod. xix. 5; Amos iii. 2; 1 Pet. ii. 9.——[n] Chap. x. 22.

NOTES ON CHAP. VII.

Verse 1. *Seven nations greater and mightier than thou*] In several places of the Hebrew text, *each* of these seven nations is not enumerated, some one or other being left out, which the Septuagint in general supply. How these nations were distributed over the land of Canaan previously to the entering in of the Israelites, the reader may see in the note on Josh. iii. 10.

Verse 2. *Thou shalt smite them, &c.*] These idolatrous nations were to be utterly destroyed, and all the others also which were contiguous to the boundaries of the promised land, provided they did not renounce their idolatry and receive the true faith: for if they did not, then no covenant was to be made with them on any secular or political consideration whatever; no mercy was to be shown to them, because the cup of their iniquity also was now full; and they must either embrace, heartily embrace, the true religion, or be cut off.

Verse 3. *Neither shalt thou make marriages, &c.*] The heart being naturally inclined to evil, there is more likelihood that the idolatrous wife should draw aside the believing husband, than that the believing husband should be able to bring over his idolatrous wife to the true faith.

Verse 6. *Thou* art *a holy people*] And therefore should have no connection with the workers of iniquity.

A special people] סגלה *segullah*,—Septuagint, λαον περιουσιον,—a *peculiar people*, a private property. The

A. M. 2553. B. C. 1451. An. Ex. Isr. 40. Sebat.

8 But [o] because the LORD loved you, and because he would keep [p] the oath which he had sworn unto your fathers, [q] hath the LORD brought you out with a mighty hand, and redeemed you out of the house of bondmen, from the hand of Pharaoh king of Egypt.

9 Know therefore that the LORD thy God, he *is* God, [r] the faithful God, [s] which keepeth covenant and mercy with them that love him and keep his commandments, to a thousand generations:

10 And [t] repayeth them that hate him to their face, to destroy them: [u] he will not be slack to him that hateth him, he will repay him to his face.

11 Thou shalt therefore keep the commandments, and the statutes, and the judgments, which I command thee this day, to do them.

12 [v] Wherefore it shall come to pass, [w] if ye hearken to these judgments, and keep and do them, that the LORD thy God shall keep unto thee [x] the covenant and the mercy which he sware unto thy fathers:

13 And he will [y] love thee, and bless thee, and multiply thee: [z] he will also bless the fruit of thy womb, and the fruit of thy land, thy corn, and thy wine, and thine oil, the increase of thy kine, and the flocks of thy sheep, in the land which he sware unto thy fathers to give thee.

14 Thou shalt be blessed above all people: [a] there shall not be male or female barren among you, or among your cattle.

15 And the LORD will take away from thee all sickness, and will put none of the [b] evil diseases of Egypt, which thou knowest, upon thee; but will lay them upon all *them* that hate thee.

A. M. 2553. B. C. 1451. An. Ex. Isr. 40. Sebat.

16 And [c] thou shalt consume all the people which the LORD thy God shall deliver thee; [d] thine eye shall have no pity upon them: neither shalt thou serve their gods; for that *will be* [e] a snare unto thee.

17 If thou shalt say in thine heart, These nations *are* more than I: how can I [f] dispossess them?

18 [g] Thou shalt not be afraid of them: *but* shalt well [h] remember what the LORD thy God did unto Pharaoh, and unto all Egypt;

19 [i] The great temptations which thine eyes saw, and the signs, and the wonders, and the mighty hand, and the stretched-out arm, whereby the LORD thy God brought thee out: so shall the LORD thy God do unto all the people of whom thou art afraid.

20 [k] Moreover the LORD thy God will send the hornet among them, until they that are left, and hide themselves from thee, be destroyed.

21 Thou shalt not be affrighted at them: for the LORD thy God *is* [l] among you, [m] a mighty God and terrible.

22 [n] And the LORD thy God will [o] put out those nations before thee by little and little: thou mayest not consume them at once, lest the beasts of the field increase upon thee.

23 But the LORD thy God shall deliver them [p] unto thee, and shall destroy them with a mighty destruction, until they be destroyed.

24 And [q] he shall deliver their kings into thine hand, and thou shalt destroy their name [r] from under heaven: [s] there shall no

---

[o] Chap. x. 15.——[p] Exod. xxxii. 13; Psa. cv. 8, 9, 10; Luke i. 55, 72, 73.——[q] Exod. xiii. 3, 14.——[r] Isa. xlix. 7; 1 Cor. i. 9; x. 13; 2 Cor. i. 18; 1 Thess. v. 24; 2 Thess. iii. 3; 2 Tim. ii. 13; Heb. xi. 11; 1 John i. 9.——[s] Exod. xx. 6; chap. v. 10; Neh. i. 5; Dan. iv. 4.——[t] Isa. lix. 18; Nah. i. 2.——[u] Chap. xxxii. 35.——[v] Lev. xxvi. 3; chap. xxviii. 1.——[w] Heb. *because.* [x] Psa. cv. 8, 9; Luke. i. 55, 72, 73.——[y] John xiv. 21.——[z] Chap. xxviii. 4.——[a] Exod. xxiii. 26, &c.——[b] Exod. ix. 14; xv. 26; chap. xxviii. 27, 60.

[c] Ver. 2.——[d] Chap. xiii. 8; xix. 13, 21; xxv. 12.——[e] Exod. xxiii. 33; chap. xii. 30; Judg. viii. 27; Psa. cvi. 36.——[f] Num. xxxiii. 53.——[g] Chap. xxxi. 6.——[h] Psa. cv. 5.——[i] Chap. iv. 34; xxix. 3.——[k] Exod. xxiii. 28; Josh. xxiv. 12.——[l] Num. xi. 20; xiv. 9, 14, 42; xvi. 3; Josh. iii. 10.——[m] Chap. x. 17; Neh. i. 5; iv. 14; ix. 32.——[n] Exodus xxiii. 29, 30.——[o] Heb. *pluck off.* [p] Heb. *before thy face;* ver. 2.——[q] Josh. x. 24, 25, 42; xii. 1, &c. [r] Exod. xvii. 14; chap. ix. 14; xxv. 19; xxix. 20.——[s] Chap. xi. 25; Josh. i. 5; x. 8; xxiii. 9.

---

words as they stand in the Septuagint are quoted by the apostle, 1 Pet. ii. 9.

Verse 8. *But because the Lord loved you*] It was no good in them that induced God to choose them at this time to be his peculiar people: he had his reasons, but these sprang from his infinite goodness. He intended to make a full discovery of his goodness to the world, and this must have a commencement in some particular place, and among some people. He chose that time, and he chose the Jewish people; but not because of their goodness or holiness.

Verse 12. *The Lord—shall keep unto thee the covenant*] So we find their continuance in the state of favour was to depend on their *faithfulness* to the grace of God. If they should rebel, though God had chosen them through his *love*, yet he would cast them off in his *justice*. The *elect*, we see, may become unfaithful, and so become *reprobates*. So it happened to 24,000 of them, whose carcasses fell in the wilderness because they had sinned; yet these were of the *elect* that came out of Egypt. Let him that standeth take heed lest he fall.

Verse 22. *Put out those nations—by little and lit-*

A. M. 2553. B. C. 1451. An. Ex. Isr. 40. Sebat.

man be able to stand before
thee, until thou have destroyed
them.
25 The graven images of their gods [t] shall
ye burn with fire: thou [u] shalt not desire the
silver or gold *that is* on them, nor take *it*
unto thee, lest thou be [v] snared therein: for
it *is* [w] an abomination to the Lord
thy God.
26 Neither shalt thou bring an
abomination into thine house, lest thou be a
cursed thing like it: *but* thou shalt utterly
detest it, and thou shalt utterly abhor it; [x] for
it *is* a cursed thing.

A. M. 2553. B. C. 1451. An. Ex. Isr. 40. Sebat.

[t] Ver. 5; Exod. xxxii. 20; chap. xii. 3; 1 Chron. xiv. 12.——[u] Josh. vii. 1, 21; 2 Mac. xii. 40.——[v] Judg. viii. 27; Zeph. i. 3.——[w] Chap. xvii. 1.——[x] Lev. xxvii. 28; chap. xiii. 17; Josh. vi. 17, 18; vii. 1.

tle] The Israelites were not as yet sufficiently numerous to fill the whole land occupied by the seven nations mentioned ver. 1. And as wild and ferocious animals might be expected to multiply where either there are no inhabitants, or the place is but thinly peopled, therefore God tells them that, though at present, by force of arms, they might be able to expel them, it would be impolitic so to do, lest the beasts of the field should multiply upon them.

Verse 25. *Thou shalt not desire the silver or gold that is on them*] Some of the ancient idols were plated over with gold, and God saw that the value of the metal and the excellence of the workmanship might be an inducement for the Israelites to *preserve* them; and this might lead, remotely at least, to idolatry. As the idols were accursed, all those who had them, or any thing appertaining to them, were accursed also, ver. 26.

CHAPTER VIII.

An exhortation to obedience from a consideration of God's past mercies, 1, 2. *Man is not to live by bread only, but by every word of God,* 3. *How God provided for them in the wilderness,* 4. *The Lord chastened them that they might be obedient,* 5, 6. *A description of the land into which they were going,* 7–9. *Cautions lest they should forget God in their prosperity,* 10–16, *and lest they should attribute that prosperity to themselves, and not to God,* 17, 18. *The terrible judgments that shall fall upon them, should they prove unfaithful,* 19, 20.

A. M. 2553. B. C. 1451. An. Ex. Isr. 40. Sebat.

ALL the commandments which
I command thee this day
[a] shall ye observe to do, that ye
may live, and multiply, and go in and possess
the land which the Lord sware unto your
fathers.
2 And thou shalt remember all the way which
the Lord thy God [b] led thee these forty years in
the wilderness, to humble thee, *and* [c] to prove
thee, [d] to know what *was* in thine heart, whether
thou wouldest keep his commandments, or no.
3 And he humbled thee, and
[e] suffered thee to hunger, and [f] fed thee with
manna, which thou knewest not, neither did
thy fathers know; that he might make thee
know that man doth [g] not live by bread only,
but by every *word* that proceedeth out of the
mouth of the Lord doth man live.
4 [h] Thy raiment waxed not old upon thee,

A. M. 2553. B. C. 1451. An. Ex. Isr. 40. Sebat.

[a] Chap. iv. 1; v. 32, 33; vi. 1, 2, 3.——[b] Chap. i. 3; ii. 7; xxix. 5; Psa. cxxxvi. 16; Amos ii. 10.——[c] Exod. xvi. 4; chap. xiii. 3.——[d] 2 Chron. xxxii. 31; John ii. 25.——[e] Exodus xvi. 2, 3.——[f] Exod. xvi. 12, 14, 35.——[g] Psa. civ. 29; Matt. iv. 4; Luke iv. 4.——[h] Chap. xxix. 5; Neh. ix. 21.

NOTES ON CHAP. VIII.

Verse 2. *Thou shalt remember all the way*] The various dealings of God with you; the dangers and difficulties to which ye were exposed, and from which God delivered you; together with the various miracles which he wrought for you, and his longsuffering towards you.

Verse 3. *He—suffered thee to hunger, and fed thee*] God never permits any tribulation to befall his followers, which he does not design to turn to their advantage. When he permits us to hunger, it is that his mercy may be the more observable in providing us with the necessaries of life. *Privations*, in the way of providence, are the forerunners of mercy and goodness abundant.

Verse 4. *Thy raiment waxed not old, &c.*] The plain meaning of this much-tortured text appears to me to be this: "God so amply provided for them all the necessaries of life, that they never were obliged to wear tattered garments, nor were their feet injured for lack of shoes or sandals." If they had carvers, engravers, silversmiths, and jewellers among them, as plainly appears from the account we have of the tabernacle and its utensils, is it to be wondered at if they also had *habit* and *sandal makers*, &c., &c., as we are certain they had *weavers, embroiderers*, and such like? And the traffic which we may suppose they carried on with the Moabites, or with travelling hordes of Arabians, doubtless supplied them with the *materials*; though, as they had abundance of sheep and neat cat-

A. M. 2553.
B. C. 1451.
An. Ex. Isr. 40
Sebat.

neither did thy foot swell, these forty years.

5 ⁱ Thou shalt also consider in thine heart, that, as a man chasteneth his son, so the LORD thy God chasteneth thee.

6 Therefore thou shalt keep the commandments of the LORD thy God, ᵏ to walk in his ways, and to fear him.

ⁱ 2 Sam. vii. 14; Psa. lxxxix. 32; Prov. iii. 12; Heb. xii. 5, 6; Rev. iii. 19.

7 For the LORD thy God bringeth thee into a good land, ˡ a land of brooks of water, of fountains and depths that spring out of valleys and hills ;

8 A land of wheat, and barley, and vines, and fig trees, and pomegranates ; a land ᵐ of oil olive, and honey ;

A. M. 2553.
B. C. 1451.
An. Ex. Isr. 40.
Sebat.

ᵏ Chap. v. 33.——ˡ Chap. xi. 10, 11, 12.——ᵐ Heb. *of olive-tree of oil.*

tle, they must have had much of the materials within themselves. It is generally supposed that God, by a miracle, preserved their clothes from wearing out : but if this sense be admitted, it will require, not one miracle, but a chain of the most successive and astonishing miracles ever wrought, to account for the thing ; for as there were not less than 600,000 males born in the wilderness, it would imply, that the clothes of the infant grew up with the increase of his body to manhood, which would require a miracle to be continually wrought on every thread, and on every particle of matter of which that thread was composed. And this is not all ; it would imply that the clothes of the parent became miraculously *lessened* to fit the body of the child, with whose growth they were again to stretch and grow, &c. No such miraculous interference was necessary.

Verse 8. A land of wheat, &c.] On the subject of this verse I shall introduce the following remarks, which I find in Mr. Harmer's Observations on the Fertility of the Land of Judea, vol. iii., p. 243.

" Hasselquist tells us that he ate olives at Joppa (upon his first arrival in the Holy Land) which were said to grow on the Mount of Olives, near Jerusalem; and that, independently of their oiliness, they were of the best kind he had tasted in the Levant. As olives are frequently eaten in their repasts, the delicacy of this fruit in Judea ought not to be forgotten ; and the oil that is gotten from these trees much less, because still more often made use of. In the progress of his journey he found several fine vales, abounding with olive trees. He saw also olive trees in Galilee ; but none farther, he says, than the mountain where it is supposed our Lord preached his sermon.

" The *fig trees* in the neighbourhood of Joppa, Hasselquist goes on to inform us, were as beautiful as any he had seen in the Levant.

" The reason why *pomegranates* are distinctly mentioned, in this description of the productions of the land of promise, may be their great usefulness in forming cooling drinks, for they are used among the Asiatics nearly in the same way that we use lemons ; see vol. ii., 145.

" *Honey* is used in large quantities in these countries ; and Egypt was celebrated for the assiduous care with which the people there managed their bees. Maillet's account of it is very amusing. ' There are,' says he, ' abundance of bees in that country ; and a singular manner of feeding them, introduced by the Egyptians of ancient times, still continues there. Towards the end of October, when the Nile, upon its

decrease, gives the peasants an opportunity of sowing the lands, *sainfoin* is one of the first things sown, and one of the most profitable. As the Upper Egypt is hotter than the Lower, and the inundation there goes sooner off the lands, the sainfoin appears there first. The knowledge they have of this causes them to send their bee-hives from all parts of Egypt, that the bees may enjoy, as soon as may be, the richness of the flowers, which grow in this part of the country sooner than in any other district of the kingdom. The hives, upon their arrival at the farther end of Egypt, are placed one upon another in the form of pyramids, in boats prepared for their reception, after having been numbered by the people who place them in the boats. The bees feed in the fields there for some days : afterwards, when it is believed they have nearly collected the honey and wax, which were to be found for two or three leagues round, they cause the boats to go down the stream, two or three leagues lower, and leave them there, in like manner, such a proportion of time as they think to be necessary for the gathering up the riches of that canton. At length, about the beginning of February, after having gone the whole length of Egypt, they arrive at the sea, from whence they are conducted, each of them, to their usual place of abode ; for they take care to set down exactly, in a register, each district from whence the hives were carried in the beginning of the season, their number and the names of the persons that sent them, as well as the number of the boats, where they are ranged according to the places they are brought from. What is astonishing in this affair is, that with the greatest fidelity of memory that can be imagined, each bee finds its own hive, and never makes any mistake. That which is still more amazing to me is, that the Egyptians of old should be so attentive to all the advantages deducible from the situation of their country ; that after having observed that all things came to maturity sooner in Upper Egypt, and much later in Lower, which made a difference of above six weeks between the two extremities of their country, they thought of collecting the wax and the honey so as to lose none of them, and hit upon this ingenious method of making the bees do it successively, according to the blossoming of the flowers, and the arrangement of nature.' "

If this solicitude were as ancient as the dwelling of Israel in Egypt, they must have been anxious to know whether *honey*, about which they took such care in Egypt, was plentiful in the land of promise ; and they must have been pleased to have been assured it was. It continues to be produced there in large

A. M. 2553.
B. C. 1451.
An. Ex. Isr. 40.
Sebat.

9 A land wherein thou shalt eat
bread without scarceness, thou
shalt not lack any *thing* in it;
a land [n] whose stones *are* iron, and out of
whose hills thou mayest dig brass.
10 [o] When thou hast eaten and art full, then
thou shalt bless the LORD thy God, for the
good land which he hath given thee.
11 Beware that thou forget not the LORD thy
God, in not keeping his commandments, and his
judgments, and his statutes, which
I command thee this day:

A. M. 2553.
B. C. 1451.
An. Ex. Isr. 40.
Sebat.

12 [p] Lest *when* thou hast eaten
and art full, and hast built goodly houses, and
dwelt *therein ;*
13 And *when* thy herds and thy flocks multiply, and thy silver and thy gold is multiplied,
and all that thou hast is multiplied ;
14 [q] Then thine heart be lifted up, and thou
[r] forget the LORD thy God, which brought

[n] Ch. xxxiii. 25.——[o] Ch. vi. 11, 12.——[p] Ch. xxviii. 47; xxxii. 15; Prov. xxx. 9; Hos. xiii. 6.——[q] 1 Cor. vi. 7.——[r] Psa. cvi. 21.

quantities: Hasselquist, in the progress of his journey from Acra to Nazareth, tells us that he found "great numbers of bees, bred thereabouts, to the great advantage of the inhabitants." He adds, "they make their bee-hives, with little trouble, of clay, four feet long, and half a foot in diameter, as in Egypt. They lay ten or twelve of them, one on another, on the bare ground, and build over every ten a little roof." Mr. Maundrell, observing also many bees in the Holy Land, takes notice that by their means the most barren places in other respects of that country become useful, perceiving in many places of the great salt plain near Jericho a smell of honey and wax as strong as if he had been in an apiary.

By Hasselquist's account it appears, that the present inhabitants of Palestine are not strangers to the use of hives. They are constructed of very different materials from ours, but just the same with the Egyptian hives. They seem to be an ancient contrivance; and indeed so simple an invention must be supposed to be as old as the days of Moses, when arts, as appears from his writings, of a much more elevated nature were known in Egypt. I cannot then well persuade myself to adopt the opinion of some of the learned, that those words of Moses, in Deut. xxxii. 13, *He made him to suck honey out of the rock, and oil out of the flinty rock*, are to be understood of his causing Israel to dwell in a country where sometimes they might find honey-comb in holes of the rock. It is very possible that in that hot country these insects, when not taken due care of, may get into hollow places of the rocks, and form combs there, as they sometimes construct them in ours in hollow trees, though I do not remember to have met with any traveller that has made such an observation. But would this have been mentioned with so much triumph by Moses in this place? The quantities of honey produced after this manner could be but small, compared with what would be collected in hives properly managed; when found, it must often cost a great deal of pains to get the honey out of these little cavities in the hard stone, and much the greatest part must be absolutely lost to the inhabitants. The interpretation is the more strange, because when it is said in the next clause, "and oil out of the flinty rock," it is evidently meant that they should have oil produced in abundance by olive trees growing on flinty rocks; and consequently, the sucking honey out of the rock should only mean their enjoying great quantities of honey, produced by bees that collected it from flowers growing among the rocks: the rocky mountains of this country, it is well known, produce an abundance of aromatic plants proper for the purpose. Nor does Asaph, in the close of the eighty-first Psalm, speak, I apprehend, of honey found in cavities of rocks; nor yet is he there describing it as collected from the odoriferous plants that grow in the rocky hills of those countries, if the reading of our present Hebrew copies be right: but the prophet tells Israel that, had they been obedient, God would have fed them with the fat of wheat, and with the rock of honey would he have satisfied them, that is, with the most delicious wheat, and with the richest, most invigorating honey, in large quantities, both for eating and making agreeable drink. Its reviving, strengthening quality appears in the story of Jonathan, Saul's son, 1 Sam. xix. 27; as the using the term *rock* to signify *strength*, &c., appears in a multitude of places. *The rock of a sword*, Psa. lxxxix. 43, for the *edge of the sword*, in which its energy lies, is, perhaps, as strange an expression to western ears.

I shall have occasion to speak of the excellence of the *grapes* of Judea in a succeeding chapter; I may therefore be excused from pursuing the farther examination of the productions of this country, upon giving my reader a remark of Dr. Shaw's to this purpose, that it is impossible for pulse, wheat, or grain of any kind, to be richer or better tasted than what is sold at Jerusalem. Only it may not be amiss to add, with respect to this country's being well watered, that the depth, תהום *tehom*, spoken of in this passage, seems to mean reservoirs of water filled by the rains of winter, and of great use to make their lands fertile; as the second word תעלתיה *tealotheiha* seems to mean wells, or some such sort of conveniences, supplied by springs; and the first word נהרתיה *naharotheiha* rivers or running streams, whether carrying a larger or smaller body of water. What an important part of this pleasing description, especially in the ears of those that had wandered near forty years in a most dry and parched wilderness! I will only add, without entering into particulars, that the present face of the country answers this description.

Verse 9. *A land whose stones* are *iron*] Not only meaning that there were iron mines throughout the land, but that the loose stones were strongly impregnated with iron, ores of this metal (the most useful of all the products of the *mineral* kingdom) being every where in great plenty.

Out of whose hills thou mayest dig brass.] As there is no such thing in nature as a *brass* mine, the word

A. M. 2553. B. C. 1451. An. Ex. Isr. 40. Sebat.

thee forth out of the land of
Egypt, from the house of bondage;
15 Who [s] led thee through that great and
terrible wilderness, [t] *wherein were* fiery serpents, and scorpions, and drought, where
there was no water; [u] who brought thee forth
water out of the rock of flint;
16 Who fed thee in the wilderness with
[v] manna, which thy fathers knew not, that he
might humble thee, and that he might prove
thee, [w] to do thee good at thy latter end;
17 [x] And thou say in thine heart, My power
and the might of *mine* hand hath gotten me
this wealth.
18 But thou shalt remember the
LORD thy God: [y] for *it is* he
that giveth thee power to get
wealth, that [z] he may establish his covenant
which he sware unto thy fathers, as *it is*
this day.
19 And it shall be, if thou do at all forget
the LORD thy God, and walk after other gods,
and serve them, and worship them, [a] I testify
against you this day that ye shall surely
perish.
20 As the nations which the LORD destroyeth
before your face, [b] so shall ye perish; because
ye would not be obedient unto the voice of
the LORD your God.

[s] Isa. lxiii. 12, 13, 14; Jer. ii. 6.——[t] Numbers xxi. 6; Hos. xiii. 5.——[u] Num. xx. 11; Psa. lxxviii. 15; cxiv. 8.——[v] Ver. 3; Exod. xvi. 15.——[w] Jer. xxiv. 5, 6; Heb. xii. 11.——[x] Chap. ix. 4; 1 Cor. iv. 7.——[y] Prov. x. 22; Hos. ii. 8.——[z] Chap. vii. 8, 12.——[a] Chap. iv. 26; xxx. 18.——[b] Dan. ix. 11, 12.

נחשת *nechosheth* should be translated *copper;* of which, by the addition of the *lapis calaminaris, brass* is made. See on Exod. xxv. 3.

Verse 15. *Who led thee through that—terrible wilderness*] See the account of their journeying in the notes on Exod. xvi. 1, &c.; Num. xxi., &c.

Fiery serpents] Serpents whose bite occasioned a most violent inflammation, accompanied with an unquenchable *thirst,* and which terminated in death. See on Num. xxi. 6.

Verse 16. *Who fed thee—with manna*] See this miracle described Exod. xvi. 13, &c.

Verse 18. *God—giveth thee power to get wealth*] Who among the rich and wealthy believes this saying? Who gives wisdom, understanding, skill, bodily strength, and health? Is it not God? And without these, how can wealth be acquired? Whose is providence? who gives fertility to the earth? And who brings every proper purpose to a right issue? Is it not God? And without these also can wealth be acquired? No. Then the proposition in the text is self-evident: it is God that giveth power to *get wealth,* and to God the wealthy man must account for the manner in which he has *expended* the riches which God hath given him.

CHAPTER IX.

The people are informed that they shall shortly pass over Jordan, and that God shall go over before them, to expel the ancient inhabitants, 1–3. *They are cautioned not to suppose that it is on account of their righteousness that God is to give them that land,* 4–6. *They are exhorted to remember their various provocations of the Divine Majesty, especially at* Horeb, 7–14; *and how Moses interceded for them, and destroyed the golden calf,* 15–21. *How they murmured at* Taberah, 22; *and rebelled at* Kadesh-barnea, 23; *and had been perverse from the beginning,* 24. *An account of the intercession of Moses in their behalf,* 25–29.

A. M. 2553. B. C. 1451. An. Ex. Isr. 40. Sebat.

HEAR, O Israel: Thou *art* to
[a] pass over Jordan this day,
to go in to possess nations
[b] greater and mightier than thyself, cities great
and [c] fenced up to heaven;
2 A people great and tall, [d] the children of
the Anakims, whom thou knowest, and *of*
whom thou hast heard *say,* Who
can stand before the children of
Anak?
3 Understand therefore this day, that the
LORD thy God *is* he which [e] goeth over before
thee; *as* a [f] consuming fire [g] he shall destroy
them, and he shall bring them down before thy

[a] Chap. xi. 31; Josh. iii. 16; iv. 19.——[b] Chap. iv. 38; vii. 1; xi. 23.——[c] Chap. i. 28.——[d] Num. xiii. 22, 28, 32, 33.——[e] Chap. xxxi. 3; Josh. iii. 11.——[f] Chap. iv. 24; Heb. xii. 29.——[g] Chap. vii. 23.

NOTES ON CHAP. IX.

Verse 1. *Thou* art *to pass over Jordan this day*] היום *haiyom, this time;* they had come *thirty-eight* years before this nearly to the verge of the promised land but were not permitted at *that day* or *time* to pass over, because of their rebellions; but *this time* they shall certainly pass over. This was spoken about the *eleventh* month of the *fortieth* year of their journeying, and it was on the first month of the following year they passed over; and during this interim Moses died.

A. M. 2553.
B. C. 1451.
An. Ex. Isr. 40.
Sebat.

face : [h] so shalt thou drive them out, and destroy them quickly, as the LORD hath said unto thee.

4 [i] Speak not thou in thine heart, after that the LORD thy God hath cast them out from before thee, saying, For my righteousness the LORD hath brought me in to possess this land : but [k] for the wickedness of these nations the LORD doth drive them out from before thee.

5 [l] Not for thy righteousness, or for the uprightness of thine heart, doth thou go to possess their land : but for the wickedness of these nations the LORD thy God doth drive them out from before thee, and that he may perform [m] the word which the LORD sware unto thy fathers, Abraham, Isaac, and Jacob.

6 Understand, therefore, that the LORD thy God giveth thee not this good land to possess it for thy righteousness ; for thou *art* [n] a stiffnecked people.

7 Remember, *and* forget not, how thou provokedst the LORD thy God to wrath in the wilderness : [o] from the day that thou didst depart out of the land of Egypt, until ye came unto this place, ye have been rebellious against the LORD.

8 Also [p] in Horeb ye provoked the LORD to wrath, so that the LORD was angry with you to have destroyed you.

9 [q] When I was gone up into the mount to receive the tables of stone, *even* the tables of the covenant which the LORD made with you, then [r] I abode in the mount forty days and forty nights, I neither did eat bread nor drink water :

10 [s] And the LORD delivered unto me two tables of stone written with the finger of God ; and on them *was written* according to all the words, which the LORD spake with you in the mount, out of the midst of the fire, [t] in the day of the assembly.

A. M. 2553.
B. C. 1451.
An. Ex. Isr. 40.
Sebat.

11 And it came to pass, at the end of forty days and forty nights, *that* the LORD gave me the two tables of stone, *even* the tables of the covenant.

12 And the LORD said unto me, [u] Arise, get thee down quickly from hence ; for thy people which thou hast brought forth out of Egypt have corrupted *themselves ;* they are [v] quickly turned aside out of the way which I commanded them ; they have made them a molten image.

13 Furthermore [w] the LORD spake unto me, saying, I have seen this people, and, behold, [x] it *is* a stiff-necked people :

14 [y] Let me alone, that I may destroy them, and [z] blot out their name from under heaven : [a] and I will make of thee a nation mightier and greater than they.

15 [b] So I turned and came down from the mount, and [c] the mount burned with fire : and the two tables of the covenant *were* in my two hands.

16 And [d] I looked, and, behold, ye had sinned against the LORD your God, *and* had made you a molten calf : ye had turned aside quickly out of the way which the LORD had commanded you.

17 And I took the two tables, and cast them out of my two hands, and brake them before your eyes.

18 And I [e] fell down before the LORD, as at the first, forty days and forty nights : I did neither eat bread, nor drink water, because of all your sins which ye sinned, in doing wick-

---

[h] Exod. xxiii. 31 ; chap. vii. 24.——[i] Chap. viii. 17 ; Rom. xi. 6, 20 ; 1 Cor. iv. 4, 7.——[k] Gen. xv. 16 ; Lev. xviii. 24, 25 ; chap. xviii. 12.——[l] Tit. iii. 5.——[m] Gen. xii. 7 ; xiii. 15 ; xv. 7 ; xvii. 8 ; xxvi. 4 ; xxviii. 13.——[n] Ver. 13 ; Exod. xxxii. 9 ; xxxiii. 3 ; xxxiv. 9.——[o] Exod. xiv. 11 ; xvi. 2 ; xvii. 2 ; Num. xi. 4 ; xx. 2 ; xxv. 2 ; ch. xxxi. 27.——[p] Exod. xxxii. 4 ; Psa. cvi. 19.——[q] Exod. xxiv. 12, 15.——[r] Exod. xxiv. 18 ; xxxiv. 28.——[s] Exod. xxxi. 18.

[t] Exodus xix. 17 ; xx. 1 ; chap. iv. 10 ; x. 4 ; xviii. 16.——[u] Exod. xxxii. 7.——[v] Chap. xxxi. 29 ; Judg. ii. 17.——[w] Exod. xxxii. 9.——[x] Ver. 6 ; chap. x. 16 ; xxxi. 27 ; 2 Kings xvii. 14.——[y] Exod. xxxii. 10.——[z] Chap. xxix. 20 ; Psa. ix. 5 ; cix. 13.——[a] Num. xiv. 12.——[b] Exod. xxxii. 15.——[c] Exod. xix. 18 ; chap. iv. 11 ; v. 23.——[d] Exod. xxxii. 19.——[e] Exod. xxxiv. 28 ; Psa cvi. 23.

Verse 5. *For the wickedness of these nations*] So then it was not by any *sovereign* act of God that these people were cast out, but for their *wickedness ;* they had transgressed the law of their Creator ; they had resisted his Spirit, and could no longer be tolerated. The Israelites were to possess their land, not because *they* deserved it, but first, because they were *less* wicked than the others ; and secondly, because God thus chose to *begin* the great work of his salvation among men. Thus then the *Canaanites were cut off*, and the *Israelites were grafted in ;* and the *Israelites*, because of their wickedness, were afterwards *cut off*, and the *Gentiles grafted in.* Let the latter not be high-minded, but fear ; *if God spared not the natural branches, take heed lest he spare not thee.* But let it be remembered that this land was originally their own, and that the present possessors had no legal right to it.

Verse 10. *Tables of stone*] See the notes on Exod xxxi. 18, and xxxii. 15, 16.

Verse 12. *Thy people—have corrupted* themselves]

A. M. 2553. B. C. 1451. An. Ex. Isr. 40. Sebat.

edly in the sight of the LORD, to provoke him to anger.

19 [f] For I was afraid of the anger and hot displeasure wherewith the LORD was wroth against you to destroy you. [g] But the LORD hearkened unto me at that time also.

20 And the LORD was very angry with Aaron to have destroyed him: and I prayed for Aaron also the same time.

21 And [h] I took your sin, the calf which ye had made, and burnt it with fire, and stamped it, *and* ground *it* very small, *even* until it was as small as dust: and I cast the dust thereof into the brook that descended out of the mount.

22 And at [i] Taberah, and at [k] Massah, and at [l] Kibroth-hattaavah, ye provoked the LORD to wrath.

23 Likewise [m] when the LORD sent you from Kadesh-barnea, saying, Go up and possess the land which I have given you; then ye rebelled against the commandment of the LORD your God, and [n] ye believed him not, nor hearkened to his voice.

24 [o] Ye have been rebellious against the LORD from the day that I knew you.

A. M. 2553. B. C. 1451. An. Ex. Isr. 40. Sebat.

25 [p] Thus I fell down before the LORD, forty days and forty nights, as I fell down *at the first;* because the LORD had said he would destroy you.

26 [q] I prayed therefore unto the LORD, and said, O Lord GOD, destroy not thy people and thine inheritance, which thou hast redeemed through thy greatness; which thou hast brought forth out of Egypt with a mighty hand.

27 Remember thy servants, Abraham, Isaac, and Jacob; look not unto the stubbornness of this people, nor to their wickedness, nor to their sin:

28 Lest [r] the land whence thou broughtest us out, say, [s] Because the LORD was not able to bring them into the land which he promised them, and because he hated them, he hath brought them out to slay them in the wilderness.

29 [t] Yet they *are* thy people, and thine inheritance, which thou broughtest out by thy [u] mighty power, and by thy stretched-out arm.

[f] Exod. xxxii. 10, 11.——[g] Exod. xxxii. 14; xxxiii. 17; chap. x. 10; Psa. cvi. 23.——[h] Exod. xxxii. 20; Isa. xxxi. 7.——[i] Num. xi. 1, 3, 5.——[k] Exod. xvii. 7.——[l] Num. xi. 4, 34.——[m] Num. xiii. 3; xiv. 1.——[n] Psa. cvi. 24, 25.——[o] Chap. xxxi. 27.

[p] Ver. 18.——[q] Exod. xxxii. 11, &c.——[r] Gen. xli. 57; 1 Sam. xiv. 25.——[s] Exod. xxxii. 12; Num. xiv. 16.——[t] Chap. iv. 20; 1 Kings viii. 51; Neh. i. 10; Psa. xcv. 7.——[u] Ver. 26; chap. iv. 34; Exod. vii. 8, 9; xiii. 3.

Debased themselves by making and worshipping an Egyptian idol. See on Exod. xxxii.

Verse 21. *I took your sin, the calf which ye had made*] See this fully explained Exod. xxxii. 20.

Verse 22. *At Kibroth-hattaavah*] See the note on Num. xi. 18.

Verse 27. *Remember thy servants, Abraham, Isaac, and Jacob*] As if he had said: "These are their descendants, and the covenant was made with those patriarchs in behalf of these." God bestows many blessings on comparatively worthless persons, either for the sake of their pious ancestors, or on account of the religious people with whom they are connected; therefore union with the Church of God is a blessing of no common magnitude. The reader will find the grand subject of this chapter explained at large in the notes on Exod. xxxi. and xxxii., to which he is particularly desired to refer.

CHAPTER X.

Moses is commanded to make a second set of tables, 1, 2. *He makes an ark, prepares the two tables, God writes on them the ten commandments, and Moses lays them up in the ark,* 3–5. *The Israelites journey from* Beeroth *to* Mosera, *where Aaron dies,* 6; *and from thence to* Gudgodah *and* Jotbath, 7. *At that time God separated the tribe of Levi for the service of the sanctuary,* 8, 9. *How long Moses stayed the second time in the mount,* 10, 11. *What God requires of the Israelites,* 12–15. *Their heart must be circumcised,* 16. *God's character and conduct,* 17, 18. *They are commanded to love the stranger,* 19; *to fear, love, and serve God,* 20, *because he had done such great things for them and their fathers,* 21, 22.

A. M. 2553. B. C. 1451. An. Ex. Isr. 40. Sebat.

AT that time the LORD said unto me, [a] Hew thee two tables of stone like unto the first, and come up unto me into the mount, and [b] make thee an ark of wood.

[a] Exod. xxxiv. 1, 2.

[b] Exod. xxv. 10.

NOTES ON CHAP. X.

Verse 1. *Hew thee two tables of stone*] See the notes on Exod. xxxiv. 1.

Verse 3. *Shittim wood*] See the note on Exod. xxv. 5, and succeeding verses, and on the parallel places in the margin.

A. M. 2553.
B. C. 1451.
An. Ex. Isr. 40.
Sebat.

2 And I will write on the tables
the words that were in the first
tables, which thou brakest, and
[c] thou shalt put them in the ark.
3 And I made an ark *of* [d] shittim wood, and
[e] hewed two tables of stone, like unto the first,
and went up into the mount, having the two
tables in mine hand.
4 And [f] he wrote on the tables, according to
the first writing, the ten [g] commandments
[h] which the LORD spake unto you in the mount,
out of the midst of the fire, [i] in the day of
the assembly: and the LORD gave them
unto me.
5 And I turned myself, and [k] came down from
the mount, and [l] put the tables in the ark
which I had made; [m] and there they be, as the
LORD commanded me.
6 And the children of Israel took their
journey from Beeroth [n] of the children of
Jaakan to [o] Mosera: [p] there Aaron died, and
there he was buried; and Eleazar his son
ministered in the priest's office, in his stead.
7 [q] From thence they journeyed unto Gudgodah; and from Gudgodah to Jotbath, a
land of rivers of waters.
8 At that time [r] the LORD separated the
tribe of Levi, [s] to bear the ark of the covenant
of the LORD, [t] to stand before the LORD to
minister unto him, and [u] to bless
in his name, unto this day.
9 [v] Wherefore Levi hath no
part nor inheritance with his brethren; the
LORD *is* his inheritance, according as the LORD
thy God promised him.
10 And [w] I stayed in the mount, according
to the [x] first time, forty days and forty nights;
and [y] the LORD hearkened unto me at that time
also, *and* the LORD would not destroy thee.
11 [z] And the LORD said unto me, Arise
[a] take *thy* journey before the people, that they
may go in and possess the land, which I
sware unto their fathers to give unto them.
12 And now, Israel, [b] what doth the LORD
thy God require of thee, but [c] to fear the LORD
thy God, [d] to walk in all his ways, and [e] to
love him, and to serve the LORD thy God with
all thy heart and with all thy soul,
13 To keep the commandments of the LORD,
and his statutes, which I command thee this
day [f] for thy good?
14 Behold, [g] the heaven and the heaven of
heavens *is* the LORD's thy God, [h] the earth
also, with all that therein *is*.
15 [i] Only the LORD had a delight in thy fathers
to love them, and he chose their seed after them,
even you above all people, as *it is* this day.
16 Circumcise therefore [k] the foreskin of

[c] Exodus xxv. 16, 21.——[d] Exodus xxv. 5, 10; xxxvii. 1.——[e] Exodus xxxiv. 4.——[f] Exodus xxxiv. 28.——[g] Heb. *words*.——[h] Exodus xx. 1.——[i] Exodus xix. 17; chap. ix. 10; xviii. 16.——[k] Exodus xxxiv. 29.——[l] Exodus xl. 20.——[m] 1 Kings viii. 9.——[n] Num. xxxiii. 31.——[o] Num. xxxiii. 30.——[p] Num. xx. 28; xxxiii. 38.——[q] Num. xxxiii. 32, 33.——[r] Num. iii. 6; iv. 4; viii. 14; xvi. 9.——[s] Num. iv. 15.——[t] Ch. xviii. 5.——[u] Lev. ix. 22; Num. vi. 23; chap. xxi. 5.——[v] Num. xviii. 20, 24; chap. xviii. 1, 2, Ezek. xliv. 28.——[w] Exod. xxxiv. 28; chap. ix. 18, 25.——[x] Or, *former days*.——[y] Exod. xxxii. 14, 33, 34; xxxiii. 17; chap. ix. 19.——[z] Exod. xxxii. 34; xxxiii. 1.——[a] Heb. *go in journey*.——[b] Mic. vi. 8.——[c] Chap. vi. 13.——[d] Chap. v. 33.——[e] Chap. vi. 5; xi. 13; xxx. 16, 20; Matt. xxii. 37.——[f] Chap. vi. 24.——[g] 1 Kings viii. 17; Psa. cxv. 16; cxlviii. 4.——[h] Gen. xiv. 19; Exod. xix. 5; Psa. xxiv. 1.——[i] Chap. iv. 37.——[k] See Lev. xxvi. 41; chap. xxx. 6; Jer. iv. 4; Rom. ii. 28, 29; Col. ii. 11.

Verse 4. *Ten commandments*] See the note on Exod. xx. 1, &c.

Verse 6. *And the children of Israel took their journey, &c.*] On this and the three following verses see *Kennicott's* remarks at the end of this chapter.

Verse 12. *Now, Israel, what doth the Lord—require of thee*] An answer is immediately given. God requires,

1. That ye *fear* him as Jehovah your God; him who made, preserves, and governs you.

2. *That ye walk in all his ways*—that, having received his precepts, all of which are good and excellent, ye obey the whole; walking in God's ways, not your own, nor in the ways of the people of the land.

3. That ye *love* him—have confidence in him as your father and friend, have recourse to him in all your necessities, and love him in return for his love.

4. That you *serve* him—give him that worship which he requires, performing it with all your *heart*—the whole of your affections, and with all your *soul*—your will, understanding, and judgment. In a word, putting forth your whole strength and energy of body and soul in the sacred work.

Verse 14. *Behold, the heaven and the heaven of heavens*] All these words in the original are in the plural number: הן השמים ושמי השמים *hen hashshamayim, ushemey hashshamayim*; *behold the heavens and the heavens of heavens*. But what do they mean? To say that the first means the atmosphere, the second the planetary system, and the third the region of the blessed, is saying but very little in the way of explanation. The words were probably intended to point out the immensity of God's creation, in which we may readily conceive one system of heavenly bodies, and others beyond them, and others still in endless progression through the whole vortex of space, every *star* in the vast abyss of nature being a *sun*, with its peculiar and numerous attendant worlds! Thus there may be systems of systems in endless gradation up to the throne of God!

Verse 16. *Circumcise—the foreskin of your heart*] A plain proof from God himself that this precept

a

A. M. 2553.
B. C. 1451.
An. Ex. Isr. 40.
Sebat.

your heart, and be no more
[l] stiff-necked.
17 For the LORD your God *is*
[m] God of gods, and [n] Lord of lords, a great
God, [o] a mighty, and a terrible, which [p] regardeth not persons, nor taketh reward:
18 [q] He doth execute the judgment of the
fatherless and widow, and loveth the stranger,
in giving him food and raiment.
19 [r] Love ye therefore the stranger: for ye
were strangers in the land of Egypt.
20 [s] Thou shalt fear the LORD
thy God; him shalt thou serve,
and to him shalt thou [t] cleave,
[u] and swear by his name.
21 [v] He *is* thy praise, and he *is* thy God,
[w] that hath done for thee these great and ter
rible things, which thine eyes have seen.
22 Thy fathers went down into Egypt [x] with
threescore and ten persons; and now the
LORD thy God hath made thee [y] as the stars
of heaven for multitude.

[l] Chap. ix. 6, 13.——[m] Josh. xxii. 22; Psa. cxxxvi. 2; Dan. ii. 47; xi. 36.——[n] Rev. xvii. 14; xix. 16.——[o] Chap. vii. 21.——[p] 2 Chron. xix. 7; Job xxxiv. 19; Acts x. 34; Rom. ii. 11; Gal. ii. 6; Eph. vi. 9; Col. iii. 25; 1 Pet. i. 17.——[q] Psa. lxviii. 5; cxlvi. 9.——[r] Lev. xix. 33, 34.

[s] Chap. vi. 13; Matt. iv. 10; Luke iv. 8.——[t] Chap. xi. 22; xiii. 4.——[u] Psa lxiii. 11.——[v] Exod. xv. 2; Psa. xxii. 3; Jer. xvii. 14.——[w] 1 Sam. xii. 24; 2 Sam. vii. 23; Psa. cvi. 21, 22.——[x] Gen. xlvi. 27; Exod. i. 5; Acts vii. 14.——[y] Gen. xv. 5; chap. i 10; xxviii. 62.

pointed out spiritual things, and that it was not the *cutting away a part of the flesh* that was the object of the Divine commandment, but the *purification of the soul*, without which all forms and ceremonies are of no avail. Loving God with all the heart, soul, mind, and strength, the heart being circumcised to enable them to do it, was, from the beginning, the end, design, and fulfilment of the whole law.

Verse 17. *God of gods, and Lord of lords*] That is, He is the source whence all being and power proceed; every agent is finite but himself; and he can counteract, suspend, or destroy all the actions of all creatures whensoever he pleases. If he determine to save, none can destroy; if he purpose to destroy, none can save. How absolutely necessary to have such a God for our friend!

A great God—mighty] האל הגבר *hael haggibbor, the mighty God;* this is the very title that is given to our blessed Lord and Saviour, Isa. ix. 6.

Verse 21. *He* is *thy praise*] It is an eternal honour to any soul to be in the friendship of God. Why are people ashamed of being thought religious? Because they know nothing of religion. He who knows his Maker may glory in his God, for without him what has any soul but disgrace, pain, shame, and perdition? How strange is it that those who fear God should be ashamed to own it, while sinners boldly proclaim their relationship to Satan!

Verse 22. *With threescore and ten persons*] And now, from so small a beginning, they were multiplied to more than 600,000 souls; and this indeed in the space of forty years, for the 603,000 which came out of Egypt were at this time all dead but Moses, Joshua, and Caleb. How easily can God increase and multiply, and how easily diminish and bring low! In all things, because of his unlimited power, he *can* do whatsoever he *will;* and he *will do* whatsoever is *right.*

ON a very important subject in this chapter Dr. Kennicott has the following judicious observations:—

"The book of *Deuteronomy* contains the several speeches made to the Israelites by Moses just before his death, recapitulating the chief circumstances of their history, from their deliverance out of Egypt to their arrival on the banks of Jordan. What in this book he has recorded as *spoken* will be best understood by comparing it with what he has recorded as *done* in the previous history; and this, which is very useful as to the other parts of this book, is absolutely necessary as to the part of the tenth chapter here to be considered.

"The previous circumstances of the history necessary to be here attended to are these. In *Exodus*, chap. xx., God speaks the *ten* commandments; in chap. xxiv. Moses, on Mount Sinai, receives the *two* tables, and is there forty days and nights; in chap. xxv., xxvi., xxvii., God appoints the service of the tabernacle; in chap. xxviii. separates Aaron and his sons for the priest's office, by a statute for ever, to him and his seed after him; in chap. xxxii. Moses, incensed at the golden calf, breaks the tables; yet he prays for the people, and God orders him to lead them towards Canaan; in chap. xxxiv. Moses carries up *two* other tables, and stays again forty days and nights. In *Numbers*, chap. iii., the tribe of Levi is selected; chap. viii., consecrated; chap. x. and xi. the Israelites march from Sinai on the *twentieth* day of the *second* month in the *second* year; in chap. xiii. spies sent; in chap. xiv. the men are sentenced to die in the wilderness during the forty years; in chap. xviii. the Levites are to have no lot nor large district in Canaan, but to be the Lord's inheritance; in chap. xx. Aaron dies on Mount Hor; lastly, in the complete catalogue of the whole march (chap. xxxiii.) we are told that they went from *Moseroth* to *Bene-jaakan*, thence to *Hor-hagidgad*, to *Jotbathah*, to *Ebronah*, to *Ezion-gaber*, to *Zin*, (which is *Kadesh*,) and thence to Mount *Hor*, where Aaron died in the *fortieth* and last year. In *Deuteronomy*, chap. ix., Moses tells the Israelites, (ver. 7,) that they had been rebels, from Egypt even to Jordan, particularly at Horeb, (ver. 8–29,) whilst he was with God, and received the tables at the end of forty days and nights; and that, after breaking the tables, he fasted and interceded for his brethren during a *second* period of forty days and nights; and this *ninth* chapter ends with the prayer which he then made. Chapter x. begins thus: 'At that time the Lord said unto me, Hew thee two tables of stone, like unto the first, and come up,' &c. And from ver. 1 to the end of ver. 5 he describes the *second* copy of the

ten commandments, as written also by God, and deposited by himself in the ark.

"After this we have now four verses, (6, 7, 8, and 9,) which not only have no kind of connection with the verses before and after them, but also, as they stand in the present Hebrew text, directly contradict that very text; and the *two* first of these verses have not, in our Hebrew text, the least connection with the *two* last of them. Our Hebrew text, (ver. 6,) says that Israel journeyed *from Bene-jaakan to Mosera.* Whereas that very text in the complete catalogue, (Num. xxxiii. 31,) says they journeyed *from Moseroth to Bene-jaakan.* Again: Aaron is here said to have died at *Mosera*, whereas he died on Mount *Hor*, the *seventh* station afterwards; see Num. xxxiii. 38. And again: they are here said to go from *Bene-jaakan* to *Mosera*, thence to *Gudgodah*, and thence to *Jotbath;* whereas the complete catalogue says, *Moseroth* to *Bene-jaakan*, thence to *Hor-hagidgad*, and thence to *Jotbathah*. But if the marches could possibly be true as they now stand in these *two* verses, yet what connection can there be between JOTBATH and the SEPARATION OF THE TRIBE OF LEVI? It is very happy that these several difficulties in the *Hebrew* text are removed by the SAMARITAN Pentateuch: for *that* text tells us here rightly that the march was from *Moseroth* to *Bene-jaakan;* to *Hagidgad;* to *Jotbathah*, to *Ebronah*, to *Ezion-gaber*, to *Zin*, (which is *Kadesh*,) and thence to Mount *Hor*, where Aaron died. Again: as the regular deduction of these stations ends with Mount *Hor* and *Aaron's death*, we have then what we had not before, a regular connection with the *two* next verses, and the connection is this: That when Aaron, the son of Amram, the son of *Kohath*, the son of LEVI, died, neither the *tribe of Levi* nor the *priesthood* was deserted, but God still supported the latter by maintaining the former; and this, not by allotting that tribe any one large part of Canaan, but separate cities among the other tribes, and by allowing them to live upon those offerings which were made by the other tribes to God himself. These four verses therefore, (6, 7, 8, and 9,) in the *same* text, stand thus: (ver. 6,) WHEN *the children of Israel journeyed from Moseroth,* and encamped in *Bene-jaakan;* from thence they journeyed and encamped at *Hagidgad;* from thence they journeyed and encamped in *Jotbathah*, a land of rivers of water: (7) From thence they journeyed and encamped in *Ebronah;* in *Ezion-gaber;* in the wilderness of *Zin*, which is *Kadesh;* and then at Mount *Hor: And* AARON DIED THERE, *and there he was buried; and Eleazar his son ministered as priest in his stead.* (8) *At that time the Lord* HAD *separated the tribe of Levi, to bear the ark of the covenant of the Lord, to stand before the Lord, to minister unto him, and to bless in his name unto this day.* (9) *Wherefore Levi hath no part nor inheritance with his brethren; the Lord is his inheritance, according as the Lord thy God promised him.*

"But however consistent these *four* verses are now with themselves, it will be still demanded, What *connection* have they with the *fifth* verse *before* them, and with the *tenth* verse *after* them? I confess I cannot discover their least pertinency here, because AARON'S DEATH and LEVI'S SEPARATION seem totally foreign to the speech of Moses in this place. And this speech *without these four verses* is a regularly connected admonition from Moses to this purpose: that his brethren were for ever to consider themselves as indebted to *him*, under God, for the renewal of the *two* tables, and also to *his* intercession for rescuing them from destruction. The words are these: (chap. x. 4,) 'The Lord wrote again the ten commandments, and gave them unto me. (5) And I came down from the mount, and put the tables in the ark, which I HAD made;—(10) Thus I stayed in the mount according to the first time, forty days and forty nights: and the Lord hearkened unto me at that time also; the Lord would not destroy thee. (11) And the Lord said unto me, Arise, take thy journey before the people, that they may go in and possess the land,' &c. But then, if these *four* verses were not at first a part of this chapter, but are evidently interpolated, there arises another inquiry, *Whether they are an insertion entirely spurious, or a genuine part of the sacred text, though removed hither out of some other chapter?* As they contain nothing singular or peculiar, are of no particular importance, and relate to no subject of disputation, they are not likely to have arisen from fraud or design; but, perfectly coinciding in sense with other passages, they may safely be considered as another instance of a large transposition [86 words] in the present text, arising from accident and want of care. And the only remaining question therefore is, *Whether we can discover*, though not to demonstration, yet with any considerable degree of *probability*, the original place of these *four* verses, that so they may be at last restored to that neighbourhood and connection from which they have been, for so many ages, separated?

"It was natural for Moses, in the course of these several speeches to his brethren in *Deuteronomy*, to embrace the first opportunity of impressing on their memories a matter of such particular importance *as the continuation of the priesthood among the Levites after Aaron's death.* And the first proper place seems to be in the *second* chapter, after the *first* verse. At chap. i. 19 he speaks of their march from *Horeb* to *Kadesh-barnea*, whence they sent the spies into Canaan. He then sets forth their murmurings, and God's sentence that they should die in the wilderness, and he ends the first chapter with their being *defeated by the Amorites*, their *weeping before the Lord*, and *abiding many days* in KADESH, which is KADESH-BARNEA, near Canaan.

"Chap. ii. begins thus: *Then we turned, and took our journey into the wilderness by the way of the Red Sea, as the Lord spake unto me:* and WE COMPASSED MOUNT SEIR MANY DAYS. Now, the many days, or long time, which they spent in *compassing Mount Seir*, that is, going round on the *south-west* coasts of *Edom* in order to proceed *north-east* from Edom, through *Moab* to *Arnon*, must include *several* of their stations, besides that eminent one at *Mount Hor*, where *Aaron died.* And as part of their road, during this long compass, lay through *Ezion-gaber*, (which was on the *eastern tongue* of the Red Sea, and the *south* boundary of Edom,) thence to *Zin*, (which is KADESH, that is, MERIBAH KADESH,) and thence to *Mount Hor*, as they marched to the north-east; so it

is probable that the five stations preceding that of *Ezion-gaber* were on the extremity of *Mount Seir*, to the *south-west*. And if their first station at entering the south-west borders of Edom, and beginning to *compass Mount Seir*, was *Moseroth*, this gives the reason wanted why Moses begins this passage at *Moseroth*, and ends it with Aaron's death at Mount Hor. And this will discover a proper connection between the four dislocated verses and the context here.—Deut. i. 46: 'So ye abode in Kadesh (*Barnea*) many days.' Chap. ii. 1: 'Then we turned, and took our journey into the wilderness by the way of the Red Sea, as the Lord spake unto me; and WE COMPASSED MOUNT SEIR MANY DAYS.'

"'For the children of Israel journeyed from Moseroth, and pitched in Bene-jaakan: from thence they journeyed and pitched in Hagidgad: from thence they journeyed and pitched in Jotbathah, a land of rivers of water: from thence they journeyed and pitched in Ebronah: from thence they journeyed and pitched in Ezion-gaber: from thence they journeyed and pitched in the wilderness of Zin, which is Kadesh: from thence they journeyed and pitched in Mount Hor, and Aaron died there, and there he was buried; and Eleazar his son ministered as priest in his stead. At that time the Lord had separated the tribe of Levi, to bear the ark of the covenant of the Lord, to stand before the Lord to minister unto him, and to bless in his name unto this day. Wherefore, Levi hath no part nor inheritance with his brethren, the Lord is his inheritance, according as the Lord thy God promised him.'

"And this paragraph being thus inserted at the end of the first verse, the second verse begins a new paragraph, thus: *And the Lord spake unto me, saying, Ye have compassed this mountain long enough; turn you northward*—through the east side of Seir (or Edom) towards Moab on the north. See ver. 4–8."—*Kennicott's Remarks*, p. 74.

These remarks should not be hastily rejected.

CHAPTER XI.

The people are exhorted to obedience from a consideration of God's goodness to their fathers in Egypt, 1–4, *and what he did in the wilderness*, 5, *and the judgment on* Dathan *and* Abiram, 6, *and from the mercies of God in general*, 7–9. *A comparative description of Egypt and Canaan*, 10–12. *Promises to obedience*, 13–15. *Dissuasives from idolatry*, 16, 17. *The words of God to be laid up in their hearts, to be for a sign on their hands, foreheads, gates, &c.*, 18, *taught to their children, made the subject of frequent conversation, to the end that their days may be multiplied*, 19–21. *If obedient, God shall give them possession of the whole land, and not one of their enemies shall be able to withstand them*, 22–25. *Life and death, a blessing and a curse, are set before them*, 26–28. *The blessings to be put on Mount* Gerizim *and the curses on Mount* Ebal, 29, 30. *The promise that they should pass over Jordan, and observe these statutes in the promised land*, 31, 32.

A. M. 2553. B. C. 1451. An. Ex. Isr. 40. Sebat.

THEREFORE thou shalt [a] love the LORD thy God, and [b] keep his charge, and his statutes, and his judgments, and his commandments, alway.

2 And know ye this day: for *I speak* not with your children which have not known, and which have not seen [c] the chastisement of the LORD your God, [d] his greatness, [e] his mighty hand, and his stretched-out arm.

3 [f] And his miracles, and his acts, which he did in the midst of Egypt unto Pharaoh the king of Egypt, and unto all his land;

4 And what he did unto the army of Egypt, unto their horses, and to their chariots; [g] how he made the water of the Red Sea to overflow them as they pursued after you, and *how* the LORD hath destroyed them unto this day;

5 And what he did unto you in the wilderness, until ye came into this place;

6 And [h] what he did unto Dathan and Abiram, the sons of Eliab, the son of Reuben: how the earth opened her mouth, and swallowed them up, and their households, and their tents, and all the [i] substance that [k] *was* in their possession, in the midst of all Israel:

7 But [l] your eyes have seen all the great acts of the LORD which he did.

8 Therefore shall ye keep all the commandments which I command you this day, that ye

[a] Chap. x. 12; xxx. 16, 20.—[b] Zech. iii. 7.—[c] Chap. viii. 5. [d] Chap. v. 24.—[e] Chap. vii. 19.—[f] Psa. lxxviii. 12; cxxxv. 9. [g] Exod. xiv. 27, 28; xv. 9, 10; Psa. cvi. 11.

[h] Num. xvi. 1, 31; xxvii. 3; Psa. cvi. 17.—[i] Or, *living substance which followed them*.—[k] Heb. was *at their feet*.—[l] Chap. v. 3; vii. 19.

NOTES ON CHAP. XI.

Verse 1. *Thou shalt love the Lord*] Because without this there could be no obedience to the Divine testimonies, and no happiness in the soul; for the *heart* that is destitute of the *love of God*, is empty of all good, and consequently miserable. See the note on chap. x. 12.

Verse 6. *What he did unto Dathan, &c.*] See the notes on Num. xvi.

Verse 8. *Therefore shall ye keep all the command-*

A. M. 2553.
B. C. 1451.
An. Ex. Isr. 40.
Sebat.

may [m] be strong, and go in and
possess the land, whither ye go
to possess it;
9 And [n] that ye may prolong *your* days in
the land, [o] which the LORD sware unto your
fathers to give unto them and to their seed, [p] a
land that floweth with milk and honey.
10 For the land, whither thou goest in to
possess it, *is* not as the land of Egypt, from
whence ye came out, [q] where thou sowedst thy
seed, and wateredst *it* with thy foot, as a garden of herbs:
11 [r] But the land, whither ye go to possess
it, *is* a land of hills and valleys, *and* drinketh
water of the rain of heaven:
12 A land which the LORD thy God [s] careth
for; [t] the eyes of the LORD thy God *are* always
upon it, from the beginning of the year even
unto the end of the year.
13 And it shall come to pass, if ye shall
hearken [u] diligently unto my commandments which I command
you this day, [v] to love the LORD
your God, and to serve him with all your
heart and with all your soul,
14 That [w] I will give *you* the rain of your
land in his due season, [x] the first rain and the
latter rain, that thou mayest gather in thy corn,
and thy wine, and thine oil.
15 [y] And I will [z] send grass in thy fields for
thy cattle, that thou mayest [a] eat and be full.
16 Take heed to yourselves, [b] that your
heart be not deceived, and ye turn aside, and
[c] serve other gods, and worship them;
17 And *then* [d] the LORD'S wrath be kindled
against you, and he [e] shut up the heaven, that
there be no rain, and that the land yield not
her fruit; and *lest* [f] ye perish quickly from off
the good land which the LORD giveth you.
18 Therefore [g] shall ye lay up these my

[m] Josh. i. 6, 7.——[n] Chap. iv. 40; v. 16; Prov. x. 27.——[o] Chap. ix. 5.——[p] Exod. iii. 8.——[q] Zech. xiv. 18.——[r] Chap. viii. 7. [s] Heb. *seeketh.*——[t] 1 Kings ix. 3.——[u] Ver. 22; chap. vi. 17. [v] Chap. x. 12.——[w] Lev. xxvi. 4; chap. xxviii. 12.——[x] Joel ii. 23; James v. 7.

[y] Psa. civ. 14.——[z] Heb. *give.*——[a] Chap. vi. 11; Joel ii. 19. [b] Chap. xxix. 18; Job xxxi. 27.——[c] Chap. viii. 19; xxx. 17. [d] Chap. vi. 15.——[e] 1 Kings viii. 35; 2 Chron. vi. 26; vii. 13. [f] Chap. iv. 26; vii. 19, 20; xxx. 18; Joshua xxiii. 13, 15, 16. [g] Chap. vi. 6; xxxii. 46.

ments] Because God can execute such terrible judgments, and because he has given such proofs of his power and justice; and because, in similar provocations, he may be expected to act in a similar way; therefore keep his charge, that he may keep you unto everlasting life.

Verse 10. *Wateredst* it *with thy foot*] Rain scarcely ever falls in Egypt, and God supplies the lack of it by the inundations of the Nile. In order to water the grounds where the inundations do not extend, water is collected in ponds, and directed in streamlets to different parts of the field where irrigation is necessary. It is no unusual thing in the East to see a man, with a small mattock, making a little trench for the water to run by, and as he opens the passage, the water following, he uses his *foot* to raise up the mould against the side of this little channel, to prevent the water from being shed unnecessarily before it reaches the place of its destination. Thus he may be said to water the ground with his foot. See several useful observations on this subject in Mr. *Harmer*, vol. i., pp. 23–26, and vol. iii., p. 411. "For *watering land* an instrument called *janta* is often used in the north of Bengal: it consists of a *wooden trough*, about fifteen feet long, six inches wide, and ten inches deep, which is placed on a horizontal beam lying on bamboos fixed in the bank of a pond or river in the form of a gallows. One end of the trough rests upon the bank, where a *gutter* is prepared to carry off the water, and the other is dipped into the water by a man standing on a stage near that end, and plunging it in with his *foot*. A long bamboo, with a large weight of earth at the farther end of it, is fastened to that end of the *janta* near the river, and passing over the gallows, poises up the *janta* full of water, and causes it to empty itself into the gutter." This, Mr. *Ward* supposes, illustrates this passage. See *Hindoo Customs, &c.*, vol. iii., p. 104. But after all, the expression, *wateredst it with thy foot*, may mean no more than doing it by labour; for, as in the land of Egypt there is scarcely any rain, the watering of gardens, &c., must have been all artificial. But in Judea it was different, as there they had their proper seasons of rain. The compound word ברגל *beregel*, *with*, *under*, or *by the foot*, is used to signify any thing under the power, authority, &c., of a person; and this very meaning it has in the sixth verse, *all the substance that was in their possession*, is, literally, all the substance that was *under their feet*, ברגליהם *beragleyhem*, that is, in their *power*, *possession*, or what they had acquired by their *labour*.

Verse 14. *The rain—in his due season, the first rain and the latter rain*] By the *first* or *former rain* we are to understand that which fell in Judea about November, when they sowed their seed, and this served to moisten and prepare the ground for the vegetation of the seed. The *latter rain* fell about April, when the corn was well grown up, and served to fill the ears, and render them plump and perfect. Rain rarely fell in Judea at any other seasons than these. If the *former rain* were withheld, or not sent in due season, there could be no vegetation: if the *latter rain* were withheld, or not sent in its due season, there could be no full corn in the ear, and consequently no harvest. Of what consequence then was it that they should have their rain in *due season!* God, by promising this provided they were obedient, and threatening to withhold it should they be disobedient, shows that it is not a *general providence* that directs

A. M. 2553.
B. C. 1451.
An. Ex. Isr. 40.
Sebat.

words in your heart and in your soul, and [h] bind them for a sign upon your hand, that they may be as frontlets between your eyes.

19 [i] And ye shall teach them your children, speaking of them when thou sittest in thine house, and when thou walkest by the way, when thou liest down, and when thou risest up.

20 [k] And thou shalt write them upon the door-posts of thine house, and upon thy gates:

21 That [l] your days may be multiplied, and the days of your children, in the land which the LORD sware unto your fathers to give them, [m] as the days of heaven upon the earth.

22 For if [n] ye shall diligently keep all these commandments which I command you, to do them, to love the LORD your God, to walk in all his ways, and [o] to cleave unto him;

23 Then will the LORD [p] drive out all these nations from before you, and ye shall [q] possess greater nations and mightier than yourselves.

24 [r] Every place, whereon the soles of your feet shall tread, shall be yours: [s] from the wilderness and Lebanon, from the river, the river Euphrates, even unto the uttermost sea, shall your coast be.

25 [t] There shall no man be able to stand before you: *for* the LORD your God shall [u] lay the fear of you and the dread of you upon all the land that ye shall tread upon, [v] as he hath said unto you.

26 [w] Behold, I set before you this day a blessing and a curse;

27 [x] A blessing, if ye obey the commandments of the LORD your God, which I command you this day:

28 And a [y] curse, if ye will not obey the commandments of the LORD your God, but turn aside out of the way which I command you this day, to go after other gods, which ye have not known.

29 And it shall come to pass, when the LORD thy God hath brought thee in unto the land whither thou goest to possess it, that thou shalt put [z] the blessing upon Mount Gerizim, and the curse upon Mount Ebal.

30 *Are* they not on the other side Jordan, by the way where the sun goeth down, in the land of the Canaanites, which dwell in the champaign over against Gilgal, [a] beside the plains of Moreh?

31 [b] For ye shall pass over Jordan to go in to possess the land which the LORD your God giveth you, and ye shall possess it, and dwell therein.

32 And ye shall observe [c] to do all the statutes and judgments which I set before you this day.

[h] Chap. vi. 8.—[i] Chap. iv. 9, 10; vi. 7.—[k] Chap. vi. 9.—[l] Chap. iv. 40; vi. 2; Prov. iii. 2; iv. 10; ix. 11.—[m] Psa. lxxii. 5; lxxxix. 29.—[n] Ver. 13; chap. vi. 17.—[o] Chap. x. 20; xxx. 20.—[p] Chap. iv. 38; ix. 5.—[q] Chap. ix. 1.—[r] Joshua i. 3; xiv. 9.—[s] Gen. xv. 18; Exod. xxiii. 31; Num. xxxiv. 3, &c.—[t] Chap. vii. 24.—[u] Chap. ii. 25.—[v] Exod. xxiii. 27.—[w] Chap. xxx. 1, 15, 19.—[x] Chap. xxviii. 2.—[y] Chap. xxviii. 15.—[z] Chap. xxvii. 12, 13; Josh. viii. 33.—[a] Gen. xii. 6; Judg. vii. 1.—[b] Chap. ix. 1; Josh. i. 11.—[c] Chap. v. 32; xii. 32.

these things, but that the very rain of heaven falls by *particular* direction, and the showers are often regulated by an *especial* providence.

Verse 18. *Therefore shall ye lay up these my words*] See chap. vi. 4-8, and see on Exod. xiii. 9.

Verse 24. *From the river*] Euphrates, which was on the *east*, to *the uttermost sea*—the Mediterranean, which lay *westward* of the promised land. This promise, notwithstanding the many provocations of the Israelites, was fulfilled in the time of Solomon, for "he reigned over all the kings from the river (Euphrates) even unto the land of the Philistines, and to the border of Egypt." See 2 Chron. ix. 26, and the note on Num. xxxiv. 12.

Verse 26. *Behold, I set before you—a blessing and a curse*] If God had not put it *in the power* of this people either to *obey* or *disobey*; if they had not had a *free will*, over which they had complete authority, to use it either in the way of *willing* or *nilling*; could God, with any propriety, have given such precepts as these, sanctioned with such promises and threatenings? If they were not *free agents*, they could not be *punished* for *disobedience*, nor could they, in any sense of the word, have been *rewardable* for *obedience*. A STONE is not *rewardable* because, in obedience to the laws of *gravitation*, it *always tends to the centre*; nor is it punishable because, in being removed from that centre, in its tending or falling towards it again it takes away the life of a man.

That God has given man a *free*, *self-determining* WILL, which cannot be *forced* by any power but that which is omnipotent, and which God himself *never will force*, is declared in the most formal manner through the whole of the sacred writings. No *argument* can affect this, while the Bible is considered as a Divine revelation; no *sophistry* can explain away its evidence, as long as the *accountableness* of man for his conduct is admitted, and as long as the eternal bounds of *moral good* and *evil* remain, and the *essential distinctions* between *vice* and *virtue* exist. If ye *will* obey, (for God is ever ready to assist,) ye shall live; if ye *will* disobey and refuse that help, ye shall die. So hath *Jehovah* spoken, and man cannot reverse it.

Verse 29. *Thou shalt put the blessing upon Mount Gerizim, and the curse upon Mount Ebal.*] The etymology of these names may be supposed to cast some

light on this institution. גרזים *gerizzim*, from גרז *garaz*, to *cut*, *cut off*, *cut down;* hence גרזים *gerizzim*, the *cutters down*, *fellers*, and *reapers* or *harvest-men*, this mountain being supposed to have its name from its great *fertility*, or the abundance of the crops it yielded, which is a possible case. Of עיבל *ebal* or *eybal* the root is not found in Hebrew; but in Arabic عبل *abala* signifies *rough*, *rugged*, *curled*, *&c.*; and أعبل *abalo*, from the same root, signifies *white stones*, and a *mountain* in which such stones are found; الأعبل *alabalo*, *the mount of white stones*. See *Giggeius* and *Golius*. And as it is supposed that the mountain had this name because of its *barrenness*, on this metaphorical interpretation the sense of the passage would appear to be the following: God will so superintend the land, and have it continually under the eye of his watchful providence, that no change can happen in it but according to his Divine counsel, so that its *fertility* shall ever be the consequence of the *faithful obedience* of its inhabitants, and a proof of the *blessing of God* upon it; on the contrary, its *barrenness* shall be a proof that the people have *departed from their God*, and that his curse has in consequence fallen upon the land. See the manner of placing these blessings and curses, chap. xxvii. 12, &c. That Gerizim *is* very *fruitful*, and that Ebal *is* very *barren*, is the united testimony of all who have travelled in those parts. See Ludolf, Reland, Rab. Benjamin, and Mr. Maundrell. Sychem lies in the valley between these two mountains.

That the land of Judea was *naturally* very fertile, can scarcely be supposed by any who considers the accounts given of it by travellers; with the exception of a few districts, the whole land is dry, stony, and barren, and particularly all the southern parts of Judea, and all the environs of Jerusalem, most of which are represented as absolutely incapable of cultivation. How then could it ever support its vast number of inhabitants? By the especial providence of God. While God kept that people under his continual protection, their land was a paradise; they lent to all nations and borrowed from none. What has it been since? A demi-solitude, because that especial blessing no longer descends upon it. No land, says Calmet, was more fertile while under the benediction of God: none more barren when under his curse. Its present state is a proof of the declaration of Moses, chap. xxviii. 23: "The *heaven* over their head is *brass*; the *earth* under their feet, *iron*." The land itself, in its present state, is an ample proof of the authenticity of the Pentateuch. Should facts of this kind be lost sight of by any who read the sacred writings?

CHAPTER XII.

All monuments of idolatry in the promised land to be destroyed, 1–3; *and God's service to be duly performed*, 4–7. *The difference between the performance of that service in the wilderness and in the promised land*, 8–11. *The people are to be happy in all their religious observances*, 12. *The offerings must be brought to the place which God appoints, and no blood is to be eaten*, 13–16. *The tithe of corn, wine, oil, &c., to be eaten in the place that God shall choose*, 17, 18. *The Levite must not be forsaken*, 19. *All clean beasts may be eaten, but the blood must be poured out before the Lord, and be eaten on no pretence whatever*, 20–25. *Of vows, burnt-offerings, &c.*, 26, 27. *These precepts are to be carefully obeyed*, 28. *Cautions against the abominations of the heathen*, 29–31. *Nothing to be added to or diminished from the word of God*, 32.

A. M. 2553.
B. C. 1451.
An. Ex. Isr. 40.
Sebat.

THESE [a] *are* the statutes and
judgments which ye shall
observe to do in the land which
the Lord God of thy fathers giveth thee to
possess it, [b] all the days that ye live upon the
earth.
2 [c] Ye shall utterly destroy all the places
wherein the nations which ye shall [d] possess
served their gods, [e] upon the high mountains,
and upon the hills, and under every green tree:
3 And [f] ye shall [g] overthrow their altars, and
break their pillars, and burn their
groves with fire; and ye shall
hew down the graven images of
their gods, and destroy the names of them out
of that place.
4 [h] Ye shall not do so unto the Lord your
God.
5 But unto the place which the Lord your
God shall [i] choose out of all your tribes to
put his name there, *even* unto his habitation
shall ye seek, and thither thou shalt come:

[a] Chap. vi. 1.——[b] Chap. iv. 10; 1 Kings viii. 40.——[c] Exod. xxxiv. 13; chap. vii. 5.——[d] Or, *inherit.*——[e] 2 Kings xvi. 4; xvii. 10, 11; Jer. iii. 6.

[f] Num. xxxiii. 52; Judg. ii. 2.——[g] Heb. *break down.*——[h] Ver. 31.——[i] Ver. 11; chap. xxvi. 2; Josh. ix. 27; 1 Kings viii. 29; 2 Chron. vii. 12; Psa. lxxviii. 68.

NOTES ON CHAP. XII.

Verse 3. *Ye shall overthrow their altars*] Where unholy sacrifices have been offered; *and break their pillars*, probably meaning statues and representations of their gods cut out of stone; *and burn their groves*, such as those about the temple of *Ashtaroth*, the Canaanitish *Venus*, whose impure rites were practised in different parts of the inclosures or groves round her temples; *and ye shall hew down the graven images*, probably implying all images *carved out of wood; and destroy the names of them*, which were no doubt at first graven on the stones, and carved on the trees, and

A. M. 2553.
B. C. 1451.
An. Ex. Isr. 40.
Sebat.

6 And [k] thither ye shall bring
your burnt-offerings, and your
sacrifices, and your [l] tithes, and
heave-offerings of your hand, and your vows,
and your freewill-offerings, and the firstlings
of your herds and of your flocks:
7 And [m] there ye shall eat before the LORD
your God, and [n] ye shall rejoice in all that ye
put your hand unto, ye and your households,
wherein the LORD thy God hath blessed thee.
8 Ye shall not do after all *the things* that we
do here this day, [o] every man whatsoever *is*
right in his own eyes.
9 For ye are not as yet come to the rest
and to the inheritance which the LORD your
God giveth you.
10 But *when* [p] ye go over Jordan, and dwell
in the land which the LORD your God giveth
you to inherit, and *when* he giveth you rest
from all your enemies round about, so that
ye dwell in safety;
11 Then there shall be [q] a place which the
LORD your God shall choose, to cause his
name to dwell there; thither shall ye bring
all that I command you; your burnt-offerings,
and your sacrifices, your tithes, and the heave-
offering of your hand, and all [r] your choice
vows which ye vow unto the LORD:
12 And [s] ye shall rejoice before the LORD
your God, ye and your sons, and
your daughters, and your men-
servants, and your maid-servants,
and the Levite that *is* within your gates: forasmuch as [t] he hath no part nor inheritance
with you.
13 [u] Take heed to thyself that thou offer
not thy burnt-offerings in every place that
thou seest:
14 [v] But in the place which the LORD shall
choose in one of thy tribes, there thou shalt
offer thy burnt-offerings, and there thou shalt
do all that I command thee.
15 Notwithstanding [w] thou mayest kill and
eat flesh in all thy gates, whatsoever thy soul
lusteth after, according to the blessing of the
LORD thy God which he hath given thee:
[x] the unclean and the clean may eat thereof,
[y] as of the roebuck, and as of the hart.
16 [z] Only ye shall not eat the blood; ye
shall pour it upon the earth as water.
17 Thou mayest not eat within thy gates the
tithe of thy corn, or of thy wine, or of thy oil,
or the firstlings of thy herds or of thy flock,
nor any of thy vows which thou vowest, nor
thy freewill-offerings, or heave-offering of thine
hand:
18 [a] But thou must eat them before the LORD
thy God in the place which the LORD thy God

A. M. 2553.
B. C. 1451.
An. Ex. Isr. 40.
Sebat.

[k] Lev. xvii. 3, 4.——[l] Ver. 17; chap. xiv. 22, 23; xv. 19, 20.——[m] Chap. xiv. 26.——[n] Ver. 12, 18; Lev. xxiii. 40; chap. xvi. 11, 14, 15; xxvi. 11; xxvii. 7.——[o] Judg. xvii. 6; xxi. 25.——[p] Chap. xi. 31.——[q] Ver. 5, 14, 18, 21, 26; chap. xiv. 23; xv. 20; xvi. 2, &c.; xvii. 8; xviii. 6; xxiii. 16; xxvi. 2; xxxi. 11; Josh. xviii. 1; 1 Kings viii. 29; Psa. lxxviii. 68.——[r] Heb. *the choice of your vows.*——[s] Ver. 7.——[t] Chap. x. 9; xiv. 29.——[u] Lev. xvii. 4.——[v] Ver. 11.——[w] Ver. 21.——[x] Ver. 22.——[y] Chap. xiv. 5; xv. 22.——[z] Gen. ix. 4; Lev. vii. 26; xvii. 10; chap. xv. 23; ver. 23, 24.——[a] Ver. 11, 12; chap. xiv. 23.

then applied to the surrounding districts. In various instances the names of whole mountains, valleys, and districts, were borrowed from the gods worshipped there.

Verse 14. *The place which the Lord shall choose*] To prevent idolatry and bring about a perfect uniformity in the Divine worship, which at that time was essentially necessary; because every *rite* and *ceremony* had a determinate meaning, and pointed out the good things which were to come, therefore *one place* must be established where those rites and ceremonies should be carefully and punctually observed. Had it not been so, every man would have formed his worship according to his own mind, and the whole beauty and importance of the grand *representative* system would have been destroyed, and the Messiah and the glories of his kingdom could not have been seen through the medium of the Jewish ritual. For uniformity in every part of the Divine worship the same necessity does not now exist; because that which was typified is come, and the shadows have all fled away Yet, when it can be obtained, how desirable is it that all sincere Christians should with *one mouth*, as well as with *one heart*, glorify their common Lord and Saviour!

Verse 15. *Thou mayest kill and eat flesh in all thy gates*] With the proviso that the blood be poured out on the ground. 1. The blood should not be eaten. 2. It should be poured out by way of sacrifice. I think this is the meaning; and not that they should pour out the blood with as little ceremony and respect as they poured water upon the ground, which is the meaning according to Calmet and others.

The roebuck, and—the hart] It is very likely that by צבי *tsebi* the *antelope* is meant; and by איל *aiyal*, the *hart* or *deer*. This is the opinion of Dr. Shaw; and from the report of travellers we learn that both these animals are found in that desert to the present day. See Harmer, vol. iv., p. 25, &c. Of the propriety of eating clean animals there could be no question, but the blood must be poured out; yet there were cases in which they might kill and eat in all their *gates*, cities, and dwellings—such as the roebuck and the hart, or all clean *wild* beasts, for these being taken in hunting, and frequently shot by arrows, their blood could not be poured out at the altar. Therefore the command appears to take in only such *tame* beasts as were used for food.

A. M. 2552. B. C. 1451. An. Ex. Isr. 40. Sebat.

shall choose, thou, and thy son, and thy daughter, and thy man-servant, and thy maid-servant, and the Levite that *is* within thy gates; and thou shalt rejoice before the LORD thy God in all that thou puttest thine hands unto.

19 [b] Take heed to thyself that thou forsake not the Levite [c] as long as thou livest upon the earth.

20 When the LORD thy God shall enlarge thy border, [d] as he hath promised thee, and thou shalt say, I will eat flesh; (because thy soul longeth to eat flesh;) thou mayest eat flesh, whatsoever thy soul lusteth after.

21 If the place which the LORD thy God hath chosen to put his name there be too far from thee, then thou shalt kill of thy herd and of thy flock, which the LORD hath given thee, as I have commanded thee, and thou shalt eat in thy gates whatsoever thy soul lusteth after.

22 [e] Even as the roebuck and the hart is eaten, so thou shalt eat them: the unclean and the clean shall eat *of* them alike.

23 [f] Only [g] be sure that thou eat not the blood: [h] for the blood *is* the life; and thou mayest not eat the life with the flesh.

24 Thou shalt not eat it; thou shalt pour it upon the earth as water.

25 Thou shalt not eat it; [i] that it may go well with thee, and with thy children after thee, [k] when thou shalt do *that which is* right in the sight of the LORD.

26 Only thy [l] holy things which thou hast, and [m] thy vows, thou shalt take, and go unto the place which the LORD shall choose:

A. M. 2553. B. C. 1451. An. Ex. Isr. 40. Sebat.

27 And [n] thou shalt offer thy burnt-offerings, the flesh and the blood, upon the altar of the LORD thy God: and the blood of thy sacrifices shall be poured out upon the altar of the LORD thy God, and thou shalt eat the flesh.

28 Observe and hear all these words which I command thee, [o] that it may go well with thee, and with thy children after thee for ever, when thou doest *that which is* good and right in the sight of the LORD thy God.

29 When [p] the LORD thy God shall cut off the nations from before thee, whither thou goest to possess them, and thou [q] succeedest them, and dwellest in their land:

30 Take heed to thyself [r] that thou be not snared [s] by following them, after that they be destroyed from before thee; and that thou inquire not after their gods, saying, How did these nations serve their gods? even so will I do likewise.

31 [t] Thou shalt not do so unto the LORD thy God: for every [u] abomination to the LORD which he hateth, have they done unto their gods; for [v] even their sons and their daughters they have burnt in the fire to their gods.

32 What thing soever I command you, observe to do it: [w] thou shalt not add thereto, nor diminish from it.

---

[b] Chap. xiv. 27; Ecclus. vii. 31.——[c] Heb. *all thy days.* [d] Gen. xv. 18; xxviii. 14; Exod. xxxiv. 24; chap. xi. 24; xix. 8. [e] Ver. 15.——[f] Ver. 16.——[g] Heb. *be strong.*——[h] Gen. ix. 4; Lev. xvii. 11, 14.——[i] Chap. iv. 40; Isa. iii. 10.——[k] Exod. xv. 26; chap. xiii. 18; 1 Kings xi. 38.——[l] Num. v. 9, 10; xviii. 19. [m] 1 Sam. i. 21, 22, 24.——[n] Lev. i. 5, 9, 13; xvii. 11.——[o] Ver. 25.

[p] Exod. xxiii. 23; chap. xix. 1; Josh. xxiii. 4.——[q] Heb. *inheritest* or *possessest them.*——[r] Chap. vii. 16.——[s] Heb. *after them.* [t] Ver. 4; Lev. xviii. 3, 26, 30; 2 Kings xvii. 15.——[u] Heb. *abomination of the.*——[v] Lev. xviii. 21; xx. 2; chap. xviii. 10; Jer. xxxii. 35; Ezek. xxiii. 37.——[w] Chap. iv. 2; xiii. 18; Josh. i. 7; Prov. xxx. 6; Rev. xxii. 18.

Verse 19. *Forsake not the Levite*] These had no inheritance, and were to live by the sanctuary: if therefore the offerings were withheld by which the Levites were supported, they of course must perish. Those who have devoted themselves to the service of God in ministering to the salvation of the souls of men, should certainly be furnished at least with all the *necessaries* of life. Those who withhold this from them sin against their own mercies, and that ordinance of God by which a ministry is established for the salvation of souls.

Verse 23. *For the blood* is *the life*] And the *life* being offered as an *atonement*, consequently the blood should not be eaten. See the notes on Lev. xvii. 11, where the subject of the *vitality* of the blood is largely considered.

Verse 31 *Their sons and their daughters they have burnt in the fire*] Almost all the nations in the world agreed in offering human victims to their gods on extraordinary occasions, by which it is evident that none of those nations had any right notion of the Divine nature. How necessary, then, was the volume of revelation, to teach men what that religion is with which God can be well pleased! The *Hindoos* to this day offer human victims to their goddess *Cali*, and at the temple of *Jaggernaut*; and yet, notwithstanding this, there are found certain persons who, while they profess Christianity, are absolutely unwilling to send the Hindoos the Gospel of Christ, because they think it would not be *politically* wise! But the wisdom of this world has ever been foolishness with God; and in spite of all this infidel policy, the word of the Lord shall have free course and be glorified.

CHAPTER XIII.

Of false prophets and their lying signs, 1–6. *Of those who endeavour to entice and seduce people to idolatry,* 7, 8. *The punishment of such,* 9–11. *Of cities perverted from the pure worship of God,* 12–14. *How that city is to be treated,* 15. *All the spoil of it to be destroyed,* 16. *Promises to them who obey these directions,* 17, 18.

A. M. 2553. B. C. 1451. An. Ex. Isr. 40. Sebat.

IF there arise among you a prophet, or a [a] dreamer of dreams, [b] and giveth thee a sign or a wonder,

2 And [c] the sign or the wonder come to pass, whereof he spake unto thee, saying, Let us go after other gods, which thou hast not known, and let us serve them;

3 Thou shalt not hearken unto the words of that prophet, or that dreamer of dreams: for the LORD your God [d] proveth you, to know whether ye love the LORD your God with all your heart, and with all your soul.

4 Ye shall [e] walk after the LORD your God, and fear him, and keep his commandments, and obey his voice, and ye shall serve him, and [f] cleave unto him.

5 And [g] that prophet, or that dreamer of dreams, shall be put to death; because he hath [h] spoken to turn *you* away from the LORD your God, which brought you out of the land of Egypt, and redeemed you out of the house of bondage, to thrust thee out of the way which the LORD thy God commanded thee to walk in. [i] So shalt thou put the evil away from the midst of thee.

6 [k] If thy brother, the son of thy mother, or thy son, or thy daughter, or [l] the wife of thy bosom, or thy friend, [m] which *is* as thine own soul, entice thee secretly, saying, Let us go and serve other gods, which thou hast not known, thou, nor thy fathers;

A. M. 2553. B. C. 1451. An. Ex. Isr. 40. Sebat.

7 *Namely,* of the gods of the people which *are* round about you, nigh unto thee, or far off from thee, from the *one* end of the earth even unto the *other* end of the earth:

8 Thou shalt [n] not consent unto him, nor hearken unto him; neither shall thine eye pity him, neither shalt thou spare, neither shalt thou conceal him:

9 But [o] thou shalt surely kill him; [p] thine hand shall be first upon him to put him to death, and afterwards the hand of all the people.

10 And thou shalt stone him with stones, that he die; because he hath sought to thrust thee away from the LORD thy God, which brought thee out of the land of Egypt, from the house of [q] bondage.

11 And [r] all Israel shall hear, and fear, and shall do no more any such wickedness as this is among you.

12 [s] If thou shalt hear *say* in one of thy

[a] Zech. x. 2.—[b] Matt. xxiv. 24; 2 Thess. ii. 9.—[c] Chap. xviii. 22; Jer. xxviii. 9; Matt. vii. 22.—[d] Chap. viii. 2; see Matt. xxiv. 24; 1 Cor. xi. 19; 2 Thess. ii. 11; Rev. xiii. 14.—[e] 2 Kings xxiii. 3; 2 Chron. xxxiv. 31.—[f] Chap. x. 20; xxx. 20.—[g] Chap. xviii. 20; Jer. xiv. 15; Zech. xiii. 3.—[h] Heb. *spoken revolt against the LORD.*

[i] Chap. xvii. 7; xxii. 21, 22, 24; 1 Cor. v. 13.—[k] Chap xvii. 2.—[l] See Gen. xvi. 5; chap. xxviii. 54; Prov. v. 20; Mic. vii. 5.—[m] 1 Sam. xviii. 1, 3; xx. 17.—[n] Proverbs i. 10.—[o] Chap. xvii. 5.—[p] Chap. xvii. 7; Acts vii. 58.—[q] Heb. *bondmen.*—[r] Chap. xvii. 13; xix. 20.—[s] Josh. xxii. 11, &c.; Judg. xx. 1, 2.

NOTES ON CHAP. XIII.

Verse 1. *If there arise among you a prophet*] Any pretending to have a Divine influence, so as to be able perfectly to direct others in the way of salvation; *or a dreamer of dreams*—one who pretends that some deity has spoken to him in the night-season; *and giveth thee a sign,* אות *oth,* what appears to be a miraculous proof of his mission; *or a wonder,* מופת *mopheth,* some *type* or representation of what he wishes to bring you over to: as some have pretended to have received a consecrated *image* from heaven; hence the origin of the *Palladium, Numa's Shields,* and many of the deities among the Hindoos. But here the word seems to mean some *portentous sign,* such as an *eclipse,* which he who knew when it would take place might predict to the people who knew nothing of the matter, and thereby accredit his pretensions.

Verse 3. *The Lord your God proveth you*] God permits such impostors to arise to try the faith of his followers, and to put their religious experience to the test; for he who experimentally knows God cannot be drawn away after *idols.* He who has no *experimental* knowledge of God, may believe any thing. *Experience* of the truths contained in the word of God can alone preserve any man from Deism, or a false religion. They who have not this are a prey to the pretended prophet, and to the dreamer of dreams.

Verse 6. *If thy brother—or thy son*] The teacher of idolatry was to be put to death; and so strict was this order that a man must neither spare nor conceal his *brother, son, daughter, wife,* nor *friend,* because this was the highest offence that could be committed against God, and the most destructive to society; hence the severest laws were enacted against it.

A. M. 2553.
B. C. 1451.
An. Ex. Isr. 40.
Sebat.

cities, which the LORD thy God
hath given thee to dwell there,
saying,
13 *Certain* men, [t] the children of Belial, [u] are
gone out from among you, and have [v] withdrawn the inhabitants of their city, saying,
[w] Let us go and serve other gods, which ye
have not known;
14 Then shalt thou inquire, and make search,
and ask diligently; and, behold, *if it be* truth,
and the thing certain, *that* such abomination
is wrought among you;
15 Thou shalt surely smite the inhabitants
of that city with the edge of the sword, [x] destroying it utterly, and all that *is* therein, and
the cattle thereof, with the edge of the sword.
16 And thou shalt gather all the spoil of it
into the midst of the street thereof, and shalt [y] burn with fire the
city, and all the spoil thereof
every whit, for the LORD thy God: and it
shall be [z] a heap for ever; it shall not be
built again.
17 And [a] there shall cleave naught of the
[b] cursed thing to thine hand: that the LORD
may [c] turn from the fierceness of his anger,
and show thee mercy, and have compassion
upon thee, and multiply thee, [d] as he hath
sworn unto thy fathers;
18 When thou shalt hearken to the voice of
the LORD thy God, [e] to keep all his commandments which I command thee this day, to do
that which is right in the eyes of the LORD
thy God.

[t] Or, *naughty men*; see Judg. xix. 22; 1 Sam. ii. 12; xxv. 17, 25; 1 Kings xxi. 10, 13; 2 Cor. vi. 15.——[u] 1 John ii. 19; Jude 19.——[v] 2 Kings xvii. 21.——[w] Ver. ii. 6.——[x] Exod. xxii. 20; Lev. xxvii. 28; Josh. vi. 17, 21.

[y] Josh. vi. 24.——[z] Josh. viii. 28; Isa. xvii. 1; xxv. 2; Jer. xlix. 2.——[a] Chap. vii. 26; Joshua vi. 18.——[b] Or, *devoted*. [c] Joshua vi. 26.——[d] Genesis xxii. 17; xxvi. 4, 24; xxviii. 14. [e] Chap. xii. 25, 28, 32.

Verse 13. *Children of Belial*] בליעל, from בל *bal*, *not*, and יעל *yaal*, *profit*;—Sept. ανδρες παρανομοι, *lawless men*;—persons *good for nothing* to themselves or others, and capable of nothing but mischief.

Verse 15. *Thou shalt surely smite the inhabitants*] If one city were permitted to practise idolatry, the evil would soon spread, therefore the contagion must be destroyed in its birth.

Verse 17. *And there shall cleave naught of the cursed thing*] As God did not permit them to take the spoils of these idolatrous cities, they could be under no temptation to make war upon them. It could only be done through a merely religious motive, in obedience to the command of God, as they could have no profit by the subversion of such places. How few religious wars would there ever have been in the world had they been regulated by this principle: "Thou shalt neither extend thy territory, nor take any spoils!"

CHAPTER XIV.

The Israelites are not to adopt superstitious customs in mourning, 1, 2. *The different kinds of clean and unclean animals*, 3–20. *Nothing to be eaten that dieth of itself*, 21. *Concerning offerings which, from distance cannot be carried to the altar of God, and which may be turned into money*, 22–26. *The Levite is not to be forsaken*, 27. *The third year's tithe for the Levite, stranger, widow*, &c., 28, 29.

A. M. 2553.
B. C. 1451.
An. Ex. Isr. 40.
Sebat.

YE *are* [a] the children of the
LORD your God: [b] ye shall
not cut yourselves, nor make any
baldness between your eyes for the dead.
2 [c] For thou *art* a holy people unto the LORD
thy God, and the LORD hath chosen thee to be
a peculiar people unto himself,
above all the nations that *are*
upon the earth.
3 [d] Thou shalt not eat any abominable thing.
4 [e] These *are* the beasts which ye shall eat:
the ox, the sheep, and the goat,

[a] Rom. viii. 16; ix. 8, 26; Gal. iii. 26.——[b] Lev. xix. 28; xxi. 5; Jer. xvi. 6; xli. 5; xlvii. 5; 1 Thess. iv. 13.

[c] Lev. xx. 26; chap. vii. 6; xxvi. 18, 19.——[d] Ezek. iv. 14; Acts x. 13, 14.——[e] Lev. xi. 2, &c.

NOTES ON CHAP. XIV.

Verse 1. *Ye* are *the children of the Lord*] The very highest character that can be conferred on any created beings; *ye shall not cut yourselves*, i. e., their *hair*, for it was a custom among idolatrous nations to consecrate their hair to their deities, though they sometimes also made incisions in their *flesh*.

Verse 4. *These* are *the beasts which ye shall eat*] On Lev. xi. I have entered into considerable detail relative to the clean and unclean animals there mentioned. For the general subject, the reader is referred to the notes on that chapter; but as there are particulars mentioned here which Moses does not introduce in Leviticus, it will be necessary to consider them in this place.

The ox] שור *shor*: BOS, fifth order *Pecora*, of the genus MAMMALIA, species 41. This term includes all clean animals of the beeve kind; not only the ox,

A. M. 2553. B. C. 1451. An. Ex. Isr. 40. Sebat.

5 The hart, and the roebuck,
and the fallow deer, and the wild
goat, and the [f] pygarg, [g] and the
wild ox, and the chamois.
6 And every beast that parteth the hoof, and
cleaveth the cleft into two claws, *and* cheweth the cud among the beasts, that ye shall
eat.
7 Nevertheless these ye shall not eat of
them that chew the cud, or of them that divide the cloven hoof; *as* the camel, and the
hare, and the coney: for they chew the cud,
but divide not the hoof; *therefore* they *are*
unclean unto you.
8 And the swine, because it
divideth the hoof, yet cheweth
not the cud, it *is* unclean unto
you: ye shall not eat of their flesh, [h] nor touch
their dead carcass.
9 [i] These ye shall eat of all that *are* in the
waters: all that have fins and scales shall ye
eat:
10 And whatsoever hath not fins and scales
ye may not eat; it *is* unclean unto you.
11 *Of* all clean birds ye shall eat.
12 [k] But these *are they* of which ye shall
not eat: the eagle, and the ossifrage, and the
ospray,

A. M. 2553. B. C. 1451. An. Ex. Isr. 40. Sebat.

[f] Or, *bison*.—[g] Heb. *dishon*.—[h] Lev. xi. 26, 27.

[i] Lev. xi. 9.—[k] Lev. xi. 13.

properly so called, but also the *bull*, the *cow*, *heifer*, and *calf*.

The sheep] שה *seh:* OVIS, fifth order Pecora, of the genus MAMMALIA, species 40; including the *ram*, the *wether*, the *ewe*, and the *lamb*.

The goat] עז *az:* CAPRA, fifth order Pecora, of the genus MAMMALIA, species 39; including the *he-goat*, *she-goat*, and *kid*. The words in the text, שה כשבים *seh chesabim*, signify the lamb or young of sheep; and שה עזים *seh izzim*, the young or kid of goats: but this is a Hebrew idiom which signifies every creature of the genus, as בן אנוש *ben enosh* and בן אדם *ben adam*, *son of man*, signify any *human* being. See Psa. cxliv. 3; Job xxv. 6.

The flesh of these animals is universally allowed to be the most wholesome and nutritive. They live on the very best vegetables; and having several stomachs, their food is well concocted, and the chyle formed from it the most pure because the best elaborated, as it is well refined before it enters into the blood. On ruminating or chewing the cud, see the note on Lev. xi. 3.

Verse 5. *The hart*] איל *aiyal*, the deer, according to Dr. Shaw; see the note on chap. xii. 15.

The roebuck] צבי *tsebi*, generally supposed to be the *antelope*, belonging to the fifth order Pecora, genus MAMMALIA, and species 38. It has round twisted spiral horns, hairy tufts on the knees, browses on tender shoots, lives in hilly countries, is fond of climbing rocks, and is remarkable for its beautiful black eyes. The flesh is good and well flavoured.

The fallow deer] יחמור *yachmur*, from חמר *chamar*, to be *troubled*, *disturbed*, *disordered:* this is supposed to mean, not the *fallow deer*, but the *bubalus* or *buffalo*, which is represented by Dr. Shaw, and other travellers and naturalists, as a *sullen*, *malevolent*, and *spiteful* animal, *capricious*, *ferocious*, and every way *brutal*. According to the Linnæan classification, the buffalo belongs to the fifth order Pecora, genus MAMMALIA, species *bos*. According to 1 Kings iv. 23, this was one of the animals which was daily served up at the table of Solomon. Though the flesh of the buffalo is not considered very delicious, yet in the countries where it abounds it is eaten as frequently by all classes of persons as the *ox* is in England. The *yachmur* is not mentioned in the parallel place, Lev. xi.

The wild goat] אקו *akko*. It is not easy to tell what creature is intended by the *akko*. Dr. Shaw supposed it to be a kind of very timorous goat, known in the East by the name *fishtall* and *serwee*, and bearing a resemblance both to the goat and the stag, whence the propriety of the name given it by the Septuagint and Vulgate, *tragelaphus*, the *goat-stag;* probably the *rupicapra* or *rock-goat*. The word is found nowhere else in the Hebrew Bible.

The pygarg] דישן *dishon*. As this word is nowhere else used, we cannot tell what animal is meant by it. The word *pygarg* πυγαργος, literally signifies *white buttocks*, and is applied to a kind of *eagle* with a *white tail;* but here it evidently means a quadruped. It was probably some kind of goat, common and well known in Judea.

The wild ox] תאו *teo*. This is supposed to be the *oryx* of the Greeks, which is a species of large *stag*. It may be the same with the *bekker el wash*, described by Dr. Shaw as "a species of the *deer kind*, whose horns are exactly in the fashion of our *stag*, but whose size is only between the *red* and *fallow deer*." In Isa. li. 20 a creature of the name of תוא *to* is mentioned, which we translate *wild bull;* it may be the same creature intended above, with the interchange of the two last letters.

The chamois] זמר *zemer*. This was probably a species of *goat* or *deer*, but of what kind we know not: that it cannot mean the *chamois* is evident from this circumstance, "that the chamois inhabits only the regions of snow and ice, and cannot bear the heat."—*Buffon*. The Septuagint and Vulgate translate it the *Camelopard*, but this creature is only found in the torrid zone and probably was never seen in Judea; consequently could never be prescribed as a clean animal, to be used as ordinary food. I must once more be permitted to say, that to ascertain the natural history of the Bible is a hopeless case. Of a few of its animals and vegetables we are comparatively certain, but of the great majority we know almost nothing. Guessing and conjecture are endless, and they have on these subjects been already sufficiently employed. What learning, deep, solid, extensive learning, and judgment could do, has already been done by the incomparable *Bochart* in his Hierozoicon. The learned

A. M. 2553.
B. C. 1451.
An. Ex. Isr. 40.
Sebat.

13 And the glede, and the kite, and the vulture after his kind,

14 And every raven after his kind,

15 And the owl, and the night-hawk, and the cuckow, and the hawk after his kind,

16 The little owl, and the great owl, and the swan,

17 And the pelican, and the gier eagle, and the cormorant,

18 And the stork, and the heron after her kind, and the lapwing, and the bat,

19 And [l] every creeping thing that flieth *is* unclean unto you: [m] they shall not be eaten.

20 *But of* all clean fowls ye may eat.

21 [n] Ye shall not eat *of* any thing that dieth of itself: thou shalt give it unto the stranger that *is* in thy gates, that he may eat it; or thou mayest sell it unto an alien: [o] for thou *art* a holy people unto the LORD thy God. [p] Thou shalt not seethe a kid in his mother's milk.

22 [q] Thou shalt truly tithe all the increase of thy seed, that the field bringeth forth year by year.

23 [r] And thou shalt eat before the LORD thy God, in the place which he shall choose to place his name there, the tithe of thy corn, of thy wine, and of thine oil, and the [s] firstlings of thy herds and of thy flocks: that thou mayest learn to fear the LORD thy God always.

24 And if the way be too long for thee, so that thou art not able to carry it; *or* [t] if the place be too far from thee, which the LORD thy God shall choose to set his name there, when the LORD thy God hath blessed thee:

A. M. 2553.
B. C. 1451.
An. Ex. Isr. 40.
Sebat.

25 Then shalt thou turn *it* into money, and bind up the money in thine hand, and shalt go unto the place which the LORD thy God shall choose:

26 And thou shalt bestow that money for whatsoever thy soul lusteth after, for oxen, or for sheep, or for wine, or for strong drink, or for whatsoever thy soul [u] desireth: [v] and thou shalt eat there before the LORD thy God, and thou shalt rejoice, thou, and thine household,

27 And [w] the Levite that *is* within thy gates, thou shalt not forsake him; for [x] he hath no part nor inheritance with thee.

28 [y] At the end of three years, thou shalt bring forth all the tithe of thine increase the same year, and shalt lay *it* up within thy gates;

29 [z] And the Levite, (because [a] he hath no part nor inheritance with thee,) and the stranger, and the fatherless, and the widow, which *are* within thy gates, shall come, and shall eat and be satisfied; that [b] the LORD thy God may bless thee in all the work of thine hand which thou doest.

[l] Lev. xi. 20.——[m] See Lev. xi. 21.——[n] Lev. xvii. 15; xxii. 8; Ezek. iv. 14.——[o] Verse 2.——[p] Exodus xxiii. 19; xxxiv. 26. [q] Lev. xxvii. 30; chap. xii. 6, 17; Neh. x. 37.——[r] Chap. xii. 5, 6, 7, 17, 18.——[s] Chap. xv. 19, 20.——[t] Chap. xii. 21.

[u] Heb. *asketh of thee.*——[v] Chap. xii. 7, 18; xxvi. 11.——[w] Ch. xii. 12, 18, 19.——[x] Num. xviii. 20; chap. xviii. 1, 2.——[y] Chap. xxvi. 12; Amos iv. 4.——[z] Chap. xxvi. 12.——[a] Ver. 27; chap. xii. 12.——[b] Chap. xv. 10; Prov. iii. 9, 10; see Mal. iii. 10.

reader may consult this work, and, while he gains much general information, will have to regret that he can apply so little of it to the main and grand question. As I have consulted every authority within my reach, on the subject of the clean and unclean animals mentioned in the law, and have detailed all the information I could collect in my notes on Lev. xi., I must refer my readers to what I have there laid down.

Verse 13. *The vulture after his kind*] The word ראה *daah* is improperly translated *vulture* Lev. xi. 14, and means a *kite* or *glede*. The word דיה *daiyah* in this verse is not only different from that in Leviticus, but means also a different animal, properly enough translated *vulture*. See the note on Lev. xi. 14.

Verse 21. *Thou shalt not seethe a kid in his mother's milk.*] Mr. Calmet thinks that this precept refers to the paschal lamb only, which was not to be offered to God till it was weaned from its mother; but see the note on Exod. xxiii. 19.

Verse 22. *Thou shalt truly tithe*] Meaning the *second* tithe which themselves were to eat, ver. 23, for there was a *first tithe* that was given to the *Levites*, out of which they paid a *tenth part* to the priests, Num. xviii. 24–28; Neh. x. 37, 38. Then of that which remained, the owners separated a *second tithe*, which they ate before the Lord the *first* and *second* year; and in the *third* year it was given to the Levites and to the poor, Deut. xiv. 28, 29. In the *fourth* and *fifth* years it was eaten again by the owners, and in the *sixth* year was given to the poor. The *seventh* year was a Sabbath to the land, and then all things were common, Exod. xxiii. 10, 11, where see the notes; and see *Ainsworth* on this verse.

Verse 26. *Or for strong drink*] What the *sikera* or strong drink of the Hebrews was, see in the note on Lev. x. 9. This one verse sufficiently shows that the Mosaic law made ample provision for the comfort and happiness of the people.

Verse 29. *And the Levite (because he hath no part nor inheritance*] And hence much of his support depended on the mere freewill-offerings of the people. God chose to make his ministers thus dependent on the people, that they might be induced (among other motives) to labour for their spiritual profiting, that the people, thus blessed under their ministry, might feel it their duty and privilege to support and render them comfortable.

CHAPTER XV.

The Sabbatical year of release, 1. *The manner in which this release shall take place,* 2–5. *Of lending to the poor, and the disposition in which it should be done,* 6–11. *Of the Hebrew servant who has served six years, and who shall be dismissed well furnished,* 12–15. *The ceremony of* boring the ear, *when the servant wishes to continue with his master,* 16–18. *Of the firstlings of the flock and herd,* 19, 20. *Nothing shall be offered that has any blemish,* 21. *The sacrifice to be eaten both by the clean and unclean, except the blood, which is never to be eaten, but poured out upon the ground,* 22, 23.

A. M. 2553. B. C. 1451. An. Ex. Isr. 40. Sebat.

AT the end of [a] *every* seven years thou shalt make a release.

2 And this *is* the manner of the release: Every [b] creditor that lendeth *aught* unto his neighbour shall release *it;* he shall not exact *it* of his neighbour, or of his brother; because it is called the LORD's release.

3 [c] Of a foreigner thou mayest exact *it again:* but *that* which is thine with thy brother, thine hand shall release:

4 [d] Save when there shall be no poor among you; [e] for the LORD shall greatly bless thee in the land which the LORD thy God giveth thee, *for* an inheritance to possess it:

5 Only [f] if thou carefully hearken unto the voice of the LORD thy God, to observe to do all these commandments which I command thee this day.

6 For the LORD thy God blesseth thee, as he promised thee: and [g] thou shalt lend unto many nations, but thou shalt not borrow; and [h] thou shalt reign over many nations, but they shall not reign over thee.

7 If there be among you a poor man of one of thy brethren, within any of thy gates in thy land which the LORD thy God giveth thee, [i] thou shalt not harden thine heart, nor shut thine hand from thy poor brother:

A. M. 2553. B. C. 1451. An. Ex. Isr. 40. Sebat.

8 [k] But thou shalt open thine hand wide unto him, and shalt surely lend him sufficient for his need, *in that* which he wanteth.

9 Beware that there be not a [l] thought in thy [m] wicked heart, saying, The seventh year, the year of release, is at hand; and thine [n] eye be evil against thy poor brother, and thou givest him naught; and [o] he cry unto the LORD against thee, and [p] it be sin unto thee.

10 Thou shalt surely give him, and [q] thine heart shall not be grieved when thou givest unto him: because that [r] for this thing the LORD thy God shall bless thee in all thy works, and in all that thou puttest thine hand unto.

11 For [s] the poor shall never cease out of the land: therefore I command thee, saying, Thou shalt open thine hand wide unto thy brother, to thy poor, and to thy needy, in thy land.

12 *And* [t] if thy brother, a Hebrew man, or a Hebrew woman, be sold unto thee, and serve thee six years; then in the seventh year thou shalt let him go free from thee.

[a] Exod. xxi. 2; xxiii. 10, 11; Lev. xxv. 2, 4; chap. xxxi. 10; Jer. xxxiv. 14.——[b] Heb. *master of the lending of his hand.* [c] See chap. xxiii. 20.——[d] Or, *to the end that there be no poor among you.*——[e] Chap. xxviii. 8.——[f] Chap. xxviii. 1.——[g] Chap. xxviii. 12, 44.——[h] Chap. xxviii. 13; Prov. xxii. 7.——[i] 1 John iii. 17.——[k] Lev. xxv. 35; Matt. v. 42; Luke vi. 34, 35.

[l] Heb. *word.*——[m] Heb. *Belial.*——[n] Chap. xxviii. 54, 56; Prov. xxiii. 6; xxviii. 22; Matt. xx. 15.——[o] Chap. xxiv. 15. [p] Matt. xxv. 41, 42.——[q] 2 Cor. ix. 5, 7.——[r] Chap. xiv. 29; xxiv. 19; Psa. xli. 1; Prov. xxii. 9.——[s] Matt. xxvi. 11; Mark xiv. 7; John xii. 8.——[t] Exodus xxi. 2; Lev. xxv. 39; Jer. xxxiv. 14.

NOTES ON CHAP. XV.

Verse 1. *At the end of* every *seven years thou shalt make a release*] For an explanation of many things in this chapter, see the notes on Exod. xxi. and xxiii., and Lev. xxv.

Verse 4. *There shall be no poor*] That is, comparatively; see ver. 11.

Verse 8. *Thou shalt open thine hand wide*] Thy benevolence shall be in proportion to his distress and poverty, and thy ability. Thou shalt have no other rule to regulate thy charity by.

Verse 9. *Beware that there be not a thought in thy wicked heart*] לבבך בליעל *lebabecha beliyaal,* thy *belial heart,* that is, thy good-for-nothing or unprofitable heart; see on chap. xiv 13.

And thine eye be evil] An evil eye signifies a covetous disposition. See the same form of expression used by our Lord in the same sense, Matt. vi. 23: *If thine eye be evil*—if thou be a covetous person. *Evil eye* is by our Lord opposed to *single eye,* i. e., a person of a liberal, benevolent mind. Covetousness darkens the soul; liberality and benevolence enlighten it.

And he cry unto the Lord against thee] What a consolation to the poor and the oppressed, that they have a sure friend in God, who will hear their cry and redress their grievances!

Verse 11. *For the poor shall never cease out of the land*] To this passage our Lord appears to allude Mark xiv. 7: *For ye have the poor with you always.* God leaves these in mercy among men to exercise the

A. M. 2553.
B. C. 1451.
An. Ex. Isr. 40.
Sebat.

13 And when thou sendest him out free from thee, thou shalt not let him go away empty:

14 Thou shalt furnish him liberally out of thy flock, and out of thy floor, and out of thy winepress: *of that* wherewith the LORD thy God hath [u] blessed thee thou shalt give unto him.

15 And [v] thou shalt remember that thou wast a bondman in the land of Egypt, and the LORD thy God redeemed thee: therefore I command thee this thing to-day.

16 And it shall be, [w] if he say unto thee, I will not go away from thee; because he loveth thee and thine house, because he is well with thee:

17 Then thou shalt take an awl, and thrust *it* through his ear unto the door, and he shall be thy servant for ever. And also unto thy maid-servant thou shalt do likewise.

18 It shall not seem hard unto thee, when thou sendest him away free from thee; for he hath been worth [x] a double hired servant *to thee*, in serving thee six years: and the LORD thy God shall bless thee in all that thou doest.

A. M. 2553.
B. C. 1451.
An. Ex. Isr. 40.
Sebat.

19 [y] All the firstling males that come of thy herd and of thy flock thou shalt sanctify unto the LORD thy God: thou shalt do no work with the firstling of thy bullock, nor shear the firstling of thy sheep.

20 [z] Thou shalt eat *it* before the LORD thy God, year by year, in the place which the LORD shall choose, thou and thy household.

21 [a] And if there be *any* blemish therein, *as if it be* lame, or blind, *or have* any ill blemish, thou shalt not sacrifice it unto the LORD thy God.

22 Thou shalt eat it within thy gates: [b] the unclean and the clean *person shall eat it* alike, as the roebuck, and as the hart.

23 [c] Only thou shalt not eat the blood thereof; thou shalt pour it upon the ground as water.

[u] Prov. x. 22.——[v] Chap. v. 15; xvi. 12.——[w] Exod. xxi. 5, 6.——[x] See Isa. xvi. 14; xxi. 16.——[y] Exod. xiii. 2; xxxiv. 19; Lev. xxvii. 26; Num. iii. 13.

[z] Chap. xii. 5, 6, 7, 17; xiv. 23; xvi. 11, 14.——[a] Lev. xxii. 20; chap. xvii. 1; Ecclus. xxxv. 12.——[b] Chap. xii. 15, 22.——[c] Chap. xii. 16, 23.

feelings of compassion, tenderness, mercy, &c. And without occasions afforded to exercise these, man would soon become a Stoic or a brute.

Verse 13. *Thou shalt not let him go away empty*] Because during the time he served thee, he made no property for himself, having been always honest towards thee; and now when he leaves thee, he has nothing to begin the world with.

Verse 14. *Thou shalt furnish him—out of thy flock*] Thou shalt give him some *cattle* to breed with; *out of thy floor*—some *corn* for *seed* and for *bread; and out of thy winepress*—an adequate provision of *wine* for present necessity.

Verse 17. *Thou shalt take an awl*] See the note on Exod. xxi. 6.

Verse 20. *Thou shalt eat it—in the place which the Lord shall choose*] Thus God in his mercy made their *duty* and *interest* go hand in hand. And in every case God acts thus with his creatures; well, therefore, might Satan ask, Doth Job serve God for naught? No! nor does God design that any man should.

Verse 21. *If there be* any *blemish*] See the notes on Lev. xxii. 20. God will have both a perfect priest and a perfect offering.

CHAPTER XVI.

The month of Abib *to be observed*, 1. *The feast of the* passover *and of* unleavened bread, 2–8. *The* feast of weeks, 9–12. *The* feast of tabernacles, 13–15. *All the males to appear before the Lord thrice in the year, none to come empty, each to give according to his ability*, 16, 17. *Judges and officers to be made in all their cities*, 18. *Strict justice shall be executed*, 19, 20. *No grove to be planted near the altar of God, nor any image to be set up*, 21, 22.

A. M. 2553.
B. C. 1451.
An. Ex. Isr. 40.
Sebat.

OBSERVE the [a] month of Abib, and keep the passover unto the LORD thy God: for [b] in the month of Abib the LORD thy God brought thee forth out of Egypt [c] by night.

2 Thou shalt therefore sacrifice the passover unto the LORD thy God, of the

[a] Exod. xii. 2, &c.——[b] Exod. xiii. 4; xxxiv. 18.

[c] Exod. xii. 29, 42.

NOTES ON CHAP. XVI.

Verse 1. *Keep the passover*] A feast so called because the angel that destroyed the first-born of the Egyptians, seeing the blood of the appointed sacrifice sprinkled on the lintels and door-posts of the Israelites' houses, *passed over* THEM, and did not destroy

A. M. 2553. B. C. 1451. An. Ex. Isr. 40. Sebat.

flock and [d] the herd, in the [e] place which the LORD shall choose to place his name there.

3 [f] Thou shalt eat no leavened bread with it; seven days shalt thou eat unleavened bread therewith, *even* the bread of affliction; for thou camest forth out of the land of Egypt in haste: that thou mayest remember the day when thou camest forth out of the land of Egypt, all the days of thy life.

4 [g] And there shall be no leavened bread seen with thee in all thy coast seven days; [h] neither shall there *any thing* of the flesh which thou sacrificedst the first day at even, remain all night unto the morning.

5 Thou mayest not [i] sacrifice the passover within any of thy gates, which the LORD thy God giveth thee:

6 But at the place which the LORD thy God shall choose to place his name in, there thou shalt sacrifice the passover at [k] even, at the going down of the sun, at the season that thou camest forth out of Egypt.

7 And thou shalt [l] roast and eat *it* [m] in the place which the LORD thy God shall choose: and thou shalt turn in the morning, and go unto thy tents.

8 Six days thou shalt eat unleavened bread: and [n] on the seventh day *shall be* a [o] solemn assembly to the LORD thy God: thou shalt do no work *therein*.

9 [p] Seven weeks shalt thou number unto thee: begin to number the seven weeks from *such time as* thou beginnest *to put* the sickle to the corn.

10 And thou shalt keep the feast of weeks unto the LORD thy God, with [q] a tribute of a freewill-offering of thine hand, which thou shalt give *unto the LORD thy God*, [r] according as the LORD thy God hath blessed thee.

A. M. 2553. B. C. 1451. An. Ex. Isr. 40. Sebat.

11 And [s] thou shalt rejoice before the LORD thy God, thou, and thy son, and thy daughter, and thy man-servant, and thy maid-servant, and the Levite that *is* within thy gates, and the stranger, and the fatherless, and the widow, that *are* among you, in the place which the LORD thy God hath chosen to place his name there.

12 [t] And thou shalt remember that thou wast a bondman in Egypt: and thou shalt observe and do these statutes.

13 [u] Thou shalt observe the feast of tabernacles seven days, after that thou hast gathered in thy [v] corn and thy wine:

14 And [w] thou shalt rejoice in thy feast, thou, and thy son, and thy daughter, and thy man-servant, and thy maid-servant, and the Levite, the stranger, and the fatherless, and the widow, that *are* within thy gates.

15 [x] Seven days shalt thou keep a solemn feast unto the LORD thy God, in the place which the LORD shall choose: because the LORD thy God shall bless thee in all thine increase, and in all the works of thine hands, therefore thou shalt surely rejoice.

16 [y] Three times in a year shall all thy males appear before the LORD thy God, in the place which he shall choose: in the feast of unleavened bread, and in the feast of weeks, and in the feast of tabernacles: and [z] they shall not appear before the LORD empty:

17 Every man *shall give* [a] as he is able, [b] according to the blessing of the LORD

[d] Num. xxviii. 19.——[e] Chap. xii. 5, 26.——[f] Exod. xii. 15, 19, 39; xiii. 3, 6, 7; xxxiv. 18.——[g] Exod. xiii. 7.——[h] Exod. xii. 10; xxxiv. 25.——[i] Or, *kill*.——[k] Exod. xii. 6.——[l] Exod. xii. 8, 9; 2 Chron. xxxv. 13.——[m] 2 Kings xxiii. 23; John ii. 13, 23; xi. 55.——[n] Exod. xii. 16; xiii. 6; Lev. xxiii. 8.——[o] Heb. *restraint;* Lev. xxiii. 36.——[p] Exod. xxiii. 16; xxxiv. 22; Lev. xxiii. 15; Num. xxviii. 26; Acts ii. 1.

[q] Or, *sufficiency*.——[r] Ver. 17; 1 Cor. xvi. 2.——[s] Chap. xii. 7, 12, 18; verse 14.——[t] Chap. xv. 15.——[u] Exod. xxiii. 16; Lev. xxiii. 34; Num. xxix. 12.——[v] Heb. *floor and thy winepress.* [w] Neh. viii. 9, &c.——[x] Lev. xxiii. 39, 40.——[y] Exod. xxiii. 14, 17; xxxiv. 23.——[z] Exod. xxiii. 15; xxxiv. 20; Ecclus. xxxv. 4. [a] Heb. *according to the gift of his hand;* 2 Cor. viii. 12. [b] Verse 10.

any of their first-born. See the notes on Exod. xii. 2, &c.

Verse 3. *Bread of affliction*] Because, being baked without *leaven*, it was unsavoury, and put them in mind of their afflictive bondage in Egypt.

Verse 11. *Thou shalt rejoice*] The offerings of the Israelites were to be eaten with festivity, communicated to their friends with liberality, and bestowed on the poor with great generosity, that they might partake with them in these sacred repasts *with joy before the Lord*. To answer these views it was necessary to eat the flesh while it was fresh, as in that climate putrefaction soon took place; therefore they were commanded to let nothing remain until the morning, ver. 4. This consideration is sufficient to account for the command here, without having recourse to those moral and evangelical reasons that are assigned by the learned and devout Mr. Ainsworth for the command. How beneficent and cheerful is the design of this institution!—*Harmer*, vol. i., p. 396.

Verse 16. *Three times in a year*] See Exod. xxiii. 14, where all the Jewish feasts are explained. See also Lev. xxiii. 34.

A. M. 2553.
B. C. 1451.
An. Ex. Isr. 40.
Sebat.

thy God which he hath given thee.

18 ᶜ Judges and officers shalt thou make thee in all thy gates, which the LORD thy God giveth thee, throughout thy tribes : and they shall judge the people with just judgment.

19 ᵈ Thou shalt not wrest judgment ; ᵉ thou shalt not respect persons, ᶠ neither take a gift : for a gift doth blind the eyes of the wise, and

pervert the ᵍ words of the righteous.

A. M. 2553.
B. C. 1451.
An. Ex. Isr. 40.
Sebat.

20 ʰ That which is altogether just shalt thou follow, that thou mayest ⁱ live, and inherit the land which the LORD thy God giveth thee.

21 ᵏ Thou shalt not plant thee a grove of any trees near unto the altar of the LORD thy God, which thou shalt make thee.

22 ˡ Neither shalt thou set thee up *any* ᵐ image, which the LORD thy God hateth.

ᶜ Chap. i. 16; 1 Chron. xxiii. 4 ; xxvi. 29; 2 Chron. xix. 5, 8.——ᵈ Exod. xxiii. 2, 6 ; Lev. xix. 15.——ᵉ Chap. i. 17; Prov. xxiv. 23.——ᶠ Exod. xxiii. 8; Prov. xvii. 23 ; Eccles. vii. 7; Ecclus. xx. 29.

ᵍ Or, *matters.*——ʰ Heb. *justice, justice.*——ⁱ Ezek. xviii. 5, 9.——ᵏ Exod. xxxiv. 13 ; 1 Kings xiv. 15 ; xvi. 33 ; 2 Kings xvii. 16 ; xxi. 3 ; 2 Chron. xxxiii. 3.——ˡ Lev. xxvi. 1.——ᵐ Or, *statue, or pillar.*

Verse 18. *Judges and officers shalt thou make*] JUDGES, שפטים *shophetim*, among the Hebrews, were probably the same as our *magistrates* or *justices of the peace.* OFFICERS, שטרים *shoterim*, seem to have been the same as our inquest *sergeants, beadles,* &c., whose office it was to go into the houses, shops, &c., and examine *weights, measures,* and the civil conduct of the people. When they found any thing amiss, they brought the person offending before the *magistrate*, and he was punished by the *officer* on the spot. They seem also to have acted as heralds in the army, chap. xx. 5. See also *Rab. Maimon in Sanhedrin.* In China,

for all minor offences, the person when found guilty is punished on the spot, in the presence of the magistrate or mandarin of justice.

Verse 21. *Thou shalt not plant thee a grove, &c.*ſ We have already seen that *groves* were planted about idol temples for the purposes of the obscene worship performed in them. (See on chap. xii. 1.) On this account God would have no groves or thickets about his altar, that there might be no room for suspicion that any thing contrary to the strictest purity was transacted there. Every part of the Divine worship was *publicly* performed, for the purpose of general edification.

CHAPTER XVII.

All sacrifices to be without blemish, 1. Of persons convicted of idolatry and their punishment, 2–7. Difficult matters in judgment to be laid before the priests and judges, and to be determined by them ; and all to submit to their decision, 8–13. The king that may be chosen to be one of their brethren ; no stranger to be appointed to that office, 14, 15. He shall not multiply horses to himself, nor cause the people to return unto Egypt, 16. Nor multiply wives, &c., 17. He shall write a copy of the law for his own use, and read and study it all his days, that his heart be not lifted up above his brethren, 18–20.

A. M. 2553.
B. C. 1451.
An. Ex. Isr. 40.
Sebat.

THOU ᵃ shalt not sacrifice unto the LORD thy God *any* bullock or ᵇ sheep wherein is blemish, *or* any evil-favouredness : for that *is* an abomination unto the LORD thy God.

2 ᶜ If there be found among you, within any of thy gates which the LORD thy God giveth thee, man or woman that hath wrought wicked-

ness in the sight of the LORD thy God, ᵈ in transgressing his covenant,

A. M. 2553
B. C. 1451.
An. Ex. Isr. 40.
Sebat.

3 And hath gone and served other gods and worshipped them, either ᵉ the sun, or moon, or any of the host of heaven, ᶠ which I have not commanded ;

4 ᵍ And it be told thee, and thou hast heard

ᵃ Chap. xv. 21 ; Mal. i. 8, 13, 14.——ᵇ Or, *goat.*——ᶜ Chap. xiii. 6.——ᵈ Josh. vii. 11, 15; xiii. 16; Judg. ii. 20; 2 Kings

xviii. 12 ; Hos. viii. 1.——ᵉ Chap. iv. 19; Job xxxi. 26.——ᶠ Jer. vii. 22, 23, 31 ; xix. 5 ; xxxii. 35.——ᵍ Chap. xiii. 12, 14.

NOTES ON CHAP. XVII.

Verse 1. *Wherein is blemish*] God must not have that offered to him which thou wouldst not use thyself. This not only refers to the perfect sacrifice offered by Christ Jesus, but to that sincerity and uprightness of heart which God requires in all those who approach him in the way of worship.

Verse 4. *If it be told thee*] In a private way by any confidential person. *And thou hast heard* of it; so that it appears to be notorious, very likely to be true,

and publicly scandalous. *And hast inquired diligently* —sought to find out the truth of the report by the most careful examination of persons reporting, circumstances of the case, &c. *And, behold, it be true*—the report is not founded on vague rumour, hearsay, or malice. *And the thing certain*—substantiated by the fullest evidence. *Then shalt thou bring forth that man,* ver. 5. As the charge of idolatry was the most solemn and awful that could be brought against an Israelite, because it affected his *life*, therefore God required that

A. M. 2553.
B. C. 1451.
An. Ex. Isr. 40.
Sebat.

of it, and inquired diligently, and,
behold, *it be* true, *and* the thing
certain, *that* such abomination is
wrought in Israel:
5 Then shalt thou bring forth that man or that
woman, which have committed that wicked
thing, unto thy gates, *even* that man or that
woman, and [h] shalt stone them with stones,
till they die.
6 [i] At the mouth of two witnesses, or three
witnesses, shall he that is worthy of death be
put to death; *but* at the mouth of one witness
he shall not be put to death.
7 [k] The hands of the witnesses shall be first
upon him to put him to death, and afterward
the hands of all the people. So [l] thou shalt
put the evil away from among you.
8 [m] If there arise a matter too hard for thee
in judgment, [n] between blood and blood, between plea and plea, and between stroke and
stroke, *being* matters of controversy within thy
gates: then shalt thou arise, [o] and get thee
up into the place which the LORD thy God
shall choose:
9 And [p] thou shalt come unto the priests, the
Levites, and [q] unto the judge that shall be in
those days, and inquire; [r] and they shall show
thee the sentence of judgment:
10 And thou shalt do according to the sentence which they of that place which the LORD
shall choose shall show thee; and
thou shalt observe to do according to all that they inform thee:

A. M. 2553.
B. C. 1451.
An. Ex. Isr. 40.
Sebat.

11 According to the sentence of the law
which they shall teach thee, and according to
the judgment which they shall tell thee, thou
shalt do: thou shalt not decline from the sentence which they shall show thee, *to* the right
hand nor *to* the left.
12 And [s] the man that will do presumptuously, [t] and will not hearken unto the priest,
[u] that standeth to minister there, before the
LORD thy God, or unto the judge, even that
man shall die; and [v] thou shalt put away the
evil from Israel.
13 [w] And all the people shall hear, and fear,
and do no more presumptuously.
14 When thou art come unto the land which
the LORD thy God giveth thee, and shalt possess it, and shalt dwell therein, and shalt say,
[x] I will set a king over me, like as all the nations that *are* about me;
15 Thou shalt in any wise set *him* king over
thee [y] whom the LORD thy God shall choose:
one [z] from among thy brethren shalt thou set
king over thee: thou mayest not set a stranger
over thee, which *is* not thy brother.
16 But he shall not multiply [a] horses to him
self, nor cause the people [b] to return to Egypt,
to the end that he should multiply horses: for-

[h] Lev. xxiv. 14, 16; chap. xiii. 10; Josh. vii. 25.——[i] Num. xxxv. 30; chap. xix. 15; Matt. xviii. 16; John viii. 17; 2 Cor. xiii. 1; 1 Tim. v. 19; Heb. x. 28.——[k] Chap. xiii. 9; Acts vii. 58. [l] Ver. 12; chap. xiii. 5; xix. 19.——[m] 2 Chron. xix. 10; Hag. ii. 11; Mal. ii. 7.——[n] See Exod. xxi. 13, 20, 22, 28; xxii. 2; Num. xxxv. 11, 16, 19; chap. xix. 4; 10, 11.——[o] Chap. xii. 5; xix. 17; Psa. cxxii. 5.——[p] See Jer. xviii. 18.——[q] Ch. xix. 17.——[r] Ezek. xliv. 24.——[s] Num. xv. 30; Ezra x. 8; Hos. iv. 4.——[t] Heb. *not to hearken*.——[u] Chap. xviii. 5, 7.——[v] Chap. xiii. 5.——[w] Chap. xiii. 11; xix. 20.——[x] 1 Sam. viii. 5, 19, 20.——[y] See 1 Sam. ix. 15; x. 24; xvi. 12; 1 Chron. xxii. 10.——[z] Jer. xxx. 21.——[a] 1 Kings iv. 26; x. 26, 28; Psa. xx. 7.——[b] Isa. xxxi. 1; Ezek. xvii. 15.

the charge should be *substantiated* by the most unequivocal facts, and the most competent witnesses. Hence all the precautions mentioned in the fourth verse must be carefully used, in order to arrive at so affecting and so awful a truth.

Verse 6. *Two witnesses*] ONE might be deceived, or be prejudiced or malicious; therefore God required *two* substantial witnesses for the support of the charge.

Verse 8. *If there arise a matter too hard for thee*] These directions are given to the common magistrates, who might not be able to judge of or apply the law in all cases that might be brought before them. The priests and Levites, who were lawyers by birth and continual practice, were reasonably considered as the best qualified to decide on difficult points.

Verse 12. *The man that will do presumptuously*] The man who refused to abide by this final determination forfeited his life, as being then in a state of *rebellion* against the highest authority, and consequently the public could have no pledge for his conduct.

Verse 15. One *from among thy brethren shalt thou set king over thee*] It was on the ground of this command that the Jews proposed that insidious question to our Lord, *Is it lawful to give tribute to Cæsar, OR NO?* Matt. xxii. 17; for they were then under the authority of a *foreign* power. Had Christ said *Yes*, then they would have condemned him by this law; had he said *No*, then they would have accused him to Cæsar. See this subject discussed in great detail in the notes on Matt. xxii. 16, &c.

Verse 16. *He shall not multiply horses*] As *horses* appear to have been generally furnished by Egypt, God prohibits these, 1. Lest there should be such commerce with Egypt as might lead to idolatry. 2. Lest the people might depend on a well-appointed *cavalry* as a means of security, and so cease from trusting in the strength and protection of God. And, 3. That they might not be tempted to extend their *dominion* by means of cavalry, and so get scattered among the surrounding idolatrous nations, and thus cease, in process of time, to be that distinct and separate people which God intended they should be and without which the

A. M. 2553.
B. C. 1451.
An. Ex. Isr. 40.
Sebat.

asmuch as [c] the LORD hath said
unto you, [d] Ye shall henceforth
return no more that way.
17 Neither shall he multiply wives to himself, that [e] his heart turn not away: neither
shall he greatly multiply to himself silver and
gold.
18 [f] And it shall be, when he sitteth upon
the throne of his kingdom, that he shall write
him a copy of this law in a book, out of [g] *that
which is* before the priests the Levites:
19 And [h] it shall be with him,
and he shall read therein all the
days of his life: that he may learn
to fear the LORD his God, to keep all the words
of this law and these statutes, to do them:
20 That his heart be not lifted up above his
brethren, and that he [i] turn not aside from the
commandment, *to* the right hand, or *to* the
left: to the end that he may prolong *his* days
in his kingdom, he, and his children, in the
midst of Israel.

[c] Exod. xiii. 17; Num. xiv. 3, 4.——[d] Chap. xxviii. 68; Hos. xi. 5; see Jer. xlii. 15.——[e] See 1 Kings xi. 3, 4.——[f] 2 Kings xi. 12.——[g] Chap. xxxi. 9, 26; see 2 Kings xxii. 8.——[h] Josh. i 8; Psa. cxix. 97, 98.——[i] Chap. v. 32; 1 Kings xv. 5.

prophecies relative to the Messiah could not be known to have their due and full accomplishment.

Verse 17. *Neither shall he multiply wives*] For this would necessarily lead to *foreign alliances*, and be the means of introducing the *manners* and *customs* of other nations, and their *idolatry* also. Solomon sinned against this precept, and brought ruin on himself and on the land by it; see 1 Kings xi. 4.

Verse 18. *He shall write him a copy of this law*] משנה התורה הזאת *mishneh hattorah hazzoth*, an *iteration* or *duplicate* of *this law*; translated by the Septuagint, το δευτερονομιον τουτο, *this deuteronomy*. From this version both the Vulgate Latin and all the modern versions have taken the name of this book; and from the original word the Jews call it *Mishneh*. See the *preface* to this book.

Out of that which is *before the priests the Levites*] It is likely this means, that the copy which the king was to write out was to be taken from the *autograph* kept in the tabernacle before the Lord, from which, as a standard, every copy was taken, and with which doubtless every copy was compared; and it is probable that the priests and Levites had the revising of every copy that was taken off, in order to prevent errors from creeping into the sacred text.

Verse 19. *And it shall be with him, &c.*] It was the surest way to bring the king to an acquaintance with the Divine law to oblige him to write out a fair copy of it with his own hand, in which he was to read daily. This was essentially necessary, as these laws of God were all permanent, and no Israelitish king could make any *new law*, the kings of this people being ever considered as only the *vicegerents* of Jehovah.

Verse 20. *He, and his children, in the midst of Israel.*] From this verse it has been inferred that the crown of Israel was designed to be *hereditary*, and this is very probable; for long experience has proved to almost all the nations of the world that *hereditary succession* in the regal government is, on the whole, the safest, and best calculated to secure the public tranquillity.

CHAPTER XVIII.

The priests and Levites to have no inheritance, 1, 2. *What is the priest's due*, 3–5. *Of the Levites that come from any of the other cities*, 6–8. *The Israelites must not copy the abominations of the former inhabitants*, 9. *None to cause his son or daughter to pass through the fire, or use any kind of divination or enchantment, as the former inhabitants did*, 10–14. *The great prophet which God promised to raise up*, 15–19. *Of false prophets*, 20; *and how to discern them*, 21, 22.

A. M. 2553.
B. C. 1451.
An. Ex. Isr. 40.
Sebat.

THE priests the Levites, *and*
all the tribe of Levi, [a] shall
have no part nor inheritance with
Israel; they [b] shall eat the offerings of the
LORD made by fire, and his inheritance.
2 Therefore shall they have no
inheritance among their brethren:
the LORD *is* their inheritance, as
he hath said unto them.
3 And this shall be the priest's due from

[a] Num. xviii. 20; xxvi. 62; chap. x. 9. [b] Num. xviii. 8, 9; 1 Cor. ix. 13.

NOTES ON CHAP. XVIII.

Verse 1. *The priests the Levites—shall have no part*] That is, says Rab. *Maimon*, they shall have no part in the *spoils* taken from an enemy.

Verse 2. *The Lord is their inheritance*] He is the portion of their souls; and as to their bodies, they shall live by the offerings of the Lord made by fire, i. e., the *meat-offering*, *the sin-offering*, and the *trespass-offering*; and whatever was the Lord's right, in these or other offerings, he gave to the priests.

Verse 3. *Offer a sacrifice*] זבחי הזבח *zobechey hazzebach*. The word זבח *zebach* is used to signify, not only an animal sacrificed to the Lord, but also one killed for *common use*. See Gen. xliii. 15; Prov. xvii. 1; Ezek. xxv. 6. And in this latter sense it probably should be understood here; and, consequently, the command in this verse relates to what the people

a

A. M. 2553.
B. C. 1451.
An. Ex. Isr. 40.
Sebat.

the people, from them that offer a
sacrifice, whether *it be* ox or
sheep; and [c] they shall give unto
the priest the shoulder, and the two cheeks,
and the maw.
4 [d] The first-fruit *also* of thy corn, of thy
wine, and of thine oil, and the first of the
fleece of thy sheep, shalt thou give him.
5 For [e] the LORD thy God hath chosen him
out of all thy tribes, [f] to stand to minister in
the name of the LORD, him and his sons for
ever.
6 And if a Levite come from any of thy
gates out of all Israel, where he [g] sojourned,
and come with all the desire of his mind [h] unto
the place which the LORD shall choose;
7 Then he shall minister in the name of the
LORD his God, [i] as all his brethren the Levites
do, which stand there before the LORD.
8 They shall have like [k] portions to eat, beside
[l] that which cometh of the sale of his
patrimony.

9 When thou art come into the
land which the LORD thy God
giveth thee, [m] thou shalt not learn
to do after the abominations of those nations.
10 There shall not be found among you *any*
one that maketh his son or his daughter [n] to
pass through the fire, [o] *or* that useth divination,
or an observer of times, or an enchanter,
or a witch;
11 [p] Or a charmer, or a consulter with familiar
spirits, or a wizard, or a [q] necromancer.
12 For all that do these things *are* an abomination
unto the LORD: and [r] because of
these abominations the LORD thy God doth
drive them out from before thee.
13 Thou shalt be [s] perfect with the LORD
thy God.
14 For these nations, which thou shalt
[t] possess, hearkened unto observers of times,
and unto diviners: but as for thee, the LORD
thy God hath not suffered thee so *to do*.
15 [u] The LORD thy God will raise up unto

[c] Lev. vii. 30–34.——[d] Exod. xxii. 29; Num. xviii. 12, 24.——[e] Exod. xxviii. 1; Num. iii. 10.——[f] Chap. x. 8; xvii. 12.——[g] Num. xxxv. 2, 3.——[h] Chap. xii. 5.——[i] 2 Chron. xxxi. 2.——[k] 2 Chron. xxxi. 4; Neh. xii. 44, 47.——[l] Heb. *his sales by the fathers.*

[m] Lev. xviii. 26, 27, 30; chap. xii. 29, 30, 31.——[n] Lev. xviii. 21; chap. xii. 31.——[o] Lev. xix. 26, 31; xx. 27; Isa. viii. 19.——[p] Lev. xx. 27.——[q] 1 Sam. xxviii. 7.——[r] Lev. xviii. 24, 25; ch. ix. 4.——[s] Or, *upright*, or *sincere*; Gen. xvii. 1.——[t] Or, *inherit*.——[u] Ver. 18; John i. 45; Acts iii. 22; vii. 37.

were to allow the priests and Levites from the animals slain for common use. The parts to be given to the priests were, 1. The *shoulder*, probably cut off from the beast with the skin on; so *Maimonides*. 2. The *two cheeks*, which may include the whole head. 3. The *maw*—the whole of those intestines which are commonly used for food.

Verse 4. *The first-fruit* also *of thy corn, of thy wine, and of thine oil, &c.*] All these *first-fruits* and *firstlings* were the Lord's portion, and these he gave to the priests.

Verse 8. *The sale of his patrimony.*] So we find that, though the Levites might have no part of the land by lot, yet they were permitted to make purchases of houses, goods, and cattle, yea, of fields also. See the case of Abiathar, 1 Kings ii. 26, and of Jeremiah, Jer. xxxii. 7, 8.

Verse 10. *To pass through the fire*] Probably in the way of consecration to Molech, or some other deity. It is not likely that their being *burnt to death* is here intended. See on Lev. xviii. 21.

Divination] קסם קסמים *kosem kesamim*, one who endeavours to find out futurity by *auguries*, using lots, &c.

Observer of times] מעונן *meonen*, one who pretends to foretell future events by present occurrences, and who predicts great political or physical changes from the aspects of the planets, eclipses, motion of the *clouds*, &c., &c. See on Gen. xli. 8.

Enchanter] מנחש *menachesh*, from נחש *nichesh*, to *view attentively;* one who inspected the entrails of beasts, observed the flight of birds, &c., &c., and drew auguries thence. Some think divination by *serpents* is meant, which was common among the heathen.

A witch.] מכשף *mechashsheph*, probably those who by means of drugs, herbs, perfumes, &c., pretended to bring certain celestial influences to their aid. See the note on Lev. xix. 26.

Verse 11. *A charmer*] חבר חבר *chober chaber*, one who uses *spells;* a peculiar *conjunction*, as the term implies, of *words*, or things, tying knots, &c., for the purposes of divination. This was a custom among the heathen, as we learn from the following verses:—

Necte TRIBUS NODIS ternos, *Amarylli*, colores:
Necte, *Amarylli, modo; et Veneris, dic*, vincula necto.
Virg. Ecl. viii., ver. 77.

"*Knit* with three KNOTS the fillets, *knit* them straight;
Then say, these KNOTS to love I consecrate."
DRYDEN.

A consulter with familiar spirits] שאל אוב *shoel ob*, a Pythoness, one who *inquires* by the means of one spirit to get oracular answers from another of a superior order. See on Lev. xix. 31.

A wizard] ידעני *yiddeoni*, *a wise one*, a knowing one. *Wizard* was formerly considered as the masculine of *witch*, both practising divination by similar means. See on Exod. xxii. 18, and Lev. xix. 31.

Or a necromancer.] דרש אל המתים *doresh el hammethim*, one who *seeks* from or *inquires* of *the dead*. Such as the witch at Endor, who professed to *evoke the dead*, in order to get them to disclose the secrets of the spiritual world.

Verse 15. *The Lord thy God will raise up unto thee*

A. M. 2553. B. C. 1451. An. Ex. Isr. 40. Sebat.

thee a Prophet from the midst
of thee, of thy brethren, like unto
me; unto him ye shall hearken;
16 According to all that thou desiredst of
the LORD thy God in Horeb [v] in the day of the
assembly, saying, [w] Let me not hear again the
voice of the LORD my God, neither let me see
this great fire any more, that I die not.
17 And the LORD said unto me, [x] They have
well *spoken that* which they have spoken.
18 [y] I will raise them up a Prophet from
among their brethren, like unto thee, and [z] will
put my words in his mouth; [a] and he shall
speak unto them all that I shall command him.
19 [b] And it shall come to pass, *that* whosoever will not hearken unto my words which he
shall speak in my name, I will
require *it* of him.
20 But [c] the prophet which
shall presume to speak a word in my name
which I have not commanded him to speak, or
[d] that shall speak in the name of other gods,
even that prophet shall die.
21 And if thou say in thine heart, How shall
we know the word which the LORD hath not
spoken?
22 [e] When a prophet speaketh in the name
of the LORD, [f] if the thing follow not, nor
come to pass, that *is* the thing which the LORD
hath not spoken, *but* the prophet hath spoken
it [g] presumptuously: thou shalt not be afraid
of him.

[v] Chap. ix. 10.——[w] Exod. xx. 19; Heb. xii. 19.——[x] Chap. v. 28.——[y] Ver. 15; John i. 45; Acts iii. 22; vii. 37.——[z] Isa. li. 16; John xvii. 8.——[a] John iv. 25; viii. 28; xii. 49, 50.

[b] Acts iii. 23.——[c] Chap. xiii. 5; Jer. xiv. 14, 15; Zech. xiii. 3. [d] Chap. xiii. 1, 2; Jer. ii. 8.——[e] Jer. xxviii. 9.——[f] See chap. xiii. 2.——[g] Ver. 20.

a Prophet] Instead of *diviners, observers of times*, &c., God here promises to give them an *infallible guide*, who should tell them all things that make for their peace, so that his declarations should completely answer the end of all the knowledge that was pretended to be gained by the persons already specified.

Like unto me] Viz., a prophet, a legislator, a king, a mediator, and the head or chief of the people of God. This was the very person of whom Moses was the type, and who should accomplish all the great purposes of the Divine Being. Such a prophet as had never before appeared, and who should have no equal till the consummation of the world.

This prophet is the Lord Jesus, who was in the bosom of the Father, and who came to *declare him* to mankind. Every word spoken by him is a living infallible oracle from God himself; and must be received and obeyed as such, on pain of the eternal displeasure of the Almighty. See ver. 19, and Acts iii. 22, 23; and see the conclusion of this chapter.

Verse 22. *If the thing follow not*] It is worthy of remark that the prophets in general predicted those things which were *shortly* to come to pass, that the people might have the fullest proof of their Divine mission, and of the existence of God's providence in the administration of the affairs of men.

THE promise contained in the 15th and 18th verses of this chapter has long been considered of the first importance in the controversies between the Christians and Jews. "Christ," says Ainsworth, "was to be a *man*, and of the stock of the Jews, by promise, because the people could not endure to hear the voice of GOD, ver. 16. And as in respect of his prophecy, so of the priesthood: *for every high priest is taken from among men*, Heb. v. 1; and also of his kingdom, as in Deut. xvii. 15: *From among thy brethren shalt thou set a king over thee like unto me*.

"1. Christ alone was like unto Moses as a PROPHET; for it is written, *There arose not a prophet in* Israel *like unto* Moses, *whom the Lord knew face to face, in all the signs and wonders which the Lord sent him to do*, Deut. xxxiv. 10, 11, 12. This therefore cannot be understood of the ordinary prophets which were raised up in *Israel*, but of Christ only, as the apostles expound it Acts ii. 22–26. 2. Christ was like unto *Moses* in respect to his office of *mediation* between God and his people, Deut. v. 5; 1 Tim. ii. 5; but greater than *Moses* as being *the mediator of a better covenant*, (or testament,) *which was established upon better promises*, Heb. viii. 6. 3. Christ was like unto Moses in *excellency*; for as *Moses* excelled all the prophets in speaking to God *mouth to mouth*, Num. xii. 6, 7, 8, so Christ excelled him and all men in that, being *in the bosom of the* Father, he hath come down from heaven and declared God unto us, John i. 18, iii. 13. 4. Christ was like to Moses in *faithfulness*, but therein also excelling; for *Moses* was faithful in God's house as a *servant*, but *Christ as the son over his own house*, Heb. iii. 2, 5, 6. 5. Christ was like to Moses in *signs* and *wonders*, wherein he also excelled *Moses*, as the history of the Gospel shows; for he was a *prophet mighty in deed and word before God and all the people*, Luke xxiv. 19. *A man approved of God among* them, *by miracles, signs, and wonders, which God did by him in the midst of* them, Acts ii. 22. For he did among them *the works which no other man did*, John xv. 24. *Unto him*, that is, not unto the diviners, wizards, or any such like, but *unto him*, and him only; as *Him thou shalt serve*, Deut. vi. 13, is expounded, *Him only*, Matt. iv. 10. And though this is principally meant of Christ in *person*, of whom God said, *Hear him*, Matt. xvii. 5; yet it implies also his *ministers*, as himself said, *He that heareth you heareth me*, Luke x. 16." To these may be added, 6. As Moses was *king* among his people, in this respect Christ is like to him, but infinitely greater; for he is *King of kings and Lord of lords*, Rev. xix. 16; 1 Tim. vi. 15. And, 7. He was like to Moses as a *legislator*. Moses gave laws to Israel by the authority and commandment of God, which the Jews have ever acknowledged as coming from the immediate inspira-

tion of the Almighty: these are contained in the Pentateuch. Christ gave a new law, the Gospel contained in the four Evangelists and Acts of the Apostles, on which the Christian Church is founded, and by which all genuine Christians are governed both in heart and life. To all which may be added, 8. That God never commissioned any human beings to give laws to mankind but Moses and Christ; and therefore, as a lawgiver, Christ *alone* resembles Moses; for to the present hour none but themselves have given laws in the name of God, which he has ratified and confirmed by the most indubitable and infallible signs, proofs, and miracles.

Dr. Jortin, in his *Remarks on Ecclesiastical History*, has drawn a parallel between Moses and Christ in a great number of particulars, which he concludes thus: "Let us search all the records of universal history, and see if we can find a man who was *so like to Moses* as Christ was, and *so like to Christ* as Moses was. If we cannot find such a one, then have we found HIM of whom Moses in the law and the prophets did write to be Jesus of Nazareth, the Son of God." On this subject see *Ainsworth*, *Calmet*, and *Dodd*, who have all marked this striking correspondence between Moses and Christ.

CHAPTER XIX.

Three cities of refuge to be appointed in the midst of the promised land; the land being divided into three parts, a city is to be placed in each, a proper way to which is to be prepared, 1–3. *In what cases of manslaughter the benefit of those cities may be claimed,* 4–6. *Three cities more to be added should the Lord enlarge their coasts, and the reasons why,* 7–10. *The intentional murderer shall have no benefit from these cities,* 11–13. *The landmark is not to be shifted,* 14. *One witness shall not be deemed sufficient to convict a man,* 15. *How a false witness shall be dealt with—he shall bear the punishment which he designed should have been inflicted on his neighbour,* 16–20. *Another command to establish the* lex talionis, 21.

A. M. 2553. B. C. 1451. An. Ex. Isr. 40. Sebat.

WHEN the LORD thy God [a] hath cut off the nations whose land the LORD thy God giveth thee, and thou [b] succeedest them, and dwellest in their cities, and in their houses;

2 [c] Thou shalt separate three cities for thee in the midst of thy land, which the LORD thy God giveth thee to possess it.

3 Thou shalt prepare thee a way, and divide the coasts of thy land, which the LORD thy God giveth thee to inherit, into three parts, that every slayer may flee thither.

4 And [d] this *is* the case of the slayer, which shall flee thither, that he may live: Whoso killeth his neighbour ignorantly, whom he hated not [e] in time past;

5 As when a man goeth into the wood with his neighbour to hew wood, and his hand fetcheth a stroke with the axe to cut down the tree, and the [f] head slippeth from the [g] helve, and [h] lighteth upon his neighbour, that he die; he shall flee unto one of those cities, and live:

6 [i] Lest the avenger of the blood pursue the slayer, while his heart is hot, and overtake him, because the way is long, and [k] slay him; whereas he *was* not worthy of death, inasmuch as he hated him not [l] in time past.

A. M. 2553. B. C. 1451. An. Ex. Isr. 40. Sebat.

7 Wherefore I command thee, saying, Thou shalt separate three cities for thee.

8 And if the LORD thy God [m] enlarge thy coast, as he hath sworn unto thy fathers, and give thee all the land which he promised to give unto thy fathers;

9 If thou shalt keep all these commandments to do them, which I command thee this day, to love the LORD thy God, and to walk ever in his ways; [n] then shalt thou add three cities more for thee, beside these three:

10 That innocent blood be not shed in thy land, which the LORD thy God giveth thee *for* an inheritance, and *so* blood be upon thee.

11 But [o] if any man hate his neighbour, and lie in wait for him, and rise up against him, and smite him [p] mortally that he die, and fleeth into one of these cities:

[a] Chap. xii. 29.—[b] Heb. *inheritest* or *possessest*.—[c] Exod. xxi. 13; Num. xxxv. 10, 14; Josh. xx. 2.—[d] Num. xxxv. 15; chap. iv. 42.—[e] Heb. *from yesterday the third day*.—[f] Heb. *iron*.—[g] Heb. *wood*.—[h] Heb. *findeth*.

[i] Num. xxxv. 12.—[k] Heb. *smite him in life*.—[l] Heb. *from yesterday the third day*.—[m] Gen. xv. 18; chap. xii. 20.—[n] Josh. xx. 7, 8.—[o] Exod. xxi. 12, &c.; Num. xxxv. 16, 24; chap. xxvii. 24; Prov. xxviii. 17.—[p] Heb. *in life*.

NOTES ON CHAP. XIX.

Verse 2. *Thou shalt separate three cities*] See on Num. xxxv. 10, &c.

Verse 3. *Thou shalt prepare thee a way*] The Jews inform us that the roads to the cities of refuge were made very broad, thirty-two cubits; and even, so that there should be no impediments in the way; and were constantly kept in good repair.

Verse 9. *Shalt thou add three cities more*] This was afterwards found necessary, and accordingly six cities were appointed, three on either side Jordan. See Josh. xxi. 1, &c. In imitation of these cities of

A. M. 2553. B. C. 1451. An. Ex. Isr. 40. Sebat.

12 Then the elders of his city shall send and fetch him thence, and deliver him into the hand of the avenger of blood, that he may die.
13 [q] Thine eye shall not pity him, [r] but thou shalt put away *the guilt of* innocent blood from Israel, that it may go well with thee.
14 [s] Thou shalt not remove thy neighbour's landmark, which they of old time have set in thine inheritance, which thou shalt inherit in the land that the LORD thy God giveth thee to possess it.
15 [t] One witness shall not rise up against a man for any iniquity, or for any sin, in any sin that he sinneth: at the mouth of two witnesses, or at the mouth of three witnesses, shall the matter be established.
16 If a false witness [u] rise up against any man to testify against him [v] *that which is* wrong:
17 Then both the men, between whom the controversy *is*, shall stand before the LORD, [w] before the priests and the judges, which shall be in those days;
18 And the judges shall make diligent inquisition: and, behold, *if* the witness *be* a false witness, *and* hath testified falsely against his brother;
19 [x] Then shall ye do unto him as he had thought to have done unto his brother: so [y] shalt thou put the evil away from among you.
20 [z] And those which remain shall hear, and fear, and shall henceforth commit no more any such evil among you.
21 [a] And thine eye shall not pity; *but* [b] life *shall go* for life, eye for eye, tooth for tooth, hand for hand, foot for foot.

[q] Chap. xiii. 8; xxv. 12.——[r] Num. xxxv. 33, 34; chap. xxi. 9; 1 Kings ii. 31.——[s] Chap. xxvii. 17; Job xxiv. 2; Prov. xxii. 28; Hos. v. 10.——[t] Num. xxxv. 30; chap. xvii. 6; Matt. xviii. 16; John viii. 17; 2 Cor. xiii. 1; 1 Tim. v. 19; Heb. x. 28.——[u] Psa. xxvii. 12; xxxv. 11.——[v] Or, *falling away*.——[w] Chap. xvii. 9; xxi. 5.——[x] Prov. xix. 5, 9; Dan. vi. 24; Hist. Sus. 62.——[y] Ch. xiii. 5; xvii. 7; xxi. 21; xxii. 21, 24; xxiv. 7.——[z] Ch. xvii. 13; xxi. 21.——[a] Ver. 13.——[b] Exod. xxi. 23; Lev. xxiv. 20; Matt. v. 38.

refuge the heathens had their *asyla*, and the Catholics their *privileged altars*. See Exod. xxi. 13, 14, and on Num. xxxv. 6, &c.

Verse 11. *If any man hate his neighbour*] See on Exod. xxi. 13.

Verse 14. *Thou shalt not remove thy neighbour's landmark*] Before the extensive use of fences, landed property was marked out by *stones* or *posts*, set up so as to ascertain the divisions of family estates. It was easy to remove one of these landmarks, and set it in a different place; and thus the dishonest man enlarged his own estate by contracting that of his neighbour. The *termini* or landmarks among the Romans were held very sacred, and were at last deified.

To these *termini* Numa Pompilius commanded offerings of broth, cakes, and first-fruits, to be made. And Ovid informs us that it was customary to sacrifice a *lamb* to them, and sprinkle them with its blood:—

Spargitur et cæso communis terminus agno.
FAST. lib. ii., ver. 655.

And from Tibullus it appears that they sometimes adorned them with flowers and garlands:—

Nam veneror, seu stipes habet desertus in agris,
Seu vetus *in trivio* florida serta lapis.
ELEG. lib. i., E. i., ver. 11.

"*Revere* each *antique stone bedeck'd with flowers,*
That *bounds the field*, or points the doubtful way."
GRAINGER.

It appears from Juvenal that annual oblations were made to them:—

——— *Convallem ruris aviti*
Improbus, aut campum mihi si vicinus ademit,
Aut sacrum effodit medio de limite saxum,
Quod mea cum vetulo *coluit puls* annua *libo.*
SAT. xvi., ver. 36.

"If any rogue vexatious suits advance
Against me for my *known inheritance*,
Enter by violence my fruitful grounds,
Or take the *sacred landmark* from my *bounds*,
Those *bounds* which, with procession and with prayer
And *offer'd cakes*, have been my *annual care.*"
DRYDEN.

In the digests there is a vague law, *de termino moto*, Digestor. lib. xlvii., Tit. 21, on which Calmet remarks that though the Romans had no determined punishment for those who removed the ancient landmarks; yet if *slaves* were found to have done it with an evil design, they were put to death; that persons of quality were sometimes exiled when found guilty; and that others were sentenced to pecuniary fines, or corporal punishment.

Verse 15. *One witness shall not rise up, &c.*] See Num. xxxv. 30.

Verse 19. *Then shall ye do unto him as he had thought to have done unto his brother*] Nothing can be more equitable or proper than this, that if a man endeavour to do any injury to or take away the life of another, on detection he shall be caused to undergo the same evil which he intended for his innocent neighbour.

Some of our excellent English laws have been made on this very ground. In the 37th of Edw. III., chap. 18, it is ordained that all those who make suggestion shall incur the same pain which the other should have had, if he were attainted, in case his suggestions be found evil. A similar law was made in the 38th of the same reign, chap. 9. By a law of the twelve Tables, a false witness was thrown down the Tarpeian rock. In short, false witnesses have been execrated by all nations.

Verse 21. *Life—for life, eye for eye, &c.*] The

operation of such a law as this must have been very salutary: if a man prized his own members, he would naturally avoid injuring those of others. It is a pity that this law were not still in force: it would certainly prevent many of those savage acts which now both disgrace and injure society. I speak this in reference to *law* generally, and the provision that should be made to prevent and punish ferocious and malevolent offences. A Christian may always act on the plan of *forgiving* injuries; and where the public peace and safety may not be affected, he should do so; but if *law* did not make a provision for the safety of the community by enactment against the profligate, civil society would soon be destroyed.

CHAPTER XX.

Directions concerning campaigns, 1. *The priest shall encourage the people with the assurance that God will accompany and fight for them,* 2–4. *The officers shall dismiss from the army all who had just built a new house, but had not dedicated it,* 5. *All who had planted a vineyard, but had not yet eaten of its fruits,* 6. *All who had betrothed a wife, but had not brought her home,* 7. *And all who were timid and faint-hearted,* 8. *The commanders to be chosen after the timid, &c., had retired,* 9. *No city to be attacked till they had proclaimed conditions of peace to it, provided it be a city beyond the bounds of the seven Canaanitish nations; if it submitted, it was to become tributary; if not, it was to be besieged, sacked, and all the males put to the sword; the women, children, and cattle to be taken as booty,* 10–15. *No such offers to be made to the cities of the Canaanites; of them nothing shall be preserved, and the reason,* 16–18. *In besieging a city no trees to be cut down but those which do not bear fruit,* 19, 20.

A. M. 2553. B. C. 1451. An. Ex. Isr. 40. Sebat.

WHEN thou goest out to battle against thine enemies, and seest [a] horses, and chariots, *and* a people more than thou, be not afraid of them: for the LORD thy God *is* [b] with thee, which brought thee up out of the land of Egypt.

2 And it shall be, when ye are come nigh unto the battle, that the priest shall approach and speak unto the people,

3 And shall say unto them, Hear, O Israel, ye approach this day unto battle against your enemies: let not your hearts [c] faint, fear not, and do not [d] tremble, neither be ye terrified because of them;

4 For the LORD your God *is* he that goeth with you, [e] to fight for you against your enemies, to save you.

5 And the officers shall speak unto the people, saying, What man *is there* that hath built a new house, and hath not [f] dedicated it? let him go and return to his house, lest he die in the battle, and another man dedicate it.

6 And what man *is he* that hath planted a vineyard, and hath not *yet* [g] eaten of it? let him *also* go and return unto his house, lest he die in the battle, and another man eat of it.

[a] See Psa. xx. 7; Isa. xxxi. 1.——[b] Num. xxiii. 21; chap. xxxi. 6, 8; 2 Chron. xiii. 12; xxxii. 7, 8.——[c] Heb. *be tender.* [d] Heb. *make haste.*

[e] Chap. i. 30; iii. 22; Josh. xxiii. 10.——[f] See Neh. xii. 27; Psa. xxx. title.——[g] Heb. *made it common*; see Lev. xix. 23, 24; chap. xxviii. 30.

NOTES ON CHAP. XX.

Verse 1. *When thou goest out to battle*] This refers chiefly to the battles they were to have with the Canaanites, in order to get possession of the promised land; for it cannot be considered to apply to any wars which they might have with the surrounding nations for political reasons, as the Divine assistance could not be expected in wars which were not undertaken by the Divine command.

Verse 2. *The priest shall approach, and speak unto the people*] The priest on these occasions was the representative of that God whose servant he was, and whose worship he conducted. It is remarkable that almost all ancient nations took their priests with them to battle, as they did not expect success without having the object of their adoration with them, and they supposed they secured his presence by having that of his representative.

Verse 5. *That hath built a new house, and hath not dedicated it?*] From the title of Psa. xxx.,—*A Psalm or Song at the Dedication of the House of David*—it is evident that it was a custom in Israel to dedicate a new house to God with prayer, praise, and thanksgiving; and this was done in order to secure the Divine presence and blessing, for no pious or sensible man could imagine he could dwell safely in a house that was not under the immediate protection of God. Hence it has been a custom in the most barbarous nations to consecrate a part of a new house to the deity they worshipped. The houses of the inhabitants of *Bonny*, in Africa, are generally divided into three apartments: one is a kind of state room or parlour; another serves for a common room, or kitchen; and the third is dedicated to the *Juju*, the serpent god, which they worship; for even those savages believe that in every house their god should have his temple! At the times of dedication among the Jews, besides prayer and praise, a feast was made, to which the relatives and neighbours were invited. Something of this custom is observed in some parts of our own country in what is called

A. M. 2553.
B. C. 1451.
An. Ex. Isr. 40.
Sebat.

7 [h] And what man *is there* that
hath betrothed a wife, and hath
not taken her? let him go and
return unto his house, lest he die in the battle,
and another man take her.
8 And the officers shall speak farther unto
the people, and they shall say, [i] What man *is
there that is* fearful and faint-hearted? let him
go and return to his house, lest his brethren's
heart [k] faint as well as his heart.
9 And it shall be, when the officers have
made an end of speaking unto the people,
that they shall make captains of the armies
[l] to lead the people.
10 When thou comest nigh unto a city to
fight against it, [m] then proclaim peace unto it.
11 And it shall be, if it make thee answer
of peace, and open unto thee, then it shall be,
that all the people *that is* found therein shall be
tributaries unto thee, and they shall serve thee.
12 And if it will make no peace
with thee, but will make war
against thee, then thou shalt besiege it:
13 And when the Lord thy God hath delivered it into thine hands, [n] thou shalt smite
every male thereof with the edge of the sword:
14 But the women, and the little ones, and
[o] the cattle, and all that is in the city, *even* all
the spoil thereof, shalt thou [p] take unto thyself;
and [q] thou shalt eat the spoil of thine enemies,
which the Lord thy God hath given thee.
15 Thus shalt thou do unto all the cities
which are very far off from thee, which *are*
not of the cities of these nations.
16 But [r] of the cities of these people, which
the Lord thy God doth give thee *for* an inheritance, thou shalt save alive nothing that
breatheth:
17 But thou shalt utterly destroy them;

[h] Chap. xxvi. 5.——[i] Judg. vii. 3.——[k] Heb. *melt.*——[l] Heb. to be *in the head of the people.*——[m] 2 Sam. xx. 18, 20.——[n] Num. xxxi. 7.——[o] Josh. viii. 2.——[p] Heb. *spoil.*——[q] Josh. xxii. 8. [r] Num. xxi. 2, 3, 35; xxxiii. 52; chap. vii. 1, 2; Josh. xi. 14.

warming the house; but in these cases the *feasting* only is kept up—the prayer and praise forgotten! so that the dedication appears to be rather more to Bacchus than to Jehovah, the author of every good and perfect gift.

Verse 7. *Betrothed a wife, and hath not taken her?*] It was customary among the Jews to contract matrimony, espouse or betroth, and for some considerable time to leave the parties in the houses of their respective parents: when the bridegroom had made proper preparations, then the bride was brought home to his house, and thus the marriage was consummated. The provisions in this verse refer to a case of this kind; for it was deemed an excessive hardship for a person to be obliged to go to battle, where there was a probability of his being slain, who had left a new house unfinished; a newly purchased heritage half tilled; or a wife with whom he had just contracted marriage. Homer represents the case of Protesilaus as very afflicting, who was obliged to go to the Trojan war, leaving his wife in the deepest distress, and his house unfinished.

Του δε και αμφιδρυφης αλοχος Φυλακῃ ελελειπτο,
Και δομος ἡμιτελης· τον δ' εκτανε Δαρδανος ανηρ,
Νηος αποθρωσκοντα πολυ πρωτιστον Αχαιων.

Iliad, l. ii., ver. 700.

"A *wife he left,*
To rend in Phylace *her bleeding cheeks,*
And an *unfinish'd mansion:* first he died
Of all the Greeks; for as he leap'd to land,
Long ere the rest, a Dardan struck him dead."

Cowper.

Verse 8. *What man* is there that is *fearful and faint-hearted?*] The original רך *rach*, signifies *tender* or *soft-hearted.* And a *soft heart* the man must have who, in such a contest, after such a permission, could turn his back upon his enemies and his brethren. However, such were the troops commanded by Gideon in his war against the Midianites; for after he gave this permission, out of 32,000 men only 10,000 remained to fight! Judges vii. 3. There could be no deception in a business of this kind; for the departure of the 22,000 was the fullest proof of their dastardliness which they could possibly give.

Verse 10. *Proclaim peace unto it.*] Interpreters are greatly divided concerning the objects of this law. The text, taken in connection with the context,) see verses 15–18,) appears to state that this proclamation or offer of peace to a city is *only* to be understood of those cities which were situated *beyond the limits of the seven anathematized nations,* because these latter are commanded to be totally destroyed. Nothing can be clearer than this from the *bare letter of the text,* unless some of the words, taken separately, can be shown to have a different meaning. For the common interpretation, the following reasons are given.

God, who knows all things, saw that they were incurable in their idolatry; that the cup of their iniquity was full; and as their Creator, Sovereign, and Judge, he determined to destroy them from off the face of the earth, "lest they should teach the Israelites to do after all their abominations," ver. 18. After all, many plausible arguments have been brought to prove that even these seven Canaanitish nations might be received into mercy, provided they, 1. Renounced their idolatry; 2. Became subject to the Jews; and, 3. Paid annual tribute: and that it was only in case these terms were rejected, that they were not to leave alive in such a city any thing that breathed, ver. 16.

Verse 17. *But thou shalt utterly destroy them*] The above reasoning will gain considerable strength,

a

A. M. 2553.
B. C. 1451.
An. Ex. Isr. 40.
Sebat.

namely, the Hittites, and the Amorites, the Canaanites, and the Perizzites, the Hivites, and the Jebusites: as the LORD thy God hath commanded thee:
18 That [s] they teach you not to do after all
their abominations, which they have done unto their gods; so should ye [t] sin against the LORD your God.
19 When thou shalt besiege a city a long
time, in making war against it to take it, thou shalt not destroy the trees thereof by forcing an axe against them: for thou mayest eat of them, and thou shalt not cut them down ([u] for the tree of the field *is* man's *life*) [v] to employ *them* in the siege:
20 Only the trees which thou knowest that
they *be* not trees for meat, thou shalt destroy and cut them down; and thou shalt build bulwarks against the city that maketh war with thee, until [w] it be subdued.

[s] Chap. vii. 4; xii. 30, 31; xviii. 9.——[t] Exodus xxiii. 33.

[u] Or, *for, O man, the* tree *of the field* is *to be employed in the siege.* [v] Heb. *to go from before thee.*——[w] Heb. *it come down.*

provided we could translate כי החרם תחרימם *ki hacharem tacharimem, thou shalt utterly subdue them*—slaying them if they resist, and thus leaving nothing alive that breathed; or *totally expel them from the land,* or reduce them to a state of slavery in it, that they might no longer exist as a *people.* This certainly made them an *anathema* as a *nation,* wholly destroying their *political* existence. Probably this was so understood by the *Gibeonites,* viz., that they either must be slain or utterly leave the land, which last was certainly in their power, and therefore, by a stratagem, they got the princes of Israel to make a league with them. When the deceit was discovered, the Israelites, though not bound by their oath, because they were deceived by the Gibeonites, and therefore were under no obligation to fulfil their part of the covenant; yet, though they had this command before their eyes, did not believe that they were bound to put even those deceivers to death; but they destroyed their *political existence,* by making them *hewers of wood and drawers of water to the congregation;* i. e., slaves to the Israelites. (See Josh. ix.) Rahab and her household also were spared. So that it does not appear that the Israelites believed that they were bound to put every Canaanite *to death.* Their *political* existence was under the anathema, and this the Hebrews annihilated.

That many of the Canaanites continued in the land even to the days of Solomon, we have the fullest proof; for we read, 2 Chron. viii. 7: "All the people of the land that were left of the Hittites, Amorites, Perizzites, Hivites, and Jebusites, who were left in the land, whom the children of Israel consumed not, them did Solomon make to pay tribute to this day." Thus Solomon destroyed their political existence, but did not consider himself bound by the law of God to *put them to death.*

Verse 19. (*For the* tree *of the field* is *man's* life) *to employ* them *in the siege*] The original is exceedingly obscure, and has been variously translated, כי האדם עץ השדה לבא כפניך במצור *ki haadam ets hassadeh labo mippaneycha bammatsor.* The following are the chief versions: *For, O man, the* trees *of the field are for* thee *to employ* THEM *in the siege*—or, *For it is man, and the tree of the field, that must go before thee for a bulwark*—or, *For it is a tree, and not men, to increase the number of those who come against thee to the siege*—or, lastly, *The tree of the field* (is as) *a man, to go before thy face for a bulwark.* The *sense* is sufficiently clear, though the strict *grammatical* meaning of the words cannot be easily ascertained: it was a merciful provision to spare all fruit-bearing trees, because they yielded the fruit which supported man's life; and it was sound policy also, for even the conquerors must perish if the means of life were cut off.

It is diabolic cruelty to add to the *miseries of war* the horrors of *famine;* and this is done where the trees of the field are cut down, the dykes broken to drown the land, the villages burnt, and the crops wilfully spoiled. *O execrable war!* subversive of all the charities of life!

THERE are several curious particulars in these verses: 1. The people had the most positive assurances from God that their enemies should not be able to prevail against them by strength, numbers, nor stratagem, because *God should go with them* to lead and direct them, and should fight for them; and against his might none could prevail. 2. All such interferences were standing proofs of the being of God, of his especial providence, and of the truth of their religion. 3. Though God promised them such protection, yet they were to expect it in the diligent use of their own prudence and industry. The priests, the officers, and the people, had their respective parts to act in this business; if they did their duty respectively, God would take care that they should be successful. Those who will not help themselves with the strength which God has already given them, shall not have any farther assistance from him. In all such cases, the parable of the *talents* affords an accurate rule. 4. Their going to war against their enemies must not deprive them of mercy and tenderness towards their brethren. He who had *built a house* and had not yet dwelt in it, who had *planted a vineyard* and had not eaten of its fruits, who had *betrothed a wife* and had not yet taken her to his house, was not obliged to go to battle, lest he should fall in the war, and the fruits of his industry and affection be enjoyed by others. He who was *faint-hearted* was also permitted to return, lest he should give way in the heat of battle, and his example have a fatal influence on others.

CHAPTER XXI.

If a man be found slain in a field, and the cause of his death be unknown, the murder shall be expiated by the sacrifice of a heifer in an uncultivated valley, 1–4. *The rites to be used on the occasion,* 5–9. *The ordinance concerning marriage with a captive,* 10–14. *The law relative to the children of the hated and beloved wives: if the son of the hated wife should be the first-born he shall not be disinherited by the son of the beloved wife, but shall have a double portion of all his father's goods,* 15–18. *The law concerning the stubborn and rebellious son, who, when convicted, is to be stoned to death,* 19–21. *Of the person who is to be hanged,* 22. *His body shall not be left on the tree all night; every one that is hanged on a tree is accursed of God,* 23.

A. M. 2553. B. C. 1451. An. Ex. Isr. 40. Sebat.

IF *one* be found slain in the land
which the LORD thy God giveth thee to possess it, lying in
the field, *and* it be not known who hath slain
him:
2 Then thy elders and thy judges shall
come forth, and they shall measure unto the
cities which *are* round about him that is slain:
3 And it shall be, *that* the city *which is*
next unto the slain man, even the elders of
that city shall take a heifer, which hath not
been wrought with, *and* which hath not drawn
in the yoke;
4 And the elders of that city shall bring
down the heifer unto a rough valley, which is
neither eared nor sown, and shall strike off
the heifer's neck there in the valley:
5 And the priests, the sons of Levi, shall
come near; for [a] them the LORD thy God hath
chosen to minister unto him, and to bless in
the name of the LORD; and [b] by their [c] word
shall every controversy and every stroke be
tried:
6 And all the elders of that city, *that are*
next unto the slain *man,* [d] shall
wash their hands over the
heifer that is beheaded in the
valley:
7 And they shall answer and say, Our
hands have not shed this blood, neither have
our eyes seen *it.*
8 Be merciful, O LORD, unto thy people Israel, whom thou hast redeemed, [e] and lay not
innocent blood [f] unto thy people of Israel's
charge. And the blood shall be forgiven
them.
9 So [g] shalt thou put away the *guilt of* innocent blood from among you, when thou
shalt do *that which is* right in the sight of the
LORD.
10 When thou goest forth to war against
thine enemies, and the LORD thy God hath
delivered them into thine hands, and thou
hast taken them captive,
11 And seest among the captives a beautiful
woman, and hast a desire unto her, that thou
wouldest have her to thy wife;
12 Then thou shalt bring her home to thine

A. M. 2553. B. C. 1451. An. Ex. Isr. 40. Sebat.

[a] Chap. x. 8; 1 Chron. xxiii. 13; Ecclus. xlv. 15.——[b] Chap. xvii. 8, 9.——[c] Heb. *mouth.*

[d] See Psa. xix. 12; xxvi. 6; Matt. xxvii. 24.——[e] Jonah i. 14. [f] Heb. *in the midst.*——[g] Chap. xix. 13.

NOTES ON CHAP. XXI.

Verse 4. *Shall bring down the heifer unto a rough valley*] נחל איתן *nachal eythan* might be translated a *rapid stream,* probably passing through a piece of uncultivated ground where the elders of the city were to strike off the head of the heifer, and to wash their hands over her in token of their innocence. The spot of ground on which this sacrifice was made must be *uncultivated,* because it was considered to be a sacrifice to make atonement for the murder, and consequently would *pollute* the land. This regulation was calculated to keep murder in abhorrence, and to make the magistrates alert in their office, that delinquents might be discovered and punished, and thus public expense saved.

Verse 6. *Shall wash their hands over the heifer*] Washing the hands, in reference to such a subject as this, was a rite anciently used to signify that the persons thus washing were innocent of the crime in question. It was probably from the Jews that Pilate learned this symbolical method of expressing his innocence.

Verse 11. *And seest—a beautiful woman*] No forcible possession was allowed even in this case, when the woman was taken in war, and was, by the general consent of ancient nations, adjudged as a part of the spoils. The person to whose lot or share such a woman as is here described fell might, if he chose, have her for a *wife* on certain conditions; but he was not permitted to use her under any inferior character.

Verse 12. *She shall shave her head*] This was in token of her renouncing her religion, and becoming a proselyte to that of the Jews. This is still a custom in the East; when a Christian turns Mohammedan his head is shaven, and he is carried through the city crying, لا اله الا الله و محمد رسول الله *la alahila allah we Mohammed resooli Allah;* "There is no God but God, and Mohammed is the prophet of God."

Pare her nails] ועשתה את צפרניה *veasethah eth tsipporneyha,* "she shall make her nails." Now whether this signifies *paring* or letting them *grow,* is greatly doubted among learned men. Possibly it means neither

a

A. M. 2553.
B. C. 1451.
An. Ex. Isr. 40.
Sebat.

house; and she shall shave her head, and [h] pare [i] her nails.

13 And she shall put the raiment of her captivity from off her, and shall remain in thine house, and [k] bewail her father and her mother a full month: and after that thou shalt go in unto her, and be her husband, and she shall be thy wife.

14 And it shall be, if thou have no delight in her, then thou shalt let her go whither she will; but thou shalt not sell her at all for money, thou shalt not make merchandise of her, because thou hast [l] humbled her.

15 If a man have two wives, one beloved, [m] and another hated, and they have borne him children, *both* the beloved and the hated; and *if* the first-born son be hers that was hated:

16 Then it shall be, [n] when he maketh his sons to inherit *that* which he hath, *that* he may not make the son of the beloved first-born before the son of the hated, *which is indeed* the first-born:

17 But he shall acknowledge the son of the hated *for* the first-born, [o] by giving him a double portion of all [p] that he hath: for he *is* [q] the beginning of his strength; [r] the right of the first-born *is* his.

18 If a man have a stubborn and rebellious son, which will not obey the voice of his father, or the voice of his mother, and *that,* when they have chastened him, will not hearken unto them:

A. M. 2553.
B. C. 1451.
An. Ex. Isr. 40.
Sebat.

19 Then shall his father and his mother lay hold on him, and bring him out unto the elders of his city, and unto the gate of his place;

20 And they shall say unto the elders of his city, This our son *is* stubborn and rebellious, he will not obey our voice; *he is* a glutton, and a drunkard.

21 And all the men of his city shall stone him with stones, that he die: [s] so shalt thou put evil away from among you; [t] and all Israel shall hear, and fear.

22 And if a man have committed a sin [u] worthy of death, and he be to be put to death, and thou hang him on a tree:

23 [v] His body shall not remain all night upon the tree, but thou shalt in any wise bury him that day; (for [w] he that is hanged *is* [x] accursed of God;) that [y] thy land be not defiled, which the LORD thy God giveth thee *for* an inheritance.

[h] Or, *suffer to grow.*——[i] Heb. *make* or *dress.*——[k] See Psa. xlv. 10.——[l] Gen. xxxiv. 2; chap. xxii. 29; Judg. xix. 24.——[m] Gen. xxix. 33.——[n] 1 Chron. v. 2; xxvi. 10; 2 Chron. xi. 19, 22. [o] See 1 Chron. v. 1.——[p] Heb. *that is found with him.*——[q] Gen. xlix. 3.——[r] Gen. xxv. 31, 33.

[s] Chap. xiii. 5; xix. 19, 20; xxii. 21, 24.——[t] Chap. xiii. 11. [u] Chap. xix. 6; xxii. 26; Acts xxiii. 29; xxv. 11, 25; xxvi. 31. [v] Josh. viii. 29; x. 26, 27; John xix. 31.——[w] Gal. iii. 13. [x] Heb. *the curse of God;* see Num. xxv. 4; 2 Sam. xxi. 6. [y] Lev. xviii. 25; Num. xxxv. 34.

but *colouring* the nails, staining them red with the *hennah,* which is much practised in India to the present day, and which was undoubtedly practised among the ancient Egyptians, as is evident from the nails of mummies which are found thus stained. The *hennah,* according to Hasselquist, grows in India, and in Upper and Lower Egypt; it flowers from May to August. The manner of using it is this: the leaves are powdered, and made into a paste with water: they bind this paste on the nails of their fingers and toes, and let it stand on all night; in the morning they are found to be of a beautiful reddish yellow, and this lasts three weeks or a month, after which they renew the application. They often stain the palms of their hands and the soles of their feet in the same way, as appears from many paintings of eastern ladies done in India and Persia, which now lie before me. This staining the soles of the feet with the *hennah* is probably meant in 2 Sam. xix. 24: *Mephibosheth had not dressed* (literally made) *his feet*—they had not been thus coloured.

Verse 15. *One beloved, and another hated*] That is, one *loved less* than the other. This is the true notion of the word *hate* in Scripture. So *Jacob* HATED *Leah,* that is, he *loved her less* than he did *Rachel;* and *Jacob have I loved, but Esau have I* HATED, that is, I have shown a more particular affection to the posterity of Jacob than I have to the posterity of Esau. See the note on Gen. xxix. 31. From this verse we see that polygamy did exist under the Mosaic laws, and that it was put under certain regulations; but it was not *enjoined,* Moses merely *suffered* it, because of the hardness of their hearts, as our Lord justly remarks Matt. xix. 8.

Verses 18–21. *The stubborn, rebellious, gluttonous, and drunken son is to be stoned to death.*—This law, severe as it may seem, must have acted as a powerful preventive of crime. If such a law were in force now, and duly executed, how many deaths of disobedient and profligate children would there be in all corners of the land!

Verse 23. *His body shall not remain all night upon the tree*] Its exposure for the space of *one day* was judged sufficient. The law which required this answered all the ends of public justice, exposed the shame and infamy of the conduct, but did not put to torture the feelings of humanity by requiring a *perpetual* exhibition of a human being, a slow prey to the most loathsome process of putrefaction. Did ever the spiking of the heads of state criminals prevent high treason?

or the gibbeting of a thief or a murderer, prevent either murder or robbery? These questions may be safely answered in the negative; and the remains of the ancient barbarism which requires these disgusting and abominable exhibitions, and which are deplored by every feeling heart, should be banished with all possible speed. In the case given in the text, God considers the land as defiled while the body of the executed criminal lay exposed, hence it was enjoined, *Thou shalt in any wise bury him that day.*

For he that is hanged is *accursed of God*] That is, he has forfeited his life to the law; for it is written, *Cursed is every one who continueth not in all things that are written in the book of the law to do them;* and on his body, in the execution of the sentence of the law, the curse was considered as alighting; hence the necessity of removing the *accursed thing* out of sight. How excellent are all these laws! How wondrously well calculated to repress crimes by showing the enormity of sin! It is worthy of remark that in the infliction of punishment prescribed by the Mosaic law, we ever find that *Mercy* walks hand in hand with *Judgment*

CHAPTER XXII.

Ordinances relative to strayed cattle and lost goods, 1–3. *Humanity to oppressed cattle,* 4. *Men and women shall not wear each other's apparel,* 5. *No bird shall be taken with her nest of eggs or young ones,* 6, 7. *Battlements must be made on the roofs of houses,* 8. *Improper mixtures to be avoided,* 9–11. *Fringes on the garments,* 12. *Case of the hated wife, and the tokens of virginity, and the proceedings thereon,* 13–21. *The adulterer and adulteress to be put to death,* 22. *Case of the betrothed damsel corrupted in the city,* 23, 24. *Cases of rape and the punishment,* 25–27; *of fornication,* 28, 29. *No man shall take his father's wife,* 30.

A. M. 2553. B. C. 1451. An. Ex. Isr. 40. Sebat.

THOU [a] shalt not see thy brother's ox or his sheep go astray, and [b] hide thyself from them: thou shalt in any case bring them again unto thy brother.

2 And if thy brother *be* not nigh unto thee, or if thou know him not, then thou shalt bring it unto thine own house, and it shall be with thee until thy brother seek after it, and thou shalt restore it to him again.

3 In like manner shalt thou do with his ass; and so shalt thou do with his raiment; and with all lost things of thy brother's, which he hath lost, and thou hast found, shalt thou do likewise: thou mayest not hide thyself.

A. M. 2553. B. C. 1451. An. Ex. Isr. 40. Sebat.

4 [c] Thou shalt not see thy brother's ass or his ox fall down by the way, and hide thyself from them: thou shalt surely help him to lift *them* up again.

5 The woman shall not wear that which pertaineth unto a man, neither shall a man put on a woman's garment: for all that do so *are* abomination unto the LORD thy God.

6 If a bird's nest chance to be before thee in the way in any tree, or on the ground, *whether they be* young ones, or eggs, and the dam sitting upon the young, or upon the eggs,

[a] Exod. xxiii. 4; Luke xv. 4–6; James v. 19, 20. — [b] Lev. xx. 4; Prov. xxiv. 11, 12; xxviii. 27. — [c] Exod. xxiii. 5.

NOTES ON CHAP. XXII.

Verse 1. *Thou shalt not see thy brother's ox or his sheep go astray*] The same humane, merciful, and wise regulations which we met with before, Exod. xxiii. 4, 5, well calculated to keep in remembrance the second grand branch of the law of God, *Thou shalt love thy neighbour as thyself.* A humane man cannot bear to see even an *ass* fall under his burden, and not endeavour to relieve him; and a man who loves his neighbour as himself cannot see his property in danger without endeavouring to preserve it. These comparatively *small matters* were tests and proofs of matters great in themselves, and in their consequences. See the note on Exod. xxiii. 4.

Verse 3. *Thou mayest not hide thyself.*] Thou shalt not keep out of the way of affording help, nor pretend thou didst not see occasion to render thy neighbour any service. The priest and the Levite, when they saw the wounded man, passed by on the other side of the way, Luke x. 31, 32. This was a notorious breach of the merciful law mentioned above.

Verse 5. *The woman shall not wear that which pertaineth unto a man*] כלי גבר *keli geber,* the *instruments* or *arms* of a man. As the word גבר *geber* is here used, which properly signifies a *strong man* or *man of war,* it is very probable that *armour* is here intended; especially as we know that in the worship of *Venus,* to which that of *Astarte* or *Ashtaroth* among the Canaanites bore a striking resemblance, the women were accustomed to appear in armour before her. It certainly cannot mean a simple change of dress, whereby the men might pass for women, and *vice versa.* This would have been impossible in those countries where the dress of the sexes had but little to distinguish it, and where every man *wore a long beard.* It is, however, a very good general precept understood *literally,* and applies particularly to those countries where the dress alone distinguishes between the male and the female. The close-shaved gentleman may at any time appear like a woman in the female dress, and the woman appear as a man in the male's attire. Were this to be tolerated in society, it would produce the greatest

A. M. 2553.
B. C. 1451.
An. Ex. Isr. 40.
Sebat.

[d] thou shalt not take the dam with
the young:
7 *But* thou shalt in any wise
let the dam go, and take the young to thee;
[e] that it may be well with thee, and *that* thou
mayest prolong *thy* days.
8 When thou buildest a new house, then
thou shalt make a battlement for thy roof, that
thou bring not blood upon thine house, if any
man fall from thence.
9 [f] Thou shalt not sow thy vineyard with
divers seeds: lest the [g] fruit of thy seed which
thou hast sown, and the fruit of thy vineyard,
be defiled.
10 [h] Thou shalt not plough with an ox and an
ass together.
11 [i] Thou shalt not wear a garment of divers
sorts, *as* of woollen and linen together.
12 Thou shalt make thee
[k] fringes upon the four [l] quarters
of thy vesture, wherewith thou
coverest *thyself*.
13 If any man take a wife, and [m] go in unto
her, and hate her,
14 And give occasion of speech against her,
and bring up an evil name upon her, and say,
I took this woman, and when I came to her,
I found her not a maid:
15 Then shall the father of the damsel, and
her mother, take and bring forth *the tokens
of* the damsel's virginity unto the elders of
the city in the gate:
16 And the damsel's father shall say unto
the elders, I gave my daughter unto this man
to wife, and he hateth her;
17 And, lo, he hath given occasions of speech

A. M. 2553.
B. C. 1451.
An. Ex. Isr. 40.
Sebat.

[d] Lev. xxii. 28.——[e] Chap. iv. 40.——[f] Lev. xix. 19.——[g] Heb. *fulness of thy seed.*——[h] See 2 Cor. vi. 14, 15, 16.

[i] Lev. xix. 19.——[k] Num. xv. 38; Matt. xxiii. 5.——[l] Heb. *wings.*——[m] Gen. xxix. 21; Judg. xv. 1.

confusion. Clodius, who dressed himself like a woman that he might mingle with the Roman ladies in the feast of the *Bona Dea*, was universally execrated.

Verse 7. *Thou shalt—let the dam go, and take the young to thee; that it may be well with thee*] This passage may be understood literally. If they destroyed both young and old, must not the breed soon fail, and would it not in the end be *ill* with them; and by thus cutting off the means of their continual support, must not their days be shortened on the land? But we may look for a humane precept in this law. The *young* never knew the sweets of *liberty;* the *dam* did: they might be taken and used for any lawful purpose, but the dam must not be brought into a state of *captivity*. They who can act otherwise must be either very *inconsiderate* or devoid of *feeling;* and such persons can never be objects of God's peculiar care and attention, and therefore need not expect that it shall be well with them, or that they shall prolong their days on the earth. Every thing contrary to the spirit of mercy and kindness the *ever blessed God has in utter abhorrence.* And we should remember a fact, that he who can exercise cruelty towards a sparrow or a wren, will, when circumstances are favourable, be cruel to his fellow creatures. The poet Phocylides has a maxim in his admonitory poem very similar to that in the sacred text:—

Μηδε τις ορνιθας καλιης ἁμα παντας ἑλεσθω·
Μητερα δ' εκπρολιπης, ἱν' εχῃς παλι τησδε νεοττους.
PHOCYL. *Ποιημα Νουθετ.*, ver. 80.

"Nor from a nest take all the birds away;
The mother spare, she'll breed a future day."

Verse 8. *A battlement for thy roof*] Houses in the East are in general built with flat roofs, and on them men walk to enjoy the fresh air, converse together, sleep, &c.; it was therefore necessary to have a sort of battlement or balustrade to prevent persons from falling off. If a man neglected to make a sufficient defence against such accidents, and the death of another was occasioned by it, the owner of the house must be considered in the light of a murderer.

Verse 9. *Divers seeds*] See the note on Lev. xix. 19.

Verse 10. *Thou shalt not plough with an ox and an ass*] It is generally supposed that mixtures of different sorts in seed, breed, &c., were employed for superstitious purposes, and therefore prohibited in this law. It is more likely, however, that there was a physical reason for this; two beasts of a different species cannot associate comfortably together, and on this ground never pull pleasantly either in cart or plough; and every farmer knows that it is of considerable consequence to the comfort of the cattle to put those together that have an affection for each other. This may be very frequently remarked in certain cattle, which, on this account, are termed true yoke-fellows. After all, it is very probable that the general design was to prevent improper alliances in *civil* and *religious* life. And to this St. Paul seems evidently to refer, 2 Cor. vi. 14: *Be ye not unequally yoked with unbelievers;* which is simply to be understood as prohibiting all intercourse between Christians and idolaters in social, matrimonial, and religious life. And to teach the Jews the propriety of this, a variety of precepts relative to improper and heterogeneous mixtures were interspersed through their law, so that in civil and domestic life they might have them ever before their eyes.

Verse 12. *Fringes*] See on Num. xv. 38.

Verse 15. Tokens of *the damsel's virginity*] This was a perfectly possible case in all places where girls were married at ten, twelve, and fourteen years of age, which is frequent in the East. I have known several instances of persons having had two or three children at separate births before they were fourteen years of age. Such tokens, therefore, as the text speaks of, must be infallibly exhibited by females so very young on the consummation of their marriage.

Verse 17. *They shall spread the cloth, &c.*] A usage of this kind argues a roughness of manners which

A. M. 2553.
B. C. 1451.
An. Ex. Isr. 40.
Sebat.

against her, saying, I found not thy daughter a maid; and yet these *are the tokens of* my daughter's virginity. And they shall spread the cloth before the elders of the city.

18 And the elders of that city shall take that man and chastise him;

19 And they shall amerce him in a hundred *shekels* of silver, and give *them* unto the father of the damsel, because he hath brought up an evil name upon a virgin of Israel: and she shall be his wife; he may not put her away all his days.

20 But if this thing be true, *and the tokens of* virginity be not found for the damsel:

21 Then they shall bring out the damsel to the door of her father's house, and the men of her city shall stone her with stones that she die: because she hath [n] wrought folly in Israel, to play the whore in her father's house: [o] so shalt thou put evil away from among you.

22 [p] If a man be found lying with a woman married to a husband, then they shall both of them die, *both* the man that lay with the woman, and the woman: so shalt thou put away evil from Israel.

23 If a damsel *that is* a virgin be [q] betrothed unto a husband, and a man find her in the city, and lie with her;

24 Then shall ye bring them both out unto the gate of that city, and ye shall stone them with stones that they die; the damsel, because she cried not, *being* in the city; and the man, because he hath [r] humbled his neighbour's wife: [s] so thou shalt put away evil from among you.

A. M. 2553.
B. C. 1451.
An. Ex. Isr. 40.
Sebat.

25 But if a man find a betrothed damsel in the field, and the man [t] force her, and lie with her: then the man only that lay with her shall die:

26 But unto the damsel thou shalt do nothing; *there is* in the damsel no sin *worthy* of death: for as when a man riseth against his neighbour, and slayeth him, even so *is* this matter:

27 For he found her in the field, *and* the betrothed damsel cried, and *there was* none to save her.

28 [u] If a man find a damsel *that is* a virgin, which is not betrothed, and lay hold on her, and lie with her, and they be found;

29 Then the man that lay with her shall give unto the damsel's father fifty *shekels* of silver, and she shall be his wife; [v] because he hath humbled her, he may not put her away all his days.

30 [w] A man shall not take his father's wife, nor [x] discover his father's skirt.

[n] Gen. xxxiv. 7; Judg. xx. 6, 10; 2 Sam. xiii. 12, 13.——[o] Ch. xiii. 5.——[p] Lev. xx. 10; John viii. 5.——[q] Matt. i. 18, 19.——[r] Chap. xxi. 14.——[s] Ver. 21, 22.

[t] Or, *take strong hold of her*; 2 Sam. xiii. 14.——[u] Exod. xxii. 16, 17.——[v] Ver. 24.——[w] Lev. xviii. 8; xx. 11; chap. xxvii. 20; 1 Cor. v. 1.——[x] See Ruth iii. 9; Ezek. xvi. 8.

would ill comport with the refinement of European ideas on so delicate a subject. Attempts have been made to show that the law here is to be understood metaphorically; but they so perfectly fail to establish any thing like probability, that it would be wasting my own and my reader's time to detail them. A custom similar to that above is observed among the Mohammedans to the present day.

Verse 22. *Shall both of them die*] Thus we find that in the most ancient of all laws adultery was punished with death in both the parties.

Verse 25. *And the man force her*] A *rape* also, by these ancient institutions, was punished with death, because a woman's honour was considered equally as precious as her life; therefore the same punishment was inflicted on the ravisher as upon the murderer. This offence is considered in the same point of view in the British laws, and by them also it is punished with *death*.

Verse 30. *A man shall not take his father's wife*] This is to be understood as referring to the case of a *stepmother*. A man in his old age may have married a young wife, and on his dying, his son by a former wife may desire to espouse her: this the law prohibits. It was probably on pretence of having broken this law, that Solomon put his brother Adonijah to death, because he had desired to have his father's concubine to wife, 1 Kings ii. 13–25

CHAPTER XXIII.

Neither eunuchs, bastards, Ammonites, *nor* Moabites, *shall be incorporated with the genuine Israelites*, 1–3. *The reason why the* Ammonites *and* Moabites *were excluded*, 4–6. Edomites *and* Egyptians *to be respected*, 7. *Their descendants in the third generation may be incorporated with the Israelites*, 8. *Cautions against wickedness when they go forth against their enemies*, 9. *To keep the camp free from every defilement, and the reason why*, 10–14. *The slave who had taken refuge among them is not to be deli-*

***vered up to his former master,* 15, 16. *There shall be no prostitutes nor sodomites in the land,* 17. *The hire of a prostitute or the price of a dog is not to be brought into the house of God,* 18. *The Israelites shall not lend on usury to each other,* 19; *but they may take usury from strangers,* 20. *Vows must be diligently paid,* 21–23. *In passing through a vineyard or field a man may eat of the grapes or corn, but must carry away none with him,* 24, 25.**

A. M. 2553.
B. C. 1451.
An. Ex. Isr. 40.
Sebat.

HE that is [a] wounded in the stones, or hath his privy member cut off, shall not enter into the congregation of the LORD.

2 A bastard shall not enter into the congregation of the LORD; even to his tenth generation shall he not enter into the congregation of the LORD.

3 [b] An Ammonite or Moabite shall not enter into the congregation of the LORD; even to their tenth generation, shall they not enter into the congregation of the LORD for ever:

4 [c] Because they met you not with bread and with water in the way, when ye came forth out of Egypt; and [d] because they hired against thee Balaam the son of Beor, of Pethor of Mesopotamia, to curse thee.

5 Nevertheless the LORD thy God would not hearken unto Balaam; but the LORD thy God turned the curse into a blessing unto thee, because the LORD thy God loved thee.

6 [e] Thou shalt not seek their peace nor their [f] prosperity all thy days for ever.

7 Thou shalt not abhor an Edomite; [g] for he *is* thy brother: thou shalt not abhor an Egyptian; because [h] thou wast a stranger in his land.

8 The children that are begotten of them shall enter into the congregation of the LORD in their third generation.

A. M. 2553.
B. C. 1451.
An. Ex. Isr. 40.
Sebat.

9 When the host goeth forth against thine enemies, then keep thee from every wicked thing.

10 [i] If there be among you any man, that is not clean, by reason of uncleanness that chanceth him by night, then shall he go abroad out of the camp, he shall not come within the camp:

11 But it shall be, when evening [k] cometh on, [l] he shall wash *himself* with water: and when the sun is down, he shall come into the camp *again*.

12 Thou shalt have a place also without the camp, whither thou shalt go forth abroad:

13 And thou shalt have a paddle upon thy weapon; and it shall be, when thou [m] wilt ease thyself abroad, thou shalt dig therewith, and shalt turn back and cover that which cometh from thee:

14 For the LORD thy God [n] walketh in the midst of thy camp, to deliver thee, and to give up thine enemies before thee; therefore shall thy camp be holy: that he see no [o] unclean thing in thee, and turn away from thee:

15 [p] Thou shalt not deliver unto his master the servant which is escaped from his master unto thee:

16 He shall dwell with thee, *even* among you, in that place which he shall choose in

[a] Lev. xxi. 17–21; xxii. 22–24.——[b] Neh. xiii. 1, 2.——[c] See chap. ii. 29.——[d] Num. xxii. 5, 6.——[e] Ezra ix. 12.——[f] Heb. *good*.——[g] Gen. xxv. 24, 25, 26; Obad. x. 12.——[h] Exod. xxii. 21; xxiii. 9; Lev. xix. 34; chap. x. 19.——[i] Lev. xv. 16.——[k] Heb. *turneth toward*.——[l] Lev. xv. 5.——[m] Heb. *sittest down*.——[n] Lev. xxvi. 12.——[o] Heb. *nakedness of any thing*.——[p] 1 Sam. xxx. 15.

NOTES ON CHAP. XXIII.

Verse 1. *Shall not enter into the congregation, &c.*] If by entering into the congregation be meant the bearing a *civil* office among the people, such as magistrate, judge, &c., then the reason of the law is very plain; no man with any such personal defect as might render him contemptible in the sight of others should bear rule among the people, lest the contempt felt for his personal defects might be transferred to his important office, and thus his authority be disregarded. The general meaning of these words is, simply, that the persons here designated should not be so incorporated with the Jews as to partake of their *civil privileges*.

Verse 2. *A bastard shall not enter*] ממזר *mamzer*, which is here rendered *bastard*, should be understood as implying the *offspring* of an illegitimate or *incestuous* mixture.

Verse 3. *An Ammonite or Moabite*] These nations were subjected for their impiety and wickedness, (see ver. 4 and 5,) to peculiar disgrace, and on this account were not permitted to hold any office among the Israelites. But this did not disqualify them from being *proselytes:* Ruth, who was a Moabitess, was married to Boaz, and she became one of the progenitors of our Lord.

Even to their tenth generation] That is, *for ever*, as the next clause explains; see Neh. xiii. 1.

Verse 12, *&c.*] These directions may appear trifling to some, but they were essentially necessary to this people in their present circumstances. Decency and cleanliness promote health, and prevent many diseases.

Verse 15. *Thou shalt not deliver—the servant which is escaped—unto thee*] That is, a servant who left an idolatrous master that he might join himself to God

A. M. 2553. B. C. 1451. An. Ex. Is. 40. Sebat.

one of thy gates, where it [q] liketh
him best: [r] thou shalt not oppress him.

17 There shall be no [s] whore [t] of the daughters of Israel, nor a [u] sodomite of the sons of
Israel.

18 Thou shalt not bring the hire of a whore,
or the price of a dog, into the house of the
LORD thy God for any vow: for even both
these *are* abomination unto the LORD thy God.

19 [v] Thou shalt not lend upon usury to thy
brother: usury of money, usury of victuals,
usury of any thing that is lent upon usury:

20 [w] Unto a stranger thou mayest lend upon
usury; but unto thy brother thou shalt not
lend upon usury: [x] that the LORD thy God
may bless thee in all that thou settest thine
hand to in the land whither thou goest to possess it.

21 [y] When thou shalt vow a vow unto the
LORD thy God, thou shalt not
slack to pay it: for the LORD thy
God will surely require it of thee;
and it would be sin in thee.

A. M. 2553. B. C. 1451. An. Ex. Isr. 40. Sebat.

22 But if thou shalt forbear to vow, it shall
be no sin in thee.

23 [z] That which is gone out of thy lips thou
shalt keep and perform; *even* a freewill-offering, according as thou hast vowed unto the
LORD thy God, which thou hast promised
with thy mouth.

24 When thou comest into thy neighbour's
vineyard, [a] then thou mayest eat grapes thy
fill at thine own pleasure; but thou shalt
not put *any* in thy vessel.

25 When thou comest into the standing
corn of thy neighbour, [b] then thou mayest
pluck the ears with thine hand; but thou
shalt not move a sickle unto thy neighbour's
standing corn.

[q] Heb. *is good for him.*——[r] Exod. xxii. 21.——[s] Or, *sodomitess.* [t] Lev. xix. 29; see Prov. ii. 16.——[u] Gen. xix. 5; 2 Kings xxiii. 7. [v] Exod. xxii. 25; Lev. xxv. 36, 37; Neh. v. 2, 7; Psa. xv. 5; Luke vi. 34, 35.

[w] See Lev. xix. 34; chap. xv. 3.——[x] Chap. xv. 10.——[y] Num. xxx. 2; Eccles. v. 4, 5.——[z] Num. xxx. 2; Psa. lxvi. 13, 14. [a] 1 Cor. x. 26; Heb. xiii. 5.——[b] Matt. xii. 1; Mark ii. 23; Luke vi. 1.

and to his people. In any other case, it would have been injustice to have harboured the runaway.

Verse 17. *There shall be no whore*] See on Gen. xxxviii. 15–21.

Verse 18. *The hire of a whore, or the price of a dog*] Many public prostitutes dedicated to their gods a part of their impure earnings; and some of these prostitutes were publicly kept in the temple of Venus Melytta, whose gains were applied to the support of her abominable worship.

Verse 19. *Usury*] See on Lev. xxv. 36.

Verse 21. *When thou shalt vow, &c.*] See on Num. xxx. 1, &c.

Verse 24. *Thou shalt not put* any *in thy vessel.*] Thou shalt carry none away with thee. The old English proverb, *Eat thy fill, but pocket none,* seems to have been founded on this law.

Verse 25. *Thou mayest pluck the ears with thine hand*] It was on the permission granted by this law that the disciples plucked the ears of corn, as related Matt. xii. 1. This was both a considerate and humane law, and is no dishonour to the Jewish code.

CHAPTER XXIV.

The case of a divorced wife, 1–4. *No man shall be obliged to undertake any public service for the first year of his marriage,* 5. *The mill-stones shall not be taken as a pledge,* 6. *The man-stealer shall be put to death,* 7. *Concerning cases of leprosy,* 8, 9. *Of receiving pledges, and returning those of the poor before bed-time,* 10–13. *Of servants and their hire,* 14, 15. *Parents and children shall not be put to death for each other,* 16. *Of humanity to the stranger, fatherless, widow, and bondman,* 17, 18. *Gleanings of the harvest, &c., to be left for the poor, stranger, widow, fatherless, &c.,* 19–22.

A. M. 2553. B. C. 1451. An. Ex. Isr. 40. Sebat.

WHEN a [a] man hath taken a
wife, and married her, and
it come to pass that she find no
favour in his eyes, because he
hath found [b] some uncleanness in
her: then let him write her a bill

[a] Matt. v. 31; xix. 7; Mark x. 4.

[b] Heb. *matter of nakedness.*

NOTES ON CHAP. XXIV.

Verse 1. *Some uncleanness*] Any cause of *dislike,* for this great latitude of meaning the fact itself authorizes us to adopt, for it is certain that a Jew might put away his wife for *any cause that seemed good to himself;* and so hard were their hearts, that Moses *suffered* this; and we find they continued this practice even to the time of our Lord, who strongly reprehended them on the account, and showed that such license was wholly inconsistent with the original design of marriage; see Matt. v. 31, &c.; xix. 3, &c.; and the notes there.

A. M. 2553. B. C. 1451. An. Ex. Isr. 40. Sebat.

of [c] divorcement, and give *it* in
her hand, and send her out of his
house.
2 And when she is departed out of his
house, [d] she may go and be another man's *wife*.
3 And *if* the latter husband hate her, and
write her a bill of divorcement, and giveth *it*
in her hand, and sendeth her out of his house;
or if the latter husband die, which took her *to
be* his wife;
4 [e] Her former husband, which sent her away,
may not take her again to be his wife, after
that she is defiled; for that *is* abomination
before the LORD: and thou shalt not cause
the land to sin, which the LORD thy God
giveth thee *for* an inheritance.
5 [f] When a man hath taken a new wife, he
shall not go out to war, [g] neither shall he be
charged with any business: *but* he shall be
free at home one year, and shall [h] cheer up
his wife which he hath taken.
6 No man shall take the nether
or the upper mill-stone to pledge:
for he taketh *a man's* life to
pledge.
7 [i] If a man be found stealing any of his
brethren of the children of Israel, and maketh
merchandise of him, or selleth him; then that
thief shall die; [k] and thou shalt put evil away
from among you.
8 Take heed in [l] the plague of leprosy, that
thou observe diligently, and do according to
all that the priests the Levites shall teach
you: as I commanded them, *so* ye shall observe to do.
9 [m] Remember what the LORD thy God did
[n] unto Miriam by the way, after that ye were
come forth out of Egypt.
10 When thou dost [o] lend thy brother any
thing, thou shalt not go into his house to fetch
his pledge.
11 Thou shalt stand abroad, and the man to

A. M. 2553. B. C. 1451. An. Ex. Isr. 40. Sebat.

[c] Heb. *cutting off*.—[d] Lev. xxi. 7, 14; xxii. 13; Num. xxx. 9. [e] Jer. iii. 1.—[f] Chap. xx. 7.—[g] Heb. *not any thing shall pass upon him*.—[h] Prov. v. 18.

[i] Exod. xxi. 16.—[k] Chap. xix. 19.—[l] Lev. xiii. 2; xiv. 2. [m] See Luke xvii. 32; 1 Cor. x. 6.—[n] Num. xii. 10.—[o] Heb. *lend the loan of any thing to*, &c.

Verse 3. *And write her a bill of divorcement*] These bills, though varying in expression, are the same in substance among the Jews in all places. The following, collected from Maimonides and others, is a general form, and contains all the particulars of such instruments. The reader who is curious may find a full account of *divorces* in the Biblioth. Rab. of Bartolocci, and the following *form* in that work, vol. iv., p. 550.

"In —— day of the week, or —— day of the month A., in —— year from the creation of the world, or from the supputation (of Alexander) after the account that we are accustomed to count by, here, in the place B., I, C., the son of D., of the place B., (or if there be any other *name* which I have, or my father hath had, or which my *place* or my father's place hath had,) have voluntarily, and with the willingness of my soul, without constraint, dismissed, and left, and put away thee, even thee, E., the daughter of F., of the city G., (or if thou have any other *name* or *surname*, thou or thy father, or thy *place* or thy father's place,) who hast been my wife heretofore; but now I dismiss thee, and leave thee, and put thee away, that thou mayest be free, and have power over thy own life, to go away to be married to any man whom thou wilt; and that no man be refused of thine hand, for my name, from this day and for ever. And thus thou art lawful for any man; and this is unto thee, from me, a writing of divorcement, and book (*instrument*) of dismission, and an epistle of putting away; according to the Law of Moses and Israel.

A., son of B., witness.
C., son of D., witness."

Verse 4. *She is defiled*] Does not this refer to her having been divorced, and married in consequence to another? Though God, for the hardness of their hearts, suffered them to put away their wives, yet he considered all after-marriages in that case to be pollution and defilement; and it is on this ground that our Lord argues in the places referred to above, that whoever marries the woman that is put away is an adulterer: now this could not have been the case if God had allowed the divorce to be a legal and proper separation of the man from his wife; but in the sight of God nothing can be a legal cause of separation but *adultery* on either side. In such a case, according to the law of God, a man may put away his wife, and a wife may put away her husband; (see Matt. xix. 9;) for it appears that the wife had as much right to put away her husband as the husband had to put away his wife, see Mark x. 12.

Verse 5. *When a man hath taken a new wife*] Other people made a similar provision for such circumstances. Alexander ordered those of his soldiers who had married that year to spend the winter with their wives, while the army was in winter quarters. See Arrian, lib. i.

Verse 6. *The nether or the upper mill-stone*] Small hand-mills which can be worked by a single person were formerly in use among the Jews, and are still used in many parts of the East. As therefore the day's meal was generally ground for each day, they keeping no stock beforehand, hence they were forbidden to take either of the stones to pledge, because in such a case the family must be without bread. On this account the text terms the mill-stone the *man's life*.

Verses 8, 9. *The plague of leprosy*] See on Lev. xiii. and xiv.

A. M. 2553. B. C. 1451. An. Ex. Isr. 40. Sebat.

whom thou dost lend shall bring
out the pledge abroad unto thee.
12 And if the man *be* poor,
thou shalt not sleep with his pledge:
13 [p] In any case thou shalt deliver him the
pledge again when the sun goeth down, that
he may sleep in his own raiment, and [q] bless
thee: and [r] it shall be righteousness unto thee
before the LORD thy God.
14 Thou shalt not [s] oppress a hired servant
that is poor and needy, *whether he be* of thy
brethren, or of thy strangers that *are* in thy
land within thy gates:
15 At his day [t] thou shalt give *him* his hire,
neither shall the sun go down upon it; for he
is poor, and [u] setteth his heart upon it: [v] lest
he cry against thee unto the LORD, and it be
sin unto thee.
16 [w] The fathers shall not be put to death
for the children, neither shall the children be
put to death for the fathers every man shall
be put to death for his own sin.
17 [x] Thou shalt not pervert the judgment of the stranger, *nor* of the fatherless;
[y] nor take the widow's raiment to
pledge:
18 But [z] thou shalt remember
that thou wast a bondman in Egypt, and the
LORD thy God redeemed thee thence: therefore I command thee to do this thing.
19 [a] When thou cuttest down thine harvest
in thy field, and hast forgot a sheaf in the
field, thou shalt not go again to fetch it: it
shall be for the stranger, for the fatherless,
and for the widow: that the LORD thy God
may [b] bless thee in all the work of thine
hands.
20 When thou beatest thine olive tree, [c] thou
shalt not go over the boughs again: it shall
be for the stranger, for the fatherless, and for
the widow.
21 When thou gatherest the grapes of thy
vineyard, thou shalt not glean *it* [d] afterward.
it shall be for the stranger, for the fatherless,
and for the widow.
22 And [e] thou shalt remember that thou wast
a bondman in the land of Egypt: therefore I
command thee to do this thing.

[p] Exod. xxii. 26.——[q] Job xxix. 11, 13; xxxi. 20; 2 Cor. ix. 13; 2 Tim. i. 18.——[r] Chap. vi. 25; Psa. cvi. 31; cxii. 9; Dan. iv. 27.——[s] Mal. iii. 5.——[t] Lev. xix. 13; Jer. xxii. 13; Tob. iv. 14; James v. 4.——[u] Heb. *lifteth his soul unto it;* Psa. xxv. 1; lxxxvi. 4.——[v] James v. 4.——[w] 2 Kings xiv. 6; 2 Chron. xxv. 4; Jer. xxxi. 29, 30; Ezek. xviii. 20.

[x] Exodus xxii. 21, 22; Prov. xxii. 22; Isa. i. 23; Jer. v. 28; xxii. 3; Ezek. xxii. 29; Zech. vii. 10; Mal. iii. 5.——[y] Exod. xxii. 26.——[z] Verse 22; chap. xvi. 12.——[a] Lev. xix. 9, 10; xxiii. 22.——[b] Chapter xv. 10; Psa. xli. 1; Proverbs xix. 17. [c] Heb. *thou shalt not bough it after thee.*——[d] Hebrew, *after thee.* [e] Verse 18.

Verse 12. *And if the man* be *poor, &c.*] Did not this law preclude pledging *entirely*, especially in case of the abjectly poor? For who would take a pledge in the morning which he knew, if not redeemed, he must restore at night? However, he might resume his claim in the morning, and have the pledge daily returned, and thus keep up his property in it till the debt was discharged; see the note on Exod. xxii. 26. The Jews in several cases did act contrary to this rule, and we find them cuttingly reproved for it by the Prophet Amos, chap. ii. 8.

Verse 15. *He* is *poor, and setteth his heart upon it*] How exceedingly natural is this! The poor servant who seldom sees money, yet finds from his master's affluence that it procures all the conveniences and comforts of life, longs for the time when he shall receive his wages; should his pay be delayed after the time is expired, he may naturally be expected to *cry unto God* against him who withholds it. See most of these subjects treated at large on Exod. xxii. 21–27.

Verse 16. *The fathers shall not be put to death for the children, &c.*] This law is explained and illustrated in sufficient detail, Ezek. xviii.

Verse 18. *Thou shalt remember that thou wast a bondman*] Most people who have affluence rose from comparative penury, for those who are *born* to estates frequently squander them away; such therefore should remember *what* their feelings, their fears, and anxieties were, when *they* were poor and abject. A want of attention to this most wholesome precept is the reason why pride and arrogance are the general characteristics of those who have risen in the world from poverty to affluence; and it is the conduct of those men which gave rise to the rugged proverb, "Set a beggar on horseback, and he will ride to the devil."

Verse 19. *When thou cuttest down thine harvest*] This is an addition to the law, Lev. xix. 9; xxiii. 22. The *corners* of the field, the *gleanings*, and the *forgotten sheaf*, were all the property of the poor. This the Hebrews extended to any part of the fruit or produce of a field, which had been forgotten in the time of general ingathering, as appears from the concluding verses of this chapter.

CHAPTER XXV.

Punishment by whipping not to exceed forty stripes, 1–3. *The ox that treads out the corn is not to be muzzled,* 4. *The ordinance concerning marrying the wife of that brother who has died childless,* 5–10. *Of the woman who acts indecently in succouring her husband,* 11, 12. *Of false weights and measures,* 13–16. *Amalek is to be destroyed,* 17–19.

A. M. 2553. B. C. 1451. An. Ex. Isr. 40. Sebat.

IF there be a [a] controversy between men, and they come
unto judgment, that *the judges*
may judge them; then they [b] shall justify the
righteous, and condemn the wicked.
2 And it shall be, if the wicked man *be*
[c] worthy to be beaten, that the judge shall cause
him to lie down,[d] and to be beaten
before his face, according to his
fault, by a certain number.
3 [e] Forty stripes he may give him, *and* not
exceed: lest, *if* he should exceed, and beat
him above these, with many stripes, then thy
brother should [f] seem vile unto thee.

A. M. 2553. B. C. 1451. An. Ex. Isr. 40. Sebat.

[a] Chap. xix. 17; Ezek. xliv. 24.——[b] See Prov. xvii. 15. [c] Luke xii. 48.——[d] Matt. x. 17.——[e] 2 Cor. xi. 24.——[f] Job xviii. 3.

NOTES ON CHAP. XXV.

Verse 1. *They shall justify the righteous*] This is a very important passage, and is a key to several others. The word צדק *tsadak* is used here precisely in the same sense in which St. Paul sometimes uses the corresponding word δικαιοω, not to *justify* or make *just*, but to *acquit, declare innocent*, to *remit punishment*, or *give reasons why such a one should not be punished;* so here the magistrates הצדיקו *hitsdiku, shall acquit*, the righteous—declare him innocent, because he is found to be *righteous* and not *wicked:* so the Septuagint: και δικαιωσουσιν τον δικαιον, *they shall make righteous the righteous*—declare him free from blame, not liable to punishment, acquitted; using the same word with St. Paul when he speaks of a sinner's justification, i. e., his acquittance from blame and punishment, because of the death of Christ in his stead.

Verse 2. *The judge shall cause him to lie down, and to be beaten before his face*] This precept is literally followed in China; the culprit receives in the presence of the magistrate the punishment which the law directs to be inflicted. Thus then *justice* is done, for the magistrate sees that the letter of the law is duly fulfilled, and that the officers do not transgress it, either by *indulgence* on the one hand, or *severity* on the other. The culprit receives nothing more nor less than what *justice* requires.

Verse 3. *Forty stripes he may give him,* and *not exceed*] According to God's institution a criminal may receive *forty* stripes; not one more! But is the institution from *above* or *not*, that for any offence sentences a man to receive *three hundred*, yea, a *thousand* stripes? What horrible brutality is this! and what a reproach to human nature, and to the nation in which such shocking barbarities are exercised and tolerated! Most of the inhabitants of Great Britain have heard of *Lord Macartney's embassy to the emperor of China*, and they have also heard of its complete failure; but they have not heard the cause. It appears to have been partly occasioned by the following circumstance: A soldier had been convicted of some petty traffic with one of the natives, and he was sentenced by a court-martial to receive *sixty* lashes! Hear my author:

"The soldiers were drawn up in form in the outer court of the palace where we resided; and the poor culprit, being fastened to one of the pillars of the great portico, received his punishment without mitigation. The abhorrence excited in the breasts of the Chinese at this cruel conduct, as it appeared to them, was demonstrably proved by their words and looks. They expressed their astonishment that a people professing the mildest, the most benevolent religion on earth, as they wished to have it believed, could be guilty of such flagrant inattention to its merciful dictates. One of the principal Mandarins, who knew a little English, expressed the general sentiment, *Englishmen too much cruel, too much bad.*"—Accurate account of Lord Macartney's Embassy to China, by an attendant on the embassy, 12mo., 1797, p. 88.

The following is Mr. Ainsworth's note on this verse: "This number *forty* the Scripture uses sundry times in cases of humiliation, affliction, and punishment. As *Moses* twice humbled himself in fasting and prayer forty days and forty nights, Deut. ix. 9, 18. *Elijah* fasted forty days, 1 Kings xix. 8; and our Saviour, Matt. iv. 2. Forty years *Israel* was afflicted in the wilderness for their sins, Num. xiv. 33, 34. And forty years *Egypt* was desolate for treacherous dealing with *Israel*, Ezek. xxix. 11–13. Forty days every woman was in purification from her uncleanness for a man-child that she bare, and twice forty days for a woman-child, Lev. xii. 4, 5. Forty days and forty nights it rained at Noah's flood, Gen. vii. 12. Forty days did *Ezekiel* bear the iniquity of the house of *Judah*, Ezek. iv. 6. *Jonah* preached, *Yet forty days and Nineveh shall be overthrown*, Jonah iii. 4. Forty years' space the Canaanites had to repent after *Israel* came out of *Egypt*, and wandered so many years in the wilderness, Num. xiv. 33. And thrice forty years the old world had Noah preaching unto them repentance, Gen. vi. 3. It was forty days ere Christ ascended into heaven after his resurrection, Acts i. 3, 9. And forty years' space he gave unto the Jews, from the time that they killed him, before he destroyed their city and temple by the Romans.

"By the Hebrews this law is expounded thus: *How many* stripes *do they beat* (an offender) *with?* With forty, lacking one: as it is written, (Deut. xxv. 2, 3,) *by number forty*, that is, the number which is next to forty, *Talmud Bab*, in *Maccoth*, chap. iii. This their

A. M. 2553.
B. C. 1451.
An. Ex. Isr. 40.
Sebat.

4 [g] Thou shalt not muzzle the
ox when he [h] treadeth out *the*
corn.
5 [i] If brethren dwell together, and one of
them die, and have no child, the wife of the
dead shall not marry without, unto a stranger:
her [k] husband's brother shall go in unto her,
and take her to him to wife, and perform the
duty of a husband's brother unto her.
6 And it shall be, *that* the first-born which
she beareth [l] shall succeed in the name of his
brother *which is* dead, that [m] his name be not
put out of Israel.
7 And if the man like not to take his [n] brother's wife, then let his brother's wife go up to
the [o] gate unto the elders, and say, My husband's brother refuseth to raise
up unto his brother a name in
Israel, he will not perform the
duty of my husband's brother.
8 Then the elders of his city shall call him,
and speak unto him: and *if* he stand *to it*,
and say, [p] I like not to take her;
9 Then shall his brother's wife come unto
him in the presence of the elders, and [q] loose
his shoe from off his foot, and spit in his face,
and shall answer and say, So shall it be done
unto that man that will not [r] build up his bro
ther's house.
10 And his name shall be called in Israel,
The house of him that hath his shoe loosed.
11 When men strive together one with an-

[g] Prov. xii. 10; 1 Cor. ix. 9; 1 Tim. v. 18.——[h] Heb. *thresheth;* Hos. x. 11.——[i] Matt. xxii. 24; Mark xii. 19; Luke xx. 28.——[k] Or, *next kinsman;* Gen. xxxviii. 8; Ruth i. 12, 13; iii. 9.——[l] Gen. xxxviii. 9.——[m] Ruth iv. 10.——[n] Or, *next kinsman's wife.*——[o] Ruth iv. 1, 2.——[p] Ruth. iv. 6.——[q] Ruth iv. 7.——[r] Ruth iv. 11.

understanding is very ancient, for so they practised in the apostles' days; as Paul testified: *Of the Jews five times received I forty* (stripes) *save one;* 2 Cor. xi. 24. But the reason which they give is not solid; as when they say, *If it had been written* FORTY IN NUMBER, *I would say it were full forty; but being written,* IN NUMBER FORTY, it means *the number which reckons forty* next after it, that is, thirty-nine. By this exposition they confound the verses and take away the distinction. I rather think this custom was taken up by reason of the manner of their beating forespoken of, which was with a scourge that had three cords, so that every stroke was counted for three stripes, and then they could not give even forty, but either thirty-nine or forty-two, which was above the number set of God. And hereof they write thus: *When they judge* (or *condemn*) *a sinner to so many* (*stripes*) *as he can bear, they judge not but by strokes that are fit to be trebled* [that is, to give three stripes to one stroke, by reason of the three cords.] *If they judge that he can bear twenty, they do not say he shall be beaten with one and twenty, to the end that they may treble the stripes, but they give him eighteen.*—*Maimon* in *Sanhedrin*, chap. xvii., sec. 2. Thus he that was able to bear twenty stripes, had but eighteen: the executioner smote him but six times, for if he had smitten him the seventh they were counted one and twenty stripes, which was above the number adjudged: so he that was adjudged to forty was smitten thirteen times, which being counted one for three, make thirty-nine. And so R. *Bechaios*, writing hereof, says, *The strokes are trebled;* that is, every one is three, and three times thirteen are nine and thirty."

Thy brother be vile, or *be contemptible.*—By this God teaches us to hate and despise the sin, not the sinner, who is by this chastisement to be amended; as the power which the Lord hath given is *to edification, not to destruction*, 2 Cor. xiii. 10.

Verse 4. *Thou shalt not muzzle the ox, &c.*] In Judea, as well as in Egypt, Greece, and Italy, they make use of beeves to tread out the corn; and Dr. Shaw tells us that the people of Barbary continue to tread out their corn after the custom of the East. Instead of beeves they frequently made use of mules and horses, by tying by the neck three or four in like manner together, and whipping them afterwards round about the *nedders*, as they call the *treading floors*, (the Libycæ areæ *Hor*,) where the sheaves lie open and expanded, in the same manner as they are placed and prepared with us for threshing. This indeed is a much quicker way than ours, though less cleanly, for as it is performed in the open air, (Hos. xiii. 3,) upon any round level plot of ground, daubed over with cow's dung to prevent as much as possible the earth, sand, or gravel from rising; a great quantity of them all, notwithstanding this precaution, must unavoidably be taken up with the grain, at the same time that the straw, which is their chief and only fodder, is hereby shattered to pieces; a circumstance very pertinently alluded to in 2 Kings xiii. 7, where *the king of Syria* is said *to have made the Israelites like the dust by threshing.*—Travels, p. 138. While the oxen were at work some muzzled their mouths to hinder them from eating the corn, which Moses here forbids, instructing the people by this symbolical precept to be kind to their servants and labourers, but especially to those who ministered to them in holy things; so St. Paul applies it 1 Cor. ix. 9, &c.; 1 Tim. v. 18. Le Clerc considers the injunction as wholly symbolical; and perhaps in this view it was intended to confirm the laws enjoined in the fourteenth and fifteenth verses of the former chapter. See *Dodd* and *Shaw.*

In *Bengal*, where the same mode of treading out the corn is used, some muzzle the ox, and others do not, according to the disposition of the farmer.—*Ward.*

Verse 9. *And loose his shoe*] It is difficult to find the reason of these ceremonies of degradation. Perhaps the *shoe* was the emblem of *power;* and by *stripping it off, deprivation* of that power and authority was repre-sented. *Spitting* in the face was a mark of the utmost

A. M. 2553. B. C. 1451. An. Ex. Isr. 40. Sebat.

other, and the wife of the one draweth near for to deliver her husband out of the hand of him that smiteth him, and putteth forth her hand, and taketh him by the secrets:

12 Then thou shalt cut off her hand, [s] thine eye shall not pity *her*.

13 [t] Thou shalt not have in thy bag [u] divers weights, a great and a small.

14 Thou shalt not have in thine house divers measures, a great and a small.

15 *But* thou shalt have a perfect and just weight, a perfect and just measure shalt thou have: [w] that thy days may be lengthened in the land which the LORD thy God giveth thee.

16 For [x] all that do such things, *and* all that do unrighteously, *are* an abomination unto the LORD thy God.

17 [y] Remember what Amalek did unto thee by the way, when ye were come forth out of Egypt;

18 How he met thee by the way, and smote the hindmost of thee, *even* all *that were* feeble behind thee, when thou *wast* faint and weary; and he [z] feared not God.

19 Therefore it shall be, [a] when the LORD thy God hath given thee rest from all thine enemies round about, in the land which the LORD thy God giveth thee *for* an inheritance, to possess it, *that* thou shalt [b] blot out the remembrance of Amalek from under heaven: thou shalt not forget *it*.

[s] Chap. xix. 13.—[t] Lev. xix. 35, 36; Prov. xi. 1; Ezek. xlv. 10; Mic. vi. 11.—[u] Heb. *a stone and a stone.*—[v] Heb. *an ephah and an ephah.*—[w] Exod. xx. 12.—[x] Prov. xi. 1; 1 Thess. iv. 6.—[y] Exod xvii. 8.—[z] Psa. xxxvi. 1; Prov. xvi. 6; Rom. iii. 18.—[a] 1 Sam. xv. 3.—[b] Exod. xvii. 14.

ignominy; but the Jews, who are legitimate judges in this case, say that the spitting was not *in* his face, but *before* his face *on the ground.* And this is the way in which the Asiatics express their detestation of a person to the present day, as *Niebuhr* and other intelligent travellers assure us. It has been remarked that the prefix ב *beth* is seldom applied to פני *peney;* but when it is it signifies as well *before* as *in* the face. See. Josh. xxi. 44; xxiii. 9; Esther ix. 2; and Ezek. xlii. 12; which texts are supposed to be proofs in point. The act of spitting, whether *in* or *before* the face, marked the strong contempt the woman felt for the man who had slighted her. And it appears that the man was ever after disgraced in Israel; for so much is certainly implied in the saying, ver. 10: *And his name shall be called in Israel, The house of him that hath his shoe loosed.*

Verse 13. *Divers weights*] אבן ואבן *eben vaaben,* a *stone and a stone,* because the weights were anciently made of stone, and some had two sets of stones, a *light* and a *heavy.* With the *latter* they bought their wares, by the *former* they sold them. In our own country this was once a common case; smooth, round, or oval stones were generally chosen by the simple country people for selling their wares, especially such as were sold in *pounds* and *half* pounds. And hence the term a *stone weight,* which is still in use, though *lead* or *iron* be the matter that is used as a counterpoise: but the name itself shows us that a *stone* of a certain weight was the material formerly used as a weight. See the notes on Lev. xix. 35, 36.

Verse 14. *Divers measures*] Literally, *an ephah and an ephah;* one *large,* to buy thy neighbour's wares, another *small,* to sell thy own by. So there were *knaves* in all ages, and among all nations. See the notes on Exod. xvi. 16, and Lev. xix. 35.

Verse 18. *Smote the hindmost of thee*] See the note on Exod. xvii. 8. It is supposed that this command had its final accomplishment in the death of Haman and his ten sons, Esth. iii., vii., ix., as from this time the memory and name of Amalek was blotted out from under heaven, for through every period of their history it might be truly said, *They feared not God.*

CHAPTER XXVI.

First-fruits must be offered to God, 1, 2. *The form of confession to be used on the occasion,* 3–11. *The third year's tithe to be given to the Levites and the poor,* 12, *and the form of confession to be used on this occasion,* 13–15. *The Israelites are to take Jehovah for their God, and to keep his testimonies,* 16, 17. *And Jehovah is to take them for his people, and make them high above all the nations of the earth,* 18, 19.

A. M. 2553. B. C. 1451. An. Ex. Isr. 40. Sebat.

AND it shall be, when thou *art* come in unto the land which the LORD thy God giveth thee *for* an inheritance, and possessest it, and dwellest therein;

2 [a] That thou shalt take of the

[a] Exod. xxiii. 19; xxxiv. 26; Num. xviii. 13; chap. xvi. 10; Prov. iii. 9.

NOTES ON CHAP. XXVI.

Verse 2. *Thou shalt take of the first of all the fruit, &c.*] This was intended to keep them in continual remembrance of the kindness of God, in preserving them through so many difficulties and literally fulfilling the promises he had made to them. God being

A. M. 2553.
B. C. 1451.
An. Ex. Isr. 40.
Sebat.

first of all the fruit of the earth,
which thou shalt bring of thy
land that the LORD thy God giveth
thee, and shalt put *it* in a basket, and shalt
[b] go unto the place which the LORD thy God
shall choose, to place his name there.
3 And thou shalt go unto the priest that
shall be in those days, and say unto him, I
profess this day unto the LORD thy God,
that I am come unto the country which the
LORD sware unto our fathers for to give us.
4 And the priest shall take the basket out
of thine hand, and set it down before the altar
of the LORD thy God.
5 And thou shalt speak, and say before the
LORD thy God, [c] A Syrian [d] ready to perish
was my father, and [e] he went down into
Egypt, and sojourned there with a [f] few, and
became there a nation, great, mighty, and
populous:
6 And [g] the Egyptians evil entreated us, and
afflicted us, and laid upon us hard bondage:
7 And [h] when we cried unto the LORD God
of our fathers, the LORD heard our voice, and
looked on our affliction, and our labour, and
our oppression.
8 And [i] the LORD brought us
forth out of Egypt with a mighty
hand, and with an outstretched
arm, and [k] with great terribleness, and with
signs, and with wonders:
9 And he hath brought us into this place,
and hath given us this land, *even* [l] a land that
floweth with milk and honey.
10 And now, behold, I have brought the
first-fruits of the land, which thou, O LORD,
hast given me. And thou shalt set it before
the LORD thy God, and worship before the
LORD thy God:
11 And [m] thou shalt rejoice in every good
thing which the LORD thy God hath given
unto thee, and unto thine house, thou, and the
Levite, and the stranger that *is* among you.
12 When thou hast made an end of tithing
all the [n] tithes of thine increase the third year,
which is [o] the year of tithing, and hast given
it unto the Levite, the stranger, the fatherless,
and the widow, that they may eat within thy
gates, and be filled;
13 Then thou shalt say before the LORD thy
God, I have brought away the hallowed things
out of *mine* house, and also have given them

A. M. 2553.
B. C. 1451.
An. Ex. Isr. 40.
Sebat.

[b] Chap. xii. 5.——[c] Hos. xii. 12.——[d] Gen. xliii. 1, 2; xlv. 7, 11.
[e] Gen. xlvi. 1, 6; Acts vii. 15.——[f] Gen. xlvi. 27; chap. x. 22.
[g] Exod. i. 11, 14.——[h] Exod. ii. 23, 24, 25; iii. 9; iv. 31.

[i] Exod. xii. 37, 51; xiii. 3, 14, 16; chap. v. 15.——[k] Chap. iv. 34.——[l] Exod. iii. 8.——[m] Chap. xii. 7, 12, 18; xvi. 11.——[n] Lev. xxvii. 30; Num. xviii. 24.——[o] Chap. xiv. 28, 29.

the author of all their blessings, the first-fruits of the land were consecrated to him, as the author of every good and perfect gift.

Verse 5. *A Syrian ready to perish* was *my father*] This passage has been variously understood, both by the ancient versions and by modern commentators. The *Vulgate* renders it thus: *Syrus persequebatur patrem meum*, "A Syrian persecuted my father." The *Septuagint* thus: *Συριαν απεβαλεν ὁ πατηρ μου*, "My father abandoned Syria." The *Targum* thus: לבן ארמאה בעא לאובדא ית אבא *Laban arammaah bea leobada yath abba*, "Laban the Syrian endeavoured to destroy my father." The *Syriac*: "My father was led out of Syria into Egypt." The *Arabic*: "Surely, Laban the Syrian had almost destroyed my father." The *Targum* of *Jonathan ben Uzziel*: "Our father Jacob went at first into Syria of Mesopotamia, and Laban sought to destroy him."

Father *Houbigant* dissents from all, and renders the original thus: *Fames urgebat patrem meum, qui in Ægyptum descendit*, "Famine oppressed my father, who went down into Egypt." This interpretation Houbigant gives the text, by taking the י *yod* from the word ארמי *arammi*, which signifies an *Aramite* or Syrian, and joining it to יאבד *yeabud*, the *future* for the *perfect*, which is common enough in Hebrew, and which may signify *constrained*; and seeking for the meaning of ארם *aram* in the Arabic أرم *arama*, which signifies *famine*, *dearth*, &c., he thus makes out his version, and this version he defends at large in his notes. It is pretty evident, from the text, that by a *Syrian* we are to understand *Jacob*, so called from his long residence in Syria with his father-in-law Laban. And his *being ready to perish* may signify the hard usage and severe labour he had in Laban's service, by which, as his health was much impaired, so his life might have often been in imminent danger.

Verse 8. *With a mighty hand, &c.*] See on Deut iv. 34.

Verse 11. *Thou shalt rejoice*] God intends that his followers shall be happy; that they shall eat their bread with gladness and singleness of heart, praising him. Those who eat their meat grudgingly, under the pretence of their *unworthiness*, &c., profane God's bounties, and shall have no thanks for their voluntary humility.

Thou, and the Levite, and the stranger] They were to take care to share God's bounties among all those who were dependent on them. The *Levite* has no inheritance, let him rejoice with thee. The *stranger* has no home, let him feel thee to be his friend and his father.

Verse 12. *The third year*, which is *the year of tithing*] This is supposed to mean the third year of the seventh or Sabbatical year, in which the *tenths* were to be given to the poor. See the law, chap.

A. M. 2553. B. C. 1451. An. Ex. Isr. 40. Sebat.

unto the Levite, and unto the
stranger, to the fatherless, and to
the widow, according to all thy
commandments which thou hast commanded
me: I have not transgressed thy commandments, [p] neither have I forgotten *them:*
14 [q] I have not eaten thereof in my mourning, neither have I taken away *aught* thereof
for *any* unclean *use*, nor given *aught* thereof
for the dead: *but* I have hearkened to the voice
of the LORD my God, *and* have done according to all that thou hast commanded me.
15 [r] Look down from thy holy habitation,
from heaven, and bless thy people Israel, and
the land which thou hast given us, as thou
swarest unto our fathers, a land that floweth
with milk and honey.
16 This day the LORD thy God hath commanded thee to do these statutes
and judgments: thou shalt therefore keep and do them with all
thine heart, and with all thy soul.
17 Thou hast [s] avouched the LORD this day
to be thy God, and to walk in his ways, and
to keep his statutes, and his commandments,
and his judgments, and to hearken unto his
voice:
18 And [t] the LORD hath avouched thee this
day to be his peculiar people, as he hath promised thee, and that *thou* shouldest keep all
his commandments;
19 And to make thee [u] high above all nations
which he hath made, in praise, and in name,
and in honour; and that thou mayest be [v] a
holy people unto the LORD thy God, as he
hath spoken.

A. M. 2553. B. C. 1451. An. Ex. Isr. 40. Sebat.

[p] Psa. cxix. 141, 153, 176.——[q] Lev. vii. 20; xxi. 1, 11; Hos. ix. 4.——[r] Isa. lxiii. 15; Zech. ii. 13.——[s] Exod. xx. 19.——[t] Exod. vi. 7; xix. 5; chap. vii. 6; xiv. 2; xxviii. 9.——[u] Ch. iv. 7, 8; xxviii. 1; Psa. cxlviii. 14.——[v] Exod. xix. 6; chap. vii. 6; xxviii. 9; 1 Pet. ii. 9

xiv. 28. But from the letter in both these places it would appear that the tithe was for the Levites, and that this tithe was drawn only once in three years.

Verse 14. *I have not—given* aught *thereof for the dead*] That is, I have not consecrated any of it to an *idol*, which was generally a dead man whom superstition and ignorance had deified. From 1 Cor. x. 27, 28, we learn that it was customary to offer that flesh to idols which was afterwards sold publicly in the shambles; probably the blood was poured out before the idol in imitation of the sacrifices offered to the true God. Perhaps the text here alludes to a similar custom.

Verse 17. *Thou hast avouched the Lord*] The people *avouch*—publicly declare, that they have taken Jehovah to be their God.

Verse 18. *And the Lord hath avouched*] Publicly declared, by the blessings he pours down upon them, that he has taken them to be his peculiar people. Thus the covenant is made and ratified between God and his followers.

Verse 19. *Make thee high above all nations*] It is written, *Righteousness exalteth a nation, but sin is a reproach to any people*, Prov. xiv. 34. While Israel regarded God's word and kept his testimonies, they were the greatest and most respectable of all nations; but when they forsook God and his law, they became the most contemptible. O Britain, even more highly favoured than ancient Israel! learn wisdom by what they have suffered. It is not thy fleets nor thine armies, howsoever excellent and well appointed, that can ultimately exalt and secure thy permanence among the nations. It is righteousness *alone*. Become irreligious, neglect God's ordinances, profane his Sabbath, despise his word, persecute his followers, and thou art *lost*. But fear, love, and serve him, and thy enemies shall be found liars, thou shalt defeat their projects, and trample on their high places.

THE form of confession when bringing the first-fruits, related ver. 4–10, is both affecting and edifying. Even when brought into a state of affluence and rest, they were commanded to remember and publicly acknowledge their former degradation and wretchedness, that they might be ever kept humble and dependent; and they must bring their offering as a public acknowledgment to God that it was by his mercy their state was changed, and by his bounty their comforts were continued. If a man rise from poverty to affluence, and forget his former state, he becomes proud, insolent, and oppressive. If a Christian convert forget his former state, the rock whence he was hewn, and the hole of the pit whence he was digged, he soon becomes careless, unthankful, and unholy. The case of the *ten lepers* that were cleansed, of whom only *one* returned to give God thanks, is an awful lesson. How many are continually living on the bounty of God, who feel no gratitude for his mercies! Reader, is this thy state? If so, then expect the just God to curse thy blessings.

CHAPTER XXVII.

Moses commands the people to write the law upon stones, when they shall come to the promised land, 1–3. *And to set up these stones on Mount* Ebal, 4; *and to build an altar of unhewn stones, and to offer on it burnt-offerings and peace-offerings,* 5–7. *The words to be written plainly, and the people to be exhorted to obedience,* 8–10. *The six tribes which should stand on Mount* Gerizim *to bless the people,* 11, 12. *Those who are to stand upon Mount* Ebal *to curse the transgressors,* 13. *The different transgressors against whom the curses are to be denounced,* 14–26.

A. M. 2553.
B. C. 1451.
An. Ex. Isr. 40.
Sebat.

AND Moses with the elders of
Israel commanded the people,
saying, Keep all the commandments which I command you this day.
2 And it shall be, on the day [a] when ye shall
pass over Jordan unto the land which the LORD
thy God giveth thee, that [b] thou shalt set thee
up great stones, and plaster them with plaster:
3 And thou shalt write upon them all the
words of this law, when thou art passed over,
that thou mayest go in unto the land which
the LORD thy God giveth thee, a land that
floweth with milk and honey; as the LORD
God of thy fathers hath promised thee.
4 Therefore it shall be when ye be gone
over Jordan, *that* ye shall set up these stones,
which I command you this day, [c] in Mount
Ebal, and thou shalt plaster them with plaster.
5 And there shalt thou build an altar unto
the LORD thy God, an altar of stones: [d] thou
shalt not lift up *any* iron *tool* upon them.
6 Thou shalt build the altar of the LORD thy
God of whole stones: and thou shalt offer
burnt-offerings thereon unto the LORD thy God:
7 And thou shalt offer peace-
offerings, and shalt eat there, and
rejoice before the LORD thy God.

A. M. 2553.
B. C. 1451.
An. Ex. Isr. 40.
Sebat.

8 And thou shalt write upon the stones all
the words of this law very plainly.
9 And Moses, and the priests the Levites,
spake unto all Israel, saying, Take heed, and
hearken, O Israel; [e] this day thou art become
the people of the LORD thy God.
10 Thou shalt therefore obey the voice of
the LORD thy God, and do his commandments
and his statutes, which I command thee this
day.
11 And Moses charged the people the same
day, saying,
12 These shall stand [f] upon Mount Gerizim
to bless the people, when ye are come over
Jordan; Simeon, and Levi, and Judah, and
Issachar, and Joseph, and Benjamin:
13 And [g] these shall stand upon Mount Ebal
[h] to curse; Reuben, Gad, and Asher, and Ze
bulun, Dan, and Naphtali.
14 And [i] the Levites shall speak, and say
unto all the men of Israel with a loud voice,

[a] Josh. iv. 1.——[b] Josh. viii. 32.——[c] Ch. xi. 29; Josh. viii. 30. [d] Exod. xx. 25; Josh. viii. 31.——[e] Chap. xxvi. 18.——[f] Chap. xi. 29; Josh. viii. 33; Judg. ix. 7.——[g] Chap. xi. 29; Josh. viii. 33 [h] Heb. *for a cursing.*——[i] Ch. xxxiii. 10; Josh. viii. 33; Dan. ix. 11

NOTES ON CHAP. XXVII.

Verse 2. *Thou shalt set thee up great stones*] How many is not specified, possibly *twelve*, and possibly only a sufficient number to make a surface large enough to write the blessings and the curses on.

Plàster them with plaster] Perhaps the original ושרת אתם בשיר *vesadta otham bassid* should be translated, *Thou shalt cement them with cement*, because this was intended to be a *durable* monument. In similar cases it was customary to set up a single stone, or a heap, rudely put together, where no cement or mortar appears to have been used; and because this was *common*, it was necessary to give particular directions when the usual method was not to be followed. Some suppose that the writing was to be in *relievo*, and that the spaces between the letters were filled up by the mortar or cement. This is quite a possible case, as the Eastern inscriptions are frequently done in this way. There is now before me a large slab of basaltes, two feet long by sixteen inches wide, on which there is an inscription in Persian, Arabic, and Tamul; in the two former the letters are all raised, the surface of the stone being *dug out*, but the Tamul is indented. A kind of reddish paint had been smeared over the letters to make them more apparent. Two Arabic marbles in the University of Oxford have the inscriptions in *relievo*, like those on the slab of basalt in my possession. In the opinion of some even this case may cast light upon the subject in question.

Verse 3. *All the words of this law*] After all that has been said by ingenious critics concerning the *law* ordered to be written on these stones, some supposing the whole Mosaic law to be intended, others, only the *decalogue*, I am fully of opinion that the (תורה *torah*) law or ordinance in question simply means the *blessings* and *curses* mentioned in this and in the following chapter; and indeed these contained a very good epitome of the whole law in all its promises and threatenings, in reference to the whole of its grand moral design. See at the end of this chapter.

Verse 4. *Set up these stones—in Mount Ebal*] So the present Hebrew text, but the Samaritan has *Mount Gerizim*. Dr. Kennicott has largely defended the reading of the Samaritan in his second dissertation on the *present state of the Hebrew text*, and Dr. Parry has defended the Hebrew against the Samaritan in his *Case between Gerizim and Ebal fairly stated*. So has *J. H. Verschuir*, in his *Dissert. Critica*. Many still think Dr. Kennicott's arguments unanswerable, and have no doubt that the Jews have here corrupted the text through their enmity to the Samaritans. On all hands it is allowed that *Gerizim* abounds with springs, gardens, and orchards, and that it is covered with a beautiful verdure, while *Ebal* is as *naked* and as barren as a rock. On this very account the former was highly proper for the ceremony of *blessing*, and the latter for the ceremony of *cursing*.

Verse 12. *These shall stand upon Mount Gerizim to bless the people*] Instead of *upon Mount*, &c., we may translate *by*, as the particle על *al* is sometimes used; for we do not find that the tribes did stand *on* either mount, for in Josh. viii. 33, when this direction

A. M. 2553.
B. C. 1451.
An. Ex. Isr. 40.
Sebat.

15 [k] Cursed *be* the man that
maketh *any* graven or molten
image, an abomination unto the
LORD, the work of the hands of the craftsman,
and putteth *it* in *a* secret *place.* [l] And all the
people shall answer and say, Amen.
16 [m] Cursed *be* he that setteth light by his
father or his mother. And all the people shall
say, Amen.
17 [n] Cursed *be* he that removeth his neighbour's landmark. And all the people shall say,
Amen.
18 [o] Cursed *be* he that maketh the blind to
wander out of the way. And all the people
shall say, Amen.
19 [p] Cursed *be* he that perverteth the judgment of the stranger, fatherless, and widow.
And all the people shall say, Amen.
20 [q] Cursed *be* he that lieth with his father's
wife; because he uncovereth his
father's skirt. And all the people
shall say, Amen.

A. M. 2553.
B. C. 1451.
An. Ex. Isr. 40.
Sebat.

21 [r] Cursed *be* he that lieth with any manner
of beast. And all the people shall say, Amen.
22 [s] Cursed *be* he that lieth with his sister,
the daughter of his father, or the daughter of
his mother. And all the people shall say,
Amen.
23 [t] Cursed *be* he that lieth with his mother-
in-law. And all the people shall say, Amen.
24 [u] Cursed *be* he that smiteth his neighbour
secretly. And all the people shall say, Amen.
25 [v] Cursed *be* he that taketh reward to slay
an innocent person. And all the people shall
say, Amen.
26 [w] Cursed *be* he that confirmeth not *all* the
words of this law to do them. And all the
people shall say, Amen.

[k] Exod. xx. 4, 23; xxxiv. 17; Lev. xix. 4; xxvi. 1; chap. iv. 16, 23; v. 8; Isa. lxiv. 9; Hos. xiii. 2.——[l] See Num. v. 22; Jer. xi. 5; 1 Cor. xiv. 16.——[m] Exod. xx. 12; xxi. 17; Lev. xix. 3; chap. xxi. 18.——[n] Chap. xix. 14; Prov. xxii. 28.——[o] Lev. xix. 14.——[p] Exod. xxii. 21, 22; chap. x. 18; xxiv. 17; Mal. iii. 5.

[q] Lev. xviii. 8; xx. 11; chap. xxii. 30.——[r] Lev. xviii. 23; xx. 15.——[s] Lev. xviii. 9; xx. 17.——[t] Lev. xviii. 17; xx. 14.——[u] Exod. xx. 13; xxi. 12, 14; Lev. xxiv. 17; Num. xxxv. 31; chap. xix. 11.——[v] Exod. xxiii. 7, 8; chap. x. 17; xvi. 19; Ezek. xxii. 12.——[w] Chap. xxviii. 15; Psa. cxix. 21; Jer. xi. 3; Gal. iii. 10.

was reduced to practice, we find the people did not stand *on* the mountains, but *over against* them on the plain. See the observations at the end of this chapter.

Verse 15. *Cursed* be *the man, &c.*] Other laws, previously made, had prohibited all these things, and penal sanctions were necessarily understood; but here God more openly declares that he who breaks them *is cursed*—falls under the wrath and indignation of his Maker and Judge. See the note on Exod. xx. 4.

Verse 16. *Setteth light by his father or his mother.*] See the note on Exod. xx. 12.

Verse 17. *Removeth his neighbour's landmark.*] See before on Deut. xix. 14, and on Exod. xx. 17. And for all the rest of these curses, see the notes on Exod. xx., and the observations at the end of it.

Verse 18. *The blind to wander out of the way.*] A sin against the sixth commandment. See on Exod. xx. 13.

Verse 26. *That confirmeth not* all *the words of this law*] The word כל *col,* ALL, is not found in any *printed* copy of the *Hebrew* text; but the *Samaritan* preserves it, and so do *six* MSS. in the collections of *Kennicott* and *De Rossi*, besides several copies of the *Chaldee Targum*. The *Septuagint* also, and *St. Paul* in his quotation of this place, Gal. iii. 10. St. Jerome says that the Jews suppressed the word, that it might not appear that they were bound to fulfil ALL the precepts in the law of Moses.

1. Dr. KENNICOTT, who contends that it was the *Decalogue* that was written on the stones mentioned in this chapter, says, "If we examine these twelve curses, they will appear to contain a strong enforcement of the *ten commands;* and it is highly probable that the curses were here proclaimed principally to secure obedience to the commandments, as will be made more clear by the following table:—

The first, second, third, and fourth Commandments.

Verse 15. Cursed be the man that maketh any graven or molten image, an abomination to the Lord, &c.

The fifth Commandment.

Verse 16. Cursed be he that setteth light by his father or his mother.

The sixth Commandment.

Verse 25. Cursed be he that taketh reward to slay an innocent person.

Verse 24. Cursed be he that smiteth his neighbour secretly.

Verse 18. Cursed be he that maketh the blind to wander out of the way.

The seventh Commandment.

Verse 20. Cursed be he that lieth with his father's wife.

Verse 21. Cursed be he that lieth with any beast.

Verse 22. Cursed be he that lieth with his sister.

Verse 23. Cursed be he that lieth with his mother-in-law.

The eighth Commandment.

Verse 17. Cursed be he that removeth his neighbour's landmark.

The ninth Commandment.

Verse 19. Cursed be he that perverteth the judgment of the stranger, fatherless, and widow.

The tenth Commandment.

Verse 26. Cursed be he that confirmeth not all the words of this law to do them."

Many will think this arrangement fanciful; and the analogy far from being natural.

2. In pronouncing these blessings and curses, the Talmud says, six tribes went up towards the top of Mount Gerizim, and six towards the top of Mount Ebal; and the priests and the Levites, and the ark stood beneath in the midst. The priests encompassed the ark, and the Levites stood round about the priests; and all Israel on this side and on that; see Josh. viii. 33. Then they turned their faces towards Mount Gerizim and pronounced the blessing, *Blessed be the man*, &c., and those on each side answered Amen! then they turned their faces towards Mount Ebal, and pronounced the curse, *Cursed be the man*, &c., and those on each side answered Amen! till they had finished the blessings and the curses; and afterwards they brought stones and built an altar. Some suppose that the Levites were divided into two grand bodies, part standing at or on Mount Gerizim, and part on Mount Ebal, and that with each division were some of the priests. The whole Dr. *Parry* supposes to have been arranged in the following manner:—

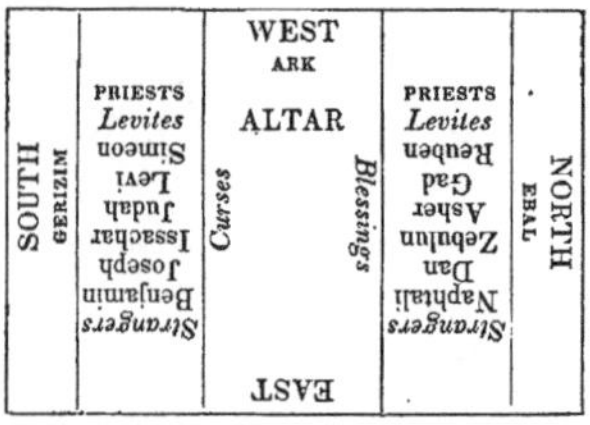
WEST
ARK
ALTAR
PRIESTS
Levites
Simeon
Levi
Judah
Issachar
Joseph
Benjamin
Strangers
PRIESTS
Levites
Reuben
Gad
Asher
Zebulun
Dan
Naphtali
Strangers
SOUTH
GERIZIM
NORTH
EBAL
Curses
Blessings
EAST

3. It is worthy of remark that Moses assigns to the children of Rachel and Leah, the two mothers of the family, the office of *blessing* the people, as being the most honourable; and these he places on Mount Gerizim. On the contrary, he assigns the office of *cursing* the people to the sons of Zilpah and Bilhah, as being the least honourable office; but with these he joins Zebulun, the youngest of Leah's sons, and Reuben, the eldest. As there must be six tribes on each mountain, it was necessary that while six of the sons of Rachel and Leah, the legitimate wives, should be employed in blessing, *two* tribes descending from the same mothers should be joined to the other *four* who proceeded from the handmaids in order to make up the number *six*. The question is, which two of the more honourable tribes should be joined to the *four* least honourable, in order to complete the number six? Zebulun is chosen, because being the sixth and youngest of all Leah's sons, he was the least honourable of those who proceeded from the free woman; and Reuben is chosen, who, though the eldest of Jacob's sons, and entitled to the birthright, had lost it by his transgression. And hence he, in his posterity, was degraded, and was obliged to pronounce the curse, *Cursed is he that lieth with his father's wife*. See Gen. xlix. 3, 4, and xxxv. 22, and the notes on both places.

4. It is strange how long the disgrace consequent on some flagrant transaction of a parent may cleave to his posterity! See this exemplified in the posterity of Reuben. Hence, with great propriety we may pray, "Remember not, Lord, our offences, nor the offences of our forefathers; neither take thou vengeance of our sins."—*Litany*. For the offences of our forefathers may be so remembered against their posterity, that God, in the course of his providence, may still keep up a controversy in *secular matters* with the descendants (though even pious) of unholy ancestors; for as all men are seminally included in their parents, they come into the world depraved with their depravity, and in some sort liable to their curses, though not so far as to affect their eternal interests without the addition of their own personal offences. Thus God may be said to visit the sins of the fathers upon the children, even unto the third and fourth generation; as he may have a controversy with the *land* for the evil which has been done in it, and for which no proper atonement has been made. Why is it that at this moment Spain is suffering the most afflictive and cruel desolations? What has she done to merit all this? Is she more wicked than all the European nations because she suffers such things? Here is the mystery: *Nations*, as such, can only be punished in this world. Look at the torrents of innocent blood shed by their ancestors in South America 300 years ago; and see now and adore the awful hand of retributive justice! (December, 1811.) We often see persons tried and afflicted, for whose distresses we can give no legitimate reason. We find others who, though they rise early, sit up late, work hard, eat the bread of carefulness, and have a full knowledge of their business, yet never get on in life. Who can account for this? Shall we say that some injustice in their ancestors has brought down the displeasure of God upon the earthly possessions that descended in that line, so that the goods *ill gotten* shall never be permitted to *multiply*? I knew an honest man, dead many years since, who by great diligence, punctuality, and integrity in his business, had acquired considerable property. Some time before his death, having by will divided his substance among his sons and his daughters, he expressed himself thus: "Children, you need not fear the curse of God on this property; every penny of it was honestly earned." Many years have since elapsed, and the blessing of God has been in the basket and in the store of all his children. Parents! leave nothing behind you that you cannot say before your God, with a clear conscience, "This has been honestly earned." If all bequests of a *contrary description* were to be deducted from last wills and testaments, the quantum of descending property would be, in many cases, small indeed.

CHAPTER XXVIII.

The blessings which God pronounces on the obedient, 1–6. *Particular privileges which the faithful shall receive,* 7–13. *The curses pronounced against the ungodly and idolatrous,* 14–19. *A detailed account of the miseries which should be inflicted on them, should they neglect the commandments of the Lord,* 20. *They shall be smitten with the pestilence,* 21; *with consumption, fever, &c.,* 22; *drought and barrenness,* 23, 24; *they shall be defeated by their enemies,* 25, 26; *they shall be afflicted with the botch of Egypt,* 27; *with madness and blindness,* 28, 29; *they shall be disappointed in all their projects,* 30; *deprived of all their possessions, and afflicted in all their members,* 31–35; *they and their king shall go into captivity,* 36, *and become a by-word among the nations,* 37. *Their land shall be unfruitful, and they shall be the lowest of all people,* 38–44. *All these curses shall come on them should they be disobedient,* 45–48. *Character of the people by whom they should be subdued,* 49, 50. *Particulars of their dreadful sufferings,* 51–57. *A recapitulation of their wretchedness,* 58–63. *The prediction that they shall be scattered among all the nations of the earth,* 64–68.

A. M. 2553. B. C. 1451. An. Ex. Isr. 40. Sebat.

AND it shall come to pass, [a] if
thou shalt hearken diligently
unto the voice of the LORD thy
God, to observe *and* to do all his commandments which I command thee this day, that the
LORD thy God [b] will set thee on high above
all nations of the earth:
2 And all these blessings shall come on thee,
and [c] overtake thee, if thou shalt hearken
unto the voice of the LORD thy
God.
3 [d] Blessed *shalt* thou *be* in the
city, and blessed *shalt* thou *be* [e] in the field.
4 Blessed *shall be* [f] the fruit of thy body,
and the fruit of thy ground, and the fruit of
thy cattle, the increase of thy kine, and the
flocks of thy sheep.
5 Blessed *shall be* thy basket and thy [g] store.

[a] Exod. xv. 26; Lev. xxvi. 3; Isa. lv. 2.——[b] Chap. xxvi. 19.——[c] Ver. 15; Zech. i. 6.——[d] Psa. cxxviii. 1, 4.——[e] Gen. xxxix. 5.

[f] Ver. 11; Gen. xxii. 17; xlix. 25; chap. vii. 13; Psa. cvii. 38; cxxvii. 3; cxxviii. 3; Prov. x. 22; 1 Tim. iv. 8.——[g] Or, *dough*, or *kneading trough.*

NOTES ON CHAP. XXVIII.

Verse 2. *All these blessings shall come on thee*] God shall pour out his blessing from heaven upon thee. *And overtake thee.* Upright men are represented as *going* to the kingdom of God, and God's blessings as *following* and *overtaking* them in their heavenly journey. There are several things in this verse worthy of the most careful observation:—

1. *If thou shalt hearken unto the voice of the Lord thy God.* The voice of God must be heard; without a *Divine revelation* how can the Divine will be known? And if not known, it cannot be fulfilled.

2. When God speaks, men must *hearken* to the words of his mouth. He who does not *hearken* will not *obey*.

3. He who *hearkens* to the words of God must *set out* for the kingdom of heaven. The curse must fall on him who *stands* in the way of sinners, and will overtake them who *loiter* in the way of righteousness.

4. Those who run in the way of God's testimonies shall have an abundance of blessing. Blessings shall *come upon them*, and blessings shall *overtake them*—in every part of their march through life they shall continue to receive the fulfilment of the various promises of God which relate to all circumstances, vicissitudes, trials, stages of life, &c., &c., each *overtaking* them in the *time* and *place* where *most* needed.

Verse 3. *In the city*] In all civil employments. *In the field*—in all agricultural pursuits.

Verse 4. *Fruit of thy body*] All thy children. *Increase of thy kine,* &c.; every *animal* employed in domestic and agricultural purposes shall be under the especial protection of Divine Providence.

Verse 5. *Thy basket*] Thy olive gathering and vintage, as the *basket* was employed to collect those fruits.

Store.] משארת *mishereth*, kneading-trough, or *remainder;* all that is laid up for *future use*, as well as what is prepared for *present* consumption. Some think that by *basket* all their property *abroad* may be meant, and by *store* all that they have at *home*, i. e., all that is in the *fields*, and all that is in the *houses*. The following note of Mr. Harmer is important:—

"Commentators seem to be at a great loss how to explain the *basket* and the *store* mentioned Deut. xxviii. 5, 17. Why Moses, who in the other verses mentions things in general, should in this case be so minute as to mention baskets, seems strange; and they that interpret either the first or the second of these words of the repositories of their corn, &c., forget that their barns or storehouses are spoken of presently after this in ver. 8. Might I be permitted to give my opinion here, I should say that the basket, טנא *tene*, in this place means their travelling baskets, and the other word משארת *mishereth*, (their store,) signifies their leathern bags, in both which they were wont to carry things in travelling. The first of these words occurs nowhere else in the Scriptures but in the account that is given us of the conveyance in which they were to carry their first-fruits to Jerusalem; the other nowhere but in the description of the hurrying journey of Israel out of Egypt, where it means the utensils in which they then carried their dough, which I have shown elsewhere in these papers means a piece of leather drawn together by rings, and forming a kind of bag. Agreeably to this, Hasselquist informs us that the Eastern people use baskets in travelling; for, speaking of that species of the palm tree which pro-

A. M. 2553. B. C. 1451. An. Ex. Isr. 40. Sebat.

6 [h] Blessed *shalt* thou *be* when
thou comest in, and blessed *shalt*
thou *be* when thou goest out.
7 The LORD [i] shall cause thine enemies that
rise up against thee to be smitten before thy
face: they shall come out against thee one
way, and flee before thee seven ways.
8 The LORD shall [k] command the blessing
upon thee in thy [l] storehouses, and in all that
thou [m] settest thine hand unto; and he shall
bless thee in the land which the LORD thy
God giveth thee.
9 [n] The LORD shall establish thee a holy
people unto himself, as he hath sworn unto
thee, if thou shalt keep the commandments of
the LORD thy God, and walk in his ways.
10 And all the people of the earth shall see
that thou art [o] called by the name of the LORD;
and they shall be [p] afraid of thee.
11 And [q] the LORD shall make thee plenteous
[r] in goods, in the fruit of thy [s] body, and in
the fruit of thy cattle, and in the fruit of thy
ground, in the land which the
LORD sware unto thy fathers to
give thee.

A. M. 2553. B. C. 1451. An. Ex. Isr. 40. Sebat.

12 The LORD shall open unto thee his good
treasure, the heaven [t] to give thee rain unto thy
land in his season, and [u] to bless all the work
of thine hand: and [v] thou shalt lend unto
many nations, and thou shalt not borrow.
13 And the LORD shall make thee [w] the head,
and not the tail; and thou shalt be above only,
and thou shalt not be beneath; if that thou
hearken unto the commandments of the LORD
thy God, which I command thee this day, to
observe and to do *them*:
14 [x] And thou shalt not go aside from any of
the words which I command thee this day, *to*
the right hand or *to* the left, to go after other
gods to serve them.
15 But it shall come to pass, [y] if thou wilt
not hearken unto the voice of the LORD thy
God, to observe to do all his commandments
and his statutes which I command thee this

[h] Psa. cxxi. 8.——[i] Lev. xxvi. 7, 8; 2 Sam. xxii. 38, 39, 41; Psa. lxxxix. 23; see ver. 25.——[k] Lev. xxv. 21.——[l] Or, *barns*; Prov. iii. 10.——[m] Chap. xv. 10.——[n] Exod. xix. 5, 6; chap. vii. 6; xxvi. 18, 19; xxix. 13.——[o] Num. vi. 27; 2 Chron. vii. 14; Isa. lxiii. 19; Dan. ix. 18, 19.

[p] Chap. xi. 25.——[q] Ver. 4; chap. xxx. 9; Prov. x. 22.——[r] Or, *for good*.——[s] Heb. *belly*.——[t] Lev. xxvi. 4; chap. xi. 14.——[u] Chap. xiv. 29.——[v] Chap. xv. 6.——[w] Isa. ix. 14, 15.——[x] Chap. v. 32; xi. 16.——[y] Lev. xxvi. 14; Lam. ii. 17; Dan. ix. 11, 13; Mal. ii. 2; Bar. i. 20.

duces dates, and its great usefulness to the people of those countries, he tells us that of the leaves of this tree they make baskets, or rather a kind of short bags, which are used in Turkey on journeys and in their houses; pages 261, 262. Hampers and panniers are English terms denoting travelling baskets, as *tene* seems to be a Hebrew word of the same general import, though their forms might very much differ, as it is certain that of the travelling baskets mentioned by Hasselquist now does.

"In like manner as they now carry meal, figs, and raisins, in a goat's skin in Barbary for a viaticum, they might do the same anciently, and consequently might carry merchandise after the same manner, particularly their honey, oil, and balm, mentioned Ezek. xvii. 17. They were the proper vessels for such things. So Sir J. Chardin, who was so long in the East, and observed their customs with so much care, supposed, in a manuscript note on Gen. xliii. 11, that the balm and the honey sent by Jacob into Egypt for a present were carried in a goat or kid's skin, in which all sorts of things, both dry and liquid, are wont to be carried in the East.

"Understood after this manner, the passage promises Israel success in their commerce, as the next verse (the 6th) promises them personal safety in their going out and in their return. In this view the passage appears with due distinctness, and a noble extent."—Observations, vol. ii., p. 181.

Verse 6. *When thou comest in*] From thy employment, thou shalt find that no evil has happened to the *family* or *dwelling* in thy absence.

When thou goest out.] Thy way shall be made prosperous before thee, and thou shalt have the Divine blessing in all thy labours.

Verse 7. *The Lord shall cause thine enemies, &c.*] This is a promise of security from foreign invasion, or total discomfiture of the invaders, should they enter the land. *They shall come against thee one way*—in the firmest and most united manner. *And flee seven ways*—shall be utterly broken, confounded, and finally routed.

Verse 8. *The Lord shall command the blessing upon thee*] Every thing that thou hast shall come by Divine appointment; thou shalt have nothing casually, but every thing, both spiritual and temporal, shall come by the immediate *command* of God.

Verse 9. *The Lord shall establish thee a holy people unto himself*] This is the sum of all blessings, to be made *holy*, and be preserved in *holiness*.

If thou shalt keep, &c.] Here is the solemn condition; *if they did not* keep God's testimonies, taking them for the regulators of their lives, and according to their direction walking in his ways, under the influence and aids of his grace, then the *curses*, and not the *blessings*, must be their portion. See ver. 15, &c.

Verse 12. *The Lord shall open unto thee his good treasure*] The *clouds*, so that a sufficiency of fructifying showers should descend at all requisite times, and the vegetative principle in the earth should unfold and exert itself, so that their crops should be abundant.

Verse 14. *Thou shalt not go aside—to the right hand or to the left*] The way of obedience is a *straight* way; it goes *right* forward; he who declines either

A. M. 2553.
B. C. 1451.
An. Ex. Isr. 40.
Sebat.

day; that all these curses shall come upon thee, and [z] overtake thee:

16 Cursed *shalt* thou *be* [a] in the city, and cursed *shalt* thou *be* in the field.

17 Cursed *shall be* thy basket and thy store.

18 Cursed *shall be* the fruit of thy body, and the fruit of thy land, the increase of thy kine, and the flocks of thy sheep.

19 Cursed *shalt* thou *be* when thou comest in, and cursed *shalt* thou *be* when thou goest out.

20 The LORD shall send upon thee [b] cursing, [c] vexation, and [d] rebuke, in all that thou settest thine hand unto [e] for to do, until thou be destroyed, and until thou perish quickly; because of the wickedness of thy doings, whereby thou hast forsaken me.

21 The LORD shall make [f] the pestilence cleave unto thee, until he have consumed thee from off the land, whither thou goest to possess it.

22 [g] The LORD shall smite thee with a consumption, and with a fever, and with an inflammation, and with an extreme burning, and with the [h] sword, and with [i] blasting, and with mildew; and they shall pursue thee until thou perish.

A. M. 2553.
B. C. 1451.
An. Ex. Isr. 40.
Sebat.

23 And [k] thy heaven that *is* over thy head shall be brass, and the earth that *is* under thee *shall be* iron.

24 The LORD shall make the rain of thy land powder and dust: from heaven shall it come down upon thee, until thou be destroyed.

25 [l] The LORD shall cause thee to be smitten before thine enemies: thou shalt go out one way against them, and flee seven ways before them: and [m] shalt be [n] removed into all the kingdoms of the earth.

26 And [o] thy carcass shall be meat unto all fowls of the air, and unto the beasts of the earth, and no man shall fray *them* away.

[z] Ver. 2.——[a] Ver. 3, &c.——[b] Mal. ii. 2.——[c] 1 Sam. xiv. 20; Zech. xiv. 13.——[d] Psa. lxxx. 16; Isa. xxx. 17; li. 20; lxvi. 15.——[e] Heb. *which thou wouldest do.*——[f] Lev. xxvi. 25; Jer. xxiv. 10.——[g] Lev. xxvi. 16.——[h] Or, *drought.*——[i] Amos iv. 9.

[k] Lev. xxvi. 19.——[l] Ver. 7; Lev. xxvi. 17, 37; chap. xxxii. 30; Isa. xxx. 17.——[m] Jer. xv. 4; xxiv. 9; Ezek. xxiii. 46.——[n] Heb. *for a removing.*——[o] 1 Sam. xvii. 44, 46; Psa. lxxix. 2; Jer. vii. 33; xvi. 4; xxxiv. 20.

to *right* or *left* from this path goes *astray* and misses heaven.

Verse 20. *Cursing*] This shall be thy state; *vexation*—grief, trouble, and anguish of heart; *rebuke*—continual judgments, and marks of God's displeasure.

Verse 21. *The pestilence cleave unto thee*] ידבק יהוה בך את הדבר *yadbek Yehovah becha eth haddaber, the Lord shall* CEMENT *the pestilence* or plague *to thee.* Sept., Προσκολλησει Κυριος εις σε τον θανατον, *The Lord will* GLUE—inseparably attach, *the death unto thee* How dreadful a plague it must be that ravages *without intermission*, any person may conceive who has ever heard of the name.

Verse 22. *Consumption*] שחפת *shachepheth*, atrophy through lack of food; from שחף *shacaph*, to be in want.

Fever] קדחת *kaddachath*, from קדח *kadach*, to be kindled, burn, sparkle; a burning inflammatory fever.

Inflammation] דלקת *dalleketh*, from דלק *dalak*, to pursue eagerly, to burn after; probably a rapidly consuming cancer.

Extreme burning] חרחר *charchur*, burning upon burning, scald upon scald; from חר *char*, to be *heated, enraged*, &c. This probably refers, not only to excruciating inflammations on the body, but also to the irritation and agony of a mind utterly abandoned by God, and lost to *hope*. What an accumulation of misery! how formidable! and especially in a land where *great heat* was prevalent and dreadful.

Sword] *War* in general, *enemies without*, and *civil broils within*. This was remarkably the case in the last siege of Jerusalem.

Blasting] שדפון *shiddaphon*, probably either the blighting east wind that ruined vegetation, or those awful pestilential winds which suffocate both man and beast wherever they come. These often prevail in different parts of the East, and several examples have already been given. See Gen. xli. 6.

Mildew] ירקון *yerakon*, an *exudation* of the vegetative *juice* from different parts of the stalk, by which the maturity and perfection of the plant are utterly prevented. It comes from ירק *yarak*, to throw out moisture.

Of these *seven* plagues, the *five* former were to fall on their bodies, the *two* latter upon their substance. What a fearful thing it is to fall into the hands of the living God!

Verse 23. *Thy heaven—shall be brass, and the earth—iron.*] The atmosphere should not be replenished with aqueous vapours, in consequence of which they should have neither the early nor the latter rain; hence the *earth*—the ground, must be wholly intractable, and, through its hardness, incapable of cultivation. God shows them by this that he is Lord of nature; and that *drought* and *sterility* are not *casualties*, but proceed from the immediate *appointment* of the Lord.

Verse 24. *The rain of thy land powder and dust*] As their *heavens*—atmosphere, clouds, &c., were to be as *brass*—yielding no rain; so the surface of the earth must be reduced to powder; and this, being frequently taken up by the strong winds, would fall down in showers instead of rain. Whole *caravans* have been buried under showers of sand; and Thevenot, a French traveller, who had observed these showers of dust, &c., says, "They grievously annoy all they fall on, filling their eyes, ears, nostrils, &c."—Travels in the East, part 1, book ii., chap. 80. The ophthalmia in Egypt

A. M. 2553.
B. C. 1451.
An. Ex. Isr. 40.
Sebat.

27 The LORD will smite thee
with [p] the botch of Egypt, and
with [q] the emerods, and with the
scab, and with the itch, whereof thou canst not
be healed.
28 The LORD shall smite thee with madness,
and blindness, and [r] astonishment of heart:
29 And thou shalt [s] grope at noonday, as
the blind gropeth in darkness, and thou shalt
not prosper in thy ways: and thou shalt be
only oppressed and spoiled evermore, and no
man shall save *thee*.
30 [t] Thou shalt betroth a wife, and another
man shall lie with her: [u] thou
shalt build a house, and thou
shalt not dwell therein: [v] thou
shalt plant a vineyard, and shalt not [w] gather
the grapes thereof.
31 Thine ox *shall be* slain before thine eyes,
and thou shalt not eat thereof: thine ass *shall
be* violently taken away from before thy face,
and [x] shall not be restored to thee: thy sheep
shall be given unto thine enemies, and thou
shalt have none to rescue *them*.
32 Thy sons and thy daughters *shall be*
given unto another people, and thine eyes

[p] Ver. 35; Exod. ix. 9; xv. 26.——[q] 1 Sam. v. 6; Psa. lxxviii. 66.——[r] Jer. iv. 9.——[s] Job v. 14; Isa. lix. 10.——[t] Job xxxi. 10; Jer. viii. 10.

[u] Job xxxi. 8; Jer. xii. 13; Amos v. 11; Mic. vi. 15; Zeph. i. 13.——[v] Chap. xx. 6.——[w] Heb. *profane*, or *use it as common meat*; as chap. xx. 6.——[x] Heb. *shall not return to thee*.

appears to be chiefly owing to a very fine sand, the particles of which are like broken glass, which are carried about by the wind, and, entering into the ciliary glands, produce grievous and continual inflammations.

Verse 27. *The Lord will smite thee with the botch*] שחין *shechin*, a violent inflammatory swelling. In Job ii., one of the Hexapla versions renders it ελεφας, the *elephantiasis*, a disease the most horrid that can possibly afflict human nature. In this disorder, the whole body is covered with a most loathsome scurf; the joints are all preternaturally enlarged, and the skin swells up and grows into folds like that of an *elephant*, whence the disease has its name. The skin, through its rigidity, breaks across at all the joints, and a most abominable *ichor* flows from all the chinks, &c. See an account of it in *Aretæus*, whose language is sufficient to *chill* the blood of a *maniac*, could he attend to the description given by this great master, of this most loathsome and abominable of all the natural productions of *death* and *sin*. This was called the *botch of Egypt*, as being peculiar to that country, and particularly in the vicinity of the Nile. Hence those words of *Lucretius*:—

Est Elephas morbus, qui circum flumina Nili
Nascitur, Ægypto in media; nec præterea usquam.
Lib. vi., ver. 1112.

Emerods] עפלים *ophalim*, from עפל *aphal*, to be elevated, raised up; swellings, protuberances; probably the *bleeding piles*.

Scab] גרב *garab* does not occur as a verb in the Hebrew Bible, but غرب *gharb*, in Arabic, signifies a distemper in the corner of the eye, (*Castel.*,) and may amount to the Egyptian ophthalmia, which is so epidemic and distressing in that country: some suppose the *scurvy* to be intended.

Itch] חרס *cheres*, a burning itch, probably something of the erysipelatous kind, or what is commonly called *St. Anthony's fire*.

Whereof thou canst not be healed.] For as they were inflicted by GOD'S justice, they could not of course be cured by *human* art.

Verse 28. *The Lord shall smite thee with madness*] שגעון *shiggaon*, distraction, so that thou shalt not know what to do.

And blindness] עורון *ivvaron*, blindness, both physical and mental; the גרב *garab*, (ver. 27,) destroying their eyes, and the judgments of God confounding their understandings.

Astonishment] תמהון *timmahon*, stupidity and amazement. By the just judgments of God they were so completely confounded, as not to discern the means by which they might prevent or remove their calamities, and to adopt those which led directly to their ruin. How true is the ancient saying, *Quos Deus vult perdere, prius dementat!* "Those whom God is determined to destroy, he first infatuates." But this applies not exclusively to the poor *Jews*: how miserably infatuated have the powers of the *continent* of Europe been, in all their councils and measures, for several years past! And what is the result? They have fallen—most deplorably fallen!

Verse 29. *Thou shalt be only oppressed, &c.*] Perhaps no people under the sun have been more oppressed and spoiled than the rebellious Jews. Indeed, this has been their portion, with but little intermission, for nearly 1,800 years. And still they *grope at noon day, as the blind gropeth in darkness*—they do not yet discover, notwithstanding the effulgence of the light by which they are encompassed, that the rejection of their own Messiah is the cause of all their calamities.

Verse 30. *Thou shalt betroth a wife, &c.*] Can any heart imagine any thing more grievous than the evils threatened in this and the following verses? To be on the brink of all social and domestic happiness, and then to be suddenly deprived of all, and see an enemy possess and enjoy every thing that was dear to them, must excite them to the utmost pitch of distraction and madness. They have, it is true, grievously sinned; but, O ye Christians, have they not grievously suffered for it? Is not the stroke of God heavy enough upon them? Do not then, by unkind treatment or cruel oppression, increase their miseries. They are, above all others, the men who have seen affliction by the stroke of his rod; Lam. iii. 1.

Verse 32. *Thy sons and thy daughters* shall be *given unto another people*] In several countries, particularly in *Spain* and *Portugal*, the children of the Jews have been taken from them by order of govern-

a

A. M. 2553.
B. C. 1451.
An. Ex. Isr. 40.
Sebat.

shall look, and [y] fail *with longing* for them all the day long: and *there shall be* no might in thine hand.

33 [z] The fruit of thy land, and all thy labours, shall a nation which thou knowest not eat up: and thou shalt be only oppressed and crushed alway:

34 So that thou shalt be mad [a] for the sight of thine eyes which thou shalt see.

35 The LORD shall [b] smite thee in the knees, and in the legs, with a sore botch that cannot be healed, from the sole of thy foot unto the top of thy head.

36 The LORD shall [c] bring thee, and thy king which thou shalt set over thee, unto a nation which neither thou nor thy fathers have known; and [d] there shalt thou serve other gods, wood and stone.

37 And thou shalt become [e] an astonishment, a proverb, [f] and a byword, among all nations whither the LORD shall lead thee.

38 [g] Thou shalt carry much seed out into the field, and shalt gather *but* little in; for [h] the locust shall consume it.

39 Thou shalt plant vineyards, and dress *them*, but shalt neither drink *of* the wine, nor gather *the grapes;* for the worms shall eat them.

40 Thou shalt have olive trees throughout all thy coasts, but thou shalt not anoint *thyself* with the oil; for thine olive shall cast *his fruit.*

41 Thou shalt beget sons and daughters, but [i] thou shalt not enjoy them; for [k] they shall go into captivity.

42 All thy trees and fruit of thy land shall the locust [l] consume.

43 The stranger that *is* within thee shall get up above thee very high; and thou shalt come down very low.

A. M. 2553.
B. C. 1451.
An. Ex. Isr. 40.
Sebat.

44 [m] He shall lend to thee, and thou shalt not lend to him: [n] he shall be the head, and thou shalt be the tail.

45 Moreover [o] all these curses shall come upon thee, and shall pursue thee, and overtake thee, till thou be destroyed; because thou hearkenedst not unto the voice of the LORD thy God, to keep his commandments and his statutes which he commanded thee:

46 And they shall be upon thee [p] for a sign and for a wonder, and upon thy seed for ever.

47 [q] Because thou servedst not the LORD thy God with joyfulness, and with gladness of heart, [r] for the abundance of all *things;*

48 Therefore shalt thou serve thine enemies which the LORD shall send against thee, in hunger, and in thirst, and in nakedness, and in want of all *things;* and he [s] shall put a yoke of iron upon thy neck, until he have destroyed thee.

49 [t] The LORD shall bring a nation against thee from far, from the end of the earth, [u] *as swift* as the eagle flieth; a nation whose tongue thou shalt not [v] understand;

50 A nation [w] of fierce countenance, [x] which shall not regard the person of the old, nor show favour to the young:

51 And he shall [y] eat the fruit of thy cattle, and the fruit of thy land, until thou be destroyed: which *also* shall not leave thee *either* corn, wine, or oil, *or* the increase of thy kine, or flocks of thy sheep, until he have destroyed thee.

52 And he shall [z] besiege thee in all thy

---

[y] Psa. cxix. 82.——[z] Ver. 51; Lev. xxvi. 16; Jer. v. 17.——[a] Ver. 67.——[b] Ver. 27.——[c] 2 Kings xvii. 4, 6; xiv. 12, 14; xxv. 7, 11; 2 Chron. xxxiii. 11; xxxvi. 6, 20.——[d] Chap. iv. 28; ver. 64; Jer. xvi. 13.——[e] 1 Kings ix. 7, 8; Jer. xxiv. 9; xxv. 9; Zech. viii. 13.——[f] Psa. xliv. 14.——[g] Mic. vi. 15; Hag. i. 6.——[h] Joel i. 4.——[i] Heb. *they shall not be thine.*——[k] Lam. i. 5.——[l] Or, *possess.*——[m] Ver. 12.——[n] Ver. 13; Lam. i. 5.

[o] Ver. 15.——[p] Isa. viii. 18; Ezek. xiv. 8.——[q] Neh. ix. 35, 36, 37.——[r] Chap. xxxii. 15.——[s] Jer. xxviii. 14.——[t] Jer. v. 15; vi. 22, 23; Luke xix. 43.——[u] Jer. xlviii. 43; xlix. 22; Lam. iv. 19; Ezek. xvii. 3, 12; Hos. viii. 1.——[v] Heb. *hear.*——[w] Heb. *strong of face;* Prov. vii. 13; Eccles. viii. 1; Dan. viii. 23.——[x] 2 Chron. xxxvi. 17; Isa. xlvii. 6.——[y] Ver. 33; Isa. i. 7; lxii. 8.——[z] 2 Kings xxv. 1, 2, 4.

---

ment, and educated in the Popish faith. There have been some instances of Jewish children being taken from their parents even in *Protestant* countries.

Verse 35. *With a sore botch*] שחין *shechin*, an inflammatory swelling, a burning boil. See ver. 27.

Verse 36–45. Can any thing be conceived more dreadful than the calamities threatened in these verses?

Verse 48. *Therefore shalt thou serve thine enemies*] Because they would not serve GOD, therefore they became *slaves* to *men*.

Verse 49. *A nation—from far*] Probably the *Romans*.

As the eagle flieth] The very animal on all the Roman standards. The *Roman eagle* is proverbial.

Whose tongue thou shalt not understand] The *Latin* language, than which none was more foreign to the structure and idiom of the Hebrew.

Verse 52. *He*—Nebuchadnezzar first, (2 Kings xxv. 1, 2, &c.,) and *Titus* next; *shall besiege thee*—beset thee round on every side, and cast a trench

A. M. 2553.
B. C. 1451.
An. Ex. Isr. 40.
Sebat.

gates, until thy high and fenced walls come down, wherein thou trustedst, throughout all thy land: and he shall besiege thee in all thy gates throughout all thy land, which the LORD thy God hath given thee.

53 And [a] thou shalt eat the fruit of thine own [b] body, the flesh of thy sons and of thy daughters, which the LORD thy God hath given thee, in the siege, and in the straitness, wherewith thine enemies shall distress thee :

54 *So that* the man *that is* tender among you, and very delicate, [c] his eye shall be evil toward his brother, and toward [d] the wife of his bosom, and toward the remnant of his children which he shall leave :

55 So that he will not give to any of them of the flesh of his children whom he shall eat: because he hath nothing left him in the siege, and in the straitness, wherewith thine enemies shall distress thee in all thy gates.

56 The tender and delicate woman among you, which would not adventure to set the sole of her foot upon the ground for delicateness and tenderness, [e] her eye shall be evil toward the husband of her bosom, and toward her son, and toward her daughter,

57 And toward her [f] young one that cometh out [g] from between her feet, and toward her children which she shall bear: for she shall eat them for want of all *things* secretly in the siege and straitness, wherewith thine enemy shall distress thee in thy gates.

A. M. 2553.
B. C. 1451.
An. Ex. Isr. 40.
Sebat.

58 If thou wilt not observe to do all the words of this law that are written in this book, that thou mayest fear [h] this glorious and fearful name, THE LORD THY GOD:

59 Then the LORD will make thy plagues [i] wonderful, and the plagues of thy seed, *even* great plagues, and of long continuance, and sore sicknesses, and of long continuance.

60 Moreover he will bring upon thee all [k] the diseases of Egypt, which thou wast afraid of; and they shall cleave unto thee.

61 Also every sickness, and every plague, which *is* not written in the book of this law, them will the LORD [l] bring upon thee, until thou be destroyed.

62 And ye [m] shall be left few in number, whereas ye were [n] as the stars of heaven for multitude; because thou wouldest not obey the voice of the LORD thy God.

63 And it shall come to pass, *that* as the LORD [o] rejoiced over you to do you good, and to multiply you; so the LORD [p] will rejoice over you to destroy you, and to bring you to naught; and ye shall be plucked from off the

[a] Lev. xxvi. 29; 2 Kings vi. 28, 29; Jer. xix. 9; Lam. ii. 20; iv. 10; Bar. ii. 3.——[b] Heb. *belly*.——[c] Chap. xv. 9.——[d] Chap. xiii. 6.——[e] Ver. 54.——[f] Heb. *after-birth*.——[g] Gen. xlix. 10.

[h] Exod. vi. 3.——[i] Dan. ix. 12.——[k] Chap. vii. 15.——[l] Heb. *cause to ascend*.——[m] Chap. iv 27.——[n] Chap. x. 22; Neh. ix. 23.——[o] Chap. xxx. 9; Jer. xxxii. 41.——[p] Prov. i. 26; Isa. i. 24.

around thee, viz., lines of circumvallation, as our Lord predicted; (see Matt. xxiv. 1, &c., and Luke xxi. 5, &c.;) *in all thy gates throughout all thy land*—all thy *fenced* cities, which points out that their subjugation should be complete, as both Jerusalem and all their fortified places should be taken. This was done literally by Nebuchadnezzar and the Romans.

Verse 56. *The tender and delicate woman*] This was literally fulfilled when Jerusalem was besieged by the Romans; a woman named Mary, of a noble family, driven to distraction by famine, boiled and ate her own child! See a similar case 2 Kings vi. 29; and see on Lev. xxvi. 29.

Verse 57. *Toward her young one—and toward her children which she shall bear*] There seems to be a species of *tautology* in the two clauses of this verse, which may be prevented by translating the last word, שליתה *shilyathah*, literally, *her secondines*, which is the meaning of the Arabic سلا *sala*, not badly understood by the Septuagint, *χοριον αυτης*, the *chorion* or exterior membrane, which invests the fœtus in the womb; and still better translated by *Luther*, die after geburth, the *after-birth*; which saying of Moses strongly marks the deepest distress, when the mother is represented as feeling the most poignant regret that her child was brought forth into such a state of suffering and death; and 2dly, that it was likely, from the favourable circumstances *after the birth*, that *she herself* should survive her *inlaying*. No words can more forcibly depict the miseries of those dreadful times. On this ground I see no absolute need for Kennicott's criticism, who, instead of ובשליתה *ubeshilyathah*, *against her secondines*, reads ובשלה *ubashelah*, *and she shall boil*, and translates the 56th and 57th verses as follows: "The tender and delicate woman among you, who would not adventure to set the sole of her foot upon the ground for delicateness and tenderness, her eye shall be evil toward the husband of her bosom, and toward her son, and toward her daughter. 57. *And she shall boil* that which cometh out from between her feet, *even her children* which she shall bear, for she shall eat them, for want of all things, secretly." These words, says he, being prophetical, are fulfilled in 2 Kings vi. 29, for we read there that two women of Samaria having agreed to eat their own children, one was actually *boiled*, where the very same word, בשל *bashal*, is used. See Kennicott's Dissertations on 1 Chron. xi., &c., p. 421.

A. M. 2553.
B. C. 1451.
An. Ex. Isr. 40.
Sebat.

land whither thou goest to possess it.

64 And the LORD [q] shall scatter thee among all people, from the one end of the earth even unto the other; and [r] there thou shalt serve other gods, which neither thou nor thy fathers have known, *even* wood and stone.

65 And [s] among these nations shalt thou find no ease, neither shall the sole of thy foot have rest: [t] but the LORD shall give thee there a trembling heart, and failing of eyes, and [u] sorrow of mind:

66 And thy life shall hang in doubt before thee; and thou shalt fear day and night, and shalt have none assurance of thy life:

67 [v] In the morning thou shalt say, Would God it were even! and at even thou shalt say, Would God it were morning! for the fear of thine heart wherewith thou shalt fear, and [w] for the sight of thine eyes which thou shalt see.

68 And the LORD [x] shall bring thee into Egypt again with ships, by the way whereof I spake unto thee, [y] Thou shalt see it no more again: and there ye shall be sold unto your enemies for bondmen and bondwomen, and no man shall buy *you*.

[q] Lev. xxvi. 33; chap. iv. 27, 28; Neh. i. 8; Jer. xvi. 13. — [r] Ver. 36. — [s] Amos ix. 4. — [t] Lev. xxvi. 36. — [u] Lev. xxvi. 16. — [v] Job vii. 4. — [w] Ver. 34. — [x] Jer. xliv. 7; Hos. viii. 13; ix. 3. — [y] Chap. xvii. 16.

Verse 64. *The Lord shall scatter thee among all people*] How literally has this been fulfilled! The people of the Jews are scattered over every nation under heaven.

Verse 65. *No ease—a trembling heart, and failing of eyes*] The *trembling of heart* may refer to their state of continual *insecurity*, being, under every kind of government, proscribed, and, even under the most mild, uncertain of toleration and protection; and the *failing of eyes*, to their vain and ever-disappointed expectation of the Messiah.

Verse 68. *And the Lord shall bring thee into Egypt again*] That is, into *another state of slavery and bondage* similar to that of Egypt, out of which they had been lately brought. *And there ye shall be sold*, that is, *be exposed to sale*, or *expose yourselves to sale*, as the word התמכרתם *hithmaccartem* may be rendered; they were vagrants, and wished to become slaves that they might be provided with the necessaries of life. *And no man shall buy you;* even the Romans thought it a reproach to have a *Jew* for a *slave*, they had become so despicable to all mankind. When Jerusalem was taken by Titus, many of the captives, which were above seventeen years of age, were sent into the works in Egypt. See Josephus, Antiq., b. xii., c. 1, 2, War, b. vi., c. 9, s. 2; and above all, see *Bp. Newton's Dissertations on the Prophecies.*

THE first verse of the next chapter, in some of the most correct Hebrew Bibles, makes the 69th of this; and very properly, as the second verse of the following chapter begins a new subject.

This is an astonishing chapter: in it are prophecies delivered more than 3,000 years ago, and now fulfilling.

O God, how immense is thy wisdom, and how profound thy counsels! To thee alone are known all thy works from the beginning to the end. What an irrefragable proof does this chapter, compared with the past and present state of the Jewish people, afford of the truth and Divine origin of the Pentateuch!

CHAPTER XXIX.

A recapitulation of God's gracious dealings with Israel, 1–8. *An exhortation to obedience, and to enter into covenant with their God, that they and their posterity may be established in the good land,* 9–15. *They are to remember the abominations of Egypt, and to avoid them,* 16, 17. *He who hardens his heart, when he hears these curses, shall be utterly consumed,* 18–21. *Their posterity shall be astonished at the desolations that shall fall upon them,* 22, 23; *shall inquire the reason, and shall be informed that the Lord has done thus to them because of their disobedience and idolatry,* 24–28. *A caution against prying too curiously into the secrets of the Divine providence, and to be contented with what God has revealed,* 29.

A. M. 2553.
B. C. 1451.
An. Ex. Isr. 40.
Sebat.

THESE *are* the words of the covenant, which the LORD commanded Moses to make with the children of Israel, in the land of Moab, beside [a] the covenant which he made with them in Horeb.

2 And Moses called unto all Israel, and said unto them, [b] Ye have seen all

[a] Chap. v. 2, 3. — [b] Exod. xix. 4.

NOTES ON CHAP. XXIX.

Verse 1. *These are the words of the covenant*] This verse seems properly to belong to the preceding chapter, as a widely different subject is taken up at ver. 2 of this; and it is distinguished as the 69th verse in some of the most correct copies of the Hebrew Bible.

Commanded Moses to make] לכרת *lichroth, to cut,* alluding to the covenant sacrifice which was offered

A. M. 2553.
B. C. 1451.
An. Ex. Isr. 40.
Sebat.

that the Lord did before your eyes in the land of Egypt unto Pharaoh, and unto all his servants, and unto all his land;

3 [c] The great temptations which thine eyes have seen, the signs, and those great miracles:

4 Yet [d] the Lord hath not given you a heart to perceive, and eyes to see, and ears to hear, unto this day.

5 [e] And I have led you forty years in the wilderness: [f] your clothes are not waxen old upon you, and thy shoe is not waxen old upon thy foot.

6 [g] Ye have not eaten bread, neither have ye drunk wine or strong drink: that ye might know that I *am* the Lord your God.

7 And when ye came unto this place, [h] Sihon the king of Heshbon, and Og the king of Bashan, came out against us unto battle, and we smote them:

8 And we took their land, and [i] gave it for an inheritance unto the Reubenites, and to the Gadites, and to the half tribe of Manasseh.

A. M. 2553.
B. C. 1451.
An. Ex. Isr. 40.
Sebat.

9 [k] Keep therefore the words of this covenant, and do them, that ye may [l] prosper in all that ye do.

10 Ye stand this day all of you before the Lord your God; your captains of your tribes, your elders, and your officers, *with* all the men of Israel,

11 Your little ones, your wives, and thy stranger that *is* in thy camp, from [m] the hewer of thy wood unto the drawer of thy water:

12 That thou shouldest [n] enter into cove nant with the Lord thy God, and [o] into his oath, which the Lord thy God maketh with thee this day:

13 That he may [p] establish thee to-day for a people unto himself, and *that* he may be unto thee a God, [q] as he hath said unto thee, and [r] as he hath sworn unto thy fathers, to Abra ham, to Isaac, and to Jacob.

14 Neither with you only [s] do I make this covenant and this oath;

[c] Chap. iv. 34; vii. 19.——[d] See Isa. vi. 9, 10; lxiii. 17; John viii. 43; Acts xxviii. 26, 27; Eph. iv. 18; 2 Thess. ii. 11, 12.——[e] Chap. i. 3; viii. 2.——[f] Chap. viii. 4.——[g] See Exod. xvi. 12; chap. viii. 3; Psa. lxxviii. 24, 25.——[h] Num. xxi. 23, 24, 33; chap. ii. 32; iii. 1.

[i] Num. xxxii. 33; chap. iii. 12, 13.——[k] Chap. iv. 6; Josh. i. 7; 1 Kings ii. 3.——[l] Josh. i. 7.——[m] See Joshua ix. 21, 23, 27.——[n] Heb. *pass.*——[o] Neh. x. 29.——[p] Chap. xxviii. 9.——[q] Exod. vi. 7.——[r] Genesis xvii. 7.——[s] Jer. xxxi. 31, 32, 33; Heb. viii. 7, 8.

on the occasion and *divided*, as is explained, Gen. xv. 18.

Beside the covenant which he made—in Horeb.] What is mentioned here is an additional institution to the *ten words* given on Horeb; and the curses denounced here are different from those denounced against the transgressors of the decalogue.

Verse 4. *The Lord hath not given you a heart, &c.*] Some critics read this verse interrogatively: *And hath not God given you a heart, &c.*? because they suppose that God could not reprehend them for the non-performance of a duty, when he had neither given them a mind to perceive the obligation of it, nor strength to perform it, had that obligation been known. Though this is strictly just, yet there is no need for the interrogation, as the words only imply that *they had not such a heart*, &c., not because God had not given them all the means of knowledge, and helps of his grace and Spirit, which were necessary; but they had not made a faithful use of their advantages, and therefore they had not that wise, loving, and obedient heart which they otherwise might have had. If they had had such a heart, it would have been God's gift, for he is the author of all good; and that they had not such a heart was a proof that they had grieved his Spirit, and abused the grace which he had afforded them to produce that gracious change, the want of which is here deplored. Hence God himself is represented as grieved because they were unchanged and disobedient: "O that there were such a heart in them, that they would fear me, and keep all my commandments always, that it might be well with them and with their children for ever!" See chap. v. 29, and the note there.

Verse 5. *Your clothes are not waxen old*] See on chap. viii. 4.

Verse 6. *Ye have not eaten bread, &c.*] That is, ye have not been supported in an ordinary providential way; I have been continually working *miracles* for you, *that ye might know that I am the Lord.* Thus we find that God had furnished them with all the means of this knowledge, and that the means were ineffectual, not because they were not properly calculated to answer God's gracious purpose, but because the people were not workers with God; consequently they received the grace of God in vain. See 2 Cor. vi. 1.

Verse 10. *Ye stand—all of you before the Lord*] They were about to enter into a covenant with God; and as a covenant implies *two parties contracting*, God is represented as being present, and they and all their families, old and young, come before him.

Verse 12. *That thou shouldest enter*] לעבר *leaber, to pass through*, that is, between the *separated* parts of the covenant sacrifice. See Gen. xv. 18.

And into his oath] Thus we find that in a covenant were these *seven* particulars: 1. The parties about to contract were considered as being hitherto *separated*. 2. They now agree to enter into a state of *close* and *permanent amity*. 3. They *meet together* in a solemn manner for this purpose. 4. A *sacrifice* is offered to God on the occasion, for the whole is a religious act.

A. M. 2553.
B. C. 1451.
An. Ex. Isr. 40.
Sebat.

15 But with *him* that standeth here with us this day before the LORD our God, [t] and also with *him* that *is* not here with us this day:

16 (For ye know how we have dwelt in the land of Egypt; and how we came through the nations which ye passed by;

17 And ye have seen their abominations, and their [u] idols, wood and stone, silver and gold, which *were* among them:)

18 Lest there should be among you man, woman, or family, or tribe, [v] whose heart turneth away this day from the LORD our God, to go *and* serve the gods of these nations; [w] lest there should be among you a root that beareth [x] gall [y] and wormwood;

19 And it come to pass, when he heareth the words of this curse, that he bless himself in his heart, saying, I shall have peace, though I walk [z] in the [a] imagination of mine heart, [b] to add [c] drunkenness to thirst:

20 [d] The LORD will not spare him, but then [e] the anger of the LORD and [f] his jealousy shall smoke against that man, and all the curses that are written in this book shall lie upon him, and the LORD [g] shall blot out his name from under heaven.

21 And the LORD [h] shall separate him unto evil out of all the tribes of Israel, according to all the curses of the covenant that [i] are written in this book of the law:

22 So that the generation to come of your children that shall rise up after you, and the stranger that shall come from a far land, shall say, when they see the plagues of that land, and the sicknesses [k] which the LORD hath laid upon it;

A. M. 2553.
B. C. 1451.
An. Ex. Isr. 40.
Sebat.

23 *And that* the whole land thereof *is* brimstone, [l] and salt, *and* burning, *that* it is not sown, nor beareth, nor any grass groweth therein, [m] like the overthrow of Sodom, and Gomorrah, Admah, and Zeboim, which the LORD overthrew in his anger, and in his wrath:

24 Even all nations shall say, [n] Wherefore hath the LORD done thus unto this land? what *meaneth* the heat of this great anger?

25 Then men shall say, Because they have forsaken the covenant of the LORD God of their fathers, which he made with them when he brought them forth out of the land of Egypt:

26 For they went and served other gods, and worshipped them, gods whom they knew not, and [o] *whom* he had not [p] given unto them:

27 And the anger of the LORD was kindled against this land, [q] to bring upon it all the curses that are written in this book:

28 And the LORD [r] rooted them out of their land in anger, and in wrath, and in great indignation, and cast them into another land, as *it is* this day.

29 The secret *things belong* unto the LORD our God: but those *things which are* revealed *belong* unto us and to our children for ever, that *we* may do all the words of this law.

---

[t] See Acts ii. 39; 1 Cor. vii. 14.——[u] Heb. *dungy gods.*——[v] Ch. xi. 16.——[w] Acts viii. 23; Heb. xii. 15.——[x] Or, *a poisonful herb.*——[y] Heb. *rosh.*——[z] Num. xv. 39; Eccles. xi. 9.——[a] Or, *stubbornness;* Jer. iii. 17; vii. 24.——[b] Isa. xxx. 1.——[c] Heb. *the drunken to the thirsty.*——[d] Ezek. xiv. 7, 8.——[e] Psa. lxxiv. 1. Psa. lxxix. 5; Ezek. xxiii. 25.——[g] Chap. ix. 14.

[h] Matt. xxiv. 51.——[i] Heb. *is written.*——[k] Heb. *wherewith the LORD hath made it sick.*——[l] Psa. cvii. 34; Jer. xvii. 6; Zeph. ii. 9.——[m] Gen. xix. 24, 25; Jer. xx. 16.——[n] 1 Kings ix. 8, 9; Jer. xxii. 8, 9.——[o] Or, who *had not given to them* any portion. [p] Heb. *divided.*——[q] Dan. ix. 11, 13, 14.——[r] 1 Kings xiv. 15; 2 Chron. vii. 20; Psa. lii. 5; Prov. ii. 22.

. The victim is *separated* exactly into *two equal parts,* the separation being in the direction of the *spine;* and these parts are laid opposite to each other, sufficient room being allowed for the contracting parties to pass between them. 6. The contracting parties *meet in the victim,* and the conditions of the covenant by which they are to be mutually bound are recited. 7. An *oath* is taken by these parties that they shall punctually and faithfully perform their respective conditions, and thus the covenant is made and ratified. See Jer. xxxiv. 18, 19, and the notes on Gen. vi. 18; xv. 18; Exod. xxix. 45; Lev. xxvi.

Verse 15. Him *that standeth here*] The present generation. Him *that is not here*—all future generations of this people.

Verse 18. *A root that beareth gall and wormwood*] That is, as the apostle expresses it, Heb. iii. 12, *An evil heart of unbelief departing from the living God;* for to this place he evidently refers. It may also signify *false doctrines,* or *idolatrous persons* among themselves.

Verse 19. *To add drunkenness to thirst*] A proverbial expression denoting the utmost indulgence in all sensual gratifications.

Verse 26. *Gods*—whom *he had not given unto them*] This is an unhappy translation. *Houbigant* renders the original words ולא חלק להם *velo chalak lahem, et quibuscum nulla eis societas,* "And with whom they had no society;" and falls unmercifully on *Le Clerc* because he had translated it, From *whom they had received no benefits.* I must differ from both these great men, because I think they differ from the text. חלק *chalak* signifies a *portion, lot, inheritance,* and God is frequently represented in Scripture as the *portion* or *inheritance* of his people. Here, therefore, I think

the original should be rendered, *And there was no portion to them*, that is, the gods they served could neither supply their wants nor save their souls—*they were no portion.*

Verse 29. *The secret things belong unto the Lord, &c.*] This verse has been variously translated. Houbigant renders it thus : *Quæ apud Dominum nostrum abscondita sunt, nobis ea filiisque nostris palam facta sunt ad multas ætates,* "The things which were hidden with the Lord our God, are made manifest to us and our children for many generations." I am not satisfied with this interpretation, and find that the passage was not so understood by any of the ancient versions. The simple general meaning seems to be this : "What God has thought proper to reveal, he has revealed ; what he has revealed is essential to the wellbeing of man, and this revelation is intended not for the *present time* merely, nor for *one people,* but for all succeeding generations. The things which he has not

revealed concern not man but God alone, and are therefore not to be inquired after." Thus, then, *the things that are hidden belong unto the Lord, those that are revealed belong unto us and our children.* But possibly the words here refer to the subjects of these chapters, as if he had said, "Apostasy from God and his truth is possible. When a national apostasy among us may take place, is known only to God ; but he has revealed himself to us and our children that we may do all the words of this law, and so prevent the dreadful evils that shall fall on the disobedient."

The Jews have always considered these verses as containing subjects of the highest importance to them, and have affixed marks to the original, לָנוּ וּלְבָנֵינוּ *lanu ulebaneynu,* "to us and to our CHILDREN," in order to fix the attention of the reader on truths which affect them individually, and not them only, but the whole of their posterity.

CHAPTER XXX.

Gracious promises are given to the penitent, 1–6. The Lord will circumcise their heart, and put all these curses on their enemies, if they hearken to his voice and keep his testimonies, 7–10. The word is near to them, and easy to be understood, 11–14. Life and death, a blessing and a curse, are set before them : and they are exhorted to love the Lord, obey his voice, and cleave unto him, that they may inherit the land promised to Abraham, 15–20.

A. M. 2553.
B. C. 1451.
An. Ex. Isr. 40.
Sebat.

AND [a] it shall come to pass, when [b] all these things are come upon thee, the blessing and the curse, which I have set before thee, and [c] thou shalt call *them* to mind among all the nations, whither the LORD thy God hath driven thee,

2 And shalt [d] return unto the LORD thy God, and shalt obey his voice, according to all that I command thee this day, thou and thy children, with all thine heart, and with all thy soul ;

3 [e] That then the LORD thy God will turn thy captivity, and have compassion upon thee,

and will return and [f] gather thee from all the nations, whither the LORD thy God hath scattered thee.

A. M. 2553.
B. C. 1451.
An. Ex. Isr. 40.
Sebat.

4 [g] If *any* of thine be driven out unto the outmost *parts* of heaven, from thence will the LORD thy God gather thee, and from thence will he fetch thee :

5 And the LORD thy God will bring thee into the land which thy fathers possessed, and thou shalt possess it ; and he will do thee good, and multiply thee above thy fathers.

6 And [h] the LORD thy God will circumcise thine heart, and the heart of thy seed, to love

[a] Lev. xxvi. 40.——[b] Chap. xxviii.——[c] Chap. iv. 29, 30 ; 1 Kings viii. 47, 48.——[d] Neh. i. 9 ; Isa. lv. 7 ; Lam. iii. 40 ; Joel ii. 12, 13.——[e] Psa. cvi. 45 ; cxxvi. 1, 4 ; Jer. xxix. 14 ; Lam. iii. 22, 32.——[f] Psa. cxlvii. 2 ; Jer. xxxii. 37 ; Ezek. xxxiv. 13 ; xxxvi. 24.——[g] Chap. xxviii. 64 ; Neh. i. 9.——[h] Chap. x. 16 ; Jer. xxxii. 39 ; Ezek. xi. 19 ; xxxvi. 26.

NOTES ON CHAP. XXX.

Verse 1. *When all these things are come upon thee, the blessing and the curse*] So fully did God foresee the bad use these people would make of their free agency in resisting the Holy Ghost, that he speaks of their sin and punishment as certain ; yet, at the same time, shows how they might turn to *himself* and live, even while he was pouring out his indignation upon them because of their transgressions.

Verse 3. *Gather thee from all the nations*] This must refer to a more extensive captivity than that which they suffered in Babylon.

Verse 5. *Will bring thee into the land*] As this promise refers to a return from a captivity in which they had been scattered among all nations, conse-

quently it is not the Babylonish captivity which is intended ; and the repossession of their land must be different from that which was consequent on their return from Chaldea.

Verse 6. *God will circumcise thine heart*] This promise remains yet to be fulfilled. Their heart, as a people, has never yet been circumcised ; nor have the various promises in this chapter been ever yet fulfilled. There *remaineth,* therefore, a rest for this people of God. Now, as the *law,* properly speaking, made no provision for the circumcision of the heart, which implies the *remission of sins,* and purification of the soul from all unrighteousness ; and as circumcision itself was only a sign of spiritual good, consequently the promise here refers to the days of the Messiah, and to

A. M. 2553. B. C. 1451. An. Ex. Isr. 40. Sebat.

the Lord thy God with all thine heart, and with all thy soul, that thou mayest live.

7 And the Lord thy God will put all these curses upon thine enemies, and on them that hate thee, which persecuted thee.

8 And thou shalt return and obey the voice of the Lord, and do all his commandments which I command thee this day.

9 [i] And the Lord thy God will make thee plenteous in every work of thine hand, in the fruit of thy body, and in the fruit of thy cattle, and in the fruit of thy land, for good: for the Lord will again [k] rejoice over thee for good, as he rejoiced over thy fathers:

10 If thou shalt hearken unto the voice of the Lord thy God, to keep his commandments and his statutes which are written in this book of the law, *and* if thou turn unto the Lord thy God with all thine heart, and with all thy soul.

11 For this commandment which I command thee this day, [l] it *is* not hidden from thee, neither *is* it far off.

12 [m] It *is* not in heaven, that thou shouldest say, Who shall go up for us to heaven, and bring it unto us, that we may hear it, and do it?

13 Neither *is* it beyond the sea, that thou shouldest say, Who shall go over the sea for us, and bring it unto us, that we may hear it, and do it?

14 But the word *is* very nigh unto thee, in thy mouth, and in thy heart, that thou mayest do it.

15 See, [n] I have set before thee this day life and good, and death and evil;

16 In that I command thee this day to love the Lord thy God, to walk in his ways, and to keep his commandments and his statutes and his judgments, that thou mayest live and multiply: and the Lord thy God shall bless thee in the land whither thou goest to possess it.

17 But if thine heart turn away, so that thou wilt not hear, but shall be drawn away, and worship other gods, and serve them;

18 [o] I denounce unto you this day, that ye shall surely perish, *and that* ye shall not prolong *your* days upon the land, whither thou passest over Jordan to go to possess it.

[i] Chap. xxviii. 11.——[k] Chap. xxxviii. 63; Jer. xxii. 41. [l] Isa. xlv. 19.——[m] Rom. x. 6, &c.——[n] Ver. 1, 19; chap. xi. 26.——[o] Chap. iv. 26; viii. 19.

this all the prophets and all the apostles give witness: "for circumcision is that of the heart, in the spirit, and not in the letter," Rom. ii. 29; and the genuine followers of God "are circumcised with the circumcision made *without hands*—by the circumcision of Christ," Col. ii. 11, 12. Hence we see these promises cannot be fulfilled to the Jews but in their embracing the Gospel of Christ. To look, therefore, for their restoration is idle and nugatory, while their obstinacy and unbelief remain.

Verse 11. *This commandment—is not hidden*] Not too *wonderful* or difficult for thee to comprehend or perform, as the word נפלאת *niphleth* implies. *Neither is it far off*—the *word* or *doctrine* of salvation shall be proclaimed in your own land; for He is to be born in *Bethlehem of Judah*, who is to *feed* and *save Israel;* and the Prophet who is to teach them is to be raised up from *among their brethren.*

Verse 12. *It is not in heaven*] Shall not be communicated in that way in which the prophets received the living oracles; but the word shall *be made flesh, and dwell among you.*

Verse 13. *Neither is it beyond the sea*] Ye shall not be obliged to travel for it to distant nations, because *salvation is of the* Jews.

Verse 14. *But the word is very nigh unto thee*] The doctrine of salvation preached by the apostles; *in thy mouth*, the promises of redemption made by the prophets forming a part of every Jew's creed; *in thy heart*—the power to believe with the heart unto righteousness, that the tongue may make confession unto salvation. In this way, it is evident, St. Paul understood these passages; see Rom. x. 6, &c.

Verse 15. *Life and good*] Present and future blessings.

Death and evil] Present and future miseries: termed, ver. 19, *Life and death, blessing and cursing.* And why were these *set before them?* 1. That they might *comprehend* their import. 2. That they might *feel* their importance. 3. That they might *choose life*, and the path of believing, loving obedience, that led to it. 4. That they and their posterity, thus choosing life and refusing evil, might be the *favourites of God* in time and eternity.

Were there no such thing as *free will* in man, who could reconcile these sayings either with sincerity or common sense? God has made the human will *free*, and there is no power or influence either in heaven, earth, or hell, except the power of God, that can deprive it of its *free volitions;* of its power to *will* and *nill*, to *choose* and *refuse*, to *act* or *not act;* or force it to sin against God. Hence man is accountable for his actions, because they are *his;* were he necessitated by fate, or sovereign constraint, they could not be *his.* Hence he is rewardable, hence he is punishable. God, in his creation, *willed that the human creature should be free*, and he formed his soul accordingly; and the Law and Gospel, the promise and precept, the denunciation of wo and the doctrine of eternal life, are all constructed on this ground; that is, they all necessarily

A. M. 2553. B. C. 1451. An. Ex. Isr. 40. Sebat.

19 [p] I call heaven and earth to record this day against you, *that* [q] I have set before you life and death, blessing and cursing: therefore choose life, that both thou and thy seed may live.

20 That thou mayest love the LORD thy God, *and* that thou mayest obey his voice, and that thou mayest cleave unto him: for he *is* thy [r] life, and the length of [s] thy days: that thou mayest dwell in the land which the LORD sware unto thy fathers, to Abraham, to Isaac and to Jacob, to give them.

[p] Chap. iv. 26; xxxi. 28.——[q] Ver. 15.——[r] Psa. xxvii. 1; lxvi. 9; John xi. 25.——[s] Chap. iv. 40; xi. 9; xii. 10.

suppose the *freedom* of the *human will:* nor could it be *will* if it were not *free*, because the principle of *freedom* or *liberty* is necessarily implied in the idea of *volition*. See on the fifth chapter and 29th verse.

Verse 19. See the note on the preceding verse.

Verse 20. *That thou mayest love the Lord*] Without *love* there can be no *obedience*.

Obey his voice] Without *obedience* love is *fruitless* and dead.

And—cleave unto him] Without *close attachment* and *perseverance*, temporary love, however sincere and fervent—temporary obedience, however disinterested, energetic, and pure while it lasts—will be ultimately ineffectual. He alone who *endures to the end, shall be saved*. Reader, how do matters stand between God and thy soul? He cannot persevere in the grace of God whose soul is not yet made a partaker of that grace. Many talk strenuously on the impossibility of falling from grace, who have not yet tasted that the Lord is gracious. How absurd to talk and dispute about the infallibility of arriving safely at the end of a way in which a man has never yet taken one hearty step! It is never among those that have the grace of God, but among those that have it not, that we find an overweening confidence.

CHAPTER XXXI.

Moses, being one hundred and twenty years old and about to die, calls the people together, and exhorts them to courage and obedience, 1–6. *Delivers a charge to Joshua,* 7, 8. *Delivers the law which he had written to the priests, with a solemn charge that they should read it every seventh year, publicly to all the people,* 9–13. *The Lord calls Moses and Joshua to the tabernacle,* 14. *He appears to them, informs Moses of his approaching death, and delivers to him a prophetical and historical song, or poem, which he is to leave with Israel, for their instruction and reproof,* 15–21. *Moses writes the song the same day, and teaches it to the Israelites,* 22; *gives Joshua a charge,* 23; *finishes writing the book of the law,* 24. *Commands the Levites to lay it up in the side of the ark,* 25, 26. *Predicts their rebellions,* 27. *Orders the elders to be gathered together, and shows them what evils would befall the people in the latter days,* 28, 29, *and repeats the song to them,* 30.

A. M. 2553. B. C. 1451. An. Ex. Isr. 40. Sebat.

AND Moses went and spake these words unto all Israel.

2 And he said unto them, I [a] *am* a hundred and twenty years old this day; I can no more [b] go out and come in: also the LORD hath said unto me, [c] Thou shalt not go over this Jordan.

3 The LORD thy God, [d] he will go over before thee, *and* he will destroy these nations from before thee, and thou shalt possess them: *and* Joshua, he shall go over before thee, [e] as the LORD hath said.

4 [f] And the LORD shall do unto them [g] as he did to Sihon and to Og, kings of the Amorites; and unto the land of them whom he destroyed.

5 And [h] the LORD shall give them up before your face, that ye may do unto them according unto all the commandments which I have commanded you.

6 [i] Be strong and of a good courage, [k] fear

[a] Exodus vii. 7; chap. xxxiv. 7.——[b] Numbers xxvii. 17; 1 Kings iii. 7.——[c] Numbers xx. 12; xxvii. 13; chap. iii. 27.——[d] Chap. ix. 3.——[e] Num. xxvii. 21; chap. iii. 28.——[f] Chap. iii. 21.——[g] Num. xxi. 24, 33.——[h] Chap. vii. 2.——[i] Josh. x. 25; 1 Chron. xxii. 13.——[k] Chap. i. 29; vii. 18.

NOTES ON CHAP. XXXI.

Verse 2. *I am a hundred and twenty years old*] The life of Moses, the great prophet of God and lawgiver of the Jews, was exactly the same in length as the time Noah employed in preaching righteousness to the antediluvian world. These *one hundred and twenty* years were divided into three remarkable periods: *forty* years he lived in *Egypt*, in Pharaoh's court, acquiring all the learning and wisdom of the Egyptians; (see Acts vii. 20, 23;) *forty years* he sojourned in the land of *Midian* in a state of preparation for his great and important mission; (Acts vii. 29, 30;) and *forty years* he guided, led, and governed the Israelites under the express direction and authority of God: in all, *one hundred and twenty years*.

Verse 3. *Joshua, he shall go over before thee*] See on Num. xxvii. 17, &c.

Verse 6. *Be strong*] חזקו *chizku*, the same word

A. M. 2553.
B. C. 1451.
An. Ex. Isr. 40.
Sebat.

not, nor be afraid of them: for
the LORD thy God, [l] he *it is* that
doth go with thee; [m] he will not
fail thee, nor forsake thee.
7 And Moses called unto Joshua, and said
unto him in the sight of all Israel, [n] Be strong
and of a good courage: for thou must go with
this people unto the land which the LORD
hath sworn unto their fathers to give them;
and thou shalt cause them to inherit it.
8 And the LORD, [o] he *it is* that doth go before thee; [p] he will be with thee, he will not
fail thee, neither forsake thee: fear not, neither
be dismayed.
9 And Moses wrote this law, [q] and delivered
it unto the priests the sons of Levi, [r] which
bare the ark of the covenant of the LORD, and
unto all the elders of Israel.
10 And Moses commanded them, saying,
At the end of *every* seven years, in the solemnity of the [s] year of release, [t] in the feast of
tabernacles,
11 When all Israel is come to
[u] appear before the LORD thy God
in the place which he shall choose,
[v] thou shalt read this law before all Israel in
their hearing.
12 [w] Gather the people together, men, and
women, and children, and thy stranger that *is*
within thy gates, that they may hear, and that
they may learn, and fear the LORD your God,
and observe to do all the words of this law:
13 And *that* their children, [x] which have not
known *any thing*, [y] may hear, and learn to fear
the LORD your God, as long as ye live in the
land whither ye go over Jordan to possess it.
14 And the LORD said unto Moses, [z] Behold, thy days approach that thou must die:
call Joshua, and present yourselves in the tabernacle of the congregation, that [a] I may give
him a charge. And Moses and Joshua went
and presented themselves in the tabernacle of
the congregation.
15 And [b] the LORD appeared in the taber

A. M. 2553.
B. C. 1451.
An. Ex. Isr. 40
Sebat.

[l] Chap. xx. 4.—[m] Josh. i, 5; Heb. xiii. 5.—[n] Ver. 23; chap. i. 38; iii. 28; Josh. i. 6.—[o] Exod. xiii. 21, 22; xxxiii. 24; chap. ix. 3.—[p] Josh. i. 5, 9; 1 Chron. xxviii. 20.—[q] Ver. 25; chap. xvii. 18.—[r] Num. iv. 15; Josh. iii. 3; 1 Chron. xv. 12, 15.

[s] Chap. xv. 1.—[t] Lev. xxiii. 34.—[u] Chap. xvi. 16.—[v] Josh. viii. 34, 35; 2 Kings xxiii. 2; Neh. viii. 1, 2, 3, &c.—[w] Chap. iv. 10.—[x] Chap. xi. 2.—[y] Psa. lxxviii. 6, 7.—[z] Num. xxvii. 13; xxxiv. 5.—[a] Ver. 23; Num. xxvii. 19.—[b] Exod. xxxiii. 9.

that is used Exod. iv. 21, ix. 15, for *hardening* Pharaoh's heart. See the notes there. The Septuagint, in this and the following verse, have, *Ανδριζου και ισχυε*, *Play the man, and be strong;* and from this St. Paul seems to have borrowed his ideas, 1 Cor. xvi. 13: *Στηκετε εν τη πιστει· ανδριζεσθε, κρατιουσθε*: *Stand firm in the faith; play the man*—act like heroes; *be vigorous.*

Verse 8. *The Lord—doth go before thee*] To prepare thy way, and to direct thee.

He will be with thee] Accompany thee in all thy journeys, and assist thee in all thy enterprises.

He will not fail thee] Thy expectation, however strong and extensive, shall never be disappointed: thou canst not expect too much from him.

Neither forsake thee] He knows that without him thou canst do nothing, and therefore he will continue with thee, and in such a manner too that the excellence of the power shall appear to be of *him*, and not of *man*.

Verse 9. *Moses wrote this law*] Not the whole Pentateuch, but either the discourses and precepts mentioned in the preceding chapters, or the book of *Deuteronomy*, which is most likely.

Some of the rabbins have pretended that Moses wrote *thirteen* copies of the whole Pentateuch; that he gave one to each of the twelve tribes, and the thirteenth was laid up by the ark. This opinion deserves little credit. Some think that he wrote *two* copies, one of which he gave to the priests and Levites for general use, according to what is said in this verse, the other to be laid up beside the ark as a standard copy for reference, and to be a witness against the people should they break it or become idolatrous. This second copy is supposed to be intended ver. 26. As the law was properly a covenant or contract between God and the people, it is natural to suppose there were two copies of it, that each of the contracting parties might have one: therefore one was laid up beside the ark, this was the Lord's copy; another was given to the priests and Levites, this was the people's copy.

Verse 10, 11. *At the end of* every *seven years—thou shalt read this law*] Every *seventh year* was a year of *release*, chap. xv. 1, at which time the people's minds, being under a peculiar degree of solemnity, were better disposed to hear and profit by the words of God. I suppose on this ground also that the whole book of *Deuteronomy* is meant, as it alone contains an epitome of the whole Pentateuch. And in this way some of the chief Jewish rabbins understand this place.

It is strange that this commandment, relative to a *public* reading of the law every seven years, should have been rarely attended to. It does not appear that from the time mentioned Josh. viii. 30, at which time this public reading first took place, till the reign of *Jehoshaphat*, 2 Chron. xvii. 7, there was any public seventh year reading—a period of 530 years. The next seventh year reading was not till the eighteenth year of the reign of *Josiah*, 2 Chron. xxxiv. 30, a space of *two hundred* and *eighty-two* years. Nor do we find any other publicly mentioned from this time till the return from the Babylonish captivity, Neh.

A. M. 2553.
B. C. 1451.
An. Ex. Isr. 40.
Sebat.

nacle in a pillar of a cloud: and
the pillar of the cloud stood over
the door of the tabernacle.
16 And the LORD said unto Moses, Behold,
thou shalt [c] sleep with thy fathers; and this
people will [d] rise up, and [e] go a whoring after
the gods of the strangers of the land, whither
they go *to be* among them; and will [f] forsake
me, and [g] break my covenant which I have
made with them.
17 Then my anger shall be kindled against
them in that day, and [h] I will forsake them,
and I will [i] hide my face from them, and they
shall be devoured, and many evils and troubles
shall [k] befall them; so that they will say in
that day, [l] Are not these evils come upon us
because our God *is* [m] not among us?
18 And [n] I will surely hide my face in that
day for all the evils which they shall have
wrought, in that they are turned unto other
gods.
19 Now therefore write ye this song for you,
and teach it the children of Israel: put it in
their mouths, that this song may be [o] a witness
for me against the children of Israel.
20 For when I shall have brought them into
the land which I sware unto their fathers,
that floweth with milk and honey; and they
shall have eaten and filled themselves, [p] and
waxen fat; [q] then will they turn
unto other gods, and serve them,
and provoke me, and break my
covenant.

A. M. 2553.
B. C. 1451.
An. Ex. Isr. 40.
Sebat.

21 And it shall come to pass, [r] when many
evils and troubles are befallen them, that this
song shall testify [s] against them as a witness;
for it shall not be forgotten out of the mouths
of their seed: for [t] I know their imagination
[u] which [v] they go about, even now, before I
have brought them into the land which I
sware.
22 Moses therefore wrote this song the same
day, and taught it the children of Israel.
23 [w] And he gave Joshua the son of Nun a
charge, and said, [x] Be strong, and of a good
courage; for thou shalt bring the children of
Israel into the land which I sware unto them;
and I will be with thee.
24 And it came to pass, when Moses had
made an end of [y] writing the words of this
law in a book, until they were finished,
25 That Moses commanded the Levites,
which bare the ark of the covenant of the
LORD, saying,
26 Take this book of the law, [z] and put it
in the side of the ark of the covenant of the
LORD your God, that it may be there [a] for a
witness against thee.

[c] Heb. *lie down*; 2 Sam. vii. 12.——[d] Exod. xxxii. 6.——[e] Exod. xxxiv. 15; Judg. ii. 17.——[f] Chap. xxxii. 15; Judg. ii. 12; x. 6, 13.——[g] Judg. ii. 20.——[h] 2 Chron. xv. 2.——[i] Chap. xxxii. 20; Psa. civ. 29; Isa. viii. 17; lxiv. 7; Ezek. xxxix. 23.——[k] Heb. *find them*; Neh. ix. 32.——[l] Judg. vi. 13.

[m] Num. xiv. 42.——[n] Ver. 17.——[o] Ver. 26.——[p] Chap. xxxii. 15; Neh. ix. 25, 26; Hos. xiii. 6.——[q] Verse 16.——[r] Verse 17.——[s] Heb *before*.——[t] Hos. v. 3; xiii. 5, 6.——[u] Amos v. 25, 26.——[v] Heb. *do*.——[w] Ver. 14.——[x] Ver. 7; Josh. i. 6.——[y] Verse 9.——[z] See 2 Kings xxii. 8.——[a] Ver. 19.

viii. 2. Nor is there any other on record from that time to the destruction of Jerusalem. See *Dodd*.

Verse 16. *Behold, thou shalt sleep with thy fathers*] שכב *shocheb*, thou *shalt lie down*; it signifies to rest, take rest in sleep, and, metaphorically, to die. Much stress cannot be safely laid on this expression to prove the immortality of the soul, or that the people in the time of Moses had a distinct notion of its separate existence. It was, however, understood in this sense by Jonathan ben Uzziel, who in his Targum paraphrases the word thus: "Thou shalt lie down in the dust with thy fathers; and thy soul (נשמתך *nishmethach*) shall be laid up in the treasury of the life to come with thy fathers."

Verse 18. *I will surely hide my face*] Withdraw my approbation and my protection. This is a general meaning of the word in Scripture.

Verse 19. *Write ye this song*] The song which follows in the next chapter. Things which were of great importance and of common concern were, among the ancients, put into verse, as this was found the best method of keeping them in remembrance, especially in those times when *writing* was little practised. Even *prose* was sometimes *sung*. The history of Herodotus was divided into NINE *books*, and each inscribed with the name of one of the NINE *Muses*, because these books were anciently sung. Homer is reported to have sung his *poems* through different Greek cities. Aristotle observes that anciently the people sung their *laws*. And Cicero observes that it was a custom among the ancient Romans to sing the praises of their heroes at the public festivals. This was the case among the northern inhabitants of Europe, particularly in Ireland and Scotland; hence the Gaelic poetry of Ossian and others. See *Dodd*; and see the note on Exod. xv. *1*, where the subject is largely treated.

Verse 21. *This song shall testify against them*] Because in it their general defection is predicted, but in such a way as to show them how to avoid the evil; and if they did not avoid the evil, and the threatened punishment should come upon them, then the song should testify against them, by showing that they had been sufficiently warned, and might have lived to God, and so escaped those disasters.

Verse 26. *Take this book of the law*] The standard copy to which all transcripts must ultimately refer:

a

A. M. 2553. B. C. 1451. An. Ex. Isr. 40. Sebat.

27 [b] For I know thy rebellion,
and thy [c] stiff neck: behold,
while I am yet alive with you
this day, ye have been rebellious against the
LORD; and how much more after my death?
28 Gather unto me all the elders of your
tribes, and your officers, that I may speak these
words in their ears, [d] and call heaven and earth
to record against them.
29 For I know that after my death ye will
utterly [e] corrupt *yourselves*, and
turn aside from the way which I
have commanded you; and [f] evil
will befall you [g] in the latter days; because
ye will do evil in the sight of the LORD, to
provoke him to anger through the work of
your hands.
30 And Moses spake in the ears of all the
congregation of Israel the words of this song,
until they were ended.

A. M. 2553. B. C. 1451. An. Ex. Isr. 40. Sebat.

[b] Chap. ix. 24; xxxii. 20.——[c] Exod. xxxii. 9; chap. ix. 6. [d] Chap. xxx. 19; xxxii. 1.

[e] Chap. xxxii. 5; Judg. ii. 19; Hos. ix. 9.——[f] Chap. xxxi. 15. [g] Gen. xlix. 1; chap. iv. 30.

another copy was put into the hands of the priests. See the note on ver. 9.

Verse 27. *While I am yet alive—ye have been rebellious*] Such was the disposition of this people to act contrary to moral goodness that Moses felt himself justified in inferring what would take place from what had already happened.

1. NEVER was a people more fully and faithfully warned, and from this very circumstance we may see that they were under no *fatal* constraining necessity to commit sin against God; they *might* have avoided it, but they *would* not. God was present to help them, till by their repeated provocations they forced him to depart: wrath therefore came upon them to the uttermost because they sinned when they might have lived to the glory of God. Those who abuse God's grace shall not only have that grace taken away from them, but shall be punished for the *abuse* of it, as well as for the *transgression*. Every sin is *double*, and must have a *twofold* punishment; for 1. Grace is resisted; 2. Transgression is committed; and God will visit for both.

2. How astonishing it is that, with such examples of God's justice before their eyes, the *Jews* should be so little affected; and that the *Gentiles*, who have received the Gospel of God, should act as if God would no more punish transgression, or that he must be so partial to *them* as to pass by iniquities for which the hand of his justice still continues heavy upon the descendants of Jacob! Let them take heed, for if God spared not the natural branches, he will not spare them. If they sin after the manner of the *Jews*, they may expect to be partakers with them in their punishments. What God does to *nations* he will do to individuals who reject his mercy, or trample under foot his grace; *the soul that sinneth*, and returns not to God by repentance and faith, *shall die*. This is a decree of God that shall never be reversed, and every day bears witness how strictly he keeps it in view.

3. The ode composed by Moses for this occasion was probably set to some lively and affecting *air*, and sung by the people. It would be much easier to keep such a *song* in remembrance, than an equal quantity of *prose*. The whole would have the additional circumstances of *cadence* and *tune* to cause it to be often repeated; and thus insure its being kept in memory. *Poetry*, though *often*, nay, *generally* abused, is nevertheless a *gift from God*, and may be employed with the best effect in his service. A very considerable part of the Old Testament is written in *poetry;* particularly the whole book of *Psalms*, great part of the prophet *Isaiah*, the *Lamentations*, and much of the *minor prophets*. Those who speak against poetic compositions in the service of God, speak against what they do not understand. All that a man hath should be consecrated to his Maker, and employed in his service; not only the *energy* of his *heart* and *mind*, the *physical force* of his *body*, but also the *musical tones* and *modulations of his voice*.

CHAPTER XXXII.

The prophetical and historical song of Moses, showing forth the nature of God's doctrine, 1–3. *The character of God,* 4. *The corruption of the people,* 5, 6. *They are called to remember God's kindness,* 7, *and his dealings with them during their travels in the wilderness,* 8–14. *Their ingratitude and iniquity,* 15–18. *They are threatened with his judgments,* 19–28. *A pathetic lamentation over them because of their sins,* 29–35. *Gracious purposes in their behalf, mixed with reproaches for their manifold idolatries, and threatenings against his enemies,* 36–42. *A promise of salvation to the Gentiles,* 43. *Moses, having finished the song, warmly exhorts the people to obedience,* 44–47. *God calls him up to the mount, that he may see the good land and then die,* 48–52.

A. M. 2553.
B. C. 1451.
An. Ex. Isr. 40.
Sebat.

GIVE [a] ear, O ye heavens, and I will speak; and hear, O earth, the words of my mouth.

2 [b] My doctrine shall drop as the rain, my speech shall distil as the dew, [c] as the small rain upon the tender herb, and as the showers upon the grass:

3 Because I will publish the name of the LORD: [d] ascribe ye greatness unto our God.

A. M. 2553.
B. C. 1451.
An. Ex. Isr. 40.
Sebat.

4 He *is* [e] the Rock, [f] his work *is* perfect: for [g] all his ways *are* judgment: [h] a God of truth and [i] without iniquity, just and right *is* he.

[a] Chap. iv. 26; xxx. 19; xxxi. 28; Psa. i. 4, Isa. i. 2; Jer. ii. 12; vi. 19.——[b] Isa. lv. 10, 11; 1 Cor. iii. 6, 7, 8.——[c] Psa. lxxii. 6; Mic. v. 7.——[d] 1 Chron. xxix. 11.

[e] 2 Sam. xxii. 3; xxiii. 3; Psa. xviii. 2, 31, 46; Hab. i. 12. [f] 2 Sam. xxii. 31.——[g] Dan. iv. 37; Rev. xv. 3.——[h] Jer. x. 10. [i] Job. xxxiv. 10; Psa. xcii. 15.

NOTES ON CHAP. XXXII.

Verse 1.—On the inimitable excellence of this ode much has been written by commentators, critics, and poets; and it is allowed by the best judges to contain a specimen of almost every species of excellence in composition. It is so thoroughly poetic that even the dull Jews themselves found they could not write it in the prose form; and hence it is distinguished as poetry in every Hebrew Bible by being written in its own hemistichs or short half lines, which is the general form of the Hebrew poetry; and were it translated in the same way it would be more easily understood. The song itself has suffered both by transcribers and translators, the former having mistaken some letters in different places, and made wrong combinations of them in others. As to the translators, most of them have followed their own fancy, from good Mr. Ainsworth, who ruined it by the most inanimate rhyming version, to certain later poets, who have cast it unhallowedly into a European mould. See the observations at the end of the chapter.

Give ear, O ye heavens] Let angels and men hear, and let this testimony of God be registered both in heaven and earth. Heaven and earth are appealed to as *permanent* witnesses.

Verse 2. *My doctrine*] לקחי *likchi*, from לקח *lakach*, to *take*, *carry away*; to *attract* or *gain over* the *heart* by eloquence or persuasive speech. Hence the Septuagint translate the word *αποφθεγμα*, an *apophthegm*, a sententious and weighty saying, for the regulation of the moral conduct. Such, properly, are the sayings in this inimitable ode.

Shall drop as the rain] It shall come drop by drop as the shower, beginning slowly and distinctly, but increasing more and more till the plenitude of righteousness is poured down, and the whole canon of Divine revelation completed.

My speech shall distil as the dew] אמרתי *imrathi*; my familiar, friendly, and affectionate speeches shall descend gently and softly, on the ear and the heart, as the dew, moistening and refreshing all around. In hot regions *dew* is often a substitute for rain, without it there could be no fertility, especially in those places where rain seldom falls. And in such places only can the metaphor here used be felt in its perfection. Homer uses a similar figure when speaking of the eloquence of Ulysses; he says, Il. iii., ver. 221:—

Αλλ' ότε δη ροπα τε μεγαλην εκ στηθεος ιει,
Και επεα νιφαδεσσιν εοικοτα χειμεριησιν—

"But when he speaks what elocution flows!
Soft as the *fleeces* of descending *snows*."

On the manner in which *dew* is produced, philosophers are not yet agreed. It was long supposed to *descend*, and to differ only from *rain* as *less* from *more*; but the experiments of a French chemist seemed to prove that dew *ascended* in light thin vapours, and that, meeting with a colder region of the air, it became condensed and fell down upon the earth. Other recent experiments, though they have not entirely invalidated the former, have rendered the doctrine of the ascent of dew doubtful. Though we know nothing certain as to the manner of its production, yet we know that the thing exists, and that it is essentially useful. So much we know of the sayings of our God, and the blessed effects produced by them: God *hath* spoken, and the entering in of his words gives light and life. See the note on Gen. ii. 6.

As the small rain] שעירם *seirim*, from שער *saar*, to be *rough* or *tempestuous*; sweeping showers, accompanied with a strong gale of wind.

And as the showers] רביבים *rebibim*, from רבה *rabah*, to *multiply*, to *increase greatly*; shower after shower, or rather a continual rain, whose drops are multiplied beyond calculation, upon the earth; alluding perhaps to the *rainy seasons in the East*, or to those *early* and *latter rains* so essentially necessary for the vegetation and perfection of the grain.

No doubt these various expressions point out that great variety in the word or revelation of God whereby it is suited to every *place*, *occasion*, *person*, and *state*; being "profitable for doctrine, reproof, and edification in righteousness." Hence the apostle says that GOD, at sundry times and in divers manners, spake in time past unto the fathers by the prophets; and in these last times has spoken unto us by his Son; Heb. i. 1, 2. By every *prophet*, *evangelist*, and *apostle*, God speaks a *particular* language; all is his *doctrine*, his great *system* of instruction, for the information and salvation of the souls of men. But some portions are like the *sweeping showers*, in which the *tempest of God's wrath* appears against sinners. Others are like the *incessant showers* of *gentle rain*, preparing the soil for the germination of the grain, and causing it to take root. And others still are like the *dew*, mildly and gently insinuating convictions, persuasions, reproofs, and consolations. The preacher of righteousness who wishes to handle this word profitably, must attend closely to those distinctions, that he may rightly divide the word of truth, and give each of his hearers his portion of the bread of life in due season.

Verse 4. He is *the Rock*] The word צור *tsur* is rendered *Creator* by some eminent critics; and خالق *khalyk* is the reading in the Arabic Version. Rab-

a

A. M. 2553. B. C. 1451. An. Ex. Isr. 40. Sebat.

5 [k] They have [l] corrupted themselves, [m] their spot *is* not *the spot* of his children; *they are* a [n] perverse and crooked generation.

6 Do ye thus [o] requite the LORD, O foolish people and unwise? *is* not he [p] thy father *that* hath [q] bought thee? hath he not [r] made thee, and established thee?

7 Remember the days of old, consider the years of [s] many generations: [t] ask thy father, and he will show thee; thy elders, and they will tell thee.

8 When the Most High [u] divided to the nations their inheritance, when he [v] separated the sons of Adam, he set the bounds of the people according to the number of the children of Israel.

9 For [w] the LORD's portion *is* his people;

[k] Heb. *he hath corrupted to himself.*——[l] Chap. xxxi. 29.——[m] Or, that they are *not his children*, that is, *their blot.*——[n] Matt. xvii. 17; Luke ix. 41; Phil. ii. 15.——[o] Psa. cxvi. 12.——[p] Isa. lxiii. 16.——[q] Psa. lxxiv. 2.

[r] Ver. 15; Isa. xxvii. 11; xliv. 2.——[s] Heb. *generation and generation.*——[t] Exodus xiii. 14; Psa. xliv. 1; lxviii. 3, 4.——[u] Zech. ix. 2; Acts xvii. 26.——[v] Gen. xi. 8.——[w] Exod. xv. 16; xix. 5; 1 Sam. x. 1; Psa. lxviii. 71.

Moses ben Maimon, in his valuable work, *Moreh Nebochim*, observes that the word צור *tsur*, which is ordinarily translated *rock*, signifies *origin*, *fountain*, *first cause*, &c., and in this way it should be translated here: "He is the first principle, his work is perfect." As he is the *cause* of all things, he must be infinitely perfect; and consequently all his works must be *perfect* in their respective kinds. As is the *cause*, so must the *effect* be. Some think the word *rock* gives a very good sense; for, as in those lands, rocks were the ordinary places of *defence* and *security*, God may be metaphorically represented thus, to signify his *protection* of his followers. I prefer the opinion of Maimon.

Verse 5. *Their spot* is *not* the spot *of his children*] This verse is variously translated and variously understood. *They are corrupted, not his, children of pollution.*—KENNICOTT. *They are corrupt, they are not his children, they are blotted.*—HOUBIGANT. This is according to the *Samaritan*. The interpretation commonly given to these words is as unfounded as it is exceptionable: "God's children have their spots, i. e., their sins, but sin in them is not like sin in others; in others sin is exceedingly sinful, but God does not see the sins of his children as he sees the sins of his enemies," &c. Unfortunately for this bad doctrine, there is no foundation for it in the sacred text, which, though very obscure, may be thus translated: He (Israel) *hath corrupted himself. They* (the Israelites) *are not his children: they are spotted.* Coverdale renders the whole passage thus: "The froward and overthwart generation have marred themselves to himward, and are not his children because of their deformity." This is the *sense* of the verse. Let it be observed that the word *spot*, which is *repeated* in our translation, occurs but *once* in the original, and the marginal reading is greatly to be preferred: *He hath corrupted to himself, that they are not his children; that is their blot.* And because they had the *blot of sin* on them, because they were *spotted* with iniquity and *marked* idolaters, therefore God renounces them. There may be here an allusion to the *marks* which the worshippers of particular idols had on different parts of their bodies, especially on their *foreheads;* and as idolatry is the crime with which they are here charged, the *spot* or *mark* mentioned may refer to the *mark* or *stigma* of their idol. The different sects of idolaters in the East are distinguished by their *sectarian marks*, the stigma of their respective idols. These sectarian marks, particulary on the forehead, amount to nearly one hundred among the Hindoos, and especially among the two sects, the worshippers of *Seeva*, and the worshippers of *Vishnoo*. In many cases these marks are renewed *daily*, for they account it irreligious to perform any sacred rite to their god without his mark on the forehead; the marks are generally *horizontal* and *perpendicular* lines, *crescents*, *circles*, *leaves*, *eyes*, *&c.*, in *red*, *black*, *white*, and *yellow*. This very custom is referred to in Rev. xx. 4, where the beast gives his mark to his followers, and it is very likely that Moses refers to such a custom among the idolatrous of his own day. This removes all the difficulty of the text. God's children have no *sinful spots*, because Christ saves them *from* their sins; and their *motto* or *mark* is, *Holiness to the Lord.*

Verse 8. *When the Most High divided to the nations, &c.*] Verses 8 and 9, says Dr. Kennicott, give us express authority for believing that the earth was very early divided in consequence of a Divine command, and probably by *lot*, (see Acts xvii. 26;) and as *Africa* is called the land of *Ham*, (Psa. lxxviii. 51; cv. 23, 27; cvi. 22,) probably that country *fell* to him and to his descendants, at the same time that *Europe* fell to *Japheth*, and *Asia* to *Shem*, with a particular reserve of *Palestine* to be the *Lord's portion*, for some one peculiar people. And this separation of mankind into three bodies, called the *general migration*, was commanded to *Noah*, and by him to his sons, so as to take place in the days of *Peleg*, about two hundred years afterwards. This general migration was prior to the partial dispersion from Babel by about five hundred years.

He set the bounds of the people according to the number of the children of Israel.] The Septuagint is very curious, Εστησεν ὁρια εθνων κατα αριθμον αγγελων του Θεου. "He established the bounds of the nations according to the number of the angels of God." The meaning of the passage seems to be, that when God divided the earth among mankind, he reserved *twelve lots*, according to the *number* of the *sons* of *Jacob*, which he was now about to give to their descendants, according to his promise.

Verse 9. *The Lord's portion* is *his people*] What an astonishing saying! As *holy souls* take GOD for *their portion*, so GOD takes *them* for *his portion*. He represents himself as happy in his followers; and they are infinitely happy in, and satisfied with, God as their

A. M. 2553.
B. C. 1451.
An. Ex. Isr. 40.
Sebat.

Jacob *is* the [x] lot of his inheritance.
10 He found him [y] in a desert land, and in the waste howling wilderness; he [z] led him about, he [a] instructed him, he

[x] Heb. *cord.*——[y] Chap. viii. 15; Jer. ii. 6; Hos. xiii. 5.——[z] Or, *compassed him about.*——[a] Deut. iv. 36.

portion. This is what is implied in being a *saint.* He who is seeking for an earthly portion, has little commerce with the Most High.

Verse 10. *He*—the Lord, *found him*—Jacob, in his descendants, *in a desert land*—the wilderness. *He led him about* forty years in this wilderness, Deut. viii. 2, or יסבבנהו *yesobebenhu, he compassed him about,* i. e., God defended them on all hands, and in all places. *He instructed him*—taught them that astonishing law through which we have now almost passed, giving them statutes and judgments which, for depth of wisdom, and correct political adaptation to times, places, and circumstances, are so wondrously constructed, as essentially to secure the comfort, peace, and happiness of the individual, and the prosperity and permanency of the moral system. Laws so excellent that they have met with the approbation of the wise and good in all countries, and formed the basis of the political institutions of all the civilized nations in the universe.

Notwithstanding the above gives the passage a good sense, yet probably the whole verse should be considered more literally. It is certain that in the same country travellers are often obliged to *go about* in order to find proper passes between the mountains, and the following extracts from Mr. Harmer well illustrate this point.

"Irwin farther describes the mountains of the desert of Thebais (Upper Egypt) as sometimes so steep and dangerous as to induce even very bold and hardy travellers to avoid them by taking a large circuit; and that for want of proper knowledge of the way, such a wrong path may be taken as may on a sudden bring them into the greatest dangers, while at other times a dreary waste may extend itself so prodigiously as to make it difficult, without assistance, to find the way to a proper outlet. All which show us the meaning of those words of the song of Moses, Deut. xxxii. 10: *He led him about, he instructed him, he kept him as the apple of his eye.*

"Jehovah certainly instructed Israel in religion by delivering to him his law in this wilderness; but it is not, I presume, of this kind of teaching Moses speaks, as Bishop Patrick supposes, but God's instructing Israel how to avoid the dangers of the journey, by leading the people about this and that dangerous, precipitous hill, directing them to proper passes through the mountains, and guiding them through the intricacies of that difficult journey which might, and probably would, have confounded the most consummate Arab guides. They that could have safely enough conducted a small caravan of travellers through this desert, might have been very unequal to the task of directing such an enormous multitude, encumbered with cattle, women, children, and utensils. The passages of Irwin, that establish the observation I have been making, follow here: 'At half past eleven we resumed our march, and soon came to the foot of a prodigious hill, which we unexpectedly found we were to ascend. It was perpendicular, like the one we had passed some hours before; but what rendered the access more difficult, the path which we were to tread was nearly right up and down. The captain of the robbers seeing the obstacles we had to overcome, wisely sent all his camels round the mountain where he knew there was a defile, and only accompanied us with the beast he rode. We luckily met with no accident in climbing this height.' p. 325. They afterwards descended, he tells us, into a valley, by a passage easy enough, and stopping to dine at half past five o'clock, they were joined by the Arabs, who had made an astonishing march to overtake them, p. 326. 'We soon quitted the dale, and ascended the high ground by the side of a mountain that overlooks it in this part. The path was narrow and perpendicular, and much resembled a ladder. To make it worse, we preceded the robbers, and an ignorant guide among our people led us astray. Here we found ourselves in a pretty situation: we had kept the lower road on the side of the hill, instead of that towards the summit, until we could proceed no farther; we were now obliged to gain the heights, in order to recover the road, in performing which we drove our poor camels up such steeps that we had the greatest difficulty to climb after them. We were under the necessity of leaving them to themselves, as the danger of leading them through places where the least false step would have precipitated both man and beast to the unfathomable abyss below, was too critical to hazard. We hit at length upon the proper path, and were glad to find ourselves in the road of our unerring guides the robbers, after having won every foot of the ground with real peril and fatigue.' p. 324. Again. 'Our road after leaving the valley lay over level ground. As it would be next to an impossibility to find the way over these stony flats, where the heavy foot of a camel leaves no impression, the different bands of robbers have heaped up stones at unequal distances for their direction through this desert. We have derived great assistance from the robbers in this respect, who are our guides when the marks either fail, or are unintelligible to us.' The predatory Arabs were more successful guides to Mr. Irwin and his companions, than those he brought with him from Ghinnah; but the march of Israel through deserts of the like nature, was through such an extent and variety of country, and in such circumstances as to multitudes and incumbrances, as to make Divine interposition necessary. The openings through the rocks seem to have been prepared by Him to whom all things from the beginning of the world were foreknown, with great wisdom and goodness, to enable them to accomplish this stupendous march." See *Harmer's Observat.*, vol. iv. p. 125.

He kept him as the apple of his eye.] Nothing can exceed the force and delicacy of this expression. As deeply concerned and as carefully attentive as man can be for the safety of his *eyesight,* so was God for the protection and welfare of this people. How amazing this condescension!

A. M. 2553. B. C. 1451. An. Ex. Isr. 40. Sebat.

[b] kept him as the apple of his eye.

11 [c] As an eagle stirreth up her nest, fluttereth over her young, spreadeth abroad her wings, taketh them, beareth them on her wings:

12 *So* the LORD alone did lead him, and *there was* no strange god with him.

13 [d] He made him ride on the high places of the earth, that he might eat the increase of the fields; and he made him to suck [e] honey out of the rock, and oil out of the flinty rock;

14 Butter of kine, and milk of sheep, with fat of lambs, and rams of the breed of Bashan; and goats, [f] with the fat of kidneys of wheat; and thou didst drink the pure [g] blood of the grape.

15 But [h] Jeshurun waxed fat, and [i] kicked: [k] thou art waxen fat, thou art grown thick, thou art covered *with fatness;* then he [l] forsook God *which* [m] made him, and lightly esteemed the [n] Rock of his salvation.

16 [o] They provoked him to jealousy with strange *gods,* with abominations provoked they him to anger.

[b] Psa. xvii. 8; Prov. vii. 2; Zech. ii. 8.——[c] Exod. xix. 4; chap. i. 31; Isa. xxxi. 5; xlvi. 4; lxiii. 9; Hos. xi. 3.——[d] Chap. xxxiii. 29; Isa. lviii. 14; Ezek. xxxvi. 2.——[e] Job xxix. 6; Psa. lxxxi. 16.——[f] Psa. lxxxi. 16; cxlvii. 14.——[g] Genesis x ix. 11.

[h] Chap. xxxiii. 5, 26; Isa. xliv. 2.——[i] 1 Sam. ii. 29.——[k] Ch. xxxi. 20; Neh. ix. 25; Psa. xvii. 10; Jer. ii. 7; v. 7, 28; Hos. xiii. 6.——[l] Chap. xxxi. 16; Isa. i. 4.——[m] Ver. 6; Isa. li. 13. [n] 2 Sam. xxii. 47; Psa. lxxxix. 26; xcv. 1.——[o] 1 Kings xiv. 22; 1 Cor. x. 22.

Verse 11. *As an eagle stirreth up her nest*] Flutters over her brood to excite them to fly; or, as some think, *disturbs her nest* to oblige the young ones to leave it; so God by his plagues in Egypt obliged the Israelites, otherwise very reluctant, to leave a place which he appeared by his judgments to have devoted to destruction.

Fluttereth over her young] ירחף *yeracheph*, broodeth over them, communicating to them a portion of her own vital warmth: so did God, by the influences of his Spirit, enlighten, encourage, and strengthen their minds. It is the same word which is used in Gen. i. 2.

Spreadeth abroad her wings, &c.] In order, not only to teach them how to fly, but to *bear* them when weary. For to this fact there seems an allusion, it having been generally believed that the eagle, through extraordinary affection for her young, takes them upon her back when they are weary of flying, so that the archers cannot injure them but by piercing the body of the mother. The same figure is used Exod. xix. 4; where see the note. The נשר *nesher*, which we translate *eagle*, is supposed by Mr. Bruce to mean the *rachama*, a bird remarkable for its affection to its young, which it is known actually to bear on its back when they are weary.

Verse 12. So *the Lord alone did lead him*] By his power, and by his only, were they brought out of Egypt, and supported in the wilderness.

And there was *no strange god*] They had help from no other quarter. The Egyptian idols were not able to save their own votaries; but God not only saved his people, but destroyed the Egyptians.

Verse 13. *He made him ride*] ירכבהו *yarkibehu*, *he will cause him to ride.* All the verbs here are in the future tense, because this is a prophecy of the prosperity they should possess in the promised land. The Israelites were to *ride*—exult, on the high places, the mountains and hills of their land, in which they are promised the highest degrees of prosperity; as even the rocky part of the country should be rendered fertile by the peculiar benediction of God.

Suck honey out of the rock, and oil out of the flinty rock] This promise states that even the most barren places in the country should yield an abundance of aromatic flowers, from which the bees should collect *honey* in abundance; and even the tops of the rocks afford sufficient support for olive trees, from the fruit of which they should extract *oil* in abundance: and all this should be occasioned by the peculiar blessing of God upon the land.

Verse 14. *Fat of kidneys of wheat*] Almost every person knows that the kidney is enveloped in a coat of the purest fat in the body of the animal, for which several anatomical reasons might be given As the kidney itself is to the abundantly surrounding fat, so is the *germ* of the grain to the *lobes* or farinaceous parts. The expression here may be considered as a very strong and peculiarly happy figure to point out the finest wheat, containing the healthiest and most vigorous *germ*, growing in a very large and nutritive grain; and consequently the whole figure points out to us a species of wheat, equally excellent both for *seed* and *bread.* This beautiful metaphor seems to have escaped the notice of every commentator.

Pure blood of the grape.] Red wine, or the pure juice of whatever colour, expressed from the grapes, without any adulteration or mixture with *water: blood* here is synonymous with *juice.* This intimates that their *vines* should be of the best kind, and their *wine* in abundance, and of the most delicious flavour.

Verse 15. *Jeshurun*] ישרון, the *upright.* This appellative is here put for Israel, and, as it comes from ישר *yashar*, he was *right, straight*, may be intended to show that the people who once not only promised fair, but were really *upright*, walking in the paths of *righteousness*, should, in the time signified by the prophet, not only revolt from God, but actually fight against him; like a *full fed horse*, who not only will not bear the harness, but breaks aways from his master, and endeavours to kick him as he struggles to get loose. All this is spoken prophetically, and is intended as a *warning*, that the evil might not take place. For were the transgression *unavoidable*, it must be the effect of some *necessitating* cause, which would destroy the turpitude of the action, as it referred to Israel; for if the evil were *absolutely unavoidable*, no blame

A. M. 2553.
B. C. 1451.
An. Ex. Isr. 40.
Sebat.

17 [p] They sacrificed unto devils,
[q] not to God; to gods whom they
knew not, to new *gods that* came
newly up, whom your fathers feared not.
18 [r] Of the Rock *that* begat thee thou art
unmindful, and hast [s] forgotten God that formed thee.
19 [t] And when the LORD saw *it*, he [u] abhorred *them*, [v] because of the provoking of his sons, and of his
daughters.
20 And he said, [w] I will hide my face from
them, I will see what their end *shall be:* for
they *are* a very froward generation, [x] children
in whom *is* no faith.
21 [y] They have moved me to jealousy with

A. M. 2553.
B. C. 1451.
An. Ex. Isr. 40.
Sebat.

[p] Lev. xvii. 7; Psa. cvi. 37; 1 Cor. x. 20; Rev. ix. 20. — [q] Or, which were *not God;* ver. 21. — [r] Isa. xvii. 10. — [s] Jer. ii. 32. — [t] Judg. ii. 14. — [u] Or, *despised;* Lam. ii. 6. — [v] Isa. i. 2. — [w] Chap. xxxi. 17. — [x] Isa. xxx. 9; Matt. xvii. 17. — [y] Ver. 16; Psa. lxxviii. 58.

could attach to the unfortunate agent, who could only consider himself the miserable instrument of a *dire necessity*. See a case in point, 1 Sam. xxiii. 11, 12, where the prediction appears in the most *absolute* form, and yet the evil was prevented by the person receiving the *prediction* as a *warning*. The case is the following:

The Philistines attacked Keilah and robbed the threshing-floors; David, being informed of it, asked counsel of God whether he should go and relieve it; he is ordered to go; and is assured of success; he goes, routs the Philistines, and delivers Keilah. Saul, hearing that David was in Keilah, determines to besiege the place. David, finding that Saul meditated his destruction, asked counsel of the Lord, thus: "O Lord God of Israel, thy servant hath certainly heard that Saul seeketh to come to Keilah, to destroy the city for my sake. Will the men of Keilah deliver me up into his hand? Will Saul come down, as thy servant hath heard? And the Lord said, He will come down. Then said David, Will the men of Keilah deliver me and my men into the hand of Saul? And the Lord said, They will deliver *thee* up. Then David and his men (about six hundred) arose and departed out of Keilah, and went whithersoever they could go: and it was told Saul that David was escaped from Keilah, and he forbore to go forth." Here was the most positive prediction that Saul would come to Keilah, and that the men of Keilah would deliver David into his hands; yet neither of these events took place, because David departed from Keilah. But had he continued there, Saul would have come down, and the men of Keilah would have betrayed their deliverer. Thus the prediction was totally conditional; and so were all these prophecies relative to the apostasy of Israel. They were only fulfilled in those who did not receive them as *warnings*. See Jer. xviii. 8–10.

The Rock of his salvation.] He ceased to depend on the *fountain* whence his salvation issued; and thinking *highly of himself*, he *lightly esteemed his God;* and having ceased to depend on him, his fall became inevitable. The figure is admirably well supported through the whole verse. We see, *first*, a miserable, lean steed, taken under the care and into the keeping of a master who provides him with an abundance of provender. We see, *secondly*, this horse waxing *fat* under this keeping. We see him, *thirdly*, *breaking away* from his master, leaving his rich pasturage, and running to the wilderness, unwilling to bear the yoke or harness, or to make any returns for his master's care and attention. We see, *fourthly*, whence this conduct proceeds—from a want of consciousness that his strength depends upon his master's care and keeping; and a lack of consideration that leanness and wretchedness must be the consequence of his leaving his master's service, and running off from his master's pasturage. How easy to apply all these points to the case of the Israelites! and how illustrative of their former and latter state! And how powerfully do they apply to the case of many called Christians, who, having increased in riches, forget that God from whose hand alone those mercies flowed!

Verse 17. *They sacrificed unto devils*] The original word שדים *shedim* has been variously understood. The Syriac, Chaldee, Targums of Jerusalem and Jonathan, and the Samaritan, retain the original word: the *Vulgate*, *Septuagint*, *Arabic*, *Persic*, *Coptic*, and *Anglo-Saxon*, have devils or demons. The *Septuagint* has *εθυσαν δαιμονιοις*, *they sacrificed to demons:* the *Vulgate* copies the Septuagint: the Arabic has شياطين *shecateen*, the plural of شيطان *Sheetan*, Satan, by which the rebellious angels appear to be intended, as the word comes from the root شطن *shatana*, he was *obstinate*, *proud*, *refractory*, *went far away*. And it is likely that these fallen spirits, having utterly lost the empire at which they aimed, got themselves worshipped under various forms and names in different places. The Anglo-Saxon has deoflum, *devils*.

New gods that *came newly up*] מקרב באו *mikkarob bau*, "which came up from their neighbours;" viz., the *Moabites* and *Ammonites*, whose gods they received and worshipped on their way through the wilderness, and often afterwards.

Verse 18. *Of the Rock* that *begat thee*] צור *tsur*, the *first cause*, the *fountain* of thy being. See the note on ver 4.

Verse 19. *When the Lord saw* it, *&c.*] More literally, *And the Lord saw it, and through indignation he reprobated his sons and his daughters*. That is, When the Lord shall see such conduct, he shall be justly incensed, and so reject and deliver up to captivity his sons and daughters.

Verse 20. *Children in whom is no faith*] לא אמן בם *lo emon bam*, "There is no *steadfastness* in them," they can never be depended on. They are *fickle*, because they are *faithless*.

Verse 21. *They have moved me to jealousy*] This verse contains a very pointed promise of the calling of the Gentiles, in consequence of the rejection of the Jews, threatened ver. 19; and to this great event it is applied by St. Paul, Rom. x. 19

A. M. 2553.
B. C. 1451.
An. Ex. Isr. 40.
Sebat.

that which is not God; they have provoked me to anger [z] with their vanities: and [a] I will move them to jealousy with *those which are* not a people; I will provoke them to anger with a foolish nation.

22 For [b] a fire is kindled in mine anger, and [c] shall burn unto the lowest hell, and [d] shall consume the earth with her increase, and set on fire the foundations of the mountains.

23 I will [e] heap mischiefs upon them; [f] I will spend mine arrows upon them.

24 *They shall be* burnt with hunger, and devoured with [g] burning heat, and with bitter destruction: I will also send [h] the teeth of beasts upon them, with the poison of serpents of the dust.

25 [i] The sword without, and terror [k] within, shall [l] destroy both the young man and the virgin, the suckling *also*, with the man of gray hairs.

26 [m] I said, I would scatter them into corners, I would make the remembrance of them to cease from among men:

27 Were it not that I feared the wrath of the enemy, lest their adversaries [n] should behave themselves strangely, *and* lest they

[z] 1 Sam. xii. 21; 1 Kings xvi. 13, 26; Psa. xxxi. 6; Jer. viii. 19; x. 8; xiv. 22; Jonah ii. 8; Acts xiv. 15.——[a] Hos. i. 10; Rom. x. 19.——[b] Jer. xv. 14; xvii. 4; Lam. iv. 11.——[c] Or, *hath burned*.——[d] Or, *hath consumed*.——[e] Isa. xxvi. 15.

[f] Psa. vii. 12, 13; Ezek. v. 16.——[g] Heb. *burning coals*; Hab. iii. 5.——[h] Lev. xxvi. 22.——[i] Lam. i. 20; Ezek. vii. 15; 2 Cor. vii. 5.——[k] Heb. *from the chambers*.——[l] Heb. *bereave*.——[m] Ezek. xx. 13, 14, 23.——[n] Jer. xix. 4.

Verse 22. *The lowest hell*] שאול תחתית *sheol tachtith*, the very deepest destruction; a total extermination, so that *the earth*—their land, and *its increase*, and all their property, should be seized; and the *foundations of their mountains*—their strongest fortresses, should be razed to the ground. All this was fulfilled in a most remarkable manner in the last destruction of Jerusalem by the Romans, so that of the fortifications of that city not one stone was left on another. See the notes on Matt. xxiv.

Verse 23. *I will spend mine arrows upon them.*] The judgments of God in general are termed the *arrows of God*, Job vi. 4; Psa. xxxviii. 2, 3; xci. 5; see also Ezek. v. 16; Jer. l. 14; 2 Sam. xxii. 14, 15. In this and the following verses, to the 28th inclusive, God threatens this people with every species of calamity that could possibly fall upon man. How strange it is that, having this law continually in their hands, they should not discern those threatened judgments, and cleave to the Lord that they might be averted!

It was customary among the heathens to represent any judgment from their gods under the notion of *arrows*, especially a *pestilence;* and one of their greatest deities, Apollo, is ever represented as bearing a *bow* and *quiver* full of *deadly arrows;* so Homer, Il. i., ver. 43, where he represents him, in answer to the prayer of his priest Chryses, coming to smite the Greeks with the *pestilence:*—

'Ως εφατ' ευχομενος· του δ' εκλυε Φοιβος Απολλων·
Βη δε κατ' Ουλυμποιο καρηνων χωομενος κηρ,
Τοξ' ωμοισιν εχων αμφηρεφεα τε φαρετρην.—
'Εζετ' επειτ' απανευθε νεων· μετα δ' ιον ἑηκε·
Δεινη δε κλαγγη γενετ' αργυρεοιο βιοιο. κ. τ. λ.

"Thus Chryses pray'd; the favouring power attends,
And from Olympus' lofty tops descends.
Bent was his *bow* the Grecian hearts to *wound;*
Fierce as he moved, his *silver shafts* resound;—
The fleet in view, he *twang'd his deadly bow*,
And *hissing fly the feather'd fates* below.
On mules and dogs the *infection* first began;
And last the *vengeful arrows fix'd in man.*"

How frequently the same figure is employed in the sacred writings, every careful reader knows; and quotations need not be multiplied.

Verse 24. They shall be *burnt with hunger*] Their land shall be cursed, and *famine* shall prevail. This is *one* of the arrows.

Burning heat] No showers to cool the atmosphere; or rather boils, blains, and pestilential fevers; this was a *second*.

Bitter destruction] The plague; this was a *third*.

Teeth of beasts—with the poison of serpents] The beasts of the field should multiply upon and destroy them; this was a *fourth:* and *poisonous serpents*, infesting all their steps, and whose mortal bite should produce the utmost anguish, were to be a *fifth* arrow. Added to all these, the *sword* of their enemies—*terror* among themselves, ver. 25, and *captivity* were to complete their ruin, and thus the *arrows of God were to be spent upon them.* There is a beautiful saying in the *Toozuki Teemour*, which will serve to illustrate this point, while it exhibits one of the finest metaphors that occurs in any writer, the sacred writers excepted.

"It was once demanded of the fourth *Khaleefeh*, (Aaly,) on whom be the mercy of the Creator, 'If the *canopy of heaven* were a BOW; and if the *earth* were the cord thereof; and if *calamities* were ARROWS; if *mankind* were the *mark* for those *arrows;* and if *Almighty* GOD, the tremendous and the glorious, were the *unerring* ARCHER; to whom could the sons of Adam flee for protection?' The *Khaleefeh* answered, saying, 'The sons of Adam must flee unto the LORD.'"

Verse 27. *Were it not that I feared the wrath of the enemy*] Houbigant and others contend that *wrath* here refers not to the *enemy*, but to God; and that the passage should be thus translated: "Indignation for the adversary deters me, lest their enemies should be alienated, and say, The strength of our hands, and not of the Lord's, hath done this." Had not God punished them in such a way as proved that his hand and not the hand of man had done it, the heathens would have boasted of their prowess, and Jehovah would have been blasphemed, as not being able to

A. M. 2553.
B. C. 1451.
An. Ex. Is. 40.
Sebat.

should [o] say, [p] Our hand *is* high,
and the LORD hath not done all
this.
28 For they *are* a nation void of counsel,
[q] neither *is there any* understanding in them.
29 [r] O that they were wise, *that* they understood this, [s] *that* they would consider their
latter end!
30 How should [t] one chase a thousand, and
two put ten thousand to flight, except their
Rock [u] had sold them, and the LORD had shut
them up?
31 For [v] their rock *is* not as our Rock,
[w] even our enemies themselves *being* judges.
32 For [x] their vine [y] *is* of the vine of Sodom,
and of the fields of Gomorrah: their grapes
are grapes of gall, their clusters
are bitter:

A. M. 2553.
B. C. 1451.
An. Ex. Isr. 40.
Sebat.

33 Their wine *is* [z] the poi-
son of dragons, and the cruel [a] venom of
asps.
34 *Is* not this [b] laid up in store with me, *and*
sealed up among my treasures?
35 [c] To me *belongeth* vengeance and recompense; their foot shall slide in *due* time:
for [d] the day of their calamity *is* at hand, and
the things that shall come upon them make
haste.
36 [e] For the LORD shall judge his people,
[f] and repent himself for his servants, when he
seeth that *their* [g] power is gone, and [h] *there is*
none shut up or left.

---

[o] Psa. cxl. 8.—[p] Or, *Our high hand, and not the LORD, hath done all this.*—[q] Isa. xxvii. 11; Jer. iv. 22.—[r] Chap. v. 29; Psa. lxxxi. 13; cvii. 43; Luke xix. 42.—[s] Isa. xlvii. 7; Lam. i. 9.—[t] Lev. xxvi. 8; Josh. xxiii. 10; 2 Chron xxiv. 24; Isa. xxx. 17.—[u] Psa. xliv. 12; Isa. l. 1; lii. 3.—[v] 1 Sam. ii. 2. [w] 1 Sam. iv. 8; Jer. xl. 3.—[x] Isa. i. 10.—[y] Or, is worse than *the vine of Sodom,* &c.—[z] Psa. lviii. 4.—[a] Psa. cxl. 3; Rom. iii. 13.—[b] Job xiv. 17; Jer. ii. 22; Hos. xiii. 12; Rom. ii. 5. [c] Psa. xciv. 1; Ecclus. xxviii. 1; Rom. xii. 19; Heb. x. 30. [d] 2 Pet. ii. 3.—[e] Psa. cxxxv. 14.—[f] Judg. ii. 18; Psa. cvi. 45; Jer. xxxi. 20; Joel ii. 14; 2 Mac. vii. 6.—[g] Heb. *hand.* [h] 1 Kings xiv. 10; xxi. 21; 2 Kings ix. 8; xiv. 26.

---

protect his worshippers, or to punish their infidelities. *Titus*, when he took Jerusalem, was so struck with the strength of the place, that he acknowledged that if God had not delivered it into his hands, the Roman armies never could have taken it.

Verse 29. That *they would consider their latter end!*] אחריתם *acharitham*, properly, *their latter times*—the glorious days of the Messiah, who, according to the flesh, should spring up among them. Should they carefully consider this subject, and receive the promised Saviour, they would consequently act as persons under infinite obligations to God; his strength would be their shield, and then—

Verse 30. *How should one chase a thousand*] If therefore they had not forgotten their *Rock*, God their *author* and *defence*, it could not possibly have come to pass that a thousand of them should flee before *one* of their enemies.

Verse 31. *For their rock*] The gods and pretended protectors of the Romans.

Is *not as our Rock*] Have neither power nor influence like our God.

Our enemies themselves being *judges.*] For they often acknowledged the irresistible power of that God who fought for Israel. See Exod. xiv. 25; Num. xxiii. 8–12, 19–21; 1 Sam. iv. 8.

There is a passage in Virgil, Eclog. iv., ver. 58, very similar to this saying of Moses:—

> *Pan Deus Arcadia mecum si judice certet,*
> *Pan etiam Arcadia dicat se judice victum.*

"Should the god Pan contend with me," (in singing the praises of the future hero, the deliverer, prophesied of in the Sibylline books,) "were even Arcadia judge, Pan would acknowledge himself to be vanquished, Arcadia herself being judge."

Verse 32. *For their vine* is *of the vine of Sodom*] The Jews are as wicked and rebellious as the Sodomites; for by the *vine* the inhabitants of the land are signified; see Isa. v. 2, 7.

Their grapes] Their actions, are *gall and wormwood*—producing nothing but mischief and misery to themselves and others.

Their clusters are *bitter*] Their *united exertions*, as well as their *individual acts*, are sin, and only sin, continually. That by *vine* is meant the *people*, and by *grapes* their *moral conduct*, is evident from Isa. v. 1–7. It is very likely that the grapes produced about the lake *Asphaltites*, where Sodom and Gomorrah formerly stood, were not only of an acrid, disagreeable taste, but of a deleterious quality; and to this, it is probable, Moses here alludes.

Verse 33. *Their wine*] Their system of doctrines and teaching, is *the poison of dragons*, &c., fatal and destructive to all them who follow it.

Verse 34. *Sealed up among my treasures?*] Deeds or engagements by which persons were bound at a specified time to fulfil certain conditions, were *sealed* and laid up in places of safety; so here God's justice is pledged to avenge the quarrel of his broken covenant on the disobedient Jews, but the *time* and *manner* were sealed in his treasures, and known only to himself. Hence it is said,

Verse 35. *Their foot shall slide in* due *time, &c.*] But Calmet thinks that this verse is spoken against the Canaanites, the enemies of the Jewish people.

Verse 36. *The Lord shall judge his people*] He has an absolute right over them as their *Creator*, and authority to punish them for their rebellions as their *Sovereign*; yet he will *repent himself*—he will change his manner of conduct towards them, *when he seeth that* their *power is gone*—when they are entirely subjugated by their adversaries, so that their *political power* is entirely destroyed; *and* there is *none shut up or left*—not one *strong place* untaken, and not one family left,

a

A. M. 2553.
B. C. 1451.
An. Ex. Isr. 40.
Sebat.

37 And he shall say, [i] Where
are their gods, *their* rock in
whom they trusted,
38 Which did eat the fat of their sacrifices,
and drank the wine of their drink-offerings? let
them rise up and help you, *and* be [k] your protection.
39 See now that [l] I, *even* I, *am* he, and
[m] *there is* no god with me: [n] I kill, and I make
alive; I wound, and I heal: neither *is there*
any that can deliver out of my hand.
40 [o] For I lift up my hand to heaven, and
say, I live for ever.
41 [p] If I wet my glittering sword, and mine
hand take hold on judgment; [q] I will render
vengeance to mine enemies, and will reward
them that hate me.
42 I will make mine arrows [r] drunk with
blood, and my sword shall devour flesh; *and*
that with the blood of the slain and of the
captives, from the beginning of
[s] revenges upon the enemy.

A. M. 2553.
B. C. 1451.
An. Ex. Isr. 40.
Adar.

43 [t] Rejoice, [u] O ye nations,
with his people: for he will [v] avenge the blood
of his servants, and [w] will render vengeance to
his adversaries, and [x] will be merciful unto his
land, *and* to his people.
44 And Moses came and spake all the words
of this song in the ears of the people, he, and
[y] Hoshea the son of Nun.
45 And Moses made an end of speaking all
these words to all Israel:
46 And he said unto them, [z] Set your hearts
unto all the words which I testify among you
this day, which ye shall command your children to observe to do, all the words of this law.
47 For it *is* not a vain thing for you; [a] because it *is* your life: and through this thing
ye shall prolong *your* days in the land, whither
ye go over Jordan to possess it.

[i] Judg. x. 14; Jer. ii. 28.——[k] Heb. *a hiding for you.*——[l] Psa. cii. 27; Isa. xli. 4; xlviii. 12.——[m] Chap. iv. 35; Isa. xlv. 5, 18, 22.——[n] 1 Sam. ii. 6; 2 Kings v. 7; Job v 18; Psa. lxviii. 20; Hos. vi. 1; Tob. xiii. 2; Wisd. xvi. 13.——[o] Gen. xiv. 22; Exod. vi. 8; Num. xiv. 30.——[p] Isa. xxvii. 1; xxxiv. 5; lxvi. 16; Ezek. xxi. 9, 10, 14, 20.

[q] Isa. i. 24; Nah. i. 2.——[r] Jer. xlvi. 10.——[s] Job xiii. 24; Jer. xxx. 14; Lam. ii. 5.——[t] Or, *Praise his people, ye nations;* or, *Sing ye.*——[u] Rom. xv. 10.——[v] Rev. vi. 10; xix. 2.——[w] Ver. 41.——[x] Psa. lxxxv. 1.——[y] Or, *Joshua.*——[z] Chap. vi. 6; xi. 18; Ezek. xl. 4.——[a] Chap. xxx. 19; Lev. xviii. 5; Prov. iii. 2, 22; iv. 22; Rom. x. 5.

all being carried into captivity, or scattered into strange lands. Or, he will *do justice* to his people, and *avenge* them of their adversaries; see ver. 35.

Verse 37. *He shall say*] He shall begin to expostulate with them, to awaken them to a due sense of their ingratitude and rebellion. This may refer to the preaching of the Gospel to them in the latter days.

Verse 39. *See now that I*—am *he*] Be convinced that God alone can save, and God alone can destroy, and that your idols can neither *hurt* nor *help* you.

I kill, and I make alive, &c.] My mercy is as great as my justice, for I am as ready to save the penitent as I was to punish the rebellious.

Verse 40. *For I lift up my hand to heaven*] See concerning oaths and appeals to God in the note on chap. vi. 13.

Verse 42. *From the beginning of revenges*] The word פרעות *paroth*, rendered *revenges*, a sense in which it never appears to be taken, has rendered this place very perplexed and obscure. Mr. *Parkhurst* has rendered the whole passage thus:—

I will make my arrows drunk with blood;
And my sword shall devour flesh,
With the blood of the slain and captive
From *the hairy head* of the enemy.

Probably מראש פרעות *merosh paroth* may be more properly translated, *from the naked head*—the enemy shall have nothing to shield him from my vengeance; the crown of dignity shall fall off, and even the helmet be no protection against the sword and arrows of the Lord.

Verse 43. *Rejoice, O ye nations*] Ye Gentiles, for the casting off of the Jews shall be the means of your ingathering with *his people*, for they shall not be utterly cast off. (See Rom. xv. 9, for in this way the apostle applies it.) But how shall the Gentiles be called, and the Jews have their iniquity purged? *He will be merciful unto his land and to his people*, וכפר *vechipper*, he *shall cause an atonement* to be made for his land and people; i. e., Jesus Christ, the long promised Messiah, shall be *crucified* for Jews and Gentiles, and the way to the holiest be made plain by his blood.

The people have long been making atonements for themselves, but to none effect, for their atonements were but *signs*, and not the *thing* signified, for the body is Christ; now the Lord himself makes an atonement, for the *Lamb of God* alone *taketh away the sin of the world*. This is a very proper and encouraging conclusion to the awfully important matter of this poem.

Israel shall be long scattered, peeled, and punished, but they shall have mercy in the latter times; they also shall rejoice with the Gentiles, in the common salvation purchased by the blood of the Saviour of all mankind.

Verse 44. *And Moses came*] Probably from the tabernacle, where God had given him this prophetic ode, and he rehearsed it in the ears of the people.

Verse 46 *Set your hearts unto all the words*] Another proof that all these awful denunciations of Divine wrath, though delivered in an *absolute* form, were only *declaratory* of what God would do IF they rebelled against him.

Verse 47. *Through this thing ye shall prolong* your *days*] Instead of being cut off, as God here threatens, ye shall be preserved and rendered prosperous in the land which, when they passed over Jordan, they should possess.

A. M. 2553.
B. C. 1451.
An. Ex. Isr. 40.
Adar.

48 [b] And the LORD spake unto
Moses that selfsame day, saying,
49 Get thee up into this [c] mountain Abarim, *unto* Mount Nebo, which *is* in
the land of Moab, that *is* over against Jericho;
and behold the land of Canaan, which I give
unto the children of Israel for a possession:
50 And die in the mount whither thou goest
up, and be gathered unto thy people; as
[d] Aaron thy brother died in Mount Hor,
and was gathered unto his people:
51 Because [e] ye trespassed
against me among the children of Israel at
the waters of [f] Meribah-kadesh, in the wilderness of Zin; because ye [g] sanctified me not
in the midst of the children of Israel.
52 [h] Yet thou shalt see the land before *thee*;
but thou shalt not go thither unto the land
which I give the children of Israel.

A. M. 2553.
B. C. 1451.
An. Ex. Isr. 40.
Adar.

[b] Num. xxvii. 12, 13.——[c] Num. xxxiii. 47, 48; chap. xxxiv. 1. [d] Num. xx. 25, 28; xxxiii. 38.

[e] Num. xx. 11, 12, 13; xxvii. 14.——[f] Or, *strife at Kadesh.* [g] See Lev. x. 3.——[h] Num. xxvii. 12; chap. xxxiv. 4.

Verse 49. *Get thee up into this mountain Abarim*] The mount of the *passages*, i. e., of the Israelites when they entered into the promised land. See the notes on Num. xxvii. 12.

Verse 50. *And die in the mount—as Aaron*] Some have supposed that Moses was translated; but if so, then Aaron was translated, for what is said of the death of the one is said of the death of the other.

Verse 51. *Ye trespassed against me—at the waters of Meribah*] See the note on Num. xx. 8.

Verse 52. *Thou shalt see the land before* thee] See Num. xxvii. 12, &c. How glorious to depart out of this life with God in his heart and heaven in his eye! his work, his great, unparalleled usefulness, ending only with his life. The serious reader will surely join in the following pious ejaculation of the late Rev. *Charles Wesley*, one of the best Christian poets of the last century:—

"O that without a lingering groan
I may the welcome word receive;
My *body* with my *charge* lay down,
And cease at once to *work* and *live!*"

It would require a dissertation expressly formed for the purpose to point out the general merit and extraordinary beauties of this very sublime ode. To enter into such particulars can scarcely comport with the nature of the present work. Drs. *Lowth*, *Kennicott*, and *Durell*, have done much in this way; and to their respective works the critical reader is referred. A very considerable extract from what they have written on this chapter may be found in Dr. *Dodd's* notes. In writing this ode the design of Moses was,

1. To set forth the *Majesty of God;* to give that generation and all successive ones a proper view of the glorious perfections of the object of their worship. He therefore shows that from his *holiness* and *purity* he must be displeased with *sin;* from his *justice* and *righteousness* he must *punish* it; and from the *goodness* and infinite *benevolence* of his *nature* he is ever disposed to *help* the *weak*, *instruct* the *ignorant*, and show *mercy* to the *wretched*, *sinful* sons and daughters of men.

2. To show the *duty* and *interest* of his *people*. To have such a Being for their *friend* is to have all possible happiness, both spiritual and temporal, *secured;* to have him for their *enemy* is to be exposed to inevitable destruction and ruin.

3. To warn them against *irreligion* and *apostasy;* to show the possibility of departing from God, and the miseries that would overwhelm them and their posterity should they be found walking in opposition to the laws of their Creator.

4. To give a proper and impressive view of the *providence* of God, by referring to the history of his gracious dealings with them and their ancestors; the minute attention he paid to all their wants, the wonderful manner in which he led, fed, clothed, protected, and saved them, in all their travels and in all perils.

5. To leave on record an everlasting testimony against them, should they ever cast off his fear and pollute his worship, which should serve at once as a warning to the world, and a vindication of his justice, when the judgments he had threatened were found to be poured out upon them; for he who loved them so long and so intensely could not become their enemy but in consequence of the *greatest* and most unprincipled provocations.

6. To show the shocking and unprecedented ingratitude which induced a people so highly favoured, and so wondrously protected and loved, to sin against their God; and how reasonable and just it was, for the vindication of his holiness, that God should pour out upon them such judgments as he had never inflicted on any other people, and so mark their disobedience and ingratitude with fresh marks of his displeasure, that the punishment should bear some proportion to the guilt, and that their preservation as a distinct people might afford a feeling proof both of the providence and justice of God.

7. To show the glory of the *latter days* in the reelection of the long reprobated Jewish nation, and the final diffusion of his grace and goodness over the earth by means of the Gospel of Christ.

And all this is done with such strength and elegance of diction, with such appropriate, energetic, and impressive figures and metaphors, and in such a powerful torrent of that soul-penetrating, pure poetic spirit that comes glowing from the bosom of God, that the reader is alternately elated or depressed, filled with compunction or confidence, with despair or hope, according to the *quick* transitions of the inimitable writer to the different topics which form the subject of this incomparable and wondrously varied ode. May that Spirit by which it was dictated give it its fullest, most durable, and most effectual impression upon the mind of every reader!

CHAPTER XXXIII.

Moses delivers a prophetical blessing to the children of Israel, 1. *The introduction*, 2–5. *Prophetic declarations concerning* Reuben, 6; *concerning* Judah, 7; *concerning* Levi, 8–11; *concerning* Benjamin, 12; *concerning* Joseph, 13–17; *concerning* Zebulun, 18, 19; *concerning* Gad, 20, 21; *concerning* Dan, 22; *concerning* Naphtali, 23; *concerning* Asher, 24, 25. *The glory of the God of* Jeshurun, *and the glorious privileges of his true followers*, 26–29.

A. M. 2553.
B. C. 1451.
An. Ex. Isr. 40.
Adar.

AND this *is* [a] the blessing wherewith Moses, [b] the man of God, blessed the children of Israel before his death.

2 And he said, [c] The LORD came from Sinai, and rose up from Seir unto them; he shined forth from Mount Paran, and he came with [d] ten thousands of saints: from his right hand *went* [e] a fiery law for them.

3 Yea, [f] he loved the people; [g] all his saints *are* in thy hand: and they [h] sat down at thy feet; *every one* shall [i] receive of thy words.

4 [k] Moses commanded us a law, [l] *even* the inheritance of the congregation of Jacob.

5 And he was [m] king in [n] Jeshurun, when the heads of the people *and* the tribes of Israel were gathered together.

[a] Gen. xlix. 28.—[b] Psa. xc. title.—[c] Exod. xix. 18, 20; Judg. v. 4, 5; Hab. iii. 3.—[d] See Psa. lxviii. 17; Dan. vii. 10; Acts vii. 53; Gal. iii. 19; Heb. ii. 2; Rev. v. 11; ix. 16. [e] Heb. *a fire of law*.—[f] Exod. xix. 5; chap. vii. 7, 8; Psa. xlvii. 4; Hos. xi. 1; Mal. i. 2.—[g] Chap. vii. 6; 1 Sam. ii. 9; Psa. l. 5.—[h] Luke x. 39; Acts xxii. 3.—[i] Prov. ii. 1.—[k] John i. 17; vii. 19.—[l] Psa. cxix. 111.—[m] See Gen. xxxvi. 31; Judg. ix. 2; xvii. 6.—[n] Chap. xxxii. 15.

NOTES ON CHAP. XXXIII.

Verse 1. *And this* is *the blessing wherewith Moses—blessed, &c.*] The general nature of this solemn introduction, says Dr. Kennicott, is to show the *foundation* which Moses had for blessing his brethren, viz., because God had frequently manifested his glory in their behalf; and the several parts of this introduction are disposed in the following order:—

1. The manifestation of the Divine glory on Sinai, as it was prior in time and more magnificent in splendour, is mentioned first.

2. That God manifested his glory at *Seir* is evident from Judg. v. 4: *Lord, when thou wentest out of Seir, when thou marchedst out of the fields of Edom, the earth trembled and the heavens dropped*, &c.

3. The next place is *Paran*, where the *glory of the Lord appeared before all the children of Israel*, Num. xiv. 10.

Instead of *he came with ten thousand saints*, by which our translators have rendered מרבבת קדש *meribeboth kodesh*, Dr. Kennicott reads *Meribah-Kadesh*, the name of a place: for we find that, towards the end of forty years, the Israelites came to Kadesh, Num. xx. 1, which was also called *Meribah*, on account of their *contentious* opposition to the determinations of God in their favour, ver. 13; and there *the glory of the Lord* again *appeared*, as we are informed ver. 6. These *four* places, *Sinai*, *Seir*, *Paran*, and *Meribah-Kadesh*, mentioned by Moses in the text, are the identical places where God manifested his glory in a fiery appearance, the more illustriously to proclaim his special providence over and care of Israel.

Verse 3. *Yea, he loved the people*] This is the inference which Moses makes from those glorious appearances, that God truly loved the people; and that all his saints, קדשיו *kedoshaiv*, the people whom he had *consecrated* to himself, were under his especial benediction; and that in order to make them a *holy nation*, God had displayed his glory on Mount Sinai, where they had fallen prostrate at his feet with the humblest adoration, sincerely promising the most affectionate obedience; and that God had there commanded them a *law* which was to be the possession and inheritance of the children of Jacob, ver. 4. And to crown the whole, he had not only blessed them as their *lawgiver*, but had also vouchsafed to be *their king*, ver. 5.

Dr. *Kennicott* proposes to translate the whole five verses thus:—

Verse 1. And this is the blessing wherewith Moses, the man of God, blessed the children of Israel before his death. And he said,

2. Jehovah came from SINAI,
   And he arose upon them from SEIR;
   He shone forth from Mount PARAN,
   And he came from MERIBAH-KADESH:
   From his right hand a fire shone forth upon them.
3. Truly, he loved the people,
   And he blessed all his saints:
   For they fell down at his feet,
   And they received of his words.
4. He commanded us a law,
   The inheritance of the congregation of Jacob.
5. And he became king in Jeshurun;
   When the heads of the people were assembled,
   Together with the tribes of Israel.

We have already seen that Dr. Kennicott reads מריבה קדש *Meribah-Kadesh*, the name of a place, instead of מרבבת קדש *meribeboth kodesh*, which, by a most unnatural and forced construction, our version renders *ten thousands of saints*, a translation which no circumstance of the history justifies.

Instead of a *fiery law*, אש דת *esh dath*, he reads, following the Samaritan version, אש אור *esh ur*, a *fire shining out* upon them. In vindication of this change in the original, it may be observed, 1. That, though דת *dath* signifies a *law*, yet it is a *Chaldee* term, and appears nowhere in any part of the sacred writings previously to the Babylonish captivity; תורה *torah*

A. M. 2553. B. C. 1451. An. Ex. Isr. 40. Adar.

6 Let Reuben live, and not die; and let *not* his men be few.
7 And this *is the blessing* of Judah: and he said, Hear, LORD, the voice of Judah, and bring him unto his people: [o] let his hands be sufficient for him; and be thou [p] a help *to him* from his enemies.

[o] Gen. xlix. 8. — [p] Psa. cxlvi. 5.

being the term constantly used to express the Law, at all times prior to the corruption of the Hebrew, by the Chaldee. 2. That the word itself is obscure in its present situation, as the Hebrew Bibles write it and *esh* in one word, אשדת *eshdath*, which has no meaning; and which, in order to give it one, the Massorah directs should be read *separate*, though written *connected*. 3. That the word is not acknowledged by the two most ancient versions, the *Septuagint* and *Syriac*. 4. That in the parallel place, Hab. iii. 3, 4, a word is used which expresses the *rays of light*, קרנים *karnayim*, *horns*, that is, *splendours*, rays, or effulgence of light. 5. That on all these accounts, together with the almost impossibility of giving a rational meaning to the text as it now satnds, the translation contended for should be adopted.

Instead of *All his saints* are *in his hand*, Dr. Kennicott reads, *He blessed all his saints*—changing בידך *beyadecha*, into ברך *barach*, *he blessed*, which word, all who understand the Hebrew letters will see, might be easily mistaken for the other; the ד *daleth* and the ר *resh* being, not only in MSS., but also in *printed* books, often so much alike, that analogy alone can determine which is the true letter; and except in the insertion of the י *yod*, which might have been easily mistaken for the apex at the top of the ב *beth* very frequent in MSS., both words have the nearest resemblance. To this may be added, that the Syriac authorizes this rendering.

Instead of לרגלך *leraglecha*, and מדברתיך *middabberotheycha*, THY *feet*, and THY *words*, Dr. Kennicott reads the pronouns in the third person singular, לרגליו *leraglaiv* and מדברותיו *middabberothaiv*, HIS *feet*, HIS *words*, in which he is supported both by the Septuagint and Vulgate. He also changes ישא *yissa*, HE *shall receive*, into ישאו *yisseu*, THEY *shall receive*.

He contends also that משה *Mosheh*, *Moses*, in the fourth verse, was written by mistake for the following word מורשה *morashah*, *inheritance;* and when the scribe found he had inserted a wrong word, he added the proper one, and did not erase the first. The word *Moses*, he thinks, should therefore be left out of the text, as it is improbable that he should here introduce his own name; and that if the word be allowed to be legitimate, then the word *king* must apply to *him*, and not to GOD, which would be most absurd. See Kennicott's first Dissertation, p. 422, &c.

Verse 6. *Let Reuben live, and not die*] Though his life and his blessings have been forfeited by his transgression with his father's concubine, Gen. xlix. 3, 4; and in his rebellion with Korah, Num. xvi. 1, &c., let him not become extinct as a tribe in Israel. "It is very usual," says Mr. Ainsworth, "in the Scripture, to set down things of importance and earnestness, by affirmation of the one part, and denial of the other; Isa. xxxviii. 1: *Thou shalt die, and not live;* Num. iv. 19: *That they may live, and not die;* Psa. cxviii. 17: *I shall not die, but live;* Gen. xliii. 8: *That we may live, and not die;* Jer. xx. 14: *Cursed be the day—let not that day be blessed;* 1 John ii. 4: *He is a liar, and the truth is not in him;* ib. ver. 27: *Is truth, and no lie;* John i. 20: *He confessed, and denied not;* 1 Sam. i. 11: *Remember me, and not forget thy handmaid;* Deut. ix. 7: *Remember, forget not;* Deut. xxxii. 6: *O foolish people, and unwise.* In all these places it is evident that there is a peculiar emphasis in this form of expression, as if he had said, *Let him* not only *not die*, but let him live in *great and increasing peace* and *prosperity*. Do not only *not forget me*, but keep me *continually* in remembrance. *He denied not*, but *confessed* FULLY and PARTICULARLY. *O foolish people*—silly and stupid, *and unwise*—destitute of all true wisdom."

And let not *his men be few.*] It is possible that this clause belongs to *Simeon*. In the Alexandrian copy of the Septuagint the clause stands thus: Και *Συμεων εστω πολυς εν αριθμω*, *and let* SIMEON *be very numerous*, but none of the other versions insert the word. As the negative particle is not in the Hebrew, but is supplied in our translation, and the word *Simeon* is found in one of the most ancient and most authentic copies of the *Septuagint* version; and as *Simeon* is nowhere else mentioned here, if not implied in this place, probably the clause anciently stood: *Let Reuben live, and not die; but let the men of Simeon be few*. That this tribe was small when compared with the rest, and with what it once was, is evident enough from the first census, taken after they came out of Egypt, and that in the plains of Moab nearly forty years after. In the first, Simeon was 59,300; in the last, 22,200, a decrease of 37,100 men!

Verse 7. *And this* is the blessing *of Judah*] Though the word *blessing* is not in the text, yet it may be implied from ver. 1; but probably the words, *he spake*, are those which should be supplied: *And this he spake of Judah, Lord, hear the voice of Judah;* that is, says the *Targum*, receive his prayer when he goes out to battle, and let him be brought back in safety to his own people. *Let his hands be sufficient for him*—let him have a sufficiency of warriors always to support the tribe, and vindicate its rights; and let his enemies never be able to prevail against him! Three things are expressed here: 1. That the tribe of Judah, conscious of its weakness, shall depend on the Most High, and make prayer and supplication to him; 2. That God will hear such prayer; and, 3. That his hands shall be increased, and that he shall prevail over his enemies. This blessing has a striking affinity with that which this tribe received from Jacob, Gen. xlix. 9; and both may refer to our blessed Lord, who sprang from this tribe, as is noticed on the above passage, who has conquered our deadly foes by his death, and whose *praying* posterity ever prevail through his might.

A. M. 2553. B. C. 1451. An. Ex. Isr. 40. Adar.

8 And of Levi he said, [q] *Let* thy Thummim and thy Urim *be* with thy holy one, [r] whom thou didst prove at Massah, *and with* whom thou didst strive at the waters of Meribah;

9 Who said unto his father and to his mother, I have not [s] seen him; [t] neither did he acknowledge his brethren, nor knew his own children: for [u] they have observed thy word, and kept thy covenant.

10 [v] They [w] shall teach Jacob thy judgments, and Israel thy law: [x] they [y] shall put incense [z] before thee, [a] and whole burnt-sacrifice upon thine altar.

11 Bless, LORD, his substance, and [b] accept the work of his hands: smite through the loins of them that rise against him, and of them that hate him, that they rise not again.

12 *And* of Benjamin he said, The beloved

[q] Exod. xxviii. 30.——[r] Exod. xvii. 7; Num. xx. 13; chap. viii. 2, 3, 16; Psa. lxxxi. 7.——[s] Gen. xxix. 32; 1 Chron. xvii. 17; Job xxxvii. 24.——[t] Exod. xxxii. 26, 27, 28.——[u] See Jer. xviii. 18; Mal. ii. 5, 6.——[v] Or, *Let them teach*, &c.——[w] Lev. x. 11; chap. xvii. 9, 10, 11; xxiv. 8; Ezek. xliv. 23, 24; Mal. ii. 7.

[x] Or, *let them put incense.*——[y] Exod. xxx. 7, 8; Num. xvi. 40; 1 Sam. ii. 28.——[z] Heb. *at thy nose.*——[a] Lev. i. 9, 13, 17; Psa. li. 19; Ezek. xliii. 27.——[b] 2 Sam. xxiv. 23; Psa. xx. 3; Ezek xx. 40, 41; xliii. 27.

Verse 8. *Of Levi he said*] Concerning the *Urim* and *Thummim* see Exod. xxviii. 30.

Thy holy one] Aaron primarily, who was anointed the high priest of God, and whose office was the most holy that man could be invested with. Therefore Aaron was called God's *holy one*, and the more especially so as he was the type of the MOST HOLY and blessed Jesus, from whom the *Urim*—all *light* and *wisdom*, and *Thummim*—all *excellence*, *completion*, and *perfection*, are derived.

Whom thou didst prove, &c.] God contended with Aaron as well as with Moses at the waters of Meribah, and excluded him from the promised land because he did not sanctify the Lord before the people.

From the words of St. Paul, 1 Cor. x. 8–12, it is evident that these words, at least in a secondary sense, belong to Christ. He is the *Holy One* who was tempted by them at Massah, who suffered their manners in the wilderness, who slew 23,000 of the most incorrigible transgressors, and who brought them into the promised land by his deputy, Joshua, whose name and that of Jesus have the same signification.

Verse 9. *Who said unto his father*, &c.] There are several difficulties in this and the following verses. Some think they are spoken of the tribe of Levi; others, of all the tribes; others, of the Messiah, &c.; but several of the interpretations founded on these suppositions are too recondite, and should not be resorted to till a plain literal sense is made out. I suppose the whole to be primarily spoken of Aaron and the tribe of Levi. Let us examine the words in this way, *Who said unto his father*, &c. The law had strictly enjoined that if the father, mother, brother, or child of the high priest should die, he must not mourn for them, but act as if they were not his kindred; see Lev. xxi. 11, 12. Neither must Aaron mourn for his sons Nadab and Abihu, &c., though not only their death, but the circumstances of it, were the most afflicting that could possibly affect a parent's heart. Besides, the high priest was forbidden, on pain of death, to go out from the door of the tabernacle, Lev. x. 2–7, for God would have them more to regard their function (as good Mr. Ainsworth observes) and duty in his service, than any natural affection whatever. And herein Christ was figured, who, when he was told that his mother and brethren stood without, and wished to speak with him, said: "Who is my mother, and who are my brethren? whosoever shall do the will of my father who is in heaven, the same is my brother, and sister, and mother;" Matt. xii. 46–50. It is likely also that Moses may refer here to the fact of the Levites, according to the command of Moses, killing every man his brother, friend, neighbour, and even son, who had sinned in worshipping the *golden calf*, Exod. xxxii. 26; and in this way the Chaldee paraphrast understands the words.

Verse 10. *They shall teach Jacob*, &c.] This was the office of the *Levites*, to teach, by their significant service and typical ceremonies, the way of righteousness and truth to the children of Israel. And of their faithfulness in this respect God bears testimony by the prophet, "My covenant was with him of life and peace," Mal. ii. 5; and, "The law of truth was in his mouth, and iniquity was not found in his lips: he walked with me in peace and equity, and did turn many away from iniquity;" ver. 6. These words are a sufficient comment on the words of the text.

Verse 11. *Bless, Lord, his substance*] The blessing of God to the tribe of Levi was peculiarly necessary, because they had no inheritance among the children of Israel, and lived more immediately than others upon the providence of GOD. Yet, as they lived by the offerings of the people and the tithes, the increase of their substance necessarily implied the increase of the people at large: the more fruitful the land was, the more abundant would the tithes of the Levites be; and thus in the increased fertility of the land the substance of Levi would be blessed.

Verse 12. *Of Benjamin—the beloved of the Lord*] Alluding to his being particularly beloved of his father Jacob, Gen. xlix. 27, &c.

Shall dwell in safety by him] That is, by the Lord, whose temple, which is considered as his dwelling-place, was in the tribe of Benjamin, for a *part* of Jerusalem belonged to this tribe.

Shall cover him all the day] Be his continual protector; *and he shall dwell between his shoulders*—within his *coasts*, or in his chief city, viz., *Jerusalem*, where the temple of God was built, on his *mountains* Zion and Moriah, here poetically termed his *shoulders*.

Some object to our translation of the Hebrew ידיד *yedid* by the term *beloved*, and think the original should be divided as it is in the Samaritan, יד יד *yad yad, the*

A. M. 2553.
B. C. 1451.
An. Ex. Isr. 40.
Adar.

of the LORD shall dwell in safety
by him; *and the LORD* shall
cover him all the day long, and
he shall dwell between his shoulders.
13 And of Joseph he said, [c] Blessed of the
LORD *be* his land, for the precious things of
heaven, for [d] the dew, and for the deep that
coucheth beneath;
14 And for the precious fruits *brought forth*
by the sun, and for the precious things [e] put
forth by the [f] moon,
15 And for the chief things of [g] the ancient
mountains, and for the precious
things [h] of the lasting hills,
16 And for the precious things
of the earth and fulness thereof; and *for* the
good will of [i] him that dwelt in the bush: let
the blessing [k] come upon the head of Joseph,
and upon the top of the head of him *that was*
separated from his brethren.
17 His glory *is like* the [l] firstling of his bullock, and his horns *are like* [m] the horns of
[n] unicorns: with them [o] he shall push the
people together to the ends of the earth: and

A. M. 2553.
B. C. 1451.
An. Ex. Isr. 40.
Adar.

[c] Gen. xlix. 25.—[d] Gen. xxvii. 28.—[e] Heb. *thrust forth.*—[f] Heb. *moons.*—[g] Gen. xlix. 26.—[h] Hab. iii. 6.—[i] Exod. iii. 2, 4; Acts vii. 30, 35.

[k] Genesis xlix. 26.—[l] 1 Chron. v. 1.—[m] Num. xxiii. 22; Psa. xcii 10.—[n] Heb. *a unicorn.*—[o] 1 Kings xxii. 11; Psa. xliv. 5.

hand, even *the hand of the Lord shall dwell for safety* or *protection*, עליו *alaiv*, *upon him*. This makes a good sense, and the reader may choose.

Verse 13. *Blessed*—be *his land*] The whole of this passage certainly relates to the peculiar fertility of the soil in the portion that fell to this tribe which, the Jews say, yielded a greater abundance of all good things than any other part of the promised land.

The precious things of heaven] The peculiar mildness and salubrity of its atmosphere.

For the dew] A plentiful supply of which was a great blessing in the dry soil of a hot climate.

The deep that coucheth beneath] Probably referring to the plentiful supply of water which should be found in digging wells: hence the Septuagint have *αβυσσων πηγων*, *fountains of the deeps.* Some suppose there has been a slight change made in the word מטל *mittal*, *for the dew*, which was probably at first מעל *meal*, FROM ABOVE, and then the passage would read thus: *For the precious things of heaven* FROM ABOVE, *and for the deep that coucheth* BENEATH. This reading is confirmed by several of Kennicott's and De Rossi's MSS. The Syriac and Chaldee have both readings: *The dew of heaven from above.*

Verse 14. *The precious fruits* brought forth *by the sun*] All excellent and important productions of the earth, which come to perfection *once* in the year. So *the precious things put forth by the moon* may imply those vegetables which require but about a month to bring them to perfection, or vegetables of which several crops may be had in the course of a year.

Verse 15. *The chief things of the ancient mountains*] ומראש הררי קדם *umerosh harerey kedem, and from the head* or top *of the ancient* or eastern *mountains*, the *precious things* or *productions* being still understood. And this probably refers to the large *trees*, &c., growing on the mountain tops, and the springs of water issuing from them. The mountains of Gilead may be here intended, as they fell to the half tribe of Manasseh. And *the precious things of the lasting hills* may signify the *metals* and *minerals* which might be digged out of them.

Verse 16. *The good will of him that dwelt in the bush*] The *favour* of him who appeared in the burning bush on Mount Sinai, who there, in his *good will*—mere love and compassion, took Israel to be his people; and who has preserved and will preserve, in tribulation and distress, all those who trust in him, so that they shall as surely escape unhurt, as the bush, though enveloped with fire, was unburnt.

The top of the head, &c.] The same words are used by Jacob in blessing this tribe, Gen. xlix. 26. The meaning appears to be that God should distinguish this tribe in a particular way, as Joseph himself was separated, נזיר *nazir*, a *Nazarite*, a consecrated prince to God, from among and in preference to all his brethren. See the notes on Gen. xlix. 25, &c.

Verse 17. *His glory* is like *the firstling of his bullock*] This similitude is very obscure. A bullock was the most excellent of animals among the Jews, not only because of its *acceptableness* in *sacrifice* to God, but because of its great *usefulness* in agriculture. There is something peculiarly noble and dignified in the appearance of the ox, and his greatest ornament are his fine *horns;* these the inspired penman has particularly in view, as the following clause proves; and it is well known that in Scriptural language *horns* are the emblem of *strength*, *glory*, and *sovereignty;* Psa. lxxv. 5, 10; lxxxix. 17, 24; cxii. 9; Dan. viii. 3, &c.; Luke i. 69; Rev. xvii. 3, &c.

His horns are like *the horns of unicorns*] ראם *reem*, which we translate *unicorn*, from the *μονοκερως monokeros* of the Septuagint, signifies, according to Bochart, the *mountain goat;* and according to others, the *rhinoceros*, a very large quadruped with one great horn on his nose, from which circumstance his name is derived. See the notes on Num. xxiii. 22; xxiv. 8. *Reem* is in the *singular* number, and because the *horns* of a *unicorn*, a *one*-horned animal, would have appeared absurd, our translators, with an unfaithfulness not common to them, put the word in the *plural* number.

To the ends of the earth] Of the land of Canaan, for Joshua with his armies conquered all this land, and drove the ancient inhabitants out before him.

They are *the ten thousands of Ephraim, &c.*] That is, The *horns* signify the ten thousands of Ephraim, and the thousands of Manasseh. Jacob prophesied, Gen. xlviii. 19, that the *younger* should be *greater* than the *elder;* so here TENS *of thousands* are given to Ephraim, and only *thousands* to Manasseh. See the census, Num. i. 33–35.

A. M. 2553. B. C. 1451. An. Ex. Isr. 40. Adar.

[p] they *are* the ten thousands of Ephraim, and they *are* the thousands of Manasseh.

18 And of Zebulun he said, [q] Rejoice, Zebulun, in thy going out; and, Issachar, in thy tents.

19 They shall [r] call the people unto the mountain; there [s] they shall offer sacrifices of righteousness: for they shall suck *of* the abundance of the seas, and *of* treasures hid in the sand.

20 And of Gad he said, Blessed *be* he that [t] enlargeth Gad: he dwelleth as a lion, and teareth the arm with the crown of the head.

21 And [u] he provided the first part for himself, because there, *in* a portion of the lawgiver, *was he* [v] seated; and [w] he came with the heads of the people, he executed the justice of the LORD, and his judgments with Israel.

22 And of Dan he said, Dan *is* a lion's whelp: [x] he shall leap from Bashan.

23 And of Naphtali he said, O Naphtali,

[p] Gen. xlviii. 19.—[q] Gen. xlix. 13, 14, 15.—[r] Isa. ii. 3.—[s] Psa. iv. 5.—[t] See Josh. xiii. 10, &c.; 1 Chron. xii. 8, &c.

[u] Numbers xxxii. 16, 17.—[v] Heb. *ceiled.*—[w] Josh. iv. 12.
[x] Josh. xix. 47; Judg. xviii. 27.

Verse 18. *Rejoice, Zebulun, in thy going out*] That is, Thou shalt be very prosperous in thy coasting voyages; for this tribe's situation was favourable for traffic, having many *sea-ports*. See Gen. xlix. 13.

And, Issachar, in thy tents.] That is, as Zebulun should be prosperous in his *shipping* and *traffic*, so should Issachar be in his *tents*—his *agriculture* and *pasturage*.

Verse 19. *They shall call the people unto the mountain*] By their traffic with the *Gentiles* (for so I think עמים *ammim* should be understood here) they shall be the instruments in God's hands of converting many to the true faith; so that instead of sacrificing to idols, they should offer *sacrifices of righteousness*.

They shall suck of *the abundance of the seas*] That is, grow wealthy by merchandise.

And of *treasures hid in the sand.*] *Jonathan ben Uzziel* has probably hit upon the true meaning of this difficult passage: "From the sand," says he, "are produced *looking-glasses* and *glass* in general; the *treasures*—the method of finding and working this, was revealed to these tribes." Several ancient writers inform us that there were havens in the coasts of the Zebulunites in which the *vitreous* sand, or sand proper for making glass, was found. See Strabo, lib. xvi.; see also Pliny, Hist. Nat. l. xxxvi., c. 26; Tacitus, Hist. l. v., c. 7. The words of Tacitus are remarkable: Et Belus amnis Judaico mari illabitur; circa ejus os lectæ arenæ admixto nitro in vitrum excoquuntur. "The river Belus falls into the Jewish sea, about whose mouth those sands, mixed with nitre, are collected, out of which *glass* is formed," or which is melted into glass. Some think that the celebrated shell-fish called *murex*, out of which the precious *purple dye* was extracted, is here intended by the *treasure hid in the sand:* this also Jonathan introduces in this verse. And others think that it is a general term for the advantages derived from navigation and commerce.

Verse 20. *Blessed* be *he that enlargeth Gad*] As deliverance out of distress is termed *enlarging*, (see Psa. iv. 1,) this may refer to God's deliverance of the tribe of Gad out of that distress mentioned Gen. xlix. 19, and to the enlargement obtained through means of Jephthah, Judg. xi. 33, and probably also to the victories obtained by Gad and Reuben over the Hagarites, 1 Chron. v 18–20

He dwelleth as a lion] Probably the epithet of *lion* or *lion-like* was applied to this tribe from their fierce and warlike disposition. And on this supposition, 1 Chron. xii. 8 will appear to be a sufficient comment: *And of the Gadites there were—men of might, men of war for the battle, that could handle shield and buckler, whose faces were* LIKE THE FACES OF LIONS, *and were as swift as the roes upon the mountains. Tearing the arm* or *shoulder with the crown of the head* seems simply to mean that no force should be able to prevail over them, or stand against them; as the *arm* or *shoulder* signifies dominion, and *the crown of the head*, sovereign princes.

Verse 21. *He provided the first part*] That is, he chose for himself a very excellent portion, viz., the land of *Sihon* and *Og*, in which this tribe had requested to be settled by the *lawgiver*, viz., Moses, from whom they requested this portion, Num. xxxii. 1–5.

He came with the heads of the people] Notwithstanding this portion fell unto them on the east side of Jordan, yet they proceeded with the *heads of the people*, the chiefs of the other tribes.

To execute the justice of the Lord] To extirpate the old inhabitants of the country, according to the decree and purpose of the Lord. See on Num. xxxii.

Verse 22. *Dan is a lion's whelp: he shall leap from Bashan.*] The Jewish interpreters observe that Bashan was a place much frequented by *lions*, who issued thence into all parts to look for prey. By this probably Moses intended to point out the strength and prowess of this tribe, that it should extend its territories, and live a sort of predatory life. It appears from Josh. xix. 47, that the portion originally assigned to this tribe was not sufficient for them; hence we find them going out to war against *Leshem* and taking it, adding it to their territories, and calling it by the name of the tribe. Jacob, in his prophetic blessing of this tribe, represents it under the notion of a *serpent in the path*, Gen. xlix. 17. The character there, and that given here, constitute the complete warrior—*stratagem* and *courage*. See the note on Gen. xlix. 17.

Verse 23. *O Naphtali, satisfied with favour*] Though this may refer to the very great fertility of the country that fell to this tribe, yet certainly something more is intended. Scarcely any of the tribes was more particularly favoured by the wondrous mercy

A. M. 2553.
B. C. 1451.
An. Ex. Isr. 40.
Adar.

[y] satisfied with favour, and full
with the blessing of the LORD!
[z] possess thou the west and
the south.
24 And of Asher he said, [a] *Let* Asher *be*
blessed with children; let him be acceptable
to his brethren, and let him [b] dip
his foot in oil.
25 [c] Thy shoes *shall be* [d] iron
and brass; and as thy days, *so shall* thy
strength *be*.
26 *There is* [e] none like unto the God of

[y] Gen. xlix. 21.——[z] See Josh. xix. 32, &c.——[a] Gen. xlix. 20.——[b] See Job xxix. 6.

[c] Or, under *thy shoes* shall be *iron*.——[d] Chap. viii. 9.——[e] Exod xv. 11; Psa. lxxxvi. 8; Jer. x. 6.

and kindness of God, than this and the tribe of *Zebulun*. The light of the glorious Gospel of Christ shone brightly here, Matt. iv. 13, 15, 16. Christ's chief residence was at *Capernaum* in this tribe, Matt. ix. 1; Mark ii. 1; and this city, through Christ's constant residence, and the mighty miracles he wrought in it, is represented as being *exalted unto heaven*, Matt. xi. 23. And it is generally allowed that the apostles were principally of the tribe of Naphtali, who were to *possess the west and the south*—to dispense the Gospel through all the other tribes. The word ים *yam*, which we here translate *west*, literally signifies the *sea*, and probably refers to the sea of Gennesareth, which was in this tribe.

Verse 24. Let *Asher* be *blessed with children*] Let him have a numerous posterity, continually increasing.

Let him be acceptable to his brethren] May he be in perfect union and harmony with the other tribes.

Let him dip his foot in oil.] Let him have a fertile soil, and an abundance of all the conveniences and comforts of life.

Verse 25. *Thy shoes* shall be *iron and brass*] Some suppose this may refer to the iron and copper mines in their territory; but it is more likely that it relates to their warlike disposition, as we know that *greaves, boots, shoes*, &c., of *iron, brass*, and *tin*, were used by ancient warriors. Goliath had greaves of brass on his legs, 1 Sam. xvii. 6; and *the brazen-booted Greeks*, χαλκοκνημιδες Αχαιοι, is one of the epithets given by Homer to his heroes; see Iliad. lib. viii., ver. 41.

And as thy days, so shall *thy strength* be.] If we take this clause as it appears here, we have at once an easy sense; and the saying, I have no doubt, has comforted the souls of multitudes. The meaning is obvious: "Whatever thy trials or difficulties may be, I shall always give thee grace to support thee under and bring thee through them." The original is only *two words*, the latter of which has been translated in a great variety of ways, וכימיך דבאך *ucheyameycha dobecha*. Of the first term there can be do doubt, it literally means, *and as thy days*; the second word, דבא *dobe*, occurs nowhere else in the Hebrew Bible: the *Septuagint* have rendered it by ισχυς, *strength*, and most of the versions have followed them; but others have rendered it *affliction, old age, fame, weakness*, &c., &c. It would be almost endless to follow interpreters through their conjectures concerning its meaning. It is allowed among learned men, that where a word occurs not as a verb in the Hebrew Bible, its root may be legitimately sought in the Arabic. He who controverts this position knows little of the ground on which he stands. In this language the root is found; دبا *daba* signifies *he rested, was quiet*. This gives a very good sense, and a very appropriate one; for as the borders of this tribe lay on the vicinity of the Phœnicians, it was naturally to be expected that they should be constantly exposed to *irruptions, pillage*, &c.; but God, to give them *confidence* in his protection, says, *According to thy days*—all circumstances and vicissitudes, *so shall thy* REST *be*—while faithful to thy God no evil shall touch thee; thy days shall increase, and thy quiet be lengthened out. This is an unfailing promise of God: "I will keep him in perfect peace whose mind is stayed upon me, because he trusteth in me;" therefore "trust ye in the Lord for ever, for in the Lord Jehovah is everlasting strength;" Isa. xxvi. 4. Some derive it from دبى *dabi, he abounded in riches*; the interpretation then would be, *As thy days* increase, *so shall thy riches*. This makes a very good sense also. See *Rosenmuller*.

Moses, having now finished what God gave him to predict concerning the twelve tribes, and what he was led in the fulness of his heart to pray for in their behalf, addresses all the tribes collectively under the names *Jeshurun* and *Israel;* and in an ode of astonishing energy and elegance describes this wondrous people, and their still more wonderful privileges. The reader will observe that, though the latter part of this chapter appears in the form of *prose* in our Bibles, yet it is written in *hemistichs* or *short metrical lines* in the original, which is the form in which all the Hebrew poetry is written; and as in other cases, so in this, it would contribute much to the easy understanding of the author's meaning, were the translation produced in *lines* corresponding to those of the original.

Verse 26. There is *none like unto the God of Jeshurun*] We have already seen the literal meaning of *Jeshurun*, chap. xxxii. 15; but besides its literal meaning, it seems to be used as an expression of *particular affection:* hence Calmet understands it as a *diminutive* of the word *Israel*. We know that τεκνοι, *sons*, in the mouth of St. John, signifies much *less* than τεκνια, which, properly translated, would be *beloved children*, a term which at once shows the helplessness of the offspring, and the tender affection of the parent. So Jeshurun may be understood here: and hence the Septuagint seem to have apprehended the full force of the word by translating it του ηγαπημενου, the *beloved one*, the object of God's especial delight.

Israel's God, and God's Israel, have no fellows. What were all the gods of the nations, even supposing they were *real* beings, in comparison of the Almighty? And what nation under heaven could be compared to the Israel of God? It was, however, from God's excellence that they derived theirs.

Rideth upon the heaven, &c.] Unites heaven and earth in thy defence and support, and comes with irre-

A. M. 2553.
B. C. 1451.
An. Ex. Isr. 40.
Adar.

[f] Jeshurun, [g] *who* rideth upon the heaven in thy help, and in his excellency on the sky.

27 The eternal God *is thy* [h] refuge, and underneath *are* the everlasting arms: and [i] he shall thrust out the enemy from before thee; and shall say, Destroy *them!*

28 [k] Israel then shall dwell in safety alone: [l] the fountain of Jacob *shall be* upon a land of corn and wine; also his [m] heavens shall drop down dew.

A. M. 2553.
B. C. 1451.
An. Ex. Isr. 40.
Adar.

29 [n] Happy *art* thou, O Israel! [o] who *is* like unto thee, O people saved by the LORD, [p] the shield of thy help, and who *is* the sword of thy excellency! and thine enemies [q] shall [r] be found liars unto thee; and [s] thou shalt tread upon their high places.

[f] Chap. xxxii. 15.——[g] Psa. lxviii. 4, 33, 34; civ. 3; Hab. iii. 8.——[h] Psa. xc. 1.——[i] Chap. ix. 3, 4, 5.——[k] Num. xxiii. 9; Jer. xxiii. 6; xxxiii. 16.——[l] Chap. viii. 7, 8.

[m] Gen. xxviii. 28; chap. xi. 11.——[n] Psa. cxliv. 15.——[o] 2 Sam. vii. 23.——[p] Psa. cxv. 9, 10.——[q] 2 Sam. xxii. 45; Psa. xviii. 45; lxvi. 3; lxxxi. 15.——[r] Or, *shall be subdued.*——[s] Chap. xxxii. 13.

sistible velocity to succour and defend thee, and to discomfit thine adversaries.

Verse 27. *The eternal God*] אלהי קדם *elohey kedem*, the *former* God; HE who was of *old*. Not like the gods which were *lately* come up. HE who ever was and ever will be; and HE who *was*, *is*, and *will be* unchangeably holy, wise, just, and merciful. See the note on Gen. xxi. 33.

Everlasting arms] As the *arm* is the emblem of *power*, and of power in a state of *exertion*, the words here state that an unlimited and unconquerable power shall be eternally exerted in the defence of God's *Church*, and in the behalf of all those who trust in Him.

Thrust out the enemy] He will expel all the ancient inhabitants, and put thee in possession of their land.

Verse 28. *Israel then shall dwell—alone*] This people shall not be *incorporated* with any other people under heaven. A prophecy which continues to be fulfilled to the very letter. Every attempt to unite them with any other people has proved absolutely ineffectual.

The fountain of Jacob] His *offspring*, shall possess a most fertile land; such was Palestine.

Verse 29. *Happy* art *thou, &c.*] אשרי *ashrey*. O the happiness of Israel! it is ineffable, inconceivable, because they are *a people saved by the Lord*—have such a salvation as it becomes the infinite perfections of God to bestow; he is their *help*—their never-failing strength, and the *shield of that help*—he *defends* their *defence*, *saves* them and *preserves* them in the *state* of salvation.

Sword of thy excellency] Or *whose sword*—his all-conquering WORD, *is thine excellency*, in its promises, threatenings, precepts, &c., &c. St. Paul, in his exhortation to the Christians at Ephesus, uses the same metaphor, *Take unto you the* SWORD *of the* SPIRIT, *which is the* WORD *of* GOD.

Thine enemies shall be found liars] Who said thou shouldst never be able to gain the possession of this good land; for thou *shalt tread on*—subdue, their *high places*—even their best fortified cities.

THE blessings contained in this chapter belong also to the spiritual Israel of God, who, according to the Divine promise, shall have a complete victory over all their spiritual foes, shall have all their inward enemies, the *whole of the carnal mind*, destroyed, (for the blood of Jesus Christ, applied by the energy of the eternal Spirit, shall not only blot out all their sin, but purify their hearts from all unrighteousness;) and thus, being delivered from their enemies, they shall love God with all their heart, and serve him in righteousness and true holiness, without fear before him all the days of their life. There are many circumstances and expressions in this ode similar to several in the prophetical blessing pronounced by Jacob on his twelve sons, Gen. xlix., for the subject is the same in both chapters; the reader is therefore requested to compare the two places, and to consider the notes on each, as they have some tendency to cast light on each other. Both these chapters constitute a part of those Scriptures which, according to St. Paul, Rom. xv. 4, were written for our learning; and, as to instruct the reader and make him wise unto salvation was the gracious design of God, we should particularly beg of him "that we may in such wise *hear* them, *read*, *mark*, *learn*, and *inwardly digest* them, that, by *patience* and *comfort* of his holy word, we may embrace and ever hold fast the blessed hope of everlasting life which he has given us in our Saviour Jesus Christ"—*Collect for the second Sunday in Advent.*

CHAPTER XXXIV.

Moses goes up Mount Nebo *to the top of* Pisgah, *and God shows him the whole extent of the land which he promised to give to the descendants of Abraham,* 1–4. *There Moses died, and was so privately buried by the Lord that his sepulchre was never discovered,* 5, 6. *His age and strength of constitution,* 7. *The people weep for him thirty days,* 8. *Joshua being filled with the spirit of wisdom, the Israelites hearken to him, as the Lord commanded them,* 9. *The character of Moses as a prophet, and as a worker of the most extraordinary miracles, both in the sight of the Egyptians, and the people of Israel: conclusion of the Pentateuch,* 10–12.

A. M. 2553.
B. C. 1451.
An. Ex. Isr. 40.
Adar.

AND Moses went up from the
plains of Moab [a] unto the
mountain of Nebo, to the top of
[b] Pisgah, that *is* over against Jericho. And
the LORD [c] showed him all the land of Gilead,
[d] unto Dan,
2 And all Naphtali, and the land of Ephraim,
and Manasseh, and all the land of Judah,
[e] unto the utmost sea,
3 And the south, and the plain of the valley
of Jericho, [f] the city of palm-trees, unto Zoar.
4 And the LORD said unto him, [g] This *is* the
land which I sware unto Abraham, unto Isaac,
and unto Jacob, saying, I will give it unto thy
seed: [h] I have caused thee to see *it* with thine
eyes, but thou shalt not go over thither.
5 [i] So Moses the servant of the LORD died
there in the land of Moab,
according to the word of the
LORD.

A. M. 2553.
B. C. 1451.
An. Ex. Isr. 40.
Adar.

6 And he buried him in a valley in the
land of Moab, over against Beth-peor: but [k] no
man knoweth of his sepulchre unto this day.
7 [l] And Moses *was* a hundred and twenty
years old when he died: [m] his eye was not
dim, nor his [n] natural force [o] abated.
8 And the children of Israel wept for Moses
in the plains of Moab [p] thirty days: so the days
of weeping *and* mourning for Moses were ended.
9 And Joshua the son of Nun was full of
the [q] spirit of wisdom; for [r] Moses had laid
his hands upon him: and the children of Israel
hearkened unto him, and did as the LORD
commanded Moses.

[a] Num. xxvii. 12; xxxiii. 47; chap. xxxii. 49.——[b] Or, *the hill*.——[c] Chap. iii. 27; 2 Mac. ii. 4.——[d] Gen. xiv. 14.——[e] Chap. xi. 24.——[f] Judg. i. 16; iii. 13; 2 Chron. xxviii. 15.——[g] Gen. xii. 7; xiii. 15; xv. 18; xxvi. 3; xxviii. 13.——[h] Chap. iii. 27; xxxii. 52.

[i] Chap. xxxii. 50; Josh. i. 1, 2.——[k] See Jude 9.——[l] Chap. xxxi. 2.——[m] See Gen. xxvii. 1; xli. 10; Joshua xiv. 10, 11.——[n] Heb. *moisture*.——[o] Heb. *fled*.——[p] See Gen. l. 3, 10; Num xx. 29; Ecclus. xxxviii. 16, 17.——[q] Isa. xi. 2; Dan. vi. 3.——[r] Num. xxvii. 18, 23.

NOTES ON CHAP. XXXIV.

Verse 1. *And Moses went up*] This chapter could not have been written by Moses. A man certainly cannot give an account of his own death and burial. We may therefore consider Moses's words as ending with the conclusion of the preceding chapter, as what follows could not possibly have been written by himself. To suppose that he anticipated these circumstances, or that they were shown to him by an especial revelation, is departing far from propriety and necessity, and involving the subject in absurdity; for God gives no prophetic intimations but such as are absolutely necessary to be made; but there is no necessity here, for the Spirit which inspired the writer of the following book, would naturally communicate the matter that concludes this. I believe, therefore, that Deut. xxxiv. should constitute the *first chapter* of the book of *Joshua*.

On this subject the following note from an intelligent Jew cannot be unacceptable to the reader:—

"Most commentators are of opinion that *Ezra* was the author of the last chapter of Deuteronomy; some think it was *Joshua*, and others the *seventy* elders, immediately after the death of Moses; adding, that the book of Deuteronomy originally ended with the prophetic blessing upon the twelve tribes: 'Happy art thou, O Israel! who is like unto thee, O people saved by the Lord,' &c.; and that what now makes the *last* chapter of *Deuteronomy* was formerly the *first of Joshua*, but was removed from thence and joined to the former by way of supplement. This opinion will not appear unnatural if it be considered that *sections* and other *divisions*, as well as *points* and *pauses*, were invented long since these books were written; for in those early ages several books were connected together, and followed each other on the same roll. The beginning of one book might therefore be easily transferred to the end of another, and in process of time be considered as its real conclusion, as in the case of Deuteronomy, especially as this supplemental chapter contains an account of the last transactions and death of the great author of the Pentateuch."—*Alexander's* Heb. and Eng. *Pentateuch*.

This seems to be a perfectly correct view of the subject. This chapter forms a very proper commencement to the book of Joshua, for of this last chapter of Deuteronomy the first chapter of Joshua is an evident *continuation*. If the subject be viewed in this light it will remove every appearance of absurdity and contradiction with which, on the common mode of interpretation, it stands sadly encumbered.

Verse 5. *So Moses—died—according to the word of the Lord.*] על פי יהוה *al pi Yehovah, at the mouth of Jehovah*; i. e., by the especial command and authority of the Lord; but it is possible that what is here said refers only to the sentence of his exclusion from the promised land, when he offended at the waters of Meribah.

Verse 6. *He buried him*] It is probable that the reason why Moses was buried thus *privately* was, lest the Israelites, prone to idolatry, should pay him Divine honours; and God would not have the body of his faithful servant abused in this way. Almost all the gods of antiquity were deified *men*, great *lawgivers*, eminent *statesmen*, or victorious *generals*. See the account of the life of Moses at the end of this chapter.

Verse 7. *His eye was not dim*] Even at the advanced age of a hundred and twenty; *nor his natural force abated*—he was a young man even in old age, notwithstanding the unparalleled hardships he had gone through. See the account of his life at the end of this chapter.

Verse 9. *Laid his hands upon him*] See on Num. xxvii. 18-23.

A. M. 2553.
B. C. 1451.
An. Ex. Isr. 40.
Adar.

10 And there [s] arose not a prophet since in Israel like unto
Moses, [t] whom the LORD knew
face to face,
11 In all [u] the signs and the wonders
which the LORD sent him to do in the
land of Egypt to Pharaoh, and
to all his servants, and to all
his land,
12 And in all that [v] mighty hand, and in all
the great terror which Moses showed in the
sight of all Israel.

A. M. 2553.
B. C. 1451.
An. Ex. Isr. 40.
Adar.

[s] See chap. xviii. 15–18.——[t] Exod. xxxiii. 11; Num. xii. 6, 8; chap. v. 4.

[u] Chap. iv. 34; vii. 19; Psa. lxxviii. 43–53.——[v] Exod. iii. 19, xxxii. 11; Deut. iv. 34; v. 15; vi. 21; vii. 8, 19.

Verse 10. *There arose not a prophet, &c.*] Among all the succeeding prophets none was found so eminent in *all* respects nor so highly privileged as Moses; with him God spoke *face to face*—admitted him to the closest familiarity and greatest friendship with himself. Now all this continued true till the advent of Jesus Christ, of whom Moses said, "A Prophet shall the Lord your God raise up unto you from among your brethren, like unto me;" but how great was this person when compared with Moses! Moses desired to see God's glory; this sight he could not bear; he saw his *back parts*, probably meaning God's *design* relative to the *latter days:* but Jesus, the Almighty Saviour, in whom dwells all the fulness of the Godhead bodily, who lay in the bosom of the Father, he hath *declared* God to man. Wondrous system of legal ordinances that pointed out and typified all these things! And more wonderful system of Gospel salvation, which is the *body, soul, life, energy,* and *full accomplishment* of all that was written in the LAW, in the PROPHETS, and in the PSALMS, concerning the sufferings and death of Jesus, and the redemption of a ruined world "by his agony and bloody sweat, by his cross and passion, by his death and burial, by his glorious resurrection and ascension, and by the coming of the Holy Ghost!" Thus ends the PENTATEUCH, commonly called the LAW of MOSES, a work every way worthy of God its author, and only less than the NEW COVENANT, the *law* and *Gospel* of our Lord and Saviour JESUS CHRIST.

Now to the ever blessed and glorious TRINITY, FATHER, WORD, and SPIRIT, the infinite and eternal ONE, from whom alone *wisdom, truth,* and *goodness* can proceed, be glory and dominion for ever and ever. Amen.

MASORETIC *Notes* on DEUTERONOMY.

The *number* of *verses* in ELLEH HADDEBARIM, Deuteronomy, is 955; the symbol of which is חנץ, in which word ץ *tsade* stands for 900, נ *nun* for 50, and ח *cheth* for 5.

The *middle verse* is the 10th of chap. xvii.: *And thou shalt observe to do all that they command thee.*

Its *Pareshioth* or larger sections are 11, the numerical symbol of which is חג *chag;* Psa. cxviii. 27: *Bind the* SACRIFICE *with cords to the horns of the altar.* In which word ח *cheth* stands for 8, and ג *gimel* for 3.

Its *Sedarim* or smaller sections are 27, the symbolical sign of which is יגיד *yaggid;* Prov. xii. 17: *He that speaketh truth,* SHOWETH FORTH *righteousness.* In which word the two י י *yods* stand for 20, ד *daleth* for 4, and ג *gimel* for 3.

Its *Perakim* or modern chapters are 34, the symbol of which is לבב *lebab;* Psa. cxi. 1: *I will praise the Lord with my whole* HEART. In which word the two ב ב *beths* stand for 4, and the ל *lamed* for 30.

The number of *open sections* is 34, of its *close sections* 124, total 158; the symbol of which is ינחילם, *yanchilem,* 148, and כבויר *cab-od,* 10. 1 Sam. ii. 8: *To make them to* INHERIT *the throne of his* GLORY. The numerical letters of the word ינחילם *yanchilem,* 148, with וד *od,* 10, taken from כבוד *cabod,* make 158, the total of its *open* and *close* sections.

The number of verses in the whole Pentateuch is 5845, the memorial symbol of which is החמה *hachammah,* Isa. xxx. 26: *Moreover the light of the moon shall be as the light of* THE SUN. In which word, the letters taken in their proper order make the sum, המחה (5 8 4 5).

The *middle verse* of the Law is Lev. viii. 8: *And he put the breastplate upon him, and he put in the breastplate the* URIM *and the* THUMMIM.

The number of OPEN *sections* in the whole Law is 290, the symbol of which is פרי *peri;* Cant. iv. 16: *Let my beloved come into his garden, and eat his precious* FRUITS.

The number of its CLOSE *sections* is 379, the symbol of which occurs in the word בשבעה *bishbuah;* Num. xxx. 10: *Or bound her soul with a bond* BY AN OATH.

Total number of all the *open* and *close* sections, 669, the memorial symbol of which is לא תחסר *lo techsar;* Deut. viii. 9: THOU SHALT NOT LACK *any thing in it.*

SECTIONS of the Book of Deuteronomy, carried on from Numbers, which ends with the FORTY-THIRD.

The FORTY-FOURTH, called דברים *debarim,* begins Deut. i. 1, and ends chap. iii. 22.

The FORTY-FIFTH, called ואתחנן *vaethchannen,* begins chap. iii. 23, and ends chap. vii. 11.

The FORTY-SIXTH, called עקב *ekeb,* begins chap. vii. 12, and ends chap. xi. 25.

The FORTY-SEVENTH, called ראה *reeh,* begins chap. xi. 26, and ends chap. xvi. 17.

The FORTY-EIGHTH, called שפטים *shophetim,* begins chap. xvi. 18, and ends chap. xxi. 9.

The FORTY-NINTH, called תצא *tetse,* begins chap. xxi. 10, and ends chap. xxv. 19.

The FIFTIETH, called תבוא *tabo,* begins chap. xxvi. 1, and ends chap. xxix. 8.

The FIFTY-FIRST, called נצבים *nitstsabim,* begins chap. xxix. 9, and ends chap. xxx. 20.

The FIFTY-SECOND, called וילך *vaiyelech,* begins chap. xxxi. 1, and ends chap. xxxi. 30.

The FIFTY-THIRD, called האזינו *haazinu,* begins chap. xxxii. 1, and ends chap. xxxii. 51.

The FIFTY-FOURTH, called וזאת הברכה *vezoth habberachah,* begins chap. xxxiii. 1, and ends chap. xxxiv. 12.

GENERAL OBSERVATIONS ON THE FIVE BOOKS OF MOSES.

We have now passed through the Pentateuch, and have endeavoured carefully to mark its important contents. Its *antiquity* sets it at the head of all the writings in the world; and the various subjects it embraces make it of the utmost consequence to every civilized part of the earth. Its *philosophy, jurisprudence, history, geography*, and *chronology*, entitle it to the respect of the whole human race; while its system of *theology* and *religion* demonstrably prove it to be a revelation from GOD. But on these topics, as many observations have already been made as the nature of a commentary professing to study brevity can possibly admit.

Of MOSES, the writer of the Pentateuch, considered as a *historian* and *philosopher*, a great deal has been said in the course of the notes on the book of GENESIS; and especially at the conclusion of the *fiftieth* chapter; to which the reader is particularly referred.

Of Moses as a *legislator*, volumes might be written, and the subject not be exhausted. What is called the *Law of Moses*, is more properly the *Law of God;* and תורת יהוה *Torath Yehovah*, the *Law of Jehovah*, is the grand title of the Pentateuch. Such a definition of this term as comports with the *nature, structure*, and *design* of the Pentateuch, has already been given in the note on Exod. xii. 40, to which the reader is requested to refer. Could we conceive Moses to have been the *author* of this system, we must consider him more than mortal: no wisdom of man has ever yet been able to invent such a code of laws.

This merit however has been disputed, and his laws severely criticised by certain persons whose interest it was to prove religion to be a cheat, because they had none themselves; and whose case must be hopeless could it be proved to be true. To some whose mental taste and feeling are strangely perverted, every thing in *heathenism* wears not only the most fascinating aspect, but appears to lay claim to and possess every excellence. These have called up Confucius, Menu, Zoroaster, and Mohammed himself, to dispute the palm of excellence with Moses! To examine the claims of such competitors, and to decide on their respective merits would require a large treatise, and my limits confine me to a sketch. To any godly, impartial mind, properly acquainted with the subject, little needs to be said; to those who are prejudiced, all reasoning is thrown away. A few words on the merit of each of these competitors must suffice.

1. To *Con fu tsee*, the great Chinese lawgiver, corruptly called *Confucius*, are attributed, in the records of his country, a number of ordinances and institutions which do honour to his times and to his people; but alas! how much of the darkness, erroneousness, and infirmity of the human mind do they exhibit! And however profitable they may be, as prudential maxims and social regulations to a certain extent, how little are they calculated to elevate or ennoble the human mind, or inspire men with a just notion of vice and virtue! Their author had no correct notion of the Divine nature; his laws had no sanction but that of *convenience* or *necessity*, and, notwithstanding their boasted excellence, have left, from the time of their promulgation to the present day, the sum total of that immense nation which profess to be governed by them, in the thickest darkness of the most degrading idolatry, closely verging upon *atheism* itself! Not so the Mosaic code; it was the *light* that lightened the universe, and the *glory* of the people who were governed by its dictates. We have the firmest ground and the most ample authority to *assert*, that the *greatest kings*, the *wisest statesmen*, the most *accomplished poets* and *rhetoricians*, the most *magnanimous heroes*, and the most *holy* and *useful people* that ever existed, were formed on the model, and brought up in the bosom and under the influence, of the Mosaic institutions. While the *Proverbs* and *Ecclesiastes* of SOLOMON, the *history* and *poetic compositions* of DAVID, the inimitable *discourses* of ISAIAH, JEREMIAH, JOEL, HABAKKUK, and others of the Jewish prophets remain, every intelligent reader will have the fullest proofs of the truth of the above *assertion*, which shrinks not under the pretence of being *hazarded;* but which must spring up in every ingenuous mind, from the fullest conviction of its own truth, after a serious perusal of the sacred code in question. All those eminent personages were brought up in the Mosaic school, and were prepared by the Pentateuch for the prophetic influence.

2. The *Institutes* of MENU, lately clothed in an English dress by the elegant hand of Sir William Jones, have been thought to stand in fair competition with the laws of Moses. I have read them carefully, with strong prejudice in their favour; and have endeavoured, to the best of my judgment, duly to appreciate their worth. I have sought for *resemblances* to the Mosaic institutions, because I thought it possible that the same God who was so fully *known in Jewry*, might have made at least a partial revelation of himself in *Hindostan;* but while I alternately *admired* and *regretted*, I was ultimately disappointed, as I plainly saw that the system in its essential parts lacked the seal of the *living God*. My readers may justly question my competency to form a correct opinion of the work under consideration—I shall not therefore obtrude it, but substitute that of the *translator*, who was better qualified than perhaps any other man in Europe or Asia, to form a correct judgment of its merits. "The work," says he, "now presented to the *European* world, contains abundance of curious matter, extremely interesting both to speculative lawyers and antiquaries; with many *beauties* which need not be pointed out, and with many *blemishes* which cannot be justified or palliated. It is a system of *despotism* and *priestcraft*, both indeed limited by law, but *artfully conspiring* to give mutual support though with mutual checks. It is filled with *strange conceits* in *metaphysics* and *natural philosophy;* with idle *superstitions*, and with a scheme of theology most *obscurely figurative*, and consequently liable to *dangerous misconception*. It abounds with *minute* and *childish formalities*, with *ceremonics* generally *absurd* and often *ridiculous;* the *punishments* are *partial* and *fanciful;* for some crimes *dreadfully cruel*, and for others *reprehensibly*

slight; and the very *morals*, though rigid enough on the whole, are in one or two instances, as in the case of *light oaths* and *pious perjury*, unaccountably relaxed."—Preface to the *Institutes* of *Menu.*

We may defy its enemies to prove any of these things against the Pentateuch. *Priestcraft* and *despotism* cannot appear under its sanction: God is King alone, and the *priest* his *servant;* and he who was prevented, by the very law under which he ministered, from having *any earthly property*, could consequently have no *secular power*. The king, who was afterwards chosen, was ever considered as God's *deputy* or *vicegerent;* he was obliged to rule according to the laws that were given by God through Moses, and was never permitted either to *change* them, or *add a single precept* or *rite* to the civil or sacred code of his country. Thus *despotism* and *priestcraft* were equally precluded. As to its *rites* and *ceremonies*, they are at once dignified and expressive; they point out the holiness of their author, the sinfulness of man, the necessity of an atonement, and the state of moral excellence to which the grace and mercy of the Creator have promised to raise the human soul. As to its *punishments*, they are ever such as the nature and circumstances of the crime render just and necessary—and its *rewards* are not such as flow merely from a principle of *retribution* or *remunerative justice*, but from an enlightened and fatherly tenderness, which makes obedience to the laws the highest interest of the subject.

At the same time that love to God and obedience to his commandments are strongly inculcated, love and benevolence to man are equally enforced, together with *piety*, which is the soul of *obedience*, *patriotism*, the life of *society; hospitality* to strangers, and *humanity* to the whole brute creation. To all this might be added that it *includes* in it, as well as *points out*, the Gospel of the Son of God, from which it receives its consummation and perfection. Such, reader, is the law of God given through Moses to the people of Israel.

3. Of the laws of *Zerdust* or *Zeratusht*, commonly called *Zoroaster*, it is unnecessary to speak at large; they are incapable of comparison with the Mosaic code. As delivered in the *Zend Avesta*, they cannot so properly be called a *system* as a *congeries* of *puerility*, *superstition*, and *absurdity;* with scarcely a *precept* or a *rite* that has any tendency to elevate the mind, or raise man from his state of moral degradation to a proper rank in civilized society, or to any worthy apprehension of the Maker and Governor of the universe. *Harmlessness* is the *sum* of the morality they seem to inculcate, with a certain superstitious reverence for *fire*, probably as the emblem of *purity;* and for *animal life*, principally in reference to the doctrine of the *Metempsychosis* or *transmigration of souls*, on which it seems to have been originally built.

4. The Koran of Mohammed is the only remaining competitor that can be supposed to be at all qualified to dispute the palm with the Pentateuch of Moses; but the pretensions of this production will be soon settled, when it is known that it possesses not one excellence, the purity and elegance of *its language* excepted, which it has not borrowed from the writings of *Moses* and the *prophets*, or the sayings of *Christ* and his *apostles*. This is a fact which none can successfully dispute, and of which the Koran itself bears the most unequivocal evidences. What can be fairly claimed as the *peculium* of the Arab lawgiver makes a motley mixture with what he has stolen from the book of God, and is in general as absurd and weak as it is on the whole false and wicked. As to the boasted *morality* of the Koran, it will have as little to exult in of this kind when the *law* and the *Gospel* have taken from it that of which they have been plundered, as the daw in the fable had when the different fowls had plucked away their own feathers, with which the vain bird had decorated herself. Mohammed, it is true, destroyed *idolatry* wherever he came; and he did the same by *true religion;* for *Judaism* and *Christianity* met with no more quarter from him than the grossest errors of pagan idolatry. To compare him with the pure, holy, disinterested, humane, and heavenly-minded Jewish legislator, would be as gross political as it would be palpable religious blasphemy. When we allow that he was a man of a deep and penetrating mind, well acquainted with the superstitious turn of his countrymen; austere, cunning, and hypocritical; a great general and a brutal conqueror, who seemed to sacrifice at no other shrine than that of his *lust* and *ambition*, we do him no injustice: the whole of his system bears the most evident proofs of imposition and forgery; nor is there a character to which imposture can lay claim that does not appear prominently in the Koran, and in every part of the Mohammedan system. The chief of these distinctive marks have already been examined in reference to the Pentateuch, in the concluding note on Exod. xviii. These are all found in the Koran, but not one of them in the Pentateuch. The Pentateuch therefore is of God; the Koran came from another quarter.

5. The different systems of the *Grecian ethic philosophers* cannot come into this inquiry. They were in general incongruous and contradictory, and none of them was ever capable of forming a *sect* that could be said to have any moral *perpetuity*.

6. The laws of *Lycurgus* and *Solon* could not preserve those states, at the basis of which they were laid; while the laws of Moses have been the means of preserving the people who held them, amidst the most terrible reverses of what are called *fortune* and *fate*, for nearly the space of 4,000 years! This is one of the most extraordinary and astonishing facts in the whole history of mankind.

7. The *republic* of *Plato*, of which it is fashionable to boast, is, when stripped of what it has borrowed from Moses, like the *Utopia* of Sir T. More, the ærial figment of a philosophic mind, *en delire;* both systems are inapplicable and impracticable in the present state of man. To persons under the influence of various and discordant passions, strongly actuated by *self-interest*, they can never apply. They have no tendency to change the moral state of society from *vice* to *virtue:* a nation of *saints* might agree to regulate their lives and conduct by them, but where is such to be found? Though Plato has borrowed much from Moses, yet he has destroyed the effect of the whole by not referring the precepts and maxims to God, by whom alone strength to fulfil them could be furnished. It is the province of the revelation of God to make the

knave an *honest* man; the *unholy* and *profane*, *pure* and *pious;* and to cause all who act by its dictates to love one another with pure hearts fervently, and to feel the finest and fullest impressions of

"The *generous mind* that's not confined at home,
But spreads itself abroad through all the public,
And feels for every member of the land."

The Pentateuch is an *original* work; nothing *like* it was ever found among the nations of the earth. Those who have asserted that its principal institutions have been borrowed from the Egyptians, neither know the Mosaic code, nor are acquainted with the Egyptian mythology. Dr. Priestley has written well on this point, and from his dissertation I shall borrow the following extracts:—

"They who suppose that Moses himself was the author of the institutions, civil or religious, that bear his name, and that in framing them he borrowed much from the Egyptians or other ancient nations, must never have compared them together; otherwise they could not but have perceived many circumstances in which they differ most essentially from them all. I shall endeavour to point out the more considerable of them.

"1. No heathen ever conceived an idea of so great an *object* as that of the institutions of Moses, which appears to be nothing less than the instruction of all mankind in the great doctrine of the unity and universal moral government of God, as the Maker of the world, and the common parent of all the human race, in opposition to the polytheism and idolatry which then prevailed, which, besides being grossly absurd in its principles, and leading to endless superstitions, threatened the world with a deluge of vice and misery. For this purpose the Hebrew nation was placed in the most conspicuous situation among all the civilized nations of the world, which were universally addicted to idolatry of the grossest kind, to divinations, necromancy, and other superstitions of a similar nature, and practised as acts of religion; some of their rites abominably licentious, and others the most shockingly cruel, as the necessary means of recommending themselves to the various objects of their worship. As all mankind imagined that their outward prosperity depended upon the observance of their respective religions, that of the Hebrew nation was made to do so in the most conspicuous manner, as a visible lesson to all the world. They were to prosper beyond all other nations while they adhered to their religion; and to suffer in a manner equally exemplary and conspicuous in consequence of their departure from it. Of this all mankind might easily judge. These great ideas occur in the sacred books of the Hebrews, and nowhere else. They are all distinctly advanced by Moses, and more fully unfolded in the writings of the later prophets. But certainly nothing so great and sublime could have been suggested to Moses from any thing that he *saw* in Egypt, or could have *heard* of in other countries.

"2. In no system of religion besides that of Moses was *purity of morals* any part of it. All the heathen religions were systems of mere *ceremonies*, on the observance of which it was imagined that the prosperity of the several states depended; and the sole business of the *priests* was to attend to the due observance of these rites, many of which were so far from being favourable to morals, that they were of the most impure and abominable nature, as is well known to all who have any knowledge of them. On the contrary, it appears, not only from the *ten commandments*, but from all the writings of Moses, and those of the prophets who succeeded him, that the purest morality, the most favourable to private and public happiness, was the principal and ultimate object of the system. The books of Moses abound with *precepts of morality*, inculcated in the most forcible manner, and they are distinguished from *laws* by having no penalty annexed to them. Such precepts as these, *Be ye holy, for I am holy;* and, *What does the Lord require of thee, but to do justice, to love mercy, and to walk humbly with thy God?* could never have been borrowed from any heathen system of religion. In this most important respect the institutions of Moses are a great *original*, and were never copied by any other lawgiver.

"3 Nowhere in all the heathen world could Moses have heard of such a proper *national worship* as that which he introduced. The Hebrew nation had not only *one* single *object* of their *worship*, in which they differed essentially from all other nations, but *one national altar*, *one* precise *ritual*, and only *one place* for the meeting of the whole nation at the public festivals. A whole tribe, a twelfth part of the nation, was set apart for services of a religious nature, and their provision made to depend in a great measure upon their performance of them, being not in lands cultivated by themselves, but in the produce of lands cultivated by others. At this one great national altar sacrifices were performed every morning and evening, in the name and at the expense of the whole nation; and the manner in which this was done was invariable, and not left to the discretion of the performers. In all other countries the places of worship were numerous; and the diversity in the modes of worship varied with the objects of them. In Egypt in particular the different *nomes* were exceedingly hostile to each other on this account. Hence arose endless and discordant superstitions.

"4. In no country besides that of the *Hebrews* were the *public festivals* expressly instituted in commemoration of such great events respecting their history and religion. It is peculiar to this nation also that the directions for the celebration of them were reduced to writing at the time of their institution, so that there could never be any uncertainty about the origin or the reasons of them. They were only three: the *passover*, on their deliverance from their state of servitude in Egypt, when the first-born of all the Egyptians were destroyed, and all theirs preserved; the *pentecost*, on the giving of the law from Mount Sinai; and the *feast of tabernacles*, in commemoration of their living in *tents* and *booths* during their travels through the wilderness. At the first of these festivals the *first-fruits* of the year were solemnly presented; at the second, the *harvest* was got in; and at the last, the *vintage* and all the greater labours of the year were closed. Among the heathen nations the festivals were numerous and perplexing. More than *sixty* were celebrated by the Athenians; the origin and reason of their institution were uncertain; and none of

them were calculated to answer any important moral purposes, but were too often the occasion, not of innocent festivity, but of intemperance and debauch. Several of the heathen festivals were celebrated in a manner the most disgusting and shocking to common modesty and common sense.

"*Sacrificing* was a mode more ancient than idolatry, or the institutions of Moses; but among the heathens various superstitious customs were introduced respecting it, which were all excluded from the religion of the Hebrews.

"In the *laws* of Moses, in which we find even the most minute circumstances of the act of sacrificing prescribed, there is no mention of any thing preceding the slaying of the animal, besides its being *sound* and of a *proper age*. It was not brought with any *garlands*. No ουλαι, or cakes of barley and salt, were put upon its *back*. No *wine* was poured upon its *horns*. No *hair* was taken from its forehead to be thrown into the fire on the altar. And nothing is said about *inspecting the entrails*, with a view to divination, which was a principal object in all the heathen sacrifices. The use that was made of the *blood* of the victims was peculiar to the Hebrew ritual; and certainly not borrowed from any heathen customs that could have been known to Moses.

"No heathens knew any thing of the *sprinkling of the blood* in the peculiarly solemn manner in which it was to be done by the Hebrew priests; and so far were they from rigorously abstaining from the *eating of blood*, that in their sacrifices to the infernal deities they partook of it as a method of feasting with them; and in the *Tauribolium* the offerer was covered with it from head to foot, and kept himself in that condition as long as he could. (As a proof of this see the note on Lev. viii. 23.) As Moses did not adopt any of the heathen customs, it is equally evident that they borrowed nothing from him with respect to sacrifices. With them we find no such distinction of sacrifices as is made in the books of Moses, such as *burnt-offerings*, *sin-offerings*, *trespass-offerings*, and *peace-offerings*, or of the *heaving* or *waving* of the sacrifices. Those particulars, therefore, he could not have had from them, whether we can discover any reason for them or not. They either had their origin in the time of Moses, or, which is most probable, were prior to his time and to the existence of idolatry.

"Had Moses copied any thing from the heathens, he would probably have introduced something of their *mysteries*, which were rites performed in secret, and generally in the night, to which peculiar privileges were annexed, and which it was deemed the greatest crime to reveal; all of them circumstances of a suspicious nature, and evidently liable to great abuse.

"The most remarkable of these mysteries were the *Eleusinian*, which were celebrated at Athens every four years, and continued nine days. Whatever these rites were, it was made death to reveal them; and if any person not regularly initiated was present at this exhibition, he was put to death without mercy.

"Nothing surely like this can be found in the institutions of Moses. There was nothing in the Hebrew ritual of worship that was any *secret*. Every thing is expressly described in the written law; and though none but priests could enter the holy place, or the holy of holies besides the high priest, every thing that was done by him there is as particularly described as what was done by the people without; and no service whatever was performed in the night except the attendance at the great altar to keep the fire in a proper state for consuming all the remains of victims; and of this no mention is made in the ritual. It is only presumed by the Jewish writers on the subject that it must have been done of course.

"Had Moses borrowed any thing from the heathens, he could not have overlooked the various modes of *divination*, sorcery, and witchcraft; their omens of a thousand kinds, their rites for consulting the dead in the art of necromancy, their distinction of days into lucky and unlucky, which constituted a great part of the religious observances of all the heathen nations, civilized or uncivilized. The Romans had even an order of priests called *augurs*, whose sole business it was to observe the flight of birds, and to make prognostications from them. But so far are we from finding in the books of Moses any thing of this kind, of which those of the Hindoos are full, that they are spoken of with the greatest contempt and abhorrence, and the pretenders to them are directed to be put to death.

"The cities of refuge have been mentioned as compared with the unlimited right of *asylum* attached to the temples of the heathens; and this may be considered as a religious as well as a civil institution. But the privileges of the *Sabbatical year* and of the *jubilee* are wholly of a civil nature, and they must have been an admirable security for personal liberty and the property of families. No Hebrew could bind himself for servitude more than *seven* years, nor could he alienate his landed property for more than *fifty*. No gift or sale could have any effect beyond this term, which was fixed for the whole nation, and did not commence at the time of every particular bargain. In consequence of this, though a family might suffer by the imprudence or extravagance of the head of it, the evil had a limit; for at the jubilee all estates reverted to the original proprietors.

"In short, no person can peruse the laws of Moses without acknowledging them to be truly *original;* and their superiority to those of other ancient nations, the most famed for their wisdom, is an evidence of their Divine origin."—*Dissertat. on the Mosaic Institutions.*

8. On this subject in general it may be just necessary to add, that the utmost that can be said of all laws merely *human* is, that they *restrain vices* through the terror of punishment. God's law not only restrains *vice*, but it infuses *virtue*. It alone brings man to the footstool of his Maker, and keeps him dependent on the strong for strength, on the wise for wisdom, and on the merciful for grace. It abounds with promises of support and salvation for the *present life*, which no false system dared ever to propose; every where Moses in the most confident manner pledges his God for the fulfilment of all the exceeding great and precious promises with which his laws are so plentifully interspersed; and while they were obedient they could say, "Not one word hath failed us of all the good things which the Lord our God spake

concerning us." Who that dispassionately reads the *Pentateuch*, that considers it in itself, and in its reference to that glorious *Gospel* which it was intended to introduce, can for a moment deny it the palm of infinite superiority over all the systems ever framed or imagined by man? Well might the Israelitish people triumphantly exclaim, "There is none like the God of Jeshurun!" and with what striking propriety does the glorious legislator add, "Happy art thou, O Israel! who is like unto *thee?* O people saved of the LORD!"

See the ZEND AVESTA, by *Anquetil du Perron*, 3 vols., 4to., Paris, 1771. CONFUCIUS SINARUM PHILOSOPHUS, by *Herdtrich*, *Couplet*, &c., folio, Paris, 1687. ZOROASTER, CONFUCIUS, et MAHOMET, comparés, par M. *Pastoret*, 8vo, Paris, 1788. The INSTITUTES of MENU, by Sir *William Jones;* and the KORAN, with Notes, &c., by Mr. *Sale*.

A SKETCH OF THE HISTORY AND CHARACTER OF MOSES.

HAVING said so much concerning the Pentateuch, there remains little room to say much concerning Moses himself, as his character is so much involved in that of his work. The genuine history of Moses is written by *himself*, and that is found succinctly detailed in the book of Exodus; *Josephus*, the *rabbins*, and the *oriental historians*, have written lives of this great man which are perfect romances; for by attempting to embellish, they have turned the whole history into ridicule. *Trogus Pompeius* has copied some of them, unless we allow that his abridger, *Justin*, is the *author* of the ill-told falsity which is found in his work. But with these relations we have no concern; and from the account written by himself, collated with the speech of St. Stephen, Acts vii., we learn the following facts:—

MOSES, the son of Amram and Jochebed, both of the tribe of *Levi*, was born A. M. 2433, B. C. 1571, while the Israelites were in a state of bondage in Egypt, and at that time under the most distressful persecution, the king of Egypt having issued an edict to destroy all the male children of the Hebrews. Added to their parental affection, his personal beauty, (Acts vii. 20,) seems to have induced the parents to hazard every thing to preserve their child's life; they therefore hid him for three months; but finding from circumstances that they could keep him secret no longer, they were determined to abandon him wholly to the care of Providence. Having provided a little vessel of bulrushes, or flags pitched, and thus rendered impervious to the water, they set him afloat on the river Nile, and sent his sister Miriam to watch the event. The daughter of Pharaoh coming to that part of the river, either to make her ablutions or to wash her clothes, seeing the vessel afloat, commanded it to be brought to her; and being struck with the helpless state and beauty of the child, judging that it belonged to one of the Hebrews, determined to preserve its life, and adopt it for her own. Miriam, his sister, who immediately appeared, but was unknown to the princess, offered her services to procure a nurse for the child from among the Hebrew women; she was accordingly employed, and Jochebed, the mother, was soon brought to the spot, and the child was immediately committed to her care, the princess being entirely ignorant of the relation that subsisted between the child and its nurse. At a proper age he was taken to the Egyptian court, and educated there as the son of Pharaoh's daughter, and was brought up in all the *learning and wisdom of the Egyptians*, and became very eminent both in words and deeds; Acts vii. 22. Here he appears to have stayed nearly *forty years*. Afterwards, in consequence of having killed one of the oppressors of his Hebrew brethren, he was obliged to take refuge in Midian, where, entering into the service of *Jethro*, a priest or prince of that country, he married his daughter Zipporah, by whom he had two sons, *Eleazar* and *Gershom*, and continued as the guardian of the flocks of his father-in-law for forty years. At the conclusion of this time God manifested himself to him while tending the flocks of his father-in-law at Mount Horeb, and gave him a commission to bring Israel out of Egypt. He went on the Divine errand, became associated with his elder brother Aaron, opened his commission to the Egyptian king, and wrought several striking miracles to prove the truth of his Divine mission. The king refusing to let the people go, God afflicted him and the land with *ten* grievous plagues; after which the people were led out, and by a most stupendous miracle passed through the divided waters of the Red Sea, which Pharaoh and his army essaying to do, were drowned. Having led the Israelites into the deserts of Arabia, commonly called the *wilderness*, God gave them the most signal manifestations of his power and goodness in a series of successive miracles, and delivered to Moses their leader that *information* and those *laws* which are contained in the Pentateuch. Having governed the people forty years in the desert, and brought them to the very verge of the promised land, he was not permitted to pass over Jordan with them, but died in the plains of Moab, while in familiar converse with his God, in the 120th year of his age. Care, labour, and years, had made no inroads upon his constitution, for it is particularly marked that *his eye was not dim, nor his natural force abated*, Deut. xxxiv. 8; that he preserved all the vivacity of youth and the vigour of manhood to a period in which, even at that time, old age made its greatest depredations upon those who had no other support than what the common course of nature afforded.

After this hasty sketch of so eventful a life as that of Moses, it may be necessary to enter more particularly into an examination of his character and conduct. This is a difficult task; but, *in* MAGNIS *voluisse* sat est.

The eulogium or character given of him by the Spirit of God, though very concise, is yet full and satisfactory: *And there arose not a prophet since in Israel like unto Moses, whom Jehovah knew face to face; in all the signs and the wonders which the Lord sent him to do in the land of Egypt, to Pharaoh, and to all his servants, and to all his land; and in all that mighty hand* (all-conquering power and influence) *and in all the great terror which Moses showed in the sight of all Israel.* Moses is called the *servant of God;* and he has farther this high character, that as a *servant* he was *faithful* to God *in all his house*, Heb. iii. 5. He faithfully discharged the trust reposed in him; and to-

tally forgetting *himself* and his own secular interest, with that also of his *family*, he laboured incessantly to promote God's honour and the people's welfare, which on many occasions he showed were dearer to him than his *own life*. Moses was in every respect a *great man*; for every virtue that constitutes genuine nobility was concentred in his mind, and fully displayed in his conduct. He ever conducted himself as a man conscious of his *own integrity*, and of the *guidance and protection of God*, under whose orders he constantly acted. He therefore betrays no *confusion* in his views, nor *indecision* in his measures; he was ever without *anxiety*, because he was conscious of the rectitude of his motives, and that the cause which he espoused was the cause of God, and that *his* power and faithfulness were pledged for his support. His *courage* and *fortitude* were unshaken and unconquerable, because his reliance was unremittingly fixed on the *unchangeableness* of JEHOVAH. He left Egypt *having an eye to the recompense of reward* in another world, and never lost sight of this grand object; he was therefore neither *discouraged* by *difficulties*, nor *elated* by *prosperity*. He who in Egypt refused to be called the son of Pharaoh's daughter, thereby renouncing the claim he might have had on the Egyptian throne, was never likely to be influenced by *secular views* in the government of the miserable *multitudes* which he led out of that country. His renunciation of the *court* of *Pharaoh* and its advantages was the amplest proof that he neither sought nor expected honour or emolument in the *wilderness*, among a people who had scarcely any thing but what they received by immediate miracle from the hand of God.

I have more than once had occasion to note the *disinterestedness* of Moses in reference to his *family*, as well as to *himself*. This is a singular case; his own tribe, that of *Levi*, he left without any *earthly possession*: and though to minister to God was the most honourable employment, yet the *Levites* could never arise to any *political* consequence in Israel. Even his *own sons* became blended in the common mass of the Levites, and possessed no kind of distinction among their brethren. Though his confidence in God was ever unshaken, yet he had a life of toil and perpetual distress, occasioned by the ignorance, obstinacy, and baseness, of the people over whom he presided; and he died in their service, leaving no other *property* but his *tent* behind him. Of the *spoils* taken in war we never read of the *portion of Moses*. He had *none*, he wanted *none*; his treasure was in heaven, and where his treasure was, there also was his heart. By this disinterestedness of Moses two points are fully proved: 1. That he was satisfied, fully so, that his mission was Divine, and that in it he served the *living God*; and 2. That he believed in the *immortality* of the soul, and the doctrine of future rewards and punishments, and therefore he laboured so *to pass through things temporal, that he might not lose the things that are eternal*. It is strange that the faith of Moses in these points should be questioned by any who had ever seriously read the Pentateuch.

The *manner* in which he bore the sentence of his exclusion from the promised inheritance, is an additional proof of his persuasion of the reality of the invisible world. No testiness, no murmuring, no expatiating on former services; no passionate entreaties to have the sentence reversed, appear in the spirit or conduct of this truly great man. He bowed to the decision of that justice which he knew could not act wrong; and having buried the world, as to himself, he had no earthly attachments; he was obeying the *will of God* in leading the people, and therefore, when his Master chose to dismiss him from this service, he was content; and saw, without *regret* or *envy*, another appointed to his office.

The *moral character* of Moses is almost *immaculate*. That he offended Jehovah at the waters of *Meribah* there can be no doubt; but in *what* the offence consisted, commentators and critics are greatly at a loss to ascertain. In the note on Num. xx. 12, I have said all that I believe *should be said* upon the point; and after all, *conjecture* is obliged to come in, to supply the place of *substantial evidence*; and the fault is so *slight*, humanly speaking, as even to glide away from the eye of conjecture itself. Had the offence, whatever it was, been committed by any *ordinary* person, it would probably have passed between God and the conscience without any *public reprehension*. But Moses was *great*, and *supereminently favoured*; and a fault in *him* derived much of its moral delinquency from these very circumstances. He did not *sanctify the Lord in the sight of the people*—he did not fully show that God himself was the *sole worker*; he appeared by his conduct to exhibit himself as an agent indispensably necessary in the promised miraculous supply; and this might have had the most dangerous consequences on the minds of this gross people, had not God thus marked it with his displeasure. This awful lesson to the *legislator* taught the *people* that their help came from GOD, and not from *man*; and that consequently they must repose their confidence in HIM alone. But this subject deserves to be more distinctly considered, as in the account given of his death this offence is again brought forth to view. God himself thus details the circumstances: "Get thee up into this mountain, and behold the land of Canaan—and die in the mount whither thou goest up, and be gathered unto thy people as Aaron thy brother, because ye trespassed against me AMONG THE CHILDREN OF ISRAEL; because ye sanctified me not in the midst of the children of Israel;" chap. xxxii. 49–51. "And Moses went up unto the mountain of Nebo, and the Lord showed him all the land; and the Lord said unto him, This is the land which I sware unto Abraham, unto Isaac, and unto Jacob, saying, I will give it unto thy seed: I have caused thee to see it with thine eyes, but thou shalt not go over thither: so Moses, the servant of the Lord, died there, according to the word of the Lord; and he buried him;" chap. xxxiv. 1–6. In the above extracts, all the circumstances relative to this event are brought into one point of view; and we see plainly the stress that is laid on the *offence* against God. YE TRESPASSED AGAINST ME AMONG THE CHILDREN OF ISRAEL—YE SANCTIFIED ME NOT IN THE MIDST OF THE CHILDREN OF ISRAEL. These words may be understood thus: The people of themselves were too much prone to take off their eye from GOD, consult their senses, and depend upon *man*; and the

manner in which Moses and Aaron performed the miracle which God commanded them to do in his name, was such as to confirm them in the carnality of their views, and cause them to depend on an *arm of flesh. Ye therefore shall not go into the promised land*, said the Lord: and the death of them both was the fullest proof to this people that it was not by might nor by power, but by the Spirit of the Lord of hosts, that their enemies were expelled, and that themselves were introduced and established in the promised inheritance. This seems to be the spirit of the whole business: and as Moses had no other end in view but the glory of God, it must have been a supreme satisfaction to his pious soul, that this end was so effectually promoted, though even at *the expense of his life.*

1. At a distant view there appears to be very little observable in the *death* of Moses; but on a nearer approach we shall find it to have been the most *honourable*, I might add the most *glorious*, with which any human being was ever favoured. As to his *death* itself, it is simply said, *He died in the land of Moab—according to the word of the Lord.* He was, as has already been observed, in familiar conversation with his Maker; and while in the act of viewing the land, and receiving the last information relative to *it*, the ancient covenant with the patriarchs, and the performance of the covenant in putting their posterity into possession of this goodly inheritance, he yielded up the ghost, and suddenly passed from the verge of the *earthly* into the *heavenly* Canaan. Thus, without the *labour* and the *delay* of passing through the *type*, he entered at once into the possession of the *antitype;* having simply lost the honour of leading the people a *little farther*, whom, with so much care and solicitude, he had brought *thus far*.

2. There is another circumstance in his death which requires particular notice. It is said, *He died—according to the word of the Lord:* the original words על פי יהוה *al pi Yehovah*, signify literally *at* (or *upon*) *the mouth of Jehovah;* which *Jonathan ben Uzziel* interprets thus: על נשיקת מימרא דיי *al neshikath meymera dayeya*, "by a kiss of the WORD of Jehovah;" and this has given rise to an ancient tradition among the Jews, "that God embraced Moses, and drew his soul out of his body by a kiss." The Targumist adds, that this was "on the seventh day of the month Adar, the same day of the same month on which he was born."

3. The last circumstance worthy of note is, that *God buried him*, which is an honour no *human being* ever received besides himself. From the tradition referred to by Saint Jude, ver. 9, it appears that *Michael*, the archangel, was employed on this occasion; that *Satan* disputed the matter with him, probably wishing the burial-place of Moses to be *known*, that it might become an excitement to superstition and idolatry; but being rebuked by the Lord, he was obliged to give over the contention; and though the place of burial was probably the *valley of the mountain* on which Moses had been conversing with God, and where he died, yet Satan himself could not ascertain the spot, and *no man knoweth of his sepulchre unto this day.*

4. It may be asked how Moses, who was bred up at an idolatrous court, which he did not quit till the fortieth year of his age, got that *acquaintance with the true God* which the apostle states him to have had; and that *faith* by which he realized spiritual and invisible things, and through which he despised all worldly grandeur and secular emolument. "*By faith*," says the apostle, "Moses, when he was come to years, refused to be called the son of Pharaoh's daughter choosing rather to suffer affliction with the people of God, than to enjoy the pleasures of sin for a season; esteeming the reproach of Christ greater riches than the treasures in Egypt; for he had respect unto the recompense of the reward," Heb. xi. 24, &c. This certainly implies a degree of religious knowledge, associated with an experimental acquaintance with Divine things, which we can scarcely ever suppose to have been at all the result of an Egyptian education. But we shall cease to be pressed with any difficulty here, when we consider the circumstance of his being providentially *nursed by his own mother*, under the authority and direction of the Egyptian princess. This gave him the privilege of *frequent intercourse with his parents, and others of the Hebrews*, who worshipped the true God; and from *them* he undoubtedly learned all the great truths of that religion which were taught and practised among the patriarchs. The circumstance of his Hebrew origin, his exposure on the Nile, his being found and adopted by the daughter of Pharaoh, were facts which could not be concealed, and must have been notorious at the Egyptian court; and when these points are considered, we need not be surprised that he never could be so identified among the Egyptians as that his Hebrew extraction should be forgotten.

That the person whom God designed to be the deliverer of his people should have been a Hebrew by birth, and have retained all his natural attachment to his own people, and yet have been brought up by Pharaoh's daughter, and had all the advantages of a highly-finished education, which the circumstances of his own family could not have afforded, is all a master-piece of wisdom in the designs of the Divine providence. Besides, Moses by this education must have been *well known*, and even *popular* among the Egyptians; and therefore the subsequent public part he took in behalf of the *Hebrews* must have excited the greater attention and procured him the greater respect both among the Egyptians and his own people. All these circumstances taken together show the manifold wisdom and gracious providence of God.

5. Thus end the *life* and the *work* of the writer of the Pentateuch, who, by the treasures of wisdom and knowledge which he has amassed in those *five* books, has enriched the whole civilized earth, and indeed greatly promoted that very civilization. His works, we may justly say, have been a kind of *text-book* to almost every writer on *geology, geography, chronology, astronomy, natural history, ethics, jurisprudence, political economy, theology, poetry*, and *criticism*, from his time to the present day. Books, to which the choicest writers and philosophers in pagan antiquity have been deeply indebted, and which were the text-books to all the *prophets;* books from which the flimsy writers against Divine Revelation have derived their natural religion, and all their moral excellence; books written in all the energy and purity of the incomparable lan-

guage in which they are composed; and finally, books which, for importance of matter, variety of information, dignity of sentiment, accuracy of facts, impartiality, simplicity, and sublimity of narration, tending to improve and ennoble the intellect, and meliorate the physical and moral condition of man, have never been equalled, and can only be paralleled by the GOSPEL of the Son of God! Fountain of endless mercy, justice, truth, and beneficence! how much are thy gifts and bounties neglected by those who do not read *this law;* and by those who, having read it, are not morally improved by it, and made wise unto salvation!

On the whole we may remark, that when God calls any person to an extraordinary work, he so orders it, in the course of his providence, that he shall have every qualification necessary for that work. This was the case with Moses: his Hebrew extraction, the comeliness of his person, his Egyptian education, his natural firmness and constancy of character, all concurred with the influences of the Divine Spirit, to make him in every respect such a person, one among millions, who was *every way* qualified for the great work which God had given him to do; and who performed it according to the mind of his Maker. SERVANT OF GOD, WELL DONE!

A GENERAL VIEW OF ALL THE SECTIONS OF THE LAW, AND OF THE PROPHETS

As read in the different Jewish Synagogues, for every Sabbath of the Year.

		PARESHIOTH, or *sections* of the LAW.		HAPHTAROTH, or *sections* of the PROPHETS.	
				Portuguese and Italian Jews.	*German and Dutch Jews.*
GENESIS.	Sec i.	בראשית Bereshith, . .	i. 1 to vi. 8. . . .	Isa. xlii. 5–21.	Isa. xlii 5-25; xliii. 10.
	ii.	תולדת נח Toledoth noach,	vi. 9 to xi. 32. . .	Isa. liv. 1–10.	Isa. liv. 1-17; lv. 1–5.
	iii.	לך לך Lech lecha, .	xii. 1 to xvii. 27. .	Isa. xl. 27–31; xli. 1–16. . . .	Ditto.
	iv.	וירא Vaiyera, . . .	xviii. 1 to xxii. 24.	2 Kings iv. 1–23.	2 Kings iv. 1–37.
	v.	חיי שרה Chaiyey Sarah,	xxiii. 1 to xxv. 18.	1 Kings i. 1–31.	Ditto.
	vi.	תולדת Toledoth, . .	xxv. 19 to xxviii. 9. .	Mal. i. 1–14; ii. 1–7.	Ditto.
	vii.	ויצא Vaiyetse, . .	xxviii. 10 to xxxii. 3.	Hos. xi. 7–12; xii. 1–11. . . .	Ditto.
	viii.	וישלח Vaiyishlach, .	xxxii. 4 to xxxvi. 43.	Obad. i. 1–21.	Hos. xii. 12-14; xiii. 1-16
	ix.	וישב Vaiyesheb, . .	xxxvii. 1 to xl. 23.	Amos ii. 1–16; iii. 1–8. . . .	Ditto.
	x.	מקץ Mikkets, . . .	xli. 1 to xliv. 17.	1 Kings iii. 15–28; iv. 1. . .	Ditto.
	xi.	ויגש Vaiyiggash, . .	xliv. 18 to xlvii. 27. .	Ezek. xxxvii. 15–28.	Ditto.
	xii.	ויחי Vayechi, . . .	xlvii. 28 to l. 26.	1 Kings ii. 1–12.	Ditto.
EXODUS.	xiii.	שמות Shemoth, . .	i. 1 to vi. 1. . . .	Jer. i. 1–19; ii. 1–3.	Isa. xxvii. 6 to xxix. 23.
	xiv.	וארא Vaera, . . .	vi. 2 to ix. 35. . .	Ezek. xxviii. 25 to xxix. 21. . .	Ditto.
	xv.	בא אל פרעה Bo el paroh,	x. 1 to xiii. 16. . .	Jer. xlvi. 13–28.	Ditto.
	xvi.	בשלח Beshallach, .	xiii. 17 to xvii. 16.	Judg. v. 1–31.	Judg. iv. 4 to v. 1–31.
	xvii.	יתרו Yithro, . . .	xviii. 1 to xx. 26.	Isa. vi. 1–13.	Isa. vi. 1–13; vii. 1–6; ix. 6 7.
	xviii.	משפטים Mishpatim, .	xxi. 1 to xxiv. 18.	Jer. xxxiv. 8–22 & xxxiii. 25, 26.	Ditto.
	xix.	תרומה Terumah, . .	xxv. 1 to xxvii. 19. .	1 Kings v. 12–18; vi. 1–13. . .	Ditto.
	xx.	תצוה Tetsavveh, . .	xxvii. 20 to xxx. 10.	Ezek. xliii. 10–27.	Ditto.
	xxi.	כי תשא Ki thissa, .	xxx. 11 to xxxiv. 35.	1 Kings xviii. 20–39.	1 Kings xviii. 1–39.
	xxii.	ויקהל Vaiyakhel . .	xxxv. 1 to xxxviii. 20.	1 Kings vii. 13–26.	1 Kings vii. 40–50.
	xxiii.	פקודי Pekudey, . .	xxxviii. 21 to xl. 38.	1 Kings vii. 40–50.	1 Kings viii. 51; vii. 1-21.
LEVITICUS.	xxiv.	ויקרא Vaiyikra, . .	i. 1 to vi. 7. . . .	Isa. xliii. 21–28; xliv. 1–25. . .	Ditto.
	xxv.	ויקרא צו Vaiyikra Tsav,	vi. 8 to viii. 36. . .	Jer. vii. 21–34; viii. 1–3; ix. 23, 24	Ditto.
	xxvi.	שמיני Shemini, . .	ix. 1 to xi. 47. . .	2 Sam. vi. 1–19.	2 Sam. vi. 1–23; vii. 1–17.
	xxvii.	תזריע Tazria, . . .	xii. 1 to xiii. 59. . .	2 Kings iv. 42–44; v. 1–19. . .	Ditto.
	xxviii.	מצרע Metsora, . .	xiv. 1 to xv. 33. . .	2 Kings vii. 3–20.	Ditto.
	xxix.	אחרי מות Acharey Moth,	xvi. 1 to xviii. 30. .	Amos ix. 7–15.	Ezek. xxii. 1–19.
	xxx.	קדשים Kedoshim, .	xix. 1 to xx. 27. . .	Ezek. xx. 2–20.	Amos ix. 7–15.
	xxxi.	אמר Emor, . . .	xxi. 1 to xxiv. 23. .	Ezek. xliv. 15–31.	Ditto.
	xxxii.	בהר סיני Behar Sinai,	xxv. 1 to xxvi. 2. .	Jer. xxxii. 6–27.	Ditto.
	xxxiii.	בחקתי Bechukkothai,	xxvi. 3 to xxvii. 34. .	Jer. xvi. 19–21; xvii. 1–14. . .	Ditto.
NUMBERS.	xxxiv.	במדבר Bemidbar, . .	i. 1 to iv. 20. . . .	Hos. i. 10, 11; ii. 1–20. . . .	Ditto.
	xxxv.	נשא Naso, ...	iv. 21 to vii. 89. . .	Judg. xiii. 2–25.	Ditto.
	xxxvi.	בהעלתך Behaalothecha,	viii. 1 to xii. 16. . .	Zech. ii. 10–13; iii. 1–13; iv. 1–7.	Ditto.
	xxxvii.	שלך Shelach, . . .	xiii. 1 to xv. 41. . .	Josh ii. 1–24.	Ditto.
	xxxviii.	קרח Korach, . . .	xvi. 1 to xviii. 32. .	1 Sam. xi. 14, 15; xii. 1–22. . .	Ditto.
	xxxix.	חקת Chukkath, . .	xix. 1 to xxii. 1. . .	Judg. xi. 1–33.	Ditto.
	xl.	בלק Balak, ...	xxii. 2 to xxv. 9. .	Micah v. 7–15; vi. 1–8. . . .	Ditto.
	xli.	פינחס Pinechas, . .	xxv. 10 to xxx. 1. .	1 Kings xx. 46; xix. 1–21. . .	Ditto.
	xlii.	מטות Mattoth, . . .	xxx. 2 to xxxii. 42. .	Jer. i. 1–19; ii. 1–3.	Ditto.
	xliii.	מסעי Masey, . . .	xxxiii. 1 to xxxvi. 13.	Jer. ii. 4–28; iv. 1, 2.	Jer. ii. 4–28; iii. 4.
DEUTERONOMY.	xliv.	דברים Debarim, . .	i. 1 to iii. 22. . .	Isa. i. 1–27.	Ditto.
	xlv.	ואתחנן Vaethchannan,	iii. 23 to vii. 11. . .	xl. 1–26.	Ditto.
	xlvi.	עקב Ekeb, ...	vii. 12 to xi. 25. . .	xlix. 14–26; l. 1–3. . . .	Ditto.
	xlvii.	ראה Reeh, ...	xi. 26 to xvi. 17. .	liv. 11–17; lv. 1–5. . . .	Ditto.
	xlviii.	שפטים Shophetim, .	xvi. 18 to xxi. 9. .	li. 12–23; lii. 1–12. . . .	Ditto.
	xlix.	תצא Tetse, . . .	xxi. 10 to xxv. 19. .	liv. 1–10.	Ditto.
	l.	תבוא Tabo, . . .	xxvi. 1 to xxix. 8. .	lx. 1–22.	Ditto.
	li.	נצבים Nitstsabim, .	xxix. 9 to xxx. 20. .	lxi. 10, 11; lxii. 1–12; lxiii. 1–9.	Ditto.
	lii.	וילך Vaivelech, . .	xxxi. 1 to xxxi. 30. .	Hos. xiv. 1–9; Micah vii. 18–20.	Isa. lv. 6–13; lvi. 1–8
	liii.	האזינו Haazinu, . .	xxxii. 1 to xxxii. 52.	2 Sam. xxii. 1–51. Some say Ezek. xvii. 22–24; xviii. 1–32.	Hos. xiv. 1–9; Joel ii. 1–27.
	liv.	וזאת הברכה Vezoth Habberachah, . . .	xxxiii. 1 to xxxiv. 12.	Josh. i. 1–18; Eccles. i.–xii. inclusive.	Ditto.

In the above chapters and verses I have, in general, followed the divisions in the best Masoretic Bibles, from which our common English Bibles will in some cases be found to differ a little.

In the synagogues the law is read entirely through in the fifty Sabbaths of their lunar year; for they join certain sections together, which are noticed at the end of the tables. But in their *intercalated* years, in which they add a *month*, they have then *fifty-four* Sabbaths, and this is one reason why we find *fifty-four Parrshahs*, and *fifty-four Haphtaras*, instead of *fifty-two*. See the concluding tables.

It has already been observed that when *Antiochus Epiphanes* conquered the Jews, about the year 168 before the Christian era, he forbade the law to be publicly read in the synagogues, on *pain of death*. The Jews, that they might not be wholly deprived of the word of God, selected from other parts of the sacred writings *fifty-four* portions, which were termed HAPHTARAS, הפטרות *haphtaroth*, from פטר *patar*, he *dismissed, let loose, opened*—for though the LAW was *dismissed* from their synagogues, and was *closed* to them by the edict of this persecuting king, yet the *prophetic writings*, not being under the *interdict*, were left *open*, and therefore they used them in place of the others. It was from this custom of the Jews, that the primitive Christians adopted theirs of reading a lesson every Sabbath out of the old and New Testaments; and on this custom the practice of the Church in our own country, in reading certain portions of the *epistles* and *Gospels* every Sunday in the year was founded.

As a proper knowledge of these *Haphtaras* or *prophetical sections* may sometimes help to fix the *chronology* of some events in the New Testament, it hath been deemed proper to give a table of them in connection with the *Pareshioth* or *sections of the law*, in the place of which they were originally read; and *with* which, ever since the days of the *Asmoneans* or *Maccabees*, they continue to be read in the various synagogues belonging to the *English*, *Portuguese*, *Italian*, *Dutch*, and *German* Jews.

From the above tables the reader will perceive that though the Jews are agreed in the sections of the *law* that are read every *Sabbath*, yet they are not agreed in the *Haphtaras* or sections from the *prophets* as it appears above, that the *Dutch* and *German* Jews differ in several cases from the *Italian* and *Portuguese*; and there are some slighter variations besides those above, which I have not noticed

TABLE I.

A PERPETUAL TABLE,

SHOWING,

Through the course of thirteen Lunar Cycles, (which embrace every possible variation,) the day of the week with which the Jewish year begins, and on which the Passover is held; as also the length of the months Marchesvan *and* Cisleu.

CYCLE CCXCIV.

Usherian year of the world.	Rabbinical year of the world.	Year of Christ.	Year of the lunar cycle.	Index.
5812	5568	1808	1	7 P 3
5813	5569	1809	2	5 d 7
5814	5570	1810	E 3	2 D 5
5815	5571	1811	4	7 P 3
5816	5572	1812	5	5 d 7
5817	5573	1813	E 6	2 D 5
5818	5574	1814	7	7 P 3
5819	5575	1815	E 8	5 P 3
5820	5576	1816	9	5 d 7
5821	5577	1817	10	2 D 3
5822	5578	1818	E 11	5 P 3
5823	5579	1819	12	5 d 7
5824	5580	1820	13	2 P 5
5825	5581	1821	E 14	7 D 3
5826	5582	1822	15	5 d 7
5827	5583	1823	16	2 P 5
5828	5584	1824	E 17	7 D 3
5829	5585	1825	18	5 P 1
5830	5586	1826	E 19	3 d 7

CYCLE CCXCV.

Usherian year of the world.	Rabbinical year of the world.	Year of Christ.	Year of the lunar cycle.	Index.
5831	5587	1827	1	2 P 5
5832	5588	1828	2	7 P 3
5833	5589	1829	E 3	5 D 1
5834	5590	1830	4	3 d 5
5835	5591	1831	5	7 P 3
5836	5592	1832	E 6	5 D 1
5837	5593	1833	7	3 d 5
5838	5594	1834	E 8	7 P 5
5839	5595	1835	9	7 P 3
5840	5596	1836	10	5 d 7
5841	5597	1837	E 11	2 D 5
5842	5598	1838	12	7 P 3
5843	5599	1839	13	5 d 7
5844	5600	1840	E 14	2 P 7
5845	5601	1841	15	2 D 3
5846	5602	1842	16	5 d 7
5847	5603	1843	E 17	2 P 7
5848	5604	1844	18	2 P 5
5849	5605	1845	E 19	7 D 3

CYCLE CCXCVI.

Usherian year of the world.	Rabbinical year of the world.	Year of Christ.	Year of the lunar cycle.	Index.
5850	5606	1846	1	5 d 7
5851	5607	1847	2	2 P 5
5852	5608	1848	E 3	7 D 3
5853	5609	1849	4	5 P 1
5854	5610	1850	5	3 d 5
5855	5611	1851	E 6	7 P 5
5856	5612	1852	7	7 D 1
5857	5613	1853	E 8	3 d 7
5858	5614	1854	9	2 P 5
5859	5615	1855	10	7 P 3
5860	5616	1856	E 11	5 D 1
5861	5617	1857	12	3 d 5
5862	5618	1858	13	7 P 3
5863	5619	1859	E 14	5 P 3
5864	5620	1860	15	5 d 7
5865	5621	1861	16	2 D 3
6866	5622	1862	E 17	5 P 3
5867	5623	1863	18	5 d 7
5868	5624	1864	E 19	2 D 5

CYCLE CCXCVII.

Usherian year of the world.	Rabbinical year of the world.	Year of Christ.	Year of the lunar cycle.	Index.
5869	5625	1865	1	7 P 3
5870	5626	1866	2	5 d 7
5871	5627	1867	E 3	2 P 7
5872	5628	1868	4	2 D 3
5873	5629	1869	5	5 P 1
5874	5630	1870	E 6	3 d 7
5875	5631	1871	7	2 P 5
5876	5632	1872	E 8	7 D 3
5877	5633	1873	9	5 d 7
5878	5634	1874	10	2 P 5
5879	5635	1875	E 11	7 D 3
5880	5636	1876	12	5 P 1
5881	5637	1877	13	3 d 5
5882	5638	1878	E 14	7 P 5
5883	5639	1879	15	7 P 3
5884	5640	1880	16	5 d 7
5885	5641	1881	E 17	2 D 5
5886	5642	1882	18	7 P 3
5887	5643	1883	E 19	5 D 1

CYCLE CCXCVIII.

Usherian year of the world.	Rabbinical year of the world.	Year of Christ.	Year of the lunar cycle.	Index.
5888	5644	1884	1	3 d 5
5889	5645	1885	2	7 P 3
5890	5646	1886	E 3	5 P 3
5891	5647	1887	4	5 d 7
5892	5648	1888	5	2 D 3
5893	5649	1889	E 6	5 P 3
5894	5650	1890	7	5 d 7
5895	5651	1891	E 8	2 D 5
5896	5652	1892	9	7 P 3
5897	5653	1893	10	5 d 7
5898	5654	1894	E 11	2 P 7
5899	5655	1895	12	2 D 3
5900	5656	1896	13	5 P 1
5901	5657	1897	E 14	3 d 7
5902	5658	1898	15	2 P 5
5903	5659	1899	16	7 D 1
5904	5660	1900	E 17	3 d 7
5905	5661	1901	18	2 P 5
5906	5662	1902	E 19	7 P 5

CYCLE CCXCIX.

Usherian year of the world.	Rabbinical year of the world.	Year of Christ.	Year of the lunar cycle.	Index.
5907	5663	1903	1	7 D 1
5908	5664	1904	2	3 d 5
5909	5665	1905	E 3	7 P 5
5910	5666	1906	4	7 P 3
5911	5667	1907	5	5 d 7
5912	5668	1908	E 6	2 D 5
5913	5669	1909	7	7 P 3
5914	5670	1910	E 8	5 D 1
5915	5671	1911	9	3 d 5
5916	5672	1912	10	7 P 3
5917	5673	1913	E 11	5 P 3
5918	5674	1914	12	5 d 7
5919	5675	1915	13	2 D 3
5920	5676	1916	E 14	5 P 3
5921	5677	1917	15	5 d 7
5922	5678	1918	16	2 P 5
5923	5679	1919	E 17	7 D 3
5924	5680	1920	18	5 d 7
5925	5681	1921	E 19	2 P 7

CYCLE CCC.

Usherian year of the world.	Rabbinical year of the world.	Year of Christ.	Year of the lunar cycle.	Index.
5926	5682	1922	1	2 P 5
5927	5683	1923	2	7 D 1
5928	5684	1924	E 3	3 d 7
5929	5685	1925	4	2 P 5
5930	5686	1926	5	7 P 3
5931	5687	1927	E 6	5 D 1
5932	5688	1928	7	3 d 5
5933	5689	1929	E 8	7 P 5
5934	5690	1930	9	7 D 1
5935	5691	1931	10	3 d 5
5936	5692	1932	E 11	7 P 5
5937	5693	1933	12	7 P 3
5938	5694	1934	13	5 d 7
5939	5695	1935	E 14	2 D 5
5940	5696	1936	15	7 P 3
5941	5697	1937	16	5 d 7
5942	5698	1938	E 17	2 P 7
5943	5699	1939	18	2 D 3
5944	5700	1940	E 19	5 P 3

CYCLE CCCI.

Usherian year of the world.	Rabbinical year of the world.	Year of Christ.	Year of the lunar cycle.	Index.
5945	5701	1941	1	5 d 7
5946	5702	1942	2	2 P 5
5947	5703	1943	E 3	7 D 3
5948	5704	1944	4	5 d 7
5949	5705	1945	5	2 P 5
5950	5706	1946	E 6	7 D 3
5951	5707	1947	7	5 P 1
5952	5708	1948	E 8	3 d 7
5953	5709	1949	9	2 P 5
5954	5710	1950	10	7 D 1
5955	5711	1951	E 11	3 d 7
5956	5712	1952	12	2 P 5
5957	5713	1953	13	7 P 3
5958	5714	1954	E 14	5 D 1
5959	5715	1955	15	3 d 5
5960	5716	1956	16	7 P 3
5961	5717	1957	E 17	5 P 3
5962	5718	1958	18	5 d 7
5963	5719	1959	E 19	2 D 5

CYCLE CCCII.

Usherian year of the world.	Rabbinical year of the world.	Year of Christ.	Year of the lunar cycle.	Index.
5964	5720	1960	1	7 P 3
5965	5721	1961	2	5 d 7
5966	5722	1962	E 3	2 D 5
5967	5723	1963	4	7 P 3
5968	5724	1964	5	5 d 7
5969	5725	1965	E 6	2 P 7
5970	5726	1966	7	2 D 3
5971	5727	1967	E 8	5 P 3
5972	5728	1968	9	5 d 7
5973	5729	1969	10	2 P 5
5974	5730	1970	E 11	7 D 3
5975	5731	1971	12	5 d 7
5976	5732	1972	13	2 P 5
5977	5733	1973	E 14	7 D 3
5978	5734	1974	15	5 P 1
5979	5735	1975	16	3 d 5
5980	5736	1976	E 17	7 P 5
5981	5737	1977	18	7 D 1
5982	5738	1978	E 19	3 d 7

TABLE II.

CYCLE CCCIII.				
Usherian year of the world.	Rabbinical year of the world.	Year of Christ.	Year of the lunar cycle.	Index.
5983	5739	1979	1	2 P 5
5984	5740	1980	2	7 P 3
5985	5741	1981	E 3	5 D 1
5986	5742	1982	4	3 d 5
5987	5743	1983	5	7 P 3
5988	5744	1984	E 6	5 P 3
5989	5745	1985	7	5 d 7
5990	5746	1986	E 8	2 D 5
5991	5747	1987	9	7 P 3
5992	5748	1988	10	5 d 7
5993	5749	1989	E 11	2 D 5
5994	5750	1990	12	7 P 3
5995	5751	1991	13	5 d 7
5996	5752	1992	E 14	2 P 7
5997	5753	1993	15	2 D 3
5998	5754	1994	16	5 P 1
5999	5755	1995	E 17	3 d 7
6000	5756	1996	18	2 P 5
6001	5757	1997	E 19	7 D 3

CYCLE CCCIV.				
Usherian year of the world.	Rabbinical year of the world.	Year of Christ.	Year of the lunar cycle.	Index.
6002	5758	1998	1	5 d 7
6003	5759	1999	2	2 P 5
6004	5760	2000	E 3	7 P 5
6005	5761	2001	4	7 D 1
6006	5762	2002	5	3 d 5
6007	5763	2003	E 6	7 P 5
6008	5764	2004	7	7 P 3
6009	5765	2005	E 8	5 D 1
6010	5766	2006	9	3 d 5
6011	5767	2007	10	7 P 3
6012	5768	2008	E 11	5 P 3
6013	5769	2009	12	5 d 7
6014	5770	2010	13	2 D 3
6015	5771	2011	E 14	5 P 3
6016	5772	2012	15	5 d 7
6017	5773	2013	16	2 P 5
6018	5774	2014	E 17	7 D 3
6019	5775	2015	18	5 d 7
6020	5776	2016	E 19	2 P 7

CYCLE CCCV.				
Usherian year of the world.	Rabbinical year of the world.	Year of Christ.	Year of the lunar cycle.	Index.
6021	5777	2017	1	2 D 5
6022	5778	2018	2	5 d 7
6023	5779	2019	E 3	2 P 7
6024	5780	2020	4	2 P 5
6025	5781	2021	5	7 D 1
6026	5782	2022	E 6	3 d 7
6027	5783	2023	7	2 P 5
6028	5784	2024	E 8	7 D 3
6029	5785	2025	9	5 P 1
6030	5786	2026	10	3 d 5
6031	5787	2027	E 11	7 P 5
6032	5788	2028	12	7 P 3
6033	5789	2029	13	5 d 7
6034	5790	2030	E 14	2 D 5
6035	5791	2031	15	7 P 3
6036	5792	2032	16	5 d 7
6037	5793	2033	E 17	2 D 5
6038	5794	2034	18	7 P 3
6039	5795	2035	E 19	5 P 3

CYCLE CCCVI.				
Usherian year of the world.	Rabbinical year of the world.	Year of Christ.	Year of the lunar cycle.	Index.
6040	5796	2036	1	5 d 7
6041	5797	2037	2	2 D 3
6042	5798	2038	E 3	5 P 3
6043	5799	2039	4	5 d 7
6044	5800	2040	5	2 P 5
6045	5801	2041	E 6	7 D 3
6046	5802	2042	7	5 d 7
6047	5803	2043	E 8	2 P 7
6048	5804	2044	9	2 D 3
6049	5805	2045	10	5 P 1

CYCLE CCCVI.				
Usherian year of the world.	Rabbinical year of the world.	Year of Christ.	Year of the lunar cycle.	Index.
6050	5806	2046	E 11	3 d 7
6051	5807	2047	12	2 P 5
6052	5808	2048	13	7 D 1
6053	5809	2049	E 14	3 d 7
6054	5810	2050	15	2 P 5
6055	5811	2051	16	7 P 3
6056	5812	2052	E 17	5 D 1
6057	5813	2053	18	3 d 5
6058	5814	2054	E 19	7 P 5

TABLE II.

Containing the whole variations in the reading of the Pareshioth, *or sections of the Law, for every year of the Jewish Cycle of 247 years.*

FIRST JEWISH EMBOLISMIC YEAR OF 383 DAYS, CONTAINING 55 SABBATHS.
INDEX, 5 D 1.

Tisri, September.		Marchesvan, Oct.		Cisleu, November.		Tebet, December.		Sebat, January.		Adar, February.	
Sabbaths of the Month.	Pareshioth.	Sabbaths of the Month.	Pareshioth.	Sabbaths of the Month.	Pareshioth.	Sabbaths of the Month.	Pareshioth.	Sabbaths of the Month.	Pareshioth.	Sabbaths of the Month.	Pareshioth.
● 5		● 6,7		● 1		● 2		● 3		● 4,5	
3	53	1	2	7	7	6	11	5	15	3	19
10	Chippur	8	3	14	8	13	12	12	16	10	20
17	Succoth	15	4	21	9	20	13	19	17	17	21
6,23	54, B.L.	22	5	28	10	27	14	26	18	24	22
24	1	29	6								

Veadar, February.		Nisan, March.		Ijar, April.		Sivan, May.		Tammuz, June.		Ab, July.		Elul, August.	
Sabbaths of the Month.	Pareshioth.	Sabbaths of the Month.	Pareshioth.	Sabbaths of the Month.	Pareshioth.	Sabbaths of the Month.	Pareshioth.	Sabbaths of the Month.	Pareshioth.	Sabbaths of the Month.	Pareshioth.	Sabbaths of the Month.	Pareshioth.
● 6,7		● 1		● 2,3		● 4		● 5,6		● 7		● 1,2	
1	23, S	7	28	5	31	4	35	2	39	1	43	6	48
8	24, Z	14	29	12	32	11	36	9	40	8	44	13	49
15	25	21	1 Pas.	19	33	18	37	16	41	15	45	20	50
22	26, P	28	30	26	34	25	38	23	42	22	46	27	51
29	27, H									29	47		

TABLE II.—CONTINUED.

SECOND JEWISH EMBOLISMIC YEAR OF 384 DAYS, CONTAINING 55 SABBATHS.
INDEX, 3 d 7.

Tisri, September.		Marchesvan, October.		Cisleu, November.		Tebet, December.		Sebat, January.		Adar, February.	
Sabbaths of the Month.	Pareshioth.	Sabbaths of the Month.	Pareshioth.	Sabbaths of the Month.	Pareshioth.	Sabbaths of the Month.	Pareshioth.	Sabbaths of the Month.	Pareshioth.	Sabbaths of the Month.	Pareshioth.
● 3		● 4,5		● 6		● 7,1		● 2		● 3,4	
5	52	3	2	2	6	7	11	6	15	4	19
12	53	10	3	9	7	14	12	13	16	11	20
19	Succoth	17	4	16	8	21	13	20	17	18	21
4,23	54, B.L.	24	5	23	9	28	14	27	18	25	22, S
26	1			30	10						

Veadar, February.		Nisan, March.		Ijar, April.		Sivan, May		Tammuz, June.		Ab, July.		Elul, August.	
Sabbaths of the Month.	Pareshioth.	Sabbaths of the Month.	Pareshioth.	Sabbaths of the Month.	Pareshioth.	Sabbaths of the Month.	Pareshioth.	Sabbaths of the Month.	Pareshioth.	Sabbaths of the Month.	Pareshioth.	Sabbaths of the Month.	Pareshioth.
● 5,6		● 7		● 1,2		● 3		● 4,5		● 6		● 7,1	
2	23	1	27, H	6	30	5	34	3	38	2	42,43	7	48
9	24, Z	8	28	13	31	12	35	10	39	9	44	14	49
16	25	15	1 Pas.	20	32	19	36	17	40	16	45	21	50
23	26, P	22	2 Pas.	27	33	26	37	24	41	23	46	28	51
		29	29							30	47		

THIRD JEWISH EMBOLISMIC YEAR OF 385 DAYS, CONTAINING 55 SABBATHS.
INDEX, 2 P 7.

Tisri, September.		Marchesvan, October.		Cisleu, November.		Tebet, December.		Sebat, January.		Adar, February.	
Sabbaths of the Month.	Pareshioth.	Sabbaths of the Month.	Pareshioth.	Sabbaths of the Month.	Pareshioth.	Sabbaths of the Month.	Pareshioth.	Sabbaths of the Month.	Pareshioth.	Sabbaths of the Month.	Pareshioth.
● 2		● 3,4		● 5,6		● 7,1		● 2		● 3,4	
6	52	4	2	2	6	7	11	6	15	4	19
13	53	11	3	9	7	14	12	13	16	11	20
20	Succotn	18	4	16	8	21	13	20	17	18	21
3,23	54, B.L.	25	5	23	9	28	14	27	18	25	22, S
27	1			30	10						

Veadar, February.		Nisan, March.		Ijar, April.		Sivan, May.		Tammuz, June.		Ab, July.		Elul, August.	
Sabbaths of the Month.	Pareshioth.	Sabbaths of the Month.	Pareshioth.	Sabbaths of the Month.	Pareshioth.	Sabbaths of the Month.	Pareshioth.	Sabbaths of the Month.	Pareshioth.	Sabbaths of the Month.	Pareshioth.	Sabbaths of the Month.	Pareshioth.
● 5,6		● 7		● 1,2		● 3		● 4,5		● 6		● 7,1	
2	23	1	27, H	6	30	5	34	3	38	2	42,43	7	48
9	24, Z	8	28	13	31	12	35	10	39	9	44	14	49
16	25	15	1 Pas.	20	32	19	36	17	40	16	45	21	50
23	26, P	22	2 Pas.	27	33	26	37	24	41	23	46	28	51
		29	29							30	47		

FOURTH JEWISH EMBOLISMIC YEAR OF 385 DAYS, CONTAINING 55 SABBATHS.
INDEX, 5 P 3.

Tisri, September.		Marchesvan, October.		Cisleu, November.		Tebet, December.		Sebat, January.		Adar, February.	
Sabbaths of the Month.	Pareshioth.	Sabbaths of the Month.	Pareshioth.	Sabbaths of the Month.	Pareshioth.	Sabbaths of the Month.	Pareshioth.	Sabbaths of the Month.	Pareshioth.	Sabbaths of the Month.	Pareshioth.
● 5		● 6,7		● 1,2		● 3,4		● 5		● 6,7	
3	53	1	2	6	7	4	11	3	15	1	19
10	Chippur	8	3	13	8	11	12	10	16	8	20
17	Succoth	15	4	20	9	18	13	17	17	15	21
24	1	22	5	27	10	25	14	24	18	22	22
		29	6							29	23, S

Veadar, February.		Nisan, March.		Ijar, April.		Sivan, May.		Tammuz, June.		Ab, July.		Elul, August.	
Sabbaths of the Month.	Pareshioth.	Sabbaths of the Month.	Pareshioth.	Sabbaths of the Month.	Pareshioth.	Sabbaths of the Month.	Pareshioth.	Sabbaths of the Month.	Pareshioth.	Sabbaths of the Month.	Pareshioth.	Sabbaths of the Month.	Pareshioth.
● 1,2		● 3		● 4,5		● 6		● 7,1		● 2		● 3,4	
6	24	5	28	3	31	2	35	7	40	6	44	4	48
13	25, Z	12	29	10	32	9	36	14	41	13	45	11	49
20	26, P	19	1 Pas.	17	33	16	37	21	42	20	46	18	50
27	27, H	26	30	24	34	23	38	28	43	27	47	25	51,52
						30	39						

TABLE II.—CONTINUED.

FIFTH JEWISH EMBOLISMIC YEAR OF 383 DAYS, CONTAINING 55 SABBATHS. INDEX, 7 D 3.

Tisri, September.		Marchesvan, October.		Cisleu, November.		Tebet, December.		Sebat, January.		Adar, February.	
Sabbaths of the Month.	Pareshioth.	Sabbaths of the Month.	Pareshioth.	Sabbaths of the Month.	Pareshioth.	Sabbaths of the Month.	Pareshioth.	Sabbaths of the Month.	Pareshioth.	Sabbaths of the Month.	Pareshioth.
● 7		● 1,2		● 3		● 4		● 5		● 6,7	
8	53	6	2	5	6	4	10	3	14	1	18
15	Succoth	13	3	12	7	11	11	10	15	8	19
22	Sab. p. Suc.	20	4	19	8	18	12	17	16	15	20
1,23	54, B.L.	27	5	26	9	25	13	24	17	22	21
29	1									29	22, S

Veadar, February.		Nisan, March.		Ijar, April.		Sivan, May.		Tammuz, June.		Ab, July.		Elul, August.	
Sabbaths of the Month.	Pareshioth.	Sabbaths of the Month.	Pareshioth.	Sabbaths of the Month.	Pareshioth.	Sabbaths of the Month.	Pareshioth.	Sabbaths of the Month.	Pareshioth.	Sabbaths of the Month.	Pareshioth.	Sabbaths of the Month.	Pareshioth.
● 1,2		● 3		● 4,5		● 6		● 7,1		● 2		● 3,4	
6	23	5	27	3	30	2	34	7	39	6	44	4	48
13	24, Z	12	28	10	31	9	35	14	40	13	45	11	49
20	25, P	19	1 Pas.	17	32	16	36	21	41	20	46	18	50
27	26, H	26	29	24	33	23	37	28	42,43	27	47	25	51,52
						30	38						

SIXTH JEWISH EMBOLISMIC YEAR OF 385 DAYS, CONTAINING 55 SABBATHS. INDEX, 7 P 5.

Tisri, September.		Marchesvan, October.		Cisleu, November.		Tebet, December.		Sebat, January.		Adar, February.	
Sabbaths of the Month.	Pareshioth.	Sabbaths of the Month.	Pareshioth.	Sabbaths of the Month.	Pareshioth.	Sabbaths of the Month.	Pareshioth.	Sabbaths of the Month.	Pareshioth.	Sabbaths of the Month.	Pareshioth.
● 7		● 1,2		● 3,4		● 5,6		● 7		● 1,2	
8	53	6	2	4	6	2	10	1	14	6	19
15	Succoth	13	3	11	7	9	11	8	15	13	20
22	Sab. p. Suc.	20	4	18	8	16	12	15	16	20	21
1,23	54, B.L.	27	5	25	9	23	13	22	17	27	22, S
29	1							29	18		

Veadar, February.		Nisan, March.		Ijar, April.		Sivan, May.		Tammuz, June.		Ab, July.		Elul, August.	
Sabbaths of the Month.	Pareshioth.	Sabbaths of the Month.	Pareshioth.	Sabbaths of the Month.	Pareshioth.	Sabbaths of the Month.	Pareshioth.	Sabbaths of the Month.	Pareshioth.	Sabbaths of the Month.	Pareshioth.	Sabbaths of the Month.	Pareshioth.
● 3,4		● 5		● 6,7		● 1		● 2,3		● 4		● 5,6	
4	23	3	27	1	30	7	Pent.	5	38	4	44	2	48
11	24, Z	10	28	8	31	14	35	12	39,40	11	45	9	49
18	25, P	17	1 Pas.	15	32	21	36	19	41	18	46	16	50
25	26, H	24	29	22	33	28	37	26	42,43	25	47	23	51,52
				29	34								

SEVENTH JEWISH EMBOLISMIC YEAR OF 383 DAYS, CONTAINING 54 SABBATHS. INDEX, 2 D 5.

Tisri, September.		Marchesvan, October.		Cisleu, November.		Tebet, December.		Sebat, January.		Adar, February.	
Sabbaths of the Month.	Pareshioth.	Sabbaths of the Month.	Pareshioth.	Sabbaths of the Month.	Pareshioth.	Sabbaths of the Month.	Pareshioth.	Sabbaths of the Month.	Pareshioth.	Sabbaths of the Month.	Pareshioth.
● 2		● 3,4		● 5		● 6		● 7		● 1,2	
6	52	4	2	3	6	2	10	1	14	6	19
13	53	11	3	10	7	9	11	8	15	13	20
20	Succoth	18	4	17	8	16	12	15	16	20	21
27	1	25	5	24	9	23	13	22	17	27	22, S
								29	18		

Veadar, February.		Nisan, March.		Ijar, April.		Sivan, May.		Tammuz, June.		Ab, July.		Elul, August.	
Sabbaths of the Month.	Pareshioth.	Sabbaths of the Month.	Pareshioth.	Sabbaths of the Month.	Pareshioth.	Sabbaths of the Month.	Pareshioth.	Sabbaths of the Month.	Pareshioth.	Sabbaths of the Month.	Pareshioth.	Sabbaths of the Month.	Pareshioth.
● 3,4		● 5		● 6,7		● 1		● 2,3		● 4		● 5.6	
4	23	3	27	1	30	7	Pent.	5	38	4	44	2	48
11	24, Z	10	28	8	31	14	35	12	39.40	11	45	9	49
18	25, P	17	1 Pas.	15	32	21	36	19	41	18	46	16	50
25	26, H	24	29	22	33	28	37	26	42,43	25	47	23	51,52
				29	34								

TABLE II.—Continued.

FIRST JEWISH COMMON YEAR OF 355 DAYS, CONTAINING 51 SABBATHS. INDEX, 5 P 1.

Tisri, September.		Marchesvan, October.		Cisleu, November.		Tebet, December.		Sebat, January.		Adar, February.	
Sabbaths of the Month.	Pareshioth.	Sabbaths of the Month.	Pareshioth.	Sabbaths of the Month.	Pareshioth.	Sabbaths of the Month.	Pareshioth.	Sabbaths of the Month.	Pareshioth.	Sabbaths of the Month.	Pareshioth.
● 5		● 6,7		● 1,2		● 3,4		● 5		● 6,7	
3	53	1	2	6	7	4	11	3	15	1	19, S
10	Chippur	8	3	13	8	11	12	10	16	8	20, Z
17	Succoth	15	4	20	9	18	13	17	17	15	21
6,23	54, B.L.	22	5	27	10	25	14	24	18	22	22, P
24	1	29	6							29	23, H

Nisan, March.		Ijar, April.		Sivan, May.		Tammuz, June.		Ab, July.		Elul, August.	
Sabbaths of the Month.	Pareshioth.	Sabbaths of the Month.	Pareshioth.	Sabbaths of the Month.	Pareshioth.	Sabbaths of the Month.	Pareshioth.	Sabbaths of the Month.	Pareshioth.	Sabbaths of the Month.	Pareshioth.
● 1		● 2,3		● 4		● 5,6		● 7		● 1,2	
7	24	5	27,28	4	34	2	38	1	42,43	6	48
14	25	12	29,30	11	35	9	39	8	44	13	49
21	1 Pas.	19	31	18	36	16	40	15	45	20	50
28	26	26	32,33	25	37	23	41	22	46	27	51
								29	47		

SECOND JEWISH COMMON YEAR OF 354 DAYS, CONTAINING 51 SABBATHS INDEX, 5 d 7.

Tisri, September.		Marchesvan, October.		Cisleu, November.		Tebet, December.		Sebat, January.		Adar, February.	
Sabbaths of the Month.	Pareshioth.	Sabbaths of the Month.	Pareshioth.	Sabbaths of the Month.	Pareshioth.	Sabbaths of the Month.	Pareshioth.	Sabbaths of the Month.	Pareshioth.	Sabbaths of the Month.	Pareshioth.
● 5		● 6,7		● 1		● 2,3		● 4		● 5,6	
3	53	1	2	7	7	5	11	4	15	2	19
10	Chippur	8	3	14	8	12	12	11	16	9	20, Z
17	Succoth	15	4	21	9	19	13	18	17	16	21
24	1	22	5	28	10	26	14	25	18, S	23	22, 23, P
		29	6								

Nisan, March.		Ijar, April.		Sivan, May.		Tammuz, June.		Ab, July.		Elul, August.	
Sabbaths of the Month.	Pareshioth.	Sabbaths of the Month.	Pareshioth.	Sabbaths of the Month.	Pareshioth.	Sabbaths of the Month.	Pareshioth.	Sabbaths of the Month.	Pareshioth.	Sabbaths of the Month.	Pareshioth.
● 7		● 1,2		● 3		● 4,5		● 6		● 7,1	
1	24, H	6	27,28	5	34	3	38	2	42,43	7	48
8	25	13	29,30	12	35	10	39	9	44	14	49
15	1 Pas.	20	31	19	36	17	40	16	45	21	50
22	2 Pas.	27	32,33	26	37	24	41	23	46	28	51
29	26							30	47		

THIRD JEWISH COMMON YEAR OF 353 DAYS, CONTAINING 50 SABBATHS. INDEX, 7 D 1.

Tisri, September.		Marchesvan, October.		Cisleu, November.		Tebet, December.		Sebat, January.		Adar, February.	
Sabbaths of the Month.	Pareshioth.	Sabbaths of the Month.	Pareshioth.	Sabbaths of the Month.	Pareshioth.	Sabbaths of the Month.	Pareshioth.	Sabbaths of the Month.	Pareshioth.	Sabbaths of the Month.	Pareshioth.
● 7		● 1,2		● 3		● 4		● 5		● 6,7	
8	53	6	2	5	6	4	10	3	14	1	18, S
15	Succoth	13	3	12	7	11	11	10	15	8	19, Z
22	Sab. p. Suc.	20	4	19	8	18	12	17	16	15	20
1,23	54, B.L.	27	5	26	9	25	13	24	17	22	21, P
29	1									29	22, 23, H

Nisan, March.		Ijar, April.		Sivan, May.		Tammuz, June.		Ab, July.		Elul, August.	
Sabbaths of the Month.	Pareshioth.	Sabbaths of the Month.	Pareshioth.	Sabbaths of the Month.	Pareshioth.	Sabbaths of the Month.	Pareshioth.	Sabbaths of the Month.	Pareshioth.	Sabbaths of the Month.	Pareshioth.
● 1		● 2,3		● 4		● 5,6		● 7		● 1,2	
7	24	5	27,28	4	34	2	38	1	42,43	6	48
14	25	12	29,30	11	35	9	39	8	44	13	49
21	1 Pas.	19	31	18	36	16	40	15	45	20	50
28	26	26	32,33	25	37	23	41	22	46	27	51
								29	47		

TABLE II.—Continued.

FOURTH JEWISH COMMON YEAR OF 355 DAYS, CONTAINING 51 SABBATHS.
INDEX, 7 P 3.

Tisri, September.		Marchesvan, October.		Cisleu, November.		Tebet, December.		Sebat, January.		Adar, February.	
Sabbaths of the Month	Pareshioth.	Sabbaths of the Month.	Pareshioth.	Sabbaths of the Month.	Pareshioth.	Sabbaths of the Month.	Pareshioth.	Sabbaths of the Month.	Pareshioth.	Sabbaths of the Month.	Pareshioth.
● 7		● 1,2		● 3.4		● 5,6		● 7		● 1.2	
8	53	6	2	4	6	2	10	1	14	6	19
15	Succoth	13	3	11	7	9	11	8	15	13	20, Z
22	Oct. Suc.	20	4	18	8	16	12	15	16	20	21, P
1,23	54, B.L.	27	5	25	9, En.	23	13	22	17	27	22, 23, H
29	1							29	18, S		

Nisan, March.		Ijar, April.		Sivan, May.		Tammuz, June.		Ab, July.		Elul, August.	
Sabbaths of the Month.	Pareshioth.	Sabbaths of the Month.	Pareshioth.	Sabbaths of the Month.	Pareshioth.	Sabbaths of the Month.	Pareshioth.	Sabbaths of the Month.	Pareshioth.	Sabbaths of the Month.	Pareshioth.
● 3		● 4,5		● 6		● 7,1		● 2		● 3,4	
5	24	3	27,28	2	34	7	39	6	44	4	48
12	25	10	29,30	9	35	14	40	13	45	11	49
19	1 Pas.	17	31	16	36	21	41	20	46	18	50
26	26	24	32,33	23	37	28	42,43	27	47	25	51
				30	38						

FIFTH JEWISH COMMON YEAR OF 353 DAYS, CONTAINING 50 SABBATHS.
INDEX, 2 D 3.

Tisri, September.		Marchesvan, October.		Cisleu, November.		Tebet, December.		Sebat, January.		Adar, February.	
Sabbaths of the Month.	Pareshioth.	Sabbaths of the Month.	Pareshioth.	Sabbaths of the Month.	Pareshioth.	Sabbaths of the Month.	Pareshioth.	Sabbaths of the Month.	Pareshioth.	Sabbaths of the Month.	Pareshioth.
● 2		● 3,4		● 5		● 6		● 7		● 1,2	
6	52	4	2	3	6	2	10	1	14	6	19
13	53	11	3	10	7	9	11	8	15	13	20, Z
20	Succoth	18	4	17	8	16	12	15	16	20	21, P
3,23	54, B.L.	25	5	24	9	23	13	22	17	27	22, 23, H
27	1							29	18, S		

Nisan, March.		Ijar, April.		Sivan, May.		Tammuz, June.		Ab, July.		Elul, August.	
Sabbaths of the Month.	Pareshioth.	Sabbaths of the Month.	Pareshioth.	Sabbaths of the Month.	Paroshioth.	Sabbaths of the Month.	Pareshioth	Sabbaths of the Month.	Pareshioth.	Sabbaths of the Month.	Pareshioth.
● 3		● 4,5		● 6		● 7,1		● 2		● 3,4	
5	24	3	27,28	2	34	7	39	6	44	4	48
12	25	10	29,30	9	35	14	40	13	45	11	49
19	1 Pas.	17	31	16	36	21	41	20	46	18	50
26	26	24	32,33	23	37	28	42,43	27	47	25	51,52
				30	38						

SIXTH JEWISH COMMON YEAR OF 355 DAYS, CONTAINING 50 SABBATHS.
INDEX, 2 P 5.

Tisri, September.		Marchesvan, October.		Cisleu, November.		Tebet, December.		Sebat, January.		Adar, February.	
Sabbaths of the Month.	Pareshioth.	Sabbaths of the Month.	Pareshioth.	Sabbaths of the Month.	Pareshioth.	Sabbaths of the Month.	Pareshioth.	Sabbaths of the Month.	Pareshioth	Sabbaths of the Month.	Pareshioth.
● 2,3		● 3,4		● 5,6		● 7,1		● 2		● 3,4	
6	52	4	2	2	6	7	11	6	15	4	19
13	53	11	3	9	7	14	12	13	16	11	20, Z
20	Succoth	18	4	16	8	21	13	20	17	18	21, P
3,23	54, B.L.	25	5	23	9	28	14	27	18, S	25	22, 23, H
27	1			30	10						

Nisan, March.		Ijar, April.		Sivan, May.		Tammuz, June.		Ab, July.		Elul, August.	
Sabbaths of the Month.	Pareshioth	Sabbaths of the Month.	Pareshioth.	Sabbaths of the Month.	Pareshioth	Sabbaths of the Month.	Pareshioth.	Sabbaths of the Month.	Pareshioth.	Sabbaths of the Month.	Pareshioth.
● 5		● 6,7		● 1		● 2,3		● 4		● 5,6	
3	24	1	27,28	7	Pent.	5	38	4	44	2	48
10	25	8	29,30	14	35	12	39,40	11	45	9	49
17	1 Pas.	15	31	21	36	19	41	18	46	16	50
24	26	22	32,33	28	37	26	42,43	25	47	23	51,52
		29	34								

TABLE III.

SEVENTH JEWISH COMMON YEAR OF 354 DAYS, CONTAINING 50 SABBATHS.
INDEX, 3 d 5.

Tisri, September.		Marchesvan, October.		Cisleu, November.		Tebet, December.		Sebat, January.		Adar, February	
Sabbaths of the Month.	Pareshioth.	Sabbaths of the Month.	Pareshioth.	Sabbaths of the Month.	Pareshioth.	Sabbaths of the Month.	Pareshioth.	Sabbaths of the Month.	Pareshioth.	Sabbaths of the Month.	Pareshioth.
● 3 5 12 19 4,23 26	 52 53 Succoth 54, B.L. 1	● 4,5 3 10 17 24	 2 3 4 5	● 6 2 9 16 23 30	 6 7 8 9 10	● 7,1 7 14 21 28	 11 12 13 14	● 2 6 13 20 27	 15 16 17 18, S	● 3,4 4 11 18 25	 19 20, Z 21, P 22, 23, H

Nisan, March.		Ijar, April.		Sivan, May.		Tammuz, June.		Ab, July.		Elul, August.	
Sabbaths of the Month.	Pareshioth.	Sabbaths of the Month.	Pareshioth.	Sabbaths of the Month.	Pareshioth.	Sabbaths of the Month.	Pareshioth.	Sabbaths of the Month.	Pareshioth.	Sabbaths of the Month.	Pareshioth.
● 5 3 10 17 24	 24 25 1 Pas. 26	● 6,7 1 8 15 22 29	 27,28 29,30 31 32,33 34	● 1 7 14 21 28	 Pent 35 36 37	● 2,3 5 12 19 26	 38 39,40 41 42,43	● 4 4 11 18 25	 44 45 46 47	● 5,6 2 9 16 23	 48 49 50 51, 52

N. B. The indexes in Table I. are set down, in the order they are there found, from the authority of Gabriel of Soranum ; but as there exist some small differences in the disposition of the indexes by different persons who have written upon this subject, a list of the variations (which are adopted by the rabbins in the construction of their calendar) is thought essentially necessary to be given here, as the following Tables are made to agree with it exactly. The variations are as below :—

A. D.	Index in Table I.	Index preferred by the Rabbins.	A. D.	Index in Table I.	Index preferred by the Rabbins.	A. D.	Index in Table I.	Index preferred by the Rabbins.
1828	7 P 3	7 D 1	1850	3 d 5	2 P 5	2009	5 d 7	3 d 5
1829	2 D 1	3 d 7	1869	5 P 1	5 d 7	2010	2 D 3	7 P 3
1830	3 d 5	2 P 5	1870	3 d 7	2 P 7	2013	2 P 5	2 D 3
1849	5 P 1	5 d 7	2008	5 P 3	5 D 1	2014	7 D 3	5 P 3

TABLE III.

To find, with the help of Table IV., *the day of the week upon which any Jewish new month or festival happens.*

1	2	3	4	5	6	7	8	9	10	11	12	13	14	15	16	17	18	19
Com Yrs.	Com. Yrs.	Emb. Yrs.	Com. Yrs.	Com. Yrs.	Emb. Yrs.	Com. Yrs.	Emb. Yrs.	Com. Yrs.	Com. Yrs.	Emb. Yrs.	Com. Yrs.	Com. Yrs.	Emb. Yrs.	Com. Yrs.	Com. Yrs.	Emb. Yrs.	Com. Yrs.	Emb Yrs
1808 L	1809 M	1810 C	1811 L	1812 M	1813 C	1814 L	1815 A	1816 M	1817 O	1818 A	1819 M	1820 K	1821 B	1822 M	1823 K	1824 B	1825 N	1826 E
1827 K	1828 H	1829 E	1830 K	1831 L	1832 D	1833 I	1834 F	1835 L	1836 M	1837 C	1838 L	1839 M	1840 G	1841 O	1842 M	1843 G	1844 K	1845 B
1846 M	1847 K	1848 B	1849 M	1850 K	1851 F	1852 H	1853 E	1854 K	1855 L	1856 D	1857 I	1858 L	1859 A	1860 M	1861 O	1862 A	1863 M	1864 C
1865 L	1866 M	1867 G	1868 O	1869 M	1870 G	1871 K	1872 B	1873 M	1874 K	1875 B	1876 N	1877 I	1878 F	1879 L	1880 M	1881 C	1882 L	1883 D
1884 I	1885 L	1886 A	1887 M	1888 O	1889 A	1890 M	1891 C	1892 L	1893 M	1894 G	1895 O	1896 N	1897 E	1898 K	1899 H	1900 E	1901 K	1902 F
1903 H	1904 I	1905 F	1906 L	1907 M	1908 C	1909 L	1910 D	1911 I	1912 L	1913 A	1914 M	1915 O	1916 A	1917 M	1918 K	1919 B	1920 M	1921 G
1922 K	1923 H	1924 E	1925 K	1926 L	1927 D	1928 I	1929 F	1930 H	1931 I	1932 F	1933 L	1934 M	1935 C	1936 L	1937 M	1938 G	1939 O	1940 A
1941 M	1942 K	1943 B	1944 M	1945 K	1946 B	1947 N	1948 E	1949 K	1950 H	1951 E	1952 K	1953 L	1954 D	1955 I	1956 L	1957 A	1958 M	1959 C
1960 L	1961 M	1962 C	1963 L	1964 M	1965 G	1966 O	1967 A	1968 M	1969 K	1970 B	1971 M	1972 K	1973 B	1974 N	1975 I	1976 F	1977 H	1978 E
1979 K	1980 L	1981 D	1982 I	1983 L	1984 A	1985 M	1986 C	1987 L	1988 M	1989 C	1990 L	1991 M	1992 G	1993 O	1994 N	1995 E	1996 K	1997 B
1998 M	1999 K	2000 F	2001 H	2002 I	2003 F	2004 L	2005 D	2006 I	2007 L	2008 D	2009 I	2010 L	2011 A	2012 M	2013 O	2014 A	2015 M	2016 G
2017 O	2018 M	2019 G	2020 K	2021 H	2022 E	2023 K	2024 B	2025 N	2026 I	2027 F	2028 L	2029 M	2030 C	2031 L	2032 M	2033 C	2034 L	2035 A
2036 M	2037 O	2038 A	2039 M	2040 K	2041 B	2042 M	2043 G	2044 O	2045 N	2046 E	2047 K	2048 H	2049 E	2050 K	2051 L	2052 D	2053 I	2054 F

The Indexes of Tables I. and II. corresponding to the letters of the above Table are as below :—

Embolismic Years.	A 5 P 3	B 7 D 3	C 2 D 5	D 5 D 1	E 3 d 7	F 7 P 5	G 2 P 7
Common Years.	H 7 D 1	I 3 d 5	K 2 P 5	L 7 P 3	M 5 d 7	N 5 P 1	O 2 D 3

TABLE IV.

TABLE IV.

To determine upon what day of the week any Jewish month commences for any given year, as also the day of the week upon which the Jews celebrate their principal fasts and festivals.

Index of the Year found in Table III.	A	B	C	D	E	F	G	H	I	K	L	M	N	O
Commencement of Tisri, or of the Jewish New-Year	5,6	7,1	2,3	5,6	3,4	7,1	2,3	7,1	3,4	2,3	7,1	5,6	5,6	2,3
Fast of Gedaliah, 3 Tisri	1	2	4	1	5	2	4	2	5	4	2	7	1	4
Fast of Atonement, 10 Tisri	7	2	4	7	5	2	4	2	5	4	2	7	7	4
Feast of Tabernacles, 15 Tisri	5	7	2	5	3	7	2	7	3	2	7	5	5	2
Hosanna Rabba, 21 Tisri	4	6	1	4	2	6	1	6	2	1	6	4	4	1
Blessings in Deut. xxxiii. read, 23 Tisri	6	1	3	6	4	1	3	1	4	3	1	6	6	3
Commencement of Marchesvan	6,7	1,2	3,4	6,7	4,5	1,2	3,4	1,2	4,5	3,4	1,2	6,7	6,7	3,4
Commencement of Cisleu	1,2	3	5	1	6	3,4	5,6	3	6	5,6	3,4	1	1,2	5
Encænia, 25 Cisleu	5	6	1	4	2	7	2	6	2	2	7	4	5	1
Commencement of Tebet	3,4	4	6	2	7,1	5,6	7,1	4	7,1	7,1	5,6	2,3	3,4	6
A fast, 10 Tebet	6	6	1	4	3	1	3	6	3	3	1	5	6	1
Commencement of Sebat	5	5	7	3	2	7	2	5	2	2	7	4	5	7
Commencement of Adar	6,7	6,7	1,2	4,5	3,4	1,2	3,4	6,7	3,4	3,4	1,2	5,6	6,7	1,2
Commencement of Veadar	1,2	1,2	3,4	6,7	5,6	3,4	5,6							
Fast of Esther, 13 Adar	5	5	2	5	4	2	4	5	2	2	5	4	5	5
Feast of Purim, 14 Adar	1	1	3	6	5	3	5	6	3	3	1	5	6	1
Commencement of Nisan	3	3	5	1	7	5	7	1	5	5	3	7	1	3
Feast of the Passover, 15 Nisan	3	3	5	1	7	5	7	1	5	5	3	7	1	3
Commencement of Ijar	4,5	4,5	6,7	2,3	1,2	6,7	1,2	2,3	6,7	6,7	4,5	1,2	2,3	4,5
33 Omer	1	1	3	6	5	3	5	6	3	3	1	5	6	1
Commencement of Sivan	6	6	1	4	3	1	3	4	1	1	6	3	4	6
Pentecost, 6 Sivan	4	4	6	2	1	6	1	2	6	6	4	1	2	4
Commencement of Tammuz	7,1	7,1	2,3	5,6	4,5	2,3	4,5	5,6	2,3	2,3	7,1	4,5	5,6	7,1
A fast, 17 Tammuz	3	3	5	1	1	5	1	1	5	5	3	1	1	3
Commencement of Ab	2	2	4	7	6	4	6	7	4	4	2	6	7	2
A fast, 9 Ab	3	3	5	1	1	5	1	1	5	5	3	1	1	3
Commencement of Elul	3,4	3,4	5,6	1,2	7,1	5,6	7,1	1,2	5,6	5,6	3,4	7,1	1,2	3,4

TABLE. V.—*Containing the order of reading the Pareshioth and Haphtaroth for ninety Jewish years, i. e., from A. M. 5572 to A. M. 5661, (both inclusive,) connected with the corresponding dates in the Christian era according to the Gregorian or New Style.*

Jewish year of the World 5572, corresponding to A. D. 1811-1812.		
Sabbaths of the Jewish year.	Saturdays of the Gregorian yr.	Pareshioth and Haphtaroth.
2 C	1811	
3 Tisri	21 Sept.	53
10	28	Chippur
17	5 Oct.	Succoth
24	12	1
1 Marches.	19	2
8	26	3
15	2 Nov.	4
22	9	5
29	16	6
7 Cisleu	23	7
14	30	8
21	7 Dec.	9
28	14	10
5 Tebet	21	11
12	28	12
	1812	
19	4 Jan.	13
26	11	14
4 Sebat	18	15
11	25	16
18	1 Feb.	17
25	8	18, S
2 Adar	15	19
9	22	20, Z
16	29	21
23	7 March	22, 23, P
1 Nisan	14	24, H
8	21	25
15	28	1 Pas.
22	4 April	2 Pas.
29	11	26
6 Ijar	18	27, 28
13	25	29, 30
20	2 May	31
27	9	32, 33
5 Sivan	16	34
12	23	35
19	30	36
26	6 June	37
3 Tammuz	13	38
10	20	39
17	27	40
24	4 July	41
2 Ab	11	42, 43
9	18	44
16	25	45
23	1 Aug.	46
30	8	47
7 Elul	15	48
14	22	49
21	29	50
28	5 Sept.	51

Jewish year of the World 5573, corresponding to A. D. 1812-1813.		
Sabbaths of the Jewish year.	Saturdays of the Gregorian yr.	Pareshioth and Haphtaroth.
7 E	1812	
6 Tisri	12 Sept.	52
13	19	53
20	26	Succoth
27	3 Oct.	1
4 Marches.	10	2
11	17	3
18	24	4
25	31	5
3 Cisleu	7 Nov.	6
10	14	7
17	21	8
24	28	9
2 Tebet	5 Dec.	10
9	12	11
16	19	12
23	26	13
	1813	
1 Sebat	2 Jan.	14
8	9	15
15	16	16
22	23	17
29	30	18
6 Adar	6 Feb.	19
13	13	20
20	20	21
27	27	22, S
4 Veadar	6 March	23
11	13	24, Z
18	20	25, P
25	27	26, H
3 Nisan	3 April	27
10	10	28
17	17	1 Pas.
24	24	29
1 Ijar	1 May	30
8	8	31
15	15	32
22	22	33
29	29	34
7 Sivan	5 June	Pent.
14	12	35
21	19	36
28	26	37
5 Tammuz	3 July	38
12	10	39, 40
19	17	41
26	24	42, 43
4 Ab	31	44
11	7 Aug.	45
18	14	46
25	21	47
2 Elul	28	48
9	4 Sept.	49
16	11	50
23	18	51, 52

Jewish year of the World 5574, corresponding to A. D. 1813-1814.		
Sabbaths of the Jewish year.	Saturdays of the Gregorian yr.	Pareshioth and Haphtaroth.
4 C	1813	
1 Tisri	25 Sept.	New yrs.
8	2 Oct.	53 [day
15	9	Succoth
22	16	Oct. Suc.
23*	17*	54, B. L.
29	23	1
6 Marches.	30	2
13	6 Nov.	3
20	13	4
27	20	5
4 Cisleu	27	6
11	4 Dec.	7
18	11	8
25	18	9, En.
2 Tebet	25	10
	1814	
9	1 Jan	11
16	8	12
23	15	13
1 Sebat	22	14
8	29	15
15	5 Feb.	16
22	12	17
29	19	18, S
6 Adar	26	19
13	5 March	20, Z
20	12	21, P
27	19	22, 23, H
5 Nisan	26	24
12	2 April	25
19	9	1 Pas.
26	16	26
3 Ijar	23	27, 28
10	30	29, 30
17	7 May	31
24	14	32, 33
2 Sivan	21	34
9	28	35
16	4 June	36
23	11	37
30	18	38
7 Tammuz	25	39
14	2 July	40
21	9	41
28	16	42, 43
6 Ab	23	44
13	30	45
20	6 Aug.	46
27	13	47
4 Elul	20	48
11	27	49
18	3 Sept.	50
25	10	51

Jewish year of the World 5575, corresponding to A. D. 1814-1815.		
Sabbaths of the Jewish year.	Saturdays of the Gregorian yr.	Pareshioth and Haphtaroth.
4 E	1814	
3 Tisri	17 Sept.	53
10	24	Chippur
17	1 Oct.	Succoth
24	8	1
1 Marches.	15	2
8	22	3
15	29	4
22	5 Nov.	5
29	12	6
6 Cisleu	19	7
13	26	8
20	3 Dec.	9
27	10	10
4 Tebet	17	11
11	24	12
18	31	13
	1815	
25	7 Jan.	14
3 Sebat	14	15
10	21	16
17	28	17
24	4 Feb.	18
1 Adar	11	19
8	18	20
15	25	21
22	4 March	22
29	11	23, S
6 Veadar	18	24
13	25	25, Z
20	1 April	26, P
27	8	27, H
5 Nisan	15	28
12	22	29
19	29	1 Pas.
26	6 May	30
3 Ijar	13	31
10	20	32
17	27	33
24	3 June	34
2 Sivan	10	35
9	17	36
16	24	37
23	1 July	38
30	8	39
7 Tammuz	15	40
14	22	41
21	29	42
28	5 Aug.	43
6 Ab	12	44
13	19	45
20	26	46
27	2 Sept.	47
4 Elul	9	48
11	16	49
18	23	50
25	30	51, 52

Jewish year of the World 5576, corresponding to A. D. 1815-1816.		
Sabbaths of the Jewish year.	Saturdays of the Gregorian yr.	Pareshioth and Haphtaroth.
2 C	1815	
3 Tisri	7 Oct.	53
10	14	Chippur
17	21	Succoth
24	28	1
1 Marches.	4 Nov.	2
8	11	3
15	18	4
22	25	5
29	2 Dec.	6
7 Cisleu	9	7
14	16	8
21	23	9
28	30	10
	1816	
5 Tebet	6 Jan.	11
12	13	12
19	20	13
26	27	14
4 Sebat	3 Feb.	15
11	10	16
18	17	17
25	24	18, S
2 Adar	2 March	19
9	9	20, Z
16	16	21
23	23	22, 23, P
1 Nisan	30	24, H
8	6 April	25
15	13	1 Pas.
22	20	2 Pas.
29	27	26
6 Ijar	4 May	27, 28
13	11	29, 30
20	18	31
27	25	32, 33
5 Sivan	1 June	34
12	8	35
19	15	36
26	22	37
3 Tammuz	29	38
10	6 July	39
17	13	40
24	20	41
2 Ab	27	42, 43
9	3 Aug.	44
16	10	45
23	17	46
30	24	47
7 Elul	31	48
14	7 Sept.	49
21	14	50
28	21	51

Jewish year of the World 5577, corresponding to A. D. 1816-1817.		
Sabbaths of the Jewish year.	Saturdays of the Gregorian yr.	Pareshioth and Haphtaroth.
5 C	1816	
6 Tisri	28 Sept.	52
13	5 Oct.	53
20	12	Succoth
23*	15*	54, B.L.
27	19	1
4 Marches.	26	2
11	2 Nov.	3
18	9	4
25	16	5
3 [illegible]	23	6
10	30	7
17	7 Dec.	8
24	14	9
2 Tebet	21	10
9	28	11
	1817	
16	4 Jan.	12
23	11	13
1 Sebat	18	14
8	25	15
15	1 Feb.	16
22	8	17
29	15	18, S
6 Adar	22	19
13	1 March	20, Z
20	8	21, P
27	15	22, 23, H
5 Nan	22	24
12	29	25
19	5 April	1 Pas.
26	12	26
3 Ijar	19	27, 28
10	26	29, 30
17	3 May	31
24	10	32, 33
2 Sivan	17	34
9	24	35
16	31	36
23	7 June	37
30	14	38
7 Tammuz	21	39
14	28	40
21	5 July	41
28	12	42, 43
6 Ab	19	44
13	26	45
20	2 Aug.	46
27	9	47
4 Elul	16	48
11	23	49
18	30	50
25	6 Sept.	51, 52

TABLE V.—Continued.

Jewish year of the World 5578, corresponding to A. D. 1817–1818.

Sabbaths of the Jewish year.	Saturdays of the Gregorian yr.	Pareshioth and Haphtaroth.
4 E	1817	
3 Tisri	13 Sept.	53
10	20	Chippur
17	27	Succoth
24	4 Oct.	1
1 Marches.	11	2
8	18	3
15	25	4
22	1 Nov.	5
29	8	6
6 Cisleu	15	7
13	22	8
20	29	9
27	6 Dec.	10
4 Tebet	13	11
11	20	12
18	27	13
	1818	
25	3 Jan.	14
3 Sebat	10	15
10	17	16
17	24	17
24	31	18
1 Adar	7 Feb.	19
8	14	20
15	21	21
22	28	22
29	7 March	23, S
6 Veadar	14	24
13	21	25, Z
20	28	26, P
27	4 April	27, H
5 Nisan	11	28
12	18	29
19	25	1 Pas.
26	2 May	30
3 Ijar	9	31
10	16	32
17	23	33
24	30	34
2 Sivan	6 June	35
9	13	36
16	20	37
23	27	38
30	4 July	39
7 Tammuz	11	40
14	18	41
21	25	42
28	1 Aug.	43
6 Ab	8	44
13	15	45
20	22	46
27	29	47
4 Elu.	5 Sept.	48
11	12	49
18	19	50
25	26	51, 52

Jewish year of the World 5579, corresponding to A. D. 1818–1819.

Sabbaths of the Jewish year.	Saturdays of the Gregorian yr.	Pareshioth and Haphtaroth.
2 C	1818	
3 Tisri	3 Oct.	53
10	10	Chippur
17	17	Succoth
24	24	1
1 Marches.	31	2
8	7 Nov.	3
15	14	4
22	21	5
29	28	6
7 Cisleu	5 Dec.	7
14	12	8
21	19	9
28	26	10
	1819	
5 Tebet	2 Jan.	11
12	9	12
19	16	13
26	23	14
4 Sebat	30	15
11	6 Feb.	16
18	13	17
25	20	18, S
2 Adar	27	19
9	6 March	20, Z
16	13	21
23	20	22, 23, P
1 Nisan	27	24, H
8	3 April	25
15	10	1 Pas.
22	17	2 Pas.
29	24	26
6 Ijar	1 May	27, 28
13	8	29, 30
20	15	31
27	22	32, 33
5 Sivan	29	34
12	5 June	35
19	12	36
26	19	37
3 Tammuz	26	38
10	3 July	39
17	10	40
24	17	41
2 Ab	24	42, 43
9	31	44
16	7 Aug.	45
23	14	46
30	21	47
7 Elul	28	48
14	4 Sept.	49
21	11	50
28	18	51

Jewish year of the World 5580, corresponding to A. D. 1819–1820.

Sabbaths of the Jewish year.	Saturdays of the Gregorian yr.	Pareshioth and Haphtaroth.
6 C	1819	
6 Tisri	25 Sept.	52
13	2 Oct.	53
20	9	Succoth
23*	12*	54, B. L.
27	16	1
4 Marches.	23	2
11	30	3
18	6 Nov.	4
25	13	5
2 Cisleu	20	6
9	27	7
16	4 Dec.	8
23	11	9
30	18	10
7 Tebet	25	11
	1820	
14	1 Jan.	12
21	8	13
28	15	14
6 Sebat	22	15
13	29	16
20	5 Feb.	17
27	12	18, S
4 Adar	19	19
11	26	20, Z
18	4 March	21, P
25	11	22, 23, H
3 Nisan	18	24
10	25	25
17	1 April	1 Pas.
24	8	26
1 Ijar	15	27, 28
8	22	29, 30
15	29	31
22	6 May	32, 33
29	13	34
7 Sivan	20	Pent.
14	27	35
21	3 June	36
28	10	37
5 Tammuz	17	38
12	24	39, 40
19	1 July	41
26	8	42, 43
4 Ab	15	44
11	22	45
18	29	46
25	5 Aug.	47
2 Elul	12	48
9	19	49
16	26	50
23	2 Sept.	51, 52

Jewish year of the World 5581, corresponding to A. D. 1820–1821.

Sabbaths of the Jewish year.	Saturdays of the Gregorian yr.	Pareshioth and Haphtaroth.
5 E	1820	
1 Tisri	9 Sept.	New yrs.
8	16	53 {day
15	23	Succoth
22	30	Sab.p.Suc.
23*	1 * Oct.	54, B. L.
29	7	1
6 Marches.	14	2
13	21	3
20	28	4
27	4 Nov.	5
5 Cisleu	11	6
12	18	7
19	25	8
26	2 Dec.	9
4 Tebet	9	10
11	16	11
18	23	12
25	30	13
	1821	
3 Sebat	6 Jan.	14
10	13	15
17	20	16
24	27	17
1 Adar	3 Feb.	18
8	10	19
15	17	20
22	24	21
29	3 March	22, S
6 Veadar	10	23
13	17	24, Z
20	24	25, P
27	31	26, H
5 Nisan	7 April	27
12	14	28
19	21	1 Pas.
26	28	29
3 Ijar	5 May	30
10	12	31
17	19	32
24	26	33
2 Sivan	2 June	34
9	9	35
16	16	36
23	23	37
30	30	38
7 Tammuz	7 July	39
14	14	40
21	21	41
28	28	42, 43
6 Ab	4 Aug.	44
13	11	45
20	18	46
27	25	47
4 Elul	1 Sept.	48
11	8	49
18	15	50
25	22	51, 52

Jewish year of the World 5582, corresponding to A. D. 1821–1822.

Sabbaths of the Jewish year.	Saturdays of the Gregorian yr.	Pareshioth and Haphtaroth.
2 C	1821	
3 Tisri	29 Sept.	53
10	6 Oct.	Chippur
17	13	Succoth
24	20	1
1 Marches.	27	2
8	3 Nov.	3
15	10	4
22	17	5
29	24	6
7 Cisleu	1 Dec.	7
14	8	8
21	15	9
28	22	10
5 Tebet	29	11
	1822	
12	5 Jan.	12
19	12	13
26	19	14
4 Sebat	26	15
11	2 Feb.	16
18	9	17
25	16	18, S
2 Adar	23	19
9	2 March	20, Z
16	9	21
23	16	22, 23, P
1 Nisan	23	24, H
8	30	25
15	6 April	1 Pas.
22	13	2 Pas.
29	20	26
6 Ijar	27	27, 28
13	4 May	29, 30
20	11	31
27	18	32, 33
5 Sivan	25	34
12	1 June	35
19	8	36
26	15	37
3 Tammuz	22	38
10	29	39
17	6 July	40
24	13	41
2 Ab	20	42, 43
9	27	44
16	3 Aug.	45
23	10	46
30	17	47
7 Elul	24	48
14	31	49
21	7 Sept.	50
28	14	51

Jewish year of the World 5583, corresponding to A. D. 1822–1823.

Sabbaths of the Jewish year.	Saturdays of the Gregorian yr.	Pareshioth and Haphtaroth.
6 C	1822	
6 Tisri	21 Sept.	52
13	28	53
20	5 Oct.	Succoth
23*	8*	54, B. L.
27	12	1
4 Marches.	19	2
11	26	3
18	2 Nov.	4
25	9	5
2 Cisleu	16	6
9	23	7
16	30	8
23	7 Dec.	9
30	14	10
7 Tebet	21	11
14	28	12
	1823	
21	4 Jan.	13
28	11	14
6 Sebat	18	15
13	25	16
20	1 Feb.	17
27	8	18, S
4 Adar	15	19
11	22	20, Z
18	1 March	21, P
25	8	22, 23, H
3 Nisan	15	24
10	22	25
17	29	1 Pas.
24	5 April	26
1 Ijar	12	27, 28
8	19	29, 30
15	26	31
22	3 May	32, 33
29	10	34
7 Sivan	17	Pent.
14	24	35
21	31	36
28	7 June	37
5 Tammuz	14	38
12	21	39, 40
19	28	41
26	5 July	42, 43
4 Ab	12	44
11	19	45
18	26	46
25	2 Aug.	47
2 Elul	9	48
9	16	49
16	23	50
23	30	51, 52

TABLE V.—Continued.

Jewish year of the World 5584, corresponding to A. D. 1823–1824.		
Sabbaths of the Jewish year.	Saturdays of the Gregorian yr.	Pareshioth and Haphtaroth.
5 E	1823	
. Tisri	6 Sept.	New yrs.
8	13	53 [day
15	20	Succoth
22	27	Sab.p.Suc.
23*	28*	54, B. L.
29	4 Oct.	1
6 Marches.	11	2
13	18	3
20	25	4
27	1 Nov.	5
5 Cisleu	8	6
12	15	7
19	22	8
26	29	9
4 Tebet	6 Dec	10
11	13	11
18	20	12
25	27	13
	1824	
3 Sebat	3 Jan.	14
10	10	15
17	17	16
24	24	17
1 Adar	31	18
8	7 Feb.	19
15	14	20
22	21	21
29	28	22, S
6 Veadar	6 March	23
13	13	24, Z
20	20	25, P
27	27	26, H
5 Nisan	3 April	27
12	10	28
19	17	1 Pas.
26	24	29
3 Ijar	1 May	30
10	8	31
17	15	32
24	22	33
2 Sivan	29	34
9	5 June	35
16	12	36
23	19	37
30	26	38
7 Tammuz	3 July	39
14	10	40
21	17	41
28	24	42, 43
6 Ab	31	44
13	7 Aug.	45
20	14	46
27	21	47
4 Elul	28	48
11	4 Sept.	49
18	11	50
25	18	51, 52

Jewish year of the World 5585, corresponding to A. D. 1824–1825.		
Sabbaths of the Jewish year.	Saturdays of the Gregorian yr.	Pareshioth and Haphtaroth.
1 C	1824	
3 Tisri	25 Sept.	53
10	2 Oct.	Chippur
17	9	Succoth
23*	15*	54, B. L.
24	16	1
1 Marches.	23	2
8	30	3
15	6 Nov.	4
22	13	5
29	20	6
6 Cisleu	27	7
13	4 Dec.	8
20	11	9
27	18	10
4 Tebet	25	11
	1825	
11	1 Jan.	12
18	8	13
25	15	14
3 Sebat	22	15
10	29	16
17	5 Feb.	17
24	12	18
1 Adar	19	19, S
8	26	20, Z
15	5 March	21
22	12	22, P
29	19	23, H
7 Nisan	26	24
14	2 April	25
21	9	1 Pas.
28	16	26
5 Ijar	23	27, 28
12	30	29, 30
19	7 May	31
26	14	32, 33
4 Sivan	21	34
11	28	35
18	4 Juno	36
25	11	37
2 Tammuz	18	38
9	25	39
16	2 July	40
23	9	41
1 Ab	16	42, 43
8	23	44
15	30	45
22	6 Aug.	46
29	13	47
6 Elul	20	48
13	27	49
20	3 Sept.	50
27	10	51

Jewish year of the World 5586, corresponding to A. D. 1825–1826.		
Sabbaths of the Jewish year.	Saturdays of the Gregorian yr.	Pareshioth and Haphtaroth.
2 E	1825	
5 Tisri	17 Sept.	52
12	24	53
19	1 Oct.	Succoth
23*	5*	54, B. L.
26	8	1
3 Marches.	15	2
10	22	3
17	29	4
24	5 Nov.	5
2 Cisleu	12	6
9	19	7
16	26	8
23	3 Dec.	9
30	10	10
7 Tebet	17	11
14	24	12
21	31	13
	1826	
28	7 Jan.	14
6 Sebat	14	15
13	21	16
20	28	17
27	4 Feb.	18
4 Adar	11	19
11	18	20
18	25	21
25	4 March	22, S
2 Veadar	11	23
9	18	24, Z
16	25	25
23	1 April	26, P
1 Nisan	8	27, H
8	15	28
15	22	1 Pas.
22	29	2 Pas.
29	6 May	29
6 Ijar	13	30
13	20	31
20	27	32
27	3 June	33
5 Sivan	10	34
12	17	35
19	24	36
26	1 July	37
3 Tammuz	8	38
10	15	39
17	22	40
24	29	41
2 Ab	5 Aug.	42, 43
9	12	44
16	19	45
23	26	46
30	2 Sept.	47
7 Elul	9	48
14	16	49
21	23	50
28	30	51

Jewish year of the World 5587, corresponding to A. D. 1826–1827.		
Sabbaths of the Jewish year.	Saturdays of the Gregorian yr.	Pareshioth and Haphtaroth.
6 C	1826	
6 Tisri	7 Oct.	52
13	14	53
20	21	Succoth
23*	24*	54, B. L.
27	28	1
4 Marches.	4 Nov.	2
11	11	3
18	18	4
25	25	5
2 Cisleu	2 Dec.	6
9	9	7
16	16	8
23	23	9
30	30	10
	1827	
7 Tebet	6 Jan.	11
14	13	12
21	20	13
28	27	14
6 Sebat	3 Feb.	15
13	10	16
20	17	17
27	24	18, S
4 Adar	3 March	19
11	10	20, Z
18	17	21, P
25	24	22, 23, H
3 Nisan	31	24
10	7 April	25
17	14	1 Pas.
24	21	26
1 Ijar	28	27, 28
8	5 May	29, 30
15	12	31
22	19	32, 33
29	26	34
7 Sivan	2 June	Pent.
14	9	35
21	16	36
28	23	37
5 Tammuz	30	38
12	7 July	39, 40
19	14	41
26	21	42, 43
4 Ab	28	44
11	4 Aug.	45
18	11	46
25	18	47
2 Elul	25	48
9	1 Sept.	49
16	8	50
23	15	51, 52

Jewish year of the World 5588, corresponding to A. D. 1827–1828.		
Sabbaths of the Jewish year.	Saturdays of the Gregorian yr.	Pareshioth and Haphtaroth.
3 C	1827	
1 Tisri	22 Sept.	New yrs.
8	29	53 [day
15	6 Oct.	Succoth
22	13	Sab.p.Suc.
23*	14*	54, B. L.
29	20	1
6 Marches.	27	2
13	3 Nov.	3
20	10	4
27	17	5
5 Cisleu	24	6
12	1 Dec.	7
19	8	8
26	15	9
4 Tebet	22	10
11	29	11
	1828	
18	5 Jan.	12
25	12	13
3 Sebat	19	14
10	26	15
17	2 Feb.	16
24	9	17
1 Adar	16	18, S
8	23	19, Z
15	1 March	20
22	8	21, P
29	15	22, 23, H
7 Nisan	22	24
14	29	25
21	5 April	1 Pas.
28	12	26
5 Ijar	19	27, 28
12	26	29, 30
19	3 May	31
26	10	32, 33
4 Sivan	17	34
11	24	35
18	31	36
25	7 June	37
2 Tammuz	14	38
9	21	39
16	28	40
23	5 July	41
1 Ab	12	42, 43
8	19	44
15	26	45
22	2 Aug.	46
29	9	47
6 Elul	16	48
13	23	49
20	30	50
27	6 Sept.	51

Jewish year of the World 5589, corresponding to A. D. 1828–1829.		
Sabbaths of the Jewish year.	Saturdays of the Gregorian yr.	Pareshioth and Haphtaroth.
2 E	1828	
5 Tisri	13 Sept.	52
12	20	53
19	27	Succoth
23*	1* Oct.	54, B. L
26	4	1
3 Marches.	11	2
10	18	3
17	25	4
24	1 Nov.	5
2 Cisleu	8	6
9	15	7
16	22	8
23	29	9
30	6 Dec.	10
7 Tebet	13	11
14	20	12
21	27	13
	1829	
28	3 Jan.	14
6 Sebat	10	15
13	17	16
20	24	17
27	31	18
4 Adar	7 Feb.	19
11	14	20
18	21	21
25	28	22, S
2 Veadar	7 March	23
9	14	24, Z
16	21	25
23	28	26, P
1 Nisan	4 April	27, H
8	11	28
15	18	1 Pas
22	25	2 Pas
29	2 May	29
6 Ijar	9	30
13	16	31
20	23	32
27	30	33
5 Sivan	6 June	34
12	13	35
19	20	36
26	27	37
3 Tammuz	4 July	38
10	11	39
17	18	40
24	25	41
2 Ab	1 Aug.	42, 43
9	8	44
16	15	45
23	22	46
30	29	47
7 Elul	5 Sept.	48
14	12	49
21	19	50
28	26	51

TABLE V.—Continued.

Jewish year of the World 5590, corresponding to A. D. 1829–1830.

Sabbaths of the Jewish year.	Saturdays of the Gregorian yr.	Pareshioth and Haphtaroth.
6 C	1829	
6 Tisri	3 Oct.	52
13	10	53
20	17	Succoth
23*	20*	54, B. L
27	24	1
4 Marchos.	31	2
11	7 Nov.	3
18	14	4
25	21	5
2 Cisleu	28	6
9	5 Dec.	7
16	12	8
23	19	9
30	26	10
	1830	
7 Tebet	2 Jan.	11
14	9	12
21	16	13
28	23	14
6 Sebat	30	15
13	6 Feb.	16
20	13	17
27	20	18, S
4 Adar	27	19
11	6 March	20, Z
18	13	21, P
25	20	22, 23, H
3 Nisan	27	24
10	3 April	25
17	10	1 Pas.
24	17	26
1 Ijar	24	27, 28
8	1 May	29, 30
15	8	31
22	15	32, 33
29	22	34
7 Sivan	29	Pent.
14	5 June	35
21	12	36
28	19	37
5 Tammuz	26	38
12	3 July	39, 40
19	10	41
26	17	42, 43
4 Ab	24	44
11	31	45
18	7 Aug.	46
25	14	47
2 Elul	21	48
9	28	49
16	4 Sept.	50
23	11	51, 52

Jewish year of the World 5591, corresponding to A. D. 1830–1831.

Sabbaths of the Jewish year.	Saturdays of the Gregorian yr.	Pareshioth and Haphtaroth.
4 C	1830	
1 Tisri	18 Sept.	New yrs.
8	25	53 [day.
15	2 Oct.	Succoth
22	9	Oct. Suc.
23*	10*	54, B. L.
29	16	1
6 Marches.	23	2
13	30	3
20	6 Nov.	4
27	13	5
4 Cisleu	20	6
11	27	7
18	4 Dec.	8
25	11	9, En.
2 Tebet	18	10
9	25	11
	1831	
16	1 Jan.	12
23	8	13
1 Sebat	15	14
8	22	15
15	29	16
22	5 Feb.	17
29	12	18, S
6 Adar	19	19
13	26	20, Z
20	5 March	21, P
27	12	22, 23, H
5 Nisan	19	24
12	26	25
19	2 April	1 Pas.
26	9	26
3 Ijar	16	27, 28
10	23	29, 30
17	30	31
24	7 May	32, 33
2 Sivan	14	34
9	21	35
16	28	36
23	4 June	37
30	11	38
7 Tammuz	18	39
14	25	40
21	2 July	41
28	9	42, 43
6 Ab	16	44
13	23	45
20	30	46
27	6 Aug.	47
4 Elul	13	48
11	20	49
18	27	50
25	3 Sept.	51

Jewish year of the World 5592, corresponding to A. D. 1831–1832.

Sabbaths of the Jewish year.	Saturdays of the Gregorian yr.	Pareshioth and Haphtaroth.
1 E	1831	
3 Tisri	10 Sept.	53
10	17	Chippur
17	24	Succoth
23*	30*	54, B. L.
24	1 Oct.	1
1 Marches.	8	2
8	15	3
15	22	4
22	29	5
29	5 Nov.	6
7 Cisleu	12	7
14	19	8
21	26	9
28	3 Dec.	10
6 Tebet	10	11
13	17	12
20	24	13
27	31	14
	1832	
5 Sebat	7 Jan.	15
12	14	16
19	21	17
26	28	18
3 Adar	4 Feb.	19
10	11	20
17	18	21
24	25	22
1 Veadar	3 March	23, S
8	10	24, Z
15	17	25
22	24	26, P
29	31	27, H
7 Nisan	7 April	28
14	14	29
21	21	1 Pas.
28	28	30
5 Ijar	5 May	31
12	12	32
19	19	33
26	26	34
4 Sivan	2 June	35
11	9	36
18	16	37
25	23	38
2 Tammuz	30	39
9	7 July	40
16	14	41
23	21	42
1 Ab	28	43
8	4 Aug.	44
15	11	45
22	18	46
29	25	47
6 Elul	1 Sept.	48
13	8	49
20	15	50
27	22	51

Jewish year of the World 5593, corresponding to A. D. 1832–1833.

Sabbaths of the Jewish year.	Saturdays of the Gregorian yr.	Pareshioth and Haphtaroth.
7 C	1832	
5 Tisri	29 Sept.	52
12	6 Oct.	53
19	13	Succoth
23*	17*	54, B. L.
26	20	1
3 Marches.	27	2
10	3 Nov.	3
17	10	4
24	17	5
2 Cisleu	24	6
9	1 Dec.	7
16	8	8
23	15	9
30	22	10
7 Tebet	29	11
	1833	
14	5 Jan.	12
21	12	13
28	19	14
6 Sebat	26	15
13	2 Feb.	16
20	9	17
27	16	18, S
4 Adar	23	19
11	2 March	20, Z
18	9	21, P
25	16	22, 23, H
3 Nisan	23	24
10	30	25
17	6 April	1 Pas.
24	13	26
1 Ijar	20	27, 28
8	27	29, 30
15	4 May	31
22	11	32, 33
29	18	34
7 Sivan	25	Pent.
14	1 June	35
21	8	36
28	15	37
5 Tammuz	22	38
12	29	39, 40
19	6 July	41
26	13	42, 43
4 Ab	20	44
11	27	45
18	3 Aug.	46
25	10	47
2 Elul	17	48
9	24	49
16	31	50
23	7 Sept.	51, 52

Jewish year of the World 5594, corresponding to A. D. 1833–1834.

Sabbaths of the Jewish year.	Saturdays of the Gregorian yr.	Pareshioth and Haphtaroth.
6 E	1833	
1 Tisri	14 Sept.	New yrs.
8	21	53 [day
15	28	Succoth
22	5 Oct.	Sab.p.Suc.
23*	6*	54, B. L.
29	12	1
6 Marches.	19	2
13	26	3
20	2 Nov.	4
27	9	5
4 Cisleu	16	6
11	23	7
18	30	8
25	7 Dec.	9
2 Tebet	14	10
9	21	11
16	28	12
	1834	
23	4 Jan.	13
1 Sebat	11	14
8	18	15
15	25	16
22	1 Feb.	17
29	8	18
6 Adar	15	19
13	22	20
20	1 March	21
27	8	22, S
4 Veadar	15	23
11	22	24, Z
18	29	25, P
25	5 April	26, H
3 Nisan	12	27
10	19	28
17	26	1 Pas.
24	3 May	29
1 Ijar	10	30
8	17	31
15	24	32
22	31	33
29	7 June	34
7 Sivan	14	Pent.
14	21	35
21	28	36
28	5 July	37
5 Tammuz	12	38
12	19	39, 40
19	26	41
26	2 Aug.	42, 43
4 Ab	9	44
11	16	45
18	23	46
25	30	47
2 Elul	6 Sept.	48
9	13	49
16	20	50
23	27	51, 52

Jewish year of the World 5595, corresponding to A. D. 1834–1835.

Sabbaths of the Jewish year.	Saturdays of the Gregorian yr.	Pareshioth and Haphtaroth.
4 C	1834	
1 Tisri	4 Oct.	New yrs.
8	11	53 [day
15	18	Succoth
22	25	Oct. Suc.
23*	26*	54, B.L.
29	1 Nov.	1
6 Marches.	8	2
13	15	3
20	22	4
27	29	5
4 Cisleu	6 Dec.	6
11	13	7
18	20	8
25	27	9, En.
	1835	
2 Tebet	3 Jan.	10
9	10	11
16	17	12
23	24	13
1 Sebat	31	14
8	7 Feb.	15
15	14	16
22	21	17
29	28	18, S
6 Adar	7 March	19
13	14	20, Z
20	21	21, P
27	28	22, 23, H
5 Nisan	4 April	24
12	11	25
19	18	1 Pas.
26	25	26
3 Ijar	2 May	27, 28
10	9	29, 30
17	16	31
24	23	32, 33
2 Sivan	30	34
9	6 June	35
16	13	36
23	20	37
30	27	38
7 Tammuz	4 July	39
14	11	40
21	18	41
28	25	42, 43
6 Ab	1 Aug.	44
13	8	45
20	15	46
27	22	47
4 Elul	29	48
11	5 Sept.	49
18	12	50
25	19	51

TABLE V.—Continued.

Jewish year of the World 5596, corresponding to A. D. 1835–1836.		
Sabbaths of the Jewish year	Saturdays of the Gregorian yr.	Pareshioth and Haphtaroth.
2 C	1835	
3 Tisri	26 Sept.	53
10	3 Oct.	Chippur
17	10	Succoth
24	17	1
1 Marches.	24	2
8	31	3
15	7 Nov.	4
22	14	5
29	21	6
7 Cisleu	28	7
14	5 Dec.	8
21	12	9
28	19	10
5 Tebet	26	11
	1836	
12	2 Jan.	12
19	9	13
26	16	14
4 Sebat	23	15
11	30	16
18	6 Feb.	17
25	13	18, S
2 Adar	20	19
9	27	20, Z
16	5 March	21
23	12	22, 23, P
1 Nisan	19	24, H
8	26	25
15	2 April	1 Pas.
22	9	2 Pas.
29	16	26
6 Ijar	23	27, 28
13	30	29, 30
20	7 May	31
27	14	32, 33
5 Sivan	21	34
12	28	35
19	4 June	36
26	11	37
3 Tammuz	18	38
10	25	39
17	2 July	40
24	9	41
2 Ab	16	42, 43
9	23	44
16	30	45
23	6 Aug.	46
30	13	47
7 Elul	20	48
14	27	49
21	3 Sept.	50
28	10	51

Jewish year of the World 5597, corresponding to A. D. 1836–1837.		
Sabbaths of the Jewish year.	Saturdays of the Gregorian yr.	Pareshioth and Haphtaroth.
7 E	1836	
6 Tisri	17 Sept.	52
13	24	53
20	1 Oct.	Succoth
27	8	1
4 Marches.	15	2
11	22	3
18	29	4
25	5 Nov.	5
3 Cisleu	12	6
10	19	7
17	26	8
24	3 Dec.	9
2 Tebet	10	10
9	17	11
16	24	12
23	31	13
	1837	
1 Sebat	7 Jan.	14
8	14	15
15	21	16
22	28	17
29	4 Feb.	18
6 Adar	11	19
13	18	20
20	25	21
27	4 March	22, S
4 Veadar	11	23
11	18	24, Z
18	25	25, P
25	1 April	26, H
3 Nisan	8	27
10	15	28
17	22	1 Pas.
24	29	29
1 Ijar	6 May	30
8	13	31
15	20	32
22	27	33
29	3 June	34
7 Sivan	10	Pent.
14	17	35
21	24	36
28	1 July	37
5 Tammuz	8	38
12	15	39, 40
19	22	41
26	29	42, 43
4 Ab	5 Aug.	44
11	12	45
18	19	46
25	26	47
2 Elul	2 Sept.	48
9	9	49
16	16	50
23	23	51, 52

Jewish year of the World 5598, corresponding to A. D. 1837–1838.		
Sabbaths of the Jewish year.	Saturdays of the Gregorian yr.	Pareshioth and Haphtaroth.
4 C	1837	
1 Tisri	30 Sept.	New yrs.
8	7 Oct.	53 [day.
15	14	Succoth
22	21	Oct. Suc.
23*	22*	54, B. L.
29	28	1
6 Marches.	4 Nov.	2
13	11	3
20	18	4
27	25	5
4 Cisleu	2 Dec.	6
11	9	7
18	16	8
25	23	9, En.
2 Tebet	30	10
	1838	
9	6 Jan.	11
16	13	12
23	20	13
1 Sebat	27	14
8	3 Feb.	15
15	10	16
22	17	17
29	24	18, S
6 Adar	3 March	19
13	10	20, Z
20	17	21, P
27	24	22, 23, H
5 Nisan	31	24
12	7 April	25
19	14	1 Pas.
26	21	26
3 Ijar	28	27, 28
10	5 May	29, 30
17	12	31
24	19	32, 33
2 Sivan	26	34
9	2 June	35
16	9	36
23	16	37
30	23	38
7 Tammuz	30	39
14	7 July	40
21	14	41
28	21	42, 43
6 Ab	28	44
13	4 Aug.	45
20	11	46
27	18	47
4 Elul	25	48
11	1 Sept.	49
18	8	50
25	15	51

Jewish year of the World 5599, corresponding to A. D. 1838–1839.		
Sabbaths of the Jewish year.	Saturdays of the Gregorian yr.	Pareshioth and Haphtaroth.
2 C	1838	
3 Tisri	22 Sept.	53
10	29	Chippur
17	6 Oct.	Succoth
24	13	1
1 Marches.	20	2
8	27	3
15	3 Nov.	4
22	10	5
29	17	6
7 Cisleu	24	7
14	1 Dec.	8
21	8	9
28	15	10
5 Tebet	22	11
12	29	12
	1839	
19	5 Jan.	13
26	12	14
4 Sebat	19	15
11	26	16
18	2 Feb.	17
25	9	18, S
2 Adar	16	19
9	23	20, Z
16	2 March	21
23	9	22, 23, P
1 Nisan	16	24, H
8	23	25
15	30	1 Pas.
22	6 April	2 Pas.
29	13	26
6 Ijar	20	27, 28
13	27	29, 30
20	4 May	31
27	11	32, 33
5 Sivan	18	34
12	25	35
19	1 June	36
26	8	37
3 Tammuz	15	38
10	22	39
17	29	40
24	6 July	41
2 Ab	13	42, 43
9	20	44
16	27	45
23	3 Aug.	46
30	10	47
7 Elul	17	48
14	24	49
21	31	50
28	7 Sept.	51

Jewish year of the World 5600, corresponding to A. D. 1839–1840.		
Sabbaths of the Jewish year.	Saturdays of the Gregorian yr.	Pareshioth and Haphtaroth.
3 E	1839	
6 Tisri	14 Sept.	52
13	21	53
20	28	Succoth
23*	1* Oct.	54, B. L.
27	5	1
4 Marches.	12	2
11	19	3
18	26	4
25	2 Nov.	5
2 Cisleu	9	6
9	16	7
16	23	8
23	30	9
30	7 Dec.	10
7 Tebet	14	11
14	21	12
21	28	13
	1840	
28	4 Jan.	14
6 Sebat	11	15
13	18	16
20	25	17
27	1 Feb.	18
4 Adar	8	19
11	15	20
18	22	21
25	29	22, S
2 Veadar	7 March	23
9	14	24, Z
16	21	25
23	28	26, P
1 Nisan	4 April	27, H
8	11	28
15	18	1 Pas.
22	25	2 Pas.
29	2 May	29
6 Ijar	9	30
13	16	31
20	23	32
27	30	33
5 Sivan	6 June	34
12	13	35
19	20	36
26	27	37
3 Tammuz	4 July	38
10	11	39
17	18	40
24	25	41
2 Ab	1 Aug	42, 43
9	8	44
16	15	45
23	22	46
30	29	47
7 Elul	5 Sept	48
14	12	49
21	19	50
28	26	51

Jewish year of the World 5601, corresponding to A. D. 1840–1841.		
Sabbaths of the Jewish year.	Saturdays of the Gregorian yr.	Pareshioth and Haphtaroth.
5 C	1840	
6 Tisri	3 Oct.	52
13	10	53
20	17	Succoth
23*	20*	54, B. L.
27	24	1
4 Marches.	31	2
11	7 Nov.	3
18	14	4
25	21	5
3 Cisleu	28	6
10	5 Dec.	7
17	12	8
24	19	9
2 Tebet	26	10
	1841	
9	2 Jan.	11
16	9	12
23	16	13
1 Sebat	23	14
8	30	15
15	6 Feb.	16
22	13	17
29	20	18, S
6 Adar	27	19
13	6 March	20, Z
20	13	21, P
27	20	22, 23, H
5 Nisan	27	24
12	3 April	25
19	10	1 Pas.
26	17	26
3 Ijar	24	27, 28
10	1 May	29, 30
17	8	31
24	15	32, 33
2 Sivan	22	34
9	29	35
16	5 June	36
23	12	37
30	19	38
7 Tammuz	26	39
14	3 July	40
21	10	41
28	17	42, 43
6 Ab	24	44
13	31	45
20	7 Aug.	46
27	14	47
4 Elul	21	48
11	28	49
18	4 Sept.	50
25	11	51, 52

TABLE V.—CONTINUED.

Jewish year of the World 5602, corresponding to A. D. 1841–1842.		
Sabbaths of the Jewish year.	Saturdays of the Gregorian yr.	Pareshioth and Haphtaroth.
2 C	1841	
3 Tisri	18 Sept.	53
10	25	Chippur
17	2 Oct.	Succoth
24	9	1
1 Marches.	16	2
8	23	3
15	30	4
22	6 Nov.	5
29	13	6
7 Cisleu	20	7
14	27	8
21	4 Dec.	9
28	11	10
5 Tebet	18	11
12	25	12
	1842	
19	1 Jan.	13
26	8	14
4 Sebat	15	15
11	22	16
18	29	17
25	5 Feb.	18, S
2 Adar	12	19
9	19	20, Z
16	26	21
23	5 March	22, 23, P
1 Nisan	12	24, H
8	19	25
15	26	1 Pas.
22	2 April	2 Pas.
29	9	26
6 Ijar	16	27, 28
13	23	29, 30
20	30	31
27	7 May	32, 33
5 Sivan	14	34
12	21	35
19	28	36
26	4 June	37
3 Tammuz	11	38
10	18	39
17	25	40
24	2 July	41
2 Ab	9	42, 43
9	16	44
16	23	45
23	30	46
30	6 Aug.	47
7 Elul	13	48
14	20	49
21	27	50
28	3 Sept.	51

Jewish year of the World 5603, corresponding to A. D. 1842–1843.		
Sabbaths of the Jewish year.	Saturdays of the Gregorian yr.	Pareshioth and Haphtaroth.
3 E	1842	
6 Tisri	10 Sept.	52
13	17	53
20	24	Succoth
23*	27*	54, B. L.
27	1 Oct.	1
4 Marches.	8	2
11	15	3
18	22	4
25	29	5
2 Cisleu	5 Nov.	6
9	12	7
16	19	8
23	26	9
30	3 Dec.	10
7 Tebet	10	11
14	17	12
21	24	13
28	31	14
	1843	
6 Sebat	7 Jan.	15
13	14	16
20	21	17
27	28	18
4 Adar	4 Feb.	19
11	11	20
18	18	21
25	25	22, S
2 Veadar	4 March	23
9	11	24, Z
16	18	25
23	25	26, P
1 Nisan	1 April	27, H
8	8	28
15	15	1 Pas.
22	22	2 Pas.
29	29	29
6 Ijar	6 May	30
13	13	31
20	20	32
27	27	33
5 Sivan	3 June	34
12	10	35
19	17	36
26	24	37
3 Tammuz	1 July	38
10	8	39
17	15	40
24	22	41
2 Ab	29	42, 43
9	5 Aug.	44
16	12	45
23	19	46
30	26	47
7 Elul	2 Sept.	48
14	9	49
21	16	50
28	23	51

Jewish year of the World 5604, corresponding to A. D. 1843–1844.		
Sabbaths of the Jewish year.	Saturdays of the Gregorian yr.	Pareshioth and Haphtaroth.
6 C	1843	
6 Tisri	30 Sept.	52
13	7 Oct.	53
20	14	Succoth
23*	17*	54, B. L.
27	21	1
4 Marches.	28	2
11	4 Nov.	3
18	11	4
25	18	5
2 Cisleu	25	6
9	2 Dec.	7
16	9	8
23	16	9
30	23	10
7 Tebet	30	11
	1844	
14	6 Jan.	12
21	13	13
28	20	14
6 Sebat	27	15
13	3 Feb.	16
20	10	17
27	17	18, S
4 Adar	24	19
11	2 March	20, Z
18	9	21, P
25	16	22, 23, H
3 Nisan	23	24
10	30	25
17	6 April	1 Pas.
24	13	26
1 Ijar	20	27, 28
8	27	29, 30
15	4 May	31
22	11	32, 33
29	18	34
7 Sivan	25	Pent.
14	1 June	35
21	8	36
28	15	37
5 Tammuz	22	38
12	29	39, 40
19	6 July	41
26	13	42, 43
4 Ab	20	44
11	27	45
18	3 Aug.	46
25	10	47
2 Elul	17	48
9	24	49
16	31	50
23	7 Sept.	51, 52

Jewish year of the World 5605, corresponding to A. D. 1844–1845		
Sabbaths of the Jewish year.	Saturdays of the Gregorian yr.	Pareshioth and Haphtaroth.
5 E	1844	
1 Tisri	14 Sept.	New yrs.
8	21	53 [day
15	28	Succoth
22	5 Oct.	Sab.p.Suc.
23*	6*	54, B. L.
29	12	1
6 Marches.	19	2
13	26	3
20	2 Nov.	4
27	9	5
5 Cisleu	16	6
12	23	7
19	30	8
26	7 Dec.	9
4 Tebet	14	10
11	21	11
18	28	12
	1845	
25	4 Jan.	13
3 Sebat	11	14
10	18	15
17	25	16
24	1 Feb.	17
1 Adar	8	18
8	15	19
15	22	20
22	1 March	21
29	8	22, S
6 Veadar	15	23
13	22	24, Z
20	29	25, P
27	5 April	26, H
5 Nisan	12	27
12	19	28
19	26	1 Pas.
26	3 May	29
3 Ijar	10	30
10	17	31
17	24	32
24	31	33
2 Sivan	7 June	34
9	14	35
16	21	36
23	28	37
30	5 July	38
7 Tammuz	12	39
14	19	40
21	26	41
28	2 Aug.	42, 43
6 Ab	9	44
13	16	45
20	23	46
27	30	47
4 Elul	6 Sept.	48
11	13	49
18	20	50
25	27	51, 52

Jewish year of the World 5606, corresponding to A. D. 1845–1846		
Sabbaths of the Jewish year.	Saturdays of the Gregorian yr.	Pareshioth and Haphtaroth.
2 C	1845	
3 Tisri	4 Oct.	53
10	11	Chippur
17	18	Succoth
24	25	1
1 Marches.	1 Nov.	2
8	8	3
15	15	4
22	22	5
29	29	6
7 Cisleu	6 Dec.	7
14	13	8
21	20	9
28	27	10
	1846	
5 Tebet	3 Jan.	11
12	10	12
19	17	13
26	24	14
4 Sebat	31	15
11	7 Feb.	16
18	14	17
25	21	18, S
2 Adar	28	19
9	7 March	20, Z
16	14	21
23	21	22, 23, P
1 Nisan	28	24, H
8	4 April	25
15	11	1 Pas.
22	18	2 Pas.
29	25	26
6 Ijar	2 May	27, 28
13	9	29, 30
20	16	31
27	23	32, 33
5 Sivan	30	34
12	6 June	35
19	13	36
26	20	37
3 Tammuz	27	38
10	4 July	39
17	11	40
24	18	41
2 Ab	25	42, 43
9	1 Aug.	44
16	8	45
23	15	46
30	22	47
7 Elul	29	48
14	5 Sept.	49
21	12	50
28	19	51

Jewish year of the World 5607, corresponding to A. D. 1846–1847.		
Sabbaths of the Jewish year.	Saturdays of the Gregorian yr.	Pareshioth and Haphtaroth.
6 C	1846	
6 Tisri	26 Sept.	52
13	3 Oct.	53
20	10	Succoth
23*	13*	54, B. L.
27	17	1
4 Marches.	24	2
11	31	3
18	7 Nov.	4
25	14	5
2 Cisleu	21	6
9	28	7
16	5 Dec.	8
23	12	9
30	19	10
7 Tebet	26	11
	1847	
14	2 Jan.	12
21	9	13
28	16	14
6 Sebat	23	15
13	30	16
20	6 Feb.	17
27	13	18, S
4 Adar	20	19
11	27	20, Z
18	6 March	21, P
25	13	22, 23, H
3 Nisan	20	24
10	27	25
17	3 April	1 Pas.
24	10	26
1 Ijar	17	27, 28
8	24	29, 30
15	1 May	31
22	8	32, 33
29	15	34
7 Sivan	22	Pent.
14	29	35
21	5 June	36
28	12	37
5 Tammuz	19	38
12	26	39, 40
19	3 July	41
26	10	42, 43
4 Ab	17	44
11	24	45
18	31	46
25	7 Aug.	47
2 Elul	14	48
9	21	49
16	28	50
23	4 Sept.	51, 52

TABLE V.—Continued.

Jewish year of the World 5608, corresponding to A. D. 1847–1848.

Sabbaths of the Jewish year.	Saturdays of the Gregorian yr.	Pareshioth and Haphtaroth.
5 E	1847	
1 Tisri	11 Sept.	New yrs.
8	18	53 [day
15	25	Succoth
22	2 Oct.	Sab.p.Suc.
23*	3*	54, B. L.
29	9	1
6 Marches.	16	2
13	23	3
20	30	4
27	6 Nov.	5
5 Cisleu	13	6
12	20	7
19	27	8
26	4 Dec.	9
4 Tebet	11	10
11	18	11
18	25	12
	1848	
25	1 Jan.	13
3 Sebat	8	14
10	15	15
17	22	16
24	29	17
1 Adar	5 Feb.	18
8	12	19
15	19	20
22	26	21
29	4 March	22, S
6 Veadar	11	23
13	18	24, Z
20	25	25, P
27	1 April	26, H
5 Nisan	8	27
12	15	28
19	22	1 Pas.
26	29	29
3 Ijar	6 May	30
10	13	31
17	20	32
24	27	33
2 Sivan	3 June	34
9	10	35
16	17	36
23	24	37
30	1 July	38
7 Tammuz	8	39
14	15	40
21	22	41
28	29	42, 43
6 Ab	5 Aug.	44
13	12	45
20	19	46
27	26	47
4 Elul	2 Sept.	48
11	9	49
18	16	50
25	23	51, 52

Jewish year of the World 5609, corresponding to A. D. 1848–1849.

Sabbaths of the Jewish year.	Saturdays of the Gregorian yr.	Pareshioth and Haphtaroth.
2 C	1848	
3 Tisri	30 Sept.	53
10	7 Oct.	Chippur
17	14	Succoth
23*	20*	54, B. L.
24	21	1
1 Marches.	28	2
8	4 Nov.	3
15	11	4
22	18	5
29	25	6
7 Cisleu	2 Dec.	7
14	9	8
21	16	9
28	23	10
5 Tebet	30	11
	1849	
12	6 Jan.	12
19	13	13
26	20	14
4 Sebat	27	15
11	3 Feb.	16
18	10	17
25	17	18, S
2 Adar	24	19
9	3 March	20, Z
16	10	21
23	17	22, 23, P
1 Nisan	24	24, H
8	31	25
15	7 April	1 Pas.
22	14	2 Pas.
29	21	26
6 Ijar	28	27, 28
13	5 May	29, 30
20	12	31
27	19	32, 33
5 Sivan	26	34
12	2 June	35
19	9	36
26	16	37
3 Tammuz	23	38
10	30	39
17	7 July	40
24	14	41
2 Ab	21	42, 43
9	28	44
16	4 Aug.	45
23	11	46
30	18	47
7 Elul	25	48
14	1 Sept.	49
21	8	50
28	15	51

Jewish year of the World 5610, corresponding to A. D. 1849–1850.

Sabbaths of the Jewish year.	Saturdays of the Gregorian yr.	Pareshioth and Haphtaroth.
6 C	1849	
6 Tisri	22 Sept.	52
13	29	53
20	6 Oct.	Succoth
23*	9*	54, B. L.
27	13	1
4 Marches.	20	2
11	27	3
18	3 Nov.	4
25	10	5
2 Cisleu	17	6
9	24	7
16	1 Dec.	8
23	8	9
30	15	10
7 Tebet	22	11
14	29	12
	1850	
21	5 Jan.	13
28	12	14
6 Sebat	19	15
13	26	16
20	2 Feb.	17
27	9	18, S
4 Adar	16	19
11	23	20, Z
18	2 March	21, P
25	9	22, 23, H
3 Nisan	16	24
10	23	25
17	30	1 Pas.
24	6 April	26
1 Ijar	13	27, 28
8	20	29, 30
15	27	31
22	4 May	32, 33
29	11	34
7 Sivan	18	Pent.
14	25	35
21	1 June	36
28	8	37
5 Tammuz	15	38
12	22	39, 40
19	29	41
26	6 July	42, 43
4 Ab	13	44
11	20	45
18	27	46
25	3 Aug.	47
2 Elul	10	48
9	17	49
16	24	50
23	31	51, 52

Jewish year of the World 5611, corresponding to A. D. 1850–1851.

Sabbaths of the Jewish year.	Saturdays of the Gregorian yr.	Pareshioth and Haphtaroth.
6 E	1850	
1 Tisri	7 Sept.	New yrs.
8	14	53 [day.
15	21	Succoth
22	28	Sab.p.Suc.
23*	29*	54, B. L.
29	5 Oct.	1
6 Marches.	12	2
13	19	3
20	26	4
27	2 Nov.	5
4 Cisleu	9	6
11	16	7
18	23	8
25	30	9
2 Tebet	7 Dec.	10
9	14	11
16	21	12
23	28	13
	1851	
1 Sebat	4 Jan.	14
8	11	15
15	18	16
22	25	17
29	1 Feb.	18
6 Adar	8	19
13	15	20
20	22	21
27	1 March	22, S
4 Veadar	8	23
11	15	24, Z
18	22	25, P
25	29	26, H
3 Nisan	5 April	27
10	12	28
17	19	1 Pas.
24	26	29
1 Ijar	3 May	30
8	10	31
15	17	32
22	24	33
29	31	34
7 Sivan	7 June	Pent.
14	14	35
21	21	36
28	28	37
5 Tammuz	5 July	38
12	12	39, 40
19	19	41
26	26	42, 43
4 Ab	2 Aug.	44
11	9	45
18	16	46
25	23	47
2 Elul	30	48
9	6 Sept.	49
16	13	50
23	20	51, 52

Jewish year of the World 5612, corresponding to A. D. 1851–1852.

Sabbaths of the Jewish year.	Saturdays of the Gregorian yr.	Pareshioth and Haphtaroth.
3 C	1851	
1 Tisri	27 Sept.	New yrs.
8	4 Oct.	53 [day
15	11	Succoth
22	18	Sab.p.Suc.
23*	19*	54, B. L.
29	25	1
6 Marches.	1 Nov.	2
13	8	3
20	15	4
27	22	5
5 Cisleu	29	6
12	6 Dec.	7
19	13	8
26	20	9
4 Tebet	27	10
	1852	
11	3 Jan.	11
18	10	12
25	17	13
3 Sebat	24	14
10	31	15
17	7 Feb.	16
24	14	17
1 Adar	21	18, S
8	28	19, Z
15	6 March	20
22	13	21, P
29	20	22, 23, H
7 Nisan	27	24
14	3 April	25
21	10	1 Pas.
28	17	26
5 Ijar	24	27, 28
12	1 May	29, 30
19	8	31
26	15	32, 33
4 Sivan	22	34
11	29	35
18	5 June	36
25	12	37
2 Tammuz	19	38
9	26	39
16	3 July	40
23	10	41
1 Ab	17	42, 43
8	24	44
15	31	45
22	7 Aug.	46
29	14	47
6 Elul	21	48
13	28	49
20	4 Sept.	50
27	11	51

Jewish year of the World 5613, corresponding to A. D. 1852–1853.

Sabbaths of the Jewish year.	Saturdays of the Gregorian yr.	Pareshioth and Haphtaroth.
2 E	1852	
5 Tisri	18 Sept.	52
12	25	53
19	2 Oct.	Succoth
23*	6*	54, B. L.
26	9	1
3 Marches.	16	2
10	23	3
17	30	4
24	6 Nov	5
2 Cisleu	13	6
9	20	7
16	27	8
23	4 Dec	9
30	11	10
7 Tebet	18	11
14	25	12
	1853	
21	1 Jan.	13
28	8	14
6 Sebat	15	15
13	22	16
20	29	17
27	5 Feb.	18
4 Adar	12	19
11	19	20
18	26	21
25	5 March	22, S
2 Veadar	12	23
9	19	24, Z
16	26	25
23	2 April	26, P
1 Nisan	9	27, H
8	16	28
15	23	1 Pas.
22	30	2 Pas.
29	7 May	29
6 Ijar	14	30
13	21	31
20	28	32
27	4 June	33
5 Sivan	11	34
12	18	35
10	25	36
26	2 July	37
3 Tammuz	9	38
10	16	39
17	23	40
24	30	41
2 Ab	6 Aug.	42, 43
9	13	44
16	20	45
23	27	46
30	3 Sept.	47
7 Elul	10	48
14	17	49
21	24	50
28	1 Oct.	51

TABLE V.—Continued.

Jewish year of the World 5614, corresponding to A. D. 1853-1854.		
Sabbaths of the Jewish year.	Saturdays of the Gregorian yr.	Pareshioth and Haphtaroth.
6 C	1853	
6 Tisri	8 Oct.	52
13	15	53
20	22	Succoth
23*	25*	54, B. L.
27	29	1
4 Marches.	5 Nov.	2
11	12	3
18	19	4
25	26	5
2 Cisleu	3 Dec.	6
9	10	7
16	17	8
23	24	9
30	31	10
	1854	
7 Tebet	7 Jan.	11
14	14	12
21	21	13
28	28	14
6 Sebat	4 Feb.	15
13	11	16
20	18	17
27	25	18, S
4 Adar	4 March	19
11	11	20, Z
18	18	21, P
25	25	22, 23, H
3 Nisan	1 April	24
10	8	25
17	15	1 Pas.
24	22	26
1 Ijar	29	27, 28
8	6 May	29, 30
15	13	31
22	20	32, 33
29	27	34
7 Sivan	3 June	Pent.
14	10	35
21	17	36
28	24	37
5 Tammuz	1 July	38
12	8	39, 40
19	15	41
26	22	42, 43
4 Ab	29	44
11	5 Aug.	45
18	12	46
25	19	47
2 Elul	26	48
9	2 Sept.	49
16	9	50
23	16	51, 52

Jewish year of the World 5615, corresponding to A. D. 1854-1855.		
Sabbaths of the Jewish year.	Saturdays of the Gregorian yr.	Pareshioth and Haphtaroth.
4 C	1854	
1 Tisri	23 Sept.	New yrs.
8	30	53 [day
15	7 Oct.	Succoth
22	14	Oct. Suc.
23*	15*	54, B.L.
29	21	1
6 Marches.	28	2
13	4 Nov.	3
20	11	4
27	18	5
4 Cisleu	25	6
11	2 Dec.	7
18	9	8
25	16	9, En.
2 Tebet	23	10
9	30	11
	1855	
16	6 Jan.	12
23	13	13
1 Sebat	20	14
8	27	15
15	3 Feb.	16
22	10	17
29	17	18, S
6 Adar	24	19
13	3 March	20, Z
20	10	21, P
27	17	22, 23, H
5 Nisan	24	24
12	31	25
19	7 April	1 Pas.
26	14	26
3 Ijar	21	27, 28
10	28	29, 30
17	5 May	31
24	12	32, 33
2 Sivan	19	34
9	26	35
16	2 June	36
23	9	37
30	16	38
7 Tammuz	23	39
14	30	40
21	7 July	41
28	14	42, 43
6 Ab	21	44
13	28	45
20	4 Aug.	46
27	11	47
4 Elul	18	48
11	25	49
18	1 Sept.	50
25	8	51

Jewish year of the World 5616, corresponding to A. D. 1855-1856.		
Sabbaths of the Jewish year.	Saturdays of the Gregorian yr.	Pareshioth and Haphtaroth.
1 E	1855	
3 Tisri	15 Sept.	53
10	22	Chippur
17	29	Succoth
23*	5* Oct.	54, B. L.
24	6	1
1 Marches.	13	2
8	20	3
15	27	4
22	3 Nov.	5
29	10	6
7 Cisleu	17	7
14	24	8
21	1 Dec.	9
28	8	10
6 Tebet	15	11
13	22	12
20	29	13
	1856	
27	5 Jan.	14
5 Sebat	12	15
12	19	16
19	26	17
26	2 Feb.	18
3 Adar	9	19
10	16	20
17	23	21
24	1 March	22
1 Veadar	8	23, S
8	15	24, Z
15	22	25
22	29	26, P
29	5 April	27, H
7 Nisan	12	28
14	19	29
21	26	1 Pas.
28	3 May	30
5 Ijar	10	31
12	17	32
19	24	33
26	31	34
4 Sivan	7 June	35
11	14	36
18	21	37
25	28	38
2 Tammuz	5 July	39
9	12	40
16	19	41
23	26	42
1 Ab	2 Aug.	43
8	9	44
15	16	45
22	23	46
29	30	47
6 Elul	6 Sept.	48
13	13	49
20	20	50
27	27	51

Jewish year of the World 5617, corresponding to A. D. 1856-1857.		
Sabbaths of the Jewish year.	Saturdays of the Gregorian yr.	Pareshioth and Haphtaroth.
7 C	1856	
5 Tisri	4 Oct.	52
12	11	53
19	18	Succoth
23*	22*	54, B. L.
26	25	1
3 Marches.	1 Nov.	2
10	8	3
17	15	4
24	22	5
2 Cisleu	29	6
9	6 Dec.	7
16	13	8
23	20	9
30	27	10
	1857	
7 Tebet	3 Jan.	11
14	10	12
21	17	13
28	24	14
6 Sebat	31	15
13	7 Feb.	16
20	14	17
27	21	18, S
4 Adar	28	19
11	7 March	20, Z
18	14	21, P
25	21	22, 23, H
3 Nisan	28	24
10	4 April	25
17	11	1 Pas.
24	18	26
1 Ijar	25	27, 28
8	2 May	29, 30
15	9	31
22	16	32, 33
29	23	34
7 Sivan	30	Pent.
14	6 June	35
21	13	36
28	20	37
5 Tammuz	27	38
12	4 July	39, 40
19	11	41
26	18	42, 43
4 Ab	25	44
11	1 Aug.	45
18	8	46
25	15	47
2 Elul	22	48
9	29	49
16	5 Sept.	50
23	12	51, 52

Jewish year of the World 5618, corresponding to A. D. 1857-1858.		
Sabbaths of the Jewish year.	Saturdays of the Gregorian yr.	Pareshioth and Haphtaroth.
4 C	1857	
1 Tisri	19 Sept.	New yrs.
8	26	53 [day
15	3 Oct.	Succoth
22	10	Oct. Suc.
23*	11*	54, B. L.
29	17	1
6 Marches.	24	2
13	31	3
20	7 Nov.	4
27	14	5
4 Cisleu	21	6
11	28	7
18	5 Dec.	8
25	12	9, En.
2 Tebet	19	10
9	26	11
	1858	
16	2 Jan.	12
23	9	13
1 Sebat	16	14
8	23	15
15	30	16
22	6 Feb.	17
29	13	18, S
6 Adar	20	19
13	27	20, Z
20	6 March	21, P
27	13	22, 23, H
5 Nisan	20	24
12	27	25
19	3 April	1 Pas.
26	10	26
3 Ijar	17	27, 28
10	24	29, 30
17	1 May	31
24	8	32, 33
2 Sivan	15	34
9	22	35
16	29	36
23	5 June	37
30	12	38
7 Tammuz	19	39
14	26	40
21	3 July	41
28	10	42, 43
6 Ab	17	44
13	24	45
20	31	46
27	7 Aug.	47
4 Elul	14	48
11	21	49
18	28	50
25	4 Sept.	51

Jewish year of the World 5619, corresponding to A. D. 1858-1859.		
Sabbaths of the Jewish year.	Saturdays of the Gregorian yr.	Pareshioth and Haphtaroth.
4 E	1858	
3 Tisri	11 Sept.	53
10	18	Chippur
17	25	Succoth
24	2 Oct.	1
1 Marches.	9	2
8	16	3
15	23	4
22	30	5
29	6 Nov.	6
6 Cisleu	13	7
13	20	8
20	27	9
27	4 Dec.	10
4 Tebet	11	11
11	18	12
18	25	13
	1859	
25	1 Jan.	14
3 Sebat	8	15
10	15	16
17	22	17
24	29	18
1 Adar	5 Feb.	19
8	12	20
15	19	21
22	26	22
29	5 March	23, S
6 Veadar	12	24
13	19	25, Z
20	26	26, P
27	2 April	27, H
5 Nisan	9	28
12	16	29
19	23	1 Pas.
26	30	30
3 Ijar	7 May	31
10	14	32
17	21	33
24	28	34
2 Sivan	4 June	35
9	11	36
16	18	37
23	25	38
30	2 July	39
7 Tammuz	9	40
14	16	41
21	23	42
28	30	43
6 Ab	6 Aug.	44
13	13	45
20	20	46
27	27	47
4 Elul	3 Sept.	48
11	10	49
18	17	50
25	24	51, 52

TABLE V.—Continued.

Jewish year of the World 5620, corresponding to A. D. 1859–1860.

Sabbaths of the Jewish year.	Saturdays of the Gregorian yr.	Pareshioth and Haphtaroth.
2 C	1859	
3 Tisri	1 Oct.	53
10	8	Chippur
17	15	Succoth
24	22	1
1 Marches.	29	2
8	5 Nov	3
15	12	4
22	19	5
29	26	6
7 Cisleu	3 Dec.	7
14	10	8
21	17	9
28	24	10
5 Tebet	31	11
	1860	
12	7 Jan.	12
19	14	13
26	21	14
4 Sebat	28	15
11	4 Feb.	16
18	11	17
25	18	18, S
2 Adar	25	19
9	3 March	20, Z
16	10	21
23	17	22, 23, P
1 Nisan	24	24, H
8	31	25
15	7 April	1 Pas.
22	14	2 Pas.
29	21	26
6 Ijar	28	27, 28
13	5 May	29, 30
20	12	31
27	19	32, 33
5 Sivan	26	34
12	2 June	35
19	9	36
26	16	37
3 Tammuz	23	38
10	30	39
17	7 July	40
24	14	41
2 Ab	21	42, 43
9	28	44
16	4 Aug.	45
23	11	46
30	18	47
7 Elul	25	48
14	1 Sept.	49
21	8	50
28	15	51

Jewish year of the World 5621, corresponding to A. D. 1860–1861.

Sabbaths of the Jewish year.	Saturdays of the Gregorian yr.	Pareshioth and Haphtaroth.
5 C	1860	
6 Tisri	22 Sept.	52
13	29	53
20	6 Oct.	Succoth
23*	9*	54, B. L.
27	13	1
4 Marches.	20	2
11	27	3
18	3 Nov.	4
25	10	5
3 Cisleu	17	6
10	24	7
17	1 Dec.	8
24	8	9
2 Tebet	15	10
9	22	11
16	29	12
	1861	
23	5 Jan.	13
1 Sebat	12	14
8	19	15
15	26	16
22	2 Feb.	17
29	9	18, S
6 Adar	16	19
13	23	20, Z
20	2 March	21, P
27	9	22, 23, H
5 Nisan	16	24
12	23	25
19	30	1 Pas.
26	6 April	26
3 Ijar	13	27, 28
10	20	29, 30
17	27	31
24	4 May	32, 33
2 Sivan	11	34
9	18	35
16	25	36
23	1 June	37
30	8	38
7 Tammuz	15	39
14	22	40
21	29	41
28	6 July	42, 43
6 Ab	13	44
13	20	45
20	27	46
27	3 Aug.	47
4 Elul	10	48
11	17	49
18	24	50
25	31	51, 52

Jewish year of the World 5622, corresponding to A. D. 1861–1862.

Sabbaths of the Jewish year.	Saturdays of the Gregorian yr.	Pareshioth and Haphtaroth.
4 E	1861	
3 Tisri	7 Sept.	53
10	14	Chippur
17	21	Succoth
24	28	1
1 Marches.	5 Oct.	2
8	12	3
15	19	4
22	26	5
29	2 Nov	6
6 Cisleu	9	7
13	16	8
20	23	9
27	30	10
4 Tebet	7 Dec.	11
11	14	12
18	21	13
25	28	14
	1862	
3 Sebat	4 Jan.	15
10	11	16
17	18	17
24	25	18
1 Adar	1 Feb.	19
8	8	20
15	15	21
22	22	22
29	1 March	23, S
6 Veadar	8	24
13	15	25, Z
20	22	26, P
27	29	27, H
5 Nisan	5 April	28
12	12	29
19	19	1 Pas.
26	26	30
3 Ijar	3 May	31
10	10	32
17	17	33
24	24	34
2 Sivan	31	35
9	7 June	36
16	14	37
23	21	38
30	28	39
7 Tammuz	5 July	40
14	12	41
21	19	42
28	26	43
6 Ab	2 Aug.	44
13	9	45
20	16	46
27	23	47
4 Elul	30	48
11	6 Sept.	49
18	13	50
25	20	51, 52

Jewish year of the World 5623, corresponding to A. D. 1862–1863.

Sabbaths of the Jewish year.	Saturdays of the Gregorian yr.	Pareshioth and Haphtaroth.
2 C	1862	
3 Tisri	27 Sept.	53
10	4 Oct.	Chippur
17	11	Succoth
24	18	1
1 Marches.	25	2
8	1 Nov.	3
15	8	4
22	15	5
29	22	6
7 Cisleu	29	7
14	6 Dec.	8
21	13	9
28	20	10
5 Tebet	27	11
	1863	
12	3 Jan.	12
19	10	13
26	17	14
4 Sebat	24	15
11	31	16
18	7 Feb.	17
25	14	18, S
2 Adar	21	19
9	28	20, Z
16	7 March	21
23	14	22, 23, P
1 Nisan	21	24, H
8	28	25
15	4 April	1 Pas.
22	11	2 Pas.
29	18	26
6 Ijar	25	27, 28
13	2 May	29, 30
20	9	31
27	16	32, 33
5 Sivan	23	34
12	30	35
19	6 June	36
26	13	37
3 Tammuz	20	38
10	27	39
17	4 July	40
24	11	41
2 Ab	18	42, 43
9	25	44
16	1 Aug.	45
23	8	46
30	15	47
7 Elul	22	48
14	29	49
21	5 Sept.	50
28	12	51

Jewish year of the World 5624, corresponding to A. D. 1863-1864.

Sabbaths of the Jewish year.	Saturdays of the Gregorian yr.	Pareshioth and Haphtaroth.
7 E	1863	
6 Tisri	19 Sept.	52
13	26	53
20	3 Oct.	Succoth
27	10	1
4 Marches.	17	2
11	24	3
18	31	4
25	7 Nov.	5
3 Cisleu	14	6
10	21	7
17	28	8
24	5 Dec.	9
2 Tebet	12	10
9	19	11
16	26	12
	1864	
23	2 Jan.	13
1 Sebat	9	14
8	16	15
15	23	16
22	30	17
29	6 Feb.	18
6 Adar	13	19
13	20	20
20	27	21
27	5 March	22, S
4 Veadar	12	23
11	19	24, Z
18	26	25, P
25	2 April	26, H
3 Nisan	9	27
10	16	28
17	23	1 Pas.
24	30	29
1 Ijar	7 May	30
8	14	31
15	21	32
22	28	33
29	4 June	34
7 Sivan	11	Pent.
14	18	35
21	25	36
28	2 July	37
5 Tammuz	9	38
12	16	39, 40
19	23	41
26	30	42, 43
4 Ab	6 Aug.	44
11	13	45
18	20	46
25	27	47
2 Elul	3 Sept.	48
9	10	49
16	17	50
23	24	51, 52

Jewish year of the World 5625, corresponding to A. D. 1864–1865.

Sabbaths of the Jewish year.	Saturdays of the Gregorian yr.	Pareshioth and Haphtaroth.
4 C	1864	
1 Tisri	1 Oct.	New yrs.
8	8	53 [day
15	15	Succoth
22	22	Oct. Suc.
23*	23*	54, B. L.
29	29	1
6 Marches.	5 Nov.	2
13	12	3
20	19	4
27	26	5
4 Cisleu	3 Dec.	6
11	10	7
18	17	8
25	24	9, En.
2 Tebet	31	10
	1865	
9	7 Jan.	11
16	14	12
23	21	13
1 Sebat	28	14
8	4 Feb.	15
15	11	16
22	18	17
29	25	18, S
6 Adar	4 March	19
13	11	20, Z
20	18	21, P
27	25	22, 23, H
5 Nisan	1 April	24
12	8	25
19	15	1 Pas.
26	22	26
3 Ijar	29	27, 28
10	6 May	29, 30
17	13	31
24	20	32, 33
2 Sivan	27	34
9	3 June	35
16	10	36
23	17	37
30	24	38
7 Tammuz	1 July	39
14	8	40
21	15	41
28	22	42, 43
6 Ab	29	44
13	5 Aug.	45
20	12	46
27	19	47
4 Elul	26	48
11	2 Sept.	49
18	9	50
25	16	51

TABLE V.—Continued.

Jewish year of the World 5626, corresponding to A. D. 1865–1866.		
Sabbaths of the Jewish year.	Saturdays of the Gregorian yr.	Pareshioth and Haphtaroth.
2 C	1865	
3 Tisri	23 Sept.	53
10	30	Chippur
17	7 Oct.	Succoth
24	14	1
1 Marches.	21	2
8	28	3
15	4 Nov.	4
22	11	5
29	18	6
7 Cisleu	25	7
14	2 Dec.	8
21	9	9
28	16	10
5 Tebet	23	11
12	30	12
	1866	
19	6 Jan.	13
26	13	14
4 Sebat	20	15
11	27	16
18	3 Feb.	17
25	10	18, S
2 Adar	17	19
9	24	20, Z
16	3 March	21
23	10	22, 23, P
1 Nisan	17	24, H
8	24	25
15	31	1 Pas.
22	7 April	2 Pas.
29	14	26
6 Ijar	21	27, 28
13	28	29, 30
20	5 May	31
27	12	32, 33
5 Sivan	19	34
12	26	35
19	2 June	36
26	9	37
3 Tammuz	16	38
10	23	39
17	30	40
24	7 July	41
2 Ab	14	42, 43
9	21	44
16	28	45
23	4 Aug.	46
30	11	47
7 Elul	18	48
14	25	49
21	1 Sept.	50
28	8	51

Jewish year of the World 5627, corresponding to A. D. 1866–1867.		
Sabbaths of the Jewish year.	Saturdays of the Gregorian yr.	Pareshioth and Haphtaroth.
3 E	1866	
6 Tisri	15 Sept.	52
13	22	53
20	29	Succoth
23*	2* Oct.	54, B. L.
27	6	1
4 Marches.	13	2
11	20	3
18	27	4
25	3 Nov.	5
2 Cisleu	10	6
9	17	7
16	24	8
23	1 Dec.	9
30	8	10
7 Tebet	15	11
14	22	12
21	29	13
	1867	
28	5 Jan.	14
6 Sebat	12	15
13	19	16
20	26	17
27	2 Feb.	18
4 Adar	9	19
11	16	20
18	23	21
25	2 March	22, S
2 Veadar	9	23
9	16	24, Z
16	23	25
23	30	26, P
1 Nisan	6 April	27, H
8	13	28
15	20	1 Pas.
22	27	2 Pas.
29	4 May	29
6 Ijar	11	30
13	18	31
20	25	32
27	1 June	33
5 Sivan	8	34
12	15	35
19	22	36
26	29	37
3 Tammuz	6 July	38
10	13	39
17	20	40
24	27	41
2 Ab	3 Aug.	42, 43
9	10	44
16	17	45
23	24	46
30	31	47
7 Elul	7 Sept.	48
14	14	49
21	21	50
28	28	51

Jewish year of the World 5628, corresponding to A. D. 1867–1868.		
Sabbaths of the Jewish year.	Saturdays of the Gregorian yr.	Pareshioth and Haphtaroth.
5 C	1867	
6 Tisri	5 Oct.	52
13	12	53
20	19	Succoth
23*	22*	54, B. L.
27	26	1
4 Marches.	2 Nov.	2
11	9	3
18	16	4
25	23	5
3 Cisleu	30	6
10	7 Dec.	7
17	14	8
24	21	9
2 Tebet	28	10
	1868	
9	4 Jan.	11
16	11	12
23	18	13
1 Sebat	25	14
8	1 Feb.	15
15	8	16
22	15	17
29	22	18, S
6 Adar	29	19
13	7 March	20, Z
20	14	21, P
27	21	22, 23, H
5 Nisan	28	24
12	4 April	25
19	11	1 Pas.
26	18	26
3 Ijar	25	27, 28
10	2 May	29, 30
17	9	31
24	16	32, 33
2 Sivan	23	34
9	30	35
16	6 June	36
23	13	37
30	20	38
7 Tammuz	27	39
14	4 July	40
21	11	41
28	18	42, 43
6 Ab	25	44
13	1 Aug.	45
20	8	46
27	15	47
4 Elul	22	48
11	29	49
18	5 Sept.	50
25	12	51, 52

Jewish year of the World 5629, corresponding to A D. 1868–1869.		
Sabbaths of the Jewish year.	Saturdays of the Gregorian yr.	Pareshioth and Haphtaroth.
2 C	1868	
3 Tisri	19 Sept.	53
10	26	Chippur
17	3 Oct.	Succoth
23*	9*	54, B. L.
24	10	1
1 Marches.	17	2
8	24	3
15	31	4
22	7 Nov.	5
29	14	6
7 Cisleu	21	7
14	28	8
21	5 Dec.	9
28	12	10
5 Tebet	19	11
12	26	12
	1869	
19	2 Jan.	13
26	9	14
4 Sebat	16	15
11	23	16
18	30	17
25	6 Feb.	18, S
2 Adar	13	19
9	20	20, Z
16	27	21
23	6 March	22, 23, P
1 Nisan	13	24, H
8	20	25
15	27	1 Pas.
22	3 April	2 Pas.
29	10	26
6 Ijar	17	27, 28
13	24	29, 30
20	1 May	31
27	8	32, 33
5 Sivan	15	34
12	22	35
19	29	36
26	5 June	37
3 Tammuz	12	38
10	19	39
17	26	40
24	3 July	41
2 Ab	10	42, 43
9	17	44
16	24	45
23	31	46
30	7 Aug.	47
7 Elul	14	48
14	21	49
21	28	50
28	4 Sept.	51

Jewish year of the World 5630, corresponding to A. D. 1869–1870.		
Sabbaths of the Jewish year.	Saturdays of the Gregorian yr.	Pareshioth and Haphtaroth.
3 E	1869	
6 Tisri	11 Sept.	52
13	18	53
20	25	Succoth
23*	28*	54, B. L.
27	2 Oct.	1
4 Marches.	9	2
11	16	3
18	23	4
25	30	5
2 Cisleu	6 Nov.	6
9	13	7
16	20	8
23	27	9
30	4 Dec.	10
7 Tebet	11	11
14	18	12
21	25	13
	1870	
28	1 Jan.	14
6 Sebat	8	15
13	15	16
20	22	17
27	29	18
4 Adar	5 Feb.	19
11	12	20
18	19	21
25	26	22, S
2 Veadar	5 March	23
9	12	24, Z
16	19	25
23	26	26, P
1 Nisan	2 April	27, H
8	9	28
15	16	1 Pas.
22	23	2 Pas.
29	30	29
6 Ijar	7 May	30
13	14	31
20	21	32
27	28	33
5 Sivan	4 June	34
12	11	35
19	18	36
26	25	37
3 Tammuz	2 July	38
10	9	39
17	16	40
24	23	41
2 Ab	30	42, 43
9	6 Aug.	44
16	13	45
23	20	46
30	27	47
7 Elul	3 Sept.	48
14	10	49
21	17	50
28	24	51

Jewish year of the World 5631, corresponding to A. D. 1870–1871.		
Sabbaths of the Jewish year.	Saturdays of the Gregorian yr.	Pareshioth and Haphtaroth.
6 C	1870	
6 Tisri	1 Oct.	52
13	8	53
20	15	Succoth
23*	18*	54, B. L.
27	22	1
4 Marches.	29	2
11	5 Nov.	3
18	12	4
25	19	5
2 Cisleu	26	6
9	3 Dec.	7
16	10	8
23	17	9
30	24	10
7 Tebet	31	11
	1871	
14	7 Jan.	12
21	14	13
28	21	14
6 Sebat	28	15
13	4 Feb.	16
20	11	17
27	18	18, S
4 Adar	25	19
11	4 March	20, Z
18	11	21, P
25	18	22, 23, H
3 Nisan	25	24
10	1 April	25
17	8	1 Pas.
24	15	26
1 Ijar	22	27, 28
8	29	29, 30
15	6 May	31
22	13	32, 33
29	20	34
7 Sivan	27	Pent.
14	3 June	35
21	10	36
28	17	37
5 Tammuz	24	38
12	1 July	39, 40
19	8	41
26	15	42, 43
4 Ab	22	44
11	29	45
18	5 Aug.	46
25	12	47
2 Elul	19	48
9	26	49
16	2 Sept.	50
23	9	51, 52

TABLE V.—Continued.

Jewish year of the World 5632, corresponding to A. D. 1871–1872		
Sabbaths of the Jewish year.	Saturdays of the Gregorian yr.	Pareshioth and Haphtaroth.
5 E	1871	
1 Tisri	16 Sept.	New yrs.
8	23	53 [day
15	30	Succoth
22	7 Oct.	Sab.p.Suc.
23*	8*	54, B.L.
29	14	1
6 Marches.	21	2
13	28	3
20	4 Nov.	4
27	11	5
5 Cisleu	18	6
12	25	7
19	2 Dec.	8
26	9	9
4 Tebet	16	10
11	23	11
18	30	12
	1872	
25	6 Jan.	13
3 Sebat	13	14
10	20	15
17	27	16
24	3 Feb.	17
1 Adar	10	18
8	17	19
15	24	20
22	2 March	21
29	9	22, S
6 Veadar	16	23
13	23	24, Z
20	30	25, P
27	6 April	26, H
5 Nisan	13	27
12	20	28
19	27	1 Pas.
26	4 May	29
3 Ijar	11	30
10	18	31
17	25	32
24	1 June	33
2 Sivan	8	34
9	15	35
16	22	36
23	29	37
30	6 July	38
7 Tammuz	13	39
14	20	40
21	27	41
28	3 Aug.	42, 43
6 Ab	10	44
13	17	45
20	24	46
27	31	47
4 Elul	7 Sept.	48
11	14	49
18	21	50
25	28	51, 52

Jewish year of the World 5633, corresponding to A. D. 1872–1873.		
Sabbaths of the Jewish year.	Saturdays of the Gregorian yr.	Pareshioth and Haphtaroth.
2 C	1872	
3 Tisri	5 Oct.	53
10	12	Chippur
17	19	Succoth
24	26	1
1 Marches.	2 Nov.	2
8	9	3
15	16	4
22	23	5
29	30	6
7 Cisleu	7 Dec.	7
14	14	8
21	21	9
28	28	10
	1873	
5 Tebet	4 Jan.	11
12	11	12
19	18	13
26	25	14
4 Sebat	1 Feb.	15
11	8	16
18	15	17
25	22	18, S
2 Adar	1 March	19
9	8	20, Z
16	15	21
23	22	22, 23, P
1 Nisan	29	24, H
8	5 April	25
15	12	1 Pas.
22	19	2 Pas.
29	26	26
6 Ijar	3 May	27, 28
13	10	29, 30
20	17	31
27	24	32, 33
5 Sivan	31	34
12	7 June	35
19	14	36
26	21	37
3 Tammuz	28	38
10	5 July	39
17	12	40
24	19	41
2 Ab	26	42, 43
9	2 Aug.	44
16	9	45
23	16	46
30	23	47
7 Elul	30	48
14	6 Sept.	49
21	13	50
28	20	51

Jewish year of the World 5634, corresponding to A. D. 1873–1874.		
Sabbaths of the Jewish year.	Saturdays of the Gregorian yr.	Pareshioth and Haphtaroth.
6 C	1873	
6 Tisri	27 Sept.	52
13	4 Oct.	53
20	11	Succoth
23*	14*	54, B. L.
27	18	1
4 Marches.	25	2
11	1 Nov.	3
18	8	4
25	15	5
2 Cisleu	22	6
9	29	7
16	6 Dec.	8
23	13	9
30	20	10
7 Tebet	27	11
	1874	
14	3 Jan.	12
21	10	13
28	17	14
6 Sebat	24	15
13	31	16
20	7 Feb.	17
27	14	18, S
4 Adar	21	19
11	28	20, Z
18	7 March	21, P
25	14	22, 23, H
3 Nisan	21	24
10	28	25
17	4 April	1 Pas.
24	11	26
1 Ijar	18	27, 28
8	25	29, 30
15	2 May	31
22	9	32, 33
29	16	34
7 Sivan	23	Pent.
14	30	35
21	6 June	36
28	13	37
5 Tammuz	20	38
12	27	39, 40
19	4 July	41
26	11	42, 43
4 Ab	18	44
11	25	45
18	1 Aug.	46
25	8	47
2 Elul	15	48
9	22	49
16	29	50
23	5 Sept.	51, 52

Jewish year of the World 5635, corresponding to A. D. 1874–1875.		
Sabbaths of the Jewish year.	Saturdays of the Gregorian yr.	Pareshioth and Haphtaroth.
5 E	1874	
1 Tisri	12 Sept.	New yrs.
8	19	53 [day
15	26	Succoth
22	3 Oct.	Sab.p.Suc.
23*	4*	54, B. L.
29	10	1
6 Marches.	17	2
13	24	3
20	31	4
27	7 Nov.	5
5 Cisleu	14	6
12	21	7
19	28	8
26	5 Dec.	9
4 Tebet	12	10
11	19	11
18	26	12
	1875	
25	2 Jan.	13
3 Sebat	9	14
10	16	15
17	23	16
24	30	17
1 Adar	6 Feb.	18
8	13	19
15	20	20
22	27	21
29	6 March	22, S
6 Veadar	13	23
13	20	24, Z
20	27	25, P
27	3 April	26, H
5 Nisan	10	27
12	17	28
19	24	1 Pas.
26	1 May	29
3 Ijar	8	30
10	15	31
17	22	32
24	29	33
2 Sivan	5 June	34
9	12	35
16	19	36
23	26	37
30	3 July	38
7 Tammuz	10	39
14	17	40
21	24	41
28	31	42, 43
6 Ab	7 Aug.	44
13	14	45
20	21	46
27	28	47
4 Elul	4 Sept.	48
11	11	49
18	18	50
25	25	51, 52

Jewish year of the World 5636, corresponding to A. D. 1875–1876.		
Sabbaths of the Jewish year.	Saturdays of the Gregorian yr.	Pareshioth and Haphtaroth.
1 C	1875	
3 Tisri	2 Oct.	53
10	9	Chippur
17	16	Succoth
23*	22*	54, B. L.
24	23	1
1 Marches.	30	2
8	6 Nov.	3
15	13	4
22	20	5
29	27	6
6 Cisleu	4 Dec.	7
13	11	8
20	18	9
27	25	10
	1876	
4 Tebet	1 Jan.	11
11	8	12
18	15	13
25	22	14
3 Sebat	29	15
10	5 Feb.	16
17	12	17
24	19	18
1 Adar	26	19, S
8	4 March	20, Z
15	11	21
22	18	22, P
29	25	23, H
7 Nisan	1 April	24
14	8	25
21	15	1 Pas
28	22	26
5 Ijar	29	27, 28
12	6 May	29, 30
19	13	31
26	20	32, 33
4 Sivan	27	24
11	3 June	35
18	10	36
25	17	37
2 Tammuz	24	38
9	1 July	39
16	8	40
23	15	41
1 Ab	22	42, 43
8	29	44
15	5 Aug.	45
22	12	46
29	19	47
6 Elul	26	48
13	2 Sept.	49
20	9	50
27	16	51

Jewish year of the World 5637, corresponding to A. D. 1876–1877.		
Sabbaths of the Jewish year.	Saturdays of the Gregorian yr.	Pareshioth and Haphtaroth.
7 C	1876	
5 Tisri	23 Sept.	52
12	30	53
19	7 Oct.	Succoth
23*	11*	54, B. L.
26	14	1
3 Marches.	21	2
10	28	3
17	4 Nov.	4
24	11	5
2 Cisleu	18	6
9	25	7
16	2 Dec.	8
23	9	9
30	16	10
7 Tebet	23	11
14	30	12
	1877	
21	6 Jan.	13
28	13	14
6 Sebat	20	15
13	27	16
20	3 Feb.	17
27	10	18, S
4 Adar	17	19
11	24	20, Z
18	3 March	21, P
25	10	22, 23, H
3 Nisan	17	24
10	24	25
17	31	1 Pas.
24	7 April	26
1 Ijar	14	27, 28
8	21	29, 30
15	28	31
22	5 May	32, 33
29	12	34
7 Sivan	19	Pent.
14	26	35
21	2 June	36
28	9	37
5 Tammuz	16	38
12	23	39, 40
19	30	41
26	7 July	42, 43
4 Ab	14	44
11	21	45
18	28	46
25	4 Aug.	47
2 Elul	11	48
9	18	49
16	25	50
23	1 Sept.	51, 52

Jewish year of the World 5638, corresponding to A. D. 1877–1878.

Sabbaths of the Jewish year.	Saturdays of the Gregorian yr.	Pareshioth and Haphtaroth.
6 E	1877	
1 Tisri	8 Sept.	New yrs.
8	15	53 [day
15	22	Succoth
22	29	Sab.p.Suc.
23*	30*	54, B. L.
29	6 Oct.	1
6 Marches.	13	2
13	20	3
20	27	4
27	3 Nov.	5
4 Cisleu	10	6
11	17	7
18	24	8
25	1 Dec.	9
2 Tebet	8	10
9	15	11
16	22	12
23	29	13
	1878	
1 Sebat	5 Jan.	14
8	12	15
15	19	16
22	26	17
29	2 Feb.	18
6 Adar	9	19
13	16	20
20	23	21
27	2 March	22, S
4 Veadar	9	23
11	16	24, Z
18	23	25, P
25	30	26, H
3 Nisan	6 April	27
10	13	28
17	20	1 Pas.
24	27	29
1 Ijar	4 May	30
8	11	31
15	18	32
22	25	33
29	1 June	34
7 Sivan	8	Pent.
14	15	35
21	22	36
28	29	37
5 Tammuz	6 July	38
12	13	39, 40
19	20	41
26	27	42, 43
4 Ab	3 Aug.	44
11	10	45
18	17	46
25	24	47
2 Elul	31	48
9	7 Sept.	49
16	14	50
23	21	51, 52

Jewish year of the World 5639, corresponding to A. D. 1878–1879.

Sabbaths of the Jewish year.	Saturdays of the Gregorian yr.	Pareshioth and Haphtaroth.
4 C	1878	
1 Tisri	28 Sept.	New yrs.
8	5 Oct.	53 [day
15	12	Succoth
22	19	Oct. Suc.
23*	20*	54, B. L.
29	26	1
6 Marches.	2 Nov.	2
13	9	3
20	16	4
27	23	5
4 Cisleu	30	6
11	7 Dec.	7
18	14	8
25	21	9, En.
2 Tebet	28	10
	1879	
9	4 Jan.	11
16	11	12
23	18	13
1 Sebat	25	14
8	1 Feb.	15
15	8	16
22	15	17
29	22	18, S
6 Adar	1 March	19
13	8	20, Z
20	15	21, P
27	22	22, 23, H
5 Nisan	29	24
12	5 April	25
19	12	1 Pas.
26	19	26
3 Ijar	26	27, 28
10	3 May	29, 30
17	10	31
24	17	32, 33
2 Sivan	24	34
9	31	35
16	7 June	36
23	14	37
30	21	38
7 Tammuz	28	39
14	5 July	40
21	12	41
28	19	42, 43
6 Ab	26	44
13	2 Aug.	45
20	9	46
27	16	47
4 Elul	23	48
11	30	49
18	6 Sept.	50
25	13	51

Jewish year of the World 5640, corresponding to A. D. 1879–1880.

Sabbaths of the Jewish year.	Saturdays of the Gregorian yr.	Pareshioth and Haphtaroth.
2 C	1879	
3 Tisri	20 Sept.	53
10	27	Chippur
17	4 Oct.	Succoth
24	11	1
1 Marches.	18	2
8	25	3
15	1 Nov.	4
22	8	5
29	15	6
7 Cisleu	22	7
14	29	8
21	6 Dec.	9
28	13	10
5 Tebet	20	11
12	27	12
	1880	
19	3 Jan.	13
26	10	14
4 Sebat	17	15
11	24	16
18	31	17
25	7 Feb.	18, S
2 Adar	14	19
9	21	20, Z
16	28	21
23	6 March	22, 23, P
1 Nisan	13	24, H
8	20	25
15	27	1 Pas.
22	3 April	2 Pas.
29	10	26
6 Ijar	17	27, 28
13	24	29, 30
20	1 May	31
27	8	32, 33
5 Sivan	15	34
12	22	35
19	29	36
26	5 June	37
3 Tammuz	12	38
10	19	39
17	26	40
24	3 July	41
2 Ab	10	42, 43
9	17	44
16	24	45
23	31	46
30	7 Aug.	47
7 Elul	14	48
14	21	49
21	28	50
28	4 Sept.	51

Jewish year of the World 5641, corresponding to A. D. 1880–1881.

Sabbaths of the Jewish year.	Saturdays of the Gregorian yr.	Pareshioth and Haphtaroth.
7 E	1880	
6 Tisri	11 Sept.	52
13	18	53
20	25	Succoth
27	2 Oct.	1
4 Marches.	9	2
11	16	3
18	23	4
25	30	5
3 Cisleu	6 Nov.	6
10	13	7
17	20	8
24	27	9
2 Tebet	4 Dec.	10
9	11	11
16	18	12
23	25	13
	1881	
1 Sebat	1 Jan.	14
8	8	15
15	15	16
22	22	17
29	29	18
6 Adar	5 Feb.	19
13	12	20
20	19	21
27	26	22, S
4 Veadar	5 March	23
11	12	24, Z
18	19	25, P
25	26	26, H
3 Nisan	2 April	27
10	9	28
17	16	1 Pas.
24	23	29
1 Ijar	30	30
8	7 May	31
15	14	32
22	21	33
29	28	34
7 Sivan	4 June	Pent.
14	11	35
21	18	36
28	25	37
5 Tammuz	2 July	38
12	9	39, 40
19	16	41
26	23	42, 43
4 Ab	30	44
11	6 Aug.	45
18	13	46
25	20	47
2 Elul	27	48
9	3 Sept.	49
16	10	50
23	17	51, 52

Jewish year of the World 5642, corresponding to A. D. 1881–1882.

Sabbaths of the Jewish year.	Saturdays of the Gregorian yr.	Pareshioth and Haphtaroth.
4 C	1881	
1 Tisri	24 Sept.	New yrs.
8	1 Oct.	53 [day
15	8	Succoth
22	15	Oct. Suc.
23*	16*	54, B. L.
29	22	1
6 Marches.	29	2
13	5 Nov.	3
20	12	4
27	19	5
4 Cisleu	26	6
11	3 Dec.	7
18	10	8
25	17	9, En.
2 Tebet	24	10
9	31	11
	1882	
16	7 Jan.	12
23	14	13
1 Sebat	21	14
8	28	15
15	4 Feb.	16
22	11	17
29	18	18, S
6 Adar	25	19
13	4 March	20, Z
20	11	21, P
27	18	22, 23, H
5 Nisan	25	24
12	1 April	25
19	8	1 Pas.
26	15	26
3 Ijar	22	27, 28
10	29	29, 30
17	6 May	31
24	13	32, 33
2 Sivan	20	34
9	27	35
16	3 June	36
23	10	37
30	17	38
7 Tammuz	24	39
14	1 July	40
21	8	41
28	15	42, 43
6 Ab	22	44
13	29	45
20	5 Aug.	46
27	12	47
4 Elul	19	48
11	26	49
18	2 Sept.	50
25	9	51

Jewish year of the World 5643, corresponding to A. D. 1882–1883.

Sabbaths of the Jewish year.	Saturdays of the Gregorian yr.	Pareshioth and Haphtaroth.
1 E	1882	
3 Tisri	16 Sept.	53
10	23	Chippur
17	30	Succoth
23*	6* Oct.	54, B. L.
24	7	1
1 Marches.	14	2
8	21	3
15	28	4
22	4 Nov.	5
29	11	6
7 Cisleu	18	7
14	25	8
21	2 Dec.	9
28	9	10
6 Tebet	16	11
13	23	12
20	30	13
	1883	
27	6 Jan.	14
5 Sebat	13	15
12	20	16
19	27	17
26	3 Feb.	18
3 Adar	10	19
10	17	20
17	24	21
24	3 March	22
1 Veadar	10	23, S
8	17	24, Z
15	24	25
22	31	26, P
29	7 April	27, H
7 Nisan	14	28
14	21	29
21	28	1 Pas
28	5 May	30
5 Ijar	12	31
12	19	32
19	26	33
26	2 June	34
4 Sivan	9	35
11	16	36
18	23	37
25	30	38
2 Tammuz	7 July	39
9	14	40
16	21	41
23	28	42
1 Ab	4 Aug.	43
8	11	44
15	18	45
22	25	46
29	1 Sept.	47
6 Elul	8	48
13	15	49
20	22	50
27	29	51

TABLE V.—Continued.

Jewish year of the World 5644, corresponding to A. D. 1883–1884.

Sabbaths of the Jewish year.	Saturdays of the Gregorian yr.	Pareshioth and Haphtaroth.
7 C	1883	
5 Tisri	6 Oct.	52
12	13	53
19	20	Succoth
23*	24*	54, B. L.
26	27	1
3 Marches.	3 Nov.	2
10	10	3
17	17	4
24	24	5
2 Cisleu	1 Dec.	6
9	8	7
16	15	8
23	22	9
30	29	10
	1884	
7 Tebet	5 Jan.	11
14	12	12
21	19	13
28	26	14
6 Sebat	2 Feb.	15
13	9	16
20	16	17
27	23	18, S
4 Adar	1 March	19
11	8	20, Z
18	15	21, P
25	22	22, 23, H
3 Nisan	29	24
10	5 April	25
17	12	1 Pas.
24	19	26
1 Ijar	26	27, 28
8	3 May	29, 30
15	10	31
22	17	32, 33
29	24	34
7 Sivan	31	Pent.
14	7 June	35
21	14	36
28	21	37
5 Tammuz	28	38
12	5 July	39, 40
19	12	41
26	19	42, 43
4 Ab	26	44
11	2 Aug.	45
18	9	46
25	16	47
2 Elul	23	48
9	30	49
16	6 Sept.	50
23	13	51, 52

Jewish year of the World 5645, corresponding to A. D. 1884–1885.

Sabbaths of the Jewish year.	Saturdays of the Gregorian yr.	Pareshioth and Haphtaroth.
4 C	1884	
1 Tisri	20 Sept.	New yrs. day
8	27	53
15	4 Oct.	Succoth
22	11	Oct. Suc.
23*	12*	54, B.L.
29	18	1
6 Marches.	25	2
13	1 Nov.	3
20	8	4
27	15	5
4 Cisleu	22	6
11	29	7
18	6 Dec.	8
25	13	9, En.
2 Tebet	20	10
9	27	11
	1885	
16	3 Jan.	12
23	10	13
1 Sebat	17	14
8	24	15
15	31	16
22	7 Feb.	17
29	14	18, S
6 Adar	21	19
13	28	20, Z
20	7 March	21, P
27	14	22, 23, H
5 Nisan	21	24
12	28	25
19	4 April	1 Pas.
26	11	26
3 Ijar	18	27, 28
10	25	29, 30
17	2 May	31
24	9	32, 33
2 Sivan	16	34
9	23	35
16	30	36
23	6 June	37
30	13	38
7 Tammuz	20	39
14	27	40
21	4 July	41
28	11	42, 43
6 Ab	18	44
13	25	45
20	1 Aug.	46
27	8	47
4 Elul	15	48
11	22	49
18	29	50
25	5 Sept.	51

Jewish year of the World 5646, corresponding to A. D. 1885–1886.

Sabbaths of the Jewish year.	Saturdays of the Gregorian yr.	Pareshioth and Haphtaroth.
4 E	1885	
3 Tisri	12 Sept.	53
10	19	Chippur
17	26	Succoth
24	3 Oct.	1
1 Marches.	10	2
8	17	3
15	24	4
22	31	5
29	7 Nov.	6
6 Cisleu	14	7
13	21	8
20	28	9
27	5 Dec.	10
4 Tebet	12	11
11	19	12
18	26	13
	1886	
25	2 Jan.	14
3 Sebat	9	15
10	16	16
17	23	17
24	30	18
1 Adar	6 Feb.	19
8	13	20
15	20	21
22	27	22
29	6 March	23, S
6 Veadar	13	24
13	20	25, Z
20	27	26, P
27	3 April	27, H
5 Nisan	10	28
12	17	29
19	24	1 Pas.
26	1 May	30
3 Ijar	8	31
10	15	32
17	22	33
24	29	34
2 Sivan	5 June	35
9	12	36
16	19	37
23	26	38
30	3 July	39
7 Tammuz	10	40
14	17	41
21	24	42
28	31	43
6 Ab	7 Aug.	44
13	14	45
20	21	46
27	28	47
4 Elul	4 Sept.	48
11	11	49
18	18	50
25	25	51, 52

Jewish year of the World 5647, corresponding to A. D. 1886–1887.

Sabbaths of the Jewish year.	Saturdays of the Gregorian yr.	Pareshioth and Haphtaroth.
2 C	1886	
3 Tisri	2 Oct.	53
10	9	Chippur
17	16	Succoth
24	23	1
1 Marches.	30	2
8	6 Nov.	3
15	13	4
22	20	5
29	27	6
7 Cisleu	4 Dec.	7
14	11	8
21	18	9
28	25	10
	1887	
5 Tebet	1 Jan.	11
12	8	12
19	15	13
26	22	14
4 Sebat	29	15
11	5 Feb.	16
18	12	17
25	19	18, S
2 Adar	26	19
9	5 March	20, Z
16	12	21
23	19	22, 23, P
1 Nisan	26	24, H
8	2 April	25
15	9	1 Pas.
22	16	2 Pas.
29	23	26
6 Ijar	30	27, 28
13	7 May	29, 30
20	14	31
27	21	32, 33
5 Sivan	28	34
12	4 June	35
19	11	36
26	18	37
3 Tammuz	25	38
10	2 July	39
17	9	40
24	16	41
2 Ab	23	42, 43
9	30	44
16	6 Aug.	45
23	13	46
30	20	47
7 Elul	27	48
14	3 Sept.	49
21	10	50
28	17	51

Jewish year of the World 5648, corresponding to A. D. 1887–1888.

Sabbaths of the Jewish year.	Saturdays of the Gregorian yr.	Pareshioth and Haphtaroth.
5 C	1887	
6 Tisri	24 Sept.	52
13	1 Oct.	53
20	8	Succoth
23*	11*	54, B. L.
27	15	1
4 Marches.	22	2
11	29	3
18	5 Nov.	4
25	12	5
3 Cisleu	19	6
10	26	7
17	3 Dec.	8
24	10	9
2 Tebet	17	10
9	24	11
16	31	12
	1888	
23	7 Jan.	13
1 Sebat	14	14
8	21	15
15	28	16
22	4 Feb.	17
29	11	18, S
6 Adar	18	19
13	25	20, Z
20	3 March	21, P
27	10	22, 23, H
5 Nisan	17	24
12	24	25
19	31	1 Pas.
26	7 April	26
3 Ijar	14	27, 28
10	21	29, 30
17	28	31
24	5 May	32, 33
2 Sivan	12	34
9	19	35
16	26	36
23	2 June	37
30	9	38
7 Tammuz	16	39
14	23	40
21	30	41
28	7 July	42, 43
6 Ab	14	44
13	21	45
20	28	46
27	4 Aug.	47
4 Elul	11	48
11	18	49
18	25	50
25	1 Sept.	51, 52

Jewish year of the World 5649, corresponding to A. D. 1888–1889.

Sabbaths of the Jewish year.	Saturdays of the Gregorian yr.	Pareshioth and Haphtaroth.
4 E	1888	
3 Tisri	8 Sept.	53
10	15	Chippur
17	22	Succoth
24	29	1
1 Marches.	6 Oct.	2
8	13	3
15	20	4
22	27	5
29	3 Nov.	6
6 Cisleu	10	7
13	17	8
20	24	9
27	1 Dec.	10
4 Tebet	8	11
11	15	12
18	22	13
25	29	14
	1889	
3 Sebat	5 Jan.	15
10	12	16
17	19	17
24	26	18
1 Adar	2 Feb.	19
8	9	20
15	16	21
22	23	22
29	2 March	23, S
6 Veadar	9	24
13	16	25, Z
20	23	26, P
27	30	27, H
5 Nisan	6 April	28
12	13	29
19	20	1 Pas.
26	27	30
3 Ijar	4 May	31
10	11	32
17	18	33
24	25	34
2 Sivan	1 June	35
9	8	36
16	15	37
23	22	38
30	29	39
7 Tammuz	6 July	40
14	13	41
21	20	42
28	27	43
6 Ab	3 Aug.	44
13	10	45
20	17	46
27	24	47
4 Elul	31	48
11	7 Sept.	49
18	14	50
25	21	51, 52

TABLE V.—Continued.

Jewish year of the World 5650, corresponding to A. D. 1889–1890.		
Sabbaths of the Jewish year.	Saturdays of the Gregorian yr.	Pareshioth and Haphtaroth.
2 C	1889	
3 Tisri	28 Sept.	53
10	5 Oct.	Chippur
17	12	Succoth
24	19	1
1 Marches.	26	2
8	2 Nov.	3
15	9	4
22	16	5
29	23	6
7 Cisleu	30	7
14	7 Dec.	8
21	14	9
28	21	10
5 Tebet	28	11
	1890	
12	4 Jan.	12
19	11	13
26	18	14
4 Sebat	25	15
11	1 Feb.	16
18	8	17
25	15	18, S
2 Adar	22	19
9	1 March	20, Z
16	8	21
23	15	22, 23, P
1 Nisan	22	24, H
8	29	25
15	5 April	1 Pas.
22	12	2 Pas.
29	19	26
6 Ijar	26	27, 28
13	3 May	29, 30
20	10	31
27	17	32, 33
5 Sivan	24	34
12	31	35
19	7 June	36
26	14	37
3 Tammuz	21	38
10	28	39
17	5 July	40
24	12	41
2 Ab	19	42, 43
9	26	44
16	2 Aug.	45
23	9	46
30	16	47
7 Elul	23	48
14	30	49
21	6 Sept.	50
28	13	51

Jewish year of the World 5651, corresponding to A. D. 1890–1891.		
Sabbaths of the Jewish year.	Saturdays of the Gregorian yr.	Pareshioth and Haphtaroth.
7 E	1890	
6 Tisri	20 Sept.	52
13	27	53
20	4 Oct.	Succoth
27	11	1
4 Marches.	18	2
11	25	3
18	1 Nov.	4
25	8	5
3 Cisleu	15	6
10	22	7
17	29	8
24	6 Dec.	9
2 Tebet	13	10
9	20	11
16	27	12
	1891	
23	3 Jan.	13
1 Sebat	10	14
8	17	15
15	24	16
22	31	17
29	7 Feb.	18
6 Adar	14	19
13	21	20
20	28	21
27	7 March	22, S
4 Veadar	14	23
11	21	24, Z
18	28	25, P
25	4 April	26, H
3 Nisan	11	27
10	18	28
17	25	1 Pas.
24	2 May	29
1 Ijar	9	30
8	16	31
15	23	32
22	30	33
29	6 June	34
7 Sivan	13	Pent.
14	20	35
21	27	36
28	4 July	37
5 Tammuz	11	38
12	18	39, 40
19	25	41
26	1 Aug.	42, 43
4 Ab	8	44
11	15	45
18	22	46
25	29	47
2 Elul	5 Sept.	48
9	12	49
16	19	50
23	26	51, 52

Jewish year of the World 5652, corresponding to A. D. 1891–1892.		
Sabbaths of the Jewish year.	Saturdays of the Gregorian yr.	Pareshioth and Haphtaroth.
4 C	1891	
1 Tisri	3 Oct.	New yrs.
8	10	53 [day
15	17	Succoth
22	24	Oct. Suc.
23*	25*	54, B. L.
29	31	1
6 Marches.	7 Nov.	2
13	14	3
20	21	4
27	28	5
4 Cisleu	5 Dec.	6
11	12	7
18	19	8
25	26	9, En
	1892	
2 Tebet	2 Jan.	10
9	9	11
16	16	12
23	23	13
1 Sebat	30	14
8	6 Feb.	15
15	13	16
22	20	17
29	27	18, S
6 Adar	5 March	19
13	12	20, Z
20	19	21, P
27	26	22, 23, H
5 Nisan	2 April	24
12	9	25
19	16	1 Pas.
26	23	26
3 Ijar	30	27, 28
10	7 May	29, 30
17	14	31
24	21	32, 33
2 Sivan	28	34
9	4 June	35
16	11	36
23	18	37
30	25	38
7 Tammuz	2 July	39
14	9	40
21	16	41
28	23	42, 43
6 Ab	30	44
13	6 Aug.	45
20	13	46
27	20	47
4 Elul	27	48
11	3 Sept.	49
18	10	50
25	17	51

Jewish year of the World 5653, corresponding to A. D. 1892–1893.		
Sabbaths of the Jewish year.	Saturdays of the Gregorian yr.	Pareshioth and Haphtaroth.
2 C	1892	
3 Tisri	24 Sept.	53
10	1 Oct.	Chippur
17	8	Succoth
24	15	1
1 Marches.	22	2
8	29	3
15	5 Nov.	4
22	12	5
29	19	6
7 Cisleu	26	7
14	3 Dec.	8
21	10	9
28	17	10
5 Tebet	24	11
12	31	12
	1893	
19	7 Jan.	13
26	14	14
4 Sebat	21	15
11	28	16
18	4 Feb.	17
25	11	18, S
2 Adar	18	19
9	25	20, Z
16	4 March	21
23	11	22, 23, P
1 Nisan	18	24, H
8	25	25
15	1 April	1 Pas.
22	8	2 Pas.
29	15	26
6 Ijar	22	27, 28
13	29	29, 30
20	6 May	31
27	13	32, 33
5 Sivan	20	34
12	27	35
19	3 June	36
26	10	37
3 Tammuz	17	38
10	24	39
17	1 July	40
24	8	41
2 Ab	15	42, 43
9	22	44
16	29	45
23	5 Aug.	46
30	12	47
7 Elul	19	48
14	26	49
21	2 Sept.	50
28	9	51

Jewish year of the World 5654, corresponding to A. D. 1893–1894.		
Sabbaths of the Jewish year.	Saturdays of the Gregorian yr.	Pareshioth and Haphtaroth.
3 E	1893	
6 Tisri	16 Sept.	52
13	23	53
20	30	Succoth
23*	3* Oct.	54, B. L.
27	7	1
4 Marches.	14	2
11	21	3
18	28	4
25	4 Nov.	5
2 Cisleu	11	6
9	18	7
16	25	8
23	2 Dec.	9
30	9	10
7 Tebet	16	11
14	23	12
21	30	13
	1894	
28	6 Jan.	14
6 Sebat	13	15
13	20	16
20	27	17
27	3 Feb.	18
4 Adar	10	19
11	17	20
18	24	21
25	3 March	22, S
2 Veadar	10	23
9	17	24, Z
16	24	25
23	31	26, P
1 Nisan	7 April	27, H
8	14	28
15	21	1 Pas.
22	28	2 Pas.
29	5 May	29
6 Ijar	12	30
13	19	31
20	26	32
27	2 June	33
5 Sivan	9	34
12	16	35
19	23	36
26	30	37
3 Tammuz	7 July	38
10	14	39
17	21	40
24	28	41
2 Ab	4 Aug.	42, 43
9	11	44
16	18	45
23	25	46
30	1 Sept.	47
7 Elul	8	48
14	15	49
21	22	50
28	29	51

Jewish year of the World 5655, corresponding to A. D. 1894–1895.		
Sabbaths of the Jewish year.	Saturdays of the Gregorian yr.	Pareshioth and Haphtaroth.
5 C	1894	
6 Tisri	6 Oct.	52
13	13	53
20	20	Succoth
23*	23*	54, B. L.
27	27	1
4 Marches.	3 Nov.	2
11	10	3
18	17	4
25	24	5
3 Cisleu	1 Dec.	6
10	8	7
17	15	8
24	22	9
2 Tebet	29	10
	1895	
9	5 Jan.	11
16	12	12
23	19	13
1 Sebat	26	14
8	2 Feb.	15
15	9	16
22	16	17
29	23	18, S
6 Adar	2 March	19
13	9	20, Z
20	16	21, P
27	23	22, 23, H
5 Nisan	30	24
12	6 April	25
19	13	1 Pas.
26	20	26
3 Ijar	27	27, 28
10	4 May	29, 30
17	11	31
24	18	32, 33
2 Sivan	25	34
9	1 June	35
16	8	36
23	15	37
30	22	38
7 Tammuz	29	39
14	6 July	40
21	13	41
28	20	42, 43
6 Ab	27	44
13	3 Aug.	45
20	10	46
27	17	47
4 Elul	24	48
11	31	49
18	7 Sept.	50
25	14	51, 52

TABLE V.—CONTINUED.

Jewish year of the World 5656, corresponding to A. D. 1895-1896.		
Sabbaths of the Jewish year.	Saturdays of the Gregorian yr.	Pareshioth and Haphtaroth.
1 C	1895	
3 Tisri	21 Sept.	53
10	28	Chippur
17	5 Oct.	Succoth
23*	11*	54, B. L.
24	12	1
1 Marches.	19	2
8	26	3
15	2 Nov	4
22	9	5
29	16	6
6 Cisleu	23	7
13	30	8
20	7 Dec.	9
27	14	10
4 Tebet	21	11
11	28	12
	1896	
18	4 Jan.	13
25	11	14
3 Sebat	18	15
10	25	16
17	1 Feb.	17
24	8	18
1 Adar	15	19, S
8	22	20, Z
15	29	21
22	7 March	22, P
29	14	23, H
7 Nisan	21	24
14	28	25
21	4 April	1 Pas.
28	11	26
5 Ijar	18	27, 28
12	25	29, 30
19	2 May	31
26	9	32, 33
4 Sivan	16	34
11	23	35
18	30	36
25	6 June	37
2 Tammuz	13	38
9	20	39
16	27	40
23	4 July	41
1 Ab	11	42, 43
8	18	44
15	25	45
22	1 Aug.	46
29	8	47
6 Elul	15	48
13	22	49
20	29	50
27	5 Sept.	51

Jewish year of the World 5657, corresponding to A. D. 1896-1897.		
Sabbaths of the Jewish year.	Saturdays of the Gregorian yr.	Pareshioth and Haphtaroth.
2 E	1896	
5 Tisri	12 Sept.	52
12	19	53
19	26	Succoth
23*	30*	54, B. L.
26	3 Oct.	1
3 Marches.	10	2
10	17	3
17	24	4
24	31	5
2 Cisleu	7 Nov.	6
9	14	7
16	21	8
23	28	9
30	5 Dec.	10
7 Tebet	12	11
14	19	12
21	26	13
	1897	
28	2 Jan.	14
6 Sebat	9	15
13	16	16
20	23	17
27	30	18
4 Adar	6 Feb.	19
11	13	20
18	20	21
25	27	22, S
2 Veadar	6 March	23
9	13	24, Z
16	20	25
23	27	26, P
1 Nisan	3 April	27, H
8	10	28
15	17	1 Pas.
22	24	2 Pas.
29	1 May	29
6 Ijar	8	30
13	15	31
20	22	32
27	29	33
5 Sivan	5 June	34
12	12	35
19	19	36
26	26	37
3 Tammuz	3 July	38
10	10	39
17	17	40
24	24	41
2 Ab	31	42, 43
9	7 Aug.	44
16	14	45
23	21	46
30	28	47
7 Elul	4 Sept.	48
14	11	49
21	18	50
28	25	51

Jewish year of the World 5658, corresponding to A. D. 1897-1898.		
Sabbaths of the Jewish year.	Saturdays of the Gregorian yr.	Pareshioth and Haphtaroth.
6 C	1897	
6 Tisri	2 Oct.	52
13	9	53
20	16	Succoth
23*	19*	54, B. L.
27	23	1
4 Marches.	30	2
11	6 Nov.	3
18	13	4
25	20	5
2 Cisleu	27	6
9	4 Dec.	7
16	11	8
23	18	9
30	25	10
	1898	
7 Tebet	1 Jan.	11
14	8	12
21	15	13
28	22	14
6 Sebat	29	15
13	5 Feb.	16
20	12	17
27	19	18, S
4 Adar	26	19
11	5 March	20, Z
18	12	21, P
25	19	22, 23, H
3 Nisan	26	24
10	2 April	25
17	9	1 Pas.
24	16	26
1 Ijar	23	27, 28
8	30	29, 30
15	7 May	31
22	14	32, 33
29	21	34
7 Sivan	28	Pent.
14	4 June	35
21	11	36
28	18	37
5 Tammuz	25	38
12	2 July	39, 40
19	9	41
26	16	42, 43
4 Ab	23	44
11	30	45
18	6 Aug.	46
25	13	47
2 Elul	20	48
9	27	49
16	3 Sept.	50
23	10	51, 52

Jewish year of the World 5659, corresponding to A. D. 1898-1899.		
Sabbaths of the Jewish year.	Saturdays of the Gregorian yr.	Pareshioth and Haphtaroth.
3 C	1898	
1 Tisri	17 Sept.	New yrs.
8	24	53 [day
15	1 Oct.	Succoth
22	8	Sab.p.Suc.
23*	9*	54, B.L.
29	15	1
6 Marches.	22	2
13	29	3
20	5 Nov.	4
27	12	5
5 Cisleu	19	6
12	26	7
19	3 Dec.	8
26	10	9
4 Tebet	17	10
11	24	11
18	31	12
	1899	
25	7 Jan.	13
3 Sebat	14	14
10	21	15
17	28	16
24	4 Feb.	17
1 Adar	11	18, S
8	18	19, Z
15	25	20
22	4 March	21, P
29	11	22, 23, H
7 Nisan	18	24
14	25	25
21	1 April	1 Pas.
28	8	26
5 Ijar	15	27, 28
12	22	29, 30
19	29	31
26	6 May	32, 33
4 Sivan	13	34
11	20	35
18	27	36
25	3 June	37
2 Tammuz	10	38
9	17	39
16	24	40
23	1 July	41
1 Ab	8	42, 43
8	15	44
15	22	45
22	29	46
29	5 Aug.	47
6 Elul	12	48
13	19	49
20	26	50
27	2 Sept.	51

Jewish year of the World 5660, corresponding to A. D. 1899-1900.		
Sabbaths of the Jewish year.	Saturdays of the Gregorian yr.	Pareshioth and Haphtaroth.
2 E	1899	
5 Tisri	9 Sept.	52
12	16	53
19	23	Succoth
23*	27*	54, B. L.
26	30	1
3 Marches.	7 Oct.	2
10	14	3
17	21	4
24	28	5
2 Cisleu	4 Nov	6
9	11	7
16	18	8
23	25	9
30	2 Dec.	10
7 Tebet	9	11
14	16	12
21	23	13
28	30	14
	1900	
6 Sebat	6 Jan	15
13	13	16
20	20	17
27	27	18
4 Adar	3 Feb.	19
11	10	20
18	17	21
25	24	22, S
2 Veadar	3 March	23
9	10	24, Z
16	17	25
23	24	26, P
1 Nisan	31	27, H
8	7 April	28
15	14	1 Pas.
22	21	2 Pas.
29	28	29
6 Ijar	5 May	30
13	12	31
20	19	32
27	26	33
5 Sivan	2 June	34
12	9	35
19	16	36
26	23	37
3 Tammuz	30	38
10	7 July	39
17	14	40
24	21	41
2 Ab	28	42, 43
9	4 Aug.	44
16	11	45
23	18	46
30	25	47
7 Elul	1 Sept.	48
14	8	49
21	15	50
28	22	51

Jewish year of the World 5661, corresponding to A. D. 1900-1901.		
Sabbaths of the Jewish year.	Saturdays of the Gregorian yr.	Pareshioth and Haphtaroth.
6 C	1900	
6 Tisri	29 Sept.	52
13	6 Oct.	53
20	13	Succoth
23*	16*	54, B. L.
27	20	1
4 Marches.	27	2
11	3 Nov.	3
18	10	4
25	17	5
2 Cisleu	24	6
9	1 Dec.	7
16	8	8
23	15	9
30	22	10
7 Tebet	29	11
	1901	
14	5 Jan.	12
21	12	13
28	19	14
6 Sebat	26	15
13	2 Feb.	16
20	9	17
27	16	18, S
4 Adar	23	19
11	2 March	20, Z
18	9	21, P
25	16	22, 23, H
3 Nisan	23	24
10	30	25
17	6 April	1 Pas.
24	13	26
1 Ijar	20	27, 28
8	27	29, 30
15	4 May	31
22	11	32, 33
29	18	34
7 Sivan	25	Pent.
14	1 June	35
21	8	36
28	15	37
5 Tammuz	22	38
12	29	39, 40
19	6 July	41
26	13	42, 43
4 Ab	20	44
11	27	45
18	3 Aug.	46
25	10	47
2 Elul	17	48
9	24	49
16	31	50
23	7 Sept.	51, 52

TABLE VI.

TABLE VI.—*Containing the year of the Jewish Lunar Cycle, the Golden Number, the first day of the Jewish Passover, Easter Sunday, and the commencement of each Jewish Year, according to the Gregorian calendar, from A. D.* 1812 *to A. D.* 1900 (*both inclusive.*)

Rabbinical year of the world.	Year from the Incarnation.	Year of the Jewish lunar cycle.	Golden Number.	First day of the Jewish Passover (15 Nisan.)	Easter Sunday.	Commencement of the Jewish year, according to the Gregorian calendar.
5572	B 1812	5	8	Saturday, March 28	March 29	September 19, 1811
5573	1813	6	9	Thursday, April 15	April 18	7, 1812
5574	1814	7	10	Tuesday, April 5	10	25, 1813
5575	1815	8	11	Tuesday, April 25	March 26	15, 1814
5576	B 1816	9	12	Saturday, April 13	April 14	October 5, 1815
5577	1817	10	13	Tuesday, April 1	6	September 23, 1816
5578	1818	11	14	Tuesday, April 21	March 22	11, 1817
5579	1819	12	15	Saturday, April 10	April 11	October 1, 1818
5580	B 1820	13	16	Thursday, March 30	2	September 20, 1819
5581	1821	14	17	Tuesday, April 17	22	9, 1820
5582	1822	15	18	Saturday, April 6	7	27, 1821
5583	1823	16	19	Thursday, March 27	March 30	16, 1822
5584	B 1824	17	1	Tuesday, April 13	April 18	6, 1823
5585	1825	18	2	Sunday, April 3	3	23, 1824
5586	1826	19	3	Saturday, April 22	March 26	13, 1825
5587	1827	1	4	Thursday, April 12	April 15	October 2, 1826
5588	B 1828	2	5	Sunday, March 30	6	September 22, 1827
5589	1829	3	6	Saturday, April 18	19	9, 1828
5590	1830	4	7	Thursday, April 8	11	28, 1829
5591	1831	5	8	Tuesday, March 29	3	18, 1830
5592	B 1832	6	9	Sunday, April 15	22	8, 1831
5593	1833	7	10	Thursday, April 4	7	25, 1832
5594	1834	8	11	Thursday, April 24	March 30	14, 1833
5595	1835	9	12	Tuesday, April 14	April 19	October 4, 1834
5596	B 1836	10	13	Saturday, April 2	3	September 24, 1835
5597	1837	11	14	Thursday, April 20	March 26	12, 1836
5598	1838	12	15	Tuesday, April 10	April 15	30, 1837
5599	1839	13	16	Saturday, March 30	March 31	20, 1838
5600	B 1840	14	17	Saturday, April 18	April 19	9, 1839
5601	1841	15	18	Tuesday, April 6	11	28, 1840
5602	1842	16	19	Saturday, March 26	March 27	16, 1841
5603	1843	17	1	Saturday, April 15	April 16	5, 1842
5604	B 1844	18	2	Thursday, April 4	7	25, 1843
5605	1845	19	3	Tuesday, April 22	March 23	14, 1844
5606	1846	1	4	Saturday, April 11	April 12	October 2, 1845
5607	1847	2	5	Thursday, April 1	4	September 21, 1846
5608	B 1848	3	6	Tuesday, April 18	23	11, 1847
5609	1849	4	7	Saturday, April 7	8	28, 1848
5610	1850	5	8	Thursday, March 28	March 31	17, 1849
5611	1851	6	9	Thursday, April 17	April 20	7, 1850
5612	B 1852	7	10	Sunday, April 4	11	27, 1851
5613	1853	8	11	Saturday, April 23	March 27	14, 1852
5614	1854	9	12	Thursday, April 13	April 16	October 3, 1853
5615	1855	10	13	Tuesday, April 3	8	September 23, 1854
5616	B 1856	11	14	Sunday, April 20	March 23	13, 1855
5617	1857	12	15	Thursday, April 9	April 12	30, 1856
5618	1858	13	16	Tuesday, March 30	4	19, 1857
5619	1859	14	17	Tuesday, April 19	24	9, 1858
5620	B 1860	15	18	Saturday, April 7	8	29, 1859
5621	1861	16	19	Tuesday, March 26	March 31	17, 1860
5622	1862	17	1	Tuesday, April 15	April 20	5, 1861
5623	1863	18	2	Saturday, April 4	5	25, 1862
5624	B 1864	19	3	Thursday, April 21	March 27	14, 1863
5625	1865	1	4	Tuesday, April 11	April 16	October 1, 1864
5626	1866	2	5	Saturday, March 31	1	September 21, 1865
5627	1867	3	6	Saturday, April 20	21	10, 1866
5628	B 1868	4	7	Tuesday, April 7	12	30, 1867
5629	1869	5	8	Saturday, March 27	March 28	17, 1868
5630	1870	6	9	Saturday, April 16	April 17	6, 1869
5631	1871	7	10	Thursday, April 6	9	26, 1870
5632	B 1872	8	11	Tuesday, April 23	March 31	16, 1871
5633	1873	9	12	Saturday, April 12	April 13	October 3, 1872
5634	1874	10	13	Thursday, April 2	5	September 22, 1873
5635	1875	11	14	Tuesday, April 20	March 28	12, 1874
5636	B 1876	12	15	Sunday, April 9	April 16	30, 1875
5637	1877	13	16	Thursday, March 29	1	19, 1876
5638	1878	14	17	Thursday, April 18	21	8, 1877
5639	1879	15	18	Tuesday, April 8	13	28, 1878
5640	B 1880	16	19	Saturday, March 27	March 28	18, 1879
5641	1881	17	1	Thursday, April 14	April 17	6, 1880
5642	1882	18	2	Tuesday, April 4	9	24, 1881
5643	1883	19	3	Sunday, April 22	March 25	14, 1882
5644	B 1884	1	4	Thursday, April 10	April 13	October 2, 1883
5645	1885	2	5	Tuesday, March 31	5	September 20, 1884
5646	1886	3	6	Tuesday, April 20	25	10, 1885
5647	1887	4	7	Saturday, April 9	10	30, 1886
5648	B 1888	5	8	Tuesday, March 27	1	19, 1887
5649	1889	6	9	Tuesday, April 16	21	6, 1888
5650	1890	7	10	Saturday, April 5	6	26, 1889
5651	1891	8	11	Thursday, April 23	March 29	15, 1890
5652	B 1892	9	12	Tuesday, April 12	April 17	October 3, 1891
5653	1893	10	13	Saturday, April 1	2	September 22, 1892
5654	1894	11	14	Saturday, April 21	March 25	11, 1893
5655	1895	12	15	Tuesday, April 9	April 14	October 1, 1894
5656	B 1896	13	16	Sunday, March 29	5	September 19, 1895
5657	1897	14	17	Saturday, April 17	18	8, 1896
5658	1898	15	18	Thursday, April 7	10	27, 1897
5659	1899	16	19	Sunday, March 26	2	17, 1898
5660	1900	17	1	Saturday, April 14	15	5, 1899
5661	1901	18	2	Thursday, April 4	7	24, 1900

EXPLANATION OF THE PRECEDING TABLES.

Before the reader enters upon the particular uses of each of the preceding tables, it will be necessary to give a detailed account of the rabbinical computation of time upon which they have been constructed. The year used by the Jews contains twelve or thirteen lunations, which are so artificially disposed that its commencement constantly happens about the time of the *autumnal equinox*. In order to effect this, they have been obliged to have recourse to the sun's revolution through the twelve signs of the zodiac, or, to speak more properly, to the quantum of time which the earth takes up in making one complete periodic revolution round the sun. This period of time, according to the rabbins, (which is the same that is used in the construction of their calendar,) is 365 days, 5 hours, 997 *chelakim*, (*points*,) and 48 moments; which, reduced to our time, is equal to 365 days, 5 hours, 55 minutes, and 25 seconds—1080 *chelakim* being contained in one hour, and 76 moments in a *chelek*. See Bibl. Rabb., Part II., p. 407.

The quantity of the synodical revolution of the moon, according to the rabbins, is 29 days, 12 hours, and 793 *chelakim*, which also reduced to our time, is equal to 29 days, 12 hours, 44 minutes, and 3⅓ seconds; and twelve times this quantity, or 354 days, 8 hours, 48 minutes, and 40 seconds, is equal to the Jewish common year, which is nearly 11 days short of the solar revolution; consequently, to keep the seasons of the year in their respective months, the rabbins employ an *embolismic* or *leap* year of 13 lunar months every second or third year, by means of which, with other corrections which will be hereafter noticed, their years are found to correspond so exactly with the Gregorian calendar as not to deviate from it materially through the course of some centuries.

In the lunar cycle of 19 years, which embraces the principal variations in the motion of the moon, they have 12 common years of 12 lunar months, and *embolismic* years of 13 lunar months; and in order that all their months may begin as nearly as possible with the day of the conjunction of the sun and moon, they have alternately, for the most part, 29 and 30 days. Thus *Tisri*, their first month, contains 30 days; *Marchesvan*, their second month, 29 or 30; *Cisleu*, 29 or 30; *Tebet*, 29; *Sebat*, 30; *Adar*, 29; *Nisan*, 30; *Ijar*, 29; *Sivan*, 30; *Tammuz*, 29; *Ab*, 30; and *Elul*, 29. In the *embolismic* year, *Adar* always consists of 30, and the *thirteenth* month, which is named *Veadar*, always of 29 days.

The reason why an *embolismic* year for the most part succeeds two common years, is evident from the circumstance of the lunar year being nearly 11 days shorter than the solar, so that in three years the latter gains from the former not fewer than about 32 days, and as only a month of 30 days is intercalated in that time, at the commencement of the lunar cycle, it is manifest that two intercalary years must sometimes happen with only one common year between. Accordingly, the 3d, 6th, 8th, 11th, 14th, 17th, and 19th years of every lunar cycle are denominated *embolismic*; see Table I. If the lunar synodic revolution consisted precisely of 29 days, 12 hours, the assigning to the Jewish months 29 and 30 days alternately, would be sufficient to fix the commencement of the different months about the day of the conjunction, *ad infinitum*; but as the synodic revolution, according to Rabbi *Adda*, contains 44 minutes 3⅓ seconds more than 29½ days, it is demonstrable that the assignment of 29 and 30 days alternately to the months must be insufficient, and in the course of a few years must produce a very sensible error.

Thus, in order to make this circumstance obvious to the lowest capacity, let the first paschal full moon in the lunar cycle be supposed to commence precisely at mid-day, then it is evident, from the quantity of a synodic revolution, as ascertained by the rabbins, that the nineteen paschal full moons which are contained in every cycle will, in this case, happen as in the following table; where the first column points out the year of the cycle; the second, the precise point of time in the lunar cycle of the respective paschal full moons; the third, the nearest corresponding day, omitting the fractional parts; and the fourth, the differences of the numbers in the third column, or in other words, the interval of time, expressed in whole numbers, which elapses between each successive paschal full moon.

1	0 days	0 hours	0 min.	0 sec.		
2	354	8	48	40	354	354
3 E	738	6	21	23	738	384
4	1092	15	10	3	1093	355
5	1446	23	58	43	1447	354
6 E	1830	21	31	26	1831	384
7	2185	6	20	6	2185	354
8 E	2569	3	52	49	2569	384
9	2923	12	41	29	2924	355
10	3277	21	30	9	3278	354
11 E	3661	19	2	52	3662	384
12	4016	3	51	32	4016	354
13	4370	12	40	12	4371	355
14 E	4754	10	12	55	4754	383
15	5108	19	1	35	5109	355
16	5463	3	50	15	5463	354
17 E	5847	1	22	58	5847	384
18	6201	10	11	38	6201	354
19 E	6585	7	44	21	6585	384
1	6939	16	33	1	6940	355

From the last column of the preceding table, it is evident that the paschal full moons happen constantly after an interval of 354, 355, 383, or 384 days, omitting the fractional parts; but the length of the Jewish year may be either 353, 354, 355, 383, 384, or 385 days. The reason of this discordance between the length of the Jewish year, and the interval between two consecutive paschal full moons, arises chiefly from the circumstance of never beginning the year on the first, fourth, or sixth day of the week. Hence, if the new moon, which regulates the commencement of the year, should happen on the 1st day of the week, the year does not begin till the following day; and if on the 4th or 6th, the commencement of the year is dated from the 5th or Sabbath. The reason why the Jews never begin their year on the first day of the week, is to prevent the occurrence of the celebration of the festival of *Hosanna Rabba* on the Sabbath day, as some parts of this festival are deemed by them incompatible with the strict observance of the Sabbath enjoined on them by the fourth commandment.

The reason why the year is never begun on the 4th or 6th days of the week, is to prevent the occurrence of the great day of Atonement on the 6th or Lord's day; for as the Jews are bound to keep this fast on the 10th of Tisri, and also to observe it as strictly as they would the Sabbath, in this case two Sabbaths as it were would come together and produce great inconvenience, as in their estimation it is not lawful to bury their dead or boil their food on either of these days.

Hence arises the necessity of adding or subtracting, from time to time, an entire day to or from the mean length of the *common* or *embolismic* year, which correction is always made in the month *Marchesvan* or *Cisleu*, just in the same manner as the intercalated day in the Gregorian calendar is always attached to the end of *February*.

From the different varieties in the length of the months *Marchesvan* and *Cisleu*, connected with the day of the week upon which the year begins, are produced *fourteen* different kinds of years among the Jews, *seven* of which are *common* years, and the other *seven embolismic*; for sometimes these two months have each only 29 days, sometimes they have each 30 days, and at other times *Marchesvan* has 29, and *Cisleu* 30 days; and the new year may commence with the Sabbath, or the 2d, 3d, or 5th day of the week.

The indexes by which these different years are distinguished in the preceding tables are for the common years, 5 P 1, 5 d 7, 7 D 1, 7 P 3, 2 D 3, 2 P 5, and 3 d 5; and for the embolismic, 5 D 1, 3 d 7, 2 P 7, 5 P 3, 7 D 3, 7 P 5, and 2 D 5. The first figure of the index denotes the day of the week upon which the year commences, thus 5 denotes the year to begin on the fifth day of the week or Thursday, 3 the third day of the week or Tuesday, &c., &c.; the letter of the index determines the length of the months *Marchesvan* and *Cisleu*; thus P stands for *perfect*, i. e., these two months are both perfect, each containing 30 days; D stands for *defective*, i. e., each of these months contains only 29 days; and a small d denotes that one of these months is defective, which in this case is always *Marchesvan*. The last figure of the index shows the day of the week upon which the passover happens, just in the same manner as the first figure denotes the day of the week upon which the year begins.

For a farther explanation of the index, let it be required to find upon what day of the week the rabbinical year of the world 5570 begins; upon what day of the week the passover is held in that year; and also the length of the months *Marchesvan* and *Cisleu*. To solve this question, we have only to refer to Table I., where we find the index of the year to be 2 D 5, i. e., the year commences on *Tuesday*, the *passover* is held upon *Thursday*, and the months *Marchesvan* and *Cisleu* are both defective, i. e., have only 29 days each.

Having premised thus much respecting the mode of constructing the Jewish calendar, we now come to explain the chief object of the preceding tables, which is to determine the order of reading the *Pareshioth* and *Haphtaroth*, or *Sections* of the *Law* and the *Prophets* for any given year. For this purpose Tables I., II., and V. are chiefly constructed. In Table I. the index for every Jewish year of the world from 5566 to 5814 (both inclusive) is given; and as these years correspond to all the years of our Lord from 1807 to 2054, both inclusive, it will be 242 years before this table, in its present form, will be entirely antiquated; and it may be rendered perpetual by affixing the same routine of indexes to the 247 years, beginning with A. D. 2055 and ending with A. D. 2301; and to the 247 years subsequent to A. D 2301, &c., &c., *ad infinitum*. Table II. contains a calendar of Sabbaths for the 14 *different kinds* of years made use of by the Jews, together with the *Pareshah* or *Pareshioth* read on the different Sabbaths of each. In the first column of the months the black circle or astronomical sign of the conjunction of the sun and moon points out the *figure* annexed to it to be the day of the week upon which the month begins, and when two numbers are affixed, it is to show that the conjunction of the luminaries corresponds to both days; the *latter* of which is always taken for the *commencement* of the *month*. All the other numbers in this column are the days of the month upon which the Sabbaths happen, except sometimes in the month *Tisri*, where two numbers occur together, the *first* of which is the *day of the week* and the *latter* the corresponding day of the month. In order therefore to find what *Pareshah* or *Pareshioth* are read on any given Sabbath, nothing more is necessary than to look into Table I. for the index of the given year, and with it to enter Table II., where against the given Sabbath, in the column of *Pareshioth*, will be found the given *Pareshah* or *Pareshioth* required.

Example I. Required the *Pareshah* or *Pareshioth* appointed to be read in the synagogue on the second Sabbath of the month Sivan, A. M. 5572. In Table I. the index for the years 5 d 7, from which it appears by Table II. that it is the second Jewish common year, and the second Sabbath of Sivan in this year is upon the 12th day of the month, over against which, in the column of *Pareshioth*, is 35, the number of the *Pareshah* required. By a reference to the list of *Pareshioth* given at the end of the commentary on the last chapter of Deuteronomy, we find that this section of the law commences with Num. iv. 21, and ends at vii. 89 of the same book. The *Haphtara* read on the Sabbath appears by the same list to be the xiiith chapter of Judges from the 2d to the 25th verse; in Table V. the 12th of Sivan, A. M. 5572, is the same with the 23d of May, 1812.

Example 2. Required the *Pareshah* or *Pareshioth* appointed to be read on the fourth Sabbath of *Tammuz*, A. M. 5584. In Table I. the index for the year is 7 D 3, which index corresponds to the fifth embolismic year in Table II., consequently the *fourth* Sabbath of *Tammuz* falls on the 28th of the month, and the *Pareshioth* for the given day are the 42d and 43d. The former commences at the second verse of the xxxth chapter of Numbers, and the latter is continued from it to the end of the book. By a reference to Table V., the 28th of *Tammuz*, A. M. 5584, answers to the 24th of July, 1824.

N. B. The figure and capital letter found in the first column of Table V. at the beginning of each Jewish year, show to which of the fourteen kinds of years, according to their disposition in Table II., the said year belongs, thus 1 C stands for the first common year; 5 E, the fifth embolismic year, &c., &c., &c.

When, in the column of *Pareshioth* and *Haphtaroth* in Tables II. and V., the word *Chippur* is affixed to any particular Sabbath, it points it out to be the great day of ATONEMENT, for which a particular service is appointed. The portion of the law read on that day begins with the 27th verse of the xxiiid chapter of *Leviticus*, and ends with the chapter. The *Haphtorah* for this day is the *book of the prophet Jonah*.

When the word *Succoth* is affixed to any particular Sabbath, if it be the 15th of *Tisri*, it is the day upon which the Feast of *Tabernacles* commences; the portion of the law for which occasion begins at the 34th verse of the xxiiid chapter of *Leviticus*. The *Haphtorah* is the xivth chapter of the *prophet Zechariah;* but on the Sabbath which follows the 15th of Tisri, if it be within the octave of the Feast of *Tabernacles*, the portion of the prophets which is read is the xxxviiith Chapter of *Ezekiel*, according to the *German Jews*, but the other Jews read from Ezek. xxxviii. 18, to xxxix. 16.

The capital letters B. L., which are affixed to the fifty-fourth section of the law in the third column of Table V., stand for *Book* of the *Law*. This section is read on the 23d of Tisri, which is contrived so as never to happen on the Sabbath, as the day upon which it is read is a time of great festivity among the Jews for their having completed the reading of the fifty-four Pareshioth, which comprise the whole book of the law.. The asterisk affixed to the 23d day of Tisri, in Table V., and its corresponding time in the Gregorian computation, is designed to show that this day happens on a week day and not on the Sabbath, as all the other days in the same columns do.

When 1 *Pas*. or 2 *Pas*. is affixed to any particular Sabbath, it is the first or second Sabbath of the passover, upon which, if the 15th of Nisan be the Sabbath day, the portion of the prophets read on the occasion is the vth chapter of Joshua, all but the first verse. If there be only *one* Sabbath in the feast of the passover, the Haphtorah is the 14 first verses of the xxxviith chapter of Ezekiel, to which some add the three following. If there be *two* Sabbaths in the feast of the passover, the latter is termed the octave, upon which they read the whole of the *Canticles*, and also the *prophet Isaiah*, from the 32d verse of the xth chapter to the end of the xiith.

When Pent. is affixed to any particular Sabbath, it is the second day of the Feast of *Pentecost*, upon which occasion the iiid, ivth, vth, and vith chapters of the prophet *Habakkuk*, together with the book of *Ruth*, are read.

Besides the 54 sections of the law which are regularly read through in the course of a Jewish year, whether it be *common* or *embolismic*, there are *four minor* PARESHIOTH which are generally read in the month *Adar* of a *common*, and in *Veadar* of an *embolismic*, year. These are שקלים *Shekalim*, זכור *Zachor*, פרה *Para*, and החדש *Hachodesh;* and are marked down in Tables II. and V. by their initial letters S, Z, P, and H. The minor Pareshah, SHEKALIM, commences with the 11th verse of the xxxth chapter of *Exodus*, and ends at the 16th verse of the same; ZACHOR begins with the 17th verse of the xxvth chapter of *Deuteronomy*, and contains the Divine malediction upon the Amalekites; PARA begins with the xixth chapter of Numbers, and ends with the chapter; and HACHODESH begins with the 10th verse of the xiith chapter of *Exodus*, and ends at the 20th verse of the same Chapter.

When the Jewish year commences on the Sabbath, (which circumstance is noticed in the third column of Table V. whenever it occurs,) Lev. xxiii. 24 and Num. xxix. 1-7 are read.

When the 25th of *Cisleu* falls on the Sabbath, the contraction *En.*, for *Encænia*, Dedication, is affixed to the number of the *Pareshah* in Tables II. and V., to show that it is the day to be held in commemoration of the altar's being *dedicated* afresh to the service of God, after its purification from its pollutions by Antiochus.

Tables III. and IV. are constructed to determine the day of the week upon which the principal Jewish Fasts and Feasts are held for any given year. One example will be sufficient to illustrate these tables. *Example*. Required the day of the week upon which the principal Jewish fasts and feasts happen in the Jewish year of the world 5573. By a reference to Table I. this year corresponds to A. D. 1813; and in Table III. in the same square with 1813 is the capital letter C, which shows that the numbers in column C of Table IV., over against the different fasts and festivals, are the days of the week required. Thus the commencement of Tisri is on the second and third days of the week; the Fast of *Gedaliah* on the 4th; the Fast of ATONEMENT on the 4th; the Feast of Tabernacles on the 2d; *Hosanna Rabba* on the 1st; the *Lætitia Legis*, or Joy for the Law, on the 3d; the commencement of *Marchesvan* on the 3d and 4th; the commencement of *Cisleu* on the 5th; the *Encænia* on the 1st; the commencement of *Tebet* on the 6th; the Fast of the 10th of *Tebet* on the 1st; the commencement of *Sebat* on the Sabbath; the commencement of *Adar* on the 1st and 2d; the commencement of *Veadar* on the 3d and 4th; the Fast of *Esther* on the 2d; the Feast of *Purim* on the 3d; the commencement of *Nisan* on the 5th; the Feast of the *Passover* on the 5th; the commencement of *Ijar* on the 6th and 7th; the 33 *Omer* on the 3d; the commencement of *Sivan* on the 1st; the Feast of *Pentecost* on the 6th; the commencement of *Tammuz* on the 2d and 3d; the Fast of the 17th of *Tammuz* on the 5th; the commencement of *Ab* on the 4th; the Fast of the 9th of *Ab* on the 5th; and the commencement of *Elul* on the 5th and 6th days of the week.

Table VI. needs little explanation; the titles of its different columns being sufficient for this purpose. The *first* column shows the year of the world according to the Jewish reckoning. The second column, the year of our Lord; the letter B in the same column shows each *Bissextile* or *Leap-year*. The 3d and 4th columns contain the *lunar cycle* and *golden numbers*. The *fifth* column shows the month and day of the month on which the Jewish passover falls, from the year 1812 to the year 1900. The *sixth* column marks the day on which *Easter* falls during the same period. The *seventh* column shows the year of our Lord corresponding with the beginning of the Jewish year in the *first* column; and also on what day of what month the Jewish year, according to the Gregorian calendar, commences. By the slightest inspection of these tables any person may at once see the day on which the Jewish passover and the Christian *Easter* falls for any year of the above period from 1812 to 1900.

On the subject of the preceding *tables* there will be doubtless various opinions among the readers of this work. Some may even think them *useless*, while others will judge them of considerable importance. The writer has only to say that no other part of the work has occasioned so much *labour* and so much *expense*. Nothing of this nature, on the same plan, has ever before met the eye of the *English* reader; nor does any other *language* afford a similar subject at once so *extensive* in the *plan*, and so *concise* in the *execution*. Those who best understand the work will perceive that it required no common *industry*, to say nothing of other requisite *qualifications*, to construct such tables, even with the extensive work of *Bartolocci's Bibliotheca Rabbinica* before him, to which the present collection of tables acknowledges high obligations. The writer could not consider his comment on the Pentateuch as even tolerably complete without such an *apparatus* as is here produced, which it is hoped every minister of the word of God will find of the utmost use to him in various matters connected with Jewish affairs; but on this subject nothing need be added, as the tables and their uses have been already so largely explained. In his prospectus the author promised "every requisite table;" and had he not added *these*, he must have considered the *pledge* given to the public not redeemed.

A CHRONOLOGY OF THE PENTATEUCH,

WITH THE

BOOK OF JOSHUA;

OR

A SYSTEMATIC ARRANGEMENT OF EVENTS,

FROM THE CREATION OF ADAM, A. M. 1, TO THE BIRTH OF PELEG, A. M. 1757, AND OF EACH SUCCESSIVE YEAR FROM THE DISPERSION OF MANKIND AT THE BIRTH OF PELEG, TO THE SETTLEMENT OF THE ISRAELITES IN THE LAND OF CANAAN. AT THE DEATH OF JOSHUA, A. M. 2561, INCLUSIVE; SYNCHRONIZED WITH THE PRINCIPAL EPOCHS IN USE AMONG THE DIFFERENT NATIONS OF THE WORLD, VIZ., THE YEAR OF THE WORLD, THE YEAR BEFORE CHRIST, THE YEAR BEFORE AND AFTER THE DELUGE, THE YEAR OF THE JULIAN PERIOD, AND THE YEAR BEFORE THE FIRST OLYMPIAD.

TO WHICH ARE ADDED,

The REIGNS of the CONTEMPORARY SOVEREIGNS of the most remarkable Monarchies, together with the Year of the Life of all the antediluvian and postdiluvian Patriarchs on record, corresponding with the Years of the principal Epochs mentioned above. Designed to save the curious reader the trouble of reducing the Years of any particular Epoch to those of another, in which he may wish to fix any Event that took place within the limits of these Tables; and to prevent the necessity of recurrence to systematic Chronologies for historic Facts in any wise connected with those mentioned in the Sacred Writings.

TABLE I.

A CHRONOLOGY OF THE BIRTH AND DEATH OF ALL THE PATRIARCHS, FROM ADAM, A. M. 1, TO REU, THE SON OF PELEG, A. M. 1787.

A. M.	B. C.	Julian Period.	Anno ante Diluvium.	Year before the first Olymp.	Year before the year of Christ, 1812.	In the YEAR of the LIFE of Adam.	Seth.	Enos.	Cainan.	Mahalaleel.	Jared.	Enoch	Methuselah.	Lamech.	Noah.	Shem.
1	4004	711	1656	3228	5816	1										
130	3874	840	1526	3098	5686	130	B									
235	3769	945	1421	2993	5581	235	105	B								
325	3679	1035	1331	2903	5491	325	195	90	B							
395	3609	1105	1261	2833	5421	395	265	160	70	B						
460	3544	1170	1196	2768	5356	460	330	225	135	65	B					
622	3382	1332	1034	2606	5194	622	492	387	297	227	162	B				
687	3317	1397	969	2541	5129	687	557	452	362	292	227	65	B			
874	3130	1584	782	2354	4942	874	744	639	549	479	414	252	187	B		
930	3074	1640	726	2298	4886	930 D	800	695	605	535	470	308	243	56		
987	3017	1697	669	2241	4829		857	752	662	592	527	365	300	113		
1042	2962	1752	614	2186	4774		912 D	807	717	647	582		355	168		
1056	2948	1766	600	2178	4760			821	731	661	596		369	182	B	
1140	2864	1850	516	2088	4676			905 D	815	745	680		453	266	84	
1235	2769	1945	421	1993	4581				910 D	840	775		548	361	179	
1290	2714	2000	376	1938	4526					895 D	830		603	416	234	
1422	2582	2132	234	1806	4394						962 D		735	548	366	
1558	2446	2268	98	1670	4258								871	684	502	B
1651	2353	2361	5	1577	4165								964	777 D	595	93
1656	2348	2366	0	1572	4160								969 D		600	98
			Anno e Diluvio.			Noah.	Shem.	Arphaxad.	Salah.	Heber.	Peleg.	Reu.				
1658	2346	2368	2	1570	4158	602	100	B								
1693	2311	2403	37	1535	4123	637	135	35	B							
1723	2281	2433	67	1505	4093	667	165	65	30	B						
1757	2247	2467	101	1471	4059	701	199	99	64	34	B					
1787	2217	2497	131	1437	4029	731	229	129	94	64	30	B				

The B signifies the year of the *birth*, and the D of the *death*, of each Patriarch.

TABLE II.—Chronology of Ancient Kingdoms

A. M.	B. C.	Julian Period.	Anno e Diluvio	Year before the first Olymp.	Kingdom of the Egyptians.	In the YEAR of the LIFE of								
						NOAH	SHEM	ARPHAXAD	SALAH	HEBER	PELEG	REU	SERUG	NAHOR
1757	2247	2467	100	1471	59 Before the foundation of this kingdom.	701	199	99	64	34				
1758	2246	2468	101	1470	58	702	200	100	65	35	1			
1759	2245	2469	102	1469	57	703	201	101	66	36	2			
1760	2244	2470	103	1468	56	704	202	102	67	37	3			
1761	2243	2471	104	1467	55	705	203	103	68	38	4			
1762	2242	2472	105	1466	54	706	204	104	69	39	5			
1763	2241	2473	106	1465	53	707	205	105	70	40	6			
1764	2240	2474	107	1464	52	708	206	106	71	41	7			
1765	2239	2475	108	1463	51	709	207	107	72	42	8			
1766	2238	2476	109	1462	50	710	208	108	73	43	9			
1767	2237	2477	110	1461	49	711	209	109	74	44	10			
1768	2236	2478	111	1460	48	712	210	110	75	45	11			
1769	2235	2479	112	1459	47	713	211	111	76	46	12			
1770	2234	2480	113	1458	46	714	212	112	77	47	13			
1771	2233	2481	114	1457	45	715	213	113	78	48	14			
1772	2232	2482	115	1456	44	716	214	114	79	49	15			
1773	2231	2483	116	1455	43	717	215	115	80	50	16			
1774	2230	2484	117	1454	42	718	216	116	81	51	17			
1775	2229	2485	118	1453	41	719	217	117	82	52	18			
1776	2228	2486	119	1452	40	720	218	118	83	53	19			
1777	2227	2487	120	1451	39	721	219	119	84	54	20			
1778	2226	2488	121	1450	38	722	220	120	85	55	21			
1779	2225	2489	122	1449	37	723	221	121	86	56	22			
1780	2224	2490	123	1448	36	724	222	122	87	57	23			
1781	2223	2491	124	1447	35	725	223	123	88	58	24			
1782	2222	2492	125	1446	34	726	224	124	89	59	25			
1783	2221	2493	126	1445	33	727	225	125	90	60	26			
1784	2220	2494	127	1444	32	728	226	126	91	61	27			
1785	2219	2495	128	1443	31	729	227	127	92	62	28			
1786	2218	2496	129	1442	30	730	228	128	93	63	29			
1787	2217	2497	130	1441	29	731	229	129	94	64	30			
1788	2216	2498	131	1440	28	732	230	130	95	65	31	1		
1789	2215	2499	132	1439	27	733	231	131	96	66	32	2		
1790	2214	2500	133	1438	26	734	232	132	97	67	33	3		
1791	2213	2501	134	1437	25	735	233	133	98	68	34	4		
1792	2212	2502	135	1436	24	736	234	134	99	69	35	5		
1793	2211	2503	136	1435	23	737	235	135	100	70	36	6		
1794	2210	2504	137	1434	22	738	236	136	101	71	37	7		
1795	2209	2505	138	1433	21	739	237	137	102	72	38	8		
1796	2208	2506	139	1432	20	740	238	138	103	73	39	9		
1797	2207	2507	140	1431	19	741	239	139	104	74	40	10		
1798	2206	2508	141	1430	18	742	240	140	105	75	41	11		
1799	2205	2509	142	1429	17	743	241	141	106	76	42	12		
1800	2204	2510	143	1428	16	744	242	142	107	77	43	13		
1801	2203	2511	144	1427	15	745	243	143	108	78	44	14		
1802	2202	2512	145	1426	14	746	244	144	109	79	45	15		
1803	2201	2513	146	1425	13	747	245	145	110	80	46	16		
1804	2200	2514	147	1424	12	748	246	146	111	81	47	17		
1805	2199	2515	148	1423	11	749	247	147	112	82	48	18		
1806	2198	2516	149	1422	10	750	248	148	113	83	49	19		
1807	2197	2517	150	1421	9	751	249	149	114	84	50	20		
1808	2196	2518	151	1420	8	752	250	150	115	85	51	21		
1809	2195	2519	152	1419	7	753	251	151	116	86	52	22		
1810	2194	2520	153	1418	6	754	252	152	117	87	53	23		
1811	2193	2521	154	1417	5	755	253	153	118	88	54	24		
1812	2192	2522	155	1416	4	756	254	154	119	89	55	25		
1813	2191	2523	156	1415	3	757	255	155	120	90	56	26		
1814	2190	2524	157	1414	2	758	256	156	121	91	57	27		
1815	2189	2525	158	1413	1	759	257	157	122	92	58	28		
1816	2188	2526	159	1412	1 From the foundation of this kingdom by Misraim, the son of Ham.	760	258	158	123	93	59	29		
1817	2187	2527	160	1411	2	761	259	159	124	94	60	30		
1818	2186	2528	161	1410	3	762	260	160	125	95	61	31		
1819	2185	2529	162	1409	4	763	261	161	126	96	62	32		
1820	2184	2530	163	1408	5	764	262	162	127	97	63	33	1	
1821	2183	2531	164	1407	6	765	263	163	128	98	64	34	2	
1822	2182	2532	165	1406	7	766	264	164	129	99	65	35	3	
1823	2181	2533	166	1405	8	767	265	165	130	100	66	36	4	
1824	2180	2534	167	1404	9	768	266	166	131	101	67	37	5	
1825	2179	2535	168	1403	10	769	267	167	132	102	68	38	6	
1826	2178	2536	169	1402	11	770	268	168	133	103	69	39	7	
1827	2177	2537	170	1401	12	771	269	169	134	104	70	40	8	
1828	2176	2538	171	1400	13	772	270	170	135	105	71	41	9	
1829	2175	2539	172	1399	14	773	271	171	136	106	72	42	10	
1830	2174	2540	173	1398	15	774	272	172	137	107	73	43	11	
1831	2173	2541	174	1397	16	775	273	173	138	108	74	44	12	
1832	2172	2542	175	1396	17	776	274	174	139	109	75	45	13	
1833	2171	2543	176	1395	18	777	275	175	140	110	76	46	14	
1834	2170	2544	177	1394	19	778	276	176	141	111	77	47	15	
1835	2169	2545	178	1393	20	779	277	177	142	112	78	48	16	
1836	2168	2546	179	1392	21	780	278	178	143	113	79	49	17	
1837	2167	2547	180	1391	22	781	279	179	144	114	80	50	18	
1838	2166	2548	181	1390	23	782	280	180	145	115	81	51	19	
1839	2165	2549	182	1389	24	783	281	181	146	116	82	52	20	
1840	2164	2550	183	1388	25	784	282	182	147	117	83	53	21	
1841	2163	2551	184	1387	26	785	283	183	148	118	84	54	22	
1842	2162	2552	185	1386	27	786	284	184	149	119	85	55	23	
1843	2161	2553	186	1385	28	787	285	185	150	120	86	56	24	
1844	2160	2554	187	1384	29	788	286	186	151	121	87	57	25	
1845	2159	2555	188	1383	30	789	287	187	152	122	88	58	26	
1846	2158	2556	189	1382	31	790	288	188	153	123	89	59	27	
1847	2157	2557	190	1381	32	791	289	189	154	124	90	60	28	
1848	2156	2558	191	1380	33	792	290	190	155	125	91	61	29	
1849	2155	2559	192	1379	34	793	291	191	156	126	92	62	30	
1850	2154	2560	193	1378	35	794	292	192	157	127	93	63	31	1
1851	2153	2561	194	1377	36	795	293	193	158	128	94	64	32	2
1852	2152	2562	195	1376	37	796	294	194	159	129	95	65	33	3
1853	2151	2563	196	1375	38	797	295	195	160	130	96	66	34	4
1854	2150	2564	197	1374	39	798	296	196	161	131	97	67	35	5

TABLE II.—Chronology of Ancient Kingdoms.—*Continued.*

A. M.	B. C.	Julian Period.	Anno e Diluvio	Year before the first Olymp.	Kingdom of the Egyptians.	Kings of Sicyon	In the YEAR of the LIFE of									
							NOAH	SHEM	ARPHAXAD	SALAH	HEBER	PELEG	REU	SERUG	NAHOR	TERAH
1855	2149	2565	198	1373	40 From the foundation of this kingdom by Misraim, the son of Ham.		799	297	197	162	132	98	68	36	6	
1856	2148	2566	199	1372	41		800	298	198	163	133	99	69	37	7	
1857	2147	2567	200	1371	42		801	299	199	164	134	100	70	38	8	
1858	2146	2568	201	1370	43		802	300	200	165	135	101	71	39	9	
1859	2145	2569	202	1369	44		803	301	201	166	136	102	72	40	10	
1860	2144	2570	203	1368	45		804	302	202	167	137	103	73	41	11	
1861	2143	2571	204	1367	46		805	303	203	168	138	104	74	42	12	
1862	2142	2572	205	1366	47		806	304	204	169	139	105	75	43	13	
1863	2141	2573	206	1365	48		807	305	205	170	140	106	76	44	14	
1864	2140	2574	207	1364	49		808	306	206	171	141	107	77	45	15	
1865	2139	2575	208	1363	50		809	307	207	172	142	108	78	46	16	
1866	2138	2576	209	1362	51		810	308	208	173	143	109	79	47	17	
1867	2137	2577	210	1361	52		811	309	209	174	144	110	80	48	18	
1868	2136	2578	211	1360	53		812	310	210	175	145	111	81	49	19	
1869	2135	2579	212	1359	54		813	311	211	176	146	112	82	50	20	
1870	2133	2580	213	1358	55		814	312	212	177	147	113	83	51	21	
1871	2134	2581	214	1357	56		815	313	213	178	148	114	84	52	22	
1872	2132	2582	215	1356	57		816	314	214	179	149	115	85	53	23	
1873	2131	2583	216	1355	58		817	315	215	180	150	116	86	54	24	
1874	2130	2584	217	1354	59		818	316	216	181	151	117	87	55	25	
1875	2129	2585	218	1353	60		819	317	217	182	152	118	88	56	26	
1876	2128	2586	219	1352	61		820	318	218	183	153	119	89	57	27	
1877	2127	2587	220	1351	62		821	319	219	184	154	120	90	58	28	
1878	2126	2588	221	1350	63		822	320	220	185	155	121	91	59	29	
1879	2125	2589	222	1349	64		823	321	221	186	156	122	92	60	30	1
1880	2124	2590	223	1348	65		824	322	222	187	157	123	93	61	31	2
1881	2123	2591	224	1347	66		825	323	223	188	158	124	94	62	32	3
1882	2122	2592	225	1346	67		826	324	224	189	159	125	95	63	33	4
1883	2121	2593	226	1345	68		827	325	225	190	160	126	96	64	34	5
1884	2120	2594	227	1344	69		828	326	226	191	161	127	97	65	35	6
1885	2119	2595	228	1343	70		829	327	227	192	162	128	98	66	36	7
1886	2118	2596	229	1342	71		830	328	228	193	163	129	99	67	37	8
1887	2117	2597	230	1341	72		831	329	229	194	164	130	100	68	38	9
1888	2116	2598	231	1340	73		832	330	230	195	165	131	101	69	39	10
1889	2115	2599	232	1339	74		833	331	231	196	166	132	102	70	40	11
1890	2114	2600	233	1338	75		834	332	232	197	167	133	103	71	41	12
1891	2113	2601	234	1337	76		835	333	233	198	168	134	104	72	42	13
1892	2112	2602	235	1336	77		836	334	234	199	169	135	105	73	43	14
1893	2111	2603	236	1335	78		837	335	235	200	170	136	106	74	44	15
1894	2110	2604	237	1334	79		838	336	236	201	171	137	107	75	45	16
1895	2109	2605	238	1333	80		839	337	237	202	172	138	108	76	46	17
1896	2108	2606	239	1332	81		840	338	238	203	173	139	109	77	47	18
1897	2107	2607	240	1331	82		841	339	239	204	174	140	110	78	48	19
1898	2106	2608	241	1330	83		842	340	240	205	175	141	111	79	49	20
1899	2105	2609	242	1329	84		843	341	241	206	176	142	112	80	50	21
1900	2104	2610	243	1328	85		844	342	242	207	177	143	113	81	51	22
1901	2103	2611	244	1327	86		845	343	243	208	178	144	114	82	52	23
1902	2102	2612	245	1326	87		846	344	244	209	179	145	115	83	53	24
1903	2101	2613	246	1325	88		847	345	245	210	180	146	116	84	54	25
1904	2100	2614	247	1324	89		848	346	246	211	181	147	117	85	55	26
1905	2099	2615	248	1323	90		849	347	247	212	182	148	118	86	56	27
1806	2098	2616	249	1322	91		850	348	248	213	183	149	119	87	57	28
1907	2097	2617	250	1321	92		851	349	249	214	184	150	120	88	58	29
1908	2096	2618	251	1320	93		852	350	250	215	185	151	121	89	59	30
1909	2095	2619	252	1319	94		853	351	251	216	186	152	122	90	60	31
1910	2094	2620	253	1318	95		854	352	252	217	187	153	123	91	61	32
1911	2093	2621	254	1317	96		855	353	253	218	188	154	124	92	62	33
1912	2092	2622	255	1316	97		856	354	254	219	189	155	125	93	63	34
1913	2091	2623	256	1315	98		857	355	255	220	190	156	126	94	64	35
1914	2090	3624	257	1314	99 Salatis, the first monarch of the shepherd dynasty.		858	356	256	221	191	157	127	95	65	36
1915	2089	2125	258	1313	100	1 Ægialeus the first monarch.	859	357	257	222	192	158	128	96	66	37
1916	2088	2626	259	1312	101	2	860	358	258	223	193	159	129	97	67	38
1917	2087	2627	260	1311	102	3	861	359	259	224	194	160	130	98	68	39
1918	2086	2628	261	1310	103	4	862	360	260	225	195	161	131	99	69	40
1919	2085	2629	262	1309	104	5	863	361	261	226	196	162	132	100	70	41
1920	2084	2630	263	1308	1	6	864	362	262	227	197	163	133	101	71	42
1921	2083	2631	264	1307	2	7	865	363	263	228	198	164	134	102	72	43
1922	2082	2632	265	1306	3	8	866	364	264	229	199	165	135	103	73	44
1923	2081	2633	266	1305	4	9	867	365	265	230	200	166	136	104	74	45
1024	2080	2634	267	1304	5	10	868	366	266	231	201	167	137	105	75	46
1925	2079	2635	268	1303	6	11	869	367	267	232	202	168	138	106	76	47
1926	2078	2636	269	1302	7	12	870	368	268	233	203	169	139	107	77	48
1927	2077	2637	270	1301	8	13	871	369	269	234	204	170	140	108	78	49
1928	2076	2638	271	1300	9	14	872	370	270	235	205	171	141	109	79	50
1929	2075	2639	272	1299	10	15	873	371	271	236	206	172	142	110	80	51
1930	2074	2640	273	1298	11	16	874	372	272	237	207	173	143	111	81	52
1931	2073	2641	274	1297	12	17	875	373	273	238	208	174	144	112	82	53
1932	2072	2642	275	1296	13	18	876	374	274	239	209	175	145	113	83	54
1933	2071	2643	276	1295	14	19	877	375	275	240	210	176	146	114	84	55
1934	2070	2644	277	1294	15	20	878	376	276	241	211	177	147	115	85	56
1935	2069	2645	278	1293	16	21	879	377	277	242	212	178	148	116	86	57
1936	2068	2646	279	1292	17	22	880	378	278	243	213	179	149	117	87	58
1937	2067	2647	280	1291	18	23	881	379	279	244	214	180	150	118	88	59
1938	2066	2648	281	1290	19	24	882	380	280	245	215	181	151	119	89	60
1939	2065	2649	282	1289	1 Bæon.	25	883	381	281	246	216	182	152	120	90	61
1940	2064	2650	283	1288	2	26	884	382	282	247	217	183	153	121	91	62
1941	2063	2651	284	1287	3	27	885	383	283	248	218	184	154	122	92	63
1942	2062	2652	285	1286	4	28	886	384	284	249	219	185	155	123	93	64
1943	2061	2653	286	1285	5	29	887	385	285	250	220	186	156	124	94	65
1944	2060	2654	287	1284	6	30	888	386	286	251	221	187	157	125	95	66
1945	2059	2655	288	1283	7	31	889	387	287	252	222	188	158	126	96	67
1946	2058	2656	289	1282	8	32	800	388	288	253	223	189	159	127	97	68
1947	2057	2657	290	1281	9	33	891	389	289	254	224	190	160	128	98	69
1948	2056	2658	291	1280	10	34	892	390	290	255	225	191	161	129	99	70
1949	2055	2659	292	1279	11	35	893	391	291	256	226	192	162	130	100	71
1950	2054	2660	293	1278	12	36	894	392	292	257	227	193	163	131	101	72
1951	2053	2661	294	1277	13	37	895	393	293	258	228	194	164	132	102	73
1952	2052	2662	295	1276	14	38	896	394	294	259	229	195	165	133	103	74

TABLE II.—Chronology of Ancient Kingdoms.—*Continued.*

A. M.	B. C.	Julian Period.	Anno o Diluvio	Year before the first Olymp.	Kings of the Egyptians.	Kings of Sicyon.	In the YEAR of the LIFE of											
							NOAH	SHEM	ARPHAXAD	SALAH	HEBER	PELEG	REU	SERUG	NAHOR	TERAH	ABRAM	SARAI, Abram's wife,
1953	2051	2663	296	1275	15 Baeon.	39 Ægialeus.	897	395	295	260	230	196	166	134	104	75		
1954	2050	2664	297	1274	16	40	898	396	296	261	231	197	167	135	105	76		
1955	2049	2665	298	1273	17	41	899	397	297	262	232	198	168	136	106	77		
1956	2048	2666	299	1272	18	42	900	398	298	263	233	199	169	137	107	78		
1957	2047	2667	300	1271	19	43	901	399	299	264	234	200	170	138	108	79		
1958	2046	2668	301	1270	20	44	902	400	300	265	235	201	171	139	109	80		
1959	2045	2669	302	1269	21	45	903	401	301	266	236	202	172	140	110	81		
1960	2044	2670	303	1268	22	46	904	402	302	267	237	203	173	141	111	82		
1951	2043	2671	304	1267	23	47	905	403	303	268	238	204	174	142	112	83		
1962	2042	2672	305	1266	24	48	906	404	304	269	239	205	175	143	113	84		
1963	2041	2673	306	1265	25	49	907	405	305	270	240	206	176	144	114	85		
1964	2040	2674	307	1264	26	50	908	406	306	271	241	207	177	145	115	86		
1965	2039	2675	308	1263	27	51	909	407	307	272	242	208	178	146	116	87		
1966	2038	2676	309	1262	28	52	910	408	308	273	243	209	179	147	117	88		
1967	2037	2677	310	1261	29	1 Europs.	911	409	309	274	244	210	180	148	118	89		
1968	2036	2678	311	1260	30	2	912	410	310	275	245	211	181	149	119	90		
1969	2035	2679	312	1259	31	3	913	411	311	276	246	212	182	150	120	91		
1970	2034	2680	313	1258	32	4	914	412	312	277	247	213	183	151	121	92		
1971	2033	2681	314	1257	33	5	915	413	313	278	248	214	184	152	122	93		
1972	2032	2682	315	1256	34	6	916	414	314	279	249	215	185	153	123	94		
1973	2031	2683	316	1255	35	7	917	415	315	280	250	216	186	154	124	95		
1974	2030	2684	317	1254	36	8	918	416	316	281	251	217	187	155	125	96		
1975	2029	2685	318	1253	37	9	919	417	317	282	252	218	188	156	126	97		
1976	2028	2686	319	1252	38	10	920	418	318	283	253	219	189	157	127	98		
1977	2027	2687	320	1251	39	11	921	419	319	284	254	220	190	158	128	99		
1978	2026	2688	321	1250	40	12	922	420	320	285	255	221	191	159	129	100		
1979	2025	2689	322	1249	41	13	923	421	321	286	256	222	192	160	130	101		
1980	2024	2690	323	1248	42	14	924	422	322	287	257	223	193	161	131	102		
1981	2023	2691	324	1247	43	15	925	423	323	288	258	224	194	162	132	103		
1982	2022	2692	325	1246	44	16	926	424	324	289	259	225	195	163	133	104		
1983	2021	2693	326	1245	1 Apachnas.	17	927	425	325	290	260	226	196	164	134	105		
1984	2020	2694	327	1244	2	18	928	426	326	291	261	227	197	165	135	106		
1985	2019	2695	328	1243	3	19	929	427	327	292	262	228	198	166	136	107		
1986	2018	2696	329	1242	4	20	930	428	328	293	263	229	199	167	137	108		
1987	2017	2697	330	1241	5	21	931	429	329	294	264	230	200	168	138	109		
1988	2016	2698	331	1240	6	22	932	430	330	295	265	231	201	169	139	110		
1989	2015	2699	332	1239	7	23	933	431	331	296	266	232	202	170	140	111		
1990	2014	2700	333	1238	8	24	934	432	332	297	267	233	203	171	141	112		
1991	2013	2701	334	1237	9	25	935	433	333	298	268	234	204	172	142	113		
1992	2012	2702	335	1236	10	26	936	434	334	299	269	235	205	173	143	114		
1993	2011	2703	336	1235	11	27	937	435	335	300	270	236	206	174	144	115		
1994	2010	2704	337	1234	12	28	938	436	336	301	271	237	207	175	145	116		
1995	2009	2705	338	1233	13	29	939	437	337	302	272	238	208	176	146	117		
1996	2008	2706	339	1232	14	30	940	438	338	303	273	239	209	177	147	118		
1997	2007	2707	340	1231	15	31	941	439	339	304	274	Peleg died A. M. 1996.	210	178	148	119		
1998	2006	2708	341	1230	16	32	942	440	340	305	275		211	179	Nahor died A. M. 1997.	120		
1999	2005	2709	342	1229	17	28	943	441	341	306	276		212	180		121		
2000	2004	2710	343	1228	18	34	944	442	342	307	277		213	181		122		
2001	2003	2711	344	1227	19	35	945	443	343	308	278		214	182		123		
2002	2002	2712	345	1226	20	36	946	444	344	309	279		215	183		124		
2003	2001	2713	346	1225	21	37	947	445	345	310	280		216	184		125		
2004	2000	2714	347	1224	22	38	948	446	346	311	281		217	185		126		
2005	1999	2715	348	1223	23	39	949	447	347	312	282		218	186		127		
2006	1998	2716	349	1222	24	40	950	448	348	313	283		219	187		128		
2007	1997	2717	350	1221	25	41	Noah died A. M. 2006. He is the last on record that lived upward of 600 years; he even outlived Nahor, one of his children of the eighth generation.	449	349	314	284		220	188		129		
2008	1996	2718	351	1220	26	42		450	350	315	285		221	189		130		
2009	1995	2719	352	1219	27	43		451	351	316	286		222	190		131	1	
2010	1994	2720	353	1218	28	44		452	352	317	287		223	191		132	2	
2011	1993	2721	354	1217	29	45		453	353	318	288		224	192		133	3	
2012	1992	2722	355	1216	30	1 Telchin.		454	354	319	289		225	193		134	4	
2013	1991	2723	356	1215	31	2		455	355	320	290		226	194		135	5	
2014	1990	2724	357	1214	32	3		456	356	321	291		227	195		136	6	
2015	1989	2725	358	1213	33	4		457	357	322	292		228	196		137	7	
2016	1988	2726	359	1212	34	5		458	358	323	293		229	197		138	8	
2017	1987	2727	360	1211	35	6		459	359	324	294		230	198		139	9	
2018	1986	2728	361	1210	36	7		460	360	325	295		231	199		140	10	
2019	1985	2729	362	1209	37	8		461	361	326	296		232	200		141	11	1
2020	1984	2730	363	1208	1 Apophis.	9		462	362	327	297		233	201		142	12	2
2021	1983	2731	364	1207	2	10		463	363	328	298		234	202		143	13	3
2022	1982	2732	365	1206	3	11		464	364	329	299		235	203		144	14	4
2023	1981	2733	366	1205	4	12		465	365	230	300		236	204		145	15	5
2024	1980	2734	367	1204	5	13		466	366	331	301		237	205		146	16	6
2025	1979	2735	368	1203	6	14		467	367	332	302		238	206		147	17	7
2026	1978	2736	369	1202	7	15		468	368	333	303		239	207		148	18	8
2027	1977	2737	370	1201	8	16		469	369	334	304		Reu died A. M. 2026.	208		149	19	9
2028	1976	2738	371	1200	9	17		470	370	335	305			209		150	20	10
2029	1975	2739	372	1199	10	18		471	371	336	306			210		151	21	11
2030	1974	2740	373	1198	11	19		472	372	337	307			211		152	22	12
2031	1973	2741	374	1197	12	20		473	373	338	308			212		153	23	13
2032	1972	2742	375	1196	13	1 Apis.		474	374	339	309			213		154	24	14
2033	1971	2743	376	1195	14	2		475	375	340	310			214		155	25	15
2034	1970	2744	377	1194	15	3		476	376	341	311			215		156	26	16
2035	1969	2745	378	1193	16	4		477	377	342	312			216		157	27	17
2036	1968	2746	379	1192	17	5		478	378	343	313			217		158	28	18
2037	1967	2747	380	1191	18	6		479	379	344	314			218		159	29	19
2038	1966	2748	381	1190	19	7		480	380	355	315			219		160	30	20
2039	1965	2749	382	1189	20	8		481	381	346	316			220		161	31	21
2040	1964	2750	383	1188	21	9		482	382	347	317			221		162	32	22
2041	1963	2751	384	1187	22	10		483	383	348	318			222		163	33	23
2042	1962	2752	385	1186	23	11		484	384	349	319			223		164	34	24
2043	1961	2753	386	1185	24	12		485	385	350	320			224		165	35	25
2044	1960	2754	387	1184	25	13		486	386	351	321			225		166	36	26
2045	1959	2755	388	1183	26	14		487	387	352	322			226		167	37	27
2046	1958	2756	389	1182	27	15		488	388	353	323			227		168	38	28
2047	1957	2757	390	1181	28	16		489	389	354	324			228		169	39	29
2048	1956	2758	391	1180	29	17		490	390	355	325			229		170	40	30
2049	1955	2759	392	1179	30	18		491	391	356	326			230		171	41	31
2050	1954	2760	393	1178	31	19		492	392	357	327			Serug died A. M. 2049.		172	42	32

TABLE II.—Chronology of Ancient Kingdoms.—*Continued.*

A. M.	B. C.	Julian Period.	Anno e Diluvio	Year before the first Olymp.	Kings of the Egyptians.	Kings of Sicyon.	Kingdom of the Argivi.	Kingdom of the Athenians.	In the YEAR of the LIFE of								
2051	1953	2761	394	1177	32 Apophis.	20 Apis.			493 SHEM	393 ARPHAXAD	358 SALAH	328 HEBER	173 TERAH	43 ABRAM	33 SARAI		
2052	1952	2762	395	1176	33	21			494	394	359	329	174	44	34		
2053	1951	2763	396	1175	34	22			495	395	360	330	175	45	35		
2054	1950	2764	397	1174	35	23			496	396	361	331	176	46	36		
2055	1949	2765	398	1173	36	24			497	397	362	332	177	47	37		
2056	1948	2766	399	1172	37	25	92 Before the foundation of this kingdom.		498	398	363	333	178	48	38		
2057	1947	2767	400	1171	38	26	91		499	399	364	334	179	49	39		
2058	1946	2768	401	1170	39	1 Thelxion.	90		500	400	365	335	180	50	40		
2059	1945	2769	402	1169	40	2	89		501	401	366	336	181	51	41		
2060	1944	2770	403	1168	41	3	88		502	402	367	337	182	52	42		
2061	1943	2771	404	1167	42	4	87		503	403	368	338	183	53	43		
2062	1942	2772	405	1166	43	5	86		504	404	369	339	184	54	44		
2063	1941	2773	406	1165	44	6	85		505	405	370	340	185	55	45		
2064	1940	2774	407	1164	45	7	84		506	406	371	341	186	56	46		
2065	1939	2775	408	1163	46	8	83		507	407	372	342	187	57	47		
2066	1938	2776	409	1162	47	9	82		508	408	373	343	188	58	48		
2067	1937	2777	410	1161	48	10	81		509	409	374	344	189	59	49		
2068	1936	2778	411	1160	49	11	80		510	410	375	345	190	60	50		
2069	1935	2779	412	1159	50	12	79		511	411	376	346	191	61	51		
2070	1934	2780	413	1158	51	13	78		512	412	377	347	192	62	52		
2071	1933	2781	414	1157	52	14	77		513	413	378	348	193	63	53		
2072	1932	2782	415	1156	53	15	76		514	414	379	349	194	64	54		
2073	1931	2783	416	1155	54	16	75		515	415	380	350	195	65	55		
2074	1930	2784	417	1154	55	17	74		516	416	381	351	196	66	56		
2075	1929	2785	418	1153	56	18	73		517	417	382	352	197	67	57		
2076	1928	2786	419	1152	57	19	72		518	418	383	353	198	68	58		
2077	1927	2787	420	1151	58	20	71		519	419	384	354	199	69	59		
2078	1926	2788	421	1150	59	21	70		520	420	385	355	200	70	60		
2079	1925	2789	422	1149	60	22	69		521	421	386	356	201	71	61		
2080	1924	2790	423	1148	61	23	68		522	422	387	357	202	72	62		
2081	1923	2791	424	1147	1 Janias.	24	67		523	423	388	358	203	73	63		
2082	1922	2792	425	1146	2	25	66		524	424	389	359	204	74	64		
2083	1921	2793	426	1145	3	26	65		525	425	390	360	205	75	65		
2084	1920	2794	427	1144	4	27	64		526	426	391	361	Terah died A. M. 2083, when Abram had completed 75 years of his life.	76	66		
2085	1919	2795	428	1143	5	28	63		527	427	392	362		77	67		
2086	1918	2796	429	1142	6	29	62		528	428	393	363		78	68		
2087	1917	2797	430	1141	7	30	61		529	429	394	364		79	69		
2088	1916	2798	431	1140	8	31	60		530	430	395	365		80	70		
2089	1915	2799	432	1139	9	32	59		531	431	396	366		81	71		
2090	1914	2800	433	1138	10	33	58		532	432	397	367		82	72		
2091	1913	2801	434	1137	11	34	57		533	433	398	368		83	73		
2092	1912	2802	435	1136	12	35	56		534	434	399	369		84	74		
2093	1911	2803	436	1135	13	36	55		535	435	400	370		85	75		
2094	1910	2804	437	1134	14	37	54		536	436	401	371		86	76		
2095	1909	2805	438	1133	15	38	53		537	437	402	372		87	77	1 ISHMAEL	
2096	1908	2806	439	1132	16	39	52		538	438	403	373		88	78	2	
2097	1907	2807	440	1131	17	40	51		539	Arphaxad died A. M. 2096.	404	374		89	79	3	
2098	1906	2808	441	1130	18	41	50		540		405	375		90	80	4	
2099	1905	2809	442	1129	19	42	49		541		406	376		91	81	5	
2100	1904	2810	443	1128	20	43	48		542		407	377		92	82	6	
2101	1903	2811	444	1127	21	44	47		543		408	378		93	83	7	
2102	1902	2812	445	1126	22	45	46		544		409	379		94	84	8	
2103	1901	2813	446	1125	23	46	45		545		410	380		95	85	9	
2104	1900	2814	447	1124	24	47	44		546		411	381		96	86	10	
2105	1899	2815	448	1123	25	48	43		547		412	382		97	87	11	
2106	1898	2816	449	1122	26	49	42		548		413	383		98	88	12	
2107	1897	2817	450	1121	27	50	41		549		414	384		99	89	13	
2108	1896	2818	451	1120	28	51	40		550		415	385		100 ABRAHAM	90 SARAH	14	
2109	1895	2819	452	1119	29	52	39		551		416	386		101	91	15	1 ISAAC
2110	1894	2820	453	1118	30		38		552		417	387		102	92	16	2
2111	1893	2821	454	1117	31	1 Ægydrus.	37		553		418	388		103	93	17	3
2112	1892	2822	455	1116	32	2	36		554		419	389		104	94	18	4
2113	1891	2823	456	1115	33	3	35		555		420	390		105	95	19	5
2114	1890	2824	457	1114	34	4	34		556		421	391		106	96	20	6
2115	1889	2825	458	1113	35	5	33		557		422	392		107	97	21	7
2116	1888	2826	459	1112	36	6	32	332 Before the foundation of this kingdom.	558		423	393		108	98	22	8
2117	1887	2827	460	1111	37	7	31	331	559		424	394		109	99	23	9
2118	1886	2828	461	1110	38	8	30	330	560		425	395		110	100	24	10
2119	1885	2829	462	1109	39	9	29	329	561		426	396		111	101	25	11
2120	1884	2830	463	1108	40	10	28	328	562		427	397		112	102	26	12
2121	1883	2831	464	1107	41	11	27	327	563		428	398		113	103	27	13
2122	1882	2832	465	1106	42	12	26	326	564		429	399		114	104	28	14
2123	1881	2833	466	1105	43	13	25	325	565		430	400		115	105	29	15
2124	1880	2834	467	1104	44	14	24	324	566		431	401		116	106	30	16
2125	1879	2835	468	1103	45	15	23	323	567		432	402		117	107	31	17
2126	1878	2836	469	1102	46	16	22	322	568		433	403		118	108	32	18
2127	1877	2837	470	1101	47	17	21	321	569		Salah died A. M. 2126.	404		119	109	33	19
2128	1876	2838	471	1100	48	18	20	320	570			405		120	110	34	20
2129	1875	2839	472	1099	49	19	19	319	571			406		121	111	35	21
2130	1874	2840	473	1098	50	20	18	318	572			407		122	112	36	22
2131	1873	2841	474	1097	1 Assis the last of the shepherd dynasty.	21	17	317	573			408		123	113	37	23
2132	1872	2842	475	1096	2	22	16	316	574			409		124	114	38	24
2133	1871	2843	476	1095	3	23	15	315	575			410		125	115	39	25
2134	1870	2844	477	1094	4	24	14	314	576			411		126	116	40	26
2135	1869	2845	478	1093	5	25	13	313	577			412		127	117	41	27
2136	1868	2846	479	1092	6	26	12	312	578			413		128	118	42	28
2137	1867	2847	480	1091	7	27	11	311	579			414		129	119	43	29
2138	1866	2848	481	1090	8	28	10	310	580			415		130	120	44	30
2139	1865	2849	482	1089	9	29	9	309	581			416		131	121	45	31
2140	1864	2850	483	1088	10	30	8	308	582			417		132	122	46	32
2141	1863	2851	484	1087	11	31	7	307	583			418		133	123	47	33
2142	1862	2852	485	1086	12	32	6	306	584			419		134	124	48	34
2143	1861	2853	486	1085	13	33	5	305	585			420		135	125	49	35
2144	1860	2854	487	1084	14	34	4	304	586			421		136	126	50	36
2145	1859	2855	488	1083	15	35	3	303	587			422		137	127	51	37
2146	1858	2856	489	1082	16	1 Thurimachus.	2	302	588			423		138	Sarah died A. M. 2145.	52	38
2147	1857	2857	490	1081	17	2	1	301	589			424		139		53	39

TABLE II.—Chronology of Ancient Kingdoms.—*Continued.*

A. M.	B. C.	Julian Period.	Anno e Diluvio	Year before the first Olymp.	Kings of the Egyptians.	Kings of Sicyon.	Kings of the Argivi.	Kingdom of the Athenians.	Year before the year of Christ, 1812.	In the YEAR of the LIFE of							
2148	1856	2858	491	1080	18 Assis.	3 Thurimachus.	1 Inachus, the first monarch.	300 Before the foundation of this kingdom.		500 SHEM	425 HEBER	140 ABRAHAM	54 ISHMAEL	40 ISAAC			
2149	1855	2859	492	1079	19	4	2	299		591	426	141	55	41			
2150	1854	2860	493	1078	20	5	3	298		592	427	142	56	42			
2151	1853	2861	494	1077	21	6	4	297		593	428	143	57	43			
2152	1852	2862	495	1076	22	7	5	296		594	429	144	58	44			
2153	1851	2863	496	1075	23	8	6	295		595	430	145	59	45			
2154	1850	2864	497	1074	24	9	7	294		596	431	146	60	46			
2155	1849	2865	498	1073	25	10	8	293		597	432	147	61	47			
2156	1848	2866	499	1072	26	11	9	292		598	433	148	62	48			
2157	1847	2867	500	1071	27	12	10	291		599	434	149	63	49			
2158	1846	2868	501	1070	28	13	11	290		600	435	150	64	50			
2159	1845	2869	502	1069	29	14	12	289		Shem died A. M. 2158. He is the last upon record that lived upwards of 500 years.	436	151	65	51			
2160	1844	2870	503	1068	30	15	13	288			437	152	66	52			
2161	1843	2871	504	1067	31	16	14	287			438	153	67	53			
2162	1842	2872	505	1066	32	17	15	286			439	154	68	54			
2163	1841	2873	506	1065	33	18	16	285			440	155	69	55			
2164	1840	2874	507	1064	34	19	17	284			441	156	70	56			
2165	1839	2875	508	1063	35	20	18	283			442	157	71	57			
2166	1838	2876	509	1062	36	21	19	282			443	158	72	58			
2167	1837	2877	510	1061	37	22	20	281			444	159	73	59			
2168	1836	2878	511	1060	38	23	21	280			445	160	74	60			
2169	1835	2879	512	1059	39	24	22	279			446	161	75	61	1 ESAU	1 JACOB	
2170	1834	2880	513	1058	40	25	23	278			447	162	76	62	2	2	
2171	1833	2881	514	1057	41	26	24	277			448	163	77	63	3	3	
2172	1832	2882	515	1056	42	27	25	276			449	164	78	64	4	4	
2173	1831	2883	516	1055	43	28	26	275			450	165	79	65	5	5	
2174	1830	2884	517	1054	44	29	27	274			451	166	80	66	6	6	
2175	1829	2885	518	1053	45	30	28	273			452	167	81	67	7	7	
2176	1828	2886	519	1052	46	31	29	272	3639		453	168	82	68	8	8	
2177	1827	2887	520	1051	47	32	30	271	3638		454	169	83	69	9	9	
2178	1826	2888	521	1050	48	33	31	270	3637		455	170	84	70	10	10	
2179	1825	2889	522	1049	49	34	32	269	3636		456	171	85	71	11	11	
2180	1824	2890	523	1048	1 Thethmosis or Amosis.	35	33	268	3635		457	172	86	72	12	12	
2181	1823	2891	524	1047	2	36	34	267	3634		458	173	87	73	13	13	
2182	1822	2892	525	1046	3	37	35	266	3633		459	174	88	74	14	14	
2183	1821	2893	526	1045	4	38	36	265	3632		460	175	89	75	15	15	
2184	1820	2894	527	1044	5	39	37	264	3631		461	Abraham died A. M. 2183.	90	76	16	16	
2185	1819	2895	528	1043	6	40	38	263	3630		462		91	77	17	17	
2186	1818	2896	529	1042	7	41	39	262	3629		463		92	78	18	18	
2187	1817	2897	530	1041	8	42	40	261	3628		464		93	79	19	19	
2188	1816	2898	531	1040	9	43	41	260	3627		Heber died A. M. 2187. He lived the longest of any upon record that was born after the Flood, and he, with some born about the same time with him, are probably alluded to in Job xv. 10.		94	80	20	20	
2189	1815	2899	532	1039	10	44	42	259	3626				95	81	21	21	
2190	1814	2900	533	1038	11	45	43	258	3625				96	82	22	22	
2191	1813	2901	534	1037	12		44	257	3624				97	83	23	23	
2192	1812	2902	535	1036	13	1 Leucippus.	45	256	3623				98	84	24	24	
2193	1811	2903	536	1035	14	2	46	255	3622				99	85	25	25	
2194	1810	2904	537	1034	15	3	47	254	3621				100	86	26	26	
2195	1809	2905	538	1033	16	4	48	253	3620				101	87	27	27	
2196	1808	2906	539	1032	17	5	49	252	3619				102	88	28	28	
2197	1807	2907	540	1031	18	6	50	251	3618				103	89	29	29	
2198	1806	2908	541	1030	19	7	1 Phoroneus.	250	3617				104	90	30	30	
2199	1805	2909	542	1029	20	8	2	249	3616				105	91	31	31	
2200	1804	2910	543	1028	21	9	3	248	3615				106	92	32	32	
2201	1803	2911	544	1027	22	10	4	247	3614				107	93	33	33	
2202	1802	2912	545	1026	23	11	5	246	3613				108	94	34	34	
2203	1801	2913	546	1025	24	12	6	245	3612				109	95	35	35	
2204	1800	2914	547	1024	25	13	7	244	3611				110	96	36	36	
2205	1799	2915	548	1023	1 Chebron.	14	8	243	3610				111	97	37	37	
2206	1798	2916	549	1022	2	15	9	242	3609				112	98	38	38	
2207	1797	2917	550	1021	3	16	10	241	3608				113	99	39	39	
2208	1796	2918	551	1020	4	17	11	240	3607				114	100	40	40	
2209	1795	2919	552	1019	5	18	12	239	3606				115	101	41	41	
2210	1794	2920	553	1018	6	19	13	238	3605				116	102	42	42	
2211	1793	2921	554	1017	7	20	14	237	3604				117	103	43	43	
2212	1792	2922	555	1016	8	21	15	236	3603				118	104	44	44	
2213	1791	2923	556	1015	9	22	16	235	3602				119	105	45	45	
2214	1790	2924	557	1014	10	23	17	234	3601				120	106	46	46	
2215	1789	2925	558	1013	11	24	18	233	3600				121	107	47	47	
2216	1788	2926	559	1012	12	25	19	232	3599				122	108	48	48	
2217	1787	2927	560	1011	13	26	20	231	3598				123	109	49	49	
2218	1786	2928	561	1010	1 Amenophis.	27	21	230	3597				124	110	50	50	
2219	1785	2929	562	1009	2	28	22	229	3596				125	111	51	51	
2220	1784	2930	563	1008	3	29	23	228	3595				126	112	52	52	
2221	1783	2931	564	1007	4	30	24	227	3594				127	113	53	53	LEVI. Archbishop Usher fixes his birth A. M. 2248.
2222	1782	2932	565	1006	5	31	25	226	3593				128	114	54	54	
2223	1781	2933	566	1005	6	32	26	225	3592				129	115	55	55	
2224	1780	2934	567	1004	7	33	27	224	3591				130	116	56	56	
2225	1779	2935	568	1003	8	34	28	223	3590				131	117	57	57	
2226	1778	2936	569	1002	9	35	29	222	3589				132	118	58	58	
2227	1777	2937	570	1001	10	36	30	221	3588				133	119	59	59	
2228	1776	2938	571	1000	11	37	31	220	3587				134	120	60	60	1
2229	1775	2939	572	999	12	38	32	219	3586				135	121	61	61	2
2230	1774	2940	573	998	13	39	33	218	3585				136	122	62	62	3
2231	1773	2941	574	997	14	40	34	217	3584				137	123	63	63	4
2232	1772	2942	575	996	15	41	35	216	3583				Ishmael died A. M. 2231.	124	64	64	5
2233	1771	2943	576	995	16	42	36	215	3582					125	65	65	6
2234	1770	2944	577	994	17	43	37	214	3581					126	66	66	7
2235	1769	2945	578	993	18	44	38	213	3580					127	67	67	8
2236	1768	2946	579	992	19	45	39	212	3579					128	68	68	9
2237	1767	2947	580	991	20	46	40	211	3578					129	69	69	10
2238	1766	2948	581	990	21	47	41	210	3577					130	70	70	11
2239	1765	2949	582	989	1 Amessis.	48	42	209	3576					131	71	71	12
2240	1764	2950	583	988	2	49	43	208	3575					132	72	72	13
2241	1763	2951	584	987	3	50	44	207	3574					133	73	73	14
2242	1762	2952	585	986	4	51	45	206	3573					134	74	74	15
2243	1761	2953	586	985	5	52	46	205	3572					135	75	75	16
2244	1760	2954	587	984	6	53	47	204	3571					136	76	76	17
2245	1759	2955	588	983	7		48	203	3570					137	77	77	18

TABLE II.—Chronology of Ancient Kingdoms.—*Continued.*

A. M.	B. C.	Julian Period.	Anno e Diluvio	Year before the first Olymp.	Kings of the Egyptians.	Kings of Sicyon.	Kings of the Argivi.	Kingdom of the Athenians.	Year before the year of Christ, 1812.	In the YEAR of the LIFE of				
										ISAAC	ESAU	JACOB	LEVI	JOSEPH
2246	1758	2956	589	982	8 Amessis.	1 Mesapus.	49 Phoroneus.	202 Before the foundation of this kingdom.	3569	138	78	78	19	
2247	1757	2957	590	981	9	2	50	201	3568	139	79	79	20	
2248	1756	2958	591	980	10	3	51	200	3567	140	80	80	21	
2249	1755	2959	592	979	11	4	52	199	3566	141	81	81	22	
2250	1754	2960	593	978	12	5	53	198	3565	142	82	82	23	
2251	1753	2961	594	977	13	6	54	197	3564	143	83	83	24	
2252	1752	2962	595	976	14	7	55	196	3563	144	84	84	25	
2253	1751	2963	596	975	15	8	56	195	3562	145	85	85	26	
2254	1750	2964	597	974	16	9	57	194	3561	146	86	86	27	
2255	1749	2965	598	973	17	10	58	193	3560	147	87	87	28	
2256	1748	2966	599	972	18	11	59	192	3559	148	88	88	29	
2257	1747	2967	600	971	19	12	60	191	3558	149	89	89	30	
2258	1746	2968	601	970	20	13	1 Apis.	190	3557	150	90	90	31	
2259	1745	2969	602	969	21	14	2	189	3556	151	91	91	32	
2260	1744	2970	603	968	22	15	3	188	3555	152	92	92	33	1
2261	1743	2971	604	967	1 Mephres.	16	4	187	3554	153	93	93	34	2
2262	1742	2972	605	966	2	17	5	186	3553	154	94	94	35	3
2263	1741	2973	606	965	3	18	6	185	3552	155	95	95	36	4
2264	1740	2974	607	964	4	19	7	184	3551	156	96	96	37	5
2265	1739	2975	608	903	5	20	8	183	3550	157	97	97 ISRAEL.	38	6
2266	1738	2976	609	962	6	21	9	182	3549	158	98	98	39	7
2267	1737	2977	610	961	7	22	10	181	3548	159	99	99	40	8
2268	1736	2978	611	960	8	23	11	180	3547	160	100	100	41	9
2269	1735	2979	612	959	9	24	12	179	3546	161	101	101	42	10
2270	1734	2980	613	958	10	25	13	178	3545	162	102	102	43	11
2271	1733	2981	614	957	11	26	14	177	3544	163	103	103	44	12
2272	1732	2982	615	956	12	27	15	176	3543	164	104	104	45	13
2273	1731	2983	616	955	1 Mephramuthosis.	28	16	175	3542	165	105	105	46	14
2274	1730	2984	617	954	2	29	17	174	3541	166	106	106	47	15
2275	1729	2985	618	953	3	30	18	173	3540	167	107	107	48	16
2276	1728	2986	619	952	4	31	19	172	3539	168	108	108	49	17
2277	1727	2987	620	951	5	32	20	171	3538	169	109	109	50	18
2278	1726	2988	621	950	6	33	21	170	3537	170	110	110	51	19
2279	1725	2989	622	949	7	34	22	169	3536	171	111	111	52	20
2280	1724	2900	623	948	8	35	23	168	3535	172	112	112	53	21
2281	1723	2991	624	947	9	36	24	167	3534	173	113	113	54	22
2282	1722	2992	625	946	10	37	25	166	3533	174	114	114	55	23
2283	1721	2993	626	945	11	38	26	165	3532	175	115	115	56	24
2284	1720	2994	627	944	12	39	27	164	3531	176	116	116	57	25
2285	1719	2995	628	943	13	40	28	163	3530	177	117	117	58	26
2286	1718	2996	629	942	14	41	29	162	3529	178	118	118	59	27
2287	1717	2997	630	941	15	42	30	161	3528	179	119	119	60	28
2288	1716	2998	631	940	16	43	31	100	3527	180	120	120	61	29
2289	1715	2999	632	939	17	44	32	159	3526			121	62	30
2290	1714	3000	633	938	18	45	33	158	3525	Isaac died A. M. 2288.	How long Esau lived after A. M. 2288 is not recorded.	122	63	31
2291	1713	3001	634	937	19	46	34	157	3524			123	64	32
2292	1712	3002	635	936	20	47	35	156	3523			124	65	33
2293	1711	3003	636	935	21		1 Argus.	155	3522			125	66	34
2294	1710	3004	637	934	22	1 Eratus, or Proetus.	2	154	3521			126	67	35
2295	1709	3005	638	933	23	2	3	153	3520			127	68	36
2296	1708	3006	639	932	24	3	4	152	3519			128	69	37
2297	1707	3007	640	931	25	4	5	151	3518			129	70	38
2298	1706	3008	641	930	26	5	6	150	3517			130	71	39
2299	1705	3009	642	929	1 Thmosis.	6	7	149	3516			131	72	40
2300	1704	3010	643	928	2	7	8	148	3515			132	73	41
2301	1703	3011	644	927	3	8	9	147	3514			133	74	42
2302	1702	3012	645	926	4	9	10	146	3513			134	75	43
2303	1701	3013	646	925	5	10	11	145	3512			135	76	44
2304	1700	3014	647	924	6	11	12	144	3511			136	77	45
2305	1699	3015	648	923	7	12	13	143	3510			137	78	46
2306	1698	3016	649	922	8	13	14	142	3509			138	79	47
2307	1697	3017	650	921	9	14	15	141	3508			139	80	48
2308	1696	3018	651	920	10	15	16	140	3507			140	81	49
2309	1695	3019	652	919		16	17	139	3506			141	82	50
2310	1694	3020	653	918	1 Amenophis.	17	18	138	3505			142	83	51
2311	1693	3021	654	917	2	18	19	137	3504			143	84	52
2312	1692	3022	655	916	3	19	20	136	3503			144	85	53
2313	1691	3023	656	915	4	20	21	135	3502			145	86	54
2314	1690	3024	657	914	5	21	22	134	3501			146	87	55
2315	1689	3025	658	913	6	22	23	133	3500			147	88	56
2316	1688	3026	659	912	7	23	24	132	3499				89	57
2317	1687	3027	660	911	8	24	25	131	3498			Israel died A. M. 2315.	90	58
2318	1686	3028	661	910	9	25	26	130	3497				91	59
2319	1685	3029	662	909	10	26	27	129	3496				92	60
2320	1684	3030	663	908	11	27	28	128	3495				93	61
2321	1683	3031	664	907	12	28	29	127	3494				94	62
2322	1682	3032	665	906	13	29	30	126	3493				95	63
2323	1681	3033	666	905	14	30	31	125	3492				96	64
2324	1680	3034	667	904	15	31	32	124	3491				97	65
2325	1679	3035	668	903	16	32	33	123	3490				98	66
2326	1678	3036	669	902	17	33	34	122	3489				99	67
2327	1677	3037	670	901	18	34	35	121	3488				100	68
2328	1676	3038	671	900	19	35	36	120	3487				101	69
2329	1675	3039	672	899	20	36	37	119	3486				102	70
2330	1674	3040	673	898	21	37	38	118	3485				103	71
2331	1673	3041	674	897	22	38	39	117	3484				104	72
2332	1672	3042	675	896	23	39	40	116	3483				105	73
2333	1671	3043	676	895	24	40	41	115	3482				106	74
2334	1670	3044	677	894	25	41	42	114	3481				107	75
2335	1669	3045	678	893	26	42	43	113	3480				108	76
2336	1668	3046	679	892	27	43	44	112	3479				109	77
2337	1667	3047	680	891	28	44	45	111	3478				110	78
2338	1666	3048	681	890	29	45	46	110	3477				111	79
2339	1665	3049	682	889	30	46	47	109	3476				112	80
2340	1664	3050	683	888	1 Orus.	1 Plemnaeus.	48	108	3475				113	81
2341	1663	3051	684	887	2	2	49	107	3474				114	82
2342	1662	3052	685	886	3	3	50	106	3473				115	83
2343	1661	3053	680	885	4	4	51	105	3472				116	84

TABLE II.—Chronology of Ancient Kingdoms.—*Continued.*

A. M	B. C.	Julian Period.	Anno e Diluvio	Year before the first Olymp.	Kings of the Egyptians.	Kings of Sicyon.	Kings of the Argivi.	Kingdom of the Athenians.	Year before the year of Christ, 1812.	In the YEAR of the LIFE of			
2344	1660	3054	687	884	5 Orus.	5 Plemmaus.	52 Argus.	104 Before the foundation of this kingdom.	3471	117 LEVI	35 JOSEPH		
2345	1659	3055	688	883	6	6	53	103	3470	118	86		
2346	1658	3056	689	882	7	7	54	102	3469	119	87		
2347	1657	3057	690	881	8	8	55	101	3468	120	88		
2348	1656	3058	691	880	9	9	56	100	3467	121	89		
2349	1655	3059	692	879	10	10	57	99	3466	122	90		
2350	1654	3060	693	878	11	11	58	98	3465	123	91		
2351	1653	3061	694	877	12	12	59	97	3464	124	92		
2352	1652	3062	695	876	13	13	60	96	3463	125	93		
2353	1651	3063	696	875	14	14	61	95	3462	126	94		
2354	1650	3064	697	874	15	15	62	94	3461	127	95		
2355	1649	3065	698	873	16	16	63	93	3460	128	96		
2356	1648	3066	699	872	17	17	64	92	3459	129	97		
2357	1647	3067	700	871	18	18	65	91	3458	130	98		
2358	1646	3068	701	870	19	19	66	90	3457	131	99		
2359	1645	3069	702	869	20	20	67	89	3456	132	100		
2360	1644	3070	703	868	21	21	68	88	3455	133	101		
2361	1643	3071	704	867	22	22	69	87	3454	134	102		
2362	1642	3072	705	866	23	23	70	86	3453	135	103		
2363	1641	3073	706	865	24	24	1 Criasus.	85	3452	136	104		
2364	1640	3074	707	864	25	25	2	84	3451	137	105		
2365	1639	3075	708	863	26	26	3	83	3450		106		
2366	1638	3076	709	862	27	27	4	82	3449	Levi died A. M. 2364. Archbishop Usher fixes the time of his death 20 years earlier.	107		
2367	1637	3077	710	861	28	28	5	81	3448		108		
2368	1636	3078	711	860	29	29	6	80	3447		109		
2369	1635	3079	712	859	30	30	7	79	3446		110		
2370	1634	3080	713	858	31	31	8	78	3445				
2371	1633	3081	714	857	22	32	9	77	3444		Joseph died A. M. 2350.		
2372	1632	3082	715	856	33	33	10	76	3443				
2373	1631	3083	716	955	34	34	11	75	3442				
2374	1630	3084	717	854	35	35	12	74	3441				
2375	1629	3085	718	853	36	36	13	73	3440				
2376	1628	3086	719	852	1 Acenchres.	37	14	72	3439				
2377	1627	3087	720	851	2	38	15	71	3438				
2378	1626	3088	721	850	3	39	16	70	3437				
2379	1625	3089	722	849	4	40	17	69	3436				
2380	1624	3090	723	848	5	41	18	68	3435				
2381	1623	3091	724	847	6	42	19	67	3434				
2382	1622	3092	725	846	7	43	20	66	3433				
2383	1621	3093	726	845	8	44	21	65	3432				
2384	1620	3094	727	844	9	45	22	64	3431				
2385	1619	3095	728	843	10	46	23	63	3430				
2386	1618	3096	729	842	11	47	24	62	3429				
2387	1617	3097	730	841	12	48	25	61	3428				
2388	1616	3098	731	840	1 Rathotis.	1 Orthopolis.	26	60	3427				
2389	1615	3099	732	939	2	2	27	59	3426				
2390	1614	3100	733	838	3	3	28	58	3425				
2391	1613	3101	734	837	4	4	29	57	3424				
2392	1612	3102	735	836	5	5	30	56	3423				
2393	1611	3103	736	835	6	6	31	55	3422				
2394	1610	3104	737	834	7	7	32	54	3421				
2395	1609	3105	738	833	8	8	33	53	3420				
2396	1608	3106	739	832	9	9	34	52	3419				
2397	1607	3107	740	831	1 Acencheres.	10	35	51	3418				
2398	1606	3108	741	830	2	11	36	50	3417				
2399	1605	3109	742	829	3	12	37	49	3416				
2400	1604	3110	743	828	4	13	38	48	3415				
2401	1603	3111	744	827	5	14	39	47	3414				
2402	1602	3112	745	826	6	15	40	46	3413				
2403	1601	3113	746	825	7	16	41	45	3412				
2404	1600	3114	747	824	8	17	42	44	3411				
2405	1599	3115	748	823	9	18	43	43	3410				
2406	1598	3116	749	822	10	19	44	42	3409				
2407	1597	3117	750	821	11	20	45	41	3408				
2408	1596	3118	751	820	12	21	46	40	3407				
2409	1595	3119	752	819	1 Ancencheres.	22	47	39	3406				
2410	1594	3120	753	818	2	23	48	38	3405				
2411	1593	3121	754	817	3	24	49	37	3404				
2412	1592	3122	755	816	4	25	50	36	3403				
2413	1591	3123	756	815	5	26	51	35	3402				
2414	1590	3124	757	814	6	27	52	34	3401				
2415	1589	3125	758	813	7	28	53	33	3400				
2416	1588	3126	759	812	8	29	54	32	3399				
2417	1587	3127	760	811	9	30	1 Phorbas.	31	3398				
2418	1586	3128	761	810	10	31	2	30	3397				
2419	1585	3129	762	809	11	32	3	29	3396				
2420	1584	3130	763	808	12	33	4	28	3395				
2421	1583	3131	764	807	1 Armais.	34	5	27	3394				
2422	1582	3132	765	806	2	35	6	26	3393				
2423	1581	3133	766	805	3	36	7	25	3392				
2424	1580	3134	767	804	4	37	8	24	3391				
2425	1579	3135	768	803	5	38	9	23	3390				
2426	1578	3136	769	802	1 Rameses.	39	10	22	3389				
2427	1577	3137	770	801	1 Rameses Miamun.	40	11	21	3388				
2428	1576	3138	771	800	2	41	12	20	3387				
2429	1575	3139	772	799	3	42	13	19	3386				
2430	1574	3140	773	798	4	43	14	18	3385				
2431	1573	3141	774	797	5	44	15	17	3384			1 AARON	
2432	1572	3142	775	796	6	45	16	16	3383			2	
2433	1571	3143	776	795	7	46	17	15	3382			3	
2434	1570	3144	777	794	8	47	18	14	3381			4	1 MOSES.
2435	1569	3145	778	793	9	48	19	13	3380			5	2
2436	1568	3146	779	792	10	49	20	12	3379			6	3
2437	1567	3147	780	791	11	50	21	11	3378			7	4
2438	1566	3148	781	790	12	51	22	10	3377			8	5
2439	1565	3149	782	789	13	52	23	9	3376			9	6
2440	1564	3150	783	788	14	53	24	8	3375			10	7
2441	1563	3151	784	787	15	54	25	7	3374			11	8

TABLE II.—Chronology of Ancient Kingdoms.—*Continued.*

A.M.	B. C.	Julian Period.	Anno e Diluvio	Year before the first Olymp.	Kings of the Egyptians.	Kings of Sicyon.	Kings of the Argivi.	Kings of the Athenians.	Year before the year of Christ, 1812.	In the YEAR of the LIFE of			
2442	1562	3152	785	786	16 Rameses Miamun.	55 Orthopolis.	26 Phorbas.	6 Before the reign of Cecrops.	3373	12 AARON	9 MOSES		
2443	1561	3153	786	785	17	56	27	5	3372	13	10		
2444	1560	3154	787	784	18	57	28	4	3371	14	11		
2445	1559	3155	788	783	19	58	29	3	3370	15	12		
2446	1558	3156	789	782	20	59	30	2	3369	16	13		
2447	1557	3157	790	781	21	60	31	1	3368	17	14		
2448	1556	3158	791	780	22	61	32	1	3367	18	15		
2449	1555	3159	792	779	23	62	33	2	3366	19	16		
2450	1554	3160	793	778	24	1 Marathon.	34	3	3365	20	17		
2451	1553	3161	794	777	25	2	35	4	3364	21	18		
2452	1552	3162	795	776	26	3	1 Triopas.	5	3363	22	19	1 JOSHUA	
2453	1551	3163	796	775	27	4	2	6	3362	23	20	2	
2454	1550	3164	797	774	28	5	3	7	3361	24	21	3	
2455	1549	3165	798	773	29	6	4	8	3360	25	22	4	
2456	1548	3166	799	772	30	7	5	9	3359	26	23	5	
2457	1547	3167	800	771	31	8	6	10 Cecrops, the first monarch.	3358	27	24	6	
2458	1546	3168	801	770	22	9	7	11	3357	28	25	7	
2459	1545	3169	802	769	33	10	8	12	3356	29	26	8	
2460	1544	3170	803	768	34	11	9	13	3355	30	27	9	
2461	1543	3171	804	767	35	12	10	14	3354	31	28	10	
2462	1542	3172	805	766	36	13	11	15	3353	32	29	11	
2463	1541	3173	806	765	37	14	12	16	3352	33	30	12	
2464	1540	3174	807	764	38	15	13	17	3351	34	31	13	
2465	1539	3175	808	763	39	16	14	18	3350	35	32	14	
2466	1538	3176	809	762	40	17	15	19	3349	36	33	15	
2467	1537	3177	810	761	41	18	16	20	3348	37	34	16	
2468	1536	3178	811	760	42	19	17	21	3347	38	35	17	
2469	1535	3179	812	759	43	20	18	22	3346	39	36	18	
2470	1534	3180	813	758	44	21	19	23	3345	40	37	19	
2471	1533	3181	814	757	45	22	20	24	3344	41	38	20	
2472	1532	3182	815	756	46	23	21	25	3343	42	39	21	
2473	1531	3183	816	755	47	24	22	26	3342	43	40	22	
2474	1530	3184	817	754	48	25	23	27	3341	44	41	23	
2475	1529	3185	818	753	49	26	24	28	3340	45	42	24	1 CALEB
2476	1528	3186	819	752	50	27	25	29	3339	46	43	25	2
2477	1527	3187	820	751	51	28	26	30	3338	47	44	26	3
2478	1526	3188	821	750	52	29	27	31	3337	48	45	27	4
2479	1525	3189	822	749	53	30	28	32	3336	49	46	28	5
2480	1524	3190	823	748	54	1 Marathus.	29	33	3335	50	47	29	6
2481	1523	3191	824	747	55	2	30	34	3334	51	48	30	7
2482	1522	3192	825	746	56	3	31	35	3333	52	49	31	8
2483	1521	3193	826	745	57	4	32	36	3232	53	50	32	9
2484	1520	3194	827	744	58	5	33	37	3331	54	51	33	10
2485	1519	3195	828	743	59	6	34	38	3330	55	52	34	11
2486	1518	3196	829	742	60	7	35	39	3329	56	53	35	12
2487	1517	3197	830	741	61	8	36	40	3328	57	54	36	13
2488	1516	3198	831	740	62	9	37	41	3327	58	55	37	14
2489	1515	3199	832	739	63	10	38	42	3326	59	56	38	15
2490	1514	3200	833	738	64	11	39	43	3325	60	57	39	16
2491	1513	3201	834	737	65	12	40	44	3324	61	58	40	17
2492	1512	3202	835	736	66	13	41	45	3323	62	59	41	18
2493	1511	3203	836	735	67	14	42	46	3322	63	60	42	19
2494	1510	3204	837	734	1 Amenophis II.	15	43	47	3321	64	61	43	20
2495	1509	3205	838	733	2	16	44	48	3320	65	62	44	21
2496	1508	3206	839	732	3	17	45	49	3319	66	63	45	22
2497	1507	3207	840	731	4	18	46	50	3318	67	64	46	23
2498	1506	3208	841	730	5	19	1 Crotopus.	1 Cranaus.	3317	68	65	47	24
2499	1505	3209	842	729	6	20	2	2	3316	69	66	48	25
2500	1504	3210	843	728	7	1 Echyteus.	3	3	3315	70	67	49	26
2501	1503	3211	844	727	8	2	4	4	3314	71	68	50	27
2502	1502	3212	845	726	9	3	5	5	3313	72	60	51	28
2503	1501	3213	846	725	10	4	6	6	3312	73	70	52	29
2504	1500	3214	847	724	11	5	7	7	3311	74	71	53	30
2505	1499	3215	248	723	12	6	8	8	3310	75	72	54	31
2506	1498	3216	849	722	13	7	9	9	3309	76	73	55	32
2507	1497	3217	850	721	14	8	10	10	3308	77	74	56	33
2508	1496	3218	851	720	15	9	11	1 Amphyction.	3307	78	75	57	34
2509	1495	3219	852	719	16	10	12	2	3306	79	76	58	35
2510	1494	3220	853	718	17	11	13	3	3305	80	77	59	36
2511	1493	3221	854	717	18	12	14	4	3304	81	78	60	37
2512	1492	3222	855	716	19	13	15	5	3303	82	79	61	38
2513	1491	3223	856	715	20	14	16	6	3302	83	80	62	39
2514	1490	3224	857	714	1 Armais.	15	17	7	3301	84	81	63	40
2515	1489	3225	858	713	2	16	18	8	3300	85	82	64	41
2516	1488	3226	859	712	3	17	19	9	3299	86	83	65	42
2517	1487	3227	860	711	4	18	20	10	3298	87	84	66	43
2518	1486	3228	861	710	5	19	21	1 Ericthonius.	3297	88	85	67	44
2519	1485	3229	862	709	6	20	1 Sthenelus.	2	3296	89	86	68	45
2520	1484	3230	863	708	7	21	2	3	3295	90	87	69	46
2521	1483	3231	864	707	8	22	3	4	3294	91	88	70	47
2522	1482	3232	865	706	1	23	4	5	3293	92	69	71	48
2523	1481	3233	866	705	The succession and reign of the Egyptian monarchs from this very uncertain.	24	5	6	3292	93	90	72	49
2524	1480	3234	867	704		25	6	7	3291	94	91	73	50
2525	1479	3235	868	703		26	7	8	3290	95	92	74	51
2526	1478	3236	869	702		27	8	9	3289	96	93	75	52
2527	1477	3237	870	701		28	9	10	3288	97	94	76	53
2528	1476	3238	871	700		29	10	11	3287	98	95	77	54
2529	1475	3239	872	699		30	11	12	3286	99	96	78	55
2530	1474	3240	873	698		31	1 Danaus.	13	3285	100	97	79	56
2531	1473	3241	874	697		32	2	14	3284	101	98	80	57
2532	1472	3242	875	696		33	3	15	3283	102	99	81	58
2533	1471	3243	876	695		34	4	16	3282	103	100	82	59
2534	1470	3244	877	694		35	5	17	3281	104	101	83	60
2535	1469	3245	878	693		36	6	18	3280	105	102	84	61
2536	1468	3246	879	692		37	7	19	3279	106	103	85	62
2537	1467	3247	890	691		38	8	20	3278	107	104	86	63
2538	1466	3248	881	690		39	9	21	3277	108	105	87	64
2539	1465	3249	682	689		40	10	22	3276	109	106	88	65

TABLE II.—Chronology of Ancient Kingdoms.—*Concluded*

A. M.	B. C.	Julian Period.	Anno e Diluvio	Year before the first Olymp.	Kings of Sicyon.	Kings of the Argivi.	Kings of the Athenians.	Year before the year of Christ, 1812.	In the YEAR of the LIFE of			
2540	1464	3252	883	888	41 Echyteus.	11 Danaus.	23 Erichthonius.	3275	110 AARON	107 MOSES	89 JOSHUA	66 CALEB
2541	1463	3253	884	887	42	12	24	3274	111	108	90	67
2542	1462	3254	885	886	43	13	25	3273	112	109	91	68
2543	1461	3255	886	885	44	14	26	3272	113	110	92	69
2544	1460	3256	887	884	45	15	27	3271	114	111	93	70
2545	1459	3257	888	883	46	16	28	3270	115	112	94	71
2546	1458	3258	889	882	47	17	29	3269	116	113	95	72
2547	1457	3259	890	881	48	18	30	3268	117	114	96	73
2548	1456	3260	891	880	49	19	31	3267	118	115	97	74
2549	1455	3261	892	879	50	20	32	3266	119	116	98	75 How long Caleb lived after A. M. 2554 is not recorded.
2550	1454	3262	893	878	51	21	33	3265	120	117	99	76
2551	1453	3263	894	877	52	22	34	3264	121	118	100 Joshua died A.M. 2561.	77
2552	1452	3264	895	876	53	23	35	3263	122	119	101	78
2553	1451	3265	896	875	1 Corax.	24	36	3262	123	120	102	79
2554	1450	3266	897	874	2	25	37	3261			103	80
2555	1449	3267	898	873	3	26	38	3260	Aaron died A. M. 2553.	Moses died A. M. 2553.	104	
2556	1448	3268	899	872	4	27	39	3259			105	
2557	1447	3269	900	871	5	28	40	3258			106	
2558	1446	3270	901	870	6	29	41	3257			107	
2559	1445	3271	902	869	7	30	42	3256			108	
2560	1444	3272	903	868	8	31	43	3255			109	
2561	1443	3273	904	867	9	32	44	3254			110	

In the foregoing chronological Tables, the numbers in the different columns are synchronical, taken collaterally, so that any event that has happened within the limits of the Tables may be found in from 10 to 17 different epochs. Thus, if the reader wishes to know in what year of the various epochs the death of Nahor the father of Abraham happened, he will at once see, by a reference to Table II., that this event took place in the year from the *creation*, according to Abp. Usher, 1997; the year before the *incarnation* 2007; in the year of the *Julian* period 2707; in the year from the *deluge* 340; and in the year before the first *Olympiad* 1231; all of which correspond with the 15th year of the reign of *Apachnas*, king of the *Egyptians*, and the 31st of the reign of *Europs*, king of the *Sicyonians*; which also correspond with the 941st year of the life of *Noah*, the 439th of that of *Shem*, the 339th of *Arphaxad*, the 304th of *Salah*, the 274th of *Heber*, the 210th of *Reu*, the 178th of *Serug*, and the 119th year of the life of *Terah*.

N. B. The numbers in Table II., pointing out the years of the life of the different Patriarchs, are all adapted to the *commencement* of the corresponding tabular years of the world; so that the year of the birth of any Patriarch is not to be referred to the A. M. corresponding to the tabular year of his life 1, but to the year immediately preceding. Thus Aaron was born some time in A. M. 2430; but at the *beginning* of A. M. 2431, Table II. shows him to have been in the *first* year of his life; yet before the conclusion of that year he entered upon his *second* year, therefore A. M. 2422 corresponds to the tabular year of his life 2.

* 9 7 8 0 2 5 9 4 8 8 7 6 7 *
ND - #0052 - 220824 - C0 - 229/152/50 - PB - 9780259488767 - Gloss Lamination